ENCYCLOPEDIA OF RELIGION

SECOND EDITION

ENCYCLOPEDIA OF RELIGION

13

SECOND EDITION

SOUTH AMERICAN INDIAN RELIGIONS
•
TRANSCENDENCE AND IMMANENCE

LINDSAY JONES
EDITOR IN CHIEF

MACMILLAN REFERENCE USA
An imprint of Thomson Gale, a part of The Thomson Corporation

THOMSON
GALE

Detroit • New York • San Francisco • San Diego • New Haven, Conn. • Waterville, Maine • London • Munich

THOMSON
GALE

Encyclopedia of Religion, Second Edition
Lindsay Jones, Editor in Chief

For more information, contact
Macmillan Reference USA
An imprint of Thomson Gale
27500 Drake Rd.
Farmington, Hills, MI 48331-3535
Or you can visit our Internet site at
http://www.gale.com

LIBRARY OF CONGRESS CATALOGING-IN-PUBLICATION DATA

Encyclopedia of religion / Lindsay Jones, editor in chief.— 2nd ed.
p. cm.
Includes bibliographical references and index.
ISBN 0-02-865733-0 (SET HARDCOVER : ALK. PAPER) — ISBN 0-02-865734-9 (V. 1) — ISBN 0-02-865735-7 (v. 2) — ISBN 0-02-865736-5 (v. 3) — ISBN 0-02-865737-3 (v. 4) — ISBN 0-02-865738-1 (v. 5) — ISBN 0-02-865739-X (v. 6) — ISBN 0-02-865740-3 (v. 7) — ISBN 0-02-865741-1 (v. 8) — ISBN 0-02-865742-X (v. 9) — ISBN 0-02-865743-8 (v. 10) — ISBN 0-02-865980-5 (v. 11) — ISBN 0-02-865981-3 (v. 12) — ISBN 0-02-865982-1 (v. 13) — ISBN 0-02-865983-X (v. 14) — ISBN 0-02-865984-8 (v. 15)
1. RELIGION—ENCYCLOPEDIAS. I. JONES, LINDSAY, 1954-

BL31.E46 2005
200'.3—dc22 2004017052

This title is also available as an e-book.
ISBN 0-02-865997-X
Contact your Thomson Gale representative for ordering information.

Printed in the United States of America
10 9 8 7 6 5 4 3 2

EDITORS AND CONSULTANTS

Editor in Chief

Lindsay Jones
Associate Professor, Department of Comparative Studies, Ohio State University

Board Members

Davíd Carrasco
Neil Rudenstine Professor of Study of Latin America, Divinity School and Department of Anthropology, Harvard University

Giovanni Casadio
Professor of History of Religions, Dipartimento di Scienze dell'Antichità, Università degli Studi di Salerno

Wendy Doniger
Mircea Eliade Distinguished Service Professor of the History of Religions, University of Chicago

Gary L. Ebersole
Professor of History and Religious Studies, and Director, UMKC Center for Religious Studies, University of Missouri—Kansas City

Janet Gyatso
Hershey Professor of Buddhist Studies, The Divinity School, Harvard University

Charles Hallisey
Associate Professor, Department of Languages and Cultures of Asia and Program in Religious Studies, University of Wisconsin—Madison

Charles H. Long
Professor of History of Religions, Emeritus, and Former Director of Research Center for Black Studies, University of California, Santa Barbara

Mary N. MacDonald
Professor, History of Religions, Le Moyne College (Syracuse, New York)

Dale B. Martin
Professor of Religious Studies, and Chair, Department of Religious Studies, Yale University

Azim Nanji
Professor and Director, The Institute of Ismaili Studies, London

Jacob Olupona
Professor, African American and African Studies Program, University of California, Davis

Michael Swartz
Professor of Hebrew and Religious Studies, Ohio State University

Inés Talamantez
Associate Professor, Religious Studies Department, University of California, Santa Barbara

Consultants

Gregory D. Alles
Associate Professor of Religious Studies, McDaniel College
Study of Religion

Sigma Ankrava
Professor, Department of Literary and Cultural Studies, Faculty of Modern Languages, University of Latvia
Baltic Religion and Slavic Religion

Diane Apostolos-Cappadona
Center for Muslim–Christian Understanding and Liberal Studies Program, Georgetown University
Art and Religion

Diane Bell
Professor of Anthropology and Women's Studies, George Washington University
Australian Indigenous Religions

Kees W. Bolle
Professor Emeritus of History, University of California, Los Angeles, and Fellow, Netherlands Institute for Advanced Studies in the Humanities and Social Sciences
History of Religions

Mark Csikszentmihalyi
Associate Professor in the Department of East Asian Languages and Literature and the Program in Religious Studies, University of Wisconsin—Madison
Chinese Religions

Richard A. Gardner
Faculty of Comparative Culture, Sophia University
Humor and Religion

John A. Grim
Professor of Religion, Bucknell University and Co-Coordinator,

Harvard Forum on Religion and Ecology
Ecology and Religion

JOSEPH HARRIS
Francis Lee Higginson Professor of English Literature and Professor of Folklore, Harvard University
Germanic Religions

URSULA KING
Professor Emerita, Senior Research Fellow and Associate Member of the Institute for Advanced Studies, University of Bristol, England, and Professorial Research Associate, Centre for Gender and Religions Research, School of Oriental and African Studies, University of London
Gender and Religion

DAVID MORGAN
Duesenberg Professor of Christianity and the Arts, and Professor of Humanities and Art History, Valparaiso University
Color Inserts and Essays

JOSEPH F. NAGY
Professor, Department of English, University of California, Los Angeles
Celtic Religion

MATTHEW OJO
Obafemi Awolowo University
African Religions

JUHA PENTIKÄINEN
Professor of Comparative Religion, The University of Helsinki, Member of Academia Scientiarum Fennica, Finland
Arctic Religions and Uralic Religions

TED PETERS
Professor of Systematic Theology, Pacific Lutheran Theological Seminary and the Center for Theology and the Natural Sciences at the Graduate Theological Union, Berkeley, California
Science and Religion

FRANK E. REYNOLDS
Professor of the History of Religions and Buddhist Studies in the Divinity School and the Department of South Asian Languages and Civilizations, Emeritus, University of Chicago
History of Religions

GONZALO RUBIO
Assistant Professor, Department of Classics and Ancient Mediterranean Studies and Department of History and Religious Studies, Pennsylvania State University
Ancient Near Eastern Religions

SUSAN SERED
Director of Research, Religion, Health and Healing Initiative, Center for the Study of World Religions, Harvard University, and Senior Research Associate, Center for Women's Health and Human Rights, Suffolk University
Healing, Medicine, and Religion

LAWRENCE E. SULLIVAN
Professor, Department of Theology, University of Notre Dame
History of Religions

WINNIFRED FALLERS SULLIVAN
Dean of Students and Senior Lecturer in the Anthropology and Sociology of Religion, University of Chicago
Law and Religion

TOD SWANSON
Associate Professor of Religious Studies, and Director, Center for Latin American Studies, Arizona State University
South American Religions

MARY EVELYN TUCKER
Professor of Religion, Bucknell University, Founder and Coordinator, Harvard Forum on Religion and Ecology, Research Fellow, Harvard Yenching Institute, Research Associate, Harvard Reischauer Institute of Japanese Studies
Ecology and Religion

HUGH B. URBAN
Associate Professor, Department of Comparative Studies, Ohio State University
Politics and Religion

CATHERINE WESSINGER
Professor of the History of Religions and Women's Studies, Loyola University New Orleans
New Religious Movements

ROBERT A. YELLE
Mellon Postdoctoral Fellow, University of Toronto
Law and Religion

ERIC ZIOLKOWSKI
Charles A. Dana Professor of Religious Studies, Lafayette College
Literature and Religion

ABBREVIATIONS AND SYMBOLS USED IN THIS WORK

abbr. abbreviated; abbreviation
abr. abridged; abridgment
AD *anno Domini,* in the year of the (our) Lord
Afrik. Afrikaans
AH *anno Hegirae,* in the year of the Hijrah
Akk. Akkadian
Ala. Alabama
Alb. Albanian
Am. *Amos*
AM *ante meridiem,* before noon
amend. amended; amendment
annot. annotated; annotation
Ap. *Apocalypse*
Apn. *Apocryphon*
app. appendix
Arab. Arabic
'Arakh. *'Arakhin*
Aram. Aramaic
Ariz. Arizona
Ark. Arkansas
Arm. Armenian
art. article (pl., arts.)
AS Anglo-Saxon
Asm. Mos. *Assumption of Moses*
Assyr. Assyrian
A.S.S.R. Autonomous Soviet Socialist Republic
Av. Avestan
'A.Z. *'Avodah zarah*
b. born
Bab. Babylonian
Ban. Bantu
1 Bar. *1 Baruch*
2 Bar. *2 Baruch*
3 Bar. *3 Baruch*
4 Bar. *4 Baruch*
B.B. *Bava' batra'*
BBC British Broadcasting Corporation
BC before Christ
BCE before the common era
B.D. Bachelor of Divinity
Beits. *Beitsah*
Bekh. *Bekhorot*
Beng. Bengali
Ber. *Berakhot*
Berb. Berber
Bik. *Bikkurim*
bk. book (pl., bks.)
B.M. *Bava' metsi'a'*
BP before the present
B.Q. *Bava' qamma'*
Brāh. *Brāhmaṇa*
Bret. Breton
B.T. Babylonian Talmud
Bulg. Bulgarian
Burm. Burmese
c. *circa,* about, approximately
Calif. California
Can. Canaanite
Catal. Catalan
CE of the common era
Celt. Celtic
cf. *confer,* compare
Chald. Chaldean
chap. chapter (pl., chaps.)
Chin. Chinese
C.H.M. Community of the Holy Myrrhbearers
1 Chr. *1 Chronicles*
2 Chr. *2 Chronicles*
Ch. Slav. Church Slavic
cm centimeters
col. column (pl., cols.)
Col. *Colossians*
Colo. Colorado
comp. compiler (pl., comps.)
Conn. Connecticut
cont. continued
Copt. Coptic
1 Cor. *1 Corinthians*
2 Cor. *2 Corinthians*
corr. corrected
C.S.P. Congregatio Sancti Pauli, Congregation of Saint Paul (Paulists)
d. died
D Deuteronomic (source of the Pentateuch)
Dan. Danish
D.B. Divinitatis Baccalaureus, Bachelor of Divinity
D.C. District of Columbia
D.D. Divinitatis Doctor, Doctor of Divinity
Del. Delaware
Dem. *Dema'i*
dim. diminutive
diss. dissertation
Dn. *Daniel*
D.Phil. Doctor of Philosophy
Dt. *Deuteronomy*
Du. Dutch
E Elohist (source of the Pentateuch)
Eccl. *Ecclesiastes*
ed. editor (pl., eds.); edition; edited by

ʿEduy. *ʿEduyyot*
e.g. *exempli gratia,* for example
Egyp. Egyptian
1 En. *1 Enoch*
2 En. *2 Enoch*
3 En. *3 Enoch*
Eng. English
enl. enlarged
Eph. *Ephesians*
ʿEruv. *ʿEruvin*
1 Esd. *1 Esdras*
2 Esd. *2 Esdras*
3 Esd. *3 Esdras*
4 Esd. *4 Esdras*
esp. especially
Est. Estonian
Est. *Esther*
et al. *et alii,* and others
etc. *et cetera,* and so forth
Eth. Ethiopic
EV English version
Ex. *Exodus*
exp. expanded
Ez. *Ezekiel*
Ezr. *Ezra*
2 Ezr. *2 Ezra*
4 Ezr. *4 Ezra*
f. feminine; and following (pl., ff.)
fasc. fascicle (pl., fascs.)
fig. figure (pl., figs.)
Finn. Finnish
fl. *floruit,* flourished
Fla. Florida
Fr. French
frag. fragment
ft. feet
Ga. Georgia
Gal. *Galatians*
Gaul. Gaulish
Ger. German
Giṭ. *Giṭṭin*
Gn. *Genesis*
Gr. Greek
Ḥag. *Ḥagigah*
Ḥal. *Ḥallah*
Hau. Hausa
Hb. *Habakkuk*
Heb. Hebrew
Heb. *Hebrews*
Hg. *Haggai*
Hitt. Hittite
Hor. *Horayot*
Hos. *Hosea*
Ḥul. *Ḥullin*
Hung. Hungarian
ibid. *ibidem,* in the same place (as the one immediately preceding)
Icel. Icelandic
i.e. *id est,* that is
IE Indo-European
Ill. Illinois
Ind. Indiana
intro. introduction
Ir. Gael. Irish Gaelic
Iran. Iranian
Is. *Isaiah*
Ital. Italian
J Yahvist (source of the Pentateuch)
Jas. *James*
Jav. Javanese
Jb. *Job*
Jdt. *Judith*
Jer. *Jeremiah*
Jgs. *Judges*
Jl. *Joel*
Jn. *John*
1 Jn. *1 John*
2 Jn. *2 John*
3 Jn. *3 John*
Jon. *Jonah*
Jos. *Joshua*
Jpn. Japanese
JPS Jewish Publication Society translation (1985) of the Hebrew Bible
J.T. Jerusalem Talmud
Jub. *Jubilees*
Kans. Kansas
Kel. *Kelim*
Ker. *Keritot*
Ket. *Ketubbot*
1 Kgs. *1 Kings*
2 Kgs. *2 Kings*
Khois. Khoisan
Kil. *Kilʾayim*
km kilometers
Kor. Korean
Ky. Kentucky
l. line (pl., ll.)
La. Louisiana
Lam. *Lamentations*
Lat. Latin
Latv. Latvian
L. en Th. Licencié en Théologie, Licentiate in Theology
L. ès L. Licencié ès Lettres, Licentiate in Literature
Let. Jer. *Letter of Jeremiah*
lit. literally
Lith. Lithuanian
Lk. *Luke*
LL Late Latin
LL.D. Legum Doctor, Doctor of Laws
Lv. *Leviticus*
m meters
m. masculine
M.A. Master of Arts
Ma ʿas. *Maʿaserot*
Ma ʿas. Sh. *Maʿ aser sheni*
Mak. *Makkot*
Makh. *Makhshirin*
Mal. *Malachi*
Mar. Marathi
Mass. Massachusetts
1 Mc. *1 Maccabees*
2 Mc. *2 Maccabees*
3 Mc. *3 Maccabees*
4 Mc. *4 Maccabees*
Md. Maryland
M.D. Medicinae Doctor, Doctor of Medicine
ME Middle English
Meg. *Megillah*
Me ʿil. *Meʿilah*
Men. *Menaḥot*
MHG Middle High German
mi. miles
Mi. *Micah*
Mich. Michigan
Mid. *Middot*
Minn. Minnesota
Miq. *Miqvaʾot*
MIran. Middle Iranian
Miss. Mississippi
Mk. *Mark*
Mo. Missouri
Moʿed Q. *Moʿed qaṭan*
Mont. Montana
MPers. Middle Persian
MS. *manuscriptum,* manuscript (pl., MSS)
Mt. *Matthew*
MT Masoretic text
n. note
Na. *Nahum*
Nah. Nahuatl
Naz. *Nazir*
N.B. *nota bene,* take careful note
N.C. North Carolina
n.d. no date
N.Dak. North Dakota
NEB New English Bible
Nebr. Nebraska

Ned. *Nedarim*
Neg. *Negaʿim*
Neh. *Nehemiah*
Nev. Nevada
N.H. New Hampshire
Nid. *Niddah*
N.J. New Jersey
Nm. *Numbers*
N.Mex. New Mexico
no. number (pl., nos.)
Nor. Norwegian
n.p. no place
n.s. new series
N.Y. New York
Ob. *Obadiah*
O.Cist. Ordo Cisterciencium, Order of Cîteaux (Cistercians)
OCS Old Church Slavonic
OE Old English
O.F.M. Ordo Fratrum Minorum, Order of Friars Minor (Franciscans)
OFr. Old French
Ohal. *Ohalot*
OHG Old High German
OIr. Old Irish
OIran. Old Iranian
Okla. Oklahoma
ON Old Norse
O.P. Ordo Praedicatorum, Order of Preachers (Dominicans)
OPers. Old Persian
op. cit. *opere citato,* in the work cited
OPrus. Old Prussian
Oreg. Oregon
ʿOrl. *ʿOrlah*
O.S.B. Ordo Sancti Benedicti, Order of Saint Benedict (Benedictines)
p. page (pl., pp.)
P Priestly (source of the Pentateuch)
Pa. Pennsylvania
Pahl. Pahlavi
Par. *Parah*
para. paragraph (pl., paras.)
Pers. Persian
Pes. *Pesahim*
Ph.D. Philosophiae Doctor, Doctor of Philosophy
Phil. *Philippians*
Phlm. *Philemon*
Phoen. Phoenician
pl. plural; plate (pl., pls.)
PM *post meridiem,* after noon
Pol. Polish
pop. population
Port. Portuguese
Prv. *Proverbs*
Ps. *Psalms*
Ps. 151 *Psalm 151*
Ps. Sol. *Psalms of Solomon*
pt. part (pl., pts.)
1Pt. *1 Peter*
2 Pt. *2 Peter*
Pth. Parthian
Q hypothetical source of the synoptic Gospels
Qid. *Qiddushin*
Qin. *Qinnim*
r. reigned; ruled
Rab. *Rabbah*
rev. revised
R. ha-Sh. *Roʾsh ha-shanah*
R.I. Rhode Island
Rom. Romanian
Rom. *Romans*
R.S.C.J. Societas Sacratissimi Cordis Jesu, Religious of the Sacred Heart
RSV Revised Standard Version of the Bible
Ru. *Ruth*
Rus. Russian
Rv. *Revelation*
Rv. Ezr. *Revelation of Ezra*
San. *Sanhedrin*
S.C. South Carolina
Scot. Gael. Scottish Gaelic
S.Dak. South Dakota
sec. section (pl., secs.)
Sem. Semitic
ser. series
sg. singular
Sg. *Song of Songs*
Sg. of 3 *Prayer of Azariah and the Song of the Three Young Men*
Shab. *Shabbat*
Shav. *Shavuʿot*
Sheq. *Sheqalim*
Sib. Or. *Sibylline Oracles*
Sind. Sindhi
Sinh. Sinhala
Sir. *Ben Sira*
S.J. Societas Jesu, Society of Jesus (Jesuits)
Skt. Sanskrit
1 Sm. *1 Samuel*
2 Sm. *2 Samuel*
Sogd. Sogdian
Soṭ. *Soṭah*
sp. species (pl., spp.)
Span. Spanish
sq. square
S.S.R. Soviet Socialist Republic
st. stanza (pl., ss.)
S.T.M. Sacrae Theologiae Magister, Master of Sacred Theology
Suk. *Sukkah*
Sum. Sumerian
supp. supplement; supplementary
Sus. *Susanna*
s.v. *sub verbo,* under the word (pl., s.v.v.)
Swed. Swedish
Syr. Syriac
Syr. Men. *Syriac Menander*
Taʿan. *Taʿanit*
Tam. Tamil
Tam. *Tamid*
Tb. *Tobit*
T.D. *Taishō shinshū daizōkyō,* edited by Takakusu Junjirō et al. (Tokyo,1922–1934)
Tem. *Temurah*
Tenn. Tennessee
Ter. Terumot
Ṭev. Y. *Ṭevul yom*
Tex. Texas
Th.D. Theologicae Doctor, Doctor of Theology
1 Thes. *1 Thessalonians*
2 Thes. *2 Thessalonians*
Thrac. Thracian
Ti. *Titus*
Tib. Tibetan
1 Tm. *1 Timothy*
2 Tm. *2 Timothy*
T. of 12 *Testaments of the Twelve Patriarchs*
Ṭoh. *ṭohorot*
Tong. Tongan
trans. translator, translators; translated by; translation
Turk. Turkish
Ukr. Ukrainian
Upan. *Upaniṣad*
U.S. United States
U.S.S.R. Union of Soviet Socialist Republics
Uqts. *Uqtsin*
v. verse (pl., vv.)
Va. Virginia
var. variant; variation
Viet. Vietnamese

viz. *videlicet,* namely
vol. volume (pl., vols.)
Vt. Vermont
Wash. Washington
Wel. Welsh
Wis. Wisconsin
Wis. *Wisdom of Solomon*
W.Va. West Virginia
Wyo. Wyoming

Yad. *Yadayim*
Yev. *Yevamot*
Yi. Yiddish
Yor. Yoruba
Zav. *Zavim*
Zec. *Zechariah*
Zep. *Zephaniah*
Zev. *Zevaḥim*

* hypothetical
? uncertain; possibly; perhaps
° degrees
+ plus
– minus
= equals; is equivalent to
× by; multiplied by
→ yields

S
CONTINUED

SOUTH AMERICAN INDIAN RELIGIONS

This entry consists of the following articles:

AN OVERVIEW
MYTHIC THEMES
HISTORY OF STUDY

SOUTH AMERICAN INDIAN RELIGIONS: AN OVERVIEW

Since the Indians of South America do not conform culturally, there is no religious uniformity among them. Despite this inconsistency, an acceptable overview can be achieved by subdividing the continent's large, geographically distinct regions into the following cultural areas.

1. *The Andes.* This mountain range stretches from present-day Colombia to Chile. The highland regions of Peru, lying between the Pacific coast region and the valleys that cut through the mountain range, were taken over in the distant past by highly advanced agrarian cultures. Among the most significant of these cultures was the Inca empire, which extended into the dawn of historical times. Direct descendants of earlier Andean cultures, the Quechua and Aymara peoples inhabit present-day Peru and Bolivia.
2. *Amazon and Orinoco rivers.* These jungle- and savanna-covered regions were conquered by tropical farming cultures. From the standpoint of cultural history, this area also includes the mountainous sections of present-day Guyana; in early historical periods, the Amazon cultural area eventually spread to the Atlantic coast. As in the past, it is now inhabited by tribes belonging to a number of linguistic families, both small and large (Tupi, Carib, Arawak, Tucano, and Pano), and by a number of linguistically isolated tribes. Together they form cultural subareas that display religious specializations.
3. *Mountains of eastern Brazil.* This region is occupied by groups of the Ge linguistic family, who practice rudimentary farming methods; they settled in these hinterlands of the Atlantic coast region, joining indigenous hunting tribes. A few of these Ge groups have survived culturally up to the present time.

CLOCKWISE FROM TOP LEFT CORNER. Sixteenth-century illuminated miniature of dancing dervishes, from the "Sessions of the Lovers." *[©Bodlein Library, University of Oxford]*; South torana at the Great Stupa at Sāñcī, India. *[©Adam Woolfitt/Corbis]*; Eleventh-century Śiva Naṭarāja from Southern India. Musée Guimet, Paris. *[©Giraudon/Art Resource, N.Y.]*; The "Wedded Rocks" at Futamigaura in Ise, Japan. *[©Werner Forman/Art Resource, N.Y.]*; Angkor Vatt, Cambodia. *[Dave G. Houser/Corbis]*.

4. *The Gran Chaco.* The bush and grass steppes of this area stretch from the Paraguay River west to the foothills of the Andes. The area was initially divided among hunters, fishers, and gatherers, and these cultures came under diverse influences from neighboring agriculturists. A series of more or less acculturated groups of the Guiacurú linguistic family (the Mataco and the Mascoy) may still be encountered at the present time.

5. *The Pampas and Patagonia.* Hunting groups wandered through these flatlands of the southern regions of South America. The extinct Pampa and Tehuelche Indians were among the peoples of this region. The Tierra del Fuego archipelago, near the Strait of Magellan, is also included within this territory. Although the inhabitants of these regions—the Selk'nam (Ona), Yahgan, and Alacaluf—are considered extinct, their culture and religion were well documented before they vanished.

6. *Southern Andes.* This area, especially its middle and southernmost regions, is populated by the agrarian Araucanians of Chile, who have prospered up to the present time. Their success has been attributed to their development of a self-sufficient culture a few decades before the Spanish invasion in the early sixteenth century. This development was the result of the influence of highly advanced Peruvian cultures, as the Inca empire progressed to the Maule River in Chile. In the eighteenth and nineteenth centuries, the Araucanians expanded eastward, but this part of the group, like its predecessors in the area, eventually became extinct.

Pronounced differences in religious phenomena appear within each of these cultural areas; these phenomena present certain discrepancies when seen together. The most outstanding contrast appears between the highly developed Andean religions, which are founded on priesthood and ruling cults, and the religious beliefs of the tribes in the eastern lowlands. Some typical examples of their forms and their respective beliefs should help to clarify their differences.

DEITIES, CULTURE HEROES, AND ANCESTORS. The tradition of a creator as the prime mover and teacher of mankind is universal among the Indians of South America (Métraux, 1949). In the majority of cases, the mythical person most often represented is not directly involved in the daily activities of mortals and therefore does not enjoy particular veneration. There is no fundamental discrepancy between this disinterested deity and the omnipotent creator whose cultic worship is integrated into a religious system; similar characteristics are attributed to both figures. A god previously venerated may fade to the position of a mythical figure, just as a mythical character can achieve cultic significance.

Under certain conditions, a creator, a culture hero, or an ancestor may rise to the position of a deity or supreme being. Such a case occurred in the old cultures of Peru with the religious figure Viracocha. Perhaps originally a culture hero of the Quechua or some other Andean people, Viracocha eventually ascended to the ranks of the highest pantheon as a result of speculation on the part of the Inca priesthood. At the beginning of the sixteenth century, Viracocha was represented in anthropomorphic sculptures that appeared in special Inca temples and was venerated through prayers and sacrificial offerings. Inti, the Inca sun god, is portrayed with a human face within a golden disk, and as the tribal god of the ruling Inca dynasty he was embodied in the Inca emperor.

The establishment of an elaborate cult for an indigenous supreme being is a typical occurrence in highly advanced cultures, but such cults are seldom found in South America outside the Andes region. When they do appear elsewhere they are likely the result of the influence of these advanced civilizations on compatible cultural and geographical situations. A report by Karin Hissink and Albert Hahn (1961) on the cultures from the lowlands of Bolivia, near the Andes, points out that the Tacana Indians of the Beni River area maintain the belief in a supreme being known as Caquiahuaca, who created the earth, human beings, animals, and plants. An old man with a white beard, Caquiahuaca lives in a cave in a mountain that bears his name and that forms the center of the world. In temples he is represented by a small beeswax figure surrounded by a series of larger wooden statues that represent the lower gods, known as *edutzi,* who assist him. As the instructor of the priest-shamans, or *yanacona,* Caquiahuaca assists them in the performance of their office, and as their master he is responsible for their religious vocation.

In addition to this, Deavoavai, the lord of the animals, also represents a creator, culture hero, and master of the dead. In his capacity as ruler of the game, Deavoavai is rooted in an earlier cultural-historical level—that of hunters, fishers, and gatherers. Such a deity is also found among other agricultural peoples, including peoples of the Amazon lowlands. Despite their reliance on an economic subsistence that has long since undergone the transition from a hunting to an agricultural base, these groups of the Amazon Basin maintain a religious emphasis that incorporates a dependence on a powerful being who controls the game, an aspect that will receive attention below. It is sufficient here to point out that within this region a relationship exists between the master of the hunted game and the supreme being, a concept first recognized by Adolf E. Jensen (1951).

Culture hero as supreme being. Konrad T. Preuss was convinced that Moma ("father") was the paramount, indeed, the only true god of the Witóto of the Putumayo area of the northwestern Amazon and that he was identified with the moon. According to creation legends among these people, Moma came into existence from the "word," that is, he was a product of magico-religious incantations and myths that are endowed with supernatural powers. He was also the personification of the "word," which he bestowed upon human beings, and the "word" was the doctrine that represented the driving force behind all religious ceremonies that Moma introduced. The original father created the earth and all things of the world from the archetype (*naino*), the "not-substance," of each individual entity. On the other hand, in a myth that explains the creation of the organic world, Moma extracts all the plants and animals from his own body. The blossoms of the food plants used by humans are evidence of his omnipotent presence, and when the trees of the earth no longer bear fruit they go to Moma in the underworld. In addition to being the moon in the heavens, he resides below as master of the dead. He was the first being to experience the suffering of death, but in the fruits of the plants he is continually resurrected.

Among the Witóto, such a representation demonstrates intensely the character of a particular form of culture hero, that is, one who is at the same time a supreme entity. Jensen applied the term *dema deity* in describing such a culture hero among the Marind-anim of New Guinea (Jensen, 1951). The distinguishing characteristics of this deity are revealed in his slaying, which occurred in primal times, and the consequent growth of all food plants out of his body.

Waríkyana supreme being. A supreme god is also manifested among the Waríkyana (Arikena), a Carib-speaking tribe of the Brazilian Guianas. The highest deity in the religion of the Waríkyana is Pura (a name that, according to the Franciscan missionary Albert Kruse, means "god"). With his servant Mura, Pura stands on the zenith of heaven's mountains and observes all things that take place below (Kruse, 1955). At the command of Pura, the rain is sent from the sky. Pura and Mura are small men with red skin and are ageless and immortal. They appeared at the beginning of the world, together with water, the sky, and the earth. In early times Pura and Mura came down to earth and created humans and animals. Because mankind did not obey the ethical precepts of Pura, he retaliated by sending a great fire that was followed by a deluge. A segment of the human race survived this catastrophe, and the Waríkyana people believe that when the end of time comes, Pura will create another holocaust. It was therefore Pura to whom prayers were directed, and in his honor a celebration took place in which manioc cakes were offered to him.

Protasius Frikel, another Franciscan, completed Kruse's description, noting that the Waríkyana view the supreme being as a reflection of the primal sun (Frickel, 1957). Pura continues to qualify as the superior god, and in addition he was also thought of as the world onto which the primal sun pours its blinding light. Pura also represents universal power, a belief that Frikel considers to be relatively recent among the Waríkyana.

In another instance, Pura is considered to be a "primordial man" or culture hero (ibid.). In any case, Pura resides in heaven and reigns over all elements. His companion and servant Mura is somehow connected with the moon and displays some features of a trickster. Such dual relationships as sun and moon, god and companion, culture hero and trickster—pairs that are often represented as twins—are encountered frequently in South American mythology. According to the Waríkyana, death is the beginning of the soul's journey to heaven, where it will be reincarnated—a journey that is modeled after the eternal cycle of the sun.

Yanoama and Mundurucú supreme beings. Kruse's work stimulated Josef Haekel to write an article about monotheistic tendencies among Carib-speakers and other Indian groups in the Guianas, as well as among those groups bordering the western areas of the Guianas (Haekel, 1958). According to Haekel's findings, reference to the name *Pura* in connection with a supreme being occurred in no other Carib-speaking tribe except the Waríkyana. To the west of their territory in the Guianas, however, the expression is used with only slight variation, even among different linguistic groups such as the isolated Yanoama (Yanonami) on the Venezuelan and Brazilian borders. According to the beliefs of some groups in Brazil, Pore is the name of a supreme being who descended to earth (Becher, 1974). Together with the moon, who is known as Perimbo, Pore established a dual relationship composed of both sexes—male and female—that was conceptually unified as a supreme entity who controls heaven, earth, and the underworld. As the most well-informed researcher of the Brazilian Yanoama, Hans Becher considers their mode of life to be strongly influenced by myths connected with the moon; the sun, on the other hand, is entirely unimportant. The awe in which these Indians hold Pore and Perimbo is so intense that they do not call on this supreme being directly. Instead, they employ the indirect services of intermediaries in the forms of plant and animal spirits (*hekura*) that reside on specific mountain ranges. Shamans identify with these spirits and when intoxicated with snuff come into contact with them.

There are strong similarities between the supreme being, Pura, of the Waríkyana and the figure of Karusakaibe, the "father of the Mundurucú" (an expression coined by Kruse, who was also a missionary among this central Tupi tribe). Karusakaibe once lived on earth and created human souls, the sky, the stars, game animals, fish, and cultivated plants, together with all their respective guardian spirits, and he made the trees and plants fruitful. Karusakaibe is omniscient: he taught the Mundurucú how to hunt and farm, among other things. He is the lawgiver of the tribe and the originator of its dual social structure. Karusakaibe is immortal. Because he was treated badly at one time by the Mundurucú, he went off to the foggy regions of the heavens. He is also credited with having transformed himself into the bright sun of the dry season. When the end of the world comes, he will set the world and all mankind on fire. But until that time he will look after the well-being of his children, the Mundurucú, who direct their prayers and offerings to him when fishing and hunting and in times of sickness. Martin Gusinde (1960) is of the opinion that Karusakaibe was once a superior god among the Mundurucú. Later his status changed to that of a culture hero.

Tupi-Guaraní supreme beings. Resonances of a supreme being concept among the Tupi-Guaraní linguistic groups are mentioned by Alfred Métraux, who was the most important specialist in their religious systems (Métraux, 1949). Among these groups, the creator often has the characteristics of a transformer, and as a rule he is also the lawgiver and teacher of early mankind. After he fulfills these tasks, he journeys westward to the end of the world, where he rules over the shades of the dead.

Among the ancient Tupinamba of the Atlantic coast and the Guarayo of eastern Bolivia, traces were found of a cult devoted to the creator, Tamoi. In Métraux's opinion, the various culture heroes, including Monan and Mairamonan) were derived from a single mythical figure—the tribal grandfather, Tamoi. The occurrence of an eclipse of the sun or the moon is a signal that according to the beliefs of the Tupinamba relates directly to the end of the world, and the men must sing a hymn to Tamoi. These eschatological beliefs are characteristic of the Tupi-Guaraní and may be connected to the messianic movements of the Tupinamba at the beginning of the Portuguese colonization period. Such movements frequently led to mass migrations in search of the mythological land of Tamoi, a region perceived as a paradise where the inhabitants share immortality and eternal youth. A similar cult devoted to the worship of the great ancestor among the Guarayo was coupled with messianic movements at the beginning of the nineteenth century. In this case, Tamoi was considered the ruler of the celestial western kingdom of the dead as well as the dominant figure at burial rites and in beliefs about the afterlife.

The most revered god of the Guaraní-Apapocuvá according to Curt Nimuendajú, the outstanding authority on this tribe at the beginning of the twentieth century, is the creator Nanderuvuçu ("our great father"). Nanderuvuçu has withdrawn to a remote region of eternal darkness that is illuminated solely by the light that radiates from his breast (Nimuendajú, 1914). He holds the means to destroy the world but retains the privilege of using this power for as long as he pleases. Because he is not concerned about the daily activities that occur on earth, no cultic practices are directed toward him. His wife Nandecy ("our mother") lives in the "land without evil," a paradise that at one time was believed to be in the east and then again in the west; this paradise also became the goal of various messianic movements of the Guaraní-Apapocuvá.

Ge solar and lunar gods. In the eastern Brazilian area, the majority of the northwestern and central Ge tribes (Apinagé, Canella, and Xerente) hold that the Sun and Moon are the only true gods. Both Sun and Moon are masculine. Though not related to each other, they are companions; the Sun, however, is predominant.

The supremacy of a solar god among the Apinagé led Jensen to the conclusion that here the mythical concept of a sun-man has a secondary identity, that is, he is also a supreme god (Jensen, 1951). To support this theory, Jensen directs attention to the fact that human begins alone have the privilege of addressing this deity as "my father." He finds additional support for this theory in the prayers that are offered to the solar god and in the role he plays in visions. An Apinagé chief spoke of an encounter he once had on a hunting expedition in which he met the sun-father in human form. The Apinagé consider the establishment of the dual organization of the tribe, as well as the placement of the two moieties within the circular settlement, to be the work of the Sun. A final supporting element observed by Nimuendajú (1939) is the Apinagé's consumption of round meat patties, which are eaten at feasts and are said to represent the sun.

At the beginning of the harvest season, a four-day dance festival is celebrated in honor of the Sun at which the dancers apply red paint to themselves in patterns representative of the sun. The Canella also publicly implore the heavenly gods, the Sun and the Moon, for rain, the safety of the game animals, the success of their harvest, and an abundance of wild fruit. In a similar manner, the Xerente call the sun "Our Creator" and pay the same devout tributes to the Sun-father as do the Apinagé. The Sun and the Moon themselves, however, never appear, but the Xerente receive instructions from these solar and lunar bodies through other celestial gods (the planets Venus, Mars, Jupiter) who are associated with the Sun and the Moon moieties. The most important ceremony of the Xerente is the Great Feast, at which a pole is erected so that the tribe members may climb to the top and pray to the Sun. At the end of the celebration, the master of ceremonies climbs this pole. Once at the top, he stretches his hand outward to the east and receives a message from a star within the constellation Orion, who acts as a celestial courier. In most cases, satisfaction is expressed and rain is assured.

The ceremonial pole as a link to the heavenly world is also believed to have been employed by the Botocudos, who were among the hunting tribes that once lived near the Atlantic Ocean but are now extinct. Their religion was apparently characterized by a belief in a supreme being in heaven, named White Head because of the image he created (the top of his head is white and his face is covered with red hair). He was also the chief of the heavenly spirits, who were known as *maret.* The *maret* spirits could be called to earth by the shaman, but in a form that is visible only to him; they also had to return to heaven in the same way. They took on the function of intermediaries between mortals and the supreme being when the shaman, through prayers and songs, turned to them in times of sickness or in an emergency. No one ever saw Father White Head face to face; although he was sympathetic toward mankind, he punished murderers and was responsible for sending rain storms.

Mother goddesses. As Métraux (1946) pointed out, the missionaries who searched for belief in a supreme being among the Indians of the Gran Chaco were not at all successful. The only mythical personality who comes close to the concept of a superior god, in Métraux's opinion, is Eschetewuarha ("mother of the universe"), the dominant deity among the Chamacoco, a Samuco group in the north Chaco region. She is the mother of numerous forest spirits as well as of the clouds. As the controller of all things, Eschetewuarha ensures that mankind receives water. In return for this favor, she expects her people to send songs to her nightly, and when such expectations are not fulfilled she punishes them. Herbert Baldus (1932), who provided in-depth information about Eschetewuarha, compares her with the universal mother of the Cágaba (Koghi), a Chibcha tribe in Colombia that had been influenced by more advanced cultures. This comparison facilitates postulating at least a phenomenological relationship between the two.

The obvious characteristics of a supreme god are apparently present in Kuma, the goddess of the Yaruro, who subsist on fishing, hunting, and gathering along the Capanaparo River, a tributary of the Orinoco in Venezuela. She is considered to be a moon goddess and consort of the sun god, who is unimportant. Kuma created the world with the help of two brothers, the Water Serpent and the Jaguar, after whom the tribal moieties were named. Although she apparently created the first two human beings herself, her son, Hatschawa, became the educator and culture hero of mankind. Kuma dominates a paradise in the west in which gigantic counterparts for every plant and animal species exist. Shamans are capable of seeing the land of Kuma in dreams and visions and are able to send their souls there. As a reliable informant explained, "Everything originated from Kuma and everything that the Yaruro do has been arranged so by her; the other gods and cultural heroes act according to her laws" (Petrullo, 1939). Métraux drew attention to the typological affinities between Kuma and Gauteovan, the mother goddess of the Cágaba, who in turn is connected with Eschetewuarha of the Chamacoco (Métraux, 1949).

Supreme beings of Tierra del Fuego. Among the people living in the southern regions of the continent, a belief in a supreme being is common in hunting and fishing tribes, especially the Selk'nam (Ona) of Tierra del Fuego and the Yahgan and Alacaluf of the Tierra del Fuego archipelago. Despite many years of European influence in this area and the astonishing similarities of their beliefs to aspects of Christianity, Métraux believed that the religion of these three tribes remained substantially independent of Christianity (Métraux, 1949). Martin Gusinde, a member of the ethnological school of Wilhelm Schmidt, provided us with research information about these tribes shortly before their cultural extinction (Gusinde, 1931, 1937, 1974). The Selk'nam, the Yahgan (Yámana), and the Alacaluf (Halakwulip) maintain belief in a supreme being who is an invisible, omnipotent, and omniscient spirit living in heaven, beyond the stars. He has no physical body and is immortal; having neither wife nor children, he has no material desires. Among the Alacaluf, the creator god is named Xolas ("star"), and despite the great distance that separates him from the earth, he concerns himself with the daily life of human beings. Through his initiative a soul is allowed to enter the body of a newborn baby; it remains in the human being until death, at which time it returns to Xolas. The Alacaluf were obliged to abstain from any form of veneration of this perfect supreme being, since any attempt to influence his will would have been fruitless. For this reason, it is not known what formal prayers were addressed to Xolas nor whether cultic practices associated with him were performed.

Watauineiwa ("ancient one, eternal one") behaved quite differently, according to the beliefs of the Yahgan. He preferred to be addressed as "my father," and he was reputed to be the lord of the world and ruler over life and death. He was an astute observer of the actions of humans and punished violations of the laws he had established in relation to morals and customs. Such rules were inculcated into the young (boys and girls concurrently) during initiation rituals, which formed the core of Yahgan religious life. In seeking contact with Watauineiwa, the individual Yahgan could draw upon numerous established prayers. A person would implore Watauineiwa, who was the controller of the game animals and of all food plants, to help him to secure his subsistence needs and would turn to Watauineiwa to ensure his continued health, to cure him of sickness, and to protect him from inclement weather and from drastic environmental changes. But Watauineiwa was also the target for harsh complaints in cases of ailments and misfortune, and in the event of death he was accused with the words "murderer in heaven."

The supreme god of the Yahgan maintained a closer contact with human beings than did Témaukel, the Selk'nam's supreme god. Témaukel ("the one above in heaven") was considered to be the originator and protector of mankind's moral and social laws, although he was otherwise uninterested in daily life on earth. Témaukel had existed from the beginning of time, but he entrusted Kenos, the first ancestor, with the final configuration of the world and the institution of social customs. In spite of the respect they accorded Témaukel, the Selk'nam prayed to him less frequently than did the Yahgan to their supreme god. Contrastingly, the Selk'nam meticulously observed the practice of throwing the first piece of meat from the evening meal out of their huts with the words "This is for him up there," an action that can be considered a form of sacrificial offering. The dead were also believed to travel to Témaukel.

Supreme beings of the Pampas, Patagonia, and the southern Andes. Although our knowledge of the religious practices and beliefs of the earlier inhabitants of the Pampas and Patagonia is sparse and relatively superficial, it is almost certain that the Tehuelche had a supreme being. Like Témaukel of the Selk'nam, the god of the Tehuelche was characterized by his lack of interest in worldly activities; he was also lord of the dead. This supreme being was, in general, sympathetic toward human beings, but there is no proof of a public cult devoted to him. Traditionally he was called Soychu. A benevolent supreme being of the same name was also found in the religious beliefs of the Pampa Indians, at least after the eighteenth century.

It would appear that the tribal religions of the southern areas of South America were, in general, marked by a belief in a supreme god. The Araucanians of the southern Andes, and in particular the Mapuche, have left behind traces of the concept of a superior god, as well as a devout veneration of him that survived well into the eighteenth century. In most instances the supreme being is referred to as either Ngenechen ("lord of mankind") or Ngenemapun ("lord of the land"). Other, more feminine descriptions may reveal an androgynous character. Ngenechen is thought of as living in heaven or in the sun and is credited with being the creator of the world as well as the provider of life and of the fruits of the earth. Although he is responsible for the well-being of mankind, he is not associated with the moral laws. An individual would turn to Ngenechen in personal emergencies with prayers, the sacrifice of an animal, or an offering of the first fruits of the harvest. A public ritual known as the Ngillatun, which has survived up to the present time among the Araucanians, consists of offering the blood of a sacrificial animal to him. Two important objects employed at this feast are the rewe, a thick, step-notched pole, and a sacrificial altar, both of which are circled by the participants at the beginning of the ceremony. In addition to the master of ceremonies, the female shaman *(machi)* takes over some of the most vital functions at the Ngillatun. With a flat drum (*kultrun*), she climbs the ceremonial pole and upon reaching the top turns to Ngenechen, who is now symbolically nearer. Métraux (1949, p. 561) and John M. Cooper (1946, pp. 742–743) have both come to the conclusion that in this instance the older features of god among the Araucanians have been conceptually modified through the centuries to conform with the concepts of the conquering Western civilization.

Earlier Spanish chroniclers viewed the thunder god Pillán as the central, if not the supreme, being of the Araucanians. Ewald Böning, in a more recent account, pointed out convincingly that the Mapuche describe Pillán in general as a powerful, extraordinary, and tremendous apparition (Böning, 1974, p. 175). Pillán primarily represents an impersonal power, but he can also manifest himself in a personal form. The concept of impersonal power seldom occurs in the mentality of the South American Indians. The Nambikwára of the Mato Grosso, for example, believe in an abstract power, known as *nande*, that is present in certain things and that contains a magic poison or a real poison. Although any individual can, to a certain extent, achieve contact with *nande*, it is the shamans above all who can manipulate this power.

NATURE SPIRITS, HUNTING RITUALS, AND VEGETATION RITES. In dealing with beliefs in a superior god, I have mentioned how the lord, or master, of the animals is one way in which the supreme being is conceptualized among South American tribes. Owing to the fact that hunting belongs to one of the oldest phases of human history, gods who are associated with this category of subsistence represent archaic beliefs. Not only do the Indians of South America believe in a master of all animals but they frequently display a belief in supernatural protectors of the various animal species. Such nature spirits characteristically display strong individualistic tendencies and are often considered to be demons (Métraux, 1949). From the standpoint of cultural history, they are related to the lord of all beasts and have affinities with him that stem from the same hunting and fishing mentality.

Tupi master of the animals. The most important representation of a master of the animals in the tropical lowlands is the forest spirit Korupira, or Kaapora, of the ancient eastern Tupi and a few primitive isolates of the Tupi tribes, as well as of the *caboclo*, or mixed race, people of Brazil. A series of recorded myths and verbal descriptions have facilitated a reconstruction of this deity.

Although the use of two names creates the impression that Korupira and Kaapora are two separate mythical figures, they are so closely related as to be nearly indistinguishable. Korupira, the master of the animals, is the protecting spirit of the beasts as well as of the forest; he punishes those who maliciously destroy the game and rewards those who obey him or those on whom he takes pity. For a portion of tobacco, Korupira will lift the restrictions that he places on the killing of his animals. Encounters in recent times with a small isolated Tupi tribe, the Pauserna Guarasug'wä, who live in eastern Bolivia, have shown that the belief in Korupira/Kaapora has survived. Kaapora originated as a human being—that is, he was created from the soul of a Guarasu Indian. He is the lord of all animals of the forest and has put his mark somewhere on each of the wild animals, usually on its ear. A hunter must turn to him with a plea to release part of the game, but he is only allowed to kill as many as he will absolutely need for the moment. In thanksgiving for his success, the hunter will leave the skin, the feet, or the entrails of the slain animal behind when he leaves the forest: by doing so he begs forgiveness from the animal for having killed it. After such reconciliations, the soul of the animal returns home to Kaapora. Presumably this tribe, like others, believes either that the spiritual owner of the game will create an entirely new animal or that the soul of the animal itself is capable of reproducing a new material form from the remains the hunter leaves behind. (The preservation of the bones of game in the so-called bone ritual appears to be widely distributed throughout South America.)

Kurupi-vyra of the Guarasug'wä is a part-animal, part-human forest spirit, but not a lord of the animals. He is, however, a possible source of help for hunters in emergencies. At such times he will lend his miraculous weapon, a hardwood wand that he himself uses to kill game, and in return he demands total obedience. Evidence of a master of the animals and a helping spirit is well documented in other regions of the South American subcontinent.

Mundurucú protective mother spirit. In the Amazon region, the idea of a lord of all animals is sometimes replaced by the belief in a lord or master of each individual animal species, and sometimes both concepts occur. Starting from the basic Tupi premise that every object in nature possesses a mother (*cy*), the Mundurucú, a Tupi-speaking group, recognize and venerate a maternal spirit of all game. She is the protector of the animal kingdom against mankind and maintains a mother-child relationship between herself and the beasts. Although she possesses a homogeneous character, she does not have a definite external form, nor does she exist as an independent personal goddess. The shaman alone knows and understands the methods for approaching her. In an ecstatic frenzy, he will feed her sweet manioc when she manifests herself in any one of her various forms (for example, as a specific type of land tortoise). The Mundurucú also attribute to each individual animal species a mother spirit that serves as a species protector.

Formerly the Mundurucú held a reconciliation ceremony at the beginning of the rainy season in honor of the guardian spirits of the game and fish. At the climax of this ceremony, two men sang songs devoted to the spirit of each animal in order to call on the spirit mothers. They performed this act while sitting in front of the skulls of numerous animals that had been taken in the hunts of the previous year. These skulls were arranged in parallel rows, according to species, in front of the men's house. Additionally, a bowl of manioc porridge was offered to the mothers of the animals to eat. When the shaman was convinced that the spirits had arrived, he blew tobacco smoke over the skulls and then, using a bamboo tube, proceeded to symbolically suck out arrowheads or bullets that had entered the spirits. Through this action the animals were pacified and the dancing could begin. Such dances, performed by the men, consisted of pantomimes of a herd of peccary, followed by representations of the tapir and other animals. This organized presentation by the Mundurucú was the most pregnant and illuminating of such ceremonies in the Amazon region.

Hunting dances. The concept of a lord, or master, of a particular species also plays an important role in the religious systems of the Carib-speaking tribes of the Guianas. This is exemplified by the frequent use of the term *father* or *grandfather* when speaking of a certain type of animal. The Taulipáng and the Arecuná of the inland regions of the Guianas believe that each individual animal type has a father (*podole*), who is envisioned as either a real or a gigantic, legendary representative of that particular species, and who displays supernatural qualities. Two "animal fathers" are especially meaningful for their hunting ritual: the father of the peccary and the father of the fish. Both of these figures were originally human shamans who were transformed into spiritual beings and became incorporated into the opening dances of the Parischerá and the Tukui, the magical hunting dances of the Taulipáng. In the Parischerá, a long chain of participants, wearing palm-leaf costumes and representing a grunting peccary herd, dance to the booming of cane trumpets or clarinets. Performing the Parischerá ensures a plentiful supply of four-legged animals, just as the Tukui dance guarantees a sufficient supply of birds and fish. Starting with a dance performed by the neighboring Maquiritaré that is similar to the Parischerá of the Taulipáng, Meinhard Schuster classified the ritual hunting dances devoted to the peccary, including those of other Carib-speaking tribes of the Guianas; he concluded that a relationship existed between these and the peccary dances of the Mundurucú (Schuster, 1976).

Animal dances devoted to the attainment of game and fish are found among other tribes of the Amazon area and the Gran Chaco. Instead of focusing on the controlling master of the animals, however, they are often directed at the soul of the animal itself. Dances in which the animals, or their spiritual master, are depicted with masks made from bast fiber, straw, or wood frequently do not belong to hunting rituals as such. Instead, they are used in conjunction with rites of passage, especially initiation and mourning feasts. This applies to the animal-mask dances of the northwestern Amazon, the tribes of the upper Xingu River, and the northwestern Ge tribes of eastern Brazil.

The jaguar. The predatory jaguar occupies a special position in the religious practices of peoples inhabiting an extensive area of South America that stretches from the coast of Brazil to the central Andes. The religious life of these peoples is dominated by activities related to the jaguar. The tribute paid the jaguar takes a number of forms: in some cases, attempts are made to pacify or to ward off the spirits of captured jaguars; in others jaguars are ceremonially killed; in yet others, the jaguar is venerated as a god.

Among the ancient Tupinamba, the cadaver of a jaguar was ornamented and then mourned by the women. The people addressed the dead animal, explaining that it was his own fault that he had been captured and killed since the trap into which he had fallen had been intended for other game. He was implored not to take revenge on human children. Among the western groups of the Boróro tribe of the Mato Grosso, who are included in the eastern Brazil cultural area, there is a dance of reconciliation performed for the slain jaguar. Such dances take place at night and consist of pantomimes of the jaguar acted by a hunter who wears a jaguar skin and is decorated with its claws and teeth. These Boróro groups believe that the soul of the jaguar will in this way be assimilated into the hunter. At the same time, the women mourn and cry emphatically to pacify the soul of the animal, which might otherwise take revenge by killing the hunter. The eastern groups of the Boróro tribe attach quite a different significance to their rites for the dead jaguar. Here the ceremonies are held in conjunction with the hunting rituals that accompany the death of an individual, and in this sense they belong to mourning rites.

Up to the beginning of the twentieth century, the Shipaya and Yuruna, Tupi-speaking tribes located on the middle Xingu River, knew of a cult dedicated to the creator of their tribe, who was known as Kumaphari. In the beginning Kumaphari had a human form, but in a state of anger he divorced himself from human beings and settled in the northern end of the world, where he became an invisible, cannibalistic jaguar. Through the shaman, who acted as a medium, the jaguar god occasionally demanded human flesh, whereupon a war party was organized for the purpose of acquiring a prisoner. The victim was shot with arrows and a portion of the body was consumed by the participants in the ritual; the remaining part was presented to Kumaphari, the jaguar god. The ceremonies practiced in this cult apparently maintained ritual cannibalistic elements found among the Tupinamba of the sixteenth century, although at that time the offering of a captured warrior to a deity was not recorded.

An active jaguar cult was also known to the Mojo, an Arawakan tribe in eastern Bolivia. The killing of a jaguar, which automatically bestowed great prestige on the hunter, was accompanied by extensive rites. During the entire night, a dance was held around the slain animal. Finally the animal was butchered and eaten on the spot. The skull, paws, and various other parts were then placed within a temple of the jaguar god, and a sacrificial drink for the benefit of the hunter was presented by the jaguar shaman. The shaman was recruited from among those men who were distinguished for having escaped alive after being attacked by a jaguar. They alone could summon and console the jaguar spirit and could allegedly turn into jaguars, a transformation known to many other Indian tribes of the Amazon region. It is justifiable to view the jaguar god of the Mojo as a "lord of the jaguars" in the same sense that the concept "master of the animals" is applied among hunting groups.

This feline predator also played a part in the religion of ancient Peru. Either a particular god possessed attributes of the jaguar, or the jaguar was an independent deity who served as the lord of the earthly jaguars and who appeared in the constellation Scorpius.

Protection from slain animals. Rituals established around various slain animals are especially obvious in eastern Brazil and Tierra del Fuego. Among the Boróro of eastern Brazil, the shaman enters a state of ecstasy after big game has been killed. In this condition he performs various activities related to the game—for example, breathing over the meat. He may also sample it before the rest of the members of the tribe partake of the meal. In this way he bestows a blessing that will protect against the revenge of the slain animal spirit (*bope*). When the Kaingán-Aweicoma (Xokleng) in the state of Santa Catarina in southern Brazil have killed a tapir, chopped greens, which are particularly favored by this animal, are spread over its head and body, which is supported upright. At the same time, the spirit of the animal is addressed with friendly words. It is asked to give a favorable report to the other animals of its kind, to report how well it was treated, and to persuade them that they too should let themselves be killed. Similarly, when a hunter of the Selk'nam of Tierra del Fuego removed the skin from a slain fox, he spoke apologetic phrases, such as "Dear fox, I am not evil-minded. I have respect and don't wish to harm you, but I am in need of your meat and your fur." By this means, the entire fox society was expected to be pacified after the loss of one of its members. The offering of such deceptions and fabrications to the slain animals is a typical archaic ritual that also finds expression among hunters in the Old World.

Plant fertility rites. I now turn to those religious rites that center around the theme of fertility, not only of planted crops but also of wild edible plants. The most impressive religious celebrations of the tribes in the lowlands of the Amazon are those held for the vegetation demons by the peoples in the northwestern section of this region. Such demons are usually, though incorrectly, identified with the worst of all demons among the ancient eastern Tupi, which demons (and their cults) are known as *yurupary* in the local vernacular (Métraux, 1949).

Among the Tucanoan and Arawakan groups of the upper Rio Negro and the basin of the Uaupés River, the Yurupary rites take place at the time when certain palm fruits particularly favored by the Indians are ripe. At the beginning of the festival, baskets of these fruits are ceremonially escorted into the village by men blowing giant trumpets. These sacred instruments, which represent the voices of the vegetation demons, are hidden from the women and children, who must therefore remain within the huts at this time. During the first part of the ceremony, in which the men scourge one another with long rods, the women are also obligated to remain within their houses. After the secret part of the ritual has ended, however, the women may join the men in feasting and drinking, which continues for several days. The purpose of this feast is to thank the demons for a good harvest and to beg them to provide a rich yield in the coming season. In former times, the so-called Yurupary rites of the Arawakan groups, the Tariana and their neighbors, incorporated the use of two matted "mask suits" made from the hair of monkeys and women. These suits, worn by a pair of dancers, were also not allowed to be seen by the women.

The underlying meaning of the Yurupary rites involves the son of Koai, the tribal hero of the Arawakan groups. Milomaki of the Yahuna (a Tucano group), on the other hand, is a sun hero with an amazing talent for singing who was responsible for having created all edible fruits. He gave these gifts to mankind, although he himself was burned to death by men for having killed members of the tribe. From the ashes of his body sprang the palm tree that provides the wood for making the large trumpets used at the feasts. The trumpets allegedly have the same tones as his voice.

Sacred wind instruments. The reproduction of the voices of supernatural beings through the use of sacred wind instruments, including wooden flutes and trumpets made from rolled bark, is an element that is, or at least was, widespread over much of tropical South America. Their use is most often connected with the expansion of the Arawakan peoples from the north to the south. In the area north of the Amazon, these instruments are utilized in cultic activities devoted to vegetation deities, whereas south of the Amazon they are a central aspect of autonomous cults that have an esoteric character, but have little connection to fertility rituals. They appear in the Flute Dance feast of the Arawakan Ipurina of the Purus River as a representation of the ghostly *kamutsi*, who reside under water and are related not only to the sun but also to the animals. The Paresi-'Kabishi, an Arawakan tribe in the western Mato Grosso, have a secret cult in which the snake demon Nukaima and his wife are represented by a huge trumpet and a smaller flute. The Alligator Jump dance of the old Mojo (an Arawakan group) is considered to be the equivalent of the snake cult of the Paresi. At the climax of this alligator cult feast, a procession is formed in which twelve men play nine-foot-long bark trumpets. Women and children are not allowed to see the proceedings; were they to do so, they would allegedly risk being swallowed by an alligator. The cultural wave responsible for the use of sacred wind instruments in the reproduction of the voices of spiritual beings apparently died out in the upper Xingu cultural area.

The flutes, which are taboo for women, are stored in special flute houses like those of the Arawakan Mehináku. They are associated with a mother spirit (*mama'e*) who has the form of a bird, the jacu (*Crax spp*), and is represented by masked dancers during the ceremonies. Among the Camayura (a Tupi group), the Jacu feast was organized for the purpose of obtaining help from three manioc *mama'e* whose assistance was needed to guarantee success with a new manioc field.

Human and plant fertility. Among the Kaua (an Arawakan group) and the Cubeo (a Tucano group) in the northwestern Amazon region, fertility rites are obviously connected with a human generative power. At the end of the masked dances, in which the dancers represent animals, the participants unite to perform the Naädö (phallus dance). They hold artificial phalluses made of bast fiber in front of their bodies, and with coital gestures they mimic the scattering of semen over houses, fields, and forests.

Farther to the west, we encounter the primal father Moma of the Witóto, a superior god who has a strong influence on the fertility of all useful plants. Moma is responsible not only for the flourishing of the planted crops, including manioc and maize, but also for useful wild fruits. In his honor, the Okima, the festival of yuca (manioc) and of the ancestors, is performed. Those under the earth are invited to participate in the festival by their worldly descendants above, who stamp their feet or beat rhythmically on the ground with "stamping sticks" that are fitted with rattles. In the ball game festival known as Uike, the soul of Moma is believed to be present within the ball, which is bounced back and forth on the knees of the persons participating. Additionally, this ball symbolically represents the fruits that are brought to the feast, the idea being that the bouncing ball makes the same movements as the fruits in the branches of the trees.

Among the Jivaroan people in Ecuador, the cult of the earth mother Nunkwi is restricted to those cultivated plants whose soul is believed to be feminine—for example, manioc. The soul of the earth mother resides within a strangely shaped stone (*nantara*) that has the power to summon Nunkwi. The association between fertility of human females and the growth of plants considered to be feminine receives obvious expression through the rule that every woman who plants a manioc cutting must sit on a manioc tuber. The same theme is expressed in the ritual for the first manioc cutting that is taken from a field whose yield is intended to be used at the Tobacco festival. The cutting is painted red, and the woman to be honored places it against her groin.

Even the *tsantsa*, the fist-sized shrunken head trophies of the Jivaroans, are connected with the fertility of the fields. The power that resides within these heads is expected to be transferred into the crops as the successful hunter, wearing the trophy around his neck, passes the fields. From the trophies the hunter also receives information concerning the fields, which he passes on to the women who tend them. The Quechua and Aymara peoples of the central Andes region frequently call upon Pachamama, the goddess of the earth, who is essentially responsible for the fertility of plants and who is believed to live underground. In addition to being connected with many celebrations, she is also associated with many daily rituals. The cult devoted to her originated in pre-Hispanic times. It has survived to the present, a persistence that is undoubtedly related to Pachamama's identification with the Virgin Mary.

For the cultural areas of eastern Brazil, the Gran Chaco, the Pampas, and Patagonia (including Tierra del Fuego), information concerning gods or spirits related to the fertility of cultivated plants is partial, has little significance, or is completely lacking.

THE SOUL, THE DEAD, AND ANCESTORS. Most of the Indian groups of South America believe that a human being has several souls, each residing in a different part of the body and responsible for numerous aspects of life. After death, each of these souls meets a different fate. One of the most interesting examples of this idea is found among the Guaraní-Apapocuvá (Nimuendajú, 1914). One soul, called the *ayvucue* ("breath"), comes from one of three possible dwelling places: from a deity in the zenith, who is the tribal hero; from "Our Mother" in the east; or from Tupan, the thunder god, in the west. In its place of origin the soul exists in a finished state, and at the moment of birth it enters the body of the individual. It is the shaman's task to determine which of the three places of origin each soul comes from. Soon after birth the breath soul is joined by another soul, the *acyigua* ("vigorous, strong"). The *acyigua* resides in the back of a person's neck and is considered to be an animal soul responsible for the temperament and impulses of that person, which correspond to the qualities of a particular animal. Immediately after death the two souls part company. The *ayvucue* of a small child goes to paradise, the "Land without Evil." The destination of the *ayvucue* of adults is another afterworld that lies just before the entrance to paradise. The animal soul or *acyigua* transforms itself into a much-feared ghost, called *angéry*, that persecutes mankind and must therefore be fought.

Research on a number of Indian tribes indicates that meticulous preservation of the bones of the dead is a widespread practice. Such action, which is similar to the preservation of the bones of hunted game, can be traced to the belief that residual elements of the soul remain in the bones after death. The conceptualization of a "bone soul" has led to the ritual consumption of bone ash from dead family members. This form of endocannibalism is practiced at the present time by different groups of the Yanoama and appears to have been relatively widespread in western South America. Among the Yanoama, we find a perception of a soul that resides outside the body of a living individual, a concept seldom documented in South America. Such a soul most often dwells in an animal, but sometimes also in plants. This type of soul may reside, for example, in a harpy eagle if the soul is that of a man, or in an otter if it belongs to a woman. The predominant element of such a concept is that of an identical life pattern: when the respective animal dies, its human counterpart will also die, and vice versa. An animal soul, usually referred to as a "bush soul," represents the alter ego of a specific individual.

Some of the fundamental beliefs in an alter ego prevalent in South America stem from within the shamanic domain. The Araucanian female shaman *(machi)* possesses an alter ego in the form of an evergreen canelo tree *(Drimys winteri)* that she tends in the forest and whose fate is intimately linked to her own. If someone discovers this tree and destroys it, the *machi* invariably dies.

Honoring the dead was an essential component within the religions of old Peru, as exemplified by the care that mummies of the ancestors were given by priests (Métraux, 1949) and by the sacrificial victims brought to them. Mummies were also taken on procession at certain festivals.

One of the few cases of a developed cult of the dead in the tropical woodlands is exemplified by the ghost dance of the Shipaya of the lower Xingu, which is the most significant religious celebration of this Tupi tribe. The souls of the dead, which are well disposed toward mankind, express a desire to the shaman—through the words of the tribal chief—that the celebration known as the Feast for the Souls of the Dead should be held. It is believed that the souls of those long dead will take possession of the shaman, who is covered with a white cotton mantle; in this form, the soul can participate in the dancing and drinking enjoyed by the living in the center of the village. When souls have borrowed the body of the shaman, his own soul lies idle in his hut. The ceremony continues for eight or more nights, during which other men who have also become the embodiment of dead souls appear in similar dance mantles.

An ancestor cult is also the focal point in the religion of the Cubeo who live in the northwest Amazon region. The soul of a dead person proceeds to the abode of the benevolent ancestors, which is located near the dwelling place of his sib, where all its dead are reunited. The ancestors are represented by large trumpets that are used not only at funeral rites but also at the initiation ceremonies for the boys of the tribe, who are whipped as these trumpets are played. The ancestors, represented by the trumpets once again, are also guardian spirits at sib gatherings. The sound they emit is believed to be a source of male strength when played during a men's bath in the river.

Among the Mundurucú in central Brazil, the large wind instruments are the embodiment of the sib ancestors when played at a particular men's feast. Like the trumpets of the Cubeo, they are not allowed to be seen by the women. At the end of the Mundurucú ceremony, a special drink made from manioc is poured into the instruments and is collected in a calabash bowl as it comes out the other end; it is then drunk by the participants. This ritual, which is looked upon as a form of spiritual communion with the ancestors, is intended as an act of reconciliation that will win their favor and help their descendants.

The combination of a memorial service for the recently dead and a commemorative ceremony for the legendary tribal ancestors can be seen in the Kwarup ritual of the Camayura, a Tupi group of the upper Xingu. The Kwarup (from *kuat,* "sun" and *yerup,* "my ancestor") centers around a number of posts, each about three feet high, outfitted and ornamented as human beings and carved from the sacred camiriva wood from which the creator, Mavutsine, allegedly fabricated the first Camayura. The chant given as people dance around these posts is the same one that Mavutsine sang as he created mankind. In the Kwarup ritual the ancestors return symbolically for the purpose of welcoming those who have recently died.

Death cults and ancestor worship also play an important role in the eastern Brazilian cultural area, particularly among the Bororo. This tribe makes a sharp distinction between nature spirits and spirits of the dead. The Boróro believe that the souls of their ancestors (*aroe*) hold a close relationship to mankind that influences and maintains its daily life. On certain social occasions, the spirits of the dead are ceremonially invoked by special shamans to whom the spirits appear and whom they enlighten in dreams. As a result of this important attachment to the spirits, the funeral rites of the Boróro are highly developed and complex. After a ceremonial hunt, the successful hunter becomes the representative of the dead man at the funeral proper, which consists of a series of established rites. Among these is a dance in which the most interesting elements are large disk-shaped bundles of wood that represent the dead person. At the same time that the dance is being performed, the deceased person's bones, which have been buried for two weeks, are exhumed and painted red with *urucú.* Feathers associated with clan colors are glued to the bones. The specially decorated skull is then displayed to the mourners. After a period of safekeeping in the house of the deceased, the basket in which the bones have been placed is sunk in a deep section of the nearby river.

Among the Ge-speaking Canella (eastern Timbira), it is the medicine men who usually establish contact with the spirits of the dead, since they are omniscient. But even those members of the tribe who do not possess particular spiritual abilities seek advice from their ancestors in emergencies. In the first phase of the initiation ceremonies for young boys in which religion is emphasized, the initiates learn how to contact the dead. This knowledge is acquired in a race in which each person to be initiated carries a wooden block that is said to be the ghost of a dead ancestor. In the funeral rituals, the men carry much larger blocks in a similar race.

The cult of the dead is not only an impressive ritual but a basic foundation of the culture of the Kaingán, the southernmost Ge tribe. The objective that lies at the core of this ritual is the elimination of the ties that connect the living and the dead. This ritual insures that the souls of the deceased will finally arrive at the resting place in the underworld, located in the west.

A cult of the dead among the indigenous people in the southern regions of South America, including the Gran Chaco and the southern Andes, contains few authentic religious elements. At a funeral, the surviving family members sponsor a large feast in honor of the dead relative. The various ceremonies that take place during this feast—for example, eating and drinking bouts, lamenting, playing of music, feigned attacks, riding games, and speeches—are intended to drive from the village the dreaded spirits of the dead or the death demons, who are responsible for the death of the tribal member, to prevent them from causing more harm. Among the people in the Gran Chaco, an attempt is made to console the dead and to pacify them in their anger at having passed away. The mourning ceremonies, which begin immediately after a person dies, are meant to serve this end. Often an invalid is set outside or buried before having actually died. Little has been recorded regarding beliefs about life of the soul after death among the peoples of the Gran Chaco.

INITIATION RITES. Among the Indians of Tierra del Fuego there is no trace of a cult of the dead to be found in the funerary practices. In this region, socioreligious emphasis was placed on rites that are generally associated with the initiation of members of both sexes and particularly on those rituals connected with the acceptance of young males into men's organizations (the Kloketen of the Selk'nam and the Kina of the Yahgan). During these rites, a chain of men came out to frighten the women. The participating men wore conical masks made from bark or animal skin that covered their heads and faces. Their bodies were painted black, white, and pink in various patterns. Although they represented specific demons and spirits of the sea, forest, and animals, there was apparently no ghost of the dead among them.

The appearance of masks so far south is correctly attributed to the extensive influence of the Tropical Forest cultural areas. Between the Tropical Forest and Tierra del Fuego, there are no gaps in the appearance of masked dances in connection with initiation celebrations, as for example the Anapösö, or Forest Spirit feast, of the Chamacoco. In this region of the Gran Chaco, the performers representing the forest spirits were elaborately decorated with feathers. These spirits are believed to have been ruled by the dog demon Pohitschio, who was the consort of the great mother, Eschetewuarha. Formerly the performers wore artistically intricate feather masks that were later replaced by sacks worn over the head with eyeholes cut in them. In either case, the women were not allowed to discover that these spirits were in reality men from their own tribe.

The Lengua of the Gran Chaco use a masked dance to represent symbolically the supernatural danger that threatens women at the onset of menstruation. In this dance, the single men, wearing rhea-feather belts and masks, approach the young women during a typical female puberty celebration. The young women believe them to be the bad spirits. They are eventually driven away by the adult women after they harass and threaten the young girls.

CONCLUSION. Because of the extreme variety of time periods from which information about these tribes is drawn, the only perspective that can be achieved in such an overview is of a diachronic nature. To close this survey of the various forms of religion, I shall briefly indicate phenomena that are particularly characteristic of the individual cultural areas.

The central Andes of pre-Columbian times is characterized by a belief in high gods and their respective cults, by the worship of ancestors and of the dead, and by agrarian rites directed to a female earth deity. The peoples of the region of the Amazon and Orinoco rivers occasionally display signs of high-god worship (Witóto, Tupi-Guaraní). Along with the vegetation cults (northwestern Amazon) that are typical of crop-cultivating peoples, there is a markedly large number of ceremonies and rites associated with deities of the hunt and of wild animals (including fish). The Ge of eastern Brazil exhibit clear signs of worship of astral deities—the Sun and Moon. The cults of the dead and of ancestors dominate much of their religious life. The Gran Chaco, by contrast, is noticeably lacking in religious ceremonies and rites in the narrow sense. First-fruit ceremonies related to hunting and fishing predominate; there are no agrarian rites. In the Pampas and Patagonia region a number of socioreligious rites are attested. The Selk'nam and Yahgan of Tierra del Fuego Archipelago believe in a high god, but there is little indication of cult worship. The regions of southern and central Andes share many aspects of religious life. The high-god cult (Ngenechen) is associated with a cultivation and fertility ritual. A highly developed form of shamanism is also prominent. Throughout South America outside the Andean region, the shaman remains the pillar of the religious life.

SEE ALSO Amazonian Quechua Religions; Ethnoastronomy; Ge Mythology; Inca Religion; Inti; Jaguars; Lord of the Animals; Mapuche Religion; Selk'nam Religion; Shamanism, article on South American Shamanism; South American Indians, articles on Indians of the Andes in the Pre-Inca Period and Indians of the Gran Chaco; Supreme Beings; Tehuelche Religion; Viracocha; Yurupary.

BIBLIOGRAPHY

Baldus, Herbert. *Die Allmutter in der Mythologie zweier sudamerikanischer Indianerstämme (Kagaba und Tumereha).* Berlin, 1932.

Becher, Hans. *Poré/Perimbó: Einwirkungen der lunaren Mythologie auf den Lebensstil von drei Yanonámi-Stämmen, Surára, Pakidái und Ironasitéri.* Hanover, 1974.

Böning, Ewald. *Der Pillánbergriff der Mapuche.* Sankt Augustin, West Germany, 1974.

Cooper, John M. "The Araucanians." In *Handbook of South American Indians,* edited by Julian H. Steward, vol. 2., pp. 687–760. Washington, D. C., 1946.

Eliade, Mircea. "South American High Gods." *History of Religions* 8 (1968): 338–354 and 10 (1970–1971): 234–266.

Frikel, Protasius. "Zur linguistisch-ethnologischen Gliederung der Indianerstämme von Nord-Pará (Brasilien) und den anliegenden Gebieten." *Anthropos* 52 (1957): 509–563.

Gusinde, Martin. *Der Feuerland Indianer.* 3 vols. Vol. 1, *Die Selknam.* Vol. 2, *Die Yamana.* Vol. 3, *Die Halakwulup.* Mödling, 1931–1974. Johannes Wilbert has translated volumes 1 and 2 as *Folk Literature of the Selknam Indians* (Berkeley, 1975) and *Folk Literature of the Yamana Indians* (Berkeley, 1977), respectively.

Gusinde, Martin. Review of *Mundurucú Religion* by Robert F. Murphy. *Anthropos* 55 (1960): 303–305.

Haekel, Joseph. *Pura und Hochgott: Probleme der südamerikanischen Religionsethnologie.* Vienna, 1958.

Hissink, Karin, and Albert Hahn. *Die Tacana: Ergebnisse der Frobenius-Expedition nach Bolivien 1952 bis 1954,* vol. 1, *Erzählungsgut.* Stuttgart, 1961.

Hultkrantz, Åke. *Les religions des indiens primitifs de l'Amérique.* Stockholm, 1967.

Jensen, Adolf E. *Myth and Cult among Primitive Peoples.* Chicago, 1973.

Kruse, Albert. *Pura, das Höchste Wesen Arikena.* Fribourg, 1955.

Métraux, Alfred. *La religion des Tupinamba et ses rapports avec celle des autres tribus Tupi-Guarani.* Paris, 1928.

Métraux, Alfred. "Ethnography of the Chaco." In *Handbook of South American Indians,* edited by Julian H. Steward, vol. 1, pp. 197–370. Washington, D.C., 1946.

Métraux, Alfred. "Religion and Shamanism." In *Handbook of South American Indians,* edited by Julian H. Steward, vol. 5, pp. 559–599. Washington, D.C., 1949.

Métraux, Alfred. *Religions et magies indiennes d'Amériques du Sud.* Paris, 1967.

Nimuendajú, Curt. *Die Sagen von der Erschaffung und Vernichtung der Welt als Grundlagen der Religion der Apapocúva-Guaráni.* Berlin, 1914.

Nimuendajú, Curt. *The Apinayé.* Washington, D.C., 1939.

Petrullo, Vincenzo M. "The Yaruros of the Capanaparo River, Venezuela." *The Smithsonian Institution, Bureau of American Ethnology Bulletin* 123 (1939): 161–290.

Schuster, Meinhard. *Dekuana.* Munich, 1976.

Trimborn, Hermann. "South Central America and the Andean Civilizations." In *Pre-Columbian American Religions,* edited by Walter Krickeberg et al., chap. 2. London, 1968.

Zerries, Otto. "Primitive South America and the West Indies." In *Pre-Columbian American Religions,* edited by Walter Krickeberg et al., chap. 4. London, 1968.

Otto Zerries (1987)
Translated from German by John Maressa

SOUTH AMERICAN INDIAN RELIGIONS: MYTHIC THEMES

South American mythology is a vast field whose purview extends linguistically and archaeologically beyond the continent proper to include the oral traditions of Panama and eastern Costa Rica as well as those of the autochthonous inhabitants of the West Indies. This article will consider myths from the point of view of religious studies and will emphasize the cosmological patterns and sacred symbolism in narratives from nonliterate South American societies of both ancient and modern times.

Since the early sixteenth century more than one thousand languages, representing a variety of linguistic stocks and many unrelated tongues, have been listed for this area—a fact that suggests that South America was populated over a great number of centuries by successive migratory groups that trekked down from Siberia, North America, and Central America. One classification of South American languages attempts to reduce hundreds of mutually unintelligible tongues to only three groups: Macro-Chibchan, Andean-Equatorial, and Ge-Pano-Carib. This classification, however, is admittedly provisional and, in the case of the last two groups, very uncertain. These migrations began more than twenty thousand years ago. The majority of early South American archaeological sites date from between twelve and fourteen thousand years ago, but quartz tools found in Brazil in 1983 have been dated at about twenty-five thousand years before the present.

The higher civilizations of ancient South America occupied the Andean region and the Pacific coast from northern Colombia to central Chile. From the point of view of mythological studies the more or less "primitive" cultures are at least as important as the higher civilizations because the less developed societies usually possess abundant collections of sacred stories. The exceeding diversity of South American aboriginal peoples has precluded the formation of a common pantheon or mythico-religious system for the whole continent. Nevertheless, since many societies have been in contact at one time or another, more than a few myths are common to several tribes. Moreover, a large number of motifs are not only found in the mythologies of different South American groups but are also known to peoples of other continents, leaving room for speculation as to whether these motifs spread through diffusion or originated independently.

Myths of Origin. South American sacred stories about how the world originated do not, as a rule, conform to the pattern of creation out of nothing by the will of an omnipotent god. Rather, they commonly depict the coming into being and unfolding of a primordial spirit. In many cases little is said about the actual genesis of the world, but a detailed description of the structure of the universe is given. This description points out the universe's tiered levels, the *axis mundi* (often in the shape of a cosmic tree), and the heavenly bodies (whose existence is mostly conceived as the product of the transformation of heroes, animals, or other creatures).

Many myths deal with characteristics of the sky, and not a few with those of the underworld. There are also many stories about the origin of night. Even more abundant than myths of world creation are those about the destruction of the world, the recurrent agents of destruction being water or fire or both.

Creation of the world. The Piaroa, who live on the south bank of the Orinoco and speak a language of the Sáliva-Piaroan family, believe that everything was created by the powers of imagination. In the beginning, they say, there was nothing at all. The first thing to appear was the sky, and then the air and the wind. With the wind, words of song were born. The words of song are the creative powers that produce thoughts and visions. Out of nothing they imagined and created Buoko, the first being, who developed in the words of song. Then Buoko imagined his sister Chejaru, and Chejaru was born. Because of this, humankind also has the power of imagination. The Piaroa say that thought is actually the only thing humans have.

The Koghi, speakers of a Macro-Chibchan language who live in the Sierra Nevada de Santa Marta, have a creation story that also underscores the spiritual nature both of the first beings and of the essence of the universe. According to this myth, creation took place in nine stages, from the bottom up. Each stage is both a cosmic level and a spiritual being called the Mother, who is sometimes accompanied by a Father or another spiritual being. The first level, which lies in darkness, is also the Sea; the second, the spiritual Tiger; the fifth, the first House of Spirit. Finally, the Fathers of the World find a huge tree and make a temple in the sky above the water. They call it the House of Spirit.

The Muisca (Chibcha) lived in the highlands of Colombia at the time of the arrival of the Spanish, and spoke a language of the Macro-Chibchan family. According to their creation myth, before there was anything in the world, it was night, and light was kept inside a great thing that, according to the Spanish chronicler who recorded the story, is the same that Europeans call God—an omnipotent, universal, ever-good lord and maker of all things. The great being began to dawn, showing the light that he had in himself, and he commenced, in that primordial light, to create. His first creations were some black birds that he commanded to go everywhere in the world blowing their breath from their beaks. That breath was luminous and transparent, and, the birds' mission accomplished, the whole world remained clear and illumined as it is now.

Cosmic levels. In many South American myths, the universe is conceived as a series of layered planes—three or four in many cases, but sometimes more. The Mataco, whose language is a member of the Mataco-Mataguayo family and who live in the Gran Chaco between the Pilcomayo and Bermejo rivers, distinguish the levels of earth, sky, underworld, and (according to some) that of another earth farther down. Originally the sky had been joined to the earth, but the Owner of the Sky separated them. Afterward, a tree grew to connect the sky and the earth. People of the earth used to climb the tree and hunt in the sky, but an old man who had been given a miserable portion of the game meat avenged himself by burning the tree. The hunters could not return; they became the Pleiades. The children of the hunters, who remained on earth, received from their mother, who was also stranded in the sky, a deerskin full of honey that she dropped from above. They grew up and became the ancestors of the present-day Mataco.

The Macuna of the Lower Pira-Parana River in the Vaupés region of Colombia, who speak a language of the Tucanoan family, think that the earth is the shape of a disk. A subterranean river is united with the earth by a whirlpool. The river is inhabited by monsters and bad spirits. Over the earth is a hot-water lake on which the sun sails from east to west in his boat every day. Over Sun Lake there is a house where the Lord of the Jaguars lives, a place that only shamans, in their flights to heaven, can reach. On top of the cosmos is a layer that covers all others like a lid. Nothing beyond it is known. The earth disk consists of several concentric zones, the innermost being the Macuna homeland. At the center, just below Sun Lake, stands a sacred mountain, which supports the firmament. No stone is taken from this mountain lest it fall, taking the sky with it. At a certain point on the earth's level is the House of the Dead. The outer zones are occupied by other Indian tribes, whites, and blacks.

Sky and underworld. The sky and the underworld are cosmic levels of special interest. They appear in myths influenced by the shamans' narratives of their ecstatic trips to the upper and lower worlds. The Marikitari, a Carib-speaking people living in the Upper Orinoco area, say that in the beginning the whole world was sky. There was no separation between heaven and earth. There was only light. In the sky dwelled good, wise people who never died; nor did they work: Food was always available. In the highest sky was Wanadi, who is still there. He gave his light to the people and they were happy. One day he said that he wanted to make people on that part of the sky called "earth." He sent a spirit who made the first people and brought them knowledge, tobacco, the maraca, and the shaman's quartz power stones. Later, an evil spirit called Orosha introduced hunger, sickness, war, and death.

The sky and the cosmic tree. Some of the myths so far recounted show a close connection between the cosmic levels and the *axis mundi,* often represented by a gigantic tree. In the Mataco myth the danger of the sky falling down is clearly pointed out. The same motif appears in many other myths of tropical forest tribes. The Ge-speaking Kayapó of central Brazil say that in the east there was a gigantic tree called End of the Sky. It supported the heavens, which in those days were parallel to the earth. After several tries, a tapir succeeded in gnawing the trunk until it broke. Then the sky drooped down at the edges, forming the celestial vault. At the place where the tree has its roots all kinds of strange beings live. When a group of people went to explore the east, they found it so frightening that they fled back home with no desire to return to the End of the Sky.

Sky, light, and darkness. Myths in which the sky, usually associated with light, is related to the origins of night are also common. The following story is told by the Cuiba, who live in the western plains of Colombia and speak a language of the Guahiboan family. In ancient times there was no night, only an endless daytime. People could not sleep. A woman who had gone out of her mind wanted to break the sky. Her husband, who was a shaman and had had a dream, warned her to be careful and not to damage the sky, which belonged to the locusts. But she paid no attention and hurled a stone that broke the sky, which was made of mud. Directly it became dark and the earth was invaded by locusts as big as iguanas. They ate the eyes of everybody except the shaman. Then the swallows, who are able to carry heavy loads, brought all the necessary mud and repaired the sky again.

Other stories about the origin of the night suggest that it was created because girls, or wives, would not grant their favors to their lovers, or husbands, since it was always daytime. A Tupi myth from central Brazil indicates that night was kept in a coconut that was opened against the formal prohibition to do so.

Sun, moon, and stars. The sun and moon play important roles in many South American myths. Their origins, like those of stars and constellations, are due in many cases to the transformation of humans at turning points or denouements in the mythical stories. Many versions of the widespread myth of the "twins and the jaguar" end with the heroes' ascending to the sky to become the sun and moon. This is perhaps the most ubiquitous myth of South America, found from Panama to the Gran Chaco and from the eastern coast of Brazil to the Amazonian forests of southern Peru, among dozens of tribes that speak mutually unintelligible languages. Different versions of this story diverge considerably, but the following summary contains a number of essential points common to a great number of stories known to widely scattered groups. A mysterious god or a civilizing hero impregnates a woman and then abandons her. While walking alone in the forest carrying twins in her womb, she is killed by one or more jaguars, but the jaguars' mother takes care of the babies and raises them. A bird or other animal tells the twins how their mother died. The twins determine to avenge their mother and prepare themselves to do so through several ordeals. They finally kill all the jaguars except one, which escapes and becomes the ancestor of present-day jaguars. After some quarreling, the twins climb to the sky, where they can be seen as sun and moon. As an example of the differences between many versions of this story, it may be mentioned that in the rich Mashco account of this tale the twins do not appear; in this case the extraordinary boy Aimarinke kills the jaguars and then goes up to heaven and becomes Yuperax, the god of lightning.

The pre-Columbian Carib of northern South America, speakers of one or another language of the extensive Carib family, were skilled navigators of the Caribbean Sea and had a rich lore about stars and constellations, some of which has survived to the twentieth century. One of their stories tells about a newly married girl who was seduced by a man in the shape of a tapir who asked her to follow him eastward to the place where earth and sky meet. Serikoai, her husband, accidentally cut off his leg with an ax and, after being cured by his mother, set out in search of his wife. He finally found her in the company of Tapir, whom he shot, severing Tapir's head. He implored his wife to return, saying that if she refused he would follow her forever. She hurried on, chased by her lover's spirit and her husband. On arriving at the earth's steep edge, she threw herself into the deep blue sky. On a clear night, one can still watch her; she has been turned into the Pleiades, with Tapir's head (the star cluster Hyades, the star Aldebaran being Tapir's red eye) close behind, and Serikoai (Orion, with Rigel indicating the upper part of her husband's sound limb) in pursuit.

MYTHS OF DESTRUCTION. Stories about the destruction of the world and humankind by a deluge—be it from excessive rain, or by high tides, or both—are fairly common in most regions of South America. Another type of myth of wholesale destruction is that of the world fire. In some cases these stories may recall actual catastrophes, but their significance seems to be symbolic of divine punishment for transgression of traditional taboos. Often, the destruction is believed to have occurred in the past; sometimes, however, the world fire is projected into the future.

The Deluge. The earliest recorded American myth of the deluge comes from the Taino, whom Columbus met on his first voyage of discovery. According to this version of the myth, a young man who wished to murder his father was banished and later killed by him. The old man kept his son's bones in a calabash where he and his wife could see them. One day they accidentally overturned the gourd and the bones turned into fish. Another day, as the man was out in the fields, four brothers, whose mother had died at their birth, took the calabash and ate all the fish. Hearing that the father was returning, they hurried to hang the vessel back in place, but it fell to the ground and broke. The water from the calabash filled the whole earth and from it also came the fish in the sea. The theme of the Deluge as a consequence of killing forbidden fish is still present among the contemporary Mataco of Argentina and southern Bolivia. In the Andean countries, Deluge myths are generaly associated with a magic mountain where humankind takes refuge. As the waters rise, the mountain also rises, thereby saving the lives of those who have reached the top. One of the best-known examples of this motif was recorded as early as the seventeenth century; its memory persists to this day among the speakers of dialects of the Araucanian language.

In the native traditions of the Huarochiri area of Peru that were collected from Quechua speakers early in the seventeenth century, the Deluge is caused by a god whose presence is not recognized by people who are reveling. Enraged, he advises a young woman who has tended him and won his friendship to take refuge on a high mountain nearby. Soon afterward, heavy rain carries the village away, leaving no one alive. Among the Kaueskar-speaking Alacaluf of southern Chile, who were once supposed to have preserved no mythology, an increasing collection of mythic tales has been gathered since the late 1970s. Among these stories is one about a devastating flood caused by the breaking of a taboo forbidding the killing of an otter. Only a young couple is saved, again by climbing a mountain.

The World Fire. The Carib-speaking Taulipáng of Venezuela connect the deluge with the world fire. They say that after the great flood, when everything had dried up, there was a great fire. All the game animals hid in an underground pit. Fire consumed everything: people, mountains, stones. That is why big chunks of coal are sometimes found in the earth. The Zapiteri, of the Mashco ethnic group of the southwestern Amazon, say that in the beginning of time it rained blood, but later the sun began to heat up and there was a great fire. The tribes of the Gran Chaco have a rich repertoire of myths about the world fire. One of these myths, from the Mataco, says that long ago the Mataco lived in great disorder. One day black clouds broke into lightning and rain began to fall. The drops were not water but fire, which spread everywhere. There were only a few survivors, among them Tokhuah the trickster, who went underground for the duration of the fire.

Many fragments have been collected of what is thought to have been a widely diffused myth of the destruction of the world by fire. According to the Tupi-speaking Apocacuva Guaraní, the World Fire was the first of four cataclysms that annihilated almost all creatures, and it will be repeated when the creator removes from under the earth the crossed beams that hold it in place. Then the earth will catch fire, a long-lasting night will set in, and a blue tiger will devour humankind.

Such Ge-speaking tribes as the Apanyekra, Apinagé, Craho, and Ramkokamekra tell stories about the beginnings, when only two persons existed, Sun and Moon, both of them male. One day Sun obtained a beautiful plumed headdress that looked like fire. Because Moon also wanted one for himself, Sun got another and threw it to Moon, warning him not to let it touch the ground; but Moon was afraid to grab it and let it fall to earth, and it immediately started to burn, consuming all the sand and many animals.

MYTHIC ANCESTORS. Different South American myths place the origin of humans at distinct levels of the universe and variously depict the human race as being born from minerals, plants, or animals. Women are sometimes assigned a separate origin. The Urus of Lake Titicaca, speakers of a language of the Uro-Chipaya family, relate that in the time of darkness the universal creator made the Chullpas, who were the first men. They were destroyed by a cataclysm when the Sun appeared, and their survivors became the ancestors of those who now call themselves Kotsuns ("people of the lake"), but are more commonly known by the name of Urus ("wild animals"), as they are called by their Aymara neighbors. The Carib-speaking Waiwai of Guyana say that before humankind existed there were on earth sky spirits, which now have the form of birds and which fly in the second heavenly layer. Some of them, however, have human form. Present-day humankind descends from the children of a woman who was one of these spirits and who, surprised while alone in the forest, was impregnated by a grasshopper-man.

The Quechua-speaking Inca of Peru had several myths of their origins that were recorded by Spanish chroniclers. According to one of these stories, the high god Vi-racocha created Alcaviza, a chieftain; and told him that after his (Viracocha's) departure the Inca noble would be born. Alcaviza resided at the place that would later become the main square of Cuzco, the capital of the Inca empire. Seven miles away, at a place called Paccaritambo ("lodge of dawn"), the earth opened to form a cave, from which the four Ayar brothers emerged, dressed in fine clothing and gold. Fearing the colossal strength of the one who had come out of the cave first, his brothers asked him to go back into the cave and fetch some golden objects that had been left behind. While he was inside, the others immured him there forever. Ayar Manco, who had come out last, took the prisoner's wife for himself. Another brother displayed big wings, flew to the sky, and from high above told Ayar Manco that the sun had ordered that he should change his name to Manco Capac ("Manco the Magnificent") and take the winged man's wife for himself. Finally the winged man turned into a stone. In the company of his only remaining brother and their wives, Manco Capac walked to Cuzco, where Alcaviza recognized from their garments that they were indeed the children of the Sun and told them to settle at whatever place they liked best. Manco Capac, the first Inca ruler, chose the site where later the Coricancha, or court of the sun, would be built. His brother went away to settle another village.

HIGH GOD. The belief in a high god conceived as omniscient and benevolent to humans rather than as an omnipotent and perfect creator (which in some cases he also is) is documented in many South American myths. It was first reported by Fray Ramón Pané in the earliest ethnological study of American Indians. He wrote that the Taino of Haiti believed in the existence of an immortal being in the sky whom no one can see and who has a mother but no beginning. At the the southernmost extreme of South America, the belief in the existence of a high god has been acknowledged among the tribes of Tierra del Fuego. The Tehuelche of Patagonia seem to have believed in a supreme being conceived as a good spirit who was also the lord of the dead. From the Araucanians (Mapuche) come testimonies of a belief, possibly autochthonous, in a supreme celestial being, Nguenechen. Very early reports say that the Tupí believed in a being they called Monan, and that they attributed to him the same perfections that Christians attribute to their God: He is eternal, and he created the heavens and the earth as well as the birds and animals.

The most famous of all South American high gods is the Andean deity Viracocha. Several etymologies have been proposed to explain the meaning of his name, among them "sea of grease" (as a rich source of life) and "lord of all created things." In any case the belief in a high creator god among the Andean peoples probably goes back to early prehistoric times. It has been suggested that Viracocha is none other than the same world creator and culture hero found in the mythology of many tribes from Alaska to Tierra del Fuego. Apparently, the ancient high god was obscured for a time by his conflation with the Inca sun god, but later the Inca were obliged to revert to the ancient high god of archaic mythologies in order to secure the support of their allies when Cuzco was threatened by other peoples. Another important Andean high god is Illapa, lord of rain, lightning, and thunder. As do some other Andean deities, Illapa hierophanically presents himself in trinitarian form comprising Illapa the Father, Illapa the Elder Son (or Brother), and Illapa the Younger Son (or Brother). Illapa's name is related to the Quechua word *illa,* meaning both "protective spirit" and "light" or "lightning."

While Illapa is a god of the Andean highlands, Con and Pachacámac belong to the Peruvian coast. Con is said to have created the sky, the sun, the moon, the earth with all its animals, the Indians, and the fish by means of his thought and breath. After having made everything, he ascended into the sky. Con was followed later by a more powerful god called Pachacámac ("world maker," or "the god who gives orders").

ORIGINS OF PLANTS AND CULTURE. The introduction of seeds for agriculture and the origins of certain staple plants and their fruits are recounted as etiological motifs in many South American myths. In Peru, several sacred personages of legendary times are credited with the creation of produce. According to an ancient story, the god Pachacámac transformed the sacrificed body of a divine being into the basic food plants of the Andean peoples.

In the traditions of the Ge-speaking Apinagé, Kayapó, Craho, and Xerenté, among the tribes of the Tropical Forest, as well as among the Mataco of the Gran Chaco, many fruits of the earth came from the heavens as gifts brought by Star Woman for her lover and his people. That is the way the Apinagé first came to know of sweet potatoes and yams and learned to plant maize and make maize cakes. The Kayapó obtained manioc, sweet potatoes, yams, and bananas through the good offices of Sky Woman, who was the daughter of Rain. Maize, however, was revealed by a little mouse who showed it to an old woman. Among the Waiwai it is said that an old woman allowed herself to be burned, and from her charred bones sprouted cassava plants of the type still in use today. In a Witóto myth an old woman who was ascending the sky in pursuit of a handsome youth fell down, transforming herself into the bitter yuca, while the young man became the sun.

In many tribal societies there are traditional stories teaching how artifacts and social intitutions first came into being. Among the Ayoré of western Paraguay and eastern Bolivia, who speak a language of the Zamuco family, there is an origin myth (or sometimes several) for every single object, whether natural or manmade. According to the Ayoré, most things originated through the transformation of an ancestor. In many cases, however, cultural objects were in the beginning owned by the ancestor who, at a certain point, gave them to humankind.

ORIGINS OF FIRE. Fire, the natural element required to transform the raw into the cooked, separates humans from animals and establishes the basis of culture; as such, it is the subject of many mythic stories, which can be broadly divided into myths about the origin of fire and myths about the origin of the techniques for fire-making. Most stories of the former group recount how, in the times of the beginnings, humans first obtained fire, either as a gift from a god or as an element stolen by a culture hero.

The greatest variety of myths about fire among South American societies probably occurs in the traditional oral literature of the Mataco. According to one of these stories, Raven was the owner of fire, and Toad, in an unsuccessful attempt to steal it, almost extinguished it. But Tokhuah, the trickster, did succeed in getting it, and, when chased away, waved his burning stick in all directions. The branches of all the species of trees that caught fire are now gathered to make drills for producing fire by friction. In another Mataco myth, Vulture, the guardian of fire, flapped his huge wings from time to time to fan the live coals. If someone attempted to take a burning piece of wood, however little, Vulture would flutter his wings with such force that the fire would flare up and the would-be thief would be burned to ashes. But according to the most widely reported version of the Mataco myth, the owner of the fire is Jaguar. In this story, Jaguar loses his fire to Rabbit, who puts live coals under his chin and runs away. Later Rabbit throws the embers in a meadow and the world begins to burn. People were thus able to obtain fire and to cook their meals, but Jaguar had to learn how to hunt and to eat his game raw. Then Tokhuah put the spirit of fire into the wood of the *sunchu* tree, which the Mataco use to make their fire-drills.

ORIGINS OF DEATH. Several types of myths about the origin of death have been noted among South American tribes. One of these may be called the "waxing and waning moon" type. The Ayoré of the Gran Chaco say that instead of following Moon, who waxes again after waning into nothing, their ancestor followed Tapir, who dies and never rises again.

The Warao of the Orinoco delta have several traditional stories representing different types of myth about the origins of death. One type concerns the "serpent and his cast off skin." It says that people lived happily on earth until one of them fell ill and died. He was buried, and the Master of the Palm-Leaf Fiber said that they should wail for their dead. The snakes immediately cried and shed their skins. That is why snakes do not die, but people do.

Another type of myth, and a very common one, attributes humanity's fate to its disobedience of a divine commandment. It is said that death and sickness came to the Warao as a punishment inflicted by the Master of Water Spirits because his daughter, who had married a Warao, had been obliged to go into the menstruation hut when she had her menses, according to the customs of her husband's village but against her will, and she died. To castigate the Indians, the water spirits caused accidents, sickness, and death.

Yet another myth type, the "ill-timed answer," is found not only among the Warao but also in Guyana and elsewhere. Once, when the world was young and animals could talk, a chief announced that Death would pass by that night. The chief added that Death would call to them first, and that a good spirit would call afterward. If they answered the second call, people would never die, but if they answered the first call, all would surely die. The chief asked everybody to stay awake, but a young man went to sleep. Night came and all was quiet. About midnight they heard a voice that they did not answer, but the young man who was sleeping woke up and answered it. From that time, people began to die.

The "malevolent decision" motif and the "shouting at and scaring away the revenant" motif sometimes overlap, as in the Mataco myth according to which there was a time when everybody lived for five hundred years and died only of old age. Three days after death they would return to life again, rejuvenated. Nevertheless, when Tokhuah, the trickster, saw Moon, who was a handsome young man with an oversized member, beginning to shine again, Tokhuah was frightened, shouting "Go away!" and threatening Moon with a stick. Moon fled upward until he reached the sky. Tokhuah did the same to those who returned from the dead, and it is surmised that because of his actions the dead do not come back to life any more.

Another widely scattered motif is the "resurrection ritual that fails." The Selk'nam of Tierra del Fuego used to say that when their hero Kenos reached old age and seemed to die, he rose up again, and caused other men who died to come back to life by washing them. Subsequently, when he decided at one point not to rise again and went into the sky and became a star, he instructed Cenuke, a powerful sorcerer, to wash old people and make them young again. But Kwanip, another powerful sorcerer, ordained that no person should be raised from the sleep of age. He hurried up to the sky where he also became a star. Since then nobody comes back from the grave.

RELATIONSHIP BETWEEN MYTH AND RITUAL. According to a well-known theory, myths recount rituals and rituals perform myths. Although this idea will hardly hold if applied to all myths and rituals, it is true that some myths relate the origins of certain rites. The southern Barasana, speakers of a Tucanoan language, tell a story of their culture hero Warimi, who in his childhood was called Rijocamacu and who always succeeded in escaping when pursued by the daughters of the supernatural Meni. One day the youngest daughter of Meni caught Rijocamacu, who instantly turned into a little baby. The girl put him to her breast. Her father approved of what she was doing, and kindled some wax, blowing on the smoke in order to chase away the spirits of the dead so that they could not frighten the baby and make him cry. Since that time, when a woman gives birth, the chief blows on the household fire and only then are the people allowed into the house. In many tales, Meni is said to have been the first to do the things that the Barasana do now.

The close relationship between myth and ritual has been established in the case of the complex of sacred stories, holy performances, and tabooed musical instruments and other items that are associated with the name *Yurupary,* known to many tribes in the western Amazon region. The stories about Yurupary differ from one tribe to another. One of these stories, told among the Macuna, was that Yurupary was an old jaguar-shaman whose female companion was Romi Kumu, another powerful being. Since he devoured many men, two ancestors decided to kill him, and they did. Afterward they burned his body; but his ashes produced a palm tree that shot quickly into the sky. The ancestors cut the palm to pieces and these became musical instruments: three male trumpets and one female flute that did not give out any sound until a hole was made to imitate the vagina of Romi Kumi. When the ancestors found Romi Kumi on an island, they stuck the flute between her legs, and that was the origin of menstruation. They gave the instruments to men, who at that time performed the agricultural work that is now performed by the women. In the Yurupary ceremonies, females are not allowed to see the instruments.

MODERN MYTHS. The myths mentioned above are ancient stories exhibiting the characteristics of South American cultures before contact with European civilization, but the creative forces of native imagination were not totally withered by the impact. Old myths were recast in new molds, making allowance for the presence of the whites and their ways. Hundreds of legends—that is, myths with some historical component— were coined in colonial times, and the process is still alive today in many areas where indigenous and foreign cultures meet. One such legend is the so-called myth of Inkarri, which has been traced to several localities in the vicinity of Cuzco, but has also been found in other areas of Peru. Its gist is that the Spanish conqueror Pizarro imprisoned and beheaded Atahuallpa, the Inca king (Span., *Inca rey* = Inkarri), but the head, which is secretly kept somewhere, is not dead, and is growing a body, which when completed will shake off the chains and fetters that hold the Inca people in bondage. Eventually, Inkarri will reestablish justice and bring back the ancient culture of the vanquished.

SEE ALSO Atahuallpa; Yurupary.

BIBLIOGRAPHY

The best collection of sources, translated into English from the Spanish, Portuguese, and other European languages, is the multivolume *The Folk Literature of South American Indians,* edited by Johannes Wilbert (Los Angeles, 1970–), published as part of the "UCLA Latin American Studies" series. Separate volumes have been devoted to the Warao (1970), Selk'nam (1975), Yamana (1977), Ge (1979), Mataco (1982), Toba (1983), Boróro (1983), and Tehuelche (1984). Extensive compilations of South American myths are Theodor Koch-Grünberg's *Indianermärchen aus Südamerika* (Jena, 1901), which does not include the Andean civilizations, and Raffaele Pettazzoni's *Miti e leggende,* vol. 4, *America Centrale e Meridionale* (Turin, 1963).

Other sources are included in more restricted ethnological studies or in anthologies devoted to Indians of a single country, such as the following works: Walter E. Roth's *An Inquiry into the Animism and Folk-Lore of the Guiana Indians* (Washington, D.C., 1908–1909), which has myths of the Arawak, Carib, and Warao; *An Historical and Ethnological Survey of the Cuna Indians,* by Erland Nordenskiöld in collaboration with Ruben Pérez Kantule, edited by Henry Wassén (Göteborg, 1938); Herbert Baldus's *Die Jaguarzwillinge* (Kassel, 1958), with myths from Brazil; Fray Cesáreo de Armellada and Carmela Bentivenga de Napolitano's *Literaturas indígenas venezolanas* (Caracas, 1975); Hugo Nino's *Literaturas de Colombia aborigen: En pos de la palabra* (Bogotá, 1978). The Taulipan and Arekuna are represented in Theodor Koch-Grünberg's *Von Roroima zum Orinoco,* vol. 2 (Stuttgart, 1924); the Marikitare, in Marc de Civrieux's *Watunna: An Orinoco Creation Cycle* (San Francisco, 1980). Myths from some tribes of the huge Amazonian area are included in C. Manuel Nunes Pereira's *Moronguêtá: Um Decameron indígena,* 2 vols. (Rio de Janeiro, 1967); Gerardo Reichel-Dolmatoff's *Amazonian Cosmos: The Sexual and Religious Symbolism of the Tukano Indians* (Chicago, 1971); Gerald Weiss's *Campa Cosmology: The World of a Forest Tribe in South America* (New York, 1975); Manuel García-Renduelas's *'Duik Múum': Universo mítico de los aguarunas,* 2 vols. (Lima, 1979); Stephen Hugh-Jones's *The Palm and the Pleiades: Initiation and Cosmology in Northwest Amazonia* (Cambridge, 1979), on the Barasana, important for the study of the Yurupary myth; Mario Califano's *Analisis comparativo de un mito mashco* (Jujuy, Argentina, 1978), based on versions from three groups of southeast Peru; Peter G. Roe's *The Cosmic Zygote: Cosmology in the Amazon Basin* (New Brunswick, N.J., 1982), on Shipibo mythology. Classic studies in Guaraní mythology are part of Alfred Métraux's *La religion des Tupinamba et ses rapports avec celle des autres tribus Tupi-Guarani* (Paris, 1928) and Curt Nimuendajú's "Die Sagen von der Erschaffung und Vernichtung der Welt als Grundlagen der Religion der Apapocuva-Guarani," *Zeitschrift für Ethnologie* 46 (1914): 284–403. For the Kamayurá and other tribes of the Upper Xingu: Orlando Villas Boas and Claudio Villas Boas's *Xingu: The Indians, Their Myths* (New York, 1973). The myth of the "twins and the jaguar," widely diffused in the Amazon, is studied in relation to early Andean civilizations by Julio C. Tello in his article "Wira Kocha," *Inca* 1 (1923): 93–320, 583–606. Two recent anthologies of Andean myths are Henrique *Urbano's Wiracocha y Ayar: Héroes y funciones en las sociedades andinas* (Cuzco, 1981) and Franklin Pease's *El pensamiento mítico* (Lima, 1982). The best edition of the Huarochiri traditions collected by Francisco de Ávila is Jorge L. Urioste's *Hijos de Pariya Qaqa: La tradición oral de Waru Chiri: Mitología, ritual y costumbres,* 2 vols. (Syracuse, N.Y., 1984). Many South American myths, or parts of them, are included in the first three volumes of Claude Lévi-Strauss's monumental *Mythologiques,* translated as *The Raw and the Cooked* (New York, 1969), *From Honey to Ashes* (New York, 1973), and *The Origin of Table Manners* (New York, 1978), also useful for its extensive bibliographies.

There is no large-scale treatment of South American mythology from the point of view of religious studies. The best overview is Harold Osborne's *South American Mythology* (London, 1968). A survey of the field since the publication of the *Handbook of South American Indians,* 7 vols., edited by Julian H. Steward (Washington, D.C., 1946–1959), is found in Juan Adolfo Vázquez's "The Present State of Research in South American Mythology," *Numen* 25 (1978): 240–276. Although dated in many respects, the *Handbook* has not been replaced as a general work of reference. Invaluable for the ethnological background to the mythology of many tribes, it also includes brief summaries on religions and mythologies, and an article by Alfred Métraux, "Religion and Shamanism" (vol. 5, pp. 559–599). The article "Inca Culture at the Time of the Spanish Conquest" by John Howland Rowe (vol. 2., pp. 183–330) provides an excellent introduction to the subject and includes sections on Inca religion and mythology. The chapters on archaeology can be updated by consulting Gordon R. Willey's *An Introduction to American Archaeology,* vol. 2, *South America* (Englewood Cliffs, N.J., 1971). The field of South American linguistics has been surveyed by different authors, among them Cestmír Loukotka in his *Classification of South American Indian Languages,* edited by Johannes Wilbert (Los Angeles, 1968).

The following periodicals have published many myths from South America: *Amérindia* (Paris, 1976–), *Anthropos* (Mödling, 1906–), *Journal de la Société des Américanistes* (Paris, 1895–), *Journal of Latin American Lore* (Los Angeles, 1975–), *Latin American Indian Literatures* (Pittsburgh, 1977–1984) *Revista do Museu Paulista* (São Paulo, 1895–1938, 1947–), and *Scripta Ethnologica* (Buenos Aires, 1973–).

New Sources

Bierhorst, John. *The Mythology of South America.* New York, 1998.

Gutiérrez Estéves, Manuel, ed. *Mito y ritual en América.* Madrid, 1988.

Fischer, Manuela. *Mito Kogi.* Quito, 1989.

Manuela de Cora, María Kuai-Mare. *Mitos Aborigenes de Venezuela.* Caracas, 1993.

Morales Guerrero, Enrique Rafael. *Mitologia Americana: Estudio preliminar sobre mitologia clásica.* Santafé de Bogoté, 1997.

Urban, Greg. *A Discourse-Centered Approach to Culture: Native South American Myths and Rituals.* Austin, 1991.

JUAN ADOLFO VÁZQUEZ (1987)
Revised Bibliography

SOUTH AMERICAN INDIAN RELIGIONS: HISTORY OF STUDY

Systematic study of South American indigenous religions began with the arrival of the first Europeans. Almost immediately after landing in the New World, scholars, priests, scribes, and soldiers began describing and assimilating the Indians' peculiar and, to them, outlandish practices for their Old World sponsors and public. The confrontation between these early explorer-chroniclers and their indigenous subjects established the basis of a religious opposition between Christian reformer and "pagan" Indian; and it is no exaggeration to say that these early accounts set the stage for all later scholarly and scientific studies of the continent's diverse religious traditions.

All early accounts of religion were driven by the practical needs of empire. For the Spaniards, the political importance of understanding and analyzing native religious belief first arose through their encounters with the powerful Inca state of highland Peru. Chroniclers such as Juan de Betanzos (1551), Pedro Cieza de León (1553), and Cristóbal de Molina (1572) among others provided vivid accounts of imperial religion and Inca state mythologies. Two concerns tempered their descriptions and choice of subject matter: the spectacle of Inca rituals and the parallels they imagined to exist between their Christian millenarian and apostolic traditions and the natives' own beliefs in a "creator god" whose prophesized return coincided with—and thus facilitated—the initial Spanish conquests in Peru. Similar messianic beliefs among the Tupi-Guaraní of eastern Brazil attracted the attention of the explorers Hans von Staden (1557) and Antonie Knivet (1591). Their writings provide fascinating accounts of Tupi religion as part of an argument intended to prove the presence of the Christian apostle Thomas in South America long before its sixteenth-century "discovery." Such early accounts inevitably strike the modern-day reader as ethnocentric. The tone of these writings is understandable, however, since their purpose was to make sense of the new cultures and peoples they met within the historical and conceptual framework provided by the Bible. Within this framework, there was only one "religion" and one true God. All other belief systems, including those encountered in the Americas, were judged as pagan. For some early theologians, the pagan practices of the South Americans placed them well outside the domain of the human. Others, however, believed the Americans were humans who had once known the true God and then somehow fallen from grace or were innocents with an intuitive knowledge of God. Early accounts of religious practices were driven by this desire to uncover evidence of the Indians' prior evangelization or intuitive knowledge of God. Catholic writers thus often interpreted the indigenous practices they observed by comparing them to such familiar Catholic practices as confession. In what is perhaps the most sympathetic account of a native religion, the Calvinist Jean de Léry made sense of the religious practices of the Brazilian Tupinambá Indians by comparing their ritual cannibalism to the Catholic Communion, in which Christians partook of the body and blood of Christ. De Léry's account suggests the extent to which all early inquiries into South American religions were inevitably colored by the religious and political lines drawn within Europe itself by the Reformation.

For Iberians, however, it was the *Reconquista* or Liberation of Catholic Spain from Moorish rule that lent the study of religion an urgent, practical tone. If Indian souls were to be recruited to the ends of the "one true religion," it was necessary to isolate and eradicate those aspects of the indigenous religions that stood in the way of conversion. Priests had to be instructed, catechisms written, and punishments devised for specific religious offenses. The ensuing campaigns to extirpate idolatries produced the first true studies of religion in the Andean highlands. Combining knowledge of Christian doctrine and missionary zeal with an increasing practical familiarity with indigenous life, theologians and priests such as José de Acosta (1590), José de Arriaga (1621), Cristóbal de Albornóz (c. 1600), and Francisco de Ávila (1608) set out to define in a rigorous and scholarly way the parameters of indigenous religion.

A few indigenous and mestizo writers sought to vindicate their culture and religion from the attacks of these Catholic campaigners, in the process contributing greatly to the historical study of Andean religion. Among the most interesting of the indigenous chronicles is an eleven-hundred-page letter to the king of Spain written between 1584 and 1614 by Felipe Guamán Poma de Ayala, a native of Ayacucho, Peru, who had worked with the extirpation campaigns. Other native accounts include the chronicle of Juan de Santacruz Pachacuti Yamqui Salcamaygua (c. 1613) and the monumental *History of the Incas* (1609), written by the half-Inca Garcilaso de la Vega. These native writers defended the goals but not the cruel methods, of Christian conversion and defended many native beliefs and practices as more just and rational than the abuses of the Spanish colonizers.

Other chronicles record European reactions to religions of the Amazonian lowlands; these include among others the travel accounts of Claude d'Abbeville (1614) and Gaspar de Carvajal, a priest who accompanied the first exploratory voyage up the Amazon River system in 1542. But if what the Europeans understood by "religion"—that is, hierarchies, priests, images, and processions—fit in well with what they found in the Andean state systems, it differed markedly from the less-institutionalized religions of the tropical forest region. Accounts of lowland religions were accordingly couched in an exaggerated language stressing atrocity, paganism, and cannibalism. Such emphases had more to do with prevailing European mythologies than with the actual religious beliefs of tropical forest peoples.

This early literature on Andean religion provided irreplaceable data about ritual, dances, offerings, sacrifices, beliefs, and gods now no longer in force—including, in the case of Guamán Poma's letter, a sequence of drawings depicting indigenous costume and ritual and, in the chronicle of Francisco de Ávila, a complete mythology transcribed in Quechua, the native language. But these colonial writings also provided a powerful precedent for religious study thereafter.

From the time of the extirpators on, religion was the salient element or institution by which indigenous peoples were judged in relation to their Christian or European conquerors. Religion, in short, became the principal index for defining the cultural and social differences separating two now adjacent populations. Such religious criteria helped shape as well the unfortunate stereotypes applied to Amazonian peoples and cultures.

Nineteenth-Century Travel and Expeditionary Literature. The interval between the seventeenth-century campaigns against idolatry and the early-nineteenth-century independence period was marked by an almost complete absence of religious studies. In Europe itself the accounts of Garcilaso de Vega, de Léry, and others provided the raw materials from which eighteenth-century philosophers crafted their highly romanticized image of the American Indian. While Jean-Jacques Rousseau (1712–1778) and others looked to the Tupinambá as a model for the "noble savage," other French philosophers held up Inca religion as an example of what an enlightened monarchy and nonpapal deist religion could look like. Although far removed from South America itself, these writings continued to influence the study of South American religions for many future generations.

With their independence from Spain in the early nineteenth century, the new South American republics became once again available to the travelers, adventurers, natural historians, and scientists who could provide firsthand observations. Whereas earlier colonial observers had approached the study of religion through the political and theological lens of empire and conversion, these nineteenth-century travelers used the new languages of science and evolutionary progress to measure the Indians' status with respect to contemporary European cultural and historical achievements. While none of these travelogues and natural histories was intended as a study of indigenous religion per se, many of them include reports on religious custom. Among the most important of these are the travel accounts of Ephraim George Squier (1877), Charles Wiener (1880), Friedrich Hassaurek (1867), and James Orton (1876) for the Andean highlands and Johann Baptist von Spix and Carl von Martius (1824), Henri Coudreau (1880–1900), Alcides d'Orbigny (1854), and General Couto de Magalhães (1876) for the Amazonian lowlands. Such descriptions were augmented, especially in the Amazon, by detailed and often highly informative accounts of "pagan" practices written by missionary ethnographers such as José Cardus (1886) in Bolivia and W. H. Brett (1852) in British Guiana (now Guyana).

This nineteenth-century literature tended to romanticize the Indians and their religions through exaggerated accounts of practices such as head-hunting, cannibalism, blood sacrifice, and ritual drinking. In these "descriptions" of religion emphasis is placed on the exotic, wild, and uncivilized aspects of the Indians' religious practices—and on the narrator's bravery and fortitude in searching them out. Such romanticizing and exoticizing, however, tended to occur unevenly. Thus whereas religions of the Amazon Basin were subject to the most exotic and picturesque stereotypes of what a tropical primitive should be, the less-remote Andean Indians were described primarily in terms of their degeneration from the glories of a lost Inca religion that was considered to be more enlightened or "pure."

Early- to Mid-Twentieth-Century Studies. The twentieth century ushered in new forms of scientific inquiry and scholarly ideals. Departing from the narrative, subjective styles of the chroniclers, travelers, and natural historians, modern writers sought to describe indigenous religion independently of any personal, cultural, or historical biases about it; subjectivity was to be subsumed to a new ideal of relativism and objectivity. These writers conform to two general yet interrelated disciplinary fields: (1) the anthropologists and historians of religion, who use a comparative and typological framework to examine the universal, phenomenological bases of religious belief, and (2) the area specialists, or Americanists, who are interested in defining the specificity and social cultural evolution of religions in the Americas.

The first group included such early scholars of lowland religions as Paul Ehrenreich (1905), Max Schmidt (1905), and Adolf E. Jensen (who later founded the Frankfurt ethnographic school, home to such important modern scholars of South American religions as Otto Zerries and Karin Hissink). Their comparativist theories proved an impetus for the later field studies of Martin Gusinde (1931–1937) in Tierra del Fuego, William Farabee (1915–1922), and Günter Tessmann (1928–1930) in the Northwest Amazon, Konrad T. Preuss (1920–1930) in both highland and lowland Colombia, and Theodor Koch-Grünberg (1900–1930) in the Orinoco and in Northwest Brazil. These field-workers wrote detailed general accounts of lowland or Amazonian religions and placed special emphasis on the analysis of iconography, mythology, and animism.

Studies of highland religion during this early-twentieth-century period tended to focus almost exclusively on antiquities. The most important of these studies are the linguistic treatises of E. W. Middendorf (1890–1892) and J. J. von Tschudi (1891) and the archaeological surveys of Max Uhle and Alfons Stubel (1892). Both Incaic and contemporary Andean materials, however, were included in the broad surveys done by the scholars Adolf Bastian (1878–1889) and Gustav Brühl (1857–1887), who were interested in comparing the religions and languages of North, South, and Central America to establish a theory of cultural unity.

The Americanists' interdisciplinary studies of indigenous religion drew on the early twentieth-century German studies and on at least three other sources as well. The first was the fieldwork during the 1920s, 1930s, and 1940s by European ethnologists such as Alfred Métraux, Paul Rivet, and Herbert Baldus as well as by American anthropologists from the Smithsonian Institution's Bureau of Ethnology. Beyond describing the general social organization, religion, ritual, and mythologies of the Indians, these men were interested in classifying the cultures and religions they found by tracing their interrelationships and linguistic affiliations. In their writings therefore a detailed account of religion is often subordinated to an overriding interest in linguistic data and material culture. For example, detailed studies of shamanism were produced by the Scandinavian ethnographers Rafael Karsten, Henri Wassen, and Erland Nordenskiöld as part of a broader comparative examination of the material culture of South America. Of these early ethnographers, the German anthropologist Curt Nimuendajú stands out both for the extent of his fieldwork among the Ge, Boróro, Apinagé, Tucano, and Tupi tribes and for the degree to which his interests in describing these groups focused on their religious and ritual life. Other important sources on religious practices during this period are provided in the accounts of missionaries and priests, such as Bernadino de Nino (1912) in Bolivia, Gaspar de Pinelli (1924) in Colombia, and Antonio Colbacchini and Cesar Albisetti (1907–1942) in Brazil.

A second group that influenced early Americanist approaches to religion was composed of ethnohistorians and archaeologists. Often hailed as the first true Americanists to work in the Southern Hemisphere, the archaeologists left a distinctive imprint on South American studies by the nature of their specialty: the study of the pre-Spanish Andean past. Excavations, surveys, and analyses of previously unstudied sites in both coastal and highland Peru by Max Uhle and Adolph Bandelier were followed by the more detailed chronological studies of Alfred Kroeber, Junius Bird, Wendell Bennett, and John Rowe. Although the chronologies and site inventories constructed by these archaeologists did not focus on religion per se, the temple structures, burials, offerings, textiles, ceramics, and other ritual paraphernalia they unearthed provided new data on the importance of religion in pre-Columbian social organization and political evolution. Interpretation of this material was facilitated by the work of ethnohistorians such as Hermann Trimborn and Paul Kirchoff. Their historical investigations of both highland and lowland religions contributed inmeasurably to an overall working definition of South American religious systems and their relation to systems of social stratification, state rule, and ethnicity.

A third and final group that helped shape Americanist studies was composed of South American folklorists, indigenists, and anthropologists. In attempting to resurrect indigenous culture and religion, *indigenista* writers of the 1930s and 1940s differed from the foreign ethnologists of these formative Americanist years. Their work was motivated largely by an explicit desire to record South American lifeways and religions before such practices—and the people who practiced them—disappeared completely. The emphasis of the *indigenista* studies on the vitality of living religious systems also served as an important counter to the archaeologists' initial influence on Americanist thinking. The prodigious group of national writers influenced by *indigenismo* subsequently compiled a vast archive of oral traditions, "customs," and ritual practices. Notable among these folklorists and anthropologists are Antonio Paredes Candia and Enrique Oblitas Poblete of Bolivia, Roberto Lehmann-Nitsche of Argentina, Gregorio Hernández de Alba of Colombia, and Jose-María Arguedas, Jorge Lira, and Oscar Nuñez del Prado of Peru. Unique among them was the Peruvian archaeologist-anthropologist Julio C. Tello. One of the most creative archaeologists working in Peru, Tello was also the only one interested in exploring the relation of the religious data he unearthed to modern-day Quechua beliefs and practices. His ethnographic publications of the 1920s are landmarks in the study of Andean religion, and his archaeological investigations of the 1930s and 1940s extended knowledge of the Andean religious mind into a comparative framework interrelating highland and lowland cosmologies and religions.

The major work to appear out of the formative period of Americanist studies is the seven-volume *Handbook of South American Indians* edited by Julian H. Steward (1946–1959). Though somewhat outdated, the *Handbook*'s articles, which cover aspects of prehistory, material culture, social organization, and ecology, still provide what is perhaps the most useful and accessible comparative source for beginning study of South American religions. Its interest for a history of religious studies, however, also lies in what it reveals about the biases informing Americanists' treatment of religion. These are (1) a preoccupation with relative historical or evolutionary classifications and the description of religious systems in terms of their similarity to, or degeneration from, a pre-Columbian standard, (2) a lowland-highland dichotomy informed by this evolutionary mode and according to which tropical forest religions are judged to be less "complex" than the pre-Hispanic prototypes formulated for the Andes by archaeologists and ethnohistorians, and (3) the comparative framework used by scholars who were more interested in discovering the cultural affinities and evolutionary links that connected different religious practices than they were in describing and analyzing the function and meaning of religious practices on a local level. The shortcomings of this dispersed and comparative focus are intimated by many of the *Handbook*'s authors, who lament the inadequacy of their data on specific religious systems.

FUNCTIONALIST AND FUNCTIONALIST-INFLUENCED STUDIES. The next group of scholars to address religious issues set out specifically to remedy this situation by studying indigenous religion in its social context. The manner in which local religious systems were treated was, however, once again tempered by the theoretical orientations of their observers. Thus the first group of anthropologists to follow the *Handbook*'s lead during the 1950s and early 1960s was influenced by the functionalist school of British anthropology. According to this theory, society is an organic whole whose various parts may be analyzed or explained in terms of their integrative function in maintaining the stability or equilibrium of a local group. Religion was considered to be a more or less passive reflection of the organic unity of a total social system. Examples of this approach are the monographs of William W. Stein (1961) on the Peruvian Andes, Allan R. Holmberg (1950) on the Siriono of lowland Bolivia, and Irving Goldman (1963) on the Cubeo of Brazil. In several cases more detailed monographs were written that focused specifically on the role of religion in indigenous social organization; these include works by Robert Murphy on the Brazilian Mundurucú, Segundo Bernal on the Paez of Colombia, David Maybury-Lewis on the Akwe-Xavante, and Louis C. Faron on the Mapuche, or Araucanians, of coastal Chile.

One variant of this functionalist approach brought out the role of religion as a means of achieving or maintaining balance between social and ecological systems. Prime examples of this approach are Gerardo Reichel-Dolmatoff's brilliant, Freudian-influenced treatments of mythology, shamanism, and cosmology among the Koghi Indians of Colombia's Sierra Nevada highlands and the Desána (Tucano) of the Northwest Amazon. Other studies of shamanism, cosmology, and hallucinogens have been carried out by the anthropologists Douglas Sharon in coastal Peru and Michael Harner in eastern Ecuador.

STRUCTURALIST STUDIES. During the 1960s and 1970s scholars began to question the passively reflective, or "superstructural," role to which much of functionalist anthropology had relegated religion as well as the simplistic and ultimately evolutionist dichotomies between the Andean and tropical forest cultures. The major theoretical impetus for this new approach came from structuralism, which proposed to analyze the affinities connecting mythologies and ritual practices and the societies in which they occurred by referring all to a pervasive symbolic or cognitive structure based on dual oppositions and on diverse forms of hierarchical organization. The pioneering works of this tradition were Claude Lévi-Strauss's studies of social organization and mythology in the Amazon basin and his four-volume *Mythologiques* (1964–1971), which presented a system for analyzing mythic narratives as isolated variants of an organizational logic whose standardized structure he invoked to explain the commonality of all North and South American modes of religious expression and social organization.

The structuralist approach has been particularly important for the study of religion. For the first time a mode of thinking—evidenced by religion and mythology—was not only taken as the principal index of cultural identity but was also seen to influence and even partly to determine the organization of other spheres of social and economic life. In its renewed focus on religion, structuralism inspired myriad studies of lowland ritual and mythology, including those by Jean-Paul Dumont, Michel Perrin, Terence Turner, Jacques Lizot, Anthony Seeger, Stephen Hugh-Jones, and Christine Hugh-Jones. These structuralist studies of mythology and social organization were completed—and often preceded—by collections of mythologies and descriptions of cosmologies (or "worldviews") by ethnographers such as Johannes Wilbert, Marc de Civrieux, Darcy Ribiero, Roberto DaMatta, Egon Schaden, Neils Fock, and Gerald Weiss. Though departing from the structuralists' methodologies, these anthropologists shared with the structuralists an interest in studying religion as an expression of social organization, society-nature classifications, and broad cultural identities.

In the Andes, where mythologies and religion were judged to be less pristine and less divorced from the ravages of historical, social, and economic change, Lévi-Strauss's theories generated interest in the study of social continuity through examination of structural forms. These studies of underlying structural continuity were based on extensive fieldwork by ethnographers and ethnohistorians such as Billie Jean Isbell, Juan Ossio, Henrique Urbano, Gary Urton, John Earls, and Alejandro Ortíz Rescaniere. These scholars have argued for the existence of a constant and culturally specific religious (as well as mythological and astronomical) structure by means of which indigenous groups have retained their cultural identity over time. Their studies of postconquest religious continuity drew on ethnohistorical models of Andean social organization, in particular R. Tom Zuidema's complex structural model of Inca social relations and ritual geographies and María Rostworowski de Diez Canseco's studies of pre-Hispanic coastal societies. Both of these ethnohistorians have emphasized the role of mythology, ritual, and religious ideology in the shaping of Andean economic and political history.

Structuralist methodology also motivated a new type of comparative study focusing on the similarities linking Andean and Amazonian religions. For example, Zuidema's structural model for Inca socioreligious organization pointed out the important similarities between this elaborate highland state system and the equally complex modes of ritual and social organization found among the Ge and Boróro Indians of Brazil. D. W. Lathrap's archaeological model for the evolution of South American social organization used similar comparative techniques to establish a common heritage of lowland and highland cosmologies. By combining this comparative insight with the historical dynamics of archaeology and ethnohistory and by assigning to religion a determinative role in the evolution of social systems, such models not only questioned but in many ways actually reversed the prevailing stereotypic dichotomy between "primitive" Amazon and "civilized" Andes.

HISTORICAL AND POSTSTRUCTURALIST VIEWS. In the final decades of the twentieth century anthropologists and other students of religion began increasingly to question the notions of unity, coherence, and continuity that had characterized much earlier work on indigenous religion. Structuralists had intepreted myth as the partial expression or transformation of mental structures that endured over time and ritual as the symbolic performance of the formal, structural principles that lent meaning to a particular culture's cosmology or worldview. Through such forms of analysis, structuralists emphasized the coherency and mobility of the structural principles expressed in the many different domains of social life. In so doing they also made important claims concerning the pervasive character of "religion" and the impossibility of drawing a definite boundary between religious and secular activities in indigenous societies.

Poststructuralist work has built on and expanded this methodological and theoretical claim that "religion" must be studied in many different and overlapping domains of social life. At the same time scholars working in the 1980s and 1990s used historical methodologies to question structuralism's claims regarding the coherency and stability of mental and symbolic structures. Because the study of indigenous societies often depended on the use of documentary sources written by Spaniards and other nonindigenous authors, history or ethnohistory has been a foundational methodology for many South Americanists. For example, Zuidema and other structualists built their models of pristine Inca and Andean religious systems through the creative, critical use of Spanish chronicles and archives. The new historical work on religion by Tristan Platt, Thomas A. Abercrombie, Joanne Rappaport, and others has drawn on ethnohistorical methods in their search for an indigenous "voice" in the colonial archive. Unlike the earlier structuralists, however, their goal was not to reconstruct the elements of a precontact society but to understand the complex role played by religion in the political worlds formed through the interaction of indigenous and European societies.

In part because of their heavy debt to structualist methodologies and perspectives, early historical anthropologies tended to approach religion as an inherently conservative domain of belief whose persistence in colonial times could be read as a form of resistance to colonial rule. Of particular importance in this respect were the studies of messianic movements as forms of religious conservatism coupled with situations of social resistance or even revolution. In the Andes such work was stimulated largely by ethnohistorical studies of colonial messianisms by the Peruvian anthropologists Juan Ossio, Franklin Pease, and Luis Millones. Other studies interpreted indigenous religious beliefs and practices as strategies for consolidating ethnic identities threatened by the encroachment of "modern" national societies. These include studies by Norman E. Whitten Jr. in Amazonian Ecuador, the mythology collections of Orlando Villas Boas and Claudio Villas Boas in the Brazilian Xingu River area, Miguel Chase-Sardi's studies of ethnicity and oral literatures in Paraguay, and William Crocker and Cezar L. Melatti in the Brazilian Amazon.

Through its emphasis on contingency, political complexity, and intrigue, subsequent work has tended to complicate the category of resistance itself, along with the dual-society models that were often implied by the concept of resistance. Stefano Varese's groundbreaking work on the Peruvian Campa or Ashaninka, based on fieldwork conducted during the late 1960s and early 1970s, provides an early example of a political anthropology of religion that emphasized the political economic contexts in which messianic movements and indigenous political resistance took shape. Other examples include the work of anthropologists Robin M. Wright and Jonathan Hill on northern Amazonian religious movements and political organization; Xavier Albó, Platt, Olivia Harris, Abercrombie, and Roger Rasnake on the colonial origins and rationality of the sacred landscapes, social practices, and authority structures through which Aymara religious practices engage issues of politics and power; and Jean Jackson and Alcida Ramos on ethnic relations and indigenous politics in the Colombian and Brazilian Amazon. Although the concept of a religious syncretism between colonial (usually Catholic) and indigenous belief systems has long been a central issue in anthropological treatments of religion, these new historical studies move well beyond the notion of syncretism to paint a more complex picture of how individuals, groups, and political movements strategically manipulate and conceptualize the semantic and epistemic divides that ideally differentiate "native" and "colonial," Indian and mestizo, resistance and accommodation.

Ethnographers have also begun to question the models of culture and meaning through which early anthropologists once defended the unity of indigenous cultural systems and the interpretation of ritual and myth. Rather than looking for the inner "meaning" hidden within religious words and practices, these ethnographies build on poststructuralist models of language and practice to explore how meaning accrues to words and practices as they unfold in time. Though focused on different areas of social production, these ethnographies hold in common the idea that "religion" is best studied across different domains of social practice rather than as a discrete symbolic system that functions to give "meaning" to other domains of indigenous experience. Thus ethnographers such as Catherine J. Allen in the Peruvian Andes have examined etiquette and sociality as lived domains in which religious belief takes hold not as an extant symbolic system but as the moral and ethical perspective that is played out through the many small routines and interactions of daily life.

Studies of Andean spatial practices and aesthetics by Urton, Nathan Wachtel, and Rappaport among others emphasized how "religious" meanings are woven into such collective material practices as wall construction and territorial boundary maintenance. Other anthropologists, such as Greg Urban and Jackson, have looked at the linguistic practices through which myths are recounted and interpreted in local social life. Finally, Michael T. Taussig's important work on the Colombian Putumayo and modern Venezuela has explored shamanism as a lens on the working of power, fear, and memory in the shaping of Colombian modernity. Taussig's work has been particularly important in that it takes the claims of indigenous religious belief and historical narrative seriously as a force in the shaping of modern Latin America. Taussig thus succeeds in questioning the spurious distinction between magical and rational thought and with it the categories of myth and history that permeated so much earlier work on South American religion.

CONCLUSION. Taken together historical and poststructuralist approaches have had the singular effect of undermining the integrity and coherency of the very categories "religion" and "indigenous" that animated so much earlier anthropology in the region. For a majority of the anthropologists and historians working in South America, it is no longer possible to speak of indigenous communities, practices, identities, or beliefs without situating them in broader regional and national histories. As the notion of indigenous religion becomes unhinged from its original location in the pristine, or supposedly pristine, life of the "Indian community," it has become possible for scholars to think critically and historically about the place of different Christian belief systems in South American indigenous life. Anthropologists have begun to study the Protestant evangelical and Catholic charismatic sects that have become so prominent in many indigenous communities of South America. Wachtel, Antoinette Fioravanti-Molinié, and others have analyzed the persistence of indigenous religious beliefs regarding threatening *ñakaqs*, or spirits who extract body fat, in contexts of uncertainty and change, including among urban indigenous groups. Similarly the category of "popular Catholicism" that was first introduced by Liberation theologists in the aftermth of Vactican II has become a stable of anthropological writing about indigenous religion, allowing for a similar extension of the category of indigenous religion to encompass a broader array of ritual practices and beliefs that are more consonant with the actual experiences of modern indigenous people living in nation states.

An important inspiration for studies focused on subaltern or indigenous groups is the new work by historians such as Sabine MacCormack on the philosophical and theological origins of South American notions of idolatry, redemption, and the miracle and Kenneth Mills on the complex political and religious forces behind the sixteenth-century campaigns against indigenous "idolatry." Through such works it becomes possible to appreciate the long route that has been traversed from early scholarly obsessions with locating a pure indigenous religion to the more historically grounded scholarship in which religious practices are at once seen as fully, even paradigmatically modern, without for that reason ceasing to be any less "indigenous."

SEE ALSO Ge Mythology; Jensen, Adolf E.; Preuss, Konrad T.; Structuralism.

BIBLIOGRAPHY

Allen, Catherine J. *The Hold Life Has: Coca and Cultural Identity in an Andean Community.* Washington, D.C., 1988. A sensitive ethnography of daily life in the Peruvian Andes, focused on the ritualized use of coca. It highlights the pervasive presence of the religious ideals and attachment to landscape that shape social interaction.

Duviols, Pierre. *La lutte contre les religions autochtones dans le Pérou colonial: "L'extirpation de l'idolâtrie," entre 1532 et 1660.* Lima, Peru, 1971. A historical study of the Catholic Church's campaign against Andean religions. It contains archival materials that describe religious practices of the time as well as an analysis of the Spaniards' motives for initiating the campaign.

Krickeberg, Walter, et al. *Pre-Columbian American Religions.* Translated by Stanley Davis. London, 1968. Contains survey articles by Hermann Trimborn and Otto Zerries. Informative for its breadth of material, it has a sample of the types of analyses used by historians of religion in the German tradition.

Lévi-Strauss, Claude. *Mythologiques.* 4 vols. Paris, 1964–1971. Translated into English by John Weightman and Doreen Weightman as *Introduction to a Science of Mythology.* 3 vols. New York, 1969. A collection and analysis of myths from the Western Hemisphere by the originator of structuralist method in anthropology. It is best read along with Lévi-Strauss's earlier works, *Tristes Tropiques* (New York, 1974) and *Structural Anthropology*, 2 vols. (New York, 1963).

MacCormack, Sabine. *Religion in the Andes: Vision and Imagination in Early Colonial Peru.* Princeton, N.J., 1991.

Métraux, Alfred. *Religions et magies indiennes d'Amérique du Sud: Édition posthume établie par Simone Dreyfus.* Paris, 1967. Métraux was one of the founding figures of Americanist studies. This collection of his articles covers nearly all the areas in which he did fieldwork, including Peru (Quechua), Bolivia (Uro-Chipaya and Aymara), the Argentinian Chaco (Guaraní), Chile (Mapuche), and Brazil (Tupi).

Mills, Kenneth. *Idolatry and Its Enemies: Colonial Andean Religion and Extirpation, 1640–1750.* Princeton, N.J., 1997.

Nimuendajú, Curt. *The Eastern Timbira.* Translated and edited by Robert H. Lowie. Berkeley, Calif., 1946. One of several detailed descriptive monographs of lowland social organization and religion produced by Nimuendajú, a German fieldworker who lived most of his life among the indigenous peoples of south-central Brazil and who adopted an indigenous surname.

Reichel-Dolmatoff, Gerardo. *Amazonian Cosmos: The Sexual and Religious Symbolism of the Tukano Indians.* Chicago, 1971. A Freudian and ecological analysis of the lowland cosmology (Tucano or Desána of the Vaupés River, Colombia) by one of Colombia's leading anthropologists. His other books, *Los Kogi: Una tribu de la Sierra Nevada de Santa Marta, Colombia*, 2 vols. (Bogotá, Colombia, 1950–1951), and *The Shaman and the Jaguar: A Study of Narcotic Drugs among the Indians of Columbia* (Philadelphia, 1975) are also considered classics in South American religious studies.

Steward, Julian H., ed. *The Handbook of South American Indians.* 7 vols. Washington, D.C., 1946–1959. A compilation of articles by archaeologists, historians, and anthropologists that provides the best overall introduction to the variety of religious forms in South America as well as to the theoretical approaches that had, up until the time of the *Handbook*'s publication, informed their study. Its seven volumes are divided by geographic area, with two volumes devoted to comparative studies.

Sullivan, Lawrence E. *Icanchu's Drum: An Orientation to Meaning in South American Religions.* New York, 1988. A wide-reaching survey of the religions of South America from the perspective of a historical of religions. It contains an unprecedentedly thorough bibliography.

Taussig, Michael T. *Shamanism, Colonialism, and the Wild Man: A Study in Terror and Healing.* Chicago, 1986. An exploration of shamanism and religious healing in the Colombian Putumayo region in the context of regional histories and experiences of violence. Offers compelling evidence of the power and presence of indigenous religious beliefs and images in the Colombian national imagination.

Tello, Julio C., with Prospero Miranda. "Wallallo: Ceremonias gentílicas realizadas en la región cisandina del Perú central." *Inca* 1, no. 2 (1923): 475–549. Written by the father of Peruvian archaeology and published in the anthropological journal he edited, this article gives detailed descriptions of indigenous ritual practices in the central highlands of Peru, comparing them with the pre-Columbian religion.

Wilbert, Johannes, and Karin Simoneau, eds. *Folk Literature of South American Indians.* 7 vols. Los Angeles, 1970–. A continuing series containing compilations of myths from the Boróro, Warao, Selk'nam, Yámana, Ge, Mataco, and Toba Indians. It contains materials from the classic, early ethnographies of these groups as well as from more recent anthropological studies. It is annotated by Wilbert, who has also published extensively on the mythologies and cosmologies of indigenous groups in the Orinoco.

Wright, Robin M. *Cosmos, Self, and History in Baniwa Religion: For Those Unborn.* Austin, Tex., 1998. An excellent example of new historical work on indigenous religion, including discussions of shamanism and its relation to mythic and historic consciousness and the Baniwas' conversion to Protestantism.

Deborah A. Poole (1987 and 2005)

SOUTH AMERICAN INDIANS

This entry consists of the following articles:

SOUTH AMERICAN INDIANS: INDIANS OF THE ANDES IN THE PRE-INCA PERIOD

The Andean region is formed by the Andes mountain range, which extends the entire length of western South America. This region can be divided into three geographically contrasting subareas: the highlands, the coast, and the eastern cordillera. In the highlands the intermontane valleys lie at altitudes of between three and four thousand meters. These valleys were the places in which the Chavín (tenth to first centuries BCE), Tiahuanaco-Huari (eighth to tenth centuries CE), and Inca (fifteenth century CE) cultures flourished. In the region along the Pacific coast, composed mostly of lowlying desert plains, life was concentrated out of necessity in the valleys formed by the rivers that drain from the highlands into the ocean. The coastal valleys in the Peruvian sector of the Andes region were the cradles of cultures such as the Moche (second to eighth centuries CE), the Paracas-Nazca (second to eighth centuries CE), and the Chimú (twelfth to fifteenth centuries CE), who devised colossal irrigation works that enabled them to bring extensive areas of desert under cultivation. The dramatic, abruptly changing topography of the eastern cordillera is covered by dense tropical vegetation. Peoples of the intermontane valleys entered this region and built the cities of Machu Picchu and Pajatén, and they terraced vast areas of the rugged, wooded hillsides to gain land for cultivation and to prevent erosion.

The sheltered agricultural cultures of the Andes have interrelated since ancient times. The areas where such cultures did not develop, although geographically "Andean," are not considered part of the Andean cultural region. The territory of the central Andes—basically equivalent to present-day Peru—became the center of the Andean cultural process. The northern Andes (parts of present-day Colombia and Ecuador) was the scene of the Quimbaya and Muisca (Chibcha) cultures and of the earlier Valdivia culture, which may have given the initial impulse to the entire high-Andean culture.

More than ten thousand years have passed since human beings first trod the Andes. The earliest settlers were hunters and Neolithic agriculturalists. By the third millennium BCE there appear incipient signs of complex cultures, such as that of Aldas on the northern coast of Peru, whose people built monumental temples. During the second and first millennia BCE, the appearance of Valdivia and Chavín represented the first flowering of developed culture, which set the foundation for the developments that eventually culminated in the Inca empire. By the time that Europeans arrived in the Americas, the Inca empire stretched for more than four thousand miles along the western part of South America, from southern Colombia in the north to Maule, in south central Chile, in the south. The empire passed into Spanish dominion in 1532, when Atahuallpa, the thirteenth and last of the Inca sovereigns, was beheaded. From then on, the breakdown of indigenous Andean cultural values is apparent.

Sources of Documentation. Study of Andean religion rests on two principle sources: the reports of early chroniclers and the archaeological documentation that presents a visual record of Andean civilizations. A number of chronicles exist that were written in the sixteenth and seventeenth centuries by Indians, mestizos, and Spaniards (who based their accounts on the reports of native informants). There are also other reports—files relating to the prosecution of cases of "witchcraft"—that remain scattered in archives, mostly unedited. The detailed reports composed by the "eradicators of idolatries" are of special value. For the most part, the chroniclers' accounts are interwoven with evident prejudices of divers origin.

Even though the archaeological and iconographic evidence is scanty, it may be that the conclusions drawn from it are founded on a firmer basis than are those derived from chroniclers' reports. Naturally, study of iconography requires specific hermeneutic methods, especially when drawings are heavily loaded with symbols or are confusingly executed. Present-day Andean religious practices (especially in rural areas), which in many cases represent survivals of the pre-Conquest Andean religious world, represent a third source of documentation.

Subsistence and Religion. The peoples of the Andes are predisposed toward mysticism and ceremonial; even today, Andeans are steeped in an elaborate religious tradition. A significant part of their intense religiosity may be explained by ecological factors: No other agricultural society in the world has had to face a more hostile environment than that of the Andes region, with its vast areas of desert, its enormous wastes, and the heavy tropical vegetation that covers the mountains' rugged eastern flanks. All physical effort, all organization of human labor, and all technological solutions are insufficient to counter the environment, to whose ordinary harshness are added nature's frequent scourges, especially droughts. This endemic state of crisis could only be exorcised, it seems, through intense magico-religious practices; only through manipulation of supernatural powers have Andean peoples believed it possible to guarantee their existence.

The dramatic situation imposed by the environment perhaps explains why Andean religiosity appears to have been unencumbered by the moralizing of other religious traditions. Rules such as "Thou shalt not steal" and "Thou shalt not commit adultery" were of course enforced, but theft and adultery were considered social offenses: It was the duty of the administrators of state law to punish offenders. There was no concept of a future expiation. The relationship between religion and morality was closest in regard to behavior toward the deities; if their worship was not properly carried out, they were affronted, resulting in a series of calamities that could be checked through prayers, weeping, and sacrifices. The hostility of nature in the Andes led to a permanently febrile state of religiosity.

Gods of Sustenance. Andean deities jointly governed both individual and collective existence by providing sustenance. Soil fertility plays a significant role in Andean religion, as demonstrated by the profuse worship given to the deities that personified and controlled the forces of nature. The gods, though individualized, form a hieratic unit and share one focus: the economic state of the people. They are conceived in the image of nature, which simultaneously separates and conjoins the creative forces, masculine and feminine. Thus the first basic division appears in the opposition of Inti-Viracocha-Pachacámac and Quilla-Pachamama. Both of these deity-configurations are creative forces, but in accordance with the social order of the sexes, the supremacy of the former, masculine element is asserted. The powerful Illapa ("thunder, weather") is also integrated into the sphere of Inti-Viracocha-Pachacámac, but, above all his other functions, Illapa directly provides life-giving rain.

Viracocha. Glimpses of a culture hero on whom divine attributes have been superimposed can be seen in the figure of Viracocha, and therefore Pierre Duviols (1977) and María Rostworowski de Diez Canseco (1983) correctly deny him the character of a creator god. Because of these same divine attributes, however, Viracocha was thought by the sixteenth-century Spaniards to resemble the God of Christianity, although Christian-Andean syncretism preserved some aspects of Viracocha's indigenous origin. Thus, according to the stories told about him, Viracocha molded humans in clay or sculpted them in stone. (They finally spring from the womb of Pachamama, "mother earth," which is sometimes represented as a cave.) On the other hand, stories about Viracocha also portray him as entering into confrontations with other divine beings and as engaged in other tasks ordinarily associated with culture heroes (for example, "teaching the created people"). Evidence of Viracocha's original character as a god of sustenance may be found in the prayer to him that was transcribed by the seventeenth-century chronicler Cristobal de Molina, in which Viracocha is presumed to be based "in thunder and tempests." Franklin Pease (1973) assigns to him outright solar and fertility attributes.

Pachacámac. The myth of Pachacámac ("animator of the world") links this Andean deity even more strongly than Viracocha with the creation of the first generation of human beings. This deity is characterized, above all, as bringing to humankind the food necessary for survival as a result of the entreaties of a primordial woman, Mother Earth. The provision of edible plants is shown in other myths: In one of these, Pachacámac disguises himself, taking the form of the sun (in some instances, the son, the brother, or even the father of Pachacámac, according to the chronicler Francisco Lopez de Gómara), who with his rays fertilizes the primordial woman, perhaps the incarnation of Pachamama. In another myth, Pachacámac kills what he has created, and this action may be interpreted as the institution of human sacrifice to nourish the food and fertility deities. When the victim is buried, his teeth sprout maize, his bones become manioc, and so on.

Inti. According to both the surviving mythic literature and the images discovered by archaeologists, the masculine creative force was incarnated in Inti, the sun. He offers heat and light, and his rays possess fertilizing powers, as is evident in the myth of Pachacámac. Mythic literature testifies to the Andeans' reliance on the power of the sun and to their anxiety that he may disappear, causing cataclysm and the destruction of humankind (an event that would be followed by the creation of a new generation of humans). This anxiety explains the redoubled prayers and supplications during solar eclipses—rituals that ended with loud cries and lamentations (even domestic animals were whipped to make them howl!). Archaeological evidence of another form of magico-religious defense against this premonition of the tragic disappearance of the sun is found in stone altars called *intihuatanas,* a word revealingly translated as "the place where the sun is tied." Inti was also associated with fertility through water, as when the sun ceases to give light, yielding to clouds and rain (which would seem a contradiction were it not for the fact that the thunder and weather god Illapa was conjoined with the sun). In visual representations, particularly those at Chavín and Tiahuanaco, Inti appears with big teardrops that surely symbolize rain. Gold was the symbol par excellence of the sun, and the robes of head shamans were covered with oscillating metal disks that reflected the sun's rays and imitated its radiance.

Pachamama-Quilla. Pachamama ("mother earth") symbolized the feminine element of divinity for the Andeans. Pachamama is incarnated as the primordial mother of mythic literature, and she is personified as Quilla, the moon. In this connection she is symbolized by silver; with this metal many representations of Pachamama were made, especially in the form of the half-moon (called *tumi*), which was one of the most important religious symbols of the Andes. The cult of Pachamama was, and still is, extensive (Mariscotti de Görlitz, 1978). Pachamama was held to be the producer of food, animals, and the first human. As primordial mother, she creates through the fertilizing action of the Sun, and she later becomes co-donor of food plants, especially maize.

The mythological literature tells of several female supernatural beings. These are likely regional versions of Pachamama. Among them are Chaupiñanca, the primordial mother of Huarochirí mythology; Illa, who appears in the mythic traditions of the Ecuadorian Andes; and Urpihuáchac, sister and wife of Pachacámac, who seems to be an expression of Cochamama, the marine form of Pachamama. To Cochamama is attributed the creation of fish and of seabirds such as the guanay, which latter act is in turn related to agricultural productivity because of the use of guano to fertilize crops.

Ancient documents show that Pachamama was individualized *ad infinitum* to guarantee the abundance of specific produce—maize, for example. Andean iconography offers representations of Pachamama incarnated in specific vegetable forms: multiple ears of maize, for instance, or groups of potatoes. In other instances these agricultural products metaphorically acquire human aspects, and they are also portrayed as being fertilized by a supernatural, anthropomorphic personage. Pachamama in her Cochamama aspect also appears to symbolize the presence of abundant water—essential for fertilizing the agricultural fields.

The symbolism of Pachamama has implications regarding the social status of women: As compared with the male element of divinity, Pachamama, the female, is clearly a passive and subaltern being. Her dependence on the male is established in the mythological literature. She uses her feminine attributes to win from the male gods favors, such as irrigation canals, that are beneficial to the collectivity. Pachamama also enshrines the modesty and passivity in sexual matters that characterizes the Andean woman to this day. The attitude of sexual modesty is to be seen in the many representations that appear to show versions of Pachamama, from the archaic terracotta figures of Valdivia to those of the late Chancay civilization of the central coast of Peru. In all these, sexual characteristics are not pronounced: The figures seem to represent almost asexual beings, and they remind one of the existence of non-Christian sexual taboos (see Kauffmann Doig, 1979a). Not only do these figures rarely stress sexual characteristics, but, curiously, they seldom portray pregnant women or women giving birth. Perhaps the anthropomorphic figures with birdlike attributes that appear on the walls of Pajatén—which figures are shown in crouching positions with spread legs—are in fact female procreators (Kauffmann Doig, 1983, p. 531). Except for the cases of sexual representations from Vicus and, especially, in Moche art (both from the northern coast of Peru), images of women found throughout the Andean culture region seem to underscore that female sexuality was marked by modesty.

Pachamama continues to play an important role in the deeply rooted peasant magic of today's Andean people. She is even venerated in Christian churches. In the Peruvian village of Huaylas, for example, Saramama (a version of Pachamama) is venerated in the form of two female saints who are joined in a single sculpture—like Siamese twins—to give visual representation to a pathetic fallacy: the symbolization of abundance that is identified in the double or multiple ears of grain that maize plants often generously produce.

Illapa. The deity Illapa (generally translated as "thunder," "lightning," or "weather") occupies a preferential place in the Andean pantheon. Much of the mythological literature makes reference to Illapa, who takes on regional names and is expressed in varying forms: Yaro, Ñamoc, Libiac, Catequil, Pariacaca, Thunapa (possibly), and so on. To refer to these beings as if they were separate would be artificially to crowd the Andean pantheon by creating too great a number of distinct deities—a trap into which many interpreters, both early and recent, have fallen. Illapa may be seen as the incarnation of Inti, the sun, in Illapa's primary mythic form of a hawk or eagle (*indi* means "bird" in Quechua), a form to which were added human and feline attributes; thus Inti-Illapa may be said to be a true binomial in the Andean pantheon.

Associated with meteorological phenomena such as thunder, lightning, clouds, and rainbows, Illapa personifies rain, the element that fecundates the earth. As the direct source of sustenance—giving rains to the highlands and rivers and rich alluvial soils to the coastal valleys—Illapa is revered in a special and universal way. Yet he is also feared: for the crash of his thunder, for lightning that kills, for catastrophic hailstorms, severe floods, and even perhaps earthquakes. The worst of his scourges is drought. Proof of Illapa's prestige is the major temple to him (individualized as the ruler of atmospheric phenomena) that stood in Cuzco, the Inca capital; according to the plan of Cuzco drawn by Guaman Poma and the description written by Molina, Illapa's temple was rivalled only by the Coricancha, the temple of the sun.

After the Conquest, Andeans fused Illapa with images of James the Apostle, a syncretism perhaps suggested by earlier Spanish traditions. In the realm of folklore, Illapa's cult may be said still to flourish in the veneration of hills and high mountains, which are the nesting places of the *huamani* (falcons) sacred to this deity. Also associated with Illapa are the *apus,* the spirits of the mountains, and the spirits of the lakes, which, if they are not worshiped, make the waves rise destructively, and which are offended if approached by someone not protected by the sacred coca leaf.

When he appears as an incarnation of, or as joined to, Inti, Illapa may be represented by a male feline with human and avian attributes. According to iconographic studies, Illapa's image as the "flying feline," or "tiger bird" (Kauffmann Doig, 1967; 1983, p. 225) is still current in the Andes, as witnessed in the oral documentation collected by Bernard Mishkin (1963) regarding Qoa, a god who is ruler of meteorological phenomena. Qoa still appears as a flying cat, his eyes throwing out lightning and his urine transformed into fertilizing rain. Pictorial representations of the "tiger bird," which have been made since the formative period, especially in Chavín and allied art (see below) have recently been related to Qoa by Johan Reinhard (1985, pp. 19–20).

ANDEAN ICONOGRAPHY. Iconographic portrayal of supernatural beings is abundant and dates back more than three thousand years. In iconographic representations, supernatural beings are configured in complex ways; their hierarchal aspects are emphasized, and some achieve the status of gods. Supernatural beings other than gods are the figures represented in Sechín and in some Chavín art. Beings with the rank of gods are found in Chavín and related cultures—Vicús, Moche, Paracas-Nazca, Tiahuanaco, Huari, and others (especially Lambayeque).

Mythological literature indicates that those male beings who fertilize Mother Earth form the topmost division of the hierarchy of the Andean pantheon, which, again, is made up of deities of sustenance. One of the most obvious expressions of the Andean gods' character as providers is the anthropomorphic wooden figure of Huari style adorned with symbols referring to basic food products that was found in the temples of Pachacámac near Lima.

The image of a conspicuously superior being is found in the initial stages of high Andean civilization (especially in Chavín and related cultures). This image, typically a human form with feline and raptorial-bird attributes, is repeated in practically all the Andean cultures that succeeded Chavín, with variations of secondary importance. At Chavín, such hierarchal figures of the highest order appear on the Raimondi Stela; although lacking human elements, the figures on the Tello Obelisk and the Yauya Stela, both Chavín in style, may also be considered as representations of the highest level of being, because of their monumental stature and fine execution. The central figure of the Door of the Sun at Tiahuanaco is an almost anthropomorphic representation of the highest-ranking god. Attributes of a culture hero are perhaps also incorporated here.

A frequently encountered image of what was perhaps the same god as the one described above (but represented in a clearer and more accessible form) is that of a hybrid being that also had a form somewhere between a feline and a bird of prey (a falcon?), represented naturalistically, in which elements of human anatomy are sometimes completely absent. This "winged feline" may be the most ancient and authentic representation known to us of an Andean god. The convoluted, baroque style of Chavín art is responsible for the fact the the "winged feline" has sometimes been identified as a caiman and sometimes as a lobster, a shrimp, or even a spider. These animals, however, do not appear in relation to the divine sphere at any later stage of Andean culture.

Supernatural beings of the highest category are to be found in representations of the culture-heroes/gods Ai-apaec and Ñaymlap and of the gods at Tiahuanaco and Paracas-Nazca. All are anthropomorphic beings that combine traits of both bird and feline; in this context they imply an evolutionary development of the older "winged feline" of Chavín. In the archetypical versions of Ai-apaec, the figure bears wings (Kauffmann Doig, 1976; 1983, pp. 362, 624). At Paracas-Nazca, one figure seems to represent an evolution from a purely birdlike body into one that incorporates human elements (Kauffmann Doig, 1983, pp. 303, 325, 331–332). Feline and ornithomorphic ingredients are evident in the large figures at Tiahuanaco and Huari; from their eyes fall large tears in the form of birds, which, since Eugenio Yacovleff (1932) and even before, have been interpreted as symbolic of the fertilizing rainwater of Pachamama (Mamapacha).

Connubial gods in which the male element radiates fertilizing solar rays are found especially in the iconography derived from Huari and, more particularly, in the valleys of Huara, Pativilca, and Casma on the coast of Peru (Kauffmann Doig, 1979a, pp. 6, 60). The examples of Inca art that have survived have but scant votive content. But both the feline and the falcon continue to occupy their place of honor among iconographic elements, as may be seen in the "heraldic shield" of the Inca rulers drawn by Guaman Poma.

FORMS OF WORSHIP. Through acts of worship, the sphere of the sacred could be manipulated to benefit humankind. The effectiveness of human intervention into the realm of the supernatural powers depended on the intensity with which the rites were performed. In the Andean world, where natural factors put agricultural production and even existence itself to a constant test, worship assumed an extraordinary intensity and richness of form. The calamities that endangered personal and collective welfare were believed to have been caused by offenses to supernatural beings and especially to a lack of intensity in worship. Offerings to the gods of sustenance and to other supernatural beings related to them complemented the cultic display. Cruel sacrifices were necessary to worship's efficacy; in times of crisis they were performed lavishly and included human sacrifices.

The diversity of forms of worship in this region was due in part to the variety of forms of divine or magical conditions that these people perceived. These conditions were in general denoted by the term *huaca,* which can be translated as "holy." *Huaca* could refer to various unusual geographical features (including special stones, hills, lakes, etc.), heavenly bodies, atmospheric phenomena, mummies, amulets, idols, and even the Inca (i.e., the ruler) himself in his capacity as a living god.

The popular form of communication with *huaca* (i.e. the entire supernatural world) was effected through the *muchay* ("worship, reverence"). *Muchay* was performed by removing one's sandals, gesticulating, throwing kisses, murmuring supplications, bowing one's shoulders in humility, puffing out one's cheeks to blow in the direction of the object worshiped, and so on. Other forms of contact with supernatural beings were made through oracles, whose traditions go back to early forms of Andean cultures, such as the Chavín. Oracles were represented in the form of idols located in sanctuaries such as the famous one of Pachacámac, near Lima; these oracles rendered predictions about important future events to shamans and priests.

To make an offering was an act of paying tribute. Offerings were made voluntarily, but they were also collected in the form of compulsory tribute, the administration of which was centralized in temples. A widespread, popular offering was *mullo,* a powder made of ground seashells, which by association was linked to fertility through water; another was coca (*Erythroxylon coca*) in the form of a masticated wad. Stone cairns in the high passes were places of worship; wads of coca would be thrown in a ritual act called Togana. The mummified dead were offered special jars containing grains, fruits, and liquids. Guinea pigs and llamas served as important sacrificial offerings.

Among sacrifices, that of young boys and girls was the most important; sometimes human sacrifice was performed by walling up a living female person. It appears that among the Inca the sacrifice of boys and girls was received as a form of tribute, called the *capaccocha,* from the provinces. The person who was to serve as the *capaccocha* was delivered to the capital city of Cuzco in great pomp; after his death, his remains were returned to his homeland and mummified; the mummy acquired votive rank and was the object of supplications for health and agricultural welfare. Necropompa (Span., "death rite") was a special type of human sacrifice that consisted of immolations (voluntary or not) that were performed on the occasion of the death of an illustrious person (Araníbar, 1961). Decapitation of human sacrificial victims had been performed since ancient times: The Sechín stone sculpture of northern Peru depicting this practice is over three thousand years old. Head shrinking was rare and there is no evidence of cannibalism in the Andean region. (Though in the myths there are a number of supernatural beings, such as Carhuincho, Carhuallo, and Achké, who are anthropophagous.) Human sacrifice, performed to achieve greater agricultural fertility, drew its rationale from the principle that the Andeans believed governed nature: Death engenders life.

The dead, mummified and revered, were expected to implore the supernatural powers for sustenance, soil fertility, abundant water, and the multiplication of domestic animals. Often bodies were buried in the cultivated fields in order to enrich them. As has recently been reported from Ayacucho, Peru, this practice survives in secret, isolated cases even to the present day: A mentally ill person is selected, intoxicated with liquor, thrown into a pit, and buried alive. Such "strengthening" rites were, according to sixteenth-century chroniclers, also practiced in laying the foundations of houses and bridges, and traces of these rites also have been recently reported from the central Andes.

Funeral rites included expressions of grief such as loud sobbing intermingled with chants in praise of the deceased; a practice that also survives in isolated areas of the Andes. The dead were mummified and taken to their tombs on stretchers. Peoples of the arid coast practiced earth burial, but in the highlands mummies were placed—singly or in groups—in *pucullos,* or *chullupas* (mausoleums that were built on almost inaccessible outcrops of rock). Individual or collective tombs were also hollowed out of extremely steep mountainsides. With few exceptions (e.g., among the Moche), bodies were buried in seated positions. Frequently the hands held the head, perhaps to simulate the fetal position. These "living" corpses were surrounded with food and drink, weapons, and other belongings meant to serve as provisions in the hereafter; some were buried with their mouths open, both to express the terror of sacrifice and to voice supplications to the gods for success in agriculture.

Religious festivals were celebrated continuously in the great plazas of Cuzco and at temples such as the Coricancha, the temple of the sun. Festivals dedicated to specific themes, especially in the context of food production, were held monthly with great pomp; the sovereign Inca presided, and guests were invited at his expense. Great quantities of *chicha* (maize beer) were consumed, drunk from ceremonial wooden vessels (*queros*).

Andeans have made pilgrimages since the remote times of Chavín, and one of the favorite *huacas,* or shrines, was the sanctuary of Pachacámac. "Natural" shrines such as those on the peaks of high mountains were also popular with pilgrims. The Collur Riti festival, a celebration that coincides with the Feast of Corpus Christi, follows ancient rites in which to this day people climb to heights of almost five thousand meters. Some of the pilgrims dress as "bear men," imitating the gestures of animals and speaking in animal-like voices; they act as intermediaries between other pilgrims and supernatural beings. Originally, the Collur Riti was dedicated to water, and even today pilgrims return to their homes with pieces of ice carved from the mountain glaciers, symbolizing the fertility imparted by water. In the past, pilgrims fasted for variable periods of time, abstaining from maize beer, *ají* (*Capsicum anuum*), and sexual intercourse.

MEDICINE AND MAGIC. Shamans use maracas in their healing rites, a practice carried on into the present by Andean *curanderos* (Span., "healers"). The *curanderos* also use hallucinogenic substances to cause them to enter the trance state.

The San Pedro cactus *(Trichocereus pabhanoi)* is a powerful hallucinogen used particularly on the Peruvian coast; it gives the *curandero* the ability to discover the cause of an illness. In the highlands the diagnosis is still made by rubbing the body of a sick person with a guinea pig or with substances such as maize powder. The cure was effected through the use of medicinal plants. Today, *curanderos* complement their ancient remedies with modern pharmaceutical products.

Divination was often performed under the influence of hallucinogens or coca. Several studies, among them those of Alana Cordy-Collins (1977) and Ralph Cané (1985) speculate that the intricate art of Chavín originated in hallucinogenic experiences.

Institutionalized worship gave rise to a rich range of folk magic. Thus, for example, there were magic love-stones *(guacangui)*. Small stone sculptures of domestic animals, used to propitiate the spirits of abundance, are still produced. Ceramic figures representing vigorous bulls *(toritos de Pucará)* are still placed on rooftops, where they signify prosperity and fertility and offer magical protection of the home.

MESSIANISM. Andean mysticism and ritual experienced a vigorous rejuvenescence some thirty years after the Spanish conquest in the form of the nativistic movement called Taqui Oncoy (see Duviols, 1977; Millones, 1964; Ossio, 1973; Curatola, 1977; Urbano, 1981). The aims of this sixteenth-century messianic movement were to drive the white invaders from the land and to reinstate the structures of the lost Inca past. The movement's power was based on the worship of *huacas,* the popular form of Andean religiosity after the Sun had lost its credibility with the defeat inflicted by the Christian God. By a kind of magic purification, Taqui Oncoy sought to free the land from European intrusion after it was no longer possible to do so by force of arms. The movement's adherents believed that, with intensified supplications and increased offerings, the *huacas* could become powerful enough to help reestablish the old order. This movement declined after ten years, but the hope of a return to the Inca past is still alive, although it is confined more and more to middle-class intellectual circles in Peru and Bolivia.

The messianic myth of Inkarri (from Span., *Inca rey,* "Inca king") should also be mentioned here. Originally recorded by José María Arguedas (1956), the myth centers on a figure, Inkarri, who is the son of the Sun and a "wild woman." According to Nathan Wachtel (1977), this archetypal "vision of a conquered people," although of native extraction, seems to be immersed in syncretism. The cult of Inkarri lacks the action that characterized the Taqui Oncoy movement. Inkarri is not an Andean god but rather a pale memory of the deified sovereign of ancient times, who after patient waiting will rise to life to vindicate the Andean world.

SEE ALSO Atahuallpa; Inca Religion; Inti; Viracocha.

BIBLIOGRAPHY

Araníbar, Carlos. "Los sacrificios humanos entre los Incas, a través de las crónicas de los siglos XVI y XVII." Ph. D. diss., University of Lima, 1961.

Arguedas, José María. "Puquio: Una cultura en proceso de cambio." *Revista del Museo Nacional* (Lima) 25 (1956): 184–232.

Cane, Ralph. "Problemas arqueológicos e iconográficos: Enfoques nuevos." *Boletín de Lima* 37 (January 1985): 38–44.

Carrion Cachot de Girard, Rebeca. *La religión en el antiguo Perú.* Lima, 1959.

Cordy-Collins, Alana. "Chavín Art: Its Shamanistic/Hallucinogenic Origins." In *Precolumbian Art History,* edited by Alana Cordy-Collins and Jean Stearn, pp. 353–362. Palo Alto, 1977.

Curatola, Marco. "Mito y milenarismo en los Andes: Del Taqui Oncoy a Incarrí: La vision de un pueblo invicto." *Allpanchis Phuturinqa* (Cuzco) 10 (1977): 65–92.

Duviols, Pierre. "Los mombies quechua de Viracocha, supuesto 'dios creador' de los evangeligadores." *Allpanchis Phuturinqa* 10 (1977): 53–63.

Favre, Henri. "Tayta Wamani: Le culte des montanes dans le centre sud des Andes péruviennes." In *Colloque d'études péruviennes,* pp. 121–140. Aix-en-Provence, 1967.

Jijón y Caamaño, Jacínto. *La religión del imperio de los Incas.* Quito, 1919.

Jimenez Borja, Arturo. "Introducción al pensamiento araico peruano." *Revista del Museo Nacional* (Lima) 38 (1972): 191–249.

Karsten, Rafael. "Die altperuanische Religion." *Archiv für Religionswissenschaft* 25 (1927): 36–51.

Kauffmann Doig, Federico. *El Perú arqueológico: Tratado breve sobre el Perú preincaico.* Lima, 1976.

Kauffmann Doig, Federico. *Sexual Behavior in Ancient Peru.* Lima, 1979. Cited in the text as 1979a.

Kauffman Doig, Federico. "Sechín: Ensayo de arqueología iconográfica." *Arqueológicas* (Lima) 18 (1979): 101–142. Cited in the text as 1979b.

Kauffmann Doig, Federico. *Manual de arqueología peruana.* 8th rev. ed. Lima, 1983.

Kauffman Doig, Federico. "Los dioses andinos: Hacia una caraterización de la religiosidad andina fundamentada en testimonios arqueológicos y en mitos," *Vida y espiritualidad* (Lima) 3 (1986): 1–16.

Mariscotti de Görlitz, Ana Maria. *Pachamama Santa Tierra: Contribución al estudio de la religión autoctona en los Andes centro-meridionales.* Berlin, 1978.

Métraux, Alfred. *Religions et magies indiennes d'Amérique du Sud.* Paris, 1967.

Millones, Luis. "Un movimiento nativista del siglo XVI: El Taki Onqoy." *Revista peruana de cultura* (Lima) 3 (1964).

Mishkin, Bernard. "The Contemporary Quechua." In *Handbook of South American Indians* (1946), edited by Julian H. Steward, vol. 2, pp. 411–470. Reprint, Washington, D.C.,1963.

Ortiz Rescaniere, Alejandro. *De Adaneva a Inkarrí.* Lima, 1973.

Ossio, Juan M. "Guaman Poma: Nueva coronica o carta al rey: Un intento de approximación a las categorías del pensamiento del mundo andino." In *Ideología mesianica del mundo andino,* 2d ed., edited by Juan M. Ossio, pp. 153–213. Lima, 1973.

Pease, Franklin. *El dios creador andino.* Lima, 1973.

Reinhard, Johan. "Chavín and Tiahuanaco: A New Look at Two Andean Ceremonial Centers." *National Geographic Research* 1 (1985): 395–422.

Rostworowski de Diez Canseco, María. *Estructuras andinas del poder: Ideología religiosa y política.* Lima, 1983.

Rowe, John Howland. "The Origins of Creator Worship among the Incas." In *Culture in History,* edited by Stanley Diamond, pp. 408–429. New York, 1969.

Tello, Julio C. "Wira-Kocha." *Inca* 1 (1923): 93–320, 583–606.

Trimborn, Hermann. "South Central America and the Andean Civilizations." In *Pre-Columbian American Religions,* edited by Walter Krickeberg et al., pp. 83–146. New York, 1968.

Valcárcel, Luis E. "Símbolos mágico-religiosos en la cultura andina." *Revista del Museo Nacional* (Lima) 28 (1959): 3–18.

Wachtel, Nathan. *The Vision of the Vanquished: The Spanish Conquest of Peru through Indian Eyes, 1530–1570.* New York, 1977.

Yacovleff, Eugenio. "Las Falcónidas en el atre y en las creencias de los antiguos peruanos." *Revista del Museo Nacional* (Lima) 1 (1932): 35–101.

New Sources

Burger, Richard L. *Chavin and the Origins of Andean Civilization.* London, 1992.

Guinea Bueno, Mercedes. *Los Andes antes de los Incas.* Madrid, 1991.

Isbell, William H., and Helaine Silverman. *Andean Archaeology.* New York, 2002.

Olsen Bruhns, Karen. *Ancient South America.* New York, 1994.

Stanish, Charles. *Ancient Andean Political Economy.* Austin, 1992.

Stone-Miller, Rebecca. *Art of the Andes: From Chavin to Inca.* London, 2002.

Von Hagen, Adriana, and Craig Morris. *The Cities of the Ancient Andes.* New York, 1998.

Federico Kauffmann Doig (1987)
Translated from Spanish by Mary Nickson
Revised Bibliography

SOUTH AMERICAN INDIANS: INDIANS OF THE COLONIAL ANDES

A number of promising points of entry beckon the student of emerging religious systems among people of indigenous descent in the colonial Andes. These beginnings include transformations within native ritual specialists' repertoires, customs surrounding death and the dead, and the expansion of elemental Catholic Christian catechization within families (and of sacramental life in general). But no feature of colonial religiosity was more vital and dynamic than the emergence of the cult of the saints as reconfigured and understood by native Andeans. The acceptance of images of Christ, the Virgin, and the other saints into the Andean religious imagination in colonial times challenges us to understand why and how new understandings emerged and developed. The capacity for mobility, inclusion, and reimagination inherent in beliefs and practices surrounding images of Christ and the saints offers up colonial Indian religion's central trunk and an analytical space from which other branches of colonial religiosity and culture can be productively studied.

Consider, first, an Andean system of meaning that appears to have encouraged native reception and understandings of Christian images: beliefs surrounding, and the interrelationships between, Andean divinities known as *huacas* (material things that manifested the power of ancestral personalities, cultural founders, and also wider sacred phenomena [Mills, 1997, chap. 2; Salomon, 1991]). There is no escaping the fact that one reads postconquest reflections upon these older phenomena, and that, as with much about the Andean past, any process of learning involves an appreciation of the needs of authors in a series of colonial presents (Graubart, 2000; Julien, 2000). Yet the fact that most understandings of *huacas* became "hybridic"—that is to say, authentically native Andean *and* influenced, to one degree or another, by the thought worlds and vocabularies of Spanish Catholic Christianity—is integral to the colonial processes and realities to be explored here. As will become abundantly clear, ideas about *huacas* and saints were soon shared not only among Spanish and Hispanicized Andean commentators, but among native devotees around sacred images. Two originally disparate systems ceased only to repeat themselves and were instead finding shared territories and conjoining to generate new understandings and religious forms (Sahlins, 1985). It is a case in which even the exceptions suggest the rule. By midcolonial times in the Andes, steadfast native opponents of the growing presence of Christian images in the hearts and minds of Indian commoners tellingly incorporated within their rejections and counterteachings the very characterizations employed against their *huacas* (Mills, 1994, pp. 106–107, *passim;* Cummins, 2002, pp. 159–160).

And one can turn, finally, to the ways in which key Christian personalities such as Christ, the Virgin Mary, and other saints were brought inside Andean imaginations and societies in colonial times. Space does not allow the concrete exemplification required, but by sampling colonial Andean transformations, a key to understanding religious change appears. It lies in doing two things simultaneously: appreciating the novelty and seriousness of the early modern Catholic project, namely total and obligatory Christianization, in the Andes as elsewhere in Spanish America; and allowing the many consequences of this enterprise of "spiritual conquest" to slip the noose of official intentions, expectations, and prescriptions. My explorations build upon what has already been proposed by others and myself about the contest and compatibility of Andean ways with aspects of Catholic Christianity; selectively, and in somewhat chronological order, these include Kubler (1946), Millones (1969, 1979), Duviols (1971, 1977), Marzal (1977, 1983] 1988), Barnadas (1987), Sallnow (1987), Platt (1987); MacCormack (1991), Dean (1996, 2002); Mills (1997, 1994, 2003), Salles-Reese

(1997), Saignes (1999), Cussen (1999), Cummins (2002), Gose (2003), and Estenssoro Fuchs (2003, 1996).

Evidence for the convergence between what one can surmise about an Andean *huaca* complex of beliefs and practices and those of the Catholic cult of the saints is compelling, especially in accounting for early transformations. But such convergences are not confining, as if pre-Hispanic understandings of *huacas* had to dictate an entire colonial aftermath of belief and action. What stands out, rather, is the unremitting dynamism of that which came to converge, a thrilling capacity for localized adaptation and translocal reproduction shown both by *huacas* (Urton, 1990; Taylor, 1987; Salomon and Urioste, eds., 1991) and by Christian images in the hands and minds of native Andean people. Saints, like *huacas,* were many and various, and they were reproducible in ways that defy simple notions of how copies and peripheries relate to originals and centers. Evidence of the often unofficial and overlapping diffusion of saintly cults and their devotional communities turns up everywhere and in ways that ought to revise not only elderly presentations of a "spiritual conquest of Indians" but also the most unidimensional portrayals of indigenous cultural agency and resistance. This brief entry emphasizes colonial Indians' complex motivations and continuing kinds of receptivity to ideas and practices that, whether sparked by non-Indian mobilizers or not, often became operative in shared and transforming colonial terms.

A Prolific Past is Perceived. An exploration of the ways in which the originally foreign power of saints was brought within and became vital parts of a colonial Andean cultural and religious system begins with conquest-era perceptions. One of the first in a series of perceptions glides past the Andean phenomena whose divine personalities and webs of relations would guide early indigenous understandings of Catholic Christian saints.

When Hernando Pizarro and other members of his advance raiding party wrote about their time in the coastal valleys of Peru just south of what became the Spanish capital of Lima in January 1533, theirs were among the first European minds with an opportunity to engage with fundamental native Andean religious forms and meanings.

Their encounter with Pachacámac, a venerable divine force of pan-Andean proportions, reveals Spanish instincts in the period immediately after the seizure of the Inca Atahuallpa in Cajamarca. Despite learning from Andean informants and from one of Pachacámac's attendants of the divinity's long oracular tradition, and of an awesome world-making and world-shaking might that had been taken carefully into account by the Incas, Pizarro and his companions were otherwise concerned. Accumulated offerings of gold and silver to Pachacámac caught their attention. They admired, too, the jewels, crystals, and corals bedecking a door at the very top of the pyramid structure.

Pachacámac himself struck the treasure seekers both as hideous and as a sad indication of the native people's gullibility. In crossing over the final threshold at the top of the pyramid, the Spaniards faced what their Judeo-Christian tradition and experience had fully prepared them to identify as an "idol." Here was a male figure carved at the top of a wooden pole. It took no effort and less theology to perceive Pachacámac as Miguel de Estete did, as a thing beneath contempt, a vile material form crafted by human hands and pilfering the adoration human beings ought to reserve only for the Christian God. The precious offerings, reportedly piled around the figure and adorning the site, showed only how much Andean peoples had been hoodwinked by an active devil who "appeared to those priests and spoke with them," conspiring to siphon "tribute" from up and down the entire coast and demanding a respect that in Incan times was rivaled only by the Temple of the Sun in Lake Titicaca (Pizarro, [1533] 1920; Estete, [c. 1535] 1924). It mattered particularly to establish whether the famous voice and oracular utterings of Pachacámac were the handiwork of the devil speaking through him or, as Hernando Pizarro sought to prove through interrogation of an Indian minister, artifice worked by the false god's attendants.

It was not long, however, before Pachacámac gave pause to different minds. Pedro de Cieza de León, who blended his own observations and inquiries with information about the coastal region gained from the Dominican Domingo de Santo Tomás, among others, can represent an uneasy transition. While still content to label his subject the "devil Pachacámac" and fascinated by tales of the vast quantities of gold and silver the "notables and priests" of Pachacámac were said to have spirited away in advance of Hernando Pizarro's arrival, Cieza also pushed harder and uncovered more (Cieza de León, [1553] 1995, pp. 214–215). His closer examinations and those of others beginning in the 1540s and 1550s began to reveal the *huacas*' multifaceted natures and interrelationships with other divine figures.

Pachacámac's divine personality offers one of the more majestic but still broadly illustrative cases in point. While consistently described across coastal and Andean regions as a predominant creative force "who gives being to the earth" (Castro and Ortega Morejón, [1558] 1938, p. 246; Santillán, [1563] 1968, p. 111b; MacCormack 1991, pp. 351–352, 154–159), he coexisted with other divine figures. The other *huacas,* too, were sometimes creative founders, oracular voices, and otherwise translocally significant. In some cases, sacred oral histories recounted these ancestral beings' origins, featured their contributions to local and regional civilization, in many cases told of their lithomorphosis into the regional landscape, and, importantly, explained their interrelationships and coexistence with other divine beings. Explanations of the natural environment and entire histories of interaction between human groups were encapsulated within the durably fluid form of the *huacas'* narratives, which themselves were remembered by ritual tellers, singers, and dancers (Salomon, 1991).

In Pachacámac's midst, Dominican friars from the convent at Chincha in the 1540s and 1550s learned much about one of these other regional ancestors and "creators," a divine figure named Chinchaycama. He was revered by the Yunga people at a certain rock from which the divinity was said to have emerged. And Chinchaycama had hardly been the only *huaca* of the Yunga. He was, rather, one of a number "who responded" to the requests and entreaties of his people. According to what the Dominicans learned and could express about this set of relationships, the Yunga made choices and assigned precedence according to their own changing requirements (including economic and environmental stress, and also political necessity). They effectively moved between *huacas* "who responded" and "this not always but only when they had need of them." This apparently selective horizontality did not much impress Spanish commentators, and it has struck at least one modern historian as an approach that treated "matters of religion somewhat casually" (Castro and Ortega Morejón, [1558] 1938; MacCormack, 1991, p. 155).

In fact, such glimpses of Chinchaycama's place within a broader picture, and of Yunga attitudes towards their *huacas,* suggest fundamental Andean religious notions. When the Incas entered this coastal region in force, with settlers from other zones, they built a shrine to their principal divinity the Sun and impressed upon others the importance of this divinity's attributes and consecration of themselves as his children. But Inca expansionism tended to incorporate rather than erase existing cults, effectively smoothing over necessary conflict and injecting themselves into longer regional mythohistoric trajectories. Cieza found that the cult of Chinchaycama continued for the natives of Chincha, operating alongside those of other divinities, including those favored by the arriving Incas (Cieza de León, [1553] 1995, p. 220). Later fragments of learning, while steadily reflecting more Cuzco-centered understandings of the historical and spiritual interrelationships between Andean divinities and the Sun, point in similar directions. Plastic and practical relationships between divine beings and between *huacas* and their peoples marked something of a ruling principle.

One such multiply informative bit of colonial learning was produced by the lawyer Hernando de Santillán amid a 1563 response to a royal *cédula* inquiring about Inca taxation. Along his purposeful way, Santillán rendered an oral tradition about Topa Inca Yupanqui on the eve of Inca expansion into the coastal valleys of the Yunga. While Mama Ocllo was pregnant with the child who would become Topa Inca, his voice was said to have issued from within her belly to inform her that a great "creator of the earth" lived on the coast, in the "Irma valley" (today the valley of Lurín, south of Lima). When Topa Inca was older, his mother told him of the experience, and he set out to find this creator. His wanderings led him to the sacred place of Pachacámac. Once in the presence of the great *huaca,* the story stresses, the Inca's gestures were those of a respectful supplicant, for he spent "many days in prayer and fasting."

After forty days, Pachacámac was said to have broken the silence, speaking from a stone. He confirmed that he was the "maker of the earth" whom Topa Inca sought. Yet Pachacámac also explained that he was not alone as this kind of force. He explained that while he had made (literally "given being") to all things "down here," that is to say on the coast; the Sun, who "was his brother," had performed the same creative function "up there," in the highlands. Delighted to hear that such an understanding had been struck, the Inca and his traveling companions sacrificed llamas and fine clothing in honor of Pachacámac. Their tone, according to Santillán's report, continued as gratitude, "thanking him [Pachacámac] for the favour he had bestowed." The Inca even asked Pachacámac if there was anything else he particularly desired. The great coastal divinity replied that since he had a "wife and children," the Inca should build him a house. Topa Inca promptly had a "large and sumptuous" house for the *huaca* constructed. But the gifting in the interests of his progeny had only begun. Pachacámac also spoke of his "four children." They, too, would require houses, shrines. One was in the valley of Mala just to the south, another in Chincha, and there was a third in the highlands, in Andahuaylas near Cuzco. A fourth child of Pachacámac was conveniently portable and would be given to Topa Inca for his safekeeping while he traveled about so that he could "receive responses to that for which he asked" (Santillán, [1563] 1968, p. 111; Rostworowski, 1992; Patterson, 1985).

Santillán's story merits both caution and close attention. Notably, privilege is granted to an Incan point of view, and to the origin of relatively recent Incan constructions at an oracular cultic center that was over half a millennium old. One is being treated to an explanatory narrative of political and religious incorporation in the interest of Incan overlordship. Scholars from a variety of disciplines have added different perspectives to show this kind of action to have been representative of how the Incas adopted certain oracular *huacas* in accordance to their need for effective regional influence and advice (Patterson, 1985; Gose, 1996; Topic et al., 2002). Yet there is a simultaneous demonstration here of the corresponding benefits of Inca sponsorship for Pachacámac and his cult: alliance and support were the surest ways to ensure that Pachacámac's "children," or new expressions, would spread across the land. In Pachacámac's case, one such expression needs no place and is to be carried about by the traveling Inca, ready to be consulted if the ruler should require a response.

The story invites us to contemplate what Andean *huacas* were and how they related to one another (Julien, 1998, esp. pp. 64–65). The matter of just how *huacas*' multiple personae, diffusions, and relationships with other divine figures might remain operative in colonial times—in cases where *huacas* endure and especially where Christian personalities enter the picture—must simply hover about us for the moment. Pachacámac's power continued to spread well beyond the regional landscape in which he was revered as a founder and creator because of developing relationships of cultic interdependence and his ability to replicate himself across time and space. Evidence of this prolific quality struck and clearly troubled Hernando de Santillán. He explained it to himself and his imagined readership in the following way: "The Devil, who speaks through them [the *huacas*], makes them believe that they [the *huacas*] have children," Santillán wrote. "And thus," he continued,

> they [native Andeans] built new houses for them, conceived of new forms of worship to the *huacas* from whom they believed themselves descended, and understood them all to be gods. Some they worshipped as men, others as women, and they assigned devotions to each one according to a kind of need: they went to some in order to make it rain, to others so that their crops would grow and mature, and to [still] others to ensure that women could become pregnant; and so it went for all other things. What happened with so much multiplication is that soon almost every thing had its *huaca.* And through the *huacas* the Devil had them [the Indians] so thoroughly deceived that herein lies the chief obstacle in that land to lodging the faith firmly among native peoples . . . to make them understand the deception and vanity of it all [reverence for these *huacas*]. (Santillán, [1563] 1968, pp. 111–112)

Other Spanish commentators reported similarly upon the Andean *huacas*' ability to enjoy multiple selves, propagate beyond original territories, take over new specializations, and win local loyalties by making themselves indispensable. Santillán himself noted the findings of his contemporary and fellow lawyer Juan Polo de Ondegardo, who claimed in 1561 to know of more than four hundred temples [*adoratorios*] within one and a half leagues of Cuzco at which offerings were actively made (Santillán, [1563] 1968, p. 112 and n. 1). Expressions of alarm were often followed by attributions of diabolic authorship seen in Santillán's account. More than a decade later, for instance, the Jesuit José de Acosta claimed to have received a priest's report in Chuquisaca (today Sucre, Bolivia) about a *huaca* named Tangatanga, whom that region's Indians believed represented three divine identities in one and one in three, like the Christian holy Trinity. "When the priest shared his astonishment at this," Acosta wrote,

> I believe I told him that the Devil always stole as much he could from the Truth to fuel his lies and deceits, and that he did so with that infernal and obstinate pride with which he always yearns to be like God (Acosta, [1590] 1962, p. 268).

Writing almost two decades later, El Inca Garcilaso de la Vega went to some trouble to point out the fragility of the evidence upon which Acosta relied. But what stands out instead is his conviction that this understanding of an Andean divinity was a "new invention" of the Indians of Chuquisaca in colonial times, "constructed after they had heard of the Trinity and of the unity of Our Lord God" (Garcilaso de la Vega, [1609] 1985, p. 54). While Garcilaso disapproves of what he depicts as a blatant effort to impress Spaniards and gain from a supposed resemblance, he raises the distinct possibility that such colonial "inventions" were commonplace among native Andeans, and without the cunning he implies.

Quite convinced of the devil's wiles, but much closer to the ground of an early colonial local religiosity than either Acosta or Garcilaso, were the Augustinian friars stationed in Huamachuco in the northern Andes in the 1550s. They met and attempted to destroy a number of provincial *huacas* in what had clearly been a bustling pre-Hispanic religious landscape but found themselves particularly embedded within the realm of a divinity named Catequil. As with Pachacámac on the central coast, the oracular fame of Catequil had been fanned by close association with the Inca dynasty and, in his case, with Huayna Capac. Despite the fact that this Inca's son, Atahuallpa, had turned against this *huaca* after unfavorable news and attempted his destruction, Catequil's essence in a large hill and high rocky cliffs proved impossible to extinguish. Because the children or expressions of Catequil had already begun to spread, sometimes with resettled people and as part of Incan political policy in the time of Huayna Capac, he had other ways to endure (Topic et al., 2002, p. 326). What is more, his pattern of cultic diffusion appears only to have continued as Catequil's tangible "pieces," or children, were spread by mobilizing devotees. A perplexed Fray Juan de San Pedro, writing on behalf of the divinity's newest enemies, the Augustinians, claimed to have discovered some three hundred of Catequil's "sons" arrayed through various towns and smaller settlements in the region. Most were particularly beautiful stones that seemed easy enough to confiscate and grind into dust, but in other ways Catequil seemed to be everywhere at once. San Pedro believed that this multiplication of "idols" had continued "after the arrival of the Spaniards in the land" (San Pedro, [1560] 1992, pp. 179–180).

As the words of these post-Pizarran commentators acknowledged, in one way or another *huacas'* cults were various and overlapping. While one divine being might remain rooted in a precise physical landscape and connected to a certain association and responsibility (often as a founding ancestor), others developed multiple roles and personalities that allowed them to transcend local beginnings and associations. In the cases of Pachacámac and Catequil, translocal significance and power were augmented by their association with members of the Inca line. Yet as the unparalleled narrative evidence collected in the late sixteenth- and early seventeenth-century province of Huarochirí would prove in the case of the cult of Pariacaca, not every important regional *huaca* with multiple identities and a vibrant supporting cast of mythohistoric "relatives" who had been important in the times of Tawantinsuyu was so actively promoted by the Incas (Taylor, ed., 1987; Salomon and Urioste, eds., 1991). In fact, Pariacaca can stand as a most famous representative for legions of other *huacas* not only in his region but across the Andes. While regionally powerful, these ancestral divinities were not so completely adopted (or rejected) by the Incas. Their intricate regional networks and transforming roles and significance for indigenous people continued deep into colonial times, especially in rural areas, where they were investigated and harassed sporadically by inspectors of native Andean religious error through the seventeenth and early eighteenth centuries (Mills, 1994; Mills, 1997).

Spanish churchmen who were commissioned as inspectors of "idolatry" in the seventeenth- and early eighteenth-century archdiocese of Lima sometimes found precisely what an earlier Santillán or Acosta might have guessed they would find among so persistently credulous a people. They found the latest, elastic work of the devil. Did it ever seem too easy to these inspectors when Indian witnesses who appeared before them sometimes confessed that they ministered to figures whom they called the devil? Part of what the devil represented in this emerging religious reality was evidence of self-Christianization, that unpredictable by-product of uneven Spanish evangelization. After all, diabolic explanations for the *huaca* complex of beliefs and practices in pre-Hispanic and emerging colonial Andean religious life had, for generations, been broadcast in Quechua in schools for the sons of regional nobles, during confession, and from the pulpits in Andean churches. Not surprisingly, the *huaca*-like appearance, nature, and competences of these reported "devils" were unmistakable and continued to change (Mills, 1997). While the wild omnipresence of these Andean devils only served to confirm many Spanish churchmen in their understanding of who had spoken through the *huacas* and made them seem so powerful to indigenous people all along, it should signal rather more to us.

What remains pertinent is the fact that the devil was an originally Spanish Christian idea that, through persistence of association and gradual processes of selective appropriation and reinvention, had been reconstituted and internalized by Indians. If reconfigured Andean "devils" had lodged inside a transforming *huaca* complex, what other originally foreign, extraordinary things encouraged by Spanish Christian efforts, and simultaneously attractive and useful to native Andeans, had also been brought within the ordinary?

A Naturalization of Images and Institutions. Some of the ways in which colonial Catholic Christianity was lived in the Andes recalled older indigenous forms and purpose, and thus encouraged a gradual transformative process. For example, when new population centers and administrative districts coincided or approximated older territorial understandings, this integrative process began with the settling of extended kin groups (*ayllus*) in new towns (*reducciones de indios).* It is impossible to generalize about the consequences. Proximity to *huacas,* and the bodies of *mallquis* too, combined with a sporadic or unevenly demanding Catholic clerical presence, encouraged everything from survivals through coexistence to innovative fusions (Mills, 1994, 1997; Gose, 2003). Even when such "new" communities failed in the wake of the late sixteenth-century epidemics, or were abandoned because of excessive tribute exactions or Spanish and mestizo interlopers, the more remote places and hamlets into which Indian families settled reflected changes. The churches and chapels that went up in very small and remote places suggested more than a hankering for "annex" or secondary parish status. "Arguments in stone," or at least in adobe blocks, could be made by native Andean Christians as well as by hopeful church officials (Brown, 2003, pp. 29–32).

Sacred images and the voluntary lay religious associations (*cofradías,* confraternities) around them sometimes coaxed new religious allegiance directly out of older ones, as in the cases in which confraternities of Indians took over the herds and lands dedicated to the kin groups' *huacas* and *mallquis.* Like Andean people at the sacrament of baptism, and like Indian towns themselves, members of the lay associations took on a saint as an advocate and protector, and these became new markers of identity and difference. But if the rise of an image-centered, confraternity Christianity was encouraged by a striking convergence of Andean needs with the arriving European institution (Celestino and Meyers, 1981; Garland Ponce, 1994), the reimagination of what came together, and the answers *cofradías* proferred to colonial lives, were just as crucial. The *cofradías* facilitated new kinds of belonging especially for displaced individuals and kin groups in parts of the colonial world where older kinship ties had fragmented or where resettlements and work regimes kept people far from their home territories. In these conditions, new generations were born. A parish and, even more, a *cofradía,* appears to have offered spaces in which members might come together for each other and themselves. Indian *cofradías* emerged in such great numbers by the late sixteenth century that churchmen worried openly about their lack of supervision. Prelates from at least the time of the Third Provincial Council of Lima (1582–1583) attempted to discourage new foundations among Indians (Vargas Ugarte, 1951–1954, vol. 1, p. 360). The discouragement was not always observed by churchmen, let alone by indigenous *cofrades,* nor did thriving lay associations of Indians fall obediently into decay. According to the Jesuit provincial Rodrigo de Cabredo, the principal Jesuit-sponsored confraternity of Indians in Potosí, that of San Salvador (sometimes called Santa Fe), boasted "more than 1,000 Indian men and women" in 1602. Contemporary observers wrote admiringly of the religious leadership of female confraternity members in particular and of the care they gave the image of the Baby Jesus in the Jesuit church ("Carta anua del año de 1602," [1603] 1986, pp. 231–233; Ocaña, c. 1599–1608, fol. 181r).

Catholic Christianity's convergence, through the saints, with structures that had guided the operations of an older *huaca* complex do not offer straight and easy answers or a singular "way" in which change occurred. In the middle of the seventeenth century, the indigenous parishioners in the town of San Pedro de Hacas, Cajatambo, revealed something of the complexity of the colonial religiosity and culture at hand. In testimonies before an investigator of their "errors" between 1656 and 1658, they explained how their local *huaca,* Vicho Rinri, was annually consulted on the eve of the Catholic festival of the town's eponymous patron. What was more, their celebrations had come to feature sacred dances, indigenous ritual confessions, and Andean offerings to Saint

Peter in the home of his standard's honorary bearer. While the officiating Spanish judge and his notary insisted that the *huaca* was being asked permission (as the devil might wish) and that the activities of the saint's guardians and the intimate sacrifices before the representation were the height of irreverence, our interpretative options should not close so readily. It seems more likely that for at least some of the parishioners of Hacas, Saint Peter had been brought within an emerging system in ways that altered but did not interrupt older religious allegiances and understandings (Mills, 1994).

Reproducibility offers another critical theme to consider. Just as important *huacas* developed multiple personalities and specializations, generating expressions of themselves in other places, so too was it common for saints to transcend their original forms, functions, and places through networks of image "copies" and shrines. In this sense, the local religious enthusiasms of Spanish Christianity for images, newly defended and refortified at the Council of Trent (Christian, 1981a, 1981b) were planted in most fortuitous soil. In some cases, *huacas* themselves were Christianized, morphing into saintly personages as their places became sacred shrines in the Catholic system (Sallnow, 1987, p. 54). Like ambitious *huacas* who, through their ministers and often out of necessity, tied their fortunes to Inca rulers or speculated through "children" in widening locations, Christ, Mary, and the other saints were amenable to being co-opted, copied, and reenergized in new environments. Many sacred images, either brought originally from Europe or made in the Andes but based upon Old World models, both capitalized on their curious novelty and shed their identity as foreigners, becoming "localized and . . . renewed" in the Andes, as elsewhere (Dean, 1996, p. 174; Gruzinski, 1990). Whether "new" expressions or faithful copies, saints became local originals, favoring a horizontal approach to religious matters similar to that which Santillán, the Dominicans, and others had so worried over among the Yunga. William B. Taylor's words on the character and development of "devotional landscapes" in colonial Mexico apply just as usefully to our understanding of how saints appealed to and worked for the colonial descendants of the Yunga and their Andean neighbors: "People were likely to be interested in more than one shrine or saint," Taylor writes, "and felt a more intense devotion to one or another at a particular time, as the array of saints' images available in most churches suggests; and devotees may never have actually visited the shrine of a favourite image or relic" (Taylor, 2004).

The working of saints' images and their copies can be partly explained through the "familiar" language and associations used most often to elucidate divine connections and expansion. Spanish, Indian, and mestizo descriptions of *huacas* as ancestors, husbands, wives, and progeny, and of themselves as the children of these beings, abound. Idioms of kinship and marriage that had symbolized interrelationships and subtle hierarchies between *huacas* and their peoples offered affectionate titles and also a vocabulary for characterizing associations between the images of saints and Christ and their colonial groupings of people. Early-seventeenth-century Aymara speakers on the shores of Lake Titicaca, for instance, were said to have bestowed the title of *mamanchic* (*mamancheq*), "mother of all," upon Francisco Tito Yupanqui's sculpture of the Virgin of the Candlemas at Copacabana (Ramos Gavilán, [1621] 1988; Salles Reese, 1997, p. 162). Similarly, their contemporaries, indigenous mineworkers and their wives and families in Potosí, flocked to a miraculous painting of Our Lady of Guadalupe from Extremadura in the church of San Francisco whom they called the *señora chapetona*, "the new lady in the land" (Ocaña, c. 1599–1608, fols. 159r). Such familiar and localizing designations abound for images of Mary (Dean, 2002, pp. 181–182), but they were not confined to her. As Thierry Saignes has found, the inhabitants of main Andean towns sometimes included (and subordinated) the sacred images of annex hamlets in a remarkably similar fashion: "the crosses and statues that decorated the village chapels were considered the 'sons-in-law' of those belonging to the church in town" (Saignes, 1999, p. 103).

The Marian images featured above are, of course, only two of many. They offer illustrative examples of the significance of multiplication and circulation and of a wider range of devotional networks across the Andean zone and early modern world. It is to ponder only an inviting surface to note that Tito Yupanqui's Our Lady of Copacabana from the early 1580s both was and was not an Andean "original." Her Indian maker famously modeled his Virgin of the Candlemas on a statue of Our Lady of the Rosary brought from Seville to the Dominican convent and church in Potosí, an image that had caught his eye and fired his devotion when he was learning his art in the silver-mining center (Mills et al., 2003, pp. 167–172). The miraculous image at Copacabana herself quickly spawned many sculpted and portrait "copies" that were enshrined in chapels across the Andes. These local copies grew more compelling to devotees by signaling their connection to the divine presence of their originals. Some began to sweat, others moved, and many were judged responsible for interceding with God to produce miracles, the narratives of which spread in the street and were broadcast from the pulpits and pages of clerical promoters and patrons. In the case of a copy of the Virgin of Copacabana among a group of disgruntled, resettled Indians in Lima's Cercado, the image reportedly cried for attention and devotion, prompting decades of contest not only over the purported miracles but over her rightful place and constituency. The intersecting roles of different Indian groups, African slaves, prelates, secular clergy, and Jesuits in this case defy simple explanations.

The image of the Virgin of Guadalupe de Extremadura painted by Ocaña in Potosí can seem a more straightforward case, that of an official purveyor's painstakingly faithful expression of a Spanish original being transplanted in the Andes. Yet the localization and rooting of a new expression here also repays closer inspection. The image's creator, the Jeronymite Diego de Ocaña, claimed to have rendered the image with the Indians' self-identification and affections foremost in mind: "Since I painted her a little dark, and the Indians are like that, they said that That Lady was more beautiful than the other images, and [that] they loved her a lot because she was of their colour." Among other aspects of his orchestration of new devotions around this image in Potosí, Ocaña quickly mobilized the Franciscan preacher Luis Jerónimo de Oré to preach to the Indians in their tongue about the history of the original Virgin of Guadalupe and about the transfer of this celestial advocate's powers through the new image to their place. (Ocaña, c. 1599–1608, fols. 159r, 163v; Mills, 2003). A miraculous narrative tradition was being added to and reshaped in Potosí as new Andean stories were being spun.

An Andean Christian Interculture. The cult of the saints offers an aspect of the Catholic Christian system that appealed to colonial native Andeans as much for its familiarity as for its access to new local powers. In highly interactive regions such as the Andean zones on which Spanish Christians began to impinge in the 1530s, that which was foreign was not unexpected. The foreign and novel might—like a new *huaca,* like the concept of the devil—require understanding initially in terms that would allow definition within emerging systems of meaning and practice. But the allure and utility of unfamiliar expressions of sacred power were tied to their perceived ability to summon valuable powers from "outside" (Helms, 1993). In time, visual expressions of Christ, the Virgin Mary, and other saints appear to have offered this kind of power for many native Andeans. Closer studies need to be made of a variety of divine personalities and sacred territories over time to understand whether the associations and competences of particular *huacas* are related in any way to the specializations of saints as advocates and if a tendency away from highly localised and specificist saints and toward generalist advocates such as the Virgin and Christ proposed by William Christian (1981) for contemporary rural Castile plays out in cultic developments in the colonial Spanish Americas. But what is clear is that the saints became principal inhabitants and powers within what Thomas Cummins has called a contested but mutual "cultural area between Catholic intention and Andean reception" (Cummins, 1995; 2002, p. 159).

Discovering how the thoughts of contemporaries can inform us on such matters—and, more often than not, interpreting their silences—offers a constant challenge. This is as true of representations of saints and their developing domains as it is of renderings of the *huacas'* pre-Hispanic natures and what had been their catchment areas. Yet even triumphant declarations about the saints that seem to skate over difficulties and ignore complex possibilities hold promise for our project. For instance, when considering the fact that the seventeenth-century Augustinian Creole Antonio de la Calancha carved up Peru into three devotional zones watched over by miraculous images of Mary that just so happened to be nurtured and championed by his religious order, it can be tempting to throw in the towel. It was, he wrote, as if the Virgin of Guadalupe in the north coastal valley of Pacasmayo, the Virgin of Copacabana in Chucuito, and the Virgin of Pucarani (toward La Paz) were divinely linked and spread apart so as "to bless [*beatificar*] the different territories in which they are venerated, and so as not to tire travelers and pilgrims when they go in search of them" (Calancha, [1638] 1974–1982, p. 1362). Yet we must view this as more than Augustinian pride and claim-making against the encroachments of other religious, and more, too, than simply a solemn register of God's designs in these friars' favor. Calancha's appeal is arguably also to native Andean devotees who he knows from experience had once moved across these very territories according to earlier divine markers and divisions.

The representations of the Jesuit provincial Rodrigo de Cabredo in 1600 as he described the work of *padres* from the Jesuit college at Cuzco in towns and villages in the region of Huamanga (modern Ayacucho) in 1599 offer an even more illuminating example for our purposes. In one place (probably San Francisco de Atunrucana), the Jesuits had set to building a new church to replace one struck by lightning and burned to the ground. In the presence of many people, including the *kuraka,* sacred images of the town's patrons San Francisco and the Baby Jesus had been enshrined and a sermon was given in commemorative thanks that local people had been freed from their blindness and the clutches of the devil. According to Cabredo:

> One of the principal fruits of this mission was teaching the Indians about the veneration (*adoración*) of images, telling them [first] not to worship (*adorar)* them as Indians do their *huacas,* and [second] that Christians do not think that virtue and divinity resides in them [the images] themselves but, rather, look to what they represent. . . . [Teaching] this [matter] is of the utmost importance, because a bad Christian with little fear of God had sowed a very pernicious and scandalous doctrine in this *pueblo,* saying many things against the honor and reverence that the images deserve.

Cabredo's emphasis falls ultimately on what was needed to "remedy the poison the Devil had sown through his minister" ("Carta anua," [1600] 1981, pp. 73–76). The notion of a wandering "bad Christian" as the devil's instrument, leading Indians astray with "pernicious and scandalous" confusions about images and *huacas,* does not fail to raise questions and suggest complications. For even if this "bad Christian" did exist, he or she appears to have found a ready audience for comparative thoughts about saints' images and *huacas,* an audience of Indians at the dawn of the seventeenth century about whom the Jesuits in Huamanga and well beyond had grown concerned.

Cross-cultural thinkers and mobilizers—contemporary people who conceptualized, influenced, and reflected religious in-betweens in the colonial Andes—offer perhaps the most remarkable indications of why and how the cult of the saints came to underpin local Andean Christianities. As dismissive as the mestizo humanist El Inca Garcilaso de la Vega had found himself in thinking over the possible interpretative needs of colonial Indians in Chuquisaca, as noted above, he did concoct a definition of the concept of *huaca* with considerably more paths into emerging colonial understandings than dead ends. At its center was a denial that people in Incan times had understood *huacas* to be gods and a hint that the appeal of Christian images and miracle stories to a native Andean might follow on naturally (Garcilaso de la Vega [1609] 1985, pp. 51–55, pp. 45–55; MacCormack, 1991, pp. 335–338). Saints, like the extraordinary ancestral beings, might be represented in forms, and stories of their deeds might be conveyed, collected, and retold by special humans.

Luis Jerónimo de Oré, the experienced Franciscan Creole whom Diego de Ocaña had recruited to preach about the Virgin of Guadalupe in Potosí in 1600, was a figure who approached such matters of possible congruence directly, in the course of evangelization. Engraved images of the Virgin begin and end his *Symbolo Catholico Indiano* of 1598, accompanied by words to guide contemplation. Mary was also a principal concern in the book itself, as Oré translated her and his faith through prayers and hymns, expounding doctrine and mysteries for Quechua-speaking Christians (Oré, [1598] 1992). The so-called anonymous Jesuit of the late sixteenth or early seventeenth century—possibly but not certainly the mestizo Blas Valera (Jesuita Anónimo [c. 1594] 1968, BNS ms. 3177; Urbano, 1992; Hyland, 2003), offers another rich case in point. He was an author immersed in a project of interpreting the Incan past as an ordered and moral anticipation for Catholic Christianity, particularly as directed by the Jesuits in structured environments such as Lima's resettled enclosure for Indians, Santiago del Cercado. Yet he had also had much else to say en route.

The Jesuit held, for instance, that the only mode of entry into Christianity that was working for native Andeans in his day amounted to self-Christianization sustained by a regular experience of the sacraments. Certainly the people benefited from priests fluent in the Quechuan language to administer to them, and they required good examples to excite their faith, just as his contemporary Acosta insisted more famously. "But when they lack someone to instruct them," the anonymous Jesuit added, "they look for ways to pick up what is required and teach it to their children." Like Oré, this Jesuit believed that native Andeans were inclined toward Catholic Christianity by their pre-Hispanic understandings and that their depth in the faith depended most upon Christianity being enlivened by careful formulations in the Quechuan language. Most Indian Christians were new and vulnerable, in his view, but this did not make them any less genuine additions to the fold. The arrival at a moment when the pace and character of religious change would depend upon the Indians' own efforts and controls was already at hand in some places, he implied, even if further work was needed on communicating key aspects of the faith.

Near the heart of such further efforts, in this Jesuit's opinion, should be "historical narration and . . . personal conversations in which the saints' lives are told and matters of virtue are treated." Picking up on what his contemporaries the Creole Oré and the peninsular Ocaña also believed and were putting into action, the anonymous Jesuit wrote that if an evangelizer's skills were such that he could translate Christian narratives into the Indians' languages, then so too could the articles of the faith, the commandments, the works of mercy, and the sacraments be rendered, allowing the arriving religion, finally, to be deeply understood. His emphasis upon the gains which might come from "*conversaciones particulares*" about the saints captures his understanding both of the intimate and horizontal manner in which the cult of the saints had already begun to enter the hearts and minds of native Andeans, and of the way that self-Christianization—daily ritual activity, communication, and developing understandings among Indian women and men, within families and lay sodalities, and between friends and acquaintances—would see this process continue. Saints could take on new Andean lives in Quechua. Only the older generation of Indians and their oral traditions seemed to present an obstacle to this vision. But for this too, the Jesuit had a suggestion. Indian children could begin "to sing before them [the adults] so that in this way they forget the ancient songs" (Jesuita Anónimo, [c.1594] 1968, pp. 80–81).

The "ancient songs" stand in here for the *huacas* and, in a certain sense, for the pre-Hispanic religious complex as a whole. This Jesuit's optimistic view of his colonial present and his faithful glimpse into the future sees a gradual substitution of one set of songs, beliefs and practices for another, the old for the new. But students of these matters are not obliged to think so instrumentally. The author's acknowledgment of what one might call a "creative tension" between modes of religious understanding and ritual remembrance in operation in the colonial Andes is more telling. He believes that a fundamental Andean religious aptitude and enthusiasm for the saints, and for their hagiographic narratives and edifying stories, had come from somewhere elastic and enduring in native Andean cultural tradition. Evidence of the survival of *huaca* cults, and their relationships and sacred histories, exists into the eighteenth century and beyond and suggests that he was correct. But what can be understood about *huacas* should not stop just here, split off, as if the study of pre-Hispanic phenomena, much less colonial "idolatry," can be separated from the culturally dialogic reality of evangelization and response and from the emergence and fruition of Andean Christianities. *Huacas,* with their multiple personalities and translocality, provided Spanish and Hispanicizing minds with ways of thinking and expressing religious relationships, and they provide colonial indigenous people with ways of understanding the images of saints and their "copies" as newly local repositories of beneficence and power.

BIBLIOGRAPHY

Acosta, José de. *De Procuranda Indorum Salute* (1588), edited by Luciano Pereña et al. Vol. 1: *Pacificación y colonización.* Madrid, 1984.

Acosta, José de. *Historia natural y moral de las Indias* (1590) Rev. ed., edited by Edmundo O'Gorman. Mexico, 1962.

"Aviso de el modo que havia en el govierno de los Indios en tiempo del Inga (Aviso de Chincha)." Transcribed and edited in María Rostworowski de Diez Canseco, "Mercaderes del valle de Chincha en la época prehispánica. Un documento y unos comentarios." In *Revista Española de Antropología Americana* 5 (1970): 135–177.

Barnadas, Josep M. "La vida cotidiana en Bolivia." In *Historia general de la Iglesia en América Latina,* edited by Enrique Dussel et al., pp. 137–145. Salamanca, 1987.

Brown, Peter. *The Rise of Western Christendom: Triumph and Diversity, A.D. 200–1000.* 2nd ed. Oxford, 2003.

Calancha, Antonio de la. *Corónica moralizada del Orden de San Agustín en el Perú* (1638) Edited by Ignacio Prado Pastor. 6 vols. Lima, 1974–1982.

"Carta anua de la provincia del Perú del año de 1599. P. Rodrigo de Cabredo to P. Claudio Aquaviva, Lima, April 20, 1600." In *Monumenta Peruana (1600–1602),* edited by Antonio de Egaña and Enrique Fernández. Rome, 1981.

"Carta anua de la provincia del Perú del año de 1602. P. Rodrigo de Cabredo to P. Claudio Aquaviva, Lima, April 28, 1603." In *Monumenta Peruana VIII (1603–1604),* edited by Enrique Fernández. Rome, 1986.

Castro, Cristóbal, and Diego de Ortega Morejón. "Relación y declaración del modo que este valle de Chincha y sus comarcanos se governavan . . ." (1558). In *Quellen zur Kulturgeschichte des präkolumbinischen Amerika,* edited by H. Trimborn, pp. 236–246. Stuttgart, 1938.

Celestino, Olinda, and Albert Meyers. *Las cofradías en el Perú, región central.* Frankfurt, 1981.

Christian, William A., Jr. *Apparitions in Late Medieval and Renaissance Spain.* Princeton, 1981a.

Christian, William A., Jr. *Local Religion in Sixteenth-Century Spain.* Princeton, 1981b.

Cieza de León, Pedro de. *Crónica del Perú: Primera parte* (1553). Lima, 1995.

Cummins, Thomas B. F. "From Lies to Truth: Colonial Ekphrasis and the Act of Crosscultural Translation." In *Reframing the Renaissance: Visual Culture in Europe and Latin America 1450–1650,* edited by Claire Farago, pp. 152–174. New Haven and London, 1995.

Cummins, Thomas B. F. *Toasts with the Inca: Andean Abstraction and Colonial Images on Quero Vessels.* Ann Arbor, Mich., 2002.

Cussen, Celia L. "El Barroco por dentro y por fuera: Redes de devoción en Lima colonial." *Anuario Colombiano de Historia Social y de la Cultura* (Bogotá) 26 (1999): 215–225.

Dean, Carolyn. "Familiarizando el catolicismo en el Cuzco colonial." In *Incas e indios cristianos. Elites indígenas e identidades cristianas en los Andes colonials,* edited by Jean-Jacques Decoster, pp. 169–194. Cuzco, 2002.

Dean, Carolyn. "The Renewal of Old World Images and the Creation of Colonial Peruvian Visual Culture." In *Converging Cultures: Art and Identity in Spanish America,* edited by Diana Fane, pp. 171–182. New York, 1996.

Duviols, Pierre. *La Lutte contre les réligions autochtones dans le Pérou colonial.* Lima, 1971.

Duviols, Pierre. "Los nombres Quechua de Viracocha, supuesto 'Dios Creador' de los evangelizadores." *Allpanchis* 10 (1977): 53–64.

Estenssoro Fuchs, Juan Carlos. "Les Pouvoirs de la Parole. La prédication au Pérou de l'évangélisation à l'utopie." *Annales* (1996): 1225–1257.

Estenssoro Fuchs, Juan Carlos. *Del paganismo a la santidad: La incorporación de los indios del Perú al catolicismo, 1532–1750.* Lima, 2003.

Estete, Miguel de. "Noticia del Perú" (c. 1535). In *Colección de libros y documentos referentes a la historia del Perú,* 2d series, vol. 8, pp. 38–39. Lima, 1924.

Garcilaso de la Vega, El Inca. *Comentarios reales de los Incas* (1609). Lima, 1985.

Garland Ponce, Beatriz. "Las cofradías de Lima durante la Colonia." In *La venida del Reino: religion, evangelización y cultura en América, siglos XVI–XX.* Cuzco, 1994.

Gose, Peter. "Oracles, Divine Kingship, and Political Representation in the Inka State." *Ethnohistory* 43, no.1 (1996): 1–32.

Gose, Peter. "Converting the Ancestors: Indirect Rule, Settlement Consolidation, and the Struggle over Burial in Colonial Peru, 1532–1614." In *Conversion: Old Worlds and New,* edited by Kenneth Mills and Anthony Grafton, pp. 140–174. Rochester, N.Y., 2003.

Graubart, Karen B. "Indecent Living: Indigenous Women and the Politics of Representation in Early Colonial Peru." In *Colonial Latin American Review* 9, no. 2 (2000): 213–235.

Gruzinski, Serge. *La Guerre de images de Christophe Colomb à Blade Runner (1492–2019).* Paris, 1990.

Helms, Mary W. *Craft and the Kingly Ideal: Art, Trade, and Power.* Austin, Tex, 1993

Hyland, Sabine. *The Jesuit and the Incas: The Extraordinary Life of Padre Blas Valera, S. J.* Ann Arbor, Mich., 2003.

Jesuita Anónimo [Blas Valera?]. "Relación de las costumbres antiguas de los naturales del Piru." In *Crónicas peruanas de interés indígena,* edited by Francisco Esteve Barba. Madrid, 1968.

Julien, Catherine J. *Die Inka.* Munich, 1998.

Julien, Catherine J. *Reading Inca History.* Iowa City, 2000.

Kubler, George. "The Quechua in the Colonial World." In *The Handbook of South American Indians,* edited by Julian H. Steward, vol. 2, pp. 331–410. Washington, D.C., 1946.

MacCormack, Sabine. *Religion in the Andes: Vision and Imagination in Early Colonial Peru.* Princeton, 1991.

Marzal, Manuel M. "Una hipótesis sobre la aculturación religiosa andina." *Revista de la Universidad Católica* 2 (1977): 95–131.

Marzal, Manuel M. *La transformación religiosa peruana* (1983). Lima, 1988.

Millones, Luis. "Introducción al studio de las idolatrías." *Letras* (Papel no. 27 del Instituto de Literatura, Universidad Nacional Mayor de San Marcos, Lima, Peru) 78–79 (1969): 5–40.

Millones, Luis. "Los ganados del señor: mecanismos de poder en las comunidades andinas, siglos XVIII y XIX." *América Indígena* 39, no. 1 (1979): 107–145.

Millones, Luis, ed. *El retorno de la huacas: Estudios y documentos sobre el Taqui Oncoy, siglo XVI.* Lima, 1990.

Mills, Kenneth. *An Evil Lost to View? An Investigation of Post-Evangelisation Andean Religion in Mid-Colonial Peru.* Liverpool, 1994.

Mills, Kenneth. *Idolatry and Its Enemies: Colonial Andean Religion and Extirpation, 1640–1750.* Princeton, 1997.

Mills, Kenneth. "Diego de Ocaña's Hagiography of New and Renewed Devotion in Colonial Peru." In *Colonial Saints: Discovering the Holy in the Americas, 1500–1800,* edited by Allan Greer and Jodi Bilinkoff, pp. 51–76. New York, 2003.

Mills, Kenneth, William B. Taylor, and Sandra Lauderdale Graham. "Making an Image and a Shrine, Copacabana, Peru (1582–1621)." In *Colonial Latin America: A Documentary History,* edited by Kenneth Mills, William B. Taylor, and Sandra Lauderdale Graham, pp. 167–172. Wilmington, Del., 2003.

Murúa, Martín de. *Historia general del Perú* (c. 1611), edited by Manuel Ballesteros Gaibrois. Madrid, 2001.

Ocaña, Diego de. Untitled, but called the "Relación del viaje de Fray Diego de Ocaña por el Nuevo Mundo (1599–1605)." Biblioteca de la Universidad de Oviedo, Spain. M-215. c 1599–1608.

Oré, Luis Jerónimo de. *Symbolo Catholico Indiano* (1598). Edited by Antonine Tibesar. Lima, 1992.

Patterson, Thomas C. "Pachacámac: An Andean Oracle under Inca Rule." In *Recent Studies in Andean Prehistory and Protohistory,* edited by D. Peter Kvietok and Daniel H. Sandweiss, pp. 169–175. Ithaca, N.Y., 1985.

Pizarro, Hernando. "Relación de Hernando Pizarro acerca de la conquista" (1533). In *Colección de libros y documentos referents a la historia del Perú,* 2nd series, vol. 3, pp. 167–180. Lima, 1920.

Platt, Tristan. "The Andean Soldiers of Christ. Confraternity Organization, the Mass of the Sun and Regenerative Warfare in Rural Potosí (18th to 20th Centuries)." *Journal de la Société de Américanistes* 73 (1987): 139–192.

Polo de Ondegardo, Juan. "Instrucción contra las ceremonias y ritos que usan los Indios conforme al tiempo de su infidelidad." In *El catecismo del III Concilio Provincial de Lima y sus complementos pastorales (1584–1585),* edited by Juan Guillermo Durán, pp. 447–455. Buenos Aires, 1982.

Polo de Ondegardo, Juan. "Los errores y supersticiones de los indios sacadas del tratado y averiguación que hizo el Lizenciado Polo." In *El catecismo del III Concilio Provincial de Lima y sus complementos pastorales (1584–1585),* edited by Juan Guillermo Durán, pp. 459–478. Buenos Aires, 1982.

Ramos Gavilán, Alonso. *Historia del santuario de Nuestra Señora de Copacabana* (1621), edited by Ignacio Prado Pastor. Lima, 1988.

Rostworowski de Diez Canseco, María. *Pachacámac y el Señor de los Milagros: Una trajectoria milenaria.* Lima, 1992.

Sahlins, Marshall. *Islands of History.* Chicago, 1985.

Saignes, Thierry. "The Colonial Condition in the Quechua-Aymara Heartland (1570–1780)." In *The Cambridge History of the Native Peoples of the Americas,* vol. 3, *South America,* part 2, edited by Frank Salomon and Stuart B. Schwartz, pp. 59–137. Cambridge, 1999.

Salles Reese, Verónica. *From Viracocha to the Virgin of Copacabana: Representations of the Sacred at Lake Titicaca.* Austin, Tex., 1997.

Sallnow, Michael J. *Pilgrims of the Andes. Regional Cults in Cuzco.* Washington, D.C., 1987.

Salomon, Frank. "Introductory Essay." In *The Huarochirí Manuscript: A Testament of Ancient and Colonial Andean Religion,* edited by Frank Salomon and George L. Urioste, pp. 1–38. Austin, Tex., 1991.

Salomon, Frank, and George L. Urioste, eds. *The Huarochirí Manuscript: A Testament of Ancient and Colonial Andean Religion.* Austin, Tex., 1991.

San Pedro, Juan de. *La persecución del demonio. Crónica de los primeros agustinos del norte del Perú* (c. 1560). Edited by Eric E. Deeds. Málaga, 1992.

Santillán, Hernando de. "Relación del origin, descendencia, política y gobierno de los Incas" (1563). *Crónicas peruanas de interes indígena,* edited by Francisco Esteve Barba, pp. 97–149. Madrid, 1968.

Taylor, Gerald, ed. *Ritos y tradiciones de Huarochirí del siglo XVII.* Lima, 1987.

Taylor, William B. "Process and Place: Toward a History of Devotional Landscapes in Mexico." Unpublished commentary for symposium on "Devotional Landscapes: Mapping the Shrines and Saints of New Spain," held at the Geographic Information Center, University of California at Berkeley, February 27, 2004.

Topic, John R., Theresa Lange Topic, and Alfredo Melly Cava. "Catequil: The Archaeology, Ethnohistory, and Ethnography of a Major Provincial Huaca." In *Andean Archaeology I: Variations in Sociopolitical Organization,* edited by William H. Isbell and Helaine Silverman, pp. 303–335. New York, 2002.

Urbano, Henrique. "Introducción." In *Antigüedades del Perú,* edited by Henrique Urbano and Ana Sánchez, pp. 7–38. Madrid, 1992.

Urton, Gary. *The History of a Myth: Pacariqtambo and the Origin of the Inkas.* Austin, Tex., 1990.

Vargas Ugarte, Rubén, ed. *Concilios Limenses (1551–1772).* 3 vols. Lima, 1951–1954.

KENNETH MILLS (2005)

SOUTH AMERICAN INDIANS: INDIANS OF THE MODERN ANDES

The Quechua and Aymara Indians of the Andes mountains are the largest group of Indians still existent in the New World. Approximately 28 million Indians and mestizos (persons of mixed Spanish and Indian descent) live along the Pacific coast and in the Andean highlands. About one-fourth of these Indians live and speak as they did before the Spanish conquest in the sixteenth century. Six million speak Quechua and approximately 1 million speak Aymara. For the purposes of this article, the religious systems of both the Quechua and the Aymara will be treated together, and both groups will be referred to, collectively, as "Andeans."

Although some Andeans have moved to large urban centers, such as La Paz, Bolivia, and Lima, Peru, the majority live in small communities (from twenty to five hundred families) scattered throughout the Andes, with a population density of three hundred persons per square kilometer of habitable and arable land. Indians live in rectangular, single-family, adobe huts with thatched gable or hip roofs. The Aymara group their huts in extended-family compounds surrounded by a wall with a central patio. For both Aymara and Quechua, marriage is monogamous, with trial marriages lasting several years. Residence is patrilocal, with bilateral inheritance among the Quechua and patrilateral inheritance among the Aymara.

Andeans practice intensive agriculture using crop rotation, irrigation, dung fertilization, and terracing of fields. They cultivate more than fifty species of domesticated plants, in a number of ecological niches: Potatoes, quinoa, and oca are grown at the highest levels of cultivatable land; corn (maize) at lower levels; and beans, squash, sweet manioc, peanuts, peppers, fruit trees, and cotton in the deep valleys and along the coast. Herders graze alpacas, llamas, and sheep on fallow fields and in high, nonarable tundra regions (14,000–17,000 ft.). Although Andeans live dispersed over wide areas, resource exchange unifies the people of different communities. The ecological band narrows as the altitude increases, so that there are many distinct communities, each utilizing the natural resources characteristic of its altitude. Because of ecological specialization, exchange of resources is very important. Andean civilization arose through these efforts to utilize many vegetational zones to furnish communities with a variety of resources.

Andeans have also adapted to this mountainous region by means of a religion that is essentially a system of ecological symbols. They use their ecological setting as an explanatory model for understanding and expressing themselves in mythology and ritual. Andeans are very close to their animals, plants, and land. Their origin myths tell how in times past llamas herded humans; in present times humans herd llamas only because of a linguistic error when llamas misplaced a suffix in Quechua, saying "Humans will eat us" instead of "We will eat humans." Andeans consider coca (*Erythoxylum coca*) a divine plant: "The leaves are like God. They have wisdom." Diviners learn about nature by chewing coca and reading its leaves. Andeans see themselves as part of nature, intrinsically affected by its processes and intimately linked with plants and animals. Moreover, Andeans believe they originated in the earth and will return to it.

Pachamama and Achachilas. Earth and mountains provide two principal Andean symbols, Pachamama and the *achachilas. Pachamama* means "mother earth," but *pacha* also refers to time, space, and a universe that is divided into heaven, earth, and a netherworld. For Andeans, time is encapsulated in space. *Pacha* is an earth that produces, covers, and contains historical events, and Pachamama symbolizes the fertile nature of the earth, which provides life. Pachamama is a universal deity, referring to all the earth and the universe because she represents the principle of nature that recycles life from death, and death from life. Pachamama is unlike the *achachilas,* the mountain spirits who represent certain peaks.

Ritually, Andeans libate Pachamama with drops of liquor before drinking and present her with three coca leaves before chewing coca. The husband places coca leaves daily into the male family members' earth shrine, an indentation within the adobe bench surrounding the inside of the patio, and the wife puts leaves under her household shrine, a table within the cooking house, so that Pachamama will provide the family with food. Diviners also offer ritual meals (*mesas*) to Pachamama during August, before Andeans begin planting. Andeans believe that the earth is open at that time and needs to be given food and drink.

Roman Catholic missioners attempted to replace Pachamama with the Blessed Mother, but this resulted in beliefs that associate the Blessed Mother with the bountifulness of the earth. For example, two major pilgrimage sites in the Bolivian Andes are La Virgen de Copacabana and La Virgen de Urkupiña. Nominally, these shrines refer to the Blessed Mother, but Andeans associate them with Pachamama and the earth (Urkupiña means "rock hill"). People travel to these shrines in August to feed Mother Earth and thus ensure an abundant harvest and an increase in flocks, offspring, or, more recently, money. This illustrates how Catholicism became syncretized with the ecological symbols of the Andean religion.

Achachilas are mountain spirits, indistinct from the mountains themselves, who are the masculine protectors of the earth and ancestors of the community. Diviners feed achachilas with ritual meals. Every Andean community has certain bordering mountains that are considered sacred: For example, the *achachilas* of La Paz, Bolivia, are the snow-crested mountains (16,000–20,000 ft.) of Illimani ("elder brother"), Mururata ("headless one"), and Wayna Potosi ("youth-Potosi"). A more traditional Aymara community, Cacachaqa, near Oruro, Bolivia, has eleven *achachilas* that together encircle it and separate it from neighboring communities. Each peak symbolizes an aspect of nature—a mineral, plant, animal, bird, or person—that is suggested by its shape and its particular resources and natural environment. Condo, a neighboring community north of Cacachaqa, shares with Cacachaqa two *achachilas,* which shows how neighboring communities are united by *achachilas.*

Throughout the Andes, there are hierarchical relationships among the *achachilas.* Ancestral *achachilas* are related to tutelary peaks of the community, the community's tutelary peaks to the region's, and the region's to the nation's. Traditionally, the metaphor for this relationship is a kinship pyramid: At the apex is the chief of the clan, followed by the heads of the major lineages and then the leaders of the local lineages. Although clans are no longer found in the Andes, lineages are important, and Andeans refer to *achachilas* in kinship terms—*machula* ("ancestor"), *apu* ("leader"), *awqui* ("grandfather"), and *tío* ("uncle"). In sum, mountains exhibit a hierarchy that is analogous to social and political systems. The worship of these mountains, then, made Andeans conscious of social, political, and natural systems.

EARTH SHRINES. Diviners are responsible for naming and feeding earth shrines (*huacas*), which are pre-Columbian in origin and are still ritually important. Earth shrines are natural openings or small holes dug into the ground through which the earth is ritually fed. They are found near passes, water holes, knobs, and rocks. Alongside the hole is usually a rock pile, where Indians place their coca quids before fresh leaves are put inside the hole. A shrine's many names may express history, humor, geography, and social relationships. For example, one earth shrine is called Jilakata's Recourse, because it was once a rest stop for Indian officials on their journey to pay tribute to the Spanish. This shrine's knob suggests its other names: Goat Corral, Bachelor's Haven, Coitus, and Chicha (corn beer) Bubble. Another earth shrine was formed, according to legend, when a certain leader expelled his sister-in-law from his land and set her upside down alongside the road. She became a rock shaped in the form of buttocks and a vagina. Today, Andean travelers place coca in the crotch of this earth shrine. Other earth shrines are dedicated to irrigation canals, agricultural fields, and livestock. An *apacheta* is an earth shrine at a mountain pass, that is, the highest point of the trail. Travelers rest at these sites, discard their coca, and pray, "With this quid may my tiredness leave me, and strength return."

Earth shrines are stratified according to ecological levels, social groupings, time, and historical epochs. Individuals have their own earth shrines; an Andean baby receives an earth shrine at birth, and must reverence it throughout his or her life. If they move from their natal village, they will periodically return to pay homage to their shrines, which continually beckon for their return until they die and are buried with their ancestors near their sacred mountain. The patrilineage has its household shrines dug into the inside and outside of the house; the community has its shrine corresponding to its level on the mountain; and the ayllu, an economically and religiously related group of communities, has its shrines up and down the mountain. Certain irrigation canals have earth shrines that are associated with the Inca civilization, and, in many villages, the chapel in the plaza is often interpreted as another earth shrine, reminiscent of the Spanish conquest. Yet the earth is the center that perdures through time, and that unifies the different places and earth shrines.

RITUALISTS. Ritual specialists of the Andes fall into two categories: diviners and sorcerers.

Diviners. Andeans frequently consult with diviners, the principal ritualists of the Andes. All Andean communities have diviners. Although they are identified from within the group by being associated with some extraordinary natural event (commonly, a bolt of lightning), they are selected as individuals for their divining skills. A typical diviner reads coca leaves by first selecting twelve perfect leaves. He marks them with insectlike bites and designates the significance of each: good luck, bad luck, community, road, a person's name, enemies, or whatever concerns the person paying for the divination. He then casts the leaves, like dice, upon a cloth to see which leaves pair with good luck and which with bad luck. If the cast is unfavorable, the participants often argue about the outcome and require another cast. Because coca leaves usually do not fall in a conclusive way, diviners are free to suggest their insights. There are many kinds of diviners: Some read the signs of nature and predict when to plant and harvest, others are skilled in social dynamics and redress conflicts, and still others understand human problems and treat mental illnesses. A few possess mystical knowledge and can reveal the inner nature of the Andean universe. Such people are highly esteemed, and Andeans travel long distances to seek them out.

Diviners conclude divinations with ritual meals (*mesas*), which are the basic rituals of the Andes. Although *mesas* vary regionally, they follow a similar pattern. A diviner sets a table (*mesa*) with a ritual cloth and scallop shells for plates, each of which is assigned an *achachila* and an earth shrine. He places a llama fetus at the head of the table for Pachamama. Next, the diviner places white llama wool, coca, llama fat, carnation petals, and animal blood on the scallop shells, beseeching the invited deities to accept the offerings. The participants imitate the diviner. There are other ritual foods, depending upon the ecological zone, but the three principal foods are coca, which symbolizes knowledge, fat, symbolizing energy, and blood (preferably from the llama), symbolizing vitality. Finally, the diviner wraps the food with the wool to make about twelve bundles (*kintos*) and ties them to the back of the llama fetus. The diviner places this in an earth shrine, and burns it, which symbolizes the consumption of the food. Andeans say that if the fire sparkles and crackles, then Pachamama and the *achachilas* have enjoyed the meal and will repay them with a good harvest.

Sorcerers. Sorcerers are different from diviners. Diviners are usually male and feed the earth shrines with llama fat, llama fetuses, and white llama wool at specific times—Wednesday and Thursday nights. They are ritualists for *achachilas,* Pachamama, and earth shrines. In contrast, sorcerers are often female and feed the wind and river with pig fat, rat fetuses, and black sheep wool on Tuesday and Friday nights. They are ritualists for the *supaya,* a term that has often been equated with the Spanish concept of the devil, although it actually refers to certain of the dead who either have not completed something in this life or have died in a strange fashion. The *supaya* belong to the netherworld of the dead (*ura pacha*), but they act in the world of the living (*kay pacha*) as living shadows. *Supaya* enter the world of the living to gather companions for the netherworld. Symbolically, they represent the consumptive forces of nature, such as death and decay, which are necessary to renew life. When someone is sick and a *supaya* is implicated, sorcerers attempt to appease him by killing and substituting the life of a llama for that of the sick person. They also offer pig fat and rat fetuses at *mesas de contra* ("misfortune tables"), so called because the ritual items are contrary to those employed by diviners in a *mesa de suerte* ("good-luck table") or *mesa de salud* ("health table"). Pig fat is inferior to llama fat because Andeans consider the pig a tropical animal that lives on fecal matter and garbage. Rat fetuses, symbolizing destructive rodents, are inferior to llama fetuses, which symbolize an animal very beneficial to Andean society.

Andeans select sorcerers by their reputation for either removing or inflicting misfortunes. Some sorcerers claim responsibility for as many as seven deaths, but others are secretive about their reputation because sorcerers are occasionally killed in revenge by victims of unsuccessful sorcery. Sorcery takes many forms in the Andes, but one way sorcerers curse people is by placing nail filings or hair of the victim inside the skulls of a cat and a dog, whose teeth are locked as if in battle, which symbolizes that husband and wife are fighting. (The breakdown of the household is a major tragedy in the Andes because it is the unit of production and subsistence.) The sorcerer hides the skulls inside the thatched roof of the victim. If the victim is aware of this, he can remove the curse by having another sorcerer perform a *mesa de contra*. Sometimes the victim has the sorcerer brought before the magistrate, who fines her and makes her take an oath not to do it again. Sorcery is taken seriously and is often the attributed cause for loss of livestock, crops, money, health, and even life.

THE AYLLU AND ITS EARTH SHRINES. The *ayllu* is basic to Andean social organization. Although *ayllus* are often based on kinship ties, they are also formed by religious, territorial, and metaphorical ties. One contemporary example is Ayllu Kaata of the Qollahuaya Indians, who live in midwestern Bolivia. Ayllu Kaata is a mountain with three major communities: Niñokorin, Kaata, and Apacheta. The people of Niñokorin are Quechua speakers who farm corn, wheat, barley, peas, and beans on the lower slopes of the mountain (10,500–11,500 ft.). The people of Kaata, who also speak Quechua, cultivate oca and potatoes on rotative fields of the central slopes (11,500–14,000 ft.). In the highlands (14,000–17,000 ft.), the Aymara-speaking people of Apacheta herd llamas and sheep. The three communities use the metaphor of the human body to understand their *ayllu:* Apacheta corresponds to the head, Kaata to the trunk, and Niñokorin to the legs. Just as the parts of the human body are organically united, so are the three levels of Ayllu Kaata.

The thirteen earth shrines of Ayllu Kaata are understood in relation to the body metaphor and to ecological stratifications. The three community shrines are Chaqamita, Pachaqota, and Jatun Junch'a. Chaqamita, a lake located to the east near the legs, is related to the sun's birth, fertility, and corn, making it a suitable shrine for Niñokorin, whose Corn Planting rite reverences this site. This lower lake is also a shrine for Curva and Chullina, neighboring *ayllus*. Earth shrines, when shared by several *ayllus*, religiously unite separate mountains, and so Qollahuaya Andeans claim that they are one people because they worship the same shrines. Pachaqota, a large lake at the head of the mountain, is the "eye" into which the sun sinks; it symbolizes death, fertilization, and llamas. On the shores of the lake, the herders of the highland community of Apacheta celebrate the All Colors rite for the increase of llamas. Pachaqota is also associated with the lakes of uma pacha (at the top of a mountain), from which animals and humans derive their existence and to which they return after death.

The Great Shrine (Jatun Junch'a), associated with the liver and the central community of Kaata, is a major shrine of Ayllu Kaata because of its central location and physiography. The Great Shrine rests on a spur, which rises from the slopes and resembles a small mountain. The Great Shrine is nourished at the rite of Chosen Field, in the middle of the rainy season, and it is also the site of a mock battle (*tinku*) between the elders and clowns during Carnival. The clowns, who sprinkle people with water, are symbolically put to death by the elders slinging ripe fruit at them.

Similar ritual battles are fought throughout the Andes: The Aymara of the Bolivian Altiplano, for example, wage theatrical warfare between the upper and lower divisions of the community. *Tinku* emphasizes the importance of contrasting pairs, and in the Andes almost everything is understood in juxtaposition to its opposite. Earth shrines, also, have meanings corresponding to binary opposition. Chaqamita and Pachaqota, for example, correspond to life and death, as well as to the rising and setting of the sun, and each term explains the other; moreover, each leads to the other.

The highlands, central altitudes, and lowlands of Mount Kaata have community shrines reflecting their ecological zones, but from the viewpoint of the *ayllu,* the community shrine is only one part of the body of the mountain. In some way every level must feed all the mountain's shrines during the *allyu* rites, such as the New Earth rite. The people of Apacheta, Kaata, and Niñokorin come together during New Earth to recreate the mountain's body. The upper and lower communities send leaders to Kaata for this rite, each bringing his zone's characteristic product: a llama or some chicha (corn beer). The llama's heart and bowels are buried in the center fields, and blood and fat are sent by emissaries to feed the earth shrines of the mountain. The body awakes to become the new earth.

The New Earth rite is one illustration, of which there are many others throughout the Andes, of how Pachamama, the *achachilas,* and earth shrines are holistically understood in terms of metaphor, ecology, and *ayllu.* The New Earth rite expresses how levels of land are understood in terms of a body with a head, heart, bowels, and legs, through which blood and fat circulate when ritualists feed the earth shrines. Specific earth shrines not only refer to specific ecologial zones but also symbolize parts of the body that holistically constitutes the *achachila* and symbolizes the social and political unity of Mount Kaata. Andeans experience the solidarity of their mountain and *ayllu* similarly to the way they experience the organic unity of their corporeal bodies. The individual's corporeal life is dependent on environmental life. Thus, the New Earth rite assures the individual's organic life by awakening Mother Earth to provide a good harvest.

RITUAL CALENDAR. Andeans insert themselves by ritual into the cycles of nature—not to control them, but to experience them and be in harmony with them. New Earth, for example, is the second of three rites dedicated to the rotative field of the year. Through these three rites the earth is gradually awakened. One year before planting, the community leaders study the fertility of the fields lying fallow to see which one is ready to begin another growth cycle of potatoes, oca, and barley. A diviner observes nature's omens and asks the neighboring mountains (*achachilas*) for their assistance. Once a field is picked, the people of the *ayllu* celebrate the rite of Chosen Field (Chacrata Qukuy) in the middle of the rainy season. Leaders dance across the field's terraces to the music of flutes, and they offer a llama fetus to the earth shrine of the selected field. The fetus brings new life to the soil, and thus the field becomes the anointed land for the year. Andeans later fertilize their plots by spreading sheep dung along the furrows where they will plant potatoes.

The rains continue to soak the anointed field, and near the end of the rainy season, in April, Andeans prepare to plow. But before the earth can be entered, it must be nurtured by the sacrifice of a grown llama during the rite of New Earth. With this rite the land is vitalized; it is opened for water, air, dung, and blood, until the time of Potato Planting, when it is covered over again. Potato Planting (Khallay Papa Tarpuna), in mid-November, is the field's final ritual, celebrated after the Feast with the Dead. According to Andean legends, the dead push the potatoes up from the inside of the earth. Also in November, people of lower levels celebrate Corn Planting (Khallay Sara Tarpuna), and at Christmastime herders sponsor their herding rituals, All Colors (Chajru Khallay). Although each rite is concerned with the animal and plant life of its zone, collectively the rites influence the corporate life of the *ayllu* and region, and leaders from the various communities participate in all of the rituals of the *ayllu* and the region.

Between the cycle of the seasons there is a day when ancestors return to the community—2 November, the Feast with the Dead. Ancestor worship remains an important part of Andean religion. Prior to the conquest, Andeans mummified the dead by wrapping them in cloth and seating them in *chullpas,* which are rock monuments above subterranean cists. The Incas dressed the mummies of their kings in fine textiles and kept them in the Temple of the Sun in Cuzco, where they were arranged in hierarchical and genealogical relationships. Today, Andeans dress the dead person for a journey, provide him or her with coca, potatoes, corn, and a candle, and bury the deceased in a cemetery near the community. Traditionally, many Andeans believe that people originate from and return to the highland lakes of the mountain. They compare death to the eclipse of the sun: Death is ecliptic, hiding the dead within the earth, where they journey with the movements of the sun, seasons, and land.

The Feast with the Dead is an annual rite of passage from the dry to the wet season and from the activity of the dead to that of the living. The dry season connotes resting; the wet season, growth. The living invite the dead to a meal when the harvest and festive times have ended and planting rituals begin. At this pivotal point in the Andean year, the dead visit the living, and then they are sent on another year's journey with their share of the harvest.

At noon on November 1, the leader of the community awakens the dead with dynamite, and for twenty-four hours the dead are served food on tables that usually have three tiers, symbolizing highlands, central altitudes, and lowlands. The arrival of a fly or the flickering of a candle signals to the living that the dead are present. The living and dead share in a meal and communicate with each other by laments and prayers. At noon the next day, everyone returns to the cemetery to place more food near the graves. Relatives of the deceased distribute food to friends, who pray for the dead relatives. Later the same afternoon, the fiesta ends with a meal and drinking.

COSMOLOGY. For Andeans, the finality of death is alleviated by their ecology. During life, Andeans become part of the land that they work: As their bodies get older, their land increases. When they die, they enter into the mountain, journey upward, and have access to the land of the dead. Moreover, the decay of their bodies enriches the land of the living. The visible levels of the living are only half of the mountain; the other half consists of the subterranean waterways of the dead.

The Andeans' worldview is an extension of the three mountain levels; they divide their universe into the heavens (*janaj pacha*), this world (*kay pacha*), and the netherworld (*ura pacha*). Each place has an ancient, a past, and a present time, to which specific beings correspond. The heavens are where the elders of lightning, sun, and stars have dwelled since ancient times; where God, Jesus, and Santiago have roamed since past times; and where dead baptized babies are descending to the *uma pacha* in present times. By their permanent and cyclical features, the heavens suggest origination and restitution, whereas the experiences of this world are temporal and consecutive. The three times of this world are symbolized by *chullpas,* the cross, and the graveyard, which refer respectively to the ancestor mummies, Jesus, and the recent dead (those who have died within three years). The ancestor mummies and the past and recent dead journey to the highlands within the subterranean waterways of the netherworld, which is the recycling area between death and life. The *supaya* are dead unable to travel because of some unfinished business. They bridge the gap between the netherworld and this world. The earth shrines denote being, space, and time, the metaphysical concepts for the universe, which are intertwined in each of the three gradient levels; thus the mountain serves as an expression of Andean cosmology.

The *uma pacha* is the point of origin and return for traditional Andeans. The highlands are the head (*uma*) of the achachila. Bunchgrass grows near the summit of the mountain, as hair on the head. The wool of the llamas that graze on this grass resembles human hair. As human hair grows after cutting, so llama wool and bunchgrass grow continually in the highlands. In a manner similar to the regeneration of hair, humans and animals originate in the highland lakes, or the eyes *(nawi)* of the *achachila.* The sun dies into these eyes of the highlands, but from the reflections within the lake come all living creatures. The lake's reflections (*illa*) are the animals and people returning from inside the earth to this world.

Animals and people originate in and return to the head of the mountain. It is the place of origin and return, like the human head, which is the point of entry and exit for the inner self. The dead travel by underground waterways to the mountain's head, the *uma pacha,* from whose lakes they can arise to the land of the living. The living emerge from the eyes of the mountain (the lakes of the *uma pacha*), journey across its head, chest, trunk, and legs (high, center, and low levels), and die in the lowlands. They are buried and return with the sun to the *uma pacha,* point of origin and return.

SICKNESS AND HEALTH. Western medicine ascribes sickness to internal disorders of the body or to the malfunctioning of organs within it, whereas Andean curing looks outside the body to the malfunctioning of the social and ecological order. Bodily illnesses are signs of disorders between the person and the land or between the person and his lineage. The diviner's role is to reveal this conflict and to redress it by ritual, which resolves the dispute or reorders the land. Diviners cure not by isolating the individual in a hospital, away from his land, but by gathering members of a sick person's social group for ritual feeding of the earth shrines of the *achachila,* because if their lineage and mountain are complete, then their body will also be complete (healthy). Community and land are inextricably bound to the physical body, and disintegration in one is associated with disorder in the other.

One illustration of how diviners interrelate environmental and social factors with sickness is the *mesa de salud* ("health table"), a commonly performed ritual in the Andes. This ritual begins with a preliminary divination session in which the diviner casts coca leaves to determine the causes of an illness. Relatives of the sick person attend and contribute to the analysis of the causes. Diviners then redress social conflicts within the lineage. If the sick person, for example, has fought with her mother-in-law, the diviner delves into the cause of this conflict and instructs the patient to gather some ritual item from the mother-in-law's household. The participants then spend several days gathering ritual items symbolic of the various altitudinal levels: chicha (corn beer) and carnations from the lowlands, potatoes from the central lands, and llama fat and a fetus from the highlands. The gathering of the ritual items reinforces the concept that health is related to the utilization and exchange of resources from different levels. Indirectly, the ritual affects health by reinforcing the need for a balanced diet. In this way, Andean ritual promotes holistic health rather than merely removing disease.

Traditionally, Andeans distinguish between *curanderos,* who cure with natural remedies, and diviners *(yachaj),* who cure with supernatural remedies. Andeans have many classes of *curanderos,* revealing a striking knowledge and classification of anatomy and an enormous list of medical paraphernalia. Because they have excelled in the practice of native medicine, Andeans have adapted to an environment that produces many stresses (hypoxia, hypothermia, malnutrition, and epidemics). Qollahuaya herbalists, for example, use approximately one thousand medicinal plants in curing. Andeans visit both diviners and herbalists for treatment of a disease, because both kinds of specialist are needed to deal with all the physical, social, spiritual, and ecological factors involved.

CHRISTIANITY. Andeans have incorporated Catholicism into their traditional way of life by stratifying it according to place and time and thus allowing it to function in ways analogous to the function of an earth shrine. For many Andeans, Catholicism is a state religion that replaced the Inca religion. Every Andean community has a chapel with a statue of a saint who is the patron protector of the village. Sculptors mold a realistic statue from plaster of paris, and seamstresses dress it with velvet and gold cloth. These statues appear almost alive, like waxworks. For some Andeans, the saint represents a white rock; for others, the saints are transformations of the dead ancestors whom they venerated during Inca times.

Annually, each village celebrates a fiesta to its saint, whose statue is paraded around the four corners of the plaza while brilliantly costumed groups dance to the music of flutes, drums, and trumpets. The official sponsor, the *preste,* walks alongside the saint, for which privilege he provides the participants with alcohol, coca, and food. Ritual and natural kin, as well as people in debt to the *preste,* contribute supplies and sponsor dance groups. For the first day or two, the fiesta is a celebration of great beauty and festivity, but by the third day it often degenerates into drunkenness and brawling. One reason is that during recent times raw alcohol has replaced the traditional beverage, *chicha,* which has a much lower alcohol content. However, alcohol and coca also relax the participants, making them susceptible to the liminal meanings of the fiesta—the basic Andean meanings being expressed in the dance, music, and ritual. These elements are highly structured and communicate underlying symbolic patterns important to Andean culture.

Although the cult of the saints reflects the importance of Catholicism in contemporary Andean culture, Andeans are only nominal Catholics: They baptize their babies primarily to prevent hailstorms and to obtain *padrinos* ("godfathers"), who provide social and political connections. Sometimes couples marry in the church, but only after a trial marriage (*iqhisiña*) to see whether the wife is fertile. Catholic catechists and Protestant missionaries have recently been converting Andeans to an evangelistic Christianity opposed to earth shrines, fiestas, and traditional Andean beliefs. Many evangelistic Protestants emphasize literacy and the reading of the Bible. Protestantism cannot be incorporated into the traditional Andean system because it tends to be comparatively barren of symbols and ritual. Consequently, converts to certain Protestant sects have radically changed their traditional cultural patterns. In sum, Catholicism has been adapted peripherally to traditional Andean religious practices, whereas evangelistic Protestantism has been very effective in changing traditional belief systems. This is because many Andeans see traditional religious practices, which reflect verticality, resource exchange, *ayllu* solidarity, and ecology, as being unimportant to modernization, with its emphasis on literacy, horizontal links, competition, and individuality.

Nevertheless, the traditional religion retains a strong hold on Andeans, who continue to look to earth and nature for their identity. Their land and their mountains continue to be their deities—not as abstract symbols but as real entities with whom they live and work and with whom they share important relations of reciprocity. For these reasons, the Andeans built a high civilization in a mountainous land that they came to worship.

Bibliography

Allen, Catherine J. "Body and Soul in Quechua Thought." *Journal of Latin American Lore* 8 (1982): 179–195. Explores the conceptual basis of "animistic" ideology, focusing on attitudes toward death and the custom of "force feeding." Excellent description of relationship between ancestors and the living.

Allpanchis Phuturinqa (Cuzco, 1969–). Published by the Instituto de Pastoral Andina, this review was founded to educate pastoral agents about Andean culture and includes many articles on Andean religion.

Arguedas, José María. *Deep Rivers.* Translated by Frances Horning Barraclough. Austin, 1978. Noted Peruvian novelist describes conflict within mestizos caught between the Andean and Spanish cultural systems. Shows how myth bridges the gulf between the magico-religious world of the Andean and the social reality of mestizo life. A penetrating book.

Arriaga, Pablo Joseph de. *The Extirpation of Idolatry in Peru* (1621). Translated by Horacio Urteaga (Lima, 1920) and L. Clark Keating (Lexington, Ky., 1968). An extirpator's manual accurately describing Andean religious practices of the sixteenth and seventeenth centuries, many of which are still found in the Andes. Shows how missioners suppressed Andean religion and attempted to replace it with Catholicism—and how Christianity got off to a bad start in the Andes.

Bastien, Joseph W. *Mountain of the Condor: Metaphor and Ritual in an Andean Ayllu.* Saint Paul, 1978. A description and analysis of rituals performed by Qollahuaya Andeans, whose diviners are famous throughout the Andes. Rituals provide the context for understanding the metaphorical relationship of Andeans with their land.

Bastien, Joseph W., and John N. Donahue, eds. *Health in the Andes.* Washington, D.C., 1981. First part contains three articles on how rituals are used to cure sick Andeans. Other parts contain environmental information concerning Andeans.

Cuadernos de investigación (La Paz, 1974). Pamphlets on Andean culture and religion published by the Centro de Investigación y Promoción del Campesinado. Especially insightful are those by Javier Albo, Tristan Platt, and Olivia Harris.

Isbell, Billie Jean. *To Defend Ourselves: Ecology and Ritual in an Andean Village.* Austin, 1978. Describes marriage, hydraulic, harvest, and fertility rituals in the village of Chuschi, Ayacucho Department, Peru. Treats the relationship between ecology and ideology through the observation and analysis of rituals.

Lewellen, Ted. *Peasants in Transition: The Changing Economy of the Peruvian Aymara.* Boulder, 1978. Analyzes the impact of Protestantism on social and economic factors of an Aymara community.

Millones Santa Gadea, Luis. *Las religiones nativas del Peru: Recuento y evaluación de su estudio.* Austin, 1979. A review of studies concerning Andean religion. Very useful for early studies on Andean religion.

Núñez del Prado, Juan Victor. "The Supernatural World of the Quechua of Southern Peru as Seen from the Community of Qotobamba." In *Native South Americans,* edited by Patricia J. Lyon. Boston, 1974. Delineates the structure of the supernatural world in southern Peru from the mythology and ethnographic data of two Quechua communities.

Orlove, Benjamin S. "Two Rituals and Three Hypotheses: An Examination of Solstice Divination in Southern Highland Peru." *Anthropological Quarterly* 52 (April 1979): 86–98. Describes two solstice divinations in Peru. Illustrates how Andeans weigh alternatives and make decisions.

Ossio, Juan M., ed. and comp. *Ideología mesiánica del mundo andino.* Lima, 1973. Compilation of articles by anthropologists and historians concerning messianism among Andean peasants. Many authors employ structuralist interpretations of Andean religion.

Paredes, M. Rigoberto. *Mitos, supersticiones y supervivencias populares de Bolivia* (1920). 3d ed., rev. & enl. La Paz, 1963. A reference book for religious practices of the Aymara.

Sharon, Douglas. *Wizard of the Four Winds: A Shaman's Story.* New York, 1978. Documents a modern shaman's view of the world. Describes mesas performed by a shaman in Trujillo Valley in the northern Andean highlands. A well-written and insightful book about Andean shamanism.

Taussig, Michael T. *The Devil and Commodity Fetishism in South America.* Chapel Hill, N.C., 1980. Discusses the social significance of the devil in the folklore of contemporary plantation workers and miners in South America. The devil is a symbol of the alienation experienced by peasants as they enter the ranks of the proletariat.

Tschopik, Harry, Jr. "The Aymara of Chucuito Peru." *Anthropological Papers of the American Museum of Natural History* 44, pt. 2 (1951):137–308. Examines how ritual establishes social equilibrium among the peasants of Chucuito, Peru. Includes detailed description of ritual paraphernalia.

Urton, Gary. *At the Crossroads of the Earth and Sky: An Andean Cosmology.* Austin, 1981. Examines the astronomical system of Misminay, Peru, to understand celestial cosmology of modern Andeans. Shows how celestial formations interrelate with the agricultural and ritual calendars.

Valdizán, Hermilio, and Angel Maldonado. *La medicine popular peruana.* 3 vols. Lima, 1922. An encyclopedia of minerals, plants, and animals used in healing and ritual.

Wachtel, Nathan. *The Vision of the Vanquished: The Spanish Conquest of Peru through Indian Eyes, 1530–1570.* Translated by Ben Reynolds and Siân Reynolds. New York, 1977. An account of the structural disintegration of Inca society and culture during the early years of the conquest. Illustrates how a present-day fiesta in Oruro, Bolivia, enacts this drama.

New Sources

Bolin, Inge. *Rituals of Respect: The Secret of Survival in the High Peruvian Andes.* Austin, 1998.

Gade, Daniel W. *Nature and Culture in the Andes.* Madison, 1999.

Larson, Brook, and Olivia Harris, eds. *Ethnicity, Markets and Migration in the Andes: At the Crossroad of History and Anthropology.* Durham, N.C., 1995.

Van Cott, Donna Lee. *Indigenous Peoples and Democracy in Latin America.* New York, 1994.

JOSEPH W. BASTIEN (1987)
Revised Bibliography

SOUTH AMERICAN INDIANS: INDIANS OF THE NORTHWEST AMAZON

In principle, the Northwest Amazon includes, as its southern limits, the region from approximately the Middle Amazon, around the mouth of the Rio Negro, to the Upper Solimões; all of the Rio Negro and its northern tributaries, including the Parima mountain range, up to the upper Orinoco Valley; and an arc connecting the Upper Orinoco to the Upper Solimões. Historically, the societies that inhabited this vast region, at least at the time of Spanish conquest in the sixteenth century, were far more numerous than they are today, and far more complex in terms of their social and political organization and interrelations amongst each other. Undoubtedly, their religious organizations and institutions were more complex as well. Sixteenth-century chroniclers left tantalizing notes describing the existence of chiefdoms and priestly societies in the Amazon floodplains region that were similar to those of the circum-Caribbean region.

The usefulness of these notes for understanding native religions at the time of conquest is, however, limited and subject to much guesswork. Scholars are not even certain which languages many of these societies spoke, much less what their religious beliefs were. Modern archaeology is just beginning to uncover the rich complexity of these societies and may, in the future, provide important elements for understanding their religions. In any case, it is certain that the vast majority of the societies of the Rio Negro, the main northern tributary of the Amazon that connects with the Orinoco via the Cassiquiare Canal, were Arawak-speaking peoples. There were also significant numbers of Tukanoan-speaking peoples in the region of the Uaupés River and its tributaries; forest-dwelling Makuan peoples in a vast region from the lower to the upper Negro; Cariban-speaking peoples on the tributaries of the upper Orinoco; and Yanomami populations in the mountainous forest regions north of the Rio Negro.

EARLY HISTORY OF THE REGION. A survey of the first historical sources and the earliest recorded traditions of the societies of Northwest Amazon indicates the widespread distribution of a ritual complex involving the use of sacred flutes and trumpets, masked dances, and the practice of ritual whipping, associated with a mythology the central themes of which included initiation, ancestors, warfare, and seasonal cycles marked by festivals. Early observers noted that this ritual complex was of central importance, and that the guardians of the sacred trumpets formed an elite priestly class with a supreme leader who was also a war chief. There are indications of ceremonial centers where rituals were celebrated among societies of different language groups.

The evolution of this complex was drastically truncated and transformed by the advance of the Portuguese and Spanish slaving commerce in the seventeenth and eighteenth centuries. Many of the most powerful chiefs were co-opted into destructive wars to obtain slaves, thus irremediably fragmenting political-religious formations, as well as leaving vast parts of the Northwest Amazon region depopulated, as people were herded into mission-run settlements, where they were forced to adapt to Western culture. By the late eighteenth century, even with a brief respite in the advance of colonization, many of the surviving societies had been introduced to Christianity and had adopted its calendric festivals, if not its belief system, into their religious patterns.

In the second half of the nineteenth century, as an early reaction to exploitation by merchants, pressures from missionaries, and the waves of epidemics that decimated the Indian population, a sequence of prophetic movements and rebellions broke out in the Northwest Amazon region. Dressing as priests and identifying themselves with Christ and the saints, prophet-shamans led the people in the "Dance of the Cross," a fusion of traditional rituals with elements of Catholicism that promised freedom from white oppression and relief from the "sins" that were believed to be causing the epidemics. While many of these movements suffered repression, the prophetic tradition continued among both Tukanoan- and Arawak-speaking peoples until well into the twentieth century in areas that escaped the attention of missionaries and government officials.

CONTEMPORARY PEOPLES AND THEIR RELIGIOUS TRADITIONS. For the indigenous peoples of the Northwest Amazon today, religion is not an institution differentiated from other aspects of their lives. When they use the term *religion*, they are generally referring to the Christian religions introduced among them in their long history of contact with nonindigenous society. When they wish to refer to their own beliefs and practices that have to do with the sacred, they generally use such phrasings as "our tradition" and "the wisdom of our ancestors." To understand these traditions, it is useful to consider four dimensions that characterize all religious traditions: cosmogony (the meaning of the beginning); cosmology (spatial and temporal structures of the universe); anthropology (the relations among living beings, including "specialists" who mediate relations with the spirits and divinities); and eschatology (the meaning of the end). This entry will seek to provide a minimum understanding of these dimensions from the rich and complex contemporary traditions of the Tukanoan-speaking peoples, the Arawak-speaking Baniwa and Kuripako, and the Maku of the Rio Negro region and its main tributaries, the Uaupés and Içana; the Yanomami of the Parima highlands on the border of Brazil and Venezuela; and the Carib-speaking Makiritare of the upper Orinoco Valley.

Tukanoans. Tukanoan-speaking peoples inhabit the rainforest region on the border of Brazil and Colombia. Although they are divided into numerous linguistic groups, they nevertheless share a body of broadly identical mythology. Religious life revolves around these myths; the importance of sacred flutes and trumpets representing the ancestors of each group; shamans and chant specialists; and a cosmology centering on the themes of mortality and immortality, death and rebirth, and the conjunction of male and female principles in the creation and reproduction of culture.

The myths explain the origins of the cosmos, describing a dangerous, undifferentiated world with no clear boundaries of space and time and no difference between people and animals. They explain how the first beings created the physical features of the landscape, and how the world was gradually made safe for the emergence of true human beings. A key origin myth explains how an anaconda-ancestor entered the world-house through the "water-door" in the east and traveled up the Rio Negro and Uaupés with the ancestors of all humanity inside his body. Initially in the form of feather ornaments, these spirit-ancestors were transformed into human beings over the course of their journey. When they reached the center of the world, they emerged from a hole in the rocks and moved to their respective territories. These narratives give the Tukanoan peoples a common understanding of the cosmos, of the place of human beings within it, and of the relations that should pertain between different peoples and between them and other beings.

The universe consists of three basic levels: the sky, earth, and underworld. Each layer is a world in itself, with its specific beings, and can be understood both in abstract and in concrete terms. In different contexts, the "sky" can be the world of the sun, the moon, and the stars; the world of the birds who fly high; the tops of mountains; or even a head adorned with a headdress of red and yellow macaw feathers, which are the colors of the sun. In the same way, the underworld can be the River of the Dead below the earth, the yellow clay below the layer of soil where the dead are buried, or the aquatic world of the subterranean rivers. In any case, what defines the "sky" or the "underworld" depends not only on the scale and context, but also on the perspective: at night, the sun, the sky, and the day are below the earth and the dark underworld is on top.

In symbolic terms, the longhouse is the universe, and vice versa. The thatched roof is the sky, the support beams are the mountains, the walls are the chains of hills that seem to surround the visible horizon at the edge of the world, and under the floor runs the River of the Dead. The longhouse has two doors: the one facing east, called the "water door," is the men's door; the other, facing west, is the women's door. A long roof beam called the "path of the sun" extends between the two doors. In this equatorial region, the underworld rivers run from west to east, or from the women's door to the men's door; completing a closed circuit of water; the River of the Dead runs from the east to the west.

The longhouse is likewise a body—the "canoe-body" of the ancestral anaconda—which, according to the myth of creation, brought the ancestors of humanity, the children of the ancestral anaconda, inside it, swimming upriver from the Amazon to the Uaupés in the beginning of time. These children are the inhabitants of the longhouse, replica of the original ancestor, containers of future generations and they themselves are future ancestors. But if the longhouse is a human body, its composition is also a question of perspective. From the male point of view, the painted front of the longhouse is a man's face, the men's door his mouth, the main beams and side beams his spinal column and ribs, the center of the house his heart, and the women's door his anus. From the female point of view, however, the spinal column, ribs, and heart are the same, but the rest of the body is inverted: the women's door is her mouth, the men's door her vagina, and the inside of the house her womb.

In the Tukanoan life cycle, there is a notion of reincarnation shared by all Tukanoans: at death, an aspect of the dead person's soul returns to the "house of transformation," the group's origin site. Later the soul returns to the world of the living to be joined to the body of a newborn baby when the baby receives its name. People are named after a recently dead relative on the father's side. Each group owns a limited set of personal names, which are kept alive by being transmitted back to the living. The visible aspect of these name-souls are the feather headdresses worn by dancers, ornaments that are also buried with the dead. The underworld river is described as being full of these ornaments and, in the origin story, the spirits inside the anaconda-canoe traveled in the form of dance ornaments.

Buried in canoes, the souls of the dead fall to the underworld river below. From there they drift downstream to the west and to the upstream regions of the world above. Women do not give birth in the longhouse, but in a garden located inland, upstream, and behind the house—also the west. The newborn baby is first bathed in the river, then brought into the longhouse through the rear women's door. Confined inside the house for about a week with its mother and father, the baby is again bathed in the river and given a name. Thus, in cosmological terms, babies do indeed come from women, water, the river, and the west.

In the Tukanoan view, *masa*, the word for "people," is a relative concept. It can refer to one group as opposed to another, to all Tukanoans as opposed to their non-Tukanoan neighbors, to Indians as opposed to whites, to human beings as opposed to animals, and finally to living things, including trees, as opposed to inanimate objects. In myths and shamanic discourse, animals are people and share their culture. They live in organized longhouse communities, plant gardens, hunt and fish, drink beer, wear ornaments, take part in intercommunity feasts, and play their own sacred instruments. All creatures that can see and hear, communicate with their own kind, and act intentionally are "people"—but people of different kinds. They are different because they have different bodies, habits, and behaviors and see things from different bodily perspectives. Just as stars see living humans as dead spirits, so also do animals see humans as animals. In everyday life, people emphasize their difference from animals, but in the spirit world, which is also the world of ritual, shamanism, dreaming, and ayahuasca visions (ayahuasca being a psycho-active liquid that is drunk on ceremonial occasions), perspectives are merged, differences are abolished, the past is the present, and people and animals remain as one.

In Amazonia, ritual specialists with special powers and access to esoteric religious knowledge are often referred to as "shamans." In order to operate successfully in the world, all adult men must be shamans to some extent. But those who are publicly recognized as such are individuals with greater ritual knowledge and a special ability to "read" what lies behind sacred narratives; they are individuals who choose to use their skills and knowledge on behalf of others, and who acquire recognition as experts. With rare exceptions, ritual experts are always men, but the capacity of women to menstruate and to bear children is spoken of as the female equivalent of shamanic power.

Tukanoans distinguish between two quite different ritual specialists, the *yai* and the *kumu*. The *yai* corresponds to the prototypical Amazonian shaman whose main tasks involve dealing with other people and with the outside world of animals and the forest. The shaman is an expert in curing the sickness and diseases caused by sorcery from vengeful creatures and jealous human beings. *Yai* means "jaguar," a term that gives some indication of the status of the shaman in Tukanoan society. The *kumu* is more a savant and a priest than a shaman. His powers and authority are founded on an exhaustive knowledge of mythology and ritual procedures, knowledge that only comes after years of training and practice. As a knowledgeable senior man, the *kumu* is typically also a headmen and leader of his community and will exercise considerable authority over a much wider area. Compared to the sometimes morally ambiguous *yai*, the *kumu* enjoys a much higher status and also a much greater degree of trust, which relates to his prominent ritual role. The *kumu* plays an important role in the prevention of illness and misfortune. He also officiates at rites of passage and effects the major transitions of birth, initiation, and death, transitions that ensure the socialization of individuals and the passage of the generations, and which maintain ordered relations between the ancestors and their living descendants. The *kumu*'s other major function is to officiate at dance feasts, drinking parties, and ceremonial exchanges and to conduct and supervise the rituals at which the sacred instruments are played, rituals that involve direct contact with dead ancestors.

The yearly round is punctuated by a series of collective feasts, each with its own songs, dances, and appropriate musical instruments, which mark important events in the human and natural worlds—births, initiations, marriages, deaths, the felling and planting of gardens, the building of houses, the migrations of fishes and birds, and the seasonal availability of forest fruits and other gathered foods. The feasts take three basic forms: *cashirís* (beer feasts), *dabukuris* (ceremonial exchanges), and rites involving sacred flutes and trumpets. The rituals involving sacred musical instruments are the fullest expression of the Indians' religious life, for they synthesize a number of key themes: ancestry, descent and group identity, sex and reproduction, relations between men and women, growth and maturation, death, regeneration, and the integration of the human life cycle with cosmic time. (For a complete description and analysis of these rites, and the symbolism of the sacred instruments, see Hugh-Jones, 1979.)

Effective missionary penetration among the Tukanoans began towards the end of the nineteenth century with the arrival of the Franciscans. The Franciscans, and the Salesians who followed them, saw native religion through the lens of their own closed religious categories. Without knowing or caring about what Tukanoan religion meant, the missionaries set about destroying one civilization in the name of another, burning down the Indians' longhouses, destroying their feather ornaments, persecuting the shamans, and exposing the sacred instruments to women and children. They ordered people to build villages of neatly ordered single-family houses and send their children to mission boarding schools, where they were taught to reject their parents' and their ancestors' ways of life.

If the missionaries were resented for their attack on Indian culture, they were also welcomed as a source of manufactured goods, as defenders of the Indians against the worst abuses of the rubber gatherers, and as the providers of the education that the Indian children would need to make the most of their new circumstances. From the 1920s onwards, the Salesians established a chain of outposts throughout the region on the Brazilian side of the frontier. At the beginning of the twenty-first century, the growing body of evangelicals apart, most Tukanoan Indians would consider themselves to be Catholics. As more and more people now leave their villages and head for urban centers in search of education and employment, life in the longhouses and the rich variety of ritual life that went with it now persists only in the memories of the oldest inhabitants. On the Colombian side of the border, the more liberal Javerians preach tolerance of Indian culture and accommodation with its values and beliefs, allowing the Tukanoans to conserve much of their traditional religion and way of life to this day.

Baniwa and Kuripako. The religious life of the Arawak-speaking Baniwa and Kuripako of the Brazil/Venezuela/Colombia borders was similarly based on the great mythological and ritual cycles related to the first ancestors and symbolized by sacred flutes and trumpets, on the central importance of shamanism, and on a rich variety of dance rituals called *pudali*, associated with the seasonal cycles and the maturation of forest fruits.

Baniwa cosmogony is remembered in a complex set of numerous myths in which the main protagonist is Nhiãperikuli, beginning with his emergence in the primordial world and ending with his creation of the first ancestors of the Baniwa phratries and his withdrawal from the world. Many of these myths recount the struggles of Nhiãperikuli against various animal-tribes who seek to kill him and destroy the order of the universe. More than any other figure of the Baniwa pantheon, Nhiãperikuli was responsible for the form and essence of the world; in fact, it may even be said that he *is* the universe.

Another great cycle in the history of the cosmos is told in the myth of Kuwai, the son of Nhiãperikuli, and the first woman, Amaru. This myth has central importance in Baniwa culture for it explains at least four major questions on the nature of existence in the world: (1) how the order and ways of life of the ancestors are reproduced for all future generations, the Walimanai; (2) how children are to be instructed in initiation rituals about the nature of the world; (3) how sicknesses and misfortune entered the world; and (4) what is the nature of the relation among humans, spirits, and animals that is the legacy of the primordial world. The myth tells of the life of Kuwai, an extraordinary being whose body is full of holes and consists of all the elements of the world, and whose humming and songs produce all animal species. His birth sets in motion a rapid process of growth in which the miniature and chaotic world of Nhiãperikuli opens up to its real-life size.

The myth of Kuwai marks a transition between the primordial world of Nhiãperikuli and a more recent human past, which is brought directly into the experience of living people in the rituals. For that reason, the shamans say that Kuwai is as much a part of the present world as of the ancient world, and that he lives "in the center of the world." For the shamans, he is the Owner of Sicknesses and it is he whom they seek in their cures, for his body consists of all sicknesses that exist in the world (including poison used in witchcraft, which is still the most frequently cited "cause" of death of people today), the material forms of which he left in this world in the great conflagration that marked his "death" and withdrawal from the world. The shamans say that Kuwai's body is covered with fur like the black sloth called *wamu*. Kuwai ensnares the souls of the sick, grasping them in his arms (as the sloth does), and suffocating them until the shamans bargain with him to regain the souls and return them to their owners.

In Baniwa cosmology, the universe is formed by multiple layers associated with various divinities, spirits, and "other people." According to one shaman, it is organized into an enormous vertical structure of twenty-five layers or "worlds"(*kuma*), there being twelve layers below "this world" *(hliekwapi)* of humans, collectively known as Uapinakuethe, and twelve above, collectively known as Apakwa Hekwapi, the "other world." Each one of the layers below the earth is inhabited by "people" or "tribes" with distinctive characteristics (people painted red, people with large mouths, etc.). With the exception of the people of the lowest level of the cosmos, and one other underworld, all other peoples are considered to be "good" and assist the shaman in his search for the lost souls of the sick. Above our world are the places of various spirits and divinities related to the shamans: bird-spirits who help the shaman in his search for lost souls; the Owner of Sicknesses, Kuwai, whom the shaman seeks in order to cure more serious ailments; the primordial shamans and Dzulíferi, the Owner of Pariká (shaman's snuff) and tobacco; and finally, the place of the creator and transformer Nhiãperikuli, or Dio, which is a place of eternal, brilliant light, like a room full of mirrors reflecting this light. The sun is considered to be a manifestation of Nhiãperikuli's body. With the exception of the level of Kuwai, all other levels are likewise inhabited by "good people." Some may "deceive" or "lie" to the shaman, but only the "sickness owner" possesses death-dealing substances used in witchcraft.

This world of humans is, by contrast, considered to be irredeemably evil. Thus, of all the layers in the universe, four are considered to be comprised of wicked people. It is remarkable how, in the context and from the perspective of the most elaborate cosmic structure thus far recorded amongst the Baniwa, the theme of evil in this world of humans clearly stands out. In shamanic discourse, this world is frequently characterized as *maatchikwe* (place of evil), *kaiwikwe* (place of pain), and *ekúkwe* (place of rot [due to the rotting corpses of the dead]), contrasting it with the world of Nhiãperikuli, which is notable for its sources of remedies against the sicknesses of this world. This world is considered to be contaminated by the existence of sorcerers and witches. Shamanic powers and cures, by contrast, are characterized in terms of the protective, beneficial, and aesthetically correct: to make the world beautiful; to make this world and the people in it better and content; to not let this world fall or end (meaning, to be covered in darkness and overrun by witches); to retrieve lost souls and make sick persons well—all are phrases that appear in shamanic discourses about journeys to the other world. In all phases of this journey, the beauty, goodness, unity, order, and truth—in a word, the "light"—of the other world (with the exception of the places of Kuwai) stand in contrast with this world of multiple pain and evil. In one sense, then, the shaman's quest would seem to be one of "beautifying" this world by seeking to create order and preventing the darkness of chaos.

In the 1950s, the majority of the Baniwa converted to evangelical Protestantism, introduced by missionaries of the New Tribes Mission. Their mass conversion was historically continuous with their participation in prophetic movements ever since the mid-nineteenth century; however, evangelicalism provoked a radical break from their shamanic traditions, as well as serious divisions and conflicts with Catholic Baniwa and those who sought to maintain their ritual traditions. Today, after half a century, evangelicalism is now the predominant form of religion in over half the Baniwa communities, although there is a growing movement among non-evangelicals to revitalize the initiation rituals and mythic traditions.

Maku. The universe of the nomadic Maku Indians of the interfluvial region in the Northwest Amazon takes the form of an upright egg, with three levels or "worlds": (1) the subterranean "world of shadows," from where all the monsters come, such as scorpions, jaguars, venomous snakes, the river Indians, and whites; (2) "our world"; that is, the forest, and (3) the "world of the light" above the sky, where the ancestors and the creator, the Son of the Bone, live. Light and shadow are the two basic substances from which all beings are composed in varying proportions. Light is a source of life. Shadow is a source of death. In "our world," leaves and fruit are the beings with the highest concentration of light, while carnivores have the highest concentration of shadow. For this reason, it is better to avoid eating carnivores and restrict one's diet to herbivores. In the world of light after death, people nourish themselves with delicious fruit juices and become eternal adolescents.

The main mythological cycle of the Maku relates the epic tale of the Son of the Bone, whose name varies with the subgroup. The myth describes the survivor of a fire that put an end to the previous creation. His attempts to recreate the world resulted in a series of blunders: conflicts, sickness, and death, all resulting from the mess left behind. After his wife is abducted by his youngest brother, the Son of the Bone leaves this world behind forever, going to live in the world of light, above the sky and the thunder, from where he sometimes emits an expression of revenge. Coincidence or not, in real life, brothers often fight among themselves, in dispute over the same women, or with their affines, in accordance with the clan system.

Yanomami. The Yanomami comprise four linguistic subgroups inhabiting the mountainous rainforests of northern Brazil and southern Venezuela. Accounts of creation vary considerably among the groups, although a common theme holds that after the destruction of the primordial world by a cosmic flood, humans originated from the blood of the Moon. The souls of deceased Yanomami, whose bone ashes are consumed during the rituals of *reahu*, are incorporated into the blood-lakes of the Moon, where they are regenerated and later reincarnated, through falling rain, to a new existence on earth.

The Yanomami word *urihi* designates the forest and its floor. It also signifies territory or the region currently inhabited. The phrase for "the forest of human beings," the forest that Omama, the creator, gave to the Yanomami to live in generation after generation, is "Yanomami land" or "the great forest-land." A source of resources, for the Yanomami, *urihi* is not a simple inert setting submitted to the will of human beings. A living entity, it has an essential image and breath, as well as an immaterial fertility principal. The animals it shelters are seen to be avatars of mythic human/animal ancestors of the first humans, who ended up assuming their animal condition due to their uncontrolled behavior, an inversion of present-day social rules. Lurking in the tangled depths of the *urihi*, in its hills and its rivers, are numerous malefic beings, who injure or kill the Yanomami as though they were game, provoking disease and death. On top of the mountains live the images of the animal-ancestors transformed into shamanic spirits, *xapiripë*. The *xapiripë* were left behind by Omama to look after humans. The entire extent of *urihi* is covered by their mirrors, where they play and dance endlessly. Hidden in the depths of the waters is the house of the monster *Tëpërësiki*, father-in-law of Omama, where the *yawarioma* spirits also live; their sisters seduce and enrage young Yanomami hunters, thereby enabling them to pursue a shamanic career.

The initiation of shamans is painful and ecstatic. During initiation, which involves inhaling the hallucinogenic powder *yãkõana* (the resin or inner bark fragments of the *Virola sp.* tree, dried and pulverized) for many days under the supervision of older shamans, they learn to "see" or "recognize" the *xapiripë* spirits and to respond to their calls. The *xapiripë* are seen in the form of humanoid miniatures decorated with colorful and brilliant ceremonial ornaments. Above all, these spirits are shamanic "images" of forest entities. Many are also images of cosmic entities and mythological personae. Finally, there are the spirits of "whites" and their domesticated animals.

Once initiated, the Yanomami shamans can summon the *xapiripë* to themselves in order for these to act as auxiliary spirits. This power of knowledge, vision, and communication with the world of "vital images" or "essences" makes the shamans the pillars of Yanomami society. A shield against the malefic powers deriving from humans and nonhumans that threaten the lives of members of their communities, they are also tireless negotiators and warriors of the invisible, dedicated to taming the entities and forces that move the cosmological order. They control the fury of the thunder and winds brought by storms, the regularity of the alternation between day and night, or dry season and rainy season, the abundance of game, and the fertility of gardens; they keep up the arch of the sky to prevent its falling (the present earth is an ancient fallen sky), repel the forest's supernatural predators, and counterattack the raids made by aggressive spirits of enemy shamans. Most importantly, they cure the sick, victims of human malevolence (sorcery, aggressive shamanism, attacks on animal doubles) or nonhuman malevolence (coming from malefic *në waripë* beings).

Makiritare. The Makiritare, Carib-speaking peoples of the upper Orinoco Valley, recount the story of their creation in the great tradition called *Watunna.* According to this tradition, the primordial sun brought the heavenly creator Wanadi into being. Through his shamanic powers, Wanadi created "the old people" and then, in his desire to place "good people" in houses on the earth, he dispatched three aspects of himself to earth. The first buried his own placenta in the earth, which gave rise to an evil being, called Odosha, who then sought to destroy every creative effort and introduced death into the world. The second aspect of Wanadi was sent to teach the people that dying is an illusion and that dreaming holds the true power of reality. He brought good people, as sounds, inside a stonelike egg to earth, where they would be born, but Odosha prevented this from happening. Wanadi then hid them in a mountain to wait until the end of the world and the death of Odosha. Wanadi's third aspect, Attawanadi, then came to earth to create the enclosed structure of the earth, which was then shrouded in the darkness created by Odosha. A new sky, sun, moon, and stars were created in this house, village, universe. Then there ensued a struggle between Odosha and Attawanadi in which Odosha is initially victorious, but Attawanadi outsmarts the evil being by assuming elusive guises. As trickster, Attawanadi thwarts Odosha's constant attempts to destroy existence in a sort of negative dialectic of the sacred. Thus cosmic history was set in motion.

Other episodes of this important cycle relate the destruction through deluge of the primordial beings and their world, and the origins of periodicity, differentiation, and bounded spaces. The deluge was the result of the killing of a primordial anaconda-monster. After this destruction, Wanadi decided to make houses and "new people," who live in a symbolic world in which, through song, ritual, and weaving, they recall these primordial events. The landscape of the Makiritare world provides constant reminders of the primordial times. The center of the universe is a lake in Makiritare territory where, in ancient times, waters poured forth from the cut trunk of the tree that originally bore all fruit. This lake contains the sea that once flooded the earth and is now bounded at the edges of the world.

Although numerous Makiritare communities converted to Protestant evangelicalism in the 1980s, many others rejected conversion, maintaining firm belief in the Watunna tradition.

Bibliography

Albert, Bruce. "Yanomami." In *Povos indígenas no Brasil.* Instituto socioambiental (Socio-Environmental Institute), 1999. Available in Portuguese and English from http://www.socioambiental.org/website/pib/epienglish/yanomami/yanomami.shtm. Basic information on Yanomami society, culture, and cosmology.

De Civrieux, Marc. *Watunna: An Orinoco Creation Cycle.* Edited and translated by David M. Guss. San Francisco, 1980. Major myth cycle of the Makiritare Indians of the upper Orinoco, collected by the author during twenty years of fieldwork.

Hugh-Jones, Stephen. *The Palm and the Pleiades: Initiation and Cosmology in Northwest Amazonia.* Cambridge, U.K., 1979. One of the earliest and most important monographs on the ritual and religious life of an indigenous peoples, the Tukanoan-speaking Barasana of the Northwest Amazon. Structuralist analysis of initiation rites, myths, and cosmology.

Pozzobon, Jorge. "Maku." In *Povos indígenas no Brasil.* Instituto socioambiental (Socio-Environmental Institute), 1999. Available in Portuguese and English from http://www. socioambiental. org / website / pib / epienglish / maku / maku.shtm. Basic information on Maku society, culture, and cosmology.

Sullivan, Lawrence. *Icanchu's Drum: An Orientation to Meaning in South American Religions.* New York, 1988. Outstanding source on native South American religions by a historian of religions. Examines the cosmogonies, cosmologies, anthropologies, and eschatologies of native peoples across the continent. Masterful work of interpretation of myths, rituals, and beliefs.

Wright, Robin. *Cosmos, Self, and History in Baniwa Religion: For Those Unborn.* Austin, Tex., 1998. Monograph on the Baniwa peoples of the Northwest Amazon, focusing on cosmogony, cosmology, eschatology, and conversion to Protestant evangelicalism.

Wright, Robin, with Manuela Carneiro da Cunha. "Destruction, Resistance, and Transformations—Southern, Coastal, and Northern Brazil (1580–1890)." In *The Cambridge History of the Native Peoples of the Americas,* Vol. 3: *South America,* edited by Stuart Schwartz and Frank Salomon, part 2, pp. 287–381. New York and Cambridge, U.K., 1999. History of three centuries of contact between indigenous societies in three regions of Brazil, and the expanding colonial frontier.

Robin M. Wright (2005)

SOUTH AMERICAN INDIANS: INDIANS OF THE CENTRAL AND EASTERN AMAZON

The vast region covered by the central and eastern Amazon may, for the purposes of this entry, be delimited by the Río Negro at the western end, the mouth of the Amazon to the east, the Guyana highlands to the north, and the central plateau of Brazil to the south. Within this region many of the great language families of South America are represented: Arawak, Tupi, Carib, Ge, and Timbira. Besides this diversity the area is also notable for some of the most complex prehistorical cultures, such as Marajoara and Santarém. This entry provides an overview of the religious systems of prehistoric and contemporary indigenous peoples as well as of peasants or *caboclos*.

PREHISTORIC CULTURES AND RELIGIOUS MANIFESTATIONS. Archaeological excavations at Marajó Island in the Amazon Delta reveal the existence of a complex society of Mound Builders spanning the period from roughly 500 to 1300 CE. The abundance of ceremonial and funerary remains on the higher mounds attests to the existence of political and ceremonial centers. Differential burials, houses for the dead, and possibly temples indicate ancestor cults. Marajoara ceramics are marked by the use of animal motifs with clear supernatural and mythical connotations that modern studies have sought to interpret in terms of Amerindian perspectivism. The symbolism of death and rebirth, shamanic motifs, binary images, abstract geometric patterns, and bodily images are all characteristic of Marajoara ceramics, indicating a complex religious system (see Schaan, 2001). Similarly the prehistoric Santarém culture at the mouth of the Tapajós was the center of a great chiefdom from the tenth century to the sixteenth century. Female fertility is a predominant element in ceramic motifs; the famous caryatid vessels display bicephalous humanlike zoomorphic figures (especially the king vulture), recalling the transformations experienced in shamanic trance or in great collective rituals using psychoactive substances in which great trumpets representing the divinities were played. Finally, mention should be made of the many cemeteries with large funerary urns discovered near the Maracá River on the lower Amazon. These urns display anthropomorphic or zoomorphic figures, with the anthropomorphic figures, often female, being seated, decorated, and painted. It has been suggested that the Maracá culture was linked to early Arawakan populations that were possibly ancestors of the Palikur.

BRIEF HISTORY OF CONTACT. The size and complexity of Amazon floodplain societies astonished the first European explorers in the mid-sixteenth century. Their populations were dense, internally stratified, and settled in extensive villages capable of producing surpluses for a significant intertribal commerce. The sociopolitical organization of what observers called "provinces" was far more elaborate than any indigenous society since then, with reports of local chiefs subordinate to regional chiefs endowed with sacred qualities, hierarchically organized lineages, sacrifice of concubines at the deaths of chiefs, ancestor cults with the preservation of the corpse through rudimentary techniques, and other evidence of social and ritual stratification.

None of this resisted the advance of the European slave hunters, spice collectors, diseases, and missionaries who, by the end of the seventeenth century, had penetrated well into the Amazon Valley. Their advance resulted in the dispersion and captivity of a majority of the riverine peoples such that the eastern Amazon was practically depopulated and infested by diseases, as mission industries and towns struggled to survive. With the depopulation of the main tributaries, expeditions penetrated ever farther into the interior to "persuade" whole populations to relocate to ethnically mixed, mission-run settlements. This process led to the formation of a neoindigenous stratum of the population, whose original cultural and linguistic differences had been neutralized, dissolving ethnic diversity into the homogeneity of generic Indians that eventually gave rise to the *caboclo* or mixed population of the region.

With the decline of colonial control by the end of the eighteenth century, many peoples withdrew from colonial settlements to reorganize and reconstitute their societies, often in new territories and with new sociopolitical and religious forms of organization. From the mid–nineteenth century until well into the twentieth, rubber extraction and exportation became the dominant form of labor organization in the Amazon, and with the severe droughts in northeastern Brazil at the end of the nineteenth century, there was a massive influx of northeastern migrants into the Amazon region. By the late twentieth century even the most isolated regions of the central and eastern Amazon, which until then had served as a refuge for many indigenous peoples, were invaded by highways, miners, and ranchers.

CONTEMPORARY INDIGENOUS RELIGIONS. The religions of several peoples will be briefly considered. Those included are the Palikur (Arawak) of the state of Amapá; the Araweté and Juruna (Tupian) of the state of Pará; the Kayapó and Xikrin (Ge) of the state of Pará; the Canela and Krahó (Timbira) of Maranhão; and the Arara (Carib) of Pará.

Palikur (Arawakan). For the contemporary Palikur, the creation and structuring of the universe and all that is part of it is the work of the Christian God. They usually disparage the beliefs of their ancestors, declaring that they were superstitions, and cite as an example the constitution of the universe in layers. In the early twenty-first century they "know that the world is round." Nevertheless they possess a vast repertoire of myths that reveals a good part of their ancient cosmology.

The myths can be divided into two categories: cosmogonic myths that tell of the emergence of the Palikur and their relations with the environment or with other ethnic groups of the region, and those myths that speak of the relation with the "beings of the other world." The myths are generally further classified into two types: "stories of the old times, of the past, a long time ago" and "false stories." They always refer to a time past, in which the "true" belief, the Christian religion, was unknown. At times, however, narrators reflect and point out that the fact in question is real and still occurs, revealing the ambiguity with which the Palikur regard the myths. It is exactly this ambiguity that has allowed for the coexistence of indigenous mythology with Christian religion, but that has not occurred with the rituals, for which reason they are no longer held. Myth is consciously relegated to an inferior position in relation to the Christian religious system.

The mythical universe appears to be divided into three layers: the world below, the terrestrial plane, and the celestial plane. The first is the mythical space par excellence, for in it dwell the supernatural spirits. Located just below the surface of the earth, its parallel position in relation to the terrestrial level facilitates contact between the two worlds, a necessary condition for the existence of the mythical world, since this plane only makes sense in connection with the world of humans. The representation of the passage between the two worlds is physical: there is a "hole" in the terrestrial level that allows for displacement from one sphere to another. The switch from one plane to another is marked by the transformation of supernatural beings that, in their world, have human form but, to come up to the terrestrial level, need to "clothe themselves" with a "cloak" that gives them animal form.

On the terrestrial level live human beings, plants, animals, and occasionally supernatural beings. This level has a topography that is analogous to this earth, about which there are many mythical narratives; however, geographical locations are fluid and vary from one narrative to another.

Finally, the celestial plane seems to be a space that is dominated exclusively by Christian cosmology—represented as Eden, inhabited by the Trinity, and reserved for the chosen, meaning those who have "accepted Jesus" before the "end of time." In terms of Palikur myths, heaven appears to be empty. But even while fragmentary, several aspects of indigenous cosmology still occupy space in this domain. The Palikur believe there are six unnamed levels. Among these, two have notable inhabitants: on the second level lives the two-headed king vulture and on the sixth is Jesus Christ, awaiting the chosen "in the celestial Eden made of gold." The other levels are described as "display windows" of purgatory, in which one sees the souls of those who do not attain eternal life. These souls are anthropomorphic, with a human body up to the neck dressed in a white cloak and the head of an animal (monkey, alligator, and so on).

In 1926 Curt Nimuendajú mentioned the existence of three heavens: Inoliku, the lowest, Mikene, and Ena. Just above the first there was a special heaven, Yinoklin, inhabited by the Yumawali spirits (or "demons," as Nimuendajú called them) of the mountains. This division of the sky by named levels does not exist now, but with small alterations, the names given to the heavens are confirmed.

Araweté and Juruna (Tupian). The guiding thread of Araweté religion is the relationship between humanity and the Máï, the immortal beings who left the earth at the dawn of time and now live in the sky. Humans define themselves as the "abandoned ones," or "forsaken," meaning those who were left behind by the gods. Humans and Máï are related as affines, for the souls of the dead are married to the gods. The Máï may, and in the long run will, destroy the earth by causing the sky to crash down. The ultimate cause of all deaths is the will of the Máï, who are conceived as being at once ideal Araweté and dangerous cannibals. The Máï are not thought of as creators, but their separation from humanity produced old age and death. Among the hundreds of types of Máï, most of which have animal names, the Máï *hete* (real gods) are those who transform the souls of the dead into Máï-like beings by means of a cannibal-matrimonial operation. That is, following its arrival in the celestial realms, the soul of the dead is killed and devoured by the Máï, after which it is resurrected by means of a magical bath and made into a godlike being who will be married to a Máï and live forever young. Besides the Máï, there are also Ani forest spirits, savage beings who invade settlements and must be killed by the shamans, and the powerful Master of the River, a subaquatic spirit who delights in kidnapping women's and children's souls, which must then be retrieved by shamans.

The most important shamanic activity is bringing down the Máï and the souls of the dead to visit the earth and partake of ceremonial meals. In these ceremonial banquets collectively produced food (honey, fish, and *cauim*, a fermented corn beverage) is offered to the celestial visitors before being consumed. The *cauim* festival is the climax of ritual life and contains religious and warrior symbolism. The leader of the dances and songs that accompany the consumption of *cauim* is ideally a great warrior, who learned the songs directly from the spirits of dead enemies. Singing is thus the heart of ceremonial life. The "music of the gods" sung by shamans and the "music of the enemies" sung by warriors are the only two musical genre known to the Araweté, and both are formed by the words of "others" quoted in complex ritual formulas.

The souls of the recently deceased often come to earth in the shaman's chants to talk to their living relatives and tell them of the bliss of the afterlife. After two generations they cease to come, for there will be no more living contemporaries who remember them; they are not ancestors, however.

Juruna cosmology has three basic coordinates. First is the opposition between life and death. This is far from being a drastic dichotomy as in Western cosmology, because there are various transitions, such as minor temporary "deaths," as in sleep, that typically take the form of dreams. The relation between life and death involves not so much the notion that if someone is dead he or she cannot be alive but rather that someone can be dead in one place but alive in another or that he or she may be alive here but already dead somewhere else. In other words, the relation is one of relative disjunction, which allows for important conjunctions. Juruna shamans used to be masters at such transitions.

Second, the world axes are formed by the oppositions between river and forest and sky and earth, each being articulated with the opposition between the presence and absence of cannibalism. The river and the sky have a positive link with cannibalism. One can say that all existence can be divided into these oppositions: human beings (river peoples and forest peoples), spirits of the dead (those living in the cliffs on the banks of the Xingu, who do not like human flesh, and those living in the sky), mammals (forest species and those living on the river bed), and so on. In addition the Juruna believe everything that exists on earth also exists in the sky, which is a kind of earth resembling that of humans. Even though the Juruna do not consider the river to be a copy of the forest, they say it can be viewed by some river inhabitants as a copy of the earth, except that the forest in their earth resembles human gallery forests, and their gardens are portions of land broken off from the river banks. Finally, there is an opposition between the viewpoints—or perspectives—of living, conscious human subjects and alien beings, such as animals, spirits, and the dead. The dynamism and complexity of Juruna cosmology depends on the confrontation between these discordant viewpoints.

Juruna shamanism used to be composed of two systems, each related to a society of the dead. Rarely was it possible for a shaman to practice both types of shamanism. The spirits of the dead inhabiting the river cliffs fear those living in the sky, whose society is composed of the souls of warriors and their leader. Indeed the Juruna fear these spirits of the sky the most, and thus this form of shamanism was considerably more powerful, dangerous, and difficult to perform. Each system of shamanism was associated with a great festival in honor of its particular category of the dead. The festival for the dead of the river cliffs was accompanied by the sound of flute music and songs performed by the dead through the mouth of the shaman. Another festival was accompanied by the music of a set of trumpets. When the Juruna offered food to the souls of warriors during their festival, they said they would rather eat the flesh of roasted Indians brought from the other world; they also refused to drink manioc beer, saying they were already drunk enough. By contrast, the spirits from the river cliffs would drink plenty after eating the meal from their hosts, spicing up the manioc beer made by Juruna women with a dose of beer brought from the other world. The last of these celebrations was held in the 1970s. Despite the changes in their ritual life, the Juruna continue to celebrate beer parties and two major festivals every year, each held for approximately one month.

Ge-Timbira. Ge-Timbira religiosity is marked by a strong dualism. That characteristic divides creation, nature and society, and the groups that make up society.

Canela. A Canela origin myth recounts that Sun and Moon walked over the land, transforming the world that already existed and thus creating the norms for social life. Sun established the norms favorable to life, whereas Moon modified them to test its imperfections. Sun created ideal men and women, whereas Moon created those with twisted hair, those with dark skin, and those seen as deformed. Sun allowed machetes and axes to work by themselves in the gardens, whereas Moon made them stop. Consequently people had to work hard to make their gardens—the origin of work. There are at least a dozen episodes of this myth that recount the beginning of death, floods, and forest fires, why the *buriti* palms are tall, why the moon has its spots, and other conditions.

Other Canela myths explain the origin of fire and corn. A boy brought fire for his people after having stolen it from the hearth of a female jaguar. Star Woman fell in love with a Canela and so came down to live for a while among his family members. During her stay she indicated that corn would grow in the forest, and she taught them that it was good to eat. This was the origin of gardens. She then returned to the sky with her mate and both transformed into twin stars, known as Castor and Pollux.

Krahó. Krahó origin myths are similar to those of the Canela. Indeed these myths seem to suggest that everything in Krahó culture, even shamanism, came from the outside. Like the Canela, the Krahó believe all of their culture was created by the twins Sun and Moon. The Krahó disapprove of the actions of Moon not only because he was less skilled than Sun but also because he insisted that Sun do what he requested, for it was from these requests that the evils that afflict humans entered the world.

Other myths tell how the Krahó studied agriculture, obtained fire, and learned the rituals and songs. Generally the myths tell the story of an individual who leaves the village and, in the world outside, learns something important, later returning to the village where he or she transmits the new knowledge. In the case of agriculture, however, a being from nature brings the knowledge of planting to the villagers and then withdraws to the outside world. The myth of Auke, which is important for understanding Krahó participation in messianic movements in the 1960s, follows the same pattern. But Auke, on entering the village, is not given the opportunity to teach the Indians what he knows, for they are afraid of him and end up violently expelling him from the village. Auke then creates white humans. Several other myths tell of individuals who, having been expelled from the village, do not return with new things that could be used by its inhabitants; rather, they stay in the world outside, transforming themselves into animals or monsters.

The Krahó have many rituals. Some are short and linked to individual life crises (such as the end of seclusion after the birth of a first child, the end of a convalescence, and the last meal of a deceased person) or to occasional collective initiatives (such as exchanges of foods and services). Others are associated with the annual agricultural cycle, for instance, those that mark the dry and wet seasons, the planting and harvesting of corn, and the harvesting of sweet potatoes. Yet other rites form part of a longer cycle, associated with male initiation, that must take place in a certain order; nowadays this cycle is difficult to reconstitute, in part because one of the rites has been abandoned. Various rites related to the annual and initiation cycles have myths that explain their origins. However, there is not a strict correspondence between the sequence of myths and that of rites, although they overlap in some ways.

The first human who acquired magical powers was carried up to the heavens by vultures, where he was cured and received powers from the hawk. There is apparently no trance among Krahó shamans, which might suggest that they are not true shamans. But each shaman explains how, like the man who went up to the sky in a myth, he was initiated through a sort of spontaneous rite of passage. He became sick and was abandoned, he was rescued by an animal (or other being) that cured him and gave him magical powers, which he tested, and then he was sent home with his new powers. In some cases there seems to occur a transformation of the shaman into the being that gives him powers, for example, the animal puts parts of his own organism into the body of the shaman, makes him eat the same food, and so on.

Kayapó. As among the Timbira, the village is the center of the Kayapó universe and the most socialized space. The surrounding forest is considered an antisocial space, where humans can transform into animals or spirits, sicken without reason, or even kill their relatives. Beings who are half-animal, half-people dwell there. The farther one goes from the village, the more antisocial the forest becomes, and its associated dangers increase. As there is always the danger that the "social" may be appropriated by the natural domain, escaping human control, the Kayapó engage in a symbolic appropriation of the natural, transforming it into the social through curing chants and ceremonies that establish a constant exchange between humans and the world of nature.

The section of forest in which the village population hunts, fishes, and cultivates land is first socialized by the attribution of place names. Thereafter human modifications of the natural world are accompanied by rituals. The opening of new gardens is preceded by a dance presenting many structural similarities to the war ritual. Opening up new gardens can be interpreted as a symbolic war against a natural rather than human enemy. Returning from the hunt, men must sing to the spirits of the game they themselves have killed in order for the spirits to remain in the forest. Each animal species designates a song that always begins with the cry of the dead animal.

Kayapó rites express basic values of their society, reflecting the image the group has of itself, the society, and the universe. Each rite translates a part of this cosmological vision and establishes a link between humans and nature, in which above all the human-animal relationship is reinforced. Kayapó rituals are many and diverse, but their importance and duration varies greatly. They are divided into three main categories: the large ceremonies for confirming personal names; certain agricultural, hunting, fishing, and occasional rites, for example, performed during solar or lunar eclipses; and rites of passage. The last are frequently solemn affairs, though short and only rarely accompanied by dances or songs. Examples of rites of passage include all ceremonies qualified by the term *merêrêmex* (people who extend their beauty), a reference to the highly elaborate way in which people decorate themselves on such occasions. Such ceremonies are group-based activities whose goal is to socialize "wild" or antisocial values. This applies to the attribution of names, a central theme of most Kayapó ceremonies; in fact personal names are borrowed from nature. Shamans enter into contact with the natural spirits and learn new songs and names from them, introducing them into culture through the large naming ceremonies.

On these occasions most of the ritual sequences take place in the village's central plaza, where an inversion of ordinary social space may be noted. The center of the village, normally organized on the basis of friendship and nonkinship, is converted into the domain of activities in which both personal family bonds and natural—and therefore "wild" elements, such as the personal names or those of killed prey—are central. The true nature of "beauty" is not only visual but also refers to an inner beauty that results from the group's activity, from the common effort required to "socialize" the names of people or of other precious objects.

Xikrin. For the Xikrin, the center of the world is likewise represented by the center of the circular village plaza, where rituals and public life in general unfold. The symbol of the center of the world and the universe is the rattle, a round, head-shaped musical instrument, played as the Indians sing and dance following a circular path that accompanies the solar trajectory. The Indians say that, when dancing, they return in time to their mythic origins, thereby recreating the energy required for the continuity and stability of the environment and the resources needed for survival, the continual reproduction of life, and the different social institutions that ensure the equilibrium indispensable to life in the community.

The Xikrin define distinct natural spaces of their universe: the earth, divided into open tracts and forest, the sky, the aquatic world, and the subterranean world. These are thought to possess distinct attributes and inhabitants, though related among themselves in different ways. The forest is home to different ethnic sets of enemies, terrestrial animals, and plants. Disrespectful appropriation of the animal world causes the fury of the spirit owner-controller of the animals who, through sorcery, regulates the predatory activities of humans. On the other hand, the forest is also the source of important attributes of Xikrin sociability, for there, in mythical times, the Indians acquired fire and ceremonial language. Clearings—places formed by the village or the swiddens—are the site for kinship and alliance relations and for the individual's socialization, in other words, for the definition of Xikrin humanity. The aquatic domain provides the possibility for strengthening physical and psychological aspects of the individual, because water causes rapid maturation through ritual immersions yet without altering the being's substance. Water is a creative element in contrast to fire, which is a transformative element. An owner-controller also exists in the aquatic domain whose relationship with humans is one of solidarity. It was the owner-controller of the waters who taught humans to cure sicknesses. Medicinal plants come from the terrestrial domain, but their knowledge and the rules for manipulating them were acquired in the aquatic world through the mediation of a shaman. The subterranean world is linked with blood, raw food, and cannibalism, representing a truly antisocial condition in which humans are prey rather than predators. It represents all that humans do not want to be. In the celestial domain, the East is the place of humanity par excellence, the place where the Xikrin originated. The Xikrin have two myths that consecrate them as inhabitants of the earth, in opposition to the sky where they originated and in opposition to the subterranean inhabitants, whom they succeeded in eliminating forever.

In Xikrin society an individual becomes a shaman after he survives an ordeal, in which he climbs a giant spider web and reaches celestial space with its eternal light, where the nape of his neck is symbolically perforated by a large harpy eagle and he thus acquires the capacity to fly. As in other native societies, the shaman has the power to transit between the human world and the natural and supernatural worlds. In life humans accumulate over time attributes from different cosmic domains, but the shaman lives, shares, and constantly communicates with these domains. In his role of intermediary, he lives in human society, shares the social world of animals and the supernatural, and has the capacity to manipulate the different domains. He negotiates with the owner-controllers of the animal world for plentiful game or an abundant catch of fish. He has the capacity to "see" in the widest sense, perceiving what is invisible to humans.

When a community has enough people and thus human resources, the cycle of rituals is continuous. During rituals individuals acquire knowledge of aspects of social organization and reproduction. Song, choreography, and decorations, which humans acquired in mythical time, are reproduced in ritual as manifestations of the present situation of humanity in the cosmos. The most important rituals are those focused on male and female naming and male initiation, consisting of five phases, each of which is symbolically related to one of the particular cosmic domains. These rituals are sometimes inserted within others, such as the new maize festival or *merêrêmei*, "beautiful festival," which takes place during the transitional period between the dry and rainy seasons; the festivals incorporating new members of a ceremonial society, such as the armadillo society; the marriage ritual or mat festival; and the funerary rituals and ritual fishing using *timbó* vine poisons. There are also newly introduced rituals, such as *Kworo-kango*, or the manioc festival, which comes from the Juruna people. At certain periods, the ritual cycle attains its climax and develops over several days with high intensity and lavish style. Ceremonial life also acts as a crucial context for the expression of the ways in which the Xikrin reflect on the relationships developed with the white world.

Arara (Carib). The history of the formation of the Arara cosmos states that the primordial cosmos was shattered after a fight occurred between two people related as *ipari* (matrilateral cross-cousins or, more generally, affines). The land on the terrestrial level now is said to be what was left over from the primeval cosmological floor that broke up and fell from the sky after the combat. That floor was also the edge of the domain where all benign beings used to live. Outside that domain, there were only malicious beasts who constantly fought, living a horrifying existence. With the shattering of the cosmos, the coexistence of all types of living beings became a necessity. Consequently extraordinary and evil creatures even now can appear on the terrestrial plane. To distinguish what is ordinary and beneficial from what is extraordinary and vicious, one must develop expertise through shamanic experiences.

As an institution Arara shamanism is dispersed, diffused, and generalized among the men. Acting as healers and agents for mediating with powerful metaphysical beings, all the men are initiated and practice at least some part of the shamanic techniques and arts. They are also responsible for ensuring, with metaphysical beings, the conditions for the hunts and rites that in turn ensure the circulation of game meat and beverages among the various subgroups. Game meat and drink make up an integral part of a system whose main axis is the native doctrine concerning the circulation of a vital substance called *ekuru.* Passing from the blood of killed animals to the earth and from there to the liquids that nourish and stimulate the growth of plants, this vital substance is the main object of desire—not only of human beings, but also of all beings who inhabit the world. Humans seek to acquire *ekuru* through the deaths of animals during the hunt and the transformation of plants into a fermented drink called *piktu*—a primordial source for acquiring these vital substances for humans.

The capacity of the earth to reprocess vital substances, transforming them into plant nutrients with which humans produce beverages, also shapes Arara funeral practices. In general the Arara do not bury their dead but construct a platform for them in the forest inside a small funeral house built especially for the occasion. Raised above the earth, the deceased gradually dries out, losing the body's vital substances that are absorbed by metaphysical beings that lurk around corpses and feed on the elements that previously gave life to the deceased. The Arara funeral is thus a kind of an eschatological exchange or reciprocity with the world's other beings. On the other hand, the circulation of *ekuru* takes place among the living through the exchange of meat for drink in the rites that follow the return of the hunters. Consequently rituals are the mode through which the circulation of vital substance conjoins various subgroups through reciprocity and mutual dependence. Through their overall symbolism, the prominent rites associated with the collective hunting trips are an efficient mechanism through which ethical and moral values become manifest and serve to constitute a native idea of their own collectivity. An intricate network of values and principles of interaction related to good conduct, kindness, solidarity, and generosity finds its primary medium of expression in the rituals.

CABOCLO RELIGION. The *caboclo* population lives in communities from the mouth of the Amazon to its headwaters and on many of its tributaries. *Caboclos* are the mixed descendants of Indians and whites, and their religiosity consists of an intermixture of the rituals and beliefs of indigenous shamanism and popular Catholicism. Both forms are ways of explaining and dealing with the powers of the universe.

The shamanic universe is populated by "enchanted beings," which were left by God as guardians of the forest, the waters, game animals, and so on. They are entities with powers of enchantment, metamorphosis, and hypnosis and can be either generous or vengeful. They include the "father" or "*caboclo* of the forest," protector of the forest; the *caipora*, responsible for game animals; and the "*caboclos* of the water," which can take humans to the bottom of rivers and streams. There are also animals (snakes, deer, and turtles) with human features that can protect, deceive, hypnotize, or make pacts.

The presence of these entities in nature makes the relations of the *caboclo* to the forest, rivers, and game highly ritualized. Daily activities, such as going into the forest or fishing, are marked by prayers or requests from the spirit entities to hunt or fish; the failure to do so could bring *panema* (bad luck), a force that infects humans, animals, or objects and makes them incapable of action. As there are procedures to cure *panema*, there are also procedures to enhance the power of the hunter, sometimes called "pacts," in which, for example, the hunter exchanges the blood of the animal for greater productivity in the hunt. The relation of the *caboclo* to nature is thus one of dependence that is kept in balance by respecting norms of relations with its inhabitants and the exploitation of its resources.

The other aspect of *caboclo* religiosity is popular Catholicism, which, far from being opposed to the supernatural beings, consists of entities and practices that are integral parts of a single religious field. In general appeals are made to the Catholic saints to deal more with human affairs, whereas the enchanted beings and pacts have relatively more to do with relations to nature. As in other regions of Brazil, popular Catholicism involves saint day festivals, collective reciting of the rosary, novenas, devotion to patron saints, and making vows. The actual presence of church representatives (priests) is infrequent in this region, as it is restricted to annual visits to administer the Sacraments.

BIBLIOGRAPHY

Capiberibe, Artionka. "Os Palikur e o Cristianismo: A construção de uma Religiosidade." In *Transformando os Deuses*, vol. 2: *Igrejas Evangélicas, Pentecostais e Neopentecostais entre os Povos Indígenas no Brasil*, edited by Robin M. Wright. Campinas, Brazil, 1999.

Castro, Eduardo Viveiros de. *Araweté: Os Deuses Canibais.* Rio de Janeiro, 1986.

Crocker, William H., and Jean Crocker. *The Canela: Bonding through Kinship, Ritual, and Sex.* Fort Worth, Tex., 1994.

Lima, Tânia Stolze. *O Dois e seus Múltiplos: Reflexões sobre o perspectivismo em uma cosmologia tupi: Mana.* Rio de Janeiro, 1996.

McEwan, Colin, Cristiana Barreto, and Eduardo Neves, eds. *Unknown Amazon: Culture in Nature in Ancient Brazil.* London, 2001.

Melatti, Júlio César. *O Messianismo Krahó.* São Paulo, Brazil, 1972.

Nimuendaju, Curt. "Os índios Palikur e seus Vizinhos." Unpublished manuscript in process of translation by Thekla Hartmann. 1926.

Schaan, Denise. "Into the Labyrinth of Marajoara Pottery: States and Cultural Identity in Prehistoric Amazonia." In *Unknown Amazon: Culture in Nature in Ancient Brazil,* edited by Colin McEwan, Cristiana Barreto, and Eduardo Neves, pp. 108–133. London, 2001.

Sullivan, Lawrence E. *Icanchu's Drum: An Orientation to Meaning in South American Religions.* New York, 1988.

Teixeira-Pinto, Márnio. *Ieipari: Sacrifício e vida social entre os índios Arara (Carib).* São Paulo, Brazil, 1997.

Turner, Terence. "The Sacred as Alienated Social Consciousness: Ritual and Cosmology among the Kayapó." In *Icanchu's Drum: An Orientation to Meaning in South American Religions,* edited by Lawrence Sullivan, pp. 278–298. New York, 1988.

Vidal, Lux Boelitz. *Morte e vida em uma sociedade indígena brasileira: Os Kayapó-xikrin do Rio Cateté.* São Paulo, Brazil, 1977.

Wagley, Charles. *Uma comunidade amazônica: Estudo do homem nos trópicos.* São Paulo, Brazil, 1977.

ROBIN M. WRIGHT (2005)

SOUTH AMERICAN INDIANS: INDIANS OF THE GRAN CHACO

The Gran Chaco (*chaco,* derived from Quechua, means "hunting land") is an arid alluvial plain in the lowlands of south-central South America. Approximately 725,000 square kilometers in area, it lies between the Andes in the west and the Paraguay and Paraná rivers in the east, and between the Mato Grosso to the north and the Pampas to the south. The scrub forests and grasslands of the Gran Chaco, though sparsely populated, were the home of numerous indigenous groups. In the main they were hunters, fishers, and gatherers, moving seasonally in search of food and practicing supplementary farming. Few still follow their traditional way of life.

The religion of the indigenous groups of the Gran Chaco can be understood through an examination of their mythic narratives, which contain their primary structures of meaning. These myths give an account of a primordial time in which an ontological modification was produced by the actions of various supernatural beings who shaped present-day cultural reality. This rupture may be caused by a lawgiver (who frequently has the appearance of a trickster), or it may be the result of infractions by ancestors or by the transformations of ancestors. Numerous supernatural beings with avowedly demonic characteristics monopolize the realm of fear and danger; their ambivalent intentions toward human beings are usually resolved through malevolent action that manifests itself in illness, culminating in the death of the individual. The general notion of power, such as the *la-ka-áyah* of the Mataco, or specific powers, such as the *uhopié* of the *Ayoré*, are the structures that ontologically define the supernatural beings as well as people who have been consecrated by them.

The spectrum of supernatural beings encompasses everything from shamans and witches, in the cases of the Guiacurú or the Mataco, to the state of "amorous exaltation" known to the Pilagá. For an integral understanding of the peoples of the Chaco it is important to consider the contributions of these special personages and states of being, which contribute a unique cultural identity to each group's cosmology. In almost all the ethnic groups of the Gran Chaco the shaman occupies the central role in religious tasks, sometimes defending and protecting, and, at other times, injuring. When engaged in healing practices, he can combine various techniques, such as singing, shaking rattles, blowing, and sucking, and can command the collaboration of familiar spirits who are generally powerful owing to their demonic nature. An important aspect of Gran Chaco religions is the idea that one or many souls are incarnated in an individual. Once the individual is dead, these souls, or spirits, enter a demonic state. Although they are directed to an established underworld, they continue to prey upon human communities.

THE ZAMUCO FAMILY. The two members of the Zamuco language group are the Ayoré and the Chamacoco of Paraguay, in the northeastern Chaco.

The Ayoré. The religion of the Ayoré (Ayoreo, Ayoreode) is expressed primarily in an extensive set of myths. All natural and cultural beings have their origins related in mythic tales, and in certain cases in various parallel myths. The morphology of the myths centers upon the metamorphosis of an ancestral figure into an entity of current reality. Each tale narrates events that occurred in primordial times and is accompanied by one or more songs, which may be used for therapeutic *(sáude)* or preventive *(paragapidí)* purposes.

Despite the abundance of tales, it is possible to classify the Ayoré myths in different cycles as they relate to a particular supernatural being or theme:

(1) *The cycle of ancestors.* Each tale in this cycle recounts events in the life of an ancestor *(nanibahai)*. These generally end with the ancestor's violent transformation into an artifact, plant, animal, or some other entity of the cosmos, and with the establishment by the ancestor of cultural prescriptions (*puyák*) governing the treatment of the new being and punishments for ignoring these prescriptions.

(2) *The cycle of Dupáde.* A celestial supernatural being, Dupáde is associated with the sun; he causes the metamorphosis of the ancestors.

(3) *The cycle of the Flood.* The tales of the Flood (*gedekesnasóri*) describe an offense inflicted on lightning by the *nanibahai,* their punishment in the form of a continual rain that inundated the world, and the survival of a few Ayoré, who became the first aquatic animals.

(4) *The cycle of "water that washes away."* These tales describe a flood (*yotedidekesnasóri*) similar to that that appears in the preceding cycle, which was caused by Diesná ("cricket"), the ruler of water.

(5) *The cycle of the Asohsná bird.* This bird (*Caprimulgidae spp*) is surrounded by numerous *puyák*. The central tale of this cycle relates the life of the female ancestor who created this bird. Asohsná is a supernatural being who established the annual ceremony that divides the year into two segments, one of which is characterized by an incalculable quantity of restrictions.

(6) *The cycle of Asningái.* This cycle relates the courage of an ancestor named Asningái ("courage"), who threw himself onto the fire, transforming himself into an animal with certain morphological characteristics. It also established the meaning of slaughter, an important institution among the Ayoré, since an individual could rise to the status of chief *(asuté)* through contamination by spilled blood.

Illness is thought to be caused in almost all cases by the individual's violation of *puyák*. The cure is entrusted to the *igasitái,* those who have knowledge of *sáude,* whose power can undo the illness through the powerful word of the ancestors. The shaman, or *daihsnái,* arrives at this state through an initiation that involves the ingestion of a strong dose of the juice of green mashed tobacco, which enables him to assume a special potency called *uhopié*. When an individual dies, the body *(ayói)* and mind *(aipiyé)* are destroyed; the soul *(oregaté)* moves to the underworld (*nahupié*).

The Chamacoco. The narrative of the Chamacoco, which recounts sacred events, is called "The Word of Ešnuwérta." This tale constitutes the secret mythology of those men who have undergone initiatory ordeals and contains the social and religious knowledge of the group. Ešnuwérta is the primordial mother. The myth is connected to the women of primordial times who were surprised by harmful supernatural beings (*axnábsero*). "The Word of Ešnuwérta" includes the actions of these *axnábsero,* characters to whom Chamacoco reality is subordinated. The physiognomy of these supernatural beings is similar to that of the Ayoré ancestors in that current reality originates from their transformations and their deaths. The distinctive characteristic of the *axnábsero* is their malignant power (*wozós*) over people.

The foundation of the social order is presented in this myth, since Ešnuwérta instituted the clans as well as the male initiation ceremonies in which the participants identify themselves with the principal deities of the myth.

The Chamacoco shaman (*konsáxa*) exercises a power appropriate to a specific region of the cosmos; for this reason there are shamans of the sky, of the water, and of the jungle. The shaman initiation begins with a vision of Ešnuwérta, who reveals the cosmos as well as the practices appropriate to the work of the shamans. Another custom originating from Ešnuwérta is called *kaamták* and has to do with a ritual offering of food; it relates to the impurity of blood, among other themes.

THE TUPI-GUARANÍ FAMILY. The Tupi-Guaraní language family includes the Chiriguano of Bolivia and the Tapuí of Paraguay.

The Chiriguano. The tale of the mythical twins Yanderú Túmpa and Áña Túmpa is the most prevalent myth among the Chiriguano (Miá) and appears in conjunction with lunar mythology. The celestial supernatural being Yanderú Túmpa made the cosmos and bestowed its goods on the Chiriguano, at the same time instructing them in cultural practices. He conceived and made Áña Túmpa, who, because of envy, attempts to undermine all Yanderú Túmpa's works. Áña Túmpa received from his maker power (*imbapwére*), which he in turn gives to other beings (*áñas*) who aid him in his malignant activities. As a result the world has undergone a profound alteration. It is now the actions of the áñas that determine the condition of the Chiriguano world, and they have introduced calamities such as illness and death. The expression *túmpa* is difficult to comprehend, but it appears to designate a quality that transforms the various entities into "state beings." The terms *áña* and *túmpa* define the supernatural nature of these beings, that is to say, they emphasize that they are extraordinary.

The shaman and the sorcerer are both initiated by the acquisition of power from the *áñas*. The initiation itself is centered on the *áñas*. Due to their ambivalence, an initiate can become a shaman (*ipáye*) if their intent is benevolent; if their intent is malevolent, the initiate receives only malignant power that causes misfortune to the people and the community.

Tapuí and Guasurangwe. The religion of the Tapuí and the Guasurangwe, or Tapieté (an offshoot of the former), does not differ essentially from that of the Chiriguano; the same structures of meaning and the same supernatural beings may be observed.

LENGUA-MASCOY FAMILY. The Lengua-Mascoy language group of Paraguay includes the Angaité, Lengua, Kaskihá, and Sanapaná peoples.

The Angaité. The religious nature of the Angaité (Chananesmá) has undergone syncretism owing to their proximity to the Mascoy and Guaranian groups. Their mythology makes reference to three levels—the underworld, the terrestrial world, and the celestial world—all of which are inhabited by supernatural beings characterized by their ambivalent actions toward humans. The deity of the dead, Moksohanák, governs a legion of demonic beings, the *enzlép,* who pursue the sick, imprison them, and carry them to the "country of the dead," which is situated in the west. At night it is even possible for them to overpower passersby. The *gabioamá* or *iliabün* act as the spirit familiars of the shaman, and with him their role is ambivalent in a positive sense. For example, they are in charge of recapturing and restoring the souls of the sick.

According to Angaité myth, fire was obtained by a theft in which a bird was the intermediary; it was stolen from a forest demon, one of the *iek'amá,* who are anthropomorphic but have only one leg. Also anthropomorphic is the soul-shadow (*abiosná*), whose eyes are its distinguishing feature. The concept of corporal material as such does not exist, except for the *iek'amá* ("living cadaver" or "skeleton"), which is what remains after death.

During the initiation process, the shaman goes into the depths of the forest or to the banks of the river, where the familiar spirits (*pateaskóp* or *enzlép*) come to him in a dream. He communicates with the familiars through ecstatic dreams and songs. His therapeutic labors include sucking harmful agents from the bodies of the sick and applying vegetable concoctions whose efficacy resides in their "bad smell." There are shamans with purely malignant intentions, such as the *mamohót,* who are responsible for tragic deaths among members of the group. The benevolent shaman is responsible for discovering the identity of the bewitching shaman and for quartering and burning the body of the victim as a restorative vengeance. The Angaité do not have "lords" or "fathers" of the species; the figures closest to this theme are Nekéñe and Nanticá, male and female supernatural beings respectively, who are anthropomorphic and whose realm is the depths of the waters.

The Lengua. The anthropogenic myth of the Lengua (Enlhít, Enslet) attributes the formation of giant supernatural beings and the ancestors of the Lengua to Beetle, who utilized mud as primary material. After giving these beings a human form, he placed the bodies of the first *enlhíts* to dry on the bank of a lake, but he set them so close together that they stuck to one another. Once granted life, they could not defend themselves against the attacks of the powerful giants, and Beetle, as supreme deity, separated the two groups. Eventually the inability of the *enlhíts* to resist pursuit and mistreatment by the giants became so grave that Beetle took away the giants' bodies. The giants' souls gave birth to *kilikháma* who fought to regain control of the missing bodies, and it is for this reason that they torment present-day humans.

The important Lengua myths include the origin of plants and fire and the fall of the world. Ritual dramatizations of the myths are part of the celebrations for female puberty (*yanmána*), male puberty (*waínkya*), the spring and autumn equinoxes, the summer solstice, war, the arrival of foreigners, marriage, and mourning.

Human reality consists of a "living soul" (*valhók*), whose dream existence is important. At death, a person is transported to *vangáuk,* which is a transitory state that leads to the *kilikháma* state. The *apyoxólhma,* or shaman, receives power (*siyavnáma*) through visions and apprenticeship to the song of the plants, whose ingestion, though lacking hallucinogenic properties, produces ritual death. Once he obtains *siyavnáma,* the shaman commands the *kilikháma,* who control numerous beings and realms of the universe. The territory of the dead *(pisisl),* situated toward the west, is the destination of the souls of the dead, although some remain close to the living.

The Kaskihá. The "masked celebration" of the Kaskihá is of particular interest. It is based on a myth that describes the origin of the festive attire following the quartering of the water deity Iyenaník. The practice of *kindáian,* which is a dance, is the only medium for invoking the power of such deities.

The Sanapaná. The rich mythic narrative of the Sanapaná focuses on the war between the heavenly world, inhabited by the ancestors (*inyakahpanamé*), and the terrestrial world, inhabited by the fox (*maalék*). The ancestors, who differ morphologically from present-day humanity, introduced the majority of cultural goods. Among the fundamental structures distinguished by the Sanapaná is the "dream," the soul's life in its wanderings separate from the body. Death is understood as theft of the soul by demonic forces, the souls of the dead that stalk during the night in forests and marshes. The demonic spirits are anthropomorphic. Some are malignant, including those whose mere appearance can cause immediate death. There are also benevolent spirits who are the familiars of shamans *(kiltongkamák)*. The shaman's initiation involves fasting and other tests.

MATACO-MAKKÁ FAMILY. The Mataco-Makká language family of the central Chaco includes the Mataco, Chulupí, Choroti, and Makká.

The Mataco. The religious universe of the Mataco *(Wichí)* centers on the notion of power (*la-ka-áyah*), which is the property of innumerable supernatural beings of demonic (*ahát*) or human *(wichí)* nature, personifications of such phenomena as the sun, moon, stars, and thunder. The Mataco recognize a dualism of body (*opisán*) and spirit (*o'nusék*) in humans. Death changes the *o'nusék* into a malevolent supernatural being.

The central character in Mataco mythic narrative (*pahlalís*), Tokhwáh, is the one who imposes cosmic and ontological order on the present-day world. The actions of this supernatural being, who has a demonic nature, are incorporated in his trickster aspect; nonetheless, he is perceived by the Mataco as a suffering and sad being. In his lawgiving role he introduces economic practices and tools; humanizes the women who descend from the sky by eliminating their vaginal teeth; institutes marriage; and teaches the people how to get drunk, to fight, and to make war. He also introduces demonic spirits who cause illnesses (*aités*) and establishes the shamanic institution (*hayawú*) and death. The most important Mataco ceremony is carried out by the shamans, in both individual and communal form, with the objective of expelling illnesses according to Tokhwáh's teachings.

The shamanic initiation includes possession (*welán*) by a demonic spirit (*ahát*) and the consequent separation of the initiate's soul (*o'nusék*), which undertakes journeys to the different realms of the cosmos. When the initiation is complete, the shaman has achieved an ontological alteration in the state of his soul—he has been transformed into a demonic being. The smoking or inhalation of the dust of the sumac (*Anadenanthera macrocarpa*) is a frequent shamanic practice.

The Chulupí. The mythology of the Chulupí (Nivaklé, Aslusláy) comprises three narrative cycles on the deities who acted in primordial times, but who then distanced themselves from humanity and the earthly world. The Xitscittsammee cycle describes a supernatural being comparable to an almost forgotten *deus otiosus.* The cycle of the supernatural being Fitsók Exíts includes prescriptions for the rites of female initiation; myths recounting the origin of women, of the spots on the moon, and of honey, among other things; and the tale of the expulsion from the universe of the supernatural creator. The Kufiál cycle relates the cataclysmic events accompanying the fall of heaven and the subsequent actions of the demiurge Kufiál, to name a few of its themes.

A structure essential to the Chulupí religion is *sič'ee,* or ultimate power, which defines and dominates a vast group of beings and actions. In effect, *sič'ee* is the strange made powerful, which can manifest itself in unexpected guises—in human or animal form, by means of a sound or a movement like a whirlwind, or as master of the spirits of the forest. The *sič'ee* plays a significant role in the initiation of the shaman (*sič'ee*): He appears to the shaman in the guise of an old man, for example, who offers the shaman power and grants him the spirit familiars called *wat'akwáis.* By fasting, enduring solitude in the woods, and drinking potions made of various plants, the initiate achieves a revelatory experience rich in visions, many of which are terrifying. The Chulupí idea of animistic reality is extremely complicated and varied, given that the soul can appear in any number of manifestations.

The Choroti. The principal cycles of the Choroti are five in number. The cycle of Kixwét describes a supernatural being, of human appearance but gigantic, whose role comprises the duplicity of both the demiurge and the trickster. The cycle of Ahóusa, the Hawk, the culture hero *par excellence,* recounts how he defeated the beings of primordial times, stealing and distributing fire and teaching humans the technique of fishing and the making of artifacts. The cycle of Woíki, the Fox, who partakes of the intrinsic nature of Kixwét and is a very important figure in indigenous cultures, contains myths describing his creation of various beings and modalities of the present-day world. The cycle of We'la, the Moon, relates the formation of the world. The cycle of Tsematakí alludes to a feminine figure characterized by her ill will toward men and her uncontainable cannibalism.

The Choroti shaman (*atew*) receives power *(i-tóksi)* from the supernatural beings *(thlamó)*, and the strength of his abilities depends on the number of familiars (*inxuélai*) he has.

The Makká. The Makká mythology can be classified as eclectic, as it demonstrates cultural contact with almost all the other indigenous groups of the Gran Chaco. The Makká cycle of the fox is similar to the narrative cycle surrounding the Mataco supernatural being Tokhwáh and demonstrates similar themes, such as the origin of women and the toothed vagina. The Makká hero Tippá, who possesses an immense penis, is somewhat reminiscent of Wéla, the Mataco moon deity.

In earlier times, power (*t'un*) was obtained by capturing a scalp, after which a complex ceremony was held in which the scalp was discarded but the soul *(le sinkál)* of the dead enemy was retained as a personal familiar, or spirit helper. This familiar would manifest itself during sleep by means of a song that even today is sung during drinking bouts. Ceremonies of drinking bouts among adults permit the regulation of power among people. The ceremony of female initiation is also important, as is true throughout most of the Gran Chaco.

The organization of the traditional religious universe was altered through the introduction of Christianity by General J. Belaieff, who brought the Makká from the interior of the Chaco to the outskirts of Asunción. The icon of Belaieff is now a central theme in Makká shamanism. Just as among the Mataco, the shaman (*weihet'x*) is charged with controlling the demonic supernatural beings (*inwomét*).

GUIACURÚ-CADUVEO FAMILY. The Guiacurú-Caduveo language family of the Gran Chaco and Brazil includes the tribes known as the Pilagá, the Toba, the Caduveo, and the Mocoví.

The Pilagá. Certain mythic cycles may be distinguished in the Pilagá mythology. One cycle describes the celestial deity Dapiči, to whom is attributed the inversion of the cosmic planes and the transference of some animals and plants to the sky. In the past, prayers were offered for his help in the most diverse activities. Another cycle describes Wayaykaláciyi, who introduced death, made the animals wild, and established hunting techniques, modifying the Edenic habits of an earlier time. Among the eminent supernatural beings is Nesóge, a cannibalistic woman who determines the practices of the witches (*konánagae*). Such characters and themes as the Star Woman and the origin of women appear in Pilagá myths.

Among the significant structures, the *payák* is the most important. This notion defines nonhuman nature, which is peculiar to supernatural beings, shamans (*pyogonák*), animals, plants, and some objects. Relations with the *payák* determine conditions in the indigenous world. Either people acquire *payák*s as familiars who aid them in their customary activities, or the *payák*s inflict suffering on them in the form of illness, the death of domestic animals, the destruction of farms, or a poor harvest of fruit from wild plants. Such concepts as the "master-dependent" (*logót-lamasék*) and the "center-periphery" *(laiñí-laíl)* allow the Pilagá to classify beings and entities according to a hierarchy of power.

The initiation of women takes place at the onset of menses. The young girl is locked in a corner of her hut and forced to fast rigorously. When males reach adolescence, they submit to scarification of their arms and legs by a shaman, and the young man is given the characteristics of the species of animal whose bone was used as a scarifier. Throughout entire lives, men continue to scarify themselves, especially when preparing for the hunt or going into battle.

The Toba. The principal themes of Toba (Kom) narrative are celestial cosmology and mythology, which appear in stories about Dapiči and the Pleiades; cataclysms; the origin of specific entities; stories of animals; stories of the trickster Wahayaka'lacigu, the lawgiver Ta'ankí, and Ašien, a supernatural being with a repulsive appearance; and encounters between Toba people and the supernatural being Nowét. The morphology of these characters, all of whom were powerful in the primordial times, fluctuates between the human and the animal.

For the Toba, the central structure of the cosmology is *nowét,* which appears in the forms of the masters of animals and of the spheres. Nowét, as a supernatural being, initiates the shamans (*pi'ogonák*) and grants them power that can be used equally to heal or to harm. Outside the shamanic sphere, all special skills—hunting, fishing, dancing, and so on—derive from power given by Nowét. Dreams are structures that have importance in the relations between humans and Nowét. Shamanic power is established by the possession of spirit familiars (*ltawá*), who help shamans cure serious illnesses, which are considered intentional and also material. Therapy combines singing, blowing, and sucking as methods of removing the harmful agent from the victim's body.

Some of the important ceremonies of the Toba are name giving, the initiation of young boys, the offering of prayers to Dapiči, matutinal prayers to the heavenly beings, and the supplications of the hunters to some supernatural being in a nowét state.

The Caduveo. Go-neno-hodi is the central deity of Caduveo mythology; he is maker of all people and of a great number of the cultural goods. His appearance is that of a Caduveo, and he is without evil intention. In his benevolence, he granted the Caduveo, in ancient times, an abundant supply of food, clothes, and utensils, as well as eternal life, but the intervention of Hawk, astute and malicious, made Go-neno-hodi modify the primordial order. Nibetád is a mythical hero identified with the Pleiades; he greeted the ancestors during the ceremony celebrating the annual reappearance of this cluster of stars and the maturation of the algaroba (mesquite).

The shamanic institution is actualized in two different individuals: the *nikyienígi* ("father"), who protects and benefits the community, and the *otxikanrígi,* the cause of all deaths, illnesses, and misfortunes in the group. Celebrations that are particularly worthy of note are the lunar ceremonies, the rites celebrating the birth of the chief's son, and the initiations of young men and women.

The Mocoví. Prominent in the scattered Mocoví material is the myth of an enormous tree that reached to the sky. By climbing its branches, one ascended to lakes and to a river. An angry old woman cut down the tree, extinguishing the valuable connection between heaven and earth.

Gdsapidolgaté, a benevolent supernatural being, presides over the world of the living. His activity contrasts with that of the witches. Healing practices among the Mocoví are the same as those of the other shamans of the Gran Chaco, with the addition of bloodletting. The Mocoví, like all the Guiacurú, believe in the honor of war and value dying in combat as much as killing. When they return from a battle they hang the heads of the vanquished on posts in the center of town and they sing and shout around them. The horse plays an important role in daily life and in the hereafter; when the owner of a horse dies, the horse is sacrificed and buried beside the owner to bear him to his final destination in the land of the dead.

ARAWAK FAMILY. The extensive Arawak family of languages includes the Chané of Argentina. Fundamental distinctions cannot be made between the corpus of Chané myths and that of the Chiriguano; similarities abound between them, particularly with respect to the figure of the shaman. There are two kinds of shamans: one with benevolent power (the *ipáye*) and another dedicated exclusively to malevolent actions that cause death (the *ipayepóci*). The *mbaidwá* ("knower, investigator") has dominion over the individual destinies of humans.

One of the most important aspects of Chané religion is the carnival of masks (also celebrated by the Chiriguano). Some of the masks are profane, representing animals and fantastic anthropomorphic characters. The sacred masks represent Áña, and these are deadly playthings that cannot be sold to travelers. When the carnival is finished, the masks become dangerous and must be destroyed.

BIBLIOGRAPHY

One can find an abundant bibliography on indigenous groups of the Gran Chaco in *Ethnographic Bibliography of South America,* edited by Timothy O'Leary (New Haven, Conn., 1963). The *Handbook of South American Indians,* 7 vols., edited by Julia H. Steward (Washington, D.C., 1946–1959), offers general characteristics on habits and customs of the peoples of this cultural area. The *Censo indígena nacional* (Buenos Aires, 1968) is restricted to the Argentine Chaco. Fernando Pagés Larraya's *Lo irracional en la cultura* (Buenos Aires, 1982) studies the mental pathology of the indigenous people of the Gran Chaco and then reviews their religious conceptions. *Scripta ethnológica* (1973–1982), a periodical published by the Centro Argentino de Ethnología Americana, Buenos Aires, contains more systematic information about the aboriginal peoples of the Gran Chaco.

There are only a few specific works that deal with particular groups; among those few are *Los indios Ayoreo del Chaco Boreal* by Marcelo Bórmida and myself (Buenos Aires, 1982). Branislava Susnik has also given attention to the Chulupí natives in *Chulupí: Esbozo gramatical analítico* (Asunción, 1968). Also worthy of mention are Miguel Chase-Sardi's *Cosmovisión mak'a* (Asunción, 1970) and *El concepto Nivaklé del Alma* (Lima, 1970). Bernardino de Nino wrote an *Ethnografía Chiriguano* (La Paz, 1912). In reference to the Caduveo culture, see Darcy Ribeiro's *Religião e mitologia Kadiuéu* (Rio de Janiero, 1950). One can also consult Johannes Wilbert's *Folk Literature of the Mataco Indians* and *Folk Literature of the Toba Indians* (both Los Angeles, 1982).

New Sources

Arce Birbueth, Eddy, et al. *Estrategias de Sobrevivencia entre los Tapietes del Gran Chaco.* La Paz, 2003.

Clastres, Pierre. *Mythologie des Indiens Chulupi.* Edited by Michael Carty and Hélène Clastres. Leuven, 1992.

Fritz, Miguel. *Los Nivaclé: Rasgos de una cultura paraguaya.* Quito, 1994.

Fritz, Miguel. *Pioneros en El Chaco: Misioneros oblatos del Pilcomayo.* Mariscal Estigarribia, 1999.

Tomasini, Alfredo. *El Shamanismo de los Nivaclé del Gran Chaco.* Buenos Aires, 1997.

Tomasini, Alfredo. *Figuras protectoras de animales y plantes en la religiosidad de los indios Nivaclé:Chaco Boreal, Paraguay.* Quito, 1999.

MARIO CALIFANO (1987)
Translated from Spanish by Tanya Fayen
Revised Bibliography

SOUTHEAST ASIAN RELIGIONS

This entry consists of the following articles:

SOUTHEAST ASIAN RELIGIONS: HISTORY OF STUDY

Southeast Asia straddles one of the two trade routes linking East Asia and the Mediterranean. For many centuries, merchants traveled through the Straights of Malacca to points further east, bringing spices, gold, and other precious commodities, and with them came religious texts, modes of ritual practice, iconographies, and other religious systems. A consequence of this strategic location is that virtually all of the major religions of the world can be found in Southeast Asia. Today by far the most common religious traditions are Theravāda Buddhism, Islam, Roman Catholicism, and the Vietnamese variant of traditional Chinese religion. Yet there are also communities of Balinese and Tamil Hindus, Protestant Christians, Sikhs, and Zoroastrians. Prior to the Second World War there were significant Jewish communities. One can also find a vast array of indigenous religions in traditionally isolated portions of the region that are either upland or on remote islands far from the trade routes.

The diversity of religion in Southeast Asia has attracted area specialists in almost all religious traditions to study the region, and the theoretical orientations and methodologies employed in the study of religion in the region are nearly as diverse as the religions of the region itself. The academic study of religion in Southeast Asia began in the early decades of the nineteenth century. The earliest works are largely descriptive. Most of them were written by colonial officials or Christian missionaries. Stamford Raffles, John Crawfurd, and Christiaan Hurgronje were among the colonial officers who made enduring contributions to the study of religion in Southeast Asia. Among the most important works by missionary scholars are Hans Scharer's studies of the indigenous religions of Kalimantan (Borneo) and Paul Bigandet's study of Burmese Buddhism. Subsequent scholars have employed a variety of philological, archeological, historical, literary-critical, political-science, and anthropological approaches. Many more general works provide important data for scholars of religion. Among the most important of these are district gazetteers and other publications of colonial governments. These often provide the only available materials for the study of the history of religion at the local level. James Scott's *Gazetteer of Upper Burma and the Shan States* (1900–1901) and John Crawfurd's *History of the Indian Archipelago* (1820) are outstanding examples. Novels and other works of fiction can also provide valuable information. A clear example is Pramoedya Ananta Toer's four-volume novel *Buru Quartet* (1996), which is a fictionalized account of the religious and cultural forces that contributed to the rise of Indonesian nationalism.

Despite this double diversity, one can detect the following general themes and questions that have shaped the academic study of religion in Southeast Asia:

- Links between scholarly agendas and the agendas of colonial and postcolonial states.
- Relations between religion and politics in traditional Southeast Asian states.
- The development of increasingly nuanced understandings of the nature of religious traditions.
- The emergence, in the last decades of the twentieth century, of a symbiotic relationship between religious studies and the social sciences, particularly cultural anthropology.

These four factors interact in very complex ways in the academic discourse about religion in Southeast Asia.

POLITICAL AGENDAS. The political agendas of colonial and postcolonial states did much to shape the development of scholarly traditions. They have influenced the topics scholars have chosen to investigate and the interpretation of their findings. The academic study of religion in Southeast Asia dates back to the early decades of the nineteenth century at a time when the British, French, Dutch, and Spanish were consolidating colonial empires. Edward Said has argued that in the Middle East, colonial scholarship was among the means through which Europeans sought to dominate and domesticate potentially hostile religious elites. Much the same can be said of colonial scholarship on Southeast Asia.

Such works as compilations of customary law and gazetteers describing local customs and periodic rituals were of immediate value to colonial officials and other resident Europeans. They remain valuable resources for scholars concerned with religious change, and are particularly important for scholars of the indigenous religions of tribes of the region. An overwhelming number of these groups converted to Christianity in the first half of the twentieth century. As their traditional religions were orally transmitted, European writings provide the only available information about those early religions.

The study of religion also provided instruments for domination in a more subtle sense. Many of the monumental works of colonial scholarship, including Stamford Raffles's *History of Java* (1817) and Paul Mus's *Barabuḍur* (1935), locate the greatness of Southeast Asian cultures in the distant past. These studies provided support for colonialist apologetics, a major theme of which was that Southeast Asian cultures had become decadent and corrupt and that benevolent Europeans were assisting these cultures with colonial rule. While intended for a European audience, these works were also read by many Southeast Asians and are in part responsible for the sense of cultural dislocation so vividly described by Toer in his novels.

Islam and Buddhism were equally misrepresented, though in very different ways. Raffles and Theodore Pigeaud went to great lengths to deny the Islamic character of Indonesian and particularly Javanese civilization. For them, Islam was a threat to colonial authority. Portraying Indonesia as a Hindu culture was part of a strategy of colonial domination. Indonesian elites educated in Dutch schools were taught that their culture and religion were an amalgamation of Hinduism and Mahayana Buddhism, and were discouraged from learning more than the rudiments of Islam. Christiaan Hurgronje, the greatest Islamicist of the colonial era, also contributed to this agenda. His studies of the Achehnese and the Southeast Asian community in Mecca were as much political briefings as they were scholarship. The Dutch were involved in a bitter war with the Achehnese and regarded Mecca as a dangerous source of rebellion.

Buddhism was misrepresented in a different way. Many of the early works on Theravāda Buddhism in Southeast Asia were written by scholars who, if not Buddhists themselves, were extremely sympathetic towards a particular understanding of Buddhism. James Scott, Harold Fielding-Hall, and others understood Buddhism as an abstract rational science of the mind with little use for spirits, gods, or what they understood as superstitious practice. They regarded what are now clearly understood as Buddhist ritual practices as either the superstitions of the lower classes or remnants of a heathen past. Like many other earlier European interpreters of Buddhism, they imagined Buddhism as they wished it to be.

The academic study of religion continues to be politically significant in the region. This is especially true of scholarship published in the languages of the region. Religious studies are not well developed in the region, but with the expansion of modern education since the end of the colonial era, studies of religion by Southeast Asian scholars have become increasingly common. Many Southeast Asian scholars of religion are trained in history; others in area, Buddhist, or Islamic studies. In many instances the lines between academic and committed scholarship is a fine one. In Southeast Asia many scholars of religion are actively engaged in political causes, movements, or parties. In addition to more traditional academic venues, intellectuals regularly publish in daily papers and weekly news magazines. Among the issues of concern to these scholars are economic development, ecological degradation, human rights, social justice, and democratization. There are no systematic studies of the writings of scholar-activists in European languages. In the Islamic societies of the region, questions concerning banking and finance are also important because of the traditional Islamic prohibition on interest. Most of this literature is inaccessible to nonspecialists because there are very few translations.

More conventional scholarship may also be pointed. Muslim Indonesia provides a cogent example. Indonesian scholars are familiar with Western scholarship that has depicted traditional cultures as being only trivially Muslim. Islamists often cite the works of Clifford Geertz as proof that their own critiques of religious traditionalists are valid. To establish the orthodoxy of their positions, traditionalists have produced countertexts that can be read simultaneously as history and theology. Zamakhsyari Dhofier's *The Pesantren Tradition* (1999) is a ready example. In this way academic scholars of religion are drawn into Southeast Asian religious discourse.

Political considerations have also influenced which communities are studied and which are not. Politically significant communities receive greater attention than minorities. Scholarly neglect of Southeast Asian Christianity, traditional Chinese religion, and Tamil Hinduism is especially apparent. Neglect of Southeast Asian Christianity is among the most serious problems confronting the field. The conversion of many tribal and Chinese people to Christianity has fundamentally altered the religious landscape of Southeast Asia. In general, there has been very little research on the interaction of religious communities in any Southeast Asian country. The religions of Myanmar (Burma) have also suffered from scholarly neglect, but for a different reason: very few scholars have been able to conduct research there since the middle of the twentieth century.

Religion, Politics, and Culture. Many scholars of Southeast Asian religions have been concerned with the role of religion in indigenous political systems and the interrelation of religion and culture. Archeologists and historians have attempted to discern the religious foundations of Southeast Asian statecraft. Of the few manuscripts that have survived from the precolonial period, a substantial number concern theories of kingship. This concern is also found in nineteenth-century texts, many of which are preserved in libraries and archives in Holland, Great Britain, and France, as well as Southeast Asia. Other important sources of the role of religion in politics include Chinese texts, inscriptions on monuments, and archeological sites, such as Pagan, Angkor, Ayutthaya, and Borobudur. George Coedes, Robert Heine-Geldern, Stanley Tambiah, and others have found that Southeast Asian kingdoms were structured as representations of Hindu or Buddhist cosmologies and that kings were often described as divine or semidivine beings. Muslim kingdoms retain some of the symbolism of the Hindu and Buddhist past and also describe Sultans as descendants of the Prophet Muhammad and as representatives of God on earth.

A substantial body of scholarship focuses on the role of traditional religious concepts in contemporary Southeast Asian politics. Benedict Anderson, Clifford Geertz, and others suggests that traditional concepts of power and authority continue to inform political discourse and the conduct of politics throughout the region. In modern Southeast Asia, religion has been used to legitimize the political programs of states, leaders, and parties, be they authoritarian or liberal.

On the Nature of Religious Traditions. For most of its history, the academic study of religion has looked to ancient, philosophically complex texts for the essence of religious traditions and has assumed that popular and contemporary variants of these texts are in some sense corrupt. This understanding of world religions is apparent in many important studies of contemporary Southeast Asian religions, including Melford Spiro's *Buddhism and Society* (1982) and Clifford Geertz's *The Religion of Java* (1960). As Boone observes, this has lead to the construction of artificial canons recognized only by Western or Western-trained scholars. The tendency to understand world religions as philosophical systems embodied in ancient texts has contributed to the view that Southeast Asian Buddhists, Hindus, and Muslims are only superficially such and that indigenous animisms remain the most important of Southeast Asian religions. This view was articulated by Raffles in the early nineteenth century and has been subject to serious criticism only since the mid-1970s.

As scholars of religion have become increasingly concerned with religion as lived experience, many have come to question the assumptions of traditional philological scholarship. As a result, there is a greater appreciation of noncanonical texts and the relation of religion to daily social life. This has lead to a creative convergence of religious studies and cultural anthropology.

Religious Studies and Cultural Anthropology. Since the 1970s the distinction between cultural anthropology and religious studies has been muted by developments in both disciplines. Earlier generations of anthropologists generally focused on exclusively oral traditions. Even those who studied Buddhists, Muslims, and other adherents of literary religions paid scant attention to religious texts. This state of affairs began to change in the 1960s and 1970s as anthropologists became increasingly concerned with systems of symbols and meanings and as scholars of religion turned their attention to contemporary versions of world religions. This convergence began in communities of scholars focused on Theravāda Buddhism and Balinese Hinduism and has progressed to the point where works by cultural anthropologists and scholars of religion are difficult to distinguish. Its greatest impact is seen in the study of Southeast Asian Islam, which has moved from the margins to the mainstream of scholarly discourse on Southeast Asian religion and the Islamic tradition more generally.

CONCLUSIONS. Southeast Asia offers a wealth of research opportunities for scholars of many disciplines concerned with the study of religion. Scholars can study particular variants of most of the major religions of the world or social and cultural systems comprising multiple religious communities, with their different religious traditions and languages.

SEE ALSO Anthropology, Ethnology, and Religion; Buddhism, article on Buddhism in Southeast Asia; Fiction, article on Southeast Asian Fiction and Religion; Hinduism in Southeast Asia; Islam, article on Islam in Southeast Asia.

BIBLIOGRAPHY

Anderson, Benedict. *Language and Power: Exploring Political Cultures in Indonesia.* Ithaca, N.Y., 1990. Explores the religious and cultural foundations in modern Indonesian political discourse and praxis.

Bigandet, Paul. *The Life or Legend of Gaudama, the Budha of the Burmese.* Rangoon, 1858.

Boon, James. *Affinities and Extremes: Crisscrossing the Bittersweet Ethnology of East Indies History, Hindu-Balinese Culture, and Indo-European Allure.* Chicago, 1990. A rich, interdisciplinary account of the history of Balinese religion and culture.

Coedes, George. *The Indianized States of Southeast Asia.* Edited by Walter Vella. Translated by Susan Cowing. Honolulu, 1968. The standard work on the Indianization of Southeast Asia from the first to the fourteenth century.

Crawfurd, John. *History of the Indian Archipelago: Containing an Account of the Manners, Arts, Languages, Religions, Institutions, and Commerce of Its Inhabitants.* Edinburgh, 1820. One of the earliest account of the territory that is now Indonesia.

Dhofier, Zamakhsyari. *The Pesantren Tradition: The Role of the Kyai in the Maintenance of Traditional Islam in Java.* Tempe, Ariz., 1999. A detailed studies of the Islamic boarding schools (*pesantren*) of east Java.

Fielding-Hall, Harold. *The Soul of a People.* London, 1898. An early British interpretation of Theravāda Buddhism in Myanmar (Burma).

Geertz, Clifford. *The Religion of Java.* New York, 1960. The classic study of popular religion in Java, though subsequent studies demonstrate that Geertz underestimated the importance Islam in Javanese culture.

Heine-Geldern, Robert. *Conceptions of State and Kingship in Southeast Asia.* Ithaca, N.Y., 1956. A classic and highly influential study of the religious orientations of premodern Southeast Asian States.

Hurgronje, Christiaan Snouck. *Mekka in the Later Part of the 19th Century: Daily Life, Customs, and Learning of the Moslims of the East-Indian-Archipelago.* Leiden, 1931. Reprint, 1970. One of the few ethnographic accounts of Muslim Mecca. It focuses on Southeast Asian Muslims resident in the holy city.

Lithai, King of Sukhothai. *The Three Worlds According to King Ruang: A Thai Buddhist Cosmology.* Translated by Frank Reynolds and Mani Reynolds. Berkeley, Calif., 1982. A translation of a Thai text describing the Theravāda Buddhist cosmos.

Luce, Gordon. *Old Burma—Early Pagan.* 3 vols. Locust Valley, N.Y., 1969–1970. A massive study of Buddhism, art, and architecture in ancient Myanmar (Burma).

Lukens-Bull, ed. *Sacred Places and Modern Landscapes: Sacred Geography and Social Religious Transformations in South and Southeast Asia.* Tempe, Ariz., 2004. Includes papers on contemporary Buddhist, Muslim and Christian sacred geographies in the region.

Mus, Paul. *Barabuḍur: Sketch of a History of Buddhism Based on Archaeological Criticism of the Texts* (1978). Translated by Alexander W. Macdonald. New Delhi, 1998.

Pigeaud, Theodore. *Java in the Fourteenth Century: A Study in Cultural History.* 5 vols. The Hague, 1960–1963. Based on a translation of an old Javanese text discover in Bali. Includes a vast amount of material on religion, culture, and politics in Indic Java.

Raffles, Stamford. *The History of Java.* London, 1817. Reprint, New York, 1965. An early description of Javanese religion and culture focusing primarily on the pre-Islamic period.

Scott, James. *Gazetteer of Upper Burma and the Shan States.* 2 vols. Rangoon, 1900–1901. Includes a vast quantity of information about northern Myanmar (Burma) shortly after the British annexation.

Smith, Bardwell, ed. *Religion and Legitimation of Power in Thailand, Laos, and Burma.* Chambersburg, Pa., 1978. Includes articles on Thai Buddhism by historian of religion Frank E. Reynolds.

Spiro, Melford. *Buddhism and Society: A Great Tradition and Its Burmese Vicissitudes.* 2d, expanded ed. Berkeley, Calif., 1982. A psychologically oriented ethnographic account of Theravāda Buddhism in Myanmar (Burma).

Tambiah, Stanley. *World Conqueror and World Renouncer: A Study of Buddhism and Polity in Thailand against a Historical Background.* Cambridge, U.K., 1976. The classical study of Buddhist notions of kingship and political authority in Thailand.

Toer, Pramoedya Ananta. *The Buru Quartet.* New York, 1996. A series of four novels (*This Earth of Mankind; Child of All Nations; Footsteps; House of Glass*) depicting the life and times of a young Dutch-educated Javanese aristocrat.

Woodward, Mark. *Islam in Java: Normative Piety and Mysticism in the Sultanate of Yogyakarta.* Tucson, Ariz., 1989. Emphasizes the Islamic character of royal and popular religion in Java.

MARK R. WOODWARD (2005)

SOUTHEAST ASIAN RELIGIONS: MAINLAND CULTURES

Mainland Southeast Asia has been termed the "crossroad of religions," for in this region, today divided into the countries of Burma, Thailand, and Laos, Cambodia (Kampuchea), and Vietnam, a large diversity of autochthonous tribal religions are intermingled with Hinduism, Theravāda and Mahāyāna Buddhism, Daoism, Confucianism, Islam, and Christianity, as well as the modern secular faith of Marxist-Leninism. Beneath this diversity there are many religious practices and beliefs that have common roots in the prehistoric past of peoples of the region. This is not to say, as have some scholars, that the historic religions are merely a veneer and that those Southeast Asians who adhere to religions such as Buddhism have been, as Reginald LeMay said of the Northern Thai, animists from time immemorial. Although certain beliefs and practices can be seen as linking peoples of the present to ancient Southeast Asian religions, they have often been reformulated to make sense within worldviews shaped by historic religions. The processes of religious change have, moreover, intensified in the wake of radical shaking of traditional orders taking place throughout the twentieth century.

Mainland Southeast Asia is not only a region of religious diversity; it is also a veritable Babel. Insofar as historical linguistics permits a reconstruction of the past, it would appear that most of the earliest inhabitants of the region spoke Austroasiatic languages ancestral to such modern-day descendants as Khmer and Mon. Many of the tribal peoples living in the highlands of central Vietnam and Laos, as well as a few groups found in northern Thailand and as far distant as Assam in India and Hainan Island belonging to China, speak Austroasiatic languages. Speakers of Austronesian languages, whose major modern-day representatives are the peoples of Indonesia, Malaysia, Micronesia, and Polynesia, as well as parts of Melanesia and Madagascar, were also present from prehistoric times in what is today southern Vietnam and the Malay Peninsula. Cham living in southern Vietnam and in Cambodia, as well as tribal peoples such as the Rhadé and Jarai in southern Vietnam, speak Austronesian languages. In the northern uplands of the region and in what is today northeastern India and southern China most peoples in prehistoric times appear to have spoken languages belonging to the Tibeto-Burman language family. The present-day Burmans and such tribal peoples as the Chin, Kachin, Lisu, Akha, and Lahu all speak Tibeto-Burman languages. Speakers of Tai (or Daic) languages seem to have originated in southern China and did not begin to settle in mainland Southeast Asia until much before the tenth century CE. Today, however, Thai (or Siamese), Lao, Northern Thai (or Yuan), and Shan—all speakers of Tai languages—constitute the major peoples of Thailand, Laos, and the Shan state of Burma, and Tai-speaking tribal peoples such as the Tho, Red Tai, Black Tai, and White Tai are found in northern Vietnam as well as northeastern Laos. Modern-day Vietnamese, which linguists assign to the distinctive Viet-Muong language family, is believed to have evolved from an Austroasiatic language that was transformed under the influence of Chinese. The distinctive Karennic languages spoken by peoples living on the eastern border of Burma and in parts of western Thailand are thought by linguists to be descendants of Tibeto-Burman stocks. Speakers of Miao-Yao languages, distantly connected to Tibeto-Burman and Sinitic language families, have migrated from southern China into mainland Southeast Asia only within the past century or so. Major migrations from China and India, spurred by the economic changes during the colonial period, also led to the introduction into the region of large numbers of speakers of Sinitic, Dravidian, and Indo-European languages.

PREHISTORIC FOUNDATIONS. People have lived in mainland Southeast Asia for as long as there have been *Homo sapiens*, and there is evidence of *Homo erectus* and even earlier hominid forms in the region as well. Paleolithic hunting-and-gathering peoples must have constructed their religious understandings of the world out of images drawn from their experiences in their environments and from the workings of the human body. Beyond this, little can be said, for there is no mainland Southeast Asian equivalent of the cave paintings of Lascaux to provide insight into the world of Paleolithic humans. It would, moreover, be quite illegitimate to project the religious beliefs of the Negritos of the Malay Peninsula, the last remaining significant groups of hunter-gatherers in the region, into the prehistoric past, for these beliefs have developed through as long a period as have other religions and have, moreover, been influenced by the religions of neighboring peoples.

The first significant evidence of religious beliefs and practices in mainland Southeast Asia comes from the period when humans in the region first began to live in settled agricultural communities. The domestication of rice, which may have taken place in mainland Southeast Asia before 4000 BCE, led to the emergence of a powerful image that was to become incorporated in almost all of the religious traditions of the region. To this day, most Southeast Asians think of rice as having a spiritual as well as a material quality; rice, like humanity, has a vital essence and is typically associated with a feminine deity. The recognition of rice as fundamental to life among most peoples in mainland Southeast Asia has been intertwined in religious imagery with the nurturing attribute of a mother.

Neolithic burial sites, many only recently discovered, are proving to be sources of knowledge about prehistoric religions in Southeast Asia. The very existence of such sites suggests that those who took so much trouble to dispose of the physical remains of the dead must have had well-formed ideas about the afterlife and about the connection between the states of the dead and the living. In the mass burial sites of Ban Chiang and Non Nok Tha in northeastern Thailand, the graves contain many items, including pottery, tools, and metal jewelry. The items found in the graves may be interpreted, on the basis of ethnographic analogy, as constituting goods believed to be used by the dead in the afterlife. In communities in northeastern Thailand today, the dead are cremated in accord with Buddhist custom, but the practice of burning personal belongings of the deceased at the same time perpetuates a pre-Buddhist tradition.

In a Neolithic burial site in western Thailand, the grave of an old man was found to contain a perforated stone disk and an antler with the tines sawed off. Per Sørensen, the archaeologist who excavated the site, believes these items may represent the headdress of a shaman; if so, they would be the earliest evidence of shamanism in mainland Southeast Asia. Shamanism must have an ancient pedigree in the region because it is found among most tribal peoples. Among the most intriguing Neolithic burial sites are ones in central Laos where large stone jars were found containing cremated human remains. This discovery suggests either that cremation predates Indian influence in Southeast Asia or that the jars were used long after they had originally been constructed as depositories of remains by peoples who had adopted the Buddhist practice of cremation.

Sites mainly in northern Vietnam and southern China dating to the first millennium BCE contain bronze drums associated with assemblages termed Dong-Son after a site in northern Vietnam. Dong-Son-type drums were later distributed widely not only in mainland Southeast Asia but in the islands of the region as well, although manufacture of the drums apparently continued to be restricted to a rather small area in northern mainland Southeast Asia. In more recent times, drums have been used by tribal peoples such as the Karen in funerary rites, and some archaeologists believe that the drums were always associated with death customs. Boat designs found on some of the Neolithic drums have been interpreted as being symbols of the means whereby souls of the dead were conveyed to the afterworld. The soul-boat image is found in a number of Southeast Asian cultures today, and a prehistoric notion may have persisted also in transformed form in the Buddhist symbol of the boat that conveys the saved across the sea of *saṃsāra* to *nibbāna* (Skt., *nirvāṇa*).

The designs on the drums, including concentric circles, frogs, birds, snakes or dragons, human figures in headdresses, buildings, and in some southern Chinese drums miniature scenes of rituals, have been variously interpreted. Some understand these as indicating a type of shamanism in which the drum played a part; others have seen them as having totemic significance. It is quite probable that at least some drum designs encode a dualistic cosmology, symbolized in part by an opposition between birds and snakes/dragons. Of particular interest are the images of buildings on piles, which may probably be regarded as a type of ritual hall or perhaps a men's house, and which are clearly related both to those found in many tribal communities today and to the *dinh,* the communal ritual hall of the Vietnamese.

There was never a uniform Dongsonian culture in northern mainland Southeast Asia. Peoples of the region in late prehistoric times were often isolated from each other by the numerous ranges of hills and must have developed distinctive religious traditions. Even though drums were widely traded throughout the region, they were most certainly put to different ritual purposes by different peoples.

An older generation of scholars, best represented by Robert Heine-Geldern, posited an underlying unity of prehistoric Southeast Asian religions that stemmed from the diffusion of a cultural complex from a single European source. While there were certainly contacts among peoples widely separated in Southeast Asia in prehistoric times, and while these contacts resulted in the diffusion of some practices and beliefs, most basic similarities must be understood to reflect the ordering of similar experiences (for example, those related to death, human fertility, cultivation of rice) that follow universal modes of human thought.

Drawing on later historical data as well as ethnographic analogy, Paul Mus, a distinguished student of Southeast Asian civilization argued that the autochthonous religions of protohistoric Southeast Asia coalesced around cults he termed "cadastral." Such cults were organized around images drawn from the local worlds of everyday experience. Spirits, such as the *nats* of various Tibeto-Burman peoples or the *phī* of the Tai, populated these worlds. Humans were able to act in their worlds because they had "vital spirits," often conceived of as multiple, as with the Vietnamese *hon,* Khmer *pralu'n,* or Tai *khwan.* These vital spirits, which only in some cases constituted souls that gained immortal states after death, could leave the body for periods of time, but unless called back and secured—a practice widely seen among many peoples in Southeast Asia—the person would weaken and die.

These cadastral cults constituted the religions of agricultural peoples who had long since made rice their staple, although some cultivated it by swidden or slash-and-burn methods and others cultivated by irrigation. Rice also was believed to possess a vital spirit. Even today, peoples as diverse as the Chin in Burma, Lawa in northern Thailand, Lao in Laos, Jarai in southern Vietnam, and Khmer in Cambodia all perform rites after the harvest to call the spirit of the rice to ensure that it will provide essential nourishment when consumed. Some peoples also believe that other beings—especially the water buffalo used for plowing in wet-rice communities and elephants used for war and heavy labor—also have vital spirits.

The cosmologies of protohistoric Southeast Asian farmers, like those of primitive peoples throughout the world, were structured around fundamental oppositions. In Southeast Asia, the oscillation between the rainy rice-growing season and the dry fallow season found expression in such religious imagery. The fertility of the rainy season is widely associated with a female deity, the "rice mother," although a male image, that of the *nāga,* or dragon, and sometimes a crocodile, is also found in many traditions. In some cases—such as among the Cham, as attested by seventh-century CE inscriptions—the female deity is a *nāgī.* The dry season finds expression in images of male creator gods associated with the sun. To this day, many peoples who have long been Buddhists still engage in rites that entail a dualistic conception of the cosmos. The Lao perform a rite toward the end of the dry season, heavy with sexual symbolism, at which they set off rockets to inform the gods that it is time to send the rains. At the end of the rainy season, when the rivers have flooded, another ceremony is held at which men compete in boat races. The boats, representing *nāgas*, serve to ensure that the earth as supreme *nāga* will accept the flood waters before they drown the rice. The concern with the power of the earth continues after the harvest when attention is turned to the Rice Mother, who is propitiated at the same time that the vital spirit of the rice is called.

The world in which protohistoric peoples lived was marked by uncertainty: Crops might fail as a consequence of late rains or devastating floods; women might be barren, die in childbirth, or lose child after child; and both men and women might die young. Hence, people wished to influence the spirits and cosmic forces that controlled fertility and life. The fundamental method of gaining the favor of spiritual powers was through sacrifices. Human sacrifice was rare in mainland Southeast Asia, although the Wa of northern Burma and southern China even in recent times took heads to offer at New Year rites. Most peoples sacrificed domestic animals, with lesser rites requiring a chicken and more important rites, a pig or even a carabao. In tribal groups such as those in Burma and northeastern India, those men who organized large-scale sacrifices and the so-called feasts of merit associated with them acquired not only the esteem of their fellows but also a spiritual quality that was believed to persist even after their death. Such tribal chiefs are assumed to be similar to what O. W. Wolters calls "men of prowess," who were the heads of protohistoric chiefdoms. What is noteworthy about the tribal chiefs, and presumably about the earlier men of the same type, is that because of the vagaries of life, their potency could never be firmly established. Attempts were made to fix this potency by making the remains of men of prowess objects of cultic attention, especially by those who succeeded them. Rough stone monuments associated with early Cham culture in southern Vietnam and upright stones found together with the prehistoric stone jars in Laos have been interpreted, by analogy with the practice by such modern tribal peoples as Chin of Burma and related groups in northeastern India, as monuments that perpetuated and localized the potency of men who had succeeded during their lifetimes in effecting a relationship between the society and the cosmos. Such monuments were to lend themselves to reinterpretation in Hindu-Buddhist terms when Indian influences began to appear in Southeast Asia.

HISTORICAL TRANSFORMATIONS. Prior to the adoption of Indian or Chinese models, there appears to have been no priesthood in any Southeast Asian society capable of enforcing an orthopraxy among peoples living over a wide area. As the ritual effectiveness of men of prowess waxed and waned, so did the relative power of the polities they headed, thus giving rise to a classic pattern of oscillation between "democratic" and "autocratic" communities found among tribal peoples such as the Kachin of Burma even in recent years. What made it possible for Southeast Asians to imagine themselves as parts of communities whose members, both living and dead, were not all known personally was the introduction of religious conceptions fixed in written texts.

Some evidence, especially from among tribal peoples in what is today southern China, suggests that writing was invented independently by Southeast Asian peoples. However, the historical fact is that the earliest written records are either in some form of Indian script or in Chinese logographs. With these borrowed writing systems came Indian and Chinese texts, rites rooted in the texts, and institutions to perform the rites and perpetuate the textual traditions.

Sinitic influences. Chinese influences appear first in conjunction with the Han conquest of what is now northern Vietnam. Between the first Han movement into the area, in 124 BCE, and 43 CE, when the Chinese suppressed a rebellion led by the legendary Trung sisters, Chinese influence appears to have lain rather lightly on the Vietnamese. From the first century CE, however, the Vietnamese came increasingly to see themselves as part of a Sinitic world, which they knew through the same texts as were used in China proper. This sense of belonging to a Chinese world remained even after the Vietnamese gained independence from China in the eleventh century.

The Chinese model was most significant for literati—the Confucian mandarinate, Mahāyāna Buddhist monks, and even some Daoist priests—who derived their cultural understanding of the world from Chinese and Sino-Vietnamese texts. As none of these literati ever attained the role of a dominant priesthood in the villages, pre-Sinitic traditions, centered on a multitude of local spirits and deities, continued to be perpetuated by spirit mediums, soothsayers, and sorcerers (*thay*). Those Vietnamese who moved out of the Red River delta in the "push to the south" that began in the thirteenth century and continued into recent times came into contact with other traditions—those of the hinduized Cham and Khmer, the Buddhist Khmer, and local tribal peoples. In part because of significant non-Sinitic influences in southern Vietnam, the impress of Chinese culture was somewhat less evident in the popular culture of that region than in that of northern Vietnam. Vietnamese in southern Vietnam have to the present often turned to non-Sinitic religious practitioners—montagnard sorcerers and Theravāda monks, for example—for help in confronting fundamental difficulties in their lives. Many of the religiously inspired peasant rebellions originating in southern Vietnam as well as some modern syncretic popular religons have drawn inspiration from non-Chinese sources. This said, Vietnamese religion in all parts of the country has assumed a distinctly Sinitic cast, being organized primarily around ancestor worship in the Chinese mode. Elsewhere in mainland Southeast Asia, only migrant Chinese and those tribal peoples such as the Hmong and Mien who have lived long in Chinese-dominated areas show similar concern with ancestor worship.

Indian influences. In those areas of mainland Southeast Asia where Indian influences first appeared in the early centuries of the common era, individuals were rarely apotheosized for being apical ancestors in a line of descent. If, however, a man (but rarely a woman) succeeded in his lifetime in demonstrating through effective action in ritual and in warfare that he possessed some charismatic quality, this quality could continue to be influential after the individual's death by giving him a cosmic body to replace his worldly one. The earliest monuments of indianized civilization in Southeast Asia appeared in significant numbers between the fourth and eighth century CE. Particular examples are Śiva *liṅgā* of the Cham in southern Vietnam, the Buddhist *semā* (Skt., *sīmā*) or boundary markers with scenes from the life of the Buddha or from the Jātakas in bas-relief found in Dvāravatī sites in northeastern Thailand, and the stupas at Beikthano and Śrīkṣetra in central Burma, Thaton in lower Burma, and Nakhon Pathom in central Thailand. These monuments can best be interpreted as having been put up to elevate a man of prowess to a divine form. Whereas an older generation of historians often associated early historical sites in mainland Southeast Asia with large kingdoms, most historians now accept that there were many petty kingdoms in the area whose power waxed and waned much as did that of the chiefdoms that preceded them. The proliferation of monuments, a pattern that climaxes in the classical civilizations of Angkor in Cambodia and Pagan in Burma, most likely represents a continuing effort by new kings, their families, and their rivals to establish their own claims to be identified with divine and cosmic power.

Influential mainland Southeast Asians who worked with Indian texts made minimal use of the Indian idea that one's place within the world was fixed at birth by some cosmic plan. The caste system did not survive the voyage across the Bay of Bengal except in a very modified form, whereby kings claimed to be *kṣatriya;* even then a man of quite lowly origins could become a *kṣatriya* by successfully usurping the throne and clothing himself in sacralized regalia.

The process of indianization in Southeast Asia included identifying a power believed to be embodied in a local shrine with divine or cosmic powers known in Indian texts. This made possible the creation of larger polities, since peoples in very different parts of a realm saw themselves as part of the same cosmos and worshiped the same gods, often gods who were also equated with the rulers. The polity was a *maṇḍala,* the "circle of a king," a domain in which a particular ruler succeeded in being viewed as the link between the world and the cosmos. The kings who founded Angkor near the Great Lake in Cambodia in the ninth century were notably successful in establishing a cult of the *devarāja,* a god-king, whose *maṇḍala* included at its height all of present-day Cambodia, the Mekong Delta of southern Vietnam, and central and northeastern Thailand. The *devarāja* cult centered on the assimilation of the king to Siva, as represented by a lingam. The capital was a place where, through erection of temples, dedicated not only to Śiva but also to Viṣṇu and other Hindu gods and to *bodhisattvas*, each king could ensure that his *maṇḍala* was a microcosm of the cosmos. While the Angkorean empire experienced a number of defeats by rulers of other *maṇḍalas,* it was not until the fifteenth century that it finally ended; by this time, the religious orientations of the populace had begun to change radically.

On the western side of mainland Southeast Asia, Burmese kings also succeeded in establishing a *maṇḍala,* that of Pagan, that between the eleventh and thirteenth centuries rivaled the splendor and power of Angkor. Although the Burmese kings promoted cults that usually equated them with the Buddha rather than with Hindu gods, the stupas and temples they built were like the Hindu and Mahāyāna temples at Angkor; they were both funerary monuments in which the kings became immortalized, albeit in this case in Buddhist terms, and recreations of the sacred cosmos. In both Pagan and Angkor, Meru, the sacred mountain that lies at the center of the universe and is also an *axis mundi,* was represented in the temple or stupa erected by a king.

The *maṇḍala* organized around a shrine that served as an *axis mundi* became the model for villages as well as capitals. In nearly every village in Buddhist Southeast Asia, a stupa has been erected. Those who contribute to its construction believe they gain merit that will ensure a better rebirth and perhaps even rebirth at the time of the next Buddha, Metteyya (Skt., Maitreya). The localized cults of the relics of the Buddha link Southeast Asians not only with early Indian Buddhism but also with the cosmographic practices of the rulers of the classical indianized states and beyond that with the cadastral cults of pre-indianized Southeast Asia.

The cult of the relics of the Buddha does not constitute the whole of Buddhism as practiced in Southeast Asia. Between the thirteenth and fifteenth centuries, missionary monks established a Theravāda Buddhist orthodoxy among the majority of peoples, both rural and urban, living in what are today Burma, Thailand, Laos, and Cambodia. In a sense, orthodox Buddhism made sense to Southeast Asians because of the pre-Buddhist idea that religious virtue is not a product solely of descent from particular ancestors but also a consequence of one's own religiously effective actions. In Buddhist terms, this idea was formulated so that people understood that although they were born with a certain karmic legacy of both merit and demerit they also continually acquire new merit and demerit from morally significant acts.

Those who became adherents of Theravāda Buddhism also retained pre-Buddhist beliefs in spirits and deities. These beliefs were given new significance in the context of a Buddhist worldview. Some of the supernatural beings were universalized and identified with Hindu deities also known to Buddhism. More significantly, spirits and deities were accorded a subordinate place within the Buddhist cosmic hierarchy generated by the law of *karman.* Beliefs in pre-

Buddhist concepts of the vital spirit—the *leikpya* of the Burmese, the *khwan* of the Tai, the *pralu'n* of the Khmer—also remained and continued to be part of ritual. These beliefs were, however, reformulated to take into account the Buddhist teaching that the soul is not immortal and that "consciousness" (Pali, *viññāṇa*) links one life with the next.

The Theravāda revolution in mainland Southeast Asia did not lead to the demise of the *maṇḍala;* on the contrary, it led local lords to demonstrate their effectiveness by claiming to be righteous rulers and validating such claims by asserting their independence or even embarking on military ventures to extend their domains at the expense of other lords. Despite the political fragmentation of premodern Buddhist societies, all could conceive of being part of a common Buddhist world. Such a conception was expressed, for example, in the recognition of important pilgrimage shrines—ones containing relics of the Buddha—that lay in other domains.

The success of Theravāda Buddhism led to a much sharper distinction between the religious traditions of the peoples of the western part of mainland Southeast Asia and those east of the Annamite cordillera. Not only were the Vietnamese becoming increasingly sinicized, but the Cham, who had once had an important indianized culture in southern Vietnam, turned from this tradition and embraced Islam, a religion that was becoming established among other Austronesian-speaking peoples in major societies of the Indonesian archipelago and on the Malay Peninsula.

Tribal peoples in Southeast Asia, mainly located in highland areas where they practiced swidden cultivation, did not remain totally isolated from the changes occurring in the lowlands. A myth among many tribal peoples in the northern part of the region tells of a "lost book" or "lost writing." The Kachin version of the myth is typical. Ninggawn wa Magam, the deity from whom humans acquired culture, called all the different tribes of humans together. To each tribe he gave a book to help them in their lives. Shans and Burmans received books written on palm leaves; Chinese and foreigners (i.e., Westerners) received books on paper; and Kachin received a book of parchment. The Kachin, not truly understanding the significance of the book, ate it and have been without writing ever since. The myth reveals a sense on the part of tribal peoples of being culturally deprived relative to those who have writing.

When tribal peoples have turned to expand their horizons, they have tended to do so through acquiring access to the literature of their lowland neighbors. The Lawa, an Austroasiatic tribal people in Thailand, see themselves as Buddhists, like their Northern Thai neighbors, but unable to practice the religion in the hills where they have no monks to instruct them. When they move down from the hills, however, they quickly transform themselves into Northern Thai. Mien, who are found more in southern China than in Southeast Asia, long ago developed a tradition of craft literacy, with ritual specialists being able to read Daoist texts in Chinese. An interesting variant on the myth is found among some Karen in Burma, who were converted in significant numbers to Christianity beginning early in the nineteenth century. Their myth tells how the book will be returned to them by foreign brothers who are identified with the Western missionaries. Even among Karen, however, more have become Buddhist than have become Christian.

Missionization—not only by Christians but in recent years by Buddhists—and the spread of modern systems of compulsory education have rendered tribal religions increasingly peripheral. So, too, have improved health care and secular education undermined beliefs in spirits that were previously elements of the religions of Southeast Asian Buddhists and Vietnamese. Moreover, as agriculture has been transformed by large-scale irrigation works and the introduction of new technology and new high-yield varieties of rice, peoples in the region have become less inclined to credit supernatural powers with the control over fertility. They may continue to perform traditional rites, but these are becoming more secular celebrations than sources of religious meaning. Nonetheless, even as the worlds of Southeast Asians are radically transformed by political-economic forces and cultural changes that have occurred over the past century and a half, there still remains among many the ancient idea of cultivating virtue through morally effective action.

SEE ALSO Ancestors, article on Ancestor Worship; Boats; Buddhism, article on Buddhism in Southeast Asia; Burmese Religion; Drums; Folk Religion, article on Folk Buddhism; Islam, article on Islam in Southeast Asia; Khmer Religion; Kingship, article on Kingship in East Asia; Lao Religion; Megalithic Religion, article on Historical Cultures; Merit, article on Buddhist Concepts; Nāgas and Yakṣas; Nats; Negrito Religions; Pilgrimage, article on Buddhist Pilrimage in South and Southeast Asia; Saṃgha, article on Saṃgha and Society in South and Southeast Asia; Stupa Worship; Thai Religion; Theravāda; Vietnamese Religion.

BIBLIOGRAPHY

Robert Heine-Geldern interprets archaeological and ethnographic evidence with reference to a diffusionist thesis that posited the source of a prehistoric "megalithic complex" in Europe. His most recent formulation of his position appears in "Some Tribal Art Styles in Southeast Asia," in *The Many Faces of Primitive Art,* edited by Douglas Fraser (Englewood Cliffs, N.J., 1966), pp. 161–214. Kenneth Perry Landon, in *Southeast Asia: Crossroads of Religion* (Chicago, 1969) and Pierre-Bernard Lafont, in "Génies, anges et démons en Asie du Sud-Est," in *Génies, anges et démons* (Paris, 1971), provide introductions to Southeast Asian religions in other than diffusionist terms. By far the most detailed comparison of beliefs and practices relating to agriculture found among peoples not only in mainland Southeast Asia but also on the islands of the region is Eveline Porée-Maspero's *Étude sur les rites agraires des Cambodgiens,* 3 vols. (Paris, 1962–1969). Also see in this connection P. E. de Josselin de Jong's "An Interpretation of Agricultural Rites in Southeast Asia, with a Demonstration of Use of Data from Both Continental and

Insular Asia," *Journal of Asian Studies* 24 (February 1965): 283–291. A general introduction to Southeast Asian religions with reference to their social context is provided in my book *The Golden Peninsula: Culture and Adaptation in Mainland Southeast Asia* (New York, 1977).

The volume *Early South East Asia: Essays in Archaeology, History, and Historical Geography*, edited by R. B. Smith and William Watson (Oxford, 1979), contains information on prehistoric and protohistoric religion; the work also has a good bibliography. H. G. Quaritch Wales's *Prehistory and Religion in Southeast Asia* (London, 1957), although dated and relying too heavily on diffusionist theory, still remains the only work to attempt a synthesis of prehistoric evidence. Per Sørensen reports on the find he interprets as evidence of prehistoric shamanism in "'The Shaman's Grave,'" in *Felicitation Volumes of Southeast-Asian Studies Presented to Prince Dhaninivat*, vol. 2 (Bangkok, 1965), pp. 303–318. The model of the "cadastral cult" was advanced by Paul Mus in *India Seen from the East: Indian and Indigenuous Cults in Champa*, translated by I. W. Mabbett and edited by I. W. Mabbett and D. P. Chandler (Cheltenham, Australia, 1975). O. W. Wolters, in *History, Culture, and Region in Southeast Asian Perspectives* (Brookfield, Vt., 1982), proposes the notion that "men of prowess" was a general type in prehistoric and protohistoric Southeast Asia. His interpretation is based, in part, on A. Thomas Kirsch's argument developed in a comparison of Southeast Asian tribal ethnography in *Feasting and Social Oscillation: A Working Paper on Religion and Society in Upland Southeast Asia* (Ithaca, N.Y., 1973). Kirsch, in turn, has elaborated on the idea of oscillation between "democratic" and "autocratic" chiefdoms first advanced by Edmund Leach in *Political Systems of Highland Burma* (Cambridge, Mass., 1954).

Vietnamese scholars have shown considerable interest in recent years in tracing the Southeast Asian origins of Vietnamese civilization. Much of their work is discussed by Keith Weller Taylor in *The Birth of Vietnam* (Berkeley, Calif., 1983). The process of "indianization" and the relationship between this process and what H. G. Quaritch Wales called "local genius" in the shaping of Southeast Asian religious traditions has been most intensively explored by George Coedès in *The Indianized States of Southeast Asia*, edited by Walter F. Vella and translated by Susan Brown Cowing (Canberra, 1968); H. G. Quaritch Wales in *The Making of Greater India*, 3d rev. ed. (London, 1974) and *The Universe Around Them: Cosmology and Cosmic Renewal in Indianized Southeast Asia* (London, 1977); O. W. Wolters in "Khmer 'Hinduism' in the Seventh Century," in *Early South East Asia: Essays in Archaeology, History and Historical Geography* and in *History, Culture and Region in Southeast Asian Perspectives* (both cited above); Hermann Kulke in *The Devaraja Cult*, translated by I. W. Mabbett (Ithaca, N.Y., 1978); and I. W. Mabbett in "Devaraja," *Journal of Southeast Asian History* 10 (September, 1969): 202–223; "The 'Indianization' of Southeast Asia: Reflections on Prehistoric Sources," *Journal of Southeast Asian Studies* 8 (March 1977): 1–14; "The 'Indianization' of Southeast Asia: Reflections on the Historical Sources," *Journal of Southeast Asian Studies* 8 (September 1977): 143–161; and "*Varṇas* in Angkor and the Indian Caste System," *Journal of Asian Studies* 36 (May 1977): 429–442. O. W. Wolters, in *History, Culture and Region in Southeast Asian Perspectives*, discusses the *maṇḍala* model, a model also discussed at somelength under the rubric of the "galactic polity" by Stanley J. Tambiah in *World Conqueror and World Renouncer* (Cambridge, 1976).

A. Thomas Kirsch in "Complexity in the Thai Religious System: An Interpretation," *Journal of Asian Studies* 36 (February 1977): 241–266; Melford E. Spiro in *Burmese Supernaturalism*, 2d ed. (Philadelphia, 1978); and Stanley J. Tambiah in *Buddhism* and the Spirit Cults in North-East Thailand (Cambridge, 1970) discuss the relationship between pre-Buddhist and Buddhist beliefs in Thai and Burmese religion. Similar attention to pre-Sinitic religious beliefs in Vietnamese religion is given by Leopold Cadière in *Croyances et pratiques religieuses des Viêtnamiens*, 3 vols. (Saigon and Paris, 1955–1958). See also Pierre Huard and Maurice Durand's *Connaissance du Viêtnam* (Paris and Hanoi, 1954).

Kirk Endicott's *Batek Negrito Religion* (Oxford, 1979) describes the religion of the last remaining major population of hunting-and-gathering people on the mainland. Karl Gustav Izikowitz's *Lamet: Hill Peasants in French Indochina* (Göteborg, 1951), Peter Kunstadter's *The Lua' (Lawa) of Northern Thailand: Aspects of Social Structure, Agriculture and Religion* (Princeton, 1965), and H. E. Kauffmann's "Some Social and Religious Institutions of the Lawa of Northwestern Thailand," *Journal of the Siam Society* 60 (1972): 237–306 and 65 (1977): 181–226, discuss aspects of religious life among Austroasiatic-speaking tribal peoples. Among the more detailed accounts of the religions of Hmong (Meo) and Mien (Yao) peoples are Jacques Lemoine's *Yao Ceremonial Paintings* (Atlantic Highlands, N.J., 1982); Guy Morechand's "Principaux traits du chamanisme Méo Blanc en Indochine," *Bulletin de l'École Française d'Extrême-Orient* 54 (1968): 58–294; and Nusit Chindarsi's *The Religion of the Hmong Ñua* (Bangkok, 1976). Theodore Stern in "*Ariya* and the Golden Book: A Millenarian Buddhist Sect among the Karen," *Journal of Asian Studies* 27 (February 1968): 297–328, and William Smalley's "The Gospel and Cultures of Laos," *Practical Anthropology* 3 (1956): 47–57, treat some aspects of religious change among tribal peoples.

New Sources

Benjamin, Geoffrey, and Cynthia Chou, eds. *Tribal Communities in the Malay World: Historical, Cultural and Social Perspectives.* Singapore, 2002.

Do, Thien. *Vietnamese Supernaturalism: Views from the Southern Region.* London, 2003.

Kipp, Rita Smith, and Susan Rodgers, eds. *Indonesian Religions in Transition.* Tucson, 1987.

Lemoine, Jacques and Chiao Chien, eds. *The Yao of South China: Recent International Studies.* Paris, 1991.

Morrison, Kathleen D., and Laura L. Junker, eds. *Forager-Traders in South and Southeast Asia: Long-term Histories.* New York, 2002.

Swearer, Donald K. *The Buddhist World of Southeast Asia.* Albany, 1995.

Tarling, Nicholas, ed. *The Cambridge History of Southeast Asia.* Cambridge, 1992.

Wijeyewardene, Gehan. *Ethnic Groups across National Boundaries in Mainland Southeast Asia.* Singapore, 1990.

CHARLES F. KEYES (1987)
Revised Bibliography

SOUTHEAST ASIAN RELIGIONS: INSULAR CULTURES

The cultures of insular Southeast Asia are made up predominantly of peoples speaking Austronesian languages, and the traditional religions of the area, despite substantial diversity and extensive borrowing from other sources, retain significant features that reflect a common origin. Linguistic evidence indicates that the point of origin of the languages of present-day Austronesians was the island of Taiwan (Formosa) and possibly also the adjacent coastal region of southeastern China. The initial expansion of the Austronesians began in the third millennium BCE and proceeded, by stages, through the Philippines and the islands of Indonesia, then east to the islands of the Pacific, and eventually west as far as the island of Madagascar.

In the first stage of this expansion, migrating Austronesian groups possessed a basic cultural technology that included the domesticated dog and pig, a knowledge of the cultivation of rice, millet, and sugarcane, and a developing craftsmanship in pottery, weaving, and barkcloth making. At a later stage in the course of this continuing expansion, the Austronesians developed further forms of cultivation involving breadfruit, bananas, taro, and yams and the use of a variety of fruit-bearing or starch-yielding palms. By this time they also possessed domesticated chickens and had developed sails for their canoes and some of the sailing techniques that were to carry them from island to island. By about 2500 BCE they had expanded through the southern Philippines and into Borneo and had begun to penetrate the islands of both eastern and western Indonesia.

Because this expansion involved a scattering of numerous small groups through thousands of islands over several millennia, it gave rise to considerable linguistic and cultural diversity. Earlier island populations were undoubtedly assimilated, although there is very little linguistic evidence on these peoples except for those in Melanesia.

Regional variation is indicated by the various linguistic subgroups of Austronesian that are currently recognized. Formosan languages are distinguished from Malayo-Polynesian languages within the Austronesian family and the Malayo-Polynesian languages are divided into (1) a western subgroup that includes the languages of the Philippines, Borneo, Madagascar, and western Indonesia as far as the island of Sumbawa, (2) a central subgroup that begins in eastern Sumbawa and comprises the languages of the Lesser Sundas and most of the Moluccas, and (3) an eastern subgroup that includes the languages of southern Halmahera and all of the languages of the Pacific.

In the course of migration, natural ecological variation as well as numerous outside influences led to the development, emphasis, or even abandonment of different elements of a general Neolithic culture. In the equatorial zones, for example, reliance on rice and millet gave way to a greater dependence on tubers and on fruit- and starch-gathering activities. As populations moved into the interior of the larger islands some sailing skills were abandoned, but a coastal or riverine orientation was generally maintained. During most of their protohistory, Austronesian populations lived in impermanent settlements and combined shifting cultivation with hunting and gathering. The development toward centralized states began on Java, on the coast of Sumatra, and in several other coastal areas that were open to trade and outside influences. Chief among these influences were religious ideas and inspiration that derived variously, at different periods, from Hinduism, Buddhism, Islam, and Christianity.

The earliest Hindu inscriptions found in insular Southeast Asia date from the fourth century CE; their location and composition, however, suggest a long period of prior regional contact with Indian religious ideas. By the fifth century, Hinduism is reliably reorted to have been established on Java, and by the sixth century, there is evidence of Buddhist influence on Sumatra and Java, with the port of Srivijaya developing into a major Buddhist center of learning in the seventh century. Javanese monuments dating from the eighth to the fourteenth centuries indicate a lively development and interrelation of Saivaite, Vaisnavite, and Buddhist traditions. By the thirteenth century, Islam had begun to spread through the islands and exert a major influence. By the fifteenth century, Catholicism had reached the region with the arrival of the Portuguese and Spanish, and by the sixteenth century, Protestantism had made its appearance with the Dutch and English. In addition, the popular traditions of Taoism and Confucianism were brought to the region by Chinese traders and settlers. Both individually and together these religions have had a profound effect in shaping religious practice in the region.

At present, 88 to 89 percent of the Indonesian population is classified as Muslim, although a significant portion of this population, particularly on Java, still adheres to traditional practices that are not considered orthodox. In the Philippines, approximately 84 percent of the population is Catholic; 3 percent is Protestant; and a further 5 percent are classified as Aglipayan, followers of an independent Philippine Christian church. Muslims constitute a small minority of approximately 5 percent in the Philippines, while Christians make up about 9 percent of the Indonesian population. In Indonesia, Bali forms a traditional Hindu-Buddhist enclave but there has occurred a recent resurgence of Hinduism on Java and elsewhere. Many members of the Chinese population of Indonesia are officially considered Buddhists, although some continue to practice forms of Taoism or Confucianism. A considerable portion are also Christian. Official statistics from Indonesia and the Philippines thus indicate only a small minority of the population in either country as official adherents of some form of traditional religion. In Sarawak and Sabah, adherents of tradition constitute a high percentage of the population of their local area, but in Malaysia as a whole they are a minority. In Brunei, similar groups form an even smaller minority.

National policies of the countries of the region affect the practice of traditional religions. Indonesia gives official recognition only to Islam, Protestantism, Catholicism, Hinduism, and Buddhism, with the result that in effect no traditional religion is regarded as a religion. In some areas a tacit tolerance of traditional practices has developed, but in general there is mounting pressure to assimilate to an officially recognized religion. On the basis of early cultural borrowings and some similarity in forms of worship, various ethnic groups have gained recognition of their traditional religion as a Hindu sect. In the Philippines, missionary efforts by both Catholics and Protestants have been directed to conversion of the remaining adherents of tribal religions. In Sarawak and Sabah, there is pressure to convert to Islam as well as to Christianity. In all the countries of the region the adherents of traditional religions are minorities whose distinct ways of life are under pressure to change. Generally, they participate only at the margins of national life.

The tribal religions of the region vary according to the groups that continue to practice them. These groups include small, often isolated peoples whose economy is based primarily on hunting and gathering with limited cultivation. Examples of such groups are the Sakkudei of the island of Siberut off the coast of western Sumatra; various wandering bands of Kubu scattered in the interior forests of Sumatra; groups of a similar kind in Kalimantan who are referred to generically as Punan; as well as a variety of other small-scale societies on other islands—the Agta and other Aeta of Luzon, the Batak of Palawan, the Da'a or To Lare of Sulawesi (Celebes), or the Alifuru groups, such as the Huaulu and Nuaulu, of Ceram in eastern Indonesia. Many of these groups, with their simplified technology, no longer possess the range of economic pursuits attributed to the early Austronesians. Other adherents of traditional religions include the unconverted members of larger, economically and socially more complex populations: some Batak, particularly Karo, from north Sumatra; Ngaju communities in Kalimantan; various Toraja peoples in Sulawesi; as well as the Sumbanese, Savunese, and Timorese in eastern Indonesia. Sumba has the distinction of being the only island in Indonesia where a majority of the population profess to follow their traditional religion.

Some of these Indonesian populations have formally established religious associations to preserve their traditional practices and some have come to be identified as followers of Hindu-Dharma, a status that affords them official government recognition. This is one possibility available to members of the Toraja "Alukta," the Batak "Pelbegu," the Ngaju "Kaharingan," and the Bugis "Towani."

In the Philippines, a majority of the indigenous peoples in the mountains of northern Luzon (among them the Isneg, Ifugao, Bontok, Ibaloi, Kalinga, and Ilongot), in Mindoro (the Hanunoo, Buhid, and Alangan), and in the interior of Mindanao (the Subanun, Bukidnon, Tiruray, Manobo, Bagabo, and Mandaya) have retained their traditional religions despite increasing missionary efforts. In Sarawak, similar tribal peoples include the Iban, Kayan, Kenyah, and Kelabit; in Sabah, the Dusun, Murut, and Lun Dayeh; all of these tribal populations and other small groups as well have undergone conversion to Christianity in varying degrees.

Other adherents of traditional religion are more difficult to classify. Some form small enclaves, often consisting of no more than a few villages, whose traditional practices represent nonacceptance of the dominant religion of their region. Such groups would include the Badui (or Kanekes) of West Java, the Tengger of East Java, and the Waktu Tiga villagers of Lombok. All of these three groups maintain special priesthoods. Badui priests are confined to an inner territorial realm, whereas among the Tengger, there is one priest for each of twenty-eight villages. Both groups claim to preserve an "Agama Budha," which refers not to a form of Buddhism but to a pre-Islamic fusion of Indic and local practice. The Tengger priests, for example, follow an ancient Saiva liturgy that is kept secret from the village population, who see their worship as an ancestral cult.

Many of the millenarian movements that have occurred in Indonesia and the Philippines can be seen as religious movements and the communities of members of these movements, such as the Kesepuhan in West Java, the Samin of Central Java, or the Rizalistas of Luzon, may also be considered as traditional religious adherents. In addition, many other individuals and groups carry on traditional rituals under nominal adherence to another formally recognized religion. On the island of Flores, for example, the people of Tana Wai Brama continue to maintain their traditional ceremonial cycle, even though they are formally classified as Catholics. The same is true for other populations, both Christian and Muslim, throughout the islands. Official statistics are therefore often misleading in assessing the extent of traditional religious adherence.

Studies of traditional religion, many of which have been written by missionaries or colonial administrators, document beliefs and practices that have since been either abandoned or modified through the process of conversion. Significant evidence on traditional religion is also derived from present practices and general conceptions that have been incorporated and retained in the major recognized religions in the course of their accommodation to the traditions of the region.

Chief among these basic conceptions and practices are the following: (1) the prevalence of complementary duality; (2) the belief in the immanence of life and in the interdependence of life and death; (3) the reliance on specific rituals to mark stages in the processes of life and death; and (4) the celebration of spiritual differentiation. All of these notions may be regarded as part of a common Austronesian conceptual heritage.

The Prevalence of Complementary Duality. Forms of complementary dualism are singularly pervasive in the religions of the region. Such dualism figures prominently, for example, in a wide variety of myths of the origin of the cosmos that combine themes of reproduction and destruction. Among the Ngaju of Kalimantan (Borneo) creation begins when the mountain abodes of the two supreme deities clash repeatedly, bringing forth the upperworld and underworld and various of its parts; in the next phase of the creation, male and female hornbills of the two deities, perched on the tree of life, renew the struggle, destroying the tree but in the process creating the first man and woman. Among the Toraja of Sulawesi the universe originates from the marriage of heaven and earth: Heaven lies upon the broad earth and, as they separate, the land is revealed and all their divine children, including the sun and moon, come forth. Among the Mambai of east Timor, a formless hermaphroditic being molds and shelters Mother Earth and Father Heaven; they separate and the pregnant Mother Earth bears the first mountain, known as the Great Father. Heaven descends upon Earth again and from their union are born the first trees and rocks and the first men and women. At each birth, the waters of the world increase, until Father Heaven eventually abandons Mother Earth, who is left to decompose and disintegrate.

Ideas of complementary duality are reflected in ideas about the principal divinity, who is often conceived of as a paired being (Mahatala/Jata among the Ngaju, Amawolo/Amarawi among the Sumbanese, or Nian Tana/Lero Wulan among the Ata Tana Ai); in ideas about categories of spirits, heroes, and other ancestral figures; in ideas about the division of sacred space: upperworld and underworld, upstream and downstream, mountainward and seaward, or inside and outside; and above all, in ideas about classes of persons and the order of participants in the performance of rituals.

Major celebrations based on this complementarity can become a form of ritual combat that reenacts the reproductive antagonisms of creation. To choose but one example, the Savunese of eastern Indonesia gather on the day preceding the night of a full moon to form male and female groups according to lineage affiliation; they position themselves at the upper and lower end of a sacred enclosure on the top of a particular hill. There they engage in ceremonial cockfighting that is timed to reach its crescendo precisely at noon. This high cosmological drama is based on a series of complementary oppositions: the conjunction of male and female, the union of the upper and lower divisions of the cosmos, and the antagonism of spirits of the mountain and sea, all of which are timed to climax when the sun is at its zenith and the moon at its fullest.

A significant feature of the traditional religions of the region is the preservation of sacred knowledge through special forms of ritual language that are characterized by the pervasive use of parallelism. Parallelism is a form of dual phraseology and, in its most canonical form, results in a strict dyadic expression of all ritual statements. The following lines, excerpted from a traditional Rotinese mortuary chant, give an idea of the parallelism of such ritual poetry:

> Delo Iuk has died
> So plant an areca nut at her foot
> And Soma Lopo has perished
> So plant a coconut at her head
> Let the coconut grow fruit for her head
> And let the areca nut grow flowerstalks for her feet.

This parallelism, which is a common feature of oral composition, resembles in form the parallelism that is to be found in the sacred literatures of other peoples of the world. (Both the *Psalms* and the *Popol Vuh* of the Quiche Maya provide good examples of such canonical parallelism.) Myths of the Batak, of the people of Nias, of the Ngaju, Kendayan, and Mualang Dayak, of the Toraja, and of a majority of the peoples of eastern Indonesia adhere to relatively strict forms of parallelism, whereas the myths of other traditional religious adherents follow freer forms of parallel compositions. In all cases, a form of duality is an essential part of the very process of composition.

Conceptions of complementary dualism continue to pervade even those societies that have adopted Hinduism, Islam, or Christianity. Balinese society is replete with dualism. The opposition between Barong and Rangda, which forms one of Bali's best-known dramatic temple performances, is a particularly striking example of complementary dualism. The Javanese *wayang,* or shadow theater, is similarly based on forms of dual opposition. Although the initial basis for many of the most important dramas was Indian, the Javanese have developed and extended these dramas to suit local conceptions. In the *Bhāratayuddha* (in the Javanese version of the Hindu epic *Mahābhārata*), the Pandawa heroes defeat and destroy their cousins, the Korawa. Yet according to the *Korawasrama,* an important Javanese text for which there exists no Sanskrit equivalent, the Korawa are resuscitated to continue their struggle with Pandawa for, as the text asserts: "How could the world be well ordered if the Korawa and Pandawa no longer existed? Are they not the content of the world?"

BELIEF IN THE IMMANENCE OF LIFE. Virtually all of the traditional religions of the region are predicated on a belief in the immanence of life. In the literature this concept is often simplistically referred to as "animism." In traditional mythologies, creation did not occur *ex nihilo:* The cosmos was violently quickened into life and all that exists is thus part of a living cosmic whole. Life is evident everywhere in a multitude of forms whose manifestation can be complex, particularistic, but also transitory. There are many different classes of beings, including humans, whose origin may be identified in some mythological account but the system is inherently open and other classes of beings may be recognized whose origin is unknown, even though their manifestation is evident. In many of the traditional religions there is no single origin of humankind. Commonly, humans either descended from a heavenly sphere or emerged from earth or sea; yet, often, the origin of some categories of humans is left unexplained. The openness of these systems does not necessarily involve indifference so much as a recognition of the limitations of human knowledge.

Although there exists an ultimate ground of identity to all manifestations of life, the traditional view makes no assumption of identity or equality among particular manifestations. The result is a general acceptance of a plurality of beings and at the same time, especially in the mystic traditions elaborated in Java, a recognition of the oneness of the individual with the whole in the commonality of life.

The traditional religions differ markedly, however, in their classification of categories or classes of beings. Priests of the Ifugao, for example, are reported to be able to distinguish over fifteen hundred spirits or deities, who are divided into forty classes. By contrast, the Rotinese recognize two broad classes of spirits—those of the inside and those of the outside—and are only concerned with naming the spirits of the inside. The traditional religions also differ significantly in attitudes to the spirit world. For some, all spirits are potentially malevolent and must be placated; in others, benevolent spirits are called upon to intervene against troublesome spirits. In the majority, however, attitudes vary according to types of spirits. The result is a kind of spiritual empiricism in which various ritual procedures are employed as experiments to see what occurs. Often this is highly individualistic: What works for one person may not work for another. In general, all traditional religions aim to achieve some form of ritual balance that accords each category of life its appropriate due.

Although rarely accorded philosophical justification except in the more consciously elaborate traditional religions, there exists the underlying assumption that, since all is part of a whole, any part can stand for the whole. Among the simplest but most common microcosmic representations of the macrocosm are rock and tree, whose union is variously interpreted as the primordial source of life and as the progenitorial conjunction of male and female. Other representations abound. Ceremonial space may be constructed to mirror the whole: Villages, houses, or ships may be symbolically arranged on a macrocosmic basis, or particular objects, such as the *kayon* that is held up to begin and end a *wayang* performance, the four-cornered *raga-raga* rack that hangs suspended in a traditional Batak house, or merely a flag and flagpole, can be vested with all-embracing cosmic significance. Frequently, the human body itself may represent the whole of the cosmos. All such representations have a potency that is centered, ordered, and ultimately diffused outward.

A fundamental feature of the traditional religions is their recognition that life depends upon death, that creation derives from dissolution. This is the emphatic theme of most myths of creation and is repeated in origin tales and in much folklore. In widespread tales of the origin of the cultivation of rice, millet, or of various tubers, for example, the first sprouts or shoots of the new crop come from the body of some ancestral figure. Moreover, since life comes from death, the ancestral dead or specific deceased persons, whose lives were marked by notable attainments, are regarded as capable of bestowing life-giving potency. Thus the dead figure prominently in the religious activities of the living and the tombs of the dead are often sources of religious benefit. In some areas, as on Sumba, the tombs of the dead occupy the center of the village; elsewhere they form the focal point of pilgrimage.

The chief sacrificial animals in the traditional religions are the chicken, the dog, and the pig (although among those populations that keep them the water buffalo is by far the most important sacrificial animal). Sacrifice generally involves creative analogies on an ordered scale. The people of Nias, who perform spectacular pig sacrifices, describe themselves as "God's pigs." In the mortuary ceremonies of the Toraja, the sacrificial water buffalo is identified with the deceased but, in other contexts, can represent the entire descent group. Among the Rotinese, as among other peoples of Southeast Asia, the water buffalo can also be analogically identified with the whole of the cosmos and sacrifice can thus be conceived as a reenactment of creation.

The entrails of chickens and the livers of pigs frequently provide a means of divination within a sacrificial context. These forms of divination, as well as others, such as the augury of birds or divination by spear, together with spirit possession form part of a complex revelatory process by which humans seek to interpret the wishes and intentions of the spirit powers.

RITUALS OF LIFE AND DEATH. The rituals of the different traditional religions of the region invariably constitute part of a continuing process or cycle and are primarily concerned with the enhancement of life, either the life of particular persons or the life of large collectivities, including that of the cosmos as a totality. Life-cycle rituals mark the process of life and death. They may be seen to begin with marriage—the union of male and female—and proceed through specific stages. Prominent among these rituals are those that mark the seventh month of a woman's pregnancy, haircutting, tooth filing, circumcision (which may have had a pre-Islamic origin but has been given increased significance through the influence of Islam), the coming of adulthood through marriage, and the formation of an autonomous household, which in many societies centers on the celebration of the completion of a house. In numerous societies, tattooing is a physical marking of this process of development and special tattoos are used to identify individuals who can claim outstanding achievements. Often tattoos are regarded as a prerequisite for admission as well as individual identification in the world after death.

Death rituals are part of the same process as those of life and in general are celebrated throughout the region with great elaboration. Death rituals are also performed in stages commencing with burial and continuing sometimes for years. Such rituals are believed to chart, or even effect, the progress of the spirit of the deceased in its journey or elevation through the afterworld. Major celebrations often occur long after initial burial, when only the bones of the deceased remain. These bones, separated from the flesh, may either be reburied in a special sepulcher or reunited in a single tomb with the bones of other members of the descent group. Often the groups involved in performing these mortuary rituals complete and reverse the exchanges that began at the marriage ceremony of the parents of the deceased, thus ending one phase and beginning the next phase of a continuing cycle. On Bali, a Hindu cremation marks a comparable stage following a similar pattern, whereas in Java and elsewhere, despite an Islamic requirement of immediate burial, the spirits of the dead are given regular offerings and the tombs of former great rulers and leaders are prominent places of pilgrimage.

A feature of many of the rituals of life and death is their botanic idiom, which reflects a common Austronesian agricultural inheritance. The rituals describe a process of planting, growing, and ripening into old age; after the harvest comes the renewal of the cycle with the planting of new seed. Thus the rituals of the life cycle often parallel those of the agricultural cycle. Conceptually they are part of the same process.

Headhunting was once a prominent feature of the social life of many of the peoples of the region. Although this form of limited warfare was given various cultural interpretations, headhunting was frequently linked in rituals to the general cycle of death and renewal. In this sense, headhunting was a form of "harvest" in which particular individuals were able to achieve great reknown.

The Celebration of Spiritual Differentiation. In the traditional religions of the region, there is no presumption of identity attached to any of the manifestations of life. Creation produced myriad forms of being and the processes of life that began in the past continue to the present. Generally, not even humankind is credited with a single origin or source of being. The result is an essential openness to life, a basic acceptance of life's many manifestations, and ultimately a celebration of spiritual differentiation.

The tendency in most traditional religions is to personalize whatever may be considered a manifestation of life. Included among such manifestations are the heavenly spheres—the sun, moon, and stars; the forces of nature—thunder, lightning, or great winds; points of geographical prominence—high mountain peaks, volcanic craters, waterfalls, caves, or old trees; places endowed with unusual significance as the result of past occurrences—sites of abandoned settlement, a former meeting place of some spirit, or the point of a past, powerful dream; and simpler iconic representations of life—ancient ancestral possessions, royal regalia, amulets, and other objects of specially conceived potency. Veneration for all such objects is accorded to the potency that the objects are considered to possess, but only as long as this potency is evident. Confrontation with any new source of unknown power requires a kind of ritual empiricism to discover precisely what is that power's appropriate due.

In social terms, these spiritual premises are conducive to notions of precedence and hierarchy. No society in the region is without some form of social differentiation. Even in the simplest of tribal societies the birth order of the children of the same parents becomes a means for such distinctions. In many societies—perhaps a majority of the societies of the region—forms and degrees of differentiation are endowed with considerable importance. The populations of many of these societies regard themselves as derived of different ancestral origins or even of different classes of creation. Thus, for example, the ranked class structures of the Ngaju of Kalimantan, of the Bugis of south Sulawesi, or of the peoples of Sumba or Tanimbar in eastern Indonesia are all predicated on distinct creations.

Equally, the same spiritual premises may promote notions of achievement. A recurrent image of life involves the metaphor of the "journey of achievement." Myths recount the founding journeys of the ancestors, folk tales extol the attainments of heroic journeys, and dreams and séances can take the form of a spiritual journey. Furthermore, many societies encourage a period of journeying in early adulthood as a means of gaining knowledge, wealth, fame, and experience.

Literally and spiritually, individuals are distinguished by their journeys. Rank, prowess, and the attainment of wealth can be taken as evident signs of individual enhancement in a life's odyssey, and this enhancement may be celebrated through major rituals, both in life and after death. In many traditional religions, mortuary rituals and the feasting that generally accompanies them are the primary indicators of a person's social and spiritual position and are intended to translate this position into a similarly enhanced position in the afterlife. These rituals invariably invoke a journey, often described as the sailing of the ship of the dead, and by these rituals the living act to accord the deceased a proper spiritual position. (Often heaven or the underworld are considered to have many layers through which the soul of the dead wanders to find its proper abode.)

In return for the performance of the mortuary ritual, the deceased ancestor becomes capable of returning benefits to the living. In ancient Java, these ideas were given an Indic interpretation in the mortuary elevation of rulers to identification with Śiva or the Buddha. Similar ideas still underlie major temple rituals on Bali, megalithic tomb building among the Sumbanese, the spectacular mortuary ceremonies and cliff burial of the Saʾdan Toraja, or the simple, less obtrusive rituals of rock and tree elsewhere in the archipelago.

Today throughout insular Southeast Asia, the basic premises of traditional religions are under challenge from religions such as Islam and Christianity that preach transcendence in place of the immanence of life and assert spiritual equality rather than celebrate spiritual differentiation. These religions are also under challenge from modernizing national governments that insist upon bureaucratic homogeneity and positive rationalism. Yet despite present pressures, traditional ways of thinking and acting continue to show remarkable resilience and continuity with the past.

See Also Balinese Religion; Batak Religion; Bornean Religions; Buddhism, article on Buddhism in Southeast Asia; Bugis Religion; Drama, article on Javanese Wayang; Islam, article on Islam in Southeast Asia; Javanese Religion; Megalithic Religion, article on Historical Cultures; Melanesian Religions, overview article; Toraja Religion.

Bibliography

A useful starting point for the study of Southeast Asian religions is Waldemar Stöhr and Piet Zoetmulder's *Die Religionen Indonesiens* (Stuttgart, 1965). A French translation of this volume is available: *Les religions d'Indonésie* (Paris, 1968). Stöhr examines various specific traits of the tribal religions of Indonesia and the Philippines on a regional basis, while Zoetmulder provides a succinct introduction to Hinduism, Buddhism, and Islam in Indonesia, together with an excellent discussion of the Balinese religion. Stöhr has since extended his general examination in *Die Altindonesischen Religionen* (Leiden, 1976). Both volumes have extensive and useful bibliographies. The general study of animism by the Dutch missionary-ethnographer A. C. Kruijt, *Het animisme in den Indischen archipel* (The Hague, 1906), is of historic interest as is the study of the Batak religion by the German missionary Johannes G. Warneck, *Die Religion der Batak* (Leipzig, 1909). Three studies of particular traditional religions by Leiden-trained anthropologists emphasizing features of complementary duality are Richard Erskine Downs's *The Religion of the Bare'e-Speaking Toradja of Central Celebes* (The Hague, 1956), Hans Schärer's *Ngaju Religion,* translated by Rodney Needham (1946; reprint, The Hague, 1963), and Peter Suzuki's *The Religious System and Culture of Nias, Indonesia* (The Hague, 1959). Roy F. Barton has provided considerable documentation on the Ifugao, including a study of their religion, *The Religion of the Ifugaos* (Menasha, 1946); Clifford Geertz has contributed enormously to the study of Java, particularly with an influential book, *The Religion of Java* (Glencoe, Ill., 1960). Our understanding of traditional religions has also been greatly enhanced by a series of recent ethnographies: Erik Jensen's *The Iban and Their Religion* (Oxford, 1974), Michelle Z. Rosaldo's *Knowledge and Passion* (Cambridge, 1980), Gregory L. Forth's *Rindi* (The Hague, 1981), and Peter Metcalf's *A Borneo Journey into Death* (Philadelphia, 1982), as well as by a number of as yet unpublished Ph.D. dissertations: Elizabeth Gilbert Traube's "Ritual Exchange among the Mambai of East Timor" (Harvard University, 1977), Robert William Hefner's "Identity and Cultural Reproduction among the Tengger-Javanese," (University of Michigan, 1982), E. D. Lewis's "Tana Wai Brama" (Australian National University, 1982), and Janet Alison Hoskins's "Spirit Worship and Feasting in Kodi, West Sumba" (Harvard University, 1984).

New Sources

Gibson, Thomas. *Sacrifice and Sharing in the Philippine Highlands: Religion and Society among the Buid of Mindoro.* London and Dover, N.H., 1986.

Kipp, Rita Smith, and Susan Rodgers, eds. *Indonesian Religions in Transition.* Tucson, 1987.

McAmis, Robert Day. *Malay Muslims: The History and Challenge of Resurgent Islam in Southeast Asia.* Grand Rapids, Mich., 2002.

Schiller, Anne Louise. *Small Sacrifices: Religious Change and Cultural Identity among the Ngaju of Indonesia.* New York, 1997.

Wessing, Robert, and Roy E. Jordaan. "Death at the Building Site: Construction Sacrifice in Southeast Asia." *History of Religions* 37 (1997): 101–121.

James J. Fox (1987)
Revised Bibliography

SOUTHEAST ASIAN RELIGIONS: NEW RELIGIOUS MOVEMENTS IN INSULAR CULTURES

Uprisings with religious content have occurred throughout insular Southeast Asian history, but religious movements show a distinctive focus. They are not anarchic protests but organized efforts, of national or international scope, to achieve reforms or some other positive objective. Such movements are apparent especially since the beginning of this century. By limiting the discussion to such movements, we can at least begin to summarize a complicated fabric of history in which local processes are as varied as they are fascinating. For the sake of simplicity, it is convenient to group the myriad insular Southeast Asian religious movements under the three streams of religious tradition from which they draw, in part, their inspiration: Buddhism and Hinduism, Islam, and Christianity. These are discussed with reference to the major island or peninsular areas of Southeast Asia: Indonesia, Singapore, Malaysia, and the Philippines.

Hindu-Buddhist Movements. The first important twentieth-century Hindu-Buddhist movement was Budi Utomo ("high endeavor") founded in 1908 by three students from the colonial Netherlands Indies medical school (STOVIA). The movement gained early adherents in other colonial technical schools, those for veterinarians and engineers, suggesting that the Western technical training was leaving the native students without any cultural or religious grounding, and that such grounding is what they sought in movements like Budi Utomo. Budi Utomo hoped to revitalize the deeply cherished Hindu-Buddhist-Javanist core of the Indonesian identity, so that a meaningful and respectable alternative could be found to the values offered by the West. Looking to India's Rabindranath Tagore and Mohandas Gandhi as inspirations in the revival of these traditions, Budi Utomo was controlled by the aristocracy and intelligentsia and never gained a broad popular following, although it had amassed some ten thousand members within a year of its founding.

Another movement, Taman Siswa ("garden of learning"), has a cultural grounding similar to that of Budi Utomo, but, unlike the earlier movement, it emphasized education. Taman Siswa was founded by Suwardi Surjaningrat, later known as Ki Hadjar Dewantara ("teacher of the gods").

Inspired by Tagore as well as such critics of Western education as Maria Montessori, Dewantara founded schools designed to restore lost traditions and identities by combining Western and Javanist-Hindu-Buddhist values. Taman Siswa schools taught the Javanese arts to encourage the child to express its inner identity, and they encouraged a family like school community in which students and teachers were mutually involved as "brothers in learning." By 1940, Dewantara had succeeded in building some 250 schools throughout the islands, some of which survive today.

A third major Hindu-Buddhist movement is really many movements and cannot be reduced to any single date of founding. These are known as *kebatinan*, from the Javanese word (of Arabic origin) *batin*, meaning "inner." Something in the range of one thousand different *kebatinan* sects now flourish, primarily on Java, most founded since the beginning of the twentieth century but rooted in practices and beliefs that go back to the beginnings of the Javanese Hindu-Buddhist civilizations in the eighth century CE.

The aim of Javanese *kebatinan* is to mute the crude feelings and perceptions of the material world in order to experience the underlying reality that is simultaneously god, self, and cosmos. The techniques are ascetic practice (abstinence from food, sleep, or sex), philosophical and psychological speculation, and meditation. Guidance in *kebatinan* meetings is provided by a teacher who is believed to possess charismatic and sacral qualities. The objective is not only to reach ultimate truth but also to balance and unify the self and, in this way, the wider society and world. Some *kebatinan* movements, such as Subud, have established branches in the West, while others, such as Sumarah, have attracted Westerners to Java; but, on the whole, *kebatinan* movements remain a quintessentially Javanese phenomenon.

While Budi Utomo, Taman Siswa, and *kebatinan* are primarily Javanese movements, Balinese Hinduism has been an important stimulus for a revival of Hindu traditions as an organized movement spreading through Java as well as Bali. Associated with this Neo-Hinduism is a Neo-Buddhism that claims as a root the only surviving folk-Buddhist population, the Tengger, who live near Mount Bromo on Java. The Indonesian Buddhist Association claims to have built ninety monasteries and acquired fifteen million adherents since 1965 (when, following the massacre of an estimated half-million so-called Communists, all Indonesians were required to declare some explicit religion or risk being branded atheistic and, therefore, Communist). These revivals, which hold massive celebrations at such revered monuments as Lara Janggrang and Borobudur, combine indigenous Bali-Java traditions with Hindu-Buddhism.

MUSLIM MOVEMENTS. Where the Hindu-Buddhist movements of insular Southeast Asia have been confined primarily to Java and Bali, the Muslim movements have ranged more widely: throughout the three thousand miles of Indonesian islands and into Singapore, Malaysia, and the southern Philippines. The stimulus for these movements was the opening in 1870 of the Suez Canal and associated increase in steamship travel, which encouraged great numbers of Southeast Asian Muslims, many of whom remained in the Near East for study, to make the pilgrimage to Mecca. By the beginning of the twentieth century, several Malay, Indonesian, Arab, and Indian citizens of insular Southeast Asia had come under the influence of the proponent of Islamic modernism, Muhammad Abduh of Cairo's al-Azhar center of learning. Returning to Singapore or other ports of embarkation and disembarkation to the Near East, these students founded schools, journals, and associations that spread through the islands and were known as the Kaum Muda ("new faction") of Southeast Asian Islam.

Pressing for a return to the fundamental truths of text and tradition, the Qurʾān and the *ḥadīth*, while rejecting the authority of teachers, scholars, and the ornate speculations of medieval Islam, modernists extolled the method of *itjihād*: analysis of the original Arabic scriptures in order to read for oneself the word of God. Paradoxically, the return to scripture stimulated an advance to modernity, at least in certain respects. Folk practices that were not in the text were excised, while proper reading was held to demonstrate an Islamic basis for modern economics, science, medicine, and law. In what they themselves termed a "reformation" *(reformasi)*, the devout Muslim could rediscover a pure identity and inspiration while equipping himself for the challenges of modernity.

Gaining impetus first in Singapore, where returning scholars founded such still-existing schools as Alsagoff, the Kaum Muda encountered resistance in Malaya but spread rapidly throughout the islands of Indonesia. Of the many Indonesian organizations standing for the Kaum Muda viewpoint, the most successful is the Muḥammadīyah, founded in 1912 by Kiai H. A. Dahlan, in the court city of Jogjakarta, Java. Muḥammadīyah worked not only to purify Islamic practice to accord with Qurʾān ic teaching but also in education and welfare, building a large system of schools as well as clinics, orphanages, and hospitals. Muḥammadīyah has been notable, too, in the strength of its women's movement, Aisjajah. Having survived periods of turmoil and repression, Muḥammadīyah now boasts some six million members.

In reaction to Kaum Muda, the so-called Kaum Tua ("old faction") took steps to cement its cherished traditions, which the reformers threatened to sweep away. In Malaya, where Islam was identified with the state, the old could be buttressed simply by stiffening the established hierarchy of Islamic officialdom. In Indonesia, lacking such an establishment, reaction took the form of a counterreformation. In 1926, Indonesian traditionalists founded the Nahdatul Ulama ("union of Muslim teachers") to withstand the threat of reformism. Ruled by a dynasty centered around a famous religious school in East Java, Nahdatul Ulama has outstripped Muḥammadīyah in gaining support from the rural masses. While Nahdatul Ulama's membership is larger, its organization is looser, and this organization has not equalled Muḥammadīyah in educational and welfare activities.

CHRISTIAN MOVEMENTS. Although significant Christian populations are found in Indonesia—especially among the

Batak, the Amboinese, the Toraja, and the Minahas—and among the Chinese throughout insular Southeast Asia, the only Christian nation is the Philippines. More than 80 percent of the Philippine population is Roman Catholic but an estimated 350 distinct Christian bodies exist there today, many of which could be termed "movements." Most significant, perhaps, is the Iglesia Filipina Independiente (IFI, or Philippine Independent Church). The foundations for this offshoot of the Roman Catholic church were laid during the Philippine revolt against Spain in 1896, but the IFI was officially founded in 1902 by Gregorio Aglipay, who became its first archbishop. When the Spanish were defeated, the Filipino priests of the IFI took over parishes held by the friars and achieved a membership of 1.5 million, or 25 percent of the Christian population. Highly nationalistic, the IFI has been known to raise the Philippine flag at the time of the consecration of the Host in the Mass.

At one time the IFI canonized José Rizal, the Filipino novelist and nationalist martyr, and other movements, too, deify Rizal as a Christ of the Malays. An example is Iglesia in Cristo, founded in 1914 by Feix Manalo and now a highly organized movement based on a special method of meditation. Another Rizalist group, Lapiang Malaya, attacked the city of Manila in 1967. Believing themselves immune to bullets, they provoked the police and military into violent reaction and thirty-three of them died. Such movements fuse Christian inspiration with nativism, nationalism, and millenarianism, often opposed to westernization, modernization, and oppression.

Religious Movements and Contemporary Society in Insular Southeast Asia. At different periods and in different places, these religious movements have contributed differently. Most of them, regardless of affiliation, were inspirational catalysts in giving rise to the striving for independence and modernity that led to the more directly political nationalist movements that began in the early twentieth century and culminated in the independence of these new nations soon after World War II. Since independence, their role has varied. In Indonesia, the Muslims have generally acted as an oppositional force complementing the government, while the Hindu-Buddhist streams have either fed into the Javanist-oriented national culture and government or provided personal fulfillment outside the governmental arena.

In Malaysia, the Muslims have identified more strongly with the government, while Hindu-Buddhism has not claimed a place in the national political culture equal to that of Hindu-Buddhism in Indonesia. In the Philippines, Islam has been oppositional, entrenched in the south against Christian incursions identified with the national polity; Christianity has been identified more with governmental authority, although Christianity, too (exemplified by such movements as the Christians for National Liberation and church support of Corazon Aquino during her rise to power in 1986), has had an oppositional role. In Singapore, the Muslims have played an oppositional role in relation to the dominant government party, but in this highly modernized, formally pluralistic society, religious movements have not played a postwar role equal to that in the other insular Southeast Asian nations.

In all of these countries, religious movements were dominant sources of nationalism and creative ferment in the early twentieth century. Later, as the impetus toward independence was seized by more purely political movements, the religious movements became relatively less important. After independence was achieved, the regimes in these countries (especially the two largest, Indonesia and the Philippines) have tended to become authoritarian, while religious movements (such as the Muslim fundamentalists) have eclipsed the Communists and others as the locus of aspiration independent of the government. The beginning of the twenty-first century could parallel the beginning of the twentieth, in that the stage is set for religious movements to resume their earlier role as a reformative force independent of the central power.

See Also Buddhism, article on Buddhism in Southeast Asia; Christianity, article on Christianity in Asia; Gandhi, Mohandas; Islam, article on Islam in Southeast Asia; Tagore, Rabindranath.

Bibliography

An outstanding account of religiously grounded uprisings before the twentieth century is P. B. R. Carey's *Babad Dipanagara: An Account of the Outbreak of the Java War, 1825–1830* (Kuala Lumpur, 1981). Other excellent accounts for Java include Sartono Kartodirdjo's *The Peasants' Revolt of Banten in 1888: Its Conditions, Course and Sequel; A Case Study of Social Movements in Indonesia* (The Hague, 1966). For Sumatra, see Christine Dobbin's *Islamic Revivalism in a Changing Peasant Economy: Central Sumatra, 1784–1847* (London, 1983).

On Budi Utomo, see Bernard H. M. Vlekke's *Nusantara: A History of Indonesia*, rev. ed. (The Hague, 1959), pp. 348–391. On Taman Siswa, see Ruth T. McVey's "Taman Siswa and the Indonesian National Awakening," *Indonesia* 4 (October 1967): 128–149; on Sumarah, David Gordon Howe's "Sumarah: A Study of the Art of Living" (Ph. D. diss., University of North Carolina, 1980); on *kebatinan*, J. A. Niels Mulder's *Mysticism and Daily Life in Contemporary Java: A Cultural Analysis of Javanese Worldview and Ethics as Embodied in Kabatinan and Everyday Experience* (Amsterdam, 1975).

For Islamic reformism in Malaya and Singapore, see chapters 2 and 3 of William R. Roff's *The Origins of Malay Nationalism* (New Haven, 1967). For Indonesia, see Taufik Abdullah's *Schools and Politics: The Kaum Muda Movement in West Sumatra, 1927–1933* (Ithaca, N.Y., 1971); my *Muslim Puritans: Reformist Psychology in Southeast Asian Islam* (Berkeley, 1978); and, specifically for Muhammadiyah, see Howard M. Federspiel's "The Muhammadijah: A Study of an Orthodox Islamic Movement in Indonesia." *Indonesia* 10 (October 1970): 57–79.

A good summary of the religious situation in the Philippines can be found in David Joel Steinberg's *The Philippines: A Singular and a Plural Place* (Boulder, Colo. 1982.)

For an overview of contemporary movements, see Robert W. Hefner's (ed.) *The Politics of Multiculturalism: Pluralism and Citizenship in Malaysia, Singapore, and Indonesia* (Honolulu, 2001); Raymond L. M. Lee's and Susan E. Ackerman's *Sacred Tensions: Modernity and Religious Transformation in Malaysia* (Columbia, S.C., 1997); and Tony Day's *Fluid Iron: State Formation in Southeast Asia* (Honolulu, 2002).

JAMES L. PEACOCK (1987 AND 2005)

SOUTHERN AFRICAN RELIGIONS

This entry consists of the following articles:

SOUTHERN AFRICAN RELIGIONS: AN OVERVIEW

There is a basic similarity in religious practice, symbols, and ideas throughout southern Africa, from Uganda to the southern sea, from the east coast to Cameroon. This is the area in which Bantu languages are spoken, and there is a link, though no absolute coincidence, between language family and religious symbolism. Some of the religious symbols of Africa also occur in Europe: The divine king of the Ganda, the Bemba, the Nyakyusa, and the Zulu appeared in the Grove of Nemi in ancient Italy and in Stuart England; but there are many other symbols of more limited provenance, such as fire, symbol of lordship or authority, and blowing out water, or "spitting," a symbol of the confession of anger and the act of forgiveness and goodwill.

Religious belief in southern Africa can best be understood through its symbolism, for religion here is expressed more through drama and poetry than through dogma or theological speculation. The invisible is embodied in tangible symbols which are bent to human purposes. Hence attention must focus on the rituals celebrated.

Among any one people there are likely to be dominant symbols which recur in one ritual after another, and full understanding of them depends upon analysis of the whole ritual cycle. Examples of such symbols are the mudyi tree (with a milky latex), which among the Ndembu represents matriliny, motherhood, and womanhood, and the plantain and sweet banana—the leaves, flowers, fruit, succoring stem—which among the Nyakyusa represent male and female respectively. These symbols are as obvious to a Nyakyusa as the skirt and trousers used to differentiate gender on washroom signs are to a European or an American.

The present tense is used for observations made during the twentieth century (with some references to earlier observers); but since rapid change is going on throughout Africa and since traditional African practice exists side by side with, and interacts with, modern Christian and Islamic practice, this article should be read in conjunction with others in the encyclopedia. What is described here is but a fragment of current religious practice in southern Africa: The symbolic systems and institutions discussed here indeed still exist widely but are not the sole beliefs or practice of whole populations.

CONCEPTS OF GOD. Throughout southern Africa there is an apprehension of God as a numinous being associated with light, brightness, and sheen. God may be represented by a high mountain glittering with snow, a tree symbolizing the mountain, or a sacred grove. There is a lively belief in the survival of the dead and in their power over the living, a power closely akin to that which living senior kinsmen have over their juniors. There is a belief in medicines—material substances which can be manipulated for good or ill, healing or murder, and which include poisons put in food as well as ointments which are rubbed on the body to make a hunter's aim true, a warrior "slippery," a candidate successful in examinations, or a choir or rugby team victorious in competition. Everywhere the power of evil is feared—a power thought to be incarnate in certain persons or familiars they control, which is called witchcraft. The notion of witchcraft involves the personification of anger, hate, jealousy, envy, lust, and greed—the negative feelings which people observe in themselves and in their neighbors. All these beliefs are general, but they appear in infinite variety, modified by kinship and political structure, by economy, and by poetic imagination, and they have changed through time.

How clearly God is distinguished from the first human, or from the founding heroes of a particular lineage, also varies with place and time. Among some peoples, at least, the distinction became clearer as outside contacts extended and the known world was no longer confined within a frame of kinship. Over many centuries Hebrew, Christian, and Islamic ideas of God, with their symbolism of monotheism and of God on high, have impinged on other ideas in Africa, notably the association of the dead with the earth; in some places a process of change may be traced over the past hundred years.

Throughout southern Africa God has been remote, approached only by exceptional priests or by the "elders." The dead are regarded as alive, and it is the shades, or ancestors, the senior dead kin, who are the mediators between humanity and divinity, communicating human needs to the divine. Prayer or direct offerings to God himself rarely occur in traditional practice, but awe of God is constantly manifested, as fear of contamination, as a distancing of humanity from God, and avoidance of such emblems of sacred power as the thunderbolt, the tree struck by lightning, and the python in the grove. One does not speak readily of God, and one speaks of him not at all if he is near. Once, when this writer was at school in London, a fellow student (later a head of state in Africa) started in his seat when this writer was so rash as to discuss lightning on a day when the Lord was muttering overhead. Unusual fecundity, such as twin birth, is also of God and fearful, hence twins and their parents are isolated from the normal village community and, because of their divine connection, they function as "herds" to drive off storms.

Gabriel M. Setiloane, himself a Methodist minister, argues cogently in *The Image of God among the Sotho-Tswana* (Rotterdam, 1976) that the first missionary to the Tswana, Robert Moffat (the father-in-law of David Livingstone), misunderstood the Tswana language (into which he translated the New Testament) and hence the Tswana experience of God. But it is John V. Taylor who shows, in *The Primal Vision,* that in Africa God is both there and not there, that he is both sought and rejected. Bishop Taylor fastens upon the "significance of this ambivalence," saying that humans have been aware of the numinous and their dependence upon it but have sought to separate themselves from it.

SHADES. Among southern African peoples shades are of two categories: the dead senior kin (male and female) of each family or lineage and the founding heroes. Family shades are relevant only for their junior kin who celebrate "rituals of kinship"; founding heroes (male or female) have relevance for political units, that is, chiefdoms, groups of chiefdoms, or regions which honor a hero and his or her descendants in "communal rituals." The ancestors of a ruling lineage, where one exists, commonly claim descent from the founding hero; or the hero may be thought of as a benefactor or prophet who left no descendants but who is celebrated in some grove or cave by a lineage or priests. The ancestors of a chief, it is believed, retain power over the country they once ruled, so in addition to rituals for founding heroes there may be a series of offerings to past chiefs.

Like God, the shades are associated with brightness, light, radiance, and whiteness. Among the Zulu and Xhosa a gray-leafed helichrysum, whose leaves and pale gold flowers both reflect light, is linked with the shades; in Pondoland "the medicine of the home" is a small, yellow-flowered senecio which gleams in the veld. The beads offered to shades and worn by a diviner, novice, or pregnant bride are white, and when an animal is slaughtered and offered to the shades, the officiants wipe their hands in the chyme, a strong bleaching agent. But again, as with God, contact with the shades is seen to be somehow contaminating. A shade must be "pushed away a little"; it must be kept from continually "brooding" over humans as a hen broods over its chicks. The dead must be separated from the living and then "brought home," that is, transformed.

Although they are numinous, the shades are held in far less awe than is God himself. To many Africans the shades are constantly about the homestead, evident in a tiny spiral of dust blowing across the yard or through the banana grove, or in the rustling of banana leaves; thought to be sheltering near the byre or in the shade of a tree, or sipping beer left overnight at the back of the great house. Their presence is so real in Pondoland that (into the twentieth century) a wife of the homestead carefully avoids the yard and the byre where men sit, even at night, lest the shades be there, and as she walks through a river associated with her husband's clan she lets her skirts trail in the water, for to tuck up her skirts would insult his shades.

The living and the dead are so closely associated in southern Africa that it is common for a man's heir (a brother, son, or sister's son) and a woman's heir (a sister, daughter, or brother's daughter) to take the property, the name, the social position, and the responsibilities of the deceased. Hence one may be told that the holder of some office—a priest, chief, king, or senior kinsman—is "Mswati the third" (or tenth, as the case may be). A founding hero frequently has a living representative in this sense, a "divine king," that is, a ruler or priest on whose health and virility the health and fertility of men, cattle, and land are thought to depend. Even into the twentieth century, a divine king who was ailing or feeble would be smothered—he must "die for the people"—and then be replaced.

Founding heroes typically are associated with a bed of reeds, from which the first man is said to have sprung; with a river source along the watershed between the Zambezi and Kongo rivers; with a pool in one of the rushing rivers of the south; with a hole in the ground (from which men and cattle emerged) on the dry edge of the Kalahari Desert; or with a grove of trees. Like family shades, heroes are of the earth and water, not of the sky. The place of celebration has moved as groups of kinsmen have moved, as chiefs have been installed and later buried, and as trees planted as boundary marks or on graves have spread into thickets.

RITUAL LIFE. Communal rituals are of various sorts, including offerings to the founding heroes, their living representatives, and chiefly descendants. Such offerings are celebrated by the leading men of the region, chiefdom, or village. The common people know little of the details; they are aware only that a celebration has taken place.

But there is also a type of purification ritual that concerns everyone. Sometimes it is linked to a celebration of first fruits; at other times it is accompanied by a military review. At the break of the rains in tropical Africa, or at the summer solstice farther south, and in any general emergency such as plague or war, the people may be called upon to purify themselves, to sweep the homesteads, throw out the old ash from hearths, and rekindle new fire. Among at least some peoples everyone is expected to "speak out," that is, to confess anger and grudges held against neighbors and kin, or against fellow priests and leading men. It is a spring-cleaning of hearts and minds as well as homesteads.

In the Swazi kingdom today—as formerly in other Nguni kingdoms and chiefdoms on the southeastern coast of Africa—all the men of the country, and many women also, gather at the time of the summer solstice to celebrate the first fruits and strengthen their king, while regiments dance and demonstrate their loyalty. The Zulu form of this ritual was powerfully interpreted by Max Gluckman (1954) as a "ritual of rebellion," but it now seems that this early analysis was based on a mistranslation. According to Harriet Ngubane (1977), a Zulu anthropologist, the key phrase used in the ritual expresses a rejection of pollution: "What the king breaks to pieces and tramples upon is a gourd that symbolizes the evil of the past year." This exactly parallels rituals farther north for "cleansing the country" in which the population of entire regions "throw out the rubbish," especially ashes from all the hearths, and distribute newly kindled fire. The Ngonde (Malawi) chant: "Let us dance, let us fight that the homesteads may be peaceful. . . . Let us throw out the ashes that death may leave the homesteads and they be at peace." Close analysis shows that such rituals symbolically cast out the anger in people's hearts. The Taita of Kenya celebrate a similar rite of casting out anger, as Grace Harris (1978) has shown.

These cleansing rites speak repeatedly of ridding the people of "the dirt" of the past year. The similarity to ancient Hebrew rituals is obvious, although published reports from southern Africa make no mention of any symbolism having to do with driving out a scapegoat. Rather, the symbols which recur here are those of heat and coolness. Heat is associated with pollution, which in turn is closely associated with anger and sexual activity; coolness is associated with rain, tranquility, and purification. These symbols are familiar to all Sotho-Tswana-speaking peoples and to others also.

Throughout southern Africa communal rituals have to do with rain, especially the dramatic "break of the rains," so eagerly awaited after the dry season. Local rituals celebrate seedtime and harvest; the firing of pasture to destroy unpalatable grass and bush which harbor tsetse flies; game drives or a fishing battue; murrain or plague; war and peace; the coronation of a chief and/or the handing over of power from one generation to the next. Details of such celebrations vary both with economy and with political structure. Regional rituals may involve the distribution of once-scarce goods, such as salt and iron tools, which in former times were brought to the shrine from beyond the boundaries of the political unit. The priests who brought the goods were sacred people: Among the Nyakyusa these priests traveled in safety, announcing their status by drumbeat. Other rituals may be connected with the growth of chiefdoms. J. Matthew Schoffeleers has written about the spread of the Mbona cult with the development of Mang'anga chiefdoms in Malawi.

KINSHIP RITUALS. Unless they concern a royal family, the rituals of kinship have no political overtones. They are celebrated on the great occasions of a person's life: at birth and death, at maturity and marriage. In southern Africa each family or lineage directs its celebrations to its own dead senior kinsmen, who are not sharply distinguished from living seniors. The living may indeed be referred to by the term for a shade as they grow old. In 1931 in Pondoland this writer heard the word *itongo* ("a shade") used in reference to an elderly father's living sister. Living as well as dead seniors are thought to bring sickness, sterility, and other misfortunes—even failure to secure a job or a residence pass—on insolent, quarrelsome, or neglectful juniors.

Family rituals vary with the economy, for the place of the shrine and the form of the offering depend upon the staple foods. Among a pastoral people the altar is the byre, the offering milk or a slaughtered animal. If the people cultivate, beer is added. Among banana-eating peoples the altar is set in a plantain grove, at the base of a succoring stem which represents the patrilineage; among hunting peoples it may be a tree or branch on which are placed trophies of the chase. To the Lele, who live on the southern edge of the equatorial forest belt, the forest is holy and is associated with men; the grassland, where villages are built, has no prestige and is associated with women. Among other peoples the cleavage is between the open pastureland or bush (the veld) and the village; or, within the village itself, between the byre and its gateway-where prayer and offerings are made and men gather—and the great hut occupied by the senior woman of the homestead. But everywhere the hearth and house, especially the doorway of the house, are sacred also, for among some peoples explicitly, and probably for all implicitly, the house represents the mother, the hearth stands for the marriage, and the doorway is the passage through which children are born. Taboos surrounding the hearth, the fire, and the whole reproductive process may be seen as an expression of the holiness of normal fertility and procreation, processes which are thought to be controlled by the shades.

Offerings to the shades consist of staple foods, especially choice foods such as a tender cut of beef eaten by the one on whose behalf prayer is made (the same cut from the right foreleg is used by peoples from Tanzania to the southern coast of Africa); a libation of fermented milk or beer; a sprinkling of flour or porridge; seeds of pulses, cucurbits, and grains. A strongly pastoral people will cling to the symbolism of slaughtering an animal—shedding blood—even when they live in a city. White goats may yet be seen grazing on the outskirts of the African quarters of Cape Town, or one may see them being led along a country road or wandering about on some modern farm where African laborers are employed. They are there to be used as offerings at times of birth or death, sickness or initiation, when meat from the butcher will not suffice; at such times informed authority turns a blind eye. The beer poured out may be made of sorghum, millet, bananas, bamboo, or even maize or cassava, which reached the coasts of Africa only in the sixteenth century and parts of the interior only in the nineteenth century.

Whatever the material used, the intention of the offering is the same: The shades are called to feast, and what is offered is a communion meal for living and dead kinsmen. If an ox has been slaughtered or much beer brewed, friends and neighbors will be asked to gather with the kinsmen, but they do not share in the sacred portions set aside for kin, who first eat and drink in a place set slightly apart from the main gathering. At an offering to the shades it is essential that kinsmen be present—the range of kin summoned depending upon the gravity of the occasion—and that they be loving and charitable to one another. Any quarrels must be admitted and resolved. This writer has heard the officiant at such a ritual urging all the kinsmen present to "drink up and speak out." Sometimes a funeral feast, or a feast celebrating the return of a prodigal son to his father, may seem like a cursing match as one after another participant admits "anger in the heart," a grudge against kinsmen. This writer heard individual women complain that they had not been received with due respect by a brother's wife when they visited and the brother's wife reply that her sister-in-law had been seen picking and stealing, taking green food from the garden as she passed through, and so forth. Unspoken anger, festering in the heart, is thought both to be the root of witchcraft and to invalidate an offering to the shades, for quarreling between kinsmen infuriates the shades.

When an offering is made, an officiant, usually the senior man of the lineage, or occasionally a dead father's sister or a grandmother of the homestead, addresses the shades, calling them by name, explaining why the offering has been made—that is, what is troubling the homestead—and requesting help. The calling of ancestors by name is in itself a form of praise, and the manner of speech is that used in the presence of a senior kinsman, or (as among the Nguni) that used to honor a chief. Prayer and praise are here barely distinguishable.

The occasions of family rituals are constant throughout the area: death and birth, especially abnormal birth such as that of twins; maturity, whether physically or socially defined; marriage; misfortune and serious illness; reconciliation after a quarrel; and the first fruits that the family celebrates after the national or regional ritual. Thanksgiving rituals also occur, particularly after escape from danger in war or hunting, or on the return home of a migrant laborer or a person released from imprisonment; and there are rituals invoking blessing for an important new tool such as a plough, but these are less general than the rituals of life crises. Everywhere the death rituals persist through time and are adapted to the new economy. In the south funeral parlors with facilities for keeping a corpse exist even in some country districts, and funerals are delayed until close kin, scattered at work centers, can gather. Sometimes the corpse of a town worker who has not visited the country for years is brought "home" to the country to be buried. Great numbers of people come to mourn, and, relative to the family's earnings, enormous sums are spent on traveling, funeral expenses, and food for guests. Many guests bring a contribution of money, but even so the family may be crippled financially. Whether a man has been buried in a Johannesburg township or a remote village, as of 1982 family status still depended on lavish expenditure just as it did among the Nyakyusa in 1935, when a hundred cattle might be slaughtered on the death of a rich chief.

Although funerals have been adapted to the new economy, they include certain traditional rites, notably a washing and purification rite after the burial and a lifting of mourning after about a year. Among the Nguni peoples of the southeast coast a commemoration dinner may replace the rite of "bringing home" the shade and implies an awareness of the continuing existence of the dead which is much greater than that experienced by many contemporary Europeans and Americans. Setiloane describes the vitality of such rites in Sotho-Tswana families of professing Christians.

All the kinship rituals, but especially funerals, are an affirmation of kinship and the unity of the extended family, and the efficacy of the ritual depends upon the presence, in love and charity, of a network of kin. Exactly who is involved varies both with the people—be they Ndembu, Bemba, Zulu, or Sotho—and with the occasion. The celebrations are a strong conservative force, for the health and well-being of the whole kinship group is thought to depend on "following the customs of the ancestors" in observing the ritual. This is evident even in a city.

Maturity rituals have many aspects; the extent to which any one aspect is stressed varies from one society to another. This article has classed maturity rituals as religious, since they are explicitly concerned with fertility, which in turn is controlled by the shades; often they involve an offering and invocation to the shades, whose blessings are sought. Frequently, perhaps always, there is a symbolic death, a period of seclusion when the novice must observe taboos associated with the world of the dead, which is followed by a rebirth after which he or she returns to ordinary life. The rituals are viewed as a proper prelude to, if not a condition of, marriage and procreation. Rituals of maturity for boys often (but not invariably) involve circumcision: Those for girls may or may not involve clitoridectomy or some lesser operation.

Circumcision is most often celebrated for a group, and those who have endured this rite together share a bond for life. The boys' group may become a unit in the army, and in areas where the political structure is based on age, its members may graduate together as elders holding legal and administrative office, and finally, as old men, share ritual functions. Where there are chiefs, a royal youth is sought to lead each circumcision group, and those circumcised with him become his closest followers. The circumcision school draws a youth out of the immediate network of kin and establishes links with scattered contemporaries and political authority, links sometimes expressed in an esoteric language known only to those initiated.

Girls' initiation, on the other hand, is most often an individual celebration at the first menstruation, and wider links with contemporaries or political authority are not treated as important. But among a few peoples, notably the Sotho-Tswana and the neighboring Venda in precolonial times, girls' initiation was a group affair with political implications; a women's regiment was linked to a men's regiment, and, like its male counterpart, it might be called out for public service.

Maturity rituals are everywhere concerned with inculcating respect for authority: respect for seniors, shades, chiefs, and respect of a wife for her husband. A man must learn to keep secrets and never reveal the affairs of his chief or the secrets of the lodge. A woman likewise must learn to hold her tongue; she must not create conflict through gossip or reveal the affairs of her husband. Often there are taboo words and riddles with a set answer, knowledge of which are taken as proof of initiation. In *Chisungu* Audrey I. Richards (1956) admirably demonstrates the use of songs, mimes, designs, and models to inculcate in a Bemba girl the proper behavior of a wife. Always the rituals instruct the novice in the behavior required of an adult man or woman, and a transformation from childish behavior to responsible behavior is expected.

The rituals assert the authority of a senior generation over a junior: The initiated secure the young novice's submission through the pain of an operation, beating, scolding, and threats, or by playing upon the novice's fear of the unseen and longing to become an honored and fertile man or woman. The ritual creates a fraternity or sorority of those who have undergone the ordeal: Those who have not undergone it are outsiders, but all who have endured are free to participate in the admonition of their juniors. A determination to use circumcision rites to bolster civil authority was made explicit in October 1981 when the Ciskei, later an "independent state" on the border of the Republic of South Africa, passed legislation empowering a chief to compel a young man to be circumcised, on the ground that "it is well known that circumcision causes irresponsible youths to behave in a responsible manner." This happened at a time when opposition by school boys and students to Ciskeian political authority was intense.

Why maturity rituals have survived among some peoples but not others, or for one sex but not the other, in fast-changing societies can only be demonstrated by analyzing historical events in particular areas. What is certain is that in some areas changes in practice have occurred since the eighteenth century, rites spreading or being abandoned; but there is also eyewitness evidence from survivors of wrecks on the southeastern coast of Africa which suggests minimal change in circumcision rites among Xhosa and Thembu peoples over three centuries.

CULTS OF AFFLICTION, SPIRIT POSSESSION, AND DIVINATION. Besides the cycle of rituals associated with families and the birth, maturity, and death of individuals, and the cycle celebrated for a chiefdom or region, there is a cycle of rituals for those individuals "called" by their shades to become diviners, or for sufferers whose sickness has been relieved by what Victor Turner has called a "ritual of affliction." Cults or guilds are formed of those who have suffered a particular travail and been cured by a particular ritual. Their experience entitles them to participate in any celebration for a sufferer of the same category. Rituals for diviners who have been called (as opposed to herbalists who learn certain medicines) and rituals of affliction are much less widespread than those for birth, maturity, and death, or those for a chiefdom or region. They are not contained within the frame of kinship or locality and seem to have proliferated with trade and travel, but of that process not much is yet known. What is certain is that among some isolated peoples (such as the Nyakyusa) these rituals do not occur at all, and among peoples with a long tradition of distant trade, such as the Shona and Tsonga, possession is often interpreted as being the work of an outsider, not that of a family shade. This phenomenon has appeared recently among the Zulu, as Harriet Ngubane (1977) has shown, and, according to John Beattie (1969), it exists among the Nyoro of Uganda as well.

Diviners are thought to be in a peculiarly close relationship with their shades, who reveal themselves in dreams and trances. Communication with the shades is fostered by cleansing and purging, observance of taboos (including sexual abstinence), fasting, isolation in the bush, offerings to the shades, and dancing to clapping or drums. The emotion is often intense when, with an insistent beat of clapping provided by a packed crowd, a novice speaks of what she has seen in dreams. In Western society the closest analogue to the diviner in this respect is the medium, and among some peoples—notably the Shona of Zimbabwe—a state of trance undoubtedly occurs. Even though it may be a stranger spirit who possesses the medium, she remains in close contact with her family shades.

Most mediums deal with the domestic problems and health of clients who come to consult them. Occasionally, however, a medium may influence public events, as did Nongqause, the Xhosa girl who in 1856 urged all Xhosa on the eastern frontier of the Cape of Good Hope to kill their cattle and destroy their grain, prophesying that when they did so the dead would rise up and sweep the whites into the sea, or the Shona medium who in 1898 urged resistance against whites in what is now Zimbabwe. During the colonial period old prophecies of the coming of whites were repeatedly recorded, and these may be seen partly as a reconciliation of old and new. To at least some Nyakyusa Christians, such prophecies were evidence of the reality—"the truth"—of ancient institutions, the prescience of past prophets. Had not the prophecy been fulfilled?

WITCHCRAFT. In southern African belief, evil does not come from the shades, who are essentially good. They discipline erring descendants, sending sickness or sterility if they have been starved (for in a real sense the shades partake of the communion meal—that is, the beer and flesh—and are satisfied by it) or neglected, not informed of a marriage, or affronted by the quarrels of their juniors. But they are concerned about the welfare of their children and are held to be the source of blessing. Rather, evil comes from another source: witchcraft. It is thought to be embodied in a serpent—a "python in the belly" (Nyakyusa), a "snake of the women" (Pondo); or it takes the form of a baboon, or a fabulous hairy being with exaggerated sexual organs (Xhosa), and so forth. Such creatures are as real in imagination as was the pitchfork-wielding Devil to the medieval European, and like him they walk the earth seeking those whom they may devour. The witch familiars (and witchcraft generally) personify the evil recognized as existing in all humans, specifically, anger, hatred, jealousy, envy, lust, greed. Even sloth appears, in the belief that certain evil people have raised others from the dead to work their fields for them.

The form of witch belief varies with the social structure, as does the relationship of victim and accused, for the points of friction in a society vary with the form of residence and economic cooperation (i.e., who lives and works together), the occasions of competition, and the location of authority. Injury is thought to come from those with whom one has quarreled: a co-wife, mother-in-law, half sibling, fellow employee, rival claimant for inheritance, affine claiming marriage cattle, litigant in court against whom judgment has been given, or fellow priest. In some societies it is mostly women, poor men, and juniors who are accused; but in societies where egalitarian values are stressed the rich man is suspect, as is the successful grower of cash crops who is thought to have attracted the fertility of his neighbors' fields to his own. The one legitimately greater than the commoner (i.e., the chief) may covet the cattle of a wealthy stock owner, who is then accused of some wrongdoing—or so outsiders have thought.

Again and again during the colonial period, "witch-finding" movements arose when some prophet would call on his people to reject evil, to purge themselves of witchcraft and medicines used for sorcery. Over large regions people in fact complied, bringing out horns of medicines or other objects to throw publicly on a pyre and implicitly or explicitly admitting evil in themselves and expressing goodwill to all. The bamucapi movement which swept through what are now Zambia, Malawi, and parts of Zimbabwe and Tanzania in 1934 was followed by a somewhat similar movement in much the same area (but with greatest influence in what is now Tanzania) between 1956 and 1964. Long before these movements arose, the Xhosa of the eastern Cape frontier had repeatedly been urged to purify themselves and reject witchcraft. In 1856 Nongqause, a sixteen-year-old medium, reported to the noted diviner Mhlakaza, her father's brother, that the shades had told her they would come to the rescue of their Xhosa descendants in their long war with whites over land on the eastern frontier, on condition that the living purify themselves and kill all their cattle. In the famine that ensued, twenty thousand people died. There is no evidence that such revivalist movements began in the colonial period: They may well have happened periodically before that, although certain characteristics of movements in colonial times, notably millennialism, were related to Christian missionary teaching.

People are known to confess to the practice of witchcraft, usually following an accusation and pressure to confess. One young mother in Pondoland explained to this writer that her baby had at first refused to nurse because she had had a witch-lover (who appeared in the form of a young man she named). The mother had then confessed, complying with the instructions of the midwives and giving her account precisely in terms of current beliefs; she was now being cleansed, and the baby was nursing all right. In some areas confessions have at times been extracted forcibly (through a poison ordeal or torture), since the recovery of the victim is held to depend upon the witch's confession and subsequent expression of goodwill toward the victim.

Ritual, Order, and the Religious Experience. Analysis of ritual is important in any study of religion, for ritual enshrines the dogma and values of participants. There is always a gap between the values expressed and everyday practice, but ideals and ideas of ultimate reality are embodied in ritual action. In southern Africa there is constant emphasis on fertility—of human beings, stock, and fields; on health; on goodwill between kinsmen and neighbors; on amity among the ruling men of the region; on respect of juniors for seniors and the responsibility of seniors toward their dependents; on the continuation of life after death.

Order exists in the universe, and the natural and social orders are felt to be interrelated: As in King Lear, disharmony in the world of humans is reflected both in the world of physical elements and in the tempest within a person's mind—in madness. If the divine king breaks a taboo, drought or flood may follow; if the ritual for a widow or a nubile girl is neglected, she may become distraught. Right order is expressed in traditional custom, and in their essence, rituals—whether positive action or negative avoidance—express the sacredness both of physiological processes, that is, menstruation, coition, parturition, and death, and of the approved relationships of men and women, old and young, leaders and followers. Both family and communal rituals are occasions of emotion, and the celebrations themselves arouse emotion, as is obvious to any observer who listens to the drumbeat and watches the dancing. Rituals, then, channel emotion and teach the mourner, the adolescent, or the parent what it is proper to feel. Nyakyusa mourners were required to express the passion of grief and fear to the men "fighting death" in the war dance and to widows, mothers, and sisters weeping violently and smearing themselves with ash and mud; but the rituals reveal little of the actual experience of the individual.

Any understanding of religious experience must come primarily from what individuals report of their own lives. Firsthand accounts are meager, but there is evidence that an awareness of the numinous exists. The talk of priests hints at their fear of a grove in which a founding hero or chief has been buried; at a communion meal of living and dead kinsmen, there is a sense that the shades are present and that the participants find satisfaction in their company; people speak of the comfort felt in a moment of danger when a man or woman has called on the shade of a parent or grandparent and sensed its presence; the fear aroused by a nightmare may be interpreted as the attack of a witch. Dreams are indeed the most common experience of the unseen, and so real that in recording the experiences of southern Africans I often had to ask, "Were you asleep or awake when this happened?" Those closest to their shades, and hence most aware of the numinous, are the hereditary priests, or rainmakers, and diviners who have been "called" and who practice as mediums.

See Also Affliction, article on African Cults of Affliction; Bemba Religion; Central Bantu Religions; Interlacustrine Bantu Religions; Khoi and San Religion; Kongo Religion; Luba Religion; Mbona; Ndembu Religion; Nyakyusa Religion; Shona Religion; Swazi Religion; Tswana Religion; Witchcraft, article on African Witchcraft; Zulu Religion.

Bibliography

To supplement the relatively few works cited in the text, the works listed herein range over all parts of the enormous area of southern Africa. Many of the books cited here were written by missionaries, who provided most of the early published evidence of the traditions of peoples in the area.

Beattie, John, and John Middleton, eds. *Spirit Mediumship and Society in Africa.* London, 1969. Firsthand accounts by trained observers of spirit mediums in thirteen African societies, with a comparative introduction.

Berglund, Axel-Ivar. *Zulu Thought-Patterns and Symbolism.* London, 1976. By far the best study of the symbolism of an Nguni people (on the southeast coast), written by a missionary who grew up speaking Zulu as a second language.

Bernardi, Bernardo. *The Mugwe: A Failing Prophet.* London, 1959. A competent account of a hereditary priest in Meru, Kenya, written by a Consolata priest who was a missionary in the area.

Callaway, Henry. *The Religious System of the Amazulu* (1870). Reprint, Cape Town, 1970. Contains valuable statements of belief by Zulu. Includes Zulu texts and English translations, with notes, by the Reverend Canon Callaway, a Zulu-speaking missionary who sought to understand traditional ideas.

Colson, Elizabeth. *The Plateau Tonga of Northern Rhodesia.* Manchester, 1962. One volume of a longterm study by an anthropologist; gives an account of ancestral spirits and rain shrines.

Crawford, James R. *Witchcraft and Sorcery in Rhodesia.* London, 1967. Based on records of court cases.

Douglas, Mary. *The Lele of the Kasai.* London, 1963. A brilliant essay on Lele symbolism, first published in African Worlds, edited by Daryll Forde (London, 1954).

Douglas, Mary. *Natural Symbols.* New York, 1970. Discusses the relationship between symbols and inner experience.

Douglas, Mary, ed. *Witchcraft Confessions and Accusations.* New York, 1970. Sets witch beliefs in comparative perspective.

Fortes, Meyer, and Germaine Dieterlen. *African Systems of Thought.* London, 1965.

Gluckman, Max. *Rituals of Rebellion in Southeast Africa.* Manchester, 1954.

Hammond-Tooke, W. David. *Boundaries and Belief: The Structure of a Sotho World View.* Johannesburg, 1981.

Harris, Grace Gredys. *Casting Out Anger: Religion among the Taita of Kenya.* Cambridge, 1978. A discussion of rejection of anger, through spraying out water or beer, as the central religious act among the Taita.

Junod, Henri A. *The Life of a South African Tribe.* 2d ed., rev. & enl. 2 vols. London, 1927. A classic by a missionary; first published as *Les Ba-Ronga* (1898; reprint, New Hyde Park, N.Y., 1962).

Kenyatta, Jomo. *Facing Mount Kenya* (1938; New York, 1962). A valuable firsthand account of Kikuyu ritual and belief.

Mbiti, John S. *African Religions and Philosophy.* New York, 1969.

Mbiti, John S. *Concepts of God in Africa.* London, 1970. Useful on the concept of time in East Africa. Makes clear that ancestors are not worshiped; offerings to them are family celebrations with the "living dead."

McAllister, P. A. "Work, Homestead and the Shades: The Ritual Interpretation of Labour Migration among the Gcaleka." In *Black Villagers in an Industrial Society,* edited by Philip Mayer, pp. 205–253. Cape Town, 1980. Evidence on a very conservative section of Xhosa on the southeast coast.

Middleton, John, and E. H. Winter, eds. *Witchcraft and Sorcery in East Africa.* London, 1963. Essays based on firsthand observation.

Ngubane, Harriet. *Body and Mind in Zulu Medicine.* London, 1977. Particularly illuminating on the ancestors and illness, pollution, color symbolism in medicine, and possession by evil spirits. An important work by an observer whose mother tongue is Zulu.

Ranger, T. O., and Isaria N. Kimambo, eds. *The Historical Study of African Religion.* Berkeley, Calif., 1972.

Richards, Audrey I. "A Modern Movement of Witch-finders." *Africa* 8 (October 1935): 448–461. Describes the bamucapi movement of 1934.

Richards, Audrey I. *Chisungu: A Girl's Initiation Ceremony among the Bemba of Northern Rhodesia.* London, 1956. The most vivid account yet written on girls' initiation; interprets symbols and explains methods of inculcating certain lessons.

Roscoe, John. *The Baganda.* London, 1911. Written by a missionary who worked closely with James G. Frazer. Includes an account of founding heroes and rituals at their shrines.

Setiloane, Gabriel M. *The Image of God among the Sotho-Tswana.* Rotterdam, 1976.

Smith, Edwin W., and Andrew Murray Dale. *The Ila-Speaking Peoples of Northern Rhodesia* (1920). 2 vols. Reprint, New Hyde Park, N.Y., 1968. Smith was a missionary, Dale a magistrate, and both were very competent linguists. They lived among the Ila of the Zambezi from 1902 and 1904, respectively, until 1914. The sections on religion are chiefly the work of Smith, who later served as president of the Royal Anthropological Institute, London. The book is a classic of early African ethnography.

Smith, Edwin W., ed. *African Ideas of God.* London, 1950. A symposium with twelve contributors and an introductory essay by Smith. Five contributors refer to southern Africa.

Swantz, Marja-Liisa. *Ritual and Symbol in Transitional Zaramo Society, with Special Reference to Women.* Uppsala, 1970. An account of the ritual and symbolism of the Zaramo of the Tanzanian coast. "Every occasion of prayer," Swantz argues, "is a restatement of the position of the family in relation to their elders and to their present leadership and authority."

Taylor, John V. *The Primal Vision: Christian Presence amid African Religion.* Philadelphia, 1963. A penetrating study based on Taylor's experience in Uganda and elsewhere in Africa.

Turner, Victor. *The Forest of Symbols.* Ithaca, N.Y., 1967. This volume was followed by Turner's *The Drums of Affliction*

(Oxford, 1968), *The Ritual Process* (Chicago, 1969), and *Revelation and Divination in Ndembu Ritual* (Ithaca, N.Y., 1975); together they constitute a profound study of Ndembu ritual and symbolism.

Willoughby, William C. *The Soul of the Bantu.* New York, 1928. Based on the experience in Botswana of a missionary who believed that "ritual is a variety of the vernacular."

Wilson, Monica. *Reaction to Conquest.* London, 1936. Includes eyewitness accounts of animal offerings and prayers to the shades.

Wilson, Monica. "Witch Beliefs and Social Structure." *American Journal of Sociology* 56 (January 1951): 307–313.

Wilson, Monica. *Rituals of Kinship among the Nyakyusa.* London, 1957. This work and its companion volume, *Communal Rituals of the Nyakyusa* (London, 1957), describe the whole cycle celebrated; they quote the texts and describe the situations on which interpretation of symbols is based.

Wilson, Monica. "Co-operation and Conflict." In *The Oxford History of South Africa,* edited by Monica Wilson and Leonard Thompson, vol. 1. Oxford, 1969. Shows that the Xhosa cattle killing of 1856 was one of a series led by prophets who urged purification from witchcraft and sacrifice to the shades.

Wilson, Monica. *Religion and the Transformation of Society.* Cambridge, 1971. Discusses the change in traditional religion as the scale of societies in Africa increases.

Wilson, Monica. "Mhlakaza." In *Les Africains,* edited by Charles-André Julien et al., vol. 5. Paris, 1977. The Xhosa cattle killing has been seen by various writers as a plot of the chiefs to drive the Xhosa to war, as a plot of the whites to destroy the Xhosa, and as a resistance movement. Little attention has been paid to its fundamental religious aspect, which is discussed here. (The text is, alas, marred by many mistakes in the French printing of names.)

MONICA WILSON (1987)

SOUTHERN AFRICAN RELIGIONS: SOUTHERN BANTU RELIGIONS

Patrilineal herdsmen and farmers belonging to the large Bantu linguistic group, which is widely spread over central and eastern Africa, moved into southern Africa in distinct waves. They appeared in the region as distinct cultural groups probably between 1000 and 1600 CE. The Sotho (Pedi, Matlala, et al.) and the related Tswana settled on the arid inland plateau where the San were hunting and the Khoi were raising livestock. The Nguni (Zulu, Swazi, and Xhosa) spread out along the southeastern coast. The Lovedu and Venda, two closely related peoples who became strongly amalgamated with the Sotho in the twentieth century, successively broke away from the Karanga in ancient Zimbabwe; the last Venda migration may have crossed the Limpopo River after 1600 CE, but their predecessors were probably among the first inhabitants of the northeastern Transvaal. The Tsonga, or Thonga, migrated in the early nineteenth century into the Transvaal, where they ran into Sotho and Venda, but their lands still lie principally in Mozambique. In spite of these people's cultural diversity, their ceremonies as well as their conceptions of the world have sprung from the same fundamental cosmology, either through derivation from a common heritage or else from interactions.

A THERMODYNAMIC CONCEPTION OF THE INDIVIDUAL AND OF THE UNIVERSE. The opposition between hot and cold is fundamental to many different rites found among the southeastern Bantu-speaking peoples. J. D. Krige and Eileen Jensen Krige have shown the importance of this opposition among the Lovedu. In effect, heat upsets equilibrium and causes dysphoria. To end severe drought, ward off the dangers associated with premature birth, and heal sickness, a cooling treatment is applied. This is also done after the birth of twins, for the whole country risks becoming dry.

The Venda also use this dialectic. Similarly, the Zulu make a sacrificer avoid warmth before undergoing an immolation to the ancestors, who are associated with water and sperm. The day before, he has to give up drinking beer, stop making love, and keep away from fire. Communication with the ancestors is possible only if all participants are cool—neither angry nor spiteful. According to the Tsonga, sick persons give off heat, as do menstruating or pregnant women and excited warriors who have just killed an enemy. The cosmic order is threatened by the birth of twins because the mother "has gone up to the sky" during pregnancy, a period of dangerous overheating inside her womb. The Pedi even recommend that pregnant women not go outside whenever it rains. The Tswana say that the hot blood of pregnant women counteracts rain medicine. Moreover, their rainmakers and chiefs must abstain from sexual intercourse throughout most of the rainy season.

The Tsonga liken the normally born baby to a pot that has not cracked when baked. The mother and child are secluded until the umbilical cord falls off. The father cannot approach his wife because she is considered to be too hot. If the baby is male, the father runs a special risk. A series of rites gradually separates the infant from the mother's burning body and integrates him into the father's sphere. The cooling process can be clearly observed during Tsonga funerals for infants. If death follows soon after birth, the body is put inside a cracked pot that is covered with a layer of ashes. If death occurs before the Boha Puri tribal integration, which allows the parents to resume sexual intercourse and is performed when the child reaches the age of one, the body is buried in a humid place. If the child dies after this rite, the funeral is conducted like that of an adult, and the corpse is buried in dry earth.

The same thermal code underlies rites of passage that, though differing in form, are basically similar. An example is the presentation to the moon. A cooling feminine principle, the moon is responsible for watching over the child's growth and is often likened to a paternal aunt. During the first new moon visible after birth, the Pedi place the baby on the ground for a few seconds, and water, symbolizing rain, is poured through the roof and onto the infant. Three months after birth, the Tsonga present the baby to the new moon, throwing a torch toward it. Once the torch goes out, the baby is separated from his or her mother and laid on a pile of ashes. This example keenly reveals the transformational process that brings these rites within a single symbolic system: the Tsonga replace rain with an extinguished torch. Moreover, whenever twins, as "sons of the sky," assist at funerals, their fontanels are smeared with ashes because they are seen as burning, hence dangerous creatures.

The Python Cult. A major divinity known as the python spirit among southeastern Bantu-speaking peoples symbolizes the coolness that is responsible for individual, social, and cosmic equilibrium. He is undoubtedly part of the most archaic Bantu cultural substratum, and both the Swazi and Venda perform ceremonies in his honor. Among the Luba in Zaire, he has a celestial manifestation, that of the rainbow. The Zulu and Luba reverse his climatic functions. Nkongolo, the Luba python, is, like the Zulu one, associated with terrestrial waters. As the rainbow, however, he burns rain rather than bringing it. In contrast, the Zulu hold the python and rainbow to be two distinct spirits whose beneficial actions with regard to water are complementary. "Coolest of all animals" according to Axel-Ivar Berglund, Python licks the fat of the black sheep that rainmakers sacrifice to him. On the other hand, the rainbow princess, iNkosazana, is the virgin daughter of the lord of heaven (and of thunderbolts), whose changing moods are dreaded by men. She intercedes so that he regularly sends gentle, soaking rain. Her rays of light plunge into the waters. Virgin girls, disguised as warriors, offer her vegetables and beer on top of a mountain forbidden to men. The feminine rainbow cult stands opposite the masculine python rite of sacrifice. Only princes may kill this venerated animal provided that they not spill its blood. Its fat goes into medicines that specialized magicians use against thunderbolts.

The rainbow princess cult is found specifically among the Nguni. Traces of it are found among the Swazi, who inaugurate the annual Ncwala ceremony during the southern summer solstice with a quest for the waters of the world. National priests lead two separate processions, one in search of river water and the other in search of seawater. Carried on a shield at the head of each procession is a ritual calabash, called "princess." These two calabashes represent the rainbow princess. This extraordinarily complex ceremony, which principally regenerates the king's mystical force, ends with a purifying bonfire that is supposed to be put out by rain.

Although the Swazi apparently have no python cult, Venda religion honors the python, and snake cults thrive among the Karanga. According to Venda cosmogony, the whole creation took place inside Python's stomach. This primordial, aquatic demiurge vomited nine creatures who roamed over the soggy earth, which was still in darkness. They became the sun, moon, and stars. Controlling fertility and rain, Python also presides over girls' puberty rites. Killing a python during the rainy season is strictly forbidden. During the dry season, its carcass is thrown into water, although the head and tail are buried in the cattle fold in order to bring prosperity. People use its fat to protect themselves from burns and to prevent fires.

Most Bantu cosmogonies are fundamentally dualistic. Thus opposite Python is Raluvhumba, who has often been mistaken for a supreme being. His name evokes the eagle, *luvumba*. Raluvhumba's voice is thunder, and during storms he is visible as a big flame. He controls the sun, which could burn the earth if it came too near. His complementarity with Python stands out in a royal ceremony that is no longer observed. After communicating with Raluvhumba in a sacred cave, the Venda king used to order his people to perform Python's dance (*tshikona*) for two nights. Much like other, neighboring societies, the Venda believe that the universe's equilibrium depends upon the joint action of two fundamental principles—water and fire, coolness and heat. Water and coolness have the advantage of having originated first; fire and heat are always menacing because they threaten life. Therefore, the Venda put out all fires when their king dies. The Lovedu do the same because the earth is "hot" whenever their queen (who is responsible for keeping the rain medicine—and keeping it cool) passes away.

These myths and rites parallel various fragmentary tales collected among the Karanga. The Korekore, a branch of the Karanga, worship Dzivaguru ("big pool"). This rain spirit lived on earth before he disappeared into a pool on a mountaintop. He was forced to vanish by the magic of a rival chief who coveted his wealth and put on red attire (the color of fire). Like the Venda Python, this vanquished spirit was the primordial ruler of the world. By going down into water, he brought darkness over the earth. His opponent had to use a new magical trick to bring the sun back. Dzivaguru said that he would accept only sheep as offerings—the same animal that the Zulu sacrifice to Python.

This tale is apparently a variation of a Hungwe myth, taken down by Leo Viktor Frobenius, that accounts for the origin of the mighty Zimbabwe kingdom, whose stone ruins are unique in the Bantu-speaking world. In olden times, a poverty-stricken people known as the Hungwe were dwelling on a mountain. They ate food raw because their chief, Madzivoa, had lost the fire that his daughters kept in a sealed horn containing oil. Hunters from the north, the Hungwe's ancestors, came into the land. They had fire and ritually smoked a pipe to sustain their magical force. Their chief gave fire to Madzivoa, married his daughter, and became the first "king" (*mambo*). Many people united around him, and even Madzivoa became his servant. The name of this fallen autochthonous chief derives from *dzivoa* ("lake" or "pool"), also found in the name Dzivaguru. These two similarly named figures met up with parallel fates at the hands of newcomers who seized their power and wealth.

The new mythical rulers of fire had to accommodate the demiurges associated with water, as told in another Karanga story collected by Frobenius. A snake spirit used to dwell in a lake on the Zimbabwe plain. The king's daughters are thought to copulate with this spirit to keep the sacred pool and rain from disappearing. The vaginas of these princesses, who enjoyed total sexual freedom, had to be continuously moist. Victims to be sacrificed for rainfall were chosen from among them. A second group of princesses had to stay chaste. They were associated with a ritual fire kept by the king's incestuous wife, Mwiza, who represents the morning star.

The Venda myth transposes these elements. Python lived with two wives. Only the first one knew his real nature and could visit him freely during daytime. The second could draw near him only at night when she was soaked. Driven by curiosity, she broke this rule and caught her husband smoking a pipe. Angrily, Python went down into a lake. To end the subsequent drought, the guilty wife had to sacrifice herself and join her husband in the water. The Venda primordial Python clearly brings to mind Zimbabwe's aquatic serpent, of whom Dzivaguru and Madzivoa are avatars.

These variant myths relate both the incompatibility of water and fire and their complementarity. The duality of the Karanga princesses with dry and moist vaginas expresses the southeastern Bantu dialectic of coolness and heat. The Venda myth about the python who secretly smoked a pipe recounts the same theme as the Hungwe one about a mysterious foreigner who drew force out of smoking and prevailed over Madzivoa, an aquatic spirit who used to keep fire in a horn. The sacrifice of the Venda Python's second wife obviously corresponds to the sacrifices demanded of the Karanga princesses. Karanga symbolism vividly distinguishes a primordial spirit associated with both terrestrial and rain waters from a ruler of fire who was his opponent or else became his ally through marriage. The Korekore see these two spirits as rivals but ultimately invoke Dzivaguru whenever there is no rain. However, this cosmogony has been obscured by the cults of possession dedicated to regional or particularistic gods. The ubiquity of these cults, borrowed from the Shona, has distracted researchers from the still-present ancient gods. In fact, Dzivaguru is the only local spirit with no medium.

The Venda, however, have made an original transposition of the ancient dualism. Python, ruler of waters, and Raluvhumba, ruler of celestial fire, are ritually complementary. In Zimbabwe, neighboring Karanga worship Mwari, a supreme being who combines the attributes of both. This "possessor of heaven" is also called Dzivaguru. Mwari's representative, the python, is venerated as a spirit of the mountains, whereas a water snake keeps rivers and springs from going dry.

COSMOLOGY AND SACRED KINGSHIP. James G. Frazer was the first to describe as "divine kingship" a political institution whose primary function is control over fertility and natural forces. I prefer to use the term "sacred kingship" because the particular chiefs who are essential to this institution are not actual gods. The Venda and Lovedu inherited the institution of sacred kingship from the Karanga while the Sotho and Tswana did not (sacred kingship is not apparently a feature of Sotho or Tswana culture despite the existence among them of some powerful military chieftaincies). The Swazi established a political and symbolic system remarkably similar to that of the Venda. Sacred kingship is widespread throughout Africa. Surprisingly constant characteristics are thus attributed to African, particularly Bantu-speaking, kings: they are uncommon beings; they take paramountcy through transgression (often incest); they are surrounded by prohibitions; and they are condemned to die early unless other victims make it possible for them to continue reigning.

The Swazi king, master of thunderbolts and of the sun, rules along with a queen mother associated with the moon and with lush vegetation. Together they control the rains. The king has the privilege of marrying his real or classificatory sisters. While young, he succeeds his father with the title "child," and when adult he takes full power by marrying the "queen of the right hand," with whom he commingles blood to become twins. But his real so-called twin is his mother. During the summer solstice, his force weakens, and the whole nation goes through a crisis. He then performs the Ncwala ceremony, which opens with the previously described quest for water. He is proclaimed "bull of the nation" after the sacrifice of an ill-treated black ox, which represents him. Following several events that alternately show his weakness and his force, he consumes the first fruits and is then disguised as the spirit of vegetation.

According to the Venda founding myth, the first two sovereigns were Sun and Moon, his twin sister as well as incestuous wife. Paradoxically, the Venda king rules with a paternal aunt (Makhadzi, a title also used to refer to the moon); an agnatic half sister takes the aunt's place during the next reign. His principal wife, often a real or classificatory sister, belongs to the royal family. The king, "light of the world," controls rain through both Python and Raluvhumba. Although no ritual marks the summer solstice, Makhadzi presides over the first-fruit ceremony.

Venda and Swazi symbolic configurations are related through transformations. In practice, the Venda put agnatic ties in place of the incestuous uterine (or twin) ties of their myth. The Swazi, on the contrary, maintain these mythical ties through a fiction. Mirrored by a queen who is the king's agnatic half sister, the Venda queen aunt obviously fills the same ritual position as the Swazi queen mother, who is a "twin" to her son. The queen of the right hand, who is both the king's wife and fictive twin, is a substitute for the queen mother. More meaningful parallels exist. The "twin body" of the Swazi kingdom expresses a great power of life; it is completed by the male *tinsila,* the sovereign's symbolic twins associated with his right and left hands. A similar pair in the Venda kingdom corresponds to the paternal uncle and agnatic half brother, respectively Makhadzi's and the queen sister's masculine doubles.

The Lovedu's mythic and historical traditions throw light upon this structural transformation of the ideal twin model. A very long time ago, Princess Dzugudini, the daughter of the king of Monomotapa, bore a son, Muhale, to her uterine brother. Their mother kept their secret, stole her husband's rain medicine, and gave it to her daughter, who fled southward with her young son. With some supporters, they reached the Lovedu land, where Muhale, who had brought fire along, founded a kingdom. The incestuous uterine couple are thus closely associated with the ritual couple formed by a son (keeper of fire) and mother (supplier of rain medicine). The Swazi have simply combined these two images to present the queen mother as her son's twin sister. Succession in the Lovedu royal house later came into the hands of women. The first queen was born out of incest between a king and his daughter. Even though the model for perpetuating sacred kingship through the union of a brother and his uterine sister (ideally between twins of the opposite sex) has shifted agnatically, the Lovedu did not adopt the Venda solution. Their rain queen reigns alone but reputedly has intercourse with a brother in order to bear an heiress.

Lovedu traditions have kept alive the incestuous marriage of sacred chiefs in the ancient Karanga civilization. The king of Monomotapa reigned with Mazarira, his sister and wife. A later account (Frobenius) states that, in ancient Zimbabwe, Mazarira was the monarch's own mother. The heir apparent lived in incest with a sister who became his principal wife with the name Mwiza (in Monomotapa, Nabwiza). When enthroned along with her brother, she lit the new ritual fire for her keeping.

Unlike the Venda one, the Karanga founding myth does not mention a primordial monarchy of the Sun and Moon twins. Moon, the first king, emerged from the primeval waters. For two years he lived chastely with Morning Star, who brought him fire and bore vegetation before being taken back by Mwari, the supreme being. Moon received a second wife, Evening Star, who invited him to have sexual intercourse. She bore mankind and animals. Moon became "ruler" (*mambo*) over a large population. Two years later, Evening Star left him to go live with Snake, master of the rains. When Moon tried to take her back, Snake bit him. Moon pined away. Rain stopped falling. His children strangled him and buried him with Evening Star who had decided to die with him. After that the children chose a new king. This myth perfectly illustrates the cosmological function of sacred kingship, here under the sign of the moon. Having lost his power over nature, the weakened king was condemned to an early death. The rulers of Monomotapa were killed whenever they showed the least physical failing, whether sickness or impotence. The following ceremony clearly associated them with the moon. At the rising of the new moon, the king had to mock fight invisible enemies in the presence of the realm's dignitaries. According to several accounts, the sacred chiefs of the Karanga and related peoples were eliminated after reigning either two or four years. In the myth, this period corresponds to the Venusian cycle. Mwiza represents Venus, the morning star. Recall that Mwiza was surrounded by chaste, dry princesses. They greeted the first rising of the morning star. On the other hand, the second group of humid princesses, who had intercourse with the snake spirit of the waters, probably had to do with the evening star.

This cosmological system obviously differs from the Venda's, even though the Karanga origins of the Venda kingdom are beyond doubt. In charge of the rains, Karanga and Venda kings are related to aquatic snake spirits. In the Venda myth, both Venusian wives belonged to Python, but only the daytime one could be with her husband whenever he smoked (i.e., used fire). The morning/evening star opposition exists but is concealed. Moreover, the Venda sovereign was not lunar. The first king was none other than Sun, whom Python vomited out. Present-day rulers proclaim to be descended from Raluvhumba, who controls thunderbolts and is symbolized by the eagle. The thunderbird's role in Karanga royal cosmogony needs to be better known. Thomas Huffman, an archaeologist, has suggested that Zimbabwe's famous stone birds represent successive rulers in the form of fish eagles. In old Zimbabwe, this brightly feathered bird was the mediator between humanity and Mwari, the celestial demiurge and congener of the Venda Raluvhumba. Recall that the Hungwe, whose name literally means "fish eagle," brought fire to the destitute folk ruled by the aquatic Madzivoa. The complementarity of the eagle and serpent restores the fundamental opposition between fire and water.

Two diverging traditions relate the origin of fire, the celestial symbol of sovereignty. The Venda king is apparently associated with the second. He went ahead of Raluvhumba when the latter appeared on earth as a big, thundering flame. The stick that the king uses to stir his porridge is called "the fire lighter."

Whereas the Karanga moon kings were killed after they reigned a short time (or whenever their physical forces failed, as in Monomotapa), the Venda kings enjoy long lives provided they do not have children after enthronement. They have to take a drug that inhibits their sexuality. Comparisons with central Africa lead to the conclusion that this practice aims at containing the king's dangerous, almost sorcerous, magical power. Among the Pende in Zaire, some sacred chiefs are forced to refrain from sexual intercourse after taking office. Lovedu ritual ascribes power over the rains to a secretly incestuous queen who had to commit suicide. It has its place in the same system of symbolic transformations, which goes back to a common ideology.

THE RITUAL COMPLEX OF CIRCUMCISION. Neither the Karanga nor the Shona practice circumcision. However, all accounts agree that this custom and its related initiation are a time-honored institution among the Sotho and Tswana, who have passed it on to the Lovedu, Venda, and Tsonga. Girls' puberty rites usually correspond to male circumcision. Girls undergo a pretended circumcision that amounts to slightly cutting the clitoris (Lovedu) or upper leg (Tswana) or to placing a knife between the legs (Pedi). The southern Sotho designate both feminine initiation and masculine circumcision with the same word (*lebello*). The Pedi, a northern Sotho people, make boys go through two successive rites (Bodika and Bogwera), but girls undergo a single collective rite (Byale). The Lovedu have adopted the latter; they call it Vyali and correlate it with the second masculine initiation. Those peoples with Karanga origins initially held only individual rites (the Venda Khoba or Lovedu Khomba) at the first menstruation.

Among the Sotho circumcision enables young men to become warriors. Each new class of circumcised youths forms a regiment in their chief's service. Although chiefs lack the attributes of sacred kings, the symbolisms of Sotho initiation and of the Swazi kingdom are strikingly close. Major Pedi chiefs keep a tribal fire that neither women nor uncircumcised boys may approach. From it initiates take a brand to light the fire that will burn continuously in the center of their circular bush camp during the dry season. After being circumcised, they gather each morning around this fire, the "little lion," and stage a feigned attack. They "pierce the laws." The solar symbolism of the lion fire is indicated by its bed lying along an east-west axis. The sun symbolizes the adult Pedi man. The "spotted white hyena" represents the lunar feminine principle but also refers to a small conical tower forbidden to those undergoing initiation. Built at the camp's eastern entry with carefully polished stones grouted with cinders, it stands alongside a smaller structure, its child. At the end of initiation, the newly circumcised follow the "hyena's tracks," a trail of cinders inside the camp, from the western entry northward to the eastern one. This path depicts the moon's apparent movement eastward, opposite to the sun's. The discovery of the hyena monument by initiates brings together pairs of opposites: sun and moon, male and female. When the masculine ceremony ends, girls who have just had their first period begin collective initiation. They experience a pretend circumcision and are secluded for a month under the authority of the chief's principal wife.

The Matlala have made interesting changes in this ceremony. The fire bed, called "lion," also lies along an east-west axis. Initiates are awakened at dawn while the morning star is shining. Since looking at the sun is forbidden during the first phase of initiation, the boys turn their faces westward. During the second phase, they look eastward and expose the right half of their bodies to the fire's heat. During this "night of change," a stake is erected and its top decorated with ostrich feathers. Greeted as grandmother, this stake replicates the Pedi's lunar monument. Throughout their retreat, initiates pretend to attack the moon. The Matlala use obviously phallic metaphors to liken the waning moon to a female elephant that has to be "stabbed" and "made to fall." Pedi initiation songs also mention a mysterious elephant, an image that instructors take explicitly to mean the dangerous menstruating woman.

Just as the lion is in opposition to the elephant, so a solar fire along an east-west axis is in opposition to the moon. This Sotho symbolism can be compared to that surrounding the Swazi lion king, associated with the sun and fire, who rules along with an elephant queen mother, associated with the moon. During the Ncwala ceremony, the weakened king runs after the summer solstitial sun. He finally has sexual intercourse with the queen of the right hand, a notorious action comparable to the solar quest for virility by newly circumcised Sotho youth. During their retreat, Pedi initiates are as weak as the Swazi king during the Ncwala. They try in vain "to run past the sun." The king's successor is chosen from among his very young sons. This child king is the only Swazi male who, at adolescence, goes through a circumcision-like ceremony. Otherwise, the Nguni do not hold circumcision or related initiation ceremonies, although they might have in the past. The Swazi seemingly concentrate the symbolism of Sotho initiation within their royal institution. The Swazi king may never drink water, just as those undergoing Sotho initiation may not. At the end of initiation, the newly circumcised jump into water while their camp is set ablaze; the Ncwala ends as the Swazi king washes while a purifying bonfire is lit. Like this king, the Pedi who have completed initiation become lions and brave warriors. Just as Pedi initiation leads to the formation of new military regiments, so the Swazi military age grades actively participate in the Ncwala, under the sign of the moon. Throughout the Sotho region, circumcision camps fall under the chiefs' direct control. The Swazi Ncwala and Sotho puberty rites are variations of the same symbolic and sociological themes.

Similarities lie even closer. Recall how the lion fire in the Pedi initiatory camp is lit. The chief's principal wife has a function like that of the Swazi queen mother—to keep rain medicine. To be wedded, she appears at sunset as all fires are put out. The fire ignited in her dwelling is used to renew the tribal fire. The fire in the chief's keeping (which he gives to those undergoing initiation) and the rain medicine kept by his principal wife (who gives birth to his successor) are both complementary and opposite. The newly circumcised youth's solar/lunar quest for a woman is also a search for rain. Strictly kept apart from the opposite sex, initiates gather around the solar lion fire during the dry season. Ritual chants invite them to follow the elephant's (woman's) tracks "when it rains," for then this animal has "no more force" and can be killed easily. Such phrases mean that a man may approach a woman only after her menstrual period. The cycle of fertility is linked to the change of seasons; menstruation suspends sexual relations and, like the dry season, falls under the sign of fire.

The Tsonga and Venda use this cosmological code. They borrowed and also adapted the institution of circumcision camps from their Sotho neighbors. A feminine elephant fire replaces the masculine lion fire in initiation camps. How should this inversion be understood? For many southeastern Bantu-speaking peoples, particularly the Swazi and Sotho, the masculine sun is complementary to the feminine moon (associated with rain and lush vegetation). But in general fire is feminine and terrestrial water masculine. Menstruation and pregnancy have to do with heat. The profound symbolic changes separating Sotho and non-Sotho circumcision rites come down to a fundamental alternative: should the ritual fire be given masculine and solar attributes or the hot properties of menstrual blood? The Sotho have made the first, the lion fire, their choice; the Tsonga and Venda have opted for the second, the elephant fire.

Moreover, the Tsonga do not put political authorities in charge of initiation. Unlike the Pedi, they entrust the ritual fire to the chief's principal wife, who keeps it burning in her dwelling in order to smoke medicine objects. Furthermore, the moon is dissociated from the sun; Moon's husband is Evening Star. For all these reasons, solar/lunar symbolism sinks into the background. Instead, all symbolism related to Tsonga circumcision is dominated by the opposition between masculine water and feminine fire, as shown by the ritual formulas taught during initiation.

Three animals successively figure in these formulas. Symbol of the circumcising knife that makes boys fit for reproduction, the crocodile "moves heavily across fords and in the rushes." The hippopotamus "opens the road for elephants toward the ford." The elephant "walks slowly on dry ground" where rain will fill her tracks. These metaphors strongly contrast the aquatic, masculine domain of the crocodile with the solid ground of the female elephant. Between these two lies the road opened up by the hippopotamus, which is associated with a virgin girl whom young boys rape. They thus open the way to the female elephant, the adult woman who becomes fertile only after menstruation, which supposedly stops with the start of the rainy season. The elephant fire is a sign of both feminine sterility and the dry season. Every day, initiates confront this fire and "stab" it with a phallic stick while they sing, "Elephant, stay calm!" Significantly, they may not drink any water during their retreat. When the camp is burned down at the end of initation, they jump into a pool as they proclaim their virility. How to interpret this sequence? Circumcision, the necessary condition for procreative functioning, falls under the sign of masculine water. Separated from this element during seclusion, initiates are brought close to a feminine fire, which they cannot extinguish before the rainy season. The symbolic space around the elephant fire in the center of the initiation camp and the crocodile's watery place outside the camp are clearly delimited. The elephant fire corresponds to menstruation, dry earth, and feminine sterility; the crocodile's watery realm to circumcision, terrestrial water, and masculine fertility.

By playing on these oppositions, the Tsonga merely adjusted Sotho symbolism to the thermodynamic code with which all their rites of passage comply. Recall that newborn Tsonga children, created inside burning wombs, undergo cooling rites and that the growth of boys is placed under the sign of the moon. Just before puberty, the ritual process is reversed, for sexuality is a new source of heat to be carefully controlled. Tsonga circumcision rites are an initiation into the mysteries of feminine fire. Circumcision definitively cuts the maternal bond and marks the beginning of a young man's search for a wife. Wives are normally taken from among pubescent girls who, excessively hot during their first menstruation, undergo a collective cooling rite, which is the reverse of the masculine ceremony. Every morning during their month-long retreat, they are led, with faces veiled, to a pool and dunked into water up to their necks. Back in the hut, they are not allowed to warm themselves near the fire. During Pedi initiation, girls are also dunked into a stream to take away heat caused by menstruation, but this occurs at sunset. The Tsonga and Venda both apply cooling treatments to lower girls' temperatures.

Solar symbolism remains a vital part of the Tsonga ceremony. Initiates leave for the place of circumcision at dawn while the morning star heralds the sun, which will pull them out of the "darkness" of childhood. In addition to putting a feminine elephant fire in place of the Pedi masculine lion fire, the Venda (and probably also the Tsonga) change its direction along a north-south axis. According to a widespread conception in southern Africa, the sun travels from its northern to its southern houses between dry and rainy seasons. Like the Pedi, the Tsonga hold initiation ceremonies during the dry season. As the southern summer solstice and the first rains draw near, the newly initiated may start "following the elephant's tracks"—fearlessly approaching women. The opposition between the elephant's dry ground and the crocodile's watery place is a sign of the changing seasons. Sexuality corresponds, as among the Pedi, to the cosmic order governed by the sun's course.

Thus the symbolic system of circumcision is based upon a kind of thermodynamics that characterizes all thought among the southeastern Bantu-speaking peoples. Moreover, circumcision resembles the *mukanda* complex of rituals that is diffused among such matrilineal Bantu-speaking peoples as the Ndembu and Chokwe in western central Africa. Consequently it brings to light a particularly interesting historical problem. Did the matrilineal societies in the region that is now comprised of Zambia, Angola, and northwest Zaire maintain a very old Bantu cultural tradition that was lost by other groups (much like the patrilineal Sotho and their near neighbors did in southern Africa)? This hypothesis cannot be dismissed *a priori*. However many arguments support another interpretation (de Heusch, 1982). It seems more plausible that the southern Bantu-speaking zone should be considered as the center of diffusion of this institution to central Africa. This type of diffusion would have taken place in the land of the Lozi, or Rotse, where the Kololo conquerors (of Sotho origin) took power in 1836. They ruled until 1864 and set up circumcision camps there that were associated with the military formation of young men. Among the Ndembu these rites also make one a warrior. Everything leads one to believe that during the nineteenth century the circumcision camps inaugurated by the Sotho conquerors were gradually adopted by neighboring populations who added to the circumcision rituals their own practice of using masks. Naturally, in each case the model is transformed from one region to another, but this transformation always takes place within the logic of symbolic thought already at work in southern Africa.

SEE ALSO Swazi Religion.

BIBLIOGRAPHY

Ashton, Hugh. *The Basuto: A Study of Traditional and Modern Lesotho.* 2d ed. London, 1967.

Berglund, Axel-Ivar. *Zulu Thought-Patterns and Symbolism.* London, 1976.

Beyer, Gottfried. "Die Mannbarkeitsschule in Südafrika, speziell unter den Sotho in Nordwest-Transvaal." *Zeitschrift für Ethnologie* 58 (1926): 249–261.

Daneel, M. L. *The God of the Matopo Hills: An Essay on the Mwari Cult in Rhodesia.* The Hague, 1970.

Gelfand, Michael. *Shona Ritual: With Special Reference to the Chaminuka Cult.* Cape Town, 1959.

Gelfand, Michael. *Shona Ritual: With Special Reference to the Makorekore.* Cape Town, 1962.

Hammond-Tooke, W. David, ed. *The Bantu-speaking Peoples of Southern Africa.* 2d ed. London, 1974.

Heusch, Luc de. *Essais sur le symbolisme de l'inceste royal en Afrique.* Brussels, 1958.

Heusch, Luc de. *The Drunken King, or The Origin of the State.* Bloomington, Ind., 1982.

Heusch, Luc de. *Mythes et rites bantous,* vol. 2, *Rois nés d'un cœur de vache.* Paris, 1982.

Heusch, Luc de. "Nouvelles remarques sur l'oncle maternel. Réponse à J. C. Muller." *Anthropologie et sociétés* 6 (1982): 165–169.

Krige, Eileen Jensen. *The Social System of the Zulu* (1936). Pietermaritzburg, 1950.

Krige, Eileen Jensen, and J. D. Krige. "The Lovedu of the Transvaal." In *African Worlds: Studies in the Cosmological Ideas and Social Values of African Peoples,* edited by Daryll Forde, pp. 55–82. London, 1954.

Krige, Eileen Jensen, and J. D. Krige. *The Realm of a Rain-Queen: A Study of the Pattern of Lovedu Society* (1943). London, 1965.

Kuper, Hilda. "Costume and Cosmology: The Animal Symbolism of the Ncwala." *Man* 8 (1973): 613–630.

Mönnig, H. O. *The Pedi.* Pretoria, 1967.

Ngubane, Harriet. *Body and Mind in Zulu Medicine: An Ethnography of Health and Disease in Nyuswa-Zulu Thought and Practice.* London, 1977.

Roumeguère-Eberhardt, Jacqueline. *Pensée et société africaines: Essais sur une dialectique de complémentarité antagoniste chez les Bantu du Sud-Est.* Cahiers de l'homme, n. s. 3. Paris, 1963.

Schapera, Isaac. *Rainmaking Rites of Tswana Tribes.* Leiden, 1971.

Stayt, Hugh A. *The Bavenda.* London, 1968.

Walk, Leopold. "Initiationszeremonien und Pubertätstriten der südafrikanischen Stämme." *Anthropos* 23 (1928): 861–966.

Warmelo, N. J. van. *Contributions toward Venda History, Religion and Tribal Ritual.* Union of South Africa, Department of Native Affairs, Ethnographical Publications, vol. 3. Pretoria, 1932.

Weischhoff, H. A. *The Zimbabwe-Monomotapa Culture in Southwest Africa.* Menasha, Wis., 1941.

New Sources

Bernardi, Nernardo. *The Mugwe: A Blessing Prophet: A Study of a Religion and Public Dignitary of the Meru of Kenya.* Nairobi, 1989.

M'Inanyara, Alfred M. *The Restatement of Bantu Origin and Meru History.* Nairobi, 1992.

Ruel, Malcolm. *Belief, Ritual and the Securing of Life: Reflexive Essays on a Bantu Religion.* New York, 1997.

LUC DE HEUSCH (1987)
Translated from French by Noal Mellott
Revised Bibliography

SOUTHERN SIBERIAN RELIGIONS.

Southern Siberia is a region covered by a large wooded band, called taiga, that stretches from the Ural Mountains to the Pacific Ocean and is bordered by two treeless zones, the tundra to the north and the steppe to the south. The taiga evokes an entire procession of images: It is here where images of impenetrable immensity and absolute refuge mix with the intimacy of nature alone. The dense mass of huge dark trees is penetrated only by the great rivers (Ob, Yenisei, Lena, and tributaries) that roll their vast waters toward the Arctic Ocean, flooding their valleys in the summer and offering their frozen surfaces as bridges in the winter.

Throughout history the natural environment has prohibited any concentration of population; people continue to live in small scattered groups and to devote themselves to various kinds of hunting, fishing, and harvesting, which causes population shifts, varying in number and distance, throughout the year. These forest groups (from small isloated ethnic groups like the Ket—1,100 in 1979—to much larger groups) belong to one or the other of two great families of the Siberian peoples: Uralic to the west of the Yenisei River and Altaic to the east. Moreover, the majority of both groups live in the zones bordering the forest; these areas serve as pastoral land, while the forest is a hunting ground. Hence, one finds ethnic groups divided between taiga and tundra or between taiga and steppe. It must be noted, however, that forest peoples of different families are more similar to each other than to steppe or tundra peoples of their own family; there are specific religious features associated with hunting life in the forest.

This distribution between taiga and tundra or taiga and steppe encourages a comparative approach, deliberately focusing on the specific religious implications of the forest, as opposed to the steppe and the tundra. However, in order to avoid the pitfall of ecological determinism, the form of societal organization and mode of thought must be considered with the natural environment (more precisely, the means of access to natural resources). This approach can also be hampered by the nature of the sources and facts themselves. The representations described in this article are those of the pre-Soviet period, that is, of the beginning of the twentieth century.

THE FOREST PEOPLES. The Uralic and Altaic families each may be divided into smaller units. The two Siberian branches of the former are the Ob-Ugrian and the Samoyed. The Ob-Ugrian people, essentially a forest-dwelling group, consists of the Khanty and the Mansi, known in the eleventh century as the Yugra to the Russians of Novgorod, who traded with them for skins and furs. After their entrance into the Russian empire in the seventeenth century they became known as the Ostiaks and Voguls, respectively. At the time of the 1979 census there were 21,000 Khanty and 7,600 Mansi (a minor increase from the 1926 figures of 17,800 and 5,700, respectively).

Because of their proximity to European Russia, the Khanty and Mansi were severely exposed to the impact of colonialism. Far worse than the burden of taxation, the appearance of new illnesses, and the exactions from civil servants were the appropriation of the best land, that bordering the rivers, by Russian peasants and the forced conversion to Orthodox Christianity; both actions provoked strong opposition. Nevertheless, rather than staging a revolt, which would be quickly crushed, some preferred submission and assimilation while others elected to escape into the depths of the forest. The traditional society of the Khanty and Mansi is organized in exogamic moieties—the "hare moiety" and the "bear moiety," each having descended through the male line from one clan, which eventually divided into many.

The Samoyed branch, settled primarily in the tundra, also has groups living in the forest: the Selkup, in particular, and a small group of the Nentsy. The Selkup (6,000 in 1926; 3,600 in 1979; called the Yenisei Ostiaks in the past when the Ket were included) were forced back from the Yenisei Valley to valleys situated farther west (Taz, Turukhan, and Yeloguy) with the onset of Russian farming. Here too, each exogamic moiety—"eagle" and "nutcracker crow"—includes several patrilineal clans divided into various territorial units.

The other major group of forest people, the Altaic family, is divided into the Turkic, Mongol, and Manchu-Tunguz branches; these comprise the principal population of eastern Siberia. The Turkic branch (722,500 in Siberia in 1979), the most important of the three, is barely represented in the forest. However, certain ethnic groups, while primarily settled in the tundra (Yakuts) or steppe (eastern Tuva, Tofa, southern Shor), are found in the adjacent mountainous forest area as well.

On the other hand, the Toj-Tuva of the upper Yenisei River, the Tofa of the Sayan Mountains, and the Shor of the Altaic forest still practiced the traditional kinds of hunting in the nineteenth century. The Tuva and Tofa combine this with the raising, riding, and milking of deer. Each clan of the Shor has its own hunting ground; any infraction of the system entails vengeance. Each Shor hunter is entitled to hunt in the grounds of his wife's clan and must share his booty with her father.

The Mongol branch is represented in the forest by the Ekhirit-Bulagat Buriats who are native to the Cisbai-kalian forests. These people were not influenced by the Mongolian empire. Although they did borrow animal breeding from their Mongolian cousins of the steppe in the sixteenth century, they have nonetheless retained an authentic hunting culture as well as the remaining visible traces of a social organization divided into exogamic moieties (Ekhirit and Bulagat), with each moiety further subdivided into several patrilineal clans.

Stemming from the Tunguz branch are the Eveny (12,000 in 1979), the various Tunguz groups along the Amur River, and the Evenki, the Tunguz of the taiga (28,000 in 1979 as compared to 38,804 in 1926). Contrary to the other Siberian peoples whose populations are concentrated in a particular region (albeit in scattered groups), they are scattered throughout all of eastern Siberia. Still identifiable in spite of a variety of lifestyles, the traditional Tunguz is a hunter, an unparalleled observer and indefatigable traveler who is also incessantly driven by the search for game. It was the Tunguz who were chosen as guides by all explorers of Siberia.

HUNTING, ALLIANCE, AND THE HORIZONTAL CONCEPTION OF THE WORLD. Considered in terms of the life they lead and the type of society in which they live, the Siberian hunters' conceptions are based on a series of principles that create a structural analogy between the social, economic, and religious domains and that inform the mechanism of the interaction of these domains. Hunting is conceived of as an alliance in which the game is equivalent to the woman: The exchanging partners in each case are on the same plane, thus the world is thought of as horizontal.

Natural beings that supply sustenance are thought to be organized, like humans, into clans and linked to each other as well as to human clans through relations of alliance and vengeance. To be outside the clan is anomalous, and brings illness, death, and other trouble; everything possible is done to avoid such an anomaly. This conception applies primarily to game that is consumed but is in general not applied either to fish or to game hunted for fur, an occupation that is engaged in to meet external demand, thus making the game simple merchandise. Although fishing is a traditional practice and often supplies an important part of their subsistence, fish is still thought of simply as food, and rarely involves the same ritual treatment as game. (On the other hand, marine mammals on the coast of the Sea of Okhotsk are considered to be hunted and not fished; they are classified under the category of consumed game.) Nor is this concept applied to gathered products, which are not conceived of as beings and which depend on a woman's activity without symbolic value. Likewise, only game that is consumed forms the subject of sociologically pertinent collective practices (hunting, ritual of consumption) and popular discourse (myths, tales, stories).

Birds appear to be particularly rich in symbolic value, a value that derives primarily from their signaling function. Thus, birds of prey and birds living on carrion, which signal the presence of game, serve as evocations of hunting. Migrators, which signal the coming and going of the seasons, evoke the voyage to the supernatural world and the circulation of souls between the world of the living and that of the dead.

Species-specific hunting and consumption restrictions are imposed upon each clan based on the mythical animal that is regarded as the clan's founder. This system has led many writers to speak of totemism, but the theory linked with this term is outdated today and even forgotten. Such a distribution of symbolic attributes—found in other places in the world—is to be understood as the clans' way of assuring networks of relationships among themselves and the necessary complementarity for general cohesion. However, the facts are insufficient to allow a systematic establishment of the roots of the symbolic exploitation of one animal species or another, except those whose relationship can be assimilated to that of a hunter and a guide (e.g., the eagle or crow).

In the representations and the ritual treatment of the slain animal, the taking of game is reduced to a taking of meat. The bones are not destroyed but are disposed of (along with the head and other parts believed to contain the vital breath of life) in such a way that the animal will be reincarnated or that another animal of the same species will appear. Seemingly out of gratitude to the animal that came to offer its flesh, the hunter treats it as a guest of honor and invites it to return. That he symbolically takes only meat and not the animal as such prevents the hunt from being likened to the murder of a member of another clan, which would unleash a chain of vengeance. It also happens that the death of the animal is recognized, but the responsibility for it is attributed to a stranger belonging to another tribe.

Just as there is a system of matrimonial alliance that legitimizes the individual's taking a wife, there is a system of economic (or one could say "food") alliance that justifies the hunter's taking of game. These two systems are often compared in detail in mythical discourse, as are their subjects and their protagonists: wife and game, the taker of wife and hunter, giver of wife and giver of game. As opposed to the others, the giver of game is an imaginary being, generally called the "spirit of the forest" and qualified as "rich." With this title and that of "owner of hunted species," he is indeed a "supernatural" power in the etymological sense of the word.

In societies divided into two exogamic moieties, the matrimonial system is one of restricted exchange, which is realized in the marriage of bilateral cross-cousins (children of both the mother's brother and the father's sister) and which amounts to an exchange of sisters. Whereas this system is sociologically simple and efficient considering the precarious conditions of life known to the Siberian hunters, it is nevertheless lacking in the constraints (debt of one side, claim from the other) necessary for its perpetuation: Partners are released immediately through the simple act of exchange. However, the system is conceived of by people who bring it into operation as though it involves three stages or three partners, thereby preventing a person from perceiving himself as both giver and taker at the same time with respect to the same partner and delaying the obligation of exchange. Thus, the taker's and giver's positions toward the same partner alternate from one generation to the next. In this way the system becomes self-perpetuating within a patrilineal line: Compensation for the wife taken by the father is a daughter of this same woman given by the son.

The hypothesis of the analogy of hunting with the matrimonial system leads both to the discovery of what compensation the hunter gives for the game he has taken and to an understanding of what are otherwise inexplicable practices: These come from the need for a third partner to create dynamics in the exchange system. The compensation for game taken is one of the same nature as the game itself—food—and is given by the hunter's wife to small tame animals (most of which belong to species that are neither hunted nor used: eagles, swans, cranes, nutcracker crows, foxes, etc.) as well as animal representations (furs, wooden figurines, etc.). The latter (Selkup, *khekhe;* Tuva, *eeren;* Buriat, *ongon;* Tunguz, *singken, sevek*), made at the time of marriage, are "fed" pieces of meat through their mouths, smeared with blood, and anointed with animal fat. In this way, the food taken from the animal world is symbolically returned. From the point of view of a tripartite system, these tame animals or animal representations occupy the taker position with respect to the hunter and the debtor position with respect to the forest spirit, the giver of game. If they are not fed, these spirits supposedly prevent the hunter from taking game and cause him and his family to fall ill and even die.

Built on an analogous model, these two systems—matrimonial and economic—also make use of mutual compensation. Frequently, the myths and tales attribute a loss in the realm of alliance (abduction of the hunter's wife or sister while he is away hunting) to excessive hunting. In the Evenk ritual called the Feast of the Bear, the taker of a wife becomes a supplier of game for his wife's brother. The numerous restrictions concerning the hunter's sexual activity before the hunt, on the one hand, and the wife's behavior (notably concerning menstrual blood) with respect to hunting weapons on the other, may also be interpreted in terms of maintaining a balance between hunting and alliance. Furthermore, in these two systems, the act of taking requires the observance of strict rules vis-à-vis the giver, such as the giving of specific offerings and demonstrating the qualities of taker. One will note that what is offered to the forest spirit (incense, tobacco, amusing stories) is intended to put him in a good mood and make him laugh, so that he will be easily persuaded to release the game: The catch involves some cunning.

Whereas these two systems and their interaction normally function autonomously, they are dependent both structurally and functionally upon the third system, shamanism, which is built on an analogous model. Based on the idea that the life of the body is subordinate to what is conveniently called the "soul" that dwells in it, this system ensures the exchange of souls between their supernatural dispensers and their natural human and animal supports. Upon death, the souls return to the spirits (which suggests the hypothesis of their reincarnation within the same clan). The artisan of this circulation is the shaman, who, it is believed, obtains the souls of game and people from their supernatural dispensers.

From the standpoint of the system, the shaman is homologous to both the wife-taker and the hunter, a fact that is often clearly demonstrated by the idea that he has a symbolic wife who is the daughter of either the forest spirit or water spirit (Selkup), or of the earth spirit Khosedam, as the Ket believe. The office of the shaman is generally transmitted through the patrilineal line, usually from grandfather to grandson; agnatic relatives oversee the rites of investiture and control the position and the exercise of the shamanic function. Thus, among the Selkup, the death of every adult blood relative entails the destruction of the shaman's drum and its replacement by a larger one. In fact, the shaman's power increases as each soul of a deceased relative rejoins the spirit world. The very presence of the shaman in the midst of his group guarantees the existence of a relationship with the soul-giving spirits. This relationship can be reinforced by certain detailed roles, such as the Buriat shaman acting as godfather to newborns and the Tunguz shaman leading the souls of the dead to the otherworld. However, the shaman's active intervention is essential whenever there is a disturbance: scarcity of game; lack of descendants; or departure of a soul, which, by leaving the body vacant, renders it sick and soon dead. The shaman, who performs a divination procedure (throwing an object that falls on the "good" or "bad" side, answering his questions "yes" or "no"), then determines the cause of the disturbance. The two major causes considered are infractions of the rules governing the exchanges (excessive or insufficient hunting or alliances, inadequate amount of food given to tamed animals and figurines, violation of taboos concerning hunting, etc.) and the death of any animal or human surviving outside the framework of the clan and thus outside the system, which results in a wandering, unintegrated soul that is consequently harmful. Mediator *par excellence,* the shaman then negotiates a return to order with the spirits, tricking them somewhat, but also giving them offerings or a new cult (for example, by making a new figurine to be fed, zoomorphic in the event of a hunting infraction and anthropomorphic in the event of a deceased outsider to be reinstated). Thus, he symbolically secures the reappearance of game, the birth of children, the return of the soul to the ailing person's body, and so on.

The taking (or retaking) of these souls cannot be realized by the shaman without the aid of what is usually called his "auxiliary spirits," equivalent to such equally essential auxiliaries as the intermediary in the marriage and the beater or guide in the hunt. He sends these spirits to search for the soul that has strayed from the sick and to track down vengeful spirits, descended from the frustrated souls of those who died violent deaths, to keep them from doing harm. The Selkup rite involving the "dark tent" is held in total darkness in the presence of the shaman's kin and consists of the shaman's proving to them his ability to stir up his auxiliary spirits and summon their services. His power increases with their number and promptness in hastening to his call. Their remuneration is found in the type of offering given them (primarily food) and, for those descended from wandering souls, in their reinstatement.

In each system, the relationship between the taker and his auxiliary has the character of a personal contract, updatable and reversible, corresponding to an exchange of services. These services, which are not identical but complementary, are not organized into a hierarchy: Thus, hunter and beater or guide have an equivalent status and an equal part regardless of the catch. This relationship between taker and auxiliary is based on the general principle of a dualist organization of the operating units from various levels, which finds expression in the very name of the Khanty-Mansi (bear, hare) or Selkup (eagle, crow) moieties (in the myths of origin, the moieties being descended either from two brothers-in-law or from two brothers, forming separate lines), in the custom of nomadic camping set up by two allied families, and so on. The Feast of the Bear, celebrated by most of these peoples, is still the totalizing ritual *par excellence,* despite some differences. There, the organization in moieties of the different units and the three systems of exchange come into play, a fact that illustrates the exceptional symbolic versatility of the bear.

While the forest world is at once aerial and terrestrial and dominates symbolic space, the aquatic world also plays an important role. The souls of the dead descend along the course of the great rivers; boats or representations of boats appear in certain funerary or commemorative rites. Because of the orientation of the rivers, both the north and downstream water are associated with death. Symmetrically, upstream water and the south have a positive connotation. Birds that migrate from the south are offered ritual receptions upon arrival and invitations to return upon leaving, as if to materialize the rebirth of life (since it is believed that they bring the souls of newborns). The simultaneous presence of quadrupeds and birds does not really affect the uniqueness of the forest, represented by the omnipresent but indivisible element that is the tree. The declivity of the rivers there does not result in a separation of "upstream" from "downstream." "Up" and "down" are not superposed positions; rather, they are contiguous in the depth of the same horizontal plane, a plane in which forest and water are essential constituents conceived of, respectively, as giver of game and giver of fish.

CATTLE BREEDING AND THE VERTICAL CONCEPTION OF THE WORLD. The notion of superposed worlds—and correlatively of a vertical liaison between them—develops from the opposition of upstream/downstream, which is reinterpreted in terms of up/down and then divided into the oppositions of sky/earth and earth/lower (or subterranean) world. This is due to the combined influence of two factors: the adoption of animal breeding and incorporation into a state organization, the Russian empire.

In that the adoption of animal breeding (or, with a subtle difference, agriculture) creates a patrimony to be handed down (herds, fields), ties of descent filiation develop and the systems of relationships tend to become vertical. Thus the alliance increasingly attempts to postpone reciprocity and begins to follow the model of a "generalized exchange" (according to which the clan from which one takes a wife is not the same as the clan to which one gives a sister). Instead of becoming segmented, the clans organize their lineages into a hierarchy. In the economic system, alimentary compensation is given to a "consecrated" or "tabooed" reindeer (or other domestic animal), fed along with its own herd but never utilized. Whereas the ritual treatment of the bones of the game animal aimed at its reincarnation on earth, the sacrifice of the domestic animal (always slaughtered in a manner different than the hunted wild animal) is intended to increase the herds of spirits. The animal gradually becomes less a being and more a product; the proportion of zoomorphic representations decreases. This ideological change, only initiated with the animal breeding in the forest, expresses itself through the obviously production-oriented breeding found in the steppe (and, to a lesser degree, in the tundra). Associated with the hierarchical centralization, it lays the groundwork for the emergence of transcendental entities and is receptive to the adoption of a world religion with dogma and clergy, such as Russian Orthodoxy or Buddhism.

It is significant that the animal breeders living in the forest consider their own shamans as decadent and the shamans of their neighbors, who remained, for the most part, dependent on hunting, as powerful. Such is the case with the Nentsy toward the Entsy, the Entsy toward the Selkup and the Ket, and with all of them toward the Tunguz. This is because in the cattle breeders' ideology the giver is now conceived of in terms of the irreversible mode of filiation and therefore acquires the status of absolute superiority. He is no longer a partner with whom one negotiates, but a master on whom one is dependent. The shaman's capacity to act is therefore necessarily reduced in principle (since he is more dependent and has fewer opportunities to negotiate). As for the spirits, the pastoral ideology organizes them into a hierarchy, multiplies and localizes them (which leads to the notion of spirit-master of separate places), and also develops supporting myths and figures of the founders and creators over the ancestors.

The Russian empire instituted Peter the Great's idea of "only one God, only one Tsar." At the same time, the Orthodox church searched for (or created) indigenous equivalents compatible with its own concepts and refused all compromise with other beliefs. The traditional spirits were lowered to the rank of "devils and demons" and confined to the underworld. The promotion of heavenly bodies (sky, sun) to the rank of supreme being owes as much to the Christian attempt to support the idea of God as to the native effort to set up a rival against it and make more powerful their traditional view of the world (since a God is conceived of as "higher" than mere ancestors).

The case of the sun (Num, Nom) among the Uralic peoples is an example of this process. Its artificially constructed image as a supreme being is vague, fluctuating, and without ritual importance. In the myths of creation attributed to it the only constant element is its opposition to Nga, its (or his) son or brother-in-law, depending upon the case, an opposition that, rather than illustrating the Christian notion of a relationship between God and the devil, is indicative of a fundamental problem of kinship among the Uralic peoples concerning the opposition between older and younger people that is the framework of the creation myths. The same is true with the Tunguz concerning the *bugha* ("sky," derived from an earlier meaning, "moose"). Relationships with the spirits are reinterpreted. That which was nothing but a reaction by the spirits (beneficial or baleful) to the treatment received from humans is radicalized into a moral opposition of good and evil. The shaman's "voyages" to the forest and aquatic worlds are replaced by an ascension into the sky or descent to the underworld. Nevertheless, the traditional pragmatic sense remains: The icons of the saints, interpreted as the souls of the dead, are "fed" in the same way as traditional representations in order to ensure the proper continuation of domestic life.

SEE ALSO Bears; Birds; Khanty and Mansi Religion; Num; Ongon; Samoyed Religion; Shamanism; Tunguz Religion; Yakut Religion.

BIBLIOGRAPHY

Delaby, Laurence. *Chamanes toungouses.* Études mongoles et sibérienes, no. 7. Paris, 1976. Analytical bibliography of Tunguz shamanism with a carefully documented general presentation.

Delaby, Laurence, et al. *L'ours, l'autre de l'homme.* Études mongoles et sibériennes, no. 11. Paris, 1980. Collection of documents and analyses on the symbolism of the bear, which serves to conceptualize "the other": the allied or the deceased. The mechanism of the alliance seen through the Evenk Feast of the Bear is analyzed by A. de Sales.

Diószegi, Vilmos, ed. *Popular Beliefs and Folklore Tradition in Siberia.* Uralic and Altaic Series, no. 57. Budapest, 1968. Collection of articles, primarily by Soviet and Hungarian authors.

Diószegi, Vilmos, and Mihály Hoppál, eds. *Shamanism in Siberia.* Translated by S. Simon. Budapest, 1978. Collection of articles on various subjects.

Donner, Kai. *Among the Samoyed in Siberia.* Edited by Genevieve A. Highland and translated by Rinehart Kyler. New Haven, 1954. The account of a long voyage through eastern Siberia from 1911 to 1913, originally published in German in 1926, is filled with ethnographical notations hitherto unpublished.

Hadjú, Péter. *The Samoyed Peoples and Languages.* Translated by Marianne Esztergar and Attila P. Csanyi. Uralic and Altaic Series, no. 14. Bloomington, Ind., 1963. A good manual and guide that reviews and classifies the knowledge on the various Samoyed groups.

Hoppál, Mihály, ed. *Shamanism in Eurasia.* 2 vols. Göttingen, 1984. Collection of articles on various subjects.

Levin, G. M., and L. P. Potapov, eds. *The Peoples of Siberia.* Translated by Stephen P. Dunn. Chicago, 1964. Historico-ethnographical encyclopedia, according only very limited space to social and religious facts.

Lot-Falck, Eveline. *Les rites de chasse chez les peuples sibériens.* Paris, 1953. General panorama organized by topic, including the clan organization of animals, rites intended to permit the "resurrection" of game, and the abundance of rules that release the hunter from guilt and legitimize his catch.

Mazin, Anatolii Ivanovich. *Traditsionnye verovaniia i obriady Evenkov-Orochonov (konets XIX-nachalo XX v.).* Novosibirsk, 1984. An excellent description of hunting rites and shamanism among a Tunguz tribe (the Orochon).

Paproth, Hans-Joachim. *Studien über das Bärenzeremoniell,* vol. 1, *Bärenjagdriten und Bärenfeste bei den tunguschen Völkern.* Uppsala, 1976. Comprehensive panorama of facts on the Feast of the Bear.

Vasilevich, G. M. *Evenki: Istoriko-etnograficheskie ocherki (XVIII-nachalo XX v.).* Leningrad, 1968. A remarkable book, the result of a long period of work on the subject of the Evenki.

Vdovin, I. S., ed. *Priroda i chelovek v religioznykh predstavle-niiakh narodov Sibiri i Severa.* Leningrad, 1976. Collection of papers devoted to religious representations about man and nature in Siberia. Contains very valuable materials.

Vdovin, I. S., ed. *Khristianstvo i lamaizm u korennogo naseleniia Sibiri.* Leningrad, 1979. Collection of articles tracing the history of religious contacts and presenting the various effects of their influence. The introduction, a global assessment of christianization, takes into account the linguistic obstacle and the refusal of Christianity to compromise with local beliefs.

Vdovin, I. S., ed. *Problemy istorii obshchestvennogo soznaniia aborigenov Sibiri.* Leningrad, 1981. Many papers in this volume concern shamanism in Siberia, based on data collected in the nineteenth and twentieth centuries.

Voyages chamaniques. 2 vols. Special issue of *L'ethnographie* (Paris), nos. 74–75 (1977) and nos. 87–88 (1982).

New Sources

Balzer, Marjorie Mandelstam. *Shamanism: Soviet Studies of Traditional Religion in Siberia and Central Asia.* Armonk, N.Y., 1990.

Buell, Janet. *Ancient Horsemen of Siberia.* Brookfield, Conn., 1998.

Diószegi, Vilmos, and Mihály Hoppál, eds. *Folk Beliefs and Shamanistic Traditions in Siberia.* Translated by S. Simon and Stephen P. Dunn. Budapest, 1996.

Jacobson, Esther. *The Deer Goddess of Ancient Siberia: A Study in the Ecology of Belief.* New York, 1993.

Martynov, Anatolii Ivanovich. *The Ancient Art of Northern Asia.* Translated and edited by Demitri B. Shimkin and Edith M. Shimkin. Urbana, 1991.

ROBERTE HAMAYON (1987)
Translated from French by Sherri L. Granka
Revised Bibliography

SOZZINI, FAUSTO PAVOLO (1539–1604), was an antitrinitarian theologian, known in Latin as Faustus Socinus. Sozzini was born in Siena on December 5, 1539. When his uncles fell under suspicion of heresy, and the Inquisition threatened the Sozzini family, Sozzini left Italy on April 21, 1561, for Lyons, France. After the death of his uncle Lelio Sozzini on May 14, 1562, Fausto acquired Lelio's manuscripts, which decisively turned his interests from literary studies to religious studies, specifically to doctrinal reform. His *Explicatio primae partis primi capitis Ioannis* (Explanation of the First Part of the First Chapter of John's Gospel), written in 1562 during his stay in Zurich and Basel, developed more fully Lelio's view of Christ as the person who revealed God's new creation by his teachings and his life.

Sozzini returned to Italy in 1563, where he served at the court of Cosimo I, duke of Florence (later grand duke of Tuscany). In 1574, after Cosimo's death, he returned to Switzerland and spent the following three years in Basel studying scripture and theology. In his greatest work, *De Jesu Christo Servatore* (On Jesus Christ, the Savior), completed in 1578, he attacked the doctrine that God requires satisfaction for human sins, argued that Christ is savior by his teachings and exemplary life, and emphasized the importance of faith, as trust in God and in Christ, as essential for salvation. In his response to Francesco Pucci (a widely traveled Italian humanist from Florence) in 1578, *De statu primi hominis ante lapsum* (On the State of the First Man before the Fall), Sozzini argued that humanity is mortal by nature; immortality is a gift of God. He next traveled to Kolozsvár, Transylvania, to attempt to dissuade the Hungarian theologian Dávid Ferenc (Francis Dávid) from his opposition to prayer to Christ (a view known as nonadorantism—that is, a denial that either religious worship or prayers for aid should be addressed to Christ). When Dávid refused to change his stance, Sozzini went on to Cracow, Poland, in 1579.

Although he was not admitted as a full member of the Minor Reformed Church of Poland (the Polish Brethren) because he did not regard adult baptism as essential for church membership, Sozzini became the outstanding theologian of that church, uniting its various groups. He wrote numerous works defending the church against attacks on its antitrinitarian theological views and its pacifist social and political views. In *De Sacrae Scripturae auctoritate* (On the Authority of Holy Scripture), which was published under a pseudonym in 1580, Sozzini used rational and historical arguments to refute the skeptical views of those who doubted the divine authority of the Bible.

In 1586, Sozzini married Elzbieta Morsztyn, who died within a year. The Inquisition cut off his income from Italy, and university students tried to kill him as a heretic. In 1589 he moved from Cracow to Luclawice. His colloquies with his followers in 1601 and 1602 at Raków presented his mature views. Sozzini died at Luclawice on March 3, 1604.

Sozzini viewed Christ as unique, a man who is divine, not by nature, but by virtue of his office, for God instructed Christ, resurrected him, and gave him all power over the church in heaven and on earth. He opposed the nonadorantism of Dávid and others, insisting on prayer to Christ for guidance and for aid. He regarded scripture as God's revelation and denied that God can be known through a natural theology. He held that humankind is mortal by nature and that only the righteous will be resurrected. At death, sinners suffer eternal extinction.

Sozzini's theological analyses and arguments elicited intense controversies, which resulted in significant changes in the thought of some Protestant theologians, particularly on the doctrine of the atonement. The Polish Brethren modified and continued his biblical, rational theology in their famous *Racovian Catechism.*

BIBLIOGRAPHY

Works by Sozzini

Alodia Kawecka-Gryczowa has provided detailed information on the original publications of Sozzini's works in *Ariańskie oficyny wydawnicze Rodeckiego i Sternac-kiego: Dzieje i bibliografia / Les imprimeurs des antitrinitaires polonais Rodecki et Sternacki: Histoire et bibliographie* (Cracow, 1974), pp. 177–187, 290–323. The principal comments on each work are in Polish and in French. Sozzini's works have been collected and reprinted as *Socini opera,* volumes 1 and 2 of *Bibliotheca Fratrum Polonorum quos Unitarios vocant* (Amsterdam, 1656). Ludwik Chmaj has added detailed notes to his Polish translation of Sozzini's correspondence, *Listy,* 2 vols. (Warsaw, 1959). Letters discovered since that date have been published in various scholarly journals.

Works about Sozzini

The Radical Reformation (Philadelphia, 1962), by George H. Williams, gives an authoritative account of the historical contexts and main themes of Sozzini's work. The most complete study available, Ludwik Chmaj's *Faust Socyn, 1539–1604* (Warsaw, 1963), is in Polish with one-page summaries in Russian and English. George H. Williams has illuminated many issues in Sozzini's theology in "The Christological Issues between Francis Dávid and Faustus Socinus during the Disputation on the Invocation of Christ, 1578–1579," in *Antitrinitarianism in the Second Half of the Sixteenth Century,* edited by Róbert Dán and Antal Pirnát (Leiden, 1982), pp. 287–321.

JOHN C. GODBEY (1987)

SPACE, SACRED SEE SACRED SPACE

SPARAGMOS SEE DISMEMBERMENT

SPEAKING IN TONGUES SEE GLOSSOLALIA

SPEECH, SACRED SEE LANGUAGE, *ARTICLE ON* SACRED LANGUAGE

SPEKTOR, YITSḤAQ ELḤANAN (1817–1896)

was an Orthodox rabbi and foremost traditional Jewish legal authority during the last half of the nineteenth century. Born in Rosh, in the Grodno district of Russia, Spektor was raised in a highly traditional milieu and as a young boy mastered the study of Talmud under the tutelage of his father, Yisra'el Isser. After his arranged marriage at the age of thirteen, Spektor went to live with his in-laws in Volkovysk, where Binyamin Diskin instructed him in rabbinics and ordained him as a rabbi. Spektor occupied his first rabbinical post at the age of twenty and served as rabbi in several Russian towns, including Nishvez and Novogrudok, centers of traditional Talmudic scholarship. In 1864 Spektor became rabbi of Kovno, where he also headed the *kolel* (advanced rabbinic academy) until his death.

Spektor's piety, his absolute command of traditional rabbinic sources and methods, and his virtually unparalleled genius in rendering Jewish legal decisions made him the communal leader of Orthodox Jewry in Russia during his day. He participated in a host of charitable and civic affairs on behalf of Russian and world Jewry, arbitrated Jewish communal disputes throughout the world, and was a staunch supporter of Jewish colonization in Palestine. In addition, Spektor attempted to defend traditional Judaism against many of the onslaughts of modernity. He himself was unable to speak Russian and was an opponent of the Haskalah (Jewish Enlightenment); he forbade the translation of the Talmud into Russian and opposed the creation of modern rabbinical seminaries where secular subjects would be taught.

Spektor's first volume of *responsa* (Jewish legal decisions), *Be'er Yitshaq* (1858), was published when he was thirty-one years old, a relatively young age for such a work. Two other collections of *responsa—Nahal Yitshaq* (1872, 1884) and *'Ein Yitsḥaq* (1889, 1895)—further enhanced his stature. His decisions, marked by an astonishing ability to cite the whole range of rabbinic literature in arriving at a judgment, display a tendency toward leniency. They remain a valuable and authoritative source for contemporary Orthodox rabbis in dealing with Jewish legal issues. The largest Orthodox rabbinical school in the United States, the Rabbi Isaac Elchanan Theological Seminary of Yeshiva University in New York, is named after him.

BIBLIOGRAPHY

The most comprehensive work yet written on Spektor's life is Ephraim Shimoff's "Rabbi Isaac Elchanan Spektor: His Life and Works" (Ph.D. diss., Yeshiva University, 1959). Samuel K. Mirsky has also written an article, "Isaac Elchanan Spektor," in *Guardians of Our Heritage* (New York, 1958), edited by Leo Jung. While both these pieces provide valuable information for an understanding of Spektor's life, a definitive critical study remains to be completed.

New Sources

Rakeffet-Rothkoff, Aaron. "Rabbi Yitshak Elhanan Spektor of Kovno, Spokesman for 'agunot.'" *Tradition* 29 (1995): 5–20.

DAVID ELLENSON (1987)
Revised Bibliography

SPELLS belong to the general context of magical thought. They consist of words or sets of words that issue a command that is efficacious merely because it has been pronounced. Spells represent one of the many techniques used to control nature and the evils arising in a given society. They are found universally and are probably as old as language itself, having been in existence since the Lower Paleolithic.

The basis of the power of spells is the primitive idea that nothing exists without a name and that to know the names of things is to possess them. Thus, to give orders with the appropriate words is to ensure success, made even more certain when the speaker is a witch, shaman, holy person, or anyone else whose profession it is to deal with mystery.

Stated in other terms, spells are all-powerful spoken formulas, words, or phrases of power. They are definitive: Once uttered, the desired chain of events is set irrevocably in motion. Each word, once enunciated, has a magical value and weight that none can control.

The order given in the spell, addressed to deities, spirits, or the forces of nature, can be creative, destructive, protective, or medicinal; it can demand triumph over an enemy, or the attainment of impossible powers or things. It can be used to break spells, cast spells, or obtain love.

CONDITIONS OF SPELLS. According to magical thought, only prayers can be spoken by anyone at any time and remain effective. Spells, by contrast, and other such magical activities, have many prerequisites. Spells in particular must be pronounced by a person who is initiated into the mysteries or endowed with supernatural powers, and who is sexually, dietetically, and socially pure. The person casting the spell must know with precision the words he or she will pronounce, the time when they must be uttered, the cardinal point toward which one will face, what one will stand or sit on, how his or her person must be arranged, the clothing, colors, ornaments, and objects to be used, the number of times one must repeat the words, and the psychological attitude and manners one must assume. Everything must be precise. As a part of religious and magical activities, spells sometimes require musical backgrounds, specially prepared settings, appropriate instruments, prudent timing, and attention to taboos that might be violated, such as sex, the lack of initiation, or impurity.

Spells can serve either collective ends, such as victory in battle, the banishing of plagues and epidemics, or the bringing of rain, or they can serve personal ends, such as the attainment of love, health, power, wealth, virility, fertility, finding out who has stolen something, or causing harm to an enemy. The former collective spells require a complex ceremony and initiates. The latter, usually carried out on a popular level, generally need only to be repeated continually or for a magical number of times.

As a general rule, spells accompany the preparation of potions, amulets, weapons, magical paraphernalia, scepters, and objects of sorcery. They are recited over sick people, addressed to the natural elements one wants to control, or murmured softly and continuously. Rarely are they repeated by large groups of people, although this does happen occasionally.

POWERFUL SOUNDS AND WORDS. Many scholars have concentrated on the study of the word as a symbol. These scholars include linguists, sociologists, anthropologists, philosophers, educators, psychiatrists, and occultists. Many of these researchers are inclined to give an onomatopoeic value to sounds: For example, /m/ and /n/ are related to the mother because of the sound made during breastfeeding; /g/ is related to water, because that is how it sounds when swallowed; and /a/ is an imperative for calling attention. Since ancient times, philosophers such as Plato (in his dialogue *Cratylus*) have remarked on how words somehow take on the form of the things they name.

Nevertheless, a serious analysis yields very few sounds or words that have the same value in all cultures. Greater universality can be found, perhaps, in the language of gestures: assenting by moving the head up and down, negating by moving it from right to left, beckoning with the arm and hand, pointing things out with the index finger or the eyes and brows, or threatening by raising a fist.

In Qabbalah, the interest in a knowledge of sounds, written letters, and words was intensified. Each sign was given a magical value that had a religious meaning and a numerical relationship. For example, the Hebrew letter *alef* became the symbol of humankind and the abstract principle of material objects; it is the trinity in unity and its numerical value is 1 (Scholem, 1974). Freemasonry also produced speculations in this field, but it assigned many meanings to the same letter. The letter *A* became an emblem of the first of the three faculties of divinity—creative power—in addition to being the abbreviation for the word *architect* (Powells, 1982). This association of the word with creation is found among many peoples of the world.

The history of religions has provided several words or short phrases that have been believed to be particularly powerful. The gnostics of North Africa, for instance, made an abundant use of talismans and incantations. Two words in particular have survived to this day: *abraxas* and *abracadabra.* The word *abraxas* represents the supreme deity and his supreme power. Numerically (a = 1, b = 2, r = 100, a = 1, x = 60, a = 1, s = 200) it adds up to 365, or the number of days in the solar year, the cycle of divine action. The word was carved into stone as a talisman and pronounced as a protective device. The word *abracadabra,* derived from the Aramaic phrase "Avreiq ʿad havraʾ " ("Hurl thunderbolts to [unto? at?] darkness"), was used to invoke the aid of the supreme spirits. Inscribed as an inverted triangle, with one less letter on each successive line, it was considered a powerful talisman.

The Jews, a people rich in esoteric and magical lore, were the inventors of Qabbalah, which includes one of the most important techniques for the numerological analysis of words and letters, intended to reveal their esoteric meaning. Four words in particular deserve mention. *Adonai,* which means "supreme lord," was spoken as an infallible invocation of aid. *Haleluyah,* translated as "hymn to the lord," also served as an invocation. *Amen* was a term that gave a full and definitive meaning to whatever was expressed. It was understood as "So be it," but with the magical sense that things could not be otherwise. Some think it was derived from invocations to Amun. *Golem* referred to the basic substance from which God created humans. When deprived of a soul, it could be used to create evil beings, who could be controlled only by pronouncing the true and secret name of God.

Within Islam, three phrases are believed by some to have a magical power. The phrase "Lā ilāha illā Allāh" ("There is no god but God") has been used to perform miracles (Idries Shah, 1968). The phrase "Allāh akbar" ("God is great") serves as a basis for white magic, and the words "Ism al-aʿẓam" are used to subjugate or subdue evil spirits.

Among Christians, the names *Christ* and *Jesus* serve to stave off evil. Roman Catholics may seek triple insurance by naming all three members of the holy family: "Jesus, Mary, and Joseph."

For Tibetan Buddhists, the phrase "Oṃ maṇi padme hūṃ" contains many occult meanings. It is believed that the first word, *oṃ,* emanates from the cosmic vibration essential to creation. Some scholars maintain that it is equivalent to the *Amin* of the Muslims and the *Amen* of the Jews. It is the basic name of the creator god. The complete phrase expresses a desire to be pure and to be part of the universal spirit.

SPELLS IN THE HISTORY OF RELIGIONS. Since ancient times people have uttered and written words, phrases, and formulas that they have believed to have some magic power or irresistible influence. Spells to ward off what is evil or undesirable and to bring about what is good or desirable are known in many cultures.

Egypt. The basic esoteric activity of the ancient Egyptians was preparation for life after death. For this purpose they developed high levels of art, magic, and religion. The preparation of a scarab, carved from semi-precious stone to replace the heart of the deceased, required that the artisan recite the following spell: "I am Thoth, the inventor and founder of medicine and letters; come to me, thou who art under the earth, rise up to me, great spirit." This spell was to be uttered without fail on a set number of days after the new moon (Idries Shah, 1968). Many similar spells are known to have been used, usually with apotropaic intent. In addition, the Egyptian *Book of Going Forth by Day* records spells that were to be used for each moment after a person's death.

Mesopotamia. The earliest Mesopotamian cultures have left very few records of their magico-religious thought. Later Assyro-Babylonian translations make it seem that one of the most crucial concerns of these peoples was the evil eye, the evil that surrounds people on all sides and affects them especially in the form of the envy of enemies. One spell against the evil eye went as follows:

> Let the finger point to the evil desires,
> the word of ill omen.
> Evil is the eye, the enemy eye,
> eye of woman, eye of man,
> eye of a rival, anyone's eye.
> Eye, you have nailed yourself to the door
> and have made the doorsill tremble.
> You have penetrated the house. . . .
> Destroy that eye! Drive out that eye!
> Cast it off! Block its path!
> Break the eye like an earthen bowl! (Garcia Font, 1963)

The old spells used in Assyrian medicine had something of a mythical nature. Take, for instance, this spell for toothache:

> After Anu made the heavens, the heavens made the earth, the earth made the rivers, the rivers made the canals, the canals made the swamps, and the swamps, in turn, made the Worm. The Worm, crying, approached Shamash, and he approached Ea, spilling tears: "What will you give me to eat and what will you give me to destroy?" "I will give you dried figs and apricots." "Of what use are they to me? Put me between your teeth and let me live in your gums, so that I can destroy the blood of the teeth and gnaw at the marrow of the gums. . . ." "Since you have spoken thus, O Worm, let Ea crush you with his powerful fist." (Hocart, 1975)

This was repeated until the pain disappeared.

Greece. The Greeks imagined their gods as having human form and character, and they occasionally ordered them to help the needy by means of magical formulas, as in the following spell addressed to Hekate:

> Come, infernal, earthly and heavenly one . . . goddess of the crossroads, bearer of light, queen of the night, enemy of the sun, friend and companion of the darkness; you who are happy with the barking of dogs and bloodshed, and who wander in the darkness, near the tombs, thirsty for blood, the terror of mortals, Gorgon,

> Mormon, moon of a thousand forms, accept my sacrifice. (Caro Baroja, 1964)

Medieval Europe. In Europe, the practitioners of witchcraft developed multiple spells for defense against enemies, always preceded by the name of God and the archangels. Terrible spells that try to control enemies have also been found. In the anonymous medieval work *Clavicula Salomonis* (Small Key of Salomo), one reads: "Man or woman! Young man or old! Whoever might be the evil person trying to harm me, either directly or indirectly, bodily or spiritually . . . MALEDICTUS ETERNAM EST, by the holy names of Adonai, Elohim, and Semaforas. Amen." After reciting this spell, a candle was extinguished as a sign of the finality of the curse.

Sudan. The Sudan covers a territory between Egypt and Ethiopia, where the magic of Egyptian antiquity and the later Muslims is mixed with primitive animistic magic. Popular sorcerers and magicians abound, openly offering their services. Frequently they exalt their own powers, which they obtain through their spells. For example, when a hunter hires one to obtain luck at hunting, the magician says: "I am a magician, all powerful in spells. What I say comes true. I say, 'Give victory to so and so.' He will have victory in all things." Afterward, the magician goes about filled with the desire that events might occur that will instill the hunter and the warrior with luck. This is accompanied by whistlelike sounds and by facing toward different cardinal points, whistling three times in each direction while holding a receptacle of water. The Sudanese believe that spells are more powerful when pronounced over running water.

The Sudanese also have spells to give power to certain leaves that are used in the preparation of medicines. The spells are recited over the leaves a specific number of times in order to bring about the desired effect.

To obtain the love of the opposite sex, the magician draws a magic circle within which the magician prepares a potion of herbs and feathers. In order to give the potion the necessary potency, the magician repeats the following spell: "I am a magician, O Pot, you contain the medicines of love, the spell of love, of passion. My heart throbs like the drum, my blood boils like water." This is repeated three times, and afterward another spell is intoned: "Bring my desire to me, my name is so-and-so, and my desire is the one whom I love." This spell requires solemnity and precision. To make it more effective, one has to open and close one's eyes four times, slowly, while saying it.

Such spells are not taught to laypersons, only to initiates. To be able to pronounce them one has to undertake a series of purifications, such as abstaining from food and sex for forty to sixty days (Idries Shah, 1968).

India. The sheer number of spells used in the sacred books of India is noteworthy in itself. The *Atharvaveda* in particular is full of them. Here will be mentioned only one, dedicated to obtaining a man's love: "By the power and laws of Varuna, I invoke the burning force of love, in thee, for thee. The desire, the potent love-spirit which all the gods have created in the waters, this I invoke, this I employ, to secure thee for me" (Idries Shah, 1968).

China. One result of China's use of ideograms is that its magic produces mostly written talismans, although spells abound, greatly influenced by their historical past. A spell written on the blade of a sword could make it invincible: "I wield the large sword of Heaven to cut down specters in their five shapes; one stroke of this divine blade disperses a myriad of these beings" (Idries Shah, 1968).

Mesoamerica. As in most cultures, magic in pre-Conquest Mexico was highly specialized, permitted only to initiates. The spells themselves prove this, since their language was comprehensible only to occultists of the time; for example, a spell for alleviating intestinal pain—very common in tropical countries—was recorded in the seventeenth century by Jacinto de la Serna:

> Ea, white serpent, yellow serpent, observe that you are damaging the coffer . . . the tendons of meat. . . . But the white eagle already goes ahead, but it is not my intention to harm or destroy you, I want only to stop the harm you cause by withdrawing . . . by stopping your powerful hands and feet. But should you rebel and disobey, I will call to my aid the pledged spirit Huactzin and also call the black chichimeco, who is also hungry and thirsty, and who rips out his intentines, to follow you. I will also call my sister, the one with the skirt of jade, who soils and disorders stones and trees, and in whose company will go the pledged leopard, who will go and make noise in the place of the precious stones and treasures: the skeletal green leopard will also accompany her. (de la Serna, [1656] 1953)

The serpents mentioned at the beginning are the intestinal maladies (intestinal worms, pinworms, tapeworms, etc.) that harm the stomach and intestines. They are threatened with the eagle, which represents the needle used to pierce the stomach for bloodletting. They are also threatened with the spirit of medicinal plants and liquids.

Modern-day spells. With the development of experimental science, one would expect magic and religion to decline. In fact all three remain active, although magic has certainly yielded ground. (Magic tends to gain ground in times of crisis.) One finds both ancient and modern spells disguised in the folk tales recorded by the brothers Grimm, such as the traditional "Magic wand, by the powers you possess, I command you to make me [rich, invisible, etc.]."

Mexico provides an interesting example of the survival of ancient spells. In pre-Conquest Mexico, death was believed to be a change of life, and it was thought that the god of the underworld, Mictlantecuhtli, was a disembodied, skeletal being with whom those who died natural deaths were united in burial. After the Spanish conquest, the figure was assimilated, ending up as a being who lends aid when the request is made in the appropriate fashion. Thus today, at the entrance to thousands of churches throughout Mexico, one can buy prayers and spells "To Most Holy Death." The most common of these tries to obtain the love of some indifferent person and says: "Death, beloved of my heart, do not separate me from your protection; do not leave him a quiet moment, bother him every instant, frighten him, worry him so that he will always think of me." This is repeated as often as possible, with the interjection of Catholic prayers.

The new mythology is even felt in the kitchen. For example, when there is some fear the the cooking will not turn out well, the following spell is recited: "Saint Theresa, you who found God in the stew, help my stew not to be [salty, burned, overcooked, etc.]." It must be admitted, however, that this and many other spells are usually said out of habit, not from a certainty that the words, through their intrinsic power, will bring the desired results. Nevertheless, a belief in the power of spells can still be found among marginal groups even today, as it has been found in the past.

See Also Incantation; Language; Magic; Names and Naming; Oṃ; Postures and Gestures.

Bibliography

Caro Baroja, Julio. *The World of Witches.* Translated by O. N. V. Glendinning. Chicago, 1984.

Cassirer, Ernst. *Language and Myth.* Translated by Susanne K. Langer. New York, 1948.

Cirlot, J. E. *Simbolismo fonetico.* Barcelona, 1973.

Garcia Font, Juan. *El mundo de la magia.* Madrid, 1963.

Hitschler, K. *Pouvoirs secrets des mots et des symboles.* Paris, 1968.

Hocart, A. M. *Mito, ritual y costumbre.* Barcelona, 1975.

Idries Shah, Sayed. *Oriental Magic.* New ed. London, 1968.

Jung, C. G. *Symbols of Transformation,* vol. 5 of *Collected Works of Carl G. Jung.* 2d ed. Edited by Gerhard Adler and translated by R. F. Hull. Princeton, N. J., 1967.

Powells, L. *La sociedad secreta y la iluminación interior.* Buenos Aires, 1982.

Scholem, Gershom. *Kabbalah.* New York, 1974.

Serna, Jacinto de la. *Manual de Ministros de Indios para el conocimiento de sus idolatrías y extirpación de ellas* (1656). Reprint, Mexico City, 1953.

Suares, Carlo. *The Sepher Yetsira: Including the Original Astrology according to the Qabala and Its Zodiac.* Translated by Vincent Stuart. Boulder, Colo., 1976.

New Sources

Ancient Christian Magic. Marvin Meyer and Richard Smith, eds. Princeton, 1999.

Betz, Hans Dieter. *Greek Magical Papyri in Translation, Including the Demotic Spells.* Chicago, 1992.

Gager, John G. *Curse Tablets and Binding Spells from Antiquity and the Ancient World.* New York, 1992.

Magic Spells and Formulae: Aramaic Incantations of Late Antiquity. Joseph Naveh and Shaul Shaked, eds. Jerusalem, 1993.

Magika Hiera: Ancient Greek Magic and Religion. Christopher A. Obbink and Dirk Obbink, eds. New York, 1991.

Selected Studies on Ritual in the Indian Religions: Essays to D.J. Hoens. Ria Kloppenborg, ed. Leiden, 1983.

Versnel, H. S. "Some Reflections on the Relationship Magic-Religion." *Numen* 38 (1991): 177–197.

Beatriz Barba de Piña Chán (1987)
Translated from Spanish by Erica Meltzer
Revised Bibliography

SPENCER, BALDWIN See GILLEN, FRANCIS JAMES, AND BALDWIN SPENCER

SPENCER, HERBERT

SPENCER, HERBERT (1820–1903), was an English philosopher who became the most influential exponent of social evolutionism. Born in Derby, England, and educated largely in an atmosphere of religious dissent (and especially influenced by Quakers and Unitarians of the Derby Philosphical Society), Spencer combined a practical bent (for railway engineering, inventions, etc.) with a constant search for scientific principles. He became assistant editor at the *Economist* in London in 1848. After an early essay (1852) on the "development hypothesis" (concerning the laws of progress), he settled on evolution as the basic principle governing all change in the universe and began propagating a theory of evolution even before Charles Darwin's *On the Origin of Species* appeared in 1859.

The core of Spencer's literary output was published in several volumes under the general title *A System of Synthetic Philosophy;* this huge endeavor was left unfinished at Spencer's death. Its bearing on religion was at least fourfold. First, the prefatory volume, called *First Principles* (1862), contains the earliest philosophic exposition of the position known as agnosticism. Proceeding beyond the fideism of William Hamilton and Henry Mansel, both of whom maintained that the existence of God was a matter of faith rather than certain knowledge, Spencer argued that the force behind the cosmic process of evolution was unknown and unknowable. Second, this work and his books *The Principles of Biology* (1864–1867) and *The Principles of Psychology* (1855–1870) defended evolution as a universal natural process of development from simple and homogenous to more complex and differentiated forms of life over millions of years. Thus Spencer became embroiled with Darwin, T. H. Huxley, and others in the debate with those who held to a literal interpretation of *Genesis* or who denied the simian ancestry of human beings. Spencer also used the evolution debate as a forum to attack the idea of established religion.

Social evolutionism was the third and most important of his system's implications for religious questions. In *The Principles of Sociology* (1876–1896), he presented a barely qualified unilineal account of religious evolution and also fleshed out the first "sociology of religion" (at least in English). Spencer thought that the origins of religion lay in the worship of ghosts or ancestors; he extrapolated this view from the balance of evidence found among "primitives," or what he had no hesitation in describing as "the lowest races of mankind." Although primitive religions had, according to Spencer, barely evolved, he believed that marks of progress could be found in the religions of the greater civilizations, and he tended to plot Greco-Roman and Hindu polytheisms, the "cruder" monotheisms of Jews and Muslims, and the relative refinements of Catholicism and Protestantism on an ascending scale, envisaging his own agnostic, scientific position as the pinnacle in the history of religious consciousness. Apart from suggesting that history reflected progress toward more mature insights and institutional complexity, Spencer outlined the kinds of religious activity worth investigation. He isolated ceremonial institutions, for example—a category in which he placed laws of intercourse, habits and customs, mutilations, and funeral rites, as well as ecclesiastical institutions.

Finally, his system also carried ethical implications. In *The Principles of Ethics* (1879–1893), and in various social essays (especially those in his book *Education: Intellectual, Moral, and Physical,* 1861), he was seen as a liberal and an "individualist" who opposed punitive child-rearing, narrow biblicist morality, and state legislation that interferes in private affairs or with the entrepreneurial spirit.

Spencer's book sales were poor during his lifetime, and he eked out a frugal existence as a London bachelor until he was taken in by two elderly women in his old age. Through the later popularization of his ideas, however, his influence was immense, especially in the United States. His work and that of E. B. Tylor were crucial in conditioning the widespread preoccupation in English-speaking scholarship with the evolution of religion. Always ready for a lively interchange with other scholars and literati, Spencer struck up close intellectual friendships with George Eliot and her companion Henry Lewes and debated with Max Müller about mythology and the origins of religion. Spencer combined cautious distinctions and vitriolic attacks in an attempt to dissociate himself from Comtism and the views propounded by Frederick Harrison, an English disciple of Auguste Comte.

Spencer's written approach to religion suffered from a certain dilettantism: His knowledge of foreign languages was limited, and his educational background provided him no basis for the in-depth study of any single historical religion. He barely traveled outside Great Britain, although his encyclopedic tendencies, as well as his ability to collect data through travelers' accounts and mission reports from all over the world, made him a precursor to the armchair scholarship associated with James G. Frazer and *The Golden Bough.*

At the turn of the twentieth century, the liveliest popularizer of Spencer's ideas was W. H. Hudson, and his most cogent critic in matters of religious sociology was Émile Durkheim. His impact has waned with the decline of social evolutionism, but his influence on cosmological theory (that of Pierre Teilhard de Chardin, for instance) and on evolution-oriented educational philosophy, especially that of John Dewey, has been more durable.

Bibliography

Other works by Herbert Spencer include *Social Statics* (1851; reprint, New York, 1954), *The Study of Sociology* (London, 1873), *The Man versus the State* (1884; reprint, London, 1950), and *An Autobiography,* 2 vols. (London, 1904). There is no monograph especially devoted to Spencer's ideas about religion, although one-half of my "The Origins of the Comparative Study of Religions" (M.A. thesis, Monash University, Clayton, Australia, 1967) analyzes these in depth. Of published works on Spencer's social theory, J. D. Y. Peel's *Herbert Spencer: The Evolution of a Sociologist* (London, 1971) and David Wiltshire's *The Social and Political Thought of Herbert Spencer* (Oxford, 1978) are the best. See also J. W. Burrow's *Evolution and Society* (London, 1966) on Spencer in the context of British evolutionist thought as a whole; Eric J. Sharpe's *Comparative Religion: A History* (London, 1975) on placing Spencer in the history of the field of comparative religion; and my "Radical Conservatism in Herbert Spencer's Educational Thought," *British Journal of Educational Studies* (1969): 267–280, on religious and philosophical assumptions underlying Spencer's views on education.

New Sources

Agnosticism: Contemporary Responses to Spencer and Huxley. Bristol, U.K., 1995.

Duncan, David. *The Life and Letters of Herbert Spencer* (1908). London, 1996.

Fitzgerald, Timothy. "Herbert Spencer's Agnosticism." *Religious Studies* 23 (1987): 477–491.

Garry W. Trompf (1987)
Revised Bibliography

SPENER, PHILIPP JAKOB

SPENER, PHILIPP JAKOB (1635–1705), is the most widely recognized representative of early Pietism. Spener was born in Rappoltsweiler, Alsace, on January 13, 1635. He grew up in a Lutheran home in which the prevailing religious atmosphere was heavily influenced by Johann Arndt's *True Christianity,* the widely beloved devotional guide of seventeenth-century Lutheranism. Thus Spener was naturally predisposed toward Arndtian piety. Being an omnivorous reader, even at a tender age, he acquainted himself early with Puritan works that had been translated into German, as well as with those coming out of the reform party within Lutheranism, the avowed aim of which was the furtherance of religious devotion and ethical sensitivity within the Lutheran churches.

After he had completed the necessary preliminary studies, Spener matriculated at the University of Strasbourg in 1651. His student life manifested what was considered, by the prevailing standards of the day, an unusually ascetic tendency, insofar as he abstained from excessive drinking, revelry, and generally rude behavior. The dominant intellectual influence upon him during his university days was exerted by his theology professor, Johann Konrad Dannhauer (1603–1666), who, among other things, deepened Spener's lifelong interest in the teachings of Martin Luther. Upon completion of his studies, Spener spent some years in travel. That he did so largely in Reformed territories seems to say something about his appreciation of the piety found in various Reformed circles. During his itinerary he visited Basel, where he studied Hebrew under Johann Buxtorf (1599–1664). At Geneva the fiery French representative of Reformed Pietism, Jean de Labadie (1610–1674), impressed Spener so much that in 1667 he published a translation of one of Labadie's edificatory tracts. During an extended visit to Tübingen he set in motion various impulses toward the development of Swabian Pietism. Upon his return to Strasbourg (1663) he worked for his doctoral degree, taught and preached, and married Susanne Ehrhardt. They had eleven children.

Spener was called to a succession of pastorates, beginning with his appointment in 1666 to the position of senior pastor at Frankfurt am Main, where his emphasis on the catechization of children and on confirmation began to evoke critical reactions. So did his introduction of private meetings among the laity for the purpose of promoting a life of personal piety. Here, too, began his correspondence with highly placed people, which gradually helped to make him the most influential pastor in Germany during his time. Then, weary of the controversies that his activities and writings had provoked, Spener accepted a call to Dresden, in Saxony, where in 1686 he became chaplain of Elector Johann Georg III. However, the elector's lack of sympathy for Spener's concerns prompted him to move to Berlin in 1691. As rector of the Church of Saint Nicholas, as a member of the Lutheran consistory, and as inspector of churches he was now at the zenith of his effectiveness. Enjoying the confidence of the ruling house of Prussia and of a large segment of the German nobility, he was instrumental in opening up many pastorates throughout Germany to the appointment of pastors with Pietist leanings. Spener died on February 5, 1705, having expressed the wish that he be buried in a white coffin, a symbol of his hope that the church on earth might expect better times.

A prolific writer, Spener published many hundreds of letters; sermons; edificatory and catechetical tracts; works on genealogy, history, and heraldry; and writings of a polemical nature. The most famous of his literary productions was his *Pia desideria,* which appeared as a preface to Arndt's *Postil* in 1675 and later was published separately at various times. In it he proposed his program for the moral and spiritual reform of individuals, church, and society, which he followed throughout his life.

The major emphases of Spener's works are typical of Pietism, namely, natural humanity's lost estate, the necessity of its religious renewal, the possibility of its conscious experience of God's regenerating and sustaining presence, the desirability of continued spiritual nourishment through worship and appropriate literature, the holy life expressed in love for God and humans, the need for religious fellowship of like-minded people, and the hope of being able to reform the church for the purpose of reshaping a sinful world. Spener was opposed chiefly because of his often expressed vision of a better future for the church, which implied that the church was in need of renewal; for his insistence on religious instruction and on a way of life calculated to be a protest against the moral laxity of the day, which in the eyes of his opponents marked him as a zealot; and for instituting private meetings (*collegia pietatis*), which were seen as having the potential to fragment the church.

BIBLIOGRAPHY

Toward the end of his life Spener published some of his writings in his *Theologische Bedencken,* 4 vols. in 2 (Halle, 1700–1702), to which Karl Hildebrand von Canstein posthumously added *Letzte theologische Bedencken,* 3 vols. (Halle, 1711). Since then many of Spener's works have been published singly, and a long series of unsuccessful attempts have been made to bring out a complete edition of his writings. Toward the end of the nineteenth century Paul Grünberg, the noted Spener scholar, edited a modernized version of Spener's *Hauptschriften* (Gotha, 1889). The Historical Commission for the Study of Pietism (Kommission zur Erforschung des Pietismus) has begun publication of a multivolume edition of *Philipp Jakob Spener Schriften,* edited by Erich Beyreuther (Hildesheim, 1979–). Spener's best-known work, his *Pia desideria,* has been translated into very readable English and supplied with an introduction by Theodore G. Tappert (Philadelphia, 1964).

The classic biography of Spener is still Paul Grünberg's *Philipp Jakob Spener,* 3 vols. (Göttingen, 1893–1906); volume 3 contains an exhaustive bibliography. The major contemporary work on Spener is Johannes Wallmann's *Philipp Jakob Spener und die Anfänge des Pietismus* (Tübingen, 1970). Martin Kruse's *Speners Kritik am landesherrlichen Kirchenregiment und ihre Vorgeschichte* (Witten, 1971), and Jan Olaf Rüttgardt's *Heiliges Leben in der Welt: Grundzüge christlicher Sittlichkeit nach Philipp Jakob Spener* (Bielefeld, 1978), are important studies of Spener's attitude toward the church government of his day and of his ethics, respectively.

F. ERNEST STOEFFLER (1987)

SPINOZA, BARUCH

SPINOZA, BARUCH (1632–1677; known as Bento in Portuguese, Benedictus in Latin) was a Jewish rational naturalist of Marrano descent and the author of a rigorously monistic interpretation of reality expressed through an interlocking chain of propositions demonstrated in the geometrical manner. Spinoza's relentless drive for the naked truth was of singular intensity, and his scientific assessment of traditional Jewish thought thoroughly uncompromising. His aim was to contemplate things as they really are rather than as we would like them to be. Anthropocentrism is peremptorily and unceremoniously banished from his philosophical purview. Despite Spinoza's unadorned style, considerable controversy still envelops the interpretation of the very foundations of his thought.

Life and Works. On July 27, 1656, Bento de Spinoza was excommunicated by the ma'amad (ruling board) of the Amsterdam Jewish community into which he had been born. His father, Mikael, had been born in Vidigere (modern-day Figueira), Portugal, and had a close personal and financial relationship with the Portuguese merchant Abraham de Spinoza of Nantes, who was both his uncle and his father-in-law. Bento was the son of Mikael's second wife, Hanna Debora, who died when the child was scarcely six. Spinoza was never trained to be a rabbi, as previously thought, and was never a full-time pupil of Sha'ul Levi Morteira, a senior instructor in Talmud-Torah Ets Hayyim, although he may have attended an adult group known as Yeshivat Keter Torah that was led by Morteira. He apparently left school at age thirteen or fourteen to work in his father's business. From 1654, the year of Mikael's death, to 1656, the firm Bento y Gabriel de Spinoza was managed by Bento and his younger brother Gabriel. In March 1656, several months before his excommunication, Spinoza decided to take advantage of a Dutch law that protected minors who had been orphaned, and dispossessed himself of his father's estate, which was heavily burdened by debts.

The manuscript of the ban, written in Portuguese, the language of all documents of the Amsterdam Jewish community, is still preserved in the municipal archives of Amsterdam but contains no signatures. Other contemporary documents suggest that young Spinoza's heretical views, which led to his excommunication, were reinforced especially by Juan (Daniyye'l) de Prado. Excommunicated in 1658, de Prado was also a member of Morteira's Keter Torah circle and had attacked biblical anthropomorphism, poked fun at the idea of Jewish chosenness, and asserted that the world was eternal and the immutable laws of nature constituted the only form of divine providence. A report of Tomas Solano y Robles to the Inquisition of August 8, 1659 also indicated that Prado and Spinoza were excommunicated because they thought the Law (Torah) untrue, that souls die with the body, and that there is no God except philosophically speaking.

The precise reasons for the excommunication of Spinoza have been much discussed and debated. Steven Nadler has argued strongly that it was Spinoza's denial of personal immortality of the soul that played the key role (*Spinoza's Heresy,* 2001). In seventeenth-century Amsterdam, four community rabbis are especially prominent, and each one of them composed treatises in defense of immortality (Isaac Aboab, Sha'ul Levi Morteira, Moses Raphael d'Aguilar, and Menasseh ben Israel). Moreover, Morteira and Menasseh tended to lump together the three doctrines that seem to have played a role in Spinoza's ban: the truth of the Torah, divine providence, and immortality. Admittedly, the Dutch may not have been unduly concerned with the goings on in the Jewish community, but what is significant here is the psychology of the community that banned Spinoza, convinced as it was of the reality of such a threat.

Jonathan Israel, on the other hand, has argued eloquently and persuasively that it was Spinoza's public and provocative repudiation of the fundamentals of Rabbinic Judaism that made it impossible for the synagogue authorities not to expel him (Israel, 2001, pp. 162–174). This is reinforced by the exceptional severity of the excommunication formula used in his case. Israel points out that if the core ideas of Spinoza's mature system were already outlined in Spinoza's *Short Treatise* (1660–1661), and if he was capable of convincing Oldenburg in 1660 that he had outflanked Cartesianism, then it seems most unlikely that if one assumes, as most scholars do, that Spinoza started his philosophical odyssey around the time of his excommunication in 1656, just four years before, that he could conceivably have reached such a level of achievement so speedily. One must conclude that he had begun his philosophical phase long before this, as indicated by various strands of evidence. Thus Jarig Jelles affirms in his preface to *Opera Posthuma* that long before the ban in 1656, Spinoza had seriously engaged the Cartesian philosophy, rebelling inwardly against the teachings of the synagogue. Similarly, the eighteenth-century historian of Amsterdam Sephardic Jewry, David Franco Mendes, stresses that, even as a boy, Spinoza vacillated in his Jewish belief as a result of his philosophical excursions. But the clearest proof, argues Israel, is what Spinoza reveals in the autobiographical passage of the *Emendation of the Intellect* (1658), where he dwells on the long inner struggle he experienced before he could tear himself loose from the double existence he had been leading, in which outward conformity was uneasily joined with inner turmoil. Spinoza was finally able to cut the Gordian knot when, by 1655, his family business was ruined and his father's estate became encumbered by sizable debts.

According to Israel, the only personage who seems likely to have guided Spinoza in a radical direction was his ex-Jesuit Latin master Franciscus van den Ende. Thus was Spinoza's precocious genius caught up in the Cartesian ferment that swept the Netherlands, and the resulting identity crisis that smoldered within him since his early teens finally came to a head through a confluence of circumstances, in 1656. The ban was consequently the inevitable outcome of a long intellectual struggle that could no longer be contained.

Apart from the report in Lucas's biography of Spinoza, which elevates Spinoza to the status of a philosopher saint, there is no evidence of an appeal by the Jewish community that Spinoza be banished from the city of Amsterdam, and no legal record of any forced exile of Spinoza. In fact, says Nadler, Spinoza appears to have been in that city throughout most of the period of his excommunication in 1656 to the beginning of his correspondence in 1661 (Nadler, 1999, pp. 156–158, 163). It also appears that sometime before early 1659 he was either staying in or making periodic visits to Leiden to study at the university there. By early 1661, Spinoza was already well known as one who "excelled in the Cartesian philosophy." Nadler further suggests that it may have been his association with university life, where all instruction was in Latin, that first moved Spinoza to use the Latinized version of his first name, Benedictus.

It is to the final years of his Amsterdam period that Spinoza's earliest philosophical writings belong. According to Nadler, following Mignini, there are good reasons for thinking that the *Treatise on the Emendation of the Intellect (Tractatus de intellectus emendatione)*, an unfinished work on philosophical method and language, is the first of Spinoza's extant philosophical treatises (Nadler, 1999, pp. 175–176). Its content and terminology suggest a dating before the *Short Treatise on God, Man and His Well-Being (Korte Verhandeling van God de mensch en des zelfs welstand)*, which he probably began sometime in late 1660 or early 1661.

To devote himself more fully to his philosophical investigations, Spinoza decided in the summer of 1661 to settle in the small village of Rijnsburg, a few miles outside of Leiden. This sleepy village had been the center of Collegiant activity in Holland, and Spinoza may have been directed there by his Collegiant friends, though its proximity to Leiden, with its university where he probably still had friends from the time he had studied there, must have added to its attraction for Spinoza. In the back of the house in which he lodged was a room where Spinoza set up his lense-grinding equipment, where in addition to lenses he also made telescopes and microscopes. Problems in optics were an abiding interest for Spinoza, and Christian Huygens, a scientist of international reputation, considered himself, Spinoza, and the mathematician Johannes Hudde to be the three leading specialists who were seeking to improve and extend the capabilities of the microscope. Huygens got to know Spinoza personally in the early 1660s and often conferred with him about scientific matters.

While Spinoza was still in Amsterdam, his friends soon became aware of the originality of his philosophical approach and persuaded him to provide them with a concise exposition of his developing ideas so they could study and discuss them. Acceding to their request, Spinoza composed a work in Latin probably sometime between the middle of 1660 and his departure for Rijnsburg. When his friends asked for a Dutch version, Spinoza reworked the text, while making many additions and revisions. Fully conscious of the novelty and daring of his thought, he urged them "to be very careful about communicating these things to others" (Nadler, 1999, p. 186). Spinoza worked on the *Short Treatise* throughout 1661 and into 1662, transcribing and emending it. This short work outlines most of the essentials of Spinoza's mature system as exhibited in the *Ethics*. Moreover, *Short Treatise*, discovered about 1860 and of which two Dutch versions are available, bears witness to the birth pangs of Spinoza's thought, which, with its strong pantheistic coloring, is still couched in language that is clearly theological. Spinoza hesitated to publish it for fear of the Calvinist theologians who might be deeply offended by it and, as Spinoza himself puts it, will "with their usual hatred attack me, who absolutely dread quarrels" (Ep. 6; Curley, 1985, p. 188; Nadler, 1999, p. 191).

In April 1663 Spinoza moved to Voorburg, near The Hague, thus gaining the advantage of proximity to a major city. Before leaving, however, he visited his old friends in Amsterdam, whereupon Jarig Jelles and Lodewigk Meyer prevailed upon him to expand his Euclidean exposition of Descartes's *Principia philosophiae* and allow its publication together with his *Cogitata metaphysica* (*Metaphysical thoughts*). This was the only book of Spinoza's to appear in his lifetime under his own name. In 1670, after Spinoza's move to The Hague, his *Tractatus Theologico-Politicus* was published anonymously under a false imprint in Amsterdam. A few months thereafter, the Reformed Church Council of Amsterdam pronounced its condemnation of the book, and a series of lesser councils and consistories swiftly followed the example. In July 1674 the Court of Holland condemned the *Tractatus* and prohibited its printing, distribution, and sale. Although the great Dutch statesman Johan De Witt seems to have preferred not to proceed to a formal provincial ban of the *Tractatus*, it is a mistake, according to Jonathan Israel, to deduce from this that he viewed it in any way favorably (Israel, 2001, pp. 277–278). A surviving fragment from a diary of the classicist Jacob Gronovius reveals that in the Dutch governing circles Spinoza was then deemed the most dangerous of the Dutch atheists and considered by De Witt a miscreant deserving imprisonment. Given the vehemence of the outcry against him, Spinoza became apprehensive when he learned that a Dutch translation of his *Tractatus* was about to be published, and he contacted his faithful friend Jelles to stop the printing. The need for caution was underlined by the trial of Adrian Koerbagh, in which the prosecutor questioned him about his relations with Spinoza and attempted to obtain from him a confession that his book contained Spinoza's teachings. Koerbagh was condemned to ten years in prison but died shortly after, in jail, in October 1669. It was Adrian's tragic end, observes Nadler, "in Spinoza's eyes a sign of collusion between the secular and the sectarian authorities, that gave him the impetus to put the final touches on his *Tractatus* and prepare it for publication" (Nadler, 1999, p. 269).

In 1672 came the French invasion of Holland and the murder of De Witt, events that cast a dark shadow on Spinoza's last years. In February 1673 he received an invitation from the elector palatine Karl Ludwig to accept a professorship at Heidelberg. Spinoza refused it for fear that it would interfere with his "further progress in philosophy," and because of his misgivings about a statement in the invitation concerning the prince's confidence that Spinoza would not misuse his freedom in philosophical teaching to disturb the public religion (Nadler, 1999, p. 313).

Late in the summer of 1675, Spinoza completed his magnum opus, the *Ethica ordine geometrico demonstrata* (*Ethics*), and went to Amsterdam to arrange for its publication. There, as he wrote to Henry Oldenburg, "while I was negotiating, a rumor gained currency that I had in the press a book concerning God, wherein I endeavored to show there is no God" (*Letter* 68, September 1675). He therefore decided to put off the publication.

Spinoza's last major work, the *Tractatus Politicus,* written in 1676–1677, abandoned the theological idiom employed in the *Tractatus Theologico-Politicus* and offered instead a straightforward analysis of aristocracy, monarchy, and democracy in an attempt to demonstrate how a stable government could be ensured. This work was unfortunately interrupted by Spinoza's death on February 21, 1677. Another late work that remained incomplete was his Latin *Compendium of Hebrew Grammar,* which he "undertook at the request of certain of his friends who were diligently studying the Sacred Tongue" (Bloom, 1962, p. 11). Spinoza was buried in the New Church on the Spuy, and his *Opera posthuma,* edited by Jelles, Meyer, and Georg Hermann Schuller, appeared in November 1677 with only the initials B. D. S.

Biblical Critique. Spinoza's excommunication left a psychological scar that explains, partly at least, much of his subsequent bitterness toward his own people and their traditions. Although his pioneering biblical critique is frequently illuminating (for example, his view that Moses did not write the Pentateuch was already openly expressed by Isaac La Peyrère, whose work *Prae-Adamitae* Spinoza possessed), much of his writing in the *Tractatus* is marred by a onesidedness that distorts his judgment. Although it is undoubtedly true that Spinoza's intended audience was a Christian one, and that this dictated his partiality toward the figure of Christ and the Apostles, the unnecessary slurs against the Pharisees and the Rabbis and the unmistakable hostility that sometimes surfaces in a number of his formulations point to the psychological effects, conscious or unconscious, of his expulsion from the Jewish community. Spinoza characterizes his new method of investigating scripture as an empirical approach that accepts the biblical text as a natural datum. Since prophecy claims to surpass human understanding, Spinoza must somehow take it at its word. For the sake of the masses, who cannot be reached by reason alone, Spinoza is willing to grant that prophecy is possible. There may be, he says, laws of imagination that are unknown to humans, and the prophets, who received their revelations from God by means of the imagination, could thus perceive much that is beyond the boundary of the intellect. Although Moses is the chief of the prophets, his eminence consisted only in his receiving his prophecies through a real voice rather than an imaginary one. In other respects, however, Moses' imagination was not especially distinguished, for he was not sufficiently aware of God's omniscience, and he perceived the Decalogue not as a record of eternal truths but as the ordinances of a legislator. Spinoza set up the figure of Christ in contrast to Moses. If Moses spoke with God face-to-face, Christ communed with him mind-to-mind (a probable allusion to the Johanine conception of Christ as the *Logos,* as noted by Leavitt in *Christian Philosophy of Spinoza* [1991]). No one except Christ received the revelations of God without the aid of the imagination, meaning Christ possessed a mind far superior to those of his fellow men. Moreover, because Christ was sent to teach not only the Jews but the whole human race, it was not enough that his mind be attuned only to the Jews; it was attuned to ideas universal and true. If he ever proclaimed any revelations as laws, he did so because of the ignorance of the people. To those who were allowed to understand the mysteries of heaven, he taught his doctrines as eternal truths. To Spinoza, the biblical doctrine of the chosenness of the Hebrews implies on their part a childish or malicious joy in their exclusive possession of the revelation of the Bible. The doctrine is to be explained by the fact that Moses was constrained to appeal to the childish understanding of the people. In truth, he claims, the Hebrew nation was not chosen by God for its wisdom—it was not distinguished by intellect or virtue—but for its social organization. Spinoza explains the extraordinary fact of Jewish survival by the universal hatred that Jews drew upon themselves. From *Jeremiah* 9:23, Spinoza deduces that the Jews were no longer bound to practice their ceremonial law after the destruction of their state. The Pharisees continued these practices more to oppose the Christians than to please God. (Spinoza's view of the Pharisees is consistently derogatory. He attributes to them economic motives in their quarrel with the Sadducees and goes so far as to say that Pontius Pilate had made concession to the passion of the Pharisees in consenting to the crucifixion of Christ, whom he knew to be innocent. Maimonides is pejoratively termed a *Pharisee,* and Spinoza dismissed his interpretation of scripture as harmful, useless, and absurd.) Moreover, on the basis of *Ezekiel* 20:25, Spinoza finds the explanation of the frequent falling away of the Hebrews from the Law, which finally led to the destruction of their state, in the fact that God was so angry with them that he gave them laws whose object was not their safety but his vengeance. To motivate the common individual to practice justice and charity, certain doctrines concerning God and humans, says Spinoza, are indispensable. These, too, are a product of the prophetic imagination, but they will necessarily be understood philosophically by those who can do so. This universal scriptural religion is distinguished both from philosophical religion, which is a product of reason and is independent of any historical narrative, and from the vulgar religion of the masses, which is a product of the superstitious imagination and is practiced through fear alone; it consists of seven dogmas. The first four concern God and his attributes of existence, unity, omnipresence, and power and will. The other three deal with people's religious acts, and seem to derive from a Christian context: human beings' worship of God, their salvation, and their repentance. Each of the seven dogmas can be understood either imaginatively, in which case they would all be false, though useful, or philosophically, in which case they would all be true. Presumably, the average individual's score would be a mixed one.

Thought. Spinoza begins and ends with God. He is convinced that upon reflective analysis individuals become immediately aware that they have an idea of *substance,* or that which is in itself and is conceived through itself. Because substances having different attributes have nothing in common with one another, and because if two things have nothing in common, one cannot be the cause of the other, then it is evident that all the entities of which humans have experience, including themselves, must, because they all have extension in common, constitute one substance. Although a human being is also characterized by thought, which has nothing in common with extension, since one is aware of one's own extension, these two attributes cannot denote two substances but must be instead two parallel manifestations of one and the same substance. Spinoza thus insists that humans have a clear and distinct idea of substance or God having at least two parallel attributes. (In *Ethics* 1.11 he defines God as consisting of infinite attributes, each one of which expresses eternal and infinite essence, but some scholars believe that Spinoza is here using the term *infinite* as a synonym for *all*, and that what he means to say in this proposition is that God exists in every possible basic way. Although he elsewhere hints that there may be more than two attributes, he stops short of saying that there are. Even more controversial is the question whether the attributes are to be understood as subjective or objective.) Although this conception of substance is ultimately derived from empirical observation, it is not dependent on any particular observation as such but follows from the analysis of ideas and is therefore a product of the power of the mind to think ideas and analyze their logical structure. It is in this sense that knowledge of substance, or God, is *a priori*, deriving essentially from an analysis of a given true definition contained within the human mind. Spinoza designates knowledges of this kind as intuitive; he ranks it as the highest form of knowledge humans have, above deductive reasoning, which is mediated by the syllogistic process, and imagination, which is based either on hearsay or random experience. For Spinoza, the only adequate or clear and distinct ideas humans possess are those related to God, simple ideas, and common notions, or axioms, and what is deduced from them. Knowledge derived from syllogistic reasoning (which yields universal knowledge) and intuitive knowledge (which represents the power of the mind itself, on which syllogistic reasoning ultimately rests) are necessarily true.

God is eternally in a state of self-modification, producing an infinite series of modes that are manifested under either of his attributes. Under the attribute of extension, there is the immediate infinite mode, motion and rest; and under thought, the absolutely infinite intellect, or the idea of God. Finally come the finite modes, or particular things. Substance with its attributes is called *natura naturans*, the creative or active divine power, whereas the entire modal system, the system of what is created, is called *natura naturata*. Spinoza's God is thus not identical with the natural world as such but only with the creative ground that encompasses it.

While others consider human actions and appetites as virtues and vices to be bewailed or mocked, Spinoza considers them natural facts to be studied and understood. Vice is impotence, whereas virtue is power. Individuals act when anything is done of which they are the adequate cause; they suffer when anything is done of which they are only the partial cause. The first law of nature (as the Stoics had already noted) is the impulse, or effort (*conatus*), by which each thing endeavors to persevere in its own being. Humans do not desire anything because they think it good, but humans adjudge a thing good because they desire it. Desire is activity conducive to self-preservation; pleasure marks its increase, pain its decrease. Spinoza offers a pioneering psychological analysis of the ways through which the human imagination acts and discusses in some detail the various laws of what he calls the association and imitation of the emotions.

Spinoza calls active emotions those which are related to the mind insofar as it acts and of which an individual is the adequate cause. Of these there are only two: desire, or the effort of self-preservation in accordance with the dictates of reason, and pleasure, or the enjoyment experienced from the mind's contemplation of itself whenever it conceives an adequate or true idea. In the conflict of emotions, weaker emotions are removed by stronger ones, as Plato had already indicated in the *Timaeus*. Knowledge of good and evil can be a determining factor only insofar as it is considered an emotion—that is, a consciousness of pleasure and pain. Inasmuch as happiness consists in humans' preservation of their own beings and they act virtuously when effecting their self-preservation in accordance with their full powers, humans must seek to maximize their power to act, which means removing their passive emotions to the greatest possible extent and substituting for them active emotions.

Spinoza suggests various remedies for the passive emotions, which he describes as mental diseases (already described by the Stoics). Since a passive emotion is a confused idea, the first remedy is to remove confusion and transform it into a clear and distinct idea. Another remedy is to realize that nothing happens except through the necessity of an infinite causal series. Humans should also endeavor to expel the many ghosts that haunt their minds by contemplating the common properties of things. Indeed, the emotions themselves may become an object of contemplation. The sovereign remedy, however, is the love of God. The mind has the capacity to cause all affections of the body to be related to the idea of God; that is, to know them by intuitive knowledge. Spinoza endeavors to demonstrate the immortality of the human mind (stripped of sensation, memory, and imagination) but insists that even during a lifetime one can experience that state of immortality which he calls blessedness and describes as union with, or love for, God. The intellectual love of God, which arises from intuitive knowledge, is eternal and is part of the infinite love with which God loves himself.

Influence on Later Thought. Among the major philosophers, Spinoza was the only one who did not found a school. During the first hundred years after Spinoza's death, his name was connected principally with the *Tractatus*

Theologico-Politicus, and as Isreal has emphsized, "no one else rivalled his notoriety as chief challenger of revealed religion") (Isreal, 2001, p. 259). Only toward the end of the eighteenth century did Spinoza begin to arouse enthusiasm among men of letters. In 1778, Johan Gottfried Herder equated Spinoza with John himself as the apostle of love, and in 1780 Gotthold Ephraim Lessing declared to Friedrich Jacobi that "there is no other philosophy than that of Spinoza" (Vallée, *Spinoza Conversations,* 1988, p. 86). Although a follower of Christian Wolff, who directed a formidable critique against Spinoza, Moses Mendelssohn hailed Spinoza as early as 1775 as a martyr for the furthering of human knowledge. As a result of the publication of Mendelssohn's *Morgenstunden* in 1785, in which he sought to attribute to Lessing a purified form of pantheism, Jacobi countered with a work called *Über die Lehre des Spinoza* ("On the teaching of Spinoza," 1785), in which he branded Spinozism as atheism and the Jewish Qabbalah as a confused Spinozism. Goethe, on the other hand, eagerly devoured Spinoza's *Ethics,* noting that it "agreed most with his own conception of nature," and that "he always carried it with him." Goethe shared two of Spinoza's most fundamental principles, his monism and his theory of necessity (Bell, 1984, pp. 153, 168). Salomon Maimon, the first to call Spinoza's system *acosmic,* spoke admiringly in his autobiography of the profundity of Spinoza's philosophy, and his first book, *Versuch über die Transendentalphilosophie* (*An essay on Transcendental philosophy,* 1790), was an attempt to unite Kantian philosophy with Spinozism. According to G. W. F. Hegel (1770–1831), there was "either Spinozism or no philosophy," and Friedrich Wilhelm Joseph von Schelling (1775–1854) wrote that "no one can hope to progress to the true and complete in philosophy without having at least once in his life sunk himself in the abyss of Spinozism" (McFarland, 1969, p. 103).

Appreciation for Spinoza in England was due especially to Samuel Taylor Coleridge, who wrote in about 1810 that only two systems of philosophy were possible, that of Spinoza and that of Immanuel Kant (1724–1804). In a letter of 1881, Friedrich Nietzsche (1844–1900) expressed his astonishment at the kinship between Spinoza's position on morality and his own, although elsewhere he is severely critical of Spinoza. Martin Buber (1878–1965) found much inspiration in Spinoza, seeing in him the highest philosophical exemplification of Judaism's unique quest for unity, but he criticized the Spinozistic attempt to depersonalize God.

In the 1850s, Shemu'el David Luzzatto stirred up a literary polemic concerning Spinoza after having been aroused by the first laudatory biography of Spinoza in Hebrew (1846), written by the poet Me'ir Letteris; by the essays of Schelling's student Senior Sachs from 1850 to 1854, in which he links together Shelomoh Ibn Gabirol, Avraham ibn Ezra, the qabbalists, and Spinoza; and by Shelomoh Rubin's *Moreh nevukhim he-hadash* (1857), which contains a positive account of Spinoza's thought. Luzzatto attacked Spinoza's emphasis on the primacy of the intellect over the feelings of the heart and his denial of free will and final causes, and called unjustified his attack on the Pharisees and on the Mosaic authorship of all of the Pentateuch. Nahman Krochmal's son, Avraham, wrote an apologetic work, *Eben ha-ro'shah* (1871), in which he defended Spinoza, whom he reverently called *Rabbenu* (Our Master) Baruch (an epithet already applied to Spinoza by Moses Hess (1812–1875) in 1837, and later also adopted by Einstein). Hermann Cohen later mounted a virulent attack against Spinoza, as impassioned as that by Luzzatto, in Cohen's "Spinoza über Staat und Religion, Judentum und Christentum" (1905; 1924, pp. 290–372).

Shortly after arriving at Sedeh Boker on December 13, 1953, in order to settle at a kibbutz in the Negev, first prime minister of Israel, Ben Gurion, published an article in the newspaper *Davar* titled "Let Us Make Amends," in which he expressed the wish "to restore to our Hebrew language and culture, the writings of the most original and profound thinker that appeared amongst the Hebrew people in the last two thousand years." The injustice that required mending was thus not the excommunication of Spinoza, since in Ben Gurion's eyes that was nothing but a historic curiosity, which in the course of time had been automatically nullified. What still needed mending was the literary cultural fact that Hebrew literature remains incomplete as long as it does not include the entire corpus of Spinoza's writings as one of the greatest spiritual assets of the Jewish nation. Ben Gurion's wish has now finally been fulfilled with the appearance of all of Spinoza's major works in Hebrew translation, and with the establishment of a Spinoza Institute in Jerusalem which holds biannual conferences devoted to Spinoza's thought. This piece of historical irony by which Spinoza's philosophical legacy has now been emphatically included in the intellectual life of Israel would undoubtedly have afforded Spinoza a measure of supreme delight. (See Dorman, 1990, pp. 154–163).

Spinoza has been regarded as the founder of scientific psychology, and his influence has been seen in the James–Lange theory of the emotions and in some of the central concepts of Freud (see Bidney, 1962). A more recent version of this kind of influence is found in the work of the noted neurologist Antonio Damasio, *Looking for Spinoza: Joy, Sorrow, and the Feeling Brain* (New York, 2003). Spinoza has also received an enormous amount of attention in the former Soviet Union. Spinoza's concept of nature as self-caused, infinite, and eternal was first singled out for comment by Friedrich Engels in his *Dialectics of Nature.* From the Soviet viewpoint, Spinoza's materialism is unfortunately wrapped in a theological garb, but his consistent application of the scientific method is seen as overshadowing "the historically transient and class-bounded in his philosophy" (see Kline, 1952, p. 33)

In America, the transcendentalists of the eighteenth century held Spinoza in very high regard. Oliver Wendell Holmes (1841–1935) read and reread Spinoza's *Ethics,* and his famous formulation that freedom of thought reached a limit only when it posed a "clear and present danger" appears to have been made under Spinoza's influence. Moreover, Spinoza had special appeal for the young American Jewish intellectuals who were children of the first wave of immigrants from eastern Europe. Morris Raphael Cohen (1880–1947) had, as a youthful Marxist, valued Spinoza the cosmopolitan who had rejected Judaism, and Lewis Feuer described Horace M. Kallen's *The Book of Job as a Greek Tragedy* (New York, 1918) as "embedded in a Spinozist matrix." Some of the greatest Jewish scientists and philosophers in modern times, such as Albert Einstein, Samuel Alexander, and Henri Bergson, also felt a deep affinity with Spinoza (see Feuer, pp. 36–79).

Bibliography

The best critical edition of Spinoza's works is that by Carl Gebhardt, *Spinoza Opera,* 4 vols. (Heidelberg, 1925; a fifth volume was added in 1987). According to Nadler, this will be superseded by an edition from the Groupe de Recherches Spinozistes. A useful edition with translation and notes of Spinoza's *Tractatus Politicus* is by A. G. Wernham, *Benedict de Spinoza, The Political Works* (Oxford, 1958). For Spinoza's Compendium of Hebrew Grammar, see Baruch Spinoza, *Hebrew Grammar,* ed. and trans. by Maurice J. Bloom (New York, 1962). A new and reliable translation of Spinoza's works by E. M. Curley is *The Collected Works of Spinoza,* vol. l (Princeton, N.J., 1985; vol. 2, forthcoming). In the meantime, there has appeared *Spinoza, Complete Works, with translations by Samuel Shirley,* edited with introduction and notes by Michael L. Morgan (Indianapolis, 2002). A comprehensive bibliography of Spinoza up to 1942 is Adolph S. Oko's *The Spinoza Bibliography* (Boston, 1964), which has been supplemented by Jon Wetlesens's *A Spinoza Bibliography,* 1940–1970, 2d rev. ed. (Oslo, 1971). See also E. M. Curley's bibliography in *Spinoza: Essays in Interpretation,* edited by Eugene Freeman and Maurice Mandelbaum (LaSalle, Ill., 1975), pp. 263–316; Wilhelm Totok's *Handbuch der Geschichte der Philosophie,* vol. 4, *Frühe Neuzeit 17* (Frankfurt, 1981), pp. 232–296; and Theo van der Werf, H. Siebrand, and C. Westerveen's *A Spinoza Bibliography, 1971–1983* (Leiden, 1984).

The best biography of Spinoza is Steven Nadler, *Spinoza: A Life* (Cambridge, U.K., 1999); supplemented by his *Spinoza's Heresy: Immortality and the Jewish Mind* (Oxford, 2001). See also A. Kasher and S. Biderman, "Why was Baruch De Spinoza Excommunicated?" In *Sceptics, Millenarians, and Jews,* edited by David S. Katz and Jonathan Israel (Leiden, 1990), pp. 98–141. For Spinoza's Marranism and his relationship to later thinkers, see Yirmiyahu Yovel, *Spinoza and Other Heretics: The Maranno of Reason and The Adventure of Immanence* (Princeton, N.J., 1989) 2 vols. Thomas McFarland, *Coleridge and the Pantheist Tradition* (Oxford, 1969); David Bell, *Spinoza in Germany from 1670 to the Age of Goethe* (London, 1984). For the Pantheism Controversy, see Frederick C. Beiser, *The Fate of Reason* (Cambridge, Mass., 1987) 44-108; and Gerard Vallée, J. B. Lawson, and C. G. Chapple, *The Spinoza Conversations between Lessing and Jacobi* (Lanham, Md., 1988). For Jewish critiques of Spinoza, see Hermann Cohen, "Spinoza über Statt und Religion, Judentum und Christentum," (1905), reprinted in Cohen's *Jüdische Schriften* (Berlin, 1924) 3.290–372; and Menahem Dorman, *The Spinoza Dispute in Jewish Thought* (Hakibbutz Hameuchad, 1990; in Hebrew). For Spinoza and modern psychological theory, see David Bidney, The Psychology and Ethics of Spinoza (reprint, New York, 1962); and Antonio Damazio, *Looking For Spinoza: Joy, Sorrow, and the Feeling Brain* (New York, 2003). For Spinoza in the former Soviet Union and in America, see G. L. Kline, *Spinoza in Soviet Philosophy* (London, 1952); and Lewis S. Feuer, "Spinoza's Thought and Modern Perplexities: Its American Career," in Barry S. Kogan, ed., *Spinoza: A Tercentenary Perspective* (Cincinnati) pp. 36-79. A good brief introduction to Spinoza is Stuart Hampshire's *Spinoza* (Baltimore, 1951). The most detailed and illuminating commentary on Spinoza's *Ethics* is Harry A. Wolfson's *The Philosophy of Spinoza,* 2 vols. (Cambridge, Mass., 1934). A comprehensive introduction and commentary (in Hebrew) on the *Short Treatise,* along with a Hebrew translation by Rachel Hollander-Steingart, can be found in *Ma'amar qatsar 'al Elohim, ha-adam, ve-oshero,* edited by Joseph Ben Shlomo (Jerusalem, 1978). A similar edition of *De Intellectus Emendatione* with Hebrew commentary is *Ma'amar 'al tiqqun ha-sekhel,* translated by Nathan Spiegel and edited by Joseph ben Shlomo (Jerusalem, 1972). Detailed analyses of Spinoza's *Theological-Political Treatise* can be found in Sylvan Zac, *Spinoza et l'Interpretation de l'Ecriture* (Paris, 1965); Leo Strauss, *Spinoza's Critique of Religion* (New York, 1965); and André Malet, *Le Traité Theologico-Politique de Spinoza et la pensée biblique* (Paris, 1966). See also the important study of J. Samuel Preus, *Spinoza and the Irrelevance of Biblical Authority* (Cambridge, U.K., 2001); Steven Frankel, "Politics and Rhetoric: Spinoza's Intended Audience in the *Tractatus Theologico-Politicus,*" *Review of Metaphysics* 52.4 (June 1999): 897–924; Steven Frankel, "The Piety of a Heretic: Spinoza's Interpretation of Judaism," *Journal of Jewish Thought and Philosophy* 11.2 (November 2002): 117–134; Shlomo Pines, *Studies in the History of Jewish Thought,* edited by Warren Z. Harvey and Moshe Idel (Jerusalem, Israel, 1997), 660–734 (The Collected Works of S. Pines, vol. 5); and Frank Leavitt, "The Christian Philosophy of Benedict de Spinoza," *Daat* 26 (1991): 97–108 (Hebrew).

Indispensable collections of documents on Spinoza's life are I. S. Révah's *Spinoza et le dr. Juan de Prado* (Paris, 1959) and "Aux origines de la rupture spinozienne," *Revue des études juives* 3 (July–December 1964): 359–431, and A. M. Vaz Dias's *Spinoza Mercator & Autodidactus* (The Hague, 1932), translated from Dutch in *Studia Rosenthaliana* 16 (November 1982) and supplemented by four related articles. A stimulating account of the social-political context of Spinoza's work is Lewis S. Feuer's *Spinoza and the Rise of Liberalism* (Boston, Mass., 1958). Two important and provocative interpretations of Spinoza from the viewpoint of contemporary philosophy are E. M. Curley's *Spinoza's Metaphysics: An Essay in Interpretation* (Cambridge, Mass., 1969) and Jonathan Bennett's *A Study of Spinoza's Ethics* (Indianapolis, Ind., 1984).

Useful collections of essays on Spinoza include *Studies in Spinoza: Critical and Interpretive Essays,* edited by S. Paul Kashap (Berkeley, Calif., 1972); *Spinoza: A Collection of Critical Essays,* edited by Marjorie Grene (Garden City, N.Y., 1973);

Speculum Spinozanum, 1677–1977, edited by Siegfried Hessing (London, 1977); *Spinoza: New Perspectives,* edited by Robert W. Shahan and J. I. Biro (Norman, Okla., 1978); *The Philosophy of Baruch Spinoza,* edited by Richard Kennington (Washington, D.C., 1980); *Spinoza, His Thought and Work,* edited by Nathan Rotenstreich and N. Schneider (Jerusalem, 1983); *Spinoza's Political and Theological Thought,* edited by C. De Deugd (Amsterdam, 1984); *God and Nature: Spinoza's Metaphysics,* edited by Yirmiyahu Yovel (Leiden, 1991); *Spinoza on Knowledge and the Human Mind,* edited by Y. Yovel (Leiden, 1994); *Desire and Affect: Spinoza as Psychologist,* edited by Y. Yovel (New York, 1999); *The Cambridge Companion to Spinoza,* edited by Don Garrett (Cambridge, U.K., 1996); *Spinoza: Metaphysical Themes,* edited by Olli Koistinen and John Biro (Oxford, 2002); *Spinoza,* edited by Gideon Segal and Y. Yovel (Burlington, Vt., 2002). For Spinoza and his relationship to Judaism, see Genevieve Brykman, *La Judeite de Spinoza* (Paris, 1972); Zeev Levy, *Baruch or Benedict: On Some Jewish Aspects of Spinoza's Philosophy* (New York, 2002); *Jewish Themes in Spinoza's Philosophy,* edited by Heidi M. Ravven and L. E. Goodman (New York, 2002). For Spinoza and the Enlightenment, see the superb study of Jonathan Israel, *Radical Enlightenment: Philosophy and the Making of Modernity 1650–1750* (Oxford, 2001); and Adam Sutcliffe, *Judaism and Enlightenment* (Cambridge, U.K., 2003). On the troubled question of whether there were qabbalistic influences on Spinoza's thought, see the good summary and analysis of this issue by Nissim Yosha, *Myth and Metaphor: Abraham Cohen Herrera's Philosophical Interpretation of Lurianic Kabbalah* (Jerusalem, Israel, 1994; in Hebrew) pp. 361–374.

DAVID WINSTON (2005)

SPIRITISM SEE AFRO-BRAZILIAN RELIGIONS; KARDECISM; NECROMANCY

SPIRIT POSSESSION

This entry consists of the following articles:

SPIRIT POSSESSION: AN OVERVIEW

Spirit possession may be broadly defined as any altered or unusual state of consciousness and allied behavior that is indigenously understood in terms of the influence of an alien spirit, demon, or deity. The possessed act as though another personality—a spirit or soul—has entered their body and taken control. Dramatic changes in their physiognomy, voice, and manner usually occur. Their behavior often is grotesque and blasphemous. Justinus Kerner, a nineteenth-century German physician and disciple of the philosopher Friedrich Schelling, describes a demonically possessed woman in his native Swabia:

> In this state the eyes were tightly shut, the face grimacing, often excessively and horribly changed, the voice repugnant, full of shrill cries, deep groans, coarse words; the speech expressing the joy of inflicting hurt or cursing God and the universe, addressing terrible threats now to the doctor, now to the patient herself. . . . The most dreadful thing was the way in which she raged when she had to submit to be touched or rubbed down during the fits; she defended herself with her hands, threatening all those who approached, insulting and abusing them in the vilest terms; her body bent backward like a bow was flung out of the chair and writhed upon the ground, then lay there stretched out full length, stiff and cold, assuming the very experience of death. (quoted in Oesterreich, 1930, p. 22)

Some of the possessed, those who suffer what the German scholar Traugott K. Oesterreich has called a somnambulistic form of possession, remember nothing of their possession. Others experience a more "lucid" form and remember it. In this case the possessed become passive spectators of an "internal" drama. Often they are said to be inhabited simultaneously or sequentially by several spirits, and their behavior varies according to the different possessing spirits. Although possession is sometimes considered desirable, as in spirit mediumship, more often, at least initially, it is considered undesirable, an affliction requiring a cure. Cures, or exorcisms, may be simple affairs involving only the exorcist and his patient, or they may be elaborate, highly theatrical performances involving the patient's whole community.

In one form or another, spirit possession occurs over most of the world. The anthropologist Erika Bourguignon found that in a sample of 488 societies 74 percent believe in spirit possession. The highest incidence is found in Pacific cultures and the lowest in North and South American Indian cultures. Belief in possession is widespread among peoples of Eurasia, Africa, and the circum-Mediterranean region and among descendants of Africans in the Americas. It occurs more frequently in agricultural societies than in hunting and gathering ones, and women seem to be possessed more often than men. However, altered states of consciousness, such as trance, are not always interpreted as spirit possession. In Bourguignon's 488 societies, 437 societies (90%) have one or more institutionalized forms of altered states of consciousness, but only 251 of these (52% of the total) understand them in terms of spirit possession.

Scholars have attempted to classify possession phenomena in many ways. Some have based their classification on the moral evaluation of the spirit. The French scholar Henri Jeanmarie argues that exorcism aims at the permanent expulsion of the possessing spirit in societies that regard the spirit as essentially evil, whereas exorcism in societies that regard the spirit as morally neutral aims at the transformation of the "malign" spirit into a "benign" one. Other scholars have looked to the cultural evaluation of the possession state itself. In *Ecstatic Religion* (1971) the anthropologist I. M. Lewis distinguishes between central and peripheral spirit possession. The former are highly valued by at least a segment of society and support the society's moral, political, and religious assumptions. In these cases possession is considered desirable, and the spirits are generally thought to be sympathetic. Peripheral possession does not support, at least directly, the moral, political, and religious order. In these cases possession is considered undesirable and requires some form of cure, and the spirits are thought to be malign. Still other scholars, such as Oesterreich, have sought the basis for classification in the phenomenology of the experience. Oesterreich divides possession into involuntary or spontaneous possession and voluntary or artificial possession.

Oesterreich's distinction plays an implicit role in many other classification systems. For example, in *Tikopia Ritual and Belief* (1967, p. 296), the anthropologist Raymond Firth distinguishes "spirit possession," "spirit mediumship," and "shamanism" on the basis of the host's control of the spirit. According to Firth, spirit possession refers to "phenomena of abnormal behavior which are interpreted by other members of the society as evidence that a spirit is controlling the person's actions and probably inhabiting his body." Spirit mediumship involves the "use of such behavior by members of the society as a means of communication with what they understand to be entities in the spirit world." The medium's behavior must be fairly regular and intelligible. Firth applies the term *shamanism* "to those phenomena where a person, either a spirit medium or not, is regarded as controlling spirits, exercising his mastery over them in socially recognized ways." In the case of spirit mediumship and shamanism, at least after the initial possession, the state of possession is often deliberately induced by inhalation of incense or mephitic fumes (as at the Delphic oracle in ancient Greece), by ingestion of drugs (as in North Africa and the Middle East) or emotionally laden substances (such as the blood of a sacrificial victim in parts of India), or by mechanical means (such as drumming, dancing, hyperventilation, or the incantation of repetitive prayers).

All these classifications impose on the reality of spirit possession a conceptual rigidity that distorts the essential fluidity of the phenomena. Often the host moves in and out of all of Firth's three states—if not in one séance then in the course of his relationship with the spirit. The anthropologist Esther Pressel found that in the African American cults of Brazil initial possessions tended to be involuntary and subsequent ones voluntary as the host gained control of his or her spirit. One Moroccan woman with whom this writer worked suffered periodic possessions in which she was very much the victim of her possessing spirit *(jinī)*. At times, however, she was able to gain some control over the spirit and convey its messages to those about her. It was rumored, though this writer never witnessed this, that she would sometimes force her possessing spirit to perform nefarious deeds for her and her secret clientele.

Too rigid a definition of spirit possession precludes recognition of its power as an authentic and believable metaphor for other conditions not usually associated by the Western observer with altered states of consciousness or with trance. For example, possession metaphors were used in Morocco to describe extreme rage, sexual excitement, love, prolonged erections, morbid depressions, and on occasion those conditions in which the subject did not want to accept the consequences of his or her own desires. In the West, possession metaphors also occur—for love, extreme anger, depersonalization, multiple personality, autonomous behavior—in short, for any experience in which the subject feels "beside himself." Such metaphors may be a residue of an earlier belief in spirit possession.

The discussion in the remainder of this article will be restricted to spirit possession as defined by Firth. Exorcisms will be divided into the permanent and the transformational. Permanent exorcisms aim at the complete expulsion of the possessing spirit; the patient is liberated from all spirit influence. Transformational exorcisms strive to change the nature of the spirit from malign to benign; as a result the relationship between spirit and host also changes. In transformational exorcisms, the patient is usually incorporated into a cult that sponsors periodic ritual occasions when the patient can again experience possession and reaffirm his relationship with his possessing spirit.

Altered States of Consciousness. An altered state of consciousness refers to any mental state subjectively recognized or objectively observed as a significant deviation from "normal" waking consciousness. Sleep, dreaming, hypnosis, brainwashing, mental absorption, meditation, and various mystical experiences are all altered states of consciousness. These states are characterized by disturbances in concentration, attention, judgment, and memory; by archaic modes of thought; by perceptual distortions, including those of space, time, and body; by an increased evaluation of subjective experiences, a sense of the ineffable, feelings of rejuvenation, loss of a sense of control, and hypersuggestibility.

The altered state of consciousness most frequently associated with spirit possession is trance (Lat., *trans,* "across," and *ire,* "to go"; cf. OFr., *transir,* "to pass from life to death"), defined as "a condition of dissociation, characterized by the lack of voluntary movement and frequently by automatisms in act and thought, illustrated by hypnotic and mediumistic conditions" (*Penguin Dictionary of Psychology,* Harmondsworth, 1971, p. 38). The subject experiences a detachment from the structured frames of reference that support his usual interpretation and understanding of the world about him. The subject is, as the Balinese say, "away," quite literally dissociated (Lat., *de,* "from," and *socius,* "companion"), removed from companionship and from society.

Ritual trance, the trance of possession, is induced by various physiological, psychological, and pharmacological means. The most common techniques involve sensory bombardment (an increase in exteroceptive stimulation), sensory deprivation (a decrease in exteroceptive stimulation), or an alternation between the two. Techniques of bombardment include singing, chanting, drumming, clapping, monotonous dancing, inhaling incense and other fumes, and experiencing the repetitive play of light and darkness. Techniques of deprivation include ideational and perceptual restrictions, blindfolding, and isolation. Fasting and other dietary restrictions, hypo- and hyperventilation (during incantations, for example), and ingestion of drugs (tobacco, cannabis, and various psychedelic substances) may also be used. Psychosocial factors—group excitement, heightened expectations, theatricality, costumes and masks, a generally permissive atmosphere, and the presence of strong behavioral models—all facilitate trance.

Although trance is considered the hallmark of possession, it is important to recognize that "possession" has been used to describe nontrance states and that the experience of possession is neither continuous nor unchanging. The possessed person moves in and out of dissociation. There are some moments of ordinary lucidity, other moments when consciousness appears to have surrendered to the possessing spirit, and still other moments of complete unconsciousness. Frequently there is a "doubling of consciousness" (*Verdoppelungserlebnis*), whereby one of the two (or more) consciousnesses looks on passively at what is happening and is quite capable of remembering what Oesterreich has called "the terrible spectacle" of possession. At other times consciousness is submerged, and the actor loses all awareness and memory of the spectacle; recall of the trance experience is confused, dreamlike, and often stereotypic. The possessed person makes frequent use of mythic plots and symbols when recounting the experience, although his tales are not as elaborate as those of the shaman describing, for example, his voyage to the netherworld.

THE POSSESSION IDIOM. The interpretation of dissociation, ritual trance, and other altered states of consciousness as spirit possession is a cultural construct that varies with the belief system prevalent in a culture. Although the relationship between spirit and host has been described in many different ways, most indigenous descriptions suggest the spirit's entrance, intrusion, or incorporation into the host. The relationship is one of container to contained. Usually, in any single culture a wide variety of metaphorical expressions are employed. The spirit is said to mount the host (who is likened to a horse or some other beast of burden), to enter, to take possession of, to have a proprietary interest in, to haunt, to inhabit, to besiege, to be a guest of, to strike or slap, to seduce, to marry, or to have sexual relations with the host. In part, this variety reflects changes in the spirit-host relationship, a relationship that should not be regarded as static, well-defined, and permanent but rather as dynamic, ill-defined, and transitory.

Although it is often of analytic significance to distinguish between the psychobiological condition of the possessed (the trance state) and the cultural construct ("spirit possession"), it should be recognized that the construct itself affects the structure and evaluation of the psychobiological condition. The construct articulates the experience, separating it from the flow of experience and giving it meaning. The experience itself instantiates the interpretive schema. The process involves the subjectification of the "external" elements, the symbols, of the spirit idiom.

It is important to stress the belief in the existence of the spirits on the part of the possessed and those about him or her in order to grasp adequately the spirits' articulatory function. The spirit idiom provides a means of self-articulation that may well radically differ from the self-articulation of the Westerner. Much of what the Westerner "locates" within the individual may be "located" outside the individual in those societies in which the spirit idiom is current. This movement inward is perhaps seen on a literary level in the gradual internalization of the "double" in nineteenth- and twentieth-century European and American literature.

Spirits, as exterior to the individual, are not projections in the psychoanalytic sense of the word. For the psychoanalyst, projection is the subject's attribution to another of feelings and desires the subject refuses to recognize in him or her self. Projection occurs only after introjection. The movement is centrifugal, from inner to outer. If "external" spirits represent as "outside" what the Westerner would regard as within, then, strictly speaking, there can be no projection, for there is nothing within to project. The movement here is centripetal, from outer to inner.

A construction of human experience so radically different from that of the Westerner is difficult to convey; nonetheless, it has been suggested by many scholars who have worked with the spirit-possessed. The anthropologist Godfrey Lienhardt, for example, refers in his study of the Dinka, a Nilotic people, to "Powers" (spirits) as extrapolations or images that are the active counterpart of the passive element in Dinka experience. Since the Dinka have no conception of mind as a mediator between self and world, the images—the powers or spirits—mediate between self and world:

> Without these Powers or images or an alternative to them there would be for the Dinka no differentiation between the experience of the self and of the world which acts upon it. Suffering, for example, would be merely "lived" or endured. With the imaging of the grounds of suffering in a particular Power, the Dinka can grasp its nature intellectually in a way which satisfies them, and thus to some extent transcend and dominate it in this act of knowledge. With this knowledge, this separation of a subject and an object in experience, there arises for them also the possibility of creating a form of experience they desire and of freeing themselves symbolically from what they must otherwise passively endure. (Lienhardt, 1961, p. 170)

Of utmost significance in both projection and articulation through "external" spirits is the status accorded the vehicle within the individual's culture. A Western paranoid who believes he or she is pursued by secret agents responds to dominant cultural images, just as does an African who believes himself hounded by ancestral spirits. Both give expression to feelings of persecution and suffer the consequences of that expression. In the first instance, the secret agents are not generally thought to exist by anyone other than the paranoid. In the second instance, the ancestral spirits are generally recognized by others. The consequences of this difference are immense. The haunted person does not necessarily suffer the same social isolation, loneliness, derision, and feelings of abandonment as does the paranoid. He or she enters a new symbolic order. The paranoid learns the language of the spirits and of possession and submits to its grammar; and is afforded the possibility of therapeutic intervention.

This is not meant to suggest that the idiom of spirit possession is more conducive to cure than the "psychological" idiom of the modern Western world. Both have their successes and failures. In societies with spirit possession some individuals articulate their experiences in terms of spirits in purely idiosyncratic ways and hence do not respond to indigenous therapeutic intervention. In *Medusa's Hair* Gananath Obeyesekere compares two patients who were exorcised at a shrine in Sri Lanka:

> One woman possessed by a demonic spirit ran around the ritual arena threatening to tear her clothes off. Her behavior was perfectly intelligible in terms of the *preta* [spirits of the dead] or demonic myth model. The other patient, a male, was pulling and pinching her skin, saying that demons were residing under it. Later on he abused the gods, the very beings who should help him to banish the demons. None of this was intelligible to the exorcist and his subculture in terms of available myth models. Demons do not get under one's skin in this culture, and it is unheard of for the gods to be abused in this manner. (Obeyesekere, 1981, p. 161)

The first patient was amenable to cure; the second was not. When Obeyesekere asked the exorcist what could be done for the second patient, the exorcist suggested taking him to a Western-trained psychiatrist! Exorcists are usually clever diagnosticians and avoid treating those patients whom they cannot cure.

The spirit idiom must be flexible enough to accommodate the individual if it is to establish itself and remain powerful. It may be composed of a highly elaborate demonology, as in Sri Lanka, Brazil, or Haiti. In these cultures the spirits have attributes and make specific demands on their hosts. In Haitian Voodoo, for example, the *lwa,* or possessing spirits, have highly developed characters. Legba, the master of the mystic barrier between men and spirits, is described as a feeble old man in rags who smokes a pipe, slings a knapsack over his shoulder, and walks painfully with a crutch. He is terribly strong, however, and anyone possessed by him suffers a violent trance. Dambala-wédo, another *lwa,* is pictured as a snake; he forces those whom he possesses to dart their tongue in and out, crawl on the ground sinuously, and fall like a boa from roof beams headfirst. Ezili-Freda-Dahomey, a sea spirit, personifies feminine grace and beauty. (She has been likened to Aphrodite.) Men and women possessed by her behave in a saucy, flirtatious manner. By contrast, in other cultures, for example in North Africa, spirits are ill defined and ambiguous. Unlike their Haitian counterparts, many North African spirits have no "biographies."

While the spirits must not be so specifically characterized as to discourage individual elaboration and specification, this does not entail that they be simply random refractions of individual desires, as some scholars, notably the German classicist Hermann Usener, have argued. The spirits must resonate with both the psychological and the social circumstances of the possessed. Psychologically, they may mirror some aspect of the individual that he refuses to accept or some desire that he denies. Or they may compensate for deficiencies in his relations with others. Thus, I. M. Lewis (1971) relates the high frequency of possession among women and marginal men to their "inferior" position in society. The spirits relate to the social world of the individual. In his study of Tikopian spirit mediumship Raymond Firth writes, "The idiom in which these personal phenomena of anxiety, conflict, illness, and recovery was couched was one in which the physical and psychological syndrome of trance was described in terms of social constructs, including notions of spirit powers and spirit action" (Firth, 1967, p. 329). Whether elaborated or unelaborated, the spirits may relate to specific social groupings. In many societies that are organized into lineages, in Africa for example, the spirits are thought to be lineage members or to have some other significant relationship with a lineage. Often they are conceived of as ancestral shades or lineage or household spirits. Diagnosis of the spirit possessed involves discovering the spirit's identity, the cause of his displeasure that led to the possession, and the nature of his demands. Therapy involves the regulation of the relationship between the possessed and the spirit. (Many anthropologists have understood this regulation as symbolic of a regulation of the possessed's "real" social relations.). In societies with looser social organizations, for example in many urban centers, the spirits are not so closely related to specific social groups. They are "open" to a larger variety of social relations, but they are not devoid of symbolic social attachment.

INITIAL POSSESSION. A first possession may be conceived of as an articulatory act. The possessed is thrust into a new symbolic order. His or her initiation frequently takes the shape of a dramatic illness—paralysis, mutism, sudden blindness, or profound dissociation—or contrary behavior, such as a wild and seemingly destructive flight into the bush or, for women, nursing the feet of a newborn infant. Many psychiatrically oriented observers have considered these symptoms to be of a hysterical nature, but careful study reveals that they may be symptoms of other forms of mental disturbance or reactions to the stresses and strains inherent in the individual's social position. Even with such dramatic symptoms, the diagnosis of possession is not necessarily immediate. There may be other options within the "medical" system of the particular society. The initial symptoms may, however, be far less dramatic. The neophyte may have been attending a possession ceremony when seized by the spirit. Such "contagious possession" has been frequently described in the literature of spirit possession. (Aldous Huxley gives a particularly readable account of contagious possession in *The Devils of Loudun,* 1952, a study of demonic possession in seventeenth-century France.)

Often the initial possession is articulated in retrospective accounts in a stereotyped manner. These may be elaborate, particularly where the possessed becomes a curer, the account providing the possessed with a culturally acceptable charter for his or her profession, or they may be a simple sentence or two. Alice Morton records the story given her by an Ethiopian curer, Mama Azaletch.

> In 1936, I was caught by a certain spirit. I ran away from my home in Bale to the desert, and there I lived in a cave. I would not see anyone or speak to anyone, and I became very wild. But there was one woman of high rank there who was interested in my case, and she would send her son to bring me beans and unsalted bread. I stayed there in that place, eating very little and seeing no one, for four years and eight months. If they had tried to take me from that cave and put me in a house with other people, I would have broken any bonds and escaped back to the desert. It was the spirit that made me wild that way. (Crapanzano and Garrison, 1977, p. 202)

Morton calls attention to Mama Azaletch's stereotypic flight into the wild, her fasting in the desert, and her renunciation of family. Mama Azaletch's story was told in both public and private. Many Moroccans with whom the writer of this article had worked had less elaborate but stereotypic stories of their "slippage" into the spirit idiom. They were at a possession ceremony, mocked the possessed or possessing spirit, and were immediately struck by the spirit.

The initiatory illness itself is an eloquent symbol, for not only does it focus attention on the possessed (who must be cured!), but it also requires definition. Such definition occurs through a variety of diagnostic and healing procedures. The initiate has to learn to be possessed and undergo exorcism. This is particularly evident where possession involves incorporation into a cult. Technically, the initiate must learn to enter trance easily, to carry out expected behavior gracefully, and to meet the demands of his spirit. Almost all reports of spirit possession emphasize the clumsiness of the neophyte and the necessity of learning how to be a good carrier for the spirit. Members of the Moroccan religious brotherhood, the Hamadsha, who mutilate themselves when in possession trance, can explain how they learned to slash their scalps with knives and halberds without inflicting serious injury. Many have serious scars from their initial possession when, as they put it, they had not yet learned to hit themselves correctly. Similar stories have been reported from Sri Lanka, Malaysia, and Fiji by adepts of the Hindu god Murukan who skewer themselves with hooks and wires. For possessions involving complex theatrical behavior, dancing, and impersonification, as in Sri Lanka or Indonesia, the learning process can be quite rigorous.

The neophyte must learn to recast conflicts in the spirit idiom and to articulate essentially inchoate feelings in that idiom, feelings of persecution or inferiority, of fear or bravado, of hatred or love. This process may proceed by trial and error, or it may occur through the guidance of a curer. The Puerto Rican Espiritistas "work" their patients through various levels of possession and develop in them, when possible, mediumistic faculties. (Such development resembles the mystic's passage through various stages of ecstasy.) The movement from initial illness to accommodation with the spirit and incorporation into the cult is often accompanied by an indeterminate period during which the possessed resists the call of the spirit and suffers depression, extreme alienation, dissociation, and even fugues. Such a period, analogous in many respects to what mystics refer to as the "dark night of the soul," may be symbolized as a period of wandering or isolation. Mama Azaletch's life in the cave may refer to such a period.

EXORCISM. Spirit possession has the tripartite ritual structure first delineated by the folklorist Arnold van Gennep in 1908. The possessed is removed from the everyday world by the possessing spirit. The possessed enters a liminal world—the world of possession, dissociation, trance—and through exorcism (which replicates the tripartite structure of possession itself) is returned to the ordinary world. Exorcisms may be permanent or "transformational." In permanent exorcism, the patient is returned to the world from which the patient came, ideally as he or she was before he was possessed. Not much is known about such patients. Have they undergone some sort of social or psychological transformation through possession and exorcism? It would seem that they have been marked by the spirit: They have been possessed, and they have been cured. In transformational exorcism, the patient is explicitly transformed. He or she has undergone a change in identity and are now, to speak figuratively, more than their self; he or she is in intimate relationship with a spirit whose demands must be recognized. Usually the possessed is incorporated into a cult, which not only provides legitimate occasions for future possessions but also supplies a new social identity. Often, as a member of such a cult, the possessed becomes an exorcist or a member of a team of exorcists.

Exorcisms may comprise little more than simple prayers or incantations sung over the possessed, as happens in Christian and Islamic contexts. Sometimes exorcisms involve torturing the possessed (pulling the ear, flagellating, or burning) until the possessing spirit has revealed its identity and demands or has released the patient. In many societies that support possession cults, the exorcisms are semipublic or public occasions. Such ceremonies tend to be highly dramatic. There is music, most frequently drumming but also music of woodwind, reed, and string instruments, and dancing, which may be simple or quite complex. In Sri Lanka and elsewhere in Southeast Asia comic or other dramatic interludes often play a role. The exorcist, the possessed, and other performers may don masks, wear special costumes, and take on the part of well-known mythic and legendary figures. The ceremonies are often accompanied by sacrifices and communal meals, and last through the night. This passage from light through darkness to light again seems to parallel the tripartite ritual movement that culminates with the "rebirth" of the patient as cured or transformed.

Patient, exorcist, and other spectators may all fall into trance. There is considerable variation in the depth and style of these trances. In some the possessed fall into an ill-defined, seemingly superficial, dreamy trance. In others they become frenetic and out of control. And in still others they take on the character of the spirit that possesses them, responding only to special songs, dancing characteristic dances, talking in a distinctive language (glossolalia), and demanding special costumes, perfumes, or objects. In many parts of the world, the possessed perform uncanny feats, such as walking over burning coals (in the Greek Anastenaria), piercing themselves with skewers and pins (the followers of Murukan in Sri Lanka, Malaysia, and Fiji), slashing their heads with knives and halberds (the Hamadsha of Morocco), playing with poisonous snakes (the rattlesnake cults of Appalachia), or stabbing themselves with swords and spears without harm (in Java, Bali, and among the Cape Malay in South Africa).

The exorcisms provide an occasion for both an individual and a transcendent drama of order and disorder, of control and the absence of control. At least in societies that consider the spirit demonic, possession reveals the underside of social, cultural, and psychological order. Possession negates the "rational" order of everyday life; it displays the world in reverse. Ritual and exorcism restore order and rationality to that world. The anthropologist Bruce Kapferer has written that in Sri Lanka the demons embody human suffering and symbolize the destructive possibilities of the social and cultural order. They provide a "terrifying commentary on life's condition and individual experience in it." They cast the individual's experience into a wider social and cultural order, and the encounter with the demonic becomes a metaphor for his or her "personal struggle within an obdurate social world" (Kapferer, 1983).

Exorcisms regulate the relationship between spirit and host. Formally, spirit possession may be understood as a series of transformations of usually negative metaphorical attributions into occasionally positive and at least ritually neutral metonymic ones in a dialectical play of identity formation. The spirit often represents what the possessed is not or does not desire. The Moroccan man who is inhabited by the female spirit ʿA'isha Qandisha is no woman; the chaste Haitian woman possessed by the promiscuous Ezili-Freda-Dahomey would disclaim any of Ezili's promiscuous desires. The host's identity and desires are here the opposite of the spirit's. During possession, however, the host becomes nearly identical with the spirits. The Moroccan man comes as close to being ʿA'isha Qandisha, a female, as possible; the Haitian woman as close to the flirtatious, saucy Ezili as possible. A negative metaphor is transformed into a positive metonym, even to the limit of identity within a very special context.

Possession cults aim to transform the relationship between spirit and host much as the Furies were transformed into the gentle Eumenides in Aeschylus's *Oresteia.* The transformation usually involves the conversion of a "wild" possession, an illness, into an institutionalized, ritualized, and periodized possession in which negative metaphorical attributes become for the occasion metonymic ones. It is as though the host were allowed to play out in a sanctioned manner who he is not and to give expression to desires that he cannot express in everyday life. This movement from metaphor to metonymy is neither direct nor simple. The changing, essentially complex relationship between host and spirit or spirits is given a sort of theatrical representation. The two may enter into conversation with one another in a friendly or inimical manner, they may struggle with each other, or the host may succumb to the spirit. Often, as in Sri Lanka, the possession includes a comic interlude that plays an important part in the exorcism itself. The comedy of exorcism, Bruce Kapferer (1983) has suggested, displays through its very irrationality the rationality of the world and allows the host to reformulate his self in accordance with that rationality. Although this movement toward the discovery or rediscovery of the rationality of the world is not immediately apparent in many simpler possessions, even these tend to bring about a transformation of the way the possessed sees his world. He takes on the view of his cult. He is attached to the demon, who becomes a primary orientation point for his understanding of himself and the world about him.

If the exorcism is successful, the patient has to become fully possessed and then released by the spirit. To be released from the spirit's influence the possessed must meet the spirit's demands, whatever they may be. In Morocco, for example, the spirit requires the host to wear certain colors, burn special incense, make regular pilgrimages to the spirit's favored sanctuaries. Often the demand includes the sacrifice of an animal with which, as the anthropologist Andras Zempléni (1984) has suggested, the spirit's host is identified. Thus the host is separated by the power of the sacrifice from the spirit with which the host has become one. So long as the possessed follows the spirit's commands, the host is blessed, protected, and generally favored. A failure to follow the commands usually leads to a renewal of the possession crisis: The host falls ill, becomes paralyzed, or is blinded. A new exorcism is then required.

Without doubt the spirit and its commands are of symbolic import to the host, resonating with significant events in the host's biography, reflecting the host's present situation, and orienting the host toward the future. The commands may symbolize adherence to the social and moral obligations and commitments the individual has in his or her everyday life; a failure to follow the commands may represent a failure to live up to these obligations and commitments; the possession may make articulate feelings that in other "psychological" idioms are described as feelings of guilt. The roles played by the spirits and their commands, by "wild" and institutionalized possessions, differ in each individual case. Generalizations tend to become overgeneralizations. The spirit idiom is subtle and, as the existentialists would say, reflects the subtility of the individual in situation. It is, of course, important to recognize that possession also plays an important role for those who witness it, providing them with an often theatrical representation, an objectification, of their cultural presuppositions, their social situation, and their psychological conditions. For them and for the possessed, possession confirms belief in the spirits. Exorcism affirms faith in a social and cultural order, an order that gives perhaps only the illusion of mastering the "irrational forces" that surround and on occasion besiege its members.

SEE ALSO Affliction; Consciousness, States of; Demons, article on Psychological Perspectives; Devils; Enthusiasm; Exorcism; Frenzy; Glossolalia; Oracles.

BIBLIOGRAPHY

Bastide, Roger. *Le condomblé de Bahia.* Paris, 1958. A detailed study of Afro-Brazilian possession.

Beattie, John, and John Middleton, eds. *Spirit Mediumship and Society in Africa.* New York, 1969. An anthology of social anthropological studies of spirit mediumship and possession in Africa.

Belo, Jane. *Trance in Bali.* New York, 1960. A detailed, descriptive study of trance in Bali.

Bourguignon, Erika. "The Self, the Behavioral Environment, and the Theory of Spirit Possession." In *Context and Meaning in Cultural Anthropology,* edited by Melford E. Spiro, pp. 39–60. New York, 1965. Anthropological consideration of the relationship between self- and spirit possession.

Crapanzano, Vincent. *The Hamadsha: An Essay in Moroccan Ethnopsychiatry.* Berkeley, Calif., 1973. An anthropological study of a Moroccan Islamic religious brotherhood whose adepts mutilate themselves when in possession trace.

Crapanzano, Vincent, and Vivian Garrison, eds. *Case Studies in Spirit Possession.* New York, 1977. An anthology of case studies of spirit possession from around the world. For a more detailed account of the arguments in this entry the reader is referred to the introduction to the book.

Firth, Raymond. *Tikopia Ritual and Belief.* London, 1967. Includes an interesting discussion of spirit possession and mediumship among these Pacific Islanders.

Goodman, Felicitas D. *Speaking in Tongues: A Cross-Cultural Study of Glossolalia.* Chicago, 1972. A study of speech patterns in trance.

Goodman, Felicitas D., Jeanette H. Henney, and Esther Pressel. *Trance, Healing and Hallucination.* New York, 1974. Three studies of trance and possession, on St. Vincent, Brazil, and the Yucatan.

Huxley, Aldous. *The Devils of Loudun.* New York, 1952. A seminovelistic study of spirit possession in seventeenth-century France.

Jeanmarie, Henri. *Dionysos: Histoire du culte de Bacchus.* 2 vols. Paris, 1951. A study of Dionysian worship in the ancient world that draws parallels with North African possession cults.

Kapferer, Bruce. *A Celebration of Demons: Exorcism and the Aesthetics of Healing in Sri Lanka.* Bloomington, Ind., 1983. A detailed symbolic anthropological study of spirit possession and exorcism in Sri Lanka.

Leiris, Michel. *La possession et ses aspects théâtraux chez les Éthiopiens de Gondar.* Paris, 1958. An insightful study of Ethiopian spirit possession by one of France's most original anthropologists and poets.

Lewis, I. M. *Ecstatic Religion: An Anthropological Study of Spirit Possession and Shamanism.* Harmondsworth, 1971. A broad social-anthropological study of possession.

Lienhardt, Godfrey. *Divinity and Experience: The Religion of the Dinka.* Oxford, 1961. A brilliant study of the religion, including spirit belief, of a Nilotic people.

Métraux, Alfred. *Voodoo in Haiti.* Translated by Hugo Charteris. New York, 1959. The classic study of Haitian Voodoo.

Monfouga-Nicholas, Jacqueline. *Ambivalence et culte de possession.* Paris, 1972. A study of possession among the Hausa of West Africa.

Obeyesekere, Gananath. *Medusa's Hair: An Essay on Personal Symbols and Religious Experience.* Chicago, 1981. A psychoanalytically oriented anthropological study of ecstasy and possession at the Hindu-Buddhist pilgrimage center of Kataragama in Sri Lanka.

Oesterreich, Traugott K. *Possession, Demoniacal and Other, among Primitive Races, in Antiquity, the Middle Ages, and Modern Times.* Translated from the German by D. Ibberson. New York, 1930. A classic compendium of case material on spirit possession.

Ortigues, Marie Cécile, and Edmond Ortigues. *Oedipe africaine.* Paris, 1966. A psychoanalytic study, owing much to Jacques Lacan, of spirit possession in Senegal.

Prince, Raymond, ed. *Trance and Possession States.* Montreal, 1958. An anthology of religious, anthropological, and psychophysiological studies of trance and spirit possession.

Sargant, William Walters. *Battle for the Mind.* Garden City, N.Y., 1957. A Pavlovian psychophysiological study of, among other things, spirit possession.

Spiro, Melford E. *Burmese Supernaturalism.* Exp. ed. Philadelphia, 1978. A study of Burmese belief in spirits and spirit possession.

Tart, Charles T. *Altered States of Consciousness.* New York, 1969. A useful anthology of psychophysiological studies.

Tremearne, A. J. N. *The Ban of the Bori: Demons and Demon-Dancing in West and North Africa.* London, 1914. An early comparative study of spirit possession among the Hausa and in North Africa.

Wirz, Paul. *Exorcism and the Art of Healing in Ceylon.* Leiden, 1954. A highly detailed account of Sinhala exorcism and curing.

Walker, Sheila S. *Ceremonial Spirit Possession in Africa and Afro-America.* Leiden, 1972. An important survey.

Zempléni, Andras. "Possession et sacrifice." *Temps de la reflexion* 5 (1984): 325–352. A carefully argued analysis of the relationship between spirit possession and sacrifice.

New Sources

Behrend, Heike, and Ute Luig, editors. *Spirit Possession: Modernity & Power in Africa.* Madison, 1999.

Caciola, Nancy. "Mystics, Demoniacs, and the Physiology of Spirit Possession in Medieval Europe." *Comparative Studies in Society and History* 42, no. 3 (1999): 268–306.

Foster, Byron. *Heart Drum: Spirit Possession in the Garifuna Communities of Belize.* Belize, 1986.

Garrett, Clarke. *Spirit Possession and Popular Religion: Fom the Camisards to the Shakers.* Baltimore, 1987.

Lambek, Michael. "Spirit Possession/Spirit Succession: Aspects of Social Continuity among Malagasy Speakers in Mayotte." *American Ethnologist* 15 (1988): 710–731.

McDaniel, June. "Possession States among the Saktas of West Bengal." *Journal of Ritual Studies* 2 (Winter 1988): 87–99.

McVeigh, Brian J. "Spirit Possession in Sukyo Mahikari: A Variety of Sociopsychological Experience." *Japanese Religions* 21 (July 1996): 283–297.

Rasmussen, Susan J. *Spirit Possession and Personhood among the Kel Ewey Tuareg.* Cambridge, U.K., 1995.

Rosenthal, Judy. *Possession, Ecstasy, and Law in Ewe Voodoo.* Charlottesville, 1998.

Smith, Frederick M. "The Current State of Possession Studies as a Cross-Disciplinary Project." *Religious Studies Review* 27, no. 3 (July 2001): 203–212.

Stoller, Paul. *Embodying Colonial Memories: Spirit Possession, Power, and the Hauka in West Africa.* New York, 1995.

Sutton, Donald S. "Rituals of Self-Mortification: Taiwanese Spirit-Mediums in Comparative Perspective." *Journal of Ritual Studies* 4 (Winter 1990): 99–125.

Wafer, Jim. *Taste of Blood.* Philadelphia, 1991.

VINCENT CRAPANZANO (1987)
Revised Bibliography

SPIRIT POSSESSION: WOMEN AND POSSESSION

Spirit possession has largely been interpreted by scholars as a phenomenon that impacts "traditional people," the poor, the uneducated, and women. The conjunction of spirit possession with oppressed or vulnerable persons has produced theories that Susan Starr Sered has called "deprivation theories" (1994, pp. 190–191) that begin with the assumption that possessions are abnormal behaviors and result from social, physical, and mental deprivations. From a feminist perspective, deprivation theories are suspect, and a revaluation of spirit possession suggests that: (1) the cross-cultural and transhistorical prevalence of accounts of spirit possession present a familiar rather than an exotic model of religious subjectivity to most human communities across the broadest spectrum of history; (2) the capacity to be possessed by an ancestor, deity, or spirit is best approached, as Sered and Janice Boddy (1989) argue, as an ability, like musical or athletic ability, although in the case of spirit possession it is likely that the person being possessed does not choose to develop the ability to receive the spirit but rather cannot choose otherwise in the face of the spirit's demands; and (3) possession is the formal root of religious experience in general, in that spirit possession is exemplary of the situation in which humans negotiate with a will that is not of human origin. These three revaluations are examined below after attending to the translational issues involved in employing spirit possession as a category of comparative study. A survey of the thematics of power found in possession studies concludes the entry.

Spirit possession can refer to a spectrum of experiences in which the person involved negotiates with or is overcome by a force such as an ancestor, deity, or spirit that employs the human body to be its vehicle for communicating to human communities. Ann Grodzins Gold provides a useful definition and discussion of the term *spirit possession* in her study of possession in rural Rajasthan (1988, p. 35): "any complete but temporary domination of a person's body, and the blotting of that person's consciousness, by a distinct alien power of known or unknown origin." This definition highlights the problem of subjectivity and agency; the possessed person is not a conscious individual but rather has a blotted consciousness and has become an instrument for the will of an alien power. While the term *spirit possession* is rarely used outside of the Western European tradition, Gold argues that the term does not "radically violate indigenous categories and does facilitate controlled comparisons with similar phenomena in other linguistic regions" (p. 39) if, she emphasizes, regional nominations are brought to bear. Applying Gold's logic, the term *spirit possession* is used below with caution, noting: (1) the importance of translating specific linguistic terms (discussed below); and (2) that the term *possession* carries with it many overdetermined connotations regarding Western notions of property and subjectivity as epitomized in the idea of a self-possessed individual.

TRANSHISTORICAL AND CROSS-CULTURAL CONTEXT. Spirit possession exists on all continents and throughout most of Western history as well. In part because of the often spectacular nature of possession accounts and because spirit possession demands a witness or a community response, we have evidence of spirit possession in legal, medical, historical, literary, and theatrical texts. As Western missionaries and academics began recording information about other cultures, the force and vivacity of spirit possession repeatedly drew authors to describe and discuss possession, producing a tremendous volume of materials. A proliferation of spirit possession ethnographies in the late twentieth and early twenty-first centuries indicates that spirit possession is a major force in a globalized world because the practice survives dislocations and relocations of culture, and women predominate in these accounts. This prevalence of material is particularly important in the study of women's religious lives because the records provide information when other references are minimal or nonexistent. Important examples include the maenads of Greek antiquity who appear in Greek tragedies such as Euripides' *Bacchae;* women possessed by the *mono no ke* spirit described in *The Tale of Genji,* a masterpiece of medieval Japanese literature (Bargen, 1997); and the *dybbukim* of medieval Eastern European Hasidic Jews described in the acclaimed play *The Dybbuk,* by S. Y. Ansky. The diaspora hosts of African and syncretic spirits found in vodou, Santería, and Candomblé in all regions of the African diaspora (Brown, 1987; Olmos and Paravisini-Gebert, 1997) have figured prominently in anthropology and literature of the diaspora. Where information is scarce about women's lives in Asia and the Pacific, we have information about Korean housewives participating in *Kut* rituals (Kendall, 1985) and the *tangki* of Taiwan (Wolf, 1992). Islamic traditions in the Middle East, Saharan Africa, Pakistan, and India describe women's predisposition to possession by *jinn* and regional spirits such as the *hantu* of Malay (Ong, 1987) and emphasize how women's possession activities are tolerated, although authorities address women's need to maintain vigilance through prayer and sanctity to avoid possession. With an increased emphasis on the study of women's lives, as well as the lives of the poor and lower castes in Hinduism has come a wave of studies of spirit possession (Egnor, 1984; Inglis, 1985; Gold, 1988; Stanley, 1988) by the gods and goddesses of Hindu traditions. In most indigenous traditions some elements of spirit possession continue to appear, as with African traditional religions (Mbiti, 1991), including those regions of Africa where Muslim and Christian influences are strong (Boddy, 1989; Maaga, 1995; Stoller, 1989 and 1995).

The controlled comparison of similar phenomena across traditions allows one to identify culturally specific models of religious subjectivity. Indigenous terms for the dynamic and role of the possessed person are rich with conceptual and rhetorical depth, related to receptivity, the mandatory element of the human's agency in a possession. In many vodou traditions the possessed person is considered to be a *chwal,* or horse, who is mounted by her spirits (Brown, 1987, p. 54), an activity that is often sexualized. In her study of Hinduism, Kathleen Erndl (1984) notes that the Goddess plays those whom she possesses and that the Punjab word for a theatrical play, *khel,* is the same word used to describe a possession. David Lan (1985, p. 59) notes that among the Korekore, a Shona group in Zimbabwe, the spirits are considered to grab their mediums, who may be referred to as *homwe,* which means "pocket" or "little bag." In all of these instances, a complex model of human agency is evoked by the notion that the human will and consciousness have been overcome, and that the human body has become receptive to the intervening agency of the possessing spirit.

RECEPTIVITY TO POSSESSION AS GENDERED ABILITY. In contrast to deprivation theories, Sered argues that women's preponderance in possession traditions can be related to their roles in nonautonomous experiences such as childbirth and their receptive role in heterosexual intercourse (1994, pp. 190–191). From this perspective, receptivity to the interventions of ancestors or deities is understood as an element of a feminine-gendered ability. From an androcentric perspective, receptivity has often been negatively evaluated as passivity, but spirit possession requires a shift in perspective critical of the claims that a self-possessed, impermeable subject is the norm of human experience. Whether male or female, possessed persons are likely to be evaluated for their receptivity. The gendered configurations of spirit possession take many forms. Women are possessed by male and female deities, men are possessed by male and female deities, and in all cases gendered tropes are employed. For example, in the Hasidic tradition (Schwartz, 1994, p. 72.), the name for the possession of a male was *ibur* (pregnant), and such a possession was highly valued by the community, while possession of women was widely interpreted to be malevolent possession by *dybbukim* and was not considered *ibur.* Helen Hardacre (1992) discusses the prominent role women have had in Japanese new religious movements founded since 1800, noting the gender transformations that were central to the theology of Deguchi Nao, whom Hardacre calls a genius of Japanese religious history. Nao was a middle-aged woman whose theology, written by her younger, male colleague while she was in a trance, turned traditional Buddhist wisdom on its head, proclaiming that Nao was The Transformed Male who signaled the arrival of a new era.

SPIRIT POSSESSION AS EXEMPLARY RELIGIOUS SUBJECTIVITY. The subjectivity of the possessed woman is radically nonautonomous, but rather than seeing this as an aberration it can be viewed as exemplifying religious subjectivity in general. The broad spectrum of roles humans have played in religious history, from mystics to prophets, are all variations on this very central theme. Hence Marilyn Robinson Waldman and Robert M. Baum (1992) compare the subjectivity of a Diola woman prophetess who reached adulthood at the beginning of World War II on the border between French Senegal and Portuguese Guinea with the subjectivity of the prophet Muḥammad in that both channeled communication from an extrahuman source to oppose the status quo. From this perspective, it is not important to create categorizations in which people can be placed; rather, the spectrum in which people experience themselves negotiating with a force of nonhuman origin is the common, formal ground of religious subjectivity in general.

What makes spirit possession unique is the degree to which the human has become an instrument for the will of the intervening agency. In terms of voice, for example, Michel de Certeau (1988) makes the following observation in his study of the seventeenth-century nuns of Loudun, whose nunnery was disrupted by a series of possessions:

> That the possessed woman's speech is nothing more than the words of her 'other,' or that she can only have the discourse of her judge, her doctor, the exorcist or witness is hardly by chance . . . but from the outset this situation excludes the possibility of tearing the possessed woman's true voice away from its alteration. On the surface of these texts her speech is doubly lost. (p. 252)

If, at the formal level, we are dealing with speech that is doubly lost, we are dealing with a model of subjectivity that is radically instrumental (as with a flute that is played, or a hammer that is wielded) rather than with an individual who is speaking. As a model of subjectivity it is the instrumentality rather than the autonomy that marks the possessed person's speech and actions. Social psychologists and ethnopsychologists have suggested that the difference found in the model of subjectivity of a possessed person and the model of subjectivity employed by modern psychology (that of an individual whose sickness is located in an individual psyche) leads to different levels of community-wide mental health. In her study of possession in India and in his study of possession in African American communities, Waxler (1977) and Csordas (1987) argue that possessions often function pragmatically to heal community problems, perhaps more effectively than modern psychiatry in some instances.

The speech of possessed persons is not only doubly lost but is often replete with critical, symbolic value, leading some ethnographers studying spirit possession to employ psychoanalytical interpretations of the speech in a way similar to the analysis of dreamwork. Willy Apollon (1999), Susan J. Rasmussen (1995), and Judy Rosenthal (1998) bring contemporary French psychoanalytic theory (Jacques Lacan) to the analysis of possessed language. Postcolonial literary scholars (Cooper, 1992; Henderson, 1993) have noted the significance of the possessed woman as a literary trope that signifies the experience of having multiple languages and heritages speak through a subject, particularly women. Spirit possession metaphorically depicts the sensibility of postcolonial subjectivity, a subjectivity that is not pure but rather spoken-through by many forces. By the turn of the twenty-first century, questions of agency, voice, and body theory had coincided with a growing effort by historians and ethnographers to produce a significant number of possession studies, granting the "Third World woman" a profound position in possession studies. Signifiers of possessed subjectivity that cross the historical spectrum of case studies include nonautonomous models of agency, heteroglossia, and volatility that attracts the attention of a community and relates to gendered notions of the ambivalent power of receptivity.

Thematics of Possession and Power. From a revalued approach to the power of possession, it is the work, war, and performance of possessions that merit analysis. In each scenario the possessed body's power is exerted in ambivalent ways, deeply implicated with the social symbolic of the community. In Malaysia, for example, indigenous possession traditions have survived, and accounts of possessed women in multination free trade zones have caught the attention of news media and scholars. Possessed women work in free trade zones. The women stop work when possessed by *hantu* (ambivalent ghosts or spirits) and weretigers (akin to werewolves) in the factories. Aihwa Ong (1987) analyzes these possessions from a feminist and materialist perspective. Similarly, in *The Devil and Commodity Fetishism in South America* (1980), Michael Taussig interprets indigenous spirits as a critical reaction to commodity fetishism in South America. The danger is that these materialist analyses dismiss the possessing ancestors or spirits as mystifications, a categorization that might be more comfortable from a materialist perspective but that elides the agency of a pouncing *hantu* or the devil in a dollar. If, on the other hand, religious subjectivity is itself understood to be a kind of work, then the efforts made by the Malay women to decrease their vulnerability to the spirits through prayer and vigilance indicates that they are working with the forces of global capitalism and the forces of possessing spirits. So also, the devils associated with the dollars of international mining companies in South America are not merely symbols to be interpreted, but rather are working forces in the religious lives of the miners.

In terms of the wars engaged by possessed women's bodies, there are two central types: gender conflict and territorial conflict. Doris Bargen (1997) argues that spirit possession was a woman's weapon in medieval Japan because a woman who was spoken-through by a possessing spirit could say things to public audiences that women were not otherwise tolerated for saying. Ann Braude (2001) discusses the spiritualism that coincided with the women's suffrage movement, noting that women who were inspired by the spirit were allowed a public forum in which to speak. These approaches can suggest that possession is a guise for political struggles. From a revalued perspective, however, the religious person is approached as a training and disciplining person, whose body is prepared to enact the will of its deity, and thus there is no viable distinction between a religious and a political struggle. In the case of the Shona in Zimbabwe, spirit possession by powerful land-governing ancestors (*mhondoro*) was largely the remit of men, but two women who were possessed by the spirit of Nehanda, a female ancestor of an early Shona dynasty, were central to the struggle for indigenous rule (Lan, 1985; Keller, 2001). In two *chimurengas,* or battles for freedom (1890 and 1950–1970), an older woman possessed by Nehanda significantly inspired and focused the fight against colonizers. The Nehanda *mhondoro* from the first *chimurenga* was tried and hung by the British, using old British witchcraft laws, but was revered for her claims that her bones would rise again to secure victory. Nehanda was revered in the songs of the socialist-inspired armies of the second, successful *chimurenga,* and the Nehanda *mhondoro* of the second *chimurenga* inherited the potent legacy of the first Nehanda. Territorial wars and gender wars have been waged through the body of a possessed woman who serves as an instrumental agency in the struggles for power that religious bodies have been trained and tempered to engage.

As Gold notes (1988, p. 37), the performative elements of possession have received great attention in Sri Lanka and across South Asia. Possessions are inherently performative. Without an audience, the possession has not effectively transpired because the possessed person is not conscious during the event to report on what has happened. Also, possessions are often violent, volatile, laden with sexual innuendo, and dramatic in the knowledge they produce. While anthropologists have invoked performance theory to explore this element of the power of possession, the question of subjectivity is again raised because performance theory largely begins with the assumption that an actor wills herself into a performative mode. Most possession traditions have rigorous tests with which they judge the validity of a possession in order to assure that it is *not* a performance by an agent. Not only are rigorous tests applied by the communities, but, as Gold notes, in Sri Lanka as well as in rural Rajasthan, the theatrical traditions of these communities show high levels of critical analysis in their employment of possessions in plays. Some plays depict fake possessions, which the entire audience recognizes as fake and laughs at, while other theatrical performances might spontaneously produce possessions that the audiences regard as authentic. Gold identifies "ethnoperformance theory" (p. 37) as the cultural backdrop against which the performative power of possession has long been analyzed by these traditions.

Viewed as a prevalent and exemplary model of religious subjectivity in general, the specific historical and geographical accounts of spirit possession provide resources for expanding the horizons against which women's religious subjectivity is understood and evaluated in the context of instrumental struggles for power and meaning.

SEE ALSO Gender and Religion, articles on Gender and African Religious Traditions, Gender and North American Indian Religious Tradition; Human Body, article on Human Bodies, Religion, and Gender; New Religious Movements; Religious Experience.

BIBLIOGRAPHY

Ansky, S. *The Dybbuk and Other Writings by S. Ansky,* edited by David G. Roskies, translated by Golda Werman. New York, 1992.

Apollon, Willy. "Vodou: The Crisis of Possession." Translated by Peter Canning and Tracy McNulty. *Jouvert* 13, nos. 1 and 2. Available from http://social.chass.ncsu.edu/jouvert/v3i12/con312.htm. Using Lacanian theory in his review of vodou studies, Apollon asks, "How can possession be made to pass through writing?"

Arthur, Marilyn. "The Choral Odes of the *Bacchae* of Euripides." *Yale Classical Studies* 22 (1972): 145–180. Arthur criticizes the argument that the Bacchic chorus is irrational and instead traces the subtle thematic development of its odes, depicting its steady and consistent power, born in part through its receptivity to Dionysos, making it powerful over Pentheus and his hypermasculine effort to resist Dionysos.

Bargen, Doris G. *A Woman's Weapon: Spirit Possession in The Tale of Genji.* Honolulu, 1997. *The Tale of Genji* is a masterpiece of medieval Japanese literature, and Bargen studies the role of spirit possession among women from an interdisciplinary perspective.

Boddy, Janice. *Wombs and Alien Spirits.* Madison, Wis., and London, 1989. An examination of Zar possession in northern Sudan.

Braude, Ann. *Radical Spirits: Spiritualism and Women's Rights in Nineteenth-Century America,* 2d ed. Bloomington, Ind., 2001. Developing the historical context in which a growing Spiritualist movement coincided with the burgeoning women's suffrage movement, Braude argues that the Spiritualist platform provided women with a place for public speaking and provided reassurances for the public regarding their recently deceased family and friends in a time of national turmoil.

Brown, Karen McCarthy. "Alourdes: A Case Study of Moral Leadership in Haitian Voudou." In *Saints and Virtues,* edited by John Hawley. Berkeley, Calif., 1987. A focused argument based on Brown's larger research project into the life of Mama Lola, a Haitian immigrant in New York City.

Chajes, J. H. "Judgements Sweetened: Possession and Exorcism in Early modern Jewish Culture." *Journal of Early Modern History* 1, no. 2 (1977): 124–169. Chajes provides the socio-historical context of Christian spirit possession and early modern Jewish spirit possession to evaluate the growing presence of possession in Jewish resources of the time.

Cooper, Caroline. "Something Ancestral Recaptured: Spirit Possession as Trope in Selected Feminist Fictions of the African Diaspora." In *Motherlands,* edited by Susheila Nasta. New Brunswick, N.J., 1992. An important analysis of spirit possession as a literary trope in African diaspora fiction.

Csordas, Thomas J. "Health and the Holy in African and Afro-American Spirit Possession." *Social Science and Medicine* 24, no. 1 (1987): 1–11. Based on interviews with a Brazilian psychiatrist who is also an initiated elder of Candomblé, this ethnopsychiatric study argues that an approach that attends to both religious and medical motives in spirit possession cults is intrinsic to the goals of contemporary medical anthropology.

De Certeau, Michel. *The Writing of History.* Translated by Tom Conely. New York, 1988. De Certeau focuses on the historiographer's problem of studying discourse that is altered using the case of the nuns of Loudun (1632–1638).

Egnor, Margaret Trawick. "The Changed Mother or What the Smallpox Goddess Did When There Was No More Smallpox." *Contributions to Asian Studies* 18 (1984): 24–45. Studying one of the most important healing deities in Madras, Mariamman, the Smallpox Goddess, Egnor discusses why Smallpox has been deified as a feminine, maternal divinity in Madras, while most of the Sinhalese disease demons took male forms. Egnor discusses the negotiated relationship between Mariamman and Sarasvati, her servant, and traces the changing role of Mariamman with the eradication of smallpox.

Erndl, Kathleen. "The Play of the Goddess: Possession and Performance in the Panjabi Cult of Seranvali." Paper presented at the Conference on South Asia, Madison, Wisconsin, 1984. Discusses the polyvalent Punjabi notion of play and applies this linguistic context to her study of goddesses who play their mediums.

Gold, Ann Grodzins. "Spirit Possession Perceived and Performed in Rural Rajasthan." *Contribution to Indian Sociology* 22, no.1 (1988): 35–63. Detailed descriptions of contrasting events of spirit possession in rural Rajasthan that Gold locates within the context of a sophisticated indigenous ethno-performance theory.

Hardacre, Helen. "Gender and the Millennium in Omoto Kyodan: The Limits of Religious Innovation." In *Religion and Society,* vol. 31, *Innovation in Religious Traditions.* Berlin and

New York, 1992. Studying the case of Deguchi Nao, a genius of Japanese religious history who began her career as a possessed woman in 1892 at the age of fifty-six, Hardacre studies the radical gender equality of Nao's symbolic universe and the limitations of that symbolic to interrupt traditional gender roles.

Henderson, Mae Gwendolyn. "Speaking in Tongues: Dialogics, Dialectics, and the Black Woman Writer's Literary Tradition." In *Aesthetics in Feminist Perspective,* edited by Hilda Heine and Carolyn Korsmeyer. Bloomington, Ind., 1993. With reference to Bakhtin, Henderson studies heteroglossia as a literary device in black women's writing.

Inglis, Stephen. "Possession and Pottery: Serving the Divine in a South Indian Community." In *Gods of Flesh, Gods of Stone: The Embodiment of Divinity in India,* edited by Joanne Punzo Waghorne and Norman Cutler. Cambersburg, Pa., 1985. Noting that the phrase "divine vessels" is used to describe clay images and "god dancers" (possessed dancers) in a Tamilnadu lineage, Inglis notes that this particular lineage is perceived to be particularly fitted for the work of making clay images in which the deities manifest themselves by making their bodies receptive to divine interventions.

Keller, Mary. *The Hammer and the Flute: Women, Power and Spirit Possession.* Baltimore, 2001. Methodological argument for comparative study of spirit possession including overview of the field and case studies of spirit possession in Malaysia, Zimbabwe, Greek antiquity, and Hasidic traditions.

Kendall, Laurel. *Shamans, Housewives and Other Restless Spirits.* Honolulu, 1985. Ethnography of Korean women whose dominant role in *Kut* rituals, both as shamans and as spectators, is an exception to their traditional roles.

Laderman, Carol. *Taming the Wind of Desire: Psychology, Medicine and Aesthetics in Malay Shamanistic Performance.* Berkeley, Calif., 1991. Interdisciplinary study of Malay shamanism highlighting the humoral aesthetic that underlies Malay shamanism and medicine.

Lan, David. *Guns and Rain: Guerrillas and Spirit Mediums in Zimbabwe.* London and Berkeley, Calif., 1985. Ethnographic study of the relationship between spirit mediums and socialist-inspired fighters during the 1960s and 1970s battle for Zimbabwe's independence from the White Rhodesian Front.

Lewis, I. M., Ahmed Al-Safi, Sayyid Hurreiz, eds. *Women's Medicine: The Zar-Bori Cult in Africa and Beyond.* Edinburgh, 1991. Tracks the dynamics and movement of women's involvement in Zar-Bori and the tension between Muslim authorities and women's practice.

Maaga, Mary. "Liminal Women: Pneumatological Practices Among West African Christians." In *Images of African Women: The Gender Problematic,* edited by Stephanie Newell. Stirling, U.K., 1995. Provides a feminist critique of Victor Turner's theory of liminality and evaluates the pneumatological practices among Christian women in the Independent Church Movement in West Africa.

Olmos, Margarite Fernández, and Lizabeth Paravisini-Gebert, eds. *Sacred Possessions: Vodou, Santeria, Obeah, and the Caribbean.* New Brunswick, N.J., 1997. Thirteen comparative and interdisciplinary studies of African-based religious systems in the Caribbean, analyzing the nature and liturgies of vodou, Santería, Obeah, Quimbois, and Gaga in specific communities in the Caribbean.

Ong, Aihwa. *Spirits of Resistance and Capitalist Discipline.* Albany, N.Y., 1987. Materialist and feminist analysis of spirit possession among indigenous Malay women working in the free trade zones of Malaysia.

Rasmussen, Susan J. *Spirit Possession and Personhood Among the Kel Ewey Tuareg.* Cambridge, 1995. An ethnography of the Air Mountain region of Niger, focusing on the unofficial but tolerated women's cult in which women are possessed by spirits called "the People of Solitude."

Rosenthal, Judy. *Possession, Ecstasy, and Law in Ewe Voodoo.* Charlottesville, Va., 1998. An ethnographic study of two orders of vodou religion (Gorovodu and Mama Tchamba) in Togo, Benin, and Ghana using indigenous interpretation and feminist-influenced Lacanian psychoanalysis.

Schwartz, Howard. "Spirit Possession in Judaism." *Parabola* 19, no. 4 (1994): 72–76. Provides a broad and generalized overview of spirit possession with specific reference to mystic traditions.

Sered, Susan Starr. *Priestess, Mother, Sacred Sister.* Oxford, 1994. A comparative study of religions in which women predominate, most of which include spirit possession practices.

Stanley, John M. "Gods, Ghosts, and Possession." In *The Experience of Hinduism: Essays on Religion in Maharashtra,* edited by Eleanor Zelliot and Maxine Berntsen. Albany, N.Y., 1988. In his study of two types of possession found in popular religion in four districts of Maharashtra, possession by ghosts and possession by gods, Stanley discusses gendered susceptibility to the entry of ghosts and gods and women's particular receptivity at times of menstruation and childbirth.

Stoller, Paul. *Embodying Colonial Memories.* London, 1995. Ethnographic study of the Hauka movement, possession by spirits that mimic the French colonialists among the Songhay of Niger.

Taussig, Michael. *The Devil and Commodity Fetishism in South America.* Chapel Hill, N.C., 1980. An ethnography of peasants in Columbia and Bolivia and their indigenous religious practices regarding the presence of the devil in the money of the capitalist developments in their regions.

Tsing, Anna L. *In the Realm of the Diamond Queen.* Princeton, 1993. An ethnography of the Meratus Dayaks of Indonesia with special attention given to Oma Adang, a female shaman, and with critical reflection on ethnography and "the gaze."

Waldman, Marilyn Robinson, and Robert M. Baum. "Innovation as Renovation: The 'Prophet' as an Agent of Change." *Innovation in Religious Traditions.* Berlin and New York, 1992. Comparing the life and times of a Diola woman prophetess and Muḥammad in terms of their respective roles within their communities as speakers of a privileged kind of communication.

Waxler, Nancy E. "Is Mental Illness Cured in Traditional Societies? A Theoretical Analysis." *Culture, Medicine and Psychiatry* 1 (1977): 233–253. Drawing from social labeling theory, Waxler interprets her comparative social psychological research in Canada and India to argue that the prognosis is brighter for a person whose community considers them possessed than is the prognosis for a person whose community considers them to be psychotic.

Wolf, Margery. *A Thrice Told Tale.* Stanford, Calif., 1992. Thirty years later, Wolf returns to field notes of an incident in which a rural Taiwanese community responded to the apparent spirit possession of a marginalized woman and explores the representational issues involved as she rewrites the incident in different academic formats.

MARY L. KELLER (2005)

SPIRITS SEE ANGELS; DEMONS; DEVILS; FAIRIES; GHOSTS; MONSTERS

SPIRITUAL DISCIPLINE. Throughout history, religious traditions have noted that those people who long for a transformative or complete understanding of themselves and of their place in the world must somehow find a teacher or set of teachings to help them along. That guide may be a person, an idea, or a set of values; whatever it is, it establishes the orientation and outlines the procedures the seekers should follow in order to make real the transformation for which they hope. Many traditions further maintain that, having found (or having hoped eventually to find) that guide, the seeker then must practice various regimens that will help him continue along the way to ultimate transformation. Such endeavors constitute spiritual discipline, the means by which people find their fullest potential in the context of any particular religious ideology.

The practice of spiritual discipline marks the notion that one who is in search of the guide is not only a human being but also a human "becoming," one on his or her way toward an ideal. Images of such discipline, therefore, often include themes of movement or passage. Mahāyāna Buddhists describe the spiritual endeavor as *bodhicaryāvatāra,* "entering the path to enlightenment"; Jewish traditions speak of religious norms as *halakhah,* "the way to go"; and traditional Hindu literatures outline the three sacred "paths," *marga,* of proper action, proper meditation, and proper devotion. Not infrequently, religious systems refer to the sacred cosmos as a whole with terms meaning "the Way," like the Chinese *dao.*

The perfection such a person seeks may take a number of forms, each reflecting the fundamental worldview presented by the pertinent religious system. It may be the fulfillment of being or the return to nonbeing; it may be personal or impersonal; it may be the enjoyment of the good life or the release of the good death. Whatever the goal, spiritual disciplines claim to offer their adherents the means by which the religious ideal may be reached.

Without discipline, the seeker founders. The Ṣūfī mystic Jalāl al-Dīn Rūmī spoke perhaps for many religious traditions besides his own when he noted that "whoever travels without a guide needs two hundred years for a two day's journey."

CONNOTATIONS OF THE TERM. The word *discipline* is a particularly apt one. To some people it rings of punishment, which in some cases is the point. But this certainly is not the primary meaning of the term, which carries a good number of connotations. The scope of its etymological cousins shows the broad applications the term can have in the study and practice of religion.

The word *discipline* may be derived through one of two ways, or, more likely, in a semantic combination of the two ways. It may come from the Latin *discere,* "to learn," and thus be directly related to the English word *disciple,* "one who follows the instructions of a teacher." *Discere* itself reflects the Indo-European root **dek-* ("take, accept"), which also appears in the English *decent, docent, docile, dogma,* and *dogmatic; doctrine, doctor* ("one who teaches doctrine"), and thus *indoctrinate;* as well as *dignity,* "to be acceptable," and *decorous,* "elegant, worthy of respect, graceful."

Perhaps the word comes from the Latin *disciplus,* "pupil," from *discapere,* "to grasp," in the sense of "to take hold of mentally" and thus "to understand." If so, then the word *discipline* derives primarily from the Indo-European **kap-* ("grab hold of") and is related to such words as the English *captivate, capture,* and *captive; accept, precept, concept;* and *participate.* Often that sense of *reception* (a related word) is described as a safe and protected experience, as would be the sense of the Germanic derivative of the root **kap-, *hafno,* appearing in the Old English *haefen,* which leads in turn to the modern English *haven,* "place of refuge."

To be disciplined, then, is to be caught up by the teachings of a guide—whether that guide be a person, an ethic, a community, a historical tradition, or a set of ideas—and to organize one's behavior and attitude according to those teachings. The person who undertakes such discipline may be understood, then, to be a disciple of that which is felt to be true, a captive of that which is valuable. Religious traditions do not tend to view this as "punishment." Rather, they generally stress the notion that this very captivity allows one to become who he or she really is, or really could be. As Zen Buddhists have long noted, one is most free when one is most disciplined.

TYPES OF SPIRITUAL DISCIPLINE. Just what kind of teacher the student follows and what type of relationship exists between the two varies from tradition to tradition and within each tradition itself, so any typological classification of spiritual disciplines runs the risk of oversimplification. Classed very generally, however, the different kinds of spiritual discipline may be understood as heteronomous, autonomous, or interactive in nature. (Within these types one can discern various modes of discipline, to which this article shall return.) These three should be understood as ideal types only: Analysis of different examples of actual spiritual endeavors will show that individual disciples and specific traditions practice a combination of all three.

Heteronomous discipline. In heteronomous discipline, the disciple submits in his or her search for realization, completion, or genuine understanding to the guidelines presented by an external authority. While this authority may be personal or impersonal in nature, the structure of the relationship between guide and disciple is often represented as objective and depicted in oppositional images: creator/creature; lord/subject; teacher/apprentice; parent/child; shepherd/sheep; wise one/foolish one; judge/judged. In obeying the commands or by imitating the paradigmatic actions of the central authority, the seeker finds the way to fulfillment and meaning.

One sees the ideals of heteronomous discipline in any account of a disciple who serves a master: the Chan Buddhist who sweeps the floor and washes the pots for his teacher; the American Indian who follows the instructions discerned in the tones of a coyote's call; the orthodox Hindu who obeys the social regulations prescribed by the Dharmaśāstras. Heteronomy is found in those cases where people find meaning and validity in their actions as defined by an external authority of some kind.

Sometimes the teacher is so distant, either in time or in space, that the disciple first must learn from a fellow, but wiser, seeker who knows the teachings if not the teacher and who, having traveled it, can illumine the difficult passage from one mode of being and understanding to another. Such is the case, for example, in the Jewish figure of the rabbi, the Christian *pater spiritualis,* the Buddhist *arhat* and *bodhisattva,* the Chinese sage, and the Siberian shaman—although the particular ideologies in which each of these figures present their teachings vary immensely.

A good example of heteronomous discipline appears in Islamic spiritual traditions. Muslims repeatedly hear in the Qur'ān the notion that a person's sole purpose in life is to serve the will of God (Allāh) by cultivating his or her potential in accordance with God's "command" (*amr*). This submission (*islām*) to God is the purpose for which God sends through prophets and revealed literatures the divine "guidance" (*hidāyah*). The central revelation, the Qur'ān, describes itself as an invitation to come to the right path (*hudan li-al-nās*) and is the source of the Islamic sacred law (*sharīʿah,* literally "the way to the water hole," an appropriate image for spiritual travelers in a desert region). Islamic tradition notes that examples of such guiding laws include what is known as *farḍ* or *wājib*—those duties and actions all Muslims must obey, such as daily prayer (*ṣalāt*), almsgiving (*zakāt*), and fasting during the holy month of Ramaḍān (*ṣawm*).

The paradigmatic disciple in this case is the prophet Muḥammad, who is said to have heard the sacred instructions from divine teachers and then to have obeyed the order to recite (*qur'ān*) those teachings to the community. Tradition holds that Muḥammad first received these lessons one night during Ramaḍān when he was visited by the angel Gabriel. After cleansing Muḥammad's body and spirit, Gabriel swept him up into the air, carrying him first to the sacred shrine at Mecca and then upward through the seven heavens to the throne of God. There, surrounded by mystic light, the Prophet received divine instructions on proper religious action, specifically the practice of the five daily prayers (*ṣalāt*), in which the Muslim is to cleanse himself and touch his forehead to the ground as he bows toward Mecca in the early morning, at noon, in midafternoon, at sunset, and in the evening. According to traditional stories, Muḥammad then returned from the heavens and shared those instructions with the human community on earth. "The key to paradise is *ṣalāt,*" Muḥammad is reported to have said; and the practice of the daily purification and prayer remains today one of the Five Pillars of Islamic faith. The four remaining pillars are *shahādah* (the profession of faith), *zakāt* (care for the unfortunate through almsgiving), *ṣawm* (fasting during the month of Ramaḍān), and *ḥajj* (pilgrimage to the Kaʿbah in Mecca).

According to Islamic mystical traditions, primarily those influenced by Ṣūfī ideologies and practices, a person intent on gaining a direct experience of God's presence and power first seeks out a teacher (Arab., *shaykh;* Pers., *pīr*) who guides the disciple (Arab., *murīd,* "one who wishes to enter [the path]") through the stages of the spiritual journey. The teacher then watches over the *murīd* carefully, for the path (*ṭarīqah*) is a long and difficult one. The master comes to know the disciple at the most intimate of levels. The master reads the student's mind and sees into the student's dreams in order to advise as the disciple moves through the anxiety and doubt inherent in the religious transformation. The master may make the *murīd* practice ascetic meditation for periods of forty days at a time and demand that the pupil direct all of his attention to God; or the master may require the student to live in a community of fellow seekers in order to benefit from the support a group can give. The master is careful to keep the disciple attentive to his or her spiritual duties as the disciple progresses through the "stations" (sg., *maqām*) on the path: repentance (*tawbah*), abstinence *(waraʿ)*, renunciation *(zuhd)*, fasting *(ṣawm)*, surrender to God *(tawakkul)*, poverty *(faqr)*, patience *(ṣabr)*, gratitude *(shukr)*, the cultivation of ecstatic joy *(basṭ)* through constraint of the ego *(qabḍ)*, and—finally—love *(maḥabbah)* and mystic annihilation *(maʿrifah)* into the being of God. Bringing the student through these stages, the Ṣūfī master shows the way to *fanā',* in which the seeker disposes of all human imperfections and takes on the qualities of the divine.

Autonomous discipline. The typological opposite of heteronomous discipline is characterized by ideologies in which the guide is said not to live or exist somewhere outside of the seeker but, rather, to inhabit the very depths of one's personal being. There, deep within the heart, the teacher rests timelessly beneath the swirling currents of the seeker's confused identity, unaffected by the vagaries of the objective world. The adept's task is to discover that inner wisdom. The discipline that arises from this notion of the guide may be called *autonomous* in nature because the aspirant's spiritual endeavors are self-contained and independent of external authority.

A good example of autonomous discipline would be the set of practices and assumptions reflected in the stories of Siddhartha Gautama's enlightenment and subsequent life as the Buddha. According to traditional accounts, the prince led a comfortable and secure life in his father's palace until, as a young man, he was shocked and utterly disillusioned with the passing enjoyments of the material world by the sight outside the royal walls of an old person, a sick person, and a corpse, sights that his father's protection had hitherto prevented him from seeing. After encountering a wandering ascetic who seemed to have attained a certain equanimity in the world of sickness and death, Gautama at age twenty-nine left his father's palace in search of a teacher who could help him understand the nature of life. He is said to have found successively two highly respected masters, but eventually left each one, unsatisfied, because he had become their equal in wisdom and yet still did not understand. He despaired of any teachings from another person, because even the most knowledgeable people did not know the full truth.

Traditional accounts say that Gautama then went alone into the forest, where he found a quiet place to fast and to control his breathing in order to enter into a trance in which he could gain transcendent knowledge. Eventually abandoning even some of these techniques because they led to what he experienced as a debilitating and therefore counterproductive physical weakness, he developed his own kind of meditation, which was neither austere nor self-indulgent. While meditating in this "middle way," he was confronted by demonic forces who tempted him, unsuccessfully, with worldly power and prestige.

Gautama is said to have entered into four successive levels of meditation (Pali, *jhāna*), each one giving him deeper awareness of the origins and nature of suffering. Finally, at the dawn ending the night of the full moon, he gained complete understanding and stood up, alone. At that point he became the Buddha, the Enlightened One. He understood what have come to be known as the Four Noble Truths: (1) that all conditioned existence is permeated by suffering; (2) that there is a cause of suffering (namely, desire); (3) that there is a way to end suffering (namely, to cease desiring); and (4) that the way to cease desiring is to follow a set of principles that became known as the Noble Eightfold Path.

Traditional Buddhist hagiographies and commentaries note that one follows that path by maintaining and practicing the following disciplines: correct views *(sammā-diṭṭhi)* to see things as they really are rather than as one wishes them to be; correct thoughts (*sammā-sankappa*), directed only to the goal of enlightenment; correct speech *(sammā-vācā),* in which one does not say anything that would harm his or other people's integrity; correct action (*sammā-kammanta*), in which one refuses to kill another creature, take what is not given, or enjoy illicit sexual relations; correct livelihood (*sammā-ājīva*), to earn a living only by ways in which living beings are not injured; correct exertion (*sammā-vāyāma*), characterized by dispassion and benevolence; correct mindfulness *(sammā-sati),* the remembrance of the Four Noble Truths; and correct meditative concentration *(sammā-samādhi),* which allows one to understand the harmful nature of selfish desire. The Eightfold Path thus combines the practice of proper wisdom (namely, correct views and thoughts), morality (correct speech, action, and livelihood), and meditation (correct mindfulness and concentration).

Buddhist tradition firmly maintains that the Buddha gained this insight by himself. Records of the Buddha's first discourse after his enlightenment note that he told his followers, "No one in any of the worlds—neither the gods, nor Māra, nor Brahmā, nor ascetics or priests or gods or human beings—had ever gained this highest complete enlightenment. I [alone] knew this. Knowledge arose in me, insight that even my mind cannot shake." No teacher is said to have given this insight to the Buddha; the implicit lesson here is that other people, too, can gain such knowledge if they cultivate autonomous discipline. Gautama himself seems to have resisted the role of a master. One text records his encouragement to others that "as wise people test gold by burning, cutting and rubbing it, so are you also to accept my teachings only after examining them and not simply out of loyalty to me" *(Jñānasāra-samuccaya* 31).

Interactive discipline. In another form of discipline, the teacher is neither completely external nor completely internal to the seeker. Rather, teaching and learning occur in a continuing and flexive process. The discipline needed here centers on a dialectical way of seeing or knowing that in itself brings the seeker to the desired transformation. Outside authority exists in the form of tradition, *ethos,* or structures of the natural world; but that authority is affected in various degrees by the hopes, worldviews, and training of the disciple. Similarly, internal authority holds sway, but it is defined and given form by external structures. Interactive discipline centers on practices that arise in an open-ended or multivalent relationship between the seeker and what he seeks.

Representative examples of interactive discipline might best come from the aesthetic arena. One thinks of a New England Shaker crafting a perfectly simple wooden chair; a *sitār* player quietly practicing a morning *rāga* in the Indian dawn; an Italian sculptor lovingly fashioning an image of the Virgin Mother out of a piece of marble. In such cases the disciple undergoes experiences in which the ideal is made real through his or her own creative power, but that ideal itself determines the form in which the disciple can make it real. Not only is there disciplined action; there is also a cultivated *interaction* between the disciple and the discipline itself.

At times the artist seems to be the effective agent in the creative process who brings his or her work to fruition through bold assertion. "This is not the moment for hesitation and doubt," Vincent van Gogh wrote of the creative process, "the hand may not tremble, nor may the eye wander, but must remain fixed on what is before one." Yet, no matter how subjective or personal this creative discipline may be, it frequently is described almost paradoxically as a participation in an impersonal event that transcends the idiosyncracies of the artist. "Everything vanishes around me," Paul Klee once noted to himself, "and works are born out of the void. . . . My hand has become the obedient instrument of a remote will." The artist cultivates a vision and undertakes a discipline in which the objective and subjective worlds converge and yet remain distinct.

Interactive discipline thus involves a kind of "attentive selflessness." Or perhaps it would be better to say that it centers on an "attentive wholeness"—for one who perfects this type of discipline is said to experience himself or herself as a creative and vital participant in the larger scope of life itself. Techniques of interactive discipline are different from those of heteronomous and autonomous discipline in that the former do not revolve around conceptual knowledge. The master is both external and internal, and neither external nor internal, to the disciple.

Interactive experience, like the artistic experience, centers on what the Japanese call *myō,* the wondrous mystery and rhythmic flow of life. One who disciplines himself or herself toward this experience seeks to know eternal truths within the mysteries of the constantly changing world. Such discipline is exemplified, to choose one of any number of possibilities, in the Japanese *haiku* tradition, in which poets compose short verses in moments of sublime understanding of the world. These poems reveal the unmediated nature of the world as it exists objectively but also the fond and attentive regard the poet holds for that world. Bashō (1643–1694) is said to have set the *haiku* tradition with this verse, translated by D. T. Suzuki:

Furu ike ya!	The old pond, ah!
Kawazu tobikomu,	A frog jumps in:
Mizu no oto.	The water's sound!

Quite typically, the images presented in *haiku* come from the ordinary world, but the terseness with which they are described comes from the poet's discerning vision of that world as an entirely remarkable place. The poet Buson (1716–1783) once exclaimed:

Tsuri-gane ni	On the temple bell
Tomarite nemuru	Perching, sleeps
Kocho kana.	The butterfly, oh!

If perfected, such interactive awareness of the world is said to lead to *satori* (enlightenment), which finds its meaning in one's everyday activities such as eating, sleeping, and moving one's body. The meaning that *satori* illumines in these activities does not come from outside; it is in the event itself. It is beingness, or life itself. Better still, it is the "is-as-it-isness" of something, the quality that in Japanese is known as *kono-mama* or *sono-mama.* It is this discipline of "seeing the isness" of the world that led the *haiku* poet Jōsō (1661–1704) to find transformative appreciation in the following image:

Mizu soko no	Under the water,
Iwa ni ochitsuku	On the rock resting,
Kono ha kana.	The fallen leaves.

Or Bashō, in a moment's notice of

Nomi shirami,	Fleas, lice,
Uma no nyo suru	The horse pissing
Makuramoto.	Near my pillow.

The freedom to experience the world as it arises from such cognitive or perceptual discipline occurs only when the poet's mind is in perfect harmony with the rhythms of life itself. "Wonder of wonders!" Hō Koji exclaimed in an eighth-century verse, "I carry firewood, I draw water!"

There are no heteronomous or autonomous authorities in this type of discipline, for to distinguish between object and subject is to bifurcate the essential unity of being. Interactional discipline takes a person beyond all dualities, including the duality of "self" and "other" or "disciple" and "master." Interactive discipline in the *haiku* tradition eventually frees the disciple from the need for a teacher. Such discipline recognizes that the guide, the way, and the wayfarer are one.

Modes of Spiritual Discipline. The three types of spiritual discipline just outlined should not be understood as mutually exclusive. Despite the autonomous ideals reflected in his early discourses, for example, even Gautama's followers directed their lives according to the instructions given them by their master and subsequently codified in the Vinaya Pitaka, a canonical collection of community rules and regulations established by the Buddha and his immediate followers. Conversely, even the Ṣūfī mystic who advances through the stages of the path under the heteronomous guidance of a shaykh finally experiences *fanā',* the annihilation of ego-consciousness that brings knowledge of the unity of reality in a state similar to that called *jam',* "unification." The Muslim, in fact, learns from the Qur'ān itself that God is "closer to man than is man's jugular vein" (50:16) and that God has placed within each person an "inner torch" *(taqwā),* which, if allowed to burn brightly, guides that person toward fulfillment. And the Japanese notion of immediacy of *myō* is said to be taught at first by a master, who teaches the student either through example or through specific instructions how to see and to experience sublime beauty himself.

In all three types of discipline, therefore, the seeker and the path on which that seeker travels are inextricably linked. Within the general parameters of these three types of spiritual discipline, one may recognize a number of ways in which the disciple actually practices the regimens deemed necessary for movement along the path. For simplicity's sake, these modes of activity can be classified in the following categories: ecstatic discipline, constructive discipline, discipline of the body, discipline of the mind, discipline of the heart, and discipline of enduring personal relationships.

It should be stated, once again, that these categories serve typological purposes only; they are not rigid classifications but general descriptive groupings of a variety of practices and ideas.

Ecstatic discipline. Many religious traditions maintain that the desired state exists outside of the human realm. It may lie in some other place such as in the heavens, across the mountains, or at the bottom of the sea; or it may take place in some other time, typically the past or the future. Whatever the case, in order to reach that extraordinary state personally or in order to be able to communicate with spirits from that other world, the seeker must somehow cultivate the ability to move out of his or her physical body, because that body is limited by the confining structures of time and space. Such out-of-the-body experience is classified generally as "ecstasy" and is attested in a variety of religious traditions throughout history.

The discipline needed to attain ecstasy typically includes practices in which the seeker deprives himself or herself of normal bodily pleasures in order to be free of his or her physical body. Such deprivational or ascetic discipline may begin with the seeker's withdrawal into solitude and spiritual tutelage under a master. It often culminates in the visitation by a guardian spirit and subsequent transformative vision or in an experience of death and resurrection.

Ecstatic discipline appears, for example, in North American Indian practices centered on what has come to be known as the vision quest. In such a quest practiced among the Thompson River Indians, for instance, a young man observed severe dietary restrictions and fasts, cleansed his spirit with such rituals as sweat bathing and immersion in a cold river, purged his body of impurities by forcing himself to vomit or by taking sacred medicines, and camped alone on a mountaintop, where he forsook sleep for nights on end. There he hoped to be visited by a guardian spirit who would teach him sacred ways and lead him through the dangers of life. The Ojibwa Indians of the Algonquin tribe near Lake Superior demanded that a boy entering puberty set up camp alone under a red pine tree, where he was to fast and to lie awake for days, waiting for a vision that would allow him to see who he was in the context of the sacred cosmos as a whole. These visions were often described as journeys taken into the worlds of the spirits, where the seeker was introduced to divine teachers who would guide him throughout his life.

Such ecstatic practices often included the seeker's ritualized symbolic death and resurrection. Shamanic initiates among the Pomo and Coast Miwok Indians of California lay on the ground and were covered with straw as if they had died and been buried; standing up and casting off the straw, the initiate was then known to have been resurrected from the dead. Among the Tlinglit Indians of coastal Alaska, a man was recognized as a potential shaman when he fell to the ground in a deathlike trance and subsequently revived.

In some instances of ecstatic discipline, the value of an enduring, rather than temporary, out-of-the-body experience lies at the very center of religious ideology itself. Perhaps the best example is that of the Tibetan traditions based on the notion of *bar do'i sems can* (or simply *bar do*), the "intermediate stage" through which a departed soul moves over the interval of forty-nine days between death and rebirth. Tibetan priests read a series of instructions—most frequently from the the *Bar do'i thos grol* (often transliterated and simplified as *Bardo Thodal,* the Tibetan *Book of the Dead)*—to the dying or dead person to help him through the dangers of the *bar do* and to help him gain a comfortable rebirth or, ideally, freedom from the cycle of rebirth itself.

Immediately upon death—in fact, before a person even knows he or she is dead—a departed soul is said first to enter the *'chi kha* state, a realm of pure light and bliss. Reading set instructions from the *Book of the Dead,* the priest tells the deceased that this is the ultimate reality and encourages the deceased to sever all emotional ties to the world left behind in order to remain free in this state. Most spirits are afraid of such freedom, however, and turn from it toward a second state known as *chos nyid,* in which the dead person encounters wondrous and beautiful creatures. The priest tells the person that these beings are images of his or her self that have been constructed through the person's own selfishness and that the person must renounce all attachment to them because they will soon turn into demonic monsters. Fearing these terrors, the person then enters a third state, *srid pa,* in which the person panics and flees into a new birth on earth as a way to avoid the horrors that have been experienced in the intermediate realm. The priest attempts to keep the person from moving through the second two of these realms—and thereby allowing the person to remain in the state of pure light and bliss—by reciting lessons and offering encouragement in the highly structured discipline of the long funerary ritual.

Constructive discipline. This mode of discipline does not seek in general to deprive the spiritual aspirant of unwanted or harmful characteristics; rather, it helps that person perfect his or her being by building on desirable characteristics that are already there.

Such constructive discipline often takes the form of personal imitation of a paradigmatic figure or figures who are said to embody desirable qualities or to have undertaken beneficial actions. Many times, therefore, such discipline takes the form of the correct performance of a ritual. "We do here what the gods did in the beginning," the priests report while explaining why they officiate at the sacred rites of Vedic India (see *Śatapatha Brāhmaṇa* 7.2.1.4). For those priests, all work performed as part of the ritual thus becomes a disciplined imitation of a divine model. So, for example, the artist who fashions the utensils and ritual paraphernalia expresses artistry in a religious context: "Those works of art produced here by a human being—[an image of] an elephant, a goblet, a sacred robe, a gold figure, a chariot—are works of art only because they imitate the art of the gods" (*Aitareya Brāhmaṇa* 6.27).

But it need not be explicit ritual behavior only that embodies the ideals and techniques of constructive discipline. Such discipline appears in any system which assumes that within the seeker lie qualities that, although perhaps dormant, can be brought to the surface so that the ideal can be made real. "Be faithful imitators of Jesus, and perfect imitators of Mary," the fifteenth-century monk Thomas à Kempis wrote to his fellow Christians in his *Imitation of Mary.* "Be simple, like the simple children of God, without deception, without envy, without criticism, without murmuring, and without suspicion." In his *Imitation of Christ,* Thomas similarly taught others to "learn to turn from worldly things, and give yourself to spiritual things, and you will see the Kingdom of God come within you" (2.1).

Elements of constructive discipline may also be seen in the Chinese, specifically the Neo-Confucian, tradition of the cultivation of sagehood. Zhangzai (1021–1077) defined the sage as one who understands the harmonious and holistic nature of oneself and one's relationship to the world. According to his teachings, a human being's essential nature (*xing*) is identical with all of nature *(tiandi),* and the sage understands the principle *(li)* that unites his essential nature with all things. According to Neo-Confucian thought, transformative understanding of this unity can be obtained through various techniques reflecting the ideology of constructive discipline. Gao Pan Long (1562–1626), for example, advocated a combination of several attitudes and practices: the cultivation of an open-minded reverence *(jing)* for all things; an intuitive exploration *(ge wu)* of the unifying principle that links the inner and outer worlds; a pervasive appreciation of the natural world; a sense of one's place in history; and a practice he generally characterized as "quiet sitting" *(jing zuo)* in which the student brings the body and mind together into a whole. Gao described this latter technique as "ordinary" *(ping chang)* because it reflects the basic unified nature of being itself.

In his *Fu qi gui* Gao notes that one may practice such quiet sitting by observing some general procedures:

> Burn incense and sit in the lotus position. . . . Try not to be lazy. After eating one must walk slowly for a hundred steps. Do not drink too much wine or eat too much meat or you will stir up the muddy waters. When resting do not take off your clothes. If you feel sleepy, then lie down. As soon as you awaken, get up.

Discipline of the body. There is a general recognition among religious traditions that the body's tendency to please its own senses tends to distract the spirit from its more ethereal tasks. Therefore, most spiritual disciplines involve the seeker's control and restraint of his or her physical body.

Christian monastic traditions provide a good example of such discipline of the body. "The life of a monk should always be as if Lent were being observed" even though "few people have the fortitude to do so," wrote Benedict of Nursia in the sixth century (*Rule of St. Benedict* 49), for "monks should have not even their bodies or their wills under their own command" (33). According to Benedict, monks were to "let one pound of bread be enough for one day, whether there be one meal only, or both dinner or supper," and "wine is not appropriate for monks at all" (39–40). Benedict nevertheless admitted, "Since it is not possible these days to convince the monks of this, let us agree at least on this: we should not drink excessively nor to the point of satiation. . . . one pint of wine a day is enough for each one" (40).

Benedict's *Rule* thus reflects the value he placed on the monk's renunciation of material goods, the primary purpose of which is to satisfy the body. "He should have nothing at all as his own: neither a book, nor tablets, nor a pen—nothing at all" (33). Six centuries later, Francis of Assisi restated and modified for his fellow monastics many of Benedict's rules, telling them, for example, "to go and sell all that they have and carefully give it to the poor," and that "all the brothers shall wear humble garments, and may repair them with sack cloth and other remnants" (*Rule of St. Francis* 3.2).

It may be, however, that the best classical example of the discipline of the body comes from the *rājayoga* tradition of India, particularly as represented by Patañjali's *Yoga Sūtra* and its principal commentaries, Vyāsa's *Yogabhāṣya* and Vācaspati Miśra's *Tattvavaiśāradī.* According to that tradition, the path to the ultimate goal of meditation practices—namely, complete autonomy (*kaivalya*)—involves eight stages or "branches" (*aṅga*) and is therefore known as the "eight-limbed discipline" (*aṣṭāṅgayoga*).

The first of the eight steps given by Patañjali is known as restraint (*yama*) and is centered on injunctions not to kill, not to lie, not to steal, not to enjoy sexual contact, and not to envy other people's possessions (*Yoga Sūtra* 2.30). The second stage is comprised of the five traditional spiritual practices (*niyama*) of cleanliness, mental equanimity, asceticism, scriptural study, and devotion to a master (2.32). At the third level, the yogin masters the various limber body postures (*āsanas,* e.g., the lotus position) that strengthen the body against the rigors of severe asceticism (2.46), some of which take many years of training before they can be practiced without the risk of dangerous injury. The fourth level consists of breath control (*prāṇāyāma*) in which the adept slows down his rate of respiration, sometimes to the point of stopping his breathing altogether for long periods of time, and in so doing releases for his disciplined use all of the life force (*prāṇa*) that is said to reside within the breath itself (2.49–51).

At the fifth stage of the eight-limbed discipline, the yogin withdraws all senses from their objects in an enstatic process known as *pratyahara,* which includes in part focusing all attention thus retrieved from external distractions on a single object—such as the spot between his eyebrows—in a technique described as *ekāgratā,* the sustained concentration on one thing *(Yogabhāṣya* 2.53). Mastering this technique gives the yogin power over all of his body, which possesses an almost immeasurable amount of energy.

The sixth level, known as *dhāraṇā,* a term that might best be translated as "mental concentration," is a form of *ekāgratā* in which the yogin, under strict guidance of a master, concentrates all powerful attention on a single sacred syllable (*mantra*) or visual diagram (*yantra*) in such a way that the mind ceases to wander about in its constant fluctuations and the yogin comes to know and experience the unity of his or her soul (*ātman*) with the soul of the universe.

In these first six stages of the eight-limbed discipline, the adept subdues and controls the instincts, desires, movements, respiration, senses, and mental activities of the physical body. This is done in order to prepare for the seventh and eighth levels of discipline, which may be said to transcend corporal existence. The seventh stage is known as *dhyāna* (deep meditation) in which the adept experiences the light of the Absolute within his or her own eternal soul. The final stage, *samādhi,* brings the yogic discipline to its fruition. At this point the yogin knows pure being, absolute consciousness, and complete bliss and is released from all suffering entailed in the cycle of rebirth.

Discipline of the mind. Many religions teach that one's mind tends to distract one from the necessities of spiritual growth and that it, like the body, must be restrained. Sometimes religious masters admonish their students not to daydream. Sometimes they scold their students for being too analytical. In either case, they encourage them to retain control over the mind.

The *Kaṭha Upaniṣad* records a mythic conversation between Naciketas, a young boy desirous of sacred knowledge, and Yama, the lord of the dead. One sees reflected in Yama's teachings the notion, cited often in ancient India, that the mind must be restrained the way a charioteer must control his horses:

> Think of the true self as [riding in] a chariot
> and that the body is the chariot.
> Think of the intellect as the charioteer
> and the mind as the reins.
>
> He who has no understanding, whose mind is out of control—
> his senses are unchecked
> Like wild horses [when unrestrained by a bad] charioteer.
> He, however, who has understanding,
> whose mind is always under control—
> his senses are checked
> Like the obedient horses [of a good] charioteer. (3.3–6)

The lord of the dead continues to teach Naciketas that the search for the absolute truth residing within the self is difficult because it "cannot be known through language, nor by the mind, nor by sight" (6.12). According to Yama, one reason it is so difficult to comprehend the nature of the self is that it has no discernible qualities or characteristics: It is "without sound, without touch, without form, imperishable . . . without taste, eternal, odorless, without a beginning and without an end, beyond the great, constant." Nevertheless, Yama asserts that "by discerning That, one is liberated from the jaws of death" (3.15).

Another Upaniṣad notes that the master should accept as a disciple only a student "whose mind is tranquil and who has attained peace. He teaches in its very truth that knowledge of *brahman* [absolute reality] by which one knows the true eternal soul" (*Muṇḍaka Upaniṣad* 1.2.12–13).

The adept who disciplines his or her mind undergoes here a kind of "unknowing" of all of the categories through which one's self, the world, and divine reality is normally understood. Part of this mental discipline involves the practice of seeing the essence of things as distinct from their form. In a classic teaching recorded in the *Bṛhadāraṇyaka Upaniṣad,* the Upaniṣadic sage Yājñavalkya repeatedly asserts (see 4.5.15, for example) that the eternal soul is "not this, not this."

Christian mystical traditions centered on the *via negativa* present similar teachings regarding the need in one's spiritual advancement to break down the categories to which one's undisciplined empirical mind clings. In his work *The Mystical Theology,* Dionysius the Areopagite (sixth century) taught that "the universal and transcendent Cause of all things is neither . . . a body, nor has He a form or shape, or quality, or quantity, or weight; nor has He any localized, visible, or tangible existence; He is not sensible or perceptible" (Happold, 1970, p. 212). Dionysius accordingly encouraged his followers to "leave behind the senses and the operations of the intellect, and all things sensible and intellectual, and all things in the world of being and nonbeing, that thou mayest arise, by knowing, towards the union, as far as is attainable, with Him Who transcends all being and all knowledge" (op. cit., pp. 216–217).

Discipline of the heart. Some religious traditions teach that the final universal truth centers on a profound, delicate, and enduring love. According to these traditions, everything that is real arises from and returns into love; and it is through the openhearted awareness of that love that one comes closer to divine truth. The cultivation of those attitudes and actions that help one see and know that love may therefore be called the discipline of the heart.

At times such discipline of the heart is described as a way of seeing the world in its sublime nature. As the Ṣūfī poet Muḥammad Gīsūdarāz (d. 1422) proclaimed,

> You look at the beautiful one and see figure and statue—
> I do not see anything save the beauty and art of the creator.

Jalāl al-dīn Rūmī (d. 1273) saw the structures of the natural world as expressions of universal love:

> If this heaven were not in love, then its breast would have no purity,
> and if the sun were not in love, in his beauty would be no light,
> and if earth and mountain were not lovers, grass would not grow out of their breast.

The Hebrew *Song of Songs* (whose verses date as early as the tenth century BCE) presents classic love imagery set in a dialogue between a bride and her bridegroom. Traditional commentaries have interpreted the relationship between the characters of the bride and groom in four ways: literally, as a man and a woman in love with each other; figuratively, as a model on which proper marriage should be based; allegorically, as the people of Israel and their god; and anagogically, as the account of an individual soul's perfected relationship to God. Whatever its reference, the love between these two finds vivid expression:

> Bride: Night after night on my bed
> I have sought my true love;
> I have sought him but not found him,
> I have called him, but he has not answered.
>
> Groom: How beautiful you are, my dearest, how beautiful! . . .
> Your lips are like a scarlet thread, and your words are delightful;
> your parted lips behind your veil are like a pomegranate cut open. . . .
> Your two breasts are like two fawns, twin fawns of a gazelle.
>
> Bride: I am my beloved's, his longing is all for me.
> Come, my beloved, let us go out into the fields to lie among the henna bushes. (3.1–7.11)

The Cistercian monks of twelfth-century Europe tended to see the religious quest as an ongoing apprenticeship in the ways of love. In his *Sermons on the Song of Songs,* Bernard of Clairvaux urged his readers to remember that "when God loves, he wants nothing else than to be loved; for he loves for no other purpose than that he may be loved, knowing that those who love him are blessed by that very love" (83.4). Christian mystics of that era often defined God in masculine and the soul in feminine terms and described the religious life as a relationship between the two. Richard of Saint-Victor, for example, outlined in *The Four Degrees of Passionate Charity* the stages through which the soul moves in its relationship to the loving God:

> In the first degree, God enters into the soul and she turns inward into herself. In the second, she ascends above herself and is lifted up to God. In the third, the soul, lifted up to God, passes over altogether into Him. In the fourth the soul goes forth on God's behalf and descends below herself.

Discipline of the heart carries the seeker further and further into the depths, or heights, of divine love. This is seen in India, too. As Kṛṣṇa (i.e., God) is reported in the *Bhagavadgītā* to have told his disciple, Arjuna:

> Through loving devotion [bhakti] he comes to know Me—my measure, and who, in very truth, I am.
> Then, knowing Me in that complete truth, he enters immediately into Me. (18.55)

Discipline of enduring personal relationships. According to some religious ideologies, religious fulfillment is best achieved through the observation of principles that serve to uphold the relationship between the human community and the deity or to maintain important familial and other interpersonal bonds.

A classical example of such relational discipline appears in the traditions centered on and developed from the Jewish notion of *mitsvah* ("commandment"; pl., *mitsvot*), a rule of discipline that is understood to have divine sanction. The rabbinic tradition of Judaism notes that God has given the people of Israel 613 *mitsvot* outlining the 248 positive instructions and 365 negative injunctions the people are obligated to honor. The most general and most familiar of the *mitsvot* are known as the Ten Commandments (see *Exodus* 20:2–14 and *Deuteronomy* 5:6–18), which combine strict monotheistic ideology with rules against destructive social behavior. According to these rules of discipline, the people of Israel are to believe in no other god but Yahveh, not to construct idols, to keep the commandments, not to misuse God's name, to observe the day of rest, to honor their parents, not to commit murder, not to commit adultery, not to steal, not to testify falsely against their neighbors, and not to be envious of other people's possessions. Rabbinic traditions are careful to say that the Ten Commandments do not exhaust *mitsvot,* and remind the people of Israel of the religious duty incumbent on all Jews, for example, to marry and have at least two children in accordance with the divine commandment to "be fruitful and multiply" (*Gn.* 1:22).

Such relational discipline finds similar expression in Paul's teachings to the hellenized Jewish-Christians at Thessalonica that the true disciple must "not [give] way to lust like the pagans who are ignorant of God; and no man must do his brother wrong in this matter, or invade his rights, because, as we have told you before with all emphasis, the Lord punishes all such offenses." Paul further noted to those disciples that we are "taught by God to love one another" in a selfless way and that "anyone who flouts these rules is flouting not man but God" (*1 Thes.* 4:4–9).

Discipline based on the maintenance of proper relationships also appears in another way in the classical Hindu notion of *varṇāśramadharma,* the sacred duties determined by one's vocation and stage of life. An entire science (*śāstra*) of such sacred duties developed in Brahmanic India in order to interpret and preserve those rules by which orthodox Hindus are to act in society.

According to the texts of that tradition, the Dharmaśāstras, society is divided into four classes (*varṇas*, sometimes translated as "castes") of people. Each *varṇa* has its own particular function, and the whole system may be understood as a symbiosis in which all parts depend on the others. The priests (*brāhmaṇas*) perform rituals that ensure the favor of the gods for specific individuals or for society in general. Warriors (*kṣatriyas*) protect the society from foreign invasions and increase its land holdings. The responsibilities of production and distribution of material goods throughout society fall to the merchants (*vaiśyas*), and the laborers (*śūdras*) perform the manual work the other classes need in order to fulfill their responsibilities.

Dharmaśāstra literatures similarly outline the four stages (*āśramas*) of one's individual life, each having its own disciplined requirements. According to a representative text, the *Mānava Dharmaśāstra* (the Laws of Manu, second century BCE), a student (*brahmacārin*) must study the Vedic scriptures under the guidance of a master until he is old enough to marry. Becoming a householder (*gṛhasthin*), one must raise a family and secure its well-being. Having carried out these responsibilities long enough to see one's grandchildren grow to be adults, one leaves the demands of family life to the children and enters the stage of the forest-dweller (*vānaprasthin*) in order to offer private oblations to his ancestors and various deities. Only if one lives long enough, and has met all of these other responsibilities, can one then become a wandering ascetic (*saṃnyāsin*) who, having finally abandoned all possessions and family obligations, seeks the inner wisdom that will bring eternal release.

SEE ALSO Asceticism; Eremitism; Ecstasy; Martial Arts; Meditation; Monasticism; Mortification; Obedience; Religious Communities, article on Christian Religious Orders; Retreat; Yoga.

BIBLIOGRAPHY

Readers interested in discussions of spiritual disciplines in several traditions not outlined above and interpreted from a variety of approaches by eminent scholars will want to consult *Papers from the Eranos Yearbooks,* vol. 4, *Spiritual Disciplines,* edited by Joseph Campbell (New York, 1960), a collection of papers read over several years at the Eranos meetings in Ascona, Switzerland.

On the development of Islamic *sharīʿah* and its relationship to personal piety, see Marshall G. S. Hodgson's *The Venture of Islam,* vol. 1, *The Classical Age of Islam* (Chicago, 1974), pp. 315–409; Fazlur Rahman's *Islam* (New York, 1966), pp. 100–116; and Frederick Mathewson Denny's *An Introduction to Islam* (New York, 1985), pp. 216–292. On Islamic spiritual traditions and mystical poetry, see Annemarie Schimmel's *Mystical Dimensions of Islam* (Chapel Hill, N. C., 1975), esp. pp. 98–227 and 287–343; Reynold A. Nicholson's *Studies in Islamic Mysticism* (Cambridge, 1921); and William C. Chittick's *The Sufi Path of Love: The Spiritual Teachings of Rumi* (Albany, N.Y., 1983). One of the better translations of the Qurʾān remains A. J. Arberry's *The Koran Interpreted* (London and New York, 1955). For an elucidating introduction to Qurʾanic thought, see Fazlur Rahman's *Major Themes of the Qurʾān* (Chicago, 1980).

Translations of traditional accounts of the Buddha's enlightenment, mostly from Pali sources, appear in E. J. Thomas's *The Life of Buddha as Legend and History,* 3d rev. ed. (London, 1949), pp. 38–96, esp. pp. 61–80, and in Edward Conze's *Buddhist Scriptures* (Harmondsworth, 1959), pp. 34–66, which is a translation of Aśvaghoṣa's Sanskrit work, *Buddhacārita* (Acts of the Buddha). For a traditional commentary on the Noble Eightfold Path, see Buddhaghosa's *Visuddimagga* 16.77–83, translated by Bhikkhu Ñyānamoli as *The Path of Purification* (Berkeley, Calif., 1976), vol. 2, pp. 583–584. For commentaries on the First Sermon, see Nalinaksha Dutt's *Aspects of Mahāyāna Buddhism and Its Relations to Hīnayāna* (London, 1930), pp. 129–202. An example of Mahāyāna Buddhist spiritual discipline can be found in Marion L. Matics's translation and study of Śāntideva's *Bodhicaryāvatāra* entitled *Entering the Path of Enlightenment* (New York, 1970). Robert C. Lester discusses Theravāda Buddhist ideals in *Theravada Buddhism in Southeast Asia* (Ann Arbor, Mich., 1973).

The quotation from Vincent van Gogh comes from *Dear Theo,* translated and edited by Irving Stone (New York, 1969), p. 114; that from Paul Klee is taken from *The Diaries of Paul Klee, 1898–1918,* edited by Felix Klee (Berkeley, Calif., 1964), p. 386.

Selections of Japanese *haiku* poetry appearing above come from D. T. Suzuki's *Zen and Japanese Culture,* 2d ed. (Princeton, 1959), pp. 215–268. See also R. H. Blyth's *Haiku,* 4 vols. (Tokyo, 1949–1952).

On the American Indian practices centered on the vision quest, see Ruth Benedict's "The Vision in Plains Culture," *American Anthropologist* 24 (1922): 1–23; Benedict's *The Concept of the Guardian Spirit in North America* (1923; Millwood, N.Y., 1974; Ake Hultkrantz's *The Religions of the American Indians* (Los Angeles, 1979), pp. 66–83; and Sam D. Gill's *Native American Religions: An Introduction* (Belmont, Calif., 1982). For personal accounts of the vision, see Gill's *Native American Traditions: Sources and Interpretations* (Belmont, Calif., 1983). On patterns of initiation in North America, see Edwin M. Loeb's *Tribal Initiations and Secret Societies* (Berkeley, Calif., 1929). The best general discussion of shamanism around the world remains Mircea Eliade's *Shamanism: Archaic Techniques of Ecstasy,* rev. & enl. ed. (New York, 1964).

Translations of the *Bar do'i thos grol* into English may be found in W. Y. Evans Wentz's *The Tibetan Book of the Dead,* 2d ed. (London, 1949), and in Francesca Fremantle and Chögyam Trungpa's *The Tibetan Book of the Dead: The Great Liberation through Hearing in the Bardo* (Berkeley, Calif., 1975). The notion of *dao* in China is discussed by Arthur Waley in *The Way and Its Power* (New York, 1958). Rodney L. Taylor offers a concise discussion of Neo-Confucian sagehood in *The Cultivation of Sagehood as a Religious Goal in Neo-Confucianism* (Missoula, Mont., 1978). The translation from Gao Pan Long's *Fu qi gui* is taken from Taylor's work.

The only available complete English translation of the *Śatapatha Brāhmaṇa* is by Julius Eggeling, *The Śatapatha Brāhmaṇa,* 5 vols., "Sacred Books of the East," vols. 12, 26, 41, 43, 44 (Oxford, 1882–1900). The *Aitareya Brāhmaṇa* has been translated by Arthur Berriedale Keith in his *Rigveda Brāhmaṇas: The Aitareya and Kausiktaki Brāhmaṇas of the Rigveda,* "Harvard Oriental Series," no. 25 (Cambridge, Mass., 1920). The best English translations of the Upaniṣads are Robert Ernest Hume's *The Thirteen Principal Upaniṣads,* 2d ed. (London, 1931), and Sarvepalli Radhakrishnan's *The Principal Upaniṣads* (London, 1953). There are many translations of the *Bhagavadgītā.* One of the best remains Franklin Edgerton's *Bhagavad Gitā* (Chicago, 1925), which includes helpful studies and a summary. Patañjali's *Yoga Sūtra* with commentaries by Vyāsa and Vācaspati Miśra has been translated by James Haughton Woods as *The Yoga-System of Patañjali* (1914), 3d ed. (Delhi, 1966).

Those interested in the writings of Thomas à Kempis might look to *The Imitation of Mary,* edited and translated by Albin de Cigala (Westminster, Md., 1948) and his far better-known *The Imitation of Christ,* translated by Leo Sherley-Price (Harmondsworth, 1953). Those wishing to read Benedict's rule have available many translations, a good one being *The Rule of St. Benedict,* edited and translated by Justin McCann (London, 1921). For Bernard of Clairvaux, see Étienne Gilson's *The Mystical Theology of Saint Bernard,* translated by A. H. C. Downes (London and New York, 1940). Translations from Dionysius the Aeropagite come from F. C. Happold's *Mysticism: A Study and an Anthology* (Harmondsworth, 1970), pp. 212, 216–217. The same is true for the translation from Richard of Saint Victor's *The Four Degrees of Passionate Charity* (see Happold, pp. 241–248, esp. p. 242). Happold's book contains short selections drawn from mystical tracts from a variety of classical religious traditions around the world.

For studies on rabbinic understanding of Jewish sacred law and custom, both written and oral, one might turn first to *The Code of Maimonides,* 15 vols. (New Haven, 1949–1980). Less imposing works include *A Maimonides Reader,* edited by Isidore Twersky (New York, 1972), and Maimonides' *Mishneh Toreh,* 3 vols., edited and translated by Moses Hyamson (New York, 1949). For other codes, see *Code of Hebrew Law: Shulḥan ʿAruk,* 5 vols., edited and translated by Chaim N. Denburg (Montreal, 1954–), or *Code of Jewish Law: Kitzur Shulhan Aruh,* 4 vols., annot. rev. ed., compiled and translated by Solomon Ganzfried and Hyman E. Goldin (New York, 1961). Otherwise, see Alan Unterman's *Jews: Their Religious Beliefs and Practices* (Boston, 1981); *A Rabbinic Anthology,* edited by C. G. Montefiore and Herbert Loewe (New York, 1974); and *The Mishnah,* edited and translated by Herbert Danby (Oxford, 1933).

WILLIAM K. MAHONY (1987)

SPIRITUAL GUIDE. Since ancient times, the figure of the spiritual guide has stood at the center of contemplative and esoteric traditions. It would appear that all such traditions stress the necessity of a spiritual preceptor who has immediate knowledge of the laws of spiritual development and who can glean from the adept's actions and attitudes his respective station on the spiritual path as well as the impediments that lie ahead. Furthermore, the guide is responsible for preserving and advancing the precise understanding of the teaching and spiritual discipline to which he is heir, including both a written tradition and an oral tradition "outside the scriptures," which at its highest level is passed on from master to succeeding master and to certain disciples according to their level of insight. The precarious nature of this transfer has been recognized by all traditions, but no one has described the situation more succinctly than the fifth Chan patriarch, who warned that from "ancient times the transmission of the Dharma has been as tenuous as a dangling thread" (Yampolsky, 1967, p. 133).

Hinduism is not alone in its insistence that the spiritual bond (*vidyāsambandha*) that exists between the spiritual preceptor (*guru*) and his disciple (*śiṣya*) is no less real than a blood relationship. Taking Socrates as the model preceptor, Kierkegaard maintained that the maieutic relationship between teacher and disciple was the highest possible relationship between man and man. Socrates, writes Kierkegaard, entered into the role of midwife, not because his thought lacked "positive content," but because he "perceived that this relationship is the highest that one human being can sustain to another" (Kierkegaard, 1962, p. 12; cf. Plato, *Theaetetus* 150).

Whether he is regarded as a midwife, *daimōn,* or *bodhisattva,* the paradigmatic feature of the spiritual guide is always his intermediate status; in a hierarchically ordered cosmos, the guide is situated in an intermediary world of subtle possibilities, between the realms of pure matter and pure spirit, between earth and heaven, or, one might say, between the exoteric and esoteric. The mythological paradigm for this idea finds expression in a variety of forms: Eros is the half-mortal, half-immortal *daimōn* of special significance to Socrates (See Plato, *Symposium* 202); in Twelver Shiism the guide is the Hidden Imām who lives unseen in the third world of the esoteric Church, a Paradise *in potentia,* between the physical and spiritual cosmos; and as Hermes, he is both the messenger of the gods and their interpreter (*hermeneutēs*), an intermediary between the terrestrial and celestial worlds who has an additional function as the "guide of the souls of the dead."

The legitimacy of the unearthly, inner guide has been vouchsafed by all traditions; but the "masterless master" who has been initiated and guided by the inner spiritual guide without first having been counseled by an outer, human guide (as in the case of Ibn al-ʿArabī, the "disciple of Khiḍr"; see Corbin, 1969) is especially rare. Hui-neng, the sixth Chan patriarch, said that if a man cannot gain awakening on his own

> he must obtain a good teacher to show him how to see into his own self-nature. But if you awaken by yourself, do not rely on teachers outside. If you try to seek a teacher outside and hope to obtain deliverance, you will find it impossible. If you have recognized the good teacher within your own mind, you have already obtained deliverance. (Yampolsky, 1967, p. 152)

On the other hand, the Indian guru Maharaj has suggested that it is the inner guru who leads the disciple to the outer guru, and it is the outer guru who reveals the inner guru (Maharaj, 1973).

ANCIENT GREECE. Pythagoras and Socrates remind us that the worthy figure of the spiritual guide is not confined to the strict forms of religion but can also be identified in various fraternities, orders, and academies whose primary concern is the self-transformation and spiritual enlightenment of their members. As is often the case with founders of religions and lineages, there are no writings that have been attributed to

Pythagoras or Socrates. The first written material on the "master" or founder of these traditions emerges often only after a long gap, so that in the instance of Pythagoras we find many of the earliest accounts idolizing and mythologizing him, attributing numerous miracles to him but remaining silent as to the essentials of his teaching.

According to Aristotle, the Pythagoreans taught that among rational beings there is that which is God, that which is man, and "that which is like Pythagoras" (Arist., frag. 192). The spiritual guide, as in the case of Pythagoras, stands between the human and the suprahuman worlds, between the mundane and the sacred; the guide is the intermediate *par excellence*, mediating energies from above and attracting disciples from below. The idea is further exemplifed by the tradition quoted by Diogenes Laertius that Pythagoras was the son of Hermes in a previous incarnation and that he received from his father a memory of all things that had happened to him (Diogenes Laertius 8.4).

The historical Pythagoras, however, remains a mystery; we have inherited a fragmentary picture of his ascetic practices, taboos, *sumbola*, and orally transmitted maxims, but nowhere does the man Pythagoras emerge.

The problem with Socrates is somewhat different. Whereas Pythagoras had no single student to organize his teaching into a "system," Socrates was followed by his disciple Plato. But the problem here is trying to separate the real Socrates, whose stature as an exemplary guide emerges even in the dialogues, from Plato's literary achievement "Socrates." Jacob Needleman's study of the *Symposium* (in *The Heart of Philosophy*, New York, 1982) reminds us of certain aspects of Socrates' personality and energy as a guide, aspects that have been long overlooked by philosophers. Socrates, as in the other dialogues, is allowed to speak for himself to the extent that he alone among Athenians admits that he does not know; he is a man who is questioning. The state of questioning once again reflects the idea of the intermediate; it represents an intermediate state of unknowing, free at least from false and unexamined views. Similarly, Alcibiades, as the "authentic" pupil of Socrates, is also alone in that, unlike the other Athenians, he is neither for nor against Socrates; many times he wishes Socrates were dead, and yet he realizes that his death should make him more sorry than glad. Alcibiades is, alas, at his "wit's end" when he enters the symposium. A glimpse of Alcibiades' estimation of Socrates is given after the former recounts his failed amorous advances:

> What do you suppose to have been my state of mind after that? On the one hand I realized that I had been slighted, but on the other I felt a reverence for Socrates' character, his self-control and courage; I had met a man whose like for fortitude I could never have expected to encounter. The result was that I could neither bring myself to be angry with him and tear myself away from his society, nor find a way of subduing him to my will. . . . I was utterly disconcerted, and wandered about in a state of enslavement to the man the like of which has never been known. (Plato, *Symposium* 219, trans. Hamilton)

Many other of Socrates' extraordinary attributes are described by Alcibiades in the dialogue, including Socrates' ridiculous and yet perfect choice of words (221), so that one might finally agree with Alicibiades that Socrates' "absolute unlikeness to any human being that is or ever has been is perfectly astonishing" (221).

JUDAISM. Although it is difficult to speculate on the figure of the spiritual guide as he might have existed in ancient Judaism, as, for example, suggested in the texts of *Psalms* and *Ecclesiastes*, the dominant figure of later times became the rabbi. The title is derived from *rav* ("master" or "teacher") and a suffix of possession; hence its literal meaning is "my master" or "my teacher." In modern times the Western world has come to regard the rabbi as a congregation leader, but his original function as a "master" is indicated in the New Testament where Jesus is frequently referred to as rabbi. Similarly John the Baptist is indicated by the title in a singular instance (*Jn.* 3:26). Jesus, when he warned his disciples not to call themselves rabbis, surely meant that this title was not to be taken lightly.

In Talmudic times the rabbi was an interpreter and teacher of the Bible and the oral law (*Mishnah*). Like many teachers in the nonmonastic traditions of the East, the rabbi derived no income from these activities but had an additional occupation that produced private income; most often he was a simple artisan or craftsman. According to doctrine, all rabbis are mutually equal, while reserving their individual freedom to give ordination to suitable disciples. However, the rabbinical mysticism of the medieval period emphasized hierarchy in other ways; to belong to the inner circle of discipleship presupposed an extraordinary degree of self-discipline. Furthermore, the most esoteric level of exegesis and transmission of teaching was reserved for the most select: "It is forbidden to explain the first chapters of *Genesis* to more than one person at a time. It is forbidden to explain the first chapter of *Ezekiel* even to one person unless he be a sage and of original turn of mind" (*Hag.* 2.1).

The title was adopted and altered to *rebe* by Hasidism in the eighteenth century. The didactic and often humorous stories told by the *rebeyim* of Poland and East Europe were passed on by tradition, so that collections exist today that faithfully reflect the scope and activity of these remarkable guides (see Buber, 1947–1948 and 1974).

CHRISTIANITY. The foundation for guidance and discipleship in the Christian tradition is naturally found in the reported actions of Christ: he called his disciples to him; they lived with him and were taught by his actions, words, and gestures.

For Christianity in general, Christ has remained the unequaled teacher, rabbi, a transcendent inner guide through whom man seeks salvation. Over and beyond this tendency toward reliance on a transcendent guide, Eastern Orthodox

Christianity has stressed the importance of the *startsy*, or elders, who guide one's spiritual and practical work. The primary texts of this tradition (called hesychasm) are contained in the *Philokalia*. They represent an unbroken tradition of practical guidance based on the teachings and disciplines of the Desert Fathers, having been written between the fourth and fifteenth centuries by spiritual masters of the Orthodox tradition. The texts show the way to awaken and develop attention and consciousness, and they describe the conditions that are most effective.

Many of the writings indicate the difficulty of accepting the vocation of spiritual guidance and attempt to discourage the false guide from destructive actions and consequences. Nilus the Ascetic (d. around 430) writes:

> But what if someone, not from any choice of his own, is obliged to accept one or two disciples, and so to become the spiritual director of others as well? First, let him examine himself carefully, to see whether he can teach them through his actions rather than his words, setting his own life before them. . . . He should also realize that he ought to work as hard for his disciples' salvation as he does for his own; for, having once accepted responsibility for them, he will be accountable to God for them as well as for himself. That is why the saints tried to leave behind disciples whose holiness was no less than their own, and to change these disciples from their original condition to a better state. (*Philokalia*, vol. l, p. 223)

Not only is there a great temptation for the more advanced monks to consider themselves as highly evolved spiritual guides or directors, but the novice must face the temptation of relying merely on himself and trusting his own judgment when he has as yet insufficient material to understand the guile and cunning of the "enemy." The monk should bring his thoughts and confessions to an elder so that he might learn the gift of true discrimination. John Cassian (d. c. 435) relates: "The devil brings monks to the brink of destruction more effectively through persuading him to disregard the admonitions of the fathers and follow his own judgment and desire, than he does through any other fault" (ibid., p. 104).

But in confessing one's thoughts and concerns there is still the pitfall of following the pseudoguide. John Cassian further encourages monks to seek out spiritual masters who truly possess discrimination and not those whose hair has simply "grown white with age." He relates: "Many who have looked to age as a guide, and then revealed their thoughts, have not only remained unhealed but have been driven to despair because of the inexperience of those to whom they confessed." *Unseen Warfare*, a text with roots in both the Western and Eastern traditions of Christianity, echoes the necessity of a qualified teacher: "A man who follows their guidance and verifies all his actions, both inner and outer, by the good judgments of his teachers—priests in the case of laymen, experienced *startzi* in monasteries—cannot be approached by the enemy" (Kadloubovsky and Palmer, 1952, p. 165).

ISLAM. It has been suggested that much of the wit, humor, and fullness of the image of the spiritual guide in the writings of the Desert Fathers and subsequent accounts of spiritual fathers in early Christianity has been gradually diluted and extracted through generations in an attempt to make the writings more generally palatable. The Ṣūfī master remains, as in the case with various Buddhist guides, a robust and vigorous man, full of life, paradox, and humor.

Shaykh or pīr. The *sharīʿah*, or divine law, is meant for all Muslims, but beyond that lies the *ṭarīqah*, or spiritual path, for the *murīd* (literally "he who has made up his will," i.e., to enter the path). In order to enter the path, it is essential that the adept find and be accepted by a spiritual master, a *shaykh* (Arabic) or *pīr* (Persian); as a *ḥadīth* (tradition) says: "When someone has no shaykh, Satan becomes his shaykh."

Many accounts are given of adepts who have undergone seeming rejection and Abūse by the master who must test the resolve and serious intent of the *murīd*. After this testing (sometimes the adept is made to wait for years), the *murīd* will only then actually begin on the path under the guidance of his master.

> The Sheikh would teach him how to behave in each mental state and prescribe periods of seclusion, if he deemed it necessary. It was well known that the methods could not be alike for everybody, and the genuine mystical leader had to have a great deal of psychological understanding in order to recognize the different talents and characters of his *murīds* and train them accordingly. (Schimmel, 1975, p. 104)

The keen attention paid by the guide to the daily activities of the adept gradually developed in the course of time to the image of the shaykh "who acutely supervised every breath of the *murīd*." The problem of finding and dwelling in the presence of an authentic shaykh is particularly acute, for the adept must choose a guide (or be chosen by a guide) who possesses the qualifications for guiding that particular disciple. "Not every *sheikh* is a master for every disciple. The disciple must seek and find the master who conquers his soul and dominates him as an eagle or falcon pounces upon a sparrow in the air" (Nasr, 1970, p. 144).

The absolute necessity of a spiritual guide is so central to the credo of Sufism that at least one biography of the Ṣūfī master Abū Saʿīd ibn Abī al-Khayr (d. 1049 CE) reports the maxim that "if any one by means of asceticism and self-mortification shall have risen to an exalted degree of mystical experience, *without having a Pīr to whose authority and example he submits himself*, the Ṣūfīs do not regard him as belonging to their community" (Nicholson, [1921] 1976, p. 10).

In this way the transmission of doctrine, method, and exercises is secured in a continuous lineage traced back through a series of dead pirs or shaykhs to the Prophet. The appearance of Muḥammad and his son-in-law, ʿAlī, at the head of a list fits in more with necessary fiction than strict historicity; the Ṣūfīs maintained they were the legitimate heirs of the esoteric teachings of the Prophet. Abū Saʿīd's lineage is traced by his biographer through ten *pīrs* to Muḥammad; the twentieth-century Ṣūfī saint Shaykh Aḥmad al-ʿAlawī (d. 1934) is credited with a "tree of spiritual mastery" including scores of generations as well as sectarian connections complex enough to require a navigator (see Lings, 1973, appendix B).

Although the shaykh has certainly undergone the ascetic and meditative training through which he guides his pupils—*dhikr* ("remembrance" [of God]), fasting, deprivation of sleep, intense physical labors, and so on—he abides in the fullness of life, active and yet detached from his actions. "The true saint," states Abū Saʿīd, "goes in and out amongst the people and eats and sleeps with them and buys and sells in the market and marries and takes part in social intercourse, and never forgets God for a single moment" (Nicholson, 1921, p. 55). For this reason the shaykh's actions often appear paradoxical or inconsistent with Islamic doctrine. Nicholson relates yet another story of Shaykh Abū Saʿīd from the *Asrār:* when the shaykh was holding one of his lavish feasts and entertainments, an arrogant ascetic—ignorant of the shaykh's novitiate and forty years' austerities—challenged him to a forty-day fast, hoping to humiliate the shaykh before his pupils and thereby earn their respect. The shaykh accepted and ate nothing while the ascetic continued to eat the small amounts of food allowed by the practice. Throughout the forty days the Ṣūfīs continued by order of Abū Saʿīd to be served delicious food while the two looked on. Finally the ascetic, no longer strong enough to perform his obligatory prayers, confessed his presumption and ignorance.

The Perfect Human Being. The idea of the Perfect Human Being *(insān-i kāmil)* seems first to have been employed by the Ṣūfī theosophist Ibn al-ʿArabī (d. 1240) and somewhat later in a more technical sense when al-Jīlī (d. between 1408 and 1417) systematized his predecessor's work. Although the idea of the Perfect Human Being has received several different treatments, a general definition might describe him as "a man who has fully realised his essential oneness with the Divine Being in whose likeness he is made" (Nicholson, 1921, p. 78). The saint *(walī)* is the highest knower of God, and consequently he occupies the highest of all human degrees, saintship (*walāyah*), as the Perfect Human Being *par excellence.* Al-Jīlī maintained that the Perfect Human Being of any period was the outward manifestation of the Prophet Muḥammad's essence, claiming that his own spiritual guide was just such an appearance. According to the system of Ibn al-ʿArabī and al-Jīlī, the Ṣūfī shaykhs are "vicegerents" of Muḥammad, invested with the "prophecy of saintship" and brought back by God from the state of *fanāʾ* ("annihilation") so that they might guide the people to God. Something of this idea is reflected in the definition by Maḥmūd Shabistarī (d. 1320) of the Perfect Human Being as he who follows a twofold movement: down into the phenomenal world and upward to the divine world of light.

Mention must also be made of the Ṣūfī master's relationship to the role of the twelfth imām, who is the Hidden Imām in both Shiism and Sufism. The Hidden Imām is the pole (*quṭb*) with whom all Ṣūfī masters are inwardly connected.

As Annemarie Schimmel writes:

> The veneration shown to the *imām* and the *quṭb*, as manifested in the mystical preceptor, is common to Sufism and Shiism. The Shia teaches: "who dies without knowing the imām of his time, dies an infidel," and Jalāluddīn Rūmī (d. 1273), though a relatively moderate Ṣūfī, said: "He who does not know the true *sheikh*—i.e., the Perfect Man and *quṭb* of his time—is a *kāfir*, an infidel." (Schimmel, 1975, p. 200)

HINDUISM. The idea of a spiritual preceptor to guide one's study of religion and philosophy has been a constant influence on the religion of India since the most ancient times. Already in the *Ṛgveda* we see him referred to as the *ṛṣi* ("seer") or *muni* (a sage, or "silent one"); as such, he is the possesser of deep spiritual insights (often resulting from performing austerities) and is considered to be the "author" of the sacred hymns. In later times we find him referred to as *ācārya, brahmāṇa,* and *svāmi* (swami), but he has most dramatically captured the attention of the West as the *guru.*

Only knowledge that was gained from a teacher was capable of successfully leading one to one's aim (*Chāndogya Upaniṣad* 4.9.3). And from *Chāndogya Upaniṣad* 6.4.1f., it appears that the spiritual guide is also necessary in order to cut through and disperse mundane, empirical knowledge and to become conscious of true spiritual knowledge.

There is also the prevalent concern for the secret transmission of esoteric knowledge. Hence, *Chāndogya Upaniṣad* 3.11.5 states that a father can teach the esoteric doctrine to "his eldest son or to a worthy pupil, and to no one else, even if one should offer him the whole earth"; see also *Aitareya Āraṇyaka* 3.2.6.9: "Let no one tell these *saṃhitās* to one who is not a resident pupil, who has not been with the teacher for at least a year, and who is not himself to become a teacher." That the pupil is often tested by the *guru* and admitted only sometimes after a novitiate or probation is attested to in several sources (e.g., *Chāndogya Upaniṣad* 8.7.3; Praśna Upaniṣad 1.2).

It would seem that the word *guru* is used in the sense of "teacher" or "spiritual guide" for the first time in *Chāndogya Upaniṣad,* but one should also point out that its original adjectival sense ("heavy one" or "weighty") is illustrative of the widespread belief that holy persons are characterized by uncommon weight, not necessarily in the outer, physical sense. Hendrik Wagenvoort and Jan Gonda have both commented on this (Gonda, 1947, 1965; Wagenvoort, 1941). Wagenvoort has shown that *guru* is etymologically related to Latin *gravis,* which is remarkable only because its derivative, *gravitas,* was frequently used in connection with the nouns *auctor* and *auctoritas.* The Latin expression *gravis auctor* ("the important or true authority") also carries the same general sense of a guru as a man of influence who takes the initiative, in other words, a man who can "do" and have an effect on others.

Although the tendency to deify the *guru* only gradually gained a doctrinal position, the idea can already be seen in the *Śvetāśvatara Upaniṣad* 6.23, which speaks of a man who has the highest love and devotion for God and for his *guru* as for God. In later times this distinction is erased so that the *guru* is identified with the gods. The great poet and mystic Kabīr (d. c. 1518) taught that the *guru* should be recognized as the Lord himself; a view echoed by Caitanya (d. 1533) and his followers. This process of deification (no doubt aided by the conception of *avatāras*) went to such extremes that the *guru* might be said to have usurped and displaced the gods in importance. Thus, the Śaiva texts teach that if Śiva becomes angry, "then the *guru* can pacify him, but if the *guru* becomes angry, no one can pacify him."

It is in relation to this theme that the idea of the "guru's grace" arose, a concept of particular force even today. Many Indian seekers feel that the mere presence of the *guru* (as in *satsang*, or keeping spiritual company) can somehow lead the pupil to liberation. This view, however, is not held universally. One can easily find numerous exceptions that suggest that the intensity of the disciple's wish for knowledge and his earnest striving are all that is necessary; the *guru*'s only true function then is to act as a messenger. Seen in this light, one can easily understand the statements that contend there is no lack of *gurus*, only of qualified and true disciples.

That the prestige and influence enjoyed by *gurus* has persisted to modern times is attested to by certain teachers of our century who possess the force and unmistakable ring of authenticity. One need only mention by way of example the writings by and about Nisargadatta Maharaj, Ramana Maharshi, and Shri Anirvan. Although in modern times there has been a great deal of speculation and criticism about the claims made by many spiritual guides of India, especially those offering their services to the West, it would be difficult and perhaps a mistake to attempt to judge those teachers on the basis of their outward actions. For no one, as Maharaj has said, could know the motives behind the actions of a truly realized *guru*. To illustrate this point, Maharaj tells the story of a *saṃnyāsin* (world-renouncing ascetic) who was told by his *guru* to marry. He obeyed and suffered bitterly. But all four of his children became the greatest saints and *ṛṣi*s of Maharashtra.

BUDDHISM. Accounts of the Buddha's early life indicate that he retired to the forest in order to receive the teaching and guidance of various celebrated hermits and teachers. However, after practicing a series of austere yogic exercises for several years, the Buddha determined that their guidance was insufficient and set out on his own to attain enlightenment. Once the Buddha attained his enlightenment he remained in a blissful state of meditation for several days and contemplated the trouble he would cause himself should he attempt to share his vision and offer guidance to a deeply deluded and ignorant mankind. He overcame this final temptation of remaining secluded and private in his vision, resolving to share his knowledge with other seekers and to guide them towards a similar transformation. It is upon this fundamental attitude that the Buddhist tradition of spiritual guidance takes its precedence.

Unlike some Indian traditions that tend to view the *guru* as an incarnation of divinity or as an intermediary to the sacred, early Buddhism emphasized the humanity of the guide and his own attainment of spiritual knowledge. The term designated by the texts for the guide or teacher is "good or virtuous friend" (Pali, *kalyāṇamitta*; Skt., *kalyāṇamitra*). The *kalyāṇamitra* provides guidance based entirely on the insight he has gained from personal experience. In one instance the *Saṃyutta Nikāya* reports that when Ānanda suggested to the Buddha that reliance on "virtuous friends" was half the holy life, the Buddha corrected him by declaring it the whole of the holy life. The same text (1:88) relates an episode in which the Buddha describes himself as the "virtuous friend" *par excellence*, as a spiritual guide who leads sentient beings to freedom from birth, old age, suffering, and death.

Bodhisattva. At the core of the development of Mahāyāna Buddhism was the role to be performed by the *bodhisattva* ("enlightenment being"). Mahāyāna doctrine argues that the old order was decidedly individualistic and that the emphasis on desiring a personal liberation, or *nirvāṇa*, was actually a hindrance to the full development of one's spiritual potentialities, stopping the larger movement toward "complete enlightment." The *bodhisattva* relinquishes his personal enlightenment and vows to work for the enlightenment of all sentient beings. After attaining the requisite insight (*prajñā*), the final stage of the *bodhisattva*'s career is devoted to the welfare of others as practiced via skillful means (*upaya*). The doctrine maintains that *prajña* without *upaya* leads to the incomplete quietistic enlightenment, while possession of *upaya* without *prajña* results in continued bondage to *samsara*. Therefore, the skillful guidance of others toward enlightenment, as an expression of compassion, becomes paramount to the spiritual progress of the *bodhisattva*; through this process of guidance something "more" is gained by him.

The employment of skillful means or technique is essentially intended for use by those spiritual guides or masters who possess a complete and perfect knowledge of the teachings and the methods of practice and who are themselves free from the delusions of the mind and emotions. The *bodhisattva* perceives through spiritual insight (*prajña*) the inner barriers and the potentialities of the pupil and can respond to each accordingly. Candrakīrti (fl. 600–650 CE) argued that contradictory teachings would naturally arise because the Buddhas were physicians rather than teachers; in considering the mental and spiritual stations of their disciples, the Buddhas would vary their teachings accordingly. The idea that the master could teach people by playing various roles while remaining inwardly free was presented in its ultimate form by the *Vimalakīrti Sūtra*, which declared that even the Māras are all *bodhisattvas* dwelling in an "inconceivable liberation" and "playing the devil in order to develop beings through their skillful means."

Lama. In what historians have termed the "second diffusion of the teaching" in Tibet, the Buddhist masters emphasized the necessity of an authoritative tradition of teaching, the validity of which was assured by direct transmission from master to disciple. The first two schools of Buddhism to appear in Tibet were the Bka'rgyudpa (Kagyüpa) and Bka'gdamspa (kadampa), founded by Marpa (d. 1096 or 1097) and Atīśa (d. 1054) respectively. With regard to the esoteric tradition of initiation and oral transmission, both schools recognize the same Indian teachers. It is also clear that the first objective of both Marpa and Atīśa was to gather around them tested disciples who would be capable of transmitting the tradition. When asked by a disciple whether scripture or one's teacher's instructions were more important, Atīśa replied that direct instruction from one's teacher was more important; if the chain of instruction and transmission is broken, the text becomes like a corpse, and no power can bring it new life. Marpa's Indian teacher, Nāropa (d. 1100), gave him similar instruction when he declared:

> Before any guru existed
> Even the name of Buddha was not heard.
> All the buddhas of a thousand kalpas
> Only came about because of the guru.
> (Nalanda Translation Committee, 1982, p. 92)

There is, perhaps, nowhere in world literature a more dramatic and haunting portrayal of the kind of guidance provided by a great master than is found in the *Life of Milarepa*, an account of Marpa's most famous disciple, Milaraspa (d. 1123). Milaraspa came to Marpa filled with remorse for the evil he had done by sorcery in his youth; he sought instruction that could free him from the karmic consequences in his future lives. But, as Lobsang P. Lhalungpa has pointed out, Marpa clearly perceived that, as a result of his previous actions, Milaraspa could not gain the desired transformation by means of any normal training. "Thus, as the condition of receiving the Dharma, Mila was required to fulfill a series of bitterly demanding and dispiriting tasks. In enforcing the great ordeals, Marpa used shifting tactics and seemingly deceitful ways" (Lhalungpa, 1977, p. x). During the so-called ordeal of the towers Milaraspa was commanded by Marpa to build single-handedly a tower. But each time Milaraspa had completed a tower, Marpa ordered him to tear it down, claiming he had not paid enough attention to the plans or that he had been drunk when he gave the "Great Magician" directions. Finally, having constructed a ten-story tower (which is still said to exist today) and at the brink of suicide, Milaraspa at last received from Marpa the secret teaching. Not just Milaraspa but Marpa's wife and several of his disciples were baffled by the apparent cruelty and irrationality of the lama Marpa, of the verbal and physical abuse he showered on Milaraspa and his seeming lack of compassion. Marpa countered the doubts of the uninitiated by saying that he merely tested Milaraspa in order to purify him of his sins.

After these trials, Marpa led his disciple through initiations and offered instruction and consultation on meditation. It is said that Milaraspa became "even greater than his teacher" and he is today remembered in Tibet as the greatest of Buddhist "saints." Later, when Milaraspa took on his own pupils, one disciple suggested that he must have been the incarnation of a Buddha or great *bodhisattva* owing to the extent of the trials and ascetic practises he had undergone and based on his great devotion to his lama. Milaraspa replied tersely that he had never heard whose incarnation he was.

Zen patriarchs and Zen masters. It has been observed that every tradition emphasizes the importance of an oral tradition of instruction for the guidance of adepts. The foundation of Chan (Jpn., Zen) Buddhism is based squarely upon this premise, as is indicated in the following verses attributed to the "founder" and first Chan patriarch in China, Bodhidharma (d. before 534):

> A special tradition outside the scriptures;
> No dependence upon words or letters;
> Direct pointing at the soul of man;
> Seeing into one's own nature, and the attainment of Buddhahood.
> (Dumoulin, 1963)

Hui-neng, the sixth patriarch, was said to have been illiterate, and it is reported in a story that is most probably apocryphal that he ordered all of the *sūtras* of his monastery thrown into a heap and burned in order to teach his disciples not to rely on word and texts but direct experience only.

The golden age of Chan in China (the period from Hui-neng's death until the persecution of Buddhism in the ninth century) was a time in which Chan masters of the most remarkable originality won the day. These were vigorous and effusive men who sought to bring their disciples to new levels of insight by demonstrating their own inexpressible experiences of enlightenment by shocking and often violent methods.

One such figure was Mazu (d. 786). A robust and unflinching presence, Mazu is described in a Chan chronicle of the period as a man of remarkable appearance: "He strode along like a bull and glared about him like a tiger." He was the first to use shouting (especially the famous cry "ho!" [Jpn., "katsu"]) as a means to shock the disciple out of his habitually duality-conscious mind. In one famous story it is related that after a typically paradoxical dialogue with one of his disciples, Mazu grabbed him by the nose and twisted it so violently that the pupil cried out in pain—and attained enlightenment.

For Mazu the important thing was not a deluded attachment to quiet sitting in meditation but enlightenment, which could express itself in everything. This was impressed upon Mazu by his own master, Huairang (d. 744). While still a student, Mazu was "continuously absorbed in mediation." On one occasion Huairang came across Mazu while the disciple was engaged in meditation and asked, "For what purpose are you sitting in meditation?" Mazu answered, "I want to become a Buddha." Thereupon the master picked up a tile and started rubbing it on a stone. Mazu asked, "What are you doing, Master?" "I am polishing this tile to make a mirror," Huairang replied. "How can you make a mirror by rubbing a tile?" exclaimed Mazu. "How can one become a Buddha by sitting in meditation?" countered the master (Dumoulin, 1963, p. 97f.).

Linji (d. 866) led his numerous disciples toward enlightenment by continuing and enlarging the use of shouting, adding to that his own favorite method of beating disciples. The "shouting and beating" Chan of Linji was not intended as punishment or random mischief. Experience had taught Linji that harsh and unexpected encounters with "reality" could lead more quickly and certainly to enlightenment than endless lectures and discourses.

An unrelenting giant among Japanese Zen masters was Hakuin (d. 1769). Born in a "degenerate" period of Buddhism in Japan, Hakuin revived the Rinzai form of Zen begun by Linji, particularly emphasizing the investigation of *kōans* and "sitting in the midst of activity." Throughout Hakuin's life he attacked forms of "silent-illumination Zen," which he consistently referred to as "dead-sitting." In his youth, Hakuin tells us, his *kōan* meditation was poor, and as a result he engaged in dead-sitting until his Zen-sickness was cured by the instruction of an insightful teacher, the hermit Hakuyu. As a result, Hakuin was totally uncompromising in his insistence of a right understanding of meditation; his ironic and acerbic tone seems to have been inherited from the harsh patriarchs and Zen masters of the past:

> How sad it is that the teaching in this degenerate age gives indications of the time when the Dharma will be completely destroyed. Monks and teachers of eminent virtue, surrounded by hosts of disciples and eminent worthies, foolishly take the dead teachings of no-thought and no-mind, where the mind is like dead ashes with wisdom obliterated, and make these into the essential doctrines of Zen. They practice silent, dead sitting as though they were incense burners in some old mausoleum and take this to be the treasure place of the true practice of the patriarchs. They make rigid emptiness, indifference, and black stupidity the ultimate essence for accomplishing the Great Matter. (Yampolsky, 1971, p. 170)

It has been argued that the ultimate purpose of the Zen master is one thing alone: to produce a disciple who can carry on the teaching and preserve the transmission of the Dharma. The lineages of many famous monks became extinct after a generation or two because they had no disciples to hand down their teachings.

The biography of Bozhang (d. 814) states: "He whose view is equal to that of his teacher diminishes by half his teacher's power. He whose view exceeds that of his teacher is qualified to transmit the teaching." Hakuin was keenly aware of the necessity of producing a worthy disciple and in fact sanctioned several of his own pupils to carry on his teaching. Armed with spiritual powers and techniques for guiding others in their quest for enlightenment, the Zen master "smashes the brains of monks everywhere, and pulls out the nails and knocks out the wedges." With typical Zen irony Hakuin describes the worthy successor he has produced who is qualified to transmit the teaching: "Without the least human feeling he produces an unsurpassedly evil, stupid, blind oaf, be it one person or merely half a person, with teeth sharp as the sword-trees of hell, and a gaping mouth like a tray of blood. Thus will he recompense his deep obligation to the Buddhas and the Patriarchs" (Yampolsky, 1971, p. 39).

SEE ALSO Authority; Leadership.

BIBLIOGRAPHY

Buber, Martin. *Tales of the Hasidim.* 2 vols. Translated by Olga Marx. New York, 1947–1948.

Buber, Martin. *The Tales of Rabbi Nachman.* Translated by Maurice Friedman. London, 1974.

Dumoulin, Heinrich. *A History of Zen Buddhism.* Translated by Paul Peachey. New York, 1963.

Gonda, Jan. "À propos d'un sens magico-religieux de skt. *guru-*." *Bulletin of the School of Oriental and African Studies* 12 (1947): 124–131.

Gonda, Jan. *Change and Continuity in Indian Religion.* The Hague, 1965.

Guénon, René. "Hermes." In *The Sword of Gnosis,* edited by Jacob Needleman, pp. 370–375. Baltimore, 1974.

Gunaratna, Henepola. *The Path of Serenity and Insight.* Columbia, Mo., 1984.

Kadloubovsky, Eugènie, and G. E. H. Palmer, trans. *Unseen Warfare, Being the Spiritual Combat and Path to Paradise as Edited by Nicodemus of the Holy Mountain and Revised by Theophan the Recluse.* London, 1952.

Kerényi, Károly. *Hermes, Guide of Souls.* Translated by Murray Stein. Zurich, 1976.

Kierkegaard, Søren. *Philosophical Fragments.* 2d ed. Princeton, 1962.

Lhalungpa, Lobsang P., trans. *The Life of Milarepa.* New York, 1977.

Lings, Martin. *A Moslem Saint of the Twentieth Century: Shaikh Ahmad al-Alawi.* 2d ed. Berkeley, 1973.

Maharaj, Sri Nisargadatta. *I Am That.* Bombay, 1972.

Nalanda Translation Committee under the direction of Chögyam Trungpa, trans. *The Life of Marpa the Translator.* Boulder, 1982.

Nasr, Seyyed Hossein. "The Sufi Master as Exemplified in Persian Sufi Literature." *Studies in Comparative Religion* 4 (Summer 1970): 140–149.

Needleman, Jacob. "The Search for the Wise Man." In *Search: Journey on the Inner Path,* edited by Jean Sulzberger, pp. 85–100. New York, 1979.

Needleman, Jacob. *The Heart of Philosophy.* New York, 1982.

Nicholson, Reynold A. *Studies in Islamic Mysticism* (1921). Reprint, Cambridge, 1976.

Palmer, G. E. H., Philip Sherrard, and Kallistos Ware, eds. and trans. *The Philokalia,* vol. 1. London, 1979.

Schimmel, Annemarie. *Mystical Dimensions of Islam.* Chapel Hill, N.C., 1975.

Yampolsky, Philip, ed. and trans. *The Platform Sūtra of the Sixth Patriarch.* New York, 1967.

Yampolsky, Philip, trans. *The Zen Master Hakuin.* New York, 1971.

STUART W. SMITHERS (1987)

SPIRITUALISM is a widespread and generally unorganized movement that arose in the United States at the end of the 1840s, was influential through the nineteenth century in the United States and elsewhere, and persists at the beginning of the twenty-first century. At its core is the belief that the living can conduct conversations with spirits of the deceased through a sensitive instrument (either a mechanical or electronic device) or a human *medium.*

Spiritualism's advent was occasioned by two events. The first was the publication of Andrew Jackson Davis's visionary cosmology and universal history, *The Principles of Nature, Her Divine Revelations, and a Voice to Mankind,* in 1847. The second was the production of audible rapping that was interpreted as coded responses of spirits to questions posed by two young sisters, Margaret and Kate Fox. Others soon reproduced the sounds during "spirit circles" or séances around the country. Spiritualists later annually commemorated the rappings as having begun on March 25, 1848.

Practitioners said Spiritualism was precipitated when spirits, including that of electrical experimenter Benjamin Franklin, established a practical "spiritual telegraph" between this world and the spirit world. Those who were not Spiritualists looked elsewhere for the sources of the movement, crediting demons, mass delusion, human folly, fraud, or simply to the influence of social and religious trends in the larger culture.

SPIRITUALISM'S THEORY AND CULTURAL BACKGROUND. The "harmonial philosophy" of Davis and his sympathizers envisioned a harmonization of past, present, and future; of matter and spirit; of reason and intuition; of men and women; and of individuals and society. It provided an ostensibly rationalist stock onto which was grafted a variety of exotic psychic phenomena, such as mesmeric trance and the Fox sisters' rappings. The result was "Modern Spiritualism," as it was called, which was optimistic about the destiny of each individual after death and of human society in the long run, and egalitarian insofar as it accepted the revelations of women, children, and others who lacked education or credentials.

Spiritualism was part of the larger culture's effort to reconcile science and religion. In the United States and Europe the intersection of matter and spirit had been explored in experiments with mesmerism. Influential books included the 1845 translation of Justinus Kerner's case study of a somnambulist, *The Seeress of Prevorst,* and the 1855 translation of Louis Alphonse Cahagnet's description of conversations with entranced clairvoyants, *The Celestial Telegraph.* The term *Spiritualism* came from mesmerism and referred to the concept of an exalted expanse opened to clairvoyants traveling without the body to realms where spirits could communicate secrets to them.

The disappearance or surrender of one's identity to another was a theme of the seventeenth-century mystical writings of Madame Guyon and Francois Fénelon, who emphasized the individual's surrender of the will to divine love. These writings were popular among American antebellum Protestant intellectuals. The Romantic movement fostered a similar surrender of the self, or hypersensitivity to spiritual or psychic "impressions." Goethe had depicted such sensitivity in his novels *The Sorrows of Young Werther* (1744) and *Elective Affinities* (1809), and it was exemplified in Bohemian wanderlust, the desire to follow personal "monitions" rather than conventional expectations. The abandonment of the self to holy enthusiasm and impulse was also encouraged in the religious revivals of the time. The Gothicism of the period resulted in the enormous popularity of Catherine Crowe's 1848 collection of stories about uncanny phenomena, *The Night-Side of Nature.*

The concern with reconciling science and religion, as well as matter and spirit, coincided with a popular interest in the newly translated writings of Swedish engineer and visionary Emanuel Swedenborg, who had conversations with spirits about their lives in other worlds that intersected with this one. Transcendentalists urged a spiritualization of the natural world, and Perfectionists suggested that the earthly could be reformed into, or revealed to be, the heavenly, stimulating seekers to set up utopian communities founded on the ideas of French socialist Charles Fourier. Also influential in the birth of Spiritualism was an efflorescence of trance visions among Shakers during the late 1830s and 1840s, which presaged many of the features of Spiritualism.

Spiritualism promoted the notion of surrendering the will to the inspiration of spirits, but it simultaneously elevated the importance of the individual's perception and judgment. It assented to testing the reality of the spirits, ranking empirical experience over traditional authority. It made a "scientific" appeal to evidence available to anyone. It also adopted the individualism and anticlericalism of the Protestant dissenting tradition, evident in the Pietistic origins of the religious groups—such as the Universalists, the Unitarians, and Quakers—among whose members Spiritualism flourished. Spiritualism, by and large, was antiauthoritarian and Spiritualists valued the liberty of individual conscience. The movement was associated with progressive politics and social theory, and was most popular in the northern United States. Southerners often saw spiritualism as one strand of a twisted skein of Yankee fanaticism that also included such causes as utopian socialism, women's rights, and the abolition of slavery.

Spiritualists accepted the naturalistic idea of geological and biological change and development, and they extended the idea to religion, which they believed also evolved and progressed. Spiritualists supposed that individuals progressed as well, continuing beyond this life into the afterlife, and Spiritualism thus expanded the realm of natural law into the supernatural. They did not view the Fox sisters' rappings or other Spiritualistic phenomena as miracles in the sense of a suspension of natural law, but they saw such phenomena as the ultimately rational—although not yet understood—effects of the interaction between this world and the higher world. The clairvoyant travels of spirit mediums also resembled the travels of naturalist explorers of exotic cultures, such as, for example, A. J. Davis's travels while in "the superior state" to the afterlife, which he envisioned as "The Summerland," a socialist community of enlightened souls. The "scientific" tendencies of Spiritualists led some of their early religious opponents to refer to them as "rationalists."

Many personal accounts described conversion to Spiritualism as a joyful liberation from a bleak Calvinist belief that the soul was powerless to affect its final disposition, or even liberation from an arid materialist belief that denied life after death. Other accounts described the adoption of Spiritualism as only a small step from the beliefs of liberal churches that already had a tenuous relationship with traditional Christian doctrine. Many Spiritualists saw themselves as "come-outers," that is, as part of a group that had left Christianity, just as their spiritual forebears had left corrupted churches. Many other Spiritualists, however, believed that they were simply finding their way back to the true core of Christianity and called themselves "Christian Spiritualists." Spiritualists were early advocates of "higher criticism" of the Bible and they were convinced that apocrypha, such as Gnostic texts, contained a true picture of Jesus's life and teachings. Spiritualists generally accepted the rococo speculations of comparative religion as it was practiced by such savants as Louis Jacolliot, who believed that the biblical story of Christ was a fiction based on the Hindu myth of Kṛṣṇa.

Traditional churches vigorously opposed Spiritualism, attributing it to the devil and equating it with previous forms of necromancy. Traditional churches also opposed Spiritualism because it made revelation deliberately open-ended and subject only to individual judgment. Spiritualism moved religion from churches, which were public places subject to the control of traditional (male) authority, to home parlors, which were private places subject to domestic (female) sentiment, or, as opponents put it, dark places where people were free of restraint. Opponents also took issue with Spiritualists' equating the authority of the Bible with that of the messages and wonders produced at séances and in other religions.

Most of the public and most scientists, with a few exceptions, treated Spiritualism as delusion, fraud, or mental disorder. Some scientists attributed séance messages to the medium's ability to read the thoughts of others in the spirit circle, rather than to the medium's ability to hear the whisperings of spirits. These scientists believed this explanation was more naturalistic.

In nineteenth-century America, Spiritualism bore the marks of the progressive wing of Protestantism. Local varieties, however, sometimes drew from other sources, such as the Spiritualism of New Orleans, which incorporated Catholicism's traditions of intercessory saints and sacraments, as well as voodoo. The Spiritualism practiced in some parts of the United States incorporated Native American methods of divination, trance induction, and spirit possession, and white mediums often discovered that their spirit guides were Indians. Modern Spiritualism was largely a phenomenon of white Americans, however, with some notable exceptions, such as Sojourner Truth and Pascal Beverly Randolph. Nevertheless, Spiritualists believed that spirit contact was at the heart of all religion, and they believed they found support for this view in the Bible, in ancient accounts of the Sibylline oracles and of prophets and druids, and in historical records of witchcraft and haunting.

Some opponents of Spiritualism argued for replacing the term *Spiritualism* with *spiritism.* As they saw it, *Spiritualism* was a word with wide application but only appropriate as a contrast to *materialism.* They insisted that *spiritism* was the proper term for what was commonly called "Spiritualism," which, according to them, was merely a submission or unhealthy attachment to spirits. Their argument had little effect on popular usage, and gained no acceptance by Spiritualists.

Spiritism, however, was used by French seer Hippolyte Léon Denizard Rivail, writing under the pseudonym Allan Kardec. Kardec's publications in the late 1850s and 1860s influenced many in the French-speaking world to accept the reality of spirit contact. They also accepted the existence of reincarnation, whereas American and English Spiritualists, at least for the first decades of the movement, rejected it.

In general, European Spiritualism was more influenced than was American Spiritualism by occult traditions, such as Hermeticism, Rosicrucianism, irregular orders of Freemasonry, and ideas from the eastern lands that Europeans had colonized. Nevertheless, American spirit mediums spread their variety of Spiritualism to Europe by lecturing and holding séances there. Maria Trenholm Hayden, for example, visited England and made an early convert of socialist Robert Owen. Daniel Dunglas Home traveled throughout Europe and gave spectacular performances, some of which powerfully affected the czarist court.

Doctrinal controversies arose within the movement: Did spirits provide tangible assistance or mere comfort? In trance, was the will erased or exalted? Was Spiritualism's essence a public platform of progressive reform, or the phenomenal manifestations of the séance? Why were revelations from trance mediums contradictory? Controversies also arose on the specifics of the afterlife (Were animals reborn there? Was retrogression possible after death?) and on the interaction between spirit and body (Did sexual prompting signal an attraction of true spiritual "affinities"?).

The Forms and Practices of Spiritualism. Spiritualists developed their own church services, with congregational singing of hymns, lectures, and Sunday schools ("lyceums") for children. Spiritualists also encouraged the development of mediums who could conduct séances or give lectures under the influence of spirits.

The séance was meant to be a ritual communion of the saints still in the flesh with those who had left it, but the séance was also meant to be a proof test of the reality of the afterlife. The earliest Spiritualists formed spirit circles similar to those that mesmerists already used to investigate "animal magnetism," where men and women touched hands around a table, forming a "magnetic battery." Mesmeric investigators had produced trance, clairvoyance, eruptions of tics or automatisms, sometimes involving writing or speaking, and the tilting of tables and levitating of people, furniture, and musical instruments. Now sitters attributed these to discarnate spirits rather than to their own manipulations of energy.

Personal messages voiced or written by the medium from the sitters' deceased friends and family were always the main products of a séance, with the sitters conducting their conversation with the spirits through the medium. But the medium might also give voice to the spirits of famous people who corrected or supplemented the ideas for which they had been known while living. Other phenomena produced at a séance might include musical sounds, disembodied voices, floating lights and phosphorescent hands, and the materialization of coins, flowers, letters, or birds. Mediums produced spirit-inspired songs, poetry, paintings, scriptures and narratives of travel to other times or worlds, revelations of hidden treasures or lucrative business opportunities, chalk messages on slate boards, spirit images on photographic plates, and novel plans for inventions and for political or social reforms. Mediums also reported the ability to read minds, to see the future, and to escape from tied ropes or locked jail cells. At séances in the 1870s and 1880s mediums might extrude from their bodies a pale diaphanous substance eventually called "ectoplasm," or they might conduct "dark cabinet materializations" in which they were locked in a cabinet and produced spectral forms who walked among the audience.

Mediums also diagnosed disease. Their reputed clairvoyance allowed them to see into a person's body to the source of illness, and, sometimes with assistance of the spirits of famous physicians, to prescribe treatment. This often included the medium's manipulation of the energy "aura" surrounding the patient's body through the laying on of hands. Many mediums made their living through healing, rather than through conducting séances or giving lectures.

Far more women than men were spirit mediums, and male mediums often characterized their sensitivity as a feminine power. Spiritualist lecturers, on the other hand, were often men, although the exceptions—such as self-styled "trance lecturers" Cora L. V. Scott Richmond, Emma Hardinge Britten, Hannah Frances Brown, Achsa White Sprague, Lizzie Doten, Ada Hoyt Foye, and Amanda Britt Spence—drew enthusiastic audiences, thrilled to see women on a platform speaking fearlessly and authoritatively.

Spiritualists believed that one feminine aspect of Spiritualism was its focus, not on the abstract intellect, but on subjective feeling and on the body. They believed that spirits had begun to affect the biological elevation of the human race by exerting spiritual influence over the conception and development of the human embryo. They also believed the spirits could free women from undesired sex, which literally degraded their offspring. Women had to be made equal to men, and each woman had to be given sole authority over when, and how often, and with whom she would have sex and children. Some Spiritualists were the first public advocates of women's reproductive rights, and Spiritualists occupied the most radical wing of the early women's rights movement.

Spiritualists made effective prophets, perhaps, but not loyal group members. They attempted to organize, but with only sporadic successes. Many were leery of setting up a hierarchy that would judge individual practices or experiences. On the other hand, they valued communion, association, and small spirit circles as aids to amplify a medium's sensitivity. In addition, groups fortified the camaraderie of believers, inculcated children in the belief in spirit communion, trained mediums, and sponsored lecturers. Local associations licensed mediums, ministers, and lecturers to protect them from ordinances against fortune telling and "jugglery." They also investigated charges of mediumistic fraud or immorality to protect Spiritualism from abuse by con artists or from embarrassment by anti-Spiritualist opponents.

Spiritualists also formed state, regional, and national associations, with varying success, and they held conventions. Propaganda for the movement was carried out by word of mouth, by experiments with séances, by lectures from traveling mediums, and by the publication of pamphlets and books. Spiritualist newspapers connected far-flung and often isolated believers into a community of faith. The most influential were *Spiritual Telegraph, New-England Spiritualist, Herald of Progress, Religio-Philosophical Journal,* and *Banner of Light.*

The first Spiritualist camp meeting was held in a field outside Malden, Massachusetts, in the summer of 1866. Camp meetings became very influential in the movement, sometimes drawing as many as twenty thousand attendees to such rural surroundings as Lake Pleasant, Massachusetts, or Cassadaga, New York (the forerunner of the center for the Spiritualist movement today at Lily Dale, New York, and the namesake for another settlement in Florida).

Spiritualism's Progress through the Nineteenth Century and Beyond. The popularity and influence of Spiritualism rose and fell. Little solid evidence exists for judging the number of Spiritualists during these years because the organizations of Spiritualism were transient, and the criteria of who counted as a Spiritualist were extremely elastic. In the United States population of thirty million on the eve of the Civil War in 1860, estimates of the number of Spiritualists have varied from a few hundred thousand to eleven million. At the time, however, both proponents and opponents of Spiritualism often accepted as reasonable the figure of two to three million Spiritualists.

By the 1880s, Spiritualism's influence had receded. Some Spiritualists defected to the newer systems of Christian Science, New Thought, and Theosophy. Some who were more politically radical were drawn into Freethought, Anarchism, and Communism, losing their religious outlook. At the same time, Spiritualism's influence had diffused through the culture, most notably in the idea of artistic and religious inspiration.

Meanwhile, Spiritualism's séance phenomena had devolved into elaborate materializations that were often indistinguishable from stage magic, inviting well-publicized exposures of fraudulent mediums by such people as magician Harry Kellar, who blazed a trail later followed by Harry Houdini. Scientists investigating Spiritualism also developed more rigorous protocols for what they began to call "psychical research," which eventually allowed the field of psychology to distance itself from the need to consider spirit as a subject for empirical research. Sigmund Freud's development of a compelling theory of the unconscious also helped render the notion of the paranormal uninteresting to psychologists, with some exceptions, notably Carl Jung. By the turn of the century, Spiritualism no longer seemed to many potential converts as a progressive, avant-garde reconciliation of religion and science, but as an antique.

Nevertheless, Spiritualism has continued throughout the world, with periodic revivals, to this day, with an umbrella organization—the National Spiritualist Association of Churches—founded in 1893, forty-five years after the Fox sisters' rappings. Interest in Spiritualism grew in England after World War I, sometimes linked to the desire by survivors for comfort and reassurance, not just concerning the fate of their loved ones who had died, but perhaps also for the old order of society. Since the late 1960s a revival of Spiritualism has taken place under the banner of the New Age movement. A strong element of theatrics, nearly always present in Spiritualism, is continued in television shows in which psychics face studio audiences in order to contact, or even "channel," the spirits.

From the beginning, Spiritualists criticized Christian miracles and superstition. Nevertheless, they also claimed as true the manifestation of physical phenomena that have yet to be empirically verified. Spiritualists sometimes said that the evidence was real but only anecdotal, and that the spirits' ability and willingness to manifest themselves were constrained by the testing requirements imposed by skeptical investigators. On the other hand, like ancient Gnosticism and present-day postmodernism, Spiritualism judged the objective, external, matter-of-fact world to be essentially devoid of truth. Truth lay instead in a dematerialized, spiritual, inner realm. One goal of Spiritualism was to demonstrate this. As a result, some Spiritualists tacitly believed that if intransigent fact had to be helped along by hidden manipulation, hoax, fiction, or impersonation in order to turn the world into, or reveal it as, or convince an observer that the world was, a magical one in which mind ruled matter, then there was little or no fault, but rather virtue, in doing so.

See Also Christian Science; New Religious Movements, article on New Religious Movements and Women; New Thought Movement; Quakers; Shakers; Swedenborgianism; Theosophical Society; Transcendental Meditation.

BIBLIOGRAPHY

Braude, Ann. *Radical Spirits: Spiritualism and Women's Rights in Nineteenth-Century America.* 2d ed. Bloomington, Ind., 2001.

Britten, Emma Hardinge. *Modern American Spiritualism: A Twenty Year's Record of the Communion between Earth and the World of Spirits.* New York, 1870; reprint, New Hyde Park, N.Y., 1970.

Buescher, John B. "More Lurid than Lucid: The Spiritualist Invention of the Word Sexism." *Journal of the American Academy of Religion* 70, no. 3 (2002): 561–593.

Buescher, John B. *The Other Side of Salvation: Spiritualism and the Nineteenth-Century Religious Experience.* Boston, 2003.

Carroll, Bret E. *Spiritualism in Antebellum America.* Bloomington, Ind., 1997.

Moore, R. Laurence. *In Search of White Crows: Spiritualism, Parapsychology, and American Culture.* New York, 1977.

Owen, Alex. *The Darkened Room: Women, Power, and Spiritualism in Late Victorian England.* Philadelphia, 1990.

Podmore, Frank. *Modern Spiritualism: A History and a Criticism.* 2 vols. London, 1902; reprinted as *Mediums of the 19th Century.* New Hyde Park, N.Y., 1963.

Taves, Ann. *Fits, Trances, and Visions: Experiencing Religion and Explaining Experience from Wesley to James.* Princeton, 1999.

John B. Buescher (2005)

SPIRITUALITY is the concern of human beings with their appropriate relationships to the cosmos. How the cosmic whole is conceived and what is considered appropriate in interacting with it differ according to worldviews of individuals and communities. Spirituality is also construed as an orientation toward the spiritual as distinguished from the exclusively material. This entry considers classic spiritualities, contemporary spiritualities, and spirituality as an alternative to religion. By the end of the twentieth century spirituality, long considered an integral part of religion, was increasingly regarded as a separate quest, with religion being distinguished from secular spiritualities. A predilection to speak of having spirituality rather than having religion indicated a change in worldview and a transition from exclusive religious traditions to inclusive, overlapping expressions of commitment to world and community.

CLASSIC SPIRITUALITIES. Each religion has a characteristic way of living in the world. Each embraces an attitude and outlook rooted in its particular worldview and has developed a set of disciplines that assists devotees in pursuing their relationship to the cosmos. Thus, one speaks, for example, of Islamic spirituality, Christian spirituality, indigenous Australian spirituality, or Hindu spirituality. By *spirituality* one denotes the characteristic sentiments and way of life of those who were born into, or came to embrace, a particular tradition. Thus, Crossroad Publishing's series, World Spirituality: An Encyclopedic History of the Religious Quest, which treats spirituality as essential to religious traditions, has published volumes on world religions and on indigenous religious traditions. However, recognizing the trend that emerged in the second half of the twentieth century of not confining spirituality to religious contexts, the series includes volumes titled *Modern Esoteric Movements* and *Spirituality and the Secular Quest.* In a preface, the series editor, Ewert Cousins, states:

> The series focuses on that inner dimension of the person called by certain traditions "the spirit." This spiritual core is the deepest center of the person. It is here that the person is open to the transcendent dimension; it is here that the person experiences ultimate reality. The series explores the discovery of this core, the dynamics of its development, and its journey to the ultimate goal. It deals with prayer, spiritual direction, the various maps of the spiritual journey, and the methods of advancement in the spiritual ascent. (Olupona, 2000, p. xii)

Spirituality regarded as a dimension of religious expression may describe the sensibility and practices of schools, orders, or denominations within a tradition. Spiritual leaders and scholars of Christianity distinguish approaches to the spiritual life of various Catholic and Protestant groups—for instance, Jesuit spirituality, Franciscan spirituality, Anglican spirituality, and Calvinist spirituality. Each spirituality employs resources of the Christian tradition (Bible reading, sacraments, prayers, good works) to develop a life based on the example of Jesus Christ and the New Testament. Similarly, each of the schools and movements within Hinduism, Buddhism, and Islam has its characteristic spirituality.

The difference between classic spirituality and those who claim to have spirituality but not religion is not so much a disagreement about what constitutes spirituality. The latter may agree with Cousins that spirituality has to do with "the deepest center of the person" and with experiences of "ultimate reality." Both see spirituality as a way of situating the self in the world. However, while the practitioners of classic spiritualities see spirituality is an aspect of religion, those on contemporary spiritual quests do not limit it in this way. Moreover, they may see their spirituality as an alternative to religion.

CONTEMPORARY SPIRITUALITIES. Contemporary spiritualities combine practices of particular religious traditions with concern for the global situation and the life of the planet. Like classic spiritualities, approaches to spirituality that were developed in the last quarter of the twentieth century are also concerned with cultivation of the self and have generated many volumes on self improvement. Contemporary spiritualities are pluralistic and diverse; they search for a global ethic, are concerned with ecology, encourage the cultivation of healthy relationships, support feminism, and pursue peace.

In *A Spirituality Named Compassion and the Healing of the Global Village, Humpty Dumpty, and Us* (1979) Matthew Fox pointed toward spirituality as an alternative to religion and, indeed, as resistance toward traditional religion. Fox was concerned with compassion as the mode of spirituality that the world needed. Aware of regional and international conflicts, some of them provoked by religious differences, he sought to discover how the members of the global community might learn to live and survive together. "Now that the world is a global village we need compassion more than ever—not for altruism's sake, nor for philosophy's sake or theology's sake, but for survival's sake" (p. 11). Thus, from within his Roman Catholic heritage, Fox began to promote what he said was "a spirituality named compassion," a spirituality that did not belong to a particular religious tradition, but that could be adopted by anyone genuinely committed to the world community. "Survival's sake," as Fox put it, is also the focus of those who, with him, advocate an ecological spirituality. For them it is not only the survival of human communities that is at stake, but also the survival of animal and plant populations and of the earth itself. "Green spirituality" has increasingly become part of religious traditions. David Kinsley, in *Ecology and Religion: Ecological Spirituality in Cross-Cultural Perspective* (1995), showed how concern with the environment becomes part of ongoing religious commitments, building on and reinterpreting the resources of existing traditions and, perhaps, adding to them. This was the concern, too, of the Harvard University Center for the Study of World Religions when in the late 1990s and early 2000s it conducted a series of conferences on "Religions of the World and Ecology." The participants reflected on the literary, doctrinal, and ritual resources that help traditions to think about and respond to the earth. Many of the contributors recognized that religions stand in need of dialogue with each other and with the disciplines of science, education, and public policy. An openness to other traditions and disciplines is a characteristic of many spiritual quests at the turn of the century.

Some, though, have sought not so much to expand traditional religious spirituality to incorporate environmental concern as to abandon traditional religious beliefs and practice in favor of commitment to the environment. Faithfulness to earth as their home, and solidarity with the creatures of the earth as their community, shape their orientation toward the world. Some call their quest and their commitment *spirituality* rather than *religion.* With a broad definition of religion, environmentally concerned spirituality could be seen as a new kind of religion—an ecological religion—but such terminology at the beginning of the twenty-first century was still in the making. All religion may have been turning to ecology as some people left behind more organized forms of religion and adopted more flexible and personal forms.

Classic spiritualities prescribed practices to help the person come closer to the ideal upheld by the religion. The self-cultivation aspect of contemporary spirituality has been presented in much popular writing, including that of Thomas Moore. In the early 1990s his trilogy on the soul—the first volume called *The Care of the Soul: A Guide for Cultivating Depth and Sacredness in Everyday Life* (1992), the second *Soul Mates: Honoring the Mysteries of Love and Relationship* (1994), and the third *The Re-Enchantment of Everyday Life* (1996)—were on the *New York Times* best-seller list. His later works have also been popular. Moore advised readers and workshop participants to attend to relationships, to cultivate a sense of place, and to make time for music. Many people who belong to organized religions and many who do not have found his nonjudgmental approach and encouragement of authenticity in daily life appealing. Yet, he has suffered scathing criticism by those who see his work as pandering to self-indulgence.

Contemporary spirituality contended with the many changes the world underwent in the second half of the twentieth century. James Conlon, the director of the Sophia Center in Culture and Spirituality at Holy Names College in Oakland, California, wrote in *The Sacred Impulse: A Planetary Spirituality of Heart and Fire* (2000) of a new vision of the world and of ways of living authentically within that vision. Expressing hope for where this would lead he asserted:

> This new vision will involve a synthesis of the wisdom of science, mystical and prophetic traditions, women, indigenous peoples, and other groups that have not previously been heard. We will strive to create a culture that will foster new energy and a zest for life, a culture based on interaction and choice, identity and purpose, images and stories, values and structures that will give renewed expression to harmony, balance, and peace. This will be a culture that celebrates diversity and pluralism at every level—pluralism revealed in the lives and stories of people and groups whose diversity is manifest in language, lifestyle, temperament, economics, and a capacity for inclusion. (pp. 30–31)

SPIRITUALITY AS AN ALTERNATIVE TO RELIGION. Among people who say that they do not have a religion but do have spirituality are some who say they once had a religion but that they outgrew it or it let them down. In North America and elsewhere, affirmation of spirituality while criticizing religion has been particularly evident in New Age groups, but has been seen, too, within traditional religions as their members search to become more attuned to contemporary circumstances. The shift in terminology that led people to say that they do not have "religion" but do have "spirituality" marked a change in consciousness, representing both a rejection of the perceived shortcomings of religion—such as inflexibility, dogmatism, and authoritarianism—and an embracing of spiritual paths that are both individual and inclusive. Moreover, this shift in terminology pointed to new visions of the world.

Those who wanted spirituality, but not religion, desired to develop themselves in their own ways. They embarked on a quest for authenticity—a quest with promise and problems. The promise lay in the potential for genuine engagement with the world in which they lived, with their own being, and with whatever they considered sacred. The problems were the dangers of self-indulgence and self-delusion against which classic spiritualities warned their devotees. The latter-day emphasis on the self may be at odds, for example, with classic Christian spirituality, which expects the Christian to be selfless in love and good works, and with the Buddhist emphasis on overcoming the self. Reflecting on the fact that many people pursue their spiritual quests without relationship to organized religion James J. Bacik urged respect for, and use of, classic religious ways when he wrote: "Individuals who pursue spiritual growth without benefit of traditional religious wisdom are in danger of adopting faddish approaches or muddling along without a clear goal or a disciplined regimen. Even those who seem to be making good spiritual progress may be missing opportunities for even greater personal growth" (1997, p. viii).

The discourses of religion and spirituality represent different, but often overlapping, understandings of self and world. The language of "religion" points to the shared past of particular groups as a basis for living now. It includes well-honed doctrines and disciplines. It tells devotees how the world is and how they should live in it. Many of the new spiritualities are eclectic, adopting texts and practices from various sources to fashion something that works for the individual. Eclecticism can be offensive to those from whom it borrows. Workshops in the United States that use Native American traditions have drawn the ire of Native people who object, for example, that their purificatory sweat lodge ceremonies have been removed from traditional social and religious contexts and inserted into the New Age seeker's repertoire. Native American scholars, including Christopher Ronwanièn:te Jocks, have called appropriators of indigenous traditions, such as Carlos Castenada and Lynn Andrews, to task for their distortion of Native traditions.

The late twentieth-century discourse of spirituality reflected the struggle of people seeking authenticity and wanting to affirm a meaning to life, but not willing to concede control over meaning to religious institutions. The disavowal of doctrine may, indeed, be a hallmark of their spirituality. Among emerging forms of spirituality were New Age, Wiccan, feminist, twelve step, and earth spiritualities. Many, too, saw spirituality expressed through sport, music, art, and other aspects of cultural life. Thus, jazz, with its improvisational direction, was seen as a manifestation of the spirit of the twentieth century. Not everyone who sought spirituality joined a group, while others went from group to group or belonged to several simultaneously. Seekers of spirituality, usually committed to authentic living, may exhibit great courage in pursuing a life that is faithful to family, friends, and environment.

At least since Friedrich Nietzsche (1844–1900), modern Western culture has spoken of the death of God or the absence of God. As the theologian Wolfhart Pannenberg noted in his Taylor lectures at Yale Divinity School, "Talk about the death or the absence of God points to the fact that the interpretation of the world, as well as the behavior of human beings in the everyday life of modern culture, gets along without reference to God" (1983, p. 71). Similarly, it seems that many human beings can get along without reference to religion, the system that in Western cultures is built around commitment to God. Roots of secular spirituality in Western cultures can be found both in ancient Greek philosophy and in Enlightenment thinkers who were concerned with linking the self to the larger whole without recourse to religion. While the classic usage of the term *spirituality* remains, the term has broadened so that in popular usage spirituality has become something that one might embrace not as a discipline of religion or as a characteristic style of religion, but instead of religion. Spirituality has come to denote a realm of concern with nonmaterial life that may include both religious and secular attitudes. Given the increasing scholarly attention in conferences and publications to the role of spirituality in contemporary culture, it is clear that the academy has recognized spirituality as a subject of study both within and independent of the study of religion.

See Also New Age Movement; Religious Experience.

Bibliography

Series

Cousins, Ewert, ed. World Spirituality: An Encyclopedic History of the Religious Quest series. Crossroad Publishing. New York, 1985–. As of 2003, there were twenty-five volumes.

Payne, Richard J., ed. The Classics of Western Spirituality series. Paulist Press. New York, 1978–. As of December 2003, there were 107 volumes in this series, most concerned with aspects of, and figures in, the Jewish, Christian, and Islamic traditions.

Tucker, Mary Evelyn, and John Grim, eds. Harvard University Center for the Study of World Religions, Religions of the World and Ecology series. Harvard University Press. Cambridge, Mass., 1997. These volumes highlight the nature spirituality that is part of all religious traditions and the challenges to traditional spiritualities occasioned by awareness of the environmental crisis.

Books

Albanese, Catherine, ed. *American Spiritualities: A Reader.* Bloomington, Ind., 2001.

Bacik, James J. *Spirituality in Action.* Kansas City, Mo., 1997.

Conlon, James. *The Sacred Impulse: A Planetary Spirituality of Heart and Fire.* New York, 2000.

Dean, William. *The American Spiritual Culture: And the Invention of Jazz, Football, and the Movies.* New York, 2002.

Fox, Matthew. *A Spirituality Named Compassion and the Healing of the Global Village, Humpty Dumpty, and Us.* Minneapolis, 1979; reprint, San Francisco, 1990.

Fox, Matthew. *Creation Spirituality: Liberating Gifts for the Peoples of the Earth.* San Francisco, 1991.

Gottlieb, Roger S. *A Spirituality of Resistance: Finding a Peaceful Heart and Protecting the Earth.* Lanham, Md., 2003.

Jocks, Christopher Ronwanièn:te. "Spirituality for Sale: Sacred Knowledge in the Consumer Age." In *Native American Spirituality: A Critical Reader*, edited by Lee Irwin, pp. 61–77. Lincoln, Neb., 1997.

Kinsley, David. *Ecology and Religion: Ecological Spirituality in Cross-Cultural Perspective.* Princeton, N.J., 1995.

Moore, Thomas. *The Care of the Soul: A Guide for Cultivating Depth and Sacredness in Everyday Life.* New York, 1992.

Pannenberg, Wolfhart. *Christian Spirituality.* Philadelphia, 1983.

Plaskow, Judith, and Carol P. Christ, eds. *Weaving the Visions: New Patterns in Feminist Spirituality.* San Francisco, 1989.

Wuthnow, Robert. *After Heaven: Spirituality in America since the 1950s.* Berkeley, 1998.

Mary N. MacDonald (2005)

SPITTLE AND SPITTING. In the past, spittle was generally believed to have magical properties. Early humans, seeing themselves at the center of the universe, perceived connections between their own bodies and cosmic bodies, gods, and demons. They related parts of their bodies to colors, plants, elements, and directions. Spittle, blood, sperm, sweat, nails, and hair became magical substances not only as a result of this unity but also because, after leaving the body, they would retain some essence of that person. Spittle could therefore be positive or negative, depending on the intent of the spitter. Spitting and blood rites have many parallels, since both involve holy fluids that signify psychic energy and are necessary for sustaining physical life. Connections are still made between body fluids and feelings: anger makes one's blood "boil"; people spit from contempt or "spit out" words in hatred; and our mouths water at the thought of some delight or become dry from fear.

In early myths, life created by spitting is equivalent to the breath of the creator or the divine word. In one version of an Egyptian creation myth, the primeval god Atum spits out his children Shu and Tefnut. Shu was the god of air (e.g., breath), Tefnut was the goddess of moisture (e.g., spittle), and the mouth was their place of birth.

In Norse mythology a being called Kvasir was formed from the spittle of the gods. To commemorate a peace treaty among them, all the gods spat into a jar, and from this mixture Kvasir was created. He was so wise that there was no question he could not answer. Later he was slain by two dwarfs who mixed his blood with honey and concocted the mead of inspiration. By cunning, the high god Odin swallowed every drop of the mead, changed himself into an eagle, and returned to the waiting gods, who were holding out vessels for Odin once again to spit out the mead. A drink of this mead bestowed the gift of poetry on men. On his flight back, however, Odin had lost some of the mead when pursued by a giant who had also assumed the form of an eagle. This part of the mead became known as the fool-poet's portion.

In this myth, the holy spittle and blood have become identical, one being transformed into the other. Mead, blood, and spittle are three familiar sources of inspiration, here combined in one myth. The Norse gods' making a covenant by spitting is related to the custom of becoming blood brothers. Similarly, to spit into each other's mouth is a way to pledge friendship in East Africa.

To transmit something of themselves, holy persons in their blessings will use some form of physical contact. Muḥammad spat into the mouth of his grandson Ḥasan at his birth. Similarly, at ordination the priest or exorcist in ancient Babylon acquired his powers by having his mouth spat into, presumably receiving the spittle of the god. Among the Luba of present-day Zaire, a candidate being initiated into the order of sorcerers drinks a brew containing spittle from each of the elders; he becomes, thereby, not only blessed with their power but also placed forever under their control.

The role of saliva as a part of healing is well known all over the world. Sometimes the emphasis is on the curative effect of the spittle itself, which is known from the fact that wounds in the mouth heal faster. The observation of wild animals licking their wounds added to this belief. Spittle of people fasting is widely reported to be particularly effective, and it has even been thought strong enough to kill snakes.

Particular significance has been attributed to the spittle of people with unique powers. In his healing, Muḥammad mixed clay with spittle. Similarly, Christ made mud of spittle and clay and anointed the eyes of a blind man, thus restoring his sight. When he spat and touched the tongue of a mute (presumably with saliva) the man could speak. Conferring power of speech on an object spat upon is found in many folk tales.

Sickness is often considered a form of possession by demons who can be exorcised by spitting. In the Babar archipelago of Indonesia, all the sick people expectorate into a bowl that is then placed in a boat to be carried out to sea. In one Buddhist tale, even sins and misfortunes vanish, if one spits upon a holy ascetic.

Spittle is also a protective agent. In southern Europe, praise is sometimes accompanied by spitting to avert the evil eye. Fear of the gods' envy makes some people spit three times, since three is a lucky number. Seeing a black cat or magpies (animals associated with witches), hearing names of dead people (for fear they might return), or smelling a bad odor (to avoid contamination) are all occasions when spitting becomes a safeguard. Before discarding hair or nails, one should spit so as to prevent their being used by witches in black magic. Because of the same belief that something of the person continues to exist in the saliva, great care was taken not to be seen spitting. Behind the custom of spitting on money found in the street lies the fear that, as a fairy gift, it might disappear.

Good luck can also be invoked by spitting. And the familiar custom of spitting on one's hands before starting a strenuous task, thus adding power, also reveals some lingering faith in the magic of spittle.

BIBLIOGRAPHY

A. H. Godbey presents a well-documented study of various customs involving spitting in his article "Ceremonial Spitting," *The Monist* 24 (January 1914): 67–91. Additional material can be found in three encyclopedic works: James G. Frazer's *The Golden Bough,* 3d ed., 13 vols. (New York, 1955), relates principles of magic and religion to local customs and rituals; *The Mythology of All Races,* 13 vols., edited by Louis Herbert Gray and George Foot Moore (Boston, 1916–1932), gives numerous examples of the spitting motif in myths throughout the world; and the *Encyclopaedia of Religion and Ethics,* edited by James Hastings, vol. 11 (Edinburgh, 1920), offers an extensive article on saliva, concentrating on superstitious beliefs.

ANNMARI RONNBERG (1987)

SPORT SEE GAMES; LĪLĀ; PLAY

SPORTS AND RELIGION.

Throughout human history, sports and religion have been closely linked. Like religion, sports convey important lessons about values and culturally appropriate behavior. The lessons they teach are similar, and both religion and sports use symbols as their primary means of communication. In most of the contemporary world, however, religion and sports occupy separate but complementary conceptual realms. Religion focuses on the idea that, as one anthropologist put it, "there is something more to the world than meets the eye" (Bowen, p. 4). In religion, that "something" is the domain of the divine or of spirit beings; in sport, that "something" is the triumph of the human spirit.

Scholars from a variety of disciplines typically describe religion as operating in the realm of the sacred and as addressing the relationship of human beings to the supernatural or the transcendent. In modern terms, sport is seen as a secular pursuit, concerned with the relationship of human beings to each other. In fact, sport and religion are closely related on a number of levels:

1. Historically, many sports developed as part of religious festivals;

2. Sport is often used as a metaphor for religious striving;
3. Sporting events evoke passionate commitment similar to that of religious festivals;
4. Religion and sport are symbolic systems that emphasize similar values and goals, including transcendence of limited personal desires in favor of nonmaterial achievements or experiences and an emphasis on cooperation and personal sacrifice for the good of the group;
5. Both religion and sport convey their message by means of powerful symbols.

NATIVE AMERICANS AND ANCIENT GREEKS. The Central American ball game, played by both the Aztec and Maya before the arrival of Spanish conquistadores in the sixteenth century, was associated with the ritual of human sacrifice. Ball courts were commonly located in the temple complex near the racks where skulls of human sacrificial victims were displayed. Players were sacrificed as food for the gods. The divine origins of the ball game are recounted in the Mayan creation myth *Popol Vuh*, which describes the defeat in a ball game of the underworld gods of sickness and death by the hero twins Hunter (Hun Hunahpu) and Jaguar Deer (Xbalanke). In *The Blood of Kings* (1986), Linda Schele and Mary Ellen Miller suggest that, among the Maya, the ritual ball game provided a conquering ruler with a means of validating his reign and a defeated rival with an opportunity to achieve an honorable death.

The four great games of ancient Greece—the Olympian, the Pythian, the Isthmian, and the Nemean —were associated with worship of the gods. The Olympian games were held in honor of Zeus, ruler of the sky, whose worship was centered on Mount Olympus, also the site of his marriage to Hera. The Pythian games were held at Delphi, the site of Apollo's oracle, and were said to have been established by the god as compensation for his killing of the great serpent Python. The Pythian games eventually came to include both physical and intellectual competitions, including musical, literary, and dramatic events. The stadium at Delphi was also the site of religious rituals.

The Isthmian games, held on the Isthmus of Corinth every second year, included poetic and musical competitions as well as athletic events. According to one legend, the Isthmian games were initiated by the Greek hero Theseus, who slew the Minotaur. Theseus was fabled to be the son of Poseidon, and the Isthmian games were dedicated to this god. The legendary origins of the Nemean games are traced to an event in which an army led by Polynices, a son of Oedipus, slew a serpent that had killed the infant Opheltes (Snake Man). The Nemean games, held in honor of Zeus, also included poetry and music competitions in addition to athletic contests.

Greek athletes were sometimes accorded the status of gods. Theogenes excelled both in boxing and the pankration, a virtually no-holds-barred sport that combined elements of boxing and wrestling. He was the son of a priest at a temple dedicated to Herakles in Thasos, on an island in the Aegean Sea. Theogenes, whose name means "god-born," claimed that he was the son of Herakles rather than the priest. Statues of Theogenes were erected at Olympia, Delphi, and Thasos. By all accounts, Theogenes was an arrogant and unpleasant man who earned the wrath of a number of enemies. During his lifetime his enemies were powerless against him, but after his death, one of them sneaked out at night and flogged his statue at Thasos. The statue fell on the man and killed him. Since the statue was guilty of the man's death, it was taken out to sea and thrown overboard. Soon afterwards, Thasos was plagued by crop failures resulting in famine. A consultation with the oracle at Delphi resulted in the order that Thasians should recall their political exiles. All living political exiles were duly recalled, but the famine continued. Another consultation with the oracle at Delphi produced the reminder that Theogenes remained at large. The statue of the athlete was restored to its base, and the famine ended.

Foot races were part of religious rituals among a number of Native American groups, and there were secret running societies throughout the Americas. Prior to the introduction of the horse by the Spanish, swift runners were important for carrying messages between groups and during times of battle. Within twenty-four hours of the landing of Hernán Cortés (1485–1547) on the east coast of what is now Mexico in May 1519, local runners had described his ship, men, horses, and guns to Moctezuma (1466–1520) at Tenochtitlán, 260 miles away. Ceremonial runners among the Mesquakie in Iowa took a vow of celibacy, adhered to strict dietary rules, and dedicated their lives to running. In many cases, runners represented their clans in races and in religious rituals. Zuni runners painted the symbol of their matrilineal clan on their chests and the symbol of their father's clan on their back. The ball was believed to hold magical power that pulled the runner along with it.

The Rarámuri, or Tarahumara (which may be translated as "foot runners"), of the Sierra Madre in Mexico incorporate wrestling matches in their Easter rituals, which are aimed at protecting God and his wife Mary from his evil rival the Devil. The Rarámuri were introduced to Roman Catholicism in the seventeenth century, and their Easter rituals exhibit a syncretism of Christianity and their own religious symbols. Since Rarámuri social life centers on the family, they cannot conceive of God as being a bachelor, because that would consign him to a lower social status. In "God's Saviours in the Sierra Madre" (1983), the anthropologist William L. Merrill states that the idea that Christ died on the cross to redeem the sins of the world makes little sense to the Rarámuri, so they have adapted his strange (to them) story to their own vision of the relationship between God and the Devil, which is that the Devil and his family threaten the well-being of God and his family. Ultimately, though they fight on behalf of God, Merrill suggests, the Rarámuri believe they must appease both God and the Devil.

CHRISTIAN AND PERSIAN THOUGHT. Even where sport is not a part of religious ritual, it is metaphorically linked to religion. The apostle Paul compared religious discipline to sport on several occasions. In his first epistle to the Corinthians he writes, "Do you not know that in a race all the runners compete, but only one receives the prize? So run that you may obtain it" (*I Cor.* 9:24). Later he includes the metaphor of boxing: "I do not run aimlessly," he writes, "I do not box as one beating the air; but I pummel my body and subdue it, lest after preaching to others I myself should be disqualified" (*I Cor.* 9:26–27). In summing up his evangelical career, Paul writes, "I have fought the good fight, I have finished the race, I have kept the faith" (*II Tm.* 4:7).

Sport involves an all-out effort toward achieving an elusive goal. Thus, it is an appropriate metaphor for the spiritual quest or for the often elusive goals of life itself. The Persian poet Nizami (c. 1141–1203 or 1217) compared life to a polo game: "The Horizon is the boundary of your polo ground, the earth is the ball in the curve of your polo stick. Until the dust of non-existence rises from annihilation, gallop and urge on your steed because the ground is yours."

HINDU DOCUMENTS. The *Ṛgveda*, perhaps the oldest of Hindu documents, draws on the chariot race as a metaphor for the pursuit of immortality. Hymn 3.31 of the *Ṛgveda* says: "Soon, Indra, make us winners of cows." Winners of chariot races won prizes of cows, whose milk is a symbol of immortality. This verse, which asks "Make us victors among men; make us more like you, O powerful one; and bring us immortality," can be interpreted, and no doubt was intended, to evoke multiple levels of meaning. In the *Ṛgveda*, milk is associated with seed, semen, and rain, all life-giving forms.

The *Upaniṣads* are Hindu sacred documents, the oldest of which may date from as early as the sixth century BCE. The *Mundaka Upaniṣad* urges readers to aim for unity with Brāhmaṇ, the creative energy underlying the universe:

> Affix to the Upanishad, the bow, incomparable, the sharp arrow of devotional worship; then, with mind absorbed and heart melted in love, draw the arrow and hit the mark—the imperishable Brāhmaṇ. OM is the bow, the arrow is the individual being, and Brāhmaṇ is the target. With a tranquil heart, take aim. Lose thyself in him, even as the arrow is lost in the target.

Though this translation by Swami Prabhavananda and Frederick Manchester refers to Brāhmaṇ as "him," Brāhmaṇ has no gender, since it is the source of all being, male and female.

JAPAN, THE UNITED STATES, AND EUROPE. In the preceding examples, sport is a metaphor for religious striving. However, Zen archery, or *kyudo,* is a ritual, a religious act. In the Japanese tradition of Zen Buddhism, the object of *kyudo* is to achieve a balance among mind, body, and bow, which gives rise to a unity that links the spirit to the target. Achieving this balance is more important than hitting the target, though hitting the target is expected to follow naturally from achieving a balance among mind, body, and bow. The ritual includes practicing correct breathing techniques to control the mental and physical force—or *ki*— believed to be centered below the navel. Proper technique ultimately leads to perfect serenity. Zen archery proceeds through eight smoothly executed stages which seem to flow as a single unit. At the sixth stage, the body of the archer is on a line with the target. The name of this stage is *kai,* or "meeting." Release of the arrow at the seventh stage is seen as an act of volition by the arrow rather than the archer:

> Like a heavy drop of water. . . that decides to be free,
> the arrow liberates itself.

The term for the seventh stage is *hanare,* or "release." At this point, it is believed that there is an explosion of energy flowing through the body of the archer.

The martial art of kung fu was believed to have been developed by the Bodhidharma (d. c. 530), the legendary founder of Zen (Chan) Buddhism at the Shaolin Monastery in China. It is said that the Bodhidharma meditated for long hours in a cave and developed *kung fu* as a means of keeping his body flexible after long, motionless meditation.

In his book *Mountaineering Essays* (1980), John Muir (1838–1914) describes his explorations with religious fervor, often using religious terminology. He writes of Cathedral Rock in California's Sierra Nevada Mountains:

> No feature, however, of all the noble landscape as seen from her seems more wonderful than the Cathedral itself, a temple displaying Nature's best masonry and sermons in stones. How often I have gazed at it from the tops of hills and ridges, and through openings in the forests on my many short excursions, devoutly wondering, admiring, longing! This I may say is the first time I have been at church in California, led here at last, every door graciously opened for the poor lonely worshiper. In our best times everything turns into a religion, all the world seems a church and the mountains altars. And lo, here at last in front of the Cathedral is blessed cassiope, ringing her thousands of sweet-toned bells, the sweetest church music I ever enjoyed. (p. 19)

This passage is comparable in religious fervor to writings of such mystics as Teresa of Ávila (1515–1582), who describes her feelings after a vision in which she was cautioned against her longing to escape city life for meditation in the desert:

> Here suddenly came upon me a recollection with an interior light so great it seemed I was in another world. And my spirit found within itself a very delightful forest and garden, so delightful it made me recall what is said in the Song of Songs: *Veniat dilectus meus in hortum suum.* (From Song of Solomon 5:1: I am come into my garden, my sister, my spouse. . . .)

MODERN SPORTS. In his book *From Ritual to Record: The Nature of Modern Sports* (1978), Allen Guttmann describes the secularization of sport as though it were a fall from grace. When it had its original close link to religion, Guttmann suggests, sport was a meaningful enterprise that upheld the noblest ideals of a group and was integral to other activities of the group. Modern sports, Guttmann writes, have become centered on the quest for quantification in the form of setting distance or other records and evaluating performance in terms of statistical data:

> The bond between the secular and the sacred has been broken, the attachment to the realm of the transcendent has been severed. Modern sports are activities partly pursued for their own sake, partly for other ends which are equally secular. We do not run in order that the earth be more fertile. We till the earth, or work in our factories and offices, so that we can have time to play. (p. 26)

In his *Homo Ludens: A Study of the Play Element in Culture* (1950), the Dutch historian Johan Huizinga describes humans as "Homo ludens," the player, and asserted that all of culture has its origins in the spontaneous activities of play. Like Guttman, Huizinga considers the rules and regulations characteristic of sports to be antithetical to the spirit of play, and he blames what he regards as the deplorable conditions of modern sports on the English. He attributes the rise of ball games to English competitions between villages and schools; to "the specifically Anglo-Saxon bent of mind" (p. 197); to the emphasis on "association and solidarity" occasioned by English social life; to the need for physical exercise in the absence of obligatory military training; and to the English terrain, which provided ideal playing fields. Huizinga sums up the English sensibility for sport: "Everybody knows the delightful prints from the first half of the 19th century, showing the cricketers in tophats. This speaks for itself" (p. 197). He adds:

> The great competitions in archaic cultures had always formed part of the sacred festivals and were indispensable as health and happiness-bringing activities. This ritual tie has now been completely severed; sport has become profane, "unholy" in every way and has no organic connection whatever with the structure of society, least of all when prescribed by the government. The ability of modern social techniques to stage mass demonstrations with the maximum of outward show in the field of athletics does not alter the fact that neither the Olympiads nor the organized sports of American Universities nor the loudly trumpeted international contests have, in the smallest degree, raised sport to the level of a culture-creating activity. However important it may be for the players or spectators, it remains sterile. The old play-factor has undergone almost complete atrophy. (p. 198)

Huizinga acknowledges that his view of modern sport may not be a popular one: "This view will probably run counter to the popular feeling of today, according to which sport is the apotheosis of the play-element in our civilization. Nevertheless popular feeling is wrong" (p. 198).

Although Guttmann agrees with Huizinga in general, he acknowledges that even modern sport sometimes has its moments of transcendence: "It is actually one of the happier ironies of modern sports that we can lose ourselves in play and forget the creative and sustaining (and restricting) social organization and cultural assumptions that have been a central concern of this book" (p. 160).

Those who bemoan the secularization of sport do not express similar criticisms of other aspects of human social life. Modern sports, which are largely the product of western Europe, have undergone secularization at the same time as other institutions. European governments became secularized as monarchs broke away from the authority of the Roman Catholic Church. The United States was founded on the ideal of separation of church and state. This was an attempt to avoid the religious rivalries and persecution that drove a number of groups to leave their European homes and settle in the land that became the United States. The French achieved their ideal of separation of church and state only in the early twentieth century, a hard-won accomplishment that in 2004 led the French government to ban religious apparel in the public schools. Modern science emerged as such thinkers as Nicolaus Copernicus (1473–1543) and Galileo Galilei (1564–1642) supplanted religious dogma with empirically derived data. At the time of the Enlightenment in the late eighteenth and early nineteenth centuries, writers such as Voltaire (1694–1778) rejected the domination of ecclesiastical authority. In the process, theater, the visual arts, literature, and music became secularized.

Scholars generally regard the secularization of government, education, science, and the arts as positive, since it liberates these institutions from the constraints of dogma and subjugation to religious hierarchies. Why then, do Guttmann and some other scholars bemoan the secularization of sport? In their view, sport alone seems to call for an alliance with an institutionalized moral and religious order. In *Sport as Symbol: Images of the Athlete in Art, Literature and Song,* Mari Womack argues that the secularization of sport is commonly viewed as degradation rather than liberation precisely because sport has retained its close symbolic ties to religion, whereas the other institutional forms have drifted further away.

Athletes may no longer be viewed as gods, but they retain their role as heroes. Athletes are held to higher standards than musicians, actors, artists, or writers. Only government officials, educators, and religious leaders excite similar degrees of outrage in the wake of scandal. American sportswriters often lament the behavior of athletes who violate cultural norms, but in fact the failures of heroes in all domains often educate us as much as their successes. Could any sermon teach the perils of arrogance and hubris better than the fictional baseball hero in Ernest Lawrence Thayer's 1888 poem, "Casey at the Bat"? In a similar situation, the real-life baseball hero Babe Ruth (1895–1948) succeeded where Casey failed. The Sultan of Swat called his shot during the fifth inning of the third game of the 1932 World Series, in what has been called "the most magnificent gesture ever made on a baseball diamond." (Durant and Bettman, p. 239). It was a grudge match between the New York Yankees and the Chicago Cubs at the Cubs' own Wrigley Field:

> The score was tied at four runs each when Babe Ruth came up to bat for the Yankees. He was greeted by a barrage of abuse from the Chicago bench. He took a strike and then defiantly pointed to the centerfield

> bleachers. He took another strike and again indicated his target as Cubs players jeered from the bench. On the next pitch, he hammered the ball to the deepest part of the centerfield bleachers, the exact spot he had indicated. Unlike Casey, the mighty Babe Ruth did not strike out. (Womack, 2003, p. 150)

In this case, Babe Ruth taught a different lesson: he defied the unsportsmanlike behavior of the opposing team and demonstrated a form of valor that is undeterred by opposition. Womack writes, "The same existential conflict that lies at the heart of religion also gave rise to the sporting contest" (2003, p. 220). "Sports symbolism," she states, "usually expresses themes of epic proportions: responsibility to oneself and others, the moral choice of Right and Wrong, the dilemmas of power, and the agony of loss and betrayal. Often, it is clear that the 'game' is life itself, played out in a hazardous universe" (2003, p. 14).

In a pluralistic society, sport makes mythological themes accessible to people from many different backgrounds. It is a fact of modern life that no one religion has a secure hold on the imagination of its adherents. No matter how strongly one believes, one knows that others do not believe. This challenges the absoluteness of one's faith. The various competing religions do not provide an overarching symbolic system that explains ultimate reality, including right and wrong, for all members of the group. Precisely because it is secularized, sport provides a symbolic system that unifies rather than divides. It addresses overarching symbolic themes, not specific theological issues. It deals not with the nature of God, but with the nature of human beings.

SEE ALSO Ballgames.

BIBLIOGRAPHY

Bowen, John R. *Religions in Practice: An Approach to the Anthropology of Religion.* 2d ed. Boston, 2002. Rather than attempting to develop a unitary definition of religion, Bowen surveys consistencies and variations in the practice of religion in a variety of contexts.

Durant, John, and Otto Bettman. *Pictorial History of American Sports.* Cranbury, N.J., 1952. The authors do not deal specifically with the relationship between sport and religion, but their richly illustrated book eloquently demonstrates the historical role of sport in American life.

Guttmann, Allen. *From Ritual to Record: The Nature of Modern Sports.* New York, 1978. Guttmann notes that sport in what he calls primitive societies was integral to other activities, whereas modern sport, with its rules and regulations, is antithetical to spontaneous play.

Harris, H. A. *Greek Athletes and Athletics.* Bloomington, Ind., 1964. Harris provides a comprehensive overview of the four Greek athletic games—the Olympic, the Pythian, the Isthmian, and the Nemean—with particular emphasis on the events held at each. He also links the athletic contests to the esteem in which athletes were held, as well as the celebration of athletic victors in the poetry of Pindar.

Hoffman, Shirl J., ed. *Sport and Religion.* Champaign, Ill., 1992. Hoffman has compiled essays dealing with various aspects of the relationship of religion to sports, including ethics, sport as ritual, the use of rituals by professional athletes, and such experiential aspects of sport as runner's high. Christianity is the only religion considered in any depth.

Huizinga, Johan. *Homo Ludens: A Study of the Play Element in Culture.* Boston, 1950. Huizinga asserts that all cultural forms arise from play, and from this he deduces that play is older than culture. He then analyzes play as a "civilizing function" with respect to law, war, poetry, philosophy, and art while taking a less positive view of sport, which he considers antithetical to the spontaneity of play.

Merrill, William L. "God's Saviours in the Sierra Madre." *Natural History* 93, no. 3 (1983). The Rarámuri (Tarahumara) of Mexico's Sierra Madre have adapted the essential message of Christianity to their own experience of the relationship between good and evil. Merrill notes that the Rarámuri see themselves as the protectors of God and his family against the designs of the Devil and his family. However, the Rarámuri consider it necessary to placate both God and the Devil.

Morford, Mark P. O., and Robert J. Lenardon. *Classical Mythology.* 4th ed. New York, 1991. The authors include a brief summary of the importance of the Olympic and Pythian games for Greek symbolism in their analysis of the complexities of relationships among the gods of Greece.

Muir, John. *Mountaineering Essays.* Salt Lake City, Utah, 1980. Muir describes in religious terms his awe at exploring the natural wonders of the West.

Scarborough, Vernon L., and David R. Wilcox, eds. *The Mesoamerican Ballgame.* Tucson, Ariz., 1991. Scarborough and Wilcox have compiled a comprehensive analysis of the ritual, representation, and social context of the Central American ball game based on the archaeological evidence, ranging from the American Southwest to Central America.

Schele, Linda, and Mary Ellen Miller. *The Blood of Kings: Dynasty and Ritual in Maya Art.* Forth Worth, Tex., and New York, 1986. Schele and Miller conclude that ball games played in the Maya sphere dramatize the military and religious might of Mayan rulers, adding that the outcome of the ball game was prearranged to result in the victory of the ruler and the sacrifice of his opponent. Thus, the symbolic victory of the ruler in the ball game dramatized his military victory over his rival on the battlefield.

Womack, Mari. "Risk and Ritual in Professional Sports." Paper presented at the meeting of American Anthropological Association Meeting, Los Angeles, California, 1981. This paper examines the conditions of risk in professional sports competition that give rise to uncertainty and anxiety. It concludes that rites of preparation aid performance in competition by giving the athlete a sense of control over his surroundings, which reduces anxiety and allows the athlete to focus on the game.

Womack, Mari. "Religion and Sport: Sacred and Secular Rituals of Conflict." UCLA Center for the Study of Religion, 1991. This paper defines aspects of contesting in sport that involve three types of opponents: the opponent in nature, the human opponent, and the enemy within. Ultimately, sport is closely allied to religion because the essence of all sport is the contest against the treacherous aspects of our selves.

Womack, Mari. *Sport as Symbol: Images of the Athlete in Art, Literature, and Song.* Jefferson, N.C., 2003. Illustrated throughout with black and white reproductions of art from a range of traditions, this book considers imagery relating to the hunt, bullfight, martial arts, ball games, racing, and contests of grace and beauty. It discusses the role of the sports hero in culture and explains the relationship of the athlete to society in general.

MARI WOMACK (2005)

SPURGEON, CHARLES HADDON (1834–1892), was an English Baptist popularly known as "the prince of preachers." The son and grandson of Congregationalist pastors, Spurgeon was converted in 1850 at a Primitive Methodist chapel and joined a Baptist church in 1851. At age sixteen, circumstances compelled him to preach unprepared in a cottage near Cambridge, England. Word of his oratorical skill and evangelical fervor spread. He was called to pastorates at Waterbeach (1852) and at New Park Street Chapel in London (1854). His preaching attracted such large crowds that it was necessary to rent public accommodations seating up to ten thousand people. In 1861 the Metropolitan Tabernacle was completed in London, and there Spurgeon ministered until his death. By age twenty-two he had become the most popular preacher of his day. He established several institutions, including orphanages and a pastors' college, the latter being the matrix for the founding of numerous churches and Sunday schools.

Although throughout his career Spurgeon preached to large audiences, his greatest immediate influence was through his weekly published sermons, numbering 3,561, which are estimated to have had more than a million regular readers. These sermons eventually amounted to sixty-three volumes, entitled *New Park Street Pulpit* (1855–1860) and *Metropolitan Tabernacle Pulpit* (1861–1917). By 1899 more than a hundred million copies of his sermons had been printed in twenty-three languages. Among his many works was the seven-volume *The Treasury of David,* a commentary on *Psalms.* He also edited a monthly magazine, *The Sword and the Trowel,* for twenty-seven years.

Spurgeon's preaching was massive in scope and narrow in doctrine. Staunchly Calvinistic, he was called by some "the last of the Puritans." From his earliest ministry until his death, he consistently maintained the gospel of grace without deference to increasingly influential high-church and liberal teachings. In 1864 his sermon against "baptismal regeneration" excited a hearty controversy that resulted in his withdrawing from the Evangelical Alliance. During the last decade of his life, Spurgeon fought against what he called the "downgrade movement," that is, the rise of higher criticism, liberalism, and rationalism within Baptist circles in England. So firmly were such views entrenched there that he withdrew from the Baptist Union in 1887, remaining independent but a Baptist until his death. Although he never sought controversy, he never shied from it. In his own words, "Controversy for the truth against the errors of the age is . . . the peculiar duty of the preacher."

Within the confines of a thoroughly evangelistic Calvinism, Spurgeon's works include such an enormous variety of topics congenial to the mainstream of orthodoxy that his writings, especially his sermons, have been valued by Christians of diverse creeds. While his influence, particularly in evangelical circles, continued through the first half of the twentieth century, in the 1960s interest in Spurgeon began to grow. All sixty-three volumes of his sermons have been reprinted, and more than 150 of his other writings are in print.

BIBLIOGRAPHY

Spurgeon's *Autobiography, Compiled from His Diary, Letters, and Records by His Wife, and His Private Secretary,* 4 vols. (London, 1897–1900), has long been out of print. An abridged and supplemented edition has appeared in two volumes: vol. 1, *The Early Years, 1834–1859* (London, 1962), and vol. 2, *The Full Harvest, 1860–1892* (Edinburgh, 1973). The standard biography is G. H. Pike's *The Life and Work of Charles Haddon Spurgeon,* 6 vols. (London, 1894). For an appreciation of Spurgeon by a noted German theologian, see Helmut Thielicke's *Encounter with Spurgeon* (Philadelphia, 1963).

DARREL W. AMUNDSEN (1987)

SRI AUROBINDO SEE AUROBINDO GHOSE

ŚRĪ VAIṢṆAVAS. The Śrī Vaiṣṇava Sampradāya, one of six major Hindu denominations devoted to Viṣṇu, is the community of those who worship Viṣṇu (also called Nārāyaṇa) in conjunction with his consort Śrī (Lakṣmī), the goddess of auspiciousness and prosperity, along with Bhūdevī, the goddess of the earth, and Nīlā, more generally known by her Tamil name of Nappinai, the human wife of the young Kṛṣṇa. The community is strongest in the South Indian state of Tamil Nadu, but it also has many adherents in the three other South Indian states and some in other parts of India. *Brahmans* are strongly represented and have most positions of leadership.

Śrī Vaiṣṇavas are adherents of the philosophy of Rāmānuja and describe their theological position as Ubhaya Vedānta, "dual theology" or "theology of the two scriptures," for, in addition to regarding as authoritative the Vedas (including the Upaniṣads) and other scriptures written in Sanskrit, the Śrī Vaiṣṇavas consider sacred the Tamil hymns of the poet-saints called the Āḻvārs (those "immersed" in God) and treat the long poem called the *Tiruvāymoḻi* as equal in value to the Upaniṣads. Both divisions of the present community trace their spiritual lineage back to still earlier *ācāryas* (teachers), and then through Nammāḻvār, the author of the *Tiruvāymoḻi,* to the Goddess, Śrī, and Viṣṇu-Nārāyaṇa himself.

The Sanskrit canon of the community includes, in addition to the Vedas, the two great epics, the treatises on social morality and ritual, and the summary of the Upaniṣadic teaching called the *Vedānta Sūtra.* These scriptures are themselves interpreted by a host of commentaries and didactic treatises in Sanskrit, and there is a corresponding, though much smaller, group of commentaries and treatises in Tamil. In both languages there are also a number of hagiographies of the Āḻvārs and *ācāryas*; greatest attention is given to Rāmānuja (traditional dates 1017–1137), who wrote only in Sanskrit but who is represented in the biographies as commenting on the *Tiruvāymoḻi* in Tamil and assigning his cousin and disciple Piḷḷān the task of producing a written commentary on this long poem. It was Piḷḷān who first called the members of the community "Śrī Vaiṣṇavas" and demonstrated the confluence of the Sanskrit and Tamil "Vedāntas." Three later commentaries are also considered authoritative.

By the end of the twelfth century there was an increasing shift in emphasis on works of a different kind, treatises on the secret meanings (*rahasyas*) of the three central mantras (ritual formulas) that specified the spiritual path and more fully discussed the doctrine of divine grace. These treatises stressed the indispensable role of Śrī as mediatrix (*puruṣakāra*). Since she is always full of maternal love, her favor should be sought first; she can persuade the Lord, who as a father must balance justice and mercy, to the side of mercy. Similarly one first humbly petitions one's own *gurū,* who is already connected with the chain of grace, for his recommendation in approaching the Lord.

The various stories about the twelve Āḻvārs assign them very ancient dates. Nammāḻvār, for example, is said to have lived some five thousand years ago, at the very beginning of the present, evil age, the *kaliyuga.* Modern historical scholarship places them from the sixth to ninth centuries CE. In contrast, the *ācāryas* are assigned dates that are accurate within one or two generations. The first *ācārya,* Nāthamuni (late ninth or early tenth century), received from Nammāḻvār in a yogic trance the entire corpus of hymns; he then arranged them to accompany Sanskrit verses in the temple liturgies. Still more stories are told about Nāthamuni's brilliant grandson Yāmuna (916–1036), but the largest part of the hagiographies focuses on the life of Rāmānuja.

The gradual splitting of the community into the Vaṭakalai ("northern culture") and Teṅkalai ("southern culture") subsects is only in part related to the relative emphasis on the Sanskrit and Tamil scriptures; the two groups understand differently the relation of divine grace to human response. Both groups affirm the primacy of divine grace in rescuing souls from their bondage in the world and maintain that all seekers of salvation should solemnly surrender, first to the goddess Śrī and then to Lord Viṣṇu. The great Vaṭakalai teacher Vedānta Deśika believed that the act of surrender gives the Lord a pretext or occasion (*vyāja*) for saving the soul, so that grace is not arbitrary. His contemporary, the Teṅkalai teacher Piḷḷai Lokācārya, on the other hand, considered it presumptuous for human beings to think they could make any contribution whatsoever to their salvation. Even "surrender," he taught, is not to be regarded as such an act; it is merely the acknowledgement of what the Lord has already done. The nicknames "monkey-hold" and "cat-hold" applied to the two groups come from a Teṅkalai source. The Teṅkalai claim that the Vaṭakalai theology likens the soul's position to that of a baby monkey, which has to hang on to its mother as she swings from tree to tree, while the Teṅkalai's own view makes the soul resemble the kitten, whose mother picks it up by the scruff of the neck without any effort on the kitten's part.

For neither group does the doctrine of grace lead to an antinomian lifestyle. On the contrary, the lives of Śrī Vaiṣṇavas are full of ritual injunctions and social obligations, but neither their good deeds nor scholarly attainments—not even emotional participation in intense devotion to God—can bring about their salvation. Their ritual act of surrender is the outward sign of a lifelong surrender of their worldly ambitions—even quite proper ones—to God's disposal. Having solemnly petitioned God's mercy, and having confidently expressed total reliance on that mercy, the devotee ought not to ask for anything else. This is clearly a difficult ideal to follow, the more so since the majority of their fellow worshipers at Viṣṇu temples are not initiated "surrendered ones" (*prapannas*) but Hindus from all walks of life who confidently ask the Lord and his consorts for all manner of material blessings.

Much of the spiritual leadership in the community is provided by various *maṭhas*, which are not communities of ascetics but groups of householder disciples of a *gurū* who becomes a *saṃnyāsin* after being chosen to head the *maṭha.* These *gurūs* perform the formal initiation of *prapatti,* bestow spiritual blessings and deliver courses of lectures on periodic tours to visit their followers, and frequently give individuals practical advice in private audiences.

The key words in Śrī Vaiṣṇava worship are *darśana,* the reverent beholding of the image form of the Lord; *smaraṇa,* the remembrance of the Lord's gracious deeds, and *seva* or *kaiṅkarya,* service to the Lord and to the Lord's disciples. While in their own homes Śrī Vaiṣṇavas perform the lengthy daily worship privately, in the 108 major Śrī Vaiṣṇava temples in South India (including the all-Indian pilgrimage center of Tirupati and the central temple at Śrīraṅgam), and in many more minor ones, they are part of a mixed company. Their joining in the Tamil and Sanskrit chanting of the liturgy is for them a confident anticipation of their participation, after this present earthly life, in the eternal chorus of praise in the Lord's heavenly home.

SEE ALSO Āḻvārs; Kṛṣṇaism; Piḻḻai Lokācārya; Rāmānuja; Tamil Religions.

BIBLIOGRAPHY

Buitenen, J. A. B. van, trans. *Yāmuna's Āgama Prāmāṇyam, or, Treatise on the Validity of Pāñcarātra.* Madras, 1971.

Gnanambal, K. "Śrīvaishnavas and Their Religious Institutions." *Bulletin of the Anthropological Survey of India* 20 (July–December 1971): 97–187.

Narasimhachari, M. *Contribution of Yāmuna to Viśiṣṭādvaita.* Madras, 1971.

Neevel, Walter G., Jr. *Yāmuna's Vedānta and Pāñcarātra: Integrating the Classical and the Popular.* Missoula, Mont., 1977.

Rangachariyar, Kadambi. *The Śrī Vaishnava Brahmans.* Madras, 1931.

Śrīnivasachari, P. N. *The Philosophy of Viśiṣṭādvaita.* 2d ed. Adyar, 1946.

Venkatachari, K. K. A. *The Manipravāla Literature of the ŚrīVaiṣṇava Ācāryas, Twelfth to Fifteenth Century A. D.* Bombay, 1978.

New Sources

Clooney, Francis Xavier. *Seeing through Texts: Doing Theology among the Srivaisnavas of South India.* Albany, N.Y., 1996.

Mumme, Patricia Y. *The Srivaisnava Theological Dispute: Mahavammuni and Vedanta Devika.* Madras, 1988.

Narayana, Vasudha. *The Way and the Goal: Expressions of Devotion in the Early Sri Vaisnava Tradition.* Washington, D.C., 1987.

Oberhammer, Gerhard. *Der "Innere Lenker" (Antaryama): Geschichte eines Theologems.* Vienna, 1998.

Seshadri, Kandadai. *Srivaishnavism and Social Change.* Calcutta, 1998.

JOHN B. CARMAN (1987)
Revised Bibliography

SSU-MA CH'ENG-CHEN SEE SIMA CHENGZHEN

STANNER, W. E. H.

STANNER, W. E. H. William Edward Hanley Stanner (1905–1981) was born in Sydney, Australia, and spent much of his childhood playing on the shores of Sydney Harbor and the surrounding bushland. On leaving school Stanner worked as a bank clerk, a job he tired of quickly, before training as a journalist. In 1926 a life-changing encounter with A. R. Radcliffe-Brown, the newly appointed foundation chair of anthropology at Sydney University, saw Stanner return to school to matriculate, eventually enrolling in a degree program with a major in anthropology and economics.

After completing his degree with first class honors, Stanner was encouraged by Radcliffe-Brown to consider a career in anthropology. He undertook his first fieldwork in the Daly River region of north Australia in 1932, and he returned to this area from 1934 to 1935 to undertake more lengthy research for his Ph.D. He would return to the Daly River region throughout his life, in the 1950s undertaking the work that would most fully inform his writings on Murrinh-pata religion.

On completing his Ph.D. at the London School of Economics under the supervision of Bronislaw Malinowski and Raymond Firth, Stanner joined an anthropological survey team in East Africa. On the outbreak of war he returned to Australia. His most noted wartime contribution was as leader of the North Australia Observer Unit. He also worked on a series of postwar reconstruction programs in Europe and the Pacific. In 1949 Stanner was appointed reader in comparative social institutions in the Research School of Pacific Studies at the newly established Australian National University, Canberra, where he remained for the rest of his working life. In the 1960s and 1970s Stanner rose to public prominence as a government adviser, and his engagements in Aboriginal affairs became more consciously political.

Stanner's works on religion, the most important being a series of essays republished in 1963 as the monograph *On Aboriginal Religion,* simultaneously serve as a broad critique of structural-functionalist approaches to the study of society and culture. He was extremely critical of earlier anthropological accounts of Aboriginal religion influenced by the work of Émile Durkheim and Radcliffe-Brown that categorized religion as merely one of a series of elements in a bounded social system. These writers had overlooked the experiential and emotional sensibilities associated with religion. Stanner argued that religion was significant in its own right, not as a subset of society or anything else. Murrinh-pata religion contained objects and symbols "beyond egotism, beyond social gain." The great symbols he observed, were "valued for their own sakes." As he sought to elucidate Murrinh-pata religious systems as "expressions of human experience of life; as essays of passion, imagination, and striving," Stanner concurrently sketched the frame of a new theoretical approach to the study of society (Stanner, 1965, p. 222). He saw human affairs not in terms of persisting social structures and enduring relations between persons in role positions, but rather as "a structure of operations in transactions about things of value." His "operational anthropology" would study real relations—"giving, taking, sharing, loving, bewitching, fighting, initiating"—and "make human sense of their cultural varieties" (Stanner, 1963, p. ii).

While seeing the definition of religion as beyond the task of anthropology, Stanner argued that Aboriginal religion must be grasped as a rich and multilayered entity: it was at once an ontological system, a moral system, a "contemporary form of thought and feeling toward the whole of reality," and "content for a devotional life" (Stanner, 1963, p. vi). He rejected Durkheim's dichotomy of secular and sacred as a framework for comprehending Aboriginal religion, arguing that it necessarily was both. Where the functionalists had offered up a desiccated view of Aboriginal religious systems as lacking imaginative and intellectual substance, or as reducible to the study of totemism, magic, and ritual, for Stanner, Murrinh-pata religious belief and practice provided a window onto all manner of aspects of Murrinh-pata being. It was in Murrinh-pata rites that one witnessed "a genius for music, song, and dance applied with skill and passion" (Stanner, 1963, p. 18). Moreover, Murrinh-pata religion was not a "dead plane of uniform changelessness" but a dynamic system, its content being enacted and articulated variably by differently gifted performers, and transformed according into the changing needs and circumstances of each generation (Stanner, 1963, p. 84).

Stanner's work contributed much to contemporary understandings of "The Dreaming," the linkage of specific Aboriginal persons, places, fauna, and flora in the present in identifiable groupings extending back to a timeless conception. Within this ontological frame, Stanner argued, there was no tension between past, present, and future. He teased out aspects of this logic and its narrative content in Murrinh-pata myth to illustrate the basis of Aborigines' acceptance of reality as a necessary connection between life and suffering. In the Murrinh-pata theory of reality, life was conceived "as a joyous thing with maggots at the centre" (Stanner, 1963, p. 37).

Critics argue that Stanner failed to fully transcend the limitations of structural-functionalism and sufficiently integrate his theoretical ideas with his ethnography. He shied away from analyzing those aspects of his material—the conjunction of religion and politics—that would have furnished the development of a theory of action. Stanner himself regarded his work as unfinished. It was a contribution to a general reappraisal of Australian Aboriginal religion that would "require the efforts of many scholars." A humanist with untiring commitment to social justice, a campaigner for land rights, a sensitive intercultural interpreter with a great gift for writing, Stanner sought to conjure up the richness and philosophical depth of Aboriginal religious systems.

Bibliography

Keen, Ian. "Stanner on Aboriginal Religion." *Canberra Anthropology* 9, no. 2 (1986): 26–50.

Morphy, Howard. "The Resurrection of the Hydra: Twenty-five Years of Research of Aboriginal Religion." In *Social Anthropology and Australian Aboriginal Studies: A Contemporary Overview,* edited by Ronald M. Berndt and Robert Tonkinson, pp. 239–265. Canberra, 1988.

Stanner, W. E. H. "The Dreaming." In *Australian Signpost: An Anthology,* edited by T. Hungerford, pp. 51–65. London, 1956; reprinted in Stanner, 1979, pp. 23–40.

Stanner, W. E. H. "Continuity and Change among the Aborigines." *Australian Journal of Science* 21 (1958): 99–109; reprinted in Stanner, 1979, pp. 41–66.

Stanner, W. E. H. *On Aboriginal Religion.* Sydney, 1963; reprint, 1966, 1989.

Stanner, W. E. H. "Religion, Totemism, and Symbolism." In *Aboriginal Man in Australia: Essays in Honour or Emeritus Professor A. P. Elkin,* edited by Ronald M. Berndt and Catherine H. Berndt, pp. 207–237. Sydney, 1965.

Stanner, W. E. H. "Reflections on Durkheim and Aboriginal Religion." In *Social Organization: Essays Presented to Raymond Firth,* edited by Maurice Freedman, pp. 217–240. London, 1967.

Stanner, W. E. H. *After the Dreaming: The Boyer Lectures, 1968.* Sydney, 1969.

Stanner, W. E. H. *White Man Got No Dreaming: Essays, 1938–1973.* Canberra, 1979.

Melinda Hinkson (2005)

STANTON, ELIZABETH CADY.

Elizabeth Cady Stanton (1815–1902) was a principal leader and philosopher of the American woman's rights movement of the nineteenth century. Her religious importance derives from *The Woman's Bible* (1895–1898), written and edited late in her career, and from her influence in inspiring feminism to a rational, antidogmatic attitude to faith.

Stanton was born in Johnstown, New York. Her father, Daniel Cady, was a prominent lawyer, congressman, and judge. When none of her brothers lived to maturity, Elizabeth wanted to become like a son to please him. Although she never succeeded in satisfying her father, her precocious intellect did gain the notice of her family's Scottish Presbyterian minister, Simon Hosack, who tutored her in ancient languages. Her father's profession also shaped her sensitivity to legal protection and political details. Shocked by women's lack of rights in divorce and custody cases, she prioritized such issues throughout her career, directly challenging traditional bastions of male authority. Her analysis and thorough articulation of structural sexism were exemplary, and they were complemented by her abilities as a polemical writer.

Stanton experienced the tumult of the Second Great Awakening preacher Charles Finney while a student at Emma Willard's school in the early 1830s. The young Elizabeth felt susceptible to his rhetoric because of her "gloomy Calvinistic training," but upon becoming one of Finney's "victims" she noted, and regretted, the "dethronement of my reason." She deemed herself saved by intellection, by science, rationality, and progress.

After her schooling was finished, Elizabeth became involved with the antislavery movement. Through her cousin, Gerrit Smith, she met her future husband, Henry Stanton (1805–1887), one of the Lane Seminary rebels and an ardent abolitionist. Though her father objected to the marriage, it went forward in 1840, with a significant change in the marriage vows: Elizabeth refused to "obey" an equal, so that command was dropped. Their honeymoon brought more substantive change, as the couple attended the 1840 World's Anti-Slavery Congress in London. Some American groups included women delegates, but the British hosts refused to seat them. However, it was here that Stanton met the Quaker Lucretia Mott, who embodied a fuller range of possibilities for women. While living in Boston, Stanton's liberal religious outlook was reinforced as she absorbed Unitarian and transcendentalist ideas, and as she met more women leaders, including Lydia Maria Child and the Grimké sisters.

Stanton's own fame blossomed with the fulfillment of plans she and Mott had formulated to hold a woman's rights conference. This finally occured in 1848, when the first

Women's Rights Convention in the United States was held in Stanton's new hometown of Seneca Falls, New York. Stanton wrote the convention's bold Declaration of Sentiments, adopting the rhetoric of the Declaration of Independence and condemning male usurpation of authority over women in matters religious, "when that belongs to her conscience and her God."

Stanton's 1850 meeting with Susan B. Anthony marked a turning point in the women's rights movement. Their ardent friendship lasted over fifty years and became one of the most productive partnerships in American political history. Due to child-care and household concerns (the Stantons had seven children), Stanton emerged as the writer of the pair, while Anthony traveled and lectured for women's rights. While they prioritized voting rights, they never made this the exclusive focus of their wider goal: recognizing women's full humanity.

During the Civil War, Anthony and Stanton formed the Loyal League, which urged the immediate emancipation of slaves. Stanton herself began to travel and speak during this period, developing into an accomplished orator. In the postwar period, however, serious splits occurred among progressive advocates of increased voting rights. Angered by what they saw as a betrayal of women by those who advanced suffrage for African American men only, Stanton and Anthony allied themselves with racist and xenophobic forces. Stanton argued explicitly for the fitness of educated white women as voters over freed slaves and immigrants, whom she caricatured as "Sambo" and "Yung Tung." Stanton's rhetoric alienated former allies, including Mott, Lucy Stone, and Wendell Phillips. This period has compromised Stanton's legacy and fueled ongoing conflict in American feminism over class and race. The woman suffrage movement broke into two competing organizations in 1869: the National Woman Suffrage Association (led by Anthony and Stanton) and the rival American Woman Suffrage Association. By the time the organizations were reunited in 1890, the woman suffrage cause was bereft of its abolitionist roots.

The visibility of the woman suffrage movement increased through the last quarter of the nineteenth century, as did its sense of its own history. With Anthony and Matilda Joslyn Gage, Stanton edited and wrote the first three volumes of the *History of Woman Suffrage* (1881–1887), an admirably exhaustive chronicle of the movement. Opposition, and occasional support, from religious leaders mark many of its pages.

Stanton had always scrutinized legal restrictions on women, but became increasingly concerned with religious limitations. In her last twenty years she wrote two major texts: her autobiography, *Eighty Years and More* (1898), and *The Woman's Bible*, which she wrote and edited. These texts reveal her religious stance. Her autobiography presents her tireless opposition to superstition and her lifelong embrace of liberal religious inquiry—her freethinking mind investigated theories of Charles Darwin, the matriarchate, and theosophy.

Stanton planned *The Woman's Bible* as a commentary and analysis on scriptural passages concerning women. She invited many women religious leaders and intellectuals to participate, but only a handful responded, fearing a backlash from a conservative religious public would damage the suffrage cause. Prominent contributors included Eva Parker Ingersoll and Gage (author of another stinging critique of patriarchal religion, *Woman, Church, and State* [1893]). In her commentaries, Stanton praises strong women (her assessment of Eve's "courage" and "ambition" is justly famous), condemns inconsistencies as "a great strain on credulity," rejects auto-validating claims of inspiration, and urges women to self-sovereignty rather than self-sacrifice. Stanton and her collaborators used humor, science, logic, common sense, and principles of justice to read against the grain of traditional biblical interpretation.

During Stanton's lifetime, *The Woman's Bible* met a chilly reception. It was parodied, denounced, or belittled by reviewers. The crushing blow came when the organization Stanton herself had led, now called the National-American Woman Suffrage Association, officially dissociated itself from the book. Despite the eloquent plea of Susan B. Anthony in her defense, this 1896 vote effectively ended Stanton's official role in the suffrage movement.

The Woman's Bible remained forgotten until the women's liberation movement of the 1970s. Feminist scholars and practitioners of religion found its method and content congenial: it was collaborative, questioned received authority, established a feminist legacy of biblical interpretation, and outlined how gender bias shaped sacred texts. However, *The Woman's Bible* has had its modern critics, particularly over its anti-Catholic and anti-Jewish biases.

At her death in 1902 many of Stanton's contemporaries memorialized her as an undaunted leader, while ignoring her analysis of belief and scripture. Yet her religious critique may well ensure her importance to future generations.

See Also Child, Lydia Maria; Gage, Matilda Joslyn; Gender and Religion.

Bibliography

Three editions of *The Woman's Bible* are available: *The (Original) Feminist Attack on the Bible (The Woman's Bible)*, edited by Barbara Welty (New York, 1974); *The Woman's Bible*: Part 1: *The Pentateuch*; Part 2: *Judges, Kings, Prophets, and Apostles*, edited by the Coalition Task Force on Women and Religion (Seattle, Wash., 1974); and *The Woman's Bible*, foreword by Maureen Fitzgerald (Boston, 1993). Kathi Lynn Kern's *Mrs. Stanton's Bible* (Ithaca, N.Y., 2001) is an excellent full-length study. Two commentary projects motivated by Stanton's Bible were published by feminist scholars on its one hundredth anniversary: *The Women's Bible Commentary*, edited by Carol A. Newsom and Sharon H. Ringe (London and Louisville, Ky., 1992; expanded ed., 1998), and *Search-*

ing the Scriptures, 2 vols., edited by Elizabeth Schüssler Fiorenza (New York, 1993–1994).

Many of Stanton's works are being issued in a proposed six-volume critical edition, with Ann D. Gordon serving as editor: *The Selected Papers of Elizabeth Cady Stanton and Susan B. Anthony,* Vol. 1: *In the School of Anti-Slavery, 1840 to 1866* (New Brunswick, N.J., 1997); Vol. 2: *Against an Aristocracy of Sex* (New Brunswick, N.J., 2000). The contemporary edition of Stanton's autobiography, *Eighty Years and More: Reminiscences, 1815–1897* (Evanston, Ill., 1993), includes essays by Gordon and Ellen DuBois.

Biographical studies of Stanton include Alma Lutz, *Created Equal: A Biography of Elizabeth Cady Stanton, 1815–1902* (New York, 1940); Elizabeth Griffith, *In Her Own Right: The Life of Elizabeth Cady Stanton* (New York, 1984), and Lois Banner, *Elizabeth Cady Stanton: A Radical for Women's Rights* (Boston, 1980). The biography assembled by her children Theodore Stanton and Harriot Stanton Blatch, *Elizabeth Cady Stanton as Revealed in Her Letters, Diary, and Reminiscences* (New York, 1922) is heavily edited and unreliable. For general background on the suffrage movement, Ellen DuBois's *Feminism and Suffrage: The Emergence of an Independent Women's Movement in America, 1848–1869,* 2d ed. (Ithaca, N.Y., 1999) remains the basic work on the period, while the book accompanying Ken Burns's documentary, Geoffrey C. Ward's *Not for Ourselves Alone: The Story of Elizabeth Cady Stanton and Susan B. Anthony* (New York, 1999), provides a good introduction for the general reader. James E. Goodman, "The Origins of the 'Civil War' in the Reform Community: Elizabeth Cady Stanton on Woman's Rights and Reconstruction" in *Critical Matrix* 1, no. 2 (1985): 1–29, presents a detailed account of the immediate post–Civil War divisions.

JENNIFER RYCENGA (2005)

STARBUCK, E. D. (1866–1947), was a prominent figure in the early academic study of the psychology of religion in the United States and the first scholar to use the phrase "psychology of religion." Edwin Diller Starbuck was born in Indiana to a devout Quaker farming family. After undergraduate work at Indiana University, he went on to Harvard University, from which he received his master's degree in 1895, and then to Clark University, where in 1897 he received his doctorate. In 1890 he was stirred by F. Max Müller's *Introduction to the Science of Religion* and decided to start studying religion. In 1893, at Harvard, he circulated two questionnaires, one on sudden conversion and the other on "gradual growth" toward religious commitment. In 1894 and 1895 he presented papers on his research before the Harvard Religious Union. After graduating from Clark University, he remained there as a fellow in the late 1890s, together with James H. Leuba.

Starbuck's 1899 book *The Psychology of Religion* was based on studies he started at Harvard under William James and continued at Clark under G. Stanley Hall; it enjoyed three editions, was reprinted several times, and was translated into German in 1909. Starbuck had the support and encouragement of James in his work, but as Starbuck himself reports in a frank autobiographical statement, there was some tension in his relationship with Hall, and mutual criticism is much in evidence.

After the turn of the century, Starbuck devoted most of his creative energy to "character training" and devised selections of fairy tales, novels, and biographies that would contribute to the moral education of the young. He taught a variety of subjects at a number of institutions, including philosophy at the State University of Iowa (1906–1930), and philosophy (1930–1938) and psychology (1938–1943) at the University of Southern California. Starbuck's important contribution remains his early survey of conversion cases, which work was immortalized by James, who used Starbuck's data in *The Varieties of Religious Experience* (1902). While the basic findings of the survey have been accepted, and seem to fit with classical and modern notions of conversion, the theoretical construction seems hopelessly naive today. Together with Hall, Starbuck regarded conversion as an adolescent phenomenon, and had the data to show it. His findings are still quoted today, and are beyond dispute, but his psychology and his definition of religion as an "instinct" no longer find serious adherents.

Starbuck's attitude toward religion was clearly positive, and he saw the importance of the psychology of religion as contributing to religious education. According to James, Starbuck's aim in starting his research in the psychology of religion was to bring about reconciliation in the feud between science and religion. According to Starbuck's autobiographical account, his interest in religion was very much an attempt to answer, via systematic study, both doubts and curiosities about religion. If one attempts an evaluation of Starbuck's work from the perspective of several generations, one might conclude that it will be remembered more by historians of the field than by practitioners. His work may belong with the classics of the field, but it must be numbered with the unread classics, even among scholars.

BIBLIOGRAPHY

Argyle, Michael, and Benjamin Beit-Hallahmi. *The Social Psychology of Religion.* Boston, 1975.

Beit-Hallahmi, Benjamin. "Psychology of Religion, 1880–1930: The Rise and Fall of a Psychological Movement." *Journal of the History of the Behavioral Sciences* 10 (1974): 84–90.

Starbuck, E. D. *The Psychology of Religion.* London, 1899.

Starbuck, E. D. "Religion's Use of Me." In *Religion in Transition,* edited by Vergilius Ferm, pp. 201–256. New York, 1937.

New Sources

Hay, David. "Psychologists Interpreting Conversion: Two American Forerunners of the Hermeneutics of Suspicion." *History of the Human Sciences* 12, no. 1 (1999): 55–73.

BENJAMIN BEIT-HALLAHMI (1987)
Revised Bibliography

STAR OF DAVID SEE MAGEN DAVID

STARS.

STARS. In all times and places, the starry night sky has both challenged and satisfied the human need to order, categorize, and standardize the unknown. In their efforts to make the night sky a familiar place, ancient civilizations imposed on groups of stars the outlines of mythical and historical figures, thus linking the celestial and terrestrial realms. The two terms used for these star groups are *constellation* and *zodiac.* Constellations are groups of stars held together by the human mind and eye. While certain of them may be related mythologically, such as the Pleiades and Orion, they are essentially autonomous and not limited in number. The zodiac is an integrated system of twelve constellations, referred to by astrological signs, that forms a backdrop to the movements of the sun, moon, and planets. Each zodiacal sign is also associated with a part of the human body and thereby serves to link the celestial and terrestrial planes. Aries, the first sign, represents the head; Pisces, the feet; the ten remaining signs between them represent other parts of the body in descending order. While scholars credit Babylonia with devising the zodiac (c. 700–420 BCE), the Babylonians themselves in their creation epic, the Enuma elish, credit the god Marduk with that invention.

The ancient Egyptians also developed an integrated system of star organization. Here, the thirty-six decans, or star groups, each ten degrees in width and each named for a deity, served two purposes. The heliacal rising (first appearance in the dawn sky) of the leading star of each decan was noted, then used to mark out the twelve-month Egyptian calendar. At night, the decans functioned as a star clock, enabling priests to know the correct time for the performance of religious observances. In this way the temporal rhythms of the earth were linked to those of the sky.

In Indian tradition the Nakṣatras, or lunar mansions, comprise another integrated system of stars. The passage of the moon through the sky was charted as the journey of the god Soma through his "resting places." Each star is thought to be inhabited by one of the twenty-eight wives with whom Soma spends one night each month.

THE SKY IN MYTH. In religions around the world, the sky symbolizes transcendence and sacrality, stretching and satisfying the human imagination. Whether it is understood as the home of the gods, the resting place of heroes, or the land of the dead, the sky is often envisioned as the transcendental model for human existence. The powers of the stars watch and guide people in life and welcome them in death. As the land of the ancestral dead, the stars represent the place of future human existence and reward. In them humans will endure forever, see and know all, thus also becoming godlike.

On the terrestrial plane, everything exists in a state of constant change. Nature is unpredictable—sometimes benign and sometimes malevolent. The sky alone remains constant, predictable, beyond change. Since the distant sky gods are usually the lawgivers of a culture, establishing order in human society, the celestial-terrestrial relationship is a reciprocal one: Humans order the uncharted night sky by imposing images on it, while the heavens, in return, impose lawful order on human society.

Catasterisms, tales in which either humans or animals achieve immortality by becoming stars, express the notion of the stars as the home of heroes. Catasterisms present a permanent image of the reward for heroic feats while providing an etiological explanation for the existence of individual stars and constellations. These tales exists in such diverse cultures as Australia, where a man becomes a star to avoid the wrath of the irate husband chasing him, and Greenland, where a group of lost seal hunters become stars. The Greeks and the Romans were the most prolific creators of catasterisms.

These stories relate that after death the soul becomes a star, a notion that originated with the Pythagoreans. The belief that only heroes become stars leads to the use of star groups such as Herakles and the Pleiades as models for heroic effort and reward. Star groups such as Andromeda and Orion, by contrast, serve as demonstrations of the lasting punishment given for the sin of hubris. The star Antinoüs was named in 132 CE in honor of Hadrian's young lover who drowned himself in the belief that he could thereby add the years allotted to him to Hadrian's life.

The Milky Way, which is frequently called the River of Heaven or the Celestial Road, is connected with the notion of the stars as the land of the dead. In Norse mythology it is the road of the ghosts going to Valhǫll; in Celtic lore it is created by Gwydion so that he can use it to seek his son's soul in the heavens; in Islam it is said that Muḥammad walked on it to reach God; in Akkad it was called the River of the Divine Lady and was traveled by ghosts; in eastern Washington state the Sanpoil Indians place the land of the dead at the end of it; the Pawnee say it is the path followed by the spirits of the dead, and the Lakota add that travel to the Spirit Land is interrupted just before arrival by an old woman who checks for wrist tattoos; those without tattoos are sent back to earth as ghosts.

TEMPLES AND THE STARS. The most concrete way to establish the importance of the stars in the ancient world is to study the alignment of temples with particular stars. As sacred structures, temples—especially those dedicated to sky gods—are designed according to a celestial pattern. In 1894 J. Norman Lockyer published his research on Egyptian temples, under the title *The Dawn of Astronomy.* With the advent of modern technology, much of Lockyer's dating has been called into question, but his general theory of celestial alignment is still operative. In England, the Americas, and the ancient Near East there is evidence of such alignment. Ancient temples were most commonly constructed in relation to the sun's position at the solstice or equinox, but there are significant instances of design with relation to individual stars.

Astral alignments are established by astroarchaeologists, who calculate the age of a site from its remains and then use computers to recreate the star patterns visible at the time the site was built. England's Stonehenge (construction started c. 2800 BCE) is a good model. There, the large standing stones were arranged against the horizon to function as foresights; smaller stones served as backsights. In order to mark the passage of the sun, the astronomer-priest would fix a spot on which to stand to observe the sunset against the foresight stones. As the sun changed its course during the year, it would set to the right or left of these stones, its extremes marking the solstice and equinox points. Stonehenge was used as an elaborate observatory for marking the important celestial events of the year. The movements of the sun, moon, planets, and important star systems such as the Pleiades and especially the heliacal risings of the stars and planets were all noted there.

The same principle was employed in Mesoamerica, most dramatically at Tenochtitlán, the political and religious capital of the Aztec, where the course of a river was altered in order to create the desired alignments for observing the rising sun at the equinox and solstice and the heliacal rising of the Pleiades. Other Mesoamerican sites were also constructed with relation to the Pleiades, as well as to the stars Capella and Sirius and the planet Venus.

Gerald Hawkins (in *Stonehenge Decoded,* Garden City, N.Y., 1965), using modern techniques, has checked Lockyer's thesis at several sites in Egypt. While disagreeing with some of Lockyer's findings, he does establish that Egyptian temples are aligned with certain stars. Edwin C. Krupp (1978) has made a connection between the alignments of the pyramids and the cult of Isis and Osiris, represented respectively by the stars Sirius and Orion. First, he notes that all stars are invisible for approximately seventy days when their light is lost in the brighter light of the sun; he finds it significant that the ancient Egyptians called this time "being in Duat" (i.e., the underworld). Krupp sees a relation between this time span and the period allotted for embalming: Seventy days were required to prepare a body for burial. Because the stars are often thought of as the land of the dead, Krupp suggests further that the shafts in the pyramids aligning with Sirius and Orion were constructed so as to allow the souls of the pharaohs to rise up to these stars, the souls' final resting place.

In North America there are few sites of astronomical interest, but where they exist the myths and legends of the people also show astronomical characteristics. The *kivas* of the Anasazi, ancestors of the modern Pueblo, show some evidence of astral alignment, and modern Pueblo rituals preserve astral timings. Among the Plains Indians, medicine wheels constructed of large and small stones arranged in the shape of a wheel with spokes establishing alignments, mark the solstices. In Saskatchewan, Canada, the Moose Mountain Medicine Wheel is also aligned to the heliacal rising of the bright summer stars Aldebaran, Rigel, and Sirius.

THE POLESTAR. Sometimes diverse cultures use similar images to describe the same star. The polestar, or North Star (the position held today by the star Polaris in Ursa Minor), because of its relative lack of motion as compared to other stars, is important for both land and sea navigation. In many cultures it is seen as the center of the universe.

Norse people believed that the gods ordered the universe by driving a spike through the earth and causing the heavens to revolve around this axis. The end of this spike was fastened to the polestar. For the Mongols, the polestar was the golden peg or nail that holds the turning heavens together. In India it is called the "pivot of the planets" and is represented by the god Dhruva, who was so immovable in his meditation that he became the polestar shining about Mount Meru, the center of the world. Because Dhruva began his meditation in a search for constancy after having been disappointed by the unsteadiness of his father's love, the star is worshiped in India as a source of constancy both in meditation and in marriage. The Mandaeans, along the Tigris and Euphrates rivers, worshiped the polestar as the central star around which all other heavenly bodies move; their sanctuaries were built so that persons entering them faced the polestar. Worshipers prayed facing it, and the dying were positioned so their feet and eyes were aligned with it.

The constancy of the polestar also led to its popularity among sailors, as the epithets Steering Star, Lodestar, and Ship Star show. (Strabo, the Greek historian and geographer of the first century BCE, attributed its use among Greek sailors to Thales, the astronomer and philosopher of the sixth century BCE.) The constant position of the polestar made it useful to land travelers as well. In Mesoamerica it was thought both to protect and to guide traveling merchants, who burned copal incense in its honor. The Arabs used the polestar to navigate across the desert and believed further that fixed contemplation of it would cure itching of the eyelids. For the Chinese, the polestar was secretary to the Emperor of Heaven and as lord of the dead punished the dead according to their deeds.

THE PLEIADES. Even in societies where little attention was paid to the stars, the movements of the Pleiades were noted. For instance, the Bantu-speaking peoples of southern Africa regulated their agricultural calendar by them, and in Bali the Pleiades and Orion were used to keep the lunar calendar. In Australia, where the first annual appearance of the Pleiades coincides with the beginning of the rainy season, the Aborigines consider these stars the source of rain and curse them if rain does not follow their appearance. In general, the last visible rising of the Pleiades after sunset is celebrated all over the southern hemisphere as beginning the season of agricultural activity.

Where myths have developed about the Pleiades, these stars are generally associated with women. In the Greco-Roman world, these stars were called the "seven daughters of Atlas," and in China they were worshiped by women and girls as the Seven Sisters of Industry. In Australia, they are seen as young girls playing instruments for a group of dancing young men, the stars of the Orion group. In the Solomon Islands they are called a "company of maidens," and among the Yurok of North America they are thought of as six women. In India they had a rich and varied identity as the nurses of Skanda, the infant god of war, and as the seven wives of the seven sages of Ursa Major. Myths in which they are depicted as wives describe the reasons for their being changed into stars as either punishment for infidelity or as a reward for fidelity. In one positive reading, the star Arundhati is considered the ideal Indian wife because her virtue was great enough to resist the god Śiva's attempt at seduction. Like the polestar, she is worshiped by married couples as a symbol of constancy.

The Pleiades also played a central role in the religious life of the Aztec. The fifty-two year cycle of their calendar was measured by the Pleiades. Indeed, legend recalls that the destruction of the world in a past age occurred at such a moment. The ceremony at the end of the cycle, the "Binding of the Years," established that the movements of the heavens had not ceased and that the world would not end but was guaranteed to last for another fifty-two years. Not only was one of the alignments of the Aztec city of Tenochtitlán to the Pleiades, but a further clue to the importance of these stars is the fact that at the time of the city's erection (c. 150 CE), the heliacal rising of the Pleiades occurred on the same day as the first of the sun's annual passages across the zenith, a day of great importance in demarcating the seasons, and the day when the sun in Mexico casts no shadow at high noon. Additionally, this was the beginning of the rainy season so important to agriculture.

The Inca called the Pleiades the "stars of summer" and believed that their appearance on the first sighting predicted the success of the crops. If the stars were large and bright when they first appeared, the crops would be successful; if they were small and dim, the crops would fail. This connection to the agricultural season in part explains the emphasis placed on the Pleiades. In Greece the Pleiades presage temperate weather: The name of one of the stars of this group, Alcyone, is connected, by derivation, with the term "halcyon days," a clement and temperate time. In ancient Greece the season safe for navigation began in May with the heliacal rising of the Pleiades and closed with their setting in late autumn. In the Hervey Islands of the South Pacific they are the favorite guides for night sailing and are worshiped by sailors.

In North America the Blackfeet use the Pleiades to regulate their most important feast, which includes the blessing and planting of the seed. The Navaho believe the Pleiades appear on the forehead of their principal deity, Black God.

SIRIUS. Regarded as one of the most important stars in ancient Egypt, Sirius played a role there similar to that of the Pleiades among the Aztec. Sirius's heliacal rising at the summer solstice coincided with the annual inundation of the Nile, thus beginning the Egyptian year. Seen as the goddess Sothis by the Egyptians, Sirius was also connected with the goddesses Hathor, Sekhet, and Isis and was generally considered to be the resting place of Isis's soul. Also called the "Nile star," Sirius had a dog for its hieroglyph and to this day is widely known as the "dog star." In ancient Rome, when the sun approached conjunction with Sirius at a festival for the protection of grain, farmers sacrificed a fawn-colored dog to the god Robigus. The Dogon of Africa also connect Sirius with a grain called po, and Po is their name for Sirius's smaller, darker companion star. That companion was first seen by Western astronomers in 1962, yet the Dogon discussed the star with Western anthropologists as early as 1940. Claiming to have known of the companion star for eight centuries, the Dogon correctly estimated that its orbit around Sirius took fifty years.

A Finnish tale explains the brightness of Sirius by the story of the lovers Zulamith the Bold and Salami the Fair: When they finally completed a bridge to each other (the Milky Way) after a thousand years of separation, they rushed into each other's arms and melted into one.

COMETS, METEORS, AND SHOOTING AND FALLING STARS. Noticeably short-lived celestial phenomena such as comets and meteors (shooting and falling stars) share in the sacred nature of the sky and add to the meaning of the "permanent" stars. The abruptness of their passage often made them seem to be omens full of meaning for good or ill. The American writer Mark Twain said of himself that he was born when Halley's comet approached the earth, and he correctly predicted his death upon its return. A comet recorded in 431 BCE gave support to the notion that Julius Caesar had become a comet upon his death a year earlier. Shakespeare made dramatic use of this idea when he wrote "When beggars die, then are no comets seen; / the heavens themselves blaze for the death of princes" (*Julius Caesar* 2.2).

In ancient Greece and Rome, comets were generally thought to portend unfortunate events. The astronomer Ptolemy (second century) said that the meanings of comets could be discerned by their individual shapes; their color revealed what they would bring (generally wind and drought), and their position in the zodiac indicated the country that would be affected. Pliny, the Roman writer of the first century CE, also believed that comets signaled disaster and specified, for example, that a comet in Scorpio portended a plague of reptiles and insects, especially locusts. Seneca the Younger, writing in the first century CE, following Aristotle, said that comets were portents of bad weather during the ensuing year.

Such ideas persisted after the rise of Christianity. In the third century CE, the church father Origen held that comets appear on the eve of dynastic changes, great wars, and other catastrophes but also may be signs of future good: He seems to have taken the star of Bethlehem, which announced Christ's birth, to be a comet. The German philosopher Albertus Magnus (d. 1280) wrote that comets signified wars and the death of kings and potentates. According to Ptolemy of Lucca (d. 1377), a comet portended the death of Pope Urban IV in 1264. The pope had sickened as soon as the comet appeared and had died three months later, on the very day it disappeared. Elizabeth I of England gained great prestige by manifesting her indifference to the comet of 1557. When her courtiers tried to deter her from looking at the dreaded object she advanced boldly to the window, declaring, "the die is thrown." Seventeenth-century Christian preachers declared that comets were sent by God to draw human beings to repentance, and as late as 1843 the Millerites thought a comet confirmed their belief in the immediate destruction of the world.

Among the Aztec similar notions prevailed. They called comets "stars that smoke" and thought they usually signified the impending death of members of nobility; the death of the ruler of Tenochtitlán followed the appearance of a comet, and another was said to have predicted the fall of Moctezuma II. The Plains Indians also connected appearances of comets with disaster and misfortune.

In the Society Islands, comets (along with meteors) were believed to be the tails of gods, and when they were seen, the people threw off their upper garments (the mark of respect shown to gods and sacred head chiefs) and exclaimed, "A god! A god!" But in Samoa comets were believed to predict the death of a chief, or some other calamity such as war or bloodshed. The Indian astronomer and astrologer Varahamihira (sixth century CE), while generally concurring with such theories, developed an elaborate system of analysis to predict the three types of events comets can bring: auspicious, inauspicious, and having mixed effects.

Shooting and falling stars, meteors, and meteorites have in common the sacred quality of having come from the heavens, whether for good or ill. Like comets they are preeminently seen as signs and portents. Ptolemy says they indicate the coming of winds and storms, while Seneca links them to violent political events. By contrast, some believed them to be connected with healing. Pliny preserved the notion that a corn may be successfully extracted at the time of a shooting star; the physician Marcellus (fourth century CE) says the same of warts, adding that if you start counting while a star is falling, the number will equal the number of years you will be free of sore eyes. In India falling stars are thought of not only as reincarnating souls traveling back to earth, but also as demons who love the night and who are connected in a negative way with the souls of the dead. Such beings are especially dangerous to pregnant women.

Among the most famous meteorites in religious history is the Kaʿbah of Mecca, which tradition says was brought to earth by the archangel Gabriel. Also important is the meteorite of the goddess Cybele of the Phrygians. It arrived in Rome in 204 BCE, when Rome was being threatened by Hannibal. The Sibylline Books, which had been consulted after a meteorite shower, foretold that a foreign army could be driven from Italy if Cybele's symbol, a meteorite, was brought to Rome. It was, and Hannibal was defeated. The Romans expressed their gratitude to the goddess by erecting a temple to her on the summit of the Palatine and held an annual celebration to commemorate her arrival.

The alignments of temples, the long history of astrological beliefs, and the abundance of myths and folktales about the stars provide ample evidence for the existence in many cultures of the notion "as above, so below." This view of the universe, in which the terrestrial and celestial realms are recognized as interrelated, has been a source of great richness to the cultural and religious experience of the human race.

See Also Astrology; Ethnoastronomy; Sky.

Bibliography

The best collection of myths surrounding the stars, constellations, and zodiac is Richard Hinckley Allen's *Star Names: Their Lore and Meaning* (1899; reprint, New York, 1963). Allen makes no attempt to synthesize his material, which is arranged in alphabetical order. For the various astral systems of the ancient world, see Robert Brown's *Researches into the Origin of the Primitive Constellations of the Greeks, Phoenicians and Babylonians,* 2 vols. (London, 1899–1900); for their scientific background, see Otto Neugebauer's *The Exact Sciences in Antiquity* (1951; New York, 1969); while Ptolemy's *Tetrabiblos,* translated by F. E. Robbins (Cambridge, Mass., 1940), remains the starting place for Western views. For the Nakṣatras and general Indian views, see *The Brihajjātakam of Varāha Mihira,* 2d ed., translated by Swami Vijnanananda (New Delhi, 1979), and Robert De Luce's *Constellational Astrology according to the Hindu System* (Los Angeles, 1963). The decans are covered by Wilhelm Gundel in *Dekane und Dekansternbilder* (Hamburg, 1936). Lynn Thorndike's *A History of Magic and Experimental Science,* 8 vols. (New York, 1923–1958), remains a valuable resource on the West up to the medieval period.

On the issue of alignments, Joseph Norman Lockyer's *The Dawn of Astronomy: A Study of Temple Worship and Mythology of the Ancient Egyptians* (1894; Cambridge, Mass., 1964), while challenged today, helped to create the field of astroarchaeology. This work is continued in *In Search of Ancient Astronomies,* edited by Edwin C. Krupp (Garden City, N.Y., 1978), which also contains excellent essays on ancient astronomy, and in *Native American Astronomy,* edited by Anthony F. Aveni (Austin, 1977), which treats archaeological sites in North and South America.

Finally, in part 4 of *The Raw and the Cooked* (1969; Chicago, 1983), Claude Lévi-Strauss provides an interesting comparison of similar myths of particular constellations, such as the Pleiades, in South America and ancient Greece.

New Sources

Aveni, Anthony F. *Stairways to the Stars: Skywatching in Three Great Ancient Cultures.* New York, 1997.

Condos, Theony. *Star Myths of the Greeks and Romans: A Sourcebook Containing the Constellations of Pseudo-Eratosthenes and the Poetic Astronomy of Hyginus.* Grand Rapids, Mich, 1997.

Evans, James. *The History & Practice of Ancient Astronomy.* New York, 1998.

Krupp, Edwin C. *Skywatchers, Shamans, & Kings: Astronomy and the Archaeology of Power.* New York, 1997.

North, John David. *Stonehenge: A New Interpretation of Prehistoric Man and the Cosmos.* New York, 1996.

SERINITY YOUNG (1987)
Revised Bibliography

STCHERBATSKY, THEODORE (1866–1942), was a Russian Buddhologist and Indologist. Fedor Ippolitovich Shcherbatskii, who signed his non-Russian writings "Th. Stcherbatsky," was born in Kielce, Poland, and died in Borovoi, Kazakhstan. He studied philology and Indology in Saint Petersburg under I. P. Minaev, Sanskrit poetics in Vienna with Georg Bühler, Indian philosophy in Berlin with Hermann Jacobi, and Sanskrit and Tibetan logic with pandits in India and lamas in Mongolia. From 1900 to 1941, Stcherbatsky taught at Saint Petersburg (later Leningrad) State University. His students included O. O. Rozenberg, E. E. Obermiller, and A. I. Vostrikov. The Russian Academy of Sciences named Stcherbatsky corresponding member (1910), academician (1918), director of the Institute of Buddhist Culture (1928–1930), and head of the Indo-Tibetan section of the Institute of Oriental Studies (1930–1942). He helped S. F. Ol'denberg produce the academy's "Bibliotheca Buddhica" series of texts, translations, and monographs (1897–), which included several of Stcherbatsky's own works.

Although Stcherbatsky wrote widely on Indology and philology, his works on Buddhist philosophy were most influential. Stcherbatsky relied on Sanskrit and Tibetan, not Pali, sources and preferred *śāstras* (scholastic treatises) to *sūtras* (canonical texts), considering them to be, respectively, technical and popular works, differing in style, not doctrine. Skeptical of the search for "original Buddhism," he investigated pluralist, monist, and idealist phases of Buddhism. Early Buddhist "pluralism" replaces substances (soul, God, matter) with innumerable, interdependent, momentary *dharmas*, which attain cessation in *nirvāṇa*. Stcherbatsky saw in later *abhidharma* literature, especially Vasubandhu's *Abhidharmakośa,* the epitome of early Buddhist philosophy. (Stcherbatsky's works emphasized traditional Buddhist scholarship and Tibetan sources but neglected modern historical criticism.) He began publishing the *Abhidharmakośa* and its commentaries in the "Bibliotheca Buddhica," summarized it in *The Central Conception of Buddhism and the Meaning of the Word "Dharma"* (1923), and translated its final section as "The Soul Theory of the Buddhists" (*Izvestiia Rossiiskoi Akademii nauk,* ser. 6, vol. 13, 1920, nos. 15, pp. 823–854, and 18, pp. 937–958).

According to Stcherbatsky, Mādhyamika "monism" sees interdependent, momentary *dharmas* as unreal or empty. Emptiness (*śūnyatā*) and interdependence (*pratītya-samutpāda*) are identified as "relativity." *Nirvāṇa* is the realization of this one reality underlying an unreal plurality. Stcherbatsky's main work on Mādhyamika, *The Conception of Buddhist Nirvāṇa* (1927), was a rejoinder to *Nirvāṇa* (1925) by Louis de La Vallée Poussin (see Guy R. Welbon's *The Buddhist Nirvāṇa and Its Western Interpreters,* 1968). Stcherbatsky later reinterpreted Mādhyamika as "relativism," reserving "monism" for the Yogacara (see the preface to *Madhyānta-Vibhaṅga: Discourse on Discrimination between Middle and Extremes,* 1936).

Yogācāra "idealism" rejects pluralism and relativism. Subject and object, separately unreal, are really inseparable. Everything exists relatively, yet relativity really exists as the true nature of consciousness. This "idealism" led to the epistemology of Dignāga and Dharmakīrti (Stcherbatsky's "Buddhist logic"), which admits only two modes of valid cognition: non-conceptual "perception," and conceptual "inference." Stcherbatsky is best known for his work on this school: his earlier *Theory of Knowledge and Logic According to the Doctrine of the Later Buddhists,* and his magnum opus, *Buddhist Logic* (2 vols., 1930–1932). Stcherbatsky, admiring both philosophers, called Dharmakirti "the Indian Kant." This comparison, and the Kantian language of *Buddhist Logic,* should be taken cautiously.

Stcherbatsky lacked sympathy for Buddhism as religion but admired Indian philosophy as rigorous philosophy. Refuting the common misconception of Indian thought as vague mysticism, his works challenge Western philosophers to acknowledge their Buddhist and Indian colleagues.

BIBLIOGRAPHY

Stcherbatsky's *Teoriia poznaniia i logika po ucheniiu pozdneishikh buddistov* (Theory of Knowledge and Logic according to the Doctrine of the Later Buddhists), 2 vols. (Saint Petersburg, 1903–1909), has been translated into German as *Erkenntnistheorie und Logik, nach der Lehre der späteren Buddhisten* (Munich, 1924) and into French as *La théorie de la connaissance et la logique chez les bouddhistes tardifs* (Paris, 1926). *Buddhist Logic,* 2 vols. (Leningrad, 1930–1932), is available in two reprint editions; other English works cited in the text are available in Indian reprint editions. The complete "Bibliotheca Buddhica" has been reprinted in Germany (1970) and in Japan (1971). For shorter Russian works in English translation, see two books edited by Debiprasad Chattopadhyaya and translated by Harish Chandra Gupta: *Papers of Th. Stcherbatsky,* "Soviet Indology Series," no. 2 (Calcutta, 1969), and *Further Papers of Stcherbatsky,* "Soviet Indology Series," no. 6 (Calcutta, 1971). The former contains bibliographical and biographical information from Russian sources, partially contradicting the obituary in the *Journal of the Royal Asiatic Society* (1943): 118–119.

New Sources

Shcherbatskoi, F. I., and V. N. Toporov, *Izbrannye trudy po buddizmu.* Moscow, 1988.

Shokhin, V. K., and Institut filosofii (Rossiiskaia akademiia nauk). *F.I. Shcherbatskoi i ego komparativistskaia filosofiia.* Moscow, 1998.

Woo, Jeson. "Oneness and Manyness: Vacaspatimisra and Ratnakirti on an Aspect of Causality." *Journal of Indian Philosophy* 28, no. 2 (2000): 225–231.

BRUCE CAMERON HALL (1987)
Revised Bibliography

STEINER, RUDOLF (1861–1925), who wrote more than 350 volumes on philosophy, science, and the arts, was the originator of an esoteric form of spiritual teaching called anthroposophy, which he defined as meaning both "knowledge of the human being" and "human knowledge." Steiner was born in Kraljevec on Murr Island, Hungary, on February 25, 1861. He was educated in Austria, lived in Germany in his middle years, and lived in Dornach, Switzerland, during the last twelve years of his life. From 1900 to 1924, in virtually every major city in Europe, he delivered over six thousand lectures, some to an audience of a dozen and others to several thousands.

From an early age, Steiner experienced access to spiritual realities, including experiences of the dead; the inner, or "etheric," forces of the plant world; and the living power of symbolic forms. At age twenty-two he was appointed editor of the natural scientific writings of Johann Wolfgang von Goethe, which were published in five volumes (1883–1897).

Beginning in 1900, at the age of thirty-nine, Steiner began to teach a Western Christian-Rosicrucian esotericism. He served as the head of the Berlin branch of the Theosophical Society from 1902 to 1911. He continued to speak about H. P. Blavatsky (1831–1891), the founder of the society, with great respect, but in contrast to the primarily Hindu-Buddhist orientation of the Theosophical Society, Steiner emphasized both the central role of Christ in the evolution of consciousness and the importance of thinking for the *karma* of the West. Steiner's doctoral dissertation, published as *Truth and Knowledge* (1892), in combination with *The Philosophy of Freedom* (1894), prepared the way for the theory of cognition that characterizes his later thought. In 1904 Steiner published two of his foundational esoteric works: *How to Know Higher Worlds* and *Theosophy.* The third foundational text from that period was *An Outline of Esoteric Science* (1909). Collectively, these three works present Steiner's fourfold theory of human nature (physical, etheric, astral, and Ego), his detailed account of the evolution of earth and humanity, guidance on the path of initiation, and his description of the workings of *karma* and rebirth. Some of the ideas in these basic anthroposophical texts can be found in Hindu and Buddhist scriptures and in the esoteric teachings of Blavatsky, but Steiner sought to establish them in the Western, specifically Christian, tradition.

In response to requests from his followers for guidance, Steiner delivered more than six thousand lectures on disparate topics in the sciences, the social sciences, the arts, education, and on many of the founders and leaders of different religious traditions. In the tradition of Goethe, Steiner showed how imaginative seeing can illuminate the natural world, especially plants and the world of color. He generated myriad insights into the inner dynamics of the natural world, including metals, crystals, plants, soil, and particularly the human body. He described in detail the effects of spiritual, astral, and etheric forces on planetary bodies, the earth, and human beings.

Steiner bequeathed a host of insights concerning color theory, painting, sculpture, and architecture. Many of his contributions in these areas are exemplified in the two Goetheanum buildings in Dornach that he designed. The first Goetheanum, for which construction began in 1913, was nearly finished when it was destroyed by fire in 1922. The second Goetheanum serves as the spiritual center for the General Anthroposophical Society. In the years 1910–1914 Steiner taught several courses on speech formation that were based on his esoteric knowledge of the human larynx, and he wrote and directed four dramas in which he attempted to use those innovations in speech to express the inner realities of human and spiritual beings. In 1912 Steiner began teaching a series of lessons for a discipline of his own invention called *eurythmy.* Using his knowledge of language and sound, he showed how the human body, particularly the limbs, can express in visible form the varied meanings of consonants, vowels, and musical notes.

Steiner posited three principal divisions of society: the economic, the political, and the spiritual-cultural. He argued that these three realms should be regarded as separate but related and of equal importance. This social theory has profound implications for Steiner's approach to education, which he placed in the spiritual-cultural sphere, essentially removed from economic and political (including governmental) influence. Steiner's attempt to develop an approach to education that would be modern, spiritual, and centered on the needs of the child dates to his lecture series of 1907, *The Education of the Child in the Light of Anthroposophy,* and it finds full expression in the Waldorf approach to education.

Waldorf Schools (named after the school in Stuttgart that Steiner founded in 1919 for the children of workers in the Waldorf-Astoria tobacco factory) employ a curriculum based on what Steiner saw as the seven-year cycles through which a child develops and on the cultivation of the child's scientific and artistic imagination. On Steiner's recommendation, Waldorf teachers strive to "receive the child in reverence, educate the child in love, and send the child forth in freedom."

Steiner delivered more than a dozen lecture series on the spiritual and esoteric revelations that he gleaned from the events depicted in the Christian scriptures. Although he emphasized that the primary spiritual path for modern humanity ought to be spiritual science, or anthroposophy, in 1922, in response to an appeal for help from German and Swiss pastors and theology students, Steiner provided the spiritual foundation for a church called the Christian Community. During Christmas week in 1923, Steiner reorganized the Anthroposophical Society with the Goetheanum as its spiritual and physical center. He died at the Goetheanum on March 30,1925.

SEE ALSO Anthroposophy; Blavatsky, H. P.; Rosicrucians; Theosophical Society.

BIBLIOGRAPHY

More than two hundred volumes by Steiner and an equal number concerning anthroposophy by other authors, including Christopher Bamford, Owen Barfield, Sergei Prokofieff, M. C. Richards, and Valentin Tomberg, are available from Anthroposophic Press/Steiner Books at www.anthropress.org. The following books are published by Anthroposophical Press/Steiner Books, Great Barrington, Massachusetts.

Bamford, Christopher, ed. *Spiritualism, Madame Blavatsky, and Theosophy.* Great Barrington, Mass., 2001.

Barnes, Henry. *A Life for the Spirit: Rudolf Steiner in the Crosscurrents of Our Time.* Hudson, N.Y., 1997.

Prokofieff, Sergei. *Rudolf Steiner and the Founding of the New Mysteries.* East Sussex, U.K., 1986.

Steiner, Rudolf. *An Autobiography—Chapters in the Course of My Life: 1861–1907.* Translated by Rita Stebbing, Herndon, Va., 1999.

ROBERT A. MCDERMOTT (1987 AND 2005)

STHIRAMATI. Although he was born in India, Indian Buddhist literature has almost nothing to say about Sthiramati (470–550). Therefore, Tibetan and Chinese sources must be relied on for information on his life. According to Tibetan Buddhist historians, Sthiramati was born in Daṇḍakarāṇya, the son of a *śūdra,* and as a child studied under Vasubandhu (c. mid-fourth to mid-fifth centuries). Both Chinese pilgrim scholars Xuanzang (600?–664) and Yijing (635–713) mention Sthiramati as one of the great Buddhist philosophers and that he was a disciple of Guṇamati (c. 420–500). In addition, in *Chengweishilun shuji,* Kuiji (632–682), a disciple of Xuanzang, gives short biographies of the ten great Buddhist masters. He includes Sthiramati and names him as a student of Guṇamati. Kuiji also reports that Sthiramati hailed from the state of Laṭā in southern India and was an older contemporary of Dharmapāla (530–561). Also, in the opening section of the Uighur translation of his *Abhidharmakośabhāṣyaṭīkā Tattvārthanāma* Sthiramati states explicitly that Guṇamati was his teacher. This is significant evidence to confirm the Chinese scholars' account that Sthiramati was a disciple of Guṇamati, not of Vasubandhu as the Tibetan historians asserted.

Both Tibetan and Chinese sources note that he dwelled at Nālandā. However, Sthiramati's name is closely associated with the city of Valabhī, and the fact that Sthiramati was one of the most renowned Buddhist masters at Valabhī is attested to by both Chinese Buddhist sources and historical documents. Regarding the dates of Sthiramati's life, Ui Hakuju suggested 470 to 550 whereas Erich Frauwallner suggested 510 to 570. Ui's date appears to be more plausible as a working hypothesis than the one established by Frauwallner because he based his calculation on Xuanzang, who, in turn relied on the dates of Dharmapāla as well as Śīlabhadra (529–645). Ui also relied on the date of Guṇamati, which he established as around 420 to 500.

EXTANT WORKS. Sthiramati is mostly known through his two extant works in Sanskrit that have been edited and partially translated into western languages: the *Madhyāntavibhāgaṭīkā* and the *Triṃśikābhāṣya.* However, the Tibetan tradition attributes thirteen works to the name Sthiramati. Among them seven are Tantric texts, although it is almost impossible to know whether the author of these works is the same Sthiramati. Of the remaining six, two are Tibetan translations of the *Madhyāntavibhāgaṭīkā* and the *Triṃśikābhāṣya,* and four are works of which the Sanskrit originals are lost, namely, *Sūtrālaṃkāravṛttibhāṣya, Pañcaskandhaprakaraṇavibhāṣa, Abhidharmakośabhāṣyaṭīkā Tattvārthanāma,* and *Ārya Mahāratnakūṭadharmaparyayaśatasāhasrikā Kāśyapaparivartaṭīkā.* The Chinese canon also contains four works under the name Anhui (Sthiramati): *Jushelun shiyishu, Dacheng zhongguan shilun, Dacheng apidamo zajilun,* and *Dacheng guang wuyunlun.* Among these the *Jushelun shiyishu* and the *Dacheng guang wuyunlun* appear to correspond respectively to the *Abhidharmakośabhāṣyaṭīkā Tattvārthanāma* and the *Pañcaskandhaprakaraṇavibhāṣa* (although they are different in contents), whereas the *Dacheng apidamo zajilun* and the *Dacheng zhongguan shilun* are works extant only in Chinese translation. Thus, in all, there are eight non-Tantric works that can be attributed with some certainty to Sthiramati.

Sthiramati was primarily a commentator and did not compose any independent treatise. His most significant contribution is in the field of Yogācāra philosophy. In his commentaries Sthiramati appears as a thinker who was mainly concerned with clarifying and systematizing Yogācāra philosophy, and, although he did have his preferences, he was not particularly interested in sectarian controversy. Sthiramati's commentaries on major Yogācāra texts, including the *Mahāyānasūtrālamkāra* and the *Madhyāntavibhāga,* show that one of his main intentions was to elucidate the Mahāyāna concept of enlightenment *(bodhi)* or buddhahood, expressed by the term *dharmadhātu,* and its soteriological implications as the ultimate goal of the Buddhist path. These issues are discussed at great length in his two larger works: the *Madhyāntavibhāgaṭīkā* and the *Sūtrālaṃkāravṛttibhāṣya.*

YOGĀCĀRA THOUGHT. Sthiramati's systematic understanding of Yogācāra philosophy is found most succinctly in his *Triṃśikābhāṣya.* According to this, ordinary people are inclined to impose the concepts of persons *(pudgala)* and phenomena *(dharma)* on the realities that in truth consist of moment-to-moment processes of cognitions (*citta* or *vijñapti*) caused by their own conditions. The view of self (or person) constitutes afflictive obstruction *(kleśāvaraṇa)* that hinders liberation *(mokṣa)* whereas the construct of phenomena leads to cognitive obstruction that hinders omniscience *(saravajñatva).* The teaching of mind-only *(cittamātra)* or cognition-only *(vijnaptimātra)* is to enable unenlightened people to understand the selflessness of persons *(pudgalanairātmya)* and the selflessness of phenomena *(dharmanairātmya).* The constructed duality of persons and phenomena *(grāhakagrāhyadvaya)* is of imagined nature *(parikalpitasvabhāva)* and is ultimately nonexistent. However, this dualistic concept is constructed based on the transformation of consciousness *(vijñānapariṇāma)* or cognition-only *(vijnaptimātra),* which is of a dependent nature *(paratantrasvabhāva).* To see that realities are cognition-only and free from the superimposition of the duality of persons and phenomena is to realize their true nature *(parinspannasvhabhāva).* Because the knowledge of the selflessness of persons is an antidote to the false view of self and because the knowledge of the selflessness of phenomena is an antidote to cognitive obstructions, to remove afflictive and cognitive obstructions is to achieve liberation and omniscience or buddhahood.

According to Sthiramati, the teaching of *vijñaptimātra* (i.e., things do not exist with intrinsic natures but are only the transformations of consciousness) is to refute the errors of the two extreme views: (1) that the objects, like consciousness *(vijñāna),* are real; and (2) that, like the objects, consciousness only exists conventionally but not ultimately.

Due to the lack of translation of his works into Chinese, Sthiramati did not get as much appreciation as Dharmapāla in the Chinese tradition. Chinese Buddhists' interpretations of Sthiramati's views on Yogācāra tend to be fragmentary and at times unfounded, and his more important contributions went unknown.

See Also Buddhism, overview article; Enlightenment; Vasubandhu; Yogācāra.

Bibliography

Frauwallner, Erich. "Landmarks in the History of Indian Logic." *Wiener Zeitschrift für die Kunde Süd und Ostasiens* 5 (1961): 125–148.

Friedman, David Lasar, trans. *Madhyāntavibhāgaṭīkā: Analysis of the Middle Path and the Extremes.* Utrecht, 1937. A translation of the first chapter.

Jacobi, Hermann, trans. *Triṃśsikavijñapti des Vasubandhu mit bhāṣya des ācārya Sthiramati.* Stuttgart, 1932.

Lévi, Sylvain. *Une systéme de philosophie bouddhique. matériaux pour l'étude du systéme Vijñaptimātra.* Paris, 1932.

O'Brien, Paul Wilfred, trans. "A Chapter on Reality from the *Madhyāntavibhāgaśāstrā.*" *Monumentica Nipponica* 9 & 10 (1953–54): 277–303; 227–269.

Tekin, Sinaşi, ed. *Abhidharma-Kośabhāṣyaṭīkā Tattvārtha-nāma. The Uigur Translation of Sthiramati's Commentary on Vasubandhu's Abhidharmakośaśāstra.* New York, 1970.

Ui Hakuju. *Anne Gohō yuishiki sanjussho shakuron.* Tokyo, 1953.

Yamaguchi, Susumu. *Sthiramati, Madhyāntavibhāgaṭīkā: Exposition systématique du Yogācāravijñaptivāda.* 3 vols. Nagoya, Japan, 1934–1937.

Cuong Tu Nguyen (2005)

STIGMATA See BODILY MARKS

STOICISM

STOICISM is a philosophy related to the ancient Greek Stoic school, which took its name from the painted "porch" (*stoa*) on the northern side of the Athenian Agora (now ruins partially excavated along Hadrianos Street), where teachers and students of the school initially met. Later, however, lessons were also held in more suitable public buildings (cf. Diogenes Laertius, 7.184).

Historical Survey. The founder of the Stoic school was Zenon (c. 335–263 BCE). Born in Cithium, Cyprus, he traveled for business to Athens in his thirties and came in contact with Socratic circles there. Zenon devoted himself to philosophy and worked out a comprehensive and ethically oriented world vision, entirely different in its ontological framework from those Plato and Aristotle had produced a few decades earlier. Having lived a successful life in Athens, whose municipality honored him with a statue, Zenon committed suicide. According to Stoic doctrine, suicide is a proper way to end one's life when circumstances (chronic illness, external pressure, etc.) prevent one from continuing to live as a wise person.

Cleanthes (c. 331–232 BCE), a student of Zenon's from Assos (not far from ancient Troy), led the school until he let himself starve to death, having reached almost one hundred years of age. Cleanthes is believed to have been interested in religion, an opinion due apparently to his famous "Hymn to Zeus" (*Stoicorum veterum fragmenta [SVF]* 1.537). In fact, Cleanthes occupied himself with a wide range of philosophical topics, including logic as well as psychology.

The third head of the Stoa was Chrysippus (c. 280–208 BCE), who came from Soli, near modern Mersin, in Cilicia (southwestern Anatolia, bordering Syria). Chrysippus was a natural scholar who wrote numerous books (only fragments are extant) by which he improved the Stoic system in all branches of philosophy. Most of what is known as Stoicism comes from him. After his death the Stoa was directed by Diogenes of Seleucia-on-the-Tigris and, later, by Antipater of Tarsus. These Stoic leaders of the first half of the second century BCE left the system set up by Chrysippus unchanged, for they were occupied in rebuking critics from rival schools, such as the Epicureans, the Peripatetics (Aristotle's followers), and especially Carneades of Cyrene, the director of the Academy (Plato's former school).

The two major Stoic figures of the following period, which August Schmekel labeled the Middle Stoa, are Panaetius of Rhodes (c. 185–c. 109 BCE) and Posidonius of Apamea, Syria (c. 135–c. 50 BCE). Both were worldly philosophers who developed friendly ties with high-ranking politicians and intellectuals in Rome. Panaetius was mainly concerned with issues of a moral and social nature; in religious matters he seems to have expressed agnostic views. Posidonius, who was endowed with an encyclopedic mind, wrote books on cosmology, geography, and history, and he restyled the Stoic system. Several tenets of Posidonius's system differed from Chrysippean "orthodoxy." For example, Posidonius accepted the existence of an "irrational" part of the soul, following a rather Platonic psychological view (*Fgm.* 150 to 169, Edelstein-Kidd). Unlike Panaetius, Posidonius also had a genuine interest in theology and religious phenomena.

During the period of Panaetius's and Posidonius's leadership, Stoicism became one of the most followed philosophical trends of late Republican and early Imperial Rome. Representative of Roman Stoicism are Vergil's *Aeneid*, Seneca's moral essays, and the emperor Marcus Aurelius's *Meditations*. All these works exhibit a consistently Stoic inspiration, although it was developed in a personal, nonprofessional way. Little is known about the internal life of the school in later times. The Athenian Stoa apparently ceased to function as a center after the mid-first century BCE, and many anonymous private teachers carried Stoic philosophy throughout the Hellenistic world. Only a few of their names have come down to us, the most famous being Epictetus of Hierapolis (Phrygia; c. 50–130 BCE), whose *Manual* was long admired as an outstanding outline of the Stoic moral attitude.

In 175 CE Marcus Aurelius established—in Athens, the cradle of ancient Greek culture—a school for the study of literature (rhetoric) and the four main philosophical trends, including Stoicism. Thus, Athens became once again the official seat of Stoicism, but no information about the names and activity of the appointed Stoic teachers has survived. This imperial school was ordered closed in 527 by the Christian emperor Justinian, after allegations that it was a haunt for pagan propaganda.

Both Jewish and Christian thinkers, including Philo, Clemens and Origen of Alexandria, Tertullian, and Augustine of Hippo, were well acquainted with Stoic philosophy and appreciated its doctrine of providence and its high ethical standards. But as a whole, Stoicism was rejected because of its alleged materialism, and Platonism seemed, for Christianity, a much better choice. Stoicism is rarely mentioned in the literature of the Middle Ages, although it should have been known through Latin sources. Additionally, it was no longer qualified as a philosophical movement or school. Only in the Renaissance did the ancient Stoa tradition find renewed appreciation. Blaise Pascal's assessment (suggested by Montaigne) of the Stoic as a person who confidently trusts in himself rather than God provoked a negative reaction from the Christian point of view. Stoic elements can be recognized in Barukh Spinoza's *Ethics* and in Immanuel Kant's moral theory.

MAIN DOCTRINES. The chief concern of ancient Stoic philosophy, as with other Hellenistic schools, was to lead human beings to happiness (*eudaimonia*), which for the Stoics consists of moral virtue (*aretē*)—that is, pursuing on every occasion what is *kalon* (good, or, originally, well-done) The wise, well-behaved person (*sophos*) enjoys perfect happiness, for he is always coherent, firm, and internally appeased (*SVF* 3.29–67; 548–588). However, the sage's art of good living (*eu zēn*, *SVF* 3.16) requires a correct understanding of the nature of things and of the place of human beings in the world.

The Stoic approach is essentially a dynamic one. Reality, or nature, is a net of mutual interactions explaining the "growth" (the original meaning of *phusis*), change, and decay of individual things. Every "real" entity must therefore be a body, because only a bodily being can act on other beings and be affected by them. The pure logical formulas are not bodily, as they do not exist anywhere (for instance, an utterance can be logically right, even though its content may never have taken place); they are simply something "one can say" (*lekton*). Yet being "bodily" does not equal being material: in this sense Stoicism is not a materialistic theory like Epicureanism. The Stoics distinguished two aspects in reality as a whole: the active and the passive. The former is a producing principle, the "force" (*dunamis*) or God—or, as Chrysippus and Posidonius put it, the "spirit" (*pneuma*). The second aspect is proper matter (*hulē*); that is, the underlying material for the spirit's activity. Both aspects are intrinsically united: the spirit includes a material component of "fire," "heat," or "ether," while matter is always pervaded and shaped by spirit (*SVF* 2.299 to 313).

As a compound of matter and spirit, the world is represented by the Stoics as an organic, harmonic, and perfect living being (*SVF* 2.633–641), in which each part has a mutual "solidarity" with all others (*sumpatheia*, *SVF* 2.475, 534, 546). The spiritual principle operating inside reality receives, in the Stoic system, various names according to its manifold functions. It is primarily the "reason" (*logos*) through which all things of the world are brought about and linked in the most rational way (*SVF* 1.85, 160, 493, 2.1051). Each phenomenon takes its own place in a serial connection of causes and effects, but the particular causal chains, heterogeneous though they may appear in detail, all hang from one single principle and deploy themselves in conformity with a world plan laid down in the Logos at the beginning; thus the interlacing of all causes displayed by reason represents the all-determining "fate" (*heimarmenē*, *SVF* 2.912–938; cf. Posidonius, *Fgm.* 377, Theiler).

Moreover, insofar as the spirit is identical with God, the Logos is the same as God's mind, and fate equals divine providence (*pronoia*). The Stoics strongly stressed the rationality of the arrangement of the world and the providential disposition of all things, aimed ultimately at the wealth of humankind; a set of Stoic arguments thereon, recycled by Christian authors, provided the bulk of what was called *theodicy* in the seventeenth century (*SVF* 2.1106 to 1186). The existing world is, for the Stoics, neither infinite nor everlasting. The same spirit that produced it once and led its development will absorb it again in its original fire in due time, by means of an all-destroying conflagration (*ekpurōsis*). Soon afterwards, another world will be shaped by it, similar to the preceding one, and so forth cyclically. This is because the spirit's Logos, and hence the resulting fate, cannot change (*SVF* 2.596–632). This theory of "eternal recurrence" is a historical antecedent to Friedrich Nietzsche's ideas.

Rival schools objected that the Stoic doctrine of fate would abolish the human freedom of the will, but the Stoics denied it. As Chrysippus explained (see Cicero, *On Fate* 18–19), fate does not have to be identified with a necessity that compels a person to do something he or she would not otherwise consent to do. Of course the environment lays down certain necessary conditions, but consent (*sunkatathesis*) to action comes from the person's own nature. Fate does not fulfill its plan automatically, but coordinates the freely chosen actions of humans with the circumstances. For instance, it was fated for Oedipus to be born, but that would not have occurred if his parents had not decided to have intercourse. Their actions were spontaneous and, at the same time, "co-destined" (*suneimarmenon*) in order to accomplish fate's end (Cicero, *On Fate* 13, cf. *SVF* 2.940). Augustine's late standpoint admitting compatibility between divine predestination and human free will was heavily influenced by this Stoic concept.

From an ethical point of view, a person's behavior, either right or wrong, depends on the strength of the soul's leading principle (*hegemonikōn*), which is the spark of universal reason. The aim of human existence is to live in accordance with reason or nature (*homologoumenōs*), that is, in a rational way. Evil doings and passions are the consequence of a degenerated rationality, not of an independent irrational faculty (*SVF* 3.456 to 480), an opinion from which Posidonius diverged. Even if fate has programmed everything, the human subject remains responsible for his or her actions and should be either blamed or rewarded by social authorities (in any case, the wicked are always unhappy). The Stoics did not believe in the immortality of the soul, but they allowed souls to survive for a while apart from their bodies, before melting away into the cosmic spirit (*SVF* 2.809 to 822).

RELIGION AND THEOLOGY. The early Hellenistic religious mentality was by no means an otherworldly one; religion was rather a consolidated social institution, and philosophy had to take it into account. The Stoa, and all other schools, recognized this common heritage and recommended that traditional polytheistic cults be preserved, although the philosopher should approach them rationally, not with superstition. Chrysippus in particular was eager to save the supposed "rational" meaning of the ancient myths, giving them an allegorical explanation, in most cases as if they were hinting at natural or astronomical phenomena—a method similar to the one already applied to the interpretation of the Homeric poems (*SVF* 2.1066–1100; see also Cornutus, *Theology*). Moreover, on behalf of the concepts of solidarity, fate, and providence, the Stoics supported the reliability of forecasts of the future both by means of divinatory techniques and through superhuman revelation in dreams and visions (*SVF* 2.1187–1216). According to Posidonius (*Fgm.* 106, Edelstein-Kidd), the godhead does not simply intervene occasionally when a forecast is sought—for instance, shaping instantly the liver of every single victim in order that it may signify something—but the cosmic *sumpatheia* and the order of fate arrange things from the beginning in such a way that a determinate liver with its natural appearance will also be a sign related to a determinate incoming event.

Theology (in the Greek sense of "talking about the gods"; see Plato, *Republic* 379a) belongs to the part of the Stoic system named "physics" (the other two parts being "logic" and "ethics"), that is, to the doctrine of reality (*phusis*). The supreme God, namely Zeus, is said in religious speech to be the all-pervading and life-giving spirit of nature. Chrysippus etymologized quite falsely the two available accusatives of the God's name, *Día* and *Zēna*, respectively, from the Greek preposition *diā* (throughout) and the verb *zēn* (to live) (*SVF* 2.1069). Zeus alone represents the ruling reason, which continues shaping the cyclically recurrent worlds. He is, in a sense, a unique eternal being. All other gods are perishable beings because they exist merely in the framework of a single world and will be wiped out, as will everything else, by the final conflagration (*SVF*, 2.1049, 1055). Of course they will reappear, exactly the same, in the subsequent cosmic cycle. These gods were thought of as earthly elements and forces, or even as stars and planets (*SVF* 1.510, 2.613, 1009, 1076).

Stoic theology is a puzzling philosophical construction, as its contemporaries pointed out (see the discussion in Cicero, *On Gods*). Since spirit and matter are but two aspects of the same reality, the godhead can also be considered a simultaneously spiritual and material being. God is both soul and body of the universe—reason, mind, and fate, and also the natural substance with all its parts, phenomena, and functions (*SVF* 2.1041, 1077, cf. Diogenes Laertius, 7.147). It is not surprising that Posidonius (*Fgm.* 369, Theiler) claimed the contemplation of heavenly bodies to be the true religious act, which uncultivated people had distorted in the worship of images. Some Stoic philosophers, however, demonstrate a less abstract idea of God and a more devotional attitude. Cleanthes, for example, spoke of Zeus as a personal ruler of the universe, whose fatal law everyone had to follow willingly; Seneca's writings exhibit a deep religious feeling, which led early Christians to imagine a friendship between him and the apostle Paul.

ALLEGED SEMITIC ROOTS. Max Pohlenz (1959) raised the question of whether Stoicism may have undergone a Semitic influence due to the Eastern origin of most of its leaders. This assumption is groundless. In the globalized Hellenistic world, the Middle East did not mean what it does in today's geopolitical context, and local provenance made little, if any, difference. The only "Semite" in the history of the Stoa was Zenon, who belonged to the Phoenician Aramaic-speaking minority of the island of Cyprus; other Stoics came from Greek colonies or from highly Hellenized areas of Asia Minor, such as Cilicia. Diogenes and Posidonius were indeed Syrian, but their native cities had been founded by Seleucid kings and populated with Macedonian military settlers. In any case, all philosophers of this age, even if they were born near Palestine (e.g., Antiochus of Ascalone, Philodemus of Gadara), had an entirely Greek education and way of life.

It is even less likely that a "Semitic" background can be understood as a source of "Jewish" influence. The Stoic "spirit" has nothing to do with biblical *ruah*, being rooted in the concept of warm breath as theorized by Greek medical science. Cleanthes' "Law of Zeus" is no philosophical Torah, because Stoic morality was not grounded in specific precepts or forbiddances. It is plausible that no Stoic teacher ever held a Bible in his hands. Posidonius, for instance, is assumed to have had somewhat anti-Jewish feelings (*Fgm.* 278, Edelstein-Kidd; 133, Theiler). One could more reasonably argue that some features of ancient Stoicism suggest Indian philosophy—the immanence of God in the universe, the conflagration, the imperturbability of the sage—but there is a lack of evidence to elaborate the issue.

SEE ALSO Cosmology; Hellenistic Religions; Logos; Monotheism; Study of Religion; Suicide; Tertullian; Zeus.

BIBLIOGRAPHY

Primary Sources

Alesse, Francesca, ed. and trans. *Panezio di Rodi e la tradizione stoica.* Naples, 1994.

Arnim, Hans Friedrich August von. *Stoicorum veterum fragmenta* (*SVF*). Reprint of 1905 edition. Stuttgart, 1978.

Cornutus, Lucius Annaeus. *Theologiae graecae compendium.* Edited by Carl Lang. Leipzig, 1881. Translated into Italian and edited by Ilaria Ramelli (Milan, 2003).

Epictetus. *Handbook of Epictetus.* Translated by Nicholas White. Indianapolis, 1983.

Epictetus. *Discourses, Book I.* Translated by Robert F. Dobbin. Oxford, 1998.

Long, A. A., and David Sedley. *The Hellenistic Philosophers.* 2 vols. Cambridge, U.K., 1987. An anthology of Stoic texts, with translations, philosophical commentary, and a full bibliography.

Marcus Aurelius. *Meditations.* Translated by Gregory Hays. New York, 2002.

Panaetius. *Panaetii Rhodii fragmenta.* Edited by Modestus van Straaten. Rev. ed. Leiden, 1962.

Posidonius. *The Fragments.* Edited by Ludwig Edelstein and Ian G. Kidd. Cambridge, U.K., 1972. Reprinted with a commentary in three volumes by Ian G. Kidd. Cambridge, U.K., 1999.

Posidonius. *Die Fragmente.* 2 vols. Edited with commentary by Willy Theiler. Berlin and New York, 1982.

Seneca. *Moral Epistles.* Edited and translated by Anna Lydia Motto. Chico, Calif., 1985.

Seneca. *Moral and Political Essays.* Edited and translated by John M. Cooper and J. F. Procopé. New York and Cambridge, U.K., 1995.

Seneca. *Dialogues and Letters.* Edited and translated by C. D. N. Costa. New York, 1997.

General Literature

Bréhier, Emile. *Chrysippe et l'ancien stoïcisme* (1910). Paris, 1951.

Colish, Marcia L. *The Stoic Tradition from the Antiquity to the Early Middle Ages.* 2 vols. Leiden, 1985.

Duhut, Jean-Joël. *Epictète et la sagesse stoïcienne.* Paris, 1996.

Gould, Josiah B. *The Philosophy of Chrysippus.* New York, 1970.

Hadot, Pierre. *The Inner Citadel: The Meditations of Marcus Aurelius.* Cambridge, Mass., 1998.

Laffranque, Marie. *Posidonius d'Apamée.* Paris, 1964.

Long, A. A. *Problems in Stoicism.* London, 1971.

Long, A. A. *Stoic Studies.* New York, 1996.

Pohlenz, Max. *Die Stoa: Geschichte einer geistigen Bewegung* (1959). 4th ed. Göttingen, Germany, 1970.

Rist, John M. *Stoic Philosophy.* London, 1969.

Rist, John M., ed. *The Stoics.* Berkeley, 1978. Includes many important essays on different topics.

Sandbach, F. H. *The Stoics.* 2d ed. London, 1989.

Schmekel, August. *Philosophie der mittleren Stoa.* Berlin, 1892.

Sharples, Robert W. *Stoics, Epicureans, and Sceptics: An Introduction to Hellenistic Philosophy.* London, 1996.

Veyne, Paul. *Seneca: The Life of a Stoic.* Translated by David Sullivan. New York, 2003.

Logic

Bobzien, Suzanne. *Die stoische Modallogik.* Würzburg, Germany, 1986.

Frede, Michael. *Die stoische Logik.* Göttingen, Germany, 1974.

Mates, Benson. *Stoic Logic.* Berkeley, 1961.

Mignucci, Mario. *Il significato della logica stoica.* Bologna, Italy, 1965.

Physics

Goldschmidt, Victor. *Le système stoïcien et l'idée du temps.* Paris, 1977.

Sambursky, Samuel. *Physics of the Stoics.* New York, 1959.

Determinism and Theodicy

Bobzien, Suzanne. *Determinism and Freedom in Stoic Philosophy.* Oxford, 1988.

Dalfen, Johannes. "Das Gebet des Kleanthes an Zeus und das Schicksal." *Hermes* 99 (1971): 173–184.

Duhut, Jean-Joël. *La conception stoïcienne de la causalité.* Paris, 1989.

Magris, Aldo. *L'idea di destino nel pensiero antico.* 2 vols. Udine, Italy, 1984–1985. See pages 514–607.

Theiler, Willy. "Tacitus und die antike Schicksalslehre." In *Forschungen zum Neuplatonismus,* pp. 46–103. Berlin, 1966.

Ethics

Campbell, Keith. *A Stoic Philosophy of Life.* Lanham, Md., 1986.

Erskine, Andrew. *The Hellenistic Stoa: Political Thought and Action.* London, 1990.

Nussbaum, Martha Craven. *The Therapy of Desire: Theory and Practice in Hellenistic Ethics.* Princeton, 1994.

Radice, Roberto. *Oikeiosis: Ricerche sul fondamento del pensiero stoico e sulla sua genesi.* Milan, Italy, 2000.

Reesor, Margaret. *The Nature of Man in Early Stoic Philosophy.* London, 1989.

Religion

Dragona Monachou, Myrto. *Stoic Arguments for the Existence and the Providence of the Gods.* Athens, 1976.

Drozdek, Adam. "Theology of the Early Stoa." *Emerita* 52 (2003): 73–93.

Frede, Dorothea, and André Laks, eds. *Traditions of Theology: Studies in Hellenistic Theology, Its Background and Aftermath.* Leiden, 2002.

Hoven, René. *Stoïcisme et stoïciens face au problème de l'au-delà.* Paris, 1971.

Stoicism and Early Christianity
Spanneut, Michel. *Le stoïcisme des Pères de l'eglise: De Clément de Rome à Clément d'Alexandrie.* Paris, 1957.

Stoicism and Gnosticism
Onuki, Takashi. *Gnosis und Stoa: Eine Untersuchung zum Apokryphon des Johannes.* Göttingen, Germany, 1989.

ALDO MAGRIS (2005)

STONES. Sacred stones have been known from the earliest times, and they occur all over the world in different cultures and religions. Often they are used as objects of sacrifice, elements in various magical rites, or instruments of divination. They may also serve practical purposes as witness or boundary stones, or as memorials; in such cases they may also evoke religious veneration. The unseen powers that are represented by such monuments are of as many different kinds as the reasons why people turn to them.

The general term *stone* includes many different objects, some of them characterized by names of Celtic origin: menhirs (tall, upright monumental stones); cromlechs (circles of standing stones); dolmens (table stones or large, flat, unhewn stones resting horizontally on upright ones); and cairns (heaps of stones). These four types as well as other monuments shaped like pillars or columns are all raised up or built by humankind (see Eliade, 1978, secs. 34ff.). But natural rocks that, in whole or in part, have peculiar or startling shapes or otherwise contrast with a flat or desolate landscape may also be venerated as sacred. Smaller, movable stones can serve as cult objects at home or can be carried as magical protection.

The symbolic meaning of sacred stones is not fixed. They may represent qualities such as firmness or barrenness but they also may represent fertility. Interpretation is made difficult by the fact that many sacred stones come to us from religions and cultures for which there is little or no literary evidence. Under such circumstances, it is understandable that historians of religion have applied many different theories to such ancient religions, speaking of ancestor cults, nature worship, fetishism, noniconic (nonfigurative) cults, animism, and dynamism. If written sources are lacking (as in the case of prehistoric times) or few (as generally occurs with ancient historic cultures), the field is open for sheer speculation. Oral traditions recorded from illiterate peoples who are still living—or who lived into comparatively recent times—contain much detailed and valuable information that may throw light on older times. Treating primitive material in this way means, however, that one adopts the much-criticized survival theory, although this theory seems to be more applicable in the case of sacred stones than in other cases. Altogether, the immensity and variety of the material illustrates well the difficulties of a phenomenological method (see Eliade, 1958, secs. 74ff.; Heiler, 1961, pp. 34ff.). In the following discussion, I shall restrict myself to observations on sacred stones from various cultures for which there is at least some literary evidence to guide the interpretation.

ANCIENT WESTERN TRADITIONS. Stones or stone pillars (Heb., *matstsevah,* from the Semitic *ntsb,* "to stand") figure prominently in the biblical story of the patriarch Jacob. When his wife Rachel died, Jacob erected a funerary stele on her grave (*Gn.* 35:20), probably as a memorial to keep her name alive. Such a pillar could also commemorate an important event, such as the pact between Jacob and the Arameans (*Gn.* 31:43ff.). However, the cultic use of stones was most common. During Jacob's flight from the wrath of Esau, God appeared to him in a dream, and he was struck with awe. Jacob took the stone that had served him as a pillow, raised it as a pillar, anointed it with oil, and called it *beit-El* (Bethel), the "house of God" (*Gn.* 28:16ff., 35:14). In this case, the stone appears to have signified the presence of God.

Such cultic pillars could be connected with altars as in *Exodus* 24:4. Such use was proscribed by the Deuteronomic Code (see, for example, *Dt.* 16:22) as a consequence of the polemics against the corresponding Canaanite cult that was condemned as the worship of pagan gods. Indeed, archaeologists have frequently overinterpreted large, upright stones from the early Palestinian excavations as cult pillars from ancient Canaan. More critical study has unveiled them as, for example, ruins of mortuary shrines or remnants of Iron Age house structures. Actual pillars were discovered at Beit She'an and the ancient city of Megiddo in Israel, and at Jubayl, the ancient Byblos, in Lebanon; their meaning, however, is still not quite clear. The earliest pillar of this kind was discovered in 1933 at ancient Mari, a site on the Middle Euphrates, now in Syria (Tell Hariri). It dates from the Old Akkadian period, circa 2300 BCE (Kennedy and Wevers, 1963).

Light may be thrown on the cult of sacred stones in the ancient Near East by the later, rich material from pre-Islamic Arabia collected by the authority on Arab paganism Ibn al-Kalbī (737–829?). Sacrificial stones are alluded to in the Qur'ān (70:43), and they are explicitly forbidden by Muḥammad (5:490–492). Observations by ancient Greek authors confirm the existence of sacred stones among the Arabs from much earlier times (Buhl, 1936; see also Clement of Alexandria, *Proprepticus* 4, 46). The rites that take place around the Ka'bah in Mecca represent a legitimated survival of the ancient worship of *'anṣāb* (stones). As elsewhere, such worship originally existed together with the veneration of trees, wooden trunks, and posts, or has been interchangeable with such veneration (Höfner, in Gese et al., 1970, pp. 359ff.).

It is uncertain whether the ancient Greek *baituloi* ("animated stones," i.e., meteorites) can be compared to the Aramaic-Hebrew *beit-El* (Fauth, 1964). But the Greek author Theophrastus (fourth century BCE) characterizes the superstitious person as one who dares not pass the already oily stones at the crossroads without prostrating himself and pouring oil on them (*Characters* 16). These quadrilateral pillars, sometimes ending in a head and surrounded by a heap of stones (Gr., *hermaios lophos*) were called "herms." This name is identical to that of the god Hermes, which etymologically means "stone." He is the stone as god or the god in stone. The various specialties of Hermes may derive from his role as god of the crossroads. As such, he is the guide of those traveling on the road and therefore a protector of commerce and illegal business. He is a messenger too, and as a guide he develops into a psychopomp who accompanies the souls of the dead to the underworld. In his connection with border stones, Hermes becomes a god of the land and thresholds and finally a patron of the entire community. The ithyphallic form of the erected stone (also observed in the Hindu *liṅgas*) represents both the fertility and apotropaic powers of the god, which in turn make him a patron of the shepherds (Herter, 1976).

There were other gods of the ancient Greek pantheon who could also be represented by either uncut or sculptured stones. To the latter belong the common sacred column, tapered to a point and called Apollo Aiguieus ("of the road"), commonly found set up in the street in front of a house door. They were anointed with oil, decorated with ribbons, and identified as altars. In the old gymnasium of Megara, the capital of the province Megaris to the west of Attica, was a small pyramidal stone that bore the name of Apollo. But the best-known sacred stone of ancient Greece was the conical stone of Apollo, the *omphalos* ("navel"), at Delphi. The poet Pindar (522–438 BCE) explains its sanctity with the belief that the sanctuary of Delphi is situated at the exact center of the earth. This interpretation might be secondary, however; the discussion of this Greek material reminds us of the difficulties of distinguishing earlier from later phases in historical development (cf. Hartland et al., 1920, p. 870, and Eliade, 1958, secs. 81f.).

MADAGASCAR. On Madagascar there exists a richly developed stone cult. The traditions explaining why these monuments were raised and the rites and practices associated with them have continued to exist right down to the present time. They present a great richness of variations, a fact that constitutes a warning against simplified reconstructions when, in other places, only archaeological memorials survive.

According to the report of a Norwegian missionary, the most common practice involving these stones takes place in the context of an ancestor cult. A man who is prominent and rich calls together his extended family before he dies and decrees as follows: "My body shall certainly die and be buried, but my spirit shall always remain with you, my children. When you are eating, set out a little food in that place where I usually eat. And what I wish for you to offer up as a sacrifice to me is the following: [At this point, he names whatever he is fondest of, such as rice, meat, liquor, eel, different kinds of fish, or honey.] And should anyone fall sick or lack for anything or suffer bad luck, then call upon us, and we shall help you. We shall protect you, sending riches, good harvests and many children." The old man lists the taboos to be observed and states where the stone or altar shall be raised and its size, which corresponds to his own importance. He himself will live in the memorial monument and accept the sacrifices. The choice of this stone, its difficult transport, and its establishment on a raised spot near the village are accompanied by many rites before the ceremonial dedication is accomplished (Ruud, 1947, pp. 117ff.). A French researcher, Charles Renel, has carefully recorded the occurrence, within the separate geographical tribal territories, of stones associated with bequests, graves, memorials, and sacrifice and the different, indigenous names that correspond to their changing appearance and varying functions. As gravestones, they are usually raised to the east on the location of the corpse's head, which is also called the grave's head. The stones are smeared with fat, flour, and the blood of sacrificed animals, and at the foot of the stone sacrificial gifts are deposited.

The older stones are generally uncut; the sculptured stones belong to more recent times. Both are called, among other things, "stone-upright" or "stone-man." Wooden scaffolding, occasionally freestanding, may sometimes have been built over them, and on these the skulls of animal sacrifices are placed. The height of the stone can vary with the social level of the deceased and sometimes directly corresponds to his physical stature; thus, the stone also acquires the character of a more or less nonfigurative statue or memorial. In this case, it may also be set up independently of the burial site. When the deceased has died in a foreign country or for other reasons has not been able to be buried, the importance of the local stone as a memorial becomes even more marked. Nevertheless, it can still be used religiously; one goes to it to make a vow, to leave a sacrificial gift, or to carry out a bloody sacrifice.

In some parts of Madagascar, wooden poles are used in place of stones and are called "intermediaries" or "transference vessels" of the spirits of the dead. A heap of stones of varying size can also be substituted for the single stone, often at the request of the deceased himself. Sometimes, passersby throw a new stone on the heap with a prayer to the unknown spirit for a fortunate journey or for protection against unknown powers reigning over the road. But most often it is relatives or fellow tribesmen who carry out this ritual piling of stones in connection with a sacrificial vow. The worship at stone heaps that are associated with particular persons is believed to promote success in love or fertility. Thus, votive gifts can consist of wooden carvings representing the male or female sexual organs, depending on the sex of the supplicant.

Other holy stones have functioned as coronation stones, for example, Stone-Holy and Stone of the Red Head in Antananarivo (formerly Tananarive). During his coronation, the king placed himself on each stone in turn to signify that his sovereignty extended over both halves of the kingdom. At the same time, the stones were associated with his ancestors, so that in touching them he assumed the strength and holiness of his forefathers. This hereditary ceremony was carried out as late as 1883 by Queen Ravanalona III, despite her conversion to Christianity.

However, not all Malagasy menhirs are connected with the dead, ancestors, or spirits. Some of them commemorate special events, certify a treaty, or mark a boundary. Such monuments are called "stones-planted." But these, too, have been dedicated with religious rituals; for example, a stone was raised in 1797 to the memory of a royal wedding that united two tribes. The king called on the Holiness of his ancestors, the Holiness of the twelve mountains, and the Holiness of heaven and earth. Then a deep pit was dug, into which the king threw a silver coin and red coral beads. After the stone had been raised, they killed a black ox with a white face and also an unruly bull. The king took their blood, smeared his forehead, neck, and tip of his tongue, and then poured the rest over the base of the stone. Meanwhile he spoke to the two tribes and commanded them to be one, just as he and his queen were one, to endure as long as the stone lasted.

Other menhirs can symbolize the royal power present and prevailing among the people. In other cases, cults center around natural cliffs of peculiar appearance that are connected with divination. For example, women come to pray for children at the "stone with Many Breasts." They smear the "breasts" of the cliff with fat, then touch their own, and throw a stone toward the protuberances of the cliff. Should it strike a large protuberance, it is said that the child will be a girl; if a small one, it will be a boy. Should the devotee come to the cliff with a health problem, a votive vow is made that is to be discharged after one has regained one's health. Hunters pray for success in the hunt to the spirit dwelling in another holy cliff said to protect wild game. Each hunter in turn whistles as he walks around the cliff; if they are all able to hold the note, it is a good omen for the presence of quarry. On their return, they sacrifice the finest wild ox as a thanks offering, burning its fat and its liver at the foot of the cliff. The meat is eaten on the spot by the hunters and their families (Renel, 1923, pp. 94–111).

THE SAMI. The holy places of the pre-Christian Sami (Lapps) in northern Scandinavia and on the Kola Peninsula have been thoroughly investigated. Five hundred and seven of them are registered in Swedish Lapland (Manker, 1957), 229 in Norway, 80 to 90 in Finland, and about 10 in Russia west of the White Sea. If restricted to the material from Sweden, the cultic sites are of various kinds: 149 hills and mountains; 108 steep cliffs, caves, springs, waterfalls, rapids, and lakes; 30 islands, skerries, peninsulas, meadows, and heaths. But the largest number consists of venerated stones or cliffs, of which there are 220. In this group, 102 examples are understood to be naturally occurring, uncut images of a deity; in only two cases are there indisputable traces of human intervention. In general, the majority are massive stones. These cult objects are called *seites*, a term of disputed meaning and origin that occurs in different dialectal forms.

Literary sources from the sixteenth century on, combined with anthropological records from the nineteenth century, provide a rich commentary on the *seite* cult, which, in some cases, has been directed toward wooden trunks, stumps, or sculptures in addition to the stone *seite.* A detailed Swedish account from 1671 describes the ritual slaughter of a reindeer behind a tent. Afterward the *seite* is approached by the Sami, who takes off his cap, bows deeply, and smears the *seite* with blood and fat from the animal. The prime cervical vertebrae, the skull, and the hoofs are offered to the deity, as are the horns, which are piled up behind the stone. In one such "horn yard" thousands of horns may be seen. The meat of the animal is eaten by the participants in the sacrifice. Then the drum tells them what kind of game they will capture and assures them of good luck with their reindeer (Manker, 1957, p. 306; cf. Holmberg, 1964, p. 109).

The god of the *seite* can also appear in human shape to his worshiper. Another seventeenth-century account tells how such a god showed himself as a tall, well-built man dressed in black like a gentleman, with a gun in his hand. A similar vision is transmitted from eighteenth-century Norway: "Then a being in human form, like a great ruler, extremely good to look at, dressed in expensive garments and trinkets, appears and sits down to take part in their meal, speaks with them and teaches them new arts, and says that he lives in the stone or mountain to which they sacrifice" (Holmberg, 1964, p. 105).

Omens are taken in connection with the sacrifice, not only with the help of the drum. From the 1670s in Finland, there is a story of a movable little stone god called Seite or Råå ("owner"). Holding this god in his hand, the Sami utters his prayers with great veneration and lists his requirements. If he then cannot lift his hand it is a bad omen, but he repeats his wishes again and again until the stone in his hand becomes so light that his hand leaps upward. When the Sami has received what he wishes, he asks the god what kind of thanks offering he wants, using the same method to get an answer (Manker, 1957, p. 314).

When compared with the stone worship of Madagascar, the Sami cult lacks a clear connection with ancestors, concerning itself instead with the "owners" of the land and the lord of animals. On the African island, the sacred stone monuments are generally erected or constructed by human hands; but in Lapland, the veneration of natural boulders, often left from the glacial epoch, predominates. The belief is common here as elsewhere that the pillars or rocks are inhabited by unseen powers, or, in Mircea Eliade's words: "The devotion of the primitive was in every case fastened on something beyond itself which the stone incorporated and expressed" (1958, sec. 74).

American Indians. Sacred rocks and stones together with their spirits are highly venerated by the Indians of both North and South America. One volcano in Ecuador has even received human sacrifices by the Puruhá. The Dakota have decorated and painted great boulders, praying to them and sacrificing dogs upon them. The Crow keep small, animal-shaped stones as powerful medicine. The Algonquin around Lake Mistassini in Canada dare not cross the waters before having sacrificed to the spirit who inhabits a massive, anomalous block. Southward, in the United States, higher, personalized gods are also believed to dwell in stones. The Kiowa in Texas possess a little stone god to whom they pray during the Sun Dance. The Tao in New Mexico venerate at the foot of a sacred mountain the "stone men" who represent two war gods. The Pueblo Indians believe that the hunter's good luck depends on his possession of stones of a curious shape.

The statuettes of the West Indian Taino consist of slightly sculptured stones that are venerated in caves. Among the South American Indians of the Andes, stone worship is very common, but stone gods are found also in the tropical region to the east. The mother goddess of the Jivaroan people in northern Peru and the supreme being of the Warao of the delta of the Orinoco are both represented by stones (Hultkrantz, 1979, pp. 60ff.).

This little catalog needs a supplementary description of the modes of worship, but it can nevertheless be compared (at least in part) with the corresponding examples from the Saami. The ecological environment of North America and Lapland is the same, both with regard to natural objects of veneration and with regard to the motives for worship, primarily to ensure good hunting and fishing.

See Also Altar; Amulets and Talismans; Crossroads; Megalithic Religion, articles on Historical Cultures and Prehistoric Evidence; Phallus and Vagina.

Bibliography

Buhl, Frants. "Nusb." In *The Encyclopaedia of Islam,* vol. 3, p. 967. Leiden, 1936.

Eliade, Mircea. *Patterns in Comparative Religion.* New York, 1958.

Eliade, Mircea. *A History of Religious Ideas,* vol. 1, *From the Stone Age to the Eleusinian Mysteries.* Chicago, 1978.

Fauth, Wolfgang. "Baitylia." In *Der kleine Pauly: Lexikon der Antike,* vol. l. Stuttgart, 1964. A very compressed, well-documented survey.

Gese, Hartmut, Maria Höfner, and Kurt Rudolph. *Die Religionen Altsyriens, Altarabiens und der Mandäer.* Die Religionen der Menschheit, vol. 10.2. Stuttgart, 1970.

Hartland, E. Sidney, et al. "Stones." In *Encyclopaedia of Religion and Ethics,* edited by James Hastings, vol. 11. Edinburgh, 1920. A group of articles covering primitive, Greek and Roman, Indian, and Semitic traditions by Hartland, Percy Gardner, William Crooke, and George A. Barton, respectively. See also R. A. W. Macalister's "Stone Monuments," in volume 11, and D. Miller Kay's "Maṣṣēbnāh," in volume 8 (1915). These articles include valuable material despite their sometimes outdated theories.

Heiler, Friedrich. *Erscheinungsformen und Wesen der Religion.* Die Religionen der Menschheit, vol. 1. Stuttgart, 1961. A rather short but good cross-cultural survey of the subject. Subsequent volumes of this voluminous series contain reliable information on stone worship: for example, volumes 5.1 (Indonesia), 5.2 (South Pacific and Australia), 7 (Old America), 18 (Celts), 20 (Tibet and Mongolia), 22.1 (Korea), 23 (Southeast Asia), and 26 (ancient Israel).

Herter, Hans. "Hermes." *Rheinisches Museum für Philologie* (Frankfurt) 119 (1976): 193–241.

Holmberg, Uno. *The Mythology of All Races,* vol. 4, *Finno-Ugric, Siberian* (1927). Reprint, New York, 1964. A classic study by a field-worker and cautious historian who is largely free from now-abandoned theories.

Hultkrantz, Åke. *The Religions of the American Indians.* Translated by Monica Setterwall. Los Angeles, 1979. A restricted phenomenological approach by a specialist. Hultkrantz has deposited a comprehensive unpublished manuscript on stone worship among the Saami (Lapps) in the Nordic Museum, Stockholm.

Kennedy, A. R. S., and John W. Wevers. "Pillar." In *Dictionary of the Bible,* 2d ed., revised by Frederick C. Grant and H. H. Rowley, pp. 772–773. Edinburgh, 1963. An instructive comparison can be made with the article in the first edition, edited by James Hastings (Edinburgh, 1909).

Manker, Ernst. *Lapparnas heliga ställen.* Stockholm, 1957. A standard work; includes an English summary, "The Holy Places of the Lapps."

Renel, Charles. "Ancêtres et dieux." *Bulletin de l'Academie Malgache* (Tananarive), n.s. 5 (1923): 1–263.

Ruud, Jørgen. *Guder og fedre: Religionshistoriskt stoff fra Madagaskar.* Oslo, 1947.

Carl-Martin Edsman (1987)
Translated from Swedish by David Mel Paul and Margareta Paul

STORM GODS

See METEOROLOGICAL BEINGS

STRAUSS, DAVID FRIEDRICH

STRAUSS, DAVID FRIEDRICH (1808–1874), German biblical critic, man of letters, and freethinker. Strauss is best known for his monumental book *The Life of Jesus* (1835). In some fifteen hundred pages, half of which are devoted to an analysis of the miracle and the death-resurrection stories in the New Testament, he argued that neither a supernaturalistic nor a rationalistic interpretation of them is credible. Rather, these narratives should be regarded as the results of a naive, primitive mentality whose natural form of expression is myth. Under the flush of religious enthusiasm, messianic fervor, and the personal influence of Jesus, the early Christians applied specifically messianic myths and legends to Jesus. In short, the "logic" of the New Testament narratives is this: "When the expected messiah comes, he will do all these miraculous things; Jesus is the messiah; therefore, Jesus must have done these things." In a concluding section of the book, Strauss explored the implications of his historical-critical work for Christian theology. He argued that it is contradictory and untenable to attribute divine predicates to a single person, Jesus, but not to the entire species, humanity. It is humanity as a whole in which the infinite incarnates itself.

The book was an immediate sensation and provoked a century-long "quest for the historical Jesus" involving much controversy over the New Testament sources and the historical inferences legitimately to be drawn from them. It is often regarded as a watershed in the development of New Testament criticism, as well as the earliest significant statement of the importance of the eschatological element in the preaching of Jesus. Even though Strauss made concessions to his critics in two later editions of the book, he bitterly withdrew these in the final, fourth edition after being denied a professorship. For a brief period in the late 1830s, he identified himself with the Young Hegelians by contributing to Arnold Ruge's journal *Hallische Jahrbücher,* but he soon became disillusioned with their political radicalism.

Even though theologically radical, Strauss was always politically conservative and unhappy with the revolutionary tendencies in German society that erupted in 1848. "A nature such as mine was happier under the old police state," he once wrote. He briefly engaged in political affairs as a member of the Württemberg Landtag but resigned after a parliamentary dispute. He wrote several biographies of well-known historical figures, and in 1864 published a more popular *Life of Jesus for the German People,* which he expected would bring him acclaim but did not. He became increasingly more nationalistic and a supporter of German unification under Bismarck.

In his last book, *The Old Faith and the New* (1873), Strauss set forward his own worldview, which he believed to be representative of his time. He argued that an educated person can no longer be Christian but can be religious in the sense of having a piety toward the cosmos. He proposed a humanistic ethic compounded with his own conservative social views. The book was attacked by Christians but even more savagely by the young Nietzsche, who thought it to be the epitome of German cultural philistinism.

BIBLIOGRAPHY

The standard German collection of Strauss's works is *Gesammelte Schriften,* 12 vols., edited by Eduard Zeller (Bonn, 1876–1878). Only three of Strauss's books are readily available in English. A new edition of George Eliot's famous translation of the fourth German edition of *The Life of Jesus Critically Examined,* edited, with critical notes and an introduction, by Peter C. Hodgson (Philadelphia, 1972), discusses and compares the various editions of the work. *In Defense of My "Life of Jesus" against the Hegelians* (Hamden, Conn., 1983) is a translation, with a very useful introduction, by Marilyn C. Massey of several of Strauss's polemical writings defending his famous work. The third is *The Christ of Faith and the Jesus of History: A Critique of Schleiermacher's The Life of Jesus,* translated and edited, with an introduction, by Leander E. Keck (Philadelphia, 1977). *A New Life of Jesus,* 2 vols., was translated anonymously in 1865 (London), and *The Old Faith and the New,* translated by Mathilde Blind, appeared in 1874 (New York); both these works have long been out of print. The most extensive and eloquent discussion of the significance of Strauss's *Life of Jesus* for nineteenth-century theology and biblical criticism is found in Albert Schweitzer's famous work *The Quest of the Historical Jesus: A Critical Study of Its Progress from Reimarus to Wrede,* translated by William Montgomery, 2d ed. (London, 1911). A useful short discussion of Strauss's significance for the Young Hegelians appears in William J. Brazill's *The Young Hegelians* (New Haven, 1970). The best biography of Strauss in English is by Horten Harris, *David Friedrich Strauss and His Theology* (Cambridge, 1973).

VAN A. HARVEY (1987 AND 2005)

STRUCTURALISM [FIRST EDITION].

In their widely read anthology of this topic, Richard T. De George and Fernande M. De George (1972) note that "bibliographies on structuralism can be virtually endless if one succumbs to the temptation to include everything related to the topic," but they claim that the following authors "are almost certain to be included in any list of structuralists" (p. vii): Karl Marx, Sigmund Freud, Ferdinand de Saussure, Roman Jakobson, Claude Lévi-Strauss, Roland Barthes, Louis Althusser, Michel Foucault, and Jacques Lacan. This may be so, but the term *structuralism* was not used before 1950, and each of the last three individuals named has repudiated the label. Moreover, the list need not begin with Marx; my own favorite protostructuralist is Giambattista Vico (1668–1744). My problem, therefore, is to indicate the core of the structuralist position within a very wide range of variation. The De Georges' formula can serve as a starting point: "An enterprise which unites Marx, Freud, Saussure and modern structuralists [is] . . . the attempt to uncover deep structures, unconscious motivations, and underlying causes which account for human action at a more basic and profound level than do individual conscious decisions" (p. xii).

HISTORY OF THE TERM. The word *structure* has a much longer academic history than does *structuralism.* The symposium papers edited by Roger Bastide (1972) explore the use of *structure* in linguistics, ethnology, art history, economics, politics, law, psychology, psychoanalysis, social psychology, sociology, and history throughout the present century. But that was not the beginning. The ambitious prospectus for Herbert Spencer's system of philosophy which dates from 1858 refers to "The Inductions of Sociology—General facts, structural and functional, as gathered from a survey of Societies and their changes" (Rumney, 1934, p. 300). What Spencer had in mind was that human societies are naturally existing whole units which can be directly observed out there in the real world. The sum of the individual members of such a society is not just an aggregate crowd but a self-sustaining totality, analogous to a biological organism, in which individuals are linked together in a network of person-to-person relationships. In the positivist tradition, Spencer assumed that there are discoverable general laws which apply to all such social organisms.

"Structural Functionalism." Structuralism of the sort associated with the name of Lévi-Strauss, which is central for the present discussion, developed within the general field of sociocultural anthropology in dialectical opposition to the "structural functionalism" postulated by Spencer, which in the early 1950s had become especially associated with the name of A. R. Radcliffe-Brown. At this period British social anthropologists used the expression *structural analysis* (and sometimes the term *structuralism* itself) to refer to the work of Radcliffe-Brown and his close associates rather than to that of Lévi-Strauss. Although this usage was dropped after 1960, the contrast is illuminating.

In Radcliffe-Brown's vocabulary *social structure* denoted a set of key, enduring relationships, perpetuated from generation to generation, which express the bonds of jural obligation that link together the individual members of a particular society. He maintained that these relationships are empirical phenomena which can be directly observed in the mutual interactions of individual members of the system. Social structure, in this sense, was considered to typify the morphology of the society in question, much as the bony structure of a vertebrate animal provides the principal basis for fitting a particular species into the Linnaean taxonomy of all species. Indeed, Radcliffe-Brown believed that a taxonomy of all human societies could be constructed from a comparison of their social structures, societies with similar social structures being placed in the same taxonomic class.

Lévi-Strauss's formulation. Claude Lévi-Strauss's radically different view of social structure was first formulated in 1945, but the nature of that difference was not immediately apparent. His 1953 conference paper entitled "Social Structure" was an attack on Radcliffe-Brown's position, but the printed discussion (Tax, 1953, pp. 108–118) suggests that none of the American and British anthropologists who heard it understood what was at issue. This is not surprising, since parts of the argument are notably obscure and oracular.

This has remained a characteristic, and perhaps essential, feature of Lévi-Strauss's numerous pronouncements about the nature of structuralism. There are many possible interpretations of his thesis, so that even his closest disciples are often at loggerheads with one another.

Perhaps the key point is that, whereas Radcliffe-Brown's social structure was "out there" in the world, supposedly accessible to direct observation, Lévi-Strauss's social structure was, as he put it, "a model in the human mind." The general idea was borrowed from Roman Jakobson's theory of distinctive features (Lévi-Strauss, 1945).

According to Jakobson, our human capacity to encode and decode sound patterns into meaningful speech forms depends on a capacity (which is innate in all human beings) to discriminate sounds as bundles of binary oppositions. For example, in English we discriminate the phoneme /p/ in *pin* from the phoneme /b/ in *bin* because, in the matrix of distinctive features representing these sounds, /p/ is unvoiced and /b/ is voiced, as shown in table 1.

Altogether there are about thirty such distinctive features, though any particular language makes use of only about half that number. The details need not concern us, though it is important to note that the speakers and auditors who encode and decode sound patterns in this way are quite unconscious of what they are doing or how they are doing it.

Lévi-Strauss initially adapted this theory to his anthropological purposes by claiming that many of the nonverbal elements of human culture—such as cosmologies, art styles, architectural design, the layout of villages, and rules concerning descent, residence, and the regulation of marriage, all of which were prominently featured in most ethnographic monographs published during the first half of the twentieth century—can similarly be broken down into sets of cultural distinctive features which are recognizable as binary oppositions. As in the case of phonology, it is the matrix combination of sets of such distinctive features which determines the characteristics of a cultural feature in any particular ethnographic setting.

In effect, Lévi-Strauss was maintaining that when anthropologists engage in cross-cultural comparison, it is not the contrast in manifestly observable social relationships that is of interest (as was maintained by Radcliffe-Brown), but rather the contrast of patterns of "relations between relations" which can be discovered by analysis yet are unconscious phenomena so far as the human actors are concerned. The theory seems to presuppose that at a very rudimentary level the variant possibilities of human culture are innate, or at any rate that human beings are innately predisposed to build up cultural constructs out of paired oppositions of a very simplistic kind, such as animate/inanimate, human/nonhuman, male/female, above/below, we/they, and symmetrical/asymmetrical.

There are other versions of modern structuralism, such as those of A. J. Greimas and Tzvetan Todorov, which similarly seem to require that the "sociologic" of the human mind contain a wide variety of innate (i.e., species-wide) binary oppositions of this sort, though there is a notable lack of consensus as to what they might be (see Hawkes, 1977, pp. 88, 95–96). Many critics would regard any such proposition as entirely implausible, but it cannot be dismissed out of hand. Shorn of its highly sophisticated elaborations, Greimas's version of distinctive-feature (*sémique*) theory requires only that the brain should have an innate propensity to make two associated types of discrimination, such that any entity held within the field of perception will always be associated with

Matrix of Distinctive Features of Speech

	Consonantal	Coronal	Anterior	Voiced	Nasal	Strident	Continuant
/p/	+	–	+	–	–	–	–
/b/	+	–	+	+	–	–	–
/s/	+	+	+	–	–	+	+
/k/	+	–	–	–	–	–	–

TABLE 1.

both its "opposite" and its "negation" (Greimas, 1966, pp. 18–29).

Furthermore, there is now increasing evidence that all normal operations of the brain are computer-like, in that information is passed from one part of the organism to another in a digital binary code of on/off signals. If your biological processes are controlled in this way, it seems highly probable that processes by which thoughts are generated in the brain are of the same general kind.

But while at one level Lévi-Strauss is arguing that the reality of culture is "a model in the mind" rather than out there in the world, he is also claiming that the patterns of relationship that can be recognized in cultural phenomena out there in the world are directly linked, by transformation, with this preexisting model in the mind. Human culture and human society are made by men, but what is made is a projection of a structure which already exists in the maker's mind.

Saussure's structural linguistics. This aspect of the theory was derived, through Jakobson, from the structural linguistics of Ferdinand de Saussure (1916), which included two further types of paired opposition, both of which have been adopted in one form or another by nearly all modern structuralists.

First, there is the notion of the linguistic sign, which is a totality composed of two interdependent parts: (1) the concept in the mind (the signified) and (2) the sound pattern on the breath, which is out there in the world and which constitutes the linguistic signal (the signifier). The concept is a transformation of the sound signal, and vice versa. It is a crucial feature of Saussure's argument that, where concepts form part of a system, they are "defined not positively, in terms of their content, but negatively by contrast with other items in the same system. What characterizes each most exactly is being whatever the others are not" (Saussure, 1983, p. 115).

Lévi-Strauss argues in exactly the same way both with regard to the relationship between the components of his cultural "model in the mind" and the components of objectively observable culture out there in the world, and also with regard to the significance of cultural elements stemming from differentiation. The meaning of any member of a set of components is determined by whatever all other members of the set are not.

The other type of paired opposition that Lévi-Strauss and most other modern structuralists have taken over from Saussure is the contrast between syntagmatic (metonymic, melodic) relations and associative (paradigmatic, metaphoric, harmonic) relations. In the first case the relations are those of contiguity: the links between elements are as in a chain. The sequence of words in a sentence provides the prototype of such a chain. In the second case the relations are those of asserted similarity: "My love is like a rose." All forms of linguistic utterance employ both these polar types of relationship, but whereas rational and scientific statements are heavily biased toward metonymy, poetic and religious utterances are biased toward metaphor.

In Lévi-Strauss's work these distinctions are particularly important for his analyses of myth, a concept which he discusses at enormous length but never defines. In practice, a Lévi-Straussian myth is almost invariably a story (or rather a set of stories) about "impossible" happenings, as when birds and animals talk like men, men fly like birds or are transformed into fish. Such transformations are metaphoric, but the society of birds, fish, or whatever which is then described is spoken of "as if" it were a society of human beings. The metaphor entails a transposition, as with a musical change of key. Social relations among real human beings are primarily relationships of contiguity depending upon metonymy; relationships among individual characters in myth are likewise metonymic. By implication, the stories are about men even when, in explicit terms, the characters are non-men. In many cases this is obvious, but the point about anthropological structuralist analysis is that intuitions of this sort can be systematized and shown to conform to unexpected regularities of pattern.

The question of validity. Admittedly, at the conclusion of a structuralist analysis the reader will often be left with a feeling that he has been told no more than what he knew already. But the exercise may still have been worthwhile, if what was originally no more than intuition has now become grounded in reason. Moreover, there are some occasions when a structuralist analysis will provide quite unexpected insights which are thoroughly convincing. The analogy with psychoanalytic procedures is very close.

But this immediately raises doubts about validity. In psychoanalysis the fact that a particular interpretation of dream material is acceptable to the dreamer does not mean that the interpretation has any truth outside the context of the immediate psychoanalytic session. Even the most celebrated examples of structuralist interpretation of myth are open to similar objections; they may be convincing, but they cannot be shown to be true in any objective sense. A hard-nosed empiricist can always find good grounds for rejecting the argument lock, stock, and barrel.

Part of this skepticism arises because of the form in which Lévi-Strauss has cast his argument. His enduring anthropological purpose was to engage in cross-cultural comparison on a very large scale. His book *Les structures élémentaires de la parenté* (1949) is concerned with most of the recorded kin-term systems of East Asia and Oceania, while his *Mythologiques* (1962–1971) ranges all over the Americas and even beyond. He therefore needed to assume that the "mind" in which his transformational structuralist "model" is located is a human universal, and it is precisely this which the skeptics find unacceptable. It is one thing to suppose that we are genetically endowed with the capacity to encode speech sounds, but it is quite another to claim that, at some abstract level, the elementary structures of total cultural systems are innate.

If, however, we take a more modest view of what structuralist analysis might reveal, many of these difficulties disappear. It is part of Lévi-Strauss's thesis that different manifest features of the same cultural system may be metaphorical transformations of the same internalized unconscious "model in the mind." For a proposition of this sort to make sense, it is not necessary for the mind in question to be an innate human universal. If the territorial scope of the generalization is restricted, it will suffice if the postulated unconscious model is located in the multiple individual minds of the members of a single society. It seems perfectly plausible that a set of individuals who have all been reared in the same cultural milieu might have the capacity to generate identical or very similar unconscious models in the mind in the way that the theory requires. But the innate components of such models could be very limited indeed.

My personal view is that structuralist method is ill adapted to cross-cultural comparison on a grand scale. It becomes illuminating for an anthropologist only when it is able to show that contrasted patterns in very different aspects of the same cultural system are logically consistent transformations/transpositions of the same abstract structure of ideas. Christine Hugh-Jones's *From the Milk River* (1979) provides an excellent example of an anthropological monograph which adapts Lévi-Straussian theory in this way. It provides a deep structuralist analysis of a single cultural system as opposed to a grand-scale rampage right across the map.

Lévi-Strauss's conservatism. The reader of this article should appreciate that, although most of the key doctrines of modern structuralism are to be found in prototypical form in the writings of Lévi-Strauss, many of his followers and imitators, especially those who have adapted the theory for purposes of literary criticism and the analysis of religious texts, have deviated from Lévi-Straussian orthodoxy on important issues.

Lévi-Strauss is a very conservative anthropologist. Unlike most of his contemporaries, he draws a sharp distinction between "primitive" and "modern" societies. He does not say that "primitive" societies are better or worse than "modern" societies, but he does assert that they are fundamentally different in kind, primarily in three binary dimensions. Primitive societies are nonliterate, nonindustrial, and "cold." They are like machines (e.g., clocks) "which use the energy with which they are supplied at the outset and which, in theory, could go on operating indefinitely . . . if they were not subject to friction and heating; . . . they appear to us as static societies with no history." On the other hand, modern societies are literate, industrial, and "hot." They are like thermodynamic machines, "they interiorize history, as it were, and turn it into the motive power of their development" (Lévi-Strauss, 1961, chap. 3).

Now Lévi-Strauss's structuralism is, as we have seen, heavily indebted to the linguistic theories of Saussure, who drew a sharp distinction between diachronic linguistics, which studies the changes of speech forms over time, and synchronic linguistics, which is concerned with structuralist issues such as the relation between thought and organized sound, and the contrast between syntagmatic and associative relations discussed above. In imitation of this dichotomy, Lévi-Strauss has insisted that his own kind of structuralist analysis is appropriate only for the synchronic study of cultural phenomena. He assumes that the cultural systems of "primitive" societies are sufficiently static to be studied as total synchronic systems in this way. By contrast, he assumes that the value attached to diachronic historical change in modern society implies that the cultural data of modern society fall outside the scope of structuralist analysis.

Lévi-Strauss's successors. Here, as elsewhere, Lévi-Strauss's doctrinal pronouncements, as well as his practical structuralist experiments, are elusive and inconsistent. With rare exceptions, he himself has confined his use of structuralist analysis to ethnographic data of the classic anthropological sort, but his imitators have not accepted this self-imposed restriction.

The first general handbook of structuralist method was Roland Barthes's *Elements of Semiology* (1964). In this book and in all his subsequent contributions to structuralist/semiotic analysis, Barthes concerned himself with materials drawn from contemporary Western culture and recent European literature.

In recent years structuralism, considered as a special style of analysis, has had a greater influence on literary criticism than on anthropology. Here, however, the formal structures discussed in the work of Lévi-Strauss and Greimas have been transformed into the Nietzschean exaggerations of Jacques Derrida's theories of poststructuralist deconstruction. Elaborations of this sort cannot be brought within the scope of the present article, though I shall make some reference to the way these writers discuss texts as objects to be interpreted and recreated by the reader rather than as channels through which an author communicates to potential readers.

Structuralist analyses of a quite conventional sort have been used with success in a number of other more immediately relevant fields. Marcel Detienne and his close colleagues have applied Lévi-Strauss's methodology to materials from ancient Greece (see Gordon, 1981); Wendy Doniger O'Flaherty (1973) has used an undiluted version of the theory to analyze a vast range of classical Indian texts; and Claude Chabrol and Louis Marin (1974), among others, have explored the applicability of the method to the analysis of biblical texts.

Continuity versus discontinuity. It is time to show why an essay on structuralism, primarily of the Lévi-Straussian sort, should have a place in an encyclopedia of religion. First, however, attention should be drawn to a modification of the more orthodox binary-opposition versions of structuralist theory which is particularly relevant in applications of this type of theory to religious materials.

Lévi-Strauss writes of reality being a model in the mind made up of a network of relations between discontinuous mental entities linked in binary pairs. But the reality which is out there in the world and which we perceive through our senses is certainly not of this kind. It is continuous in both time and space. It is not naturally made up of separate things and separate events; the appearance of discontinuity is imposed on our experience by the way we perceive it and, more particularly, by the way we use words to describe it. We feel that there is a disjunction between day and night because we have these two words, *day/night*, linked in binary opposition; in our ordinary experience, however, daytime just fades into nighttime and vice versa.

Structuralist theorists have handled this incompatibility between the continuities of experience and the discontinuities of conceptual thinking in a variety of ways, but several anglophone writers, including Mary Douglas (1966), Victor Turner (1969), and myself (1976) have emphasized the relevance of the arguments of Arnold van Gennep (1909).

Van Gennep originally applied his arguments to rituals marking a change of social status. In the world of experience out there, time is continuous. When a husband dies, there is no chronological discontinuity between the moment when his wife is his wife and the subsequent moment when she has become his widow. But in social time things are quite different: society imposes an intermediate stage of mourning when the wife/widow is removed from ordinary social relations and is subject to various kinds of restrictions. During this intermediate phase she is subject to taboo and is treated as a sacred person.

Van Gennep's insight can be generalized in a variety of ways. First, it is empirically the case that social transitions nearly always have a triadic structure which van Gennep himself described as (1) the rite of separation, (2) the marginal state (*rite de marge*), and (3) the rite of aggregation. Second, it is also an empirical fact that not only is the marginal state regularly marked by taboo, but that all forms of holiness, whether applied to particular persons or particular places or particular times, can be shown on analysis to be marginal; they represent an interface between two nonholy categories which we are thereby able to perceive as separated from each other. The argument is that, at the level of the model in the mind, the impression of disjuncture is achieved either by suppressing all consciousness of the ambiguities that lie at the margin or by treating the margin as belonging to a different order of reality: sacred-extraordinary-supernatural versus profane-ordinary-natural.

Implications for the Study of Myth and Ritual. To judge by the titles of their books, structuralist authors are quite centrally concerned with the analysis of myth, but they rarely explain what they mean by this elusive concept, and the definitions that have been offered are seldom mutually compatible. I must therefore offer my own.

To live comfortably in society, every individual must have access to a cosmology—an ordered set of topological, physical, and metaphysical ideas which make sense of immediate experience. The cosmology is not naturally known; it is given to us by the conventional assumptions of the cultural system in which we live; it is taught to us as part of the complex process by which we are transformed from animals into socialized human beings. Furthermore, as an adjunct to learning what the cosmos is like, we also learn how to behave in particular contexts of time and place and interpersonal relationship. These rules of behavior likewise derive from the process of individual socialization.

Both the cosmology and the rules of behavior have to be justified. They are justified by stories about the past which explain how things came to be as they are, and by stories of a rather similar kind which provide precedents for culturally approved behavior or, alternatively, precedents for the supposedly dire consequences of ignoring local cultural conventions. The entire corpus of such validating stories is myth.

Universal versus local applicability. Viewed in this way, myth has moral value. It is sacred for those who accept the validity of the cosmology and the associated customary rules, but in itself it is of strictly local validity. Anthropologists like me who accept the empirical evidence that there are no cultural universals which are not entirely trivial are likely to reject the view of Lévi-Strauss, Freud, and many others who argue that there is a universal human mythology associated with universal, unconscious motivations shared by all individual human beings.

It is important to notice that there is nothing in this context-restricted, functionalist definition implying that myth is fanciful or untrue in a realistic, positivist, historical sense. This point needs emphasis and exemplification.

The biblical story of the garden of Eden is a myth for devout Jews and Christians because of its cosmological and moral implications, and not because it contains such "untrue" incidents as God and the serpent both conversing with Adam and Eve. Likewise, the stories that are told about the signing of the Magna Carta at Runnemede near Windsor in 1215 are myth for all contemporary anglophone upholders of parliamentary democracy. In this case there is very little in the basic story which is obviously untrue (in the talking-serpent sense). Indeed, some parts of it are demonstrably true in a historical sense, since copies of the original document still exist. Yet the story is nonetheless a myth, because it is made to serve as a precedent for customary political conventions which are still significant in the societies in question.

In this approach to myth, the social context in which the stories are told is fundamental; a myth story isolated from its proper context is devoid of meaning. It follows that those who think about myth in this way are bound to regard Lévi-Stauss's extraordinary four-volume *Mythologiques* as largely a waste of time, since the whole exercise is devoted to the cross-cultural comparison of very abbreviated versions of manifestly untrue stories completely isolated from their very diverse original social settings.

Some of the myth analyses which Lévi-Strauss published prior to 1962 took note of a functional (contextual) factor, but in his later work he seems to assume that myth is an undifferentiated, species-wide phenomenon which the human mind is predisposed to generate, in much the same way as it is predisposed to generate speech. He seeks to show how the patterning and combination of myth stories are capable of conveying meaning, but the meaning in question is very general and not context-determined. The superficial differences between the myths of various cultures are treated as comparable to the differences of phonology and grammar in different human languages. At the level of innate capacity, the deep structure is always the same. The myths that appear in ethnographic records are all transformations of a single universal myth which, like phonology, is structured according to a system of distinctive features based on binary oppositions. It follows that the themes with which this mythology is concerned are ultimately human universals of a physiological kind such as sex, metabolism, orientation, and life/death, rather than the solution of local, culturally determined moral issues.

This view of what mythology is about will not be congenial to anthropologists who feel that their basic concern is with cultural diversity, but it is not necessarily unacceptable to the students of universalist religions who may likewise feel that the metaphysical reality to which religion responds is always the same reality, no matter what its cultural form may be. And even those who, like me, believe that myth has a local rather than a universal significance, have much to learn from Lévi-Strauss about the way the messages conveyed by myth are embedded in the patterning and structure of the presentation, rather than in the manifest content of the stories themselves.

This contrast of view among structuralists as to whether myth has universal or local significance is also found in their view of ritual. For the universalists, ritual equates with non-verbal communication; what can be said about it is not very different from what can be said about language as verbal communication. The study of ritual is seen as a branch of a more general zoological field, the study of animal behavior. By contrast, those who see ritual as a localized, culturally determined phenomenon link it quite directly to the local mythology and to particular rather than general cosmological assumptions. Myth and ritual are mutual transformations; each validates the other in its local setting. But in either case the generalizations of the structuralists concerning binary oppositions, transformations, combinations, metonymic and metaphoric associations, and marginal states can prove illuminating.

Myths and rituals as related sets. One particular structuralist proposition is especially relevant for my present purposes: the thesis that mythical stories or sequences of ritual behavior can never be decoded when considered in isolation but only when considered as related sets. A myth story does, of course, always have a manifest meaning considered as a folk tale or as a record of an incident in history. In the same way, an isolated ritual sequence can always be viewed as a dramatic performance which the local customary rules require to be performed at a particular time and place. But the structuralists assume that there is always another deeper, unconscious meaning which is of equal or perhaps greater significance. The structuralist thesis is that such deeper meanings are apprehended by the listener to a myth, or by the participant-observer in a ritual situation, at a subliminal, aesthetic or religious level of consciousness. Structuralist analytical procedures are supposed to make such hidden meanings explicit.

The structuralists' thesis is that the auditor of a myth (or the participant in a ritual) is able to take account of many other myths and rituals with which he or she is familiar. The interpretation applied to the text of any particular story will then be influenced by the moral and aesthetic implications of other such stories.

Thus, devout Jews and Christians will associate any particular story from the Old Testament with a host of other stories both canonical and noncanonical, and it is the structure of the total set of such stories which carries implication. Invariably, analyses of myth in the structuralist manner derive their inferences from a comparison of a number of different stories treated as members of a single set. At the end of the analysis, it is the differences and not the similarities among the stories that prove to have been treated as significant.

This goes right back to the grounding of structuralism in phonological distinctive-feature theory: it is finely discriminated differences between sounds which allow us to discriminate the words of which they form a part, as for instance *bin/pin.* But there are great practical difficulties. In phonology the units that are discriminated fall within a limited set of possible phonemes specified by a limited set of phonological distinctive features. But if we use this mental process as a model for the analysis of myth, we need first to agree about the units of discussion. Within any particular story, how is the overall text to be cut up into segments for purposes of comparison? And among several stories which differ in detail but which seem to have a certain overall similarity, how is the analyst to decide whether any particular story is or is not a member of the same set? The structuralists' failure to formulate any rules about how such questions should be answered seems, on the face of it, to be a very serious defect in their methodology.

In practice, the procedure is intuitive. For those who consider that a structuralist methodology is appropriate to the analysis of religious literature, one obvious set of primary units consists of all the stories in the Bible, while another such set is provided by all the stories about Śiva in the classical Vedic and Puranic literature of the Hindus. The bulk of the materials thus specified is enormous; any practical analysis would have to restrict the scope of the investigation still further by *ad hoc* criteria. But it is easier to justify arbitrary limits of this sort than Lévi-Strauss's universalist practice, which allows him to put into one set stories drawn at random from any part of the world and any cultural context.

It should be noted that the arbitrariness of structuralist analysis connects up with certain of the arguments of poststructuralist literary criticism. Myths (however defined) and sacred books and works of art in general, including music, drama, dance, and the plastic arts, can be regarded as text without authors. The message in the text is what the reader (or auditor or participant-observer) discovers. It is treated as the word of God, but it is an aesthetic response, something in the reader's own unconscious mental processes, which makes the discovery. Thus any "text" is polysemic, a multiple combination of signs; it has many possible meanings, and no particular possibility has any special authenticity that the others lack.

This is what makes sectarian diversity in literary religions so very common. The devotees may all share the same sacred book, but there are vast numbers of different ways to put an authentic interpretation on what it contains. Structuralist and poststructuralist theorizing have provided a sort of rational explanation for this all-too-obvious phenomenon of history.

Prerequisites for structural analysis. A convincing structuralist analysis of even a very abbreviated set of texts takes up a great deal of space, so that in an article of this sort exemplification is hardly possible. The following three prerequisites are essential.

1. The total text under consideration must contain a number of separate segments (stories) which differ in detail but which are also in some respects similar. Taken together, these similar stories form a set. The items in the set can be compared and contrasted. A case in point is provided by the four Gospels of the New Testament. At a certain level each of the Gospels tells the same story, yet the details differ and are in some respects radically contrasted. Whereas orthodox Christian biblical criticism has assumed that these contradictions are of minor significance, or can be satisfactorily explained away to leave a residual unitary account of what really happened in real historical time, the structuralist assumes that it is precisely in the differences that the message of the Gospels, considered as a set, is likely to be found. Within the total text thus considered, all parts of the text have equal value; it is quite inappropriate to the method to discriminate among different kinds of story element under such labels as *parables, historical narratives,* and *folk tales* (see Leach and Aycock, 1983, chap. 5).

2. The major segments (stories) must themselves be segmentable into elements (incidents in the stories, motifs). There is a pattern of relationships between the elements in any one story. The patterns differ in the different stories. The analysis calls for a comparison of these differences. In other words, as in phonology, the coding of the total system is assumed to be a structure of relationships between relationships.

3. The establishment of the patterns and the contrasts between them call for close attention to very fine details in the texts under consideration. Ideally, the analysis should take account of every detail; it is a presupposition of the distinctive-feature thesis that, while the text may contain redundancies, it cannot contain accidents. Every detail adds something to the cogency of the message.

Examples of structuralist analysis. Multifaceted structuralist analyses often turn out to be more interesting than those confined to a single dimension. As we have seen, the structuralist thesis is that the fundamental pattern of the structure under examination is "in the mind." The patterns that can be observed out there in the world of cultural experience—in speech or written text or musical performance or ritual sequences, in the design of works of art and buildings, or in the layout of cultural space—are all transformations of the same mental structure. Thus, at one remove, they should also be transformations of each other. If structuralist analysis has application to religious studies, its principal value might be to give unexpected insight into how the aesthetic imagination is able to carry out these transformations from one artistic medium to another.

All this is very laborious. The linguistic analogy is with the parsing of a sentence, first into words related in a grammatical structure, and then into phonemes related in a phonological structure, and then into the patterns of distinctive features that constitute the phonemes. The skeptic needs to be persuaded that the demonstration of such a fine-grain hierarchy of relations could possibly be worthwhile.

I would not myself want to suggest that skepticism should be wholly abandoned, but I recommend a close reading of O'Flaherty's *Asceticism and Eroticism in the Mythology of Śiva* (1973), taking special note of the pull-out Chart of Motifs and of the complexities of Appendix A (pp. 319–320), which together show what I mean by saying that, in structuralist analysis, it is assumed that the message is embedded in relationships between relationships. This is a one-dimensional study, but it is a very distinguished example of its kind.

My own favorite definition of myth is that of Julius Schniewind: "Mythology is the expression of unobservable realities in terms of observable phenomena" (Bartsch, 1953–1962, p. 47). This puts myth at the very core of all forms of religious expression. In the five pages of her concluding chapter, O'Flaherty provides as good an argument as any that I know for saying that a structuralist analysis of a corpus of mythology can show us how these unobservable realities become apprehensible through close familiarity with a set of stories which on the face of it are mutually contradictory.

But the determined skeptic can find reassurance in the fact that competent structuralists analyzing the same materials seldom arrive at the same conclusions. Chabrol and Marin's *Le récit évangelique* (1974) is a multiauthored structuralist monograph on the theme of the New Testament parables. Their work derives its theoretical basis from the semiotic theories of A. J. Greimas. Leach and Aycock's *Structuralist Interpretations of Biblical Myth* (1983, chap. 5) is a much shorter structuralist essay but is also concerned with New Testament parables, and the underlying theory is similar in many respects. The argument which Chabrol offers in his essay "De la sémiotique en question" (Chabrol and Marin, 1974, pp. 193–213) overlaps at many points with what I have been saying in the present article. Yet with the possible exception of Chabrol himself (see p. 135), the various French authors all agree that *parable* is a meaningful genre for structuralist purposes, while I, in the work cited above, argue quite specifically that it is not. A critical comparison of the arguments offered in these two, in some ways very similar, contributions might be of value for those who find the structuralist/semiotic treatment of religious texts too slippery to handle.

Conclusion: The Sistine Chapel. I shall conclude by offering the skeleton of part of one of my own essays showing how works of art, literary texts, and church practice can be combined in a meaningful structural pattern.

The nine main panels in the ceiling of the Sistine Chapel in the Vatican are of world renown. They are grouped in three sets of three, a cross-reference to the Holy Trinity. At the altar end, God as Creator and Light of the World appears alone without man; at the opposite end are three panels depicting Noah/Adam, the sinful but potentially redeemable man without God. At the center are three scenes where man and God are together: the creation of Adam, the creation of Eve, and the temptation of Adam and Eve and their expulsion from paradise.

The Sistine Chapel, which is the personal chapel of the pope, is dedicated to the Virgin Mary of the Assumption as Queen of Heaven. The Virgin in this role is the Second Eve; she also stands for the church itself. In the center panel the figure of the newly created Eve is at the exact center of the entire ceiling. In the panel depicting the Fall, the serpent coiled around the tree of life is doubled and effectively cruciform. It has two humanoid heads. One, which forms a branch to the left, is that of the temptress who grasps the voluptuous but still innocent Eve by the hand. The other, which forms a branch to the right, is that of the angel armed with the flaming sword which drives the now haggard sinners into the wilderness. The face of the serpent-temptress is like that of the newly created Eve, but it looks in the reverse direction; the face of the voluptuous, innocent Eve is that of the uncreated Eve who appears wrapped in the womb of time in the panel showing the creation of Adam. According to a medieval legend, the cross on which Christ died was cut from the tree of life that had grown in the garden of Eden.

The cruciform depiction of this tree with its double-headed serpent was originally positioned so as to be directly above the screen dividing the secular antichapel from the sacred chapel proper. In a more ordinary church of the period, this position would have been filled by a crucifix standing above the rood screen.

The theme of the double-headed serpent turned into a crucifix recurs in the corner panel to the right of the altar, where the manifest depiction is the story of the healing of the sinful Israelites smitten by a plague of serpents in the wilderness. In this case there is a direct cross-reference to the passage in the *Gospel of John* that reads: "And as Moses lifted up the serpent in the wilderness, even so must the Son of man be lifted up: That whosoever believeth in him should not perish, but have eternal life" (*Jn.* 3:14–15).

This is only a partial outline. Even in minimally convincing form, full analysis calls for an essay substantially longer than the whole of the present article. Many of the themes in this analysis have also appeared in other interpretations of Michelangelo's iconography, but some are a peculiar product of structuralist methodology. Some art historians, theologians, and literary critics find the results convincing. Such is the only justification which I can put forward for structuralism in general. If some readers of structuralist analyses feel that they have thereby gained insights which they did not have before, the exercise has been worthwhile.

BIBLIOGRAPHY

In no sense at all should the bibliography which follows be regarded as a guide to the literature of structuralism, or even to that part of structuralist literature concerned with religious studies. It simply lists references mentioned in the foregoing article. Those who wish to pursue the fundamentals further could hardly do better than to consult the richly annotated twenty-six page bibliography and reading guide appended to Hawkes's *Structuralism and Semiology* (cited below), though since its publication there has been a further huge expansion of the relevant literature.

Barthes, Roland. *Éléments de sémiologie.* Paris, 1964. Translated by Annette Lavers and Colin Smith as *Elements of Semiology* (New York, 1964). A good guide to the fundamentals of Saussure's structuralism, though the terminology in the English version is very confusing.

Bartsch, Hans Werner, ed. *Kerygma and Myth: A Theological Debate.* 2 vols. Translated from German by Reginald H. Fuller. New York, 1953–1962. A discussion of Rudolf Bultmann's views concerning mythology in the New Testament.

Bastide, Roger, ed. *Sens et usages du terme structure dans les sciences humaines et sociales.* 2d ed. The Hague, 1972. A set of papers offered at a colloquium held in Paris under the patronage of UNESCO in January 1959. Émile Benveniste notes that the term *structuralism,* which he puts between inverted commas or in italics, is so recent that it is not included in a French dictionary of linguistic terminology published in 1951.

Chabrol, Claude, and Louis Marin, with the collaboration of Alain J. Cohen, Christian Mellon, and François Rastier. *Le récit évangélique.* Paris, 1974. A collection of structuralist essays in the manner of A. J. Greimas that are concerned with biblical materials, especially New Testament parables.

De George, Richard T., and Fernande M. De George, eds. *The Structuralists: From Marx to Lévi-Strauss.* New York, 1972. An anthology showing that a common structuralist theme can be found in work by Marx, Freud, Saussure, Jakobson, Lévi-Strauss, Barthes, Althusser, Foucault, and Lacan. The introduction offers a helpful overview.

Douglas, Mary. *Purity and Danger: An Analysis of Concepts of Pollution and Taboo.* London, 1966. Contains, as chapter 3, the author's well-known but badly flawed essay "The Abominations of Leviticus," which has had considerable influence on later discussions of biblical food taboos.

Gennep, Arnold van. *The Rites of Passage* (1909). Translated from French by Monika B. Vizedom and Gabrielle L. Caffee. London, 1960. Van Gennep's theory has been greatly extended by later authors; the original is now of historical interest only.

Gordon, R. L., ed. *Myth, Religion and Society.* Cambridge, 1981. Representative essays by an important group of French classical scholars (Marcel Detienne, Louis Gernet, Jean-Pierre Vernant, and Pierre Vidal-Naquet) who employ structuralist techniques of analysis. With an introduction by R. G. A. Buxton and an extensive and valuable bibliography.

Greimas, Algirdas Julien. *Sémantique structurale: Recherche de méthode.* Paris, 1966. An early work by an influential structuralist theorist. Not recommended for novices.

Hawkes, Terence. *Structuralism and Semiology.* New York, 1977. The best short guide to the subject in the English language. Excellent bibliography.

Hugh-Jones, Christine. *From the Milk River: Spatial and Temporal Processes in Northwest Amazonia.* Cambridge, 1979. An ethnographic account of the Barasana Indians of the Vaupes region of Colombia that successfully combines the empirical approach of traditional British social anthropology and an idealist model-in-the-mind style derived from the structuralism of Lévi-Strauss. See also the companion volume by Stephen Hugh-Jones, *The Palm and the Pleiades: Initiation and Cosmology in Northwest Amazonia* (Cambridge, 1979).

Jakobson, Roman, and Morris Halle. *Fundamentals of Language.* The Hague, 1956. Most of Jakobson's huge oeuvre is somewhat inaccessible for the ordinary reader. This well-known work contains a useful but incomplete account of phonological distinctive-feature theory.

Leach, Edmund. *Genesis as Myth and Other Essays.* London, 1969. All the essays in this collection apply a structuralist style of analysis to biblical materials. The title essay, which dates from 1961, was one of the earliest of this genre.

Leach, Edmund. *Culture and Communication: The Logic by Which Symbols Are Connected; An Introduction to the Use of Structuralist Analysis in Social Anthropology.* Cambridge, 1976. The long-winded full title of this widely read work is self-explanatory. The range is narrower and rather different from Hawkes's comparable *Structuralism and Semiology.* Chapter 18 is entitled "The Logic of Sacrifice."

Leach, Edmund, and D. Alan Aycock. *Structuralist Interpretations of Biblical Myth.* Cambridge, 1983. Five essays by Leach and two by Aycock on themes comparable to those in Leach's *Genesis as Myth and Other Essays.*

Lévi-Strauss, Claude. "L'analyse structurale en linguistique et en anthropologie." *Word: Journal of the Linguistic Circle of New York* (1945): 33–53. An English version, somewhat revised, appears as chapter 2 of Lévi-Strauss's *Structural Anthropology,* translated by Claire Jacobson and Brooke Grundfest Schoepf (New York, 1963). The 1945 version was Lévi-Strauss's first thoroughgoing application of structuralist method. His debt to Roman Jakobson is explicit. This essay introduced the celebrated, though much criticized, concept of "the atom of kinship."

Lévi-Strauss, Claude. *Les structures élémentaires de la parenté.* Paris, 1949. The first magnum opus of anthropological structuralist literature. Its merits and limitations are still hotly debated by professionals in the field.

Lévi-Strauss, Claude. "Social Structure." In *Anthropology Today: An Encyclopedic Inventory,* edited by A. L. Kroeber, pp. 524–553. Chicago, 1953. Now only of historical interest. Connects with Tax's *An Appraisal of Anthropology Today.*

Lévi-Strauss, Claude, in collaboration with Georges Charbonnier. *Conversations with Claude Lévi-Strauss* (1961). Translated from French by John Weightman and Doreen Weightman. London, 1969. A series of radio interviews given when Lévi-Strauss was at the peak of his celebrity.

Lévi-Strauss, Claude. *Mythologiques.* 4 vols. Paris, 1964–1971. Translated by John Weightman and Doreen Weightman as *Introduction to a Science of Mythology,* 4 vols. (London, 1970–1981). An obsessional masterpiece reminiscent of the unabridged edition of James G. Frazer's *The Golden Bough.* Nonspecialists can find the important parts of the argument published elsewhere in shorter form.

O'Flaherty, Wendy Doniger. *Asceticism and Eroticism in the Mythology of Siva.* London, 1973. A successful adaptation of Lévi-Strauss's method of myth analysis to a large body of classical Indian textual material.

Rumney, Jay. *Herbert Spencer's Sociology*. London, 1934.

Saussure, Ferdinand de. *Cours de linguistique générale*. Lausanne, 1916. Translated, with annotation, by Roy Harris as *Course in General Linguistics*, edited by Charles Bally and Albert Sechehaye, with the collaboration of Albert Reidlinger (London, 1983). The best English edition of a major structuralist classic.

Tax, Sol, et al., eds. *An Appraisal of Anthropology Today*. Chicago, 1953. Lévi-Strauss's "Social Structure" is discussed on pages 108–118.

Turner, Victor. *The Ritual Progress: Structure and Anti-Structure* (1969). Ithaca, N.Y., 1977. Although Turner is often called a structuralist, his style of analysis differs widely from that of Lévi-Strauss.

EDMUND LEACH (1987)

STRUCTURALISM [FURTHER CONSIDERATIONS]. In 1970, Sir Edmund Leach wrote in his book about Claude Lévi-Strauss (1908–) that structuralism was held by many to be a new philosophy. "Lévi-Strauss," he stated, "is regarded among the intellectuals of his own country as the leading exponent of 'Structuralism,' a word which has come to be used as if it denoted a whole new philosophy of life on the analogy of 'Marxism' or 'Existentialism.' What is this 'Structuralism' all about?" (1970, p. 15). Leach has answered the question himself in a number of publications. His characterization may certainly be an apt impression of what was "in the air" in the 1960s. Later this was to change, but it is not quite off the mark to say that post-structuralism—sometimes presented as postmodernism—has since been highly advertised as much more than a method or a fashion; it has been heralded as grasping the very spirit of the age. It may seem so if one discusses the latest trends in late modern societies, but when applied to religion and the study of religion, the attractiveness of the latest intellectual fashions fade. Religions and religious traditions are much more conventional, traditional, and ritualized than late modern trends and fashions, and it therefore makes good sense to study religions and matters pertaining to religion in a structuralist framework.

It is the basic premise of structuralism that human sociocultural products, such as language and religion, are sign systems in which any entity becomes meaningful only in relation to the system and its rules and against a structured background. The structures and rules are mostly followed unconsciously. Ironically, post-structural phenomena may thus also be analyzed in structuralist terms.

Thus, structuralism is by no means exhausted as an approach to human cultural and social formations. The long philosophical debate over whether the structures retrieved in analysis are preeminently to derive from minds producing culture or are to be located in the products themselves dissolves to an extent in a structuralist perspective. That is because all cultural products, be they language, symbolism, religion, or any other aspect of culture, are and must be structured if they are to be understandable by and meaningful to other humans. This leads to an evaluation of structuralism as more than simply one method among others of equal standing. It has been suggested by Peter Caws (1997) that structuralism may indeed be *the* philosophy for the human sciences. That the term *structuralism* covers a wide array of subjects is evident from the introduction by John Lechte in his *Fifty Key Contemporary Thinkers* (1996) to many of the prominent thinkers in the history of the structuralist movement, from the earliest inspirations to the later postmodernist phases.

REVISIONS AND CRITICISMS. As scholars pick up the structuralist tradition as an approach in the study of religion, they are able to review, revise, and continue to develop the structuralist approach. Although the earlier stage of structuralist scholarship was much concerned with exegeses of the most "canonical" writing of, especially, Lévi-Strauss, subsequent research has not been uncritical of the "masters," and it has also been able to advance and transform the initial inspirations and to solidify and justify the structuralist paradigm (Johnson, 2003).

One of the critical points in the early structuralist period was a rather consistent criticism concerning the validity and replicability of structural analysis and the more practical issues of method: How does one proceed and where are structures to be found? Are they part of the "native's reality"—are they in the human mind or in sociocultural products? Are they conscious or subconscious representational models or are they analytical and explanatory models made by the analyst? Leach's suspicion was quite clear:

> In all his writings Lévi-Strauss assumes that the simple first-stage "model" generated by the observer's first impressions corresponds quite closely to a genuine (and very important) ethnographic reality— the "conscious model" which is present in the minds of the anthropologist's informants. . . . It seems all too obvious that this initial model is little more than an amalgam of the observer's own prejudiced presuppositions. (1970, p.12)

Leach also remarks that Lévi-Strauss "consistently behaves like an advocate defending a cause rather than a scientist searching for ultimate truth" (1970, p. 12). Although "ultimate truth" seems outside the range of human knowledge, the implications are clear enough. On the other hand, since the days when it was necessary to defend structuralism as a new approach, analyses have proved quite fruitful in many areas of the human sciences, from social anthropology to media studies to biblical scholarship. As Stanley J. Tambiah has illustrated in his *Edmund Leach* (2002), Leach's own production is a fine example of this fruitfulness, especially in relation to cultural codes, classificatory systems, and ritual formations. Further, it should be emphasized that semiotics, discourse analysis, and a range of other approaches would have been unthinkable without the influence of structuralism.

As the structuralist theoretical inspiration has proved highly consequential for many of the human sciences, a number of works have appeared that critically review and revise the earlier reading and understandings of the groundbreaking effort of the founders. Among these, Paul J. Thibault's *Re-reading Saussure* (1997) stands out as he demonstrates how Saussure's ideas about language were not simply formal and abstract but much more concerned with how meaning is produced in social life. Thibault thoroughly criticizes the more conventional readings of Saussure. Roy Harris's work is also highly interesting for its analyses of the ways in which Saussure's intellectual legacy has been handled.

STRUCTURALISM AS METHOD AND THEORY IN THE STUDY OF RELIGION. Jeppe Sinding Jensen's article "Structure" in *Guide to the Study of Religion* (2000) traces the development of structuralism in the human sciences with a special emphasis on the ramifications for the study of religion. Hans H. Penner forcefully advocates structuralist theory for the study of religion in his *Impasse and Resolution: A Critique of the Study of Religion* (1989). Penner disproves the thesis set forth by Leach and others about the probable weakness concerning the validity and replicability of structuralist methodology. Penner demonstrates how scholarship on, for example, Buddhism and Hinduism has benefited from structuralist analyses by discovering the underlying regularities of the symbolic systems. However, the most central issue in structuralist analysis is myths and mythologies. Here, Penner agrees with Lévi-Strauss, writing that "it is very dangerous if not erroneous to view myths as symbolic representations of actual social realities or of some cultural psyche, whatever that may mean. Furthermore, it is also a mistake to study myths as concealing some hidden 'mystical' meaning. The meaning of a myth is given in its concrete relations with other versions. Thus, it is clearly a misunderstanding to call this type of analysis reductionistic" (p. 176). In his later anthology, *Teaching Lévi-Strauss* (1998), Penner took up the problem of teaching structuralism, which has been fraught with difficulties arising from the many criticisms and misunderstanding of Lévi-Strauss's work: "From my own study of this thought I believe it is fair to say that the charges of 'anti-history,' 'idealism,' and the impossibility of verifying or falsifying his work are simply false. Nevertheless, these charges were leveled at the very beginning of his publications and as usual they were then used by many who seem to have not read his publications. . . . For many in the study of religion he was simply put down as a 'reductionist'" (p. x).

Others have wanted to know how one could "prove" the existence of structures, and many simply confused structure as an abstract term for a set of relations with more empirical manifestations of systems and design, such as the structure of government or of a building, for example. Earlier structuralists were suspected by their more empiricist counterparts of being too philosophical, idealist, or rationalist, and thus of generating scholarship that was not grounded in "reality."

STRUCTURALISM IN EMPIRICAL STUDIES. Over the years, more empirical and subject-oriented research in a structuralist frame of mind has replaced the style of the earlier programmatic and more technical essays. Structuralism has become ordinary, legitimate, and mainstream in the study of religion to the extent that terms such as "structural," "structuralist," or "structuralism" do not appear in the title of works that draw on the structural heritage. There are certain traits that can disguise the fact that an argument in the study of religion has come from structuralism, including: notions of systemic relations and of synchronicity; the idea of there being no firm foundations and definite pristine historical origins; and the absence of single or direct references for meanings and semantic contents. It is also a structuralist idea that elements and meanings are neither fixed nor given but always depend on relations to other elements and meanings—that is, the notion of systemic relations between elements. A further trait of a hidden structural argument occurs when the text metaphor is extended to cover actions and institutions, which thus become "readable" because of the rules of composition (constitutive and regulatory) that govern their functions. Another keyword is *transformation,* which structualists use instead of *change* or *influence* to stress the way in which something novel is always created or produced in relation to a given structure; thus, it can also be shown that, for example, syncretism is not simply a hodge-podge of singular elements but a cultural creation with certain structural properties.

An instructive empirical example of "implicit structuralism" is given by Louise Bruit Zaidman and Pauline Schmitt Pantel in *Religion in the Greek* City (1994). In their study of the Greeks' "figuration of the divine," they point out that a remarkable feature of Greek culture is:

> the large degree to which all their systems of representation—pantheons, myths, visual images—were mutually supportive. If there was a logic at work behind the constitution of the pantheon and the elaboration of myths, this was no less true of the creation of the visual images of the divine that populated the Greek city. Moreover, these systems of representation cannot be separated from the rituals which gave expression to the underlying systemic structures. It is clearly impossible, for example, to study a statue in isolated abstraction from the ritual use to which it was put. (p. 228)

Other religions and cultures of the Indo-European language family have been subjected to various structural approaches from early on, as in the approach of Georges Dumézil concerning the relations between the ideological roles of rulers, warriors, and peasants in the mythologies of traditional Indo-European societies. However, Old Norse mythology has also proven a field well-suited to structural analysis. The value of structural analysis in the study of myth, ritual, and other sociocultural institutions in the Hindu religious traditions has also been demonstrated. Thus, whenever we talk about such issues as the Confucian concept of *li* (propriety), the Muslim system of *tahara* (purity), or similar sets of sociocultural codes of conduct, we may perceive the validity of structural approaches. E. Thomas Lawson and Robert N. McCauley demonstrate in *Rethinking Religion* (1990) that this goes for rituals as well. In a number of studies of religious traditions, implicit structuralism has made its impact. This may also be in the mode of a pragmatic structuralism working from the positions of Michel Foucault and Pierre Bourdieu. In some areas, such as studies of the Muslim tradition, these inspirations have made an obvious impact—Talal Asad's *Genealogies of Religion* (1993) is an example. The "systematicity" argument may of course be overstated, and there is a problem if one suggests that entire systems should be present in every human actor's individual mind—and consciously so. This is not the case, for the structuralist argument presupposes that competence is largely unconscious, in the sense that speakers may talk without explicit knowledge of the linguistic rules they obey or violate.

The Survival of Structuralism in Semiotics and Semantics. It is frequently assumed that the advent of post-structuralism indicated the demise of structuralism. This may have been the case in literary theory and criticism, where other reading strategies have replaced structural analysis. But, there is even a "post" post-structuralism—or is there? As it turns out, post-structuralism is a continuation of structuralism, but with an emphasis on self-critical and reflexive thought. However, the field has been bursting with near-perplexing jargon, and the consequences for the human and social sciences of applying postmodernist theory have been quite uncertain to many. It is understandable when scholars of religions are uneasy with post-structuralism and postmodernist skepticism about realism and the idea that all claims to truth are but power games. Students of religion are quite sensitive to the differences between religious and scholarly discourse. The crucial questions also involve the problem of representation, that is, about who speaks how about whom, and here the "post" movements present both problems and solutions. There is the problem that profound difference makes us all different, while at the same time it also makes us all equal—and game for comparison and analysis.

Semiotics, the study of signs and signification, also arose out of the structuralist milieu, and in the French tradition it represented, as "structural semantics," attempts toward developing a formal science of meaning. In the study of religion, semiotics evolved into a more practical approach, demonstrating the heuristic capacities of the methodology. The field of biblical studies has, on the whole, proven fertile ground for structuralist and semiotic analyses, as witnessed by the appearance of journals such as *Semeia: An Experimental Journal for Biblical Criticism* and *Linguistica Biblica*. In a more general vein, Richard Parmentier's *Signs in Society* (1994) concerns semiotics in the anthropology of culture.

Semantics, the study of meaning in philosophy and linguistics, is also generally an heir to structuralist notions, as the general theory of meaning in the wake of analytic philosophy has turned towards holistic perspectives, as shown in Jensen's "On a Semantic Definition of Religion" (1999). This is also forcefully demonstrated in *Language, Truth, and Religious Beliefs* (1999), edited by Nancy K. Frankenberry and Hans H. Penner, a reader on relevant positions for this discussion. How semantics and structuralist thought have converged on the philosophy of language is also the topic of Jaroslav Peregrin's important work, *Meaning and Structure* (2001), in which a number ofpostanalytic philosophical and holist positions are reviewed. Holistic methodology is consonant with the general structuralist tenet that elements of a system (words, terms, concepts, and so on) do not have meaning in themselves but only in relation to other elements and the larger system that they constitute—such as in a language or a "form of life," as Ludwig Wittgenstein later termed the preconditions for mutual understanding. What goes for conceptual systems in general also goes for the study of religion, as the notions, models, and theories employed in that activity are also interdependently defined.

In direct relation to methodology in the study of religion, mention must be made of Gavin Flood's *Beyond Phenomenology* (1999), where the author proposes a shift in philosophical basis away from the subject and toward a philosophy of signs as the "first philosophy" for the study of religion. This idea is precisely in accordance with the fundamental tenets of the structuralist paradigm.

Meanings, Minds and Symbolic Worlds. Holistic and structuralist theory is also opposed to the "mentalist" point of view, where meanings must necessarily and only be located in individual minds. However, the thought that meanings are somehow related to what individuals "have in mind" is obvious, not only from common experience, but also on the basis of cognitive theories and research; however, the precise way in which symbolic systems, meaning, and the mental and cognitive are related is a complex question over which there is considerable controversy. The concept of the "human mind," as used by Lévi-Strauss and others, has caused consistent confusion, since in French it would mostly refer to something social and public, but in English it would refer to a mental realm. There is no doubt, however, that the "universes of the mind," as they have been called by the semiotician Yuri Lotman (1990), must not only be in minds, but must also be abstract systems of signs so that they may "circulate" between minds and thereby be involved in the creating of worlds of meaning.

All this may seem suggestive of idealism. If so, it is not a problem. For, as Peter Caws argues in his *Structuralism* (1997), "a form of idealism that may be philosophically suspect if applied to the world of nature may be exactly appropriate when applied to the world of society, since although the existence of nature cannot reasonably be supposed to be dependent on minds (the New Physics to the contrary notwithstanding), the existence of society as society can" (p. 17). It is only when humans invent, construct, and make some things "count as" other things that society, culture, and language come into existence—with art, politics, money, rules about ritual purity, and all that it takes to make human and symbolic worlds meaningful. And in making those worlds, we also make ourselves—would we be thoughtful humans if we were not full of thoughts?

Bibliography

Asad, Talal. *Genealogies of Religion: Discipline and Reasons of Power in Christianity and Islam.* Baltimore, 1993. Post-structural analyses on religion and power.

Biardeau, Madeleine. *Histoires de poteaux: Variations védiques autour de la déesse hindoue.* Paris, 1989. Structural studies in ancient Indian cosmology.

Bourdieu, Pierre. *The Logic of Practice.* Translated by Richard Nice. Cambridge, U.K., 1990. On human practice and society as structured and structuring.

Caws, Peter. *Structuralism: A Philosophy for the Human Sciences.* Atlantic Highlands, N.J., 1997. In-depth reflections on structuralism in the human sciences.

Davidsen, Ole. *The Narrative Jesus: A Semiotic Reading of Mark's Gospel.* Aarhus, 1993. A semiotic analysis of biblical text.

Davis, Colin. *After Poststructuralism: Reading, Stories, and Theory.* London, 2003. Critical reflections on the fate of post-structuralism.

Doniger, Wendy. "Post-modern and—colonial—Structural Comparisons." In *A Magic Still Dwells: Comparative Religion in the Postmodern Age,* edited by Kimberley C. Patton and Benjamin C. Ray, pp. 63–74. Berkeley, Calif., 2000. On comparison and and postmodernism in the study of religion.

Flood, Gavin D. *Beyond Phenomenology: Rethinking the Study of Religion.* London, 1999. Methodological reflections on the study of religion from a philosophy of language perspective.

Frankenberry, Nancy K., and Hans H. Penner, eds. *Language, Truth, and Religious Belief: Studies in Twentieth-Century Theory and Method in Religion.* Atlanta, 1999. Anthology of important essays on language and meaning aimed at students of religion.

Harris, Roy. *Saussure and His Interpreters.* New York, 2001. Analyzes the influence of Saussure's linguistic theory.

Jensen, Jeppe Sinding. "On a Semantic Definition of Religion." In *The Pragmatics of Defining Religion: Contexts, Concepts, and Contests,* edited by Jan G. Platvoet and Arie L. Molendijk, pp. 409–431. Leiden, Netherlands, 1999. Structural, semantic, and semiotic theories in relation to the definition of religion.

Jensen, Jeppe Sinding. "Structure." In *Guide to the Study of Religion,* edited by Willi Braun and Russell T. McCutcheon, pp. 314–333. London, 2000. Review of issues concerning structure and structuralism in the study of religion.

Jensen, Jeppe Sinding. *The Study of Religion in a New Key: Theoretical and Philosophical Soundings in the Comparative and General Study of Religion.* Åarhus, Denmark, 2003. The comparative study of religion redefined in a philosophy of language perspective.

Johnson, Christopher. *Claude Lévi-Strauss: The Formative Years.* Cambridge, U.K., 2003. Lévi-Strauss's early biography as a history of structuralism.

Leach, Edmund. *Claude Lévi-Strauss.* New York, 1970. Classic work on Lévi-Strauss and structuralism in anthropology.

Lechte, John. *Fifty Key Contemporary Thinkers: From Structuralism to Postmodernity.* London, 1994. Concise catalog of the most prominent names in the development of structuralist theory.

Lotman, Yuri M. *Universe of the Mind: A Semiotic Theory of Culture.* Bloomington, Ind., 1990. A theory of relations between language, semiotics and culture.

Lawson, E. Thomas, and Robert N. McCauley. *Rethinking Religion. Connecting Cognition and Culture.* Cambridge, U.K., 1990. Language-theoretical and cognitive views on ritual forms and structures.

Malamoud, Charles. *Cooking the World: Ritual and Thought in Ancient India.* New York, 1996. Structural study of ancient Indian cosmology and practice.

Parmentier, Richard J. *Signs in Society: Studies in Semiotic Anthropology.* Bloomington, Ind., 1994. Theoretical studies on the role of semiotics in anthropology.

Penner, Hans H. *Impasse and Resolution. A Critique of the Study of Religion.* New York, 1989. Critical introduction to structuralism as a method for the study of religion.

Penner, Hans H., ed. *Teaching Lévi-Strauss.* Atlanta, 1998. An introduction to Lévi-Strauss's work with responses by critics.

Peregrin, Jaroslav. *Meaning and Structure: Structuralism of (Post)analytic Philosophers.* Aldershot, U.K., 2001. The position of structuralism in recent philosophy of language.

Potter, Jonathan. *Representing Reality: Discourse, Rhetoric, and Social Construction.* London, 1996. Critical responses to postmodernist theory.

Rosenau, Pauline Marie. *Post-modernism and the Social Sciences: Insights, Inroads, and Intrusions.* Princeton, 1992. Critical analysis of the position of postmodernism in social science.

Ross, Margaret Clunies. *Prolonged Echoes: Old Norse Myths in Medieval Northern Society,* vol. 1, *The Myths.* Odense, Denmark, 1994. On structures in Old Norse myth and cosmology.

Tambiah, Stanley J. *Edmund Leach: An Anthropological Life.* Cambridge, U.K., 2002. Biography of Leach, written as a history of structuralism in British social anthropology.

Thibault, Paul J. *Re-reading Saussure: The Dynamics of Signs in Social Life.* London, 1997. Critical reappraisal of Saussure's theoretical legacy.

Zaidman, Louise Bruit, and Pauline Schmitt Pantel. *Religion in the Ancient Greek City.* Translated by Paul Cartledge. Cambridge, U.K., 1994. Structures in ancient Greek religion.

Jeppe Sinding Jensen (2005)

STUDY OF RELIGION

This entry consists of the following articles:

AN OVERVIEW
THE ACADEMIC STUDY OF RELIGION IN AUSTRALIA AND OCEANIA
THE ACADEMIC STUDY OF RELIGION IN EASTERN EUROPE AND RUSSIA
THE ACADEMIC STUDY OF RELIGION IN JAPAN
THE ACADEMIC STUDY OF RELIGION IN NORTH AFRICA AND THE MIDDLE EAST
THE ACADEMIC STUDY OF RELIGION IN NORTH AMERICA
THE ACADEMIC STUDY OF RELIGION IN SOUTH ASIA
THE ACADEMIC STUDY OF RELIGION IN SUB-SAHARAN AFRICA

STUDY OF RELIGION: AN OVERVIEW

Unlike theology, the academic study of religion seeks to provide accounts of the world's religions from perspectives that have no confessional (religious) ground or agenda. As an empirical pursuit, it is concerned with understanding and explaining what people actually think and do without establishing or enforcing norms for that thought and behavior. It takes the entire universe of religions as its object of study; classically educated scholars were once fond of quoting the Roman playwright Terence (c. 186–159 BCE), a freed slave from North Africa: *"homo sum; nihil humanum mihi alienum puto"* ("I am a human being; I consider nothing human foreign to me"). It also aspires to treat all religions equally. Of course, these characterizations are subject to critical interrogation, both in terms of the degree to which individual works live up to them and the degree to which they are themselves philosophically defensible.

Despite the field's universal reach, Europeans and North Americans have tended to conceive of the study of religion ethnocentrically. Although the objects of study—religious people—have been universal, the subjects—the people doing the studying—have not. When they did not physically reside in Europe or North America, they were intellectually, if not biologically, of European or North American descent. They studied religions—as a young scholar in the Middle East recently described his professional activity in correspondence with this author—from a Western perspective.

The pervasiveness of European and North American political and economic colonialism and cultural influence gives some credence to this conception. Nevertheless, a view of the academic study of religion excessively centered on the so-called West also takes several risks. It risks ignoring antecedents of that study in various parts of the globe that predate or do not depend upon the European Enlightenment. It risks neglecting vigorous traditions of that study that are emerging in various parts of the world. And it risks impoverishing that study by looking only to Europe and North America for theoretical and methodological inspiration. In other words, it confines the academic study of religion not within the boundaries of a religious community, as in the case of theology, but within those of a culture or civilization.

The entries that follow treat the academic study of religion throughout the world. It has seemed expedient to divide the articles in terms of large geographical regions arranged alphabetically, but one should remember that these regions are themselves somewhat artificial. The entries seek to address how religious studies has come into being in different ways in different academic settings. They treat the contribution of scholars in each region to the study of religions that are found outside as well as within the regions. Thus, the entry on South Asia, for example, treats the manner in which South Asians have studied religions, not the study of South Asian religions. The remainder of this entry offers more general observations about the emergence of the study of religion, its development, and its methods.

THE EMERGENCE OF THE ACADEMIC STUDY OF RELIGION.

According to a well-worn German cliché, *Religionswissenschaft*—the comparative study of religion, the history of religions, the academic study of religion—is a child of the Enlightenment. Insofar as this cliché invites us to disregard intellectual developments outside of Europe, it issues an invitation that we should decline. But it does begin to identify the conditions under which the academic study of religion appeared in Europe, and in doing so it invites us to reflect more generally on the conditions under which that study has emerged.

There are many kinds of knowledge about religions. Before the emergence of the academic study of religion, people learned about their own religions from people such as relatives, neighbors, priests, shamans, teachers, preachers, monks, nuns, and maybe even philosophers and theologians. They learned about other religions from similar sources, along with proselytizers, apologists, polemicists, and heresiologists, who provided information about the practices and beliefs of other people but also gave reasons either to adopt those beliefs and practices, to disregard them, to fear them, or even to persecute and kill the people who adhered to them. In addition, travelers like Herodotos (c. 484–between 430 and 420 BCE), Xuanzang (602–664), and Ibn Battuta (1307–1377), at times less interested in specific religious agendas, provided knowledge of the practices and beliefs of people who lived in more remote lands. All of these people and others as well, such as foreign service officers and journalists, may provide information about religions, but that information does not in itself constitute the academic study of religion. In order for that study to emerge, at least three conditions need to be met.

First, the academic study of religion encompasses only certain kinds of knowledge, namely, those kinds associated with institutions devoted to the professional production and dissemination of knowledge, such as universities. These kinds of knowledge derive their authority in part from the application of approved procedures. Scholars self-consciously pursue methods that are presumed to eliminate mistakes and errors that plague ordinary knowledge and/or that produce accounts that have the appearance of greater-than-average sophistication. These kinds of knowledge also derive their authority in part from various forms of institutional validation: material support for those who produce and transmit knowledge by approved means; the certification of those who have mastered both the techniques and content of the produced knowledge; and the codification and preservation of the knowledge produced—either in human memory, as in the case of *sūtras* and *śāstras,* or via external media such as handwritten, printed, or, increasingly, electronic books and journals. One condition for the emergence of the academic study of religion, then, is the development of such institutions of knowledge, as has happened for example among Mahāyāna Buddhists in north India in the first few centuries CE, in the Middle East toward the end of the first millennium CE, and in Europe beginning in the thirteenth century CE.

The mere existence of institutions such as universities is not, however, sufficient for the emergence of the academic study of religion. In Europe, for example, an interval of over half a millennium intervened between the development of the medieval universities and the emergence of the academic study of religion. (By contrast, in sub-Saharan Africa that study has been a component of such institutions almost from the very beginning.) At least two other conditions are necessary.

The first of these conditions requires thinkers to class practices, claims, and forms of association together in ways similar to the ways in which they are classed together by the term "religion" in English and other European languages today, and then to view the resulting set as a proper object for study by a distinct group of scholars. Martin Riesebrodt has argued that this classification is not as culturally limited as it may at first seem. He has pointed out that people have grouped together phenomena that German (and English) speakers think of as religious even without having a generic notion of religion. For example, Aśoka's edicts treat *brāhmaṇas* (early Hindus) and *śrāvaṇas* (early Buddhists, Jains, and other renouncers) as if they belonged to the same class. Polemicists at Chinese courts during the first millennium CE also thought of Buddhist, Daoist, and Confucian teachings as of similar kind. Nevertheless, the manner in which such classes are conceptualized—whether as *dharm[a]* in Sanskrit-based languages, *din* in Arabic, *shukyō* in Japanese, or something else—may present difficulties for the emergence of the academic study of religion. For example, the traditional institutionalized study of *dharma,* whose sense in Sanskrit we might convey by terms such as *statute, ordinance, law, duty, justice, virtue,* and *morality* as well as *religion,* bears little resemblance to anything that we would know as either the academic study of religion or theology, as even a passing acquaintance with the *Dharmaśāstras* makes clear. Abrahim Khan suggests that this term's meaning has in fact hampered the emergence of the academic study of religion as a single, independent academic pursuit in India. Japanese scholars in the Meiji era and later wrestled with the meaning of the term "religion" in a somewhat different way. In order to endorse the politically desirable view that Japan was a secular state, they had to separate into religious and nonreligious spheres beliefs and practices that had customarily been classed together as Shintō. In the second half of the twentieth century, Africans, reacting to imported European concepts, questioned the extent to which the term "religion" really worked in African contexts. Although in North America and Europe the academic study of religion is fairly widely established today, some scholars in that region, too, have questioned the extent to which the category "religion" is applicable across cultures. In doing so, they have seemed to call the legitimacy of that study as a distinct field into question.

The combination of the institutionalization of knowledge and the identification of religion as a fit object of study does not inevitably lead to the emergence of the academic study of religion. It might just as well lead to apologetics, as happened in Middle Eastern and European universities during the medieval period, or to a global theology or religious philosophy, such as the *philosophia perennis* that attracts thinkers around the world today. At least one further condition is necessary for the emergence of the academic study of religion. That is the relinquishing of interest in establishing traditional religious claims and turning instead to understanding and explaining religious phenomena, regardless of provenance, through nonconfessional models. Herodotos displays something of this attitude, in the absence of the other two conditions, when he remarks that all people know equally (little?) about the gods, so he is simply going to talk about human affairs and customs.

Academic communities may adopt these pluralistic, humanistic projects via different tracks. In contexts within which one religion, such as Christianity or Islam, is considered to be uniquely true, an important step between apologetics and the academic study of religion may be the conviction that all religions share a basic core, rooted somehow in the essence of humanity. This step is transitional, because it leaves in place a tension between the concerns of a global religious philosophy or theology on the one hand, and understanding and explaining religions through nonconfessional models on the other. Europe and its cultural descendants largely followed this track. European thinkers such as Herbert of Cherbury (1583–1648) responded to the wars of religion by formulating the notion of a "natural religion" common to all people. The Romantics responded to Enlightenment rationality by celebrating universally human "intimations of immortality" and of other religious profundities. Both laid the foundations for the emergence of a comparative study of religion whose character as a global theology was expressed well in the dying words of an early Swedish scholar who also happened to be a Lutheran archbishop, Nathan Söderblom (1866–1931): "I know God exists; I can prove it from the history of religions." Tensions between the comparative study of religion as a global theology and an academic study of religion that is more self-consciously humanistic remain especially strong in North America, in part as a result of the profound influence once exercised by Mircea Eliade (1907–1986).

In contexts in which traditional claims to religious exclusivity are lacking and all religions are somehow seen as manifestations of religious truth, a different track for the emergence of the academic study of religion is probably necessary. That is because in these contexts it would simply be a task of the local equivalent of theology or religious philosophy to elucidate the common core of truth that all religions share. Precisely what forces have stimulated a shift to the use of nonreligious models in these areas remains a question for future research. One certainly cannot overlook the importance of external stimuli, especially in regions that were heavily colonized (sub-Saharan Africa) or that saw themselves engaged in military and cultural competition with Europeans and U.S. Americans (Japan). At the same time, it may not do justice either to scholars who have urged the adoption of humanistic models or to their situations simply to refer to them as "westernized." On the one hand, "Western" models of education, such as Britain introduced into colonized Africa, were actually heavily theological. On the other, some non-Westerners like early Japanese scholars of religions have criticized Westerners for blurring the distinction between the academic study of religion and theology.

DEVELOPMENT OF THE ACADEMIC STUDY OF RELIGION. The preceding section contains unmistakable resonances with the thought of Max Weber, especially his notions of routinization, rational-bureaucratic authority, and the disenchantment of the modern world. Of the three conditions discussed above, however, perhaps only the second is actually distinctively modern, and that only if we extend modernity back into the immediate post-Reformation period, as historians of philosophy usually do. Nevertheless, the emergence of the academic study of religion as a result of the confluence of these three conditions is in fact a modern—or more recent—development. Individual entries will summarize regional histories in more detail. Here it may be helpful to venture a few signposts.

A tradition common in Europe and North America attributes the birth of the "science of religion," as it was called, to the comparative philologist Friedrich Max Müller (1823–1900), who referred to it for the first time in the 1867 preface to his *Chips from a German Workshop.* Nevertheless, several factors complicate this birth story. First, Europeans before Müller had done philological, ethnographic, and theoretical work that might just as well be considered a part of the academic study of religion, e.g. the work of Eugène Burnouf in the study of Buddhism. Second, inasmuch as Müller's own vision of the science of religion, informed by German idealism, sought a scientific means to religious truth, it is not clear that his science is precisely what we mean by the study of religion. Third, traditions in the Middle East, Japan, and perhaps elsewhere, too, that predate Müller's talk can claim equal regional significance in moving toward a science of religions. In short, the birth of this field of study is attributable not to a single event but to an extended and complex series of events in several regions.

One major player in the European buildup to the study of religion was philology. During the humanist movement of the fifteenth century, Europeans learned Greek and Hebrew and critically edited ancient biblical manuscripts. In the late eighteenth and nineteenth centuries they followed a similar pattern with regard to a broader range of materials. They learned the "classical" languages of the Middle East and Asia and set themselves to work on the "sacred books" written in these languages, a move that some connect with a residual Protestantism. They further deciphered ancient writing—hieroglyphics, cuneiform—and opened new vistas in what they saw, somewhat oddly, as their own antiquity, especially prebiblical civilizations in the Middle East and the linkage of European languages to Sanskrit and Old Iranian. Within Europe incipient cultural nationalisms, inspired in part by J. G. Herder (1744–1803), stimulated the collection, and at times the wholesale invention, of local folklore. At the same time, ethnographic reports of ideas and practices elsewhere—custom reserves for Bronislaw Malinowski (1884–1942) the honor of being the first actual anthropological fieldworker—poured into Europe. European thinkers filtered all this material through mental sieves that sought to retrieve the essence of religion and its earliest or primal forms, resulting in once well-known theories such as fetishism, solar mythology, totemism, animism, pre-animism or dynamism, primitive monotheism, and the magic-religion-science schema of James George Frazer (1854–1941). These theories, in turn, provided a context for the reflection of thinkers such as Emile Durkheim (1858–1917), Max Weber (1864–1920), and Sigmund Freud (1856–1939).

Alongside philological, ethnographic, and folkloristic studies, liberal Protestant theology played a major role in the development of the academic study of religion in Europe and North America. Inspired by Friedrich Schleiermacher (1768–1834), liberal theologians attempted to rescue Christianity from the critical results of natural science, history, and ethnography by appealing to a supposedly universal religious experience of which Christianity was the supreme manifestation. The result in the first half of the twentieth century was a phenomenology of religion as developed by Nathan Söderblom, Rudolf Otto (1869–1937), Friedrich Heiler (1892–1967), Gustav Mensching (1901–1978), Gerardus van der Leeuw (1890–1950), and their associates, and, with less Christian emphasis, the similar endeavors of thinkers like C. G. Jung (1875–1961) and Mircea Eliade. While philologists, ethnographers, and folklorists were often content to work within academic units defined either by language and culture (e.g., East Asian Languages and Civilizations) or by a more general method (e.g., Cultural Anthropology), the phenomenologists generally favored the placement of the academic study of religion in a single, autonomous academic unit or department.

Although the political convictions of individual scholars varied, none of these moves happened in a political vacuum. For example, Michel Despland has discussed the relationship between the policies of the July Monarchy in France and a hermeneutically oriented study of religious texts. David Chidester has noted similarities between Britain's management of colonized peoples and its management of their religions. What Europeans and North Americans have noticed less, perhaps, is how the encounter looked from the other side.

Colonial mastery provided Europeans with ready control over an extremely wide variety of materials not so easily available to the colonized. It provided the motivation to study those materials by making knowledge of the people to whom they had belonged desirable. It also provided a safe space from which scholars could examine the materials but ignore the claims they made—or even become enamored with them without surrendering any real sense of identity or control. At the beginning of the twentieth century colonial endeavors presented Japanese scholars with similar opportunities, although their range was more limited.

For the colonized the situation was different. Quite aside from possessing different histories of the formulation and organization of knowledge, people on the receiving end of the colonial project did not need to develop academic fields to learn about the "sacred books of Europe." Missionaries were more than willing to provide that knowledge, even if colonial governments did not always appreciate their efforts. And far from being able to study the claims and practices of the colonial rulers from the detached perspective of a supposedly disinterested, value-free science, colonized people were forced to define themselves over against claims by representatives of a dominant power that threatened to undercut their traditional identity and destroy their intellectual autonomy.

The early leaders in the academic study of religion were in fact the Europeans, with help from the Japanese and North Americans. Nevertheless, it would be simplistic to see the study of religion merely as a colonialist enterprise. It may also be seen as in part a response in the arena of reflection on religion, and not always the dominant one, to fundamental infrastructural changes that made colonialism as well as nationalism possible: the increasing compression of space and time as a result of ever more rapid technologies of transportation and communication. The results of this space-time compression include increased personal contacts between peoples previously separated, closer economic, political, and cultural interdependence, and substantial increases in the scale of institutions of knowledge as well as manufacturing and trade. This compression facilitated the appearance of an academic study of religion not simply by granting greater access to data but also by making confessional frames for knowledge less convincing—although they certainly remained convincing to many—and creating a context in which knowledge of religion not limited by confessional boundaries became more desirable. It did so under the shadow of increased nationalism and colonialism, which both resulted from and enforced inequitable control of new technologies as well as intellectual and cultural activities.

From a long perspective, what may be remarkable about the institutionalization of the academic study of religion is not that it first took place in Europe, Japan, and North America but how quickly it occurred all over the world. (That occurrence should not be isolated from the simultaneous emergence of many other aspects of contemporary life, from scientific medicine to weapons technology.) The institutionalization of the study of religion came in two waves. The first wave occurred in the late nineteenth and early twentieth centuries, when Europeans along with North Americans and Japanese took the lead in establishing university positions and programs (Lausanne 1871; Boston 1873; Tokyo 1903) as well as professional societies (United States 1890 [dissolved ten years later], Europe [International Association for the History of Religions] 1900, Japan 1930) for the study of religion. (In 1905 only the Tokyo chair carried the title "science of religion.") Research and publication were, of course, the inevitable concomitants of such foundations—in one sense they were their *raison d'être*—symbolized but certainly not exhausted in the English-speaking world by the massive *Sacred Books of the East* series. The second wave, which came in the third quarter of the twentieth century in the wake of decolonization and the cold war, was much more wide-ranging. It saw the development of programs for the academic study of religion in sub-Saharan Africa; Australia, New Zealand, and Oceania; Latin America; and to a limited extent South Asia and the Middle East, along with the founding of new programs in Europe as well as a burgeoning of programs in the United States.

These efforts have met with varying success. Despite a long tradition, Japan has programs in the academic study of religion in only about one percent of its universities; by contrast, by the 1970s the corresponding number in the United States was about one third. Such efforts have also encountered a variety of challenges. For example, programs in sub-Saharan Africa have suffered from a lack of infrastructure as well as a loss of intellectual talent to more prosperous parts of the globe. In most places a primary challenge has come from dominant religions and ideologies. French institutions have been adamantly secular for over a century, but elsewhere in Western Europe dominant programs in Christian theology have outdone the academic study of religion in competition for scarce resources and public status; for example, in the United Kingdom the leading programs have been in so-called new universities (Lancaster, Manchester, Stirling), and a similar pattern is visible to some extent in Germany (Bayreuth, Bremen), despite traditions in older universities (Berlin, Bonn, Marburg, Tübingen). Programs in Eastern Europe and China have had to negotiate a state ideology antagonistic to religion, while programs in the United States, which blossomed during the cold war, have needed to negotiate a state ideology whose opposition to "godless communism" favored religious commitment. In the Middle East, space-time compression has brought about a very different relationship with the rest of the world: the rerouting of formerly vigorous, intercontinental trade either around or, in the case of air travel, over the region and a shift to oil as a source of wealth, often actually or seemingly controlled by foreigners. This context has encouraged a religiously defined cultural loyalism. Although some programs in the academic study of religion have arisen in the region, most work takes place in the context of the presumed superiority of Islam as God's final revelation.

The academic study of religion has often justified itself in terms of its public utility. For example, in Japan before 1945 some advocated pursuing it as a contribution to national unity. In postcolonial Africa scholars turned to the study of indigenous religions as a means to foster independent political and cultural identities. More broadly, Mircea Eliade aspired to revive culture through the formulation of a "new humanism."

At the beginning of the twenty-first century scholars of religions were pursuing yet another public role: providing the general public and more specifically mass communications media with reliable information about religions (Japanese scholars after the Aum Shinrikyō attacks; ReMID in Germany and INFORM in the United Kingdom; the information bureau of the American Academy of Religion). In addition, many countries have been wrestling with ways to make their traditions of religious education in schools more pluralistic. Although some have adopted a pluralistic confessional approach, as in Germany, where students choose an education in either Catholicism, Protestantism, or a more general ethical culture, others, such as South Africa, have at least proposed replacing confessionally based education with a pre-university public education in the academic study of religion.

Methods and Issues in the Academic Study of Religion. There is still very little by way of a universally acknowledged theoretical or methodological canon in the academic study of religion. One positive result is that the field admits a considerable amount of creativity. Another result, however, is that the remarks that follow will inevitably be idiosyncratic, reflecting regional and personal preferences at least as much as any greater unity. They touch briefly upon commonalities that unite the academic study of religion, methods and theories of that study, and recent trends.

Commonalities. In the English-speaking world, there has been considerable uncertainty about both the name and character of the academic study of religion. In the last one hundred years scholars have called this pursuit the science of religion, comparative study of religion(s), history of religion(s), religious studies, (more colloquially) world religions, and the academic study of religion(s). The terminology used in this set of entries, "the academic study of religion," remains ambiguous. For example, in those parts of the world where Christianity is the dominant religion, biblical studies are traditionally a part of theology. As sometimes practiced, however, biblical studies might just as well be seen as a highly developed subfield within the academic study of religion.

Uncertainty about the name of this study finds a reflection in uncertainty about its character. Is it an academic discipline, united in the application of a specific method, or is it an unruly, polymethodic field, including any and every academic pursuit that somehow treats religious data? Is the object of study—"religion"—a category sui generis, which must be studied on its own terms, or does it conveniently bring together elements from different areas of life, permitting the reduction of the religious to the nonreligious? Is the goal to understand human religious insights or symbols as they come to expression in human speech and action, as one understands the meanings of books, or is it rather to provide explanations for various occurrences along the lines of the social and natural sciences? Does one require a special sympathy for religion in order to make sense out of it, or is one required to be an outsider—a "methodological" if not actual atheist or agnostic—in order to see clearly? Arguments about these and similar questions have perhaps generated more heat and smoke than they have light. Nevertheless, one might detect a trend in the late twentieth and early twenty-first centuries toward a conception of the study of religions that is polymethodic, explanatory, at least methodologically agnostic, and sees religion simply as a convenient category.

If the efforts of a century and a half have had uncertain results in precisely denoting or defining the academic study of religion, they have been somewhat more successful in creating a common language for it. Scholars have abandoned earlier, almost Linnaean attempts to group religions into meaningful classes—natural religions, national religions, prophetic religions, ethical religions, world religions, and so on—as a preliminary to locating them in grand developmental schemas. They have also abandoned attempts, inspired by Hegel, to identify the essence of each religion in a simple term or proposition (for example, Zoroastrianism as "the religion of struggle," Christianity as the "religion of love" [van der Leeuw]). But other efforts have been more successful. Consider the matter-of-factness with which we now speak of various religions as givens—Hinduism, Buddhism, Daoism, Shintō, and so on—where, at least from a Christian or Muslim perspective, these now distinct religions were once simply paganism and idolatry. Scholars have also created the rudiments of a technical vocabulary, in which the terms *myth, ritual, rite of passage, sacrifice,* and perhaps *symbol* may be the most widely successful terms. Other terms that were once prominent, such as *experience, numinous, sacred,* and *profane,* not to mention older creations like *totem* and *taboo,* now seem characteristic of disputed or discarded positions. Since the 1980s, however, studies have appeared that vigorously seek to deconstruct these common categories, both in terms of descriptive and conceptual inadequacy and political disutility. Although these studies often present compelling analyses, they have as yet had only a limited effect on actual linguistic usage. Scholars now seem, however, to be abandoning the term "myth."

Methods and theories. At the beginning of the twenty-first century there is some consensus that the academic study of religion is a polymethodic field. There is also some consensus about some of the "approaches" or "perspectives" that this field contains. Almost invariably mentioned, along with other approaches, are history, psychology, sociology, and comparative studies or phenomenology; the meaning of the last term varies considerably. Although one might define these approaches primarily in terms of problems and theories, in the way, for example, physicists and sociologists delineate their fields, scholars of religions have generally begun instead with the ideas of "great thinkers," for example, William James (1842–1910), Sigmund Freud, and C. G. Jung for psychology; Karl Marx (1818–1883), Max Weber, and Émile Durkheim for sociology; Gerardus van der Leeuw and Mircea Eliade for phenomenology. Work in the related field of anthropology has received similar treatment, although the "great thinkers" there may be somewhat more recent (Bronislaw Malinowski, E. E. Evans-Pritchard [1902–1973], Claude Lévi-Strauss [b. 1908], Clifford Geertz [b. 1926]).

In addition to knowing the ideas of these "great thinkers" and their epigones, the common expectation today is that scholars of religion will also know the languages of the people whose religions they study. Such expectations provide a clue to the methods that scholars of religions actually employ. Work in the field tends to depend upon textual analysis, ethnographical observation, or both, combined with a generous amount of theorizing to set the context for the application of these methods. It less frequently analyzes nonverbal artifacts with the methods of archaeology, art history, and musicology, a tendency some attribute to a residual Protestantism. Such a modus operandi assures that scholars are attuned to the richness of their data. It also means, however, that work in the field tends to consist of anecdotal observations coupled, in the best instances, with sophisticated reasoning. Scholars of religions have had relatively little interest in the formulation of generalizations based on a statistical analysis of data. They tend to regard such generalizations as overlooking complexity and to relegate them to the "social scientific" study of religion, located in other academic departments, professional associations, and journals.

Trends. Readers looking for specific topics that interest scholars in the academic study of religion probably do best to consult the topical outline of this encyclopedia, but it may be helpful here to note some broader trends. One is the increasing specialization that has taken place over the last one hundred years. The demand that scholars possess sophisticated linguistic and cultural knowledge, coupled with the increase in the number of people who have such knowledge for different languages and cultures, has resulted in specialization by areas, such as South Asian religions, Islam, and Buddhism, along with subdivisions of these larger groups, like Vedic studies, contemporary Islam, and Japanese Buddhism. Other kinds of specialized groupings—women and religion, religion and literature—exist, although they often straddle the divide between the academic study of religion and theology. Specializations defined by applying specific methods to theoretical issues, as in, for example, the distinction between physical and organic chemistry, are much less common.

A second trend has been an emerging tension between two broad orientations within the field, critical theory and science. The former is the more established, growing out of the field's traditional interpretive interests and relying heavily on the French "philosophers of 1968," such as Jacques Derrida (1930–2004) and Michel Foucault (1926–1984), as well as postcolonial thought, most notably, perhaps, the thought of Edward Said (1935–2003). These scholars have focused on the conditions in which knowledge is produced, critiquing claims to objectivity and universal validity. They embrace a wide variety of positions, but among common tendencies we might note the following: the conviction that knowledge is a culturally limited social construction; an emphasis on the inevitable distortions of translation tending to an assertion of incommensurability between languages, cultures, and communities; the interrogation of the cultural rootedness of the categories and methods of scholarship; the deconstruction of general groupings in favor of particularity and difference; an interest in the corporeal and material as opposed to the ideational that presupposes at the same time as it critiques a Cartesian dualism or Platonic idealism; a preference for the marginal, variously defined by race, gender, class, and other categories as well; the identification of political, economic, and social domination as the actual if unstated goal of social science and scholarly endeavors more broadly; an insistence upon plurivocity and an experimentation with nontraditional, non-monographic literary forms; and—despite the generalizations implicit in some of the preceding characteristics—a rejection of the possibility of formulating adequate generalizations about cultural materials.

More recently, voices have arisen claiming to produce just the sorts of knowledge that the critical theorists find untenable. This trend has been strongest, perhaps, among those who claim to have found in cognitive science a ground for universals that transcend the limitations of social construction. (Cognitive science itself arose as an alternative to behaviorism in psychology and philosophy.) When those who favor science do not simply dogmatically insist upon science as the most compelling form of contemporary knowledge, they may emphasize considerations like the following to justify their approach: the large amount of shared mental content which the intersubjective communication that we appear to observe presupposes; the evolutionary demands that require communication and commensurability for the survival of the species; the ability of controlled, cross-cultural experimentation to establish adequate generalizations about universal mental structures; the need to postulate these structures in order to explain various human abilities, such as the learning of language; the tendency of critical-theoretical accounts to overlook commonalities and overstate differences and so make generalizations seem implausible; the apparent logical fallacies, such as the genetic fallacy of rejecting categories on the basis of their prior history, and self-contradictions within the critical theorists' approach; and the tendency of critical theorists to exempt their own scholarly efforts from the scathing criticisms that they direct at others. At present the lines between critical theory and science are sharply drawn, and it is impossible to predict what the future of this tension might be.

Finally, one might note a growing awareness of the global character of the academic study of religion, as witnessed in part by the entries that follow. The International Association of the History of Religions now boasts affiliates in such diverse places as Cuba, Indonesia, Nigeria, and New

Zealand and has been very active in hosting conferences outside of Europe and North America. The International Committee of the American Academy of Religion has sought to foster connections between scholars in North America and other parts of the world. The impetus for both sets of activities remains, however, largely European and North American.

One would anticipate that a growing self-consciousness among scholars of religions in regions outside Europe and North America would lead them to explore their own traditions of knowledge about religions which predate European contact, as literary scholars have begun to do (e.g., Ganesh N. Devy, *After Amnesia: Tradition and Change in Indian Literary Criticism* [Bombay, 1992]; cf. Japan; North Africa and the Middle East). At the same time, scholars will need to reflect critically on the extent to which a regionalized view of the academic study of religion will remain expedient. For example, are South Asian scholars fascinated with Marx "Westernized," or does that label, or more broadly does the consideration of the academic study of religion region by region, obscure what may be alternative and ultimately more compelling interests uniting groups of scholars across regional boundaries?

Bibliography

Braun, Willi, and Russell T. McCutcheon, eds. *Guide to the Study of Religion.* London, 2000.

Chidester, David. *Savage Systems: Colonialism and Comparative Religion in Southern Africa.* Charlottesville, Va., 1996.

Chidester, David. *Christianity: A Global History.* New York, 2001.

Connolly, Peter, ed. *Approaches to the Study of Religion.* London, 1999.

Despland, Michel. *L'émergence des sciences de la religion. La Monarchie de Juillet: un moment fondateur.* Paris, 1999.

Devy, Ganesh N. *After Amnesia: Tradition and Change in Indian Literary Criticism.* Bombay, 1992.

Jordan, Louis Henry. *Comparative Religion: Its Genesis and Growth.* Edinburgh, 1905.

Kippenberg, Hans G. *Die Entdeckung der Religionsgeschichte: Religionswissenschaft und Moderne.* München, 1997.

Lincoln, Bruce. *Theorizing Myth: Narrative, Ideology, and Scholarship.* Chicago, 1999.

Michaels, Axel, ed. *Klassiker der Religionswissenschaft: Von Friedrich Schleiermacher bis Mircea Eliade.* 2d ed. Munich, 1997.

Preus, J. Samuel. *Explaining Religion: Criticism and Theory from Bodin to Freud.* Atlanta, 1996.

Sharpe, Eric J. *Comparative Religion: A History.* 2d ed. La Salle, Ill., 1986.

Taylor, Mark C., ed. *Critical Terms for Religious Studies.* Chicago, 1998.

Wasserstrom, Steven M. *Religion after Religion: Gershom Scholem, Mircea Eliade, and Henry Corbin at Eranos.* Princeton, N.J., 1999.

Gregory D. Alles (2005)

STUDY OF RELIGION: THE ACADEMIC STUDY OF RELIGION IN AUSTRALIA AND OCEANIA

Aside from literature reinforcing the Christian and Jewish ways of life, studies in religion in the Oceanic region began with reports on the customs and beliefs of "savage" or "native" peoples in and near European colonies. Along with the published diaries of early explorers, whose observations were highly cursory, most of the early commentators were missionaries, including the Spanish Jesuit Juan Antonio Cantova, who wrote about the Caroline Islands as early as the 1720s; William Ellis of the London Missionary Society, who documented various Polynesian cultures by 1829; and the German Lutherans Carl Ottow and Johann Geissler, who described the New Guinea Biak people in 1857. In addition, visitors who utilized missionary informants—such as the French captain François Leconte, who wrote about northern New Caledonia in 1847—also recorded events of interest to the study of religion in the region.

Pioneer Missionaries' Reports. Although evangelization was their main priority, many pioneer missionaries were surprisingly interested in gaining knowledge of the peoples they encountered. Such concepts as *mana* and *taboo,* destined to stimulate Western theories about the origins of religion, hailed from the Pacific mission field. In the 1770s, after Captain James Cook's brief notations on the meaning of taboo in Tahiti and Hawai'i, the term became associated with biblical prohibition in evangelistic discourse and was thereafter incorporated into European vocabularies. The priest-academic Robert Codrington introduced the notion of mana as manipulated "spirit power" after investigating Banks Islander beliefs (New Hebrides, now Vanuatu) in the 1870s, at a time when he headed the Anglican Melanesian Mission. Totemism became an acclaimed feature of Aboriginal (and thereby very primitive) religion; the earliest significant account of an Australian native protecting an animal (a *goanna*) as his "brother" was made by a London Missionary Society delegate in 1834. Ideas about high gods, again important for origins theories (e.g., Andrew Lang in the 1890s), arose out of Aboriginal talk of the All-Father, which was in all likelihood an innovative indigenous concept to make sense of missionary teachings about the one God.

That Polynesia could match Europe and Asia for sacralized royalty, moreover, was made plain by the Hawaiian king Kalakaua's eulogistic *Legends and Myths* (1888). With this background, a professional competitiveness sometimes arose when secular anthropologists entered the region. There was no love lost, for example, between the Lutheran Carl Strehlow, a missionary to the Aranda in central Australia, and Baldwin Spencer, the leader of the 1894 Hort Expedition and later Chief Protector of the Aborigines (1911–1912), who divulged many secrets about Aranda religion that Strehlow had honored. In another case, Bronislaw Malinowski, allegedly the first true field anthropologist, was told nothing about the coastal Mailu by his initial host, the London Missionary Society missionary William Saville (1914–1915), who wanted to write up his own findings. Disappointed,

Malinowski moved on to the Trobriand Islands. Although Oceania was home to a quarter of the world's discrete religions and research material was plentiful, this professional tension lasted through the years leading up to World War II.

In a number of places, missionary scholarship was utterly determinative. For example, the Dutch relied on church initiatives to carry missionaries into Irian Jaya, the far and dangerous frontier of Indonesia. The church also had a singular influence across equatorial Polynesia as illustrated by the work of Wyatt Gill in Rarotonga (the capital of the Cook Islands) and Father Sebastian Englert on Easter Island. Elsewhere a mixture pertained, and government-sponsored anthropology was sometimes evident. In the more colonized Polynesia, for example, the one-time British governor of New Zealand, Sir George Grey, adopted a policy of collecting Maori lore that lasted up until the 1890s, and during the 1910s the U.S. Bureau of Indian Affairs, otherwise focused on mainland cultures, encouraged Nathaniel Emerson to document the Hawaiian *hula.* Between World War I and World War II, Francis Williams, the most reputable of all government anthropologists, worked in coastal parts of Australia's Territory of Papua (now Papua New Guinea), although his brief included cooperation with the missions. The Anglican cleric Adolphus Elkin, who served as a professor of anthropology at the University of Sydney from 1934 to 1956 and founded the journal *Oceania,* was welcomed by the Australian government as adviser on Aboriginal issues during the 1940s.

EARLY INTELLECTUALS. Interest in the wider world of comparative religion came late in the colonial histories of Australia, New Zealand, and also Hawai'i, which matched other southeast Pacific museum constructions with its own Bernice P. Bishop Museum as early as 1885, before American annexation. A key impetus to study other religions was provided by the Theosophical Society, starting in Australia by 1895 and possessing an impressive center in Sydney during the 1910s. In New Zealand during the 1920s, a circle of study formed around Elsdon Best, cofounder of the *Journal of the Polynesian Society* in 1898, who likened the Maori cult of Io to a removed Gnostic-looking deity with layers of beings that separated him from the earth. At the same time, more critical scholarship emerged: The Australian surgeon Grafton Elliot Smith became a chief instigator of the Egyptocentric Diffusionist school in the 1920s, after having been anatomy professor in Cairo, and Samuel Angus of Scotland, a graduate of the universities of Princeton and Berlin (under Adolf von Harnack, 1851–1930, and Gustav Adolf Deissmann, 1866–1937), took up a professorship in New Testament and historical theology at the University of Sydney in 1915 and quickly emerged as an eminent authority on Greco-Roman mystery religions.

This coming and going of "imported" and "exported" intellectuals was typical well into the post–World War II period. Scholars writing on non-Christian traditions usually arrived from outside. Among provocative Germanics was the economist Kurt Singer, who wrote from Sydney that the Zoroastrian stress on the battle between good and evil added to problem of human conflict, and Peter Munz, who sought to better the theories of myth formulated by James G. Frazer (1854–1941) and Claude Lévi-Strauss (b. 1908) from Dunedin, New Zealand. British scholars Raynor Johnston (comparative mysticism) and John Bowman (Samaritans) went to Melbourne, and George Knight (Semitics) went first to Dunedin and later to Suva, the capital of Fiji. In return, Australia and New Zealand lost various experts in Christianity to overseas postings, including the theologian Colin Williams to Yale University, where he became dean of the divinity school; the church historian George Yule to the University of Aberdeen; the New Testament specialists John O'Neill and Graham Stanton to the University of Edinburgh and Cambridge University, respectively; and the interfaith specialist John D'Arcy May to Dublin University. Some expatriate dons came as long-term (and often highly productive) visitors; yet, as time went on, homegrown scholarship firmed up and the Pacific eventually became established on its own as a region of scholarly prowess.

EARLY ACADEMIC PROGRAMS. With university courses in Asian studies—especially on Middle Eastern and Indic civilizations—being set in place during the late 1950s and the 1960s, the time was ripe for historical and comparative studies of religions to enter the academic forum. Among the faculty of Australian National University's new oriental studies program were Indologist A. L. Basham, Buddhologist Jan De Jong, and Islamicist Antony Johns, as well as the region's leading scholar in the sociology of religion, Hans Mol. Similar studies were also implemented at the University of Melbourne, where the journal *Milla wa-Milla: The Australian Bulletin of Comparative Religion* made its appearance in 1961 and the first of the Charles Strong Lectures, designed by a liberal Protestant cleric to be on non-Christian traditions, took place. These were followed up by the publication of *Essays on Religious Traditions of the World,* initiated in 1970 by the Anglican priest George Mullens, a scholar in Japanese Buddhism. The first department of religious studies in the region, however, was not institutionalized until 1971, and then at Victoria University in Wellington, New Zealand, although New Zealand's programs at the University of Canterbury in Christchurch, New Zealand, and the University of Otago in Dunedin foreshadowed this, with Albert Moore's 1966 University of Otago lectureship in the history and phenomonology in religion being the discipline's first generically significant appointment for Australasia. The foundation professor at New Zealand's University of Wellington was Lloyd Geering, a renowned liberal Christian theologian.

Intriguingly, Geering remains the only memorable classic-looking theologian born and bred in the whole South Pacific region. Theologically engaged Australians who possess genuine international acclaim have simply not worked on mainstream matters—John Eccles's work on synaptic theory and Charles Birch's work in process thought are two obvious cases. However, Australia is a more secular country, and Eric Sharpe, the first chair of the religious studies department at the University of Sydney (1977–1996), was by no means a practicing theologian. Sharpe secured the Sydney chair primarily on the basis of his work *Comparative Religion: A History* (1975). This volume established him as one of the world's leading methodologists in the comparative and historical study of religions, a reputation that emanated from Australia and was consolidated by such later works as *Understanding Religion* (1983) and *Nathan Söderblom and the Study of Religion* (1990).

An Englishman, Sharpe had strong connections to the University of Manchester (especially John Hinnells) and Lancaster University (especially Ninian Smart) and served as chair of the history of religion department at Sweden's Uppsala University from 1980 to 1981. Although Sharpe could have been enticed back into the transatlantic center of theoretical debate, he decided to remain in Australia and consolidate his new department. He consistently published research on Western interpretations of Hinduism and brought to Sydney brahmin Indologist Arvind Sharma, who founded the journal *Religious Traditions* in 1978 and the *Journal of Studies in the Bhagavadgītā* in 1981. Sharpe also continued conducting historical studies of Christian missionary approaches to other religions. At the 1988 Chicago symposium on his opus, Sharpe acquitted himself artfully against younger critics' suggestions that he was a closet theologian, and as the years went on he defined himself more as an historian of ideas about religion than anything else. Interestingly, in 1995 his first academic appointee and protégé Garry Trompf took a chair in the History of Ideas beside him at the University of Sydney.

Trompf had previously held the first of two lectureships in religious studies in Australia, in the not-yet-independent Territory of Papua New Guinea, where he taught alongside the Semiticist and fellow Australian Carl Loeliger. Australia's north was to yield the earliest formal developments in the discipline, with the first autonomous department emerging at the University of Queensland in 1975, before Sharpe arrived in Sydney. Although begun under the early leadership of the Englishman Eric Pyle, Queensland was to wait until 1981 for an established chair. That the Australian-born Francis Andersen took the position was significant nationally, but it was also indicative of the weight of interests in the department. He was a fine biblical scholar amid others, including the American Edgar Conrad as a fellow commentator on Hebrew prophetism and the Irishman Seán Freyne and the German-Australian Michael Lattke as scholars of New Testament times. Queensland, however, was also to secure a special reputation for Buddhist studies. Buddhism had already been of wide attraction, including the popular writings by the early feminist-lawyer Marie Byles from 1957 to 1965, the founding of the *Journal of the Oriental Society of Australia* in Sydney in 1963, and the various textual studies and translations, especially those of Peter Masefield. Special distinction was also given to the work of the Australian Philip Almond on the history of Buddhism's Western interpretations and Rod Bucknell's work on meditative practice.

Almond, who succeeded Andersen as professor after the latter moved to the University of California at Berkeley, can be credited with a distinctly Australian contribution to the theory of religion. He was crucial among revisionist thinkers in deconstructing Western scholarly reifications and popular representations of significant Eastern traditions. In *The British Discovery of Buddhism* (1988), he argued that Buddhism, as it is popularly defined in most textbooks, was a Western invention. At a slightly later stage, Almond went on to ponder the Victorians' invention of Islam, and his work compared with Edward Said's deconstruction of Orientalism. In other writings, especially *Mystical Experience and Religious Doctrine* (1982) and those appealing to the methodological insights of Rudolf Otto (1869–1937), Almond doubted that mysticism could be apprehended with the kinds of objectivist treatment beginning to dominate his discipline.

At the University of Sydney, research into the religions of Oceania was a forte, with Trompf returning to Australia in 1978. Like Sharpe and Almond, Trompf was, admittedly, better equipped to write on Western theoretical ideas. A practicing historian who later served as a professor of history at the University of Papua New Guinea from 1983 to 1985, he was the beneficiary of a very strong tradition of religious history in Australia, if one considers such lights as the German Hermann Sasse, the Britisher John McManners, the New Zealander Edwin Judge, and the Australian Bruce Mansfield, who founded the internationally acclaimed *Journal of Religious History* from Sydney in 1960. This background helps explain Trompf's books on Western historiography and religious ideas, particularly his volumes on *The Idea of Historical Recurrence* (1979). However, prior training in prehistory and ethnohistory and over ten years of intensive research in Melanesia (Fiji, Papua New Guinea, Solomon Islands, Vanuatu, and New Caledonia) allowed him to produce the first major monographs—*Melanesian Religion* (1991) and *Payback* (1994)—to address one of the most complex religious scene in the world. A distinctively homegrown contribution to the theory of religion developed from these combined interests that dealt with "the logic of retribution" (i.e., those aspects of religious life concerned with revenge, reciprocity, and the explanation of events in terms of praise and blame, reward and punishment).

Scholarship set on understanding Melanesia's religious life seems to have involved one of the largest conglomerates of social-scientific endeavor ever undertaken. Important theoretical positionings were forged out of the region's great cultural diversity: the Polish anthropologist Bronislaw Malinowski's school of functionalism derived from his Trobriands research; the English proto-structuralist A. M. Hocart read Fijian chieftainship as a basic model of sacral leadership; in his studies in Houailou, New Caledonia, Lévi-

Strauss's predecessor Maurice Leenhardt framed early body theory as a self-awareness process running from cosmomorphism to anthropomorphism; the Hungarian Géza Róheim and the Englishmen John Layard tried substantiating Freudian and Jungian insights, respectively, from coastal Papua and Malekula; and Margaret Mead (1901–1978) and Gregory Bateson worked together to formulate theories of gender and social divisiveness from the Sepik area. Important contributions to particular religio-ethnologic issues have also been drawn from Melanesia, mainly by European and American researchers. Topics that have been addressed include headhunting by Jan van Baal, cannibalism by Marshall Sahlins, grand ceremonial exchanges by Andrew Strathern, initiatory disclosures by Fredrik Barth, ritual homosexuality by Gilbert Herdt, sorcery by Reo Fortune and the Australian Michele Stephen, and sacral legitimation of leadership by Jean Guiart and Maurice Godelier. Melanesian cargo cultism produced various theories, such as cosmic regeneration by Mircea Eliade (1907–1986), proto-nationalism by the neo-Marxist Peter Worsley, the dream of a perfected reciprocity by Kenelm Burridge, new explanations of a changing cosmos by Peter Lawrence, a rite of passage into modernity by Patrick Gesch, and a search for salvation by John Strelan. The conversion processes among Melanesians also attracted mission historians such as the Australians Niel Gunson on Polynesia, David Hilliard on the Solomons, and David Wetherell on Papua; missiologists such as the eminent Australian scholar Alan Tippett, as well as Theo Ahrens, Ennio Mantovani, Friedgard Tomasetti, Darell Whiteman, and Mary MacDonald; and analysts of indigenizing Christianity such as John Barker and the Australian Bronwyn Douglas. Part of Trompf's vision has been to assess Melanesian religion in all its aspects to find the means of representing all this scholarship synoptically and to facilitate indigenous scholarly writing on religion.

An early graduate of the Sydney department, Tony Swain confirmed its strength in indigenous studies by writing the first exhaustive account of theories about Australian Aboriginal religion and the first history of Aboriginal religion since outside contact in *A Place for Strangers* (1993). He questioned Eliade's stress on cosmic axis and accounted for more diffuse notions of space and one's belongingness to land. He also disputed that there were any traditional Aboriginal notions of Mother Earth and denied that high gods were honored before outside pressures from Melanesia and then white colonization. Again, Swain benefited from important predecessors that included, aside from those already mentioned, the Australians Ronald Berndt and Ted Strehlow (both with German backgrounds), W. E. H. Stanner of Australian National University, and the Victorian Max Charlesworth. Swain and Trompf's *Religions of Oceania* (1995) revealed the extraordinary international interest in the Pacific religious scene. Sometimes disproportionate group interest is found, such as Germanic scholarship on the Aborigines and Americans on Micronesia, but some unusual individual achievements by outsiders stand out. For example, the Italian Valerio Valeri wrote a detailed account of Hawaiian religion; the German Hans-Jürgen Greschat wrote a thorough ethnography of taboo; and the Finn Jikka Siikala wrote an authoritative account of new religious movements in central Polynesia.

ACADEMIC PROGRAM DEVELOPMENT. Other intellectual and institutional developments within the whole Australo-Pacific region make for a complex story. In Victoria, programs for studying religion were successively established at LaTrobe University, Deakin University, and Monash University. At LaTrobe the sinologist Paul Rule researched Western images of Confucianism; Gregory Bailey studied ancient Indian ideologies; and the Australian dean of patristics, Eric Osborn, researched select pre-Nicene Church Fathers. Deakin possessed the philosophers Max Charlesworth and Ian Weeks. Charlesworth, who had already taught a religious studies course at Melbourne University as early as 1970—basically in the philosophy of religion—was to institutionalize his dream as professor at Deakin (in Geelong) and he went on to write incisively about methodology issues in *Religious Inventions* (1997). In Victoria, interestingly, there has been sympathy for the idea of a *philosophia perennis* behind spiritual traditions, revealed not only in Kenneth Oldmeadow's fine exposition, *Traditionalism: Religion in the Light of Perennial Philosophy* (2000), but also among philosophers attracted by Eastern, especially Indian, metaphysics, including Ian Kesarcodi-Watson and Purussotima Bilimoria, founder of Australian Society for Asian and Comparative Philosophy and editor of the journal *Sophia*.

Further afield in Australia, Adelaide is most important. With the change in institutional status that produced the University of South Australia came the largest department of religion studies in the country in 1991. This was spearheaded by Professor Norman Habel, the brilliant expositor of the book of Job and founder of the Earth Bible project. With liberal philosophical theologian Vincent Hayes, he founded the Australian Association for the Study of Religions in 1975, which came to oversee the Charles Strong Lectures and built up its own publications, including the journal *Australian Religion Studies Review*, first published in 1988. The Association's concern with a variety of religions demarcated it from the Theological Association of Australia and New Zealand, which is linked to the journals *Colloquium*, *Australian Biblical Review*, and *Pacifica*.

New Zealand benefited from Paul Morris, who returned to Wellington from Britain in 1993 to take over the chair from Geering. Already established in Judaic studies, Morris went on to edit impressive collections on modernity and postmodernity (and New Zealand religious verse). He worked with James Veitch, a critical thinker inspired by Geering with an eye for crises produced by environmental degradation and ideologies of terror. Also worthy of mention are the well-known Africanists Elizabeth Isichei, who was for a time at Wellington, and Harold Turner, who has worked primarily from Britain. Other New Zealand scholars of note are Albert Moore, an authority on religious art; Brian Colless, a patrologist; and Peter Donovan, an instructor in philosopher of religion. Of journals published in New Zealand, Auckland's *Prudentia* stands out, although its special issues brought together classicists, philosophers, theologians and religionists from across the Tasman Sea and were dominated by Australians, especially the patrologist Raoul Mortley and the historian of philosophy David Dockrill.

Although Mark Jurgensmeyer wrote his first book on religion and politics, *The New Cold War?* (1993), from the University of Hawai'i, in the Pacific Islands more broadly the history and phenomenology of religion has chiefly focused on traditional and changing religious life. Although they also have pastoral agendas, the Melanesian Institute's journals *Catalyst* and *Point* provide valuable information, and the Micronesian Seminar, a research institute founded by the Catholic Church in 1972, contributes to scholarship in the north Pacific. The CORAIL colloquia in Nouméa have been a key outlet for research in French dependencies, as fixtures in Hawai'i have been for American scholars, such as the East-West Center and Brigham Young University's journal *Pacific Studies.* Overall, indigenous writing in religion has been more consistently theological; major forums are the *Journal of Melanesian Theology* and *Journal of Pacific Theology.*

Biblical Scholarship. To conclude, one cannot underestimate the continuing strength and color of biblical scholarship in Australasia (e.g., authors such as Robert Maddox, John Painter, Robert Barnes, and the controversial Barbara Thiering), and their impact on religious institutions. The same may be said of regional church (and school) historians (e.g., Ian Breward, Hilary Carey, and Susan Emilsen) and public-policy philosophers (e.g., Graham Little and Robert Gascoigne). Apart from the more comparativist volume *Reclaiming Our Rites* (1994), most feminist and gender-related works about religion betray women's hopes for greater opportunities within the Christian churches. Even Aboriginal womanist writers such as Anne Pattel-Gray and Lee Skye have been theologically oriented. Although the creation of religious studies departments threatened divinity boards, theological colleges held their own, and in some universities, theological studies discovered new life (e.g., Flinders, Monash, and the Australian Catholic University). Pauline Allen from the Australian Catholic University was rewarded with the presidency of the International Patristics Association in 2003 for groundbreaking (and liturgically relevant) publications on early Christian prayer and spirituality.

Much sociology of religion has been crucial for religious organizations to ponder their constituencies and demographic possibilities. Over and above valuable theoretical work on religion as identity and anchorage—such as *Identity and the Sacred* (1976)—Hans Mol heralded the more statistical approach found with Alan Black, Gary Bouma, Trisha Brombery, and Philip Hughes. Some sociology is more internationalist: Rowan Ireland on Brazilian spirit movements; Rachael Kohn on self religions, and the Sydney branch Center for Millennial Studies on comparative chiliasm. Impressive empirical and clinical work in Australia also led to the publication of the *International Journal of the Psychology of Religion* by Lawrence Brown of the University of New South Wales in 1991. Intense research into ancient Gnosticisms by Samuel Lieu, Majella Franzmann, and Iain Gardner, and into later esoterico-theosophic currents by Gregory Tillett and John Cooper, have been reflected in the Australian cofounding of the monograph series *Gnostica* in 1997. Interest in religion and science was greatly boosted by cosmologist Paul Davies' arrival in Adelaide in 1990, and religion and politics received a boost with the introduction of the monograph series *Religion, Politics, and Society* in 2001. Clearly, at the beginning of the twenty-first century, the critical study of religions is most certainly in blossom in Australia and Oceania.

See Also Australian Indigenous Religions, overview article; Christianity, article on Christianity in Australia and New Zealand; Transculturation and Religion, article on Religion in the Formation of Modern Oceania.

Bibliography

Barnes, Robert. "Religious Studies and Theology: A Short Historical Survey, 1850 to the Present." In *Knowing Ourselves and Others: The Humanities in Australia into the 21st Century*, edited by Anthony Low, vol. 2, ch. 24. Canberra, Australia, 1998.

Osborn, Eric. *Religious Studies in Australia since 1958.* Sydney, Australia, 1978.

Trompf, Garry. "A Survey of New Approaches to the Study of Religion in Australia and the Pacific." In *New Approaches to the Study of Religion*, edited by Peter Antes, Armin Geertz, and Randi Warne, sect. 2, ch. 4. Berlin, 2004.

Garry W. Trompf (2005)

STUDY OF RELIGION: THE ACADEMIC STUDY OF RELIGION IN EASTERN EUROPE AND RUSSIA

In most European countries, the study of religion developed during a period of transition between the nineteenth and twentieth centuries. It was a time when scholars were attempting to categorize and examine the full range of human activities. The study of religions emerged then as a specifically modernistic, empirically oriented discipline focusing on culture, and concerned first and foremost with the human being. Individual researchers gained academic standing and recognition not by reason of nationality or citizenship but rather by virtue of their academic credentials, their interests and affinities for specific schools of thought, as well as by trends within the field of religious studies—all factors that have little to do with geopolitical principles. In an examination of the course of the development of religious studies in Europe, which may be subdivided into the continent's eastern and western spheres, much depends on political developments in Europe during the Cold War period. European religious studies stands in an objectively identical context: over the course of many centuries, Europe's religious situation was determined by a single religion, and this fact also restricted, in a fundamental way, the modes of access to religion that were open to theoretical and methodological research.

In contrast, it was European expansionism that brought knowledge of non-European religions, and which consequently contributed decisively to the creation of a common material basis for research within the field of religious studies. With the exception of Soviet Russia, this religious-scientific material was appraised in the other countries now designated as "eastern European" by such methods commonly deployed by religious-studies scholars in general. These include comparative methods, religious-historical methods, religious-phenomenological methods, religious-critical methods, and others. Moreover, with these methods, similar results were also achieved. Only after 1945, when these states came under Soviet domination, did the situation change. This change was due to the application of powerful political and ideological constraints. As a result, however, no distinctively Eastern European variant of religious studies has come into existence, and Eastern Europe was also thereby prevented from becoming a place of academic self-identification. On the contrary, the academic study of religion was eradicated almost entirely behind the Iron Curtain, though it did manage to retain a certain form in Poland. It was replaced during the Cold War era by the ideology of so-called scientific atheism.

The Emergence of Religious Studies in Eastern Europe and Russia. The beginnings of religious studies in Eastern Europe, as elsewhere on the continent, occurred during the last third of the nineteenth century, when new efforts were undertaken in religious research. These new directions were influenced by new currents of thought, including positivism and evolution theory, as well as from the positive impact of new information from the ethnological, religious-historical, and archaeological spheres. However, the study of religion was not established as an institution (i.e., as a relatively independent field of academic investigation) until the period following World War I. Therefore, in the comparison to Western Europe, the scientifically ascertainable history of religious studies in Eastern European countries is shorter by approximately two generations of researchers. However, this applies primarily to Poland, the Czech Republic (formerly Czechoslovakia), and to some extent even in Hungary. But in Russia, and in a large portion of the Balkans, the academic study of religion studies was not firmly established as an institution until the political changes that came after 1989. Consequently, the development of religious studies in the eastern half of Europe must be viewed in an entirely different manner from its progress in Western Europe.

The early history of religious studies in Poland, the Czech Republic, and Hungary is connected with an interest in folklore that emerged in the nineteenth century. Scholars sought traces of religious traditions and mythologies in ancient folk legends. The tradition of comparative mythology—from which, in the first half of the twentieth century, the methods of the comparative study of religion arose—is rooted here. One must count among the best-known researchers of this period in Poland the ethnologist and religious historian Jan Aleksander Karlowicz, the historian of Christianity Ignacy Radlinski, and the Asian studies specialist Andrzej Niemojewski. In the Czech Republic the ethnologically oriented mythology researchers František Ladislav Čelakovský and Josef Jungmann were noteworthy pioneers. In Hungary, the academic exploration of religion was fostered from the circle of theologically educated members of the clergy, and was characterized as strongly Christian. In the middle of the nineteenth century, the study of religion had traditionally been identified with apologetics. Occupying the preeminent place among Hungarian researchers of this time are the linguist Zsigmond Simonyi, who also translated into Hungarian for the first time the work of Max Müller in 1876, and the founder of Islamic studies in Hungary, I. Goldziher. It was Goldziher who made the first mention in Hungary, in 1881, of a new discipline called comparative religious studies.

The truly formative period of religious studies occurred in the years after World War I, and developments in Eastern Europe revealed specific trends pertinent to each country. Even the conceptualizing of religious concepts proceeded in a different manner. The differences are strictly tied to the disparate historical development of these countries. For example, a long-standing Protestant tradition prevailed in the Czech Republic, but Poland was shaped by the strictest Roman Catholicism. Thus even the fundamental conception of religious studies, not to mention an understanding of other religions, differed between the two lands. Schematically expressed, in the Czech Republic religion was considered a component of public culture, and from the very beginning one devoted oneself to the investigation of religion, from differing technical points of view. Thus linguistics, historical sciences, psychology, ethnology, and religious philosophy all played a role, but this was true of theology only to a lesser degree. This diversity of approaches has exerted a profound influence, which extends down to the present time and finds expression in the quest for answers to the questions of what the scientific study of religion is, how one can classify it, and by which rationality paradigm it is sustained. The supreme embodiment of this quest is the work of the actual founder of Czech academic religious studies, the Indologist Otakar Pertold, who in 1920 published *Základy všeobecné vědy náboženské* (Foundations of the universal study of religion).

Religious studies in Poland, by contrast, tended toward a Catholicized view, which understood religion in several more distinctive forms as the phenomenon *sue generic*, and in religious history worked with the conception of Christianity as the exemplar. There also arose the so-called leizistic study of religion, that is, freethinking and anti-clerical religious studies, which attempted to examine religions objectively in their plurality, free of any religion-based bias. This inner split endured in Poland into the twenty-first century. Catholicism exerted a similarly formative influence on the development of Hungarian religious studies. The study of religion was conducted only within the theological seminaries and institutions, and efforts in the direction of a secular research, such as the suggestion by Ernst Troeltsch that an independent college for the academic study of religion be established at every university, were strictly rejected. Among those who rejected a secularized study of religion was the Catholic professor Aladár Zubriczky, who concerned himself with the parallels between Christianity and other religions, and who viewed Christianity as the veritable paragon of what a religion should be.

During the period between the two world wars, academic activities in these three countries kept apace with those in other comparable states (e.g., the Netherlands, France, and Finland), and had good prospects for further development. However, the decisive break came after World War II, when Eastern Europe came under Soviet domination. At that point, the academic study of religions was prohibited and suppressed. In places where the study of religion was already in existence in the form of established institutions—as for example in the Czech Republic—these institutions were uprooted. Scientific atheism became the sole method according to which the essential nature of religions was to be interpreted. In many cases religious-studies researchers were personally persecuted, driven from the universities by the dozens, and forced into punitive hard labor; the Czech historian of religion Záviš Kalandra, who specialized in ancient Slavic mythologies, was even sentenced to death in a sham trial and executed in 1950.

As a consequence of these developments, the academic study of religion almost totally vanished from Eastern European academic life for the next four decades, and survived only in theological seminaries and institutions, where it was pursued under the guise of the theological disciplines. Specifically, this development went forward in Poland, where internal political forces were not as thoroughly devastating as elsewhere in the Soviet bloc and where, consequently, the publication of religious-scientific works as well as translations remained a possibility. In principle, it can be said that this period entailed significant setbacks, not only because of the near-total extermination of religious studies as a field, but also because of the further theologization of religious studies in those places where it partially survived. This resulted in great difficulties in the theoretical-methodological realm and in the struggle to achieve self-understanding in which religious studies engaged after the sweeping political changes that occurred after 1990.

The time after the change was one of revival for the academic study of religion. There had been evidence that it was still nominally active, though dormant, back in the late 1960s during a period of political thaw, and again thanks to developments that occurred when Soviet leader Mikhail Gorbachev instituted a policy of perestroika in the 1980s. Because of this, religious studies as a discipline was able to officially establish itself relatively quickly. Religious-studies departments returned to the universities; national societies for the academic study of religion were established; magazines, books, and translations in the field of religious studies were published; attempts were also made to re-establish international academic contacts. However, the relatively long cultural isolation into which the totalitarian states had been driven, which was true of the academic research in general within these countries as well, had a lingering negative impact on the field which endured into the twenty-first century.

In Soviet Russia, the development proceeded along far different lines. From the year 1917 onwards, the doctrine of scientific atheism was regarded as sacrosanct, and its declared goal was not knowledge, but rather the total abolition of religion from social life, along with every tradition having anything in common with religion. As attested by the literature of the era, research was not supposed to have been "objective"—that is, as impartial as possible—but rather was to direct itself according to the principles of the class struggle, and thus in accordance with subjective-ideological interests. Although there were attempts at a so-called "Marxist study of religion," such as Dmitrii Modestovich Ugrinovich's 1973 work *Introduction to the Theoretical Study of Religion*, these political restrictions were not overcome until the latter part of the 1990s. However, after the formation of the Russian Federation in 1993, an entirely different set of problems arose. These involved legal measures vis-à-vis religious liberty, freedom of conscience, the position of the churches in society, and the role of churches in religious and ethical instruction within the schools. Consequently, the establishment of religious studies as a field along standard academic principles was persistently delayed.

CONTRIBUTIONS. In spite of these unfavorable conditions, a large number of religious-academic works by Eastern European scholars have been published since the first two decades of the twentieth century. Individual researchers concerned themselves with a wide range of problems from the history of religion. There also emerged highly specialized schools of Polish and Czech Arab/Islamic studies, as well as Polish, Hungarian and Czech Asian studies; moreover, both Czech Egyptology and Hungarian Tibetan studies are well-known throughout the academic world. Separate Jewish, Hindu, Buddhist, and biblical fields of study are all well developed. The psychology of religion, sociology of religion, and religious geography are also established in the field. A certain peculiarity makes for an ongoing interest in the philosophy of religion as an auxiliary discipline. Philosophy of religion admittedly belongs to the philosophical rather than religious-scientific disciplines, but it is nonetheless highly valued; this is due to its conceptual nature, and to the possibility of taking advantage of its theoretical-methodological approaches.

Among Hungarian researchers, the following should be mentioned: Károly Kerényi, *Einführung in das Wesen der Mythologie* (Introduction to the nature of mythology, written with Carl Jung, 1951); *Die Religion der Griechen und Römer* (The religion of the Greeks and Romans, 1963); Sándor Bálint, *Tamulmányok a magyar vallásos népélet köréböl* (Essays on folk religion in Hungary, 1943); Instván Hahn, *Istenek és népek* (Gods and peoples, 1968); *Hitvilág és történelem: Tanulmányok az ókori vallások köréböl* (Religion and history: Essays concerning ancient religions, 1982); Imre Trencsényi-Waldapfel, *Vallástörténeti tamulmányok* (Studies on the history of religion, 1959); and Sir Mark Aurel Stein, *Innermost Asia: Detailed Report of Exploration in Central Asia, Kansu and Eastern Iran* I–IV, 1921.

From among the many Polish contributions, the following should be mentioned: Tadeusz Margul, *Sto lat nauki o religiach świata* (One hundred years of the scientific study of religion, 1964); Franciszek Adamski, editor, *Socjologia religii* (Sociology of religion, 1983); Zgymunt Poniatowski, *Religia i nauka* (Religion and science, 1960); Jan Szmyd, *Teorie i doświadczenie* (Theory and proof, 1966); and Witold Tyloch, editor, *Current Progress in the Methodology of the Science of Religion,* 1984; *Studies on Religions in the Context of Social Sciences: Methodological and Theoretical Relations,* 1990.

In the Czech Republic there arose, among others, Josef Tvrdý, *Filosofie náboženství* (Philosophy of religion, 1921); Frantisek Lexa, *Náboženská literatura staroegyptská* I-II (Ancient Egyptian religious literature, 1921); Vincenc Lesný, *Buddhismus* (Buddhism, 1948); Josef Kubalík, *Dějiny náboženství* (The history of religion, 1984); Dusan Zbavitel, *Hinduismus a jeho cesty k dokonalosti* (Hinduism and its path to perfection, 1993); Zbynek Žába, *Les Maximes de Ptahotep,* 1956; *Rock Inscriptions of Lower Nubia,* 1968; Miroslav Verner, *Ancient Egyptian Monuments as seen by V. R. Prutky,* 1968; Bretislav Horyna and Helena Pavlincová, *Filosofie náboženství* (Philosophy of religion, 1999); *Dějiny religionistiky* (The history of religious studies, 2001); Dusan Lužný, *Náboženství a moderní společnost* (Religion and modern society, 1999); and Luboš Bělka, *Tibetský buddhismus v Burjatsku* (Tibetan Buddhism in Buryatia, 2001).

Works devoted to the conceptualizing of religious studies, and of religious ideas, merit careful attention. The first theoretical-methodological work in Eastern Europe was Pertold's book *Základy všeobecné vědy náboženské* (Foundations of the universal study of religion). This author considers religion to be an emotion-based awareness of dependence on that which currently transcends the limits of all possible human knowledge. Under the influence of positivism and evolution theory, he distinguished between so-called primitive religions (i.e., ancestor worship, animism, pre-animism, fetishism, shamanism), theistic religions (i.e., polytheistic and monotheistic religions), and new religious forms that come into existence through the decay of monotheism (sects, magic, folk religion). He subdivided the scientific study of religion into what he called concrete religious studies, which deals with religious facts, and so-called abstract religious studies, whose task is to classify and evaluate the knowledge gained from the history of religion.

The first introduction to religious studies after World War II appeared in Poland with Poniatowski's *Wstęp do religioznawstwa* in 1959. This work was essentially oriented toward religious theory to accommodate the interest of the Polish Academy's workgroup for religious theory, which was created in 1957. In the Czech Republic, only one introduction was written prior to 1989, *Nástin religionistiky* (Overview of the scientific study of religion) from Jan Heller and Milan Mrázek in 1988. This, however, is written from a theological point of view. The first introduction that conformed to the requirements of the academic study of religion was Horyna's 1994 work *Úvod do religionistiky* (Introduction to the study of religions). Here the scientific study of religion was represented in a manner comparable to that of other standard works of Western European scholarship; questions of religious-scientific theory were stressed, as well as questions concerning the internal structuring of religious studies, its conceptual foundations, and religious-scientific metalanguage. In Russia, theoretical problems of religious studies have been reflected with delay and with many obscurities; this was a legacy of Marxist ideology.

SCHOLARLY ORGANIZATIONS AND PUBLICATIONS. Colleges for the scientific study of religion first came into existence in Poland and the Czech Republic shortly after World War I. The first college for the history of religion dates back to 1918 at Poland's University of Lublin; its dean was Josef Archutowski. The first college for religious studies came into existence in 1923 at the Wolna Wszechnica Polska in Warsaw, with Stefan Czarnowski as its dean. In 1937, Wiesław Niemczyk appointed himself the first professor of religious studies in Poland at the University of Warsaw. In the Czech Republic, Pertold appointed himself the first professor of comparative religious studies at Charles University in Prague, where the College of Religious Studies was established in 1934 within the philosophy department. However, this college was dissolved by Communist order in 1948, so that no direct line of successorship exists between it and the post-1989 colleges.

Pertold attempted to incorporate Czech religious studies into international research circles, and participated in the year 1912 in the Fourth International Congress for the History of Religion in the Dutch city of Leiden. His work, however, went unrecognized until 1990 at the Sixteenth Congress of the International Association for the History of Religions (IAHR) in Rome, where the newly established Czech Society for Religious Research was admitted to the regular membership ranks. In contrast, the Polish Society for the Scientific Study of Religion dated back to 1958, and had been admitted to IAHR ranks at the Twelfth Congress in Stockholm, Sweden. In other Eastern European countries, the scientific study of religion as an institutionalized field of university education existed neither during the period of Communist rule nor prior to that time. It was only after 1990 that the scientific study of religion began to develop in a dynamic fashion. In Hungary, there are three colleges for religious studies: at the Catholic College in Vác, at the University of Pécs, and at the University of Szeged, which emerged as the center of Hungarian religious studies. The Romanian Society for the History of Religion (RAHR) is a member of the IAHR. The situation is also similar in Russia—although here the circumstances are in part unclear—and in the former Soviet Union satellite states of Lithuania, Estonia, Latvia, and the Ukraine, though swift academic advances occurred during the post-1989 era.

Professional journals in the field of religious studies are published in almost all Eastern European countries. The most traditional of these periodicals is the Polish publication *Euhemer. Przegląd Religionznawczy* (Euhemer. Representation of the scientific study of religion), which was founded in 1957 and since 1991 has appeared under the title *Przegląd Religionznawczy* (Representation of the scientific study of religion). In 1991, the specialist publishing house NOMOS was established in Krakow, Poland, to issue technical literature in the field of religious studies. The leading Czech journal is *Religio. Revue pro religionistiku* (Journal for the scientific study of religion), founded in 1939; it serves as the central organ of the Czech Society for the Scientific Study of Religion, which is headquartered in Brno. At Masaryk University in the same city, the periodical *Religionswissenschaft* (Religious Studies) is also published, which brings together the most important religious-scientific works from both domestic and foreign contributors. After the break-up of the former Czechoslovakia into two independent states in 1993, the Slovak Society for Religion Research—publisher of the periodical *Hieron*—became an independent entity. At the University of Szeged in Hungary, the journal *Vallástudományi periodika* (Religious-Scientific Periodical) is available in an online version (http://www.vallastudomany.hu/liminalitas/index.php).

PERSPECTIVES. Religious-scientific cooperation in the eastern European countries—as in the whole of Europe—is hampered by enormous linguistic and cultural differences. It seems unlikely that a supra-national Eastern European religious-scientific organization could come into existence, and the individual representatives of religious studies in the former Eastern bloc countries show no initiative in this direction. The IAHR and the European Association for the Study of Religions (EASR) serve as the common foundation for cooperation. The same diversity prevails in a thematic sense. Over the course of time, the political differences that caused academic progress in Eastern Europe to lag were remedied. The research focuses on the history of religion, new religious movements in Europe, enculturation of non-European religions in Europe, which include Buddhism, Islam, Asian religions, and new religious phenomena.

The significance attached to the theory of religious studies is also constantly increasing; its identity problems, which have to do with the deficient methodological equipment; deductive procedures; object and meta-theory; principles of epistemological formalization; the logic of linguistic means of expression, particularly in religious-scientific definition procedures; criteria-formation in the realm of the semantic completeness of religious-scientific concepts; possibilities for the creation of disciplinary, fundamental, and practice-oriented religious-scientific axiomatics.

The question "What is the scientific study of religion?" is pursued with the same seriousness as is the question "What is religion?" Furthermore, the more recent history of Western religious studies is being absorbed, and instruction concerning methodological difficulties—and their possible resolution—is being sought within it. It is possible to conclude that there is no longer any significant difference between European religious studies in the eastern and western halves of the continent, or in any case that if differences do remain they are few in number. This is true as regards topics and the dynamics of development, as well as social resonance. Few seem cognizant of these facts, however. For example, in the most recent and modern introduction to religious studies, written by Hans G. Kippenberg and Kocku von Stuckrad (Munich 2003), not a single word is devoted to Eastern European religious studies.

SEE ALSO Comparative Religion; Marxism; Politics and Religion, article on Politics and Christianity; Positivism.

BIBLIOGRAPHY

Bronk, Andrzej. *Nauka wobec religii.* Lublin, Poland, 1996. Summarizes the theoretical foundations of conceptions of religion in the history of religious studies; focuses on the epistemological foundations of religiology.

Doležalová, Iva, Luther H. Martin, and Dalibor Papoušek, eds., *The Academic Study of Religion During the Cold War: East and West.* New York, 2001. Conference book from the convention of the same name; contains important contributions made to the field of religious studies in Eastern Europe during the period 1948–1990, together with some new perspectives that emerged after 1990.

Horyna, Břetislav. *Úvod do religionistiky.* Prague, 1994. The standard work on religious studies in the Czech Republic, with an overview of the theories of religion, of the scientific study of religion, of methodologies, and of technical history.

Horyna, Břetislav, and Helena Pavlincová. *Dějiny religionistiky. Antologie.* Olomouc, Czech Republic, 2001. Anthology of the most important among contemporary religious-scientific contributions across all of Europe, including an analysis of the methodological foundations of individual researchers. Serves as the East European parallel to Waardenburg's and Whaling's *Approaches.*

BRETISLAV HORYNA (2005)

STUDY OF RELIGION: THE ACADEMIC STUDY OF RELIGION IN JAPAN

The study of religion in Japan is probably best known to Western people for D. T. Suzuki and the Kyoto School.

However, it would be too Orientalistic to assume that the modern Japanese study of religions has been predominated by Zen Buddhist philosophy with a somehow mystical method of intuition. Japanese students majoring in *shūkyōgaku* (the study of religion) have been reading classic and contemporary works that are more or less similar to those on the reading lists at Western graduate schools. Moreover, the earliest Japanese scholars of religion regarded themselves as more scientifically objective than their Western counterparts who were struggling to detach themselves from the influence of Christian theology. Although those Japanese scholars were, in reality, far from ideologically neutral, the establishment of the study of religion as a nonconfessional university department (at Tokyo Imperial University in 1905) and of an academy of religion (in 1930) were quite early in comparative terms. In addition, the ninth Congress of the International Association for the History of Religions took place in Tokyo in 1958. Nevertheless, the study of religion has never been granted a high status in Japan. Whereas the number of academy members had reached 2,000 by the end of the twentieth century, less than ten universities had departments of *shūkyōgaku*, that is, only 1 percent of all four-year universities and colleges in Japan. This paradoxical position of the Japanese study of religion reflects the sociopolitical contexts of religion in modern Japan.

Prehistory of the Study of Religion. It is commonly accepted that the modern study of religion in Japan started in the Meiji era (1868–1912), after Japan opened its doors to the Western world. The Japanese word for religion, *shūkyō,* was also coined at the beginning of the era as a translation of the Western term. This does not mean that there were neither precursors of *shūkyōgaku* nor concepts similar to religion before Japan became fully exposed to Western culture. Nakamoto Tominaga (1715–1746) is one of the Japanese scholars who developed comparative, historical, and critical approaches to religion without Western influences. Tominaga's rational thinking derived from Confucian education, which was promoted by the Tokugawa government. Rather than defending Confucianism, however, Tominaga compared it with Buddhism and Shintō, and then attempted to present a new teaching that surpassed all three. Like the Western thinkers of the Enlightenment, he criticized existing religions by exposing the historically conditioned nature of their ideas and scriptures.

Tominaga's comparative study of religion was not unique; it was a common practice among scholars at that time to consider Shintō, Buddhism, and Confucianism as related concepts. However, there was no fixed word, like the later *shūkyō* (religion), that placed them in a single category. Sometimes people called them *kyō* ("teaching") in order to emphasize their doctrinal aspects; at other times they used a word with more practical connotations, *dō* (*tao,* "way").

This terminological ambiguity indicates that a generic category called religion was not yet needed. Japanese scholars in those days did not ask the question that was central to the Enlightenment and gave rise to the modern study of religion in the West: what is the essence of religion? Nor was there any further development in methodology, in contrast to the West, where the methodology of the humanities was polished through imitating and challenging the methods of the rapidly progressing natural sciences. Although the Japanese did access the abundant data about the various religions found within their religiously pluralistic country, they did not embark on the systematic study of comparative religion by themselves.

A drastic change to this situation came about at the outset of the Meiji era. "Religion" was developed as a formal concept, initially to serve political and juridical needs. In order to integrate the country as a nation-state, the Meiji government adopted an imperial system and chose Shintō as its moral guideline. The government then defamed Buddhism, which was once amalgamated with Shintō, while reaffirming the long-standing ban on Christianity. At the same time, however, the government strove to modernize Japan by following Western systems, and in so doing it soon realized that religious freedom was regarded as one of the requirements of a modern society. The government was pressed to permit the freedom of religion yet sought to maintain the special status of Shintō. It managed to solve this problem by making rhetorical use of the concept of religion. The concept, which was an import from the West, was modeled after Christianity, in particular belief/doctrine-centered Protestantism. In light of this definition of religion, Shintō, which mostly consisted of ritual practices, was termed non-religious. The government declared that Shintō was not a religion, but a system of state rituals superior to individual religions. "Non-religious" was promoted as a positive virtue rather than implying something less than a religion. This was the rhetoric used to legitimize what later was called State Shintō. The government insisted that it was different from state religion and thus compatible with freedom of religion. Not all Japanese were convinced by this reasoning, and a heated dispute arose when the *Kyōiku chokugo* (Imperial rescript on education) was enacted in an effort to infuse all schoolchildren with national morality shaped by Shintō ideas.

Scholars debate what other effects were caused by the conceptualization of religion in the Meiji society. The consensus is that practice-based folk religions were suppressed, being categorized as superstitions. Established religions such as Buddhism imitated the modern features of religion epitomized in Protestantism for the sake of survival. In addition, Japan was unique among the cultures encountering the modern West in the failure of Christian missionaries to expand Christianity in the country, which was supposed to be perfectly religious already, according to the newly adopted concept of religion. It was under these circumstances that the study of religion gradually took its form in Japan.

Early Developments (1905–1945). Toward the end of the nineteenth century, universities modeled after Western, particularly German, institutions began to be founded in Japan. While there were a number of private universities, some of which had either Buddhist or Christian backgrounds, a few national universities were granted a leading position in research and teaching. In 1890 Tetsujirō Inoue (1855–1944) delivered a lecture on comparative religion and Eastern philosophy at Tokyo Imperial University, Japan's first national university. In 1905 Masaharu Anesaki (1873–1949) was appointed to the first professorship in religious studies at the university, and the first department for the study of religion was established. Other national universities, which were independent of any religious organization, followed suit. The early scholars emphasized the importance of free inquiry and a comparative approach.

Nevertheless, their scholarly research was guided by significant practical concerns alongside the scientific ideal of objectivity. The fundamental question about the nature of religion had been evoked in the debate on the legitimacy of State Shintō, and the public came to expect scholars of religion not only to offer a professional definition of religion but also to present a blueprint for religion's future. Their recommendations varied. Inoue supported the Imperial rescript on education in the debate. His goal was to replace all religions with national morality and rational philosophy. He believed that existing religions would become outdated in the process of modernization.

While rationalist scholars such as Inoue thought that society would ultimately be able to dispense with religion, most scholars of religion, including Anesaki, hoped to secure the role of religion in contemporary and future society. They therefore defended religion against modern secularism. Still, it was self-evident to almost all of them that religion could serve to consolidate and expand their new nation-state, and in that aspect of national loyalty they were not much different from right-wing nationalists who promoted the Imperial rescript on education.

In this process of describing religion in comparison to other categories such as education and morality, they came to presuppose the *sui generis* quality of religion, and different scholars presented various universal definitions of religion, which were also assumed to be its origin. Their views of religion can be described, overall, as psycho- or subject-centered. For example, Manshi Kiyozawa (1863–1903) defined religion as "a mental faculty or disposition which enables man to apprehend the Infinite" (in *The Skeleton of Philosophy of Religion,* an essay in English distributed to attendees at the World Parliament of Religions held in Chicago in 1893). Many Japanese scholars, even those with religious affiliations, regarded the divine being as a projection of human feelings, desires, or life forces. Interestingly, they did not think that such views would undermine religion. They were in fact optimistic about religion, believing in its evolution. Although these tendencies were distinct, it is difficult to discern how many of them were derived from their contemporary Western thoughts or from the indigenous tradition of Buddhism or animistic Shintō.

Twenty-five years after the first department for the study of religion was established, The Japanese Association for Religious Studies was founded, the first nationwide academic organization in the field. At that time there were strong antireligious movements inspired by Marxism, which was one of the causes that led scholars of religion to unite to defend religion. During the same period Japan became an imperialistic power and started to expand its colonies from Korea to other parts of Asia. In a parallel to Western scholarship, Japanese scholars developed ethnographic studies based on fieldwork in the new colonies in Asia, aware that studying the religions of diverse ethnic groups would serve Japan's colonial policy. It is often pointed out that the Kyoto School, the well-known group of religious philosophers from Kyoto Imperial University, justified Japanese imperialism with their ideas of Buddhism as postmodern, post-Western wisdom. Scholars of religion who supported Japanese imperialism ideologically were not limited to the Kyoto School, however. Moreover, many scholars found their freedom of research being increasingly restricted.

DEVELOPMENTS SINCE 1945. With the end of the Second World War, it was publicly admitted that State Shintō was, indeed, a religion. The Shintō Directive, which specified the occupation policy on religion, was issued in 1945 to abolish the entire system of State Shintō. At the same time the imperial family was demythologized to allow a democracy to be established. In the postwar period the influence of the United States became immense, both politically and culturally. It was ironic, therefore, that many Japanese remained skeptical about religion throughout the Cold War, despite their living in a capitalistic society. Traumatic memories of religious totalitarianism continue to influence the Japanese to separate religion from politics, to an extent that they often feel uncomfortable about the religious aspect of U.S. politics, often called the civil religion of the United States. In addition, opinion polls indicate that a large number of Japanese have a strong distrust of any religious organization.

Under these circumstances, the scholars of religion in postwar Japan became more careful to maintain scientific neutrality than had been the prewar scholars, who were socially engaged in defending religion. This neutral attitude culminated in the work of Hideo Kishimoto (1903–1964), a leading postwar scholar who sharply contrasted the study of religion as a purely empirical science with the study of theology. It does not mean that the postwar study of religion had no perspectives. Many scholars took an interest in minor, or what are called "little," religious traditions, the religions of the populace, whereas prewar scholars more often investigated the religious elites. This new tendency reflected the politically liberal atmosphere that spread through the humanities and social sciences in the 1950s. It was also a result of differentiating the study of religion itself from studies of Buddhist, Shintō, or Christian religions that focused on textual studies and elitist traditions. It may also be true that cross-religious categories like folk religion were more suited to comprehending the syncretic pluralism of Japanese religions.

In these respects, the Japanese study of religion has many things in common with the history of religions, a term often used to describe a humanistic tradition within the study of religion in the West. Nonetheless, most Japanese scholars have never identified themselves as historians of religions in this sense. The reason for this may be largely institutional. Since the study of religion has been a small field, it has never become too compartmentalized; those researching new religious movements, for example, worked closely with field workers studying folk religions. In addition, Japanese scholars in other departments such as sociology used to pay little attention to religion due to the pervasive indifference to religion in Japan. Rivalry with those scholars also helped to unite the field.

Because of these factors, the Japanese study of religion developed by embracing psychology, sociology, anthropology, and other approaches to religion. In the process, Japanese scholars readily adopted Western theories such as functionalism and structuralism, but they also found Christian influences in the Western study of religion and elaborated original theories of religion from their point of view. To take a few examples, whereas the Western study of religion used to emphasize the mind or the mind-body dichotomy in religion, Kishimoto rehabilitated the aspect of the body in religion as seen in ascetic practices, and Keiichi Yanagawa (1926–1990) presented a definition of religion as human relationships, in sharp contrast to the monotheistic idea of religion.

The Japanese study of religion differs from its Western, and particularly American, counterparts in a number of other respects. The Japanese scholarly view of religion tends to be ritual-centric rather than myth-centric. Studying myth is relatively unpopular partly because of the sensitive nature of Japanese mythology, which was once believed to be the historical truth about the origins of the imperial family, and partly because of the lack of a strong tradition of Greco-Roman classical studies. Instead, the study of rituals such as festivals and shamanic practices is prevalent. It is also noteworthy that the philosophy of religion has always been much more existentialistic, as represented by the Kyoto School tradition, than Anglo-American. In addition, the study of religion in Japan used to center more on modernization than secularization. Although secularization did become a central theme in the sociology of religion, it was the problem of modernization that evoked lively cross-disciplinary discussions in postwar Japan. Scholars first ascribed the problems of the prewar political system to the immaturity of Japan as a modern society. Long discussions followed as to whether Japan had remained half feudalistic or had achieved modernization in its own unique way. It was in this context that Robert Bellah's *Tokugawa Religion,* which analyzed the relationships between Japanese religious ethics and industrialization, attracted attention.

The debate on modernization was, in a sense, a question of Japanese identity. The postwar quest for national identity was satisfied on a popular level by Japanese studies (*nihonjinron/nihonbunkaron*), which overly emphasized the uniqueness of Japanese culture, including religion, based on the stereotypical contrast of the Orient and the Occident. On a more academic level, Japanese folklore studies, a neighboring field to religious studies founded by Kunio Yanagita (1875–1962), has most often been charged with ethnocentrism. It is considered to have originated in the Kokugaku (National Learning) movement, a nativistic movement based on philological study of Norinaga Motoori (1730–1801), an apologist for Shintō. At the same time, the work of Yanagita, who had been a private scholar, was reevaluated in the context of the counter-culture movements in the late 1960s and 1970s as an alternative to the established modern sciences of the universities.

The counterculture movements led to postmodernism in the 1980s. The trend was best embodied by Shinichi Nakazawa (b. 1950), a scholar of religion who had a Carlos Castenada-like experience with a guru in Tibet and later wrote books that combined his experiences with postmodern thought like that of Julia Kristeva. Whereas the Western postmodern study of religion tended to be critical of religion from a Freudian or a Marxist perspective, its Japanese equivalent could slide into Buddhist supremacism. This echo of wartime ideology resurrected a tough question as to whether the idea of the triumph of Eastern thought over Western thought was a mere reversal of Orientalism or if it had a certain validity.

It was no accident, therefore, that the new religion Aum Shinrikyō grew during the decade. Aum's release of Sarin gas in Tokyo subway stations in 1995 profoundly shocked Japanese scholars of religion. The incident forced them to seriously reconsider what the public role of the study of religion should be. Despite the overall lack of interest in religion among the Japanese public, new religious movements had been active, and the study of new religious groups had become quite popular in the postwar period. Scholars of religion treated new religions as Western historians of religions were treating indigenous religions, reevaluating them on their own merits instead of dismissing them as primitive. Accordingly, after Aum's gas attack, they faced criticism for having been standing on the side of new religions.

The postcolonial critique also raised the same question about the social role of the study of religion. Scholars started looking closely at diversity within the minor religious traditions, particularly in terms of gender and ethnicity, and problematizing the long neglect of oppressed minorities both by society and by the academy. Japanese feminist and gender-based studies of religion derive from the second wave of Japanese feminism in the 1970s. Interest in these studies has been high despite the twin difficulties of male domination of Japanese religious traditions and the lack of interest in religion within Japanese feminist movements.

In order to study the ongoing interactions between contemporary society and religions, new scholarly organizations were established in the 1990s. The most notable is the Japanese Association for the Study of Religion and Society (JASRS), founded in 1993. The International Institute for the Study of Religion (IISR), originally set up in 1953, was also reorganized in 1993, along with the Religious Information Research Center (RIRC).

At the beginning of the twenty-first century, popular issues in the mainstream of the Japanese study of religion include religion in practice *(seikatsu no shūkyō)*, globalization/localization and religion, religion and violence, and the concept of religion and Orientalism. New impulses are emerging from the question of whether the study of religion should be more socially engaged rather than assuming neutrality. The responses to this question range from critical approaches following Saidian-Foucaultian reflections about knowledge and power to religious approaches following Nakazawa's attempt to guide the individual's spiritual quest.

Last but not least, all Japanese universities have recently been asked to reform themselves structurally to become more globally competitive. This movement is represented by the Twenty-First Century Center of Excellence (COE) program, a funding system that rewards selected universities and research institutions. The program is administered by the Japan Society for the Promotion of Science with the support of the Japanese government. It encourages research that will directly contribute to society, which has promoted the idea of applied sciences even among traditional humanistic disciplines; the study of bioethics is one example within the field of religious studies. With this new focus, the study of religion is once again facing a challenge to serve public and national interests without losing its critical stance.

BIBLIOGRAPHY

Primary sources in English

Anesaki Masaharu. *Buddhist Art in Its Relation to Buddhist Ideals, with Special Reference to Buddhism in Japan.* Boston, 1915, reprint, New York, 1978.

Anesaki Masaharu. *History of Japanese Religion, with Special Reference to the Social and Moral Life of the Nation.* London, 1930, reprint, 1995.

Bellah, Robert N. *Tokugawa Religion: The Values of Pre-Industrial Japan.* New York, 1957; reprint, London, 1985.

Katō Genchi. *A Study of Shinto: The Religion of the Japanese Nation.* London, 1926; reprint, 1971. Genchi Katō (1873–1965) initiated the study of Shintō from the perspective of comparative religion.

Kishimoto Hideo. "An Operational Definition of Religion." *Numen* 8 (1961): 236–240.

Kishimoto Hideo. "Religiology." *Numen* 14 (1967): 81–86.

Tominaga Nakamoto. *Emerging from Meditation.* Translated and edited by Michael Pye. London, 1990.

Uno Enkū. *Religious Rites and Ceremonies Concerning Rice-Planting and Eating in Malaysia.* Tokyo, 1942. Enkū Uno (1885–1949) is one of the early Japanese scholars of religion. This ethnographical essay has its background in Japanese imperialism in Asia.

Yabuki– Keiki, editor. *Rare and Unknown Chinese Manuscript Remains of Buddhist Literature Discovered in Tun-Huang Collected by Sir Aurel Stein and Preserved in the British Museum.* Tokyo, 1930. Keiki Yabuki (1879–1939), himself belonging to the Jōdoshū Buddhist tradition, was one of the pioneers who incorporated the study of religion into Buddhist studies. He is famous for his studies on the teaching of the three stages, but his works are not available in English.

Yanagawa Keiichi. "Matsuri no kankaku." *Shūkyō kenkyū* 49 (1976): 223–242. Available in English as "The Sensation of Matsuri" from http://www2.kokugakuin.ac.jp/ijcc/wp/cpjr/matsuri/yanagawa.html.

Yanagita Kunio. *About Our Ancestors: The Japanese Family System.* Tokyo, 1970; reprint, Tokyo, 1988.

Yanagita Kunio. *The Legends of Tono.* Tokyo, 1975.

Secondary sources in Western languages

Isomae Junichi. "The Discursive Position of Religious Studies in Japan: Masaharu Anesaki and the Origins of Religious Studies." *Method and Theory in the Study of Religion* 14, no. 1 (2002): 21–46.

Japanese Association for Religious Studies. *Religious Studies in Japan.* Tokyo, 1959. A commemorative volume from the Ninth International Congress for the History of Religions.

Kawahashi Noriko, and Masako Kuroki. "Editors' Introduction: Feminism and Religion in Contemporary Japan." *Japanese Journal of Religious Studies* 30, no. 3/4 (2003): 207–216. This entire volume is dedicated to feminist and gender studies of religion in Japan.

Matsumoto Shigeru. *Motoori Norinaga 1730–1801.* Cambridge, U.K., 1975; reprint, Ann Arbor, Mich., 1995.

Prohl, Inken. *Die "spirituellen Intellektuellen" und das New Age in Japan.* Hamburg, Germany, 2000. A critique of Shinichi Nakazawa and other popular religious-spiritual scholars such as Yasuo Yuasa.

Pye, Michael. "Japanese Studies of Religion." *Religion* 4 (1975): 55–72.

Pye, Michael. "Modern Japan and the Science of Religions." *Method and Theory in the Study of Religion* 15, no. 1 (2003): 1–27. This article, along with "Religious Studies in Japan" by Tamaru, provides a general view of the Japanese study of religion, with a special focus on its prehistory.

Reader, Ian. "Dichotomies, Contested Terms, and Contemporary Issues in the Study of Religion." 2004. Available from http://www.japanesestudies.org.uk/discussionpapers/Reader2.html. This article touches on the concept of religion in Japan in light of recent theoretical discussions.

Rotermund, Hartmut O. "Les sciences des religions au Japon." In *Le Grand Atlas des Religions.* Paris, 1988.

Shimazono Susumu. "The Study of Religion and the Tradition of Pluralism." *Japanese Journal of Religious Studies* 9, no. 1 (1982–1983): 77–88. This article discusses the influence of religious pluralism on the Japanese study of religion.

Snodgrass, Judith. *Presenting Japanese Buddhism to the West: Orientalism, Occidentalism, and the Columbian Exposition.*

Chapel Hill, N.C., 2003. This book closely examines presentations by Japanese Buddhists at the World Parliament of Religions in Chicago in 1893. Opinions are divided as to whether the World Parliament of Religions was a major contributor in the formation of the study of religion in Japan.

Staggs, Kathleen M. *In Defense of Japanese Buddhism: Essays from the Meiji Period by Inoue Enryō and Murakami Senshō.* Microfilm, Ann Arbor, Mich., 1987. Both Enryō Inoue (1858–1919) and Senshō Murakami (1851–1929) had a Jōdo Shinshū Buddhist background and applied a modern method of free inquiry to Buddhist and religious studies. Inoue also published unique works on the superstitious aspects of folk religion.

Tamaru Noriyoshi. "Religious Studies in Japan: A Preliminary Report." In *The Notion of "Religion" in Comparative Research: Selected Proceedings of the 16th IAHR Congress,* edited by Ugo Bianchi. Rome, 1994.

Primary sources in Japanese

Anesaki Masaharu. *Shūkyōgaku gairon* (An Introduction to the Study of Religion). Tokyo, 1900.

Anesaki Masaharu. *Fukkatsu no Shokō* (The Dawn of Revival). Tokyo, 1904.

Kishimoto Hideo. *Shūkyōgaku* (The Study of Religion). Tokyo, 1961.

Yanagawa Keiichi. *Gendai nihonjin no shūkyō* (Religions of Contemporary Japanese People). Kyoto, 1991.

Secondary sources in Japanese

Isomae Junichi and Hidetaka Fukasawa, eds. *Kindai nihon niokeru chisikijin to shūkyō* (Intellectuals and Religion in Modern Japan). Tokyo, 2002. A detailed biographical work on Anesaki with critical essays and a comprehensive catalogue of his writings.

Shimazono Susumu, and Yoshio Tsuruoka, eds. *Shūkyō saikō* (Reconsidering the Concept of Religion). Tokyo, 2004. This contains a few articles on the concept of religion in Japanese contexts.

Suzuki Norihisa. *Meiji shūkyō shichō no kenkyū* (The Trends of Religious Thought in the Meiji Era). Tokyo, 1979.

Tamaru Noriyoshi, ed. *Nihon no shūkyō gakusetsu* (Theories of the Study of Religion in Japan). Vol. 1, Tokyo, 1982; vol. 2, Tokyo, 1985. A collection of articles on early Japanese scholars of religion, such as Seiichi Hatano (1877–1950), Enkū Uno (1885–1949), and Chishin Ishibashi (1886–1947). Limited availability.

SAKOTO FUJIWARA (2005)

STUDY OF RELIGION: THE ACADEMIC STUDY OF RELIGION IN NORTH AFRICA AND THE MIDDLE EAST

The academic study of religion in North Africa and the Middle East builds upon a long and rich tradition of comparison and analysis of the history, beliefs, and practices of different religious communities. Most of the major universities in the region currently teach the comparative study of religion within an Islamic studies curriculum, whether or not the university and its programs are intended to be secular. Despite the relatively limited visibility of the comparative study of religions in regional institutions, the scholarly discipline can be traced back to a vigorous and creative scholarship that flourished at least as early as the tenth century.

The disciplinary approach and institutional organization of the study of religion in the Middle East and North Africa is based largely on a scholarly tradition developed in the premodern period, particularly during the eleventh, twelfth, and thirteenth centuries. Several well-known scholars wrote far-reaching and influential works during this period that still serve as the basic textbooks for the contemporary university study of religion.

AL-BĪRŪNĪ. Perhaps the single best example of the study of religion within Islamic civilization comes from the penetrating works of al-Bīrūnī (973–1050). Attached to the Ghaznavid court in what is today Afghanistan, al-Bīrūnī produced two important works studying ancient and contemporary religions. The first, titled *Book of the Remains from Bygone Centuries,* contains al-Bīrūnī's account of pre-Islamic civilizations. The second, titled the *History of India,* is an encyclopedic catalog and analysis of the culture of South Asia. The information in al-Bīrūnī's study of India comes both from firsthand observations in northwest India and from his extensive study of Sanskrit and related Indian languages and texts. Combing both ethnographic and textual research, al-Bīrūnī's work is primarily descriptive, though a rudimentary analytical framework utilizing more generic categories such as "ritual" and "belief" is evident from al-Bīrūnī's observations.

MILAL WA NIHAL. Most influential in many contemporary university programs in comparative religion is a body of scholarship known under the Arabic term *al-Milal wa al-Nihal,* roughly translated as "Sects and Heresies" and is often understood as heresiographical or doxographical in nature, though individual authors provide different rationales for their works. In general, this scholarship presents an overview of beliefs attributed to different groups both historically and contemporaneous with the writers. These beliefs are often grouped into three broad categories: Islamic beliefs and sects, beliefs and sects of "People of the Book" (Arabic, *ahl al-kitāb*) or "revealed" religions, and everything else, including other religions and philosophers. Sometimes this categorization is reduced to Muslim and non-Muslim beliefs, as in the work of Fakhr al-Dīn al-Rāzī in which he discusses Jews, Christians, Mazdaeans, dualists, Sabians, and philosophers.

Ibn Hazm. Abū Muḥammad Alī Ibn Aḥmad, known as Ibn Ḥazm (994–1064) was one of the most prolific writers on other religions and their relationship to Islam. In his *al-Milal wa al-Nihal* work, Ibn Ḥazm discusses doctrines pertaining to Islam, Mazdaeans, Christians, Brāhmaṇs, Jews, various philosophers, dualists, and others. The book is organized according to specific topics rather than particular religious groups, but the topics themselves are loosely arranged according to what Ibn Ḥazm sees as sectarian divisions arising from adherence to certain beliefs. For example, Ibn Ḥazm has a general section on Christianity followed by more specific discussion of the nature of Christ, those who deny prophethood and the angels, and the difference between miracles and magic. In his discussion of Judaism Ibn Ḥazm mentions that the Jews reject the trinitarianism of Christians but faults them for using a Torah that does not contain an accurate record of the revelation given to Moses. Zoroastrians are faulted for insisting upon the prophethood of Zoroaster while denying the equality of other prophets.

Ibn Ḥazm spends considerable attention detailing examples of how the stories of the prophets in the Jewish Torah and the Christian New Testament contradict what is known from the Qurʾān and Islamic tradition. In addition to his criticism of the sources and redaction of the Bible used by Jews and Christians, Ibn Ḥazm wrote extensively on Islamic law. He was a strong proponent for the notion that the Qurʾān and the *sharīʿah* derived from it superseded all earlier older legal codes, to the extent that the revelation of the Qurʾān abrogated all parts of the Bible that it did not specifically confirm. Although he is apparently well informed about the different religious ideas he catalogs, Ibn Ḥazm's main interest is in a defense of Islam as providing a holistic interpretation of the world fully compatible with history and rationality. His *al-Milal wa al-Nihal* work also includes a section mentioning what is known about certain biblical prophets and the veneration due to them, followed by discussions of beliefs concerning the creation of heaven and hell, the resurrection of the dead, the punishment of the tomb, and repentance. In his final sections he treats a number of individual issues not necessarily associated with any particular group such as visions, the created nature of certain things, and the relationship of body and soul.

Abū al-Maʿālī. Abū al-Maʿālī Muḥammad bin ʿUbayd Allāh (c. 1092) produced one of the earliest Persian works in the *al-Milal wa al-Nihal* tradition. His book, titled *Explication of Religions,* treats a number of religions that came before Islam, including ancient Arab religion, Greek philosophy, Judaism, Christianity, Zoroastrianism, Mazdakism, and Manichaeism. He separates this group of religions from "idolatrous" religions such as Hinduism. Abū al-Maʿālī's main focus in the book appears to be his conviction that all people, even non-Muslims, hold a belief in a creator being, which he claims proves the existence of God.

Shahrastānī. Muḥammad bin ʿAbd al-Karīm al-Shahrastānī (1086–1153) lived near Khurāsān and wrote a well-known *al-Milal wa al-Nihal* work. Shahrastānī states that he wrote the book in an attempt to document "the religious beliefs of all the world's people." Shahrastānī divides these religious beliefs into two main categories: ideas derived from revealed books and ideas derived from elsewhere. The first category is further subdivided into Muslims and People of the Book. People of the Book include the Jews (Kairites, Isawiyah, Samaritans), Christians (Chalcedonians, Nestorians, Jacobites), and the people of a "false book" such as the Zoroastrians and the dualists, under which category he places the Manichaeans. The second category of beliefs originating from nonrevealed sources includes the Sabians of Harran, philosophers (Greek and Islamic), pre-Islamic Arab religions, and the beliefs of Indians (Brāhmaṇs, adherents to spirits, star worshipers, and idol worshipers). He follows this by a brief discussion of philosophical ideas among the Indians.

The longest section in the book is that on the philosophers and their ideas. Shahrastānī describes the different religious ideas within the Islamic framework of revealed and nonrevealed corresponding to the general Qurʾanic notion of the People of the Book following prophets with divine messages. Shahrastānī conceives of God as a unitary being from whom creation proceeds in a fashion that gained him as reputation as adhering to Nizarī Ismāʿīlī doctrines of emanation and incarnation. This allows him to see truth in ideas derived both directly and indirectly from God. A similar approach is found in the *Ḥikmat al-khālidah* of Miskawayh and the *Ṭabaqāt al-umam* of Saʿīd al-Andalusī, where it is argued that God gave each of the world's peoples certain intellectual and civilizational gifts that they retain despite their straying from the directly revealed truths of Islam.

History. Medieval Muslim historians often write about the history of different religions. In the course of his history of the world, for example, Muḥammad bin Jarīr al-Ṭabarī (839–923) recounts numerous traditions from both Muslim and pre-Islamic sources concerning the religious beliefs and practices of Iran, Arabia, Egypt, Mesopotamia, and the Fertile Crescent. Later historians, such as Ibn al-Athīr, built upon Ṭabarī's work and repeated much of his information, sometimes with their own additions. Other historians provide detailed historical backgrounds to explain the origins of religious groups present in their time. Aḥmad b. Abd al-Qādir al-Maqrīzī (1364–1442), well-known historian of Egypt, includes an especially long section on the different groups among the Jews of his time. He uses a variety of medieval, late antique, and Hellenistic sources, including the medieval Hebrew translation of Josephus.

Stories of the Prophets. Equally important are the historical and mythological accounts pertaining to what is called the "Stories of the Prophets" in Muslim histories and Qurʾān commentaries. Although regarded as "Muslim" prophets by these writers, the cycle of stories associated with such pre-Islamic figures as Abraham, Moses, and Jesus were told often in conscious comparison to Jewish and Christian accounts of the same figures. Scholars such as Ibn Kathir specifically compare passages from the Bible and from Jewish and Christian interpretation with the Qurʾān and its interpretation by Muslims. In addition to major prophetic figures, other characters also appear in these stories, including Samson, St. George, and the Seven Sleepers. Such scholarship frequently reflects a relatively sophisticated approach to textual criticism and the burgeoning of a sort of comparative mythology.

Travel and Geography. The approach and content of most *al-Milal wa al-Nihal* and historical scholarship is focused on literary sources and doctrinal questions. Descriptions of practices, largely drawn from ethnographic-type observations comparable to those found in the histories of Herodotus, can be found in the large collection of travel accounts produced by Arab and Muslim scholars in the medieval period but continuing through to the nineteenth century.

One of the best-known travelers is Ibn Baṭṭūṭa (1304–1368) who left from Tangiers and traveled throughout the Middle East, East Africa, Asia Minor, Central Asia, India, Sri Lanka, Bengal, Sumatra, and China. Ibn Baṭṭūṭa's travel account, as well as those of many others, are expanded journals of pilgrimage journeys. During the travels described in his account, Ibn Baṭṭūṭa made pilgrimage to Mecca at least four times. Ibn al-Jubayr (1145–1217) was one of the first to leave a long account of his journeys in the Middle East while on pilgrimage to Mecca, which includes his firsthand observations on the beliefs and practices he encountered. Travel accounts and guides written for pilgrims visiting regional sites in Syria, Lebanon, and Palestine, such as those of al-Harawī and Ibn al-Ḥawrānī, constitute a valuable record not only of Muslim practices and beliefs but also myths and rituals associated with certain sites by other religious groups in the area.

Other scholarship focused on geography includes a great deal of information on religious practices and beliefs. Scholars such as Yāqūt, Ibn al-Faqīh, and al-Bakrī compiled geographical dictionaries that contain a wealth of information derived from a variety of sources on the religious traditions associated with certain cities, shrines, mountains, and places of pilgrimage. Scholars such as al-Qazwīnī produced works examining the "wonders" (*ʿajāʾib*) of the world, compiling and comparing mythologies associated with different locations, often utilizing historical, linguistic, and ethnographic approaches. Other early "wonders" accounts focused specifically on India and China. Similar approaches can be found in the large collection of works focused on the "virtues" (*faḍāʾil*) of cities such as Jerusalem, Damascus, and Mecca. These *faḍāʾil* works bring together from various types of sources historical and mythological traditions associated with the origins of sanctuaries, certain ritual practices, and beliefs connected to particular peoples and locations.

JEWISH AND CHRISTIAN STUDIES OF ISLAM. Jewish and Christian scholars also wrote extensively on Islam, and on their own religions, not always with the simple aim of discrediting others but rather in formation of their own distinct identity. This is particularly true where the Muslim majority was and is still in close contact with large non-Muslim minorities, in Spain, Yemen, Egypt, Lebanon, and the Fertile Crescent. Much of this went on in the area of comparative scriptural exegesis, with Jews, Christians, and Muslims interpreting what amounts to a common scriptural tradition, though the identity and authority of different texts (i.e., Qurʾān, Bible) was often the issue in such discussions. This sort of more direct polemic continues today and is not often overt, strongly influenced by perceptions of the political situation between Israel and the Palestinians.

MODERN AND CONTEMPORARY STUDY OF RELIGION. In the modern period, many state-sponsored and private universities include the comparative study of religion as part of the regular curriculum. There are few independent departments devoted to the comparative study of religion, with the exception of departments of *daʿwa* (proselytizing) at some regional universities. Separate departments of *daʿwa* can be found at some universities such as the Islamic University of Medina and the Department of Daʿwa and Religious Fundamentals (*uṣūl al-dīn*) founded in 1991 at the Umm al-Qura University of Mecca. The curriculum emphasizes the comparative study of religions as a means to allow students to contextualize their own religious traditions within a global religious community.

The Amir ʿAbd al-Qadir University in Constantine, Algeria has a Department of Creed and Comparative Religion (al-ʿAqīdah wa Muqārinah al-Adyān). Ain Shams University in Cairo offers the comparative study of religious traditions within the various language and literature departments in the Faculty of Arts, including the languages of Islamic nations, and Hebrew language and literature. The Center for Oriental Studies at the University of Cairo offers a number of courses and a publication series in Comparative Religion. The University of Mauritius offers a degree program in history and heritage studies that incorporates Islamic studies into a broad spectrum of cultural and religious influences on Mauritius history. Individual courses teaching Islamic studies within a comparative, liberal arts framework can also be found at the University of the United Arab Emirates, Sidi Muḥammad b. ʿAbdallah University in Fes, the American University of Beirut, Sultan Qabus University in Musqat, Bogazici University in Istanbul, and the American University of Cairo.

Uṣūl al-dīn. Other universities devote departments and colleges to the general study of religion, within the framework of an Islamic studies curriculum. The department of *uṣūl al-dīn* at the University of Jordan, for example, teaches the standard subfields within Islamic studies, including *al-Milal wa al-Nihal* studies as well as individual courses in comparative religion and Muslim-Christian dialogue. A similar curriculum exists university-wide at Omdurman Islamic University in the Sudan, and al-Quds University in Jerusalem includes an Islamic studies department within liberal arts and a separate Islamic Research Center established in 1987 with a broad, comparative scope. Within its *uṣūl al-dīn* faculty, al-Azhar University offers a comparative curriculum devoted to the study of religions (Christianity, Judaism, Hinduism, pre-Islamic Arab religions, Buddhism, Confucianism, and ancient Egyptian religions) with courses examining the origins of religion, the connections between religion and society, and the history and importance of the study of different religions from an Islamic perspective.

***Sharīʿah* colleges.** Most comparative studies of religion within the universities of the Gulf region are housed within separate colleges devoted to the study of *sharīʿah* (Islamic law) and Islamic studies. The department of *uṣūl al-dīn* in the College of Sharīʿah at the Imam Muḥammad bin Saʿud University was established in the 1950s. The faculty of *sharīʿah* and *uṣūl al-dīn* at the King Khalid University was founded in 1976, and in the 1990s Islamic studies (including the comparative study of religions under the heading of *al-Milal wa al-Nihal*) was moved into the College of Sharīʿah and Islamic Studies at Kuwait University. Iranian universities, such as the Bu Ali Sina University and Shiraz University offer degree programs in Islamic law through the faculties of law at each institution.

Despite their separate institutionalization, these colleges of *sharīʿah* and Islamic studies are often more akin to a North American "divinity school" with a more diverse curriculum than a "seminary"-style college. Other colleges of *sharīʿah* and Islamic studies are more strictly preprofessional, however. The Salahaddin University in Arbil, Iraq, was established in 2003 with the aim of preparing *imāms* for service in the Kurdistan region of Iraq. The faculty of *sharīʿah* and Islamic studies at Yarmouk University in Irbid, Jordan, was established in 1991, merging the then existing Islamic Studies Center into a college designed for professional training. A similar situation pertains to the college of *sharīʿah* at al-Ahqaf University in the Ḥaḍramawt region of Yemen.

CHALLENGES AND CURRENT TRENDS. Today the basic focus of most regional programs in the comparative study of religion is historical and doctrinal. The more differentiated conception of religion as inclusive of practices and beliefs outside of canonical texts and officially sanctioned venues has suffered in the modern period. Modern Muslim scholars of religion tend to isolate what they consider to be religion (Arabic, *dīn*) from tradition and culture (Arabic, *turāth, thaqāfah*). The broad view taken by premodern travelers, historians, and *al-Milal wa al-Nihal* scholars, as well as the more self-critical approach to canonical Islamic texts and doctrines, has largely been replaced by a less complex cataloging of accepted beliefs and practices.

The major challenge facing the study of religion in Arab universities is the perception that comparison and theoretical models represent a challenge to indigenous methods and approaches to the study of religion. This is particularly evident in the defensive and protective posture taken by scholars of the major foundational subjects in classical Islam, especially the historical study of the Prophet Muḥammad and the interpretation of the Qurʾān. Such a defensive stance sometimes has the unfortunate result of stifling discussion and use of the rich comparative approaches developed by premodern Muslim scholarship.

Scholars trained largely in European and North American institutions have introduced innovative approaches to regional studies of religion. This includes, for example, perspectives adopted from the history of religions, text-critical studies, philosophy of religion, and anthropology. Scholars using such approaches are not always successful given the institutional and intellectual barriers in regional universities. Reactions range from the establishment of institutions to the publication of monographs criticizing particular schools of thought and individuals, but sometimes reactions have taken the form of threats and outright violence against particular individuals. The banning of certain publications, both classical and modern, is not uncommon in the region, including the expurgation of passages from classical texts and modern textbooks for K–12 education.

Where European and American models have been most influential is in the areas of archaeology and textual-historical studies. Archaeologists from the King Saʿūd University in Riyadh, for example, have produced a number of excellent analyses of pre-Islamic Arabian religion, and indigenous scholarship on antiquities in other areas, especially Egypt and Jordan, is world class. The German approaches associated with *Religionswissenschaft* and *Religionsgeschichte* are more easily integrated into regional curricula, perhaps because of the emphasis, familiar from the classical Islamic tradition, upon history and doctrine. Within the context of other disciplines, religion is treated with more theoretical ingenuity, as a variable in anthropological, art historical, and political scientific studies.

Centers for comparative religion. Since the 1970s a number of initiatives have created regional centers and brief runs in journals and other periodicals devoted to the relations of Muslims and non-Muslims. Most of this has focused on Muslim-Christian dialogue, such as the programs at the Centre d'Études et de Recherches Économiques et Sociales in Tunis, the joint visits between the Vatican and al-Azhar officials, and the Seminar on Islamic-Christian dialogue founded in Tripoli, Libya, in 1976. These initiatives, however, appear to have been more concerned with political relations than with the academic study of religion.

More recently, as a reaction to the more insular attitude of some regional scholars, a number of regional institutions and centers specifically devoted to the comparative study of religions have been established. A prime example of this is the Royal Institute for Interfaith Studies (Arabic, Maʿhad al-Malakī li-Dirāsāt al-Dīnīyyah) founded by Prince Ḥasan bin Talal in 1994 in Amman, Jordan. The RIIFS, devoted primarily to the study of Judaism, Christianity, and Islam, publishes quarterly journals in English and Arabic and sponsors lectures and visiting scholars from around the world. Other state-supported and private institutions in the region have begun to cultivate more active and creative programs in the comparative study of religion as a means to broaden both academic and popular conceptions of religious identity and civil cooperation.

Another example of this is the Department of Theology and Religions at Qum University in Iran, founded in 2001 with the stated aim of "highlighting the role of religion in dialogue among civilizations. . .for the purpose of understanding one another. . . ." Associated centers in Iran include the Institute for Dialogue among Religions in Tehran and the Bureau for Knowledge and Religions at the Research Center for Human Sciences and Cultural Studies. Since 2001, al-Azhar University has introduced an English-language unit for Islamic studies, and Tashkent Islam University implemented a revised curriculum in the study of world religions. This corresponds with the growing number of Turkish and North African universities that have begun to offer a curriculum aimed explicitly at participating in dialogue with non-Muslim societies.

Such initiatives should not be seen as novel undertakings but rather represent a reinvigoration of the fertile indigenous tradition of the comparative study of religion from the classical Islamic period.

BIBLIOGRAPHY

Adang, Camilla. *Muslim Writers on Judaism and the Hebrew Bible: From Ibn Rabban to Ibn Hazm.* Leiden, 1996.

Broadhurst, R. J. C. *The Travels of Ibn Jubayr.* London, 1952.

Ernst, Carl. *Following Muḥammad: Rethinking Islam in the Contemporary World.* Chapel Hill, N.C., 2003.

Gibb, H. A. R. *The Travels of Ibn Battuta.* 2 vols. Cambridge, U.K., 1958–1962.

Ḥasan, Muḥammad Khalīfah. *ʿAlāqah al-Islām bi-l-adyān al-ukhrā.* Cairo, 2003.

Ibn Hazm, Ali bin Ahmad. *al-Fiṣal fī al-milal wa al-ahwa' wa al-nihal.* 3 vols. Edited by A. Shams al-Din. Beirut, 1999.

Kafafi, Mohamed Abdul Salam, trans. *The Bayan al-Adyan by Abu'l-Maʿali Muḥammad ibn ʿUbayd Allāh.* London, 1949.

al-Maqrīzī, Aḥmad b. ʿAbd al-Qādir. *al-Mawaʿiz wa al-Iʿtibar fi dhikr al-khiṭaṭ wa al-athār.* 2 vols. Cairo, 1892.

Meri, Josef W. "A Late Medieval Syrian Pilgrimage Guide: Ibn al-Hawrani's al-Isharat ila amakin al-ziyarat (Guide to Pilgrimage Places)." *Medieval Encounters* 7 (2001): 3–78. Based on edition by Bassam al-Jabi. Damascus, 1981.

Monnot, G. "Les écrits musulmans sur les religions non-bibliques." *MIDEO* 11 (1972): 5–48.

Nanji, Azim, ed. *Mapping Islamic Studies: Genealogy, Continuity, and Change.* Berlin, 1997.

Palacios, H. Asín. *Abenházam de Crodoba y su historia critica de las ideas religiosas.* Madrid, 1927–1932.

Sachau, Eduard, trans. *Chronolgie orientalischer Völker.* Leipzig, Germany, 1878. Translated into English as *The Chronology of Ancient Nations* (London, 1879).

Sachau, Eduard, trans. *Al-Beruni's India.* 2 vols. London, 1888–1910.

al-Shahrastānī, Muḥammad bin ʿAbd al-Karīm. *al-Milal wa al-nihal.* 2 vols. Edited by A. Mahna and A. Faʿur. Beirut, 2001.

al-Ṭabarī, Muḥammad bin Jarīr. *Ta'rīkh al-rusul wa al-mulūk.* Edited by M. J. de Goeje. 16 vols. Leiden, Netherlands, 1879–1901. English translation of section on pre-Islamic period: *The History of al-Tabari:* Volume 1: *From Creation to the Flood,* translated by Franz Rosenthal (Albany, N.Y., 1989); Volume 2: *Prophets and Patriarchs,* translated by William Brinner (1987); Volume 3: *The Children of Israel,* translated by William Brinner (1991); Volume 4: *The Ancient Kingdoms,* translated Moshe Perlmann (1987).

Waardenburg, Jacques, ed. *Muslim Perceptions of Other Religions: A Historical Survey.* New York, 1999.

Wasserstrom, Steven. *Between Muslim and Jew: The Problem of Symbiosis under Early Islam.* Princeton, N.J., 1995.

Wheeler, Brannon. *Prophets in the Quran: An Introduction to the Quran and Muslim Exegesis.* London, 2002.

BRANNON WHEELER (2005)

STUDY OF RELIGION: THE ACADEMIC STUDY OF RELIGION IN NORTH AMERICA

North American intellectuals, poets, and scholars have shown considerable enthusiasm in exploring religion dating back to the nineteenth century. This spirit flourished in scholarly, theological, philosophical, and artistic investigations.

THE EARLY ROOTS OF THE ACADEMIC STUDY OF RELIGION. Academic study in the nineteenth century was often tied to Christian theological interests and institutions, but this is not to say that all religious study was simply apologetics. Early scholars in the emerging field of North American comparative religions included James Freeman Clark (Harvard Divinity School), who published *Ten Great Religions: An Essay in Comparative Theology* in 1871. Between the 1860s and 1900 several religiously oriented university chairs were appointed at places such as Harvard, Boston University, Princeton, and Cornell—Clark's appointment as "Professor of Natural Religion and Christian Doctrine" at Harvard being one example. Although these chairs did not represent a full-fledged comparative religion such as was emerging in Europe, they did portend a trend away from singly theological reflections and apologetics. In addition to Clark, other scholars included W. D. Whitney, James Freeman Clarke, and George Foot Moore. In 1892 T. W. Rhys Davids, a British scholar of Buddhism, was invited to lecture at the newly established "American Lectures on the History of Religions," a joint venture among several colleges and universities. In the same year the University of Chicago established a department devoted to the study of comparative religion.

Outside of universities, Ralph Waldo Emerson (and other transcendentalists), Walt Whitman, and John Burroughs represent just a few of the voices among amateur Orientalists, philosophers, poets, and theologians interested in religious experience, mysticism, religious psychology, and religious pluralism. On the level of popular culture, Chicago's World Parliament of Religions in 1893 offered a plurality of different Christian congresses and lectures and introduced many Americans to what became the earliest understandings of Buddhist Theravāda and Zen as well as Hindu Vedānta. These events and thinkers held the common interest in religion and trust in "modern" scholarly methods to reveal the origins, meanings, and truths of the myriad human behaviors deemed religious.

These forces—as well as a plurality of religious groups examining their own theology— created a diversity of ideas, interpretations, and reflections on institutional religions (such as Christianity and Buddhism), on religious texts (such as the *Bhagavadgītā* and the Bible), and on the role of religious practices and claims in society (such as religion and law or psychology of religion).

This early phase of amateur and academic study of religion was wide-ranging, yet disciplinary identity and overall theoretical coherence were still in development. Often uneasy (even antagonistic) mixtures of theology, history, and social sciences evolved in this early academic study of religion. Even though clear disciplinary identity was lacking, active study proceeded in several areas. Unique among these was the American school of psychology of religion. Stanley Hall (1884–1924)—trained at Wilhelm Wundt's laboratory of experimental psychology in Leipzig—brought European psychology to the United States and set the stage for the development of an original American psychology of religion by James H. Leuba (1868–1946), Edwin Diller Starbuck (1866–1947), William James (1842–1910), and others. Positivism and American "pragmatism" were this new psychology's orientation, questionnaires and surveys became one of its primary methods, and the psychology of religious conversion was one of its early foci. Leuba addressed conversion from the psychological point of view and as a scientific rationalist in his 1896 dissertation in psychology (written at Clark University under Stanley Hall). Starbuck and James, from different perspectives, were more accepting of transcendental realities and distinctly "religious" experience, but nonetheless their approaches were thoroughly scholarly in Starbuck's *The Psychology of Religion* and James's *The Varieties of Religious Experience.*

Another fruitful area of research was in the emerging discourses of American anthropology. North American scholars and professional (and amateur) ethnologists had a long encounter with indigenous Americans. Franz Boas, Robert H. Lowie, Paul Radin, Alfred L. Kroeber, and Clyde Kluckhohn (to name a few) all showed significant interest in religious aspects of Native American cultures (worldviews, ceremonies, and myths). Boas (1858–1942) at Columbia University trained numerous anthropologists (Lowie, Radin, and Kroeber among them) who tended to work from the basic assumption that understanding native cultures required careful study of their "religions" (rituals, myths, and customs). The influence of Native American studies and American anthropology had wider impact than just the Americas, being of interest to both anthropologists and scholars of religion in Europe. Whereas such thinkers as the French Lucien Lévy-Bruhl tended toward the philosophical and theoretical, American anthropologists contributed a strong emphasis on empirical fieldwork and (following Boas), a keen sense of history, and even a distrust of overtheorizing the data.

One of the peculiarities of American higher education is that the major universities have not been—and arguably still are not—state institutions as they have been in most parts of the world. The development of divinity schools at such institutions as Chicago, Harvard, Yale, and Princeton led the early- and mid-twentieth-century development of the academic study of religion. Whereas social sciences (psychology, anthropology, sociology) were contributing both data and theories to the study of religion, it was often these divinity schools that led the self-conscious pursuit for an American "comparative religion" or "history of religions." Harvard and Chicago are two notable examples, training many of the historians and comparativists who populated the many departments of religious and cultural studies of the 1960s, 1970s, and following decades.

Religious Studies and Related Disciplines. Following the lead of these divinity schools, "religious studies" emerged as an academic discipline during the 1960s and 1970s in private and state universities. Religious studies include disciplinary approaches such as anthropology, sociology, history, and philology. Other approaches are geographic or chronological, such as religion in America, East Asian cultures and religions, and ancient Near Eastern studies. Others are drawn from doctrinal or community boundaries, such as Buddhist, Hindu, Islamic, or Christian studies.

After World War II, following the earlier interests of Clark, James, and Boas and even such thinkers as John Dewey, several new voices and schools of thought spoke from within the emerging field of religious studies. Prominent among them were Erwin R. Goodenough (Yale), Wilfred Cantwell Smith (Harvard), Joachim Wach (responsible for the program at Brown and for shaping the program at the University of Chicago), Mircea Eliade (following Wach at the University of Chicago), and the Scottish-born Ninian Smart (University of California, Santa Barbara). From different perspectives, their approaches tended to treat the topic of religion as a self-generated category whose study was an act of interpretation and understanding. Their interests (philosophy, sociology, history, and phenomenology) and area studies backgrounds (Christianity, Hinduism, and Buddhism) varied. Eliade was particularly prominent among these mid-century voices. He tended to look at religious products (myths and rituals) as manifestations of sacred (or mystical) reality that originated outside of human experience. Thus he collected vast amounts of diverse cultural material into general categories, such as "myth," as exemplified in his *Patterns in Comparative Religion* (1958). Even though this kind of study brought together broadly divergent materials into overarching categories, there was also a strong sense of contextual history in the Chicago school of the history of religions. The Chicago journal *History of Religions,* begun in 1961 at the height of Eliade's prominence, has tended to publish detailed and context-rich historically grounded studies.

The approaches of these mid-century thinkers varied widely but might be described as treating religious institutions and behaviors as phenomena similar to literature, a music composition, or a performance. Following the analogy of the arts, a particular religious ritual must be interpreted (appreciated, criticized) much like a musical performance or an artifact. Study of this kind might include, for example, encouraging the practice of Zen meditation in addition to studying Zen texts on meditation or interviewing Zen monks. Ninian Smart referred to this kind of study as "participatory" and insisted that the study of religion need be polymethodic and interdisciplinary because in order to understand religion the scholar must be simultaneously inside and outside of the subject of study. Smith, Eliade, and Smart all argued that the academic study of religion needed to be a broad utilitarian and humanistic study and not some kind of strictly (and only) objective historical study of particular traditions.

The mid-century study of religion also boasted several "popular" trends in books and media. The works of the literature scholar Joseph Campbell and the Bollingen Foundation are examples of the extensive study of comparative mythology that—although occurring outside of religious studies or divinity schools—brought a vast amount of religious materials to popular audiences in books and media, such as Campbell's *Hero with a Thousand Faces* and *The Masks of God* and the PBS series *Moyers: Joseph Campbell and the Power of Myth.* While many scholars of religion view Campbell's work as "popular" and "literary" instead of historical or scholarly, this does not downplay the influence of such work in bringing comparative religious materials to large audiences (many of whom might never have studied religion in universities). The religion scholar Huston Smith, author of *The World's Religions: Our Great Wisdom Traditions* (1958) and other textbooks and general works on religion, hosted film and television presentations of religions and the psychology of religious experiences that, like Campbell's work, presented comparative religions to large popular audiences.

At the same time American social scientific studies of religion viewed religion not as self-generated phenomena understandable only on its own terms but as a cultural product. Human beings generate the varied religious practices and beliefs that they employ for a variety of contingent, political, personal, and social purposes. This kind of science is described as reductive: it examines religion not as a special subject but as a product of social life that can be explained with the same intellectual tools as other human phenomena, such as political parties, psychological pathology, or marketing trends. Although this orientation grew out of American social scientific concerns for "religion in culture," it echoed in many ways Europe's "scientific study of religion" more than the "history of religions" and "religious studies" common in North American divinity schools and religious studies departments. Some of the North American scholars who approached religion in these ways included Peter Berger, Thomas Luckmann, Bryan Wilson, and Robert Bellah as well as others in sociology who devoted significant attention to the study of religion. The works of Clifford Geertz, Mary Douglas, and Victor Turner contributed both description and theory to the anthropological study of religion.

CONTEMPORARY TRENDS. The intermixture of humanities and social sciences approaches and the additions of original approaches from cultural studies in the late twentieth- and early twenty-first centuries has led to considerable diversity in the discussions and discourses on religion. It is not possible to collect a canon of a dozen authors and thereby gain an overview of North American academic approaches to religion. In this broadly diverse and creatively rich context, all scholars share, in principle, an insistence on intellectual rigor and critical self-awareness. The lack of an all-encompassing theme in the field reflects the shared insistence on focusing on religion in specific historical contexts (regardless of the analytical and intellectual methods employed). Significant in this American trend is the plethora of critical examinations of the role of subjectivity in all productions of knowledge (in universities and popular culture). Scholars of previous generations often critically examined political authority or religious truth claims, yet they sometimes failed to use these same critical methods to examine their own productions of knowledge about complex human phenomena (whether religion, culture, or politics). Beginning from different backgrounds and presuppositions, contemporary scholars employ the principle of contesting and examining everything, not just the subject matter but also scholarship and the academy itself.

The combination of area study with the study of disciplinary history is a primary manifestation of this trend toward rigorous disciplinary self awareness. Steven M. Wasserstrom (Judaic studies), Robert A. Orsi (religion in America), Sam D. Gill (religion and cultural studies), and many others practice this new trend in their scholarship and published works. Wasserstrom's *Religion after Religion: Gershom Scholem, Mircea Eliade, and Henry Corbin at Eranos* (1999) carefully explores the mystical and poetic influences on the formation of the discipline in the works of three scholars (of Judaism, history of religions, and Islamic studies respectively). Part of understanding how to practice the study of religion is through understanding the genealogy of the study itself in North America. Gill's *Storytracking: Texts, Stories, and Histories in Central Australia* (1997) presents several aspects of the contemporary trend to careful contextual research and self-critique. *Storytracking* presents the worldview of Australian Aboriginal religion by applying the Aboriginal peoples' own methods of narrative to the study of Australian Aboriginal culture and thereby also provides critique of previous scholarship that distorted the data. As such it provides both an original study of Aboriginal culture and a critique of the academic study of religion.

Bruce Lincoln (myth, ritual, and ideology), Charles Long (religion in the contemporary world), and Jonathan Z. Smith (Judaism's myth and ritual) are prominent scholars and teachers who reflect on the topic of religions and the study of religions and contribute significant applications of these reflections and theories to area studies. These three thinkers' contributions cover extensive and detailed philological, historical, and cultural studies touching almost all aspects of the academic study of religion from ancient Israel, Africa, and Europe to contemporary religious, political, and cultural issues in North America and abroad. Diana L. Eck (Hinduism and religious pluralism) and Martin Marty (Christianity and religion in the contemporary world) continue and defend the humanistic concerns of the mid-century thinkers that religion is a kind of personal, irreducible human experience also through careful awareness and critique of previous scholarship and through specific contributions to Hindu and Christian studies.

Some scholars directly pursue this disciplinary self-awareness by addressing the theoretical basis of the academic study of religion and the constitution of the field (especially under the rubrics of method, theory, or metatheory). In many cases these approaches focus less on critiquing the discipline through specific area studies than on the academic study of religion itself as their area study. Some prominent voices are Hans Penner, Donald Wiebe, Catherine Bell, and Russell McCutcheon.

Contributions continue to come from outside of religious studies as well. Examples include Edward Said (postcolonial theory) and Talal Asad (anthropology, especially religion and secularism in the Middle East), whose writings contribute to specific study of the Middle East while also providing extensive theoretical and philosophical contributions on the study of culture. Works from such contributors include Asad's *Formation of the Secular: Christianity, Islam, Modernity* (2003), which is of interest to anthropologists, scholars of religion, and area specialists, and a broad general readership as well. Rodney Stark (sociology, especially rational choice theory of religion) represents different, strictly social scientific principles by offering comprehensive social scientific theories to explain religion.

At one time the study of religion could be divided into either history or sociology or according to intellectual trends, such as functionalism, structuralism, or phenomenology. There is no single or dominant trend in the contemporary study of religion, although postcolonial studies, critical theory, performance studies, religion and ecology, feminism, subaltern studies, and cognitive science inform the traditional orientations of history, philology, and the social sciences. As a field religious studies constantly battles to remain relevant to the wider public and maintain rigorous scholarly study while also being subject to intellectual, political, and cultural fads, trends, and moods.

INSTITUTIONAL TRENDS IN COLLEGES AND UNIVERSITIES. In the late 1960s and early 1970s colleges and universities established departments of religious studies as part of larger cultural trends. The "red scare" and anticommunist political mood encouraged interest in and defense of religion as a defining feature of the democratic cultures. It was also a time of assertive revivalism, creativity, and change within traditional American religious communities. Vatican II and liberal Protestant theology revitalized Christian interests in "religion." A new conservatism that emphasized historical and textual study also emerged. The 1960s counterculture was fascinated with so-called exotic traditions, such as Buddhism and yoga, and also antitraditional explorations of occultism. Changing immigration policies and patterns, the proliferation of media, international affairs, and geopolitical interests in the Middle East and Asia all contributed to a vast increase in international and multicultural interests. U.S. and Canadian trends in higher education reflected these social and intellectual trajectories, and the result was an explosion of liberal arts and cultural studies programs (religious, women's, ethnic, and others).

By the 1970s institutional boundaries were drawn more strictly between theology and the secular study of religion. Conservative Protestant colleges remained committed to theological study of religion focused on the active promotion of their particular religious views. Roman Catholic colleges and universities tended before the 1970s to offer courses in theology but generally did not offer majors and minors in the study of religion. Since that time many Catholic institutions have developed religion programs, and although in many ways unlike the conservative Protestant colleges, they are generally aimed at preparing students for occupations within religious industries (churches and counseling). Mainline Protestant colleges developed along parallel patterns with public institutions, adopting ecumenical outlooks and secularizing trends (such as in the divinity schools mentioned above).

During the 1980s and afterward programs expanded to include a broader range of approaches, especially those of the social sciences and cultural studies. Religious studies scholars now regularly employ fieldwork, ethnography, statistical analysis, demographics, cultural criticism, and performance studies. These developments have extended the boundaries of religious studies beyond traditional categories, such as "scripture" or "Hinduism." Women's issues, the politics of religious violence, religion and medicine, and religion and the body are particular examples of these transformations.

After the 1980s some programs in religious studies continued to grow and prosper, whereas others suffered due to political changes and fiscal constraints in higher education. Changes in public and private funding and the adoption of corporate business models by many universities have caused departments and programs to defend their existences based on costs and enrollment. In these environments religious studies programs must compete with other departments for students, funding, and faculty appointments. Many programs have coped with these fiscal realities by shifting their emphasis away from competing for majors and minors through reframing their place within university-wide programs, such as providing courses for general education, multicultural and international initiatives, and other circumstances in which religious studies is not the students' major program of study.

A different trend in the study of religion is the formation of centers that focus on religious topics but draw faculty from numerous departments. Such centers capitalize on the inherent interdisciplinary nature of the field drawing on scholars from multiple disciplines. Harvard's Center of the Study of World Religions, Toronto's Department and Center for the Study of Religion, and the University of Chicago's Martin Marty Center (and institute devoted to relating the scholarly study of religion to wider public audiences) are three examples. There has also been a rise of "centers" that focus on a geographic area (culture, religions, politics, history, and languages). An example is the Center for Sikh and Punjab Studies at the University of California, Santa Barbara. Some centers focus on an issue, such as conflict studies or women's studies, or a specific time period. For example, Trinity College's Leonard E. Greenberg Center for the Study of Religion in Public Life focuses on religion in the contemporary world. Other disciplines and cultural studies programs also contribute significant studies of religious subject matters. One example is the Department of Cultural Studies and Comparative Literature at the University of Minnesota.

PROFESSIONAL ORGANIZATIONS, PROJECTS, AND PUBLICATIONS. Professional organizations in the study of religion arrange conferences (regional, national, and international), disseminate information, support various publications (books, conference volumes, and journals), and publicize the field. The American Academy of Religion (AAR), founded in 1909 and incorporated in 1964, includes scholars from several disciplines and promotes reflections and teachings focusing on a critical understanding of religious traditions, issues, questions, and values. The AAR collects and publishes data and statistics about theology and religious studies programs and sponsors the publication of the *Journal of the American Academy of Religion (JAAR)*. The North American Association for the Study of Religion (NAASR), formed in 1985, is devoted to historical, comparative, structural, theoretical, and cognitive approaches to the study of religion. The NAASR is affiliated with the International Association for the History of Religions (IAHR). Its journal *Method and Theory in the Study of Religion (MTSR)* examines theoretical issues and pedagogical and research methods. The Canadian Corporation for Studies in Religion (CCSR) is a consortium of several other academic societies in the field of religious studies (including the Canadian Society for the Study of Religion and the Canadian Society of Biblical Studies). It coordinates research and publications and was originally formed in 1971 to coordinate research among the different societies and to publish the bilingual (French and English) journal *Studies in Religion/Sciences Religieuses (SR)*. The Society for the Scientific Study of Religion (SSSR) was founded in 1949 by scholars in religious studies and social sciences. Its *Journal for the Scientific Study of Religion (JSSR)* generally focuses on sociological approaches to the study of religion. There are additional organizations that support or publish academic studies of religion either from outside the field (such as those devoted to anthropology or literature) or from area studies within the field. Area and topical studies organizations are numerous. Examples include the Society of Biblical Literature (SBL), the American Schools of Oriental Research (ASOR), and the Society for Tantric Studies (STS). Numerous other journals publish religious studies topics, such as *History of Religions*, *Religion*, and *Journal of Hebrew Scriptures*.

Publications are an intense area of academic interest. In addition to scholarly monographs, edited works, and journals, North Americans have contributed significantly to the publication of encyclopedias, dictionaries, and textbooks in the field of religion. Encyclopedias of religion, religion and nature, religion and ecology, mythology, ritual, Christianity, and many area studies works have been published in single- and multivolume sets and electronically. Textbooks arranged topically, geographically, and historically offer a broad and creative area of introductory and advanced sourcebooks for scholars and students. North America has been a leading contributor in this last area, offering, for example, Mark Taylor's edited text, *Critical Terms for Religious Studies* (1998), and Daniel L. Pals's *Seven Theories of Religion* (1996).

BIBLIOGRAPHY

"AAR Guide for Reviewing Programs in Religion & Theology." Academic Relations Task Force, 1999.

Bell, Catherine. *Ritual: Perspectives and Dimensions.* New York, 1997.

Braun, Willi, and Russell T. McCutcheon, eds. *Guide to the Study of Religion.* London, 2000.

Cady, Linell E., and Delwin Brown, eds. *Religious Studies, Theology, and the University: Conflicting Maps, Changing Terrain.* Albany, N.Y., 2002.

Capps, Walter H. *Religious Studies: The Making of a Discipline.* Minneapolis, 1995.

De Vries, Jan. *Perspectives in the History of Religions.* Translated by Kees W. Bolle. Berkeley, Calif., 1977.

Fitzgerald, Tim. *The Ideology of Religious Studies.* New York, 1999.

Gill, Sam. "The Academic Study of Religion." *Journal of the American Academy of Religion* 62, no. 4 (1994): 965–975.

Jensen, Jeppe Sinding, and Luther H. Martin, eds. *Rationality and the Study of Religion.* Aarhus, Denmark, 1997. See pp. 136–144.

Lincoln, Bruce. *Theorizing Myth: Narrative, Ideology, and Scholarship.* Chicago, 1999.

Lincoln, Bruce. *Holy Terrors: Thinking about Religion after September 11.* Chicago, 2002.

Marty, Martin. "You Get to Teach the Study of Religion." *Academe* 82, no. 6 (1996): 14–17.

McCutcheon, Russell T. *Critics Not Caretakers: Redescribing the Public Study of Religion.* Albany, N.Y., 2001.

Sharp, Eric J. *Comparative Religion: A History.* 2d ed. La Salle, Ill., 1986.

Smith, Jonathan Z. *To Take Place: Toward Theory in Ritual.* Chicago, 1994.

Smith, Jonathan Z. "Religious Studies: Whither (Wither) and Why?" *Method and Theory in the Study of Religion* 7, no. 4 (1995): 407–413.

Wiebe, Donald. *The Politics of Religious Studies.* New York, 1999.

JEFFREY C. RUFF (2005)

STUDY OF RELIGION: THE ACADEMIC STUDY OF RELIGION IN SOUTH ASIA

The locus for the academic study of religion in South Asia is found in a network of university departments and scholarly sites rather than in departments of religious studies or comparative religion within individual universities. The network also includes scholars located in nonuniversity settings: theological institutions, research institutes in social sciences, and specialized scholarly centers with a tradition of respected publications in academia.

The South Asian region includes at least 330 state-supported universities, of which 275 are in India, 17 in Pakistan, 18 in Bangladesh, 15 in Sri Lanka, and 5 in Nepal.

Institutions with a multidisciplinary focus in India include the National Institute of Advanced Studies (natural and social sciences and technology) and the Christian Institute for the Study of Religion and Society in Bangalore; the Centre for the Study of Developing Societies in Delhi; and the Indian Institute of Advanced Studies in Shimla. Pakistan has the Christian Study Centre, located at Rawalpindi, an ecumenical research and fact-finding site focusing on Islamization, interfaith dialogue, women and minorities, and conflict prevention and management among different religious groups in the region. In Sri Lanka the Ecumenical Institute for Study and Dialogue, located in Colombo, offers Buddhist studies, comparative religion, and studies of church and society. Scholars at these institutions have produced distinguished comparative and interpretive studies related to the different religious traditions of South Asia.

The South Asian strand of this field, beginning in a Western historical context, has for its antecedents in South Asia a form of study expressed most notably by two North Indian rulers. One is the emperor Aśoka (c. 265–238 BCE), who sought to respect and protect all religions, and the other is the emperor Akbar (1542–1605 CE), whose religious dialogues at Fatehpur Sikri encouraged debates among different religions with a view to synthesizing them into a single religion. In modern times the South Asian strand of the academic study of religion can be usefully delineated in the context of three historical conferences held between 1960 and 2003 in Marburg in Germany and in Bangalore and Delhi in India.

THE IAHR CONGRESS, MARBURG, 1960. The International Association for the History of Religions Congress was held in Marburg, West Germany, in 1960. The prospect of holding an IAHR Congress in India was raised by Swami B. H. Bon Maharaj, the rector of the Institute of Oriental Philosophy in Vrindavan, India. In March 1960 he had founded the Indian national group that sought and obtained affiliation with IAHR. This proposal was unwelcome to some of the European members because they felt the Indian representatives were confused about the history of religion as an academic field. As R. J. Zwi Werblowsky's report on the congress noted, South Asian representatives showed what others considered to be a misunderstanding of Western scholarship in their failure to distinguish between studying religion and the study of religion. The Indian scholars felt their own tradition of philosophizing about religion and studying it as part of a religious discipline should be known to the West.

The parochial views expressed at the congress failed to do justice to the South Asian intellectual tradition, which has a long association with historical research and scientific thought. That tradition has produced monographs and scholarly papers in Indology, archeology, history, and sociology relating to functional and causal questions on matters that now fall under the category of the study of religion. Still the objective study of religion, as opposed to a moral study, has been slow to gain recognition in South Asian academia, and the region has a comparatively insignificant representation at international conferences on the academic study of religion. India's secularist politics are largely responsible and have provided a model for its universities. The Indian constitution, though tolerant of all religions and showing sensitivity to religious values, explicitly prohibits favoring any one of India's many religious traditions. This prohibition caused a reluctance among state-funded institutions to introduce religion as a subject in their curricula.

The avoidance of religion in any state-funded college curriculum can be seen as early as 1882, when a government commission recommended teaching the principles of natural theology, which favored no single religious tradition, in public and private colleges. One of the commission members objected on the grounds that this, far from satisfying the religious camp, would be a step backward on the secular side. In 1903 the Indian Universities Commission rejected the idea of introducing a course on the theology of any one religion into the state curriculum. Later commissions sought to preserve the religious neutrality of the state while becoming more sympathetic to religious studies. A commission chaired by Sarvepalli Radhakrishnan in 1948–1949 pointed out that to be secular did not mean to be religiously illiterate. The report of the Secondary Education Commission (1952–1953), headed by A. L. Mudaliar, agreed that secularism did not mean there was no place for religion. The Sri Prakasa Committee (1959–1960) report recommended an objective, comparative, and systematic study of the important religions of India. The report of the Kothari Commission (1964–1966) drew a distinction between religious education and education about religion and suggested establishing chairs in comparative religion at the universities at a time when the debate in North America was just beginning as to whether the academic study of religion should remain a secular study independent of religio-theological approaches.

THE BANGALORE CONSULTATION, BANGALORE, 1967. The study of religion in Indian universities was addressed at the

1967 Bangalore Consultation, a milestone event in the academic study of religion in South Asia. Two of the presentations were by the North American scholars John Carman and Wilfrid Cantwell Smith, who respectively considered the study of religion at Indian universities and in a global context. Presentations at the conference helped move discussion among Indian academics to a more critical and analytical level. The paper by T. M. P. Mahadevan, the director of the Centre for Advanced Study at the University of Madras, outlined principles governing the teaching of religion at the university level. One of them was the encouragement of "the method of objective criticism." He also recommended that "the stress should be on the teaching of moral and spiritual values, and not on dogmas and particular rituals" (Seminar on the Study of Religion in Indian Universities, 1968, p. 55). The effort to reconcile two opposite and contradictory approaches, the secular and the religio-theological, reverberated in presentations calling for the establishment of comparative religion as a university subject.

The prevailing view conceived of the study of religion as a means of promoting moral and spiritual values. Much-needed perspective was added by the inaugural address, presented by the vice chancellor of Bangalore University, V. K. Gokak, who pointed out that if the objective of teaching religion was to promote spiritual values, then it could not be done through either an eclectic philosophical approach dealing with "elements of reality that each philosophic system accepts" or the scientific study of religion that "refines away the essence of religion itself to vanishing point the awareness of spirit and all that it implies" (Seminar on the Study of Religion in Indian Universities, 1968, pp. 28, 30). By recalling that the scientific study of religion already operated in the context of existing departments of history and sociology, the inaugural address took the position that the study of religion should serve "secularity or tolerance, not spirituality" (Seminar on the Study of Religion in Indian Universities, 1968, p. 32). The presentation by J. L. Mehta of the Centre of Advanced Study in Philosophy at Banaras Hindu University proposed that one of the tasks of the study of religion in India was to aid in understanding the "other . . . within the complex fabric which is the heritage of the Hindu student of religion" and that for such an understanding "detached and disciplined academic energy and attention" are required (Seminar on the Study of Religion in Indian Universities, 1968, pp. 39, 40).

What is important to note about the level of dialogue that characterized the Bangalore Consultation is that it was accomplished in concert with scholars from North America and showed Indian scholars to be mindful of the Western intellectual tradition. In particular Mehta's presentation, referring to the task of coming "to closer grips with the truths of other religious traditions" and of understanding one's own religious and cultural tradition, introduced a discussion of hermeneutic as a methodology in the study of religion (Seminar on the Study of Religion in Indian Universities 1968, p. 39). In this respect, the reflections at the conference approximated the discussion occurring outside India on the direction and scope of the academic study of religion.

Comparative religion. The Bangalore Consultation involved more than theoretical discussions of the study of religion. It also marked a shift to the use of the term *comparative religion,* which implied a preference for a study of the different religions of India. That perspective introduced the element of dialogue as a methodology suited to learning about other religions' traditions from the perspective of their own adherents and representatives. The impetus for this conceptualization arose from the dialogue between Indian and Western scholars who wanted to see a recognition of India's moral and religious values. Carman and Smith stressed the importance of understanding the outward expression of a religious tradition and its inner meanings for its adherents, for whom the traditions may have supreme significance. Methodologically this approach is unlike that taken by either philosophy or theology, both of which are concerned with ideas rather than their adherents. A dialogue allows room to consider the views of the reflective and articulate practitioner. In this respect comparative religion became a method in the study of religion as well as a discipline. Ultimately, however, it did not gain any significant momentum among South Asian institutions of learning.

Smith was among the advocates of this method, and in 1965 he recommended to the Kothari Commission that chairs and degrees in comparative religion be established. The University Grants Commission and the Education Commission accepted his recommendation, which was implemented at Punjabi University at Patiala and at Visva-Bharati University at Santiniketan in its philosophy department. A comparative religion department was already in place at Osmania University as a result of a 1949 reorganization, but due to lack of support from the university, it was later divided into two independent departments: Islamics and Indology.

Radhakrishnan, chair of the 1948–1949 University Education Report, characterized comparative religion in his *East and West in Religion* as a means for different religions to share their visions, insights, hopes, fears, and purposes. He also believed comparative religion could serve as a prophylactic against claims of exclusivity by any one religious tradition. This functional view was later accommodated by Smith's conceptualization of comparative religion as both a discipline and a subject. But the momentum for establishing comparative religion as a university discipline ultimately rested on asking and finding answers to the fundamental question of what religion really is. Given that only a handful of South Asian universities offer courses on religion at undergraduate and postgraduate levels, it may well be that the question has failed to become as important to scholars in South Asia as it is to their Western counterparts.

Still the drive to have comparative religion instituted as a discipline within a university setting persists in South Asia and may perhaps be due largely to the Indological works and wider academic interests of F. Max Muller, who is associated with the founding of comparative religion as a scholarly discipline.

Hindrances to the academic field. One reason the South Asian approach to the study of religion differs from the Western approach is that the South Asian worldview sees *dharma* or religion configured in a different way. The dichotomy between the sacred and the secular does not exist in South Asia as it does in the West. Among Western academics, the study of religion is understood to deal with the outward expressions of a social reality and the production of data about it. The tendency in South Asia is to focus on understanding the inner meaning of that social reality in peoples' lives and in that respect comes to be seen and taught as an aspect of Indian philosophy. It approximates in the West that which is known as philosophical theology, having philosophy as its academic mother.

Another factor mitigates against the establishment of religious studies departments in Indian universities: aspects of religion as a subject matter are already considered by various different departments, thus making a separate department redundant. The field of anthropology, for example, is frequently occupied with aspects of the study of religion. But anthropologists generally have little interest in understanding religion as a phenomenon, and their study seldom shifts from descriptive accounts to explanatory and theoretical ones. On the other hand, there is little significant momentum in existing comparative religion departments to broaden the study as a subject matter and a discipline comparable to that found in the West.

THE IAHR REGIONAL CONFERENCE, DELHI, 2003. The Indian Association for the Study of Religion (IAHR) Regional Conference took place in Delhi, India, in December 2003. One of its aims was to restructure and strengthen the Indian Association for the Study of Religion in recognition of the fact that India was comparatively underrepresented in the scholarly study of religion on the international level. The restructuring of the existing national association was intended to encourage wider participation in the study of religion beyond a handful of scholars working in anthropology, especially on tribal and folk religions.

The conference, whose theme was "Religions and Cultures in the Indic Civilization," brought together some three hundred scholars, roughly 20 percent from the West. Many of the participants focused attention on the relevance of the study of religion and its future direction. In the inaugural session Bhikhu Parekh delivered an address titled "The Role and Place of Religion," which was followed by Ashis Nandy's "A Modest Plea for Learning the Language of Religion." In one workshop four papers dealt with teaching a basic course on the academic study of religion in an Indian context. In another session the theme was promoting the study of religion in Indian universities. Papers presented included "Political Implications of Changes in Religious Demography in India," "Language and Religion as Sites of Struggle," "Women Regaining a Lost Legacy: The Restoration of Bikkhuni Order in Sri Lanka," suggesting a shift away from a normative to a nonnormative approach as practiced at secular universities in the West. Interestingly the majority of participants came from outside departments of comparative religion or philosophy. Conference participants expressed interest in establishing an Indic studies network, raising hopes that a stronger South Asian presence will emerge to make a distinct contribution to the academic study of religion.

RELIGIOUS STUDIES IN MODERN SOUTH ASIA. Thirteen institutions of higher learning on the Indian subcontinent offer one or more courses on the study of religion as a subject either at the undergraduate or at the postgraduate level, according to the 2003–2004 *Commonwealth Universities Handbook*. India has a total of nine universities that offer degrees either at the undergraduate, masters, or doctoral level. This does not include schools focusing on a specific religion or tradition. Sri Lanka has two universities that offer courses in the study of religion at the undergraduate level. In Pakistan only the Lahore School of Management, in its social science department, offers a course at the undergraduate level. In Bangladesh there is growing interest in courses and programs on world religions. Dhaka University in Bangladesh established a Department of World Religions in 2000, offering two-year master's and master of philosophy degrees. Small private universities in Bangladesh also offer programs in comparative religion.

In the Muslim world of South Asia, the academic study of religion is comparatively slow in gaining recognition. Most teaching focuses on the classical and modern perspectives of Islamic thought and contemporary movements and issues related to the Muslim world. Interfaith dialogue is limited to Islamic forms of religious consciousness and the desire to perpetuate traditional Islamic values without going beyond a normative approach. As Smith suggested at the Bangalore Consultation in 1967, "Muslim society here is on the whole too frightened to be interested in other men's faith; and too bewildered to ask systematic questions about its own."

Religion and politics. The emergence of national politics in the postindependence era in South Asia has historicized and contextualized academic study of religion on the subcontinent. In particular religion has become intertwined with nationalist politics, resulting in religious communalism, the rejection of the concept of a modern nation-state as understood in the West, and resistance to modernization and secularization as indicators of social development. For some, religion has become a means to overcome a disenchantment with modernity and to reinstate South Asia's cultural and spiritual heritage. Neither political Islam nor political Hinduism can be discounted in the subject matter of academic studies of religion. Nor can the temper of such religious movements, linked to transcendent values, be understood solely in terms of Western democratic models of party politics or polity.

The phenomenon of religion in South Asia has become subject matter for scholars not only in political science but also in economics, geography, sociology, and cultural studies. Many have a Marxist orientation seldom found among academics in the West. Thus the study of religion in South Asia is characterized by certain broad themes reflected by contemporary scholars, such as Madhu Kishvar and Asgar Ali Engineer, and in some of the works presented at the 2003 Delhi Conference cosponsored by IAHR. Themes include women's and minority rights, nationalism and identity, diaspora and ethnicity, peace and conflict studies, rethinking of secularization and globalization with respect to Indic cultural heritage, and ethnic politics and religious empowerment.

History and the future. Historical context distinguishes South Asian concepts of the study of religion from either the North American or European approaches. As a secular state, India is impartial to expressions of religion in its secular institutions of learning. It has a history of resisting the study of religion as a subject matter but allows for the study of the phenomenon under existing departments, such as sociology and anthropology. In this unique environment South Asian scholars from different disciplinary fields will undoubtedly continue to bring their unique perspectives and worldviews to the study of religion, approaching it from a historical, phenomenological, and structural perspective. Those with a philosophical bent may move the study from descriptive accounts to explanation and theory. The inseparable connection between religion and philosophy explored by scholars such as Sarvepalli Radhakrishnan, T. R. V. Murti, T. M. P. Mahadevan, Daya Krishna, and Muhammad Iqbal continues as a tradition of scholarly investigation. Methodological and theoretical studies have their antecedents in studies by scholars such as K. N. Jayatilleke, Ananda Coomaraswamy, M. N. Srinivas, Aziz Ahmad, Fazlur Rahman, and T. M. Madhan.

Though the prospect of a burgeoning rise of departments of religion in South Asia, and, for that matter, of student enrollment, seem dim, the indications are promising for an increased interest in the academic study of religion: interaction and dialogue occurring between Western and South Asian academics at international conferences, visiting scholar arrangements, and joint academic projects and publications. In such encounters each side clearly becomes exposed to the influence of the other, thereby keeping alive in the academic study of religion the idea of comparative religion as method and discipline, and providing impetus for the rethinking and reconceptualizing of the engagement between the philosophy of religion and the history of religions.

Bibliography

Association of Commonwealth Universities. *Commonwealth Universities Yearbook.* London, 2002–2003. Provides information for each British Commonwealth country on its higher education institutions, structure of degree programs and diplomas, developments and initiatives, and departmental specializations.

Conference on Religions and Cultures in the Indic Civilization. Available at www.indicreligions.com. Lists speakers and the titles of their addresses, panels, abstracts, and critical comments on the academic quality of the conference held in New Delhi, December 18–21, 2003.

Pye, Michael, ed. *Marburg Revisited: Institutions and Strategies in the Study of Religion.* Marburg, Germany, 1989. Reports on the study of religion, primarily in European and African regions.

Radhakrishnan, Sarvepalli. *East and West in Religion.* London, 1948; reprint, 1958. Offers a perspective as early as the 1930s on the conceptualizing of religion by distinguished Indian scholars in the field.

Seminar on the Study of Religion in Indian Universities. *Study of Religion in Indian Universities: A Report on the Consultation Held in Bangalore in September 1967.* Bangalore, India, 1968. Includes papers presented by John B. Carman, V. K. Gokak, J. L. Mehta, T. M. P. Mahadevan, Hasan Askari, and Wilfrid Cantwell Smith; the recommendations of the seminar; a list of participants; and a copy of the program.

Werblowsky, R. J. Zwi. "Marburg, and After" *Numen* 7–8 (1960–1961): 215–220. A report on the Marburg Congress and reasons for resisting the suggestion to hold the Congress in India.

Abrahim H. Khan (2005)

STUDY OF RELIGION: THE ACADEMIC STUDY OF RELIGION IN SUB-SAHARAN AFRICA

The academic study of religion has emerged as a vibrant discipline in some parts of sub-Saharan Africa. Although the discipline was heavily influenced by developments in western Europe and North America, it had gained a distinctive identity by the 1980s. The region made significant contributions to the overall character of religious studies, particularly in the area of method and theory in the study of indigenous religions. Scholars in sub-Saharan Africa interacted with the dominant questions that have shaped the field. Operating in a context characterized by a plurality of religions, they offered valuable reflections on the character of religion. Some scholars from outside the African context also settled in the region and used the richness of the material on religion to explicate the significance of the complex phenomenon. Notable local and regional traditions of the study of religion were established in sub-Saharan Africa by the late 1990s. Although significant differences could be identified in the execution of the task in this vast region, the emphasis on the importance of religion to Africans was a salient point uniting scholarly reflections. Most scholars in the academic study of religion devoted their resources to an analysis of the three dominant religious traditions. Studies on African traditions, Christianity, and Islam constituted the bulk of the material on religious studies in sub-Saharan Africa. Abstract methodological reflections were limited, perhaps reflecting the abundance of the data on religion.

Many scholars in the study of religion argued that religion was a critical variable in efforts to understand the lives of most Africans. The academic study of religion was predicated on the assumption that religion was central to most endeavors to establish the meaning of existence in an African context. In this pursuit, multiple methodological strategies were employed. Sociological, psychological, anthropological, and phenomenological approaches were used to locate the significance of religion to Africans. African scholars provided impressive descriptions of the major religions, alongside other migrant religions like Hinduism, Buddhism, and others. In their edited volume *The Historical Study of African Religion, with Special Reference to East and Central Africa* (1972), Terence O. Ranger and Isaria N. Kimambo bemoaned the lack of historical sensitivity in the study of indigenous religions. However, this criticism was taken seriously and African scholars produced many impressive monographs on the history of the various religions of Africa by the late 1970s. Although this review concentrates on the efforts of scholars based in departments of religious studies, it is important to acknowledge that creative writers, political scientists, and scholars based in other departments made valuable contributions to the study of religion in Africa.

The Emergence of Religious Studies in Sub-Saharan Africa. While the academic study of religion became an established academic discipline in many African universities by the latter half of the twentieth century, various categories of writers had provided useful information on the religions of Africa much earlier. Travelers, missionaries, amateur ethnologists, and other nonspecialists had written reports on various aspects of religion in Africa in the nineteenth century. Although indigenous religions suffered at the hands of casual observers, the earlier writers preserved valuable information. Missionaries like Henri A. Junod (1863–1934), who operated in Mozambique from 1907 onward, provided sound descriptions of local religious beliefs and practices. Earlier, John William Colenso (1814–1883), who was ordained as the bishop of Natal in 1853, had identified Zulu names for god in the context of a general theory of comparative religion. By the time the discipline found its way to African shores, the reality of religious pluralism had anticipated it.

The academic study of religion in sub-Saharan Africa is inextricably intertwined with the political history of the region. The experience of colonialism, from around 1880 to 1960, shaped traditions of the study of religion for most African nations. Former British colonies tended to have lively departments of religious studies because religious education was popular in secondary schools, whereas in Francophone countries such traditions were suppressed. Similarly, religious studies departments did not emerge in former Portuguese colonies like Angola and Mozambique. Zambia provided a unique case of a former British colony that did not develop a department of religious studies, although the faculty of education at the University of Zambia at Lusaka offered courses on aspects of the discipline.

Historical experiences like the struggles for political independence and assertions of nationhood in the postcolonial period are indelibly printed on the study of religion in the region. After the realization of the importance of education for Africans by both missionaries and the colonial state, colleges and universities were gradually established. Most of the universities were instituted after World War II, although Fourah Bay College in Freetown, Sierra Leone, was founded by the Church Missionary Society in 1827. In Kampala, Uganda, Makerere University, later to be influential in the study of indigenous religions, started off as a technical college in 1922. Although initially university colleges in African countries were affiliated to universities in metropolitan centers, the decolonization process in the 1960s led to the emergence of national universities in independent countries. Such universities promoted the study of religion for ideological purposes.

It is worthwhile to observe that some departments of religious studies were established in West Africa before any such departments existed in Britain. Scholars from outside Africa were influential in the setting up of nonconfessional departments of religious studies. Geoffrey Parrinder was instrumental in the creation of the religious studies department at the University College of Ibadan in Nigeria in the late 1940s. Noel King was actively involved in the emergence of the department for the study of religions at the University of Ghana, Legon. Harold Turner and Andrew Walls taught at the University of Nigeria, Nsukka, before the civil war in 1967. They went on to have impressive academic careers in Europe, using their knowledge of the religious situation in Africa.

The dominance of missionaries in the field of education contributed to the greater attention that Christianity enjoyed in the study of religion in sub-Saharan Africa. Many departments concentrated on church history and theology, reflecting their earlier identity as departments of theology. Most scholars were themselves adherents of Christianity or Islam, engendering the committed approach. However, most African countries renamed departments of theology or divinity as departments of religious studies to reflect the pluralist environment that had been established in most countries. They also placed special emphasis on the study of indigenous religions in an effort to develop a distinctive African identity.

Contributions. The achievements of African scholars in the study of religion may be located in many areas. However, the most notable areas include theoretical reflections on the meaning of religion, critique of the centrality of scripture, and suggesting new approaches to the study of religion. African scholars also put the study of indigenous religions firmly on the agenda of religious studies. African scholars refined the debate on insiders and outsiders in the study of religion by insisting that they were better placed to understand traditional religions, as opposed to European scholars. In the 1960s and 1970s, African scholars like John S. Mbiti, E. B. Idowu, Kwesi Dickson, and others published significant works on various aspects of indigenous religions. Other West and East African scholars maintained that African scholars were strategically located to provide objective descriptions of the religions of their own people.

African scholars questioned the definition of religion as the opposition between the sacred and the profane. In his *African Religions and Philosophy* (1969), Mbiti remarks that such a distinction did not apply to traditional African contexts, where religion permeated all spheres of life. This initiated debate over whether the Western definition of religion satisfied the criterion of cross-cultural applicability.

Religious studies in the West have tended to emphasize scripture in the world's religions. Frederick Maximilian Muller (1823–1900) initiated the interest in scripture with *The Sacred Books of the East* (1879–1910). African scholars drew attention to the absence of sacred writings in indigenous religions, noting that these religions remained vibrant nonetheless. Thus, the presence of scripture did not accord a religion any special status, African scholars maintained. This led to some relativization of the significance of scripture in the discipline.

African scholars also highlighted the importance of oral traditions to the study of religion. While textual analysis had featured prominently in religious studies in the West, no such texts existed in most parts of Africa. The historical study of indigenous religions had to grapple with the issue of oral sources. Fieldwork became a critical aspect of religious studies in Africa. Other researchers into African Independent Churches, such as Marthinus Daneel and Gerardus Oosthuizen, also used this approach. Some African scholars who participated in indigenous religious practices, such as the traditional healer and anthropologist Gordon Chavunduka of Zimbabwe and Wande Abimbola, an Ifa priest and Nigerian scholar, also drew attention to the body of knowledge that was found in indigenous religions. They called for alternative approaches that were not dependent on Western models of scientific rationality.

In their descriptions of the various religions of Africa, scholars in Africa have also sought to discern the meaning of religion. In his *Religion and Ultimate Well-Being: An Explanatory Theory* (1984), the South African scholar Martin Prozesky concludes that the search for ultimate well-being was the driving force behind religion. Laurenti Magesa (1997) also argues that indigenous religions were inspired by the search for abundant life. Detailed descriptions of the religions of Africa and methodological reflections were part of the African contribution.

Major Challenges. The religious commitment of most African scholars resulted in theological works that sought to promote Christianity or Islam. African phenomenological scholars like Jacob Olupona and Friday Mbon of Nigeria and J. S. Kruger of South Africa protested against the encroachment of theology in the 1980s. Earlier, Okot p'Bitek had criticized the application of Christian concepts in *African Religions in Western Scholarship* (1971). The hegemony of Christian and, to a lesser extent, Islamic theology remained intact. Subservience to Western methodologies and research interests by some African scholars also stifled creativity.

The shortage of books and journals threatened the viability of religious studies in the region. Many departments operated with ill-equipped libraries. Significant journals like the *Journal of Religion in Africa* were inaccessible to most students and lecturers. Most established scholars relocated to Western countries such as Canada, the United Kingdom, and the United States in search of better career opportunities. Poor remuneration and oppressive regimes contributed to such developments. The worst affected countries included Nigeria, Kenya, Zimbabwe, and others—countries that had developed impressive traditions in the academic study of religion. However, institutions in some countries, such as South Africa, Botswana, and Namibia, managed to retain their staff. In most parts of the continent, departments of religious studies have struggled to justify their relevance amid incessant calls by governments to reduce costs. Between 2003 and 2004, South African departments of religious studies were forced to merge.

Gender imbalances have also been noticeable in the discipline in the region. Few female scholars have participated, with Christian theologians dominating. Mercy Amba Oduyoye of Ghana, Isabel Phiri of Malawi and South Africa, and Musa Dube of Botswana analyzed the religious experiences of African women in the late 1990s. The shortage of scholarships in religious studies, as opposed to theology, resulted in the low numbers of African female scholars of religion.

Institutionalization of the Academic Study of Religion in Sub-Saharan Africa. The study of religion took place at various levels of educational achievement during different historical periods. Arabic schools, bible colleges, and primary and secondary schools offered subjects that provided some knowledge about the religious context. Teacher training institutions introduced students to the various religions of the world by emphasizing the divergent approach, which does not seek to convert students to a specific religion. In some countries, such as Zimbabwe, the diploma in religious studies has offered graduates a number of career opportunities in the civil service and the private sector. The effects of HIV/AIDS in sub-Saharan Africa in the 1990s and beyond has led some nongovernmental organizations to recruit graduates trained in the study of religion.

Aspects of the academic study of religion were also found in some church-sponsored universities and theological colleges in the 1980s. Although Christianity received preferential treatment, comparative religion was an integral part of the curriculum. In southern Africa some theological colleges sought to establish associate status with national universities in an effort to maintain high academic standards. Courses on the history of religions exposed students to religious pluralism. Although the popularity of the discipline varied among the different countries, it continued to attract significant numbers of students.

Scholarly Organizations and Publications. The high number of lecturers in the discipline facilitated the emergence of scholarly organizations. These included the Nigerian Association for the Study of Religions, founded in 1976; the Association for the Study of Religions in Southern Africa, initiated in 1979; and the African Association for the Study of Religions (AASR), formed in 1992. The AASR has regional chapters and publishes a newsletter that keeps African scholars abreast of developments in the field. It has also sponsored a few monographs and books that are widely distributed in Africa. Other theologically oriented organizations like the Association of Theological Institutions in Southern Africa and the Ecumenical Association of Third World Theologians have contributed to the publication of some valuable monographs on Christianity and indigenous religions. These regional groupings have facilitated interaction across national boundaries and rescued the study of religion from narrow nationalistic agendas.

Despite the shortage of books, some impressive initiatives have been witnessed on the publication front. Following the demise of apartheid in South Africa, a number of texts that sought to describe religious pluralism in the country were published, such as Martin Prozesky and John W. de Gruchy's edited volume *Living Faiths in South Africa* (1995). Launched in the 1990s in Malawi, the Kachere book series sought to capture the religious scene in the country, covering aspects of Christianity, indigenous religions, and other themes. In Kenya, Acton Publishers, an initiative by the scholar Jesse N. K. Mugambi, was launched in 1992. Mambo Press of Zimbabwe publishes books on religion in the region. Scholars like James Amanze of the University of Botswana, Peter Kasenene in Swaziland and Uganda, and Patrick Maxwell in South Africa produce material within the discipline of religious studies. Monographs and articles on Islam, indigenous religions and churches, new religious movements, and other aspects of religion in Africa are also being produced.

Among African countries in the 1990s, South Africa had the highest number of journals that appeared consistently. These include the *Journal for the Study of Religion, Missionalia, Religion and Theology, Scriptura,* and others. Although some of the journals have a theological slant, they publish useful articles on the academic study of religion. In Nigeria, the journal *Orita* has defied the odds and continues to publish articles on the three dominant religions.

Contextualization. Although some scholars, such as Donald Wiebe in *The Politics of Studying Religion* (1998), have insisted on a rigid separation between the discipline and communities of faith in the region, close cooperation has existed since the 1960s. Organized religious groups have used scholarly services, with scholars responding to the felt needs of the communities among whom they operated. They have also published on those issues that were relevant to their contexts. Religious violence in Nigeria precipitated research into the role of religion in curbing extremism. The reality of HIV/AIDS in the region in the 1990s prompted research into the appropriation of religion in the struggle against the pandemic. In their pursuit of contextual relevance, most African scholars have remained in dialogue with scholars from other parts of the world through publications, conference attendance, and other modern communication facilities.

Despite major challenges, the academic study of religion in most parts of sub-Saharan Africa continue to be encouraging. In their investigations into the religions of Africa and methodological reflections, African scholars provide alternative interpretations regarding the nature and purpose of religious studies. Although they can be abrasive in the study of indigenous religions and militant in protesting against their peripheral position in global religious studies, they are contributing to the shape of the field. Their commitment to producing works of high quality in contexts characterized by resource deficiencies provides indications that a new era of promise is dawning on the academic study of religion. Often marginalized and portrayed as uncritical consumers of methodological tenets developed elsewhere, scholars in sub-Saharan Africa are taking up the challenge of interpreting the significance of religion as full members of the guild.

BIBLIOGRAPHY

Amanze, James. *African Traditional Religion in Malawi: The Case of the Bimbi Cult.* Blantyre, 2002. Describes the vibrancy of a specific African indigenous religion.

Chidester, David. *Savage Systems: Colonialism and Comparative Religion in Southern Africa.* Charlottesville, Va., 1996. This study highlights the power imbalances between indigenous African people and Europeans, as well as the contestation regarding the concept of "religion."

Hackett, Rosalind I. J. "The Academic Study of Religion in Nigeria." *Religion* 18 (1988): 37–46. Describes the development of religious studies in Nigeria.

Kasenene, Peter. *Religion in Swaziland.* Braamfontein, 1990. A description of the religious situation in Swaziland.

Magesa, Laurenti. *African Religion: The Moral Traditions of Abundant Life.* New York, 1997. An analysis of the centrality of morality to the indigenous religions of Africa and how they seek to promote well-being.

Mbiti, John S. *African Religions and Philosophy.* London, 1969. A useful text that highlights efforts to bring some sense of unity to the disparate indigenous religions of Africa.

Muller, Frederick Maximilian. *The Sacred Books of the East.* Oxford, 1879–1910. Provides insights into the centrality of scripture in the academic study of religion in the West.

p'Bitek, Okot. *African Religions in Western Scholarship.* Kampala,1971. This work captures the insistence by African scholars that they are best placed to study the indigenous religions of Africa.

Platoon, Jan, James Cox, and Jacob Olupona, eds. *The Study of Religions in Africa: Past, Present, and Prospects.* Cambridge, U.K., 1996. A comprehensive analysis of the study of the various religions of Africa, including reflections on methodology.

Prozesky, Martin. *Religion and Ultimate Well-Being: An Explanatory Theory.* London, 1984. An effort to locate the central theme that runs across religious traditions of the world.

Prozesky, Martin, and John W. de Gruchy, eds. *Living Faiths in South Africa.* New York, 1995. A description of the religions of South Africa in their plurality.

Pye, Michael, ed. *Marburg Revisited: Institutions and Strategies in the Study of Religion.* Marburg, Germany, 1989. See contributions by Peter McKenzie, "The History of Religions in Africa," pp. 99–105, and Jan Platvoet, "The Institutional Environment of the Study of Religion in Africa South of the Sahara," pp. 107–126.

Ranger, Terence O., and Isaria N. Kimambo. *The Historical Study of African Religion, with Special Reference to East and Central Africa.* London, 1972. Highlights the value of historical research to the study of African indigenous religions.

Ter Haar, Gerrie. *Faith of Our Fathers: Studies in Religious Education in Sub-Saharan Africa.* Utrecht, 1990. Outlines developments within the study of religions in sub-Saharan Africa.

Uka, E. M. *Readings in African Traditional Religion: Structure, Meaning, Relevance, Future.* Bern, 1991. Provides useful discussions of some of the key methodological issues in the study of African indigenous religions.

Wiebe, Donald. *The Politics of Religious Studies: The Continuing Conflict with Theology in the Academy.* New York, 1998. Captures the argument that theology should not be allowed to infect religious studies.

EZRA CHITANDO (2005)

STUPA WORSHIP. The Sanskrit term *stūpa* first occurs in the Vedas, where it conveys the meaning "knot of hair, top," or "summit." It is unclear how the term came to be used by Buddhists to refer to the mounds erected over the relics of Śākyamuni Buddha, but this usage can be traced back to early Buddhism, as can the practice of worship at stupas. The Jains too built stupas, but these postdate the earliest Buddhist structures. The terms *thūpa* (*thūba*) and *dhātugabbha* (Skt., *dhātugarbha*) are attested in Pali sources. This latter term derives from references to the Buddha's relics as a *dhātu* ("element") and to the dome or "egg" (*aṇḍa*) of the stupa as a *garbha* ("womb" or "treasury").

According to the *Mahāparinibbāna Suttanta,* after Śākyamuni Buddha achieved final *nirvāṇa* his body was cremated and stupas were erected to receive his remains. Śākyamuni's cremation and the installation of his relics in stupas are probably historical facts. The early Buddhists erected stupas because they believed that Śākyamuni had freed himself from the cycles of birth and death. Had Śākyamuni died and remained within those cycles it would have been pointless to build a stupa for him, for not only would the place of his rebirth be unknown, but one could not have expected him to act on the requests of his believers. According to the *Mahāparinibbāna Suttanta,* stupas could be built to receive the remains of the following four types of people (known as *thūparahā,* "worthy of stupas"), all of whom had transcended the cycles of birth and death (*saṃsāra*): *tathāgata*s (buddhas), *paccekabuddha*s (self-enlightened buddhas), *tathāgatassa sāvakā*s ("hearers of the Buddha"), and *rājā cakkavatti*s ("universal rulers").

Such sages could be enshrined in stupas because they had entered *nirvāṇa.* In the Āgamas, such people were said to have realized *diṭṭadhamma-nibbāna* ("*nirvāṇa* in this world") or *saūpadisesa-nibbāna* ("*nirvāṇa* with remainder"). *Nirvāṇa* was also called the "*dharma* realm" (*dhammadhātu*). Such terms suggest that *nirvāṇa* was not always viewed as extinction but often as an actual state or realm a person enters upon realizing enlightenment.

When the Buddha died, he was said to have entered *parinibbāna* ("complete *nirvāṇa*") or *anupādisesanibbāna-dhātu* ("*nirvāṇa* without remainder"). Thus, even after the Buddha died he was not viewed as having completely ceased to exist; rather, he was thought to exist in the realm of *nirvāṇa.* Consequently, believers could worship and offer their prayers to him through the medium of the stupa. It was at this time that the belief that the Buddha could respond to the petitions of his worshipers probably developed. If "*nirvāṇa* without remainder" had been considered a completely quiescent state, then such responses by the Buddha would have been impossible. Thus, the people who worshiped at Buddhist stupas seem to have believed that the Buddha continued to be active. This belief later led to Mahāyāna doctrines about the *dharmakāya*'s activity in the world.

During the early period of Buddhism offerings to the Buddha's relics (*śarīra-pūjā*) were made by laypeople. According to the *Mahāparinibbāna Suttanta,* the Buddha was asked by Ānanda what type of ceremony should be held for the Buddha's remains. The Buddha replied, "You should strive for the true goal [*sadattha*] of emancipation [*vimokṣa*]." The Buddha thus prohibited monks from having any connection with his funeral ceremonies and instead called upon wise and pious lay believers to conduct the ceremonies. According to this same text, it was the Mallas of Kusinārā who conducted the cremation. The Buddha's remains were then divided among eight tribes in central India and stupas were built.

Closely related to the stupa in functional terms is the *caitya* (Pali, *cetiya*). *Caitya*s are similar to stupas, although originally the two were distinct entities. In Buddhism, the term *caitya* referred originally to a place that was sacred. In the *Mahāparinibbāna Suttanta caitya*s are described as places that men and women of good families "should see so that feelings of reverence and awe will arise." Four of these are mentioned in the text: the Buddha's birthplace at Lumbinī, his place of enlightenment at Bodh Gayā, the site of his first sermon at the Deer Park (in Banaras), and the place where he entered "*nirvāṇa* without remainder" (Kuśinagara). Because the pilgrims who visited these sites were called *caitya-cārika,* the sites must have been known as *caitya*s. Sacred objects of worship that helped people remember the Buddha were both present at and themselves identified as *caityas*. For example, in Bodh Gayā pious pilgrims could worship at the bodhi tree or the Adamantine Seat (*vajrāsana*) on which the Buddha sat when he realized enlightenment. Because the stupa was an object of worship, it too could be called *caitya.* The difference between stupas and *caityas* is explained in the *Mohesengqi lü* (*Mahāsāṃghika Vinaya*): "If the Buddha's relics are enshrined, the site is called a *stūpa;* if the Buddha's relics are not enshrined, it is called a *caitya*" (T.D. 22.496b). This explanation suggests that by the time the Vinaya of the Mahāsāṃghikas was compiled, *caityas* and stupas had the same exterior shape. As time passed, the Buddha's relics became increasingly difficult to obtain and other objects were enshrined when stupas were constructed. Thus, the distinction between stupas and *caityas* gradually vanished.

After the Buddha's death, stupa worship became increasingly popular. With King Aśoka's (r. 268–232 BCE) conversion to Buddhism, stupa worship spread throughout India. Aśoka ordered that the eight stupas erected after the Buddha's death be opened and that the relics within them be removed, divided, and enshrined in the many new stupas that he had commissioned to be built throughout India. These events are described in the *Ayuwang zhuan* (*Aśokarājāvadāna;* T.D. 50.102b) and in the *Ayuwang jing* (*Aśokarājā Sūtra*?; T.D. 50.135a–b). In the records of his travels in India, the Chinese Buddhist pilgrim Xuanzang mentions the stupas constructed by Aśoka, many of which have been identified in modern times by archaeologists.

THE FORMATION OF BUDDHIST ORDERS AROUND STUPAS. Little is known about the history of stupa worship during the 250 years between Aśoka's reign and the rise of Mahāyāna Buddhism at approximately the beginning of the common era. However, archaeological evidence from this period indicates that stupas were built in many areas in India and that stupa worship was a growing practice. Clearly, religious orders must have formed around some of these stupas and doctrinal developments reflecting the increasing importance of stupa worship undoubtedly occurred. Although most of the stupas are in ruins today and little is known of these doctrines, the new teachings associated with stupa worship contributed much to the rise of Mahāyāna Buddhism.

Buddhism has long been formulaically defined in terms of the so-called Three Jewels: the Buddha, the Dharma, and the Order (*saṃgha*). Apart from the Mahīśāsaka and Dharmaguptaka schools, which held that the Buddha was a part of the jewel of the *saṃgha,* most schools argued that the Three Jewels were distinct elements, with stupas belonging to the jewel of the *saṃgha.* In fact, stupas and sects (i.e., the monastic order) do seem to have developed separately. Economic considerations played a role in this doctrinal debate. Given that the Three Jewels were separate, alms donated to the jewel of the Buddha could only be used for the jewel of the Buddha (i.e., stupas), not for the jewel of the Order (i.e., Buddhist sects). Thus, monks were not allowed to use items that had been offered at stupas, that is, to (the jewel of) the Buddha.

Originally, stupas were institutions independent of the Hīnayāna schools. Archaeological evidence reveals that the stupas were constructed and administered by lay believers and were not affiliated with any particular school or sect. However, as stupas worship continued to flourish, stupas came to be constructed within monastic compounds and monks began to worship at them. Yet even after stupas came to be affiliated with sects in this way, alms given to the stupa still had to be used for the stupa alone and could not be used freely by the monks. Monks who had received the full Vinaya precepts *(upasampadā)* were not allowed to live within the confines of stupas or to take custody of their assets. Thus, although a stupa might be affiliated with a particular sect, a clear distinction was maintained between the property and site of the stupa and those of the order of monks. However, as stupa worship became more popular and more alms were offered at stupas, the schools suffered adverse economic effects. To counter this, the schools argued that little karmic merit would result from such offerings; some even openly opposed stupa worship.

Once a stupa accumulated alms, believers began to live around it and use the food and clothing that had been offered at it. These believers, who were considered religious specialists in their own right, probably assisted pilgrims who came to the stupa by finding lodgings for them, giving instructions about worship, and explaining the carvings of the Buddha's life and of the *jātakas* ("birth tales") inscribed there. They probably preached about the greatness of Śākyamuni's personality, compassion, and power to help save sentient beings and formulated doctrines concerning these subjects that were independent of sectarian (*nikāya*) opinion. Of course, these doctrines differed from those that had been originally preached by Śākyamuni.

The religious specialists who lived around the stupas resembled monks and nuns in many ways. They served as leaders of orders, teaching lay believers and receiving alms from them. However, although these religious specialists led lives similar to those who had abandoned the life of a householder, they still were not monks (*bhikṣus*). Because they had not taken the full set of precepts *(upasampadā)*, they did not belong to the jewel of the *saṃgha* and thus were permitted to live at the stupas.

Because they felt that certain religious experiences were necessary if they were to teach others, these religious specialists not only taught lay believers but also engaged in strict religious practices. Consequently, they imitated the practices performed by Śākyamuni Buddha and strove to attain an enlightenment identical to that which Śākyamuni had experienced. Because Śākyamuni had been called a *bodhisattva* before he had realized enlightenment, they too called themselves *bodhisattvas*. The term *bodhisattva,* which had originally been used to refer to the period of practice prefatory to becoming a Buddha, was now used to refer to *all* religious practitioners who, unlike Hīnayāna devotees, aspired to realize the supreme enlightenment of the Buddha rather than arhatship.

The orders of religious practitioners that sprang up around the stupas were thus vitally interested in two major doctrinal themes: the Buddha's ability to save sentient beings and the types of practices that would enable people to realize Buddhahood. The religious activities of these *bodhisattvas* eventually led to the development of Mahāyāna Buddhism. Indeed, it is difficult to conceive of these doctrines developing among Hīnayāna monks. Because Hīnayāna monks respected Śākyamuni Buddha as a great teacher and believed that he taught the path of the arhat for their enlightenment, they probably would not have used a term such as *bodhisattva* to refer to themselves because it would have placed them on a level equal to that of Śākyamuni. In following the practices of the arhat, they had little reason to be concerned with new doctrines about the ways in which the Buddha could save sentient beings. However, lay believers, who were unable to follow the austere regimen of the monks, would have been vitally interested in teachings about how the Buddha could save them. The new doctrines that developed in the orders around the stupas did not stress the importance of observing the full set of precepts and performing all the practices required of a monk; rather, in these doctrines, a form of Buddhism for lay believers, one that emphasized faith (*śraddhā*) in the Buddha, was described.

MAHĀYĀNA BUDDHISM AND STUPAS. At least some varieties of Mahāyāna Buddhism arose from the orders around stupas. Stupa worship continued to develop even after Mahāyāna Buddhism had begun to take form. Although the orders associated with stupas are not clearly described in Mahāyāna literature, the existence of such groups can be clearly inferred from these texts. Only a few do not mention stupa worship. The "Chapter on Pure Practices" of the *Buddhāvataṃsaka Sūtra* contains a detailed description of *bodhisattva* practices, many of which focus on stupa worship (T.D. 9.430ff.). According to the *Ugradatta-paripṛcchā* and the *Daśabhūmikavibhāṣā, bodhisattvas* could practice either at stupas or in the forest (Hirakawa, 1963, pp. 94–98). They were to meditate and perform austerities in the forest, but if they became ill, they were to return to a stupa in a village to be cured. Thus, *bodhisattvas* went to stupas for many reasons besides worship, including recovering from illness, nursing the sick, making offerings to teachers and saints (*āryapudgala*), hearing discourses on doctrine, reading scriptures, and preaching to others.

Stupas were more than objects of worship. They also served as centers for Mahāyāna practitioners, with quarters for devotees located nearby. These early Mahayanists abandoned their lives as lay believers, wore monastic robes, begged food, read sūtras, and studied doctrine under the guidance of preceptors. They also meditated, worshiped, and prostrated themselves at the Buddha's stupas. An important part of stupa worship was the circumambulation of the stupa (usually three times) while chanting verses in praise of the Buddha.

Two types of *bodhisattvas* are mentioned in early Mahāyāna texts: monastic (i.e., renunciant) *bodhisattvas*, who lived and practiced at the stupas, and lay (i. e., householder) *bodhisattvas*, who made pilgrimages to the stupas in order to worship at them. Lay *bodhisattvas* placed their faith in the Three Refuges (or Three Jewels), observed the Five Precepts (*pañca śīlāni*) or the Eight Precepts (*aṭṭhaṅgikaṃ uposathaṃ*), and performed religious practices. In many ways, their practices resembled those of Hīnayāna lay believers. However, the two groups had very different objectives in their practice. While Hīnayāna lay believers (m., *upāsaka;* f., *upāsikā*) sought a better rebirth, Mahāyāna lay *bodhisattvas* strove to attain buddhahood and based their practices on the Mahāyāna position that helping others results in benefits for oneself.

Bodhisattvas often observed a set of Mahāyāna precepts called the Path of the Ten Good Acts (*daśakuśala-karma-pathā*). However, according to some later Mahāyāna texts, monastic *bodhisattvas* were to receive full monastic ordination (*upasampadā*). Thus, at a later date monastic *bodhisattvas* began to use the complete set of precepts from the Vinaya for their ordinations. In such cases, they probably did not use monks from the Hīnayāna sects as their preceptors (*upādhyāya*), because qualified preceptors could be found in the Mahāyāna orders.

According to the *Saddharmapuṇḍarīka Sūtra,* worshiping and making offerings at stupas were practices that led to buddhahood. In the *Upāyakauśalya-parivarta* (Chapter on expedient means), a variety of practices leading to buddhahood are discussed. These include not only the practice of the six perfections (*pāramitās*) but also the building of stupas, the carving of images, and acts of worship and offering made at stupas (T.D. 9.8c–9a). Because the realization of buddhahood was the primary goal of Mahāyāna practice, stupa worship clearly had a close relationship to Mahāyāna beliefs.

The stupa also provided a model for many elements in Amitābha's Pure Land (Sukhāvatī). The Pure Land was said to have seven rows of railings (*vedikā*); railings were an important architectural component of the stupa. Other elements of stupas were also found in descriptions of the Pure Land, including rows of *tāla* trees (*tāla-paṅkti*), lotus ponds (*puṣkariṇī*), halls (*vimāna*), and towers (*kūṭāgāra*). Thus, the portrayal of the Pure Land was apparently based on an idealized view of a large stupa. Moreover, according to the early versions of the *Emituo jing* (the smaller *Sukhāvatīvyūha Sūtra*), the *bodhisattva* Dharmākara vowed that anyone who worshiped or made offerings at stupas would be reborn in his Pure Land (T.D. 12.301b). This vow was eliminated in later versions of the sūtra, suggesting that, as time passed, Amitābha worship developed independently of stupa worship.

The evidence from these sūtras suggests that the relationship between Mahāyāna Buddhism and stupa worship was very close. Even the Perfection of Wisdom literature, which emphasized the memorization and copying of sūtras, did not deny that merit was produced by offerings at stupas. Rather, it maintained that stupa worship produced less merit than copying the scriptures. Thus the origins of the Perfection of Wisdom tradition as well are related to stupa worship.

SEE ALSO Buddhism, Schools of, article on Mahāyāna Philosophical Schools of Buddhism; Nirvāṇa; Relics; Temple, articles on Buddhist Temple Compounds.

BIBLIOGRAPHY

For a detailed study of the role of the stupa in the formation of Mahāyāna Buddhism, see my article "The Rise of Mahāyāna Buddhism and Its Relationship to the Worship of Stūpas," *Memoirs of the Research Department of the Tōyō Bunko* 22 (1963): 57–106. André Bareau's "La construction et le culte des stupa d'après les *Vinayapiṭaka*," *Bulletin de l'École Française d'Extreme Orient* 50 (1962): 229–274, provides a wealth of detail on Buddhist cultic life at the stupas, as does Prabodh Chandra Bagchi's "The Eight Great Caityas and Their Cult," *Indian Historical Quarterly* 17 (1941): 223–235. For the *Mahāparinibbāna Suttanta*, see the translation by T. W. Rhys-Davids in volume 3 of *Dialogues of the Buddha*, in "Sacred Books of the Buddhists," vol. 4 (1921; reprint, London, 1973), pp. 71–191.

HIRAKAWA AKIRA (1987)
Translated from Japanese by Paul Groner

SUÁREZ, FRANCISCO (1548–1617), was a Spanish Jesuit philosopher, theologian, and jurist. Francisco de Suárez was born on January 5, 1548, at Granada, where his father was a wealthy barrister. Destined by his family to an ecclesiastical career, he prepared for it by studying canon law at the University of Salamanca. In 1564 he joined the Society of Jesus. From 1566 to 1570 he was a student of theology at the same university at a time when it was undergoing a lively Thomist revival.

In 1571, the year before he was ordained priest, Suárez was assigned to teach philosophy at Segovia, and over the next decade he taught both philosophy and theology at various Jesuit colleges in Castile, including Valladolid, where he delivered a set of celebrated lectures on the first part of Thomas Aquinas's *Summa theologiae*. Called to Rome in 1580, he continued the series at the Roman College, where his subject was the second part and where, it is said, Pope Gregory XIII was occasionally in attendance. Uncertain health brought Suárez back to Spain in 1585, to Alcalá, and here his lectures on the *Summa*, specifically on the third part, were concluded. He transferred to Salamanca in 1592, and in 1597, at the instance of Philip II of Spain (now also king of Portugal), he went to Coimbra, where he taught until 1616. He died a year later in Lisbon.

Suárez's first published work, *De deo incarnato*, which grew out of his lectures on the third part of the *Summa*, appeared in 1590, and his last, *De defensione fidei*, a tract directed against the views on the divine right of kings held by James I of England, in 1613. In between he published eleven other works, of which the most popular and influential, *Disputationes metaphysicae* (1597), went through eighteen editions in the course of the seventeenth century. Ten more works were published posthumously before 1655, under the direction of the Portuguese Jesuits. The passage of time did not lessen interest in Suárez's writings; editions of his *Omnia opera* were published in Venice in 1747 and in Paris in 1856.

Suárez's thought was expressed always within a scholastic context, and he professed to be a Thomist. Certainly the work of Thomas Aquinas was basic to his own, but he often deviated from classical Thomism, a fact stressed particularly during the Thomist revival of the early twentieth century. Suárez, for example, did not admit the real distinction between essence and existence, and his metaphysics was more a self-contained whole than a mere elaboration of Aristotle. He viewed philosophy in any case as a basis for theological research.

In the quarrel between the Jesuits and the Dominicans over the problem of the relationship between grace and free will he took no formal part, though during the crisis of the first decade of the seventeenth century he was active behind the scenes promoting the more liberal Jesuit position. Similarly, he did much to establish the moral school of probabilism, which was later associated with Jesuit confessional practice. As a jurist Suárez did much to elaborate the notion of penal law and the juridical force of custom. He was a powerful advocate of the principle of subsidiarity in civil society, and he insisted that the powers of the state were rooted in the free consent of the governed. His doctrine of *ius gentium*, based upon the precept of universal love that transcends national or racial divisions, contributed to the development of international law.

Suárez was probably the greatest of all the Jesuit theologians, and as such he has had continuing importance within the intellectual life of the Catholic church. But he was influential far beyond his own order or his own communion. Spinoza, Leibniz, Berkeley, and Vico have all acknowledged their debt to Suárez. The title given him by Pope Paul V—Doctor Eximius ("distinguished scholar")—seems even now appropriate.

BIBLIOGRAPHY

For a good synopsis of Suárez's teaching, see René Brouillard's article "Suarez, François," in *Dictionnaire de théologie catholique* (Paris, 1941). A longer study, with biographical details, is Raoul de Scorraille's *François Suarez de la compagnie de Jésus*, 2 vols. (Paris, 1912–1913). Two useful special studies are *Francisco Suárez: Addresses in Commemoration of His Contribution to International Law and Politics*, edited by Herbert Wright (Washington, D.C., 1933), and José Hellín's *La analogía del ser y el conocimento de Dios en Suárez* (Madrid, 1947).

MARVIN R. O'CONNELL (1987)

SUBALTERN STUDIES. What does it mean when a peasant resistance movement and a religious movement are one and the same phenomenon? In the last three decades, three different themes have surfaced in the interface between the study of religion and Subaltern Studies: (1) the idea of religion as a function of the Marxist/Gramscian view of early Subaltern Studies; (2) the changing debates about religion as the Subaltern Studies project became more involved with cultural studies, postmodernism, and the postcolonial project; and (3) the approach to Subaltern Studies within the study of religion.

THE IDEA OF RELIGION AS A FUNCTION OF THE MARXIST/GRAMSCIAN VIEW OF EARLY SUBALTERN STUDIES. Subaltern Studies began in India with an explicitly but not exclusively Marxist and Gramscian focus. It analyzes and advocates for the "bottom layer of society" by challenging capitalist logic (Spivak, 2000, p. 324); thus it has both a negative task of undoing capitalist assessment of the underclass as well as a positive task of describing acts of agency and independence and resistance. Inspired in part by the work of E. P. Thompson, and carried on by the work of scholar and editor Ranajit Guha, the publication of the nine-volume series *Subaltern Studies* comprises a great bulk of the theoretical and topical work. Subaltern Studies began in the late 1970s and early 1980s with Indian, European, and American scholars who turned toward understanding peasant consciousness in India, in so far as any and all consciousness was a product of material conditions. Consciousness, here, is broadly viewed by Subaltern writers in the traditional Marxian sense as a manner of thought determined by one's place in the production system; yet at the same time, these writers also view consciousness as a form of subjectivity which can and does develop modes of resistance to that system. Since then, the concerns of Subaltern Studies have blossomed into a global phenomenon with strong institutional support from mainstream academia in Africa, South America, Ireland, and China, as well as India, Europe, and America. Moreover, Subaltern Studies' focus is no longer exclusively South Asian, but spans communities around the globe, and scholars in the field produce articles written in a large variety of vernacular languages besides English.

Subaltern Studies has been confronted from the very beginning with the problem of how to account for the ongoing role of religion, and the related issues of caste and kinship, in a nonessentializing way. Its source of intellectual inspiration, Antonio Gramsci, as well as others, were careful to point out that, in the absence of a socialist party to support the peasant class, religion was not simply self-deception or false consciousness. Rather, religion could be viewed as "a specific way of rationalizing the world and real life," and "a framework of real political activity" (Gramsci, 1971, pp. 326–327, 337). E. P Thompson, who addressed the Subaltern Studies conference in its formative stages, also reminded Subaltern Studies thinkers that one should not be surprised at the persistent role of loyalties of religion as well as of caste and kinship in shaping working–class consciousness (Thompson, 1991, p. 92). Indeed, as Rajnarayan Chadavarkar argued, the very presence of these factors made the idea of a working class in India a completely different enterprise than that of Thompson's England, inspired as it was by the artisan class and peculiarly British challenges of polity and organization (Thompson, 2000, p. 57).

In light of this Gramscian tension between acknowledging the role of religion in peasant consciousness and being careful not to reify it, early Subaltern Studies showed varying approaches to the topic. As early as 1974 R. Hilton argued in a European context that the capacity for organization in pursuit of social and political demands arose naturally from the experience of peasant. Thus, by implication, religious rites closely linked to agricultural cycles and subsistence needs, such as rainmaking ceremonies in times of drought and ceremonies to contain epidemics, gave expression to the collectivity of the Indian peasant village (Hilton, in Landsberger, 1974).

Others argued that to invest in the idea of strong primordial ties to community, religion, caste, and kinship is to obscure the complexity of the urban working classes in India. For them, it was not a matter of simple transfer, of bringing a simple, rural peasant consciousness to the factories in urban centers throughout the subcontinent. The conflicting identities, catalyzed by industrial competition as well as by the influences of urban neighborhoods, regionalisms, and nationalisms, must also be added to the mix. Such complexities demanded a culturally specific sociological discipline whereby religion could never play a primordial, but only a contingent, role (Chandravarkar).

Other Subaltern Studies scholars focused on how activists attempted to appropriate religious imagery for their own ends. Gyan Pandey's study of the *swaraj* (self-rule) movement and Shahid Anin's study of the Gorakhpurians' interpretation of Gandhi are excellent examples of this approach (Pandey; Amin). Gyan Pandey argues that peasant movements such as the Eka and the Kisan Sabha in 1921 were not Congress-inspired and therefore "top down," but rather motivated by a structure of land ownership that led to land shortages and high rents. Relatedly, Amin specifically addresses the ways popular peasant culture is made out of religious symbolism. In Amin's view, Gorakhpur villagers did not simplistically respond to the "holy man" Mahatma Gandhi, but rather developed a kind of millennialism whereby *swaraj* figured directly as a form of local political agency.

These early attempts to deal with religious aspects of peasant consciousness led to the problem of the Subaltern Studies' relationship to conventional Marxist theory. Early on, Partha Chatterjee argued that peasant modes of being cannot be called simply class consciousness, but are more complex types of consciousness and practice (Chatterjee, 1983, pp. 58–65). Rosalind O'Hanlon also put forward the view that changes in religion, as well as other essentialized categories, such as caste or nation, present the scholar with "the problem of mapping what on the surface look like fundamental transformations of mentality." She also noted that Subaltern Studies must trace the origins of such transformations in their relationship to the state or to organized religions, without slipping into a rigid teleology or a denial of historical specificity (O'Hanlon, 2000, pp. 92–93).

CULTURAL STUDIES, POSTMODERNISM, AND THE POSTCOLONIAL PROJECT. This concern grew even stronger as Subaltern Studies became deeply inflected with postmodern cultural studies, especially in the United States. Many assessments of this trend trace its beginnings to the publication of Edward Said's *Orientalism,* a hugely influential work concerned with Western intellectual tradition's representation of its colonial subjects, particularly those in the Middle East. Said's *post-Orientalist* perspectives then combined with contemporary postmodern concerns with textual and discourse analysis; through this confluence *postcolonial* studies became the reigning episteme through which much of the Subaltern was then studied. Leading writers in the field of postcolonial studies, such as Homi Bhabha, Gayatri Spivak, Gyan Prakash, Dipesh Chakrabarty, and many others, are concerned with philosophical issues of cultural representation. From this postcolonial perspective, they have argued forcefully for several basic changes in the study of Third World histories: (1) explorations of cultural difference (inspired in part by Jacques Derrida's (1930–2004) idea of *differance*); (2) nonessentialized cultural categories; and (3) the writing of a postfoundationalist as well as a postnationalist historiography (Chakrabarty, 1992, pp. 1–26; Chakrabarty, 2000; Spivak, 1985, pp. 120–130 and 330–363; Bhabha, 1994; Prakash, 1992, 1994, 1996). Among many other priorities, these writers state the need for writing a history which is influenced neither philosophically by an idea of a single cultural mind which applies to all members of a society, nor anachronistically by a false idea of a unifying nation or set of origins set somewhere in a hoary past.

Given these views, many subaltern writers are overtly suspicious of disciplines and fields such as religious studies in the Western academy. Such a field is, in their view, prone to hegemonic and essentializing constructions of the *other* under a dominant institutionalized gaze. However, subaltern theorists are also concerned amongst themselves about the reification of religion in their own writings. Some later postmodern writers, such as Dipankar Gupta, have criticized the tendency in subaltern writers to attribute primordiality to the masses, or to assume a traditional consciousness, or even primordial loyalties of religion, community, kinship, and language (Gupta, 1985). Many subaltern writers have wondered aloud whether subaltern ideas of a moral community, albeit in the guise of folk religious values of peasant community, are nonetheless well on their way to yet another essentializing category. If peasant or worker consciousness can be reified and severed from history in this way, why not caste, nation, or religious community? Thus, the problem remains. As one Subaltern Studies critic put it, although many subaltern writers accept the autonomy of peasants, their accounts are ultimately not that different from the processes of Sanskritization, Islamicization, or popularization—ideas which have all come under fire for essentializing and reifying historical processes of change (Bayly, 2000, p. 122). How can subaltern writing avoid the problem of making the community an "it" with firm boundaries and, as Marxist secularists increasingly suspect, expressing a sympathy for the religious as a way of defining that community (Spivak, 2000, p. 326)?

SUBALTERN STUDIES WITHIN THE STUDY OF RELIGION. The reaction of the religious studies scholarly community to Subaltern Studies has been markedly different from the reaction of Subaltern Studies to it; one might even go so far as to say that they are "mirror images" of each other. Although the Subaltern school, even in its more marked "cultural studies" form of later years, is mostly ambivalent, if not downright hostile, to the idea of religion as a category of analysis, religious studies students have welcomed the category of the subaltern wholeheartedly. Indeed, they have embraced much of the Gramscian tradition with fairly enthusiastic vigor in two significant ways: (1) Subalternist writing can further define and criticize religious studies' own Orientalist perspectives, both colonial and postcolonial; and (2) more postcolonial writing in Subaltern Studies can help religious studies scholars to nuance their descriptions of the cultural identity of the religious groups with whom they concern themselves.

Marxist scholars of religion such as Bruce Lincoln, Timothy Fitzgerald, and Russell T. McCutcheon, would certainly embrace Subaltern Studies as part of a larger, generally Marxist perspective with which to criticize religious practices as one among many forms of cultural hegemony (Lincoln, 1994; Fitzgerald, 2000; McCutcheon, 2001, 2003). Although differing in outlook, these thinkers see this kind of critique as the primary obligation of the scholar. Others are concerned with Subaltern Studies' later, more postmodern incarnations: Richard King's work, *Orientalism and Religion: Post-Colonial Theory, India and the Mystic East* (1999), masterfully outlines some of the issues in the relationship between religious and postcolonial studies.

Many scholars of religion, such as those mentioned above, as well as their numerous area-studies counterparts, would not fundamentally disagree with the premises of later Subaltern School works on religion, such as those essays found in the 1992 volume of Subaltern Studies: Partha Chatterjee's study of the Ramakrishna movement as a religion of urban domesticity; Terence Ranger's study of the Matobo in South Africa; and Saurabh Dube's study of the construction of mythic communities in Chhattisgarh (Chatterjee, 1992; Ranger, 1992; Dube, 1992). Each of these essays attempts to combine class, caste, and religious consciousness in such a way that, even if class concerns win out, the dynamics of particularly religious world views have been thoroughly analyzed. Relatedly, many scholars of religion have used Subaltern Studies as a way to analyze the colonial strategies of missionary movements, such as Malagasy Christianity (Larson), Latin American and other Spanish Colonial Catholicisms

(Rabasa, 2000; Rafael, 1998), and the interactions of Christianity with indigenous traditions in India (Dube, 1998; Clarke, 1998).

In addition, Subaltern Studies provides a remarkably suitable framework to study the resistant practices of particular religious groups in the category of contemporary subaltern, such as South Asian Muslims in America (Mohammad–Arif, 2002), Dalit traditions in India, Native American (Arnold, 2001; Bays and Wacker, 2003) or Santeria traditions in North America (Hackett, 1999; Harding, 2000; Campbell, 1987;), or minorities in China (Dirlik, 1996; Gladney, 2003). This intellectual move has also gained institutional support, for instance with the American Academy of Religion's 2004 initiative, "Contesting Religion and Religions Contested: The Study of Religion in a Global Context." In addition to the already established Indigenous Religious Traditions group, the project's major concerns include the funding of studies from below, the representation and inclusion of Third World scholars, and the examination of the effect of the study of religion on the communities it has engaged, particularly communities from traditionally disempowered populations. Another move toward institutional support was Claremont-McKenna's initiative, "Theorizing Scriptures," inaugurated by Vincent Wimbush in 2004. In this conference, scriptural interpretation "from below" is acknowledged and engaged as a serious intellectual endeavor. Here, the view of scriptural hermeneutics held by Native-American, African American, Australian, Latino, Dalit, Chinese, Muslim, and many other less mainstream religions is given voice and careful analysis. This initiative also highlights women's voices of scriptural interpretation, thus joining critiques of Subaltern Studies that call for a more explicit focus on gender than has been the case in the past three decades (Spivak, 1991, 2002).

Whatever the nascent institutional support for the study of these forms of agency, for many scholars religion plays a central role in certain kinds of resistance—one that cannot be ignored. Indeed, one scholar, Sathianathan Clarke, has gone so far as to coin the term *Subaltern theology* to describe the particular political and religious practices of Dalit Christians against both Hindu and state hegemony. Oddly enough, this explicitly religious usage is somewhat consonant with Gayatri Spivak's rather remarkable statement that "subaltern theology" (religious thought as a form of political resistance) cannot be ignored, for if it is, then Subaltern Studies becomes a matter of law enforcement rather than "agency in the active voice" (Spivak, 1999). This historical moment represents a rather tense and at the same time fruitful crossroads between the two fields, where both Marxist and religious studies scholars struggle to understand religion when it emerges as a form of resistant and political agency in its own right.

BIBLIOGRAPHY

What follows is a basic overview of major works and authors in the field, whose bibliography is now voluminous. For a basic introduction to the major authors in Subaltern Studies,see Ania Loomba, *Colonialism/Postcolonialism* (London, 1998); David Ludden's *Reading Subaltern Studies* (Delhi, India, 2001); and Ranajit Guha, ed. *A Subaltern Studies Reader (1986–1995)* (Minneapolis, Minn., 1997). *Key Concepts in Post Colonial Studies,* by Bill Ashcroft, Gareth Griffiths, and Helen Tiffin (London, 1998), is also helpful for basic terminology, as is Bart Moore–Gilbert's *Postcolonial Theory: Contexts, Practices, and Politics* (London, 1997). Vinayak Chaturvedi's *Mapping Subaltern Studies and the Postcolonial* (London, 2000) gives an excellent historical overview of the field, as do the introductions to the nine volumes of the Subaltern Studies Series.

For a review of the turn to the postmodern, begin with Edward Said's *Orientalism* (New York, 1978), as well as the significant reviews by James Clifford (*History and Theory* 19:2 [1980]: 204–223), Victor Browbeat (*American Scholar* [Autumn, 1979]: 532–541), and J. H. Plumb (*New York Times Book Review* [February 18, 1979]: 3.28). Said's own "Orientalism Reconsidered" in *Race and Class* 7:2 [1985]: 1–15) gives some of his own thoughts about the pitfalls of the post-Orientalist project. Major monographs in the 1990s include Nicholas Dirks, ed., *Colonialism and Culture* (Ann Arbor, Mich., 1992); Homi Bhabha, *The Location of Culture* (New York, 1994); Partha Chatterjee, *The Nation and its Fragments: Colonial and Postcolonial Histories* (Princeton, 2004); Gyan Prakash, *After Colonialism: Imperial Histories and Postcolonial Displacements* (Princeton, 1995); Arif Dirlik, *The Postcolonial Aura: Third World Criticism in the Age of Global Capitalism* (Boulder, Colo., 1997); Gayatri Spivak, *A Critique of Postcolonial Reason: Toward a History of the Vanishing Present* (Cambridge, Mass., 1999); and Dipesh Chakrabarty, *Provincializing Europe: Postcolonial Thought and Historical Difference* (Princeton, N.J., 2000). Numerous essays and more specialized monographs have appeared from these authors in the early 2000s as well. Major critiques of the Subalternist/postcolonial project include that of Aijaz Ahmad, *In Theory: Classes, Nations, and Literatures* (London, 1992), and Sumit Sarkar, *Writing Social History* (Delhi, India, 1997), especially "The Decline of the Subaltern in Subaltern Studies."

Amin, Shahid. "Gandhi as Mahatma: Gorakhpur District, Eastern UP, 1921–22." In *Subaltern Studies III,* edited by Ranajit Guha, pp. 1–61. Delhi, 1984.

Arnold, David. "Famine in Peasant Consciousness and Peasant Action: Madras 1876–78." In *Subaltern Studies III,* edited by Ranajit Guha, pp. 62–115. Delhi, 1984.

Arnold, Philip. *Eating Landscape: Aztec and European Occupation of Tlalocan.* Boulder, Colo., 2001.

Bayly, C. A. "Rallying Around the Subaltern." In *Mapping Subaltern Studies and the Post Colonial,* edited by Vinayak Chaturvedi, pp. 116–126. London, 2000.

Bays, Daniel H., and Grant Wacker, eds. *The Foreign Missionary Enterprise at Home: Explorations in American Cultural History.* Tuscaloosa, Ala., 2003.

Campbell, Horace. *Rasta and Resistance: From Marcus Garvey to Walter Rodney.* Trenton, N.J., 1987.

Chakrabarty, Dipesh. "Postcoloniality and the Artifice of History: Who Speaks for 'Indian' Pasts?" *Representations* 37 (1992): 1–26.

Chakrabarty, Dipesh. *Colonizing Europe.* Princeton, N.J., 2000.

Chatterjee, Partha. "Peasants, Politics, and Historiography: A Response." *Social Scientist* 11.5 (1983): 58–65.

Clarke, Sathianathan. *Dalits and Christianity: Subaltern Religion and Liberation Theology in India.* Delhi, 1998.

Dirlik, Arif. "Chinese History and the Question of Orientalism." *History and Theory* (December, 1996).

Donaldson, Laura, and Kwok Pui Lan. *Postcolonialism, Feminism, and Religious Discourse.* New York, 2002.

Dube, Saurabh. *Untouchable Pasts: Religion, Identity, and Power among a Central Indian Community, 1780–1950.* Albany, N.Y., 1998.

Fitzgerald, Timothy. *The Ideology of Religious Studies.* New York, 2000.

Gladney, Dru. *Dislocating China: Muslims, Minorities and other Subaltern Subjects.* Chicago, 2003.

Gramsci, Antonio. *Selections from the Prison Notebooks of Antonio Gramsci.* Edited and translated by Quintin Hoare and Geoffrey Nowell Smith. London, 1971.

Guha, Ranajit, ed. *Subaltern Studies I.* Delhi, 1982.

Guha, Ranajit, ed. *Subaltern Studies III.* Delhi, 1984.

Guha, Ranajit, ed. *Subaltern Studies VI.* New Delhi, 1989.

Gupta, Dipankar. "On Altering the Ego in Peasant History: Paradoxes of the Ethnic Option." *Peasant Studies* 13.1 (fall, 1985): 9–20.

Hackett., Rosalind. *Art and Religion in Africa.* New York, 1999.

Harding, Rachel, et al., eds. *A Refuge in Thunder: Candomble and Alternative Spaces of Blackness.* Bloomington, Ind., 2000.

Hilton, R. "Peasant Society, Peasant Movements and Feudalism in Medieval Europe." In *Rural Protest: Peasant Movements and Social Change.* Edited by H. A. Landsberger. London, 1974.

King, Richard. *Orientalism and Religion.* London, 1999.

Landsberger, H. A., ed. *Rural Protest: Peasant Movements and Social Change.* London, 1974.

Larson, Pier M. "Capacities and Modes of Thinking: Intellectual Engagements and Subaltern Hegemony in the Early History of Malagasy Christianity." *American History Review* 102, no. 4 (October, 1997): 968–1002.

Lincoln, Bruce. *Authority: Construction and Corrosion.* Chicago, 1994.

Mallon, Forencia E., "The Promise and Dilemma of Subaltern Studies: Perspectives from Latin American History." *American Historical Review* (December 1994): 1491–1515.

McCutcheon, Russell T. *Critics Not Caretakers: Redescribing the Public Study of Religion.* Albany, N.Y., 2001.

McCutcheon, Russell T. *The Discipline of Religion: Structure, Meaning, Rhetoric.* New York, 2003.

Mohammad-Arif, Aminah. *Salaam America: South Asian Muslims in New York.* London, 2002.

O'Hanlon, Rosalind. "Recovering the Subject: Subaltern Studies and the Histories of Resistance in Colonial South Asia." In *Mapping Subaltern Studies and the Post Colonial,* edited by Vinayak Chaturvedi, pp. 72–115. London, 2000.

Pandey, Gyan. "Peasant Revolt and Indian Nationalism: The Peasant Movement in Awadh, 1919–1922." In *Subaltern Studies I,* edited by Ranajit Guha. Delhi, 1982.

Prakash, Gyan. "Postcolonial Criticism and Indian Historiography" *Social Text* 31 (1992): 8–19.

Prakash, Gyan. "Subaltern Studies as Postcolonial Criticism." *American Historical Review* 99.5 (1994): 1474–1490.

Prakash, Gyan. "Who's Afraid of Postcoloniality?" *Social Text* 9.14.4 (1996): 187–203.

Rabasa, Jose. *Inventing America: Spanish Historiography and the Formation of Eurocentrism.* Norman, Okla., 1993.

Rabasa, Jose. *Writing Violence on the Northern Frontier: The Historiography of New Mexico and Florida and the Legacy of Conquest.* Durham, N.C., 2000.

Rafael, Vincente. *Contracting Colonialism: Translation and Christian Conversion in Tagalog Society under Early Spanish Rule.* Ithaca, N.Y., 1988.

Spivak, Gayatri. "Can the Subaltern Speak: Speculations on Widow Sacrifice." *Wedge* 7/8 (winter/spring 1985): 120–30.

Spivak, Gayatri. "Feminism in Decolonization." *differences* 3.3 (1991): 139–170.

Spivak, Gayatri. "The New Subaltern: A Silent Interview." In *Mapping Subaltern Studies and the Post Colonial,* edited by Vinayak Chaturvedi. London, 2000.

Stephens, Julie. "Feminist Fictions: A Critique of the Category 'Non–Western Woman' in Feminist Writings on India." *Subaltern Studies VI,* edited by Ranajit Guha. New Delhi, India, 1989.

Tharu, Susie. "Response to Julie Stephens." *Subaltern Studies VI,* edited by Ranajit Guha. New Delhi, 1989.

Thompson, E. P. *Customs in Common.* New York, 1991.

Thompson, E. P. "The Making of the Working Class: E. P. Thompson and Indian History." In *Mapping Subaltern Studies and the Post Colonial,* edited by Vinayak Chaturvedi. London, 2000.

LAURIE LOUISE PATTON (2005)

ŚUBHĀKARASMHA (637–735), Indian monk and missionary, was the founder of the Zhenyan school in China. Śubhākarasṃha (Chin., Shanwuwei) arrived in the Chinese capital, Chang'an, in 716. A missionary of Vājrayana Buddhism, he was followed in 720 by Vajrabodhi and his disciple Amoghavajra. The three *ācāryas* ("teachers") established Zhenyan as the dominant form of Buddhism at the court.

Śubhākarasṃha was born a prince in a small royal family near Magadha in North India, supposedly a descendant of Śākyamuni's uncle, Amṛtodana. The family migrated to Orissa, where Śubhākarasṃha's succession to the throne at age thirteen plunged him into a struggle with his brothers. Although victorious, Śubhākarasṃha's piety led him to renounce the throne in favor of his elder brother, and he became a monk. He led a life of wandering, seeking out teachers in the "south seas," and he learned the craft of making stupas and other castings. Making his way to the monastic university of Nālandā, Śubhākarasṃha became a disciple of Dharmagupta and was initiated into the Vajrayāna teachings of the *dhāraṇīs*, *yoga,* and the Three Mysteries. He debated with heretics and finally was sent by Dharmagupta as a missionary to China.

After his arrival in Chang'an, the emperor Xuanzong (r. 713–756) lodged Śubhākarasṃha in the Ximing Temple. There, Śubhākarasṃha translated a text aimed at the procurement of wealth, which apparently led to the emperor's order impounding the monk's Sanskrit manuscripts. Sometime later the texts were returned and the monk Yi Xing was ordered to assist in Śubhākarasṃha's translation work. The emperor was especially interested in texts dealing with magical and astronomical lore. In 724 Śubhākarasṃha accompanied the emperor to the eastern capital, Loyang, and was commissioned to translate the *Mahāvairocana Sūtra* (T.D. no. 848), which, along with the *Sarvatathāgatatattvasaṃgraha* (T.D. no. 866), translated by Vajrabodhi, forms the basis of East Asian Vajrayāna. Yixing composed the first six of seven volumes of the *Commentary* (T.D. no. 1796) on the *Mahāvairocana Sūtra* before he died. The final volume (T.D. no. 1797) was completed by the Korean monk known in Chinese as Bukesiyi. The massive *Commentary* contains Śubhākarasṃha's oral explanations of passages in the *Mahāvairocana Sūtra* and represents a creative interpretation of the Vajrayana for a Chinese milieu. Śubhākarasṃha also translated the *Susiddhikāra Sūtra* (T.D. no. 893), a compendium of rituals. In 732 Śubhākarasṃha petitioned the emperor, requesting that he be allowed to return to India, but his request was denied and he died in 735. Śubhākarasṃha's body was embalmed and a stupa erected in his honor near the Longmen caves.

Śubhākarasṃha's importance lay in his translation into Chinese of key texts of the Vajrayana tradition, including the *Mahāvairocana Sūtra* and the *Susiddhikāra Sūtra,* and in his establishment of the Zhenyan school in the Chinese court. Through his oral teachings contained in the *Commentary,* Śubhākarasṃha initiated a tradition of careful adaptation of Indian Vajrayana ideas and practices for the East Asian milieu. In its original, and in its revised edition of Wengu and Zhiyan, the *Commentary* was a source of creative interpretation for both Zhiyan and, later, Japanese Shingon and the Esoteric branches of Tendai. Finally, Śubhākarasṃha applied his supernormal "powers" *(siddhi)* as a means of building political support for Zhenyan. He was a *siddha,* or "wonderworker," as well as a translator, and his exploits caught the imagination of both courtiers and masses. Years after his death, emperors and officials visited his tomb to pray for rain.

SEE ALSO Mahasiddhas; Zhiyan.

BIBLIOGRAPHY

The biographies of Śubhākarasṃha, Vajrabodhi, and Amoghavajra have been translated and carefully annotated by Zhou Yi Liang in his "Tantrism in China," *Harvard Journal of Asiatic Studies* 8 (March 1945): 241–332.

New Sources

Chen, Jinhua. "The Construction of Early Tendai Esoteric Buddhism: The Japanese Provenance of Saicho's Transmission Documents and Three Esoteric Buddhist Apocrypha Attributed to Subhakarasimha." *Journal of the International Association of Buddhist Studies* 21, no. 1 (1998): 21–76.

Orzech, Charles D. "Seeing Chen-yen Buddhism: Traditional Scholarship and the Vajrayana in China." *History of Religions* 29 (1989): 87–114.

Yamamoto, C., and International Academy of Indian Culture. *Mahavairocana-Sutra: Translated into English from Ta-p'i lu che na ch'eng-fo shen-pien chia-ch'ih ching, the Chinese Version of Subhakarasimha and I-hsing, A.D. 725.* New Delhi, 1990.

CHARLES D. ORZECH (1987)
Revised Bibliography

SUFFERING

SUFFERING. Suffering may be defined as the experience of organisms in situations that involve physical and mental pain, usually attended by a sense of loss, frustration, and vulnerability to adverse effects. As a fact of sentient life, pain is a phenomenon concomitant to existence itself and yet, on the human level at least, it is one that is inextricably linked with the sense of one's individuality. As such, pain can only be defined subjectively, and because of its implications for the survival of the individual, the experience of pain often provokes questions about the meaning of life itself.

The effort to understand the meaning of pain is natural, as is the human attempt to mediate painful experiences through recourse to secular or religious symbol systems. A major reason for the enormous influence of science and technology and the esteem in which they are currently held lies in their success in giving human beings power, or the illusion of power, over forces that adversely affect them. However, while science, technology, and social institutions have done much to alleviate suffering, these means, even at their most beneficent, can eliminate only some aspects of pain, but not all.

Thus suffering, more than any other fact of human life, raises the philosophical questions that religion is customarily called upon to answer. When stricken with grief, we question the purpose of life and look for meaning in a universe that harbors such pain. Traditionally, religions have responded to the problem of suffering in two ways: first, by trying to place the human experience of pain within the context of an overall understanding of the universe and, second, by showing ways to overcome or transcend suffering through faith, piety, appropriate action, or change in perspective. Within this broad response, religions have worked out varied systems of answers to the questions and challenges posed by the problem of human suffering.

JUDAISM. Jewish tradition reflects a number of approaches to an assessment of the nature and meaning of suffering and offers a selection of options for transforming painful experiences in order to make them comprehensible. Basically, Judaism sees suffering as man's vulnerability to the negative effects of any number of occurrences over which he has little or no control; in other words, much suffering arises simply from being human.

In a brief review of some of the Jewish explanations for the fact of suffering, two categories emerge. The first attributes suffering either to sin or to ignorance of the right path that should be followed; the second postulates that suffering may attend spiritual progress.

It has been generally recognized in rabbinic Judaism that suffering is largely due to one's own misconduct. Numerous passages throughout both biblical and rabbinic literature indicate that suffering results from wrongdoing and is thus a punishment for sin (*Prv.* 22:8). A direct relationship exists between suffering and wrongdoing, on the one hand, and between joyfulness and right action, on the other. Suffering may also arise from a misconception about the true nature of the self, which leads to a course of action that is ultimately self-destructive rather than self-fulfilling. In the stories of Jacob and Joseph, for instance, suffering comes about because one does something fundamentally wrong or alien to one's being. In such cases, suffering may function as the means by which one comes to terms with one's true self. This view suggests that self-knowledge, as well as a proper understanding of the world and of truth, can come only through struggle and through becoming sensitized to things that one would not have been fully aware of without first having suffered.

Many rabbinic and biblical passages indicate that suffering does not simply punish, but also serves an educational purpose. For example, *Deuteronomy* 4:20 reads: "He brought you out of the iron furnace of Egypt to be his people." Here, Rashi (Shelomoh ben Yitshaq, 1040–1105) interprets "iron furnace" to mean a furnace made of iron for the purpose of refining a precious metal such as silver or gold. Samuel David Luzzatto comments that it is a furnace for smelting iron, emphasizing the purificatory purpose of suffering. We find a similar idea in *Jeremiah* 11:4 and in *Isaiah* 48:10, which states: "Behold, I have refined thee but not with silver, I have chosen thee out of the furnace of affliction." Suffering gives special insight and leads to self-transcendence and concern for others; without suffering, man is insensitive and given to self-interest and self-centeredness. As *Exodus* 23:9 admonishes: "Do not oppress a stranger, for you know the feelings of a stranger, since you, yourselves, were strangers in the land of Egypt."

There is another way in which suffering is understood in Jewish tradition: one may suffer not because one has done wrong but, on the contrary, because one has done right. Here a distinction is made between suffering that results from sin and suffering that results from acting virtuously. Having recognized one's responsibilities through one's own suffering, one is confronted with a new form of suffering that arises from the assumption of the burdens of others. In this respect, suffering is a necessary part of the burden of ascent, since it results from the assumption of tasks that the righteous take upon themselves. Acting virtuously necessarily entails suffering—not a slight, passing discomfort, but intense, agonizing suffering. The doctrine of chastisements of love affirms that God gives special burdens to those who have an unusual capacity to endure them. The righteous bear the burden of ascent; according to *Psalms* 11:5, "The Lord tries the righteous." In a rabbinical interpretation of this text, Rabbi Yonatan writes:

> The Lord tries the righteous (Ps. XI, 5). The potter does not test cracked vessels; it is not worthwhile to tap them even once because they would break; but he taps the good ones because, however many times he taps them, they do not break. Even so God tries not the wicked, but the righteous. Rabbi Joe b. Hanina said, "The flax dealer who knows that his flax is good pounds it for it becomes more excellent by his pounding and when he knocks it, it glistens the more. But when he knows that his flax is bad, he does not knock it at all, for it would split. So God tries, not the wicked, but the righteous." R. Elazar said, "A man had two cows, one strong and one weak. Upon which will he lay the yoke? Surely upon the strong. So God tests the righteous." (*Gn. Rab.*, 32.3)

The idea that those who are able to bear the burden are the ones who should carry it is interpreted by Henry Slonimsky to be the heart of the Midrashic teaching on suffering. He states: "The answer to the question why the good must suffer for the inadequacies of the world would be the fact that the world is growing, developing, and therefore inevitably defective, and there must be someone noble enough to assume the burden, as exemplification of a new insight, namely that nobility obligates, noblesse oblige" (Slonimsky, 1967, p. 39). Taking on the burdens of others can only be done by those individuals who are made capable by their own experience and understanding of suffering. Several *midrashim* indicate how dear and precious are these shattered ones of God. In the name of Rabbi Abba' bar Yudan, the Midrash states: "Whatever God has declared unfit in the case of an animal he has declared desirable in the case of man. In animals he declared unfit the 'blind or broken or maimed or having a wen' [*Lv.* 22:22], but in man he has declared the broken and contrite heart to be desirable." Also, Rabbi Yehoshu'a ben Levi said, "He who accepts gladly the sufferings of this world brings salvation to the world" (B. T., *Ta'an.* 8a).

A sublime individual response to suffering is seen in an incident in Rabbi Zusya's life:

> When Rabbi Shemlke and his brother visited the *maggid* of Mezritch, they asked him the following. "Our sages said certain words which leave us no peace because we do not understand them. They are that men should praise and thank God for suffering just as much as for wellbeing, and receive it with the same joy. Will you tell us how we are to understand this, Rabbi?" The *maggid* replied, "Go to the House of Study. There you will find Zusya smoking his pipe. He will give you the explanation." They went to the House of Study and put their question to Rabbi Zusya. He laughed. "You certainly have not come to the right man! Better go to someone else rather than to me, for I have never experienced suf-

> fering." But the two knew that, from the day he was born to this day, Rabbi Zusya's life had been a web of need and anguish. Then they knew what it was to accept suffering with love. (Buber, 1947, pp. 217–218)

Innumerable *midrashim* embrace the doctrine of vicarious suffering. With regard to the *Song of Songs*, Raba states: "As the dove stretches out her neck to the slaughter, so do the Israelites, for it was said, 'For thy sake we are killed all day long' (*Ps.* 44:22). As the dove atones for sins, so the Israelites atone for the nation."

In this process of the transformation of the world through vicarious suffering, the role of the suffering individual and that of the prophet become linked with the idea of the suffering people. This concept appears in the passages in *Isaiah* 53 on the suffering servant, who is the great symbol of vicarious suffering. The controversy over whether the phrase *suffering servant* refers to an individual or to the people as a whole can be resolved once it is seen that it stands for both: the prophet is to the people as Israel is to the nations. Just as the nations resist the witness of Israel, so the people resist the word of the prophet.

Jewish tradition affirms that there is a correlation between one's suffering and one's actions, that suffering is self-inflicted. There is, therefore, a just order of things, in the sense that evil acts bring about evil consequences. However, in late biblical and postbiblical Judaism, the doctrine of immortality and resurrection was introduced to account for the suffering of the innocent, which saves the justice of God by positing perfect retribution and reward in the world to come. It is often suggested that the wicked flourish because they are allowed to consume, while still in this world, whatever reward may be due to them, and the righteous suffer because they are exhausting whatever penalties they may have incurred. In qabbalistic (mystical) Judaism, the doctrine of reincarnation was accepted as a means of solving this problem, in that human souls were given repeated chances to atone in this world before a final judgment.

Nevertheless, Judaism finds suffering to be a very harsh, crippling, and disastrous experience—one that a person should strive to avoid whenever possible. Throughout their long history of suffering, persecution, exile, torture, and death, the Jewish people have wrestled with the perplexing problem of why they seem to have experienced such a degree of suffering. Even "the resolve to observe the commandments was, in itself, the cause of death and suffering" (Urbach, 1975, p. 442). Faced with the choice of disobeying God or submitting to the ultimate suffering of martyrdom, the rabbis refused to be swayed into any kind of masochistic fervor; they still realistically recognized how dreadful suffering is. All sufferings, as well as terrible martyrdoms, were not simply acquiesced to, but fiercely questioned.

Jewish teaching clearly acknowledges that there is great injustice in the world and great suffering on the part of the innocent. The pain and death of children is a frequent example, as is the slaughter of millions in wars, political upheavals, and concentration camps. Jewish tradition deals with this problem of mass suffering, of the undifferentiated fate of the innocent and the guilty, by claiming that this is an unfinished world in which justice and peace are not given, but have to be won. Suffering is a necessary part of completing this world, and the individuals who take up the burden of striving to perfect it also suffer.

Such a concept, however, does not explain why God would so constitute the world, nor does it fully account for the sufferings of those ordinary people who are caught up in wars, earthquakes, or other human or natural catastrophes. Therefore, a tendency can be found in the rabbinic tradition to consider the problem of suffering as one of the areas beyond full human comprehension. In the popular tractate *Avot* (c. 200 CE), a portion of the Mishnah, Rabbi Yanna'i states: "It is not in our power to explain either the prosperity of the wicked or the affliction of the righteous" (4.19). The terrible death by torture of the venerable 'Aqiva' ben Yosef at the hands of the Romans (second century CE) illustrates the point. It is said that, on Sinai, Moses was granted a vision of the learning and wisdom of 'Aqiva' in expounding Torah and then was given another vision of the rabbi's martyrdom. When Moses protested to God, "Master of the Universe, is this the Torah and this its Reward?" he was told, "Be silent, for this is the way I have determined it" (B. T., *Men.* 29b).

God also suffers: he is a God who cares for his creatures and yet is unable to prevent their suffering. He is so intimately concerned with human destiny that what men and women do affects him directly: "In their afflictions I was afflicted" (*Is.* 63:9; cf. *Ps.* 91:15, *Gn.* 6:5–6). This is also poignantly illustrated in various *midrashim* where God is pictured as weeping and needing consolation because of all the suffering and tragedy in the world: "When God remembers his children who dwell in misery among the nations of the world, he causes two tears to descend to the ocean and the sound is heard from one end of the world to the other" (B. T., *Ber.* 59a).

CHRISTIANITY. Many of the same responses to suffering found in Judaism are also quite understandably evidenced in Christian thought. For example, the statement in *Proverbs* 22:8 that one brings about one's own suffering ("He that soweth iniquity shall reap calamity") is paralleled in *Matthew* 26:52: "They that take the sword shall perish with the sword." In his letter to the Galatians, Paul concurs: "Whatsoever a man soweth, that shall he also reap" (*Gal.* 6:7). Numerous passages, both in the New Testament and in other Christian writings, indicate that suffering is the just payment for sin. Such a penalty may even come in the form of a swiftly executed death sentence, as in the cases of Ananias and Sapphira (*Acts* 5:1–11) and the profanation of the eucharist (*1 Cor.* 11:29–30). However, in *John* 9:3, Jesus specifically rejects the notion that suffering is always the result of sin, asserting that a man's blindness was caused neither by his own nor his parents' sin.

Explicit both in the New Testament and in other Christian literature is the secondary understanding that suffering may serve a disciplinary function. As Paul states: "Suffering produces endurance, and endurance produces character, and character produces hope" (*Rom.* 5:3–4). Such learning experiences are designed to conform the Christian to the image of Christ himself. This sense of suffering as a way in which God disciplines believers is echoed both in *Hebrews* 12:3–13 and in *James* 1:2–4. A corollary concept, which is also present in Jewish thought, holds that suffering may also be seen as a preventive dose of spiritual medicine, intended, as it were, to forestall the germination of sin.

Christianity absorbed other interpretations of suffering that are Jewish in origin. For example, in the Jewish tradition, suffering is a part of the prophetic situation that is a characteristic of the burden of ascent. In a development of this idea, *Acts of the Apostles* 20:23 states that Paul's sufferings—stonings, imprisonments, and other afflictions—resulted from his missionary activity. Paul himself states that the sufferings he endured resulted from his faithfulness to his task of bringing the Christian message to the whole world.

Upholding one's beliefs, it was acknowledged, would bring on the opprobrium of the world. The writer of *Matthew* warns: "Then they will deliver you up to tribulation, and put you to death; you will be hated by all nations for my name's sake" (*Mt.* 24:9); and, "They will deliver you up to councils and flog you in their synagogues" (*Mt.* 10:17). *Acts* relates that the apostles who had been imprisoned and beaten "left the presence of the council, rejoicing that they were counted worthy to suffer dishonor for the name" (*Acts* 5:41). Not just individuals, but whole Christian communities were persecuted and suffered for their beliefs.

From a Christian perspective, suffering is something that is both inevitable and welcome—something to be confronted rather than avoided. In *2 Corinthians* 12: 9–10, Paul exults: "Most gladly therefore will I rather glory in my infirmities, that the power of Christ may rest upon me. Therefore I take pleasure in infirmities, in reproaches, in necessities, in persecutions, in distresses for Christ's sake, for when I am weak, then I am strong." The sense that suffering is inescapable appears in Jesus' experience in the Garden of Gethsemane, where on the eve of his crucifixion, he prays: "Father, if thou be willing, remove this cup from me; nevertheless, not my will, but thine, be done" (*Lk.* 22:42).

In both Christianity and Judaism, the peak of suffering is reached when an individual (or a people) prefers to give his or her own life rather than transgress God's commandments or forsake and repudiate true religion. Many passages in Jewish literature are devoted to martyrologies (especially those detailing the martyrdoms of Rabbi ʿAqivaʾ and of Ḥaninaʾ ben Teradyon), noting the martyrs' strong affirmations of faith at the time of their deaths. Christianity relates similar examples of the religious courage of the faithful, most notably Jesus himself. In the gospels of Matthew and Mark, Jesus asks, "My God, why hast thou forsaken me?" (*Mt.* 27:46, *Mk.* 15:34); in the gospel of Luke he adds, "Father, forgive them, for they know not what they do" (*Lk.* 23:24). According to all three accounts, Jesus died as a martyr to his messianic mission.

Paul's theme of the necessity of sharing in the sufferings of Christ (*Rom.* 8:15) as a prerequisite of sharing in the glories of Christ was carried to extremes by some of the early church fathers. Ignatius of Antioch went so far as to suggest that martyrdom is the only way to become an authentic Christian and thus ensure one's arrival in the presence of God. In fact, Ignatius willingly embraced his own martyrdom to the extent that he encouraged his fellow believers not to do anything that might prevent it from taking place, so convinced was he of the necessity of imitating "the passion of my God" in order to ensure his salvation.

Jesus represents the Gospel's embodiment of the concept of the suffering servant. Seeing Jesus not only as the suffering servant, but also as the Messiah, the Gospel writers fuse these two roles into a synthesis that does not, however, occur in the Hebrew scriptures, where the two remain distinct. A corollary to this fusion of the Messiah and suffering servant is the view of Christ's crucifixion as a vicarious atonement both for the sinful nature of humankind as well as for the sinful acts of each individual: "The Son of man came not to be ministered unto, but to minister, and to give his life as a ransom for many" (*Mk.* 10:45; see also *Jn.* 1:29, 3:5). The writers of the synoptic gospels view Jesus as the Messiah who has been sent into the world to bring about repentance and salvation and to usher in God's kingdom. Jesus' prediction of his own passion occurs throughout the synoptic gospels: his particular passion that is depicted at the end of each gospel portrays him as the being who, by his suffering, crucifixion, and resurrection, becomes the symbol through whom human beings may hope for a similar fate for themselves.

A different and distinctively Christian (as opposed to Jewish) view of suffering can be found in the Pauline writings. In working out his theology, Paul strives to answer certain questions concerning the role of suffering. First, why is there suffering in a world created by a good God who cares for and loves his creatures? Second, why must God not only allow the suffering of his chosen, but why must the best—like Job, or the suffering servant, or the prophet—suffer such grievous fates? Most particularly, for the Christian, why must God's plan include the passion, suffering, and death of the individual designated to be the only begotten Son of God, Jesus the Christ?

In his discussion of Pauline theology in *Theology of the New Testament,* Rudolf Bultmann writes: "The death and the resurrection of Christ are bound together in the unity of one salvation-occurrence: 'he who died' is also 'he who was raised up' (*Romans* 8:34; *2 Corinithians* 5:15, 13:4). Similarly, 'as God raised Christ, so He will also raise us' (see *1 Corinthians* 6:14, *2 Corinthians* 4:14)." Bultmann then claims that the incarnation is also a part of that one single salvation process, referring to biblical assertion that "he who gave himself up to die is no other than the preexistent Son of God" (*Phil.* 2:6ff., *2 Cor.* 8:9, *Rom.* 15:3). According to Bultmann, the incarnation is never accorded a meaning independent of the crucifixion.

In fact, Christ's death is seen as the merger of propitiatory and paschal sacrifices. As a propitiatory sacrifice, Christ's blood expiates sin and achieves forgiveness for the believer (*Rom.* 3:25). That Jesus' death was viewed by the early church as such a propitiation is seen in the liturgy of the Lord's Supper (*1 Cor.* 11:24), not merely in Palestinian congregations, but also in the newly evangelized Hellenistic churches. Jesus' death is also viewed as significant for the congregation of the people of God as a paschal sacrifice (*1 Cor.* 5:7, *Heb.* 13:12). The vicarious nature of that sacrifice is reiterated in *2 Corinthians* 5:21: "He made him who was unacquainted with sin to become sin in our stead."

Christ died in the place of all, then, and for the sake of all. According to Paul's view, Christ's death is not to be seen either as a merely propitiatory or vicarious sacrifice, but as a colossal cosmic occurrence. Salvation signifies release from death and sin. This release from sin, in turn, is seen in terms of release from the law. Hence, centuries later, Bultmann could claim that the sacrifice of Christ's death does not merely cancel the guilt and punishment of sin, but also is the means of release from law, sin, and death. Bultmann believes that Paul viewed the powers of the age in a gnostic light, and in this sense the Redeemer becomes a cosmic figure and his body a cosmic entity. Thus, those who are bound up with him in one body share in a redemption from the sinister powers of this world.

For Paul, apparently, Christ Jesus is the means by which the suffering of this world, man's inherent sinfulness, and death itself can be overcome. By being at one with he who suffered, a person is able to finally achieve a state that is free both from suffering and from death. In *2 Corinthians* 1:5, Paul avers: "As we share abundantly in Christ's suffering so through Christ we share abundantly in comfort too." More explicitly, in *Philippians* 3:8–10, he asserts: "I have suffered the loss of all things . . . in order that I may gain Christ and may be found in Him . . . that I may know him and the power of his resurrection and may share his sufferings, becoming like him in his death, that if possible I may attain the resurrection from the dead." At present, he who is one with—or in the body of—Christ will indeed continue to suffer. He has the promise, however, that he will not be left to suffer continually, but will eventually overcome that suffering through his faith in Christ. Christ himself is the evidence that, as he overcame suffering and death, so may the worshiper.

In his letter to the Romans, Paul exposes man's plight—bondage to the law of sin—which makes a man a miserable wretch groaning for deliverance from the body of death. In Christ, however, man achieves true freedom through the law of the spirit of life. Thus, salvation is to be seen as an eschatological occurrence insofar as it is not merely a historic fact, but a reality that is continually being renewed in the present. Hence, the prospect of overcoming sin, suffering, and death is available to those who decide to reorder their previous self-understandng and their past existence from one of egocentrism to one of radical surrender to the grace of God through Christ.

In short, according to Paul, it was necessary for Jesus to have been incarnated, crucified, and resurrected—that is, to have suffered and died—because this is the only way in which the individual might believe that his own suffering and death can, through faith in the risen Christ, be overcome. A god who simply promises redemption cannot engender the same depth of conviction as a God who not only promises but, as it were, delivers. God's birth into a human body and his suffering, together with his resurrection, are evidence of the possibility that believers, too, can hope to transcend sin, suffering, and death.

ISLAM. Islamic views of suffering may be categorized broadly under two headings. The first is that of suffering as the punishment for sin; the second, of suffering as a test or trial. The Qurʾān repeatedly stresses that all who do evil will be punished for their actions in this world and the next. This doctrine is associated with an emphasis on the perfect justice of God, which is to be vindicated on Judgment Day, when the evildoers will be thrown into the fires of Hell (surah 52). Sin is associated with disbelief, which is the root of misconduct. Unbelievers suffer as they learn of their mistakes. Thus, the punishment of sin through suffering may serve an educational function—namely, to show unbelievers the truth of God's word. The idea that lack of belief is a root of evil reveals a central precept of Islam on the subject of suffering. This precept may be expressed as the belief that evil is found within man, and that subsequently the punishment of suffering is also found there. It is written in the Qurʾān: "God dealeth not unjustly with [unbelievers]; but they injure their own souls." Just as sin is inextricable from punishment in the moral system of Islam, the unbeliever always condemns himself to suffer, for, in the final analysis, disbelief is the greatest suffering—the suffering of the soul.

Equally important to the Muslim perspective on suffering is the idea that suffering is a test of man's belief. This concept is premised upon the belief that the true Muslim stands by his faith despite his woes. Suffering not only tests men's strength of faith, it also reveals their hidden feelings, allowing God to look into the innermost depths of their souls. The judgment of and distinction between the righteous and the impious are central to God's universe. As the Qu'ran points out, God "hath created the heavens and the earth . . . that he might prove you, and see which of you would excel in works" (surah 11). Suffering is incorporated into the fabric of the world and is instrumental to the purposes of God. Suffering both separates good and evil men and serves as the punishment and teaching for the unbeliever.

The response to suffering that Islam advises is a complex one and is essentially different from either the Jewish or Christian viewpoint. In Islam, suffering is not a welcome way of proving one's faith, as in Christianity; neither is it something that should be avoided whenever possible, as in Judaism. Rather, Islam sees suffering as a necessary though unfortunate component of man's life that should be alleviated where possible and endured otherwise.

According to Bowker (1970), Islam advocates both an active and a passive response toward suffering: one should not only endure one's own suffering, but also perform good works to alleviate the suffering of others. Both responses are required of the true believer. The passive response to suffering is based on the idea of suffering as a test of one's belief in God. One must live through suffering, accepting it as God's will and having faith that God will not force any soul beyond its capacity. Nonetheless, one should not surrender to fatalism when facing suffering, but should always keep hope and faith in God. This opinion is implied by the Qur'ān's argument against suicide: God's plans will justify and vindicate the righteous in the end, and to deny this by suicide is to blaspheme against him.

The active response to suffering is grounded in the Islamic belief that man is the cause of his own suffering. Islam considers good those things that rid the world of suffering. The man who helps others is a righteous man; the true believer is revealed by his good works as well as by his acceptance of suffering. Moreover, if suffering is punishment for sin, then doing good works will alleviate this punishment.

Within Islam there is a problematical contradiction between the belief in God's omnipotence and recognition of the existence of suffering. All suffering is believed to be part of God's overall design, and is thought to have a distinct and undeniable purpose. This has tended to lead to a determinist view of existence; the free will of man is questioned. Such a tendency was prominent in the early period of the development of Islam but was later challenged by several schools of thought. The Qur'ān is ambigous on this issue and points to both the designs of God and the free will of man as causes for suffering.

SEE ALSO Cosmology; Four Noble Truths; Holocaust, article on Jewish Theological Responses; Karman; Myth; Ordeal; Saṃsāra.

BIBLIOGRAPHY

Barth, Karl. *Credo.* New York, 1962.

Bowker, John. *Problems of Suffering in Religions of the World.* Cambridge, 1970.

Buber, Martin. *Tales of the Hasidim,* vol. 1, *The Early Masters.* New York, 1947.

Bultmann, Rudolf. *Theology of the New Testament.* 2 vols. New York, 1951–1955.

Goguel, Maurice. *The Life of Jesus.* New York, 1933.

Hartshorne, Charles, and William L. Reese. *Philosophers Speak of God.* Chicago, 1953.

Kittel, Gerhard. "Nomos." In *Theological Dictionary of the New Testament.* Nashville, 1967.

Kümmel, Werner George. *Promise and Fulfillment.* New York, 1973.

Ladd, George E. "The Kingdom of God: Reign or Rule?" *Journal of Biblical Literature* 81 (1962): 230–238.

Leibowitz, Nehama. *Studies in Shemot.* Jerusalem, 1976.

Rowley, H. H. *Submission in Suffering.* Cardiff, 1951.

Schuon, Frithjof. *Understanding Islam.* Baltimore, 1972.

Slonimsky, Henry. *Essays.* Cincinnati, 1967.

Urbach, E. E. *The Sages.* 2 vols. Jerusalem, 1975.

JACK BEMPORAD (1987)

SUFISM.

One of the truly creative manifestations of religious life in Islam is the mystical tradition, known as Sufism. The term derives most probably from the Arabīc word for wool *(ṣūf)*, since the early ascetics of Islam (Ṣūfīs) are said to have worn coarse woolen garments to symbolize their rejection of the world.

ORIGINS. Muslim mystical writers such as Abū Bakr al-Kalābādhī (d. 990/5) and ʿAlī al-Hujwīrī (d. 1071/2?), nonetheless, have proposed a number of etymologies for Ṣūfī: *ṣaff,* "rank," implying that Ṣūfīs are an elite group among Muslims; *ṣuffah,* "bench," alluding to the People of the Bench, the intimates of the prophet Muḥammad who gathered at the first mosque in Medina; *ṣafa'*, "purity," focusing on the moral uprightness essential to the Ṣūfī way of life. The resolution of the etymological debate is less critical than the recognition that the terms *Ṣūfī* and *Sufism* evoke complex layers of meaning in Islam, including the denial of the world, close association with the Prophet and his message, and a spiritual attainment that raises one to a rank of unique intimacy with God.

Some earlier Western scholars of Sufism concluded that mysticism is incompatible with the Muslim perception of an almighty, transcendent God with whom one shares little intimacy. In their opinion Ṣūfī mysticism was born of Islam's contact with other major world religions, especially Christianity and Buddhism. This theory is no longer considered viable for two reasons: First, the Qurʾanic perception of the relationship of the individual to God is quite complex, highlighting both immanence and transcendence, and second, while no one denies that Islam evolved in a religiously pluralistic environment, one need not conclude that phenomena common to both Islam and other traditions are therefore derivative.

The vision of the God-man relationship in the Qurʾān offers a study in contrasts. On the one hand God is the almighty creator and lord of the cosmos who sustains the universe at every moment (Qurʾān 10:3 ff.); men and women are but servants—finite, vulnerable, and prone to evil (2:30 ff. and 15:26 ff.). God is both lawgiver and judge (surahs 81 and 82); whatever he wills comes to be (2:142; 3:47; 3:129; 5:40; 13:27). Servants of God are enjoined to embrace his will, not question its import, for men and women will be rewarded or punished according to their deeds. To breach the lord-servant *(rabb-ʿabd)* relationship leads easily to the cardinal sin of *shirk,* substituting some other power for that of God.

On the other hand the inaccessibility of the transcendent Lord must be understood in the context of those Qurʾānic verses that speak of his abiding presence both in the world and in the hearts of the faithful. For did he not actually breathe his own spirit into Adam at creation (Qurʾān 15:29, 38:72)? And is he not closer to man than his own jugular vein (50:16)? God's presence is all-pervasive, for to him belong the East and the West, the whole of creation,

> . . . and wherever you turn, there is God's face. Truly God is omnipresent, omniscient. (2:115)

The Qurʾān enjoins on every Muslim the practice of recollecting God (33:41), for the peaceful heart is one in which the remembrance of God has become second nature (13:28–29). The most crucial Qurʾānic verse for Ṣūfīs, however, describes the establishment of the primordial covenant between God and the souls of men and women in a time before the creation of the cosmos:

> And when your Lord took from the loins of the children of Adam their seed and made them testify about themselves (by saying), "Am I not your Lord?" They replied, "Yes, truly, we testify!" (7:172)

This unique event, which confirms the union between God and the souls of all men and women, has become known in Ṣūfī literature as the "Day of *Alast,*" the day when God asked "Alastu bi-rabbikum" ("Am I not your Lord?"). The goal of every Muslim mystic is to recapture this experience of loving intimacy with the Lord of the Worlds.

The experience of mystical union need not, therefore, be seen as foreign to Islam. On the contrary, interior spiritual development becomes a concern at a relatively early date in the writings of important Qurʾān commentators. Of the two traditional methods of Qurʾanic exegesis predominating in Islam, *tafsīr* emphasizes the exoteric elements of the text: grammar, philology, history, dogma, and the like, while *taʾwīl* stresses the search for hidden meanings, the esoteric dimensions of the Qurʾanic text. It is among Ṣūfīs (and Shīʿī Muslims) that *taʾwīl* has found special favor.

Early commentators such as Muqātil ibn Sulaymān (d. 767) often combined literalist and allegorical methods depending on the nature of the verse in question. More important is the contribution of the sixth imam of the Shīʿah, Jaʿfar al- Ṣādiq (d. 765), who stressed not only the formal learning of the commentator but also his spiritual development. An individual's access to the deeper meanings of the Qurʾān is dependent, therefore, on his or her personal spiritual development. Since text and commentator interact dynamically as living realities, the Qurʾān reveals more of itself to the extent that the Muslim makes progress in the spiritual life. The power of the text is such that for many later Ṣūfī commentators such as Sahl al-Tustarī (d. 896) simply hearing the recitation of the sacred text could induce ecstatic states in the soul of the listener.

The Ascetic movement. The early catalysts for the development of mysticism in Islam, however, were not all spiritual in nature. The dramatic social and political changes brought about by the establishment of the Umayyad dynasty in the mid-seventh century also played a pivotal role. The capital of the empire was moved from Medina to the more opulent and cosmopolitan Damascus, and the rapid spread of Islam introduced enormous wealth and ethnic diversity into what had originally been a spartan, Arab movement. In reaction to the worldliness of the Umayyads, individual ascetics arose to preach a return to the heroic values of the Qurʾān through the abandonment of both riches and the trappings of earthly power. The three major centers of the ascetic movement in the eighth and ninth centuries were Iraq, especially the cities of Basra, Kufa, and Baghdad; the province of Khorasan, especially the city of Balkh; and Egypt.

Ḥasan al-Baṣrī. A leading figure of the period was Ḥasan al-Baṣrī, who was born in Medina in 642 but settled in Basra, where he died in 728. Ḥasan was renowned for his almost puritanical piety and exceptional eloquence. At the heart of his preaching was the rejection of the world (*al-dunyā*), which he described in a letter to the Umayyad caliph ʿUmar ibn ʿAbd al-ʿAzīz (r. 717–720) as a venomous snake, smooth to the touch, but deadly. Ḥasan contrasts this world of transiency and corruption with the next world, which alone is a realm of permanence and fulfillment.

The extreme to which Ḥasan's anti-worldly stance led him is reflected most vividly in this same letter where he implies that the creation of the world was a mistake. From the moment God first looked on his handiwork, Ḥasan insists, God hated it. Such a theological position runs counter to the basic understanding of the value of creation that Islam shares with Judasim and Christianity. As *Genesis* 1:31 affirms, "God saw all that he had made, and it was very good." To speculate on the origins of Ḥasan's gnosticlike condemnation of the material world would take us beyond the objectives of this present article; suffice it to say that ambivalence toward materiality remained a significant aspect of later Islamic mysticism. The impact of gnostic ideas, however, continued to mold later Sufism, especially in the eastern provinces of the empire. The work of Henry Corbin has done much to open for the student of Sufism this complex world of Ṣūfī, and especially Ismaʿīlī, gnosis.

Ḥasan al-Baṣrī's asceticism, although world-denying, did not entail the total abandonment of society or social structures. On the contrary, Ḥasan functioned as the moral conscience of the state and fearlessly criticized the power structures when he felt they overstepped moral bounds. He eschewed the role of the revolutionary and refused to sanction movements designed to overthrow irreligious politicians. In Socratic fashion, Ḥasan preferred to work for the ruler's change of heart through persuasion, not violence. Ḥasan's dedication to ascetic ideals did not, moreover, lead him to forsake family life. He married and raised a family, albeit in straitened circumstances. While Ḥasan al-Baṣrī is considered a pivotal figure in the early development of Sufism, he is also noted as a transmitter of traditions (*ḥadīth*) and as a defender of human freedom in the early theological debates of Islam.

Ibrāhīm ibn Adham. While there are some extant written materials attributable to Ḥasan al-Baṣrī, textual sources for the lives and teachings of many early ascetics are of questionable value. Often the dearth of authentic historical sources makes it difficult, if not impossible, to distinguish between facts and pious embellishments. A prime example is the life of the famous ascetic Ibrāhīm ibn Adham (d. 770?). Ibrāhīm was said to be a prince of the formerly Buddhist city of Balkh; he gave up his throne in order to pursue the path of asceticism. Some Western commentators have pointed to the possible parallel between his life story and the Buddha legend.

The fables about Ibrāhīm highlight his generosity, altruism, and, most important, his complete trust in God *(tawakkul).* Ibrāhīm's quietism, however, did not lead him to depend on others for his subsistence. He preferred to work and scorned those who relied on begging. It would seem to be fact that he served in two naval battles against the Byzantines; while fighting in the second, he lost his life.

Many tales of Ibrāhīm's life stand out because of the ascetic practices they describe. He cherished ridicule and humiliation; more startling is his joyous acceptance of physical abuse—bloody beatings, being dragged by a rope tied round his neck, being urinated upon, and the like. Clearly such stories are later additions by hagiographers. Nonetheless these grotesque, seemingly masochistic acts are accepted as integral elements of his life history by many Ṣūfī writers. And such tales have helped to shape later authors' understandings of asceticism in this early period of Sufism.

Rābiʿah al-ʿAdawīyah. The actual transition from asceticism to true love mysticism in Islam is documented in the spiritual theory of one of the first great female Ṣūfīs, Rābiʿah al-ʿAdawīyah (d. 801). Sold into slavery as a child, she was eventually freed because of the depth of her piety. Rābiʿah's focus was not on asceticism as an end in itself, but rather on its ability to help foster a loving relationship with God. Asceticism was only one of the means necessary for the attainment of union; to make ascetic practices themselves the goal, and not intimacy with the Beloved, was, in her estimation, a distortion of the Ṣūfī path.

The love Rābiʿah nurtured was completely altruistic; neither fear of Hell nor desire for Paradise were allowed to divert her gaze from the Beloved.

Rābiʿah's vision of altruistic love (*maḥabbah*) and mystical intimacy *(uns)* are preserved in beautiful prayers and poems attributed to her. These represent some of the earliest aesthetic expressions of mystical experience in Islam.

One particularly vivid body of fables scattered throughout the Muslim sources centers on the spiritual rivalry between Rābiʿah al-ʿAdawīyah and Ḥasan al-Baṣrī. The problem with these tales, however, is that they describe a relationship that was historically improbable. Ḥasan died in 728, when Rābiʿah was at best in her early teens. Despite its questionable historicity, the Ḥasan-Rābiʿah cycle provides a valuable insight into male-female relationships in early Ṣūfī circles.

In the vast majority of these didactic tales Rābiʿah's spiritual insight and emotional maturity set her far above her male rival, Ḥasan, whose naiveté and presumptuous self-confidence are held up to ridicule. On occasion the conflict is described in actual male-female terms, with Ḥasan and his male Ṣūfī companions insisting that no woman has the ability to match a man's spiritual perfection. While Rābiʿah proves them wrong beyond the shadow of a doubt, there remains the fact that her success is due partially to the abandonment of the traditional female role and the assumption of more male characteristics. For example, she is said to have repeatedly refused Ḥasan's marriage proposals and remained celibate and childless throughout her life.

Dhū al-Nūn al-Miṣrī. A number of early Ṣūfīs such as Rābiʿah evinced a sophistication of esthetic expression and theoretical speculation that laid a solid foundation for later work by Ṣūfī mystics. Pivotal figures such as Dhū al-Nūn al-Miṣrī (d. 859) were both poetic stylists and theoreticians. Although no complete text of his mystical writings has survived, many of his logia, prayers, and poems have been preserved by later writers. He was master of the epigram and an accomplished poetic stylist in Arabic. The full force of his literary talent comes to light, however, in his prayers.

The child of Nubian parents, Dhū al-Nūn was born in Upper Egypt at the end of the eighth century. While many of the factual details of his life are often indistinguishable from pious fiction, a reliable kernel of historical data emerges. Although he lived in Cairo, Dhū al-Nūn traveled extensively, and during one of his sojourns in Baghdad, he ran afoul of the caliph al-Mutawakkil (r. 847–861). The confrontation was sparked by his refusal to accept the Muʿtazilī doctrine of the createdness of the Qurʾān. For this act of defiance, Dhū al-Nūn was imprisoned; during his heresy trial, however, he so affected the caliph with his *apologia* for the Ṣūfī life that al-Mutawakkil released him unharmed.

The preserved sayings of Dhū al-Nūn attest to the profundity of his mystical insight and to the skill with which he developed terminology and structures to analyze the mystical life. He excelled at elucidating the nuances of the various stages *(maqāmāt)* and states *(aḥwāl)* encountered by the mystic along the Ṣūfī path. To him is attributed the first construction of a coherent theory of *maʿrifah,* spiritual gnosis, which he contrasts with *ʿilm,* the more traditional path of discursive reason.

A pivotal aspect of Dhū al-Nūn's mysticism is the *coincidentia oppositorum,* the "conjunction of opposites." The God who pours out his love upon the faithful Ṣūfī wayfarer is, in Dhū al-Nūn's view, the same God who afflicts his lover with pain and torment. God is, at one and the same time, *al-muḥyī,* "the giver of life," and *al-mumīt,* "the one who kills." Legend has it that at his death the following words were found inscribed on his forehead:

> This is the beloved of God,
> who died in God's love.
> This is the slain of God,
> who died by God's sword.

Mystical ecstasy. The evolution of ascetic and theoretical principles to guide the Ṣūfī wayfarer, and the growing sophistication of aesthetic expressions of love mysticism were not the only signs of a maturing mystical tradition in Islam. An additional area of creative exploration by a number of ninth- and tenth-century Ṣūfīs centered on refining the understanding of what actually constitutes the goal of mystical experience.

Rābiʿah's articulation of the primacy of love in mystical union provided a general framework for discussion; it did not, however, resolve the most vexing question. Does union entail the complete obliteration of the lover's soul in the Beloved or is the object of mysticism a loving relationship in which both lover and Beloved preserve their independence? Expressed more technically, of what do the experiences of mystical annihilation (*fanāʾ*) and persistence in union (*baqāʾ*) consist?

Abū Yazīd al-Bisṭāmī. The debate was brought to a head in dramatic fashion by a number of mystics whose ecstatic utterances provoked and scandalized the traditional elements both within and without the Ṣūfī movement. One of the earliest ecstatics was Abū Yazīd (known also as Bāyazīd) Ṭayfūr ibn ʿĪsā al-Bisṭāmī (d. 874), who lived in seclusion at Bisṭām in the province of Qūmis. Few details of his life are known, but it is said that he was initiated into the subtleties of mystical union by one Abū ʿAlī al-Sindī and that he developed a friendship with Dhū al-Nūn.

Muslim hagiographers and spiritual writers have preserved, nevertheless, many of the ecstatic utterances *(shaṭaḥāt)* attributed to Abū Yazīd. These sayings differ from earlier Ṣūfī expressions of union because of their seeming affirmation of the total identification of lover and Beloved. Cries of "Subḥānī!" ("Glory be to me!") and "Mā aʿẓaMā shaʾnī!" ("How great is my majesty!") shocked the uninitiated because they smacked of *shirk,* associationism, and aroused many Muslims' suspicions that Sufism was a heretical movement.

In a famous text, considered spurious but existing in several versions, Abū Yazīd vividly describes his reenactment of the Prophet's night journey *(miʿrāj)* as a mystical ascent during which his "I" is gradually absorbed into the "He" of the Beloved. Eventually "He" and "I" become interchangeable, for in reality the attributes of Abū Yazīd's essence have been subsumed into God.

This particular understanding of mystical annihilation *(fanāʾ)* is characteristic of Abū Yazīd's mystical theory. Complete *fanāʾ* is attained only after the most arduous stripping away of one's attributes. Nothing is spared, neither personality nor spiritual attainments. Abū Yazīd compares the process to the snake's struggle to slough off its skin, or to the blacksmith's violent manipulation of red-hot iron. The mystic experiences the most dramatic shifts of emotion and spiritual experience; the soul vacillates between the expansive rapture of *basṭ,* in which the self appears literally to fill a room, and the implosion of *qabḍ,* in which the self seems reduced to the size of the tiniest sparrow.

Because of the apparent extremism of his ecstatic utterances, al-Bisṭāmī was revered by later Ṣūfīs as the advocate of the path of intoxication (*sukr*) in contrast with the path of sobriety (*ṣaḥw*) associated with the famous Baghdad Ṣūfī Abū al-Qāsim al-Junayd (d. 910). The division between sober and intoxicated Ṣūfīs was to remain an important one throughout the history of Islamic mysticism.

Al-Ḥallāj. Despite their dramatic power, the ecstatic utterances of Abū Yazīd al-Bisṭāmī are overshadowed by those of the most famous of the Baghdad mystics, Ḥusayn ibn Manṣūr al-Ḥallāj. He was born in 857 at al-Ṭūr, in the Iranian province of Fārs. His initiation into Sufism began early in life, while he was still a teenager. For more than twenty years he lived in seculsion and was trained by a number of the great Ṣūfī masters of the period: Sahl al-Tustarī, ʿAmr al-Makkī, and al-Junayd.

Eventually, however, al-Ḥallāj broke away from his teachers and became an itinerant preacher. His wanderings led him through Arabia and Central Asia to the Indian subcontinent. He came into contact with sages and mystics from a number of other religious traditions who expanded the horizons of his own religious experience. As he continued to mature spiritually al-Ḥallāj attracted increasingly larger numbers of disciples. He became known as *ḥallāj al-asrār,* "the carder of consciences," a play on the family name al-Ḥallāj, which meant "cotton carder."

The core of al-Ḥallāj's preaching was a call to moral reform and to the experience of intense union with the Beloved. Among al-Ḥallāj's poetic and prose writings, one phrase stands out as the paradigmatic expression of mystical ecstasy, his famous "Anā al-Ḥāqq!" ("I am the divine Truth!"). To the ears of non-Ṣūfīs and of more sober elements in Sufism, al-Ḥallāj's self-divinizing cry was tantamount to *shirk,* if not a bald rephrasing of the Christian notion of incarnation *(ḥulūl).*

It is very doubtful that al-Ḥallāj wished to be considered primarily a metaphysician. Consequently the charges leveled against him were due to misperceptions of the intent of his mystical expressions. It would remain for later Ṣūfīs to articulate philosophically a doctrine of identity between God and creation. Al-Ḥallāj's expressions of ecstasy, on the contrary, are part of a tradition whose main goal was to celebrate the transforming power of the experience of mystical union with the Beloved; secondarily the concern was to contribute to the growing body of technical terminology and theoretical speculation about the nature of mysticism.

Many scholars have considered al-Ḥallāj's proclamation of unique intimacy with the divine to be one of the main causes of his eventual imprisonment and execution at the hands of the Abbasid authorities. There is no doubt that al-Ḥallāj's ecstatic utterances and his reinterpretation of certain elements of Islamic ritual practice were objects of violent criticism by many of the religious hierarchy. His execution, however, was as much the result of politics as of mysticism.

Al-Ḥallāj's insistence on announcing publicly his vision of mystical union transgressed a cardinal principle of the great Ṣūfī masters of his generation. The accomplished mystic was never to divulge to the uninitiated experiences that were beyond their comprehension; the true nature of union was to be discussed only with one's fellow adepts or not at all. Such elitism did not conform to al-Ḥallāj's more populist notion of mysticism. For his lack of prudence he was ostracized by his former teacher al-Junayd and was branded a political threat and rabble-rouser by the secular authorities.

Finally, al-Ḥallāj found himself embroiled in caliphal politics during the reign of al-Muqtadir (908–932). He was lionized and defended by one vizier and condemned by the next, protected by the caliph's mother, but finally sentenced to death by the son. Al-Ḥallāj spent about eight years in prison before he was eventually executed in 922. The gruesome details have been recorded by his disciples: Al-Ḥallāj was flogged, mutilated, exposed on a gibbet, and finally decapitated. The body was then burned. For al-Ḥallāj, however, death was not a defeat; on the contrary, he desired fervently to become a martyr of love. Al-Ḥallāj was convinced that it was the duty of the religious authorities to put him to death, just as it was his duty to continue to preach aloud the unique intimacy he shared with the divine:

> Kill me, my trusted friends,
> for in my death is my life!
> Death for me is in living, and
> life for me is in dying.
> The obliteration of my essence
> is the noblest of blessings.
> My perdurance in human attributes,
> the vilest of evils.

The creativity of al-Ḥallāj's work is reflected perhaps most strikingly in his ingenious use of the science of opposites. In his *Kitāb al-ṭawāsīn* al-Ḥallāj describes his two role models in mysticism as Iblīs (the devil) and Pharaoh. Both suffered condemnation at the hands of God, al-Ḥallāj attests, yet neither swerved from his appointed course. The Qurʾanic text affirms on several occasions that Iblīs, who was chief of the angels and the most dedicated of monotheists, was commanded by God to bow to the newly created Adam. He refused, despite God's threat to condemn him forever, and chose, like al-Ḥallāj, to become a martyr of love.

> My refusal is the cry, "Holy are you!"
> My reason is madness, madness for you.
> What is Adam, other than you?
> And who is Iblīs to set apart one from the other?

All three are outcasts who have transgressed the law to attain a higher goal. Yet the reason for the transgression is each one's love relationship with God, which functions as a higher law for the perfected Ṣūfī.

> My friend and my teacher are Iblīs and Pharaoh. Iblīs was threatened with the fire, but he did not go back on his preaching. And Pharaoh was drowned in the Red Sea, but he did not acknowledge any mediator at all. . . . And if I were killed, or crucified, or if my hands and feet were cut off, I would not go back on my preaching.

ʿAyn al-Quḍāt. An even more subtle treatment of the science of opposites (*coincidentia oppositorum*) is evident in the work of another martyr-mystic of Islam, ʿAyn al-Quḍāt al-Hamadhāni, who was born in western Iran in 1098. He proved himself a brilliant student as a young man, mastering the traditional Islamic religious sciences. He was also recognized for the quality of his literary style in both Arabic and Persian. The most influential Ṣūfī master in his spiritual formation was Aḥmad al-Ghazālī (d. 1128), a preeminent teacher and the brother of the most famous mystic-theologian in Islam, Abū Ḥamid al-Ghazālī (d. 1111). Aḥmad's own contribution to Sufism is considerable, especially his classic treatise on mystical love, *Sawanih.*

As ʿAyn al-Quḍāt's fame grew, his disciples increased and, like al-Ḥallāj, he soon incurred the wrath of the religious and political authorities. He was accused of a number of heretical ideas, the most serious being the claim that there was a complete identity between the Creator and his creation. Imprisoned in Baghdad, ʿAyn al-Quḍāt was later transferred to his native city of Hamadhān where he was put to death in grisly fashion in 1131; he was only thirty-three years of age.

The conjunction of opposites, according to ʿAyn al-Quḍāt, is reflected in the very notion of the God of Islam. One need look only to the Muslim confession of faith (Shahādah) for confirmation: "Lā ilāha illā Allāh" ("There is no god but God!"). *Lā ilāha* ("there is no god") is the realm of the malevolent divine attributes, which spawn falsehood and which seduce the soul of the mystic away from the truth.

To pass from *lā ilāha* to the realm of *illā Allāh* ("but God") requires that the Ṣūfī wayfarer confront God's chamberlain, who stands guard at the threshold of *illā Allāh.* Who is this chamberlain? None other than the devil Iblīs.

In the same way that al-Ḥallāj in his *Kitāb al-ṭawāsīn* purports that the devil Iblīs is a model of piety, ʿAyn al-Quḍāt employs this paradoxical motif to dramatize the tension of opposites in God. He links Iblīs with Muḥammad, claiming that both are but different aspects of the same divine reality. Iblīs is described as the black light of straying while Muḥammad is the white light of truth and gnosis; both spring, however, from the same attribute of God, namely his power. Muḥammad is the guiding light of God's power while Iblīs is its destructive fire.

Perhaps the most creative symbols employed by ʿAyn al-Quḍāt to capture the conflict within God are those of the curl and the mole that lay upon the face of the Beloved. The lock of hair that hangs in an arrogant curl over the cheek of the Beloved enjoys a privileged state of intimacy. Instead of driving away the seeker from the threshold of *illā Allāh* with the sword of divine power, or deceiving the soul with black light, the Iblīs-curl distracts and seduces the Ṣūfī with the amorous gestures of the coquette, thus entangling the soul in lesser spiritual attainments.

The image of the Iblīs-curl must, of course, have its Muḥammad counterpart. In addition to the curl, the mistress possesses another mark of beauty, a black mole on the cheek that is equated with Muḥammad. Both curl and mole, however, spring from the face of God; the curl is seducer while the mole is the guide to Truth.

All of the paradoxical images used by ʿAyn al-Quḍāt—the tension between curl and mole, black light and white light, between *lā ilāha* and *illā Allāh*—point to the fact that God himself is the source of paradoxes. Moreover ʿAyn al-Quḍāt is convinced that both poles of the paradox must be experienced if one is to attain true spiritual gnosis:

> Unbelief and faith are two veils beyond the throne between God and the servant, because man must be neither unbeliever nor Muslim.

MYSTICAL LITERATURE. The science of opposites, with its rich symbolism and provocative speculation, appealed only to a small number of Ṣūfīs because of the level of intellectual sophistication it demanded and because of its esoteric quality. In contrast, beginning in the late ninth century, a number of texts began to appear that were aimed at a broader spectrum of the Muslim faithful and functioned as training guides for men and women interested in cultivating mystical experience.

The manual tradition. The emphasis of the manuals was not on the arcane dimensions of Sufism, but on its accessibility and its conformity with Islamic orthodoxy.

One of the earliest manuals addressed to a Ṣūfī novice is the *Kitāb al-riʿāyah* (Book of consideration) of Abū ʿAbd Allāh al-Ḥārith ibn Asad al-Muḥāsibi (d. 857). He is remembered particularly for his skill in developing the examination of conscience as an effective tool for advancement in the spiritual life.

Among the classics of this genre of religious literature in Sufism are the *Kitāb al-taʿarruf* (Book of knowledge) of Abū Bakr Muḥammad al-Kalābādhī (d. 990 or 995), the *Kitāb al-lumaʿ* (Book of concise remarks) of Abū Naṣr ʿAbd Allāh ibn ʿAlī al-Sarraj (d. 988), *Al-risālah al-qushayrīyah* (The Qushayrīan letter) of Abū al-Qāsim ʿAbd al-Karīm al-Qushayrī (d. 1074), the *Kashf al-maḥjūb* (Unveiling of the veiled) of ʿAlī ibn ʿUthmān al-Jullābī al-Hujwīrī (d. 1071/2?), and the *Qūt al-qulūb* (Nourishment of the heart) of Abū Ṭālib Muḥammad ibn ʿAlī ibn ʿAṭīyah al-Ḥārithī al-Makkī (d. 996).

Spiritual guidance. Doubtless the primary goal of these manuals was to serve as guides for novices newly embarked upon the Ṣūfī path. The literary structure reflected this; often the conceit was that of the master writing to, or answering the questions of, a particular disciple. The internal composition of the texts varies considerably from one author to the next. Some are collections of insights strung together like random pearls; others, such as the *Kashf al-maḥjūb* of al-Hujwīrī, present a coherent and systematic analysis of Sufism.

Earlier Ṣūfīs had relied heavily on the personal relationship of master (shaykh, pir) with disciple (*murid, ṭālib*) to provide the guidance necessary for spiritual progress. But as the number both of disciples and of famous shaykhs increased, written manuals became invaluable supplements to personal spiritual direction. The manuals preserved the teachings of many of the greatest Ṣūfī guides and made their wisdom available to a larger number of the brethren. While Ṣūfī manuals never supplanted the master-disciple relationship, they did attain a permanent place of influence and honor among Muslim mystics.

In addition to providing spiritual guidance, the Ṣūfī manuals also addressed a number of subsidiary issues of critical importance. The first was the need to legitimize the place of Sufism in the broader spectrum of Islamic religious life. To this end authors such as al-Kalābādhī and al-Qushayrī made deliberate efforts to demonstrate that Sufism was in conformity with the orthodox theological synthesis, namely Ashʿarism. Al-Sarrāj as well took pains to prove that Sufism was completely in tune with the Qurʾān, *ḥadīth,* and Islamic legal tradition (*sharīʿah*).

A further cause of heightened tension between Ṣūfīs and the champions of orthodoxy concerned the possible conflict between the roles of Ṣūfī saint and traditional prophet. Sunnī Islam presumed that prophethood was the pinnacle of spiritual perfection, exemplified by Muḥammad himself. To substantiate this claim, Muslim theology asserted that all prophets possessed the special gift of impeccability (*ʿiṣmah*); each had the power, moreover, to perform a unique miracle (*muʿjizah*) in order to verify his mission.

Some Ṣūfīs, on the other hand, suggested that sainthood was an even more elevated spiritual rank than prophethood because it presumed a unique intimacy with the divine. Most manual writers, however, evolved a less polemical stance, one designed to reinforce the mainstream character of Sufism. They concluded that the highest level of sainthood was only the first level of prophethood. While the prophet was impeccable from birth, the saint was only protected (*maḥfūẓ*) from committing serious sin, and this only after he or she had attained sainthood. Whereas the miracles of the prophets were unique and indisputable, the miracles of the saints (*karāmāt*) were repeatable and subject to satanic influence.

A common objective of all the Ṣūfī manuals is to analyze in depth the various stages and states that make up the Ṣūfī path. Stages are considered by spiritual writers to be levels of permanent growth in the mystical life; states represent the more transient emotional and psychological experiences associated with the various stages. The process of scrutinizing in analytic fashion the stages and states of mystical experience resulted in the creation of a sophisticated technical vocabulary that provided a basis for common discourse among Ṣūfīs of every generation.

The exploration of the stages and states of mystical experience resulted, as well, in the development of highly refined theories of spiritual psychology. Ṣūfī psychologists aimed first and foremost at providing trainees with the means to gain control over the *nafs,* or lower soul (see surah 12:53), which was identified as the satanic element within men and women. Al-Makkī describes the *nafs* as arrogant, deceptive, envious, a beast that wallows in excess.

The Ṣūfī novice was not helpless, however, in his confrontation with the *nafs.* Men and women possessed an angelic force (*malak*) sent by God to do battle with the *nafs* in the arena of the heart (*qalb*). As al-Muḥāsibī indicates, both *malak* and *nafs* employ similar weapons, notably the various internal impulses (*khawāṭir*) that arise in the heart urging one to good or evil.

On occasion the various movements in the heart are quickly identifiable either as the satanic whisperings (*waswasah*) of the *nafs* or as the impulses of the *malak.* Much more difficult, however, are those times when the origin of the *khawāṭir* is unclear. For the devil-*nafs* excels at deluding the soul of the Ṣūfī and seducing him or her to actions that, while not sinful, deflect the Ṣūfī from the road to the greater good. It is in dealing with these spiritual dilemmas that the techniques of Ṣūfī psychology articulated in the manual tradition demonstrate their subtlety and true sophistication.

Al-Ghazālī. The effort of many of the manual writers to legitimize Sufism's place in Islam culminates in the work of a man whose contribution to the Islamic religious sciences ranges far beyond mysticism. Abū Ḥāmid Muḥammad ibn Muḥammad al-Ghazālī was born at Ṭūs near the modern Iranian city of Mashhad in 1058. His early training was in jurisprudence (*fiqh*), but he soon excelled in theology (*kalām*) and eventually in Arabic philosophy (*falsafah*), which was exemplified by the Neoplatonism of al-Fārābī and Ibn Sīnā (Avicenna).

A recurring theme in al-Ghazālī's work is the relationship between reason and revelation. The great Arab philosophers tilted the balance in favor of reason, insisting that truth was attainable without the aid of revelation. The conclusions arrived at by philosophers, however, did not always conform to the standard orthodoxy derived from the Qur'ān. For example, dogmas on the creation of the world from nothing, the resurrection of the dead, God's knowledge of particulars as well as universals—all were called into question by the philosophers.

Al-Ghazālī championed the truth of revelation over that of philosophical speculation. He was not, like some fundamentalist extremists, antiphilosophical however. On the contrary, al-Ghazālī's fascination with philosophical logic is manifested in many of his works, for he was convinced that philosophy could contribute substantially to Muslims' understanding of law and theology. It was only against the excesses of philosophy that he railed in his *Tahāfut al-falāsifah* (The incoherence of the philosophers), not against philosophical reasoning per se.

Al-Ghazālī's influence was enhanced by the political support he received from the ruling authorities, especially the Seljuk vizier Niẓām al-Mulk, who appointed him professor at the Niẓāmīyah *madrasah* in Baghdad in 1091. It was during his professorship at Baghdad, however, that a personal crisis radically transformed the future shape of al-Ghazālī's career. Whereas his earlier concerns had been with more theoretical and speculative issues, the focus now shifted to the role of religious experience in the life of the Muslim.

In 1095 al-Ghazālī experienced what can only be called an emotional and psychological breakdown. As he described it later in his autobiography, *Al-munqidh min al-ḍalāl* (The deliverer from error), his state of anxiety left him almost catatonic. He suffered terrible doubts about his ability to arrive at any religious truth; more important he was overwhelmed by the emptiness of external religious ritual and law. Al-Ghazālī abandoned his teaching career and sought a solution to his doubts in Sufism, which, he hoped, would provide him with the personal experience of truth or *dhawq* (lit., "taste").

The success of his quest is attested by his later writings, which foster the integration of an interior life with the life of external observance. Alone, each leads either to excess or to spiritual myopia; together, however, they constitute a life of balance and dynamic spiritual growth. To this end al-Ghazālī wrote what was to be his most influential work, the *Iḥyā' 'ulūm al-Dīn* (Revivification of the religious sciences), which epitomizes his vision of Islamic life and which remains an integral part of the training of Muslim scholars to this day.

After eleven years of absence from teaching, al-Ghazālī was persuaded to return once again to the classroom by the vizier Fakhr al-Mulk, son of his late patron, Niẓām al-Mulk. His second career lasted only several years, for he retired to a Ṣūfī convent at Ṭūs before his death in 1111. The measure of his impact on the intellectual life of Islam is impossible to calculate. In the history of Sufism, however, he is especially remembered for having contributed substantially to the acceptance of mystical experience as an integral dimension of Islamic religion.

Other genres. In addition to the Ṣūfī manuals, other important genres of mystical literature developed in the classical period. Fables, epigrams, epic poems, poetry, aphorisms, all were creative vehicles for mystical expression. Early Qurʾān commentators and street preachers had focused on the lives of the prophets for inspiration. This spawned the *Qiṣaṣ al-anbīyaʾ* (Tales of the prophets), collections of lively didactic stories, often with moral themes. In similar fashion the lives of famous Ṣūfīs were assembled by mystical writers into biographical dictionaries, which evolved into important companion volumes to the manuals.

Despite the fact that authors rarely distinguished between historical fact and pious fiction, these hagiographic compendia are crucial for current knowledge of the lives and teachings of the great masters of classical Sufism. Individual compilers, moreover, offer important critiques of a number of Ṣūfī movements, mystical theories, and the like.

The first systematic history of the lives of Ṣūfī mystics is ascribed to Abū ʿAbd al-Raḥmān al-Azdī al-Sulamī (d. 1021). His *Ṭabaqāt al-ṣūfīyah* (Generations of the Ṣūfīs) became the basis for the expanded versions of two later Ṣūfīs, the *Ṭabaqāt al-ṣūfīyah* of Abū Ismāʿīl Abd Allāh Anṣarī (d. 1089) and the *Nafaḥat al-uns* (Wafts of pleasure) of Nūr al-Dīn ʿAbd al-Raḥmān ibn Aḥmad Jāmī (d. 1492). The most comprehensive work of Ṣūfī hagiography, however, is the prodigious, multivolume *Ḥilyat al-awliyāʾ* (Necklace of saints) of Abū Nuʿaym al-Iṣfahānī (d. 1037). Later writers continued the tradition, including Farīd al-Dīn ʿAṭṭār (d. 1221?) with his *Tadhkirat al-awliyāʾ* (Biographies of the saints).

ʿAbd Allāh Anṣarī and the epigram. Many of these authors excelled at more than one genre of mystical literature. ʿAbd Allāh Anṣarī of Herat, a city in present-day Afghanistan, for example, is noted for important works on mystical theory but most especially for his epigrams, the *Munajat* (Intimate conversations). This tiny book, a milestone in Ṣūfī literature, is the *vade mecum* of countless Persian-speaking Muslims. Although the text appears deceptively simple it contains the kernel of Ansari's complex vision of mystical union.

To appreciate Anṣarī's contribution to Islamic mysticism, it is essential to place him in the context of the theological debates that resulted in the classical synthesis of al-Ashʿarī (d. 935) and his school. Controversies arose in the ninth century over differing interpretations of the Qurʾanic verses dealing with freedom and predestination, the nature of divine attributes, and the origins of good and evil. The most influential group defending radical freedom and moral responsibility were the Muʿtazilah, whose views were strongly influenced by Greek thought. Since human beings are responsible for their deeds, they insisted, God cannot be blamed in any way for human turpitude. Reward and punishment are absolutely just because God himself is just. Furthermore God's justice requires that actions have an intrinsic moral worth that can be recognized by men and women.

The logic of the Muʿtazilī view, nevertheless, was challenged by verses in the Qurʾān itself that emphasize God's complete omnipotence and question human beings' ability to determine their fates, for God "leads astray whomever he wills and guides whomever he wills" (16:93). A solution proposed by al-Ashʿarī and his followers was to choose neither radical freedom nor complete predestination, but rather to affirm both as true. This use of paradox as a hermeneutical tool permeates both theology and mysticism in Islam.

It must be admitted, however, that al-Ashʿarī's views leaned more in the direction of predestinarianism than of freedom. He was a staunch proponent of God's complete control over human actions; freedom is little more than God's willingness to allow people to participate in their determination of their fate. It is God alone who first creates human actions and then ascribes them to humans.

Even secondary causality is called into question because to assert that nature functions independently according to its own laws seems to ascribe to nature an independent power separate from God, a position smacking of *shirk.* In defending God's absolute omnipotence, furthermore, al-Ashʿarī was obliged to deny the intrinsic goodness or evil of human actions. An action is good or evil only because God has determined it to be so. Lying, for example, is evil because God has so decreed; if he changed his mind lying would be right.

Anṣarī's theological views were even more conservative than those of al-Ashʿarī. As a follower of Aḥmad ibn Ḥanbal (d. 855), Anṣarī defended the most literalist interpretations of the Qurʾān. Whereas the Muʿtazilah allegorized the anthropomorphic descriptions of God's attributes in the Qurʾān, and the Ashʿarīyah affirmed their existence, albeit in a way beyond the grasp of human reason, Anṣarī and the Ḥanabīlah insisted that the verses must be taken at face value. Consequently his positions appeared even more paradoxical than those of the more moderate Ashʿarīyah.

As Anṣarī indicates in the *Munājāt,* God commands people to obey him and then prevents their compliance. Adam and Eve, for example, are seduced not by Satan, but by God. Their seduction is predestined and they are obliged to particpate. Despite the seeming victimization of humans by God, however, the Ṣūfīs are not to conclude that they are absolved of responsibility for their evil deeds. Paradoxical as it may sound, Anṣarī recommends that the true attitude of the devoted mystic is that taken by Adam and Eve when they were confronted with the tragedy of their sin. They realized they were God's pawns but blamed themselves for the deed: "And they both said, 'O Lord, we have wronged ourselves!'" (surah 7:23).

Anṣarī moves naturally in the *Munājāt* from a discussion of the paradoxical tension between freedom and predestination to that between good and evil. And he reflects an attitude toward ethics that is characteristic of many of the ecstatic Ṣūfīs: Whatever God wills for the mystic, be it blessing or curse, intimacy or separation, is good because it comes from God. Such a stance runs counter to the mainstream ethics of Sunnī Islam, which locate the guide for human action and the determination of moral worth in the synthesis of Qurʾān, *ḥadīth,* and *sharīʿah.*

For the perfected Ṣūfī, however, there is a higher law, namely the love relationship, that determines action and provides the means to evaluate the goodness or evil of particular behavior. The upshot is that, for the Ṣūfī elite, certain practices are permissible that would be disproved according to the religious law of the community.

Such an attitude has often been cited as proof of the dangerous antinomian tendencies endemic to Sufism. On closer examination, however, such behavior is not that far removed from the classical Ashʿarī synthesis. Al-Ashʿarī, as has been seen, claims that actions are good or evil because God determines them to be so; moreover, if he changed his mind about a particular action its moral worth would change. What one finds in the behavior of a number of Ṣūfīs is, in fact, the acting out of this hypothetical case, for the Ṣūfī elite insist that the quality of their love relationship with the divine raises them to a higher tier of ethics, one at times radically different from the lower tier. Anṣarī counsels the Ṣūfī to move beyond the everyday concerns with reward or punishment, and beyond the common notions of good and evil. The goal is to please the Beloved; that is what constitutes the good.

Anṣarī goes so far as to claim that the lover-beloved relationship moves one to a plateau on which even the five pillars of Islam appear superfluous. The pilgrimage to Mecca is an occasion for tourism; almsgiving is something that should be left to philanthropists; fasting is an ingenious way to save food; and ritual prayers should be left to old crones. The focus of the mystic should not be the laws and ritual structures of the Islamic community (*ummah*); it is the love relationship that supersedes all.

Anṣarī is a dramatic example of the mystic whose basic theological and religious conservatism do not bar him from the most exuberant expressions of union. He is not, however, alone in perceiving that the Ṣūfī adept must often move beyond the constraints of Islamic law. Abū Saʿīd ibn Abī al-Khayr (d. 1089) of Mayhana in Khorasan, for example, mirrors as well the same paradoxical approach to religious practice. He began his life as a violent ascetic, isolating himself from normal social intercourse and faithfully observing the obligations of the law. It is said that he was discovered by his father hanging upside down in a pit, reciting the Qurʾān.

At the age of forty, however, Abū Saʿīd attained gnosis (*maʿrifah*) and his actions changed dramatically. He and his followers became renowned for their feasting. In place of ritual prayer, communal Ṣūfī devotions were substituted. Once, when questioned by a non-initiate about his attitude toward the pillars of Islam, especially the pilgrimage to Mecca, he replied that it was a waste of time to travel so far simply to circumambulate a stone house (the Kaʿbah). Rather, the sacred cube should circumambulate him! These statements, shocking though they were to non-Ṣūfīs and even to some of the more sober mystics, were not intended to flout the law. On the contrary, the privileged spiritual elite understood their behavior as that which was enjoined on them by the Beloved.

The mathnavī: Farīd al-Dīn ʿAṭṭār. The epigrams of ʿAbd Allāh Anṣarī, succinct and accessible to a wide range of people, are in sharp contrast with the poetic genre of *mathnavī,* which was introduced into Sufism by the Ghaznavid poet Ḥakīm Abū al-Majd Majdūd ibn Adam Sanāʾī (d. 1131?). The rhyming couplets of the *mathnavī* had previously been made famous in secular literature by the renowned Persian poet Firdawsi in his *Shāh-nāmah* (The epic of the kings). The general structure of Sanāʾī's mystical *mathnavīs,* the most famous of which is the *Ḥadīqat al-ḥaqīqah* (The garden of truth), is imitated by later Ṣūfī authors. The framework consists of mystical teachings interspersed with illustrative fables, anecdotes, proverbs, and the like. The different *mathnavīs* vary, however, in length, the quality of their style, and in the organization and development of their themes.

Important as Sanāʾī's introduction of the *mathnavī* into Sufism was, he is not remembered as a great stylist. For a true master of the *mathnavī* form one must turn to the Persian poet and spiritual guide, Farīd al-Dīn ʿAṭṭār (d. 1221?). ʿAṭṭār lived most of his life in and around the city of Nishapur, near the modern Iranian city of Mashhad. It is reported that he was killed during the Mongol sack of the city. His name indicates his occupation, that of apothecary, and it appears that he continued in his profession even as he composed his mystical treatises.

It is evident from ʿAṭṭār's work that he was a man learned in both the religious sciences and secular literature. He demonstrates enormous perspicacity in his treatment of the subtleties of the spiritual life. ʿAṭṭār's success, however, is due equally to the fact that he possessed the requisite literary skills to mold his ideas into an aesthetic whole of genuine quality. ʿAṭṭār is poet, storyteller, and spiritual theorist; he entertains, cajoles, and leads the reader through numerous levels of spiritual awareness.

Of his *mathnavīs* the best known is the mythic fable *Manṭiq al-ṭayr* (The conference of the birds). The text operates on a number of levels. On the surface it is a lively fable about a group of birds who decide to seek out their king, the Sīmurgh, of whom they have only the barest recollections. The journey is long and arduous, the path uncertain. Many birds abandon the quest out of weakness, apathy or fear; others perish along the way. Finally thirty birds arrive at the palace of the Sīmurgh. This event constitutes the pun on which the story is based, for "thirty birds" in Persian is *sī murgh.*

The far more serious level on which the fable operates is that of an elaborate analysis of the Ṣūfī path. Asceticism, illumination, and finally union are explored in depth. The internal structure of the work resembles an ascending spiral staircase. The bird-souls progress upward, often returning to an earlier point, except now at a more advanced level. The birds are not uniform souls but mirror a variety of human personality types. Their strengths and difficulties reflect, moreover, the issues faced by a wide variety of Ṣūfī seekers.

The overall power of the work is due to its meticulous organization. It is necessary to study the text closely to appreciate the care with which ʿAṭṭār develops his multileveled thematic structure. The last section of the work describes the seven valleys through which the tested remnant must pass in order to reach the Simurgh. The final valley is that of *fanāʾ*, "annihilation," where the thirty birds merge with their beloved Simurgh as the moth merges with the flame.

Lyric and mathnavī: Jalāl al-Dīn Rūmī. Despite ʿAt-tar's obvious literary and analytic skills, his work is surpassed by the greatest of the Persian mystical poets, Jalāl al-Dīn Rūmī (known as Mawlānā, "our master"). Rūmī was born in Balkh in 1207, the son of Bahāʾ al-Dīn Walad, who was himself a noted legist, teacher, and spiritual guide. Around 1219, however, Bahāʾ al-Dīn left Balkh because of the threat of invasion by the Mongols. The family set out on pilgrimage to Mecca, passing through the city of Nishapur where, it is reported, Bahāʾ al-Dīn and his young son met ʿAṭṭār, who predicted Rūmī's future greatness.

Bahāʾ al-Dīn settled eventually in Konya in Anatolia (known as Rūm, hence the name Rūmī). He was warmly received by the ruling Seljuk authorities and resumed his career as teacher and shaykh. Following in his father's footsteps, Jalāl al-Dīn became well versed in the Islamic religious sciences and philosophical theology. After Bahāʾ al-Dīn's death in 1231, Jalāl al-Dīn assumed his father's teaching post.

Rūmī's Ṣūfī training progressed in serious fashion under the tutelage of Burhān al-Dīn Muḥaiqqiq, one of his father's disciples. The critical moment in Rūmī's spiritual development, however, was his meeting in 1244 with Shams al-Dīn of Tabriz. For two years they were inseparable, Rūmī finding in Shams the vehicle through which to experience the true ecstasy of mystical love. Their relationship was a source of jealousy and scandal among Rūmī's family and followers. Abruptly, Shams departed Konya for parts unknown.

Rūmī was disconsolate, but, with the help of his son Sulṭān Walad, he engineered Shams's return. Rūmī's rekindled joy was shortlived, however, because Shams disappeared for the last time in 1248, and there is persuasive circumstantial evidence that Shams was murdered, perhaps with the connivance of Rūmī's family.

The intense love relationship Rūmī shared with Shams was the catalyst for the creation of some of the most extraordinary poetry in the Persian language. Rūmī was prolific; his poetic verses number close to forty thousand, collected in a work that bears the name of his beloved, the *Divāni Shams-i Tabrīzī*. He is a master of imagery, ranging from the mundane realities of food, weaving, and the like to more subtle treatments of nature, music, and religious symbols. Prominent, of course, is the image of Shams, "the sun," in whose brilliance and intensity Rūmī loses himself. Both the agony of separation and the exhiliration of union ebb and flow throughout his poetry. The emotions evoked run the gamut of human experience. Rūmī does not hesitate to shock; anger, cruelty, and vulgar sexuality share the stage with the ecstasy of annihilation in the Beloved, proving that the Ṣūfī quest must not be romanticized. Love not only has the potential to fulfill; it also destroys.

Rūmī's other masterpiece, his *Mathnavī-yi maʿnavī* (Spiritual Couplets), was written at the urging of his cherished disciple Ḥusām al-Dīn Chelebī. Ḥusām al-Dīn, like many Ṣūfīs of the period, discovered in the *mathnavīs* of Sanāʾī and ʿAṭṭār a wealth of spiritual wisdom. It was imperative, Ḥusām al-Dīn believed, for his revered shaykh to preserve his teachings in similar fashion for posterity. Thus Rūmī was persuaded to dictate his *Mathnavī* to Ḥusām al-Dīn, who transcribed the text and read it back to his master for correction. The final product is substantial, six books totaling almost thirty thousand verses. Several of Rūmī's lesser works—letters, discourses, and sermons—have been preserved as well.

Whereas ʿAṭṭār's works, especially his *mathnavīs*, are noted for their clear structural development, those of Rūmī resemble more the stream-of-consciousness style. One must be steeped in Rūmī's work before daring to analyze his thought.

The statement is often made that Rūmī's *Mathnavī* is the Qurʾān of the Persians. While the main point is the enormous popularity the text has had, and continues to have, in the Persian-speaking world, there is another level on which the comparison is apt. The Qurʾān communicates itself primarily in individual, sometimes self-contained, units, not as a structured whole. Similarly, many segments of the *Mathnavī* have an internal unity of their own. Yet the sections of the text are strung loosely together like a string of pearls of different sizes, shapes, and hues. Themes appear and disappear, only to be addressed again from a different perspective. To seek out a unifying structural element in the *Mathnavī* is perhaps to do an injustice to the intent of the author. Its appeal lies in its fluidity and allusiveness. True, this can be frustrating at times; frustration, however, soon turns to fascination as the reader is lured once again into the complex web of Rūmī's thought.

GNOSIS AND IBN ʿARABĪ. The history of mysticism in Islam is replete with individuals of brilliance and creativity. Among these exceptional personalities, however, one stands out from the rest because of his unique genius. Abū Bakr Muḥammad ibn al-ʿArabī al- Ḥātimī al-Ṭāʾī was born at Murcia in Muslim Spain in 1165. He is honored with the titles "Al-Shaykh Al-Akbar" (*"doctor maximus"*) and "Muḥyī al-Dīn" ("the revivifier of religion"). Eventually he came to be known under the name Muḥyī al-Dīn ibn ʿArabī.

While still a child, Ibn ʿArabī and his family moved to Seville, where he received the greater part of his education in the traditional Islamic religious disciplines. He was greatly influenced in his spiritual development by two female Ṣūfīs, especially Fāṭimah of Cordova. A great deal of his mystical insight, however, evolved from visionary experiences, the first occuring during an illness in his youth. Throughout his life he continued to have visions on which he placed a great deal of reliance.

Ibn ʿArabī's visionary bent is equally evident in his claim to have been initiated into Sufism by the mythic figure Khiḍr, a mysterious being, said to be immortal, associated with a Qurʾānic fable (*sūrah* 18) and pre-Islamic legends. Khiḍr is renowned in Sufism as a saint and guide of exceptional spiritual power; to be chosen as one of his disciples is a rare privilege.

In his early twenties Ibn ʿArabī traveled extensively throughout Spain and North Africa and broadened his intellectual perspectives. He describes a unique meeting in Cordova with the greatest of the Muslim Aristotelian philosophers, Ibn Rushd (known as Averroës in the Latin West). The encounter is heavy with symbolism, for Ibn Rushd represents the total reliance of philosophers on reason *(ʿaql)*, while Ibn ʿArabī champions gnosis *(maʿrifah)* as the only means to experience the fullness of truth.

In 1201 Ibn ʿArabī left Spain and North Africa for the last time, undertaking travels that brought him to many important centers of Islamic learning. In 1223 he settled in Damascus, where he remained until his death in 1240. His mausoleum continues to be an important pilgrimage center.

Ibn ʿArabī is unique because he was both an original thinker and synthesizer. Many of his ideas resonate with earlier intellectual developments in Sufism and in philosophical theology. His greatness, however, lies in his ability to systematize Ṣūfī theory into a coherent whole with solid metaphysical underpinnings. Ibn ʿArabī, therefore, should not be viewed as an eccentric outside of the mainstream, but rather as the genius who was able to gather together various strains of mystical philosophy and to mold them into an esthetic whole.

The corpus of Ibn ʿArabī's work is massive, which complicates considerably any attempt at a comprehensive analysis of his thought. In addition his style is often dense, reflecting the esoteric nature of his ideas. Two of his most influential works are *Al-futūḥat al-makkīyah* (The Meccan revelations), which he was ordered to write in a visionary experience while on pilgrimage, and *Fuṣūs al-ḥikam* (The bezels of wisdom).

Waḥdat al-Wujūd. The central concept in Ibn ʿArabī's system is *waḥdat al-wujūd,* "unity of being." Scholars have debated whether Ibn ʿArabī intends this term to describe a monist system, where nothing exists but the One. An affirmative response does not indicate, however, a dramatic shift in Muslim metaphysics because, in reality, Ibn ʿArabī is only taking the Ashʿarī synthesis to its logical extreme. The Ashʿarī insistence on God's total omnipotence and control over the universe implies that God is the only true agent. It is not illogical, therefore, to suggest, as Ibn ʿArabī does, that God must also be the only true existent.

The divine essence in itself is completely transcendent; it is, in fact, unknowable, the *lā ilāha* ("there is no god") of the Muslim confession of faith. This plane of unconditioned unity (*aḥadīyah*), however, is not the only plane on which divine reality exists. The plane of oneness (*wāḥidīyah*) is characterized by a unity in plurality, a unity in which the qualities of all possible existents reside. Once again the ultimate solution is paradox. The divine is undifferentiated and totally transcendent; yet in the divine are discovered the qualities of all potential beings.

Reality, therefore, is tiered, a progression of spiritual manifestations. Ultimate reality is the *theos agnostos,* the "unknown God," from which emerge the different planes of divine existence, culminating in the God of revelation, Allāh, the *illā Allāh* ("but God"), of the confession of faith. The creation of the cosmos occurs, not out of nothing (*creatio ex nihilo*) as traditional Western theology would have it, but because of the yearning of the unknown God to escape from isolation. A *ḥadīth* dear to Ṣūfīs encapsulates God's intent: "I was a hidden treasure and I desired to be known, so I created the creation in order that I might be known."

Creation, therefore, is the manifestation of the One in the plurality of created beings. God's sigh of longing breathes forth the universe, the mirror in which he comes to know himself. The agency through which the cosmos is produced is the divine creative imagination. The process is not static but dynamic, for in the same way that God exhales, he inhales, drawing creation back to its source in the One. Gnosis for the Ṣūfī, therefore, entails progress along the path from illusion (the naive conviction that he is an independent reality distinct from God) to insight into creation's identification with God's self-revelation.

The Perfect Human Being. The mirror that the One projects forth is not uniformly polished. The created being in which the Absolute becomes most fully conscious of itself is man. And there is in every generation *al-insān al-kāmil,* the Perfect Human Being, who is the link between Absolute Being and the created realm. Through the mediacy of the Perfect Human Being the dynamic process of emanation and return takes place. In fact, the process would be impossible without that being, the most perfected Ṣūfī, the *quṭb* ("pole"), the axis around which the cosmos revolves.

Ibn ʿArabī's emanationist view of creation reinterprets, moreover, the traditional understanding of the goal of mysticism in Islam. Many early Ṣūfīs described the path as a growth in loving union between a soul, which retains its essential independence, and the Beloved who, while being the source of creation, is distinct from it. For Ibn ʿArabī and his followers, the goal is not primarily love but wisdom, to move from the illusion of plurality to the gnostic insight that one has always been, and will continue to be, totally united with the source of all being.

Waḥdat al-wujūd has enormous implications, furthermore, for the Ṣūfī understanding of human freedom and ethics. Nothing manifests itself in creation unless God wills it. This is an axiom of both Ibn ʿArabī and traditional Islam. In Ibn ʿArabī's system, the archetypes of all potential beings exist in the One. When these potential realities are actualized in the illusory realm of plurality, they function completely in accord with their celestial archetypes. In the realm of the created world, therefore, individual free choice is illusory. All change is predetermined by the archetype of the particular reality. Freedom exists only insofar as all creatures participate in the freedom of the One, with which they are ultimately identified.

Ethics, in addition, must be seen in the light of the determinative power of the celestial archetypes. In the realm of creation, the law (*sharīʿah*) delineates what actions are in accord with God's revelation. From the perspective of the One, however, all actions are good since they are manifestations of the divine creative imagination and are in accord with the celestial archetypes. Culpability is relative because it is operative only in the realm of created illusion. Eventually all return to the undifferentiated One; thus there is no eternal reward or punishment in the traditional sense.

The complexity of Ibn ʿArabī's thought defies summation in a few brief paragraphs. Nor have scholars in the field yet gained sufficient mastery of his work to unravel his convoluted and sometimes contradictory ideas. What is clear, however, is the pervasive influence of Ibn ʿArabī and his school on later Sufism. Disciples such as Ṣadr al-Dīn Qūnawī (d. 1274) in Anatolia and commentators on his work such as ʿAbd al-Raḥmān ibn Aḥmad Jāmi (d. 1492) in Persia disseminated his ideas throughout the Islamic world.

ṢŪFĪ FRATERNITIES. The history of Sufism is much more than the history of mystical theory and expression. There is a significant social dimension to Islamic mysticism that must be explored if the picture is to be complete. Even many of the early Ṣūfīs, individualists though they were, sought out the advice and counsel of their fellow wayfarers. From the very beginning, therefore, companionship (*ṣuḥbah*) was considered essential for progress in the spiritual life.

Fluid interaction among Ṣūfīs soon evolved into the more structured relationship of master and disciple, adding a new level of social complexity. Not only would disciples visit their masters, but many also took up residence with them. The earliest formal Ṣūfī convent seems to date from the latter part of the eighth century CE, on the island of Abadan.

Political changes in the Islamic empire contributed to the stabilization of Ṣūfī institutional structures. In the mid-eleventh century the Seljuks wrested control of the Abbasid caliphate from the Shīʿī Buyids. The Seljuks were staunch Sunnīs who took over the religious educational system of the *madrasahs* in order to reindoctrinate the intelligentsia with Sunnī orthodoxy. The public support they provided for Ṣūfī establishments afforded the Seljuks more control over the type of Ṣūfī piety inculcated in the new recruits, but at the same time, government patronage ensured the survival of the various Ṣūfī institutions.

By the thirteenth century, several types of Ṣūfī establishments had evolved, each with a different general purpose. The *ribāṭ* was a residence or training center, which originated in the Arab regions of the empire. *Khānqāhs* were similar establishments rooted in the more persianized environment of Khorasan; they eventually spread, however, into the Arab centers. The more serious training took place in the *zāwīyahs*, which usually housed a teaching shaykh; *khalwah* is the name given to the retreat of a single Ṣūfī or dervish. (Dervish is derived from the Persian word for Ṣūfī, *darvīsh,* "poor," "beggar.")

More important than the physical environment in which Ṣūfīs congregated is the evolving infrastructure of the Ṣūfī communities themselves. In the eleventh century, fluid organizations continued to predominate; their common link was the desire for *ṣuḥbah* and for the guidance of a shaykh. Frequently, a master and his disciples remained a cohesive social unit only until the death of the master, after which the group disbanded.

By the thirteenth century the situation had altered significantly. Many Ṣūfī groups became self-perpetuating social organizations whose central focus was the founder and his teaching. No longer was the survival of the group dependent on a particular living shaykh; authority was passed from shaykh to disciple, thus providing a stable structural basis for the continued growth and development of the community. The new master was the chief custodian of the founder's spiritual legacy and, on occasion, an innovator in his own right.

Silsilahs. These stable social organizations came to be called *ṭarīqahs* ("ways"), known in English as Ṣūfī orders, fraternities, or brotherhoods. Each founding shaykh had his *silsilah* ("chain"), his spiritual lineage which contributed substantially to his stature in the Ṣūfī community. The *silsilah* is, more precisely, a genealogy, tracing the names of one's master, of one's master's master, and so on back through history. Often a prominent shaykh would have been initiated more than once, by a number of illustrious Ṣūfīs, thus adding additional stature to his spiritual pedigree.

There are two main *silsilah* groups, which later subdivided into literally hundreds of Ṣūfī fraternities. The first chain, generally considered the more sober of the two, traces its links back to Abū al-Qāsim al-Junayd, the famed spiritual guide from whom al-Ḥallāj eventually broke away. The second, and more intoxicated, *silsilah* derives from the first great Ṣūfī ecstatic, Abū Yazīd al-Bisṭāmī. These designations are very general, and membership in either group indicates only a spiritual genealogy, not necessarily an actual attitude toward mystical experience.

The members of the Bisṭāmī branch are often called Malāmati, "blameworthy." The appellation, however, can be overstressed, for it does not mean that they scorned Islamic law. On the contrary, many were meticulous in their observance. But eventually the name came to describe, in broad terms, those Ṣūfīs who eschewed completely all of the public trappings of Sufism and of piety in general; they were characterized by the virtue of absolute sincerity (*ikhlāṣ*). The Malāmatīyah rejected Ṣūfī initiation and the guidance of a shaykh, nor would they engage in public devotional practices common to Ṣūfīs. Whatever ritual acts they performed were carried out in private. Their individualism made them appear to some as suspicious and marginal. The Malāmatīyah, nevertheless, should be clearly distinguished from the Qalandarīyah, or wandering dervishes, many of whom did engage in practices that made mockery of the religious law and of traditional morality.

The centrality of *silsilah*s in Ṣūfī fraternities is not completely unique. One discovers an analogous emphasis in the *ḥadīth* literature, where the literary structure of a *ḥadīth* has two parts: the chain of transmitters *(isnād)* and the body of the text (*matn*). According to Muslim tradition, the authenticity of the *ḥadīth* is guaranteed by the reliability of the *isnād*. In the same way that the power of sacred word in the *ḥadīth* has been preserved by the chain of transmitters, so too do the teachings and powers of a particular shaykh remain alive through his *silsilah*.

Whether or not the *isnād*s are historically reliable is not a question that need be discussed here. Suffice it to say that the importance of *isnād*s for Muslims is to ground *ḥadīth*s solidly in the period of the original revelation. Thus there can be no question that the teachings of the *ḥadīth*s are innovations; rather *ḥadīth*s are but more detailed insights into God's will already expressed in general terms in the Qurʾān.

In similar fashion the *silsilah*s of Ṣūfī shaykhs provide them with religious legitimacy. Even though the Ṣūfī orders may vary considerably in their teachings and attitudes toward mystical experience, they each can claim, through their spiritual genealogies, to be solidly based upon the foundations of Sufism.

Veneration of saints. The institutionalization of *ṭarīqah*s and the emphasis on *silsilah*s enhanced substantially the religious and political position of the master. Whereas in the past the shaykh functioned primarily as an expert and confidant, he now became a repository of spiritual power as well. A shaykh's lineage did not provide simply a list of teachers; it implied that the spiritual power of each of these great Ṣūfīs had been transmitted to this last member of the line.

The shaykhs of the great Ṣūfī orders, therefore, took on superhuman qualities. They became known as *awliyāʾ* (sg., *walī*), intimates or friends of God. Their spiritual perfection raised them far above the level of their disciples and of the masses of Muslim faithful. The spread of Ibn ʿArabī's teaching, particularly the notion of the Perfect Human Being, which was elaborated upon by Ibn ʿArabī's intellectual disciples, especially by ʿAbd al-Karīm ibn Ibrāhīm al-Jīlī (d. 1428), provided an intellectual framework within which to explain this cosmic role of the saintlike shaykh. Many of the shaykhs of important orders were acknowledged by their followers as the *quṭb*, the "pole" or "axis" around which the cosmos revolves, the Perfect Human Being, the point at which the divine Creative Imagination most fully manifests itself in the world of illusion. The fact that a number of individuals claimed this status at one and the same time was cause for a certain amount of friction and rivalry among the powerful fraternities.

The concept of *quṭb* is linked by Ibn ʿArabī and his predecessors with a whole hierarchy of cosmic beings. Al-Hujwīrī describes them as the officers of the divine court, made up of three hundred *akhyār* ("excellent ones"), forty *abdāl* ("substitutes"), seven *abrār* ("piously devoted ones"), four *awtād* ("pillars"), three *nuqabāʾ* ("leaders"), and one *quṭb* (known also as *ghawth,* "succor"). Ibn ʿArabī's hierarchy is somewhat different in structure. The *quṭb* is joined by two *aʾimmah* ("guides"), four *awtād,* seven *abdāl,* twelve *nuqabāʾ*, and eight *nujabāʾ* ("nobles"). The cosmic hierarchy, regardless of its particular description, is the spiritual power through which the order and continued existence of the cosmos are ensured.

The term *walī* is often translated as saint; this is misleading because there is no religious hierarchy in Islam empowered to canonize individuals as saints, as one has, for example, in Roman Catholicism. Rather, the status of *walī* is attained through public acclamation. There are, nevertheless, analogies between Christian saints and Muslim *awliyāʾ*, insofar as both possess spiritual power that is capable of being transmitted to disciples or devotees. In Islam this power is called *barakah* ("blessing"). The *barakah* of a *wali* has the potential to transform an individual spiritually as well as to provide concrete material blessings. *Barakah* should be understood as concretely as possible. It is often transmitted through the power of touch, similar to the laying on of hands or the application of relics, practices common in other religious traditions of the West.

The perfected shaykhs are objects of veneration both during their lives and after their deaths. It is generally accepted that they possess the power of miracles (*karāmāt*), although their miracles are subject to satanic influence in a way that the miracles of prophets are not. The extraordinary powers of the *awliyāʾ* are not diminished in any way after their death; on the contrary, their intercession often appears more efficacious. Consequently the tombs of great Ṣūfī *awliyāʾ* are vibrant pilgrimage centers to this day.

Ritual practice. Much has been said thus far about the shaykhs of Ṣūfī orders. What were the general patterns of life of the members of these communities? It is difficult to generalize because of the different character of the various brotherhoods. There are, however, some areas of commonality. The full members of the fraternities committed themselves in obedience to the shaykh, who initiated them into the order and bestowed upon them the patched frock (*khirqah*), the sign of their entry onto the Ṣūfī path. They were encouraged to subject themselves completely to the master's will, to be like dead bodies in the hands of the body-washers. Some members of orders remained celibate while others married; some lived lives of extreme poverty while others had a very comfortable existence. Common to most of the Ṣūfī fraternities were ritual practices called *dhikr* ("remembrance") and *samāʿ* ("audition").

Dhikr. The impetus for the practice of *dhikr* is derived from those Qurʾanic verses that enjoin the faithful to remember God often. Among Ṣūfīs this duty evolved into a complex exercise performed by an individual or group. Many fraternities put their own particular stamp on the *dhikr* exercise. Most *dhikr* techniques, however, involve the rhythmic repetition of a phrase, often Qurʾanic, in which one of the names of God appears. In Islam, Allāh has one hundred names, ninety-nine of which are known; the hundredth name is hidden. Certain Ṣūfīs who ascribed to themselves the rank of *quṭb* claimed to have been blessed with this most precious secret.

The more sophisticated methods of *dhikr* usually involve breath control, body movements, and a number of other complex techniques to gain control over the five senses as well the psyche and imagination. In some Ṣūfī groups, such as the Naqshbandīyah, *dhikr* is a private exercise. The goal is to move from vocal *dhikr* to silent *dhikr,* with each stage representing a more intense level of union with the Beloved until, at the final stage, *dhikr* moves to the innermost recesses of one's being and one can no longer distinguish between the one remembering and the Remembered.

Samāʿ. Like *dhikr, samāʿ* has become identified with Ṣūfī ritual practice. It involves listening to music, usually with a group. The music is often accompanied by Qurʾān chants and/or the singing of mystical poetry. The recital is intended to spark a mystical experience within the auditors. Those most affected by the *samāʿ* rise up to dance in unison with the music. Depending on the Ṣūfī group, the dance can be a marvel of aesthetic movement or the frenetic writhings of the seemingly possessed.

From its inception *samāʿ* has been controversial among Ṣūfīs. No one questions the efficacy of chanting the Qurʾān. The doubts arise with music and the singing of mystical love poetry. Music and singing were considered by many shaykhs to be amoral: neither good nor evil by nature. *Samāʿ* possesses the power, however, to engulf the spirit of the disciples and to seduce them to immoral behavior. Consequently many shaykhs, if they approve of *samāʿ* at all, insist that only accomplished Ṣūfīs be allowed to participate. Novices are warned to beware.

Dhikr and *samāʿ* have served an important function outside of the ranks of the full-fledged members of the Ṣūfī orders. The theoretical developments in Sufism from the thirteenth century onward were shaped by the work of Ibn ʿArabī and his interpreters. The complex and esoteric nature of this school of Ṣūfī thought, however, placed it far beyond the reach of most Muslims. It was the ritual exercises of the orders that helped fill the gap and minister to the immediate spiritual needs of the faithful. Thus Sufism came to represent, for many, not abstruse theory but concrete practice that was accessible to all.

The emphasis on *dhikr* and *samāʿ* has helped to blur the distinction in popular Sufism between mystical experience that is attained after serious spiritual training and experience that is self-induced. Unsophisticated sessions of *dhikr* and *samāʿ*, to this day, often consist of self-hypnosis, hysteria, drug-induced states, and other violent emotions that pass for mystical experience. Despite accusations of vulgarization, *dhikr* and *samāʿ* remain important emotional outlets in the Muslim community and are unique sociological events during which various levels of society find themselves interacting on an equal footing. And in the hands of spiritual adepts, *dhikr* and *samāʿ* remain potent tools for creating an ambiance in which to attain heightened levels of religious experience.

The widespread interest in *dhikr* and *samāʿ* among the Muslim faithful has resulted in increased membership in the Ṣūfī fraternities. These new members, however, should more properly be called affiliates. They perhaps take some training from a shaykh; their primary vehicle for contact with the group, however, is attendance at periodic sessions of *dhikr* and *samāʿ*. Otherwise they lead the normal life of a layman or woman. In parts of the Islamic world today, membership in one Ṣūfī order or another has become for many a social obligation, even though those so affiliated have little interest in, or understanding of mysticism.

Particular orders became associated with different strata of society, geographical regions, and guilds. The Suhrawardīyah, for example, were extremely influential in court circles in thirteenth-century Delhi, while orders such as the Bektāshīyah and Khalwatīyah in Turkey had a more popular appeal. The identification of order with social group became so complete that one could be said to be born into a particular fraternity. This did not, however, prevent an individual's eventual shift from one order to another.

The orders: individual characteristics. The role of the shaykh and the ritual exercises of *dhikr* and *samāʿ* are integral elements in almost all of the Ṣūfī orders. The distinctive personalities of the fraternities, however, are as significant as their similar structures and practices. The contrasts are often striking. In Anatolia, for example, the Mawlawīyah (or Mevleviye) and the Bektāshīyah represent opposite ends of the spectrum.

Mawlawīyah and Bektāshīyah. The Mawlawīyah trace their *silsilah* to the mystic and poet Jalāl al-Dīn Rūmī. Rūmī himself, however, did not establish a formal *ṭarīqah* during his lifetime; rather, it was his son, Sulṭān Walad, who took upon himself the task of organizing the order. The Mawlawīyah are known for their aesthetic sophistication, both in ritual practice and in mystical poetry. The order's particular identity is derived, of course, from Rūmī's *Mathnavī* and the *Divāni Shams-i Tabrīzī.*

Perhaps the most famous aspect of the Mawlawīyah is its ritual *samāʿ*, an exquisite combination of music, poetry, and whirling dance (hence their name in the West, "Whirling Dervishes"). It is hard to capture in words the refinement of the choreography. The rhythmic, turning movements of the adepts are mesmerizing and executed with a subtle grace and precision equal to the best of European classical dance. The serene faces of the Ṣūfīs, moreover, reflect the depth of the spiritual rapture achieved by the practitioners.

In contrast, the Bektāshīyah takes its name from a shadowy figure, Ḥajjī Bektāsh of Khorasan (d. 1337?). At first the group was loosely organized, but by the fifteenth century it had developed a highly centralized structure. The Bektāshīyah are noted for their syncretism; the rituals and beliefs of the order represent an amalgam of Shiism, Byzantine Christianity, esoteric cults, and the like. By the end of the sixteenth century, the Bektāshīyah had become associated with the Janissary corps, an elite military unit of slave-soldiers established by the Ottoman sultan Murād I (1360–1389). Despite the heterodox practices of the Bektāshīyah, their identification with the powerful and much-feared Janissaries provided them with security from persecution by the orthodox religious authorities. Where the Mawlawīyah attracted a more educated elite, the Bektāshīyah appealed to the less literate masses who were fascinated with the magic-like rituals and political power.

Suhrawardīyah and Rifāʿīyah. In Iraq, as well, there arose two fraternities with diametrically opposed interpretations of religious experience. The genealogy of the Suhrawardīyah begins with Abū al-Najīb al-Suhrawardī (d. 1168), who was a disciple of Aḥmad al-Ghazālī. Abū Najīb is the author of an important rulebook for novices, *Kitāb ādāb al-muridīn* (Book of the manners of the disciples). The text evinces Abū Najīb's long experience as a director; his rules are strict and comprehensive, yet attuned to the human frailties of the young and untutored.

The fraternity that bears the name Suhrawardi was founded by Abū al- Najīb's nephew, Shihāb al-Dīn Abū Ḥafṣ ʿUmar al-Suhrawardī (d. 1234). Shihāb al-Dīn, the author of the extremely influential work, *ʿAwārif al-maʿarif* (Masters of mystical insights), is remembered in Ṣūfī circles as a great teacher. Teaching, in fact, became a characteristic note of the fraternity. The Suhrawardīyah made significant inroads into the Indian subcontinent, where its ranks included such important figures as Bahāʾ al-Dīn Zakarīyā of Multan (d. 1268).

While the ethos of the Suhrawardīyah is characterized by serious training in the classical Ṣūfī tradition, the Rifāʿīyah or "Howling Dervishes" focus primarily on dramatic ritual. This fraternity springs from the marshlands of southern Iraq, where its founder, Aḥmad ibn ʿAli al-Rifāʿī (d. 1182), spent most of his life. Contemporary observers describe vividly the bizarre practices engaged in by members of the fraternity: fire-eating; piercing ears, hands, necks, and penises with iron rings; biting heads off live snakes, and so forth. Clearly the appeal of the Rifāʿīyah is primarily emotional.

Shādhilīyah. A fine example of a fraternity that responded to the religious needs of the larger community while cultivating a solid intellectual base in mystical theory is the Shādhilīyah. Abū al-Ḥasan al-Shādhilī (d. 1258) began his religious career at Tunis, where he was well known as a preacher. It was there that he founded his order in 1227. Impelled by a vision, he traveled eastward and settled eventually in Egypt, where the Shādhilīyah order came to flourish.

The most famous of the early Shādhilī shaykhs is not the founder but the third leader of the group, Ibn ʿAṭāʾ Allāh (d. 1309). He was born in Alexandria and spent his early years in the study of *ḥadīth* and the law. Ibn ʿAṭāʾ Allāh's training in the traditional religious sciences made him wary of any involvement with Sufism. His attitude eventually mellowed, and for twelve years he placed himself under the direction of the second shaykh of the order, Abū al-ʿAbbās al-Mursī (d. 1287), whom he eventually succeeded.

Ibn ʿAṭāʾ Allāh's writings epitomize the spirit of the Shādhilīyah order. On one hand his work is very much in the intellectual tradition of the Ibn ʿArabī school. For example his book, *Laṭāʾif al-minan* (Subtle graces), written in defense of the fraternity and its practices, emphasizes the exalted role of the shaykh as *walī* and *quṭb.* On the other hand, the true genius of Ibn ʿAṭāʾ Allāh is most evident in his collected aphorisms, the *Ḥikam* (Maxims). They remain to this day one of the most popular Ṣūfī texts in the Islamic world. Combining the erudition of the scholar with the vibrant, persuasive language of the enthusiast, Ibn ʿAṭāʾ Allāh succeeds in communicating complex ideas in a way that is accessible to a wide range of individuals. Like the *Munājāt* of ʿAbd Allāh Anṣarī, the *Ḥikam* of Ibn ʿAṭāʾ Allāh must be savored time and time again, for their richness seems almost inexhaustable.

In the same way that Ibn ʿAṭāʾ Allāh, through his writings, made the Sufism of the orders more accessible to larger numbers of Muslims, his fraternity as a whole adopted a structural form more in tune with the lives of the laity. Whereas some brotherhoods insisted on the abandonment of one's profession and even of family life, the Shādhilīyah allowed its members to remain involved in the secular world. In this respect, they were precursors of a similar development in the Christian West, when, in the sixteenth century, Ignatius Loyola founded the Society of Jesus, or Jesuits, whose members contrary to traditional monastic structures, were intent on fostering *contemplatio in actione,* contemplation while remaining fully involved in the secular world. Ibn ʿAṭāʾ

Allāh's *Ḥikam* has a place of honor in Islamic spirituality equal to that of Loyola's *Spiritual Exercises* in Christianity.

There is not sufficient space to describe even briefly all of the great *ṭarīqahs* that have become part of mainstream Sufism since the thirteenth century. The Qādirīyah, whose eponymous founder, ʿAbd al-Qādir Jīlāni (d. 1116), is perhaps the most widely revered saint in all of Islam; the Naqshbandīyah, whose stern Sunnī spirit, disseminated in Central Asia and the Indian subcontinent, has spawned political movements and great poets such as Mīr Dard (d. 1785); the music-loving Chishtīyah, Kubrawīyah, and so forth—all have played pivotal roles in the formation of Islamic religious life.

Decline of the orders. The nineteenth and twentieth centuries, however, have not been kind to Sufism, especially the Sufism of the orders. A number of factors contributed to the decline: the general secularization of world culture; colonialism, with its concomitant critique of Islamic religion and society; the response of Islamic modernism; and the rise of Islamic fundamentalism.

The changing political climate had profound effects on the Ṣūfī orders. In Turkey, for example, they were abolished by Mustafa Kemal Atatürk in 1925 because they represented to him all that was corrupt and backward about Islam. Atatürk was in the process of transforming Turkey into a modern nation state from the rubble of the Ottoman empire. The traditional power of the Ṣūfī shaykhs and orders was incompatible with nationalism; the orders, therefore, were eliminated as public institutions.

At times, however, the orders were not victims of political change but its instigators. The Tijānīyah of West Africa and the Sanūsīyah of North Africa are prime examples. The Tijānīyah were militant revivalists. They fought bravely against the French in West Africa and eventually established a kingdom of their own during the latter part of the nineteenth century.

The Sanūsīyah were similarly fundamentalist and militant. For decades they were at odds with Italian colonial power in North Africa. As a counterbalance they sided with the British who eventually invested the shaykh of the Sanūsīyah with authority in the region. The transformation of the shaykh into king of Libya and the accompanying solidification of political power eventually led to the decline of the Sanūsīyah as a Ṣūfī movement.

Despite the fact that many nineteenth- and twentieth-century Ṣūfī groups reflected fundamentalist tendencies, they still became the objects of attack by the ultra-orthodox, of whom the Wahhābīyah of Saudi Arabia are but one example. Among such groups, any ritual practice not explicitly sanctioned by religious law is anathema. The very premise on which Sufism is based, namely union with God, is rejected as un-Islamic. One sees today in many of the most vibrant Islamic revivalist movements a similar tendency to espouse the most puritanical forms of literalist religion. In such a world Sufism has little place.

In the Indian subcontinent, the involvement of many hereditary pirs (i.e., shaykhs) with Sufism has been based, in the modern period, more on family status, wealth, and influence than on any serious interest in mysticism. A backlash was inevitable. Muhammad Iqbal, one of the fathers of modern Muslim intellectual life in the subcontinent, rejected Sufism because of the corruption he perceived. He also reacted strongly against the Ṣūfī doctrine of *waḥdat al-wujūd*, because it entailed the negation of the self: If the self is nonexistent, why confront the problems of human existence? Nevertheless, his *Reconstruction of Religious Thought in Islam*, published in 1930, reflects Ṣūfī emphases on interiority, although his goal was to reinterpret Islam in humanistic terms that harmonized the spiritual and material realms of existence.

Attacks on Sufism are not new; they have occurred throughout the history of the tradition. The dramatic decline of Sufism in the modern period, however, is due as much to external as to internal forces. The intimate contacts between the Islamic world and the European West resulted in virulent critiques of Islamic religious practice, especially devotionalism. Muslim reactions were varied: Some accepted the critique and mimicked Western secular societies (Atatürk's Turkey, for example); some reasserted their identity by returning to what was believed to be true Islam, devoid of Ṣūfī accretions (the Wahhābīyah, for example); others, such as the Muslim modernist Muhammad ʿAbduh and his successors, proposed various more moderate plans for the adaptation of Muslim society to the demands of the modern world.

All of these responses, however, possessed anti-Ṣūfī elements, for most rejected Ṣūfī ritual practice and devotionalism as either non-Muslim or antimodern. Moreover, the power of the Ṣūfī shaykhs over masses of the faithful was seen by most to be counterproductive to modernization and to the development of a functioning secular state, for the shaykhs were often perceived as proponents of superstition, religious emotionalism, and outmoded power structures.

Mysticism in modern Islam is not an arid wasteland but rather more like a fallow field. There have been important modern teaching shaykhs such as Aḥmad al-ʿAlawī (d. 1934), whose influence is still felt in North Africa. Moreover, the popular piety of Sufism still flourishes in many parts of the Islamic world, including North Africa, Egypt, the Indian subcontinent, and Indonesia. The great tradition of vernacular poetry, established by master artists such as the Turkish mystic Yunus Emre (d. 1321), continues to produce a rich literature. Central Asia, the Indian subcontinent, Africa, Indonesia—every corner of the Islamic world has produced its local poet-saints.

Doubtless Sufism has become increasingly more identified with popular ritual practice than with formal spiritual training. The transformation of Sufism into a mass movement could not help but lead to a certain vulgarization. There continue to arise, nevertheless, individual masters whose commitment to the path is reminiscent of the great figures of the classical period. Classical Ṣūfī literature survives because it still has the ability to touch the spirits of modern men and women. It is in this continued interaction between shaykh and *murīd* that hope for the future of Sufism resides.

SEE ALSO Darwīsh; Dhikr; Folk Religion, article on Folk Islam; Ghazālī, Abū Ḥāmid al-; Ḥallāj, al-; Ibn al-ʿArabī; Madrasah; Mawlid; Miʿrāj; Nubūwah; Nūr Muḥammad; Rūmī, Jalāl al-Dīn; Samāʿ; Ṣuḥbah; Ṭarīqah; Walāyah.

BIBLIOGRAPHY

By far the best introduction to Sufism in English is Annemarie Schimmel's *Mystical Dimensions of Islam* (Chapel Hill, N.C., 1975). Other introductory texts of interest are A. J. Arberry's *Sufism: An Account of the Mystics of Islam* (1950; reprint, London, 1979) and Reynold A. Nicholson's *The Mystics of Islam* (1914; reprint, London, 1963). The most astute treatment of the development of early Sufism, especially its relationship to Qur'ānic exegesis, is Paul Nwyia's *Exégèse coranique et language mystique* (Beirut, 1970).

There are a number of monographs dealing with one or other of the early Ṣūfī ascetics. Margaret Smith's two works, *Rābiʿa the Mystic and Her Fellow-Saints in Islam* (Cambridge, 1928) and *An Early Mystic of Baghdad: A Study of the Life and Teaching of Ḥārith b. Asad Al-Muḥāsibi, A. D. 781–A. D. 857* (1935, reprint, New York, 1973), are both excellent, as well as Nicholson's study of Abū Saʿīd ibn Abī al-Khayr in *Studies in Islamic Mysticism* (1921; reprint, Cambridge, 1976).

There are two excellent English translations of Ṣūfī manuals, Nicholson's translation of al-Hujwīrī's *Kashf al-Maḥjūb: The Oldest Persian Treatise on Sufism,* 2d ed. (London, 1936), and Arberry's translation of al-Kalābādhī's *Kitāb al-taʿarruf* under the title *The Doctrine of the Sufis* (Cambridge, 1935). Several chapters of Seyyed Hossein Nasr's *Ṣufi Essays* (London, 1972) deal with stations and states and the master-disciple relationship.

No study of the ecstatics in Sufism is complete without Louis Massignon's extraordinary work on al-Ḥallāj, translated into English by Herbert Mason as *The Passion of Al-Ḥallāj: Mystic and Martyr of Islam,* 4 vols. (Princeton, N. J., 1982). Carl W. Ernst's *Words of Ecstasy in Sufism* (Albany, 1984) is extremely helpful as well. Reynold A. Nicholson's *The Idea of Personality in Sufism* (1964; reprint, Lahore, 1970) is a lucid exploration of the psychology of ecstatic utterances.

There is an excellent translation by Wheeler Thackston of Anṣarī's *Munājāt* in *The Book of Wisdom and Intimate Conversations,* translated and edited by Wheeler Thackston and Victor Danner (New York, 1978). The premier scholar of Anṣarī is Serge de Laugier de Beaurecueil, whose bibliography of Anṣarī provides much useful information and some fine translations: *Khwādja ʿAbdullāh Anṣarī, 396–481 H./ 1006–1089: Mystique Ḥanbalite* (Beirut, 1965).

There are a number of fine translations of ʿAṭṭār's *mathnavīs*: *The Ilāhī-nāma or Book of God,* translated by J. A. Boyle (Manchester, 1976); *Le livre de l'épreuve (Musībatnāma),* translated by Isabelle de Gastines (Paris, 1981); and *The Conference of the Birds,* translated by Afkham Darbandi and Dick Davis (London, 1984). The best comprehensive study of ʿAṭṭār and his work remains Helmut Ritter's *Das Meer der Seele* (Leiden, 1955).

Henry Corbin has written extensively on Islamic gnosticism, Islamic Neoplatonism, and Ibn ʿArabī. Works such as *Creative Imagination in the Ṣūfism of Ibn ʿArabī* (Princeton, N.J., 1969) demonstrate his extraordinary erudition and propose provocative syntheses that must be evaluated with care. A new translation of Ibn ʿArabī's *Fuṣūṣ al-ḥikam* by R. W. J. Austin under the title *The Bezels of Wisdom* (New York, 1980) is excellent. Toshihiko Izutsu's comparative study of Sufism and Taoism, *A Comparative Study of the Key Philosophical Concepts in Sufism and Taoism* (Tokyo, 1966), also serves as an excellent introduction to Ibn ʿArabī's thought. Finally, in his *Studies in Islamic Mysticism* (1921; reprint, Cambridge, 1976) Reynold A. Nicholson provides a very lucid analysis of the idea of the Perfect Human Being as it originated with Ibn ʿArabī and was later developed by al-Jīlī.

The best translations of Rūmī's work are by Reynold A. Nicholson, especially *The Mathnawi of Jalālu'ddin Rūmī,* 8 vols. (London, 1925–1971). Annemarie Schimmel's *The Triumphal Sun: A Study of the Works of Jalāloddin Rumi* (London, 1978) is a solid introduction to his writings, as is William C. Chittick's *The Sufi Path of Love: The Spiritual Teachings of Rumi* (Albany, N.Y., 1983). Schimmel's *As Through a Veil: Mystical Poetry in Islam* (New York, 1982) places Rūmī in the wider context of the poetic tradition in Sufism.

There are many studies of individual Ṣūfī orders. The best general work, however, is J. Spencer Trimingham's *The Sufi Orders in Islam* (New York, 1971). The role of the fraternities in the Indian subcontinent is extremely well presented in Annemarie Schimmel's *Islam in the Indian Subcontinent* (Leiden, 1980). An English translation by Victor Danner of Ibn ʿAṭā' Allāh's *Ḥikam* can be found in Thackston and Danner's *The Book of Wisdom and Intimate Conversations* (cited above). A superb French translation and commentary of the same text, together with a thorough analysis of the early development of the Sha-dhilīyah can be found in Paul Nwyia's *Ibn ʿAṭā'Allāh et la naissance de la confrérie šādilite* (Beirut, 1972). One of the more interesting treatments of a Ṣūfī in the modern period is Martin Lings's study of the life and writings of Shaykh Aḥmad al-ʿAlawī, *A Moslem Saint of the Twentieth Century,* 2d ed. (Berkeley, Calif., 1973).

PETER J. AWN (1987)

ṢUḤBAH (lit., "companionship"). In mystical parlance, *ṣuḥbah* can refer to (1) a mystic's return from seclusion (*ʿuzlah*) to human society; (2) the company of the spiritual mentor, which a new entrant to the mystical fold needs for spiritual training; and (3) social contact with all human beings. The value of *ṣuḥbah* was first to be appreciated when those near the Prophet became known as *ṣaḥābah* ("companions"), since they had the privilege of being in his company. Thereafter mystics looked upon the "company" of a superior mystic-master as a way to spiritual development. The spiritual guide (pir or shaykh) came to occupy a high position on account of his capacity to influence the thought and character of those who came near him.

Abu al-Ḥasan al-Hujwīrī (d. 1079) identified three types of companionship that he considered inseparable and interconnected: (1) companionship with God, the awareness of God's presence at all times, which controlled and determined every detail of external behavior; (2) companionship with one's own self, which dictated the avoidance in one's own company of all that was improper in the company of others and unbecoming in the presence of God; and (3) companionship with fellow creatures. Operating within such a comprehensive concept of *ṣuḥbah*, mystical writings include the totality of a mystic's life—prayers and penitence, travels, sojourns in hospices, dealing with fellow mystics, relations with kin and friends, methods of earning a livelihood, marriage or celibacy—as aspects of that person's *ṣuḥbah*. As such, the principles of *ṣuḥbah* came to determine mystical actions in all their details, and many brochures and treatises were written on the subject. Notable works include al-Junayd's *Taṣḥīḥ al-irādah* (The rectification of discipleship), Aḥmad ibn Khadrūyah Balkhī's *Al-riʿāyah bi-ḥuqūq Allāh* (The observance of what is due to God), and Muḥammad ibn ʿAlī Tirmidhī's *Ādāb al-murīdīn* (Rules of conduct for disciples). Al-Sulamī's *Kitāb ādāb al-ṣuḥbah* (Book on the rules of company), al-Qushayrī's *Risālah* (Epistle), al-Hujwīrī's *Kashf al-maḥjūb* (The unveiling of the veiled), and Abu al-Najīb Suhrawardī's *Ādāb al-murīdīn* neatly consolidate all the information available in earlier works.

In the initial stages of mystical development in Islam, the term *ṣuḥbah* was used in a limited sense to mean the company of the mystic teacher only; elaborate rules of residence and discipline were developed later. When Sufism came out of its first phase, designated by Reynold A. Nicholson as "the period of the Quietists," the value of companionship was emphasized and seclusion was considered of little significance in the building up of a spiritual personality. In mystical discipline, companionship and seclusion were paired as complements and supplements to each other. Shaykh Abū al-Ḥasan ibn Muḥammad al-Nūri (d. 907) remarked: "Beware of secluson for it is connected with Satan, and cleave to companionship for therein is the satisfaction of the merciful God." Among the eleven veils that have to be lifted before gnosis can be attained, Al-Hujwīrī considered companionship the ninth. Meticulous care in the performance of duties pertaining to *ṣuḥbah* could lift this veil and make gnosis possible.

Islamic mysticism, particularly before the organization of the Ṣūfī orders (*ṭuruq;* sg., *ṭarīqah*), considered travel an essential part of mystical discipline. The rules of *ṣuḥbah* therefore deal with both residents (Pers., *muqīmān*) and travelers (Pers., *musāfirān*). Regarding those who undertook travel as part of their spiritual training, rules were laid down about articles they took along, people with whom they could keep company, places where they could stay, and the way they had to conduct themselves while staying in a mosque, in a Ṣūfī center, or in an educational institution (*madrasah*). The main principle governing behavior in all these spheres was that a mystic did not forget God while involved in any of these activities and could utilize travel as a means for breaking undue attachment to material assets and family, for learning to live with complete resignation to the will of God, and for trying to develop a spirit of adjustment to different conditions of life and company.

Life within the Ṣūfī centers is similarly defined by elaborate rules of *ṣuḥbah*. Residents had to share responsibility for running the center; travelers were treated as guests for three days but after that they too were obliged to do some work to lighten the burden of the permanent residents. The Ṣūfī centers that provided facilities for *ṣuḥbah* were of different types: *khānagāhs* where separate accommodation was generally provided for all inmates; *jamāʿat-khānahs*, where all lived a communal life under one roof and slept on the ground; *zāwiyahs* and *dāʾirahs*, smaller institutions where persons of one affiliation lived in order to devote their time to meditation. Mystics following different masters laid down principles of *ṣuḥbah* according to the basic teachings of the order to which they belonged, but the *ʿAwārif al-maʿārif* of Shaykh Shihāb al-Dīn Suhrawardī (d. 1234) was generally accepted as the model on which *khānagāh* life could be organized and the basic objectives of *ṣuḥbah* achieved.

SEE ALSO Khānagāh.

BIBLIOGRAPHY

For a brief mention of *ṣuḥbah* in the larger context of Ṣūfī thought and practice, see Annemarie Schimmel's *Mystical Dimensions of Islam* (Chapel Hill, N.C., 1975). Al-Hujwīrī's discussion of *ṣuḥbah* can be found in *The Kashf al-Mahjúb, the Earliest Persian Treatise on Sufism*, translated by Reynold A. Nicholson, new ed. (1936; reprint, London, 1976), pp. 334–366. Abū al-Najīb Suhrawardī's *Kitāb ādāb al-murīdīn* has been translated in abridged form by Menahem Milson as *A Sufi Rule for Novices* (Cambridge, Mass., 1975). Important compendia of Ṣūfī practice available in Arabic include al-Qushayrī's *Al-risālah al-qushayrīyah* (Cairo, 1966), Shihāb al-Dīn Suhrawardī's *ʿAwārif al-maʿārif* (Beirut, 1966), and al-Sulamī's *Kitāb ādāb al-ṣuḥbah* (Jerusalem, 1954).

KHALIQ AHMAD NIZAMI (1987)

SUHRAWARDĪ, SHIHĀB AL-DĪN YAḤYĀ.

Shihāb al-Dīn Yaḥyā ibn Ḥabash ibn Amīrak Abū al-Futūḥ Suhrawardī (AH 549–587/1170–1208 CE) was born in a village near Zanjan, a northern Iranian city. He began his studies at an early age when he went to the city of Maragheh to study philosophy with Majd al-Dīn al-Jīlī, and then traveled to Iṣfahān, where he pursued his advanced studies in philosophy and *al-Baṣāʾir* (The observations) of ʿUmar ibn Salān al-Sāwī with Ẓāhir al-Dīn al-Fārsī.

Suhrawardī traveled to Anatolia and Syria, where he met Malik Ẓāhir, son of the famous Ṣalāḥ al-Dīn Ayyūbī, in Aleppo in 1200. Suhrawardī's openness to other religious traditions, especially Zoroastrianism, as well as his keen intelligence and esoteric orientation, antagonized the orthodox jurists at Malik Ẓāhir's court, who declared Suhrawardī to be a heretic. They asked Malik Ẓāhir to put Suhrawardī to death, and when he refused they signed a petition and sent it to Ṣalāḥ al-Dīn Ayyūbī, who ordered his son to have Suhrawardī killed. Malik Ẓāhir reluctantly carried out his father's order and Suhrawardī was killed in 1208. For this reason he has received the title *al-Maqtūl* (the Martyr).

Not much is known about Suhrawardī. It is said that he lived somewhat of a monastic life and shied away from people. One day he would dress in court style and the very next day as a wandering dervish. Suhrawardī lived at a time when the influence and power of the rationalist theologians (Muʿtazilites) had been substantially curtailed by the more faith-based Ashʿarites. While the debate among the advocates of intellectual sciences continued, philosophical and theological schools were also challenged by the mystics of Islam, the Ṣūfīs. At the center of these controversies stood Avicenna (Ibn Sīnā) with his powerful philosophical paradigm. Avicenna's philosophy by Suhrawardī's time had lent itself to different interpretations, and this brought about a number of schools that were essentially Avicennian, though each emphasized different aspects of his ideas.

First, there was the purely Aristotelian aspect of Avicenna's philosophy. Next, there were exponents of theology (*kalām*) who found Avicenna's logic and metaphysics to be a useful means of analysis and therefore adopted them. Finally, there was the mystical aspect of Avicenna, which received less attention than his rationalistic writings. In these types of writings, such as *Ḥay ibn Yaqẓān* and the final chapter of the *Ishārāt*, the mystical and Neoplatonic aspects of Avicenna's philosophy are most apparent. Suhrawardī was well aware of such writings. For example, in his *al-Ghurba al-gharbiyah* (The occidental exile) he continues Avicenna's story using some of the same metaphors.

Suhrawardī's project was to bring about a rapprochement between rationalism, mysticism, and intellectual intuition within one single philosophical paradigm and to bridge the deep division between different schools in the Islamic intellectual tradition. He called his school of thought *al-ḥikmah al-ilahiyyah* (transcendental philosophy) or *Ḥikmat al-ishrāq* (philosophy of illumination), and it is for this reason he has been called "Shaykh al-ishrāq" (Master of Illumination). Suhrawardī argued that the application of reason as a means of discovering the truth is limited, and that one has to rely on an experiential wisdom to comprehend the truth completely. In a mystical state, Suhrawardī compared his findings through logic and discursive reasoning to his mystical vision; he accepted those that corresponded with one another, and others he rejected. For Suhrawardī, reason, mystical experience, and intellectual intuition are ultimately reconcilable.

Suhrawardī's writings are diverse (i.e., Peripatetic, mystical, and illuminationist [*ishrāqī*]). They include his four large treatises that are of doctrinal nature: *al-Talwiḥāt* (The book of intimation), *al-Muqawamāt* (The book of opposites), *al-Muṭāraḥāt* (The book of conversations), and finally *Ḥikmat al-ishrāq* (The philosophy of illumination), which is his magnum opus. The first three of these works are written in the tradition of the Peripatetics, with commentaries and criticism of certain Aristotelian concepts, such as the epistemic function of definition.

There are shorter works, some of them written in Arabic and some in Persian. These works are also of a doctrinal nature and should be regarded as further explanations of the larger doctrinal treatises. They are: *Hayākil al-nūr* (Luminous bodies), *Alwāḥ ʿimādiyah* (Tablets of ʿImād al-Dīn), *Partaw nāmah* (Treatise on illumination), *Iʿtiqād fī -al-ḥukamāʾ* (On the faith of the hakims), *al-Lamaḥāt* (The flashes of light), *Yazdān shinākht* (Knowledge of the divine), and *Bustān al-qulūb* (The garden of the heart).

Suhrawardī wrote a number of treatises of an esoteric nature in Persian. These initiatory narratives contain highly symbolic language and incorporate Zoroastrian and Hermetic symbols, as well as Islamic ones. These treatises include: *ʿAql-i surkh* (Red intellect), *Āwāz-i par-i Jibrāil* (Chant of the wing of Gabriel), *Qiṣṣat al-ghurba al-gharbiyah* (Story of the occidental exile), *Lughat-i murān* (Language of the termites), *Risālah fī ḥalāt al-ṭufūliyyah* (Treatise on the state of childhood), *Rūzī bā jamāʿat-i Ṣufiyān* (A Day among the Ṣūfīs), *Ṣafir-i simūrg* (The Sound of the griffin), *Risālah fi -al-miʿrāj* (Treatise on the nocturnal ascent), and *Partaw nāmah* (Treatise on illumination). These treatises are intended to demonstrate the journey of the soul toward unity with God and the inherent yearning of humans toward gnosis (*maʿrifah*).

There are also a number of treatises of a philosophic and initiatic nature. These include his translation of *Risālat al-ṭaīr* (Treatise of the birds) of Avicenna and the commentary in Persian on Avicenna's *Ishārāt wa-al-tanbihāt*. There is also his treatise *Risālah fī ḥaqīqat al-ʿishq* (Treatise on the reality of love), which is based on Avicenna's *Risālah fi-al-ʿishq* (Treatise on love) and his commentaries on verses of the *Qurʾān* and the *ḥadīth*. Also, it is said that Suhrawardī may have written a commentary upon the *Fuṣūṣ* of al-Fārābi, which has been lost. Finally, there is the category of his liturgical writings, *al-Waridāt wa-al-taqdisāt* (Invocations and prayers), which consists of prayers, invocations, and litanies.

Bibliography

For more information concerning Suhrawardī's life, see Ibn Abī ʿUṣaybiʿāh, *ʿUyūn al-anbāʾ fī ṭabaqāt al-aṭibbāʾ*, edited by August Muller (Konigsberg, Germany, 1884); Ibn Khallikān, *Wafayāt al-a ʿyān*, edited by I. ʿAbbās (Beirut, 1965); Shams al-Dīn Shahrazūrī, *Nuzhat al-arwāḥ wa Rawḍat al-afrāḥ fī taʾrīkh al-ḥukamā wa-al-falāsifah*, edited by Khurshīd Aḥmad, vol. 2 (Hyderabad, India, 1976); and Mehdi Amin Razavi, *Suhrawardi and the School of Illumination* (London, 1993).

For the major texts of Suhrawardī's writing, see *Opera Metaphysica et Mystica*, vols. 1 and 2, edited with an introduction by Henry Corbin (Istanbul, 1945 and 1954). *Opera Metaphysi-*

ca et Mystica, vol. 3, edited with an introduction by S. H. Nasr (Istanbul, 1970). See also S. H. Nasr, "Suhrawardī: The Master of Illumination, Gnostic and Martyr," translated by William Chittick, *Journal of the Regional Cultural Institute* 2 (1969), pp. 209-225. S. H. Nasr, *Three Muslim Sages: Avicenna, Suhrawardī, Ibn ʿArabī* (Cambridge, Mass., 1964), pp. 52–82; S. H. Nasr, "Shihāb al-Dīn Suhrawardī al-Maqtul," in *A History of Muslim Philosophy,* edited by M. M. Sharif (Wiesbaden, Germany, 1963), pp. 372–398. For Suhrawardī's political orientation, see Hossein Zi'ai, "The Source and Nature of Political Authority in Suhrawardī's Philosophy of Illumination" in *The Political Aspects of Islamic Philosophy: Essays in Honor of Muhsin S. Mahdi,* edited by Charles E. Butterworth (Cambridge, Mass., 1992), pp. 304–344; and Jaʿfar Sajjādī, *Shihāb al-Dīn Suhrawardī wa sayrī dar falsafah-yi ishrāq* (Tehran, 1984).

MEHDI AMINRAZAVI (2005)

SUICIDE. The topic of religiously motivated suicide is a complex one. Several of the major religious traditions reject suicide as a religiously justifiable act but commend martyrdom; among them are Judaism, Christianity, and Islam. These religions distinguish between actively willing to end one's life in suicide and passively accepting one's death as the divine will by means of martyrdom at the hands of another. Nonetheless, the actions of some of the early Christian martyrs and the deaths of the Jews at Masada in 74 CE blur this distinction.

In contrast to religiously motivated suicide one may speak of heroic and altruistic suicide, the act of a person who decides that he or she has an ethical responsibility to die for the sake of community or honor. One must also differentiate between religiously motivated suicide and suicide that may be virtually forced upon an individual by the norms of society and may constitute either a duty or a punishment. One thinks of *satī,* widow burning in India, and of *seppuku,* self-disembowelment, when it occurred as a punishment in Japan. In these cases too, however, no simple distinction holds true. *Satī* became an accepted practice within medieval Hinduism, upheld by the brahmans, and accounts indicate that even into modern times it was often a voluntary practice. By her self-sacrifice the widow both achieved an honored status for herself and atoned for the sins and misdeeds of herself and her husband. *Seppuku* was often the voluntary last act of a defeated warrior who chose to demonstrate both his fealty to his lord and his mastery over himself.

Like the major Western traditions, both Buddhism and Confucianism condemn suicide, but there are examples of self-immolation by Buddhist monks and of the seeking of honorable death by Confucian gentlemen. In contrast to these traditions, Jainism regards favorably the practice of *sallekhana,* by which a Jain monk or layperson at the end of his lifetime or at the onset of serious illness attains death by gradual starvation.

These few examples demonstrate the complexity of the topic of religiously motivated suicide and the difficulty in distinguishing it from martyrdom or sacrifice, on the one hand, and from heroic or altruistic suicide, on the other. In addition, the occurrence in 1978 of the mass suicides at Jonestown, Guyana, raises the question of the relation between religious motivations for suicide and general fear of persecution, combined with mass paranoia. This question applies equally well to the mass suicide of Jews faced with persecution in York, England, in 1190 and to the mass suicides of Old Believers in Russia in the late seventeenth century.

On the whole, what may be termed religiously motivated suicides constitute but a small proportion of the total number of suicides. In his classic work *Le suicide,* Émile Durkheim discussed the social causes for egoistic, altruistic, and anomic suicides. His work and that of many other scholars demonstrate that suicide has most often occurred for reasons other than religious ones. These include the desire to avoid shame, to effect revenge, to demonstrate one's disappointment in love, and to escape senility and the infirmities of old age. Suicide as a means of avoiding shame and upholding one's honor was considered a creditable act in societies as different as those on the Melanesian island of Tikopia, among the Plains and Kwakiutl Indians of North America, and in ancient Rome.

Scholars have argued that the incidence of and attitude toward suicide are largely dependent on the individual's and society's view of the afterlife. Where death is perceived as a happy existence, scholars such as Jacques Choron believe, there is an inducement to suicide. In the first known document that apparently reflects on suicide, the Egyptian text entitled *The Dialogue of a Misanthrope with His Own Soul,* death is seen as attractive because it will lead to another and better existence. The tendency toward suicide is strengthened when suicide is regarded either as a neutral act or as one worthy of reward. Suicide rates also increase when this life is regarded as no longer acceptable or worthwhile. For example, Jim Jones, the founder of the Peoples' Temple, urged his followers in Guyana to commit suicide in order to enter directly into a new and better world, where they would be free of persecution and would enjoy the rewards of the elect. In the Jonestown community, suicide on a mass scale was appreciated as a religiously justifiable act that would be rewarded in the afterlife.

ANCIENT GREEK AND ROMAN CIVILIZATION. While the ancient Greek writers and philosophers did not consider suicide an action that would lead to a better existence, they did see it as an appropriate response to certain circumstances. The fact that Jocasta, the mother of Oedipus, chose to commit suicide upon learning of her incestuous relationship with her son was understood and appreciated by the ancients as an appropriate response to a disastrous situation. Heroic suicide in the face of a superior enemy and the choice of death to avoid dishonor or the agony of a lengthy terminal illness were accepted as justifiable actions. Through the voice of Socrates, Plato in his *Phaedo* did much to form the classical attitude toward suicide. Socrates himself chose to drink the hemlock, but he also affirmed the Orphic notions that humans are placed in a prison from which they may not release themselves and that they are a possession of the gods. The decision to commit suicide is thus an act against the gods, depriving them of their prerogative to end or to sustain human life. The key word for both Plato and Socrates is *necessity.* A person may appropriately end his life only when the gods send the necessity to do so upon him, as in fact they did to Socrates. Plato's disciple, Aristotle, argued even more strongly against suicide. He regarded it as an offense against the state, since by such an act a person fails to perform his obligations as a citizen. Thus it became a social outrage—a view that has continued to dominate thought in the West until the most recent times.

Whereas the Pythagoreans and Epicureans opposed suicide, the Stoics regarded it favorably under certain circumstances. The Stoic was obliged to make a decision that properly addressed the demands of the situation; at times the decision might be to commit suicide. Both Zeno and his successor, Cleanthes, are reported to have done so.

Heroic suicide and suicide to avoid dishonor or suffering became frequent within the society of the Roman empire. Seneca, in particular, moved beyond the insistence on a divine call or necessity for suicide to the assertion that suicide at the appropriate time is a basic individual right. For Seneca, the central issue was freedom, and he affirmed that the divine had offered humankind a number of exits from life; he himself chose to exercise the right to suicide. His successor, Epictetus, placed more limits on suicide, stressing again the belief that one must wait for the divine command before acting: The suffering that is a normal part of daily life for much of humanity does not of itself constitute a sufficient reason for suicide—although exceptional pain and suffering offer justifiable cause. For Epictetus, Socrates was the best model and guide in deciding when one might legitimately choose to end one's life.

JUDAISM. Whereas suicide was at the very least tolerated, and often applauded, among the ancient Greeks and Romans, the Hebrew people disapproved of it. Judaism draws a clear distinction between suicide, which it defines as self-murder, and martyrdom, which it defines as death on behalf of one's faith and religious convictions. Nonetheless, the Hebrew scriptures, which contain few references to dying by one's own hand, do describe several instances of heroic suicide. The king Abimelech, gravely wounded by a woman, called upon his armor-bearer to kill him (*Jgs.* 9:52–54). Although he did not literally kill himself, his command to his aide may be regarded as effecting what he could not perform himself, so that he might not die in dishonor. The death of Samson (*Jgs.* 16:28–31) may certainly be judged a heroic suicide, since by his act he brought about the demise of a large number of the enemy Philistines. The gravely injured Saul fell upon his own sword in order to avoid a disgraceful death at the hands of his enemies (*1 Sm.* 31:4), and his armor-bearer, who had failed his master's request to kill him, then fell upon his own sword. The death of Ahithophel, the counselor to David and then to David's son Absalom, would appear to be a suicide motivated by disgrace. When Absalom refused to follow the advice Ahithophel gave him regarding his battle with David, Ahithophel returned home, set his affairs in order, and hanged himself (*2 Sm.* 17:23). The last suicide recorded in the Hebrew scriptures, the death of the king Zimri, occurred because of the loss of a decisive battle (*1 Kgs.* 16:18).

Although Hebrew scriptures do not explicitly forbid suicide, the Judaic tradition came to prohibit it, partly in the belief that God alone gives life and takes it away, and partly on the basis of the sixth commandment, which forbids unjustified homicide. However, rabbinic law regards persons committing suicide as most frequently being of unsound mind and thus not responsible for their actions. Under these circumstances, they may still receive normal Jewish burial rites. Furthermore, suicides committed under duress, as for example to avoid murder, idolatry, or adultery, were considered blameless and indeed even praiseworthy. The mass suicide at Masada in 74 CE and other mass suicides in Europe during the Middle Ages were considered in this light.

Concerning Masada, the historian Josephus Flavius recounts, on the basis of the report of a few survivors, that on the eve of the Roman assault on that hill the leader of the vastly outnumbered Jewish resistance, Elʿazar ben Yaʾir, called the community together and reminded them of their vow not to become the slaves of the Romans. That night many of the soldiers killed their families and committed suicide. Others drew lots to decide who would kill his fellows and then die by his own hand. It is impossible to say how many of the more than nine hundred defenders allowed themselves to be killed and how many ended their lives by suicide. In spite of the Jewish prohibition against suicide, Masada came to be regarded as a heroic sacrifice, and it remains a living symbol of a people's response to oppression.

Although accounts of individual suicide within Judaism are rare, there are examples of mass suicides during times of persecution. During the First Crusade, in 1096, Jews who had obtained sanctuary in the bishop's castle at Worms chose mass suicide over baptism; similar instances of suicide to avoid baptism occurred in various Rhineland towns, such as Mayence, and in York, England, where in 1190 some 150 Jews set fire to the building in which they had sought safety and then consigned themselves to the flames. Yet other instances of mass suicide occurred during the Black Death, when popular superstition blamed the outbreak of the plague on the Jews. Although abuse and persecution were certainly major motivating factors during the periods of the Crusades and the Black Death, these mass or multiple suicides appear to have arisen from a deep religious desire to remain true to the faith. They point again to the difficulty in distinguishing between, on the one hand, suicides motivated by fear of persecution and, on the other, suicides motivated by religious convictions and ideals, deaths that in the latter case the tradition judges to be acts of martyrdom. Certainly the deaths at Masada must be regarded as both faithful obedience to religious affiliation and identity and the culmination of a desire to give the Jews' enemies a hollow victory.

Christianity. Christianity repudiates suicide on much the same biblical grounds as does Judaism. The only suicide recorded in the New Testament is that of Jesus' betrayer, Judas Iscariot; it is described in such a way as to indicate that it was a sign of repentance for his deed (*Mt.* 27:3–5). The church father Tertullian referred even to Jesus' death as voluntary—a description approximating that of suicide, since clearly a divine being controls his own life. In his book *Conversion* (1962), Arthur Darby Nock points to the "theatricality" present in some of the actions of the early martyrs, as in "the frequent tendency of Christians in times of persecution to force themselves on the notice of the magistrates by tearing down images or by other demonstrations" (p. 197). Bishop Ignatius of Antioch, writing to his fellow Christians in Rome, pleaded that they do nothing to hinder his martyrdom but allow him to be consumed entirely by the beasts. But whereas Tertullian asserted that only martyrs would reach paradise before the Parousia, Clement of Alexandria sought to stem the tide of those rushing to martyrdom by differentiating between self-motivated suicide and genuine martyrdom for the faith.

In his *City of God,* which appeared in 428 CE, the church father Augustine wrote against suicide in a way that became determinative for the tradition. He discussed various situations in which a Christian might find himself or herself, and concluded that suicide is not a legitimate act even in such desperate circumstances as those of a virgin seeking to protect her virtue. Augustine argued that suicide is a form of homicide, and thus prohibited by the sixth commandment; that a suicide committed in order to avoid sin is in reality the commission of a greater sin to avoid a lesser; and that one who commits suicide forfeits the possibility of repentance. Subsequent church councils, as well as such eminent theologians as Thomas Aquinas in the thirteenth century, sided with Augustine. Suicide, in contrast to martyrdom, came to be regarded as both a sin and a crime. Dante placed suicides in the seventh circle of the inferno in his *Divine Comedy,* and popular opinion throughout Christian Europe regarded suicides in the same light as witches and warlocks. Indeed, their corpses were treated in a similar manner: Suicides were frequently buried at crossroads with stakes driven through their hearts to prevent their ghosts from causing harm. The last recorded instance of such a burial in England occurred in 1823, and the law mandating confiscation of the property of a convicted suicide remained on the books until 1870.

In spite of ecclesiastical censure, religious impulse did lead to suicides, sometimes on a mass scale. Some thirteenth-century Cathari or Albigensians may have chosen suicide by starvation. Even more dramatic are the accounts of the Old Believers *(raskol'niki)* in late-seventeenth-century Russia who chose death by fire over obedience to liturgical changes introduced by the archbishop Nikon, with the subsequent backing of the tsars. According to tradition, on several occasions one to two thousand people who had been besieged by government troops, as at Paleostrovskii monastery in 1688, locked themselves within chapels or monasteries and burned them to the ground, consigning their own bodies to the flames.

Although martyrdom as a testimony to one's faith continues to be honored within Christianity, suicide as an individual act undertaken for nonreligious motives is regarded as a sin, and until recently it was regarded as a crime unless done in ignorance of its implications or in a state of lunacy. Few Christian theologians and philosophers challenged this view. John Donne, who served as dean of Saint Paul's in London, was a notable exception. In his book *Biathanatos,* written in 1608 but not published until 1644, Donne challenged the Augustinian belief that suicides cannot repent; he argued that a totally negative attitude toward suicide places limitations on the mercy and charity of God. New attitudes toward suicide were subsequently expounded by a variety of philosophers such as David Hume, who argued that suicide is not a crime. However, although the Christian attitude toward suicide may now be characterized as more compassionate than during earlier periods, the act of suicide, in contrast to martyrdom, continues to be regarded as a serious sin.

Islam. Islam joined Judaism and Christianity in prohibiting suicide (*intiḥār*) while glorifying those who die the death of a martyr *(shahīd)* or witness to the faith. While scholars debate whether or not the Qurʾān itself specifically forbids suicide, they agree that the *ḥadīth,* the traditions that preserve the words of the Prophet on a wide variety of issues, prohibit suicide. According to these sources, Muḥammad proclaimed that a person who commits suicide will be denied Paradise and will spend his time in Hell repeating the deed by which he had ended his life. By the tradition's own standards, religiously motivated suicide is an impossibility, since the taking of one's own life is both a sin and a crime. Nonetheless, as with Judaism and Christianity, the line between suicide and martyrdom is not clear. Since it is believed that the Muslim martyr who dies in defense of the faith is rewarded with immediate entrance into Paradise, where he or she will enjoy great pleasures and rewards, it would not be surprising if some Muslims readily participated in battles even when badly outnumbered, in the hope that they might die while fighting.

Within Islam the Shīʿī sect emphasizes the self-sacrifice and suffering of its imams, the successors to Muḥammad. The death of Ḥusayn, the grandson of the Prophet, and the third imam, was regarded by his followers as an act of voluntary self-sacrifice that could be termed a religiously motivated death. Although he died on the battlefield, his death was subsequently interpreted as a goal he both desired and actively sought; the passion play enacted as the climax of ʿĀshūrāʾ (tenth of Muḥarram) depicts his death as actively willed. In a translation of this play (*Muhammedan Festivals,* edited by G. E. von Grunebaum, New York, 1951) Husayn says: "Dear Grandfather [Muḥammad], I abhor life; I would rather go visit my dear ones in the next world" (p. 92). Within Shiism, and the Ismāʿīlī sect, Ḥasan-i Sabbāḥ in the twelfth century formed the order of the Assassins, which was devoted to establishing its own religious and governmental autonomy, in part by killing both Crusaders and Sunnī Muslims. The death of a member of this order was regarded not as a suicide, even when his mission had been one almost certain to result in his death, but rather as a glorious martyrdom that would earn him both the veneration of society and the delights of Paradise. The tradition cites many accounts of a mother who rejoiced on hearing of the death of her son, only to put on mourning clothes when she learned subsequently that he had not died and thus had not attained the glorious state of martyrdom.

HINDUISM AND JAINISM. In discussing Judaism, Christianity, and Islam, this article has pointed to the close relationship between suicide and martyrdom and the difficulty frequently encountered in distinguishing between them. Regarding the religions of the East, the difficult issue is the relation between suicide and sacrifice. In Hinduism, the Brāhmaṇas laid the foundation for religiously motivated suicide by declaring that the fullest and most genuine sacrifice is that of the individual's self. The *Śatapatha Brāhmaṇa* outlines the procedure by which one renounces the world, forsaking one's belongings and departing into the forest. Certainly Hinduism affirms that suicide must be a thoughtful decision—as in the resolve of a person to end the sufferings of old age—or that it must be a religiously motivated act. One Upaniṣad condemns those who attempt suicide without having attained the necessary degree of enlightenment. The Dharmasūtras firmly prohibit any suicide other than one religiously motivated. In ancient and medieval Hinduism a number of methods of committing suicide were regarded favorably, such as drowning oneself in the Ganges, jumping from a cliff, burning oneself, burying oneself in snow, or starving oneself to death. Various places of pilgrimage, such as Prayāga (present-day Allahabad) or Banaras, were seen as particularly auspicious places for ending one's life.

Two types of suicide in Hinduism, very different in form and intention, are worthy of special examination. The first is the death by suicide of the enlightened person, the world renouncer. Such a person, in his or her quest for release from *saṃsāra,* has been devoted to increasingly difficult acts of penance and to a thorough study of the Upaniṣads. Once this person has attained the goal of freedom from all desires, he or she may begin the great journey in the direction of the northeast, consuming nothing other than air and water. According to the lawgiver Manu, a brahman might also follow this procedure when beginning to be overcome by a serious illness.

The second form of suicide in Hinduism that deserves special attention is *satī,* widow burning. It appears to have been a form of suicide motivated by both social and religious considerations. Although the custom is not unique to India, it nonetheless was practiced there most frequently and over the longest period of time. The practice may go back as far as the fourth century BCE, but it began to grow in popularity only after about 400 CE. According to Upendra Thakur in his study *The History of Suicide in India,* "*satī* in its latest forms was a mediaeval growth though it had its germs in ancient customs and rituals" (1963, p. 141). The practice of *satī* might take one of two forms. In one, *sahamaraṇa,* the woman ascended the funeral pyre and was burned alongside the corpse of her husband. In the second, *anumaraṇa,* when the wife learned that her husband had died and his body had already been cremated, she would ascend the pyre and die alongside his ashes, or with some belonging of his. Certainly, at least in some cases, *satī* was motivated by genuine feelings of grief and affection on the part of the widow. Although the practice remained voluntary, in some areas social pressure may have made *satī* more the rule than the exception. No doubt the practice also gained popularity because the life of a widow was both lonely and degrading. On the other hand, the blessing or curse of a woman on her way to perform *satī* was believed to be very powerful, and her act of sacrifice was believed to purify both herself and her husband. Thus, although the act of *satī* may not always have been religiously motivated, it did have its religious reward. The British, during their rule of India, made a determined effort to abolish the practice, finally outlawing it as homicide in 1829.

Perhaps the tradition that most explicitly condones religiously motivated suicide is Jainism. Following the teaching of their saint Mahavira, who lived in the sixth century BCE, the Jain monk and the Jain layperson lead, in differing degrees, a rigorously ascetic life in order to attain liberation and to free the soul from karma. Members of the laity as well as monks are encouraged to practice *sallekhanā* (austere penance), in order to attain a holy death through meditation. Jains believe it is their duty to prevent disease or the infirmities of old age from undermining the spiritual progress they have attained through asceticism and meditation. Jainism prescribes strict rules for when *sallekhanā* is appropriate. As Padmanabh S. Jaini indicated in his book *The Jaina Path of Purification,* Jainism distinguishes between impure suicide, by which the passions are increased, and pure suicide, the holy death attained with "inner peace or dispassionate mindfulness" (Jaini, 1979, p. 229). *Sallekhanā* involves gradual fasting, often under the supervision of a monastic teacher, until the stage is reached whereat the individual no longer consumes any food or drink and thus gradually attains death by starvation. Jains perceive *sallekhanā* to be the climax of a lifetime of spiritual struggle, ascetic practice, and meditation. It allows the individual to control his own destiny so that he will attain full liberation or at the very least reduce the number of future reincarnations that he will undergo.

BUDDHISM AND CONFUCIANISM. Turning to Buddhism and Confucianism, one finds that suicide is legislated against in both traditions, but that there are notable exceptions involving religiously motivated suicide. Gautama Buddha, in his personal search for salvation, deliberately chose against the practice of fasting unto death. Nonetheless, under certain extraordinary circumstances, Buddhists see religiously motivated suicide as an act of sacrifice and worship. Indications of this positive attitude toward suicide, or self-sacrifice, are found in some of the accounts of the Buddha's previous lives contained in the Jatakas (Birth Tales). The stories of the Buddha's previous lives as a hare *(Śaśa Jātaka)* and as a monkey *(Mahākapi Jātaka)* both describe suicide as an act of self-sacrifice to benefit another, and only in the story of the monkey does this act lead to death. Another famous account is that from the *Suvarṇaprabhāsa,* a Mahāyāna *sūtra,* which describes the suicide or sacrifice of the Buddha, during his life as the prince Mahāsattva, in order to feed a hungry tigress unable to care for herself. Following this model, Buddhism in its various forms affirms that, while suicide as self-sacrifice may be appropriate for the person who is an *arhat,* one who has attained enlightenment, it is still very much the exception to the rule.

Confucianism based its attitude toward suicide on another consideration, that of filial piety and obligation. The person who commits suicide robs his ancestors of the veneration and service due them and demonstrates his ingratitude to his parents for the gift of life. The duty of a gentleman is to guide his life according to *li,* the code or rules of propriety. In rare cases, suicide was required of the gentleman who failed to uphold these rules. In some instances a gentleman might commit suicide to protest improper government, since above all a gentleman was obliged to uphold the virtue of humaneness. Thus, in these unusual instances suicide was the correct way to demonstrate adherence to the precepts of Confucianism.

Although the Japanese tradition of *seppuku,* or *harakiri,* should be regarded in its voluntary form as heroic rather than as religiously motivated suicide, it nonetheless does contain certain religious elements. The standard by which all acts of *seppuku* (disembowelment) were judged was set by the heroic Minamoto Yorimasa during a desperate battle in 1180. While suicide was usually performed as an individual act by a noble warrior or *samurai,* there are examples in Japanese history of mass suicides, such as that of the forty-seven *ronin* who accepted the penalty of *seppuku* in order to avenge the death of their lord in 1703.

While Christian missionaries in Japan, from the time of the arrival of the first Jesuits, sought to prevent *seppuku,* the Zen Buddhist tradition continued to regard it as a form of honorable death. The selection of the *hara,* or belly, as the point at which the sword was plunged into the body reflected the belief that the abdomen is the place where one exercises control over one's breathing and is, indeed, the central point of self-discipline. More generally, as Ivan I. Morris states in his book *The Nobility of Failure,* the abdomen was considered in the Japanese tradition as "the locus of man's inner being, the place where his will, spirit, generosity, indignation, courage, and other cardinal qualities were concentrated" (Morris, 1975, p. 367). Thus, by committing oneself to the performance of *seppuku,* which became a clearly defined ritual, one demonstrated in this final act the greatest degree of self-control, discipline, and courage.

CONCLUSION. This article has focused directly on religiously motivated suicide. It has omitted references to suicide among elderly Inuit (Eskimo) and among young Tikopia islanders, to cite only two examples from a vast number of possibilities. In these cases, as in many others, although the suicides may be heroic or altruistic, they do not demonstrate a clear religious motivation. Suicides by reason of financial failure, or loss of honor or of a loved one, occur among the Kwakiutl and Iroquois Indians, as well as among Bantu-speaking peoples of Africa. Occurrences of suicide are not limited by geography or time, but of the many suicides that have taken place throughout the ages, only a small proportion can be judged to be religiously motivated.

The examples of religiously motivated suicide discussed here demonstrate the wide variety of forms and purposes that the act may take. Many of the examples, from both East and West, illustrate the difficulty in distinguishing between suicide that is religiously motivated and suicide that is motivated by heroism, altruism, or fear of persecution and suffering. The deaths at Jonestown in 1978 raise anew the problem of how to differentiate between religiously motivated suicide and suicide induced by paranoia and terror. There is no simple distinction between suicide and martyrdom, on the one hand, or between suicide and sacrifice, on the other. In formulating these distinctions and in evaluating the morality and religious value of certain acts that result in death, each person brings to bear his or her own religious and ethical values and tradition. Such personal judgment must, however, be conjoined with the awareness that what may be perceived by one observer as needless self-sacrifice or even self-murder may be judged by another as the noblest example of religiously motivated suicide in behalf of beliefs, values, or tradition.

SEE ALSO Martyrdom.

BIBLIOGRAPHY

There is a vast literature on suicide, but relatively little of it focuses on the act as religiously motivated. Any student of the topic must begin with Émile Durkheim's *Le suicide,* translated by John A. Spaulding and George Simpson as *Suicide: A Study in Sociology* (New York, 1951). It is the classic work on the varieties of suicide analyzed from a sociological viewpoint. Jacques Choron's chapters on "Suicide in Retrospect" and "Philosophers on Suicide" in his volume *Suicide* (New York, 1972) are quite helpful in understanding the place of suicide in the West at different times. A volume edited by Frederick H. Holck, *Death and Eastern Thought: Understanding Death in Eastern Religions and Philosophies* (Nashville, 1974), contains several chapters that refer to suicide. Alfred Alvarez also discusses the themes of religious motivation for suicide and religious prohibition of the act in his book *The Savage God:*

A Study of Suicide (London, 1971). He includes personal reflections on his own suicide attempt, and describes his friendship with the poet Sylvia Plath, who committed suicide in 1963.

Among the older studies of the topic, still useful are *Suicide: A Social and Historical Study* by Henry Romilly Fedden (London, 1938) and *To Be or Not to Be: A Study of Suicide* by Louis I. Dublin and Bessie Bunzel (New York, 1933).

There are relatively few sources that consider religiously motivated suicide in specific traditions. For the Western religious traditions, the reader should refer to the bibliography of the article *Martyrdom* as well as to the various primary sources mentioned throughout this article. In addition, for Judaism, the reader will find useful Yigael Yadin's *Masada: Herod's Fortress and the Zealots' Last Stand* (New York, 1966) and Cecil Roth's *A History of the Jews in England* (Oxford, 1941), which discusses the events at York. On Christianity, particularly informative is Samuel E. Sprott's *The English Debate on Suicide from Donne to Hume* (La Salle, Ill., 1961). William A. Clebsch has prepared a new edition of John Donne's work, translated as *Suicide* (Chico, Calif., 1983), with a very helpful introduction. Robert O. Crummey presents a fascinating account of suicides among the Raskol'niki in his book *The Old Believers and the World of Antichrist: The Vyg Community and the Russian State, 1694–1855* (Madison, Wis., 1970). See especially his chapter entitled "Death by Fire." On Islam, the most useful secondary source remains Franz Rosenthal's "On Suicide in Islam," *Journal of the American Oriental Society* 66 (1946): 239–259. For the Assassins, one should consult the comprehensive historical account by Marshall G. S. Hodgson in *The Order of Assassins: The Struggle of the Early Nizârī Ismâʿīlīs against the Islamic World* (1955; New York, 1980).

For the Eastern traditions, in addition to the volume edited by Holck and the primary texts mentioned in the article, the following books are useful sources for individual traditions. For Hinduism, see both the older account by Edward Thompson, *Suttee: A Historical and Philosophical Enquiry into the Hindu Rite of Widow-Burning* (London, 1928), and the more comprehensive study by Upendra Thakur, *The History of Suicide in India: An Introduction* (Delhi, 1963). For Jainism, Padmanabh S. Jaini offers a detailed account of *sallekhanā* in his book *The Jaina Path of Purification* (Berkeley, 1979). The Buddhist account entitled "The Bodhisattva and the Hungry Tigress" may be found in the volume edited by Edward Conze, *Buddhist Scriptures* (Harmondsworth, 1959). For the Japanese attitude toward suicide and death, see the fascinating work by Ivan I. Morris, *The Nobility of Failure: Tragic Heroes in the History of Japan* (New York, 1975), and for the study of *seppuku* among the warrior class, see *The Samurai: A Military History* by S. R. Turnbull (New York, 1977).

New Sources

Buddhism

Jan, Yün-Hua. "Buddhist Self-Immolation in Medieval China." *History of Religions* 4 (1965): 243–268. A survey of Chinese Buddhist texts providing justifications of religious suicide.

Lamotte, Etienne. "Le suicide religieux dans le bouddhisme." *Bulletin de la Classe des Lettres et des Sciences de l'Académie royale de Belgique* 51 (1965). 156–168. A monographic study by the foremost scholar of classic Buddhism.

McCutcheon, Russell. *Manufacturing Religion.* Oxford, 1997. See the pp. 167–177 for the self-immolations of the Vietnamese Buddhist monks, providing a non-historical political explanation which is unreliable from the religious-historical point of view.

Hinduism

Bosch, Lourens P. van den. "A Burning Question: Sati and Sati Temples as the Focus of Political Interest." *Numen* 37 (1990): 174–194. The issue is situated in the context of religion's definition.

Weinberger-Thomas, Catherine. *Ashes of Immortality: Widow-Burning in India.* Chicago, 1999. A radically new interpretation of satī based on fieldwork in northern India as well as extensive textual analysis.

New Cults

Introvigne, Massimo. "The Magic of Death: The Suicides of the Solar Temple." In *Millennialism, Persecution, and Violence. Historical Cases* edited by Catherine Wessinger. Syracuse, N.Y., 2000, pp. 287–321.

Kabazzi-Kisiniria, S. Deusdedit, R. K. Nkurunziza, and Gerald Banura. *The Kanungu Cult-Saga. Suicide, Murder or Salvation?* Kampala, Uganda, 2000.

Mayer, Jean-François. *Il Tempio Solare.* Turin, Italy, 1997.

Nesci, Domenico Arturo. *The Lessons of Jonestown. An Ethnopsychoanalytic Study of Suicidal Communities.* Rome, 1999. The author is a professional psychoanalyst and psychiatrist but writes as a humanist

Wessinger, Catherine. *How the Millenium Comes Violently. From Jonestown to Heaven's Gate.* New York and London, 2000.

Islam

Cook, David. "Suicide Attacks or 'Martyrdom Operations' in Contemporary Jihad Literature" *Nova Religio: The Journal of Alternative and Emergent Religions.* 6, no. 1 (2002): 7–44.

MARILYN J. HARRAN (1987)
Revised Bibliography

SUKKOT is the Hebrew name for the Jewish autumnal festival, also called the Festival of Booths, or Tabernacles. Sukkot begins on the fifteenth day of the month of Tishri and lasts for seven days, followed by an eighth day called ʿAtseret (possibly meaning "assembly"; see *Lv.* 23:36, *Nm.* 29:35). (Outside Israel, ʿAtseret is observed also on the ninth day.) Thus, according to Jewish tradition, there are really two distinct but interconnected festivals: Sukkot proper and Shemini ʿAtseret ("eighth day of ʿAtseret"). The Sukkot rituals are carried out only on Sukkot proper; two are essential. The first is to dwell in booths or tabernacles (*sukkot;* sg. *sukkah*) as a reminder of the dwellings in which the Israelites lived at the time of the Exodus from Egypt (*Lv.* 23:33–44). The second is derived from the biblical verse regarding four plants: *lulav* (palm branch), *etrog* (citron), *ʿaravot* (willows), and *hadassim* (myrtles) (*Lv.* 23:40). It is traditionally understood that these four plants are to be ritually held in the hand. Sukkot, as the culmination of the three pilgrim festivals, is the season of special rejoicing (*Dt.* 16:13–17) and is referred to in the liturgy as "the season of our joy."

THE SUKKAH. The main symbol of the festival is a hut, having at least three walls, no roof, but covered with leaves or straw. During the seven days of the festival, all meals are eaten in the *sukkah.* Many Jews, especially those living in warm climates, sleep there as well. In addition to the biblical reason, medieval thinkers saw the command to dwell in the *sukkah,* a temporary dwelling, as a reminder to man of the transient nature of material possessions, and an exhortation that he should place his trust in God. According to the mystics, the *sukkah* is visited on each of the seven days by a different biblical hero—Abraham, Isaac, Jacob, Moses, Aaron, Joseph, and David. It is the custom among many Jews to recite a welcoming formula to these guests (*ushpizin*) as if they were real persons visiting the *sukkah.*

THE FOUR SPECIES. The rite of the four plants consists in taking them in the hand during the synagogue service and waving them above and below and in the four directions of the compass. The stated reason is to dispel harmful "winds" and to acknowledge God as ruler over all. Various interpretations have been given of why it is commanded to take these four plants. For example, it has been said that they represent the human backbone, heart, eye, and mouth, all of which must be engaged in the worship of God. Moses Maimonides (1135/8–1204) treated these as homiletical interpretations and suggested as the true reason a means of thanksgiving to God for the harvest. The harvest motif is also observed in the custom of having a procession in the synagogue while holding the four plants on each day of Sukkot. During the procession the Hoshaʿnah ("save now") prayer for a good harvest in the year ahead is recited. On the seventh day there are seven processions, hence the name of the day, Hoshaʿnah Rabbah ("great Hoshaʿnah"). At the end of the service on this day, the ancient custom of beating bunches of willows on the ground follows. On Shemini ʿAtseret a special prayer for rain is recited. In a later development within Jewish tradition, Hoshaʿnah Rabbah is seen as setting the seal on the judgment made on Yom Kippur, so that the day is a day of judgment with prayers resembling those offered on Yom Kippur. There is a folk belief that if a person sees his or her shadow without a head on the night of Hoshaʿnah Rabbah, that person will die during the year.

SHEMINI ʿATSERET. The last day of the festival has acquired a new character from medieval times. The weekly Torah readings—from the beginning of *Genesis* to the end of *Deuteronomy*—are completed on this day and then immediately begun again, so that the day is both the end and the beginning of the annual cycle. The day is now called Simḥat Torah ("rejoicing of the Torah"). In the Diaspora, Simḥat Torah falls on the second day of Shemini ʿAtseret (23 Tishri). In Israel, Simḥat Torah coincides with the one-day celebration of Shemini ʿAtseret on 22 Tishri, the day also observed by Reform Jews, who no longer observe the additional second day of festivals traditionally observed by Diaspora Jews. The person who has the honor of completing the reading is called the "bridegroom" of the Torah, and the one who begins the reading again is the "bridegroom" of *Genesis.* On this joyful day the scrolls of the Torah are taken in procession around the synagogue, and the "bridegrooms" invite the congregation to a festive repast.

BIBLIOGRAPHY

Two useful books on the Sukkot rituals and customs are Isaac N. Fabricant's *A Guide to Succoth,* 2d ed. (London, 1962), and Hayyim Schauss's *The Jewish Festivals: History and Observance* (New York, 1973).

New Sources

Rubenstein, Jeffrey L. *The History of Sukkot in the Second Temple and Rabbinic Periods.* Atlanta, 1995.

Ulfgard, Håkan. *The Story of Sukkot: The Setting, Shaping, and Sequel of the Biblical Feast of Tabernacles.* Tübingen, 1998.

Yaged, Moshe. "The Biblical Readings for the Festival of Sukkot—Their Influence on Simhat Torah." *Journal of Jewish Music and Liturgy* 10 (1987–1988): 1–5.

LOUIS JACOBS (1987)
Revised Bibliography

SUMERIAN RELIGION SEE MESOPOTAMIAN RELIGIONS

SUN. There can hardly be anyone on earth who has not been profoundly aware of the apparent progress of the sun across the heavens and who has not related to it, either personally or as a numinous force. The rising and setting of the sun provides one of the primal dichotomies, parallel to those between day and night, light and darkness, warmth and cold, life and death, *yang* and *yin.* Night is mysterious, dangerous, akin to the darkness of the womb. Daylight symbolizes renewed life, truth, logic. In modern thinking, the sun often stands for individual consciousness, and the moon (or night) for the unconscious, the ocean, or the feminine principle. In children's drawings, a happy scene includes a huge round sun with rays like hair. Unhappy and frustrated children produce an entirely black sky. Mentally disturbed patients often draw their own bodies as the sun's disk, complete with arms and legs like rays.

In classical poetry birth is described as "reaching the shores of light." In the *Eumenides* of Aeschylus, the conflict is between the fearsome Furies, avengers of the mother's blood, who constantly invoke the "dark mother," and the shining Apollo, revealer of truth and righteousness (and symbolic of paternal predominance). The west, where the sun sets, in most rituals represents death; the east, where the sun rises, life and birth. Even Neanderthal burials were oriented according to east and west. When a Greek priest faced north in sacrifices, the right hand, stretched toward the east, represented the fortunate side, the left, the "sinister."

In many primitive mythologies, the sun is an object tossed up or hung in the sky by mortals or trickster figures.

The Hopi Indians claim that they made their sun themselves, by throwing into the sky a shield made of buckskin together with a fox skin and a parrot's tail to make the colors of sunrise and sunset. The San of Africa believe that the sun was once a mortal who gave out light from his armpit. In order to make the light brighter, some children threw him into the sky, whereupon he became round and shines now for all humankind. Among the Tatars, the culture hero Porcupine took some fire on his sword and threw it up into the sky to make the sun. For the moon, he thrust his sword into the water; thus the sun is hot and the moon cool. The famous American Indian trickster Coyote is said to have sent the wolf to bring him fire to make the sun. In one of the Oceanic myths that describe life beginning inside a shell, the creator, Spider Woman, opened the shell and then threw up two snails to make the sun and moon. In Norse mythology the sun and moon are sparks from Muspelheim, the realm of fire. The gods, however, anthropomorphized them and set them to drive chariots across the sky.

In more sophisticated societies, the luminaries were set in the heavens by the high god. Sometimes, they represented his eyes. In ancient Egypt the sun was sometimes called the eye of Re; in northern Europe, the eye of Óðinn (Odin); in Oceania, the eye of Atea.

The creation myth of Mesopotamia, *Enuma elish,* relates how the conquering god Marduk, who had solar characteristics himself, "set up stations for the gods in the sky, determining the year by setting up the zones." According to the *Book of Genesis* "God made the two great lights, the greater light to rule the day, and the lesser light to rule the night. . . . And God set them in the firmament of the heavens to give light upon the earth, to rule over the day and over the night, and to separate the light from the darkness" (1:16–18). In Plato's great myth the *Timaeus,* "the Demiurge [the creator] lit a light which we now call the sun. . . to shine through the whole heaven and to enable the living creatures to gain a knowledge of numbers from the uniform movements. In this way there came into being night and day, the period of the single most intelligent revolution" (39c). Thus the Demiurge, having set out all the heavenly bodies, put them in motion and brought time into being.

More often, the sun is anthropomorphized, sometimes as a female but more frequently as a male. He crosses the sky by the appropriate means of locomotion. In ancient Sumeria, he walked. In ancient Egypt, he sailed in a boat like the ones on the Nile, in company with some of the other gods and the pharaoh. When the horse was domesticated, about the beginning of the second millennium BCE, the sun drove a chariot pulled by white or flaming horses. The horse, the sacred animal of the Indo-Europeans, was one of the animals most closely connected with the sun and was often sacrificed to it. Another creature associated with the sun was the bird—a falcon, raven, or eagle, or, of course, the fabulous phoenix, which dies and is born again from the fire every five thousand years. The wings of birds are attached to the sun's round form to produce the winged disk so common in solar iconography. In Africa and India the tiger and especially the lion are sun animals; in the Americas, the eagle and the jaguar. Leo is the zodiacal sign for the fiercest summer month; the lion is the royal animal on all the kingly architecture of the ancient Near East. The many representations of a lion attacking a bull may, some have surmised, reflect the heat of summer routing spring, represented in the zodiac by Taurus, the bull, or the paternal cult, attacking the female horned moon.

Eclipses of both sun and moon were experienced with great dread. The Tatars believed that an eclipse meant that the sun was attacked by a vampire who lived in a star. In Norse myth the sun was pursued by a supernatural wolf who will devour it when the world ends. The ancient Egyptians believed that a demon—the Chinese, a dragon—was attacking the sun. Some North American Indian tribes, on the other hand, believed that the sun and moon were eclipsed when they held their infants in their arms. In Tahiti it was believed that eclipses occurred when the sun and moon were mating.

Many devices were employed to "cure" eclipses, such as the beating of drums or the making of other loud noises or the shooting of arrows at the sun. "Snaring the sun" is one of the most widespread sun myths in Oceania and North America. This is one of the exploits of Maui, the Polynesian culture hero, for instance, who caught the sun and beat it so that it would not go so fast. It has been conjectured that stories of this kind are explanations for the solstices, when the sun is perceived to stand still for several days. The high cultures of the Inca and of Mesoamerican peoples were familiar with the stations of the sun, and the Pueblo measured sunrise points on the eastern horizon to divide the year. The Zuni used as a gnomon an erect slab with a solar effigy on top, and the sun temple at Cuzco, like Greek temples, was so oriented that the sun at the solstice would penetrate the shrine.

There seems to be no doubt that the impressive monument at Stonehenge in England was set up to mark the solstices and equinoxes as well as the stations of the moon. New carbon 14 readings indicate that Stonehenge is at least as old as the first pyramids, ruling out influence from the East on its construction. In view of the tremendous labor involved in moving and setting the megaliths, which occurred in three stages several centuries apart, there can hardly be any question that religious motivation was involved. Diodorus Siculus, writing in the first century BCE, described a "spherical temple to Apollo among the Hyperboreans," which may be a reference to Stonehenge as a great temple to the sun. Recent research has turned up other observatories in Scotland, the Orkneys, and even in Carnac in Brittany. Gold and bronze disks engraved with crosses and spirals, daggers and horse trappings with the same designs, and amber disks with gold rims, all contemporary with the last phase of Stonehenge, have been found in the British Isles and in Scandinavia. It is tempting to imagine a crowd of people, each carrying a sun amulet, waiting for the summer sunrise at Stonehenge.

A spectacular object confirming northern sun worship is the famous disk found in Trundholm in northern Zealand, plated with gold and decorated with circles and spirals; it is set on wheels and drawn by a bronze horse, probably one of a pair. In all the Scandinavian countries have been discovered objects and rock carvings decorated with disks, boats, and scenes of humans raising their arms to a disk. Sometimes there are men in the shape of disks, carrying weapons. These have been interpreted as solar deities or mortals wearing the sun's emblem. The wheel, the boat, the cross in a circle, and the swastika (a moving wheel) can all be seen as sun symbols.

The summer solstice in northern Europe today is marked by bonfires and the rolling downhill of flaming wheels, as it was no doubt millennia ago. The winter solstice is a time to encourage the sun to grow again, represented by the burning of the Yule log, the Ḥanukkah light, and the lighted candles of Saint Lucy in Sweden. The boar's head at the Christmas feast represents the old year, or the old sun, and the suckling pig with the apple of immortality in its mouth is the new sun.

It was the tendency of nineteenth-century scholars to search for a single key to the understanding of all mythology. One of the most popular of these keys was the concept of the sun hero, a ubiquitous figure who was either the sun itself or an offspring of the sun. It has become clear over the years that all myths cannot be traced to one source. Yet there are some elements of myth that do seem to have solar references in common, perhaps formulated by the ancients at the time when astral religion invaded the Mediterranean world. It has been pointed out (by Joseph Campbell, for instance, in *The Hero with a Thousand Faces*) that in most myths heroes have one divine parent and that they wander about on the earth and make at least one trip to the underworld. Also, most myths describe a wandering sun, which goes under or behind the earth at night, and in most myths the divine parent is perceived as a sun figure. One instance is the Greek Perseus, whose mother, an underground divinity, was impregnated by a shower of gold, the sun's metal. Another is the Irish Cú Chulainn, who is explicitly a son of Lugh Lamfhada, "Lugh of the long hands," an epithet that is reminiscent of the long rays that end in human hands pictured at Amarna in Egypt. Lugh was a god of brightness and the sky and, like Apollo, master of all crafts. He fought at the mythical battle of Moytura, where he vanquished his grandfather, the giant Balor, who had one eye in the middle of his forehead, like the cyclopes, who were also sun figures. The Welsh counterpart of Lugh is Lleu Llaw Gyffes, or Lludd. Lludd had a temple at Lydney in England near the Severn where he is portrayed, perhaps through Roman influence, as a young man with a solar halo driving a chariot. The Samson of *Genesis,* a mighty and short-tempered Herakles figure, has a name derived from the Hebrew word for "sun." Samson's fight with a lion, and his birth, which is connected with a supernatural figure who vanishes in flames, seem to point to other solar connections.

Homer's Odysseus has been interpreted as a sun figure, since he wanders for nine years, which is the period the Greeks used to correlate solar and lunar calendars. He finally reaches his Penelope, who weaves by day and unravels by night. Most replete with sun details, however, is the story of Herakles, son of the sky god Zeus, who wanders the earth to perform his deeds, returns unhurt from the underworld, dies in a fire, and is taken up to heaven. He not only lives on in heaven but also has a shade who lives on in the underworld. Herakles' labors were perhaps limited to twelve (although others have been recorded) in order to fit them into the zodiac.

As an all-seeing eye who travels the world, the sun acquired the character of a spy for the gods and therefore a stern judge of humankind. When the heavenly bodies began to be seen as parts of a well-ordered and consistent system, more pure and dependable than that of the old gods, the sun, an obvious leader in the sky, took his place as a symbol of the newly emerging royal power. Thus, organized cults of the sun are strongest in the great civilizations, which were often kingships. A new sense of power and organization, as well as a new sense of justice, found its central source in kingship, just as the harmony of the heavens was centered in the sun. "It is a remarkable coincidence," writes Jacquetta Hawkes, "that a discovery and an invention attendant on the creation of Bronze Age civilization came just in time to provide symbols of the sun gods and their temples. These were gold and the wheel" (Hawkes, 1962, p. 73). Since its discovery, gold has been the royal metal, as well as the sun's. The sun royal was adopted by all kings but never so completely as by the Sun King, Louis XIV (r. 1643–1715). Elizabeth II of England at her coronation in 1952 wore a golden gown under her robe, and her archbishop prayed that her throne "may stand fast in righteousness forevermore, like the sun before her and as the faithful witness in heaven." One must thus look to the high civilizations and imperial kingships to find the most highly developed cults of the sun.

Ancient Egypt. Very early in its history, somewhere in the fourth millennium BCE, Egyptians broke away from a moon calendar and organized time around the heliacal rising of the star Sirius, which occurs about July 19. This date coincided with the yearly inundation of the Nile, the most important period in the agricultural life of a country that has no rainfall and no seasons. From that time on the year was divided into twelve months of thirty days each, with a five-day intracalendrical period. Whether or not this arrangement affected the religious life of the Egyptians, as some have argued, the sun in various aspects became the dominant figure in Egyptian religious life, combining with, and in some cases supplanting, other deities.

One of the earliest manifestations of the sun was the falcon god Horus, who appears on the famous palette of Narmer, the unifier of the two lands that became Egypt. Horus was probably an ancient sky god, seen as a soaring bird who was manifest in the sun itself; he was known as Re-Harakhty, the god of the horizon, or sunrise. He was at first the son of the sky goddess Hathor (in Egypt the sky is female and the earth male). Later, as the tendency to group the important gods into families developed, he was known as the son of Osiris, the god of fertility and the underworld. Osiris' sister-wife, Isis, mourns for her dead husband and secretly raises their son Horus to do battle with Osiris' murderer, his brother Seth. In this family, the sun god, Re, was combined with an older creator god, Atum. In Heliopolis, a temple compound just north of modern Cairo near the old capitol of Memphis, a powerful priesthood built up the cult of Re-Atum, beginning at least in the fourth dynasty (2600 BCE). This is the period in which were built the first great pyramids, which pointed toward the sun. In the mythology developed at Heliopolis, the creator Re-Atum produced land from the surrounding waters. A mound in the temple was known as the Ben-Ben and was supposed to represent the semen of Re. Out of his own substances the creator god made sky and earth, air and water, and finally the four divinities: Osiris, Seth, and Isis and Nephthys, their wives.

The powerful priesthood at Heliopolis proclaimed the pharaoh the son of the Sun. It seems likely that the earlier pharaohs had themselves represented the Sun, and that they lost power under the growing influence of the priesthood. It was also possible for the priests to control the selection of the pharaoh's divine successor from among his offspring.

The history of ancient Egypt is neatly divided into the Old, Middle, and New Kingdoms, with two intervening periods of anarchy. After the first intermediate period, a new royal house arose in the south, at Thebes. There, Re was combined with a local god, Atum, the "Hidden One," probably representing the air. This god flourished throughout the New Kingdom, when Egyptian power spread into Asia. The great temples at Karnak and Luxor testify to the power and enormous wealth of the sun cult.

The sun was usually pictured as sailing across the sky in a boat, with various attendants and sometimes with the pharaoh himself. At other times the sun is seen sailing up the leg and belly of the sky goddess, who bends over the earth or straddles it in the form of a cow. Or the sun was swallowed at night by the sky mother and is born each morning from between her thighs. The sun was symbolized by a falcon but more notably by the mythical phoenix, which alighted on the Ben-Ben every five hundred years, was consumed in fire, and rose again. Another important symbol of the sun was the scarab, the dung beetle Khepri, which supposedly created itself by rolling its eggs in balls of dung. The obelisks, as well as the gold-topped pyramids, point toward the sun. On the early squat obelisk of the fifth dynasty, the sun is pictured as creator of life and lord of the seasons.

In the reign of Amunhotep III (1417–1439 BCE), the actual disk of the sun, called the Aton, began to appear as a numinous symbol. It was the pharoah's son Amunhotep IV (1379–1362 BCE), however, who attempted, in one of the great religious revolutions of history, to convert the entire nation to monotheistic worship of the Aton as sole god. Whether he was religiously motivated or whether he wished to break the power of the enormously wealthy priesthood, he sought to abolish all other worship in favor of the Aton, the sun's disk. He changed his name to Akhenaton ("Aton is satisfied") and built a new capital at Amarna. In this city he supported a new school of art, which pictured him in naturalistic style with his beautiful wife Nefertiti and his five daughters, all under the brilliance of the sun, which reached down to earth with long rays ending in human hands. Akhenaton has left a well-known hymn to the Aton as creator of all the beauties of the world: "How manifold are your works. They are mysterious in men's sight, O sole incomparable god, all powerful. You created the earth in solitude as your heart desires. Men you created, and cattle, whatever is on earth." Akhenaton's revolution failed, and after his mysterious death the priesthood reclaimed their power, and a young man (probably his son-in-law) resumed the worship of Amun, adopting the name of Tut-Ankh-Amun (or Tutankhamen).

MESOPOTAMIA. In the land between the Tigris and Euphrates rivers, where are found the earliest traces of urban living, writing, kingship, and an organized priesthood, the sun was at first subordinate to the moon. To the first recorded inhabitants, known as the Sumerians, the chief god was An, a sky god who had retired from active control and left the rule of the universe to his son, Enlil, the Air. A son of Enlil was the important moon god, Nanna, whose children were the Sun—Utu—and the Evening Star—Inanna. In Sumerian times, the regions were divided into a series of independent cities, each devoted to the worship of a patron god. Only two minor cities, Larsa and Sippar, worshiped Utu, the Sun.

The Semitic-speaking states that followed the Sumerians took over the religious organization they found, calling the moon Sin and the sun Shamash. In that dangerously torrid land, the sun was considered a baleful god. But since he traveled continually across the sky, he was considered a spy for the high gods and a stern judge of humankind. Travelers prayed to him before setting out on a journey, and armies before an expedition. He was thus a warrior god and leader of armies. In the quest of the hero Gilgamesh for the secret of immortality, it was the Sun who guided him on his journey. Originally the Sun walked across the heavens; in later times he rode a cart drawn by onagers, wild asses from the desert. Still later, the horse drew the Sun's chariot. The Sun in his chariot appeared in the morning at the eastern gate on the Mountain of Sunrise, in the evening arrived at the Mountain of Sunset, and then passed through to the underworld. Because of his appearance in the underworld, the Sun was sometimes pictured in company with Tammuz, the Mesopotamian dying god, who dies and is reborn. There was very little concern for judgment of the dead in Mesopotamia, and Shamash's character as judge was thus reserved for the upper world. At Ur, it was the Sun who punished a corrupt judge for taking bribes and oppressing the people.

Shamash was the god of oracles and was supposed to inscribe the signs that the diviners read in the intestines of sheep. Soothsayers claimed they were descended from a king of Sippar, who lived before the flood; the diviners were the most prestigious of the priests in that city of the Sun. From Assyrian times are preserved a number of questions asked of the Sun concerning the state and the royal family. The diviner read the answers in the entrails of dissected sheep. Probably a result of this activity was the Sun's power to control witches and demons.

Shamash was also invoked to heal the sick, free captives from bondage, and help women in labor. One prayer reads, "O Shamash, lofty judge . . . may the knot that impedes her delivery be loosed . . . may she bear. May she remain in life and walk in health before the godhead." The Sun, in other words, brings the unborn to light. He was also asked to deliver victims of spells, curses, and ghosts: "O Shamash, may I be strong and face the authors of my enchantment!"

The sun god is pictured as an old man with a long beard; sunbeams radiate from between his shoulder blades. He is seen sitting on a throne or sometimes on a horse. His special symbols are a four-pointed star in a disk with flames shooting out from between the points of the star and, of course, the winged disk, which was set above representations of royalty.

The study of heavenly bodies, conducted in Mesopotamia from at least 2000 BCE, led to a belief in an ordered universe and in the important position of the sun among the planets. Thus, with the rise of centralized imperial power in Assyria and Babylonia, the sun came into prominence as a symbol of royal power. The lawgiver Hammurabi (c. 1750 BCE) calls Shamash "great judge of heaven and earth" and proclaims that it was from Shamash that he received his laws. The sun god is seen seated on a throne, handing Hammurabi a ring and a staff. The sun temple at Babylon was known as "the house of the judge of the world."

Warlike Assyrians claimed Shamash as a great god of battles, almost the same as their own Ashur. Assyrian kings called themselves "suns of the world." Marduk, hero of the New Year festival at Babylon and a grandson of the high gods, is shown as a heavily bearded god with sun rays emanating from his shoulders. Thus the Sun in Mesopotamia, first perceived of as judge, lawgiver, and governor of magic, illness, and prophecy, grew into an image of the Sun Royal.

THE INDO-EUROPEANS. About the beginning of the second millennium BCE, people speaking related languages spread across western Asia into Europe, bringing similar pantheons into India, Iran, Asia Minor, and most of Europe. Their high god was a sky god—Dyaus, Pitar, Zeus, or Jupiter. But in many cases this high god tended to fade out of the pantheon, leaving the universe to his offspring, sometimes the sun god. This process, known as solarization, brought the sun to the fore as creator and ruler of the gods.

The most cherished animal of the Indo-Europeans was the horse, and they perhaps introduced the chariot to the western world. From this time on the sun is pictured as driving a chariot across the sky, and the horse became one of the sun's animals, often sacrificed to him.

In ancient Indian and Iranian texts appear the names *Varuṇa* and *Mitra,* which seem to mean respectively "the sky" and "the light of day." Mitra faded out in India, but in Iran, as Mithra, he was the subject of many hymns in the sacred writings, the Avesta. Mithra is said to represent celestial light, which appears before sunrise on the mountains, whence it crosses the sky in a chariot. He is said to be neither sun, moon, nor star, but with his hundred eyes he constantly keeps watch on the world. None can deceive him, so he is viewed as a god of truth and righteousness. He is the enforcer of oaths and contracts and is also called "lord of the wide pastures who giveth abundance and cattle." He combats the forces of evil, spies out his enemies, swoops down and conquers them, and is the ally of the faithful in their wars. Thus Mithra, though not identified with the sun, shares all the attributes of the Mesopotamian Shamash. When the Persians conquered Babylon the name *Mithra* was translated as *Shamash.* A large number of the names of Persian aristocrats are compounds of *Mithra.*

The Greek historian Herodotus relates that the Persians sacrificed to the sun as well as to earth, fire, and water and that leprosy was thought of as punishment for a sin against the sun (*Histories* 1.138). When Xerxes was leading his huge army through Asia Minor to attack Greece, he waited on the Asiatic shore until sunrise and then poured a libation from a golden cup, which he threw together with a golden scimitar into the sea (7.54). Xerxes' army was accompanied by a riderless chariot drawn by eight white horses, which Herodotus says was sacred to Zeus, the sky god. It was followed by a chariot of the sun, also drawn by white horses. Herodotus also tells us that along the route were led horses that were intended to be sacrificed to the sun. Horse sacrifices have been recorded from India to Ireland and have commonly accompanied the coronation of kings.

A true sun hymn occurs in the Avesta: "Unto the undying, swift-horse sun be propitiation and glorification. . . . When the sun rises up, the earth, made by Ahura, becomes clean. . . . Should the sun not rise up, the demons would destroy all things." Every layman in ancient Persia was required to recite a prayer to the sun at sunrise, at noon, and at three in the afternoon. Persian deities were established in Lydia, Cappadocia, and Armenia by Iranian officials, and it is probably through Persian influence that the sun god became prominent in places like Emesa, Baalbek, and Palmyra in Syria.

In India, the same divinities, Varuna and Mitra, are called in the *Ṛgveda* "kings of gods and men." They drive chariots across the sky and live in heavenly palaces with a thousand gold columns and a thousand doors. Ten hymns of the *Ṛgveda* are devoted to the sun under the name of

Sūrya, who seems to represent the actual disk of the sun. Sūrya had the power to drive away darkness, witches, and evil dreams; he is also a healing god, particularly effective against jaundice. He is the husband of Dawn and drives a chariot, sometimes with one and sometimes with seven horses. Another name for the sun is *Savitṛ.* Sometimes it is said that the sun is Savitṛ before his rising and Sūrya afterward. Savitṛ "brings all men and animals to rest; men lay down their work and birds seek their nests." Among other names given to the sun in the ancient poems is that of Viṣṇu, because "he strode across the sky in three giant steps" to ward off demons from humankind. Viṣṇu, of course, came to be one of the three great gods of Hinduism, the one especially benevolent to humankind.

ANCIENT GREECE. In Hesiod's *Birth of the Gods* (c. 750 BCE) Helios is the son of Hyperion, also a sun figure, and is the brother of the Moon (Selene) and of the Dawn (Eos). He is not included in the family of Olympians who came into prominence after Homer and Hesiod (from about 800 BCE), but belongs to an older, less-well defined group that was closely connected with natural phenomena. In Homer (c. 800 BCE), Helios reveals to Hephaistos the adultery of his wife, Aphrodite. In the Demeter myth he reports that Hades has carried off to the underworld Demeter's daughter, Persephone. The chariot of the sun is mentioned not in Homer but in the so-called Homeric Hymns (c. 700 BCE). Demeter stands before the chariot as she begs for help. According to the Homeric *Hymn to Helios,* "as he rides in his chariot, he shines upon all men and deathless gods, and piercingly he gazes with his eyes from his golden helmet. He rests upon the highest point of heaven until he marvelously drives down again from heaven to the Ocean." The poet Mimnernus (c. 630 BCE) describes the sun as floating back through the subterranean ocean in a golden bowl made for him by the divine smith Hephaistos. These descriptions laid the foundations for the hundreds of depictions of the sun in his chariot in Greek art, continuing into Roman times.

As in Mesopotamia, the Sun in Greece is involved in oaths and is a god of vengeance. In Aeschylus, Prometheus, bound upon his crag, calls upon "the all-seeing circle of the sun" to witness his woes. In *Oedipus of Colonus,* by Sophocles, Creon drives his brother-in-law out of the house so that "the sun may not look upon such a wretch." Cassandra in Aeschylus's *Agamemnon* calls upon the Sun for vengeance on her murderers. Medea in Euripides' play makes Aegeus swear by earth and sun that he will protect her. In the *Argonautica* of Apollonius Rhodius (third century BCE) she swears by the Sun and Hekate. In the *Iliad,* 19.196, a boar is sacrificed to Zeus and the Sun in confirmation of an oath.

There was little direct worship of the sun in ancient Greece, though there are traces of earlier rites. Plato says the earlier Greeks made obeisance to the rising and setting sun. Pausanias in his guidebook to Greece (second century BCE) mentions several shrines to the sun in remote places. For instance, the people of a little town north of Corinth, when suffering from a plague were told by the Delphic oracle to sacrifice a goat to the Sun. When they did, and the plague stopped, in gratitude they sent a bronze goat to the oracle, which many people, says Pausanias, thought was the Sun itself. Corinth itself was originally sacred to the Sun and, according to Pausanias, was called Heliopolis ("city of the sun"). Later the Sun gave the city to Aphrodite.

The island of Rhodes, however, had a true cult of the sun, influenced perhaps by the sun worship of the East. In legend, the island was brought up out of the sea to compensate Helios for his exclusion from the heavenly lottery. It was on Rhodes that Helios loved the nymph Rhoda and begot the seven wise men of the ancient world. An impressive festival of the sun, held on Rhodes every four years, included athletic games and a chariot race. Every year the Rhodians threw into the sea a chariot drawn by four horses. The famous colossus of Rhodes, one of the seven wonders of the world, erected in 284 BCE, was a figure of the sun god. Pliny recounts that it was 105 feet high and that one of its fingers was larger than most statues. It was thrown down by an earthquake sixty-six years after it was erected.

In addition to being an all-seeing eye and god of vengeance, the sun in Greece has a connection with magic. Among his children were Aeetes, king of Colchis, Circe, the witch of the *Odyssey,* and Pasiphae ("all-shining"; perhaps a reference to the moon), who bewitched her husband, Minos of Crete. Most famous of the sun's lineage is Medea, daughter of Aeetes, whose enchantments form the plot of Euripides' play.

The *Odyssey* tells the story of the cattle of the Sun, which were taboo to mortals. They roamed on the island of Trinacria, seven herds of fifty each, tended by two daughters. Odysseus had been warned not to touch the cattle, but his marooned sailors were starving and killed and ate some. The flesh on the spits writhed and lowed. The Sun appealed to Zeus for vengeance and threatened to go down and shine in the underworld if he were not appeased. Zeus therefore hurled a thunderbolt, which destroyed the ship and left only Odysseus alive in the water. These cattle have been interpreted in various ways: Some say that they are the clouds that gather at sunrise and sunset, and Aristotle thought they stood for the days of the lunar year.

In ancient Greece, Apollo was a god of prophecy, sickness, healing, and death. He is connected by the historian Herodotus with the Hyperboreans, people of the north or east, who sent mysterious offerings to Apollo at Delphi. From the fifth century BCE on, there are suggestions that link Apollo to the sun. The best known myth of the sun from ancient Greece is the story of Phaethon, who begged to drive the chariot of the sun, lost control of it, and would have scorched the earth if he had not been killed by a thunderbolt. In a fragment of Euripides, the mother of Phaethon says that the true name of the sun is *Apollo,* meaning "the destroyer," since he had destroyed her son. The Orphic poets, as well as the Cynic philosopher Crates (c. 300 BCE), called the sun

Apollo. Cornutus, writing about Greek mythology in the first century BCE, says that the sun is Apollo and the moon is his sister Artemis. In Roman times, after the names of the Greek gods reached Italy, this identification was taken for granted. The first Roman emperor, Augustus, favored the worship of Apollo, built a temple to him on the Palatine, and had the poet Horace, in his secular hymns, speak of the sun as Apollo and the moon as Diana (identified often with Greek Artemis).

As the intellectual life of philosophy developed, the Olympians lost their appeal. Philosophers substituted for them the "visible gods," the fixed heavenly bodies. In Plato's *Laws* (10.3) Socrates prays to the rising sun. Star lore from Mesopotamia combined with Greek mathematics to produce astrology, which gave impetus to the tendency to believe that the heavens had a meaningful relationship with humans. Many philosophers opposed astrology, but the Stoics embraced it as an example of the pantheism they advocated. The sun was obviously the most important of the planets, and in the growing mysticism of the Roman era became the final destination of souls freed from the wheel of fate.

ANCIENT ROME. As in Greece, sun festivals are rare in ancient Rome, but there are indications of the early worship of Sol Indiges, that is, an original and native god. There was a public sacrifice to this god on the Quirinal on the ninth of August. Varro's book on agriculture (first century BCE) says he will mention not the city gods but those who are the best guides of the farmer, the sun and moon, "whose seasons are observed at seedtime and harvest." Varro believed that the Sabine king Tatius, a contemporary of the founder Romulus, brought to Rome the worship of the sun and moon. He also stated that the ancient family of the Aurelii (whose descendants founded the cult of Sol Invictus) came from the Sabine country and that their name was originally Ausel, the Sabine word for "sun."

The sun and moon were deities of the chariot races. It is possible that the famous "October horse" ritual, held on the ides of October, was originally a sacrifice to the sun. This ritual involved a sacrifice of the outside winning horse; a similar ritual occurred in March, and thus these rituals marked the planting and the harvest seasons. The Sun had a temple on the Aventine near the Circus, from which spectators could watch the races. The Sun's image in gold was on the roof, since it was not proper to display the Sun indoors. It was to that temple that offerings were made when a conspiracy against Nero was revealed, since the Sun had discovered the plot (Tacitus, *Annals* 15.74). Augustus, returning from the conquest of Egypt, brought with him two obelisks with inscriptions declaring that he dedicated them to the sun, one of which he set up in the Campus Martius and the other in the Circus. They are now in the Piazza di Monte Citorio and the Piazza del Popolo.

Under the empire, various forms of sun worship spread into Rome from the East, imported both by slaves and by the Roman legions. The cult and mysteries of Mithra were the most widespread of these, apparently first taken up by soldiers of Pompey from Cilician pirates. The cult was obviously derived from the older Iranian cult, but from the two intervening centuries that separate these cults little is known about Mithra; the cult spread, however, to all areas of the empire. It involved initiation in a simulated cave; immortality was promised to initiates as a reward for the soldierly qualities of courage and discipline. Some astral features were collected along the way, and the degrees of initiation were known by the names of the planets. Mithra, who was said to be a special comrade or son of the sun, was born from a rock and sacrificed a bull, from which all creation sprang. After his deeds on earth were accomplished, he partook of a special love feast with the sun god before being carried up to heaven in a fiery chariot. The initiates imitated the love feasts in *mithraea,* underground shrines, which can still be found wherever the legions went. In death they were to be carried to the sun in Mithra's chariot. It became traditional for steles of the emperor to depict this journey upward in the sun's chariot.

One of the more lurid incidents in the late Roman empire involved the short reign of a young man who called himself Elagabalus, or Heliogabalus, after his god. A relative of Septimius Severus (r. 193–211 CE) on his Syrian wife's side, the youth was the hereditary priest of a sun god who was worshiped at Emesa in Syria in the shape of a black meteorite. After the death of Severus and his son Caracalla, the ladies of the court contrived to have the youth named emperor, though he was then only fourteen years old. He brought his black stone to Rome and built for it a magnificent temple on the Palatine. In front of his temple every day the youth burned incense, poured wine, offered bloody sacrifices, and—most difficult for the Romans to accept—danced Oriental dances. According to the time-honored fate of unsuitable emperors, the young man was assassinated after four years of rule.

The final victory at Rome of the sun god came about through the emperor Aurelian, who in 270 CE assumed the task of reconquering those parts of the empire that had defected. Aurelian's mother is said to have been a priestess of the Sun in the village in which he was born, from the old Sabine family of the Aurelii. The time was ripe for a new supreme deity who would symbolize imperial power, the person of the emperor, and the new astral religion. Aurelian found such a god in Palmyra, the oasis city in the Syrian desert. Aurelian dedicated a fortune in gold, silver, and jewels from his plunder to restore the temple of the Sun in Palmyra. In 274 CE he established Sol Invictus ("the invincible sun") as the official religion of the Roman empire, and was the first emperor to wear Oriental robes and the diadem, a sun symbol. Sol Invictus continued as supreme god and patron of emperors until Constantine, who started his reign as a sun worshiper and later turned the empire over to Christianity. The coins of Aurelian and of succeeding emperors show the Sun offering the ruler, as Preserver of the World, a globe.

The Sun portrayed in these coins is not Oriental; he has the features of the Greek Apollo, wearing a crown with solar rays. Sometimes he drives a chariot drawn by four horses. Such coins read: "To the Invincible Sun, companion of Augustus."

Julian, called the Apostate, in his brief reign (359–362) tried to bring back the worship of the sun. "From my childhood," he writes in his prose hymn to the sun, "an extraordinary longing for the rays of the sun penetrated my soul" (*Hymn to King Helios* 130c). The Neoplatonists, with whom Julian identified the leading philosophical school of the late empire, believed in one supreme ineffable god but were able to accept the sun as a symbol, "offspring of the first god." According to Julian, "His [Helios's] light has the same relation to the visible world as truth to the intelligible world" (ibid., 133a). Julian recognized three aspects of the sun god: the sun of the intelligible world, of the intellectual world, and of the sensible world, which last he identified with Mithra.

The birthday of Sol Invictus and of Mithra were celebated on December 25, close to the time of the winter solstice. In 353 or 354 CE Pope Liberius set this date as the Feast of the Nativity, and a few years later he founded the Church of Santa Maria della Neva, now known as Santa Maria Maggiore, which became the center of the Roman celebration of Christmas. The Nativity gradually absorbed or supplanted all the other solstice rites. Solar imagery came increasingly to be used to portray the risen Christ (who was also called Sol Invictus), and the old solar disk that had once appeared behind the head of Asian rulers became the halo of Christian saints. Excavations under Saint Peter's Basilica, undertaken in hope of finding the tomb of Peter, found a very early Christian mosaic that showed Christ driving a chariot, with rays above his head.

JAPAN. The national religion of Japan, Shintō, is an extraordinary combination of myth, national feeling, ancestor worship, and highly sophisticated mysticism. Japanese writers on the subject assert that theoretical analysis in the Western style is quite unsuitable for Shintō; it is rather a system of rites, feelings, and intense poetic appreciation. There is no doubt that the performance of the rites has over the centuries given the Japanese people a confidence in themselves and their place in society and the universe. The sun appears on the Japanese flag today, but the epithet "Land of the Rising Sun" was perhaps invented by the Chinese.

Japanese cosmogony, first recorded in the seventh century CE, relates how the islands came to be formed out of the primeval waters by a celestial couple, who gave birth to many other natural features. When the wife was burned and died in giving birth to fire, her husband, fleeing from the sight of her decomposing body, stopped to purify himself, and in the process produced from his right eye the Sun (female) and from his left eye the Moon (male). The Moon plays very little part in the mythology, but from the nose of the original husband was produced Susano-o no Mikoto, who represents violence, earthly qualities, and death, while the sun goddess, Amaterasu, stands for light and purity. Susano-o no Mikoto, realizing that the earth could only be created and peopled if the two powers cooperated, tried to force his way into the abode of Amaterasu, whereupon she hid in a cave and left the world in darkness. There are a number of caves in modern-day Japan that are identified as the cave where the goddess hid herself. Eventually the other gods persuaded Amaterasu to emerge. Among the sacred regalia they employed to ensure her emergence was a mirror—the mirror that is said to be part of the ritual at the famous Ise Shrine.

Shintō teaching maintains that Amaterasu and Susano-o no Mikoto represent not good and evil but complementary qualities that are necessary to produce life on earth. Eventually the world as it stands was completed, and Amaterasu became the ancestor of the first emperor of Japan. The sun goddess is the center of Shintō worship, which is intended to bind the people together in reverence for her earthly representative. The goal of Shintō is the maintenance of harmony among humankind, nature, and the gods. The greatest reality visible in the heavens becomes the symbol of the greatest reality known and revered on earth.

The earliest records of Shintō derive from the seventh century BCE, when writing was introduced, but the roots of the system may stretch much further back. In the Middle Ages, it was much influenced by Buddhism, but the two became distinct in the eighteenth century. In 1946, the American occupation forces demanded that the emperor renounce his divine status as part of their abolition of the state religion. It appears that the formal renunciation has had little effect on the symbolic relationship that has endured for centuries between the sun goddess and the imperial family. On the other hand, the retreat of state Shintō, which had highly politicized overtones and which was the basis for a fanatical militarism, in a sense returned the religion to the people. The priests, without government support, turned to the population. When it became time for the reconstruction of the Grand Shrine at Ise, which is prescribed every twenty years, there was an unprecedented outpouring of donations from the entire populace. More than fifty million people contributed to the rebuilding of the shrine in 1953, even more in 1973.

The rituals have continued and the emperor has participated in the divine nature of his ancestors by praying for the well-being of his people. In the great ceremonies at the end of June and December (the solstices), the imperial families and ministers of state pray for purification from sin for the entire country.

THE AMERICAS. Many native North Americans regarded the Sun as their supreme deity. In the Plains, the Crow thought of themselves as descendants of the Sun and swore by it. In lower Mississippi, the Natchez maintained a total theocracy; their priest-chieftain was a substitute on earth for their supreme being, the Sun. For the Pueblo, the Sun is a powerful deity but subordinate to others, such as the Corn Goddess. They perform ceremonies at the summer solstice to slow down the sun and at the winter solstice to hasten his progress toward spring. It is presumed that these rites are a projection of the same religion that is a basis for the sun cults of the high cultures of Mexico and Peru.

Mesoamerica. The Maya of Mesoamerica developed a complex civilization that to date has not been entirely revealed to modern researchers. There are still discoveries to be made in the huge structures now in ruins; they are probably not cities in a real sense but religious establishments where a priestly caste expended tremendous energies on mathematical study and on astronomical observations. They invented a sign for zero and produced two complicated calendars, which come together every fifty-two years. The site of one of their complexes was itself a huge calendar by which they could determine solstices and equinoxes. Since the Maya hieroglyphics have not been entirely deciphered, and since many of their sacred books were destroyed by the Spaniards, there is no clear picture of their complex religious pantheon, which involved four aspects for each deity (for the four points of the compass), or of the characteristics of their gods, which changed from one area to another. The supreme deity seems to have been a sky god, pictured as an old man with a Roman nose; he often performed as a sun god and was married to the Moon. Rain gods and fertility gods were also part of the pantheon. It is still unknown why the Maya civilization collapsed, although many theories, such as climactic change, conquest, or peasant revolt, have been suggested.

In the tenth century CE, conquering Toltec from Tula in central Mexico moved into Maya territory, took over the city of Chichén Itzá, together with many of the Maya achievements. The Toltec brought with them their culture hero, the Feathered Serpent, but also their belief that the sun god died every night and had to be resuscitated every morning with human blood. They established two priestly warrior groups, the Eagles, representing the sun in the daytime, and the Jaguars, representing the sun in the underworld. A frieze at Chichén Itzá from Toltec times shows members of the groups presenting a human heart to the sun. The sacrifice was often succeeded by a cannibalistic feast in which pieces of the victim, if he had been a great warrior, were passed out to the elite. A priest donned the skin of the victim and danced before the people.

The Toltec had perhaps been driven out of the valley of Mexico by the Aztec, who settled on islands in Lake Texcoco and built their elaborate city Tenochtitlán on the site that is today known as Mexico City. They took over from their predecessors the temple architecture, their fifty-two-year calendar, and the sacrifice to the sun, which they carried to even more grisly lengths. On some occasions as many as twenty thousand victims were sacrificed on the sun pyramid. The Aztec believed that on their journey north, their sun god, Huitzilopochtli, who took the form of a hummingbird, led them in the day, and the fearsome Tezcatlipoca, the sun of the underworld, led them at night. A third form of the sun represented the physical disk of the sun, under the name of Tonatiuh. He appears on the huge calendar stone, thirteen feet across, that is now in the Museo Nacional de Antropología. This stone pictures the four suns that the Aztecs believed had existed before them and the fifth, under which they lived. The former suns had been destroyed by storms, floods, and darkness, and the present sun, represented by Tonatiuh, was to end in an earthquake. The whole calendar is circled by fire serpents, which the Sun uses to fight his enemies at night. The entire religion of the Aztec was suffused with the battle between light and darkness and life and death. The universe, they believed, would fall into ruins if they did not feed the "skeleton" sun every morning as he rose.

It seems to have been the priesthood, possibly under the influence of psychedelic drugs, who drove the armies to seek increasing numbers of conquests in order to provide prisoners for the sacrifices. Huitzilopochtli is said to have proclaimed, "My principal purpose in coming and my vocation is war." All young Aztec were educated for war and taught to endure pain. There is a story told of the gladiatorial battle that followed the morning sacrifice in which a captive was tied to a stone and given four staves to defend himself against two Eagle and two Jaguar knights. Once, a captive miraculously won his battle and was released, but he returned to die on the stone so that he would not lose the privilege of accompanying the sun across the sky every morning. In the afternoon, the sun was followed by women who had died in childbirth, for they had also died "taking a man prisoner."

Peru. In Mexico the Sun became one of the most bloodthirsty of all divinities, but the sun god of the Inca of Peru was an autocratic but paternalistic deity, who planned for the welfare of his people while controlling their every action. In the high civilization of Peru, the sun again symbolized royal power; images of the sun were emblazoned with the most lavish display of the sun's metal ever seen. In Peruvian society there was no trade in (as there was among the Aztec) nor use for metal, except for extravagant adornment of the gods and royal personages.

A number of Spanish chronicles have recorded Inca rule as one of the most orderly and regulated in the world. All land was owned by the state and was divided into church, state, and peasant holdings. Inca territory was divided into four quarters ruled by governors, who were subordinate to the emperor, the son of the Sun. The emperor controlled the priesthood, usually making his brother high priest.

The leading tribes that formed the Inca empire seem to have arrived in Cuzco from somewhere around Lake Titicaca. Their legend told that the founder and his sister, children of the Sun, were set down by their father on an island in the lake. The first emperor is said to have been sent by his father, the Sun, to establish a city at the place where the golden wand the Sun carried struck the ground. This site was Cuzco, at eleven thousand feet above sea level. It was apparently the custom for each new emperor to build his own palace, so that the site became a maze of buildings, temples, and palaces, lavishly decorated with gold. In the main square, the Inca emperor himself was enthroned during festivals. From that square it was possible to see the sun columns on the hills east and west, markers of the solstices. The mummified figures of past emperors were seated, robed in gold, around the temple of the Sun, with their wives between them. The temple was called the Place of Gold and was so arranged that sunrise fell on a gold-sheathed solar disk and filled the whole temple with reflected light. On festival days the mummies were paraded around the city, preceded by the emperor on a palanquin, honored as if he were a god. Tradition held that the emperor married his sister, who represented the moon, but a large number of "virgins of the Sun" were available to him, so that he had many descendants. These were the "children of the Sun," the rulers of the bureaucracy, who paid no taxes. Others of the virgins were used for sacrifice or kept in seclusion, weaving or making brew.

The temple also housed the gods of conquered peoples, who were allowed to visit their gods and pay homage to them, although there was a strong missionary pressure on them to honor the sun god. By practicing efficiency and good military discipline, the Inca established an empire that stretched from Ecuador to northern Chile and that had just reached its height at the time of the Spanish conquest.

In the last century of the empire one of the Inca, by the name of Pachacuti, introduced a new high god, Viracocha, as creator. The legend relates that Pachacuti had a vision that prompted this religious revolution. He came to believe that the sun worked too hard on his daily journey to have created the universe. Viracocha may have been a local god from another tribe. Another possibility is that the new god was more acceptable to some of the conquered people, such as the Chimú of the coast, who worshiped the moon and the sea. It is recorded that they complained, "The sun is dangerous to us." A gold statue of the new deity was placed in the Sun's temple as an addition to its other resplendent embellishments.

Great Inca festivals consisted of dances, processions, prayers, and sacrifices, usually of llamas and guinea pigs but sometimes of human beings. The four chief festivals were those of the solstices and the equinoxes, the most important of which was the winter solstice. On this day, considered New Year's Day, all fires were relit by a piece of cotton kindled by the sun's rays. The relit fire was used for the sacrifices and then handed over to the Virgins of the Sun to be guarded until the next year. If the day was cloudy, the fire had to be kindled by friction and there was great anxiety among the people. At the summer solstice, the population gathered in the central square clothed in feathers and golden robes to watch the Inca emperor pour a libation to the Sun from a golden vase.

The priesthood, like all the other members of Inca society, were organized in a strict hierarchy. Many were engaged in divination and in curing the sick. They divined by reading the intestines of llamas and the flight of birds. To cure the sick, they engaged in rites of exorcism. Public confessions were an important part of religious life. Anyone who was malformed or had lost children was considered to have sinned against the Sun and to have disobeyed the Inca emperor. It was necessary for the sinner to confess; he would then be given a penance by the priest and be purified in running water. Anyone who did not confess was believed to be destined for a place deep in the earth where there were only stones for food. Those who confessed, as well as those who had led blameless lives, were promised a happy afterlife in the Sun's heaven. The Children of the Sun and the Inca emperor himself were, as a matter of course, believed to live with the Sun forever.

SEE ALSO Amaterasu Ōmikami; Avesta; Light and Darkness; Mithraism; Saura Hinduism; Sol Invictus; Winter Solstice Songs.

BIBLIOGRAPHY

Since there are few books devoted entirely to the religious and mythological aspects of the sun, most of the material must be extracted from religious writings, encyclopedias, and histories of the religion of the different regions. A highly respected source for ancient Rome is Franz Altheim's *History of Roman Religion* (New York, 1938). Of the many works on Egyptian religion, a good summary is Ann Rosalie David's *The Ancient Egyptians* (London, 1982). The *Dictionnaire des antiquités grecques et romaines,* vol. 4, edited by Charles Daremberg and Edmond Saglio (Paris, 1911) contains an article "Sol" by Franz Cumont, which treats both Greek and Roman sun worship with a wealth of detail. A comprehensive picture of the religion of Britain and Ireland can be found in Jan de Vries's *Keltische Religion* (Stuttgart, 1961). An essay called "The Sun and Sun Worship," in *Patterns in Comparative Religion* by Mircea Eliade (New York, 1958), provides many insights into various aspects of the subject. The article "Christmas," in the *Encyclopaedia of Religion and Ethics,* edited by James Hastings, vol. 3 (Edinburgh, 1910), details the many theories on the origin of the solstice festivals. A very lengthy chapter on the sun in James G. Frazer's *The Worship of Nature* (London, 1926) is packed with data from primitive sources and makes a point of criticizing the pansolism of the nineteenth century. In *The Chariot of the Sun* (New York, 1969) Peter Gelling and Hilda R. Ellis Davidson have produced a useful account of sun worship in the Bronze Age in northern Europe. *Man and the Sun* (New York, 1962) by the archaeologist and historian Jacquetta Hawkes is an accurate and sensitive treatment of sun worship in the ancient world and the Americas. Unfortunately, it does not contain a bibliography or notes. Jean Herbert, in *Shintō* (London, 1967), presents a worthy effort to make the Japanese cult available to the Western world. It contains many translations of ancient literature and more recent Japanese commentaries. In *The Religions of the American Indians* (Berkeley, 1979), Åke Hultkrantz gives a concise but thorough summary of the beliefs of the American Indians, both north and south. A work on astroarchaeology, *In Search of Ancient Astronomies,* edited by Edwin C. Krupp (Garden City, N.Y., 1978), treats, among others, the work of Atkinson, Hawkins, and Thom on the megaliths of the British Isles. The most recent and fullest account of the religions of the ancient Near East is to be found in Thorkild Jacobsen's *The Treasures of Darkness: A History of Mesopotamian Religion* (New Haven, Conn., 1976). An extremely useful collection of material from all over the world, both ancient and primitive, is the *Mythology of All Races,* 13 vols., edited by Louis H. Gray (Boston, 1916–1932), published under the auspices of the Archaeological Institute of America. Martin P. Nilsson brings to his *Geschichte der griechischen Religion,* 3d ed., 2 vols. (Munich, 1967–1974), a wealth of information from archaeology and comparative religion. Still the most complete collection of mythological material is to be found in *Ausführliches Lexikon der griechischen und römischen Mythologie,* edited by W. H. Roscher (1866–1890; Hildesheim, 1965), in articles entitled "Helios," "Sol," and "Sonnenkulten." The "Sacred Books of the East" series, containing the religious writings of India and Persia collected by F. Max Müller in 1884, has been reissued (Delhi, 1965). Maarten J. Vermaseren, in *Mithras, the Secret God* (New York, 1963), presents a detailed account of the cult of Mithra in the Roman world.

New Sources

Aldhouse-Green, Miranda. *The Sun-Gods of Ancient Europe.* London, 1991.

Bailey, Adrian. *The Caves of the Sun: The Origin of Mythology.* London, 1997.

Fideler, David. *Jesus Christ, Sun of God; Ancient Cosmology and Early Christian Symbolism.* Wheaton, Ill.., 1993.

Goodison, Lucy. *Death, Women, and the Sun: Symbolism of Regeneration in Early Aegean Religion.* London, 1989.

Heilbron, J. L.. *The Sun in the Church: Cathedrals as Solar Observatories.* Cambridge, Mass., 2001.

Hornung, Erik. David Lorton, trans. *Akhenaten and the Religion of Light.* Ithaca, N.Y., 1999.

Orcutt, William Tyler. *Sun Lore of All Ages: A Collection of Myths and Legends Concerning the Sun and Its Ages.* San Diego, Calif., 1999.

Saran, Anirudha. *Sun Worship in India: A Study of the Deo Sun-Shrine.* New Delhi, 1992.

Taylor, J. Glen, ed. *Yahweh and the Sun: Biblical and Archeological Evidence for Sun Worship in Ancient Israel.* Sheffield, U.K., 1994.

Titcomb, Sarah. *Aryan Sun Myths: The Origin of Religions.* San Diego, Calif., 1999.

JEAN RHYS BRAM (1987)
Revised Bibliography

SUN DANCE [FIRST EDITION] is currently used as a generic term having reference to a rich complex of rites and ceremonies with tribal variations specific to at least thirty distinct tribal groups of the North American Plains and Prairie. Although tribal variations of beliefs, traits, and the structuring of ceremonial lodges are significant and of great importance to the groups concerned, there are nevertheless sufficient similarities to justify use of the generic term. Since these distinct tribal groups represent at least seven mutually unintelligible language families, understandably there is also present the once-universal sign language, a rich means by which even subtle and complex matters could be communicated to all the tribes. Traditionally the peoples have been divided into four major groupings: the northern tribes; the southern tribes; the village, or eastern, tribes; and the Plateau, or western, tribes. Each tribe within these groups gives the Sun Dance its own specific term, which has reference to particular ritual emphases. The Shoshoni and Crow, for example, refer to the complex as the Thirst Lodge, or Thirst Standing Lodge; for the Cheyenne it is the Medicine Lodge; and for the Siouan peoples it is known as the Dance Gazing at the Sun.

The precise tribal origin of the Sun Dance within the North American Plains groups cannot be determined with certainty, in part because calendric rites of world and life renewal involving sacrificial elements and shamanic-type acts of healing are very widespread throughout North America. Leslie Spier's extensive yet inconclusive study (1921) suggested that the complex possibly originated among—or diffused from—the Arapaho and Cheyenne. In terms of more ancient origins outside North America there are compelling parallels with the Tunguzic peoples of Siberia, who had new year festivals of renewal with ritual emphasis on a world tree as axis joining heaven and earth; offerings made of ribbons and sacrificed animal skins were made to this tree. Other shamanic elements described by A. F. Anisimov involve the rhythmic power of drums, the inducing of trances, visions, and curing ceremonies, all of which are strongly reminiscent of the North American Plains Sun Dance traits (Anisimov, 1963).

It is unfortunate that the early anthropological accounts of Native American religious practices were usually flat, ignoring or paying insufficient attention to the spiritual realities underlying religious beliefs and practices as the peoples themselves understood them. The rich values and sacred meanings encoded within cultural forms such as the arts, crafts, and architecture were also largely ignored. Even Robert Lowie, who was very familiar with the early history of the Crow Sun Dance, was able to write in 1915 that the Sun Dance "in large measure served for the aesthetic pleasure and entertainment of the spectators." The Swedish scholar Åke Hultkrantz, commencing his early studies in 1947, challenged these prevailing reductionist perspectives; by giving proper recognition to religious beliefs and practices of primal origin and by integrating the perspectives and methodologies of both anthropology and the history of religions, an approach now found increasingly within current ethnohistorical studies. It is essentially this approach that is respected in the following descriptions.

The rich diversity of beliefs and traits specific to the Sun Dance traditions in some thirty distinct tribal groups, each of which manifests varying levels of acculturation and creative adaptions, can hardly be encompassed within a brief essay. Judicious selection must therefore be made of essential elements across a fair sampling of tribal groups. Attention will also be given to contemporary movements among many Native American peoples for revitalization of traditional sacred values and practices. Indeed, it is primarily the Sun Dance that, as its popularity increases, is acting as model and stimulus for traditionalist movements extending even to non-Plains tribes and to disenchanted non-Native Americans who are seeking examples of what true religious traditions really are.

GENERAL DESCRIPTION. The major Sun Dance celebrations take place for all the tribal groups in late June or early July, "when the sage is long" and "the chokecherries are ripe," or, as some put it, in "the moon of fattening." In the times when these peoples were nomadic pasturalists, the grasses of the prairies would during these months be sufficient to feed the great herds of horses belonging to the tribal bands, who often were joined in the circles of camps with allied tribes. These springtime ceremonies (in the past they may have been held earlier than June) were actually the climax of an annual cycle of minor rites and meetings of many types. Among the Crow, for example, "prayer meetings" take place regularly at the time of the full moon; among all the tribes, groups of singers meet periodically around their drums in order to practice and to instruct younger singers in the extremely difficult and subtle Sun Dance songs, many of which have been faithfully transmitted from ancient times. There are also contemporary songs that have come out of an individual's sacred experiences or that have been learned from other tribes, for today there is much exchange of songs and other cultural elements in the course of the more popular pan-Indian summer powwow circuit. However, all songs that are used in the Sun Dance lodge must accord with particular styles and rhythms, since clear distinctions are made between ceremonial and social dance songs.

Given the complex logistics of the Sun Dances, with encampments of large numbers of people, many people volunteer or are selected during the year to fulfill a wide range of duties. Usually a sponsor coordinates the many details and materials for the construction of the sacred lodge or the provision of the feast at the end of the ceremonies, both of which are accomplished at considerable expense and sacrifice. The most important person however, is the spiritual leader, a "medicine person," who is guardian of the sacred lore and who usually has received special powers through the vision quest (or who may have received the authority to lead the ceremonies from a retiring elder who has passed on his sacred powers). These spiritual leaders have traditionally been recognized as holy people, for they know and live the sacred traditions and have powers for curing those who are ill in body or spirit. Such shamanic figures have been greatly respected as leaders within the tribe, or they have been feared because of the great strength of their mysterious powers. Such leaders should not be considered as belonging only to the past, however, for new leaders are taking their places. Indeed, there are today a growing number of such leaders, including younger men and women who have attempted to become acculturated within the dominant society but, often finding this to be a process of diminishing returns, have gone back to the wise elders for help in reestablishing traditional values in their contemporary ways of life.

Those who participate in the actual ceremonies within the sacred lodge are often individuals who were previously in situations of extreme danger, perhaps as members of the armed forces in wars the United States has conducted overseas, and who vowed that if they should survive they would participate in the next Sun Dance upon returning home. Paradoxically, their experiences in foreign wars have acted as a stimulus for the continuation, and indeed intensification, of the Sun Dance traditions into the present.

To those sacrificing in the lodge for the first time are assigned mentors who are experienced in the Sun Dance rituals and who—having known the suffering of being without food or water for a period of three or four days—are able to counsel and give support to the novice in the lodge. Other camp duties are taken care of by special "police" who see that proper conduct and respect for sacred matters are observed, functions once fulfilled by the warrior societies. A camp crier is also named, who has the responsibility of encircling the camp on horseback in the very early mornings and in the evenings, of chanting instructions to the people, or of giving useful information concerning the day's activities. On occasion such criers might relate humorous incidents, intending to bring great laughter from the circles of lodges, or from the wall tents used today. For in Plains life, now as in the past (and even in the context of the most serious affairs), humor has a legitimate and effective purpose—not just the momentary relief of tensions accompanying the enactment of sacred rites, but also the opening of the human person to deeper modes of understanding.

LODGE CONSTRUCTION. Once the Sun Dance encampment has been established at an appropriate place where there is good water and pasturage, the first ritual act is to select a special cottonwood tree with branches forking at the top. The tree is then cut in a ceremonial manner, the first blow of the ax often being given by a young woman who has been chosen for her virtue and purity (if any man present knows that she has been unfaithful he has the right and obligation to denounce her publicly). The tree must be felled in a specific direction and is not allowed to touch the ground; it is then carried on poles, with songs, ritual acts, and prayers performed along the way. The cottonwood tree is finally placed in a hole prepared at the center of what will be the sacred lodge, which is itself at the center of the encampment. The selected tree is now understood as the axis at the center of the world. It links heaven and earth, thus giving the people access to spiritual realities and conveying the images of the center and the heavens above, together with their larger implications. For most peoples who practice the Sun Dance, this special tree is understood as a "person." In a way akin to human participation in the sacrifice, the tree transmits to those who sacrifice in the lodge the cooling powers of the moisture it has gathered from the stream near which it grew, and then it dies.

The tree thus recapitulates the major themes of the Sun Dance, which involve the alternations of dry and moist, ignorance and wisdom, and death and life—for if there is to be life there must also be death. Once the tree has been ceremonially raised, offerings are placed at its base, and in its fork is put a nest of cherry or willow branches in which may be placed sacred offerings or, often, rawhide effigies. Colored ribbons, signifying heaven and earth, may be tied high on the tree's forking branches. Each tribal group has its own color symbolism and specific manner of dressing the tree. Among the Crow, for example, the head of a bull buffalo is placed, facing east, on the tree, and in the branches there is an eagle, both symbols recapitulating the theme of heaven and earth. Around the tree as spiritual center the circular lodge is then constructed in accord with symbolical variations specific to each of the tribal groups.

The general architectural design for most tribal Sun Dance lodges is the central tree around which are twenty-eight vertical, forked poles associated with the twenty-eight days of the lunar month. This circle of forked poles is then joined together by horizontal poles laid into the upright forks. In addition the Shoshoni, Crow, and Arapaho lodges have twenty-eight very long poles extending from the forks at the circumference and then all laid into the crotch high on the central tree, a structure that resembles a spoked wheel. The Siouan lodges do not have poles radiating out from the center; a distinctive feature of their lodge, in accord with their ceremonial usage, is the construction of a continuous overhead shade arbor around the inner periphery of the lodge. All styles of lodges, however, have entryways facing the east, the place of the rising sun, and brush is usually placed loosely around the outer walls for the greater privacy of the participants within. For all tribal groups, the lodge is not merely understood as a "symbolic model" of the world, but rather it is the world, universe, or created cosmos. Since construction of the lodge recapitulates the creation of the world, all acts in this process are accompanied by prayers and powerful songs associated with ancient myths of origin and creation. The occasion, reminiscent of a primordial time, is solemn, dignified, and of great beauty.

Around the sacred lodge in concentric circles the camps of family units are set up in accord with long-established protocol. At Sun Dance encampments the doorways of many tipis or wall tents are not toward the east, as is customary in daily usage, but rather toward the sacred lodge and tree at the center of the circle. To the west of the sacred lodge there are usually special tipis in which private ceremonies take place exclusively for those who will sacrifice in the lodge. Sweat lodges are also set up, but apart from the camp circle, so that those who have made their vows may be purified before entering the lodge.

Typical Performances. Even though there are many commonalities in all Plains Sun Dance ceremonies, there are also tribal variations that are of great importance to the peoples concerned. In the Siouan form, for example, which has been described by the Lakota Black Elk in *The Sacred Pipe* (Brown, 1952), there are at least two distinctive and central sacrificial elements, one of which is described by the Lakota term for the Sun Dance, *wiwanyag wachipi* ("dance gazing at the sun"). Here, during one complete daylight cycle, the dancers, who are also observing a total fast, move periodically around the inner periphery of the lodge in sunwise manner so that they are always gazing at the sun—a cause, no doubt, of intense suffering.

A second Lakota or Siouan emphasis, also involving sacrificial elements, is the practice of certain dancers, in accord with earlier vows, to have the muscles of the chest pierced by the presiding spiritual leader, who inserts wooden skewers by which they are tied with raw-hide thongs to the central tree. These people then dance, encouraged by the drums and the songs of warriors (brave songs), pulling back on the thongs until the flesh and muscles tear loose. In addition to elements of self-sacrifice, there are spiritual implications of being physically tied to and thus identified with the tree as sacred center. A similar theme is also expressed by the ceremony wherein individuals have skewers inserted into both sides of the shoulders and into the muscles of chest and back. The thongs are then attached to posts set up to represent the four directions. The individual is thereby identified with the center in relation to the four horizontal directions of space. Such sacrificial acts are not just of former times, but are in increasing use today among a number of Siouan peoples. In distinction from prevailing traits and themes of the Siouan Sun Dance, which are strongly reminiscent of elements from earlier military complexes, the Arapaho, the Cheyenne, and the tribes of the Blackfeet Confederation place emphasis on rites of world and life renewal, employing ritual objects that include sacred medicine bundles whose contents have reference to the origins of the tribes.

Finally, emphasis should be given to critical elements in the history of the Sun Dance and to a modified Sun Dance movement that originated among the western Shoshoni and has been transmitted to the Crow. In 1881 the United States government attempted to ban all Sun Dances, believing that they were "demoralizing and barbarous." It was not until 1904, however, that the dances were rigorously prohibited by the Commissioner of Indian Affairs. However, because these ceremonies were central to spiritual needs, they continued to be practiced in secret or in modified forms by almost all the Plains tribes with the exception of the Crow, who had already abandoned the ceremonies in 1875. One of the still continuing modified Sun Dances was that of the Wind River Shoshoni, whose version spread to the Northern Ute in 1890, to the Fort Hall Shoshoni and Bannock in 1901, and to the Shoshoni of Nevada in 1933. With the Indian Reorganization Act of 1934, however, open practice of the dances commenced, but now in forms that gave greater emphasis to spiritual elements rather than to the extreme tortures associated with the earlier military societies.

In 1941 the charismatic Shoshoni Sun Dance leader John Truhujo brought the Sun Dance back to the Crow through the support of the tribal superintendent Robert Yellowtail. A tradition that had been abandoned for more than sixty-six years was thereby reinstated. In January of 1985 Truhujo died at the age of approximately 105, having transferred his sacred powers to Thomas Yellowtail, brother of the former superintendent. It is the Sun Dance in this particular form, faithfully led by Thomas Yellowtail to the present time, that has become for the Crow, as well as for many other tribes, an example and stimulus giving continuity and viability to the essentials of the spiritual heritage of the Plains peoples.

In this Shoshoni/Crow Sun Dance the dancers take positions in arbors that surround the inner periphery of the lodge, with the presiding spiritual leader, or "medicine man," always at the west. Women, who are allowed within the lodge to fast, take places slightly to the north of the east-facing entrance. The large ceremonial drum and the alternating teams of drummers and singers have their place a little to the south of the entrance, and they are surrounded by strong-voiced older women who help to sing the sacred songs. The dance's spiritual force resides in the movements of the fasting participants, who for the three or four days' duration of the ceremony are always oriented to the central tree, toward which they dance as often or as little as they wish. They blow on eagle-bone whistles tipped with eagle down, as if they themselves were eagles; then they dance backward to their stalls, still facing the central tree. The rhythmic movements of the dancers are dignified, and their concentration on the tree is continual and intense; for them this is the center and source of life, and the lodge symbolizes the totality of creation. In the course of the ceremonies, participants often receive sacred visions; when they sleep—never for more than a few hours at a time—dreams of special meaning may come.

An especially powerful and beautiful ceremony central to the Sun Dance takes place every morning just before sunup, when all the dancers, under the direction of the group's spiritual leader, face the direction of the rising sun, moving slowly to the beat of the drum and blowing softly on eagle-bone whistles. As the sun rises the drum and the sunrise greeting-song come to a crescendo. Eagle plumes tied to the wrists of the dancers are held out to the sun's first rays and are then touched to parts of the body so that the dancer may receive purifying blessings. Once the sun is above the horizon, the dancers sit wrapped in their blankets while very ancient sacred songs are sung and communal prayers are offered. On the second or third day of the dance, people who are ill come into the lodge and stand at the sacred tree to receive help from the spiritual leader, who prays over them and often draws out the illness with the aid of an eagle-wing fan. Accounts of cures are legion. At the conclusion of the Sun Dance, water that has been blessed is ceremonially passed around among the participants, who have taken no food or water since they first entered the lodge. Thereafter, many people from the camp bring valuable gifts into the lodge, sometimes even horses loaded with blankets and beadwork, which are given away to particular persons who are called forward to receive them. The dancers themselves usually complete the ceremonies with a purifying sweat bath at a nearby creek or river, and in the evening there may be a special feast for all.

The power of sacred traditions of primal origin cannot be compromised by time, place, or number of participants, for in themselves the values and realities concerned are of timeless and universal validity. Though a world of other priorities ignores or neglects such values they may nevertheless be rediscovered as still enduring, even increasing in meaning into the present day. The history of the Plains Sun Dance is continuing witness to this reality.

Bibliography

Anisimov, A. F. "The Shaman's Tent of the Evenks and the Origin of the Shamanistic Rite." In *Studies in Siberian Shamanism*, edited by Henry N. Michael, pp. 84–123. Toronto, 1963. An excellent example of Siberian shamanic elements reminiscent of shamanic phenomena in North America.

Brown, Joseph Epes, ed. *The Sacred Pipe.* Norman, Okla., 1953. An especially useful work; chapter 5 presents descriptions of the Lakota Sun Dance by the sage Black Elk.

Dorsey, George A. *The Arapaho Sun Dance.* Chicago, 1903.

Dorsey, George A. *The Cheyenne*, vol. 2, *The Sun Dance.* Chicago, 1905. Dorsey's books define in great ethnographic detail and with excellent plates and diagrams most elements of the Arapaho and Cheyenne Sun Dance as they obtained at the turn of the century.

Hultkrantz, Åke. *Belief and Worship in Native North America.* Syracuse, 1981. Chapter 4 presents an excellent treatment of the symbolical language encoded in the Wind River Shoshoni Sun Dance Lodge.

Jorgensen, Joseph G. *The Sun Dance Religion.* Chicago, 1972. This work contains much valuable information on the Ute and Shoshoni Sun Dances, but its theory that these were redemptive movements following the collapse of the Ghost Dance of 1890 is open to question.

Lowie, Robert H. *The Sun Dance of the Crow Indians.* New York, 1915. Good ethnographic documentation of the early forms of the Crow Sun Dance; omits many of the religious and spiritual elements.

Powell, Peter J. *Sweet Medicine.* 2 vols. Norman, Okla., 1969. One of the best accounts of the Cheyenne Sun Dance rites and beliefs, with close attention given to religious symbolism and the people's sacred history.

Spier, Leslie. "The Sun Dance of the Plains Indians: Its Development and Diffusion." *Anthropological Papers of the American Museum of Natural History* 16 (1921): 451–527. An early, inconclusive study of the origins of the Sun Dance.

Voget, Fred W. *The Shoshoni-Crow Sun Dance.* Norman, Okla., 1984. The best account of the renewal of the Crow Sun Dance under the influence of the Shoshoni Sun Dance leader, John Truhujo.

Walker, James R. *The Sun Dance and Other Ceremonies of the Oglala Division of the Teton Dakota.* New York, 1917. The best and most comprehensive account of the early forms of the Sun Dance among the Lakota.

JOSEPH EPES BROWN (1987)

SUN DANCE [FURTHER CONSIDERATIONS].

The Plains Indian Sun Dance is typically a ceremony of about twelve days duration. Three to four days of this period consist of the dance itself, danced by men (and, increasingly, women) who commit themselves to a self-sacrificing discipline of abstinence from both food and water throughout the dance. Typically, the four days before the dancing are set aside as a period of preparation and purification and the four days following are set aside for a series of ceremonies that bring the whole to a close.

The historical tradition was to hold the Sun Dance in an elevated place, usually on a plateau. With the advent of the reservation era and federal prohibitions against observing the ceremony, the sites were often moved to sheltered and hidden places in physical depressions in the landscape where the ceremony could avoid easy detection.

The Sun Dance in the contemporary period has functioned as a stimulus for the growing traditionalist movement in many tribal communities, and it continues to be appealing to many non-Indians who are disenchanted with their own religious traditions. To the regret of many Indian leaders and scholars, this same attraction has influenced a transformation of Native American traditions toward a certain mimicry of the religious traditions disavowed by their white adherents. The relatively famous (or infamous) Lakota Sun Dances can attract hundreds of dancers, all ready to go to the tree and offer their flesh for the piercing rite. At the same time there are a plethora of other Sun Dances held that are so small as to render them invisible in the non-Indian landscape.

Enormous commitments of resources and time are always a factor in the ceremony. Even the smallest Sun Dance requires the sustained efforts of a variety of people: to cut timbers and leafy coverings for the shade arbor for supporters; to cut wood and then tend the fire day and night for the duration of the ceremony; to collect the necessary "medicines" needed to sustain the dance and provide healing to those who come; to provide and prepare the food to feed the people; and to complete a great variety of other detailed tasks.

In most tribal traditions, the ceremony can be completed with the fulfillment of a commitment by a single dancer, the tree, and a single singer. In reality, while the number of dancers may have always been small historically, the full number of participants regularly included the whole of a tribe's community in these various supporting roles. Lakota peoples, for instance, would congregate annually in the Black Hills for the Sun Dance as a ceremony that brought together all of the disparate bands. In the modern world it has become commonplace for as many as a hundred or more to commit to dancing this strenuous and demanding ceremony.

The Sun Dance is traditionally a men's ceremony. The single most characteristic feature is the sustaining of life or, as Lakota people often say, "That the people might live." The blood that flows in the piercing rite of many tribal traditions marks the ceremony as a male rite. Indeed, this sacrifice has been characterized as men's attempt to gain some sense of equality with women and their natural life-giving character signified by the monthly flow of blood in menstruation. If women bring new life into the community, men contribute to the maintaining of life through the Sun Dance ceremony.

While much of the professional literature misrepresents the piercing as self-torture or self-mutilation, for Indian communities it is always seen as a personal sacrifice offered on behalf of the people. In any event, participants invariably report that the piercing itself is not the most difficult aspect of this demanding ceremony, but rather comes as a climactic resolution that brings relief to the tension of one's prayers. The real focus of the ceremony is always the prayers of the dancers.

Many Sun Dance leaders emphasize strongly that, like all other key ceremonies, the Sun Dance ought always be done according to the direction of a particular vision given to someone in a particular time and place. Hence, each Sun Dance is a discrete phenomenon. One constant in all tribal variants is that there is a tree. Everything else is based on the particular vision and can vary from tribe to tribe and from one Sun Dance leader to another within a tribe.

Many tribes continue to practice a form of the Sun Dance that is still a tribal ceremony. That is to say that the tribal community sponsors only one Sun Dance each year and that it is a ceremony performed by and for the tribe as a whole. The ceremony held at Ethete, Wyoming, is an example. A high percentage of the Northern Arapaho population is involved, and the tribe's government extends certain privileges to those who are principal participants. These ceremonies function in the modern world as spiritual events that provide social cohesion for the tribe.

Other tribes, particularly the Siouan group of Lakota and Dakota, have engaged in a substantial transformation of their ceremonial life and its intent. One could argue that these tribes have moved towards the individualization represented by missionary Christianity. As such, these Sun Dance ceremonies tend today to proliferate into individual and family events that can even be seen as competing with one another for adherents. These ceremonies form around specific spiritual leaders, and many are increasingly open to anyone, Indian or non-Indian, who will make the personal commitment to a particular spiritual leader.

Ultimately, the proliferation of Sun Dances on Lakota reservations reflects back the denominational variety of missionary religion, which has historically functioned to divide

Indian communities and to break down tribal cohesion by introducing Western religious choice and the paradigm of denominationalism. It can also be argued, of course, that traditional Lakota culture allows for the making of these sorts of leadership choices. While leadership was hereditary, it was always possible for any members of a band or group to follow another leader should they decide that they disagreed with the direction of leadership.

In any case, the contemporary result has been that there is no longer a "Lakota" tribal Sun Dance; instead, more than two dozen Sun Dances have been reported at the Oglala reservation at Pine Ridge over a single recent summer, with a similar number at the neighboring Rosebud and Cheyenne River reservations. The shift, however, has become more pronounced as Lakotas and Dakotas have invited more and more non-Indians as participants into their tribal ceremonial rites.

Bibliography

Holler, Clyde. *Black Elk's Religion: The Sun Dance and Lakota Catholicism.* Syracuse, N.Y., 1995.

White, Phillip M. *The Native American Sun Dance Religion and Ceremony: An Annotated Bibliography.* Westport, Conn., 1998.

Tink Tinker (2005)

SUNDANESE RELIGION. Although the Sundanese of West Java, Indonesia, consider themselves Muslims, many pre-Islamic ideas still permeate their religious life. A key point in understanding Sundanese relations to the supernatural is the relationship between the soul and a creative or generative power that animates the universe. This power, *anu ngayuga* ("that which creates") is limited and is contained to varying degrees in the elements that make up the cosmos. The amount of power in a person is determined by ancestry and the time, place, and conditions of birth. It may further wax or wane according to the state of ritual or moral purity of the person (see Anderson, 1972).

Soul. The Sundanese have two ideas of soul: *nyawa* and *semangat.* Other words such as *roh* and *jiwa* are occasionally used, but these are adoptions from the Arabic and Sanskrit, respectively, and overlap in meaning between *nyawa* and *semangat. Nyawa* is simply life or breath, existing only while the person lives. *Semangat,* on the other hand, is that aspect of soul that connects a person to the ancestors and gives him or her various capabilities and strengths. It is the whole of a person's spiritual life. Provencher (1975) relates *semangat* to the Melanesian and Polynesian mana.

The *semangat* belongs with the person, but may occasionally leave if frightened or if a taboo is broken. In this case the person's soul must be coaxed back, or illness and death may follow. The *semangat* is also considered to be able to travel away from a person during sleep, making it dangerous to awaken him suddenly, and may further transmigrate and enter an animal such as a tiger.

The amount of *semangat* in a person is not constant but may be added to through study, especially of sacred texts and magic, as well as through the acquisition of sacred objects and heirlooms. It may also be diminished through impure and worldly actions. There must be an inner balance between the *semangat* and the social persona of the person. Too much or too little of it to fit the situation makes the person uncomfortable and may lead to disquietude or illness. These last two aspects of *semangat* are much like the cosmic power mentioned above, and one may see semangat, then, as the unique expression of cosmic creative power (*anu ngayuga*) in individuals.

Semangat is located throughout the body, although it seems to be focused on the navel. The Sundanese take care to bury brushed-out hair and nail clippings, as these are parts of the person and thus contain soul substance that may be used against one in magic. Amulets are worn around the waist, protecting the center of the soul.

The placenta *(ari ari)* is considered to be the elder sibling of the person. It is also believed that the same placenta comes back to the mother as she bears each successive child, creating a spiritual or soul bond between siblings.

The father, who planted the seed and made the body, is responsible for its physical maintenance. The soul is said to come from the mother, and she is responsible for the spiritual makeup of the child. For this reason there is a *tali batin* (spiritual tie) between the mother and her children and between the children via the shared placenta.

This connection goes back to the ancestors as well. Ancestral graves are visited and the ancestors are notified when a ritual is to take place or when one goes on an extended journey. Ancestral spirits may also be consulted in times of need. They are often associated with a particular piece of land. Traditionally, people were buried on family land, and inherited land could not be sold to outsiders. Placentas, especially those of infant girls, are also often buried on family land, with which the soul is thus intimately connected (Mus, 1975).

Ancestral souls may also be called on for aid in times of trouble, in which case the ancestor may appear in the form of a tiger. Deceased rulers are said to guard their realms in this form; shamans are said to be able to take on tigrine form while curing.

The Wider Supernatural World. The shaman (*dukun, kuncen*) is the vehicle for dealing with the wider supernatural world. Aside from being human soul stuff, cosmic power is also found in animals, plants, and the like. Like ancestral graves, places such as caves and mountains can be strongly imbued with it. Since this power is amoral, it may be dangerous to ordinary people. Through their craft, shamans are able to interact with these forces and thereby protect the community.

Ordinary people may make requests from these powers, which are often manifested as spirits or magical animals, after being introduced by the *kuncen*. Incense is burned and magical formulas (*jampes*) pronounced, after which the supplicant awaits the arrival of the power. If the power grants the petitioner's request, it may demand in return that the petitioner agree to be turned into a pig, a monkey, or a snake after death or that a human life be sacrificed to it annually.

Other supernatural forces include place spirits (*jurigs*), which may be seen as disembodied bits of cosmic power. They tend to exist on boundaries such as the water's edge or in secluded, quiet places. One does not make requests of these spirits, but only takes care not to bother them excessively. They are said to be generally harmless, though some delight in frightening people, and one type of water spirit (*lulun samak*) sometimes grabs people and drowns them.

Also to be reckoned with are the *silumans*, the spirits of those who have died an unnatural death; and the *kuntianaks*, the spirits of women who have died in childbirth. *Silumans* often inhabit caves and are then said to be the entities that make such places foreboding. The *kuntianak* is a danger to women who are about to give birth by causing difficulties that may lead to the woman's death; she would then become a *kuntianak* herself. For this reason, an expectant mother must take special precautions, such as carrying a sharp metal instrument and not going near the water alone during the last month of her pregnancy. Further magical precautions are taken by the *paraji*, the midwife.

Like the *jurig*, the *siluman* and *kuntianak* may be seen as disembodied cosmic power. This power is dangerous because it must be contained, and in its search for an envelope may possess a person. For this reason also, these powers are found in caves because caves make good containers.

Plants are also imbued with cosmic power—especially rice, trees, and bamboo. Rice, which is the personification of the rice goddess Dewi Sri, is said to have a soul. Care must be taken not to offend the goddess, and offerings are made both in the rice field and in the storage room (*goah*). Offerings in the field are made by the *wali puhun*, the shaman who ensures the fertility of the field. When cutting down trees or large bamboo, permission must be asked from the spirit inhabiting either the area or the tree; otherwise this spirit is likely to cause mischief or to possess someone.

CEREMONIES. Most ceremonies are conducted inside the house, which may be seen as a model of the cosmos itself. Ancestral spirits are invited to these ceremonies and thereby both add their power to the event and give it their blessing. The core of all ceremonies is the *hajat*, a ceremonial meal. Here the shaman, speaking for the householder, states the purpose of the occasion. Blessings from God (Allāh) are invoked, incense is burned while magical formulas are spoken, and then the food is consumed.

Each year on the birthday of the prophet Muḥammad, a *hajat* is held during which heirlooms and amulets are cleaned and restored. These items are said to contain cosmic power that may be added to by chanting over them during the ritual. On the same night, graves visited for help during the year are chanted over in order perhaps to infuse them with the power inherent in the Prophet's birth. This is also a good night to call up one's tiger ancestor, as such spirits are about, on their way to the ancient center of the Sundanese kingdom of Pajajaran at Pakuan near Bogor.

SEE ALSO Islam: Islam in Southeast Asia; Southeast Asian Religions, article on Insular Cultures.

BIBLIOGRAPHY

Anderson, Benedict R. O'G. "The Idea of Power in Javanese Culture." In *Culture and Politics in Indonesia*, edited by Claire Holt, pp. 1–69. Ithaca, N.Y., 1972.

Hasan Mustafa, Hajī. *Over de Gewoonten en Gebruiken der Soendanezen.* Translated into Dutch by R. A. Kern. The Hague, 1946.

Hidding, Klaas Aldert Hendrik. *Ñi Pohatji Sangjang Sri.* Leiden, 1929.

Hidding, Klaas Aldert Hendrik. *Gebruiken en Godsdienst der Soendaneezen.* Batavia, 1935.

Mus, Paul. *India Seen from the East.* Clayton, Australia, 1975.

Provencher, Ronald. *Mainland Southeast Asia: An Anthropological Perspective.* Pacific Palisades, Calif., 1975.

Rikin, Wesley Mintardja. *Ngabersihan als Knoop in de Tali Paranti.* Leiden, 1973.

Sell, Hans Joachim. *Der Schlimme Tod bei den Völkern Indonesiens.* The Hague, 1955.

Wessing, Robert. *Cosmology and Social Behavior in a West Javanese Settlement.* Papers in International Studies, Southeast Asia Series, no. 47. Athens, Ohio, 1978.

New Sources

Glicken, Jessica. "Sundanese Islam and the Value of Hormat: Control, Obedience, and Social Location in West Java." In *Indonesian Religions in Transition*, edited by Rita Smith Kipp and Susan Rodgers, pp. 238–252. Tucson, 1987.

Newland, Lynda. "Under the Banner of Islam: Mobilising Religious Identities in West Java." *Australian Journal of Anthropology* 11, no. 2 (2000): 199–222.

Newland, Lynda. "Of Paraji and Bidan: Hierarchies of Knowledge among Sundanese Midwives." In *The Daughters of Hāritī: Childbirth and Female Healers in South and Southeast Asia*, edited by Geoffrey Samuel and Santi Rozario, pp. 256–278. London, 2002.

Noorduyn, J., and A. Teeuw. "The Ascension of Sri Ajnyana: A Local Form of Saivism in an Old Sundanese Allegorical Poem." In *Society and Sulture of Southeast Asia: Continuities and Changes*, edited by Lokesh Chandra, pp. 283–298. New Delhi, 2000.

ROBERT WESSING (1987)
Revised Bibliography

SUNDÉN, HJALMAR. Hjalmar Sundén (1908–1993) was a Swedish psychologist of religion. Sundén was born in Eksjö, Sweden, the son of a lieutenant-colonel and a homemaker. The peak of Sundén's academic career came late in life. He became a professor at the age of fifty-nine and retired eight years later, a much-appreciated mentor and friend to half a dozen postgraduates, some of whom became professors in the psychology of religion. Sundén remained active as a writer and speaker at symposia, enjoying great academic success during the last twenty-five years of his life. He died at the age of eighty-five.

Sundén was educated in Stockholm, at Norrmalm upper-secondary school and University College, obtaining his master of philosophy degree in 1930. He continued his studies at Uppsala, where he graduated from the Faculty of Theology. His rare gift for languages—he spoke German, French, and English fluently—made it easy for him to learn Hebrew, ancient Greek, and Latin. After only two years of study he received his master's degree in theology in 1932. The following year he was ordained a priest in the Swedish Lutheran Church.

Sundén was given a personal chair in the psychology of religion at the University of Uppsala by special parliamentary decree in 1967, after having worked for years as a priest, a teacher of religion in secondary schools, a psychologist in the state police academy, a psychologist of religion at the University of Stockholm, and a docent in the history of religion, including the psychology of religion, at Uppsala. He was a brilliant speaker, in demand all over Sweden. His lecture tours gave him profound knowledge of the questions that concerned ordinary people. Far removed from scholastic exercises, he always had a deep empathy and respect for ordinary popular piety. This approach and insight proved to be decisive in his later research and academic career.

In his doctoral thesis on the philosopher Henri Bergson, *La théorie bergsonienne de la religion* (1940), Sundén critically reviewed the then-prevailing theories in relation to Bergson's two sources of morality and religion: one rooted in intelligence that also results in science and its static, mechanistic ideal, and the other based on intuition, finding expression in the free creativity of art and philosophy and the mystical experience of the saints. It was the latter that caught the eye of the future psychologist of religion and occupied his thoughts for the rest of his life—his last article was on Teresa of Avila.

Sundén asked simple but profound questions. How is it that people experience existence as religious? Why is it that some people conceive of existence in terms of pure chance, some speak of the interplay of contingencies, while still others prefer to use the word *fate*? Then there are those who perceive an intention in the experiential, contact with the "other" or "another." How is an experience of the world in religious terms psychologically possible?

The answers to these questions are to be found in Sundén's main contribution to the psychology of religion, his magnum opus *Religionen och rollerna* (Religion and roles, 1959). Here he elucidates his understanding of religious experience through role theory, which is based on the discovery that all sacred texts contain descriptions of pious people who have acted in relation to God or gods. The biblical tradition provides people with behavior and role models of how Christians have been in dialogue with God and experienced his presence. When reading the *Psalms*, people are inadvertently absorbed into the mythic figure of David, thereby finding themselves within a specific interactional system, the human role in relation to the divine partner, God. The thinking is: as God saved then, he will also do so now if people trust and rely on him. No matter how hopeless the situation may seem, the promises are eventually expected to be fulfilled.

Contrary to previous theories, Sundén argues that religious experience does not consist of specific feelings, nor is it independent of cultural tradition. It does not emerge from empty nothingness or from any inner mysterious psychic layer. It is rather a matter of perception, the process whereby sensory stimulation is translated into organized or meaningful experience: the intuitive recognition of an existential "truth." Learning is a decisive factor, providing *un système aperceptif* for the soul to be touched and moved by a personal living God. Religious experience is thus reproducible and not the subjective phenomenon to which some scholars have wanted to reduce it.

Sundén integrated the structural-analytic, the interactionist, and the perceptual analytical models from the major research traditions within the social sciences into a psychology of religion, and he based this on his profound knowledge of the history of religions and contemporary theories and methods. His great knowledge of religious texts, and his empathy for them, enabled him to fashion role theory into a powerful hermeneutical tool, especially for the psychological interpretation of autobiographies and other types of personal documents, such as diaries, journals, and letters.

Sundén has rightly been regarded as the founder of the psychology of religion in the Nordic countries. When his magnum opus was translated into German as *Die Religion und die Rollen* (1966), his ideas quickly found fertile soil in Germany, the Netherlands, and Belgium, as well as in the United States in the late 1980s. For many years Sundén chaired the International Association for the Psychology of Religion. His role theory has had the same influence among European psychologists of religion as Gordon Allport's religious-orientations theory had among American psychologists.

BIBLIOGRAPHY

Hjalmar Sundén has written extensively on role theory, but the most elucidating of all his presentations still remains the first essay he ever wrote on the subject in his collection *Sjuttiotredje psalmen och andra essäer* (Psalm seventy-three and other essays; Stockholm, 1956). For those who cannot read Swedish, his article "Saint Augustine and the Psalter in the Light of Role-Psychology," published in the *Journal for the Scientific Study of Religion* 26, no. 3 (1987): 366–412 (an issue dedicated entirely to Sundén's role theory), provides an eloquent substitute.

Holm, Nils G. "Role Theory and Religious Experience." In the *Handbook of Religious Experience,* edited by Ralph W. Hood, pp. 397–420. Birmingham, Ala., 1995. This essay provides a thorough presentation of Sundén's role theory.

Holm, Nils G. "An Integrated Role Theory for the Psychology of Religion: Concepts and Perspectives." In *The Psychology of Religion: Theoretical Approaches,* edited by Bernard Spilka and Daniel N. McIntosh, pp. 73–85. Boulder, Colo., 1997. In this essay, Holm elaborates Sundén's role theory towards an analysis of what he calls an "inner existence space."

Holm, Nils G., and J. A. Belzen, eds. *Sundén's Role Theory: An Impetus to Contemporary Psychology of Religion.* Åbo, Finland, 1995. Sundén's pupils collected their latest essays in the memory of their mentor and friend.

Källstad, Thorvald, ed. *Psychological Studies on Religious Man.* Uppsala, Sweden, 1978. Festschrift dedicated to Sundén on his seventieth birthday.

Sundén, Hjalmar. *Religionen och rollerna.* Stockholm, 1959. German: *Die Religion und die Rollen: Ett psykologiskt studium av fromheten* (*Eine psychologische Untersuchung der Frömmigkeit*). Translated by Herman Müller and Suzanne Öhman. Berlin, 1966.

Wulff, David. *Psychology of Religion: Classic and Contemporary Views.* New York 1991.

René Gothóni (2005)

SUNNAH. In every "founded" religious tradition, maintaining proximity to the founder has been an important source of legitimacy and authority, just as arguments about how to establish that proximity have been a source of conflict. In the Islamic tradition, the word *sunnah* has been the focal point of such issues. A word with a very old history in the Arabic language, *sunnah* comes from a root that is concretely associated with honing or molding, with something firmly rooted, like a tooth (*sinn*). *Sunnah,* by extension, came to mean habitual practice, customary procedure or action, norm, standard, or "usage sanctioned by tradition."

Early Evolution. Among pre-Islamic Arabs, *sunnah* had the force of what anthropologists would call "tribal custom," that is, the generally agreed upon "thing to do" in matters of piety, morality, and social activity. In fact, it was the *sunnah* of the prophet Muḥammad's Arab compeers that initially led them to reject him, since the habitual social and spiritual practices of their ancestors were incompatible with his vision and demands. And it was his reinterpretation of their *sunnah* that helped him win them over, for he "reminded" them successfully that what they took to be true tradition (polytheism, for example) was what modern scholars would call "invented tradition," and that the true *sunnah* of their ancestors was the same Abrahamic ethical monotheism that he was announcing, in that he called upon his listeners to fulfill Abraham's moral contract with the one God.

The Qurʾanic revelations themselves did not establish an unequivocal meaning for *sunnah.* They referred either to the *sunnah* of those of old (the wrongheaded customs of Muḥammad's Arab brethren) or to the *sunnah* (or *sunan,* pl.) of God, namely his punishment of that other *sunnah.* The Qurʾān's flexible usage of the word *sunnah* never disappeared, but *sunnah* quickly came to be associated with the exemplary, imitable, normative words, deeds, and silent approval of the Prophet himself, whose behavior was assumed to be consistent with all previous prophets. In the sense of Muḥammad's exemplary pattern, *sunnah* took on an extraordinarily positive coloration and a predominant place in Muslim piety. The *sunnah* of the Prophet *(sunnat al-nabī)* began to preempt tribal *sunnah*; the new "tribe," the Muslims, acquired a new pattern of established practice. That development, along with the simultaneous revelation of the sacred text, the Qurʾān, *through* Muḥammad produced one of these dynamic paradoxes that have enriched the histories of all the major religions: the relationship between Muḥammad's roles as vehicle of revelation and as exemplar of the most important *sunnah.* Muḥammad was only a man, receiving but not authoring God's word. Yet that word was difficult to follow without its bearer's example and explication; the Qurʾān itself urged Muslims to follow God and his Messenger. Although the injunction not to deify Muḥammad was taken seriously, he was still a man set apart from others by his special intimacy with God and his role as the Seal of the Prophets. Some may also have attributed to him the special, magical powers they would have previously expected from any holy person. In his mission, Muḥammad was, more than many prophets, both messenger and exemplar, because he was a temporal as well as spiritual leader. There was always a thin line between emulation and veneration, between making him an ideal exemplar and dehumanizing him into a perfect man. One could imitate him, but not completely, because he was too special; but one could not make him so special that he was not human. Within this range, myriad authentic pious responses have flourished.

Furthermore, although scriptural religions have always developed sources of commentary that involve the founder, Muslims relied unusually heavily on Muḥammad. They produced a massive, multifunctional, multifaceted corpus of "news" or "reports" (*ḥadīth*) from the companions of the Prophet, whose humanness, though exceptional, had to be maintained. It is true that the *ḥadīth* did not establish Muḥammad as an exemplar apart from his role as bearer of revealed truth; but, ironically, it was the very denial of his divinity that made him so imitable, that allowed personal details to accumulate to a level almost unmatched in the history of religion, with the possible exception of the personality of Mohandas Gandhi. Ironically, too, it may have been the very size of the corpus that not only encouraged selectivity but also promoted, and reflected, disagreement about the norms to be derived from it.

Sunnat al-Nabī. In time, and especially under the pressure of practical necessity, the two parts of Muḥammad's mission coalesced into two separate oral and written bodies of texts: (1) revelation (*waḥy*), that is, divine word or Qurʾān; and (2) inspired prophetic example *(sunnat al-nabī).* The most common literary vehicle of the *sunnat al-nabī*, the *ḥadīth*, functioned to maintain proximity to Muḥammad's *sunnah* in much the same way as the *ayyām*, a pre-Islamic literary form for preserving noble tribal exploits, had kept tribal *sunnah* alive. The early Muslim community, whose *sunnah* was based on that of Muḥammad, preserved the *sunnat al-nabī* through the memorization and transmission of *ḥadīth*. Some Muslims said that *sunnat al-nabī* had been revealed along with the Qurʾān, as has sometimes been said of the oral law and the written law (Torah) in Judaism; others have even relied on *sunnah* more than on the Qurʾān.

The range covered by the *sunnat al-nabī* was as broad as that of oral law too: food and eating, manners, clothing and jewelry, hygiene and grooming, social behavior, forms of greeting, and etiquette, as well as weightier religious, political, or economic matters. Consequently, the *sunnah* of the Prophet and the early community came to play a major role in the development of the Islamic legal system (*sharīʿah*) and systematic discussion about God (*kalām*). (This usage of the term *sunnah* should not be confused with the technical sense in which it is also used within the *sharīʿah* for a certain level of permissibility of acts.)

Sunnah also came to function in various extralegal, extratheological ways. The quoting of *ḥadīth* could have a performatory quality: the mere act of citing an apt *ḥadīth* could help one manage a given situation or display one's piety. Through literary presentations of Muḥammad's life pattern, or *sīrah*, which also came to be the name of a biographical genre, the *sunnah* was spread even wider. The use of *ḥadīth* as primary sources for the writing of historical narrative became common. Muḥammad's various roles, especially that of societal reformer, became paradigms for the behavior of many later leaders. At the popular level and especially among Ṣūfīs (mystics), Muḥammad became the soul's guide and the perfect universal human, showing people how to behave in the presence of God; numerous poetic genres emerged to capture this side of him. Above all, the cultivation of the *sunnat al-nabī*, not just in legally binding matters but in the smallest details of mundane daily existence, took on the salvific quality present in orthodox Jews' observance of *ḥalakhah* (law).

Until recently, most Western scholars have focused on the authenticity and reliability of these materials. There is an old academic tradition that views the *ḥadīth*-based picture of the *sunnat al-nabī* as a *post hoc* creation of the second and particularly third centuries of Islam, when the major authoritative collections of *ḥadīth* were compiled. More recent scholarship has argued that *ḥadīth* emerged very early, in written as well as oral form, and that the very earliest Muslim community assumed sincerely that its *sunnah* was continuous with that of the Prophet.

Scholars have also disagreed about how closely to connect *ḥadīth* and *sunnah*. Although the derivation of *sunnah* for legal purposes depended heavily on the study and explication of *ḥadīth*, the two were not coterminous. The *ḥadīth* were simply verbal reports, tens of thousands of them, about something Muḥammad said or did. They contained many, many potential norms or standards, but those had to be derived or actualized to have legal force. Some matters that were traditionally agreed upon as *sunnah* were contradicted by particular *ḥadīth* or had no basis in *ḥadīth*. Furthermore, individual Muslims could easily disagree with one derivation of a norm and prefer another or prefer one *ḥadīth* to another or reject one and accept another. Finally, the *ḥadīth* format came to be used for conveying all sorts of information not directly related to the life of the Prophet.

As the *sunnah* gradually acquired the meaning of the received, recognized, normative practice of Muḥammad and, to an extent, his companions, its opposite came to be represented by the word *bidʿah* (literally, "starting new," "innovation"). It first became significant as a critique of the behavior of the Marwanid caliphs (685–750), who were seen to have deviated from the ideal of Muḥammad and his companions. Some Muslims always used the word in a negative way—to refer to something beyond the parameters of the acceptable. For others, *bidʿah*, like *sunnah*, can be good or bad—bad if it contradicted the accepted *sunnah*, good if it was consistent with it, even if not contained in it, and promoted the good of the community.

Western scholars often translate *bidʿah* as "heresy" when applied by Muslims to unacceptable religious practices and beliefs. However, "heresy" obscures the pragmatic bent of the Islamic tradition in favor of a dogmatic bent more appropriate to a tradition such as Christianity, which had, unlike Islam, institutionalized theological ways in order to judge and control deviation. The charge of *bidʿah* referred not so much to the content of beliefs as to their practical consequences; it was often made by rulers to reprove certain members of society and dissuade them from adopting socially appealing ideas that disrupted the status quo.

SUNNĪ AND SHĪʿĪ. During the first 120 years of Islamic history, disagreements emerged about how best to derive, understand, and be true to the Prophet's *sunnah*. Through a series of internal conflicts, sides and positions shifted frequently. By the time the Abbasid dynasty of caliphs overthrew and replaced the Umayyads (750), two major orientations had begun to crystalize, both of which were addressed by the Abbasid platform. For some, Muḥammad's unifying and law-giving function was primary to his *sunnah* and would be best preserved if his community (*jamāʿah*) were kept together at all costs, in two ways: (1) by providing a system of rules (*sharīʿah*) as close as possible to those he brought, with a body of learned men (*ʿulamāʾ*) to manage it; and (2) by providing a "nomocratic" leader (*khalīfah*) who would "stay close" to Muḥammad by uniting the community physically, by guaranteeing its security, and by ensuring a proper Muslim environment through protection of the *sharīʿah* and its learned managers. Muḥammad's charismatic function would not be imitated by a person but, rather, routinized in the law.

Another group found proximity to Muḥammad in a different device—physical descent. For them, maintaining proximity to his *sunnah* depended on recapturing his intimacy with God and his closeness to and divinely guided designation of a relative, his cousin and son-in-law ʿAlī, to succeed him. Although they too gathered *ḥadīth*, established *sunnah*, and worked out shariah, for them it was all unusable without a continuation of the charismatic interpretation the Prophet had provided. They had sought, unsuccessfully, to provide the community with a theocratic ruler (*imām*) who could incorporate the nomocratic functions of the *khalīfah* but whose legitimacy would not depend on doing only that. Muḥammad's charismatic function would not be duplicated by the *imāms* but, rather, transformed and kept alive by them on the basis of their special inherited inner skills.

Although affection for the family of the Prophet was diffused throughout the Muslim community, this group carried partisanship further. In their hearts and minds, certain descendants of the Prophet through his cousin ʿAlī (*imāms*) partook of Muḥammad's special qualities; yet they suffered and were frequently martyred at the hands of wrongful rulers. The passing over of ʿAlī for the caliphate the first three times it was awarded and the martyrdom of the third of their line, Ḥusayn ibn ʿAlī, at the hands of the fifth caliph, Yazīd (r. 680–683), as well as subsequent misfortunes, predisposed them to support the Abbasids, who claimed to represent the innate right of the family of the Prophet over those who had usurped it.

However, after they came to power, the Abbasids rejected the special claims of this group, which had generally been known as the partisans (*shīʿah*) of ʿAlī, in favor of the nomocratic style favored by the majority, who styled themselves "the people of the *sunnah* and the community" (*ahl al-sunnah wa-al-jamāʿah*). Although the short form Sunnī stuck to them, as did Shīʿī to the others, nomenclature should not imply that only they were committed to *sunnah* and *ḥadīth* as sources of knowledge. Rather, they established proximity to the *sunnah* by maintaining a consensual *jamāʿah*, whereas the Shi'ah stayed close to it by resisting the decisions of the misguided *jamāʿah* and by trying to substitute what they saw as a more profound, esoteric understanding and style of leadership.

Subtle interpretations aside, however, "Sunnī" came to stand, in different senses, for the majoritarian, mainstream, "orthoprax" style of Islamic piety, especially among those who adhered to it (more than 90% throughout history). By the time of the influential legal theorist and schematizer al-Shāfiʿī (d. 820), an unsystemic and sometimes imaginative derivation and use of *ḥadīth* about Muḥammad's and his community's *sunnah* had become commonplace among the several early Jamāʿī-Sunnī "schools" of *fiqh* (jurisprudence), as had many other legal techniques. Simultaneously, intellectually important movements like Shiism and Muʿtazilī rationalism had developed modes of reasoning that downplayed the authority of a *ḥadīth*-borne *sunnat al-nabī*.

Responding to these and other factors, al-Shāfiʿī sought to rationalize and circumscribe the legitimate roots or sources (*uṣūl*) of jurisprudential deliberation. These he limited to a hierarchy of four, each of which had a fixed relationship to the one(s) before: Qurʾān, *sunnah*, *ijmāʿ*, and *qiyās*. The starting point had to be the Qurʾān. However, where the *sunnah* could explain or supplement revealed truth, it became a second source by virtue of a frequent Qurʾanic injunction, "Obey God and his Messenger." The *sunnah* had to be based on *ḥadīth* traceable back to the Prophet himself or a companion through the supporting (*isnād*) of an unbroken chain (*silsilah*) of reliable transmitters. Thus did al-Shāfiʿī solidify for Jamāʿī-Sunnīs Muḥammad's role as uniquely authoritative exemplar.

Furthermore, where the entire community, as represented by its learned men (*ʿulamāʾ*), had reached consensus (*ijmāʿ*), that too became law if it was consistent with the first two sources. In justifying the use of *ijmāʿ*, al-Shāfiʿī had recourse to a famous *ḥadīth*, "My community will never agree on an error." *Ijmāʿ* sometimes sanctioned, for example, the Arab custom of male and female circumcision, which in turn came to be known as *sunnah* too. Finally, the *ʿulamāʾ* could make adaptive extensions of the first three sources by using personal judgment limited to analogy (*qiyās*) to something in the other three sources. They were equipped to perform their functions not because they possessed any innate characteristics but because they had acquired, through devoted study of Qurʾān and *ḥadīth*, the knowlege (*ʿilm*) of what is right.

Deserving of comment is the relationship between this approach to *ḥadīth* and *sunnah* and *tradition*, a word that is often used to translate them. Al-Shāfiʿī's *ḥadīth*-oriented approach was actually antitraditionalist. By insisting on the use of texts in the form of *ḥadīth* that were traceable to Muḥammad, he was restricting the role "tradition" had been playing among legists because, by the second Islamic century, many things that had become "traditional" among legists had no textual base or were contradicted by the texts.

Al-Shāfiʿī's approach should more properly be viewed as "textualist": he accepted practices not because they were customary but because they were documented. Not long after his death, the *ḥadīth* began to be compiled into a series of six major authoritative collections. Although some of them may have reflected "traditions" in the narrower sense, the impact of this whole series of developments was to control the traditional in favor of what was based on a text and to undermine contemporary rulers' attempts to legitimize custom based on the court rather than *sunnah* based on *ḥadīth*.

Emergence of schools. Gradually, four major Jamāʿī-Sunnī "schools" (sg., *madhhab*; pl., *madhāhib*) of law, all influenced by al-Shāfiʿī's system, formed around the teachings of four leading early figures: Ahmad ibn Ḥanbal (780–855), Mālik ibn Anas (715–795), Abū Ḥanīfah (699–767), and al-Shāfiʿī himself. Eventually, standardization set in to the point at which, by the fourteenth century, no further significant variation was anticipated—a situation expressed by the phrase "the closing of the gate of *ijtihād*" (individual inquiry).

Sharīʿah-oriented Jamāʿī-Sunnism came to focus on the establishment of communal consensus and the maintenance of the public order—in worship, in marketplace behavior, or on the highways and frontiers. Judges (*qāḍīs*) judged what was brought to their attention, not what they ferreted out privately. Books of law focused on ritual obligations (summarized by the five pillars—confession of faith, daily prayer, alms, fasting during the month of Ramaḍān, and pilgrimage to Mecca) as well as on family and personal status law and economic and political matters. This style of piety came to accept as ruler (*khalīfah*) whomever the great majority of the community accepted and to define him as guarantor of physical security and provider of an atmosphere in which the *sharīʿah* could prevail.

Some Jamāʿī-Sunnīs also used *ḥadīth* and *sunnah* as the basis for *kalām* (speculative discussion about God), although others viewed *kalām* itself as *bidʿah*, by virtue of its presumptuous attempt to prove what had already been revealed as true. By the eleventh century, two major *ḥadīth*-oriented schools—the Māturīdī (named after Abū Manṣūr al-Māturīdī, d. 944) and the Ashʿarī (named after Abū al-Ḥasan al-Ashʿarī, d. 935)—had won out over more rationalistic groups such as the Muʿtazilah. The Ashʿarīyah and Māturīdīyah emphasized emotional faith as opposed to the mere assent of intellectualized belief and relied on Muḥammad's own faith and the *ḥadīth* that expressed it as the best guides. They favored an exoteric (*ẓāhirī*) style of reading the Qurʾān and *ḥadīth*. Although they insisted on the unity of God, they accepted the existence of his attributes as mentioned in the Qurʾān, asserting that those attributes were not part of his essence. They emphasized that God exercised power over human action through continuous atomistic creation, though they did not remove the power of human choice altogether. They set limits on speculation by accepting many difficult Qurʾanic points outright, without regard to how they were true.

Sufism. Despite the emphasis of Jamāʿī-Sunnīs on *sharīʿah*, they also began by the twelfth century to partake of mystical piety (Sufism), partly because of the accomplishments of al-Ghazālī (d. 1111), the *kalām* teacher and self-styled Ṣūfī. Al-Ghazālī managed to make a place in Jamāʿī-Sunnī legalism for the more spiritualized, ineffable qualities of the Ṣūfīs. Organized groups of Ṣūfīs (*ṭarīqahs*) of great scope and variety gradually appeared and expanded so that by the sixteenth century much if not most of the adult male Sunnī population may have belonged to one or the other of these groups.

Jamāʿī-Sunnīsm has been described as the "piety of solidarity." Its emphasis on the universal applicability and accessibility not only of the Qurʾān but also of Muḥammad's *sunnah* has promoted remarkable cultural homogeneity among the many diverse peoples who have come under the Islamic umbrella during the past fourteen centuries.

SEE ALSO Caliphate; Ḥadīth; Imamate; Muḥammad; Nubūwah.

BIBLIOGRAPHY

Two Arabic sources available in English translation give textured evidence for how the *sunnah* evolved: Alfred Guillaume's *A Translation of [Ibn] Isḥāq's Sīrat Rasūl Allāh* (1955; reprint, Lahore, 1967) is an early biography of Muḥammad that shows how accounts of his life and portrayal of his *sunnah* did not depend on *ḥadīth* alone; *Islamic Jurisprudence: Al-Shāfiʿī's Risālah,* translated by Majid Khadduri (Baltimore, 1961), offers a classic statement on the role of *ḥadīth* in formulating *sharīʿah.*

Although many excellent works have been written about *sunnah* and *ḥadīth*, William A. Graham's *Divine Word and Prophetic Word in Early Islam* (The Hague, 1977) is particularly useful. In this pathbreaking study, Graham argues that the role of Muḥammad's *sunnah* as a norm goes back to his own lifetime and that it developed much more continuously than past scholars have thought. Ignácz Goldziher's *Muslim Studies*, 2 vols., translated by C. R. Barber and S. M. Stern (Chicago, 1967), is an erudite study of various aspects of Islam and a good example of a legalistic approach to *ḥadīth* and *sunnah*; Goldziher tends to be skeptical about their reliability, however. The first chapter of volume 1 is especially useful. Another important work is Nabia Abbott's *Studies in Arabic Literary Papyri*, 2 vols. (Chicago, 1957–1967), a detailed study of early Islamic written texts. Professor Abbott includes evidence that *ḥadīth* were committed to writing much earlier than scholars had previously argued. See also A. J. Wensinck's article "Sunna," in *Shorter Encyclopaedia of Islam* (Leiden, 1974); James Robson's "Tradition, the Second Foundation of Islam," *Muslim World* 41 (1951): 22–33; and Josef van Ess's *Zwischen Ḥadīth und Theologie* (Berlin, 1975).

For Shīʿī developments and approaches to *sunnah* and *ḥadīth*, S. H. M. Jafri's *The Origins and Development of Shiʿa Islam* (London, 1979) is a solid chronological history of Twelver Shiism, with a good analysis of the Twelver attitude to and concern for *sunnah.* Marshall G. S. Hodgson's "How Did the Early Shiʿa Become Sectarian?" *Journal of the American Oriental Society* 75 (1955): 1–13, is a seminal article that manages to convey the fluidity of pre-Abbasid politics as well as the reasons for the consolidation of Twelver Shiism in the late eighth century.

On *bidʿah*, see D. B. Macdonald's article "Bid'a" in *Shorter Encyclopaedia of Islam* (Leiden, 1974), a brief survey with good basic information and unfortunately few nuances, and Bernard Lewis's "Some Observations on the Significance of Heresy in Islam," *Studia Islamica* 1 (1953): 43–63, a more subtle interpretation of *bidʿah* than usual, in a nondogmatic context.

MARILYN ROBINSON WALDMAN (1987)

ŚŪNYAM AND ŚŪNYATĀ. "Empty," "open," "devoid," "nothing," and "nonexistent" are words used to translate the term *śūnyam.* "Emptiness," "openness," "nothingness," "nonsubstantiality," "relativity," and "the inexhaustible" have been used to translate *śūnyatā.* These two terms, of major importance in Buddhism, have been used to express a philosophical idea, a focus of meditation, a religious attitude, and a manner of ethical action. "Emptiness" may thus indicate deprivation (or self-substantiated reality in conventional experience), a complex implicit interrelatedness of all existing things, or blissful perfect freedom (from anxiety, anger, and pain). As general religious terms, *śūnyam* and *śūnyatā* are used in an attempt to indicate and incite an awareness of "the way things really are" (*yathābhūtam*). The complexity of the concept expressed as "emptiness" derives from the recognition in Buddhism that teaching the truth about life is urgent for alleviating suffering, but that implicit in thinking and speaking resides a tendency to create an illusion (of self-sufficient realities) that is itself the cause of that suffering. The teaching of "the emptiness of things" is a medicine for the spiritual illness seen wherever there is greed, hate, and self-delusion; it is a response to a universal, problematic condition that is found in particular specific forms and thus requires different kinds and levels of correction. Assertions about the empty nature of existence pertain to different objects of concern, for example, conventional phenomena, the basic (usually hidden but more fundamental) causal factors of existence, the highest mode of perceiving phenomena, or the nature of everything. Similarly, different Buddhist schools have recognized the value of different interpretations but have judged the value of a particular interpretation on a scale from the most superficial understanding (for beginners) to the most profound (for spiritual adepts). In all the interpretations and explanations, however, there is a clear recognition that the notion of emptiness is closely tied to the practice of perceiving existence in an "empty manner," which, in turn, results in behavior typified by patience, compassion, strength of character, and morality.

Teaching of Emptiness as Part of the Bodhisattva Path. During the second century BCE, Buddhist teachers in India emphasized "emptiness" as a basic description of the nature of existing things. They were known as "teachers of emptiness" (*śūnyavādins*). Their approach to enlightenment is dramatically portrayed in the Prajñāpāramitā Sūtras (The perfection of wisdom discourses). These *sūtras* maintain that the teaching and meditation training of the contemporary traditional masters, as depicted in the analysis of the Abhidharma Piṭaka, resulted in only a partial enlightenment. The Abhidharma masters had insight only into the emptiness of "the self" and general empirical phenomena, which they could perceive by breaking up conventional perceptions of oneself and "the objective world" into their fundamental causal factors (*dharmas*). While reviewing the *dharmas* was recognized to be a monastic skill that provided the foundation for the cultivation of nonattachment to the self and the world, the "teachers of emptiness" held that such a review, with its emphasis on attaining *nirvāṇa* by avoiding attachment to the "constructed world," could itself become a subtle attachment. To prevent attachment to *dharma* analysis and the expectation of an individual *nirvāṇa* they insisted that even the *dharmas*, together with their identifying characteristics, had to be seen as empty. All distinctions, including those between *nirvāṇa* and the world in flux (*saṃsāra*) and between enlightenment and non-enlightenment, were empty of inherent characteristics. The emptiness of all things is a significant part of the Bodhisattva Path to enlightenment in Mahāyāna (Great Vehicle) Buddhism (which developed in northern India and spread to China, Korea, Japan, and Tibet). This path is a spiritual training that begins with instruction of the Buddha's Middle Way to avoid attachment to "the appearances of the world" and acquisition of self-constricting energy (*karman*). The path includes putting the teaching into practice (perhaps through many lifetimes and even aeons of time) by meditation, by moral action that results in "seeds of virtue," and eventually by the formation of "the thought of enlightenment" (*bodhicitta*) and the earnest resolution (*praṇidhāna*) to work for the welfare of all living beings. Progress on the path includes the perfection of charity, morality, effort, and wisdom. A distinguishing character of this wisdom is that the recognition of emptiness is combined with compassion for all living beings. Such wisdom is cultivated through a skill (*upāyakauśalya*) to fully engage the conditioned world (*saṃsāra*) without being tainted by its evil, delusion, and compulsive drivenness toward pain. The Bodhisattva Path is elaborated in subsequent centuries in such texts as the *Madhyamakāvatāra* (Entering the Middle Way) by Candrakīrti (sixth century CE), the *Śikṣāsamuccaya* (Compendium of Precepts) by Śāntideva (eighth century CE), and the *Bhāvanākrama* (The course of spiritual development) by Kamalaśīla (eighth century CE). In claiming to perfect the meditational practice of the Abhidharma masters within the Indian Buddhist community, the composers of the Prajñāpāramitā Sūtras claimed—as did the composers of such other early Mahāyāna discourses as the *Saddharmapuṇḍarīka Sūtra* (Lotus of the good law discourse) and the *Vimalakīrtinirdeśa Sūtra* (Exposition by Vimalakīrti)—that their teaching of emptiness was consistent with, and indeed the deepest comprehension of, the earliest recorded doctrine of the Buddha. The earlier recorded discourses (*nikāyas*) had already used the notion of emptiness to describe the ephemeral quality of phenomena, especially the lack of permanence and self-existence of perceived objects. During meditative quieting of the mind, and through a descriptive analysis of the many factors that constitute perceived objects, the monk sought to remove mental and emotional disturbances that arose from false expectations of permanence. Though everyday phenomena "exist" in a composite, conditioned manner, they are empty of anything that is permanent or self-existent. In articulating this path of nonattachment to mental, emotional, or material "things," the *nikāyas* use designations such as "empty," "impermanent," and "nonessential"; however, they are aware that in conventional speech an assertion implies the denial of its opposite claim. To avoid such implications they also warn that enlightenment is not the same as holding a *view* of emptiness, of nonexistence rather than existence, of "it is not" rather than "it is." Rather, one should avoid clinging to ideas or apprehensions that divide one's experience into "is" and "is not," "being" and "nonbeing," or "if not this, then that." The path to enlightenment, expounded by the "teachers of emptiness" in the Prajñāpāramitā Sūtras, absorbed the earlier Buddhist recognition that the self and objects of perception are empty of self-existence. The "teachers of emptiness" extended the awareness of the empty nature to everything. Thus the *dharmas* (causal factors of existence), the Buddha's teaching, the path to liberation, the beings who seek liberation, liberation, and "emptiness as a teaching" were all viewed as being empty—all viewed in an empty manner. The Bodhisattva Path was described as "no-path" or "non-coursing"; the Buddha's position was "having no place to stand." The attainment of enlightenment was "no-attainment." There was no defilement, no purification; no arising and no dissipation of existence; and no release from existence to attain *nirvāṇa*—because all these are empty of self-substantiated reality, inherent characteristics, and essential value. This kind of teaching was meant neither for the "worldling" attached to the things of existence nor even for a novice in the Buddha's Middle Way. Such people as these might become fearful and despondent or might interpret the teaching as a nihilistic view or simply as a negative expression of a transcendent essentialism. Only courageous pursuers of truth who had accumulated a resource of spontaneous virtue and clarity of perception could see that such "non-coursing" implies complete interrelatedness with all living beings and that the deepest cognition of emptiness is expressed as compassion.

THE MĀDHYAMIKA SCHOOL. The effort to formulate and justify the insight that all things are empty while living in a spontaneous, comprehensively caring manner was systematized differently by two Indian schools of Buddhism, the Mādhyamika ("middle way") and the Yogācāra ("yoga practice") schools. Nāgārjuna (late second century CE) is often regarded as the founder of the Mādhyamika school. The invocation of one of his major writings, the *Mūlamadhyamakākarikās* (The Fundamentals of the Middle Way), includes a summary of "eight negations" that has epitomized the emptiness teaching for subsequent generations: no origination, no dissipation; no permanence, no ending; no differentiation, no identity; no coming (into existence), no going (from existence). Throughout this work, Nāgārjuna analyzes basic philosophical notions and views, for example, causal conditions, time, *karman,* self (*ātman*), the fully enlightened one (*tathāgata*), and *nirvāṇa.* He shows that none exists in the sense of self-sufficient existence (*svabhāva*) and, thus, that each is empty (of self-sufficient existence). At the same time, he demonstrates that all phenomena exist because emptiness is the same as dependent co-origination (*pratītya-samutpāda*). As radical relational existence, emptiness is identical to existence. Contrary to the claim of his opponents that to designate everything as "empty" is to say that nothing exists, Nāgārjuna insists that one can account for changing existence or enlightenment only if one recognizes that these lack self-existent reality (i.e., emptiness as dependent co-origination).

To perceive all existing things as dependently co-originating, or empty, requires a shift from the conventional mode of perception. Conventional experience divides the world into likes and dislikes, desires and fears, and "you" and "me" as separate entities. This hides the fact that these perceptions can exist only in interrelationship. To perceive through the deep awareness of emptiness, people must become aware of how they construct attachments and fears while perceiving, conceptualizing, and judging. Concepts and language create the places for sensations and emotions "to reside." Therefore, they are a prime focus for dissipating attachments. Nāgārjuna and his followers in the Mādhyamika school use a critical dialectic to show how concepts that presume to describe independent, self-sufficient reality are illusory. The general structure of this dialectic is to assert that any self-subsistent, independent entity is unchanging and unrelated; to claim that such an entity accounts for any phenomenon in the continually changing world is either logically contradictory or contrary to common experience. Likewise in this dialectic is a rejection of the common assumption that any denial of something logically requires the opposite positive assertion. That is, when denying that an entity has "being," a person implicitly asserts that the entity has "nonbeing." Thus in the Mādhyamika dialectic a common argumentative procedure is the denial of "four alternatives" *(catuṣkoti).* For example, in discussing the nature of the perfectly enlightened one (*tathāgata*), Nāgārjuna states: "One can say neither 'empty' nor 'non-empty'; nor both, nor neither. The purpose of these designations is for communication only" (*Mūlamadhyamakakārikās* 22.11). The religious significance of the critical dialectic is to show the "non-abiding" character of "the way things are." The empty character of existence cannot be encapsulated in language or in any perception that implicitly assumes permanent essential qualities or substances. By dislodging a person's hope that language or logic can capture the empty, or intrinsically relational dynamic of existence, one can avoid the delusion of permanence as a condition for happiness and serenity. The use of logic to justify the emptiness of experienced "things," juxtaposed with the assertion that language distorts a true cognition of emptiness, led to the doctrine of two levels or modes of truth. The notion of two modes of truth recognizes that logic, metaphor, or verbal description has use in conventional day-to-day experience but that such conventional use also hides and distorts a deeper (or higher) cognition known through an immediate, direct, intuitive awareness. For the Mādhyamika, emptiness was the object of highest knowledge and, at the same time, accounted for the possibility of the conditioned, conventional forms in everyday life. However, to say that emptiness is "the object" of knowledge does not mean at the highest level of truth that emptiness exists as a separate entity. This is the realization of the "emptiness of emptiness." Because "the two modes of truth"—like everything else—are related but distinct, the systematic formulation of how they were to be defined and related became a focus of much subsequent discussion and writing throughout the millennia. Within the Mādhyamika school and between various schools or lineages of teaching in India, Tibet, China, Korea, and Japan, there were various understandings of the two levels of truth and the meaning of emptiness in the context of realizing the highest truth. Within Mādhyamika, the subschool called Prāsaṅgika (from *prasaṅga,* a logical method of "necessary consequence") stressed the distorting character of all concepts and logic. Its adherents applied their rigorous "consequential dialectic" to all concepts that purported to express the highest truth, in order to dislodge any pretense of language to do so. Language and logic are, nevertheless, important tools to show the self-contradictory and distortional character of conceptual formulation. In his *Prasannapadā* (Clearly worded commentary), on Nāgārjuna's *Mūlamadhyamakakārikās,* Candrakīrti advocates this position, emphasizing that the awareness of emptiness is the destruction of *all* views or formulations. Even the negation of self-existent reality *(svabhāva)* is not a positive cognition of anything. In his commentary, Candrakīrti argues against Bhāvaviveka, an important spokesperson for the other Mādhyamika subschool, the Svātantrikas ("Independents"). The Svātantrikas held that language and logic cannot express the most profound aspects of the highest truth but that some assertions express the truth of emptiness more accurately than others. Further, the accurate statements are amenable to verification within conventional rules of logical justification. This discussion continued outside India, especially in the development of Tibetan Buddhist lineages. For example, the Prāsaṅgika position was elaborated by the Sa skya and later by the Rnying ma pa commentators, while the Svātantrika position was advocated by the Dge lugs pa lineage, including the great master Tsong kha pa (1357–1419 CE). The Tibetan monasteries developed their own lineages by drawing on ideas and interpretations from various earlier schools. They attempted to synthesize the teachings from different sources and thus develop a more complete view, while the Prāsaṅgika view is said to be the basis for knowing emptiness and is found in all four divisions of the *tantras* ("deep meaning texts").

THE YOGĀCĀRA SCHOOL. The ideas of the other major Indian school of Mahāyāna Buddhism, the Yogācāra, were systematically formulated during the fourth century CE by the two monks Asaṅga and Vasubandhu. Like the Mādhyamikas, the Yogācāras also recognize that all phenomena are empty (i.e., conditioned, without selfsubsisting reality). However, they insist that the "courser in wisdom" should positively affirm the ultimate reality of consciousness. It is consciousness that is empty and that knows in an empty or delusive manner. All living beings, Asaṅga claims in his *Madhyānta-vibhaga* (Distinguishing between the middle and extremes), have the capacity to pervasively construct "that which is not there" (*abhūta-parikalpa*). This capacity artificially divides the interdependent world into many dualities, for example, subject and object, being and nonbeing. The elimination of dualistic fabrication is true emptiness. Consciousness, in Yogācāra reflection, is the comprehensive reality and is composed of three kinds of reality: completely fictive or illusory (*parikalpita-svabhāva*), dependent or conditioned (*paratantra-svabhāva*), and truly real or nondual (*pariniṣpanna-svabhāva*). Through the practice of the Bodhisattva Path the illusory reality is recognized for what it is: nonexistent. This recognition purifies the conditioned existence, which itself is not a real object but a modality of consciousness. When this is realized, the nonduality (or emptiness) of all things is manifest and exists as the ultimate reality (*paramārtha sat*). Whereas the Mādhyamikas stress that both the conditioned forms and the unconditioned reality are empty, the Yogācāras emphasize that the true reality is neither empty nor nonempty.

Another aspect of the Yogācāra emphasis on consciousness, found in several Indian discourses that contributed to the Mahāyāna understanding of ultimate reality, was the notion of the "matrix of enlightened reality" (*tathāgata-garbha*). Vasubandhu had described the basis of multiple kinds of consciousness as a "store consciousness" (*alaya-vijñana*). This store consciousness contains both pure and impure "seeds" (*bījas*) that influence subsequent consciousness. Similarly, the *tathāgata-garbha* is the womb, or matrix, from which pure consciousness in the manifested world arises. Such a Mahāyāna text as the *Srīmālādevī-siṃhanāda Sūtra* (The lion's roar of Queen Srimala) equates the *tathāgata-garbha* with emptiness. Here "emptiness" means both "being devoid of impurities" and the natural "power of enlightenment" to produce nonattached consciousness in worldly forms. The ultimate nature of the *tathāgata-garbha* is perfect purity. It is manifested in forms as well as being the formless reality. However, enlightened reality—also called "the Buddha nature"—is said to be nonempty in respect to the virtues of Buddhahood, which are manifested in the phenomenal world. Insofar as there is a strong emphasis on enlightened reality, which is manifest in particular concrete forms, the *tathāgata-garbha* is said to be neither simply empty nor simply nonempty. In India during the second half of the first millennium CE, in China beginning in the fifth century CE, and in the development of the Tibetan lineages, Buddhist scholars developed several formulations of the relation between the conditioned and the unconditioned realities, between the pure and the impure conditioning influences, and between emptiness and conditional form.

EMPTINESS IN CHINESE AND JAPANESE SCHOOLS. In China the Mādhyamika school maintained a teaching lineage for several centuries from the fifth century CE on as the Sanlun ("three [middle way] treatises") school. The teachings of the Mādhyamika were studied in Japan from the seventh century CE on but without a separate community following a lineage succession. The Yogācāra doctrine was transmitted to China through the translation of texts and a lineage of teachers that became known as the Faxiang ("characteristics of dharma") school. This school was transmitted to Japan during the seventh and eighth centuries CE, where it was known as the Hossō school. The Chinese Mahāyāna Buddhists, during the fifth and sixth centuries, wrestled with the cognition of emptiness first in relation to Neo-Daoist notions of nothingness (*kong*), which implied that emptiness is a primary source from which all phenomenal forms arise. In the flowering of Buddhism in China (from the sixth century CE through the first half of the ninth century CE), Buddhist scholars understood emptiness within the context of the broadbased Chinese philosophical problem of the relation between the substance or foundation *(ti)* of everything and its function or appearance *(yong)* in the changing world. Within the Sanlun school, contrasting understandings of this relation between substance and function are found in the writings of Sengzhao (374–414 CE) and of Jizang (549–623 CE). Sengzhao assumed the identity of substance and function, affirming that emptiness is the foundation of all things that appear through dependent co-arising and is the nature of insight that recognizes the illusory (empty) character of phenomena; thereby the enlightened person abides in non-abiding (emptiness) and moves (in an empty manner) in conditioned existence. Jizang, on the contrary, held that substance and function need to be clearly distinguished, and emphasized that the highest truth is manifest when the conventional truth is negated. Emptiness is basically the dialectical negation of both being and nonbeing and of both affirmation and negation. The highest truth is known in conditioned existence when names and characteristics of things are negated or transcended in nonphenomenal awareness. During the sixth and seventh centuries CE, the Chinese Buddhists synthesized the notions of emptiness, multiple kinds of truth (reality), and dependent co-arising within a cosmological context in developing two distinctly Chinese schools or teaching lineages. These were Tiantai, formulated by Zhiyi (531–597 CE), and Huayan, systematized by Fazang (643–712 CE). Both are attempts to relate substance and function in one harmonious and interrelated matrix of reality. Chih-i held that there was a threefold truth—the empty *(kong)*, the provisional (*jia*), and the middle *(zhong)*—and that these three parts are reciprocally identical and simultaneous. Rather than view the truths in a lower-to-higher order, he presented them as different modalities of one universal consciousness. While they appear to be separate processes, he maintained, in their deepest character of interrelatedness they are one undifferentiated matrix whose principle is beyond dualistic or linear comprehension. Fazang held that the "nature of things" was emptiness, by which he meant the harmonious interdependent co-arising of particular, concrete phenomena. Such a universe is "the body of the *tathāgata.*" Rather than devaluing particular phenomena because they are conditioned (non-eternal), his system insists that each has supreme value in its interrelatedness to everything else. Fazang held that the three natures (levels of awareness) proposed by Yogācāra teachers are intrinsically interrelated, and together form a whole, because they are all empty. The most profound nature is the incomprehensible "suchness" (formless emptiness), which is also the emptiness of the interrelatedness of conditioned existence (dependent co-origination); this, in turn, is also the non-self-substantial (empty) nature of illusory mental construction. To know the intrinsic emptiness ("suchness") of all forms is the highest awareness. However, most people do not see the complex emptiness of everything. At a lower level of awareness, one can also say that the evil and pain experienced in the world represent only the potential for realizing incomprehensible "suchness" and that the *tathāgata-garbha* causes the transformation of enlightenment in particular minds and moments of consciousness. Nevertheless, in reality, the world is an inconceivably vast expression of emptiness that is the glorious manifestation of unchanging fullness, an overbrimming potential of "openness." Another very important expression of emptiness is found in the "Meditation school," which is known as Chan in China and Zen in Japan. The focus in Chan communities has been, and is, on "the practice of emptiness." The basic negation of concepts as inadequate communication of "the way things are" and an emphasis on quieting the mind and extending the empty mode of perception into daily life continue the themes found in the Bodhisattva Path as portrayed in the Prajñāpāramitā Sūtras. Zen masters have commented on these discourses as well as on the central Mādhyamika and Yogācāra treatises and on the poems and comments of previous Zen masters. Zen is the practice of manifesting "the Buddha mind," which is also "no-mind." The realization of "no-mind" is the loss of attachment to conventional perceptions, theoretical concepts about reality, and self-images. In that state of awareness, a Zen practitioner is directly confronted with emptiness—not as an idea or as the denial of an idea but as "what is at that moment." Many Zen masters have emphasized that the notion of emptiness is misleading or useless when it is used to describe a distinctive quality of experience. At the same time, "emptiness" is prominently used as a focus of meditation, in which the meditator is called on to "become emptiness." Basically, it is a mental tool to dissipate attachment to images and concepts. In the contemporary discussion of cross-cultural philosophy and interfaith dialogue in which Buddhists are involved, the notion of emptiness and the negating dialectic are important points of engagement with other philosophies. The empty perception of "the way things are" has been compared with the critique of reason given by the eighteenth-century German philosopher Immanuel Kant and with the distorting character of language described by the twentieth-century philosophers Ludwig Wittgenstein and Martin Heidegger. The claim that all things are dependently co-originated is compared with similar concepts in "process philosophy," as expounded, for example, in Alfred North Whitehead's *Process and Reality.* The notion of emptiness forms a central concern in the philosophical thought of the contemporary Japanese philosophers Nishida Kitarō and Nishitani Keiji as they discuss the nature of goodness, existence, and selfhood in a cross-cultural philosophical context. In interfaith dialogue, emptiness is a major topic in the Christian and Buddhist discussion of the nature of ultimate reality, human nature, and religious awareness. Likewise, the empty apprehension of oneself that is best manifested in compassion is compared with mystical disciplines that require the love of others found in various religious traditions. As a fundamental and multidimensional concept, emptiness continues to engage reflective people who pursue the tantalizing question of the nature of things.

SEE ALSO Ālaya-vijñāna; Bodhisattva Path; Buddhism, Schools of, article on Tibetan and Mongolian Buddhism; Buddhist Philosophy; Chan; Dharma, article on Buddhist Dharma and Dharmas; Huayan; Mādhyamika; Nāgārjuna; Nirvāṇa; Numbers, article on Binary Symbolism; Prajñā; Pratītya-samutpāda; Soteriology; Tathāgata-garbha; Tiantai; Yogācāra; Zen.

BIBLIOGRAPHY

A good historical introduction to the development of the "teaching of emptiness" in India is Edward Conze's *Buddhist Thought in India* (London, 1962); his translations of the Prajñapāramitā Sūtras, especially *The Perfection of Wisdom in Eight Thousand Lines and Its Verse Summary* (Bolinas, Calif., 1973), are basic for understanding how the term "empty" functions in communicating the Bodhisattva Path. A standard philosophical analysis of Indian Mādhyamika thought, emphasizing the logical dialectic, is T. R. V. Murti's *The Central Philosophy of Buddhism,* 2d ed. (London, 1970), and a useful linguistic and philosophical analysis of the translation of the Indian Madhyamika into Chinese thought is found in Richard H. Robinson's *Early Mādhyamika in India and China* (Madison, Wis., 1967). In my book *Emptiness: A Study in Religious Meaning* (New York, 1967) I compare the religious language structure of the term "emptiness" and the Indian Mādhyamika dialectic with other kinds of religious expression in order to delineate their religious meaning. A collection of essays edited by Minoru Kiyota, *Mahāyāna Buddhist Meditation* (Honolulu, 1978), contains several excellent essays on the meaning of emptiness in Buddhist theory and practice in India, Tibet, China, and Japan. An introduction to the understanding of emptiness within the meditative practice of Tibetan Buddhism is *Practice and Theory of Tibetan Buddhism,* edited and translated by Geshe Lhundup Sopa and Jeffrey Hopkins (New York, 1976). A lengthy explanation of the realization of emptiness according to the texts and oral traditions of the Prāsaṅgika-Mādhyamika tradition in Tibet is Jeffrey Hopkins's *Meditation on Emptiness* (London, 1983). Two different and complementary interpretations of emptiness in Huayan Buddhism are found in Garma C. C. Zhang's *The Buddhist Teaching of Totality* (University Park, Pa., 1971) and Francis H. Cook's *Huayan Buddhism* (University Park, Pa., 1977). A classic introduction to the Zen negation of mental images is D. T. Suzuki's *The Zen Doctrine of No-Mind* (London, 1949), which is also found in an abbreviated form in *Zen Buddhism: Selected Writings of D. T. Suzuki,* edited by William Barrett (Garden City, N.Y., 1956). Nishitani Keiji's *Religion and Nothingness,* translated by Jan van Bragf (Berkeley, Calif., 1982), is a prime example of a contemporary philosophical use of the notion of emptiness to explore the deepest awareness of existence.

New Sources

Burton, D. *Emptiness Appraised: A Critical Study of Nagarjuna's Philosophy.* Richmond, U.K., 1999.

Hopkins, J. *Emptiness in the Mind-Only School of Buddhism: Dynamic Responses to Dzong-ka-ba's The Essence of Eloquence: I.* Berkeley, 1999.

Hopkins, J., and E. Napper. *Meditation on Emptiness.* Boston, 1996.

Ichimura, S. *Buddhist Critical Spirituality: Prajña and Sunyata.* Delhi, 2001.

King, R. *Indian Philosophy: An Introduction to Hindu and Buddhist Thought.* Washington, D.C., 1999.

Napper, E. *Dependent-Arising and Emptiness: A Tibetan Buddhist Interpretation of Madhyamika Philosophy Emphasizing the Compatibility of Emptiness and Conventional Phenomena.* Boston, 2003.

Viévard, L. *Vacuité (Sunyata) et Compassion (Karuna) dans le Bouddhisme Madhyamaka.* Paris, 2002.

Williams, P., and A. Tribe. *Buddhist Thought: A Complete Introduction to the Indian Tradition.* New York, 2000.

FREDERICK J. STRENG (1987)
Revised Bibliography

SUPERNATURAL, THE. Mysterious occurrences and beings that habitually or occasionally impinge upon one's everyday experience are called "supernatural." It is commonly said that belief in the supernatural characterizes all religions and that belief in the supernatural wanes in modern societies.

HISTORICAL DEVELOPMENT OF THE NOTION. The term *supernatural* was given wide currency by Thomas Aquinas (1225–1274) and the Scholastics, but it had numerous antecedents in the idiom of the Hellenistic thinkers and church fathers. Neoplatonists in particular accumulated superlatives to speak of the realm of the divine: It was above the highest heaven, beyond the world, and even beyond being. Christians spoke of God as being above nature: He had not grown out of anything but was eternally self-subsistent. They also spoke of Christ as bringing to humankind benefits that were above nature, that is, benefits that were beyond what human beings could reach with their own powers. This link between grace and the supernatural became firmly entrenched in scholastic theology. Thomas taught that in the Fall humanity was hurt in its very nature (that is, weakened as a being) and lost its supernatural gifts, especially its access to the vision of God. God, according to Thomas, in his grace gratuitously heals the wounds (and thus restores to humans what naturally belongs to them) and reopens humanity's path to his supernatural end, thus restoring access to the added bliss of life with God. This theology expresses a constant theme in the Christian faith: The natural and the supernatural are at odds; the sacred and the profane are estranged. God, who is quite separate and distinct from the world, is not responsible for this state of affairs, and his intention is to rectify it. Nature and supernature will, in time, be reconciled.

The word *supernatural,* however, left the confines of the schools and began to lose its precise technical meaning. It became associated with the unusual, the marvelous, the surprising. Robert Lenoble (1968) has shown a continuity, from antiquity to the present day, in what he calls "marvel psychology." Popular thought makes rough distinctions between what is natural, what is artificial, and what is miraculous: Water flows down into valleys, human beings build dams, and the Virgin diverts floods from villages when dams break down. What characterizes common thinking about the subject is uncertainty about the precise borders between the natural, the artificial, and the miraculous. When the dam breaks down, does it do so by itself, through wear and tear, or because some man has put explosives in it or some woman has cast a spell upon it? And does the water spare the village because of its situation—the village is on high land—or because of divine intervention? While medieval theologians had used the term *supernatural* to refer to the moral and spiritual dynamics of salvation, ordinary Christians came to call supernatural any extraordinary occurrence that could not be accounted for by the usual explanations at hand.

The scientific revolution of the seventeenth century radically transformed the idea of cognition. With the mechanistic revolution came, certainly for some human beings, a precise knowledge of the limits of the natural. "Natural" causes have come to explain increasing amounts of experience, and it is commonly assumed that in time, natural causes will be found for events that currently resist explanation. Nature is seen to be a rigid, coherent system that works like a clock, does not pursue moral ends, and is indifferent to human aspirations. Modern humans know how to build dams that are fail-safe; they know for sure that those dams cannot be destroyed by spells; and they do not count on the Virgin to intervene in the event of an accident. Nature, then, always works according to rigorous laws and, by definition, excludes the miraculous. (The older nature was malleable: It was quite willing to see God—who ruled over it—reorder its workings momentarily or locally to bring about a miracle for some special purpose.) At first, the new nature was deemed to magnify God even more than the older one: Its strict regularity and its order seemed to testify to the awesome grandeur of its creator. That it was not a model and had nothing to teach humanity was deemed at first only to serve the interests of the dialogue between man and God. René Descartes (1596–1650) taught that human beings and God are alike in that both are spirits. The human being, a finite spirit, cannot create *ex nihilo,* but like an engineer, can shape everything: The whole of nature is matter in his hands (Lenoble, 1968).

At the same time, however, for reasons that had to do with the aftereffects of the wars of religion, the rise of the modern state, and the new demands for social conformity, the Baroque taste spread in Christian lands. What was infinite, awesome, powerful, overwhelming, and stunning was considered to convey a sense of God. Religious architecture and furniture became calculatedly impressive; oratory became stately. Miracles as powerful disruptions of nature's laws appeared, then, necessary to the cause of religion. Many theologians thus taught that human beings must regard the supernatural as contrary to nature: God, they said, intervenes providentially, and occasionally suspends the course of nature; he also reveals supernatural truths that humans must obediently accept even though their truth is not manifest to one's unaided reason. Rare were the theological voices like that of William Law (1686–1761), who taught that "there is nothing that is supernatural but God alone." Since it was evident that nature would always be what Newton said it was, salvation tended to become less cosmic and more interior. Nature and grace remained isolated: Humans would enjoy redeemed existence only in heaven. Eighteenth-century philosophers such as Voltaire, Hume, and Gibbon, for their part, gave currency to the idea that the supernatural was a notion accepted only by the ignorant and the credulous.

The far-reaching impact of the Baroque on sensibilities may be observed in the novel, a literary form whose real development began in the eighteenth century. The supernatural, the Gothic, and the fantastic were predominant themes in early examples of this mass-appeal genre. Suspense, terror, and pleasure were sustained by stories of desolate houses, mysterious dogs, vampires, murderous plants, doomed infants, premature burials, and preternaturally lascivious monks. An abundance of torture, carnality, magic, and solitary horror placed the protagonist and the reader in a world totally unlike the safe everyday middle-class world, and kept them thrilled, constantly on the verge of terrifying doom or unspeakable bliss. There was also a constant epistemological suspense, a specifically modern feature in fantastic tales: Were the events or apparitions caused supernaturally, or were they in reality some clever manipulation of appearances? The protagonist's and the reader's senses of reality were kept constantly off balance, precisely at a time when science and society worked together to give them a world as safe as possible (Penzoldt, 1952). The entry of the supernatural into literature raised interesting questions: Did readers who enjoyed these novels believe in the existence of supernatural beings and the possibility of supernatural occurrences? One might agree that people believe anything while they are reading it, but what happens to their belief when they are not reading but instead dealing and coping with their everyday world?

Application of the Notion to the Study of Religious and Cultural Systems. Among scholars of the nineteenth century it came to be commonly admitted that belief in what Herbert Spencer has called "the supernatural genesis of phenomena" characterized religious people. All religions were said to feature belief in supernatural beings. Émile Durkheim (1858–1917) noted that religion thrives on the sense of things surpassing human knowledge, and he quoted Spencer's reference to the omnipresence of something inscrutable. But Durkheim also stressed that the idea of the supernatural appeared only very late in religious evolution, and that many

Christians were confident that God and nature were as one, or that dogma and reason fully agreed. The idea that belief in the supernatural was characteristic of religion remained, however, firmly entrenched. Lucien Lévy-Bruhl (1857–1939) in his early influential work argued that the primitive mind believed in "mystical," not "physical," influences, whereas practically all contemporaries recognize a clear line of demarcation between the supernatural (rejected by all except the credulous) and the data furnished by everyday ordinary sense experience and the broad light of day. R. R. Marret (1866–1943) confirmed that the notion gives a good minimal definition of religion. He classified the supernatural according to negative modes (taboo) and positive modes (mana). The sense of the supernatural, Marret stressed, is an existential and affective reality, a response to the extranormal and the uncanny, and is thus not related to a reasoned theory of nature. "Power belongeth unto God," and the sense of the supernatural is the sense of the nearly overwhelming presence of great power. Paul Radin (1883–1959) argued against Lévy-Bruhl and spoke of the supernatural as arising against a background of inevitable fears (stemming from economic and psychic insecurity) that he found to be present in all human beings, primitive and modern. He saw in the modern West a decline in religion and in recourse to supernatural beings for help, because other means of emphasizing and maintaining life values were available and on the ascendant. Revision of the initial positivist separation between credulous and rational people reached a climax with Lévy-Bruhl's famous reversal, recorded in his *Notebooks* (posthumously published in 1949): "Primitives reject contradiction, just as we do, when they perceive it." Lévy-Bruhl developed comparative epistemology, according to whose tenets anthropologists were to compare modes of thought, psychic capacities, and mental categories without assuming at the outset that they themselves were in possession of a language that could adequately give an account of everything other minds did (Needham, 1972).

While this should be admitted, scholars today should still try to speak adequately of the varieties of admittedly extreme and nonverifiable languages people have recourse to when they express their reaction to situations that have powerful impact on them but remain opaque in their meaning, or desperately baffling in their consequence. Light can be derived from recent developments in anthropology that have profited from comparative studies in mythology, literature, and folklore. In all cultures stories abound, ranging from myths to folk legends, that tell the adventures of heroes in a world or worlds teeming with supernatural beings and awe-inspiring circumstances.

Consider the example of the *Odyssey,* a fairly typical tale. (Supernatural occurrences there, however, are among the milder ones, and the range of unusual creatures is somewhat narrow: There is a shortage of evil spirits and demons such as abound in other types of literature.) In his travels Odysseus has to deal with (1) the remote but supreme authority of the king of the gods; (2) the support or enmity of powerful gods who have influence at court (Athena); (3) the support or enmity of powerful gods who rule in some corner of the world (Poseidon); (4) minor gods or goddesses (Calypso, who enjoys a perpetual vacation at her seashore home); (5) human beings with magical powers (Circe); (6) monstrous beings with terrifying powers (the Sirens); (7) powerful giants (the Cyclops); and (8) very unusual human beings (the lotus-eaters, who are more strange than ordinary foreigners). The hero himself is endowed with exceptional powers of endurance and prowess at the bow; he performs an extraordinary feat (he returns from Hades) and thus represents here the ninth type of being. Other heroes in such tales can fly, change their size, and so on. All nine types of beings may be called supernatural or said to have supernatural traits, although all may also be characterized by terms other than *supernatural.* Only the first three are the object of religious devotion or have cults. The fourth type, while divine, may be outside the religious world. Sirens and witches have powers ordinary human beings do not have, while giants (like dwarfs) have only their unusual size in their favor.

There is thus a whole range of modes of being and modes of power, finely shaded, for all these beings, and a whole range of appropriate human responses to them. The hero is the person best equipped to survive in this perilous world, who possesses an appropriately wide range of skills and attitudes. Senior gods are to be honored with sacrifices and piety. Sirens are simply to be avoided. One can do business with the Cyclops, but the game is dangerous. Transactions with Calypso and Circe are profitable and agreeable, provided the hero keeps them at arm's length or has some special protection. There is also a whole range of modes of belief, and only one part of it is appropriately labeled religious belief. The hero does not believe in Zeus in the same way that he believes in the Sirens. And it should not be immediately clear to us what it means to attribute belief to the bards who recite such tales and to the audiences that hear them. Whether a man believes in Zeus may be tested: Does he perform the appropriate ritual, and does he exhibit the appropriate attitudes? But how can one verify behaviorally a belief in sirens? How often are human beings confronted with apparently beautiful women half visible above reefs? Needham (1972) has successfully argued that statements of belief are the only available evidence of the phenomenon. Both theologians and anthropologists, he maintains, have taken too much for granted and have been too quick to specify what beliefs other people have and what difference these beliefs make.

Belief in anything, including supernatural beings, is thus a very elusive phenomenon. The Dorze of Ethiopia say that the leopard became a Christian and so eats no meat on the fast days of the Coptic church. Nevertheless, they watch their cattle just as carefully on those days. And they are baffled when the anthropologist professes to see a contradiction in this. So what does go on in their minds when they say the leopard fasts on Wednesdays and Fridays? Among contemporaries, not everyone who reads horoscopes will profess belief in them, and among those who do profess such a belief, how many are actually to be found making a decision on a primarily astrological basis? It would be safer to characterize religion by attitudinal factors and ritual practice rather than by belief. And any statement of belief should be taken with a grain of salt. People like, for adaptive or escapist purposes, to tell and hear stories that provide a map clarifying the configuration of forces in the world, that show modes of coping with those forces, and that do not demand any firm commitment to belief and ensuring action. Children everywhere acquire their bearing in reality from fairy tales. What beliefs they fleetingly entertain or settle on matter less than the inferences they learn to draw about possible realities. The highly imaginative stories of primitives abound in wit and irony and cannot be pinned down with the psychology of belief common among sober scientists (whose thinking often reflects the easy and moralistic recourse to expressions of belief characteristic of early modern theologians).

Systematic Considerations. The human being has in its favor a quick mobile mind, but it is frail and its body is destined to contract disease and, ultimately, to die. Men and women are thus constantly the potential victims of aleatory events that can be painful to them. Fearful of impending disasters, they seek the protection of stronger human beings. As infants and children they start life with such protection. Later they attach themselves to strong persons whom they count on to be successful and wise so that they themselves can live in a secure world, one without interstices from which unpredictable attacks might come. When successful, these strong ones ward off actual dangers. When unsuccessful, as they inevitably will be, the strong ones, if wise, will be an authority providing cognitive and affective reassurance: Yes, loss and pain have occurred, but they are on the right path; it was inevitable, some good may come of it, and, in any case, there is lasting value in the new attitude gained and the new turn taken (Sennett, 1980). Priests, who are typical examples of strong ones, are also thinkers. They teach survival skills and provide ritual and verbal comfort when these skills fail, as necessarily they must. Strong ones are therefore in touch with suitable explanations that ideally can help in those boundary situations that occur when one's ordinary world falls apart.

Strong ones, in turn, feel themselves in touch with a strength or with other real and enduring strong ones who are beyond society, beyond this world, be they spirits, gods, God, history, or "the way things are." The label "supernatural" is appropriately attached to that strength or those preeminently strong beings that are not within the daily and social range of interaction. The authority of the social strong ones is thus always transitory and relative, more or less plausible. The limits to their authority stem from one's own willingness or ability to trust them; but one's trust rests on one's sense of their reliability: Are they in touch with the enduring strength so that they can help one to keep in touch with it, or do they devour one's trust for their own petty human benefit?

The modern concept of nature and natural causes firmly supports a reality principle: When physically sick (or, today, even when anxious) people mainly turn to scientific medicine. Fear of and belief in supernatural agencies do not color in any significant way their sense of what is feasible in their embodied condition. But people hold on to some nonscientific health lore passed on through oral, unofficial channels, and nostalgically transmit recipes for more natural care of the human body and its ailments. Alternative "soft" medicines prosper. In matters of wealth, prestige, and happiness there is no scientific establishment that rules over one's expectations; unproved arts and pleasurable illusions abound. The reality principles that set limits to one's desires are socially determined: Rules are prescribed according to what is socially admitted, rewarded, or punished.

Human beings want both to be believed and to be understood, but usually not at the same time and not by the same people. Individuals want their words and their symbols (1) to be believed and accepted and (2) to create reality, a safe common reality that is not limited to the individual alone. Thus, individuals want to be supported and upheld, but they also want to be understood. They want to share something of their complex and problematic rapport by means of their words and symbols. Thus individuals want the liveliness of their consciousness to be acknowledged. When they want to be believed, they construct presumably strong structures (which are cemented by or rest upon strong ones) that they then deconstruct in the process of understanding. The characteristic feature of modern society is not fewer beliefs in supernatural beings but the variety of strong ones turned to and included in one's world for different purposes and at different times, and the variety of the structures of plausibility that buttress them.

Thus, somewhat polytheistically, in matters of health people turn to state-supported hospitals and the health-food stores of the counterculture; they believe in public schools and in private ones; they read mainstream literature and avant-garde poems; they watch television and go to art films; they attend institutionalized churches and buy books about spirituality in the free market of ideas. Alternative modes of knowledge prosper in the margins left by the dominant scientific or nonscientific modes. The symbolization of humanity's relation to the ultimate conditions of its existence is no longer the monopoly of any group explicitly labeled "religious." And, heroic or not, humans, like the hero of many folk tales, have no permanent master to guide their steps through all the perils of life. Everyone must encounter directly the Circes and Poseidons of this world. At different times they turn to different masters for help and protection. But in the present libertarian society the quality of their services is uncertain, and, in any case, the good ones can help only as long as one asks them to.

See Also Holy, Idea of the; Sacred and the Profane, The; Transcendence and Immanence.

Bibliography

Bellah, Robert N. *Beyond Belief: Essays on Religion in a Post-Traditional World.* New York, 1970. A collection of articles by a leading sociologist of religion. Especially noteworthy are those on religious evolution, on belief, and on symbolic realism.

Douglas, Mary, and Aaron Wildavsky. *Risk and Culture: An Essay on the Selection of Technological and Environmental Dangers.* Berkeley, 1982. The illustrations are drawn from a specific contemporary issue, but the essay shows well how culture achieves some protection against danger.

Lenoble, Robert. *Esquisse d'une histoire de l'idée de nature.* Paris, 1968. The classic history of the ideas entertained about nature.

Lubac, Henri de. *Surnaturel: Études historiques.* Paris, 1946. Essays on the idea of the supernatural in Christian theology.

Needham, Rodney. *Belief, Language, and Experience.* Oxford, 1972. A brilliant introduction to problems in comparative epistemology.

Penzoldt, Peter. *The Supernatural in Fiction.* 1952; New York, 1965. An excellent account of the supernatural novel.

Sennett, Richard. *Authority.* New York, 1980. The best analysis of authority as bond in modern society.

Turner, Victor. "An Ndembu Doctor in Practice." In *Magic, Faith and Healing,* edited by Ari Kiev. New York, 1964. A classic account of a supernatural healing practice.

Waardenburg, Jacques. *Classical Approaches to the Study of Religion: Aims, Methods and Theories of Research,* vol. 1, *Introduction and Anthology.* Paris, 1973. The classic anthology of the major statements by the founders of the modern study of religion, including Spencer, Durkheim, Lévy-Bruhl, Marret, and Radin.

New Sources

Auerbach, Nina. *Our Vampires, Ourselves.* Chicago, 1995.

Berger, Peter. *A Rumor of Angels: Modern Society and the Rediscovery of the Supernatural.* New York, 1990.

Edmundson, Mark. *Nightmare on Main Street: Angels, Sadomasochism, and the Culture of the Gothic.* Cambridge, Mass., 1997.

Karlsen, Carol. *The Devil in the Shape of a Woman: Witchcraft in Early New England.* New York, 1987.

Kieckhefer, Richard. *Magic in the Middle Ages.* New York, 1989.

Lehmann, Arthur, and James Meyers, comp. *Magic, Witchcraft, and Religion: An Anthropologic Study of the Supernatural.* New York, 1989.

Nelson, Victoria. *The Secret Life of Puppets.* Cambridge, Mass., 2002.

Schmidt, Jean-Claude. *Ghosts in the Middle Ages: The Living and the Dead in Medieval Society.* Chicago, 1998.

Michel Despland (1987)
Revised Bibliography

SUPERSTITION. *Superstition* is a judgmental term traditionally used by dominant religions to categorize and denigrate earlier, less sophisticated or disapproved religious attitudes and behavior. A belief is perceived as superstitious by adherents of a particular religious orthodoxy, and it is from their perspective that the category acquires its meaning. An anthropological description of the same belief would use different, nonjudgmental language drawn from the perspective of people engaged in the beliefs and practices condemned as superstitious by others. The use of the term *superstition* is inevitably pejorative rather than descriptive or analytical, for superstition is defined in opposition to a given culture's concept of true religion. Its specific meanings vary widely in different periods and contexts, so that a survey of its historical application rather than an abstract definition is the best approach to the concept of superstition.

Origin and Classical Usage. The classical world criticized certain religious behaviors as irrational, or as reflecting an incorrect understanding of both nature and divinity. Greek writers from Theophrastus to Plutarch mockingly described a cringing, obsessive fear of the gods (*deisidaimonia*) as an inappropriate religious attitude. Roman philosophers sometimes echoed this theme, but the etymology of the Latin word *superstitio* (from *superstes,* "surviving, witnessing") indicates a separate evolution from a possibly neutral meaning of divination to a pejorative term. According to Émile Benveniste, *superstitio* included the idea of surviving an event as a witness and referred originally to divination concerning the past, the power to witness a distant event as though it were present. In its earliest Latin literary usage by Plautus and Ennius, *superstitio* was already a negative term describing divination, magic, and "bad religion" in general. Cicero gives a concrete example, explaining that "those who spent whole days in prayer and offered sacrifices, that their children might outlive them, are called superstitious" (*On the Nature of the Gods* 2.28). For classical Roman observers like Seneca, Lucretius, and Cicero, *superstitio* meant erroneous, false, or excessive religious behaviors stemming from ignorance of philosophical and scientific truths about the laws of nature. Such ignorance was associated with the common people (*vulgus*) and with the countryside (*pagus*), so that superstitious behavior had a social locus in the uneducated, lower orders of Roman society. As the empire expanded, the term *superstitio* was applied to exotic foreign religions of which the Romans disapproved, such as the Egyptian cult of Isis and later the Jewish sect of Christianity. Its meaning became more collective, referring to the "religion of others" in pejorative terms rather than to an individual Roman's inappropriate or exaggerated religious attitudes.

Early Christianity. The early Christians adopted this collective meaning, turning the category of superstition back on the Romans. In the period after the second century, pagans and Christians reciprocally condemned each other's religious beliefs and ceremonial practices as the superstitious cult of false deities. But the militant monotheism of Christianity intensified the negative meanings of these charges. The church fathers interpreted Roman statues as idols, their sacrifices as offerings to the devil, and their oracles as the voices of demons. Such false beliefs did not deserve the name of religion, for, as Lactantius explained, "religion is the worship of the true, superstition is that of the false" (*Divine Institutes* 4.28). Wishing to condemn the pagans out of their own mouths, Augustine of Hippo quoted Cicero's description of superstitious attitudes among the Romans, but he rejected Cicero's distinction between religion and superstition as an inadequate attempt "to praise the religion of the ancients which he wishes to disjoin from superstition, but cannot find out how to do so" (*City of God* 4.30). This use of *superstitio* to categorize the whole of classical pagan religion as idolatrous and even demonic constitutes a basic core of meaning that persists throughout the common era.

MEDIEVAL CHRISTIANITY. The religions of the Germanic tribes were perceived in a similar way by the Christian missionaries who undertook the conversion of these so-called barbarians in the period following the fall of the Roman Empire. The cure for their idolatry and superstition was baptism and the acceptance of Christianity as the true religion. But even after the evangelization of whole tribes, attitudes, beliefs, and practices associated with pre-Christian religions persisted. Early medieval denunciations of such paganizing observances in sermons and treatises against the *superstitiones rusticorum* were frequent. The epistle *On the Correction of Rustics* (c. 572) by Bishop Martin of Braga condemned popular magical practices, divination, and the worship of "rocks, trees and springs" as apostasy to the devil. Not all superstition was rustic, however. Martin also rejected the use of Latin calendrical vocabulary, since the days of the week were named after pagan gods (in his view demons) like Mars, Jove, and Venus. The limited, local success of such polemics is witnessed by the fact that Portuguese, alone among the emergent European vernaculars, purged this ancient vocabulary under church pressure.

The difficulties of weaning newly evangelized peoples from their old ways led Pope Gregory I (590–604) to suggest a gradualist approach to their conversion. Writing to Augustine of Canterbury, a missionary in England in the early seventh century, he acknowledged that "it is doubtless impossible to cut out everything at once from their stubborn minds" (Bede, *History of the English Church and People* 1.30). Gregory proposed that heathen shrines be reconsecrated as churches and that existing days of celebration be adapted to the Christian calendar. The Feast of Saint John the Baptist, for instance, was fixed on the former date of a midsummer festival. These syncretic fusions of old and new religious observances were often the target of later reformers' campaigns against "pagan survivals" within Christianity. Throughout the medieval period, church councils and synods condemned paganizing and superstitious observances in an effort to complete the process of Christianization by enforcing more orthodox standards.

Scholastic theologians brought the analysis of superstitious error to a new level of thoroughness and sophistication. Thomas Aquinas (1225–1274) defined superstition as "the vice opposed to the virtue of religion by means of excess . . . because it offers divine worship either to whom it ought not, or in a manner it ought not" (*Summa theologiae* 2.2.92.7). The idea of "undue worship of the true God" revived the classical meaning of exaggerated or overscrupulous religious behavior, now seen as occurring within Christianity rather than wholly or partially outside of it. Aquinas's systematic exposition also classified idolatry, divination, and magical practices in general as superstitious by virtue of the inappropriate object (demons rather than God) toward which they were directed. The Scholastic theory of the diabolical pact as the causative mechanism behind magical effects assured that superstition in its medieval version was perceived as neither "harmless" nor inefficacious. Even if a magical procedure did not directly invoke the power of the devil to gain its ends, it nevertheless drew on forces outside those controlled or sanctioned by the church and was therefore presumptively diabolical.

The gradual extension of the medieval Inquisition's jurisdiction to include cases of superstition as well as heresy was a turning point in the European attitude toward magical beliefs. Founded in the early thirteenth century to combat organized heretical groups such as the Waldensians and the Albigensians, the Inquisition was initially empowered to hear only those cases that involved an explicit diabolical pact and therefore "manifestly savored of heresy." Infrequent fourteenth-century sorcery trials involved literate men accused of conjuring demons or casting spells by using the techniques of learned, ritual magic associated with handbooks like the *Key of Solomon*. By the fifteenth century, however, the theory of the implicitly diabolical pact was invoked to extend inquisitorial jurisdiction to the magical activities of the illiterate population. As a result, the "new crime" of witchcraft emerged in this period, combining existing peasant beliefs in the possibility of magical harm (*maleficium*) with the scholastic theory of the implicit diabolism of all magical effects.

While customary law in many parts of Europe had treated magical harm (*maleficium*) like any other crime causing physical harm to persons, livestock, or crops, without attention to the fact that such harm was alleged to have occurred through magical means, the new theological approach focused directly on the means employed, not the end pursued. All magical activity implied that the perpetrator had obtained the power to achieve those effects by apostasy to the devil. Superstitious offenses were no longer simply the topic of pastoral reprimand by bishops and synods. By the late Middle Ages such activities had been criminalized, and they were increasingly prosecuted in both secular and church courts during the late sixteenth and the seventeenth century.

This campaign against popular magic emphasized those activities that were, in Aquinas's terms, superstitious by virtue of their presumptively diabolical object. The humanist and Protestant reform movements of the early sixteenth century stressed another meaning of the term *superstition*. Many traditional Catholic religious observances were now judged superstitious because of the "inappropriate manner" in which they offered worship to God. The Catholic humanist reformer Desiderius Erasmus (1466–1536) denounced the externalized ceremonialism of the late medieval church as a superstitious deformation of the true religion. His *Praise of Folly* satirized clerical attachment to repetitious prayer, fasting, and other ascetic practices as well as popular devotion to relics, saints, and shrines. A character in his *Colloquies* observes that "Of all Our Ladies, I like best Our Lady of Walsingham," to which his companion replies, "And I Our Lady of Mariastein." These attitudes constituted, in Erasmus's view, a series of distractions from the central moral teachings of Christianity. People might travel to see a saint's bones, he complained, but they did not attempt to imitate the saint's holy life.

CATHOLICISM AND THE PROTESTANT REFORMATION. The Protestant Reformation intensified humanist critiques of Roman Catholicism. Starting with Martin Luther's attack on indulgences in the *Ninety-Five Theses* (1517), the new theology of justification by faith rather than by works provided the theoretical basis for rejecting Roman Catholic reliance on external devotions as "works righteousness." To John Calvin, superstition was the "pharisaical opinion of the dignity of works" maintained by the "false religion" of Rome. Having rejected most of the ceremonial aspects of Catholicism, from holy water and saints' cults to transubstantiation and the Mass, Protestants of all denominations agreed in their denunciations of the papist religion as magical and superstitious. The term was also used to describe backsliding within the reformed camp, whether high-church fondness for vestments and incense or lingering attachments to rosaries and shrines among the less advanced segments of the population. In the extensive vocabulary of sixteenth-century religious polemics, one of the most common charges was that of superstition.

Although the Roman Catholic Church had finer lines to draw in deciding what was and was not superstitious, a parallel effort to identify and eliminate popular "ignorance and superstition" became a major preoccupation after the Council of Trent (1545–1563). Responding in part to humanist criticism, the church discouraged exaggerations of orthodox observances, such as the "desire for fixed numbers of candles and Masses" described as superstitious in the Tridentine decrees. The definition adopted by the Council of Malines in 1607 expressed the Counter-Reformation position: "It is superstitious to expect any effect from anything, when such an effect cannot be produced by natural causes, by divine institution, or by the ordination or approval of the Church." This ultimately jurisdictional approach left intact the indulgences and exorcisms condemned as "ecclesiastical magic" by the Protestants, but it rejected popular magic by asserting an institutional monopoly on access to the supernatural.

Following the anti-Protestant heresy trials of the mid-sixteenth century, the Holy Offices of Spain and Italy turned their attention to the suppression of popular beliefs and practices categorized as superstitious. Trials for magical healing, divination, and love magic occupied a prominent place in inquisitorial prosecution throughout the seventeenth century. This campaign against superstition occurred in different forms in both Protestant and Catholic countries as part of a wider "reform of popular culture," a systematic attempt by members of the clerical and lay elites to raise the religious and moral level of the European population. Historical studies of early modern Europe have shown that these efforts to suppress popular magical beliefs were not wholly successful; the persistence of magical assumptions among the peasantry has also been documented by twentieth-century anthropological field studies.

ENLIGHTENMENT AND POST-ENLIGHTENMENT ATTITUDES. If the Protestant Reformation viewed the entire Roman Catholic religion as superstitious, the radical anticlerics of the French Enlightenment used the term in an even wider sense, dismissing all traditional religions as superstitious. Voltaire's *Philosophical Dictionary* (1764) asserts that "superstition was born in paganism, adopted by Judaism and infested the Christian church from the beginning." In place of the fanaticism and intolerance associated with organized religion, the *philosophes* proposed a "natural religion" that would acknowledge a supreme being but regard his creation as sufficient revelation. The scientific study of nature was thus proposed as a new cultural orthodoxy, and the concept of superstition was redefined to fit this frame of reference. From "bad religion" it came to mean "bad science," assuming its modern sense of misplaced assumptions about causality stemming from a faulty understanding of nature. Thus magical beliefs and practices continue to be regarded as superstitious, although the original religious sense of the diabolical efficacy of such practices has been replaced with a scientific sense of the impossibility of magical effects in a universe governed by natural law.

SEE ALSO Folklore; Folk Religion; Magic.

BIBLIOGRAPHY

A general history of Western concepts of superstition has yet to be written. Such a history can be reconstructed with the aid of the primary materials presented by Lynn Thorndike in *A History of Magic and Experimental Science,* 8 vols. (New York, 1923–1958), and by Henry C. Lea in *Materials toward a History of Witchcraft,* 3 vols. (New York, 1939).

A succinct, careful review of the etymology and history of the term in classical Roman literature is provided by Denise Grodzynski in "Superstitio," *Revue des études anciennes* 76 (January–June 1974): 36–60. In *The Cult of the Saints: Its Rise and Function in Latin Antiquity* (Chicago, 1981), Peter Brown argues convincingly against interpreting the cult of saints as a superstitious deformation of the original Christian message.

The uses of the concept in medieval canon law and ecclesiastical literature receives thorough, systematic attention in Dieter Harmening's *Superstitio: Überlieferungs- und theoriege-*

schichtliche Untersuchungen zur kirchlich-theologischen Aberglaubensliteratur des Mittelalters (Berlin, 1979). The medieval condemnation of learned and popular magic as superstitious is the subject of Edward Peters's *The Magician, the Witch, and the Law* (Philadelphia, 1978).

The Protestant expansion of the term during the Reformation to include Roman Catholicism is described by Jean Delumeau in "Les réformateurs et la superstition," in *Actes du Colloque l'Amiral de Cologny et Son Temps* (Paris, 1974), pp. 451–487. Keith Thomas provides a magisterial analysis of the survival and suppression of magical beliefs after the Reformation in *Religion and the Decline of Magic: Studies in Popular Beliefs in Sixteenth and Seventeenth Century England* (New York, 1971). The sixteenth-century effort to achieve a "reform of popular culture" is described as a "battle between Carnival and Lent" by Peter Burke in *Popular Culture in Early Modern Europe* (New York, 1978). The Roman Catholic campaign against superstition is examined by M. O'Neil, "*Sacerdote ovvero strione:* Ecclesiastical and Superstitious Remedies in Sixteenth Century Italy," in *Understanding Popular Culture,* edited by Steven L. Kaplan (New York, 1984).

E. William Monter chronicles the prosecution of superstitious offenses by post-Reformation religious orthodoxies and describes also the Enlightenment assault on superstition and religious intolerance in *Ritual, Myth and Magic in Early Modern Europe* (Athens, Ohio, 1983). A study of the meaning of superstition in the modern world is undertaken by Gustav Jahoda in *The Psychology of Superstition* (London, 1969).

New Sources

Meyer, Birgit, and Peter Pels. *Magic and Modernity: Interfaces of Revelation and Concealment.* Stanford, Calif., 2003.

Parish, Helen, and William G. Naphy, eds. *Religion and Superstition in Reformation Europe.* Manchester and New York, 2002.

Trachtenberg, Joshua. *Jewish Magic and Superstition: A Study in Folk Religion* (1939). Philadelphia, 2004.

MARY R. O'NEIL (1987)
Revised Bibliography

SUPREME BEINGS are divinities whose nature reveals a unique quality of being—generally, a transcendent spiritual power—in a culture's religious system. Such divine beings figure in many different religious systems, yet they manifest values and symbolic associations that display remarkable similarities. The first section of this article presents, in a general way, the power, attributes, and values common to a large number of supreme beings. The second section illustrates these features by referring to specific historical forms of supreme beings. The final section summarizes the history of scholarly interpretations of the origin, nature, and meaning of these singularly important and complex supernatural beings.

GENERAL FEATURES. A supreme being is generally described in symbolic terms that reflect the values most highly appraised in a specific historical situation. Considering the complexities of any culture's history, it is extraordinary that a comparative discussion of the nature of supreme beings constantly returns to the same cluster of religious ideas. Without prejudice to one or another aspect of supreme being highlighted in one historical moment or another, this article presents here a general view of the kinds of power and value revealed in supreme beings. It should be noted that the intricacies of history make general statements a source of great controversy. The supremacy of these divine figures marks with an appropriate intensity the heat of debate over their origin, nature, and form. Since each supreme being is a creative and unique composition of elements, the attributes described herein best serve to define the general category of supreme being, and, as shall be seen, apply to specific beings only in one degree or another.

The power of supreme beings is inherently ambivalent, because they manifest their potent omnipresence in a passive mode. Unlike the activities of culture heroes, which are abundantly described in epic cycles of myth, the presence of supreme beings is generally acknowledged in mythology only in brief accounts. In contradistinction to the dramatic activities of vegetation deities, totems, ancestors, and solar and lunar divinities, supreme beings occupy almost no place in scheduled public cults. It has long been acknowledged that sky divinities, or "high gods," admirably reveal many of the central attributes and powers of supreme beings.

Not limited to any single sphere of concern or influence (e.g., fertility of plants or of animals), supreme beings are omnipresent and omnipotent, but, by that very fact, they remain uninvolved with particular activities. Their power—unreckoned by time, unbounded by space—applies to all spheres of life and not to any one alone. Great power and presence reside in a supreme being's inactive transcendence of historical particularities. This remoteness relates to the power of permanence that often reveals itself in symbolisms of the sky and heavenly heights. Standing immutable since before time began, supreme beings remain uninvolved with change. Their steadfastness and eternity go hand in hand with their relative withdrawal from the detailed alterations of historical circumstances. The uniqueness of their infinite character is often portrayed in myth as a kind of loneliness. By their very nature, they stand apart from creation. Nevertheless, they seldom withdraw altogether from the world; they withdraw only to that level that suits their infinite, omnipotent, omniscient character.

Transcendence enables supreme beings to see and to know everything. This strongly colors the nature of their spiritual force: By seeing and understanding all, they can do everything. In keeping with their passive nature, it is the omniscient thought of supreme beings that "actively" expresses their infinite knowledge. As creators, supreme beings create preeminently, but by no means exclusively, by the power of thought or word alone—*creatio ex nihilo*. Their word is creatively powerful.

If supreme beings know all things in the world and even think them into existence, such knowledge is not reciprocal. Knowing everything, they often pass beyond the comprehension of lesser beings. Once again, paradox pervades the nature of supreme beings. Present everywhere, they remain inaccessible. Seeing all, they may remain invisible. In relation to knowledge, supreme beings are the clearest revelation of mystery—a sacred meaning that can never be exhaustively known, despite its uninterrupted presence. Full knowledge of a supreme being always remains hidden. In this connection, supreme beings are often associated with religious specialists and esoteric societies, whose knowledge of special mysteries is made known in elaborate and secret initiations.

The majestic omnipresence of supreme beings involves them in all that is. Their involvement with being as such takes several particular expressions. They may create the universe directly, or they may create it indirectly through supernatural agents over whom they exercise control. In religious systems in which supreme beings have not bequeathed creation to the guardianship of other supernatural beings, they may be viewed as sustaining all life, assuring the fruitfulness of creation, or owning all that exists. As the foundation of all that is real, they may be the sovereign upholders of the world order, rulers of all beings, and even providers of moral commandments and socioethical mores. As guarantors of good order, supreme beings punish transgressions in passive ways, by withholding fertility (famine), health (epidemic), or the process of the seasons (drought). As creators and maintainers of life, they fertilize the vital forms of the universe. Although a supreme being may be prayed to spontaneously by individuals at any time and in any place, public invocation is often limited to times of calamity when life itself seems threatened.

One response consonant with the enigmatic, transcendent, and passive power of supreme beings is the human tendency to replace them with other religious conceptions. In fact, supreme beings per se do not usually dominate the religious imagination. When myths recount the withdrawal to the transcendent heights appropriate to their nature, they are replaced in importance by more active religious forms: gods who specialize in fertilizing activity, vegetation deities, storm gods, culture heroes, divine twins, ancestors, the dead, world rulers, theological abstractions of virtues, or metaphysical principles of cosmic law. The passive is overtaken by the active. Transcendent station yields to the processes of the concrete world. Infinity gives way to the here and now. Yet, supreme beings reveal the very meaning of transcendence and infinity in all its forms: omnipresence, omniscience, omnipotence.

HISTORICAL FORMS. Although essential elements of the power and structure of supreme beings may be recognized and isolated for the sake of analytic discussion, it must be acknowledged that they have appeared across human history in complex forms that differ greatly in specific composition from one culture to another. Their manifestations are not limited to one or even several places on the globe. Nor does geographic distribution entirely explain the process of the historical development or diffusion of this religious idea. No matter how marginal to the history of technological development a culture might appear to be (e.g., the hunting cultures of Tierra del Fuego), that culture's complex notions of supreme being give evidence of a lengthy and complicated history. There appear to be no social or economic factors that determine, in cause-and-effect fashion, the compound of elements that constitute the form through which a supreme being reveals itself in a culture. After lengthy debate among scholars, little doubt remains that sophisticated theologies of supreme being predate the introduction, through missionary or colonial influence, of theological ideas from historical monotheisms. Because arguments based solely on geographic and historical evidence have failed to be convincingly clear, the survey of supreme beings presented here follows the logic of the structures that are evident in the forms of supreme beings themselves. Structures exemplified briefly include (1) attributes, (2) activities, (3) relationships to other divinities, and (4) the place of supreme beings in cult.

Attributes. Even when the forms of supreme beings are only poorly outlined, they are more than vague supernatural forces. Supreme beings are divine persons, with names and epithets that convey their attributes and reveal something about their nature. In addition to personality, their characteristics include celestiality, primordiality, and omniscience; associations with creation and death; remoteness and symbolic means of access; and their tendency to be replaced by other concepts.

Celestiality. The names of numerous supreme beings refer to their connections with the sky. Among the Samoyeds, the supreme being is called Num ("sky"). Along the Australian coast in the vicinity of Shoalhaven Bay, the name *Mirirul* ("sky," or "he who is in the sky") indicates the supreme beings found among the Yuin and their neighbors. In Africa, one of the names for the supreme being of the Galla and other Oromo peoples is Waq ("sky"), as in the phrases *guraci waq* ("dark sky") and *waka kulkullu* ("calm sky"). He is also called Cólok ("the sky"). Among some Ewe peoples, the universal father is called Dzingbe ("sky"); his wife is the earth. Northeast of the Ewe live the Akposo people, who call the supreme being Uvolovu ("the high one," or "the regions above"). Among the Selk'nam hunters of Tierra del Fuego, the name of the supreme being is Témaukel ("the one up there"), although this name is seldom uttered aloud. In its place, one uses the circumlocution *so'onh-haskan* ("dweller in the sky") or *so'onh kas pémer* ("he who is in the sky"). Among the Tsimshian south of the Tlingit, an irascible supreme being named Laxha (also called Laxhage or Laha, "sky") deluges the earth. The Haida of Queen Charlotte Islands call the supreme being Siñ or Sing ("bright sky"). The connection of supreme beings with the sky is not exhausted by the direct translations of their names. More important, in accounts that describe them as dwelling in the sky, or as expressing themselves through celestial elements such as the stars and the rains, these associations are extended.

Primordiality. Another large number of names refer to the antiquity of supreme beings, who often reveal, as part of their own nature, the meaning of what is primordial, most fundamental, a part of the nature of existence from its earliest beginnings. Primordiality is thus part of a supreme being's nature. The Yahgan of Tierra del Fuego call their supreme being Watauineiwa ("the primeval," or "the ancient one"). The Botocudo of eastern Brazil believe in a supreme being who lives in heaven and is called Old Man or Father White-head. During the great August sacrifices in Cuzco, Viracocha, the supreme being of the Inca, was praised as the one "who exists from the beginning of the world to its end."

Omniscience. A large body of epithets refers to the omniscience and omnivoyance of supreme beings. Baiame, supreme being of the Kamilaroi, Wiradjuri, and Euahlayi of New South Wales, sees and hears everything, especially at night, with his many eyes and ears. Daramulun, according to the Yuin, can observe all human action from his position in heaven. In Assam, the Khasis of the Mon-Khmer nucleus of Indochinese peoples believe in a female supreme being and creator who dwells in heaven and who sees and hears all that happens on earth. On Madagascar, the supreme being Andriamanitra sees all those things that lie hidden. In the Avesta, Ahura Mazdā is described as *vouru casani* ("widely seeing").

The clarity of a supreme being's knowledge may be manifested in the light of the bright sky, which, by virtue of its own luminosity, sees and knows all existence that lies below. The Altai Tatars call upon their supreme being as the Ak Ajas ("white light"). The Khanty refer to Ajas Kan ("the bright leader"). Buriats speak of the dwelling of their celestial god as "a house ablaze with silver and gold." For the Mansi, Tārem is a "good golden light on high." In Sumerian, the divinity is described as *dingir* ("shining, bright"), and in Akkadian, *ellu* expresses the same meaning.

Cosmogonic power. Other names refer to supreme beings as the source of all life and power. The Warao of the Orinoco Delta refer to Kanobo ("great father") as the author of life. Also in Venezuela, the Yaruro people believe in a great goddess who created the world. Everything sprang from her, and everything living returns to the western paradise where she now lives. The Caliña and Galibi peoples from the Surinam coast maintain that the goddess Amana ("she without a navel") was not born but has lived forever. All life comes from her, for she begets and contains everything that comes to be. Her twin sons assist in creation. The supreme deity of the Koghi (Cágaba) of Colombia is also a universal mother who gives birth to all creation. She rules the cycles of life, death, and rebirth for all creatures. The mother is omnipresent. Life is an intrauterine existence. Among the Mbyá, a Guaraní people of Paraguay, the supreme being gives life to the world and continues to extend goods in the form of game and health. The Tupinamba of the southern Brazilian coast conducted a search for the land of Tamoi, the supreme being whose name means "great father." He created life and now governs a distant paradise wherein there is no death. In Australia, the supreme being's role as life-giver is recognized in the epithets extended to Baiame, who is addressed as Mahmanmu-rok ("our father") among the Kamilaroi and as Boyjerh ("father") among the Euahlayi. Among the Yuin, Daramulun is spoken to as Papang ("father"). The Kurnai use Mungan-ngaua ("our father") as the proper name of their supreme being.

Specific references to supreme beings as creators occur in many cultures. By way of brief illustration one may mention examples from North America, Oceania, Africa, Australia, and South America.

Native American creator gods include Awonawilona, the Zuni supreme being whose solar associations are sublimated almost to the point of becoming a speculative philosophical principle of life. He creates the clouds and the waters of the world from the breath of his own heart. Tirawa Atius of the Pawnee lives above and beyond the highest heaven. The wind is his breath. Tcuwut Makai, supreme being of the Pima, dwells in the west, governing rain and winds. His first creation was crushed when he pulled the sky too close to the earth. In his second attempt, he fixed the stars and the Milky Way in the sky. Ahone is a sky-dwelling creator of sun, moon, and stars. The existence of belief in him is documented among peoples of the Virginia Colony in 1610. He had no cult to speak of; instead, sacrifices were made to Oke, a god who punished people with hurricane winds to make their crops suffer.

In Oceania, one may call attention to Tangaroa (Tangaloa, Ta'aroa, and many other variants), a widely known Polynesian divinity of the sea; Agunua, the supreme spirit of San Cristobal in the Solomon Islands; Yelafaz, the anthropomorphic sky-dwelling god of Yap; Djohu-ma-di-hutu ("lord above"), believed in by the Alfuri of Molucca; Qat, lunar supreme being of the Banks Islands; Hintubuhet ("our bird-woman"), supreme being in New Ireland; and Ndengei (Degei), the great serpent-god of Fiji. Ndengei usually lies immobile in his cave on Mount Kauvandra on the northeast coast of Viti Levu, but occasionally, when he is stirred, he causes earthquakes and heavy rains.

African supreme beings who are creators include Deng, the omniscient "free-divinity" of the Dinka people, who is identified as Nhialic Aciek ("god the creator"). The term *nhial* ("up," or "above") is associated with multiple modes of supernatural expression. Among the Western Dinka, Deng has no shrines but is honored in sacrifice together with Nhialic ("divinity itself," an appellation applied to Deng) and the ancestors. Also in Africa, one may point to Cagn, the mantis-shaped creator of the San people; Kosane, the vaguely defined supreme being of the Venda; Ọlọrun, high god of the Yoruba; Katonda, supreme being of the Ganda; Lugaba, supreme creator divinity of the Hima; and Ngai, supreme being of the Maasai.

In South America, too, there is no shortage of supreme beings who are creators. Among them one may mention Pelepelewa, god of the Trio of Surinam; Kamuscini, the talking sky-god of the Bakairi; Karu of the Mundurucú of the Tapajós River; and El-al, a supreme being known in Patagonia. In Australia, one finds many creator supreme beings celebrated in scholarly literature. Among those not mentioned above are Bunjil of the Kulin, Nurrundere of the Narrinyeri, Mangarrara of the Larrakia people, and, as a collective name for the high god of the Aboriginal peoples of southeastern Australia, the All-Father.

Such examples by no means exhaust the number of supreme beings whose complicated nature includes the role of creator. The supreme beings mentioned above seem principally interested in the creation of the sky, the stars, the earth, and meteorological phenomena. They concern themselves with the creation of vegetation only in a secondary way. However, other creators, a smaller group of supreme beings, interest themselves particularly in the creation of trees, vines, herbs, grasses, and other forms of vegetation.

In general, this second group is more dramatically involved with rain than with other, more ethereal celestial elements. Among many such supreme beings one may mention uNkulunkulu of the Zulu peoples; Bego Tanutanu, the creator of the landscape, source of foods, plants, and instruments of culture at Buin in the southern Bougainville straits; Tsui //goab, Khoi celestial god who unites the clouds and swells the rains; Teharonhiawakhon, the Iroquois twin divinity who holds heaven at two points (or with his two hands); and Yuskeha, the parallel Huron divinity who sends good weather for crops and enjoys sexual relations with Ataentsic ("she whose body is ancient"), who is also called "the dark one" (i.e., the earth). One notices that supreme beings who are creators of vegetation tend to absorb or acquire attributes more commonly seen among culture heroes, specialized deities of vegetation, and storm gods.

Control over life is also reflected in the supreme beings' ability to end life when they will. For example, among the Yámana of Tierra del Fuego, the supreme being is called "slayer in the sky"; among the Maidu of north-central California, he is also called "a slayer." Supreme beings often figure in deaths that are mysterious, summary, and sudden. Celestial supreme beings strike humans with their thunderbolts. The Semang of Kedah believe that the supreme being Kari created everything except the earth and humankind. These last were fashioned by Ple, a subordinate deity. Kari sees everything from on high and punishes humans by dropping on them a flower from a mysterious plant. Where the flower lands, fatal lightning strikes. The Apapocúva-Guaraní supreme being, Nanderuvuçu ("our great father"), withdrew long ago into a distant dark country where the only light that exists comes from within his chest. Eventually, it is believed, he intends to destroy the world and thereby bring about the end of time.

Remoteness. More often than not, the sky is the principal manifestation of supreme being. From this preponderance of historical facts has come the term *high god,* over whose origin and nature the controversy surrounding supreme being once raged. Scholars have made clear the fact that supreme being is not a simple personification of the "natural" object, the sky. Rather, a supreme being is a distinct divine personality who reveals himself or herself in the power of the sky. Many peoples are careful to make the same distinction in various ways, speaking of their supreme being as dwelling beyond the sky, or as the invisible sky that lies beyond the visible one, or as wearing the sky for a vestment. Puluga, in the Andaman Islands, is said to reside in heaven. The sky is his house. For Baiame, an Australian high god, the sky is a campground, brightened with stars that serve as campfires and traversed by the river of the Milky Way. Num, the Samoyed divinity whose name means "sky," lies in the seventh heaven, but he cannot be a simple personification of the natural sky, for he is also believed to be the earth and the sea. For many Ewe-speaking populations, the blue color of the heavens is a veil that Mawu uses to shield her face, and the clouds are her clothing.

Because a supreme being dwells in inaccessible heights and displays a passive and transcendent character, his outline tends to be left undefined. Although his personality is awesome and powerful, he often avoids dramatic action in favor of inert omnipresence. He may remain mysterious and vaguely delineated. Such is the case with Moma ("father"), the supreme being of the Witóto of Colombia. Associated closely with the power of the word in rituals and chants, he created all things in the world from the mere "appearance" (*naino*) of each thing's "nonexisting substance." Moma calls himself Nainuema ("he who is or possesses what is not present," that is, illusive appearance). According to the Witóto, Moma captured the specter of appearances in his dream and pressed it to his breast until he could transform it into the earth. Earthmaker, supreme being of the Winnebago, comes to consciousness in the primordium in order to make the world keep still. He then remains aloof. What Earthmaker was like, or what there was before he came to consciousness, the Winnebago do not know. The Pawnee contend that Tirawa Atius ("father on high") is in everything. However, no one is able to know what he looks like.

The remoteness of the power of a supreme being may even be portrayed as indifference. When the passivity of a supreme being is exaggerated to the point of his extreme withdrawal from creation, he takes the form of a *deus otiosus,* a god who has retired himself and his unique powers from the active world. He no longer captures the religious imagination in the commanding way of more dramatic supernatural beings. He may, nevertheless, remain the ground for all created and creative possibilities. The Lenape (Delaware), a southern Algonquin group, believe that Gicelamu'kaong ("he who created us through his thought") entrusted his supernatural responsibilities to subordinate beings: the winds, the lord of animals, the sun, the moon, and the thunder. He then withdrew to the twelfth heaven. Nonetheless, he looks over human activities, especially the longhouse ceremonies, for the center post of the cult house is the staff that he keeps in his hand. Témaukel remains rather indifferent to the affairs of the Selk'nam of Tierra del Fuego. He did not complete the work of creation but deputized Kénos, the mythical ancestor, to raise the sky and provide moral instruction. He now lives in the stars. Absent from cult, he still interests himself in moral behavior and punishes the wayward with sickness and premature death. The pre-Zoroastrian conception of Ahura Mazdā depicted him as a divine being who creates only through the mediation of the *spenta mainyu* ("good spirit").

The paradoxical coupling of power and passivity within the supreme being of the sky may be made known in sexual terms. Or the coupling of power and passivity may be expressed in terms of the alternations of the bright sky of day and dark sky of night. Thus Puluga, though omniscient, knows the thoughts within human hearts only in the light of day. In the Banks Islands, it is believed that at the beginning night did not exist. Qat spread the night over the earth so that creation remained obscure. However, after a while the situation did not suit him, and, with a red obsidian knife (dawn), he cut into the darkness. The rays of sunlight that enter through the roof of a house are said to be his spears. Among a western group of San, the supreme being, called Kággen, produces darkness by spreading the bile that spills when he splits open the gallbladder of an antelope. Upset by the darkness, he creates the moon.

The power of transcendent height is continued in the supreme beings who dwell on the tops of mountains. Well known are Mount Olympus of Greek mythology and Haraberazaiti in Iranian belief. In Palestine, Mount Tabor and Mount Gerizim stand as high holy places. Himinbjörg ("heaven's mountain") figures importantly in the Norse Eddas. Ngenéchen, divinity of the Araucanians of Chile and Argentina, lived on top of volcanoes with his wife and children. In the same area, the god Pillán, who lives on mountains in the middle of the sky, seems to have served as a model for Ngenéchen.

Just as mountains symbolically express access to the transcendent realms of infinite power, so other paradigmatic symbols reveal the place of contact with the otherwise inaccessible source of life. In particular, the cosmic tree or world tree is a startling image of access to the dwelling of the high god. Flathead Indians believe that the roots of the cosmic tree reach down into the dwelling place of the evil being, Amtep. At the upper end lies Amotken ("the old one"), a good celestial creator. Rites are often celebrated in connection with an image of the cosmic tree. Thus, during the Turco-Tatar horse sacrifice, the shaman carries the soul of the victim to Ülgen, the supreme being, by scaling nine notches cut into a birch tree. Ascending the tree, the shaman reports his voyage through the nine heavens. Contact between this world and the celestial powers is reflected also in images of the Milky Way, the ladder reaching to heaven, and the liana. The *climax* ("ladder") in the mysteries of Mithra had seven rungs fashioned of seven different metals. Cultures in North America, Oceania, Africa, and ancient Egypt all possess myths concerning ascent to heaven along a cosmic ladder.

In Misminay, near Cuzco in Peru, the Milky Way is conceived of as a stream of semen that flows through the center of celestial space just as the Vilcanota River, its terrestrial counterpart, flows through the center of the earth. As the Milky Way encircles the world, it descends into the ocean in the west, absorbing the earth's waters, and travels underground to rise in the eastern sky. Taking the form of rain, fog, and hail, the heavenly water-semen falls into the headwaters that feed the Vilcanota River. The Milky Way also contains female elements, the *yana phuyu* ("dark spots"), which are the sources of various animal species.

Celestial bodies and elements are often portrayed as the more active constituents and expressions of a supreme being himself. Nurrundere, thunder-voiced god of the Australian Narrinyeri, produces the rainbow when he urinates. The Xhosa of southern Africa believe that hail falls when Utikxo arms himself for battle. On Timor, monsoon rains come forth from Usi Neno, a supreme being with strong solar aspects, as a result of the effort he expends in his intercourse with Usi Afu, goddess of the earth. In Indonesia, in the Ambon Islands, the supreme being called Upu Lanito ("lord heaven") sets stars in the sky as a sign that he has gone to warn the sun and moon about an impending attack of *nitu* ("spirits"). There are abundant accounts that describe the sky as the face of a supreme being; the sun and moon are his eyes.

It shall be seen that the more active divinities tend to specialize in one life-giving activity or sphere (e.g., crops, animals, the dead, military organizations, cosmic laws, or the laws of a kingdom) rather than to remain, as do supreme beings, vague and passive sustainers of life in general. In many instances, their activities are expressed in independent mythologies of active supernatural beings who overshadow the remote and transcendent supreme being. The end result is that there exist religious systems wherein the supreme being is supplanted by more active and specialized deities or, alternatively, wherein the formal expression of the supreme being itself is presented not as remote and transcendent but as quite intensely involved with the specific life processes of the universe. In the latter case, the form of the supreme being absorbs attributes from other important and more active supernatural beings like the culture hero, the trickster, or fertility gods.

Activities. It has been seen that supreme beings are supreme by virtue of their unique nature, not necessarily by virtue of their achievements or exploits. Supreme being, by its very nature, underlies all that is; its character stands in a direct relationship to what exists, what is ontologically true. In this connection, supreme beings are often invoked as witness to oaths, as witness to what is. In northwestern Sumatra, among the Batak peoples, reference is made to Debata. When he smiles, his mouth opens to reveal his teeth in the form of lightning. He is invoked in oaths taken over serious matters. He punishes perjury with bolts of lightning. On Ceram, people swear to the truth by Upu Langi ("lord heaven") and his female counterpart, Upu Tapene. Otherwise, there seems to be no regular cult offered to them. Swahili speakers frequently testify to the truth of an assertion by swearing to "Mungu mmoja" ("the one god") or by saying "Mungu anaona" ("God is watching").

By no means are supreme beings always portrayed as creators. Nevertheless, cosmogonic activity is the single activity that befits their foundational character, their role as the ground of all existence. Some supreme beings leave no room for doubt about their cosmogonic activity. Their powerful thought alone brings the world into being. Such is the manner in which Wakonda, the Omaha supreme being, created the world. At first, all things were in his mind. The same is true of the Winnebago creator, Earthmaker. Creation proceeds from his thought. When he wishes something, it comes to exist, just as he wishes. It has already been seen how the Witóto supreme being, called Nainuema ("he who is appearance only"), ties a phantasm to his breast with his dream-thread in order to create the world. The Maidu of California believe that Ko'doyanpe ("earth namer") brought about creation after long and intense thought. Likewise, Dasan, the high god-ancestor of the northern Pomo, called the world into being with his words. Whether such sublime notions are preserved from the most archaic traditions or whether they are the fruit of more recent theological speculations that have purified and rarefied earlier ideas is a matter of some dispute.

As evident in several examples above, supreme beings' involvement with creation may be more subtle and complicated. They may take responsibility only for the initial creative impulse toward form, leaving the final shaping of the world to other supernatural beings, especially to a "transformer," or culture hero. In many cases, the supreme being is only indirectly involved in creation. He engenders, empowers, or presides over those beings who create the world and its creatures. His creative activity remains supervisory. In other instances, he may create in cooperation (or in competition) with other powerful beings. In any case, a supreme being appears to be more than a rational "first cause" of creation. Life and existence, as a whole, stem from and are maintained in accordance with his own inner nature. I do not speak here of a necessary pantheism or emanationism, since a supreme being is a distinct personality who remains distinguishable from creation.

Regardless of the degree of his active participation in creation, once the universe exists a supreme being's major job is done. He then "retires" at some remove, often to the heavenly heights, where he devotes himself to the passive and transcendent pursuits of maintaining and sustaining life. He may thus leave the world to powers who preside directly over specific domains that are less than cosmogonic in scope and whose activities—the accomplishment and functioning of specific world processes—make sense in a world that already exists. Myths often recount the withdrawal of the high god as the event that marks the end of the primordium.

Relationship to other divinities. A supreme being rarely occupies the dominant position in a pantheon or a divine hierarchy. Once creation has ended, if indeed he was involved actively in the cosmogony, the supreme being yields the mythical stage to more active beings whose personalities are more clearly delineated.

A supreme being's link to the very foundations of being is often expressed in temporal terms (for example, he may exist before the other gods exist). Consequently, in the cases in which more active beings take over the religious imagination, his eventual passivity in relation to them may be expressed in terms of old age and its inactive fragility. In the Akkadian text *Enuma elish,* the primordial couple, Apsu and Tiamat, now grown old, are nettled by the noise and games of younger divinities, by whom they are eventually destroyed. The god El, as reported in the Ugaritic texts, is weak and senile. While in his palace in Mount Tsafon, El is attacked by Baal. The younger god not only usurps the previously dominant position of the supreme being but routs him to the farthest reaches of creation. In explicitly sexual terms, younger gods may deprive a supreme being entirely of his no longer exercised potency by castrating him. Ouranos, the Greek cosmocrat and husband of Gaia (Ge), was castrated by his son and successor Kronos. This event interrupted the unbroken coitus between sky and earth during the primordium. When his sexual organs were tossed into the sea, Aphrodite came into being. In the Hurrito-Hittite theogony, which appears to bear North Syrian and Sumerian influences, Alalu was replaced by the god Anu. After nine years had passed, Anu himself was attacked by Kumarbi, who bit Anu's loins. Swallowing part of the god's sexual organ, Kumarbi became pregnant with three children. These violent divine beings express attributes quite different from those of the unchanging supreme beings. Their dynamism tends to alienate still further from myth and cultic activity the transcendent and passive character of supreme beings. Supreme beings are thus often obscured and their power eclipsed.

As is characteristic in the above examples, the younger, "champion" divinities who usurp a supreme being's position are often associated with the fertility of fields and animals. In their connection with agriculture and fecundity, they are often known in the violent but necessary manifestations of weather and storm gods. Their character is bound up with tempestuous change, the violence of concrete life processes that make fertility of seed and stock possible but unforeseeable. Such violence is one important aspect of Indra, hailed as "bull of the world," "lord of the plow" *(śiraspati),* and "master of the fields" *(ūrvavapati).* He uses his *vajra* (thunderbolt) to kill the monstrous Vrta and thereby release the waters. Also in South Asia one finds Parjanya, son of the sky and god of hurricanes. He unleashes the rains and assures fertility for animals, crops, and humans. In Iran, the meteorological divinity Verethraghna is dramatic and fertilizing. As illustrated by creators specializing in vegetation, the form of a supreme being may itself contain aspects of these fecundator beings. In such cases supreme beings maintain a more active role in the mythic imagination, but at the cost of losing something of their unchanging nature.

On the one hand, the passive involvement of a supreme being in the very ground of being in all its forms may give rise, eventually, to his usurpation or transformation by dynamic figures specializing in one or another specific life form or process: fertility and fecundator gods. On the other hand, in a parallel but separate development, a supreme being's supervisory capacity, his general omniscience passively expressed, may develop into more active and concrete expression in the form of a sovereign god. Whether such a sovereign god is the result of a process in which a supreme being, for example a sky god, absorbs the traits of a cosmocrat, or vice versa, must be reviewed on a case-by-case basis. In all these cases, however, the emphasis of the resultant form no longer falls on the supreme being's transcendent supervision of the universe but on his active guardianship of the norms of world order.

Certain sovereign divinities enforce the most general cosmic or "natural" laws inherent in the structures of the universe. Varuṇa, called Sahasrākṣa ("thousand-eyed") in the *Ṛgveda,* is the universal king *(saṃraj),* who guards the norms of world order. By virtue of his own nature, his power is over all existence. Unlike the champion gods of fertility, who violently conquer their specialized domains, Varuṇa reigns through his innate relationship to *ṛta* (the cosmic, ethical, and ritual order of the universe) and through his mastery of magico-spiritual influence (*māyā*), which allows him to bind with his "nets," "ropes," and "knots" those who transgress that order. In other cases, a sovereign divinity may be interested less in cosmic processes than in human moral action. In such instances, he may send forth moral commandments and laws and punish breaches of the ethical order. As sovereign, a supreme being may even interest himself in the details of socioethical behavior, upholding the proper performance of customs and mores.

The cosmic pillar that upholds the universe, or the *columna universalis,* is often associated with the sovereign being, himself the upholder of cosmic order. As an *axis mundi,* like the cosmic tree and mountain, it points to aspects of the sovereign that preserve celestial powers and associations. During their Winter Ceremonial, the Kwakiutl people of the northwest American coast wrap a cedar "cannibal pole" in red-cedar bark to endow it with *nawalak* ("supernatural power"). Projecting through the roof of the house, the forty-foot post is considered to be the Post of the World and the insignia of the great divinity Baxbakualanuxsiwae ("man-eater at the mouth of the river"). It is an image of the great copper pole that upholds the heavens and provides passage between the spatial realms of the cosmos. The Saxons maintained a cult of a cosmic pillar called Irminsul, one image of which Charlemagne destroyed in the village of Eresburg in 772. It was the "pillar of the universe" that supported all existing things. Horace reports the existence of such a pillar and similar associated beliefs among the Romans. In Vedic India, as reported in the first book of the *Ṛgveda,* a similar pillar was called the *skambha.* The Achilpa, an Aranda group of Australia, carry a sacred pole that they call *kauwa-auwa,* and they wander in the direction in which it leans. It is a replica of the pillar fashioned by the god Numbakula who, after covering it with blood, ascended along the *kauwa-auwa* until he disappeared into the sky.

Cult. In his most removed form, as noted above, a supreme being usually inspires no regular public cult. A relative absence of cult seems to characterize many of those celestial supreme beings whose passivity borders on otioseness. To a great degree this is true of Thakur (among the Santāl of India), Synshar (among the Khasis), Kari (among the Semang), Sammor or Peng (among the Sakai of the Malay Peninsula), Pirman (among the Benwa-Jakun of Johore), Tuhan Allah (also among Jakun groups), Muladjadi (among the Batak of central Sumatra), Petara (among the Sea Dyaks of Borneo), Opo-geba-snulat (on the Indonesian island of Buru), Lowalangi (on the island of Nias in Indonesia), Hintubuhet (in New Ireland), Ndengei (in Fiji), Takaro (on Malo Island, near Malekula), Gueggiahora (among the Camacâes in Bahia, Brazil), Wendé (among the African Kaguru), Zame Asizame Ôyô (among the Fang of West Africa), Mpambe (among the Anjanja south of Lake Malawi), Ruwa (among the Chagga of Mount Kilimanjaro), and Yelafaz (on the island of Yap).

In fact, those celestial supreme beings who do call forth a regular cult seem to be exceptional cases. Among them are Agunua, venerated at Haununu on the southwest coast of San Cristobal in the Solomon Islands, and Tabuarik, who, together with his lightning-wife, De Itji, is celebrated in a cult that features sacred stones (for instance, on Nikunau in the Gilbert Islands). More often supreme beings are invoked spontaneously, and even frequently, by individuals or by a community in extreme circumstances of famine, earthquake, drought, and so on. When this irregular aspect of worship first came to scholarly attention, it led investigators to undervalue the importance of supreme beings. Unable to take seriously the profound truth of myth, early investigators were incapable of seeing that the absence of regular public cult was related to the supreme beings' associations with the ground of all being.

A supreme being is often associated with initiatory societies that focus on the knowledge of mysteries. In such secret initiations, many of a supreme being's celestial attributes are maintained. Such appears to be true among Native American tribes of California who possessed what was called the Kuksu cult, wherein the masked initiates impersonated spirits of the dead. The sound of a bull-roarer imitated the voice of the supreme being and other spirits. The area in which this secret society flourished coincides roughly with the area in which there are clearly delineated concepts of a high god (e.g., among the Maidu). However, this connection is a complicated one. Among the Yahgan of Tierra del Fuego, the *ciexais* puberty initiations involve themselves deeply with Watauineiwa, the supreme being who established them. In the *kina*, the secret society rituals of the Yahgan, however, no mention is made of him. Nor does the supreme being figure in the Selk'nam esoteric initiations (*klóketen*), on which the Yahgan probably modeled the *kina*. Although knowledge of a supreme being may be transmitted, refined, and reshaped in secret societies, it is unwarranted to draw the more general conclusion that supreme beings are the creation of such elites.

Among those supreme beings who merge with or yield to more active forms, there exists a tendency toward a more scheduled public cult. This can be seen in cults dedicated to solarized supreme beings. Although solarized supreme beings share something of the sacrality of the sky, their potency and periodic activity often highlight the manifest rational order of regulated life processes, which outshines the mysterious and unfathomable order of being commonly associated with celestial supreme beings.

Summary. The attributes and powers of supreme beings, often reflected in their very names, are most clearly made known in sky divinities. The activity that best suits the infinite and omnipotent nature of supreme beings is the creation of the world. Often, but not always, they create the world through thought, a *creatio ex nihilo,* which is in keeping with their passive nature. After creation, a supreme being often retires on high and becomes even more transcendent a power. When supreme beings do take a more active role, their form tends to merge with or yield to other divine forms. Such is true, on the one hand, with sovereign divinities who ruled the world and, on the other hand, with fecundators and "champion" divinities. Knowledge of a transcendent and mysterious supreme being is often better preserved in initiatory secret societies than in the public cults that surround the more active expressions of sun god, storm god, or meteorological beings.

There is no doubt that many forms of supreme being, as known today, have been influenced by the religious ideas of historical monotheisms. Such contacts reveal themselves in the very names of many supreme beings, not to mention the influences brought to light in careful study of the histories and religious ideas of cultures around the globe. However, the impact of such historical change ought not to be exaggerated. In the first place, no culture's religious ideas have remained without change through history. Even those forms held by scholars to be most archaic give evidence of complicated historical processes that involve borrowing, deterioration, new inspiration, and reconstitution. The contemporary era ought to be seen as a further instance of a much larger historical process. In the second place, in those areas where absorption of ideas from monotheisms is clearly evident, one does not generally find inert imitations of monotheisms but lively new syntheses, often in terms that are best understood as part of the religious history of a local culture's conception of supreme being.

SCHOLARLY THEORIES. In the development of the discipline of history of religions, the investigation of supreme beings has occupied a special place. For more than a century, three factors have especially affected the scholarly debate about the nature of supreme beings: the provenance of the materials studied; the dogmatic concerns of the investigators, whether theological or scientific; and the judgments in vogue regarding the nature of religious expressions. On the most general plane, one may distinguish four important positions taken during the study of supreme beings over the past 120 years.

Four main views. The first point of view, exemplified in the work of Leopold von Schroeder, interested itself in the sky gods known through sacred texts in the Indo-European family of languages. Interest in such exalted forms of supreme being was eclipsed when attention turned to the ethnographic data pouring in from cultures outside the Indo-European sphere. This second position, developed most successfully by E. B. Tylor, held that it was impossible to see supreme being as anything but a most recent religious form in human history. Tylor considered the idea of supreme beings to be a rational elaboration of simpler and earlier religious notions. The third perspective began with Andrew Lang, who called attention to the authentic existence of supreme beings outside Indo-European and ancient Near Eastern culture history, principally in Aboriginal Australia. Taking his cue from Lang, Wilhelm Schmidt carried on an intense and comprehensive investigation of supreme beings in traditional cultures of the Americas, Oceania, Australia, Asia, and Eurasia.

Regardless of their judgment on the antiquity and meaning of the various forms of supreme being, these three views of the issue never succeeded in detaching the inquiry into the nature of supreme being from the question of the appearance of historical monotheism with its concomitant theological constructs of revelation, creator (or first cause of creation), and moral rectitude. A historicist search for simple origins, an exaggerated rationalism in defining religion, and a dismal appraisal of the nature of myth are common to all three approaches.

It fell to Raffaele Pettazzoni to take a fourth position by reinstating a consideration of the supreme being of the sky, this time in a framework that treated the history of monotheism as a particular, even if related, historical instance. Drawing upon data from all over the world, Pettazzoni centered his research on what were called the "primitive" religions. Taking Pettazzoni's insight about the celestial being as a starting point, Mircea Eliade has presented a morphology of supreme beings that serves as the foundation for his comparative historical studies of religion. In addition to these general positions and their principal protagonists, a large number of scholars interested themselves in one or another specific aspect of the problem and contributed to the understanding of supreme beings.

Early studies. During the nineteenth century many scholars of religion investigated religious texts from cultures in the Indo-European language family. Their main concerns were philological. When they investigated the meaning of specific religious images and forms, they took a special interest in those forms that were associated with natural phenomena. Nevertheless, the comparative philology of Indo-European languages pointed to the existence of a supreme sky god. The identification of the Indo-European radical *deiwos* ("sky") in designations meaning "god" (for example, in Old German *tivar,* Lithuanian *diewas,* Latin *deus,* Iranian *div,* and Sanskrit *deva*) lent support for a theory like that of Charles Ploix, who contended in *La nature des dieux: Études de mythologie greco-latine* (1888) that the sky was the principal subject of myth and religion.

In this way, the nineteenth-century attempt to discover a theory of origins of religion in natural phenomena made way also for a sky-dwelling supreme being. Unfortunately, a shallow understanding of myth in general led to the conclusion that supreme beings were merely personifications of one or another natural phenomenon. In *Die Herabkunft des Feuers und des Göttertranks* (1859), Adelbert Kuhn gave a privileged place to meteorological phenomena such as rain, lightning, storms, and thunder, holding that these celestial phenomena were responsible for the development of mythological themes.

In *Die Geschichte der Religion* (1869), Otto Pfleiderer also laid great stress on the importance of a celestial supreme being. He considered the sky god a natural starting point for the development of monotheism. By postulating that the origins of religion lay in the personification of natural phenomena in the heavens and by hypothesizing about the connection between the sky god and monotheism, he provoked reactions from investigators with theological concerns. E. G. Steude, in *Ein Problem der allgemeinen Religionswissenschaft und ein Versuch einer Lösung* (1881), argued that early belief in a sky god, although a vague form of monotheism, might easily degenerate into polytheism through the personification of other celestial phenomena. Therefore, "primitive" belief in a supreme being ought not to be judged a true monotheism.

F. Max Müller, the foremost spokesperson of the school of nature mythology, attempted to avoid the theological pitfalls by positing the origin of religion in an innate capacity of the human soul to respond to the infinite. Consequently, in his studies of comparative mythology Müller placed great stress on those objects that are wholly intangible and that best express infinity: the sun, the dawn, and the sky. The experience of the infinite made available in the contemplation of these intangible objects (*numina*) ultimately gave rise to their designation by name (*nomina*). Through a "disease of language," the named objects were personified as gods, whose exploits were recounted in myths. According to Müller, the origin of supreme being lies neither in polytheism nor in monotheism but in what he termed "kathenotheism," the tendency of the religious perception to treat any particular god as the only one in any specific moment.

Much of the early interest in Indo-European supreme beings culminated some years later in the work of Leopold von Schroeder. In the first volume of his *Arische Religion* (1914), he presents in an exhaustive fashion the instances of supreme sky beings: Indian Dyaus-pitr, Latin Jupiter, Greek Zeus Pater, Scythian Zeus-Papaius, Illyrian Daipatures, and Thraco-Phrygian Zeus-Pappos. However, by the time von Schroeder's useful collection of researches had been gathered together, the investigation of supreme beings in the history of religions had already passed beyond the relatively narrow confines of Indo-European texts. An increasing amount of reliable ethnographic data and a better awareness of the enormity of culture history demanded that the question be debated on wider grounds. Rather than a contribution to the general history of supreme being, von Schroeder's work became a masterful synthesis of a generation of research by specialists in only one area of religion.

Evolutionary theories. At the end of the nineteenth and the beginning of the twentieth century, when scholars turned systematic attention to the history of religions outside Indo-European cultures, interest in the nature and meaning of supreme being waned. In their enthusiasm for evolutionary theories of the development of human ideas, various schools of scientific thought placed the concept of supreme being on the opposite end of history from the origin of religious thought. The idea of supreme being and its manifold forms were thus deprived of the prestige of origins.

Sir John Lubbock, for example, contended that the earliest stages of human development gave evidence of a total absence of religion. Religious inclinations began with a belief in fetishes and arrived at the concept of a supreme being only after passing through the intervening stages of totemism, worship of nature, shamanism, and anthropomorphism (idolatry). In a similar way, Herbert Spencer attributed the origin of religious ideas to a vague belief in ghosts, which culminated in ancestor worship. The worship of distinguished ancestors eventually gave rise to the notion of supernatural beings. Ultimately, the concept of supreme being was the outcome of a lengthy historical process of reflection on human personalities such as a chief famous for strength and bravery, a medicine man of high esteem, or a stranger with superior knowledge of arts and inventions.

Various evolutionary theories found it inconceivable that an exalted notion of supreme being could exist in antiquity. Instead, religious history was seen as a development from simple ideas to more complex ones. In this way, the "origin" of supreme beings was postulated in animal totems, rudimentary human emotions, the human will at work in primitive magic, or a vague universal magic force.

The most popular of these theories was that of animism, set forth by E. B. Tylor in *Primitive Culture: Researches into the Development of Mythology, Philosophy, Religion, Art and Custom* (1872). For Tylor, the idea of supreme being was only the last in a long series of developments of religious ideas, which ultimately began with the idea of the human soul. The doctrine of a supreme being emerged only in the "later stages" of human history after it had been transformed, rationally projected on nature, and developed throughout a stage of ancestral worship and idolatry. Eventually it emerged in the form of a "pure" spirit that took its place in a polytheistic pantheon over which it gradually stood supreme.

The enthusiasm that greeted animism and other evolutionary theories succeeded in displacing scholarly interest in supreme beings. In placing the idea of supreme being in the most recent stages of human history, these theories implied or stated explicitly that the concept of supreme being was introduced into the cultures of Aboriginal Australia, Africa, and Native America by Christianity or Islam. In the opinions of these evolutionary theorists, the concept of supreme being was not an authentic local tradition. Scarcely heard in the din of scientific enthusiasm were opinions like those of the theologian C. von Orelli. Examining beliefs in supreme beings in Africa, Australia, and North America in his *Allgemeine Religionsgeschichte* (1899), von Orelli concluded that the original form of religion was a monistic belief in a celestial divinity, whose nature was known through revealed truth.

Andrew Lang. A disciple of Tylor, Andrew Lang called for a reconsideration of supreme beings in the light of materials from southeastern Australia as reported by A. W. Howitt. Lang pointed to the authentic existence of the idea of supreme being among Australian Aborigines, Andamanese pygmies (Negritos), and certain peoples of Africa and the Americas, whose life-ways were deemed most simple and whose religious ideas were therefore considered most archaic. He thus questioned one of the fundamental presuppositions of the animistic theory.

Lang never abandoned totally the evolutionary scheme, but he did challenge its overall simplicity. He argued that the idea of supreme being stood quite apart from the religious conceptions of soul and spirit that emerged in response to such phenomena as death, illness, and dreaming. A supreme being was an entity with a quality of being unique unto itself. It could not be an elaboration of earlier and simpler notions, for, in some cases, the idea of supreme being exists where no evidence of ancestor worship is found.

In *The Making of Religion* (1898), Lang presents the supreme being as a deathless "maker" of all creation that is not fashioned by human hands. Lang considered the idea of supreme being a sublime religious conception that the human intellect was capable of conceiving at any stage of its historical development. Though recognized by the religious intellect, a supreme being was a creative power that the imagination eventually encrusted with mythical elements. Consequently, although the conception of a creator was exalted, the forms into which mythic fancy cast supreme beings were often erratic and degrading.

Lang's insistence on the authentic existence of a sublime supreme being in the religious thought of cultures that animists deemed "lower" or "savage" races met with little success during his lifetime. Nor was his the only voice to fall on deaf ears. As early as 1860, in his second volume of *Anthropologie der Naturvölker*, Theodore Waitz-Gerland had argued for the existence of an indigenous African religion whose ideas of supreme being were so exalted that they approached the limits of monotheism. In his *History of Religion* (1906), A. Menzies, too, had concluded that there existed a widespread belief in a vague and remote divinity who managed the world but found no place in cult, but he was not sure how archaic the form was.

Wilhelm Schmidt. In the very year of Lang's death, Wilhelm Schmidt published the first volume of *Der Ursprung der Gottesidee* (1912), a twelve-volume work that was to occupy him for the next forty years. An ethnologist of uncommon energies and linguistic abilities, Schmidt studied supreme beings in a comprehensive fashion. Although he acknowledged his debt to Andrew Lang for having recognized the existence of supreme beings outside historical monotheisms, his main thrust was to situate the study of supreme beings in a more accurate historical framework than the one provided by an ideology of evolution.

Following Fritz Graebner and Bernard Ankermann, Schmidt attacked theories of a unilinear and evolutionary development of religious history. He argued convincingly that human history was a more complicated reality. In the place of simple unilinear development, Schmidt, following the trend of continental historical tradition, proposed the existence of a number of culture circles (*Kulturkreise*), each with distinctive ecological, economic, political, social, and ideological components that developed in relative independence of one another. By first delineating the characteristics of supreme beings found in each culture circle and by comparing those traits seen to be common to distinct culture circles, Schmidt hoped to arrive, through reliable empirical and historical methods, at that original configuration of the idea of God existing in the common archaic culture (*Urkultur*). In this way, Schmidt argued that the contemporary societies of Oceania, Africa, the Americas, and Asia ought not to be ranked in any temporal order on a unilinear time line. On the other hand, features common to many of them pointed to the existence of a temporally earlier culture of shared beliefs.

Like Lang before him, Schmidt emphasized the moral and rational capacities, reflected in the conceptions of supreme beings, of those peoples who had been dubbed "savage" or "primitive." In fact, Schmidt exaggerated the importance of rationality in the nature of religion, for he held that supreme beings were inextricably bound to the rational process of inquiry into the first causes of the universe.

By studying those features common to the religions of African and Asian pygmies, Schmidt postulated the existence of shared religious beliefs stemming from the earlier historical stratum that he called the religion of Archaic Pygmy Culture *(Religion der Pygmäischen Ur-kultur)*. Abstracting from American and Arctic materials in the same manner, Schmidt outlined the beliefs in a supreme being that characterized a hypothetical Archaic Arctic-American Culture. Finally, by comparing his constructions of Archaic Pygmy and Arctic-American cultures with religious beliefs in southeastern Australia, Schmidt postulated the "historical outlines" of earliest belief in a supreme being.

What Schmidt found in the reconstructed primordial culture was a supreme being whose nature satisfied all human needs, in particular, the need for a rational first cause of the universe and its creatures. In this way, the supreme being was viewed as the father and founder of social realities, the family, and kin alliances as well as the author of moral realities in his role as lawgiver and ethical judge, who is himself free from all moral corruption. Schmidt argued that the belief that the supreme being was a protective father, supportive of the virtues of trust and love, provided archaic humans with the capacity to live and work toward supramundane goals. Rendering labor significant and providing a sense of responsibility, the belief in a supreme being proved to be an effective impetus for the forward struggles of human history.

Thus, the supreme being of Archaic Culture was the lord of human history because he was seen to fill all time and was the source of the beginnings of human life as well as the judge at its end. Furthermore, since the supreme being was believed to fill all the space of the universe, Archaic Culture could conceive of the existence of only one supreme being, unique and without peer. This being reigned as sovereign over all peoples of the earth. In short, through his historical investigation of ethnographic data, Schmidt contended that the religion of the most archaic human culture was a primordial monotheism (*Urmonotheismus*), whose existence could best be explained through a primordial revelation (*Uroffenbarung*) of the supreme being itself at the beginning of time.

Recognizing that the high god is found in contemporary cultures with less frequency than in the primordial culture, and acknowledging that the contemporary high god is often absent from scheduled cult and manifest in many obscure forms, or even supplanted by other divine figures, Schmidt atributed this degeneration to the very march of history, to the effects of change on human life and thought. Lang had made the same point. Where Lang had attributed the withdrawal of the high god to the cloak of mythic fancy put on over time, Schmidt also considered the economic and social realities of culture history. Thus, the experiences of matrilineal agrarian societies stressed the importance of a female supreme being, lunar associations, and blood sacrifices. Patrilineal totemic cultures contributed emphases on solar symbolism of a male supreme being. Patriarchal cattle-breeding cultures underlined the supreme being as a sky god, the highest in a pantheon of ranked beings increasingly associated with natural phenomena. Through such a historical process, the kernel idea of a primordial supreme being weakened over time, even while the images of supreme being multiplied themselves in number and breadth of special application. History took its greatest toll on the idea of supreme being in those cultures with a long history of ethnological change. For this reason, Schmidt laid great stress on the study of cultures that remained on the margins of technological change.

Schmidt's historical extrapolations from ethnographic materials drew criticism from anthropologists. His assertions of the existence of a primordial monotheism and revelation disturbed theologians. From the point of view of history of religions, Schmidt's greatest shortcoming would prove to be his lack of appreciation of religious elements other than strongly rational ones. In short, although he helped break the stranglehold of evolutionary theories and renewed serious study of supreme being, he continued a rational tradition of interpretation that found it impossible to appreciate the many existential dimensions of myth subsequently disclosed by a more profound hermeneutics of religion. For these reasons, his ideas never gained widespread acceptance. Nevertheless, Schmidt's mammoth studies of supreme beings stand as a monument to his industry and to the existence of the concept of supreme beings in the general history of cultures.

In Schmidt's wake. A distinguished school of culture history grew up around the researches of Wilhelm Schmidt. Although his disciples were very careful to emend or even to reject his historical conclusions about a primordial Archaic Culture and his theological conclusions about a primordial monotheism, they did continue to hold that the investigation of supreme beings outside monotheism constituted a high priority of research. In particular, the researches of Willhelm Koppers, Josef Haeckel, and Martin Gusinde confirmed the importance of the position of supreme beings in many of the cultures that Schmidt had studied.

Reactions to Schmidt came from both theological and ethnological quarters. In general, his critics raised their objections on the basis of material from one special field or another. For the most part, however, other investigators—Preuss, Radin, Lowie, Söderblom, and van der Leeuw among them—agreed with Schmidt in recognizing the existence and importance of a supreme being in many cultures around the world.

In "Die höchste Göttheit bei den kulturarmen Volkern" (1922), Konrad T. Preuss claimed that supreme beings did not form a late stage of human development but rather the foundation of human thought. In *Glauben und Mystik im Schatten des höchsten Wesens* (1926), Preuss pointed out that the separate ideas concerning the world are woven into a universal scheme personified by the supreme being of the sky. Paul Radin, in *Primitive Man as Philosopher* (1927), put forward the idea that a supreme being was a creation of a special type of religious person, one inclined toward intellectual reflection. Speculative thought inclined itself toward an unapproachable, abstract divinity, absent from cult and from the contamination of mythic fancy. Radin opposed this sublime figure to the figure of the transformer, a nonethical, materialistic, and dynamically dramatic figure who fascinated the more pragmatically inclined religious mind. Robert H. Lowie, who examined supreme beings in his *Primitive Religion* (1924), was not so much concerned with the historical origin of the idea of supreme being. Admitting its antiquity, he insisted on the need to consider it as an idea on its own merits, quite apart from notions of spirit, ghost, ancestor, or *mana.*

Nathan Söderblom, a great specialist in Iranian religions, also abandoned the quest for the historical origins of religion in favor of a threefold typology of religions distinguishing ethnic religion from mysticism of infinity and from prophetic revelation. He denied any connection between what he termed "primitive high gods" and the supreme beings of monotheisms. Since the high gods remained remote from their world and absent from cult, they appeared to him to be abstract reflections upon the origin of creation. Far from being true divinities, they were a rational construct of an "originator" (*Urheber*). In *Das Werden des Gottesglaubens: Untersuchungen über die Anfänge der Religion* (1926), he postulated a different origin in human experience for the idea of a supreme being in the religions "of the Book." In these traditions, prophets interpreted their experience of a divine will making itself felt in both the legal and political arenas of daily life as an experience of the supreme (that is, most powerful and authoritative) being. This contrasts with the primitive notion of supreme being, which was, in his view, developed in response to questions about the origins of things.

Gerardus van der Leeuw employed several of Söderblom's key concepts in his treatment of supreme beings in "Die Struktur der Vorstellung des sogenannten Höchsten Wesens" (1931). Later, in *Phänomenologie der Religion* (1933), van der Leeuw extended the basic cognitive categories that Söderblom thought lay behind the concept of supreme being into a more refined Gestalt psychology of religion. The supreme beings outside monotheisms were an outgrowth of the basic cognitive structure of origination. Following Preuss, van der Leeuw also argued that these supreme beings, these high gods, preserved the world order by serving as systematic expressions of the mystical unity on which the conception of the world of everyday experience was grounded.

Like Söderblom and Preuss, van der Leeuw considered the question of the nature and structure of supreme beings in isolation from the history of the idea and the historical situations of particular expressions of supreme beings. An intrinsic element of such supreme beings is their otiosity, their remoteness. Whatever form a supreme being may take, whether sky god, weather god, or animal in form, it is always a form that remains in the background of the religious psyche. According to van der Leeuw, the supreme being created the world but now remains uninvolved with it in any practical way. He is looked upon as a being who in the past accomplished something extraordinary but who will never act in such a way again. Whereas Andrew Lang and Wilhelm Schmidt believed that the supreme being suffered mythic distortions accrued throughout history, van der Leeuw argued that the supreme being, as a structure of the religious psyche, exists outside history.

Raffaele Pettazzoni. It was Raffaele Pettazzoni who proposed that ambivalence is an essential component of the structure of supreme beings. Reappropriating the historical vision of Giovanni Battista Vico, who emphasized that every religious phenomenon is also a "genomenon" (something with a temporal history of development) and that the truths of human history are especially accessible through ideas forged in the symbolic terms of their time ("verum et factum convertuntur"), Pettazzoni embarked on an enormous study of the historical expressions and forms of supreme beings. Nonetheless, he respected the efforts and contributions of phenomenologists, who studied the forms of supreme beings in their essential structures.

The essentially ambivalent structure of supreme beings emerged from Pettazzoni's study of their historical forms. On the one hand, one finds relatively inactive creators who have retired to inaccessible regions once their acts of creation have been accomplished. On the other hand, one finds in history testimonies to supreme beings who are extremely dynamic overseers of the moral order. These active and omniscient sky gods often intervene directly in the course of human affairs by punishing transgressors of the statutes of social order with the weapons of weather and flood so characteristic of their own tempestuous natures.

Over the course of time, Pettazzoni argued, these historically separate features combined into a basic phenomenological structure of a dualistic nature. Their common meeting ground is the sky. Pettazzoni pointed out the primordial and cosmic quality of the remote and inactive creator. In his view, those features of a supreme being that emphasize his transcendence of the world are best suited to express his conservation of the very conditions that guarantee its existence and endurance. Once the world is fashioned, the function of the creator can only be to prolong its duration and ensure its stability. Further action would endanger it. Creativity and passivity are thus indissolubly, if paradoxically, linked with one another. In this way, Pettazzoni rejected the hypothesis of Andrew Lang and Wilhelm Schmidt that the remoteness of the creator is a historical development of mythic fantasy.

On the other hand, criticizing the view held by van der Leeuw and Söderblom, which claimed that the dynamic features of supreme beings are foreign to the otiose figure of a primordial creator, Pettazzoni asserted that moral omniscience is also fundamental to the structure of supreme being. The capacity for moral supervision renders a supreme being morally relevant to historical and social order. Arguing that it is not only the God of historical monotheism who actively involves himself in the course of human events, Pettazzoni documented the existence of all-seeing, celestial supreme beings in Australia, Asia, Indonesia, Melanesia, Africa, and the Americas. Cultures in all of these places provide evidence of the existence of an ambivalent supreme being, both passive creator and omniscient sky god, who oversees the moral order and who is inclined to cede his place to more specialized forms of weather divinities.

Pettazzoni's contribution to the study of supreme beings was his positive evaluation of myth. Rather than viewing it as a degeneration or trivialization of a pure and primordial rational idea, Pettazzoni considered myth the most suitable vehicle for the expression of the sublime and exalted truth contained in the nature of the transcendent and omniscient supreme being. The full existential meaning of supreme being is manifest in myth as in no other form of rational discourse.

Mircea Eliade. In several of his studies in the history of religions, Mircea Eliade has given priority to the investigation of supreme beings. In his great morphological treatise, *Patterns in Comparative Religion* (1958), the nature and meaning of supreme being becomes the foundation stone for his approach to the study of religion. Observing the results of earlier investigations, Eliade concludes that in every instance supreme being is a complex figure representing a very involved historical process of religious experiences, revelations, and theoretical systematizations. Nonetheless, Eliade agrees with Pettazzoni that supreme being best manifests its unique spiritual quality as a hierophany of the sky. Height and infinite space become especially suitable manifestations of what is transcendent and supremely sacred. Such supreme beings are primordial; they preexist the world as it is now known, and they act as creators who are beneficent and eternal. They establish the order of creation and become the upholders of its laws. Consequently, Eliade holds that supreme beings are more than simple hierophanies of the sky. Instead, they possess a quality of being that is uniquely their own.

Eliade's special contribution to the study of supreme beings is his illumination of the process of their withdrawal or disappearance. He draws attention to the fact that myth often narrates the withdrawal of a supreme being to remote heights, whence he presides over the larger contours of life, destiny, and the afterlife of the soul, without, however, assuming any dominant role in public cult. In retirement, supreme beings are often replaced by other religious forms: by divinities of nature, by ancestors, by powers of fertility, by solar or lunar divinities, and so forth. Eliade contends that this tendency to give way to more concrete and dynamic forms is an essential element of the stucture of supreme being.

Further, Eliade holds up the withdrawal of supreme beings as the exemplary model for the very process of the religious imagination in history. Considering "the sacred" as a structure of human awareness, he points to its historical occultation or withdrawal even as it manifests itself in concrete and, one could say, profane forms. The withdrawal of the supreme manifestation of being and the occultation of its fullness before active but more circumscribed divine appearances lead to a process of experimentation with sacred forms. This process constitutes the history of religious experience: a religious quest for the full manifestation of supreme being, which myth describes as existing "in the beginning."

Eliade has made a historical application of his morphological analysis of supreme beings in *Australian Religions: An Introduction* (1973), in several articles on South American religions, and in *A History of Religious Ideas* (1978–1986) as well as in other works. At first, Eliade draws attention to the replacement of supreme beings by other divine forms that share the celestial sacrality of supreme being even though they lose something of its transcendent omnipotence: weather, storm, solar, and lunar gods as well as universal sovereign gods who reign from on high. To this extent he develops suggestions made by Pettazzoni. However, his more general point is that supreme being is replaced in the religious imagination by a range of epiphanies of elementary life forces that come to compose a cosmic sacrality: water, stone, earth, vegetation, and animals. These epiphanies reveal themselves as particular modes of being of which a supreme being is the fullest manifestation. Because of this relationship to supreme being no longer fully manifest in history, each cosmic religious form tends, by "imperial" expansion of its meaning to all realms of life, to express itself as a revelation that, like supreme being, includes all other possibilities. However, these limited revelations are, by their very nature, incapable of expressing fully the sacred. They provoke the need for the experience of other forms.

Concluding remarks. Understanding the nature, structure, and meaning of supreme beings outside monotheism has remained a priority for scholars who study religion in a comparative and historical frame of reference. The study of this important being has played a singular role in expunging several futile assumptions that plagued the early stages of investigation. Specifically, the naive premises that the origins of religion might be found in a single simple cause, that valid religious experience might be exhausted through rationalistic explanations, and that religious history is a unilinear progressive development had all to be abandoned. In their place, the study of supreme beings has substituted a deeper appreciation of the complexities of human experience in all cultures and in all times and a more profound understanding of the wider existential dimensions of mythic truth.

In particular, better acquaintance with supreme beings has underscored not only the inestimable value of the religions of Asia, Africa, Oceania, the Americas, and archaic cultures but also the inescapable need to know them well in order to understand the religious experience of humankind.

SEE ALSO Ahura Mazdā and Angra Mainyu; All-Father; Animism and Animatism; Axis Mundi; Cosmogony; Deus Otiosus; El; Eliade, Mircea; Evolution, article on Evolutionism; God; Jupiter; Kulturkreiselehre; Lang, Andrew; Leeuw, Gerardus van der; Lowie, Robert H.; Mawu-Lisa; Meteorological Beings; Mountains; Müller, F. Max; Num; Num-Tūrem; Pettazzoni, Raffaele; Polytheism; Preuss, Konrad T.; Radin, Paul; Schmidt, Wilhelm; Shangdi; Sky; Söderblom, Nathan; Spener, Philipp Jakob; Tangaroa; Tian; Tylor, E. B.; Ülgen; uNkulunkulu; Varuṇa; Viracocha; Zeus.

Bibliography

General Works

A number of important studies treat the general investigation of supreme beings on a large scale. In addition to their theoretical and historical value, these works also provide ample bibliographies on the subject. Mircea Eliade's *Patterns in Comparative Religion* (New York, 1958) deals at length with the question of supreme beings in chapter 2, "The Sky and Sky Gods." There follow twelve pages of bibliography containing some three hundred entries grouped by geographic and culture area. For a brief synthesis of Raffaele Pettazzoni's view on the issue, see his "The Supreme Being: Phenomenological Structure and Historical Development," in *The History of Religions: Essays in Methodology,* edited by Joseph M. Kitagawa and Mircea Eliade (Chicago, 1959), pp. 59–66. Other important works by Pettazzoni include *Dio: Formazione e sviluppo del monoteismo nella storia delle religioni* (Rome, 1922); "Allwissende höchste Wesen bei primitivsten Völkern," *Archiv für Religionswissenschaft* 29 (1930): 108–129, 209–243; and *L'onni-scienza di Dio* (Turin, 1955). A wealth of material is contained in the eleven thousand pages of Wilhelm Schmidt's *Der Ursprung der Gottesidee,* 12 vols. (Münster, 1912–1955). Other general works central to the discussion of supreme beings include Nathan Söderblom's *Das Werden des Gottesglaubens: Untersuchungen über die Anfänge der Religion,* 2d ed. (Leipzig, 1926); Gerardus van der Leeuw's "Die Struktur der Vorstellung des sogenannten Höchsten Wesens," *Archiv für Religionswissenschaft* 29 (1931): 79–107; Carl Clemen's "Der sogenannte Monotheismus der Primitiven," *Archiv für Religionswissenschaft* 27 (1927): 290–373; and Paul Radin's *Monotheism among Primitive Peoples* (London, 1924).

Specific Studies

Most of the recent works on the subject make no attempt to encompass the wide parameters of the nature and meaning of supreme beings. Any list of these studies specializing in the supreme being of one culture area could become inordinately long. The following works, not included in the bibliographies of the general treatises cited above, serve as illustrations of the kind of works that bring clarity to the state of the question in their particular field.

China

David N. Keightley, "The Religious Commitment: Shang Theology and the Genesis of Chinese Political Culture," *History of Religions* 17 (1978): 211–225. Joseph Shih, "The Notion of God in the Ancient Chinese Religion," *Numen* 16 (1969): 99–138. Homer H. Dubs, "The Archaic Royal Jou Religion," *T'oung pao* 46 (1958): 217–259.

Oceania

Hans Schärer, *Ngaju Religion: The Conception of God among a South Borneo People,* translated by Rodney Needham (The Hague, 1963). Anicetus B. Sinaga, *Toba-Batak High God: Transcendence and Immanence* (St. Augustin, West Germany, 1981).

Africa

E. E. Evans-Pritchard, *Nuer Religion* (Oxford, 1956). Godfrey Lienhardt, *Divinity and Experience: The Religion of the Dinka* (Oxford, 1961). John S. Mbiti, *African Religions and Philosophy* (New York, 1969). Charles H. Long, "The West African High God: History and Religious Experience." *History of Religions* 3 (1964): 328–349.

South America

Mircea Eliade, "South American High Gods, Part I," *History of Religions* 8 (1968–1969): 338–354. Mircea Eliade, "South American High Gods, Part II," *History of Religions* 10 (1970–1971): 234–266. Arthur Andrew Demarest, *Viracocha: The Nature and Antiquity of the Andean High God* (Cambridge, Mass., 1981). Ana Maria Mariscotti, "Die Stellung des Gewittergottes in den Regionalen Pantheen der Zentralanden," *Baessler-Archiv* (Berlin), n. s. 18 (1970): 427–436.

Mesoamerica

Miguel León Portilla, *La filosofía nahuatl estudiada en sus fuentes,* 2d ed. (Mexico City, 1959). Bodo Spranz, *Göttergestalten in den mexikanischen Bilderhandschriften der Codex Borgia-Gruppe* (Wiesbaden, 1964). Mercedes Olivera de Vazquez, "Los 'dueños del agua' en Tlaxcalcingo," *Boletin del Instituto Nacional de Antropología e Historia* (Mexico City) 35 (1969). Ferdinand Anders, *Das Pantheon der Maya* (Graz, 1963).

North America

Josef Haekel, "Kosmischer Baum and Pfahl in Mythus und Kult der Stämme Nordwestamerikas," *Wiener völkerkundliche Mitteilungen* 6 (1958): 3–81. Åke Hultkrantz, "The Structure of Theistic Beliefs among North American Plains Indians," *Temenos* 7 (1971): 66–74. Åke Hultkrantz, *Religions of the American Indians,* translated by Monica Setterwall (Los Angeles, 1979).

Australia

E. A. Worms, "*Djamar,* the Creator," *Anthropos* 45 (1950): 641–658. T. G. H. Strehlow, "Personal Monototemism in a Polytotemic Community." In *Festschrift für A. E. Jensen,* edited by Eike Haberland et al. (Munich, 1964), pp. 723–754. Mircea Eliade, *Australian Religions* (Ithaca, N.Y., 1973).

New Sources

Egwu, Raphael. *Igbo Idea of the Supreme Being and the Triune God.* Würzburg, 1998.

Global God: Multicultural Evangelical Views of God. Edited by Aida Besancon Spencer and William David Spencer. Grand Rapids, Mich., 1998.

Gupta, V. P. *Cult of Mother Goddess: A Global Perspective.* Delhi, 1999.

Hodgson, Janet. *God of the Xhosa: A Study of the Origins and Development of the Traditional Concepts of the Supreme Being.* Cape Town and New York, 1982.

Motz, Lotte. *Faces of the Goddess.* New York, 1997.

Pruett, Gorden E. *As a Father Loves His Children: The Image of the Supreme Being as Loving Father in Judaism, Christianity and Islam.* Bethesda, Md., 1994.

Ryan, Patrick. "'Arise, O God:' The Problem of 'gods' in West Africa." *Journal of Religion in Africa* 11/3 (1980): 161–171.

Schwartz, O. Douglas. "Hardship and Evil in Plains Indian Theology." *American Journal of Theology & Philosophy* 6/2–3 (1985): 102–114.

Spirituality and the Brain. Is God a Figment of the Imagination? Films for the Humanities & Sciences. Princeton, 2002.

Tovagonze, Venance. "God-Concept: 'Supreme Being' in African Tribal Religions." *Journal of Dharma* 17 (1992): 122–140.

LAWRENCE E. SULLIVAN (1987)
Revised Bibliography

SŪRDĀS (also called Sūr Dās and Sūradāsa; c. 1483–1563), a North Indian devotional poet. Known for his brilliant *padas* (lyrics) in the Braj dialect of Hindi, Sūrdās is one of the most popular poets of Kṛṣṇa *bhakti* (devotion) in the North Indian heartland.

The traditionally accepted story of his life has come down through the hagiographic accounts of the Vallabhite sect of Kṛṣṇa *bhakti,* which claims Sūrdās as the first of its "eight seals"—eight poets who lived during the early days of the sect and whose compositions are part of the sect's daily liturgy. According to these accounts, Sūrdās was born near Delhi in 1478, the same year as Vallabhācārya, the founder of the sect, and, like him, was of the Sārasvat Brāhmaṇ caste. Reputedly blind from birth, he was endowed with miraculous gifts of clairvoyance as well as great musical talent. At a young age, he left home to become an ascetic, eventually settling near Agra. There he composed devotional songs and attracted a following. In 1510 Vallabhācārya came through on one of his preaching tours and met Sūrdās. Until that time, all of Sūrdās's compositions had been of the *vinaya* type—hymns of supplication and humble pleas for salvation. Vallabhācārya taught him the story of Kṛṣṇa as embodied in the tenth chapter of the *Bhāgavata Purāṇa,* instructed him in his doctrines, and enjoined him to sing about the *līlā* (divine play) of Kṛṣṇa. He then brought Sūrdās to the sect's newly established Shrīnāthjī temple in Govardhan and put him in charge of composing songs for the liturgy. In this setting, where he spent the remainder of his life, Sūrdās composed the *Sūrsāgar,* a retelling of the *Bhāgavata Purāṇa* in twelve chapters of verse. He died, according to Vallabhite sources, shortly before the death of Vallabhācārya's son, Viṭṭhalnātha, in 1585, his life thus spanning that of both the founder of the sect and his immediate successor.

Serious scholarly doubt has been cast on this account. Another nonsectarian Hindu tradition suggests that Sūrdās's dates are 1483 to 1563, that he was by caste a Bhāṭ (panegyrist), and that he became blind only later in life. The issue is further complicated by references in Muslim sources to a renowned singer named Sūrdās at the court of the emperor Akbar (r. 1556–1605). The somewhat subordinate ranking of this Mughal Sūrdās—he is far less celebrated than his father, a certain Rāmdās—and a disagreement among the royal choniclers as to whether Rāmdās hailed from Gwalior or Lucknow makes it unlikely, however, that this Sūrdās is the same as the renowned Vaiṣṇava poet. The early-seventeenth-century *Afsānah-i-Shāhāñ* of Muḥammad Kabīr also mentions a Sūrdās, who is referred to as a performer at the court of the Afghan ruler Islām Shāh (r. 1545–1555). This Sūrdās—who sounds more likely to be "our" man—is included in a select list of "accomplished scholars and poets" whose luster was intended to burnish the reputation of Islām Shāh a half century or more later. Sūrdās is the only non-Muslim to be included in the group.

This image of Sūrdās as a court poet is entirely at variance with the Vallabhite account that has become so standard. But the most serious challenge to the Vallabhite view comes not from alternate biographies, Vaiṣṇava or otherwise, but from the textual history of the *Sūrsāgar* itself. Though the present-day standard edition of nearly five thousand *padas* is indeed divided into twelve chapters following the *Bhāgavata Purāṇa,* the oldest extant manuscripts, which contain only a few hundred *padas,* are not. Nor do the older manuscripts follow the Vallabhite liturgical calendar, use the characteristic theological terminology of the sect, or group the *vinaya* lyrics at the beginning as a distinct genre. The present-day *Sūrsāgar* is thus the product of gradual addition to an original core of episodic lyrics, and of the imposition of a systematic framework by a self-conscious sectarian tradition. A critical edition prepared by Kenneth E. Bryant in cooperation with Vidyut Aklujkar and others is shortly to be published and will force a radical reevaluation of the text, at least in scholarly circles.

Despite the incorporation of Sūrdās into the history and liturgy of the Vallabhite community, his importance as a religious figure extends far beyond the sectarian. His name has become a household word used to refer to blind persons, especially blind mendicant singers, while the *Sūrsāgar,* whose lyrics are sung by Indians of all sectarian persuasions, is considered one of the literary and devotional treasures of the Hindi-speaking area. Sūrdās's lyrics touch on all aspects of the Kṛṣṇa story, but he is best known for his depiction of Kṛṣṇa's childhood and adolescence. Among the poems on Kṛṣṇa's childhood, those dealing with Kṛṣṇa as the butter thief are among the favorites. Also popular are the lyrics that describe the irresistible attraction of Kṛṣṇa's flute-playing and how it draws the cowherd women *(gopīs)* from their homes. Sūrdās's second most beloved theme is that of the pain of separation *(viraha)* felt by Rādhā and the cowherd women after Krishna leaves them and settles in Mathura, resuming the royal station he was forced to abdicate at birth. Among these *viraha* poems are the famous "bee songs," in which the cowherd women mock the cold monistic philosophy of Kṛṣṇa's emissary Uddhav and assert the superiority of their loving personal devotion to Kṛṣṇa. Sūrdās's third most popular theme is that of *vinaya,* in which he turns from dramatic third-person description and narration to the intimate first-person voice of the devotee praying to his god for salvation, sometimes humbly, sometimes with reckless abandon. The *Sūrsāgar* also contains *padas* that plumb Kṛṣṇa's activities as a mature adult—stories associated with the great *Mahābhārata* epic—as well as a number that celebrate Rāma and Sītā, as in the *Mahābhārata*'s parallel epic, the *Rāmāyaṇa.*

Finally, there are poems that function as verbal icons, as in the following example. Here, one young woman catches a glimpse of Kṛṣṇa playing his flute Muralī and shares her vision with a friend, likening her mind and eyes to two birds: the *chātak,* which survives on raindrops, and the *chakor,* which lives on moonbeams:

Look, friend: look what a mass of delight—
For my *chātak*-bird mind, a cloud dark with love;
 a moon for my *chakor*-bird eyes.
His earrings coil in the hollows of his neck,
 gladdening his tender cheeks,
As crocodiles might play on a nectar pond
 and make the moonlight shudder in their wake.
A wealth of elixir, his mouth and lips,
 and little Muralī perched in his hands
Seems to be filling that pair of lotus vessels
 with still more of that immortal liquid.
His deep-toned body, sheathed in brilliant silk,
 glitters with a garland of basil leaves
As if a coalition of lightning and cloud
 had been ringed by parrots in flight.
Thick locks of hair; a lovely, easy laugh;
 eyebrows arched to a curve—
To gaze upon the splendor of the Lord of Sūr
 is to make one's wishes lame.
Hawley and Bryant, *Sūr's Ocean,* §41

The *Sūrsāgar* is a work of remarkable range, yet it is important to keep in mind that, at least until the eighteenth century, it was composed entirely of independent lyrics such as the one above, most of them quite short and all of them intended to be sung. The poet's task was not to retell a sustained narrative but to allow his audiences to experience familiar episodes in a fresh way, either by introducing some novel vignette or perspective, by phrasing his poems as puzzles, by assembling metaphors and allusions in new ways, or by seducing his listeners into a langorous lethargy from which he could then awake them. The hagiographer Nābhādās, writing early in the seventeenth century, summed up the views of many subsequent listeners, performers, and critics when he observed that what set Sūrdās apart was his status as a poet's poet: "What poet, hearing the poems Sūr has made, will not nod his head?"

See Also Bhakti; Hindi Religious Traditions; Kṛṣṇa; Poetry, article on Indian Religious Poetry; Vaiṣṇavism, article on Bhāgavatas.

Bibliography

For a brief overview of the traditional understandings of Sūrdās and his relationship to the Vallabhite sect, see S. M. Pandey and Norman Zide's "Sūrdās and His Krishna-*Bhakti,*" in *Krishna: Myths, Rites, and Attitudes,* edited by Milton Singer (Chicago, 1966), pp. 173–199. Vrajeśvara Varmā's *Sūrdās,* 2d ed. (Allahabad, India, 1979), is a balanced and thorough study of Sūrdās's life and poetry. *Pastorales par Soûr-Dâs,* translated and edited by Charlotte Vaudeville (Paris, 1971), contains representative *padas* and a critical introduction. Kenneth E. Bryant's *Poems to the Child-God* (Berkeley, Calif., 1978) is a rhetorical study of Sūrdās's poetic strategies and breaks new ground in the analysis of Indian devotional poetry. In "The Early *Sūr Sāgar* and Growth of the Sūr Tradition," *Journal of the American Oriental Society* 99, no. 1 (January–March 1979): 64–72, John Hawley presents for the first time the manuscript evidence that challenges the traditional view of the *Sūrsāgar.* Other essays by Hawley on various aspects of Sūrdās's life and works are collected in his *Sūr Dās: Poet, Singer, Saint* (Seattle, Wash., 1984); these are supplemented by a further set that appear in *Three Bhakti Voices* (Delhi, 2005). The most extensive translations of poems attributed to Sūrdās are by Jaikishandas Sadani (*Rosary of Hymns,* New Delhi, 1991), A. J. Alston (*The Divine Sports of Krishna,* London, 1993), Krishna P. Bahadur (*The Poems of Sūradāsa,* Delhi, 1999), and J. P. Srivatsava (in *Medieval Indian Literature: An Anthology,* vol. 2, edited by K. Ayyappa Paniker, New Delhi, 1999). The most ambitious critical assessment by Indian authors writing in English is K. C. Sharma, K. C. Yadav, and Pushpendra Sharma's *Sūradāsa: A Critical Study of His Life and Work* (Delhi, 1997).

The standard edition of the *Sūrsāgar,* upon which many authors rely, is the Nagari Pracharini Sabha's *Sūrsāgar,* 2 vols. (Varanasi, India, 1948, with subsequent reprints). Partial editions have also been produced by Javāharlāl Chaturvedī (Calcutta, 1965) and Mātāprasād Gupta (Agra, India, 1979). A full-scale critical edition of Sūrdās poems that can be traced to the sixteenth century has recently been completed by Kenneth Bryant and will be published as volume two of *Sūr's Ocean* (forthcoming). In the first volume of that work, John Hawley provides a translation and poem-by-poem analysis of compositions included in the Bryant edition, with extensive introduction. Bryant and Gopal Narayan Bahura have performed a valuable service by publishing a facsimile edition (*Pad Sūradāsajī kā,* Jaipur, India, 1982) of the earliest extant manuscript containing poems attributed to Sūrdās. Written at Fatehpur in 1582, it contains 239 Sūrdās *padas.*

Karine Schomer (1987)
John Stratton Hawley (2005)

SŪRYA See SAURA HINDUISM

SUSANO-O NO MIKOTO, one of the major deities in Japanese mythology, offspring of Izanagi and Izanami, and brother of Amaterasu. The meaning of the word *susano-o* is interpreted as either "a terrible man," or "the man of Susa," with *susa* read as a place-name. (*Mikoto* is a suffix used for a respected person or deity.) The character of Susano-o is extremely complex because he is an amalgam of several local and national deities. Although this deity personifies evil, several of his acts have an unmistakably beneficent character.

Susano-o caused the most dramatic event in Japanese mythology when he angered Amaterasu. He first aroused her wrath by emptying his bowels in the palace. But when Amaterasu was injured as a result of Susano-o's misbehavior she forthwith entered the Rock Cave of Heaven, and having fastened the Rock Door, dwelt there in seclusion. Eight hundred myriad deities then gathered to consider how to lure her out and restore light to the world. Their solution was to have Ame no Uzume, a female deity, perform an erotic dance in front of the cave. This caused laughter among the deities, and Amaterasu, curious about the noise outside, opened the door a crack and peered out. Then Tajikara no Kami (god of strength) took her by the hand and led her out, and the radiance of the supreme deity filled the universe. For his role in provoking this event, the deities punished Susano-o on the sacred ground. They cut off his beard and his fingernails and toenails, and expelled him from the heavenly world. Because of the banishment of Susano-o, the evil deity, a good crop was expected in the coming new season.

In this myth, Susano-o plays a negative role, but his later activities are more positive. Following his expulsion from the realm of the gods, Susano-o descended to the province of Izumo, which was located in western Honshu, the main island of Japan. There he learned that an eight-headed serpent appeared in Izumo each year to devour a young girl. Susano-o intoxicated the serpent with liquor and killed it. As he cut into the serpent's body, the blade of his sword broke. Thinking this strange, he cut open the flesh and discovered a sword within. The sword, called Kusanagi no Tsurugi, became one of the Three Imperial Regalia. After this incident, Susano-o became the ancestor god of Izumo.

Susano-o is also the most important deity of northern Kyushu. Three female descendants of Susano-o were enshrined at Munakata, a religious center of that region. Thus there is a link between the Munakata and Izumo shrines, not only because Susano-o was the ancestor god of the female deities but also because Ōkuninushi, the son of Susano-o, married Takiribime, one of the three Munakata deities. The Munakata deities also had ties to western Honshu, for the deity enshrined at Itsukushima, near present-day Hiroshima and south of Izumo, is Itsukushima-hime, one of the three Munakata deities.

This geographical pattern suggests that Susano-o and his children were the deities of northern Kyushu and the western tip of Honshu. In sharp contrast, Amaterasu was originally the goddess of Yamato Province in central Japan. Susano-o and Amaterasu might therefore represent two separate political forces before the emergence of a unified Japanese kingdom—the one centered in northern Kyushu, the other in Yamato. When the rival forces merged, the myths were combined as they are found today in the *Nihongi* and the *Kojiki*. The *Kojiki* states that when Susano-o went to the heavenly world, there was consternation and alarm. Amaterasu said of the ascent of Susano-o that there was "surely no good intent. It is only that he wishes to wrest my land from me." Her reaction is understandable if the two deities were rivals before they were united as brother and sister.

Susano-o was also the god of the sea. Itsukushima-hime, one of his three daughters, was also enshrined at Okinoshima, located in the Tsushima Strait north of Kyushu. In ancient times, when the government sent missions to Korea or China, prayers for a safe voyage were offered at Okinoshima. This supports the *Nihongi*'s description of Susano-o as ruler of the sea.

SEE ALSO Amaterasu Ōmikami; Izanagi and Izanami; Japanese Religions, article on The Study of Myths.

BIBLIOGRAPHY

Aston, W. G., trans. *Nihongi: Chronicles of Japan from the Earliest Times to A. D. 697* (1896). Reprint, 2 vols. in 1, Tokyo, 1972.

Aston, W. G. *Shinto: The Way of the Gods* (1905). Reprint, Tokyo, 1968.

Chamberlain, Basil Hall, trans. *Kojiki: Records of Ancient Matters* (1882). 2d ed. With annotations by W. G. Aston. Tokyo, 1932; reprint, Rutland, Vt., and Tokyo, 1982.

Matsumura, Takeo. *Nihon shinwa no kenkyu.* Vol. 2. Tokyo, 1955.

Philippi, Donald L., trans. *Kojiki.* Princeton, 1969.

KAKUBAYASHI FUMIO (1987 AND 2005)

SŪTRA LITERATURE.

SŪTRA LITERATURE. The Sanskrit term *sūtra* means "a thread"; it is also used, however, to refer to a short, aphoristic sentence and, collectively, to a work consisting of such sentences. Sūtra literature, as distinguished from *śāstra* literature, is in prose. The *sūtra* style, characterized by *laghutva* ("brevity, conciseness"), is a mnemonic device that attempts to condense as much meaning as possible into as few words, even syllables, as possible.

The most important sūtra texts in the context of the religious literature of India are the Kalpasūtras. The term *kalpa* has been variously explained by different traditional and modern scholars, but can best be rendered as "ritual." *Kalpa,* together with *śikṣā* (phonetics), *chandas* (prosody), *nirukta* (etymology), *vyākaraṇa* (grammar), and *jyotiṣa* (astronomy), is one of the six Vedāṅgas, or branches of learning auxiliary to the Vedas. The Kalpasūtras are closely connected with the individual Vedic schools (*śākhās*). (Even though not all the texts have survived, it may be assumed that at one time each Vedic school had not only its own *saṃhitā, brāhmaṇa, āraṇyaka,* and *upaniṣad* but also its own *kalpa-sūtra.*) There are three main classifications of Kalpasūtra: Śrautasūtras, Gṛhyasūtras, and Dharmasūtras.

The ritual performances described in the Śrautasūtras distinguish themselves by their—often extreme—complexity. First, in addition to the *yajamāna* (patron of the sacrifice) and his wife, for whose benefit the ritual is performed, *śrauta* ritual can involve the presence of up to sixteen specialized priests. Second, it requires an elaborately laid-out sacrificial area in which three sacred fires are kept burning continually. Third, *śrauta* ritual includes not only *ekāha* ("one-day-long") ceremonies but also *ahīna* rituals, which last up to twelve days, and *sattra* "sessions," which can extend over several years. Large sections of the Śrautasūtras are devoted to the Agniṣṭoma sacrifice, which is the prototype (*prakṛti*) for many variant forms of soma sacrifices collectively called *jyotiṣṭoma,* among which are the seventeen-day-long Vajapeya and the Rājasūya, the royal consecration. Other well-known *śrauta* rituals are the sacrifices to the new and full moons (Darśapūrṇamāsau), the horse sacrifice (Aśvamedha), and the animal sacrifice (Paśubandha). Some Śrautasūtras end in more or less independent appendices called *sulbasūtras*; because they describe the exact layout of the sacrificial area (*vedi*), they are, in effect, the earliest Indian texts on geometry and mathematics.

In addition to rites that are part of the daily life of the householder and rituals on such occasions as building a house or digging a tank, the Gṛhyasūtras principally deal with the *saṃskāras*. These are the rites of passage that guide a Hindu through the various stages of his life, from conception until death, especially the Upanayana (his second birth, at which time he begins the study of the Veda and is invested with the sacred thread) and marriage. Many topics treated in the Gṛhyasūtras also appear in the Dharmasūtras, although the latter expand their teachings to cover all the duties and obligations of the different *asramas* ("stages of life") and *varṇas* ("classes of society"). The Dharmasūtras, in prose, are considered to be the precursors of the versified Dharmaśāstras.

Treatises in sūtra style also form the basic texts for the six Hindu *darśanas* (orthodox philosophical systems). They are Jaimini's *Pūrvamīmāṃsā Sūtras,* Bādarāyaṇa's *Uttaramīmāṃsā Sūtras,* or *Vedānta Sūtras,* Gautama's *Nyāya Sūtras,* Kaṇāda's *Vaiśeṣika Sūtras,* Kapila's *Sāṃkhya Sūtras,* and Patañjali's *Yoga Sūtras.* Some of these philosophical sūtras are so concise that they have lent themselves to divergent interpretations, and they have thus become the authoritative texts for very different philosophical systems. Bādarāyaṇa's sūtras, for example, are the common source for all later schools of Vedānta, including Śaṇkara's Advaita, Rāmānuja's Viśiṣṭādvaita, and Madhva's Dvaita. The sūtra style was also adopted in certain Buddhist and Jain scriptures.

The area of sūtra literature in which the ideal of brevity and conciseness has been realized most perfectly is the grammatical literature, which technically belongs to the Vedāṅgas, mentioned earlier. Pāṇini's *Aṣṭādhyāyī* not only uses as few words as possible; it has recourse to all kinds of devices to abbreviate the sūtras, such as the replacement of longer grammatical terms with shorter symbols. The commentators on Pāṇini's work go to great length to account for the presence and meaning of each and every syllable in the *Aṣṭādhyāyī.*

It would be misleading to suggest specific dates for the Kalpasūtras and for sūtra literature generally. The texts clearly belong to the end of the Vedic period, and they are thought to be earlier than the epic period. Allowing for exceptions belonging to earlier or later dates, the major part of the sūtra literature may be safely situated in the second half of the first millennium BCE.

SEE ALSO Śāstra Literature.

BIBLIOGRAPHY

The most recent, informative, and comprehensive book on the Kalpasūtras is Jan Gonda's *The Ritual Sutras* (Wiesbaden, 1977), vol. 1, pt. 2, of *History of Indian Literature,* edited by Jan Gonda. Some of the Gṛhyasūtras and Dharmasūtras are available in English translation in volumes 2, 14, 19, and 30 of the series "Sacred Books of the East" (Oxford, 1879–1910), edited by F. Max Müller.

New Sources

Dharmasutras: The Law Codes of Apastamba, Gautama, Baudhayana, and Vasishtha. Annotated text and translation by Patrick Olivelle. Delhi, 2000.

LUDO ROCHER (1987)
Revised Bibliography

SUZUKI, D. T. (1870–1966), also known as Suzuki Daisetsu Teitarō, Buddhist scholar, prolific author, and itinerant lecturer, remains the single most important figure in the popularization of Zen in the twentieth century. At the time of his death in 1966, Suzuki had authored dozens of volumes on Zen and Buddhism in English and had produced an even greater oeuvre in his native Japanese. His writings on Zen remain influential in the West, and translations of his work into Korean, Chinese, and other Asian languages have contributed to a resurgence of popular interest in Zen throughout East Asia. Suzuki's accomplishments as a scholar, popularizer, and evangelist are remarkable, given that his philological skills were acquired largely on his own and that he had no formal credentials as a Zen teacher. (Whereas he was a serious lay practitioner, he neither ordained as a priest nor received Dharma transmission.) He owed his success to his considerable intellectual and linguistic gifts, his seemingly boundless enthusiasm and energy, his prodigious literary output, and his having the right message at the right time.

EARLY YEARS. Born Suzuki Teitarō in the town of Kanazawa (Ishikawa prefecture) on October 18, 1870, Suzuki was the youngest of five children. (The name Daisetsu or "great simplicity" was given to him later by his Zen teacher Shaku Sōen [1859–1919].) Suzuki's family belonged to the Rinzai sect of Zen, but Suzuki credited his own serious interest in Buddhism to the influence of his high-school mathematics teacher Hōjō Tokiyori (1858–1929), a student of the Zen master Imakita Kōsen (1816–1892). Hōjō was also responsible for introducing Zen to Nishida Kitarō (1870–1945), a classmate and friend of Suzuki who would later emerge as Japan's preeminent modern philosopher.

Suzuki's father, a physician, died soon after Suzuki's fifth birthday, and in 1889 Suzuki was forced to leave school and a probable career in medicine owing to his family's ongoing financial difficulties. Suzuki made a living for a while as a primary school English teacher and in 1891 entered the Tokyo Senmon Gakkō, later renamed Waseda University. Later that same year, at the urging of his friend Nishida, Suzuki transferred to Tokyo Imperial University, and at the same time began to practice Zen with Kōsen at Engakuji, an important Rinzai monastery in Kamakura. When Kōsen died in 1892, Suzuki continued his Zen practice under Kōsen's successor, Shaku Sōen.

Both Kōsen and Sōen were pivotal figures in the revival of Zen following the government-sanctioned persecution of Buddhism in the 1870s. Progressives like Kōsen and Sōen sought to broaden Buddhism's appeal, opening the doors of their monasteries to laypersons, encouraging secular education, and promoting an ecumenical attitude toward other Buddhist schools. (Sōen himself spent three years in Ceylon studying Pali Buddhism with Kōsen's blessing.) Suzuki took advantage of the liberal atmosphere at the Engakuji *zendō* (meditation hall), and it was through Sōen that Suzuki, who had considerable facility in English, became familiar with Occidental writings on Buddhism.

INFLUENCES. Suzuki's life took a turn in the early 1890s when he became acquainted with the writings of Paul Carus (1852–1919), an offbeat German philosopher and writer who had emigrated to the United States and was working as a writer and editor for Open Court Press in La Salle, Illinois. Suzuki's contact with Carus came by way of Sōen, who met Carus at the 1893 Chicago World's Parliament of Religions. (Sōen attended as a member of the Japanese Buddhist delegation, and his speech to the Parliament had been translated into English by Suzuki.) Carus was in Chicago covering the Parliament for his journal, *Open Court*, and was so impressed by Sōen and the other Buddhist representatives that he became an ardent champion and exponent of Buddhism in his publications. Soon after the Parliament Carus sent Sōen some of his books, including a somewhat bowdlerized compendium of Buddhist scriptures entitled *Gospel of Buddha* (1894). Sōen, who knew little English, passed the *Gospel* on to Suzuki, who was immediately taken by Carus's depiction of the Buddha as an eminently rational figure who eschewed religious institutions and meaningless ritual. Suzuki produced a Japanese translation of the *Gospel* and wrote to Carus expressing praise for his understanding of Buddhism. Carus responded by sending Suzuki more of his publications, including his book *The Religion of Science* (1893). Shortly thereafter, at Suzuki's request, Sōen wrote to Carus saying that Suzuki "has been so greatly inspired by your sound faith which is perceptible in your various works that he earnestly desires to go abroad and to study under your personal guidance." Carus agreed at once to Sōen's request and promised to help Suzuki pay for the trip by offering him employment as his personal assistant.

It is not surprising that Suzuki, a talented student of Western philosophy and a lay practitioner of Zen, should have been attracted to Carus's writings. Carus was passionately devoted to the reconciliation of science and religion, and his approach to Buddhism rendered it wholly commensurate with the modernist, rationalist, and scientific outlook that dominated university campuses in Meiji, Japan.

Suzuki arrived in America in 1897 and went on to spend some eleven years in La Salle, earning his keep as translator and proofreader at the Open Court Press. His life there was by no means easy—he was obliged to perform domestic services for the Carus household and he was provided with little remuneration for the long hours he put in at the press. By the time Suzuki was ready to return to Japan, he appears to have grown disillusioned with his eccentric host, and he rarely mentions Carus in later writings.

Whatever Suzuki's personal relationship may have been with his employer, Carus's philosophy left its mark on him. Carus's interest in monism, his evolutionary approach to religion, and his attempt to reconcile religion and science are all in evidence in Suzuki's later writings on Buddhism. But Carus was not the only influence on Suzuki during his years in La Salle. Open Court Press published two leading intellectual journals, *Open Court* and *The Monist*, and through them Suzuki encountered the writings of many prominent philosophers of the day, including Charles Sanders Peirce (1839–1914) and William James (1842–1910). James's book *The Varieties of Religious Experience* (1902) was responsible in part for Suzuki's later emphasis on Zen as a form of religious mysticism predicated on "pure experience."

Upon returning to Japan in 1909, Suzuki held a series of lectureships in English at Gakushuin (1909–1921) and Tokyo Imperial University (1909–1914). In 1911 he married Beatrice Erskine Lane (1878–1939), a native of Newark, New Jersey, and graduate of Radcliffe College and Columbia University, whom Suzuki had met four years earlier in the United States. The two had a son named Paul, but not much more is known about Suzuki's relationship with his wife. Clearly, they had many interests in common: in addition to having studied Western philosophy with William James and Josiah Royce, Lane was a Theosophist and student of religious mysticism. In Japan she turned her attention to Shingon, a school of Japanese Esoteric Buddhism, and went on to publish some of the earliest work on the subject in English.

Suzuki shared his wife's interest in theosophy, and in the 1920s their Japanese home served as a meeting place for a branch of the Order of the Star in the East. (The Order, an offshoot of the Theosophical Society founded in 1911, continued until 1929 when it was disbanded by its spiritual leader, Jiddu Krishnamurti [1895–1986].)

Theosophy was fashionable at the time, as was Swedenborgianism, a Christian movement based on the writings of the Swedish mystic and theologian Emanuel Swedenborg (1688–1772). Suzuki was enamored of Swedenborg for several years and was instrumental in the introduction of Swedenborgianism to Japan, both as an active member of the Japanese Swedenborg Society and as translator of four of Swedenborg's works. In 1910 Suzuki traveled to London to attend the international Swedenborg conference in the capacity of "Vice President," returned again in 1912 to continue his work for the Swedenborg Society, and in 1913 wrote his own Japanese introduction to Swedenborg's life and teachings, dubbing him "the Buddha of the North." Whereas his passion for Swedenborg later cooled, his interest in Christian mysticism did not; his writings following the war are filled with appreciative discussions of the medieval Dominican mystic Meister Johannes Eckhart (c. 1260–1327/8).

In 1921 Suzuki moved to Kyoto to take a position as Professor of Buddhist Philosophy at Otani University, a university affiliated with the Shin denomination of Japanese Buddhism. (Suzuki had a life-long interest in Shin Pure Land teachings and published many works touting the unity of Zen and Pure Land thought.) Inspired in part by his experience with *Open Court* and *The Monist,* at Otani Suzuki launched the journal *Eastern Buddhist,* which was intended to serve as a non-sectarian vehicle for the propagation of Mahāyāna Buddhism. "Our standpoint," wrote Suzuki in the second issue of *Eastern Buddhist,* "is that the Mahāyāna ought to be considered one whole, individual thing and no sects, especially no sectarian prejudices, to be recognized in it, except as so many phases or aspects of one fundamental truth. In this respect Buddhism and Christianity and all other religious beliefs are not more than variations of one single original Faith, deeply embedded in the human soul" (Suzuki, 1921, p. 156).

PHILOSOPHY OF ZEN. Virtually all of Suzuki's later writings are attempts to elucidate this "one single original Faith," which he would come to understand as grounded in a transcultural, transhistorical, nondual religious experience lying at the core of all the major religions. The word "Zen," insists Suzuki, refers precisely to this singular transformative experience. That is to say, Zen is not Buddhism, not religion, not philosophy, not really anything that can be talked about at all. In his *An Introduction to Zen Buddhism* Suzuki writes: "Zen has no God to worship, no ceremonial rites to observe, no future abode to which the dead are destined, and, last of all, Zen has no soul whose welfare is to be looked after by somebody else and whose immortality is a matter of intense concern with some people. Zen is free from all these dogmatic and 'religious' encumbrances" (Suzuki, 1934, p. 14).

The claim that true Zen is free of the trappings of religion might seem commonplace to contemporary students of Buddhism, but it is nonetheless a rather peculiar way to characterize a tradition that placed tremendous emphasis on monastic ritual and liturgy, on funerary rites for the welfare of the deceased, on literary accomplishment, and on the formal veneration of a host of buddhas, *bodhisattvas,* and religious patriarchs. Suzuki's characterization of Zen as something that transcends religious and cultural differences must be understood as the result of his life-long effort to synthesize a variety of religious and philosophical traditions, both Buddhist and non-Buddhist, Eastern and Western. If his presentation of Zen seems unremarkable to us today, it testifies to the enduring legacy of Suzuki and his intellectual heirs.

Suzuki's claim that Zen refers to a universal mystical experience is considered by many modern scholars and Zen masters alike as an oversimplification, however well intentioned. More troubling, however, is Suzuki's insistence that Zen constitutes the very essence of Japanese culture. Suzuki began emphasizing the connection between the Japanese cultural experience and the experience of Zen in the 1930s as part of his claim that the Japanese are more evolved spiritually than other peoples, including their Asian neighbors. Japanese life is, according to Suzuki, inherently "Zen-like," and thus the Japanese are naturally predisposed to Zen understanding.

Suzuki's attempts to ennoble Japanese culture must be understood within the context of the times—his writings on the subject first appear just as Japan's imperial ambitions were reaching new heights, and their armies were driving deeper into Korea, Manchuria, and China. Suzuki's extensive writings touting the innate spirituality of the Japanese, and linking this spirituality with the warrior ethos, were in keeping with popular sentiments of the day. (The Zen establishment was, on the whole, an enthusiastic supporter of Japanese colonial expansion.) As the war progressed, so did the extravagance of some of Suzuki's claims. In 1944, for example, between trips to the air-raid shelter, Suzuki wrote a book called *Japanese Spirituality,* which argued that true Zen is not a product of China, much less India, but rather emerged out of the meeting of Buddhism and Japanese culture in the Kamakura period. Suzuki was fully aware of the Indian and Chinese roots of Zen, having written extensively on the topic, but here he insists that true Zen is not a "natural expression" of those cultures, and thus it was not until Zen came to Japan that it was fully realized. Besides, in Suzuki's mind Zen had long since disappeared on the continent. In so far as such statements would have lent credibility to Japan's sense of spiritual mission in Asia, Suzuki could understandably be construed as supporting the ongoing military campaign.

After the Japanese defeat, Suzuki claimed to have been opposed to the war; he said that he believed losing the war was in Japan's own best interests. Private letters to friends written prior to the war substantiate Suzuki's claims: they express his reservations about Japanese militarism, and his disgust with excessive public displays of patriotic zeal. Nevertheless, some Japanese intellectuals such as Umehara Takeshi (1925–) took umbrage with Suzuki: if Suzuki was so opposed to the war effort, why did he—a student of Zen who claimed to have attained satori—not speak out openly?

IMPACT. Be that as it may, Suzuki's lifelong effort to impart his love of Zen and Japanese culture must be deemed a resounding success. Following the war he continued to travel to Europe and America, sometimes for extended periods of time. He was a popular lecturer, speaking at college campuses around the world, and from 1951 to 1957 he held a series of professorships at Columbia University. And he was, above all else, an indefatigable writer, producing over thirty volumes in English and even more in Japanese. Whereas much of Suzuki's writings were intended for a popular audience, he did make substantial contributions to Buddhist scholarship. His three-volume study of the *Laṅkāvatāra Sūtra* published in the 1930s, for example, remains the most comprehensive work on the subject to date, and Zen scholars continue to consult his editions of important Dunhuang manuscripts.

Suzuki's work made a significant impact not only among those interested in the study of religion, but also among theologians, philosophers, writers, artists, and musicians. In his preface to *Outlines of Mahāyāna Buddhism* Alan Watts reported that as early as 1927 James Bissett Pratt had observed "there are two kinds of cultured people: those who have read Suzuki and those who have not" (Suzuki, 1963, p. xv). By the 1950s there seem to have been relatively few of the latter, as is evident from the flattering profile of Suzuki in the August 31, 1957, issue of the *New Yorker*. His influence on the beat poets is well known. According to William Barrett in his *Zen Buddhism: Selected Writing of D. T. Suzuki*, the German philosopher Martin Heidegger (1889–1976) remarked, "If I understand this man correctly, this is what I have been trying to say in all my writings" (Barrett, 1956, p. xi). Suzuki's English works, such as *Zen and Japanese Culture* (first published as *Zen Buddhism and Its Influence on Japanese Culture*, 1938)—a book that unapologetically celebrates the unique spiritual gifts of the Japanese and the sublime affinity between Zen and Japanese martial culture—continue to capture the imagination of new generations of readers. Whereas more traditional Zen teachers may dismiss Suzuki for his intellectualism or for his lack of proper Zen credentials, they have Suzuki to thank for the currency of Zen in the West.

BIBLIOGRAPHY

Abe Masao. *A Zen Life: D. T. Suzuki Remembered.* New York, 1986.

Barrett, William. *Zen Buddhism: Selected Writings of D. T. Suzuki.* New York, 1956.

Faure, Bernard. *Chan Insights and Oversights: An Epistemological Critique of the Chan Tradition.* Princeton, 1993.

Sharf, Robert H. "The Zen of Japanese Nationalism." In *Curators of the Buddha: The Study of Buddhism under Colonialism*, edited by Donald S. Lopez, Jr., pp. 107–160. Chicago, 1995.

Suzuki D. T. *An Introduction to Zen Buddhism.* Kyoto, 1934.

Suzuki D. T. *Essays in Zen Buddhism: First Series.* London, 1949; reprint, New York, 1961.

Suzuki D. T. *Zen and Japanese Culture.* Princeton, 1959.

Suzuki, D. T. *Outlines of Mahāyāna Buddhism.* New York, 1963.

Suzuki D. T. *Suzuki Daisetz zenshū* [Collected Works of Suzuki Daisetsu Teitarō]. 32 vols. Tokyo, 1968–1971.

Suzuki D. T. *Japanese Spirituality.* Translated by Norman Waddell. Tokyo, 1972.

Suzuki D. T. *Swedenborg: Buddha of the North.* Translated by Andrew Bernstein. Swedenborg Studies, no. 5. West Chester, Pa., 1996.

Switzer, A. Irwin, and John Snelling. *D. T. Suzuki: A Biography.* 1st ed. London, 1985.

ROBERT H. SHARF (2005)

SUZUKI SHŌSAN (1579–1655) was a Japanese Buddhist monk known for his advocacy of *Niō-zazen*, a meditative technique drawing upon both Zen and Pure Land methodologies. Shōsan was a bodyguard retainer *(hatamoto)* of Tokugawa Ieyasu and fought in the crucial battles that gave the Tokugawa family control of all Japan. In 1620, a few years after Ieyasu's death, Shōsan tonsured himself as a Zen monk, favoring the Sōtō sect. Yet he never formally became affiliated with any sect and soon set himself up as the master of a small temple and meditation center called Onshinji some miles out of Okazaki, near Asuke, his birthplace. After six or seven years there, he moved to the Edo (Tokyo) vicinity, where he lived the rest of his life as a semi-itinerant teacher and writer.

Although Shōsan was well known in Zen circles, his influence was negligible for two reasons: He never became an official member of any sect, and his meditational methods and emphasis were nontraditional. He became widely known then and later for his so-called *Niō-zazen*. This "method" takes its name from Shōsan's use as models for meditation the images of the two fierce warrior-gods (Niō) that guard the entrance of many Buddhist temples in Japan, rather than the quietly seated Nyorai image. He also suggested as a model Fudo, the "angry" Buddha portrayed as wreathed in flames and with sword and lasso in either hand.

The reasons for this advocacy are given clearly by Shōsan. For beginners in meditation—and he considered every contemporary, including himself, as such—the Nyorai model was too passive. It did not embody the fierce energy necessary for successfully engaging in the hand-to-hand combat with one's self-love, which is essential for productive meditation. Hence he recommended setting the back teeth, tightly clenching the fists, scowling with a warrior's fierce glare, and repeating the Pure Land Nembutsu vigorously, all the while thinking, "I am about to die."

Although unique to Shōsan, *Niō-zazen* was not simply a casual mixture of Pure Land and Zen methodologies, as his detractors in both sects have alleged. Rather, it was a tangible embodiment of his dominant conviction that the Buddhist *dharma* must be made available to the masses in the most effective form, regardless of sectarian tradition. He was persuaded that Buddhism was being misperceived and bypassed as a passive, other-worldly faith in favor of "practical" and "useful" Confucianism. *Niō-zazen* was one way of combating this. But even more fundamentally, he sought to integrate Buddhism into the daily life of samurai, farmer, artisan, and merchant. He preached the inherent sanctity of all honest labor as Heaven's appointment for earthly life. By so regarding it, and by combining daily activities with the continual saying of the Nembutsu, one could cut off evil thoughts, accumulate merit, and begin to walk the Buddha's way toward enlightenment. Hence he preached that all work could be made into Buddha work; that is, into genuine religious discipline.

This fusion of the sacred and the secular in daily life, made practical and specific in its form, was Shōsan's most important contribution to Buddhism. It is not to be seen as a mere assertion of the innate sacrality of the secular and the profane, regardless of religious tradition. It is an assertion of the potential sacredness of all human effort and a strong protest against a Buddhism interpreted as otherworldly detachment in the name of a religious transcendence of time and space.

BIBLIOGRAPHY

The English-language discussions of Suzuki Shōsan are meager. There is one volume, *Selected Writings of Suzuki Shōsan,* translated by Royal Tyler (Ithaca, N.Y., 1977), which is a serviceable treatment with substantial footnotes and a brief introductory treatment of Shōsan. Hajime Nakamura has dealt briefly with him in *A History of the Development of Japanese Thought,* vol. 2, *From 592 to 1868* (Tokyo, 1967), and "Suzuki Shōsan, 1579–1655, and the Spirit of Capitalism in Japanese Buddhism," *Monumenta Nipponica* 22 (1967): 1–14. Two essays, "Suzuki Shōsan, Wayfarer" and "Selections from Suzuki Shōsan," translated by Jocelyn and Winston King, appear in the *Eastern Buddhist* 12 (October 1979). See also my chapter "Practising Dying: The Samurai-Zen Death Techniques of Suzuki Shōsan," in *Religious Encounters with Death,* edited by Frank E. Reynolds and Earle H. Waugh (University Park, Pa., 1977), pp. 143–158, and my *Death Was His Kōan: The Samurai-Zen of Suzuki Shōsan* (Berkeley, Calif., 1985), which is a substantial treatment of Shōsan's life, thought, meditational method, and embodiment of Tokugawa social and religious values.

New Sources

Braverman, Arthur, trans. and ed. *Warrior of Zen: The Diamond-Hard Wisdom Mind of Suzuki Shosan.* New York, 1994.

WINSTON L. KING (1987)
Revised Bibliography

SVENTOVIT was the four-headed "god of gods" (*deum deus*) of the pre-Christian northwestern Slavs. His name, **Sventovit,* is variously written—as *Sventovit, Svantevit, Suatovitus,* and, in the *Knythlingasaga* (c. 1265), *Svantaviz*—but his cult is precisely described in the *Gesta Danorum* (14.564) of Saxo Grammaticus (late twelfth century).

The center for the worship of Sventovit was in Arkona, on the Baltic island of Rügen. In the center of town was the citadel-temple, a wooden structure of consummate workmanship, built with logs and topped by a red roof. Inside the surrounding fence was a barbican, whose four posts stood free of the outer walls of the temple and adjoined some of the beams of the roof. The inner chamber, partitioned by heavy tapestries, held an enormous statue of Sventovit. Its four heads and necks were joined together: facing north, south, east, and west, they apparently corresponded to the four columns of the barbican. The faces were beardless and the hair short. The statue's right hand held a drinking horn inlaid with various metals; the left was set akimbo. A close-fitting mantle, reaching to the idol's knees, was made of several kinds of wood. The idol stood on the temple floor, with its base hidden in the ground below. Nearby lay the god's bridle and saddle, along with an enormous sword whose blade and scabbard were richly chased and damascened with silver.

A retinue of three hundred horsemen served Sventovit, and the plunder they won in war went to the head priest. Saxo mentions that tribute was paid not only by the Wends but also by the Scandinavians. In time, a treasure of incredible value was amassed; when the Christian Danes stormed Arkona in 1168, they removed the statue and carried away seven boxes of treasure, including two gold beakers.

A white horse consecrated to Sventovit was venerated as an incarnation of the god himself. Success or failure in war was foretold through the horse in the following manner: three rows of palings or lances were laid by the priest in front of the temple; if the horse stepped across the first row with its right foot first, the omen was favorable. The prophetic role of the horse in the divination ceremonies of the northwestern Slavs is confirmed by its magic function in Russian popular tradition, particularly by the traditional horse epithet, *veshchii* ("seer"), which has an exact correspondence in the Avesta.

Shortly after harvest, a great festival was held in honor of Sventovit. Cattle were sacrificed, and prophecies were made from the quantity of mead that remained in the drinking horn held by the god: if the liquid had diminished during the previous year, a bad harvest was predicted for the next. At the end of the ceremony, the priest poured the old liquid out at the god's feet and refilled the vessel, asking the god to bestow victory on the country and to increase its wealth. Then a man-sized festal cake was brought in. Placing the cake between himself and the people, the priest asked if he was still visible; if the people answered in the affirmative, the priest expressed the wish that they would not be able to see him the next year. This ceremony was believed to ensure a better harvest for the following year. (Similar customs of foretelling the future from gigantic cakes are known among Belorussians and Russians in the twentieth century.)

Disposition of the Sventovit idol from Rügen is unknown. In 1857 a carved wooden post was discovered in Zbruch, near Husjatyn in southeastern Poland, that bears a striking resemblance to Saxo's description. Carved on all four sides, in four registers, it shows four terminal figures, one of which holds a drinking horn. Another four-headed statue, called Chetyrebog ("four-god"), stood in Tesnovka, near Kiev, until 1850. Prehistoric stone stelae depicting the same god, helmeted and holding a cornucopia in the right hand, and occasionally with a horse engraved on the back, are known from various Slavic territories. A stela from Stavchany, in the upper Dniester Basin, can be dated to the fourth to sixth century CE, but most of the finds are accidental and undated.

West Slavic four-headed military gods were variously named, but in fact they probably represent one multifaceted god, the archetypal Indo-European god of heavenly light. The gods Svarozhich, Iarovit, Porovit, and Sventovit, worshiped in West Slavic temples of the eleventh and twelfth centuries, seem to represent the seasonal aspects of the sun: the winter or "young" sun (Svarozhich), the spring sun (Iarovit), the summer sun (Porovit), and the harvest sun (Sventovit). The Roman Janus Quadrifons ("four-faced") is a parallel, as is the Iranian four-faced warrior god Verethraghna.

BIBLIOGRAPHY

Berlekamp, Hansdieter. "Die Ausgrabungen auf Kap Arkona, 1969–1970." In *Berichte über den II. Internationalen Kongress für slawische Archäologie*, vol. 3, pp. 285–289. Berlin, 1970.

Dyggve, Ejnar. "Der Holztempel Svantevits und der schuchhardtsche Baubefund zu Arkona." In *Berichte über den V. internationalen Kongress für Vor- und Frühgeschichte.* Berlin, 1961.

Máchal, Jan. "Slavic Mythology." In *The Mythology of All Races,* vol. 3, edited by Louis H. Gray and George Foot Moore, pp. 217–330. Boston, 1918.

Palm, Thede. *Wendische Kultstätten: Quellenkritische Untersuchungen zu den letzten Jahrhunderten slavischen Heidentums.* Lund, 1937.

Rosen-Przeworska, J. "La tradition du dieu celtique à quatre visages chez les Protoslaves et les Slaves occidentaux." *Antiquités nationales et internationales* 4, no. 14–16 (April–December 1963): 65–69.

Schuchhardt, Carl. *Arkona, Rethra, Vineta.* Berlin, 1926.

Zakharov, Alexis A. "The Statue of Zbrucz." *Eurasia Septentrionalis Antiqua* 9 (1936): 336–348.

New Sources

Kapica, F. S. *Slavyanskije tradicionnije verovanija, prazdniki i rituali* (Slavic traditional beliefs, festivities and rituals). Moscow, 2001.

Shaparova, N. S. *Kratkaya enciklopedija slavyanskoj mifologii* (A short dictionary of Slavic mythology). Moscow, 2001.

Tokarev, S. A. "Mifi narodov mira (World myths)." *Bolshaya Rossijskaya Enciklopedija,* vol.1–2. Moscow, 1998.

MARIJA GIMBUTAS (1987)
Revised Bibliography

SWAMINARAYAN MOVEMENT.

Chronologically located between the "*bhakti* renaissance" of the medieval period and the early to mid-nineteenth-century Hindu revivalism of colonial India, the Swaminarayan movement is a devotional tradition rooted in Vaiṣṇavism and arising out of Gujarat in western India. The spread and transnational growth of specific Swaminarayan sects demonstrate how a regional expression of Hindu devotionalism, in accommodating to larger political and social changes, has succeeded in providing meaningful ways of being Hindu in the diasporic context.

SWAMINARAYAN ORIGIN NARRATIVE. All Swaminarayan sects connect their devotional tradition to the historical person of Sahajanand Swami (1781–1830 CE), who was born near Ayodhya, Uttar Pradesh, in northern India. His biography is the basis for the Swaminarayan origin narrative, one that combines hagiography with historically confirmed persons, events, and places.

According to Swaminarayan tradition, the young Sahajanand Swami was known as Ghanshyama. Following the death of his parents when he was eleven years old, he embarked on a phase of wandering. He attracted attention for his textual knowledge (evidenced by his winning debates with older religious scholars), asceticism (adoption of *brahmacarya* vows of celibacy), and performance of austerities *(tapas),* an example of which involved standing on one leg for four months while clad only in a loincloth. At the age of nineteen, Ghanshyama, now known as Nilkantha, arrived in Saurashtra, the peninsular area of southern Gujarat. Here he encountered Mukhtananda Swami, the senior ascetic of a group whose head preceptor *(guru),* Ramananda Swami, was temporarily away. He asked Mukhtananda the questions he had asked during his encounters with ascetics throughout India; receiving satisfactory answers, Nilkantha ended his period of wandering. On October 28, 1800, he was initiated by Ramananda Swami and given two names, "Sahajanand" and "Narayan Muni." Not long thereafter Ramananda Swami, in spite of opposition from his followers, designated the young Sahajanand Swami as his successor.

The beginning of the Swaminarayan movement dates to 1801 when Sahajanand Swami became the leader of Ramananda's group. Swaminarayan literature records that "Swami Narayan" quickly became known for his teachings, which emphasized moral, personal, and social betterment. He traveled throughout the Gujarat region, outlining his behavioral expectations along gender lines and according to social groups, from laity to ascetics and political leaders. Though his followers record that he was against caste, Sahajanand Swami's teachings did not openly advocate the dissolution of caste or the abandonment of commensal rules. For both laity and ascetics, he supported *varṇāśramadharma,* or the fulfillment of duties according to caste, social class, and gender. He prescribed nonviolence, abstinence from intoxicants, strict vegetarianism (including no onion or garlic), sexual continence, and frugal living. Sahajanand Swami's social reform centered on the "uplift" of all peoples and ranged from the promotion of literacy for men and women to providing assistance to famine sufferers. By age twenty-five, he had an order of five hundred male *sādhus* (ascetics) who, notwithstanding the special rules requiring ascetics to avoid all contact with women, were responsible for spreading his message and consolidating the growing numbers of Swaminarayan *satsaṅgīs* (devotees).

During Sahajanand Swami's lifetime Gujarat came under British control. The Swaminarayan movement became further known for its campaigns against early child marriage, widow immolation *(satī),* and female infanticide, all practices that had excited concern among the indigenous intelligentsia and colonial administrators of the established Bengal Presidency. Because of his reputation for being a social progressive, Sahajanand Swami attracted the interest of and subsequently met Bishop Reginald Heber, the Lord Bishop of Calcutta, and John Malcolm, governor of the Bombay Presidency. By the time of his death at the age of forty-nine on June 1, 1830, Sahajanand Swami was considered by his many *satsaṅgīs* to be *Bhagavān* (Lord) Swaminarayan, the highest manifestation of reality.

The Original Swaminarayan Movement. From its early days, the Swaminarayan movement was noted for its organizational capacities and rationalized methods for transmitting its practices and prescriptions. *Sādhus* compiled Sahajanand Swami's discourses, maintained records of his activities, and collected together commendatory letters written by colonial administrators. Among his innovations, Sahajanand Swami established an institutional structure that provided for the perpetuation of the Swaminarayan *satsaṅg,* the community of followers-in-truth. Two administrative seats *(gāddī),* outlined in the *Lekh,* a text written by Sahajanand Swami, were established by dividing India into northern and southern juridical territories. The Ahmedabad temple was designated administrative head of the northern seat and the Vadtal temple, the center for the southern seat. Being celibate, Sahajanand Swami installed two nephews as *ācāryas* (preceptors) in the administrative seats and specified that the sons of the *ācāryas* would preserve these hereditary positions. The two hereditary lines and *gāddīs* still exist, although the migration of devotees has necessitated their merger into one organization (the International Swaminarayan Satsang Organization) for the overseas communities. The *ācāryas* oversee the temples, *sādhus,* and *satsaṅgīs* in their respective *gādis.* Further duties include the administration of the Swaminarayan *mantra* for new male initiates, installation of temple icons, and management of the *gāddī*'s material wealth.

Another distinction of the Swaminarayan movement is the clear separation of men and women *(strī-puruṣa maryādā)* in all temple activities and to some extent in social life as well. Swaminarayan temples have separate entrances for men and women. Though women can take the vow of celibacy, there is no comparable order of *sādhvīs* (female renunciates). The wives of *ācāryas* have substantial duties paralleling their husbands: they are responsible for teaching and overseeing the activities of women *satsaṅgīs* and for administering the Swaminarayan *mantra* (for women only).

Whereas the early *satsaṅgīs* were from a wide variety of castes and class backgrounds, later members came increasingly from the emerging Patidar farmer caste, who were finding commercial success in agriculture and entrepreneurial activities. In the years following Sahajanand Swami's death, the cooperative relationship between Swaminarayan *ācāryas, sādhus,* and householders and the British allowed for favorable reciprocation such as temple land grants and festival permits. Scholars of modern Gujarat history are critical of this cooperation, arguing that the Swaminarayan movement's alignment with the British reflected its bias toward promoting its own caste and class interests at the expense of other groups either unable or unwilling to yield to Anglo-colonial hegemony. Indeed, Swaminarayan history does not show much evidence of protest against the colonial presence.

New Swaminarayan Sects. As it happened, the greatest schism in the Swaminarayan movement was prompted not by outsiders but came from within. In 1906 a *sādhu,* Swami Yagnapurushdas, left the Vadtal temple. In 1907 he established the first new Swaminarayan sect, the Bochasanwasi Shri Akshar Purushottam Swaminarayan Sanstha (BAPS). Headquartered in Ahmedabad, Gujarat, BAPS claims over one million followers worldwide including both laity and ascetics. With its religious leaders and membership drawn from a wide caste background, caste distinctions in this new sect are of less concern than in the original Swaminarayan *gāddīs.* As part of its social reform activity, BAPS has established temples and charitable projects in *dalit* (formerly referred to as Untouchables or *harijan*) and *adivasi* (autochthonous groups or tribal communities) villages in Gujarat. More so than the original sect, BAPS is a global movement and, early on, it embraced new technologies to support its transnational growth. It runs a large publishing house and music recording studio, and employs systematic methods for training *sādhus* and laity in Swaminarayan *bhakti.* Additionally, BAPS upholds the movement's connection to social reform through a variety of programs and campaigns, such as anti-addiction and anti-dowry events, disaster relief, temple building, and the sponsorship of public festivals. BAPS activities are not always without controversy, as in its open support of the Sardar Sarovar dam project in Gujarat. For its supporters, the Sardar Sarovar dam and the multi-dam Narmada Valley Development Project of which it is a key component are intended to increase power capacity and provide irrigation, cleaner drinking water, and flood control; for its opponents, the dam is environmentally and socially disastrous and is purchased at the cost of submerging a high percentage of *dalit* and *adivasi* villages. The wealthy BAPS organization is criticized by dam opponents for acting to protect its class interests, including those of its land holding members. In response, BAPS followers who are familiar with the Narmada controversy point to the various village relocation and community rehabilitation projects voluntarily instigated and funded by BAPS.

In addition to BAPS's break from the original Swaminarayan *satsaṅg,* other schisms have occurred. In 1966 a handful of East African BAPS followers broke away and founded the Yogi Divine Society. Additionally, *sādhus* from the original movement have left to form their own institutions that sometimes (e.g., Swaminarayan Gurukuls) but not always (e.g., Swaminarayan Gadi) retain an affiliation with their *gāddī.*

Swaminarayan Texts and Their Interpretation. Two core texts, the *Vachanamritam (Vacanāmṛta)* and *Shiksha-*

patri (Śikṣāpatrī), provide the foundation for Swaminarayan *bhakti.* Other important texts include hagiographies *cum* histories such as the *Satsangijivanam,* which elaborate on Sahajanand Swami's life story and teachings. The *Vachanamritam* is the first Gujarati vernacular text and consists of 262 discourses given by Sahajanand Swami between 1819 and 1829 and recorded by senior *sādhus.* The *Shikshapatri,* authored by Sahajanand Swami in 1826 and originally written in Sanskrit, is a listing of 212 precepts, a code of behavior for Swaminarayan followers. As the most accessible of Swaminarayan texts, the *Shikshapatri* is also the most controversial: its precepts range from the practical to the political, from matters of bodily hygiene and money management, to advice on coping with unjust rulers. This small manual is accountable in part for the "puritanical" image of the Swaminarayan movement.

The philosophical foundation for Swaminarayan devotionalism is the *viśiṣṭādvaita,* or qualified non-dualism, of Rāmānuja (1017–1137 CE). Sahajanand Swami expanded Rāmānuja's delineation of three separate and eternal existential entities into five, namely *parabrahman, brahman, māyā, īśvara,* and *jīva,* but was most focused on the relationship between *parabrahman, brahman,* and *jīva.* As explained in the *Vachanamritam, parabrahman* (synonymous with *puruṣottama*) is the highest existential entity and is never formless: it possesses the power of immanence and action *(antaryāmīśakti)* and manifests itself in a distinctly human form. *Brahman* (synonymous with *akṣara* and *akṣarabrahman)* is the second-highest reality and, in its formless state, is known as *akṣaradhāma,* the all-prevading and unfathomable abode of *parabrahman* and all released *jīva. Jīva* (also *ātman*) stands for the eternal, indivisible, and genderless entity, often translated as *soul.* Swaminarayan devotionalism offers release *(mokṣa)* attainable not through textual knowledge or correct ritual practices but through the recognition that Sahajanand Swami is himself *puruṣottama,* that is the highest existential reality, who appears in human form, and who resides in *akṣaradhāma.* As the highest reality, Sahajanand Swami is thus not an *avatāra* or descended form of a higher entity but the ultimate creator of all entities.

The most significant differences between the various sects in the Swaminarayan movement rest in the interpretation of who is *puruṣottama* and how to understand the relationship between this eternal entity with human-like form and *satsaṅgīs* whose devotional activities are motivated by the possibility that each individual *jīva* can potentially achieve eternal existence in *akṣaradham,* alongside *puruṣottama.* The *Vachanamritam, Shikshapatri,* and iconic representations in the six original Swaminarayan temples point to Kṛṣṇa (Krishna) as *puruṣottama,* the foremost entity to whom devotion must be directed. For original sect members, this does not necessarily disrupt the conviction that Sahajanand Swami is also *puruṣottama,* that is, Lord Swaminarayan, rather than an *avatāra* of Krishna. *Satsaṅgīs* explain this inconsistency by noting that Sahajanand Swami was careful to make his divinity known only to those who were ready for this revelation. For the BAPS community, there is no ambiguity regarding the identities and relationship of *puruṣottama* to *akṣara,* the resolution of this distinction being the basis for the sect's founding.

In contrast to the textual interpretations of the original Swaminarayan *gāddī,* BAPS founder Swami Yagnapurushdas expounded a return to the "correct" understanding of Lord Swaminarayan's teachings, specifically that Sahajanand Swami is *puruṣottama* and his immanence is always present on Earth in the form of *akṣara* or *akṣarabrahman,* the "living guru." *Akṣara* is thus conceptualized as having two states, one with and one without form. In BAPS, the importance given to *akṣara* as form distinguishes its textual interpretation from the original *gāddīs. Akṣara* with form is visible and tangible as the contemporaneous living *guru,* the one who embodies *puruṣottama's* immanence. Referred to variously as *akṣaraguru* and *akṣarabrahman* and commonly translated as "god-realized saint," the living guru and form of *akṣara* is always male.

For BAPS *satsaṅgīs,* it is contact with the personal and living form of *akṣara* and the constant maintenance of devotional attitudes to this form that allows for *mokṣa.* By recognizing *akṣara* in its manifest form, *jīva,* clothed in human form and impaired by bodily emotions and senses, can acquire the knowledge necessary for escaping the conditioning of *māyā.* In Swaminarayan devotionalism, *māyā* is understood, at the most general level, to be primordial matter *(prakṛti)* or that which conceals the knowledge required for *jīva* to attain *mokṣa,* the liberation from *saṁsāra,* the cycle of rebirth. Often translated as illusion, *māyā* is also associated with causing egoism, bodily desires, and wordly attachments, all barriers to achieving release. The *satsaṅgī's* hope is to achieve this release in the current lifetime and thereafter to exist as *brahmarūpa,* in identification with *brahman,* in *akṣaradhama,* alongside *puruṣottama* and *akṣara.* In Swaminarayan *viśiṣṭādvaita,* the ultimate reality, *puruṣottama,* never merges with *akṣara* or with lower existential entities.

BAPS followers do not follow the *ācāryas* and temples of the original *gāddīs* but have constructed temples to reflect their interpretation of Swaminarayan *viśiṣṭādvaita.* Also, a lineage of *akṣaragurus,* or living *gurus,* has been retroactively traced back to Gunatitanand Swami, a *sādhu* who lived during Sahajanand Swami's lifetime. The *guru* provides the template for ideal devotional behavior and through him devotees can achieve awareness of their eternal *jīva.* The most recent living *guru* is Pramukh Swami who, in 1971, became the "religious and spiritual" head of BAPS.

On Devotional Practices. Membership in the Swaminarayan movement begins with a brief verbal initiation followed by the devotee's acceptance of the Swaminarayan *mantra.* The devotee then agrees to live a life according to specifications outlined in the core Swaminarayan texts.

The Swaminarayan ritual calendar as well as its ritual practices, vocabulary, and gestures are similar to those found among the Vallabha Saṃpradāya and in Vaiṣṇavism in general. (Founded by Vallabha in the sixteenth century, the Vallabha Saṃpradāya is a Hindu devotional sect that remains influential in Gujarat and includes many wealthy merchants and other business-oriented caste groups among its followers.) *Satsaṅgīs* perform daily offerings *(pūjā)* to the iconic representation *(mūrti)* of Lord Swaminarayan kept in the home. For BAPS followers, *pūjā* includes the pictorial forms of the *guru* lineage and a reading selection from *Swami ni Vato,* a collection of brief sayings by Gunatitanand Swami. All *satsaṅgīs* must dress modestly, wear a double-stranded necklace of beads, and apply sectarian marks on their foreheads, with the women's mark differing from the men's. Besides regular participation at temple events, *satsaṅgīs* are also expected to contribute a portion of their annual income to the temple.

The *Vachanamritam* outlines four categories of action for helping devotees strengthen their devotionalism. Much of temple-based discourse and many events revolve around assisting *satsaṅgīs* to reflect upon and act on these suggestions:

1. Remain within the expectations and rules for moral living.
2. Develop a deep attachment to Lord Swaminarayan and *sādhus.*
3. Control mental and physical senses.
4. Develop knowledge of Swaminarayan philosophy.

The most tangible means for attaining and expressing correct devotional postures is to perform *seva,* service and resources that are volunteered. "Doing *seva,*" *satsaṅgīs* note, helps them to transcend bodily desires and focus more intensely on the glory of the highest existential reality, *puruṣottama.* Female followers are especially visible as *seva* volunteers and this has contributed to dramatic changes, particularly in the BAPS sect. In BAPS, women have parallel leadership positions and activities to men. Women manage their groups and sponsor their own events and publications. Though sometimes frustrated at the gender segregation and their inability to have direct contact with *guru* and *sādhus*, women consider theirs a privileged position, of having a god-realized *guru* who powerfully guides them from a distance.

CONTEMPORARY ISSUES. Coinciding with the migration of Gujarati peoples, the Swaminarayan movement has also expanded beyond India. Its religious and lay leaders are focused on the needs of Hindus in the diaspora who are creating permanent rather than temporary lives outside of India. BAPS, through its worldwide network of more than five hundred temples and a large "volunteer" base, is by far the most visible sect in the Swaminarayan movement. Since it's founding, BAPS and its living *gurus* have traveled to wherever Gujaratis have gone, openly addressing immigrant-diaspora issues of resettlement, cultural loss, and community building. This has resulted in the creation of programs that were not needed in the Gujarat context, such as Gujarati language classes and festivals to promote "Hinduism." BAPS Swaminarayan communities in the United States and Great Britain now have resident *sādhus* who teach and administer temple activities. North of London, a BAPS traditional-style marble and stone temple with an attached exhibition hall attracts upwards of ninety thousand visitors during Hindu new year celebrations. Similar "traditional" temple complexes were completed in Chicago, Illinois, and Houston, Texas. In Gandhinagar, Gujarat, an elaborate monument, exhibition, and research center known as Akshardham was the site of a terrorist attack in 2002. Swaminarayan sites and their polished presentation of "Hinduism" are clearly attracting notice, owing to a visibility reflective of the movement's diasporic wealth and organized management structure.

What is remarkable is the degree to which BAPS, and to a lesser extent the original Swaminarayan *gādis,* have translated the injunction for moral living and reform into a larger transnational project, one that positions Swaminarayan *bhakti* as synonymous with a reified sense of "Hinduism." This equation promotes a problematic conceptualization of religion, one that uncritically conflates it with culture, language, and geography and offers a seamless portrait of Hindu traditions. The contemporary Swaminarayan movement thus appears sympathetic to pro-Hindu fundamentalist sentiments. While this connection is disputed by its leaders, what is less refutable is the movement's growing base of immigrants who are attracted to representations of an essentialized Hinduism. The Swaminarayan movement has, in spite of its restrictive codes of behavior, endured for over two centuries: its newer communities demonstrate how politics of religious nationalism and the needs and desires brought on by diasporic living can spur accommodations to, rather than retreat from, external changes.

SEE ALSO Bhakti; Rāmānuja; Vaiṣṇavism; Vallabha.

BIBLIOGRAPHY

Brent, Peter. *Godmen of India.* London, 1972. Contains account of author's meeting with the English translator of the *Vachanamritam,* H. T. Dave, and Swami Jnanjivandas, the third living *guru* in the Bochasanwasi Shri Akshar Purushottam Swaminarayan Sanstha.

Dave, H. T. *Shree Swaminarayan's Vachanamritam.* Bombay, 1977; reprint, Ahmedabad, India, 1989. First complete English translation of Sahajanand Swami's discourses from the BAPS perspective.

Dwyer, Rachel. "Caste, Religion, and Sect in Gujarat: Followers of Vallabhacharya and Swaminarayan." In *Desh Pardesh: The South Asian Presence in Britain,* edited by Roger Ballard, pp. 165–190. London, 1994. A clear exposition of the caste composition of Gujarat and a comparative look at two Gujarati Vaiṣṇava religious sects, the Swaminarayan movement and Vallabha's Puṣṭimārga Saṃpradāya.

Hardiman, David. "Class Base of Swaminarayan Sect." In *Economic and Political Weekly* (September 10, 1988): 1907–1912. Critical examination of the Ahmedabad *gāddī* of the original Swaminarayan movement. Argues that the activities and attitudes of this *gāddī* stem from its narrow caste base.

Heber, Reginald. *Narrative of a Journey through the Upper Provinces of India, from Calcutta to Bombay, 1824–1825,* vol. 2. Philadelphia, 1828. A record of his diary, the second volume contains Bishop Heber's encounter with Sahajanand Swami in March 1825. The Bishop's conversation with the "Hindoo reformer" as well as his descriptions of the meeting have been deployed by the Swaminarayan movement as proof of its founder's impact on the colonial presence in Gujarat. As a historical record, this diary confirms the positive impression that the original Swaminarayan movement and its founder made on a Christian emissary and his countrymen.

Kim, Hanna Hea-Sun. "Being Swaminarayan: The Ontology and Significance of Belief in the Construction of a Gujarati Diaspora." Ph.D. diss., Columbia University, New York, 2001. An ethnographic exploration of the Bochasanwasi Shri Akshar Purushottam Swaminarayan Sanstha based on fieldwork conducted in the United States, United Kingdom, and India. Looks at the ways in which followers think about and participate in Swaminarayan devotionalism and draws closer attention to female followers and their engagement with Swaminarayan prescriptions of behavior. Provides comprehensive bibliography for BAPS publications.

Monier-Williams, Monier. "The Vaishṇava Religion, with Special Reference to the *Śikshā-Pātrī* of the Modern Sect called Svāmi-Nārāyaṇa." *Journal of the Royal Asiatic Society of Great Britain and Ireland,* n.s., 14 (1882): 289–316. Written after Monier-Williams, Boden Professor of Sanskrit at Oxford, had toured the Gujarat region in 1875. Though its language and tone are reflective of the author's Orientalist perspective, this article does contain an early portrait of the Vadtal Swaminarayan *gāddī* during a Hindu new year celebration.

Monier-Williams, Monier, ed. "Sanskrit Text of the *Śikshā-Pātrī* of the Svāmi-Nārāyaṇa Sect." *Journal of the Royal Asiatic Society of Great Britain and Ireland,* n.s., 14 (1882): 733–772. Includes the full Sanskrit text of the *Shikshapatri* given to Monier-Williams by the *ācārya* of the Vadtal *gāddī* in 1875. Also includes Monier-Williams's English translation, which, when compared to the English translations by the sects in the Swaminarayan movement, reveals striking elisions and differing transliterations.

Mukta, Parita. "The Public Face of Hindu Nationalism." *Ethnic and Racial Studies* 23, no. 3 (May 2000): 442–466, argues that diasporic Hindus in the United Kingdom are fostering religious nationalism through temples and temple-sponsored activities. Polemical in tone, the article critiques the activities of the London BAPS temple.

Pocock, David. *Mind, Body, and Wealth: A Study of Belief and Practice in an Indian Village.* Oxford, 1973. An incisive ethnographic look at various Hindu sects in Gujarat. Included is an introduction to the original Swaminarayan community, its founder, and its central texts. This book is notable for its early effort to refrain from using the word *religion* in order to avoid an artificial separation of Hindu practices from other areas of social life.

Pocock, David. "Preservation of the Religious Life: Hindu Immigrants in England." *Contributions to Indian Sociology,* n.s., 10, no. 2 (1976): 341–365. An ethnographic encounter with the Bochasanwasi Shri Akshar Purushottam Swaminarayan Sanstha community in London, this is useful for its observations of BAPS in its early diasporic formation. Certain points are remarkably prescient and others, when combined with more recent data (cf. Kim, 2001), underscore the transformative capacity of this community, most notably reflected in profound changes in the role of women.

Shukla, Sandhya. "Building Diaspora and Nation: The 1991 'Cultural Festival of India'." In *Cultural Studies* 11, no. 2 (1997): 296–315. Pointed critique of diasporic South Asians and their modes of identity and ethnicity-making. Article directs attention to the BAPS-sponsored "Cultural Festival of India," the first national event for the American Swaminarayan community.

Williams, Raymond Brady. *Religion of Immigrants from India and Pakistan: New Threads in the American Tapestry.* Cambridge, U.K., 1988. Provides a closer look at Gujarati Swaminarayan communities in the United States, including the original Swaminarayan and Bochasanwasi Shree Akshar Purushottam Swaminarayan Sanstha sects.

Williams, Raymond Brady. *An Introduction to Swaminarayan Hinduism.* Cambridge, U.K., 2001. A revised and updated version of an earlier text, *A New Face of Hinduism: The Swaminarayan Religion,* Cambridge, U.K., 1984. The most comprehensive and accessible English-language source by a non-Swaminarayan devotee on the history and religious philosophy of the Swaminarayan movement. Contains a wealth of details particularly with respect to the administration and organization of the dominant Swaminarayan sects. This focus, which is necessarily a male one owing to the gender segregation in the lay and religious hierarchy, is enriched by Williams's first-hand interviews with the male religious leadership in the major sects of the Swaminarayan movement.

Primary materials and websites

Texts and other printed materials by the founder, principal religious leaders, and followers of the Swaminarayan Movement are generally available outside of India at the larger temples connected to the different Swaminarayan sects. Though all sects use the same core texts (e.g., *Vachanamritam, Shikshapatri),* translations reflect their sectarian orientation. In addition to books and other published media, the web sites for the two largest Swaminarayan sects offer explanatory essays and updates on current temple and community activities. The web site for the original Swaminarayan *gāddīs* is www.moksha.akshardham.org. The web site for the Bochasanwasi Shri Akshar Purushottam Swaminarayan Sanstha is www.swaminarayan.org.

HANNA H. KIM (2005)

SWAMI VIVEKANANDA SEE VIVEKANANDA

SWANS. Related to the elements of both air and water, the swan is a symbol of breath, spirit, transcendence, and freedom. In many religious traditions it is interchangeable with the goose or duck in signifying the soul. Swans connote both death beneath the waters and rebirth, or victory over death, in the air. The complexity of the symbol is reflected in its alchemical representation as the union of opposites, the mystic center.

A prominent motif among origin myths is the cosmogonic dive, in which a swan or other aquatic bird is sent by God to the depths of the primordial waters to bring back the "seed of earth," from which God creates the world. This image existed in manifold versions among prehistoric populations of northern and eastern Europe and, from the third millennium BCE, among the peoples of America.

In Hindu iconography the swan personifies *brahman-ātman,* the transcendent yet immanent ground of being, the Self. Brahmā is often depicted borne on a swan, the divine bird that laid upon the waters the cosmic egg from which the god emerged. Variations of this image are common in Bali and Sri Lanka. The *paramahamsa* ("supreme swan" or gander) represents freedom from bondage in the phenomenal sphere and is a term of honor addressed to mendicant ascetics. The *haṃsa* bird is carved on the ornamental bands of Kesava temple at Somnathpur, erected in 1268 and dedicated to Viṣṇu.

In ancient Egypt, swans were associated with the mystic journey to the otherworld, as they are in the shamanistic religions of North Asia. In ancient Greece, priests of the Eleusinian mysteries were regarded as descendants of the birds; after their immersion in the purifying waters they were called swans. Vase paintings of the fifth century BCE show the swan as their attribute. In its amatory aspect, the swan was sacred to Aphrodite and Venus and was the form assumed by Zeus as Leda's lover.

As a solar sign, the swan was the sun god's vehicle in Greece; it was assimilated to the *yang* principle in China and inscribed on one of the wings of Mithra, the Persian god of light. In Celtic myths, swan deities represent the beneficent, healing power of the sun. In the ancient religion of the Sioux Indians of the North American Plains, birds are reflections of divine principles, and the sacred white swan symbolizes the Great Spirit who controls all that moves and to whom prayers are addressed.

An ambivalent symbol in Judaism, the swan (or the duck or goose) is conspicuous on ceremonial objects although categorized as a bird of defilement in the Bible. In the Christian tradition, it symbolizes purity and grace and is emblematic of the Virgin. The belief that swans sing with their dying breath has linked them with martyrs.

Folklore is rich in legends of swan maidens and swan knights. Believed to have been totemistic figures and original founders of clans, the half-human, half-supernatural beings who metamorphosed into swans became images of spiritual power. The skiff that carried the archangelic grail knight Lohengrin, a savior sent by God to overcome evil, was drawn by a swan. The motif of the swan maiden or knight is widely disseminated in mythology and ritual throughout Europe, India, Persia, Japan, Oceania, Africa, and South America.

The bird's sweet song has made it a perennial metaphor in the arts. The Egyptians associated it with the harp; the Greeks, with the god of music; and the Celts deemed its song magical. Shakespeare was known as the Swan of Avon; Homer, the Swan of Maeander; and Vergil, the Mantuan Swan. Ever since Plato had Socrates aver that swans "sing more merrily at the approach of death because of the joy they have in going to the god they serve," the term *swan song* has been an epithet for an artist's last work.

SEE ALSO Horses; Prehistoric Religions.

BIBLIOGRAPHY

Bachelard, Gaston. *L'eau et les rêves: Essai sur l'imagination de la matière.* 4th ed. Paris, 1978. A poetic and psychological meditation on the symbolic meaning of the swan in literature and poetry. The author's views are based mainly on poetry and dreams but are cognate with sacred and archaic myths.

Brown, Joseph Epes, ed. *The Sacred Pipe: Black Elk's Account of the Seven Rites of the Oglala Sioux.* Norman, Okla., 1953. The swan as symbol of the Great Spirit; the concept of birds as reflections of divine principles.

Campbell, Joseph. *The Flight of the Wild Gander.* New York, 1969. An examination of the complex of motifs in which the swan, interchangeable with the gander, is linked to the flight of the entranced shaman and to the *brahman-ātman* with which the yogin seeks to identify.

Eliade, Mircea. *Zalmoxis, the Vanishing God: Comparative Studies in the Religions and Folklore of Dacia and Eastern Europe.* Chicago, 1972. The relation of the swan to prehistoric myths of the cosmogonic dive.

ANN DUNNIGAN (1987)

SWAZI RELIGION.

The Swazi are part of the vast Bantu-speaking population of southern Africa, and their rich cultural heritage is a fusion of Nguni and Sotho elements. Prior to the incursion of colonial and Western influences they were Iron Age horticulturalists and cattle pastoralists, organized into centralized chieftancies. Polygyny and patrilineal descent characterize the kinship system.

The Swazi developed their particular national identity under a dual monarchy represented by a hereditary king of the Nkosi Dlamini clan and a queen mother (the mother of the king or, if she is dead, a surrogate). Unlike other African kingdoms that came under British colonial rule, the Swazi were never conquered by direct force, and much of their traditional culture survived and flourished under the leadership of King Sobhuza II (1899–1982). A direct lineal descendant of the founder of the royal Dlamini dynasty, Sobhuza was internationally acknowledged in 1968 as king and head of the newly created, independent state of Swaziland.

In 1982 approximately half a million Swazi lived in the Kingdom of Swaziland, an arbitarily demarcated country of 6,705 square miles wedged between the Republic of South Africa and the People's Republic of Mozambique. This tiny kingdom, the heartland of traditional culture, is ecologically diverse and rich in natural resources. Its wealth includes fertile soils, abundant perennial bush pasturage, forests alive with wondrous trees and wild animals, precious minerals, and four major rivers and several streams. Some 40 percent of all land, the legacy of colonial concessions, is owned by whites. Although few Swazi are able to support themselves with agriculture or pastoralism and most rely on wage labor, they remain deeply attached to their ancestral lands and to their cattle. The land is vested in the king as trustee for the nation, and its use is allocated by hereditary chiefs to heads of homesteads. Throughout the region, the king and queen mother are renowned for their knowledge of ritual "to work the rain," the symbol of fertility and "the water of life."

Swazi traditionalists perceive a majestic order in their universe, one alive with powers, *emandla* (a collective noun that has no singular). These powers continue through time and are not bound by space. They appear in diverse forms and operate with varying degrees of potency. They are *in* substance rather than *of* substance; in water, not of water; in earth, not of earth; in man, not of man. Among the Swazi, no rigid division is drawn between natural and supernatural. No substance is considered immutable. Sacred and secular are shifting dimensions of a total reality in which human behavior may influence the elements as much as the elements influence the human condition. Between them there is perpetual and dynamic interaction.

The Swazi have no elaborate myth of creation. The world is there, mysterious and wonderful. In the symbolic system of the Swazi, there is a diversified hierarchy of powers connecting humans to each other and to the cosmos. In the mythical distance is Mvelamqandi ("who-appeared-first") generally described as a power "above," unapproachable, unpredictable, of no specific sex. He/she is sometimes identified with, and sometimes distinguished from, Mkhulumqandi, the first *mkhulu,* a term applied to a grandfather, symbolic mediator between those living on the earth and those "below," the ancestors, *emadloti.* Mvelamqandi occasionally sent as his messenger Mlendengamunye, the "one-legged" (interpreted as oneness, unity), who descended in a thick mist and whose appearance, visible only to women and children, portended the coming of *fever,* a generic term for a variety of illnesses; thus Mlendengamunye had to be propitiated with symbolic sacrifices. He was last seen in the reign of King Mbandzeni (1875–1889), during a period of early missionary activity. Although Mvelamqandi, Mkhulumqandi, and Mlendengamunye are no longer mentioned in prayer or sacrifice, Swazi theologians, including Sobhuza, have referred to these three divinities, as well as to other powers in the pantheon—such as the rainbow, titled Inkosatana ("the princess"); the lightning, titled Inyoni ("the bird"); and a water serpent, titled Inyoka Yemakhandakhanaa ("the snake with many heads")—to emphasize a sacred and hierarchical order of the cosmos.

The earth is seen as stationary; the calendar of religious events, both national and domestic, is regulated by the visible movements of the sun against fixed points on the horizon and by its position in relation to the waxing and waning of the moon. The divinity of the king is associated with the sun—radiant, burning, source of both heat and light, journeying across the sky in a more or less regular path twice a year, controlling the seasons and the productive activities of nature. The moon has its own internal dialectic, associated with fertility, femininity and growth, decline and rebirth. Ceremonies to introduce a person into the fullness of a new status take place when the moon is growing or when it is full. A ceremony that temporarily isolates a man from his fellows is held in the period of the moon's decline and darkness.

The earth, mother to the living and the dead, must be approached with reverence. When a person dies, all in the homestead are prohibited from digging, plowing, or planting, or in other ways "wounding" the earth until the body has been buried and the mourners purified. When Sobhuza died in late August 1982 (the time of the first rains), such prohibitions were imposed throughout the kingdom until the rising of the third moon. The fact that rain did not fall for several weeks afterward and that the country was threatened by drought and famine was interpreted as a reaction to this disturbance in the balance between human actions, the ancestors, and cosmic powers.

The king and the queen mother together represent the physical embodiment of sacred power, as indicated by their traditional titles, *ingwenyama* ("the lion") and *indlovukah* ("the she-elephant"). These are two of the most powerful animals in nature: the lion—male, father of many cubs, aggressive, carnivorous; the she-elephant—maternal, matriarchal, stable, firm, herbivorous, mother of one calf after a long period of gestation. Together the two monarchs are spoken of as "a twin," a mysterious, unequal double, united in a relationship riddled with ambivalence. Their everyday actions—eating, drinking, bathing, dressing—are circumscribed by taboos, and they receive unique treatment to endow them with the "shadow of sovereignty."

At the observable, sociological level, the queen mother and king live in separate homesteads; hers is the sacred center, his is the administrative capital. Their duties are complementary; the balance of power is delicate, and tension between them is believed to endanger the physical condition of the country. The most sacred objects are in the care of the queen mother, and the king must come to the shrine of the nation to address his royal ancestors and offer sacrifices. The correct performance of rituals takes considerable time, concentration, and self-discipline. While the secrets of specific rituals are known to appointed representatives of historically associated clans, only the king is "owner" of all.

Swazi religion sanctions enjoyment of the material and physical: food, women, and dancing. It does not idealize poverty or place a value on suffering as a means to happiness or salvation. To deal with the hazards of life—failure of crops, unfaithfulness of women, illness and ultimate death—the culture provides a set of optimistic notions and positive, stereotyped techniques that are especially expressed through the ancestral cult, the vital religion of the Swazi.

In the ancestral cult, the world of the living is projected into the world of spirits *(emadloti),* who continue the patterns of superiority and inferiority established by earthly experiences as man or woman, old or young, aristocrat or commoner.

Swazi believe that the spirit, or breath, has an existence distinct from that of the flesh. When a person dies, both flesh and spirit must be correctly treated to safeguard the living and show appropriate respect for the dead. Mortuary ritual varies according to both the status of the deceased and his or her relationship with different categories of mourners. The flesh is buried in a cattle kraal, hut, cave, or royal grove. The spirit, after a brief period of aimless wandering, is ritually "brought back" at a sacrificial feast to the family circle.

For conservatives, irrespective of rank or age, the ancestors are an integral part of the reality of routine daily life. Their presence is all-pervasive; their relationships to each category of members of the kinship circle—married, unmarried, agnates, and in-laws—affect the language, movements, and clothing of the living. This is particularly conspicuous in the laws of "respect" governing the behavior of a married woman, the outsider brought in to perpetuate the husband's lineage (e.g., she must avoid speaking any word containing the first syllable of the names of particular senior male in-laws; she must not walk in front of the entrance to the shrine or through the cattle kraal). Visitors, on entering a homestead, on receiving food or other hospitality, praise the headman, not as an individual, but by reciting the names of his clan; clan praises are ancestral commemorations.

It is through the ancestors that Swazi confront the universal issues of mortality and morality. *Emadloti* represent continuity through fertility. They may appear in dreams, or they may materialize temporarily as "snakes" (e.g., the king as a terrifying mamba, the queen mother as a beautiful lizard, a wife as a harmless green garden snake).

Illness and other misfortunes are frequently attributed to the ancestors, but Swazi believe that *emadloti* do not inflict sufferings through malice or wanton cruelty. The mean husband, the adulterous wife, the overambitious younger brother, the disobedient son may be dealt with directly or vicariously by the spirits, who thus act as custodians of correct behavior and social ethics. Ancestors punish, they do not kill; death is brought about by evildoers *(batsakatsi),* who are interested in destroying, not in perpetuating, the lineage or the state. If an illness originally divined as sent by the *emadloti* later becomes fatal, evildoers are assumed to have taken advantage of the patient's weakened condition. Ancestors have greater wisdom, foresight, and power than the rest of mankind, but they are not considered omnipotent.

Swazi have no class of ordained priests, and the privileged duty of appealing to the *emadloti* rests with the head of the family. The father acts on behalf of his sons; if he is dead, the older brother acts on behalf of the younger. In this patrilineal society, ancestors of a married woman remain at her natal home, approachable only by her senior male kinsmen. Contact is usually made through the medium of "food" (meat, beer, or tobacco snuff); the dead, who are said to be often hungry, "lick" the essence of the offerings laid at dusk on an altar in the shrine hut and left overnight.

Emadloti are spoken of with respect and fear, and they are routinely addressed with the formality demanded by living elders. But they are not adored or worshiped. They are approached as practical beings, and appeals to them are sometimes spontaneous and conversational, interspersed with rebukes and generally devoid of gratitude. There is no conflict between the ethics of the ancestral cult and the mundane desires of life. Swazi desire the ends they say the *emadloti* desire for them.

Interpreting the messages of the ancestors is the task of diviners (*tangoma*), the main specialists in deep, esoteric knowledge. They are called upon to reveal the cause of illness or misfortune (the particular offense or the specific ancestor who must be "remembered" or appeased), and they indicate, but do not carry out, the cure (ritual sacrifice, purification, or medical treatment). *Tangoma* work in collaboration with specialists in medicines *(tinyanga temitsi),* but whereas the latter acquire their knowledge voluntarily and deliberately, each diviner is "entered," often against his or her will, by an ancestral spirit who takes control.

The training of diviners is lengthy and arduous. They suffer both mentally and physically, and when they finally qualify, "reborn like the new moon," their entire being has changed. Dressed in the strange costume of their new calling, they demonstrate their powers in a public séance, accompanying their performances with inspired songs and dances. Techniques of divination vary; some diviners use material objects (bones, shells, roots), while others rely on "feel" or verbal cues. There is no fixed hierarchy of diviners, and reputations fluctuate. Though some individual diviners are recognized as frauds and others are seen as fallible, perception through possession by the ancestors is never challenged.

Diviners, who are often of exceptional intelligence, perform within the legal framework of religion. In this capacity they practice against evildoers (witches and sorcerers) who act illegally, in secret and horrible ways, some through an innate propensity for evil, others through deliberate use of material substances, including poisons and parts of the human body. Political leaders and other aristocrats employ medicine men and diviners to bolster their positions, but are actively discouraged from becoming either medicine men or diviners themselves, since this would interfere with their administrative duties and does not fit into their ascribed status. The Ingwenyama is believed to have deeper knowledge than any of his subjects and to be able to detect and destroy evildoers by virtue of his royal blood reinforced by unique royal potions.

The king and his mother take the lead in the cycle of national rituals. The most dramatic and illuminating example is the Ncwala, a ritual which grows in elaboration and potency as the king increases in power. If the king dies and his successor is a minor, a very attenuated ceremony, known as the Simemo, is performed. (On Sobhuza's death, the council selected as his heir a boy of fourteen years.) Traditionally, the first full Ncwala should be performed when the young king reaches full manhood and is married to two ritual queens.

Ncwala is divided into two parts, Little Ncwala and Big Ncwala. Little Ncwala, which opens when the sun reaches its resting place in the south and the moon has waned, lasts two days and symbolizes the break with the old year. Big Ncwala, which opens when the moon is full and lasts six days, symbolically revitalizes the king and fortifies the nation against evildoers within the country and enemies outside its borders. In the liminal period, sacred dances and songs are practiced throughout the country, ritual costumes are prepared, and sacred ingredients are collected by national priests. Swazi participants, as well as foreign analysts, interpret the complex ritual at various levels of meaning.

Ingwenyama is recognized as the "owner" of Ncwala. Anyone else who attempts to "dance Ncwala" is judged guilty of treason. Politically, Ncwala is a reflection of rank in which major social categories—princes, chiefs, queens, councillors, and warriors in age regiments—are visibly distinguished from each other by sacred costumes and perform distinctive roles in the service of Ingwenyama as symbol of the nation. At another level, Ingwenyama is mystically identified with the miraculous and ever-changing powers in nature—the sun and the moon, not as separate elements but in their interaction. The king's body is bathed with "waters of all the world" drawn from rivers and from the ocean by two groups of national priests, each group carrying a sacred gourd titled Inkosatana, "the princess," which is also the title of the rainbow. Ingwenyama "bites" of the green foods of the new year and also of the organs of a fierce black bull which has been thrown and pummeled to the rhythm of a lullaby by a regiment of "pure youths who have not yet spilled their strength in children."

The king appears in the ceremonies in a variety of unique clothing, whether it be a penis sheath of ivory on his naked body or, as at the climax of the main day, an indescribably elaborate costume of bright green, razor-edged grass and evergreen shoots. With his face half hidden by a cap of black plumes over a headband of lion skin, he is an awe-inspiring creature of the wild.

On the final day of the ritual, the day of purification, relics of the past year are burned on a pyre in the sibaya (cattle kraal) of the capital village, and rain, symbolizing the blessing of the ancestors, must fall to extinguish the flame and drench the rulers and their people.

A complementary and less elaborate women's ritual, Mhlanga (from the word for "reed," a symbol of fertility), centers on the queen mother. Each winter, unmarried girls are sent on a pilgrimage to marshy areas to cut the long supple reeds needed to repair the fences surrounding the enclosures of the queen mother and the queens. The reeds must be golden ripe, not brittle, the tassles full, and the seeds not yet dispersed. The girls wear brief costumes to reveal their beauty and purity, and singing and dancing are essential for the performance. The king must be present; the girls are feasted and the ancestors offered their share.

Although early missionaries who preached the Protestant ethic condemned traditional Swazi beliefs and practices, Swazi rulers were interested in learning the new religion. From their point of view, the ancestral cult is not incompatible with the basic tenets of Christianity, only with the specific applications of the tenets that missionaries have made.

Sobhuza never identified himself with any specific denomination, but his role as priest-king of the entire country was increasingly recognized during his reign not only by independent African churches, but by some of the more conventional congregations as well. Queen mothers have retained their affiliation with individual churches while at the same time carrying out their traditional ritual duties. Priests of independent churches participate in Ncwala, and members of any denomination may hold services in the Lobamba National Church, an impressive structure completed in 1978 in the ambience of the ritual capital. The extent to which this symbiotic process will continue is unpredictable. As long as the myth of the Swazi divine kingship retains a political hold over the Swazi, this will be ritualized in the Ncwala. If the myth is abandoned and Swazi kingship ends or is made subordinate to other myths with different loyalties and interests (such as individual equality), both the ritual and the underlying political meaning of the Ncwala will be lost. But judging from the histories of other African societies, the Swazi will hold to their belief in the ancestors and in diviners.

BIBLIOGRAPHY

There is as yet no full-length study of Swazi religion, although a general monograph by Brian Allan Marwick, *The Swazi* (Cambridge, 1940), does include a chapter titled "Religion and Magic." A very rich store of information on Swazi beliefs, rituals, and symbols is contained in books and articles I have written: among them, *An African Aristocracy: Rank among the Swazi* (Oxford, 1947) is a detailed account of the traditional political system and its economic and religious institutions; *The Swazi: A South African Kingdom* (New York, 1963) is a case study with an interpretive chapter on religion; *So-bhuza II: Ngwenyama and King of Swaziland* (London, 1978) is a biography of a traditional king which illustrates the importance of religion as an attribute of modern Swazi kingship. The close relationship between Swazi kingship and the independent church movement is well documented by Bengt Sundkler in *Zulu Zion and Some Swazi Zionists* (Lund and Oxford, 1976).

My study "A Ritual of Kingship among the Swazi," *Africa* 14 (1944): 230–256, also included in *An African Aristocracy*, is a detailed ethnographic account of Ncwala based on participant observation and texts. The ritual has received different interpretations by scholars with diverse theoretical approaches. The most significant of these studies are Max Gluckman's *Rituals of Rebellion in Southeast Africa* (Manchester, 1954), which emphasizes political and social functions; T. O. Beidelman's "Swazi Royal Ritual," *Africa* 36 (October 1966): 373–405, which interprets the cosmological system and makes use of Jungian psychology; and Luc de Heusch's *Mythes et rites bantous*, vol. 2, *Rois nés d'un coeur de vache* (Paris, 1982), which sets the Ncwala in a broad comparative framework built on a brilliant, Lévi-Straussian analysis of sacred kingship in Africa.

New Sources

Cummergen, Paul. "Zionism and Politics in Swaziland." *Journal of Religion in Africa*, 30 (2000): 370–386.

Hall, James. *Sangoma: An Odyssey into the Spirit World of Africa.* New York, 1994.

Kasanene, Peter. *Swazi Traditional Religion and Society.* Mbabane, 1993.

HILDA KUPER (1987)
Revised Bibliography

SWEARING SEE VOWS AND OATHS

SWEDENBORG, EMANUEL (1688–1772), was a multifaceted genius, scientist, and visionary. He was born in Stockholm, Sweden, on January 29, and he died in London on March 29. Paradox surrounds Swedenborg's intellectual legacy. The scientific and philosophical works that brought him the acclaim of his contemporaries have largely been forgotten. The contributions that he made to the Swedish Board of Mines and the House of Nobles were significant, but like the efforts of most bureaucrats and politicians they were intended to have an immediate and practical impact on policy, not history. Thus, despite his genius, Swedenborg's exemplary life would attract scant notice, apart from his revelatory claims and his voluminous religious writings. He published his writings anonymously for almost twenty years and never attempted to gather a following. Nonetheless, after his death, followers devoted to his religious works appeared first in Europe and then around the world.

EDUCATION OF SCIENTIST AND CIVIL SERVANT. Swedenborg was born into wealth and privilege; both of his parents came from mine owning families. His father, Jesper Swedberg (1653–1735), was ordained into the ministry of the Lutheran Church in 1682. In 1703 he was elevated to bishop and served in Skara until his death in 1735. He name was changed to Swedenborg upon ennoblement in 1719. Jesper Swedberg had pietistical leanings, believed in the importance of works as well as faith, and had both a hymnbook and a translation of the Bible condemned by church censors.

Emanuel Swedenborg matriculated at the University of Uppsala, from which he graduated in 1709 with a degree in philosophy. From 1710 until 1715 he traveled in Europe with a principle focus on studying mathematics and astronomy. On his trip abroad, he also learned various practical skills, including engraving and instrument making. In addition he wrote three volumes of poetry, and before returning home he wrote down descriptions of fourteen inventions, including a submarine, an air pump, and a fixed-wing aircraft.

Upon his return to Sweden in 1715, he began publishing *Daedalus Hyperboreus*, Sweden's first scientific journal. In addition, he became an assistant to the great inventor and mechanical genius Christopher Polhem (1668–1751). Together they served King Karl XII by working on various engineering projects. In recognition of Swedenborg's contributions to the realm, the king named him Extraordinary Assessor of the Board of Mines. The death of Karl XII in Fredrikshald in 1718 brought an end to Sweden's era as a great power. Swedenborg was ennobled in 1719 by Queen Ulrika Eleonora (1688–1741).

The death of Karl XII ushered in what is called in Sweden "the age of freedom" and the renunciation of the King's policies. The new political climate also put Swedenborg's commission as assessor in doubt. Determined to be seated, in 1720 Swedenborg traveled to Europe to study mining techniques. After his return to Sweden he took up his life as a noble and author, and after 1724 as a bureaucrat, having finally been granted a position as a regular assessor and given a salary. In this position he was one of seven men responsible for Sweden's important mining industry. The members of the Board of Mines set policies, inspected mines for safety, tested the metals produced for quality, set prices, and adjudicated law suits. Swedenborg served on the board for twenty-three years. Appointed president of the Board of Mines in 1747, he declined the appointment and resigned from the board in order to devote himself to his spiritual mission.

NATURAL PHILOSOPHER. With his career finally established, Swedenborg turned his mind to understanding scientifically the riddle of creation and the purpose of self-conscious life. In 1734 he took a leave of absence from the Board of Mines to publish his *Opera philosophica et mineralia* (*Philosophical and Mineralogical Works*) in Liepzig. Swedenborg's cosmology is indebted in part to the philosophy of René Descartes (1596–1650). In a series of studies culminating in *Principia rerum naturalium* (*The Principia; or the First Principles of Natural Things*, 1734) Swedenborg presented a theory about the origin of the universe. Starting from a mathematical point of departure, he envisioned the planetary system as developing a series of complicated particle combinations. Swedenborg tried to integrate the soul into this consistently mechanistic structure, and in *De infinito* (*The Infinite*, 1734) he presented his future research program "to prove the immortality of the soul to the very senses themselves."

This empirical intention led him into an extensive study of contemporary physiology and anatomy, as well as both ancient and modern philosophy. The first result of this effort was the publication of *Oeconomia regni animalis* (The economy of the animal soul's kingdom, 1740–1741). Dissatisfied with his initial effort, believing that he had not been sufficiently thorough, he began again. He published three volumes of *Regnum animale* (The animal soul's kingdom, 1744–1745) before abandoning the project.

Religious Crisis and Spiritual Call. It was during this publishing trip abroad that Swedenborg experienced a profound spiritual crisis during the 1743 to 1744 period. The crisis began in dreams that he recorded in a journal for his own personal use. Discovered in 1859, it is known today as *The Journal of Dreams.* In it, he not only recorded his dreams, he interpreted them. He discovered his sin of pride and arrogance, he prayed, he sought forgiveness, and he found himself held in the bosom of Christ. He recorded intense temptations that affected both his body and his spirit. Drawn deeply inward, he understood that he must follow Christ in all things. He put aside his scientific work, obeying a divine commission to write down and publish the true meaning of the scriptures, in order to make them universally available. Swedenborg's spiritual call can be viewed as either a disjunction in or a culmination of his own intellectual journey.

Returning to Sweden he focused on studying the Bible in Hebrew, searching for the key to its internal or spiritual meaning. Swedenborg had earlier developed a doctrine of correspondences, according to which all phenomena of the physical world have their spiritual correspondences. He wrestled with the meaning of the story of creation and the nature of God. He discovered that in the Bible, words used in one place correspond to words used in another place, and finally he grasped the idea that the garden in *Genesis* does not refer to the natural creation of the earth and the universe, but to the spiritual process of human regeneration. *Genesis* details this spiritual process through which every individual can return to and be conjoined with the one God, the Lord Jesus Christ, to eternity. Swedenborg documents this in the eight volumes of the *Arcana coelestia* (Secrets of heaven, 1749–1756). In this work Swedenborg states that what he writes about heaven and eternal life is true, because his eyes and spirit have been opened and "I have seen, I have heard and I have felt."

Religious Teachings, Controversy, and Impact. The focus of Swedenborg's religious teachings is not on the crucifixion and the sacrifice of Jesus, the only begotten son of God, to atone for the sins of humanity, but on the risen Lord Jesus Christ who overcame the world. According to Swedenborg, the Christian interpretation of the Trinity and redemption led over time to the complete separation of faith and charity, or belief and works, in the Christian churches. This necessitated the Last Judgment and the Second Coming. According to Swedenborg, the Last Judgment was a spiritual event that occurred in 1757. It made possible the Second Coming for everyone who is drawn to understand the spiritual meaning of the new heaven and the new earth, described in the *Book of Revelation* and spiritually opened by means of correspondences. Like the Last Judgment, the Second Coming was also a spiritual event for Swedenborg. It was announced in the spiritual world on June 19, 1770, by the twelve disciples who had followed Christ in the world. The record of the announcement was published in *True Christianity* (1771), thus making it an historical event, and it becomes an internal and personal event whenever its truth is accepted by an individual.

Swedenborg's religious writings, set down in eighteen different works, indicate that humanity now lives in a new age in which every one can freely choose his or her spiritual destiny. The spiritual world, which encompasses heaven, the world of spirits, and hell, is inhabited solely by men and women who have lived on this earth or other planets in the universe. In the sight of the Lord, the heavens appear as one "grand man." Individuals find their place there by discovering their dominant affection or love. No one is cast down into hell or raised into heaven apart from the life they have led and chosen here on earth. However, it is not necessary to know about Swedenborg, his teachings, or the new church to achieve eternal salvation. It is only necessary to live a good and useful life within the framework of the many spiritual truths available around the globe.

For twenty-seven years Swedenborg attended to his call to write and publish his new revelation "fresh from heaven." He never attempted to develop a following or organize a church. He initially published his works anonymously, but several clairvoyant experiences that occurred in public revealed his extraordinary powers. Soon Swedenborg and his books became a focus of discussion and conversation in Europe. Immanuel Kant (1724–1804) became so interested that he ordered a complete set of the *Arcana coelestia* (Heavenly secrets, 1749–1756). Although in private correspondence, Kant spoke in a positive tone about Swedenborg and his experiences, in 1766 he published *Dreams of a Spirit-Seer,* in which he ridiculed Swedenborg and his metaphysics. Kant's critique set the stage for the central controversy surrounding Swedenborg's religious writings, which concerns whether they are what Swedenborg claims they are. Were the works divinely revealed to him, or are they the product of an overactive imagination? Swedenborg's writings have inspired the founding of churches by those who believe that the divine had a hand in them, but they are derided as the product of a mentally unstable man by those who believe that they sprang from Swedenborg's own imagination. A third possible approach to them, particularly attractive to students of religion, is that Swedenborg drew on esoteric practices and traditions to shape his religious corpus.

Despite the controversy surrounding the precise nature of their inspiration, Swedenborg's religious writings have had a profound impact on Western literature and the arts, in large part because of the doctrine of correspondences. To cite one example, in 1972 Joshua C. Taylor, the director of the National Gallery in Washington, D.C., testified to the importance of Swedenborgianism in American art in the catalogue that accompanied an exhibit entitled *The Hand and the Spirit,* which took place at the University Art Museum in Berkeley, California. In the catalogue Taylor identified several categories of religious art in America, but said that he found no sect or set of beliefs that provided an impulse toward art, particularly in the nineteenth century, with one exception—Swedenborgianism. Taylor wrote: "only Swedenborgian teaching had a direct impact on art, and this was through its link with a complex philosophical view of perception and aesthetic judgement which suggested not narrative themes but a spiritual context for artistic form" (Dillenberger, 1972, p. 14).

In 1908, and with great pomp and ceremony, Swedenborg's remains were brought back to Sweden and laid to rest in Uppsala Cathedral. The Swedish government, not without controversy, financed an elegant sarcophagus to hold the simple wooden coffin brought from London. The red granite memorial, approved by the Riksdag (the Swedish parliament), was carved to honor Swedenborg the scientist, despite the fact that his worldwide reputation, even then, rested on his revelations and religious writings. The parliament's decision not withstanding, Swedenborg's religious writings continue to shape the human spirit around the world in prayer, poetry, paintings, story, and song.

See Also Swedenborgianism.

Bibliography

The Swedenborg Foundation in West Chester, Pa., is publishing the New Century Edition of the Works of Emanuel Swedenborg, with Jonathan Rose as series editor. The first title to be released in the series was *Heaven and Hell* (2000), translated by George F. Dole. Other series titles include a one-volume edition, also translated by Dole, of Swedenborg's *Divine Providence* and *Divine Love and Wisdom* (2003).

Heaven and Hell (2000). This book gives a detailed description of life after death. *Divine Providence and Divine Love and Wisdom* (2003). This book provides insight into the spiritual laws governing human life, and insight into the divine purpose and order of creation.

Benz, Ernst. *Emanuel Swedenborg: Visionary Savant in the Age of Reason.* Translated by Nicholas Goodrich-Clarke. West Chester, Pa., 1949; reprint, 2002. A biography that examines Swedenborg's place within the rational and esoteric currents of the eighteenth century.

Bergquist, Lars. *Swedenborg's Dream Diary.* Translated by Anders Hallengren. West Chester, Pa., 1989; reprint, 2001. The most recent examination of Swedenborg's dream diary with an attempt to connect his dreams to his social world and life.

Dillenberger, Jane, and Joshua C. Taylor, *The Hand and the Spirit: Religious Art in America 1700–1900,* Berkley, Calif., 1972. An exhibit catalog exploring American religious art during the eighteenth and nineteenth centuries.

Dole, George F., and Robert H. Kirven. *Scientist Explores Spirit: A Biography of Emanuel Swedenborg.* West Chester, Pa., 1992. A highly readable and clear short biography of Swedenborg.

Hanegraaff, Wouter J. *New Age Religion and Western Culture: Esotericism in the Mirror of Secular Thought.* Leiden, 1996. An innovative exploration of the esoteric roots of the New Age Movement with attention to Swedenborg's role in the transformation of perspective.

Johnson, Gregory, ed. *Kant on Swedenborg: Dreams of a Spirit-Seer and Other Writings.* Translated by Gregory R. Johnson and Glenn Alexander Magee. West Chester, Pa., 2002. A reassessment of Kant's view of Swedenborg suggesting Kant's indebtedness to and use of Swedenborg in his own philosophy.

Jonsson, Inge. *Emanuel Swedenborg.* Translated by Catherine Djurklou. New York, 1971. A modern intellectual history of Swedenborg's thought, connecting his thought to neo-Platonism and Descartes, as well as linking Swedenborg's philosophy and theology.

Lamm, Martin. *Swedenborg.* Stockholm, 1915. This work has been translated into German (Leipzig, 1922) and French (Paris, 1936); it was translated into English by Thomas Spiers and Anders Hallengren as *Emanuel Swedenborg: The Development of His Thought* (West Chester, Pa., 2000). A pioneering biography of Swedenborg that places his thought within the framework of Western literary and intellectual history.

Sigstedt, Cyriel. *The Swedenborg Epic: The Life and Works of Emanuel Swedenborg.* London, 1952; reprint, 1981. A detailed biography of Swedenborg that draws on the enormous document collection assembled by the Swedenborg Scientific Association during the first half of the twentieth century.

Williams-Hogan, Jane. "The Place of Emanuel Swedenborg in Modern Western Esoteric Tradition." In *Western Esotericism and the Science of Religion,* edited by Antoine Faivre and Wouter J. Hanegraaff, pp, 201–252. Leuven, Belgium, 1998. An exploration of Swedenborg's religious system within the framework of the five characteristics of esotericism as defined by Antoine Faivre, as well as a response to Swedenborg's thought by important figures in modern Western Esotericism.

Jane Williams-Hogan (2005)

SWEDENBORGIANISM, often referred to as the New Church or the Church of the New Jerusalem, is a global religious movement based upon the theological writings of Emanuel Swedenborg (1688–1772). When Swedenborg died in London on March 29, 1772, his spiritual legacy was to be found in the books and manuscripts he left behind. His spiritual journey as a revelator began in 1744 when, at the end of a profound personal spiritual crisis, he responded to what he believed was a call from Jesus Christ to serve him. As he began to study the Bible in Hebrew, Greek, and Latin, he concluded that the Bible was written in correspondences, and became convinced that he had been called to reveal its internal or spiritual sense. His biblical exegesis laid the foundation for a new, written revelation. By the time of his death he had published eighteen titles. His first theological work, *Arcana Coelestia* (1749–1756) or *Secrets of Heaven* was published in eight volumes. It presents the spiritual or internal sense of the biblical books of *Genesis* and *Exodus.* Also included in his corpus are works titled *Heaven and Hell* (1758),

Last Judgment (1758), *Divine Love and Wisdom* (1763), *Divine Providence* (1764), *Revelation Unveiled* (1766), *Love in Marriage* (1768), and *True Christian Religion* (1771).

Swedenborg's print runs were large for the eighteenth century. It is known that in 1758 he published five books with print runs of one thousand each. He also distributed them widely, sending them to church officials in several countries, as well as offering them for sale. Still, at the time of his death there were perhaps only a handful of individuals who accepted his teachings in Europe. No organizations existed, established by him or others, to promote his new Christianity. Swedenborg was one of the last authors to write exclusively in neo-Latin; his works, therefore, required translation into the vernacular to reach the growing number of newly literate individuals. Prior to 1800, some of his works had been translated into German (1765), English (1770s), French (1782), and Russian (1780s).

Establishment of the New Church. Despite the obstacles to spreading Swedenborg's message, his religious writings had gained a sufficient following, particularly in England, by the end of the 1770s that organized reading circles developed among the artisans and industrial workers of Lancashire just as the cotton industry was taking off. By the mid 1770s copies of the translation of *Heaven and Hell* by William Cookworthy (1705–1780) and Thomas Hartley (1707–1784) began to circulate in the villages and hamlets surrounding Manchester. The development of the reading circles was due in part to the sensational claims made by Swedenborg in the book that he had "seen and heard" what lay beyond death's door. But as the sensationalism subsided, those who remained interested in the theology were supported by the efforts of John Clowes (1743–1831), rector of Saint John's Anglican Church in Manchester, an early believer in and translator of Swedenborg's writings.

According to Robert Hindmarsh (1759–1835), another early believer, Swedenborgian minister, historian, and author of *Rise and Progress of the New Jerusalem Church in England, America, and Other Parts* (1861), these small circles in Lancashire not only read and discussed what Swedenborg had written, but they soon began to worship together based on the new vision of Christianity found in Swedenborg's writings. Their focus was on worshiping the one divinely human God, the Lord Jesus Christ, who is considered to be a visible God who contains the invisible, as the physical human body contains within it the invisible soul. Swedenborg, in *True Christian Religion* (1771), acknowledges the trinity in God. He wrote, "These three, the Father, Son, and the Holy Spirit, are three essential components of one God. They are one the way our soul, our body, and the things we do are one." In initiating worship, these early believers had grasped the central, indeed fundamental, teaching of Swedenborg's theology that God is one in essence and person and that the Lord Jesus Christ is that God. In addition, Swedenborg's teachings emphasize the following ideas: the reality of the spiritual world and the rationality of its operation; the spiritual nature of the last judgment, which Swedenborg claimed took place in 1757; the essential spiritual nature of human beings; the correspondence between the spiritual world and the natural world; human freedom in spiritual things; the marriage of love and wisdom in the Lord and thus in all creation; the essential partnership of faith and charity found in a life of use; and the sacred nature of marriage.

John Clowes had ordered a copy of Swedenborg's *Vera Christiana Religio* (True Christian Religion) in 1773 upon the recommendation of his solicitor. Upon receiving it, he put it aside, only picking it up to read months later, just before he was to leave on an extended trip. He saw the words *Divinum Humanum* (divine human) and closed the book. Several days later his recollection of these words was accompanied by a deep sense of peace. This experience reoccurred daily. Finally, with a sense of urgency, he broke off his journey and returned home to read the book that seemed to be calling to him. Clowes wrote that after reading Swedenborg's book, all his theological questions had been answered. Clowes immediately became actively involved in the work of translation, as well as seeing to the publication and distribution of Swedenborg's writings. He also assumed the role of shepherd to the groups that began to emerge in Lancashire. He remained active in this work until his death, although he never separated from the Anglican Church in which he served as a pastor. In fact, Clowes lamented the move to form a separate "New Church" organization promoted by Robert Hindmarsh in London.

Hindmarsh, a printer by trade and a member of John Wesley's Methodist movement, had frequently heard Swedenborg's writings discussed in the circles in which he lived and worked. In 1782 he was given two of Swedenborg's writings, *Heaven and Hell* and *The Commerce between Soul and Body* (1769). Many years later, Hindmarsh wrote that after reading them, he was immediately convinced of their heavenly origins. Late in 1783 he circulated an advertisement calling for any interested readers of Swedenborg to meet on December 5. Four of the five men who came to the meeting formed the nucleus of the London Theosophical Society devoted to the study and publication of Swedenborg's writings.

The fifth man, James Glen (1749–1814), a plantation owner in South America, soon left for the New World carrying copies of Swedenborg's writings with him. He stopped in Boston and Philadelphia, giving lectures in both cities and leaving behind books for sale. Even though he was just passing through, Glen's efforts made a significant contribution to the development of Swedenborgianism in the newly formed United States.

By 1787, when the New Church (the name, from *Revelation* 21:2, often taken by Swedenborgian churches) was formally established in England, there were six groups in Lancashire and the founding society in London. One of the remarkable sociological facts of the establishment of this organization is that it was founded by individuals who had never personally known Swedenborg. Those who developed the rituals for worship and the organizational structure were attracted to the message of the theology, rather than to the man who had written it.

The British Conference of the New Church, as it was officially named, was an offshoot of the London Theosophical Society, which by 1787 had approximately one hundred members drawn from various ranks in British society and including individuals from a variety of countries who resided in London. Their religious backgrounds were also diverse, coming from a wide range of Christian confessions, including Anglican, Methodist, Baptist, Calvinist, and Dissenters. Among them were also individuals who were mystics, Quakers, deists, or agnostics. This Theosophical Society, which predates the organization founded by H. P. Blavatsky and Henry Steel Olcott in 1875, was an organization whose membership had widely different interests in Swedenborg's religious writings. Some members believed that they were divinely given revelation from God and thus were to become over time the source of renewal for Christianity. Among this group, however, some believed that renewal first should be attempted within existing Christian confessions, while others felt that it was more in keeping with the message to form a new and separate organization. Other members were interested in Swedenborg's writings in order to learn the secrets through which spirits could be contacted.

Those who wished to form a separate organization asked that a vote be taken in order to proceed. Losing the vote by a small margin, these members decided to go ahead with plans to form a new church. Hindmarsh led this movement. Clowes hastened to London to dissuade them from making such a move. Unconvinced, the separatists went ahead with their plans and, on July 31, 1787, fourteen men and two women gathered to celebrate the sacraments of baptism and the holy supper in the name of the Lord Jesus Christ, and thereby established the New Church. According to Hindmarsh's record in *Rise and Progress,* "All those present declared themselves to be 'of the Lord's New Church in its outward and visible form on Earth.'" On June 1 the following year they completed the establishment of a new church when two men were ordained into the priesthood. Although other Swedenborgian or New Church organizations have developed in different countries around the world since 1788, all of them acknowledge some form of direct or indirect indebtedness to the actions taken by the men and women present at these foundational ceremonies.

The operational structure of this new organization was far from clear. In order to proceed, it was determined that a national conference of believers should be called to establish common beliefs, principles of association, and forms of worship. A circular was sent out that included forty-two resolutions of belief to be affirmed at a conference to be held at a chapel in London's East Cheap section in April 1789. On Easter Monday that year, approximately eighty men and women gathered at the chapel to attend the five-day conference, which ran from April 13 to 17. Among those present was the poet William Blake (1757–1827) and his wife, Catherine. Both signed the conference minute book acknowledging their assent to the thirty-two propositions drawn from the religious writings of Swedenborg that had been discussed and affirmed during the conference. Among other things, the approved resolutions stated that "the Theological Writings of the Honorable Emanuel Swedenborg are perfectly consistent with the Holy Word; they also contain the Heavenly Doctrines of the New Church, which he [Swedenborg] was enabled by the Lord to draw from the Holy Word, while under the Inspiration and Illumination of his Holy Spirit."

The last of the resolutions called for the group to meet again in April of the following year. On the agenda for subsequent conferences was the need to approve a liturgy consistent with Swedenborg's teachings, as well as principles of organization that would likewise be drawn from Swedenborg's revelation. Harmony reigned during this first general conference of the New Church, but the same spirit did not prevail in the gatherings that followed. The underlying issue that developed among conference participants was the growing attachment of certain members to opposing models of church governance—congregational versus hierarchical.

British Conference of the New Church. The issue was not resolved until the general conference of 1815, when the congregational model favored by the majority was no longer challenged. By that time there were three societies in London, thirty societies in Lancashire, and ten others in Great Britain. The British Conference has convened every year since that date with the various congregations and societies sending delegates. In 1815 the conference also adopted a presidential form of government with a one-year renewable term. This form of government persisted within the British Conference until 1970, when the length of the presidential term became five years. In 1900 the British Conference had seventy-three societies with a total membership of 6,337. They ran eleven day schools, which served 4,375 students, and they had over 7,000 children in attendance at their Sunday schools.

From its beginning until the middle of the twentieth century, the British Conference not only served the New Church in Great Britain, but also believers and congregations throughout the British colonies. It was a source of theological training, ministers, and hymnals and other printed material for groups in Australia, New Zealand, South Africa, and Nigeria. At the beginning of the twenty-first century these groups form independent associations, although history and tradition connect them to the British Conference. The largest of these groups (approximately 15,000 members) is the New Church of Southern Africa, founded by David Mooki (1876–1927) in 1911. It was run as a mission of the British Conference for many years, creating its own theological school in Orlando, Gauteng. The New Church of Southern Africa became independent in 1970, under the leadership of Obed S. D. Mooki (1919–1990), son of the elder Mooki. The president holding office in 2000 was Paul S. Kenene.

During the first half of the nineteenth century, the clergy of the British Conference were trained through a tutorial system. A theological school was established in London in 1865 in order to standardize training. It moved to Radcliffe, a suburb of Manchester, in 1984 to be closer to the geographical center of the membership. A congregational system of government had been chosen to enhance local control. A consequence of this system was that salaries of the clergy were paid by the local congregations without any assistance from the national body. As a result, recruiting men for the ministry was difficult, because in many locations with small congregations an adequate living could not be guaranteed. Thus, the British Conference throughout its history has had more congregations than ministers to serve them. This difficulty was at least technically addressed by opening the ministry to women in 1998. But the challenges of secularization and modernization could not be overcome simply by recruiting women into the ministry. Organizational and constitutional changes were initiated in 1999 in an attempt to meet these difficulties head on. The conference has thus become more centralized and more reliant on the Internet for all types of communication, including recruitment of new members and instruction in the theological school. According to its vision statement, the British Conference has also chosen to be inclusive and nonjudgmental, while at the same time it seeks to stimulate spiritual growth by applying the writings of Swedenborg to life.

From 2001 to 2002, the British Conference of the New Church had the following statistical profile: 1,148 members, 29 worshiping congregations, and 7 groups; there were 25 ministers, of whom 14 were retired or no longer in active service, and 44 lay worship leaders.

The Swedenborgian Church of North America. The Swedenborgian Church of North America was organized as the General Convention of the Church of the New Jerusalem in Philadelphia, Pennsylvania, in May 1817. At that time there were approximately 360 receivers of Swedenborg's teachings in the United States, located in seventeen different societies. The issues before the convention were to establish a permanent organization that could oversee the needs of the already existent congregations; to assist in the development of new ones; to regularize ordination; and to support missionary efforts. Delegates assembled in Philadelphia from five states: New York, Pennsylvania, Maryland, Virginia, and Ohio. Two foreigners also attended the Philadelphia convention, one from Scotland and one from Sweden.

The General Convention's adoption of a congregational form of government was natural, due to the democratic temper of early America, and because the congregations had existed prior to the central organizing body, as had also been the case in England. A proposal to consider a hierarchical form of government was placed on the agenda during the 1820s, but it was never actively considered. The General Convention organized itself into regional associations, and delegates from the associations attended the annual convention and conducted the business of the church. To oversee the work, officers were selected. At the first convention a president was chosen; the next year the position of vice president was also established, but it was not until the eleventh annual convention that a financial report was submitted for approval. This basic system of government still frames the work of the Swedenborgian Church of North America.

The doctrinal principles outlined by the General Convention emphasized "knowledge of the Lord in his Divine Humanity," because church members believed it is the fundamental principle of all true religion. These principles also emphasized sharing one's faith with others so that the Lord's kingdom might come through the practice of the divine teachings of charity, good works, and love for each other. Attention was paid to the recruiting of sincere men to the ministry, and a system of licensing and ordination was created that persisted until a theological school was established in Waltham, Massachusetts, in 1867.

Controversy emerged within the General Convention of the Church of the New Jerusalem when, after the American Civil War, some ministers and church members with a belief in a hierarchical form of government began to press their views. Rebuffed by the General Convention, they formed their own theological school in Philadelphia in 1876. The inability of the two groups to find a mutually acceptable solution led to a schism in 1890.

The high point of growth for the General Convention in the nineteenth century was in 1890. In that year the annual reports listed 154 societies, 119 ministers, and 7,095 members. During the nineteenth century the convention's doctrinal emphasis on inward and individual spiritual development fit well into the American spirit. The teachings were a particularly unique source to learn more about human psychology and motivation. There was a strong identification of the membership with the teachings of Swedenborgianism, and Swedenborgian thought and teachings were absorbed into the broader American culture, helping to create what John Humphrey Noyes (1811–1886), historian and founder of the Oneida Community, called "Swedenborg's century." Samson Reed's (1800–1880) *Observations on the Growth of the Mind* (1826), a book based on Swedenborg's principles, suggested that changing times originate in a changing mind. Reed's work had a far-reaching impact. It appealed to Ralph Waldo Emerson (1803–1882), and Emerson's good friend, the English author Thomas Carlyle (1795–1881). It inspired Emerson's masterwork *Nature* (1836), and Emerson included Swedenborg in his essay "Representative Men" (1850). Carlyle wrote that Swedenborg's new spiritual philosophy would soon leaven all religious thought.

Swedenborg was also an important source of inspiration for Edgar Allan Poe (1809–1849) and Walt Whitman (1819–1892). Both men broke important ground by bringing new psychological insights into the very structure of their art, as did the celebrated landscape artist George Inness (1825–1894), a member of the Swedenborgian Church and a man who used Swedenborg's teachings on the correspondences of color and form to shape his spiritualized landscapes.

This convergence of psychology and Swedenborgianism was an obvious strength for the development of the General Convention in the nineteenth century. However, as psychology became an independent, nonreligious discipline, what had been a unique Swedenborgian contribution to American culture became more widely available in a secularized form. This affected the growth of the General Convention.

In the twentieth century, the General Convention of the Church of the New Jerusalem became the Swedenborgian Church of North America. It maintained its congregational structure, with a president (elected for a three-year term, eligible to serve one additional consecutive term), a vice president, recording secretary, and treasurer. Those who serve in the latter three offices are elected for one-year renewable terms. Together, these officers, plus three ministers and six laypeople, constitute the General Council that governs the church. In addition there is a Council of Ministers that supervises the pastoral and theological matters of the church.

The Swedenborgian Church of North America is known as the liberal "branch" of the New Church in North America. It is a member of the National Council of Churches, and it has attempted to meet the challenges of secularization by adapting to the enlightened values of Western postmodern society. It supports environmental causes and has policies that welcome diversity and inclusiveness. The Swedenborgian Church of North America has ordained women since 1975 and does not view a person's sexual orientation as an impediment to ordination.

In 1999 the Swedenborgian Church of North America closed its theological school, the Swedenborgian School of Religion in Newton, Massachusetts, and the property was sold. In 2001 the Swedenborg School of Religion formed a partnership with the Pacific School of Religion in Berkeley, California. The program, supervised by the Pacific School's Swedenborg House of Studies, offers a master of divinity degree, as well as a certificate of theological studies in conjunction with the Pacific School. Distance education is a feature of the program, and the holdings of the library have been integrated into the database of the Graduate Theological Union in Berkley. This move has brought the theological education of the Swedenborgian Church of North America under the umbrella of one of the most progressive Christian theological schools in the United States.

Statistics for the Swedenborgian Church of North America reported in their journal, *The Messenger*, for the year 2001 are as follows: the church had a total membership of 1,926, of which 1,431 were listed as active. They had 40 churches, 34 active ministers, and congregations in the United States, Canada, and Guyana.

The General Church of the New Jerusalem. The General Church of the New Jerusalem, unlike the British Conference and the Swedenborgian Church of North America, has an episcopal form of church government. It was legally established in 1897 after withdrawing from the General Convention in 1890. The principles of what was called the "Academy Movement" within the General Convention led to the schism and separation. The members of the Academy Movement believed that the theological writings of Emanuel Swedenborg constituted the third testament of the Christian Bible. That is, they believed that Swedenborg's writings were not merely divinely inspired revelation, but were, in fact, the word of God. Like the Old Testament and the New Testament, they were the third part of the divine word. Just as the sign on the cross calling Jesus "the king of the Jews" was written in Hebrew, Greek, and Latin, so, according to the General Church of the New Jerusalem, the Old Testament was written in Hebrew, the New Testament in Greek, and the third and final testament was produced in Latin. Secondly, they believed that the theological writings of Swedenborg prescribed a hierarchical form of church government with three degrees of the priesthood. And thirdly, they believed in the necessity of educating children based on principles drawn from these same theological works. Thus, even prior to separation from the General Convention, they had established schools from the primary grades through high school and college, culminating in a theological school for the training of priests.

The schism was based on principle, but it also came about as a result of the clash of strong personalities and political maneuvering within the organization of the General Convention of the Church of the New Jerusalem. Once separated from the convention, the dominance of Bishop William H. Benade (1816–1905) created new difficulties within the fledging organization. Finally, the members of the Advent Church that Benade had formed withdrew from him and established a new organization in 1897—the General Church of the New Jerusalem. The scope of the organization was international from its inception. Congregations in Canada and Great Britain joined with those in the United States in support of the principles of the Academy Movement. These principles, developed by Benade, were maintained by the new organization, but his autocratic style of leadership was rejected. A group numbering 347 participated in the move to withdraw from the General Convention. In 1900, just three years after incorporation, the General Church of the New Jerusalem had an international membership of 560. Because it was founded on principle rather than propinquity or nationality, it competed with both the American General Convention and the British Conference for members.

The General Church of the New Jerusalem created an organization in which theological and ecclesiastical matters were separated from financial ones. The bishop was to supervise the spiritual life of the church but a lay board of directors was to supervise it financially. Furthermore, instead of adopting a binding constitution, the organization decided to write a document titled "The Order and Organization of the

General Church of the New Jerusalem." Originally published in 1914, it has been revised six times since that date. The last revision occurred in 1999, when the language of the document was made gender inclusive. The decision not to write a constitution was made so that the organizational structure of the General Church of the New Jerusalem could be more responsive to the membership as it grew and developed. Furthermore, given the difficulties of its own foundation, those involved did not want any form of organization that would prevent future generations from making changes they might deem necessary for the life of the church.

Council and assembly are also important governmental principles for the General Church of the New Jerusalem. The bishop and the ministers all have lay councils that meet with them on a regular basis. In addition, every four or five years, all the members of the church get together at a general assembly to make important decisions. These councils and assemblies are governed by the principle of unanimity, with doubt signaling the need to delay decision making.

Education is a word that is synonymous with the Academy Movement and the General Church. This Swedenborgian organization has made education one of its highest priorities; however, in 1995 evangelization became an equivalent priority when an Office of Evangelization was established. Due to its origins in the Academy Movement, the General Church was a school before it became a church. The Academy Movement organized a theological school in 1876, when several ministers who were proponents of academy principles were no long welcome to teach at the theological school in Waltham, Massachusetts. Soon the Academy Movement not only ran a theological school in Philadelphia, but also a college and high school. These institutions moved to Bryn Athyn, Pennsylvania, in the 1890s and were still in operation in 2003. The international character of the General Church of the New Jerusalem has helped to create an international student body at all of its schools, but particularly at the college. In 2000, students came from more than seventeen countries, including Brazil, Canada, France, Korea, Sri Lanka, Sweden, and the United Kingdom.

The General Church of the New Jerusalem is considered the most conservative of the New Church organizations. By 2003, for example, it still did not ordain women. Nonetheless, it is the most diverse both racially and nationally. An unpublished study by Jane Williams-Hogan in 1998 showed that the British Conference had a minority membership of 5 percent, the Swedenborgian Church of North America had a 1½ percent minority membership, and the General Church of the New Jerusalem had 11 percent.

Although nowhere is it mandated that members of this church live together in communities, in practice this is also a characteristic of the General Church of the New Jerusalem. Communities have developed around existing General Church schools, or individuals will band together to form a community and a school. In the year 2000 the General Church operated ten elementary schools, six of which are located in New Church communities in the United States and Canada. In addition, there is a New Church elementary school in South Africa, and one was established in Ghana in 1999. Two preschools were established that same year in Denver, Colorado, and Ivyland, Pennsylvania.

A statistical profile of the General Church of the New Jerusalem in 2000 indicated a membership of 4,585, with a total international community of approximately 14,000, including minors, young adults, and adults who attend church services but who have not signed the rolls. The church had 92 public places of worship in 2000—57 in the United States, 8 in Canada, and 27 outside of North America. These groups were served by a total of 99 active and retired clergymen.

The Swedenborgian Movement Worldwide. Other Swedenborgian organizations exist in the world beyond the three discussed above. In 2003 independent New Church groups existed in Australia, France, Japan, Kenya, Nigeria, the Philippines, Russia, South Africa, Sri Lanka, and the Ukraine, among other places. It is interesting to note, however, that from its inception the Swedenborgian movement has developed organizationally primarily within the framework of English-speaking countries. The three organizations discussed in this article not only developed in Great Britain and the United States, but they also chose to establish theological schools. Although other theological schools have subsequently been established outside of the United States and England, these have all been developed through the missionary efforts of English-speaking organizations.

Many of these independent Swedenborgian organizations have been started as a result of an individual reading one of Swedenborg's theological writings and discovering the divine within it. The reader has then determined to form a church or religious organization in response. This pattern occurred in Great Britain, France, Russia, and Sweden in the eighteenth century; in Australia, Canada, New Zealand, and the United States in the nineteenth century; in Brazil, Nigeria, South Africa, Japan, Korea, and Ghana in the twentieth century; and already in the twenty-first century in the Philippines and Sri Lanka. While the membership numbers are not large, these groups nonetheless represent a different mechanism of conversion than that of a personal encounter with believers, *gurus*, or some other religiously inspired charismatic person. Conversion occurs after reading a book, after which the individual often attempts to find other similarly interested people or organizations. Writing to book publishers is a common method by which these individuals find existing organizations and fellow believers. Thus, Swedenborg's method of spreading his message by publishing and distributing books, although it is no longer the only method used to recruit new members, has been surprisingly effective.

See Also Swedenborg, Emanuel.

BIBLIOGRAPHY

Block, Marguerite Beck. *The New Church in the New World: A Study of Swedenborgianism in America.* New York, 1932.

Evans, Jean. *A History of the New Church in Southern Africa, 1909–1991, and a Tribute to the Late Reverend Obed S. D. Mooki.* Johannesburg, South Africa, 1991.

Hindmarsh, Robert. *Rise and Progress of the New Jerusalem Church in England, America, and Other Parts.* London, 1861.

Robinson, I. A. *A History of the New Church in Australia, 1832–1980.* Melbourne, 1980.

Williams-Hogan, Jane. *A New Church in a Disenchanted World: A Study of the Formation and Development of the General Conference of the New Church in Great Britain.* Ann Arbor, Mich., 1985.

Williams-Hogan, Jane. "Contemporary Swedenborgian Religious Organizations: A Comparative Sociology Analysis." Unpublished paper presented at a Plenary Session of the 12th International CESNUR Conference, Turin, Italy, September 10–12, 1998.

Williams-Hogan, Jane. "Discovering the Two Faces of Religious Charismatic Action—Traditional and Modern: A Model." In *Approaching Religion,* part 1, edited by Tore Ahlbäck, pp. 273–304. Åbo, Finland, 1999.

Williams-Hogan, Jane. *Swedenborg e la Chiese swedenborgiane.* Torino, Italy, 2004.

JANE WILLIAMS-HOGAN (2005)

SWORDS SEE BLADES

SYMBOL AND SYMBOLISM.

[*This entry presents a history of the study of symbolism: issues, theories, and approaches. For an explanation of symbols from various religious traditions, see* Iconography.]

Understanding symbolism as a particular mode of religious thought begins with some consideration of what one means by the term. Most generally, a symbol is thought of as something that stands for something else. However, it is not a simple matter to identify the particular mode of "standing for" that provokes an observer to call something a symbol, as opposed to any of the other terms we use to designate figurative devices, like *sign, figure, metaphor, image, receipt, token,* or *allegory,* to name just a few. Although different definitions have been used throughout the long history of semiotics, a certain consistency exists in the characteristics thought to be specific to "symbol" (Greek *sumbolon,* late Latin *symbolum,* Italian *simbolo,* German *Symbol,* French *symbole*). These defining characteristics have consistently granted the idea a special relevance to religion. While various objects have been called symbols—including the purely arbitrary signifiers used in mathematical or scientific notation and, in the ancient period, the tokens of identity used in diplomacy and as markers of business agreement—a large subset of these appear in contexts that deal specifically with figuration of the divine. In particular, a symbol, as opposed to other forms of signification, tends to be understood as a representational mechanism that renders transcendent realities into tangible forms.

This article surveys the general outlines of the study of symbolism by proceeding historically, highlighting certain key contributions relative to the study of religion and focusing attention on some of the main theoretical issues.

POINTS OF ORIGIN. Though the Romantics created the modern apotheosis of the symbol, they did not invent the idea. The symbol has a rich premodern history, which, while not determinative, renders comprehensible certain habits of thought that animate the concept's later history. The term originated in Greek. The neuter noun, *sumbolon,* is formed from the verb *sumballein* (prefix *sun* + the verb *ballein*), which can mean many things but whose least marked sense is "to put" things "together." In 1931, Walter Müri disproved conclusively the notion that the noun is derived from the notion of a thing "put together" with something else. Philological considerations argue against this interpretation and also against the idea that symbol indicated, from its inception, an unspecific and general association between things. (This sense would have required *sumblêma,* which is uncommon and attested very late.) Neuter nouns in omicron formed from other *-ballein* verbs consistently mark the *instrument by which* the action of the verb is completed. Consequently, if the noun had actually been derived from the verbal sense of "put together," it would have yielded the sense of a device used to put other things together, and this suggestion turns out to be awkward in the face of attested ancient usage.

The neuter noun in the classical period regularly designated one of the two halves of a deliberately broken piece of material (a terracotta shard, for example) that were distributed to the two parties to an agreement in order to provide a secure authentication, at some future date, of their original arrangement. One sense of the verb *sumballein* stands out clearly, given knowledge of the philological parallels, as the best explanation of the evidence for the noun. The verb has a well-attested sense of "to agree," which positions the symbol as a device by which agreement is completed. Symbols seal the deal, so to speak. In the classical age, this context is by far the most common. Symbols appear as authenticating markers in many different fields, including in hospitality arrangements, in business, and in diplomacy. Although this background sets, at first glance, a kind of intuitively satisfying background for understanding the later history of a representational device, on closer inspection, it is too humble to have served as the origins for the master concept of figuration that appears later. A "receipt" and a "passport" are, after all, a far cry from a mode of representation that mediates between humans and the divine. Two other contexts need to be considered; these will explain the ways in which a narrow term of authentication gains a broader meaning and will show that symbols had, even in their earliest days, certain unique representational powers.

First, in the mystery religions and famously among adherents of the Pythagorean sects, the term *sumbolon* designates a particularly significant kind of authentication. It is the secret password or short, enigmatic verbal formula that verifies membership in a particular cult. These symbols carried the added power to authenticate a cult member as he or she ascended a ladder of spiritual wisdom. Knowledge of the secret symbol allows a person to gain access to higher tiers of enlightenment. In the deepest expression of this aspect, the symbol can be used after death to give the deceased access to the regions of the blessed, where souls live in splendor after their separation from their bodies. These symbols are indeed passports but ones that facilitate the movement of humans toward the divine, and so set up conditions more congenial to the later development of the idea. This background underlies the early Christian usage of the Latin *symbolum* for the Apostle's Creed.

The second important context for understanding the symbol's later history is in the field of divination. A different Greek term, the masculine *sumbolos,* which emerges from a different sense of the originating verb *sumballein,* applies here. In addition to the idea of agreement, the verb carries a meaning of "to meet." Again, on philological parallels, the masculine noun in omicron indicates a thing or person doing the action of meeting, and so comes to indicate that which one meets. In the field of divination, chance meetings of many kinds played an important role, and *sumbolos* is the most general term for these. Because of the prominence of the neuter form (and of neuter forms in the language of divination more generally) the masculine term tends to become assimilated to the neuter. By the classical period, it had outgrown its specific use to describe an ominous chance meeting and had become a general term for a divine sign of any kind. The symbol as divine sign forms the second important background idea to the later development of the concept. In a kind of mirror image of the symbol in the Mysteries, the divine sign also facilitates movement of the divine toward the human. In both contexts, human aspirations for the divine are expressed in concrete form.

These early manifestations of the notion of the symbol contain two important aspects. First, a current of secrecy is present throughout. The symbol marks a form of sign that brings something to light, and yet it means something that is not apparent to the uninitiated. In other words, the symbol has an esoteric or "closing" function, as well as an exoteric or "disclosing" one. Later theories of the symbolic will tend to preserve this esoteric dimension and draw on the power that secrecy always bestows. In addition, the symbol in the mystery context points to a performative dimension to symbolic representation. It has the power to enact a change in the one who wields it.

On these bases, the term *symbol* came into slightly broader use around the Mediterranean in the wake of Alexandrian Hellenization after the third century BCE. In addition to divine omens of all kinds, as well as magico-religious cultic formulas, the term designated allegorical representations of the divine in poetic texts, and cultic manifestations of divinities with their traditional accoutrements, such as accompanying birds or distinctive dress. These two developments show the newfound usefulness of the notion of the symbol in conceptualizing the ways in which divinities (which in a Hellenistic context could make increasingly extravagant claims to transcendence) might somehow be captured in more tangible forms. This use is an abrupt departure from the classical practice and is surely due to the influence of the usages in divination and in the mysteries. So the symbol began to describe that particular mode of representation through which, for example, Homer's all-too-corporeal gods or traditional cultic forms of anthropomorphic divinities might relate to a transcendent divine principle as it was beginning to be understood. It is perhaps not a surprise that a parallel (and pivotal) context emerged in the *Greek Magical Papyri,* in which a symbol meant a magical amulet or token. It marked a divinely charged material object that had some sort of numinous power to produce tangible effects here on earth. It was intended to describe a reproduction of the divine in material form rather than a representation per se.

SYMBOLS IN LATE ANTIQUITY. In late antiquity, the symbol took on a new life, one that marked a crucial stage in its development. The post-Plotinian Neoplatonists explicitly married the Pythagorean password to enlightenment, the omen, the material representation that renders the traditional god in tangible form, the allegorical representations of the divinities in poetic texts, and the amulet of the magicians in order to produce a systematic theory of the symbol as a master device of representation. The first stage in this development begins with the work of Iamblichus (c. 245–c. 325), who followed Plotinus' lead in making philosophy a soteriological pursuit. Drawing on the Pythagoreans for inspiration, he claimed that different levels of knowledge required different forms of discourse. Scientific knowledge might be reached adequately through likenesses and images, but esoteric wisdom of the divine superstructure of the cosmos required a secret language of symbols. In his *On the Mysteries,* Iamblichus further develops this idea in relation to what he saw as the secret symbolic language of the Egyptians. Knowledge of the hieroglyphs was spotty in late antiquity, and ignorance of this language contributed greatly to its perceived capacity to carry the most profound wisdom. Iamblichus also devoted a great deal of attention to justifying a form of ritual praxis, part of his comprehensive philosophical-religious discipline, in which symbols play a critical part. They are required to activate the rituals; more specifically, they are the material items or secret language that invokes the divine presence. This notion implies that symbolic figuration relies not on mimetic imitation but on the invocation of true presence.

These developments led to the work of the great follower of Iamblichus, Proclus (d. 485). Proclus created a highly developed symbol theory that played a central role in his metaphysics, his theory of ritual, and his views on figuration of the divine in language or in the arts. All the post-Plotinian

Neoplatonists understood that the transcendent principle of the universe, the One, radiated out from itself the whole of the universe, with each successive layer of reality imitating what had come immediately before it. This view made the cosmos a kind of cascading theophany. Yet they also tried to comprehend Plato's famous conundrum that representation is always and everywhere a movement away from, rather than closer to, the truth. The Neoplatonists had to work within two views: that the material world is a theophany and that it is a shadow world of hopelessly decayed imitation. More often than his predecessors, Proclus uses the "symbol" precisely to resolve this tension. In his theory, most clearly articulated in his *Commentary on the Republic,* symbolic figuration does not involve imitation based on resemblance—in other words, Plato's objections do not apply to it. Instead, the symbol reproduces the real presence of its referent; it operates according to invocation and not according to imitation. Drawing on an apothegm he knew from the *Chaldean Oracles,* a text of dubious provenance that became a holy book for the Neoplatonists, Proclus stated that as the higher orders create the cosmos through imitation, they sow "symbols" throughout it. Proclus thought these symbols were nodes of divine radiance nestled within our tragically decayed world of imitations. These secret symbols can be harnessed by the knowledgeable poet, philosopher, or ritual practitioner, in order to render the divine in a suitable material form. This theory allows him to construct a defense of Homer, construct a metaphysics that mediates between the divine source and its mundane effluxions, and develop an explanation for how the divine might actually be made present in ritual praxis.

While Proclus is not particularly well known in the wider contemporary history of ideas, his thought regarding the symbol has had a long-standing and definitive influence. Certain key Romantic philosophers recovered his corpus in the eighteenth century, and their theories will be discussed below. Proclus's ideas also greatly influenced a person who became the single most important authority on figuration of the divine for medieval readers of the Bible. Shortly after Proclus's death, a body of work emerged that came to be attributed to Dionysius the Areopagite, Paul's convert mentioned in *Acts* 17:34. This pseudepigraphical collection of texts reinvented Proclus's theories of symbolism to help the early Christians understand the representation of the divine in cult, in texts, and in Dionysius' emanationist metaphysics. Dionysius reworked Proclus's theories for an understanding of the Christian sacraments (in the *Ecclesiastical Hierarchy*), hierarchical tiers of beings (in the *Celestial Hierarchy*) and the places in Scripture where the divine is figured in physical and sometimes even entirely corporeal form (in the *Divine Names*). Dionysius's mystical hermeneutics applied to all aspects of the divinely infused world, from scripture to church to cosmos. When his corpus was translated by John Scotus Eriugena in the ninth century, it quickly became the authoritative guide for medieval clergy trying to understand how the Scriptures could assign tangible qualities to the transcendent godhead. (The corpus also served as a guide for Christian mysticisms of many varieties across medieval Europe, both in the east and the west.) In his *Summa theologica,* Thomas Aquinas cites Dionysius some seventeen hundred times, more often than any other writer except Augustine of Hippo.

The Romantic movement. The turning point for contemporary interest in symbolic theory, and the most convenient point at which to begin a brief account of its modern life, occurred around the middle of the eighteenth century, among a group of thinkers and literary figures who have come to be known collectively as the Romantic movement. Their concern with symbols—charged by their reading of the late-antique Neoplatonists, but less the outcome of any single current of symbolic theory than a constellation of ideas scattered throughout the disciplines of Western academia—was one aspect of their general spirit of resistance against what they perceived as the dangerous excesses of eighteenth-century rationalism. With the Romantics, the "symbol" grew in importance and became the most prominent vehicle for the view that figuration, now considered in its most general terms, is a root process defining the human being and, importantly, that figuration, considered as a mental process, resides in a position of priority over even rational thought itself.

One of these Romantics, Johann Georg Hamann (1730–1788) reflected the general mood, though not the academic rigor of the times, in arguing the merits of poetic discourse as the "mother tongue of humanity." In protest against Kant, this most difficult and oracular of Romantic authors saw the perfection of knowledge not in abstraction but in symbols, since symbols enable one to view all the phenomena of nature and history as revelations of a divine communication. His contemporary, Johann Gottfried Herder (1744–1803), who was taught by both Kant and Hamann, was more balanced in his approach to the Enlightenment and its representatives. For Herder, the task of aesthetics lay in the search for a universal logic of artistic symbolization; to this end, he developed his own theory of the evolution of language, giving a central role to folk poetry. His use of Jean-Jacques Rousseau's (1712–1778) model of human growth as an analogy for the course of history and its progress away from the childlike innocence of the "noble savage" was widespread in the Romantic movement. Similarly, Novalis (Friedrich von Hardenberg, 1772–1801) also defended the primacy of imagination and poetry as a means to produce the symbolism of a higher reality, and he drew special attention to the "magical" power of symbolic words. Among theorists of literature, Samuel Taylor Coleridge (1772–1834), influenced by F. W. J. Schelling (1775–1854) and the late-antique Neoplatonists, found the symbol to be a powerful representational tool that had the unique capacity to grasp the transcendent in physical, palpable form. The symbol, he thought, becomes "consubstantial" with its referent.

Together with Georg Christoph Lichtenberg (1742–1799), a physicist with a mystical bent who was actually anti-

Romantic, the self-avowed psychological novelist Karl Philip Moritz (1757–1793) merits mention for drawing attention to dreams as symbolic expressions of the inner self. The first major achievement in this area came after the turn of the century, with Gotthilf Heinrich Schubert (1780–1860), whose views of the dream as an abbreviated hieroglyphic language later earned him recognition by Freud as a forerunner of modern psychological dream interpretation. The work of Carl Gustav Carus (1789–1869) on dream interpretation has more immediate links to modern psychology, however, because of the extensive and systematic use he made of the notion of an unconscious mind, a notion that incidentally was widespread among the Romantics. Carus's distinction between relative and absolute layers of the unconscious, and his argument for a participation of the latter in a sort of universal, pantheistic life force reflected in dream symbols, were an inspiration to theories later developed by Jung after his break from Freud.

One side effect of the Romantic movement—perhaps the one that, more than any other, carried the attention to symbolism over into the nineteenth century—was the variety of opinion it sparked among classical mythologists, both among those sympathetic to the Romantics and those opposed. Scholars such as Samuel Clarke (1675–1729), Johann Ernesti (1707–1781), Christian Heyne (1729–1812), and Johann Hermann (1772–1848) reinterpreted the gods and heroes of ancient Greece as symbols expressing a primitive level of philosophy or psychology. The very tools of allegoresis that the medieval theologians—following a tradition going back to the Greek philosophers and literary critics—had used to reveal the hidden wisdom of the ancient myths were used to discredit its symbolic importance. Moritz, among others, objected to the reductionism in such interpretation and argued for the primacy of understanding the historical conditions of classical antiquity. The complaints of Jacques Antoine Dulare (1775–1835) against "symbolizing" what were basically pragmatic cults and beliefs typified the new and more empirical approach to the symbol that was gaining strength. This foment of opinion generated many later efforts to link a personal meaning of symbols to a general morphology of nature myths, such as are described in the work of Georg Ferdinand Frobenius (1849–1917) and Paul Ehrenreich (1855–1914).

One key figure, whose systematic treatment of symbols united the influences of the Romantic movement with the study of classical mythology, was Georg Friedrich Creuzer (1771–1858). Creuzer was steeped in late antique ideas about the symbol. He produced editions of Proclus and other key Neoplatonists which helped to re-awaken the Neoplatonic spirit of the symbol. Employing a comparative approach that used materials from Egypt, Greece, and Rome, as well as India and Persia, he tried to develop a theory of symbolism that would at once respect the pragmatic meaning of symbols as carriers of concrete tradition (including the scientific) and the religious meaning of symbols as the force to unify (*sun-ballein*) spirit and matter. Objections to Creuzer's work, however, in particular to his attempt to show the influence of Oriental symbolism on Christian symbolism, arose on every side, the most devastating of them from the pen of the classicist Johann Heinrich Voss (1751–1826). Even scholars in the early twenty-first century often deny Creuzer the important place he deserves in the history of the study of symbolism.

Perhaps the best known of the Romantic students of symbolism is Johann Jakob Bachofen (1850–1887). A historian devoted to the non-literate ancient world, he turned to myth as a guide to understanding the distant past, and from there developed a highly particularized exegesis of symbols. While Bachofen appears to have carried on his work independently of Dulare and Creuzer, he shared their concern for developing a universal, abstract theory of the symbol rooted in the facts of history. For him, the fundamental theme of the ancient myths—and hence also the basis for the symbols that myths interpret—was that of gynecocracy, or mother right. Although modern scholarship has since discredited this idea, along with most of his other historical arguments, the remarkable imagination and suggestiveness of Bachofen's work has kept it alive among those concerned with a general theory of the symbol.

THE SYMBOLISTS. The Symbolist movement was one of literary esotericism that formed among a group of French poets in the final two decades of the nineteenth century. The leading thinker was Stéphane Mallarmé (1842–1898); after his death, it virtually came to an end. Although its roots may be traced to the philosophies of Hegel and Schopenhauer, the Aesthetic movement in England, and the mystical writings of Swinburne, the movement took shape basically as a reaction against the impact of scientific realism on the literary arts.

Unlike the Romantics, who had been more concerned with the interpretation of specific symbols or the development of a general theory about symbolization processes, the Symbolists were preoccupied with creating symbols of ideal beauty appropriate to their age. While the Romantics were overtly political and public—the idea of the "noble savage" that was so dear to them provided part of the intellectual backdrop to the French Revolution—the Symbolists deliberately withdrew from the vulgar sentiments of public life. Theirs was a quasi-metaphysical, highly theoretical attempt to idealize absolute Beauty, to promote its contemplation, and at the same time to create it by restoring a musical sense to poetry and by using highly symbolic terms. Given to theorizing about symbols in esoteric terms, as these thinkers were, it is no surprise that their influence was restricted. In other respects, too, the major proponents of the movement seemed intentionally to flout existing traditions. Mallarmé used Christian ritual symbolism to erect a metaphysics designed to explain symbols. Charles Baudelaire (1821–1867), who may be credited as the first poet to exalt the value of symbols, did so by inverting the symbols of Christianity into a sort of diabolism. Paul Verlaine (1844–1896) also gave more popular form to the principles of Mallarmé by locating them within a Christian context. In fact, however, all of the Symbolists stood firmly outside of the Christian frame in their search for an alternate center to their aesthetic-mystico-religious sensibility: ideal Beauty.

Although the Symbolist movement was short-lived, and its theories have long since fallen out of favor, it did have an impact on symbolism in literature by cross-fertilizing it with anthropology, classics, and religion. The American counterpart of the movement, represented by writers such as Edgar Allen Poe, Herman Melville, and Henry James, as well as European post-Symbolists such as Rainer Maria Rilke and William Butler Yeats, shared many of the Symbolists' instincts about the mystical dimension of symbolism. Despite the movement's lack of influence on the study of symbols then being undertaken by philosophers and anthropologists, its reorientation from the objective world of facts to the evocative, psychological power of symbols brought the symbolic process itself to the surface, thereby foreshadowing developments in the twentieth century.

THE RISE OF MODERN ANTHROPOLOGY. By Bachofen's time, the influence of the Romantic movement on the study of symbols had begun to wane. Ethnological data gathered directly from primitive societies was beginning to accumulate, and the empirical method for the study of symbols, including those of the ancient world, was becoming more disciplined. Important work was done by Lewis H. Morgan (1818–1881) on Native American sacrificial rites; by William Robertson Smith (1846–1894) on Semitic sacrifice; by Henry Clay Trumbull (1830–1903) on the comparative study of sacrifice in India, China, the Near East, Africa, and Central America; by John Ferguson McLennan (1827–1881) on marriage symbolism; and by N. D. Fustel de Coulanges (1830–1889) on the influence of religious symbols on ancient Greek and Roman civil institutions. These and other works of the period contained a new rigorous approach to analyzing the data, coupled with an attempt to translate the meaning of symbols into abstractions more suitable to the modern critical mind.

This new scientific approach did much to demystify the study of occult and secret symbolic traditions, as well as to open the way to a more objective study of sexual symbolism in primitive culture and religious rites. The censure that Creuzer and Dulare had encountered a century before began steadily to weaken.

No doubt the most important figure of this period is Edward Burnett Tylor (1832–1917), rightly credited as the founder of modern cultural anthropology. Tylor's contribution to the study of the symbol has no direct links to the Romantics. Drawing instead from mid-nineteenth-century British philosophy, which had been rocked by evolutionary theory, he formulated a rather rationalistic and often condescending view of symbols. The myth-making faculty of primitive peoples that F. Max Müller and the brothers Grimm had helped to rediscover interested Tylor as a potential clue to the evolutionary development of mind, and led him to uncover a fundamental animism at the source of the symbolic process.

Another important influence on symbol theory at the time was James G. Frazer (1854–1941). His monumental study on the notion of the slain god, *The Golden Bough*, which had grown out of his work on nature symbolism and relied heavily on insights from Robertson Smith, not only influenced students in all fields of symbolism, but also affected scholars of literature. The sheer scope and wealth of Frazer's achievement, however, tended to overshadow the lack of development in his theory of symbols. And, as had Tylor, he bypassed important questions raised by the Romantics and the Symbolists.

At the start of the twentieth century, interest in symbolism continued to strengthen and to gain respectability among academics. Typical of this trend was Franz Boas (1858–1942), whose work on primitive art symbols led him to a number of interesting but controversial conclusions about the relationship between religious ideas and the literalization of natural symbols. The major influence at the time, however, came from the work of Émile Durkheim (1858–1917). Turning away from the nineteenth-century bias toward treating symbols as discrete entities with meanings in themselves—and thus turning his back on the Romantics and the Symbolists alike—Durkheim sought to uncover their social implications. He did not care very much about any inner reality in symbols, nor did he care where they came from; he was interested only in their effect on the society that used them. To this end, he proposed the revolutionary idea of viewing society as a system of forces conditioned by the symbolizing process: symbols were social because they preserved and expressed social sentiments. In assuming that non-empirical symbolic referents must be distorted representations of empirical reality, many critics later argued, Durkheim had viewed symbols too narrowly and failed to appreciate their polyvalent structure. While his concern with symbolic referents may have prevented him from exploring the wider reaches of symbolic significance, the boldness of his hypothesis laid a challenge before students of the symbol that retains its force in the early twenty-first century.

A. R. Radcliffe-Brown (1881–1955) owed much to Durkheim in the former's approach to symbols as meanings that give expression to sentiments in individuals in order to regulate collective needs or preserve relations and interests important to a particular society. Despite Radcliffe-Brown's numerous intuitions and descriptive distinctions, as well as a more scrupulous grounding in direct fieldwork than his predecessor, his work suffers from a certain lack of theoretical clarity by comparison.

Bronislaw Malinowski (1884–1942) shared many of Radcliffe-Brown's views, but Malinowski approached symbols with a keener sensitivity to their linguistic implications and a more complex theoretical understanding of them.

Rather than viewing words as having meaning in themselves, he saw them as entirely relative to their context, where they both communicate conventions and organize behavior. Like all symbols (of which they are the prototype), words modify the human organism in order to transform physiological drives into cultural values. Although Malinowski confused speech with language, and so was driven to generalizations that contemporary linguistic theory no longer accepts, his main concern was in classifying and interpreting symbolic forms to show how the process of symbolization affects the formation and function of culture. He succeeded in undoing the generalized symbolic interpretations of myths that some anthropologists had inherited from the Romantics.

R. R. Marett (1866–1943) attempted to trace the origins of religion to pre-animist beliefs in superhuman forces, but these efforts were armchair investigations from a scholar who preferred common sense to actual work in the field. Despite their limitations, however, his reports had high literary value and considerable influence on many other theoreticians working in symbolic theory. Lucien Lévy-Bruhl (1857–1939), most often remembered for his attempt to relate the origins of religion to a "prelogical" primitive mind that shared in the realities of nature by means of what he called participation mystique—a position that he retracted later in life—also deserves credit for highlighting the need to study symbolic thought and behavior.

Although the contributions of these pioneers continue to be recognized and supported by field studies, scholars hold many diverse opinions as a result of increased sensitivity to the complexities of symbol theory. Social scientists have become increasingly aware of the methodological assumptions underlying their own behavior and of the effects of psychological factors, the critical apparatus of philosophical hermeneutics, and advances in linguistic theory.

Victor Turner (1920–1983) developed an important theory of symbolism from his studies on ritual in the late twentieth century. Particular symbols can be understood, he argued, only by setting them in their wide "action-field context," considering their immediate role in ritual, and observing the particular patterns of behavior associated with them. Turner saw this series of expanding contexts as giving meaning to the symbol; furthermore, he focused attention on the context of the interpreter. His approach helped to clarify the distinctions between exegetical meaning (given by indigenous informants), operational meaning (derived from observation of a symbol's use), and positional meaning (deduced from its place in the totality of symbols). The psychological functions that Turner accorded symbols—to guard against excessive emotion and to serve as a catharsis to express feelings—initially were controversial but now have become commonplace.

Ever since Durkheim, anthropologists have emphasized the pivotal role of social structure (as both matrix and offspring) in the symbolic process, but the concrete forms of many symbols have caused scholars to investigate the ways that these symbols reflect the visible world of nature. In his researches on Semitic religions, Robertson Smith suggested that symbols of divinity, even those clearly wrought by human hands, were originally drawn from earth symbols. Mary Douglas has taken a more developed and inventive approach to natural symbols,, linking the origins of symbolization to the structure and processes of the human body. She reminds her colleagues that the modern study of symbols needs to consider symbols generated by social structures that may alienate people from themselves, from one another, and from the earth.

Modern anthropological theory owes much to Claude Lévi-Strauss and his research in linguistics and depth psychology, particularly in the realm of myth and symbol. Instead of the functional approach championed by Malinowski, or the more traditional symbolic approach that described symbols primarily in terms of their meanings, Lévi-Strauss's structuralism resurrected interest in myths and symbols as phenomena more basic than the meanings they convey, the social functions they fulfill, or the social systems that give them shape. Symbols belong to their own systems, he asserted, within which they are subject to certain basic relationships and patterns of transformation. His attempt to locate a universal human nature in some common, relatively stable mental structures underlying all variations in behavioral expression has helped to revive the Romantics' quest for a generalized theory and to preserve sensitivity to insights in symbolic theory developed in other disciplines.

Depth Psychology. Although some Romantics and others developed psychological theories of the symbol in the nineteenth century, these theories did not gain prominence until the twentieth century, notably in the work of Freud and Jung.

Sigmund Freud (1856–1939) founded his psychoanalytic movement on a theory of symbols whose refinement he pursued throughout his life. Freud used the dream symbols of the neurotically disturbed as fundamental data for his theories of how one's perception of the past is distorted, displaced, condensed, and filtered according to the internal conscious and unconscious dynamics of the psyche. So startling and compelling were his ideas that by the early years of the twentieth century they had become essential lessons for students of symbolism. W. H. R. Rivers (1864–1922) and Charles Seligman (1873–1940), both British, were among the first anthropologists to incorporate his ideas into their ethnographic work. In 1935, Jackson Lincoln made a daring application of Freud's method of dream interpretation to primitive culture; after him, Géza Róheim (1891–1953) used Freud's ideas in his studies of myth and folklore. Freud's concept of condensation, applied early on by Edward Sapir (1894–1939), has appeared in the work of such contemporaries as Victor Turner and Mary Douglas. Even those who, like Malinowski, were repelled by Freud's neglect of social factors, or who, like Lévi-Strauss, rejected the primacy Freud gave to the sexual meaning and etiology of symbols, have had to acknowledge the significance of unconscious factors in the formation of myths and symbols.

Carl Gustav Jung (1875–1961) had less influence than Freud on students of symbolism, but his research continues to stimulate interdisciplinary studies, and it has won respect in many depth psychology circles which are inimical to Freud. By seeing symbols not merely as private symptoms of unresolved repressions, but as expressions of the psyche's struggle for realization and individuation, Jung encouraged a more positive assessment of many neglected esoteric and mystical traditions from both East and West. His ideas affected the work of the Sinologist Richard Wilhelm (1873–1930) and the Indian scholar Heinrich Zimmer (1890–1943). In contrast to Freud, Jung has not attracted much attention from philosophers, but he has offered certain anthropologists, such as Paul Radin (1883–1959), a balance to Freud's excesses. Mythologists such as Joseph Campbell and Károly Kerényi (1897–1973), as well as numerous critics of art and literature such as Herbert Read (1893–1968) and Maud Bodkin, bear the stamp of Jung's symbolic theory clearly in their work. Although his methods of scholarship and use of data were controversial, both during his lifetime and afterward, Jung remains a testament to the power exerted by the study of symbolism over the inquiring intellect.

PHILOSOPHY AND RELIGIOUS STUDIES. Although philosophers and theologians have been interested in the problem of symbols since the time of the Neoplatonists, twentieth-century symbolic theory became something of a cottage industry among philosophers interested in or influenced by the field of semiotics.

Charles Sanders Peirce (1839–1914) took the first important step in this direction. His distinctions among the terms sign, symbol, index, and icon posed a number of fundamental questions that continue to intrigue many philosophers; in fact, his research provided a stimulus for anthropologists and historians to forge similar distinctions in their own work. In 1923, C. K. Ogden and I. A. Richards published *The Meaning of Meaning,* which disseminated Peirce's categories and stimulated interest in his ideas. American philosopher C. W. Morris also incorporated new insights from semantics and social psychology into the sphere of philosophical logic.

Ernst Cassirer's (1874–1945) work was much more ambitious in scope. He viewed the philosopher's task as the quest for the human spirit at work in culture, and coupled this outlook with his neo-Kantian leanings to produce a theory of "symbolic forms" as the basis to all human apprehension of the world. Although Cassirer's apparent neglect of criteria for verification has made him easy prey to later generations of scholars, his attempt to develop a consistent theory of mind grounded in the symbolic function represents a bold step beyond the purely logical frame of Peirce. His most notable successor in this regard has been Susanne Langer, best known for her aesthetic theory.

Among contemporary philosophers who have grappled impressively with the legacy of symbolic theory and with data from psychoanalysis, anthropology, and linguistics, the work of Paul Ricoeur stands out for the wide influence it has enjoyed among students of religion. For Ricoeur, "thought" needs something to "think about," and what it thinks about are symbols. The proper task of philosophy is hermeneutics, which he understands as the recovery of meaning through attention to the symbol-making function that begins with language and carries over into every person's attempt to be rational.

Religious studies in the twentieth century have become so closely bound to the study of symbols and the symbol-forming process that one is almost unthinkable without the other. The role that Mircea Eliade (1907–86) played in this chapter of Western intellectual history is hard to overestimate. In an impressive array of studies in the history of religions ranging from primitive societies to esoteric traditions, Eliade gradually constructed a comparative view of the phenomenon of symbolism that at once incorporates the gains of other disciplines and informs them with fresh insight.

The study of symbolism has also left its impression on modern theological studies. By introducing the philosophical hermeneutic tradition into biblical research, Rudolf Bultmann (1884–1976) redefined the domain of scriptural studies. In the area of systematic theology, Paul Tillich (1886–1965), whose dependence on existential hermeneutics is equally apparent, though at a more abstract level, argued throughout his work for the positive and indispensable role that symbolism plays in religious language. Conversely, he tried to show how the place of the symbol in human culture argues for the notion of an "Unconditioned" as a universal solvent of human consciousness.

GENERAL SYMBOLIC THEORY. A symbol usually is something concrete and particular that represents something else, usually abstract and generalized. The symbol often becomes a focal point for thoughts and emotions associated with its referent, or a trigger for associated habits. While the symbol itself is typically easily perceived, its referent may not be. Indeed, theorists commonly define a symbol in such a way that its referent is unclear, particularly with the powerful and lasting religious symbols, which generally resist direct connection to a single definable referent.

Theories of symbolism can be differentiated according to the factors that are judged to be formative in the symbolizing process (such as tradition and convention, biological needs and processes, the occurrence of natural phenomena, the structure of the human psyche, and divine hierophanies and revelations). A common, though largely tacit, assumption in most modern theories of symbolism is that the capacity to generate and use symbols is a core technology unique to the human species. This assumption exists as a prerequisite for, rather than an epiphenomenon of, the capacity for higher-order mental activity. Cassirer made this point forcefully in referring to symbolization as the root of all social communication, calling human beings *homo symbolicus.* Susanne Langer extended the argument further, viewing symbolization as one of the most basic and primitive functions of mind. Symbols appear not only in rational, discursive thought and behavior but also in the arts, which Langer attempts to define as varieties of "virtual" behavior. Theorizing of the symbolic process, therefore, typically involves theorizing of the structure of the psyche itself in order to explain how meaning is created and handed down as humans reproduce. The British linguistic analysts and those of the Vienna Circle also contributed to symbolic theory: they were concerned with discovering the invariable patterns by which meaning enters into human communication and with disposing of the distorted patterns by which meaning is turned into nonsense. Moreover, Freud's point of departure in the neurotic symptom and Jung's search for archaic, archetypal patterns both represent attempts to describe the universal structure of mind in terms of symbol-making processes.

The Meaning of Religious Symbols. The problem of symbolic meaning introduces a consideration of hermeneutics and of semiotic logic. To the extent that they invoke a hermeneutics, religious symbols ask the scholar to consider what qualities—subjective, objective, or both—define a symbol as religious. Next, the researcher must determine whether a possible religious symbol is actually functioning as a living symbol or should instead be classified as some other form of communication. What works as a symbol in one age may, even within a given tradition, cease to be relevant in the next age. Naturally, the same precept applies to differences among various cultural settings, and even among individuals. Problems like these underlie the distinction between a synchronic study of symbols, which seeks to locate a symbol within a certain living context or fund of symbols, and a diachronic approach, which looks for invariable patterns in religious symbolism. While many anthropologists take the synchronic approach, Lévi-Strauss represents the diachronic approach. His work on patterns of binary opposition has tried to bracket the question of the concrete meaning of symbols in order to concentrate on the deep structure of the symbol-making mind. Most students of the religious symbol part from him on this point. Many, in fact, would say that Lévi-Strauss himself subsequently departed from this position by arguing that one cannot clarify the process of signification without beginning with the concrete meaning of concrete symbols.

Turning to semiotics, religious symbols raise equally fundamental questions. Early in the twentieth century, the Swiss linguistic theoretician Ferdinand de Saussure (1857–1913) set the tone for much of general symbolic theory. He had three objectives: to identify the signifier, to determine just what it is signifying, and to describe the mechanism by which the signifying process takes place. Yet another aspect, one that Saussure purposefully neglected in his own work, has proved to be essential to many of the most creative modern studies of religious symbolism: namely, the nature and extent of the relationship between signifier and signified, apart from the actual mechanism by which it is established.

Mircea Eliade made one of the boldest attempts to describe this relationship in terms appropriate to religious symbolism. Echoing the Symbolists and Romantics, Eliade contended that the symbol reveals certain dimensions of reality that would otherwise elude understanding. For him, these deeper dimensions are disclosed not only through the reflection of the interpreter of the symbols, but also in the "internal logic" of the symbols. This idea, however, depends on the premise that there is something contained "in" the symbol that is being disclosed. He and Rudolf Otto, call this embedded something "the sacred," a reality of an order distinct from the natural and possessed of a power beyond humans' comprehension and control. This shift away from the knowing subject does not deny the opening assertion that symbols are constituted as such subjectively, nor that they are basically cultural phenomena. Rather, it moves away from the anthropological approach to one that seeks to remove the arbitrariness from the symbol, through an assertion that the symbol reveals something *else,* something outside the closed system of human cultural production. This attitude opens a path to understanding "natural symbols" that goes beyond investigations into the natural capacity of mind, and establishes symbolic conventions in order to capture invariable patterns of meaning that those conventions communicate.

Jung's research into "natural symbols" gradually deflected his mature work away from models of the psyche and questions of physiology toward a search for "archetypal" patterns of meaning by which symbols could be classified and interrelated. Although his early work with Freud had convinced him of the need to see the symbolic process at work in the psychic appropriation of physiological processes, Jung eventually placed greater emphasis on the religious and spiritual significance of universal patterns that appear in the individual experience of symbols.

Opinions vary widely regarding the general nature, classification of forms, and function of symbolism in culture and psyche, and the problems multiply when considering the actual interpretation of particular symbols. The topic is commonly divided into two areas: a general hermeneutics, or rules for interpreting symbols, and actual exegesis within a given hermeneutics. Many scholars have attempted to produce universally applicable lexicons of symbols purporting to decode the secrets of dreams, religious imagery, esoteric traditions, and the like. A philosophical approach to hermeneutics that is more congenial to scholarly endeavors and closer to the goal of the Romantics is Ricoeur's restatement of one of the symbol's oldest characteristics: that a symbol both reveals and conceals—that it possesses both a symptom-hiding and a truth-proclaiming dimension. In this view, meaning and the interpretation of meaning are essential and complementary moments in the general phenomenology of the symbol: interpretation involves refining the symbol and looking to the interpreter to reveal everything condensed in the symbol. The symptomatic dimension of the symbol, for Ricoeur, finds its clearest exponent in Freud, who attempted to reduce all symbols to some repression of desire. (Ricoeur found Jung too obscure and difficult to follow.) To Freud's "hermeneutic of suspicion," which is basically a process of "demystification," Ricoeur adds a hermeneutic standpoint long preserved in the West through Christian interpreters of the words of the scriptures: opening oneself up to the inexhaustible "kerygmatic" (teaching) capacity of the symbol.

THE ENDURANCE OF SYMBOLS. The idea of the symbolic has proved compelling across the centuries and over many disparate cultures. This may have as much to do with what the symbol hides as with what it puts on display. Among the different types of figuration of which humans have conceived, symbols most consistently promise revelation—but they earn this capacity through an equal and opposite tendency to mystify. From the early passwords of the mystery religions, to the secret hermeneutics of Pseudo-Dionysius, to the Romantics' vehicles toward the transcendent, to Eliade's promise of divine disclosure, the symbol is a repository for the perennial desire of humans to see their gods. Since direct revelation lies out of reach, one settles for an image, a representation that is usually called a symbol. At the same time, the more this mode of figuration promises, the more it takes away. Clouds of mystery thicken around the signified to the precise degree that the signifier comes more clearly into view. At last, face-to-face always turns out to be not yet.

Although symbols are a human creation, they seem to have a life of their own, describing a dimension of human experience that stubbornly resists humans' control. Consequently, they have become especially relevant in a world that has developed increasingly elaborate conceptions of its own utter self-containment. Technological advances and expansion of knowledge—dizzying over the mere forty lifetimes that separate us from the classical Greeks—stand as impediments to even entertaining the idea of human limitation. But the symbol endures, ready to reassert, via a rich language of human imagination and through a process that operates at the root level of human experience, the infinite expanse against which humans' most magnificent achievements must always, in the end, be measured.

SEE ALSO Cassirer, Ernst; Eliade, Mircea; Iconography; Images, article on Images, Icons, and Idols; Jung, C. G.; Langer, Susanne; Myth, overview article.

BIBLIOGRAPHY

Among the most extensive and readily accessible bibliographies on symbolism are those included in Juan Eduardo Circlot, *A Dictionary of Symbolism,* translated by Jack Sage (1962; 2d ed., New York, 1971), and Raymond Firth, *Symbols: Public and Private* (Ithaca, N.Y., 1973). Circlot's lengthy introductory essay offers a helpful overview of symbolic theory, particularly as it pertains to the interpretation of esoteric material. The first six chapters of Firth's masterful work constitute the perhaps most comprehensive treatment available of the rise and development of anthropological work on symbols; in addition, he covers the range of opinion regarding the relationship between symbol and myth. Other helpful sources are the introduction of C. M. Bowra in *A Heritage of Symbolism* (1943; reprint, New York, 1961), which contains a brief but authoritative account of the French Symbolists; and Otto Gruppe, *Geschichte der klassischen Mythologie und Religionsgeschichte während des Mittelalters im Abendland and während der Neuzeit* (Leipzig, 1921) and Jean Pépin, *Mythe et allégorie: Les origenes grecques et les contestations judéo-chrétiennes* (Paris, 1976), which contains detailed information on numerous thinkers in Western history who came to symbolic theory by way of classical mythology. For more information on the classical background, see Peter T. Struck, *Birth of the Symbol: Ancient Readers at the Limits of their Texts* (Princeton, N.J., 2004).

An important study of the religious-symbolic qualities attributed to the written word is Alfred Bertholet's *Die Macht der Schrift in Glauben und Aberglauben* (Berlin, 1949). Harold Bayley's *The Lost Language of Symbolism,* 2 vols. in 1 (1912; reprint, London, 1974), despite its age, remains a classic study of the origin of symbolic folklore surrounding the emblem, including much material of directly religious interest.

Myth, Symbol, and Reality, edited by Alan M. Olson (Notre Dame, Ind., 1980), presents a good overview of the range of current symbolic theory; Jacques Waardenburg's notes provide a good deal of useful bibliographical material. A study by John Skorupski, *Symbol and Theory: A Philosophical Study of Theories of Religion in Social Anthropology* (Cambridge, U.K., 1976), draws careful attention to the contribution that recent British philosophy has made to clarifying the conflicts in anthropological opinion. Philip Pettit, *The Concept of Structuralism* (Berkeley, Calif., 1975) and Peter Munz, *When the Golden Bough Breaks: Structuralism or Typology?* (London, 1973) are both short but extremely helpful guides to the debate surrounding the work of Lévi-Strauss and its relationship to linguistic theory. In the latter half of his book, Munz does a particularly noteworthy job of isolating the principal theoretical problems faced by psychology, metaphysics, and mythology in trying to explain the symbolic process. In a provocative little book, *Rethinking Symbolism,* translated by Alice L. Morton (Cambridge, U.K., 1975), Dan Sperber argues forcefully against the underlying assumption of much current theory about symbols' meaning—in particular the ideas of Freud, Lévi-Strauss, and Turner—on the grounds that they work without meaning at all.

The opening chapter of Mircea Eliade's *Images and Symbols: Studies in Religious Symbolism* (New York, 1961) is a helpful introduction to the basic philosophical position he has maintained rather consistently throughout his work; also see Eliade's "Methodological Remarks on the Study of Religious Symbolism" in *The History of Religions: Essays in Methodology,* ed. Mircea Eliade and Joseph M. Kitagawa (Chicago, 1959). In *Freud and Philosophy* (New Haven, Conn., 1970), Paul Ricoeur lays out in detail his own theory of symbolism, in contrast not only to Freud's psychoanalysis but also to other philosophical schools. A straightforward history of modern hermeneutics that aids in connecting symbolism with contemporary Christian theology and exegesis work has been done by Richard E. Palmer in *Hermeneutics: Interpretation Theory in Schleiermacher, Dilthey, Heidegger, and Gadamer* (Evanston, Ill., 1969). For a concise account of Paul Tillich's position and its major objections to psychological, sociological, and philosophical approaches to the symbol, see his essay "The Religious Symbol," *Daedalus* 87 (1958): 321. Jacques Ellul's *The New Demons,* translated by C. Edward Hopkins (New York, 1975), offers a good taste of his longstanding campaign against the mindless absorption of the sacred symbols of religious tradition into technological modes of thought. Gabriel Vahanian's *God and Utopia* (New York, 1977) and David A. Martin's *The Breaking of the Image* (New York, 1980) present contrasting but more positive approaches to the question of the future of religious symbolism in a technological society.

For some recent trends among sociologists of religion who are interested in the subject of symbolism, see the *Proceedings of the Fourteenth International Conference on Sociology of Religion,* Strasbourg, 1977. Jolande Jacobi's *Complex, Archetype, Symbol in the Psychology of C. G. Jung,* translated by Ralph Manheim (Princeton, 1959), and a special issue of *Rivista di psicologia analitica* (no. 2, 1971) both provide handy introductions to the Jungian approach to the symbol. The volumes of the *Eranos Jahrbuch* (Zurich, 1934–) and *Symbolon* (Basel, 1960–) are a good source of information for current interdisciplinary work going on in the interpretation of ancient and modern symbolism, both Eastern and Western.

PETER T. STRUCK (2005)

SYMBOLIC TIME is understood to be the temporal form that organizes the symbols of a religious system into an order of periodicity. The analysis of symbolic time extends the understanding of religion as a symbolic system, so that the major functions of time within the system may be taken into account: (1) the time intrinsic to the formation of religious symbols and to the ritual performance (i.e., the time that is internal to the sacred event), (2) the connection that symbolic time has with the history and dynamic of a religious social bond, and (3) the time that is specific to the intentional life of the individual.

INTENTIONAL CHARACTER OF SYMBOLIC TIME. Symbolic periodicity encompasses, in its temporal structure, both change and duration, implying a sheer sequence of symbolic events and also a type of internal correlation of events and symbols that reflects the functional unity of the interval of time and the continuity of its structure.

The calendrical structure of the symbolic system has a complexity that differs from that of a means of time reckoning or chronology. The temporal order of symbolic events is quite different from the abstract concept of time as a continuous quantity infinitely divisible into successive parts that are homogeneous and impenetrable (Hubert and Mauss, 1909, p. 190). When compared with the chronological succession of cosmological time units, the symbolic performative system of festivals within a given culture or historical religion appears to be discontinuous and to have an uneven distribution over the sequence of the year. An order of precedence among religious festivals emphasizes a single festival, or set of festivals, around which the entire calendrical performance of the symbolic system is organized and that is replicated as the periodical structure of the religious year. Calendrical periodicity has an order that is temporally specific and reflects the dynamics of the symbolic function. It cannot be adequately analyzed by means of a descriptive model of the immediate empirical form of cyclic repetition.

The analysis of symbolic time may be pursued by linking the periodical structure of the religious symbols to the relational character of the symbol itself. It is possible to identify the dominant symbols that constitute the paradigmatic structure of a symbolic system and to identify their symbolic components and processual aspects, which define the dynamic movement of symbolic time.

A dominant symbol is a processual unity of word, semiotic transformation of an object of mediation, and action. It is structured as a relation that mediates a dynamic order of reality. Each symbolic feature is formed in such a way as to be a relational structure that binds two or more polarities to each other. As a unity, the religious symbol is generated within the dynamic of a relation between the subject and God, or an ultimate reality that has the capacity to condition the life of the subject. In their complex temporal features, symbols are the work of reason and the structures of perception, the dynamics of value, and the form of action in an intentional condition that comes into being when a constitutive relation between polar subjects appears as a new possibility or a new necessity.

In this sense, religious symbols are structures that are formed in the course of action and in the elaboration of experience. Symbol formation is present in the mental activity of the individual from the earliest stages; it is the way by which the relation with reality is established. But the temporal analysis of the type of processual structures that are differentiated by the religious symbol shows that the relation may not be defined simply in terms of subjectivity or in terms of intersubjective exchange. The central structure of a religious symbol defines the condition itself of "being in relation," the condition that shall be called *intentionality* or *intentional bond;* a symbol articulates the effective relation that conditions the life of the intentional subjects.

Symbols differentiate the direct expression and performance of the bond that relates the subject with the intentional object. The symbolic bond has a polar structure: It is constituted both by the orientation of the subject toward the object and by the way in which the object is determinant and active in the intentional life of the subject. The symbol is also performative because it elaborates the cognitive and dynamic structure of the intentional relation itself.

Symbolic time in its specifically religious form is the result of a temporal elaboration of the intentional exchange with an ultimate reality. This temporal elaboration represents a dynamic, generative process. In fact, symbols are temporally correlated in such a way as to constitute the nascent state of a bond with an intentional reality and to resolve unviable conditions in that relation. This article shall call the temporal development and articulation of symbols within a symbolic system the *figura.*

As the specific modality of the bond, a religious "public" symbol and the figura have a temporally complex structure. The symbol does not define exclusively or simply a subjective or intersubjective perception of and orientation toward a significant reality. Nor does the symbol, as the synthesis of the intentional process of a bipolar dynamic, present merely the synthetic form of probability of a logical inference. Instead, being the structure that defines the dynamic of an effective relation of the intentional bond, the "public" symbol is a temporal relation of relations in the sense that it defines the transformation by which the subjective perception emerges into a form of reciprocity, which is constitutive of an intentional bond.

This process of transformation to public intentional form corresponds to the epigenesis of a new intentional and social reality and to the cultural creations that have produced, through time, a vital bond. The path from a subjective to a "public" symbol progresses through a symbolic innovation, differentiated by the figura. It traces into specific structures of dominant symbols and into their temporal correlation a sheer sequence from past to future of temporal symbolic modalities, from the original insight to a condition of vital presence to a new structural orientation of action that expresses the time and the creative character of the bond. The religious figura, itself, has an historical formation that has come about through the actions of founders, the creativity of individuals and collective movements that have produced innovation within a tradition of forms of religious relation. The temporal dimension is intrinsic to the public symbol because it corresponds to the dynamic structure of the intentional relation, to its unity and transformation.

Symbols are generated within the intentional relation and constitute necessary structures and functions by which the new reality becomes and remains intentional. Formed within the intentional exchange, symbols are complex facts that differentiate the generative force of relation. They elaborate the internal principle of causality, the order of necessity, and the temporal logic that is stated within an intentional reality.

Because the symbol is both temporal and intentional, it is possible to interpret the symbolic or religious system not primarily as a system of signification, as analogical representation, nor simply as a set of metaphors, but as a processual structure that elaborates the forms of the "condition of being in relation" and the dynamics of the nascent state that is created within the ultimate intentional relation. The connotative and denotative features of signification that the symbol clearly presents may, consequently, be seen to be functions of the primary structure of the symbol as intentional relation.

The temporal function indicates that the symbol is the constant empirical constituent of the intentional relation. The religious symbol is a temporal artifact specific to the dynamic generated in the intentional relation. It is not an independent object but the temporal creativity in which the actual intentional event has its passage to a public, new bond. This applies not only to the individual symbol but also to the symbolic system as it is shaped by the interrelation of sacred text, symbolic forms of intentional exchange, and symbolic action.

Three theoretical elements, therefore, define symbolic time, namely, figura, periodicity, and intentional epigenesis. The "figura" is the set of symbols that are temporally correlated into a periodical system, and it is the original central structure of time within the intentional event. For this reason, the figura is the minimal unit of analyis of the symbolic temporal function. Periodicity defines the correlation of the symbols within a temporal interval. Intentionality, as the relational character of the symbols, is the epigenetic process, the nascent state of an intentional bond.

The temporal function of the figura is the dynamic process of a presence that has an intentional character. In the development from the first insight to an intentional bond, the figura is directed toward the resolution of the tension between those factors that are generative of an intentional bond and those that move in a contrary direction and finally destroy the bond or reduce its vitality. The formation of a figura and its performance is the result of a sequence of historical choices and actions related to the formation and selection of symbolic institutional structures. The figura reflects the experience of long periods of trial and error in the historical formation of a religious tradition, a sacred history, and a people. The intentional character of the figura becomes most evident in the language and action of the sacrifice and in the formulation of the sacred bond.

By formalizing the "relational" aspect of the symbols and of the development of the figura and by correlating it with the symbolic, sequential, and performative movement of the figura, one may specify the intentional character of periodicity presented by symbolic time.

Intentional Epigenesis and Formation of the Figura. The process of formation of the religious bond within a sacred history corresponds to the development of symbolic structures of a divine encounter and union. Defined in its relational character both of divinization and of incarnation, the development is a process of transcendence that has the temporal structure of a total object relation. The total object relation is an intentional action that transforms the bond from subjective to public. It is a nascent state within the intentional event that guides the passage from an inadequate modality of relation (in which the subject attempts to appropriate the value of life represented by the object and to negate the intentional value of the object and the constitutive and vital character of the relation) to a modality of the bond in which the object is restored to its original value as object of relation. With this epigenetic movement, both subject and object come to be recognized in their wholeness as vital to the bond, and the bond becomes a creative condition of intentional life.

In theological or religious language, the epigenetic sequence is often expressed in terms of the transformation from death to life, from darkness to light, from slavery to freedom through a time and history of salvation.

A total object relation allows the recognition of the other as total object. This is achieved by means of a resolution of the dynamics and structural intentional modalities of a partial object relation that are destructive or appropriative of the object and therefore inadequate to the condition of reciprocity of an intentional bond. This occurs through a creative intentional initiative (gift, sacrifice) in which the intentional dynamics of the partial object relation are transformed from appropriative to reciprocal and through models of thought and action that sustain intentional reciprocity in the creation of sociocultural institutions that express the bond. It follows from this that the nascent state and the epigenesis of a total object relation, in its temporal symbolic structure, is a sequence of intentional positions that build a symbolic intentional bond. Each passage from one intentional position to another is guided, in its unity, by particular dominant symbols.

The temporal correlation of the dominant symbols is the order of successive creations of the intentional relation; this develops the nascent state into a vital form of life and corresponds to the sacred history of the bond.

The initial stages of the sequence are not merely incidental to the development of a vital cultural and institutional bond. They are, instead, the necessary elements, stages, and modalities of the temporal process of the bond itself.

Symbolic time is a generative symbolic form. It traces and differentiates a specific way by which human action, in a given intentional bond, both at the level of the individual and of the collectivity, becomes intentionally creative. The nascent state related to the figura is a process of formation of something new, the specific event of the coming into being of an intentional bond, a dynamic covenant that constitutes a new order of possibility and the creation of new cultural and institutional forms. The figura is the generative time of an intentional public bond that has been brought about by a transformation of the structure of intentional relations and by the symbolic and institutional elaboration of intentional existence.

The intentional character of the figura within the development of a sacred history is differentiated as the paradigmatic action, the symbolic agent (identified as founder, hero, or prophet), and the normative order of intentional life. Symbolic time is, therefore, interior to the intentional relation of the bond, and symbols are structures that both differentiate and connect the initial perception of reality to the elaboration of concrete forms of relation and to their articulation through time.

RITUAL PERFORMANCE. The figura, as it is represented by a calendrical order, makes use of three types of temporal parameters: time units, rules of symbolic performance, and sets of festivals or rituals. The "time units" are periodical intervals normally related to astronomic measurements of the solar and lunar year, the solstices and equinoxes, the month, the week, and the day. The set of performative rules defines the logic of interrelation of the symbolic features of word, action, and object in the form of intentional exchange and coordinates the different symbols in such a way as to express the intentional structure of the figura through its temporal periodical performance. Festivals are symbolic public actions that have a mythic and ritual structure.

The features of the three main temporal parameters are correlated so that a condition of time is created that is periodical. The temporal coordination of the dominant symbols is ritualized in a calendrical, repetitive form.

The different festivals and their distribution, which is, as has been seen, uneven and discontinuous through the year, correspond to the calendrical coordination of specific events of the epigenetic sequence. These events are correlated into a performative paradigm that has the pattern of a "fact coming into being" (*fait naissant*). This performative pattern, which structures the individual ritual and permeates the periodicity of the figura, has a tripartite structure consisting of a phase of separation and destructuration, of limen, and of restructuration and organization into a new relationship (van Gennep, 1960; Turner, 1969). In the first phase the ritual subjects become detached from their former modalities of intentional relation and from their structural expression; in the last phase a new cultural and structural bond is created in which the individual and the collectivity express a new intentional modality. The celebration of the intentional bond occurs in the liminal phase of the ritual and is centered in the performance of the sacrifice. The central phase is liminal and transitional: The ritual actors are freed from structural or social definition while they acquire a new symbolic definition.

The performative paradigm of the figura elaborates the three main phases and conditions of the epigenetic sequence that are intrinsic to the formation of a bond: the originating occasion and condition of the fact coming into being, which carries with it the resolution of modalities that are contrary to the bond, the definition of the bond through the sacrifice, and the public and historical structures instituted by the bond. The whole corresponds to the nascent state and to the process of adaptation within the intentional bond.

Every festival, and indeed the figura as a whole, creates a confrontation between the new and the old, between viable and unviable modalities of the bond. Through the performative pattern, the figura roots the continuity of the cultural symbolic institution in a constant dynamic process.

THE PERIODICITY OF THE FIGURA. The figura is predicated on the correlation of the epigenetic and performative paradigms. In the case of the Christian tradition, the figura is centered on the three initiatory sacramental symbols of baptism, Eucharist, and confirmation. The epigenetic model is defined in terms of transformation from a condition of death to one of life. The transformation is elaborated in a structural and dynamic sequence of active and passive exchanges between God and humanity. The line of action of God toward humans initiates the sequence and is coordinated—in a dialogical structure—with a complementary line of action of humans toward God. Initiated by gift, the sequence passes through a creative intentional crisis that is specified in the sacrifice and leads, at the end of the process of transformation, to a differentiation of a total object relation. The performative model of the festivals of Easter time (which articulates the three dominant sacramental symbols and which is central to the religious year) constitutes an order of relation between intentional events that have been differentiated through the "history of salvation" from creation and the original relation with God to the constitution of the covenant.

From the point of view of the epigenetic performative sequence, the order of "events" in a sacred history derives its significance and constitutive character not primarily from the chronological aspect of the sequence but from its relation to the dynamics and transformations of the intentional bond and from the conditions of continuity of that bond. Together the two complementary models, the epigenetic and the performative, constitute the periodical order of a religious figura which, in its temporal unity, sustains the dynamic continuity of the intentional relation. The three phases of the ritual process translate each of the three epigenetic positions and the sequence as a whole, which develops the institutional forms of the intentional relation into the performative pattern of a fact coming into being.

The sacrifice is at the center of the figura both in the epigenetic sequence and in the performative process. As the point of qualitative change in the creation of the bond, the sacrifice is the active resolution of what is contradictory to the bond and the affirmation of a new condition of total object relation. In the ritual process, the sacrifice specifies the structural differentiation of the intentional bond in its "coming into being." The ritual process may be described as a performative sequence that has an epigenetic function.

The performative articulation of symbols and festivals creates the temporal order of the positions of epigenesis through the ritual sequence while maintaining the explicit connection of each festival and dominant symbol with the central symbolic position elaborated by the sacrifice. This results in a periodical correlation of the different symbols with the transformative structure of the sacrifice. While festivals mark the change related to the symbolic positions, the sacrifice renews the central dynamic of the nascent state of the bond. This periodical process of the figura creates a "dynamic state," which corresponds to the complex intentional relation of the bond.

The calendrical system elaborates the periodical temporal order of the figura, which is ritually performed in the interval of the year through a set of festivals. Recurrent intervals of the year, like the week or the day, offer a rhythmic movement of religious time repeating in ritual form the central paradigm of the figura.

The performance of the figura, which is the original central structure of time, is also the anamnesis and memorial of the foundation of the bond. The historical formation of the calendar shows a progressive differentiation of a set of festivals, which is correlated to the central structure of the figura and which celebrates the apotheosis of the historical founder, the unity of the people of the covenant, and the celebration of those events that have been most significant for the historical continuity and development of the bond. The two orders of time, the periodical symbolic structure of the bond and the celebration of the continuity and the tradition of the bond, are frequently positioned along two discrete temporal axes within the periodical interval of the year. For example, the epigenetic performance may be positioned on the lunar axis; the celebration of the historical formation of the tradition may be positioned on the solar axis. But the religious calendar expresses primarily the order of the temporal epigenetic symbols.

The intentional bond creates and sustains an objective order of relations that is linguistic, institutional, and normative. Although it may appear to be independent of the time of epigenetic performance, this symbolic institutional order has an inherently temporal structure and is ruled by the timelike order of the figura.

The figura is dynamic rather than static, synchronic as well as diachronic; it is related to the event but in such a way that the event may be understood as a nascent state and the creative element of history and continuity. The figura is not an ahistorical archetype, nor is it a rigid whole, obeying some closed formal principle. It is, instead, connected to the history of religious interpretation and ideas; it is internal to the process of formation of intentional action and to that of the social bond. The figura expresses a form of causality that is specific to the intentional character of the historical event.

The individual is directly active in forming and performing the figura but the figura is the way toward the bond for the individual. By defining the dynamic structure of the bond, the figura traces an initiatory path toward the public character of experience. The time of the figura becomes the time and depth of the religious structure of mind of the individual.

The symbolic time system within a culture may present a broad range of historical variation. By the way in which the polar aspects of the figura are emphasized, a tradition may differ in style and in institutional form. For example, Manichaeism and other forms of religious dualism explain the confrontation inherent in the intentional relation as a conflict between two opposite and independent systems of reality and two orders of time. Other religious systems, such as Judaism, connect the religious polarities into one order of relation and correlate the intentional confrontation with the time itself of the intentional bond.

Particular historical styles within one religion, while maintaining the temporal integrity of the figura, may differ in the interpretation and emphasis that they give to the epigenetic or to the performative orders of symbolic time or to one of the dominant symbols. But the religious figura is simultaneously a transformative nascent state and a living tradition. Symbolic time, by sustaining a system of religious reciprocity, an intentional vision, and a processual articulation of reality, is structured in its development and unity as an epiphany of intentional life.

See Also Calendars; Ritual.

Bibliography

Mircea Eliade's *Cosmos and History: The Myth of the Eternal Return* (New York, 1954) remains the fundamental study of periodical return to the mythical time of the origin. Henri Hubert and Marcel Mauss, in "La représentation du temps dans la religion et la magie" in their *Mélanges d'histoire des religions* (Paris, 1909), pp. 189–229, first described the qualitative nature of calendrical time. The performative structure of the ritual process is analyzed in Arnold van Gennep's classic work of 1909, *The Rites of Passage* (Chicago, 1960), and in Victor Turner's *The Ritual Process: Structure and Anti-Structure* (Chicago, 1969). Francesco Alberoni has made a significant contribution to the understanding of dynamic structures of the nascent state in *Movement and Institution* (New York, 1984). Symbolic intentionality is presented in relation to the Christian liturgical year in my book *Tempo symbolico: Liturgia della vita* (Brescia, 1985). Henri-Irénée Marrou offers a thoughtful approach to the theological interpretation of time and history in *Théologie de l'histoire* (Paris, 1968). For an illuminating analysis of studies of time in ancient cultures and of the concept of periodicity in historiography, see Arnaldo Momigliano's "Time in Ancient Historiography," in his *Essays in Ancient and Modern Historiography* (Middletown, Conn., 1977). Clifford Geertz's *The Interpretation of Cultures* (New York, 1973) makes an important contribution to the study of religion as a symbolic system. The temporal forms within narrative are discussed by Paul Ricoeur in *Time and Narrative* (Chicago, 1984).

New Sources

Baumgarten, Albert I., ed. *Apocalyptic Time.* Leiden and Boston, 2000.

Bradshaw, Paul F., and Lawrence A. Hoffman. *Passover and Easter: The Symbolic Structuring of Sacred Seasons.* Notre Dame, Ind., 1999.

Dario Zadra (1987)
Revised Bibliography

SYMEON THE NEW THEOLOGIAN (949–1022)

SYMEON THE NEW THEOLOGIAN (949–1022) was a Christian mystic. Symeon is called "the New Theologian," first because, like John the Evangelist, he speaks of mystical union with the Trinity, and, second, because Gregory of Nazianzus, known as "the Theologian," had also written passionately on the Trinity. Symeon's personal life and his writings reflect a good deal of the polemical, because he considered himself a zealot battling the fossilized segments of the institutional church for a return to radical gospel Christianity. That he, as all mystics who articulated their experiences in writings, would be branded as a dangerous reformer walking the slender line between orthodoxy and heresy is not surprising. His ardent, passionate nature, plus the genuinely rare mystical graces that he had experienced, compounded to "force" him, as he confessed, to share his mystical experiences freely with others.

Symeon was born at Galatia in Paphlagonia (in Asia Minor) in 949. This was the time of the powerful Macedonian dynasty, which had given the Byzantine empire its greatest periods of peace and expanding prosperity. Symeon's parents, Basil and Theophano, belonged to the Byzantine provincial nobility, which had won favor with the administration and had acquired some modicum of wealth.

There are two main sources of knowledge about Symeon's life: the *Life* written by his disciple, Nicetas Stethatos, and the writings of Symeon himself. Symeon's uncle Basil brought him to the imperial court of Constantinople, where he continued his secondary education. Refusing to pursue higher studies, he was taken under direction by a holy monk of the Stoudion monastery in Constantinople, who allowed him to enter the monastery in his twenty-seventh year.

The fervent life of the novice under the guidance of his charismatic spiritual director caused jealousy among the monks, and Symeon transferred to the neighboring monastery of Saint Mamas. Here he made great progress in learning and in spiritual perfection, and within three years he was tonsured monk, ordained priest, and elected abbot. By his discourses (*catecheses*) to his monks, he strove to lead them into a greater consciousness of God's presence indwelling them, but not without stirring up great opposition, especially from Stephen, archbishop of Nicomedia and chief adviser to the patriarch of Constantinople. Stephen emphasized reason, philosophy, and rhetoric in his theology; Symeon's theology was charismatic and apophatic, stressing a mystical and interior way of negation that doubts the capacity of reason to comprehend mystery.

Under attack, and desirous of more solitude for prayer and writing, Symeon resigned as abbot in 1005. Four years later, the official circle of theologians headed by Stephen succeeded in having Symeon exiled to a small town called Paloukiton, near Chrysopolis on the Asiatic shore of the Bosporus. There he passed thirteen years in the small monastery of Saint Marina in prayer and writing, dying in 1022.

Symeon, as one of the most "personal" writers in Byzantine spirituality, reveals himself in his writings in all his sinfulness and ecstatic joy in union with God. His central work can justly be considered his thirty-four discourses, *Catecheses.* As these were preached before a live audience of his fellow monks of Saint Mamas, usually during the morning office of matins, they represent a genre unique in Byzantine spirituality. Two characteristics shine forth in this writing. One sees a most traditional presentation of classical themes common to all the Greek fathers who wrote on the spiritual life of ascesis and contemplation. But on the other hand, one finds a new and insistent accent on the operations of the Holy Spirit to effect the end of the spiritual life and of all Christian ascesis and contemplation, namely, greater mystical union with the indwelling Trinity.

Other writings of Symeon developed around key theological issues as he engaged in controversy with Stephen and other official "scholastic" Byzantine theologians. In these writings Symeon is not exhorting monks but is struggling to combat the heavy rational theology that he felt was destroying true Christianity. His writings collected in *Theological Treatises* form an integrated series focusing on the unity of the Trinity.

The fifteen writings collected in *Ethical Treatises* are much more uneven. The first two treatises deal with the economy of God's salvation; the following nine (numbers 3–11) form a fairly unified presentation of Symeon's doctrine on mysticism; the last four (numbers 12–15) deal with a variety of subjects of a more practical nature concerning the way in which ordinary people in the world can attain salvation.

Symeon's *Practical and Theological Chapters* is a collection of ideas about a variety of topics, probably notes gathered by him on points touching the ascetical and contemplative life of Christians. But it is Symeon's *Hymns of Divine Love,* which he completed shortly before his death in 1022, that will place him in the ranks of the greatest mystics of all time. These are fifty-eight hymns without any unifying theme or system of mystical theology, but they show clearly Symeon's own mystical experiences through the power of poetic rhythm. His mystical experiences and personal love toward Jesus Christ are expressed in a language rarely surpassed by other mystics except those who, like Symeon, had to resort to poetry, as did John of the Cross, to convey the intensity of such ecstatic mystical union. Each hymn is a poetic composition of great power and beauty that can ignite in the reader a desire to strive to attain such "endless light" as Symeon must have enjoyed.

In Symeon were combined the two predominant currents within Eastern Christianity of the earlier centuries. One was the mystical school of the Desert Fathers, which stressed the Semitic concept of a total experience of God and humanity in the *locus Dei,* the place of God in the person called in biblical language the "heart." The second approach was the intellectual mysticism of the Alexandrian school of Clement of Alexandria, Origen, and Evagrios of Pontus. The accent here was on the human mind, which, when purified of the hold of the sensible world of passions, was able to "see" God in an interior light. In addition to producing this synthesis, Symeon was an innovator in writing candidly of his own mystical experiences and in presenting these as normative for all Christians.

Symeon may be judged in the light of his unique, powerful, and affective personality as against the formalism that had suffocated much of the charismatic and mystical elements in the church of Constantinople. His works were rooted in the great traditions of the Eastern Christian fathers, both dogmatically and mystically and, as such, present a balanced Christian mystical theology.

BIBLIOGRAPHY

The critical Greek text with a French translation of Symeon's main works can be found in volumes 51, 96, 104, 113, 122, 129, 156, 174, and 196 of *Sources chrétiennes* (Paris, 1957–1973). An English translation of *Catéchèses* by C. J. de Catanzaro is available in *Symeon the New Theologian: The Discourses* (New York, 1980) in "The Classics of Western Spirituality." My translation of *Hymnes* is in *Hymns of Divine Love by St. Symeon the New Theologian* (Penville, N.J., 1975). Discussion of Symeon's life and thought can be found in my *The Mystic of Fire and Light: St. Symeon, the New Theologian* (Penville, N.J., 1975).

GEORGE A. MALONEY (1987)

SYNAGOGUE. The origins of the synagogue are obscure and will probably never be known. This is in part because the synagogue developed in a nonrevolutionary manner, its significance recognized only once it was a well-established institution of Jewish life. A hint of the original function of this institution may be found in its most prominent Greek and Hebrew names used in antiquity, *sunagōgē* and *beit knesset.* Both refer to an assembly or house of assembly. Numerous theories have been propounded to explain the origins of this institution. The most venerable of these places the origins of the synagogue in Babylonia (modern Iraq) during the sixth century BCE. There, "by the waters of Babylon," this theory suggests, the exiled Judeans assembled to "sing the Lord's song in a strange land" (*Ps.* 137). *Ezekiel* 11:16, "Though I removed them far off among the nations, and though I scattered them among the countries, yet I have been a lesser sanctuary to them for a while in the countries where they have gone," has often been cited in support of this thesis. This approach has roots that go back at least to the medieval period in Babylonia (modern Iraq), and it was developed further by Christian Hebraists beginning in the seventeenth century in their attempt to find biblical antecedents for later Jewish practice. More recent theories place the origins of the synagogue in third-century BCE Egypt, asserting that Jewish "prayer places" (*proseuchē*) described in inscriptions were in fact the earliest synagogues, or elsewhere in the Western Diaspora. These approaches assert the priority of exile and hence distance from the Jerusalem Temple as a determining factor in the formation of the synagogue. In recent years the origins of the synagogue in biblical Israel have been asserted. According to this theory, the Second Temple–period synagogue was the descendant of the "gate of the city" of biblical times. None of these approaches is supported by sufficient data.

An approach that is more clearly supported by the available evidence suggests that the synagogue as a place for religious ritual was a development of the later Second Temple period. This approach begins with the fact that institutions known as "synagogues" are clearly evidenced in literary and archaeological sources from the first century CE, and it cautiously assumes a development that occurred before synagogues were mentioned in literary texts without asserting a specific moment when the first synagogue appeared. A long prehistory is assumed by *Acts of the Apostles* 15:21, by Josephus Flavius (*Against Apion* 2.175), and by the ancient rabbis (e.g., *t. Megillah* 2:12), all of whom assert the existence of synagogues in hoary biblical antiquity. The factors occasioning the earliest development of the synagogue were shared by other communities in the Greco-Roman world. The general trend toward smaller religious communities that existed side by side with the major cults of each city was adopted by Jews in Palestine and in Diaspora settings. This phenomenon may be evidenced in Egypt as early as the third century, if the "prayer places" (*proseuchē*) known from epigraphy were in any way similar to "prayer places" known from the writings of the first-century Egyptian scholar Philo of Alexandria. A Jewish "prayer place" from the second century BCE was discovered on the Greek island of Delos. We have no idea what kinds of "prayer" took place in these early "prayer places." By the first century (and undoubtedly much earlier) the increasing significance of Scripture and its interpretation in Second Temple–period Judaism set the liturgical frame for these synagogues. This focus on Scripture and scriptural interpretation is expressed early on in the public ceremony of reading and interpreting the Pentateuch described in *Nehemiah* 8, a Persian-period text that exercised a profound influence upon later synagogue practice.

The best evidence for synagogues during the first century is a monumental inscription found just south of the Temple Mount in Jerusalem by R. Weill in 1913–1914. This Greek inscription translates:

> Theodotos, son of Vettenos the priest and synagogue leader (*archisynagogos*), son of a synagogue leader and grandson of a synagogue leader, built the synagogue for the reading of the Torah and studying of the commandments, and as a hostel with chambers and water installations to provide for the needs of itinerants from abroad, which his fathers, the elders and Simonides founded.

The *terminus ad quem* for the inscription is the destruction of Jerusalem by the Romans in 70 CE. It provides evidence of three generations of priestly synagogue leaders. The liturgical focal point for this, and for every other Second Temple–period text that has been recovered, is scriptural study. This is clearly the element that distinguished synagogue liturgy, both for Jews and non-Jews. Philo describes the Sabbath liturgy of an Essene "synagogue" in Palestine:

> For that day has been set apart to be kept holy and on it they abstain from all other work and proceed to sacred places (*hierous. . .topous*) that they call synagogues (*sunagogai*). There, arranged in rows according to their ages, the younger below the elder, they sit decorously as befits the occasion with attentive ears. Then one takes the books (*biblous*) and reads aloud and another of especial proficiency comes forward and expounds what is not understood. . . .

Luke 4:16–30 and the *Acts of the Apostles* 13:15–16 provide additional early illustrations of public Scripture reading and explication in synagogues. It is unknown whether other liturgical acts were performed in synagogues at this time, though ample numbers of later Second Temple–period Jewish prayer texts are extant.

It is likely that the earliest synagogue buildings (like many after them) were simply rooms within domestic structures with no special renovations, and hence are unidentifiable archaeologically. Five purpose-built or purpose-renovated buildings that might be identified as later Second Temple–period synagogues have been excavated in Israel. These were uncovered at Masada, Gamla, Herodian, Kiryat Sefer, and Modi'in. Other supposed synagogues, at Magdala, Capernaum, and Jericho, are far less likely. Gamla is the earliest synagogue. This large public building was built on the eastern side of Gamla, next to the city wall. Built of local basalt, this structure is rectangular (13.4 by 17 meters). The main entrance was on the west, with an exedra and an open court in front of it. The center of the hall was unpaved and surrounded (except for the main entrance) by stepped benches. The synagogue at Masada is a ten-meter-square room that was converted by the Jewish rebels who inhabited this desert fortress from 66 to 74 CE. The rebels added banks of benches on each wall, and a small room on the northwestern wall within which were found fragments of the books of *Deuteronomy* and *Ezekiel.* The literary definition of the first-century synagogue as a house of assembly where Scripture was studied is uniquely paralleled in this structure. At Herodian a room was converted by Jewish rebels with the addition of benches that were similar to those at Masada. The synagogues at Kiryat Sefer and Modi'in are small freestanding structures with benches lining the walls. It seems likely that these communal buildings served as synagogues as well, though there is no epigraphic evidence to support this identification.

LATE ANTIQUITY: THE LATE ROMAN AND BYZANTINE PERIODS. Evidence for synagogues during the second through the fourth centuries is mostly literary. Rabbinic literature from Palestine and from Sassanid Babylonia (modern Iraq) present synagogues as regular features of the Jewish communal landscape. Early rabbinic (Tannaitic) literature mentions a broad range of activities that took place within synagogues. These included the recitation of Aramaic translations of the Torah reading (*m. Megillah* 4:6,10), Torah blessings (*t. Kippurim* 3:18), sounding of the ram's horn (*shofar*) on the new year (*m. Rosh Hashanah* 3:7), use of the palm frond (*lulav*), myrtle, willow, and citron (*ethrog*) on the feast of Tabernacles (*m. Sukkah* 3:13; *t. Sukkah* 2:10), recitation of the *Book of Esther* reading on the Feast of Esther (Purim), possibly even by women (*m. Megillah* 2:4), recitation of the *hallel* psalms (*t. Pesahim* 10:8), eulogies (*t. Megillah* 2:18), public oaths (*m. Shevuot* 4:10), local charity collection (*t. Shabbat* 16:22; *t. Terumah* 1:10; *t. Baba Batra* 8:4; Matt. 6:2), communal meals (*m. Zavim* 3:2; *m. Bekhorot* 5:5). By the third century they were also used as elementary schools (*y. Megillah* 3:4, 73a). Rabbinic literature suggests the development of an increasingly standardized public liturgical tradition, important elements of which were enacted within synagogues (e.g., *m. Berakhot* 7:3). Rabbinic public prayer (the "public" defined as a quorum of at least ten men) took place in formal thrice-daily sessions as well as in the context of communal meals. This format continues to this day. In liberal Jewish communities the quorum now includes women. In antiquity there was considerable variation in custom dependent on locality and scholar, modern scholars differing on the balance between variation and standardization. Rabbinic liturgy was built around the recitation of the "Shema (*Deut.* 6:4–9, 11:13–21; *Num.* 15:37–40) and its blessings" together with the Eighteen Benedictions (also known as the "Standing prayer," the *Amidah*) morning and evening, and the Eighteen Benedictions with accompanying liturgy in afternoon prayers. Prayer times, though not the content of these rituals, were associated with the times of the Temple sacrifices. By the third century public prayer was described homiletically as being equivalent in efficacy to sacrifices in the Temple, although the notion of the rebuilding of the Jerusalem Temple was never questioned in liturgical terms until the advent of modern Reform Judaism. In rabbinic times synagogue prayer and the preexisting public reading of Scripture melded into a single liturgical structure. The Torah was publicly read, with attendant blessings, in the morning and afternoon services on the Sabbath and festivals and on Monday and Thursday mornings. A reading from the prophets (the *haftarah*) accompanied the Sabbath morning and festival Torah reading. Scripture reading was simultaneously translated into Aramaic (later concretized in *Targum* texts such those preserved in *Targum Neofiti* and *Targum Onkelos*), a tradition that was popular into the early Middle Ages and is still followed by Yemenite Jews. Various cycles for reading Torah existed in antiquity. Palestinians generally completed the entire Pentateuch in something more than three years, while Babylonians read on a yearly cycle. The Babylonian custom is followed in all traditional communities today.

The increase in synagogue functions was paralleled by the developing notion that synagogues were in some way holy. Mishnah *Megillah* 3:1–3 describes the centrality of Scripture within the synagogue, as well as the transient holiness ascribed to this institution by the early rabbis. At the focal point of the synagogue, this text suggests, was the Torah scroll, which stood at the top of a hierarchy:

> The people of a town who sold their town square: They must buy a synagogue with its proceeds; If they sell a synagogue, they must acquire a (scroll) chest. If they sell a (scroll) chest, they must acquire cloths (to wrap sacred scrolls). If they sell cloths, they must acquire books (of the Prophets and Writings). If they sell books, they must acquire a Pentateuch (scroll). But, if they sell a Pentateuch, they may not acquire books (of the Prophets and Writings). And if they sell books, they may not acquire cloths. And if they sell cloths, they may not acquire a chest, And if they sell a chest, they may not acquire a synagogue. And if they sell a synagogue, they may not acquire town square.

Tosefta *Sukkah* 4:6 projects a second-century Palestinian reality onto a great synagogue in Alexandria. This text focuses attention upon a large podium (*bimah*) upon which the biblical texts were read, with no mention of a Torah shrine. An ideal synagogue is described in Tosefta *Megillah* 21–23, which establishes categories that set the parameters of Jewish legal discussions of synagogue architecture for the next two millennia. At the same time it suggests a second focal point within synagogues: orientation toward Jerusalem.

> The Community leader (*hazan ha-knesset*) arises to read, someone stands until the time when he reads. How do the elders sit? Facing the people, their backs to the *qodesh*. When they set down the (Scroll) chest—its front is toward the people, its back to the *qodesh*. The *hazan ha-knesset* faces the *qodesh*. All the people face the *qodesh*. For it is said: "and the congregation was assembled at the door of the tent of meeting (Lev. 8:4)." The doors of the synagogue are built on the eastern side, for thus we find in the Tabernacle, for it is said: "Before the Tabernacle toward the east, before the tent of meeting eastward (*Num.* 3:38)." It is only built at the highest point of the town, for it is written: "Above the bustling (streets) she (wisdom, i.e., Torah) calls out (Prov. 1:21)."

The location of the synagogue and some of its internal arrangement are articulated through reference to the biblical Tabernacle and the Temple of Jerusalem. Alignment toward Jerusalem as focused through a Torah cabinet became basic to synagogue architecture, as did the notion that the ideal synagogue should be higher than the surrounding structures (the latter having generally been kept in the breach). The identification of the synagogue with the Temple was a developing concept throughout antiquity and the medieval period. By the third century the cabinet (*teva*) was being called *arona* (cabinet, reminiscent of the Ark of the Covenant), and its curtain *parokhta,* reminiscent of the Temple curtain. There is no evidence for the physical separation of men and women in ancient synagogues, though a social distinction existed. Physical gender separation is known beginning during the early Middle Ages, when it was seen as an expression of the holiness of the synagogue due to its conceptual relationship with the Temple (where gender separation sometimes occurred).

The dual foci—the scrolls as local cult object along with a more subtle physical alignment in the direction of Jerusalem—became ideologically significant features of almost all synagogues until modern times. While the standard codes of Jewish law all legislate that the synagogue interior be aligned toward the Torah shrine on the Jerusalem wall of the synagogue, local realities were far more complex even in the most rabbinically oriented medieval and early modern communities.

Archaeological evidence for purpose-built synagogues begins to appear during the late third or early fourth century, becoming quite common between the fifth and ninth centuries. Undoubtedly there were many other buildings that are archaeologically unidentifiable as synagogues. More than one hundred synagogues are known archaeologically from the Land of Israel, and another ten structures have been discovered that served Diaspora communities. At least 150 Diaspora synagogues are known from literary and archaeological sources. The earliest extant late-antique synagogue is also one of the most important. The synagogue discovered at Dura Europos, a city in the Syrian desert, is the earliest yet discovered, and among the most important. Excavated in 1932, the Dura synagogue was built as a renovated private dwelling. Sometime before 244–245 this dwelling was renovated as a synagogue. The largest room was renovated for this purpose, with a large Torah shrine built on the western (Jerusalem-aligned) wall and benches around the walls. The façade of the Torah shrine was decorated with the image of the Jerusalem Temple, flanked on the right by the Binding of Isaac (which according to *2 Chronicles* 3:1 took place on "Mt. Moriah," the Temple Mount) and on the left by a seven-branched menorah, a palm frond (*lulav*), and citron (*ethrog*). There was some other painting, lost in a massive renovation of the synagogue that took place in 244–245. At that time the walls were completely covered with paintings drawn from the Hebrew Bible and read through the prism of Jewish biblical interpretation (midrash). Sixty percent of the paintings have been preserved. Themes are generally heroic, reflecting such themes as the Discovery of Moses by the Daughter of Pharaoh, the Crossing of the Read Sea, the Tribes encamped around the Tabernacle, Ezekiel's Vision of the Dry Bones, and Esther before King Ahasveros. The paintings show profound parallels with traditions preserved in rabbinic literature, as do Aramaic and Persian inscriptions on the paintings and a Jewish liturgical parchment found near the synagogue. The Dura synagogue has been interpreted as a forerunner of Christian art and as evidence for a supposed late-antique "nonrabbinic Judaism." The evidence is actually much closer to rabbinic tradition than most contemporary scholars have suggested.

Archaeological evidence for synagogues increases from the fourth century onward. Synagogues conforming to three main architectural types were constructed by Jews in late antique Palestine: the broadhouse (e.g., Horvat Shema, Eshtemoa), the "Galilean-type" basilica (e.g., Capernaum, Kefar Baram), and longhouse basilicas (e.g., Hammath Tiberias B, stratum 2a), which from the latter fifth or sixth century onward often were apsidal (Beth Alpha, Na'aran).

The interior space of most of these synagogues was aligned toward a permanent Torah shrine, which usually stood on the Jerusalem-aligned side of the synagogue. The basilica form was used by both Jews and Christians beginning around the turn of the fourth century. "Broadhouse-type" synagogues have benches built around the interior walls, focusing attention upon the center of the room. The broadhouses from the Hebron Hills (e.g., Eshtemoa, Khirbet Susiya) form a regional type. The entrances of these halls were aligned toward the east. The eastward alignment is perhaps modeled upon the Temple, and parallels Tosefta Megillah 3:23. The interior of the synagogue hall was aligned toward the Torah shrine, which stood on the Jerusalem-aligned wall.

Galilean-type basilicas are architecturally related to the narrow gable churches of nearby Syria. Like these churches, most Galilean-type synagogues were entered through three portals. A unique feature of these synagogues is the arrangement of the interior columns. Columns were constructed on the northern, eastern, and western sides of the hall. This served to focus attention on the interior of the southern, Jerusalem wall with its three portals. Scholars have posited that Torah shrines were constructed between the doors on the Jerusalem wall at Capernaum, Chorazin, and Meiron. In an instructive parallel, S. D. Goitein notes that in synagogues in Yemen two entrances flank the Torah shrine on the Jerusalem wall and that this arrangement existed in a synagogue in medieval Hebron.

Basilical synagogues were constructed throughout the Land of Israel. In "basilica-type" synagogues the visitor might cross the expanse of the atrium, sometimes a narthex, and the nave, to reach the Jerusalem-aligned wall. At the center of this wall was the building's focal point, the Torah shrine, which often stood upon a raised platform. Following contemporary church architecture, synagogues from the late fifth century onward often included an apse on the Jerusalem wall that housed the Torah shrine, and the platform was often surrounded by a low partition (called in Christian context a "chancel screen") decorated with Jewish iconography.

The art of Palestinian synagogues, particularly decorated mosaics, is an integral part of the late Roman and Byzantine artistic tradition. The synagogue at Beth Alpha contains the most completely preserved Byzantine period mosaic and well exemplifies this tradition. It builds on iconography well known from the Hammath Tiberias B, 2a mosaic, with its images of the zodiac and a panel containing a Torah shrine flanked by two menorahs. The Beth Alpha mosaic is divided into three panels. As at Hammath Tiberias, closest to the Torah shrine of the synagogue is a panel containing the image of a shrine flanked by lighted menorahs. In the center is a zodiac wheel, personifications of the seasons in the corners, and unique to this building, closest to the entrance to the synagogue, the image of the Binding of Isaac (*Genesis* 22).

Zodiacs and some other images are often labeled in Hebrew, the language of Scripture and most liturgy, even as dedicatory inscriptions appear in Aramaic and Greek. At Beth Alpha the narrative of the scene is glossed with biblical citations in Hebrew. Biblical themes in other synagogues include David (Gaza), Daniel in the Lion's Den (Na'aran and Khirbet Susiya), and Gerasa (Noah's Ark, labeled in Greek). Sepphoris contains the Angelic Visitation to Abraham (*Genesis* 18), the Binding of Isaac, Aaron before the Tabernacle, and other cultic imagery. Jews continued to use images of the zodiac long after Christians abandoned this imagery, owing to the significance of the heavens and constructions of time in Jewish thought and liturgy.

Archaeological remains of late-antique synagogues show important parallels to contemporaneous liturgical and rabbinic texts. This is particularly evident in inscriptions, where formulae show clear relationships with literary sources. A very significant example is the Rehov inscription, discovered in the narthex of a sixth-century synagogue. This twenty-nine-line inscription, which deals with local agricultural law, is the earliest extant physical evidence of a rabbinic text. Increased decoration of the physical environment of Palestinian synagogues paralleled the development of increasingly complex liturgical texts. Professional poets composed prayers for each Sabbath and festival according to the local reading cycles. These texts (*piyyutim*) were often quite complex. Named poets appear from the fourth century onward, beginning with Yosse ben Yosse, Yannai, Eleazar son of Rabbi Qallir, Yehuda, and Yohanan the Priest. These homiletic texts strongly parallel public homilies (*midrashim*) and traditions in Targumic literature. There is no theme in synagogue art that does not find important parallels in these literatures. The tradition of virtuoso poets preparing liturgical compositions for synagogue performance continued through the Middle Ages, particularly (though hardly exclusively) in areas of Italy and Northern Europe that continued elements of the Palestinian liturgical tradition.

Known Diaspora synagogues during this period conform to local architectural norms. What unifies them are the presence of a large Torah shrine and often images of menorahs. Other than Dura, the most impressive extant Diaspora synagogues were uncovered in Ostia Antica, the ancient port of Rome, and in Sardis in Asia Minor. The Ostia synagogue building was first constructed toward the end of the first century of the Common Era, though it is not known whether it served as a synagogue at this point. The use of the building as a synagogue went through two stages. It was enlarged during the second and third centuries, then enlarged further and partly rebuilt at the beginning of the fourth. The entrances in the façade of the basilica from the second through third centuries are aligned toward the east-southeast, perhaps in the direction of Jerusalem. A stepped podium stood on the wall opposite the main entrance. A Latin and Greek inscription from this phase makes mention of a shrine for the Torah:

> For the well-being of the emperor! Mindus Faustus established and built (it) and set up the ark (*keiboton*) of the Holy Torah (*nomo hagio*).

During the fourth century the southernmost entrance portal on the eastern wall of the synagogue was sealed and replaced with a large freestanding Torah shrine. This Torah shrine is structurally contiguous with images of shrines in wall paintings and gold glasses discovered in the Jewish catacombs of Rome and with images on oil lamps discovered in Ostia.

The Sardis synagogue is the largest and the grandest synagogue yet uncovered, its main hall measuring fifty-four by eighteen meters. It has been estimated that the synagogue could accommodate one thousand people. This impressive building, the largest synagogue known before the modern period, was part of the municipal center of Sardis and taken over by the Jewish community and remodeled as a synagogue during the fourth century. It formed the southern side of the civic center of Sardis. The remodeling included the installation of two aediculae on stepped podia on the eastern wall of the synagogue and the construction of a podium in the center of the hall. The significance of these aediculae is made clear both by their prominence and by an inscription found near them that reads "Find, open, read, observe." Another Greek inscription refers to the Torah shrine as the *nomophylakion,* "the place that protects the Torah." A molding from the synagogue contains both an inscribed menorah and the image of a Torah shrine with its doors open to show scrolls stacked horizontally within it.

We know little of the liturgies of Jews in the western Diaspora. John Chrysostom describes synagogue customs in fourth-century Antioch as part of his polemic *Against the Jews,* aimed against Judaizers within his community. These include blowing the ram's horn on Rosh Hashannah, walking barefooted and fasting on Yom Kippur (known from rabbinic literature), and incubation in synagogues. He also knows that Jews and non-Jews considered synagogues to be holy places, the sanctity of the place being construed as deriving from the presence of biblical scrolls. Chrysostom suggests that reading of *Psalms* was important to synagogue liturgy. Inscriptions, most notably a Greek rendition of *Psalm* 135:25 discovered in ancient Nicaea (today Iznik in Turkey) supports this. These characteristics (other than incubation) were also prevalent in synagogues in Palestine and in Sassanian Iraq that are described in the Babylonian Talmud. The great significance of Torah shrines and images of shrines full of scrolls suggests the centrality of Scripture within Diaspora communities, as it was for communities in the Land of Israel.

MEDIEVAL AND MODERN SYNAGOGUES. Liturgies during medieval and modern times were largely based upon models developed already in classical rabbinic literature. While significant differences exist between Ashkenazic (Central and Eastern European) rites, Sephardic (Spanish and Portuguese) rites, Italian, and the rites of Jews in the lands of Islam, the differences are far outweighed by the continuities. Modern liturgies maintain continuity to the extent that each movement sees itself as bound by Talmudic tradition. The interior furnishings of synagogues also follow ancient models as preserved in rabbinic sources. These include a large permanent Torah shrine (called *aron ha-qodesh,* "Holy Ark" by Ashkenazim; *hekhal,* "shrine," by Sephardim), generally on the

Jerusalem-aligned wall of the synagogue and a platform for reading Scripture.

In all periods of Jewish history, the physical structure of the purpose-built synagogue buildings generally followed the styles prevailing in contemporary non-Jewish architecture. Neither early rabbinic literature nor later medieval and modern rabbinic scholars focused on the architectural aspects of the synagogue. Architects, however, were confronted with a major liturgical problem. Since two major components of the synagogue were the Torah shrine and the platform (*bimah*) from which it was read, the spatial relationship between the two had to be resolved. The sixteenth-century Sephardic legalist Joseph Caro (1488–1575) reflects on this tension. Caro debates whether the platform must be placed in the center of the hall or whether it could be joined with the Torah shrine, usually on the Jerusalem-aligned side of the building. Caro writes: "the placement [of the *bimah*] in the center is not required, rather everything depends upon the locality and the time. . ." (*Kesef Mishneh* to Maimonides' *Mishneh Torah* 11:3). Solutions (and nonsolutions) differed from community to community. In Central Europe, for example, the center of attention was the *almemor,* the reading podium, which dominated the entire space. In baroque and rococo Italy, however, a harmonious solution was found between the reading podium and the Torah shrine by placing them at opposite ends of the hall, connected by a broad and open central aisle. Seating was placed on the sides. In such a way neither dominated but both contributed to a sense of balance.

MEDIEVAL AND PRE-EMANCIPATION SYNAGOGUES. Much of what we know about synagogues in Byzantine Palestine and under medieval Islam is derived from the documents discovered in the repository of the medieval Ben Ezra Synagogue in old Cairo (Fostat), itself an exceptional example of synagogue architecture under Islam. Archaeological evidence for medieval European synagogues is widespread beginning near the turn of the first millennium. The famous Worms synagogue, built in 1175, is generally accepted by scholars as the oldest surviving medieval synagogue. Although the original was destroyed by the Nazis, a faithful reconstruction now stands in its place. Its double-nave building, patterned after Romanesque chapter houses of convents and monastic refectories suggest a model that is found in such later Ashkenazic synagogues as the famous late thirteenth-century Altneuschul of Prague, the old synagogue of Kraców (in the suburb of Kazimierz), and those of Regensburg, in Bavaria, and Buda (now part of the city of Budapest). The *almemor (bimah)* in these synagogues predominated: it stood in the center between two columns or piers.

There are two synagogues extant in Toledo, Spain, albeit transformed into churches after the expulsion in 1492: the five-aisled synagogue later known as Santa María la Blanca and the synagogue later known as El Tránsito. In style Santa María la Blanca resembles twelfth-century Moroccan mosques. El Tránsito was built around 1357 by Shemu'el ha-Levi Abulafia, treasurer to King Pedro the Cruel of Castile. Its ornamental plasterwork with Hebrew inscriptions and Mudéjar designs is especially noteworthy. The Sephardic (Spanish-Portuguese) synagogue of Amsterdam, designed by the Dutch architect Elias Bouman around 1675, became the prototype for synagogues for the entire Sephardic world. The Amsterdam synagogue, a large, galleried basilican hall, was clearly inspired by neighboring Protestant churches.

The many rural wooden synagogues in Poland, Lithuania, and the Ukraine, most destroyed by the Nazis, are most interesting. Dating from the seventeenth to the nineteenth centuries, these wooden synagogues, probably constructed by anonymous Jewish craftsmen, had intricate multicolored painted interiors. In many of them, four wooden columns supported the interior domed *bimah.* Numerous synagogues are extant from this period from Islamic countries, India, and elsewhere in Asia and the Americas. Among the most exotic is a synagogue known only from drawings dated 1722 by a Jesuit missionary. The synagogue of Kaifeng, China, was built in a local vernacular architecture and furnishings. A raised *bimah* stood at the center of the prayer hall, with a Torah shine aligned toward Jerusalem on the western wall.

MODERN SYNAGOGUE ARCHITECTURE. During the nineteenth century, when Jews in Western Europe were emancipated and American Jews strove for full acceptance, prominent architects, some of whom were Jewish, built large and impressive synagogues as statements of the new status of Jews in Western society. These synagogues were often built in neo-Islamic and neo-Byzantine styles (although sometimes the Romanesque was employed), ostensibly to emphasize the Eastern origins of Judaism. Neoclassical synagogues were also constructed, especially in America at the turn of the twentieth century as an alternative to Christian and Moslem architecture and as a statement of a developing Jewish-American synthesis.

In the modern period, many innovations have been introduced to synagogue architecture, particularly within liberal communities. Separate seating for women has been eliminated in liberal synagogues, thus generally making balconies or separate rooms unnecessary. In America, Reform (and today, many Conservative) synagogues are referred to as "temples," originally in an attempt to distance their communities from traditional beliefs in the messianic return to Zion and the rebuilding of the Jerusalem Temple and to avoid the term "synagogue," which had negative connotations in Christian circles. Prayer services became far less participatory and hierarchical, following Protestant liturgical models. This was expressed architecturally through the construction of a single podium at the focal point of the synagogue, which housed a Torah shrine, a reading table (often turned toward the congregation rather than toward the shrine), and a speaking lectern. During the postwar years daring experimentation by such leading architects as Frank Lloyd Wright and Erich Mendelssohn employed a modernist aesthetic for American synagogue buildings. Synagogues were consciously integrated into their surroundings, and the maximum use of glass brings nature into the sanctuary. Recent years have seen a turning away from the monumentality of the nineteenth- and twentieth-century edifices. Synagogue architecture in America has become far less monumental, responding to a current the focus on "spirituality" and "community." The central *bimah* has reappeared in liberal synagogues (and reasserted itself within Orthodox contexts), as more participatory and less hierarchical liturgical forms have emerged.

See Also Judaism, overview article.

Bibliography

Fine, Steven. *Art and Judaism During the Greco-Roman Period: Toward a New "Jewish Archaeology."* Cambridge, 2005. In addition to presenting a liturgical analysis of ancient synagogue remains and further reflection on the notion of synagogue holiness, Fine discusses the significance of ideology and influence of ancient synagogue architecture in the construction of American neoclassical synagogues.

Fine, Steven, ed. *Sacred Realm: The Emergence of the Synagogue in the Ancient World.* New York, 1996. Essays by Fine, E. Meyers, L. Rutgers, L. Feldman, R. Hachlili, and A. Shinan survey the history, literature and archaeology in the ancient world.

Grossman, Susan, and Rivka Haut, eds. *Daughters of the King: Women in the Synagogue.* New York, 1992. Essays in this volume discuss both the history of women's participation in synagogue life and more recent developments in North American Jewish communities.

Gruber, Sam. "Archaeological Remains of Ashkenazic Jewry in Europe: A New Source of Pride and History." In *What Athens Has to Do with Jerusalem: Essays in Classical, Jewish, and Early Christian Archaeology in Honor of Gideon Foerster,* ed. L. Rutgers, pp. 267–301. Louvain, 2002. The most recent and comprehensive study of archaeological remains of early European synagogues.

Gruber, Sam. *American Synagogues: A Century of Architecture and Jewish Community.* New York, 2003. A general presentation of the history and architecture of synagogues in America during the twentieth century.

Gutmann, Joseph. *The Jewish Sanctuary.* Leiden, Netherlands, 1983. An introduction to the synagogue, its art and architecture.

Jarrassé, Dominique. *Synagogues: Architecture and Jewish Identity.* Paris, 2001. This survey of synagogue architecture is refreshing both because it is not focused on the United States, but on synagogues of the Islamic world and Asia.

Krinsky, Carol H. *Synagogues of Europe.* New York, 1985. Krinsky surveys the architectural history of the synagogue in Europe.

Lambert, Phyllis, ed. *Fortifications and the Synagogue: The Fortress of Babylon and the Ben Ezra Synagogue, Cairo.* Montreal, 2001. An in-depth study of the Ben Ezra synagogue in Cairo, this collection throws considerable light on the history of the synagogue during the medieval and modern periods in the lands of Islam.

Levine, L. I. *The Synagogue: The First Thousand Years.* New Haven, Conn., 2000. A handbook for the study of the synagogue from its origins to the rise of Islam.

Reif, Stefan C. *Judaism and Hebrew Prayer.* Cambridge, U.K., 1993. A survey of the history of Jewish prayer from its origins to the modern period.

Joseph Gutmann (1987)
Steven Fine (2005)

SYNCRETISM [FIRST EDITION].

The term *syncretism* usually refers to connections of a special kind between languages, cultures, or religions. This term is most frequently used in the history of religions, where a special effort has been made to give it a more precise meaning.

History and Usefulness of the Concept. The term *sugkrētismos* first occurs in Plutarch (*Moralia* 490ab). It was probably based on *sugkrētos* (Ionian form of *sugkratos,* "mixed together") and was explained by popular etymology or by Plutarch himself as referring to the behavior of the Cretans who, despite the discord habitual among them, closed ranks when an external enemy attacked them. Early interpretations, which reversed the relation between coinage and meaning, may be left aside. Discussions of the term in the *Suda* (4.451), the *Etymologicum magnum* (732.54f.), and Erasmus's *Adagia* (27) and *Epistolae* (3.539) are based on Plutarch's explanation, which was thus transmitted to the modern period. Efforts at reconciliation between Molinists and Thomists in the sixteenth century and between Lutherans and Calvinists in the seventeenth century can be criticized as syncretist. The first application of the term to a situation in the history of religions probably ocurred in an anonymous review (of an edition of Minucius Felix) that appeared in Fraser's *Magazine for Town and Country* (London, 1853, vol. 47, p. 294). Thereafter it appeared rather frequently in the science of religion and historical theology of the second half of the nineteenth century. Hermann Usener (*Götternamen,* 1896; 1928, pp. 337–340) rendered it as "mishmash of religions" (*Religionsmischerei*). In German, *Mischerei,* unlike *Mischung* ("mixture, blending"), has negative overtones, and in fact Usener regarded the phenomenon of syncretism as an unprincipled abandonment of the faith of the Fathers, even though it was at the same time a necessary transitional stage in the history of religions. Later on, the word came to be used mostly without negative overtones, but it continued to be applied in all sorts of ways.

As an explanatory category. Precise application makes it clear that no definition of syncretism is possible without a specific context and that the term cannot serve as an adequate description of homogeneous sets of phenomena. It is possible, nonetheless, to use the concept of syncretism as a category of historico-genetic explanation. It makes possible a critique of the Romantic ideological contrast between syncretism and pure national tradition or, as the case may be, uncontaminated popular religion. In addition, it is a useful heuristic tool for tracking down otherwise hidden antecedents of historical facts, as well as for identifying the phenomenon of syncretism itself as something (requiring later definition) that can in turn be an antecedent for subsequent factual situations. The concept also contributes to a sociopsychological clarification of a readiness for the balancing, subordination, superordination, and unification of truth.

As a description of phenomena. In the use of the concept of syncretism there is no *adaequatio intellectus et rei* ("correspondence of mind and object"). The concept is in principle a tool for interpretation and as such is in principle independent of the term inherited from antiquity. Agreement must be reached on what the term is to mean here and now. The parties to the agreement must see to it that the constituents of the concept are close enough to one another, despite the diversity in the phenomena, that a unity of type is preserved. An individual connection is not to be described as syncretist when taken in isolation but only when it is seen as an element in a complex unity.

Typology of Phenomena. Since it is not possible to apply the concept of syncretism in a universal, univocal way, a typology is needed. For present purposes we may propose two main headings, as follows.

Relations between complex wholes. A complex unity or whole can be any coherence of mental elements and of actions, representations, or objects related to these elements, which has the function of giving human beings an irreducible explanation of their world, as well as norms that are likewise not further reducible. The coherence can take sociological form in an organization or institution, though it need not; in its intellectual expression it can be presented as a system but may also take some other doctrinal form.

Relations between particular components. Particular components of a religion (e.g., its gods) can also be linked to one another in various ways. They can be identified; new relations can be established between them; various shifts may occur within a pantheon due to encounters with another pantheon. Such particular relations, which are established quasi-organically (at least at the popular level) and anonymously, presuppose relations between complex units or wholes. But a particular component can also be the creation of a literary author. Here the establishment of particular relations can be undertaken by individuals and without any connection in principle with more comprehensive encounters between cultures and religions, even where the latter have occurred. Many an author has established his own syncretism (e.g., in the Hellenistic age of late antiquity certain Pythagoreans, astrologers, Orphics, Physikoi, the various compilers of the Hermetic corpus and the sibylline and Chaldean oracles, the Tübingen theosophists, alchemists, Lukianos of Samosata, Aelius Aristides, Numenius of Apamea, Porphyry, Iamblichus, and Sallust).

The Late-Twentieth-Century State of Scholarship. When the concept of syncretism is used in describing phenomena, the application of the term is still not the result of an analysis; rather, it serves as a disparaging judgment on certain manifestations, a judgment assumed to be obvious. The adjective *syncretic*, used in this way, occurs in countless treatises on religions, where it designates both simple and complex phenomena; its definition is taken for granted and various inferences are drawn from it. Only in the 1970s were initial efforts undertaken to distinguish between the concept and the array of phenomena.

Subsequent stages in scholarship are represented by the conferences on the problem that were held in Äbo (1966), Göttingen (Reinhausen) and Strasbourg (both in 1971), Santa Barbara (1972), and Besançon (1973). These have led to various consensuses. The present article attempts simply to advance the consensus, but it cannot promise any certain results.

System and history. The concept of syncretism can be used to describe either a state or a process. It is used in the first way if, for example, an entire religion—or its particular components or traits—are described as a syncretism or as syncretic. In this case the concept is applied statically to describe a state or condition in which the characteristics of the object are systematically correlated among themselves.

The concept is used processually when we speak of a syncretic tendency or development, or of a development that will end in syncretism. Syncretism is here understood as a process which extends through time and in which gradations or stages of development are to be distinguished. This may be called a dynamic concept of syncretism. An attempt has been made to capture this dimension of syncretism in neologisms like *syncretization.*

Syncretism in History. It follows from the above that a project for a "history of syncretism" would be inappropriate. All that can be done is to point out constellations in the general history of religions that have made possible what historians may, under certain conditions, call "syncretism." The syncretic results of these constellations as such are not initially cohesive in respect to content, although such cohesiveness may of course occur. The location of such results under the concept of syncretism depends on a genetic and typological analysis. At the present time such an analysis can only take the form of a classification. The present article is therefore organized along classificatory lines, but within the classes suggested the examples offered will be in chronological order.

Presuppositions. Religious entities that were originally separate can come together in such a way that a syncretism results. The first possible result is that what is superimposed predominates, while what is older survives. This happened, for example, in the Nabatean and Palmyrene religions of the Hellenistic period, and in the associations that arose as a result of Christian missionization in Africa. A second possibility is that the substratum continues to exercise dominance; for example, the Sumerian substratum in relation to the Akkadian superimposition, the Celtic substratum in relation to the Roman superimposition, and perhaps the Germanic eschatology in relation to a superimposed Oriental one. A third possibility is that a balance may be established between the various components, as, for example, in Manichaeism or in some pseudo-Islamic sects (such as Ahl i Haqq, the Druze, the Yesids). In addition to a syncretism of what was originally separate, there is a syncretism of elements from related sources. Jewish, Christian, Islamic, and Marxist eschatologies, for example, are all related, yet each of them developed into something so independent of the others that the few attempts, mostly of a literary kind, which have been made to fuse them or reduce them to a common denominator can, with reservations, be called syncretist.

Syncretism in religion need not be accompanied by syncretism in other areas. In principle, the coincidence and non-coincidence of diverse syncretisms occur with equal frequency. Though it seems odd to speak of a "mixed" language or of a "mixed" culture, since any culture in principle always has heterogeneous precursors, there are nonetheless examples of such that will clarify what is meant. The mixed Jewish-German culture of the Middle Ages also used a mixed language, Yiddish. But a cultural syncretism need not be accompanied by a linguistic syncretism; for example, on the islands of Japan, continental Asian and oceanic insular cultures have mingled, but the Japanese language has remained homogeneous. Conversely, a linguistic syncretism need not be matched by a cultural one; thus a certain form of Persian-Turkish literary language is in the service solely of Islamic culture.

Analogous relations exist between cultural and religious syncretisms. An example of the coincidence of a syncretic culture with a syncretic religion can be seen in hellenized Egypt, especially in the cult of Serapis and possibly also in modern nativist movements in some regions that were colonized by Western societies. A cultural syncretism is to be found, to a certain measure, for some time after the migration of the Israelites into Canaan; yet there was no corresponding religious syncretism, and where such threatened to occur, the prophets resisted it.

A linguistic syncretism matched by a religious syncretism often occurs when a language is pidginized or creolized in a group in which tribal religion has to some extent been amalgamated with Christianity. On the other hand, a linguistic syncretism was not accompanied by a religious syncretism when a Hebrew-Aramaic language was used for discussion in Rabbinic Judaism; nor was a religious syncretism accompanied by a linguistic syncretism in the mystery religions of late antiquity with their *hieros logos* only in Greek.

Symbiosis. A social presupposition for the rise of a syncretism can be the coexistence of various groups. It may be hypothesized that there were coexistences like this even in prehistoric times, insofar as inferences regarding that period can be made from the nonliterate cultures of modern times. The matrilinear traits observable, until their recent disappearance, in many food-growing cultures were ascribed to groups possessing a developing economy in the Neolithic period; scholars even went so far as to regard the transition to production through food cultivation as a cultural fact attributable to women.

Closer observation showed, however, that food-collecting and grain-harvesting peoples and early food cultivators exhibited a characteristic that was typical of hunters—namely, the relating of a group of people to a particular animal. There is thus the possibility that from the outset food was collected or was grown and harvested not only for human consumption but for animal consumption as well. The conclusion would be not that the relations of human groups to certain animals and their relations to certain plants were antecedently connected but rather that the two types of cultures and their modes of religious expression were fused.

The situation is clearer in cases where there is written evidence. In Asia Minor and Media in the first century CE worshippers of the Iranian goddess Anāhitā lived together with worshipers of the Greek goddess Artemis, and this symbiosis led to a limited syncretism. Other symbioses in the same part of the world did not, however, lead to any syncretism. Symbioses are to be presupposed prior to many other and varied linkings of divinities throughout the Hellenistic world. The doctrines espoused by modern messianic movements in Africa, Asia, and Latin America have demonstrably been shaped by the contacts of ethnic groups with representatives of Western civilization; the preaching of missionaries has played an important but by no means isolated role here.

Acculturation. If we locate the fact of symbiosis in the larger context of the systems in which those living together are socialized and to which a great many subsystems also belong, we may speak of acculturation. Once movements of conquest became imperial in scope (e.g., the Achaemenid dynasty and the empires of Alexander the Great, the Romans, the Spaniards, and the English), they brought diverse cultures into contact; the conflation of tradition that resulted for one of the two sides could repeatedly lead to syncretisms.

Superposition. The most extensive example of this was probably the migration of the Aryans into the Asiatic subcontinent, which was already inhabited by non-Indo-European peoples. Depending on local circumstances, we may speak of a sanskritization of the Dravidian part of India, of a hierarchization of castes, and so on. In any case, Hinduism—the Hinduism of the epic and Puranic period and thereafter—became a religion very different from that of the Vedas. The comprehensiveness of which its representatives boast is one aspect of its syncretist character.

Parallel phenomena. Not every symbiosis, acculturation, or superposition, however, has led to a syncretism. Other formations may have resulted, the names of which are often, and misleadingly, used as synonyms for *syncretism.*

Synthesis. Although J. D. Droysen and others have called Hellenism a mixed culture, it was not syncretic throughout. The ideas of Droysen and later scholars who speak of Hellenism as a reconciliation of cultures or an integration of cultures into a higher unity are better represented by the term *synthesis*, which in turn is to be understood as a complex of synthetic phenomena. This can correctly be taken to mean that there were as many kinds of Hellenism as there were cultures that established links of one or other kind with Greek culture. Egyptian, Babylonian, and Iranian Hellenism were the principal types, and most of the cults within each of the three were synthetic in character after the manner of Hellenistic Judaism or many of the city-state cults in the empires of the Seleucids and Antigonids. Syncretist formations in religion were special cases in these various Hellenisms.

Evolution. This term designates a process, internal to a system, that produces new elements and that is irreversible. The new elements can then become the center of a new unity and thus of a new system. The result of the process is a new religion, but this new religion is not syncretic. It was in this way that Buddhism arose out of the previous religious systems in India and not by way of a clash between Brahmanism and alien systems. The Bahāʾī religion and even its precursor, Babism, arose because their founders took over, from the Twelvers, the institution of the imam, or mediator of revelation; non-Islamic elements played no part in this process.

Harmonization. Theosophists in particular incline to the conviction that all religions are true and lead to union with God. Thus Ramakrishna (1834–1886) said that he had tried all religions (i.e., Hinduism, Islam, and Christianity) and had found that all were moving toward the same God in different ways. The founders and adherents of other neo-Hindu reform movements hold similar views. Comparable tenets are also found frequently in the broad stream of tradition flowing from ancient Gnosticism via the Neoplatonism of the Middle Ages and Renaissance (Neoplatonism was concerned to harmonize philosophy and religion rather than various religions) to modern anthroposophy. The claim is usually not made that all religions teach the same thing, nor are the lines of demarcation between them removed. But a harmony is establihed among them by the claim that they are all seeking the same goal. This assertion includes an emphasis on the unity of the goal (e.g., God), which is comparable to presuppositions of unity that can in other circumstances lead to a syncretism. In the cases mentioned here, however, no syncretism has resulted.

Consequences. When a religio-historical development has in fact reached a syncretistic stage, its syncretistic character is usually not communicated to the subsequent stages. To this extent it is correct to say that syncretism is always a transitional phase. Here again various kinds are to be distinguished.

Transformation. An example that was significant on the scene of world history because it accompanied the expansion of Islam was the dehellenization of the Orient. This process occurred not only in religion but also in the area of material culture, with which archaeology and aesthetics deal; in the institutions of government; and even in ideas. Once the languages spoken in Asia Minor and the Semitic, Iranian, and Egyptian languages spoken in various regions began to assert themselves again, after the spread of Greek culture in the cities of the East in approximately the second century CE, their revival did not bring a return to prehellenistic conditions but rather a transformation, or metamorphosis, of the synthetic and at times syncretistic character of Hellenism into a new unity. This unity operated in the direction of homogeneity, although analytically viewed it was itself not homogeneous and it did not, on that account, become uniform.

Earlier, a complex process of transformation had likewise given rise to the Christianity of the apostolic and postapostolic ages. Despite the multiform derivation of many of its basic concepts and views, this Christianity was not a syncretist religion (with, for example, rabbinic and Hellenistic Judaism as two of its chief components). The same must be said of Catholicism, which came into being after a further transformation, namely, a now non-Judaic Hellenization of Christianity. In a similar manner, various forms of Eastern Christianity developed that can no longer be described as Hellenistic and certainly not as syncretic; this development took place not only in the Nestorian and Monophysite churches, but in smaller churches as well.

Manichaeism and orthodox Zoroastrianism, among other religions, emerged in a region in which Baptist, Syrian Christian, and Zurvanite elements were in close but undefined proximity. Manichaeism was, in addition, syncretic, but the syncretism was held in check by systematization. Zoroastrianism was not syncretic. Even elements that from an analytical standpoint were not Iranian appeared in it as Iranicized, although there was no question of "absorption."

Disintegration. If the component parts that produced a syncretic formation had been independent for a sufficiently long time or if they continued to have an independent existence alongside the syncretism, they also tended to reassert themselves in a perceptible way within it. To the extent that this happened, the syncretist structure fell apart. Thus not only did the various Eastern Hellenistic societies undergo dehellenization, but there were also Greek reactions against them. From the eighth century onward in Japan there were syncretist unions of Shintō and Mahāyāna Buddhism, but people visited temples of each separate religion as well as temples shared by both; the result was a continuing awareness of the difference between the two. With the exception of Ryōbu Shintō, which did not break up until the fourteenth century and then did so for political reasons, these syncretisms did not last long, although the symbiosis of Shintō devotees and Buddhists continued.

Absorption. When a superimposed level does not ultimately lose out to the subordinate level—as frequently happens—but remains dominant, absorption occurs. Thus, for example, it is very likely that the sky god of the invading Greeks became heir to the many mountain gods of the pre-Greek period. In a way, faith in Yahveh, who rules from Sinai, absorbed the faith of nomads from the tribes of Abraham, Isaac, and Jacob in the God of their fathers as well as belief in the Canaanite high god El.

Connections between Complex Unities. Whole religions may be confronted with one another in processes of acculturation and superposition. This happened when the religion of the Greek city-state met local religions in Asia Minor, the Fertile Crescent, Iran, and Egypt. Ever since scholars began to pay closer attention to the consequences of Alexander's expedition, the "syncretism of antiquity" has been regarded as the classic instance of syncretism in the history of religions. It is to be noted, however, that the result of the confrontation was not simply new, limited syncretic religions along the whole line. Rather, the few institutionalized or organized religious systems of which this can be said already presupposed partial and more diffuse areas of syncretism. In many cases, the rise of such diffuse areas was promoted when the Greek conviction of the oneness of truth encountered a type of thinking that was imprecise in its concepts and tended to focus on the pictorial.

Between religions. In relations between the Sumerians and the Akkadians, only the process just described above occurred. On the other hand, the religio-political effort of Sargon of Akkad (r. c. 2350–2294 BCE) and his daughter to unite the Sumerian and Semitic religions was of a different nature. Its thrust was to remove the distinction between originally different religious systems, in order that, contrary to what happened in Israel, the opposition between the incoming Semitic and native Sumerian religions, and thus their latent or open competition, might disappear.

In tenth-century China, theological systems were created out of Confucianism, Daoism, and Buddhism. There already existed a widespread popular conviction, which impacted on everyday life, that these three religions complemented each other and even intended the same thing.

Within religions. In Egypt the systems and mythologies of the gods that were represented by originally different priesthoods underwent a variety of combinations when individual districts were united, although the combinatory process did not occur solely under these conditions. Theologians among the priests felt impelled by the universalist claims of their local gods to assimilate, for example, the cosmogonies of Heliopolis and Hermopolis, Heliopolis and Memphis, Hermopolis and Memphis, Memphis and Thebes. A similar process occurred in the formation of the imperial cult of Marduk at Babylon, but opportunities of this kind were far more numerous in Egypt and lasted far longer. The Egyptian-Hellenistic syncretism of the Ptolemaic period was therefore perhaps the richest of the syncretisms that arose in the confines of Alexander's empire.

The example of Egypt has led scholars to speak of syncretism also within Iranian and Greek religion. But the concept is not appropriate here. On the other hand, there were many instances of intrareligious syncretism in India: the myths of the gods Savitṛi, Indra, Vāyu, Aryaman, Rudra, Agni, Sūrya, and Yama could be regarded as the same amid numerous variations, while both Vaiṣṇavism and Śaivism incorporated many other Hindu traditions.

Combination of Particular Elements. The reference here is to combinations established among, for example, rites, ideas, symbols, divinities, persons, writings, and so on. Either one element is enriched by other meanings or it continues to exist alongside other elements. But even this juxtaposition can take various forms and indicate either latent competition or reciprocal completion.

Addition. When the dividing line between diverse elements is removed (and with it the competition between them), but one element does not absorb the other, the result is a combination whose components not only are evident to the modern student but must also have been recognizable by the devotees of the time. That sort of thing happened both within individual religions and between religions. In Egypt, for example, one kind of eternity (*nhh*) was assigned to the god Re, another (*dt*) to the god Atum. The result was the god Re-Atum. Something comparable occurred frequently in Hellenism. The addition of Baal of Doliche to a Jupiter already assimilated with Zeus produced Jupiter Dolichenus, and so forth.

Theocrasies—combinations of gods—presuppose additions. They occur when for practical purposes one god is fused with another in the eyes of his worshipers, even though there may be no identification at the conceptual level. In the many half-theriomorphic gods of Egypt a tendency to blur the borderlines between forms and concepts is already recognizable. A number of the major Egyptian divinities arose in this manner, but the names of many lesser gods were also combined, and either kept their separate determinatives or were written with a common determinative.

Similar theocrasies occurred, though less frequently, among all the peoples of the ancient Near East. The demonstrable reason often was that polytheism caused difficulties for the faithful. But politics may also have been present in the background, especially in the encounter of different peoples. At the instigation of the Egyptian magnate the Uza-Hor-Resnet (a Persian collaborator) the Persian king Cambyses II (r. 528–522 BCE) prostrated himself before the image of Neith of Sais and had sacrifices offered to her in her temple as mother of Re (and therefore of the living pharaoh), as well as to Osiris (and therefore to the pharaoh after his death). One might assume that in honoring these divinities he actually intended to honor the corresponding Iranian divinities: the goddess later promoted by Artaxerxes II (r. 405–359 BCE) under the name *Anāhitā*, and the *fravashi* of the king. The Egyptian may also have composed the canal inscription in which Darius the Great (r. 521–486 BCE) describes himself as son of Neith and thus establishes a link with this goddess that the Iranian king did not have with Anāhitā. As a result, the character of Anāhitā likewise changed in the ensuing period.

This first instance of an international theocrasy preceded the many theocrasies of the Hellenistic age. Among these, the Alexandrian triad of Sarapis, Isis, and Harpocrates calls for special attention. Sarapis developed out of Osiris, Apis, and probably a "Hades Jupiter Dis" of Asia Minor into the god of an imperial cult that Ptolemy I (r. 323–285 BCE), with the aid of priests, philosophers, and masters of ceremonies, established for the Egyptians and Greeks of his empire. Isis "of a thousand names," the "manifestation in a single form of goddesses and gods," could in principle absorb every form on her peaceful triumphal march. Harpocrates, her underage son, who was an aspect of Horus, was equated with many other youthful gods and finally with Herakles.

A new divinity, Hermes Trismegistos, arose through a fusion of Hermes, the Greek god of fortunate inventions, and Thoth, the divine scribe of the Egyptians. This new god became the focus of an entire corpus of writings and remained the master and guarantor of esoteric knowledge down to the Renaissance.

Philo Byblius tells us of Greco-Canaanite theocrasies. Greco-Aramaic-Iranian theocrasies were wide-spread in the East, while theocrasies in general were rarer in the West; the latter included ancient Spanish-Phoenician or Celtic-Roman.

Forms of worship. When one rite adopts components from another rite, forms of worship are combined. But because the basic stock of possible ritual actions is relatively small, external influence in this area is often indistinguishable from the action of factors already present in the tradition. This situation is clearest in the area of the Christian liturgy and, indeed, from the beginning as far as the sacraments are concerned. Because ablution rituals of all kinds were so widespread, it is often unclear whether baptism was an act that stood out—because of its initiatory nature—in a series of already-existing ablutions, or whether the ablutions represented secondary repetitions of an originally unique act of baptism.

Baptism thus provides a fundamental example of the difficulty of clearly establishing a connection between various rites. Jewish proselyte baptism, for example, probably originated within Judaism and was not taken from outside baptist movements of the kind that lived on in the rites of the Elkesites and the Mandaeans. Christian baptism, for its part, rather than having been derived from that same external environment, represented an acceptance and development of the baptism of John, which itself was part of the Jewish milieu, but had acquired an eschatological dimension.

On the other hand, baptism clearly entered the Mithra mystery cults from outside, probably from Christianity. The ceremonies of many African independent churches and of the cargo cults of Melanesia are fusions of Protestant liturgies and ethnic cults. The cult of Umbanda in Brazil is a combination of the liturgy of the Catholic Mass with West African rituals.

Parallelization. The paralleling of elements is most easily practiced when one is persuaded of the unity of truth. If truth is one, diverse names do not point to real differences but may be shown to be simply different names for the same thing. This is the path very clearly taken by Greek thinkers, and in this respect Roman thought followed Greek. Primary among the various modes of parallelization is that of interpretation.

Interpretation. *Interpretatio graeca* and *interpretatio romana* were long regarded as a principal presupposition, or even as a principal phase, of syncretism itself. This is understandable in view of the wide diffusion of both. Behind these two "interpretations," however, there was in most instances no real theocrasy but only a tendency toward it. This tendency was most widespread in literature, so that we may speak first of all of a literary syncretism. In Porphyry, for example, the Arimanius Deus ("the god who apes") is learnedly interpreted as *antimimos daimon.* Apollo appears in place of Mithra (probably in order to show the harmony between Greeks and Persians) on votive tablets in the Fire Sanctuary of Persepolis during the time of Alexander. Helios stands for Mithra in Xenophon and probably also in Plutarch (unless he stands here for Ohrmazd), in relief sculptures of the Parthian period, and so on.

Greek interpretation claimed to be interested, though not exclusively, in those individual traits of the alien object that already seemed familiar. The Roman renaming of the Greek gods was also clearly a form of interpretation. But a new kind of *interpretationes Romanae* occurred once Rome had destroyed the Seleucid and Ptolemaic empires and conquered regions belonging to the Celts and the Germans. Thenceforth interpretations no longer simply established parallels, as they did among the Greeks; rather there was always present to some degree a subordination of the local god to the corresponding Roman god. The counterexample of the Hebew Yahveh, who refused even to be interpreted as Jupiter, throws light on the exclusive character of Roman interpretation and the resultant tendency to theocrasy. Interpretations of Yahveh occurred only on the fringes of Judaism, as, for example, in Elephantine (an island in the Nile), or among the Hypsistarians where, characteristically, interpretation was rendered possible only by using the Greek equivalent of the biblical El 'Elyon (Hypsistos). Appropriative interpretations of other traditions reached their high point in gnosticism, where the conviction of the unity of truth had become a faith in the unity of redemption that would not allow any division. For this reason, gnostic systems also provide the most impressive instances of the various kinds of syncretism. These were always preceded by an *interpretatio gnostica.*

Equivalence. Clearly, equivalence is a presupposition in all forms of parallelization, in identification and theocrasy, and in the syncretism of complex unities. But it acquires a special developmental significance when unities, or elements of them, are assigned different values and are conceived as ways to the same goal, with the stipulation that one of them leads to the goal more effectively than the others. This type of valuation has found a place in the philosophy of religion, for example, in that of Śaṅkara (c. 738–822 CE), who speaks of a graduated way to God. The early Christian doctrine of a *praeparatio evangelica* (preparation for the gospel) among the Greeks and the Jews likewise belongs here to some extent, though it loses its syncretist character due to its apologetic function in relation to Judaism and paganism. On the other hand, a developmental or evolutionary equivalence is frequently admitted in the later stages of many religions (for example, post-Islamic, post-Christian, and post-Shintō), and, more generally, in numerous new entities of the present time, which, despite their claims to a higher truth, are forced to admit that the truth-claims of their predecessors have a relative validity.

Amalgamation. This term describes a fusion that is more irreversible than a simple *mingling*. The term mingling is more appropriate as a description of the phenomenon of syncretism. This is due to the origin of the term in ancient physics, in which there was much discussion of combinations, mixtures, and fusions, while the problem of the mass or quantity that an element may no longer have if it is truly part of a mixture remained ultimately unresolved. This is very much in keeping with the dissolubility of a syncretism, which can become operative at any time. *Amalgamation*, on the other hand, describes a borderline case of syncretism and to that extent is by and large equivalent to *synthesis*.

Exchange of qualities. First mention belongs here to the exchange of qualities between the *bodhisattvas* of Mahāyāna Buddhism and the spirits and demons (including the kami of Shintō) of the peoples proselytized by this version of Buddhism. It is not a matter of equivalent figures, so that we cannot speak of parallelization or addition. Nor is it a matter of gods on both sides though gods might arise from the process. The *bodhisattvas*, now outfitted with qualities derived from the relevant folklore, had the important function of showing that redemption, for which the redemption accomplished by the Buddha paves the way, is present in the traditions of the proselytized peoples. To this end the figures involved must resemble one another; on the other hand, they have no personal core, but rather their characteristics are interwoven as in a jigsaw puzzle.

Identification. Wherever there is no theocrasy, identification, which in principle supposes the same degree of identity on both sides, exists. It is difficult, however, to see that the logical process represented by identification has actually been at work in the linking of religious traditions. At most it can be said that in literary syncretisms, the authors of which have been trained in logic, identifications do occur, for example, between central concepts of spirit, or between these and personifications.

SYNCRETIST RELIGIONS. These are the high points of syncretic processes inasmuch as they are not the first realizations of syncretism but already presuppose less organized syncretic fields. Such religions are as it were "metasyncretisms" or "second-level" syncretisms.

Mystery religions. "Mystery" as a cult form did not as such have a syncretist character. This is clear from the so-called mysteries of the ancient world: the Eleusinian mysteries, the mysteries of the Cabiri of Samothrace, or, in the pre-Hellenistic period, those of Orpheus, Dionysos, and Cybele. Nonetheless, the kind of mystery worship in which the most important factor was the conformity in destiny between the initiate and his or her deity did foster the development of syncretic mystery religions in the Hellenistic period. The Isis mysteries of Egypt presupposed the faith in Osiris that had already acquired syncretic ties (though not related to the mysteries) in the Serapis cult of the Ptolemies. The Mithra mysteries of Asia Minor did not presuppose any ancient Iranian mystery but only the god Mithra as such, albeit a Mithra equated with Sol and Helios. In this instance, the second-level syncretism emerged through the addition of a further link with a mystery type of worship native to Asia Minor. Something similar is to be said of the mysteries of Sebazios, who had been an ancient Phrygian or Lydian god, and of Jupiter Dolichenus, who had been the Baal of Doliche. Once the basic idea of the mysteries of Cybele and Attis was integrated into the context provided by the idea of the so-called dying and rising gods, these mysteries acquired a different character than they had had before the introduction of agriculture into Asia Minor.

Manichaeism. Syncretisms that were part Babylonian, part Iranian, part Christian Hellenism were presupposed by Manichaeism. Its founder, Mani, effected a further syncretism by creating a unique system in which previously existing linkages were interrelated in an entirely new and original way. Manichaeism could therefore be described, depending on those being addressed, as true Christianity, true gnosis, true Zoroastrianism, true shamanism, true Buddhism, and even true Taoism. At times these missionary efforts gave rise to new syncretistic formations. There is doubt whether the latter repeat earlier syncretisms—for example, the part played by Buddhism in the rise of Manichaeism is disputed—or, on the contrary, that they represent "third-level" syncretisms. To a certain extent, therefore, Manichaeism was the supreme syncretism, and it is not surprising that, given its power of suggestion, people saw medieval Bogomilism and Catharism as revivals of it. The latter, however, represented something different, namely, transformations of Paulicianism that retained to some extent a dualistic character, but were not on this account to be classified as properly syncretist.

Gnosticism. Only Valentinianism and Sethianism can be compared with Manichaeism in their degree of systematic formulation. The other Gnostic doctrines were not systems but myths; all however, were syncretic in the same degree, despite differences in content. All were also preceded by Greco-Oriental syncretisms, though this does not mean that Greek teaching on spirit is to be understood as forming the nucleus of the gnostic doctrine of redemption. Central to the Gnostic concept of redemption was the idea of a redeemer who himself needed redemption; around this spiritual nucleus the syncretic contents of the various Gnosticisms were organized in very diverse ways. Such phenomena could arise even on the fringes of Judaism, although Judaism by its nature provided the fewest necessary presuppositions. On the other hand, the process readily occurred in the Greco-Oriental religions. Second-level syncretisms made their appearance in the structure of the myths, in the peculiar character of the redeemer figures, and in the way history and the world were conceived. The result was a basic pattern that has recurred in the various Gnosticisms down to the modern period, although this does not mean that all the details of these later Gnosticisms derive from ancient Gnosticism.

Middle Ages. Here I mean to speak of "Middle Ages" in both the West and the East, despite the fact that the line of demarcation from the modern period, which alone makes the term meaningful, is not the same in the East as in the West. The unbroken transmission of the alchemy of late antiquity down to the Renaissance, the uninterrupted continuity of *heikhalot* mysticism and the Qabbalah as a broad stream within the Jewish tradition, and the ever-possible revival of Neoplatonic thought meant that new syncretisms could constantly arise; these would be comparable to the ones that occurred in the period when alchemy, Jewish mysticism, and Neoplatonism first appeared. In many instances (for example, Ramón Lull (c. 1232–1315), related traditions from the Islamic world were added, although in Lull's case any basically syncretist pattern disappeared due to the level of conceptual abstraction. The same is true of Agrippa (1486–1535) in relation to Jewish mysticism and of Paracelsus (1493–1541) in relation to Neoplatonism. In the milieus of these two men, however, there were popular forms of both white and black magic that can be described as syncretic. In the East, syncretisms of a new kind arose in various places. First mention belongs here to the connections between an already syncretic Hinduism and a nonsyncretic Islam, fostered in part by the religious policy of Akbar (1542–1605). This ranged from the so-called Muslim brahmans (via interactions between Muslims and Hindus at common festivals and common shrines in the Punjab and the Sultanates of Delhi) to the formation of a syncretistic organization, Sikhism. In the Near East, the continuance of ancient syncretisms despite the superposition of Islam led to syncretisms with the latter, as among the Druze, the Shamsīyah, the Yesid, the Ahl-i Ḥaqq, and in some Turkish orders of dervishes. In missionary Buddhism there arose the connections, mentioned earlier, between the *bodhisattvas* and the spirits (or demons) of Central Asiatic, Chinese, and Japanese folklore.

Modern age. The acculturation process of the nineteenth and twentieth centuries has likewise produced new syncretisms that focus either on a utopian future or on a present that is in need of improvement. Among the former type, the cargo cults of Melanesia, Micronesia, and Polynesia are intelligible only against the background of Christian missionary activity. These cults materialize the objects of the Christian hope proclaimed by the missionaries and turn them into forms of tangible prosperity imported from outside; they thus produce numerous new interpretations of Christ and other biblical figures in the light of indigenous saviors. The equal or higher status that these cults give to their own mythical tradition as compared with the Bible leads inevitably to the development of new myths that retain only a formal likeness either to Christian legend or their own older myths.

A similar situation is discernible in the so-called African independent churches, especially when ancestor worship and initiation are combined with Christian veneration of the saints and with baptism. Further linkages lead to a mythical topography into which the biblical topography can be incorporated and to a parallel-structured eschatological geography.

Of the new supraregional institutions of the present time, some are less syncretistic, others more; the most syncretistic is the Unification Church, in which old Korean shamanistic, Mahāyāna Buddhist, and Presbyterian contributions are still recognizable.

Other modern syncretic movements focus on a present that is in need of improvement. In Brazil the Catholic ecclesial tradition, Pentecostalism, and African and Indian cults, as well as, in some cases, an academic formation in the mythology of European classical antiquity, all had to come in contact in order that the great syncretic religions—Candomblé, Macumba, and Umbanda—might arise. The syncretic teaching on spirits and gods found in these religions can be interpreted in terms of Christian veneration of the saints or of Indian, African, or even Greek mythology. A common orientation to a Buddhist king and a socialist party leader, whose charisma ensured the prosperity of the country, led to a Buddhist-Marxist syncretism in Burma. In Vietnam, contacts between Buddhism, Christianity, and popular religion led to the establishment of a new organized religion, Cao Dai.

CONCLUSION. It can be stated as a principle that syncretism, where verifiable, is a late stage in a particular epoch of the history of religions. It will therefore always contain truth-claims, inasmuch as insight gained at last into the relativity of all that has preceded makes it possible to compare, combine, and interchange elements from the tradition. A tolerant attitude to all that is of value in the world is thus a basic condition for the rise of any syncretism, as well as a basic virtue of the human being who is shaped by syncretism and in turn supports it. In addition, however, an enormous intellectual power is required in order to cement all the elements together into a new type of tradition and, further, to maintain the combination of the erudite and the popular.

SEE ALSO Gnosticism; Hellenistic Religions; Hermetism; Manichaeism; Mystery Religions; New Religious Movements.

BIBLIOGRAPHY

Modern study of the topic was inaugurated by Richard Reitzenstein and H. H. Schaeder in their classic *Studien zum antiken Synkretismus aus Iran und Griechenland* (Leipzig, 1926). The investigation begun there has been continued in a series of symposia: *Syncretism: Based on Papers Read at the Symposium on Cultural Contact, Meeting on Religious Syncretism Held at Abo on the 8th–10th of September 1966, edited by Sven S. Hartman* (Stockholm, 1969); *Les syncrétismes dans les religions grecque et romaine: Colloque de Strasbourg, 9–11 juin 1971* (Paris, 1973); *Synkretismus im syrisch-persischen Kulturgebiet: Bericht über ein Symposion in Reinhausen bei Göttingen in der Zeit vom 4. bis 8. Oktober 1971*, edited by Albrecht Dietrich (Göttingen, 1975); *Les syncrétismes dans les religions de l'antiquité: Colloque de Besançon, 22–23 octobre 1973*, edited by Françoise Dunand and Pierre L. Lévêque (Leiden, 1975); and *Religious Syncretism in Antiquity: Essays in Conversation with Geo Widengren, edited by Birger A. Pearson* (Missoula, Mont., 1975). A recent approach to the topic can be found in Ulrich Berner's *Untersuchungen zur Verwendung des Synkretismus-Begriffes* (Wiesbaden, 1982). The historical situations in which syncretisms can arise are best described in Mircea Eliade's monumental *A History of Religious Ideas* (Chicago, 1978–1986).

Many volumes are devoted to the critical appraisal of syncretist materials in the series "Études préliminaires aux religions orientales dans l'Empire romain," edited by Maarten J. Vermaseren (Leiden, 1967–1981). The theme was also the subject of a special research area undertaken from 1968 to 1981, the results of which were published in the series "Göttinger Orientforschungen"; see especially Joachim Spiegel's *Die Götter von Abydos: Studien zum ägyptischen Synkretismus* (Wiesbaden, 1971); Wolfgang Schenkel's *Kultmythos und Märtyrerlegende: Zur Kontinuität des ägyptischen Denkens* (Wiesbaden, 1977); Brigitte Altenmüller's *Synkretismus in den Sargtexten* (Wiesbaden, 1975); and Maria Theresia Derchain-Urtel's *Synkretismus in ägyptischer Ikonographie: Die Göttin Tjenenet* (Wiesbaden, 1979). In addition to the works on Egypt, the series offers a general study: *Synkretismusforschung: Theorie und Praxis*, edited by Gernot Wiessner (Wiesbaden, 1978). The principle of syncretism is also discussed in Richard Merz's *Die numinose Mischgestalt* (Berlin, 1978).

Hypotheses regarding an ancient syncretism in Greece and Iran are defended by Otto Kern in *Die Religion der Griechen*, vol. 1, *Von den Anfängen bis Hesiod* (Berlin, 1926), and vol. 2, *Die Hochblüte bis zum Ausgang des fünften Jahrhunderts* (Berlin, 1935), and by Sven S. Hartman in *Gayomart: Étude sur le syncrétisme dans l'ancien Iran* (Uppsala, 1953). Descriptions of syncretism in India can be found in almost every study on the religions of India. On late antiquity, see, in addition to the symposia mentioned above, Christoph Elsas's *Neuplatonische und gnostische Weltablehnung in der Schule Plotins* (Berlin, 1973). On South America, see Lindolfo Weingärtner's *Umbanda: Synkretistische Kulte in Brasilien, eine Herausforderung für die christliche Kirche* (Erlangen, 1969); Ulrich Fischer's *Zur Liturgie des Umbandakultes* (Leiden, 1970); and Horst H. Figge's *Geisterkult: Besessenheit und Magie in der Umbanda-Religion Brasiliens* (Freiburg, 1973).

For a discussion on syncretism in Africa, see Raymond Rozier's *Le Burundi: Pays de la vache et du tambour* (Paris, 1973). On Japan, see Joseph M. Kitagawa's *Religion in Japanese History* (New York, 1966) and J. H. Kamstra's *Encounter or Syncretism: The Initial Growth of Japanese Buddhism* (Leiden, 1967). On syncretism within a variety of Buddhist cultures, see *Buddhist Backgrounds of the Burmese Revolution*, by Emanuel Sarkisyanz (The Hague, 1965), and *Buddhism in Ceylon and Studies in Religious Syncretism in Buddhist Countries*, edited by Heinz Bechert (Göttingen, 1978).

On the Christian position regarding the problem, consult Willem Adolph Visser't Hooft's *No Other Name: The Choice between Syncretism and Christian Universalism* (London, 1963). On the dispute concerning syncretism within the Protestant church, see Otto Ritschl's *Die reformierte Theologie des 16. und 17. Jahrhunderts in ihrer Entstehung und Entwicklung* (Göttingen, 1926).

CARSTEN COLPE (1987)
Translated from German by Matthew J. O'Connell

SYNCRETISM [FURTHER CONSIDERATIONS].

Syncretism belongs with several other terms in the study of religions, such as *myth*, *magic*, or *religion*, that derive from Greek or Latin words but have a complex semantic history in which the meaning of the ancient Greek or Latin word is relatively unimportant when compared to the adoption and resemantization of the term in modern scholarly discourse. In the case of syncretism, Erasmus's adaptation and Latinization of Greek *synkrētismós* (Plutarch, the *Suda* lexicon) into *syncretismus* paved the way for later usages. Erasmus adopted the term in its ancient meaning of "banding together of Cretans" as a proverbial term to designate an alliance of unlike partners based on usefulness, not on mutual attraction, and he applied it to the changing coalitions in the religious fights of his own time (*Adagia* 1.1.11) or to the necessity of humanist scholars to close ranks against their ideological enemies (*Letter* 947 to Melanchthon, from 1519). After Erasmus the term radically changed its meaning. When reused in Protestant sources in its French and English adaptations, it referred to the closing of ranks among different groups of reformed Christians, especially Lutherans and Calvinists, despite their considerable doctrinal differences and under the pressure of their common enemy, the papacy, and it was used to censure this closing of the ranks as bizarre and unacceptable. Although in these texts the intended meaning was "a behavior like that of Erasmus's beleaguered Cretans," it was quickly understood as "unprincipled blending of theological and liturgical truth (ours) and falsehood (theirs) under outside pressure." This negative use and meaning resurfaced in the nineteenth-century missionary polemics against native influences on Christianity, and it survives in contemporary Catholic discourse about ecumenism and any other "relativisms" (Joseph Cardinal Ratzinger). In a more descriptive sense, but still with negative connotations, the term became prominent in the scholarly language of historians of religion, philosophers, and linguists in the latter half of the nineteenth century. In the study of religions, it was mainly used to describe the later stages of Greek and Roman religions, with their many imports from Near Eastern cultures (J. Réville, *La religion à Rome sous les Sévères,* 1886) or its identification of divinities such as Asclepius and Zeus (*"synkretismus oder religionsmischerei,"* H. Usener, *Götternamen,* 1895 [1949], p. 337); as a precursor, J. A. Hartung had described the reception of Greek elements into Roman religion as *Vermischung* (*Die Religion der Römer,* 1836, p. 249). But as early as in the 1880s it was used in other religions, such as Talmudic Judaism or Avestan religion (see *Journal of the American Oriental Society* 11 [1887]: 114, or 16 [1894]: 76). From the perspective of a church historian following the church's traditional evaluation, Adolf von Harnack used the concept to characterize gnosticism (*Lehrbuch der Dogmengeschichte,* vol. 1, 1886; see A. Hilgenfeld, "Religionsmischung," *Zeitschrift für wissenschaftliche Theologie* 33 [1890]: 1). Negative connotations are obvious, and "syncretistic" almost equals "heretical." Thus, *syncretism* was and still is used as a normative term. Its scholarly use as a descriptive term creates the same complex problems as the use of the term *magic:* it has proved almost impossible to free it entirely from normative connotations.

Two assumptions underlie the descriptive usage: religions can be understood as autonomous entities, and purity is their early ("original") stage; in a simple evolutionary concept, syncretism (impurity) is seen as a later phenomenon (lucid in G. van der Leeuw, *La religion dans son essence et ses manifestations,* 1948, pp. 167 ff., 589–593). This appropriation of elements from other, especially Asian religious cultures was often viewed as a sign of weakening ("effete times," *Journal of the American Oriental Society* 11 [1887]: 114) and a result of the population mix in the great urban centers of later antiquity ("syncretism and cosmopolitanism," *Journal of the American Oriental Society* 11 [1887]: 16, and [1894]: 76). Subtexts are the negative view of city life in an industrialized society whose ideals were still derived from a rapidly disappearing rural life, and the equally negative view of the Semitic East as a foil to Greekness, Romanness, or Christianity (e.g., M. Olender, *Les langues du paradis,* 1989, pp. 75–111 on Ernest Renan). Political implications are evident, and it would be interesting to compare the contemporary development of the terms *nation* and *nationalism*: the rise of two major European nation-states, Germany and Italy, falls into the same period as the rise of the term *syncretism.* In an interesting inversion, the term also characterized the religious imperialism of the Roman emperors who appropriated foreign cults as part of a strategy of homogenizing the empire ("all the varieties of mankind . . . restamped at the Caesarean mint," *Frazer's Magazine for Town and Country* 47 [1853]: 294): this prepared for its critical use in colonial history.

As a scholarly term, *syncretism* has been used for describing a wide variety of phenomena, such as the influence of one religion on another (Christian or Islamic influence on African religions), the interpenetration of two religious systems (such as Sumerian and Assyrian religion), the mutual influence of local religions (as in ancient Egyptian religion), the appropriation of foreign divinities (such as Mithra in Rome), or the combination of different divinities into one entity (such as Zeus and Asclepius). Some of these phenomena were viewed as unconscious, others could be seen as a conscious blending of religious elements; usually, however, an evolutionary approach prevailed that had no interest in individual agents of syncretism. The usefulness of the term was debated well before Karsten Colpe's above entry in this encyclopedia, and the debate continues, with good reasons. A successful scholarly term is an instrument that enables succinct comparison between phenomena that are viewed as related; in order to do so, it has to have a precise content and its meaning has to find wide agreement in the scholarly community. If the content is vague and fuzzy, comparison is impossible, and if the community does not agree on the definition, communication outside a narrow circle of initiates breaks down.

RECENT APPROACHES. In the years after Colpe's entry (and already before that), the term underwent more and sometimes radical criticism; some of the critics rejected it in favor of another term.

Redefinition. A first approach insisted on the extreme fluidity of the concept and its lack of definition, which reduces its heuristic value. Instead of rejecting the term altogether, several critics paralleled Colpe's own move to redefine the term. Perhaps the most interesting proposal is Ulrich Berner's (1992, 2001). Using Niklaus Luhmann's system theory, Berner differentiates between the religious system (such as Greek religion, or Christianity) and the elements of this system; he regards religions as systems whose elements—both their own form and their relationship to the overall system—are constantly changing. He defines *syncretism* not as the result of a process (as many earlier scholars had done) but as the process itself. This leads him to locate syncretism on both levels of the system: syncretism acts either between different religious systems (say between Shintoism and Christianity) or between single elements of the same system (say between two Greek divinities); for the latter process, he also proposed to use the term *rationalization,* leaving *syncretism* to designate processes between different religious systems. On both levels, he then introduced several other terms to deal with phenomena that traditionally were also called syncretism.

This approach to religious terminology shares its problems with many comparable approaches in which a traditional but vague term is retained with a new and specific definition: it has to find a consensus group that shares its meaning. In the case of syncretism, such a consensus has not been reached. In Colpe's proposal the term remains so loose, despite the initial definition, as to comprise a large group of different phenomena; in Berner's case, one might argue that it would be easier to replace *syncretism* with yet another new term than to retain it in its strictly confined meaning; in fact, Berner also uses *systematization* to denote processes that affect entire religious systems. Berner's insistence on syncretism as a process, however, has become crucial; other scholars, as we shall see presently, shared this evaluation.

A similar development occurred in anthropology. Anthropologists were less susceptible to the notion of pure cultures than historians of religion, and early on they subscribed to a descriptive use of the term. But anthropologists also began to realize that such a description would make sense only when applied to a process, "syncretization," not to a state: syncretism as a state would call for its opposite, pure culture, but such a pure culture exists only at the end of an almost infinite regression towards hypothetical origins; all known past and present cultures are syncretistic (Stewart and Shaw, 1994, pp. 7–9; Johnston, 2002, pp. 71ff).

Rejection. More recently, scholars rejected the term altogether. Following the lead of recent cultural studies, especially Homi Bhabha (*The Location of Culture*, 1994) who in turn followed the pioneering work of the colonial historian Edward Said, these scholars reject the assumption that religions are autonomous entities or systems that can at some point react with each other; they rather focus on the constant interaction of single elements in a continuum where interaction takes place both at the zones of contact and at every possible other place as well; in Luhmann's sense, then, we would have to enlarge the system to global size. Boundaries are not the result of intrinsic processes but they are set from outside, usually through hierarchically superior and powerful agents that delineate national religions (versus foreign religions), orthodoxies (versus heresies), or correct religions (versus native distortions in a colonial setting). The discourse on syncretism is thus inevitably political, and the descriptive term "syncretism" is replaced by "hybridity" to express this acephalous interaction of elements in a potentially global system. Up to now, the term and its concomitant methodology have been applied to the question of gnosticism (King, 2003) or the formation of Christianity and rabbinic Judaism (Boyarin, 1999, p. 8).

This approach builds on the insight that religions are not autonomous entities (Joachim Wach, *Religionswissenschaft. Prolegomen zu ihrer wissenschaftlichen Grundlegung*, 1924, p. 86) and succeeds in taking the criticism against the term *syncretism* seriously; in a move that is similar to the rejection of the term *magic* as a "semantic trap" (M. Wax and R. Wax, *Current Anthropology* 4 [1963]: 495–513), the description makes use of a new term. Two problems will have to be addressed in future research. One is the simple fact that traditional terminology is surprisingly resistant and inert (or, perhaps less surprisingly, the scholarly community as such is conservative), as the case of *magic* demonstrates. The other, more serious question is whether a model that deals with culture can be transferred to religion without modifications and adaptations: is religion an integral and equal subsystem of culture, or do its elements behave in a different way?

Middle ground. In between these two opposing views lies a third approach that on the surface looks like a compromise, although it is somewhat prior to the introduction of the term *hybridity*. It starts from the same discontent with *syncretism* as a very vague descriptive term with a normative life of its own and the view that there are no religions that would be entirely autonomous entities. All religious phenomena in a given society have always been open to interactions not only from inside the system (Berner's "rationalization") but from the outside, which lead to changes in single elements or in the entire system. Thus, as a descriptive category of religious or cultural phenomena, syncretism would be unnecessary, not the least because it is a category that is based on an evolutionary understanding of culture and religion: these phenomena are defined by their origin. Nevertheless, in this approach the concept is retained in two distinct ways: as describing processes of religious change and in a discourse of syncretism; these discourses necessarily involve the workings of power and of agency (Stewart and Shaw, 1994).

The first way became a focus of scholarly interest in the later quarter of the twentieth century, and it lacked a distinct vocabulary. Agreeing with Berner's restriction of "syncretism" to processes only, this approach opens itself to the same problem as the first, that is, to the necessity of defining the term in a rather specialized way, which therefore potentially reduces its communicative value. The second interest is a critical and historical one and reflects the self-reflexive state of contemporary religious studies that it shares with most other fields in cultural and social studies that also led to the rejection of the term. The two ways of dealing with the term and the underlying reality seem in a somewhat precarious combination; there is no self-evident path leading from syncretism as a process to syncretism as a discourse.

EXEMPLIFICATION. An example might highlight the advantages and problems in the different approaches. I shall not select one of the well-known areas of syncretism as outlined above by Colpe but deal with two very distinct phenomena, the creation of new religious movements and the formation of divine personalities.

Invention of a new religion. In the past, the term was applied with preference to new religious entities, either to define them or to characterize their creation. A case in point is the Roman mysteries of Mithra. A single actor, the anonymous inventor of Mithraism, created it in a conscious act of bricolage by taking over elements from what he regarded as an exotic religion (Persian) but acting inside his own cultural and religious matrix and reacting to concerns in this very society (Beck, 1998, pp. 115–128). One could call this creative process *syncretism* and agree that the term has to be confined to comparable processes, such as the formation of single gnostic bodies or even the creation of Mormonism, or one could define the term *hybridity* to denote these same processes. The decision is more one of political correctness than of scholarly gain, and in both cases, it involves the redefinition of a broader term from another field.

Formation of a divine personality. Another area that traditionally made use of the term *syncretism* is the formation of divine personalities. A complex case is the Greek god Zeus. Linguistic and functional analysis has shown that Zeus has homologues outside Greece, in various other Indo-European religious cultures; whatever the exact mechanisms of the diffusion of Indo-European speakers were, Zeus's Indo-European ancestry is well established. The way in which Greek Zeus appeared in poetry and in the cults and images between 700 BCE and 400 BCE is considerably more complex. He presides over the present cosmic order in a succession of rulers since the beginning of cosmogony and theogony. In a story that depends on several Near Eastern succession myths, he fought a battle of wits with Prometheus, a member of the earlier generation of gods and protector of humans whose stories were influenced by those of Mesopotamian Ea/Enki. In order to secure his power, he fought a monster with snake features: this resonates with several Near Eastern foundation myths; the later story of how he was attacked and temporarily defeated by Typhon is connected with the Syrian Mount Kasios, where Baal Zaphon was worshiped. Like many Semitic Baalim and Anatolian weather gods, Zeus was the god of rain, storms, and lightning whose preferred place of worship was mountaintops. Thus, a considerable number of Near Eastern stories helped to shape the early Greek myths of Zeus, as Near Eastern mountain cults shaped the cult of Zeus on mountaintops. The transfer mechanism of stories is clear: through direct or indirect contact, a Near Eastern story was adapted and reshaped by an early Greek singer; the reshaping was conditioned by the singer's creativity, the specific circumstances of his performance, and the expectations of the audience. The mechanism of cult transfer is less clear, but presumably some of the stories in turn created cults. Furthermore, most early Greek communities worshiped Zeus, and their local stories legitimated and explained their cults. These local stories and cults interacted with those of their neighbors; the stories were sometimes picked up by itinerant singers and incorporated into their narrative. Early Greek images of Zeus in the shape of a walking god brandishing a thunderbolt resonated with Syrian or Anatolian images of local Baalim and with Egyptian monumental statues. In an inverse movement, gods in other language areas were read as Zeus: Baalim in Syria; local weather gods in Anatolia, who in Greek inscriptions appeared as Zeus, often with the local name as an epithet; Tinia in Etruria; Jupiter in Rome.

This narration assumes several processes of interaction to have taken place and several categories of agents to have been consciously or unconsciously active: the transfer of narrations from the ancient Near East to Greece, from Asian storytellers, scribes, priests, and ordinary people telling stories to Greek merchants, travelers and, finally, itinerant singers who diffused them to Greek audiences; the transfer of local Greek stories from one place to another by singers who made it part of their repertoire; the foundation of specific cults or the change of local rituals through the agency either of a singer's tale or a neighbor's cult; the manufacturing of images by Greek craftsmen after images seen by travelers and merchants in the East or dedicated in a Greek sanctuary by Greek and Eastern merchants, travelers, and religious specialists; the identifications of a local god with Zeus by travelers such as Herodotus who wanted to understand and explain to their audience a foreign god by translating his name, by Greek settlers who wanted to worship a local god under a name they knew, by members of local elites in Anatolia, Etruria, and Rome who intended to enhance the prestige of their cult by adding stories and images from Greece, or by local craftsmen looking for pictorial traditions that they lacked in their local setting. These agents and interactions created the traditions of local and Panhellenic storytelling, iconography, and cult.

Using the language of syncretism, one would have to speak of two basic forms of syncretism, external and internal, between systems and within a system. But to do this would mean to drastically simplify the description of the various processes and thus to lose a rich heuristic and descriptive arsenal; it seems better to create new and more specific terms than to redefine *syncretism* to include just one type of process.

More problems arise when we try to define the boundaries of the systems: do we have to respect the boundaries set by the locals, or do we impose them from our point of view, and if so, what are the criteria used? The boundaries that Greeks themselves defined were shifting over the period we focused on, from the city (*polis*) to the tribe, to all Greeks as a unit; the shifts resulted from political developments inside Greece. Modern definitions of boundaries usually follow language or political structure, thus replicating the model of the modern nation-state: Greek religion as an autonomous entity was the religion of the people who spoke Greek or of the territory over which Greeks ruled; this expanded the system when, as a consequence of Alexander's conquests, Greek became the language of the entire Eastern Mediterranean world, whereas it would collapse when the Romans took over. More recently, scholars resignedly accepted the *polis* as the basic unit of religion and ended up with a vast plurality of Greek religions. This verges towards a *reductio ad absurdum*: any religious contact between two cities could be called syncretism.

CONCLUSIONS. Syncretism was heavily discussed in the 1970s and 1980s; then, the debate slowed down. Colpe's hope that scholars could agree on one meaning proved unfounded; and since the term still has its polemical meaning in present-day church language, it is unlikely that such an agreement is imminent. In this situation it might be more useful not to use the term at all, even though no replacement is in sight. As *hybridity* with its origin in the discourse of colonial history suggests, the underlying problems of cultural identity and autonomy are too sensitive to lend themselves to neutral descriptions and formalizations; it is likely that the coexistence of several scholarly communities with their own terminology will persist for some time.

BIBLIOGRAPHY

Theoretical studies

Berner, Ulrich. *Untersuchungen zur Verwendung des Synkretismus-Begriffes.* Göttingen, Germany, 1982.

Berner, Ulrich. "Synkretismus." In *Handbuch religionswissenschaftlicher Grundbegriffe,* vol. 5, pp. 143–152. Stuttgart, Germany, 2001.

Motte, André, and Vinciane Pirenne-Delforge. "Du 'bon usage' de la notion de syncrétisme." *Kernos* 7 (1994): 11–27.

Siller, Hermann Pius, ed. *Suchbewegungen. Synkretismus—kulturelle Identität und kirchliches Bekenntnis.* Darmstadt, Germany, 1991.

Stewart, Charles, and Rosalind Shaw, eds. *Syncretism/Anti-syncretism: The Politics of Religious Synthesis.* London and New York, 1994.

Select examples of recent usage

Baines, John. "Egyptian Syncretism. Hans Bonnet's Contribution." *Orientalia* 68 (1999): 199–214.

Beck, Roger. "The Mysteries of Mithras: A New Account of Their Genesis." *Journal of Roman Studies* 88 (1998): 115–128.

Blázquez, José María. "El sincretismo en la Hispania Romana entre les religiones indigenas, Griega, Romana, Fenicia y Mistéricas." In *Religiones en la España Antiqua,* pp. 29–82. Madrid, 1991. (Originally published in 1981.)

Boyarin, Daniel. *Dying for God: Martyrdom and the Making of Christianity and Judaism.* Stanford, Calif., 1999.

Burkert, Walter. "Migrating Gods and Syncretism. Forms of Cult Transfer in the Ancient Mediterranean." In *The Howard Gilman International Conferences,* vol. 2: *Mediterranean Cultural Interaction,* edited by Asher Ovadiah, pp. 1–21. Tel Aviv, 2000.

Johnson, Paul Chistopher. *Secrets, Gossip, and Gods. The Transformation of Brazilian Condomblé.* Oxford, 2002.

King, Karen L. *What Is Gnosticism?* Cambridge, Mass., 2003.

Lambert, Wilfred G. "Syncretism and Religious Controversy in Babylonia." In *Aufsätze zum 65. Geburtstag von Horst Klengel,* vol.1, pp. 159–162. Berlin, 1997.

Martin, Luther H. "Why Cecropian Minerva? Hellenistic Religious Syncretism as System." *Numen* 30 (1983): 131–145.

FRITZ GRAF (2005)

SYRIAC ORTHODOX CHURCH OF ANTIOCH.

The Syriac Orthodox Church and its dependency in India, along with the Coptic, Armenian, Ethiopian, Malankara, and Eritrean Orthodox Churches, make up a communion now called Oriental Orthodox, erroneously called "Monophysite" in the past. These churches did not accept the Council of Chalcedon (451 CE) and its Christological definition that proposed two natures in Christ and so fell out of communion with the rest of the Christian world. But they never accepted the classical Monophysite position of Eutyches, who affirmed that the humanity of Christ was absorbed into his single divine nature. They affirm the perfect humanity as well as the perfect divinity of Christ, inseparably and unconfusedly united in a single divine-human nature of Christ's person. In Christology these churches follow Severus of Antioch and also Cyril of Alexandria, who spoke of the "one incarnate nature of the Word of God." Long known as Syrian Orthodox, in April 2000 this church's Holy Synod changed its official name in English to the Syriac Orthodox Church of Antioch in order to avoid confusion with Syrian nationality.

HISTORY. Antioch was one of the largest cities in the ancient eastern Mediterranean and became an important political, military, cultural, and commercial center after it was incorporated into the Roman Empire in 64 BCE. It became the Greek-speaking capital of the Roman province of Syria, where most of the inhabitants in the countryside spoke Syriac, a dialect of Aramaic. A Christian community formed at Antioch early in the common era; according to *Acts* 11:26, it was here that the followers of Jesus were first called Christians, and a strong case has been made that the *Gospel of Matthew* was composed in the city. Both Peter and Paul spent time in Antioch; Paul and Barnabas later set out from the city on their missionary journeys after the local prophets and teachers agreed with the undertaking.

Ignatius of Antioch (c. 35–c. 107 CE) provided in his writings the first evidence of a monarchical episcopacy at Antioch, although the Antiochians themselves have traditionally viewed Peter as their first bishop. In the second and third centuries CE a number of heresies arose and caused unrest in the community, including Gnosticism, docetism, Montanism, and Novatianism. Yet these early centuries also saw great scholars and thinkers, such as Paul of Samosata (third century CE), Theodore of Mopsuestia (c. 350–428 CE), and Diodore of Tarsus (d. 394 CE), all three of whom the Syriac Orthodox now regard as heretics. John Chrysostom (c. 354–407 CE) came from the Greek-speaking city church.

The leadership of the Syriac Church was decimated by the persecution that broke out under Diocletian around 304 CE. But by the time of the Council of Nicaea (325 CE) the metropolitanate of Antioch had largely recovered, having six Roman provinces under its jurisdiction (Palestine, Phoenicia, Coele-Syria, Arabia, Mesopotamia, and Cilicia) with sixty-six bishops and ten rural bishops. Edessa, rather than Antioch, was now the center of Syriac Christianity, and its catechetical school, called the Athens of the Aramaic world, flourished until the Byzantine emperor Zeno destroyed it in 489 CE. The center then moved to Nisibis.

Increased efforts by the Byzantine emperors to Hellenize the Syriac-speaking population in the countryside—where the "one nature" Christological formula was widely accepted—met with stiff opposition there and also in Egypt. Resistance began in 449 CE with the Second Council of Ephesus (called the "Robber Council" in the West) and exploded after Chalcedon's adoption of the "two nature" formula in 451 CE. In spite of efforts by the Byzantine emperors to impose Chalcedonian orthodoxy, in the end only about half of the faithful of the ancient Antiochian Patriarchate (located mostly in the Hellenized urban areas) accepted Chalcedon. They eventually adopted the Byzantine rite and become what is in the twenty-first century the Greek Orthodox Patriarchate of Antioch. The other half, more representative of the Syriac-speaking faithful of the interior, never accepted Chalcedon, retained their Syriac liturgical tradition, and evolved into the Syriac Orthodox Church.

By the end of the fifth century CE the Syro-Egyptian revolt found a great champion in Severus, patriarch of Antioch (c. 465–538 CE), under whose influence the Synod of Tyre (513–515 CE) formally rejected the Chalcedonian formula. Byzantium sought to crush the movement through ruthless persecution. In 518 CE the Second Council of Constantinople deposed and anathematized Severus, who then fled to Egypt.

In 521 CE Emperor Justin expelled all non-Chalcedonian monks and clergy and drove the Syriac Church into the wilderness. This contributed to a renaissance of Syriac monasticism, which was characterized by devotion to vigorous asceticism and solitude. One Syriac monastic, Saint Simeon Stylites (c. 389–459 CE), had spent years alone on top of a column, introducing a unique form of Syriac asceticism known as *stylitism*; this practice continued well into the Middle Ages.

In 544 CE the Syriac priest Jacob Baradeus was ordained bishop through the influence of Ḥārith ibn Jabalah, king of the Arabs (c. 529–569 CE), with the support of Empress Theodora (a Syrian) in Constantinople. Bishop Jacob Baradeus is credited with reviving the Syriac Orthodox hierarchy by ordaining some twenty-seven bishops and hundreds of priests and deacons. Because of Bishop Jacob's pivotal role in preserving the church for future generations, its detractors began much later to call the church "Jacobite." But this name was never accepted by the Syriac Orthodox themselves because of its suggestion that Jacob had been the founder of their church.

The Persian invasions began when Chosroes I (reigned 531–579 CE) sacked Antioch in 540 CE and were repeated in 614 CE; by 616 CE both Syria and Egypt had fallen to the Persian Sassanids. The Persians deported large numbers of Syriac Christians to Mesopotamia, where they were joined by Christians disaffected from the local (Nestorian) church of the East. The Syriac Church reorganized itself during this period, and great centers developed at Seleucia-Ctesiphon (Mesopotamia) and again at Edessa. In 629 CE the Byzantine emperor Heraclius, who was an Edessan, drove out the Persians and resumed persecution of the Syriac Orthodox.

In 636 CE the Arabs conquered Syria. The new Islamic Empire, cultured and tolerant, especially after Muʿāwiya, the first Umayyad caliph (661–680 CE), shifted its capital to Damascus, improved the legal status of the Syriac Orthodox, and allowed them to organize themselves separately in Mesopotamia with their own metropolitan with authority over all the faithful east of the Euphrates. Marutha of Tagrit (629–649 CE) was the first bishop to hold this office, having received from the patriarch the title "maphrian of the East." These metropolitans were elected by the bishops of the area and enjoyed a high level of autonomy, even for a time ordaining the patriarchs. (The maphrians were nominated by the patriarchs after 793 CE, and the office became defunct in 1848.) The great center of the church's scholarship was now at the monastery of Kenneshre on the Euphrates. Perhaps its most famous graduate was Jacob of Edessa (633–708 CE), the ascetic scholar and exegete who revised the Syriac Old Testament and the Syriac liturgy.

The Umayyad caliphate of Syria was replaced in 750 CE by the Abbasid caliphate, and in 762 CE the capital was moved to the newly founded city of Baghdad. Under the Abbasids, and also from 969 to 1043 CE, when the Fatimid caliphate ruled Syria from Egypt, there was periodic persecution of Christians and some signs of corruption in the hierarchy and the monasteries. Many Christians converted to Islam. Seljuk Turks conquered Jerusalem and Damascus in the eleventh century. In 1092 the Turkish Empire collapsed, and from 1098 to 1124 the Latin Crusaders occupied Antioch and Jerusalem.

Nevertheless in the twelfth century the Syriac Church had 20 metropolitan sees, 103 bishops, and millions of believers in Syria and Mesopotamia. Sultan Ṣalāḥ al-Dīn (Saladin), who defeated the Crusaders and took over Palestine from them, was supportive of culture and encouraged learned Christians. An outstanding leader and scholar at this time was Patriarch Michael the Great (1126–1199), whose *Chronicle* remains an important source of Syriac Orthodox history. The turbulent thirteenth century, wracked by invasions of Latin Crusaders from the West as well as of Mamluk Turks and Mongols from the East, also produced a number of pivotal figures, including the chronicler and philosopher Gregory Bar Hebraeus (1226–1286), maphrian of the East. The Syriac Orthodox Church grew to more than two hundred dioceses at this time; decline set in around 1401 with the attack by Tamerlane, the Turkic conqueror.

In the seventeenth century a majority of the Thomas Christians of the Malabar Coast in India turned to the Syriac Orthodox Church and asked it to send them bishops in reaction to the reforms and Latin practices that the Portuguese had imposed on them at the Synod of Diamper in 1599. This had led to the Coonen Cross revolt in 1653 and an effort to receive pastoral oversight from a church that would allow them to maintain their ancient traditions. This new relationship was formalized during the visit of Mar Gregorios, Syriac metropolitan of Jerusalem, to India in 1664. The group then formed an autonomous church within the Syriac Patriarchate.

By this time the church in Syria had dwindled to about twenty bishops from probably more than two hundred in the thirteenth century. Capuchin and Jesuit missionaries began to work among the Syriac Orthodox and received many of them into the Catholic Church. The Catholic group chose Bishop Andrew Akhijan as its patriarch in 1662, but he had no successor after his death in 1702. A Catholic patriarchate was permanently established only in 1782, when Syriac Patriarch Michael Jarweh declared himself Catholic and took refuge in Lebanon. The Orthodox then elected a new patriarch of their own, and the two lines have continued into the twenty-first century.

In the nineteenth century, in the Ottoman Turkish Empire, Kurds assaulted Syriac Christians with large-scale massacres in 1843, 1846, and 1860. In 1861 the Levant came under the protection of the French, who worked to strengthen the Catholics. During and immediately following World War I, as the Ottoman Empire was collapsing, tens of thousands of Syriac Orthodox died as a result of massacres and expulsions.

Protestant missionaries in the Middle East since 1819 have also drawn many Syriac Orthodox into their faith communities. Migrations to Europe and the Americas further depleted their numbers, with many of the émigrés joining other churches, Protestant or Catholic.

MODERN TIMES. The nineteenth and twentieth centuries were turbulent times for the Syriac Orthodox in the Middle East, and the struggle for survival became more and more intense. The headquarters of the Patriarchate, which had been in Antioch until 1034, at Mar Barsauma monastery until 1293, and at Der Zafaran monastery until 1933, moved to Homs in 1933 and then to Damascus in 1959. Headed in 2003 by Mar Ignatius Zakka I Iwas (b. 1933, elected 1980), the church has a total of 25 bishops and about 500,000 members. The Syriac Orthodox Church in the twenty-first century has an established hierarchy in Syria, Lebanon, Iraq, Jordan, Turkey, India, the United States, Canada, and Australia. There is also an Archdiocese of Central Europe and the Benelux countries based in the Netherlands, an archdiocese and patriarchal vicariate within the Metropolitanate of Sweden and Scandinavia based in Södertälje, Sweden, and an archdiocese in Germany.

Some theological education is still provided by the monasteries, but Saint Ephrem Syriac Orthodox Seminary is the Patriarchate's major theological school. It was founded in Zahle, Lebanon, but moved to Mosul, Iraq, in 1939. It moved back to Zahle in the 1960s and relocated to Atchaneh, near Beirut, in 1968. The outbreak of civil war in Lebanon forced the removal of the students to Damascus, Syria. New facilities for the seminary at Sayedniya, near Damascus, were consecrated by the Syriac patriarch on September 14, 1996.

The Syriac monastic tradition, nearly wiped out by the invasions of Tamerlane, survives in the Tur Abdin region of southeastern Turkey. There are two sizable complexes at Der Mar Gabriel and Der Zafaran with a total of about fifteen monks and four communities of nuns in the area. There are monasteries in Jerusalem, near Mosul in Iraq, in the Netherlands, in Germany, and in Switzerland. There is also a monastery with about sixty monks connected with the seminary in Sayedniya, Syria. The Syriac patriarch has also created a new order of nuns, the Virgins of Saint Jacob Baradeus, which has about fifteen members. The order's headquarters is in Atchaneh, Lebanon, and there are additional communities in Damascus and Baghdad.

The Syriac Church in India suffered a split in 1912, when a group composing about half of its members declared itself autocephalous (independent) of the Syriac Patriarchate and elected its own catholicos. They and those who had remained loyal to the Patriarchate were reconciled in 1958, when the Indian Supreme Court declared that only the catholicos subject to the Syriac patriarch and bishops in communion with him had legal standing. But in 1975, after the catholicos broke relations with Damascus, the Syriac Patriarchate excommunicated and deposed him and appointed a rival, causing the community to split again. In June 1996 the Supreme Court of India rendered a decision declaring that, whereas there is only one Orthodox Church in India whose spiritual head is the Syriac patriarch, the autocephalous catholicos alone has legal standing as the head of the church in India. Unfortunately this did not reconcile the two communities, whose dispute has become embittered. In 2003 the two sides were more or less evenly divided with about one million adherents each.

ECUMENICAL ACTIVITY. The Syriac Orthodox Church has been an active participant in the modern ecumenical movement; it has been a member of the World Council of Churches since 1960 and was a founding member of the Middle East Council of Churches. In most of the theological dialogues it has acted in concert with the other Oriental Orthodox Churches. It has had a long-standing relationship with the Anglican Communion in the Middle East and India; the Oriental Orthodox and Anglicans reached a Christological agreement in 2002.

The Syriac Orthodox Church also participated in unofficial consultations with the Eastern (Byzantine) Orthodox Churches from 1964 to 1971 and in an official joint commission from 1985 to 1993. In addition the Syriac Orthodox patriarch signed a joint statement with the Greek Orthodox patriarch of Antioch on November 12, 1991, that sanctions much closer relations between the two churches, including a substantial level of sacramental sharing.

Relations with the Catholic Church have improved dramatically, as was shown by the signing of common declarations by Pope Paul VI and Patriarch Ignatius Jacob III in 1971 and by Pope John Paul II and Patriarch Ignatius Zakka I Iwas in 1984. The second declaration states that past schisms and divisions concerning the doctrine of the incarnation "in no way affect or touch the substance of their faith." It also authorized their faithful to receive the sacraments of penance, Eucharist, and anointing of the sick in the other church when access to their own clergy is materially or morally impossible and outlined broad areas of pastoral cooperation. In addition a direct bilateral theological dialogue between the Catholic Church and the Malankara Syrian Orthodox Church began in 1989. It issued an agreement on interchurch marriages in 1993.

LITURGY. The Syriac Orthodox liturgical tradition, often called West Syrian, drew upon translations of Greek texts from Jerusalem and Antioch and added Syriac-language material from Edessa, largely poetry and hymns. It is one of the richest ancient Christian liturgical traditions, with about one hundred Eucharistic prayers, three baptismal liturgies, and poetic sets of daily offices and festal liturgies now available in English (few of which are in use). The choir has not replaced the congregation in worship, as it has in the Byzantine tradition. The principal anaphora (Eucharistic prayer) is that of Saint James, which is rooted in the Jerusalem tradition and attained its present form at the end of the fourth century CE. Many of the hymns in use come from Ephraem the Syrian, the great fourth-century CE ascetic and poet.

BIBLIOGRAPHY

Atiya, Aziz S. *A History of Eastern Christianity.* London, 1968.

Brock, Sebastian, and David G. K. Taylor, eds. *The Hidden Pearl: The Syrian Orthodox Church and Its Aramaic Heritage.* Rome, 2001.

Chaillot, Christine. *The Syrian Orthodox Church of Antioch and All the East: A Brief Introduction to Its Life and Spirituality.* Geneva, 1998.

Daniel, David. *The Orthodox Church of India.* 2d ed. New Delhi, 1986.

McCullough, W. Stewart. *A Short History of Syriac Christianity to the Rise of Islam.* Chico, Calif., 1982.

Moffett, Samuel H. *A History of Christianity in Asia,* vol. 1: *Beginnings to 1500.* New York, 1992.

Paulos Gregorios. *The Orthodox Church in India: An Overview.* Delhi and Kottayam, India, 1982.

Paulos Gregorios. "Syrian Orthodox Church of Antioch." In *The Encyclopedia of Religion,* 1st ed., edited by Mircea Eliade, vol. 14, pp. 227–230. New York, 1987.

Sélis, Claude. *Les Syriens orthodoxes et catholiques.* Turnhout, Belgium, 1988.

Trimingham, J. Spencer. *Christianity among the Arabs in Pre-Islamic Times.* New York, 1979.

RONALD G. ROBERSON (2005)

SZOLD, HENRIETTA

SZOLD, HENRIETTA (1860–1945), was a Zionist leader and a founding president of Hadassah, the leading women's Zionist organization in the United States. Born in Baltimore, Maryland, the eldest child of Benjamin Szold and Sophia (Schaar) Szold, she was educated by her father, a rabbi, and in local schools, graduating first in her high school class. She subsequently taught, wrote articles in the Jewish press, and organized night classes for east European Jewish immigrants in Baltimore before leaving for Philadelphia in 1893 to work for the Jewish Publication Society of America (founded 1888). There, she edited and translated important volumes of Judaica, indexed Heinrich Graetz's *History of the Jews,* and for a time compiled the *American Jewish Year Book.* In 1903 she attended classes at Jewish Theological Seminary of America in New York. In 1909, after her first love, Louis Ginzberg, professor at the seminary, married another woman, she traveled to Palestine, where her Zionist commitments were renewed. In 1910, she became secretary of the Federation of American Zionists, and two years later joined with other women to found Hadassah on a nationwide basis. After 1916, she devoted her full attention to the organization and spent considerable time in Palestine involved in its medical and educational endeavors as well as broader Zionist affairs. She spent her last years directing the efforts of Youth Aliyah, the movement established to save Jewish youngsters in Nazi-occupied Europe by bringing them to Palestine.

Henrietta Szold espoused a Jewish way of life that was at once deeply religious, strongly ethical, and broadly tolerant. Her religious practices and outlook were shaped by Conservative Judaism, but she followed an independent course, evinced considerable interest in Jewish religious writings by women, and insisted on her right to recite the Qaddish prayer in memory of her mother, as well as to fulfill other Jewish religious obligations traditionally restricted to men. Impelled by her religious values as well as her lifelong pacifism, she associated during her last years with Jewish thinkers in Palestine who sought Arab-Jewish rapprochement and advocated a binational state. Her example of Jewish social activism coupled with her fostering of traditional Jewish ideals has inspired Jewish women throughout the world, particularly those associated with Hadassah.

BIBLIOGRAPHY

Henrietta Szold's writings and letters remain scattered; for a small selection, see Marvin Lowenthal's *Henrietta Szold: Life and Letters* (New York, 1942). A brief but penetrating overview of Szold's life and career by Arthur Hertzberg appears in *Notable American Women,* edited by Edward T. James et al. (Cambridge, Mass., 1971). Full-length studies include Alexandra Lee Levin's *The Szolds of Lombard Street: A Baltimore Family, 1859–1909* (Philadelphia, 1960), which covers her early life, and two critical biographies: Irving Fineman's *Woman of Valor: The Life of Henrietta Szold, 1860–1945* (New York, 1961) and Joan Dash's *Summoned to Jerusalem: The Life of Henrietta Szold* (New York, 1979).

New Sources

Gidal, Nachum Tim. *Henrietta Szold: A Documentation in Photos and Text.* Jerusalem, 1997.

JONATHAN D. SARNA (1987)
Revised Bibliography

T

ṬABARĪ, AL- (AH 224/5–310; 839–923 CE), fully Abū Jaʿfar Muḥammad ibn Jarīr al-Ṭabarī, was an Islamic religious scholar and historian. Born in Āmul in Ṭabaristān, northern Persia, just south of the Caspian Sea, al-Ṭabarī reports that by the age of seven he had learned the Qurʾān by heart, by the age of eight had qualified as a prayer leader (*imām*), and by the age of nine was studying traditions from Muḥammad. At the age of twelve he set off on the proverbial Muslim quest for knowledge, first by attending school in Rayy (in what is now Tehran) and then, in 855, setting off for Baghdad, likely in hopes of studying with the famous traditionist Aḥmad ibn Ḥanbal, who, however, died in that same year just before al-Ṭabarī's arrival. After a number of sojourns in other cities in Iraq, Syria, Palestine, and Egypt, he settled in Baghdad and devoted his life to scholarly pursuits involving teaching and writing. Al-Ṭabarī is reported to have written over twenty works, although differentiating individual books is sometimes problematic because of the suspicion that some works may be known under a variety of titles. According to various anecdotes, al-Ṭabarī avoided taking any positions of administrative responsibility, despite the urging of government officials and colleagues, and devoted his energies purely to his work. Stories are told of him writing forty pages a day for forty years, and while the accuracy of the numbers is doubtful given their symbolic value, his dedication to his work is apparent in the level of his output.

Al-Ṭabarī was an impressively prolific polymath. He wrote on such subjects as poetry, lexicography, grammar, ethics, mathematics, and medicine, although none of his works on these topics has survived. His fame today rests primarily upon his writings in the fields of history, the Qurʾanic sciences, and law. The scope of his accomplishments in the first two fields is especially significant given the unique value of his two main works, the world history entitled *Taʾrīkh al-rusul wa-al-mulūk* (The history of the prophets and the kings) and the commentary (*tafsīr*) on the Qurʾān entitled *Jāmiʿ al-bayān ʿan taʾwīl āy al-Qurʾān* (The gathering of the explanation of the interpretation of verses of the Qurʾān).

Al-Ṭabarī's *Jāmiʿ al-bayān ʿan taʾwīl āy al-Qurʾān* is, at least superficially, a voluminous compendium of traditional matter concerned with the meaning of each verse of the

---

CLOCKWISE FROM TOP LEFT CORNER. The Golden Pavilion, or Kinkakuji, in Kyoto, Japan. *[©Dallas and John Heaton/Corbis]*; Thor's hammer amulet, tenth century. National Museum of Iceland, Reykjavik. *[©Werner Forman/Art Resource, N.Y.]*; Tenth- to twelfth-century stone carving of Chacmool near the Temple of the Warriors at Chichen Itza in Mexico. *[©Kevin Schafer/Corbis]*; Temple of Hatshepsut in Luxor, Egypt. *[©Dallas and John Heaton/Corbis]*; Nepalese Tārā. *[©Christie's Images/Corbis]*.

Qurʾān, presented in sequence following the text of scripture. Some 35,000 traditions (with a significant degree of duplication present in actual interpretational material) going back to the first Islamic century (seventh to eighth centuries CE) are cited. Al-Ṭabarī was also a creative scholar, however, and his editorial function in compiling this type of information cannot be ignored. Any reports of Qurʾanic interpretation attributed to Muqātil ibn Sulaymān (d. 767), for example, are omitted, presumably because of his tarnished reputation as a reliable source. In general, al-Ṭabarī omits any information that was rejected by the consensus of the community at his time. In addition, al-Ṭabarī virtually always notes which interpretation of a given verse he prefers, and he is given to supporting his contentions with philological analysis or poetical evidence not necessarily connected with any report from a traditional authority. He also discusses matters of dogmatics and law, in some instances in a detailed manner and on a sophisticated level. The theological outlook in his work is in keeping with the mainstream of Baghdad thought at the time, following in the legacy of Ibn Ḥanbal, although his opinions did, on occasion, evoke some protest among local rival scholars. His theological position is also evidenced in two independent works, *Ṣarīḥ al-sunnah* (The essence of correct practice), a brief profession of faith (*ʿaqīdah*) written in response to accusations of incorrect belief on al-Ṭabarī's part by his contemporaries; and a fragment of his work on the "principles of religion," *uṣūl al-dīn*, entitled *Tabṣīr fī maʿālim al-dīn* (An instruction concerning the characteristics of religion), which was directed to the inhabitants of his hometown of Āmul regarding sectarian opinions that were emerging in the area.

Each section of *Jāmiʿ al-bayān* commences with a quotation from the Qurʾān, generally a verse or a thematic unit. Traditions are then cited, complete with their chains of authority *(asānīd;* singular: *isnād)* substantiating the transmission of the report; the traditions are grouped according to different possibilities of interpretation for the passage in question. The citation of these groups of traditions is frequently preceded by a statement such as, "Interpreters differ concerning the meaning of God's having said that. . . ." Following the enumeration of all attested interpretations, al-Ṭabarī usually gives his own preference, saying, "In my opinion, the best of the statements is the following. . . ," and he argues the case on the basis of parallel Qurʾanic passages, grammar, poetry, theology, or whatever seems appropriate to make his point.

Al-Ṭabarī also appended a fairly extensive introduction to *Jāmiʿ al-bayān* entitled *Risālat al-tafsīr* (The epistle on interpretation), in which he sets forth some principles of interpretation along with a discussion of the standard disputed issues concerning the Qurʾān (the language of the Qurʾān, the notion of the seven readings of the text, and the collection of the Qurʾān). He argues for a concept of the "obvious" (*ẓāhir*) meaning of the Qurʾān, rather than metaphorical or figurative renderings, as the only legitimate mode of interpretation. This "obvious" meaning of a text can be overridden only by a positive indication of the necessity to do so, as by a tradition that is fully authoritative and convincing. Otherwise the *ẓāhir* meaning, defined as "what predominates in practice," *al-ghālib fī-al-istiʿmāl*, must be accepted. Al-Ṭabarī also compiled as a separate work a massive collection and evaluation of textual variants to the Qurʾān, *Kitāb fī-al-qirāʾāt* (A book on the variant readings), which still exists today in manuscript form.

As a historian, al-Ṭabarī equaled his accomplishments as a Qurʾanic exegete. His *Taʾrīkh al-rusul wa-al-mulūk*, which exists today in fifteen printed volumes, is said to be a greatly abbreviated version of al-Ṭabarī's original plan. The work commences with the creation and the era of the biblical patriarchs, details some early rulers of Israel and Persia, and then moves on to Sassanid history. As might be expected, the text becomes far more detailed after this portion. For the life of Muḥammad, the first four caliphs of Islam, the Umayyad dynasty, and the Abbasid rulers up to 915, it is organized year by year. The aim of the work was to document world history leading up to Muḥammad, and then to trace the continuity of the experiences of the Muslim community in the following years. Like his Qurʾān commentary, this work is traditionally oriented in structure, although here al-Ṭabarī's editorial role is more clearly limited to selection, arrangement, and documentation of the material cited; rarely do the editor's own words intrude.

Al-Ṭabarī's respect for his method of simple presentation results in much duplication, such that historical records conveying similar material are found frequently. This results from the inclusion of reports that stem from different sources, all of which were judged by al-Ṭabarī to be trustworthy in the *isnād* of their transmission and thus intrinsically valuable. His history telling, therefore, is not linear but a conjunction of varying accounts. Al-Ṭabarī's editorial role does at least allow him to support his own regional and partisan positions within the broad scheme of Islamic history. *Taʾrīkh al-rusul wa-al-mulūk* quickly became famous in the Islamic world, with later writers using it as the basis for even more comprehensive works and others working at extending its chronological dimensions and also translating it into Persian and Turkish.

Al-Ṭabarī attempted to strike out on his own in the juristic field. He formed a school of law (called the Jarīrīyah after his father), but it quickly fell into obscurity after his death, since it was not substantially different from the school of al-Shāfiʿī, to which al-Ṭabarī originally belonged. Fragments of a large work that al-Ṭabarī wrote on law, *Ikhtilāf al-fuqahāʾ* (The disagreement among the jurists), which details the opinions of great jurists of early Islam, as well as of a collection of *ḥadīth* entitled *Tahdhīb al-āthār* (The revised compilation of the traditions), still exist, but those works represent only a small portion of his overall scholarly output in the area.

Al-Ṭabarī is considered a master of historical writing and of *tafsīr*, and in subsequent generations he was seen as the most important intellect of his age, a *mujtahid*. He gained this stature not only because of his prodigious output but also because of his critical acumen, especially as displayed in *Jāmiʿ al-bayān*. The *tafsīr* is also the earliest complete and extensive work of its type available today (although other briefer but earlier works do still exist), and the history has been a major source for all reconstructions of events in early Islam, since it is, like the *tafsīr*, the earliest comprehensive compilation of historical reports for the Islamic period. Considering the importance and value of the works, it is somewhat surprising that few complete manuscript copies have survived to the present (scattered single volumes are available in numerous libraries, however) and that, until the end of the nineteenth century, the complete work of the *tafsīr* was believed lost. Perhaps because of the voluminous nature of the texts, they remained works suitable only for other scholars; later summaries and translations of the works became particularly important and, in some ways, eclipsed the original work, even though al-Ṭabarī's fame as a historian and religious scholar remained intact.

BIBLIOGRAPHY

Taʾrīkh al-rusul wa-al-mulūk was published under the general editorship of M. J. de Goeje with the title *Annales quos scripsit Abū Djafar Moḥammed ibn Djarīr aṭ-Ṭabari*, 15 vols. (Leiden, 1879–1901). Other editions were printed in Cairo in 1909 and in 1960–1965. The entire work has been translated into English in thirty-nine volumes, *The History of al-Ṭabarī* (Albany, N.Y., 1985–1999), volume 1, *General Introduction, and From the Creation to the Flood*, translated and annotated by Franz Rosenthal (1989), provides a detailed survey of al-Ṭabarī's life, works, and accomplishments. For an understanding of the scope of al-Ṭabarī's history, see Claude Gilliot, "Récit, mythe, et histoire chez Tabari: Une vision mythique de l'histoire universelle," *Mélanges de l'institut dominicain d'études orientales du Caire* 21 (1993): 277–289; and Chase F. Robinson, *Islamic Historiography* (Cambridge, U.K., 2003). A full treatment of al-Ṭabarī's history and studies about it is found in Franz-Christoph Muth, *Die Annales von aṭ-Ṭabarī im Spiegel der europäischen Bearbeitungen* (Frankfurt, 1983).

Al-Ṭabarī's commentary (*tafsīr*) on the Qurʾān, *Jāmiʿ al-bayān ʿan taʾwīl āy al-Qurʾān*, was first published in Cairo in 1903 and again in 1905; a new Cairo edition was begun in 1954. A summary translation has been published in French by Pierre Godé, *Commentaire du Coran* (Paris, 1983), in five volumes, and a portion, through *sūrah* 2, verse 103 (including the introduction), is available in English as *The Commentary on the Qurʾān, by Abū Jaʿfar Muḥammad b. Jarīr al-Ṭabarī, Being an Abridged Translation of Jāmiʿ al-bayān ʿan taʾwīl āy al-Qurʾān*, with an introduction and notes by J. Cooper, edited by Wilferd Madelung and Alan Jones (Oxford, 1987). A fundamental study on this work is Otto Loth, "Tabari's Korancommentar," *Zeitschrift der Deutsche morgenländischen Gesellschaft* 35 (1881): 588–628. Harris Birkeland, *The Lord Guideth: Studies on Primitive Islam* (Oslo, 1956), provides a detailed study of the structure of the traditions cited by al-Ṭabarī. Herbert Berg, *The Development of Exegesis in Early Islam: The Authenticity of Muslim Literature from the Formative Period* (Richmond, U.K., 2000), uses al-Ṭabarī's *tafsīr* as a source of data to discuss the issue of the reliability of the ascription of material to early authorities. Claude Gilliot, *Exégèse, langue, et théologie en Islam: L'exégèse coranique de Tabari (m. 311/923)* (Paris, 1990), is a masterful study of al-Ṭabarī's exegetical approach; it is supplemented by Gilliot's articles "Exégèse et sémantique institutionelle dans le commentaire de Tabari," *Studia Islamica* 77 (1993): 41–94, and "Mythe, recit, histoire du salut dans le commentaire coranique de Tabari," *Journal Asiatique* 282 (1994): 237–270.

On al-Ṭabarī's *ḥadīth* work, see Claude Gilliot, "Le traitement du *Ḥadīṯ* dans le *Tahḏīb al-āṯār* de Tabari," *Arabica* 41 (1994): 309–351. Al-Ṭabarī's creed is translated in Dominique Sourdel, "Une profession de foi de l'historien al-Ṭabarī," *Revue des études islamiques* 36 (1968): 177–199.

ANDREW RIPPIN (2005)

ṬABĀṬABĀʾĪ, ʿALLĀMA. Muḥammad Ḥusayn Ṭabāṭabāʾī (1903–1981) was arguably one of the most prominent Shīʿī Muslim scholars of the twentieth century; he was given the honorific title *ʿAllāma*, a testimony to the extent and depth of his knowledge in the Shīʿī tradition of Islamic scholarship.

Ṭabāṭabāʾī was born into a family of Shīʿī *ʿulamāʾ* (Islamic scholars) in Tabrīz, northwest of Iran, in 1903. In 1918, after finishing his primary education, he entered the field of religious studies and, until 1925, he studied Arabic grammar, logic, principles of Islamic jurisprudence, Islamic law, theology, and philosophy. In 1926 he settled in Najaf, the most famous Shīʿī seminary *(ḥawza)* in Iraq at that time, in order to complete his higher studies, attaining a license to perform *ijtihād*—independent reasoning and deduction based on the principles and sources of Islamic law.

He returned to Tabrīz, his birthplace, in 1934. In 1946, due to the political situation in the northwest of Iran, which at that time was under the influence of the Soviet Union, he went to the city of Qum, where he resumed his scholarly research. In Qum he taught Islamic philosophy and Qurʾanic studies for the rest of his life and became one of the greatest contemporary masters in these two disciplines.

Ṭabāṭabāʾī was a prolific writer in both Arabic and Persian. His work had a profound impact on contemporary Shīʿī thought, principally through his contribution to four areas: Qurʾanic commentary and interpretation, philosophy, mysticism, and sociocultural debate.

Ṭabāṭabāʾī successfully revitalized the discipline of Qurʾanic exegesis *(tafsīr)*, making this one of the core subjects of the curriculum within the seminary of Qum. His own monumental commentary on the Qurʾān, *al-Mīzān fī Tafsīr al-Qurʾān*, is ample evidence of his mastery of all the sciences required for in-depth Qurʾanic interpretation.

Al-Mīzān appeared at a time when standards of scholarship in Shīʿī seminaries were determined by the discipline of jurisprudence *(fiqh)*. Those who were involved in other fields, such as *tafsīr,* were considered weak both in scholarly and social terms. The reason was that although in the seminaries the discipline of *fiqh* was dominated by Uṣūlī thought, *tafsīr* was still strongly influenced by the rival Akhbārī school, which places primary stress upon the narration of traditions (*aḥādīth* or *akhbār,* pl. of *khabar,* "report"). Thus, *tafsīr* was not given very much importance. Ṭabāṭabāʾī succeeded in radically changing this state of affairs, such that *tafsīr* is now considered one of the major disciplines within Shīʿī seminaries. The key interpretive principle applied by Ṭabāṭabāʾī in his commentary is that of interpreting verses of the Qurʾān through other verses of the Qurʾān. According to him, in order to obtain an understanding of the objective meaning of the Qurʾān, the interpreter must set aside all personal ideas and opinions and make an effort to understand and interpret the verses of the Qurʾān only in the light of other Qurʾanic verses. Although this method was used in part by various schools of interpretation, it was Ṭabāṭabāʾī who articulated and employed this method most successfully, making it the very cornerstone of his interpretive hermeneutic. He wrote *al-Mīzān* over a period of eighteen years, from 1954 to 1972. Originally written in Arabic in twenty volumes, it has been translated into Persian, and the first six volumes have been translated into English.

Ṭabāṭabāʾī also played a significant role in elevating the status of Islamic philosophy in Shīʿī circles, and particularly within Iran; he contributed to the process by which philosophy became once again a major focus of teaching and research. Although he was a master in Mullā Ṣadrā's philosophical school, *al-ḥikmah al-mutaʿāliyah* (transcendent theosophy), he avoided the mixing of philosophy with the traditional, transmitted sources, the Qurʾān and *ḥadīth,* that characterizes the works of Mullā Ṣadrā's school of philosophy. Ṭabāṭabāʾī insisted on maintaining a clear distinction between these two disciplines, as is clearly expressed in his philosophical works *Bidāyat al-ḥikma* (The beginning of philosophy) and *Nihāyat al-ḥikma* (The ultimate end/goal of philosophy).

His contribution to Islamic mysticism, known in its Shīʿī form as *ʿirfān,* consisted in his teaching of one of the principal sources of this approach, that is, the school of Muḥyī al-Dīn Ibn al-ʿArabī. He succeeded in his efforts, despite strong opposition from many exoteric Shīʿī scholars of his time. The emergence in the Shīʿī seminary of Qum of a new generation of scholars well-versed in the mysticism of Ibn ʿArabī is in large part due to his influence.

Ṭabāṭabāʾī was also actively involved in sociocultural debates about Islam. After World War II, the influence of modernism and Marxism on traditional Iranian society was increasing. Ṭabāṭabāʾī devoted several books and articles to discussing key issues arising out of these confrontations between modernism and tradition—such as the status of religion in the modern world, the rights of women, and the weakness of materialistic philosophy. Between 1958 and 1977 Ṭabāṭabāʾī had an important series of scholarly and philosophical debates with Henry Corbin, the renowned French scholar of Islamic thought. He also encouraged his students to participate in sociocultural debates; among those students, one should mention such figures as Murtaḍā Muṭahharī and Muḥammad Ḥusayn Bihishtī, who went on to play important roles in Iran's Islamic revolution in 1979.

The influence of Ṭabāṭabāʾī on Shīʿī thought generally remains very strong; at present most of the masters of Islamic philosophy, mysticism, and interpretation of the Qurʾān in the seminaries of Iran were his students. In addition to the above-named students, one should also mention such towering figures as S. J. Āshtiyyānī, Ayatollah Javādī Āmulī, and Ayatollah Ḥasanzādih Āmulī, who are now known as the leading experts in Iran in interpretation of the Qurʾān, Islamic philosophy, and *ʿirfān.* Seyyed Hossein Nasr was also one of Ṭabāṭabāʾī's students, and it was through Nasr that Ṭabāṭabāʾī was introduced to the English-speaking world, with his translation of Ṭabāṭabāʾī's *Shīʿa dar Islam,* as *Shiʿite Islam,* in 1975. Ṭabāṭabāʾī died on November 15, 1981.

SEE ALSO Ibn al-ʿArabī; Mullā Ṣadrā.

BIBLIOGRAPHY

Works by Ṭabāṭabāʾī

Al-Mīzān fī Tafsīr al-Qurʾān. 20 vols. Beirut, 1974.

Shiʿite Islam. Translated and edited by Seyyed Hossein Nasr. London and Albany, N.Y., 1975. Includes Ṭabāṭabāʾī's biography and bibliography.

The Qurʾān in Islam: Its Impact and Influence in the Life of Muslims. Translated by A. Yates. Blanco, Tex., and London, 1987.

Islamic Teaching: An Overview. Translated by R. Campbell. New York, 1989. Includes a translation of the author's brief autobiography.

Al-Mīzān: An Exegesis of the Qurʾān. Vols. 1–7. Translated by Syed Saeed Akhtar Rizvi. Tehran, 1983–1992.

Studies

Al-Awsī, ʿAlī. *Al-Ṭabāṭabāʾī wa Manhajuh fī Tafsīrih al-Mīzān.* Tehran, 1985.

Miṣbāḥ, Muḥammad Taqī. "Naqsh ʿAllāma Ṭabāṭabāʾī Dar Nihḍat Fikrī Hawzah ʿIlmiyyah Qum." In *Yādnāmih Mufassir Kabīr Ustād ʿAllāma Sayyid Muḥammad Ḥusayn Ṭabāṭabāʾī,* edited by A. Mīyānajī, pp. 135–144. Qum, Iran, 1982.

Nasr, Seyyed Hossein. "Ṭabāṭabāʾī, Muḥammad Ḥusayn." In *The Oxford Encyclopedia of the Modern Islamic World,* vol. 4, edited by John L. Esposito, pp 161–162. Oxford, 1995.

Qurʾānic Research Quarterly 9–10 (1997). Issue devoted to Ṭabāṭabāʾī.

MOHAMMAD JAFAR ELMI (2005)
REZA SHAH-KAZEMI (2005)

IMAGES AND THE BODY

One of the few generalizations about religion that may be safely declared is that the practice of belief is always, in one way or another, a firmly embodied affair, transpiring in the medium of the human body. Even in the hands of the most zealously ascetic or scholastic adherents, religion's deep register is the body that is denied, cloaked, disciplined, or scorned. In less repressive religious cultures, the body is celebrated as the vessel of memory, the bearer of social status, the medium of divine presence, and the richly adorned display of fecundity, transport, joy, or sexual union.

The human body offers manifold possibilities to act as the medium of belief. Costume for ritual occasions such as prayer or recitation of holy writ **(a)** shapes personal performance by investing the individual with the solemnity of public display. More permanent changes to the body, such as tattoos, make personal statements that link the individual to a variety of communities—some of them ethnic or racial, but also the associations of tattoo wearers linked through tattoo shops, clubs, newsletters, and magazines. Religious iconography, such as

(a) A Jewish boy reads from the Torah at his bar mitzvah. *[©Nathan Nourok/ Photo Edit]*

that displayed on the back of the woman shown here **(b)**, operates across the lines of many subcultures.

In addition to the decoration of the body itself, artists everywhere have made use of the human form in objects and images that allow endless permutations of meaning. The Luba people of the Democratic Republic of the Congo carve figural stools **(c)** for the complex array of seating arrangements that structure the hierarchy of the privileged members of the Luba court. The stools consist of female figures (but can also be abstract forms) upholding the sitter, which is a male chief or a member of the royal court. The female body possesses the power of birth-giving and serves as the vessel containing the spirit of the king. Past kings remain invested in their stools. The features of the female figure, particularly the patterns of scarification, are material texts that encode royal history. Luba women are believed to hold the taboos and restrictions of kingship within their bodies and as such serve as the figures symbolically holding up the kings.

(b) ABOVE. A cross and the opening words of *Psalm 23* tattooed on a woman's back. *[©Steve Chenn/Corbis]* **(c)** RIGHT. Luba caryatid stool of carved wood, Democratic Republic of the Congo. *[©Christie's Images/Corbis]*

The material forms of religious practice are found to address all aspects of human embodiment. Four objects from South Pacific societies make this clear. Drumming is part of the liturgical life of peoples as far apart as Oceania, native North America, Africa, and Mongolia. As an accompaniment to song and dance, the drum helps to celebrate key ritual occasions, such as funerals or the completion of a house or canoe among peoples in Papua New Guinea **(d)**. The steady beat of the drum structures chant and resonates through the body, harmonizing the group that sings clan songs, initiates youth, or performs the lamentation of burial. The drum is an instrument that evokes bodily participation in the social life of ritual. No less a part of ceremony is the painting of the body. Dishes such as the one reproduced here **(e)** were used in Papua New Guinea to mix pigments. It has been suggested that since the figures on such dishes represent clan animals and ancestors, using them for the mixing of colors applied to the body may have been part of a ritual absorption of clan

(d) Above. A hand drum from East Sepik province in Papua New Guinea, wood, fiber, shell, animal hide, and pigment. *[Masco Collection; photograph by Dirk Baker]* **(e) Left.** A pigment dish from East Sepik province in Papua New Guinea, wood, fiber, and pigment. *[Masco Collection; photograph by Dirk Baker]*

or ancestral spirits into the very body of the participant. On the island of New Zealand, richly carved objects were used to attend to other aspects of the body. A carved wooden bar, called *paepae* **(f)**, may have been part of the ritualizing of excreting waste. It has been suggested that such a device was bitten by someone using a latrine as the final act of elimination, providing a cleansing of taboo caused by excretion. The Maori also used another type of carved device, the feeding funnel **(g)**. It was forbidden for food to touch the lips of chiefs while they healed from the application of tattoos. The feeding funnel allowed the chief to eat semi-liquid food. The elaborately tattooed faces on the outside of the funnel may correspond to the power the funnel seeks to preserve in the tattooed face of the chief who ate with the funnel.

(f) **Top.** A *paepae* of carved wood and haliotis shell, New Zealand. *[Masco Collection; photograph by Dirk Baker]* **(g)** **Left.** A Maori feeding funnel (*koropata*) of carved wood and haliotis shell, New Zealand. *[Masco Collection; photograph by Dirk Baker]*

Religious practices mine the human body for its rich metaphorical significance. Olmec artists produced marvelous ceramic figures of infants **(h)**, whose interpretation remains inconclusive, but which have been linked to funerary practices, shamanistic rites, and fertility ceremonies. For example, small figures shown in the care of old women have led some to believe that the infant figures helped shamans perform rites effecting cures or healthy births. Other forms of evidence associate the sculptures of infants with sacrificial rites that transformed the infants into rain and vegetation, thus procuring seasonal regeneration and agricultural fertility. One authority indicates that the ceramic figures themselves may have been used in such rites, or may represent the children who were sacrificed. In either case, infancy meant rebirth and the remarkable skills of Olmec artists at naturalistic rendition of the infant's gesture and fleshy forms no doubt enhanced the efficacy of the rite.

If images of infants could assist with the renewal of nature in ancient Olmec culture, a visual practice at the beginning of the Common Era among Egyptians sought to ensure an individual's life after death. The practice involved affixing realistic portrayals of individuals to their mummified bodies in order for their spirits to recognize themselves and reside in the body after death **(i)**. These portraits were commissioned during the lifetime of

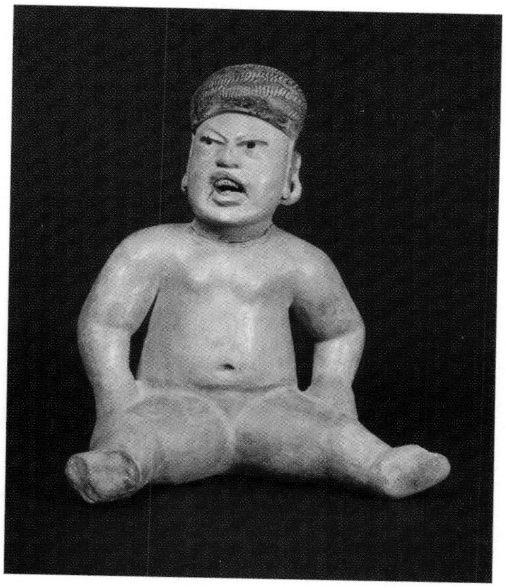

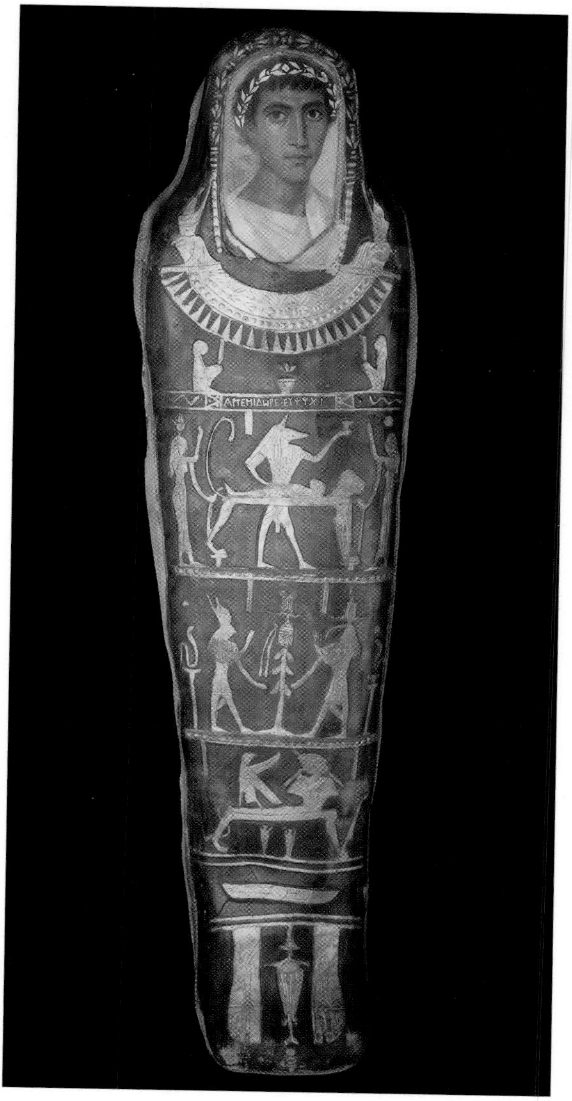

(h) **Top.** An Olmec figure, 1200–900 BCE, Mexico. *[©Kimbell Art Museum/Corbis]* **(i)** **Right.** A mummy case with a portrait of Artemidorus, Hawara, Egypt, Roman period, c. 100–120 CE. *[©HIP/Scala/Art Resource, N.Y.]*

the individual and displayed at home, then used in the preparation of the body after death. This close association of image and body may have been incorporated into Christian practice, which found an important place for the relics of saints and martyrs. The fifteenth-century bust of Saint Margaret of Antioch **(j)** recalls the early fourth-century saint who defeated a dragon, which is seen here lying docilely beneath her hand. She was martyred during the reign of Diocletian, one of the last pagan emperors of late antiquity. Now missing is the relic of the saint that occupied the compartment in the figure's chest. Margaret's dedication to assisting women in labor made her popular in the Middle Ages and the infantile size of the dragon may dramatize her power to soothe the pain of childbirth.

Another martyred woman, Daphne, was portrayed by the artist Kiki Smith in a way that recalls the torture of Christian saints. According to Ovid, Daphne was metamorphosed into a laurel tree in order to be delivered from the amorous pursuit of Apollo. When she prayed "change and destroy the body which has given too much delight," her human flesh changed to bark, limbs, and

(j) ABOVE. Nicolaus Gerhaert and workshop, *Bust of Saint Margaret of Antioch*, c. 1465–1470, walnut. ***[Lucy Maud Buckingham Medieval Collection, 1943.1001 overall; photograph by Robert Hashimoto; reproduction, The Art Institute of Chicago]*** **(k) RIGHT.** Gian Lorenzo Bernini, *Apollo and Daphne*, 1624, marble. ***[©Scala/Art Resource, N.Y.]***

leaves (Ovid, *Metamorphoses*, bk. 1). Smith portrays the body of the helpless nymph crucified by her own wish. Although Ovid indicates that it was the malice of Cupid that inflicted love upon the chaste girl by piercing Apollo with his fated arrow, Daphne blames her body for inciting desire. Smith leaves us to wonder why the body of a woman suffers as the victim of the male assault of desire. By contrast, the Baroque sculptor Gian Lorenzo Bernini produced a virtuoso performance in marble **(k)** in which the viewer is intended to marvel at the sensuous transformation of marble into flesh as well as marble into tree limbs and foliage, almost without pausing to consider the injustice done to Daphne.

The violent stilling of desire occupies a great deal of religious energy. Hinduism, like Christianity, possesses a long-established ascetic tradition in which practitioners deny themselves physical comforts, dress, and possessions, and take only the least amount of nutrition, as in the case of the Indian Sādhu or holy man shown here **(l)**. One of the oldest aspects of Christianity is mortification of the flesh. In the later Middle Ages and the early modern period, visual contemplation of Christ's suffering was one of the primary forms of Christian spirituality. Following the Protestant Reformation, a reassertion of images of suffering—portraying Christ, his disciples, and the saints—were designed to invite devout viewers to direct their attention and devotion to the self-effacing merits of Christ **(m)** and

(l) ABOVE. An Indian sādhu and a woman at prayer in Vārāṇasī. *[©David Samuel/Corbis]* **(m)** LEFT. Giovanni di Paolo, *Christ Suffering and Christ Triumphant*, later fifteenth century, portrays the two aspects of Christ, demonstrating the doctrine of salvation afforded by his sacrifical death on the cross and his power over death as final judge. *[©Scala/Art Resource, N.Y.]*

(n) Giovanni Francesco Guercino, *Saint Peter Martyr*, oil on canvas, seventeenth century. Holding the symbolic palm of martyrdom and calmly posing with the instrument of his death lodged in his head, the saint receives the reassurance of divine acceptance from two angels. *[©Scala/Art Resource, N.Y.]*

his martyred followers **(n)**. At times this imagery was especially graphic in order to jolt viewers to attention and to elicit from them an empathic response accompanied by remorse and self-incrimination. The sacrifice and pain undertaken by Christ and the saints were the means of human salvation and were to be regarded with solemn gratitude.

Bibliography

Clifton, James. *The Body of Christ in the Art of Europe and New Spain, 1150–1800.* Munich and New York, 1997.

Coe, Michael D., et al. *The Olmec World: Ritual and Rulership.* Princeton and New York, 1995.

Posner, Helaine. *Kiki Smith.* Boston, 1998.

Roberts, Mary Nooter, and Allen F. Roberts. *Memory: Luba Art and the Making of History.* New York and Munich, 1996.

Wardwell, Allen. *Island Ancestors: Oceanic Art from the Masco Collection.* Seattle and Detroit, 1994.

David Morgan (2005)

TABERNACLES, FEAST OF SEE SUKKOT

TABOO

TABOO is a social prohibition or restriction sanctioned by suprasocietal (innate) means or a socially sanctioned injunction alleged to have the force of such a prohibition. Taboo stands at the intersection of human affairs and the forces of the larger universe. Generally it is determined by divine or animistic mandates; but it may involve "punishment" by inherent circumstances as well, for instance, the real, but exaggerated, danger of genetic damage to the offspring of incestuous unions implied in the incest taboo of American folk culture.

The word *taboo* (from the Tongan *tabu,* a variant of the more general Polynesian term *tapu* and the Hawaiian *kapu*) reached the West through Captain James Cook's account of his third voyage. He was introduced to the term at Tongatapu, in the Tonga, or Friendly, Islands, and commented that the word had a very comprehensive meaning but generally signified a thing that is forbidden (Webster, 1942, p. 5). In fact, the general Polynesian usage implies that what is *tapu* is interdicted through its relation to the sacred, or its relation to cosmic forces. *Tapu,* then, relates the cosmic to human actions, and the realm of *tapu* amounts to a comprehensive system of religious mandate controlling individual and social life.

In Polynesian religion, *tapu* has the function of segregating persons, objects, or activities that are divine or sacred, or those that are corrupt or polluting, from the common, everyday realm. Thus chiefs, high-ranking persons, and their lineages were surrounded with *tapu*; the heads of all persons, and especially of chiefly persons, were *tapu*; but also the clothing and sleeping places of women in their menstrual periods were dangerous to men, who were *tapu* in relation to them (Best, 1905, p. 212). An "eating *tapu*" required men and women, and often all classes of persons of unequal status, to eat separately, or even to have their food prepared separately and with different utensils.

Consecrational *tapu* applied in circumstances of worship and labor performed for the gods and temples, and those involved entered a *tapu* state, which had to be neutralized later. Life-crises events (birth, marriage, illness, death) involving chiefly persons, wars, and fishing expeditions imposed community-wide restrictions on common activities, including the preparation and eating of food, movement, the lighting of fires, and noisemaking. *Tapu* could also be invoked through appealing to the gods to enforce a prohibition on some object, crop, or piece of land; in the Marquesas Islands a chief could taboo land in this way by calling it his "head." A temporary taboo laid on crops, trees, or fishing grounds was called a *rahui* (Handy, 1927, p. 46).

Tapu, as a state of sacred interdiction, stands in contrast to the neutral, or common, state, *noa* (whatever is free from *tapu* restriction). Fresh as well as salt water was used throughout Polynesia for the removal and neutralizing of *tapu* and of polluting influences harmful to one's *tapu* (Handy, 1927, pp. 51–55). Fire and heat were also used ritually against baneful influences, especially spirits. Many communities maintained a "sacred water" or spring specifically for the removal of *tapu.*

The cosmic principle or force behind the restrictions and prohibitions of *tapu* is conveyed in the general Polynesian conception of *mana. Mana* is invisible and abstract, knowable only through its efficacy and through its manifestation in things, yet it is universal. Like the Arabic *barakah, mana* combines sacredness with the sense of "luck" or "power" in the most encompassing terms. Chiefs, chiefly persons and their possessions and doings, and rites involving the gods are *tapu* because they are suffused with *mana.* The danger of polluting influences is that they may discharge the *mana* of persons or objects that are more highly endowed; common persons, on the other hand, run the risk of being struck or overcome by *mana* greater than theirs. *Tapu* may be seen as the "insulator" between unequal degrees of *mana.* Thus Handy suggests that electricity may serve as a useful analogy in illustrating the nature of the concept of *mana* (ibid., p. 28), though of course it is fundamentally a religious rather than a naturalistic concept.

Even modern curers and others who have recourse to its manipulation consider *mana* distinct in its operation from the world of ordinary life processes, exchanges, and human interaction. Curers who use *mana* may not accept compensation in money (MacKenzie, 1977). As a universal power, *mana* is evidenced in every kind of efficacy: a woodcarver manifests *mana* in his talents and in the tools and circumstances of his work, and canoe makers, gardeners, curers, sorcerers all have their *mana,* capable of being lost or dispersed unless the proper *tapu* are observed. Of these examples of *mana* the chiefly *mana* is the highest and most concentrated, and it poses a serious danger for the unprotected commoner.

As an abstract and generalized conception of power, *mana* is analogous to Lakota *wakan,* Iroquois *orenda,* and other concepts of power found among indigenous North American groups. The term is by no means universal among Austronesian-speaking peoples, though many have cognate notions. Among the major world religions *mana* has counterparts, perhaps, in the Islamic notion of *barakah,* the Hindu notion of *sakti,* and possibly in the Greco-Christian concept of *charisma.*

The notion of the "psychic unity of mankind," that is, that human cultures everywhere must pass through certain necessary stages of evolutionary growth, allowed speculative writers around the turn of the twentieth century to draw conspicuous examples of primitive religious concepts from particular ethnographic areas and universalize them. The Polynesian notions of *tapu* and *mana* lent themselves extraordinarily well to this search for the epitomizing evolutionary trait, for they were already quite abstract and, in Captain Cook's phrase, "very comprehensive" in their meanings.

Early anthropologists deemed taboo noteworthy, for it marked the point where a religious idea (*mana*) affected the norms and regulation of everyday life. Breach of a taboo meant divine or other suprasocietal sanctions; hence, taboos, or a system of taboos, outlined the spiritual mandate and boundaries for social existence.

In the evolutionary model for primitive religion that emerged in the decades immediately before and after 1900, taboo played the role of archetypal religious rule, or mandate; as *mana* did of generalized supernatural force, or power; and as totemism did of collective or individual identification with supernatural (or quasi-natural) entities. Thus emerged the alliterative formula "totem and taboo" as an encompassing rubric for primitive religion, to which Freud turned in seeking socially expressed equivalents for psychological states.

In the writings of Émile Durkheim, and among his followers in the schools of French and British social anthropology, *taboo* came to have the sense of a largely social restriction, or mandate, through the Durkheimian proposition that the religious and the supernatural were the means by which society took account of its own existence—worshiped itself. If, in other words, the suprasocietal forces of the world around us are nothing more than the reflection of society itself, then taboo, however it may be regarded by the members of a society, is ultimately social in its origin. Even in this understanding of it, however, *taboo* carries a somewhat stronger connotation than mere "law" or "rule," for taboos are special instances in which social constraints are referred directly to the religious manifestation of the social rather than to a secular authority.

The modern sense of *taboo* has acquired a certain ambiguity through the widespread acceptance of a socio-centric interpretation. Thus, depending on whether one accepts a formal, cultural, or a sociological understanding of the prohibition, the sanctions upon it will be, respectively, divine and innate, or human and social.

But the issue of the sanctioning force behind a taboo involves only a partial appreciation of the distinctiveness of this kind of prohibition. Taboo differs from abstract, codified law in the degree to which the prohibited object or act is specified and developed into a symbol, or even a fetish, of the prohibition itself. Taboo is not so much a system of regulations as it is a scheme of negative differentiation, in which the fact of prohibition and the prohibited act or object itself obscure the reasons for a prohibition. In this regard, the early theorists who saw "totem and taboo" as interlinked bases of "primitive thought" drew attention to a significant relation between them. For taboo designates items in order to prohibit them, whereas totemic representation is based on affinities between social units and phenomenal entities. Yet the practice of exogamy (marrying outside of one's totemic group), once felt to be an integral part of totemism, comprehends both of these at once, for it places a marriage taboo on those who share affinities with the same entity.

Thus taboos serve to control and channel human interaction and collective activity through a system of negative differentiation, marking out certain persons, objects, and occasions by specifying what may not be done to, with, or on them. Words used as names are sometimes tabooed when a person holding the name undergoes a change in status. In the Marquesas and Society islands, a common word included in the name of a king or heir apparent would be tabooed and also replaced in everyday language. When a king of Tahiti assumed the name *Pomare,* the word *po* ("night") was replaced in common speech by *rui,* and *mare* ("cough") was changed to *kare* (Webster, 1942, p. 301). Similar taboos are found among the Zulu and the Malagasy. Among the Tiwi of northern Australia, the name of a person who has died, together with the common-noun equivalent of that name, and all the names that the deceased had bestowed upon others, together with their equivalents, are tabooed for ordinary use and transferred to a sacred language (Lévi-Strauss, 1966, pp. 209–210).

Taboos on name use, and often on any sort of interaction, are frequently encountered in the norms for kin relationship. In Papua New Guinea these are so common that the Pidgin term for "relative by marriage" is simply *tambu* ("taboo"). The extreme case, widespread in Aboriginal Australia and New Guinea, is a taboo involving total avoidance between a man and his wife's (or future wife's) mother. A relationship is set up between them precisely by their not interacting, one that forces them to communicate solely through the bridal exchanges. Thus the tabooing or, in this case, the negative differentiation of relationship creates the basis for future relationships by creating a marriage. Further taboos of affinity control and direct the subsequent course of the relationship by restricting overfamiliarity among other kinspeople brought into contact by the marriage.

Taboos on specific kinds, classes, or styles of food and on food preparation are perhaps the most commonly encountered of all human prohibitions. Many peoples who have no general term for "taboo" have a word for "food taboo." Food restrictions, probably universal in human cultures, often conceal (or initiate) preferences or are themselves disguised as health precautions. Well-known examples include the Hebraic prohibition against using the same utensils for preparing meat and dairy products, the Hebraic and Islamic restrictions against eating the meat of animals that have been incorrectly slaughtered and against eating pork, and the Hindu ritual distinction between *pakkā* foods, prepared in clarified butter, and *kaccā* foods, boiled in water. Among the Kaluli of Mount Bosavi in Papua New Guinea, an elaborate system of food taboos operates to prevent relationships among cultural domains that must not be mixed. Married men and women must not eat fresh meat, and smoked meat is available only through exchanges with in-laws; thus, bonds will form through marriage links rather than with single hunters (Schieffelin, 1976, p. 71).

Mourning restrictions most often take the form of taboos, ranging from prohibitions on speaking of, or using the names of, the deceased, through those on the use of the house or property of the deceased, to severe injunctions of seclusion (for widows or widowers). In parts of the Pacific, there are restrictions against washing or self-adornment, and often the mourners must wear relics. In traditional China, specific degrees of mourning behavior were specified according to one's relationship to the deceased. Among the Yi people of Yunnan Province in China visitors are prohibited from entering a compound where there are newborn infants or piglets, where someone is gravely ill, or where someone has died. Immediately upon a person's death, among the Usen Barok of New Ireland, a taboo called the *lebe* goes into effect: no gardening can be done, no fires can be made, and no arguments will be tolerated until the conclusion of the final mourning feast, up to a week later. It is also forbidden to utter a cry of lament until the mourners hear the first squeals of the pigs being slaughtered for the first feast.

Taboos surrounding ritual or worship are often the severest of all, for they involve mediation with the very forces that are understood to mete out the sanctions. The major ritual of the Daribi of Papua New Guinea concerns the placating of an unmourned and angry ghost, who possesses the *habu* ritualists in the process. Any deviation from the prescribed format of the ritual results in the affliction of the offenders with the dread *habu* illness, a malign act of possession that is merely the intended therapeutic possession gone awry (Wagner, 1972, p. 156). Food taboos accompanying the Chihamba ritual among the Ndembu of Africa keep the participants from "eating Chihamba" or the characteristics associated with this spirit (Turner, 1975, pp. 71–72). The sense of ritual indiscretion as mediation gone wrong is conveyed by the Navajo belief that ghosts cause people to do the opposite of whatever has been decreed in taboos.

The emphasis of a taboo, however negatively it may be phrased, is always upon the thing, act, or word tabooed. We tend to contemplate the object of the taboo itself in a search for motives, or possibly origins, for the prohibition. Thus, for instance, pork is a potential carrier of trichinosis, mothers-in-law have many potential conflicts of interest with their sons-in-law, and interbreeding among close relatives may lead to the expression of deleterious recessive genes. The difficulty with this sort of literalistic thinking can be seen in these examples. Taboo is usually indirect; its real object is not so much what is forbidden as it is the cultural and social circumstances affected by the prohibition. The Kaluli do indeed say that the juices of fresh meat are unhealthy for women and that their husbands should avoid it out of compassion. But the taboo on the eating of fresh meat for married persons serves to force them into the painstaking and appropriate activity of preparing and exchanging smoked meat with relatives by marriage. It aligns with a number of other taboos to restrict interaction to culturally appropriate categories.

The Daribi, in another example, actually have no experience of disagreeable mothers-in-law, for a married person is never allowed to see the mother-in-law, much less speak with her. But the taboo forces each party to be especially aware of the other and to funnel their efforts into organizing the exchanges that must pass between the two sides. An effective relationship is formed through the principle of "not relating"! Finally, what we know as the "incest taboo" is actually the summation of a number of particular kin relationships, which are of differing extent and content in different cultures. What may be considered to be incestuous, or a relative, or a relationship, varies from one culture to another. But the fact of kin regulation through restriction, or kin taboo, if you will, is common to all cultures, for it is the essence of kinship. Hence, whether its prohibitions are imposed by men or gods, taboo incorporates the regulatory imperative of culture itself.

See Also Evolution, article on Evolutionism; Power; Purification.

Bibliography

Best, Elsdon. "The Lore of the Whare-Kohanga." *Journal of the Polynesian Society* 15 (1906): 147–162. An early, but classic, discussion of *mana* and pollution in Maori lore.

Handy, E. S. Craighill. *Polynesian Religion.* Honolulu, 1927. A dated, but synoptic, summary, with comprehensive sections on *mana* and *tapu.*

Lévi-Strauss, Claude. *La pensée sauvage.* Paris, 1962. Translated anonymously as *The Savage Mind* (London, 1966). A challenging and highly original treatment of the symbolism of differentiation and classification.

MacKenzie, Margaret. "*Mana* in Maori Medicine: Rarotonga, Oceania." In *The Anthropology of Power,* edited by Raymond D. Fogelson and Richard N. Adams, pp. 45–56. New York, 1977. An engaging and illuminating account of the use of *mana* in a modern, mechanized society.

Schieffelin, Edward L. *The Sorrow of the Lonely and the Burning of the Dancers.* New York, 1976. A well-written ethnographic exploration of an exotic worldview, including a comprehensive investigation of food taboos.

Turner, Victor. *Revelation and Divination in Ndembu Ritual.* Ithaca, N.Y., 1975. A mature consideration of ritual and ritual prohibition by a foremost modern authority on the subject.

Wagner, Roy. *Habu: The Innovation of Meaning in Daribi Religion.* Chicago, 1972. A discussion of the symbolism of taboo and ritual prohibition in a New Guinea society.

Webster, Hutton. *Taboo: A Sociological Study.* Stanford, Calif., 1942. A highly detailed documentation of taboos and related ethnographic usages in a somewhat dated scholarly style.

Roy Wagner (1987)

TAFSĪR

TAFSĪR is an Arabic word meaning "interpretation"; it is, more specifically, the general term used in reference to all genres of literature which are commentaries upon the Qurʾān.

Tafsīr and Related Terms. The word *tafsīr* is used only once in the Qurʾān (25:33), but this is not overly surprising, for most technical terms involved in Muslim exegesis have been derived and adapted either from the field of rhetoric or from the legal tradition. In the case of *tafsīr* the word appears to have evolved from a description of a poetic figure in which one hemistich contains an explanation of the preceding one.

There is much discussion in various Arabic sources concerning the precise meaning of the term *tafsīr* and its relationship to other technical words such as *maʿānī, taʾwīl,* and *sharḥ,* all of which connote "interpretation" in some way. Historically, *maʿānī,* literally "meanings," appears to have been the earliest major term used for the title of works of interpretation; *taʾwīl,* literally related to the notion of "returning to the beginning," was introduced perhaps late in the third century AH (early tenth century CE) as the general term for works of Qurʾānic interpretation, only to have been supplanted in the eleventh century CE by *tafsīr. Sharḥ* seems to have been reserved primarily for profane purposes such as commentaries on poetry, but it was also employed for Qurʾanic super-commentaries. The prime focus of a dispute which took place probably in the early tenth century and which involved such central figures of early exegesis as Abū Jaʿfar al-Ṭabarī (d. 923 CE) and al-Māturīdī (d. 944) was the differentiation of *tafsīr* from *taʾwīl.* Both of these major exegetes, note, used the word *taʾwīl* in the title of their commentaries upon the Qurʾān: *Jamiʿ al-bayān ʿan taʾwīl āy al-Qurʾān* (The gathering of the explanation of the interpretation of the verses of the Qurʾān) and *Taʾwīlāt al-Qurʾān* (The interpretations of the Qurʾān), respectively. The basic question at stake concerned the ways in which traditional material could be employed to provide exegetical data. *Taʾwīl,* in the understanding of some scholars, was interpretation which dispensed with tradition and was founded upon reason, personal opinion, individual research, or expertise, whereas *tafsīr* was based upon material *(ḥadīth)* transmitted through a chain of authorities from the earliest period of Islam, preferably from Muhammad himself or at least from one of his companions. However, the point was certainly never clear, because other proposed differentiations between *taʾwīl* and *tafsīr* glossed those simple edges. Muqātil ibn Sulaymān, an early exegete (d. 767), for example, implies a distinction between *tafsīr* as what is known on the human level and *taʾwīl* as what is known to God alone. According to a similar notion, *tafsīr* applies to passages with one interpretation and *taʾwīl* to those with multiple aspects. And, of course, a further complication is indicated by the very title of al-Ṭabarī's *tafsīr:* that is, *taʾwīl* could be used for a work that was quite tradition-oriented, at least in basic form. A further suggestion is that the dispute over *tafsīr* and *taʾwīl* is to be traced back to the earliest sectarian disputes in Islam, between the general community and the followers of Muḥammad's son-in-law and cousin, ʿAlī ibn Abī Ṭālib (d. 661), known as the Shīʿah, who wished to appropriate the word *taʾwīl* for reference to interpretation of "concealed" (i. e., esoteric) parts of the Qurʾān as demanded by Shīʿī doctrine.

It should also be noted that the terms *tafsīr* and *taʾwīl* were not in fact the exclusive property or concern of Muslims; Jews and Christians writing commentaries on the Bible in Arabic used both words. The Jewish theologian Saʿadyah Gaon (d. 942) titled his Arabic translation of the Pentateuch *Tafsīr basīṭ naṣṣ al-Tūrāh* (The simple interpretation of the text of the Torah), and the Copt Butrus al-Sadamanti in about the year 1260 wrote *Al-muqaddimah fī al-tafsīr* (Introduction to interpretation), which formed a part of his overall work on the interpretation of the New Testament Passion narratives. These are only two examples of use of the word *tafsīr* for scriptural interpretation outside Islam; many other similar instances could be cited.

PURPOSE OF TAFSĪR. Interpretation aims to clarify a text. *Tafsīr* takes as its beginning point the text of the Qurʾān, paying full attention to the text itself in order to make its meaning clear. It also functions simultaneously to adapt the text to the present situation of the interpreter. In other words, most interpretation is not purely theoretical; it has a very practical aspect of making the text applicable to the faith and the way of life of the believers. The first of these two interpretive aspects is generally provoked by insoluble problems in meaning, by insufficient detail, by intratextual contradiction, or by unacceptable meanings. Interpretation that fits the text to the situation serves to align it with established social custom, legal positions, and doctrinal assertions.

Other practical reasons can also be cited for the initial creation of *tafsīr* as an entity. As Islam expanded, it was embraced by a large number of people who did not know Arabic; interpretation, sometimes in the form of translations (although this was officially frowned upon) and other times in a simple Arabic which did not contain the ambiguities and difficulties of the original scriptural text, fulfilled the purpose of allowing easier access to the book. In addition, there was the basic problem of the text itself and how it was to be read. The early Arabic script was defective in its differentiation of letters of the alphabet and in the vocalization of the text; although eventually there arose an official system of readings *(qirāʾāt)* which gave sanction to a basic seven sets of vocalizations of the text (with further set variations still possible to some extent), in the earliest period a greater freedom with regard to the text seems to have been enjoyed. This freedom extended to the consonantal structure of the text and was legitimized through the notion of the early existence of various codices of the Qurʾān, each with its own textual peculiarities. Differences between these versions and the later, official ʿUthmanic text (as far as theses could be cited by the exegetes), as well as the variations created by the different official vocalization systems, then demanded explanation and justification in order to establish claims that a particular reading provided the best textual sense. The end result was that *tafsīr* acted to establish a firm text of scripture within what became the set limits of the *qirāʾāt.*

ORIGINS OF TAFSĪR. Traditionally it has been held that *tafsīr* arose as a natural practice, originating with Muḥammad and then continuing organically from that point forward; the earliest material has thus become known as *tafsīr al-nabī* ("the interpretation of the Prophet"). Various companions of Muḥammad and some early believers are also seen as the major figures who started interpreting the Qurʾān and teaching people exactly what their understanding of the text was; central among them was ʿAbd Allāh ibn ʿAbbās (d. 687?), who gained the title *tarjumān al-Qurʾān,* "the interpreter of the Qurʾān."

A debate rages in the scholarly literature on the nature of early *tafsīr,* most especially over the idea of opposition to the activity itself in the early Islamic period. This notion was first isolated by Ignácz Goldziher in *Die Richtungen der islamischen Koranauslegung* (Leiden, 1920); on the basis of traditional Muslim reports concerning the caliph ʿUmar (d. 644) and his punishment of a certain person (variously identified) for interpreting unclear passages of the Qurʾān, Goldziher concluded that interpretation of Qurʾanic verses dealing with historical legends and eschatology was illegitimate. Harris Birkeland in *Old Muslim Opposition against Interpretation of the Koran* (Oslo, 1955) rejected this contention on the basis of his own evaluation of the traditional reports, which suggested to him certain contradictions, especially over the identity of the flogging victim and over whether such punishment was in keeping with ʿUmar's character. Birkeland has argued that, rather than general opposition to *tafsīr,* there was no opposition at all in the first Muslim century, that strong opposition arose in the second century, and that thereafter the activity of *tafsīr* was brought into and under the sphere of orthodox doctrine and requirements. In particular, strict methods were introduced for the transmission of the information, which formed the core of interpretational procedure, and in this way, *tafsīr* gained total acceptance. Nabia Abbott, in an excursus to her *Studies in Arabic Literary Papyri II: Qurʾānic Commentary and Tradition* (Chicago, 1967), reasserted Goldziher's isolation of early opposition on the basis of traditional information that the person in question certainly existed and that flogging was in keeping with the character of ʿUmar. For Abbott, however, the opposition was limited to the interpretation of a specific category of unclear verses *(mutashābihāt),* a claim that she based on the traditional biographical material, which indicates that those people who are mentioned as opponents of *tafsīr* in fact transmitted much material themselves. Therefore, for Abbott, the only opposition to *tafsīr* that ever existed was that connected with the ambiguous or unclear verses. Precisely what is to be understood by the "unclear verses," however, is glossed over in this argument. Exegetes never have agreed and never will agree on which verses are unclear, or even on what that expression means. Some things are unclear to one person while they are perfectly clear to another, often because of a different (especially religious) perspective on the material.

The major problem with all of these discussions is the lack of substantial evidence, with the result that the entire argument remains speculative. Manuscript evidence for *tafsīr* barely reaches back to the third century AH (ninth century CE), at which point several genres of commentary had already emerged. Much of the material found in these texts seems to have originated in a popular worship context (such as semiliturgical usage or sermons) or in the storyteller environment provided by wandering preachers *(quṣṣāṣ)* and their didactic, homiletic sermonizing, which aimed to improve the religious sentiments of the uneducated majority of people. In other words, producing entertaining tales was a key to the development of *tafsīr.* From this point of view, the whole discussion of the origins of *tafsīr* as conducted by Goldziher, Birkeland, and Abbott is rendered rather redundant.

LEGITIMATION OF TAFSĪR IN THE QURʾĀN. While the Qurʾān does not explicitly state that it should be interpreted, commentators have been able to justify their profession over the centuries by reference to the text itself. The most famous and the most problematic passage applied in this way is *sūrah* 3:5–6, the terminology of which has been referred to several times in the preceding sections:

> It is He who has sent down to you the book in which are clear verses [*muḥkamāt*] that are the essence of the book and others that are unclear [*mutashābihāt*]. As for those in whose hearts is a perversion, they follow the unclear part, desiring dissension and desiring its interpretation *[taʾwīl].* But no one knows its interpretation *[taʾwīl]* except God. And those firm in knowledge say: "We believe in it; all is from our Lord." Yet none remember except men who understand.

This passage establishes two categories of interpretation, perhaps most easily viewed as "clear" *(muḥkam)* versus "unclear" *(mutashābih).* Many different translations and identifications have been put forth for the latter, some of which render the category hermeneutically trivial (e.g., identification of the "mysterious letters" which precede various *sūrahs* as the *mutashābihāt*), while others prove more valuable (e.g., identification of all verses with more than one interpretive aspect as *mutashābihāt*). Even more crucial, however, was the punctuation of the verse. The original Arabic text provides no indication of where stops and pauses should be taken; as a result, it was also possible to render the latter part of the pericope:

> But no one knows its interpretation except God and those firm in knowledge who say: "We believe in it; all is from our Lord."

With such a reading, the interpretive task was not limited to the rather trite exercise of making totally plain the already clear verses; the unclear verses, too, became targets for the commentators, and with that concept defined in some appropriate manner, the way was opened for the creation of a *tafsīr* on every verse of the Qurʾān.

EMERGENCE OF TAFSĪR LITERATURE. It seems fairly certain that written *tafsīr* works began to emerge in the second century AH at the latest. Documentation starts to proliferate toward the end of that period, and various modes of analysis (e.g., attention to the convergent lines of transmission of a text) also suggest this as the earliest verifiable period. The emergent literature itself can be analyzed into various categories which not only display the distinctive literary qualities and differences of the texts but also suggest an overall relative historical ordering of them. The five sequential categories suggested by John Wansbrough in his *Quranic Studies: Sources and Methods of Scriptural Interpretation* (Oxford, 1977) are narrative (aggadic), legal (halakhic), textual (masoretic), rhetorical, and allegorical. While the historical sequence itself may be open to some debate, the categorization itself is, in true scientific fashion, functional, unified, and revealing.

Narrative tafsīr. Narrative *tafsīr* is exemplified in the text by Muqātil ibn Sulaymān, which has subsequently been given the title *Tafsīr al-Qurʾān* (Interpretation of the Qurʾān), although that is unlikely to have been the original name, and is also embodied in various sections of the work by Ibn Isḥāq (d. 768), *Sīrat Rasūl Allāh* (The life of the messenger of God). The creation of an edifying narrative, generally enhanced by folklore from the entire Near Eastern world (including the heritages of Byzantium, Persia, and Egypt, but most especially that of the Judeo-Christian milieu) is the main feature of such commentaries. Adding detail to otherwise sketchy scripture and answering the rather mundane questions which the curious mind will raise when confronted by a contextless scriptural passage are the central concerns of this genre. In fact, the actual narrative seems to be of prime importance; the text of scripture remains underneath the story itself, often subordinated in order to construct a smoothly flowing narrative.

For the first part of *sūrah* 2:189 ("They are asking you about the new moons. Say: 'They are appointed times for the people and the pilgrimage'"), Muqatil tries to provide the answers for the curious reader. Just who is asking? Why did they ask? Precisely what did they ask? This type of approach is the essence of aggadic *tafsīr.* Muqatil provides the following comment on the verse:

> Muʿādh ibn Jabl and Thaʿlabah ibn Ghanamah said: "O Messenger! Why is it that the new moon is just visible, then it appears small like a needle, then brightens until it is strong, then levels off and becomes a circle, only to start to decrease and get smaller, until it returns just as it was? Why does it not remain at a single level?" So God revealed the verse about the new moons.

The identification of the participants and the precise question being asked (provided in a marvelously naive and therefore entertaining manner) are specified. The overall interpretation of the verse becomes clear through this supplying of contextual material.

Legal tafsīr. Muqātil ibn Sulaymān once again is a focal point in the development of legal interpretation. Here, the arrangement of the material becomes the prime indicator of the genre; whereas in narrative interpretation the order of scripture for the most part serves as the basic framework, for the legal material a topical arrangement is the definitive criterion. The fact that the actual content of Muqātil's legal *tafsīr,* entitled *Tafsīr khams mīʾah āyah min al-Qurʾān* (The Interpretation of Five Hundred Verses of the Qurʾān), is probably derived from his narrative *tafsīr* reveals that the prime criterion is indeed the form of the work.

Muqātil's text covers the following topics: faith, prayer, charity, fasting, pilgrimage, retaliation, inheritance, usury, wine, marriage, divorce, adultery, theft, debts, contracts, and holy war. This range of topics gives a fair indication of the nature of much of the material in the Qurʾān which was found to be of legal value.

Textual tafsīr. Activities centered on explanations of the lexicon of scripture, along with its grammar and variant readings, are the focus of textual commentaries. One of the earliest texts devoted to this type of analysis is that of the philologist al-Farrāʾ (d. 822) entitled *Maʿānī al-Qurʾān* (The meanings of the Qurʾān), a fairly technical work which primarily explains the difficult points of grammar and textual variants. The work of Abū ʿUbayd (d. 838), *Faḍāʾil al-Qurʾān* (The merits of the Qurʾān), is similar, although it is divided by topic rather than following the Qurʾanic order, as does the work of al-Farrāʾ. Earlier simple texts also exist, including that by Muqātil ibn Sulaymān, *Kitāb al-wujūh wa-al-naẓāʾir* (The book of [word] senses and parallels), and al-Kisāʾī (d. 804), *Mushtabihāt al-Qurʾān* (The resemblances of the Qurʾān), both of which are devoted to semantic analysis of the text. Muqātil's text compiles lists of word usages according to the number of senses of meaning *(wujūh)* of a given word; al-Kisāʾī's work is similar but deals with phrases rather than individual words.

Rhetorical tafsīr. Concern for the literary excellencies of scripture is the focal point of works such as that by Abū ʿUbaydah (d. 824), *Majāz al-Qurʾān* (The literary expression of the Qurʾān), although the origin of this type of analysis may well be in textual exegesis (with a grammatical focus) rather than in a purely literary type. The impetus for its development as a separate genre, however, was the nascent notion of the miraculous character of the Qurʾān and the literary evidence for it. While this became a full doctrine only in the fourth century AH, its exegetical roots are to be found here. The work *Taʾwīl mushkil al-Qurʾān* (The interpretation of the difficulties in the Qurʾān), by Ibn Qutaybah (d. 889), proves to be an important transition point between this earliest rhetorical analysis based upon grammatical and exegetical niceties and that of the later doctrine of the miraculous character or inimitability of the Qurʾān *(iʿjāz).* In these texts attention is paid to the literary qualities of the Qurʾān which place it outside the norm of Arabic prose and poetry; various poetical figures are isolated, for example, are subjected to analysis for meaning, and, in many cases, are then compared with older Arabic poetry.

Allegorical tafsīr. Support for dissident opinion in Islam was generally found *ex post facto* through the expediency of allegorical interpretation. Supported through a terminological differentiation of the *ẓāhir* as *historia,* "literal," and the *bāṭin* as *allegoria,* "symbolic," the Ṣūfī *tafsīr* of Sahl al-Tustarī (d. 896) exemplifies this trend in the earliest period. No attempt is made in this work, however, to provide an overall allegorical interpretation; rather, it takes isolated passages from the text of scripture and views them in light of mystical experience. The order of scripture is followed in al-Tustarī's text as it now exists, although the initial compilation may not have followed any such order. About one thousand verses (out of some sixty-two hundred) in the Qurʾān are covered in this manner.

The commentary itself, which is structured piecemeal and reads in a disjointed fashion, contains much more than straightforward allegorical interpretation: legends of the ancient prophets, stories about Muḥammad, and even some about the author of the work himself also find their place. Nor is any overall pursuit of mystical themes to be found; indeed, its general nature is fragmentary. The esoteric portions of the text are formed around typically Ṣūfī meditations on the Qurʾān, each taking a key word from the text. Allegorical interpretation in this case becomes as much a process of thematic association as one of textual commentary.

Consolidation of Classical Tafsīr. It is with the fourth century AH (tenth century CE) that true works of *tafsīr* emerge, combining in various ways the five formative elements I have described above. The first landmark of this type of *tafsīr* is that of al-Ṭabarī, *Jāmiʿ al-bayān ʿan taʾwīl āy al-Qurʾān,* which gathers together in a compendium reports from earlier authorities dealing with most aspects of the Qurʾān. Verse-by-verse analysis is provided, each detailed with virtually every major interpretational trend (except sectarian). The material supplied in this manner is given in its full form, complete with the chains of transmitters for each item of information to lend the weight of tradition to each statement. This type of work is classically called *tafsīr bi-al-maʾthūr* ("interpretation by tradition"), as opposed to *tafsīr bi-al-raʾy* ("interpretation by opinion"), but the categories are misleading. Al-Ṭabarī provides his own personal interpretation, both implicitly by his editorial selection of material and explicitly by stating his opinion where different trends of interpretation exist, sometimes even going against the entire thrust of tradition and providing his own point of view; in this sense, this work, too, is *tafsīr bi-al-raʾy.*

In the centuries after al-Ṭabarī, *tafsīr* as an activity increased and became more and more sophisticated and, in some cases, reached voluminous quantities. Al-Māturīdī, Abū al-Layth al-Samarqandī (d. 983?), al-Thaʿlabī (d. 1035), and al-Wāḥidī (d. 1075) are all prominent people who in the fourth and fifth centuries AH produced volumes of *tafsīr,* sometimes, as in the case of al-Wāḥidī, in multiple editions.

Theological concerns begin to make a greater impact upon *tafsīr* in this period; it is a trend which culminates in the production of the most famous Qurʾān commentaries in the Muslim world, those of the rationalist Muʿtazilī al-Zamakhsharī (d. 1144), the philosopher Fakhr al-Dīn al-Rāzī (d. 1209), and the Sunnī traditionalist al-Bayḍāwī (d. sometime between 1286 and 1316). Debates rage among these authors, and many others, over the central questions of Islamic theology and the various positions to be found in the Qurʾān. Topics covered include free will and predestination, the attributes of God, the nature of the Qurʾān, the imposition of the tasks of the law, the nature and extent of the hereafter, and so forth. The Muʿtazilī al-Zamakhsharī opts for interpretation based upon reason in his commentary *Al-kashshāf ʿan ḥaqāʾiq ghawāmiḍ al-tanzīl* (The unveiler of the realities of the secrets of the revelation). Apparent contradiction between verses of the Qurʾān are resolved in favor of the Muʿtazilī doctrines of the unity and justice of God. Al-Bayḍāwī produced an edited version of the text by al-Zamakhsharī in his *Anwār al-tanzīl wa-asrār al-taʾwīl* (The lights of the revelation and the secrets of the interpretation), removing in the process most of the Muʿtazilī tendencies and compressing the material into an even more concise form. Al-Rāzī's unfinished *tafsīr, Mafātīḥ al-ghayb* (The keys of the unknown), discusses the Qurʾān in terms of a rationalist philosophy which for the most part involved a rejection of the Muʿtazilī position and argued in support of orthodoxy. Humans, for al-Rāzī, are predetermined, and God's freedom and power cannot be confined by human rationality.

Encyclopedist *tafsīr* works in the tradition of al-Ṭabarī also continue with writers such as Ibn Kathīr (d. 1373), al-Shawkānī (d. 1839), and al-Ālūsī (d. 1854). The opposite trend toward distillation reaches its peak, in popular terms, with the *Tafsīr al-Jalālayn* of Jalāl al-Dīn al-Suyūṭī (d. 1505) and Jalāl al-Dīn al Maḥallī (d. 1459).

Specializations within Classical Tafsīr. While the all-encompassing commentary marks the highlight of exegetical activity in the classical period, the field of specialized Qurʾānic sciences was emerging at the same time, providing a number of subdisciplines within *tafsīr.* Some of these are continuations of the earliest developments; others arise under new impetuses. General compendia of information on these sciences arise in the discipline known as *ʿulūm al-Qurʾān* ("the sciences of the Qurʾān"), represented by such works as *Nukat al-intiṣār li-naql al-Qurʾān* (Gems of assistance in the transmission of the Qurʾān), by al-Bāqillānī (d. 1012); *Al-burhān fī ʿulūm al-Qurʾān* (The criterion for the sciences of the Qurʾān), by al-Zarkashī (d. 1391); and *Al-itqān fī ʿulūm al-Qurʾān* (The perfection about the sciences of the Qurʾān), by al-Suyūṭī. The topics gathered in these books are also subjects of separate monographs by a wide variety of writers; these topics include *naskh,* abrogation of legal passages of the Qurʾān; *asbāb al-nuzūl,* the occasions of revelation of individual verses and surahs of the Qurʾān; *tajwīd,* recitation of the Qurʾān; *al-waqf wa-al-ibtidāʾ,* pauses and starts in recitation of the Qurʾān; *qirāʾāt,* variants to the text of the Qurʾān; *marsūm al-khaṭṭ,* the writing of the Qurʾān; *aḥkām,* the laws of the Qurʾān; *gharīb,* the strange or difficult words in the Qurʾān; *iʿrāb,* the grammar of the

Qurʾān; *qiṣaṣ al-anbiyāʾ,* the stories of the prophets; and *iʿjāz,* the inimitability of the Qurʾān. As these topics indicate, it is indeed difficult to separate developed *tafsīr* from both legal concerns *(fiqh)* and grammar *(naḥw).*

SECTARIAN TAFSĪR. Parallel to the development of mainstream Sunnī Muslim *tafsīr* in the classical period, works arose from various other Muslim groups, each pursuing its own particular sectarian aim and, once again, attempting to make the Qurʾān relevant to its own particular point of view and situation.

Shiism. For the Shīʿah in general, the authority of the imams who descended from ʿAlī ibn Abī Ṭālib was ultimate in matters of interpretation of the Qurʾān. While *ḥadīth* traditions circulated in Sunnī circles were generally accepted, this material was often supplemented or corrected on the authority of the imams. The category of the *mutashābihāt* was particularly useful to the Shīʿah, for a number of appropriate "unclear" verses could be understood as referring to ʿAlī and his family. Such verses were also useful for "discovering" stridently critical comments concerning the early leaders of the Muslim community, namely Abū Bakr (d. 634), ʿUmar, and ʿUthmān.

The earliest Ithnā ʿAsharīyah or Twelver Shīʿī *tafsīr* in existence today appears to be the somewhat fragmentary commentary of ʿAlī ibn Ibrāhīm al-Qummī (d. tenth century) with the ascribed title *Tafsīr al-Qurʾān;* other prominent works include *Al-tibyān fī tafsīr al-Qurʾān* (The explanation in interpretation of the Qurʾān), by Muḥammad ibn al-Ḥasan al-Ṭūsī (d. 1067), and a major commentary which is a compendium of information comparable to that of al-Ṭabarī, *Majmaʿ al-bayān li-ʿulūm al-Qurʾān* (The collection of the explanation of the sciences of the Qurʾān), by Abū ʿAlī al-Ṭabarsī (d. 1153 or later).

Allegorical interpretation is favored in Shīʿī *tafsīr* as a process of looking for the "inner" meaning in many passages. The special way of applying this method is to find references to ʿAlī and his family, which, of course, serves to promote Shīʿī claims to power and legitimacy. For example, in al-Qummī's *tafsīr,* the notion of Islam itself is defined not simply as submission to God but also as submission to the authority of the line of imams. The use of textual variation is also present in some works, although whenever the Shīʿah have been powerful in political affairs and fully institutionalized, such notions have generally been rejected as anti-status quo. This was already true to some extent in the eleventh century but became even more so with the rise of the Safavids in the sixteenth century. The specific argument occurred over whether some of the Qurʾān had been changed, or even omitted by ʿUthmān when he ordered its compilation, in order to undermine Shīʿī claims. Passages referring directly to ʿAlī had been erased, it was suggested. Al-Qummī argues, for example, that there are verses in the Qurʾān where "letters have been replaced by other letters," and he says that there are places where "verses contradict what God has sent down" (that is, they contradict or at least do not support Shīʿī beliefs). Al-Ṭabarsī argues, however, that the only change that has occurred in the Qurʾān concerns the overall order of the text itself and not its contents. One common textual variant which does receive wide acceptance among Shīʿī commentators concerns the word *ummah* ("community"), which is believed to be properly read *aʾimmah* ("leaders") or imams *(aʾimmah* being the plural of *imām* and having the same basic consonantal structure as *ummah).*

The Shīʿah, like the Muʿtazilah, looked to the Qurʾān for support of the rationalist theological doctrines that were a key element of their belief system: free will and the created Qurʾān. Their interpretational method, therefore, is similar to that employed by al-Zamakhsharī. The Ismāʿīlīyah likewise employed the Qurʾān as a reference point for their theologizing; the group's esoteric leanings, often characterized as extreme, are not witnessed in many texts but are found, for example, in the fragmentary *Mizāj al-tasnīm* (The condition of *tasnīm)* by Ismāʿīl ibn Hibat Allāh (d. 1760). In general, the Ismāʿīlī movement sees the outer meaning of the Qurʾān as only the symbol of the true inner meaning. The imam of the age, who has in him the true, full revelation, adapts the Qurʾān to the spiritual and mental condition of humanity through interpretation; eventually, people will be brought to the true and full meaning of the text, which is essentially the knowledge of the unity of God. Such is the presupposition with which all Ismāʿīlī *tafsīr* approaches the text.

The more recent Bahāʾī movement establishes its clear Islamic heritage through the existence of works of *tafsīr* written in Arabic by Sayyid ʿAlī Muḥammad al-Shīrāzī (1819–1850). Known as the Bāb, or "gate," he claimed to have initiated a new prophetic cycle and became the focal point of the movement which developed later as the Bahāʾī. Among his works are commentaries on *sūrahs* 12, 108, and 113 of the Qurʾān. In general these are marked by a spiritualistic interpretation of eschatology, including the notions of paradise, hell, death, and resurrection, all of which are taken to refer to the end of the prophetic cycle as well as the end of the physical world (although the latter is recreated by God in each prophetic cycle).

Sufism. Directly related to Shīʿī *tafsīr* in general is Ṣūfī interpretation, which provides a mystical speculation upon the Qurʾān. This interpretation usually justifies itself through reference to mystical activities believed to have been practiced and supported by Muḥammad. Sahl al-Tustarī, mentioned above, probably represents the earliest example of this tendency. Abū ʿAbd al-Raḥmān al-Sulamī (d. 1012) compiled his *Ḥaqāʾiq al-tafsīr* (The truths of interpretation) from various Ṣūfī authorities and other important personalities. All of the material can be considered allegorical, since it is devoted to finding the inner meaning of each passage as it relates to the mystical quest. A typical example is found in the interpretation of sura 17:1, the classical reference to Muḥammad's "night journey" to heaven, which is taken as a reference to each mystic's ascent to the higher levels of consciousness. Another prominent Ṣūfī, Abū Ḥamīd al-Ghazālī (d. 1111), did not write a commentary on the Qurʾān as such but found many occasions on which to record his approach to the text of scripture from the point of view of the intellectual Ṣūfī. For al-Ghazālī as for most other mystics, the Qurʾān works on two levels: the practical and the cognitive. The former applies to the inner self and its purification without neglect of the outer activities, while the latter is a meaning found through inner experience in light of mystical thought, and it can be reached only through firm knowledge of the practical or outer aspects. ʿAbd al-Razzāq al-Qāshānī (d. 1330?) compiled perhaps the most widely known Ṣūfī *tafsīr,* although it has often been mistakenly attributed directly to his teacher, the famous Muḥyī al-Dīn ibn al-ʿArabī (d. 1240), and thus is usually known under the title of *Tafsīr Ibn al-ʿArabī* (The interpretation of Ibn al-ʿArabī). As with al-Ghazālī, the outer principles of religion are not to be forgotten, although within the context of the *tafsīr* they certainly become submerged under allegorical interpretation, here seen in terms of the esoteric inner meaning as well as the symbolism of real events in the world.

EMERGENCE OF MODERN TAFSĪR. The rise of colonialism and the impact of Western thought in the eighteenth and nineteenth centuries certainly did not spell the end of *tafsīr* activity; in fact, at various times, the modern world has provoked more and more voluminous commentary upon the Qurʾān. Modern *tafsīr* is no different in basic impetus from its classical counterpart; it, too, desires to fit the text of scripture to the conditions of the era contemporary with the interpreter.

The impact of science has perhaps been the major factor in creating new demands and also the element of contemporary life to which much early modern *tafsīr* made its response. Muslims had not understood the true message of the Qurʾān, most modernists argued, and had therefore lost touch with the true scientific, rational spirit of the text. Out of this basic point several elements have emerged that unite all modernist interpretations: (1) the attempt is made to interpret the Qurʾān in the light of reason ("to interpret the Qurʾān by the Qurʾān," as it is frequently phrased) rather than with all the extraneous material provided by tradition in the form of *ḥadīth* reports and earlier commentaries; "Back to the source" often becomes the motto of such approaches; (2) the attempt is made, through the expediency of interpretation, to strip the Qurʾān of all legendary traits, primitive ideas, fantastic stories, magic, fables, and superstition; symbolic interpretation is the primary means for such resolutions; (3) the attempt is made to rationalize doctrine as found in or as justified by reference to the Qurʾān.

The earliest focal point of modernist *tafsīr* activity arose in India. Shāh Walī Allāh (1703–1762) is often seen as the precursor of the Indian reformist movement, but that trend reached its true blossoming with the Indian civil servant and educator Sayyid Ahmad Khan (1817–1898), who wrote the first major explicitly modernist *tafsīr,* entitled simply *Tafsīr al-Qurʾān.* His commentary was directed toward making all Muslims aware of the fact that Western influence in the world required a new vision of Islam, for Islam as it was actually practiced and believed in by most of its adherents would be seriously threatened by modern advances in thought and science. Where, therefore, was the true core of Islam to be found? How was its center to be defined? For Ahmad Khan, these questions were to be answered through reference to the Qurʾān, which, if it were properly understood through the use of the powers of reason, would provide the necessary answers. The basis of the required social and educational reforms, for example, were to be found in the Qurʾān. By returning to the source of Islam, the religion would be revitalized and the future would be secure.

In the Arab world, Muḥammad ʿAbduh (1849–1905), a vigorous champion of educational reform, also wrote a commentary on the Qurʾān, commonly called *Tafsīr al-Manār* (The interpretation of al-Manār), which was completed after his death by his pupil Rashīd Riḍā (1865–1935). Not overly modernistic in outlook, ʿAbduh's *tafsīr* does, however, urge the moderate use of rationality in matters of theology and tries to demonstrate that the Qurʾān is to be read primarily as a source of moral guidance applicable to the modern situation. The spiritual aspect of the Qurʾān was most important to ʿAbduh, and he, like many commentators in the past, was quite prepared to leave certain matters in the Qurʾān unexplained and to concentrate on their mysteriousness rather than to suggest resolutions for interpretational difficulties.

This type of interpretation continues more recently in the Arab world, represented, for example, by the intellectual spokesman for the Egyptian Muslim Brotherhood, Sayyid Quṭb (1906–1959), who in his work *Fī ẓilāl al-Qurʾān* (In the shade of the Qurʾān) interprets the text according to his own particular ideological leanings. India, too, has produced many such commentaries; examples are Abū al-Kalām Azād (1888–1959), whose Urdu work *Tarjumān al-Qurʾān* (The interpretation [or translation] of the Qurʾān) emphasized the notion of the unity of humankind while its author faced the rising tide favoring the formation of Pakistan, and Abū al-Aʿlā Mawdūdī (1903–1979), the author of *Tafhīm al-Qurʾān* (The meaning of the Qurʾān), who uses the Qurʾān to establish a blueprint for a future Islamic society in Pakistan to be formed through his political party, Jamāʿat-i Islāmī.

The impact of Western science is perhaps the most notable aspect of modern commentaries. Both Ahmad Khan and ʿAbduh were intent on encouraging their compatriots to embrace the scientific outlook of the West in order to share in the progress of the modern world. Often this effort involved little more than simply stating that the Qurʾān enjoins its readers to seek and use rational knowledge, but at other times it also involved the historical claim that Islam had developed science in the first place and had then passed it on to Europe, so that in embracing the scientific outlook in the present situation Muslims were only reclaiming what was truly Islamic. A more distinctive trend in *tafsīr* emerges also, however, primarily in the person of Ṭanṭāwī Jawharī (1870–1940) and his twenty-six-volume work, *Al-jawāhir fī tafsīr al-Qurʾān* (Jewels in the interpretation of the Qurʾān). God would not have revealed the Qurʾān, so the argument goes, had he not included in it everything that people needed to know; science is obviously necessary in the modern world, so it should not be surprising to find all of science in the Qurʾān when that scripture is properly understood. Jawharī also makes reference to the classical notion of the miraculous character or inimitability of the Qurʾān *(iʿjāz),* which he takes to refer primarily to the content of the text in terms of its knowledge concerning matters which are only now becoming clear to humankind. Since the scientific knowledge contained in the text is proof of its miraculous character, references are found in the Qurʾān for numerous modern inventions (electricity, for example) and scientific discoveries (the fact that the earth revolves around the sun).

Western thought has also influenced *tafsīr* in another way, although perhaps not so dramatically in terms of its popular acceptance as has "scientific" exegesis; the emergence of modern literary-philological-historical criticism has, thus far, played a fairly minor role but most certainly has found its supporters. ʿĀʾishah ʿAbd al-Raḥmān, a university professor in Morocco who writes under the name Bint al-Shāṭiʾ, represents a development of this line. This modern interpretation is not a resurrection of the philological type of commentary associated with al-Zamakhsharī, for example, who, although he wrote with great critical acumen, is for most modernists too full of unnecessary material which is seen to be a hindrance to understanding in the modern world; rather, ʿAbd al-Raḥmān pursues a straightforward approach, searching for the "original meaning" of a given Arabic word or phrase in order to understand the Qurʾān in its totality. This process does not involve the use of material extraneous to the Qurʾān itself, except perhaps for the use of a small amount of ancient poetry, but rather it uses the context of a given textual passage to define a word in as many overall contexts as it occurs. Neither the history of the Arabs nor that of the biblical prophets nor scientific topics are to be found in the Qurʾān because providing such material is not seen to be the task of the text. The purpose of the narrative elements of the Qurʾān is to provide moral and spiritual guidance to the believers, not to provide history or "facts." Within the Muslim world, the attempt to demythologize scripture—as in this approach—marks the beginnings of an incorporation of a type of modern critical scholarship developed in the context of biblical studies; its future at this point, however, remains uncertain.

See Also Biblical Exegesis; Iʿjāz; Qurʾān; Scripture.

Bibliography

On the principles of interpretation there is little material available specifically for the Muslim context; works on Jewish *midrash* are, however, most useful. Reference should be made to Géza Vermès's "Bible and Midrash," in volume 1 of *The Cambridge History of the Bible,* edited by Peter R. Ackroyd and C. F. Evans (Cambridge, 1970); this essay has been reprinted in Vermès's *Post-Biblical Jewish Studies* (Leiden, 1975). Also see Renée Bloch's "Midrash," in volume 5 of the *Supplement au dictionnaire de la Bible,* edited by Louis Pirot and others (Paris, 1957); an English translation by Mary Howard Callaway has been published in *Approaches to Ancient Judaism,* edited by William S. Green (Missoula, Mont., 1978).

Four books are fundamental to the modern study of *tafsīr: Die Richtungen der islamischen Koranauslegung* (Leiden, 1920), a collection of Ignácz Goldziher's lectures delivered in 1913, has yet to be replaced as a general overview of the subject; Theodor Nöldeke's *Geschichte des Qorāns,* vol. 2, *Die Sammlung des Qorāns,* 2d ed. (Leipzig, 1919), contains, especially on pages 123–192, much valuable and basic material; John Wansbrough's *Quranic Studies: Sources and Methods of Scriptural Interpretation* (Oxford, 1977) is essential to the study of the formation and early development of *tafsīr* and to all discussions of terminology and genres of exegetical literature; volume 1 of Fuat Sezgin's *Geschichte des arabischen Schrifttums* (Leiden, 1967) records most of the known Arabic works of *tafsīr* up to the fifth century AH.

Jane I. Smith's *An Historical and Semantic Study of the Term "Islām" as Seen in a Sequence of Qurʾān Commentaries* (Missoula, Mont., 1975), discusses the works of seventeen exegetes on specific verses of the Qurʾān and at the same time provides useful introductions to the lives and works of the individuals. On Ṣūfī *tafsīr* two excellent works exist: Paul Nwyia's *Exégèse coranique et langage mystique* (Beirut, 1970) and Gerhard Böwering's *The Mystical Vision of Existence in Classical Islam: The Qurʾānic Hermeneutics of the Ṣūfī Sahl al-Tustarī, d. 283/896* (New York, 1980). The latter discusses both textual and thematic matters in exemplary fashion.

Modern *tafsīr* has been analyzed by J. M. S. Baljon in *Modern Muslim Koran Interpretation, 1880–1960* (Leiden, 1961) and by J. J. G. Jansen in *The Interpretation of the Koran in Modern Egypt* (Leiden, 1974); both works provide basic yet informative overviews of the subject and bring Goldziher's work up to the present day.

Not many works of *tafsīr* have been translated, primarily because of their overly technical nature. Helmut Gätje has compiled extracts from various exegetes and arranged them thematically for the use of students in his *Koran und Koranexegese* (Zurich, 1971), translated by Alford T. Welch as *The Qurʾān and Its Exegesis* (Berkeley, 1976). Full works of *tafsīr* which have been translated are very few: *The Tales of the Prophets of al Kisāʾī,* translated by Wheeler M. Thackston (Boston, 1978), a book of the *qiṣaṣ al-anbiyāʾ* genre, and *The Recitation and Interpretation of the Qurʾān: Al-Ghazālī's Theory,* translated by Muhammad A. Quasem (London, 1982), are two worthwhile texts. Attention should be paid to *The Life of Muhammad: A Translation of Ishaq's "Sīrat Rasūl Allāh"* (1955; reprint, Lahore, 1967), by Alfred Guillaume for the passages of early *tafsīr* which are contained in it; reference to these is, however, unfortunately not facilitated by an index of Qurʾānic verses in the translation. Translations of two chapters from the *Tafsīr* of al-Bayḍāwī are available. These are primarily intended for students of Arabic, since the discussion frequently tends to revolve around the sense of a given Arabic word or grammatical construction; *Bayḍāwī's Commentary on Surah 12 of the Qur'ān,* edited by A. F. L. Beeston (Oxford, 1963), is the most accessible of such texts. Modern *tafsīr* has not been served well by translation either, although the following are available: *The Meaning of the Qur'ān,* 8 vols., translated by A. A. Maududi (Lahore, 1967–1979); Abū al-Kalām Āzād's *Tarjumān al-Qur'ān,* 2 vols., translated and edited by Syed Abdul Latif (New York, 1962–1967), and Sayyid Quṭb's *In the Shade of the Qur'ān,* translated by M. A. Salahi and A. A. Shamis (London, 1979).

Further bibliography on *tafsīr* can be found in my article "The Present Status of *Tafsīr* Studies," *Muslim World* 72 (July–December 1982): 224–238.

ANDREW RIPPIN (1987)

TAFTĀZĀNĪ, AL- (AH 722–791? / 1322–1389 CE), more fully Sa'd al-Dīn Mas'ūd ibn 'Umar al-Taftāzānī; master of a range of intellectual disciplines including theology, philosophy, metaphysics, logic, grammar, and rhetoric, as well as fundamental principles of jurisprudence and Qur'anic exegesis. Born in Taftāzān, Khorasan, he is renowned for the breadth and quality of his scholarship, though little is known about his personal life. His writing career started at the age of sixteen, and before his death his works were known and studied from the eastern part of the Muslim world to Egypt in the West. Al-Taftāzānī's eminence in scholarship was noticed and recognized in his lifetime by the Mongol rulers, especially the famous Timur Lenk (Tamerlane), by whom he was personally honored.

Al-Taftāzānī's best-known work is probably his commentary on the creed of al-Nasafī (d. 1142 CE), *Sharḥ al-'aqā'id al-Nasafīyah,* still studied in major Muslim seminaries. His work on the fundamental principles of Islamic law, *Sharḥ al-talwīḥ 'ala al-tawḥīd li-matn al-tanqīḥ fī uṣūl al-fiqh,* was published in Beirut in 1983. Because he wrote commentaries on Ḥanafī as well as Shāfi'ī works of jurisprudence his biographers differed as to which school of law he belonged to. The same was true in terms of his theological position. His commentary on al-Nasafī's *'Aqā'id* (written in 1367) led some to consider him a Māturīdī in view of his apparent espousal of their doctrines: for example, he viewed creation *(takwīn)* as eternal and an essential attribute of God, accepted the doctrine of free will, viewed the Qur'ān as an expression of God's eternal self-speech (a position also adopted by the later Ash'arīyah), and rejected the possibility of actually seeing God in the afterlife. Despite these apparent Māturīdī leanings, his *Maqāṣid* and *Sharḥ al-Maqāṣid* (written in 1383) reveal him to be an Ash'arī. Clearly his was a mediating position in which he demonstrated independence of thought and a resistance to legal or doctrinal classification.

BIBLIOGRAPHY

Brockelmann, Carl. *Geschichte der arabischen Literatur,* vol. 2. 2d ed. Leiden, 1949. See also the supplement to volume 2 of the first edition. Leiden, 1938.

Elder, Earl Edgar, trans. *A Commentary on the Creed of Islam: Sa'd al-Dīn al-Taftāzānī on the Creed of Najm al-Dīn al-Nasafī.* 2 vols. Translated with introduction and notes. New York, 1950.

Ibn Khaldūn. *Muqaddimah: An Introduction to History.* 2d ed. Translated by Franz Rosenthal. Princeton, 1967. See volume 3, pages 117, 315.

Storey, C. A. "Al-Taftāzānī." In *The Encyclopaedia of Islam.* Leiden, 1913–1934.

Taftāzānī, Mas'ūd ibn 'Umar al-. *Maqāṣid al-ṭālibīn fī uṣūl al-dīn,* and *Sharḥ al-Maqāṣid.* Istanbul, 1887.

Taftāzānī, Mas'ūd ibn 'Umar al-. *Sharḥ al-'aqā'id al-Nasafīyah fī uṣūl al-dīn wa-'ilm al-kalām.* Edited and introduced by Claude Salāma. Damascus, 1974. For further bibliographical references, see Salāma's introduction.

WADI Z. HADDAD (1987)

TAGORE, RABINDRANATH (1861–1941), poet, novelist, playwright, composer, and spiritual leader, is best known as the winner of the 1913 Nobel Prize for Literature and one of India's greatest modern poets. Yet he was also a complex figure who embodied many of the deepest religious and political tensions of late colonial India. As his friend E. J. Thompson described him, Tagore had a kind of dual soul, torn between his love of solitude, contemplation, and art and his commitment to social action (Thompson, 1921).

Born in Kolkata to a wealthy Bengali Brāhmaṇ family, Tagore was the son of Debendranath Tagore, a leader in the influential Hindu reform movement known as the Brāhmo Samāj and a key figure in the "Bengal Renaissance" of the nineteenth century. Although he later became critical of the movement, the universalistic and humanistic ideals of the Brāhmo Samāj had a lasting impact on Rabindranath Tagore's thought.

Tagore was a poet from an early age, composing his first piece at age eight. He was not, however, a spirit to be restrained by conventional educational institutions, and he left school at fourteen to study at home. Though a lover of the great Sanskrit poets like Kalidasa and the devotional lyrics of the Bengal Vaiṣṇavas, Tagore was also deeply influenced by nineteenth-century English poets, perhaps above all by the English romantics like John Keats and Percy Bysshe Shelley, whose reverence for nature and ideal of the creative artist can be seen throughout Tagore's work.

In 1890 Tagore took charge of the family estates in Shelidah (modern Bangladesh), where he came to admire the simple daily life, natural beauty, and folk culture of rural Bengal. Here he also first came into contact with the Baūls, a group of wandering spiritual "madmen" who reject the outward trappings of institutional religion and instead seek the indwelling "man of the heart," the elusive presence of the divine that dwells within every human body. The Baūls' iconoclastic "religion of man" (*manusher dharma*) had a lasting influence on Tagore's spiritual ideals. Called by some the "greatest of the Baūls," Tagore was a key figure in the popularization of Baūl music and spirituality as an icon of Bengali folk culture.

Tagore described his own spiritual vision as a "religion of the artist." Rejecting the rigidity and superficiality of institutional religions, including that of the Brāhmo Samāj, he based his "poet's religion" on a vision of the creative unity among God, humanity, and nature. Just as the One Divine Creator manifests himself in the infinite forms and beauty of nature, so too the individual artist reflects that diversity and returns it to divine unity through poetry, music, and art.

Tagore's literary output is astonishing in its breadth and diversity. In addition to poetry in various genres, he wrote novels, short stories, essays, political articles, and songs while also composing music and painting. He began translating his works into English, and his first attempt, *Gitanjali* (Song offerings; 1913), won the Noble Prize for Literature in 1913. Praised by W. B. Yeats as lyrics "expressing in thought a world I have dreamt of all my life," these songs helped give Tagore an international reputation and introduced Bengali literature to the world (Yeats 1913: xiii).

Unfortunately Tagore has so often been subject to hagiography and aesthetic idealization that it is often forgotten that he was, in his early life, also deeply involved in nationalist politics. As an active participant in the Swadeshi (Our Country) movement, he played an important role in the struggle for independence from British rule in the years up to 1907. He, however, grew disillusioned with the elitism and increasing violence of the movement and so gradually retreated from the political sphere into the inner domain of poetry, art, and spirituality.

This profound disillusionment with the violence of the nationalist movement and the retreat into an inner realm of spirituality is poignantly expressed in his novel *The Home and the World* (*Ghare-bāire;* 1919). One of Tagore's darkest works, it centers on the terrorist violence of 1907 and the ultimate failure of violent revolt as a means to independence. At the same time it also expresses Tagore's own ambivalent status, torn between home and world, between the inner realm of art and spirituality and the outward realm of public action.

Even after his withdrawal from political action Tagore continued to speak on social and political issues, if only in a sort of "antipolitical" way. In 1917, shocked by the horrors of World War I, Tagore also delivered a series of lectures in Japan and the United States that leveled a scathing attack on the "madness of nationalism" (Kopf 1979: 301). A monstrous and dehumanizing force spreading through the globe, nationalism had in Tagore's eyes only succeeded in stripping human beings of their individuality and ended in violent self-destruction.

In addition to his importance as a poet, artist, and political figure, Tagore was also deeply concerned with education. He founded Shantiniketan (the "abode of peace"), one of India's most original examples of alternative pedagogy. Dismayed by the stifling structures of traditional education in British India, Tagore turned instead to the model of the *tapovanas* or forest hermitages. Classes at Shantiniketan were held outdoors, in the shade of trees, emphasized the arts, and fostered the ideal of creative unity central to Tagore's own philosophy.

Tagore's influence remains evident in contemporary India not only in his homeland, where he is a cultural icon, but throughout the country and beyond. The composer of the national anthems of both India and Bangladesh, he is also one of the most widely published authors of the twentieth and twenty-first centuries. However, perhaps his most lasting relevance lies in his encounters with religious violence and terrorism in colonial India. His reflections on the "madness of nationalism" are no less relevant for the twenty-first century, as religious violence has by no means ended but arguably only grown more intense and destructive. It is more than a little ironic that the same country that sings his lyrics in its national anthem should remain torn by the very religious nationalism that Tagore so deplored.

SEE ALSO Bengali Religions; Hinduism; Poetry, article on Indian Religious Poetry.

BIBLIOGRAPHY

Tagore's works exist in many editions and translations, among them the Oxford Tagore translations (Oxford, U.K., 2002–2004) and the Rabindranath Tagore Omnibus (New Delhi, 2003). A thorough biography of Tagore in English is Krishna Dutta and Andrew Robinson, *Rabindranath Tagore: The Myriad-Minded Man* (New York, 1995). Older works include Edward John Thompson, *Rabindranath Tagore: His Life and Work* (Calcutta, India, 1921); and Krishna Kripalani, *Rabindranath Tagore: A Biography* (Calcutta, India, 1980). Useful discussions of Tagore's role in modern Indian religion and politics include David Kopf, *The Brahmo Samaj and the Shaping of the Modern Indian Mind* (Princeton, N.J., 1979); Stephen N. Hay, *Asian Ideas of East and West: Tagore and His Critics in Japan, China, and India* (Cambridge, U.K., 1970); and Hugh B. Urban, *Tantra: Sex, Secrecy, Politics, and Power in the Study of Religion* (Berkeley, Calif., 2003), chap. 3.

HUGH B. URBAN (2005)

ṬĀHIRAH SEE QURRAT AL-ʿAYN ṬĀHIRAH

TAI CHEN SEE DAI ZHEN

T'AI-CHI SEE TAIJI

T'AI-HSÜ See TAIXU

TAIJI.

In the *Yi jing* (Book of Changes; a wisdom book in ancient China that is widely believed to have been a major source of inspiration for Confucianism and Daoism), the term *Taiji* ("great ultimate") signifies the origin and ground of Heaven and earth and of all beings. It is the Great Ultimate that is said to engender or produce yin and yang, the twin cosmic forces, which in turn give rise to the symbols, patterns, and ideas that are, indeed, forms of yin and yang. The interaction of the two modalities of these cosmic forces bring about the eight trigrams that constitute the basis of the *Yi jing.* Combining any two of the eight trigrams, each of which contains three broken (yin) and three unbroken (yang) lines, forms one of the sixty-four hexagrams. These are taken as codes for all possible forms of change, transformation, existence, life, situations, and institutions both in nature and in culture. The Great Ultimate, then, is the highest and the most fundamental reality, and is said to generate and underlie all phenomena.

However, it is misleading to conceive of the Great Ultimate as the functional equivalent of either the Judeo-Christian concept of God or the Greek idea of Logos. The Great Ultimate is neither the willful creator nor pristine reason, but an integral part of an organic cosmic process. The inherent assumption of this interpretation is that the universe is in a dynamic process of transformation and, at the same time, has an organic unity and an underlying harmony. The universe, in Joseph Needham's understanding, is well-coordinated and well-ordered but lacks an ordainer. The Great Ultimate, so conceived, is a source or root, and is thus inseparable from what issues from it.

It was the Song-dynasty neo-Confucian master Zhou Dunyi (Zhou Lianxi, 1017–1073) who significantly contributed to the philosophical elaboration of the notion. In his *Taijitu shuo* (Explanation of the diagram of the Great Ultimate), strongly influenced by the cosmology of the *Yi jing,* Zhou specifies the cosmic process as follows: the Great Ultimate through movement and tranquility generates the two primordial cosmic forces, which in turn transform and unite to give rise to the Five Agents or Five Phases (*wuxing,* water, fire, wood, metal, and earth). When the five vital forces *(qi),* corresponding to each of the five "elements" (agents or phases), interact among themselves and reach a harmonious order, the four seasons run their orderly course. This provides the proper environment for the Five Agents to come into "mysterious union." Such a union embraces the two primordial cosmic forces, the female and the male, which interact with each other to engender and transform all things. The continuous production and reproduction of the myriad things make the universe an unending process of transformation. It is in this sense, Zhou Dunyi states, that "the Five Agents constitute a manifestation of *yin* and *yang,* and *yin* and *yang* constitute a manifestation of the Great Ultimate." This is the basis for the commonly accepted neo-Confucian assertion that the Great Ultimate is embodied both singly by each thing and collectively by all things.

It has been documented that Zhou's *Taijitu shuo* grew out of a long Daoist tradition. Indeed, it is believed that Zhou received the diagram itself from a Daoist master: Daoist influences are evident even in his explanatory notes. His introduction of the term "the Non-Ultimate" or "the Ultimate of Non-being" *(wuji)* generated much controversy among Song and Ming dynasty Confucian thinkers because the notion "non-ultimate" or "non-being" seems closer to the Daoist idea of nothingness than the Confucian concept that the human world is real. However, by defining human spirituality in terms of the notion that it is "man alone who receives the cosmic forces and the Five Agents in their most refined essence, and who is therefore most sensitive," Zhou clearly presents a philosophical anthropology in the tradition of Confucian humanism.

A similar attempt to read a humanist message into the seemingly naturalistic doctrine of the Great Ultimate is also found in the writings of Shao Yong (Shao Kangjie, 1011–1077), perhaps one of the most metaphysical Confucian masters of the Song dynasty. Shao's cosmology is presented as the numerical progression of the one to the many: "The Great Ultimate is the One. It produces the two (*yin* and *yang*) without engaging in activity. The two (in their wonderful changes and transformations) constitute the spirit. Spirit engenders number, number engenders form, and form engenders concrete things" (Chan, 1969, pp. 492–493). Shao further maintains that the human mind in its original state is the Great Ultimate. If one's mind can regain its original calm, tranquility, and enlightenment it has the capacity to investigate principle *(li)* to the utmost. The mind can then fully embody the Great Ultimate not only as the defining characteristic of its true nature but also as an experienced reality, a realized truth. This paradoxical conception that the Great Ultimate is part of the deep structure of our minds but that it can be fully realized only as a presence in our daily lives is widely shared among neo-Confucian thinkers.

Zhu Xi (1130–1200), in a rationalist attempt to provide an overall cosmological and metaphysical vision, defines the Great Ultimate as "nothing other than principle," or, alternately, as "merely the principle of Heaven and earth and the myriad things." Perhaps inadvertently, Zhu Xi restricted the Great Ultimate so as to acknowledge its function as the ground of all beings but not necessarily its role in the generation of the universe. However, there is fruitful ambiguity in Zhu Xi's position. In response to the challenging question as to whether the Great Ultimate must split into parts to become the possession of each of the myriad things, Zhu Xi employed the famous Buddhist analogy of moonlight scattered upon rivers and lakes. That there is only one moon in the sky does not prevent its being seen everywhere without losing its singularity and wholeness. Zhu Xi further depicts the Great Ultimate as having neither space nor form. The

Great Ultimate, although symbolizing the principle of activity and tranquility, is not directly involved in the creative transformation of the universe. Nevertheless, like Zhou Dunyi and other neo-Confucian thinkers, Zhu Xi insisted that the truth of the Great Ultimate must be personally realized through moral self-cultivation: the truth of the Great Ultimate is not simply knowledge about some external reality but a personal knowledge rooted in self-awareness in the ethico-religious sense.

In the folk tradition, the symbol of the Great Ultimate carries a connotation of mysterious creativity. The spiritual and physical exercise known as *Taiji quan* (a form of traditional Chinese shadowboxing) is still widely practiced. This slow, firm, and rhythmic exercise disciplines the body and purifies the mind through coordinated movements and regulated breathing. It is a remarkable demonstration that cosmological thought can be translated into physical and mental instruction for practical living without losing its intellectual sophistication. After all, in the Chinese order of things, to know the highest truth is not simply to know about something but to know how to do it properly through personal knowledge.

SEE ALSO Confucianism; Li; Yinyang Wuxing; Zhou Dunyi; Zhu Xi.

BIBLIOGRAPHY

Chan, Wing-tsit. *A Source Book in Chinese Philosophy.* Princeton, 1969. See chapters 28, 29, and 31.

Fung Yu-lan. *A History of Chinese Philosophy.* 2 vols. Princeton, 1952–1953. See volume 2, pages 435–442, 457–458, and 537–545.

Graham, A. C. *Two Chinese Philosophers.* London, 1958.

Needham, Joseph. *Science and Civilisation in China.* 5 vols. Cambridge, 1954–.

Tu Wei-ming. *Humanity and Self-Cultivation: Essays in Confucian Thought.* Berkeley, 1979. See chapter 5, pages 72–76.

TU WEI-MING (1987)

TÁIN BÓ CUAILNGE

TÁIN BÓ CUAILNGE (The cattle raid of Cuailnge) is the longest and the most famous of the early Irish heroic tales. It exists in three recensions. The first of them is preserved in *Lebhor na hUidhre* (The book of the dun cow), dated circa 1100 CE, and in the Yellow Book of Lecan, a late fourteenth-century manuscript. The second is preserved in the Book of Leinster, written in the mid-twelfth century, and the third in two manuscripts of the fifteenth and sixteenth centuries. However, as with many other early Irish tales, the date of the earliest extant manuscript provides only a *terminus ante quem* for the first recording as well as for the composition of the text, and even in the first recension of *Táin Bó Cuailnge* there are several linguistic strata which make it possible to trace the earlier written history of the tale back to the seventh or eighth century. This recension seems to have been compiled about the middle of the eleventh century from at least two variant written versions dating from about the ninth century, but may also have drawn upon sources in oral tradition. On linguistic and other grounds Rudolf Thurneysen (1921) concluded that the saga may have been recorded for the first time in the middle of the seventh century. Moreover, there is a poem composed not later than the seventh century in which the supernatural woman Scáthach addresses the principal hero of *Táin Bó Cuailnge*, Cú Chulainn, and foretells, cryptically and laconically, some of the main events of the tale; but whether the poet was drawing upon an oral tradition or a written version of the tale is uncertain.

In its extant form, the story tells of an attack on the province of Ulster organized by Ailill and Medhbh, king and queen of Connacht, and supported by the rest of Ireland. The object of the attack is to carry off the great bull of the Ulster people, the Donn Cuailnge ("the brown bull of Cuailnge"). Such was the prestige of *Táin Bó Cuailnge* in early medieval Ireland that it generated an extensive complex of ancillary tales and traditions and came to be accepted by native men of learning as the classic statement of the heroic ethos.

As it stands, the saga reflects something of Irish political conditions at the beginning of the historical period (fifth century) or earlier, but some scholars have suggested that its original theme was the rivalry of two bulls. The background to this rivalry is given in a separate tale: the bulls had formerly been magical swineherds who had quarreled and passed through a series of metamorphoses before reaching their actual form. Bruce Lincoln has argued that the account of the fight between the bulls at the end of *Táin Bó Cuailnge* is a reflex of an Indo-European cosmogonic myth: "a man . . . and a bull . . . are killed and dismembered, and from their bodies the world is constructed" (*Priests, Warriors, and Cattle*, Berkeley, 1981, pp. 86–92). However, several difficulties remain to be resolved before this attractive hypothesis can be accepted.

BIBLIOGRAPHY

Carney, James. "Early Irish Literature: The State of Research." In *Proceedings of the Sixth International Conference of Celtic Studies*, pp. 113ff. Dublin, 1983. This lecture refers to recent philological studies on the early history of *Táin Bó Cuailnge.*

O'Rahilly, Cecile, ed. *Táin Bó Cúailnge from the Book of Leinster.* Dublin, 1967.

O'Rahilly, Cecile, ed. *Táin Bó Cúailnge: Recension I.* Dublin, 1976. This and the preceding entry refer to the two main recensions of the saga. Both recensions provide an introduction and translation.

Thurneysen, Rudolf. *Die irische Helden- und Königsage bis zum siebzehnten Jahrhundert.* 2 vols. (Halle, 1921). See pages 96ff. This is the classic study of *Táin Bó Cuailnge* and the Ulster cycle in general. The approach is predominantly textual and philological; the main shortcoming is its inadequate comprehension of the oral and mythological dimensions of early Irish literary tradition.

PROINSIAS MAC CANA (1987 AND 2005)

TAIPING ("great peace" or "great equity") denotes a pan-Chinese social ideal and utopian slogan of rebels and dynasty founders. *Ping* ("level, balanced, just, harmonious"), *daping* ("great peace"), or *taiping* ("supreme peace") first appear in Confucian texts of the pre-Han (pre-206 BCE) era. There these terms denoted the ideal state of the world that had existed in high antiquity and that could again be brought about by a sage ruler who practiced the proper rites and music (*Daxue, Li ji*). The term never implied social equality in a modern sense but rather referred to a society where, as Xunzi defined it, each individual occupies the place that he should and fulfills his task according to his capacities. At the same time, Great Peace was not limited to human society but denoted a cosmic harmony that resulted in a seasonal climate, plentiful harvests, and longevity of all living beings (*Chunqiu fanlu, Yantie lun*). It was a state in which all the concentric spheres of the organic Chinese universe, which contained nature as well as society, were perfectly attuned, communicated with each other in a balanced rhythm of timeliness, and brought maximum fulfillment to each living being.

During the Han dynasty (206 BCE–220 CE), Great Peace became the social ideal of the official Confucian state doctrine (which it remains to this day). However, when the Han declined, "Great Peace" became the slogan also of popular movements of revolt inspired by Daoism. Daoism had earlier found a place for the concept in its own philosophy. The Daoist philosopher Zhuangzi (fourth century BCE) had called a government that conformed to the order of nature *taiping*, an idea that was in no contradiction to the Confucian definition of the term. The Daoist popular movements were opposed not to the ideal of Great Peace but to the dynasty that subscribed to it and had failed to bring it about. Thus, *taiping* cannot be called a "revolutionary" ideal, although two of the greatest social upheavals in Chinese history are called Taiping rebellions.

Twice during the Han period, a group of *fangshi* ("masters of [esoteric] techniques") presented at court a *Taiping jing* (Classic of Great Peace). It was rejected because of its Daoist tenor. This or a similar *Classic of Great Peace* became the sacred scripture of the first Taiping or "Yellow Turban" Rebellion (184 CE), which eventually brought down the Han empire. This scripture, still extant in a revised version (probably sixth century), elaborates the messianic element in the Taiping tradition: the Great Peace that the princes of high antiquity brought about through a Daoist government of "nonintervention" (*wuwei*) is a state that will be recreated in the near future as a result of revelations by a divine messenger called Celestial Master (Tianshi). The religious originality of this view lies in its substitution of the Confucian virtues and rites with Daoist spiritual exercises and other methods of longevity as the means by which to reach Taiping.

The rebellion of 184 was crushed, but it engendered a messianic ideology that flourished during the Period of Disunion (220–581), was rekindled in all subsequent periods of upheaval, and formed the basis of Daoist as well as Buddhist messianism and eschatology in China. This Taiping ideology centered around the expectation that a divine or human sage ruler, the Perfect Lord of Great Peace (Taiping Zhenjun), emissary of Heaven, will appear on a prophesied date at the height of a period of cosmic chaos and human suffering. He will save the elect (*zhongmin*, the "seed people") from the demonic forces sent to destroy all evildoers, and will usher in the reign of Great Peace (as related in the *Dongyuan shenzhou jing*). Even in this religious setting, the messianic kingdom is often no more and no less than a glorious new Chinese dynasty, although in some Daoist traditions it is developed into a paradisiacal utopia.

Dynasty founders, especially those of the Tang, 618–906, and the Ming, 1368–1644, tapped this messianic tradition by casting themselves in the role of the sage ruler of Taiping. Ten times in Chinese history Taiping was chosen as the name of a reign period (*nianhao*). Emperor Taiwu of the Northern Wei called both himself and a period of his reign (440–452) "Perfect Lord of Great Peace."

The second Taiping rebellion (1850–1865) was the most powerful of several great uprisings toward the end of the Manchu dynasty. In 1851, the visionary rebel leader Hong Xiuquan (1813–1864) from Canton proclaimed the Heavenly Kingdom of Great Peace (Taiping Tianguo) with himself as Emperor of Great Peace (Taiping Tianzi). His religion was a combination of Chinese traditions with many elements from Protestant Christianity (monotheism, ten commandments, Sunday worship, iconoclasm, condemnation of "Chinese idol-worship"). Hong called himself the younger brother of Jesus Christ. God had endowed him with imperial legitimation (in the shape of a seal), with the (Daoist) power to kill demons (a sword), and with divine scriptures (revelation in Chinese religion is always in the form of writing). The Taiping theocracy established in Nanjing was destroyed in 1864, but the Taiping ideal lives on in Daoism and in most of the modern Chinese syncretist religions.

SEE ALSO Daoism, overview article; Millenarianism, article on Chinese Millenarian Movements.

BIBLIOGRAPHY

The basic texts on the Taiping ideal of antiquity and the Daoist Taiping Dao movement are presented in Werner Eichhorn's "Tai-ping und Tai-ping Religion," *Mitteilungen des Instituts für Orientforschung* 5 (1957): 113–140; see also Max Kaltenmark's "The Ideology of the Tai-ping ching," in *Facets of Taoism*, edited by Holmes Welch and myself (New Haven, 1979), pp. 19–52. On medieval Daoist messianism, see my article "The Image of the Perfect Ruler in Early Taoist Messianism: Lao-tzu and Li Hung," *History of Religions* 9 (1969–1970): 216–247, and "Taoist Messianism," *Numen* 31 (1984): 161–174. The religion of the nineteenth-century Taiping Tianguo *movement is the subject of a detailed monograph by Vincent Shih, The* Taiping Ideology (Seattle, 1967).

New Sources

Prazniak, Roxann. *Of Camel Kings and Other Things: Rural Rebels against Modernity in Late Imperial China.* Lanham, Md., 1999.

Spence, Jonathan D. *God's Chinese Son: The Taiping Heavenly Kingdom of Hong Xiuquan.* New York, 1996.

ANNA SEIDEL (1987)
Revised Bibliography

TAIWANESE RELIGIONS.

The term *Taiwanese religions* is used here to describe the religious beliefs and practices of the people who inhabit Taiwan, regardless of their ethnic or sub-ethnic backgrounds. Taiwan has long been recognized for its diverse range of religious traditions. As different groups of Taiwanese have attempted to find meaningful ways to confront life crises, social disorder, natural disasters, and a sense of injustice, they have created a wide range of beliefs and practices, each with its own distinctive background and characteristics. This diversity befits Taiwan's historical development as an island situated in a key commercial and strategic location, and justifies the use of the plural form in considering its religious traditions.

HISTORICAL OVERVIEW. Taiwan was first settled by Aboriginal peoples of Austronesian (Malayo-Polynesian) origin, with significant immigration from the Chinese mainland only beginning by the seventeenth century. During the Qing dynasty (1644–1911), the island was largely a frontier region that never became fully integrated into the Chinese empire. However, Han Chinese migrants brought their gods over from China, and worshipped them in various compatriot, territorial, and commercial temples. Various Chinese sectarian movements, as well as Christianity, also began to spread in developed areas of Taiwan, but it appears that no eminent Buddhist or Daoist figures came to the island at this time.

During the colonial era (1895–1945), when Taiwan was ruled by Japan, the island enjoyed a prolonged period of urbanization and industrialization, which laid a firm foundation for its economic development. Taiwanese religious traditions flourished during most of this era, despite policy shifts from laissez-faire (1895–1915) to regulation (1915–1930s) to efforts to co-opt Buddhism and Christianity while suppressing sectarian movements and temple cults under a "temple-restructuring" campaign enacted during the "Japanization" movement (1930s–1940s).

Taiwan became a province of the Republic of China (ROC) in 1945, and the Nationalist (Guomindang) government relocated to Taiwan in 1949 after its defeat in the Chinese civil war. Many prominent religious specialists followed the Nationalists over from China during these chaotic years, including eminent Buddhist monks, the Daoist Celestial Master (Tianshi), leaders of sectarian traditions such as the Way of Unity (Yiguan Dao), and Christian missionaries. More recently, Tibetan Buddhists and members of new Japanese religions have begun to proselytize in Taiwan. While the state kept a close watch on these movements during the early decades of the postwar era, the end of martial law in 1987 marked the beginning of a new era of religious development.

At the beginning of the twenty-first century, Taiwan boasts one of the most dynamic religious environments in East Asia. In contrast with China, where religion is only gradually emerging from the shadow of long-term oppression by a totalitarian regime, Taiwanese religions are thriving and even expanding. Freedom of religion has always been guaranteed under the ROC Constitution, Article 13 of which clearly states, "the people shall have freedom of religious beliefs." However, now that Taiwan has developed into a democracy, people can practice the religious tradition of their choice without fear of state suppression. Members of any religious faith are free to congregate and introduce their belief systems to others, while previously outlawed sectarian movements now operate openly and continue to expand. The legitimacy of Taiwan's religious traditions can also be seen in the formation of the Taiwan Association of Religious Studies, which was founded on April 18, 1999, and has attracted the membership of dozens of students, faculty, and religious specialists from both Taiwan and other countries.

Another striking facet of religion in Taiwan is that economic growth and technological development have not resulted in the decline of religious practice; on the contrary, many educated men and women who surf the web on a daily basis apparently feel no qualms about practicing religion, and many large religious organizations and temples have their own websites.

ABORIGINAL RELIGIONS. Taiwan's most venerable religious traditions are those of its Aboriginal peoples, who are usually classified by place of residence as Plains Aborigines and Mountain Aborigines. Long-term processes of acculturation and even assimilation have diluted the aborigines' religious traditions, which generally centered on ancestor worship, lifecycle rituals, and annual festivals. Moreover, numerous aborigines have converted to Christianity, especially Presbyterianism. Some Aboriginal beliefs and practices have survived, however, and are gaining increasing recognition from scholars and government officials. These religious traditions continue to play important roles in aAboriginal life, and also serve as a vital force in the reformation of aborigine identity.

BUDDHISM. Historical evidence indicates that no eminent Buddhist monks came to Taiwan during the Qing dynasty, although some monks did make the journey across the Taiwan Straits from southern China in order to help manage temples in Taiwan that were constructed by the state or local communities. During the colonial era, lay Buddhists and members of the *saṃgha* attempted to evade state control by actively cooperating with Japanese Buddhists. Some subordinated their sacred sites administratively to Japanese Buddhist lineages. Others formed religious associations that pledged their loyalty to the colonial authorities, including the Patriotic Buddhist Association, the Buddhist Youth Association, the Taiwan Friends of the Buddhist Way, and largest and perhaps most important of all, the South Seas Buddhist Association. Nevertheless, Chinese Buddhists monastics managed to preserve many of their core beliefs and practices, and did not copy their Japanese brethren to the extent of getting married, eating meat, and drinking wine.

The postwar era has witnessed the growth of four prominent Buddhist organizations: the Buddhist Association of the Republic of China, which until the 1960s served as the state-approved and sole representative of Buddhists in Taiwan; the monastic order known as the Buddha's Light Mountain (Foguangshan), which was founded by Venerable Master Xingyun (Hsing-yun; b. 1927) and promotes a form of humanistic Buddhism advocated by the reformer Taixu (1890–1947); the Compassionate Relief Merit Society (Ciji gongdehui), which was founded in 1966 by Master Zhengyan (Cheng-yen;b. 1937) and has gained renown worldwide for its charitable works; and Dharma Drum Mountain (Fagushan), which was founded by Venerable Master Shengyan (Sheng-yen; b. 1930) and emphasizes the importance of meditation and self-cultivation. The number of lay Buddhists in Taiwan has also increased since the 1960s, but since most Taiwanese tend to identify themselves as "Buddhists" regardless of whether or not they have been initiated into this religious tradition, the exact number of practicing Buddhists in Taiwan is nearly impossible to quantify. One new development has been the growing influence of exiled Tibetan monks of the Tantric Buddhist sect, who have attracted a sizeable following in Taiwan since the 1980s. The Dalai Lama visited the island in 1997 and 2001.

DAOISM. Daoist practice can be bifurcated into monastic and nonmonastic traditions, both of which have played important roles in the history of Chinese religions. In Taiwan, however, the former tradition has almost no presence. The nonmonastic tradition is far more influential, especially the Celestial Master movement, the leader of which has the authority to bestow ordination registers on Taiwanese Daoist masters. A number of Daoist traditions that arose in southern China are also prevalent in Taiwan, including the Lüshan, Pu'an, and Sannai movements. Hoklo and Hakka masters from China's southern provinces of Fujian and Guangdong transmitted these different forms of Daoism to Taiwan during the eighteenth and nineteenth centuries, and scholars are only beginning to fully appreciate the variation in distribution and practice among Daoist masters belonging to different sub-ethnic groups, particularly in terms of their liturgical traditions.

After the sixty-third Celestial Master Zhang Enpu followed the Nationalist government into exile in 1949, he attempted to restructure Taiwanese Daoism by founding the Daoist Association of the Province of Taiwan and the Daoist Assembly of the Republic of China. However, these organizations have exerted only a limited influence on the Daoist movements mentioned above. Their liturgical traditions, including exorcistic and healing rites as well as mortuary rituals, are still frequently performed today, and Daoist masters continue to play key roles in communal festivals, particularly those involving Daoist offerings (*jiao*; often referred to as "rites of renewal").

CHRISTIANITY AND OTHER FOREIGN RELIGIONS. The first Christian missionaries arrived in Taiwan during the early years of the seventeenth century. These included Spanish Catholics who proselytized in the north and Dutch Protestants who proselytized in the south. However, they do not appear to have attracted many converts, and ended up being driven out of Taiwan by Koxinga (1624–1662). No subsequent missionizing efforts took place until the second half of the nineteenth century. Spanish Dominicans attempted to preach the gospel among Plains Aborigines in the hills and mountains of southern Taiwan, and educate catechists by opening a seminary and training school, but these efforts were largely unsuccessful until the early twentieth century. English and Canadian Presbyterians exerted a far more significant influence throughout Taiwan. Among the most renowned Presbyterian missionaries of that era were Dr. James L. Maxwell (1836–1921) and Dr. George L. Mackay (1844–1901). Both combined proselytizing and healing: Maxwell was an unordained medical missionary, while Mackay pulled teeth and built hospitals. Like the Dominicans, the Presbyterians were most successful in attracting converts among Taiwan's Plains Aborigines, and were unable to make any inroads in Mountain Aborigine communities until the 1930s. Despite initial slow growth and cases of persecution, the Presbyterians were able to gain a significant following for a number of reasons, including having women accompany their missionary husbands (which allowed them to interact far more freely with Han Chinese and Aboriginal women), printing Bibles that used a romanized form of Southern Min (Taiwan's main local dialect), and publishing a journal entitled *The Church News* beginning in July 1885. Now named the *Taiwan Church News*, this journal is still being published today, and may be the oldest church newspaper in East Asia. Education also played an important role in Presbyterian missionizing efforts, with the Tainan Theological College being formally founded in 1880, and middle schools and girls' schools being set up during the late nineteenth century as well.

Christianity flourished during much of the colonial era, as the Japanese were initially tolerant of a religion that they saw as representing Western modernity. The Dominicans founded the Blessed Imelda School for Girls in 1917 in Taipei, and also established catechist schools in central and southern Taiwan, as well as the Santa Infancia of Holy Childhood Orphanage in the south. In addition, Methodist evangelists like Dr. John Sung (1901–1944), who converted thousands of followers throughout Asia, proselytized in Taiwan. Japanese Christians also came to Taiwan, including members of the Japanese Anglican (Episcopal), Congregational, Methodist, and Presbyterian churches. The colonial era also witnessed the development of two indigenous Christian churches: the Holiness and the True Jesus.

The Presbyterians continued to build and manage hospitals, as well as the Happy Mount Leprosy Colony (founded in northern Taiwan in 1934). Presbyterian theological colleges in northern and southern Taiwan also thrived, while the Reverend William Campbell (1841–1921) founded a school for the blind in southern Taiwan in 1900 to 1901. Missionary efforts to preach the gospel were further facilitated by the on-going translation and publishing of scriptures in romanized Southern Min. Other dedicated evangelists like Campbell N. Moody (1866–1940), who preached in over 900 of 1,100 villages in one county, also proved instrumental to the continuing growth of the Presbyterian movement. Presbyterian leaders made great efforts to develop their church's self-sufficiency by training local clergy and establishing a united Presbyterian church (the Presbyterian Church of Taiwan). This took the form of a synod, with presbyteries in the north and south of the island serving as equal partners. This self-sufficiency helped the Presbyterian Church of Taiwan survive the difficult years of the late colonial and early postwar era.

During the 1930s, Christian believers engaged in a series of tense confrontations with the colonial authorities over politically charged issues such as whether Christians should worship at Shintō shrines. Roman Catholics decided to attend, and English Presbyterians acquiesced as well, but Canadian Presbyterians were adamant in refusing to take part. All Christian movements eventually lost control of schools and other church properties by the 1940s. Many foreign missionaries left Taiwan, while others were expelled; local Christians were harassed, and some detained. In 1943, all local churches were absorbed into the Japanese-run Christian Church of Taiwan, and many churches suffered during the Allied bombing of Taiwan. By the end of World War II, however, English and Canadian Presbyterian missionaries had begun to make plans to return to the island.

Taiwan's churches kept a low profile during the early years of the postwar era, particularly after the February 28 indicent of 1947, during which thousands of Taiwanese were massacred by Nationalist forces intent on suppressing a local uprising. From 1965 to 1985, however, the Presbyterian Church of Taiwan began to publicly criticize the cultural policies of Taiwan's Nationalist government, while also advocating Taiwanese identity. The Presbyterian Church of Taiwan resisted attempts to promote Mandarin as a national language at the expense of local dialects, and continued to publish Bibles using Southern Min romanization, even after thousands of copies were confiscated. Some leaders, such as the Reverend Kao Chun-min, went to prison for their beliefs. At the same time, however, the Presbyterian Church of Taiwan and other churches managed to survive and even grow due to the Nationalist policy of opening Taiwan's doors to Western missionaries, including Anglicans, Baptists, Catholics (Jesuits, Vincentians, and the Catholic Missionary Society of America, also known as the Maryknoll Order), Jehovah's Witnesses, Lutherans, Methodists, Mormons, Pentecostals (mainly members of the Assemblies of God), and the Unification Church. However, most missionaries belonging to these churches did not speak Southern Min, and unlike the Presbyterian Church of Taiwan made little headway outside of Taiwan's major cities. Indigenous churches also grew during the postwar era, particularly Holy Spirit, which belongs to the Pentecostal movement.

Christianity in Taiwan is thriving at the beginning of the twenty-first century. Roman Catholicism made a remarkable comeback in Taiwan after 1949, when multitudes of Catholic clergy and believers followed the Nationalists to the island, thereby infusing local Catholicism with new strength and vigor. According to government statistics, as of June 2001 there were 1,135 Catholic churches, 677 clergymen, and 664 foreign missionaries in Taiwan serving nearly 300,000 believers. By that same date, the Protestant congregation had expanded to approximately 605,000 members, with 3,609 churches, 2,566 ministers, and 1,087 foreign ministers. Of these, over 220,000 were members of the Presbyterian Church of Taiwan, which has begun to focus its efforts on social welfare and environmental protection. The Presbyterian Church of Taiwan was active in organizing relief efforts after the devastating earthquake on September 21, 1999, and the church worked alongside other Christian organizations, such as the Chinese Christian Relief Association, to help local communities engage in reconstruction efforts.

Other foreign religions in Taiwan include Islam, Judaism, Bahā'ī, Tenrikyō, and Mahikarikyō. The largest of these is Islam. Approximately twenty thousand Muslims accompanied the Nationalist government to Taiwan in 1949, the majority of whom were soldiers, civil servants, or food-service workers. As of June 2001 Taiwan was home to approximately 53,000 Muslims, as well as thirty-four mullahs and six mosques.

SECTARIAN RELIGIONS. By the eighteenth century, sectarian movements composed mostly of lay Buddhist believers had begun to make their presence felt in Taiwan. Subsequently labeled "vegetarian religions" (*zhaijiao*) by the Japanese colonial authorities, these sects featured a membership of men and women who identified themselves as adhering to a form of Buddhism that exists apart from and is superior to that of the ordained Buddhist clergy. In terms of practice, believers generally perform a variety of Buddhist rituals, but adopt a strict diet that requires abstaining from meat and five types of pungent roots (onions, chives, leeks, scallions, and garlic). Many vegetarian sects became popular due to their willingness to perform rites for the dead, often at rates cheaper than those charged by ordained Buddhist and Daoist specialists. Some sects also featured latent millenarian doctrines, an issue that gained the attention of the colonial authorities after a millenarian-inspired uprising in 1915 known as the Xilai An Iincident. In order to survive the subsequent crackdown, some members of vegetarian sects organized the Taiwan Buddhist Dragon Flower Association (Fojiao Longhua hui) in order to demonstrate their allegiance to the island's Japanese overlords. Today, although many Taiwanese have adopted different forms of vegetarian diets, the overall influence of vegetarian movements is declining due to the rapid growth of the Buddhist organizations mentioned above.

The latter half of the nineteenth century was a period of rapid growth for other sectarian groups that practiced spirit-writing, published morality books, and congregated at sacred sites often referred to as "phoenix halls" (*luantang*). Some scholars refer to such sects as "Confucian," while some groups have not hesitated to use this term as an autonym. The question of exactly how "Confucian" these movements really are is difficult to resolve because this term has long been used to describe a wide variety of phenomena, including temples founded by state or local elites that are dedicated to the worship of Confucius, secular organizations that stress Confucian teachings, such as the Confucius-Mencius Society, and a wide range of sectarian groups, such as the Divine Teachings of the Confucian Tradition (Ruzong shenjiao). Modern sects in China and Taiwan have not hesitated to use the term *Confucian* to describe their tenets and practices, but for these groups, Confucianism includes unique and syncretic interpretations of key Confucian philosophical texts, as well as a distinctive liturgical style that differentiates them from other similar and hence competing groups.

Many sects that practice spirit-writing or publish morality books remain highly popular in Taiwan today. Perhaps the largest and best-known movement is the Way of Unity, which spread to Taiwan from China during the postwar era and features an eclectic religious doctrine that draws upon both traditional Chinese religious teachings and other major world religions like Christianity, Islam, Judaism, and Hinduism. Outlawed during the first decades of the postwar era, it is now a flourishing movement. According to government statistics, as of June 2001 there were 3,218 large or medium-sized Yiguan Dao temples in Taiwan, with 2,326 temple priests serving approximately 887,000 believers. However, these numbers may be somewhat inflated, and the Way of Unity has undergone a series of schisms during the postwar era, meaning that this data should not be seen as reflecting a single coherent religious movement. Other popular sectarian groups include Li-ism (Doctrine of Order), which like the Way of Unity was transmitted from China to Taiwan after 1949, as well as a wide range of groups generally referred to as "new religions" (*xinxing zongjiao*) that arose during the postwar era, particularly following the lifting of martial law. One of the best known of these groups is the Religion of the Yellow Emperor (Xuanyuan jiao), which was formally founded in Taiwan in 1957 by a legislator named Wang Hansheng. This sect attempts to promote Chinese nationalism, and preaches a syncretic philosophy combining elements of Confucianism and Daoism. Other charismatic yet controversial leaders, including Lu Shengyan, Miaotian, Qinghai, and Song Qili, have formed sectarian associations that have attracted large numbers of dedicated followers but have yet to eclipse more established religions in terms of numbers of believers and overall influence.

COMMUNAL RELIGIOUS TRADITIONS. Of Taiwan's many various beliefs and practices, communal religious traditions centering on temple cults and festivals remain the most popular and the most prevalent. Temples continue to play an integral role in individual, family, and community life, and temple cults have retained their importance as sites for daily worship, community service, and massive festivals. Membership in a temple cult is ascriptive, and does not require any form of initiation, so it is impossible to accurately calculate the exact number of men and women who belong to communal religious traditions. However, every year hundreds of thousands of Taiwanese (including many members of the religious traditions discussed above) donate money to local temples and take part in their festivals.

Most deities worshipped in temple cults in Taiwan were transmitted to the island from China, but there are also cults to indigenous deities, particularly local heroes and the unruly dead. Taiwan's most ubiquitous deity is the Earth God (Tudi gong), whose temples dot every urban and rural community. Other popular deities include Mazu (originally the goddess of the sea, now worshipped as an all-powerful protective deity) and the Royal Lords (*wangye;* originally plague deities, but now invoked to counter all manner of calamities). These and other deities are worshipped for their ability to provide health and prosperity, while their temples and festivals contribute to the formation of local social structures and a sense of identity.

One particularly fascinating phenomenon of the postwar era has been the steady popularity of cults associated with the unruly dead or eccentric deities, such as the Buddhist monk Crazy Ji (Jigong or Jidian), who gained renown for his spiritual powers despite a distinct penchant for eating meat, drinking wine, and hanging out with prostitutes. Such cults were extremely active during the Everybody's Happy (Dajia le) lottery craze of the 1980s. The inauguration of a Lotto lottery in January 2002 has prompted a new wave of worship of Taiwan's unruly gods, although the current fervor has been somewhat tempered by the fact that more and more Taiwanese are choosing to rely on computer programs to try to predict winning numbers.

Another important development is that temples are no longer strictly local entities, but now play important roles on the national stage as well. The Nationalist government actively attempted to discourage temple cults during the 1960s and 1970s (for example, in 1968, the Ministry of the Interior promoted a series of guidelines to regulate local religion entitled "Promoting Frugality in Folk Sacrifices"), a policy that only began to change during the 1980s and has now been almost completely abandoned. Today's political elites increasingly appreciate the constructive roles temples play in Taiwanese society, and now limit any state intervention to sponsoring local festivals while also attempting to regulate their contents. In addition, the modernization of Taiwan's infrastructure and liberalization of the mass media has resulted in popular pilgrimage sites being able to exert an island-wide influence.

At the same time, since Taiwan began to democratize during the 1980s, temple cults have been more than passive observers of modernization and changing state policies; they now play activist roles in community life by building libraries and community centers, sponsoring cultural activities, such as chess tournaments and classes in traditional fine arts, and engaging in a wide range of charities. Presidential and legislative candidates network with local elites and strive to attract grassroots support by campaigning at temples to popular local deities, while some aspiring politicians have attempted use temple cults to advance their own interests against those of the state. One example of the intense and also complex links between religion, politics, and identity in contemporary Taiwan involves the abortive attempt by a prominent Mazu temple known as the Zhenlan Gong to undertake a direct pilgrimage to the goddess's ancestral temple in Fujian during the spring and summer of 2000, a move that challenged the policies of the then newly elected government of President Chen Shui-bian.

The flourishing of Taiwan's many religious traditions should come as no surprise to those who have studied the history of Chinese culture during the late imperial and modern eras. Religious associations and their sacred sites have long constituted one of the most important public spaces in Asian societies, and have been key arenas where elites and representatives of the state vied to assert or reinforce their dominance over local culture and society. In Taiwan today, democratization has further enhanced the importance of religion in community life, and prompted representatives of the state to be more proactive in terms of interacting with the island's religious traditions. A similar process may be beginning in China, where local communities are slowly beginning to reassert their autonomy and religious networks are once again functioning as a second government in the sense of providing services and mobilizing the population. The extent to which the growth of local religious traditions may have a long-term impact on modern Chinese society remains to be seen, but the outpouring of new ethnographic work on China, as well as the continuing efforts of scholars researching Taiwan and Hong Kong, should give us a more comprehensive perspective on this issue in the future.

SEE ALSO Buddhism, article on Buddhism in China; Chinese Religion, overview article; Christianity, article on Christianity in Asia; Daoism, overview article.

BIBLIOGRAPHY

A massive corpus of Chinese-language scholarship on Taiwanese religions has been published since the mid-1980s. Good introductions to this subject may be found in Chang Hsun and Jiang Tsann-terng, eds., *Taiwan bentu zongjiao yanjiu daolun* (Taipei, 2001), and Chang Hsun and Jiang Tsann-terng, eds., *Taiwan bentu zongjiao yanjiu de xin shiye han xin siwei* (Taipei, 2003). Some Western-language works also provide valuable introductions to Taiwan's religious traditions, including Philip Clart and Charles B. Jones, eds., *Religion in Modern Taiwan: Tradition and Innovation in a Changing Society* (Honolulu, 2003); Paul R. Katz and Murray A. Rubinstein, *Religion and the Formation of Taiwanese Identities* (New York, 2003); and Robert P. Weller, *Alternate Civilities: Democracy and Culture in China and Taiwan* (Boulder, Colo., 1999). See also a special issue of *The China Quarterly* 174 (June 2003), edited by Daniel L. Overmyer, entitled *Religion in China Today.* Scholars can also keep up with developments in the field by visiting the websites of the Taiwan Association of Religious Studies (tars.org.tw/tars.htm) and the Society for the Study of Chinese Religions (www.indiana.edu/~sscr).

Those who wish to learn more about Taiwan's historical development before exploring its religious traditions should begin by consulting Murray A. Rubinstein, ed., *Taiwan: A New History* (Armonk, N.Y., 1999), which provides a fine overview of the island's history. Stevan Harrell and Huang Chun-chieh, eds., *Cultural Change in Postwar Taiwan* (Boulder, Colo., 1994) treats the island's recent cultural development, while Melissa J. Brown, *Is Taiwan Chinese? The Impact of Culture, Power, and Migration on Changing Identities* (Berkeley, 2004) considers important issues of ethnicity and identity. Useful background information about Taiwan may also be found on the Formosa website prepared by the Reed Institute (academic.reed.edu/formosa/formosa_index_page/formosa_index.html), as well as on Taiwan's Government Information Office website (www.gio.gov.tw/taiwan-website/index.html).

Those wishing to begin their research by reading relevant secondary literature should consult the following bibliographies: Laurence G. Thompson, *Chinese Religion in Western Languages: A Comprehensive and Classified Bibliography of Publications in English, French, and German through 1980* (Tucson, Ariz., 1985); Laurence G. Thompson and Gary Seaman, *Chinese Religions: Publications in Western Languages,* Vol. 2: *1981–1990* (Ann Arbor, Mich., 1993); Thompson and Seaman, *Chinese Religions: Publications in Western Languages,* Vol. 3: *1991–1995* (Ann Arbor, Mich., 1998); and Thompson, Seaman, and Zhifang Song, *Chinese Religions: Publications in Western Languages,* Vol. 4: *1996–2000* (Ann Arbor, Mich., 2002). Another key source of information is the bibliography prepared by Philip Clart (web.missouri.edu/~religpc/bibliography_CPR.html), which is updated on a regular basis. For a thorough bibliography of Chinese-language and Japanese-language scholarship, see Lin Meirong, ed., *Taiwan minjian xinyang yanjiu shumu* (*zengding ban*), rev. ed. (Nankang, Taiwan, 1997).

A great deal of research has been done on Taiwan's Aboriginal peoples and their religious traditions, but relatively little has been published in English. A good place to start is John R. Shepherd's *Statecraft and Political Economy on the Taiwan Frontier, 1600–1800* (Stanford, Calif., 1993), which provides an excellent account of Taiwan's Plains Aborigines. Numerous scholars at the Institute of Ethnology, Academia Sinica, such as Huang Ying-kuei and Pan Ing-hai, have published extensively on Aboriginal religion in both Chinese and English, and scholars may keep track of their results by visiting the Institute of Ethnology website (www.sinica.edu.tw/ioe/english/index.html) and reading the Institute's *Taiwan Journal of Anthropology.* Useful background information may also be found in a special report on Taiwan's aborigines in *Cultural Survival Quarterly* 26, no. 2 (2002), available at www.culturalsurvival.org/publications/csq/index.cfm?id=26.2. See also the Council of Indigenous Peoples website (www.apc.gov.tw/en/).

Taiwanese Buddhism has been extensively studied by local scholars, with numerous important books and articles by Jiang Tsann-terng and Lu Hui-hsing. For accounts in English, one should start with Charles B. Jones, *Buddhism in Taiwan: Religion and the State, 1660–1990* (Honolulu, 1999), as well as Julia C. Huang, "Recapturing Charisma: Emotion and Rationalization in a Globalizing Buddhist Movement from Taiwan," Ph.D. diss. (Boston University, 2001).

Early research on Taiwan's Daoist traditions was initially undertaken by scholars like Kristofer M. Schipper and Liu Chiwan, but now much of the most important work is being done by Lee Fong-mao. John Lagerwey's *Taoist Ritual in Chinese Society and History* (New York, 1987) provides a detailed account of Taiwan's liturgical Daoist traditions, while Kenneth Dean's *Taoist Ritual and Popular Cults of Southeast China* (Princeton, 1993) contains invaluable information on their origins and links to communal religious traditions in the province of Fujian.

A sizeable group of Taiwanese scholars has published in Chinese on Taiwan's sectarian movements, including Cheng Chihming, Chiu Hei-yuan, Li Shih-wei, Lin Pen-hsuan, Sung Kuang-yu, and Wang Chien-ch'uan. Among the most valuable studies published in English are David K. Jordan and Daniel L. Overmyer, *The Flying Phoenix: Aspects of Chinese Sectarianism in Taiwan* (Princeton, 1986), and Philip A. Clart, "The Ritual Context of Morality Books: A Case Study of a Taiwanese Spirit-writing Cult," Ph.D. diss. (University of British Columbia, 1996). See also Clart's "Confucius and the Mediums: Is there a 'Popular Confucianism'?" *T'oung Pao* 89, nos. 1–3 (2003): 1–28. Barend ter Haar's *The White Lotus Teachings in Chinese Religious History* (Leiden, 1992) contains a path-breaking analysis of the historical background of these movements.

Overviews of the history of Taiwanese Christianity include Hollington K. Tong's *Christianity in Taiwan: A History* (Taipei, 1961) and William Jerome Richardson's "Christianity in Taiwan under Japanese Rule, 1895–1945," Ph.D. diss. (Saint John's University, New York, 1972), which also contains useful appendices listing the names of all missionary personnel in Taiwan during the colonial era, as well as an annotated bibliography of relevant primary sources. See also Murray A. Rubinstein's classic study, *The Protestant Community on Modern Taiwan: Mission, Seminary, and Church* (Armonk, N.Y., 1991). Useful essays on Taiwanese Christianity may also be found in Daniel H. Bays, ed., *Christianity in China: From the Eighteenth Century to the Present* (Stanford, Calif., 1996), as well as Stephen Uhalley Jr. and Xiaoxin Wu, eds., *China and Christianity: Burdened Past, Hopeful Future* (Armonk, N.Y., 2001).

An impressive amount of research on Taiwan's communal religious traditions has been published from the 1960s and 1970s to the present day. Some of the most important early scholarship was undertaken by Stephan Feuchtwang, David Jordan, Daniel Overmyer, and Wang Shih-ch'ing. Among the most representative works of that era are David K. Jordan's *Gods, Ghosts, and Ancestors: Folk Religion in a Taiwanese Village* (Stanford, Calif., 1972), and P. Steven Sangren's *History and Magical Power in a Chinese Community* (Stanford, Calif., 1987). Important essays were also published in Arthur P. Wolf, ed., *Religion and Ritual in Chinese Society* (Stanford, Calif., 1974), and G. William Skinner, ed. *The City in Late Imperial China* (Stanford, Calif., 1977).

More recently, a new generation of researchers led by scholars like Chang Hsun, Lin Fu-shih, Lin Mei-rong, Mio Yuko, P. Steven Sangren, Donald Sutton, Robert Weller, and James Wilkerson has begun to shed additional light on Taiwan's communal religious traditions. Some of the most important publications in English include Allessandro Dell'Orto, *Place and Spirit in Taiwan: Tudi Gong in the Stories, Strategies and Memories of Everyday Life* (London and New York, 2002); Marc L. Moskowitz, *The Haunting Fetus: Abortion, Sexuality, and the Spirit World in Taiwan* (Honolulu, 2001); Meir Shahar, *Crazy Ji: Chinese Religion and Popular Literature* (Cambridge, Mass., 1998); Meir Shahar and Robert Weller, eds., *Unruly Gods: Divinity and Society in China* (Honolulu, 1996); and Donald Sutton, *Steps of Perfection: Exorcistic Performers and Chinese Religion in Twentieth-Century Taiwan* (Cambridge, Mass., 2003).

PAUL R. KATZ (2005)

TAIXU (1890–1947), Chinese Buddhist reformer, founder of the Wuchang Buddhist Institute and the Buddhist journal *Haichaoyin,* and active participant in various Buddhist movements. Taixu's lay name was Lü Peilin. Born in Haining in Zhejiang, he became a monk of the Linji school of Chan Buddhism at the age of sixteen. Buddhist scriptures as well as the radical political writings of Liang Qichao and others inspired him to act for the reformation of Chinese Buddhism. He tried to put his reform programs into practice by founding the Fojiao Xiejin Hui (Association for the Advancement of Buddhism) in 1912, but the association was short-lived owing to opposition from conservative Buddhists. In 1917 Taixu visited Taiwan and Japan. Later, he established the Enlightenment Society (Jueshe) at Shanghai with the help of some eminent Chinese. The society organized public lectures and disseminated knowledge of Buddhism through its own publications. Taixu next made a preaching tour of several cities in China and in Malaya. In 1920 he founded the Buddhist periodical *Haichaoyin.* He established the Wuchang Buddhist Institute in 1922, the first modern Buddhist seminary in China. In 1923, Taixu and a few followers founded the World Buddhist Federation, which included among its members Inada Eisai and K. L. Reichelt. Two years later he led the Chinese Buddhist delegation to the Tokyo Conference of East Asian Buddhists. In 1927 he became the head of the Minnan Buddhist Institute. During that year, he associated with the Chinese Nationalist leader Chiang Kai-shek, who financed Taixu's world tour in 1928. The Chinese Buddhist Association was founded by Reverend Yuanying (1878–1953) at Shanghai in 1929, but Taixu's early relation with it was not cordial, though he was on its standing committee. In 1930 he founded the Sino-Tibetan Buddhist Institute in Chongqing; this became the headquarters of the Chinese Buddhist Association in the war years, 1937 to 1945. During the war, Taixu led a Chinese Buddhist mission of goodwill to Burma, India, Ceylon, and Malaya to win support and sympathy for China, and he was awarded a medal by the Chinese government for his contributions to the war effort. His influence on Nationalist leaders declined after the war, and he died on March 12, 1947. His writings were published posthumously in thirty-three volumes.

Since the late nineteenth century, Chinese Buddhism has been under constant pressure from the government and from intellectuals. In 1898 a high official proposed that 70 percent of monastic buildings and their income should be taken over to finance the public school system. Although this was not put into practice, and although the Buddhists managed at times to put off or soften anti-Buddhist threats, the idea of using Buddhist property to finance education arose again in 1928 and 1942. Taixu's suggestions for reform were part of the Buddhist reaction to public pressure. As a compromise, Taixu suggested in 1942 that 40 percent of monastic income be used for educational and charitable institutions run by the Buddhists in exchange for government protection of monastic property, but his suggestion had no effect on either side.

Taixu's attempts to reform and modernize Chinese Buddhism were to some extent successful. A number of prominent scholars and religious leaders were trained at the academies and libraries that he founded, and his lectures and writings helped create a more positive public attitude toward Buddhism. But his larger dream of a worldwide Buddhist movement, and his plan for reorganizing Buddhist institutions throughout China never materialized during his lifetime. His ideas were often viewed by the conservative Buddhist establishment as radical and unacceptable. They cooperated with him reluctantly in times of crisis but were always opposed to his ideas on monastic affairs. Yet, viewed from a historical perspective, his program of reform and modernization (the establishment of Buddhist academies, journals, foreign contacts, and so forth) can be seen to have created new patterns for Chinese Buddhism.

The religious thought of Taixu falls in the mainstream of Chinese Buddhism. It recognizes that all sentient beings possess the Buddha nature and are subject to the law of causation. The operation of cause and conditions is universal and incessant, and all worldly phenomena are based on that operation. If one follows the five Buddhist precepts, a happy life in this world is achievable. This happy life is, however, not lasting; it is subject to change. One must therefore strive for a higher wisdom and thus attain *nirvāṇa*. When one realizes that there is neither self nor object and that only the mind is universal and unlimited, one will work for the salvation of all sentient beings so that they too may become Buddhas. Taixu's contribution is his adoption of a new terminology and a modern style of writing, thus tuning the old philosophy to the new thought in China. He often used words like *revolution, evolution, science, democracy, philosophy,* and *freedom,* as well as other concepts popular in his time. Although he may not always have used these terms with a clear understanding of their modern meaning, by incorporating them into the context of Buddhism he made the tradition continue to appeal to young people at the beginning of the twentieth century.

BIBLIOGRAPHY

The most complete and competent account of Taixu is the chronological biography compiled by Yinshun, *T'ai-hsü ta-shih nien-p'u* (1950; reprint, Taibei, 1973). Taixu's autobiographical writings, including *T'ai-hsü tsu-chuan* (rev. ed., 1945), can be found in the collection of his writings, *T'ai-hsü ta-shih ch'üan-shu,* vols. 29–30 (1953; reprint, Taibei, 1973). Holmes Welch's chapter on the monk in his *The Buddhist Revival in China* (Cambridge, Mass., 1968), pp. 51–57, is overly critical. See also Paul E. Callahan's "T'ai-hsü and the New Buddhist Movement," *Papers on China* 6 (March 1952): 149–188, and the entry on Taixu in the *Biographical Dictionary of Republican China, 1911–1949,* edited by Howard L. Boorman (New York, 1970). Selections from Taixu's writings in English translation can be found in his *Lectures in Buddhism* (Paris, 1928) and Chou Hsiang-kuang's *T'ai-hsü: His Life and Teachings* (Allahabad, India, 1957).

New Sources

Fu, C.W.-h. and S. A. Wawrytko. *Buddhist Ethics and Modern Society: An International Symposium.* New York, 1991.

Long, Darui. "An Interfaith Dialogue between the Chinese Buddhist Leader Taixu and Christians." *Buddhist Christian Studies* 20 (2000): 167–189.

Pittman, Don A. "The Modern Buddhist Reformer T'ai-hsu on Christianity." *Buddhist Christian Studies* 13 (1993): 71–83.

JAN YÜN-HUA (1987)
Revised Bibliography

TALIESIN. The ninth-century *Historia Brittonum,* usually attributed to "Nennius," names Taliesin as one of a famed group of Welsh poets of the latter half of the sixth century. The thirteenth-century *Book of Taliesin* contains a body of poetry of diverse origins and different dates that the scribe presumably associated with Taliesin, but modern research has isolated some twelve poems that are regarded as his authentic work. These are heroic court poems sung to royal patrons and to Urien, Owain, and Gwallawg, kings of the sixth-century northern British kingdoms of Rheged and Elmet.

The early medieval Welsh poet was a complex persona, and Taliesin acquired the status of a vaticinatory poet (perhaps conflated with the figure of Myrddin/Merlin) and purveyor of esoteric and learned lore, both bardic and Christian. Many of the poems in the *Book of Taliesin* reflect this role, which is given a specific context in the *Story of Taliesin (Hanes Taliesin).* Although found in manuscript copies of the sixteenth century and later, this composite tale is certainly earlier. The first part relates how the witch Ceridwen concentrated her learning in three drops of a brew which she prepared for her son. At the crucial moment of fulfillment they fell onto the hand of a serving lad, Gwion Bach, who sucked his scalded finger and acquired the knowledge and bardic power intended for the son. In the ensuing pursuit Gwion and Ceridwen undergo several metamorphoses until the lad is swallowed as a seed of corn by Ceridwen in the guise of a hen to be reborn nine months later. He is taken up by Elffin, named Taliesin, and soon reveals his precocity as poet and sage. The rest of the tale recounts his feats of learning at the court of the sixth-century king Maelgwn Gwynedd.

Poems of the *Story of Taliesin* are spoken by Taliesin, but those in the *Book of Taliesin,* though lacking this specific context, nevertheless refer to similar circumstances and are to be dated to the tenth century. One such poem alludes to Taliesin's creation by the wizards Math and Gwydion, characters found in the Four Branches of the *Mabinogi;* another relates his transforming of trees into warriors in the Battle of Goddau. The poem titled *The Spoils of Annwn* refers to the poet's return as one of the survivors of Arthur's disastrous attack on the otherworld, an episode underlying the Second Branch, which names Taliesin and a survivor. This early stratum of Taliesin's legend links him not with historical characters of the sixth century but with purely mythological figures and episodes. In later bardic tradition, Taliesin becomes the archetypal inspired poet.

Bibliography

Trioedd Ynys Prydein: The Welsh Triads, 2d ed. (Cardiff, 1978), edited by Rachel Bromwich, gives a concise discussion of the sources and offers scholarly opinion, while Ifor Williams's *Chwedl Taliesin* (Cardiff, 1957) analyzes the development of the Taliesin legend. Patrick K. Ford edits the text of the legend, *Ystoria Taliesin* (Cardiff, 1992) and in his introduction he discusses its themes; he translates the story in his *The Mabinogi and Medieval Welsh Tales* (Berkeley, 1977). See also Juliette Wood, "The Elphin Section of Hanes Taliesin," *Etudes Celtiques* 18 (1981): 229–244, and "The Folklore Background of the Gwion Bach Section of Hanes Taliesin," *Bulletin of the Board of Celtic Studies* 29 (1982): 621–634. Marged Haycock has published a number of important articles on the nonhistorical Taliesin material in the Book of Taliesin, including "Preideu Annwn and the Figure of Taliesin," *Studia Celtica,* 18/19 (1983–1984): 52–78, "Cadair Ceridwen," in Iestyn Daniel and others, eds., *Cyfoeth y Testun* (Cardiff, 2003), 148–175, "The Significance of the Cad Goddeu Tree List in the Book of Taliesin," in M. J. Ball et al., editors, *Celtic Linguistics* (Amsterdam, 1990): 297–331, "Taliesin's Questions," *Cambrian Medieval Celtic Studies* 33 (1997): 19–80.

Brynley F. Roberts (1987 and 2005)

TALISMANS See AMULETS AND TALISMANS

TALMUD.

In form, the Talmud is an extended, multivolume elaboration of selected tractates of the Mishnah, but it must be emphasized that the contents of the Talmud go far beyond its ostensible base. No subject of interest to the ancient rabbis failed to find its way into this immense body of teaching, and for that reason no question arising in later centuries was deemed outside the range that Talmudic teaching might legitimately claim to resolve. A document that seemed merely to elucidate an older text eventually became the all-embracing constitution of medieval Jewish life.

The Mishnah supplied the overall format for the Talmud. Like the former, the Talmud is divided into tractates, which in turn are divided into chapters and then into paragraphs. Each phrase of the Mishnah is discussed, analyzed, and applied for as long as the editors of the Talmud have materials to supply; when such materials are exhausted (sometimes after very long and quite wide-ranging digressions), the discussion simply moves on to the next phrase or paragraph. The digressions can be such that one loses track of the Mishnaic passage under discussion for pages at a time, but the Talmud always picks up again from its base text when the next section begins.

Origins and Development. Very soon after it began to circulate, the Mishnah of Yehudah ha-Nasi' (compiled c. 200 CE) assumed a central place in rabbinic study. As time went on, the structure and content of the Mishnah—the meaning and the sequence of its paragraphs—determined the manner in which the growing accumulation of rabbinic lore was organized. Non-Mishnaic legal materials (the so-called outside traditions; Aram., *baraitot*) were studied primarily in connection with their Mishnaic parallels, and an entire supplementary collection (Tosefta) that followed the Mishnah's own sequence of orders, tractates, and chapters was compiled. Similarly, post-Mishnaic rabbinic teachings—of law, morality, theology, and so forth—were remembered and discussed primarily as the consecutive study of Mishnaic tractates called them to mind, so that most such teachings eventually came to be linked with one or another specific passage (or, occasionally, several) in the earlier collection.

In this way, great compilations of rabbinic teaching, each in the form of a loose exposition of the Mishnah, came into being. Evidence suggests that various centers of rabbinic study developed their own such collections, though in the end only one overall collection was redacted for the Palestinian centers and one for Babylonia. For several generations, the collections remained fluid. Materials were added, revised, or shifted. Free association led to the production of extended discourses or sets of sayings that at times had little to do with the Mishnaic passages serving as points of departure. Early materials tended to be brief explanations of the Mishnah or citations of parallel texts, but later rabbis increasingly commented as well on remarks of their predecessors or other non-Mishnaic materials. Numerous scholars have seen in the developing tradition two sorts of material: brief, apodictic statements of law and much longer dialectical explanations of the specific laws and their underlying principles. Such discussions in turn eventually gave rise to a new generation of legal dicta, and these in turn provoked new efforts at dialectical complication. Thus the Talmudic tradition grew.

The Hebrew word *talmud* and its Aramaic equivalent *gemara'* both mean "study." Each term had other meanings at various times, but in the end *gemara'* came to be the name of the vast Mishnah commentary that had taken shape, and *talmud* the name of the combined text (Mishnah plus *gemara'*) that eventually emerged. The rabbis of the immediate post-Mishnaic period (third to fifth centuries CE) are called *amora'* from the Aramaic *'mr,* "say, discuss"), because their characteristic contribution to the developing tradition was the extended discussion of the Mishnah they produced.

Through a process that can no longer be traced with certainty, the text of the *gemara'* underwent periodic reshaping until finally the two Talmuds as we now know them came into being. It should be emphasized that early rabbinic Torah study was oral, so that the *gemara'* was not so much a fixed text as a more-or-less accepted formulation of accumulated lore. There is therefore no reason to assume that there ever was an authorized "original text" of the Talmud, and there may have been parallel recensions of these collections from the earliest stages of their history preserved in different localities. There is still no altogether accepted standard text, and even the relatively uniform wording of recent centuries has much to do with the eventual predominance of European over Asian and North African Jewry and the standardization that inevitably followed the invention of printing.

The Jerusalem, or Palestinian, Talmud. The so-called Jerusalem Talmud (Heb., *Talmud Yerushalmi*) is really the work of the rabbinic academies of the Galilee; it was substantially completed by the middle of the fifth century. The Jerusalem Talmud covers the first four orders of the Mishnah with the exception of two tractates (*Avot* and *'Eduyyot*); in the last two orders, only half of tractate *Niddah* has Palestinian *gemara'*. The Jerusalem Talmud is characterized in general by brevity and an absence of editorial transitions and clarifications. Its discussions frequently seem laconic and elliptical and often take the form of terse remarks attributed to one or another amora with no connective phrasing at all between them. Occasionally, however, such comments are built up into a more integrated dialectical treatment, with objections raised and answered, contradictions cited and resolved, and biblical proof texts adduced as the editors see fit.

The Babylonian Talmud. According to tradition, the redaction of the Babylonian Talmud (Heb., *Talmud Bavli*) was completed by the amoraim Ashi and Ravina' around the year 500. It is clear, however, that the distinctive features of this Talmud in contrast to the other are the work of several generations of mostly anonymous rabbis who came after these authorities and are collectively known as the savoraim (from the Aramaic root *svr,* "consider, hold an opinion"), that is, those who reconsidered the Talmudic text and established its final version. Thanks to the labors of these latter revisers, the Babylonian Talmud is far more thoroughly worked out than the Palestinian. Its arguments are replete with a sophisticated technical terminology for introducing source materials, considering objections and counterobjections, offering refutations and defending against them, and so forth. In addition to their detailed contributions, the savoraim also composed entire sections of the Talmud; in particular, the extended discussion at the beginning of many tractates is attributed to them. In general, the literary superiority of the Babylonian Talmud, its far greater logical clarity, and its considerably larger bulk can be attributed to the savoraim of the sixth and seventh centuries. The Talmud in its current form did not exist until these had done their work.

While the Jerusalem Talmud treats the entire first order of the Mishnah, the Babylonian Talmud has *gemara'* only for the first tractate (*Berakhot*), which deals with liturgy; the rest of the order treats agricultural rules that were not considered applicable outside the Holy Land. On the other hand, and harder to explain, the great bulk of the fifth order, which regulates the long-destroyed Temple cult and is not to be found in the Jerusalem Talmud, has very substantial Babylonian *gemara'*. Otherwise, with minor exceptions, the two Talmuds cover the same parts of the Mishnah.

LATER DEVELOPMENTS. Over the several centuries following the appearance of the two Talmuds, the Babylonian Talmud gradually eclipsed the other. This predominance was rationalized by the claim that the Babylonian Talmud was the more recent, so that its editors already knew the Jerusalem Talmud and could include its acceptable teachings in their own work and suppress those portions for any reason found unworthy. In retrospect, however, it is clear that such a claim was part of the propaganda of the Babylonian geonim of the last centuries of the first millennium CE in favor of their own authority and against the rival authority of the rabbis of the Land of Israel. The eventual predominance of the Babylonian Talmud throughout the Diaspora and even in the Land of Israel probably is to be explained through reference to such factors as the relatively stronger ties of the rising communities of North Africa and Spain to Babylonian Jewry and the relatively more severe decline of Palestinian Jewry, especially under the onslaught of the Crusades. Those parts of Europe, especially Italy, that retained strong ties with the community in the Land of Israel apparently maintained a tradition of study of the Jerusalem Talmud, but by the beginning of the second millennium this process had run its course. From then on, "the Talmud" always meant the Babylonian. It was taken for granted that issues of Jewish law should be resolved by reference to the Babylonian Talmud, not the Palestinian, and that the latter could provide rulings only in cases where the Babylonian Talmud was silent or ambiguous.

Once the primacy of the Babylonian Talmud was established, this primacy was continually reinforced. The Babylonian Talmud received more attention. It was studied by more scholars, it became the subject of more and of better commentaries; it was copied more often and more carefully by larger numbers of scribes. The result is that modern scholars have a more solidly established text of the Babylonian Talmud and a more fully developed exegetical tradition with which to work. Modern critical study of the Jerusalem Talmud has much more fundamental analytical and restorative work to accomplish before a reliable and comprehensible text becomes available.

It should be noted as well that the power of the medieval Christian church affected the development of the Talmud in two important ways. Periodic waves of seizure and destruction reduced the number of Talmud manuscripts available in certain parts of Europe. The most important of these waves took place in thirteenth-century France and in Italy at the time of the Counter-Reformation; the last burning of the Talmud occurred in Poland in 1757. Occasionally thousands of copies of the Talmud or of Talmudic digests and commentaries were destroyed at a time. In addition, Jewish efforts to avoid such destruction often led to voluntary or involuntary submission of the Talmud to censorship by church authorities. As a result, much early rabbinic discussion of Jesus or the Christian religion has been lost or must now be recovered from scattered manuscripts.

TALMUDIC RELIGION. Despite its vast size and scope, the Talmud is not without focus. Certain themes and certain styles of argument and discourse strongly predominate in its pages, and as a result both the religion of the Talmudic sages themselves and the forms of Judaism based on the Talmud that flourished during the Middle Ages are more compatible with certain types of spirituality than with others.

The role of law. Well more than half of the Babylonian Talmud and more than three quarters of the Jerusalem Talmud are devoted to questions of law. The Mishnah itself takes the form of a law code, and Talmudic discussions are chiefly concerned with clarifying, extending, and finding new applications for the provisions of Mishnaic law. This concentration on law is related to the ancient rabbis' role in their communities, where they usually served as judges, teachers, or public administrators. Rabbinic piety came to be organized around gratitude for the law and joy in its fulfillment. The law was understood to be a divine gift, and observance of its provisions was seen as the appropriate response to this generosity. To observe the law meant to strengthen one's link to its giver, and in developing the law into a huge accumulation of detailed regulations covering all aspects of day-to-day living, rabbinic teachers sought to multiply occasions for strengthening this link. Study of the law was both the highest intellectual activity in which a Jew might engage and also a practical activity designed to further this expansion of opportunity. Enlarging the scope of the law was not felt to be adding to an already heavy burden; on the contrary, it increased the portion of one's life that could be conducted in response to the voice of God.

The role of study and intellect. While the Mishnah looks like a law code, however, in fact it is probably something other; its numerous unresolved disputes, its sporadic use of biblical proof texts, and its occasional narratives all reflect the value of study as a religious ritual in its own right, and eventually the activity of studying God's law was as important in Talmudic religion as was the content of that study. Even before the Talmud was completed, this enhancement of study as religious rite had led to the creation of an elaborate set of legal corpora, most of which were identified by the name of the master to whom the discrete opinions in each corpus were attributed. The well-known Talmudic penchant for hair-splitting dialectics reflects the rabbis' concern that each of these sets of teachings be internally consistent on the one hand and significantly different from any other such set on the other. Hence the frequency with which the Talmud records the chains of transmission by which individual sayings were passed on. Hence the steadily growing integration of teachings from widely disparate fields of law into a single web, and the often forced effort to find unifying principles behind teachings that seem to have nothing to do with one another. Hence, as well, the relative lack of interest in the personalities of early masters, except, paradoxically, for those few who became the subject of frequently incredible legends.

This intellectual tendency had several important consequences for Talmudic religion. It gave rabbinic studiousness a scholastic tinge that continued to sharpen as later centuries wore on. It made text commentary an important genre of religious literature; a standard edition of the Talmud even today contains several classical commentaries on the page along with the text and many, many more at the back of the volume. Rabbinic intellectualism turned into disciplined argument; the interplay of proof and refutation became a holy activity. It also gave primacy to the correct formulation of sacred texts and recitations; this in turn had important effects on Talmudic and post-Talmudic conceptions of prayer, meditation, and inward spirituality.

TALMUDIC LEARNING AND RELIGIOUS AUTHORITY. In the ancient rabbis' view there was a connection between their emphasis on learning and the role of leadership to which they aspired. It was taken for granted that only the Torah, when properly and sufficiently studied and understood, could enable the people of Israel to become the "kingdom of priests and holy nation" (*Ex.* 19:6) that God intended them to be. This in turn meant that only those properly and sufficiently learned in Torah should be allowed to assume leadership over the community, since only such leaders could be trusted to guide the people in a divinely ordained direction.

Inherent in Talmudic and post-Talmudic Judaism is the assumption that Torah learning (once the Talmud was complete, this meant Talmudic learning) is the only proper criterion by which the leaders of the community should be selected. Whenever conditions permitted, rabbis sought to institutionalize their authority over the community. In the early period, this meant reaching an accommodation with the real rulers of the community (e.g., the Roman empire or, in Babylonia, the allegedly Davidic dynasty of the exilarchs). Later, it meant assuring that internal Jewish courts should be dominated by rabbis and that Talmudic law should govern those aspects of life where Jews maintained internal autonomy (marriage and divorce, religious ritual, educational institutions). Although rabbinical authority was not without challengers, it was never overthrown in principle until the breakdown of Jewish self-government, which began in the late eighteenth century and continued into the nineteenth.

Talmud Study as Religious Experience. Rabbis saw their own teaching as "oral Torah." They believed the contents of the Talmud represented a part of the revelation to Moses that had been kept oral but faithfully transmitted for centuries before its inclusion in the text of the Talmud. The name *Talmud,* in fact, can be understood as a short form of the common phrase *talmud Torah,* or "Torah study." Thus to study Talmud was in fact to let oneself hear the word of God, and to add to the accumulation of commentaries, digests, codes, and the like was to make one's own contribution to the spread of divine revelation in the world. To learn Torah was thus a kind of sober mysticism, a reliving of the events at Sinai, while to add to the growing body of "oral" law was to share in a divine activity. Already in the Talmud God is depicted as studying Torah several hours per day (B. T., *ʿA. Z.* 3b), but the kinship between the rabbi and God was felt to be even stronger. By increasing the amount of Torah in the world, the rabbi could do what previously only God had been held able to accomplish.

Thus the text of the Talmud became the center of an activity believed to be the most Godlike available to human experience. Everyone (in practice this meant every male) could study some Torah, and no one was considered incapable of adding a few original thoughts to a study session. Talmud study became a widespread activity among later Jewish communities. The degree of commitment to this activity might vary, from the ascetic twenty-hour-per-day devotion of the secluded scholar to one-hour-per-week popular learning on Sabbath afternoons. The climax of a boy's education was the point at which he was ready to learn *gemaraʾ*. Such "learning" continues even in the present time, even after the functioning authority of Talmudic law has all but disappeared. It represents the most powerful and the most durable inheritance of classical Judaism.

See Also Biblical Exegesis, article on Jewish Views; Halakhah; Mishnah and Tosefta.

Bibliography

The history and current state of critical scholarship about the two Talmuds is comprehensively reviewed in two essays in *Aufstieg und Niedergang der römischen Welt,* vol. 2.19.2 (Berlin and New York, 1979): Baruch M. Bokser's "An Annotated Bibliographical Guide to the Study of the Palestinian Talmud," pp. 139–256, and David Goodblatt's "The Babylonian Talmud," pp. 257–336. Both have been reprinted in *The Study of Ancient Judaism,* vol. 2, edited by Jacob Neusner (New York, 1981). Several of Neusner's students also produced longer examinations of the work of particular modern scholars; he collected these in *The Formation of the Babylonian Talmud* (Leiden, 1970). Readers can also consult Strack-Stemberger, *Introduction to the Talmud and Midrash* (revised edition, Minneapolis, 1992).

Neusner has also investigated the religious implications of conceiving of Torah study as a holy activity and the theological implications of rabbinic intellectuality; see his concise *The Glory of God Is Intelligence* (Salt Lake City, Utah, 1978). A more popular effort of the same sort is Morris Adler's *The World of the Talmud* (New York, 1958). See also my own "Talmud," in *Back to the Sources,* edited by Barry W. Holtz (New York, 1984), pp. 129–175.

Robert Goldenberg (1987 and 2005)

TAM, YAʿAQOV BEN MEʾIR

TAM, YAʿAQOV BEN MEʾIR (c. 1100–1171), leading Jewish halakhic scholar, known as Rabbenu ("our teacher") Tam from the biblical description of the patriarch Jacob as *tam* (*Gn.* 25:27), a word often translated as "quiet," with the connotation of a studious, scholarly person. The scion of a learned rabbinical family, he was the grandson of Rashi (Shelomoh ben Yitsḥaq, 1042–1105), the most prominent Talmudic commentator, and the brother of Shemuʾel ben Meʾir, the Rashbam. He was himself the greatest of the founders of the Tosafist school of Talmudic commentators in the twelfth to fourteenth centuries.

In his commentaries Tam employed the method of comparative examination of the Talmudic texts, aiming to explain contradictions and inconsistencies while elucidating the passages. He was against making any corrections in the traditional text of the Talmud unless there was absolutely no other way of understanding a particular passage. His concerns encompassed practical legal and religious applications as well as a theoretical understanding of the Talmudic system. He generally opposed current usages that seemed contrary to Talmudic teachings and customs and also did not allow deviation from ancestral practices. His reasoned legal decisions were based on the Talmud itself and not on the varying needs of the time, although he sometimes resolved contradictions between the Talmud and the religious and legal practices of the day by reinterpreting the traditional texts.

Tam was accepted by his contemporaries as the greatest scholar of his generation. Many disciples flocked to study with him from France and Germany and even as far away as Italy, Bohemia, and Russia; through them, his teachings and opinions circulated throughout Europe, reaching even to Spain. Considered the central halakhic authority of the age, he received halakhic and Talmudic questions and problems from all parts of Europe. By virtue of his position he issued various regulations *(taanot)* for the Jewish communities of the time. Tam's *responsa* (answers to questions posed) and comments on the Talmud were accepted as authoritative by later generations, especially among Western (Ashkenazic) orthodox Jewry.

His main work is *Sefer ha-yashar* (Vienna, 1811), which includes his halakhic *responsa* (annotated Berlin, 1898) and his *novellae,* or comments, on the Talmud (annotated Jerusalem, 1959). The book as we have it is a later unedited collection from the original with additions from other authors. However, the greater part of his teachings are not included in this work but are scattered throughout the *tosafot* and the collections of *responsa* and decisions of his time.

See Also Tosafot.

Bibliography

No monograph on Yaʿaqov ben Meʾir Tam has appeared in English. Three important discussions of Tam's life and influence are my own "Yaḥaso shel Rabbenu Tam le-beʿayot zemano," *Zion* 19 (1954): 104–141; Viktor Aptowitzer's *Mavoʾ le-sefer Raʾavyah* (Jerusalem, 1938), pp. 357–366; and chapter 3 of E. E. Urbach's *Baʿalei ha-tosafot,* 4th ed. (Jerusalem, 1980).

New Sources

Langer, Ruth. "Kalir Was a Tanna: Rabbenu Tam's Invocation of Antiquity in Defense of the Ashkenazi Payyetanic Tradition." *HUCA* 67 (1996): 95–106.

Shalom Albeck (1987)
Revised Bibliography

TAMIL RELIGIONS.

The term *Tamil religions* denotes the religious traditions and practices of Tamil-speaking people. Most Tamils originated and continue to live in India's southernmost area, now known as the state of Tamil Nadu; however, millions of Tamils have migrated to other parts of India, especially to its large cities, as well as abroad, particularly to Malaysia, Singapore, Sri Lanka, Madagascar, Australia, Great Britain and, more recently, to the United States and Canada. Many emigrant Tamils retain elements of a cultural, linguistic, and religious tradition that predates the Christian era and has experienced a complex interaction of influences from Dravidian, Sanskritic, and heterodox sources. At its apex between the eighth and fifteenth centuries, the Tamil region was the major center of Hindu civilization and, indeed, one of the major centers of civilization in the world. Today, while most Tamils remain essentially Hindu, some Tamils have embraced elements of Islam and Christianity.

Early Tamil Religion. A Neolithic cattle-herding culture existed in South India several millennia prior to the Christian era. By the first century, a relatively well-developed civilization had emerged, still largely pre-Hindu and only marginally sanskritized. It is described in some detail in Tamil texts such as the *Tolkāppiyam* (a grammar written around the start of the Christian era) and by the "Caṅkam" poets—an "academy" of poets who wrote in the first two centuries CE. This culture was essentially Dravidian in nature.

The origins of the Dravidians are still a matter of dispute, but the South Indian culture known to current researchers by the first century was probably based largely on the Neolithic cultures that developed in the area. However, these cultures were influenced in prehistoric times to varying degrees by the filtering of some remnants of a Negroid culture originating in East Africa; by migrations from the eastern Mediterranean world refracted through the Elamite and Indus civilizations; by a megalithic culture that made its way into Southwest India by the eighth century BCE; and by a people sometimes called "Proto-Australoid" who came into the subcontinent by way of northeastern India from the Malay peninsula.

The religious life of the Tamil civilization of Cankam times gave evidence of no significant mythological or philosophical speculation nor of any sense of transcendence in a bifurcated universe. Rather, it was oriented by a fundamental veneration of land and a sense of the celebration of individual life. Colorful flora and fauna were extolled and ascribed a symbolic significance that bordered on the sacred; for example, peacocks, elephants, and the blossoms of various trees were used as images for the basic realities of individual and cosmos. Earth's color and fertility were affirmed. Indigenous deities were venerated in field and hill, reflecting the attributes of the people in that zone and presiding over functions typical to their respective areas; thus, the god Murukan̲ presided over hill and hunt and battled the malevolent forces of the hills, while Vēntan̲ oversaw the pastoral region and afforded it rain.

"Possession" is one of the most common ways in which the gods were believed to manifest themselves—both in their priests and in young women. Worship of the gods sometimes occurred in a special place—in the clearing of a field or the bank of a river, for example, where a small pillar or *kantu* was set up to represent the deity. The cult of the hero was a common feature of this period as evidenced by the erection of numerous hero stones (*naṭukkals*) over the graves of fallen heroes, be they hunting warriors or tribal chieftains. Urn burial, a remnant of megalithic culture, was used occasionally, especially after the death of the chieftain or hero.

The city was not foreign to this early culture and by the third century CE, at least, religious imagery reflected an urban setting. Poets likened the urban chieftains and warriors to the gods and spoke of urban festivals. Some of the earlier gods were merged together in an urban setting, even while continuing their earlier functions in extra-urban contexts. Rituals, however, often continued to reflect a seasonal or folk character: In the hills, garlanded young women are said to have danced, intoxicated, with priests (*vēlan̲s*) of Murukan̲ (*Cilappatikāram* 24), while in the plain, at the onset of monsoons, after harvests and transplantings, bathers gambolled in the waters, were garlanded and smeared with sandal, often astride elephants or horses, and drank intoxicating beverages (*Paripāṭal* 6, 7, 10).

The early character of Tamil religion, in sum, was celebrative and relatively "democratic." It embodied an aura of sacral immanence, sensing the sacred in the vegetation, fertility, and color of the land. The *summum bonum* of the religious experience was expressed in terms of possession by the god, or ecstasy. Into this milieu there immigrated a sobering influence—a growing number of Jain and Buddhist communities and an increasing influx of *brahmans* and other northerners.

The Heterodoxies. By the third century BCE, pockets of Jains and Buddhists were settling in the deep South. Some may have migrated across the straits from Sri Lanka; others came southward during the reign of Aśoka, the Mauryan emperor. By the first century CE, both had established settlements and built small institutions and shrines known as *paḻḻis*. Although both Jain and Buddhist monks tended to live outside the cities for centuries—the Jains often in rock caves and the Buddhist monks in monastic communities—their impact on Tamil country increased, enhanced by the influx and influence of lay members. The politics and literature of Tamil country were influenced by Jain and Buddhist savants, especially between the fourth and seventh centuries CE. Consequently, the dominant mood of religion in Tamil country for some three centuries reflected Jain and Buddhist values. There was little emphasis on theism or indigenous sacred places. Sobriety and self-effacement became a respected way of life, especially for the elite.

The Hinduization of Tamil Country. Beginning in the third century CE, migrating *brahmans* and other persons influenced by Vedic and epic traditions were also becoming a part of the Tamil landscape. In the early cities, chieftains who sought to enchance their status employed *brahman* priests to perform Vedic rituals as had been the case in the north during the epic period. It was in the seventh century, however, that Hindu Sanskritic culture and religion merged with the indigenous Tamil society, leading to a pervasive hinduization of Tamil country and the emergence of a new and creative Hindu civilization.

The first significant feature of the "Hindu age" in Tamil India was the rise of devotional poetry (*bhakti*) in the vernacular language during the seventh, eighth, and ninth centuries. Poets who were followers of Śiva (Nāyaṉārs) and of Viṣṇu (Āḻvārs: literally, those who are "immersed") popularized these two deities throughout Tamil country. These poets were drawn from all walks of life, though over half of them were of *brahman* or of royal background. At first, their attacks on Jains and Buddhists tended to be virulent, especially in the case of the Śaiva Tiruñanacambantaṉ. But by the mid-eighth century, Hindu devotionalism had taken a significant hold in Tamil country and the poets could afford to take a more accommodating attitude toward the declining Jain and Buddhist presence.

Between the years 650 and 940 the twelve Vaiṣṇava poet-saints (Āḻvārs) wrote some four thousand verses, which were eventually canonized in the *Nālāyira-divyaprabandham* (The four thousand divine verses) edited in the tenth century by Nāthamuni, the first major *ācārya*, or sectarian teacher, of Vaiṣṇavism. Of the earlier Āḻvārs, the most prolific was Kalikaṉṟi (800–870), also known as Tirumaṅkai, who wrote 1,227 verses combining militant, heroic, and erotic imagery with the anguish of separation from his lord. The ninth- and tenth-century Āḻvārs associated primarily with western Tamil country include Viṭṭuciṭṭaṉ, known as Periyāḻvār ("great Āḻvār"), who wrote 473 verses largely from the standpoint of the deity's mother expressing fondness for the child Kṛṣṇa. Periyāḻvār's daughter Kōtai, popularly known as Āṇṭāḻ ("she who rules the lord"), wrote 173 verses. Often erotic, they focused on Kṛṣṇa as an adolescent from the viewpoint of a *gopī* who spends time with the Lord in his inner chamber. Finally, Caṭakōpaṉ or Āḻvār Māṟaṉ (880–930), also known affectionately as Nammāḻvār ("our own devotee"), wrote 1,296 verses that combine passionate devotion for Kṛṣṇa with the metaphysics of Vedānta, the philosophical system of Vaiṣṇava *brahmans*. Nammāḻvār has come to be seen as the most authoritative of the Āḻvārs for the Sri Vaiṣṇavas.

While tradition claims there were sixty-three Śaiva poet-saints (Nāyaṉārs)—perhaps in response to the traditional sixty-three saints of Jainism—there were in fact only eight who were poets of repute, while another Śaiva poet of the period, Māṇikkavācakar, who was important for the shaping of Śaiva devotionalism, was not accepted as a Nāyaṉār for several centuries. The earliest of the Nāyaṉārs was probably a woman, Kāraikkāl Ammaiyār (seventh century CE), who renounced worldly pleasures for devotion to Śiva. Tirumūlar (eighth century CE) is noted for his 3,000-verse philosophical treatise, *Tirumantiram*, which interprets Sanskrit Agamic and Tantric material into Tamil. The best known and most prolific of the Nāyaṉār poets were the three whose poetry makes up the first seven sections of the *Tēvarām*, the Tamil Śaiva canon. Two of these are seventh-century figures: Tirunāvukkaracar, better known as "Appar," or "Father," and his younger contemporary, Campantar or Tiruñāṉacampantar, who is generally believed to have been a child prodigy uttering all his poetry before the age of sixteen; the third poet is the ninth-century (?) Cuntaramūrtti. However, perhaps the best of all the Śaiva poets of these three centuries was the ninth-century Māṇikkavācakar, for whom the religious experience was like ecstasy and "madness" when one was possessed by Śiva. Māṇikkavācakar's use of erotic imagery apparently was a major factor in keeping him from being accepted as a poet of the Śaiva canon until at least the twelfth century, when Cēkkiḻār included him in his *Periyapurāṇam*, the mythical hagiography of the Śaiva saints.

The religion propagated by the *bhakti* poets used epic and puranic mythology selectively and gave it a locus in Tamil India. A number of basic themes were stressed: (1) the supremacy, greatness, even terror of Śiva or Viṣṇu, coupled nonetheless by the deity's grace and compassion for those who were devoted to him; (2) the concrete and available presence of the god in his specific sacred places and, hence, the desirability of pilgrimage, festival, and temple ritual; (3) the affirmation of the individual in the experience of *bhakti* or devotion to god and the possibility of anyone's attaining the god's grace regardless of one's station; (4) the sense of community among the god's devotees and the merit in serving and being in such company; (5) the celebration of the experience of the god as the highest attainment of religion.

Tamil *bhakti* reflected many strands of religion at once. While it incorporated, on the one hand, certain aspects of Jain and Buddhist values (e.g., a sense of community among devotees; hospitality to fellow devotees; and the possibility of spiritual attainment irrespective of social or economic backgrounds); on the other hand, it directly confronted these heterodoxies with a vigorous theism; an affirmation of the phenomenal world as God's creation; and the importance of the devotional experience and of pilgrimage to the deity's special places. This *bhakti* movement reaffirmed elements of early Tamil religious perspectives: the emphasis on celebration, ecstasy, even possession by the god; the importance of the individual in religious experience; and the affirmation of the land and its special places. At the same time, Tamil *bhakti* illustrated the importance of a number of elements of post-Vedic orthodox, Sanskritic Hindu religion: the full-blown theism and mythology of the epics and Purāṇas, the spawning of temple-oriented ritual centered by *devapūjā* (worship through the icon), increased emphasis on liberation as the ultimate aim in religion, and others.

The centerpiece of Tamil *bhakti,* nonetheless, remained the personality of the god and his relationship with individual human beings. The god's exploits were recited selectively; his awesome and terror-inspiring character (as with Śiva) or his miracle-working one (as with Viṣṇu), was invoked. Yet at the same time, his grace *(aruḷ),* love *(anpu),* and wooing of devotees was variously portrayed. The devotee, for his part, learned to attain the god's grace. The relationship was variously described as that of lover to a beloved; friend to friend; parent to child. The relationship generally differed in Śaiva and Vaiṣṇava *bhaktas*: For the former, a certain individuality of the devotee was thought to be retained in the devotional relationship with the god—a relationship said to be that between sun and light or flower and fragrance. In Vaiṣṇava *bhakti,* on the other hand, the loss of the devotee's selfhood in relation to the divine was stressed and the surrender of the one to the other celebrated.

Religion in the Medieval Period. From the eighth through the fifteenth century much of Hindu civilization was centered in Tamil India, where a prolific religious literature emerged in both Tamil and Sanskrit. In addition to the devotional literature, a number of ritual treatises were prepared in this region, including many of the Śaivāgamas, those texts used by Śaiva sects, as well as those of the Vaiṣṇava sects, the Pāñcarātrāgamas and Vaikhānasāgamas. Portions of several Purāṇas were authored by anonymous Tamil scholars and regional recensions of others prepared. Not least important of the literary corpus emerging after the twelfth century were the *Tālapurāṇas,* or mythological stories of temple sites throughout Tamil country.

In addition to the literature, Tamil India became the scene for an explosion of temple construction, incorporating an architecture that became characteristically Dravidian. There was also prolific sculpting in stone, and, during the years of the Cōḻa reign, in bronze. These architectural and sculpturing styles, together with the texts in which they were canonized, became the model for much of the architecture in city and temple building to be found in Southeast Asia from Burma to Cambodia. Another important achievement of the "medieval" centuries was the development of Hindu thought and of several philosophical schools. The religious history of this era is perhaps most easily divided into three periods: The Pallava (575–900); Cōḻa (900–1300); and Vijayanagar (1300–1700) periods.

The Pallava period. The Pallava period takes its name from the dynasty founded by Siṃhaviṣṇu and is best understood as a transitional or foundation era. In addition to the founding of *bhakti* sects devoted to Śiva and Viṣṇu, the period is characterized by the start of the South Indian tradition of temple-building in permanent stone. Canons for the building of these structures were developed and included the classical Dravidian forms of the *vimāna* or central tower and the *maṇṭapa* or main hallway. The temple assumed the symbolic character both of a microcosm and of the human form, and became the major focus for ritual events. Temple icons and the deities they represented were ascribed the attributes of kingship, while rituals addressed to the icon increasingly assumed the character of the giving of gifts to a king.

Another important development of this period was the growth of Brahmanic settlements in South India. These rural settlements, which came to be known as *brahmadeyas*, were granted by Tamil landowners as emblems of the alliances that had developed between the two communities. The *brahmadeyas* became major loci of Sanskrit learning and culture and radiated Sanskritic influence into virtually all of Tamil life even while its *brahman* residents were being tamilized.

It is this period also that marks the life and work of Śaṅkara (788–820) and Bhāskaran, his contemporary. The former was especially instrumental in making Advaita (monism) attractive to intellectuals, and in substantially grounding the speculative tradition in the Upaniṣads, thereby strengthening the Brahmanic option in its dispute with Buddhist thought.

The Cōḻa period. The Cōḻa period (900–1300) was characterized by the formalization and systematic Sanskritization of religion. Śaivism received special favor under the aegis of the Cōḻas; hence, there was construction and enlargement of Śaiva temples. These temples were symbols of the official state cult that overwhelmed or incorporated into themselves many of the lesser village cults. (One of the few major "folk" deities to survive and increase in strength in this period was the Goddess, whose cultus and symbols were permitted to flourish and increase in popularity.) The temples were at first characterized by the tall *vimāna* or central tower, but eventually by the building of several ornate *gopuras* or entranceways at each site. The temple, further, became a center for economic exchange, storage of land and goods, and social interaction, as well as a symbol of political liaison between kings, sectarian leaders, and landowners. A considerable literature known as *Talapurāṇas*, purporting to relate to the mythic history of temple sites, began to develop.

Another religious institution emerging to prominence in the Cōḻa period was the *maṭam* (Skt., *maṭha*) or monastic center. The *maṭam* became a center of spiritual learning especially for non-*brahmans,* though it often assumed economic and political power as well. The *brahmadeya* or *brahman* settlement continued to be the locus of much Sanskritic learning, radiating Brahmanic influence throughout the region.

Systematization in textual form continued in both Śaivism and Vaiṣṇavism. This was expressed in the continued formalization of ritual texts—the Śaivāgamas for Śaiva sects and the Pāñcarātrāgamas and Vaikhānasāgamas for Vaiṣṇavism—and in philosophical treatises. Śaiva Siddhānta proved to be the philosophical systematization of the Śaiva religious experience. It was formally expressed in forty terse Tamil verses by the thirteenth-century poet Meykaṇṭār (Meykaṇṭa Tēvar), and was known as the *Śivajñānabodham* (*Civañāṉapōtam*). A verse commentary, known as the *Śivajñānasiddhiyār,* was written by his disciple Aruṇanti Śivācariyar. Śaiva Siddhānta speaks of three realities—the lord (*pati*), the human soul (*pacu;* Skt., *paśu*), and the three bonds of human existence (*pāca;* Skt., *paśa*). In Śaiva Siddhānta the soul was to be freed from the bonds of *karman* (the law of cause and effect), *māyā* (the over-valuing of the phenomenal world), and *āṇava* (self-orientation) in order to become permanently attached to (and hence share the quality of) the lord Śiva.

Vaiṣṇava speculation, meanwhile, reached new heights during this period thanks largely to the work and thought of Yāmuna (918–1038), Rāmānuja (1017–1137), and Madhva (1199–1278). A central concern of these *ācāryas*, or preceptors, was that of affording a philosophical foundation for the devotional experience and hence in describing the relationship between the deity and the devotee, primarily in the form of surrender (*prapatti*). Yāmuna extolled the greatness of the lord and described the abject need of the devotee; Rāmānuja affirmed this theme but went on to argue for the "qualified" nature of supreme existence (*viśiṣṭādvaita*) in contradistinction to Śaṅkara's more radical monism. Madhva, in contrast to the exponents of Śaṅkara's system, argued for the reality and plurality of the world and the difference between the self and *brahman.* For each of these thinkers, *brahman* was perceived in terms of a personal deity.

The twelfth century was the period in which perhaps the greatest Tamil poet lived. Kampaṉ, the "imperial poet," master of style and form, is best known for his transcreation of Vālmīki's *Rāmāyaṇa.* While borrowing extensively from the content and style of the Sanskrit epic, Kampaṉ's version, nonetheless, creatively adapts the finest of Tamil poetics, and locates the story in a distinctively Tamil landscape.

It was during the Cōḻa period that the influence of Hindu (and especially Śaiva) thought, which had started spreading into Southeast Asia under the Pallavas and Guptas, became more pronounced. *Brahmans,* now perceived as skilled and versatile advisers to kings, were to be found in such city-states as Polonnāruva (Sri Lanka), Pagan (Burma), Ayutthayā (Thailand), Angkor Wat and Angkor Thom (Cambodia) and Madjapahit (Java). These *brahmans* and other Hindu immigrants transported notions of divine kingship and cosmology; thus the architecture of capital cities, palaces, temples, and even the biers of dead kings, as well as some of the rituals in the courts of Southeast Asia, came to reflect motifs canonized in Śaivāgama texts of the Cōḻa period.

The Vijayanagar period. With the decline of the Cōḻa line and the rise of the Vijayanagar hegemony, whose capital was in Andhra Pradesh, shifts occurred in the character of religion in Tamil India. While the Vijayanagars, through political alliances, succeeded in keeping the expanding Islamic empire from making major political inroads in the South, there were nonetheless increasing Muslim influences. From the tenth century onward pockets of Muslims settled into small communities along the Tamil and Malabar coasts and radiated influence outward from these centers, and by the fourteenth and fifteenth centuries occasional military expeditions had led to brief periods of Muslim rule in several portions of Tamil country.

Another important political development of the Vijayanagar period, due in part to the increase in military capability, was the rise of local and supralocal rulers known as *nāyakkas*, who sustained pockets of political stability under suzerainty of the Telugu Vijayanagars. These *nāyakka* domains often led to the patronage of local Hindu institutions and the enhancement of local temples and festivals. The rise of the *nāyakka* system in Tamil country also led to change in the role of *brahmans* and temples in the region. The *brahmadeya* declined in power and *brahmans* were no longer given gifts to the degree that had been true in the Cōḻa period. Yet *brahmans,* especially Telugu *brahmans,* became important consultants in military and ritual affairs, and the temples, their deities, and their festivals came increasingly to express the reciprocities, including gift giving and the exchange of honors, that had been a part of the Cōḻa sociopolitical order.

The Cōḻa period was a time for the formalization and institutionalization of religion, especially of Śaivism, into temples and literary texts written primarily in Sanskrit. In the post-Cōḻa period the vernacular once again became the chief medium for religious expression, and thus the more popular forms of Hinduism found expression across the Tamil region. Tamil Hinduism during the Vijayanagar period thus was characterized by resurgent devotionalism and increased participation in temple rituals and festivals by a broader spectrum of people. One might speak of this new era as the "silver age" of Tamil *bhakti.*

The harbinger of this post-Cōḻa trend was Aruṇakirinātar (c. 1475–1550). His poetry was characterized by an ingenious use of meter and sound as an accompaniment to dance; by a skillful combination of Sanskrit and Tamil terms, albeit in a Tamil idiom that celebrated its very Tamilness; by lavish praise of Murukaṉ and that deity's consorts and sacred places; and by a call both to egalitarian issues and to a devotion to God. Aruṇakir likened the religious experience to a profound silence.

By the seventeenth and eighteenth centuries *bhakti* literature had mushroomed. Such poets as Tāyumāṉavar, Kacciyapaciva, and Kumārakurupara celebrated the mythology, sacred places, and devotionalism of Śaivism. Tamil *Tālapurāṇas,* or mythologies of temple sites, proliferated in the fifteen and sixteenth centuries, each purporting to describe the mythical history and grandeur of local temples by localizing and re-enforcing themes that had been part of the Tamil landscape for centuries, especially the sacrality and power of land and waters. The role of the Goddess was an important theme in these temple myths, especially her identity with the land and the necessity to channel her considerable power into the patterns of normative theism.

The late Vijayanagar period saw a resurgence of temple construction. The number of temples almost tripled in the two centuries between 1550 and 1750. While the construction of Śaiva temples was relatively moderate, particularly in eastern portions of the Tamil region, temples to Viṣṇu, the Goddess, and Śiva's sons Murukaṉ and Gaṇeśa proliferated much more rapidly than in earlier centuries, especially in western portions of the region. Further, these temples more frequently became the arena for public events, including marriages and festivals. Festivals such as the Cittarai festival (April–May) in Madurai and the Mahānavamī festival (September–October) in Vijayanagara were described by commentators in the fifteenth and sixteenth centuries as enormous celebrations and paradigmatic events. Such festivals came to express a wide range of social and religious realities; relationships between castes and sectarian groups; the role of the king as presiding presence, warrior *par excellence,* and agent of prosperity; celebration of harvest or significant seasonal transition; and the reenactment of the career of the deity and the extolling of him or her as celestial prototype of the king and cosmic ruler. Extant temples were enlarged, *gopura*s, or entranceways, were donated by numbers of wealthier families, and the temple environs took on the character of a miniature city.

These centuries were also a time when some Sanskrit Purāṇas and epic literature were transcreated into Tamil. In the seventeenth century, for example, the Tamil version of the *Skanda Purāṇa* appeared, giving to the epic deity a flavor that incorporated all his appropriate Tamil heritage.

Another form of *bhakti* literature that proliferated by the sixteenth and seventeenth centuries was a form of poetry known as *piḷḷaitamil,* which worshiped the deity in the form of a child. While the Āḻvār Āṇṭāḷ was apparently the first poet to celebrate in Tamil the childhood of Kṛṣṇa, there is increased use of this form of poetry in both Vaiṣṇava and Śaiva contexts. In this type of *bhakti* the poet often assumes the form of the deity's parent and equates the stages of childhood to rhythms of the cosmos and of the poetic medium.

However, there was also a religious countermovement to be found in Tamil country during much of this period. Primarily between the tenth and fifteenth centuries a cryptic "antiestablishment" form of religion found its expression in the poetry and lifestyle of persons known as *cittar*s (Skt., *siddha*s). Primarily Śaiva, the *cittar*s were nonetheless committed to the notion that Śiva or Civan was not to be worshiped in iconic form but rather as the supreme limitless one who was virtually identifiable with individual life-forms (*jīvanātman*). Theirs was a lifestyle therefore given to *yoga,* bodily disciplines, meditation, and healing practices. Temple cults, iconic worship, caste, and Brahmanism were criticized, and such notions as *karman* and reincarnation deemphasized. Rather, the body was believed to be temple and microcosm, and internal power the noblest of virtues. In their poetry, natural objects became images of the individual's spiritual quest: The dancing snake, for example, could be seen as the individual's personhood or spirit, and the bee came to represent the life force. Pattiṉāttar II (fourteenth-fifteenth centuries) and his disciple Pattirakiriyar, on the other hand, were more pessimistic: Life is tragic, the body filthy, and the beauty of women detestable. The human is a frustrated beggar who longs to be delivered and liberated by God. This is a mood that appears, to varying extents, in the writings of Aruṇakirinātar (fifteenth century), Tayumāṉavar (1706–1744), and Rāmaliṅka Cuvāmikal (nineteenth century).

In summary, the Vijayanagar period was a time when religion subtly reaffirmed Hindu and Tamil identities in the wake of the extensive Sanskritization of the Cōḻa period and in the face of Muslim and Telugu influence throughout the period. Literary and architectural expressions of religion reflected a resurgence of devotionalism and participation. The cultus of the Goddess had become widespread and devotional Vaiṣṇavism and Śaivism were resurgent, most frequently expressing themselves in worship of the deity's childhood, the building of shrines, and the incorporation of aspects of popular religion. In the meanwhile the tradition had also produced a self-critical movement, focusing on the body as medium of worship and raising questions about the public cultus.

PRE-MODERN PERIOD. By the seventeenth century European influence had begun to leave its impact on Tamil culture and religion. As early as the fourth century Christians had inhabited areas along the southwest coast. Pockets of Jewish merchants settled in such western cities as Cochin where, by the eleventh century, they had negotiated extensive privileges and rights with local rulers. While these groups remained economically active in the area now known as Kerala, they tended to be socially insular and their impact on Tamil-speaking peoples was marginal. By the late sixteenth century, however, Christian missionaries had begun to influence Tamil letters and lifestyle more actively: Enrique Enriquez, a Portuguese Jesuit who was in southwestern India from 1546 to 1600, sought to prepare catechisms and grammars in Tamil in such a way as to make a permanent impact on the development of Christian Tamil theological vocabulary and to create a Catholic fishing community. Roberto de Nobili, a Jesuit who spent much of his life in Madurai after arriving in Goa in 1605, sought to present Christian scriptures and thought as extensions and fulfillments of Tamil Brahmanism. Constantine Beschi, a Jesuit who was in Madurai from 1710 to 1747, made original contributions to Tamil literature.

The first of the Protestant missionaries was Bartholomaus Ziegenbalg, who arrived in Tranquebar in 1706. He wrote relatively sympathetic manuscripts on the religious life of South India and continued the process of translating the Bible and Christian ideas into Tamil. Christian Schwartz, who arrived in 1750, served an important role as mediator between local rulers and British officials. Others, such as Johann Fabricius, who died in 1791, and the nineteenth century's Bishop Caldwell, were instrumental in developing a dictionary and comparative Dravidian grammar respectively, implements that increased the exchange of ideas between the English and Tamil worlds. In the nineteenth century G. U. Pope's translation of Māṇikkavācakar and Henry Whitehead's description of Tamil village religion helped make elements of the Tamil religious landscape better known to Tamils as well as to the English-speaking world, even though the work of neither was free of the Western/Christian bias of the authors. This sort of interpretive work continued into the twentieth century with the scholarship of C. G. Diehl and others.

An indigenous Tamil Christianity emerged during these centuries that included not only the conversion of large groups of people from the lower strata of the social order in specific villages or districts, but also the development of such articulate Tamil spokesmen for the "new" religion as H. A. Krisna Pillai, Vedanayagar Sastriar, and A. J. Appasamy. Christian hospitals, schools, colleges, orphanages, and presses dotted the Tamil landscape and influenced the shape of Tamil Hindu responses.

Quite apart from the attempts at Christianization that accompanied the European presence were other forms of westernization that influenced the shape of religion in Tamil country. On the one hand, there were those Westerners who romanticized the Hindu tradition. Most notable of these was Annie Besant (1847–1933; active in India between 1894 and 1920), who established the international headquarters of the Theosophical Society in Madras and became both an active defender of Hindu values and a crusader for reform. On the other hand, there were tendencies to criticize or undermine traditional patterns of life and religion in the area. These included a range of activities from the relatively virulent "preaching missions" sponsored by missionaries to the more subtle acts of discrimination and exploitation associated with colonialism.

Still another dimension of religion evident in the premodern period that had an impact on current religious life was the continuing practice of indigenous village and folk forms of worship. Encouraged by the relative eclecticism of the Vijayanagar period, folk forms of religion became increasingly apparent and influential on the more literate forms of religion. Local deities designed to protect village and field and representing the social stratification of their worshipers have been an important part of the Tamil religious landscape even into the present century. These include such deities as Aiyanār, who has been a protector deity of Tamil villages since at least the eighth century; Karappacāmi, the black "servant" god, and various regional *viraṉs* (hero-warriors). Such deities as these are sometimes ascribed exploits of resistance to British forces in local mythology. Local goddesses such as Mariammaṉ are considered personifications of the world's natural forces and hence are propitiated lest pestilence or national catastrophe befall. During the mid-twentieth century many such deities have become linked to the "great tradition" of Hinduism, particularly as those strata of society for whom these deities were paradigmatic have been integrated with the larger social order.

THE PRESENT. The Tamil religious response to the impact of the West has been expressed in a great variety of ways. Some of these have been characteristic of neo-Hinduism throughout India. There has been some adaptation of strategies (e.g., the use of preaching missions and the development of benevolent institutions) and of ideas from British and Christian sources. There has been the syncretistic combination of ideas drawn selectively both from within the tradition and from Christian or Western sources; most commonly, these "mosaics of religion" have been created by individuals and by certain *gurus* and their groups. Sarvepalli Radhakrishnan (1888–1975) may be the best known of those southern thinkers of the twentieth century who have reaffirmed elements of the Hindu tradition in ways that interweave Western ideas.

However, the last century and a half has been characterized by a rebirth of Tamil self-consciousness. The discovery, translation, and interpretation of Tamil languages and literature by Westerners has encouraged a resurgence of regional and ethnic pride among Tamils. Classical Tamil texts have been recovered and republished. Tamil devotional literature has been memorized and is invoked as the standard of ideal religion, albeit interpreted and used selectively. Shrines have been renovated and their mythical antiquity extolled. Often, regional traditions and myths assume precedence over national ones. Thus even though brahmanization continues to occur as folk and village culti are Hinduized, and although various Anglicizations have been accepted as normative, the Tamil and non-*brahman* roots of religious practice are perpetuated and practiced with fervor. As Tamils, especially non*brahmans,* have migrated abroad in search of economic opportunities, they have taken with them to Malaysia, Sri Lanka, East Africa, Madagascar, and North America self-perceptions and religious lifestyles.

The character of much of this Tamil religion in the modern era is aptly described as neo-*bhakti.* Participation in festivals and pilgrimages at temple sites has increased geometrically. Renovation of some temples deemed significant began in the latter part of the nineteenth century; they began to welcome all spectra of society in the 1920s, and they have become more accessible by transportation systems since the 1930s. Deities such as Murukaṉ have attained enormous popularity throughout the region for a variety of reasons, among which are his appeal to all spectra of society; his presumed Tamil antiquity and identity; and his amalgamation of much of the religious symbolism that has been part of Tamil cultural history. In more recent decades, local goddesses such as Mariammaṉ have been increasingly brahmanized and made part of the great Hindu tradition even while retaining ties to local sites and folk culture. Aiyyappan, whose prototypical shrine is in Kerala, has nonetheless attracted increasing numbers of Tamil worshipers who see in him Tamil roots, genuine power, and an invitation to a sense of community that transcends caste. Various forms of ancient ritual continue to be practiced in the homes of the orthodox even while accommodations are made to the exigencies of commerce and contemporary life. At the same time, public pressures to "streamline" and "democratize" religion have led to the de-brahmanization of ritual in some temples and the privatization of some religious practices. Yet in many respects, religion is as much a part of the contemporary Tamil consciousness as it has ever been.

SEE ALSO Āḻvārs; Besant, Annie; Bhakti; Buddhism, article on Buddhism in India; Gaṇeśa; Goddess Worship, article on The Hindu Goddess; Hindu Tantric Literature; Indian Religions, articles on History of Study and Rural Traditions; Indus Valley Religion; Jainism; Kingship; Kṛṣṇaism; Madhva; Māṇikkavācakar; Meykaṇṭār; Murukaṉ; Radhakrishnan, Sarvepalli; Rāmānuja; Rāmāyaṇa; Śaivism, articles on Nāyaṉārs and Śaiva Siddhānta; Śaṅkara; Sinhala Religion; Southeast Asian Religions, article on Mainland Cultures; Temple, article on Hindu Temples; Vaikhānasas; Vaiṣṇavism, article on Pāñcarātras; Yāmuna.

BIBLIOGRAPHY

Carman, John B. *The Theology of Rāmānuja.* New Haven, Conn., 1974. The most thorough single study of the eleventh-century Hindu theologian, couched in discussion of the implications of studying a religious system from outside a tradition.

Clothey, Fred W. *The Many Faces of Murukaṉ: The History and Meaning of a South Indian God.* The Hague, 1978. A phenomenological analysis of how a god reflects the cultural history of the Tamil people.

Nilakanta Sastri, K. A. *Development of Religion in South India.* Bombay, 1963. Though dated and focusing on Sanskritic and Brahmanic expressions of religion, this book remains the only attempt at a comprehensive history of religion in South India.

O'Flaherty, Wendy Doniger. *Śiva: The Erotic Ascetic.* Oxford, 1981. While this book makes no reference to Tamil religion, it is a structural analysis of much of the mythology of Śiva gleaned from puranic texts focusing on themes of eroticism and asceticism.

Reiniche, Marie-Louise. *Les dieux et les hommes: Étude des cultes d'un village du Tirunelveli, Inde du Sud.* Paris, 1979. An important study of cultic life in a Tamil village and how deities reflect social and cultural realities therein.

Shulman, David. *Tamil Temple Myths.* Princeton, N.J., 1980. A bold, comprehensive examination of Tamil *Talapurāṇas* (myths about a temple's origin), centering on the interconnecting motifs of goddess, land, power, and sacrifice.

Singer, Milton. *When A Great Tradition Modernizes.* New York, 1972. A sociologist's reflection, based primarily upon Tamil India, on the impact that the processes of modernization have on religion.

Smith, H. Daniel. *A Descriptive Bibliography of the Printed Texts of the Pāñcarātrāgama.* 2 vols. Baroda, 1975–1980. An annotated description of some of the most important ritual texts of the Pāñcarātrāgama school of Śrī Vaiṣṇavism.

Stein, Burton. *Peasant State and Society in Medieval South India.* Oxford, 1980. The definitive and comprehensive description of "medieval" South Indian history, including an analysis of the role of religious institutions throughout the period.

Stein, Burton, ed. *South Indian Temples.* New Delhi, 1978. Essays on the sociological, political, and economic role of temples in medieval Tamil country.

Tiliander, Bror. *Christian and Hindu Terminology.* Uppsala, 1974. A description of how, by choice of Tamil and Sanskrit words in the translation process, early missionaries created a Tamil Christian vocabulary.

Welbon, Guy, and Glenn E. Yocum, eds. *Religious Festivals in South India and Sri Lanka.* New Delhi, 1982. A wide-ranging and useful series of essays incorporating philological and anthropological studies in the festival experience of South Indians, primarily of Tamil-speaking peoples.

Whitehead, Henry. *The Village Gods of South India.* 2d ed., rev. & enl. Delhi, 1976. Though written by a missionary and first published early in this century, this book has remained a "classic" description of village religion in nineteenth-century Tamil India.

Yocum, Glenn E. *Hymns to the Dancing Śiva.* New Delhi and Columbia, Mo., 1982. A comprehensive study of the most important of the Tamil Śaiva poets, the ninth-century Māṇikkavācakar.

Zvelebil, Kamil V. *The Smile of Murukan: On Tamil Literature of South India.* Leiden, 1973. The most comprehensive survey to date of Tamil literature, including chapters on many who had a religious impact: *bhakti* poets, the *cittar*s, Kampan, and Arunakiri.

FRED W. CLOTHEY (1987)

TAMMUZ SEE DUMUZI

TANGAROA

TANGAROA is the most important of the "departmental" gods of Polynesia. In his many cognates, he was worshiped by most Polynesians as the chief god and creator of the world. His popularity, however, depended chiefly on his role as ruler over the ocean. Tangaroa stands as the origin and personification of all fish; his offspring are the creatures of the sea. Tangaroa was often appealed to by seafarers and fisherman, and, under the title Tangaroa-whakamautai, he was recognized by the Maori of New Zealand as the controller of the tides.

MYTHOLOGICAL CONTEXT. The souls of the Polynesian ancestors live on in the spirit land of Hawaiki, which is the symbolic place of origin of the Polynesian people. Ancestor deification was probably the original form of Polynesian religion. While some of the gods' names were common throughout the Pacific islands, most Polynesian gods were strictly local deities. The Polynesian deities have been classified into four groups: supreme, "departmental," tribal, and family. The departmental gods were classified according to the aspect of nature they ruled. The major departmental gods—Tane, Rongo, Tu, and Tangaroa—were often portrayed in eastern Polynesian mythology as the sons of Rangi ("sky") and Papa ("earth"). Areas of authority were distributed among the four departmental gods, who, together with the tribal ancestors, constituted the pantheon of the earliest Polynesian mythology and who were shared by many island groups.

The parentage of these deities was often traced to ancestors: like the gods of Greek mythology, the Polynesian departmental deities had once been living persons with human desires and passions. The process of creating gods continued in Polynesia until the advent of Christianity in the Pacific islands during the early nineteenth century. In general, the study of Polynesian myths and religious beliefs has been dependent upon source materials from early missionaries, who were not free from prejudice. The religion and mythology of the Maori of New Zealand, however, were systematically studied and therefore constitute an important exception.

TANGAROA'S ROLE. In New Zealand, Tangaroa appears to have been venerated under several names, such as Tangaroa-nui, Tangaroa-ra-vao, Tangaroa-mai-tu-rangi, Tangaroa-a-mua, Tangaroa-a-timu, and Tangaroa-a-roto. On other Polynesian islands, Tangaroa was known as Ta'aroa, Tangaloa, Tanaroa, and Kanaloa. Tangaroa's role varied because major gods were often fused with local or family deities. Tangaroa did, however, continue to exist as an independent major god in most of the Polynesian myths, and a distinct Tangaroa cult developed in parallel to other common worship practices. This cult apparently flourished on the islands where there was an affinity between gods and eponymous ancestors. On some islands, there remains only scant information about Tangaroa, but his former importance is proven by his appearance in many *fagu* (sacred) chants:

> O Tangaroa in the immensity of space
> Clear away the clouds by day
> Clear away the clouds by night
> That Ru may see the stars of heaven
> To guide him in the land of his desire (Buck, 1938)

Tangaroa was portrayed as the supreme being in western and central Polynesia, but he was worshiped as the god of the sea. In the Samoan Islands, Tangaroa was essentially a creator—the being who formed the islands or who raised them up from the depths of the sea. In Tongan mythology, Tangaroa appeared as the sky god. Tui Tonga, the founder of the Tongan royal family, was respected as having descended from Tangaroa. He was therefore held to be sacred and to possess great powers that were attributed to semidivine chiefs. Though Tangaroa was also referred to as the supreme being and first cause in Samoa, the Society Islands, and Hawai'i, the complex was almost absent from the belief system of the Polynesian marginal islands according to E. S. Craighill Handy (1927).

In the Cook Islands, Tangaroa and Rongo are said to have been the twin children of the primal parents Papa and Atea ("heaven"). Tangaroa is said to have taken a wife, Hina, in the Cook Islands—a conjunction that was held throughout Polynesia. On Easter Island, the Ariki Mau ("great chief") was the possessor of *mana* ("power") that was transmitted down the genealogical line from the ancestral gods Tangaroa and Rongo. On Samoa, Rongo is said to be the offspring of Tangaroa and Hina. Thus the roles of the gods, as well as their names, frequently vary from region to region.

There is a striking contrast to the above in the interpretation given Tangaroa in the Marquesas Islands, where Tangaroa was elevated into a divinity who battled Atea for supremacy. A creation myth of the Marquesas, however, contains many references to Tangaroa as merely a god of the sea and winds. It is plausible that the status of Tangaroa declined under the growing influence of Christian missionaries on the islands. In Hawaii, where he is called Kaneloa, Tangaroa was less important than the other departmental gods. This lack of status may have been due to the fact that the people of Hawaii later arranged their pantheon to conform with the Christian triadic pattern, using Kane (Tane), Ku (Tu), and Lono (Rongo) to form a trinity.

EFFECTS OF CHRISTIANIZATION. As might be expected, the advent of the Europeans led to radical changes in Polynesian religions. In the Austral, Society, Tuamotu, and Gambier islands, the people still know Tangaroa as the god of the sea. Polynesian contact with Europeans, however, and the eventual conversion of many islanders to Christianity destroyed the old gods' religious authority. Why, then, is Tangaroa the sole "survivor" among the many Polynesian gods? The answer is tied to the fact that for the Polynesians, descendants of great seafarers, the ocean is vitally important. The music-loving Polynesians continue to sing their old chants even though they no longer fully understand the role that the texts had played in their religious traditions. The old *fagu* chants, still known in the extreme eastern end of the Tuamotu Islands, offer a sketch of the creation myths and of some of the religious concepts that existed before the advent of Christianity. These chants contain not only the name of Tangaroa but also the names of other gods; even ancestral gods often appear in parodies. But, in general, the gradual disintegration of traditional island society has coincided with the death of the Polynesian gods.

Radical change was enhanced by the modernization of island societies after World War II. In the 1960s, Tangaroa was mentioned in only one of the parody chants that was used on the occasion of welcoming visitors to the eastern Tuamotus:

> We descend from Tangaroa Manini, we are ready for you
> We love you Manini, with blessings
> Has come to our land. (Hatanaka, 1976)

It may be that one day even the name of Tangaroa will no longer be known to the Polynesian people; then all of the gods will have returned to the land of Hawaiki.

BIBLIOGRAPHY

Buck, Peter H. *Vikings of the Sunrise.* New York, 1938.

Handy, E. S. Craighill. *Polynesian Religion.* Honolulu, 1927.

Handy, E. S. Craighill. *History and Culture in the Society Islands.* Honolulu, 1930.

Hatanaka, Sachiko. *A Study of the Polynesian Migration to the Eastern Tuamotus: Preliminary Report.* Kanazawa, Japan, 1976.

SACHIKO HATANAKA (1987)

TĀNGRI SEE TENGRI

TANG YONGTONG (1893–1964) was an eminent scholar of the history of Chinese Buddhism. A native of Huangmei County in Hubei Province, China, Tang studied in Beijing and graduated from Quinghua University in 1917. In order to pursue his studies he went to the United States in the following year, where he specialized in philosophy, Sanskrit, and Pali at Harvard University. Tang received his master's degree in 1922 and returned to China, where he began a teaching career that spanned four decades.

By the 1940s, Tang was already well established in the philosophy department of Beijing University, becoming its chairman and eventually being named dean of the College of Humanities. In addition to his research on Buddhism and Indian philosophy, Tang was an expert on the school of thought known as *xuanxue* ("dark learning"), which flourished during the Wei and Jin dynasties (third and fourth centuries CE). He also lectured on such Western philosophical traditions as rationalism and empiricism, having studied European philosophy during his years abroad. In 1947 Tang was named an academician of the Central Research Institute, and thereafter returned to the United States to give a series of lectures at the University of California.

Firmly rejecting suggestions that he go to Taiwan following the establishment of the People's Republic in 1949, Tang actively took part in academic affairs in the newly established People's Republic. He was appointed chairman of the Council for Academic Affairs and vice-president of Beijing University, and was elected a member of the Academic Society of the Chinese Academy of Sciences. In addition, Tang was a member of the Standing Committee of the first, second, and third National People's Congresses.

Consonant with both Marxist theory and contemporary scholarship in the social scientific study of religion, Tang focused more on the historical and social impact of Buddhist thought than on its religious influence. His principal works include *Hanwei liang Jin Nanbeichao fojiao shi* (A history of Buddhism from the Han and Wei Dynasties to the Northern and Southern Dynasties), *Suitang fojiao shigao* (A history of Buddhism in the Sui and Tang Dynasties), and *Yindu zhexue shilue* (A concise history of Indian philosophy). Through his academic work and official posts Tang influenced an entire generation of Chinese students of Buddhism.

BIBLIOGRAPHY

Cihai: Zhexue fence. Shanghai, 1980.

Tang Yongtong. *Tang Yongtong quan ji.* 7 vols. Shi Jia Zhuang, China, 2000.

Tang Yongtong xueshu wenjhi. Beijing, 1983. Selected works of Tang Yongtong with full bibliography and biographical sketch.

REN JIYU (1987 AND 2005)

TANLUAN (traditional dates 476–542, but more probably c. 488–554) was the author of the first known systematic work to be produced in China on Pure Land (Chin., Jingtu) Buddhism, that branch of the Buddhist tradition that emphasizes faith in the Buddha Amitābha (Buddha of Limitless Light; Chin., Emituofo; Jpn., Amida) and rebirth in Sukhāvatī ("land of bliss"), Amitābha's paradisiacal realm in the western quarter of the universe, as a means of attaining enlightenment. Tanluan's writings were a major textual source for the Japanese monk Shinran (1173–1262), the founder of the Jōdo Shinshū, which therefore regards Tanluan as one of its major patriarchal figures.

According to his biography in the *Xu gaoseng zhuan* (Further Biographies of Eminent Monks), Tanluan was born in the north, near Wutai Shan in Shansi Province, and studied Buddhism in his youth. Following a serious illness, however, he took up the pursuit of techniques of immortality recommended in various Daoist texts. His quest eventually led him to a supposed encounter with Tao Hongjing (456–536), the eminent Six Dynasties alchemist and master of the Maoshan Daoist tradition, who allegedly transmitted to him ten fascicles of "scriptures of the immortals" (*xian cjng*). On his way north again Tanluan stopped in Luoyang, where the Indian monk and translator Bodhiruci is said to have introduced him to the *Guan wuliangshou jing* (Scripture on the Visualization of the Buddha Amitābha). Bodhiruci remarked to him at the time that Amitābha (known also by his alternate Sanskrit name, Amitāyus, Buddha of Limitless Life) was the "greatest immortal" (*da xian*), given his ability to lead beings out of the realm of rebirth altogether. This historically questionable episode is nonetheless suggestive of the close link that must have been popularly perceived between the soteriological goals of Daoism and some of the Buddhist traditions, a link that may have contributed to the rapid growth in popularity of the Amitābha cult in Tanluan's time. In the aftermath of this encounter Tanluan devoted himself to the study of the Pure Land scriptures, eventually gathering around himself a group of devotees to Amitābha.

Many Daoist and Buddhist works are attributed to Tanluan, but only two, both of which are Buddhist, are unquestionably authentic. The first, a systematic treatise, is generally known by the abbreviated title *Wangsheng lun zhu* (Notes on the Treatise on Birth [in the Pure Land]; T. D. no. 1819). The second, the *Zan Emitofoji* (Canticles on Amitābha; T. D. no. 1978), is an apparently liturgical work. The *Lun zhu* is Tanluan's commentary (*zhu*) to the so-called *Sukhāvatīvyūhopadeśa** (*Wuliangshou jing yupotishe yuansheng ji*), a collection of Buddhist-style hymns (Skt., *gāthā*), with autocommentary, attributed uncertainly to Vasubandhu. Tanluan's commentary proceeds carefully *au pied de la lettre,* with only a few insertions external to the format of "Vasubandhu's" text. His general intent is to show how one may achieve liberation by availing oneself of the pure *karman* of Amitābha, which is freely dispensed to all who seek it in accordance with a series of resolves (*pranidhana*) taken by this Buddha while still the *bodhisattva* Dharmākara.

Drawing on the *Larger Sukhāvatīvyūha Sūtra,* the *Smaller Sukhāvatīvyūha Sūtra,* and the *Guan wuliangshou jing,* Tanluan shows how the power of Amitābha is effective for all beings who call upon him in faith, even for laypersons who cannot meditate or for those sunk in immorality. Faith in, and worship of, Amitābha is accomplished through what Tanluan (imparting his own classification to "Vasubandhu's" discussion) termed the "five gates of recollection" (*wu nianmen*): bodily worship (i. e., bowing, etc.); vocal praise (especially, but not exclusively the invocation of his name, i. e., *nianfo* practice); wholehearted resolve to be reborn in the Pure Land; visualization (*guan*) of the delights of the Pure Land; and "turning toward" (*huixiang*), a purposely ambiguous term that means both turning toward beings while the practitioner is still in *samsara,* so as to give them the religious merit gained through one's own practice and, having been born in the Pure Land, turning back toward beings by being reborn in *samsara* in order to liberate others.

Tanluan's demonstration of these simple practices is sophisticated and profound, being based heavily upon the *Mahāprajñāpāramitā Śāstra* (a commentary on the *Perfection of Wisdom Scripture* attributed to Nāgārjuna), but it is not necessary to understand the demonstration in order to use the practice. The *upāya* (skill in means) involved is that of the passionate longing for heavenly delights. The Pure Land is depicted *as if* it were a heaven of sensual delight (i. e., a *devaloka,* or realm of a deity), but in fact it is outside of the phenomenal world of *saṃsāra.* It is not a phantasm, however: "It exists extra-phenomenally," says Tanluan, and is by its inner nature pure in every respect, even in respect of discursive thought. Thus, when one dies and, through Amitābha's power, is reborn in the Pure Land and sees Amitābha there as its lord, one is actually "not born." One's desires take on the Pure Land's nature of desirelessness as the water of rivers takes on the saltiness of the sea when it runs into it. One's passionate longing for delight is extinguished "like ice mixed with fire: The fire [of the passions] goes out, and the ice [of the Pure Land's delights] disappears." Thus, one has effectively achieved *nirvāṇa* and one functions like a *bodhisattva* of the upper levels (i. e., a *bodhisattva* who has achieved the state of nonretrogression), ever remaining fixed in the *dharmakāya* (unmanifest Buddha nature) yet constantly manifesting bodies in all the worlds where Buddhist teachers are needed, "like the sun that remains in the sky yet is reflected in hundreds of rivers and pools."

Tanluan was virtually ignored in China, but his influence in Japan has been considerable since Shinran's time. Shinran used the *Lun zhu* as the major source of his *Kyōgyōshinshō,* a collection of proof texts on Pure Land Buddhism, and composed his own *San Amidabu-tsuge,* which was closely based on Tanluan's *Zan Emitofo ji.* Shinran built his even simpler practice of gratefully rejoicing in *already having been* liberated by the power of Amitābha on the intellectual foundation provided by Tanluan.

See Also Amitābha; Jingtu; Nianfo; Shinran; Tao Hongjing.

Bibliography

For an excellent introduction to Tanluan's thought and its influence on the Pure Land tradition in China, see Mochizuki Shinkō's *Chūgoku jōdo kyōrishi* (Kyoto, 1964). Fukuhara Ryōgon's *Ōjō ronchū no kenkyū* (Kyoto, 1978) and Mikogami Eryū's *Ōjō ronchū kaisetsu* (Kyoto, 1969) contain valuable analyses of the *Wangsheng lun zhu,* as does my own "Tanluan's Commentary on the Pure Land Discourse: An Annotated Translation and Soteriological Analysis of the *Wangshenglun Zhu*" (Ph. D diss., University of Wisconsin, 1973). For a discussion of the influence of Tanluan's thought on Japanese Pure Land Buddhism, see Bandō Shōjun's "Shinran's Indebtedness to Tanluan," *The Eastern Buddhist* n. s. 4 (May 1971): 72–87, and, more fully, my "Shinran's Proofs of True Buddhism: Hermeneutics and Doctrinal Development in the *Kyōgyōshinshō's* use of Tanluan's *Lunzhu,*" in *Buddhist Hermeneutics,* edited by Donald S. Lopez, Jr. (Honolulu, forthcoming).

ROGER J. CORLESS (1987)

T'AN-LUAN SEE TANLUAN

TANNAIM.

The term *tanna* is used to refer to an authority of the Mishnah and its related works, in contradistinction to *amora,* referring to a sage of the *gemara'*. The word derives from the Aramaic *teni* ("to repeat") and by extension means "to learn" or "to teach."

The tannaim were the sages of rabbinic tradition who lived immediately before, and then during the century and a half following, the destruction of the Temple in Jerusalem (70 CE). This period is traditionally divided into five or six generations. The most prominent authorities of the period included Hillel, Gamli'el the Elder, Yoḥanan ben Zakk'ai, Gamli'el of Yavneh, Eli'ezer ben Hyrcanus, 'Aqiva' ben Yosef, Me'ir, and Yehuda ha-Nasi'. The period ends with the generation of Yehuda ha-Nasi', the editor of the Mishnah (c. 200 CE), although the following generation in Palestine is one of transition. The division in Babylonia is clearer, though the amora Rav is occasionally spoken of as having tannaitic authority.

The texts that record the traditions of these sages are termed *tannaitic,* and they include the Mishnah, the Tosefta, the halakhic *midrashim,* and a broad variety of traditions preserved in the Jerusalem and Babylonian Talmuds. Traditions that are ascribed tannaitic authority are introduced, almost without exception in the Babylonian Talmud but with frequent exception in the Jerusalem Talmud, with a set of technical vocabulary that employs the root *tny.* Such traditions are termed *baraitot* (sg., *baraita'),* meaning "traditions outside, or excluded from, the Mishnah" (from Aramaic *bar,* "outside").

The tannaitic texts, particularly the Mishnah but to a significant extent the *baraitot* as well, form the basis of later rabbinic legal deliberations. These texts were tested, interpreted, and sometimes emended by the amoraim, and they were in a very real sense accorded the authority of canon. The tannaim often became great legendary figures who were thought to have experienced, and sometimes even instigated, miracles.

The term *tanna'* is secondarily used to refer to the professional repeater or reciter of the rabbinic schools who functioned during both the tannaitic and amoraic periods, even into the centuries that followed (the amoraic period ended c. 500 CE). The *tanna'* may also have been referred to as *roveh* ("repeater"), later confused with *rabbah* ("the great").

The official traditions of the rabbinic schools were oral. The functionaries who memorized the official texts were the *tanna'im,* who were in all respects living books. The process of committing the official text to memory most likely occurred in the following way. First, the master would decide upon the version of the tradition to be taught. He would then call upon his *tanna',* who would be asked to recite the tradition a great many times until its memorization was secure. At that time other *tanna'im* might be called in, for whom the first *tanna'* would then recite the tradition. He would test their memorization, and in this way the version of the text would be secured in the mouths of increasing numbers of *tanna'im.*

Such a method constituted genuine publication. There are several accounts in Talmudic literature in which the *tanna'* is consulted to clarify the official version of a tradition. When the *tanna'* testified to the reading of a text, his testimony was deemed authoritative. Even the Mishnah's editor, Yehuda ha-Nasi', is reported to have consulted his *tanna'* for a proper reading, and this particular *tanna'* is spoken of as having a "tested" or "revised" version of the Mishnah.

Because the *tanna'* was depended upon to provide published traditions, without commentary and without emendation, the *tanna'im* were apparently chosen for their phenomenal memories, not their intelligence. An overly intelligent *tanna';* might have been tempted to emend a text if he thought it to be problematic. One sage speaks of a *tanna'* as "a basket filled with books" (B.T., *Meg.* 28b), that is, filled with information but not able to do much with it. A popular saying declares that "the *tanna'* recites and doesn't know what he is saying" (B.T., *Soṭ.* 22a). Still, some of the greatest sages also acted as *tanna'im.* In addition, the potential fallibility of oral publication was widely recognized, and it is probably for this reason that *Avot* 3.7 warns strongly against any interruption during one's repetition exercises.

The traditions of certain schools were thought to be especially reliable. This was true of the schools of Hiyya' and Oshaya', Palestinian sages of the transitional generation following the compilation of the Mishnah. The former of these teachers is also spoken of as being a repeater for Yehuda ha-Nasi'.

SEE ALSO Beit Hillel and Beit Shammai; Eli'ezer ben Hyrcanus; Gamli'el of Yavneh; Gamli'el the Elder; Me'ir; Mishnah and Tosefta; Yehuda ha-Nasi'; Yoḥanan ben Zakk'ai.

BIBLIOGRAPHY

Jacob N. Epstein provides a comprehensive review of the terminologies that identify tannaitic sources; see *Mavo' le-nusaḥ ha-Mishnah,* 2 vols. (1948; reprint, Jerusalem, 1964), pp. 813ff. The authoritative review of the tannaitic process is Saul Lieberman's "The Publication of the Mishnah," in his *Hellenism in Jewish Palestine* (1950; reprint, New York, 1962), pp. 83–99. Lieberman was the first to frame the process in terms of publication. Also extremely useful, despite its flaws, is Birger Gerhardsson's *Memory and Manuscript,* translated by Eric J. Sharpe (Uppsala, 1961), pp. 93–112.

New Sources

Berger, Michael S. *Rabbinic Authority.* New York, 1998.

Kalmin, Richard Lee. *The Sage in Jewish Society in Late Antiquity.* New York, 1999.

Melamed, Ezra Zion, ed. *Midreshe halakhah shel ha-Tanaim be-Talmud Yerushalmi.* Jerusalem, 2000.

DAVID KRAEMER (1987)
Revised Bibliography

TANTRISM

This entry consists of the following articles:

TANTRISM: AN OVERVIEW

The term *tantrism* is a nineteenth-century western invention, coined to refer to what were considered to be a body of heterodox religious teachings, first discovered by European scholars in Indian works called *Tantras.* Although there is no term in any Asian language for tantrism, it continues to be applied by scholars to a bewilderingly diverse array of esoteric precepts and practices attested across much of South, Inner, and East Asia from the sixth century CE down to the present day.

The most salient phenomena common to all tantrisms are the use of *maṇḍalas, mantras,* and ritual practices in order to map, organize, and control a universe of powerful beings, impulses, or forces in pandemonium. Here, it is important to note that the specifically tantric use of *maṇḍalas, mantras,* and initiations first emerged in India as a religious response to or reflection of a situation of anomie. With the fall of the imperial Guptas in about 550 CE, much of the Indian subcontinent was plunged into a centuries-long period of feudalism, in which multiple, shifting political "centers" were in constant flux, passing under the control of a series of often low-caste rulers whose claim to dominion over a territory was, from the standpoint of orthodox religious polity, illegitimate. In order to legitimate their power, these newly arisen rulers called on a variety of religious specialists to ritually consecrate them with tantric *mantras,* transforming them into divine kings, and their conquered territories into equally consecrated *maṇḍalas* of royal power. Ronald M. Davidson has encapsulated this feudal dynamic:

> In the medieval military culture, the apotheosis of the king served his strategy of divine right to the assumption of power, irrespective of his actual lineage. However, the process of divine royalty conversely implied the royalty of divinity, so the apotheosis of rulers entailed the feudalization of the gods. . . . [T]he great and local deities of the period . . . occupied positions in metaphysical space analogous to the positions controlled by their devotees in terrestrial space, with all the attendant rights and responsibilities. At the same time, lesser divinities became understood as representatives of the imperial divinity, who protected them in a complex exchange of divine services, just as the vassals owed allegiance and loyalty to the monarch through the exchanges of goods, services, land, and booty. (*Indian Esoteric Buddhism,* 2002, pp. 71–72.)

When one bears in mind the Indian feudal context within which tantrism emerged out of preexisting Hindu, Buddhist, and Jain religious systems, a number of specifically tantric terms and practices become comprehensible. These include the use of *mantras* (secret spells) as "weapons" (*śastras*), "missiles" (*astras*), and "armor" (*kavaca*); ritual practices of "binding the directions" (*dig-bandhana*) as a means to securing a consecrated space from invasion by demonic forces; the construction of tantric *maṇḍalas* on the model of fortified palace-citadels; multiple associations of tantric goddesses with warfare; the bearing of royal weapons or scepters (*vajras*) by tantric initiates; the tantric "acts" (*karmas*) of pacification, subjugation, immobilization, enmity, eradication, and liquidation; and the narrative use of the language of conquest (both military and sexual) in tantric discourse in general. Here, the original tantric practitioner par excellence was not the traditional religious specialist—a Brāhmaṇ priest or a Buddhist or Jain monk—but rather the king, as exemplary member of the laity. Much of the early history of tantrism is intertwined with the emergence of a new type of lay religious specialist, "shamanic" ascetic practitioners who identified themselves, through their supernatural powers, with royal gods and divine kings. To these latter, they offered a variety of services and products, including spells and potions for the control of women, the attainment of wealth, and the annihilation of enemies; spirit possession; magical healing and manipulation of the dead, demons, and other entities; future-telling; and so on. In Hindu and Buddhist circles, these tantric supermen were called "Perfected Beings" (*Siddhas, Mahāsiddhas*) and "Virile Heroes" (*Vīras*); among Śvetāmbara Jains, the "Teachers" (*Sūris*) of the Kharatara Gaccha sub-sect have played an analogous role.

GEOGRAPHICAL SPREAD OF TANTRISM. The origins of tantrism are Indian. All authentic tantric lineages—of deities, scriptures, oral teachings, and teachers—claim to extend back to Indian scriptures. The founders of every major tantric tradition, school, or sect either trace their guru-disciple lineages back to an Indian source, or are considered to be incarnations of bodhisattvas whose cults first arose in India. The exploded pantheons of tantrism—principal multi-headed and multi-armed deities proliferating into *maṇḍalas* of families or clans—are generally Indian, or at least traceable to Indian prototypes. The great bulk of tantric legends concerns Indian Siddhas and Mahāsiddhas. The hieratic language of tantrism generally remains the Sanskrit of medieval India, so that for any lineage-based tantric body of practice to be considered legitimate in Chinese, Japanese, Korean, or Tibetan tantric traditions, its translated root text has had to be traceable back to a Sanskrit original. In these translated sources, *mantras*—whose efficacy resides in their sound shape—will not be translated, but rather frozen (at least in theory) in the original Sanskrit. Furthermore, Sanskrit characters form the basis of the hieratic *siddham* script employed in Chinese and Japanese tantric *maṇḍalas* and texts. The yogic practice that is so central to tantrism is also of Indian origin (albeit influenced by Daoist techniques).

Tantrism has persisted and quite often thrived across much of Asia since its Indian origins in the middle of the first millennium of the common era. Its practitioners have lived in India, China, Japan, Tibet, Nepal, Bhutan, Pakistan, Sri Lanka, Korea, and Mongolia, as well as in the "Greater India" of medieval Southeast Asia: Cambodia, Burma, and Indonesia. The medieval history of South Asian Hinduism, Buddhism, and Jainism is saturated with tantrism. In Hindu India, the Pāñcarātra, Gauḍīya Vaiṣṇava, Sahajiyā, Pāśupata, Kāpālika, Śaiva Siddhānta, Siddha Kaula, Yoginī Kaula, Krama, Trika, Śrīvidyā, Paścimāmnāya, Nāth Siddha, and Śākta movements, orders, and sects have all been tantric or heavily colored by tantrism since the medieval period. Medieval Jain tantric works such as the tenth-century *Jvālinī Kalpa* resembled coeval Hindu and Buddhist Tantras in every way but for the names of the deities who were the objects of their ritual practice. Although Buddhism disappeared from the subcontinent in the thirteenth century, India (including present-day Pakistan) was the cradle of Buddhist tantrism in its Mahāyāna, Mantrayāna, and Vajrayāna forms, which were exported into Mongolia, Nepal, Bhutan, China, Korea, Japan, and Tibet. Certain of the Yoginī Tantras of early Buddhist tantrism originated in the Swat Valley of present-day Pakistan, and the tenth-century *Kālacakra Tantra,* an important Vajrayāna work, was likely written by an author living in the same region. Tibetan Buddhism is nearly entirely a Vajrayāna tradition: this applies to the four major existing schools (the Rnying ma [Nyingma] pas, Bka' brgyud [Kagyu] pas, Sa skya [Sakya] pas, and Dge lugs [Geluk] pa), as well as to specific forms of practice, such as Rdzogs chen (the "Great Perfection" practice unique to Nyingma). The ritual of the medieval Chinese state was tantric, and China was the medieval changing-house for nearly every Buddhist tantric tradition transmitted to Japan, Korea, and Mongolia. In China, tantrism has persisted, since the twelfth century CE, within Daoist ritual practice. In Japan, all of the eight traditional schools of Buddhism have a tantric pedigree: of these, the Shingon and Tendai schools have persisted as Japan's most successful exponents of "Pure Buddhist Esotericism." In Southeast Asia, Cambodian inscriptions indicate the presence of Hindu tantric specialists there in the early medieval period; the medieval kings of Bali underwent Hindu tantric initiations, and present-day Balinese Hinduism continues to display its Indian tantric origins.

From 1642 until the exile of its Dge lugs (Geluk) pa leadership in 1950, Tibet was a tantric Buddhist theocracy. Today, the constitutional monarchies of Nepal and Bhutan are the world's sole surviving "tantric kingdoms," with their state ceremonial comprised of tantric liturgies and rituals and nearly all of their deities tantric. One of these, Bhairava, is a tantric god found in every part of Asia, and worshipped in a tantric mode by Hindus, Jains, and Buddhists alike. Similarly, the originally Indian tantric gods Tārā, Ambikā, Akṣobhya, Mahākāla, Gaṇeśa, Avalokiteśvara, and Skanda, as well as numerous groups of multiple tantric deities, are found throughout much of Asia.

FUNDAMENTALS OF TANTRIC PRACTICE. Tantric practice consists of a set of ritual and meditative strategies for accessing and appropriating the energy or enlightened consciousness of the absolute godhead that, coursing through the universe, infuses its creatures with life and the potential for salvation. Humans in particular are empowered to realize this goal through strategies of embodiment—that is, of causing that supreme energy, essence of *nirvāṇa,* or quality of buddhahood to become concentrated in one or another sort of template or grid (a *maṇḍala* or *mantra,* the human body, or a ritual structure)—prior to its internalization in or identification with the individual microcosm. This they may do by appropriating elements of this world (which is real and not an illusion) such as words, images, bodies, and substances, into rituals that collapse subject and object, thereby projecting them into a realization of their inherent buddha nature or Śiva-self.

Drawing on its feudal Indian origins, tantrism also remains a body of practice with explicit this-worldly aims: the control of all of the beings located in the universal power grid, including lesser gods, living people, the dead, animals, and demons. While much of tantric practice has become sublimated into tame forms of "pure esotericism," it must be recalled that the great volume of early tantric texts were devoted to sorcery—that is, to magical techniques for controlling other beings against their will. Such remains the primary goal of tantrism as it continues to be practiced on a popular level throughout much of Asia.

The key to understanding tantric practice is the *maṇḍala,* the energy grid that represents the constant flow of divine and demonic, human and animal impulses in the universe, as they interact in both constructive and destructive patterns. This grid is three-dimensional, in the sense that it locates the supreme deity (god, goddess, celestial buddha, bodhisattva, or enlightened *tīrthaṃkara*)—the source of that energy and ground of the grid itself—at the center and apex of a hierarchized cosmos. All other beings, including the practitioner, will be situated at lower levels of energy/consciousness/being, radiating downward and outward from the elevated center point. Because the deity is both transcendent and immanent, all of the beings located at the various energy levels on the grid participate in the outward flow of the godhead, and are in some way emanations or hypostases of the deity himself (or herself).

This is particularly the case with the tantric guru, the preceptor from whom a practitioner receives instruction and initiation, and with whom tantric practitioners frequently identify the godhead at the center of the *maṇḍala.* Here, the guru, as an already fully realized or empowered tantric being, plays a pivotal role, linking the human with the divine. In certain tantric traditions, the male guru's female consort—variously called the Yoginī, Ḍākinī, "Action Seal," or "Lotus Maiden"—is equally exalted as she is identified with the supreme female godhead. It is in this particular context that sexualized ritual may be brought to the fore in tantric initiation: the female consort, as the embodiment of the divine, transmits to the initiand the transformative energy and wisdom of the godhead through her sexual emissions, which are considered to be liquid gnosis. In this way, the initiand becomes a member of the divine family or clan of both his guru and the godhead at the center of the *maṇḍala*.

Crucial to the initiation process as well as to many other types of tantric practice is the notion that within the gross body of the human microcosm there is a subtle, yogic body that is the mesocosmic replica of the divine dyad, the supreme godhead in its male and female manifestations. This body, comprised of energy channels and centers, drops and winds, is itself a *maṇḍala*: viewed from above, the vertical central channel of the subtle body would appear as the center point of the *maṇḍala*, with the various energy centers aligned along that channel being so many concentric circles, wheels, or lotuses radiating outward. As such, initiation and all forms of yogic practice involve, once again, an effort on the part of the practitioner to return to the elevated center point of the emanated *maṇḍala*. Movement toward the center, effected through a combination of external ritual and internal meditative practices, basically entails harmonizing one's own energy or consciousness level with that of the (deities of the) circle in which one finds oneself. First encountered as obstacles, these divine, demonic, or animal impulses are eventually overcome, and transformed into positive sources of energy that carry one closer and closer to the deity at the center. Alternatively, one may, having overcome them, also coerce those same potentially destructive lower-level beings to do one's bidding, through various ritual technologies.

THE INSTITUTIONALIZATION AND DOMESTICATION OF TANTRISM. As its sociopolitical contexts have changed, so too has the content of tantrism, with persons from a broader range of society appropriating and adapting its rituals and their attendant metaphysics to their specific needs and aspirations. In general terms, this has taken the form of an institutionalization of tantrism by Hindu Brāhmaṇs and Buddhist monks on the one hand and, on the other, the domestication of its base from lay elites (kings, aristocrats, and Siddhas) to wider strata of householder society. In spite of periodic reformations or revivals of "primitive" tantrism in various parts of the Asian world, both of these trends have had the effect of draining tantrism of its original specificities, of making institutional forms of tantrism look more like the broader, conventional, or orthodox religious contexts in which they have been embedded.

Many of the original tantric masters understood speech to be a performative act, and intentionally subverted conventional language in their teachings and use of *mantras* as a means to effect a breakthrough in their disciples' perception of reality. Among their disciples were members of the literati, who committed these speech acts into writing, writings that were in turn anthologized, codified, commentated on, and systematized into texts and canons of texts. Tantric *mantras*, which were originally secret spells for coercing a wide range of supernatural entities into doing one's bidding, became "semanticized" into the phonematic manifestations of powerful gods and compassionate buddhas, who could be accessed through the *mantras'* proper pronunciation. The term *mūdra* ("seal"), which originally referred to the sealing together of male and female bodies in sexual union, came to refer to complex hand and finger positions to be maintained while meditating, or to the parched grain that Hindu practitioners consume as a tantric sacrament. The *homa* fire sacrifice rituals of early tantrism, which often involved the offering of human and animal blood and gore to ravening demonic entities, became sublimated into either yogic practice or the meditative burning away of impediments to liberation or salvation in the fire of gnosis. More fundamentally, the tantric ritual arena came to be sealed off from the powerful but dangerous entities and forces of the original tantric universe, with the pandemonium of the real world walled out from the quiet center or the monastic cell or household shrine.

Orthodox Hindu and Buddhist hermeneutical strategies neutralized the heterodox and heteroprax content of early tantrism by interpreting it in a variety of ways. On the one hand, much of what was objectionable in the externals of tantric practice was internalized into yogic, meditative, or imaginative techniques. On the other, such practices were marginalized into the purview of a limited elite—the Siddhas and Vīras of tantric legend and their emulators—with more conventional, devotional, salvation-oriented practice recommended for the religious mainstream of monks, priests, and householders. Here, there was a trade-off between danger and efficacy, purity and power in the world, in which circumspection was strongly advised to all but a select few. It was the dangerous content of the early tantric rituals that most distinguished them from those found in the orthodox Buddhist Sūtra literature and the Hindu Vedas: but for those who dared to undertake them, and transact in prohibited substances (sexual fluids, unclean or proscribed food) with problematic beings (outcaste women, minions of the spirit world) through heterodox practices (sexualized initiation rituals, sorcery), self-transformation could be instantaneous rather than the result of several lifetimes of practice.

BIBLIOGRAPHY

Davidson, Ronald M. *Indian Esoteric Buddhism: A Social History of the Tantric Movement.* New York, 2002.

Faure, Bernard. *The Red Thread: Buddhist Approaches to Sexuality.* Princeton, N.J., 1998.

Goudriaan, Teun, and Sanjukta Gupta. *Hindu Tantric and Śakta Literature.* Wiesbaden, Germany, 1981.

Gupta, Sanjukta, Dirk Jan Hoens, and Teun Goudriaan. *Hindu Tantrism.* Leiden, Netherlands, 1979.

Harper, Katherine Anne, and Robert Brown, eds. *The Roots of Tantra.* Albany, N.Y., 2002.

Kværne, Per. "On the Concept of Sahaja in Indian Buddhist Tantric Literature." *Temenos* 11 (1975): 88–135.

Nandi, Ramendra Nath. *Religious Institutions and Cults in the Deccan.* Delhi, 1973.

Robinson, James, trans. *Buddha's Lions: The Lives of the Eighty-Four Siddhas.* Berkeley, Calif., 1979.

Samuel, Geoffrey. *Civilized Shamans: Buddhism in Tibetan Societies.* Washington, D.C., 1993.

Snellgrove, David. *Indo-Tibetan Buddhism: Indian Buddhists and Their Tibetan Successors.* 2 vols. Boston, 1987, 1995.

Strickmann, Michel. *Mantras et mandarins: Le bouddhisme tantrique en Chine.* Paris, 1996. (English translation forthcoming.)

White, David Gordon. *Kiss of the Yoginī: "Tantric Sex" in Its South Asian Contexts.* Chicago, 2003.

White, David Gordon, ed. *Tantra in Practice.* Princeton, N.J., 2000.

DAVID GORDON WHITE (2005)

TANTRISM: HINDU TANTRISM

Tantrism must certainly rank as among the most problematic and controversial categories in the study of religion generally and the study of Hinduism specifically. Virtually every proposition about Tantrism is disputed, ranging from its origins and distinctive traits to the evaluation of its place in the history of religions. Herbert Guenther, one of the last century's greatest scholars of the subject, once observed that Tantrism is "probably one of the haziest notions and misconceptions the Western mind has evolved." Often enough one encounters completely contradictory statements concerning Tantrism in the scholarly literature. As one modern observer puts it, the term is a sort of "floating signifier . . . gathering to itself a range of contradictory qualities." Because of this some have argued that there is no real referent to the words *Tantrism* or *Tantric* and therefore such terms should be abandoned entirely. Others choose to retain the terminology, albeit not without reservations.

We may start with the problematic nature of the name *Tantrism* itself. The term derives from the Sanskrit root *tan-*, "to extend, stretch, expand." *Tantra* thus can mean "succession," "unfolding," "continuous process," or "extension." The term appears already in the Vedic *Shrauta Sūtras* (c. fifth century BCE) in the sense of a "ritual framework" or "interweaving of rites," and *Tantrism* does indeed refer often enough to a certain type of ritual practice. The term is also used in the sense of an "extension" or "expansion of knowledge," or the "weaving" of various threads into a text; it can also be used as a synonym for a "system," or "system of thought," or a "compendium." Certain texts in the Hindu tradition are thus labeled *Tantras* (one common definition within the indigenous tradition is "a scripture by which knowledge is spread"), although not all of these "Tantras" can be regarded as "Tantric," and other texts that may indeed be so regarded are called by different names (e.g., Āgamas, Nigamas, and Samhitas).

A practitioner of Tantra is known as a *tāntrika* or a *sādhaka.* The Tantric adept is termed a *siddha* or "accomplished one." The ritual and meditative method or path distinctive to Tantra is called a *sādhana* ("performance leading to a goal"), which is supposed to result in the attainment of certain "powers" (*siddhis*). As a path that often entails physical practices, Tantricism overlaps considerably with the Hindu traditions of yoga: one sometimes encounters the term *tantra-yoga* and a Tantric practitioner is frequently called *yogin* or *yoginī.*

Many scholars argue that there is, however, no indigenous Indian term that corresponds to *Tantrism*; that is to say, there was in the native tradition no recognition of a unified school or system or religious sect called *Tantrism.* Under this view, the word and conceptual apparatus that usually clings to it is entirely of foreign invention. David Gordon White has contended, however, that the term *Tantrism* does closely correspond to the scholastic tradition of ritual exegesis embodied in the textual corpus known as the *Tantraśāstra* (Theoretical treatises on Tantra), the most famous of which is the *Tantraloka* of Abhinavagupta (eleventh century CE).

One should also note, as we have above, that the adjective *tāntrika* ("Tantric") does appear in Sanskrit texts, in some cases to contrast a form of belief and practice to the more "orthodox" or "Vedic" (*vaidika*) forms of Hinduism. In some of the non-Tantric Sanskritic texts, *vaidika* refers to forms of practice suitable for *brahmans* and others of the higher classes, while the *tāntrika* rites are relegated to the lower castes. In the Tantric texts, unsurprisingly, the *tāntrika* path is defined very differently. Some contrast the wise *tāntrika,* whose knowledge penetrates to the true meaning of things, to the superficial *vaidika.* One text defines this form of practice in the following way: "He by whom the senses are conquered and whose mind is fixed . . . he whose intellect is still with regard to his own affairs or those of others . . . this, in short, is said to be the *tāntrika* method."

The origins of Tantricism are, like virtually everything else about the phenomenon, also contested. Some think Tantrism originated in Buddhist circles. Indeed, the oldest known "Tantric" texts are Buddhist; the *Guhyasamāja Tantra,* attributed to Asaṅga, dates back perhaps to the third century CE. Other scholars, however, presume Hindu origins for this form of religious belief and practice. Andre Padoux (1987) states unequivocally that "Tantrism is fundamentally a Hindu phenomenon."

Given the paucity of historical materials and the general uncertainty involved in the subject, the question of whether Tantrism was originally Hindu or Buddhist will probably never be resolved. What is sure is that Buddhist and Hindu Tantrism share much by way of doctrine, imagery, and practice, and they apparently cross-fertilized each other over the course of centuries. Within Hinduism per se, there are also Tantric strains within most of the major divisions of that tradition—Vaiṣṇava, Śaivite, and Śākta (the latter is often regarded in its entirety as "Tantric").

The term *Tantrism* thus refers to a broad movement, probably originating in the middle centuries of the first millennium CE, which spread into Hindu, Buddhist, and (to a lesser extent) Jain traditions. This "movement" (some prefer to envisage Tantrism as simply an attitude) is usually conceptualized as encompassing activities (symbolically imagined or ritually enacted) normally prohibited in the bourgeois India of the time, including some form of sexual intercourse (although the sexual component is often minimal in such groups and is, in any event, to be understood within a larger symbolic and ritual contextual framework).

Tantrism in its origins was, then, fundamentally a set of reinterpretations of the various existing religious traditions of India. It was also often perceived—both in historical India and the modern West—as controversial if not dangerous and degenerate. As Hugh Urban (2003) has written, for most understandings of Tantrism (both popular and scholarly, Indian and Western), the key element is "the very *extremity* of Tantra, its radical Otherness."

HISTORY OF THE STUDY AND REPRESENTATION OF TANTRISM. For many modern specialists, the category is now viewed as inextricably bound up in the prejudices and cultural psychodynamics of the Westerners who, it is argued, "invented" it in the nineteenth century. Some of the early Western scholars of Tantrism seemed aware of the constructionist nature of their label. Arthur Avalon (also known as John Woodroffe), one of the pioneers of Tantric studies, wrote in 1922 that "the adjective *tantric* is largely a Western term." Once constructed, however, "Tantrism" took on a life of its own and often served as a screen onto which outsiders projected either their deepest anxieties and fears or their desires and hopes.

Tantrism for many was the most degenerate and peripheral form of Indian religion. When it was first "discovered" by Westerners at the end of the eighteenth century, it was almost universally regarded as the most horrifying example of the excesses of Indian religiosity. Otherwise put, *Tantrism* was the label placed on those practices Westerners regarded as most abhorrent. Such views were only strengthened in the Victorian era where Tantrism was all but equated with illicit sexuality. The "so-called Tantric religion," writes one such Victorian, is essentiality nothing more than a cult where "nudity is worshipped in Bacchanalian orgies which cannot be described." Already by this time the standard stereotypes of "Tantrism"—and ones that have often endured to this day—were in place. What was definitive of this debased form of Hinduism was sexual licentiousness, as well as the consumption of prohibited substances, such as liquor, beef, and aphrodisiacs. In sum, as the nineteenth-century Indologist H. H. Wilson would opine, Tantrism stood "for all that is abominable in the present state of Hindu religion."

In the twentieth century some scholars arose to proclaim the exact opposite: that Tantrism was, in fact, both the root and crowning achievement of Indian religiosity. Avalon regarded Tantrism as both "orthodox" (meaning, for him, "Aryan" or "Vedic") and in conformity to science. As for the sexual components of this form of Hinduism, Avalon would write that "There is nothing 'foul' in them except for people to whom all erotic phenomena are foul" (1975, p. 134). Other Western Indologists, including Heinrich Zimmer, would also champion the cause of Tantrism as the ideal religion for the modern age—creative, life-affirming, sensuous. For Mircea Eliade, Tantrism represented the "autochthynous heart of aboriginal India" and "reveals an experience that is no longer accessible in a desacralized society—the experience of a sanctified sexual life" (1959, p. 172; 1970, p. 201). It is, according to Eliade, in Tantrism that the opposition of the sacred and profane is finally resolved.

Such views, positive and negative, in the West were echoed in India. Many of the reformers of the so-called Neo-Hindu movement of the nineteenth and early twentieth centuries specifically targeted Tantrism as the prime example of how far Hindus have fallen from the purity of the golden age of Vedic origins. For many of the leaders of what is sometimes called the "Hindu renaissance," Tantrism represented everything wrong with Hinduism and for all that was an embarrassment about India in relation to the West. Vivekananda, in his nationalistically inspired opposition to Tantra, claimed it was "un-Indian," with origins in Central Asia and Tibet.

For other Indians, however, Tantricism represented the very best of the Indian religious heritage. Perhaps the greatest of all the modern Indian saints and mystics, Ramakrishna, seems to have been a Tantric practitioner. On the other end of the spectrum, Tantrism's association with radicalism, subversion, and transgression made it appealing to Indian revolutionaries in the extreme wings of the nationalist movement of the late nineteenth and early twentieth centuries. For revolutionary nationalists like Aurobindo Ghose (in his early years), Tantric symbols and deities (especially the terrifying figure of the Tantric goddess Kālī) became sources of revolutionary inspiration. And for others, like the Marxist scholar N. N. Bhattacharyya, Tantrism represented evidence for an ancient classless society based on matriarchy and the worship of the Mother Goddess that was largely eclipsed by the patriarchal, caste-oriented Vedic culture and its legacy.

Among the many controversies regarding Tantra found in the scholarly literature, there is also dispute about whether Tantrism has been relegated to peripheral or tangential status vis-à-vis "real" Hinduism, or, conversely, whether the fascination with Tantricism—bordering on obsession—has blown out of all proportion its place in the study of that religion. Paul Muller-Ortega (1989) and Douglas Brooks (1990) both argue that, despite the apparent vogue and interest in Tantrism, it is nevertheless the unwanted "stepchild" of Indology—a persistence source of shame and embarrassment, and thus neglected and poorly attended to. On the other hand, Hugh Urban contends that "Tantrism has in fact been central to both academic and popular discourse about India in the twentieth century. Indeed, it has in many cases clearly been exaggerated and exploited" (2003, p. 8).

The Origins, History, and Traditions of Hindu Tantra. Andre Padoux observed that "the history of Tantrism is impossible to write" due to the paucity of data (and, it could be said, by virtue of the definitional uncertainty as what counts as "Tantrism"). Such pessimism has not changed much. Urban has reiterated that "the historical origins of the vast body of traditions that we call Tantra are today lost in a mire of obscure Indian history and muddled scholarly conjecture" (2003, p. 23).

Scholars have nevertheless put forth two very different narratives to account for the possible sources of Tantrism. The first locates the earliest "Tantrism" in the Indus Valley civilization, here conceived as a matriarchal culture complete with goddess worship, fertility rites, and proto-yogic practices. When Aryan invaders destroyed the Indus Valley civilization, Tantrism supposedly went underground, where it survived among the tribal groups at the periphery of Indian culture but also as the "autochthonous substratum" of later Hinduism. According to this account, Tantrism then reemerges a thousand years later in texts of the middle centuries of the first millennium, but only as the Sanskritized, elitist expression of a continuous and fundamentally popular form of Indian religion.

A quite different narrative assumes that Tantrism derives from the Aryan or Vedic religion itself. From this point of view, Tantrism is in essence the outgrowth of the intellectual and religious elite, and not based on a popular movement (let alone "autochthonous substratum") within Hinduism. Scholars adhering to this position cite the fact that the texts in which the beliefs and practices of Tantrism are first encapsulated are written in Sanskrit, and not in any popular vernacular.

A third, and mediating, possibility for accounting for the origins of Tantrism is to see it as the combination of both autochthonous and Vedic roots, or perhaps a synthesis of shamanic and magical practices (possibly originating in Central Asia) and the mystical speculations characteristic of the *brahman* elite.

All such attempts at locating the temporal and cultural origins of Tantrism remain theoretical and speculative. The geographical origins of the Tantric movement of the middle centuries of the Common Era is no less fraught with uncertainty. Although many of the centers of the Tantric movement were located in the frontier or border areas of India (e.g., Kashmir and Assam), other equally important geographical locales for Tantric expressions include Andhra, Kerala, Madhya Pradesh, and Orissa. There does not seem to be one central place from which Tantrism sprung.

There is also no conclusive evidence of Hindu Tantras in the period before 800 CE, although most scholars agree that the classical form of Hindu Tantrism originated at least two or three centuries before that. Stone inscriptions indicate that Tantric deities were worshiped in the fifth century and many agree that Tantrism was well established by the sixth or seventh centuries CE. While there is little precisely dated evidence available, it seems that the period from the eighth or ninth century to the fourteenth century was one in which Tantrism flourished in India. Most of the texts regarded as "Tantric" (the Tantras, Samhitas, and Āgamas) date from this period, as do many temples and some of the greatest thinkers of the Tantric traditions (e.g., Abhinavagupta).

Already in the medieval period and then in subsequent centuries, the Tantric movement exerted influences on all forms of Hinduism. It has been noted that the pantheon of present-day Hinduism is largely comprised of Tantric deities. Tantrism also left its imprint on the temples, iconography, and rituals of the more "mainstream" Hinduism. Indeed, as we have seen, some scholars believe that the influence of Tantrism was so great that virtually all of Hinduism from medieval times forward can be understood as "Tantric." Mainstream Hinduism, under this view, is more "Tantric" than not.

But despite the huge influence of Tantrism on the theology, arts, iconography, temples, and rituals of the orthodox or mainstream religion, most Hindus have not in the past and would not now regard themselves as *tāntrikas*. The esoteric nature of much of the practice together with the initiatory structure of many of the Tantric groups have insured that membership of self-identified Tantric practitioners would always be limited, even while "Tantric" influences on Hinduism have been pervasive. The secretive and esoteric nature of many Tantric groups has also, in India as in the West, helped to generate a dubious reputation for Tantrism. In much of today's India, the label carries the same negative connotations it has borne for so long in the West. Brooks observes that "The word 'Tantra' in vernacular languages [of India] . . . is frequently used to conjure notions of black magic, illicit sexuality, and immoral behavior" (1990, p. 5).

"Tantrism," writes Padoux, "is essentially sectarian." The main division of sects in Hinduism as a whole consists of the worshipers of Viṣṇu (Vaiṣṇavas), the worshipers of Śiva (Śaivas or Śaivites), and those who worship the Goddess, in one or another of her many forms, as the supreme deity (the Śāktas). There are Tantric sects within each of these main divisions, although the Tantric groups within the Śaivite and Śākta groupings regard Śiva and Śakti as inseparable and therefore are not themselves clearly distinguishable according to these sectarian divisions. There is also considerable similarity between the terms *Tantrism* and *Śāktism*; while groups labeled in these two ways are not identical, they do intersect and often overlap.

Among the Vaiṣṇavas, the Pāñcarātra sect (with origins circa sixth century CE) was heavily influenced by the Tantric movement, although today most members of this sect do not consider themselves as Tantric practitioners. The Vaiṣṇava-Sahajiyās of Bengal, however, remain close in spirit to other forms of Tantrism. The Sahajiyās, who flourished especially between the sixteenth and nineteenth centuries, worship Viṣṇu in the form of Kṛṣṇa and his lover Rādhā. The poems of the Sahajiyā Tantrics are replete in erotic imagery, and practitioners use devotional singing and dancing to try to induce a state of mystical ecstasy envisioned as the union of the god and his consort.

It is, however, most especially in certain of the Śaivite sects that we find the classical instantiations of what is called *Tantrism.* One of the earliest of the Śaivite groups, the Pāśupatas (dating to perhaps the second century CE), emphasized radical asceticism and bizarre or disreputable behavior (thought to be in imitation of the wild divine ascetic, Śiva) in the pursuit of supernatural powers or *siddhis*. Other early Śaivite sects that display Tantric tendencies include the Kāpālikas and the Kālāmukhas, about whom little is known because no texts from these groups survive. Contemporary reports about them, however, insist on their outrageous, scandalous behavior and socially abhorrent practices. As their name indicates, the Kāpālikas ("skull-bearers") probably used human skulls as begging bowls, were said to frequently practice in cemeteries, and may have engaged in ritualized sex. While evidence is scanty, it seems that such early Śaivite Tantrics embraced practices that subverted conventional morality and embraced controversial methods in the service of power and liberation.

Another set of Śaivite Tantric practitioners were known as the Nātha Siddhas (also known as the Kānphaṭās, or "split-ears"). They were also called the Gorakhnāthis due to the name of their founder, Gorakhnāth or Gorakṣa, who was supposedly the author of many of the Tantric texts of the *haṭhayoga* tradition. The aim of these practitioners was that of many other Tantrics, the state of liberation in this lifetime known as *jīvanmukti,* here thought to be achievable through the distinctive practices of yoga entailing breath control and retention and the "regression" of sexual energy and fluids.

Special mention must be made of the great philosopher of the "non-dual" Śaivism of Kashmir, Abhinavagupta (born c. 950 CE), who is responsible for many philosophically sophisticated and systematic Tantric treatises written in Sanskrit. One of the most famous of these is entitled the *Tantrāloka* (Elucidation of the Tantras), a commentary or exegesis of the Tantras. David White has argued for the importance of Abhinavagupta in the systematization and rationalization of Tantra. In his exegesis of the esoteric rites of Tantric practice, Abhinavagupta "sublimates, cosmeticizes, and semanticizes many of its practices into a type of meditative asceticism whose aim it was to realize a transcendent subjectivity. In the process, he transforms ritual from a form of 'doing' to a form of 'saying'" (2003, p. 16).

For some, then, Hindu "Tantrism" has been understood as referring to a particular kind of sect within Hinduism. In recent years, however, there has also arisen a tendency to envision it as an extremely widespread, even ubiquitous, trait of Indian religions in general. Eliade, for example, writes that "from the fifth century CE onward Tantrism becomes a pan-Indian 'fashion.' One meets it everywhere in innumerable different forms" (1970, p. 200). If, however, Tantrism is found everywhere within Hinduism, "in innumerable different forms," then what, if anything, constitutes its distinctiveness?

A Survey of Definitional Traits. It is generally agreed that there is no one body of doctrines and practices shared by all forms of Hindu Tantrism, and most scholars now also believe that a search for a unitary definition of *Tantrism* is futile. What we refer to as *Tantrism* is not so much a unified tradition but a loose grouping of particular texts, traditions, practices, and doctrines that differ in some regards from each other and overlap considerably with other "non-Tantric" currents within Hinduism. At best, then, there are elements that may be regarded only as characteristic, but not definitive, of Tantrism. Tantrism cannot be defined in terms of one or more standard traits but only in a "polythetic" manner in which any particular instance participates in one or more of a set of "family resemblances."

As a way to familiarize readers with what scholars have meant by "Hindu Tantrism," the following list of definitional traits may be useful. Many—indeed most—of these traits do not fit all instances of what has been called *"Tantrism."* Some of them are hotly contested by scholars (as noted below), but each has appeared in the scholarly literature as at least partially definitive of the phenomenon.

Non-Vedic or extra-Vedic in origin or scriptural authority. The ritual practices and methods for attaining religious goals in Tantrism are often characterized as "non-Vedic" (by which is meant, to some extent, "unorthodox" or at least "new," "unprecedented"). Tantric rituals and most of the distinctive worldview associated with Tantrism do not appear in Vedic texts nor in the strictly Brahmanic or *"smārta"* traditions that represent themselves as closely based on the Veda. Tantric texts, like the Vedas, do claim to be revealed from a transcendent source, but often enough there is no attempt to link the legitimating origin of Tantric practice back to the Vedas—as is indeed the case with the more orthodox traditions of Hinduism.

Tantrism, in other words, often represents its revelations as "new," or rather "newly revealed." This hitherto secret knowledge is said to have now become available because it is especially suitable for the *kali* age, the present era of degeneration when previously revealed methods and wisdom are no longer realizable by corrupt humans. As we have seen, the orthodox traditions themselves sometimes draw a distinction between *vaidika* and *tāntrika* rituals and practitioners and, in this way, the Tantric traditions agree.

This possible trait for what goes into constituting a group as "Tantric" does not preclude the claims sometimes made in Tantric texts to Vedic legitimacy, which may have in some cases been introduced at a later date in order to facilitate acceptance of Tantrism by the more orthodox Hindus. Nor does it necessarily deny that certain features of Tantrism, especially the emphasis on correlations and connections between the body, seen as a microcosm, and the universe as a whole or the macrocosm, at least resemble (if not derive) from modes of thought that may be characterized as "Vedic" (see below). What the emphasis on the non- or extra-Vedic character of Tantrism does begin to point to is Tantrism's controversial and "unorthodox" nature.

Controversial or antinomian practices. It is indeed the radical and transgressive methods prescribed by certain groups in the history of Indian religion that are often enough assumed, at least in part, by the label *Tantric.* For some groups, this has meant antisocial ascetic practices, such as eschewing clothing and ordinary hygiene, meditating in cemeteries, and carrying human skulls as begging bowls, as well as practices involving human corpses and the worship of deities in gruesome, terrifying forms. For others it has meant engaging in ritualized sex and the exchange of bodily fluids, or rituals that call for the ingestion of otherwise prohibited substances. In all cases, the purpose of such antinomian behavior seems to have been in one way or another to transcend the world of dualities (including "pure" and "impure," "good" and "bad").

Among the best known of these controversial practices is the ritual of indulging in what are called the five elements or principles (*pañcatattvas*) or the "five M's" (referring to the Sanskrit letter with which each of the five begins). This practice forms the core of the so-called "left-handed" path (*vāmamarga*) of Tantrism. Members of the group form a circle of alternating males and females, which represents the cosmos or *maṇḍala.* Having ritually constituted each male as the god and each female as the goddess (and the embodiment of the female energy known as *śakti*), practitioners then make what are regarded as sacrificial offerings to the divine within. These offerings consist of substances normally forbidden in caste Hinduism: meat (*mamsa*), fish (*matsya*), alcohol (*madhu*), and parched grains (one of the meanings of term *mudrā,* and perhaps indicating some kind of aphrodisiac). The ceremony culminates in the "fifth M," ritual intercourse or *maithuna,* which epitomizes the transcendental unification and resolution of all opposites. This kind of practice could also, however, be done entirely imaginatively within meditation, following the "right handed" path.

Esoteric Tantric groups thus claimed to be able to engage in practices that for the uninitiated would result in the most disastrous karmic ends. Such a path is termed "heroic" (*vira*) and dangerous in that it intentionally confronts head-on the most deep-seated desires and the most repulsive of aversions in the attempt to rise above both. Through various meditative and ritual techniques, the Tantric practitioner could "do whatever fools condemn" and rid himself "of passion by yet more passion":

> So, with all one's might, one should do Whatever fools condemn, And, since one's mind is pure, Dwell in union with one's divinity. The mystics, pure of mind Dally with lovely girls, Infatuated with the poisonous flame of passion That they may be set free from desire. By his meditations the sage . . . draws out the venom (of snakebite) and drinks it. He makes his deity innocuous, And is not affected by the poison. . . . When he has developed a mind of wisdom And has set his heart on enlightenment There is nothing he may not do To uproot the world (from his mind). . . . Water in the ear is removed by more water, A thorn (in the skin) by another thorn. So wise men rid themselves of passion By yet more passion. (*Cittaviśuddhiprakaraṇa,* Embree, 1988, pp. 24–38)

An anti-ascetic and anti-renunciatory attitude and a positive attitude toward the body. Tantrism has often been viewed as a kind of reaction to the renunciatory and ascetic strains in Hinduism. From the time of the ancient Upaniṣads, asceticism and world renunciation were usually thought to be more or less essential in the quest for liberation or *mokṣa.* Such an attitude is accompanied by a fundamentally negative evaluation of the body and its desires.

The "first characteristic" of Tantrism, according to Eliade, is its anti-ascetic attitude. The body is "revalorized" in Tantric circles and "acquires an importance it had never before attained in the spiritual history of India . . . The Upanishadic and post-Upanishadic pessimism and asceticism are swept away. The body is no longer the source of pain, but the most reliable and effective instrument at man's disposal for 'conquering death'" (1970, p. 227).

In Tantrism, the physical body becomes the vehicle and microcosmic locus of powers that can be tapped and enjoyed as the means to liberation. As such, the body must be kept healthy and strong, and a very different understanding of desire emerges. Tantrism sometimes represents itself as the "easy" path in which desire is not renounced but utilized on the road to salvation. As one text puts it, "No one succeeds in attaining perfection by employing difficult and vexing operations; but perfection can be gained by satisfying all one's desires."

Madeleine Biardeau has summed up *Tantrism* as "an attempt to place *kama,* desire, in every meaning of the word, in the service of liberation . . . not to sacrifice this world for liberation's sake, but to reinstate it, in varying ways, within the perspective of salvation" (cited in Padoux, 1987, p. 273) Thus *Tantrism* here means the use of desire to gain both worldly and supernatural "enjoyments" (*bhukti* or *bhoga*) as well as powers (*siddhis*) and to attain the state of liberation in this very lifetime and in the embodied state. The this-worldly is not renounced but rather reintegrated into the soteriological quest.

Such a view of the Tantric embrace of the body, desire, and sensuality must also be contextualized by the often equally characteristic trait of an emphasis on ritual and the use of yoga or mental and physical "discipline" in Tantric groups. Desire—especially in its most powerful form, sexual desire—is not simply indulged in Tantric practice but rather is harnessed and "disciplined" by ritual or yogic methods. "The 'easiness' of the tantric path is more apparent than real," writes Eliade. "The fact is that tantric road presupposes a long and difficult *sadhana*" (1970, p. 206).

Religious use of sexual intercourse. David White has stated that "sexual ritual practice is the sole truly distinctive feature of South Asian Tantric traditions. All of the other elements of Tantric practice . . . may be found elsewhere" (2003, p. 13). We have seen above how ritualized sex is integrated into the "left-handed" forms of Tantric practice and how "desire" is not to be avoided but utilized. The ritualized or even "yogic" sex of traditional Indian Tantric practice at least theoretically has nothing to do with simply indulging one's desires, let along with the orgiastic and lascivious. It rather takes place secretly under what might be called "laboratory conditions" and within a context where all the participants are advanced practitioners. The event is totally sacralized; the participants are all fully divinized beforehand and the act of intercourse is to be envisioned not as sex at all but as the unification of all polarities, and most especially the union of Śiva and Śakti, the passive and active principles of the cosmos. Such a union is thought to represent or indeed actualize absolute reality itself.

The purpose of the ritual is not climax in its conventional sense of self-gratification, and indeed sometimes orgasm is prohibited in this yogic form of sex. The goal is rather the experience of cosmic union, the highest and ultimate end of Tantric practice. As Georg Feuerstein (1998) notes, in opposition to the lurid notion of "Tantric sex" sometimes current among outsiders, "There is nothing glamorous about Tantric sexual intercourse."

Esotericism and secrecy. Given the controversial nature of Tantric groups, a high premium was (and may very well still be) placed on secrecy. Many, if not most, of the practices characteristic of "Tantrism" were traditionally carried out privately, away from the gaze of the uninitiated. Practitioners were aware of the disapproval that would accompany public knowledge of certain of their rituals. Texts warn of the dire consequences that will befall those who reveal the secrets to outsiders. Tantric methods are also often said to be extremely dangerous to those who practice them without proper initiation and guidance, and therefore on these grounds too they should be kept from the awareness of the general public.

The esoteric nature of Tantrism was insured in part by its initiatory structure. Only those who had gained the permission of the Tantric master or *gurū* and who had undergone what can be very complex initiation or consecration (*dīkṣā*) ceremonies were eligible to learn the secrets of a particular sect. In opposition to the Vedic or Vedic-based orthodox groups, Tantric practice was typically open to initiates of all castes and both genders. "Initiation, secrecy, and the necessity of a spiritual master are essential Tantric traits," according to Padoux.

Another way in which the esoteric knowledge and practices of Tantrism were protected was through its elaborate system of symbols and especially by the utilization of an enigmatic and highly ambiguous form of language that renders many texts unintelligible to outsiders (and that provides endless difficulties for scholars trying to decipher such discourse). This form of writing is sometimes termed *sandhya bhasa* or "twilight speech" to indicate its capacity to convey within it two different meanings at once, and also to point to the paradoxical and ultimately indescribable qualities of esoteric realizations. Twilight speech may thus have as its original purpose not only to protect secrets but also to indicate that ordinary language is incapable of expressing the deep truths of Tantra.

Homologies and correlations between the macrocosm and the body regarded as a microcosm. The idea that the cosmos in its entirety, the macrocosm, is replicated or represented within the very body of the practitioner (conceived of as a microcosm) is frequently encountered in Tantrism and, indeed, is a necessary assumption for much of Tantric ritual and meditative practice. The positing of correlations between the body and the world, between the microcosm and macrocosm, between the human and the divine, and between the beings and actions involved in ritual and the cosmic entities, energies, and processes—all these are more or less necessary presuppositions for other elements of the worldview and practices of Tantrism.

In spirit, at least, if not in the specifics, this notion of a potentially discoverable nexus of resemblances linking the human, the ritual, and the cosmos is identical to that of Vedism, culminating in the Upaniṣadic equation of the Self (*ātman*) and the macrocosmic principle of unity (the *brahman*). As such, the idea that Tantrism is entirely or pervasively "non-Vedic" and "unorthodox" must be qualified.

The positing of a mystical physiology or "subtle body" and the projection of divinities into the body. An essential part of the idea of the body as a microcosm was the typically Tantric conceptualization of an "inner" or "subtle" body and an intricate science of veins, channels, winds or energies, and centers that comprise what one may call a mystical anatomy or physiology.

While there are vague correspondences between the structure and elements of this subtle body and the anatomical organs and endocrine system of the physical body, the two are not identical. Thus, for example, the various centers or chakras ("wheels," so called because they are envisioned as whirling circles) of the mystical body (some traditions count five of these, others seven) are located near, but are not identified with, parts of the physical body: the crown of the head, between the eyebrows, at the areas of the throat, heart, navel, and sexual organ, and at the base of the spinal column. Each of these centers forms the locus of a complex set of imagery; each is said to contain lotuses of different colors and shapes, different Sanskrit letters or *mantras,* geometrical designs, deities, cosmological elements and entities, and so forth. Each chakra, in other words, is a tremendous potential source of cosmic power of a certain sort. Taken together these centers within the human body contain the universe as a whole.

Linking together and springing forth from these centers is a vast system of tens of thousands of *nadi*s—veins, nerves, currents, or channels—the most important of which is a "central channel" (*sushumna*) surrounded on either side by two other *nadi*s called the *ida* (on the left) and *pingala* (on the right), the latter of which, among other things, is correlated with the moon and the sun. Running through these channels are various "winds" or energies known as *prāṇa*s.

Tantric practice, especially but not exclusively in its more meditative forms, consists of realizing the cosmic nature of this subtle body and then tapping into its transformative powers. This is done initially by imaginatively projecting divinities and powers into the body (the practice is called *nyāsa*), thereby homologizing it with the Tantric pantheon in order to realize and awaken these forces within. This process is often accompanied by the use of sacred and powerful syllables called "seed" or *bīja mantras* and the use of secret gestures called *mudrā*s.

But the real centerpiece of such meditation is the awakening of the energy, force, or power within the practitioner's being called *śakti* (the female and active principle of the universe) or *kuṇḍalinī* (envisioned as a snake coiled at the base of the spine). As one text puts it, "As a door is opened with a key, so the *yogi* opens the door of liberation by awakening the *kuṇḍalinī.*" This cosmic power, once aroused, is moved up through the central channel where it passes through, one by one, each of the chakras and invigorates the dormant powers within them. This results in the attainment of progressively higher states of consciousness and ability by the practitioner. When the *kuṇḍalinī* reaches the chakra at the crown of the head—the divine seat of the god Śiva—the female *śakti* is said to be reunited with the male principle. This is equated with liberation for the practitioner, a state that is said to be accompanied by "great bliss" and ecstasy.

Many scholars regard this mystical physiology as distinctive to Tantra, especially the notions that the active force in the universe (*śakti,* conceived as the Goddess) is present also in each individual in the form of *kuṇḍalinī.* The identification with and appropriation of the power of the Goddess, and the emphasis on tapping the *śakti/kuṇḍalinī* power within one's body, forms what some would regard as an essential element in what we call *Tantra.*

Distinctive goals: The attainment of *siddhis* and the realization of liberation in this lifetime (*jīvanmukti*). While all forms of Hinduism seek the goal of liberation or release from the bonds of *saṃsāra,* one of the features shared by most Tantric groups is the urgency with which that quest is imbued. Indeed, some scholars have focused on the "experiential" nature of Tantrism as its distinctive quality, its emphasis on practice over doctrine and on results above all. Tantric practitioners typically seek, in this very lifetime and in this very body, the experience of unity or oneness ("nonduality"), of "spontaneity" (*sahaja*), or of "moving through the void" (*khecarī*), which is most commonly known as "liberation in this life" (*jīvanmukti*). While there are, as we have seen, many and various methods for attaining this goal, the conceptualization of the goal itself in these terms is perhaps one of the most basic commonalities shared by Tantric groups.

The liberated Tantric practitioner, the "accomplished one" or *siddha,* is, according to one text, free from the "pairs of opposites" or all duality, no longer bound by the forces of *karma,* unconquerable, "without inhalation and exhalation," invulnerable to all weapons, and immortal. Other extraordinary powers (the "accomplishments" or *siddhi*s) are also sought and supposedly realized along the way to the ultimate goal. These include the ability to fly, to know the past and future, to decipher the languages of animals, realize one's previous lives, read the thoughts of others, become invisible, and so on. In some texts, abilities such as these are summarized as the eight "great powers" (*mahāsiddhi*s): miniaturization, magnification, levitation, extension, irresistible will, mastery, lordship over the universe, and fulfillment of all desires.

MODERN WESTERN APPROPRIATIONS OF HINDU TANTRA. The problems inherent in the study of Tantrism have been further compounded by the widespread interest in and appropriation of the term *Tantra* to identify certain modern and Western New Age beliefs and practices. This form of "Neo-Tantrism" may or, more often, may not have anything much in common with the Tantrism practiced traditionally in India. Neo-Tantrism is, however, often represented by its adherents and supporters as both "ancient" and "Indian," perhaps in part as a means to legitimate its blend of spirituality and sexuality, sacred transcendence and materialistic indulgence. Furthermore, Tantrism has also appealed to, and been appropriated by, some modern Western feminists. Tantrism's supposed matriarchal roots, its elevation of goddess figures, its emphasis on the female power or *śakti,* its "embodiedness" or valorization of the body and physicality, and the supposed equality of the genders in its ritual practices—all these traits have endeared Tantrism to a certain segment of modern feminist spirituality.

Neo-Tantrism first emerged as part of the spirituality associated with the counterculture of the 1960s. An important cross-culturally transitional figure was Bhagawan Shree Rajneesh (also known as Osho), an Indian *gurū* who attracted a largely Western following with an eclectic philosophy revolving around his particular vision of "Tantra": "Tantra does not believe in improving your character . . . Tantra says—if you are greedy, be greedy . . . If you are sexual, be sexual, don't bother about it at all" (1974, p. 190). His teachings, he claimed, were particularly suitable for modern Westerners, an "iconoclastic brand of spirituality" or a "religionless religion" that does not deny or repress life and the body but rather affirms and expresses sensuality and physicality.

Since Rajneesh, New Age groups claiming to be in one way or another Tantric have multiplied and spread. The internet is replete with sites offering "Tantric sex," "sex magic," "sacred sex," "spiritual sex," and so forth—all under the umbrella of Tantrism. Neo-Tantrism, it has been argued, represents the ideal religion for consumer society, embracing the most materialistic and hedonistic desires and repositioning them as "spiritual" and as the means for achieving transcendence.

This new twist in the already extremely complex history of the phenomena called *Tantric* has provoked yet more controversy among scholars of Tantrism. Most view the appearance of neo-Tantrism as a trivializing perversion of the "authentic" Tantric traditions. For these observers, neo-Tantrics have mistaken, among other things, the "sexualization of ritual" of traditional Tantrism for the "ritualization of sex." Or, otherwise put, they have (intentionally or not) blurred the distinction made in the Indian tradition between the science of Tantra (*tantraśāstra*) and the science of erotics (*kāmaśāstra*)—the former entailing the use and transformation of desire in the service of liberation, whereas the latter's goal is the fulfillment of desire as one of the "ends of life" of a householder. One scholar thus refers to the "pathetic hybrid of New Age 'Tantric sex.'" For other observers, however, the neo-Tantrism of the modern West is just another incarnation of the infinitely protean, and always contestable, category of Tantrism.

SEE ALSO Buddhist Books and Texts, articles on Canon and Canonization; Goddess Worship; Hindu Tantric Literature; Kuṇḍalinī; Maṇḍalas, article on Hindu Maṇḍalas; Mantra; Mudrā.

BIBLIOGRAPHY

Avalon, Arthur (John Woodroffe). *Introduction to Tantra Sāstra.* 6th ed. Chennai, India, 1973.

Avalon, Arthur (John Woodroffe). *Shakti and Shakta.* 8th ed. Chennai, India, 1975.

Bharati, Agehananda. *The Tantric Tradition.* London, 1965.

Bhattacharya, Benyotosh. *The World of Tantra.* New Delhi, 1988.

Brooks, Douglas Renfrew. *The Secret of the Three Cities: An Introduction to Hindu Śākta Tantrism.* Chicago, 1990.

Dasgupta, S. *Obscure Religious Cults.* 3d ed. Calcutta, 1969.

Dimock, Edwin C. *The Place of the Hidden Moon: Erotic Mysticism in the Vaisnava-Sahajiya Cult of Bengal.* Chicago, 1966.

Eliade, Mircea. *The Sacred and Profane: The Nature of Religion.* New York, 1959.

Eliade, Mircea. *Yoga: Immortality and Freedom.* Princeton, N.J., 1970.

Embree, Ainslie T., ed. *Sources of Indian Tradition,* vol. 1. New York, 1988.

Feuerstein, Georg. *Tantra: The Path of Ecstasy.* Boston, 1998.

Guenther, Herbert. *The Tantric View of Life.* Berkeley, 1972.

Gupta, Sanjukta, Jan Dirk Hoens, and Teun Goudriaan. *Hindu Tantrism.* Leiden, 1979.

Lorenzen, David N. *The Kapalikas and Kalamukhas.* New Delhi, 1972.

Muller-Ortega, Paul Eduardo. *The Triadic Heart of Śiva: Kaula Tantricism of Abhinavagupta in the Non-Dual Shaivism of Kashmir.* Albany, N.Y., 1989.

Padoux, Andre. "Tantrism: An Overview." In *The Encyclopedia of Religion,* edited by Mircea Eliade, vol. 13, pp. 272–274. New York, 1987.

Rajneesh, Bhagwan Shree. *Tantra: The Supreme Understanding.* Poona, India, 1974.

Urban, Hugh. *Tantra: Sex, Secrecy, Politics, and Power in the Study of Religion.* Berkeley, 2003.

White, David Gordon. *The Alchemical Body: Siddha Traditions in Medieval India.* Chicago, 1996.

White, David Gordon. *Kiss of the Yogini: "Tantric Sex" in its South Asian Contexts.* Chicago, 2003.

White, David Gordon, ed. *Tantra in Practice.* Princeton, 2000.

BRIAN K. SMITH (2005)

TANYAO (mid-fifth century CE), Chinese Buddhist monk and central figure in the revival of Buddhism after its suppression by the Northern Wei dynasty (385–534). Little is known about the early life of Tanyao except that he was eminent monk in the non-Chinese Bei Liang kingdom (397–439, in what is now Gansu province) before it was conquered by another non-Chinese kingdom, the Northern Wei.

As was the case in many of the northern dynasties, Buddhism was popular among the rulers of the Northern Wei. Thus when Tanyao arrived in the Northern Wei capital of Pingzheng (modern Datong), he found allies among the many Buddhists at the imperial court, the most prominent of whom was Crown Prince Huang. But Huang's father, the reigning emperor Taiwudi, came under the influence of an anti-Buddhist clique led by the Daoist adept Kou Qianzhi and the Daoist literatus Cui Hao, both openly hostile toward Buddhism. In 446 the emperor instituted a series of repressive measures against Buddhism, culminating in the issuance of an edict for its wholesale proscription.

The guiding hand behind the edict, which among other things ordered the execution of every monk in the realm, was Cui Hao, who effected it by taking advantage of the emperor's fury upon discovering a cache of weapons in a monastery in the city of Chang'an, a fact that the emperor took to be evidence of Buddhist complicity in a rebellion he had only recently suppressed. Other officials at court, including Kou Qianzhi, presented memorials urging the amelioration of the harshest points of the edict, thus delaying its actual promulgation and allowing monks time to flee or return to lay life, Tanyao resisted giving up the robe until the concerned crown prince convinced him of the prudence of this action, but he nevertheless maintained the sacerdotal paraphernalia in secret.

Kou Qianzhi died in 448, and in 450 Cui Hao was executed along with his entire clan for including unsavory aspects from the lives of the emperor's ancestors in the official history of the dynasty that he had been commissioned to write. With the passing of this duo, anti-Buddhist strictures began to relax. But full restoration occurred only after the assassination, by a eunuch, of Taiwudi in 454 and the accession of his grandson, Wenchengdi.

Buddhism had been subject to state control since the beginning of the dynasty, when Emperor Taizu granted the Chinese monk Faguo the official title of *daoren tong* (director of monks). In that capacity Faguo set a precedent in Chinese Buddhist history by identifying the emperor with the Tathāgata and requiring monks to bow down to him, an act in clear violation of monastic precedent. The *daoren tong,* which was abolished with the proscription of Buddhism, was revived with the restoration under a new name—the *jianfu cao* (office to oversee merits), a name later changed to *zhaoxuan si* (office to illumine the mysteries)—and presided over by a Kashmiri called Shixian. The new office was the center of a network, more finely woven than ever before, of governmental control over religious affairs.

Tanyao was Shixian's successor and held the post, now called the *shamen tong* (office of the *śramaṇa* superintendant), for more than twenty years. It was he who took advantage of the augmented interpenetration of government and religion to expand and glorify the Buddhist church.

One of his first important accomplishments was to persuade the new emperor, who was anxious to reverse the karmic effects of his grandfather's crimes, to undertake the costly project of chiseling into the walls of the Yungang caves (a few miles west of the capital) massive images of Buddhas and *bodhisattvas*, works still considered some of the greatest achievements of Chinese Buddhist art. The first group of caves (nos. 16–20 on modern charts) contains five Buddhas, one seventy feet tall, representing the first two emperors of the dynasty; the then-reigning emperor Wenchengdi; his father, Crown Prince Huang (who never reigned); and the infamous Taiwudi. The association of the imperial family with Buddhism could not have been represented in more intimate terms.

Another step taken by Tanyao to expand the influence of Buddhism was the establishment of Saṃgha Households (*sengji hu*) and Buddha Households (*fotu hu*). A Saṃgha Household was a voluntary association of a certain number of families responsible for paying sixty bushels of grain to the local branch of the *shamen tong.* That office then stored the grain for distribution to the poor in times of famine. Those Saṃgha Households faithfully fulfilling their responsibility were exempted from taxation.

Buddha Households consisted of a group chosen from among criminals or slaves who as bondsmen of the monastery had the responsibility of cultivating its fields and maintaining its buildings and grounds. With numerous monasteries under construction under Tanyao's leadership, amnesty after amnesty was granted to provide them with Buddha Households.

The Saṃgha Households and the Buddha Households were important for other reasons as well. On the one hand, they served the state by opening up new lands for cultivation during the years when war-induced underpopulation left so much land uncultivated that there were frequent famines. They also lightened the government's burden of supporting prisoners. On the other hand, they provided the church with a source of revenue and a pool of potential converts.

In addition to his many administrative accomplishments, Tanyao also translated scripture. His translations of the *Saṃyuktaratnapiṭaka Sūtra* (*Za baocang jing*), completed with the assistance of Indian monks in 462, and the compilation *Fu facang yinyuan zhuan,* both containing many stories in the Jātaka and Avadāna genres, provided edifying themes for sculptors working in the Yungang caves.

SEE ALSO Kou Qianzhi.

BIBLIOGRAPHY

For the traditional account of Tanyao's life, see his biography in Daoxuan's *Xu gaoseng zhuan* (T.D. 50.427c–428a). Tsukamoto Zenryū's authoritative study of the Northern Wei period, *Shina Bukkyōshi kenkyū: Hokugi hen* (Tokyo, 1942), includes a wealth of valuable material on Tanyao and his intellectual and political milieu. The chapter on Tanyao has been translated by Galen E. Sargent as "The Śramaṇa Superintendent T'an-yao and His Time," *Monumenta Serica* 16 (1957): 363–396. See also Leon Hurvitz's *Wei Shou on Buddhism and Taoism* (Kyoto, 1956), a translation of the *Shilao zhi,* and Tsukamoto Zenryū's *Daisekibutsu* (Tokyo, 1953).

New Sources

Huntington, John C. "The Iconography and Iconology of the 'Tan Yao' Caves at Yungang." In *Oriental Art* (1986): 142–159.

Tsukamoto Zenryū. *A History of Early Chinese Buddhism: From Its Introduction to the Death of Huiyuan.* Translated by Leon Hurvitz. Tokyo, 1985.

MIYAKAWA HISAYUKI (1987)
Revised Bibliography

T'AN-YAO SEE TANYAO

TAO-AN SEE DAO'AN

TAO AND RE SEE DAO AND DE

TAO-CH'O See DAOCHUO

TAO HONGJING

TAO HONGJING (456–536 CE), a polymath scholar of Daoism, was largely responsible for establishing the textual corpus of the Maoshan or Shangqing (Highest Clarity) lineage, of which he is recognized as the tenth patriarch. Tao's contributions to the study of pharmacology and alchemy in China are also of singular importance, and during his own lifetime he was recognized for his authoritative knowledge of calligraphy and astrological calculations. Born near the southern imperial capital of Jiankang (modern-day Nanjing), Tao was the scion of a leading family of gentry officials with a long history of service to the southern courts since the fall of the Han dynasty (206 BCE–220 CE).

The Tao family had marital links to some of the most important Daoist figures in Southern China, including the great scholar Ge Hong (283–343 CE), but Hongjing's mother and grandfather were both Buddhists. Despite these religious affiliations, Tao's early training was Confucian. He completed several commentaries on Confucian classics at an early age, and his dedication to scholarship soon earned him a reputation at court. By his early twenties he had achieved modest success in official service, being appointed "reader in attendance" to imperial princes. His intellectual and scholastic accomplishments garnered him much respect and allowed him to move freely in the élite social circles and literary salons of Jiankang.

During the period of mourning for his mother between 484 and 486, Tao began his formal initiation into Daoism. He became a disciple of Sun Youyue (398–489 CE), abbot of the Xingshi Temple in Jiankang. Sun had, in turn, been a disciple of Lu Xiujing (406–477 CE), the main systematizer of the Lingbao ritual liturgy. Sun possessed textual artifacts of the Maoshan revelations passed on by Lu, and he allowed Tao to view them. These texts had been produced between 364 and 370 CE by a visionary named Yang Xi (330–c. 386) living in the area of Maoshan (Mount Mao), southwest of the imperial capital. Yang claimed that he had received the texts from a number of "perfected immortals" (*zhenren*), residents of the Heaven of Highest Clarity (*Shangqing tian*). The message of the perfected was a synthesis of Celestial Master's Daoism, and elements of the southern occult traditions, such as represented in the work of Ge Hong. Alchemy and apotropaic ritual is much in evidence, but the texts pointed towards the future of Daoism with their tendency toward techniques of internal cultivation, such as visualization meditation.

The style and content of the Maoshan manuscripts, as well as their calligraphy, made a deep impression on Tao, and he began searching for more examples, making a trip in 490 to the eastern regions (present-day Zhejiang) for that purpose. Two years later, in 492, he renounced secular life altogether and retired to live at Maoshan. With the help of imperial sponsorship, Tao built a hermitage there, which he named the Huayang Observatory (*Huayang guan*). He assembled some disciples, and began the work of reconstructing the Shangqing scriptural corpus.

Tao's first major project was the compilation of the *Dengzhen yinjue* (Secret formulae for ascending to perfection). Most of this work is now lost, but originally it was a large collection of technical material derived from Yang Xi's revelations. It was intended for Tao's disciples, for whom he added copious annotations. The two works for which Tao Hongjing is best know seem both to have been completed in the same year, 499. The *Zhengao* (Declarations of the perfected), is a compendium of the Maoshan revelations themselves. It includes correspondence between Yang Xi and his patrons, and records of conversations between Yang and his perfected guests, as well as information on the secret geography of the Maoshan area. The *Zhengao* also contains many poems, ostensibly composed by the perfected. The ecstatic style of these poems was to be influential, particularly during the later Tang dynasty (618–907 CE).

Continuing a tradition passed down from his father and grandfather, Tao also compiled his *Bencao jing jizhu* (Collected notes on the classic of pharmacopoeia). This was an expanded and annotated version of the oldest work of Chinese pharmacopoeia, *Shennong bencao jing* (Shen Nong's classic of pharmacopoeia). Tao doubled the number of entries in the earlier classic and also reorganized the material according to more rational criteria. Although this work comes down to us only in fragmentary form, it had an enormous impact on traditional Chinese medicine because it brought order and reason to a tradition in disarray. It also facilitated the systematic incorporation of *materia medica* into Chinese medical practice.

In 502 a new dynasty, the Liang, replaced the previous Qi dynasty (479–502 CE). Fortunately, Tao Hongjing enjoyed a close personal relationship with Wudi (464–549 CE), the first Liang emperor. This ensured continued imperial support for Tao's work, even when Wudi, a fervent Buddhist, proscribed Daoism in 504. It was in the same year, 504, that Wudi commissioned Tao to undertake alchemical experiments on his behalf. Tao expended a great amount of time and energy in his attempts to produce elixirs according to recipes described in the Shangqing scriptures. Tao's careful notes on his research are the earliest extant records of alchemical experimentation in China. His work also strengthened the relationship of alchemy to Daoism.

During the latter part of his life, Tao Hongjing remained based at Maoshan, but made an extended trip to the southeast, to the area of modern Fujian province. He continued his alchemical experiments on the trip, but it may be that he was also motivated by anticipation of a messianic apocalypse, such as predicted in certain Shangqing texts. While on that excursion, Tao made the acquaintance of Zhou Ziliang, a young man who became his disciple. Zhou was a visionary after the model of Yang Xi, and played host to some of the same perfected beings. In 515, at the age of only twenty,

Zhou committed ritual suicide in response to a divine summons received in the course of his visions. Tao submitted a textual record of Zhou's activities and visions, entitled *Zhoushi mingtongji* (The record of Master Zhou's communication with the unseen world), to the imperial court in 517.

Tao Hongjing's involvement with Buddhism is often overlooked. Tao had early exposure to the religion via his mother and grandfather. Throughout his lifetime he continued to befriend Buddhist priests, and was actively involved in debates over Buddhism's nature and significance. It is claimed that the founder of Chinese Pure Land Buddhism, Tanluan (476–542 CE), studied Daoist arts and herbalism with Tao. In 513 Tao formally took Buddhist vows and when he died, about a month before his eightieth birthday in 536 his disciples followed his instructions and arranged for an equal number of Daoist and Buddhist priests to attend his funeral.

Tao Hongjing's legacy is multifaceted. His work on pharmacopoeia and medicine was of great consequence for the later development of Chinese medical practice. His alchemical studies were also highly influential, due especially to the methodical and empirical spirit that he brought to them. In terms of the history of Chinese religions however, the institutional and textual foundation that he laid for the Maoshan or Shangqing school had the greatest lasting impact. The semimonastic community that he established at Maoshan was to provide the base upon which the success of the Shangqing school was built during the succeeding Tang dynasty, a time during which Daoism was favored with its greatest popularity among the Chinese elite.

SEE ALSO Alchemy, article on Chinese Alchemy; Daoism, overview article and articles on Daoist Literature and The Daoist Religious Community.

BIBLIOGRAPHY

Mugitani Kunio. "Tō Kōkei nempo kōryaku." *Tōhō shukyō* 47 (1976): 30–61; 48 (1976): 56–83. An excellent source for biographical information on Tao Hongjing. Relates Tao's life to other political and cultural events of the day.

Needham, Joseph, and Lu Gwei-Djen. "Spagyrical Discovery and Invention: Physiological Alchemy." In *Science and Civilization in China*, vol. 5: *Chemistry and Chemical Technology*, pt. 5, pp. 210–220. Cambridge, U.K., 1983. Section *h*, discusses historical aspects of Tao Hongjing's involvement with alchemy.

Needham, Joseph, et al. "Pandects of Natural History (*Pen Tsao*)." In *Science and Civilization in China*, vol. 6: *Biology and Botanical Technology*, sect. 38, pp. 220–263. Cambridge, U.K., 1986. Discusses early Chinese pharmacopoeia and Tao's contributions to it.

Robinet, Isabelle. *La révélation du Shangqing dans l'histoire du taoïsme.* 2 vols. Paris, 1984. A detailed study of the Maoshan revelations and the Shangqing textual corpus. Volume 2 contains an extensive annotated listing of Shangqing texts and their content.

Robinet, Isabelle. *Taoist Meditation: The Mao-shan Tradition of Great Purity.* Translated by Norman Girardot and Julian Pas. Albany, N.Y., 1993. Excellent general study of Shangqing meditation.

Strickmann, Michel. "The Mao Shan Revelations: Taoism and the Aristocracy." *T'oung-pao* 63 (1977): 1–64. Discussion of the social and historical context of the Maoshan revelations. Contains a translation of Tao's account of the dispersion of the Shangqing manuscripts.

Strickmann, Michel. "On the Alchemy of T'ao Hung-ching." In *Facets of Taoism: Essays in Chinese Religion*, edited by Holmes Welch and Anna Seidel, pp. 123–192. New Haven, Conn., and London, 1981. Still the best English-language source for Tao Hongjing's life and religious activities. Special focus on Tao's alchemical practice and its significance.

Strickmann, Michel. *Le Taoïsme du Mao Chan: Chronique d'une révélation.* Paris, 1981. Strickmann's book-length discussion of the Maoshan revelations and the Shangqing textual legacy. The annotated reconstruction of the Shangqing textual corpus is less extensive than Robinet's, but is still very useful.

T. C. RUSSELL (2005)

T'AO HUNG-CHING SEE TAO HONGJING

TAO-SHENG SEE DAOSHENG

TAPAS. The Sanskrit term *tapas,* from *tap* ("heat"), was in ancient India an expression of cosmic energy residing in heat, fervor, and ardor. Through anthropocosmic correspondences established in early Vedic sacrificial traditions *tapas* became one of the key concepts of South Asian religions and the accepted term in Sanskrit and other Indic languages for ascetic power, especially a severely disciplined self-mortification that produces both personal and cosmic results.

A wide range of religious expressions concerning *tapas* appears already in the *Ṛgveda.* The gods Agni, the sacrificial fire, and Sūrya, the sun, both possess heat inherently, whereas *tapas* is generated within the warrior deity Indra and his weapons as a concomitant of heroic fury in battle. Indra's heated rage may be connected to certain proto-Indo-European warrior-cult phenomena; Ṛgvedic references to ascetics who handle fire, as well as other references to sweating as an initiatory technique, may be connected with pre-Vedic ecstatic or shamanic experiences. *Tapas* can be a weapon itself, used by Indra, for example, to encircle Vṛtra, or employed, perhaps ritually, by enemies of priests who pray to Indra and Varuṇa for protection (*Ṛgveda* 10.167, 7.82). In Hymn 9.113 the ritual production of divine *soma* is accomplished by *tapas,* faith, order, and truth. But perhaps the most influential Ṛgvedic speculations on *tapas* occur in such late cosmogonic hymns as 10.129 and 10.190, where *tapas,* existing prior to both divine and human beings, is linked in the procreative process with primordial desire (*kāma*), mind, order, and truth, a cosmic association that served as a template for late Vedic soteriologies as well as post-Vedic popular mythologies. Finally, the *Ṛgveda* reveals that the ancient sages and godlike ancestors also embody this cosmic fervor, the *ṛṣis* sitting to perform *tapas* (10.109), and the *pitṛs* ("ancestors") attaining their invincible places in the heavens by means of *tapas* (10.154).

It is in the *Yajurveda* recensions, the *Atharvaveda,* and the several Brāhmaṇas that *tapas* receives full recognition: the human body becomes a metaphor of sacrificial fire and *tapas* is simultaneously the means to and the experience of transformation. The Vedic student (*brahmacārin*), according to *Atharvaveda* 11.5, generates such powerful *tapas* that it fills his teacher, the gods, and the three worlds. *Tapas* is primal energy ready to be drawn upon by the knowledgeable, the adept, and the aggressively self-disciplined. Prajāpati, lord of creatures, continues, in the Brāhmaṇas, the older impersonal cosmogony involving *tapas* and blends with it the personal one of self-sacrificing Puruṣa (*Ṛgveda* 10.90): overcome with desire (*kāma*), Prajāpati discharges in heated procreation, exhausting himself into the substance of the universe by repeated emission. That this striving to create by self-heating provided a ritual model is clear from the many correspondences defining the Vedic sacrificer, who maintains the created worlds by laborious ritual (*karman*); he is simultaneously identified with the sacrificial fire, Agni, and Puruṣa-Prajāpati, as he undergoes spiritual regeneration. The way is now clear for ascetic technique to replicate, and in some ways to replace, sacrificial technique. Both are performances on an exhaustive, even painful scale: procreative on a sexual model, yet requiring chastity; bearing personal cosmic fruits, results that can be stored; and burning away, by inner heat, those impurities that are hindrances to transcendent, immutable being. *Śatapatha Brāhmaṇa* 10.4.4 is an illustration of the Brahmanic bond between cosmogony through sacrifice, and transcendence (rebirth) through ascetic perseverance, all declared in Prajāpati's thousand-year *tapas.*

The Upaniṣads further explore these mysterious connections in the heat of sexuality, hatching, ripening, digestion, strife, grief, rage, ecstasy, and mystical vision. The way is opened for a normative *tapas* practiced by every religious seeker in the third stage (*āśrama*) of life, and thus a modification or lay version of the extreme *tapas* professed by the ascetic bent upon world- and self-conquest. In the texts of the Jains and Buddhists, in various traditions of yoga and Tantra, and in popular myths and folklore collected in the Sanskrit epics and Purāṇas, a profile emerges of ascetic *tapas.* By degrees of fasting, chastity, silence, meditation, breath-control, and difficult postures, usually practiced in solitary vigil in forests and mountains, the yogin or *tapasvin* "heats the three worlds." His techniques include a "five-fires" position (sitting naked between four fires beneath the midsummer sun), immersing himself in a river in midwinter, and remaining unsheltered in monsoon rains.

The ascetic, like the sacrificer, demonstrates his interior fire as a cosmic force capable of recreating, reordering, or dismissing the world. So powerful is this religious model that much of the dramatic tension of post-Vedic mythology is provided by world-threatening *tapas* produced from ascetic ardor. Gods, goddesses, demons, kings, heroes, married sages, celibate yogins, young children, even animals perform *tapas.* The god Brahmā produces by *tapas*; Śiva's *tapas* and magical fire alternately create and destroy; Pārvatī maintains *tapas* for 36,000 years; a host of demons (*asuras* and *daityas*) concentrate on world domination by *tapas*; the Pāṇḍava heroes exercise *tapas* in forest exile. *Tapas* and *kāma* cooperate in keeping the created world together; erotic desire poses the strongest threat to ascetic world-transcendence, and therefore repression and lust together with self-control and self-abandon provide antiphonal parallels to the ancient Indra-Vṛtra cosmic opposition, a cooperative discord that threads the drama of creation and recreation.

Whereas Hinduism routinized *tapas* into ordinary observance of fasts, meditations, and yogalike practices, and Buddhism elected a middle path between austerity and indulgence, Jainism perfected *tapas* in both lay and monastic careers as a means of burning off old *karman* and blocking accretions of new *karman.* In Jainism and in some traditions of Tantric yoga *tapas* survives today as disciplined self-mortification and as an internal experience of transformation.

SEE ALSO Agni; Indra.

BIBLIOGRAPHY

The best contextual discussion of *tapas* in Brahmanic initiation, sacrifice, cosmogony, and eschatology is by Mircea Eliade in *A History of Religious Ideas,* vol. 1 (Chicago, 1978), esp. pp. 220–238. See also his *Yoga: Immortality and Freedom,* 2d ed. (Princeton, 1969), pp. 106–114, 330–341. Chauncey J. Blair's *Heat in the Rig Veda and the Atharva Veda* (New Haven, 1961) has analyzed the root *tap,* its derivatives, and other words concerning "heat" in two Vedic texts. I discuss the religious significance of *tapas* as fire and heat in the Vedic tradition in my book *In the Image of Fire: Vedic Experiences of Heat* (Delhi, 1975), esp. chaps. 4–5. In *Asceticism and Eroticism in the Mythology of Śiva* (London, 1973) Wendy Doniger O'Flaherty provides penetrating analyses of some forty-five motifs, primarily in the Purāṇas, on creative and destructive *tapas* and so forth; see motifs 8, 10, 18, 25, 36, 39, 45. On *tapas* in Jain monastic traditions, see Padmanabh S. Jaini's *The Jaina Path of Purification* (Berkeley, 1979), esp. pp. 250–251; for lay traditions, see R. H. B. Williams's *Jaina Yoga: A Survey of the Mediaeval Śrāvakācāras* (London, 1963), pp. 238–239.

New Sources

Bronkhorst, Johannes. *The Two Sources of Indian Asceticism.* Bern, 1993.

Kaelber, Walter O. *Tapta-Marga: Asceticism and Initiation in Vedic India.* Albany, N.Y., 1989.

Keemattam, Augusthy. *The Hermits of Rishikesh: A Sociological Study.* New Delhi, 1997.

Yadavaprakasa. *Rules and Regulations of Brahmanical Asceticism: Yatidharmasamuccaya of Yadava Prakasa.* Albany, N.Y., 1995.

DAVID M. KNIPE (1987)
Revised Bibliography

TAPU SEE POLYNESIAN RELIGIONS; TABOO

TAQĪYAH

TAQĪYAH ("safeguarding, protection") and *kitmān* ("concealment") are terms applied, primarily in the Shīʿī branches of Islam, to two broader types of religious phenomena: (1) the "prudential concealment" of one's allegiance to a minority religious group in danger of persecution and (2) the esoteric "discipline of the arcane," the restriction of a spiritual reality or mystery (or its symbolic form) only to those inwardly capable of grasping its truth.

JURIDICAL AND ETHICAL DIMENSIONS. The classical discussions found in all Islamic legal schools are based on various Qurʾanic verses (16:106, 3:28, 40:28, etc.) permitting the neglect of certain religious duties in situations of compulsion or necessity. In each school an elaborate casuistry was developed, detailing the special conditions for such exceptions. However, the crucial practical question for Shīʿī groups, given the endangered minority position of the Shīʿī imams and their followers from earliest Islamic times onward, was that of concealing the outward signs of their Shīʿī allegiance (for example, their distinctive forms of the ritual prayer and profession of faith) under threatening circumstances. Hence, Shīʿī legal discussions of *taqīyah* traditionally focused on this aspect, emphasizing, for example, surah 16:106, which was taken to describe the divine forgiveness of a companion of the Prophet, ʿAmmār ibn Yasīr, who had been forced to deny his faith by the idolators of Mecca.

Sunnī polemics against Shiism have traditionally stressed this narrowly prudential aspect of *taqīyah,* portraying it as a sign of moral or religious hypocrisy, passivity, and the like. However, neither that polemic (which overlooks the central theme of martyrdom and heroic resistance in Shīʿī piety and sacred history) nor the narrowly ethical reasonings of the legal schools (including those of the Shīʿah) accurately conveys the distinctively positive symbolic function of *taqīyah:* for the Shīʿah themselves, and like the martyrdom of so many imams and their supporters, it is a perennial and fundamental form of "witnessing" their essential role as the faithful spiritual elite of Islam, and not simply another communal sect or school.

SPIRITUAL AND ESOTERIC DIMENSIONS. This uniquely Shīʿī conception of *taqīyah* (or *kitmān*) as a high spiritual duty, rather than a pragmatic necessity, is grounded in a large body of reported sayings *(ḥadīth)* of the first Shīʿī imam, ʿAlī ibn Abī Ṭālib (d. AH 40/661 CE), and other early imams (notably Muḥammad al-Bāqir and Jaʿfar al-Ṣādiq) which repeatedly stress the positive, essential role of *taqīyah* as an integral part of religion *(dīn)* and true piety (*taqwā;* see Qurʾan 49:13). In Shīʿī tradition, the concept of *taqīyah* is intimately bound up with the fundamental role of the imams, and their initiates, as the divinely instituted guardians of the esoteric wisdom or "hidden secret" *(sirr maknūn)* constituting the essential spiritual core and intention of the Qurʾanic revelation. In this context, *taqīyah* refers primarily to the initiate's strict responsibility to divulge the forms of that spiritual knowledge only to those rare individuals capable of perceiving (and safeguarding) their inner truth.

Similar assumptions of esotericism—especially the basic distinction between a public level of formal "belief" and ritual practice, and a higher level of contemplative insight and perception accessible only to a spiritual or intellectual elite—were equally fundamental to such widespread (though by no means specifically Shīʿī) Islamic spiritual traditions as Sufism and the philosophic schools. Those assumptions, along with corresponding practices, came to be pervasive not only in the high literate culture (for example, Ṣūfī mystical poetry) but also in social domains not involving strictly "religious" activities. Moreover, the social and political conditions underlying *taqīyah* in Shīʿī circles, and such later offshoots as the Druze or Nuṣayrīyah, likewise encouraged similar precautionary developments among other minority religious groups or sects, whether Islamic (certain Ṣūfī *ṭarīqahs*, religio-political "brotherhoods," and so forth) or non-Islamic. Hence, "*taqīyah*-like" phenomena—whether or not justified in specifically Shīʿī terms—have continued to form an essential, if still relatively unstudied, dimension of religious and social life in many regions of the Islamic world down to the present day.

BIBLIOGRAPHY

For the classical Islamic legal sources, see R. Strothmann's "Taḳīya," in *The Shorter Encyclopedia of Islam* (Leiden, 1961), which includes non-Shīʿī treatments; Hamid Enayat's *Modern Islamic Political Thought* (Austin, 1982), which touches on contemporary Shīʿī political reinterpretations; and especially Etan Kohlberg's "Some Imāmī-Shīʿa Views on *Taqiyya,*" *Journal of the American Oriental Society* 95 (1975): 395–402, with extensive bibliographic references. Henry Corbin's *En Islam iranien,* 4 vols. (Paris, 1971–1972; English translation in preparation), contains numerous translated canonical sayings of the Shīʿī imams concerning *taqīyah* and its esoteric underpinnings, as well as later developments; see index under *ketmān* and *taqīyeh.* For illustrations from later Shīʿī thought and references to parallel phenomena in other Islamic traditions such as philosophy and Sufism, see my work *The Wisdom of the Throne* (Princeton, 1981). References to the actual social manifestations of *taqīyah* at any period are usually fragmentary (given the very nature of the phenomenon) and must be gleaned from autobiographies, travelers' reports, and so on. Excellent illustrations for nineteenth-century Iran may be found in Comte de Gobineau's *Les religions et les philosophies dans l'Asie centrale,* 2d ed. (1863; reprint, Paris, 1971), and Edward Granville Browne's *A Year amongst the Persians* (1893; reprint, Cambridge, 1959). For representative developments in the Indian context, see Azim Nanji's *The Nizārī Ismāʿīlī Tradition in the Indo-Pakistan Subcontinent* (Delmar, N. Y., 1978).

JAMES WINSTON MORRIS (1987)

TĀRĀ (Tib., Sgrol ma) is a Buddhist deity who represents the female counterpart of the *bodhisattva* Avalokiteśvara. She appears as the savior of the world whenever people are in distress and thus is known in Tibet, where she has gained great popularity, as the Great Savioress. By the time Mahāyāna and Vajrayāna Buddhism were firmly established in Tibet, Tārā had become one of the most important female deities, one whose influence was reflected back as the very source of the Tibetan people. One tradition has it that Avalokiteśvara and Tārā, in the semblance of a monkey and a rock demoness, had monkey offspring who gradually became humans, thus accounting for the origin of the Tibetans. As the *śakti* of the Buddha Amogasiddhi, Tārā also personifies "all-accomplishing wisdom."

Tārā is said to represent the very essence of loving devotion, extending her loving care to the bad as well as the good. She always accompanies the faithful in their religious practices; hence, it is customary in monastic communities to meditate on the *maṇḍala* of Tārā (Sgrol ma Dkyil 'khor). However, it is difficult to determine whether, during the early spread of Buddhism, the influence of Tārā extended beyond the court or scholarly circles.

It is the opinion of some scholars that the cult of Tārā was brought to Tibet by Atīśa (982–1054). As evidence of this, they point to the tradition that holds that Atīśa's trip to Tibet and his meeting with 'Brom ston pa were predicted by a *yoginī* whom Atīśa met under the tutelage of Tārā, and to Tārā's alleged appearance before Atīśa at Mnga' ris, where he met 'Brom ston. However, tradition has it that when Srong bstan sgam po (d. 649) received the Nepalese princess Bhrikutī and the Chinese princess Wencheng as his brides, they brought Buddhist images and other objects with them. In later times, these two princesses were believed to have been incarnations of the green, or prosperous, and white, or helpful, Tārā. If this latter tradition is accepted then the introduction of Tārā into Tibet predates the arrival of Atīśa. However, it can scarcely be doubted that it was Atīśa who gave new emphasis to the cult of Tārā, to whom he was especially devoted.

It is difficult to determine exactly when and how the cult of Tārā emerged. Tārā shares many mythic parallels with Brahmanic deities. For example, Durgā and Tārā hold several names in common. Thus, although some scholars claim the priority of one over the other, it seems impossible to determine whether the cult of Tārā has a Brahmanical origin or a Buddhist origin. The early sculptural representations of Tārā seem to point to a sixth-century beginning for the image of the Buddhist Tārā. These early images, found in caves such as Ellora, Aurangabad, and others, depict a placid form in contrast to the fierce representation of her corresponding Hindu goddess. Later, however, Tārā in her Mahāmāyāvijayavāhinī, or fierce, aspect is conceived as a war goddess in the manner similar to that of the Hindu Devī. The iconic representations seem to indicate that Tārā in her early and simple form is seated and possesses two arms and two hands. As time passes, her iconic representations became more complex: not only is there an increase in the numbers of heads, arms, and hands, but the number of accessory figures attending her gradually increases. Another feature of her iconic representation is her appearance with four—Amogasiddhi, Ratnasambhava, Amitābha, and Akṣobhya—of the Five Buddhas (the fifth being Vairocana). In these representations, Tārā usually, but not always, appears in colors corresponding to the colors of these Buddhas. The complexity of her iconic representation can be appreciated through a careful study of the *Sādhanamālā,* the *Niṣpannayogāvalī,* and other texts.

Tārā is said to manifest herself in five forms for the benefit of her worshipers. She takes on the five forms of the protective goddesses—Mahāpratisarā, Mahāmāyūrī, Mahāsāhasrapramardanī, Mahāsītavatī, and Mahāmantrānusārini—in order to protect beings from all sorts of earthy troubles and miseries. Her protective power is categorized as defense against the "eight great terrors" *(aṣṭamahābhaya),* poetically expressed in verse by Candragomin. In time, the "eight great terrors," the perils of elephants, lions, fire, serpents, robbers, fetters, sea monsters, and vampires, were each assigned their own Tārā, and the depiction of eight Tārās became a popular subject for artists.

Tārā has been propitiated and invoked in various ways, for various reasons, by various people. Many of her devotees hope for relief from a variety of worldly ills. For example, Candragomin, feeling sorry for a beggar woman who had no means to arrange for her daughter's marriage, is said to have prayed with tears in his eyes to a picture of Tārā. The image thereupon became a real Tārā who took off her ornaments made of various jewels and gave them to Candragomin, who in turn gave them to the beggar woman. Asvabhāva composed a long eulogy to Bhaṭṭārikā Ārya Tārā when his disciples were bitten by a poisonous snake, whereby the snake encountered great pain. He then sprinkled water charmed with a Tārā mantra on his disciples and the poison came out of their wounds.

The cult of Tārā that was reintroduced to Tibet during the second diffusion of Buddhism did not become the exclusive property of any one sect. Indeed, in the course of time the cult of Tārā found its way into most of the countries where Mahāyāna Buddhism spread.

SEE ALSO Avalokiteśvara; Buddhism, article on Buddhism in Tibet.

BIBLIOGRAPHY

Beyer, Stephan, *The Cult of Tārā: Magic and Ritual in Tibet.* Berkeley, 1973. An extremely comprehensive study on the cult of Tārā that gives both textual and practical examples of Tārā worship and the way in which the divine power of Tārā can be acquired.

Blonay, Godefroy de. *Matériaux pour Servir à l'Histoire de la Déesse Buddhique Tārā.* Paris, 1895.

Chandra, Lokesh. *Hymns to Tārā.* New Delhi, 1967.

Chattopadhyaya, Debiprasad, ed. *Tāranātha's History of Buddhism in India.* Translated from Tibetan by Lama Chimpa and Alaka Chattopadhyaya. Simla, India, 1970. Events related to Tārā are discussed throughout this religious history of Buddhism in India.

Ghosh, Mallar. *Development of Buddhist Iconography in Eastern India: A Study of Tārā, Prajñas of Five Tathāgatas and Bhakti.* New Delhi, 1980.

Kumar, Pushpendra. *Tārā: The Supreme Goddess.* Delhi, 1992.

Mullin, Glenn H., ed. *Meditations upon Arya Tārā.* By the First, Fifth and Seventh Dalai Lamas. Dharamsala, 1978.

Mullin, Glenn H., ed. *Six Texts Related to the Tārā Tantra.* By the First Dalai Lama. New Delhi, 1980.

Rinpoche, Zopa. *Tārā: The Liberator.* Boston, 1993.

Rituals for the Practice of the Sarvadurgatipariśodhana, Avalokiteśvarasadhana, Tarasadhana, and Usnisavijaya Teachings. By various Masters of the Phan-po Nalendra tradition. New Delhi, 1978.

Sastri, Hiranand. *The Origin and Cult of Tārā.* New Delhi, 1977.

Sircar, Dines Chandra, ed. *The Śakti Cult and Tārā.* Calcutta, 1967. Proceedings of lectures and seminars organized by the U.G.C. Centre of Advanced Study in the Department of Ancient Indian History and Culture, University of Calcutta. Contains twelve papers on Śakti and six papers on Tārā. A useful guide to the various problems related to a study of Tārā.

Taranatha, Jo-nan-pa. *History of the Tārā Cult in Tantric Buddhism.* Translated and edited by David Templeman. Dharamsala, 1981.

Taranatha, Jo-nan-pa. *The Origin of Tārā Tantra.* Translated and edited by David Templeman. Dharamsala, 1981.

Tromge, Jane. *Red Tārā Commentary: Instructions for the Concise Practice known as Red Tārā: An Open Door to Bliss and Ultimate Awareness.* Junction City, Calif., 1994.

Tulku, Chagdud, trans. *Red Tārā: An Open Door to Bliss and Ultimate Awareness.* Junction City, Calif., 1991.

Wayman, Alex. "The Twenty-One Praises of Tārā: A Syncretism of Caivism and Buddhism." *Journal of Bihar Research Society* 45, nos. 36–43 (1959).

Willson, Martin. *In Praise of Tārā: Songs to the Saviouress.* Boston, 1986.

Yeshe, Lama Thubten. *Cittamani Tārā: A Commentary on the Annuttarayoga-tantra Method of Cittamani Tārā.* Arnstorf, 1980.

Yeshe, Lama Thubten. *Cittamani Tārā: An Extended Sadhana.* Translated and edited by Martin Willson. Boston, 1993.

LESLIE S. KAWAMURA (1987 AND 2005)

TARASCAN RELIGION. The Tarascan Indians, speakers of a genetically unaffiliated language, created one of the major empires of pre-Conquest Mexico, rivaling and successfully repulsing the Aztec. Like the latter, they had a complex religious hierarchy, a priest-king, and a developed system of rites, myths, and religious legends. During and following the Spanish conquest in the sixteenth century, however, more than 90 percent of these people were destroyed in a holocaust of slaughter, disease, and slave labor. In the early twenty-first century about ninety thousand Indians (about two-thirds Tarascan speaking)—surrounded by non-Tarascans—live on in the high, cool, green Sierra Tarasca, where they subsist by various combinations of lumbering, arts and crafts, fishing, farming (mainly maize), and raising livestock. Immediate to moderately extended families are grouped into villages of several hundred to several thousand persons. Factional rivalries within the villages are exceeded by the nearly ubiquitous intervillage hostilities, and both, like the rivalries between families, are balanced by a strong ethic of familial and communal solidarity and the integrative function of religious ritual.

Tarascan history is still reflected in today's religious culture. Prehistoric ritual groups such as the "moon maidens" and mythical symbols such as deer masks and "the tigers" figure in the fiestas. But the main historic source of Tarascan religion is Spain of the sixteenth and seventeenth centuries—evident not only in "the Moors" and other ritual actors in Tarascan religious fiestas but also in the dogmatically simple focus on Saint Francis and the holy family brought to them by Franciscan missionaries, notably the great humanist Don Vasco de Quiroga. Tarascan religious practice, whatever its sources, is marked by aesthetic integration, perhaps above all in the music of its many bands, and the diagnostic Dance of the Little Old Men (hunched, red-masked figures who alternate between hobbling on canes and jigging with adolescent energy).

A major axis of Tarascan religion lies in individual rites of passage. Baptism, ideally, takes place a week after birth: A man and a woman, usually spouses, become the child's godparents and, more important, the ritual co-parents (Span., *compadre;* Tarascan, *kúmpa*) of the child's parents. At two or three subsequent rites, notably that of confirmation, the parents acquire additional but less valued *compadres* who, in particular, help with obligations in religious ritual. The major individual rite, the wedding, includes a ceremony in a Roman Catholic church and a great deal of folk religious ritual—conspicuously the climactic and widespread *kúpera* dance between the couple and their siblings and cousins, who successively dance up to each other, exchange drinks, and lightly scratch each others' faces with rose thorns. This wedding also invokes and creates ties of ritual kinship (kinship and religious ritual are largely thought of and acted out in terms of each other). Death is celebrated by a night-long wake, with much drinking, and a funeral procession through the entire village. (If the deceased was an infant or a child, the body is borne on a table.)

The main way the Tarascan relates to the supernatural, however (aside from individual sorcery and witchcraft), is through familial and communal ritual. Every town stages an annual fiesta for its patron saint; most towns organize four to six such affairs each year, each for a different saint; and at least one town, Ocumicho, puts on a fiesta every month—with a correspondingly great expenditure of time and energy. These fiestas are run by elected officials or *cargueros* (Span., "load bearers"), who, with the support of dozens or even scores of kin or ritual kin, may spend huge amounts of pesos on the bands, elaborate fireworks, alcohol, ceremonial dishes, Catholic masses, livestock for slaughter, and other elements of the fiesta. While these expenses are often said to be ruinous, the average person is quite ready to incur them, or at least resigned to them because of the social status they imply. Also, the debts can be a source of prestige that links the *carguero* into a larger human network. In some of the more conservative towns the offices of the different saints are ranked in terms of prestige, forming a sort of "ceremonial ladder," in which the *carguero* who sponsors the associated fiestas gradually ascends a series of metaphorical rungs. Although most *cargueros* are men, women do most of the work of organizing and preparation. Some annual fiestas—for example, to Our Virgin of the Assumption—are purely religious, but the great majority involve commercial and market functions (these functions constitute the primary emphasis of some festivals).

Religious ritual is diagnostically regional. Some fiestas are essentially local—for example, that of Saint Cecilia in tiny San José, where many of the men actually are musicians. But people are aware of fiestas and practices in their entire region as well, and a large number of fiestas are pan-Tarascan, either because they attract many pilgrims or because the day is celebrated in the several villages where a given saint is patron, as in the cases of the popular San José and San Francisco. All Saints and All Souls days are observed in all towns by quiet vigils with flowers and bread figures at the graves of the recently deceased. In Janitzio, on the other hand, a thousand candle-bearing canoes hover around the island during the night of November 1. An individual whose personal saint coincides with that of a village often makes a pilgrimage, or at least says a special prayer. (Prayer generally focuses on help with practical, personal problems such as illness or jealousy and envy, and so is inextricably intertwined with the culture's pervasive witchcraft and sorcery.)

A notable feature is the great variation in the religious autonomy of a village, which is reticulated closely with its political orientation and economic standing. At one extreme the annual and personal rituals (baptism, confirmation, marriage, and the wake) are managed by local societies and religious specialists (who, for example, may know an oration by heart). A priest may come to a village once a month (or even less often), or the person or persons concerned may go to the county seat for the priest's ministrations. Some villages categorically refuse to allow a priest to participate in such sacred matters as the construction of a new church or the organization of a passion play because they realistically fear financial loss. At the other extreme a local priest may be active and highly influential not only in religious ritual but also in local politics—to the extent of controlling the external relations of the village. The grass-roots role of the priest is so important because the Tarascan do not in general own or read the Bible or other religious literature (with the exception of a few thousand Protestants, limited to a few pueblos, who do have a superb Tarascan translation of both Testaments). The Tarascan concern is not with doctrine, argument, theology, or texts, but with a costly ritual and its economic, social, and political implications.

Nevertheless, the Tarascan share a network of explicit and implicit understandings, symbols, and attitudes that have been synthesized and transmitted largely by word of mouth. Every village, family, and individual holds to a different subset of these beliefs—pagan, local, Catholic, and secular—but there is cohesion in the area as a whole. This is in large part due to the fiestas. "Because of the fiestas," modern industry has attracted few Tarascan; "because of the fiestas," Protestant missionaries have made few converts; agrarian reform has had to compromise with the fiestas; and work and the family are strongly motivated by their roots in the fiestas. Fiestas, not as symbols or surface phenomena only, but as vivid, primary experiences, are the basis of Tarascan religion.

BIBLIOGRAPHY

Beals, Ralph. *Cherán: A Sierra Tarascan Village.* Washington, D.C., 1946.

Bechtloff, Dagmar. *Bruderschaften im Kolonialen Michoacár: Religion Zwischen Politik und Wirtschaft in Interkulturellen Gesellschaft.* Münster, 1992.

Becker, Marjorie. *Setting the Virgin on Fire: Lázaro Cárdenas, Michoacán Peasants, and the Redemption of the Mexican Revolution.* Berkeley, Calif., 1995.

Carrasco Pizana, Pedro. *Tarascan Folk Religion: An Analysis of Economic, Social, and Religious Intersections.* New Orleans, 1952.

Foster, George M., assisted by Gabriel Ospino. *Empire's Children: The People of Tzintzuntzan.* Washington, D. C., 1948.

Foster, George M. *Culture and Conquest: America's Spanish Heritage.* New York, 1960.

Friedrich, Paul. "Revolutionary Politics and Communal Ritual." In *Political Anthropology,* edited by Marc J. Swartz, Victor Turner, and Arthur Tuden, pp. 191–220. Chicago, 1966.

Relación de las ceremonias y ritos y población y gobierno de los Indios de la provincia de Michoacán (1541). Morelia, Mexico, 1977. A facsimile reproduction of manuscript c. IV.5 in the Escorial Library, El Escorial, Spain, with transcription by José Tudela and introduction by José Corona Núñez.

Ribera Farfan, Carolina. *Vida neuva pavra Tarecuato: cabildo y parroquía ante la nueva evangelizacion.* Zamora, Mich., 1998.

Verástique, Bernardino. *Michoacán and Eden: Vasco de Quiroga and the Evangelization of Western Mexico.* Austin, Tex., 2000.

Zantwijk, Rudolph A. M. van. *Servants of the Saints: The Social and Cultural Identity of a Tarascan Community in Mexico.* Assen, Netherlands, 1967.

PAUL FRIEDRICH (1987 AND 2005)

TARASIOS (c. 730–806), patriarch of Constantinople from 784 to 806. Tarasios was born to a prominent family in Constantinople. His father, Georgios, had served as a judge and prefect (mayor) of the capital. Tarasios was excellently trained in theology and secular learning, which helped him to rise in both the civil and ecclesiastical ranks. During the reign of Leo IV and his wife Irene, Tarasios was chief secretary (*protoasikritis*) of the imperial court, perhaps from 775 to 784, when he was ordained and elevated to the patriarchal throne. His speedy elevation to the ranks of the priesthood was not unusual in the Byzantine church even though it was objected to by several iconophiles.

As patriarch, Tarasios became instrumental in the convocation of the Second Council of Nicaea in 787, which condemned iconoclasm. Not only was he the power behind the council, but it was on that occasion that the right of presiding over a council was transferred entirely to the patriarch. Tarasios, a prudent man, proved moderate in his policies toward both the problems of the imperial house and the iconoclastic controversy. His moderation was perceived as laxity, and Tarasios was attacked by the rigorous monastic party of Theodore of Studios.

Tarasios fostered the building of social welfare institutions, including a hospital and homes for the poor. He restored good relations with Rome and upon his death was honored by both the Greek and the Latin churches. Only a few of his letters and a sermon survive. His biography, which constitutes an important source for the period, was written by Deacon Ignatios.

Bibliography

Sources for Tarasios's writings are *Patrologia Graeca*, edited by J. P. Migne, vol. 98 (Paris, 1860), cols. 1423–1500, containing his *Apologeticus ad populum*, *Epistolae*, and *Oratio;* and *Les Régestes des actes du patriarcat de Constantinople*, edited by Venance Grumel, vol. 1 (Istanbul, 1936), pp. 12–22. References to Tarasios may be found in Hans Georg Beck's *Kirche und theologische Literatur im byzantinischen Reich* (Munich, 1959), p. 489; Iōannēs Karaiannopoulos's *Pegai tēs Buzantines historias*, 4th ed. (Thessaloniki, 1978), p. 215; and S. Efstratiades's *Hagiologion tēs orthodoxou ekklesias* (Athens, 1935), pp. 445–446.

DEMETRIOS J. CONSTANTELOS (1987)

ṬARFON (late first and early second centuries CE), Palestinian tanna. A Jewish resident of Lod, he was the teacher of Yehudah bar Il'ai and a prominent leader of the generation of rabbis active at the seaside town of Yavneh after the destruction in 70 CE of the Temple in Jerusalem.

There are two strands within the traditions associated with Ṭarfon. One group of traditions makes Ṭarfon subservient to his colleague ʿAqivaʾ ben Yosef and occasionally mocks Ṭarfon for foolishness in his behavior or opinions. A second group of traditions cites Ṭarfon's actions as precedents for the rulings of Yehudah bar Ilʿai and appears to have been formulated by Yehudah's disciples.

In establishing the criteria for legal decisions on the performance of religious obligations, Ṭarfon emphasized the importance of deed over intention, of formal action or objective fact over subjective thought. This posture differs sharply from that of ʿAqivaʾ, who placed greater emphasis on the role of intention. In several instances Ṭarfon's view is included in the text as a foil for the authoritative opinion of ʿAqivaʾ.

Ṭarfon's major rulings frequently concern rituals performed by priests. In matters of dispute he consistently ruled in favor of the priestly families. He ruled, for instance, that a priest may receive gifts of heave-offerings of wine and oil from a householder throughout the year, an economic advantage for the priest. Ṭarfon's dicta emphasized that the priests could play a central role in the life of the Jews even after the destruction of the Temple.

SEE ALSO Tannaim.

Bibliography

Joel Gereboff's *Rabbi Tarfon: The Tradition, the Man and Early Rabbinic Judaism* (Missoula, Mont., 1979) presents a systematic study and analysis of all the materials concerning this rabbi. In *Tannaitic Symposia* (in Hebrew), 3 vols. (Jerusalem, 1967), Israel Konovitz collects all the references to Ṭarfon in rabbinic literature.

New Sources

Willems, Gerard F. "Le Juif Tryfon et rabbi Tarfon." *Bijdragen* 50 (1989): 278–292.

TZVEE ZAHAVY (1987)
Revised Bibliography

ṬARĪQAH. The Arabic word *ṭarīqah*, meaning a road or path, also signifies a "mode" or "method" of action as well as a "way" or code of belief. In the context of Sufism, *ṭarīqah* refers to both the path of spirituality itself—"the way"—and the manner of traveling (*sulūk*) along this path as the wayfarer passes through various stages (*manāzil*) and stations (*maqāmāt*) in the quest to approach nearer to God.

More concretely, however, *ṭarīqah* (and its plural, *ṭurūq*) is used as a generic term for the various organized brotherhoods or Ṣūfī orders that direct this spiritual quest into a particular code of practices pursued in a communal setting. It is in this sense that the word *ṭarīqah* is most frequently used: a confraternity founded around the figure or the memory of a charismatic figure of spiritual authority. *Ṭarīqahs* are arranged hierarchically around loyalty and obedience to a living guide or master, following fixed rites of initiation, observing specific spiritual practices and a code of etiquette, typically centered in a physical structure other than a mosque (e.g., a shrine, lodge, hospice, retreat), and financed by pious endowments *(waqf)* of real property and income.

A number of these *ṭarīqah* brotherhoods date their development into formal institutions to the twelfth and thirteenth centuries; in the succeeding centuries they became geographically and culturally more pervasive and more structurally defined. These *ṭarīqahs*—some regional, others widely distributed, but few of them highly centralized—developed into a rich and diverse complex of religious associations throughout the Middle East, North and sub-Saharan Africa, Arabia, Central Asia, South and Southeast Asia, and China and in the twentieth century in Europe, North America, and Australia. They were influential not only in the popularization of Sufism but in the spread of Islam as a religion; sometimes they have also fostered resistance movements or developed into political forces in their own right.

Beyond this the influence of the *ṭarīqahs* has been manifold: they add an emotional, psychological, and spiritual dimension to devotional practice, in many cases by integrating poetry and music, the visual arts, and mystical contemplation into religious life; they contribute to the intimacy of social life; they are associated with trade and craft guilds; they have provided staging posts and hospices for travelers and merchants; and they maintain shrines and other facilities by means of charitable endowments. They have also served as credit and finance institutions, thus contributing to commerce and a stable network of trade throughout the Muslim world, especially along the great distances of the Silk Road across Central Asia to China and in the maritime trade of the Indian Ocean.

Though their influence as institutions waned somewhat over the nineteenth and twentieth centuries, a wide and vibrant variety of *ṭarīqah* institutions still exist in various forms in both urban and rural locales.

ORIGINS AND EARLY DEVELOPMENT. The use of the word *ṭarīqah* in the writings of al-Junayd (d. 910), al-Ḥallāj (d. 922), al-Sarrāj (d. 988), al-Hujwīrī (d. 1072), and al-Qushayrī (d. 1074) denotes a method of moral psychology for the guidance of individuals directing their lives toward a knowledge of God. In early Sufism the term *ṭarīqah* was thus understood as a method or path by which an individual passing through various psychological stages in the obedience to and practice of the law (*sharīʿah*) proceeds from one level of knowledge of God to a higher one with the ultimate reality of God (*ḥaqīqah*) as the goal. Although Sufism has been accused of advocating or permitting an antinomian path, the *ṭarīqah* orders for the most part held to the belief in the primacy of *sharīʿah* (which is itself etymologically related to another root for road or path). As Jalāl al-Dīn Rūmī's famous Persian mystical poem, *Mathnawī*, expresses it:

> *Sharīʿah* is like a candle lighting the way. You must take this candle in hand before the way can be traveled. Having set out on the way, your walking is *ṭarīqah*, and when you arrive at your destination, that is truth (*ḥaqīqah*, the real, or God).

The institutional elaboration of this path derived from a spiritual impulse that established itself early in Islam. It originates in part from a mystical hermeneutic applied to the lexicon of the Qurʾān, investing particular verses and scenes with special significance, and from the intense, passionate spirituality evident in the *sīrah* of the Prophet and some of his companions. It was an impulse that grew stronger in the seventh and eighth centuries with the emergence of what Marshall Hodgson (1974) has described as "the piety-minded opposition" to the luxury, worldliness, and nepotism of the Umayyad caliphate and later dynasties. The mystical traditions of Sufism emerged from this piety-minded alternative to both the political and the religious establishments. Islamic spirituality has also reemerged at various historical junctures, especially the colonial period, in the form of counterculture, protest, or even militant resistance movements.

This religious quest for interior purity and control over the self (*nafs*), the slaying of which was described by later Ṣūfīs as the greatest of human struggles (*jihād-i akbar*), fell heir to the rich spiritual traditions of Hellenism and Christianity in the eastern Mediterranean. In the manner of the desert monks and other ascetics in Syria and Egypt, some Muslims began to wear a distinctive habit of coarse wool (*ṣūf*). The term *ṣūfī* was used as early as the eighth century CE to describe a man wearing such wool garments, and *ṣūfīyah* is attested in the following century in reference to groups or nascent communities of such Ṣūfīs.

SPIRITUAL EXERCISES. Early Islamic spirituality emphasized reliance upon God through the practice of poverty (*faqr*). Indeed two words for a "poor person," dervish (Persian *darwīsh*) and fakir (Arabic *faqīr*), retain their association with Ṣūfī asceticism. Techniques of the Ṣūfī *via purgativa* included fasting, seclusion (*khalwah*), a daily calling oneself to account for one's behavior (*muḥāsibah*), and scrupulous introspection (*murāqabah*) with a view to weeding out impure intentions. Ṣūfīs also spent much time in personal devotions, performing vigils, litanies (*aḥzāb*), and intimate prayers (variously called *wird, munājāt, duʿāʾ*) in addition to the prescribed ritual prayers (*ṣalāt*).

Some contemplative or ecstatic exercises came to be performed in groups, such as the ceremonial *dhikr*, or "remembrance" of God, involving the repeated and rhythmic recitation of words and phrases—usually attributes of God derived from the Qurʾān or forms of the Shahādah—often in combination with controlled breathing. Another group ceremony was the *majlis-i samāʿ* (listening session or concert). As early as 850 CE there were *samāʿ* houses in Baghdad in which the Ṣūfīs could listen to music and let themselves be drawn into mystical states. *Samāʿ* might also feature the chanting or singing of poetry on spiritual themes, accompanied by music, to which the listeners might respond with rhythmic movement. Although similar to dancing, such responses were conceived as either a deliberate form of motive meditation or as an uncontrollable response to an ecstatic state. Most of the *ʿulamāʾ* rejected *samāʿ* as an impious practice (in part because of the associations of music and dance with royal courts and dancing slave girls) and it was not universally accepted among the *ṭarīqahs*, though many Ṣūfī manuals defend it when properly regulated. Some orders also hold communal ceremonies involving the piercing of body parts with skewers or knives in trance-like states to induce or demonstrate the achievement of ecstatic states.

COMMUNAL LIFE. The nucleus from which the *ṭarīqahs* developed was the relationship established between master and adept. This mirrored the teacher-student relationship in the *madrasahs* or the master-apprentice relationship in the urban craft guilds (from whose ranks the *ṭarīqahs* drew much of their membership). A popular preacher or revivalist, a healer, a visionary mystic, an ascetic or other holy man might draw a number of devoted listeners to hear lectures or to experience the charisma and spiritual energy (*barakah*) of his presence. This might develop into a lasting relationship between a spiritual guide (*murshid*), or elder (Arabic, *shaykh*; Persian, *pīr*), directing his seeker (*murīd*). Prior to the twelfth century the relationship of such disciples to one another was typically unstructured, though they might travel together when accompanying the master on a journey and either do odd jobs or beg to support themselves. Some groups, such as the Karrāmīyah (based on the teachings of the ascetic preacher Ibn Karrām, d. 869), apparently evolved into more systematic movements.

Ṣūfī teachers who acquired a wider reputation were eventually able to set up hospices or lodges of their own to accommodate students. One of the earliest, a "small cloister" (*duwayrah*), was established by the ascetic ʿAbd al-Wāḥid ibn Zayd (d. c. 750) on the island of ʿAbbādān in the Persian Gulf and continued to operate after his death. Other similar institutions at about this time are described as existing in eastern Persia, in Damascus, on the Byzantine frontier, and in Alexandria and North Africa.

As a fraternity grew, it might move from the master's private house or shop to a separate compound, which could include a hall for devotional exercises, a large kitchen for guests and disciples, a small mosque, and possibly a school. Larger centers included living quarters for some initiates, either individual cells or a larger dormitory. Often such centers grew up around the tomb of the founder of the *ṭarīqah* or a local shrine visited by pilgrims. The names of these centers or retreats varied according to location and function, typically *zāwiyah* and *ribāṭ* in the Maghreb; *tekke* in Anatolia and the Balkans; *khānaqāh,* a Persian word, throughout Iran and India (sometimes as *khānagah*) as well as in Egypt and the Levant (as *khānqāh).* The Persian word *dargāh* (literally "threshhold" but used for the royal court or palace) is also found, particularly in India. The Chishtīyah *shaykhs* in India prefer to use their own personal residence, designated as a "community home" (*jamāʿat-khānah*), to avoid the adepts becoming entangled in the mundane distractions of administering a large center and its endowments.

Some such *khānaqāh* centers kept open house, while others might be visited only by appointment. The *shaykh* lived with his family in one quarter, saw his disciples at fixed hours, and led the five daily prayers. Some *khānaqāhs* were large and could accommodate both long- and short-term visitors. The Saʿīd al-Suʿadāʾ in Egypt, founded by Saladin (Ṣalāḥ al-Dīn) in 1173, accommodated three hundred dervishes, and contemporary chronicles record how every Friday people gathered round to gain blessings by watching them leave the compound for the Friday noon prayer.

The communal life of the *ṭarīqah* had obvious attractions. Congregational prayer gave strength and warmed faith, collective pursuit of spiritual exercises created an encouraging environment, and communal worship ceremonies like *dhikr* and *samāʿ* fostered mystical experience. The communal setting of the *ṭarīqah* also led to greater formalization of the relationship between the *shaykh* and his disciples. Favored disciples enjoyed close companionship and conversation with the *shaykh,* pursued in some of the *ṭarīqahs* through the technique of *tawajjuh,* or total face-to-face concentration. This was practiced by the disciple concentrating on his *shaykh* as he performed the *dhikr* or by the *shaykh* who reciprocated by concentrating on his disciple, entering his heart and guiding him.

The spiritual authority of the *ṭarīqahs* and their *shaykhs* are certified by a *silsila*, or "chain" of transmission, which (in a parallel to the *isnād* of a *ḥadīth* report) certify the founder of the order's link to a presumed oral tradition of interpretation handed down the generations from the Prophet. These *silsilas*, not all of them historically plausible, function as spiritual geneaologies and naturally diverge according to the date, birthplace, and heritage claimed by the founder of the particular *ṭarīqah.* Most, however, converge on Jaʿfar al-Ṣādiq (d. 765) and trace their way back to Muḥammad through his cousin and son-in-law ʿAlī, who thus holds a special mystical significance for both Sunnā and Shīʿī Ṣūfīs.

A master of outstanding spiritual authority and charisma might create so strong an impression on his followers that his method and the community of disciples attached to him continued after his death. His mantle, literally symbolized by the bestowal of a ceremonial patchwork cloak (*khirqah*), was passed to one or more of his chosen disciples, who inherited his authority and continued his work either in the home *khānaqāh* or in an ancillary one in another city. This new *shaykh,* who might be chosen from among the elder *shaykh*'s sons, appointed by the *shaykh,* or elected, was succeeded in turn by one of his disciples. In this way a line of transmission of authority and *barakah* was established, so that the spiritual power of the founding *shaykh* could be transmitted forward to future generations of disciples.

A new disciple then did not become simply the follower of a *shaykh.* He made his oath of allegiance both to his *shaykh* and to the founder of the line of transmission to which his *shaykh* was heir. By so doing he gained the right to have knowledge of the special *dhikr* formulas distinctive to the order and to share in the spiritual power of the entire line of transmission. Thus to the relationship between teacher and disciple (joined by their mutual desire to draw closer to

God) was added the component of initiation into a source of spiritual insight and power that extended over generations.

Most Ṣūfī orders insisted on the necessity of a living guide to follow the *ṭarīqah*, but there were exceptions. Some Ṣūfīs, calling themselves Uwaysīs after the example of Uways al-Qaranī (a contemporary of the Prophet who only met him in a dream), claimed to have been initiated or illuminated through a dream or vision of a past master rather than through the guidance and presence of a living master. Qalandarī dervishes underwent an initiation ritual that included shaving the face (including eyebrows) and head but normally practiced their wandering, mendicant, and antinomian lifestyle without direction from a *shaykh*.

THE *ṬARĪQAH* AS AN ESTABLISHED INSTITUTION. The *madrasah* system of education, by licensing professors, formalizing the curriculum, and subsidizing students, succeeded in professionalizing the legal discipline in the eleventh and twelfth centuries CE. In the thirteenth century the Abbasid caliph al-Nāṣir encouraged the spread of young men's chivalric societies (the *futūwwa* orders), establishing an interest in and conveying legitimacy on the idea of urban fraternal organizations. These institutional models must also have suggested themselves to the Ṣūfī communities. If the community of disciples of a particular Ṣūfī master survived and replicated itself for a generation or more after the death of the founder, it would often become known as the "method," or *ṭarīqah*, of its eponymous founder, as, for example, "the method of Najm al-Dīn Kubrā," or Ṭarīqat al-Kubrāwīyah. It has been supposed that the development of the *ṭarīqah* orders into formal religious institutions centered around a lodge or shrine, following a fixed rule, and projected to continue functioning indefinitely began in the twelfth century (as some of the orders' *Silsilahs* claim). Commonly, however it was the children or grandchildren of the founding *Shaykhs*, rather than the *Shaykhs* themselves, who organized the disciple communities into institutional orders, a process that can be clearly documented for the late thirteenth and fourteenth centuries. Later in the Ottoman period the *ṭarīqah* institutions become corporate entities with subbranches that were sometimes described by a different generic term, *ṭā'ifah* (plural, *ṭawā'if)* as "societies."

Despite the esoteric character of the theosophy they promulgated, the ideas and rituals of the *ṭarīqahs* attracted the masses with the hope of obtaining spiritual and temporal benefits from the sanctity and spiritual power of the great figures in the orders, from the tombs in which they were buried, and from the places and relics with which they were associated. Thus the *ṭarīqahs* became great communities, comprising all strata of society, offering something to the educated and uneducated alike, fostering devotional poetry and music, tolerating a wide range of folk practices, yet preserving and extending a great tradition of spirituality. They likewise played a major social role. Their hospices (*khānaqāhs*) offered lodging to travelers, medical treatment for the sick, and help for the poor. They also became centers for popular devotion. They extended their membership by granting associate tertiary status to individuals who, while living outside the community, practiced their normal trades, performed the daily prayers in the *ṭarīqah* environment under the direction of the *shaykh* and took part in *dhikr* exercises, litanies, or *samā'* sessions.

INITIATION RITUALS. Most of the *ṭarīqahs* have similar rituals of admission, although degrees of fervor, sincerity, and integrity have varied over time and place. An initiation, a great event in the life of both the initiate and the community, is marked by a day of festival. A model initiation ceremony described in one of the manuals for the Qādirīyah *ṭarīqah* is described as follows. The candidate first performs ritual ablutions; he then prays two *rak'ahs* and sits facing the *shaykh* with his knees pressed together. Clasping his *shaykh*'s right hand, he recites the opening *sūrah* of the Qur'ān followed by a series of formulas invoking blessings upon the Prophet, and the various *silsilas*, especially those of the Qādirīyah line, by which his *shaykh* establishes his authority. Afterward the *shaykh* has him repeat, phrase by phrase, a formula containing various components: a prayer asking God's forgiveness; a testimony that the vow he is taking is that of God and his apostle; recognition that the hand of the *shaykh* is that of 'Abd al-Qādir, founder of the order; and a promise that he will recite the *dhikr* as the *shaykh* requires him to do. The *shaykh* then utters a prayer and recites the Qur'anic verse of allegiance: "Those who vow their allegiance to you, vow their allegiance to God; the hand of God is upon their hands. Thus whoever violates it, violates himself, but whoever fulfills what he has promised God he will undertake, God will give him a mighty reward" (48:10). Alternately verse 16:91 is used: "Fulfill the pact of God once you have made a pact with him."

SOCIAL ETHICS AND ETIQUETTE. The number of manuals filled with stories illustrating and enjoining delicate, tactful, and respectful behavior on the *ṭarīqah* initiates demonstrates a remarkable sensitivity to etiquette and propriety. One of the earliest treatises on the norms of proper behavior among members of a *ṭarīqah*, Abū al-Najīb al-Suhrawardī's *Ādāb al-murīdīn* (The manners of the disciples) dates from the twelfth century CE. It is representative of practices in a number of orders and elaborates an etiquette of great sensitivity. Apart from its intrinsic interest, it demonstrates the primacy of human values and courtesy over rigorous ascetic practices and complex theosophical ideas in the brotherhoods. It also shows clearly that the *ṭarīqahs* did not see themselves as subsects outside the regular religious disciplines.

The work classifies religious scholars into three groups (in practice these were not fixed identities but points on a continuum of religious orientation with considerable overlap): traditionalists, jurists, and (Ṣūfī) *'ulamā'*. The traditionalists are the watchmen of religion, who deal with the external meaning of *ḥadīth*. The jurists are the arbiters of religion, whose specialty is their ability to make legal inferences. The Ṣūfīs in turn base their lives and conduct on both groups of specialists and refer to them in case of difficulties. Tradition and law are the basis for their lives, including both their inner modes of spirituality and their outward behavior. In the description of this outward behavior one sees an extraordinary concern for personal relations in both family and community life: patience with the ignorant, compassion with one's wife and family, agreement with brethren. Openness, modesty, and humility are the ideals. The movements of tongue, ear, eye, heart, hands, and feet are to be directed to charity.

Meticulous attention is given to the details of social behavior, personal cleanliness, modesty in dress, and restraint in eating. The brethren at any hospice should exercise great care in their treatment of guests. As host, the *shaykh* should encourage them to overcome their shyness at the table and offer them whatever food he is able to provide. The guest, for his part, should sit where he is directed, be pleased with what is given to him, and not leave without excusing himself. The host should then accompany the departing guest to the door of the house. In certain circumstances joking is permitted, provided that slandering, mimicry, and nonsense are avoided. This practice is supported by a tradition relating words attributed to ʿAlī: "When the Prophet saw one of his friends distressed, he would cheer him up by joking."

The Role of Women. ʿAbd al-Raḥmān Al-Sulamī's (d. 1022) compilation of the lives of women Ṣūfīs attests to the involvement of many women besides the famous celibate saint Rābīʿah al-ʿAdawīyah (d. 801). Ibn ʿArabī (1165–1240) also writes about the miracles of Ṣūfī women, one of whom was his teacher. In Tunisia there is a shrine for a thirteenth-century woman saint, ʿĀʾisha al-Mannūbīyah, whom oral tradition asserts to have been a disciple of al-Shādhilī, and Ṣūfī women healers in contemporary India or Uzbekistan attract many informal disciples.

Although outstanding exemplars of female chastity and purity in life or in literature have been upheld as saints and Ṣūfī heroines, in which role they become public figures as honorary "men" *(rijāl),* the wayfarer along the *ṭarīqah* is conventionally assumed to be male. A rather misogynistic attitude can be found in some Ṣūfī writings, including the view that women (as well as children and the entaglements of supporting a household) are distractions from the path of true spiritual struggle.

The *ṭarīqah* orders operate in the public sphere, which has historically been a male domain in most Muslim societies, whereas women's religious organizations tend to operate in the domestic sphere. In Saljūq Anatolia and probably elsewhere female members of ruling families cultivated relationships with Ṣūfī teachers, often financing the construction of their lodges, as dedicatory inscriptions attest. This probably gave aristocratic women considerable influence in the promotion of specific orders, but it would appear that, as in a mosque, women usually attended talks or other ceremonies at Ṣūfī lodges in a segregated gallery or behind a curtain or grille. There is also documentary evidence of the wives or female servants of *shaykhs* serving Ṣūfī brotherhoods in some capacity behind the scenes, and the daughters of various *shaykhs* were married into the families of political or community leaders, solidifying membership and backing for the *ṭarīqah.*

After World War II women *shaykhas* directing circles of exclusively female disciples were noted among established Ṣūfī orders in Soviet Central Asia and the Caucasus, including the Naqshbandīyah and Qādirīyah of Daghestan, though this development was condemned by the Muslim Spiritual Board of the North Caucasus. In the late 1970s western Ṣūfī women in northern California met with an elder Mevlevi initiate from Turkey who encouraged their efforts; as a result some Ṣūfī organizations in North America and in Turkey have begun not only accepting female disciples but even holding integrated ceremonies. However, in Turkey it is more common for women to participate in female-only *dhikr* ceremonies in the homes of individuals. The public participation of women in the *ṭarīqah* environment (or the *madrasah* system) is not well documented for the medieval period. In the absence of contrary evidence, it can be assumed that the integrated public participation of women in the *ṭarīqah* orders is a development of the late twentieth century.

The *ṭarīqah*s of the thirteenth through the fifteenth centuries are the culminating point in a shift from an individualistic, elitist, ascetic spirituality to a corporate, congregational organization with a place for individuals representing a whole range of spiritual attainment and every stratum of society. There may be an inclination to see in them a counterpart to the religious orders that developed in the Christian tradition from the fifth century onward and that also channeled a large part of the impulse for solitary asceticism into an institutional framework. The analogy is only partly valid, for the two types of organization were different. The *shaykh* of a *zāwiyah* did not have the administrative authority of an abbot, nor did the *ṭarīqah*s have the same centralized government and formal lines of communication that linked the houses of the Benedictine order, for example. While the *ṭarīqah*s were, in one meaning of the term, corporate, they did not become corporations in the Western sense.

Individual *Ṭarīqah*s. There are over two hundred *ṭarīqah*s, and in fact many more if the numerous branches and subdivisions are counted. The selection presented here is intended to show aspects of their individuality as reflected in the social classes to which they made their appeal, their attitudes toward government authority, their spiritual exercises and theosophy, and the circumstances in which they flourished.

Qādirīyah. The Qādirīyah *ṭarīqah* is commonly viewed as the first of the brotherhoods to emerge in the form of a structured organization, and it is still operating in the early twenty-first century. It began in Baghdad but eventually established itself as far afield as Yemen, Egypt, Sudan, the Maghreb, West Africa, India, and Southeast Asia. It claims

ʿAbd al-Qādir al-Jīlānī (1088–1166) from the region of Gīlān near the Caspian Sea in Iran as its founder, tracing its *silsila* through al-Junayd. ʿAbd al-Qādir was a Ḥanbalī legal scholar—a follower of the strictest, most literalist school of Islamic law—and was invested with the Ṣūfī habit by the founder of the first Ḥanbalī *madrasah.* Although he was a stern teacher, ʿAbd al-Qādir has become perhaps the most famous saint in the Islamic world, and stories of his miracles abound from Java to Morocco. His tomb in Baghdad has remained a place of pilgrimage for members of the brotherhood to the twenty-first century, with pilgrims—many of them from the Indo-Pakistan subcontinent, where the Qādirīyah was introduced in the late fourteenth century—remaining there for weeks, silently sweeping his sanctuary with little brooms. Old Sindhi songs tell how ʿAbd al-Qādir's spiritual realm extends through every town and region between Istanbul and Delhi.

The Qādirīyah had a very catholic appeal; all strata of society from ruler to peasant found a place within it. In popular belief ʿAbd al-Qādir was a renewer of Islam, and among members of the order there is a well-known story that he discovered a man by the wayside on the point of death and revived him. The "man" then revealed that he was the religion of Islam. The order, it should be noted, was to play a particularly important role in the Islamization of West Africa.

Rifāʿīyah. Slightly later than the founding of the Qādirīyah, the establishment of the Rifāʾīyah order in southern Iraq is credited to Aḥmad al-Rifāʾī (d. 1182). Although never as popular as the Qādirīyah, it was widespread in Antaolia by the fourteenth century and is still represented there and in Egypt. It is distinguished by one of its ritual practices, a particularly loud recitation of the *dhikr,* which led members to be known as the Howling Dervishes.

Suhrawardīyah. One of the oldest *ṭarīqahs* is the Suhrawardīyah, named after its founder, Abū al-Najīb ʿAbd al-Qāhir al-Suhrawardī (d. 1168), author of the above-mentioned *Ādāb al-murīdīn,* and also a professor of Shāfiʿi law at the Niẓāmīyah college in Baghdad. Significantly he was a pupil of Aḥmad al-Ghazālī (d. 1126), younger brother of the great Abū Ḥāmid al-Ghazālī (d. 1111), who helped win acceptance for the Ṣūfī dimension of Islam within the wider Islamic community. The influence and scope of the order was extended and given its decisive character by ʿAbū al-Najīb's fraternal nephew and student, Shihāb al-Dīn Abū Ḥafṣ ʿUmar al-Suhrawardī (1145–1234), whose treatise *ʿAwārif al-maʿārif* (Masters of mystical insights) became a standard work on the theory of Ṣūfī devotion.

The Abbasid caliph al-Nāṣir built a *ribāṭ* for Shihāb al-Dīn and his disciples in 1203 and appointed him as the caliphal envoy to the Ayyūbid rulers of Egypt and Syria in 1208 and then to the Saljūqs of Asia Minor in 1221. Shihāb al-Dīn Suhrawardī's disciples spread from Asia Minor and Syria through Persia and northern India, and it was they who established the Suhrawardīyah brotherhood on a permanent footing. Its origins, however, are credited to Abū al-Najīb and his nephew, Shihāb al-Dīn, who also figure in the *silsila* of the Kubrawīyah brotherhood as teachers of its founding figures, Najm al-Dīn Kubrā (d. c. 1220) and Najm al-Dīn Rāzī (d. 1265). The Suhrawardīyah became one of the most prominent and influential brotherhoods, though it subdivided into numerous branches after the fourteenth century.

Mawlawīyah. The Mawlawīyah order, more commonly known by its Turkish adjectival form, Mevlevi, takes its name from the title Mawlawī (my master), by which the Persian mystic poet Jalāl al-Dīn Rūmī (1207–1273) was addressed. His community of disciples in Konya was systematized into an order by Sulṭān Walad (d. 1312), Rūmī's son, who built a shrine dome (*türbe*) over Rūmī's resting place. From this base Sulṭān Walad and his son, Ūlū ʿĀrif Chalabī, established Mevlevi lodges throughout Anatolia, each with its own deputized *shaykh.*

As a boy Rumi had lived with his father, Bahāʾ al-Dīn-i Walad (d. 1231), a visionary and mystically minded Ḥanafī preacher (*wāʿiẓ*), in the small town of Wakhsh (in modern-day Tajikistan) and then in Samarqand before migrating to Anatolia. Though Bahāʾ al-Dīn is seen as the seminal figure of the order, his importance has been exaggerated in the hagiographical accounts of his life (the Ṣūfī genre of biography typically casts its subjects in a miraculous light, emphasizing their importance and spiritual authority). Bahāʾ al-Dīn apparently had a small handful of disciples in Khorasan but enjoyed no great reputation before accepting the patronage of the Saljūq sultan in Konya, who established a *madrasah* for him, which functioned more as a Ṣūfī center than a college of law. When Bahāʾ al-Dīn died, one of his old disciples came from Khorasan to take charge of the Konya disciples, a role Rūmī eventually assumed after he had completed studies of law in Syria and a period of seclusion. Rūmī also cultivated relations with the Konya Saljūqs and developed a following of his own but temporarily abandoned this role late in 1244 after meeting Shams al-Dīn Tabrīzī, an itinerant and iconoclastic Ṣūfī with some training in Shāfiʿī *fiqh,* with whom Rūmī spent an intense period of *ṣuḥbah* and seclusion. The encounter and the eventual disappearance of Shams from Konya led Rūmī to an ecstatic form of love mysticism expressed through poetry and *samāʿ,* extravagantly praising Shams, though subsequent figureheads of the disciple community, Ṣalāh al-Dīn Zarkūb (d. 1258) and Husām al-Dīn Chalabī (d. 1284), are also praised. Rūmī's extraordinary output of Persian poetry in his *Mathnawī* and *Dīwān* has been recited widely, from Bosnia to Bengal and throughout Central Asia, inspiring many Ṣūfīs of various *ṭarīqah* affiliations to imitate or comment upon it.

The Mevlevi *ṭarīqah* operated primarily in the territories of the Ottoman Empire, where it became a wealthy corporation with close ties to the imperial court. It was a hereditary order and, thanks to its central organization, did not fragment, though its character did change somewhat in the mid–sixteenth century, when Dīwānah Muḥammad Chalabī and Yūsuf Sīnachāk introduced Shīʿī influences into the order. The Mevlevi order promoted calligraphy and Persian literature, though it operated almost exclusively in Turkish- or Arabic-speaking environments. In later years there seems to have been much overlap between Mevlevi membership and that of other Anatolian orders, such as the Bektāshīyah, founded around the same time, and the Khalwatīyah, founded in the fourteenth century, both of which appeared more active by the twentieth century than the Mevlevis.

After serving 1001 days in the kitchen of the Mevlevi lodge, initiates were permitted to participate in the characteristic "turning" ceremony, a meditative graceful spinning performed in distinctive robes and hats to the accompaniment of a musical ensemble, usually consisting of a singer/reciter and a variety of instruments, almost always including drums and a reed flute. Beginning in the late eighteenth century, a visit to one of the Mevlevi lodges to observe one of these so-called Whirling Dervish ceremonies became an important part of European tourists' experience of Istanbul.

Shādhilīyah. Rather different in character is the Shādhilīyah, founded by Abū al-Ḥasan al-Shādhilī of Tunis (1196–1258), who traveled widely in the Maghreb and Spain, finally settling in Alexandria, where he died. In contrast to both the Rifāʿīyah and the Mawlawīyah, this *ṭarīqah* practices internalized and silent devotions. Thus its appeal is individualistic, focusing on the development of private prayer. Nonetheless the emphasis of Abū al-Ḥasan's teaching was against the solitary and the institutional life alike, and he urged his followers to realize their yearning for God through faithful attention to their daily responsibilities in society. They were not enjoined to beg or even to live in voluntary poverty; Egyptian sources refer to the Shādhilīs' tidy attire, which distinguished them from many of the other Ṣūfīs thronging the streets of Cairo. The Shādhilīyah of Yemen are also credited with discovering the value of brewed coffee beans as a means of staying awake during periods of night prayer.

This order has no special theosophical ideas apart from the fact that members are held to have been predestined to join it from pre-eternity. Rather, the goal is a deep yet sober spirituality, drawing on al-Muḥāsibī, the teacher of al-Junayd, on al-Makkī and his *Qūt al-qulūb* (The nourishment of the heart), and on the spiritual teaching of al-Ghazālī in the fourth volume of *Iḥyāʾ ʿulūm al-dīn* (The vivification of the religious sciences). Its teaching is subtle and not directed at the masses, as can be seen from the *Ḥikam* (Maxims), an enduring classic of Ṣūfī spirituality written by Abū al-Ḥasan's immediate successor, Ibn ʿAṭāʾ Allāh al-Iskandarī (d. 1309). This work, a collection of 262 brief sayings followed by four short treatises and a number of prayers, has generated numerous commentaries in many of the languages of the Muslim world.

Like many of the orders, the Shādhilīyah produced a variety of local offshoots all over the Muslim world. Among them, the Ḥāmidīyah Shādhilīyah is one of the modern orders that still attracts and provides a basic spiritual formation for many Egyptians. The appeal of the Shādhilīyah extends primarily to the officials and civil servants of the middle class, whose responsibilities, values, and attitudes are embodied in the order's attention to detail. Even after the Atatürk government prohibited Ṣūfī orders in Turkey in 1925, the Shādhilīyah retained its attraction for the middle class. It has also gained a following among some European Muslims.

Chishtīyah. India was particularly fertile ground for the development of the *ṭarīqahs*, and it is impossible to write the history of Islam in the subcontinent without a detailed study of them. Along with the Suhrawardīyah, the Chishtīyah was among the earliest *ṭarīqahs* operating in India, and the first to originate in the subcontinent. It was founded by Muʿīn al-Dīn Chishtī (d. 1236), a native of Sīstān, who had been for a time a disciple of Abū Najīb al-Suhrawardī. He arrived in Delhi in 1193 and then moved to Ajmer, an important city in newly conquered Rajputana, where he founded a *khānaqāh*. Niẓām al-Dīn Awliyāʾ (d. 1325) spent fifty years extending the Chishtīyah throughout India by dispatching hundreds of his own disciples from his center in Delhi. The simplicity and ardor of Chishtī teaching, their extreme hospitality and charity, and their readiness to welcome guests without discrimination attracted many followers. In fact the Chishtīyah illustrates in an exemplary manner the extraordinary contribution of the *ṭarīqahs* to the Islamization of the subcontinent.

At first the adherents kept their distance from government, but later they developed a close association with the Mughal court. Salīm (later Jahāngīr), the heir apparent of Emperor Akbar (d. 1605), was born in the home of a Chishtī *shaykh*, and in gratitude Akbar commissioned a splendid *dargāh* for the Chishtīyah in Fatehpur Sikri. Jahāngīr himself decorated the Chishtī city of Ajmer with beautiful buildings of white marble, and Jahānārā Begum (d. 1681), daughter of Shāhjahān and Mumtāz Maḥall, wrote about the life of Muʿīn al-Dīn Chishtī and requested to be buried in his shrine compound. The Chishtīyah, like other *ṭarīqahs* in India, contributed immensely to the development of literature in the vernacular languages, and a Chishtī, ʿAbd al-Raḥmān, who lived during the reign of Awrangzīb (1658–1707), is regarded as the greatest mystical poet in the Pashto language. This *ṭarīqah* was noted for its active encouragement of the practice of *samāʿ*, an example followed by various other orders in South Asia, where the genre of Ṣūfī music known as Qawwālī, which Fateh Ali Khan and other performers popularized around the world in the 1980s, developed.

Naqshbandīyah. Bahāʾ al-Dīn-i Naqshband (1318–1388) traces his mystical heritage through Amīr Kulāl, a spiritual adviser to Tīmūr (Tamerlane), to the Persian-speaking Central Asian lineage of Ṣūfīs, the Khwājagān, initiated by Abū Yūsuf ʿAlī Hamadānī (d. 1140). Bahāʾ al-Dīn founded the Naqshbandī *ṭarīqah* in Bukhara, which he left only three times: twice for pilgrimage to Mecca and once to meet with the ruler of Herat, Muʿizz al-Dīn Ḥusayn, to whom he taught the Naqshbandī principles. His tomb, surrounded by a large shrine complex, is a place of pilgrimage. From here the *ṭarīqah* spread geographically, coming to rival the popularity and influence of the Qādirīyah. It was to have an important role in Central Asia and India and also developed branches in Afghanistan, Iraq, Turkey, China, Sumatra, the Riau archipelago, Java, and other Indonesian islands. The order still has a strong following scattered over the length and breadth of the Muslim world. In the late eighteenth century Ma Ming-Hsin, who had become a Naqshbandī-Jahrī while on pilgrimage to Mecca, returned to Kansu Province in China to found the politically important "New Teaching" movement. In the first Indonesian elections in 1955, a Sumatran Naqshbandī was elected to the national parliament as the sole representative of the Ṭarīqah political party.

Bahāʾ al-Dīn-i Naqshband rapidly established connections between his *ṭarīqah,* the trade and craft guilds, and the merchant houses, so that as his spiritual influence grew, so did his wealth. The order soon gained a position of power in the Timurid court and, assuming a custodial role over government, supervised the administration of religious law. Indeed under the leadership of Khwājah Aḥrār of Herat (1404–1490), the Naqshbandīyah virtually dominated political life in Central Asia. It was his conviction that "to serve the world, it is necessary to exercise political power"; in other words, it is necessary to maintain adequate control over rulers in order to ensure that they implement the divine law in every area of life.

Unlike the Chishtīyah and those who followed their example, the Naqshbandīyah recited their *dhikr* silently and banned music and rhythmic movements. They believed that through *dhikr* without words one could achieve a level of contemplation in which subject and object became indistinguishable and the individual soul returned to God as it had been before creation. Among their techniques of meditation was concentration on their *shaykh*; another practice was regular visitation of saints' tombs in the hope that, by concentrating on the spirit of the departed *shaykh,* they would increase their spiritual strength.

The Naqshbandīyah was a moderate order that did not demand heroic austerities; like the Shādhilīyah, it regarded spiritual purification and education of the heart as more productive than harsh mortification designed to conquer the lower soul. It taught a middle way, that the mean between excessive hunger and excessive eating was the safest. The true fast consists of keeping the mind free from the food of satanic suggestions. Despite its essential sobriety, this method proved congenial to the poets of the time, and by the beginning of the eighteenth century all the leading poets in the Indo-Persian style were either members of the Naqshbandī *ṭarīqah* or under its influence.

The order played an important role in the religious and political history of Mughal India as leaders of a movement of reaction against the syncretist Dīn-i ilāhī (Divine Religion) of the emperor Akbar. An important figure in this reaction was Aḥmad Sirhindī (d. 1624), who was initiated into the order by its *shaykh,* Khwājah Bāqī Billāh, in 1600. The order remained involved in political developments, including a strong reaction against Hindu practices, up to 1740. The Naqshbandī Shāh Walī Allāh (1703–1762), enrolled concurrently in the Qādirīyah, became the greatest reformer of eighteenth-century Delhi and one of the leading figures in the renewal of Islam; his influence contributed to reform movements in the nineteenth century and beyond.

In Sulaymānīyah in Iraqi Kurdistan, Mawlānā Khālid Baghdādī (d. 1827) established a subbranch of the Naqshbandī order, which developed an independent character as the Khālidīyah. It absorbed most of the other Naqshbandī branches in the Middle East and displaced the Qādirīyah *ṭarīqah* in Kurdistan. It cultivated relations with the Ottoman elite and fought for the Turks in the Russo-Turkish War. Later implicated with opposition to the Turkish Republic, it was closed down with the rest of the Ṣūfī orders in Turkey in 1925. After the Iraqi revolution in 1958, the Khālidīyah shifted its operations to Iranian Kurdistan until the Iranian Revolution of 1979.

The literature of the Naqshbandīyah *ṭarīqah* is written in Persian, and one of the great Persian mystical poets, ʿAbd al-Raḥmān Jāmī (d. 1492), was integrally involved in the order. Because of its Sunnī loyalties, however, the Naqshbandī inroads in Persia were uprooted in the sixteenth century by the Shīʿī Safavid dynasty, paradoxically itself tracing its lineage to a Sunnī Ṣūfī teacher, Ṣafī al-Dīn of Ardabīl (1252–1334). His descendants eventually converted the order to Shiism, built it into a militant movement, and ultimately conquered Iran in the late fifteenth century, establishing a long-lived dynasty during which the country was converted to Shiism.

Niʿmatullāhīyah. Most of the Ṣūfī fraternities discussed here were founded and developed in a Sunnī environment. Shāh Niʿmat Allāh Walī (d. 1430), the eponymous founder of this *ṭarīqah*, was a Sunnī, though descended from the Prophet through the Shīʿī lineage of Ismāʿīl, son of Jaʿfar al-Ṣādiq. He studied in Shiraz and traveled widely among Ṣūfī circles in the Arabic-speaking Middle East before establishing several lodges of his own in Central Asia, where he came into competition with the Naqshbandīs. After Tīmūr grew suspicious of his aims and banished him from Transoxania, Shāh Niʿmat Allāh moved to Herat and finally settled in Māhān, from where he promoted the theosophy of Ibn ʿArabī in his prolific and popular writings and poetry, winning many followers in the area of Shiraz and Kirmān. His son, Khalīl Allāh, was invited to South India by Aḥmad Shāh Bahmān in 1436, establishing a further Niʿmatullāhī following among the Deccani aristocracy. Exactly how the order took on a Shīʿī character is obscure, but the Safavid ruler and ardent Shīʿī Shāh Ismāʿīl appointed a Niʿmatullāhī *shakyh,* Mīr Niẓām al-Dīn, as the chief religious official of the Safavid domain in 1512. Though the Safavid house intermarried with Niʿmatullāhīs, the order lost favor under Shāh ʿAbbās when it was implicated in a rebellion. It was only revived in the eighteenth century by help sent from the Deccani branch of the *ṭarīqah* in the person of Maʿṣūm ʿAlī-Shāh, who had gained a large following throughout Central Iran. He was executed in 1797 at the behest of Shīʿī scholars implacably opposed to Sufism.

In the nineteenth century the Niʿmatullāhīyah of Iran broke into several branches, represented in the early twenty-first century principally by the Ṣafī-ʿAlīshāhīs and the Sulṭān-ʿAlīshāhīs, both of which were encouraged under the Pahlavi dynasty. In 1974 the order was brought to the West, where it was represented by Javad Nurbakhsh as Khaniqahi-Nimatullahi.

Tijānīah and Sanūsīyah. The eighteenth-century revival movements of Shāh Walī Allāh in India and Muḥammad ibn ʿAbd al-Wahhāb in Arabia had a counterpart in the *ṭarīqah*s. Sometimes this revival was expressed in the reform of existing orders, sometimes in the development of suborders, sometimes in the appearance of new ones. The generation of orders in fact never ceased. In North and West Africa, for example, between 1500 and 1900 at least twenty-eight *ṭarīqah*s emerged, one-third originating in Morocco. Here it is sufficient to draw attention to two that were to play an important role in Islamic revival movements in the Sudan, Egypt, and North and West Africa. The first was the Tijānīyah, based in what is now Algeria and Morocco, and the other the Sanūsiyah in Libya.

The founder of the Tijānīyah was Abū al-ʿAbbās Aḥmad al-Tijānī (1737–1815). He spent several years studying in Fez, then he studied in Abyaḍ for five years, and in 1773 he went to Mecca and Medina and finally to Cairo, where he studied under various *shaykhs,* one of whom suggested that he found a *ṭarīqah.* He then returned to Fez, where, although he continued to travel extensively, he maintained his center.

The demands of the order are exclusive, and members may not join any other order. The Tijānīyah have their own formulas for *dhikr,* to be recited as many as a hundred times at particular points in the day. They are further distinguished from many of the other orders by their submission to established government, even where this has been non-Muslim. Thus throughout the French occupation of Algeria, they remained for the most part on good terms with the French authorities. When the emir ʿAbd el-Kader, a Qādirī named after the founder of the order, attempted to enlist them in a struggle against the French in 1836, the Tijānī chief refused, saying it was their purpose to live a religious life in peace. The emir then marched on their town and demanded that they submit to him, but they again refused and, although outnumbered, resisted a siege for eight months, took refuge in another town, and in the following year offered moral and material aid to the French.

This *ṭarīqah* won adherents in Egypt, Arabia, and other parts of Asia and still enjoys a strong following in parts of Africa formerly under French rule. In the first half of the nineteenth century it was propagated in French Guinea by ʿUmar Tal after his return to Dinguiray (which became one of the most important religious cities in the region), where it took over and displaced the Qādirīyah tradition.

Sīdī Muḥammad ibn ʿAlī al-Sanūsī was born in Algeria in 1791. From 1821 to 1828 he lived in Fez, where he studied Qurʾanic exegesis, *ḥadīth,* and jurisprudence. Traveling for the pilgrimage, he remained in Mecca from 1830 to 1843, founding his first *zāwiyah* there in 1837. On leaving Mecca he settled in Cyrenaica, where he founded additional *zāwiyah*s. After his death in 1859 the order was continued by his two sons, Sīdī Muḥammad al-Mahdī (1844–1901), his successor, and Sīdī Muḥammad al-Sharīf (1846–1896). Al-Sanūsī left detailed instructions relating to initiation into his order, and his devotional writings became the basis of the Sanūsī routines. At the same time all his activities were imbued with a rigorous work ethic. He inspired his followers to work together to build roads, to form trade cooperatives, to undertake irrigation projects, and to establish agricultural communities.

In fact such activities were integral to the work of many *ṭarīqah*s, such as the Tijānīyah and its offshoot in Senegal, the Murīd movement. The discipline of the brethren had a counterpart in the discipline of a trade guild or corporation. Likewise the tremendous vitality of the nineteenth-century *ṭarīqah*s was also channeled into political activity, especially diplomatic negotiations with the European powers. Throughout this period it is clear that they operated as an invisible international network attempting to protect the cultural and religious identity of Islam against the European powers. The same Emir ʿAbd el-Kader who tried to involve the Tijānīyah in an uprising against the French had received an *ijāzah* (license) to found his own branch of the Qādirīyah when he led the 1832 revolt against the French in Algeria and proclaimed a *jihād.* Captured by the French in 1847, he wrote to Napoleon III in 1865, petitioning him to mediate with Czar Alexander II on behalf of the release from prison of a Naqshbandī-Khālidī Ṣūfī *shaykh* in Daghestan, Imām Shāmil (1796–1871), who had been imprisoned for taking part in a *jihād* movement against the Russian Empire in the northern Caucasus.

There are also grounds for seeing a Sanūsī inspiration in the late nineteenth-century Achehnese war against the Dutch, just as there had been a strong international Naqshbandī movement behind resistance to the Dutch in West Sumatra and other parts of the Indonesian archipelago. These influences, inspirations, networks, and personalities thus ranged between Algeria and the Caucasus, Cyrenaica, Malaya, Indonesia, and East and West Africa, with the hub of the network at Mecca, where the *shaykhs* of the various regional establishments of the orders met and pooled information and ideas.

Tradition and Change. In spite of this political vitality, the influence of the *ṭarīqahs* was reduced to a minimum after the reformist movement inaugurated by Jamāl al-Dīn al-Afghānī and Muḥammad ʿAbdūh resulted in an intensive campaign against them. There had been movements against the *ṭarīqahs* before, yet a relative balance between the strength of their supporters and their opponents had prevailed. In the early twentieth century, however, there was a qualitative change and a definite shift in balance as the convergence of various factors militated against the *ṭarīqahs* in a special way.

The reform movement was inspired in part by nineteenth-century European secular rationalism and in part by a renewed emphasis upon the rationalist or puritanical understanding of Islam by movements such as Wahhabism (which led eventually to a ban on Ṣūfī orders in Saudi Arabia). As a result many of the practices of the order were seen not only as idolatrous innovations—such as the celebration of the birthdays of deceased saints, the honoring of their tombs, and certain forms of meditation—but also as harboring superstitions that disgraced Islam by making it appear contemptible to Europeans. Dervishes were also associated with the use of narcotics (to induce ecstasy) and with the practice of pederasty, a habit attested in Ṣūfī sources from the medieval period though not sanctioned by the official code of the *ṭarīqahs*. Moreover since the reformists believed the *ṭarīqahs* attracted people to otherworldliness and magic instead of challenging them to face reality, they considered it a root cause of the backwardness of Muslims. Muḥammad ʿAbdūh and Rashīd Riḍā, for example, while accepting the ethical and spiritual ideas of Sufism (as per al-Ghazālī), regarded every aspect of the *ṭarīqahs* as degenerate, and in Turkey under Atatürk they were outlawed altogether.

Abuses were easy to find. Some *shaykhs* believed that holiness was hereditary; certain heads of orders regarded great wealth as a right, an outward manifestation of the spiritual favors they had received. *Barakah* (the blessing a *shaykh* and his *silsila* could give) was something to be bought and sold. Moreover despite the international networks so characteristic of the *ṭarīqahs*, many individual *shaykhs* remained too attached to family clan and local traditions to respond to the rise of nationalism.

Modernization and secularization also undermined the social and economic foundations of the *ṭariqahs*. Employment now required training in public institutions created by the state rather than the parochial education offered by *ṭarīqah* schools and "study circles" *(ḥalaqāt)*. Clubs and associations took over the social role of the *ṭarīqahs*, and industrialization weakened the trade and craft guilds with which they had been formerly associated. There were also rival religious organizations: for example, in Egypt, the Muslim Brotherhood, because of its dispersion into local groups, was able to offer the community individual guidance and service that had previously been the province of the *ṭarīqahs*. Moreover the local orientation of many branches of the orders made them appear irrelevant to communities increasingly related to the outside world.

If modernity has weakened the traditional membership base and structure of the *ṭarīqahs* and governments have regulated or curtailed their functions, they nevertheless retain vitality and the potential to adapt to changed circumstances. It is striking that in Indonesia, for example, the reformist-oriented anti-*ṭarīqah* party, the Masyumi, which during the 1950s appeared to reflect the dominant Islamic ethos, was eclipsed by the traditional, adaptive *ṭarīqah*-tolerant group, the Nahdatul Ulama. Research on African *ṭarīqahs* shows that they contribute to social stability and, in a very special way, to the work ethic. The Murīdīyah of Senegal, born in an African environment, is an example of the moral authority and social dedication of a modern *ṭarīqah*. Equally important, various offshoots of the Naqshbandī order in former Soviet territories, such as Daghestan and Chechnya, have become numerous and influential.

The *tariqahs* still play an important social and political role in addition to the enrichment they bring to the spiritual lives of millions of people. Traditional celebrations like the *mawlids*, or saints' birthdays, often sponsored by *ṭarīqah* associations, remain extraordinary public events and displays of devotional fervor in India. This is also true in Egypt, where the Supreme Council of Ṣūfī Orders estimated in 1989 that between three and five million people belonged to one of the seventy-three registered orders. The interest in theosophical Sufism has also increased, largely because it jumped across confessional boundaries in the twentieth century as Western scholars engaged with the Ṣūfī tradition, first in the form of translations of Ṣūfī poetry, then as the object of metaphysical study (for example, in the Eranos seminars in Switzerland). In the West, Sufism was offered as the "perennial philosophy" and popularized as a method of spiritual psychology by Idries Shah and others.

Finally, Ṣūfī poetry found a broader commercial audience. Following the earlier example of Hazrat Inayat Khan, Meher Baba, and other teachers who came to the United States from India and elsewhere to establish disciple communities, the traditional *ṭarīqah* orders have also responded to this "New Age" receptivity. Traditional orders have established branches or subbranches in Europe and the United States, including the Khaniqahi Nimatullahi, Shādhilīyah (counting René Guénon among its members), Naqshbandi-Haqqani, and Jerrahi Order of America. Previously interrupted traditions have also been successfully revived or recreated by Western devotees, as is the case of the Mevlevi Order of America and the Threshold Society, which do not, however, require their members to be Muslims. These Western *ṭarīqah* branches purchase centers, appoint *shaykhs,* train disciples, teach classes, sponsor festivals and academic conferences, and maintain a presence on the internet. Meanwhile new orders, such as the MTO or Maktab-i ṭariqat-i Uwaysī, founded by Shah Maghsoud Angha (d. 1980), are actively promoted among diaspora communities and indigenous

Westerners. The International Association of Sufism, a nonprofit organization founded by Nahid Angha and Ali Kianfar in 1983, attempts not only to promote Sufism but to foster dialogue among the various organizations and orders of Sufism and to undertake pan-*ṭarīqah* activities.

Of equal significance is the renewed interest upon the part of educated urbanites in the Middle East in Sufism as a tolerant and inner-directed expression of Islamic spirituality, in contrast to fundamentalist or Islamist formulations of religion. For example, there was a significant surge of interest in the teachings of Rūmī and the practices of the Mevlevis throughout the 1980s and 1990s among young people in Iran, who saw him as representative of an expansive and tolerant understanding of Islam. The Turkish Ministry of Culture also promotes Rūmī and the Mevlevis as representatives of the great cultural and spiritual heritage of that country.

The historical importance of the *ṭarīqah*s is profound. After the fall of Baghdad to the Mongols in 1258, they helped maintain communication and intellectual interchange across the Arabic-, Turkish-, and Persian-speaking regions. They had a stabilizing role in critical periods of change and political uncertainty, and as new political centers of power became established, notably the Mughal and Ottoman Empires, they either associated themselves with the ruling classes or became a significant element in the social fabric of the new polity. Far from being rivals to the *ʿulamāʾ*, the founders of the *ṭarīqah*s and their successors, the great Ṣūfī *shaykhs* were masters of the law, and their spiritual exercises were a further dimension of their competence in *fiqh*, not a substitute for it. In India in particular their contribution to a creative acceptance of Islam and faithful observance of the norms of Islamic law—the Naqshbandī-inspired reform movement in seventeenth-century Delhi is a notable example—is enormous.

The new centers of political authority both recognized them as the standard-bearers and exemplars of the norms of religious behavior and provided them with ample opportunities to gain wealth, power, and influence. Given such acceptance, they added a richness and color, a vitality, and an emotional intensity to every stratum of religious and social life. Their cultural significance as promoters of literature and music and their role in Islamizing the vernaculars of many regions of the Muslim world have likewise been enormous.

SEE ALSO Attention; Bisṭāmī, Abū Yazīd al-; Dance; Darwīsh; Dhikr, Ghazālī, Abū Ḥāmid al-; Ibn al-ʿArabī; Ibn ʿAṭāʾ Allāh; Islam, articles on Islam in Central Asia, Islam in South Asia, Islam in the Caucasus and the Middle Volga; Islamic Law, article on Sharīʿah; Islamic Religious Year; Khusraw, Amīr; Madhhab; Madrasah; Mosque; Mysticism; Niẓām al-Dīn Awlīyā; Retreat; Rūmī, Jalāl al-Dīn; Samāʿ; Sufism; Ṣuḥbah; Sunnah; Walāyah; Waqf.

BIBLIOGRAPHY

General Works

Literature in English, German, French, Arabic, and Turkish on the *ṭarīqah* orders and Islamic sainthood is extensive and is causing a significant reevaluation of views. The selective bibliography focuses on works in English. Spencer Trimingham's *The Sufi Orders in Islam* (New York, 1971; reprint 1998), though now somewhat dated, remains the standard handbook on the subject. Readable scholarly overviews of the history and practices of the *ṭarīqah*s are in some general works on Sufism, including Carl Ernst's *The Shambhala Guide to Sufism* (Boston, 1997) and William Chittick's *Introduction to Sufism* (Oxford, 2000). Alexander Knysh's *Islamic Mysticism: A Short History* (Leiden, 2000), conceived as a reference work, provides a detailed history of the theory and praxis of Sufism, including the orders, systematically presented. John Voll, "Sufism: Sufi Orders," in *The Oxford Encyclopedia of the Modern Islamic World*, edited by John L. Esposito (Oxford, 1995), provides an excellent précis and is especially good on the role of the *ṭarīqah*s in resistance to colonialism. Specialist bibliographies are in the articles on the individual brotherhoods and their founding figures in Ehsan Yarshater, ed., *Encyclopaedia Iranica* (New York, 2001–), and H. A. R. Gibb et al., *The Encyclopaedia of Islam*, 2d ed. (Leiden, 1960–). The articles "Ṭarīqa" and "Taṣawwuf" in the latter are especially important and comprehensive. Alan Godlas's online article "Sufism—Sufis—Sufi Orders: Sufism's Many Paths," available from www.arches.uga.edu/~godlas/Sufism.html, contains extensive scholarly information about the *ṭarīqah* organizations, complete with links to Ṣūfī teachers, orders, and subbranches on the web.

Sources

Abū al-Najīb al-Suhrawardī's *Ādāb al-murīdīn* is available in the abridged translation of Menahem Milson as *A Sufi Rule for Novices* (Cambridge, Mass., 1975). See also H. Wilberforce Clarke, trans., *The ʿAwarif u'l-maʿarif by Shahab-u'd-Din b. Muhammad Suhrawardi* (New York, 1973).

Special Studies

Abbas, Shemeem. *The Female Voice in Sufi Ritual: Devotional Practices of Pakistan and India.* Austin, Tex., 2002.

Abun-Nasr, Jamil. *The Tijaniyya: A Sufi Order in the Modern World.* Oxford, U.K., 1965.

Baldick, Julian. *Imaginary Muslims: The Uwaysi Sufis of Central Asia.* New York, 1993. A précis and analysis of a history of the Uwaysi tradition written circa 1600.

Bashir, Shahzad. *Messianic Hopes and Mystical Visions: The Nūrbakhshīya between Medieval and Modern Islam.* Columbia, S.C., 2003.

Bennigsen, Alexandre, and S. Enders Wimbush. *Mystics and Commissars.* London, 1985. Excellent coverage of the Ṣūfī brotherhoods of the Caucusus and Central Asia, including their development after the 1917 revolution.

Bos, Matthijs van den. *Mystic Regimes: Sufism and the State in Iran, from the Late Qajar Era to the Islamic Republic.* Leiden, 2002. An anthropological approach to the Niʿmatullāhī brotherhood, focusing on the twentieth-century relations of the competing Ṣafī-ʿAlīshāhī and Sulṭān-ʿAlīshāhī branches and their connection to the Iranian state.

Buehler, Arthur. *Sufi Heirs of the Prophet: The Indian Naqshbandiyya and the Rise of the Mediating Sufi Shaykh.* Columbia, S.C., 1998. Traces the history of the Naqshbandis, the impact of colonialism and modernity, and the changing construction of spiritual authority of Naqshbandi *shaykhs* in South Asia.

Clarke, Peter B. *West Africa and Islam: A Study of Religious Development from the Eighth to the Twentieth Century.* London, 1982.

Clayer, Nathalie. *Mystiques, état et société: Les halvetis dans l'aire balkanique de la fin du Xve siècle à nos jours.* Leiden, Netherlands, 1994.

Cornell, Rkia Elaroui, ed. and trans. *Early Sufi Women.* Louisville, Ky., 1993. A translation of the earliest collection of the vitae of Ṣūfī women, by al-Sulamī (d. 1021), with introduction on the role of women in Sufism.

Cornell, Vincent. *Realm of the Saint: Power and Authority in Moroccan Sufism.* Austin, Tex., 1998.

DeWeese, Devin. *Islamization and Native Religion of the Golden Horde.* University Park, Pa., 1994. Describes the role of the Yasawiyya in the Islamization of the Central Asian steppes.

Ernst, Carl W. *Eternal Garden: Mysticism, History, and Politics at a South Asian Sufi Center.* Albany, N.Y., 1992. A study of the role of Sufism and Ṣūfī shrines in the Deccan and their influence on Indian political history and conversion to Islam, based upon the Chishtis of Khuldābād.

Ewing, Katherine Pratt. *Arguing Sainthood: Modernity, Psychoanalysis, and Islam.* Durham, N.C., 1997. Explores the post-colonial construction of Ṣūfī identity, particularly the figure of the Pīr and the Qalandar, on the basis of fieldwork done in Lahore, Pakistan.

Gilsenan, Michael D. *Saint and Sufi in Modern Egypt: An Essay in the Sociology of Religion.* Oxford, 1973.

Gramlich, Richard. *Die schiitischen Derwischorden Persiens.* 3 vols. Wiesbaden, 1965–1981.

Gramlich, Richard. *Die Wunder der Freunde Gottes: Theologien und Erscheinungsformen des islamischen Heiligenwunders.* Stuttgart, 1987.

Gramlich, Richard. *Weltverzicht: Grundlagen und Weisen islamischer Askese.* Wiesbaden, 1997.

Hodgson, Marshall G. S. *The Venture of Islam.* Chicago, 1974.

Hoffman, Valerie. *Sufism, Mystics, and Saints in Modern Egypt.* Columbia, S.C., 1995. Includes an examination of the role of women and a comparison with elements of spirituality shared in common with Coptic Christianity.

Huda, Qamar-ul. *Striving for Divine Union: Spiritual Exercises of Suhrawardī Ṣūfīs.* London, 2003.

Johansen, Julian. *Sufism and Islamic Reform in Egypt: The Battle for Islamic Tradition.* Oxford, 1996. Includes translations of the Egyptian government's 1976 and 1978 ordinances concerning the Ṣūfī orders.

Jong, F. de. *Turuq and Turuq-Linked Institutions in Nineteenth Century Egypt.* Leiden, 1978.

Jong. F. de, and Bernd Radtke, eds. *Islamic Mysticism Contested: Thirteen Centuries of Controversies and Polemics.* Leiden, 1999.

Karamustafa, Ahmet. *God's Unruly Friends: Dervish Groups in the Islamic Later Middle Period, 1200–1550.* Salt Lake City, Ut., 1994. Discusses the history and practices of Qalandars and non-affiliated Ṣūfīs and dervishes.

Karrar, Ali Salih. *The Sufi Brotherhoods in the Sudan.* Evanston, Ill., 1992.

Lapidus, Ira. *Muslim Cities in the Later Middle Ages.* Cambridge, Mass., 1967.

Lewis, Franklin. *Rumi: Past and Present, East and West.* Oxford, 2000. Chapter 10 in particular deals with the history of the Mevlevi order.

Lewisohn, Leonard, ed. *The Heritage of Sufism.* 3 vols., 2d ed. Oxford, 1999. A number of articles in these volumes discuss individual brotherhoods in the Persianate world.

Lifchez, Raymond, ed. *The Dervish Lodge: Architecture, Art, and Sufism in Ottoman Turkey.* Berkeley, Calif., 1992. An excellent study of the physical structures maintained by various Ṣūfī organizations in Anatolia and their functions.

Martin, Bradford G. *Muslim Brotherhoods in Nineteenth Century Africa.* Cambridge, U.K., 1976.

Massignon, Louis. *Essai sur les origines de lexique technique de la mystique musulmane.* 3d ed. Paris, 1968.

McChesney, R. D. *Waqf in Central Asia: Four Hundred Years in the History of a Muslim Shrine, 1480–1889.* Princeton, N.J., 1991.

Naguib al-Attas, Syed. *Some Aspects of Sufism as Understood and Practised among the Malays.* Singapore, 1963.

Netton, Ian Richard. *Sufi Ritual: The Parallel Universe.* Richmond, U.K., 2000.

O'Fahey, Rex. *Enigmatic Saint: Ahmad Ibn Idris and the Idrisi Tradition.* Evanston, Ill., 1990.

Pinto, Desiderio. *Piri-Muridi Relationship: A Study of the Nizamuddin Dargah.* New Delhi, 1995.

Popovic, Alexandre, and Gilles Veinstein, eds. *Les ordres mystiques dans l'Islam: Cheminements et situation actuelle.* Paris, 1986.

Qureshi, Regula. *Sufi Music of India and Pakistan: Sound, Context, and Meaning in Qawwali.* Cambridge, U.K., 1986; reprint Chicago, 1995.

Raudavere, Catharina. *The Book and the Roses: Sufi Women, Visibility, and Zikir in Contemporary Istanbul.* Istanbul, 2002.

Rizvi, Saiyid A. A. *A History of Sufism in India.* 2 vols. New Delhi, 1983.

Schimmel, Annemarie. *Mystical Dimensions of Islam.* Chapel Hill, N.C., 1975.

Schimmel, Annemarie. *My Soul Is a Woman: The Feminine in Islam.* Translated by Susan Ray. New York, 1997.

Sirriyeh, Elizabeth. *Sufis and Anti-Sufis: The Defence, Rethinking, and Rejection of Sufism in the Modern World.* Richmond, U.K., 1999. A geographically wide-ranging study of Muslim and colonial European reactions to popular Sufism as well as the reshaping of Sufism from the eighteenth century to the twenty-first century.

Taylor, Christopher. *In the Vicinity of the Righteous: Ziyāra and the Veneration of Muslim Saints in Late Medieval Egypt.* Leiden, 1999. Discusses the role of visitation of saint's tombs in Egypt and its historical connection with the rise of the *ṭarīqahs*.

Vikør, Knut. *Sufi and Scholar on the Desert Edge: Muḥammad b. ʿAlī al-Sanūsī and His Brotherhood.* London, 1995.

Werbner, Pnina, and Helene Basu. *Embodying Charisma: Modernity, Locality, and Performance of Emotion in Sufi Cults.* London, 1998. Analyzes the rituals of local Ṣūfī shrines and centers in India, Pakistan, and Bangladesh.

Wolper, Ethel Sara. *Cities and Saints: Sufism and the Transformation of Urban Space in Medieval Anatolia.* University Park, Pa., 2003.

Zarcone, Thierry, Ekrem Işin, and Arthur Buehler, eds. *Journal of the History of Sufism.* Istanbul, 2000–. Vols. 1–2 cover the Qādirīyah order.

A. H. Johns (1987)
F. D. Lewis (2005)

TATAR RELIGION See INNER ASIAN RELIGIONS

TATHĀGATA.

In pre-Buddhist India, the term *tathāgata* designated a liberated sage. Unlike other titles for Gotama Buddha common in Pali scriptures such as *bhagavan* (blessed one) and *jina* (victorious one), the Buddha often used the term *tathāgata* to refer to himself. As George Bond has noted, three etymologies for it are prominent in Theravāda texts: (1) *tathā-gato,* meaning "one who has gone thus," who has attained *nirvāṇa* like all prior buddhas, freed from the conditioned, distorted mentalities and sufferings of mundane existence; (2) *tatha-āgato,* meaning "one who has come thus," who has reached the attainment achieved by all buddhas of prior ages, propelling him to come as the universal teacher for this age; and (3) *tatha-āgato,* meaning one who has come to the final truth of things and shows the way to that truth.

To call Gotama Buddha *tathāgata* was to identify him as a type, the latest in the line of perfect buddhas from past ages, highlighting his attainment as supreme for this age. All *tathāgatas* are said to be one in their essential attainments, including four peerless types of fearlessness, ten powers of pervasive knowing (such as knowledge of the causal order, of the capacities, dispositions and destinies of living beings, and of the methods of spiritual development appropriate for each one), six types of perfected supernormal awareness, unconditional compassion, thirty-two exemplary marks of physical perfection, and other excellences.

In line with the first and third etymologies of *tathāgata* above, to call Gotama *tathāgata* was to designate him the personification of the *dharma,* of the truths and attainments that he had realized. Thus, what made him a *tathāgata* was his *dharma-kāya* (Pali, *dhamma-kāya*), his body of *dharma* attainments, made manifest through the physical signs and charismatic powers of his material body, his *rūpa-kāya.*

In line with the second etymology of *tathāgata,* "one come thus as universal teacher," to call Gotama *tathāgata* was also to designate him the most worthy and karmically weighty object of reverence and offerings. The Buddha, his community and teaching, were generously supported by the offerings of devotees during his lifetime. After physical death, the physical embodiment and presence of the Buddha (*rūpa-kāya*) was represented to the world in sacred reliquary mounds containing his relics (stupas), which became focal objects of offering and circumambulation, symbolically reenacting the ways that Gotama's devotees had offered reverence to him as reported in scriptures. By ritually affirming the Buddha's continuing presence in the world as symbolic container (*rūpa-kāya*) of his all-knowing mind (*dharma-kāya*), stupas, and later buddha images, symbolically affirmed the Buddha's continuing power for this world, enabling devotees through the centuries to establish their own relationship to the Buddha at those sacred sites. Stupas and images provide physical supports both for rituals of offering and blessing and for meditations that vividly bring to mind the Buddha's qualities and powers (*buddhānusmṛti*). Thus, in the early centuries after the Buddha's final nirvāṇa, connotations of *tathāgata* informed the emerging two *kāya* paradigm of buddhahood and religious practices centered upon it.

In several Abhidharma schools prior to the rise of Mahāyāna Buddhist movements, saṃsāra and nirvāṇa were framed as a fundamental dualism, nirvāṇa understood as an unconditioned reality totally beyond the dependent origination of conditioned life, attained by cutting off the inmost causes for the five aggregates of conditioned life, for all components of mind and body, through long practice of the path. The pre-Mahāyāna etymologies of *tathāgata* noted above express that dualism: "thus gone" to nirvāṇa beyond the conditioned arising of saṃsāra, "thus come" from that transcendent attainment to reveal the path of liberation before passing totally beyond the world at final nirvāṇa.

But in the centuries after Gotama Buddha's physical passing, within some Buddhist communities, the ritual and meditative practices mentioned above that symbolically affirmed the continuing presence and power of the Buddha's nirvāṇa in this world, together with further developments in practice and philosophy, gradually shifted doctrinal formulation of a Buddha's nirvāṇa toward non-dualism. A Buddha's nirvana was thus understood to be fundamentally undivided from this world in its pervasive awareness, spiritual power and liberating activity. This reformulating of a buddha's nirvāṇa began to take doctrinal expression in Mahāsāṃghika schools a few centuries after the Buddha's *pari nirvāṇa,* and was much further developed in Mahāyāna texts from the first century BCE onward, where it became formalized as the doctrine of the "unrestricted" (all-active) nirvāṇa of the buddhas (*apratiṣṭhita-nirvāṇa*). In this formulation, a buddha's nirvāṇa was said to far exceed that of his arhat disciples, because it comprised not only freedom from bondage to conditioned causes of suffering, but also freedom to unleash vast and endless liberating activity for living beings.

Several factors contributing to this reformulation of nirvāṇa took expression in Mahāyāna scriptures of the early centuries CE, including the emergence of a new Mahāyāna cosmology; a nondual ontology of emptiness; and further development in practices and doctrines of devotion, compassion, and nondual awareness.

Influenced in part by the new meeting of cultures and cosmologies in the Kuṣāṇa Empire of Central Asia of the early centuries CE, and in part by a new emphasis upon many persons taking up the bodhisattva path (all of whom would generate their own realm of buddha activity as fruition of that path), Mahāyāna scriptures expressed a new Buddhist cosmology of numerous *tathāgatas* simultaneously inhabiting different universes in all directions, often in radiant pure realms attended by celestial bodhisattvas (not just appearing individually from age to age). In many Mahāyāna scriptures, the yogic powers of Buddha Gotama or advanced bodhisattvas opened devotees' perception to visions of cosmic *tathāgatas* such as Amitābha, Akṣobhya, and Vairocana, whom devotees ritually reverenced and praised, to whom they made manifold offerings, and from whom they received manifold radiant blessings. Scenes expressing this are prominent, for example, in the *Avataṃsaka sūtra* collection, several *Prajñāpāramitā- sūtras, Vimalakīrti, Śuraṃgamasamādhi, Samādhirāja,* and *Saddharmapuṇḍarīka.*

In such scriptures, visual or oral encounters with cosmic *tathāgatas* often precede or follow a bodhisattva's realization of transcendental wisdom (*prajñāpāramita*), the nondual awareness of *tathāgatas* and advanced bodhisattvas that discern the emptiness of all phenomena (*śūnyatā*), their lack of substantial, independent existence. The empty nature of phenomena, because known by the *tathāgatas* just thus, is frequently referred to as "thusness" (*tathatā*). Although all conditioned phenomena continually change, their intrinsically empty nature never changes, is unconditioned and undivided, like space. Whereas pre-Mahāyāna Abhidharma schools taught penetrating insight (*vipassana*) to cut off the dependent origination of conditioned phenomena and thus attain the unconditioned peace of nirvāṇa beyond them, Mahāyāna texts taught that the very nature of conditioned phenomena was unconditioned emptiness (*śūnyatā*), thusness (*tathatā*), intrinsic peace. Hence, these texts proclaimed, to realize ordinary phenomena as empty, intrinsically quiescent, is to realize nirvāṇa as undivided from saṃsāra.

One way to express this Mahāyāna metaphysic of nondualism was through playful reinterpretation of previous Buddhist etymologies for *tathāgata.* Thus, the Buddha declares in the *Aṣṭasāhasrikā* (eight-thousand-verse) *Prajñāpāramitā sūtra,* "*Tathāgatas* (literally ones who have 'thus gone' or 'thus come') certainly do not come from anywhere, nor do they go anywhere. For indeed thusness (*tathatā*) is unmoving, and the *Tathāgata* is thusness" (Makransky, p. 32). *Tathāgatas* are those whose awareness has become nondual with thusness, who thereby abide in the ultimate, unmoving nature of all phenomenal comings and goings, the undivided, empty, nirvāṇic dimension of this world.

This implies that the awareness through which a buddha or bodhisattva transcends bondage to saṃsāra is also intimate with saṃsāra. To know all living beings nondually through undivided thusness is to sense all beings through boundless, unconditional compassion and love. The bodhisattva path to buddhahood is therefore described as a synergy of deepening wisdom of emptiness (*prajñāpāramita*) and compassionate activity for beings (*puṇya,* spiritual merit). Bodhisattvas, by thereby accumulating vast wisdom and merit, under the guidance and protection of the *tathāgatas,* generate luminous pure realms from which to enact their own salvific activity as they become *tathāgatas* upon completion of their path. Thus, the *tathāgatas,* viewed from above as celestial powers and from below as the fruition of the bodhisattva path, spontaneously radiate blessings and salvific activities and manifestations throughout their domains, making the liberating power of saṃsāra nirvāṇa available to beings in saṃsāra as the compassionate outflow of their knowledge that nirvāṇa and saṃsāra are ultimately undivided.

Because, Mahāyāna texts say, thusness (*tatāhta*) as the empty nondual reality of all things is undivided, the term *tathāgata* now also connotes undividedness among the *tathāgatas* in their essential realization of it, referred to as *dharmakāya.* Likewise, in thusness, all living beings are undivided from the *tathāgatas* and possessed of a primordial purity of awareness that constitutes an innate potential for enlightenment, referred to as the *tathāgata essence* of beings (*tathāgata-garbha*), their intrinsic buddha nature. The ontological oneness of buddhas in nondual thusness supports a communion of *tathāgatas* and celestial bodhisattvas in their visionary manifestations (witnessed in Mahāyāna scriptures by interactions among visionary *tathāgatas*), which—when informed by the teaching of buddha nature—opens into a communion with all living beings. Reverent gestures of bowing and offering are given vivid ritual forms in liturgies such as the seven-part offering practice at the end of the *Gaṇḍavyūha sūtra,* which includes praise, offering, confession, ritual rejoicing, ritual requests, bodhisattva resolutions to attain enlightenment for beings, and dedication of merit to all, while receiving radiant blessings from all the holy beings. Such practices express deepening communion with and participation in the salvific activity of the *tathāgatas* and bodhisattvas in and through the luminous, empty ground of thusness in which all are ultimately undivided.

Elements of such liturgical materials were taken up by Buddhist practice communities of Central Asia, East Asia, and Tibet as means to collect merit and wisdom for the path, to receive blessings and inspiration from the *tathāgatas* and celestial bodhisattvas, and to mediate their power to surrounding communities for healing, protection, prosperity, auspiciousness, and well-being. In this way, practices mediating the power of *tathāgatas* and bodhisattvas became an important part of the activity of Mahāyāna monastic institutions of medieval India, East Asia, and Tibet, whose social, economic, and political support by local communities was motivated in part by communal desires for the application of such ritual power to meet social needs.

See Also Buddha; Perfectibility.

Bibliography

For a summary of key Theravāda sources on *tathāgata,* see George Bond, "Tathāgata," in *Encyclopedia of Religion,* volume 14

(New York, 1987). For examples of early Buddhist and Theravāda ritualization of the Buddha's nirvāṇa as presence and power within saṃsāra, see John Strong, *The Legend of King Aśoka* (Princeton, N.J., 1983), and Kevin Trainor, *Relics, Ritual, and Representation in Buddhism* (New York, 1997). For Asian Buddhist practices mediating the power of *tathāgatas* and bodhisattvas, see Alan Sponberg, "Meditation in Fa-hsiang Buddhism," Daniel Stevenson, "Four Kinds of Samadhi in Early T'ien-t'ai Buddhism," and David Chappel, "From Dispute to Dual Cultivation: Pure Land Responses to Ch'an Critics," in *Traditions of Meditation in Chinese Buddhism*, edited by Peter Gregory (Honolulu, 1986); Raoul Birnbaum, *The Healing Buddha* (Boston, 1989); Glenn Wallis, *Mediating the Power of Buddhas* (Albany, N.Y., 2002); David McMahan, *Empty Vision* (New York, 2002); and Richard Payne and Kenneth Tanaka, eds., *Approaching the Land of Bliss* (Honolulu, 2003). On this subject see also the Princeton University series: *Buddhism in Practice* (Princeton, N.J., 1995), *Religions of India in Practice* (Princeton, N.J., 1995), *Religions of China in Practice* (Princeton, N.J., 1996), edited by Donald S. Lopez, Jr., and *Religions of Japan in Practice* (Princeton, N.J., 1999), edited by George J. Tabane, Jr. For systematic perspectives on *tathāgata*, especially within Mahāyāna traditions, see Edward Conze, *Buddhist Thought in India* (Ann Arbor. Mich., 1973); Paul Griffiths, *On Being Buddha* (Albany, N.Y., 1994); John Makransky, *Buddhahood Embodied* (Albany, N.Y., 1997); and Paul Williams, *Mahāyāna Buddhism* (New York, 1989).

JOHN MAKRANSKY (2005)

TATHĀGATA-GARBHA. Early monastic Buddhism emphasized the reality of "selflessness" *(anātmatā)* as the essential nature of all beings. The "ignorance" *(avidyā)* at the root of suffering in the samsaric life cycle was said to be the misperception of a fixed and independent "self" *(ātman)* within a selfless, wholly relative person. The overcoming of the delusion of self was called "wisdom" *(prajñā)*, and it was commonly explained as the "wisdom of selflessness." However, the earliest sermons of the Buddha are replete with such expressions as "mastery of the self is the real mastery," "he who conquers his own self is the supreme warrior," and so forth. Self-control was a prime goal of the early Buddhist monk or nun. Thus, the term *self* had two distinct connotations. In one, it referred to a fixed, independent, self-substance, and in the other, it referred to the living, empirical, continuum of the person; the former was denied and the latter, clearly presupposed.

With the rise of the messianic Buddhism of the "universal vehicle" (Mahāyāna), both sides of this ambiguity were developed in various ways. The "self" that was thought not to exist was equated with "intrinsic reality" *(svabhāva)*, "intrinsic identity" *(svalakṣaṇa)*, and "intrinsic objectivity" *(svarūpa)*. Its systematic denial was expanded beyond "subjective selflessness" *(pudgala-nairatmya)* to encompass "objective selflessness" *(dharma nairātmyā)*, which was understood as equivalent to "emptiness" *(śūnyatā)*. Notions concerning the other "self," the living, empirical personality that was acknowledged to exist, developed into two major concepts, "enlightenment-spirit" *(bodhicitta)*, and "Buddha essence" *(tathāgata-* or *sugata-garbha)*. The "spirit of enlightenment" concept dates from the earliest Mahāyāna scriptures (first century BCE); its systematization was begun by the scholastic master Nāgārjuna (c. second century CE). The second dates from the second and third centuries CE), with the emergence of the later Mahāyāna scriptures such as the *Laṅkāvatāra Sūtra*, the *Saṃdhi-nirmocana Sūtra*, the *Tathāgatagarbha Sūtra*, the *Srī-māladevī Sūtra* and the *Mahāparinirvāṇa Sūtra*. It was systematized by the Yogācāra masters Maitreyanātha, Asaṅga, and Vasubandhu during the fourth and fifth centuries CE.

The enlightenment-spirit *(bodhicitta)* theory eventually began to reflect the original ambiguity of the Buddha's use of *self*, by employing the scheme of "two realities" *(satya-dvaya)*, the absolute and the relative. The absolute spirit was equated with the wisdom of selflessness, and the relative spirit with the loving mind seeking the welfare of all beings. The perfection of the absolute spirit was thought to result in the achievement of the *dharmakāya* ("truth body") of Buddhahood, and the perfection of the relative spirit in the achievement of the *rūpakāya* ("form body") of Buddhahood, with its heavenly *saṃbhoga* ("beatific") and earthly *nirmāṇa* ("emanation") bodies. An important point is that the duality between the two spirits, as between the two realities, only obtains from the relative perspective. In the enlightened view, the two are ultimately the same: wisdom and compassion are one, the absolute is no different from the relative, and truth is equivalent to form. This is summarized in Nāgārjuna's famous statement, "Emptiness [is] the essence of compassion" ("Śūnyatā-karuṇā-garbham").

Against this background, we can understand the emergence of the Buddha-essence doctrine. The Absolute Truth Body *(dharmakāya)* of the Buddha is transcendent and eternal, yet omnipresent and immanent in every atom of infinity. Thus, from a Buddha's perspective, all beings are already immersed in the "truth-body realm" *(dharmakāyadhātu)* and persist in suffering only because they do not know their own actual situation. Each being's presence in the truth-realm is the *essence* of each; it is each one's essential participation in Buddhahood. Thus, each has an essence of Buddhahood, that is, a Buddha essence within him or her that is one's very selflessness or "natural ultimate freedom" *(prakṛti-parinirvāṇa)*. One's critique, through *prajñā*, of the misknowledge of self and the resultant realization of selflessness amounts to the removal of the obscurations of the Buddha essence and the revelation of the natural luminosity of the Buddha realm.

To refer to the useful compendium of sources written by the Tibetan scholar Bu ston (1290–1364), the *Tathāgatagarbha Sūtra* gives nine similes of the Buddha essence: like a Buddha in a closed lotus, like the honey in the comb, like the grain in the husk, like gold in ore, like treasure buried beneath a pauper's house, like a tree-seed in its sheath, like a Buddha-image wrapped in a filthy cloth, like a world monarch amid the impurities of the womb, and like a golden image contained within its clay mold. Of these nine similes, the first three are said to indicate the *dharmakāya* in its senses of "absolute" and "element" *(dhātu)*, the simile of the golden image to indicate "suchness" *(tathatā)*, and the remaining five to indicate the "spiritual gene" *(gotra)*, an important equivalent concept in which one's inherent Buddhahood is conceived of as a genetic cause of the *dharmakāya.*

The *Mahāparinirvāṇa Sūtra* reveals the Buddha essence of all beings as permanent, happy, omnipresent, pure, and free, for this is how beings appear in a Buddha's vision. The *Avataṃsaka Sūtra* extends its visionary theme of the mutual interpenetration of all things to illustrate how the Buddha wisdom exists in the mind of every being as each one's jewel-like essential perfection. The *Aṅgulimālīya Sūtra* states that "the Buddha essence is the reality, the absolute body, the permanent body, the inconceivable body of the transcendent Lord. . . . It is the self." The *Laṅkāvatāra Sūtra* mentions the Buddha essence and equates it with the "fundamental consciousness" *(ālaya-vijñāna)*, the basic seat of ignorance underlying the six usual consciousnesses and the afflicted mentality *(kliṣṭamanas)* in the idealist psychology of that scripture. Finally, the *Śrīmāladevī Sūtra* mentions the Buddha essence as indispensable both to the process of enlightenment and to the afflicted world.

The apparent contradiction between these revelations and the earlier teachings that all beings are impermanent, miserable, selfless, and impure is addressed in the scriptures themselves by referring to the two realities and the two perspectives, using the hermeneutical concepts of "interpretable meaning" *(neyārtha)* and "definitive meaning" *(nītārtha)*. The Buddha uses his "skill in liberative technique" *(upāyakauśalya)* to teach according to the abilities of his disciples. The notion of an "intention" *(abhiprāya* or *abhisaṃdhi)* underlying a teaching is introduced to explain the Buddha's various strategies. Buston extracts a number of such "intentions" from the texts. The *tathāgata-garbha* doctrine is taught in order to (1) eliminate despair and generate effort, giving the practitioner hope of attaining liberation; (2) eliminate pride and produce respect for others; (3) eliminate absolutistic reifications and nihilistic repudiations and produce wisdom.

In the *Laṅkāvatāra Sūtra,* Mahamati asks the Buddha how his Buddha-essence teaching differs from the "supreme-self" teaching of the *brahmans.* The Buddha replies:

> The perfect Buddhas have taught the Buddha essence intending emptiness, reality-limit, *nirvāṇa,* non-creation, signlessness, and wishlessness. For the immature to be free of their terror of selflessness, they teach the realms of non-conceptuality and non-appearance by the gateway [i.e., teaching] of the Buddha essence. . . . They teach the essence to attract those heterodox persons who are too deeply attached to their "self" notions to awaken to the profound enlightenment. (*Laṅkāvatāra Sūtra,* ed. P. L. Vaidya, Darbhanga, 1959, p. 33)

And in the *Mahāparinirvāṇa Sūtra* the Buddha tells a story about his meeting with five hundred ascetics who admired his beauty and inner composure and wanted to follow his teaching, but were afraid because they thought he was a nihilist; he reassured them that he was not a spiritual nihilist by teaching them the Buddha-essence doctrine.

Among the great Indian treatises, Maitreyanātha's *Ratnagotravibhāga* is the locus classicus of the systematic exposition of the Buddha-essence doctrine. It is elucidated by Asaṅga and Vasubandhu in great detail, without departing from the basic principles given in the scriptures above. On the basis of this treatise, the Jonaṅ order of Tibetan Buddhism developed an elaborate theory of the Buddha essence, connecting it to various Tantric ideas. In Tantrism as well, the Esoteric concept of the "indestructible drop" *(akṣayabindu)* as the basis of transmigration and Buddhahood and the life essence of a living being is extremely similar to the Buddha-essence doctrine. Philosophically, the Tibetans tended to the explanation given in the *Laṅkāvatāra Sūtra* that the *tathāgata-garbha* theory referred to selflessness in a manner soothing to those still unprepared for the more radical denial of self.

In East Asia, the notion of the *tathāgata-garbha* enjoyed great popularity. In a treatise attributed to the Indian Aśvaghoṣa, known in East Asia by the translated title *Dasheng qixin lun* (Awakening of faith in the Mahāyāna), the idealistic idea of mind as world-creator is wedded to the *tathāgata-garbha* doctrine to elevate the *tathāgata-garbha* to the status of a divine mind responsible for the creation of the world of transmigration as well as the attainment of liberation and enlightenment. The Chinese master Jing ying Huiyuan (523–592 CE) developed an elaborate idealistic *(vijñānavāda)* Buddhology on this basis. His theories were critiqued by the Centrist (Mādhyamika) master Jizang (549–623), who sought to avoid the theistic implications of doctrines such as Huiyuan's. Later systematizers such as Zhiyi of the Tiantai school, Fazang of the Huayen school, and many of the greatest Chan masters used the Buddha-essence doctrine in various ways, sometimes with an Idealist (Yogācāra) twist, at other times with a Centrist (Mādhyamika) twist. In modern East Asian Buddhism, the doctrine is again serving Buddhist popularizers and dialogists as a strategy for reassuring cultures where "soul" theories are traditional.

It is noteworthy that the English popularization "Buddha nature" comes from the East Asian writers, for the Chinese *hsing* can be read as "nature," whereas the Sanskrit *garbha, dhātu,* or *gotra* cannot be stretched without considerable effort from the meanings "essence," "element," or "gene," respectively, to that of "nature."

SEE ALSO Ālaya-vijñāna; Buddhist Philosophy; Nirvāṇa; Soul, article on Buddhist Concepts; Tathatā.

BIBLIOGRAPHY

See David S. Ruegg's *La théorie du tathāgatagarbha et du gotra* (Paris, 1969), Diana Y. Paul's *Philosophy of Mind in Sixth Century China* (Stanford, Calif., 1984), and Takasaki Jikidō's *A Study on the Ratnagotravibhāga (Uttaratantra), Being a Treatise on the Tathāgatagarbha Theory of Mahāyāna Buddhism* (Rome, 1966). Buston's compendium of sources on *tathāgata-garbha* has been translated by Ruegg as *Le traité du tathāgatagarbha de Bu ston Rin Chen Grub, traduction du De bzin gsegs pa'i snin po gsal zin mdzes par byed pa'i rgyan* (Paris, 1973).

New Sources

Brown, B. E. *The Buddha Nature: A Study of the Tathagatagarbha and Alayavijñana.* Delhi, 1991.

Hookham, S. K. *The Buddha Within: Tathagatagarbha Doctrine according to the Shentong Interpretation of the Ratnagotravibhaga.* Albany, N.Y., 1991.

King, Richard. "Is 'Buddha-Nature' Buddhist? Doctrinal Tensions in the Srimala Sutra—an Early Tathagatagarbha Text." *Numen* 42 (1995): 1–20.

Lopez, Donald S., Jr., ed. *Buddhism in Practice.* Princeton, 1995.

Takasaki, Jikido. "The Tathagatagarbha Theory Reconsidered: Reflections on Some Recent Issues in Japanese Buddhist Studies" *Japanese Journal of Religious Studies* 27, nos. 1–2 (2000): 73–83.

ROBERT A. F. THURMAN (1987)
Revised Bibliography

TATHATĀ. According to the *Dasheng qixin lun* (The Awakening of Faith in Mahāyāna), "suchness" (Skt., *tathatā* or *bhūtatathatā;* Chin., *chen-ju;* Tib., *de bźin nyid)* denotes the totality of reality in both its transcendental and phenomenal aspects. It establishes the oneness and unity of the absolute and relative spheres and expresses the totality of all things *(dharmadhātu).* Suchness is held to exist in all beings and thus to undergo no changes either in its perfect or defiled state: its nature remains uncreated and eternal. All events and things of *saṃsāra* (i.e., all *dharmas*) make their appearance in the form of individualizations or mental constructions as a consequence of the beginningless continuity of the subconscious memory *(smṛti)* of past experiences acquired during previous existences. It is through the elimination of all mental projections that the world construed in the mind *(citta)* ceases to make its appearances. When seen in this radically transformed way, all things in their essential nature escape and defy any explanation or description because they are free and beyond distinction, remain unchanged, and are characterized by their absolute sameness *(samatā),* which precludes any transformation, destruction, or distinction. Since they cannot be explained in any way, their verbal or conceptual descriptions must be regarded as mere representations; they do not denote realities. All things remain ever as they are; they are such *(tathā)* as they are, and it is their Suchness *(tathatā),* free of all attributes, that expresses the nature of their oneness and totality.

Suchness can only be understood through the inner realization that the true nature of existence does not manifest itself through dichotomous appearances: knower-known, subject-object, perceiver and perceived. The notion of Suchness embraces two aspects, the immutability, purity, and totality of all things, on the one hand, and the activities that evolve within *saṃsāra,* on the other. However, these two aspects of Suchness denote fundamentally one and the same reality. They cannot be considered as two separate entities; rather, they are simply representations of Suchness "operating," as it were, in its transcendental and phenomenal spheres. When equated with *śūnyatā* ("emptiness"), *tathatā* represents the absolute negation of all phenomena and their attributes. Thus, in its metaphysical aspect it has nothing in common with the conditioned and defiled world. It stands beyond and above the impurity and relativity of *saṃsāra.* Suchness remains free and undefiled; it cannot be comprehended precisely because it comprises within itself the totality of things and because its nature escapes conceptual categorization.

Saṃsāra, the sphere of defilement and imperfection, has no beginning but it can be brought to an end. Suchness, which is eternal, pure, and perfect by nature, is present in *saṃsāra* but it remains obscured by defilements. Yet while it is in the sphere of phenomenal existence that Suchness and *saṃsāra* coincide, they are neither identical nor distinct from one another. *Saṃsāra* makes its appearance as a chain of dependently originating phenomena issuing from the *tathāgata-garbha* ("womb of the Tathāgata"), which represents, as it were, the personified principle that stands between the absolute sphere, which is transcendent to human thought, and the relative sphere, which is pervaded by imperfections. When absolute reality becomes manifest in the relative world it projects itself as, or is called, the store-consciousness *(ālaya-vijñāna),* which contains within itself two opposite principles. One is the principle of nonenlightenment and the inclination to perpetuate the cycle of samsaric existences; the other is the principle of enlightenment, which represents the highest quality and state of mind, free of all subjectivity.

When it is devoid of all attributes and conceptual projections, the mind may be compared to space insofar as it is ubiquitous and constitutive of the unity of all things. This universally perfect mind, enlightenment itself, constitutes the *dharmakāya* ("Dharma body, Dharma essence") of all the Tathāgatas. The mind aware of its perfect and pure nature abides in the state of enlightenment, yet so long as it is restricted and obscured by ignorance it remains in the state of nonenlightenment. In other words, perfect enlightenment is embedded in phenomenal existence through the presence of *prajñā* ("transcendental wisdom") and through the law of retribution *(karman).* By perfecting and unveiling *prajñā,* and through the performance of meritorious acts, the element of enlightenment within the mind becomes purified and freed from karmic residues and wisdom becomes manifested in its fullness as the *dharmakāya.* The impurities and mental projections that obscure the mind in its nonenlightened state are produced under the influence of *avidyā* ("ignorance"). It is ignorance that induces the appearance of all mental constructs. When ignorance is subdued and eliminated it is merely the "reenlightened" wisdom that shines forth. Ignorance, although it is the cause of all mental states and projections that obscure the clarity of enlightenment, is nonetheless inherently present in enlightenment. Here again, the two are neither identical nor nonidentical. Just as waves are present on water stirred by the wind, so are mental projections stimulated by the "winds" of ignorance. Once ignorance is eliminated, the mental "waves" subside and the purity of the mind in its enlightenment-essence remains undisturbed.

The nature of perfect and timeless enlightenment is characterized as unattainable by any means within the relative sphere. When enlightenment is totally free of all hindrances *(kleśāvaraṇa* and *jñeyāvaraṇa)* and of the store-consciousness *(ālaya-vijñāna),* which becomes entangled in phenomenal events, it remains pure and immutable in its nature. Yet at the same time, this pure and unhindered enlightenment unfolds itself and becomes manifest as a *tathāgata* (i.e., a Buddha), or in some other form, in order to bring living beings to spiritual maturation. Pure and perfect enlightenment may be spoken of as being present and manifest in the phenomenal sphere precisely as nonenlightenment when, owing to the mind's ignorance, the true nature of Suchness is not fully perceived. In this sense, the state of nonenlightenment has no true existence of its own; it can only be considered in relation to perfect enlightenment, which, as nonenlightenment, is obscured by ignorance. Thus, perfect enlightenment, which remains unchanged and unimpeded at all times, is not really produced (it is ever present within all things) but rather becomes manifested through and within the defiled world that has evolved under the influence of ignorance. A full understanding of the Suchness of all things depends on the degree of the mind's purity and the mind's ability to perceive it. Ordinary people, overwhelmed by defilements and hindrances, do not perceive the nature and presence of Suchness. On the other hand, the Tathāgatas understand it perfectly.

All beings are innerly endowed with Suchness and with all the innate impulses necessary to eradicate imperfections and defilements and to pursue the path of moral activities. From the moment that beings give rise to the thought of enlightenment *(bodhicitta)* until the moment they attain Buddhahood they are protected and guided by the *bodhisattvas* and *tathāgatas*, who assume various manifestations in order to guide them along the path. Suchness, although variously described as the effulgence of wisdom, as true knowledge or pure mind, as tranquil, pure, eternal, and immutable, nevertheless remains free of all distinctions and attributes precisely because all things are of "a single taste," a single reality unaffected by any modes of particularization or dualism.

Sources of the *tathatā* theory include such canonical works as the *Laṅkāvatāra, Śrīmālādevīsiṃhanāda,* and *Tathāgatagarbha Sūtras*, and several other Mahāyāna works including the *Dasheng qixin lun.* The theory of *tathatā,* although present within the writings of both the Mādhyamika and (especially) Vijñānavāda schools, has never been represented by a separate tradition. It has nonetheless exercised influence on philosophical and religious speculation and was particularly and predominantly present in the latest phases of Buddhist writings known as the Tantras.

See Also Ālaya-vijñāna; Nirvāṇa; Prajñā; Soteriology; Śūnyam and Śūnyatā; Tathāgata-garbha.

Bibliography

The authorship of the *Dasheng qixin lun (Mahāyānaśraddhotpāda Śāstra)* is one of the most vexed questions in the textual history of Mahāyāna Buddhism. Although the work is traditionally attributed to Aśvaghoṣa, the Indian Buddhist writer and poet of the first or second century CE, many scholars have doubted this attribution, and some believe the work to be of Chinese origin. See especially Paul Demiéville's "Sur l'authenticité du *Ta tch'eng k'i sin louen,*" in *Bulletin de la Maison Franco-Japonaise* 2 (1929): 1–79, and Walter Liebenthal's "New Light on the *Mahāyāna-Śraddhotpāda Śāstra,*" *T'oung pao* 46 (1958): 155–216. Regardless of this question, the text has exercised great influence on the development of Buddhism in China and continues to be studied to this day in Japan. Two translations of the work, which contains a full and readily comprehensible exposition of *tathatā,* are D. T. Suzuki's *Aśvaghoṣa's Discourse on the Awakening of Faith in the Mahāyāna* (Chicago, 1900) and Yoshito S. Hakeda's *The Awakening of Faith, Attributed to Aśvaghoṣa* (New York, 1967).

Two studies of the *Ratnagotravibhāga mahāyana-uttaratantra,* an important source for theories of *tathāgata-garbha* and *tathatā,* are Eugene Obermiller's *The Sublime Science of the Great Vehicle to Salvation, Being a Manual of Buddhist Monism* (Leiden, 1931) and Takasaki Jikidō's *A Study on the Ratnagotravibhāga (Uttaratantra)* (Rome, 1966). A highly technical discussion of these topics can be found in David Seyfort Ruegg's *La théorie du tathāgatagarbha et du gotra* (Paris, 1969). See also Alex and Hideko Wayman's translation of the *Śrīmālā Sūtra, the Lion's Roar of Queen Śrīmālā: A Buddhist Scripture on the Tathāgatagarbha Theory* (New York, 1974), which contains a concise doctrinal exposition in the introduction.

New Sources

Jñanasribhadra, Ye shes dpal bzang po, et al. *Sei nyuryogakyo chu.* Kyoto, 1993.

Sharf, R. H. *Coming to Terms with Chinese Buddhism: A Reading of the Treasure Store Treatise.* Honolulu, 2002.

Sutton, F. G. *Existence and Enlightenment in the Lankavatara-Sutra: A Study in the Ontology and Epistemology of the Yogacara School of Mahayana Buddhism.* Albany, N.Y., 1991.

Suzuki, D. T. *Studies in the Lankavatara Sutra.* New York, 2000.

Tanabe, G. J. *Religions of Japan in Practice.* Princeton, 1999.

Tadeusz Skorupski (1987)
Revised Bibliography

TATTOOING See BODILY MARKS

TAUBES, JAKOB.

TAUBES, JAKOB. Jakob Taubes was born in Vienna on February 25, 1923. In 1937, as a result of the appointment of his father, Zwi Taubes, as chief rabbi to Zürich, he moved to Switzerland and survived the Nazi persecution. In 1943 he became a rabbi. In 1947 he completed his studies in philosophy at Zürich and published *Abendländische Eschatologie* (Western Eschatology).

In 1948 he moved to the United States, where he married Susan Anima Feldman. He obtained a post at the Jewish Theological Seminary in New York, where he worked with Louis Finkelstein, S. Libermann, and Lewis L. Strauss. In 1949 he met Gershom Scholem (1897–1982). However, his association with Scholem was not successful: personal and theoretical reasons led to a quick breakdown in their relations.

He returned to the United States in 1953 and after being awarded a Rockefeller scholarship he spent the next two years at Harvard University. In the academic year 1955–1956 he taught at Princeton University. In 1956 he was a professor of history and philosophy of religion at New York's Columbia University, where he remained for ten years. He met Peter Szondi (1893–) and Theodor Adorno (1903–1969). In 1966 he was appointed as the chair of Jewish studies at the Freie Universität Berlin, a post that he held until 1979, when he took charge of the new Department of Hermeneutics. During this same period he taught at the Maison des Sciences de l'Homme in Paris. In Berlin Taubes became an icon of the student movement.

Along with Jürgen Habermas (1925–) and Dieter Heinrich (1927–), he was editor of the *Theorie* series of Suhrkamp. In 1983 the first of the three-volume *Religionstheorie und Politische Theologie* was published and dedicated to Carl Schmitt (1888–1985), whom Taubes had met in 1978 and with whom he had remained in touch. The history of this working relationship was the subject of his book *Gegenstrebige Fügung*. In 1987 the Heidelberg Seminar on the *Letters to the Romans* took place and was eventually published under the title *Die politische Theologie des Paulus*. After being ill on a number of occasions and spending time in nursing homes, he died on March 21, 1987.

Taubes's work was based on identifying a link between religion and politics. Beginning in the early 1980s he prepared work that would lead to the three-volume *Religionstheorie und Politische Theologie*, an endeavor that had actually begun in the 1950s when, after producing a work on political philosophy and theology, he published two studies (*Theology and Political Theory* and *On the Symbolic Order of Modern Democracy*), the product of a detailed study of Schmitt's works; or earlier when, in *Abendländische Eschatologie*, the only book published during his life, he attempted to return to the problem of political theology, the source of which he identified in the origins of Jewish theocracy. In this work, a year after the publication of *Lebendiges Judentum* (Living Judaism; the book by Zwi Taubes, in which the Zionist standpoint appears as the only means of escape for European Jewry), there is no reference to the *so'ha*; however, the whole work is based on the need to question the historical position reached without resorting to the solution proposed by his father. A forerunner of the debate that followed concerning modernity, despite being referred to by Karl Löwith (1897–1973) in *Meaning in History* (1949), *Abendländische Eschatologie* remained forgotten for a long time. The work is an attempt to examine the position in Western history of the need for fulfillment specific to apocalyptics. It is divided into four parts: the first identifies in Jewish apocalyptics and their Gnostic expression "the essence of eschatology"; the second is devoted to the "history of apocalyptics"; and the third and fourth volumes are concerned with its definition, first theologically and then philosophically, in modernity.

The history of philosophy and political theology are the two pivotal themes of his work and they find full expression in Paul's (c. 3–c. 66) Messianism. At first Taubes attempted to redefine the idea of Messianism in a different way from Scholem; thus, in the seminar on the *Letters to the Romans*, in an answer to the views of Friedrich Nietzsche (1844–1900), Sigmund Freud (1856–1939), Karl Barth (1886–1968), Schmitt, Walter Benjamin (1892–1940), and Scholem himself, he returns Paul to his Jewish roots, believing that Paul's antinomic Messianism, first of all, was the only way to attain the fulfillment of the original apocalyptic requirement of the end of history, without thereby resorting to a dualist Gnostic or Marcionite solution, and also that it represented the most appropriate way of dealing with the question of Law, either the Torah or the Nomos, which nonetheless found its most complete expression in Schmitt's concept of sovereignty. In short, through Paul, Taubes produces a detailed Messianic account of the two main problems of the postmodern age: the end of history and the end of sovereignty. In his opinion, following in the footsteps of Benjamin, Pauline Messianism produced an upheaval of political theology and a radical reconsideration of the history of philosophy.

BIBLIOGRAPHY

Works by Jakob Taubes

Religionstheorie und Politische Theologie. Munich, 1983–1987.

Ad Carl Schmitt: Gegenstrebige Fügung. Berlin, 1987.

Abendländische Eschatologie. Munich, 1991.

Die politische Theologie des Paulus. Munich, 1993.

Vom Kult zur Kultur. Munich, 1996. A collection of essays.

Il prezzo del messianesimo: Lettere di Jacob Taubes a Gershom Scholem e altri scritti. Macerata, Italy, 2000, with an unpublished seminar on Benjamin's thesis.

Messianismo e cultura. Milan, 2001.

Other Sources

On Taubes, see Norbert W. Bolz and Wolfgang Hübener's collection *Spiegel und Gleichnis: Festschrift für Jacob Taubes* (Würzburg, 1983), Richard Faber, Eveline Goodman-Thau, and Thomas Macho's collection *Abendländische Eschatologie: Ad Jacob Taubes* (Würzburg, 2001), and also the monograph by Elettra Stimilli, *Jacob Taubes: Sovranità e tempo messianico* (Brescia, Italy, 2004).

ELETTRA STIMILLI (2005)

TAULER, JOHANNES (c. 1300–1361), German Dominican and mystic. Born at Strasbourg, Tauler entered the convent of the Strasbourg Dominicans as a young man and was probably a student, and certainly a disciple, of Meister Eckhart. Living at a time of political upheaval, aggravated by the social excesses that came in the wake of the Black Death, Tauler was distinguished by a remarkable sobriety of language and thought, a refusal of extremism, and a profound understanding of human nature, which did not keep him from being a demanding spiritual guide. His surviving sermons, all in German, were preached to Dominican nuns, written down, copied, and sent to other convents eager for spiritual nourishment, then often in scarce supply.

Primarily a pedagogue and a "master of life," Tauler takes as his starting point a carefully defined conception of "man as being really like three men *(Menschen)*, though remaining one": the sensible man, with sensations, perceptions, imagination, action, and sensible will; the rational or intellectual man, capable of abstract thought, conceptualization, and deduction; and the higher, or interior and essential man, the "depth" *(Grund)* from which the spark emerges and in which the birth of God takes place.

The spiritual life starts with sensible devotion (images of the life, death, and resurrection of Christ) and a love that is felt strongly at the time of the first "conversion" of the heart, often with a degree of exaltation that approaches intoxication. But such devotion and love, though useful, remain "in nature," and there follows a lengthy period in which the person advances with difficulty, under the guidance of reason as it exercises discernment, often amid obscurity and aridity when reduced to its own powers and sustained by naked faith. If the person perseveres, this period brings a detachment that will do away with all obstacles to the unmediated encounter with God. In this process an experienced teacher is needed. If God wills it, the person will attain supernatural contemplation, a pure gift that cannot be merited.

In addition to Bernard of Clairvaux, William of Saint-Thierry, and Meister Eckhart, Tauler drew on Christian (Dionysius the Areopagite) and non-Christian (Proclus) Neoplatonism. Tauler exercised an extensive influence in the Germanic countries (as a young man, Luther read and reread him) and also—through Latin translations and complex channels—on Spanish and French spiritual writers.

BIBLIOGRAPHY

An exhaustive bibliography of works published before 1961 is in *Johannes Tauler: Ein Deutscher Mystiker,* edited by Ephrem Filthaut (Essen, 1961), pp. 436–479. A bibliography of works from 1961 until 1969 is in *Bibliographisches Handbuch der Deutschen Literaturwissenschaft,* vol. 1, edited by Clemens Köttelwesch (Frankfurt, 1973). For 1969 through 1973 there is *Bibliographie der Deutschen Sprach- und Literaturwissenschaft,* edited by Hildegard Huttermann, Clemens Köttelwesch, and Heinz-Georg Halbe (Frankfurt, 1973). The original texts of Tauler's sermons are published as *Sermons de Tauler,* 2 vols., edited by A. L. Corin (Liège, 1924–1929). A critical edition was produced by Ferdinand Vetter as *Die Predigten Taulers,* "Deutsche Texte des Mittelalters," vol. 11 (Berlin, 1910). A. L. Corin has translated the sermons into French in three volumes, *Sermons de Tauler* (Paris, 1927–1935), and Georg Hofmann has produced a German edition in two volumes, *Sämtliche Predigten* (Freiburg, 1983). An English translation by Maria Shrady is available as *Johannes Tauler: Sermons* (New York, 1985). Selections from Tauler have been translated and edited by Eric Colledge and Sister M. Jane, O.P., as *Spiritual Conferences* (Saint Louis, 1961). A brief secondary source on Tauler is James M. Clark's *The Great German Mystics* (Oxford, 1949), pp. 36–54, with bibliography, pp. 114–117.

CLAIRE CHAMPOLLION (1987)
Translated from French by Matthew J. O'Connell

TAʿZIYAH, more fully known as *taʿziyah-khvānī* or *shabīh-khvānī,* is the Shīʿī passion play, performed mainly in Iran. The word itself is derived from the Arabic *ʿazāʾ,* "mourning," and the *taʿziyah* performance marks the death of Ḥusayn, the grandson of the prophet Muḥammad and the third imam of the Shīʿah, who was brutally murdered, along with the male members of his family and a group of followers, while he was contesting his hereditary right to the caliphate. The horrors of this hot and bloody scene, which took place on the plain of Karbala near the Euphrates on ʿĀshūrāʾ, the tenth day of the Muslim month of Muḥarram, in AH 61/680 CE, became the prototype of Shīʿī martyrdom.

Beginning in the middle of the tenth century, annual parades held in Baghdad during the month of Muḥarram vividly portrayed the fate of the martyrs, loudly lamented by attending crowds. When the Safavid monarch made Shiism the state religion of Iran in the sixteenth century, these demonstrations became highly elaborate, featuring men, on caparisoned horses and camels, acting the role of martyrs with bloody wounds and gruesome injuries. Floats were also constructed to depict the various events at Karbala, and the entire parade was accompanied by funerary music while bystanders wailed and beat their breasts. Contemporaneously, the lives, deeds, and sufferings of Ḥusayn and other Shīʿī martyrs were also treated in a book entitled *Rawḍat al-shuhadāʾ* (The Garden of the Martyrs), which in turn gave rise to readings called *rawẓah-khvānīs,* or "garden recitations" in Persian. It was from a combination of the Muḥarram parades and the *rawẓah-khvānī* that the *taʿziyah* drama emerged in the middle of the eighteenth century.

Nowadays, *ta'ziyah* can be performed throughout the year, but originally it was staged only in the month of Muḥarram and the following month of Ṣafar. From the crossroads and public squares where they were first presented, *ta'ziyah* performances soon moved to caravansaries and private houses, and then to a special type of theater called *takīyah* or *Ḥusaynīyah*. Over the next century and a half theaters of various sizes and constructions were built, reaching enormous proportions in the elaborate Takīyah Dawlat (State Theater) built by Nāṣir al-Dīn Shāh in the 1870s.

In all these performance areas or playhouses the main action takes place on a raised circular or square platform around which the audience is seated on the ground, but the movement of the actors in and around the audience preserves the traditional interaction of performers and spectators in the Muḥarram celebrations. Audience participation is so intense that men and women weep and mourn as though the historical scenes before them were taking place in the immediate present.

The protagonists, dressed predominantly in green, sing their parts, while the villains, who wear red, speak their lines. Symbolic stage properties, such as a bowl of water to represent a river, are improvised according to need, particularly in the villages, where costumes are few. The director/producer is omnipresent on the stage as prompter, property man, and regulator of the actors, musicians, and viewers. Villagers and townsmen participate when professional actors are scarce, but troupes of actors travel from place to place, with men playing the women's roles. Parts are often passed from father to son in family groups: acting is a hereditary trade.

The Islamic Revolution of 1978–1979 utilized the Ḥusayn paradigm and was carried out in accordance with the Shīʿī calendar. The stationary rituals such as *ta'ziyah* and the *rawẓah-khvānī* served as political rallies at which the assembled people were stimulated by speakers who mixed the Karbala mourning slogans with political ones. The digressions and the comparisons of the plight of Ḥusayn with the contemporary political, moral, and social situation have long been a tradition at these rituals and can evoke in the audience a particular social and religious climate which can move the audience to political action.

Ta'ziyah reached its peak in Iran in the second half of the nineteenth century. In the 1960s and 1970s, because of overt westernization and other social and political factors, the performances, which had been an urban creation, retreated to the rural areas. The fate of this original theater form in the world of Islam is now uncertain. The Shīʿah of the Caucasus (part of Iran until the early nineteenth century) and of Iraq and southern Lebanon know it on a more limited scale. Innovative Western theater directors and producers are now very much interested in the *ta'ziyah* as a means of breaking down the barriers that divide the audience from the actors in Western theater.

On the Indian subcontinent the name *ta'ziyah* is given to a symbolic miniature reproduction of Ḥusayn's tomb as well as of the tombs of other Shīʿī martyrs. These *ta'ziyahs* are not literal facsimiles of any particular tomb but imaginary recreations. Usually made of bamboo and/or sticks covered with colorful paper and papier-mâché, these structures resemble Indian architecture more than the architecture of Western Asia, where the original tombs were built. The *ta'ziyahs* are carried in processions (during the months of Muḥarram and Ṣafar) and are housed in *imām-bārahs* and private houses, including those of Sunnī Muslims. They may be small enough for two men to carry or immense structures carried by many people. At the conclusion of the procession some of the *ta'ziyahs* may be buried in a local "Karbala ground." Other models, known as *ẓarīḥs*, are made of durable material, generally silver, and are not carried in processions or buried.

See Also ʿĀshūrāʾ; Rāwẓah-khvānī.

Bibliography

Chelkowski, Peter, ed. *Tá'ziyeh: Ritual and Drama in Iran.* New York, 1979.

Pelly, Lewis. *The Miracle Play of Hasan and Husain* (1879). Reprint, Farnborough, U.K., 1970.

PETER CHELKOWSKI (1987)

TEARS

TEARS have always played important roles as symbols and signs in religious life around the world, yet they have only recently begun to attract significant scholarly interest. From the tears shed in love and longing for the absent Kṛṣṇa by the *gopis* (milk maidens) in Brindavin to those shed by Shiʿi Muslims during the annual remembrance of the martyrdom of al-Husayn; from the tears of compunction of Christian mystics to "the welcome of tears" of the Tapirapé people of central Brazil (in which friends literally bathe each other when meeting), tears are ubiquitous in the world's religions. A general overview of tears in the history of religions based on a general phenomenology of tears enables us to appreciate many of symbolic associations tears have had in diverse religious traditions, as well as their many uses in religious rituals. No attempt is made here to exhaust the diverse examples of ritualized tears in the history of religions. Instead, what follows is a brief discussion of some of the central functions tears, or the acts of weeping, crying, and lamentation, have served in religious ritual activities, as well as in narrative, pictorial, and dramatic representations.

The Phenomenological Nature of Tears. Defined in physical terms, tears are a transparent saline liquid secreted from the lachrymal ducts around the eyes. The physiological functions of tears are to keep the cornea moist, wash away irritants from the eyes, and, with the antibacteriological agents they contain, fight infection of the eyes. It is not these physiological functions but rather the symbolic import of tears, the various meanings that people have attributed to them, and the diverse ways that tears have been ritualized that are important for the history of religions. In a pedantic sense, tears are a human universal, for all healthy persons have the ability to shed tears. Yet, in the study of tears in the history of religions, not all tears are identical; the meaning of specific tears is culturally and historically negotiated and renegotiated over time and space. The meaning attributed to specific tears depends upon a number of situational elements and specific sociocultural expectations. Local constructions of gender, class, age groupings, and occupational roles, for instance, can all affect the meaning of tears, as well as the value and appropriateness of specific acts of crying tears. For a supposedly dispassionate Buddhist monk, for instance, crying over a death might be considered inappropriate, whereas this would not bring any censure for a lay person.

The following basic phenomenological characteristics are worthy of note:

1. tears are a salty liquid;
2. tears flow from the eyes down the face;
3. tears are an extruded bodily product;
4. tears cross the bodily boundary of inside/outside;
5. tear-filled eyes produce blurred vision; and
6. tears are often, but not always, unwilled and uncontrolled.

Because they are liquid, tears often are associated with water, as well as with other bodily fluids such as blood and milk; because they flow downward, they are associated with streams, waterfalls, and rain; and because they are saline, sometimes they are associated with the sea or ocean. In this manner, tears are connected to broader symbolic complexes. Yet, it is difficult to imagine disembodied tears because of their immediate association with the human body and, more specifically, with the head and the body. Marcel Mauss (1872–1950), one of the leaders of the Durkheimian school of sociology, first pointed out that in societies and religions around the world, the human body is a primary site of symbolization and social control (Mauss, 1935, 1979). The human body as a whole, specific body parts (e.g., the head, arms, feet, stomach, genitals), body orifices, and bodily products often become religiously or ideologically overdetermined signs. That is, the names of body parts metaphorically come to refer to more than their physiological referents, while they also carry positive or negative connotations. As such, they are discursive sites of multiple, competing, and even contradictory ascriptions of meaning and valuations. In addition, the body is frequently a physical site of ritual work designed to transform it, enculturate it, or otherwise control it.

Tears are a bodily product that is extruded from the body, like blood, sweat, urine, feces, vomit, mucus, spittle, mother's milk, and seminal fluids. All of these are symbolically charged substances. However, the specific cultural and historical understanding of the human body as such, the differences posited among specific kinds of bodies, and the cultural valuations that are attached to specific body parts and bodily products all help to determine how these symbolically charged things are viewed (positively or negatively) and how they are related to each other. Less often noticed are the ways these and related social factors affect how the human body and its products are subjectively experienced by individuals.

Mary Douglas famously argued that "the body can stand for any bounded system. Its boundaries can represent any boundaries which are threatened and precarious" (Douglas, 1966, p. 115). As an extruded liquid, tears cross the bodily boundary of inside and outside. They flow from the realm of the invisible to that of the visible, and from the hidden or private sphere to the public sphere. As Arnold van Gennep noted many years ago, liminal states, sites, and activities, including the crossing of boundaries, are ambivalent and inherently dangerous (Van Gennep, 1960). When the boundary is bodily, issues of purity and pollution arise almost inevitably. Thus, in an important sense, tears are liminal; they move and exist betwixt and between two distinct states or spaces, and therefore they are "natural symbols" of transitions or passages. These passages may be spatial or temporal, or both. Not surprisingly, ritual tears are often shed at important rites of passage, such as weddings and funerals, as well as on more common occasions of parting or reunion.

The liminal nature of tears enables them to serve as a symbolic means of mediation between persons (living or dead), between an individual and society, between the inner world and the outer world, and so forth. In this sense, tears play an important sociopolitical function in mediating (and potentially transforming) power relations between humans, divine and human beings, and the dead and the living. In crossing the boundary of the body, bodily products have a transgressive potential that often makes them dangerous, polluting, or disgusting. The ancient Indian text *The Laws of Manu* includes tears in a long list of bodily products that are polluting. In many cultures blood becomes polluting when it flows outside a body (e.g., as menstrual flow), but in other instances—or, better, in the case of other bodies—blood may be said to have positive power, as in the ritual bleedings the Aztec and Mayan kings performed on themselves in order to reinvigorate the cosmos. Unlike most other bodily products, though, tears are usually considered to be polluting. Indeed, perhaps because of the function they play in washing the eyes, they are widely believed to be purifying and even to possess healing powers.

In many cases, instead of becoming a polluting substance by transgressing the boundary of the individual human body, tears function as a sign of a problem with the social body. Seemingly uncontrolled weeping produces a disheveled body, which itself symbolizes a disordered or chaotic social body. Thus, tears may imply that proper social boundaries have been transgressed, or that a desired interpersonal relationship has been ruptured. At the same time, tears can function as an invitation to the other party to repair a broken relationship, or as an appeal for rectification of a problem.

Another potential meaning of tears that is suggested by their crossing the bodily boundary of inside/outside bears mention: Tears may serve as a sign of ecstasy—an out-of-body state or psychosomatic experience. This is why tears are often associated with mystical experience in religions around the world, including Jewish Qabbalah, Christian mysticism, and Sufism. Alternatively, tears may be taken as a sign that a spirit or deity has entered a body and possessed it. In the religious services of Pentecostal Christians, for example, the descent of the Holy Spirit into the body of a believer is signaled by glossolalia (speaking in tongues), the loss of full consciousness, and frequently by copious tears flowing down the face. The absence of tears may also be a sign that a human body has been possessed. During the Spanish Inquisition in Europe, suspected witches were sometimes ordered to cry. Because the ability to cry tears was considered to be a mark of human nature, the inability to produce them on command signaled that a demonic nature inhabited the witch's body.

Healthy eyes bring light into the dark cavernous human body and the mind, providing crucial information about conditions in the exterior world. In the West, the eyes have long been called "windows to the soul." Although this metaphor is culturally specific, reflecting on the phenomenology of windows enables us to appreciate the symbolic associations drawn in the West between windows, eyes, and tears. A transparent window provides outsiders with visual access to an interior space, while simultaneously providing insiders with visual access to the exterior. As such, windows are a passive medium for visual activity across a boundary demarcating an interior and an exterior space. Eyes are like windows insofar as they, too provide visual access to both the interior and exterior of the human body. In sharp contrast, tears cross the bodily boundary of inside and outside in one direction only: Tears flow out of the eyes, not into them. The unidirectional nature of the flow of tears informs the widespread belief that tears carry information about the interior world of an individual (or, at times, of a group) out to the broader world. Tears are believed to be signs of interior and otherwise invisible states, most commonly affective or spiritual states. However, as noted earlier, the determination of the meaning of specific tears is also affected by the local religious and medical understanding of the body. For instance, in the Western humoral theory of the body, which held sway from the time of Galen in the second century CE until the Renaissance, tears were taken to be a symptom of the changing balance of the five humors in the body. Similarly, melancholy, which was characterized by uncontrollable bouts of crying, was considered to be the result of excess humidity in the body.

Unlike transparent windows and healthy eyes, which allow clear vision across boundaries, tearful eyes produce blurred vision. Phenomenologically, this blurred vision of the outside world suggests the blurring of boundaries and differences. Thus, ritual tears shed in mourning over a deceased person may blur the boundary between the dead and the living. Similarly, ritual tears may dissolve other spatial and temporal boundaries. The participants in the annual Shiʿi devotional rites of Muharram, for instance, weep in order to return to the time and the place of the martyrdom of al-Husayn at Karbala. Recalling this aspect of the phenomenology of tears also helps us to better understand the phrase "dissolve into tears." When an individual dissolves into tears, verbal speech is no longer possible, but the entire body "speaks." Collective weeping can produce a psychosomatic experience of communion.

Another aspect of the phenomenology of tears has long caused problems for students of religion. Tears are often seemingly spontaneous emotional responses to external stimuli or memories. When understood to be a spontaneous and unwilled affective response to joy, anger, frustration, and so on, crying appears to be a natural and universal human emotional response and therefore, precultural in nature. Although feelings or emotions have a subjective immediacy and reality, they have no observable or objective physical reality per se. Feelings have to be expressed—in a grimace, a smile, a frown, a cry, rolling of the eyes, and so on—in order to be communicated to others. Tears, though, are literally expressed in the sense that lachrymal fluid is squeezed out of the body. This characteristic allows actual tears to provide apparent objective evidence of subjective states and of otherwise hidden psychosomatic conditions.

The problem historians of religions faced was that ritualized weeping is clearly not spontaneous; it is choreographed. Ritual weepers, professional and nonprofessional as well, can often turn their tears on and off at will. Some Western scholars found this disconcerting; others found it to be confirmatory evidence of the presumed duplicitous and insincere nature of "primitives." Yet others, perhaps influenced by the Protestant suspicion of the "empty" rituals of the Roman Catholic Church, sought to distinguish between "real" tears and artificial or false ones. A. R. Radcliffe-Brown in his famous anthropological study *The Andaman Islanders* (1922) noted that there were two types of weeping: (1) weeping as a spontaneous expression of feeling; and (2) weeping as "required by custom." Following Durkheim's argument in *The Elementary Forms of the Religious Life* (1912), Radcliffe-Brown largely dissociated ritual weeping from individual emotions of grief, sadness, and so on. Functionalists followed Radcliffe-Brown in arguing that, rather than being provoked by a strong emotion such as grief, the tears shed in ritual contexts primarily served to evoke feelings of social solidarity. Here, too, they developed a claim made by Durkheim, who asserted that ritual weeping produced a collective sense of "effervescence" that helped to restore and strengthen proper social relations.

The functionalist interpretation of ritual weeping is not completely wrong; ritual tears serve multiple purposes, including creating a shared emotional state. However, insofar as this line of argument suggests that spontaneous tears are "real," whereas ritual tears are not, it is misleading. In effect, to distinguish true and false tears in this way is to universalize the Western bourgeois and Protestant privileging of the individual as the ultimate locus of value. Moreover, it prematurely forecloses serious inquiry into the distinct local discourses about tears and the body. Finally, to imply that "primitives" are hopelessly controlled by "custom" is to deny that they can willfully act for their own intents and purposes. It also ignores the ways in which people everywhere at times use the cultural expectations concerning emotional displays for specific purposes. Nevertheless, it is important to recognize that social and cultural "feeling rules" do inform ritualized weeping and other affective displays. Cultural capital is often gained by following such affective scripts, but we must also take account of those affective displays that challenge the status quo.

Tears as Substance, Sign, and Symbol. Tears sometimes function as a powerful substance in religious ritual practices or in myths. That is, the actual physical tears themselves are believed to have specific powers. In the Middle East, for example, tears have been collected in tiny glass bottles for their healing qualities for thousands of years. Two examples illustrate how one aspect of the phenomenology of tears—their salinity—has been adapted to local ecological and agricultural conditions in symbolic form. During the annual dry season, as well as in periods of extended drought, the Aztecs performed rain rituals which incorporated sacrifice and ritual weeping. More than being mere expressions of grief, it was believed that the saline tears shed by participants produced rain by flowing down to the moist and rotting underworld where fresh water was trapped. Like the salt water of the sea, tears had the power to desiccate the land and to wither the crops. Just as Aztec agricultural practices required them to control and direct the salt water from the great Mexican basin in order to irrigate crops with fresh water, tears, too, were controlled and ritually directed. The ritual tears flowed down, causing the release and counter flow of fresh productive water from underworld springs.

These Aztec ritual tears recall those shed by Susano-o, a Japanese deity, in a myth recounted in the *Kojiki* (712 CE). Like the Aztec rituals, the Susano-o myth cycle is closely related to the local ecology, agricultural cycle, and irrigation practices. After the death of Izanami, the spouse of Susano-o's father, and her descent to the underworld, Susano-o was appointed to rule the realm of the ocean (a variant found in the *Nihon shoki* [720 CE] says the underworld). Susano-o, however, refused: "He wept and howled until his beard extended down over his chest for a length of eight hands. His weeping was so violent that it caused the verdant mountains to wither and all the rivers and waters to dry up" (Philippi, 1968, p. 72) Here, too, salty tears shed over the dead threaten to destroy the fertility of the land.

Although tears are sometimes powerful substances, more often they function as highly charged symbols and signs. As signs, ritual tears exaggerate human emotions and interpersonal relationships for dramatic effect. Mourning rites often include ritual weeping, with stylized performances of grief. Weeping here may be an expression of felt emotion, but it need not be. It may also help to create a sense of social solidarity, as Durkheim first suggested, but frequently ritual weeping publicly displays the social and moral status of the deceased and his or her family. One might say that in many cultures ritual tears are the measure of the man. The death of a great man (however that be defined) provokes intense and extensive weeping, whereas a dead man for whom few people weep risks being perceived to have been a "small" man in many ways. Similarly, weeping for the bride in marriage rites marks a rite of passage, a separation of a woman from her natal family, and her reincorporation into a new family. The sadness in parting may be real, but we must also note that the "worth" of a bride may also be measured in part by the depth of feelings of loss that are publicly displayed by relatives.

Ritualized tears also are used strategically or politically to "say" things by those who are powerless or who occupy a socially inferior position. In the ancient Near East, for example, a widow, orphan, or resident alien could get a hearing from the king by calling out to him, throwing herself prostrate before him, and crying. In II *Samuel* 14 is an example of this: Joab asks a woman to dress as a widow and approach King David to appeal for his mercy on Absalom. The ruse succeeds precisely because of the cultural expectation that a good king is one who protects the weak, the powerless, and the poor. Not to respond to the tearful pleas of a widow could open the king to whispered criticism and even his branding as a bad ruler. Significantly, in the Psalms and elsewhere King David himself reportedly shed copious tears of the same sort as this "widow"; that is, King David's ritual tears participated in the same cultural politics of affective display. However, in this case, when David wept and appealed to Yahweh, he effectively placed himself in the inferior and debased position relative to God, whereas he was in the superior position relative to the widow. In other words, insofar as God was imagined as a king writ large, even human kings had to appeal to Him through the same sort of stylized affective display.

Scholars have only begun to investigate the ritual display of emotions and, alternatively, the control of them. We will fully appreciate such rituals, and understand the rich multitude of literary and artistic representations of tears, only by carefully noting how specific aspects of the phenomenological nature of tears have been exploited, adopted, and adapted by specifically situated persons in their own efforts to create religious and moral worlds of meaning. Medieval Japanese poets often equated tears with the dew, employing the poetic conceit of "dew on [one's] sleeves," for instance, to suggest the tears shed by a sensitive person. Although the Japanese poets stressed the ephemeral nature of the dew and tears (and, by extension, human feelings), the evidence of the history of religions speaks to the ubiquitous presence of tears over time and space.

SEE ALSO Aztec Religion; Blood; Eye; Gennep, Arnold van; Head, article on Symbolism and Ritual Use; Human Body, article on Myths and Symbolism; Liminality; Mauss, Marcel; Rain; Rites of Passage; Water.

BIBLIOGRAPHY

Christian, William A. "Provoked Religious Weeping in Early Modern Spain." In *Religious Organization and Religious Experience,* edited by John Davis, pp. 97–114. London, 1982.

Corrigan, John, ed. *Religion and Emotion: Approaches and Interpretations.* New York, 2004.

Douglas, Mary. *Purity and Danger: An Analysis of the Concepts of Pollution and Taboo.* London, 1966.

Durkheim, Emile. *The Elementary Forms of the Religious Life.* London, 1912.

Ebersole, Gary L. "The Function of Ritual Weeping Revisited: Affective Expression and Moral Discourse." *History of Religions* 39 (2000): 211–246.

Mauss, Marcel. "Techniques of the Body." In Marcel Mauss, *Sociology and Psychology,* translated by Ben Brewster. London: 1979, originally published in 1935.

PhIlippi, Donald L., trans. *Kojiki.* Tokyo, 1968.

Radcliffe-Brown, A. R. *The Andaman Islanders.* London, 1922, revised ed. 1933.

Urban, Greg. "Ritual Wailing in Amerindian Brazil." *American Anthropologist* 90 (1988): 385–400.

Van Gennep, Arnold. *The Rites of Passage.* Chicago, 1960, originally published 1909.

Wolfson, Eliot W. "Weeping, Death, and Spiritual Ascent in Sixteenth-Century Jewish Mysticism." In *Death, Ecstasy, and Other Worldly Journeys,* edited by John J. Collins and Michael Fishbane, pp. 209–247. Albany, N.Y., 1995.

GARY L. EBERSOLE (2005)

TECUMSEH (1768–1813) or Tecumtha ("Shooting Star," the celestial panther), a Kispoko Shawnee born near the Mad River in western Ohio, devoted his life to intertribal movements resisting American expansionism and its devastating effects on American Indian communities. Because he and his compatriots fought during a period when power shifted decisively toward the U.S. nation-state, historians have asserted that theirs was a lost cause. Of course during Tecumseh's lifetime no one could have known this. For many American Indians living in the interior, inter-tribal resistance not only made sense, it was a well-established political tradition energized by powerful spiritual and cultural values. This tradition influenced Tecumseh even as it enabled him to influence Indians from the Great Lakes to the Gulf Coast.

During the mid-eighteenth century, the Delaware prophet Neolin had called for a radical break with things European. Based on his visions, Neolin urged Native Americans to regain their independence, to wean themselves from the worst aspects of the fur trade, and to regain the old arts of self-sufficiency. He influenced Pontiac, leader of a massive anti-British uprising in 1762 that involved Anishinaabes, Ottawas, Potawatomis, Menominees, Hurons, Delawares, Shawnees, Senecas, Mesquakies, Kickapoos, Macoutens, Weas, Sauk, and Miamis.

This movement, like many that followed, had emerged in a context already strongly shaped by extensive contact and trade with Europeans. In these contact-zones, diverse peoples moved across and depended upon multi-dimensional networks of cross-cultural ties to engage in reciprocal forms of exchange. New kinds of political figures, alliance chiefs, helped mediate between non-hierarchical Native American villages and imperial authorities. Over time, political, material, and cultural hybridity became the norm, not the anomaly. Tensions and conflicts abounded, but Indians had an essential place in this dynamic world and, most important, could compel non-Natives to come to terms with them.

When this balance shifted, as European settlement expanded and the population of non-Natives soared, Native Americans faced a serious crisis. In region after region, the newcomers became less interested in Indian trade or showing reciprocity within hybridized "middle grounds," and far more interested in acquiring Indian land, through any means necessary. On the so-called frontier new forms of Indian-hating spread along with calls for the extermination of Native Americans. Relations, always tense, became polarized and racialized. Facing this new situation, American Indian prophets like Neolin called for religiously motivated resistance.

A few decades later and further into the interior, a Mohawk prophetess named Coocoochee inspired Native Americans of the Ohio and Great Lakes region to fight to rid their lands of the intrusive American presence. Indeed, on November 4, 1791, in western Ohio, Miamis, Shawnees, Delawares, Potawatomis, Ottawas, Chippewas, Wyandots, Mingos, and Cherokees defeated a large army led by General Arthur St. Clair. Tecumseh certainly learned about this remarkable Indian victory over the Americans.

During his twenties, Tecumseh participated actively in the Chickamaugan revolt in the Southeast. Like many Shawnees, Tecumseh had strong ties to the region. His mother was Creek and he had children with a Cherokee woman. The Chickamaugans comprised dissident Cherokees, Creeks, Shawnees, and ex-Tories. Disgusted with established tribal leaders and distressed by settler incursions onto Indian lands, they built new intertribal towns near the Tennessee River. In 1789, while fighting at their side in a Cumberland raid, Tecumseh saw his beloved older brother Cheeseekau (Pepquannakek, "Shawnee Warrior") killed. Subsequent setbacks brought an end to the Chickamauga revolt a few years later. The American opposition was simply too strong in the Southeast. The same was true in the Ohio country. In 1795 at the Treaty of Greenville, Shawnee leaders and others ceded about two-thirds of what is now Ohio to the Americans.

After 1795, in the Ohio country and in the Southeast, power continued to shift toward the Americans, but in an accelerated manner. During this period, the newly settled states of Kentucky (1792) and Tennessee (1796) acted like a great geopolitical wedge cutting into Indian country. On the one hand, this "wedge" acted as a barrier that made traditional intertribal diplomacy and exchange between northern and southern Indians more difficult and treacherous. On the other hand, Kentucky and Tennessee provided staging grounds for the next wave of invasion and settlement into regions that would eventually be known as the Old Northwest and Old Southwest. New cessions of tribal lands, north and south, chipped away at the remaining land base of interior Indians. By 1810, in the Old Northwest, settlers outnumbered Indians nearly four to one. As newcomers threatened to displace Indians and destroy all forms of reciprocal exchange (the so-called "middle ground"), a new prophetic movement emerged among the Shawnees. It was led by Tecumseh's younger brother Lalawethika (The Rattle).

Lalawethika (1775–1836) realized his own prophetic destiny in 1804 when he awakened from a trance. He had received a revelation directly from the Creator. This experience transformed Lalawethika. He stopped drinking and took a new name, Tenskwatawa, the Open Door. Echoing the messages of previous prophets, Tenskwatawa spoke against dependency, alcohol consumption, and land cessions, and in favor of intertribal solidarity, temperance, and reform. He disliked the fact that missionaries and other agents of American culture encouraged Native men to work in the fields growing food crops. In his eyes, only women tended domestic crops full time. Real men shed blood in the forest. Tenskwatawa charged several people among the Delawares with complicity with evil spirits. This witch-hunt led to the execution of several people, including two annuity chiefs, who had close ties to the Americans or Christian missionaries.

Other modes of internal reform were less violent, but also revealed tensions within tribal communities, between accommodationists and rebels, and between Native Americans and Americans. Tenskwatawa and Tecumseh organized an intertribal village first at Greenville (now in Ohio), then at Prophetstown on the Upper Wabash river (now Indiana). These towns attracted men and women from a dozen or so tribes, including Potawatomis, Ottawas, Ojibwas, Menominees, Winnebagos, Kickapoos, Sacs, and Foxes. Inevitably, this gathering, no matter how peaceful its intent, excited fear and mistrust among white authorities and the chiefs closely allied to them.

Tensions increased still further with the 1809 signing of the Treaty of Fort Wayne, which ceded more than 2.5 million acres of Indian land. The Delaware, Potawatomi, Miami, and other Indian leaders who signed were condemned by Tecumseh and Tenskwatawa. The lands in the western country were common property among all the tribes, and a sale was void unless made by all the Tribes. his brother concurred. Sounding an anti-colonial note that reflected increased racial consciousness, Tenskwatawa taught that whites were not created by God, but by a lesser spirit. Tenskwatawa and Tecumseh advocated Indian solidarity against the American invasion. As the War of 1812 approached, they also carefully considered allying with the British to gain military support. Eventually they did so, only to be gravely disappointed.

Tecumseh also sought support from southern tribes. In 1811, Tecumseh, accompanied by a Mequashake Shawnee prophet named Seekaboo, traveled among Chickasaws, Choctaws, and Creeks to promote pan-tribal cooperation and anti-American militancy. Their only success came among the Creeks, a strong nation increasingly vexed by trade debts, settler incursions, land cessions, internal class divisions, and meddling federal Indian agents. To show their solidarity with northern nations, rebel Creeks danced the Dance of the Indians of the Lakes. They also attacked leaders closely connected with U.S. government officials.

Within two years, the Creek anti-colonial movement attracted nine thousand participants, about half of the entire Creek nation. When a Creek civil war erupted between the rebel Redsticks and their accommodationist opponents, Americans in surrounding states and territories seized the conflict as an opportunity to invade Creek country, ostensibly in behalf of the "friendly" Indians. American armies and militias crushed the Redstick faction and, with the war's close in 1814, exacted huge land cessions from the entire Creek nation, friend and foe alike.

By then Tecumseh himself was dead, killed in the Battle of the Thames, near Moraviantown in Canada, on October 5, 1813. Two years earlier, as Tecumseh recruited support in the South, an army led by William Henry Harrison had destroyed Prophetstown. With these and other defeats, Tecumseh's and Tenskwatawa's movement ended.

In some ways, however, the comprehensive religio-political challenge that their movement embodied continued to trouble Americans. Among other things, Americans who wrote about this movement and its leading figures found it much easier and popular to divide in their representations what had been united in practice. In novels, plays, histories, and speeches, white writers split religion and politics, divorced passion from reason, contrasted Tenskwatawa with Tecumseh. They demonized the prophet, who continued to live for more than two decades after the war, as the font of all of kinds of irrational excesses, the one who foolishly led his followers into the disastrous Battle of Tippecanoe (November 7, 1811). And they mythologized his brother Tecumseh, now safely dead, as a romantic, but doomed, warrior who thought strategically and fought nobly, all for nought. In sum, white writers celebrated Tecumseh as a singular genius, though one handicapped by his brother's incompetence.

These simplistic stereotypes obscured the complex realities. In fact, some Native Americans in the South remembered Tecumseh as a prophet himself. And it is clear that he and Tenskwatawa both drew upon key ideas from previous intertribal resistance movements, movements that had fused prophetic teachings with political goals to rally Native communities facing new forms of domination. In other words, Tecumseh fought with everything he had to defend the cultural and political sovereignty of American Indians.

BIBLIOGRAPHY

Dowd, Gregory Evans. *A Spirited Resistance: The North American Indian Struggle for Unity, 1745–1815.* Baltimore, 1992.

Edmunds, R. David. *The Shawnee Prophet.* Lincoln, Nebr., 1983.

Martin, Joel. *Sacred Revolt: The Muskogees' Struggle for a New World.* Boston, 1991.

Sugden, John. *Tecumseh: A Life.* New York, 1997.

White, Richard. *The Middle Ground: Indians, Empires, and Republics in the Great Lakes Region, 1650–1815.* New York, 1991.

JOEL W. MARTIN (2005)

TEHUELCHE RELIGION.

[*This entry discusses the religious system of the Aónikenk, or southern Tehuelche Indians.*] Known as the Aónikenk ("southerners"), the southern Tehuelche Indians inhabited the region of Argentine Patagonia, which extends east and west from the Atlantic Ocean to the foothills of the southern Andes and north and south from the Chubut River (43° south latitude) to the Strait of Magellan. The ethnographic data used in this essay come primarily from fieldwork done in the 1960s, when the surviving Aónikenk population was estimated to number about two hundred, although barely seventy were still speaking their own language, which is part of the Araucana-chon family.

Until their final biological, social, and cultural annihilation—due to pressures exerted by the Araucanian peoples to the north and to European conquest and colonization during the nineteenth century—they were nomadic hunters with set patterns of movement, encampments, and territories. Their displacements were subject to seasonal variations: summer hunting in the coastal region was accompanied by a certain social dispersion, whereas the western areas of Aónikenk territory were associated with more stable winter settlements and some degree of population concentration. The Aónikenk were subdivided into three groups, with a varying number of exogamous patrilineages; their residential pattern was patrilocal. There are numerous gaps in our knowledge of the religious system of the southern Tehuelche, but an imposing, if fragmentary, mythology stands out. By the time travelers began to be familiar with Aónikenk mythology, it had already begun to disintegrate, in part because it was forbidden to share it with outsiders.

COSMOLOGY. The mythic chronology speaks of four ages. The chaos of the first age is expressed in the image of a deep sea (the Flood?) or of a thick, wet darkness. During the second era, the high god—known variously as Weq.on ("truthful one"), Kooch ("heaven"), the Old One, and the Everlasting One, among other paraphrases—creates and gives order to the cosmic elements. Third is the epoch of Elal, the young god who shapes the earth, performs the ontological schism between undifferentiated and differentiated reality, and makes possible present-day human life with his ordering of technoeconomic, social, ritual, and ethical phenomena. His actions cover the end of the mythic era and mark the transition to the fourth age, the present one.

The cosmology describes the world as a system of four superimposed strata: the celestial sky, the atmospheric sky, the earth, and the subterranean region. The first is considered to be the highest, the second and third are rated ambiguously, and the last stratum is ranked the lowest. The cardinal points are rated similarly: the east is the best, the north and south are ambiguous, and the west is very bad.

RITUAL. No form of cult to the high god is recorded. The women possessed a repertory of sacred songs, dedicated to Elal and to Moon and Sun and their daughter, that were transmitted matrilineally. The canonical and reduplicated form of periodic exhortations given before hunting expeditions, which were uttered loudly by the chief of the local group, suggests the transformation of an ancient prayer addressed to Elal, inventor of hunting weapons and techniques.

Moon is the feminine deity who rules over periodic and alternating processes: menstruation, gestation, the life cycle, and the tides. During the new moon and eclipses, the members of the community would assemble behind their tents looking to the east; the women intoned the song of the deity and addressed prayers to her, begging her to "return to illuminate the world," to grant them health, longevity, and good luck.

The song to the daughter of Sun and Moon was included in a rite for regulating high tide. This rite is related to an episode of Elal's cycle that associates the tides with the daughter's animistic states. According to it the goddess was transformed into a siren; her excitement over the maternal apparition was linked to high tide during the first quarter of the moon, and her unhappiness during the last quarter to low tide. The life cycle was marked by rites of passage: birth, puberty initiation, marriage, and death were culturally meaningful milestones. The events of the life of Elal symbolically reflect these experiences, suggesting in both instances evolutionary stages of understanding, with special powers gained at each stage.

The ritually and mythically significant classification of colors is based on the white-red-black triad. The highest opposition sets up white and black as symbols of life and death (or concealment), respectively. Newborn babies were ritually painted white, while gravediggers (a strictly female role) were painted black. The lowest opposition, according to a hypothesis formulated by Carlos J. Gradin (1971, p. 113), contrasted the attraction of favorable aspects, denoted by white, with the rejection of the malefic, indicated by red; in contextual terms, however, the two colors complemented each other through their shared protective nature. Gradin's hypothesis reaffirms the sequence of colors used in therapeutic and funerary rites, where red accompanies the segregative phase, staving off the dangers entailed by impurity, and white accompanies the reincorporative phase, capturing the virtues to which a renewed condition allows one to aspire.

PANTHEON. The Aónikenk deities' spheres of activity and their relationships of complementarity and exclusion present a confusing panorama, which I will attempt to clarify. Elsewhere, I have noted processes of superimposition and transposition of attributes from the high god to other deities (Siffredi, 1969–1970, p. 247): for example, Elal possesses omnipotence and creativity as well as characteristics of a culture hero, while atmospheric phenomena are assigned to Karuten ("thunder"), a being of the atmospheric sky who is subordinated to Elal. The role of judge of the dead is assigned to the dyadic deity High God/Seecho; the high god judges how well the ethical ideal has been realized by the deceased, while Seecho, the "old woman" goddess, seconds his judgment. She admits to the afterworld—the eastern celestial sky—those among the dead who have tattoos on their left forearms (formerly such tattoos were the mark of initiates) and throws into the ocean those who lack tattoos. The belief that the dead were reunited with Elal and the high god in the eastern celestial sky, a land that knows neither penury nor illness, was well established. Elal moved definitively there after finishing his acts on earth, mounted on the swan goddess Kukn, the young goddess who assists Elal in many of the cycle's most important events.

The dyad Elal/Kukn displays a similar structure to that of the dyad High God/Seecho. The connection and hierarchical relationship between both dyads appears in the fact that the genesis and permanence of Elal's and Kukn's powers are ascribed to the high god. The secondary role and the spatial liminality of both feminine deities—expressed by their placement in the atmospheric sky—symbolically confirms the social dominance of men. The resulting tetrad, articulated along the criteria of age and sex (Old God/Old Goddess-Young God/Young Goddess), suggestively resembles the composition of Araucanian divine tetrads.

A similar coincidence between Tehuelche and Araucanian belief can be seen in a dualism that goes back to the primary confrontation between high, portrayed by the high god, and low, represented either by darkness *(tons)* or by the deep sea *(xóno);* high and low are the foundations of Order and Chaos. This dialectic extends over a vast semantic field in which roles, states, orientations, luminosity, numerical properties, zoological and color classifications, and behavioral and cognative qualities converge. One pole links the celestial deities, life, healing, shamans, the masculine, east, day, evenness, water birds, herbivores, white, red, temperance, and wisdom—all of which contrast with the chthonic beings, death, illness, witches, the feminine, west, night, oddness, carrion birds, carnivores, animals that live in dens, fish and sea mammals, black, intemperance, and ignorance.

MYTHOLOGY. The southern Tehuelche anthropogony includes motifs that relate to the differentiation of the human species and to the origin of copulation, marriage, and death. The beginning of Aónikenk people is accounted for in two ways. One is that Elal modeled male and female genitals out of clay into which he then blew the breath of life; another is that a role reversal between sea and land animals converted the former into the Aónikenk. Since land creatures were turned into marine fauna, the Aónikenk attribute the taboo on eating fish to this second mythical account.

The cosmogony recounts that the high god abandons his typical inactivity to begin the work of creation, which results from acts that are not always deliberate or conscious. One version of Aónikenk cosmogony contrasts the high god with *xóno,* the aquatic chaos that covered almost all primordial space except for a small piece of land in the valley of the Senguer River, in which the high god, little by little, grew larger. This region, the true "cosmic center," contains the palpable signs of divine action (i.e., certain topographical features) and is also the setting for the fabulous birth of Elal and for his acts on earth.

Manuel Llaras Samitier's versions of Aónikenk cosmogony (in Wilbert, 1984, pp. 17–18) contrast Kooch with *tons,* ubiquitous darkness. Saddened by his overwhelming solitude, Kooch's tears generate the "bitter sea" and his breath creates the wind that dispels darkness. The creation of Sun and Moon also plays a part in the darkness's attenuation. The amorous coupling and uncoupling of Sun and Moon evoke the rhythmic succession of darkness and light. Such images express the establishment of a temporal ordering by means of the alteration of day and night and of spatial ordering through the regulation of the cosmic elements: light, wind, and clouds.

THE CYCLE OF ELAL. Elal is the fruit of the union of antinomial conditions: his father, one of the chthonic monsters engendered by *tons,* devours his pregnant mother, one of the clouds created by Kooch. Elal's maternal grandmother rescues and raises the newborn Elal. Two testimonies enlivened the Aónikenk's memories: a bottomless spring, risen from the corpse of the Cloud, Elal's mother, marks the spot where Elal was born, appropriately called Beautiful Water. The red dawns observed from high vantage points reaffirmed for the Aónikenk this primordial shedding of blood.

Elal symbolically represents a mediation between heavenly and chthonic, the mythical and the present era, nature and culture. His quasi-earthly condition is in harmony with the formation of a world on a human scale. His mediation of the chthonic realm, for purposes of giving it order, is evident in the battles against cannibalistic giants, whose peculiarity lay in the vulnerability of their heels, a complementary and converse trait to that shown by the solar people, whose mouths operate as anuses. Elal's slaying of the ogres, beginning with his own father, culminates in their petrification. They can thus be observed by the Aónikenk in the immutable form of rocks or fossil remains.

The mediation of the high aspect is developed during Elal's celestial journey to the region of Sun and Moon, his future in-laws. The couple show their hostility by assigning him to perform deadly trials for a three-day period—not unlike the Aónikenk's shaman's apprentice, who was required to spend three days of initiation in caves—before giving him their daughter. Unlike other suitors, Elal is able to carry out all the trials with the help of Kukn, the swan goddess.

In sociological terms, Elal's unsuccessful marriage to the daughter of Sun expresses the risks of extreme exogamy. Conversely, the cycle's next episode, in which Elal's grandmother attempts to seduce him, highlights the Aónikenk's abomination of incest in that the grandmother is transformed into a mouse and condemned to live underground. The gravity and eschatological meaning of this is supported by one old Aónikenk woman's assertion: "My grandmother trod on the mouse whenever she saw it, because it was to blame for the departure of her powerful grandson, whom she had raised."

The transition between the mythical and present eras is understood as the passage from predifferentiated to clearly defined reality. The Aónikenk believed that the earth emerged from the unformed sea, which was forced to the east by Elal's unfailing arrows. Elal's comings and goings from west to east, resembling the Aónikenk's seasonal migrations, endowed their habitat with the contrasting topography of mountains, woods, plateaus, valleys, lakes, rivers, and islands. The image of an almost empty sky is opposed to that of one peopled with constellations representing earthly animals and objects, a tradition shared by many hunting peoples. Molded by Elal, the constellations constitute visible guides for human action.

The schism between animal, human, and divine natures is marked by the confinement of each to a defined sphere. Although there is room for mediation between these spheres through shamans and witches, easy communication disappears after the mythical era. A rock with the imprints of Sun's feet—probably a reference to the petrographs of the "footprint style" (2500 BCE) of southern Patagonian rupestrian art (Gradin, 1971, p. 114)—locates the site where Sun, exiled by Elal, was supposed to have helped himself up in order to climb to the sky.

Temporally, the homogeneity of the original, predifferentiated reality—eternal life, continuing winter, and the unformed sea—is contrasted with the periodicity and alternation suggested by the appearence of the driving forces of the cycle of death and reproduction, of seasonality (and each season's specific activities), and the movements of the tides. In ontological terms, the lack of differentiation between the many primordial beings and things—indicated by their shared humanoid condition—is set against the delineation of specific identities. On a sociological plane, the antisocial and incestuous nature—or the "meanness"—of the primordial humanoids is contrasted with human sociability based on the adequate sharing of goods, collaboration in hunting, sexual division of labor based on complementarity, prohibition of incest, and the exogamy of the local group. On an ethical plane, the formation of an Aónikenk ideal focused on courage, industriousness, tolerance, hospitality, respect for the property of others, and reserve in front of outsiders.

CONCLUSION. We are now witnessing the deplorable annihilation of this ethical ideal, extending throughout the southern Tehuelche religious system. Although in mythical terms the Aónikenk recognized the shock of the changes wrought by Europeans and their own consequent frustration, they did so merely by becoming aware of, and not by actively resolving, the conflict.

The absence of revivalist or revitalizing reactions would have been compensated for, at the very least, by mythical reflection on the meanings of alcoholism, of being deprived of their hunting lands, and of having to submit to foreign power. Incorporated as part of the cycle of Elal, the Aónikenk's great penury is reflected in the final impotence of the once-powerful deity. Thus one sees a religiosity that, since it is unable to form new relationships, is signaling the demise of its foundations as a rationale for cultural practice.

I hope in this article to have begun to fulfill, in at least a limited fashion, the mission entrusted by the last of the Aónikenk: that of revealing and spreading their "Word," which they knew would outlast their own lifetime and that of their gods, annihilated by history.

SEE ALSO Mapuche Religion.

BIBLIOGRAPHY

The most complete compilation of Tehuelche mythic texts and narratives can be found in *Folk Literature of the Tehuelche Indians,* edited by Johannes Wilbert and Karin Simoneau, "UCLA Latin American Studies," no. 59 (Los Angeles, 1984). Johannes Wilbert's introduction (pp. 1–13) provides a rigorous history of Tehuelche folk literature studies. Among the versions contributed by authors to the compilation can be recommended those obtained by Tomás Harrington (text 49), Rodolfo M. Casamiquela (texts 4, 69, 80, 95, and 104), and Marcelo Bórmida and me (texts 5, 11, 22–24, 28–44, 46–48, 50–56, 58–60, 62–64, 66–68, 70–73, 75, 78, 79, 83, 85–94, 96–102, and 105–110); these versions meet the appropriate heuristic requirements in regard to collection, transcription, identification of informants, and genealogical proofs. Undoubtedly, the versions contributed by Manuel Llaras Samitier (texts 1–3, 8–10, 12–14, 25, 45, 65, and 74), especially the cosmogonic ones, are the richest, although unfortunately they do not always meet the above requirements.

The cultural links between certain southern Tehuelche, northern Tehuelche, and Selk'nam (Ona) mythic themes are outlined by Marcelo Bórmida and me in "Mitología de los Tehuelches meridionales," *Runa: Archivo para las ciencias del hombre*

(Buenos Aires) 12 (1969–1970): 199–245. For a comparison of these elements with those contained in the anthropogonies of the Gran Chaco, see Edgardo J. Cordeu's and my "En torno a algunas coherencias formales de las antropogonías del Chaco y Patagonia," *Relaciones de la Sociedad Argentina de Antropología* 5 (1970): 3–10. An interesting literary analysis that excerpts an episode from the cycle of Elal and reformulates it in its context was done by Juan Adolfo Vázquez in "Nacimiento e infancia de Elal: Mitoanalisis de un texto Tehuelche meridional," *Revista iberoamericana* (Pittsburgh) 95 (April–June 1976): 201–216. For a typological-comparative analysis of the deities and hierophanies and a summary exposition of the rites of passage and shamanistic and witchcraft conceptions and practices, see my "Hierofanias y concepciones mítico-religiosas de los Tehuelches meridionales," *Runa: Archivo para las ciencias del hombre* 12 (1969–1970): 247–271. Carlos J. Gradin makes many valid suggestions on the magico-religious meaning of southern Patagonian rupestrian art in "A propósito del arte rupertre en Patagonia meridional," *Anales de arqueología y etnología* (Cuyo, Argentina) 26 (1971): 111–116. A reconstruction of the mythico-religious components of the Aónikenk habitat can be found in my own "Aspectos mítico-religiosos de los Tehuelches meridionales (Aonik'enk): El Habitat," *Boletín del Centro Argentino de Estudios Americanos* (Buenos Aires) 1 (January–April 1968): 49–54.

New Sources

Aguerre, Ana M. *Las Vidas de Panti: En la Tolderia Tehuelche del Rió Pinturas y el Despues, Provincia de Santa Cruz, Argentina.* Buenos Aires, 2000.

Bernal, Irma, and Mario Sánchez Proaño. *Los Tehuelches y otros cazadores australes.* Buenos Aires, 1988.

Casamiquela, Rodolfo M. *En pos del Gaulicho.* Rio Negros, 1988.

McEwan, Colin, Luis A. Borrero, and Alfredo Prieto. *Patagonia: Natural History, Prehistory, and Ethnography at the Uttermost End of the Earth.* London, 1997.

Nacuzzi, Lidia R. *Identidades impuestas: Telhuelches, Aucas y Pampas en el norte de la Patagonia.* Buenos Aires, 1998.

Pérez Bugallo, Rubén. *Pillantun, estudios de etno-organología patagónica y pampeano.* Buenos Aires, 1993.

Alejandra Siffredi (1987)
Translated from Spanish by Erica Meltzer
Revised Bibliography

TEILHARD DE CHARDIN, PIERRE.

Pierre Teilhard de Chardin (1881–1955), a French Jesuit, was a distinguished scientist of human origins, a Christian mystic, and a prolific religious writer. Prohibited by his church from publishing any nonscientific works, his philosophical and theological writings were printed only after his death, though they circulated clandestinely before. His major opus, *Le Phénomène humain*, appeared in 1955 and was an immediate best-seller. The English translation, introduced by Julian Huxley, was titled *The Phenomenon of Man* (1959), later more accurately retranslated as *The Human Phenomenon* (1999). Throughout his life, Teilhard de Chardin reflected on the meaning of Christianity in the light of modern science, especially in relation to evolution. He was concerned with the social, cultural, and spiritual evolution of humankind, as well as the place of religion, spirituality, and mysticism in an increasingly global society marked by pluralism and convergence. Some of his thoughts parallel those of the Hindu evolutionary thinker Sri Aurobindo.

Biography. Born on May 1, 1881, in Sarcenat near Clermont-Ferrand, France, Pierre Teilhard de Chardin was the fourth of eleven children of an ancient aristocratic family of the Auvergne. His father was a gentleman farmer with scientific and literary interests; his mother was a great-grandniece of Voltaire. Brought up in a traditional Catholic milieu marked by a vibrant faith, Teilhard's pantheistic and mystical leanings were already evident in childhood. His devout mother shared his interest in mysticism, whereas his father encouraged the collection of fossils, stones, and other specimens, laying the foundations for his son's future scientific career.

After an excellent education at a Jesuit boarding school, Teilhard entered the Jesuit novitiate at the age of eighteen. Deeply torn between an equally passionate love for God and the natural world, he resolved his crisis of faith by realizing that the search for spiritual perfection could be combined with that for scientific understanding. When the Jesuits were exiled from France, he continued his theological studies at Hastings in the South of England (1902–1905; 1908–1912), where he was ordained in 1911. From 1905 to 1908 he taught physics and chemistry to mainly Muslim pupils at a Jesuit school in Cairo. There he first discovered his great attraction to the desert and the East, leading him later to write with great lyrical beauty about cosmic and mystical life, culminating in his spiritual classics "Mass on the World" (1923) and *The Divine Milieu* (1927).

Henri Bergson's *Creative Evolution* (1907), which saw the world immersed in an immense stream of evolutionary creation, revealed to Teilhard the meaning of evolution for the Christian faith. Overflowing with the presence of the divine, the living world was experienced by Teilhard as an all-encompassing cosmic, mystical, and "divine milieu." These deeply mystical experiences were followed by scientific studies in Paris, interrupted by World War I, during which Teilhard served as a stretcher-bearer in a North African regiment at the Western Front. Living through the fiercest battles, miraculously never wounded, he found himself part of a pluralistic "human milieu," which led him to speculate about the growing oneness of humanity. These reflections grew later into the new idea of the "noosphere" (sphere of mind), an immense web of inter-thinking and interaction that connects people around the globe, hailing a new stage in human evolution. Almost daily encounters with death moved Teilhard to leave an "intellectual testament," communicating his vision of the world, which in spite of its turmoil he saw as animated by and drawn towards God. He began to write a series of stirring essays, published posthumously as *Writings in Time of War* (1968). Little known, these were seminal for his later work and provide one of the best introductions to his thought.

Teilhard completed his studies in geology and paleontology after the war. Following the brilliant defense of his doctorate in 1922, he was elected president of the French Geological Society and appointed to the chair in geology at the Institut Catholique in Paris, where he could publicly expound his ideas about evolution and Christianity. This soon led to difficulties with his church, which continued throughout his life. Because of these difficulties, he was glad to join a fossil expedition in China in 1923, where he traversed much of the Mongolian Desert. China soon became a place of almost permanent exile, and he spent most of his scientific career there (1926–1946) after his license to teach at the Institut Catholique was revoked in 1925 as a result of a paper he wrote on evolution and original sin. Teilhard first worked with Jesuit fellow scientists in Tianjin, and he then became a member of the Chinese Geological Survey in Beijing, where he collaborated in the discovery of the skull of the 200,000-year-old Peking Man at Zhoukoudian. His scientific work brought him into contact with leading paleontologists of his time and involved numerous expeditions across Asia, including trips to India, Indonesia, Myanmar, Sri Lanka, Vietnam, and Japan, as well as regular travels between East and West.

The unforgettable experience of World War I was followed by the equally formative discovery of the vast continent of Asia with its variety of peoples and cultures. Many of Teilhard's essays were written in China, as were his two main books, a practical treatise on spirituality, *The Divine Milieu*, and his best known, though most difficult work, *The Human Phenomenon*, which he wrote from 1938 to 1940. Teilhard met some of his best friends in China among American and European scientific colleagues; he also first encountered the American sculptor Lucile Swan in Beijing, with whom he formed a deep, intimate friendship that lasted until the end of his life.

Teilhard returned to Paris after World War II and attracted a considerable following for his ideas. In 1948 he was invited as a candidate for the chair of paleontology at the Collège de France, but fearing further difficulties with the Vatican, his order refused permission. Not being allowed to lecture in public or publish his writings, he accepted a research post at the Wenner-Gren Foundation for Anthropological Research in New York in 1951, and made two trips to fossil sites in South Africa. Lonely and suffering, he spent the last years of his life mostly in New York, where he died in 1955 on Easter Sunday (April 10), as had been his wish. He is buried in the Jesuit cemetery at Saint Andrews on the Hudson.

The posthumous publication of his works raised much interest and controversy due to the exploratory nature, complexity, and unfamiliar terminology of his new ideas, but also due to the challenge of his unifying global vision. Although harshly dealt with by church authorities, Teilhard gained loyal support from several members of his order, especially Henri de Lubac and René d'Ouince, his longtime superior, who described him as "a prophet on trial" in the church of his time.

The Human Being, the World, and God. Teilhard's method is based on a particular kind of phenomenology, different from that of other disciplines. It emphasizes the study of all phenomena by relating outer to inner "seeing." Such seeing involves the correlation of scientific knowledge of the outer world with a unifying inner vision, whereby the world is seen as held together by "Spirit." This holistic approach leads to a profound transformation of the seeing person and the world as seen, for seeing more implies being more.

Teilhard's thought is profoundly ecological—he saw human beings as an integral part of cosmos and nature, humankind as part of life, and life as part of the universe. In this dynamic and organic perspective the human being is not a static center, but "the axis and leading shoot of evolution." The rise of evolution is an immense movement through time, from the development of the atom to the molecule and cell, to different forms of life, to human beings with their great diversity. This evolutionary rise toward greater complexity leads in turn to a greater "within" of things, an increase in consciousness and reflection. The idea of greater interiority emerging within more complex organic structures is described as the "law of complexity-consciousness," sometimes called "Teilhardian law," and it is recognized as one of Teilhard's master ideas.

Cosmic, human, and divine dimensions are closely interwoven. Each is involved in a process of becoming, or genesis, and all are centered in Christ. Whereas *cosmogenesis* refers to the birth of the cosmos, *anthropogenesis* and *noogenesis* refer specifically to the emergence of human beings and the birth of thought. These are closely studied by modern science, whereas *Christogenesis*, or the birth of God in Christ as an event of cosmic significance, can be seen only through the eyes of faith. Cosmic and human evolution are moving onward to a fuller disclosure of Spirit, culminating in "Christ-Omega." The outcome of this forward and upward process cannot be taken for granted but involves human responsibility and co-creativity. For this reason, Teilhard was much concerned with moral and ethical choices, with the hope and energy needed for creating the right future for humanity and the planet, as expressed in *The Future of Man* (1964). Working for the future and helping in "building the earth" is an important educational task that entails a change of mind and heart in people. Teilhard inquired into the resources of spiritual energy needed to create a better quality of life, greater human integration, and a more peaceful and just world. Although there are thousands of engineers calculating the material energy reserves of the planet, Teilhard inquired about "technicians of the Spirit" who can supply the necessary spiritual energy to sustain the life of individuals and the entire human community.

Here, the spiritual heritage of world faiths and philosophies is most important, providing some of the most valuable spiritual energy resources. Human beings are responsible for their further self-evolution and a greater unification of the human community, but these goals need ultimately spiritual, rather than merely material, resources, and the greatest of these spiritual resources is love. The noosphere as a sphere of thought—surrounding the globe like the atmosphere as a layer of air or the biosphere as layer of life—can also be interpreted as an active sphere of love through which greater bonds of unity, of "amorization," are created between human beings. Teilhard was convinced that people must study the phenomenon of love as the most sacred spiritual energy resource in the same way that they study all other phenomena in the world. Love is so central in his thinking that Teilhard's entire corpus can be interpreted as a metaphysic of love. Yet he also called for a rigorously scientific approach to the energies of love, just as the sociologist Pitirim Sorokin proposed a scientific analysis of the production of "love-energy" in the human community, so necessary for its self-transformation.

Teilhard's dynamic understanding of God is sometimes compared to that of process philosophy and is best described as panentheism. His deeply mystical approach to God is expressed in his spiritual writings, such as *The Divine Milieu* and *The Heart of Matter* (1978). It centers above all in the person of Christ, whom Teilhard experienced as a cosmic and universal reality. He spoke of the "three natures" of Christ: human, divine, and cosmic. His numerous reflections on the universal, cosmic Christ contain important suggestions for a new Christology, never systematically developed. Teilhard spoke of the ever-present, ever-greater Christ, expressing a strongly Christocentric vision of faith that was grounded in a pan-Christic mysticism. As he often used the image of fire and heart, drawn from the Bible and the Christian mystics, Teilhard's spirituality can also be described as a fire-and-heart mysticism, at once profoundly modern and ancient. In its affirmation of the world as God's creation, it belongs to the kataphatic rather than apophatic type of Christian mysticism, expressing a strong affinity with contemporary creation spirituality.

Mircea Eliade saw Teilhard de Chardin's specific genius in celebrating the sacredness of the cosmos. However, the cosmos cannot be seen in isolation from the social and spiritual bonds of humanity, animated by the powers of all-transforming love and seeking a higher form of union. Scattered across Teilhard's writings exists a general theory about religion as the driving force in human evolution. Central to the phenomenon of religion and spirituality is the phenomenon of mysticism, experienced in a variety of forms across different religious traditions and culminating in a mysticism of love and action.

Teilhard's vision of the world represents a unique blend of science, religion, and mysticism. Central to it are the ideas of the noosphere and the divine milieu—the first belonging more to a secular context, the second to a deeply religious context—as well as ideas about spiritual energy, and the transformative powers of love. The essayistic, fragmentary nature of Teilhard's work, with its profusion of ideas and fluidity of language, marks him more as a postmodern than a traditional thinker. Insufficiently well known, and often cited out of context, his work contains challenging reflections on God, the world, humanity, science and religion, ecological responsibilities, interfaith encounter, and the convergence of religions. Teilhard's work also explores a greater unification, or "planetization," of humanity; the place of the feminine and love in creating greater unity; and the central importance of spirituality and mysticism. Some of his thoughts are insufficiently developed and opaquely expressed; others must be criticized for certain elements of exclusiveness and Eurocentrism. Yet his ideas are said to have influenced the founding debates of the United Nations, several documents of the Second Vatican Council, Christian-Marxist dialogue, discussions on futurology, and discussions concerning the World Wide Web, whose patron he is sometimes said to be. Others have called Teilhard a New Age prophet, yet such a description ignores the profoundly Christian core of his vision.

Teilhard's mysticism of action is directed towards the creative transformation of the outer and inner world, and it is based on the deepest communion with God, intimately present throughout creation. Teilhard's powerful affirmation of the incarnation and his brilliant vision of the universal, cosmic Christ within an evolutionary perspective provide inspiring ideas for a reinterpretation of the Christian faith in the modern world, governed by an ongoing scientific and spiritual quest. Theologians will be interested in his understanding of God, Christ, and creation; scholars of religion will gain from his reflections on the place of religion, especially mysticism, in human evolution; and scientists are attracted to the newly emerging possibilities of the noosphere and the as yet unexplored energies of love for achieving profound personal and social transformation.

Bibliography

Pierre Teilhard de Chardin's religious and philosophical works were published posthumously in French between 1955 and 1976 in thirteen volumes entitled *Oeuvres* (Éditions du Seuil, Paris). Their English translations appeared between 1959 and 1978. Also published were numerous volumes of letters, extracts from his diaries, and the collection of his previously published scientific papers, *L'Oeuvre scientifique*, edited by Nicole and Karl Schmitz-Moormann, 11 vols. (Olten, Switzerland, 1971).

Teilhard presents his evolutionary system in its most complete form in *The Phenomenon of Man* (London and New York, 1959), now available in a much-improved translation by Sarah Appleton-Weber, *The Human Phenomenon* (Brighton, U.K., and Portland, Ore., 1999). To understand the full intent of this work, one should first read Teilhard's classic treatment of Christian spirituality in *The Divine Milieu* (London and New York, 1960; reprint, translated by Siôn Cowell, Brighton, UK, 2004), followed by the theological essays in *Science and Christ* (London and New York, 1968) and *The Heart of Matter* (London and New York, 1978). Many readers find the easiest entry into Teilhard's thought through his vivid letters, especially *Letters from a Traveller*, edited by Claude Arragonès (London, 1966), or through his early, very lyrical work *Writings in Time of War* (London, 1968) and the selected essays in *Hymn of the Universe* (London and New York, 1965). This also contains his famous "The Mass on the World," originally written in 1923. Of particular appeal among his other works are *The Future of Man* (London and New York, 1964), *Human Energy* (London and New York, 1969), and *Christianity and Evolution* (London and New York, 1971).

A helpful reference work has been provided by Siôn Cowell, *The Teilhard Lexicon* (Brighton, UK, and Portland, Ore., 2001), the first English-language dictionary of Teilhard de Chardin's writings and vocabulary. Claude Cuénot's biography, *Teilhard de Chardin* (London and Baltimore, 1965), with its rich documentation and detailed bibliography of Teilhard's publications, is an indispensable resource, but not as readable as the shorter life by Mary Lukas and Ellen Lukas, *Teilhard* (New York and London, 1977), or the illustrated biography by Ursula King, *Spirit of Fire: The Life and Vision of Teilhard de Chardin* (Maryknoll, N.Y., 1996). The vicissitudes of Teilhard's life, especially the censure of his writings, have been amply documented by his Jesuit superior, René d'Ouince, in *Un prophète en procès*; vol. 1, *Teilhard de Chardin dans l'église de son temps* (Paris, 1970). Among numerous commentators the Jesuit Henri de Lubac must rank as one of the best; his early study *The Religion of Teilhard de Chardin* (London, 1967) is especially helpful. Another Jesuit, Thomas M. King, offers a searching analysis of Teilhard's mystical experience in *Teilhard's Mysticism of Knowing* (New York, 1981), undertaken from a different perspective by Ursula King in *Towards a New Mysticism: Teilhard de Chardin and Eastern Religions* (London and New York, 1980), which examines Teilhard's views on Eastern and Western religions in a converging world, including his new mysticism of action. R. C. Zaehner's *Evolution in Religion: A Study in Sri Aurobindo and Pierre Teilhard de Chardin* (Oxford, 1971) provides an insightful comparison between a Hindu and Christian approach to the evolutionary reinterpretation of two different religious traditions; see also Ursula King, "Teilhard de Chardin and the Comparative Study of Religions" in Christopher Lamb and Dan Cohn-Sherbok, eds., *The Future of Religion: Postmodern Perspectives, Essays in Honour of Ninian Smart* (London, 1999), pp. 54–76. J. A. Lyons's *The Cosmic Christ in Origen and Teilhard de Chardin* (Oxford, 1982) analyzes Teilhard's innovative passages on Christ's "three natures" and his traditional roots in Greek patristics. An earlier overall theological synthesis was undertaken by Christopher F. Mooney, *Teilhard de Chardin and the Mystery of Christ* (New York, 1966).

Well worth studying are *The Letters of Teilhard de Chardin and Lucile Swan*, edited by Thomas M. King and Mary Wood Gilbert (Washington, D.C., 1993), especially for their detailed coverage of his China years and his friendship with Swan. Mathias Trennert-Hellwig, *Die Urkraft des Kosmos: Dimensionen der Liebe im Werk Pierre Teilhard de Chardins* (Freiburg, Germany, 1993) provides the most comprehensive study of Teilhard's dynamic vision of love. A comparison with Pitirim Sorokin's ideas on love is found in Ursula King, "Love – A Higher Form of Human Energy in the Work of Teilhard de Chardin and Sorokin," *Zygon* 39, no. 1 (2004): pp. 77–102.

The diffusion and critical reception of *The Divine Milieu*, especially in France, has been closely examined by Hai-Yan Wang, *Le phénomène Teilhard: L'aventure du livre Le Milieu Divin* (Paris, 1999). A wide-ranging discussion of Teilhard de Chardin's spirituality is found in Pierre Noir's "Teilhard de Chardin," *Dictionnaire de spiritualité: Ascétique et mystique, doctrine et histoire*, vol. 15, pp. 115–126 (Paris, 1991); selected texts on spirituality have been thematically grouped in *Pierre Teilhard de Chardin: Writings, Selected, with an Introduction by Ursula King* (Maryknoll, N.Y., 1999). The background, semantic context, and importance of Teilhard de Chardin's noosphere concept in relation to contemporary scientific discussions are extensively documented in *The Biosphere and Noosphere Reader: Global Environment, Society, and Change*, edited by Paul R. Samson and David Pitt (London, 1999). The relevance of Teilhard de Chardin's work, especially in relation to contemporary cosmology and ecology, is evident from the essays in *Teilhard in the 21st Century: The Emerging Spirit of Earth*, edited by Arthur Fabel and Donald St. John (Maryknoll, N.Y., 2003).

Ursula King (2005)

TEKAKWITHA, KATERI (c. 1656–1680), native American convert to Christianity. Tekakwitha was born in the Iroquoian town of Gandahouhague, near present-day Fonda, New York. Her father was Mohawk, and her mother Algonquin, a captive adopted into the Turtle clan after a raid. When she was four years old Tekakwitha survived an attack of smallpox that killed her immediate family. The disease weakened her eyesight, and she afterward exhibited a general tendency to withdraw from social contact. By 1667, when Tekakwitha first encountered Jesuit missionaries, she was already inclined to a way of life that Christianity sanctioned. Indian townspeople exerted strong pressure to make her conform to native ways, but she persisted in her new interest. This determination culminated on Easter Day, 1676, when she was baptized by Jacques de Lamberville, S.J. The following year, local opposition to her Catholicism mounted, and she fled the region to take refuge with other Catholic Indians living along the Saint Lawrence River in Upper Canada.

Tekakwitha settled at Caughnawaga, or La Prairie de la Madeleing, an intertribal village of Christian Indians bound together more by religious allegiance than by tribal heritage. There she quickly established a reputation for austere self-denial and pious virtue. From her First Communion at Christmas 1677, until her death less than three years later, the maiden impressed all about her with her modest fervor and ardent prayers. Beset with a frail constitution, she worked as best she could in village gardens, fasted two days per week, administered flagellations, and kept a private vow of chastity. In 1678 she began a quasi-convent patterned after the Hospital Sisters of Montreal, but such rigors hastened her own end. Her death enhanced local stories about her exemplary conduct, and Indian as well as French neighbors made a shrine of her gravesite. Many were inspired by her extraordinary life, and in 1932 she was nominated for sainthood. On October 22, 1980, John Paul II pronounced her blessed, thus acknowledging her as an example of Catholic piety in colonial New France.

BIBLIOGRAPHY

Buehrle, Marie E. *Kateri of the Mohawks.* Milwaukee, 1954.

Fisher, Lillian M. *Kateri Tekakwitha: The Lily of the Mohawks.* Boston, 1996.

Lecompte, Edouard. *An Iroquois Virgin: Catherine Tekakwitha.* New York, 1932.

Lecompte, Edouard. *Glory of the Mohawks: The Life of the Venerable Catharine Tekakwith.* Milwaukee, 1944.

HENRY WARNER BOWDEN (1987 AND 2005)

TEKHINES. Tekhines, a Yiddish word from the Hebrew *Teḥinnot,* "supplications," are Jewish private devotions and paraliturgical prayers in Yiddish written by both women and men but recited primarily by women. As texts in the vernacular, tekhines are important sources for the history of popular Judaism in the seventeenth, eighteenth, and nineteenth centuries, and they are particularly useful in studying the history of women's religion.

Most Jewish men of the period attained basic literacy in Hebrew, and a few elite went on to full mastery of the classic literary tradition. Only a small number of women, however, learned more than the rudiments of Hebrew, and those central and eastern European Jewish women who could read usually were literate only in the vernacular Yiddish. Jewish liturgy and other devotional and scholarly works were written by men and were almost always in Hebrew, making them inaccessible to most women. Furthermore because women were excluded from most areas of public religious leadership and participation (they could not serve as rabbis, cantors, judges, or advanced teachers and did not count in a quorum for public prayer), they left behind a scant literary legacy. Tekhines therefore, as an enormously popular devotional genre, allows scholars a valuable window into women's religious lives.

In books of tekhines each individual prayer begins with a heading that describes when and sometimes how it should be recited: "A pretty tekhine to say on the Sabbath with great devotion"; "A tekhine that the woman should pray for herself and her husband and children"; "A confession to say with devotion, not too quickly; it is good for the soul"; "When she comes out of the ritual bath"; "What one says on the Eve of Yom Kippur in the cemetery"; "When the shofar is blown on Rosh Hashanah, say this." Scholars are divided as to whether these prayers were meant for women as a substitute for the Hebrew liturgy or as a supplement, recited as occasional and voluntary prayers. Although some tekhines were intended to be recited in the synagogue and a few were written for male worshippers ("A lovely prayer for good livelihood to be said every day by a business man"), the majority were associated with women's spiritual lives in the home: prayers to be recited privately on each day of the week and on Sabbaths, festivals, fasts, and new moons; for the three so-called "women's commandments" (namely lighting Sabbath candles, removing a small portion of bread dough with a prayer recalling the priestly tithes in the ancient Temple in Jerusalem, and observing menstrual avoidances and purification); for pregnancy and childbirth; for visiting the cemetery; for private grief such as childlessness and widowhood; for recovery from illness; for sustenance and livelihood; and for confession of sins. Tekhines framed women's domestic lives and roles as sacred, and they also connected them with the grander themes of Jewish thought, especially the hope for the messianic redemption and the end of exile.

BACKGROUND. During the sixteenth and seventeenth centuries new rituals and genres of religious literature emerged whose audience was a sort of intellectual middle class. This development parallels the emergence of similar literature in Christian Europe, enabled in part by the rise of publishing after the invention of the printing press. Guides to the ethical life, books of pious practices, and new liturgies and rituals, often in abridged and simplified form, were published both in Hebrew, for an audience of men with a basic education in classical Jewish texts, and in Yiddish, the vernacular, for women and nonscholarly men. Many of these new publications (including the Hebrew *teḥinnot,* or supplemental prayers for men) developed out of and popularized a mystical pietism that had originated among the sixteenth-century qabbalists of Safed in Palestine. Tekhines allowed women to participate in this pietistic revival and its popular literature. By contrast, however, tekhines published in the eighteenth and nineteenth century show little evidence of influence from Hasidism, the great eastern European Jewish religious revival movement that originated in the mid–eighteenth century.

HISTORY OF THE GENRE. Although there are some handwritten tekhines, most of them were professionally printed. The earliest versions—a few small, anonymous collections—appeared in the late sixteenth century in Prague. Two main groups of tekhines exist, however: those that were printed in western Europe in the seventeenth and eighteenth centuries, which, although published anonymously, were probably written or compiled by men for women, and those that appeared in eastern Europe in the seventeenth, eighteenth, and early nineteenth centuries, often with named authors, some of which were written or compiled by women.

Most western European tekhines were published in collections addressing many topics, either in small books or as appendices to Hebrew prayer books. The first major collection (containing thirty-six prayers), titled simply *Tekhines,* was published in Amsterdam in 1648; reprints, expansions, and additional collections followed. In the mid–eighteenth century a comprehensive collection containing 123 prayers emerged, titled *Seyder tkhines u-vakoshes* (Order of supplications and petitions, 1762), although there may be one or two earlier editions. This tekhine was reprinted many times, with alterations, over the next 150 years, first in western and later in eastern Europe. The western European texts not only depict the holiness to be found in the domestic and mundane activities of a wife and mother, but they also describe for women the angels, the patriarchs, the heroes of Jewish history, and the ancient Temple that stood in Jerusalem.

The earliest eastern European tekhines were published in Prague. *Eyn Gor Sheyne Tkhine* (A very beautiful tekhine, c. 1600) is one of the first to claim female authorship: it is attributed to "a group of pious women." Two other Prague imprints, one from the beginning of the eighteenth century and the other from 1705, are also attributed to women: Rachel, daughter of Mordecai Sofer of Pinczow, and Beila, daughter of Ber Horowitz. Like many other eastern European texts, all three of these Prague tekhines were quite short, and each of them dealt with a single subject, such as a tekhine "to be recited with devotion every day." One notable work, however, *Seyder Tkhines* (Prague, 1718), was written by a man—Matthias ben Meir, the former rabbi of Sobota, Slovakia—explicitly for a female audience. "My dear women," he writes, ". . . I have made this tekhine for you in Yiddish, in order to honor God and . . . to honor all the pious women. For there are many women who would gladly awaken their hearts by saying many tkhines." This work contains thirty-five prayers addressing a variety of topics.

Except for the Prague imprints, the eastern European tekhines were usually small pamphlets printed on bad paper with crabbed type, often with no imprint, making their bibliographic history difficult to trace. Books of tekhines originating in eighteenth-century eastern Europe, especially in Galicia, Volhynia, and Podolia (now parts of Poland, Belarus, and the Ukraine), tended to deal with a smaller number of subjects (such as the high holidays and the penitential season), were often written by a single author, and were usually fewer than twenty pages. Because a significant number of these authors were women, these texts capture women's voices directly. Important examples include: *Tkhine imohes* (Tekhine of the [biblical] matriarchs), for the Sabbath before the new moon, by Leah Horowitz (eighteenth century), which argues for the power of women's prayer and quotes from rabbinic and qabbalistic sources; *Tkhine imohes fun rosh khoydesh elul* (Tekhine of the matriarchs for the new moon of Elul [and the entire penitential season], n.d.) by Serl, daughter of Jacob ben Wolf Kranz (the famed Preacher of Dubno, 1741–1804), which calls on the four biblical matriarchs (Sarah, Rebecca, Rachel, and Leah) to come to the aid of the worshipper and plead her case before the heavenly court; and *Shloyshe sheorim* (The three gates), attributed to the legendary Sarah bas Tovim (who probably lived in Podolia in the eighteenth century), which contains three sections: one for the three "women's commandments," one for the high holidays, and one for the Sabbath before the new moon. In contrast to the western European texts, some eastern European tekhines suggest that women should take part—in some fashion—in such traditionally male activities as synagogue prayer and Torah study.

By the mid–nineteenth century the genre had undergone significant changes. Jews in central and western Europe had largely abandoned Yiddish; books comparable to tekhines were published first in Germanized Yiddish, then in German in Yiddish characters, and finally in German. These texts expressed an entirely new sensibility, however, influenced by the rising ideal of the bourgeois family, with its stress on sentiment and emotional family ties and its new definition of gender roles. Similarly in eastern Europe the ideal of the bourgeois family came into play but in a rather different fashion. *Maskilim,* "enlighteners," or men who wished to reform eastern European Jewish life, wrote tekhines to reach the "benighted" traditional women with their reform program. Unlike earlier tekhine authors, female or male, they scorned their audience and the genre. Often because they thought they could sell more books, they attributed their works to female authors, either those who had actually written tekhines a century earlier or to creations of their own imagination. (Because the maskilic practice of using female pseudonyms was well known, earlier scholars were skeptical of any attributions to female authorship. Many seventeenth- and eighteenth-century women authors have been authenticated, however.) In addition to these newer maskilic tekhines, older texts and collections—both those that were originally published in western Europe and those printed in eastern Europe—continued to be reprinted in eastern Europe in numerous editions, although they are often revised or garbled by the printers.

SIGNIFICANCE. The tekhines reveal a whole world of women's religious lives, concerns, customs, and settings for prayer. These texts are deeply spiritual, no less than the complex and esoteric works produced by qabbalists and Hasidic masters. The women (and men) who composed these prayers for women addressed the spiritual issues of their day, whether on the level of domestic piety or national redemption. The tekhines themselves are at home in the literature produced for the intellectual middle class of this period; they fit well among the guides to the upright life, books of customs, condensed guides to pious practices, and digests of mystical teachings that were read by householders and artisans. Indeed the tekhines show how much women belonged to this intellectual and spiritual world. Finally, the tekhines provide worshipers with a direct experience of passionately emotional individual prayer that is mostly absent from the more collective and formalized male worship experience.

MODERN DEVELOPMENTS. As the use of Yiddish declined among emigrants from eastern Europe in the late nineteenth century and the twentieth century and the Yiddish-speaking heartland was destroyed by the Holocaust, the genre of tekhines nearly disappeared, except among Hasidim and other isolated traditional, Yiddish-speaking populations. After the 1980s, however, the tekhines aroused new interest among both scholars and members of the Jewish public. Jewish women in particular have sought to find a usable past in which to root themselves. Orthodox women have turned to the traditional tekhines as a direct expression of their predecessors' spirituality. This movement has occurred despite the fact that, unlike their European ancestors, many young Orthodox women in the United States in the early twenty-first century are well-educated in the Hebrew prayer book and classical sources in Hebrew and may not speak or read Yiddish at all. Liberal Jewish feminists have also sought role models in the historical tekhines uncovered by scholars, and many of them have also written and published new tekhines, some of which have been incorporated into new editions of Conservative and Reconstructionist prayer books.

SEE ALSO Gender and Religion, article on Gender and Judaism; Judaism, articles on Judaism in Northern and Eastern Europe to 1500 and Judaism in Northern and Eastern Europe since 1500; Liturgy.

BIBLIOGRAPHY

Kay, Devra. *Seyder Tkhines: The Forgotten Book of Common Prayer for Jewish Women.* Philadelphia, 2004.

Kratz-Ritter, Bettina. *Für "fromme Zionstöchter" und "gebildete Frauenzimmer."* Hildesheim, Germany, 1995.

Weissler, Chava. *Voices of the Matriarchs: Listening to the Prayers of Early Modern Jewish Women.* Boston, 1998.

CHAVA WEISSLER (2005)

TEKKE SEE KHĀNAQGĀH

TELEVISION SEE RELIGIOUS BROADCASTING

TEMPLE

This entry consists of the following articles:

TEMPLE: HINDU TEMPLES

"The Indian temple, an exuberant growth of seemingly haphazard and numberless forms," wrote Stella Kramrisch in 1922, "never loses control over its extravagant wealth. Their organic structure is neither derived from any example seen in nature, nor does it merely do justice to aesthetic consideration, but it visualizes the cosmic force which creates innumerable forms, and these are one whole, and without the least of them the universal harmony would lack completeness" ("The Expressiveness of Indian Art," *Journal of the Department of Letters,* University of Calcutta, 9, 1923, p. 67). This intuitive understanding of the temple's structure and significance has been fleshed out and confirmed by Kramrisch and others in the years since those words were penned.

AXIS, ALTAR, AND ENCLOSURE. Hindu temples are built to shelter images that focus worship; they also shelter the worshiper and provide space for a controlled ritual. Between the fifth and the fifteenth century CE, Hindu worshipers constructed stone temples throughout India, but sacred enclosures of another sort had been built centuries before. Tree shrines and similar structures that enclose an object for worship (tree, snake, *liṅga,* pillar, standing *yakṣa,* all marked by a vertical axis) within a square railing, or later within more complicated hypaethral structures, have been illustrated in narrative relief-sculptures from the first few centuries BCE and CE. Whatever the variations, these structures mark a nodal point of manifestation, as does Viṣṇu in reliefs from the fifth century CE that show him lying on the cosmic ocean, with a lotus that springs from his navel supporting Brahmā, who proceeds to generate the universe.

In creation myths and in the imagery of the lotus, as in the structure of Mauryan monolithic pillars (from the third century BCE), the cosmic axis separates heaven from the waters. Creation flows from this nodal point toward the cardinal directions, producing a universe that is square, marked by the railing-enclosure of these early shrines, by the *harmikā* (upper platform) of the Buddhist stupa, and by the edges of the brick altar used for sacrifice. The *Āpastamba Śulbasūtra,* a text probably of the fourth century BCE, comments that "though all the earth is *vedi* [altar], yet selecting a particular part of it and measuring it they should perform the *yajña* ['sacrifice'] there" (6.2.4). The identity of the altar and the entirety of creation is thus established quite early, and this configuration of vertical axis, square altar, and enclosure persists in Indian architecture to demonstrate the participation of each monument in the cosmogonic process.

DIAGRAM OF CONSTRUCTION. The Vāstupuruṣa Maṇḍala—the square diagram on which the altar, temples, houses, palaces, and cities are founded—also outlines creation (see figure 1). The myth of the *vāstupuruṣa* portrays the first sacrifice, in which a demon is flayed and his skin held down by divinities who ring the diagram (*padadevatās*; lit., "feet deities"). In the center is the "place for *brahman*"—the formless, ultimate, "supreme reality." The use of this diagram for the construction of houses and the laying out of cities on a grid of eighty-one squares (nine by nine) is recorded in a chapter on architecture in Varāhamihira's sixth-century CE text, the *Bṛhat Saṃhitā;* the use of a grid of sixty-four squares (eight by eight) as a special case for the construction of temples (figure 1) is recorded in a separate chapter.

Cave, Mountain, and Shelter. By the early centuries CE the use of anthropomorphic images to focus worship had moved from "substratum" cults into mainstream Hinduism and into Buddhism. Early Hindu images often represented cosmic parturition—the coming into present existence of a divine reality that otherwise remains without form—as well as "meditational constructs," to use T. S. Maxwell's phrase. The representation of the Buddha became permissible with the emergence of two new conceptions: the Buddha in cosmic form, replacing or supplementing the stupa as focus for meditation, and the *boddhisattvas*, figures who mediate between the aspirant and the ultimate reality of nonexistence. Behind anthropomorphic imagery in India, however, is always an ultimate reality without form.

Early shelters for anthropomorphic images were of several types: apsidal brick structures resembling the *caitya-gṛhas* of the Buddhists, elliptical structures perhaps suggesting the "cosmic egg," open altars and hypaethral structures (both extending earlier aniconic formulas), small stone *chatrīs* (umbrellas or pavilions), cave shrines, and eventually temples with towers. Rock-cut shrines of the early fifth century CE (particularly those at Udayagiri, near Vidiśa, in central India), present two imperative metaphors for the temple: the sanctum as womb *(garbha)* in which the seed of divinity can be made manifest, and the temple as mountain. As the cave opens up the earth, so the sanctum opens up the temple.

If existing cave shrines emphasize the cave metaphor, an inscription dated 423/4 CE from Gaṅgadhāra in western India already compares a temple there to "the lofty peak *(śikhara)* of the mountain Kailāśa," and the so-called Pārvatī Temple at Nachna of about 465 CE ornamentally rusticates its exterior walls to suggest Kailāśa's piled rocks and animal-filled grottoes. The metaphors of cave and mountain for sanctum and temple are explicit in inscriptions and texts, but it is the concept of divinity made manifest and the practice of devotional worship *(bhakti)* that make the temple possible. The cosmic mountain and its womb/cave ultimately shelter a tender divinity, in the form of an image, and must open out to include and give shelter to the worshiper, who approaches the central point of cosmic manifestation along a longitudinal axis.

Iconicity of Architectural Form. In North India, the fifth century CE saw experimentation in the means by which architecture could supply shelter to images. Small cave shelters were excavated (Udayagiri), cavelike cells were constructed (Sāñcī), structures with towers were built in impermanent materials (Gaṅgadhāra), and stone "mountains" were built (as at Nachna) with cavelike sanctums. Some temples began to show multiple and variant images of the central divinity on the walls (Maḍhia), and others became complexes by adding subsidiary shrines to shelter other deities (Bhumara, Deogarh). Such a proliferation of images can be seen as a product of the Hindu conception of cosmic parturition: if divine reality is formless, through the process of creation it takes an infinity of forms in this (created) world; though the

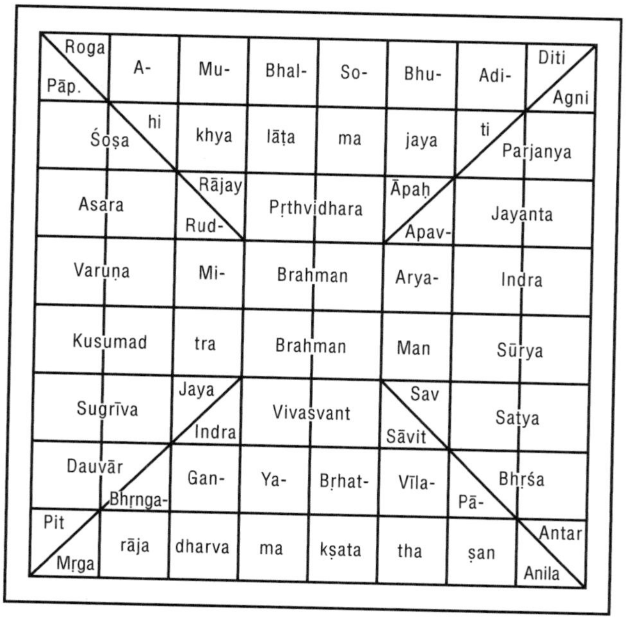

FIGURE 1. Vāstupuruṣa Maṇḍala. Ritual diagram for temple construction as described in Varāhamihira's *Bṛaht Saṃhitā;* sixth century CE.

individual may choose one divinity as "trunk" for worship, others take up appropriate positions as "branches."

Only in the sixth century did such experiments lead to a North Indian temple form that was complete in its symbolism and architectural definition. On plan, the North Indian temple grows from the Vāstupuruṣa Maṇḍala (see figure 1): its corners are those of the square *vedi*; its walls are half the width of the sanctum in thickness (as prescribed in the *Bṛhat Saṃhitā*); at its center is the *brahmasthāna.* The outer walls begin to acquire projecting planes that measure the dimensions of the interior sanctum and the "place for *brahman.*" The central projections on the wall now and then show closed doorways but most often frame secondary images (*parśvadevatās*) that extend and differentiate the form of the divinity within. In elevation, these planes continue up through the superstructure as bands that curve in to meet a square slab at the top of the temple, from which a circular necking projects. The necking supports a large, circular, ribbed stone *(āmalaka)* that takes the form of an *āmala* fruit and normally is crowned by a stone waterpot *(kalaśa)* from which leaves sometimes sprout.

The imagery (and its iconicity) is explicit. Just as the block of the temple's walls projects planes outward in order to display the images that make its sacred content manifest, so too the temple "grows" in altitude, marking the process of cosmic parturition by its form. The womb of the temple, its sanctum *(garbhagṛha)*, provides the dimension for an *uttaravedi* ("upper altar") that terminates the tower (some seventh-century shrines show this altar as a shallow, pillared platform at the top of the curvilinear superstructure). Extending the dimensions of the *brahmasthāna*, the necking above this *vedi* takes the form of the emerging "world pillar" *(axis mundi)*, which passes symbolically through the sanctum with the body of the temple as its sheath.

As North Indian architecture evolves between the sixth and the thirteenth centuries, the plan of the temple shows more and more offsets, the walls gain more images, and the central tower of the temple becomes clustered by other, miniature towers, increasingly giving the effect of a mountain peak through specifically architectural means. If this variety of constructional forms, buttresses, and images "body" forth reality in the manifest world, the ribbed *āmala* stone at the top of the temple, much like the staff that sprouts in *Tannhäuser*, presents the ripening seed's potentiality for fruition. Both the pot with germinating seeds that is buried under the foundation and the vase finial placed on top of the temple as an act of final consecration ritually help to perpetuate cycles of cosmic growth and fruition.

PALACE, HUT, AND FORTRESS. The temple thus combines physically the pillar that marks the axis of cosmic parturition, the altar of sacrifice taking the shape of the created universe, and the need for shelter of the tender divinity and the human worshiper; it unites the cosmic mountain and potent cave. South Indian temples, built in stone from the seventh century CE, give emphasis to the temple's role as shelter for anthropomorphic divinities by retaining throughout their evolution a terraced, palatial form crowned by a domed *śikhara* that has the shape of the ascetic's hut. As early as the Ājīvika caves in the Barabār Hills of Bihar, dating from the third century BCE, the hut of the living ascetic had been an architectural form appropriate for presenting the concept of sacred potentiality.

The temple is called *prāsāda* ("palace") in North India, and the architectural veneer of its superstructure, in both north and south, allude to forms of palace architecture. In the north, these have been completely subordinated to the temple's vertical ascent, becoming body for the altar that still presents itself at the top of the temple, open to the sky. In the south, deities sheltered within the temple's compact, palace-like structure increasingly took on the accoutrements of a secular ruler, through ritual and the cycle of festivals. While divinity in the form of images (*mūrtis*) could take on qualities of royalty, and kings did validate their role by patronage of temples, the king was considered a reflection of divine order principally through the quality of his actions and the nature of his responsibilities, not by divine right.

If the temple is palace for divinity, it also is fortress, protecting the world from disorder and chaos. Corners are "attended with evils" according to the *Bṛhat Saṃhitā* (53.84), and "the householder, if he is anxious to be happy, should carefully preserve Brahman, who is stationed in the center of the dwelling, from injury" (53.66). In the puranic legend of Śiva conquering the three worlds, he frees three "cities" of demons, making them his devotees and transforming the cities into his temples. In fact, images of Guardians of the Quarters (*dikpālas*) are placed on the corners of temples from about the seventh century, and a number of geometric experiments with plans based on the rotation of squares seem to play on the fort as a form for temple architecture.

Large temples in South India often enclose the sanctum in a series of ambulatory paths and walls that simulate rings of fortification around a walled city, and in fact use the eighty-one-square *maṇḍala* appropriate for the city, with a single square at the center surrounded by concentric rings of squares, to define the temple's plan. If practice in South India increasingly emphasized the royal personality of the divinity and his relation to his subjects and kingdom by use of great festival processions, it also began to surround temples and contiguous sections of the city with walls pierced by gateways (*gopuras*) that became the focus of patronage themselves.

ACCESS AND ASPIRANT. The Hindu temple must also act as access and approach for aspirants and worshipers. This role changes the temple from a centralized, bilaterally symmetrical structure (reflecting the nature of the cosmogonic process) to one with a defined longitudinal axis. On that axis the worshipers approach their personal divinity within the sanctum; but also on that axis the aspirants increasingly can place themselves, in halls built for that purpose, as if under the umbrella of the sacrificer, positioning themselves for ascent. "The whole intention of the Vedic tradition and of the sacrifice is to define the Way *(mārga)* by which the aspirant . . . can ascend [the three] worlds," wrote Ananda K. Coomaraswamy. "Earth, Air, and Sky . . . compose the vertical Axis of the Universe. . . . [These are] the Way by which the Devas first strode up and down these worlds . . . and the Way for the Sacrificer now to do likewise" ("*Svayamātṛṇṇā*: Janua Coeli," in *Coomaraswamy*, vol. 1, *Selected Papers: Traditional Art and Symbolism*, ed. Roger Lipsey, Princeton, 1977, pp. 465–467, 470). The temple is as much a monument to the procession of time as it is a static model of the cosmos or a marker of its origin. *Padadevatās* ringing the *vāstumaṇḍala* (grid) are identified with the asterisms (*nakṣatras*) of the lunar calendar, and the temple both helps generate and acts as a focus for the ritual time of the festival calendar. Personal ritual within the temple involves both approach and circumambulation, and movement by the aspirant through time toward release had to be a recognized part of the architect's program for the temple.

All sides of the temple allow access to the divinity through imagery, but the entry that pierces and makes ritual approach possible, most frequently on the east, is given increasing importance and architectural definition as temples evolve. Halls for ritual and assembly are added along this axis and sometimes used for dance or music to entertain the divinity, but often they serve simply as shelters for approach. One common and potent configuration places the sanctum (sometimes surrounded by an enclosed ambulatory path) behind a closed hall that may also be fronted by an open hall and an entry pavilion.

In the Kaṇḍarīya Mahādeva Temple at Khajuraho (c. 1025–1050), for example, space for the worshiper within the closed hall takes the same dimensions as the sanctum, with parallel rings of the *maṇḍala* defining walls of the sanctum, the space within the hall, ambulatory walls, and the outer enclosure. Ceilings in such halls imitate the canopy over the ritual sacrificer; this intention is made architecturally clear in some cases by having a separately defined pavilion within the hall over the central platform, as at Sinnar in Maharashtra or at the great Jain temple at Ranakpur. The ritual fire can be placed in this position, and worshipers gather there as much to carry out ritual as to face the image of the deity.

The Temple in the Human Image. In such an architectural context, *yogin* and god are equal participants: the place of divine manifestation and the path of the aspirant have been given consubstantiality along the temple's longitudinal axis; sanctum and sacrificer's space both have become altars manifesting supreme reality in human form. In the Hindu temple, the axis of cosmic creation and the ritual path for release of the aspirant/worshiper/sacrificer *(yajamāna)* meet; the temple shares in the image of the "Supernal Man" (Puruṣa). As Kramrisch has written, "Puruṣa, which is beyond form, is the impulse towards manifestation" ("The Temple as Puruṣa," in *Studies in Indian Temple Architecture*, ed. Pramod Chandra, New Delhi, 1975, p. 40). This is true whether that manifestation is of the cosmos, of divine forms, or of human potential.

See Also Iconography, article on Hindu Iconography; Maṇḍalas, article on Hindu Maṇḍalas.

Bibliography

Bhattacharyya, Tarapada. *The Canons of Indian Art.* Calcutta, 1963. A pioneering modern work on India's architectural texts.

Coomaraswamy, Ananda K. "Early Indian Architecture: II, Bodhi-Gharas." *Eastern Art* 2 (1930): 225–235. In this series Coomaraswamy establishes a basis for understanding the forms of early Indian architecture.

Kramrisch, Stella. *The Hindu Temple.* 2 vols. Calcutta, 1946. Kramrisch's monumental work lays out, as no other, the ritual and metaphysic of the temple and establishes a groundwork for the analysis of standing monuments.

Meister, Michael W. "Maṇḍala and Practice in Nāgara Architecture in North India." *Journal of the American Oriental Society* 99 (1979): 204–219. An article that demonstrates through the analysis of standing monuments the practical applicability of the ritual *vāstumaṇḍala.*

Meister, Michael W., ed. *Encyclopaedia of Indian Temple Architecture*, vol. 1, pt. 1, "South India, Lower Drāviḍadēśa." Philadelphia, 1983. The first in a series of volumes intended to cover the full spread of India's temple architecture with technical detail.

Meister, Michael W. "Śiva's Forts in Central India." In *Discourses on Śiva*, edited by Michael W. Meister, pp. 119–142. Philadelphia, 1984.

Meister, Michael W. "Measurement and Proportion in Hindu Temple Architecture." *Interdisciplinary Science Reviews* 10 (1985): 248–258.

Sarkar, H. *Studies in Early Buddhist Architecture of India.* New Delhi, 1966. Brings to light the results of new excavation and research on early forms of Indian sacred architecture.

Stein, Burton, ed. *The South Indian Temple.* New Delhi, 1978. A collection of essays succinctly dealing with the South Indian temple as a sociological institution.

New Sources

Michell, George. *The Hindu Temple: An Introduction to Its Meaning and Forms.* Chicago, 1988.

Royal Patrons and Great Temple Art. Edited by Vidya Dehejia. Bombay, 1988.

Michael W. Meister (1987)
Revised Bibliography

TEMPLE: BUDDHIST TEMPLE COMPOUNDS IN SOUTH ASIA

During the life of the Buddha (sixth to fifth century BCE), he and his disciples were sheltered by lay followers near various urban centers in North India. After his death, according to Buddhist tradition, his body was given royal cremation, and relics were distributed among eight city-states, which then established royal burial mounds (stupas) incorporating these relics in order to memorialize him. Two centuries later the Mauryan emperor Aśoka (r. c. 270–230 BCE) is said to have reopened these stupas to distribute the relics more widely in his attempt to spread the Buddha's teachings; Buddhist tradition relates that Aśoka established 84,000 stupas throughout the empire.

Compounds in South Asia. Though shelters for the monks and stupas as monuments to memorialize the Buddha and his teaching defined the physical requirements of Buddhist architecture for many centuries, symbolic and ritual requirements gradually transformed such elements into what properly can be called Buddhist temple compounds.

Stupas and stupa-shrines. A stupa originally was used to mark the relics of the Buddha or one of his principal disciples, as well as significant objects (such as the Buddha's begging bowl) or places related to his life or sanctified by his presence. At the same time, however, the structure of such a memorial stupa incorporated cosmogonic and cosmological references relating to a point or place of cosmic origination (the egg, *aṇḍa*), to a vertical axis marking cosmic parturition, and to the cardinal orientation of the created universe. Rituals related to such cosmogonic and cosmological beliefs must have been carried out around large stupas such as those constructed at Sāñcī, Taxila, or Amarāvatī. Small stupas, set up by laity as well as by members of the Buddha's order (*saṃgha*), were often used as votive markers of a follower's devotion. A major complex such as that at Sāñcī grew to include large stupas, monastic establishments, clusters of votive monuments, and eventually temples enshrining objects intended for devotional worship. Large free-standing stupas as ritual centers continue to mark major Buddhist sites in South Asia, as well as in Myanmar, Nepal, Tibet, and Sri Lanka.

Initially, the Buddha himself, as a great teacher who had transcended the cycle of birth and rebirth through his teachings, was not the focus of devotional practice. The stupa, however, standing both for his presence and for a Buddhist and Indian conception of universal order, took on its own devotional aspect; shelters were constructed for the stupa and its worshipers, as in the structural stupa-shrine at Bairat or the excavated (rock-carved) stupa-houses (*caityagṛha*) at Guntupalli and Junnar.

From these early enclosed stupas evolved a major type of Buddhist structure, the *caitya* hall, housing an object used as a focus for worship (*caitya*). These *caitya* halls are typically apsidal structures with a central nave and side aisles; a stupa is placed prominently (and mysteriously) within the apse. The structural examples are known only from their foundations, but a number of rock-carved *caitya* halls survive in the Western Ghat mountains.

The earliest of these, at Bhājā, Bedsa, and Kondane date from the second or first centuries BCE; the largest, at Kārlī, from the first century CE; the latest, at Ellora, from perhaps the early seventh century CE. Located on trade routes and patronized by merchants and others from nearby urban centers, these large establishments also provided monastic cells for wandering monks and abbots, and sheltered pilgrims and travelers. At Bhājā, the abbot's cave has a veranda guarded by large images of the sun and rain gods, Sūrya and Indra; the individual monastic cells at Kaṇherī, scattered across a hillside outside of Mumbai, have stone beds and pillows, verandas, and grilled windows, each carefully located to take advantage of views through the neighboring hills to the harbor beyond. Both nuns and monks inhabited these cells, and helped to sponsor them, forming a community of followers who served the site and eventually might die and be memorialized there.

In the early centuries of the Common Era, much sectarian debate occurred within Buddhism over the role of the stupa—whether its function was primarily votive, memorial, or cultic. The concept of the transcendent Buddha with emissaries (*bodhisattvas*) to assist the devotee led to the introduction of images of the Buddha for worship; at the site of Nāgārjunikoṇḍa (third to fourth century CE) excavations have revealed a complex that combines a large, freestanding stupa, a monastic dormitory (*vihāra*), and a pair of apsidal *caitya* halls facing each other, with a stupa in one apse and an image of the Buddha in the other. In fifth-century *caitya* halls excavated at the great Buddhist cave site of Ajantā, an image of the Buddha, placed against the apse-stupa as if emerging from it, is a standard part of the complex. In cave 29, a gigantic image of the Buddha, reclining at the moment of his death and transcendence, fills the left wall of the cave as well, his feet placed toward the apse and his head toward daylight at the entrance.

Ajantā has more than thirty-two rock-cut Buddhist caves placed along the face of a horseshoe-shaped gorge; several date between the first century BCE and the first century CE. Two of these early caves and two dating from the fifth century CE are *caitya* halls; the remainder take a *vihāra* form. The concept of a cosmic Buddha, still accessible to his monastic aspirants, led to a significant change in the nature of such a Buddhist establishment, however.

The Buddha's body. That the Buddha in his cosmic body could both be visible to worshipers and live among the members of his *saṃgha* is the mystery of later Buddhism. Friar Bala, the high-status monk who set up the earliest images and inscribed images at both Sārnāth and Śrāvastī late in the first century CE, called them *bodhisattvas*—the Buddha returned to the worshiper, his "body made of mind" (*manomaya*). A third image, at Kauśāmbī, was dedicated by Buddhamitrā, a nun. Such images were set up under umbrellas marked with cosmological signs, on thrones at the base of trees, within railings as were other open-air *caityas,* in association with previously built stupas or those in *caitya* halls, and ultimately in temple-shelters of their own.

Monasteries and monastic shrines. For many centuries after the death of the Buddha, monastic retreats were provided principally for the assembly of monks during the rainy season, but such places took on other functions over time, becoming retreats for lay travelers and eventually centers for learning. Foundations at Taxila in the northwest and at the important Buddhist university of Nālandā in Bihar show monastic complexes in the shape of rectilinear compounds with cells enclosing a central shared court. Monks lived in these cells much as students live in a Banaras Hindu University dormitory today.

Early monastic caves, carved in conjunction with major *caitya* halls (as at Bhājā and Kārlī), show cells arranged along verandas set into the surface of the rock. Gradually such rock-carved sites began to mimic constructed monastic compounds, with cells surrounding an "open" court encased in the rock (the actual cave ceilings over these courts were painted to resemble cloth coverings hung as shelters from sun and rain).

At Ajantā, side-by-side with fifth-century CE apsidal *caitya* halls, members of the royal Vākāṭaka court had similar monastic caves excavated but added to them an enlarged hall on axis with the cave entrance, in which an image of the cosmic Buddha was enshrined. These *vihāra* caves thus served as votive "temples," donated by the Vākāṭaka kings and their ministers, as well as residences for high members of the *saṃgha.*

BUDDHIST EXPANSION. In the region of Gandhāra in the northwest, through which Buddhism spread toward Central Asia, large monastic compounds also had associated stupas, sometimes placed in the center of the court, as well as a *gandhakuṭī* (sweet-smelling chamber) among the monks' rooms assigned as the residence of the Buddha. Gandhāran sculptural reliefs also show thatch-domed structures with arched entrances, which shelter small stupas or relic containers as if for worship. These "vernacular" wooden or wattle-and-daub *caitya* shrines are sometimes depicted built on large platforms with a long central flight of steps and corner pillars marking the compound as if equivalent to the large ritual stupas built in this region, as that at Saidu Sharif. Clusters of votive stupas, as at Bhājā and Kaṇherī, sometimes have inscriptions assigning each to a particular deceased member of the monastic community.

Relic shrines and Buddhist retreats. As Buddhism spread to the northwest and south in the first centuries BCE, relic shrines became a significant component of monastic and ritual compounds. In Gandhāra in the northwest, these could be simple shed-shelters placed in association with large ritual stupas, or they could take the form of relic stupas with enclosed chambers giving access to relic caskets. In South India, carved reliefs also sometimes depict circular thatch-domed shelters that frame reliquary urns. The cult of relics—of the Buddha and of his monastic followers—gave a major impetus to the process of conversion and the spread of Buddhism in both regions.

One first-century BCE relief from an early Buddhist stupa site in Karnataka, Kanganhalli, uniquely depicts a stepped embankment with pilgrims, much like the steps of the *ghāt* (tank) excavated at the important Buddhist center of Nāgārjunakoṇḍa. Four sacred structures shown lined up at the top consist of a solid stupa, a stupa set on a circular platform that has a visible reliquary shrine within, a sacred tree shrine, and what seems to be a large stepped altar.

Other fragmentary reliefs from Kanganhalli represent the model for all Buddhist compounds, the *vihāra* and "sweet-smelling" huts of the Jetavana garden into which the Buddha and his followers took retreat. More detailed than similar narrative depictions from Barhut, these reliefs from Kanganhalli show simple gates and compound walls, an ox-cart bringing coins to be spread out in payment, simple ascetics' huts (presumably the *gandhakuṭī* and *kosambakutī* hut for monks from Kosambī), a tree shrine, an altar marked with footprints, a "walking path" for the Buddha, and a large tapering multistoried central assembly hall (*vihāra*).

Landscape, statehood, and pilgrimage. The siting of Buddhist compounds was of utmost importance. Located along trade and pilgrimage routes from an early period, Buddhist establishments served merchants and coreligionists as way stations in the wilderness, retreats in proximity to urban centers, and markers at sites (*tirthas*) sacred to other groups. If the Jetavana garden was one model, the miracle at Śrāvastī where the Buddha manifest himself in a multitude of forms provided a rationale. Stupas, monasteries, *caitya* halls, and relic shrines all formed part of a natural landscape mapped by pilgrims, merchants, monks, and nuns. The stupas on Sāñcī hill; *caitya* halls and monasteries in Ajantā's horseshoe gorge; retreats carved into the Western Ghat mountains; the manmade embankment (*ghāt*), tanks, and shrines laid out along a river at Nāgārjunakoṇḍa; monasteries marching up the valleys through Swat; all intentionally partake of nature and integrate themselves within a landscape. That we are largely unable to reconstruct initial principles of Buddhist planning should not detract us from understanding that the result was intended to be what one scholar has described as a *mesocosm*—a sacred landscape in the living world.

A pilgrimage and political complex such as that at Bamiyan, Afghanistan—as famous for its frescoes as for the two giant Buddha statues destroyed in 2001 by the Taliban—can well exemplify the extent to which a Buddhist compound could incorporate and model the world. Long before the explicit rendering of buildings as cosmic maps (*maṇḍalas*), as in Tibet, was common, Buddhist sites in South Asia less formally "centered" nature to bring the universe alive. At Bamiyan, a long cliff with mountains looming behind is honeycombed with pilgrim's caves. Two gigantic standing Buddha statues were carved into the cliff some distance apart by the seventh century CE; a third reclining image of the Buddha's *mahāparinirvāṇa* was also recorded by pilgrim accounts. The cliff's facade was a single canvas, dwarfed by the landscape of the valley, but to visit these images in ritual order according to one scholar was to retrace the spiritual career of the historical Buddha Śākyamuni. Bamiyan's valley became the "compound" within which ambulation and pilgrimage occurred, as by extension did the kingdom of Bamiyan and the human-occupied Jambudvīpa continent cited so frequently in early Buddhist inscriptions and texts. Also in this valley in front of these images, according to the seventh-century CE Chinese visitor Xuanzang, the king performed a state ritual (the Pañcavārṣika) in which he gives up his wealth and "body" and then has them restored. By doing so each year he guaranteed the well-being of the assembled community.

BUDDHIST TEMPLES. Bodh Gayā, the site in Eastern India at which the historical Buddha is said to have achieved enlightenment, reflects successive changes in Buddhist belief and practice. Under the present *bodhi* tree rests a stone altar set up in the time of Aśoka Maurya to mark the place of the Buddha's enlightenment. The tree and altar are surrounded by a modern railing mimicking the form of an ancient tree shrine, but railing pieces from the Śunga period (second to first centuries BCE) remain nearby. Such open enclosures set around objects of worship (trees, pillars, images of nature spirits, stupas) represent pre-Buddhist practices that were absorbed into the iconography of popular Buddhism. Set next to the tree shrine is a large and restored brick temple of the seventh century CE, pyramidal in shape, its surface ornamented to suggest a multi-terraced palatial structure not unlike the *vihāra* represented in the Kanganhalli relief. A large image of the Buddha is enshrined within the present structure for worship. A relief on a second- to third-century CE terra-cotta plaque from Kumrāhār demonstrates that an earlier shrine in much the same form was already there by that period. Though such a Buddhist temple structure was based exclusively on Indian palatial forms, its conceptualization already suggests a model for the later pagoda temples that range from Nepal through East Asia, although these draw on a different architectural language for their sheltering roofs. The distinctive importance of Bodh Gayā is attested by numerous votive miniature representations of this temple from along trade and pilgrimage routes into southeast Asia.

Terraced "temples" of a different sort were built across North India, most notably at Kumrāhār, Paharpur, and Lauṛīya Nandangaṛh. These structures, suggesting temple-mountains, featured cruciform bases with reentrant angles, on which stood either stupas or temple structures. The temples, and sometimes the stupas, had shrines facing the cardinal directions. The great terraced temple at Paharpur was also set within an enormous monastic court.

The most extensive representation of such terraced temple structures is found among the monuments scattered across the vast plains of Burma, particularly at Pagan. The Ananda temple there has a cruciform plan, interior ambulatories, and a central temple-like superstructure dating originally from the early eleventh century.

Cosmological compounds. The grandest expression of such an architectural conception within the Buddhist tradition, and one that reflects an increasingly perceived relationship between a manifest cosmic order and the responsibilities of Buddhism to provide visible aids to the aspirant struggling toward release, was the monument at Borobudur in Java, begun in the eighth century, but undoubtedly with South Asian prototypes. Though we are told that the compound underwent four periods of construction, with changing, possibly even conflicting, conceptions of its final design, one overriding metaphysical interpretation seems ultimately to emerge. In the opinion of most scholars, its five square terraced galleries covered by sculpture and its three upper circular terraces set with seventy-two perforated stupas and crowned by a solid stupa (with two empty chambers) were meant to incorporate and represent a Buddhist metaphysics, both cosmological and ontological, through which aspirants could ultimately find their way to release. In Cambodia as well, where Khmer rulers patronized both Hindu and Buddhist structures, the association of the king with the *bodhisattva* Lokeśvara reflected the former's role as representative of such a cosmic order on earth.

From their simple beginnings as shelters for aspiring monks to memorialize a past teacher, Buddhist compounds became cosmogonic and cosmological monuments, accommodating both state structures and lay rituals, and eventually restoring the Buddha to his worshipers as a cosmic presence, accessible to monks and laity for devotion as well as instruction. Indeed, they became institutions to mold human aspiration as permanent in form as the urban society the Buddha once had renounced. This transformation reflected the strength, pragmatism, and flexibility of the Buddha's teachings and provides some explanation for the success of Buddhism's great missionary expansion from India into other parts of the Asian world.

Bibliography

Bareau, André. "La construction et le culte des stūpa d'apré le *Vinayakapiṭaka.*" *Bulletin de l'École Francaise d'Extreme-Orient* 5 (1962): 229–274. A presentation of textual evidence for interpreting the uses put to the stupa within Indian Buddhism.

Coomaraswamy, Anada K. *Essays in Early Indian Architecture,* edited by Michael W. Meister. New Delhi, 1992. Classic documentation and interpretive essays on the representation of early India architecture in Buddhist sculpture.

Dehejia, Vidya. *Early Buddhist Rock Temples.* Ithaca, N.Y., 1972. Concise, scholarly survey of the early Buddhist rock-cut tradition in India.

Dumarcay, Jacques. *Borobudur.* Oxford, 1978. A significant analysis by the architect responsible for the conservation of the Borobudur monument.

Dutt, Sukumar. *Buddhist Monks and Monasteries of India.* London, 1962. A pioneering study connecting Buddhist compounds and their users.

Faccenna, Domenico. *Saidu Sharif I (Swat, Pakistan);* vol. 2: *The Buddhist Sacred Area: The Stūpa Terrace.* Rome, 1995. Preliminary excavations report on a type-setting stupa and monastery complex in Swat.

Gutschow, Niels. *The Nepalese Caitya: 1500 Years of Buddhist Votive Architecture in the Kathmandu Valley.* Stuttgart, Germany, and London, 1997. An environmentally and culturally sensitive study of stupa complexes in Nepal.

Klimburg-Salter, Deborah E. *The Kingdom of Bāmiyān: Buddhist Art and Culture of the Hindu Kush.* Naples, Italy, 1989. Interpretive exploration of the site and setting for the giant Buddha images and related caves at this important pilgrimage center in Afghanistan.

Levy, Robert I. *Mesocosm: Hinduism and the Organization of a Traditional Newar City in Nepal.* Berkeley, Calif., 1990. A significant anthropological investigation of the mental space of urban planning in traditional Nepal.

Meister, Michael W. "Notes Toward the Study of Representations of Early Indian Architecture, Kanganhalli." In *Prasadam: Recent Researches on Archaeology, Art, Architecture and Culture,* edited by S.S. Ramachandra Murty, D. Bhaskara Murti, and D. Kiran Kranth Choudary. New Delhi, 2004. Important excavated evidence for early Buddhist compounds.

Mitra, Debala. *Buddhist Monuments.* Calcutta, 1971. A general but detailed and well-informed survey of both Buddhist belief and monuments in India by a past director general of the Archaeological Survey of India.

Sarkar, H. *Studies in Early Buddhist Architecture in India.* Delhi, India, 1966. An important study bringing together research and the results of recent excavations.

Schopen, Gregory. *Bones, Stones, and Buddhist Monks: Collected Papers on the Archaeology, Epigraphy, and Texts of Monastic Buddhism in India.* Honolulu, 1997. A significant repositioning of lay and monastic popular practice surrounding monuments away from Buddhist canonical texts.

Slusser, Mary Shepherd. *Nepal Mandala: A Cultural Study of the Kathmandu Valley.* Princeton, N.J., 1982. A magisterial introduction to the cities, monuments, and history of this once closed Himalayan kingdom.

Stone, Elizabeth Rosen. *The Buddhist Art of Nāgārjunakonda.* Delhi, 1994. Definitive study of archaeological evidence from the most important region for early Buddhism in southern India.

MICHAEL W. MEISTER (2005)

TEMPLE: BUDDHIST TEMPLE COMPOUNDS IN EAST ASIA

Symbols of the Buddha and precursors of Buddhist monuments appeared in China in the Western Han dynasty (206 BCE–9 CE). During the Eastern Han (23–220 CE), Buddhist images and places to worship them had made their way to the Chinese capital and many provincial regions. By the fourth century CE multicultural monastic communities practiced Buddhism in China's westernmost regions, including oasis towns in what are today Xinjiang Uighur Autonomous Region and Gansu province. By the next century, temple compounds had sprung up in cities, towns, and secluded, mountainous areas in every part of China, and Buddhism and its architecture had reached the Korean peninsula. By the end of the sixth century, the religion flourished in all three East Asian countries—China, Korea, and Japan.

In general, the movement of Buddhism and the temple compound was eastward, initially from India to Central Asia, to China, to Korea, to Japan, but occasionally transmission of architecture and ideas occurred via alternate routes that bypassed Central Asia or Korea, for instance. Wherever Buddhism went, the temple compound was the core of both monastic and religious communal life. Its size and complexity increased with time, such that new sects gave rise to new architectural forms and building arrangements. Patronage often was a direct reflection of imperial interest in the faith. Constructed almost exclusively with local materials, the architecture of temple compounds was adapted to every climate and region of East Asia. Yet through two millennia of history, the core structure and the primary purposes of the Buddhist temple compound as a setting for Buddhist worship and education have remained constant.

TEMPLE COMPOUNDS IN CHINA. Buddhist temple compounds presented the first serious challenge to the highly developed, coherent, codified, and even rigid Chinese architectural system. For more than two thousand years prior to the appearance of Buddhism, individual Chinese structures had been supported by timber frames made of primarily straight pieces of wood. By the time Buddhism entered China, cantilevers in the form of bracket sets had been introduced to help support the weight of large, prominent roof eaves, and ceramic tile had become the primary material for roof coverings. The system was employed for emperors and commoners alike, in palaces and ritual halls of the sovereign, humble dwellings, and altars that were built by both groups. Ground plans of all these structures were almost invariably four-sided, the one exception being ritual halls that excavations suggest had circular and octagonal rooms. Principles of axiality and four-sided enclosure dominated Chinese construction; the latter was so important that it was almost impossible to find a structure without an arcade-enclosed courtyard adjoining or in front of it. Buildings and space multiplied along orthogonal lines, sometimes joined by arcades, in either direction. Except for watchtowers or gate-towers, before the entry of Buddhism, Chinese buildings were one-story high. These principles of Chinese construction and space would influence and usually govern imperial and religious building across East Asia until the twentieth century.

Construction in China's first Buddhist centuries. Three fundamental architectural forms of early Indian Buddhist construction—stupa, *caitya*, and *vihāra*—had to be accommodated by the Chinese system in order for Buddhist temple compounds to exist. All three were achieved during the centuries of disunion between the fall of the Han dynasty in 220 and reunification under the Sui in 581. During this period, many of the non-Chinese rulers of small and short-lived dynasties and kingdoms were eager patrons of a religion whose origins were as foreign on Chinese soil as were they. By the end of the sixth century, Buddhism had become the dominant religion in every region of China and its borders.

The most striking symbol of Buddhism on the Chinese landscape was the tower-like structure known as a *pagoda*, the Western name of the East Asian version of the stupa. The stupa had already undergone transformation along the route eastward across Central Asia from its initial Indian form of a circular plan with an egg-shaped dome capped by a balustrade-enclosed *harmikā* to a taller, occasionally four-sided monument. Its primary purposes as a relic mound, either for the remains of a Buddhist or other sacred relics or to mark a sacred place or event in the history of the faith, remained the same. At least five versions of the pagoda stood as parts of Chinese temple compounds before the beginning of the Tang dynasty (618–907). Three examples of pagodas with four-sided plans are represented by the single-story, nearly square Four-Entry Pagoda at Shentong Monastery in Licheng, Shandong, restored in 611; the multistory pillar-pagoda whose perimeter decreases story by story from base to top; and the multistory pillar-pagoda of uniform perimeter dimensions from first story to last. The latter two are found near centers of Buddhism in China that included major clusters of Buddhist worship caves. Both forms of pillar-pagoda had roof eaves marking each story. The fourth and fifth pagoda types taper in size from base to roof. One has an octagonal and the other a dodecagonal ground plan. Numerous octagonal pagodas survive from every period of Chinese history, but the only surviving, and only known, twelve-sided pagoda was built at Songyue Monastery on Mount Song, Henan, in 523. All pagodas of the early period have replicas on their exterior facades of the doors, windows, and corbel bracketing found on contemporary Chinese wooden architecture. Those that survive are brick or stone masonry.

Joining the pagoda as a focal point of worship in an early Chinese temple compound was the Buddha hall, in which were enshrined the main devotional images of the worship complex. Worshipers could enter Buddha halls, in contrast to pagodas, which sometimes could be entered but in other instances had imagery carved on the exterior and were circumambulated during worship. The earliest extant wooden Chinese Buddha halls are from the eighth and ninth centuries. From excavated remains and written descriptions we know that Buddha halls of the sixth and seventh centuries were rectangular in plan and of one story.

The site of Yongning Monastery in the Northern Wei (493–534) capital at Luoyang in Henan province is one of the most extensively excavated and described temple compounds of the early period of Buddhist architecture in China. Its rectangular wooden pagoda soared 161 meters in nine stories. Each side of each story was supported by ten pillars and had three doors and six windows. The doors were vermilion lacquer, held in place with golden nails. Golden bells hung from each corner of each level. The Great Buddha hall directly to its north was fashioned after the main hall of audience of Luoyang palace. It contained a three-meter-tall golden Buddha. Also following imperial architecture, Yongning Monastery was enclosed by a 212-by-301-meter mud-earth wall, 3.3 meters thick, with a gate on each side. Its main gate, seven bays across the front, was 66 meters high and rose three stories. The others were two stories high. Records inform us that Yongning Monastery had a thousand bays of rooms, among which were monks' quarters, towers, pavilions, and the main Buddha hall and pagoda behind one another at the center. Yongningsi (temple compound) was just one of 1,367 Buddhist structures or temple compounds in the Northern Wei capital during its forty-year history. The main southern capital in Jiankang (present-day Nanjing) had 480 monasteries during the third through sixth centuries. Although not all received the kind of imperial patronage lavished on Yongning Monastery, whether converted from residences, built anew, or expanded from earlier structures, every temple compound had a pagoda and Buddha hall, and usually at least an entry gate and one enclosing corridor joined to the gate or surrounding the two main structures. All were Chinese versions of the *vihāra,* the second Buddhist structural type imported from India. Like their Indian predecessors, most contained residential architecture for monks, and, even more so than in India, the Chinese Buddhist temple compound was a group of courtyard-enclosed spaces. Unlike many Indian *vihāra,* pagodas projected above the low walls of temple compounds, and were sometimes the only feature that made it possible to distinguish a Chinese temple compound from a palace complex.

The last architectural form inherited from Indian Buddhist temple compounds was the *caitya.* In China, the *caitya* took the form of a rock-carved worship cave. The Chinese had occasionally carved tombs into natural rock prior to the entry of Buddhism. In at least one instance—the panorama of rock-carved imagery from the Han dynasty at Lianyungang in Jiansu province—Buddhist deities are believed to have been carved into the face of rock. The concept of worship in a cave-temple, however, was inherited from India by way of Central Asia. Cave-temples with relief sculptures and paintings decorating their interiors, along with freestanding temples in oases along the Silk Routes, were seen by Chinese merchants before the fall of the Han dynasty. By the end of the fourth century, cave-temples in the vicinity of Dunhuang in Gansu province showed a unique blending of Chinese and South Asian structure and iconography. Structural and decorative features of cave-temples in Xinjiang and Gansu continued to bear signs of the native communities of monks and merchants from every part of Asia as late as the tenth century. Most famous among cave-temple monasteries are, from west to east, Kizil, Kumtura, and Bezeklik in Xinjiang; the Mogao and other cave-temple groups in the Dunhuang region, and Maijishan in Gansu province; and Yun'gang, Tianlongshan, Xiangtangshan, Longmen, and Gongxian in the north central Chinese provinces of Shanxi, Hebei, and Henan. Additional cave-temples studied in the twentieth century Gansu, the Ningxia Hui Autonomous Region, southeastern China, and Liaoning in the Northeast is giving way to the redating and refinement of chronologies for all of China's cave-temples.

The transmission of Buddhism and the rock-carved temple compound never followed a clear or direct path from South to East Asia during the five centuries (fifth to tenth) during which the architectural form flourished in Central Asia and China. Features of Chinese architecture, notably the ceramic tile roof and pillar-supported structure raised on a high platform with bracket sets, appeared in the murals and in reliefs at each of the sites named above by the fifth or sixth century. Often these indicators that Buddhism had entered the Chinese sphere existed alongside worshipers whose non-Chinese ethnicity was emphasized in the paintings or sculpture. Even after the facial features of figures that decorated the walls of Chinese *caitya* halls had become Sinified, elements of South Asian architecture persisted. One of the most common decorative features in Chinese cave-temples is the pointed, horseshoe-shaped arch called a *caitya* arch.

Temple compounds after 800 CE. The impermanence of wooden architecture has meant that rock-carved cave-temples, paintings of temple compounds on the walls of cave-temples, and excavated remains provide the most reliable evidence of comprehensive Buddhist worship space before the tenth century. Eight individual Buddha halls have been identified from the period 782 to 966, most with original images and some with wall paintings. Six are in Shanxi province, one is in Hebei, and one in Fujian. All but one are of the humble variety, with three or five bays across the front, indicating that their temple compounds either were not recipients of imperial patronage or were constructed in times of political and budgetary turmoil.

In China, the most important temple compounds, including rock-carved worship caves, were commissioned by the emperor or empress, often in or near national capitals, sometimes near their burial sites and other times on sacred Buddhist peaks. Second-grade temple compounds often were commissioned by prefectural governments. Third-grade monasteries would be founded by princes and princesses, high-ranking nobility, or wealthy merchants. The same groups patronized temple compounds in Korea and Japan. The least distinguished temple compounds were built by local funds of private individuals.

The greatest temple compounds of the Sui dynasty (581–618) dominated their capital city Daxing (Chang'an under the Tang dynasty, today Xian). Daxing Mountain Monastery spanned an area 525 by 562 meters. Dachangding Monastery was three times as large, with eastern and western divisions and a pagoda that soared more than 97 meters. It was still common at this time and in the subsequent Tang dynasty for imperial residential architecture to be transformed into Buddhist temple compounds. The residence of the prince of Wei, son of the second Tang emperor, was transformed in 658 into a monastery with more than four thousand bays of rooms and thirteen major Buddhist halls arranged around ten courtyards.

By the Tang dynasty, it is possible to associate building plans with Buddhist ceremonies. Halls used for ordination of Zhenyan (Jpn., Shingon) monks were divided into front and back spaces; the private back space was used for the initiation rite in which the Womb and Diamond World *maṇḍalas* were removed from the wall and placed on a low central table or on the floor. Other halls had a central altar with images where the pagoda-pillar had stood in cave-temples, and an enclosing ambulatory defined by pillars. Both hall types and full-scale monasteries are depicted in Buddhist murals and paintings on silk of the period.

From the Song, Liao, and Jin dynasties of the mid-tenth through mid-thirteenth centuries, monasteries with numerous types of buildings survive all over China. A pagoda or multistory pavilion and main Buddha hall remained the most important structures in most Chinese temple compounds from this period. Sometimes the two were on a building line that dominated the temple compound. Temple compounds of the period with pagodas or pavilions at their focus include Dule Monastery in Yi county, Hebei, whose pavilion and front gate are dated 984; Fogong Monastery in Ying county, Shanxi, whose 67-meter pagoda, the tallest wooden pagoda in China today, dates to 1056; and Fengguo Monastery in Yi county, Liaoning, whose main hall was built in 1013. At Fengguo Monastery, a law (*dharma*) hall for expounding the Buddhist scriptures stood on the main building line with the 48.2-by-25.13-meter main hall and pavilion behind the front gate. East and west of the central line were pavilions to the Three Vehicles (*triyāna*) and Amitābha Buddha. A covered, pillar-supported arcade of 120 bays enclosed Fengguo Monastery. Longxing Monastery in Zhengding, Hebei, which was begun by imperial Song patronage shortly after the establishment of the dynasty in 960 and whose buildings were repaired or restored during the next century, included an even longer line of main structures: a hall to the Sixth Patriarch, a hall to Śākyamuni Buddha, an ordination platform, and a pavilion to Avalokiteśvara known as Dabei or Foxiang Pavilion, which stood on the main axial line behind the front gate. In addition, pairs of side halls, pavilions, and towers framed each major courtyard in front of one of the axially-positioned structures.

The pairing of pagodas and pavilions on either side in front of a main hall became standard in tenth- to thirteenth-century Chinese Buddhist temple compounds. Shanhua Monastery in Datong, Shanxi, consisted of a front gate, a hall of the three deities, and a main hall along its main building line, along with two pairs of halls and a pair of pavilions joined to the covered arcade that enclosed it. One of the pavilions at both Shanhua and Longxing monasteries contained the temple compound's sūtra collection. A standard feature in Chinese monasteries of this middle period, the sūtra hall was often a pavilion or other multistory structure.

By the Southern Song dynasty (1127–1279), the majority of temple compounds were dedicated to the Chan sect. The major monasteries of this meditational form of Buddhism were dominated by seven halls arranged along a north-south line: a front gate, a Buddha hall, a Vairocana hall, a law hall, front abbot's quarters, abbot's quarters, and a room for seated meditation. Buildings for mundane affairs, such as storage halls and dormitories, filled the space on either side of the main building line. Monks' quarters sometimes contained a single huge bed on which monks meditated and slept. Other monasteries of the period had a hall dedicated to the five hundred arhats (*luohan*). In addition to accounts by Chinese pilgrims and records kept at the monasteries, knowledge of Southern Song monasteries such as Tiantongsi is preserved in accounts of Japanese Buddhist pilgrims to south China. An important account is the illustrated record of Gikai, who visited the five headquarters of Chan Buddhism in Zhejiang and Jiangsu provinces, including Ayuwang (King Aśoka) Monastery in Mingzhou, in 1259.

By the thirteenth century, great variety was found in monastery architecture in China. When a monastery contained three main buildings, for instance, the most important Buddha hall could be right behind the main gate or last in line. The lack of consistency can in part be explained by the presence in China of numerous Buddhist sects and by an increasing syncretism in Buddhist and Daoist worship that gave rise to new sects. Often a twelfth- or thirteenth-century Buddhist temple compound was architecturally indistinguishable from a Daoist temple compound on the exterior; upon entering, however, statues and paintings confirmed the temple's affiliation. In addition, Daoist precincts could be constructed at Buddhist monasteries and Buddhist precincts at Daoist temple compounds. Guangsheng Monastery in Hongdong, Shanxi, contains a Buddhist and a Daoist hall constructed in the first quarter of the fourteenth century.

By the fourteenth century, Lamaist Buddhism had pervaded the Chinese landscape. The most representative structure of a Lamaist Buddhist temple compound in China is the bulb-shaped pagoda known as a *dagoda*, often painted white. The Lamaist pagoda of Miaoying Monastery, built in 1279, and the one in Beihai Park, built in 1651, still rise above much of the rest of Beijing's architecture. Lamaist temple compounds dominated the regions of China adjacent to Tibet, in particular areas of Sichuan, Ningxia Hui, and Qinghai, as well as Inner Mongolia. Patronized by the Manchu rulers of the last Chinese dynasty, Qing (1644–1911), some of the most creative architecture of China's last three imperial centuries stands at Lamaist temple compounds.

Traditional Buddhist monasteries never disappeared from China. Chan monasteries continued to be built and restored into the last Qing century, especially at sacred locations, such as the Four Great Peaks; Wutai in Shanxi province, dedicated to Mañjuśrī; Putuo, the island off the coast of Ningbo, dedicated to Avalokiteśvara; Emei in Sichuan, dedicated to Samantabhadra; and Jiuhua in Anhui, dedicated to Kṣitigarbha. The later temple compounds of traditional sects retained axial arrangements and often were larger than their pre-fourteenth-century predecessors. These temple compounds included two new hall types, the diamond hall and the hall of divine kings, both of which also were incorporated into Lamaist construction in China. Also new in fourteenth-century temple compounds were brick "beamless" halls that were a sharp contrast to the ubiquitous wooden buildings of Chinese construction.

TEMPLE COMPOUNDS IN KOREA. Buddhism entered Korea from China officially in 372. Although not every Chinese Buddhist sect became popular in Korea, most were known there. Thus Korean Buddhist temple compounds contained the standard structures of Chinese monasteries. A standard plan in a Korean Buddhist temple compound, a plan that is equally common in China, includes an entry gate with a pair of divine kings on each side, followed by a law hall and main hall, and often additional halls behind or on the sides of this core group. As in China, almost all Korean temple compounds have Buddha halls and pagodas. Rock-carved cave-temples also are found in Korea, but are much rarer than in China.

Korea's best-known Buddhist temple compounds are Pulguksa and Sŏkkuram, both outside Kyŏngju, capital of the united Silla kingdom (668–935). Pulguksa consists of a front gate with two halls directly behind it, and smaller halls dedicated to buddhas or *bodhisattvas* in their own precincts. The entry and most of the enclosing corridors of the monastery are elevated on stone foundations. Pulguksa's twin pagodas, similarly, are made of stone, the predominant Korean material of early pagodas. Sŏkkuram is Korea's most famous rock-carved Buddhist cave-chapel. The site with the greatest concentration of Buddhist rock-carved niches and worship spaces in Korea is Namsan (southern mountain), also in the vicinity of Kyŏngju. In addition to thousands of images, Namsan has a pair of stone pagodas. The largest temple compound in Korea is T'ongdo, located between Kyŏngju and Pusan. One of the most noteworthy is Haein Monastery, which has been destroyed and rebuilt seven times; Haein Monastery houses an extensive set of woodblocks for the printing of Buddhist scriptures and the *Tripiṭaka Koreana.*

TEMPLE COMPOUNDS IN JAPAN. Although rock-carved cave-temples were never constructed in Japan, more pre-ninth-century wooden architecture from Buddhist temple compounds survives there than in any other East Asian country. Among remains from the Asuka and Nara periods (552–784 CE) are main Buddha image halls known in Japanese as *kondō* (literally, "golden hall"), octagonal halls that commemorate men important in a temple compound's history; multistory pagodas, including two miniature pagodas; lecture halls for teaching the scriptures; and gates, enclosing corridors, a sūtra repository, a monks' dormitory, and a refectory. Through these structures, as well as excavated remains and literary descriptions, temple compounds of the first Buddhist centuries in Japan, as well as China and Korea, have been reconstructed. It is known, for example, that three arrangements dominated temple compounds in Japan in the first Buddhist centuries. At Shitennōji in Osaka, the pagoda and hall are on an axial line, the arrangement implemented in China at Yongning Monastery, as well as in the temple compounds at Miruksa (early seventh century) of the Silla kingdom and Gumgangsa (sixth century) of the Paekche kingdom of Korea. At Japan's Hōryūji, whose four oldest buildings date to around 700, and at Kawaharadera, the pagoda and main Buddha hall were placed side by side. At sixth-century Asukadera, south of Nara in Asuka, three main Buddha halls enclosed a dominant central pagoda on all but the south side. Yet another Nara-period plan included twin pagodas on either side in front of the main hall. Each of these plans is suggested by excavated remains in Korean kingdoms of the sixth and seventh centuries; they are also seen in murals dating from the seventh and eighth centuries on the walls of cave-temple compounds in China after Dunhuang. Expansive temple compounds of eighth-century Japan, including Hōryūji and Tōdaiji, inform us of yet more kinds of structures that survive in rebuilt versions—bell and drum towers used to keep time and call monks to prayer, halls for ceremonies of certain moons of the lunar year, ordination halls, and treasure repositories. Temple compounds could also include shrines to monks or monk-founders, halls to individual buddhas or *bodhisattvas*, gardens, bathhouses, and anything else that offered full-service life and education to the monastic and sometimes lay community.

Coincident with the move of the main capital to Heian (Kyoto) at the end of the eighth century, esoteric Buddhist sects, particularly Tendai and Shigon, both transmitted by monks who had traveled to China to study their teachings, rose in Japan. In contrast to the temple compounds of the seventh and eighth centuries that dominated Japan's capital cities, early Heian-period monasteries had smaller buildings located in remote, often mountainous settings. Thereby, the clergy were kept distant from court affairs. Muroji in Nara prefecture, Daigoji and Jingoji on the outskirts of Kyoto, and many of the monasteries of the sacred Buddhist peak Koya, trace their origins to this period. So does the Eastern Monastery, Tōji, in Kyoto. Although buildings of temple compounds in the middle part of the Heian period remained small in comparison to their Nara counterparts, decoration became lavish. The change corresponded to the surge in Pure Land Buddhism, whose monasteries often included a re-creation of the Buddha's paradise, or Pure Land, in the form of a hall with a lotus pond in front of it. The Phoenix Hall of the Byōdōin in Uji, once the residence of one of Japan's wealthiest families, and the Golden Hall of Chūsonji in Hiraizumi are typical Fujiwara-period (951–1086) monastery buildings. By the end of the Heian period, however, much less ornate temple compounds became popular: one-bay square halls dedicated to Amitābha Buddha of the Western Paradise were common.

Austere construction characterized temple compounds of the next period of Japanese history, named Kamakura (1185–1333) after the location of its capital, when the power of government lay in the hands of the military ruler known as the *shogun.* Austerities suited to a militaristic age were compatible with Zen Buddhism, a meditational sect, which became popular across Japan beginning in the thirteenth century. Like Esoteric and Pure Land Buddhism, Zen was transmitted from China. Yet even from the twelfth, thirteenth, and fourteenth centuries, when Chan (Jpn., Zen) flourished in South China, few temple compounds survive intact, in contrast to the scores of Zen temple compounds with original structures in Japan. Zen temple compounds are known for two-story entry gates where portrait statues of the sixteen arhats were installed on the second floor. The main Buddha hall of a Zen temple compound, where public ceremonies were enacted, was known as *butsuden.* Other assemblages of monks took place in the law hall. Both in Kamakura and later in Kyoto in the fourteenth through sixteenth centuries, Zen temple compounds consisted of public reception space, used chiefly by the main abbot; abbot's quarters; halls for study and meditation; a hall for sūtra recitation; a hall dedicated to the monastery founder; and usually gardens. The abbot's quarters traced its origins to a humble one-bay square hut *(hōjō),* the kind of dwelling used by the earliest Indian Buddhists, but these became increasingly important and lavish by the end of the twelfth century. Yet another hall type of Zen temple compounds was the *shariden,* the relic hall. Examples of all these structures remain in Kamakura and most survive at one of the best examples of a Zen temple compound, the Tōfukuji in Kyoto. Two styles of Kamakura temple compounds originated on China's southeastern coast. They were differentiated by the names Indian style and Tang (or Chinese) style, even though their buildings used Chinese components from base to roof. Other temple architecture of the period and as late as the fifteenth century was designated Japanese (native) style and mixed style.

The return of the shogunate to the Japanese capital in Kyoto ushered in the Muromachi age (1338–1573), a period of luxurious living represented by the Silver Pavilion and the Golden Pavilion. Each was a devotional-meditational-reception hall for the private use of the shogun at his residential-religious building complexes. The in-town shogunate residences also included tea huts and Zen meditational gardens, sometimes made largely of rocks. The Muromachi period was the last age of great innovation in Buddhist temple architecture in Japan.

Temple compounds survive, are restored, and built anew in China, Korea, and Japan today. After a millennium-and-a-half of history, they are still centers of Buddhist education, worship, and communal life.

BIBLIOGRAPHY

Prip-Moller, Johannes. *Chinese Buddhist Monasteries: Their Plan and its Function as a Setting for Buddhist Monastic Life.* Copenhagen, 1937.

Seckel, Dietrich. *The Art of Buddhism.* Translated by Ann Keep. New York, 1968.

Soper, Alexander. *The Evolution of Buddhist Architecture in Japan.* Princeton, N.J., 1942.

Steinhardt, Nancy S., ed. and expander. *Chinese Architecture.* New Haven, Conn., 2002.

Suzuki Kakichi. *Early Buddhist Architecture in Japan.* Translated by Mary N. Parent and Nancy S. Steinhardt. Tokyo, New York, and San Francisco, 1980.

Zhongguo jianzhu yishu quanji, vol. 12: *Fojiao jianzhu.* Pt. 1: *The North,* edited by Cao Changzhi. Beijing, 2002; Pt. 2: *The South,* edited by Ding Chengpu. Beijing, 1999.

Zhongguo meishu quanji, vol. 4: *Zongjia jianzhu,* edited by Sun Dazhang and Yu Weiguo. Beijing, 1991.

NANCY SHATZMAN STEINHARDT (2005)

TEMPLE: BUDDHIST TEMPLE COMPOUNDS IN TIBET

The area covered by Tibetan Buddhist culture—which extends from the Tibetan Autonomous Region of China into neighboring Chinese provinces and into adjacent parts of India, Nepal, Bhutan, and Burma (Myanmar)—shares a common architectural tradition. The basic units are the temple and the stupa. Temples may stand alone either in open countryside or in a village or town, or more commonly they may, singly or in a group, form the core of a monastic community, or sometimes of a fortified palace complex. Stupas, usually modest in size, are ubiquitous features of the landscape. Occasionally a stupa of massive proportions will dominate a monastery or temple site.

The architectural style of Tibetan Buddhism is distinctive and as such has been exported to Mongolia and parts of China, and to Tibetan refugee communities around the world. The style has been created over some fourteen centuries as an eclectic mix from a variety of sources. Basic design concepts of plan and elevation—*vihāra, maṇḍala,* multistoried construction—derive largely from India, often via Nepal. The main inspiration for building materials and techniques, as well as some of the decoration, has been the domestic farmhouse architecture of Tibet itself, with its many regional variations. Economic conditions dictate the use of native labor—essentially drawn from the local peasant farming population—for erecting and maintaining the main structure of religious buildings, which follow the local farmhouses in their reliance on heavy load-bearing outer walls of layered mud, mud brick, or rough stone. Internally the ceilings and flat roofs are supported by wooden columns, beams, and joists, the timbers for which may have to be imported from a distance. These factors in turn determine the form, finish, and size of walls, room spaces, and other architectural elements of temples, which from the constructional point of view can be regarded as oversized farmhouses. Temples are however distinguished from farmhouses by decorative embellishments that have originated in India, Nepal, Kashmir, China, and Mongolia and have often been executed by craftspeople imported from those countries.

The First Spreading of Buddhism: Jo khang (Jokhang) and Bsam yas (Samye). Buddhism is traditionally held to have been introduced into Tibet in the early seventh century. A major landmark in the process was the foundation of the still extant Jo khang temple in Lhasa by the Nepalese wife of King Srong btsan sgam po (Songtsen gampo, r. c. 618–641). While the story is heavily obscured by legend its essentials are plausible. The Jo khang, built on a level site and facing in the direction of Nepal, follows the *vihāra* layout so common in the architecture of the Kathmandu Valley. A three-storied range of chambers faces inward toward a rectangular inner courtyard, which, unlike its Nepalese prototypes, is covered with a flat roof. Light is admitted through a skylight onto the main image of the Buddha, which occupies a chamber in one of the shorter sides opposite the entrance porch.

While the outer walls and much of the present woodwork are entirely of the farmhouse-derived Tibetan type, the older columns, brackets, and door frames are compatible with the seventh-century Nepalese style, suggesting the participation of craft workers from Nepal. The four small-pitched roofs perched on the flat top of the building, with their complex wooden bracketing and gilded metal covering are instantly recognizable as of Chinese inspiration, almost certainly executed by Chinese artisans. At least one of them is known to have been added in the fourteenth century.

The inward-looking chambers of the Jo khang are occupied by chapels containing images of Buddhist divinities and a variety of mural paintings, both iconic and narrative in subject matter. An additional circumambulation corridor was later added round the whole building, and further concentric circumambulation routes lead round the streets outside and toward the outskirts of the city of Lhasa, reinforcing the supreme position of the Jo khang at the center of Tibetan religious life.

The other major religious complex founded in Tibet during the first spreading of Buddhism is Bsam yas, some 120 kilometers southeast of Lhasa, built by King Khri Srong lde btsan (Trisong detsen, ruled c. 755–797) in about 770 as the home of the country's first monastic community. Its layout, based on the *maṇḍala* with explicit cosmic symbolism, is strikingly different from that of the Jo khang. A central building of three superimposed temple chambers containing images of buddhas and divinities (the stories were originally built or decorated in Tibetan, Indian, and Chinese style respectively) represents Mount Meru at the center of the universe in Indian cosmology, looking outwards across a low surrounding wall representing concentric rings of mountains and lakes. Outside this, symmetrically placed at the quarters and intermediate directions, are four directional stupas and variously shaped small temples representing the sun and moon and the four earthly continents. The whole is surrounded by a quasi-circular wall. Living quarters for monks and other ancillary buildings are not part of the symbolic plan, as is normally the case in later buildings. The foundation of Bsam yas marks the inauguration of Buddhism as the state religion of Tibet under the King as a kind of cosmocrator. Its plan was allegedly inspired by the monastery of Odantapuri in Bihar, India, and may also owe something to the example of a temple at Wutaishan in China; there are also interesting parallels with the roughly contemporary palace-city of Baghdad. While the main structures of the present buildings at Bsam yas are original, the complex, like the Jo khang, has suffered periods of damage and neglect, most recently in the Cultural Revolution (1966–1976), and much of the woodwork and decoration dates from later periods.

The Second Spreading of Buddhism: Tabo and Alchi. After the collapse of the early Tibetan empire in the years after 842 CE, Buddhism was on the defensive in a politically fragmented country and little is known of architectural activity except for the mention of a few temples which, if genuine, must have been very small. Datable building programs begin again in 996 with the Western Tibetan complexes of Tabo and Mtho lding (Tholing, the latter largely destroyed in the Cultural Revolution). Generally, individual temples of this period are much smaller than the Jo khang or Bsam yas, and are built in small groups within walled compounds. While the details of a number of temple compounds from this period are known, by far the best preserved are those at Tabo and Alchi, both now in India.

The main temple at Tabo (Himachal Pradesh, India) is externally an unprepossessing single-story mud-brick chamber with no windows or external decoration. Internally however it displays a sophisticated arrangement of the deities of the Vajradhātu *Maṇḍala*, crafted in stucco and fixed part way up the internal walls of the single chamber. The image of the central buddha, Vairocana, is moved along the axis from the entrance porch toward the rear of the chamber, and in a small space behind it is the image of Amitābha, of whom Vairocana is an emanation. Thus the use of height to convey symbolically a progression to more supramundane levels at

Bsam yas is replaced by movement along an axis. Height is however used to differentiate the mural paintings of the internal walls, which cover historical and narrative themes lower down and iconic subjects higher up. The flat roof of the chamber is supported in the usual fashion by wooden columns to leave a central space suitable for the communal rituals of the monks. This practical requirement henceforth very commonly dictates the form of the Tibetan temple chamber. Conceptually it can be seen as both a *maṇḍala*, housing a conventional set of divine images, and as a *vihāra*, with the images represented as statues or paintings looking into a central space from the sides, and the main image at the far end opposite the entrance. Both types of plan are sanctioned in the Tibetan Buddhist scriptures: the *vihāra* mainly in the Vinaya texts of monastic discipline, and the *maṇḍala* in the Tantras. Details of the carpentry recall styles from lower down the Himalayan valleys, from whence most of the timber probably came.

While the assembly hall at Alchi in present-day Ladakh (India) resembles the main temple of Tabo, the Sumtsek or temple of three diminishing stories there reworks some of the themes touched upon above. Of uncertain date, perhaps eleventh to twelfth century, it is of *maṇḍala*-like plan with four projections, one of them occupied by the entrance porch and the other three- by four-meter high stucco images of *bodhisattvas* whose heads project above the ceiling into the gallery of the next story. The small central space is occupied by a stupa: too small for communal worship it was used like a few others of its type for individual Tantric initiations. Just as remarkable as the plan and elevation of the temple are its paintings, which cover the entire inner surface in luxuriant profusion. As at Bsam yas and Tabo, symbolic use is made of height, with more mundane scenes and subjects below, more transcendental ones above. Carpentry details at Alchi strongly resemble those in the architecture of the Kashmir Valley (now surviving only in stone), whence some of the craftsmen are known to have traveled.

TRANSITION: SHALU. The temple compound of Shalu near Shigatse in south-central Tibet illustrates the transition from the style of the second spreading of Buddhism to the mature style, sometimes called the Dge lugs (Geluk) pa style, which had evolved by the fifteenth to sixteenth century and continues to this day.

The original temples at Shalu, from the early eleventh century, comprised a pair of single windowless chambers sharing a party wall and known as the "twin chapels," whose ceilings are each supported by four wooden columns remarkable in this period for their height, about six meters. They faced across what was presumably an open space toward a two-story temple, nowadays made up of a chamber traversed by the main entrance passage, with a chapel devoted to the goddess of wisdom (Prajñāpāramitā). The capitals and bracketing between the columns and ceilings of all these early temples show interesting experiments that bring together elements of both Chinese- and Indian-derived carpentry.

In the late thirteenth century, additional single-story temples were constructed along the sides of the compound to create an enclosed central courtyard. This paved the way for a complete transformation of the complex in the early fourteenth century, made possible by the connections of the local princes with the hierarchs of the nearby principality of Sa skya (Sakya), who had been appointed viceroys of Tibet by the Yuan (Mongol) dynasty of China. Lavish patronage was available in the form of financing and the services of mural painters, carpenters, and tile-makers sent from China. The painters were from an imperial atelier set up some decades earlier by the famous Nepalese artist and sculptor Aniko. Thus the construction of this phase of Shalu was a true international effort, as has frequently been the case in Tibetan architecture. Raw materials for tile glazing and painting must have been imported from China, while timber was transported from across the Himalayas.

The central courtyard was roofed over to create a columned assembly hall lit by a central skylight. Over the chapels on each of the four sides was erected a Chinese pavilion of traditional wooden construction with a pitched roof of green glazed tiles, looking onto the central roof terrace in the fashion of the Jo khang. The whole was surrounded by a two-story circumambulation corridor. Internal surfaces not already painted were covered with mural paintings, where some of the earliest Chinese influence within Indo/Nepalese-derived Tibetan art can be seen.

By this time the distinctive Tibetan wooden entablature of column, bracket, beam, and joist had evolved and was used in the lower parts of the building. In the upper Chinese pavilions, however, Chinese bracketing and other carpentry details are exactly those found in contemporary Chinese architecture.

THE DGE LUGS PA STYLE. The basic temple layout exemplified at Shalu was much utilized after the government was taken over by the Dalai Lamas of the Dge lugs pa or Yellow Hat order of Tibetan Buddhism in the mid-seventeenth century. There was however a strong tendency to move the sites of temples and monasteries away from the river plains of earlier times to defensive hilltop positions. From there they could dominate the surrounding landscape not only visually and symbolically, but in some cases also militarily, in times when armed conflict between Buddhist monastic orders and their backers was not unknown. In some cases the temple and monastery merged with the fortified palace, so strong was the interconnection between religion and politics. The most outstanding examples of this process are the Potala palace of Lhasa and the *dzongs* of Bhutan, though there have been many others.

The Potala was begun by King Srong btsan sgam po in 637. In a development of the basic *vihāra* layout, a rectangular ground-floor assembly hall is surrounded by inward-looking cells over which are superimposed stories of further cells to leave a galleried and open central inner terrace over the hall. The internal spaces are mostly dedicated as chapels, monastic rooms, and Dalai Lama's living apartments or funerary stupas. The adjoining Red Palace to the east was erected by the last regent of the fifth Dalai Lama from 1690 to 1694 to incorporate the latter's mausoleum. Courtyards, monastic living quarters, access ramps, and defensive end bastions completed the complex. While it is defensible and has indeed been besieged a number of times, it is doubtful whether its main purpose was defense so much as a visual symbol of the religio-political center of the Tibetan polity.

The *dzongs* of Bhutan (the main ones located at Ha, Thimphu, Punakha, and Tongsa, and dating from the seventeenth to the twentieth centuries), while built around a monastic core, had defense as a principal purpose. Each was intended as a center of civil, military, and religious administration for its surrounding valley complex. Within a mighty enclosing and elongated rampart are typically two courtyards: a public courtyard near the single entrance, separated by a towering central temple of three to five stories from an inner monastic courtyard.

The external appearance of religious buildings has been largely standardized, with outer walls tapering inward toward the top, and whitewashed to contrast with black-framed windows. The style closely resembles that of the local farmhouses, even to the extent of incorporating the roof parapets of stacked brushwood or other fuel and animal fodder as a fossilized element in religious buildings usually painted red. There are local variations—for instance in Bhutan the window frames are more elaborate and brightly painted and the temples are provided with overhanging pitched wooden roofs, but even here the red horizontal band is present in painted form. Stylized banners and standards of textile or, more commonly, gilded metal, of Indian, Nepalese, or Mongolian derivation adorn the roofs of temples, the more important of which may still be marked with small Chinese-style gilded pavilions. Internally the tapering wooden columns that support beams via elongated voluted brackets, all brightly painted, have also been largely standardized.

THE STUPA: RGYAL RTSE (GYANTSE). Tibetans conventionally recognize eight designs of stupa, relating them to episodes in the life of the Buddha. In practice all but the type commemorating the enlightenment are rare. However there are a few examples of the "stupa of many doors," the most remarkable being that in the town of Rgyal rtse, the so-called Kumbum, which dominates its temple complex. Built from 1427 to 1439 by the local princes, it is unusual in that all five stories of the stepped base, the dome, and the spire are hollowed out into chapels containing a rich variety of images and wall paintings. Thus the form of the stupa is fused with that of an elaborate Tantric *maṇḍala.*

BIBLIOGRAPHY

Chayet, Anne. *Art et archéologie du Tibet.* Paris, 1994. General account of Tibetan architecture in its cultural and artistic setting.

Denwood, Philip. "Architectural Style at Shalu." In *Tibetan Art: Towards a Definition of Style,* edited by Jane Casey Singer and Philip Denwood, pp. 220–229. London, 1997. Analysis of the successive building phases of Shalu Monastery.

Goepper, Roger. *Alchi, Ladakh's Hidden Buddhist Sanctuary: The Sumtsek.* London, 1996. Lavish documentation of the temple and its mural paintings.

Guise, A., ed. *The Potala Palace of Tibet.* London, 1988.

Khosla, Romi. *Buddhist Monasteries in the Western Himalaya.* Kathmandu, Nepal, 1979. Study by an architect of a well-defined region (Ladakh and northern Himachal Pradesh) with unusually accurate plans.

Klimburg-Salter, Deborah E. *Tabo: A Lamp for the Kingdom.* Milan, Italy, 1997. Thorough historical account and well-illustrated documentation of the contents of this temple.

Ricca, Franco, and Erberto Lo Bue. *The Great Stupa of Gyantse: A Complete Tibetan Pantheon of the Fifteenth Century.* London, 1993. Thorough textual and visual documentation.

Richardson, Hugh Edward. "The Jo-khang: 'Cathedral' of Lhasa." In *Essais sur l'art du Tibet,* edited by Ariane Macdonald, pp. 157–188. Paris, 1977.

PHILIP DENWOOD (2005)

TEMPLE: BUDDHIST TEMPLE COMPOUNDS IN SOUTHEAST ASIA

Buddhists in Southeast Asia have established temple compounds of importance since ancient times. In Java, significant complexes were built in the eighth and ninth centuries (in Central Java) and in the eleventh to fifteenth centuries (in East Java), prior to the spread of Islam. In mainland Southeast Asia, where Theravāda Buddhism is practiced today, the development of Buddhist temples can be traced from early historical times through the present.

Because so many temple compounds have included dwelling places for monks, it is sometimes held that it is preferable to speak of monasteries, rather than temples. Since, however, monastic establishments are in general places of public worship, either term is acceptable. Temple compounds can include the same elements found in India: the stupa, which need not contain an actual relic of the Buddha; a sanctuary or a hall holding a principal Buddha image; and housing for monks. In the living traditions of Burma (Myanmar) and Thailand (together with Laos and Cambodia), special importance is attached to halls that can accommodate public worship and to those that provide for monastic ceremonies a space that is necessarily demarcated by ritual boundary stones. Sometimes these halls are distinct, sometimes one in the same.

In this entry, a survey of developments in Southeast Asia follows descriptions of three complexes of particular distinction and ambition: Borobudur in Central Java (eighth to ninth centuries); the Nagayon in Pagan, Burma (eleventh century); and Wat Phra Chettuphon in Bangkok, Thailand (eighteenth to nineteenth centuries).

BOROBUDUR. Borobudur, or Chandi Borobudur, is a unique monument, the profundity of which has been widely acknowledged, even in the absence of general agreement about its interpretation. It may be regarded as a stupa elevated upon a sequence of terraces, as in such later structures as the twelfth-century Dhammayazika at Pagan (where the terraces bear reliefs depicting Buddhist birth stories) and the Kumbum in Gyantse, Tibet (where niches on the terraces hold images of deities in the Vajrayāna pantheon). Its Indian antecedents are obscure. In complexity, quality of workmanship, and expressiveness, Borobudur surpasses these later buildings and perhaps all other Buddhist monuments.

The original 160 relief panels encircling the lowest quadrangular story were covered with stone blocks, apparently before the monument reached its ultimate shape, as a result of a need to prevent subsidence. These reliefs depict scenes of cause and effect, such as appropriate punishments for evil deeds. Above are four stories generally referred to as galleries. Each of these can be circumambulated by a visitor entering from one of the four axial stairs, and each contains a major series of narrative reliefs on the inner wall, with reliefs of lesser importance on the outer wall. The height of the outer wall prevents views out to the landscape. In the first gallery, the primary 120 panels depict the life of the Buddha through his enlightenment; directly below, the reliefs depict Buddhist tales, both *jātakas* and *avadānas.* On the second and third galleries, the primary reliefs depict the *Gaṇḍavyūha Sūtra,* specifically the visits of the pilgrim Sudhana to "good friends," who provide instruction in Mahāyāna Buddhist doctrine according to Avataṃsaka tenets, and Sudhana's arrival at the Tower of Maitreya, characterized in the text as a fantastic architectural structure that provides a visualization of the nature of the *dharmadhātu,* the "truth realm" or phenomenal world as perceived by buddhas. The reliefs of the fourth and topmost gallery are devoted to the Samantabhadra vows, a text describing miraculous visions and committing the pilgrim to the *bodhisattva* path, and to the vow to remain in the world, aiding suffering creatures until all beings can enter *nirvāṇa* together. Overlooking each of these four galleries are life-sized buddha images in niches (in all, 368 images); these are differentiated according to direction on the first three galleries; over the fourth gallery, all the buddhas execute a teaching gesture.

After the fourth gallery, the visitor enters a "plateau," above which rise three concentric terraces, which hold a total of seventy-two (thirty-two, twenty-four, and sixteen) perforated stupas with diamond-shaped and square openings, through which is visible a life-sized sculpture of the Buddha performing the teaching gesture known as *dharmacakra mudrā.* Crowning the monument is a much larger central stupa, which is solid. From these terraces the visitor has a view over the landscape.

The reliefs of the covered base and the four galleries present a straightforward pilgrimage along the *bodhisattva* path of Mahāyāna Buddhism. The significance of the upper terraces, on the other hand, is less clear. Older interpretations draw conclusions from points of connection with Buddhist cosmology, seeing in the half-hidden buddhas of the perforated stupas a move toward the invisibility of the topmost "formless realm" of the Buddhist cosmos. One recent interpretation argues that the upper terraces represent an ideal world, contrasting with and paralleling the real world of the galleries, and that the perforated stupas convey higher meditational experience in two ways. The openings in the stupas are actually the shapes of the breaths of the meditator, who is paying visits on the terraces to the planets and stars, the moon, and the sun. Secondly, if the stupas were gilded and reflected each other and the visitor, they would have conveyed the nature of the *dharmadhātu,* in which enlightened ones perceive phenomena as resembling a hall of mirrors. It may be that originally Borobudur was to be crowned with a sanctuary that would have stood for the Tower of Maitreya as illustrated in the third-gallery reliefs. A change of plan resulted in the terraces with perforated stupas, unique in the Buddhist world, but paralleling chakras ("circles," psychic centers within the human trunk) of lotuses with thirty-two, twenty-four, and sixteen petals, like those found in the Tantric texts that were soon to dominate Indian monastic centers.

THE NAGAYON. The Nagayon, a relatively small temple constructed in the late eleventh century, is one of the oldest buildings in the ancient capital of Pagan, Burma. Constructed of brick and stucco, it reflects older traditions of northern India and Bangladesh, and its spire takes the form of the *śikhara* of the northern Indian Hindu shrine. There are three interior spaces: a hall, an ambulatory, and a sanctuary. Ten niches in the hall hold sculptures depicting important events in the life of the Buddha. On the inner and outer walls of the ambulatory, which encircles the sanctuary, beside murals (originally) illustrating the Buddha's life and birth stories, are sixty niches with sculptures. Twenty-eight of these niches hold a sequence of images of buddhas, representing the historical Buddha Gautama and his twenty-seven predecessors in the distant past. In a panel below each buddha of the past appears a small-scale figure who represents the contemporary incarnation of Gautama hearing a prediction regarding future buddhahood. For instance, the Buddha Dipankara informed the hermit Sumedha that he would become a buddha after innumerable eons. From the darkened ambulatory, the visitor enters the sanctuary, in height nearly double that of the ambulatory; it has small clerestory windows through which, under the right conditions, light falls upon the head of the tall standing central Buddha image, with magical effect.

A passage found in Sanskrit *avadāna* texts describes a miracle of the Buddha: the Buddha smiles, rays of light emerge from his eyeteeth, ascend to the higher heavens and descend to the earth, and then return to the Buddha's mouth. This passage is found also in an inscription of the reigning Burmese king, Kyanzittha (1084–1111). The Buddha smiled because he was about to predict to his disciple Ānanda the reign of Kyanzittha himself. Therefore the visitor to the Nagayon, having pondered the giving of predictions in the sculptures of the ambulatory, enters the sanctuary to find dramatically re-created the Buddha's smile, the miracle of the light rays, and, it is implied, a prediction.

WAT PHRA CHETTUPHON. The Holy Chettuphon Monastery, which occupies an extensive compound adjacent to the royal palace in Bangkok, does not aspire to present the sort of ultimate experiences a pilgrim can find at both Borobudur and the Nagayon. It is, on the other hand, an encyclopedic monastery, constructed in such a way as to encompass all Buddhist thought, as well as history and the learned sciences. Chettuphon is the Thai pronunciation of Jetavana, a compound presented to the Buddha by one of his patrons, where the Buddha spent nineteen rainy seasons. The monastery is commonly known as Wat Pho, a memory of its pre-1791 name, the Bodh-ārāma, "Enlightenment Park." The monastery is divided into two main walled sections, one consisting of dwelling places for the abbot and for hundreds of monks, the other, which will be briefly described here, of dozens of buildings, some commemorative in nature, some for public worship, and some for instruction, all either aligned or hierarchically arranged. Nearly all the structures in the monastery were constructed in the course of building campaigns by two monarchs, Rama I (r. 1782–1809) and Rama III (r. 1824–1851).

The primary structure is the *uposatha* (sabbath) hall (in Thai, the *bōt*), a massive rectangular building (the exterior measures 51 by 29 meters; the interior, 31 by 19 meters) entered from the east, and housing a large image of the Buddha at the western end. A *bōt* is a structure necessarily surrounded by a set of eight ritual boundary stones *(sīmā)* that permanently set aside a sacred space. Only in the *bōt* may the monks recite the 227 rules of the discipline, which they must do twice a month, and only in the *bōt* may ordinations be held.

Second in importance to the *bōt* is a group of four stupas to the west, uncharacteristically set slightly askew from the *bōt* axis but still positioned in such a way that the worshiper in the *bōt* who pays homage to the main image is also honoring the stupas that lie beyond. The main stupa holds the remains of a Buddha image dedicated in 1503 at the principal royal monastery in the former capital of Ayutthaya (abandoned in 1767 following a war with Burma); the three other stupas commemorate kings Rama II, III, and IV. Further west stands the library.

Themes of royal commemoration and of the heritage of the former capital of Ayutthaya (1351–1767) number among the many layers of meaning at Wat Phra Chettuphon. Rama I's ashes were installed by Rama IV under the pedestal of the main image in the *bōt.* Encircling the outer wall of the *bōt* are 152 marble narrative relief panels depicting the Indian epic the *Rāmāyana,* beginning with the abduction of Prince Rāma's beloved Sītā by the demon king and ending with some of the victory battles by Rāma's forces in Lanka. These reliefs spread the message that righteous kings make Buddhist monasticism possible, and they may also have had an esoteric content, alluding to stages of meditation. (They also reinforced the monastery's position as a center of learning and literary culture in the reign of Rama III.) The image placed inside the main stupa is not the only old image at Wat Phra Chettuphon; in fact, in the primary and secondary galleries that surround the *bōt* there are rows of hundreds of bronze seated buddha images brought from Ayutthaya and cities further north by Rama I.

Other layers of meaning involve specifically Buddhist messages. Easily explicable systematic intent is found in at least some of the four *vihāra* (Thai, *wihān;* image hall) that surround the *bōt* and are connected by the primary and secondary galleries. The main image in the northern *wihān,* for instance, shows the Buddha seated in a forest as an elephant and a monkey bring him offerings, while the original murals and inscriptions were devoted to the thirteen ascetic practices, solitary forest pursuits that contrast with the communal activities of the urban monastery, which are apparently connoted in the southern *wihān.* The western *wihān,* lying between the *bōt* and the stupas, originally held murals depicting the stories of the Buddha's hair relic and of his footprints—that is, of the tangible legacies he bequeathed. The subject matter of these murals is out of the ordinary; in the most common schemes, as found in image halls, the Buddha's defeat of the army of the devil is depicted on the eastern (or entrance) wall, Buddhist cosmology on the western wall (behind the principal image), and the life of the Buddha or the stories of the last ten of his previous existences on the side walls.

Wat Phra Chettuphon, unlike Borobudur or the Nagayon, provides no single climactic experience. It has been argued, however (by Chot Kanlayanamit, a twentieth-century traditional Thai architect), that the ornamental elements of Thai image halls and stupas are characterized by quietude, lightness, and levitation, three qualities that themselves convey the character of Buddhist meditation and spiritual ascent.

HISTORICAL OVERVIEW. The history of Buddhist temples in Southeast Asia can to some degree be reduced to the history of elements mentioned so far: the stupa, the sanctuary, and the image hall, which may or may not also be an *uposatha* hall. Additional elements include the library and dwelling places for monks. The history is greatly complicated, however, by variations and changes in the relative importance of these elements and by the fact that for the earlier periods no evidence survives of wooden structures, either free-standing or erected upon brick platforms.

In Java, aside from the exceptional Borobudur, stone sanctuaries dominate surviving temple sites. In Central Java, sanctuaries, including single-chambered, triple-chambered, and cruciform types, held various configurations of buddhas and *bodhisattvas.* During the East Javanese period, stone sanctuaries accommodated deities seen as participating in a Buddhist-Hindu syncretism, and they frequently bore narrative relief sculptures on the exterior, illustrating Javanese texts. The situation in classical Cambodia was somewhat similar; in form, Buddhist sanctuaries were indistinguishable from Hindu ones until the construction at Angkor of the Bayon (c. 1200), which has giant faces on its towers. Scholars still debate the original meaning of these faces, but traditional Cambodian thought connects them with the Brahmā gods of the higher levels of the Buddhist cosmos.

In Pagan, Burma (eleventh to thirteenth centuries and later), many of the temples have configurations similar to the one seen at the Nagayon. The much larger Ananda (c. 1100) takes the form of four Nagayon-like temples back-to-back, emanating from a solid brick core. Sculptures depicting the life of the Buddha are placed in niches in interior corridors, where the play of light has a role somewhat like that found at the Nagayon. The exterior is encircled by glazed terracotta panels at ground level depicting the army of the devil and worshiping gods in a giant reenactment of the events of the night of the Buddha's enlightenment; on the tiered roof, hundreds of panels illustrate the Buddha's previous lives. At Pagan subsequently, the interest in interior light disappeared, and the massive two-storied temple developed. There were also brick monastic dwellings in the city, arranged as cells around a court (as in northern India), as well as giant stupas functioning as focal points for worship. The most important great stupa surviving today in Burma is the Shwedagon in Rangoon, which houses the Buddha's hair relic.

The brick-and-stucco temple traditions of Pagan did not last into modern times. Instead, the characteristic Burmese monastic building, a long rectangular structure raised on stilts, has its roots in the indigenous wooden architecture of Southeast Asia. It has an exterior platform and three main sections, each surmounted with pyramidal roofs: the sanctuary, which is a room beneath a tiered spire (*pyathat*; Skt., *prāsāda*); a multipurpose room, or reception hall; and a storeroom. The east-west orientation is the opposite of older (and elsewhere, standard) practice; the sanctuary is at the eastern end, and the Buddha image faces west. In the multipurpose room (20 by 15 meters in some cases), which has a dais of its own for Buddha images, monks gather for chanting in the morning, instruction is given to novices, the public may attend twice-monthly holy day services, and monks and novices sleep on bedrolls stored away during the day. The *uposatha* hall, which generally has a masonry foundation, is called a *thein (sīmā).* Since most monasteries lack a *thein*, monks attend a neighboring establishment for services twice a month.

As a rectilinear masonry image hall spacious enough for congregational worship, the *bōt* (*uposatha* hall) at Wat Phra Chettuphon has many antecedents, not only in Thailand but also in Cambodia and Vietnam. What was new at the time of construction was the designation of the principal hall as the *bōt.* In earlier practice, the *bōt* was a secondary structure of more modest dimensions, primarily for the use of monks (and traditionally, in northern Thailand, access was denied to women). Over the past two hundred years, the Wat Phra Chettuphon pattern has become standard. In the older pattern, the main hall (*wihān*) is the place where the twice monthly holy day services are held; at these, monks chant, lay people may take a vow to follow the behavioral precepts, and a sermon is given. (Ordinarily, older women form the major portion of the audience at these services.) Public services can also be held, however, in a *sālā*, sometimes a wooden building on stilts, sometimes an open-air pavilion.

An early rectilinear hall from the seventh to ninth century was excavated in central Thailand at U Thong. A simple brick platform, 28 by 5 meters, it evidently had a wooden superstructure. A much more elaborate prototype for the independent but aligned structures of later times can be seen at the Buddhist temple site of Dong-duong in Vietnam (c. 900), where an image hall (37 by 15 meters) lies directly in front of other buildings further west, including a sanctuary. The early Sukhothai *wihān* (north-central Thailand) had dimensions more square; the *wihān* at Wat Saphan Hin (late thirteenth century) measures 25 by 20 meters, was hardly raised off the ground, and housed a giant stucco standing Buddha. By the early fifteenth century this type of *wihān* had been replaced by a more longitudinal one with high plinth. In central and north-central Thailand, the principal *wihān* tended to be aligned with a stupa or, frequently, with a tower called a *prāng*, an adaptation of the Cambodian sanctuary tower (but having no enterable sanctuary).

BIBLIOGRAPHY

Chihara, Daigoro. *Hindu-Buddhist Architecture in Southeast Asia.* Translated by Rolf W. Giebel. Leiden, 1996.

Chōt Kanlayānamit. "Sathāpattayakam bǣp thai dœ̄m." In *Laksana thai lēm 1 phūm lang*, edited by Khụkrit Prāmōt, pp. 296–414. Bangkok, 1982. For a brief summary of Chōt's views on Buddhist aesthetics, see Hiram W. Woodward Jr. et al., *Sacred Sculpture of Thailand* (Baltimore, Md., 1997), page 25.

Dumarçay, Jacques. *The Temples of Java.* Translated and edited by Michael Smithies. Singapore, 1986.

Dumarçay, Jacques, and Michael Smithies. *Cultural Sites of Burma, Thailand, and Cambodia.* Kuala Lumpur, and New York, 1995.

Duroiselle, Chas, ed. *Epigraphia Birmanica, Being Lithic and Other Inscriptions of Burma.* Archaeological Survey of Burma, vol. 1, pt. 2. Rangoon, 1960. The text and translation of Kyanzittha's inscription (the great inscription of the Shwezigon Pagoda, Pagan) appears on pages 90–129.

Fraser-Lu, Sylvia. *Splendour in Wood: The Buddhist Monasteries of Burma.* Trumbull, Conn., 2001.

Gosling, Betty. *A Chronology of Religious Architecture at Sukhothai: Late Thirteenth to Early Fifteenth Century.* Ann Arbor, Mich., 1996.

Kinney, Ann R. *Worshiping Siva and Buddha: The Temple Art of East Java.* Honolulu, 2003.

Luce, Gordon H. *Old Burma—Early Pagàn.* 3 vols. Locust Valley, N.Y., 1969–1970.

Matics, K. I. *A History of Wat Phra Chetuphon and its Buddha Images.* Bangkok, 1979.

Pichard, Pierre. "Le hall d'ordination dans le monastère thai." *Bulletin de l'École Française d'Extrême-Orient* 87 (2000): 125–149.

Pichard, Pierre, and Francois Lagirarde, eds. *The Buddhist Monastary: A Cross-Cultural Survey.* Paris, 2003.

Strachan, Paul. *Pagan: Art and Architecture of Old Burma.* Whiting Bay, U.K., 1989.

Woodward, Hiram W., Jr. "On Borobudur's Upper Terraces." *Oriental Art* 45, no. 3 (1999): 34–43. This article includes brief summaries of interpretations of Borobudur.

HIRAM WOODWARD (2005)

TEMPLE: DAOIST TEMPLE COMPOUNDS

It is difficult to say what was the first Daoist structure in China or when or where it was built. It seems certain that large Daoist temple complexes were not erected during the age of the philosophers Laozi in the sixth century BCE or Zhuangzi in the fourth to early third century BCE. By the early centuries of the Common Era, Daoist architecture was constructed in China, although even then it may not have been explicitly associated with a codified doctrine or what we today think of as religious practices. The ambiguity is inherent in attempts to define Daoism itself. Certainly Daoist temple compounds are groups of buildings that contain images of identifiable Daoist deities and are backdrops for Daoist rituals and worship. Yet sacred mountains and other elements of the landscape or natural settings, with little or no architecture, may provide equally fervent settings for worship of Daoist deities or may be worshipped themselves. Rustic retreats and grottoes may offer architectural environments for an ascetic's meditation or an alchemist's practice, and they may be structural appendages to more traditional temple compounds.

Although worship of native or popular deities or natural elements or spirits that come to be part of the Daoist pantheon predates the arrival of Buddhism in China in the Han dynasty (206 BCE–220 CE), it was the presence of monumental Buddhist architecture and its imagery that gave the greatest impetus to the Daoist temple compound. After the Han dynasty, the forms and functions of Daoist architecture in China directly reflected the styles and purposes of Chinese Buddhist buildings and the interior images they were designed to house. Male and female Daoist clergy came to be trained and reside in monastic settings. As a result, from the outside, the pillar-supported halls with ceramic tile roofs arranged in lines, the covered arcades that connect and enclose them, and the plaster walls that surround them are usually indistinguishable from those of a Buddhist temple compound. In addition, beyond the main, central image halls are libraries, stele pavilions, dining halls, dormitories, and shrines and tombs to lay leaders and reknowned transcendants associatied with the temple compound, features also found in a Buddhist monastic setting. Occasionally, a temple compound includes halls for both Buddhist and Daoist worship.

The name is one of the first clues that a temple compound is Daoist. Among religious architecture in China, two suffixes almost invariably define Daoist structures. The first is *guan*, often translated as "abbey." *Guan* is the third character in the name of Beijing's most famous Daoist temple compound, Baiyun guan (White Cloud Abbey). A Daoist temple compound of higher status takes *gong*, a term borrowed from imperial architecture and meaning "palace," as its last character. Yongle Gong, the Palace of Eternal Joy, is Daoism's most famous *gong*. Both *guan* and *gong* are basically equivalent to the Buddhist *si* (monastery or temple compound). Other terms are shared with Buddhist and Confucian temple architecture in China. *Miao*, for example, is an individual temple in either a Buddhist or a Daoist temple compound, but *miao* is also used to refer to a Confucian temple compound (Kong[zi]miao). *An* can be both a Daoist or Buddhist nunnery or, when it refers to a small religious complex, it may be translated as "hermitage." *Ci*, or "shrine," is a veneration temple and may be part of a larger Buddhist, Daoist, or Confucian compound, or it can refer to the compound itself, such as Jinci, the Daoist Jin Shrine complex.

In all likelihood, Daoist masters conducted ceremonies and rituals in temple compounds in the Han dynasty, but no archaeological evidence of them has been found. The best architectural evidence of Daoist practice in the early centuries of the Common Era survives in Sichuan and a few regions of adjacent provinces. Cliff tombs, particularly in Pengshan and Leshan, both in Sichuan province, are replete with images in relief sculpture of one of early Daoism's most popular deities, the Queen Mother of the West, said to be capable of bestowing the elixir of immortality. Textual records inform us that Daoist rites took place in *zhi*—a term borrowed from the secular tradition in which it means a place where governing occurs—and in *jingshi*, or "chambers of quietude." Other terms, *dong* (caves or grottoes), *dongtian* (literally, "cavern heavens"), and *fudi* (blessed plots), are also found in historical texts and religious writings, but none is described. The assumption that Daoist temple compounds existed is based primarily on the large numbers of their Buddhist counterparts—1,367, in the capital city Luoyang at the end of the fifth century—and countless cave-temples in cities and at pilgrimage sites in the centuries following Han.

Only by the Sui-Tang period (581–907) is it certain that Daoist temple compounds were present in China's cities and the countryside. The capital city of Sui and Tang—Daxing, and then Chang'an—housed ten Daoist abbeys at the end of the sixth century and sixteen in the middle of the eighth century. At least four Daoist temple compounds stood within the walls of Tang Chang'an's two palace complexes. Both the Great Ultimate palace complex and the Great Luminous palace complex had a hall dedicated to the Three Purities, Daoism's most popular trinity, and auxiliary structures. In 741, Tang emperor Xuanzong (Minghuang) (r. 712–756), established a temple (*miao*) to Laozi in Chang'an, in the secondary capital Luoyang, and in each prefectural capital. Later the same year, he built a hall for the worship of Laozi in his Flourishing Celebration palace complex. Following this precedent, even the non-Chinese ruler Abaoji (r. 907–926), whose successor would found the Liao dynasty (947–1125), built at least one Daoist abbey in his first capital in Inner Mongolia. Under the non-Chinese dynasty Jin (1115–1234), important construction took place at Tianchang Abbey (today White Cloud Abbey in Beijing), where building had begun during the Tang dynasty. The oldest extant wooden building from a Daoist temple complex survives at Five Dragons Temple in Ruicheng, Shanxi province. It is dated by inscription to the year 831.

More than a dozen buildings from the eleventh through thirteenth centuries, a period of syncretism among the three faiths, survive at Daoist temple compounds. Premier among them is Sage Mother Hall at the Jin Shrines in Taiyuan, Shanxi province, built between 1023 and 1032. Today a complex of more than thirty buildings, in the Zhou dynasty (1150–256 BCE) a shrine to Prince Shu Yu, son of Zhou King Wu, stood there. The shrine to Shu Yu's mother, the Sage Mother, is marked by beams that span eight rafter lengths (the greatest span of the period), gilt dragons that wind around the front columns, and a fish pond covered by a cruciform bridge in front. All are examples of the most eminent building standards of eleventh-century China. Although clearly having ties to China's imperial tradition, the Daoist context is underscored by the worshippers who come to the shrine to pray for help from the Sage Mother and to pray for rain from the nearby springs. Further associations between the shrines and Daoism are the presence of grottoes to Laozi, the Three Purities, the Three Heavens, and Yellow Emperor; shrines to the Three Pruities, the Eastern Peak, Three Sages, and Lu Ban, the Chinese patron deity-hero of architects; pavilions to the Daoist immortal Lü Dongbin, the Three Officials, and Zhenwu, the Supreme Emperor of Dark Heaven; temples (*miao*) to the god of wealth, Dragon King, spirits of the mountains, god of war, and god of the earth; and a palace complex to the god of literature.

The Temple to the Earth God (Houtumiao) in Wanrong, Shanxi province, focused on a Daoist deity but heavily patronized by the imperial family, was a similar temple compound of the Song dynasty (960–1279). Built in 1006 but destroyed by flood waters in the sixteenth century, its nine-bay, multistoried main hall, the central focus of five courtyards of architecture, is believed to have resembled an imperial palace of Song times. Its plan is believed to have been nearly identical to that of the Daoist Temple to the Earth God compound in Dengfeng, Shanxi, that survives in a post-Song version. Halls to the Three Purities, dated 1016 and 1176, stand at abbeys known as Xuanmiaoguan in Putian, Fujian province, and Suzhou, Jiangsu province, respectively. Both possessing the broadly sloping roof eaves of southeastern Chinese buildings of the Song dynasty, the former is today a middle school and the latter a tourist site. Jade Emperor Temple and Two Immortals Abbey are also among the Daoist temple compounds in Shanxi province where both architecture and sculpture survive in their eleventh- and twelfth-century forms. Two Song emperors were intimately involved with Daoism and Daoist construction. Zhenzong (r. 998–1023) ordered the construction of Abbeys to Celebrate the Heavens (Tianqingguan) throughout his empire. The equally prolific patron Huizong (r. 1101–1125) had Genyue (Northeast Peak), an artificial Daoist paradise of mountains, streams, and landmasses, built at his capital city, in addition to numerous Daoist temple complexes there and throughout China. More than thirty Daoist temple complexes were built in the Southern Song (1127–1279) capital city, today Hangzhou.

Several of China's most important premodern buildings remain at Daoist monasteries from the period of Mongolian rule (1267–1368). Three superlative halls and a gate stand at the Yongle Palace in southern Shanxi, a building complex dedicated to the popular twelfth- and thirteenth-century Daoist sect, Quanzhen. Paintings of the Three Purities and their entourages, the immortal Lü Dongbin, and the twelfth-century founder of Quanzhen Daoism, Wang Zhe (1113–1170), cover the interior walls of the three main halls, making this site the largest repository of Daoist painting in China. An even more splendid building, the Hall of Virtuous Tranquility, was built by imperial order at the Temple to the Northern Peak in Quyang, Hebei province, in 1270. Its white marble approach and balustrade, as well as its roof eaves and bracketing, are believed to be the closest extant examples of China's imperial building tradition of the thirteenth century. The Temple to the Water God, alternately known as the Dragon King, is an example of humbler Daoist architecture but with equally extraordinary murals. Among them are paintings of the Dragon King and his court and an itinerant dramatic troop that performed there in the fourteenth century.

Post-fourteenth-century Daoist temple complexes survive in every city and town of China today and across the Chinese countryside. Some of the most impressive Daoist temple compounds are on sacred peaks, among which Mount Tai and Mount Wudang are probably the most famous. Located in Shantung province, Taishan, the Eastern Peak, was considered the abode of life-giving forces, including those that controled the fate of the Chinese emperor, as well as the site to which dead souls return. In imperial times more than 250 temple compounds stood on the mountain, with Dai Temple, dedicated to the god of the mountain itself, the most austere. Inside Dai Temple, the god of Mount Tai is enthroned in the yellow robes of a Chinese emperor, and the emperor's journey from his capital to Taishan is painted on the interior walls. Wudangshan, in Hubei province, is where Daoists believed Zhenwu, the Perfected Warrior, attained immortality. Because the Yongle emperor (r. 1403–1424) believed Zhenwu had come north to help him attain the Chinese throne from his uncle, he patronized enormous temple complexes across the mountain. With time, many of the palaces and abbeys have burned or otherwise been destroyed, including the Golden Hall. Many consider the Purple Empyrean Palace, dedicated to the Jade Emperor, whose buildings rise step by step along the ascent to the top of the peak, the most dramatic temple complex on Mount Wudang.

Among urban temple compounds, Azure Ox (Qingyang) Palace in Chengdu, Sichuan province, is exemplary. Founded at the site where Laozi is said to have transcended to immortality, the Tang emperor Xuanzong stopped there to worship Laozi in 751. In addition to Laozi, civil and military officials, the Eight Daoist Immortals, the Three Purities, and Tang rulers are all focal deities in Azure Ox Palace's halls. The recipient of several later imperial visits, the temple compound was destroyed and rebuilt in every successive dynasty.

Today, Daoist temple compounds are especially active in Taiwan. The Pointing Southward Palace (Zhinangong), dedicated to Lü Dongbin and Quanzhen Daoism, floats on a mountain above the village of Mucha. Yet in spite of the large numbers of Daoist temple compounds throughout China, individually they are more reflective of the architectural concerns of their times of origin and locations than specifically Daoist features. Except for the occasional placement of images such as the Three Purities on a roof ridge, little of the exterior marks a temple compound as Daoist. Only upon entering its halls and identifying deities such as the Three Purities, the Perfected Warrior, Jade Emperor and his entourage, Eight Immortals, or Dragon King can one be certain of the Daoist affiliation of a temple compound that in most ways blends into the framework of traditional Chinese architectural space.

SEE ALSO Daoism, overview article; Iconography, article on Daoist Iconography.

BIBLIOGRAPHY

Chavannes, Édouard. *Le T'ai chan: Essai de monographie d'un culte chinois.* Paris, 1910. Outstanding investigation of the mountain and related cult.

Goodrich, Anne Swann. *The Peking Temple of the Eastern Peak.* Nagoya, Japan, 1964. Account of an active Daoist temple complex visited by the author during her years in Beijing, 1930–1932. Includes details about the numerous Daoist divinities associated with the site.

Jing, Anning. *The Water God's Temple of the Guangsheng Monastery: Cosmic Function of Art, Ritual, and Theater.* Leiden, 2002. Investigation of the Daoist temple Shuishenmiao (Temple of the Water God, Temple of the Dragon King) that proposes relations between its murals, ritual, and particularly supplications for water in the region.

Katz, Paul. *Images of the Immortal: The Cult of Lü Dongbin at the Palace of Eternal Joy.* Honolulu, 1999. Study of the history of Yongle Gong (Palace of Eternal Joy) that proposes links between its siting and murals and Daoist ritual.

Steinhardt, Nancy S. "Taoist Architecture." In *Taoism and the Arts of China,* edited by Stephen Little and Shawn Eichman, pp. 56–75. Chicago, 2000. Catalogue of the most spectacular and important exhibition of Daoist art ever mounted.

Yoshioka, Yoshitoyo. "Taoist Monastic Life." In *Facets of Taoism,* edited by Holmes Welch and Anna Seidel, pp. 229–252. New Haven, Conn., 1979. Description of the author's experiences at Baiyun guan in Beijing from 1940 to 1946.

NANCY SHATZMAN STEINHARDT (1987 AND 2005)

TEMPLE: CONFUCIAN TEMPLE COMPOUNDS

The architecture of Confucianism is built in honor of men. It is dedicated to Confucius (551–479 BCE), sage, moral leader, and philosopher of the ancient state of Lü in Shandong province, or his disciples and their teachings. Confucian monuments are distinct from other Chinese religious structures in their avoidance of images. Images may be enshrined in a Confucian temple, and over time, the influence of other religions in which deities are worshiped has led to limited use of Confucian statues as icons. In the purest form of the religion, however, tablets on which the name of the Confucian is inscribed serve as the focus of veneration and Confucius, his relatives, or other Confucians are honored by a visit to the site or by participation in a ceremony. Confucian temple compounds can be dedicated to civil (in contrast to military) officials in general, as well as to individual paragons of moral or state virtue.

During his lifetime, Confucius (Kongzi [Master Kong] or Kong Qiu [family name Kong, personal name Qiu] in Chinese) established a school for the teaching of his principles of good government in Qufu, capital of his home state of Lü. In 478 BCE, a year after his death, disciples built a temple in Qufu to honor their teacher. The few records about this temple inform us that it was a three-part structure containing Confucius's clothes, instruments, carriage, and books. For the next 2,500 years, Qufu would be the location of many of China's most important Confucian temple compounds. Even today, it is difficult to walk down a street of Qufu without coming upon architecture dedicated to Confucius or his disciples, or commemorating an important spot in Confucian history.

By traditional Chinese calculation, Qufu traces its association with the principles of Confucianism to the so-called Yellow Emperor who lived in the twenty-seventh century BCE. Legend records that the Yellow Emperor was born about four kilometers east of Qufu. In the twenty-sixth century BCE, the son of the Yellow Emperor made Qufu his capital. In the twelfth century BCE, the duke of Zhou, brother of the emperor and the highest-ranking state official, was considered a paragon of governance by moral virtue. His principles of good government were highly regarded by Confucius. A temple dedicated to the duke of Zhou has stood in Qufu since the first millennium BCE.

In the second century BCE, the Chinese emperor offered animal sacrifices at the temple built by Confucius's disciples when passing through the state of Lü. The following century, the emperor conferred posthumous titles on Confucius. In the second century CE, the relation between emperor and temple was further strengthened when government officials were appointed to maintain it.

By the Tang dynasty (618–907), imperial rites were conducted at a memorial service for Confucius. This extraordinary reverence for someone who was not a member of the imperial family was unprecedented in Chinese history. Beginning in the late fourteenth century, after the Mongol regime fell and China was returned to native hands, memorial services to Confucius were conducted biannually at Qufu's Confucian temple compound. As had been the case in ancient times, the fortunes of the empire were linked to recognition of the ideal relation between ruler and subject described in Confucian texts. Thus until the rule of the Manchus beginning in the mid-seventeenth century, a Confucian temple could be erected only through explicit imperial decree. During the Manchu (Qing) dynasty (1644–1911), temples honoring Confucius, his teachings, and civil officials came to be built in every province and in most major cities.

The first statue of Confucius is said to have been placed in a hall of the Qufu temple compound during repairs of 539. The date is logical, for the sixth century in China was one of widespread patronage of Buddhist architecture and its accompanying imagery. Still, until the ninth century the Confucian Temple was modest in comparison to Buddhist temple compounds or the emperor's palace. The ninth-century temple complex in Qufu consisted of a front gate, main hall, two side halls, and a residential hall behind them.

The most major changes in the status of the temple compound in Qufu were coincident with the further elevated status of the Kong family in the Song dynasty (960–1279). Already in the first century BCE, a descendant of Confucius had received the title of marquis and a fief at Qufu. In 1055, amid a wave of renewed interest in Confucius's writings known as neo-Confucianism, the emperor enfeoffed a forty-sixth-generation descendant of Confucius as the duke of Yansheng and awarded him and his descendants fourteen hectares of land. Like honors bestowed on the temple, this hereditary succession of a duke has no parallel in Chinese history. Before the end of the Song dynasty, the Confucian temple compound consisted of three courtyards of buildings enclosed by a covered arcade of 316 bays.

In premodern times, the main south gate of the temple was the south gate of the city of Qufu. The temple complex today consists of nine courtyards of architecture. Among them are three main halls, one main pavilion, an altar, three shrines, two side halls, two minor halls, and two studies, for a total of 446 bays of buildings. Stretching more than a kilometer from south to north, the space is punctuated by fifty-two archways. The names of structures often are references to Confucius or Confucian writings. Striking Metal and Vibrating Jade Gate, built in 1538, recalls a line in Mencius's writings comparing the completion of a musical performance to the view that Confucius's thought is a summation of all philosophies of sages that came before him. The Gate of the Great Mean, in the fourth courtyard and surviving in its Qing dynasty form, is named for the Confuciuan text, *Doctrine of the Mean.* Lingxing Gate is a reference to a star in the constellation Ursa Major and thus a symbol that Confucius was a star who had come down to earth. Other gates are named Augmenting Truth and Harmony of the Written Language.

The two most impressive halls of the Confucian temple compound in Qufu stand near the center of the main building axis. Star of Literature Pavilion, a name intended to link Confucius with the constellation of the god of literature. The 23-meter high, multistory library with three sets of roof eaves towers above the rest of the temple compound in the fifth courtyard. When the emperor visited Qufu, he fasted and bathed in courtyards east and west of Star of Literature Pavilion in preparation for sacrifices to honor the sage. Behind Star of Literature Pavilion is a wide courtyard with thirteen stele pavilions arranged in two rows. They were built to house fifty-three tablets presented to the temple compound by emperors from each period from Tang through Qing.

The second focal building, Dacheng (Great Achievement) Hall, dominates the seventh courtyard. Measuring 45.8 by 24.9 meters at the base and 24.8 meters in height, the size, double set of yellow ceramic tile roof eaves, and dragons entwined on the front columns compare only with the Hall of Great Harmony of the Beijing Forbidden City or the Hall of Heavenly Favors at the tomb of the first Ming emperor. East of the Great Achievement Hall courtyard is a building where offerings were made to five generations of Confucius's ancestors; to the west is a hall for paying homage to Confucius's parents. Also in this courtyard is the Apricot Altar, erected in 1018 at a spot where Confucius is said to have taught.

Directly behind the Great Achievement courtyard is a smaller but similar building dedicated to Confucius's wife Qiguan. At one time she was revered together with her husband in the same building, but in 1018 a Song emperor erected a separate shrine for her. The position of the husband's hall in front of his wife's follows the pattern for imperial residential architecture in the Forbidden City. The focus of the last courtyard is the Hall of Relics of the Sage. It contains 120 stone stelae depicting events in Confucius's life.

From the exterior, the individual buildings and their arrangement around courtyards are difficult to distinguish from the architecture of other prominent imperial and religious complexes. Names of gates and halls, the prevalence of tablets with names of those revered in contrast to statues, and associations with literate Chinese culture or remembered events are signs that the temple compound is Confucian. An unobtrusive wall, for example, is a revered spot because in the third century BCE when the ninth generation of Confucius's descendants lived in Qufu, books were hidden inside the wall when troops of the First Emperor came to the city to burn classical writings.

In one important way, architecture of the Qufu Confucian temple is unique. Since the ninth-generation descendants of Confucius, the temple has been adjacent to the mansion of the Kong family. Descendants of Confucius resided in the mansion for seventy-seven generations, until the founding of the People's Republic of China. Through the centuries, the rank and influence of the chief resident of the Kong family mansion rose to the equivalent of prime minister. He was the leader of all *wen*, or civil officials, and was allowed to ride his horse inside the Forbidden City. He owned tax-exempt "sacred fields" from which income was used in Confucian ceremonies. He was even allowed to sell official titles.

Confucius's tomb and those of his parents are also in Qufu. So is the academy where Confucius taught and temples to Confucius's disciples Mencius, Yanzi, and Zengzi. Mencius's residence and tomb, and his parents' tomb, are there as well.

The most famous Confucian temple compound outside Qufu is in Beijing. One of the few Confucian temples constructed during the period of Mongolian rule in China, in the late thirteenth century, the majority of buildings date from the Qing dynasty. A stone tablet at the entrance orders civil and military officials to descend from their horses or sedan chairs as a sign of respect for the sage. Consisting of two parallel building lines, passage through the central gate was a privilege allowed only to the Chinese emperor. The eastern side of the compound is occupied by six successive courtyards, the back two parallel, which contain a shrine to Confucius; tablets recounting the 700-year history of scholars who achieved success in the national exams; the Great Achievement Gate; the multi-roofed Great Achievement Hall containing a central wooden tablet whose Chinese and Manchu inscriptions glorify Confucius, a pair of flanking tablets on either side of it dedicated to Confucius's four most important disciples, and eight more tablets for less eminent sages lower and behind them; the Hall for Reverence to Confucius's Ancestors with tablets for members of five generations who preceded him; a library; and a shrine to officials. The western sector has only three courtyards, all focused on the central one that houses the imperial academy. Built by the Mongols for the education of imperial and other select children, in the eighteenth century the structure was rebuilt and named Biyong Palace to recall the name of the place where princes and official sons were educated in the Chinese capital at the time of Confucius. The multi-eaved, elevated structure is enclosed by a circular moat and further surrounded by a marble balustrade, following the pattern of the imperial academy in Confucius's day and of the Temple to Heaven complex where the emperor performed annual sacrifices in the name of the state in Ming and Qing times. Originally all structures had gray roof tiles but they were replaced with golden ones in the eighteenth century.

Today, some of the most active Confucian temple compounds are in Taiwan. The best-known one is in the capital, Taipei, but two others have older buildings of greater architectural importance. The Confucian temple compound in the southern city of Tainan was built by the son of Zheng Chenggong (Koxinga, 1624–1662), a Japanese-born, anti-Manchu commander who retreated to the southern island after the Manchus overthrew the Ming dynasty in 1644 and who subsequently led the resistance that chased the Dutch away in 1661. Its most important building, Great Achievement Hall, contains a wooden tablet honoring Confucius and sixteen tablets dedicated to famous sages. The Confucian Temple in Zhanghua, in central Taiwan, first built in 1716, was carefully restored in the 1970s and is today a premier example of eighteenth-century southeastern Chinese architecture.

The most important event at a Confucian temple is the celebration of Confucius's birthday, which usually occurs on September 28. Wearing the costumes of civil officials, attendants carrying ax-shaped weapons, fans, umbrellas, and instruments in the style of those from Confucius's day perform music and dances

Confucian temples survive in many other major Chinese cities. Many have been used as schools throughout history and a few are educational institutions today. Some towns have a corresponding temple complex for military officials, or *wu*, the most famous of which is in Yuncheng, Shanxi province.

SEE ALSO Chinese Religion, overview article; Confucianism, overview article.

BIBLIOGRAPHY

Han Baode. *Zhanghua Kongmiao de yanjiu yu xiufu jihua.* Taizhong, Taiwan, 1976. Detailed account of the restoration of the Confucian temple in Zhanghua, including a general discussion of Confucian temples and excellent drawings of the Zhanghua buildings.

Kang Yuancuo. *Kongshi zuting guangji* (1311). Taipei, 1970. The most important text about the Confucian shrine at Qufu, including drawings of the site and building plans.

Kong Xiangmin and Wei Jiang. *Qufu.* Shandong, 1982. Guidebook to Qufu and its Confucian monuments, largely pictorial, prepared by a descendant of Confucius.

Pan Guxi, ed. *Qufu Kongmiao jianzhu.* Beijing, 1987. The most thorough architectural analysis of every structure in the Confucian temple compound of Qufu.

Shryock, John K. *The Origin and Development of the State Cult of Confucius.* New York, 1932. A history of Confucianism in China that makes reference to Confucian architecture.

Wilson, Thomas A. *On Sacred Grounds: Culture, Society, Politics, and the Formation of the Cult of Confucius.* Cambridge, Mass., 2003. Nine essays that seek to understand the role of Confucius and Confucianism through Chinese history.

NANCY SHATZMAN STEINHARDT (1987 AND 2005)

TEMPLE: ANCIENT NEAR EASTERN AND MEDITERRANEAN TEMPLES

Modern writers use the term *temple* in different ways. Applied to Near Eastern religion, it refers to a complete architectural complex, including a shrine with the cult statue. Applied to Greek, Etruscan, and Roman architecture, *temple* refers to the equivalent of this shrine, and the whole complex is termed *sanctuary*.

EGYPT. Modern scholars have traditionally divided Egyptian temples into several types, according to their functions. The two principal are "divine" temples, the residence of a god or gods, and "mortuary" temples, the place for rituals, offerings, and sacrifices for a deceased king. Ancient Egyptians, however, did not see the functions, plans, symbols, and rituals of their temples quite so separately and distinctly as modern taxonomies would suggest. Thus, "divine" temples could also serve for the worship of the king, while "mortuary" temples were often used for a joint cult of the king and the god. Accordingly, these modern divisions are currently being questioned.

Recent excavations show that the earliest temples date back to the Early Dynastic period (c. 3185–2630 BCE). These temples were still quite simple in their plan, generally consisting of an open court followed by a shrine made of mud-brick, which contained the cult statue. During the Old Kingdom (c. 2630–2160 BCE) stone was introduced as a building material, especially for royal cult complexes. In contrast, shrines for the gods remained modest in scale and materials. During the Middle Kingdom (c. 2040–1650) the state took an unprecedented interest in temples, which were erected for the gods in all the major cult places of Egypt. Stone was regularly used as a building material, and there was a particular emphasis on figural decoration. During that period, the plan that became characteristic of the divine cult complexes of the New Kingdom (c. 1550–1075 BCE) appeared. This is the plan that we now usually associate with the Egyptian temple, mainly because in no other period of Egyptian history has the construction of monumental temples been more intensive than it was during the New Kingdom.

The Egyptian temple of the New Kingdom was set apart from the outside world by a massive enclosure wall made of mud-brick and without decoration. This wall was a boundary between order and disorder; it transformed the temple into a fortress against chaos. Within this enclosure was the pylon (a modern term derived from the ancient Greek word for "gateway"), a monumental entrance built of stone which consisted of a gateway flanked by two towers. This pylon was decorated on the outside with reliefs representing the king hunting or defeating his enemies in battle. Only the king, the priests, and, on some ritual occasions, representative commoners, were admitted beyond this gateway, and then only after having performed a ritual of purification. After the pylon was a large open-air court surrounded by columns. This court led to the most sacred part of the temple, where access was restricted to the king and certain selected priests.

The first room of this part of the temple was the hypostyle hall, an enclosed, basilica-like space whose roof rested on numerous rows of close-set columns. This hall was like a vestibule, which gave access to a series of chambers with different functions. One contained small tables and stands for offerings and sacrifices. Another had the sacred boat of the god, installed atop a platform. One housed the cult statue, closed in a shrine. Because the statue was the very being of god, its shrine was the heart of the temple, the holy of holies. In the inner area of the temple there could be also shrines for divinities associated with the principal god, storerooms for the paraphernalia of ritual, and rooms with administrative purposes.

What is characteristic about this architecture is that rooms and unroofed spaces, which were always rectangular, were disposed in exact sequence according to an axial alignment from the entrance pylon to the inner chambers. The courts were unroofed, though often surrounded by a colonnade; the inner parts were completely roofed and increasingly in shadow. The roof level decreased as the floor level rose. All these solutions enhanced a sense of mystery that culminated in the heart of the temple.

The precise arrangement of this plan varied from temple to temple, with some larger and more complex than others. As time went on, temples could be greatly expanded with additional sections (most frequently, a new pylon, followed by an additional open-air court). This was the result of the desire for personal display of individual kings, who by transforming famous temples reasserted their primary role in Egyptian religion and society. The degree of complexity possible for an Egyptian temple can be illustrated by the Temple of Amun at Karnak, one of the most important, which has been added to and altered over millennia. Elements go back to the Middle Kingdom (presumably obliterating even earlier construction) and extended down to the Ptolemaic and Roman periods (Figure 1 shows a portion of the final arrangement). Complex though it is, in principle it is the same as the smaller temples which share its twenty-five-hectare precinct.

Both texts and images give us an idea about the rituals performed in these temples. The daily ritual consisted in tending the cult statue, which was cleaned and provided with clothes, food, drink, and other offerings. This daily ritual in essence provided the god with the needs of life, which were thought to be the same as those of humans. In theory, it was the king who performed this daily ritual, because he was, in theory, the sole priest; for this reason, only the king is depicted in the wall decorations performing the appropriate actions. In fact, the daily ritual was performed by the priests, the vicars of the sacerdotal power of the king, who thus acted on his behalf. Another ritual that took place in temples, and which was performed on the occasion of many religious festivals, was the procession of the god from the inner part to the open-air court. The cult statue, closed in a shrine, was mounted on a barque borne on the shoulders of the priests, or sometimes carried on a sledge. It was enveloped in incense and accompanied by dancers, singers, and instrumentalists to the open-air court. Here the god met visiting gods, while the assembled worshipers, including common people, could glimpse the shrine and ask the god within for oracular responses.

MESOPOTAMIA. Our knowledge of Mesopotamian temples is seriously limited by the fact that they were built in mudbrick. For this reason, only a few of them have been preserved above the level of the foundations, and none in its entire elevation.

Temples from the fourth millennium BCE have been documented. They could be very large, and they had generally a tripartite plan, consisting of a *cella* (the space that contains the cult statue) at the center and subsidiary rooms off either side. The *cella* included altars and offering-tables, and it could be entered from different sides of the building. Very often, multiple recesses and buttresses were used to add some variety to the exterior (and sometime even to the interior) of the building, by creating contrasts in light and shadow.

In plan, the temples of the third millennium BCE are characterized by their continuity with the preceding period. There was, however, a marked tendency to set them apart from the rest of the settlement. They were constructed on top of high platforms and enclosed with high walls. Sometimes there was an outer enclosure that included, along with the temple and the inner enclosure, other shrines and probably offices for the temple administration. In the inner court around the temple there were stores and workshops: their location gives clues about the part played by temples in the economy of this region. In these temples the gods were believed to be present in their cult statues, which stood in front of a niche at one end of the cella. Near the niche were an altar and an offering-table, and along the walls stood the statues of the worshipers, represented with their hands clasped.

Near the end of the third millennium, the habit of setting the temples apart, in a high position, culminated in the placing of some of them at the top level of ziggurats, the most conspicuous landmarks of Mesopotamian towns. Whether all ziggurats had temples at their top level, however, remains unclear, because of the poor state of preservation of these monuments. For the same reason, we know nothing of the architecture of these "high temples"—as in the case of the ziggurat built by Urnammu at Ur, which is generally restored with a single room, but incorrectly so. In the absence of specific texts, it is also difficult to have an idea of the rituals performed in these "high temples," or to understand what correlation they might have had with the buildings found at the base of the ziggurats in the same sacred enclosure. From Herodotus, the Greek historian of the fifth century BCE, we are informed that in the ziggurat at Babylon one of the rituals was a sacred marriage between a priestess and the god, which took place at night. Yet, this was clearly not the only ritual performed in the temple, but only the one that captured the attention of the historian.

After the fall of Ur, a temple of Ishtar-Kititum was built at Ishchali (nineteenth to the eighteenth century BCE). The large structure (about 100 by 65 meters) stood on a platform and had a rectangular plan articulated around two open courts. Three entrances framed by towers gave access to the interior: two on the south side, leading into the open courts, and one on the east side, in relation to a secondary temple located to the north of the main complex. The main shrine was located at the western end and was elevated with respect to the rest of the temple. This shrine was accessible from the smaller court, and consisted of an ante-cella, a broad, shallow *cella* with a niche for the cult statue, and a treasury on the back. This building condensed the previous, Mesopotamian tradition, but it also introduced features that would be characteristic of temples built in Mesopotamia during the Assyrian (c. 1350–612 BCE) and Neo-Babylonian periods (c. 612–539 BCE).

AEGEAN IN THE BRONZE AGE. Places set aside for the cult of the divinity can be recognized in the material remains of the Bronze Age, in Crete as well as on the Greek mainland. The Cretans worshiped at shrines of various types. Natural caves were used for the deposit of offerings. The peaks of certain mountains were also sites of sanctuaries—some simply defined by enclosure walls, others given a number of rooms, usually rectangular—in which large stones served as altars. Thick layers of ash show that bonfires were lit, which would have been visible from sanctuary to sanctuary. The use of these sanctuaries ended abruptly, perhaps as a consequence of the cataclysmic eruption of the volcano of Thera in the fifteenth century BCE. Finally, there were sanctuaries in the palaces of the Cretan kings, shrine rooms marked by central pillars, with the symbolic double ax. These rooms were small and shallow, functioning as a focus for offerings rather than for any form of congregational ritual. It is likely that other parts of the palace complexes served ritual functions, including the bull-leaping depicted in Cretan art, but here the interaction of religion and architecture is, at best, uncertain: clearly none of it constitutes a temple in the normal sense.

Sanctuaries on the Greek mainland were probably influenced by Cretan practice. One at Mycenae consisted of a set of small, irregularly shaped rooms containing benches on which offerings could be placed, along with terracotta figurines apparently intended as representations of the deity, a goddess. There was also a mural painting of her. Such shrines are found in the fortified sites close to the walls and gateways; they seem to have had a special role in the protection of the community. The possibility of religious functions in the palaces cannot be excluded.

GREECE. There are few remaining traces of religious practice during the Protogeometric period (1050–900 BCE), when cult buildings were generally small. An exception is the large building with apsidal plan surrounded by wooden posts at Lefkandi, in Euboea (1000 BCE). The function of this short-lived building was funerary, for in the main space were buried a warrior, a woman, and a number of horses.

Temples built during the Geometric period (900–700 BCE) were generally modest in scale and simple in plan. The temple of Apollo at Dreros (c. 700), in Crete, consisted of a rectangular room preceded by a shallow porch. In the middle of the *cella* two posts flanked a central hearth, and against the back wall was a bench with three bronze statues, the cult images of Apollo, Leto, and Artemis. What is remarkable about this temple, and other buildings of the same period, is that sacrifices took place inside, near the cult image. The arrangement of the interior with a central hearth flanked by posts is reminiscent of the halls in Mycaenean palaces.

In the Orientalizing period (700–600 BCE) temples were monumentalized. Their size was significantly increased, durable materials were introduced, and the *cella* (*naos*) was often surrounded by a row of columns, the peristyle. This feature, according to recent excavations in the temple of Artemis at Ephesus, was introduced in the second half of the eighth century. Most likely, the inspiration came from Egypt, where columns played a prominent role in the design of temples.

The use of stone instead of wood for columns and entablature led to the establishment of distinctive orders. In the Archaic period (600–480 BCE) the Doric order was characteristic of mainland Greece, south Italy, and Sicily, and the Ionic was characteristic of the Aegean and Asia Minor; however, geographical distinctions were not completely rigid, and whether these orders had an ethnic connotation remains a question. During the same period, the erection of monumental temples was particularly intense in Asia Minor and the west. In both areas the Greeks were surrounded by other cultures, and monumental temples might have been a means to reassert the cultural identity of the communities responsible for their erection. Among the temples in Asia Minor, three stand out for their colossal size: the temples of Hera at Samos (c. 560 BCE, rebuilt c. 530 BCE), of Artemis at Ephesus (c. 560–470 BCE), and of Apollo at Didyma (c. 550–520 BCE). These temples were surrounded by two, even three rows of columns, and must have seemed like a forest of stone. The temples at Ephesus and Didyma are also characteristic because their core was not the *cella* with the cult statue, but an open-air court (*sekos*), which at Didyma included the shrine with the cult statue and a spring sacred to Apollo. The most interesting feature of temples built in the Greek West was a special room called the *adytum*, placed at the end of the *cella* and separated from it by a wall with a doorway. This special room apparently served to house the cult statue. The need for this innermost sacred chamber has been explained by the possibility that the rest of the *cella* was regularly used for the performance of collective rituals, but there is no evidence to support this view.

The main monumental temples of the fifth century BCE were built in mainland Greece. One was the temple of Zeus at Olympia (472–456 BCE), and the other was the Parthenon (447–438 BCE), erected along with other religious buildings on the Athenian Acropolis according to a comprehensive site plan.

The Parthenon, dedicated to Athena, is probably the most famous, certainly the most lavishly decorated, but not the largest of Greek temples (see Figure 3). The temple, built upon the remains of an unfinished predecessor destroyed by the Persians in 480 BCE, has seventeen Doric columns on each long side and eight at both short ends, and it measures overall some 31 by 70 meters. It has two rooms, the eastern *cella*, which housed the chryselephantine statue of Athena made by Pheidias, and the western "rear room," which held the valuable offerings. Between these two rooms and the peristyle there are two shallow porches, the *pronaos* and *optisthodomos,* compressed here to the advantage of the *cella.* The traditional interpretation of the Parthenon as a temple has been recently called into question, for it had very little cult associated with it, and no connection with the major public festivals. However, this building was clearly designed as and regarded as a temple in Classical Antiquity.

During the Late Classical period (400–323 BCE), the building of temples lost much of its appeal in mainland Greece and the Greek West. Only a few were built on a monumental scale, and the majority were reduced in size. Asia Minor is an exception: parallel to a renaissance of the Greek cities of the region there was a revival of Ionic architecture. The Artemision at Ephesus was rebuilt on the same colossal scale as its archaic predecessor. Meanwhile, new cities, such as Priene, strained their energies and economic resources to have temples that would leave a mark on the cityscape.

Temples built during the Hellenistic period (323–31 BCE) were essentially similar to those of the Classical period, though they might have been constructed in regions conquered by Alexander the Great that were not Greek in origin. The more florid Corinthian order was occasionally used. In these areas the traditional, non-Greek religious practice had to be respected. In Egypt, for example, the ruling Macedonian Greek dynasty of the Ptolemies assiduously built temples in the traditional Egyptian manner described above, with only a few innovations.

The Greek temple was the house of the god, because it served to shelter the cult statue. It was not a congregational building, for the congregation (which at the chief festivals of major cults was very large) gathered round the open-air altar for prayers and sacrifices. Like the crowds, the cult statue overlooked these performances at the altar. Temples were normally oriented to face the point at which the sun rose on the day of the festival. Though some cult statues were large and valuable, the rooms in which they stood did not have to be particularly spacious. Even in the largest temples a surprising portion of the total area was taken up by external embellishment. This emphasis on the exterior of temples does not mean that access to them was reserved for a privileged few. Literary evidence suggests that even if specific restrictions existed (based on days, ethnicity, and gender), entry by ordinary people into the *cella* was not unusual, especially for the purpose of praying, which was considered more effective when done before the cult statue. Temples also served as storerooms for objects, particularly those of value, offered to the gods.

Etruria. In the beginning, cult practice was performed in the open air. The earliest shrines, dating back to the seventh century BCE, had the same plan as residential houses, and they could also be incorporated into a larger palace. By the end of the seventh century BCE, temples consisted of a simple, rectangular *cella* with the opening on a short side. This new plan was still similar to contemporary domestic architecture. The traditional Etruscan temple was defined in the second half of the sixth century BCE. The building was set on a high podium and was accessible only by flights of steps or ramps on the main front. It had a quadrangular or rectangular plan and was always articulated in two areas: a deep open *pronaos* with two or three rows of widely spaced columns (front), and one or three *cellas*—depending on the number of divinities worshipped—which were generally flanked by outer passages. The rear of the temple was closed, and there was no peristyle on all four sides, as in Greek temples. Again, the houses of the elite provided the model for this plan. Temples were differentiated from residential architecture by their position on top of high podia. For the columns a new order was introduced, called Tuscanic after Vitruvius: the shaft was unfluted, but the capital was similar to the Doric. The elevation of these temples looked sturdy to later, Roman writers, and this impression was certainly suggested by the short columns, the wide eaves of the roof, and the heavy external terracotta decoration. Ancient literary sources link the definition of the Etruscan temple with the monumentalization of Rome under the rule of the Etruscan family of the Tarquinii. In fact, the largest Etruscan temple known to us is the three-*cella* temple dedicated in 509 BCE, under Tarquinius Superbus, to the triad Jupiter Optimus Maximus, Juno, and Minerva on the Capitoline Hill in Rome. Other monumental temples were built in Etruria between the end of the sixth and the beginning of fifth century BCE, and they all conformed to the same basic type. The same can be said of temples built in the first half of the fifth century BCE, when the erection of temples was most intense in the history of Etruscan cities, and of temples built or rebuilt during the fourth century BCE.

What is characteristic of the Etruscan temple is the deep *pronaos*, the podium, and the great emphasis on the front. This strict frontality also dictated the axial planning of the areas and altars in front of the temples, and would remain characteristic of Roman religious architecture. Most likely, this disposition, as well as the orientation of the temples—generally to the south—strongly depended on cult practice and religious beliefs. We know that the Etruscans had rules for the placing of altars and sacred areas, and that the augurs played a significant role. This might have also been the case for the temple. The *cella* of the Etruscan temple housed the cult statue of the god, and most likely, in this culture, as in Greece and in the ancient Near East, the temple served as his or her house. However, in consideration of the positioning of the temple on a high podium, and of the restriction of the access to the stairs on the front, admission to the temple must have been very limited, unlike in Greek temples.

Rome. Roman temples inherited the strictly frontal emphasis and high bases of Etruscan temples. Early Roman temples were built in the Etruscan manner, but little survives from this period. It is unlikely, however, that there were any significant improvements in design or construction before the Second Punic War at the end of the third century BCE, when the first temples made entirely of stone were erected. Thereafter, Rome was increasingly involved in the affairs of the Hellenistic East, and Roman buildings were influenced by Hellenistic forms, particularly the Corinthian order, though temples still retained the essential Etruscan arrangement with high bases and steps only at the facade. Plans were conservative, with columns across the facade only, or, if extended along the sides, terminating in front of a wall across the back. Occasionally the Romans adopted the full surrounding colonnades of Greek temples. Although temples were commissioned by a variety of individuals during the republic, under the empire, patronage was mainly under the imperial family. Under Augustus and the Julio-Claudian emperors (27 BCE–68 CE), temples in Rome changed their appearance. Marbles of various types were introduced for the internal and external decoration, and the Corinthian order became canonical for both columns and entablature. In the years immediately after the Julio-Claudian dynasty, temples did not play a primary role in the general layout of sanctuaries, and were also scaled down. However, a revival of temple architecture took place in the period at the end of the second and the beginning of the third century CE. To this period date major enterprises in the city of Rome, such as the Pantheon (see below); the construction of many new temples in North Africa, such as the one in the honor of the Severan family in Leptis Magna (216 CE); and, finally, the completion of ambitious projects in the Roman East, such as the sanctuary at Baalbek (see below). By contrast, between the second half of the third and the beginning of the fourth century CE, the temple endured a crisis that culminated with the erection of the new Christian basilicas during the Constantinian period (306–337 CE).

In essence, the Roman temple functioned like the Greek as the house of the god and the storeroom of his or her offerings. It could also serve for the cult of the emperor and his family. Burnt sacrifices were made at an altar, which was usually placed immediately in front of the temple at the bottom of the steps so that worshipers faced the altar (and the temple) rather than surrounding it. Where possible, the temple stood in a colonnaded precinct, which also emphasized the axial symmetry. Roman temples, however, showed greater concern than the Greek for the use of the *cella* as a room. The Roman *cella* often occupied a greater portion of the total area, was wider, and was invariably freed from encumbering internal supports for the roof, a consequence of better carpentry techniques and the availability of better timber. This enhancement of the *cella* does not signify congregational use in the full sense, but the temples were certainly used for gatherings, which might have been political rather than fully religious in character—meetings of the senate, for example.

These developments culminated in the best preserved of all Roman temples, the Pantheon in Rome, built by the emperor Hadrian (117–138 CE) to replace an earlier building of Augustus' time (see Figure 4). Dedicated to all the gods, it is circular rather than rectangular. It had a conventional precinct and porch, but the *cella*, 150 Roman feet in diameter, was roofed with a concrete dome. Light was admitted, for deliberate effect, through an opening in the center of the dome.

In the provinces of the empire, temples sponsored by the authorities usually imitated those of Rome. They most often employed local building techniques and, usually, local materials, but they were essentially similar to Roman prototypes. Local tradition, however, often influenced form. This is very clear in Egypt, where Egyptian-style temples were still being built under the Romans. In Greece and part of the east the relationship was different, because Roman temples themselves were already influenced by Greek form and served similar religious concepts. Here the local tradition was architectural rather than religious, and was not insisted upon. Roman temples on high bases were built, some distinctly frontal, but there was a more ready tendency towards fully colonnaded arrangements, when money was available. The Roman East was wealthy—Asia Minor and Syria in particular—and some temples of the Roman period were quite splendid. The major Greek cities were already well provided for—Artemis of Ephesus (Diana of the Ephesians) still had the temple last rebuilt for her in the fourth century BCE—and new building was mostly concerned with the political cult of Rome and with individual emperors (Trajan, for example, at Pergamum). Pergamum also possesses, in the sanctuary of Asklepios patronized by the emperor Caracalla, a unique example of a temple based on the Pantheon at Rome.

The most splendid of these temples in the Roman East is that dedicated to Jupiter at Heliopolis, the Roman military colony at Baalbek in Lebanon. A huge temple stands on a high podium in the Roman tradition. On the podium is a Greek-type stepped base. The surrounding Corinthian colonnade is arranged in the East Greek (Ionic) manner with a wider central spacing at each end. In the *cella* (now ruined) was a shrine structure with a cult crypt underneath (better preserved in the neighboring so-called Temple of Bacchus) serving local religious ritual. Outside was a tall tower altar of eastern type. Eastern influences can be detected in the architectural decoration, such as Persian-style bulls on the frieze. Finally, the temple was given a precinct (never completed) and forecourt with a gateway building flanked by towers which derives from local, not Roman, concepts.

SEE ALSO Architecture; Iconography, articles on Egyptian Iconography, Greco-Roman Iconography.

BIBLIOGRAPHY

Arnold, Dieter. *Die Tempel Ägyptens. Götterwohnung, Kultstätten, Baudenkmäler.* Zurich, 1992.

Boëthius, Axel. *Etruscan and Early Roman Architecture.* Harmondsworth, U.K., 1978.

Burkert, Walter. "The Meaning and Function of the Temple in Classical Greece." In *Temple in Society*, edited by Michael V. Fox, pp. 27–47. Winona Lake, Ind., 1988.

Colonna, Giovanni, ed. *Santuari d'Etruria.* Milan, 1985.

Dinsmoor, William Bell. *The Architecture of Ancient Greece.* 3d ed. London, 1950.

Frankfort, Henri. *The Art and Architecture of the Ancient Orient.* 5th ed. New Haven, Conn., 1996.

Gros, Pierre. *L'architecture romaine.* 2 vols. Paris, 1996-2001.

Gruben, Gottfried. *Griechische Tempel und Heiligtümer.* 5th ed. Munich, 2001.

Hägg, Robin, and Nanno Marinotos, eds. *Greek Sanctuaries.* London and New York, 1993.

Heinrich, Ernst. *Die Tempel und Heiligtümer im Alten Mesopotamien.* Berlin, 1982.

Hellmann, Marie-Christine. *L'architecture grecque*, vol. 1, Paris, 2002.

Lawrence, Arnold W. *Greek Architecture.* 5th ed. Revised by R. A. Tomlinson. New Haven, Conn. 1996.

Martin, Roland. *Greek Architecture*, New York, 1998.

Shafer, Byron E., ed. *Temples of Ancient Egypt.* Ithaca, N.Y., 1997.

Tomlinson, R. A. *Greek Sanctuaries.* London, 1976.

Ward-Perkins, J. B. *Roman Imperial Architecture.* Harmondsworth, U.K., 1981.

R. A. TOMLINSON (1987)
CLEMENTE MARCONI (2005)

TEMPLE: MESOAMERICAN TEMPLES

The most common form of sanctuary in Mesoamerica is the temple-pyramid-plaza, that is, the peculiar combination of an elevated foundation, almost always artificially built, with a temple on the upper platform. Usually adjoining this unit at the base of the access staircase is a series of open spaces (plaza, esplanade, altar platform). This basic combination was perpetuated for over twenty-five centuries, with several constants that gave it relative coherence within an extremely varied panorama and allowed it to be integrated into larger and more complex architectural clusters.

STRUCTURES. The embryonic form of this temple combination can be found in the principal mounds built from compressed soil or from *adobe* (sun-dried brick) by the Olmec in areas around the Gulf of Mexico, such as San Lorenzo (in the present-day Mexican state of Veracruz) and La Venta (in Tabasco) between 1200 and 900 BCE. Associated with a thrust toward monumentality that reflected the cultural vigor in Mesoamerica at the end of the Preclassic period (600 BCE–200 CE), the temple-pyramid-plaza soon spread to other regions. Thus, in the central plateau of Mexico we find, as antecedents to the Pyramids of the Sun and the Moon in Teotihuacan, the large, elongated mounds of Totimehuacan (Puebla) and the superimposed circular platforms (150 meters in diameter) in Cuicuilco, in the southeast corner of the Valley of Mexico. In the northern part of Petén (Guatemala), in the heart of the Maya area, the massive pyramids of El Mirador, with their apexes emerging from the dense forest, foreshadow the great Maya temples of Tikal in the same region.

Together with this tendency toward monumental building there was a great preoccupation with architectural permanence. This concern was reflected in the emergence of large retaining walls for the compressed fill of earth and rubble. These walls constituted the solid nucleus of the pyramid, and their taluses tended to follow the natural sloping angle of the fill. The access staircase, generally the only one placed on the axis of the temple, was initially incorporated into the general mass of the pyramid itself. With the passing of time it tended to project outward, frequently bordered by two *alfardas,* or flat ramps, which in turn often projected slightly beyond the steps or, according to local or regional style, assumed more complex shapes. In the same manner, the sides of the pyramid could be decorated with large masks or other sculptures or ornamented rhythmically with moldings, notably variations on the talus panel (*tablero-talud* or *talud-tablero,* a panel, or *tablero,* usually framed with moldings, that projected from the slope). These architectural elements, together with the proportions, divisions, and other formal characteristics of the foundation, define the principal masses of the structure and highlight their respective horizontal or vertical features.

Finally, the temple itself, which usually occupies the upper platform of the pyramid, evolved from a simple hut to a more elaborate building made of masonry. Depending on the region, it was covered with a flat roof supported by wooden timbers and surrounded by low parapets or, as can be observed among the Maya, with vaulting made up of different types of projecting (corbeled) arches. Various types of panels, moldings, and sculptures enrich the temple silhouettes, which could be crowned with more or less massive roof combs, as in the case of Classical Maya architecture, or with sculptured finials distributed at regular intervals on the outside perimeter of the parapet in the style of a battlement. Such finials can be observed in the architectural tradition of Mexico's central plateau from the period of Teotihuacán until the Spanish conquest.

INTERPRETATIONS. From the Spanish chroniclers of the sixteenth century we learn that in spite of the staircases, which were usually wide and well proportioned in relation to the whole (and independent of the scale, large or small, of the rooms inside), the sanctuary that usually topped each pyramid for the most part remained closed to the common mortal. This observation seems to indicate that, at least in its community aspects, worship was conducted outdoors, either on the upper platform of the pyramid in front of the main entrance to the sanctuary or, if there was one, on the altar platform in the center of the plaza located at the foot of the pyramid, where the congregation gathered.

Naturally, there are a few exceptional cases in which the pyramid was conceived without a temple. If in fact worship was essentially an outdoor activity, the interior space of the sanctuaries, relatively large in Mexico's central plateau, Oaxaca, and other regions of Mesoamerica, could be reduced to very small dimensions, apparently without undermining its sacred character. This is particularly evident in the Maya area, where the width of the interior spaces fluctuates on the average between three meters and seventy-five centimeters, as we can see when we compare, for example, a temple in Palenque, in southern Mexico, with one in Tikal. There are, however, extreme cases, such as Building A in Nakum (Petén), where the narrow chambers measure only fifty and forty-two centimeters in width (perhaps to function as a "loudspeaker" that dramatically amplified the voice of the priest). Such considerations likewise help to explain those full-scale simulated temples in the Rio Bec region of Campeche, which are sometimes crowned by two or three solid "towers." These towers, incorporated into the mass of a low, functional building, in turn constitute versions of compressed pyramids, complete with simulated staircases. This imitation of the temple-pyramid was not detrimental to the symbolic meaning of certain privileged parts of the building, such as the staircase, the sides of the tower, the main doorway (or its upper frieze alone), and the roof comb.

The primary function of the Mesoamerican pyramid was to elevate the temple; occasionally it served as a ruler's mausoleum (as in the outstanding example of Palenque). However, the pyramid could lack a temple altogether (as in the twin-pyramid complexes of Tikal), or it could have twin staircases leading to two clearly differentiated temples (as occurs during the last three centuries before the Spanish conquest).

The Mesoamerican tradition of not razing buildings to the foundation before undertaking new construction is fortunate for archaeology. As a result of much remodeling, expansion, and superimposing, which on occasion generated artificial acropolises (the particularly high and compact clusters of buildings that resulted from centuries of adding new layers of construction, as found at the North Acropolis of Tikal), the remains of temples, dismantled only to a certain height to become part of the fill for a new building, reappear bit by bit from their burial ground to tell us the history of their city, their gods, and their rulers. While the effigies of deities (as well as the sacrificial stone) speak to us about a place designed for rituals, other features, particularly among the Maya (where we find so many roof combs, stelae, and other dynastic records), suggest the self-glorification of a ruling prince.

SEE ALSO Iconography, article on Mesoamerican Iconography; Pyramids, overview article.

BIBLIOGRAPHY

Three general surveys with good photographs and an appreciation of architectural aesthetics may be recommended: Doris Heyden's and my *Pre-Columbian Architecture of Mesomamerica* (New York, 1975), Henri Stierlin's *Maya* (Fribourg, 1964), and Stierlin's *Mexique ancien* (Fribourg, 1967).

PAUL GENDROP (1987)
Translated from Spanish by Gabriela Mahn

TEMPLE SOLAIRE. The Order of the Solar Temple, a European esoteric movement, shocked European public opinion with its mass suicides and homicides of 1994, 1995, and 1997, and it had a crucial effect on subsequent anticult activity by various European governments.

THE ARGINY MOVEMENT. A whole group of new religious movements flourish with foundational mythologies connected to the medieval Knights Templars. Most trace their origin to the Order of the Temple founded in 1805 by Bernard-Raymond Fabré-Palaprat (1777–1838), a French physician and Freemason. After Palaprat's death, the movement went through a number of schisms, and by 1950 more than one hundred small neo-Templar bodies were in existence throughout the world. New groups emerged during the 1950s, some of them claiming mystical experiences in which their founders were directly initiated as Knights Templars from the spirit world by ascended "Masters of the Temple."

Jacques Breyer (1922–1996), a prolific French esoteric author, claimed to have had such an experience with two companions on June 12, 1952, in the ruins of Arginy Castle in France. These events led to the establishment of the Sovereign Order of the Solar Temple (Ordre Souverain du Temple Solaire, or OSTS). In the 1960s Julien Origas (1920–1983), an interpreter who had served four years in jail for his wartime activities as a Nazi collaborator, became associated with the Arginy movement, and established the Renewed Order of the Temple (Ordre Rénové du Temple, or ORT) as an independent but related branch of the OSTS. On March 21, 1981, the leaders of OSTS and ORT converged in a mystical ceremony in Geneva on the premises of a third organization, also recognized by Breyer as part of the Arginy movement: the Golden Way Foundation, established by Joseph Di Mambro (1924–1994). The ceremony was—according to Di Mambro—at least as important as the Arginy experience, and was later cited as the founding date of the Order of the Solar Temple.

THE ORDER OF THE SOLAR TEMPLE. Di Mambro was born in Pont-Saint-Esprit (Gard, France) in 1924. A jeweler by trade, in 1956 he joined AMORC, the Ancient and Mystical Order of the Rosy Cross. He left it around 1970, joined the Arginy movement, and—after a minor skirmish with French justice in 1971 for writing bad checks—moved to Annemasse, near the Swiss border. He later moved to Switzerland, where in 1973 he started a full-time career as teacher of yoga and occult philosophy. He also became the founder of several occult societies. In 1982 Di Mambro's Golden Way Foundation was joined by Luc Jouret (1947–1994), a popular Belgian homeopathic doctor who had established a practice in Annemasse. The Amenta Club (later renamed Atlanta), a circle established by Jouret for his clients and friends, became a vehicle for disseminating Di Mambro's ideas. Di Mambro also introduced Jouret to Origas, and the Belgian doctor quickly ascended to a leadership position in the ORT.

When Origas died in 1983, Jouret claimed to have been designated as his heir and as leader of the ORT, but his claims were challenged by the Origas family. Jouret and Di Mambro eventually left the ORT and established the International Order of Chivalry-Solar Tradition, more commonly known as the Order of the Solar Temple (Ordre du Temple Solaire, or OTS). By this time they operated a system of Chinese boxes. People initially attended Jouret's speeches organized by the Amenta and Atlanta Clubs. Those most interested were invited to join the Arcadia Clubs. The most dedicated members of the Arcadia Clubs were eventually invited to join the true secret organization, the OTS. By 1989 (possibly the year of its maximum success) the OTS had 442 members, most of them in French-speaking countries (only sixteen in the United States). Jouret had considerable success in Quebec as a motivational speaker, especially at Hydro-Québec, the public hydroelectric utility of the province, where he recruited fifteen executives and managers for the OTS between 1987 and 1989.

By this time, the theme of an imminent end of the world (originating from certain ideas of Breyer, but including new elements about UFOs and extraterrestrials) was a central part of OTS teaching. When the OTS apocalyptic worldview was discovered behind the facade of Jouret's motivational speeches, the group started to experience strong and organized opposition.

THE TRAGEDY. In 1991 the Martinique branch of ADFI (Association pour la défense des familles et de l'individu, the largest French anticult organization) denounced the conversion of wealthy Martinicans to the OTS and their eventual move to Quebec. ADFI-Martinique was able to join forces with Rose-Marie Klaus, a disgruntled Swiss OTS ex-member whose husband Bruno had left her within the frame of new "cosmic" marriage rearrangements introduced by Di Mambro and allegedly dictated by the ascended Masters. Eventually, Klaus's determined opposition made inroads: Jouret found it increasingly difficult to be invited as a motivational speaker, and in February 1993 the Canadian police started investigating the Solar Temple. On March 8, 1993, two OTS members, Jean-Pierre Vinet and Hermann Delorme, were arrested as they were attempting to buy semiautomatic guns with silencers, illegal weapons in Quebec. A warrant for arrest was also issued against Luc Jouret, at that time in Europe. In fact, the arms deal had been arranged by a police informant engaged in a sting operation. The prosecution ended with a "suspended acquittal" and a minor fine for Jouret, Vinet, and Delorme (with the latter leaving the OTS following the incident). Rose-Marie Klaus managed to have lurid accounts of the "cult of the end of the world" published in the media. Vinet was fired from his position at Hydro-Québec, and police investigations were launched in France and Australia, where Di Mambro had some financial interests, later grossly exaggerated by sensationalist accounts in the press.

It is not easy to determine whether the preparation for a "transit" of the core members of the OTS to another planet (through suicide) was started before or after the first Canadian police actions in 1993. The first versions of the texts about the transit (proclaiming that the end of the world was near, and that it was eminently reasonable to leave planet Earth in search of salvation on the star Sirius or on another faraway planet) were probably written at about the time the Canadian investigation was started in February 1993. That same year the OTS was confronted by two major factors of internal stress. In Quebec, dissension about Jouret's leadership erupted, and Robert Falardeau, an officer with the Quebec Ministry of Finances, replaced him as Grand Master (with Jouret remaining an important international leader). In Europe, Di Mambro had serious health problems. A number of French and Swiss members had left the OTS in 1993, wondering whether their money had not mostly been spent to support the leader's luxurious lifestyle. Worst of all, rumors began circulating in 1990 that the most secret and sacred experience of the OTS—visible manifestations of the Masters of the Temple—were, in fact, holographic and electronic tricks stage-managed on behalf of Di Mambro by a loyal member, Antonio (Tony) Dutoit. These rumors led Di Mambro's son, Elie, to quit the OTS. Dutoit and his wife eventually confirmed the rumors, distanced themselves from Di Mambro, and in 1994 named their newborn baby Christopher Emmanuel. This was particularly intolerable for Di Mambro, who considered the name Emmanuel to be reserved for his own daughter, who was named Emmanuelle, but was addressed in the OTS as "Emmanuel," as if she were male. Emmanuelle—allegedly conceived by Dominique Bellaton, Di Mambro's mistress, through cosmic intercourse with an ascended Master—was regarded as the embodiment of the cosmic Christ. As a consequence, Di Mambro become persuaded that the infant Christopher Emmanuel Dutoit was the antichrist and another omen of the imminent end of the world.

Within this climate, Di Mambro had a paranoid reaction to the police investigations, and set in motion the chain of events eventually leading to the "departure." It is unclear when exactly messages from the Masters and from a "Heavenly Lady" channeled by Di Mambro and by Camille Pilet (1926–1994)—the most prominent and wealthy businessman in the OTS and the alleged reincarnation of Joseph of Arimathea—started preparing the Templars for a "transit" out of this world, but preparations probably began around 1990. It is also unclear when (probably in 1993) an inner core of members learned that the transit would not involve a spaceship or other extraterrestrial vehicle, but would be a mystical suicide. At any rate, on October 4, 1994, fire destroyed Joseph Di Mambro's villa in Morin Heights, Quebec. Among the ruins, the police found five charred bodies. Three of these people—the Dutoits and their infant son—had been stabbed to death before the fire. Having perpetrated or at least supervised the killings in Morin Heights, which probably took place on September 30, Joël Egger and Dominique Bellaton (the mother of the "genuine" cosmic child) joined forty-six other OTS members and children of members in Switzerland. In the early morning of October 5, the police found all of them dead in two OTS centers in Cheiry (canton of Fribourg) and Granges-sur-Salvan (canton Valais). Twenty-three bodies were found in Cheiry and twenty-five in Granges-sur-Salvan, along with the remains of the devices programmed to start the fires that almost destroyed both OTS centers. From the lengthy investigation of the Swiss police and judiciary, it seems that most of those dead in Cheiry were murdered, while at least half of those found in Granges-sur-Salvan committed suicide. But the dichotomy between suicide and murder is only part of the story. Documents left by the Temple suggest that along with murdered traitors and core members strong enough to understand the full implications of the transit, there were also weaker Templars. The latter did not oppose the idea of the transit (although they may have understood it as something different from a suicide), but they needed "help" to accomplish it.

Interestingly, after the murders and suicides few former members reinterpreted the OTS from the anticult perspective, and the majority continued to express sympathy for the organization. It seems that Di Mambro had explicitly planned the survival of some "witnesses" by establishing the ARC (Association for Cultural Research for the external world, but in fact the Association Rosy-Cross) in Avignon on September 24, 1994. One of the speakers at the Avignon meeting was a well-known French conductor, Michel Tabachnik, who had joined the OTS some years earlier and had been an occasional speaker with Jouret in Quebec. The only public figure to survive the 1994 tragedy, he was accused by a sensationalist press of being the secret leader of the OTS or at least Di Mambro's successor. Although he was acquitted in a criminal trial in France in 2001, Tabachnik's musical career was compromised.

Notwithstanding the continued police interest in what was left of the OTS, a second "transit" happened on December 23, 1995, when sixteen OTS members and three of their children were found dead in the Vercors mountains, near Grenoble, France. In a third incident, discovered on May 23, 1997, in Saint-Casimir, Quebec, another five members of the OTS—including Bruno Klaus, the former husband of vocal apostate Rose-Marie Klaus—committed suicide. While only a handful of persons who regard themselves as members of the OTS or the ARC remain alive in Europe or Quebec after the third incident, further suicides cannot be ruled out as long as some people continue to share the OTS ideology and regard the "transit" as both reasonable and desirable.

SEE ALSO Movement for the Restoration of the Ten Commandments of God; New Religious Movements, overview article and articles on New Religious Movements and Millennialism and New Religious Movements and Violence.

BIBLIOGRAPHY

Hall, John R., and Philip Schuyler. "The Mystical Apocalypse of the Solar Temple." In *Millennium, Messiahs, and Mayhem: Contemporary Apocalyptic Movements*, edited by Thomas Robbins and Susan J. Palmer, pp. 285–311. New York, 1997. An early scholarly approach.

Introvigne, Massimo. "The Magic of Death: The Suicides of the Solar Temple." In *Millennialism, Persecution, and Violence: Historical Cases*, edited by Catherine Wessinger, pp. 138–157. Syracuse, N.Y., 2000.

Introvigne, Massimo, and Jean-François Mayer. "Occult Masters and the Temple of Doom: The Fiery End of the Solar Temple." In *Cults, Religion, and Violence*, edited by David G. Bromley and J. Gordon Melton, pp. 170–188. New York, 2002. An assessment of the tragedy's meaning.

Mayer, Jean-François. *Der Sonnentempel: Die Tragödie einer Sekte.* Updated ed. Freiburg, Germany, 1998. The standard scholarly approach.

Mayer, Jean-François. "'Our Terrestrial Journey Is Coming to an End': The Last Voyage of the Solar Temple." *Nova Religio: The Journal of Alternative and Emergent Religions* 2, no. 2 (April 1999): 172–196.

MASSIMO INTROVIGNE (2005)

TEMPTATION. Approaches to the complex phenomenon of temptation are as diversified as are cultures, worldviews, the self-understanding of men and women, the concept of sin, and so on. But behind all the astonishing differences there might well be discovered agreement on one point: that the center of human temptation is egocentricity, and genuine love is its victor. In the Judeo-Christian tradition, reflection on temptation arises in the quest for the sources of evil, which leads to a questioning of both God's nature and the nature of humankind. However, for the Hebrews, these questions were further complicated because of their own negative reactions to earlier solutions put forth by their neighbors. A continuing theme in Israel's history is the belief that their neighbors were tempting them to abandon faith in Yahveh and the law of Moses. Consequently, they must destroy those who were or could become such a temptation. This sad pattern reappears in Christianity as a motive for the crusades, inquisitions, and the burning of so-called witches. Christians were thus diverted from the actual, horrifying temptations that drew them away from humanness, love of neighbor, and even from the true image of God as a merciful Father of all.

The problem of temptation seems to resist a rational, conceptual approach. Perhaps the most adequate approach to its historical study is by way of its symbols. The prototype of these symbols and myths is the *Genesis* story of Adam and Eve. Similar symbols are to be found in most African cultures. It seems that with these stories there is not yet the question of original sin but, rather, the more basic question: what is the response of humanity when confronted with evil?

The Fall of Adam and Eve—of humanity in general—and its consequences are presented in the first twelve chapters of *Genesis*. There we see Cain tempted to do violence, a temptation to which he yields, killing his brother. The increase in violence finds its symbol in Lamech, whose warlike attitude is reflected also in his relationship with women. Finally, the world is so flooded with sin that Noah can withstand it only with utmost difficulty.

However, while a one-sided, legalistic understanding of faith and morality warned against the temptation of disobedience, it remained blind to the temptation to disown the prophetic tradition and blind to unjust structures and the unjust exercise of authority, which today's Christians sharply denounce as "institutionalized temptations."

All too often in Christendom the tendency prevailed to condemn any form of doubt about religious and moral doctrines and traditions, while today many Christians pray that God may grace them with the courage to doubt at the right point and, thus, to be preserved from the disgraceful temptation of choosing a false security over the sincere search for truth. Some Christians seem not to care much about the existential question of whether they are truly on the road to salvation, but for Martin Luther and many other Christians of all denominations, it has been a matter of faith to fight desperately against such a temptation.

In Western religions there have always been conflicting trends between those who gave primacy to the fight against temptations arising from one's own heart and those who gave first place to fighting unjust and dehumanizing structures as the main sources of temptation. There were and still are those who are overly optimistic about the individual's battle against temptation and, at the same time, pessimistic about changing immoral society. Today many who call for renewal of church institutions fall into the temptation of overlooking the interwovenness of persons and society and the difficulty of achieving simultaneously the ongoing individual conversion and the changing and healing of public life, including church structures.

For many religious people in the West it is still difficult to recognize the enormous temptation involved in renouncing one's own responsibility and yielding to anguish instead of making clear decisions about the Christian's mission to be salt to the earth. One aspect of this all-pervasive temptation is easy conformity to a culture of greed, consumerism, and a wasteful style of life.

Christians are awakening only gradually to the temptation to waste our human and ecological resources. Many are struggling with the temptation to render indiscriminate military service and grant one's own government a blind presumption of righteousness in respect to armaments, arms sales, and military actions. Perhaps here, however, we are beginning to perceive a major shift in Western Christianity's approach to the theme of temptation.

DEFINITION OF TEMPTATION. For Immanuel Kant, temptation is the paradoxical expression of the human person, destined by nature for the good yet inclined to do evil. He defines temptation as a challenge to live one's freedom for good in the purest way.

In the Septuagint, and consequently in Christian tradition, the Greek word *peirasmos* indicates quite different concepts in different contexts. Often it refers to sinful people "tempting God," murmuring against him and challenging him in unbelief and distrust (cf. *Ex.* 17:1–7). The New Testament, too, warns against this temptation of humans "to tempt God," to challenge him (*1 Cor.* 10:9), to defy him in disobedience (*Heb.* 3:8), to request from him miraculous interventions at a whim or for purposes of self-exaltation (cf. *Mt.* 4:7: "You are not to put the Lord your God to the test").

Most frequently, however, the word *temptation* is used to describe humans being tempted in various ways. Two forms of *peirasmos* have to be distinguished carefully. One concerns the various troubles and trials seen as an opportunity, or *kairos,* for the believer to strengthen his faith, his endurance, and, finally, his capacity to share in Christ's redemptive suffering. *James* 1:2–3 describes this kind of *peirasmos:* "Whenever you have to face trials of many kinds, count yourselves supremely happy in the knowledge that such testing of your faith breeds fortitude, and if you give fortitude full play you will go on to complete a balanced character." Sometimes only the victorious conclusion of such a trial allows the positive evaluation of the event, as in *James* or, even more evidently, in the beatitudes (*Mt.* 5:11–12, *Lk.* 6:21–23).

The other kind of *peirasmos* refers to temptation in the sense of endangering salvation, that is, when the person is assaulted from within and/or from without by godless powers aimed at his downfall. The Lord exhorts us to pray that we may not be brought to such dangerous tests: "And lead us not into temptation" (*Mt.* 6:13, *Lk.* 11:4). Christ warns his disciples that his own terrible trial can become for them a dangerous test: "Stay awake, all of you; and pray that you may be spared, that you may not enter into temptation" (*Mk.* 14:38).

Martin Luther is particularly anxious that we do not confuse those tests in which God guides us through the trial from beginning to end with those temptations into which we walk self-confidently from the start and thus expose ourselves to the danger of downfall.

TEMPTATION AND THE TEMPTER. While the scripture warns us against the tempter in his various disguises, the main emphasis is on our own "heart," our personal response to temptations. The Bible calls on Christians to take responsibility by consistently rebuking the sinner who wants to exculpate himself by inculpating others.

Temptation arises from within. *James* is most explicit: "Temptation arises when a man is enticed and lured away by his own lust" (1:14). Here the author of *James* follows the main line of the synoptic Gospels, as when Jesus calls for change of heart, for purification of one's inmost thoughts and desires: "It is from within men's hearts that evil intentions emerge" (*Mk.* 7:20). *James* speaks of *epithumia* ("desire"), which in the Jewish thought of the time referred to the ambivalent impulses and inclinations (or *yetser*) assigned to Adam and Eve in rabbinic literature to explain their capacity for being tempted. Augustine's term *concupiscence* does not correspond exactly to *yetser.* While the Hebrew scriptures and rabbinic literature try to understand human vulnerability to temptation as *epithumia,* Augustine believes temptation to be based on our heritage of sin from Adam. We may understand concupiscence as that inner inclination for temptation and sin, the intensity of which depends on unrepented sins, the weakness or lack of a fundamental option for God and for the good, and the attraction to sin that comes from a sinful world around us, where the sins of the past continue to poison the human environment.

This same idea is present also in thought about the struggle that exists in our inmost being between *sarx* and *pneuma* (or "body" and "spirit"). For Paul, temptation manifests in our lower nature, the body, and is supported by the collective selfishness and arrogance present in all humanity. The *sarx*—and with it, temptation—loses power to the degree that we are renewed and guided by the *pneuma.*

God does not tempt anyone. *James*'s great concern that "God is untouched by evil" (1:14) already existed in Jewish wisdom literature. The main concern of the oldest Israelite tradition, however, was the absolute rejection of any kind of dualism: God has absolute sovereignty. The distinction found in this tradition between being "put to the test" by dangerous temptation or by trials destined to purify or refine had not yet been neatly elaborated.

A striking example is in a comparison of the story of David's temptation regarding a census, as told in *2 Samuel* with the later story in *1 Chronicles.* The first account says, "The anger of Yahveh once again blazed out against the Israelites, and he incited David against them. 'Go,' he said, 'take a census of Israel and Judah'" (*2 Sm.* 24:1). In those days a census was considered an attack on God's prerogative to give increase to his people. Hence David was punished by a pestilence that diminished the nation. The author of *1 Chronicles* is more careful about the image of God as one of absolute goodness; he gives another version: "Satan rose against David to take a census of the Israelites" (*1 Chr.* 21). In this later tradition monotheism had become so firmly established that the introduction of a tempter inimical to God's people was not to be feared.

The wisdom literature provided helpful distinctions and directions of thought. The authors were careful not to allow the sinner any exoneration and to avoid any contamination by dualism. Their greatest care was to show God's wisdom in the sovereign government of world and history.

Temptation, uncomfortable as it may be, is an ingredient of life. Those who put their trust in God will overcome it, and it serves moral growth in their life. God does not incite to evil, but he allows both suffering and temptation as tests for the virtuous. "God has put them to the test and proved them worthy to be with him; he has tested them like gold in a furnace, and accepted them as holocausts" (*Wis.* 3:5). The sinner has no excuse, since he falls because of lack of love and fear of God. Those who truly adhere to God will make good use of freedom.

This is succinctly expressed by Jesus, son of Sirach: "Do not say, 'the Lord is responsible for my sinning,' for he is never the cause of what he hates. Do not say, 'it was he who led me astray,' for he has no use for a sinner. The Lord hates all that is foul, and no one who fears him will love it either. He himself made him in the beginning, and left him free to make his own decisions. . . . To behave faithfully is within your power" (*Sir.* 15:11–16).

The serpent and the woman in *Genesis* 3. The narrative of the fall is an anthropological myth of great depth and complexity. Its symbols express ancient Israelite reflections on the origin of evil. It depicts in a lively way the diversionary rhetoric of the sinner, who always needs a scapegoat for his own vindication. Adam attempts to use Eve as his scapegoat, while Eve blames the serpent. Some see in the role attributed to Eve a deeply ingrained misogyny in the Yahvistic authors. Paul Ricoeur may come closer to the intention of the narrative when he writes in his *La symbolique du mal* (Paris, 1960) that the woman here is not so much the "second sex" as, rather, an expression of the human being's frailty, man's as well as woman's (vol. 2, p. 239). The story exposes the sin of Adam more than that of Eve, because it unmasks Adam's domineering attitude toward the woman (*Gn.* 3:16). In the fall, man too must confess: "This is flesh of my flesh." There is a solidarity in both salvation and perdition.

Why is the serpent introduced to allow man to exonerate himself? We can respond that the very mechanism of exculpation is part of sinful man, since when he confesses his sin humbly before the merciful God, he finds no need to accuse others. Yet there is still more in this anthropological metaphor. The serpent is also a creature, one that is "the most subtle of all the wild beasts God has made" (*Gn.* 3:1). It becomes a metaphoric presentation of man's subtle pursuit of his egotism and his no less subtle self-defense and self-belying mechanisms (cf. Philbert Avril, *Délivre-nous du mal,* Paris, 1981, p. 23).

Ricoeur thinks that this is also the way James's epistle explains the self-deceptive concupiscence. The serpent is a part of ourselves as long as we have not the strength of truth to unmask the shrewdness of our exonerating maneuvers. It might also symbolize "the chaotic disorder in myself, among us and around us" (*La symbolique du mal,* vol. 2, p. 242). That would bring into the whole vision of the first twelve chapters of *Genesis* a sharper awareness of the various dimensions of solidarity in either good or evil, including the cosmic dimension and the need for humans to decide one way or the other.

While theologians and preachers during the last centuries frequently identified the serpent of *Genesis* with Satan or the devil, there seems to be a growing consensus among biblical scholars and theologians that in the early tradition reflected in *Genesis* 3, nobody thought or spoke of Satan, the personified Evil One. In his 1937–1938 work *Creation and Fall: A Theological Interpretation of Genesis 1–3 and Temptation,* Dietrich Bonhoeffer was insisting already that this narrative has no need of *diaboli ex machina.* The serpent symbolizes the ambiguity of people, their human relationships, and their environment.

Satan and his helpers. Satan interests us here only in relation to temptation. What does the tempter add to the understanding of temptation? In the older tradition, Satan never appears; it is God who tests man and calls him to decision (Seesemann, 1968, p. 25). In the *Book of Job,* we find God testing man in much the same way as he tested Abraham. The successful end is decisive: the person who counts on God will overcome temptation. What is new in *Job* is that God acts through intermediary forces.

The nebulous Satan here has nothing to do with the super-Satan of the Persian religion or with the apocalyptic and threatening "prince of darkness" of later writings in Judaism and Christianity. This Satan is a not very effective literary effort meant to exonerate God from appearing as the source of evil. Such a Satan becomes a real threat to the sufferer through those "friends" who, having a false image of God, judge the sufferer to be one who deserves such punishment. For the sufferer, these friends are indeed Satan's cruelest helpers. Even Christ on the cross was exposed to them: the pseudo-religious people who insulted him. Job's victory over this temptation occurs because of his trustful adoration of the ever greater God.

The shrewd Satan who tempts Jesus in the desert embodies the insidious temptation put to Christianity in the first and following centuries. The misuse of the Bible by cleverly twisting its words to create false meanings tempted people away from the faith.

Satan represents also the terrible temptation of a too earthly understanding of the messianic hope of Israel and the mission of Christ. This is seen strikingly when Jesus rebukes Peter for refusing to believe in a suffering and humble servant-Messiah: "Away with you, Satan; you are a stumbling-block to me, because the way you think is not God's but man's" (*Mt.* 16:23).

Satan at his most shameless—asking Jesus to adore him—mirrors the vain self-glorification of the earthly powers of the time, particularly in the divinization of the Roman emperors. The figure of Satan should not turn attention away from these perennial temptations but should emphasize the superhuman dimension. It is a sharp warning against belittling any situation of temptation.

As we saw in *Genesis* 3, for the believer there is no way of denying guilt by pointing to a tempter or to the devil. Aware of the powers of darkness in their mysterious solidarity of perdition, the followers of Christ put their trust in God and make the wholehearted decision for his reign, a reign of justice, peace, and love. They put on "all the armor which God provides to stand firm against the devices of the devil" (*Eph.* 6:10). They will not only avoid being tempters in any way, helpers of the powers of darkness, but will commit themselves to active and generous membership in a solidarity of salvation.

This was the mind of the early church in an integrated discourse on the Christian's decision for Christ and for battle against temptations arising from the gnostic and Manichaean trend toward speculations on angelic and demonic hierarchies. We find this sobriety still in Thomas Aquinas. But in the following centuries great parts of Western Christianity indulged in fantastic speculations about witches and a slavish fear of devils as well as ritual exorcisms of them, while lacking trust in God and making no firm decision for an all-embracing solidarity.

Today there is a strong reaction, partially in favor of the original sobriety and partially in indifference to the figure of Satan, whereby the vast dimensions and blinding powers of evil are lost to sight. Referring to Ernst Bloch, Leszek Kolakowski, in his *Gespräche mit dem Teufel* (3d ed., Munich, 1977), wonders whether some Christians realize the depth and cosmic dimensions of evil. Reading Kolakowski one thinks of the devilish temptation to expect a paradise of peace in the midst of ever increasing conflict and hatred.

The Christian discourse on the tempter points to the great temptations arising from bad example and evil "friends" who initiate the inexperienced into the skills of crime and corruption. The diabolic temptation seeks directly the moral corruption of others. It is masterfully described in the famous novel *Les liaisons dangereuses* (1782) by Choderlos de Laclos. Laclos exposes both the superficial optimism of the Enlightenment and the libertinism of the time preceding the French Revolution. The book aroused much anger in its time, since it disclosed the truth of fallen humans, who can go to the limits of malice and cunning in tempting others, especially those devoted to virtue. But even to those most skilled and aggressive tempters there come moments when humanness somehow shines through, insinuating "that malice does not constitute a hopeless and irrevocable fact in human existence" (Knufmann, 1965, p. 202).

This idea was theologized by Origen, who wanted to leave open the hope that after a long duration of "eternity" even the devil and his helpers might be converted and saved by the divine power of *apokatastasis.* Origen's thought, problematic as it may be, opposed tenaciously the dualism of Manichaeism. Sinners—even the tempter and his helpers—because they are God's creatures, keep, somehow, a remnant of goodness. The theory also intended to emphasize that no sinner on earth should be considered a hopeless case.

For many contemporary Christians this thought is unacceptable in view of the diabolical crimes in our times. Mohandas Gandhi, however, thought that the coherent and thorough spirituality of *satyāgraha* ("doing the truth in love") could hope to change even persons like Adolf Hitler and Joseph Stalin into *satyāgrahins*. For Gandhi, "it is an article of faith that no man has fallen so low that he cannot be redeemed by love" (quoted by Pie-Raymond Reagmey in *Nonviolence and the Christian Conscience,* London, 1966, p. 199). This optimism is not a blindness to the horrifying evil present in humans but a recognition of the power of their spirit, enkindled and guided by the universal spirit to overcome such evil at all costs. It may be one of the most diabolic temptations of Western people not to consider this opportunity and be willing to pay its price in order to overcome the diabolically vicious circle of nuclear madness.

Psychological Perspectives. Psychoanalysis and psychotherapy have made major contributions to a better understanding of the mechanisms of various temptations. We note especially the ego-defense mechanism of repression (unconscious forgetting or prevention of consciousness) of what is too difficult to face consciously. It could be, for instance, a call to a more truthful search for life's deeper meaning. Repression usually works through a security complex which refuses to let reality challenge it.

Karl Menninger notes that temptations and sins arise from the "huge world of the unmanifest" (1973, p. 221). The "unmanifest" includes not only whatever the filter of repression is hiding but also unconfessed guilt feelings which often become confused with real guilt. On this point, Menninger refers to the Bible: "If we say we have no sin, we deceive ourselves, and the truth is not in us" (*1 Jn.* 1:8).

The result of the individual and collective temptation to deny sin and guilt is frequently undefinable anguish, feelings of senselessness, and/or despair about human freedom and dignity. The deeper source of these temptations is an unwillingness "to do the truth in love," thereby hindering truth from setting us free (cf. *Jn.* 8:31–41).

Another ego-defense is the tendency to project one's own evil inclinations on another, on some villain. In her work with children, psychotherapist Christine Lutz found that the healing and growth of moral sense progressed when the children realized that what they saw in others was, to a great extent, a projection of their own shortcomings (*Kinder und das Böse: Konfrontation und Geborgenheit,* Stuttgart, 1980).

Depth psychology has studied the mechanism of aggression. On the one hand, there is the danger of trying to repress it instead of channeling it wisely. On the other hand, there is the uncontrolled and mutually contagious mechanism that leads to the vicious circle of aggressive challenges and aggressive reactions. Although psychology suggests that it is sometimes liberating to allow one's anger an honest expression, Menninger rightly warns: "But there is always a temptation to use it as a whip, and what begins as a device for relief continues as a weapon for aggression" (1973, p. 144).

Sociological Perspectives. The broad theological expression "sin of the world" is given sharper contours in modern studies on "institutionalized temptation." In his book *Our Criminal Society* (Englewood Cliffs, N.J., 1969), Edwin M. Shur has an apt formulation: "In a sense, existing patterns of crime represent a price we pay for structuring society as we have structured it" (p. 9). In a society and culture that emphasize "having" over "being," with an educational system oriented to personal success and a whole economic system that encourages increasing consumption, people yield thoughtlessly to temptations, and nobody feels guilty. "No one thinks sin was involved" (Menninger, 1973, p. 120). The "respectable crimes" of the wealthy and powerful, their unpunished corruption, and their clever manipulations are constant incitement for others to further injustice and dishonesty in smaller matters. The little thief is caught and condemned to a prison system in which massive temptations are forced upon inexperienced transgressors of the law.

The people of wealthy countries have adopted lifestyles inseparably connected with the predatory exploitation of the earth's resources and pollution of the environment. Here we see temptations of planetary dimensions that increase the tensions between countries of free enterprise and those of massive state capitalism. How many horrifying temptations are involved in the arms race, the arms trade, and, above all, the nuclear threat! One source of the massive "institutionalized temptations" is the lack of prophetic voices; another is the unwillingness to pay earnest attention to those voices that might be heard.

Theological Perspectives. In a brief synthesis of theological perspectives that recur continuously, the point of departure for the Christian is Jesus having been tempted as we are: "Since he himself has passed through the test of suffering, he is able to help those who are meeting their test now" (*Heb.* 2:18). The church fathers stressed the point that it was after his baptism that Jesus underwent the temptation, and they connect this with the final test of his passion. Similarly, those baptized in Christ can best face temptation and suffering by putting their trust in Christ and holding fast to their baptismal commitment.

Jesus overcame temptation not just by enduring the suffering it brought but by making this very suffering the supreme sign of God's love and saving solidarity. That this love is the goal of all Christians is revealed by gospels that unmask the temptations involved in clinging to laws while betraying the covenant, now understood as the supreme law of unselfish, all-embracing love between God and humankind.

Another biblical direction is to combat evil by doing good, to overcome violent injustice by doing the truth of love in nonviolent commitment (cf. *Rom.* 12:21; *1 Thes.* 5:15; *1 Pt.* 3:9; and above all, *Mt.* 5). For believers, all temptations—but particularly those arising from the vicious circle of violence—are a challenge to sanctity, to redemptive love. An unrenounceable perspective grows out of Paul's understanding of the combat between *sarx* and *pneuma,* whereby false images of love and freedom are exposed by searching wholeheartedly for true love aided by the promptings of the spirit (cf. *Gal.* 5:13, 6:2).

See Also Apocatastasis; Evil; Fall, The.

Bibliography

There are innumerable books and articles concerning the temptation of Jesus and, in that light, temptation in general. The following books merit special attention: Ernest Best's *The Temptation and the Passion: The Markan Soteriology* (Cambridge, 1965) and Jacques Dupont's *Les tentations de Jésus au désert* (Paris, 1968). Both books contain excellent bibliographies. A comprehensive presentation of the church fathers' explanation of the biblical texts and their application to the understanding of Christian life is found in Santino Raponi's *Tentazione ed Esistenza Cristiana* (Rome, 1974). On the biblical use of the term *peirasmos,* see Heinrich Seesemann's *Theological Dictionary of the New Testament,* edited by Gerhard Friedrich (Grand Rapids, 1968), vol. 6, pp. 23–36. See Horst Beintker's study *Die Überwindung der Anfechtung bei Luther* (Berlin, 1954) for an overview of Martin Luther's approach to temptation from the perspective of the doctrine of justification by faith. Helmut Thielicke's *Theologie der Anfechtung* (Tübingen, 1949) is representative of a good part of Protestant theology's discussion of the issue. Also important is Dietrich Bonhoeffer's *Creation and Fall: A Theological Interpretation of Genesis 1–3 and Temptation* (1937–1938; New York, 1965). While at times emphasizing the power of Satan, Bonhoeffer never allows for man's exculpation. His ideas seem to reflect the time of great affliction for the church in Germany.

Of the numerous studies about the impact of a poisoned environment and a defective culture and society on temptation, Reinhold Niebuhr's *Moral Man and Immoral Society* (New York, 1932) and Edwin M. Shur's *Our Criminal Society* (Englewood Cliffs, N. J., 1969) are noteworthy. In his much-read book, *Whatever Became of Sin?* (New York, 1973), Karl Menninger points to the mechanisms and temptations of denying sin and thus, also, human freedom and responsibility. C. S. Lewis attempts to unmask real temptation in his widely known book *The Screwtape Letters* (New York, 1946). Helmut Knufmann reflects on novelists' treatment of temptation as a theme in his book *Das Böse in den Liaisons Dangereuses de Choderlos de Laclos* (Munich, 1965).

New Sources

Brewer, Talbot. "The Character of Temptation: Towards a More Plausible Kantian Moral Philosophy." *Pacific Philosophical Quarterly* 83 (June 2002): 103–131.

Schiavo, Luigi. "The Temptation of Jesus: The Eschatological Battle and the New Ethic of the First Followers of Jesus in

Q." *Journal for the Study of the New Testament* 83 (June 2002): 103–131.

Sorabji, Richard. *Emotion and Peace of Mind: From Stoic Agitation to Christian Temptation.* New York, 2000.

BERNHARD HÄRING (1987)
Revised Bibliography

TEN COMMANDMENTS. The Ten Commandments (or the Decalogue) appear twice in the Hebrew scriptures, at *Exodus* 20:1–17 and at *Deuteronomy* 5:6–21. There are differences between the two listings, but the order and the general contents are substantially identical. The commandments may be grouped as follows:

- *Commandments 1–3:* God's self-identification, followed by commandments against the worship of other gods, idolatry, and misuse of the divine name (*Ex.* 20:1–7, *Dt.* 5:6–11).
- *Commandments 4–5:* Positive commands to observe the Sabbath and to honor parents (*Ex.* 20:8–12, *Dt.* 5:12–16).
- *Commandments 6–7:* Prohibitions of violent acts against neighbors, namely, killing and adultery (*Ex.* 20:13–14, *Dt.* 5:17–18).
- *Commandments 8–10:* Prohibitions of crimes against community life, namely, stealing, testifying falsely, and hankering after the life and goods of neighbors (*Ex.* 20:15–17, *Dt.* 5:19–21).

In the Jewish and Christian communities the order has occasionally varied, and the numbering has varied considerably, especially in the different Christian communions. Tables listing the various enumerations can be found in works by Harrelson (1980) and Nielsen (1968). The prologue with which the list opens, both in *Exodus* and in *Deuteronomy,* belongs to the Ten Commandments: "I am the Lord your God, who brought you out of the land of Egypt, out of the house of bondage." In the oldest listing of the "Ten Words" (*Ex.* 34:28), the prologue may not have appeared, but it became attached to the list early in Israel's history, setting the demands of God into the context of divine grace and mercy.

The origin of the Ten Commandments is traditionally traced to Moses. There is no adequate reason to doubt the accuracy of the tradition, even though the present form of the Ten Commandments is considerably later than Moses' time. None of the individual commandments, which were probably originally brief, pithy prohibitions of actions ruled out in principle, requires a dating later than the time of Moses. The grouping of the ten may belong to the time when the tribes of Israel had settled in Canaan and maintained ties across tribal lines; some scholars would assign the collection to a later time, perhaps to the ninth century BCE. The closest analogies to the Ten Commandments in the Hebrew scriptures appear in the curse ritual of *Deuteronomy* 27:15–16 and in portions of the section of the Torah sometimes called the "Book of the Covenant" (*Ex.* 20:23–23:33). See, for example, *Exodus* 21:15–17, where short, categorial legal pronouncements appear.

The Ten Commandments are alluded to in a number of places in the Hebrew scriptures, in the Qumran literature, and in the New Testament, although they are rarely quoted exactly and do not appear at all in a complete listing outside of *Exodus* and *Deuteronomy.* The prologue is found in a number of places (*Hos.* 13:4, *Ps.* 81:10/11), and there are lists of some of the prohibitions in several places (*Hos.* 4:2, *Mk.* 10:17–22 and parallels). But the fundamental outlook of the Ten Commandments is characteristic for the Jewish and Christian communities through the centuries. God will not have the divine name and selfhood profaned, for the Creator remains free and sovereign over against the creation. God demands rest from labor as well as labor, and he will not tolerate the mistreatment of elderly parents by adult children. God claims authority over human life and demands respect for life on the part of all. God will not permit the violation of the extended life of human beings in their social and institutional relations.

The Ten Commandments became a fixed part of Christian catechetical practice and worship. Less prominent in Islam, they are implicit in much that Muḥammad taught. In the course of Christian history they have frequently contributed to narrowness of vision and legalism. Yet it seems likely that they have contributed much more by way of positive guidance to the community. Negatively put categorical statements of this sort provide moral orientation of the community, the defining characteristics of a people, showing what is simply not allowed. The Ten Commandments require positive statements of what idolatry means, what murder is, how the Sabbath is to be observed, and the like. They constitute not so much a constriction of human freedom as an invitation to the community to claim its proper freedom within the confines of what would be ruinous for it.

SEE ALSO Israelite Law, overview article; Israelite Religion.

BIBLIOGRAPHY

Greenberg, Moshe. "Decalogue." In *Encyclopaedia Judaica,* vol. 5. Jerusalem, 1971.

Harrelson, Walter. *The Ten Commandments and Human Rights.* Philadelphia, 1980.

Nielsen, Eduard. *The Ten Commandments in New Perspective.* Naperville, Ill., 1968.

Stamm, J. J., with M. E. Andrew. *The Ten Commandments in Recent Research.* 2d ed. Naperville, Ill., 1967.

WALTER HARRELSON (1987)

TENDAISHŪ. The Japanese Tendai School takes its name from the Tiantai (Japanese, Tendai) School in China, which was located on Mount Tiantai. Japanese monks carefully studied the Tiantai texts they obtained in China, but after the ninth century CE relatively little exchange occurred between the Chinese and Japanese schools. As a result, Japanese Tendai developed in ways that were frequently distinct from its Chinese antecedent. In the following paragraphs the institutional development of the school is discussed, followed by some of its doctrinal developments.

INSTITUTIONAL HISTORY. Tendai was initially based on writings by the Tiantai exegetes Zhiyi (538–597 CE) and Zhanran (711–782 CE) that had been brought to Japan by Jianzhen (Japanese, Ganjin, 688–763 CE). The de facto founder of the school, Saichō (767–822 CE, also known by his posthumous title Dengyō daishi) was able to obtain these texts while he was practicing on Mount Hiei and was so impressed by them that he traveled to China to obtain better copies. When Saichō returned from China in 805 CE, he found that the court was more interested in the Esoteric Buddhist *(mikkyō)* doctrines he brought back than in Tiantai doctrine. As a reward for performing Esoteric rituals to heal the emperor's illness, Saichō was awarded two yearly ordinands by the court; this marks the establishment of the school. Saichō's understanding of Esoteric Buddhism did not equal that of Kūkai (774–835 CE), founder of the Shingon school, who returned to Japan in 806 CE. As a result the Tendai monks Ennin (794–864 CE) and Enchin (814–891 CE) traveled to China, where they spent more time studying Esoteric Buddhism than Kūkai, brought back more texts than Kūkai, and introduced new rituals that appealed to patrons from the imperial family and the noble classes. Consequently, the school flourished and successfully competed with Shingon.

Still a small group of monks 120 years after Saichō's death, the Tendai school was significantly less influential than its long-time rival, the Hossō school. Although it had enjoyed sporadic successes, particularly under Ennin and Enchin, the school had sunk into a period of decline. Tendai was revived and came to dominate the Japanese Buddhist world during the administration of Ryōgen (912–985 CE). When many of the buildings on Mount Hiei burned down in 966 CE, shortly after he had assumed the leadership of the school as *zasu*, Ryōgen obtained funding to rebuild them from Fujiwara Morosuke (908–960 CE), the power behind the throne. In return for Morosuke's support, Ryōgen ordained Morosuke's son Jinzen (943–990 CE) and designated him as the next Tendai *zasu*. Jinzen's relatives later assumed many leadership positions in the Tendai school and controlled many of the lands that Morosuke had given to Tendai; they performed Esoteric rituals to insure their clan's continuing domination of the Japanese political scene.

Ryōgen also renovated Tendai education through a system of debate. Tendai scholar-monks were expected to memorize vast amounts of literature, to be able to recite passages relevant to doctrinal problems, and then to resolve any contradictions between the texts. Monks who excelled at this were given high appointments by the court. As a result Tendai finally came to dominate Hossō and Shingon. Ryōgen was also responsible for improvements to Tendai Esoteric rituals, making them more elaborate or using them in new ways to attract the patronage of the nobility.

The introduction of the nobility into the governance of Tendai resulted in a number of significant changes in Tendai. Noble lineages came to control a number of cloisters, called *monzeki*, thereby limiting access for commoners to the positions of authority in Tendai. The transmission of special Esoteric rituals and secret doctrines within such lineages contributed to increasing factional tendencies within Tendai. Separate lineages representing both Esoteric and Exoteric teaching formed. In addition, the lands controlled by Tendai institutions had to be administered and protected, resulting in special classes of monks who performed these functions.

Tendai monks had engaged in factional disputes with Hossō and Shingon monks from early in Tendai history. These factional tendencies eventually turned inward, partially because of competition among lineages for patronage and control of the Esoteric rituals that appealed to the nobility. The origins of this particularly virulent dispute began with a debate over who should succeed Saichō's disciple Gishin (781–833 CE) as *zasu*. The factions eventually coalesced around those who traced their lineages back to two of the great figures of Tendai Esoteric Buddhism, Ennin and Enchin. The connection with Esoteric Buddhism was not accidental, because this tradition valued the integrity of ritual lineages that preserved secrets connected with the performance of rituals. Because the rituals were conducted for the nobility, considerable economic advantages accrued to those who could preserve the secrecy of their lineage. Arguments continued to revolve around appointments as *zasu* and abbots of major temples until the monks in Enchin's lineage were forced to withdraw from Mount Hiei and make Onjōji (also known as Miidera), located at the foot of Mount Hiei, their base late in the tenth century, near the end of Ryōgen's tenure as *zasu*. The tensions between the two groups continued to erupt sporadically in subsequent centuries, occasionally resulting in bloodshed and the burning of each other's temples. Both groups were further subdivided into ritual and doctrinal lineages that used oral transmissions (*kuden*) to propagate their teachings and ritual practices.

The Tendai educational system was so influential during the medieval period that virtually all of the founders of the Kamakura schools of Buddhism received their early training in Tendai institutions. Several, such as Hōnen (1133–1212) and Eisai (1141–1215), remained Tendai monks for most of their lives.

The end of much of Mount Hiei's secular power came in 1571 as part of Oda Nobunaga's (1534–1582) efforts to reunify Japan. To do so he had to eliminate rival political and military powers. Because Tendai had long been involved in Japanese politics through the many monks with noble lineages, Oda ordered his troops to make an example of Mount Hiei. They burned all of the mountain's monasteries and killed as many monks, women, and children as they could find. Tendai influence was eventually reestablished, though never to the extent it had enjoyed earlier, by Tenkai (1536?–1643), who obtained the support of Tokugawa Ieyasu (1542–1616), the first military ruler of the Tokugawa period. Tenkai gathered many of the surviving Tendai texts, reinstituted the Tendai educational system and its associated rituals, established Nikkō as a mausoleum for Ieyasu and his descendants, and founded Kan'eiji as the equivalent of Mount Hiei in the new capital, Tokyo.

During the middle of the Tokugawa period, a movement to reform the Tendai school by changing the ordination system was begun by Myōryū (1637–1690), a monk who had first been ordained in the Rinzai Zen tradition and then converted to Tendai after reading through the Buddhist canon. Myōryū noted that Saichō had stated that *bodhisattva* monks should first be ordained with the Mahāyāna *bodhisattva* precepts from the *Brahmā's Net Sūtra* (*Fanwangjing*), a Chinese Buddhist apocryphal text. According to Saichō, monks were then to be ordained with the 250 precepts used by all monks in East Asia from *Four-Part Vinaya* (*Sifenlu*) after they had finished twelve years of practice on Mount Hiei. Until that point almost all Tendai monks had rejected the *Sifenlu* precepts. Myōryū and his disciple Reikū (1652–1739) gained the patronage of ordained members of the imperial family and the military government to advance their case. Another monk, Shinryū (b. 1711), eventually criticized the reform movement, and the military government ordered that all Tendai monks were to be ordained with only the *bodhisattva* precepts. Even though the effort to reinstitute Hīnayāna ordinations failed, other parts of the reform movement succeeded, including a 1689 prohibition on an Esoteric ritual and oral transmission that affirmed that all desire, just as it is, was ultimate truth (homage to the profound tenet, *genshi kimyōdan*). The decline of *hongaku* thought and a renewed emphasis on Chinese Tiantai doctrine followed.

Following World War II and the installation of laws allowing more freedom to religion, Tendai split into approximately twenty groups, largely because of institutional and economic reasons, the most important of which is still called Tendaishū. It maintains two colleges that contribute to the training of its monks, Taishō University in Tokyo and Eizan gakuin at the foot of Mount Hiei. In addition, a few monks still practice assiduously on Mount Hiei, with an occasional monk undergoing twelve years of seclusion at the Pure Land Chapel (Jōdoin), the site of Saichō's mausoleum. Others circumambulate Mount Hiei (*kaihōgyō*), treating it like a *maṇḍala*, for periods ranging up to seven years. Those who complete the seven-year practice (an average of one person a decade) are lionized as living buddhas. The Tendai constantly walking meditation, a continuous ninety-day circumambulation of Amida Buddha, has also been revived. Since the 1990s, women have been playing a more significant role, receiving training and occasionally becoming abbesses of temples. On a more popular level, the school has instituted a campaign with the slogan "Light up your corner," based on a quotation from one of Saichō's works. It also sponsored a number of interfaith peace conferences while Yamada Etai (1895–1994) was head of the school.

Like other schools of Japanese Buddhism, modern Tendai is beset by a number of basic problems. The school must figure out a means to educate and inspire young monks, many of whom become monks because they come from temple families, not because they are excited about Buddhism. Poor temples in the country need better support and are short of monks. The role of women, both temple wives and nuns, is not clear. Tendai needs to find better ways of reaching out to both current and potential parishioners. Tendai programs in social welfare are not clearly defined. Such problems are not unique to Tendai, but their solutions will certainly affect the future of the school.

Doctrinal Issues. After Saichō returned from China, he wrote a document describing the lineages of the teachings he received in China: Tendai, Esoteric Buddhism, *bodhisattva* precepts, and Chan. Besides these, several other doctrinal movements came to play important roles within Tendai, including Pure Land, Shinto (Sannō Shintō), and an extension of Tendai doctrine that is referred to by twentieth-century scholars as "original enlightenment thought" (*hongaku shisō*). In the following discussion these are surveyed under the rubrics of Tendai and original enlightenment, Esoteric Buddhism, *bodhisattva* precepts, and Pure Land.

Tendai doctrine. Chinese Tiantai doctrine regarded the *Lotus Sūtra* as the Buddha's highest teaching. In fact, the school was sometimes called the Tendai Hokkeshū (Tendai Lotus school). This sūtra was used to harmonize the various teachings within Buddhism (*kaie*), demonstrating that all other forms of Buddhism were expedient means leading up to the universal teaching of One-vehicle to salvation. However, the *Lotus Sūtra* could also be used to reject expedient teachings in favor of the ultimate teaching (*haigon ryūjitsu*). Much of later Tendai doctrinal history consists of how monastic scholars combined other Buddhist teachings with those of the *Lotus Sūtra*, using both the inclusive and the exclusive approaches to expedient teachings.

The majority of Saichō's writings were polemical, defending his position against the claims of Hossō monks. When he died at the comparatively young age of fifty-five, he had not systematized his views on a variety of issues, including the interpretation of the *bodhisattva* precepts and how Esoteric and Exoteric Buddhism had the same purport. His successor, Gishin, who had accompanied Saichō to China, did not even mention these issues in a handbook of Tendai doctrine he submitted to the court. Some of Saichō's disciples tried to remedy these deficiencies by writing sets of questions to their Chinese counterparts (Tōketsu), but in many cases the two sides seemed to be talking past each other. The unfinished quality of Saichō's positions turned out to work in Tendai's favor. The ninth century was marked by remarkable creativity as Tendai monks traveled to China in search of new teachings and clarification.

Although much of Japanese Tendai doctrine is based on the three major works by Zhiyi and their commentaries by Zhanran, Japanese monks did much more than simply write commentaries that reflected Chinese concerns and interpretations. Instead, they had their own concerns in reading and interpreting Chinese texts, sometimes taking passages out of context and pushing them in new directions. Most of Saichō's writings had been polemical attacks on Hossō and defenses of Tendai in which he sometimes took terms from Chinese texts and gave them a new emphasis. Occasionally he used terms that had not appeared before. For example, terms such as *sokushin jōbutsu* (the realization of buddhahood with this very body), *jikidō* (direct path), and *sōmoku jōbutsu* (the realization of buddhahood by trees and grasses) were found in Chinese Tiantai texts, but in Japanese Tendai they received a new emphasis. At first Japanese monks attempted to enlist Chinese help in clarifying these teachings, writing letters to China in which they asked about doctrine, but eventually Japanese Tendai doctrine developed in unique ways, helped by the paucity of direct contact between Chinese Tiantai and Japanese Tendai after Enchin's travels. Japanese monks explored these issues through a debate system in which they might take issues out of context and develop them in new ways.

From the late Heian period to the middle of the Edo period, much of Tendai thought was concerned with a movement that has been called *hongaku* thought by twentieth-century scholars. The locus classicus of the term *hongaku,* often translated as "original enlightenment," is in a Chinese apocryphal text, the *Dasheng qixin lun* (Awakening of faith in the Mahāyāna), where it is found with two other terms, *shikaku* (realized enlightenment) and *fukaku* (nonenlightenment). *Hongaku* referred to the concept that all sentient beings had an intrinsic quality of enlightenment that provided the bases for both realized enlightenment and nonenlightenment. Through assiduous practice a person could realize enlightenment and leave nonenlightenment. The term *hongaku thought* is a modern term used to refer to Japanese Tendai texts that discuss the implications of original enlightenment, often adopting a position that affirms this world just as it is without any need for practice. The dissociation of original enlightenment and realized enlightenment is epitomized by the mythical claim that Ryōgen bestowed *hongaku* teachings on his student Genshin (942–1017) and teachings about realized enlightenment on his student Kakuun (953–1007), thereby suggesting that *hongaku* could be interpreted as an independent term instead of in association with practice.

The development of *hongaku* thought has often been characterized as a degenerate phase of Tendai because it is characterized by the flagrant disregard of historical precedent, the production of texts attributed to major Tendai figures of the past, and a seeming disregard for traditional (and sometimes for all) forms of practice. However, *hongaku* texts exhibited a wide variety of attitudes toward traditional doctrine and practice. Some, such as those written by Kōen (1263–1317) of the Kurodani lineage (discussed below) advocated the reestablishment of Saichō's twelve-year period of seclusion. Other texts, such as the *Shinnyokan* (Discernment of suchness) required little more than a firm belief that one was already a buddha. A number of strategies were employed in *hongaku* texts to justify creative doctrinal positions, including the creation of sources, secret oral transmissions, word play, and associations of unrelated terms. These innovative teachings were justified by regarding subjective interpretations (often called mind discernment or *kanjin*) above doctrines that relied on Scripture.

More traditional forms of Tendai scholarship continued to survive during this period. Figures such as Hōchibō Shōshin (1131?–1215?) and Jitsudō Ninkū (1307–1388) wrote commentaries, essays, and debate manuals that displayed meticulous care with historical sources. Shōshin in particular was known for his careful differentiation of Chinese and Japanese doctrinal views.

Tendai Esoteric Buddhism. Tendai's most immediate problem after Saichō's death was competing with the Esoteric Buddhist tradition represented by Kūkai's Shingon school. The Tendai school occasionally used the term *Shingon school* to refer to its Esoteric teachings. The two Esoteric traditions are sometimes differentiated by calling Tendai Esoteric Buddhism "Taimitsu" and Kūkai's school "Tōmitsu"; however, Tōmitsu is usually referred to as the Shingon school. Much about the Esoteric traditions Saichō received in China and his understanding of them remains obscure; in fact, the texts Saichō is said to have received in China may have been written by Annen (841–889? CE) to bolster Tendai claims to Esoteric lineages. However, Saichō's insistence on the agreement of the purport of the Perfect Teaching and Esoteric Buddhism has been a hallmark of Taimitsu. The inferiority of Saichō's transmission of Esoteric Buddhist ritual led to Tendai monks such as Ennin traveling to China, where he studied for nine years, from 838 to 847 CE. He collected 508 texts in 802 fascicles, more than Kūkai, studied the Sanskritic *siddhaṃ* script, and brought back new rituals. He also established a Dhāraṇī Hall in which the ritual of Abundant Flames (*shijōkōhō*) was to be performed to protect the emperor and the state, thus giving Tendai the ritual apparatus to compete successfully with Tōmitsu at court. Ennin also wrote the first major commentaries on the *Vajraśekhara Sūtra* and the *Susiddhikara Sūtra.* Along with the *Mahāvairocana Sūtra,* these three major texts form the basis of the threefold system of Esoteric Buddhism upon which Taimitsu was based. Enchin studied in China from 853 to 858 CE under the Chinese Esoteric Buddhist master Fazhuan, the same master Ennin had trained under, and also brought back a large number of texts and ritual traditions. Enchin was the author of a number of texts that explained the connection between Esoteric Buddhism and Tendai. For example, he argued that the *Mahāvairocana Sūtra* should be classified with the *Lotus Sūtra* in the Tendai system of five periods.

Esoteric Buddhism was eventually systematized by Annen. Although he did not travel to China, Annen collected all of the texts and practices he could and strove to explain and reconcile the differences he encountered. In addition, he was acutely aware of Kūkai's tradition and defended Tendai interpretations against criticisms from Tōmitsu sources, even as he borrowed elements of Kūkai's teachings.

Tendai Esoteric Buddhism is marked by several factors that differentiate it from Shingon. While Shingon argues for the nonduality of the Womb and Diamond-realm *maṇḍalas*, Tendai added another tradition, that found in the *Susiddhikara Sūtra* (*Soshitsujikyō*). This gave Taimitsu added elements of practice that helped it compete with Tōmitsu. Saichō had argued that the *Lotus Sūtra* and Esoteric Buddhism had the same import; in contrast, Kūkai had given Tendai and the *Lotus Sūtra* relatively low rankings in his classification of doctrine. Later Tendai monks had striven to clarify the Tendai view. Saichō's student Kōjō (779–858 CE) developed an Esoteric ritual for the *Lotus Sūtra.* Ennin argued that all of Buddhism could be encompassed in "One Great Perfect Teaching" (*ichidai engyō*), a classification that identified the essence of all teachings. However, he also needed to differentiate teachings in a hierarchical manner. Because the *Lotus Sūtra* claimed that it was a hidden teaching revealed only as the end of Śākyamuni's life, it could be interpreted as a hidden or Esoteric teaching. At the same time, because the *Lotus Sūtra* did not have the ritual elements found in Esoteric texts, Ennin argued that, although both the *Mahāvairocana Sūtra* and the *Lotus Sūtra* were doctrinally the highest teaching, only the *Mahāvairocana Sūtra* included the most superior practices.

Annen further refined these teachings with a classification called the "four ones": one Buddha, one time, one place, and one teaching. Like Ennin's One Great Perfect Teaching, Annen stressed the unity of Buddhist teachings. This teaching was based on the identity of the *dharmakāya* with the entire cosmos and the teaching that the *dharmakāya* preached. Annen also had to explain how Buddhism could be classified in a hierarchical fashion, which he did by adding a fifth category—Esoteric teachings—to the traditional fourfold Tendai doctrinal system: Hīnayāna, shared, distinct, and Perfect teachings. Esoteric teachings were thus given the highest position. Annen so identified Tendai with Esoteric teachings that he used the term *Shingon* (mantra) to refer to his teachings.

The agreement of the *Lotus Sūtra* and Esoteric Buddhism can be seen in Tendai discussions of several doctrines. Saichō based his argument on the realization of buddhahood with this very body (*sokushin jōbutsu*) on the story of the realization of the eight-year-old Nāga girl in the *Lotus Sūtra.* In discussions by later Tendai monks, the definition of this rapid realization changed to become more radically sudden, with Esoteric elements sometimes added. Tendai discussions of the preaching of the *dharma*-body (*hosshin seppō*) emphasized how the various bodies of the Buddha were ultimately combined; thus the preachings of Śākyamuni could be included as aspects of the preaching of the *dharma*-body. In both of these doctrines the Tendai position differed from that found in the Shingon school. Although Annen's work marks the high point of the systematization of Taimitsu thought and practice, later monks continued to refine it, and a number of separate ritual lineages emerged.

The most important text for Taimitsu has been the commentary of Yixing (683–727 CE) on the *Mahāvairocana Sūtra.* Tendai used a different recension of the text, the fourteen-fascicle *Darijing yishi*, than the Shingon school, which used the twenty-fascicle *Darijing shu.* Although the two recensions did not differ significantly doctrinally, ritual differences were evident.

Esoteric Buddhism also decisively influenced two other traditions: the practice of circumambulating mountain peaks (*kaihōgyō*) and the Sannō tradition of Shinto. *Kaihōgyō* is said to have begun with the monk Sōō (831–918 CE), who established a temple called Mudōji on Mount Hiei as the base for the practice. In its fully developed form a practitioner (only men perform this practice) takes a vow to travel on set courses for one thousand days spread over seven years. Traveling the course is compared to traveling through a *maṇḍala*, with the practitioner paying homage to deities at around three hundred sites. After seven hundred days of circumambulation, the practitioner undergoes a nine-day period without food, water, sleep, or lying down. He then completes the practice, extending his circumambulation down to Kyoto. Upon completing the practice, he is received by the emperor. Once a practitioner has taken a vow to begin the practice, he is not permitted to end his austerities early. In fact he carries a knife to end his life if he cannot finish the practice.

The Tiantai school in China honored a deity who protected its headquarters. In a similar manner, Hie taisha was established at the foot of Mount Hiei as the focal point of a cult to honor the deities that protected the Tendai school on Mount Hiei. As time passed the numbers of shrines and deities increased. By the Kamakura period deities were considered manifestations of various buddhas and *bodhisattvas.* Tendai doctrine was used to give the system more coherence. The term *Sannō* (mountain king) by which this form of Shintō was known consisted of two characters, the first made up of three vertical strokes joined by a single horizontal stroke and the second consisting of three horizontal strokes and one vertical stroke. The very name of the cult called to mind the unity of the three truths. The separation of Shintō and Buddhism during the Meiji Restoration resulted in the independence of the Sannō cult from Tendai.

Precepts and monastic discipline. Near the end of his life, Saichō proposed that the *Four-Part Vinaya* ordination traditionally used throughout East Asia be abandoned as inferior Hīnayāna and that a Mahāyāna ordination based on the Mahāyāna *bodhisattva* precepts found in the *Brahmā's Net Sūtra* and *Lotus Sūtra* be substituted for it. Neither source had been compiled with the objective of serving as the basis of monastic discipline. Perhaps in recognition of this, Saichō had proposed that his monks receive a "provisional Hīnayāna ordination" after spending twelve years on Mount Hiei. This would have enabled the monks to participate in monastic assemblies with monks from other schools. One week after his death the court approved Saichō's proposal, but his premature death had prevented him from specifying how this change was to be implemented.

During the subsequent centuries the precepts were interpreted in a variety of ways based on these sources. For example, *Questions and Answers on the Rules for Students* (*Gakushōshiki mondō*), a later text attributed to Saichō, claimed that the precepts were primarily based on the *Lotus Sūtra*, a text that actually contained little in the way of explicit instructions concerning monastic discipline. Monks could violate the precepts as long as they adhered to the *Lotus Sūtra*, a vague requirement. During the late Heian period and the Kamakura period a number of monks attempted to introduce stricter interpretations of the precepts. Shunjō (1166–1227) traveled to China, learned that Tiantai monks were still ordained with the precepts from the *Four-Part Vinaya*, and returned to Japan to introduce the practice to Tendai. He was criticized by other Tendai monks for deviating from Saichō's plan and had to make his headquarters at Sennyūji in Kyōto.

The monks in the Kurodani lineage of Tendai combined the *Lotus Sūtra* with the precepts of the *Brahmā's Net Sūtra*. Ejin (d. 1289) and Kōen revived monastic discipline by following Saichō's instructions for a twelve-year period of sequestration on Mount Hiei. At the end of that period a monk received a "consecrated" ordination (*kaikanjō*), which was based on *hongaku* thought. Sitting side by side with his teacher in a scene reminiscent of the two buddhas that appeared together in the *Lotus Sūtra*, the student was told that he had realized buddhahood with his current body. The tradition, however, carried the seeds of its own degeneration because the new "buddha" was told that he could create new precepts and teachings as needed.

Ninkū, who was active in both the Tendai and Seizan sect of the Jōdo School, relied on a commentary on the *Brahmā's Net Sūtra* by Zhiyi and detailed sets of temple rules to restore monastic discipline. A key part of his agenda was identifying the *Brahmā's Net* precepts as a Perfect teaching and thus as profound as the *Lotus Sūtra*. He also argued that the *Brahmā's Net* precepts should not be interpreted in terms of Esoteric Buddhism and Pure Land, thereby preserving the integrity of the precepts. When they had been interpreted in terms of these other traditions, the argument could be made that the recitation of the Buddha's name *(nembutsu)* or a magical incantation *(dhāraṇī)* would vanquish huge amounts of bad karma.

Finally, as mentioned above, during the Tokugawa period several monks from the Anrakuritsuin on Mount Hiei attempted to require all Tendai monks to undergo ordinations based on the *Four-Part Vinaya* but were eventually defeated. Thus Saichō's reform of monastic discipline led to a wide variety of interpretations of the precepts, many of which contributed to the lax observance of monastic rules.

Pure Land. The ninety-day constantly walking meditation, one of the four meditations described by Zhiyi, focuses on the circumambulation of an image of Amida (Amitābha) accompanied by the recitation of Amida's name, progresses to a visualization of the Buddha, and concludes with a contemplation on emptiness. This meditation provided the ritual basis of Tendai Pure Land but was performed only infrequently according to Zhiyi's directions on Mount Hiei. Although Saichō had specified that all four of Zhiyi's types of meditation be practiced on Mount Hiei, he did not live long enough to put the constantly walking meditation into effect. Ennin brought the first Pure Land practices used on Mount Hiei when he returned from China, a practice called the Uninterrupted Recitation of the Buddha's Name (*fudan nembutsu*) from Wutai Shan, China, that was based on rituals instituted by Fazhao (d. 820? CE). These practices consisted of the recitation of the *Omituojing* (Sūtra on Amitābha) rather than the much simpler recitation of the Buddha's name mentioned in the constantly walking meditation. The practice generally lasted only seven days, shorter than the ninety days required by Zhiyi, and became popular in Japan. It was more concerned with extinguishing the karmic effects of wrongdoing and being reborn in the Pure Land than with the discernment of emptiness. Thus from the beginning Tendai Pure Land ranged over a variety of possible practices and goals, from meditations that focused on a realization of emptiness or the Pure Land in this life and world to oral recitations that resulted in rebirth into a paradisiacal Pure Land when one died. This ambiguity was reflected in the term *nembutsu*, which could refer to either a meditation on the Buddha or the recitation of his name.

Genshin, the most able Tendai exegete of the tenth century, systematized Tendai Pure Land thought. Although he was skilled in doctrinal topics, including Hossō and logic, he is primarily remembered for his authorship of the *Ōjō yōshū* (Essentials of rebirth in the Pure Land), a text that included many of the ambiguities in practice and goal mentioned above because the practices could be used by a variety of people. The text included vivid descriptions of the hells and Pure Land that influenced many. Temples such as the Byōdōin reflected efforts to create architectural images of the Pure Land. Genshin's text also included discussions of deathbed rites and doctrinal issues connected with Pure Land. It had an immediate effect leading to the formation of several organizations devoted to Pure Land practice, including the Assembly for the Advancement of Learning (Kangaku-e) and the Assembly for the Concentration on the Twenty-five Bodhisattvas (Nijūgo zanmai-e), groups that included both lay and monastic practitioners. Pure Land practices were later spread by a variety of men with Tendai affiliations, including Kōya (903–972 CE) and Ryōnin (1072–1132), founder of the Yūzū nembutsushū. Hōnen, founder of the Jōdoshū, spent most of his life as a Tendai monk, and Shinran (1173–1263), founder of the Jōdo Shinshū, was trained on Mount Hiei.

Some Tendai practitioners considered Pure Land practices easier because the recitation of the Buddha's name could be done by anyone and vanquished large amounts of bad karma. For other practitioners, Pure Land practice was difficult. Uncertainty about whether one's rebirth into the Pure Land was assured led some to focus incessantly on the purification of their thoughts. Salvation was only ensured at death when the practitioner died comfortably with a mind focused on the Buddha. Such fervent practice sometimes led to vivid dreams and visions of the Pure Land, events that were often recorded in the biographies of those reborn in the Pure Land (*Ōjōden*).

Pure Land practices in Tendai were not conducted separately from other practices. A popular saying, "Recitation of the *Lotus Sūtra* in the morning and the recitation of the Buddha's name (*nembutsu*) at night," reflects the typical Tendai attitude. Esoteric Buddhist practices were sometimes mixed with Pure Land rituals because Amida was found in various maṇḍalas. Moreover when Tendai followers stressed the oral recitation of the *nembutsu*, the contemplative aspect was also present. The emphasis on creating a Pure Land in this world coexisted with beliefs in rebirth in a Pure Land located far from this one. In addition, Tendai monks such as Ninkū and Shinzei (1443–1495) emphasized that the precepts must be observed while the *nembutsu* is chanted. Tendai views of Pure Land thus differed in important ways from Jōdo and Jōdo Shin traditions, which argued that the recitation of the Buddha's name was the only way to salvation.

SEE ALSO Tiantai.

BIBLIOGRAPHY

Adolphson, Mikael S. *The Gates of Power: Monks, Courtiers, and Warriors in Premodern Japan.* Honolulu, 2000.

Dobbins, J. C. "A Brief History of Pure Land Buddhism in Early Japan." In *Engaged Pure Land Buddhism: Challenges Facing Jōdo Shinshū in the Contemporary World: Studies in Honor of Professor Alfred Bloom*, edited by Kenneth Tanaka and Eisho Nasu, pp. 113–165. Berkeley, Calif., 1998.

Fukuda Gyōei. *Tendaigaku gairon.* Tokyo, 1959.

Groner, Paul. "The *Lotus Sūtra* and Saichō's Interpretation of the Realization of Buddhahood with This Very Body (*sokushin jōbutsu*)." In *The Lotus Sūtra in Japanese Culture*, edited by George J. Tanabe Jr. and Willa Tanabe, pp. 53–74. Honolulu, 1989.

Groner, Paul. "The *Fan-wang ching* and Monastic Discipline in Japanese Tendai: A Study of Annen's *Futsū jubosatsukai kōshaku.*" In *Chinese Buddhist Apocrypha*, edited by Robert E. Buswell Jr., pp. 251–290. Honolulu, 1990.

Groner, Paul. "Shortening the Path: The Interpretation of the Realization of Buddhahood in This Very Existence in the Early Tendai School." In *Paths to Liberation: The Mārga and Its Transformations in Buddhist Thought*, edited by Robert E. Buswell Jr. and Robert M. Gimello, pp. 439–474. Honolulu, 1992.

Groner, Paul. *Saichō: The Establishment of the Japanese Tendai School.* Honolulu, 2000.

Groner, Paul. *Ryōgen and Mount Hiei: Japanese Tendai in the Tenth Century.* Honolulu, 2002.

Groner, Paul. "Jitsudō Ninkū on Ordinations." *Nichibunken Japan Review* 15 (2003): 51–75.

Hazama Jikō. *Nihon Bukkyō no kaiten to sono kichō.* 2 vols. Tokyo, 1948–1953. Vol. 2 contains a discourse on the Tendai thought of Original Enlightenment.

Hazama Jikō. *Tendaishū shi gaisetsu.* Edited by Ōkubo Ryōjun. Tokyo, 1969.

Misaki Ryōshū. *Taimitsu no kenkyū.* Tokyo, 1988.

Ōkubo Ryōshun. *Tendai kyōgaku to hongaku shisō.* Kyōto, Japan, 1998.

Ōkubo Ryōshun. *Taimitsu kyōgaku no kenkyū.* Kyōto, Japan, 2004.

Rhodes, Robert. "The *Kaihōgyō* Practice of Mt. Hiei." *Japanese Journal of Religious Studies* 14, nos. 2–3 (1987): 185–202.

Shimaji Daitō. *Tendai kyōgakushi.* Tokyo, 1929.

Stone, Jacqueline I. *Original Enlightenment and the Transformation of Medieval Japanese Buddhism.* Honolulu, 1999.

Sueki Fumihiko. *Heian shoki Bukkyō shisō no kenkyū: Annen no shisō keisei wo chūshin to shite.* Tokyo, 1995.

Tamura Kōyū. *Saichō kyōgaku no kenkyū.* Tokyo, 1992.

Uesugi Bunshū. *Nihon Tendai shi.* 2 vols. Nagoya, Japan, 1935.

Weinstein, Stanley. "The Beginnings of Esoteric Buddhism in Japan." *Journal of Asian Studies* 34, no. 1 (1974): 177–191.

PAUL GRONER (2005)

TENGRI. The earliest attested occurrence of a word in an Altaic language is the transcription into Chinese of the word *tengri* in the *Qian Han shu* (*juan* 94). It has kept this or a related form (*tenggeri, tanara, tängri, tanri, tari*, et al.) down to the present day. Etymologically, the word appears to be linked with a verb that means "to turn." It has been used continuously, not only by the "shamanistic" or "animistic" Turco-Mongols but also by those who have adopted universal religions. I shall concern myself here only with its meaning in the former case.

The original use of the word *tengri* was in designating the physical sky, as in such statements as "The sun is in the sky" or "The clouds darken the sky." This long-held meaning eventually was lost. With the deification of the sky, the word took on two other interpretations as well, either that of sky god or the more vague sense of "god," "deity," and, adjectivally, "celestial" and "divine." It is not always possible to determine whether *tengri* is being used as an adjective or a noun.

Deities Named Tengri. At the same time that Tengri the sky god emerges (second half of the first millennium CE), Old Turkic inscriptions mention various deities named Tengri, but little information is available on these. Yol Tengri is the "god of roads or paths" or "god of luck" (*yol* has these two meanings), Öd Tengri is the "god of weather"; there is a Tengri who lies among the reeds as well. No evidence indicates the nature of the relationship between these characters and the sky god. Any attempt to make such a determination is complicated by the fact that the same inscriptions more often refer to much greater divine powers that were never called *tengri*. "Venerated" or "worshiped" celestial bodies also were never called *tengri*.

From toponymy and foreign sources, we know that in certain cases mountains are called *tengri* (for example, Tengri Tag, "celestial mountain"; Chin., Tianshan), as are some lakes (for example, Tengri Nor, "celestial lake," in Mongolia). To add to the confusion, an eleventh-century observer, Maḥmūd al-Kāshgharī, remarked that the word *tengri* applies to everything that appears enormous—a huge tree, for instance. Knowing this, it is no surprise today to see the sky god, who has a greatly attenuated reality, gradually replaced by great deities who are often called Tengri. Even if one has every reason to believe that the word is an adjective, does this usage not make a god out of a divine being or object? Such is the case with certain shamans, like the one who enthroned Chinggis Khan, Teb Tenggeri ("very celestial"); certain sorcerers ("a holy old woman"); the nation ("my sacred nation"); and most of the khans ("my holy khan"). In fact, there was a Türk sovereign who had no name but Tengri Khan (*r.* 734–741). Finally, scholars are unsure to what extent something called "blue" (in Turkic languages, *kök;* Mong., *köke*), in the sense of an attribute of the sky, is to be identified with God. Examples of this usage are found among the Turkic peoples and among the Mongols; as, for instance, in the case of the Mongol emperor Möngke: Köke Möngke ("blue eternal").

The Sky God. The modern Turco-Mongol peoples who have preserved their ancient religion have less of an interest in the sky god than previously. Most often, the sky is the abode of a celestial god, sometimes anthropomorphized, who has numerous assistants—his sons and daughters, his wife, and many others. The sky is divided into levels, generally seven according to the supposed number of planets. Even in areas where Russian Orthodoxy or Buddhism has had little influence, there are many unstable *tengris*, a fact that corresponds perfectly to the traditional ideology. All attempts to classify them are wholly imposed from without and lack foundation in the tradition. As for the sky god, in areas where belief in him persists, he is nonetheless considered to be very distant. The Altaic tribes call him Tengere Kaira Khan ("merciful lord sky"), but his sons and assistants hold the real power, notably the power of creation: they are Bai Ülgen alone or together with Kysogan Tengere and Mergen Tengere. The great god of the Yakuts is Iuriung Aĭyy Toĭon ("white lord creator") or Aĭyy Toĭon. It is believed that he gradually became a *deus otiosus.* In fact, it appears that he has always been such for the masses. As early as the tenth century, Balik Bayat, "supreme old one" or "supreme wealthy one," is regarded as the creator. I must point out, however, that the ancient cosmogonies are inconsistent and that the problem of origins has only recently been addressed. When creation was later attributed to the sky god, it seems likely that it was in response to questions posed by Muslims or Christians.

The active sky god is an imperial creation that concerns only the imperial religion: the people devoted attention to him only in times when imperial power was sufficient to command widespread obedience to the deity. Occasionally, sincere devotees of the sky god would appear. Such mystics were claimed to be "slaves of Tengri," but no Islamic influence can be discerned in this appellation. The sky god appears already before the common era among the Xiongnu, then later, continually, in all the great political formations up to the fourteenth century. Under the Türk (sixth to eighth century) and under the Mongols (thirteenth to fourteenth century), he is particularly visible. The former call him "blue," "elevated" or "above," and "endowed with power"; the latter add to these qualities that he is "eternal," a characteristic supposedly long implied.

It is not an exaggeration to say that no other deity has responded so much to the needs of his loyal followers. The Turco-Mongol emperor first wanted to gather all those of his race, then the entire world. His god was national (the Tengri of the Türks and Mongols), then universal and unique. There is but one god in the sky and one sole sovereign on earth: such is the ideology. It represents a desperate but unsuccessful effort to promote monotheism; the other deities remained alive in the minds of the people and were more or less associated with the sky god. Even so, the sky god is as predominant as the emperor himself, who "comes from him," "resembles him" (and is sometimes his son), conducts privileged conversations with him, receives and transmits his orders, conquers in his name, names dignitaries in his name, rewards and punishes with death (the only punishment of Tengri, used often against those who revolt), distributes to everyone, man or beast, *kut*, a vitality that brings happiness, and *ülüg*, luck. Nevertheless, the sky god can do without the emperor when he is weakening or has lost his divine mandate. In such a case he "applies pressure," or sends his messengers: an eagle, an enigmatic angel, some rays of light often accompanied by "dazzling daughters," or the animal guides, particularly the wolf, who are none other than the imperial ancestors. Anyone can talk to the sky god, but shamans are forbidden to have closer relationships with him than the prince does: any pretension of having such a relationship will lead to the shaman's destruction. In contrast, great respect is shown to all those who are specialists in spirituality, notably to foreign priests who are protected and exempted from taxes on the condition that they pray for the emperor's longevity.

It appears that in ancient times the Tengri cult thrived for only short periods; nevertheless, it developed rapidly. Sacrifices of white horses or other animals were offered to Tengri annually or daily, usually on fixed dates or during special events. Prayer itself spread and became an essential element in the Tengri cult in the thirteenth century. Great orisons were conducted by the sovereign from an elevation where, over a period of time lasting from one to three days, he continually bowed in prayer to the sky with bare head and loosened belt. It has always been common practice to go around in a circle on horseback: this is called "going around the sky."

It is a common belief among practitioners of the Tengri cult that souls reside in Tengri before their incarnation and that the souls of the deceased return to him. In fact, when a death is announced, one says "He flew off" or "He became a gyrfalcon." The destination is specified: "He climbed to the sky with his body" and "In the sky you will be as among the living." However, beliefs probably concern particularly great personages and those who will be needed in the beyond to serve them.

SEE ALSO Buriat Religion; Chuvash Religion; Mongol Religions; Turkic Religions; Ülgen.

BIBLIOGRAPHY

For the most part, the sky god of the Altaic peoples has been studied in works relative to their religion, particularly contemporary beliefs. Wilhelm Schmidt, in his perspective of primitive monotheism, accords Tengri an eminent place in *Der Ursprung der Gottesidee,* vols. 9–12 (Münster, 1949–1955). Paul Pelliot has written primarily a linguistic work: "Tängrim> Tärim," *T'oung pao* 37 (1944): 165–185. The only monograph is my "Tängri: Essai sur le ciel-dieu des peuples altaïques," which appeared in four parts plus additional notes in *Revue de l'histoire des religions* 149 (January–March 1956): 49–82, (April–June 1956): 197–230; 150 (July–September 1956): 27–54; (October–December 1956): 173–212; and 154 (July–September 1958): 32–66.

New Sources

Birtalan, Ágnes. *Die Mythologie der Mongolischen Volksreligion.* Stuttgart, 2000.

Rona-Tas, Andras. "Materialien zur alten Religion der Turken." In *Synkretismus in den Religionen Zentralasiens: Ergebnisse eines Kolloquiums vom 24.5. bis 26.5.1983 in St. Augustin bei Bonn,* edited by Walther Heissig and Hans-Joachim Klimkeit, pp. 33–45. Wiesbaden, 1987.

JEAN-PAUL ROUX (1987)
Translated from French by Sherri L. Granka
Revised Bibliography

TENRIKYŌ. A monotheistic Japanese religion established in 1838, Tenrikyō preaches a doctrine of world renewal and individual salvation. Its founder, Nakayama Miki (1798–1887), received a revelation from Tenri Ō no Mikoto (also known as Oyagami, or "God the parent"), and became Kami no Yashiro ("the living shrine of God"). According to Tenrikyō church tradition, God revealed himself through Nakayama in order to deliver people from individual sufferings and social evils, and to prepare the way for the *kanrodai sekai* ("perfect divine kingdom"), in which humankind will enjoy *yōkigurashi* ("joyous and blissful life") in union with God the Parent. Tenrikyō spread rapidly throughout Japan during the tumultuous eclipse of the Edo period (1600–1868).

HISTORY. The eldest daughter of Maekawa Masanobu and his wife Kinu, Maekawa Miki (later, Nakayama Miki) became a pious devotee of Pure Land Buddhism early in life. Although she wished to become a nun, in obedience to her parents' wishes she married Nakayama Zembei in 1810. In her marriage she affirmed the values of worldly life through moral compassion toward others and devotion to Shintō deities. The revelation she experienced in her forty-first year resulted in a dedication to almsgiving, leading her family into extreme poverty. She affirmed her credibility by working miracles, teaching that divine protection was attainable only through a life of sincere piety. Her mission to achieve the new world order of *kanrodai sekai* was misunderstood by many, and she and her followers were persecuted for many years, she herself being imprisoned several times.

Despite intensifying persecution, Nakayama wrote two books, the *Mikagurauta* and the *Ofudesaki,* taught her disciples the movements for the Kagura Zutome ("salvation dance service"), the essential rite in Tenrikyō, and determined the location of the *jiba,* the sacred spot that is believed to be the original birthplace of humans. On the morning of January 26, 1887, she urged her disciples to perform the Kagura Zutome (which had been prohibited by the police), asking them to decide for themselves whether the laws of humankind or those of God are supreme. As they performed the service around the Kanrodai, a symbolic monument erected at the *jiba,* Nakayama died. Her followers believed that she had passed from a corporeal to a spiritual state, remaining in her sanctuary and helping them to realize God's kingdom in this world. Nakayama's ascension to this new state, together with the *hinagata* ("model life") she exemplified, became the focal point of the Tenrikyō faith.

After her passing, God spoke through Iburi Izō (1833–1907), Nakayama's most trusted disciple. The *Osashizu* was compiled from revelations made to him and fostered the emergence of a structured Tenrikyō church system. Tenrikyō was sanctioned by the government and officially classified as one of the sects of Sect Shintō in 1888. The church was then forced to alter its teachings and activities to conform to government policies. Nevertheless, Nakayama's teachings were retained intact and spread throughout Japan by 1895. Missions were established in the United States in 1896, in Taiwan in 1897, in Korea in 1898, and in China in 1901. After World War II, with the guarantee of religious freedom under the 1947 Constitution, the Fukugen ("restoration of the original teachings") movement was carried out to purify Tenrikyō teachings, which had been distorted by the influences of Shintō and state nationalism. This movement marked a step toward a redefinition of Tenrikyō as distinct from Sect Shintō. By the 1980s, Tenrikyō had approximately three million followers, with 16,664 churches and 20,039 mission stations scattered worldwide. Tenrikyō also operates social and cultural institutions, including a university, a library, a museum, a publishing house, a hospital, and an orphanage.

DOCTRINE. Tenri Ō no Mikoto ("lord of heavenly reason"), as revealed through Nakayama, is the creator of the world, and is also defined as the *moto no kami* ("original god") and the *jitsu no kami* ("true god"). God has ten attributes, which are manifested symbolically as *tohashira no kami* ("ten deities"), each representing a particular aspect of God working in the physical world. God is further posited as Tsukihi ("sun and moon") and finally as Oyagami ("God the parent"), revealing his pantheistic and immanent nature as well as his transcendental and personal existence. He is the god of parental love, who created the world in order to enjoy seeing the harmonious life of human beings. Believing in neither original sin nor the fall of man, Tenrikyō holds that the revelation was necessary to rectify human selfishness, which is contrary to God's original intent. The revelation occurred through three preordinations—the soul, the place, and the time—which are historically manifested in the soul of Nakayama, the *jiba* (the place of the original creation), and the time of revelation. This triad comprises the core of the Tenrikyō doctrine, and emphasizes the historical inevitability of the revelation.

Tenrikyō defines human physical existence as a *kashimono-karimono* ("something lent or borrowed," i.e., from God) and death as a *denaoshi* ("restart"). The progressive purification of the human heart is recognized through the process of reincarnation. Its ethical teaching is founded upon the doctrine of *yattsu no hokori* ("eight dusts"), consisting of *oshii* ("grudge"), *hoshii* ("covetousness"), *nikui* ("hatred"), *kawaii* ("selfish love"), *urami* ("enmity"), *haradachi* ("fury"), *yoku* ("greed"), and *kōman* ("arrogance"). These are defined as pollutants to be cleansed in order to uncover one's true nature and attain a state of *makoto-shinjitsu* ("sincere piety"). Salvation requires three activities. Receiving *osazuke* ("the holy grant") is the most important rite; it enables one to be reborn at the *jiba* and to become an agent of God to help others through prayers. Performing *hinokishin* ("daily service") in one's given social position is another means to achieving personal maturity. Last, frequent pilgrimages to the *jiba* are urged to renew one's faith and to enjoy a blissful and joyous life in union with God.

SCRIPTURES. The essential Tenrikyō canonical texts are the *Mikagurauta* (Songs for the sacred dance), the *Ofudesaki* (Tip of the divine writing brush), and the *Osashizu* (Divine directions), the first two personally written by Nakayama under divine inspiration and the third revealed through Iburi. Written between 1866 and 1875, the *Mikagurauta* consists of five sections. The first three comprise the verses for the Kagura Zutome service. The fourth, containing eight verses, and the fifth, consisting of twelve stanzas of ten verses each, are the songs for the Teodori (Sacred Dance) service. Revealed to Nakayama between 1869 and 1882, the *Ofudesaki* is composed of seventeen parts comprising 1,711 verses written in the 5-7-5-7-7-syllable *waka* style. This scripture introduces the basic creed of Tenrikyō and elucidates the creation of the world, the nature of God, the significance of the *jiba* and the Kanrodai, and the importance of the Kagura Zutome.

The *Osashizu,* a large collection of directions revealed to Iburi from 1887 to 1907 after Nakayama's passing, is divided into two categories: *kokugen* (prophesies and directions to meet the exigencies of salvation) and *ukagai no sashizu* (directions in response to individual inquiries). The *Osashizu* contains concrete and detailed instructions concerning church organization and personal conduct, and offers Tenrikyō adherents guidance for solving the problems of daily life.

SEE ALSO New Religious Movements, article on New Religious Movements in Japan.

BIBLIOGRAPHY

The Doctrine of Tenrikyō. Sponsored by the Tenrikyō Church Headquarters. Tenri, 1972.

Fukaya Tadamasa. *Fundamental Doctrines of Tenrikyō.* Tenri, 1973.

Mikagura-uta: The Songs for the Tsutome. Translated by the Tenrikyō Church Headquarters. Tenri, 1972.

Nakayama Shōzen. *On the Idea of God in Tenrikyō Doctrine.* Tenri, 1962.

Ofudesaki, the Tip of the Divine Writing Brush. Sponsored by the Tenrikyō Church Headquarters. Tenri, 1971.

Straelen, Henry van. *The Religion of Divine Wisdom.* Tokyo, 1954.

Tenri Daigaku Oyasato Kenkyujo. *Tenrikyō jiten.* Tenri, 1977.

Tenrikyō: Its History and Teaching. Edited by the Tenrikyō Church Headquarters. Tenri, 1966.

Tenrikyō Kyōkai Hombu, comp. *Osashizu.* 7 vols. Tenri, 1966.

Tenrikyō Year Book 1981. Sponsored by the Tenrikyō Church Headquarters. Tenri, 1981.

New Sources

Kisala, Robert. "Contemporary Karma: Interpretations of Karma in Tenrikyo and Rissho Koseikai." *Japanese Journal of Religious Studies* 21 (1994): 73–91.

Morishita, Saburo Shawn. *Teodori: Cosmological Building and Social Consolidation in a Ritual Dance.* Rome, 2000.

UEHARA TOYOAKI (1987)
Revised Bibliography

TERESA OF ÁVILA

TERESA OF ÁVILA (1515–1582), epithet of Teresa de Ahumeda y Cepeda, Christian saint, Spanish mystic, religious reformer, and author of religious classics. Teresa was born at Ávila in the Castilian region of Spain on March 28, 1515, the third child of Don Alonso Cepeda, a moderately wealthy merchant. She was a spirited child, and early in life she began to manifest deep religious feelings. When she was seven she and her eleven-year-old brother ran away from home, intending to go to the country of the Moors and offer themselves for martyrdom. Later, writing about the episode in her *Life,* she said that she had done this because she "wanted to see God." However, the adventure ended abruptly a few meters outside the walled city of Ávila when the two children met their uncle, who promptly took them home.

In her early teens Teresa took a great interest in clothes, read romantic stories, and apparently had a romance with a cousin. When she was fifteen her mother died at the age of thirty-three, having produced nine children, and her father sent Teresa to board at Our Lady of Grace Convent, a kind of finishing school for girls from comfortable families. She remained there for a year and a half, and during that period her contact with the Augustinian nuns prompted her to start thinking about a religious vocation.

Illness forced Teresa to leave the school, and she went to live with a sister to recuperate. She began to visit the Carmelite Convent of the Incarnation in Ávila to talk about becoming a nun. One of the nuns later recalled the charm and beauty of the nineteen-year-old Teresa. In 1535, at the age of twenty, Teresa entered the Convent of the Incarnation, where she remained for twenty-eight years until she left to found her own reformed Carmelite convent. At the time of Teresa's entrance the convent had 140 nuns, and although the reform movement was to emanate from it, there was nothing scandalous about life there; it was simply a comfortable and not particularly demanding existence. The nuns, especially those from affluent families, lived in a suite of rooms, often attended by a servant. They were able to visit freely outside the convent, and they spent long hours each day in the parlor visiting with outsiders. Teresa lived this type of life until she was about forty, when she experienced what she called her "conversion" while reading the *Confessions* of Augustine. From that point until the end of her life, she followed a rigorous personal program of discipline and prayer that culminated in frequent religious experiences in which she saw the Lord and heard him speak. Teresa herself described these experiences as "intellectual visions and locutions."

For seven years after her "conversion" Teresa continued to live at the Incarnation, but she began to plan the establishment of a small Carmelite convent that would follow the original Carmelite rule of 1209, which had been mitigated by Eugenius IV in 1435. She claimed that she had been encouraged to do this in her visions, but at first, there was much opposition from the nuns in the convent and other ecclesiastics. She finally obtained permission from Rome, and on August 24, 1562, along with four other nuns, she established in Ávila a convent of discalced Carmelite nuns. The word *discalced* (lit., "without shoes") referred, in the religious parlance of the time, to a reformed group that usually went barefoot or in sandals. Teresa's reformed convent in Ávila was dedicated to Saint Joseph, and the nuns who lived there followed the original Carmelite rule, rather than the mitigated one observed at the Incarnation. This meant a much stricter observance of such conventual disciplines as fasting, silence, and restriction of contact with outsiders.

Teresa, who now called herself of Teresa of Jesus, remained at that first convent for just over four years, a time later described as "the most restful years of my life." Her original intention had been to establish only that single reformed convent, but in 1567 the Carmelite general, Giovanni Rossi, on a visitation from Rome, approved Teresa's work and commanded her to establish other convents. During the next fifteen years she would personally found about one convent per year in Spain, and after her death similar reformed Carmelite convents were established all over the world.

While she was still a nun at the Incarnation, Teresa began writing an account of her life, a task she completed during the first years of her reform. She always called it her *libro grande,* but it was only the first effort in an impressive body of Christian literature. These works, never originally intended for general publication, were written at odd moments during a busy career of religious administration. She wrote four major prose works, a series of shorter works, poems, and numerous letters, of which 445 are extant. Principal among these works are *Foundations,* which describes her adventures in founding convents, *Way of Perfection,* which explains prayer, and *Interior Mansions,* which describes the dimensions of spiritual and mystical growth. Her works are considered Christian masterpieces, and she is undoubtedly one of history's great authorities on mysticism.

Teresa also developed the idea of establishing religious houses of reformed Carmelite men. She obtained permission from the general in Rome and in 1568 opened the first monastery of reformed Carmelite friars at Duruelo, twenty-five miles from Ávila. One of those original friars was Juan de Yepes y Alvarez, who was to be known to history as John of the Cross. Soon there were reformed Carmelite monasteries all over Spain, and eventually they spread around the world.

In 1582 Teresa founded the last of her fifteen convents, at Burgos. On her return trip to Ávila she was taken ill and stopped at her convent at Alba de Tormes. At sixty-seven, suffering from uterine cancer, she died there on October 4, 1582. Paul V beatified her in 1614; Gregory XV canonized her in 1622; and Paul VI, who called her "the light of the universal church," declared her a doctor of the church in 1970.

BIBLIOGRAPHY

Teresa's own writings constitute the fundamental source for her life and doctrine. The standard editions are *The Complete Works of Saint Teresa of Jesus,* 3 vols. (New York, 1946), and *The Letters of Saint Teresa of Jesus* (Westminster, Md., 1949), both translated and edited by E. Allison Peers from the critical Spanish edition of Silverio of Saint Teresa. *Saint Teresa of Ávila* (Milwaukee, 1943), by William T. Walsh, is a full and standard biography of her life, while Marcelle Auclair's *Saint Teresa of Avila* (New York, 1953) combines splendid scholarship with excellent literary style. John Beevers's *Saint Teresa of Avila* (Garden City, N. Y., 1961) is a fine and insightful short study of her life. E. Allison Peers's *Handbook to the Life and Times of Saint Teresa and Saint John of the Cross* (Westminster, Md., 1954) provides invaluable information about the social and religious milieu in which Teresa lived.

PETER T. ROHRBACH (1987)

TERTULLIAN (160?–225?), Quintus Septimius Florens, first Christian theologian to write extensively in Latin. An African, Tertullian laid the foundations for Western theology through the range of issues he addressed and his precise formulations. Although he became an adherent of the Montanist sect, his thought exerted much influence on Cyprian, bishop of Carthage (248–258), and later Latin authors.

LIFE. Little is known of Tertullian's life. Data supplied by Jerome in his *Lives of Famous Men* (392–393) were apparently inferred from remarks in Tertullian's own writings and are now generally discounted by scholars. Probably born and reared in Carthage, he received an excellent education and was considered one of the luminaries of his day. Although he employed considerable legal jargon and argument in his writing, he probably cannot be identified with the jurist Tertullianus whose opinions were cited in the *Digest* and *Codex Justinianus.* His extensive legal knowledge would have come from classical education.

Tertullian converted to Christianity around 193 to 195, doubtless attracted by the discipline of Christians, especially their willingness for martyrdom. His unusual gifts, education, and commitment quickly propelled him into a position of leadership, but, contrary to Jerome's assumption, he was never ordained a presbyter or elder in the Carthaginian church, identifying himself several times in his writings as a member of the laity. He did, however, preach or teach, for several of his writings are sermons.

Sympathetic by inclination with the rigorous views of discipline held by the Montanists, a charismatic sect that originated in Phrygia about CE 170, Tertullian veered toward that sect as the catholic church in North Africa moved away from it. For him this entailed no radical shift in views, but rather a hardening of certain ones held earlier on remarriage, flight to avoid persecution, and repentance for serious sins—all of which, as a Montanist, he prohibited absolutely. His new affiliation notwithstanding, he continued as the chief spokesman against gnosticism and Marcionism and as the major theologian in the West until Augustine.

After several years in the Montanist camp Tertullian separated from them and formed a sect of his own called Tertullianists, which still existed in Augustine's heyday (c. 400–430). This schism could well have resulted from the growing tendency of Montanists to make exaggerated claims for their founder Montanus, as Tertullian was horrified by any ideas that were not thoroughly orthodox.

Throughout his career Tertullian belonged to the literary circles in Carthage. In his writings he cited numerous classics, perhaps drawn in part from anthologies but certainly also from works he knew in depth. As a stylist, he surpassed both Jerome and Augustine. He was a creative and passionate debater whose erudition and technique place him in the second Sophistic movement. The exact date of his death is unknown.

WRITINGS. Tertullian's writings, thirty-one of which are extant, are notoriously difficult to date. They were once neatly divided into pre-Montanist, or catholic, and Montanist, according to "Montanistic" allusions. Recent studies, however, have demonstrated Montanist leanings not only in Tertullian but in early North African Christianity, hence this method has been discarded and the dating of many works revised.

The writings range across a wide spectrum, but they can be conveniently grouped under the headings of apologies for Christianity, treatises on the Christian life, and antiheretical works. In the summer of 197, Tertullian drafted two apologies, *To the Nations* and *Against the Jews,* the latter intended for Christian readers but never completed. Shortly thereafter, he revised *To the Nations* and published it as the finely argued and highly stylized *Apology,* his best-known work. In *On the Testimony of the Soul* he departed from his custom of citing scriptures and elaborated a purely psychological argument set out briefly in chapter 17 of the *Apology.* Years later, in 212, he reiterated in summary form arguments of the *Apology* in an appeal addressed to Scapula, proconsul of Africa, to halt the persecution of Christians.

Tertullian reflected a characteristic rigorist bent in the sermons and treatises on Christian life he composed throughout his brief career; his tone merely became sterner in Montanist days. In what is probably his earliest writing, *On the Shows,* dated 196 or early 197, he explained why Christians should not attend pagan games, theatrical productions, or contests. He saw no hope for the person who attended, for "he openly 'denies,' who gets rid of the distinctive mark by which he is known." To go from church to the shows is to go "from sky to stye." In *On Idolatry* he widened his prohibitions. Christians had to live with pagans, he said, but they did not have to sin with them. In *On the Dress of Women,* at least part of which was composed in his catholic years, he urged Christian women to set themselves apart from pagan women in clothing, adornment, hair style, and even in the way they walked. About the same time he exhorted Christians in *The Martyrs* to view prison as a place of withdrawal from the corrupt world and their imprisonment as discipline for heavenly citizenship.

In other treatises titled *On Baptism, On Prayer, On Repentance, On Patience,* and *To His Wife*—now dated between

198 and 203—Tertullian exhibited similar tendencies to distinguish Christian from pagan life. Those being baptized should come not to have sins forgiven, he insisted, but "because they have *ceased* sinning." For those who sin after baptism martyrdom is "a second baptism." In some contrast to his later stance in *On Modesty,* written about 210 or 211, Tertullian reluctantly followed the *Shepherd of Hermas* (c. 140) in permitting repentance for serious sins following baptism, but he openly expressed admiration for the Montanist prohibition of second marriages and refusal to grant forgiveness to fornicators or adulterers. In *To His Wife* he urged her, first, not to remarry if he should die, but then, if she should nevertheless marry again, not to marry a pagan. *On Modesty* classified second marriages, whether after the death of a spouse or not, "the same as adultery" and labeled Hermas "the shepherd of adulterers." In *On Patience* Tertullian lauded patience as the Christian virtue *par excellence,* especially in the face of death and martyrdom.

During his Montanist years, Tertullian sharpened the lines separating Christian and pagan. In *On the Wearing of the Laurel Wreath* he set forth the rule that whatever scriptures do not explicitly permit is forbidden. Since wearing the laurel was of pagan origins, it was idolatrous and thus prohibited for Christians, as was military service. In *On Flight in Persecution* Tertullian negated the more humane view presented in *To His Wife* and *On Patience* and sternly forbade escape. Persecution is God's, not the devil's, will, thus no Christian should flee. He saved his harshest words, however, for the Valentinian gnostics who encouraged the faithful to flee persecution. Their teaching he called the "scorpion's sting" in a work bearing that title. In *On Exhortation to Chastity* and *On Monogamy* the formidable rigorist stoutly defended the Montanist insistence on a single marriage and preference for celibacy. Christian perfection, he argued, descended from virginity from birth, to virginity from the new birth, to continence within marriage. Against the Marcionites, however, Tertullian did affirm the sanctity of marriage. In *On Fasting* he commended also the zeal of Montanists for more fasts. In *On the Veiling of Virgins* he urged virgins to take the veil and flee the temptations of the world.

Apart from his curious defense of his wearing the pallium as an appropriate Christian "philosopher's" dress, the remaining writings of Tertullian are antiheretical. Here, too, Tertullian manifested his separatist inclinations. "What has Jerusalem to do with Athens, the church with the academy, the Christian with the heretic?" he demanded to know. Like Irenaeus, he proceeded to set forth the "prescription" that heresy represented a departure from the truth that Christ delivered to the apostles and they to apostolic churches. He reiterated the point in the polemic *Against Hermogenes,* in which he countered the view that God created the soul from preexistent matter. In a more extensive work, *On the Soul,* Tertullian again took up his cudgels against the philosophers, "those patriarchs of the heretics." Although grudgingly admitting that some philosophers had happened on the truth, he himself insisted on obtaining truth from revelation, including that obtained through Montanist seers. A prophetess, for instance, confirmed his (and the Stoics') concept of a corporeal soul. In his five books *Against Marcion,* the longest of his writings, and in the treatises *On the Flesh of Christ* and *On the Resurrection of the Flesh* he repudiated Marcionite and Valentinian views as being of pagan origin. Similarly, the polemic *Against the Valentinians* ridiculed the Valentinian system for inconsistencies and contradictions characteristic of pagan philosophies. Finally, in *Against Praxeas* he rejected modalism in godhead on the grounds of inconsistency and its conflict with "the rule of truth."

THOUGHT. Tertullian labored assiduously to defend Christianity from the culture of his day. With that end in view he accentuated the authority of the rule of truth, a summary of the faith, and of the Bible interpreted more or less literally but with careful reference to context and his own situation. He also invented ecclesiastical Latin. These factors notwithstanding, he in no way equaled Irenaeus, whose treatise *Against Heresies* he invoked often, in development of a biblical theology. On the contrary, he drew many of his basic presuppositions from Stoicism and thus laid the ground for a distinctive Latin theology. His enduring contribution lay in his gift for finding apt formulas to state particular truths of faith.

Stoicism influenced Tertullian's concept both of God and of the soul as corporeal. He asserted that nothing can exist without a body. Thus, even though God is spirit, God is also body. So also is the soul corporeal. If it were not corporeal, it could not desert the body.

From this important assumption Tertullian deduced another: the transmission of sin through generation. Every human soul is a branch of Adam's soul; therefore, every soul inherits characteristics of Adam's soul, including sin. Tertullian, however, did not add to this a conclusion Augustine reached, that is, that guilt is also inherited.

In his refutation of modalism Tertullian won a victory for the Logos Christology of the apologists and Irenaeus. The first to use the term *Trinitas* ("trinity"), he argued that one God is simultaneously Father, Son, and Holy Spirit, not successively, as Praxeas held. Simultaneity is possible if the Trinity is "one substance in three persons": "three, however, not in unchangeable condition, but in rank; not in substance, but in attitude; not in office, but in appearance;—but of one nature and of one reality and of one power, because there is one God from whom those ranks and attitudes and appearances are derived in the name of Father and Son and Holy Spirit." At the same time Tertullian recognized that to say the Son is "of one substance" with the Father poses a problem for his humanity and might lead, as it did later, to confusion as to the Son's personhood. Anticipating later debate, he repudiated the idea of a mixing or confusion of natures in some *tertium quid.*

On some matters of doctrine Tertullian's Montanism left a mark, although it is difficult to say exactly what the mark was, since both Montanism and Tertullian adhered rather closely to primitive Christian views. Most significant was his acceptance of the eschatological framework of Montanist thought. According to this, the age of the Paraclete promised in *John* 14:16 was inaugurated by Montanus and the prophets Priscilla and Maximilla. The dawning of this dispensation signaled a time of new prophetic revelations and of greater Christian discipline—fasting, prohibition of second marriages, and willingness to suffer martyrdom. Christ was expected to return soon and set up his millennial kingdom with headquarters at Pepuza in Phrygia, Montanus's hometown. In the interim the church would be divided. On the one side were the psychics, on the other the pneumatics. The former, catholics, would not accept the discipline of the new prophecy; the latter, Montanists, would. In line with this understanding of the church, the Montanist Tertullian shifted his views of ministry so as to give a greater weight to prophecy.

Given his allegiance to Montanism, a sect increasingly regarded as heretical, it is remarkable that Tertullian had so great an impact on later Christian theology. This must have been due not to his personality but to his unquestioned orthodoxy on most matters and his genius for coining just the right phrase.

SEE ALSO Montanism.

BIBLIOGRAPHY

An excellent critical edition of the whole corpus of Tertullian's writings now exists in the *Corpus Christianorum,* Series Latina, vols. 1 & 2 (Turnhout, Belgium, 1954). A complete translation can be found in *The Ante-Nicene Fathers,* vols. 3 & 4 (Grand Rapids, Mich., 1956). Numerous recent works have debated critical problems regarding Tertullian's life and thought. A searching examination of biographical and literary matters is to be found in Timothy D. Barnes's *Tertullian: A Historical and Literary Study* (Oxford, 1971). A valuable older work, by James Morgan, *The Importance of Tertullian in the Development of Christian Dogma* (London, 1928), is in need of updating. Most recent studies have focused on particular aspects of Tertullian's theology, but Gerald L. Bray's *Holiness and the Will of God: Perspectives on the Theology of Tertullian* (Atlanta, 1979) has attempted a more comprehensive treatment. T. P. O'Malley's *Tertullian and the Bible: Language-Imagery-Exegesis* (Utrecht, 1967) also supplies helpful insight into this important aspect of Tertullian's writings.

E. GLENN HINSON (1987)

TESHUB was the Hurrian god of the storm. His name, also spelled *Teshshub, Te,* and *Teya,* is attested in theophoric Hurrian personal names in documents from Mesopotamia, Syro-Palestine, and Anatolia. Since the few Hurrian religious texts from outside the Hittite sphere are still somewhat poorly understood, most of what we know about the god, his mythological roles, and his cult is from Hittite Anatolia.

During the last two centuries of the Hittite kingdom (c. 1400–1200 BCE) Teshub was the chief god of the pantheon, with his cult center at Kummiya. He was the son of Anu (An), the sky god. His wife was the goddess Hebat. He had four brothers: Aranzakh (the Tigris River), Tashmishu, and two others whose names are unknown, and a sister, Shawushka, who was the goddess of love and war. Teshub and Hebat had a son, Sharruma, and a daughter, Allanzu.

Teshub is represented anthropomorphically in low relief on the rock walls of the sanctuary of Yazilikaya, near Bogazköy (Bittel, 1975, pp. 167–169), standing upon two unnamed anthropomorphic mountain gods and holding a club in his right hand. At the head of a procession of male deities, he meets and faces his wife, Hebat, the principal goddess of the pantheon, who heads a procession of goddesses. Around Teshub are represented other members of his immediate family. His size and position on the relief are in keeping with his rank as the chief god of the Hittite empire, but otherwise his dress and complements are those of a normal Hittite storm god.

In the mythological texts Teshub is always referred to by one of the two cuneiform signs for "storm god," not by the name Teshub. In the first myth of the so-called Kumarbi cycle, usually titled *Kingship in Heaven* (English trans. in Pritchard, 1969, pp. 120f.), Anu, who had usurped the throne of kingship over the gods from Alalu, is driven from his throne by Alalu's son Kumarbi. During the struggle Kumarbi bites off Anu's penis and swallows it. Anu curses Kumarbi and promises that from the seed thus implanted in Kumarbi five gods will be born, to defeat and depose him. The first one mentioned (and therefore the eldest) is Teshub.

In the sequel, called the *Song of Ullikummi* (ibid., pp. 121ff.; Güterbock, 1951–1952), the god Kumarbi, whom Teshub has displaced as head of the pantheon, seeks to overthrow him by means of a stone monster named Ullikummi, whom Kumarbi had engendered through having sexual intercourse with a huge boulder. Thus the pattern of the offspring of a former king of the gods overthrowing his father's successor, which was set in *Kingship in Heaven,* continues. Teshub is first defeated by the monster and must hide, but he eventually triumphs with the help of the god Ea (Enki).

A prayer of King Muwatallis is addressed principally to Teshub, called the Storm God of Kummanni. Although this is the only prayer in the Hittite archives addressed primarily to Teshub, other Hittite prayers contain sections in which subordinate deities—Teshub and Hebat's children or grandchildren, and once even Teshub's bull, Seri—are asked to intercede with Teshub or Hebat for the person praying. The Hittite archives also contain descriptions of religious festivals in honor of Teshub and Hebat (Laroche, 1971, pp. 123ff.).

BIBLIOGRAPHY

Bittel, Kurt, et al. *Das hethitische Felsheiligtum Yazilikaya.* Berlin, 1975.

Gurney. O. R. *Some Aspects of Hittite Religion.* London, 1977.

Güterbock, Hans G. "The Song of UlliKummi." *Journal of Cuneiform Studies* 5 (1951): 135–161 and 6 (1952): 8–42.

Laroche, Emmanuel. *Recherches sur les noms des dieux hittites.* Paris, 1947.

Laroche, Emmanuel. *Catalogue des textes hittites.* Paris, 1971.

Pritchard, J. B., ed. *Ancient Near Eastern Texts relating to the Old Testament,* 3d ed. Princeton, 1969.

Steiner, G. "Gott: Nach hethitischen Texten." In *Reallexikon der Assyriologie und vorderasiatischen Archäologie,* edited by D. O. Edzard et al., vol. 3, pp. 547–575. Berlin and New York, 1957.

New Sources

Deighton, H. J. *The "Weather-God" in Hittite Anatolia: An Examination of the Archaeological and Textual Sources.* Oxford, 1982.

Haas, Volkert. *Geschichte der hetitischen Religion.* Leiden, 1994.

Hoffner, Harry A., Jr. *Hittite Myths.* Atlanta, 1990. Translations of texts related to the Storm god Teshub.

HARRY A. HOFFNER, JR. (1987)
Revised Bibliography

TEXTILES.

Processing fiber into thread and transforming those threads into fabrics, possibly the oldest human technology, first appear on the cultural horizon during the Neolithic period, between twelve and fifteen thousand years ago. Not until the sixth millennium BCE, however, do fragments of textiles excavated at sites in central Europe and the Middle East provide evidence for their inclusion in ritual or religious contexts. These grave furnishings and occasional finds from refuse dumps suggest purpose and intent; however, the archaeological record is far from complete. The documentation of the actual meanings of many ritual practices involving fabric is, in most cases, relatively recent. Despite differences in time and space and the fact that few causal links exist among the cultures discussed here, the practices involving textiles in religious rites and ceremonies can be considered in three broad categories: (1) symbolic meanings associated with textiles, (2) ritual functions for textiles within religious practices, and (3) links between the sacred and the profane realms.

TEXTILES AS SYMBOLS. In most societies that developed textile technologies, cloth and its production served as metaphors for life. In Greek mythology, for example, three goddesses known as the Moirai controlled the lives of mortals. The Fates, as they are more commonly known, include Clotho the spinner, who creates the web of life; Lachesis, who measures its length; and Atropos, who cuts it. The physical act of interlacing prepared threads on a frame to create textiles is a powerful symbol. The spinning of thread, its winding onto bobbins, and the warping of the loom symbolize conception, gestation, and birth. The process of weaving evokes the vicissitudes of life, growth, and maturity. Cutting the cloth from the loom can symbolize death, but more frequently it symbolizes rebirth and renewal because the process creates an object that can then be used.

In parts of South Asia and the South Pacific the physical form of a newly woven cloth is tubular because the warp yarns are continuous and form an uninterrupted circle between the two beams of the loom. When the cloth is finished only a small section of the warp yarns remains unwoven. For normal use the textile is cut open across this area. The rich metaphorical potential of the continuous yarns in the uncut cloth became obvious to diverse groups within the Indonesian archipelago. Among the Sasak tribes on the island of Lombok in eastern Indonesia, three sacred tubular cloths are made for a child at birth by the eldest woman weaver in the family. These are stored in a sacred area of the house until needed. In the course of the hair-cutting, circumcision, and marriage rites, the warps of these textiles are cut. Although deceptively modest in appearance, these red, yellow, black, and white striped cotton textiles are endowed with significance affecting the general well-being of individuals. Farther west, on the island of Bali, the more elaborate *geringsing,* decorated with double ikat-patterns, have similar metaphorical significance. *Geringsing* also have a circular warp that must be cut to form a cloth. A single cloth, which may take over a year to produce, accompanies an individual throughout each life-crisis ceremony; ultimately it serves as a funeral pall for the corpse.

The associations with female textile "producers" reflect other, more nuanced cultural meanings. Across the ages dowries have involved fine textiles and the presumption that these specialized fabrics embodied a bride's skills to provide for and clothe the family. Entire industries in many parts of the world, like those still flourishing in Morocco, cater to the wedding trade and, despite their patriarchical commercialization, are evidence of the link between textiles and life processes. The productive and fructifying qualities associated with women are transferred to dowry textiles, which in turn function as fertility symbols. When juxtaposed with male symbols in metal or agricultural products, textiles evoke a complementary polarity, a polarity well illustrated in the archaeological and ethnographic record. The second-century CE graves of Dian nobles excavated in Southwest China at the sites of Shizaishan and Lijaishan, for example, contained bronze models of looms, other weaving tools, and sewing boxes in female graves; comparable male burials were furnished with bronze weapons and models of agricultural tools.

Together, tools or weapons and textiles symbolized completion and ideals of cosmic harmony. Echoes of this notion are found in legends of the ancient Mediterranean and Asian worlds that personified the annual conjunction of two stars within the Milky Way as the weaving maiden and the herdsman.

RITUAL USES FOR TEXTILES. In Jewish tradition the tassel or tzitzit at each corner of a man's tallith, which is worn as an undergarment, consists of eight strings and five knots wrapped in specific ways to equal the numerical value of one of the names of god. The numerical value of the word *tzitzit* (together with the eight strings and five knots on each corner) adds up to 613, the number of mitzvoth, or obligations, in the Torah.

Binding. Present-day Hindu practice continues to use a thread or cord as the symbol of renewal, creating a closed circle that ties the worshiper to the principles of the faith. During *Upanayana,* a rite-of-passage ceremony, sacred cords are placed over the shoulders of adolescent boys to signify their eligibility for education within the caste tradition. For the brahman caste the thread is cotton; for the *kṣatriya* (warrior or ruler) caste the cord is hemp; for the *vaiśya* (artisan or merchant) caste the cord is wool. Women also use the sacred thread within rituals. For example, at the annual festival of the goddess Gauri, a cotton thread sixteen times the woman's height is wound into a skein and laid before images of the goddess. Later the skein is worn around the neck, then buried or burned.

Ritual bonding frequently uses textiles. The priest's stole that drapes the joined hands of a couple during the marriage ceremony in the Western and Eastern Christian Church in effect becomes the tie that binds man to woman and the couple to the church, reinforcing the sanctity of marriage. In many Muslim societies ritual bonding occurs when the bridal couple is invited to sit on a shared mat or textile. Among the Batak tribes of northern Sumatra the climax of the traditional marriage ceremony is the enveloping of the couple in a single textile by the bride's father. Other members of the immediate family are also wrapped in shawls during the course of the ceremony, further emphasizing the bonds this event celebrates.

Offering. Literally hundreds of blankets, bolts of cloth, and other utilitarian textiles, as well as great quantities of nontextile domestic and ritual goods, were amassed by extended family groups among the tribes of the northwest coast of North America for potlatch feasts. They were presented to guests or burned in extravagant demonstrations of exchange. In contemporary revivals, commercial cloth and clothing are exchanged. Although less dramatic, the imported Chinese white silk scarves patterned with Buddhist symbols and the simple Indian white cotton gauze scarves used by Tibetan Buddhists convey a similar sense of offering and sacrifice. In the wool-producing regions of the Tibetan Plateau these exotic imports were tokens of exchange between individuals upon meeting and offerings to images. Tibetans also offer rectangles of cotton cloth block-printed with prayers to the elements as acts of devotion. Flown from poles, suspended on lines, or tied to the roofs of temples and shrines, these textiles are literally destroyed by the winds that activate intercessions with the gods.

Funeral customs provide other insights into textile-offering practices. Although knowledge of the actual practice is far from complete, the archaeological record for pharaonic Egypt and pre-Columbian Peru is spectacular. The dry climates of the Egyptian desert and of coastal Peru have preserved vast quantities of textiles used in burial. Egyptians wrapped mummies of the dead in fine linen. Complete wardrobes of clothes and household linens, reflecting the status and means of the individual in life, were also interred to provide the comforts of this earth in the next world. Along the dry south coast of Peru, pre-Columbian mummy bundles of aristocrats contain numerous finely woven and embroidered sets of wool and cotton clothes as well as large quantities of other fine textiles.

In China, where silk was a principal trade commodity as well as the imperial standard for the payment and collection of taxes, silk textiles played a major role in life and death. Throughout the centuries the number and quality of burial clothes reflected the status of the individual in life. The remarkably well-preserved chambered tomb of the Lady Dai at Mawangdui, Changsha, which dates from about 160 BCE, contained over twenty-seven items of silk apparel, including some twelve coats, forty-six rolls of uncut silk, and numerous silk wrappers and bags. During the later imperial period the custom of preparing clothes especially decorated with characters meaning "long life" (the so-called *shufu,* or "longevity" coats) arose, but burial clothes mainly copied an individual's official wardrobe, which designated rank at court. Archaeology has also revealed abuses of the rules of entitlement, such as the garments recovered from the tombs of Xu Fan (1463–1530) and his wife from Taizhou, Jiangsu province, in which the wive's robes outranked those of her husband by two ranks.

Although there are instances of funeral textiles recycled from life, such as the bridal garments used for the burials of Chinese women, which reflected a most exalted status in the rigid patriarchial society that largely ignored women, most were specially acquired for burial. The obligation and expense for a Confucian funeral were borne by the next generation of the family. By contrast, nineteenth-century aristocrats on the island of Timor in eastern Indonesia devoted considerable amounts of time and money to amassing quantities of prestige textiles for their own burials.

Sacrifices do not always involve fabrics of the greatest economic or aesthetic value. For some cultures specific textiles are produced for shrouds. The traditional burial clothing of Jews is a set of simple, untailored linen garments. In Bali the sacred cloths called *bebali* are in effect token textiles made only for offering. Loosely woven, they are too fragile for use; most are too small to function as clothing for the living. During the late imperial period in China and continuing into the twenty-first century, sets of paper clothes and models of bolts of silk are as offerings to the dead for the next life.

Textile offerings were important in rituals honoring personified deities. In pharaonic Egypt images of gods within cult temples were centers of elaborate ceremonies that imitated human life. Gods were awakened in the morning, fed, bathed, and clothed, taken on festive outings, and put to bed at night, not unlike the pharaoh, the living manifestation of god on earth. Aqllawasi (House of Chosen Women), often referred to as Virgins of the Sun, was a cloistered community of Quechua noble women devoted to the cult of the Sun God. Among their duties was the weaving of clothing for the ruler or Inka, the embodiment of the Sun God on earth. Perhaps the most celebrated textile offering of antiquity was the annual Panathenaia in Athens, an event commemorated on the inner frieze of the Parthenon. The climax of the festival was a procession carrying the costly new peplos made by the women of Athens to the Acropolis and the presentation of this garment to the cult image of Pallas Athena.

Offerings of clothing to temple images were frequent occurrences throughout Buddhist, Hindu, Daoist, and Confucian Asia. In late imperial China, for example, where the giving of prestige cloths marked the New Year as well as birthday celebrations, many of the city gods were presented on these occasions with new robes, cut especially large and often without side seams, a fact frequently recorded in pious inscriptions by donors.

Icons. In some cultures textiles themselves are venerated. The effigies of the hearth deities worshiped by nomadic Mongols were made entirely of felt. These special effigies, called *ongot,* one identified as male, the other female, were kept inside the yurt. In Buddhism, before the development of a rich figural iconography following the second century CE, images of the Buddha's attributes, including his mantle and his throne with its textile-covered cushion, served the faithful as a symbolic focus for worship. The legend and the numerous illustrations of Veronica's veil or the much-celebrated linen shroud preserved in the cathedral at Turin, which bears a human image said to be that of the crucified Christ, are two examples of venerable textiles from the Christian tradition. Among Muslims the presentation of the cloth cover from a saint's tomb is a means of conveying blessings on an honored visitor.

Among the Toraja tribes of central Sulawesi, a group of sacred textiles called *ma'a* and *sarita* embody spiritual power. These textiles are heirlooms handed down through families; they are used for display on many ritual and ceremonial occasions. Some of these textiles are of local manufacture, but many are made of imported Indian cotton cloth that has been painted with Torajan symbols.

In Tibet, *maṇḍalas* depicting various deities in the Buddhist pantheon were constructed in the appliqué technique from Chinese silks and other exotic fabrics donated to monasteries. The most impressive examples were the gigantic *maṇḍalas* measuring over twenty meters in length that were displayed once a year against the facade of the Potala in Lhasa.

Creation of a sacred place. The place where a ritual or ceremony is performed may have a temporal as well as a spatial dimension. The suspension of normal time to create a temporal framework in which humans can commune with the supernatural can be aided by textiles in several ways. For example, the repeated use of textiles or sets of textiles, such as the red vestments and altar furnishings employed in the Western Christian Church within the same context over time (e.g., for feast days of martyrs), emphasizes a sense of ritual cycle that is permanent despite the passage of real time. The use of the same textile within a sequence of events, as is done with the *geringsing* cloths from the island of Bali, achieves for the participant a sense of suspended animation. A third sense of ritual time is embodied in the notion of transformation: special furnishings or clothing can dramatize the transformation of a place into the presence of a god or of the individual into a servant or intermediary of the god.

Textiles also have spatial functions, creating a sacred precinct within a larger profane context. On the most fundamental level, textiles can provide a focus for ritual. The act of spreading a cloth, whether it is the simple linen textile that covers the top of the Christian altar or the elaborately patterned silk covers for the Buddhist incense tables, transforms a table into an altar.

The *kiswah,* the most important textile in Islam, covers the Ka'bah in Mecca, a square granite structure that immures the Black Stone. The stone itself predates the founding of Islam, but it became the most sacred relic of the religion and the focus of Muslim pilgrimage to Mecca. The *kiswah* is made of black silk with Qur'anic inscriptions woven or embroidered in gold. Covering a cubical structure roughly twelve meters high, the *kiswah* is a dramatic indicator of a sacred precinct. It is replaced annually, and the older textile is cut into pieces that are sold as relics.

Textiles suspended over a ritual area transform the space beneath to offer real or symbolic protection. Some are portable, like the wedding canopies common to many faiths. In effect they transform any space beneath them into a ritual area and are reused as occasion demands. Other canopies convey cosmological meaning. Those placed over altars or above images in Christian or Buddhist buildings, for example, serve as metaphors for heaven, contrasting the visual universe or firmament with the larger perceived but invisible heaven beyond.

The pierced quatrefoil canopy called *yunjian* in Chinese, meaning "cloud collar," which is placed on the apex of Mongol felt yurts, is of central Asian or southern Siberian origin. Its four pendant points promote spatial orientation with the cardinal points of the compass; the hole at the top is called a sky door and symbolizes the gate to heaven, through which the earth axis passes. The application of this shape around the necks of garments, which also arose on the steppe, conferred a notion of cosmic orientation to the wearer.

Fabric may also cover the area on which ritual occurs. Mats and carpets indicate places for prayer and meditation in most Asian cultures, which did not develop elaborate furniture for sitting but lived primarily on the floor. For example, small square woolen carpets decorated with Buddhist symbols were commonly used by Buddhist monks in Tibet. High-ranking clergy, however, often sat on silk-covered cushions.

Some floor coverings promote ideas of spatial orientation. Within many of the powerful agrarian empires across the world, the precise arrangement of specific floor coverings and other furnishings within a ritual area ensured the success of the ceremony. A fourth-century BCE text, the *Shujing* (Book of history), describes the proper procedure for setting up the offerings for the burial of a prince, with detailed instructions concerning the appropriate carpet, offering table, and sacrifice for each of the cardinal points within the tomb area. In other instances single textiles function as spatial indicators: the organization of motifs in certain Mongol, Turkish, and Chinese carpets within the rectilinear confines of the textile imply a correct alignment.

The most famed ritual floor covering, the so-called Muslim prayer carpet, is traditionally decorated with an arch at one end echoing the *miḥrāb* niche in the mosque, which orients prayer toward Mecca. However, the function of these carpets is independent of decoration, since they provide a spatial substitute for worship within a mosque to assist the faithful in discharging the obligation of prayer five times a day. No specific carpets are prescribed for the mosque floor. If anything were to be considered the first religiously prescribed floor covering, it would be the simple plaited palm-leaf mat used by nomadic Arabs. But once Islam came into contact with the artistically sophisticated cultures of western Asia, custom and taste dictated design. Historically, many carpets were merely decorative; however, some were undoubtedly used for prayer within the home.

Textiles have served as portable shrines for nomadic peoples, and some of these textile environments survive among settled populations. The *mahmal* tents used during the Muslim pilgrimage to Mecca are one example.

Textile curtains act as screens shielding sacred ritual areas and guarding access to them. Although a distancing device, these textiles afford the celebrants a ritual dramatic effect when they are suddenly parted to reveal mystery. The ark curtain or *parochet* (Hebrew, *parokhet*) is the main ritual textile within Jewish practice. Its precedents can be found in the tabernacle described in chapter 26 of *Exodus*. This record of one of the most celebrated of the portable ritual-textile environments profoundly influenced the ritual trappings of later Jewish and Christian practice. Within Ashkenazic tradition the standard *parochet* consists of a prestige cloth framed between two pillars and a lintel, a device previously thought to relate to sixteenth-century title pages from printed books. The form may well have more ancient precedents, however, recalling times when practice demanded large curtains hung between architectural bays to subdivide areas of worship. Archaeological evidence from the third-century CE synagogue at Dura-Europos in Syria reveals that a large curtain divided the area in front of the Torah shrine from the congregation. This custom of using curtains to subdivide spaces within religious and secular architecture was widespread in the Near East and the Mediterranean during classical times.

This pattern influenced early Christian worship as well. In the early centuries of the Christian era, large curtains were used to articulate space within the church or meeting room to accommodate different audiences. Part of the building was accessible to nonbelievers, and other provisions were made for those under instruction but not yet baptized. The faithful were divided into groups, with men and women occupying different areas; the clergy had an area around the altar. In the West large curtains disappeared from the interiors of religious buildings with the rise of the Romanesque architectural style around the year 1000. The *parochet* and the tabernacle veils of the Western Christian Church are humble reminders of times when interiors were lavishly decorated with textiles.

Large curtains remained in use in the Eastern Christian Church for a time, but the development of the iconostasis on which icons were displayed gradually replaced the portable curtains separating the sanctuary from the nave. The amphithyron, a smaller curtain that hung behind the central doors of the iconostasis, is all that remains of the more elaborate curtaining systems. Only in Ethiopian churches practicing Coptic rites do large dividing curtains survive.

The notion of concealment is present at other levels as well, particularly in practices that shield sacred paraphernalia from the eyes of the uninitiated or from direct contact with the profane hand. In the Christian Church the chalice and the Host, as well as many of the accoutrements used in the service, are only revealed at the appropriate moment in the ritual; at other times they are veiled from sight. The Torah mantles, made of the most costly silk and gold-enriched fabrics, the simple tie-dyed silk curtains that hang in front of the painted images of Tibetan Buddhist *maṇḍalas*, and the elaborately embroidered *epitaphios sindon* of the Greek Orthodox rite, which veils the chalice and paten, serve identical functions.

Textile Links between the Sacred and the Profane Realms. Throughout history textiles have conveyed both symbolic and economic meaning. Before the industrial age reduced most textiles to the realm of disposable consumer goods, all textiles possessed real value as the product of the labor invested in cultivating, spinning, dyeing, and weaving. These labor factors, as well as the materials, skills, and ritual meanings, conferred prestige that could be transferred. Many religious organizations relied on cloistered workshops to produce liturgical textiles. These establishments were often managed by women, whose textile production calls to mind specialized dowry manufacture. Some particularly time-consuming specialized techniques associated with these workshops are like pious acts of devotion embodying repetitive invocations and blessings. During the seventeenth and eighteenth centuries, secular schools for young noble women—like the Smol'nyi Institute founded by Catherine the Great and the Maison royale de Saint-Cyr established by Madame de Maintenon—were modeled on cloistered ateliers. These schools produced fine textiles for the church as well as for aristocractic households, as evidenced by the surviving fabrics dating from the late Medieval period. The largest number of textiles used within religious ceremony have neither ritual function nor meaning as religious symbols. Rather, their purpose is self-consciously decorative. Whether temporary or permanent, these textiles enhance ritual through splendid display. These decorations often featured fabrics that had been transformed from secular uses for the purpose. Many churches encouraged the donation of secular prestige textiles by the faithful as a meritorious deed, and this cache of prestige goods was available for recycling. Particularly valuable textiles were often used to wrap relics and other sacred items before placing them in reliquaries for storage. In the West many examples of the medieval silks survive only from these contexts.

Banners and hangings announce the special character of ritual space. They can be carried in procession or used for interior display. Most of these objects are showy and made of lightweight materials; some, such as the banners used in Buddhist temples, have long streamers that add movement as well as color to ritual space. Banners bearing images of deities convey popular iconography and may serve an informal educative function, but in general they are difficult to distinguish from comparable secular decoration.

Textiles that adorn the interior walls of worship halls, like the wall paintings many of them replaced, are commonly didactic. The painted cotton temple hangings from northern India, for example, often depict stories from Hindu mythology. Many of the tapestry sets woven for religious institutions in medieval Europe illustrate the lives of the saints or depict apocalyptic visions. In the West the popularity of such monumental textiles lapsed with the rise of the Gothic architectural style. The Graham Sutherland tapestry at Coventry Cathedral is an outstanding example of the twentieth-century revival of tapestry weaving that has affected contemporary Western Christian Church decoration.

Carpets may cover the floors, cushioning bare feet as in the mosques of Islam, decorate the space before the altar as in Christian practice, or wrap the pillars of the worship hall as in Tibet and China. In most cases these lavish displays are more apt to result from pious donation of secular goods than from ritual requirements.

A vast range of covers for lecterns, reading desks, books, scrolls, cushions, kneelers, and furniture utilize fine textiles. Textile valances enhance architectural settings. The *kapporet* (cover) placed over the Torah curtain transforms the Torah shrine into the mercy seat of the Ark of the Tabernacle. In East Asian religious contexts, elaborately embroidered valances were often added to the niches in which image shrines were placed. Some of these were special commissions donated to the temples. One popular Chinese Buddhist valance type was made as a patchwork by members of the congregation from personal textiles or from temple supplies of donated textiles.

In the same way that most vestments used by religions throughout the world were derived from secular clothing, many of the decorative textiles that have become associated with ritual also have secular origins. One group of textiles in particular, however, remains virtually unchanged from its secular usage. Cloths of state, throne covers, footstool covers, umbrellas, and baldachins are statements of secular political power. They designate rank and position within the clergy (of Western Christian traditions, Judaism and Buddhism) for purposes of prestige and control rather than ritual.

SEE ALSO Clothing; Kaʿbah.

BIBLIOGRAPHY

In the absence of a comprehensive investigation of textiles used in ritual and ceremony, information is scattered in many sources, and data are inconsistent from culture to culture. General references to the roles textiles play in ritual are in Michael V. Angrosino's *The Culture of the Sacred* (Prospect Heights, Ill., 2004), and Catherine M. Bell's *Ritual Theory, Ritual Practice* (New York and Oxford, 1992). A number of papers that cover the aspects of ritual textiles are in Lynne Milgram and Penny Van Esterik, eds., *The Transformative Power of Cloth in Southeast Asia* (Toronto, 1994), and Textile Society of America, *Sacred and Ceremonial Textiles, Proceedings of the Fifth Biennial Symposium of the Textile Society of American, Chicago, Illinois, 1996* (Minneapolis, 1997).

For the Christian Church, scholarship has focused largely on vestments. Identification of nonvestment textiles used in Christian ritual is in J. Wickham Legg's *Notes on the History of the Liturgical Colours*, Transactions of the St. Paul's Ecclesiological Society (London, 1882), and in Legg's *Church Ornaments and Their Civil Antecedents* (Cambridge, U.K., 1917). Among the best explanations of the origins and uses of textiles in Jewish ritual is Barbara Kirshenblatt-Gimblett's *Fabric of Jewish Life* (New York, 1977). This exhibition catalog to the collection of ritual and ceremonial textiles in the Jewish Museum collection is well illustrated and contains a good bibliography.

Specific aspects of the use of textiles within ancient and historical Western religious contexts are in Elizabeth Grace Crowfoot, "The Clothing of a Fourteenth-Century Nubian Bishop," pp. 43–51; Veronika Gervers, "An Early Christian Curtain in the Royal Ontario Museum," pp. 56–81; and Donald King, "How Many Apocalypse Tapestries?," pp. 160–167; all of which are in *Studies in Textile History: In Memory of Harold B. Burnham*, edited by Veronika Gervers (Toronto, 1977). In addition, this Festschrift contains Rita Bolland, "Weaving the *Pinatikan*, a Warp-Patterned *Kain Bentenan* from North Celebes," pp. 1–17, and John E. Vollmer, "Archaeological and Ethnographical Considerations of the Foot-Braced Body-Tension Loom," pp. 343–354, both of which discuss non-Western textiles. R. B. Serjeant's *Islamic Textiles: Material for a History up to the Mongol Conquest* (Beirut, 1972), which was originally published serially in *Ars Islamica* 9–14 (1942–1951), is the basic reference for Islamic textiles. A good source for both Islamic and East Asian carpets is M. S. Dimand's *Oriental Rugs in the Metropolitan Museum of Art* (New York, 1973). In addition to the catalog to the Metropolitan Museum's considerable collection, this volume includes a series of essays documenting the use of carpets in Asia as well as their earliest appearances in the West.

One of the best references for the East Asian region in English is J. J. M. de Groot's *The Religious System of China: Its Ancient Forms, Evolution, History, and Present Aspect, Manners, Customs, and Social Institutions Connected Therewith* (Leiden, 1892–1910). This six-volume study remains one of the best standard references on traditional religious practices in China. Leonardo Olschki's *The Myth of Felt* (Berkeley, Calif., 1949) contains a perceptive essay on the significance of this material in traditional Mongol society. Articles by international scholars documenting ritual use of textiles throughout the Indonesian Archipelago are in Mattibelle Gittinger, ed., *Indonesian Textiles: Irene Emery Roundtable on Museum Textiles, 1979 Proceedings* (Washington, D.C., 1980). Other Asian practices are dicussed in Alice Beck Kehoe's *Shamans and Religion* (Prospect Heights, Ill., 2000); and Rosemary Crill, Steven Cohen, and Ruth Barnes, *Court, Temple, and Trade: Indian Textiles in the Tapi Collection* (Mumbai, India, 2002). References to textiles within the Tibetan context are in the five-volume catalog by the Newark Museum, *Catalogue of the Tibetan Collection and Other Lamaist Articles in the Newark Museum* (Newark, N.J., 1950–1971).

References to New World practices are in Laurie Adelson and Arthur Tracht, *Aymara Weavings: Ceremonial Textiles of Colonial and Nineteenth-Century Bolivia* (Washington, D.C., 1983), and Ann Pollard Rowe and John Cohen, *Hidden Threads of Peru: Q'ero Textiles* (Washington, D.C., 2002).

JOHN E. VOLLMER (1987 AND 2005)

TEZCATLIPOCA ("the smoking mirror") was one of the four Aztec creator gods who arranged the universe and set the cosmic ages in motion through periodic celestial battles. Tezcatlipoca was sometimes cast as the supernatural antagonist of Quetzalcoatl, the deity associated with cultural creativity, urban order, and priestly wisdom. Yet Tezcatlipoca has the most overwhelming power and protean personality of any Aztec deity. Among his aspects were Itztli, a calendar god; Tepeyolotl, an ancient jaguar-earth god; Ixquimilli-Itztla-coaliuhqui, a god of punishment; and Omacatl, the spirit of revelry. His many forms reflect the omnipotent character of numinous forces in Aztec religion. The range of Tezcatlipoca's power is perhaps best represented in his designation as "the enemy on both sides."

As in all pictorial representations of Mesoamerican deities, Tezcatlipoca's costume contains elements crucial to his identification. His primary emblem, a smoking mirror made of obsidian, is often depicted as a circular disk with a shaft through it and two curling forms representing smoke attached to the edges. The mirror emblem is located either in the deity's headdress or in place of one foot. According to one source, his foot was bitten off by an earth monster during the struggle for the creation of the world. On the social level, this emblem of the smoking mirror was intimately associated with the divine power of the Aztec *tlatoani* (king).

Tezcatlipoca's specific ritual significance was expressed in the great annual festival of Toxcatl. In book 2 of Fray Bernardino de Sahagún's *Historia general de las cosas de la Nueva España* (compiled 1569–1582; also known as the Florentine Codex), we learn that for a full year prior to Toxcatl, Tezcatlipoca's *ixiptla* (deity impersonator) lived in the Aztec capital in complete splendor and honor, treated as a great lord. Usually a captive warrior, the *ixiptla* had to be physically perfect in size, proportion, skin color, and beauty. By women he was called "tall one, head nodder, handful of stars." He moved regally about the capital dressed in flower headdresses and luxurious ornaments, carrying his smoking pipe and flute and speaking graciously to all who greeted him. Twenty days prior to his sacrifice at the height of Toxcatl, the *ixiptla* was given four beautiful maidens in marriage. Following his heart sacrifice to the Sun, his head was strung on the public skull rack in the main ceremonial center of Tenochtitlán. Of the dramatic turnabout in the life of Tezcatlipoca's impersonator, the Florentine Codex states: "And this betokeneth our life on earth. For he who rejoiceth, who possesseth riches, who seeketh and coveteth our lord's sweetness, his gentleness—riches and property—thus endeth in great misery. For it is said, 'None come to an end here upon earth with happiness, riches and wealth'" (trans. Anderson and Dibble, vol. 2, p. 69).

According to the sacred historical traditions of the Aztec, which trace back to the paradigmatic kingdom of Tollan (900–1100 CE), Tezcatlipoca, a great sorcerer, drew uncanny powers from his obsidian mirror in a struggle against the Toltec priest-king Topiltzin Quetzalcoatl ("our young prince the feathered serpent"). Topiltzin Quetzalcoatl was tricked into drunkenness and sexual incontinence, which led to the utter collapse of his well-ordered city-state. Several primary sources suggest that the conflict between the great king and his magical antagonist was centered on Tezcatlipoca's desire to replace animal and insect sacrifice with human sacrifice.

BIBLIOGRAPHY

Brundage, Burr C. *The Fifth Sun: Aztec Gods, Aztec World.* Austin, 1979. See especially Brundage's insightful chapter, "The Quality of the Numinous" (pp. 50–79), and his detailed discussion of the deity in "Tezcatlipoca" (pp. 108–126).

Sahagún, Bernardino de. *Florentine Codex: General History of the Things of New Spain,* vol. 2, *The Ceremonies.* Translated by Arthur J. O. Anderson and Charles E. Dibble. Santa Fe, N. Mex., 1951. This remarkable translation is one of the richest sources for the study of Aztec religion, in that it contains a detailed description, provided by Aztec elders shortly after the Conquest, of the great ceremony of Toxcatl, which was dedicated to Tezcatlipoca. It provides the reader with a vivid example of the complex and contradictory forces symbolized by Tezcatlipoca.

New Sources

Barjau, Luis. *Tezcatlipoca: Elementos de una teología nahua (Tezcatlipoca: Elements of a Nahua Theology).* Mexico City, 1991.

Miller, Mary and Karl Taube. *The Gods and Symbols of Ancient Mexico and the Maya.* London, 1993.

Olivier, Guilhem. *Moqueries et metamorphoses du'an dieu aztèque: Tezcatlipoca, le "Seigneur au miroir fumant" (Mockeries and Metamorphasis of an Aztec God: Tezcatlipoca, the 'man of the smoking mirror').* Paris, 1997.

DAVÍD CARRASCO (1987)
Revised Bibliography

THAI RELIGION. Thailand must be counted as one of the preeminent Buddhist countries in the world. Official figures place the percentage of Buddhists in a population of 47 million in 1980 as more than 95 percent. If those, mainly of Chinese and Vietnamese extraction, who follow Mahāyāna and Confucian traditions are excluded from the census category of Buddhists, wherein they are officially subsumed, still well over 90 percent of the populace of Thailand can be counted as adherents of Theravāda Buddhism. Despite the apparent uniformity of religion that such a characterization suggests, there are many facets of Thai religion. As different sectors of the Thai populace have attempted to find meaningful ways to confront fundamental problems of disease and death, threats of social disorder, and experienced or perceived injustices, they have turned to different types of religious practice, each with its own distinctive history. Although these different types can be said in some basic sense to belong to an encompassing tradition of Thai Theravāda Buddhism, they are still sometimes in tension with each other.

TRADITIONAL THAI RELIGION. In 1292, Ramkhamhaeng (Rāma Khamhaeng), the king of the principality of Sukhōthai in what is today north-central Thailand, put up a stele on which was recorded the first known text in any Tai language—that is, in any of the languages spoken by the ancestors of such modern-day peoples as the Lao, the Yuan (Northern Thai), and the Siamese (Central Thai). The inscription is notable for being the first historical evidence that Tai-speaking peoples had become adherents of Theravāda Buddhism. Prior to the thirteenth century, Tai-speaking peoples living in northern mainland Southeast Asia and in southern China had followed animistic traditions based on beliefs in a realm of spirits *(phī)* and deities *(thǣn)* and in a vital essence *(khwan)* that made human beings, rice, and certain animals more than mere physical organisms. Some Tai-speaking peoples such as the Red Tai, or Tho living in northern Vietnam and northeastern Laos, remained animistic until at least the middle of the twentieth century. Others, such as the Siamese, the Yuan of northern Thailand, the Lao of Laos and northeastern Thailand, the Shan of Burma, and the Lue of southern China and northwestern Laos, while retaining beliefs in spirits and a vital essence, also came to understand the world in terms of the Buddhism of the Pali tradition.

Initially, Buddhism among the Tai, as among other peoples in mainland Southeast Asia, appears to have centered primarily on the cult of relics. The enshrinement of such relics in stupas and the placement of images and other reminders of the Buddha served to establish the presence of the Buddha in the domains *(muang)* of the Tai. Having accepted the Buddha, the Tai were open to the teachings of missionary monks belonging to what has been termed the "forest monastery" tradition who traveled from domain to domain in the fourteenth and fifteenth centuries. One of the most important consequences of the work of these monks was the establishment of *wats* (temple-monasteries) in villages as well as in court centers. The members of the *sangha* (Skt., *saṃgha*), or order of monks, who lived in these monasteries popularized the Dhamma, the doctrines of Buddhism, by using texts written in the vernacular rather than in Pali, the canonical language of the Theravāda tradition. Among the most influential were the *Sermon on the Three Worlds,* written by a prince of Sukhōthai in the middle of the fourteenth century, and sermons in the form of *suttas*, written probably in northern Thailand in the fifteenth century, that tell of the "blessings" *(ānisaṃsa)* acquired through ritual acts.

In the Buddhist worldview adopted by the Tai, all sentient beings—human, animal, demonic, and divine—are understood to be situated along a continuum of relative suffering, the place they occupy on the continuum being determined by the consequences of *kamma* (Skt., *karman;* Thai, *kam*)—that is, consequences of actions performed in previous existences. The differences among human beings—male and female, ruler and peasant, rich and poor, beautiful and ugly, healthy and sickly—can also be interpreted with reference to the theory of *kamma.* Tai continued to believe in a personal vital essence *(khwan),* in spirits *(phī),* in gods—now construed in Hindu-Buddhist terms as *devatā* (Thai, *thē-wadā*), as well as in "fate" or cosmic influence—notions adapted from Indian thought and conceived of as *khrọ̄?* (from Skt., *gṛha,* astrological mansion or the place of a planet in the zodiac) or *chatā* (from Skt., *jāta,* "born"). These beliefs, however, related to proximate, not ultimate, causes of fortune and misfortune. One's *kamma* ultimately determined whether one could be successful in securing one's wandering vital essence, in propitiating spirits, in worshiping the deities, or in dispelling cosmic influences.

A significant change of one's position along the continuum of suffering could only be accomplished through accumulating merit *(puñña;* Thai, *bun)* and not acquiring demerit *(pāpa;* Thai, *bāp).* To "make merit" *(tham bun)* as a layperson one was to offer alms *(dāna;* Thai, *thān)* to the *sangha.* A male could also make significant merit through becoming a member of the *sangha* and subjecting himself to the monastic "discipline" *(vinaya;* Thai, *winai).* To avoid demerit one was to observe a code of morality *(sīla;* Thai, *sīn)* that ensured that one would transcend ignorance and resist the temptation to act so as to fulfill one's lust, greed, or anger. The consequences of immoral behavior—such as punishment in hell *(naraka;* Thai, *narok)*—as well as of moral and meritorious action—such as rebirth in heaven *(sagga;* Thai, *sawan* from Skt. *svarga)* and eventual rebirth on earth at the time of the next Buddha, Śrī Ariya Maitreya (Thai, Phra Sī Ān)—were detailed graphically in such sermons as the popular tale of the travels of the monk Mālaya to hell and heaven.

These Buddhist ideas, as well as the articulation of these beliefs with notions deriving from the pre-Buddhist past of the Tai, were organized into three major popular religious traditions followed by Tai-speaking peoples living in what is today Thailand. To this day, the ritual practices of the Siamese of central Thailand, the Yuan of northern Thailand, and the Lao of northeastern Thailand, while sharing some basic similarities, remain distinctive.

The Buddhist worldview adopted by Tai peoples shaped their orientation toward society. Fundamental to this order was the division between the sexes. The ideal Buddhist man should become a member of the *sangha* in order to pursue the Path. In practice, very few Tai men ever became members of the *sangha* for life, but it became the norm among all peoples living in premodern Thailand for young men to spend at least a lenten period of three months as either a novice or a monk. For women, a connection was made between the secular role of woman as mother and woman as nurturer for the religion. The hierarchical order of traditional society was understood in terms of differences in the karmic legacies that each person was assumed to have been born with.

Most monks in premodern Thailand acted primarily to preserve and transmit the local religious traditions of the communities where they lived. Although they traced their lineage to the "forest monastery" monks of the fifteenth century, there is no evidence to suggest that monks during the period between the fifteenth and nineteenth centuries were known for withdrawing from the world to devote their lives to meditation. Some monks, however, lived in monasteries that served as centers of study of the Dhamma. It was these monks who kept alive a tradition of Pali scholarship as well as of composition of vernacular religious texts. These centers were supported mainly by rulers of the traditional kingdoms or by lords of domains subordinate to the kings.

Kings and lords of premodern Tai realms and domains were held in popular belief to have the right to rule because they "had merit" *(mī bun);* that is, they had inherited at birth a large store of positive consequences of *kamma* from previous incarnations. They were expected to display their meritoriousness in their conspicuous support of the religion and in ensuring the peace and order of the worlds over which they held sway. This concept of merit can be seen to be similar to the Mahāyāna notion of compassion shown by *bodhisattvas* toward the world. Some Tai kings did claim to be *bodhisattvas*, but such a claim was far less common in Tai kingdoms than in those of premodern Burma.

In the major premodern Tai kingdom, the Siamese kingdom of Ayutthayā (1350–1767), court traditions, especially after the fifteenth century, showed strong Brahmanic influences, influences introduced from Angkor, which the Siamese had conquered. When the new Siamese kingdom with its capital at Bangkok was founded in 1782, its first rulers downplayed the Brahmanic state cult in favor of such Buddhist activities as unifying the *sangha,* restoring the scriptures, and sponsoring public almsgiving. At the end of the nineteenth century, King Chulalongkorn (c. 1868–1910) restored many Brahmanic state rites in an effort to enhance the image of the monarchy. The observance of some of these rites persisted even after a coup in 1932 transformed Siam into a constitutional monarchy, but by the second half of the twentieth century they had assumed a more dramaturgical than religious significance.

CONTEMPORARY RELIGION IN THAILAND. Religion as practiced by the peoples living in what was to become modern Thailand was rarely rendered problematic to its adherents. Only when the world collapsed, as it did following the destruction of Ayutthaya by the Burmese in 1767, did people question the efficacy of traditional practice for making sense of their lives. The period between the fall of Ayutthaya and the founding of Bangkok in 1782 is notable for the appeal that Buddhist millennialism held for many. Millennial experimentation was brought to an end, however, when in 1782 General Cakkrī deposed the then-reigning monarch, Taksin, who claimed to be a *bodhisattva.* Cakkrī, as Rama I (1782–1809), the founding ruler of the present dynasty, laid the foundations for a new order by restoring peace throughout the kingdom and, indeed, by extending his political control even farther than his predecessors. He moved to purify the religion by purging the *sangha* of monks who were deemed not to be observing the Vinaya (disciplinary code), by convening a Buddhist council to ensure that the Tipiṭaka (Skt., Tripiṭaka), the Buddhist scriptures, were available in an error-free Pali form, and by promoting the study of both the scriptures and commentarial literature written in Pali.

The new order established by Rama I proved to be fertile ground for the development of a major reform movement led by a man who would become King Rama IV, better known as Mongkut. Mongkut, who served as a monk between 1824 and 1851, was stimulated by his conversations with Christian missionaries and other Westerners who had begun to come to Siam to search for what could be taken as the essential elements of Buddhist practice. He became the leader of a small coterie of monks who spurned what they considered to be "superstitious" accretions in traditional practice and turned to Pali scriptures and commentaries to find the basis for "true" Buddhism. When Mongkut became king (r. 1851–1868), his associates in the *sangha* became the vanguard of a new fraternity, one called the Dhammayuttika-nikāya ("the fraternity of those who adhere to the Dhamma"), in contrast to the larger fraternity, the Mahānikāya (Mahanikai), of monks who continued to follow traditional practice.

Under King Chulalongkorn, Mongkut's son and successor, leading Dhammayuttika monks, and especially Prince Wachirayān (Vajirañāṇavarorasa), another of Mongkut's sons and the head of the Dhammayuttika fraternity, were given effective authority over the whole of the *sangha* in Chulalongkorn's domains. Prince Wachirayān, even before he became prince patriarch *(sangharāja)* in 1910, was able with the backing of the king to bring monks from the several different local Theravāda traditions into a single national order. Prince Wachirayān also instituted reforms throughout the *sangha* on the basis of Mongkut's and his own interpretations of Pali texts. The religious reforms instituted by Prince Wachirayān became the basis for what might be termed officially sanctioned orthodoxy in contemporary Thai Buddhism.

Under King Chulalongkorn, Siam began a transformation into a modern state. To meet the threat of colonial expansion by the British and the French, Chulalongkorn instituted administrative reforms that entailed the replacement of local lords by centrally appointed officials who adhered to common bureaucratic norms. So long as Siam was ruled by absolute monarchs, however, it still retained an important characteristic of the traditional state; that is, order depended upon the personal efficacy of the monarch. This traditional characteristic was eliminated in the "revolution" of 1932, during which a group of nonroyal "promoters" forced King Prajadhipok (r. 1925–1935) to accept a constitution that proclaimed Thai sovereignty to rest not in the monarch but with the people as a nation.

Although the name Siam persisted for a time after 1932, modern Thailand can be said to have begun in this year. The revolution of 1932 focused attention on the question of who made up the national community of Thai, a question that emerged in the wake of large-scale migration of Chinese to Thailand, the integration of peoples of different traditions into a single state, and the drawing of clear territorial boundaries around the state as a consequence of pressures from neighboring colonial powers. Since 1932, successive governments have made use of a unified *sangha* and a statewide system of compulsory education to inculcate in the populace the idea that Thai nationalism is rooted in what is taken to be a common Buddhist heritage.

Both the reformation of Buddhism led by the Dhammayuttika fraternity and the emergence of state-sponsored Thai Buddhist nationalism served to stimulate a self-consciousness in many Thai about their religion. This self-consciousness, in turn, stimulated yet further changes in Thai religion. While the refiguration of Theravāda thought begun by Mongkut early in the nineteenth century reached a climax in the works of Prince Wachirayān, works that still today form the basis of religious studies carried out by most monks, a number of monks have continued to pursue significant theological inquiries. By far the most influential of contemporary Buddhist thinkers is Phutthathāt Phikkhu (Buddhadāsa Bhikkhu), who lives at a center called Sūan Mōk ("garden of liberation") in southern Thailand. Phutthathāt (b. 1906) has sought in lectures and writings to interpret the Dhamma with reference to the theologies of other religions, most notably Zen Buddhism, and with reference to the experiences of Thai living in a much more secularized world than did their forebears. Writing for a more learned audience, the monk known under the title of Phra Rātchawaramunī (Rājavaramunī)—given name Prayut (b. 1941)—has sought also to make the Buddhist message relevant to modern life. His *Phutthatham (Buddhadhamma)*, published in 1982, has been acclaimed as one of the most significant works on Theravāda ethics ever written.

The radical reformulation of Buddhist practice also begun by Mongkut and the founders of the Dhammayuttika fraternity has been carried yet farther by some monks. Ācān Man Phūrithattha (Bhūridatto Thera), a Lao-speaking Dhammayuttika monk from northeastern Thailand who died in 1949 at the age of 78, concluded early in his life that to follow the Path to ultimate salvation, one must withdraw from the world and devote one's life to meditation. His life as a *dhūtanga,* or wandering ascetic, became the model for many other monks. A number of his disciples, and the disciples of his disciples, known in Thai and Lao as *ācān* (Skt., *ācārya*), or teachers, have achieved fame as meditation masters and strict followers of the Dhamma. A new interest in the significance of meditation for Buddhist practice has also been strongly encouraged by a number of non-Dhammayuttika monks and lay masters. Phutthathāt's center, Sūan Mōk, and satellite centers elsewhere, like the forest retreats of the *ācān,* attract many laypersons as well as monks who wish to learn to meditate. In the 1950s Phra Phimonlatham (Vimaladhamma Thera; given name Āsatha), a high-ranking monk from Wat Mahāthāt, a major temple-monastery in Bangkok, introduced and worked to popularize a form of *vipassanā* ("insight") meditation that he had learned from a master in Burma.

Prior to the death of Prime Minister Sarit Thanarat in 1963, Thai governments considered the burgeoning popularity of meditation monks as potentially, if not actually, threatening to establishment Buddhism. Since the mid-1960s, however, the disciples of Ācān Man in particular have been accorded increasing official support, and the king and queen have been conspicuous in their patronage of these monks and in their attendance at the funerals of Ācān Man's major disciples. Forest monasteries today are popular retreats for urban laypersons who seek to temper their active involvement in the world with a detachment that comes from meditation practice. Meditation centers have also been established in Bangkok and other cities, not only by monks but also by the laity. Among the most famous lay masters is Ācān Nāēp, a woman. Since the late 1970s, Phimonlatham has also undertaken a program to stimulate the popularity of insight meditation in rural communities as well as in the cities and towns.

Although what might be termed the "meditation movement" has been accommodated to establishment Buddhism in Thailand, other movements have emerged in reaction to official orthodoxy and to government-sponsored Thai Buddhist nationalism. Millennial uprisings in northeastern Thailand in 1901–1902 and resistance in the 1920s and 1930s by Khrūbā Sīwichai (Siri-vijoyo Thera), a highly revered popular northern Thai monk, to the authority of the state-appointed *sangha* hierarchy were precursors to contemporary religious dissent in Thailand. In the mid-1950s and especially in the 1970s, a number of monks emerged as conspicuous critics of government policies. While most of these "political monks" could be considered leftists, there were also a number associated with right-wing causes. Of particular note is Kittiwutthō Phikkhu (Kittivuḍḍho Bhikkhu), who gained notoriety in the mid-1970s for arguing that killing communists was not murder as understood in Buddhist terms and thus did not produce demerit. Although only a few monks have taken active roles in Thai politics, there are many lay Buddhist leaders who have contributed to a widening discourse on the salience of religious values for public life. Among the best known of what might be termed "social gospel" Buddhists is Sulak Sivarksa, who has exerted significant influence through his numerous essays and the organizations he has helped to create.

Members of the laity have also assumed leadership roles in the many cults that have emerged and continue to emerge in contemporary Thailand. The typical cult is one in which a spirit medium (who typically would be a woman) is believed able to gain the assistance of her control spirit to aid a client who is ill or otherwise in distress. Some cults have assumed a wider significance; the most famous of recent years is one known under the name Samnak Pū Sawan (Center of the Heavenly Ancients). The male leader of this cult claimed to be the vehicle for the spirits of a number of famous men in Thai history, including a former patriarch of the *sangha.* As it developed, the belief system of the cult became increasingly syncretic, uniting Christian, Muslim, and Chinese elements with magico-Buddhist ones. In the late 1970s, the cult, which had gained thousands of followers, including several high-ranking military officers, took on a distinctly political cast as its leader sought to use it for promoting an international peace center that he would head. In 1981 the government attempted to arrest him, but he disappeared before the arrest was effected.

Although the ecumenicalism of the Samnak Pū Sawan movement was idiosyncratic, more significant connections between Thai Buddhism and other religions in Thailand have evolved in recent years. A number of Protestant and Catholic leaders have joined with Buddhist leaders in religious dialogue and in human rights activities. The smallness of the Christian population (about 0.6 percent of the total) has perhaps helped to encourage relatively good relations between Christians and Buddhists. In contrast, Muslims (who account for about 4 percent of the population) have found it much more difficult to relate to Buddhists. A Muslim-Buddhist dialogue may, nonetheless, prove to be a means leading to a reconstrual of Thai civil religion in other than strictly Buddhist terms.

Life in Thailand in the twentieth century has become increasingly secularized and rationalized as more and more aspects of experience are interpreted with reference to bureaucratic regulations, market transactions, technological processes, and scientific medicine. While these processes of change have led many Thai to turn away from traditional religious practices as being no longer significant to their lives, they have also served to make people aware of those experiences that do not make sense in terms of secular, rational meanings. It is the awareness of those illnesses that do not respond to modern medicine, of increasing disparities in wealth and power, of the potential collapse of order as occurred in Kampuchea, that leads many Thai to consider what ritual and ethical practices are most meaningful to them. This religious consciousness is what gives contemporary Thai religion its dynamic character.

See Also Buddhism, article on Buddhism in Southeast Asia; Folk Religion, article on Folk Buddhism; Kingship, article on Kingship in East Asia; Mongkut; Saṃgha, article on Saṃgha and Society in South and Southeast Asia; Southeast Asian Religions, article on Mainland Cultures; Theravāda.

Bibliography

The collection *Religion and Legitimation of Power in Thailand, Laos, and Burma,* edited by Bardwell L. Smith (Chambersburg, Pa., 1978), contains several essays that trace the history of Thai religion and discuss the relationship between Buddhism and power in both traditional and contemporary Thailand. A. Thomas Kirsch's "Complexity in the Thai Religious System: An Interpretation," *Journal of Asian Studies* 36 (February 1977): 241–266, provides a good introduction to traditional Thai religion. Stanley J. Tambiah's *World Conqueror and World Renouncer* (Cambridge, 1976) traces the history of Thai religion with reference to *sangha*-policy relations and his *Buddhism and the Spirit Cults in North-East Thailand* (Cambridge, 1970) details the elements of traditional religious practice as still found in a Lao-speaking community in northeastern Thailand.

A major source for traditional Buddhist cosmology as understood by the Thai is *Three Worlds According to King Ruang: A Thai Buddhist Cosmology,* translated with an introduction and notes by Frank E. Reynolds and Mani B. Reynolds (Berkeley, 1982). Lucien M. Hanks, Jr., considers the implications of Buddhist cosmological beliefs for Thai society in his "Merit and Power in the Thai Social Order," *American Anthropologist* 64 (1962): 1247–1262. For discussions of gender ideas as shaped by the traditional Buddhist worldview of Tai peoples, see my essays "Mother or Mistress but Never Monk: Buddhist Notions of Female Gender in Rural Thailand," *American Ethnologist* 11 (May 1984): 223–241, and "Ambiguous Gender: Male Initiation in A Buddhist Society," in *Gender and Religions: On the Complexity of Symbols,* edited by Caroline Bynum, Stevan Harrell, and Paula Richman (Boston, 1956). The best study of the religious reforms of the nineteenth century is Craig J. Reynolds's "The Buddhist Monkhood in Nineteenth Century Thailand" (Ph. D. diss., Cornell University, 1973). See also Reynolds's "Buddhist Cosmography in Thai History, with Special Reference to

Nineteenth-Century Culture Change," *Journal of Asian Studies* 35 (February 1976): 203–220, and A. Thomas Kirsch's "Modernizing Implications of Nineteenth Century Reforms in the Thai Sangha," *Contributions to Asian Studies* 8 (1975): 8–23.

The structure and ritual practices of established Thai Buddhism are discussed in Kenneth E. Wells's *Thai Buddhism: Its Rites and Activities* (1939; reprint, Bangkok, 1960). Jane Bunnag's *Buddhist Monk, Buddhist Layman: A Study of Urban Monastic Organization in Central Thailand* (Cambridge, 1973) describes establishment Buddhism as she observed it in the old capital of Ayutthayā. On the government's control and use of the Thai *sangha* in the twentieth century, see Yoneo Ishii's "Church and State in Thailand," *Asian Survey* 8 (October 1968): 864–871; my "Buddhism and National Integration in Thailand," *Journal of Asian Studies* 30 (May 1971): 551–567; J. A. Niels Mulder's *Monks, Merit and Motivation,* 2d rev. ed. (DeKalb, Ill., 1973); Somboon Suksamran's *Political Buddhism in Southeast Asia: The Role of the Sangha in the Modernization of Thailand,* edited by Trevor O. Ling (London, 1977); and Tambiah's *World Conqueror and World Renouncer.*

The theology of Phutthathāt is examined at some length by Louis Gabaude in "Introduction à l'herméneutique de Buddhadasa Bhikku" (Ph. D. diss., Sorbonne, 1979); also see Buddhadāsa's *Toward the Truth,* edited by Donald K. Swearer (Philadelphia, 1971). Phra Rātchawaramunī's *Phutthatham* (Bangkok, 1982) has been reviewed at some length by Sulak Sivaraksa in the *Journal of the Siam Society* 70 (1982): 164–170. The role of Ācān Man, his disciples, and other meditation masters in Thailand have been analyzed by Stanley J. Tambiah in *The Buddhist Saints of the Forest and the Cult of Amulets* (Cambridge, 1984). Also see Jack Kornfield's *Living Buddhist Masters* (Santa Cruz, Calif., 1977).

My article "Millennialism, Theravāda Buddhism, and Thai Society," *Journal of Asian Studies* 36 (February 1977): 283–302, discusses the major millennial uprising in modern Thai history. Somboon Suksamran in *Buddhism and Politics in Thailand* (Singapore, 1982), as well as in his earlier *Political Buddhism in Southeast Asia,* Tambiah in *World Conqueror and World Renouncer,* and several of the essays in *Religion and Legitimation of Power in Thailand, Laos and Burma* (all cited above), discuss political monks. Sulak Sivaraksa's *A Buddhist Vision for Renewing Society* (Bangkok, 1981) brings together several of the author's essays written in English. On religious and ethical self-consciousness of some Thai in the context of political-economic change, see also my article "Economic Action and Buddhist Morality in a Thai Village," *Journal of Asian Studies* 42 (August 1983): 851–868.

New Sources

Benjamin, G., C. Chou, and Institute of Southeast Asian Studies. *Tribal Communities in the Malay World: Historical, Cultural and Social Perspectives.* Singapore, 2002.

Hayashi, Y. *Practical Buddhism Among the Thai-Lao.* Melbourne, 2003.

Hughes, J. *Faces of Culture: Explorations in Anthropology.* Queensland, 1993.

Kamala, T. *Forest Recollections: Wandering Monks in Twentieth-Century Thailand.* Honolulu, 1997.

Keyes, C. F., et al. *Asian Visions of Authority: Religion and the Modern States of East and Southeast Asia.* Hononlulu, 1994.

Mulder, N. *Inside Thai Society: Religion, Everyday Life, Change.* Chiang Mai, Thailand, 2000.

Rhum, M. R. *The Ancestral Lords: Gender, Descent, and Spirits in a Northern Thai Village.* DeKalb, Ill., 1994.

Taylor, J. L. *Forest Monks and the Nation-State: An Anthropological and Historical Study in Northeastern Thailand.* Singapore, 1993.

CHARLES F. KEYES (1987)
Revised Bibliography

THEALOGY. In 1979 Naomi Goldenberg first used the word *thealogy* to denote feminist discourse on the Goddess (*thea*) rather than God (*theo*), proclaiming in her book *Changing of the Gods* (1979) that "we are about to learn what happens when father-gods die for a whole generation" (p. 37). Although father-gods are, in fact, alive and well in the world's religions, thealogy has become widely known to scholars of religion and gender and of emergent religion as a provocation to a spiritual and political shift away from the androcentric (male-centered) theological paradigm. Instead, thealogy offers a group of largely participant, experientially grounded texts that explore the many dimensions of female becoming: that of the Goddess, of women, and of nature as encompassing both of these.

Although thealogy is a product, at least in part, of the neo-romantic hippie movement of the 1960s and 1970s, it is also and more immediately a feminist project. Like Christian and Jewish feminist theology, thealogy developed from both the nineteenth-century proto-feminist vision of the feminine as a redemptive locus of moral and spiritual value and the sexual egalitarianism of the second wave secular women's movement. Rejecting the wholesale secularism of early second wave feminism, but drawing on the separatist elements of radical feminism, thealogy developed the feminist criticism of religion as the divinization of masculinity (patriarchy having, as Kate Millet once put it, "God on its side") not to relinquish the divine as such, but to repudiate exclusively masculine models of the divine.

Insofar as it serves the contemporary Goddess movement, thealogy might be said to be the discourse of a new women's religion (one of the very few living women's religions in the world today). Thealogy has emerged from a network of groups and journals, and from a small but growing academic literature with a predominantly North American, British, German, and Australasian readership. Although thealogy can now be studied in universities up to the doctoral level, it is itself resistant to the reintroduction of any totalizing monotheism or to any merely feminized conception of God. Rather, it is derived from feminist reflection on women's experience and on the sacral power of femaleness. There is no authoritative tradition or corpus to which the thealogian must defer. It is a nonprofessional, non-normative discourse both producing and produced by spiritual feminist ritual practice and celebration.

Thealogy's focus on female moral, spiritual, symbolic, and biological difference and its privileging of the divine and human bond between mothers and daughters have made it hospitable to lesbians and any who protest the erasure of the Goddess and her replacement by an exclusively male God styled as king, lord, father, or as a nonpersonal power whose transcendental otherness empties the natural, embodied world of its value. It is notable, however, that thealogy is not without its male adherents and sympathizers. These are especially to be found in the pagan elements of the men's spirituality movement and in modern Witchcraft, or Wicca—arguably the only Western religion that honors the female as an embodiment of the divine. Indeed, thealogy is often, but not invariably, a function of feminist Wicca, where women ritually align their energies with those natural and biological forces whose "Goddess-power" can be channeled or "drawn down" to the purposes of creative change.

However, not everyone in the Goddess movement is willing to espouse a thealogy. There is little doubt that a significant proportion of Goddess feminists would regard thealogy as the arrogation of their experience by an elite minority of feminist academics. Precisely because it is a discourse, thealogy might also seem epistemically superfluous—women already find and know the Goddess in the processes of their own embodiment and in the very fabric and energies of the natural world immediately around them.

The Distinction Between Thealogy and Feminist Theology. Thealogy is something of a boundary discourse. There are those on the gynocentric or woman-centered left of Jewish and Christian feminism who would want to term themselves *theo/alogians* because they find the vestiges of the Goddess or "God-She" within their own traditions as Hochmah, Shekhinah, Sophia, and other "female faces" of the divine. Others would consider thealogy to be inherently pagan in that paganism already honors a female natural/divine principle (albeit one whose powers are balanced by a male generative principle). Paganism also celebrates the transformatory power of female sacrality and repudiates the monotheistic (masculine) legal dispensation of salvation and (masculine) saviors offering redemption from the sin that is so often premised on a redemption from female sexuality.

While it shares much of paganism's religious orientation, thealogy and late-twentieth-century feminist theology have in common an original political impetus and an ecofeminist, relational, inclusivist attempt to reclaim women's history and female experience—especially that of mothers. Both thealogy and feminist theology are in sharp opposition to patriarchal conflict and economics. There is, however, a long-standing and regrettable mutual hostility between some Goddess feminists and Christian feminists. The latter are critical of thealogy's supposed accommodation of goddesses who represent patriarchal constructs of the feminine that are subordinate to male deities. Christian and other feminists are also critical of what they consider to be thealogy's escapist historiography and its tendentious interpretation of traces of goddess worship in texts and landscapes. Thealogy's supposed ethical polarization of the masculine and the feminine is also rejected as unduly essentialist. For feminists in the biblical traditions, God may be like a mother, but is not herself the Mother. Likewise, thealogy's celebration of a divinity whose will is located in and mediated by natural forces, as well as its apparent detachment of women from the history of thought and culture, is widely considered by other feminists (both secular and religious) to be unhelpful to the cause of women. An ecological account of femaleness and of change seems to confirm the traditional patriarchal derogation of women as subrational and properly marginal to the political and historical process.

Christian and Jewish feminist theology countermands the gynophobia and misogyny of its traditions, persevering with faiths considered originally or essentially liberative. Thealogy, by contrast, argues that these traditions cannot make sense of or do justice to a woman's personal and collective experience; patriarchal religion is not merely inhospitable to women but also spiritually and politically harmful.

Concepts of the Goddess. Thealogy can be monotheistic, polytheistic, or nontheistic in character. The nonsystematic, nondogmatic fluidity of its conception of the Goddess allows it to move freely between technical distinctions considered, in any case, to be artificial. Most thealogy, however, postulates a single Goddess—"the Goddess"—in whom all the female divinities named in the world's past and present religions inhere. She is one who might be petitioned and who might reveal herself to the subject in dreams, visions, and the imagination.

The Triple Goddess invoked by feminist Wicca is probably the most characteristic of popular thealogy. Here the Goddess wears three aspects: maiden, mother, and crone. Considered the first of the world's religious trinities, the Triple Goddess hypostatizes the three aspects or stages of women's lives as they pass through girlhood into maturity and motherhood and on into postmenopausal old age. The Triple Goddess exemplifies how all change—both creative and destructive—is part of a cyclic and interdependent natural/divine economy. Incorporating all possibilities, she is not omniscient, morally perfect, or omnipotent.

For others—especially the thealogical avant-garde of the late 1970s and 1980s—the Goddess is not a real external divinity but a psychologically and politically liberating archetype offering women a new sense of self-worth. A variation on this theme is the view that the Goddess—the power and dance of being—is inseparable from the fullness of a woman's own becoming. Mary Daly, for example, uses the word *Goddess* as a metaphor or "verb" naming women's post-patriarchal self-realization and active participation in the powers of female being. Since thealogy can be contingent upon its author's shifting emotions and stage of life, thealogians are generally content to subscribe to a fluid combination of all of these views.

Carol P. Christ and Starhawk are the world's most influential thealogians. While Starhawk's thealogy informs and emerges from the communal political context of San Francisco's Reclaiming Network, Carol Christ's work offers the most focused thealogical discussion. Like many other Goddess feminists, Christ disowns goddesses who are or have been revered in patriarchal religions as mere aspects or attributes (sometimes violent or death-dealing) of a supreme male deity or who are subordinate to other male gods. Instead, in *Rebirth of the Goddess* (1997, pp. xv–xvi), she experiences and theorizes the Goddess as the reconnective power of intelligent embodied love that is the ground of all being: a source of hope and political and ecological healing that will reunite the world and the divine. Her foundational article "Why Women Need the Goddess" (1979) enumerates the reasons why women realize their spiritual and political power from celebration of the Goddess. However, for Carol Christ, the Goddess is also one to whom one might pray and who cares about the individual. Most recently, her book *She Who Changes* (2003) offers a relational thealogy that draws on the process philosophy of Charles Hartshorne to reimagine the changing world as the body of Goddess/God.

THEALOGICAL HISTORY AND ETHICS. Thealogy construes the historical process as belonging to the nonlinear history of nature, which is itself a natural history of the Goddess and therefore of each female body. The female body—whether that of a woman or the earth itself—is a generative site of the transformative power of which time itself is a part. But since patriarchy is founded upon the continual historical and psychological "murder" of the Goddess and the appropriation of her power, history also has a temporal sequence: a history of erasure and suppression, whose knowing is mediated not so much through textual evidence as by one's ontological and physical situation in the landscape and sites associated with the Goddess. Thealogical history tells an archaeological, political, and ecological story of which the subject's own story is an inalienable part.

Although thealogical time is primarily and essentially nonlinear, its periodizations are derived from the work of feminist scholars such as Marija Gimbutas, Merlin Stone, Barbara Walker, and others who claim, on largely archaeological grounds, that the female divine was originally universally revered in apparently peace-loving matrifocal cultures dating from about 30,000 BCE. By about 2000 BCE invasions of Indo-European warriors were destroying the cult of the Great Mother, which went underground by the fifth century CE with the ascendancy of early Christianity, only to reemerge in the priestesshoods and individuals who have discovered the Goddess in the late twentieth century. This temporal scheme has a narrative and psychological function in helping women to "remember" a time when their sacral, biological, and cultural power was revered.

Yet not all thealogians are persuaded that this historiography is a necessary condition of thealogy; even those inclined to support the thesis of a primary and universal cult of the Goddess also allow that its value may be less historical than inspirational. It may be that a primary function of thealogical historiography is to offer a mythography that relativizes patriarchal religion and politics as neither original nor necessary to the world order, but rather an ecologically and spiritually unsustainable aberration.

It is arguable that thealogy's organicist conception of life is inimical to the establishment of ordinary ethical obligations and norms. The thealogical construal of creation and destruction as a single natural/divine process organically regulated by change rather than law can appear to weaken the distinction between good and evil. Traditional religious notions of human transcendence and perfectibility become, at best, otiose. Nonetheless, evil is not entirely naturalized by thealogy. The ecological connections between all living things and the meta-intelligence of nature impose a consequentialist practical ethic of restraint, generosity, and care. Cast as patriarchy itself, evil is politicized and prophetically named in ritualized direct action as the domination and exploitation of the Goddess/earth that tears the life-giving connections of her web and all that depends on it.

SEE ALSO Feminist Theology; Gender and Religion, overview article and article on History of Study; Goddess Worship; Paganism, Anglo-Saxon; Patriarchy and Matriarchy; Wicca; Witchcraft.

BIBLIOGRAPHY

Christ, Carol. "Why Women Need the Goddess: Phenomenological, Psychological, and Political Reflections." In *Womanspirit Rising: A Feminist Reader in Religion*, edited by Carol Christ and Judith Plaskow. New York, 1979; reprint, 1992. An influential article that draws on the work of Clifford Geertz to outline the religious, political, and psychological reasons why women should, in its author's view, turn to Goddess spirituality.

Christ, Carol. *Rebirth of the Goddess: Finding Meaning in Feminist Spirituality*. Reading, Mass., 1997. Exemplifies thealogy's commitment to academic research that derives meaning from the significant interconnections between theory and the scholar's own spiritual journey.

Christ, Carol. *She Who Changes: Re-Imagining the Divine in the World*. New York, 2003. Draws on the process philosophy of Charles Hartshorne to present a thealogy in which the relational power of "Goddess/God" is immanent in a changing world.

Daly, Mary. *Outercourse: The Be-Dazzling Voyage*. London, 1992. An autobiographical approach to radical feminist philosophy, in which the post-Christian "leap beyond patriarchal religion" that Daly makes in her earlier books is further elaborated.

Eller, Cynthia. *Living in the Lap of the Goddess: The Feminist Spirituality Movement in America*. Boston, 1993. Provides an overview of the Goddess tradition and a detailed phenomenological account of the feminist Spiritualist movement in the United States.

Griffin, Wendy, ed. *Daughters of the Goddess: Studies of Healing, Identity, and Empowerment.* Lanham, Md., 2000. A collection of predominantly theoretical essays written by American and British Goddess feminists writing as academics, practitioners, or both.

Goldenberg, Naomi. *Changing of the Gods: Feminism and the End of Traditional Religions.* Boston, 1979. A groundbreaking thealogical text, using Jung and other thinkers to urge women to envision the end of patriarchal religions and to experience liberation through new woman-centered spiritualities such as feminist Wicca.

Long, Asphodel "The One or the Many: The Great Goddess Revisited." *Feminist Theology* 15 (1997): 13–29. Examines the different conception of female deity in the contemporary Goddess movement.

Mantin, Ruth. "Can Goddesses Travel with Nomads and Cyborgs? Feminist Thealogies in a Postmodern Context." *Feminist Theology* 26 (2001): 21–43. Correlates postmodern feminist accounts of female subjectivity and identity with the thealogical poetics of the "spiraling" journey of the female self.

Raphael, Melissa. *Thealogy and Embodiment: The Post-Patriarchal Reconstruction of Female Sacrality.* Sheffield, U.K., 1996. A study of Goddess feminism's construal of the female body's transformative power.

Raphael, Melissa. *Introducing Thealogy: Discourse on the Goddess.* Sheffield, U.K., 1999; Cleveland, 2000. An accessible introduction to Goddess feminist thealogy, historiography, politics, and practice.

Reid-Bowen, Paul. "Reflexive Transformations: Research Comments on Me(n), Feminist Philosophy, and the Thealogial Imagination." In *Gender, Religion, and Diversity: Cross-Cultural Perspectives,* edited by Ursula King and Tina Beattie, pp. 190–200. London and New York, 2004. A discussion of thealogy and Goddess feminism by a committed male feminist.

Salomonsen, Jone. *Enchanted Feminism: Ritual, Gender, and Divinity Among the Reclaiming Witches of San Francisco.* London and New York, 2002. Discusses Starhawk's teaching and her continuing influence since the formation of the Reclaiming Collective in 1979. Includes ethnographic descriptions and a theological discussion of the beliefs and practices of their new religious movement.

Starhawk. *The Spiral Dance: A Rebirth of the Religion of the Great Goddess.* New York, 1979. A pivotal work of thealogical historiography in which Starhawk presents Wicca as a Goddess-worshipping religon that empowers women today.

MELISSA RAPHAEL (2005)

THEATER SEE DANCE; DRAMA

THECLA was the most popular female saint after Mary in early Christianity. Thecla was widely remembered as a disciple of the apostle Paul in Asia Minor (modern Turkey). The original source for the Thecla legend was the second-century *Acts of Paul and Thecla,* which reports her story as follows: When Paul comes to Thecla's hometown of Iconium preaching a gospel that emphasized the virtue of celibacy, Thecla abandons her plans for marriage and follows the apostle. This countercultural action provokes the anger of her fiancé, her family, and the local governor, who together conspire to have her burned at the stake. Thecla is saved only when a miraculous thunderstorm quenches the flames. Later, after being reunited with Paul, she is sexually assaulted on the road to Antioch by a prominent citizen of that city. She manages to rebuff her attacker, but he arranges to have her thrown to the beasts in the local arena. While in custody she receives support from a rich female patron, and in the arena she is defended by a lioness and survives the attacks of lions, bears, and bulls. She finally throws herself into a pool filled with ravenous seals, which are struck dead by a flash of lightning, and she baptizes herself in the water. After the awestruck governor releases her, she dresses herself in male clothes and begins to travel and teach the gospel after the fashion of Paul. Ultimately, Thecla takes her final rest at the town of Seleucia (modern Silifke, Turkey).

The North African writer Tertullian (*On Baptism* 17, c. 200 CE) provides the first external reference to the *Acts of Paul and Thecla.* He reports that it was composed by an Asian presbyter, but certain details in Thecla's story have prompted speculation about the folkloric origins of her legend. The prominence of female characters and the details of their social relations have led some scholars to argue further that the *Acts of Paul and Thecla* may have had roots in the storytelling practices of ascetic women. While such origins ultimately remain uncertain, Tertullian gives evidence that early Christian women appealed to Thecla's example to "defend the liberty of women to teach and to baptize" (*On Baptism* 17).

By the fourth and fifth centuries, devotion to Thecla as a saint and ascetic exemplar had become a widespread phenomenon in the Mediterranean world. The focal point of this devotion was her pilgrimage shrine, Hagia Thekla at Seleucia. Ancient sources describe large numbers of monks who lived in the vicinity and managed the shrine, including a community of female virgins in residence within the sanctuary area. Modern excavations at the site have uncovered the remains of three basilicas, a large public bath, and a number of cisterns. A flurry of architectural adaptation at the site in the late fifth century attests its rapidly growing popularity among Christian pilgrims.

Thecla's shrine was also the recipient of literary patronage. Later writers produced expanded versions of her legend, including accounts of her "martyrdom" at Seleucia—specifically, how she finally escaped her persecutors by disappearing into a large rock while still alive. The story was meant to validate the local veneration of Thecla as a true martyr, despite the absence of her bodily relics. The rock into which she sank became a local cultic marker, the site of the altar in her church. Finally, collections of miracle stories also documented the experiences of pilgrims who came to the shrine in search of healing, among them women from a wide range of social backgrounds.

The cult of Saint Thecla—that is, the social practices, institutions, and material artifacts that marked the lives of actual devotees—was not limited to Hagia Thekla at Seleucia. From Gaul to Palestine, devotion to Thecla was expressed through literature and art: her visual image appears on wall paintings, clay flasks, oil lamps, bronze crosses, wooden combs, stone reliefs, golden glass medallions, and textile curtains.

One region for which there is wide-ranging evidence of Thecla devotion is Egypt. Athanasius of Alexandria (c. 300–373 CE) refers to Thecla extensively in his writings to Alexandrian virgins, and his rhetoric presupposes that his female ascetic readers were already intimately familiar with Thecla's example. During the theological controversies of the fourth century, this community of women was exiled to the distant Kharga Oasis in the Western Desert of Egypt. Ancient wall paintings of Thecla that still survive in local cemetery chapels may provide evidence for the funerary practices of those ascetic women at the oasis. Alexandrian devotion to Thecla is also witnessed by the production of monastic *Lives* modeled after her example—among them, a series of legends about early Christian transvestite saints (monastic women who disguised themselves as men). Near Alexandria, a satellite shrine to Saint Thecla was established near the pilgrimage center dedicated to the Egyptian Saint Menas. Numerous pilgrim flasks with the image of Thecla paired with Menas survive from that site. Finally, the cult of Thecla was thoroughly "Egyptianized" in late antiquity with the production of new namesake martyr legends connected with locales in the Nile Valley.

Other regions have provided more scattered material evidence for Thecla devotion. Fourth-century golden-glass medallions with the image of Thecla among the beasts have been discovered at a cemetery in Köln, Germany. A church and catacomb in Rome are named after Saint Thecla, but no specific images or artifacts survive that might give information about her local cult in late antiquity. In Syriac Christianity, despite a lack of nontextual artifacts from antiquity, a rich literary tradition has been preserved, including a homily given by Severus of Antioch (c. 465–538 CE) on the feast day of Saint Thecla, and at least eleven manuscripts of the *Acts of Paul and Thecla*, the oldest dating to the sixth century CE. Finally, in North Africa, red ceramic pottery from the late fourth or early fifth century portrays the anonymous image of a female martyr, stripped to the waist and praying with arms outstretched between two lions. The details of the iconography have led some to argue that the figure is Thecla; however, it could just as easily be the representation of a namesake African martyr. A similar case appears on the gravestone of an Egyptian woman named Thecla, where the deceased is portrayed in the image of her patron saint.

The evidence for namesakes of Saint Thecla is fairly abundant in late antiquity, and the practice of naming one's child after the saint provides yet another window into the religiosity of her devotees. This religiosity was ultimately grounded in an ethic of imitation. Whether they were mothers or virgins, early Christian women who participated in Thecla's cult commonly saw themselves as striving to imitate her virtues as a female saint and martyr.

BIBLIOGRAPHY

Burris, Catherine, and Lucas van Rompay. "Thecla in Syriac Christianity: Preliminary Observations." *Hugoye: Journal of Syriac Studies* 5, no. 2 (2002): 1–14. Available from http://syrcom.cua.edu/Hugoye/Vol5No2/HV5N2BurrisVanRompay.html.

Dagron, Gilbert, ed. *Vie et miracles de Sainte Thècle.* Brussels, Belgium, 1978.

Davis, Stephen J. *The Cult of St. Thecla: A Tradition of Women's Piety in Late Antiquity.* Oxford, 2001.

Davis, Stephen J. "Crossed Texts, Crossed Sex: Intertextuality and Gender in Early Christian Legends of Holy Women Disguised as Men." *Journal of Early Christian Studies* 10, no. 1 (2002): 1–36.

Hennecke, Edgar, and Wilhelm Schneemelcher, eds. *New Testament Apocrypha*, vol. 2: *Writings to the Apostles, Apocalypses, and Related Subjects.* Rev. ed. English translation edited by Robert McLachlan Wilson. Cambridge, UK, and Louisville, Ky., 1992. See pages 239–246.

Lipsius, Richard A., and Max Bonnet, eds. *Acta Apostolorum Apocrypha.* Leipzig, Germany, 1891. Text in Greek and Latin. See pages 235–272.

MacDonald, Dennis R. *The Legend and the Apostle: The Battle for Paul in Story and Canon.* Philadelphia, 1983.

Nauerth, Claudia, and Rüdiger Warns. *Thekla: Ihre Bilder in der frühchristlichen Kunst.* Wiesbaden, Germany, 1981.

van den Hoek, Annewies, and John J. Herrmann Jr. "Thecla the Beast Fighter: A Female Emblem of Deliverance in Early Christian Popular Art." *The Studia Philonica Annual* 13 (2001): 212–249.

STEPHEN J. DAVIS (2005)

THEISM is the philosophical worldview that perceives the orders of existence (physical things, organisms, persons) as dependent for their being and continuance on one self-existent God, who alone is worthy of worship. Theists differ among themselves about the nature of God and the relation of God to these orders, but they close ranks against deists, who, in principle, exclude revelation and divine intervention in world order, and against pantheists, who identify God with these orders. Theists hold that God, transcendent creator of the orders, remains an indivisible unity as he sustains them in accordance with their capacities and his ultimate purposes.

In formulating their views, philosophical theists remind themselves of the many obstacles that impede the human search for the true, the good, the beautiful, and the holy. They distinguish between the ultimate mystery of being and mysteries that vanish as human understanding increases. Aware that the last word on the mystery of being is beyond their grasp, they pursue the best clues to the relation of the ultimate reality to themselves and the quality of their existence. In the history of theism and of monism, it is almost invariably claimed that immediate experiences of the divine are the most authentic, inspiring sources of truth about the ultimately real, and that these religious experiences take priority over claims based on rational, moral, and aesthetic experience.

However, since religious experients, including seasoned mystics, make conflicting claims about what is revealed, most philosophical theists (hereafter referred to simply as "theists") will take into account the claims based on religious insight but will not grant them arbitrary priority over other interpretations of experience. Broadly speaking, the drift in theistic thinking is toward improving insight into the nature of God and the attributes that are essential for conveying his transcendence and immanence. This essay, in the main, stresses the drift of these reflections without expounding paradigm arguments as such, even as they have been articulated by great theists.

Ontological Argument. When Anselm, archbishop of Canterbury (1093–1109), formulated the ontological argument for God, he was expressing an invincible conviction: the human intellect is, in fact, gripped by at least one idea that, clearly understood, proves the knower's kinship with the ultimate reality as inherently one and good. Anselm's fascinating proposal is that every mind has the idea of a perfect being, namely, of "that than which nothing greater can be conceived" (*Proslogium,* chap. 2). The uniqueness of this idea is missed by any opponent who counters that to argue thus is like deducing the existence of an island from the idea of a perfect island; after all, any island, to be an island, must be perfect. But the idea of a perfect island is not "that than which nothing greater can be conceived," namely, a self-existent being.

Proponents deduce that this one self-existent being is intrinsically immutable, omnipotent, omniscient, and good. These attributes dominate their interpretations of the perfection of this transcendent God's immanence in the world orders. The conclusion of the ontological argument is not grounded in interpretations of human experiences of sense and of value. Indeed, the mind's awareness of perfection is the guiding norm for evaluating claims based on these dimensions of human experience. Nevertheless, theists, whether or not they are sufficiently impressed by the ontological proof, usually explore the family of ideas associated with perfect being in order to help resolve conflicts that do originate in experiences of sense and of value.

Cosmological Argument. The cosmological argument for God centers attention on the explanation of the dependable regularity of changes among the countless beings that make up the spatiotemporal world and constitute it an orderly whole (a cosmos). The cosmological theist emphasizes that the cause-and-effect connections (and other relations) in this world are contingent and not self-existent, that they cannot of themselves ground the cosmic order assumed in so much theory and practice. The Theist therefore proposes that this, or any, cosmic order is the product of a self-existent cause. For without such a cause, the successions of beings and events, having no reliable frameworks of their own, are in fact happenstance. Moreover, the cosmos is a collective whole whose unity is actually contingent, unless the succession of beings and events is grounded in the activity of a self-existent cause. Such a cause is not one supreme being alongside other beings, and it cannot be conceived adequately on the model of any dependent being.

The argument thus far presented allows all contingent beings to be modes of the One, which is consistent with forms of monism. But, for reasons to be noted, the theist holds that the cause, although immanent in all orders, must not be conceived as absorbing them, as in panentheism, nor identified with them, as in pantheism.

While some theists regard such cosmological conclusions as logically demonstrative, most theists regard them as more reasonably probable than alternative explanations of the cosmos. "More reasonably probable" does not mean statistically probable, however. Because there can be no observation of a series of world orders (as there can be of, say, repeated throwings of dice), there can be no calculation of mathematically probable trends. After all, cosmological theists seek the explanatory ground for trusting connections (including statistical calculations) that underlie the uniformity of nature.

Some critics of cosmological theists charge that they commit the fallacy of composition in affirming that a whole of contingent parts must itself be contingent. For example, they contend that a whole of overlapping, contingent beings and events may logically be an everlasting cosmos. To this a cosmological theist replies that to explain cosmos by self-existent cause is, in fact, not to commit the fallacy of composition. Surely, there is no fallacy in concluding that a group composed of blind members is never more than a totality of blind individuals. Similarly, a whole composed of intrinsically contingent beings and relations cannot be other than contingent. Moreover, the theist points out that a continuous, everlasting contingency is still contingency and certainly no substitute for a whole, unified by a self-existent cause.

Theists and monists agree that the self-existent cause (the One) is indivisible and immutable. Were it composite or changing in any way, we would be back seeking an adequate ground for dependable change. Other philosophical considerations influence the theist's and monist's differing conceptions about the immanence of the transcendent One. But they agree, in principle, that analogical inferences from the dependent orders can serve as pointers to the nature of the One. They both discourage the mythological mode of anthropomorphism in depicting the One. And it is on the foundation of the self-existent, immutable One as the essence of perfection that they proceed to refine conceptions of the transcendent One in itself and in its immanence within the dependent orders.

Thus, both theists and monists agree that the self-existent One is incorporeal, since corporeal being is limited by its spatial nature. But is this incorporeal One to be conceived as a person? For example, is its nature compatible with the influential, first formal definition of a person as proposed by Boethius (c. 480–525): "an individual substance of a rational nature" (*Against Eutyches* 6)? The line of reasoning that favors belief in the personhood of the One is fundamental also to the cosmological argument for the self-existent, immutable cause: any successive change cannot be a succession independent of an unchanging, unifying agent. Furthermore, a succession cannot be known as a succession apart from a nonsuccessive experient of succession. In the last analysis, reasoning itself is not possible without a time-transcending unity, free from limitations of corporeal composition. The self-existent cause is best conceived, therefore, as an unchanging, indivisible Person.

However, monists in the West (e.g., Plotinus, Spinoza, Hegel, F. H. Bradley) and in the East (especially Indian exponents of Advaita Vedānta, from Śaṅkara in the ninth century CE to Sarvepalli Radhakrishnan in the twentieth century) developed the concept of incorporeal unity, but they considered the attribution of any concept of a person to the suprapersonal One as misleading. The theist, nevertheless, contends that an infinite Person, inherently and fully rational, is the least misleading view of the contemporaneous One. Can the adherent of the suprapersonal One intelligibly deny that the One is self-aware and aware of all that is (omniscient)? Moreover, can we avoid theoretical shipwreck if the very insistence on the fathomless depths of the One leads to the conclusion that the finite person's ideals of logic and of truth, goodness, and beauty bear, in principle, no trustworthy clue to the nature of suprapersonal unity?

Nor does the theist stop here. The spearhead of the theist's rejection of an all-absorbing One is the conviction that the individual person experiences free will to choose between alternatives within his powers. The theist stresses that without free will it makes no sense to refer to conclusions as true or false. For a conclusion that cannot be drawn from a relatively free, impartial weighing of evidence for and against hypothesis is nothing but the outcome of the regnant play of factors in the knower. Such an outcome is one event among other events and is neither true nor false.

Furthermore, if personal free will is nullified, so is the difference between moral good and moral evil, since each depends on a person's having the free will to choose between alternative courses of action deemed to be good or evil. It is such freedom of will that is vital to the theist's conception of a person's responsibility to other persons and to his interpretation of a person's relation to the physical, the subpersonal orders of being, and to God himself.

Hence, when the theist is told that the orders of being are ultimately machinelike and indifferent to the values of persons, or that the whole framework of things is a logical network that allows for no (supposedly capricious) free will, or when mystical union with the One is taken as indubitable evidence that a person is in fact only a particular center of God's being, the theist will stand by a person's experience of limited free will while pointing out the theoretical and moral consequences of its denial. This stand is basic to his conception of the Creator as person.

Although theists are not of one mind as to the self-existent Person's relation to the order of physical things and of subpersonal living beings, they concur that God creates persons out of nothingness *(creatio ex nihilo)*. This concept, unthinkable to any Greek or Indian philosopher, is admittedly mysterious, but what is posited must be understood in its context. *Creatio ex nihilo* does not mean that God, as it were, takes nothing and makes what he creates therefrom. Rather, he creates what did not exist prior to his creative act. God does not create from being(s) independent of him, nor does he create from his own being; the created orders do not emanate from his being. God creates persons to be free within their potential and in relation to the other orders. The Indian philosopher Rāmānuja (c. 1017–1173) argued against the absorption of persons in the distinctionless One *(brāhman)*, as held in the prevailing *advaita* (nondualist) philosophy of Śaṇkara—although, in the end, he, too, insisted on their ultimate union with the suprapersonal One.

Does the creation of persons, free to develop their own potential and, within limits, their own environments, not conflict with the attribute of God's omnipotent will? No, since God's creating of free persons is self-imposed and is, therefore, an instance of God's omnipotence.

But may not a person's use of freedom influence the fulfillment of God's purposes? On this, theists disagree, depending, in good part, on their conception of God's other attributes. It is worth noting that often, when it seems that God's attributes in effect conflict with each other, theists warn that God's attributes must not be isolated from each other, since this would violate the indivisibility of God's being. The application of this doctrine here supports the view that God's self-imposed creating of persons as free and not as puppets will not issue in the thwarting of his purposes.

But, if the attribute of God's omniscience is defined as God's knowing all that is, has been, and will be, must not God's foreknowledge be limited (and his power affected) by a person's freedom? What can it mean to affirm human freedom of choice if God knows in every instance and in every detail what any person will choose? Some theists take omniscience to mean that the Creator knows all there is to know (including all the options possible and available). They cannot understand how the freedom of persons at the point of choice is compatible with foreknowledge of what the choice will be, let alone compatible with the necessary fulfillment of the omnipotent God's will. Their theistic opponents, however, urge that the creation of free persons should not be interpreted as curtailing either God's power or his knowledge in any way that would limit his control of all there is and will be. They argue that we should not impose on the perfect, timeless Person the conditions of temporal succession to which finite persons are limited in knowing. They suggest that something like human intuitive knowing "all at once," which differs markedly from discursive inference "from one meaning to the other," provides a more helpful clue to God's knowing.

It is plain that the self-existent Creator, whose immutable transcendence is contemporaneous with his immanence in the temporal world, leaves theists with theoretical tensions. But they find these tensions more acceptable than the identification of all that exists with the One.

Teleological Argument. In advancing the concept of the contemporaneous cause as Creator-Person, the theist implies his conviction that causal order is best understood in terms of some goal. Such teleological thinking examines composite things and series of events that strongly suggest design, namely, the cooperation of parts that produce one kind of goal and not another. The spring of a watch is best understood in terms of its relation to the other parts that, along with it, effect the purpose of the watch. So, also, although every animate cell has its own order, understanding of that cell is increased once its contribution to the orderly function of the whole organism is specified.

Accordingly, the teleological argument for God does not arbitrarily add purposeful goal seeking to nonpurposive causes. It centers attention on the designs that can be reasonably inferred as causal patterns when they are viewed in the context of unifying goals. For theists moving from cosmological considerations to teleological understanding, the controlling conviction is that the physical, the organic, and the human orders are most reasonably understood as fitting together within the comprehensive purpose of the Creator. Moreover, teleological theists hold that the inanimate and subhuman orders are so created as to provide for the good of persons, persons who can and should realize that they live in God's world, a training ground for the life to come.

Insofar as theists expound and defend a teleological argument that calls to mind a Creator-Architect-Carpenter who provides the specific physical environment for specific biological species and who does so to suit the created endowments of persons, they continue to encounter strong opposition from scholars who draw on scientific data to support their conviction that no such planned creation and no such Creator is tenable. Charles Darwin's *On the Origin of Species* (1859) spurred on the explanation of present organic structures as consequences of gradual modifications that favored the survival of the fittest. Other scientific discoveries relevant to the theory of evolution and scientific and philosophical interpretations of pertinent new data have enlarged the area of confrontation between teleologist and nonteleologist.

The teleological theist argues, however, that, even granting explanation of evolution in terms of the survival of the fittest, it is the arrival of the fit that still calls for teleological explanation. Nonetheless, the Darwinian theory of evolution led many theists to emphasize the demands of moral consciousness and religious consciousness as independent sources of belief in God.

Wider Teleological Argument. All the more significant is the comprehensive rethinking of teleological theism that has produced a "wider teleological argument," a position that has developed systematically in the context of historical philosophic issues. The outstanding statement of this position is in the two volumes of *Philosophical Theology* (1928–1930) by Frederick R. Tennant. Tennant defends the irreducible unity of the person and explores the cognitive limits of knowledge based on a person's sensory and nonsensory capacities; he concludes that no dimension of personal experience can arrive at logically coercive beliefs.

Tennant does not assume that a nonteleological view of the universe is already established. Nor is our world, as known, more reasonably explained as the product of ultimate, random variations or chance happenings. Rather, such knowledge as we guide ourselves by is the joint product of continuing human interaction with an amenable framework of things. Accordingly, to postulate planning in the ultimate collocation of things is to understand better what the human search for truth and values presupposes, namely, the basic relevance of cognitive activities to the order of things. Thus, "If Nature evinces wisdom, the wisdom is Another's" (Tennant, 1930, p. 107).

This wider teleology is articulated when Tennant points out that the nonbiological, physical order does not itself require either the existence or the progressive evolution of species. Yet, the drift of subhuman evolution allows for the arrival of the new order of conscious-self-conscious persons, for whom "survival of the fittest" does not adequately account. Persons, in turn, cannot exist unless their comprehensive reasoning with regard to the other orders guides their moral efforts to improve the quality of their individual and communal survival.

Tennant does not exclude the inspirational value of religious experiences from the chain of evidence for the Creator-Person. But, in his analysis of the varieties of religious experience, he does not find the immediate, uninterpreted knowledge of God to warrant the conclusion that religious experience should be independent of criticism grounded in the rational and moral dimensions of experience. Religious experience with all its suggestiveness is not given cognitive priority, but it does serve as an important confirmatory link in the chain of evidence, reasonably interpreted.

All in all, then, the claims to reasonably probable knowledge are the more reliable insofar as they can be viewed as joint products of persons interacting with each other in their ongoing interchange with their total environment. No one link in this chain of evidence for cosmic teleology is, by itself, strong enough to justify the conclusion that the Creator-Person is immanent in the orders of being. Consequently, the wider teleological argument is to be judged for its reasonableness as a cumulative whole. But this is no cause for alarm, since, to take an example from the scientific realm, the hypothesis of biological evolution is accepted as a cumulative whole despite weaker and missing links of evidence. Accordingly, the theoretical backbone of the broader teleological theism is its more reasonable interpretation of human experience cumulatively viewed.

Moral Argument. There are theists sympathetic with Tennant's wider teleology who hold that his view of the ethical link simply does not do justice to the experience of the moral consciousness. Their crucial contention is that the value judgments of persons, although related to their desires and feelings, are not experienced as originating in them. Rather, the irreducible moral consciousness becomes increasingly aware of an objective order of values that exerts imperative authority over persons' lives. This unique, normative order, not dependent on human desiring and not descriptive of actual processes in the natural world, is most coherently interpreted as expressive of the Creator's goodness.

In sum, according to this moral argument for God, an unconditional, universal order of values is gradually revealed not only as morally imperative for persons but necessary in their struggle for fulfillment. Most reasonably understood as rooted in God's nature, it is this objective order of values that is the strongest link in any argument for a God worthy of worship. Indeed, without this independent source of normative values, the cosmological and teleological arguments do not suffice to assure the goodness of God.

Tennant, however, provides an elaborate critique of this account of the moral consciousness and the objectivity of value judgments. He argues that to root value-experience in desires and feelings does not, of itself, justify the charge that value judgments are relativistic. He interprets the objectivity and universality of value-experiences and value judgments as joint products of each person's interaction with at least the natural and social orders. It is the most coherent organization of such value judgments that is, indeed, the capstone of the wider teleological argument. For now, persons, experiencing and organizing their values as joint products of their interaction with orderly trends not of their own making, can better interpret the immanent direction of the collocation of things. Hence, the progressive appreciation of the conditions of the qualitative range of value-experiences remains the normative insight into what kind of personal growth this kind of world fosters.

Theoretical Problems. Whichever of the above approaches to God is most acceptable to the traditional theist, central to his vision remains the perfection of the self-existent, transcendent Creator, immanent in his creations and, especially, in the optimum development of morally autonomous persons. This vision of "absolute" perfection poses obstinate theoretical problems for the theist himself, as he tries to clarify the dynamics of the perfection of an immutable Creator-Person who is immanent in his temporal, changing creation. This article confines itself to three questions of especial concern to theists. Adequate discussion of these alone would require analysis of other knotty metaphysical issues (such as the ultimate nature of space and time or the specific nature of God's relation to the spatiotemporal world).

The first question is "How can God be immutable and yet immanent in a changing world, let alone in the kind of changing relations that obtain between him and developing moral agents?" The theist invariably does not flinch as he grants that this theoretical conflict is intrinsic to the theistic transcendent-immanent situation. For a perfect Creator cannot create without creating dependent, imperfect beings; and he will not annul the will of persons free to choose changes within their power. Nevertheless, while thus holding that there is no intelligible bridge from the changing created realms to the immutable Creator, the theist urges that God's immutability is not to be conceived in rigid and timeless mathematical fashion. He does suggest analogies within human experience that render the impasse less stark, such as those concentrated moments in which the past and future seem to fuse with a timeless, transcendent unity.

The second question moves the first into perhaps the most sensitive area of the theist's belief: the passibility of God, that is, God's responsiveness to human need. If God's immutable perfection is appropriately responsive to the created orders in their kind, how can he be unchanged and unchangeable? If he is unchanged and unchangeable, how can he be anything but impassive to the moral struggle of persons? What can it mean to say that he appropriately responds to their situations (that he "knows," "suffers," "redeems," or "liberates") without enduring any change himself? Here the theist, avoiding anthropomorphism, urges us to realize that the Creator-Person will not, in the nature of the case, undergo the psychic states of persons and suffer as we do.

Nevertheless, the moral-religious thrust of the theist's resistance to both deism and monism is at stake, for he defends the concept of a morally free person who is ultimately responsible to God, a God who "knows" and is appropriately responsive to the ranges of human striving. Can this person-to-Person relation be honored by a God who, in his immutability, does not change at all in response to even the worthy appeals of his repentant creatures? In the face of this impasse, some theists hold that God's immutability is compatible with his passibility, if his responses to need are conceived as the overflow of his essence and, hence, neither diminish nor improve it.

The third question is "In view of the amount and quality of evils, how can one reasonably believe in a Creator who, omniscient and limited by nothing beyond or within himself, is perfect in purpose and accomplishment?" The response of the theist depends to some extent upon what he claims to be the pearl of great price in the human ideal of the good. There are differences among theists on this matter, but the exposition here takes as vital to all theistic views of the ideal good the freedom of persons to choose, within limits, their own destiny. Such freedom does not exist in a vacuum; indeed, it would be powerless without a network of order that helps a person to know the good and evil consequences of his actions. Without such freedom a person would not experience the profound satisfaction of building the character so essential to the conservation and increase of values available to him as he develops.

So important is this pearl that the theist, never unaware of the maldistribution of values and disvalues, is poignantly mindful of the undeserved and vicious evils inflicted by man's inhumanity to man and by natural forces beyond human control. He is not given to holding that evil is illusory, or that it exists as a privation of goodness. But neither will he minimize a fact that becomes the foundation of his thinking about evil. Evil, in the last analysis, has no independent power of its own; it lives parasitically on the good. The theist's trust in the goodness of the Creator-Person is, therefore, grounded in this priority in the very nature of things. This fact also fortifies his belief in a personal immortality that is not an external addition to life in this imperfect world but is, rather, the extension of the creative goodness of God.

Even if all this be granted, serious concerns persist. Can it be conceded, even to so acute a theist as Tennant, that a Creator-Person, both omnipotent and omniscient, cannot, in the collocation and governance of things, create water that quenches thirst but does not drown? Again, it may be granted that, without the possibility of evil, persons would not experience the qualities of creativity resulting from their developing virtues. Nevertheless, would a Creator who is all-good, omnipotent, and omniscient create a world in which so much "nondisciplinary evil" occurs? Nondisciplinary evils are evils that, as far as we can see, are not instrumental to the realization of other values. They are those evils that undermine even the most heroic moral effort; they finally fell the oak that has weathered many storms. They, too, are parasites upon the good, but whatever the source, they are the irreducible evils that defy being classified as means to some good.

The traditional theist now reminds us of our keyhole vision in this life. To other theists, this appeal to ignorance is unavailing. After all, it is open to opponent and exponent alike. These "finitistic" theists, determined to explain the evidence at hand as reasonably as possible, reexamine the concept of perfection presupposed by traditional theists. They suggest that the impasses of transcendence-immanence ultimately hinge on the assumption that perfection necessarily excludes all temporality and change in the self-existent Creator. Why must we hold, finitists ask, that self-existence necessitates God's immutability in every respect? Why cannot perfection characterize a transcendent, self-existent Creator who expresses his purposes in the temporal orders without danger of becoming the victim of the changes required? Indeed, why suppose that only immutable perfection is worthy of worship?

In any case, finitistic theists contend that the actual course of natural and human history is more reasonably explained if the Creator-God's omnipotence and immutability are limited in the interest of his creative goodness. And his moral perfection consists in God's conservation and renewal of value realization despite recalcitrant conditions within his own being. This Creator-Person, thus limited in power by uncreated conditions within himself, creates and recreates situations most consistent with his purposes.

The specific way in which the morally perfect Creator-Person is limited in power depends upon the particular theist's conception of God's immanence in the inorganic, organic, and personal orders and, especially, on that theist's view of God's relation to persons as individuals and in community. Finitistic theists, however, cannot tolerate, theoretically, the conception of a self-existent Creator limited by any being(s) completely independent of his own will. Such theists vary in their description of the recalcitrant factor(s) that are inherent in the self-existent Creator. But the basic thrust of their views inspires the worship of a God who, dealing creatively with recalcitrance, continues to create, in accordance with his concern that the conditions for creativity be preserved and increased at every level possible.

Such finitistic theism saves transcendence from the pantheistic absorption of persons. At the same time, it is free from the dangers of a theism that, in the name of immutable perfection, sets up impasses that encourage the conception of a deistic Creator who knows not the quality of continuing, creative caring.

See Also Atheism; Deism; Monism; Pantheism and Panentheism; Proofs for the Existence of God; Theodicy; Transcendence and Immanence.

Bibliography

The books in this highly select bibliography contain, each in its own scope, the needed expansion, significant particularity, and helpful context for explication of the condensed discussion of central topics in this article. The suggestions in the next paragraph include comprehensive cultural and religious background for the theistic themes focused on in the main presentation. Elaboration on these themes, with an eye to the variety of interpretations, is provided in the remaining suggestions.

Arthur O. Lovejoy's *The Great Chain of Being: A Study of the History of an Idea* (Cambridge, Mass., 1942) is a fascinating study of the historical roots and the growth of ideas involved in this article. Alfred E. Taylor's "Theism," in the *Encyclopaedia of Religion and Ethics,* edited by James Hastings, vol. 12 (Edinburgh, 1921), is a classic historical analysis of theistic philosophy in the West up to the early decades of the twentieth century. Étienne Gilson's *L'esprit de la philosophie médiévale,* 2 vols., 2d ed. (Paris, 1944), translated by A. H. C. Downes as *The Spirit of Medieval Philosophy* (New York, 1936), emphasizes the assimilation of Greek philosophical ideas by formative Christian thinkers such as Augustine, Aquinas, Bonaventura, and Duns Scotus. James D. Collins's *God in Modern Philosophy* (1959; reprint, Westport, Conn., 1978) examines critically much of the modern debate. In chapter 8 of *Indian Philosophy,* 2d ed., vol. 2 (London, 1927, 1931), Sarvepalli Radhakrishnan expounds the main tenets in the monistic system of Śaṅkara, and, in chapter 9, he contrasts these with the theism of Rāmānuja. Annemarie Schimmel's *Gabriel's Wing: A Study into the Religious Ideas of Sir Muḥammad Iqbal* (Leiden, 1963) gives a vivid account both of Islamic thought and culture and of the reevaluation of the essential tenets of Islam by the poet-philosopher Iqbal; further, it provides a comprehensive bibliography.

See H. P. Owen's *Concepts of Deity* (New York, 1971) for discriminating definitions of attributes of the traditional theistic God and for contrasts with dominant themes in the work of six twentieth-century thinkers; this book includes a select bibliography. The studies by Eric L. Mascall, *He Who Is,* rev. ed. (London, 1966), and *Existence and Analogy: A Sequel to "He Who Is"* (1949; reprint, New York, 1967), are standby expositions of theistic issues. Milton K. Munitz's *The Mystery of Existence: An Essay in Philosophical Cosmology* (New York, 1965) is included here for its searching critique of theistic approaches to mystery.

John Hick's "Ontological Argument for the Existence of God," in *The Encyclopedia of Philosophy,* edited by Paul Edwards, vol. 5 (New York, 1967), is an able exposition of the argument (with solid bibliography). The specific analyses in *The Ontological Argument,* edited by Alvin Plantinga (London, 1940), provide welcome context. John Laird's *Theism and Cosmology* (1940; reprint, Freeport, N.Y., 1969) examines metaphysical issues relevant to the God of theism. *The Cosmological Arguments: A Spectrum of Opinion,* compiled and edited by Donald R. Burrill (Garden City, N.Y., 1967), includes noteworthy excerpts from classical discussions of both the cosmological and the teleological arguments as well as commentary by recent and contemporary philosophers. *Natural Theology: Selections,* edited with an introduction by Frederick Ferré (Indianapolis, 1963), is an abridged version of William Paley's *Natural Theology, or Evidences of the Existence and Attributes of the Deity Collected from the Appearances of Nature* (London, 1802). The judicious introduction frees Paley's underlying teleology from shallow stereotypes. Frederick R. Tennant's *Philosophical Theology,* vol. 1, *The Soul and Its Faculties* (Cambridge, 1928), and vol. 2, *The World, the Soul, and God* (Cambridge, 1930), is probably the most broadly based, yet closely reasoned, study, to date, issuing in a teleological theism. The most systematic critique of it is Delton L. Scudder's *Tennant's Philosophical Theology* (New Haven, 1940).

For systematic presentation of ethical ideas and their objectivity in relation to other arguments for God and his attributes, there are few works that equal William R. Sorley's *Moral Values and the Idea of God,* 3d rev. ed. (Cambridge, 1918). Herbert J. Paton's *The Modern Predicament* (London, 1955) is lucid in its exposition and evaluation of the issues evoked by a moral approach to God's nature and attributes. Edward H. Madden and Peter H. Hare's *Evil and the Concept of God* (Springfield, Ill., 1968) finds both traditional and finitistic theistic explanations of evil inadequate. Edgar S. Brightman's *A Philosophy of Religion* (1940; reprint, Westport, Conn., 1969) includes a comprehensive survey of philosophic issues, a brief historical exposition of absolutistic and finitistic theism, and his defense of a "finite-infinite" God. It also provides an extensive bibliography and a helpful lexicon. John Hick's *Evil and the God of Love,* 2d ed. (London, 1977), explores traditional and recent accounts of evil and defends an Irenaean view. S. Paul Schilling's *God and Human Anguish* (Nashville, 1977) stands out for its well-annotated account of various historical and recent explanations of excess evil as well as for his own temporalistic theism.

New Sources

Basinger, David. *The Case for Freewill Theism.* Downers Grove, Ill., 1996.

Beaty, Michael, ed. *Christian Theism and the Problems of Philosophy.* Notre Dame, Ind., 1990.

Cowan, Paul, and Paul Moser, eds. *The Rationality of Theism.* New York, 2003.

Craig, William Lane, and Quentin Smith, eds. *Theism, Atheism, and Big Bang Cosmology.* New York, 1995.

Frame, John. *No Other God: A Response to Open Theism.* Nashua, N.H., 2001.

Morris, Thomas. *God and the Philosophers: The Reconciliation of Faith and Reason.* New York, 1994.

O'Connor, David. *God and Inscrutable Evil: In Defense of Theism and Atheism.* Lanham, Md., 1998.

Smart, J. J. C. and John Haldane. *Atheism and Theism.* 1996; rpt. Malden, Mass., 2003.

PETER A. BERTOCCI (1987)
Revised Bibliography

THEOCRACY means "rule by God" and refers to a type of government in which God or gods are thought to have sovereignty, or to any state so governed. The concept has been widely applied to such varied cases as pharaonic Egypt, ancient Israel, medieval Christendom, Calvinism, Islam, and Tibetan Buddhism.

The word was first coined in the Greek language (*theokratia*) by the Jewish historian Josephus Flavius around 100 CE. Josephus noted that while the nations of the world were variously governed by monarchies, oligarchies, and democracies, the polity of the Jews was theocracy. This, he thought, went back to Moses, who was not attracted by the model of these other polities and therefore "designated his government a theocracy—as someone might say, forcing an expression—thus attributing the rule and dominion to God" (*Against Apion* 2.165).

From Josephus's coinage the term found its way into modern languages, though most early uses were references to the government of ancient Israel, and thus faithful to the original context. The poet John Donne, in a sermon of 1622, stated that the Jews had been under a theocracy, and the Anglican bishop William Warburton, in his *Divine Legation of Moses Demonstrated* (1737–1741), engaged in a long discussion of Israelite theocracy.

Impetus for wider use of the word came from G. W. F. Hegel's *Philosophy of History,* where the term was employed to describe that early phase of ancient oriental civilization in which there was no distinction between religion and the state. In the later nineteenth and early twentieth centuries, the term became what Karl Mannheim called a *Kampfbegriff,* by which "enlightened" contempt for "priest-ridden" societies could be expressed. It was with something of this force that it was used by W. E. H. Lecky in his *History of Rationalism* (1865) and by Brooks Adams in *The Emancipation of Massachusetts* (1887).

Theocracy has not become a rigorously defined concept in either social science or the history of religions, although the term is frequently used in historical writing. This is probably because it does not name a governmental system or structure, parallel to monarchy or democracy, but designates a certain kind of placement of the ultimate source of state authority, regardless of the form of government. In biblical studies, where the notion of theocracy has had its longest currency, it has probably also been used with the greatest consistency and fruitfulness.

This article deals with the various meanings that the term theocracy may be usefully given, with examples relevant to each meaning: hierocracy, or rule by religious functionaries; royal theocracy, or rule by a sacred king; general theocracy, or rule in a more general sense by a divine will or law; and eschatological theocracy, or future rule by the divine.

HIEROCRACY. *Theocracy* has often been used as a term to describe societies where the clergy or priests rule, but this is not the exact denotation of the word, and another word, hierocracy, is available for such situations. Some have called this "pure" theocracy. Among such theocracies, a distinction can be made between those in which the religious functionaries who exercise rule are priestly in character and those in which they are more prophetic-charismatic.

Theocracies of this type have not been very numerous. Several of the stages in the history of ancient Israel exemplify it: the early period, beginning with the Sinai covenant and continuing with the leadership of Moses and Aaron; the religious confederation of the tribal amphictyony; and the charismatic (though occasional) leadership of the Judges down to the time of Samuel. Thus, Israel had strongly theocratic elements, in the sense of rule by religious functionaries. Centuries later, after the return from exile in the late sixth century BCE, a theocracy emerged with the priestly leadership of the generations after Ezra. The priestly theocratic pattern became so important among the Jews at this time that the later Hasmoneans legitimated their rule by claiming the high priesthood. This was the case until the end of the rule of Alexander Yannai over the small Jewish state in 67 BCE.

This kind of theocracy has been rare in Christianity, which grew up as a clandestine religion at odds with a hostile state. Nonetheless, a kind of theocracy in the sense of priestly rule appeared in the Papal States of central Italy and lasted for over a millennium (756–1870). However, this situation was not usually thought of as a prototype of the ideal but, rather more pragmatically, as a way of securing the independence of church authority, centered in Rome, from interference and control by secular powers. Another Christian example of pure theocracy can be found in the early years of the Latter-Day Saints, or Mormons, in the United States, where the prophetic leaders (first Joseph Smith and then Brigham Young) exercised religious and temporal authority in the life of the community, both in earlier settlements and then in Salt Lake City.

The early years of Islam, under the prophet Muḥammad and his first successors, the caliphs, were also theocratic in the sense that there was rule by the religious leadership, though it was not a priestly but a prophetic-charismatic leadership. It is, however, difficult to say at exactly what point the caliphate ceased to be a primarily religious institution.

Tibetan Buddhism has often been cited as an example of priestly theocracy. After the thirteenth century, Tibet was ruled by various elements of the Buddhist priesthood; in the seventeenth century, the Dge lugs pa sect gained the temporal rule of the land and governed through the Dalai and Panchen lamas, as successive incarnations of Avalokiteśvara and Amitābha Buddha, respectively, until the Chinese Communist invasion destroyed this pattern in 1959. The Dalai Lama was the principal ruler from his capital at Lhasa, and administration was exercised by him (or by a regent ruling in his name when a new Dalai Lama was being sought) through a cabinet composed partly of monks.

Many short-lived communal and revolutionary movements inspired by religion have functioned as pure theocracies. Examples of this include the Taiping Rebellion in China in 1858; the seizure of Khartoum in the Sudan by a claimant to the role of the Mahdi in 1885; and the People's Temple of Jim Jones, which was established in Guyana in 1977, only to end in mass suicide.

ROYAL THEOCRACY. Rule by a king thought to possess divine status or power, or to be entrusted by God with authority over the earth, is a second kind of theocracy. Such sacred kingship has many ramifications beyond what can be considered in relation to the concept of theocracy. Traditional Japan was ruled by such a royal theocracy, the emperors being regarded as descendants of the sun goddess Amaterasu. Some societies of the ancient world were theocratic in this sense: the ancient Mesopotamian kings were regarded as chosen servants and regents of the gods, and the Egyptian pharaohs were thought to be directly descended from the sun god, who had created the earth and had at first ruled it personally, later ruling it through them. In both Egypt and Mesopotamia, as well as among other ancient peoples, kings also fulfilled many important roles in ritual, thus acting as intermediaries between men and the gods. Analogies have frequently been drawn between ancient Near Eastern sacred monarchy and Israelite kingship, but such inferences should be drawn with caution, especially since Israel's monarchy had been established within the time of Israel's historical memory and had been opposed by a school of thought that felt that Yahveh alone should be recognized as king (1 *Sm.* 8:6–22, *Hos.* 8:4, 13:10–11). However, Israelite monarchy borrowed some of the theocratic features of its Near Eastern predecessors, especially elements of court ritual. Still, Israel under the monarchy was a royal theocracy, for the kings were considered to be the anointed and chosen servants of Yahveh and the earthly representatives of Yahveh's theocratic authority.

Monarchy as the fulfillment of a sacred role of divine regency also appeared in Christianity. The most obvious examples have been in Eastern Christianity, both Byzantine and Russian, in which the imperial office was regarded as God-given, and the emperor regarded as God's representative on earth in all temporal matters, as well as in the external affairs of the church. In Byzantium, the distinction between the religious and the secular was not as sharply drawn as it usually was in the West, and the Byzantine emperor had certain liturgical prerogatives that were closed to the layperson. Such sacred kingship also appeared in Western Christianity among the early Germanic kings who ruled after the dissolution of the Roman empire, and especially in the rule of Charlemagne. It reappeared with some of the Holy Roman emperors who sought to counter the claims of papal theocracy after the eleventh-century Gregorian reform, and at the courts of Henry VIII and Louis XIV.

General Theocracy. A third type of theocracy, by far the most common, is that more general type wherein ultimate authority is considered to be vested in a divine law or revelation, mediated through a variety of structures or polities. In a sense, both priestly and royal theocracies may be of this sort: for example, in Israelite monarchy the Law stood as an authority beyond that of the king at the time of the Josianic reform; Byzantine emperors in spite of their choice by God were subordinate to the principles of revealed truth; and even the Egyptian god-kings were supposed to rule according to the eternal principles of *maat,* or justice. Theocracy in this third sense has been quite common as a conception in such universalizing religions as Christianity and Islam, where there has often been a thrust toward bringing the whole human sphere under the aegis of the divine will; but it has also appeared in some ancient and tribal societies where the laws and customs of the people are understood to be revealed by the gods, as in some of the ancient Greek city-states.

Historical conditions have made this type of theocracy less common in Christianity than might otherwise have been the case; in earliest Christianity, theocracy was ruled out by the sharp dichotomy between the church and a hostile world that prevailed in Christian thinking, and in modern times, secularization has rendered otiose any program for the rule of Christian norms over all of society. Furthermore, some kinds of Christian thinking about society—for example, the two-kingdom theory of Lutheranism; Christian Aristotelianism, which grants to the state a basis in its own right; and the modern acceptance of the separation of church and state—have weakened the theocratic impulse.

In Christianity, the two most commonly cited examples of this kind of theocracy have been medieval Roman Catholicism and some of the Calvinist societies of the sixteenth and seventeenth centuries.

Earlier medieval thought looked upon the spiritual and the temporal as two coordinate powers under God, with their own separate structures of rule. After the Gregorian reform of the eleventh century, however, papal theorists sought to divest the temporal overlord of his sacred character and promoted the view that the church, through the pope, was sovereign in all temporal affairs, even if this sovereignty were not exercised directly but through secular rulers whom the church had the authority to direct, judge, or remove. This papal theocracy reached its height in the early thirteenth-century pontificate of Innocent III, who made good his claim to have the authority to dispose earthly powers when he disciplined various European monarchs, including King John of England. Defenders of papal theocracy, however, made even more far-reaching claims in the next century, asserting that the popes, as vicars of Christ on earth, exercised all the prerogatives of Christ's heavenly kingship, which was both royal and priestly, and were, theoretically, not only the possessors of all earthly political sovereignty but the ultimate owners of all property. Late medieval developments, including the papal captivity and schism, the rise of conciliarism, and nationalism, led to the decline of effective papal theocracy.

Theocracy has often been attributed to the government of certain Reformed or Calvinist states, whether Zurich under Huldrych Zwingli, Geneva under John Calvin, England under Oliver Cromwell, or Puritan Massachusetts. In none of these cases was there a hierocratic theocracy, since in most of them the clergy were less likely to hold public office than they had been previously—for example, Cromwellian England abolished church courts and the House of Lords with its bishops, and the Massachusetts Bay Colony forbade the clergy to serve as magistrates. Even in Geneva, the clergy had only an advisory role in checking and balancing the civil government. But all of these societies had an ideal, well expressed by the Strasbourg theologian Martin Bucer in his *De regno Christi,* of a holy community on earth in which the sovereignty was God's and in which the actual law should reflect the divine will and the government seek to promote the divine glory. In the Puritan examples of Cromwellian England in the 1650s and Massachusetts Bay in the first generations of its settlement, there was both a hearkening after Old Testament theocratic patterns and a sense of the importance of government entrusted to truly regenerate persons—or the saints—in an effort to create a holy commonwealth. In fact, however, rule was exercised in both cases more through a godly laity than through the clergy, and in both Cromwellian England and Puritan Massachusetts the state had considerable power in church affairs.

It is also in this general sense of theocracy that Islam ought to be considered theocratic. Islam grew up as a religious community that was its own state, and thus from the beginning there was no distinction of church and state; rather, there was a unitary society under God's revealed rule and law. Islam was much less a church than a theocratic state, but as a theocracy, it was laical and egalitarian, with traditions neither of sacred kings nor of a powerful priesthood. The basis of this divine rule is to be found in *sharīʿah,* or law, which provides for a pattern of life uniting all the aspects of human existence—political, social, religious, domestic—into a grand whole under divine rule. Such rule has been variously exercised in Islamic history, but the *ʿulamaʾ* as well as the caliphs and, in Shiism, the imams have been important in its application. Many modern Islamic revival movements, reacting against Western aggression and internal decline, have tended toward the repristination of the theocratic elements in Islam; this was true of the Wāhhābīyah in the eighteenth and nineteenth centuries and has been true of many contemporary movements.

Eschatological Theocracy. A fourth kind of theocracy is eschatological, centering on visions of an ideal future in which God will rule. Restoration eschatology and messianic ideas in ancient Israel were of this type. In Christianity, such eschatological theocracy appeared in the beliefs of the medieval followers of Joachim of Fiore, who anticipated the emergence of a third age in which all would be perfect, and in the beliefs of the sectarians of seventeenth-century England, such as the Seekers, Quakers, or Fifth Monarchists, who dreamed of a coming millennial age when Christ would rule. Such modern offshoots of Christianity as the Jehovah's Witnesses and the Unification Church of Sun Myung Moon present recent examples of groups anticipating an earthly reign of Christ. Islamic eschatology centering on the figure of the Mahdi has occasionally begotten similar hopes.

See Also Charlemagne; Constantine; Dalai Lama; Imamate; Israelite Law, article on State and Judiciary Law; Kingdom of God; Kingship; Shiism.

Bibliography

There is no single, synoptic account of the whole range of theocratic phenomena. Among general studies of religion, Gustav *Mensching's Soziologie der grossen Religionen* (Bonn, 1966) and *Soziologie der Religion,* 2d ed. (Bonn, 1968), pp. 79f., 112, and 155–158, take interest in the notion of theocracy. Among the many studies of sacred kingship in the ancient world, Henri Frankfort's now classic text *Kingship and the Gods: A Study of Ancient Near Eastern Religion* (1948; reprint, Chicago, 1978) is a good place to begin. Thomas L. Brauch, "The Emperor Julian's Theocratic Vocation," *Society of Biblical Literature Seminar Papers* 25 (1986): 291–300, examines theocracy in the late Roman pagan revival. For a general account of theocracy and ancient Israel, see John W. Wevers's "Theocracy" in the *Interpreter's Dictionary of the Bible,* vol. 4 (Nashville, 1962), pp. 617–619. D. Otto Plöger deals with Daniel, Joel, and other examples of late Israelite eschatology in *Theokratie und Eschatologie* (Neukirchen, West Germany, 1959). For the concept of theocracy in Philo, Maimonides, traditional Rabbinic thought, and modern Israel, see Gershon Weiler, *Jewish Theocracy* (Leiden, 1988). For Tibetan theocracy, see Franz Michael and Eugene *Knez's Rule by Incarnation: Tibetan Buddhism and Its Role in Society and State* (Boulder, Colo., 1982). Dieter Georgi, *Theocracy in Paul's Praxis and Theology* (Minneapolis, 1991), uses theocracy as a conceptual tool for interpreting the apostle Paul. For royal theocracy in Byzantium, see Deno John Geanakoplos's *Byzantine East and Latin West* (Oxford, 1966), especially chapter 2. Among many treatments of medieval papal thought, the following deal extensively with the theme of theocracy: *La théocratie: L'église et le pouvoir au moyen âge* by Marcel Pacaut (Paris, 1957); *L'idée de la royauté du Christ au moyen âge* by Jean Le Clercq (Paris, 1959), especially chapters 1, 7, and 8; and *Church State and Christian Society at the Time of the Investiture Contest* by Gerd Tellenbach (1959; reprint, New York, 1979).

A number of authors investigate Reformation and Puritan theocracy: Robert C. Walton in Zwingli's *Theocracy* (Toronto, 1967); E. William Monter in *Calvin's Geneva* (New York, 1967), especially chapter 6; Harro Höpfl in *The Christian Polity of John Calvin* (Cambridge, 1982); George L. Hunt in *Calvinism and the Political Order* (Philadelphia, 1965); Rene Paquin in "Calvin and Theocracy in Geneva," *ARC, The Journal of the Faculty of Religious Studies, McGill* 28 (2000): 91–113; Aaron B. Seidman in "Church and State in the Early Years of the Massachusetts Bay Colony," *New England Quarterly* 18 (1945): 211–233, which seeks to set the record straight on theocracy in the colony; Avihu Zakai, in "Theocracy in New England: The Nature and Meaning of the Holy Experiment in the Wilderness," *Journal of Religious History* 14 (1986): 131–151; and Jerald C. Brauer in "The Rule of the Saints in American Politics," *Church History* 27 (September 1958): 240–255, which also discusses theocratic impulses in later American history. For a study of the Quakers and theocracy, see Thomas G. Sanders's *Protestant Concepts of Church and State* (New York, 1964), pp. 125–178. The theocratic aspects of Islam are variously alluded to in Ruben Levy's *The Social Structure of Islam,* 2d ed. (Cambridge, 1957), and E. I. J. Rosenthal's *Political Thought in Medieval Islam* (1958; reprint, Cambridge, 1968); Majid Fakhry deals with some modern revivals of theocratic thinking in "The Theocratic Idea of the Islamic State in Recent Controversies," *International Affairs* 30 (October 1954): 450–462. Modern Iran is examined in Mehran Kamrava, *The Political History of Modern Iran: From Tribalism to Theocracy* (Westport, 1992). Legal and ethical issues are explored in Lucas A. Swaine, "How Ought Liberal Democracies to Treat Theocratic Communities," *Ethics* 111 (January 2001): 302–343.

Dewey D. Wallace, Jr. (1987 and 2005)

THEODICY. Why do the righteous suffer? Why do the wicked prosper? Why do innocent children experience illness and death? These are ancient questions, but they have been given new poignancy in our day by the events of the European Holocaust. The fact that many who died in the Holocaust were devout Jews or Christians also poses a special problem for the faiths to which these victims belonged. Traditionally, Jews and Christians have affirmed God's goodness and his absolute sovereignty over history. But how can this faith be reconciled with suffering on the scale for which Auschwitz is the symbol?

THEORETICAL POSITIONS. The effort to answer questions of this sort is commonly referred to as *theodicy.* The term was apparently coined by the philosopher Gottfried Leibniz (1646–1716) and is a compound of the Greek words for God *(theos)* and justice *(dikē).* Theodicy may thus be thought of as the effort to defend God's justice and power in the face of suffering. Theodicies result from this effort: they are specific explanations or justifications of suffering in a world believed to be ruled by a morally good God.

The theodicy problem. The "problem of theodicy" arises when the experienced reality of suffering is juxtaposed with two sets of beliefs traditionally associated with ethical monotheism. One is the belief that God is absolutely good and compassionate. The other is the belief that he controls all events in history, that he is both all-powerful (omnipotent) and all-knowing (omniscient). When combined with some other implicit beliefs—for example, the belief that a good being would try to prevent suffering insofar as he is able—these various ideas seem contradictory. They appear to form a logical "trilemma," in the sense that, while any two of these sets of ideas can be accepted, the addition of the third renders the whole logically inconsistent. Thus, it seems that it can be affirmed that God is all-good and all-powerful, but not also that there is suffering in the world. Similarly, the fact of suffering can be affirmed along with God's goodness, but the insistence on God's omnipotence appears to render the whole ensemble of beliefs untenable. Theodicy may be thought of as the effort to resist the conclusion that such a logical trilemma exists. It aims to show that traditional claims about God's power and goodness are compatible with the fact of suffering.

Alternative definitions. Some writers have tried to expand the term *theodicy* beyond its classical Western philosophical and theological usage. The sociologist Max Weber, for example, sought to redefine the term in order to render it applicable to religious traditions that do not involve belief in one just, all-powerful deity. In Weber's usage, *the theodicy problem* referred to any situation of inexplicable or unmerited suffering, and *theodicy* itself referred to any rationale for explaining suffering. This wider definition has value for the comparative study of religion. Nevertheless, without neglecting other religious responses to suffering, I shall here be using the term *theodicy* in its classical sense, as the effort to defend God's justice and power in a world marred by suffering.

Dissolutions of the theodicy problem. One reason for holding to the narrower definition of theodicy is that it allows us to see that theodicy in its classical sense is very much a feature of ethical monotheism. Theodicy in this sense does not arise in traditions that fundamentally deny or reject any one of the three major sets of ideas that form the theodicy problem: the belief in God's goodness, the belief in his power, or the belief in the real occurrence of suffering. Religious positions that fundamentally dissolve the problem may be classified according to which of the three basic beliefs they do not accept.

Denials of God's justice. Some religious positions avoid theodicy by denying that God (or the gods) is morally good. Very few religious traditions openly hold God to be evil, although Wendy Doniger O'Flaherty, in her book *The Origins of Evil in Hindu Mythology* (Berkeley, 1976), has argued that at least one important motif in Hindu mythology traces suffering to the gods' pettiness and fear of human power. More common than an outright denial of the deity's justice, however, is the claim that God's justice is somehow qualitatively different from our ordinary human ideas of right and wrong. Words like *justice* or *goodness* when applied to God have no relation to their meaning when applied to human beings. What would be regarded as wickedness on the part of a human being—for example, the slaughter of children—may not be unjust where God is concerned. We shall see that this view has had some currency in Islam and in Calvinist Christianity.

Denials of God's omnipotence. Rather than compromise the divine goodness, some religious traditions have avoided theodicy by qualifying the divine power. This view is especially characteristic of religious dualisms, which explain the fact of suffering by positing a power or principle of disorder that wars incessantly with God for control of the world. In Zoroastrianism, for example, imperfections and suffering in this world are traced to an ongoing cosmic struggle between the good deity, Ahura Mazdā (Ōhrmazd), and his evil antagonist, Angra Mainyu (Ahriman). Similarly, the gnostic religion Manichaeism explained suffering in terms of a struggle between a "spiritual" god of goodness and light and an evil "creator" demon associated with darkness and matter.

Apart from dualism there are other ways by which religions can deny God's omnipotence. One of the most important of these is found in Buddhism, where suffering is traced to the automatic operation of the moral law of retribution known as *karman.* I shall return to *karman* in connection with Buddhist teaching as a whole, but for now it may be noted that *karman* eliminates the need to justify God (or the gods) in a world of suffering because it places that suffering almost wholly beyond divine control.

Denials of the reality of suffering. The final major way by which to avoid the problem of theodicy is to deny the third component in the trilemma, that is, that there really is suffering in the world. This position may seem impossible since unhappiness, illness, and death are all around us. Yet in various ways, religious thinkers and religious traditions have sometimes denied the ultimate reality or significance of suffering. The philosopher Spinoza, for example, affirmed that the world seems filled with evil only because it is regarded from a narrow and erroneous human point of view. From the divine perspective, however, the world forms a necessary and perfect whole. Some Hindu thinkers have also denied the reality of suffering by advocating adoption of the divine point of view. According to the Vedantic tradition, what we call evil or suffering is really an aspect of *māyā,* the cosmic principle of dynamism and individuation. This principle is not ultimate, and the sage who attains the divine perspective sees *māyā* as an illusory process that does not really affect the eternal soul. This teaching renders the world of suffering inconsequential.

Classical theodicies. Those familiar with the Western religious traditions may be unpersuaded by these various dissolutions of the theodicy problem. They may find that some of these positions, such as the denial that God is just in humanly understandable terms, seriously jeopardize a religious faith based on belief in God's goodness. Other dissolutions may seem to ignore the importance of the evil that God seeks to overcome or may erode confidence in God's ability to master that evil. Yet we have seen that the alternative position—affirmation of God's absolute goodness and power in a world of serious suffering—appears to be illogical. Defenders of ethical monotheism, however, have usually refused to accept this apparent illogicality. With varying degrees of self-consciousness, they have maintained that the alleged contradiction between monotheism and suffering does not exist. This view underlies the specific theodicies that have been elaborated to defend belief in a just and all-powerful God.

The key to these positions is an understanding of what it means to say that God is omnipotent. Typically, it is argued that while God can do anything he wills himself to do and anything that is capable of being done, he cannot do what is logically impossible. This is not because his power is limited but only because what is logically impossible cannot really be thought or conceived. Thus, God cannot make a "square circle," and we cannot ask or desire him to do so, because the very idea of a square circle is nonsense. Only the accident of language that makes a "square circle" seem as possible as a "seedless apple" leads us to think that God's inability here represents some limit to his power.

With this as a basis, it is further argued that the claim that God's goodness and power are logically incompatible with suffering is not correct, because it is not true that an all-good, all-powerful being would necessarily eliminate all suffering from the world. What is true is that such a being would want to bring about the greatest state of goodness in the world. But creating such a state may involve the creation of some specific goods whose existence logically entails the possibility of certain evils, and these evils may be the source of the suffering we see around us.

The enterprise of theodicy, therefore, essentially involves the identification of those eminently valuable goods whose existence may entail certain states of suffering or evil. Proponents of specific theodicies usually contend that a world without these goods would be of lesser value than one that contains them, and so God is morally justified in having created a world in which these goods, with their attendant evils, exist.

While those involved in the enterprise of theodicy frequently focus on one good or the other in their defense of God, theodicy is inherently an eclectic activity. A variety of distinct values and arguments are commonly advanced to defend God's goodness. Some of the major theodicies listed here are not even theodicies in the most precise sense since they involve less the identification of specific values whose existence justifies suffering than the assertion that such values might exist. In any case, none of these classical theodicies is necessarily exclusive of the others, and adherents of ethical monotheism usually hold several of the following positions.

The free-will theodicy. One of the most powerful and most frequently adduced explanations of suffering is the free-will theodicy. Those who hold this position maintain that a world containing creatures who freely perform good actions and who freely respond to their creator's goodness is far better than a world of automatons who always do what is right because they cannot do what is wrong. Now, while God can create free creatures, if they are truly free he cannot causally determine what they do. To create a creature freely capable of doing what is morally right, therefore, God must create a creature who is also capable of doing what is morally wrong. As it turned out, some of the free creatures God created have exercised their freedom to do wrong, and this is the source of the suffering we see around us. Some of this suffering is directly caused by these wicked beings, while some results when they are justly punished by God for their conduct.

As easily stated as this theodicy is, it has many complexities, and it has frequently been challenged. Recent debate has been especially vigorous. Philosophers such as Antony Flew and J. L. Mackie, for example, have questioned the link in this argument between free will and the possibility of wrongdoing. Since the conduct of free beings is not unshaped by causal factors, they contend, God might have molded human nature and the physical environment in such a way that free beings never do wrong. Or, they argue, since it is logically possible for any free being never to do wrong, there is nothing illogical in God's having created a whole race of free beings none of whom ever does wrong. However, other philosophers, notably Nelson Pike and Alvin Plantinga, have rejected these arguments, claiming either that they run counter to our commonsense understanding of freedom, which involves essentially an idea of nondetermination by causal forces, or that they mistakenly derive from ambiguities in what it means to say that God can create free beings who never do wrong. While it is true, they would say, that God can create a race of free beings none of whom ever happens to do wrong, it is not true that God can create free beings and bring about their never doing wrong. Whether wrong is done depends on the beings themselves. This leads these philosophers to the conclusion that God must expose the world to the possibility of suffering and evil if he chooses to create beings who are genuinely free.

A more traditional and long-standing objection to the free-will theodicy is that it does not apparently handle the problem of natural (or physical) evil as opposed to moral evil. Moral evil may be thought of as states of suffering traceable to the agency of free beings, such as war, racism, or genocide. Natural evil is that evil or suffering that is not traceable to acts or volitions of free beings, including such things as earthquakes, floods, and pestilence. Even if it is granted that this distinction is not sharp (some of the damage wrought by earthquakes, for example, is the result of shoddy construction techniques and other forms of human ignorance or avarice), clearly there are instances of suffering utterly beyond human control. Because this suffering is not traceable to human abuse of freedom, these critics contend, God must ultimately be held responsible for its existence.

Defenders of the free-will theodicy have responded to this objection in various ways. They have sometimes traced natural evil to the agency of demonic beings (fallen angels or Satan) whose own malevolence results from a perverse exercise of free will. They have also sometimes argued that natural evils are ongoing punishments for wrongful acts by humankind's first parents, so that suffering is a result of Original Sin. Despite occasional efforts at their revival, these responses have little currency today. As a result, many proponents of the free-will theodicy find themselves forced to turn elsewhere to supplement their defense of God. They frequently resort to one of the educative theodicies.

Educative theodicies. The force of the educative theodicies lies in their ability to justify at least some of the suffering experienced by innocent persons. This suffering exists, it is argued, because it serves to enrich human experience, to build moral character, or to develop human capacities.

Within the broad assertion that suffering has educative value, at least several distinct claims can be identified. It is sometimes maintained, for example, that modest suffering enhances our appreciation of life's satisfactions (as separation from loved ones can enrich moments spent with them). On a far deeper level, it is argued that even very serious suffering can toughen us to adversity and can help us develop depth of character, compassion, or new capabilities. Finally, it is common in this connection to stress the value of a world based upon regular laws of nature. Certainly, much suffering results from the operation of natural laws. Had God wished to, he might have created a world in which no regular laws existed—a world in which the flames threatening a sleeping family suddenly turned cool. But such a world, it is argued, would be a magical garden with little opportunity for growth in human knowledge. The human race would forever remain in intellectual infancy. This explanation in terms of natural laws is also sometimes advanced to explain the puzzling problem of animal suffering.

These educative theodicies are important, but their limits are apparent. Many of life's satisfactions do not require suffering to be enjoyed. Good health can be appreciated without the experience of disease. It is true, and perhaps profoundly true, that serious suffering can stimulate the development of our capacities and character. But this is not always so. Sometimes suffering embitters, diminishes, or destroys people. Finally, while growth in our understanding of nature's laws is valuable, we must ask whether this knowledge can be justified if its price has been the wasting of lives down through countless generations. What kind of education is it, some ask, that kills so many of the students?

Eschatological (or recompense) theodicies. Many of the difficulties of the educative theodicies derive from the brevity of human life. If an individual's existence were to continue beyond death, some of these problems might be overcome. Then, unmerited or unproductive suffering might be placed in a larger context of experience and meaning. Eschatological theodicies are based on the conviction that human life transcends personal death and that the righteous eventually receive their full reward. (It is also frequently maintained that the wicked receive appropriate punishment.) These theodicies differ from one another on the question of just when or how such recompense occurs. The *eschaton* ("last thing") can be envisioned as a historical epoch that begins at the end of history, a time when the righteous are resurrected in renewed bodies. Or it can be understood as an eternal heavenly realm that one enters after death. In either case, eschatological theodicies assume that the blissful future life more than compensates for present suffering.

Eschatological theodicies clearly play an important part in reconciling many religious believers to the fact of suffering. Nevertheless, this kind of theodicy faces many difficulties today. Some persons regard the idea of an afterlife as incredible. Others reject the idea that future bliss can compensate for present misery. They point out that while suffering may come to an end, the painful memory of suffering endures. Such novelists as Dostoevskii, Camus, and Elie Wiesel have also asked whether anything can compensate for the massive suffering inflicted on children during the persecutions of recent times.

Theodicy deferred: The mystery of suffering. Long before Auschwitz, religious believers recognized that any effort to justify severe suffering in terms of identifiable values risks trivializing the enormity of human anguish. Rather than renounce their faith in God's justice and power, however, some of these believers have chosen to deny that the mystery of suffering can be fully understood. They have preferred to defer comprehension and to trust in God's ultimate goodness and sovereignty. Frequently they have connected this with their eschatological expectations and have looked forward, not just to recompense but to a final understanding of God's purposes in the world.

Very often, those who stress the mystery of suffering also emphasize the limited nature of human understanding and the enormous differences that exist between God and humans. This position should not be confused, however, with the view that God's justice is somehow qualitatively different from our own. The latter perspective dissolves the problem of theodicy by placing God beyond moral accountability, whereas the view discussed here insists that God's justice will ultimately be vindicated. Faith is not the belief in a God beyond justice but the belief that God's justice will finally be upheld.

Communion theodicies. Emphasis on the mystery of suffering and the need to defer our understanding of it may help to sustain religious faith in the face of evil; but it also imposes new burdens on that faith, because human beings may come to regard themselves as pawns in a cosmic game, and God may come to be viewed as distant and indifferent. To offset this, religious traditions have sometimes presented suffering itself as an occasion for direct relationship, collaboration, and even communion with God.

Several related positions may be identified here. One refuses to accept the seeming distance of God in the mystery of suffering by insisting on God's presence with the sufferer in the midst of anguish. God is a *compassionate* God, who *suffers with* his creatures and who is most intensely present when he seems farthest away. This position may not explain why God allows suffering in the first place, but it comforts and sustains the believer in the moment of trial. Moreover, since God is a suffering God, suffering also affords the believer a unique opportunity to obey and to imitate his creator. Those who suffer for a righteous purpose do God's will and make known his presence in the world. Suffering thus provides the most intense opportunity for collaboration and communion between God and humankind.

With this emphasis on communion, the enterprise of theodicy comes full circle. That which first threw open to question God's goodness and power, the bitter suffering of innocent persons, now becomes the supreme expression of love between God and humans. Unlike the mystical dissolutions of the theodicy problem that were looked at earlier, the fact of suffering is not here denied. Instead, the reality of suffering and its importance in human life are heightened. But suffering itself is transvalued: what is usually viewed as an experience to be avoided is now seen as an opportunity for intense religious fulfillment.

TEACHINGS ON THEODICY IN THE HISTORY OF RELIGIONS. These theoretical positions on suffering and theodicy are not just abstract logical possibilities. They find concrete expression in the life and teachings of historical religious communities. Religions may even be characterized in terms of which of these theoretical positions they favor. While all of these positions may have some presence in a tradition, one or another is usually emphasized and serves as a distinguishing trait. Even closely related traditions like Judaism and Christianity evidence their uniqueness by subtle preferences among these different theodicies.

Judaism. In Jewish tradition, the theodicy problem is addressed not only in Hebrew scriptures but in rabbinic teachings.

Biblical foundations. The Hebrew scriptures provide the basis for both Jewish and Christian theodicies. With varying degrees of emphasis, they contain many of the positions we have reviewed. However, the free-will theodicy is probably to the fore. This view is firmly anchored in the account of history given in *Genesis,* where a world created as "good" or "very good" by God is viewed as corrupted by human sinfulness. From the first deliberate but unnecessary transgression of the divine commandment by Adam and Eve, we follow a process of recurrent and accelerating wrongdoing that vitiates the goodness of nature and that pits person against person. While the account in *Genesis* does not answer all the questions that troubled later thinkers (why, for example, God chose to create human beings in the first place), it does place primary blame for both natural and moral evil on humankind's abuse of freedom.

Much the same view is conveyed in the portions of the Bible that were influenced by the Deuteronomic writer and the early prophets. Here, suffering is explained in simple retributive terms: loyalty to the moral and religious conditions of the covenant brings prosperity and peace; wickedness brings plague, famine, and war. Since the prophetic literature often aims to summon the sinful nation to covenantal obedience, it is recognized that the connection between conduct and its consequences is not always immediate. The result is an immanent eschatological theodicy based on confidence in a prompt, future balancing of moral accounts. Thus said Isaiah (*Is.* 3:10–11):

> Tell the righteous that it shall be well with them, for they shall eat the fruit of their deeds. Woe to the wicked! It shall be ill with him, for what his hands have done shall be done to him.

This simple equation between suffering and punishment was not unchallenged in biblical thinking, and the disasters of the period from the Babylonian exile onward, when the Israelites were often most intensely loyal to the covenant, forced an explanation of seemingly innocent suffering. In wisdom literature, especially the *Book of Job,* the older theodicy is rejected. Job is an innocent man, blameless and righteous in every way; yet he suffers (*Jb.* 1–2). The prose epilogue, apparently appended at a later date, seeks to maintain the retributive schema by suggesting that Job is eventually more than compensated for his trials (42:10–17), but the book's most decisive response to suffering borders on a radical dissolution of the theodicy problem. Answering Job out of a whirlwind, God asks, "Where were you when I laid the foundations of the earth?" (38:4). A litany of God's mighty deeds in nature and history follows, with the suggestion that man is too puny a creature to question his maker's justice. Job repents his presumption: "I have uttered what I did not understand, things too wonderful for me, which I did not know" (42:3).

The *Book of Job* may be read as an abandonment of the very effort to comprehend God's justice, as an assertion that a creature cannot ask its maker to render account. Or, less radically, it may be read as a deferred theodicy—not the claim that God is unjust or beyond justice but that we are unprepared here and now to fathom God's righteous ways.

The repeated assertions of God's control of the wicked support this interpretation. In any case, the more radical stance, amounting to a dissolution of the theodicy problem, finds expression elsewhere in the wisdom literature. *Ecclesiastes,* for example, repeatedly emphasizes the obscurity of God's ways in dealing with humans. Occasionally the text despairs of there being any justice in the world: "one fate comes to all, to the righteous and the wicked, to the good and the evil" (*Eccl.* 9:2).

These dramatic responses of the wisdom tradition are not the only positions of the exilic and postexilic period. In some of the later prophetic writings, especially in "Second Isaiah," a complex, new theodicy appears: the idea of the suffering servant. This is the innocent "man of sorrows," an "offering for sin" who bears the sins of others and is "wounded for our transgressions" (*Is.* 53:3–10). Just who this figure is remains unclear. Is he the prophet himself or some other charismatic figure? Is he the nation as a whole or a righteous remnant? Whatever the answer, this idea embodies a new theodicy, combining the free–will theodicy with elements of the educative and communion theodicies. Suffering is still produced by sin, but the servant suffers vicariously. He bears his stripes to absorb the punishment of others, to highlight and communicate the consequence of sin and God's wrath against it. His suffering teaches others and is also a unique form of service to God. Finally, in a bid to the eschatological theodicy, it is promised that this servant will ultimately have his reward. He will be given a "portion with the great" and will "divide the spoil with the strong" (*Is.* 53:12).

In the latest texts of the Hebrew Bible, as well as in many writings of the intertestamental period, these eschatological and recompense themes move to the fore with the appearance of apocalyptic writings, such as the *Book of Daniel.* In these, history is viewed as moving toward a final cosmic resolution, when God will smash the empires of the wicked and raise the righteous dead to "everlasting life" (*Dn.* 12:2). The Hebrew scriptures thus draw to a close with a reassertion of the ultimate connection between suffering and sin.

Rabbinic teaching. Many of the motifs found in the Hebrew scriptures are continued in rabbinic thinking. Foremost once again is the free–will theodicy and the link between suffering and sin: "If a man sees that painful suffering visits him," says the Talmud, "let him examine his conduct" (B.T., *Ber.* 5a). Or again, more radically, "There is no suffering without sin" (B.T., *Shab.* 55a). It follows from this that any apparent discrepancy between conduct and its reward must be overcome or denied. Eschatology becomes acutely important. The righteous may look forward to the world to come *('olam ha-ba'),* where all inequities will be overcome and the wicked must fear hell (Gehenna). Whatever observable suffering one experiences may be regarded as expiation of those inevitable sins that all human beings commit. Suffering thus prepares one for final reward: "Beloved are sufferings, for as sacrifices are atoning so is suffering atoning" (*Mekilta' de Rabbi Yishma'e'l* 2. 280).

This stress on the positive value of suffering is emphasized in a series of rabbinic teachings that go beyond the view of suffering as retribution and emphasize its educative dimensions or the opportunity it provides for obedience to God and communion with him. Sometimes, for example, suffering is seen as having disciplinary value. Frequently alluded to is *Proverbs* 3:11, which teaches that God is like a father who chastises a well-loved son. ʿAqiva' ben Yosef, martyred by the Romans in the Bar Kokhba Revolt, is said to have laughed during his torture. When asked by his tormentor why he did this, ʿAqiva' replied that all his life he had been reciting the Shemaʿ, the ritual formula in which the pious Jew is commanded to love God with all his heart, soul, and might, and now, amidst his tortures, he realized that he had finally been given the opportunity to fulfill this commandment. For ʿAqiva', as well as for many Jews who looked to him, suffering becomes an occasion for divine grace. Amidst suffering, these Jews came to see the presence of a God whose purpose, at a price in suffering to himself and to his people, was to render Israel a holy community.

Christianity. The crucifixion of Jesus clearly forms the focal point for all Christian thinking about suffering. But the interpretation of this event varies widely in Christian thinking, as do the theodicies that it brings forth.

The New Testament. Although the problem of suffering is everywhere present in the earliest Christian writings, what theodicies we can identify in the New Testament writings are largely implicit. Expectedly, many of the theodicies we examined in the context of biblical and rabbinic thought are clearly assumed. Particular emphasis, for example, is given to aspects of the free-will theodicy. It is true that the crucifixion provides for Christians decisive evidence that not all who suffer are guilty. Nevertheless, the death of Jesus is also the result of almost every form of human wickedness. Factionalism, nationalism, militarism, religious hypocrisy, greed, personal disloyalty, and pride all conspire here to effect the death of an innocent man.

The fact that Christ is clearly blameless provokes the further question of why he should be allowed to suffer at all. At least several answers appear throughout the New Testament, some of which are also applicable to other innocent victims. On one level, in many New Testament texts a qualified dualism makes its appearance. Evil and suffering are traced to the agency of demonic forces or to Satan (e.g., *Mk.* 5:1–13; *Mt.* 9:32–34, 12:22–24). On another level, the eschatological theodicy is vigorously reasserted, with Christ's resurrection furnishing proof that the righteous are able to vanquish all the forces of wickedness and to surmount suffering and death. The apostle Paul typically insists that the Resurrection is a source of personal hope and confidence for all who follow Christ (*1 Cor.* 5:15–19; *2 Cor.* 4:14). Side by side with this, and found everywhere from the Gospels to *Revelation,* is a vivid apocalyptic expectation. Christ is the "Son of man" whose life (and death) will usher in the kingdom of God. In this kingdom, worldly hierarchies of reward will be overturned: "Many that are first will be last and the last will be first" (*Mk.* 10:31; *Mt.* 5:19).

Also running through many texts are elements of the educative theodicy. The letter to the Hebrews and the letter of James sound the note that suffering is sent by God as a test and a discipline of those he loves (*Heb.* 12:3–13; *Jas.* 1:2–4, 12). Paul continues this theme, adding to it elements of a communion theodicy. Christians should rejoice in suffering because it produces endurance, character, and hope (*Rom.* 5:3–5). Suffering also presents the opportunity to imitate Christ (*1 Cor.* 11:1), who has shown that power is made perfect not in strength but in weakness (*2 Cor.* 12:9). This emphasis on Christ's fellow-suffering is a constant theme in Paul's letters.

Finally, in Paul's writings we find an important extrapolation from the free-will theodicy: emphasis on the universality of sin and the universal deservedness of suffering. This theme is not altogether new—it has deep roots in biblical and Jewish thought—but it is radicalized by Paul, especially in his *Letter to the Romans* (3:9–10, 23). The implications of this teaching for the theodicy problem are dramatic. Since all are sinners, what is extraordinary is not that some suffer in a world ruled by God, but that anyone is spared the divine wrath (*Rom.* 9:22–24). The fact that not all are punished is explained in terms of God's grace being manifest in Christ's vicarious suffering and in God's willingness to suspend the punishment for sin (*Rom.* 3:24). This teaching clearly builds on dimensions of theodicy encountered in the Hebrew scriptures, including the suffering servant motif (now applied singularly to Christ). Nevertheless, it has the effect of revolutionizing Christian thinking about theodicy by converting the mystery of suffering into the mystery of divine grace.

Subsequent developments. It is impossible to review briefly all the contributions of later Christian thinking to theodicy. Suffice it to say that the major lines of thought build upon those established in the New Testament. Paul's ideas, especially, play a major role. Augustine (354–430) developed Paul's suggestions into a fully elaborated doctrine of original sin. According to Augustine, Adam and Eve's transgression and punishment, "sin and its penalty," are to be viewed as passed on to their descendants through sexual reproduction. Because everyone thus "merits" punishment, emphasis is on God's grace and his election of those who are spared a just fate. Election itself is explained in terms of divine predestination, in accordance with which God has eternally decreed who shall be spared the punishment merited by all.

This position clearly does not solve the theodicy problem entirely, and in some respects the problem is sharpened in a new way. The question becomes not why human beings have incurred suffering but why God, in his foreknowledge and power, should have allowed the whole disastrous course of events proceeding from the Fall to have occurred in the first place. Sometimes the legitimacy of this question is denied. In Calvinism, for example, Paul's admonitions against questioning the creator (*Rom.* 9:19–21) are expanded to a doctrine that places God altogether beyond measurement by human justice. With this denial of God's accountability, the theodicy problem is dissolved. Not all Christians, however, have accepted this extreme view, and repeated efforts have been made to explain and to justify God's creation of beings capable of sin.

In his book *Evil and the God of Love* (London, 1977), John Hick argues that at least two major responses to this question may be identified in the Christian tradition. One is traceable to Augustine and constitutes the historically dominant line of thinking about the problem. (A similar view, for example, is taken by Thomas Aquinas and many other Catholic theologians.) It begins by explaining evil in creation not as a substantial reality in itself (as the Manichaeans had contended) but as an aspect of nonbeing. Thus, evil does not stem from God but represents the unavoidable and nonculpable absence of his goodness or presence in mere "created" things (the doctrine of evil as a *privatio boni*). Why God should have created free human beings is explained aesthetically in terms of the desirability of his creating a graded hierarchy of being. Once created and given every inducement for obedience, however, human beings nevertheless inexplicably turned away from God toward nonbeing. As a result, they have been justly punished, and the suffering that results (within a retributive theory of punishment) is fitting, as is the eternal damnation of those not rescued by God's grace. Indeed, the whole outcome is sometimes justified by Augustine in terms of its overall moral balance and aesthetic perfection.

Contrasted with this view is a position that Hick associates with Irenaeus (c. 130–202) but that also has resonance in the writings of Friedrich Schleiermacher (1768–1834) and F. R. Tennant (1866–1957). It, too, traces suffering to the abuse of freedom. But its explanation of the place of both freedom and transgression in the divine plan is quite different from that of the Augustinian tradition. Here the Fall is fully within God's intention. God has knowingly created imperfect beings who are distanced from the divine splendor and destined to fall, but he is justified in doing this because he has the moral purpose of affording these beings the opportunity for growth and free development so that they may establish a mature personal relationship with him. In this view, the world is a "vale of soul making" and it is possible to apply to the Fall the words of the Easter liturgy: "O felix Culpa quae talem ac tantum meruit habere redemptorem" ("O fortunate crime, which merited such and so great a redeemer!"). A further implication of the Irenaean theodicy, in Hick's view, is that it casts doubt on older retributive theories of punishment that may justify the consignment of some persons to eternal suffering in hell. The Irenaean theodicy suggests a more generous "universalist" eschatology, which sees all who have lived as eventually becoming "children of God."

Hick himself expresses a strong preference for this view. While not all contemporary Christian thinkers share this preference, it is reasonable to say that there exists among contemporary Christian theologians a predilection to stress God's moral purpose in creating free beings and to see God himself as personally involved in the venture and risk of human freedom.

Islam. In his book *The House of Islam* (1975), Kenneth Cragg observes that because of its emphasis on God's transcendence, Islam "does not find a theodicy necessary either for its theology or its worship" (p. 16). With one or two important qualifications, this is a reasonably accurate assessment of the state of theodicy in a tradition that insists on surrender to the divine will (one meaning of *islām*) and finds it blasphemous to hold that God is accountable to human moral judgments. Nevertheless, while theodicy has not been a major preoccupation of Muslims, there are, especially in the earliest texts, implicit efforts to understand the sources of suffering and why God might allow it to exist.

The Qur'ān. We know that one of the most persistent explanations and justifications of human suffering traces that suffering to free creatures' abuse of their freedom. At first sight, this free-will theodicy seems to have little footing in the Qur'ān because of its repeated emphasis on God's sovereignty and his absolute control over human behavior. In *sūrah* 6:125, for example, we read:

> Whomsoever God desires to guide, He expands his breast to Islam; whomsoever he desires to lead astray, He makes his breast narrow, tight. . . .

Or again, in 61:5:

> When they swerved, God caused their hearts to swerve;
> and God guides never the people of the ungodly.

Although passages like these shape the later emphasis on predestination in Islamic thought, they may not have this meaning in the Qur'ān. For one thing, these utterances are frequently used to explain the recalcitrance of Muḥammad's opponents, and thus are more properly understood as affirmations of God's ultimate control of the wicked than as philosophical disquisitions on freedom. In addition, these passages are offset by many others in which a substantial measure of human freedom, initiative, and accountability is assumed. "He leads none astray save the ungodly," says surah 2:24, while *sūrah* 4:80 makes what seems to be an explicit statement of the free-will theodicy:

> Whatever good visits thee, it is of God; whatever evil visits thee is of thyself.

In addition, the Qur'ān displays two other themes associated with the free-will theodicy. One is a view of suffering as a test of righteousness. More than once the question is asked, "Do the people reckon that they will be left to say 'We believe,' and will not be tried?" (29:1; 3:135; cf. 14:6; 2:46). Because such testing can sometimes lead to martyrdom and death, the Qur'ān also supports a vivid eschatological expectation. Those who withstand the test shall have their reward. All human deeds are said to be recorded in books kept by the angels. These will be opened following the general resurrection on the day of judgment *(yawm al-dīn)*. Those whose record is wanting shall descend to the Fire, while the righteous shall dwell in the Garden *(al-jannah)* where their bliss is depicted in spiritual as well as vividly material terms (surah 9:74; 75:23; 52:24; 56:17f.; 76:11–21).

Later developments. If the Qur'ān's perspective on suffering and its implicit theodicy display substantial similarity to some familiar positions in the Hebrew Bible and New Testament, subsequent Islamic thought strikes off on a path of its own. From the eighth century CE onward, the free-will position becomes involved in a series of bitter disputes between the Mu'tazilī school of "rationalists," or "humanists," and more orthodox defenders of God's sovereignty (including his role as sole creator of human acts). Entangled in extraneous political conflicts, this debate continued for several centuries, until the victory of the orthodox position through the work of Abū al-Ḥasan al-Ash'arī (d. 935 CE) and others. What emerged was an extreme predestinarian position, according to which not only suffering or blessedness but the acts and volitions that lead to them are totally in the hands of God. Al-Ash'arī himself tried to secure some limited room for human responsibility through a doctrine of "acquisition," according to which acts proceed from God but attach themselves to the will of the individual. Nevertheless, this teaching remains overwhelmingly deterministic. An oft-quoted tale presenting an imaginary conversation in heaven between God, an adult, and a child captures the resulting orthodox view. The child asks God, "Why did you give that man a higher place than myself?" God replies, "He has done many good works." The child then asks, "Why did you let me die so young that I was prevented from doing good?" God responds, "I knew that you would grow up to be a sinner; therefore, it was better that you should die a child." At that instant a cry arises from all those condemned to the depths of hell, "Why, O Lord! did you not let us die before we became sinners."

In the context of such determinism, all responsibility for good and evil devolves upon God himself. Lest it be thought, however, that God may legitimately be accused of injustice, Islamic orthodoxy hastens to add that in his sovereignty, God may not be subjected to human moral judgment. God's command is itself the defining feature of right, and what God wills can never be morally impugned. The great medieval theologian Abū Ḥāmid al-Ghazālī (d. 1111) affirms that "there is no analogy between his justice and the justice of creatures. . . . He never encounters any right in another besides himself so that his dealing with it might be a doing of any wrong."

This emphasis on God's omnipotence does not mean that Muslims (any more than Calvinists) view God as a capricious despot. On the contrary, their constant affirmation is that God is "merciful and compassionate." Yet in the encounter with suffering, a human's response must not be to complain, to question, or even to try to defend God. Hence, for Islamic orthodoxy at least, theodicy remains an undeveloped dimension of the religious life. Its place is taken by the sentiment conveyed by the Qurʾānic formula "Ḥasbunā Allāh" ("God is sufficient unto us").

Hinduism and Buddhism. It would ordinarily not be advisable to lump together any treatment of such complex traditions as Hinduism and Buddhism. But where the issue of theodicy is concerned, this approach has much to recommend it since it emphasizes the fact, already mentioned, that both traditions share a common perspective on suffering. This is the view that suffering derives from the operation of the automatic law of moral retribution known as *karman* working in conjunction with a process of reincarnation. In his *Sociology of Religion* (Boston, 1963), Max Weber characterized *karman* as "the most radical solution of the problem of theodicy" (p. 147), but this reflects Weber's own broader use of the term *theodicy* to cover any explanation of suffering. In fact, because *karman* traces suffering to one's own thoughts and deeds, and because it denies the gods any involvement in or control over the process of suffering, it is not a theodicy in our sense at all. Rather, it is a fundamental dissolution of the theodicy problem as we encounter it in ethical monotheism.

How decisive a resolution of the problem of suffering are the combined teachings of *karman* and reincarnation may be illustrated by a famous tale concerning the assassination of Mahāmoggallāna, a respected disciple of the Buddha. When the Buddha was asked to explain Moggallāna's brutal death, he replied that, while undeserved in terms of his present life, it was altogether suited to his conduct in a previous existence. In that life, said the Buddha, Moggallāna had been guilty of cruelly killing his elderly parents. (This tale is reprinted in Henry Clarke Warren's *Buddhism in Translation,* New York, 1963, pp. 221–226.) The implication of this tale is that in a world ruled by *karman* there is no such thing as "innocent suffering." All suffering (even animal suffering) is deserved. We have seen that the free-will theodicy has sometimes tended toward this same conclusion, but in all the Western traditions where this theodicy has been espoused, there have always been voices affirming the reality of innocent suffering. In Hinduism and Buddhism, however, these voices have been silenced by a drive toward the total and lucid explanation of worldly suffering afforded by *karman.*

A further implication of this teaching is that the gods may be neither blamed nor appealed to when suffering occurs. In Buddhism, belief in *karman* helps explain the subordinate place of God or the gods in the schema of salvation. Not only may divinity be attained by any righteous individual, but the gods themselves, through sins that create bad *karman,* may plunge from their lofty state. As a result, it makes no sense to look to the gods for release from suffering, since they are as subject to suffering as anyone else. Nor can they be held responsible for what suffering occurs.

Hinduism appears somewhat less certain about these conclusions. In the earlier Vedic texts, the gods are sometimes presented as powerful, righteous figures who reward and punish human beings and to whose compassion one may appeal. Varuṇa, in particular, bears many of the marks of a supreme deity, and it is possible to see here an implicit free-will theodicy with human suffering traced to transgression of God's righteous law. Nevertheless, these lines of thought are not developed in later Hindu thinking, and in the post-Vedic period, when *karman* moves to the fore, even the gods are subordinated to it. According to one tradition of Hindu mythology, for example, the god Indra slays a wicked brahman, but, in so doing, he becomes subject to the moral penalty for brahmanicide. In an effort to free himself of this burden, Indra ends by inflicting suffering on human beings. Thus, even the goodness of the gods is compromised as they find themselves powerless before the operation of this moral law of cause and effect. It is true that in popular and mythological traditions the gods are frequently seen as able to free themselves from the effects of *karman.* They are also viewed as able to benefit their devotees. But what power they have in this regard does not usually extend, within the world of *karman,* to helping human beings escape automatic punishment for serious sin.

Neither can the gods be held responsible in these traditions for the shape of reality. Buddhism explicitly denies the gods any role in creation. The universe is conceived of as an ongoing, eternal, and cyclical process of becoming, and only an error on the part of the first-born god Brahma allows him to think himself its creator. Hinduism gives a more active role to the gods in this cyclic process of evolution and devolution. The world proceeds from Viṣṇu and is actively brought forth by Brahmā. But this process is not understood in moral terms. Instead, creation is a process whereby every potentiality within the great God is allowed to manifest itself in the world of differentiation. This means that everything in creation, blessings and suffering, the gods and the demons, all good and all evil, represent the working out of the divine plenitude. If creation is conceived in anthropomorphic terms at all, it is not a morally intentioned act for which God is accountable but an expression of the deity's spontaneous creativity or play *(līlā).*

There is, therefore, in neither of these traditions any question of morally justifying the gods, and there is no real theodicy. Instead, the paramount religious questions become how (in popular Hinduism especially) one can procure some favor from the gods, how one can produce good *karman,* and how, finally, one can altogether escape *saṃsāra,* the world of karmicly determined becoming. This latter question becomes particularly important when it is realized that within *saṃsāra* suffering is virtually inescapable. While deeds that generate good *karman* may lead to prosperity or bliss in some future life, it is almost certain that such a state will not endure. Because every transgression brings its penalty, and because those who are spiritually or materially well placed are more likely to transgress, existence in *saṃsāra* is an endless shuttle between momentary respite and prolonged misery.

We need not review in detail here the various Hindu and Buddhist answers to the question of how one may escape *saṃsāra.* These answers constitute the core teachings of their traditions. They range from Hinduism's stress on the profound recognition that one's soul *(ātman)* is identical with Being-itself *(brahman),* and hence basically unaffected by the flux of becoming, to Buddhism's opposing insistence that there is no eternal soul capable of being affected by *saṃsāra* (the doctrine of *anātman*). Despite the enormous differences between these teachings, they have much in common: suffering is viewed as endemic to the world process, and the goal is extrication from this process. Suffering is not a reason for praising or blaming God. The legacy of *karman* thus colors Indian thought from beginning to end, from its conception of the problem of suffering to that problem's resolution. Within this intellectual context, theodicy in its classic sense finds little room for development.

CONCLUSION. Along with the corrosive effect of modern scientific knowledge, the problem of innocent suffering poses one of the greatest challenges to ethical monotheism in our day. In the wake of the mass suffering of this epoch, some have rejected such monotheism, agreeing with the remark by Stendahl that "the only excuse for God is that he does not exist." Others have been drawn to various dissolutions of the theodicy problem, ranging from the Eastern stress on *karman* to an extreme fideism that abandons the insistence on God's justice.

Before rejecting ethical monotheism or the theodicies it has stimulated, however, it is worth keeping in mind that both spring from a profound moral intentionality. Ethical monotheism expresses the conviction that a supreme power guides reality and that this power is characterized by righteousness and love. Theodicy is the effort to sustain this conviction in the face of innocent suffering. Theodicy, therefore, is often less an effort to provide an account of the immediate facts of experience than an expression of hope and confidence that despite worldly reverses or human resistance, goodness and righteousness will triumph. Theodicy may not violate the requirements of logic, nor may it ignore the experienced reality of suffering. Theodicy's deepest impulse, however, is not to report the bitter facts of life but to overcome and transform them.

This essentially moral motivation should be kept in mind as we evaluate theodicies and their alternatives. Various dissolutions of the theodicy problem, from denials of God's power or justice to denials of the reality of suffering, may seem intellectually satisfying, but they may have moral implications we hesitate to accept. Theodicies, too, are subject to a moral test. If some older theodicies, such as reliance on the harsh idea of original sin, are no longer widely held, this may reflect their moral inadequacy. Conversely, theodicies that still attract attention are those that draw upon and deepen our moral self-understanding. The idea that God is committed to the perilous enterprise of creating free, mature human beings exemplifies this approach. This theodicy draws on certain aspects of our deepest moral experience—for example, the experienced relationship between parents and children—and uses these to illuminate the relationship between God and his creatures. Unless this ultimate moral basis and intention is kept in mind, neither theodicy's purpose nor its persistence will be well understood.

SEE ALSO Afterlife; Evil; Free Will and Predestination; Holocaust, The, article on Jewish Theological Responses; Karman; Līlā; Saṃsāra; Suffering.

BIBLIOGRAPHY

Useful surveys of classic Western philosophical and theological discussions of theodicy can be found in John Hick's *Evil and the God of Love,* 2d ed. (London, 1977), S. Paul Schilling's *God and Human Anguish* (Nashville, 1977), and David Ray Griffin's *God, Power, and Evil: A Process Theodicy* (Philadelphia, 1976).

Some of the most important classic discussions of this problem include Augustine's treatment of the issue in his *Confessions,* bk. 7, chaps. 3–5 and 12–16, in his *Enchridion,* chaps. 3–5, and in *The City of God,* bk. 11, chaps. 16–18, and bk. 12, chaps. 1–9. Thomas Aquinas has a very similar discussion in his *Summa theologiae,* first part, questions 47–49, as does John Calvin in his *Institutes of the Christian Religion,* bk. 1, chaps. 1–5 and 14–18, bk. 2, chaps. 1–5, and bk. 3, chaps. 21–25. The great medieval Jewish philosopher Mosheh ben Maimon (Maimonides) also advances a theodicy in his *Guide of the Perplexed,* pt. 3, chaps. 11 and 12, which relies heavily on the connection between wrongdoing and suffering.

Modern philosophical discussion of theodicy has its start with Leibniz's *Essais de théodicée sur la bonté de Dieu, la liberté de l'homme, et l'origine du mal* (1710), translated by E. M. Huggard as *Theodicy: Essays on the Goodness of God, the Freedom of Man, and the Origin of Evil* (London, 1952). On the other side, penetrating criticisms of theism and theodicy are offered by David Hume in his *Dialogues Concerning Natural Religion* (1779) and by John Stuart Mill in his *Three Essays on Religion* (1874).

In this century, debate in this area has been especially vigorous. Important theological discussions include Nels Ferré's *Evil and the Christian Faith* (New York, 1947), Austin Farrer's *Love Almighty and Ills Unlimited* (Garden City, N. Y., 1961), and the works by Hick, Schilling, and Griffin mentioned above. A critique of these and other efforts at theodicy is offered by Edward H. Madden and Peter H. Hare in their *Evil and the Concept of God* (Springfield, Ill., 1968).

Influential criticisms of theism and the free-will theodicy have been advanced by Antony Flew in his essays "Theology and Falsification" and "Divine Omnipotence and Human Freedom," in *New Essays in Philosophical Theology,* edited by Antony Flew and Alasdair MacIntyre (London, 1955), and by J. L. Mackie in his article "Evil and Omnipotence," *Mind,* n. s. 64 (1955): 200–212. This last essay is reprinted along with rejoinders by Nelson Pike and Ninian Smart in *God and Evil* (Englewood Cliffs, N. J., 1964), edited by Pike. Responding to these discussions, Alvin Plantinga provides a powerful defense of theodicy in general and of the free-will theodicy in particular in his *God and Other Minds* (Ithaca, N. Y., 1967), chaps. 5 and 6, and in his *God, Freedom and Evil* (London, 1975).

The problem of evil and the issue of theodicy has also had an important place in fictional writing during the modern period. Particularly noteworthy are Fedor Dostoevskii's *The Brothers Karamazov,* translated by David Magarshack (London, 1964), esp. bk. 5, chap. 4; Albert Camus's *The Plague,* translated by Stuart Gilbert (New York, 1948); and Elie Wiesel's *Night,* translated by Stella Rodway (London, 1960).

A sign of how much the problem of theodicy is a Western concern is that no comparable body of literature exists on the theodicy problem in Islam, Hinduism, or Buddhism. Nevertheless, there are some discussions worth noting. Max Weber's treatment of theodicy in his *Religionssoziologie* (Tübingen, 1922) is a pioneering effort to look at the problem of suffering and theodicy in a comparative context. This essay is translated as "Theodicy, Salvation, and Rebirth" in Weber's *Sociology of Religion,* translated by Ephraim Fischoff (Boston, 1963). Weber's view is critically examined and developed by Gananath Obeyesekere in his article "Theodicy, Sin, and Salvation in a Sociology of Buddhism," in *Dialectic in Practical Religion,* edited by E. R. Leach (Cambridge, 1968).

A good survey of the problem of suffering in diverse religious traditions (and in Marxism) is provided by John Bowker's *Problems of Suffering in Religions of the World* (Cambridge, 1970). Both Arthur L. Herman's *The Problem of Evil and Indian Thought* (Delhi, 1976) and Wendy Doniger O'Flaherty's *The Origins of Evil in Hindu Mythology* (Berkeley, 1976) contain useful information on the diversity of responses to suffering in Indian religious traditions.

Unfortunately, there is less explicit discussion of this issue in Islamic writings or in writings about Islam, and what sources do exist are largely in Arabic. The best available review of this issue is the doctoral dissertation of Eric Lynn Ormsby, *An Islamic Version of Theodicy: The Dispute over Al-Ghazālī's "Best of All Possible Worlds"* (Princeton University, 1981). Brief mentions of this problem may also be found in Kenneth Cragg's *The House of Islam,* 2d ed. (Encino, Calif., 1975) and W. Montgomery Watt's *What Is Islam* (London, 1968). Watt's *Free Will and Predestination in Early Islam* (London, 1948) is an influential discussion of the deterministic themes that have tended to minimize the presence of theodicy in this tradition. On the other side of the issue, Jane I. Smith and Yvonne Haddad's *The Islamic Understanding of Death and Resurrection* (Albany, N. Y., 1981) provides a useful review of the themes of accountability and recompense that form an implicit theodicy in this tradition.

New Sources

Adams, Marilyn McCord. *Horrendous Evils and the Goodness of God.* Ithaca, N.Y., 1999.

Adams, Marilyn McCord, and Robert Merihew Adams. *The Problem of Evil.* New York, 1990.

Alford, C. Fred. *What Evil Means to Us.* Ithaca, N.Y., 1997.

Basinger, David. "The Problem with the 'Problem of Evil.'" *Religious Studies* 30 (1994): 89–97.

Boyd, Gregory. *God at War: The Bible and Spiritual Conflict.* Downers Grove, Ill., 1997.

Leaman, Oliver. *Evil and Suffering in Jewish Philosophy.* New York, 1995.

Pinn, Anthony. *Why Lord? Suffering and Evil in Black Theology.* 1995; rpt. New York, 1999.

Rowe, William, ed. *God and the Problem of Evil.* Blackwell Readings in Philosophy. Malden, Mass., 2002.

Sands, Kathleen. *Escape from Paradise: Evil and Tragedy in Feminist Theology.* New York, 1998.

Swinburne, Richard. *Providence and the Power of Evil.* New York, 1998.

RONALD M. GREEN (1987)
Revised Bibliography

THEODORE OF MOPSUESTIA

THEODORE OF MOPSUESTIA (350–428), Christian biblical exegete and theologian. Theodore was born in Antioch about the same time as John Chrysostom, who became his friend and fellow student. Since Theodore belonged to the noble class, he attended courses given by the most renowned professor of rhetoric at that time, Libanius. He was later admitted to the Asketerion, the famous school near Antioch, of Diodore (later bishop of Tarsus) and Karterios. Even after his ordination as bishop of Mopsuestia, in Cilicia, he occasionally lectured at the school, where his reputation as a teacher attracted such distinguished pupils as Rufinus, Theodoret of Cyrrhus, and Nestorius. His work in uprooting the remnants of polytheism in his province was very successful.

Theodore wrote widely on various subjects, but only a part of his literary production has been preserved. A pioneer in biblical exegesis, he basically followed the hermeneutic principles of his teacher Diodore, although he diverged from them in some important points. He showed greater confidence in his personal understanding than in the authority of traditional hermeneutics, with the result that he rejected the canonicity of many books of scripture.

Only four of his commentaries have been preserved: *On the Twelve Prophets,* parts of *On the Psalms, On John,* and *On the Epistles of Paul.* In all of these he uses critical, philological, and historical methods and rejects the Alexandrian method of allegorical interpretation. Also of great importance are his *Catechetical Homilies,* which were discovered in a Syriac translation.

As an indefatigable combatant against the heresies of his time, Theodore's attention was particularly directed toward Apollinaris of Laodicea. Theodore's dogmatic fragments that have been preserved, especially *On the Incarnation,* are directed against him. Theodore's extreme position on the two natures of Christ is largely a response to Apollinaris's teaching about the mutilation of Christ's human nature. Following the Antiochene line of thought, which combined the spiritual element with the material in such a way that they are not confused, Theodore admitted that the two natures of Christ are perfect and also remain two. His only concession on this subject was to conceive a single person only in reference to the union of the two natures; in this case the being of the person is not in essence, but in God's will, and the union is not natural but moral. Accordingly, Mary, the mother of Christ, is only nominally *theotokos,* mother of God.

As an Antiochene, Theodore stressed the great importance of the human contribution to salvation, which he developed beyond the position of the Antiochene school. He ascribed all human achievements to free will, thus destroying the meaning and the importance of original sin. He also attributed free will to Jesus Christ, who, according to this understanding, is subject to sin, believing thereby that Christ's perfection would be worthy of greater estimation. In this area he was a forerunner and probably a teacher of Pelagius.

Because of these doctrines, and especially because of his position as a forerunner of Nestorianism, Theodore was the posthumous victim of strong polemics. Some of his writings together with his doctrine on the incarnation were condemned by Justinian and by the Second Council of Constantinople (533).

BIBLIOGRAPHY

The edition of Theodore's texts in *Patrologia Graeca,* edited by J.-P. Migne, vol. 66 (Paris, 1847), is incomplete. Editions of individual works with better, although fragmentary, texts are his commentary on *Psalms, Le commentaire de Théodore de Mopsueste sur les Psaumes, I–LXXX,* edited by Robert Devreesse (Vatican City, 1939); his commentary on the Prophets, *Theodori Mopsuesteni commentarius in XII prophetas,* edited by Hans Norbert Sprenger (Wiesbaden, 1977); the Syriac text of his commentary on the *Gospel of John* with a Latin translation, *Comentarius in Evangelium Ioannis Apostoli,* 2 vols., edited by J.-M. Vosté, *Corpus Scriptorum Christianorum Orientarium,* vol. 115 (in Syriac) and vol. 116 (in Latin) (Louvain, 1940); his commentary on the epistles of Paul, *In epistolas B. Pauli commentarii,* 2 vols., edited by Henry B. Swete (1880–1882; reprint, Farnborough, 1969); and the commentaries *On the Nicene Creed* and *On the Lord's Prayer and on the Sacraments of Baptism and the Eucharist,* "Woodbrooke Studies," vols. 5 and 6 (Cambridge, 1932–1933), which include the Syriac texts and English translations edited by Alphonse Mingana.

Theodore's life and work is discussed in Leonard Patterson's *Theodore of Mopsuestia and Modern Thought* (New York, 1926); Robert Devreesse's *Essai sur Théodore de Mopsueste,* "Studi e testi," vol. 141 (Vatican City, 1948); and Rowan A. Greer's *Theodore of Mopsuestia, Exegete and Theologian* (London, 1961). A recommended study of his theology is Richard A. Norris's *Manhood and Christ: A Study in the Christology of Theodore of Mopsuestia* (Oxford, 1963).

PANAGIOTIS C. CHRISTOU (1987)

THEODORE OF STUDIOS

THEODORE OF STUDIOS (759–826), theologian and monastic reformer of the Byzantine church. Born to an aristocratic family in Constantinople, Theodore received an excellent secular and religious education under the close supervision of his mother, Theoktiste, and his mother's brother, the abbot Platon.

Eighth-century Byzantine society was greatly disturbed by the Iconoclastic Controversy. Theodore's family had sided with the Iconophiles, those who favored the use of icons in Christian worship. His uncle Platon was a leader against the Iconoclasts, and Theodore followed in his footsteps, as a result of which he suffered persecution and was sent into exile three times.

When the persecution of the Iconophiles ceased under Emperor Leo IV, many monks, including Platon, returned to Constantinople. Under his influence, Theodore's family moved in 780 to Bithynia, where they established a monastic community on their estate of Fotinou, not far from the village of Sakkoudion. Here Theodore was ordained a priest in 787 or 788 and his monastic career began. In 794 Platon resigned as abbot in Theodore's favor. When Theodore became abbot, he reorganized the monastery according to the rule of Basil of Caesarea (c. 329–379), and the Sakkoudion community prospered for a while with a hundred monks. Because of Saracen raids in Bithynia, Theodore and most of his community were allowed by the patriarch in 798 or 799 to move to the monastery of Studios in Constantinople.

Under Theodore's leadership, the Studios monastery underwent a period of renaissance and exerted great influence on Byzantine society. It had more than seven hundred monks and perhaps as many as a thousand. Theodore became one of the most powerful men in Constantinople and found himself in conflict with both emperors and patriarchs. He tried to integrate monasticism and society and engage monks not only in spiritual matters but in social welfare activity, in hospitals, in *xenones* (hospices), and in work among the needy.

Theodore was a prolific author of doctrinal, apologetic, canonical, and ascetic theology. He also wrote poetry, homilies, and letters. His doctrinal and apologetic works defend the use of icons as part of the christological teachings of the church and stress that the event of the Incarnation fully justifies the use of iconography. His canonical and ascetic works aimed at the improvement of monasticism's image and discipline. His poetry includes many church hymns and liturgical services which remain in use, as well as iambic epigrams for different nonreligious occasions. His homilies delivered on various feast days and ecclesiastical occasions display style and logic. Theodore's letters, addressed to private persons, monks, emperors, other state dignitaries, popes, and patriarchs, are an important biographical source. More than 550 of them survive.

Theodore's significance is twofold. First, his writings constitute a mirror of eighth- and early ninth-century Byzantium. Second, his life reveals agonistic efforts to free the church from imperial influence. In this he was more concerned with an orderly and moral society than with mystical theology, more attuned to the legalisms characteristic of Roman theology than to the spiritual aspirations of the Christian East.

BIBLIOGRAPHY

Sources

Cozza-Luzi, Giuseppe, ed. *Novae patrum bibliothecae,* vols. 8 and 9. Rome, 1871 and 1888. In volume 8, see especially part 1, pages 1–244; in volume 9, see especially part 1, pages 1–318, and part 2, pages 1–27.

Garzya, A. "Epigrammata." *Epeteris hetairias Buzantinon spoudon* (Athens) 28 (1958): 11–64.

Migne, J.-P., ed. *Patrologia Graeca,* vol 99. Paris, 1860.

Trempelas, Panagiotes N. *Ekloge Orthodoxou Hellenikes Humnographias.* Athens, 1949. See pages 220–231.

Studies

Beck, Hans Georg. *Kirche und theologische Literatur im byzantinischen Reich.* Munich, 1959. See pages 491–496.

Gardner, Alice. *Theodore of Studium: His Life and Times.* London, 1905.

Marin, Eugène. *Saint Théodore, 759–826.* Paris, 1906.

Mpalanos, Demetrios S. *Hoi Buzantinoi ekklesiastikoi sungraph-eis.* Athens, 1951.

Papadopoulos, Chrysostomos. "Ho Hagios Theodoros Stoudites." *Epeteris hetairias Buzantinon spoudon* (Athens) 15 (1949): 1–27.

New Sources

Cholij, Roman. *Theodore the Studite: The Ordering of Holiness.* New York, 2002.

DEMETRIOS J. CONSTANTELOS (1987)
Revised Bibliography

THEODORET OF CYRRHUS (c. 393–c. 458), bishop, theologian, and church historian. Theodoret was born in Antioch to wealthy Christian parents. From early childhood he devoted himself to learning and study. After the death of his parents, he entered the monastery at Apamea. In 423, against his will, he was elected bishop of Cyrrhus, east of Antioch. The young, successful bishop was imbued with an apostolic zeal for christianization. In an attempt to show the superiority of Christianity, he wrote at this time *The Healing of the Greek Passions,* which was directed toward pagan intellectuals.

As an Antiochene, at the outbreak of the Nestorian dispute, Theodoret sided with Nestorius (who accepted two distinct natures in Christ) and refused to condemn him at the Council of Ephesus (431). Theodoret's *Pentalagion* and *A Refutation of Twelve Chapters of Cyril,* neither of which is fully extant, reflect his criticisms of Cyril of Alexandria's attack on Nestorius. Theodoret contributed decisively to the compromise of 443 and probably wrote the declaration of faith of that union, but the peace move did not last long. Theodoret wrote his *Eranistes* in 447 in opposition to Eutyches (who taught one nature in Christ). The Robber Synod of 449, which affirmed Eutyches' position, deposed Theodoret, who retreated from his see until the new rulers, Marcian and Pulcheria, restored him in 450.

Theodoret's condemnation of Nestorianism before the Council of Chalcedon (451) prompted the council to acknowledge him as orthodox. Theodoret, like the council, rejected both those who sought to distinguish the existence of two persons in Christ and those who maintained, as Eutyches did, that the divinity and humanity of Christ became one nature (see Theodoret's *Epistle* 119). Theodoret's activities after 451 are unknown, and it is likely that he died around 458. The Second Council of Constantinople (553), convened to settle the dispute that became known as the Three Chapters Controversy, condemned Theodoret's writings against Cyril, but Theodoret himself was not condemned as a heretic.

Theodoret's literary output covers important areas of the life and activity of the church. In addition to the works already mentioned, Theodoret wrote the apologetic *On Providence* (c. 436), ten discourses delivered at Antioch, and *On Chrysostom* (incomplete). Along with the several dogmatic writings referred to above, *On the Holy and Undivided Trinity* and *On the Incarnation of the Lord*—which have been falsely attributed to Cyril of Alexandria—were actually composed by Theodoret, as were *An Exposition of the True Faith* and *Questions and Answers for the Orthodox,* both wrongly attributed to Justin Martyr. *Libellus against Nestorius* is falsely attributed to Theodoret.

Along with Theodore of Mopsuestia, Theodoret is regarded as the principal exegete of the theological school of Antioch and as one of the most important interpreters of scripture. His *Ecclesiastical History* (449–450) continues Eusebius's work of the same title and covers the period from 323 to 428. *History of Divine Love* (or *Ascetic Citizenship*) presents the lives of male and female ascetics in Syria. *Summary of Heretical Slander* (c. 453) presents in its first four discourses all the heresies up to the time of Eutyches, and, in the second part, the exceptional *Summary of Divine Dogmas.* Some 230 letters written by Theodoret are preserved, and they are an important source of the history and dogma of Christianity in the fifth century.

BIBLIOGRAPHY

The collected works of Theodoret, edited by J. L. Schulze and J. A. Noesselt, are available in *Patrologia Graeca,* edited by J.-P. Migne, vols. 80–84 (Paris, 1859–1864). Available in English is Theodoret's *A History of the Monks of Syria,* translated by R. M. Price (Kalamazoo, 1985). See also M. Richard's "L'activité littéraire de Théodoret avant le Concile d'Éphèse" and "Notes sur l'evolution doctrinale de Theodoret," *Revue des sciences philosophiques et théologiques* 24 (1935): 83–106 and 25 (1936): 459–481. G. Bardy's article on Theodoret in the *Dictionnaire de théologie catholique,* edited by A. Vacant et al. (Paris, 1946), is a valuable secondary source.

THEODORE ZISSIS (1987)
Translated from Greek by Philip M. McGhee

THEODOSIUS (c. 347–395), Roman emperor (379–395). In the worst disaster since the days of Hannibal the Roman army and the emperor Valens were wiped out near Hadrianopolis by the Goths in August 378. The senior surviving emperor, the young Gratian, summoned from his

Spanish homeland a certain Theodosius who was elevated as emperor in January 379 at the age of 33. His first task was to come to terms with the barbarian invaders. He allowed them to settle and used them as federated troops. He dealt with the other military threat, Persia, by establishing a policy of coexistence that yielded a century of peace.

Since religious stability was accepted as the architectonic element through which the empire was held together, it occupied Theodosius's continuous attention. It is not easy to tell exactly how much of subsequent imperial policy was initiated by the emperor himself. It may be supposed that his influence on the laws was direct and strong; on the councils and church affairs generally it was indirect and deeply affected by practical politics as well as by those around him. These included women of the household, episcopal politicians, and court officials.

In 380 Theodosius was baptized (possibly in connection with a serious illness), despite the fact that people of his class ordinarily postponed baptism until they were beyond the occasions for sin inherent in public office. Accordingly, he was the first emperor brought up in a Christian family who was a fully initiated and believing Christian for the greatest part of a long reign. As a full member of the church, it was his duty to assist in church affairs. Further, the theory was beginning to take shape of the pious Christian monarch who, as *persona* ("personification") of the laity and of the body politic, prepared and made possible the oblation offered by the priests; he also, in some sense, represented the mind and heart of the body of Christ. (This idea was taken over not only by the Byzantine monarchies but may be detected in monarchical thinking in France, Britain, and Russia.)

In February 380, possibly even before his baptism, Theodosius issued an edict (Theodosian Code 16.1.2) commanding all people to walk in the way of the religion given by Peter to the Romans, and more recently exemplified by Damasus of Rome (d. 384) and Peter of Alexandria (d. 381). Those who hold the Father, Son, and Holy Spirit to be one godhead in equal majesty are catholic Christians. Others are heretics who will be struck by the divine vengeance as well as by the imperial action undertaken according to heaven's arbitration. In January 381 Theodosius followed this up with a law stating that everywhere the name of the one supreme God was to be celebrated and the Nicene faith observed (16.5.6). A person of Nicene faith and a true catholic is one who confesses the omnipotent God, and Christ his son, God under one name, and who does not violate the Holy Spirit by denial. The law quotes parts of the creed promulgated by the Council of Nicaea (325) and then interprets it in accordance with the teachings of the Cappadocian fathers, one of whom, Gregory of Nazianzus, had been ratified in his position as bishop of Constantinople by Theodosius.

In May 381 a council of 150 bishops met at Constantinople. (A sister council met at Aquileia in Italy, but it is not possible to determine the exact interrelationship of the two.) The creed associated with Constantinople took up and reaffirmed the teaching of the Council of Nicaea with modifications in keeping with the teachings of Athanasius and other Fathers, who had upheld the Nicene faith during a half century of civil war inside the church. Without the *filioque* clause (which says that the Holy Spirit proceeds "also from the Son" and is a later Western addition), it remains one of the great central affirmations of faith acceptable to most Christians. The canons of the council give precedence to Rome as the see of Peter but insist that Constantinople, as the new Rome, must have appropriate standing. No doubt the decisions were made by the council itself, but the emperor and his ecclesiastical policymakers had largely determined who was to be present and what issues were on the agenda.

The beliefs adumbrated by the laws and the council had immediate implications. Trinitarian heretics, like the various followers of Arius, were cajoled and coerced. People who in the minds of the legislators insulted God by apostatizing from Christianity or following the teachings of Mani were fiercely attacked. A mere decade was to pass before pagans (a contemporary word designating followers of the old Greco-Roman ways of worship) also became the object of this zeal for conformity. During this reign the independent status of the Jews was maintained despite mob and demagogic attacks, but later they, too, met the Theodosian logic.

During these years of policy-making, Theodosius had made Constantinople the definitive capital of his empire and, since the murder in 383 of Gratian, his senior colleague, had permitted Maximus, a staunch Nicene Christian, to govern the far western end of the empire. Italy was nominally under the rule of the young Valentinian II, whose powerful mother, Justina, was friendly to the Arians and earned the title "Jezebel" from Ambrose. In 387, Maximus invaded Italy and Justina's family fled to Thessalonica. Theodosius, whose wife Flaccilla had died in 385, visited them there and married the daughter Galla, thereby absorbing the claims of the dynasty of Valentinian. Obviously, much else became subsumed in his ambition to found a lasting dynasty with control of the whole Roman world. In an easy victory, he defeated Maximus and sent his pagan barbarian general Arbogast over the Alps to govern the far west on behalf of Valentinian.

Late 388 found Theodosius in Italy, the last person to rule de facto from the Atlantic to the Euphrates. It was not long before he came into collision with Ambrose, the bishop of Milan. At Callinicum, on the Persian border, a Christian mob had destroyed a synagogue, and Theodosius, as became a Roman magistrate, ordered the bishop to rebuild it. Ambrose forced the emperor to rescind the order. Then, in the latter part of 390, Ambrose imposed excommunication and public penance on the emperor for ordering a blood bath at Thessalonica that had resulted in the deaths of ten to fifteen thousand people. During mass on Christmas Day 390, the emperor was reconciled.

These events had a tremendous effect on the emperor. He seems to have determined, as his laws express, to cooperate with zealous Christian leaders to prevent further insult to heaven by barring the pagan cults. Until now, legislation had not worsened the pagan position, and the commando raids by Christian monks and mobs had been kept in some check. In 391 and 392, Theodosius caused surviving pagan sacrifices at Alexandria and Rome to cease and proscribed domestic cults (16.10.10–11). The world-renowned Temple of Serapis at Alexandria was destroyed by monks led on by the local bishop, while Roman officials stood by. Riots by the Christian mobs, fueled by the promise of spoils, spread like wildfire. Alarmed, the pagan aristocrats in the west looked for allies.

In May 392 Valentinian II died mysteriously. Arbogast elevated a certain Eugenius to the position of emperor and in 393 invaded Italy. The western pagans offered their help and were enthusiastically received. The struggle was likened by both sides to that of Jupiter and Hercules versus Christ. As Theodosius tried to enter Italy through the valley of the Frigidus River in September 394 his enemies gave battle. He was facing defeat when the bora, a violent Adriatic wind, sprang up from behind him. Both sides took this as showing that God was on Theodosius's side. The panic-stricken pagans died at their posts or fled.

At the time of his triumph in January 395, gout and death overtook Theodosius. He was survived by his son Arcadius in the East where the East Roman (Byzantine) Empire lived on until the Turks struck down the last Christian emperor in the gateway of Constantinople in 1453. In the West, his young and feeble son Honorius sat enthroned. The Goths sacked Rome in 410; within the century the Western Empire had collapsed and the medieval papacy had emerged.

Despite his title, Theodosius the Great was a mediocre man who completed the work of Diocletian and Constantine and put together a scheme of survival for the East Roman Empire. Behind its fortifications, Western civilization gained time to take shape. Thanks to the religious policy of Theodosius, his predecessors back to Constantine, and his successors down to his redoubtable granddaughter Pulcheria (399–453), certain features of the Greek, Hellenistic, Roman, African, and ancient Near Eastern heritages that might otherwise have been excluded were decisively imbibed by Christianity. This process created and presented a face of Christianity that for centuries has obscured its innate affinity with the powerless, the underprivileged, and the non-Western, as well as its heritage of detestation of coercion, violence, and triumphalism.

BIBLIOGRAPHY

The text of the Theodosian Code can be found in *Theodosiani Libri XVI,* 3 vols. in 2, edited by Theodor Mommsen and Paul M. Meyer (Berlin, 1905), and translated into English by Clyde Pharr, in *The Theodosian Code* (Princeton, N.J., 1952). See also Jill Harries and Ian Wood, eds., *The Theodosian Code* (Ithaca, N.Y., 1993), and John F. Matthews, *Laying Down the Law: A Study of the Theodosian Code* (New Haven, Conn., 2000). On the Emperor himself, Adolf Lippold's *Theodosius der Grosse, und seine Zeit,* 2d ed., enl. (Munich, 1980), is a thoroughly researched study of most aspects of Theodosius's policies. See also Wilhelm Ensslin, *Die Religionspolitik des Kaisers Theodosius d. Gr* (Munich, 1953), and Stephen Williams and Gerrard Friell, *Theodosius: The Empire at Bay* (New Haven, Conn., 1995).

A monograph in English central to the question of Theodosius's role in Christianity is my *The Emperor Theodosius and the Establishment of Christianity* (Philadelphia, 1960). Jörg Ernesti's *Princeps Christianus und Kaiser aller Römer: Theodosius der Grosse im Lichte zeitgenössischer Quellen* (Schöningh, 1998) is a highly detailed and full discussion of the literature as a whole. Important related discussions can also be found in Kenneth G. Holum's *Theodosian Empresses* (Berkeley, Calif., 1982) and J. F. Matthew's *Western Aristocracies and Imperial Court, A. D. 364–425* (Oxford, 1975). Related themes are taken up in Tony Honoré, *Law in the Crisis of Empire, 379–455 AD: The Theodosian Dynasty and its Quaestors with a Palingenesia of Laws of the Dynasty* (Oxford, 1998), and Bente Kiilerich, *Late Fourth Century Classicism in the Plastic Arts: Studies in the So-Called Theodosian Renaissance* (Oxford, 1993).

This reign saw the beginning of the effulgence of intellect, holiness and charity, associated with such names as the Cappadocians, the Bethlehem women and Jerome, the desert Mothers and Fathers, Augustine and Monica, Ambrose, the Priscillianists, Martin of Tours, and the Pelagians. Each has an extensive bibliography that interlinks with that of the Emperor. See also Incontro di studiosi dell'antichità cristiana, *Vescovi e Pastori in Epoca Teodosiana* (Rome, 1996). A good visual aid is also offered in the film "Trials and Triumphs in Rome: Christianity in the 3rd and 4th Centuries," directed by Bob Bee (Princeton, N. J., 1999).

NOEL Q. KING (1987 AND 2005)

THEOLOGY

This entry consists of the following articles:

THEOLOGY: COMPARATIVE THEOLOGY

Historically, the term *comparative theology* has been used in a variety of ways. First, it sometimes refers to a subsection of the discipline called "comparative religion" wherein the historian of religions analyzes the "theologies" of different religions. Second, within the discipline variously named "the science of religion," *Religionswissenschaft,* or "history of religions," some scholars have used the term *comparative theology* to indicate one aspect of the discipline. F. Max Müller, for example, in his *Introduction to the Science of Religion,* used the term to refer to that part of the "science of religion" that analyzes "historical" forms of religion, in contrast to *theoretic theology,* which refers to analysis of the philosophical conditions of possibility for any religion. As a second example, in 1871 James Freeman Clarke published a work entitled *Ten Great Religions: An Essay in Comparative Theology,* which concentrated on the history of religious doctrines in different traditions.

Problems and Possibilities. On the whole, contemporary scholars in history of religions or religious studies do not use the term *comparative theology* in Müller's or Clarke's senses, and these earlier usages are therefore now of more historical than current disciplinary interest. In the contemporary scholarly world, the term can be understood in two distinct ways. First, it may continue to refer to a comparative enterprise within the secular study of history of religions in which different "theologies" from different traditions are compared by means of some comparative method developed in the discipline. Usually, however, *comparative theology* refers to a more strictly theological enterprise (sometimes named "world theology" or "global theology"), which ordinarily studies not one tradition alone but two or more, compared on theological grounds. Thus one may find Christian (or Buddhist or Hindu, etc.) comparative theologies in which the theologian's own tradition is critically and theologically related to other traditions. More rarely, comparative theology may be the theological study of two or more religious traditions without a particular theological commitment to any one tradition. In either theological model, the fact of religious pluralism is explicitly addressed, so that every theology in every tradition becomes, in effect, a comparative theology.

In principle, the two main approaches are complementary and mutually illuminating: any comparative enterprise within history of religions (or comparative religion)—that is, a secular or scientific study—will interpret theologies as material to be further analyzed from the perspective of, and by means of, the comparativist criteria of that discipline. Any theological attempt at comparative theology—that is, from within the context of belief—will interpret the results of history of religion's comparisons of various theologies by means of its own strictly theological criteria.

The fact that theology itself is now widely considered one discipline within the multidisciplinary field of religious studies impels contemporary theology, in whatever tradition, to become a comparative theology. More exactly, from a theological point of view, history of religions, in its comparativism, has helped academic theology to recognize a crucial insight: that on strictly theological grounds, the fact of religious pluralism should enter all theological assessment and self-analysis in any tradition at the very beginning of its task. Any contemporary theology that accords theological significance (positive or negative) to the fact of religious pluralism in its examination of a particular tradition functions as a comparative theology, whether it so names itself or not. The history and nature of this new, emerging discipline of comparative theology as theology bears close analysis.

A difficulty with the phrase *comparative theology* is that *theology* may be taken to describe a discipline in Western religions but not necessarily in other traditions. Indeed, the term *theology* has its origins in Greek religious thought. Historically, theology has functioned as a major factor within the religious discourse of Christianity that has been influenced by Hellenistic models—and, to a lesser extent, within that of Islam and Judaism. Any enterprise that is named "comparative theology," therefore, must establish that the very enterprise of theology is not necessarily a Greco-Christian one.

To assure this, two factors need clarification. First, to speak of "theology" is a perhaps inadequate but historically useful way to indicate the more strictly intellectual interpretations of any religious tradition, whether that tradition is theistic or not. Second, to use *theo logia* in the literal sense of "talk or reflection on God or the gods" suggests that even nontheistic traditions (such as some Hindu, Confucian, Taoist, or archaic traditions) may be described as having theologies in the broad sense. Most religious traditions do possess a more strictly intellectual self-understanding.

The term *theology* as used here does not necessarily imply a belief in "God." Indeed, it does not even necessarily imply a belief in the "high gods" of some archaic traditions, nor the multiple gods of the Greeks and Romans, nor the radically monotheistic God of Judaism, Christianity, and Islam. Whatever the appropriate term used to designate ultimate reality may be, that term is subject to explicitly intellectual reflection (e.g., the term *sacred*, as in the "dialectic of the sacred and the profane" in the great archaic traditions, as analyzed by Mircea Eliade; the term *the holy*, suggested as the more encompassing term, in distinct ways, by Nathan Söderblom and Rudolf Otto; the term *the eternal*, as suggested by Anders Nygren; the term *emptiness*, as used in many Buddhist traditions; or the term *the One*, as in Plotinus; etc.). Insofar as such explicitly intellectual reflection occurs within a religious tradition, one may speak of the presence of a theology in the broad sense (i.e., without necessarily assuming theistic belief). However useful it may be for the purposes of intellectual analysis, the term *theology* should not be allowed to suggest that the tradition in question names ultimate reality as "God"; or that the tradition necessarily considers systematic reflection on ultimate reality important for its religious way. (Indeed, in the case of many Buddhist ways, "systematic" reflection of any kind may be suspect.) "Theology," thus construed, will always be intellectual, but need not be systematic. With these important qualifications, it is nonetheless helpful to speak of "comparative theology" as any explicitly intellectual interpretation of a religious tradition that affords a central place to the fact of religious pluralism in the tradition's self-interpretation.

Among the theological questions addressed by a comparative theology may be the following. (1) How does this religion address the human problem (e.g., suffering, ignorance, sin), and how does that understanding relate to other interpretations of the human situation? (2) What is the way of ultimate transformation (enlightenment, emancipation, salvation, liberation) that this religion offers, and how is it related to other ways? (3) What is the understanding of the nature of ultimate reality (nature, emptiness, the holy, the sacred, the divine, God, the gods) that this religion possesses, and how does this understanding relate to that of other traditions?

Such comparative theological questions may be considered intrinsic to the intellectual self-understanding of any religious tradition or way, and one may thus speak of the implicit or explicit reality of a "comparative theology." More specific proposals will result from particular comparative theological analyses; for example, the suggestions of a radical unity among many religions (Frithjof Schuon, Huston Smith, Henry Corbin), or suggestions that one may have a Christian or Hindu or Buddhist or Jewish or Islamic comparative theology (Wilfred Cantwell Smith, Raimundo Panikkar, Masao Abe, Ananda Coomaraswamy, S. H. Nasr, Franz Rosenzweig, et al.). All these more particular proposals, however, are based on theological conclusions that have followed an individual theologian's comparative assessment of his or her own religious tradition and other traditions. Prior to all such specific theological proposals, however, is the question of the nature of any comparative theology from within any religious tradition.

In general terms, therefore, comparative theology always accords explicit theological attention to religious pluralism, despite radical differences in theological conclusions. In methodological terms, contemporary comparative theology provides an intellectual self-understanding of a particular religious tradition from within the horizon of many religious traditions. It is a hermeneutical and theological discipline that establishes mutually critical correlations between two distinct but related interpretations: on the one hand, the theological interpretation of the principal religious questions given a context of religious pluralism in an emerging global culture; on the other, an interpretation of the responses of a particular religious tradition to that pluralism.

As this general methodological model clarifies, the comparative theologian cannot determine before the analysis itself what ultimate conclusions will occur, for example, that all religious traditions are either finally one or irreversibly diverse, or that a particular tradition must radically change or transform its traditional self-understanding as the result of pluralism. It is clear that to start with an explicit (and usually, but not necessarily, positive) assessment of religious pluralism challenges the position of traditional theology, which argued, implicitly or explicitly, that the fact of religious pluralism (and therefore of a comparative hermeneutical element as intrinsic to the theological task) was of no intrinsic importance for theological interpretation. A contemporary Christian comparative theology, for example, will inevitably be different from a Hindu or Jewish or Islamic or Buddhist comparative theology. But, just as important, each of these emerging comparative theologies will be different from all those traditional theologies which disallowed a comparative hermeneutics within the theological task, either explicitly (through claims to exclusivism) or implicitly (by denying its usefulness). There is as yet no firm consensus on the results of "comparative theology," but it is possible that those engaged in this increasingly important task may come to agree on a model for the general method all comparative theologians employ. The further need, therefore, is to reflect on this method. First, however, it is necessary to review the historical precedents for this emerging discipline.

HISTORY: PREMODERN DEVELOPMENTS. For reasons of clarification and space, this historical survey will be largely confined to Western traditions where strictly theological issues have been especially acute. Westerners should not forget, however, that other traditions (especially those of India) have struggled for a far longer period and with great philosophical sophistication with the question of religious pluralism. (See Surendranath Dasgupta, *A History of Indian Philosophy*, 5 vols., Cambridge, 1922–1955, and Eric J. Sharpe, *Comparative Religion: A History*, London, 1975.)

Monotheistic religions until early modernity. Although the term *comparative theology* is not employed in discussions of the premodern period, comparative elements in traditional Western philosophies and theologies were present, in positive and negative ways, in the premodern period. In the Jewish, Christian, and Islamic traditions, the insistence upon the exclusivity of divine revelation led, on the whole, to a relative lack of interest in analyzing other religions, save for polemical or apologetic purposes. This lack of interest was based (especially in the prophetic trajectories of those religions) on an explicitly and systematically negative assessment of other religions or ways from the viewpoint of scriptural revelation. Attacks on the ancient Canaanite religions by the prophets of Israel in the Hebrew scriptures are the clearest among many examples of this "exclusivist" development. Still, as modern scholarship has shown, the borrowings by ancient Israel from other religious traditions, or those by early Islam from Jews, Christians, and "pagans," suggest a more complex scenario than traditional Jewish, Christian, and Islamic exclusivist theological interpretations suggest. Moreover, there are elements (especially in the wisdom tradition) that suggest more positive appraisals of other religious traditions (e.g., the covenant with Noah, the *Book of Ecclesiastes*, universalist tendencies in the New Testament, as in *1 Timothy* 3–5). Other exceptions are found in the Logos tradition of Philo Judaeus in Judaism and the distinct but related Logos traditions of three Christian theologies (Justin Martyr, Clement of Alexandria, Origen). The esoteric and gnostic strands in all three monotheistic traditions challenged orthodox biblical theologies through more syncretic theologies, which were sometimes based on a belief in an original (and shared) revelation. The use of ancient Greek and Roman philosophical sources in the theologies of all these traditions also provides some partial exceptions to exclusivist emphases.

Yet even the use of Plato, Aristotle, the Stoics, and the Neoplatonists in Jewish, Christian, and Islamic theologies was strongly conditioned by the framework of the received traditions, especially traditional theological interpretations of the subsidiary position of philosophical reason to revelation (Ibn Sīnā, Maimonides, Thomas Aquinas). Inevitably, the use of the "pagan" philosophies of ancient Greece in Jewish,

Christian, and Islamic theological self-understanding generated some comparativist interests in all these monotheistic theologies—but these were usually colored by traditional apologetic and polemical concerns. The greatest exception to this general rule may be found among Islamic thinkers, especially al-Sharastānī (d. 1153), whose treatise *The Book of Sects and Creeds* provides a comparative theological analysis from an Islamic perspective of most of the major religions of the then-contemporary world. Most Christian theologies, for example, did not agree with Tertullian's implied negative response to his famous rhetorical question, "What has Athens to do with Jerusalem?"

The most common understanding on the part of Christian theology was that the use of philosophical resources did not necessitate any assessment of the religions to which these "pagan" philosophers may have held. For example, the use of Middle Platonism and Neoplatonism by Christian theologians emerged at those locations (e.g., Alexandria) where the relationship of Neoplatonism to the mystery religions and occult practices was weakest in the ancient world. Hence theologians like Origen and Clement could appeal to Middle Platonic philosophy without comparativist analyses of the explicitly cultic practices sometimes associated with Middle Platonism and Neoplatonism. The dominant comparative question for Christian theology (and, in their distinct but related ways, for Jewish and Islamic theologies) was the relationship of theology to philosophy, of revelation to reason. There was little explicit theological interest in comparativist religious analyses—again save for the traditional apologetic and polemical treatises on the "pagans."

Ancient Greece and Rome. Provided that a particular religion did not interfere with civic order, the ancient Greeks and especially the Romans were generally more tolerant of religious differences than were the monotheistic religions. This tolerance, in certain somewhat exceptional circumstances, gave rise to some interest in the fact of religious diversity. Among the classical Greeks, the major writer with an interest in comparativism is undoubtedly the great historian Herodotos. His work demonstrates remarkable concern with non-Greek religions (especially the religions of the Egyptians, Persians, and Babylonians), as well as with the religious diversity within the Greek world itself. As a "comparativist," his "syncretist" sympathies are equally clear. His most notable successor in these interests (especially as regards Egyptian religion) is Plutarch.

The Stoics were the first in the West to attempt to establish the existence of common beliefs within the diversity of beliefs in the ancient world. They did so through their invention of the term *religio naturalis* ("natural religion"). The most famous work of what might be called comparative theology in the ancient world remains Cicero's famous dialogue *De natura deorum*, in which the theologies and philosophies of the Stoics, Epicureans, and Academics are discussed. (Cicero's great dialogues encouraged comparativist interest in later ages as well—witness David Hume's use of him as a model for his *Dialogues Concerning Natural Religion.*) The Stoics also developed allegorical methods of interpreting the ancient myths and gods (e.g., Zeus interpreted as the sky, Demeter as the earth). These methods were later employed by some Jewish (e.g., Philo) and many Christian theologians as an implicitly comparativist, hermeneutic method of scriptural interpretation. Comparativist interests may also be noted in the writings of Varro and comparative elements are evident in texts with other major interests—for example, Strabo's *Geography* and Tacitus's *Germania.* In the medieval period, the outstanding figure with comparativist interests was the Christian philosopher-theologian Nicholas of Cusa.

Early Western modernity. The Renaissance, of course, occasioned new interest in the works of antiquity, including the classical mythologies. The most remarkable expression of this interest can be found in the speculations on the existence of an original revelation in all religions, in the texts of the Christian thinkers Marsilio Ficino, Giovanni Pico della Mirandola, Giordano Bruno, and others. These men not only revived the ancient myths for Christian theological purposes but also argued for the "esoteric tradition" as the common stream present in all the known religions of both antiquity and the modern world.

The age of Western exploration in the fifteenth, sixteenth, and seventeenth centuries stimulated new interest not only in the religions of antiquity but also in the newly observed religions of the Americas and those of Asia. The most remarkable example of an exercise in "comparative theology" during this period remains the work of a Jesuit missionary to China, Matteo Ricci, whose positive assessment, on Christian theological grounds, of Confucianism is unique. Indeed, Ricci's letters and reports, although unsuccessful with authorities at Rome, were, in the eighteenth century, deeply influential upon the interest in Chinese religion among such thinkers as Leibniz, Voltaire, Christian Wolff, and Goethe. The comparative theological interests of the Enlightenment were characteristically addressed to classical Confucianism (somewhat bizarrely interpreted as eighteenth-century "natural religion"), rarely to Daoism or Chinese Buddhism.

With the advent of historico-critical methods, the comparative theological interests of Western thinkers shifted in both their approach and in the areas of their dominant interest. The Romantic thinkers (e.g., Johann Gottfried Herder) analyzed distinct cultures as unitary expressions of the unique genius of particular peoples. This interest encouraged the development of historical studies for each religion as unitary and unique. Earlier negative assessment by Enlightenment thinkers of what they had named "positive religions" (as distinct from a presumed common "natural religion") yielded, in the Romantics, to a positive comparativist assessment of particular religious traditions and cultures. The simultaneous nineteenth-century historical interest in the ancient Near East spurred renewed comparativist interest in the religions of ancient Assyria, Babylonia, and Egypt.

The rise of interest in Indian religions, moreover, paralleled both Western colonial expansion and the scholarly development of Indo-European studies in the expanding search for the sources of Western culture. Indeed, in the nineteenth century that interest in Indian religious traditions arose not only among scholars in Indo-European studies but also among philosophers with little strictly scholarly competence, but with strong comparative theological interests—such as the American Transcendentalists (Emerson, Thoreau, et al.) and the German philosopher Arthur Schopenhauer. With the emergence of historical consciousness, the transition from ancient, medieval, and early-modern comparative theological interests to a more complete modernism may be said to have begun.

The modern period. The crucial intellectual development in the rise of comparative theology in the modern period was the emergence of historical consciousness and historico-critical method. The recognition of the historically conditioned character of religious traditions led to a crisis of cognitive claims for Western Christian and Jewish theologians. The Enlightenment's hope that a universal "natural religion" could be abstracted from all "positive" (i.e., particularist) religions was a hope shared, in different ways, by most thinkers of the period, including both the Christian philosophers Leibniz and Kant and the Jewish thinker Moses Mendelssohn.

But the combined force of Romanticism's fascination with past cultures as living and unique wholes expressive of particular peoples and the scholarly development of historico-critical methods and a resultant historical consciousness led to a widespread awareness of the need to incorporate that historical sense in all the exercises of reason, including philosophy and theology. Thus Western philosophy and theology, by becoming historically conscious, became implicitly (and often explicitly) comparativist as well.

The two major thinkers who initiated this comparative philosophy and theology—although it is important to recall that neither ever so named it—were Friedrich Schleiermacher and G. W. F. Hegel. Schleiermacher, a Reformed theologian, developed a Christian theology that deeply influenced all later Christian theology, among other reasons because it incorporated explicitly comparative elements. Schleiermacher defined religion as "the sense and the taste for the Infinite" and, later and most influentially, as "a feeling of absolute dependence"; as such, religion is the central reality for humankind. Moreover, in his Christian theology he attempted a comparison of religions. He argued for the superiority of the monotheistic over the polytheistic religions and for the superiority of the "ethical monotheism" of Christianity over the "ethical monotheism" of Judaism and the "aesthetic monotheism" of Islam. The details of Schleiermacher's controversial theological arguments are less important here than his insistence that Christian theology should include genuinely comparative elements.

Schleiermacher's great contemporary and rival, Hegel, had a similarly controversial influence on the development of historical and comparative elements in philosophy (and, to a lesser extent, in Christian theology). Hegel's complex developmental-dialectical model for philosophy demanded, on intrinsic philosophical grounds, a systematic and comparativist account of the major civilizations and the major religions. The thrust of his argument was that Spirit itself (at once divine and human) had a dialectical development that began in China and moved through India, Egypt, Persia, Israel, Greece, and Rome to the "absolute religion" of Christianity. This last reached its climax in German Protestantism and in his new dialectical philosophy. Hegel's formulation of the intellectual dilemma for comparative theology and comparative philosophy is an attempt to show the "absoluteness" of one religion (Protestant Christianity) by relating it explicitly to a developmental and comparative (i.e., dialectical) schema. This attempt to demonstrate absoluteness proved influential upon both Western Christian theology and secular philosophy.

Although the comparativist conclusions of both Schleiermacher and Hegel are generally accorded little weight among contemporary philosophers and theologians, their joint insistence on the incorporation of comparativist elements into both Christian theology and secular philosophy has proved enormously influential. In the twentieth century, their most notable Christian theological successor has been Ernst Troeltsch. Troeltsch engaged in several disciplines: he was a major historian of Christianity, a sociologist of religion, an interpreter of the new comparative "science of religion," an idealist philosopher of religion, and an explicitly Christian theologian. His ambitious theological program has proved more important for its methodological complexity and sophistication than for any particular theological conclusions. Troeltsch insisted throughout his work in these different disciplines that Christian theology as an academic discipline must find new ways to relate itself critically not only to its traditional partner, philosophy, but also to the new disciplines of sociology of religion and the general science of religion. Troeltsch became, in sum, the systematic theologian of the newly emerging "history-of-religions" school of Christian theology centered at the University of Göttingen.

It is also notable that Troeltsch shifted his earlier theological judgment on the "absolute superiority" of Christianity among religions to a later position in which he held that Christianity was only "absolute" for Westerners. This controversial theological conclusion was based, above all, on Troeltsch's conviction (as a historian) of the unbreakable relationship of a religion to its culture. This was true, for Troeltsch, even for such relatively culture-transcending religions as Christianity and Buddhism. This theological conclusion of merely relative absoluteness was also warranted by Troeltsch's conviction that it is impossible to assess the relative value of a religion through objective or neutral criteria that are independent of the diversity of particular cultural and religious values. Similar comparative theological enterprises (generally without Troeltsch's methodological sophistication and without his conclusion of the merely relative superiority of Christianity for Westerners) may be found in both liberal Protestant and Catholic modernist theologies in the early twentieth century.

However, the relative optimism, as well as the comparativist theological interests, of both the liberal Protestant and Catholic modernist theologians soon disappeared. In Catholicism, the end came through the intervention of Rome. Among Protestants, it occurred through the collapse of liberal optimism following World War I. The major theological alternative for Protestant thought at that time (generally called dialectical theology, or neo-Reformation theology) was found in the work of Karl Barth. Barth rejected most of the liberal Protestant theological program, including its comparativism. He held that Christian theology was a discipline not intrinsically related to the larger question of the nature of religion (including Christianity as a religion). Christian theology was determined only by the question of the meaning of God's self-revelation in the Word of Jesus Christ. As such, any Christian theological interest in comparativist analyses of religions was improper to the strictly theological task.

Barth's great theological contemporaries Rudolf Bultmann and Paul Tillich, however, continued to include some major historical and comparative emphases in their distinct and non-Barthian formulations of dialectical theology. Indeed, at the end of his long career, and influenced by his seminar work with Mircea Eliade, his colleague at the University of Chicago, Tillich returned explicitly to his earlier Troeltschian interest in history of religions in an important lecture entitled "The Significance of History of Religions for Systematic Theology" (1965). Other Christian theologians, moreover, continued and refined aspects of the program set forth by Troeltsch. It is notable that three of the most important founders of the discipline known as phenomenology of religion in the modern period, Nathan Söderblom, Gerardus van der Leeuw, and Rudolf Otto, were also Christian theologians who incorporated their phenomenological and historical work on religion into their constructive proposals for Christian theology.

Even granted these notable and important exceptions, however, Christian theology of the period between the wars largely abandoned its earlier comparativist interests: in Roman Catholic theology through the suppression of modernism and the revival of scholasticism; in Protestant theology through the ascent of Barthian dialectical theology. These developments tended to remove Christian theology from its earlier intellectual alliance with the "scientific" study of religion. Both Protestant dialectical theology and Roman Catholic scholastic theology gave relatively little attention to comparativism.

However, a comparativist theological analysis within the Barthian perspective, designed to show the radical contrast of Christian revelation to that of other religions, may be found in the notable work of Hendrik Kraemer, especially in his detailed study of other religions, *The Christian Message in a Non-Christian World* (1938). In Roman Catholic theology (especially in the work of Jean Daniélou and Henri de Lubac), moreover, the "return to the sources" movement of the *nouvelle théologie* of the 1940s and 1950s engaged in historical and comparative work on the relationships of non-Christian religions and philosophies to historical Christianity in the scriptural, patristic, and medieval periods.

This scholarly work helped set the stage for the affirmative declarations on the world religions by Rome both during and after the Second Vatican Council (1961–1965). Roman Catholic theologians (most notably Karl Rahner and Hans Küng) began to include comparativist elements in their Catholic theological proposals. In Jewish theology, an earlier notable comparativist theological enterprise was achieved by the great Jewish theologian Franz Rosenzweig with his development of a "two-covenant" theme.

In our own period, many Christian theologians have returned to the kind of comparativist theological program initiated by Schleiermacher and Hegel and refined by Troeltsch. Without necessarily accepting the conclusions of earlier comparative theologies, and without abandoning the strictly theological gains of dialectical theology, many contemporary ecumenically oriented Christian theologians (whether Protestant, Catholic, or Orthodox) are concerned to include explicitly comparativist elements within their theologies. There are, at present, many alternative proposals for how this might best be accomplished. Among Christian comparative theologians these include the "theology of the history of religions" proposal of Wolfhart Pannenberg; the Christian theologies of religious pluralism of John Cobb and Raimundo Panikkar that allow for mutual and radical self-transformation; proposals of Hans Küng and Langdon Gilkey for dialogue among the religions as intrinsic to all Christian theological self-understanding; proposals for a "global" or "world" theology by Wilfred Cantwell Smith, a thinker who is both a Christian theologian and a historian of religion; a proposal for radical rethinking of Christianity's traditional christological claims by the Protestant theologian and philosopher of religion John Hick and the Catholic theologian Paul Knitter; explicitly comparative theological proposals based on the pluralism within the Christian tradition as a central clue to a pluralism among all religions (George Rupp); and revisionary comparative proposals for different religious models (saint, sage, etc.) from a Christian theological perspective (Robert C. Neville). Comparative theologies in other traditions have also been developed, such as the Hindu global theologies of Swami Vivekananda and Ananda Coomaraswamy, the Buddhist comparative theology of Masao Abe, and the Islamic global theology of the sacred of S. H. Nasr.

Important comparativist theological elements may also be found in the modern period in the philosophers Ernest

Hocking and F. S. C. Northrup, the historian Arnold Toynbee and the psychologist C. G. Jung. Each of these thinkers, although not a theologian, exerted a powerful comparativist influence upon many theological enterprises.

General Theological Method and the Possibility of a Shared Method for Comparative Theology. As contemporary theologians in a religiously pluralistic world grope for new, inevitably tentative formulations of a paradigm to guide their deliberations and inform their expectations, they are confronted with the question of method. Theological method must always be a secondary matter for comparative theology, subsidiary to concrete interpretations of the specific symbols of a particular religious tradition. Method—precisely as a necessarily abstract, heuristic guide—must always be secondary to the concrete interpretations of each particular theology. But the secondary also serves. Reflection on method serves the common cause of all concrete comparative theologies by bringing into sharper focus the principles behind the common search for a new paradigm—principles that are often obscured in the present sharp conflict among particular proposals and conclusions in this emerging discipline. The abstract does not merely extrapolate from the concrete; the abstract also enriches the concrete by highlighting and clarifying what is essential.

It is helpful, therefore, to reflect on what kind of general theological method may be shared by contemporary comparative theologians despite otherwise sharp differences among them. The present hypothesis can be described by four premises. First, comparative theology must be a reinterpretation of the central symbols of a particular religious tradition for the contemporary religiously pluralistic world. Second, a new paradigm for comparative theology must be so formulated that the interpretations of a tradition can no longer be grounded in older, classicist bases but must rely on new foundations that incorporate both past tradition and the present religious pluralism. Third, in keeping with the demands of an emerging globalism and a pluralistic world, theologians in all traditions must risk addressing the questions of religious pluralism on explicitly theological grounds. Fourth, it follows from these first three premises that contemporary theologians must engage in two complementary kinds of interpretation of a tradition—those now known as the "hermeneutics of retrieval" and the "hermeneutics of critique and suspicion." There is no innocent interpretation, no unambiguous tradition, no history-less interpreter. There is no merely abstract, general "situation" and no theological method that can guarantee certainty. There is only the risk of comparative theological interpretation itself: the risk of interpreting the great symbols in all the traditions for the present pluralistic situation and then presenting those interpretations to the wider global theological community and the wider community of religious studies for criticism.

This general model can be made more specific by introducing the following definition of a shared theological method in the new situation: any theology is the attempt to establish mutually critical correlations between an interpretation of a particular religious tradition and an interpretation of the contemporary situation.

Thus, contemporary theology as a discipline shares with history of religions, the humanities, the social sciences, and, more recently, the natural sciences, a turn to reflection on the process of interpretation itself. For theology is one way to interpret the elusive, ambiguous, and transformative reality named, however inadequately, "religion." Theology is not merely a synonym for any interpretation of religion but rather bears its own methodological demands and its own criteria. It is necessary, therefore, to clarify this definition of theology and to show how it can yield a common model for a theological method, one appropriate to a contemporary comparative theology in any tradition.

Theologians interpret the claims to meaning and truth in the religious classics of a particular tradition for a new situation. The religious classics are theologically construed as human testimonies to some disclosure of ultimate reality by the power of ultimate reality itself, as that power is experienced by human beings. The questions to which such testimonies respond are the fundamental "limit-questions" of the ultimate meaningfulness or absurdity of existence itself. Religious questions are questions of an odd logical type, emerging at the limits of ordinary experience and ordinary modes of inquiry (ethical, aesthetic, political, scientific). Like strictly metaphysical questions, the fundamental questions of religion must be logically odd, since they are questions concerning the most fundamental presuppositions, the most basic beliefs about all knowing, willing, and acting. Like strictly metaphysical questions, religious questions must be on the nature of ultimate reality. Unlike metaphysical questions, religious questions ask about the meaning and truth of ultimate reality, not only in itself but also as it relates existentially to human beings. The religious classics, therefore, are theologically construed as testimonies by human beings who cannot but ask these fundamental limit-questions and, in asking them seriously, believe that they have received an understanding of or even a response from ultimate reality itself: some disclosure or revelation bearing a new and different possibility of ultimate enlightenment, or some new way to formulate the questions themselves, or some promise of total liberation that suggests a new religious way to become an emancipated human being through a grounded relationship to that ultimate reality which is believed to be the origin and end of all reality.

It is not the case, of course, that theology has only become hermeneutical in the modern period. However, the explicit concern with hermeneutics after Schleiermacher has been occasioned, among Westerners, by the sense of cultural distance from the religious traditions caused by the seventeenth-century scientific revolution and the eighteenth-century Enlightenment. This sense of distance has been intensified by the emergence of historical consciousness (as expressed by Troeltsch and Joachim Wach), and the development of the great liberation movements and their attendant hermeneutics of suspicion (with respect to sexism, racism, classism, etc.). And it has been still further intensified by the Western sense of cultural and religious parochialism stimulated by the emerging pluralistic and global culture as well as by the tensions, conflicts, and possibilities present in North-South and East-West relationships. The epoch-making events of modernity have brought about a need for explicit reflection on the hermeneutical character of all the religious disciplines, including the hermeneutical developments (as elucidated by Wach, Mircea Eliade, Joseph M. Kitagawa, Charles H. Long, et al.) in history of religions and the widely recognized hermeneutical character of all theology.

In order to understand the present situation of radical religious pluralism, theologians must interpret it theologically. Interpretation is not a technique to be added on to experience and understanding but is, as Hans-Georg Gadamer and Paul Ricoeur argue, anterior and intrinsic to understanding itself. This is especially the case for any theological interpretation of the contemporary situation. For theology attempts to discern and interpret those fundamental questions (finitude, estrangement, alienation, oppression, fundamental trust or mistrust, loyalty, anxiety, transience, mortality, etc.) that disclose a religious dimension in the contemporary situation.

Paul Tillich described this hermeneutical character of theology as the need for an explicit analysis of the given "situation," that is, for a creative interpretation of our experience which discloses a religious dimension (for example, of cultural pluralism itself). It is possible to distinguish, but not to separate, the theologian's analysis of the "situation" from his or her analysis of a particular religious tradition. Theologians, in sum, interpret both "situation" and "tradition." In some manner, implicit or explicit, they must correlate these two distinct but related interpretations. Like any other interpreter of the contemporary pluralistic situation, and like any other interpreter of the religious questions in that situation, the theologian brings some prior understanding to the interpretation—an understanding influenced by the historical givens of a particular religious tradition. A Buddhist comparative theology, for example, will inevitably be different from a Jewish comparative theology.

The clarification of the emerging discipline called "comparative theology" follows from this brief analysis of theology itself as an academic and hermeneutical discipline. In the sense outlined above, theology is an intrinsically hermeneutical discipline that interprets intellectually a particular tradition in a particular situation. Further, any interpretation of a tradition will always be made in and for a particular situation. In classical Western hermeneutical terms, this means that every act of interpretation includes not only *intelligentia* ("understanding") and *explicatio* ("explanation"), but also *applicatio*, an application of the interpretation to its context that is at the same time a precondition to any understanding and interpretation.

A properly theological interpretation of the contemporary situation demands that those fundamental religious questions cited above be raised, for the responses to them by a particular religious tradition are the primary, strictly theological, means of interpreting that tradition (e.g., an interpretation of the way of Buddhist enlightenment as the response to a fundamental situation of suffering and a fundamental state of inauthentic existence seen as "ignorance"; an interpretation of the Christian creed of faith, hope, and love as a response to the fundamental situation of suffering and an existential state of inauthentic existence seen as sin). Internal to each theological interpretation of each religious tradition, moreover, is a theological assessment and identification of the normative elements of that religion (e.g., identification of the proper canons of the religion, of the proper role of "tradition," of the proper role of modern historical research, etc.).

Any theology, therefore, involves the development of a set of mutually critical correlations between two distinct but related interpretations: an interpretation of the tradition and an interpretation of the contemporary situation. But it is important not to presume that a tradition will always supply adequate responses to the questions suggested by the contemporary situation. Rather, as the qualifying phrase "mutually critical" suggests, the theologian cannot determine before the concrete interpretation itself whether the traditional responses of a religion are adequate to the contemporary situation.

In strictly logical terms, the concept of "mutually critical correlations" suggests a number of possible relations between the theologian's two somewhat distinct interpretations: (1) identities between the questions prompted by and the responses to the situation and the questions and responses given by the tradition (as in many liberal and modernist Christian theologies); (2) similarities-in-difference, or analogies, between those two interpretations (as in many Neo-Confucian "theologies"); and (3) radical disjunctions, or more existentially, confrontations, between the two (as in the Hindu and Buddhist insistence on the necessity of the reality of a "higher consciousness"); or the radical dialectic of the sacred and the profane in archaic ontologies; or the radical correction of traditional self-interpretations of a religion after the emergence of historical consciousness.

In properly general and heuristic terms, therefore, theology is an intellectual enterprise that may now be described more exactly as the hermeneutical attempt to establish mutually critical correlations between the claims to religious meaningfulness and truth of a religious tradition and the claims to religious meaningfulness and truth within the historical situation for which that tradition is being interpreted.

This general model of theology as an intellectual discipline within religious studies may be further specified to demonstrate how "comparative theology" both fits and challenges it. Comparative theology fits the model insofar as it also demands that the theologian attempt to establish mutually critical correlations between the claims to religious meaning and truth in the same two sets of interpretations. What renders any theology within a particular tradition explicitly comparative, however, is a substantive (and not merely methodological) change in the interpretation of the contemporary situation. Any comparative theology in a particular tradition will insist on theological grounds that religious pluralism in the contemporary situation must receive explicit theological attention. Insofar as that crucial hermeneutic and theological change of focus is made at all, the theological task is notably altered. For now the different questions and responses of the various religions present in the contemporary pluralistic situation must be explicitly and comparatively analyzed as part of the task of any theological interpretation in any tradition. A sense of the cultural parochialism of traditional theological interpretations of both situation and tradition is likely to follow. A confrontation with any traditional, purely exclusivist, interpretation of the one tradition is also likely—just as earlier confrontations with traditional interpretations were occasioned by the emergence of historical and hermeneutical consciousness. A sense of the need for any comparative theological interpretation to take account of the comparative analyses of history of religions is also likely to arise, with the result that comparative theology will also recognize the need for the kind of interdisciplinary discourse found in "religious studies."

Comparative theology is an emerging discipline with as yet no firm consensus on conclusions, but with a possible agreement on the revised method of correlation that it implicitly employs. It is a branch of the general field of religious studies that must learn from the comparative method used in the study of history of religions, by reflecting on the results of those studies in explicitly theological ways. Traditional theological self-interpretations in all traditions are likely to undergo radical revisions—indeed, even at this early stage in the discipline, such revisions are visible. The final conclusions for any tradition's self-understanding in a religiously pluralistic world will be determined only by further, concrete comparative theological studies in and among all the traditions. Yet this much is clear: any contemporary comparative theology in any tradition must relate itself explicitly to the comparative studies of theologies in history of religions and to the theological dialogues among the religions. It must also explicitly raise the traditional theological questions of meaning and truth that earlier, secular comparative enterprises were legitimately able to "bracket."

In sum, comparative theology, as theology, is an academic discipline that establishes mutually critical correlations between the claims to meaningfulness and truth in the interpretations of a religiously pluralistic situation and the claims to meaningfulness and truth in new interpretations of a religious tradition. The central fact of religious pluralism, as well as the existence of religious studies (especially history of religions), has challenged all theologies in all traditions to become explicitly comparative in approach. The future is likely to see the evolution of most traditional theologies into comparative theologies in all non-fundamentalist traditions. With that development, the conflict in interpretations among various models and differing conclusions among contemporary comparative theologians may eventually yield to a disciplinary consensus for all theology. Any theology in any tradition that takes religious pluralism seriously must eventually become a comparative theology.

See Also Comparative-Historical Method; Hermeneutics; Religious Diversity; Truth.

Bibliography

Systematic Views

The following list of contemporary publications in English is representative (but by no means exhaustive) of theological work that functions, implicitly or explicitly, as comparative theology.

Hick, John. *God and the Universe of Faiths.* New York, 1973.

Hick, John, and Brian Hebbletwaite, eds. *Christianity and Other Religions.* Philadelphia, 1980.

Küng, Hans. "The Challenge of the World Religions." In his *On Being a Christian,* translated by Edward Quinn, pp. 89–118. Garden City, N.Y., 1976.

Panikkar, Raimundo. *Myth, Faith and Hermeneutics: Toward Cross-Cultural Religious Understanding.* New York, 1979.

Panikkar, Raimundo. *The Unknown Christ of Hinduism.* 2d ed., rev. & enl. Maryknoll, N.Y., 1981.

Pannenberg, Wolfhart. "Toward a Theology of the History of Religions." In his *Basic Questions in Theology,* translated by George H. Kehm, vol. 2, pp. 65–118. Philadelphia, 1971.

Rahner, Karl. "Christianity and the Non-Christian Religions." In his *Theological Investigations,* vol. 5, pp. 115–134. Baltimore, 1966.

Rupp, George. *Beyond Existentialism and Zen: Religion in a Pluralistic World.* Oxford, 1979.

Schuon, Frithjof. *The Transcendent Unity of Religions.* Rev. ed. Translated by Peter Townsend. New York, 1975.

Smart, Ninian. *Beyond Ideology: Religion and the Future of Western Civilization.* New York, 1981. See pages 17–68.

Smith, Huston. *Forgotten Truth: The Primordial Tradition.* New York, 1976.

Smith, Wilfred Cantwell. *The Meaning and End of Religion.* New York, 1963.

Smith, Wilfred Cantwell. *Religious Diversity.* Edited by Willard G. Oxtoby. New York, 1976.

Smith, Wilfred Cantwell. *Towards a World Theology: Faith and the Comparative History of Religion.* Philadelphia, 1981.

Additional Sources

The reader interested in further background and bibliography for the historical sections of this article will find references and much of the early history recounted here in Eric J. Sharpe's influential study *Comparative Religion: A History* (London, 1975). I have followed Sharpe's work in several of the more historical sections. The reader may refer to that work for further detail. Among earlier works, see also Morris Jastrow's *The Study of Religion* (London, 1901) and Joachim Wach's *The Comparative Study of Religions* (New York, 1958). For more recent materials and invaluable bibliographies, see Mircea Eliade's magisterial *A History of Religious Ideas,* 3 vols. (Chicago, 1978–1986). See also *The History of Religions: Essays in Methodology,* edited by Mircea Eliade and Joseph M. Kitagawa (Chicago, 1959), and Jacques Waardenburg's *Classical Approaches to the Study of Religion: Aims, Methods and Theories of Research,* 2 vols. (The Hague, 1973–1974).

Representative of modern, influential tests in the emerging discipline of comparative theology, the following works are worthy of special attention:

Hegel, G. W. F. *Lectures on the Philosophy of Religion.* 3 vols. Translated by E. B. Speirs and J. B. Sanderson. London, 1895; reprint, Atlantic Highlands, N.J., 1968.

Hocking, William E. *Living Religions and a World Faith.* New York, 1940; reprint, New York, 1975.

Northrop, F. S. C. *The Meeting of East and West.* New York, 1946; reprint, Woodbridge, Conn., 1979.

Radhakrishnan, Sarvepalli. *The Hindu View of Life.* London, 1927; reprint, London, 1980.

Radhakrishnan, Sarvepalli. *Eastern Religions and Western Thought.* 2d ed. Oxford, 1975.

Schleiermacher, Friedrich. *On Religion: Speeches to Its Cultured Despisers.* Translated by John Oman from the third edition. London, 1894; reprint, New York, 1955.

Schleiermacher, Friedrich. *The Christian Faith.* Edited by H. R. Mackintosh and J. S. Stewart. Edinburgh, 1928; reprint, New York, 1963.

Tillich, Paul. *The Future of Religions.* Edited by Jerald C. Brauer. New York, 1966.

Toynbee, Arnold. *An Historian's Approach to Religion.* New York, 1956.

Troeltsch, Ernest. *The Absoluteness of Christianity and the History of Religions.* Translated by David Reid. Richmond, Va., 1971.

New Sources

Barnhart, Bruno, and Joseph Wong. *Purity of Heart and Contemplation: A Monastic Dialogue between Christian and Asian Traditions.* New York, 2001.

Benin, Stephen. *The Footprints of God: Divine Accommodation in Jewish and Christian Thought.* Albany, N.Y., 1993.

Bloom, Harold. *Omens of Millennium: The Gnosis of Angels, Dreams, and Resurrection.* New York, 1996.

Leeming, David, and Jake Page. *God: Myths of the Male Divine.* New York, 1996.

Neusner, Jacob, Bruce Chilton, and William Graham. *God: The Formative Faith and Practice of Judaism, Christianity, and Islam.* Boston, 2002.

Obeyesekere, Gananath. *Imagining Karma: Ethical Transformation in Amerinidian, Buddhist, and Greek Rebirth.* New York, 1996.

Right, J. Edward. *The Early History of Heaven.* New York, 2000.

Viswanathan, Gauri. *Outside the Fold: Conversion, Morality, and Belief.* Princeton, N.J., 1998.

DAVID TRACY (1987)
Revised Bibliography

THEOLOGY: CHRISTIAN THEOLOGY

The word *theology* always means discourse or speech about God. But which God is meant and what does this God do? Plato, in his *Republic,* assigns *theologia* to the poets (379a5); by *theology* he means narratives about the gods and theogonies. Aristotle contrasts the "theologians," who offer mythological explanations of the world, with the "philosophers," or "physiologists," who look for the explanation of things within things themselves. On one occasion he divides "theoretical" philosophy into three parts: mathematics, physics, and theology, this last being identical with "first" philosophy, or metaphysics (*Metaphysics* 6.1025a). Toward the end of the second century BCE, Panaetius of Rhodes distinguished three kinds of theology and was followed in this by Varro, whom Augustine cites (*City of God* 6.5): mythological, "natural" or philosophico-cosmological, and civil or political. "Civil theology" or "political theology" referred to the cult of the Caesars.

Among Christians, the first applications of the term *theology* to knowledge of the God in whom they believed occur in the writings of Origen (d. 254). For Eusebius of Caesarea (d. 339), *theologia* no longer applied to paganism at all but designated exclusively the knowledge of the Christian God and of Christ. Eusebius was also familiar with the distinction that would become classic among the Greeks and would be known to the Latin Middle Ages as well, between *theology,* which means discourse about the inner life of God, and *economy,* meaning God's activity for our salvation, which includes Christ, church, sacraments, and eschatology. Proclus (d. 485), the Greek philosopher, wrote an *Elements of Theology,* a treatise on the ultimate principles of reality.

In the West, *theologia* was for a long time used only infrequently; other terms prevailed, such as *sacra scriptura* ("sacred scripture"), *sacra erudito* ("sacred knowledge"), and *divina pagina* ("divine pages"). Thomas Aquinas (d. 1274) preferred *sacra doctrina* ("sacred doctrine"). But in his time, *theologia,* which Peter Abelard (d. 1142) had used as the title of a work on Christian dogma in its entirety, meant the knowledge elaborated and taught in the faculty of the same name. Our modern use of the term was thus established.

HISTORICAL DEVELOPMENT. Theology exists because the godhead is revealed in historical actions or events, the meanings of which are conveyed in language or inspired writings. The words of a sage, even one who is "inspired," are not enough. The writings provide food for a meditation of a sapiential kind that is geared to the conduct of human life. God revealed the relationship he wants to establish with man and in the process was also self-revelatory.

Before the end of the first century after the Hijrah, Islam was already discussing the dilemma of predestination and free will. Next to be discussed were the last things and the salvation of unbelievers who were in good faith. In these discussions and in the texts of the mystics were to be found only fragments of a theology. While Judaism had too lofty an idea of God's absoluteness to make an effort to investigate his nature, it did gather into the Talmud the discussions and interpretations of the rabbis; it developed an apologetic for dealing with Islam; it reflected on the anthropomorphisms of the Bible; and it produced great religious philosophers (e.g., Maimonides, d. 1204).

Christians for their part not only had inherited the Jewish scriptures and the revelatory deeds that these scriptures narrate and explain; they also found themselves confronted with the fact of Jesus Christ. First an object of faith, this fact became also an object of thought. It was a complex fact: a man who is Son of God, dead yet living, weak yet Lord. It demanded that God be seen as Father of a Son, the two of them acting through a Holy Spirit who is at once immanent in the "hearts" of the faithful and transcendent over them. Help in expressing these ideas was found in the Stoicism of the day, which was widespread even among slaves. This philosophy provided the idea of a Logos and a Spirit *(pneuma)* that permeated the cosmos, kept it in motion, and quickened minds as well. On the other hand, to take this approach was to cosmologize God and turn the Logos and Pneuma into subordinate intermediaries between God and the things of the world. Before the Council of Nicaea (325), even Christians who proved their fidelity by martyrdom had been influenced by these ideas and had formulated their faith in an unsatisfactory manner. Various interpretations publicly expressed were judged to cast doubt on essential aspects of the object of faith. The result was that an orthodoxy—true praise, true faith—emerged and, with it, the beginnings of a reflection on faith and in faith or, in other words, something of a theology.

Faith, which is already in the realm of thought, must necessarily express itself in an active way. It looks for coherence among many facts and elements that, however diverse, all come from the same God who is carrying out a homogeneous plan. Since faith is also fidelity, and therefore orthodoxy, it develops in response to deviations. Since it has to do with mysterious realities that are irreducible to the facts grasped by our sciences and are very complex, the very assent of faith is accompanied by the questioning that Augustine and Thomas Aquinas call *cogitatio:* "Credere est cum assentione cogitare" ("To believe is to assent while thinking"). When this reflection in faith ceases to be occasional and becomes systematic, it is theology.

This process began in the East. Schools of higher-level catechesis were established there; in these schools the quest was for gnosis, that is, a deepening both of knowledge and of Christian life. "True gnosis," as it is called by Irenaeus (*Against Heresies* 4.33.8), fights the false gnosis of Basilides and Valentinian in the name of the authentic tradition guaranteed by apostolic succession. This true gnosis is in accordance with reason (3.12.11). The Didaskalion, or Catechetical School, of Alexandria was headed by Clement and then by Origen, who in his *On First Principles* gives the first complete theological statement that is linked to a philosophical culture. As a result, he distinguished what we now call dogma and theology. In contrast to platonizing Alexandria, Antioch, another great Christian metropolis, practiced a more historical and literal reading of the scriptures. At Nisibis and Edessa, on the other hand, Ephraem of Syria (d. 373) theologized in a poetical and lyrical way that was alien to Greek culture.

The second half of the fourth century and the first half of the fifth saw in both the East and West a flowering of geniuses and saints: the Fathers. These included Athanasius (d. 373), Basil of Caesarea (d. 379), Gregory of Nazianzus (d. 391), Gregory of Nyssa (d. 395), Chrysostom (d. 407), and Cyril of Alexandria (d. 444), in the East; and in the West, Hilary (d. 367), Ambrose (d. 397), Jerome (d. 420), Augustine (d. 430), and Leo I (d. 461). These men defended and lent luster to the Christian faith chiefly by a rational explanation of scriptures that focused on the Christian mystery and made use of typology. In Origen's thought, and that of some others, typology is pushed to the point of allegory. Even at this time, however, there were signs of a difference in the way theological activity was carried on in the Greek East and in the Latin West, at least beginning with Augustine in the West.

The Latin fathers (including Augustine) regarded the literary and philosophical culture of the patristic age (Second Sophistic, Platonic, and Stoic) to be a human formation of the Christian although it was acquired in the pagan schools of the time. Basil, Gregory of Nazianzus, and Chrysostom insisted on the value of this formation, while Julian the Apostate denied Christians access to it to prevent their being weakened by it. The Fathers engaged in argument chiefly in order to invalidate the conclusions drawn by heretics, but they did not use philosophical concepts and arguments in order to develop new theses that went beyond the traditional faith. From the philosophers, and especially from Platonism, they borrowed certain broad ideas and expressions but little with conceptual content new to their faith. They saw the philosophers rather as fathers of heresies. This did not prevent later philosophical borrowings by John of Damascus (d. 749), Photios (d. about 891), Cerularios (d. 1058), and Michael Psellus (d. 1078?). Even today, however, Orthodox theology dutifully follows the Fathers. The nineteenth canon of the Trullan Synod (692) says "The church's pastors must explain scripture in accordance with the commentaries of the Fathers." While the medieval and modern West has been receptive to many questions and currents of thought and has even formulated new dogmas, thus making the proof from tradition difficult and complicated, Eastern Christianity has kept a kind of direct contact with its patristic tradition. It derives its faith directly from the liturgy, in which that tradition finds expression. When the attempt was made on numerous occasions to introduce into Eastern Orthodoxy a creative appeal to reason, especially because of the influence of the West and in imitation of it, there was a reaction. Thus there was a reaction against John Italus, who succeeded Michael Psellus as head of the University of Constantinople; the seventh article of his condemnation in 1082 reads "Cursed be those who devote themselves in depth to the sciences of the Hellenes and do not use these simply to exercise the mind but instead adopt their sterile opinions." The reaction was even more vigorous in the fourteenth century when, after the great Latin classics had been translated into Greek, rationalist and humanist claims roused the opposition of Gregory Palamas (d. 1359), who developed a new systematization of the spiritual tradition of the Greek East. Since the fourth century this tradition had devoted itself to reflection on the incarnation of the Word and the divinization of creatures, to the union of the divine and the human, the uncreated and the created. This was the background for the two great debates peculiar to the East—the iconoclastic struggle, which was the final phase of the christological controversies (union of the spiritual and the sensible), and the debate over Palamism (divinization, communication of God to the human creature, and rejection of any rationalism in theology)—the victorious outcome of which is celebrated by the Feast of Orthodoxy. Established in 843, this feast commemorates the restoration of icon worship and Orthodox rejection of the theological rationalizers.

There have been other developments in Orthodox theology; for example, in the nineteenth century, the influence of G. W. F. Hegel and Friedrich Schelling in Russia. But even in fairly personal systematizations this theology has remained faithful to its special character. It is not a simple intellectual exercise but a call to live in a personal way the truth revealed by Jesus Christ and proclaimed in the faith of the Orthodox church, which draws its life and inspiration from the Holy Spirit. Theoretical knowledge must be integrated with life experience and with prayer that is practiced as part of the church community and in its liturgical celebration.

The Latin fathers differ very little from the Greeks. However, beginning with Anselm and continuing throughout Scholasticism, a favorite formula of Augustine's became the motto for an exercise of reason in theology that is peculiar to the medieval West. In Augustine, reason and faith supply each other with nourishment within the unity of contemplation, in accordance with his formula: "Intellige ut credas, crede ut intelligas" ("Understand that you may believe, believe that you may understand"; *Sermons* 43.9). The second part of this formula has often been expressed by means of *Isaiah* 7:9: "Nisi credideritis non intelligetis" ("Unless you believe, you shall not understand"; Septuagint and Vulgate). Augustine himself focuses less on the duality of the two spheres than on the union of the two activities or ranges of activity in reaching the fullness of truth. For truth in itself is one. It exists in the triune God; it is to be found in the Wisdom of God that has come to us in sensible form in Jesus Christ. On our side, there is an *intelligere,* or knowing, that prepares for and nourishes faith, and an *intellectus,* or understanding, which is the fruit of a devout and loving faith that makes use of the resources and analogies supplied by nature and reaches the *intellectus fidei,* or understanding of faith, so that "what faith grasps the mind sees" (*On the Trinity* 15.27.49).

The *intellectus fidei* of Anselm (d. 1109) is not quite the same as that of Augustine. Anselm means a use of reason on the basis of faith ("I desire to gain some understanding of your truth which my heart believes and loves"), but reason, for him, has the power to discover at its own rational level the necessary connection that gives the truth of faith its objective coherence. That is what he means by understanding what we believe; this is true of the existence of God and it is true of redemption, which we can think out "as though we knew nothing about Christ."

The monastic theology of Bernard of Clairvaux, who was nineteen years old when Anselm died, is quite different in character: a theology of the spiritual struggle and of the life of mystical union as experienced in the cloister. However, from Anselm and the theologians at Bec came the initiatives, timid at first, that produced Scholasticism. Anselm of Laon was a disciple at Bec. He in turn had Abelard for a pupil, but the pupil was too gifted and too aware of his gifts to find satisfaction at Laon. Abelard inaugurated what became systematic theology and the dialectical method of bringing together opposed theses that call for a solution. This method of the *quaestio* (interrogation) was applied in commentaries on Peter Lombard's *Book of Sentences,* which was to be the textbook for the teaching of theology down to the sixteenth century. The teaching was done in schools or universities and came to be known as "Scholasticism."

Scholastic theology had very great practitioners in Bonaventure and Thomas Aquinas (both of whom died in 1274). Thomas's intention was to search out and express, with the help of analysis, the perceived order of things and reason, an order determined by God. That which revelation discloses to us provides the starting point, of course, but the Scholastic also had a fearless trust in the rational mind as trained in the school of Aristotle. Profound insights, rigorous arguments, honesty about the data, and sureness of Catholic sensibility have made Thomas the "Common Doctor" of the Catholic church. Following the Augustinian tradition, Bonaventure insisted more on the interior supernatural enlightenment and transformation that are necessary conditions for understanding sacred doctrine.

Although opposed to one another as realist and nominalist, John Duns Scotus and William of Ockham in the fourteenth century were at one in criticizing the trust in speculative reason when this takes God and Christian realities for its object. Ockham marked the beginning of the *via moderna* which was introduced in the universities in the fifteenth century. The development of a theology marked by abundant discourse and nice distinctions led by way of reaction to spiritual currents and a mysticism that were unrelated to dogma (Thomas à Kempis, *Imitation of Christ*). But another and different current was also born: humanism with its cultivation of the ancient languages, its criticism of Scholasticism, its publication of texts that printing carried far and wide. Martin Luther (d. 1546) was heir to all three currents: Ockhamist voluntarism, mystical inwardness, and the textual resources of humanism. Nonetheless, he would mark a new beginning.

The Protestant Reformation led, in Catholic theology, to the development of a scholarly apologetics (e.g., the *Controversiae* of Bellarmino, 1621); the criticisms of the *philosophes* likewise elicited an abundant apologetic production in the eighteenth century and down to the first third of the twentieth. Theology found itself faced with new activities of critical reason: history, science of religions, critical exegesis, psychology of religion. The serious urgency of the questions thus raised led to the modernist crisis. There had been creative minds that cultivated a healthy openness to modernity as well as close ties with tradition (Johann Adam Möhler, Matthias Joseph Scheeben, John Henry Newman), but the chief fruit of the Catholic restoration that the nineteenth century found necessary was a renewed scholasticism possessing little creativity. Once the modernist crisis was past, theology regained its vitality from a renewed sense of the church, a renewed contact with its own sources (Bible, Fathers, liturgy), and with the questions raised by twentieth-century thinkers (ecumenism, problems of unbelief, theology of liberation, and so on).

Luther began his Reformation with a reform of theology. In reaction to Scholasticism and Aristotle he eliminated philosophical concepts and expressed the religious relationship of salvation in biblical terms. The object of his theology is man as sinful and lost and God as the one who justifies and saves him; a "theology of the cross," not a theology of the inner ontology of God; a theology that draws its life not from a symbiotic relationship with metaphysics but from pure faith in the gospel of grace, which is consonant with the spirit of scripture. Luther himself did not compose a comprehensive systematic treatise. His disciples made up for the lack by their *loci communes,* or dogmatic expositions (Melanchthon, 1531; Chemnitz, 1591; Gerhard, 1610–1625; Hutter, 1619). John Calvin produced his *Institutes of Christian Religion* as early as 1536, but he also commented on scripture daily. Protestant theology took the form of an exposition of what the church ought to be teaching in the light of its biblical norm and also in the light of the church's own past. Thus Luther and, to an even greater extent, Melanchthon and Calvin, referred back to the Fathers and especially to the ancient symbols or creeds and the first four ecumenical councils.

Starting at the end of the sixteenth century, Lutherans reintroduced into theology the metaphysics of Aristotle along with that of Francisco Suárez. Seventeenth-century Lutheran orthodoxy was much like Catholic Scholasticism. In the eighteenth century, however, two divergent currents exercised their influence: Pietism, which expressed theology in terms of personal experience, and rationalism, which interpreted religion and God in terms of man and not of God and rejected the heteronomy involved in supernatural faith. An example of this theology based solely on reason is Julius Wegscheider's *Institutiones theologiae Christianae dogmaticae* (Institutes of Christian dogmatic theology; 1815). The culture of the day had cut itself off from the faith as celebrated by the church. Some philosophers who had begun as theologians (Fichte, Hegel, Schelling) treated religion as a branch of their philosophy. Friedrich Schleiermacher (d. 1834) took up these challenges and ushered in a new era of Protestant theology. He asserted the originality of religion, which is not to be identified with either metaphysics or morality: "The essence of religion is neither speculation nor action, but intuition and feeling," and specifically the feeling of dependence, which constitutes our relation to God. Jesus Christ gave supreme expression to this feeling, and a community of believers took shape that found its origin in him. Theology, for Schleiermacher, is the sum total of scientific knowledge without which the life of the Christian community could not be ordered.

All subsequent Protestant schools of theology—the confessional, the orthodox, the liberal, as well as the contemporary restoration in the form of a return to the Reformers under the influence of Karl Barth (d. 1968)—have depended on Schleiermacher. Rejecting a simple description of what is believed and preached *(Glaubenslehre),* Barth began with the sovereignty of God's word understood as an act of God. The Bible as such is not the word of God, but only a testimony to the acts through which God spoke and ultimately to Jesus Christ, who is God's Word made flesh. The word can be received only in faith, which is the act by which God (the Holy Spirit who bears witness within us) enables us to understand when he speaks. This word has given rise in the course of history to the special community, the church, whose mission is to confess its faith in the word of God within the circumstances of the particular historical moment. At this point theology comes on the scene. Theology is the reflective critical act by which the church goes back over the word it speaks and the confession it makes of Jesus Christ; the purpose is to test the truthfulness of that word and confession, that is, their conformity to the word of God as attested in scripture. This theology has three parts: does the Christian word come from Christ? (biblical theology); does it lead to Christ? (practical theology); is it in conformity with Christ? (dogmatic theology).

The whole of Protestant theology is, of course, not reducible to Barth, and not all Protestant theologians accept his radicalism. Thus, while the pragmatism of William James (d. 1910) is not a genuine theology, the dogmatic theology of Emil Brunner (d. 1966) admits the validity in theology of a natural knowledge of God. There are even strict Calvinists in Holland, Scotland, and France, who allow a value to a natural knowledge of God. Paul Tillich (d. 1965) sought to bridge the gap between the modern mentality or culture and Christianity by establishing a correlation between the ultimate questions raised by human beings and the ever new challenge of the word of God. His work elicited an enormous response.

Catholic theologians for their part carry on their work not only under the supervision of a teaching authority but also in the context of a fidelity and a continuity that is provided by a tradition developed through the centuries. Protestant theologians, on the other hand, are bound solely by the word of God and think under their own responsibility. They do, however, have the aid of the faithful witnesses who have gone before them and of their church's profession of faith. Many Protestant theologians work within a confessional dogmatics that derives its norms from the creedal documents and classical writings of their churches. In our time we find, for example, Werner Elert, Paul Althaus, and Edmund Schlink among the Lutherans, and Auguste Lecerf and G. G. Bekouwer in the Reformed church.

Since its beginnings Anglican theology has endeavored to integrate three tendencies and has been unwilling to abandon completely any one of them: a traditional and "Catholic" tendency (Fathers, liturgy, episcopate), a Protestant and Puritan tendency, and a rational and critical tendency (history; in extreme cases, certain "modernist" theses). One or other tendency may dominate in a given age or in a particular author but without excluding the other values and while endeavoring to remain in a *via media.* Thus a writer like Richard Hooker (d. 1600) resists the Calvinist tendency but rejects a number of Roman positions (papacy, transubstantiation) and remains closely associated with the political structure of the nation. After him it is the "Caroline divines" who are the classical authors of Anglo-Catholicism, which was revitalized in the nineteenth century by the Oxford Movement (1833–1845). In the interval, however, the seventeenth and eighteenth centuries had been marked by a rational and liberal current of thought (Latitudinarianism), and then by the "evangelical" movement (John Wesley, Methodism). After 1860, rational criticism began to be heard, but this was also the time of the Oxford Movement and ritualism; the second half of the century saw the appearance of great scholars now classical in biblical and patristic studies. In the twentieth century, Anglican theology has focused chiefly on Christology, on the vital ecumenical questions of the day (church, ministry), and on the problems of modern society. On the whole, Anglican theology is a theology that always seeks a balanced outlook. It endeavors to express the realities of Christian existence but without pressure from a Roman-style teaching authority.

The Practice of Theology. Theology is discourse through which believers develop and express the content of their faith as confessed in the church; to this end the theologian uses the resources of the culture and focuses on the questions asked by the mind of the time. This activity involves the theologian, who is first of all a believer, in a series of intellectual operations, such as those analyzed by Bernard Lonergan (d. 1984). The theologian's starting point is the witness given to God's revelation of the divine plan and mystery in the Bible, tradition, and the current life of the faithful; the theologian attempts to lay out, explain, and communicate the rich and complex content found in this witness. In addition to the labor required in handling the great mass of data, theologians face two major difficulties. (1) How are they to express supernatural mysteries when they have at their disposal only concepts and terms from our earthly experience? (2) How are they to overcome the dislocation between ancient testimonies that reflect histories and cultures no longer ours, and the needs and desires of our own day?

The answer to the first question is to be found in analogy. Certain terms contain an inherent imperfection and limitation: the Bible calls God a "rock," a "lion," a "fortress." These are metaphors expressing not the being of God but God's relation to us and the divine manner of acting. The Bible uses such language because it is concerned primarily with what God is *for us* and we for God. Other terms, however, do not inherently, or in their very notion *(ratio),* contain any imperfection, even though they exist only imperfectly in us: being, intelligence, wisdom, goodness, truth, substance, person, and so on. These terms are open to infinity. They can be applied to God, although we do not fully understand the nature of their existence in God. In the case of many of these concepts and terms, however, only positive revelation allows us to predicate them of God. Without revelation we would not have thought of applying to God such terms, for example, as *father, son,* and *generation* (for a discussion of this last, see Thomas's *Summa contra gentiles* 4.11).

The answer to the question concerning the dislocation of past and present is supplied by hermeneutics. This enables the theologian to express the meaning of a traditional statement in the language of the day and in response to present needs. But in the form hermeneutics takes today it is not restricted to the expressing of traditional statements in the language of contemporary culture and in response to its needs. Nor is theology a body of knowledge *organized* on the basis of an objectivist reading of the revealed "given" (scripture, dogma, tradition); it is not what Dietrich Bonhoeffer criticized, even in Barth, as "revelational positivism." The act of theologizing is an act of interpretation that actualizes the meaning of revelation, the event that is Jesus Christ, and the church's experience, and makes these relevant to contemporary believers. The danger in this process is to introduce the subject into the object in such a way that we substitute our ideas and questions for those of God. Hermeneutics can turn into a way of evading the authority that imposes itself on the subject. Was there not something of this in certain of the moral and allegorical readings of scripture by the early Fathers? Texts, after all, intend to say something. A text is not simply a stimulus to an existential decision (the demythologization program of Rudolf Bultmann). And there are certain objective norms—dogma, the ecclesial community's profession of faith: "The living tradition whose agent is the interpreting community defines a hermeneutical field that excludes erroneous or arbitrary interpretations" (Claude Geffré). It is true, however, that the inheritance is open to rereadings which are not simply repetitions.

Theology as science. Theology claims the status of a science, and this claim is supported by its publications and its place among the university disciplines. Its status as a science is justified (1) because it has a specific object given to it by the foundational events of Christianity, which were historically real; and (2) because it employs a specific method for taking possession of this datum and organizing its complex content in a coherent intellectual way. This method, moreover, is not naive but critical, making use of the rational disciplines that study the religious fact: history, philology, critical exegesis, psychology, sociology, sociology of knowledge, and so forth. Theology is thus able to enter into competition with these disciplines, which, because they offer various interpretations of religious facts, are in danger of being reductionist. Theologians, however, must maintain the twofold fidelity mentioned above. They would cease to be theologians if they were to betray the originality of the faith, even as they employ the methods of other disciplines to analyze it. Theology may not, therefore, be reduced to a philosophy of religion. Contrary to David S. Adam, in his essay "Theology," philosophy of religion is not "the highest stage or form of theology" *(Encyclopaedia of Religion and Ethics,* edited by James Hastings, vol. 12, 1921, p. 299). The philosophy of religion analyzes the religious fact and reflects on religious experience as thematized in religions. This is, after all, one area of human experience. The philosophy of religion may therefore have the same material object as theology. It differs from the latter, however, (1) because it does not consider the objects of belief—the mysteries—as such, but studies religion as an activity, along with its conditions and the categories it uses, and (2) because it does not take revelation as a normative source of true propositions. On the other hand, unlike the science of religions or even religious psychology, the philosophy of religion is not purely descriptive. It studies the whole range of religious activity in order to discover the rational structures implied in it, examines these in a critical way, and sometimes strives to provide a critical justification of them. Theology goes further: it pursues its task while certain about the supernatural reality of what faith asserts.

Parts and forms of theology. Considered in its own proper nature, theology has some constituent parts. Materially, it includes various statements its object calls into being, for example, doctrines concerning the Trinity, Christology, the sacraments, ecclesiology, and Mariology. Formally it includes positive theology and speculative theology. Positive and speculative theology are two parts, or phases, that must not be separated but must rather be cultivated together. They incorporate the necessary appropriation of the "given" (the positive phase) by a scientifically competent study of the sources (scripture, monuments of tradition, magisterium, experience of the Christian people and of mankind generally) and the act of contemplation (the speculative phase) leading to the organization of a developed and communicable discourse.

Dogmatic theology and moral (or practical) theology are two different types of knowledge, but since no mystery is proposed for our belief except insofar as it is a source of salvation for us, the faith that seeks understanding (dogmatic theology) finds in this understanding the rules for our living (morality or ethics). In Protestant theology, practical theology includes what Catholics call pastoral theology, and even ecclesiology. In the fifteenth century, when Scholasticism was getting lost in purely logical or dialectical subtleties, writings on spiritual or mystical theology multiplied in isolation, being connected less with the mysteries than with spiritual experience. Pietism played a comparable role in seventeenth and eighteenth century Protestantism. The separation was not a fortunate one; it pointed to a lack of spiritual depth in scholastic methodology. Similarly, we must not distinguish or separate "kerygmatic theology"—the communication of the essential gospel message—from dogmatic theology, a position proposed in 1936 in Austria by Franz Lackner. There must certainly be a connection between knowledge and a life-giving communication of a message. This connection is the problem of the apostolate and may call for an output of adapted works of theology, but it must not be turned into a division of theology.

The term *negative theology* comes from the unknown author at the end of the fifth century who wrote under the name of Dionysius the Areopagite (Pseudo-Dionysius). *Apophatic theology* would be a better term. This is not a special theology but a way of respecting the "unknowableness of God" (which is the title of a work of John Chrysostom). In it positive statements are put negatively, as in the Chalcedonian christological definition: "a union without confusion, without separation."

It is commonly assumed today that one person's work can no longer embrace all areas of theology because theology has become so comprehensive and complex and requires such a variety of knowledge. We may think, however, of the work of Barth, Michael Schmaus, and others. It is even more legitimately acknowledged that theology can no longer claim to control the culture through an all-embracing body of knowledge, as it could do in the West in the thirteenth century. It might more accurately be said that a pluralism is required in a world that has grown complex and secularized and in which ideas are exchanged without any possible compartmentalization. It should be observed, however, that there has always been a pluralism in theology: Alexandria and Antioch; Augustinianism, Thomism, and Scotism; realism and nominalism; pietism and rationalism; liberalism and confessional tradition; and so on. Pluralism is valuable. It is a quality of unity itself, provided the unity involves plenitude and communion. Nevertheless, all theology is required to be faithful to the apostolic confession of faith.

Contemporary theology. In contemporary theology three dimensions or functions in particular are being developed.

1. In a world of secularized cultures, fundamental theology is being developed as a critical justification of the foundations of faith and therefore of theology. It has replaced the apologetics of a bygone time. Apologetics sought to provide rational proof of the suitability and existence of a revelation, and of the divine authority of

the Roman Catholic magisterium. Fundamental theology, however, starts with the facts of the Christian message and shows its meaning and the way in which it meets the needs of the contemporary world. Christianity represents one existential possibility. We can see immediately that this approach is very close to the idea of theology as a hermeneutic and is subject to the danger, mentioned earlier, of giving too large a place to human subjectivity.

2. In dealing with contemporary men and women, theologians must take them in their real situations and with their real dimensions, and thus fundamental theology allies itself to a "political theology" (J.-B. Metz; Jürgen Moltmann). The latter seeks to overcome the "privatization" characteristic of bourgeois religion and establish itself as critic of society in the name of suffering and the cross of Jesus Christ; in so doing it brings a message of hope and Christian eschatology. Latin American "theology of liberation" examines the situation of the poor, who are deprived of their rights and their dignity, and determines the "given" which is to serve as a starting point for rethinking God, Christology, and the church and its mission (Gustavo Gutiérrez). The practice of struggle becomes a matrix within which theological reflection develops. The same is true, with modifications, of the theologies directed to the liberation of all those who are oppressed or excluded from a place in history: black theology, African theology, feminist theology.

3. Ecumenism has its theological literature, its periodicals, its meetings, but it is above all a dimension of every vigorous theology today. The name "ecumenical theology" is given more specifically to a well-informed reflection on ecumenism and its purpose and methods, to a theological study of the World Council of Churches, or to the subject matter of a professorship in *Konfessionskunde:* the study of the Christian churches in their history, worship, theology, and life. It is no longer possible to theologize without taking account of ecumenical questions and of the contributions of all the churches, the theological originality of each, and the confessional life of each. As theology reexamines the sources of particular Christian beliefs and continues to develop in a pluralistic setting, it is becoming "metaconfessional"; chapters on particular subjects in works of theology are sometimes written by theologians from different churches. Closely associated with the ecumenical outlook is a critical attitude toward "dogmatism"—a dogmatic fundamentalism that has no sense of the historical development of dogmas.

All churches have their traditions. Many have norms for orthodoxy and the regulation of life. The work of the theologian is a specific ministry alongside the ordained or hierarchical pastoral ministry; it continues the ministry of the *didaskaloi,* the teachers, in the New Testament and the early church. The two ministries are subject to the same rule of apostolic faith and serve the same believing people and in the same world, but their tasks and responsibilities differ. Theologians are dedicated to research; they associate with intellectual and cultural innovators; they claim a legitimate freedom to be innovators themselves. The hierarchic pastors, who are responsible for keeping communities united in orthodox faith, intervene at times in the theologians' work, depending on the discipline of the various churches. Many churches have institutions and laws for settling such conflicts.

SEE ALSO Atonement, article on Christian Concepts; Attributes of God, article on Christian Concepts; Canon; Christian Ethics; Church; Councils, article on Christian Councils; Creeds, article on Christian Creeds; Eastern Christianity; Enlightenment, The; Heresy, article on Christian Concepts; History, article on Christian Views; Humanism; Icons; Jesus; Justification; Mary; Merit, article on Christian Concepts; Neoplatonism; Philosophy, article on Philosophy of Religion; Platonism; Proofs for the Existence of God; Protestantism; Reformation; Roman Catholicism; Scholasticism; Trinity.

BIBLIOGRAPHY

For further elaboration of the topics addressed above, see my "Theologie," *Dictionnaire de théologie catholique* (Paris, 1946), vol. 15, pp. 341–502. This essay has been partially translated as *A History of Theology* (Garden City, N.Y., 1968). See also my *La foi et la théologie* (Tournai, 1962).

From among the many books on theological method, see Johannes Beumer's *Theologie als Glaubensverständnis* (Würzburg, 1953), which follows the program outlined by Vatican I, and Bernard J. F. Lonergan's *Method in Theology* (New York, 1972). See also Henry Duméry, Claude Geffré, and Jacques Poulain's "Théologie," *Encyclopaedia universalis* (Paris, 1968), vol. 15, pp. 1086–1093.

On the history of the conception and practice of theology, see "Théologie," by Duméry and others, listed above; *Klassiker der Theologie,* edited by Heinrich Fries and Georg Kretschmar, vol. 1, *Von Irenäus bis Martin Luther* (Munich, 1981), and vol. 2, *Von Richard Simon bis Dietrich Bonhoeffer* (Munich, 1983); R. P. C. Hanson's *Allegory and Event: A Study of the Sources and Significance of Origen's Interpretation of Scripture* (Richmond, Va., 1959); and René Arnou's "Platonisme des Pères," *Dictionnaire de théologie catholique* (Paris, 1933), vol. 12, which defends Origen against the accusation of having given Platonism precedence over the pure Christian message. Also valuable are E. P. Meijering's *Orthodoxy and Platonism in Athanasius: Synthesis or Antithesis?* (Leiden, 1968) and Josef Hochstaffl's *Negative Theologie: Ein Versuch zur Vermittlung des patristischen Begriffs* (Munich, 1976).

The Greek and Latin fathers started the elaboration of theological treatises on the basis of scripture; this development is discussed in Aloys Grillmeier's "Vom Symbolum zur Summa: Zum theologiegeschichtlichen Verhältnis von Patristik und Scholastik," in *Kirche und Überlieferung,* edited by Johannes Betz and Heinrich Fries (Freiburg, 1960), pp. 119–169. Because of their documentation and clarity, the works of Martin Grabmann are still required reading: *Die Geschichte der scholastischen Methode,* 2 vols. (1909–1911; reprint, Basel,

1961), and *Die Geschichte der katholischen Theologie seit dem Ausgang der Väterzeit* (Freiburg, 1933). For Anselm, see G. R. Evans's *Anselm and Talking about God* (Oxford, 1978); for Thomas Aquinas, consult the stimulating studies of M.-D. Chenu, *La théologie comme science au troisième siècle,* 2d ed. (Paris, 1943), translated as *Is Theology a Science?* (New York, 1959), and *Introduction à l'étude de saint Thomas d'Aquin* (Montreal, 1950); for Bonaventure, see Georges H. Tavard's *Transiency and Permanence: The Nature of Theology According to St. Bonaventure* (New York, 1954).

In the modern age one of the most important developments has been the emphasis intellectuals have put on history. See, for example, *Historische Kritik in der Theologie: Beiträge zu ihrer Geschichte,* edited by Georg Schwaiger (Göttingen, 1980). For a discussion of Catholicism, John Henry Newman remains a model that is unfortunately too little known; see, for example, Thomas J. Norris's *Newman and His Theological Method: A Guide for the Theologian Today* (Leiden, 1977). One of the many interesting studies of the crisis of modernism, which, however, errs in reducing it to an almost orthodox liberalism, is Thomas M. Loome's *Liberal Catholicism, Reform Catholicism, Modernism* (Mainz, 1979). Two important books on contemporary theology are *Bilan de la théologie du vingtième siècle,* 2 vols. (Paris, 1970–1971), edited by Robert van der Gucht and Herbert Vorgrimler, and *Theology in Transition: A Bibliographical Evaluation of the "Decisive Decade," 1954–1964* (New York, 1965), edited by Elmer O'Brien.

On the general characteristics of Orthodox theology, there are several noteworthy articles, now rather old, by competent specialists. See, for example, articles by Aurelio Palmieri, *Studi Religiosi* 2, no. 2 (1902): 115–135, and 2, no. 4 (1902): 333–351; and Venance Grumel, *Echos d'Orient* 30 (1931): 585–596. For the cultural climate of Eastern Christianity, see Endre von Ivanka's *Hellenisches und Christliches im frühbyzantinischen Geistesleben* (Vienna, 1948). The best of today's specialists is doubtless John Meyendorff; see his *Byzantine Theology: Historical Trends and Doctrinal Themes,* 2d ed. (New York, 1979), and his studies of Gregory Palamas. On the fourteenth- and fifteenth-century debate between the hesychast spiritual tradition and humanist rationalism, see Gerhard Podskalsky's *Theologie und Philosophie in Byzanz* (Munich, 1977). Philip Sherrard's *The Greek East and the Latin West: A Study in the Christian Tradition* (London, 1959) perhaps rigidifies and oversimplifies the differences, but this work has some stimulating things to say on the approach to the mystery of God.

In Protestant theology two introductions may be mentioned: Karl Barth's *Evangelical Theology: An Introduction* (New York, 1963) and Roger Mehl's *La theologie protestante* (Paris, 1966). Richard H. Grutzmacher's *Textbuch zur systematischen Theologie des 17. bis 20. Jahrhunderts,* 3d ed. (Leipzig, 1935) provides an excellent collection of representative texts from German theologians. The following books are also very useful: Wilhelm Gass's *Geschichte der protestantischen Dogmatik in ihrem Zusammenhange mit der theologie überhaupt,* 4 vols. (Berlin, 1854–1867); Isaak Dorner's *Geschichte der protestantischen Theologie* (Munich, 1867), translated as *History of Protestant Theology,* 2 vols. (1871; reprint, New York, 1970); and Otto Pfleiderer's *The Development of Theology in Germany since Kant and Its Progress in Great Britain since 1825* (London, 1890).

The Anglican classics have been collected in the eighty-eight volumes of the "Library of Anglo-Catholic Theology" (Oxford, 1841–1863); extracts with bibliography are given in P. E. More and F. L. Cross's *Anglicanism* (London, 1935). On the same tradition, see A. M. Allchin's *The Spirit and the Word: Two Studies in Nineteenth Century Anglican Theology* (New York, 1963). Vernon F. Storr's *The Development of English Theology in the Nineteenth Century, 1800–1860* (London, 1913) is regarded as a classic. It may be complemented by L. E. Elliott-Binns's *English Thought, 1860–1900: The Theological Aspect* (Greenwich, Conn., 1956) and Arthur M. Ramsey's *From Gore to Temple: The Development of Anglican Theology between Lux Mundi and the Second World War, 1889–1939* (London, 1960).

On the practice of theology, see, in addition to the works by Congar and Lonergan already cited, E. L. Mascall's *Existence and Analogy* (London, 1949) and his *Words and Images: A Study in Theological Discourse* (New York, 1957). On the relation of theology to the scientific spirit, see Thomas F. Torrance's *Theological Science* (London, 1969).

On the hermeneutical movement, see Hans-Georg Gadamer's *Wahrheit und Methode* (Tübingen, 1965), translated as *Truth and Method* (New York, 1975); René Marlé's *Le problème théologique de l'herméneutique,* 2d ed. (Paris, 1968); Jean Greisch, Karl Neufeld, and Christoph Théobald's *La crise contemporaine: Du modernisme à la crise des herméneutiques* (Paris, 1973); *Le deplacement de la théologie* (Paris, 1977) by J. Audinet and others; and various issues of *Revue des sciences religieuses* (Strasbourg), especially the volumes for 1977, 1978, and 1982.

Of the many works of theological discourse by the oppressed, only a few can be mentioned here: by several authors, *Théologies du tiers-monde* (Paris, 1977) and *Théologie de la libération en Amérique Latine* (Paris, 1974), which has been translated as *Liberation Theology in Latin America* (New York, 1982); Gustavo Gutiérrez's *Teología de la liberación* (Lima, 1971), translated as *The Poor and the Church in Latin America* (London, 1984); James H. Cone's *A Black Theology of Liberation* (Philadelphia, 1970); Bruno Chenu's *Dieu est noir: Histoire, religion et théologie des Noirs américains* (Paris, 1977); Gerald H. Anderson's *Asian Voices in Christian Theology* (Maryknoll, N. Y., 1976); Tharcisse Tshibangu's *Le propos d'une théologie africaine* (Kinshasa, 1974); and Raymond Facelina and Damien Rwegera's *Théologie africaine: Bibliographie internationale, 1968–1977* (Strasbourg, 1977).

For ecumenical theology, see Gustave Thils's *La "théologie oecuménique": Notion, formes, démarches* (Louvain, 1960) and the very extensive documentation in Siegfried Wiedenhofer's "Ökumenische Theologie (1930–1965): Versuch einer wissenschaftsgeschichtlichen Rekonstruktion," *Catholica* (Münster) 34 (1980): 219–248.

For a critique of "dogmatism," see Josef Nolte's *Dogma in Geschichte: Versuch einer Kritik des Dogmatismus in der Glaubensdarstellung* (Freiburg, 1971) and my *Diversités et communion* (Paris, 1982), which raises the basic question enunciated in the title.

New Sources

Davaney, Sheila Greeve. *Divine Power: A Study of Karl Barth and Charles Hartshorne.* Philadelphia, 1986.

Gorringe, Timothy J. *A Theology of the Built Environment.* Cambridge, 2002.

Guntin, Colin E., ed. *The Cambridge Companion to Christian Doctrine.* Cambridge and New York, 1997.

Hauerwas, Stanley. *The Wilderness Wanderings: Probing Twentieth-Century Theology and Philosophy.* Boulder, Colo., 1997.

Heffner, Philip J. *The Human Factor: Evolution, Culture, and Religion.* Minneapolis, 1993.

Ingraffa, Brian D. *Postmodern Theory and Biblical Theology: Vanquishing God's Shadow.* Cambridge and New York, 1995.

Kamitsuka, David G. *Theology and Contemporary Culture: Liberation, Postliberal, and Revisionary Perspectives.* Cambridge and New York, 1999.

Kaufman, Gordon D. *God, Mystery, Diversity: Christian Theology in a Pluralistic World.* Minneapolis, 1996.

Parratt, John, ed. *A Reader In African Christian Theology.* Denver, 2002.

Pelikan, Jaroslav. *The Melody of Theology: A Philosophical Dictionary.* Cambridge, Mass., 1988.

Yves Congar (1987)
Translated from French by Matthew J. O'Connell
Revised Bibliography

THEOSOPHICAL SOCIETY. Founded in 1875 in New York City, the Theosophical Society is an organization whose name was chosen to align it with the larger theosophical tradition. This tradition embraced Neoplatonism, Gnosticism, medieval mystics like Meister Eckhart and Nicholas of Cusa, Renaissance philosophers like Giordano Bruno and Paracelsus, and Romantic mystics and philosophers like Jakob Boehme and Friedrich Schelling as well as wider religious philosophies like Vedānta, Mahāyāna Buddhism, Qabbalah, and Sufism. The Theosophical Society functions as a bridge between East and West, emphasizing the commonality of human culture.

The First Generation. Among the sixteen persons who participated in the formation of the Theosophical Society, two were notable for their roles in its future development: Helena Petrovna Blavatsky (1831–1891), a charismatic Russian of upper-class family, and Henry Steel Olcott (1832–1907), an American lawyer and journalist. Blavatsky was the energetic force that brought the society into existence, and she remained its chief theoretician throughout her life. At the age of eighteen, to escape the bonds of an unwanted marriage, she began her world travels, in the course of which she circumnavigated the globe and became familiar with a wide range of intellectual and mystical traditions. In 1873 she moved to New York, eventually meeting Olcott in Chittenden, Vermont, at Spiritualist meetings he was reporting for a New York newspaper. The Theosophical Society subsequently grew out of evening gatherings held in Blavatsky's New York apartment, at which papers and conversation about arcane matters attracted a small company of intellectuals. Blavatsky's first significant publication was *Isis Unveiled* (1877); her major book is *The Secret Doctrine* (1888), setting forth a cosmology; her most readable work is *The Key to Theosophy* (1889). Her periodical articles (in English and French, but excluding those in Russian) fill fourteen volumes of *Collected Writings* (1950–1991).

Olcott provided the organizing force that held the Theosophical Society together. During the American Civil War he had investigated procurement fraud for the military, and his early writings covered agriculture, insurance, and Spiritualism. He became the first president of the society and held that post until his death. He also became a champion of civil rights for the Ceylonese in Sri Lanka, where he remains a national hero; a promoter of education for the common people of Sri Lanka and India; and a key figure in the Buddhist revival, espousing an ecumenical Buddhism.

Three years after the Theosophical Society's founding, Olcott and Blavatsky left New York for Bombay, arriving there in 1879. A short-lived alliance with the Hindu reform movement of the Ārya Samāj failed because both sides misunderstood the basic orientation of the other. But Olcott and Blavatsky enjoyed a considerable popularity with some native Indians and members of the British raj, Blavatsky particularly among the latter for her ability to produce phenomena, such as the materialization of objects, and for her claim to be in touch with human teachers of extraordinary abilities.

In 1882 the Theosophical Society acquired property in southern India at Adyar, on the outskirts of Madras (now Chennai) where the Adyar River flows into the Bay of Bengal, property that is still the international headquarters of the society. In 1885 Blavatsky left India after an investigation by a staff member of the Society for Psychical Research (SPR) resulted in a report calling her an imposter, although the report was later shown by another member of the SPR to have been biased and flawed (Harrison, 1997). Blavatsky eventually settled in London, where she spent the last four years of her life producing the major body of her writings.

Meanwhile the Theosophical Society continued to grow, with national sections (semiautonomous bodies) being formed within the international organization. The first three sections were established in the United States (1886), England (1888), and India (1891).

Later Generations. The most important person in the Theosophical Society's history after Blavatsky and Olcott was Annie Wood Besant (1847–1933). Already a proponent of free thought as well as an activist and the most famous woman orator in England, Besant met Blavatsky after reviewing the latter's book *The Secret Doctrine* for an English periodical. Besant joined the Theosophical Society just two years before Blavatsky's death and was almost immediately recognized as Blavatsky's spiritual successor. Besant became international president of the society upon Olcott's death in 1907.

Shortly after Blavatsky's death a disagreement arose about the role within the Theosophical Society of William Quan Judge (1851–1896), who was one of the society's original organizers and who had become the chief executive of the American section. As a result in 1895 most of the members and branches in the United States seceded from the parent society and formed an independent organization that is now headquartered in Pasadena, California. The parent society soon reestablished itself in the United States through lecture tours by Besant and others.

Besant was a supporter of Indian independence within the British Empire, and she became the first woman and the only non-Indian to serve as president of the Indian National Congress. Besant was also a vigorous promoter of education and of human and animal welfare. With her colleague Charles Webster Leadbeater (1854–1934), she added significantly to the body of Theosophical literature and sponsored the young Jiddu Krishnamurti (1895–1986), who later became an independent religious philosopher.

During the second generation the presentation of Theosophy focused on Indic and particularly Hindu spirituality in a Westernized form. Besant and Leadbeater also promoted several Western traditions interpreted in Theosophical terms, particularly Christianity through the Liberal Catholic Church and Freemasonry through a French-derived form of Co-Masonry that admitted women on equal footing with men. Besant also organized the Order of the Star in the East to promote Krishnamurti as the spokesperson for a new world teaching. These ancillary movements were organizationally autonomous but had overlapping memberships and leaderships with the Theosophical Society.

The Theosophical Society had its largest membership and influence during the 1920s. The 1929 decision of Krishnamurti to dissolve the Order of the Star and withdraw from the role envisioned for him, coupled with the effects of the Great Depression and World War II, reduced public awareness of the society. The society fared badly under totalitarian regimes, whether of the right or the left, being outlawed and persecuted in Francisco Franco's Spain, Adolf Hitler's Germany, Joseph Stalin's Russia, and other dictatorships. Yet Krishnamurti went on to become an important spiritual teacher in the late twentieth century, and the Theosophical Society continued under able leaders. Besant was followed in the presidency by an Englishman, George Arundale (1934–1945); a Sri Lankan, Curuppumullage Jinarajadasa (1945–1953); an Indian, N. Sri Ram (1953–1973); another Englishman, John Coats (1973–1979); and another Indian, Radha Burnier (1980–), daughter of Sri Ram. In the early twenty-first century the society has branches in some seventy countries and a membership of approximately thirty-two thousand.

THEOSOPHY. The Theosophical Society has no requirement of belief or practice for its members other than subscription to its three "objects" and a way of life not incompatible with them. These objects are:

> To form a nucleus of the universal brotherhood of humanity, without distinction of race, creed, sex, caste, or color
>
> To encourage the study of comparative religion, philosophy, and science
>
> To investigate unexplained laws of nature and the powers latent in humanity.

In addition to these objects a body of teachings has evolved that attempts to state in present-day terms concepts called the ancient wisdom, the perennial philosophy, or simply theosophy. These concepts, which are not incumbent on members of the society, although they are widely espoused by members, have no official statement. The concepts may include such ideas as the following, each with ethical implications:

- There is only one ultimate reality, of which all existent things are expressions. Theosophy is philosophically monistic, with implications of human equality (formulated in the society's first object) and concern for animal welfare (resulting in the practice of vegetarianism for ethical reasons and the avoidance of other animal exploitation).
- The orderliness of the world is expressed in cyclical patterns, which can be seen in all aspects of reality from the macrocosm to the microcosm, including the reincarnation of an individual human consciousness in a long series of lives. The belief that an individual has lived or will live in bodies of both sexes and of various races and cultures fosters an understanding of and respect for human differences.
- The orderliness of the world is based on a principle of causation called karma, which operates in both material and moral realms, positing for every action a corresponding reaction, both physical and ethical. The fact that every action by a person has unavoidable consequences is a basis for practical morality: to do harm to another is to generate harm for oneself; to do good to another is to ensure good for oneself.
- World history follows an evolutionary pattern, not only of material forms but of intellect and spirit, governed by both causes and purposes. Evolution is teleological, and consequently human life is meaningful and purposeful, a recognition of which aids successful living.
- All objects in the universe are imbued with consciousness of some sort, and consciousness evolves through the ages so that, for example, mineral consciousness becomes successively vegetative, animal, human, and eventually something beyond human. Furthermore the interconnection and interdependence of all consciousness implies an ecological rather than exploitative approach to life.
- The final purpose of evolutionary development is that the ultimate reality may become conscious of itself

through its expression as the world (similar to the philosophy of Alfred North Whitehead), and the purpose of human life is to further that evolutionary development by a conscious participation in it. All individuals have a high and serious calling, which may be responded to by carrying out the duties of their stations in life.

- Human beings are assisted in fulfilling the purpose of their lives by the teachings and examples of sages, prophets, saints, avatars, or bodhisattvas; but the responsibility for that fulfillment and the impulse to meet it arise from within the individual, who is responsible for his or her own salvation. A means to fulfill one's purpose for being is an intelligent and spiritually sensitive activism, tempered by the realization that one's knowledge of the world and of oneself is still severely limited, making humility and tolerance the best guideposts to ultimate success.

Extensions and Influences. For a small and nonproselytizing organization, the Theosophical Society has had some notable effects. Offshoots of the parent society, headquartered at Adyar, Chennai, India, include the Theosophical Society with international headquarters at Pasadena, California (the direct descendant of the Judge group); the United Lodge of Theosophists; the Temple of the People at Halcyon, California; the Anthroposophical Society, which began as the German section of the Theosophical Society; the Buddhist Society U.K., which began as the Buddhist Lodge of the Theosophical Society; the Arcane School, Lucis Trust, and other organizations springing from Alice Bailey (1880–1949), who was an employee of the Theosophical Society; and a number of organizations often loosely categorized as New Age.

The concepts of the Theosophical Society have affected modern life especially in the areas of religious and social reform, art, literature, and what may loosely be called spirituality. Olcott was a leading force in the modern Buddhist revival, as was a protégé of his, Anagārika Dharmapāla (1864–1933), who founded the Maha Bodhi Society to preserve Buddhist sites and to extend Buddhism. Besant's prominence in Indian politics and in social movements inspired a number of others in India, England, and the United States to promote reform, especially for women's rights. An earlier Theosophical exponent of woman's rights was Matilda Joslyn Gage (1826–1898), American feminist and coauthor with Elizabeth Cady Stanton and Susan B. Anthony of the *History of Woman Suffrage* (1881–1887). Wassily Kandinsky framed his theory of nonobjective art in Theosophical terms, citing Blavatsky in his manifesto, *Concerning the Spiritual in Art* (1912); another pioneer in abstraction, Piet Mondrian, developed the neoplastic style of art on Theosophical principles. The Irish literary revival was influenced by Theosophy, particularly in the person of its chief exponent, William Butler Yeats. On a more general level, the Theosophical Society popularized such concepts as reincarnation, karma, and the aura as well as practices such as yoga and the complementary healing technique called Therapeutic Touch.

See Also Anthroposophy; Besant, Annie; Blavatsky, H. P.; Olcott, Henry Steel; Steiner, Rudolf.

Bibliography

Blavatsky, Helena Petrovna. *Isis Unveiled: A Master-Key to the Mysteries of Ancient and Modern Science and Theology.* 2 vols. London, 1877; reprint, Wheaton, Ill., 1972. The author's first major work, which established her reputation as a figure in nineteenth-century esotericism.

Blavatsky, Helena Petrovna. *The Secret Doctrine: The Synthesis of Science, Religion, and Philosophy.* 2 vols. London, 1888; reprint, 3 vols., Wheaton, Ill., 1978. The author's major work, a commentary on the otherwise unknown *Stanzas of Dzyan,* dealing with the origin of the universe (cosmogenesis) and of the human species (anthropogenesis) and including essays on symbolism and contemporary science.

Blavatsky, Helena Petrovna. *The Key to Theosophy: Being a Clear Exposition, in the Form of Question and Answer, of the Ethics, Science, and Philosophy for the Study of Which the Theosophical Society Has Been Founded.* London, 1889; reprint, Pasadena, Calif., 1995. One of the author's last works, a presentation of her ideas for the general reader.

Blavatsky, Helena Petrovna. *Collected Writings.* 15 vols. Compiled and edited by Boris de Zirkoff. Wheaton, Ill., 1950–1991. A collection of all known periodical articles and some other incidental writings by Blavatsky, with an extensive index by Dara Eklund as vol. 15.

Blavatsky, Helena Petrovna. *The Letters of H. P. Blavatsky,* vol. 1: *1861–1879.* Edited by John Algeo. Wheaton, Ill., 2003. The beginning of a collection of all of Blavatsky's known correspondence, this volume contains letters written before she settled in India in 1879, with extensive background essays and notes.

Ellwood, Robert. *Theosophy: A Modern Expression of the Wisdom of the Ages.* Wheaton, Ill., 1986. A popular presentation of basic Theosophical concepts as viewed by a religion scholar who is also a Theosophist.

Harrison, Vernon. *H. P. Blavatsky and the SPR: An Examination of the Hodgson Report of 1885.* Pasadena, Calif., 1997. An examination by an expert in forgery of the 1885 report submitted to the Society for Psychical Research, which branded Blavatsky as a fraud, concluding that the report was biased and that the crucial handwriting evidence was misinterpreted.

Olcott, Henry Steel. *Old Diary Leaves: The True Story of the Theosophical Society.* 6 vols. New York, 1895–1935; reprint, Adyar, India, 1974–1975. The founder-president's recollections of events between 1874 and 1898, originally published partly as journal articles that were later collected.

Prothero, Stephen. *The White Buddhist: The Asian Odyssey of Henry Steel Olcott.* Bloomington, Ind., 1996. A biography of Olcott focusing on his interactions with the Buddhist community and his role in the modern Buddhist revival, especially in Sri Lanka, where he became a national hero.

John Algeo (2005)

THERAVĀDA.

The term *Theravāda Buddhism* refers, first, to a "school" and closely related "orientations" within the history of Buddhist monasticism and, second, to forms of Buddhist religious, political, and social life in various Buddhist countries. Although these two aspects of Theravāda Buddhism must be distinguished, they overlap and interact in various ways at different points in Theravāda history. In the present article, the specifically monastic aspects will receive priority, but reference will be made to the civilizational dimension as well.

What is the best way to identify the school and the related orientations that should appropriately be considered under the Theravāda rubric? This is a very difficult question, and there is no answer that proves appropriate in all circumstances. For our purposes, however, the following characterization may be helpful. The Theravāda school and orientations within Buddhist monasticism are those that have been self-consciously identified with the "Way of the Elders" (Skt., Sthaviravāda; Pali, Theravāda) and have maintained Pali as the language in which they have preserved what they hold to be the authentic teaching of the Buddha. Within the larger divisions of the Buddhist community, the Theravāda is the sole surviving member of the so-called Eighteen Schools, the eighteen (by traditional reckoning) *nikāyas* that together made up what its detractors would come to call Hīnayāna Buddhism, the "lesser vehicle" to salvation. With the other Hīnayāna schools, the Theravāda shares a soteriology centered around the figure of the *arahant* (Skt., *arhat*), forms of community life strictly regulated by the Vinaya, or code of monastic conduct, and a canon that rejects the authenticity of the Mahāyāna *sūtras*. Theravāda remains today, as it has been for nearly a thousand years, the dominant Buddhist tradition in Sri Lanka (Ceylon), Burma, Thailand, Laos, and Cambodia.

Once this way of identifying the scholastic expressions and orientations of Theravāda Buddhism has been established, the identification of Theravāda forms of Buddhist civilization is much easier. Quite simply, Theravāda forms of Buddhist civilization are those that have been strongly influenced by the Theravāda school (including its conceptions and prescriptions relevant to society as a whole as well as to the monastic community) and heavily supported by Theravāda monks.

The recognition of these two dimensions of Theravāda Buddhism, and the specification of very general criteria for identifying each of them, does not resolve the very serious problems involved in generating an adequate historical description. It does, however, establish parameters that will facilitate the discussion.

ORIGINS AND EARLY DEVELOPMENT. Theravāda Buddhism, like other forms of Buddhism, had its origin in the life of the early Buddhist community. However, during the earliest stages of Buddhist development schools had not yet crystallized in any formal sense. Although the claim to represent the earliest Buddhism is doctrinally important, none of the schools that developed later can be considered, on the basis of purely historical scholarship, to be the sole inheritor and preserver of the original form of Buddhist teaching and practice.

The first centuries. We know that not longer than 110 years after the death of the Buddha the different emphases that existed within the earliest community culminated in a major schism. The school known as the Mahāsāṃghika ("those of the great assembly") was more populist in its attitude toward doctrinal matters, disciplinary practices, and modes of communal organization. By contrast, the Sthaviravāda school was more conservative in its approach to doctrine and practice and was more hierarchical in its patterns of community life.

Although a Theravāda tradition using Pali as its sacred language probably existed in the earliest days, its differentiation from other related traditions at this point was still quite nascent. The preferences for versions of the received tradition according to language or dialect were, as far as we know, not yet correlated with particular differences in doctrinal or practical orientation. Nor had the issues that later led to the more refined scholastic divisions been formulated in any hard and fast way.

Similarly, it is impossible to identify "Buddhist civilization," much less its Theravāda form, during the first centuries of Buddhist history. This is not to say that the Buddhist tradition generally, and the Theravādins in particular, did not have civilizational aspirations. From texts dating to this period, it seems clear that they did. But at this point the opportunity for implementation had not yet arisen.

Aśoka and after. By the period of the reign of Aśoka (third century BCE) the initial division of the Buddhist community into those of the "Great Assembly" and those of the "Way of the Elders" had subdivided further. Exactly how many groups existed, what range of languages or dialects were used to preserve their Master's teachings, and how sharply these groups were divided remains problematic. But according to Theravāda accounts dating from at least the fourth century CE, Aśoka himself sponsored a council that clarified the major differences.

According to these later accounts, Aśoka requested that a Buddhist council be held under the leadership of his monastic preceptor, a Theravāda monk named Moggaliputtatissa. At this council, the Theravādins claim to have bested their opponents in heated debates on numerous disputed issues. Not only was the Third Council supposed to have upheld the Theravādins' orthodoxy but also to have resulted in the expulsion of the defeated heretics from the *saṃgha* (Pali, *sangha*), or monastic order. The lack of corroboration from non-Theravāda sources casts doubt on the ecumenical character of the Third Council; however, most scholars accept that some sort of council was held.

Further Theravāda accounts record that Aśoka sponsored Buddhist missions that traveled beyond the frontiers of his considerable empire. These accounts date the founding of the Theravāda school in Southeast Asia and Sri Lanka to

Aśoka's missions to Suvaṇṇabhūmi (CE, Southeast Asia) and Tambapaṇṇi (CE, Sri Lanka), respectively. Aśoka's Pillar Edicts corroborate only that he sponsored the mission to Tambapaṇṇi. Other inscriptional evidence, however, supports the chronicles' accounts about a mission to Himavanta (typically identified with the Himalayan areas), whereas again the Pillar Edicts are silent. Therefore, the chronicles' accounts about a mission to Suvaṇṇabhūmi may well be accurate.

There is no substantial reason to doubt that by Aśoka's time the Theravādins formed a distinctive group within the Buddhist *sangha*. They preserved the teachings of the Buddha in Pali through their oral tradition; by the Third Buddhist Council or shortly thereafter, the Theravādins held their own positions on specific points of doctrine and practice. They also actively contributed to the Buddhist missionary activity during the third and second centuries BCE. It may nevertheless be premature to speak of Theravāda's influence as having achieved civilizational scale apart from its role within the Indian *sangha* as a whole. During the centuries that followed Aśoka's death, the Theravāda tradition continued to spread its influence in India, but as one school among many (eighteen is the traditional number given). Specific information remains scanty.

Sri Lanka and the Dhammadīpa tradition. In Sri Lanka, however, the situation was quite different. Within this distinctive provincial area, Theravāda traditions became firmly established and prospered. The Pali chronicles compiled and preserved by the Sinhala monks, inscriptions, and extensive archaeological remains make it possible to reconstruct a comparatively full picture of Theravāda Buddhism in the Sri Lanka of the first century BCE.

For example, the Pali chronicle written in fifth-century Sri Lanka and known as the *Mahāvaṃsa* (Great Chronicle) records the momentous decision to commit the Theravāda canon, preserved and transmitted for centuries by oral tradition, to writing. According to the *Mahāvaṃsa*, between the years 29 and 17 BCE Sri Lanka was threatened by foreign invasion and famine, and the Theravāda monks feared that the monastic community would be dispersed and the oral tradition broken and lost. In an effort to prevent this, they gathered together and committed to writing the Tipiṭaka (Skt., Tripiṭaka; "three baskets"), that is, the Buddhist canon. As a result, this aspect of the tradition was solidified in a basic form that has remained largely intact through Theravāda history.

The first two Piṭakas, or "baskets," are the Sutta Piṭaka, which contains sermons, discourses, and sayings attributed to the Buddha, and the Vinaya Piṭaka, which contains stories about the Buddha that introduce rules concerning the conduct for monks and nuns and the proper functioning of the monastic order. These two baskets comprise many strata of traditions ranging in dates from the time of the Buddha himself up to at least the time of Aśoka. Most of the material that they contain is present also in the traditions preserved by other Buddhist schools in various forms of Prakrit and Sanskrit, sometimes in slightly different form and often much embellished.

However, in the case of the third Piṭaka, called the Abhidhamma, or "Higher Teaching," the situation is quite different. Here we have a collection of seven compositions, each unique to the Theravāda school. These seven compositions represent a relatively late scholastic formulation, compiled possibly during the Aśokan or early post-Aśokan period. Together they present and summarize Buddhist teachings in a systematic form that differentiates Theravāda scholasticism from that of the other schools that were developing during the same period. This Theravāda distinctiveness is perhaps most explicitly expressed in the *Kathāvatthu*, an Abhidhamma text attributed to Moggaliputtatissa and associated with the Third Council. In this forensic and polemic text over two hundred Theravāda positions are defended against opposing doctrines. For example, the doctrine of *anatta* ("no-self") is defended against an opponent who asserts the existence of some kind of continuing personal entity (a view usually associated with the Pudgalavāda school); the doctrine of *anicca* (momentariness) is defended against an opponent who affirms the existence of past, present, and future times (a view usually associated with the Sarvāstivāda school); and the attainments of the *arahants* (Skt., *arhats*; fully perfected saints) are defended against opponents who questioned their perfection (a view associated most often, but not exclusively, with the Mahāsāṃghikas).

There is strong evidence to suggest that before the beginning of the common era an extensive tradition of commentaries on many portions of the Pali Tipiṭaka already existed in the Sinhala vernacular. To what extent the original forms of these commentaries were brought to Sri Lanka by the legendary missionaries of Aśokan times is unclear. Nor can we be sure to what extent these commentaries were composed in India in Pali and subsequently translated into Sinhala and to what extent they were actually composed or adapted in Sri Lanka. Since none of these commentaries has survived in its early Sinhala form, the contents cannot be determined with certainty. We know only that before the beginning of the common era a significant corpus of Tipiṭaka commentaries, preserved in Sinhala, formed an integral component of the Theravāda tradition in Sri Lanka.

By this time, too, Theravāda Buddhism in Sri Lanka had become a civilizational religion. It may be, as the later chronicles maintain, that the civilizational character dates to the time of the Aśokan missionaries to Sri Lanka. Said to have been the son of Aśoka, the monk named Mahinda (Skt., Mahendra) supposedly succeeded in his missionary goal of establishing the Theravāda lineage in Sri Lanka and converting the Sinhala king, Devānaṃpiyatissa. Shortly thereafter, according to the texts, Aśoka's daughter, the nun Sanghamittā, brought to Sri Lanka the ordination lineage for women. King Devānaṃpiyatissa is credited with founding the famous Mahāvihāra monastery, which not only encompassed the king's capital within its boundaries, but later housed the monks who authored the chronicles that we now possess.

Another possible point for the emergence of Theravāda as a civilizational religion is the reign of the Sinhala hero, King Duṭṭhagāmaṇī (r. 161–137 BCE). According to the fifth-century *Mahāvaṃsa* account (whose preeminent hero is Duṭṭhagāmaṇī, as opposed to the fourth-century *Dīpavaṃsa* account, whose hero is Devānampiyatissa), Duṭṭhagāmaṇī sought to evict the South Indians who had established their hegemony in northern Sri Lanka. While still a prince he organized a campaign in which the struggle to establish centralized rule and the struggle to establish Theravāda Buddhism as the "national" religion became closely identified. With the victory of Duṭṭhagāmaṇī and his construction of the Mahāthūpa (a funerary mound that enshrined relics of the Buddha and formed a key monument within the Mahāvihāra's monastic complex) in the capital of Anurādhapura, the civilizational character of Theravāda found a powerful vehicle of expression. Certainly, by the end of the first century BCE, after the Pali scriptures had been committed to writing, the Theravāda ideal of Sri Lanka as the Dhammadīpa, the "Island of the Dhamma," seemed well-developed not only in Sri Lankan religious and political institutions, but in Sinhala identity as well.

THERAVĀDA BUDDHISM IN GREATER INDIA. The history of Theravāda Buddhism in India and Southeast Asia during the first millennium CE continues to be extremely obscure. We know that Theravādins held sway in a number of important Buddhist centers in India, especially in Andhra Pradesh and Tamil Nadu. And we also know that several of the most famous Theravāda scholars were of Indian origin and, among these, some did their primary work in Indian monasteries.

In Southeast Asia, specifically among the Burmese of Lower Burma and the Mon peoples of Lower Burma and Thailand, the Theravāda tradition became firmly rooted and exerted a significant civilizational influence. Later legends trace the founding of this tradition to Soṇa and Uttara, the two missionaries reportedly dispatched to Suvaṇṇabhūmi by Moggaliputtatissa. The first archaeological evidence of Buddhism's presence has been found along inland and coastal trade routes, and dates to early in the first millennium CE. In Lower Burma inscriptions have been found that confirm a preeminent Theravāda presence in Pyu/Burmese royal centers beginning from the fifth century CE, and some sort of Theravāda influence is attested in Pagan somewhat later. In Thailand, similar evidence indicates that the Theravāda tradition was an important, perhaps central, religious element in the Mon civilization of Dvāravatī that flourished over a wide area of central, northern, and northeastern Thailand from the sixth to the eleventh century. Such sources notwithstanding, information concerning the kind or kinds of Theravāda Buddhism that existed among the Burmese and Mon is virtually nonexistent. Moreover, there is little data that illumines the relationship between the various Theravāda traditions and the other schools—notably other Hīnayāna schools that used Sanskrit as their sacred language—that were also very influential throughout the mainland areas of Southeast Asia.

In Sri Lanka, literary and archaeological remains provide many more details regarding local Theravāda history. According to fifth-century chronicle accounts, the first major division within the Theravāda *sangha* in Sri Lanka occurred soon after the Pali Tipiṭaka was commited to writing, probably between 29 and 17 BCE. A famous monk named Mahātissa evidently built, with royal support, an impressive new monastery in Anurādhapura. Sometime thereafter, monks of the long-established Mahāvihāra fraternity (by whose account this story is preserved) accused Mahātissa of violating the monastic discipline and tried to expel him from the *sangha.* Monks loyal to Mahātissa then formed the fraternity of the Abhayagiri monastery, which became for some time the Mahāvihāra's archrival. The Abhayagiri lineage maintained independent institutional traditions that eventually gave rise to branch monastic communities as far distant as Java.

Like the Mahāvihāra, the Abhayagiri came to include an order of nuns among its residents. These nuns seem to have been very active and were responsible for transmitting the women's ordination lineage to China in the fifth century. With an extensive network of affiliated monasteries, the Abhayagiri controlled its own sizable collection of wealth and property. This new fraternity also came to possess its own version of the Pali Tipiṭaka, its own distinctive version of certain aspects of Theravāda doctrine, and its own interpretation of particular points of monastic discipline. In addition—in contrast to their Mahāvihāra rivals—the Abhayagiri *nikāya,* like the communities that supervised the great monastic universities of India, welcomed into their midst monks from other Hīnayāna schools, and from various Mahāyāna and, later, Tantric traditions as well.

This willingness of the Abhayagiri Theravādins to welcome Mahāyāna adherents into their company generated, some three centuries after its founding, a schism within its own ranks. In the middle of the fourth century three hundred monks declared their aversion to the presence of Mahāyāna monks at the Abhayagiri, withdrew from that fraternity, and formed an independent group that came to be known as the Jetavana fraternity. The new Jetavana *nikāya* acquired affiliated monasteries and also considerable land and other wealth. But compared to the Mahāvihāra and Abhayagiri *nikāyas,* the Jetavana remained relatively small. From time to time, it became associated with particular doctrinal and disciplinary interpretations of its own, but a sustained distinctive orientation never emerged to compete seriously with its two rivals. Although by the end of the third century the Theravāda *sangha* in Sri Lanka had become divided, certain tendencies remained common to all three *nikāyas.* For example, the Theravāda scholasticism that blossomed during the fifth century drew scholars from the Mahāvihāra and from other *nikāyas* as well.

The most influential scholar associated with this efflorescence, if not Theravāda scholasticism generally, was Bhadantacariya Buddhaghosa. Probably a native of northern India, Buddhaghosa traveled to Sri Lanka in order to translate the Sinhala commentarial tradition, preserved by the Mahāvihāravāsins, into Pali, which by this time was recognized as the lingua franca of the international Theravāda community. Buddhaghosa's industriousness during his residence at the Mahāvihāra produced a rich and extensive corpus of Pali commentarial literature that became a fundamental resource for subsequent scholarship and practice throughout the Theravāda world. In addition, Buddhaghosa produced a comprehensive meditational guide and doctrinal summary known as the *Visuddhimagga* (The Path of Purification). Rich with historical anecdotes, the *Visuddhimagga* remains an authoritative resource for Theravāda scholars and adherents from his own time to the present. Although there is no corroborating evidence, a Southeast Asian tradition records that Buddhaghosa traveled to Burma late in his life and that his influence inaugurated a renascence of Burmese Theravāda.

Two monks from South India, Buddhadatta, a younger contemporary of Buddhaghosa, and Dhammapāla, his successor, also made significant contributions to the new literature in Pali. And many scholars believe that it was a monk from the Abhayagiri monastery who composed a manual entitled *Vimuttimagga* (The Path of Liberation), which, while not as wide-ranging, was nevertheless remarkably parallel to Buddhaghosa's *Visuddhimagga.* Some scholars suggest there may be a common source for both of these manuals that has parallels or variations in India as well.

Another movement in Sri Lanka that drew interested monks from all Theravāda *nikāyas* was ascetic in character and led to the rise of at least two prominent groups. The first group, known as the Paṃsukūlikas ("those who wear robes made from rags"), began to play an important role during the seventh century and continued to be noted in historical records until the eleventh and twelfth centuries. Although little is known about the group, it is quite possible that at least some of the Paṃsukūlikas were strongly influenced by Tantric trends that were becoming increasingly prominent throughout the Buddhist world, including Sri Lanka.

The second group, which attracted many proponents, especially from among the Mahāvihāravāsins, first began to be mentioned in tenth-century records. Referred to as *āraññikas* ("forest dwellers"), these monks declined to reside in the rich monasteries of the capital and established their own monastic centers in the countryside. They adopted a more stringent discipline than their urban contemporaries, and emphasized more rigorous modes of scholarship and meditation.

Throughout the entire first millennium CE, as Sri Lankan Theravāda Buddhism developed its monastic teaching and modes of practice, it also developed various civilizational aspects of its orientation. There was often serious and sometimes destructive competition between segments of the monastic community for royal support in particular and lay support in general. Serious disagreements among different Theravāda groups concerned various matters such as the propriety of monastic land ownership and wealth, the status and authority of the king, the appropriateness of various forms of ritual practice, and the like. But despite the differences, several general trends emerged. For example, over the course of the millennium monastic institutions controlled increasing amounts of land and accumulated increasing amounts of wealth. With regard to royalty, the Theravāda notion of kingship became gradually more exalted until, by the end of the period, the king was generally portrayed as a *bodhisatta* (future Buddha). Various relics of the Buddha, especially the tooth relic and the alms bowl relic, came to be regarded as palladia of the kingdom, and also became centers around which large-scale "national" festivals were celebrated.

THE GREAT REVIVAL AND BEYOND. During the first centuries after the turn of the second millennium CE, the center of gravity in the Theravāda world shifted significantly to the east. In India, Buddhism, including Theravāda Buddhism, succumbed almost completely to the pressures exerted by Hinduism and Islam. But in Sri Lanka, Burma, and Thailand, Theravāda gained new vitality and spread to new areas. Establishing centers in the Mekong Valley, the Theravādins attained preeminence by the mid-fourteenth century both among the Khmer (Cambodians) and the Lao.

At the beginning of the period Theravāda fortunes were at a low ebb. In Sri Lanka, the Theravāda *sangha* had suffered serious setbacks as a result of Cōḻa invasions from South India and the collapse of the hydraulic civilization of northern Sri Lanka. In Southeast Asia, the Pyu-Burmese and Mon civilizations in which the Theravādins had played a major role had lost much of their vitality. During this period, the kingdom of Pagan seemed to be more oriented toward Hinduism and Sanskritic forms of Buddhism than toward Theravāda. And with hegemony over most of what is now Thailand, the powerful and expansive Khmer court at Angkor was strongly oriented toward Hinduism and Mahāyāna Buddhism.

Accounts of the beginnings of the Theravāda resurgence that occurred in the latter half of the eleventh century vary according to the tradition that has preserved them. However, one primary fact stands clear both in Sri Lanka and in Burma: Theravāda became the favored tradition at the major centers of political power. In Sri Lanka this occurred after the explusion of the Cōḻa invaders and the restoration of Theravāda-oriented Sinhala royalty by Vijayabāhu I. In Burma, it occurred through the conquest of the Mon by King Aniruddha of Pagan, his introduction of Mon Theravāda monks and their traditions to Pagan, and the subsequent recognition in Pagan of the preeminence of the Theravāda *sangha.*

Sri Lanka. In Sri Lanka, the revitalized Theravāda tradition was given an important new direction in the twelfth century when, during the reign of Parākramabāhu I, a major reform and reorganization of the *sangha* was implemented. Parākramabāhu I requested the Mahāvihāra-oriented *āraññikas*, who had begun to appear on the scene two to three centuries earlier, to preside over a council. The goal of the council, not dissimilar from the goals of previous but less successful royal policies, was to purify and unify the Sri Lankan *sangha*. This time a number of factors contributed to success. On one hand, the *nikāyas* had been weakened by the recent confiscation of monastic property by King Vikramabāhu I (r. 1111–1132) and, on the other, there was a respite in the warring between Sinhala and South Indian groups.

The council "purified" the *sangha*, which meant that the code of proper monastic conduct was ascertained and monks who refused to comply were expelled. The reforms then unified the *sangha* by bringing all the remaining factions (and it is clear there were many) together into a single communal order. In so doing, the reforms provided the basis for a new structure of ecclesiastical organization that was established either at that time or shortly thereafter. The new system involved the appointment, by the king, of a *mahāsvami* or *sangharāja* to act as the monastic head of the *sangha* as a whole, and also the appointment (under him) of two *mahāsthaviras* to supervise the *gāmavāsin*, or village-dwelling monks, and the *vanavāsin*, or forest-dwelling monks (also called *āraññikas*), respectively.

The reform movement that the council expressed and abetted also generated a tremendous burst of literary creativity that matched and perhaps even exceeded the literary achievements of Buddhaghosa and others some seven centuries earlier. This new literary efflorescence had two very important dimensions. The first was the production, primarily by a monk named Sāriputta—a leading figure at the council who later seems to have held the position of *mahāsvami*—and his disciples, of a whole new strata of Pali literature. The new Pali compositions included a series of subcommentaries on the commentaries of Buddhaghosa, especially on Vinaya; also included were a number of very important texts dealing with the lineages or histories (*vaṃsa*) of various relics of the Buddha and monuments to him, as well as the more wide-ranging historical chronicles that brought the narrative of the *Mahāvaṃsa* up to date. This new literary dynamism also generated new genres of Pali and Sinhala literature that were often permeated with devotional themes. This literature vividly expressed the new reformist concern to convey the Theravāda message in linguistic and religious idioms acceptable both to monastic and lay constituencies in the countryside as well as in the urban centers.

This reformed tradition by and large remained preeminent and creative in Sri Lanka up to the coming of the Portuguese in the fifteenth century, and persisted for some centuries thereafter. The *sangha* retained its symbiotic relationship with the Sinhala kings, and the monasteries acquired new lands and wealth. However, during the period after 1500, when the authority of the indigenous Buddhist kingdom was increasingly confined to the inland highlands, the *sangha* suffered a serious erosion of standards. By the early eighteenth century, the level of monastic scholarship and discipline had reached a very low level indeed.

Burma. In Southeast Asia, the resurgence of Theravāda proceeded rather differently. At the time King Aniruddha came to the throne in Pagan (eleventh century) the Mon in Lower Burma preserved a very ancient Theravāda tradition associated with the Aśokan missionaries Soṇa and Uttara. Through the reforms initiated by Aniruddha and his monastic preceptor, Shin Arahan, and renewed by his successor, King Kyanzittha, a strong Theravāda tradition was established in Upper Burma and given powerful royal support. In the twelfth century a further reformist element was introduced at Pagan by a monk named Chapaṭa, who had gone to Sri Lanka during the reign of Parākramabāhu I and had been reordained in the newly purified and unified Sri Lankan *sangha*. Thus, by the end of the twelfth century, when the Pagan dynasty was still a very powerful force, the Theravāda tradition had become firmly established as the preeminent religion in Burma. What is more, the three major subtraditions that were to coexist and compete with one another through the entire premodern period—those associated with Lower Burma, Upper Burma, and Sri Lanka—were all more or less firmly in place.

The Burmese monastic reforms, which in some respects corresponded to those that had been implemented in twelfth-century Sri Lanka, took place when the fifteenth-century Mon king named Dhammaceti assumed the throne in Lower Burma. Formerly a monk, King Dhammaceti sponsored a delegation of eighteen monks to be reordained in Sri Lanka. When these monks returned, Dhammaceti insisted that all those within his realm who wished to remain in the *sangha* be reordained by the new fraternity. Following this "purification" and unification process, the king proceeded to establish a monastic hierarchy whose responsibility it was to maintain strict adherence to the Vinaya rules. King Dhammaceti's efforts served to emphasize the influence of Sinhala monastic traditions in Burma. Moreover, his activities gave impetus to a new tradition of Pali Abhidhamma scholarship and commentaries that has been a hallmark of Burmese Buddhism ever since.

Thailand, Cambodia, and Laos. Farther to the east, the Theravāda resurgence developed later than it had in Burma. The first hint that an expansion of Theravāda influence might be in the offing came from the report that one of the five monks who accompanied Chapaṭa on his journey to Sri Lanka in the late twelfth century was a member of the royal court of Angkor. However, it is not until the latter part of the thirteenth century that hard evidence becomes available. Based on the report of a Chinese visitor, Theravāda—possibly with connections both to Mon and Sinhala traditions—had become one of the major factors in the religious life at the Khmer/Cambodian capital at Angkor.

The newly established (thirteenth-century) Thai kingdoms of Lānnā in northwestern Thailand and Sukhōthai in central Thailand assumed the reigns of power from their Mon predecessors in areas formerly defined by the ancient Dvāravatī civilization. Like their Mon predecessors, the Thais also venerated Theravāda traditions. But during the mid-fourteenth century, Mon Theravāda traditions had to make way for a Sinhala reformist movement that spread from a center at Martaban in Lower Burma to several Thai capitals including Ayutthayā, Sukhōthai, and Chiangmai (Lānnā).

Theravāda monasteries continued to proliferate throughout the region. By the latter part of the fifteenth century the Lānnā capital of Chiangmai had emerged as one of the major intellectual centers in the Theravāda world. In central Thailand, where the locus of power gradually shifted from Sukhōthai to Ayutthayā, the Theravāda presence was consolidated. Farther east in Cambodia, Theravāda gradually displaced the deeply entrenched traditions of Hinduism and Mahāyāna Buddhism, a transition facilitated by the abandonment of the old capital of Angkor in the mid-fifteenth century. According to chronicle accounts, Theravāda became the preeminent tradition in Laos beginning with the conversion of a Laotian prince during his exile in the court of Angkor in the mid-fourteenth century. He subsequently became the ruler of the powerful Laotian kingdom of Luang Prabang. Through the entire area during this period, appropriation of reformist Theravāda influence from Sri Lanka continued. Indeed, by the beginning of the sixteenth century, reformist Sinhala fraternities dominated in all of the major royal centers and in many of the lesser ones as well.

Throughout the later premodern period in Southeast Asia there were a number of Theravāda kingdoms that held sway over various geographical areas for varying periods of time. A succession of such kingdoms constituted and fostered a loosely linked "national" tradition in Burma, and a more stable Thai kingdom was governed from Ayutthayā. A series of leading Theravāda kingdoms succeeded one another in Laos, and in Cambodia still another royal center was established. Since the pattern and development of Theravāda religion, both monastic and civilizational, varied from area to area and from kingdom to kingdom, generalizations are necessarily problematic. However, at least two important characteristics can be observed across the entire area.

First, monastic history, punctuated as it has been by reform movements, has necessarily also been subject to the considerable tensions intrinsic to that process. In Southeast Asia a continuing tension, more or less explicit, characterized relations between reformist movements and other Theravāda traditions that continued to coexist with them. Reformist groups vied with each other and indigenous groups over the purity and authenticity of their monastic observances. An extremely sensitive matter, monastic factionalism could readily be interpreted as a sign of the king's inability to maintain order in his kingdom (and often was). By way of demonstrating their authority to rule, royal sponsors had to act judiciously to balance the often contradictory demands of monastic purity and unity.

Generally speaking, the reformists were associated with Sinhala fraternities and sooner or later with royal sponsors. On the other hand, the Theravāda fraternities that resisted these reforms (fraternities that were often themselves the products of earlier reforms) typically maintained their own traditions about monastic discipline and the propriety of monastic wealth. In some instances these latter groups preserved texts and practices originally derived from Sanskrit Buddhist schools that had once exerted considerable influence in the area. They were often involved with localized modes of sacrality and were very resistant to attempts from the capital to exert centralized authority. In addition, they often utilized both Pali and vernacular texts, as well as mystical and magical modes of practice, that were clearly Tantric in character. It should be noted, however, that beliefs in the magical power of properly intoned sounds—especially Pali words—to effect order or secure protection seem to have been common to both groups.

The second characteristic of the premodern Theravāda tradition throughout Southeast Asia was the distinctive manner and extent of its civilizational role. Like the Theravāda *sangha* in Sri Lanka, the Theravāda *sangha* in Southeast Asia maintained symbiotic relationships with the various kings who ruled in specific areas. The *sangha* supported the veneration of *thūpa*s and Buddha images that had connections with political and social life at every level. Also like the Theravāda *sangha* in Sri Lanka, the *sangha* in Southeast Asia developed a textual tradition in Pali and in the various vernaculars (some translated, some originally composed) that addressed the religious, social, and moral concerns of all groups from court to village. But in Southeast Asia there was a special practice that further enhanced the civilizational impact of Theravāda, namely, the temporary participation of a significant segment of the male population in the life of the monastic order. In some areas this involved a temporary ordination as a novice. In other areas it involved temporary ordination, or several temporary ordinations, as a full-fledged member of the Order. But whatever form this practice took, it provided the context for a monastic acculturation that has given the societies of Burma, Thailand, Cambodia, and Laos their distinctive Theravāda flavor.

THERAVĀDA BUDDHISM SINCE 1750. During the past two and a half centuries Theravāda Buddhism has retained its basic structure, and the major regional traditions have maintained many of the particularities that had come to characterize them during premodern times. However, during this period there have been important developments in the Theravāda world, some the result of internal dynamics and others the result of the external pressures of colonialism and "modernity." Since most of these developments have appeared throughout the Theravāda world, we will pursue our discussion thematically. However, since these developments took very different forms in different areas, it will be necessary to give careful attention to regional and national differences.

In the monastic context the stage was set for the developments of the modern period by major reforms that were implemented in each of the three major Theravāda regions. In Sri Lanka the relevant reform took place in the middle decades of the eighteenth century. Centered in the independent kingdom of Kandy and led by the *sangharāja* named Välivita Saranamkara, this movement received royal support. Believing their ordination lineage to be defective, the reformers invited Thai monks to Sri Lanka to reintroduce an authentic Theravāda lineage. Through their efforts a new Siyam (Thai) *nikāya* was established.

Later in the eighteenth century King Bodawpaya (r. 1781-1819) succeeded in uniting Burma under his rule and in establishing a considerable degree of royally regulated discipline within the Burmese *sangha.* Through his efforts Bodawpaya officially resolved the long-standing and rancorous dispute between monastic factions about the proper way of wearing the monastic robes. Having more or less unified the *sangha,* Bodawpaya's reforms established the basis for the Thudhamma segment of the Order that has continued to include the majority of Burmese monks.

In Indochina the corresponding reforms were sponsored by King Rāma I, the founder of the Thai kingdom of Bangkok. Having claimed the throne after a period of severe disruption following the destruction of the former Thai capital of Ayutthayā, the first ruler of the new Cakkrī dynasty introduced a series of reforms that unified the *sangha* and strengthened discipline within its ranks. This more or less unified fraternity—later called the Mahanikāya—has never lost its majority position within the Thai *sangha.* In Cambodia and Laos closely related, although less reformed, Mahanikāya fraternities were dominant at the beginning of the modern period and have held that position ever since.

During the nineteenth century there emerged within the *sangha* in each area a major competing faction or factions. In Sri Lanka two competing fraternities appeared on the scene—the Amarapura *nikāya* (so called because it received its new ordination lineage from the branch of the Burmese *sangha* that was recognized at the Burmese capital of Amarapura) and the Rāmañña *nikāya* (so called because it received its new ordination lineage from the Mon *sangha* that had its center in the Rāmañña country of Lower Burma). The Amarapura *nikāya* came into being because ordination in the Siyam *nikāya* had quickly become limited to members of the highest (*goyigama*) caste. Although the intrusion of caste distinctions into the Theravāda *sangha* in Sri Lanka was not a new phenomenon, such discrimination led, in the early nineteenth century, to the formation of a competing fraternity. This new fraternity was—and remains today—a rather loose confederation of several smaller groups from various other castes that are especially prominent in southwestern Sri Lanka.

The Rāmañña *nikāya* was established in 1864 when a group of monks with a more uncompromising attitude toward any kind of caste distinctions within the *sangha* and a more "modernist" approach to all aspects of Buddhist teaching and practice formed their own independent fraternity. ("Modernist" in this article refers to a skeptical attitude toward traditional beliefs regarding cosmology, the existence of gods and spirits, and the efficacy of rituals.) Although this stricter and more modernist Rāmañña *nikāya* has remained by far the smallest of the Sinhala fraternities, it has nevertheless exerted considerable influence on the Buddhist community in Sri Lanka.

During the nineteenth century many of the same factors and orientations were present in Burma as in Sri Lanka, but a different kind of political and social context led to a much greater proliferation of *nikāya* and similar groups called *gaings*. In Burma, much more than in Sri Lanka, the nineteenth-century British conquest disrupted the fabric of social life. In response to a disrupted environment, numerous small, more tightly organized groups formed alongside the majority Thudhamma monks who continued to accept the authority of the royally sponsored Thudhamma Council through the reign of King Mindon Min (d. 1878). These various groups both complemented one another and competed with each other for purity of monastic observance and its attendant lay support. Among these groups the Thudhamma monks and the Shwegyin fraternity came to play the most important role. In comparison with the Thudhamma monks, the Shwegyin group succeeded in maintaining a more rigorous level of scholarship and discipline. The Shwegyin and the other smaller reformist communities, although less explicitly "modernist" in their orientation than the Rāmañña fraternity in Sri Lanka, had close affinities with it.

In western Indochina during the nineteenth century a single new *nikāya,* the Thammayut, emerged to complement and compete with the established Mahanikāya fraternity. The Thammayut (Dhammayuttika) *nikāya* was founded in Thailand in the mid-nineteenth century by the future king Mongkut (Rāma IV) during his more than twenty years in the *sangha.* Clearly modernist in its orientation, the group received its ordination lineage from the same Mon tradition to which modern-oriented reformists in other Theravāda countries also turned. But unlike the Rāmañña fraternity in Sri Lanka and the Shwegyin fraternity in Burma, the Thammayut fraternity received special support from Thailand's unconquered monarchy all through the late nineteenth and early twentieth centuries. This, plus the closely related fact that its members were drawn largely from the highest levels of the Thai elite, enabled it to exert a powerful influence on the much larger Mahanikāya. The Thammayut's favored status and elite membership also enabled it to play an important role in drawing provincial traditions into the central Thai *sangha,* and in extending central Thai influence into the *sanghas* of Cambodia and Laos as well.

Thus, by the beginning of the twentieth century the various fraternities that still constitute the Theravāda *sangha*s in Sri Lanka and Southeast Asia had already come into being. But there is one related twentieth-century development that should also be mentioned, namely the very tentative and controversial reemergence of the order of nuns. For almost a millennium the order had not existed in the Theravāda context, although in some Theravāda areas there were many, typically older women who adopted a celibate mode of life and frequented the monastic environs. But in recent years a few determined women from Theravāda countries have gone to Taiwan, where they have been ordained into the lineage of nuns that had been transmitted from Sri Lanka to China in the fifth century. The number of such nuns in Theravāda countries is currently still minuscule, and the authenticity of their ordination is not recognized by the great majority of Theravāda monks and laity. But the seeds for a possible revival have clearly been planted.

During the modern period these essentially monastic developments have been complemented by a number of civilizationally oriented movements, all of which have drawn on long-established Theravāda traditions. But at the same time they have appropriated and adapted these traditions in new ways. Four movements may be cited as examples.

1. Millenarian movements, which constitute the first example, may be subdivided into at least two major types. The first type, which has appeared primarily in Burma and other Southeast Asian countries, is represented by more mystical, politically passive movements that have at their respective centers a cult devoted to a charismatic personage (sometimes identified with the future Buddha Metteyya) who is expected—at some very indefinite future time—to usher in a new age. The second type is represented by more activist movements that have arisen in periods and contexts where crises of power have occurred. Such politically active millenarian movements appeared in Sri Lanka and Southeast Asia during the period of British and French colonial conquest. They have appeared within the colonial context itself—most notably in the famous Saya San rebellion in Burma. They have also appeared when indigenous governments (particularly in Burma and Thailand) have sought to extend their authority into outlying areas.

2. A closely related set of movements that has been particularly strong in Southeast Asia has involved the cultivation of meditational practice. Many of these movements have coalesced around charismatic individuals who have achieved advanced meditational states and are in some instances rumored to be *arahants*, or fully perfected saints. Often in such cases these meditationally advanced individuals make their power available to their followers in the form of appropriately blessed amulets and other sacred objects. On the other hand, many of the movements in this set emphasize the importance of meditation for all. Special forms of practice have been developed for less committed monks and for the laity. Numerous lay-oriented meditation centers have been set up in Burma where the contemporary meditational emphasis began to take form in the early twentieth century, in Thailand where lay meditation has enjoyed great popularity in recent years, and increasingly in Sri Lanka as well.

3. A third set of movements that have had a significant impact are those that can be characterized as "modernist" in the specific sense noted above. In the monastic context, modernist concerns were very much involved in the formation of several of the monastic fraternities that developed in various Theravāda countries during the nineteenth century. Equally important, major lay movements with modernist ideologies have appeared and taken root. In Sri Lanka in the late nineteenth century, Anagārika Dharmapala and those who shared his views emphasized a "this-worldly" mode of lay asceticism (Anagārika is a title designating a lay ascetic) and rejected many traditional Buddhist beliefs and practices as superstitious and useless. During and since Dharmapala's time many other modernist movements and associations have developed among the laity all across the Theravāda world, particularly in the urban areas. The influence of these movements and associations has been most evident in Sri Lanka and Thailand, but they have been—at certain points—active components in the Theravāda communities in Burma and, to a lesser extent, in Cambodia and Laos as well. It is also important to note that several of these modernist movements and associations have been instrumental in the establishment and maintenance of a significant Buddhist ecumenical organization known as the World Fellowship of Buddhists.

4. Considering Theravāda Buddhism's civilizational character, it is not surprising that it became involved in the political processes and ideological trends that have affected the various Theravāda countries during the nineteenth and twentieth centuries. In Sri Lanka and Burma certain segments of the Theravāda community, including the monastic community, became very deeply involved with movements for national independence. These same groups were also involved with attempts, during the postindependence period, to build new, democratically structured societies that would be both Buddhist and socialist. In the 1950s such hopes were strongly expressed in the context of the 2,500th anniversary of the Buddha's death, celebrated in 1956. These celebrations included a much-heralded "sixth" Buddhist Council that was sponsored by the Burmese government of U Nu.

Since the late 1950s the situation in both countries has changed considerably. In Sri Lanka the early hopes for Buddhist nationhood have been seriously eroded, and a nonsocialist government has come to power. Moreover, some Sinhala spokesmen representing both the left and the right have used a Buddhist idiom in the rhetoric surrounding communal violence between the Sinhala majority and the substantial Tamil minority. In Burma the hopes for Buddhist nationhood also dimmed, and the military government that took over in the early 1960s—despite its nominal support for Buddhist socialism—sought to keep Buddhism isolated from the mainstream of national life. But in the Burmese case it should also be noted that in recent years the military government has taken a significantly new tack by initiating a reform of the monastic order that is intended to "purify" it, demonstrate government interest in monastic affairs, and open channels of communication between the government and the *sangha*.

Further east, the interactions between Theravāda Buddhism, politics, and ideology have been equally important but quite different in character. In Thailand the affinity between the Theravāda tradition and nationalism has been as strong as in Sri Lanka or Burma. But since Thailand was never conquered by a Western nation, this affinity has resulted in a basically cooperative relationship between Buddhism and the established government, and a rather stable continuation of the traditional symbiotic relationship between the *sangha* and state. In recent years Buddhism has become closely associated with capitalist development, while socialism—Buddhist or otherwise—has remained on the political and ideological periphery.

In Cambodia and Laos an early continuity with the received tradition was followed by a break that has been both dramatic and devastating. The continuity that characterized the religio-political situation during the colonial period was made possible by the fact that the French—who were the colonial overlords in the area—chose to rule at a distance and to leave the established religious and political order largely intact. The radical break was, of course, the result of the disruption caused by the war that racked the area in the late 1960s and early 1970s, and by the victory of the Communists in both countries. In Cambodia, the Communist devastation of Buddhism during the Pol Pot regime (1975–1980) was widespread and brutal. In Laos (and, since 1980, in Cambodia), the approach of the Communist authorities has been considerably more restrained; but even in these contexts traditional Buddhist institutions have suffered serious damage and traditional Buddhist values have been directly and severely challenged.

THERAVĀDA TODAY. Theravāda Buddhism remains very much alive in Sri Lanka and Southeast Asia, both as a monastic tradition and as a civilizational force. The *sangha*, despite its many problems, carries on its traditions of Pali scholarship and meditational practice. It continues to produce persons with intellectual substance and spiritual prowess. And it continues to generate movements (often conflicting movements) aimed at monastic reform, spiritual development, and societal well-being.

In addition, Theravāda Buddhism continues to exert its influence on the institutions and values of the societies in the traditionally Theravāda areas. This influence takes quite different forms in Sri Lanka, where ethnic differences often involve religious differences; in Burma, where the nation's leaders have sought to insulate the populace from many aspects of "modernity"; in Thailand, where the pace of "modernization" is rapid indeed; and in Cambodia and Laos, where Theravāda Buddhism has been "disestablished" by recently installed Communist governments. But in each instance Theravāda Buddhism continues to provide meaning in the everyday life of its adherents.

SEE ALSO Arhat; Aśoka; Buddhaghosa; Buddhism, article on Buddhism in Southeast Asia; Burmese Religion; Duṭṭhagāmaṇī; Khmer Religion; Kingship, article on Kingship in East Asia; Lao Religion; Moggaliputtatissa; Mongkut; Saṃgha; Sinhala Religion; Southeast Asian Religions, article on Mainland Cultures; Thai Religion; Vinaya; Worship and Devotional Life, article on Buddhist Devotional Life in Southeast Asia.

BIBLIOGRAPHY

Unfortunately there is no one book that adequately covers Theravāda Buddhism as a whole. Perhaps the most comprehensive single study for the premodern period is Kanai Lal Hazra's *History of Theravāda Buddhism in South-East Asia* (New Delhi, 1982), which touches on Indian and Sri Lankan developments as well. This book needs to be supplemented by other works that deal with particular aspects of the tradition, such as Wilhelm Geiger's *Pali Literature and Language*, 2d ed., translated by Batakrishna Ghosh (Delhi, 1968); John C. Holt's *Discipline: The Canonical Buddhism of the Vinayapitaka* (Delhi, 1981); John Ross Carter's *Dhamma: Western Academic and Sinhalese Buddhist Interpretations* (Tokyo, 1978); Stephen Collins's *Selfless Persons: Imagery and Thought in Theravāda Buddhism* (Cambridge, 1982); Winston L. King's *Theravāda Meditation* (University Park, Pa., 1980); and Bhikkhu Nyanatiloka's *Guide to the Abhidhamma-pitaka*, 3d ed., revised and enlarged by Nya-naponika Thera (Kandy, 1971). Many of the civilizational aspects are covered in two related books edited by Bardwell L. Smith, *Religion and Legitimation of Power in Sri Lanka* and *Religion and Legitimation of Power in Thailand, Laos, and Burma* (both, Chambersburg, Pa., 1978). Similar themes are explored in Heinz Bechert's three-volume *Buddhismus, Staat und Gesellschaft in den Ländern Theravāda-Buddhismus* (Frankfurt, 1966–1973). Two other studies written for more general audiences are Robert C. Lester's *Theravāda Buddhism in Southeast Asia* (Ann Arbor, 1973) and Donald K. Swearer's *Buddhism and Society in Southeast Asia* (Chambersburg, Pa., 1981).

Because of vast translation efforts, primarily by the Pali Text Society, the nonspecialist has access to a large body of Theravāda literature. Virtually the entire Tipiṭaka has been translated into English and is included in either the "Sacred Books of the Buddhists" or the "Translation Series" of the Pali Text Society. Among the most important postcanonical texts that are available in English are Wilhelm Geiger's translation of *The Mahāvaṃsa, or The Great Chronicle of Ceylon* (London, 1964); Bhikkhu Ñyanamoli's translation of Buddhaghosa's fifth-century work, *The Path of Purification*, 2d ed. (Colombo, 1964); and Frank E. Reynolds and Mani B. Reynolds's translation of Phya Lithai's fourteenth-century cosmological treatise, *Three Worlds according to King Ruang* (Berkeley, 1982).

A useful introduction to the Theravāda tradition in Sri Lanka is provided in *Two Wheels of Dhamma*, edited by Bardwell L. Smith, Frank E. Reynolds, and Gananath Obeyesekere, "American Academy of Religion Monograph Series," no. 3 (Chambersburg, Pa., 1973). This introduction should be supplemented by the R. A. L. H. Gunawardhana's excellent *Robe and Plough: Monasticism and Economic Interest in Early Medieval Sri Lanka* (Tucson, 1979) and Kitsiri Malalgoda's *Buddhism in Sinhalese Society, 1750–1900* (Berkeley, 1976). For two books that deal with quite different dimensions of the "contemporary" tradition, see Michael Carrithers's *The Forest Monks of Sri Lanka: An Anthropological and Historical Study* (Delhi, 1983) and Richard F. Gombrich's *Precept and Practice: Traditional Buddhism in the Rural Highlands of Ceylon* (Oxford, 1971).

The most comprehensive overview of Theravāda Buddhism in Burma is provided by Melford E. Spiro in his *Buddhism and Society: A Great Tradition and its Burmese Vicissitudes* (New York, 1970). Serious students will also want to consult E. Michael Mendelson's very important study, *Sangha and State in Burma: A Study of Monastic Sectarianism and Leadership*, edited by John Ferguson (Ithaca, N.Y., 1975); Emanuel Sarkisyanz's *Buddhist Backgrounds of the Burmese Revolution* (The Hague, 1965); and Manning Nash's *The Golden Road to Modernity: Village Life in Contemporary Burma* (New York, 1965).

The Theravāda tradition in Thailand has been comprehensively studied by Stanley J. Tambiah in a trilogy of excellent books: *World Conqueror and World Renouncer* (Cambridge, 1976), *Buddhism and the Spirit Cults in North-East Thailand* (Cambridge, 1970), and *The Buddhist Saints of the Forest and the Cult of Amulets* (Cambridge, 1984). Other items of interest include Donald K. Swearer's *Wat Haripuñjaya* (Missoula, Mont., 1976) and our "Sangha, Society and the Struggle for National Integration: Burma and Thailand," in *Transitions and Transformations in the History of Religions: Essays in Honor of Joseph M. Kitagawa*, edited by Frank E. Reynolds and Theodore M. Ludwig (Leiden, 1980), pp. 56–88.

Studies that deal with Theravāda Buddhism in Laos and Cambodia are much less adequate and are virtually all in French. The best introductions are probably the articles on Buddhism in the collections edited by René de Berval in *France-Asie* entitled *Présence du royaume Lao* (Saigon, 1956), translated by Mrs. Tessier du Cros as *Kingdom of Laos* (Saigon, 1959), and *Présence du Cambodge* (Saigon, 1955). Two books that provide overviews of sorts are Marcel Zago's *Rites et cérémonies en milieu bouddhiste Lao* (Rome, 1972) and Adhémard Leclère's *Le bouddhisme au Cambodge* (Paris, 1899). The most important new studies are three short but erudite works by François Bizot that highlight an important Tantric influence in the Pali Buddhist traditions in Cambodia and draw implications for our understanding of the Theravāda tradition more generally. These have appeared under the titles *Le figuier à cinq branches* (Paris, 1976), "Le grotte de la naissance," *Bulletin de l'École Française d'Extrême-Orient* 66 (1979); and *Le don de soi-même* (Paris, 1981).

Further bibliographical information—including annotations of many of the works cited here—can be obtained by consulting the relevant sections in *Guide to Buddhist Religion* by Frank E. Reynolds et al. (Boston, 1981), or in Reynolds's "Buddhism," in *A Reader's Guide to the Great Religions*, edited by Charles J. Adams, 2d ed. (New York, 1977), pp. 156–222.

New Sources

Andaya, Barbara Watson. "Localising the Universal: Women, Motherhood, and the Appeal of Early Theravada Buddhism." *Journal of Southeast Asian Studies* 33 (February 2002): 1–31.

Anderson, Carol. *Pain and Its Ending: The Four Noble Truths in the Theravada Buddhism Canon.* Richmond, U.K., 1999.

Berkwitz, Stephen C. "History and Gratitude in Theravada Buddhism." *Journal of the American Academy of Religion* 71 (September 2003): 579–605.

Burford, Grace G. *Desire, Death, and Goodness: The Conflict of Ultimate Values in Theravada Buddhism.* New York, 1991.

Carter, John Ross. *On Understanding Buddhists: Essays on the Theravada Tradition in Sri Lanka.* Albany, 1993.

Gombrich, Richard Francis. *Theravada Buddhism: A Social History from Ancient Benares to Modern Columbo.* New York, 1988.

Holt, John Clifford, Jacob N. Kinnard, and Jonathan S. Walters. *Constituting Communities: Theravada Buddhism and the Religious Cultures of South and Southeast Asia.* New York, 2003.

Leve, Lauren G. "Subjects, Selves, and the Politics of Personhood in Theravada Religion in Nepal." *Journal of Asian Studies* 61 (August 2002): 833–861.

Swearer, Donald K. *Becoming the Buddha: The Ritual of Image Consecration in Thailand.* Princeton, 2004.

Trainor, Kevin. *Relics, Ritual and Representation in Buddhism: Rematerializing the Theravada Tradition.* New York, 1997.

FRANK E. REYNOLDS (1987)
REGINA T. CLIFFORD (1987)
Revised Bibliography

THÉRÈSE OF LISIEUX (1873–1897), epithet of Thérèse Martin, French Carmelite nun and Catholic saint. Thérèse was the youngest of nine children born to Louis and Zélie Martin. When Thérèse was eight her family moved to the small Norman town of Lisieux, where she was to spend the remainder of her life, with the exception of one pilgrimage to Rome shortly before she entered the convent. Within a few years of the family's arrival in the town, Thérèse's two older sisters became nuns at the cloistered convent of Discalced Carmelites in Lisieux, and at an early age Thérèse decided to join them. Her first application to enter the convent, made when she was fourteen, was rejected on account of her age, but at fifteen she entered the convent.

In the cloister Thérèse exhibited unswerving fidelity to the Carmelite rule and unfailing kindness to the convent's twenty-five nuns, some of whom had quite unattractive personalities. However, the full dimensions of her spiritual life became evident only in her posthumously published autobiography. Eighteen months before her death she manifested signs of a fatal tubercular condition, and her last months were plagued by extreme pain and even nagging temptations against faith. She died at the age of twenty-four, exclaiming, "My God, I love you."

During the last years of her life Thérèse wrote her memoirs in three separate sections, mostly at the request of the convent's superior. One year after her death the memoirs were published under the title *L'histoire d'une âme* (The Story of a Soul). The simple book, written in epistolary style, is a candid recounting of her own unfailing love for and confidence in the goodness of God, and it achieved instant and enormous popularity in translations into many languages. In the next fifteen years alone more than a million copies were printed. This worldwide response prompted the Holy See to waive the usual fifty-year waiting period, and Thérèse was beatified in 1923 and canonized in 1925. In the bull of canonization, Pius XI said that she had achieved sanctity "without going beyond the common order of things."

BIBLIOGRAPHY

Of the many English translations of *L'histoire d'une âme,* perhaps the most readable is Ronald Knox's *Autobiography of St. Thérèse of Lisieux* (New York, 1958), which is done in Knox's usual felicitous style. Other of Thérèse's writings are contained in *Collected Letters of St. Thérèse of Lisieux,* edited by Abbé André Combes and translated by Frank J. Sheed (New York, 1949). For a short but incisive biography, see John Beevers's *Storm of Glory* (New York, 1950); for a more critical study, see my book *The Search for St. Thérèse* (Garden City, N. Y., 1961).

PETER T. ROHRBACH (1987)

THERIANTHROPISM is a term derived from the Greek compound of *thēr* ("wild beast") and *anthrōpos* ("human") and is usually used to denote a deity or creature combining the form or attributes of a human with those of an animal. As an analytic category, it has little salience, since scholars have variously included under its rubric not only animal-headed gods, were-animals, mythological demihumans and monsters (such as centaurs, sphinxes, and minotaurs) but also examples of animal impersonation in rituals, spirit possessions by animals, mythological beings of animal aspect but human character (such as the North American Indian figure Coyote), and anthropomorphic gods (such as Zeus and Dionysos) who sometimes transform themselves into animals. Ideas about the supernatural linkage of humans and animals are probably universal—even in cultures with anthropomorphic monotheism, there are ideas of were-animals, therianthropic demons, and the possession of human souls by animals. Visual or literary images of therianthropic beings can be found in virtually all of the world's cultures, where they contrast with and complement representations of other forms of supernatural beings.

HISTORICAL INTERPRETATIONS. Discussions of therianthropy were most prevalent during the nineteenth century, when the idea of a part human, part animal deity was seen as a critical development stage in human history, midway between the totemic identification of hunter and prey that was supposed to characterize savage religions and the anthropomorphic deities of civilization. The occurrence of therianthropic deities was interpreted either as a survival of savage ideas in later religions or as the result of a historical diffusion of these more advanced representations of the divine from their Egyptian/Mesopotamian point of origin. The fact that most therianthropic figures known at that time came from the civilizations of the Middle East, where most of the archaeological research was being conducted, and that these civilizations were seen as midpoints between savagery and civilization gave added weight to the idea that therianthropy was a partial progress toward a rational, anthropomorphic religion. (Interestingly, Plato uses an account—one that is probably spurious—of a rural Arcadian cult of lycanthropy to contrast with the rational religions of urban Athens.)

CONTEMPORARY INTERPRETATIONS. The categorical distinctions between primitive and civilized mentalities that provided the rationale for developmentalist interpretations of religious history have not been supported by anthropological research, and most contemporary interpretations of therianthropic symbolism take a semiotic approach to the subject. Animals are seen as emblems of principles, as vehicles for symbolically expressing existential truths about the human condition. Therianthropic images juxtapose two principles in a unified being. Thus, it is not the animality of the image that is important but its duality, its ambiguity, its nature as a dialectic category that simultaneously contrasts and synthesizes two opposing metaphorical principles—images of noncontiguous categories made continuous (culture-nature, wild-domesticated, rational-emotional, independent-submissive, etc.). Therianthropic images, given their nature as a category of representation betwixt and between other categories, as a category whose elements are neither separate nor unified, are frequently associated with rituals of transition and liminality (as in initiation rites and carnivals) or with the intermediate stages of creation, when the world is in neither its primal nor its finished state.

Only as the psychology of religion and the theory of symbolism permit the development of new modes of understanding can we hope to deal with the historical and theological questions that are posed by differentiating therianthropic images of the divine from those that are theriomorphic or anthropomorphic. All three kinds of images may exist simultaneously in the psychologies, if not the artistic representations, of the world's peoples. Therianthropic ideas simultaneously differentiate and synthesize the qualities that define humanness with those that define the nonhuman other, and they may not represent significantly different, historically traceable, understandings of the nature of divinity so much as conventional representations of a universal religious phenomenon.

See Also Animals; Shape Shifting.

Bibliography

Therianthropism is discussed by Joseph Campbell, who takes a diffusionist approach to the topic, in *The Way of the Animal Powers* (New York, 1983).

Stanley Walens (1987)

THESMOPHORIA.

The Thesmophoria was an annual women's festival widely celebrated in ancient Greece. In most areas it took place in autumn, at the season of plowing and sowing, and it was held in honor of the grain goddess Demeter and her daughter Persephone. Fertility of crops and of women was evidently the essential theme.

The Athenian form of the ritual is the best known. Here the festival occupied three days. On the first day the women went up to the sacred grove of Demeter Thesmophoros, set up an encampment there, out of sight of all males, and made some preliminary sacrifices. On the second day they fasted, sitting humbly on the ground, as Demeter was said to have fasted in grief over the abduction of her daughter. This abstinence was probably understood as a kind of purification in preparation for the main ceremonies. The third day featured pomegranates to eat, obscene jesting, and perhaps flagellation—all things associated with fertility. Piglets were slaughtered, and parts of them, it seems, were cooked and eaten; substantial portions, however, were thrown into *megara,* deep holes in the earth, together with wheat cakes shaped like snakes or like male genitals, and an otherwise unknown goddess, Kalligeneia, whose name means "fair birth," was invoked. At some stage—perhaps the night before—certain women who had for three days observed purity restrictions climbed down into the hole, and while others clapped, brought out the decayed remains of the previous year's offerings. These were ceremoniously carried out of the camp and set forth on altars. (The Thesmophoria itself took its name from this "bringing of the deposits.") If a farmer took a little portion of the remains and mixed it in with his seed corn, he was supposed to get a good crop. This element of primitive agrarian magic suggests that the Thesmophoria's origins lay in a remote past.

See Also Demeter and Persephone.

Bibliography

A full and judicious discussion can be found in Martin P. Nilsson's *Griechische Feste von religiöser Bedeutung* (Leipzig, 1906), pp. 313–325. Walter Burkert's *Griechische Religion der archaischen und klassischen Epoche* (Stuttgart, 1977), translated as *Greek Religion* (Cambridge, Mass., 1985), concentrates on the main features and their interpretation. Ludwig Deubner's *Attische Feste* (Berlin, 1932), pp. 40–60, remains the most detailed study of the Athenian Thesmophoria, but one of its main conclusions (that the pigs were deposited at a different festival in the summer) is strongly disputed. H. W. Parke's *Festivals of the Athenians* (Ithaca, N.Y., 1977) follows Deubner on this point. For primitive customs of fertilizing fields with the remains of sacrificial victims, see chapter 7 of James G. Frazer's *Spirits of the Corn and Wild,* 2 vols., part 5 of *The Golden Bough,* 3d ed., rev. & enl. (London, 1912).

New Sources

Brumfield, Allaire Ch. *The Attic Festivals of Demeter and Their Relation to the Agricoltural Year.* New York, 1981.

Clinton, Kevin. "The 'Thesmophorion' in Central Athens and the Celebration of the 'Thesmophoria' in Attica." In *The Role of Religion in the Early Greek Polis: Proceedings of the Third International Seminar on Ancient Greek Cult, Organized by the Swedish Institute at Athens, 16–18 October 1992,* edited by Robin Hägg, pp. 111–125. Stockholm, 1996.

Nixon, L. "The Cults of Demeter and Kore." In *Women in Antiquity: New Assessments,* edited by Richard Hawley and Barbara Mary Levick, pp. 75–96. London, 1995.

Prytz, Johansen J. "The Thesmophoria as a Women's Festival." *Temenos* 11 (1975): 78–87.

Sfameni Gasparro, Giulia. *Misteri e culti mistici di Demetra.* Rome, 1986. See especially pages 223–284.

Versnel, Hendrik S. "The Roman Festival for Bona Dea and the Greek Thesmophoria." In *Inconsistencies in Greek and Roman Religion. 2. Transition and Reversal in Myth and Ritual,* pp. 235–260. Leiden, 1993.

M. L. West (1987)
Revised Bibliography

THEURGY

(from the Greek *theourgia*) means literally something like "actuating the divine" and refers to actions that induce or bring about the presence of a divine or supernatural being, whether in an artifact or a person. It was a practice closely related to magic—not least in its ritual use of material things, sacrifices, and verbal formulas to effect the believer's fellowship with the god, demon, or departed spirit. It is distinguished from ordinary magical practice less by its techniques than by its aim, which was religious (union with the divine) rather than secular. Use of the term *theourgia*—as well as of the related *theourgos,* referring to a practitioner of the art—arose in the second century CE in Hellenistic circles closely associated with the birth of Neoplatonism. The practice was commended and followed, in the third and later centuries, by certain Neoplatonist philosophers and their disciples.

The origins of this movement can be traced, in all probability, to a work called the *Chaldean Oracles,* plausibly attributed to the reign of Marcus Aurelius (161–180). A collection of obscure and pretentious oracular utterances written in Homeric hexameters, this work, now known only in fragments, was apparently assembled (if not composed) by one Julian the Chaldean or (perhaps more likely) by his son Julian the Theurge. Much of its content is quasi-philosophical, and its account of the first principles shows affinities with the thought of the Pythagorean philosopher Numenius, who was teaching around the middle of the second century. It also contained, however, prescriptions for theurgic rites and indications of the "sights" that they produce, for example, "a formless fire whence a voice proceeds" (frag. 146).

Concerning the value of such practices, there was significant disagreement among Neoplatonist thinkers. Plotinus himself, it is now agreed, either knew or thought nothing of the *Chaldean Oracles.* His way to human fulfillment in the divine was the way of *theoria* ("contemplation"), not that of *theourgia.* It was his disciple Porphyry who was the first among philosophers to give some status to the practice of theurgy. In spite of the severe criticisms of it that he had leveled in his *Letter to Anebo,* Porphyry came, according to Augustine (*City of God* 10.9f.), to acknowledge a theurgy whose aim was purification of the soul and that produced "appearances of angels or of gods." At the same time Porphyry insisted that the value of such practices was strictly limited. What they purified was not the intellectual soul, but only its lower, pneumatic adjunct, which is adapted to visions of spirits, angels, and inferior deities; they had no power to bring people into the presence of Truth itself. Presumably Porphyry continued to believe, with Plotinus, that it is only the practice of virtue and of philosophical contemplation that raises the soul to fellowship with the supreme God.

This conviction was not shared, however, by Porphyry's own disciple, the Syrian Iamblichus (d. 325), who, in his long treatise *On the Mysteries,* replied to the strictures expressed by his teacher in the *Letter to Anebo.* According to Iamblichus, there exists, in theurgy, a mode of fellowship with the divine that is independent of philosophical thought and that "those who philosophize theoretically" do not achieve. "What effects theurgic union is the carrying through of reverently accomplished actions which are unspeakable and transcend any intellectual grasp, as well as the power of mute symbols which only the gods understand" (*On the Mysteries* 2.11).

This debate, however, did not end with the exchange between Iamblichus and his teacher. In his youth the emperor Julian was a disciple of the philosopher Eusebius, who taught that "the important thing is purification [of the soul] through reason" and who condemned wonder-working. Julian, however, was more impressed in the end by the teaching of one Maximus, who, by burning incense and reciting a formula in the temple of Hecate, caused the statue of the goddess to smile and the torches in her hands to blaze; the emperor-to-be accordingly adopted Maximus as his teacher (Eunapius, *Lives of the Philosophers and Sophists* 474).

What the practice of theurgy involved becomes plain from the text of Iamblichus's treatise itself. There he defends and interprets a variety of rites and practices that involve either the use of offerings or tokens of some sort or the various phenomena that accompany divine possession. It is plain, however, that in his mind the practices he explains can be understood and entered into—and indeed function—at more than one level. True theurgy, he suggests, is, "the summit of the priestly art" and is reserved "to a very few"—those, indeed, who "share in the theurgic gods in a way which transcends the cosmos," because they "go beyond bodies and matter in service of the gods, being made one with the gods by a power which transcends the cosmos" (*On the Mysteries* 5.20–5.22). For all this, however, there is little new or unfamiliar in the phenomena he alludes to, from the "enthusiasm" of the Corybantes to the sacrifice of animals. He refers, for example, to levitation as one manifestation of possession by a god. He is also familiar with situations in which the theurgist makes use of a medium (*ho dechomenos*), and both he and the medium—and sometimes the assembled spectators—see the "spirit [*pneuma*] which comes down and enters" the one who is possessed (3.6). In another vein, he refers to theurgic use of hollow statues that are filled with "stones, herbs, animals, spices, [and] other such holy, perfect, and godlike things," so as to create a receptacle in which the god will be at home (5.23). Though this practice seems to have been especially favored by late classical practitioners of theurgy, it clearly draws on widespread and ancient practices of sympathetic magic.

What is interesting and new, then, in Iamblichus's account of *theourgia,* as over against *theoria,* is precisely the terms in which he understands and defends it. For one thing, it is plainly his conviction that theurgy is not a matter of manipulating the gods. Over and over again he denies that material objects or circumstances, or psychological states of human subjects, can supply the explanation of theurgic phenomena, which by their nature transcend the capacity of such causes. Similarly, he denies that the power of the gods is compelled by human agency. The presence of the human soul with the gods is effected through a gift of divine agencies—through their universal self-bestowal. It is this self-bestowal that empowers the invocations and actions of the theurgist, which reach out to the transcendent by reason of "assimilation and appropriation" to their object (3.18). Behind this conception there lies, of course, a rationalized concept of universal sympathy, which emphasizes not merely the interconnectedness of things at the level of the visible cosmos but also the presence and participation of all finite realities in their immaterial ground, the divine order. At the same time, however—and somewhat paradoxically, in view of this insistence on the mutual indwelling of the various levels of reality—Iamblichus insists that "the human race is weak and puny . . . possessed of a congenital nothingness," and that the only remedy for its error and perpetually disturbed state is to "share as far as possible in the divine Light" (3.18). Thus the practice of theurgy, through which the gods themselves bestow their light and presence, is the one hope of humanity. Iamblichus had lost not the philosophy so much as the faith of a Plotinus.

In Christian circles, the term *theourgia* and its derivatives came into use in the writings of Dionysius the Areopagite (Pseudo-Dionysius), himself a student of the Neoplatonist Proclus, who, after Iamblichus, was the weightiest philosophical advocate of theurgic practice. In Dionysius, however, the term is employed in the sense required by the Christian doctrine of grace: theurgy is not the effect of a natural and universal sympathy between different orders of being, but the self-communicating work of the divine. For Dionysius, Jesus is "the Principal [*archē*] of all hierarchy, holiness, and divine operation [*theourgia*]." The priesthood, by imitating and contemplating the light of the higher beings—who are, in their turn, assimilated to Christ—comes to be in the form of light, and its members are thus able to be "workers of divine works [*theourgikoi*]." The operative sense of Dionysius's use of the term is captured later by Maximus the Confessor, for whom the (new) verb *theourgein* means "to divinize"; he uses it in the passive voice to denote the effect of divine grace conferred through Christ.

Bibliography

Dodds, E. R. "Theurgy and Its Relation to Neoplatonism." *Journal of Roman Studies* 37 (1947): 55–69. Reprinted in *The Greeks and the Irrational* (Berkeley, 1951), pp. 283–311.

Iamblichus of Chalcis. *Les mystères d'Égypte.* Edited by Édouard des Places. Paris, 1966.

Lewy, Hans. *Chaldaean Oracles and Theurgy: Mysticism, Magic and Platonism in the Later Roman Empire.* 2d rev. ed. Paris, 1978, with a preface by Michel Tardieu.

New Sources

Blumenthal, Henry I., and E. Gillian Clark, eds. *The Divine Iamblichus, Philosopher and Man of Gods.* Bristol, 1993.

Bregman, Jay. "Judaism as Theurgy in the Religious Thought of the Emperor Julian." *Ancient World* 26 (1995): 135–149.

Di Pasquale Barbanti. Maria. *Proclo tra filosofia e teurgia.* Catania, 1983.

Finamore, John F. "Plotinus and Iamblichus on Magic and Theurgy." *Dionysius* 17 (1999): 83–94.

Fowden, Garth. *The Egyptian Hermes: A Historical Approach to the Late Pagan Mind.* rev. ed. Princeton, 1993. See Chapters 5 and 6.

Hadot, Ilsetraut. "Die Stellung des Neuplatonikers Simplikios zum Verhältnis der Philosophie zu Religion und Theurgie." In *Metaphysik und Religion. Zur Signatur des spätantiken Denkens. Akten des Internationalen Kongresses vom 13.–17. März 2001 in Würzburg,* ed. by Theo Kobusch and Michael Erler, pp. 323–342. Munich, 2002.

Iamblichus. *De Mysteriis.* Translated with an introduction and notes by Emma C. Clarke, John M. Dillon, and Jackson P. Hershbell. Leiden, 2004.

Johnston, Sarah Iles. *Hekate Soteira: a Study of Hekate's Roles in the Chaldaean Oracles and Related Literature.* Atlanta, 1989.

Johnston, Sarah Iles. "Riders in the Sky: Cavalier Gods and Theurgic Salvation in the Second Century A.D." *Classical Philology* 87 (1992): 303–321.

Leppin, Hartmut. "Proklos. Der Philosoph als Theurg." In *Gelehrte in der Antike. Alexander Demandt zum 65. Geburtstag,* edited by Andreas Goltz, Andreas Luther and Heinrich Schlange-Schöningen, pp. 251–260. Cologne, 2002.

Majercik, Ruth. *The Chaldean Oracles.* Leiden, 1989.

Saffrey, Henri-Dominique. "La théurgie comme phénomène culturel chez les néoplatoniciens (IV-V siècles)." *Koinonia* 8 (1984): 161–171.

Shaw, Gregory. "Theurgy as Demiurgy. Iamblichus' Solution to the Problem of Embodiment." *Dionysius* 12 (1988): 37–59.

Shaw, Gregory. *Theurgy and the Soul. The Neoplatonism of Iamblichus.* University Park, Pa., 1995.

Sheppard, Anne. "Proclus' attitude to theurgy." *Classical Quarterly* 32 (1982): 212–224.

Tardieu, Michel. "La gnose Valentinienne et les Oracles Chaldaïques." In *The Rediscovery of Gnosticism. Proceedings of the International Conference on Gnosticism at Yale, New Haven, Conn. March 28–31 1978, I: The School of Valentinus,* ed. by Bentley Layton, pp. 194–237. Leiden 1980.

Theiler, Willy. *Die chaldaïschen Orakel und die Hymnen des Synesios.* Halle, 1942 (reprinted in *Id. Forschungen zum Neuplatonismus,* Berlin 1966, pp. 252–301).

Trouillard, Jean. *La mystagogie de Proclus.* Paris, 1982.

Van Lifferinge, Carine. *La Théurgie. Des Oracles Chaldaïques à Proclus.* Liège, 1999.

Richard A. Norris (1987)
Revised Bibliography

THIASOI is a term in Greek religious cults that designates the followers or adherents of a deity who, as a more or less formally organized group, participate in communal and private celebrations. While the Sanskrit root-word *dhiyaindhas* denotes devout and reverent supplication, the Greek term *thiasos* has become most strongly associated with the orgiastic and ecstatic frenzy of the worshipers of Dionysos, with features made famous through Euripides' *The Bacchae,* such as omophagia (tearing animals apart and eating their raw flesh). The Dionysian *thiasoi* comprise such groups as the Maenads and Thyiads, which during the winter months performed their frenzied dances in trancelike states beyond "civilized" regions (i.e., cities and temple precincts) in the "wilderness," in order to reenact the mythic fate of Dionysos himself (who was torn apart by Titans) as well as to reawaken the god of spring and fertility. While the *thiasoi* may have originated with the celebrations of any deity of the *polis,* after the fifth century BCE they seem to become more privatized, to be divorced at the same time from any specific sanctuary, and to lose their gender-specific separation of initiation rituals through which an individual becomes conversant with the mystery.

Thiasoi could be interpreted as the sometimes more public, sometimes more esoteric and secret fraternities, guilds, or clubs that are devoted and dedicated to any deity: in short, they are cult associations. Most commonly these associations were segregated by gender and age: as we find female attendants of Dionysos, we have also male clubs such as the Corybantes and Curetes for Zeus. The tendency toward dramatic representation and enactment of a deity's mythic deeds appears in all such cult associations. All of them seem to have used such paraphernalia as masks and costumes.

Thiasoi may be closely related to such phenomena as women's and men's initiation clubs as found in the form of secret societies in many extant cultures. The Greek understanding would have come close to such dramatization of mythic events through imitation and identification: Plato mentions that the human *thiasoi* imitate their divine prototypes (Plato, *Laws* 815b). The initiation ordeals and actions of some cult associations can be historically verified, while the content and existence of many other such organizations must remain conjectural, such as the Idaean Dactyls, the Telchines, or the Cyclops, which could all have been mythic representations of existing secret craft associations of smiths.

What *is* certain is the development from purely religious and mystical cult associations to guild and craft associations (*technitai*), which continue to have religious characteristics. These guilds enjoyed many privileges, such as the right to asylum and freedom from taxation or military service. They were led by a priest of the Dionysos cult. In many ways the Greek development of clubs organized by gender and age seems to run a similar course, from mystical initiation and dramatic enacting of sacred history to rational organization of crafts and guilds, as we find in the development of fraternities and sororities in the history of Christianity.

Bibliography

Burkert, Walter. *Griechische Religion der archaischen und klassischen Epoche.* Stuttgart, 1977. Fine summary of the diverse interpretations of religious associations.

Der kleine Pauly: Lexikon der antike. 5 vols. Munich, 1964–1975. Encyclopedic collation on the basis of *Paulys Realencyclopädie*; emphasizing the secularization of religious associations in Hellenistic times.

New Sources

Avram, Alexandru. "Der dionysische thiasos in Kallatis: Organisation, Repräsentation, Funktion." In *Religiöse Vereine in der römischen Antike. Untersuchungen zu Organisation, Ritual und Raumordnung*, edited by Ulrike Egelhaaf-Gaiser und Alfred Schäfer, pp. 69–80. Tübingen, 2002.

Gentili, Bruno. "Il Partenio di Alcmane e l'amore omoerotico femminile nei tiasi spartani." *Quaderni Urbinati di Cultura Classica* 22 (1976): 59–67.

Kloppenborg, John S. "Collegia and Thiasoi: Issues in Function, Taxonomy and Membership." In *Voluntary Associations in the Graeco-Roman World*, edited by John S. Kloppenborg and Sthephen G. Wilson, pp. 16–30. London-New York, 1996.

L'association dionysiaque dans les sociétés anciennes. Actes de la table ronde organisée par l'École française de Rome (Rome 24–25 mai 1984). Paris, 1986.

Schlesier, Renate. "Die Seele im Thiasos: zu Euripides, Bacchae 75." In *Psukhe - Seele - Anima: Festschrift für Karin Alt zum 7. Mai 1998*, ed. by Jens Holzhausen, pp. 37–72. Stuttgart, 1998.

Villanueva Puig, Marie-Christine. "Le cas du thiase dionysiaque." *Ktèma* 23 (1998): 365–374.

Klaus-Peter Köpping (1987)
Revised Bibliography

THOMAS À KEMPIS

THOMAS À KEMPIS (1379/80–1471), also known as Thomas Hemerken, late medieval Christian mystic. Born in the German town of Kempen, near Cologne, Thomas at age fourteen entered one of the schools of the Brethren of the Common Life in the Dutch city of Deventer and spent the rest of his long life in the Netherlands. Ordained to the priesthood in 1413, he entered an Augustinian monastery near Zwolle, where he remained until his death. A reputed portrait of Thomas carries this inscription: "In all things I sought quietness and found it only in retirement and books." Whether or not the portrait is indeed one of Thomas, the legend is one that accurately describes him.

His lasting fame proceeds from the book *Imitation of Christ.* While its authorship cannot be firmly established and has been disputed by many scholars, the preponderance of opinion is that Thomas was the author. A devotional manual for personal spiritual growth and development, *Imitation of Christ* has been an influential guide to personal piety for persons as different as Samuel Johnson and John Wesley. The number of known editions far exceeds two thousand.

The fifteenth century saw a reaction against what was felt to be the excessively intellectual quality of medieval scholasticism. *Imitation of Christ* reflects these feelings in its marked Christocentricity and its insistence upon experience rather than reason, and it presents a kind of piety that has appealed far beyond the Middle Ages. It shares many basic assumptions with eighteenth-century Protestant pietism and was an influential work for this movement, particularly in England and Germany.

The reputation of the book has diminished in the twentieth century because of its innate quietism. The social implications of the gospel and the activism that it might require find no support in Thomas's book. But wherever Christianity is seen as consisting primarily in personal devotion and private piety, the work's traditional reputation still holds.

Apart from *Imitation of Christ*, Thomas's writings have attracted little lasting attention. His *Small Alphabet for a Monk in the School of God* is in much the same vein as *Imitation.* A number of biographies of leaders in the Brethren of the Common Life breathe the same spirit but have never attained the same popularity.

Scholars have disagreed rather sharply about the relationship of Thomas to later movements, such as the Protestant Reformation. Albert Hyma argued that there was direct continuity between him and his school and Martin Luther. R. R. Post, on the other hand, maintained that the discontinuity was far greater than the continuity, especially in the way Thomas insisted on the virtues of monastic life. No definite answer is possible. Whatever his influence on Luther and Erasmus, it is known that *Imitation* was the favorite book of Ignatius Loyola, the founder of the Society of Jesus.

For the most part Thomas simply ignored the peculiarities of later medieval theology, concentrating instead on his own inner experience. It is for this reason that the popularity of *Imitation of Christ* has far transcended the author's time and place. A devotionalist rather than a theologian, Thomas has had a continuing appeal to persons of similar disposition.

BIBLIOGRAPHY

Hyma, Albert. *The Brethren of the Common Life.* Grand Rapids, Mich., 1950.

Hyma, Albert. *The Christian Renaissance: A History of "Devotio Moderna."* 2d ed. Hamden, Conn., 1965.

Post, R. R. *The Modern Devotion: Confrontation with Reformation and Humanism.* Leiden, 1968.

Schaff, David S. *The Middle Ages from Boniface VIII, 1294, to the Protestant Reformation, 1517,* vol. 5, pt. 2, of *History of the Christian Church.* New York, 1910.

HOWARD G. HAGEMAN (1987)

THOMAS AQUINAS

THOMAS AQUINAS (Tommaso d'Aquino, 1225–1274), Italian Dominican theologian, doctor of the church, patron of Roman Catholic schools, and Christian saint. One of the most important and influential scholastic theologians, Thomas is seen by the Roman Catholic church as uniquely "her very own" (Pius XI). He has been honored with the scholastic titles Doctor Communis (thirteenth century) and Doctor Angelicus (fifteenth century), among others.

LIFE AND WORKS. The youngest son of Landolfo d'Aquino, lord of Roccasecca and Montesangiovanni and justiciary of Emperor Frederick II, and his second wife, Teodora of Chieti, Thomas had five sisters, three older brothers, and at least three half brothers. The family castle of Roccasecca, where Thomas was born, midway between Rome and Naples, was on a mountain in the northwest corner of the kingdom of Sicily. Sicily was ruled by the Hohenstaufen emperor Frederic II (1194–1250), who was in almost continual warfare with the papal armies of Honorius III (1216–1227), Gregory IX (1227–1241), and Innocent IV (1243–1254). Divided political and religious loyalties rendered the position of the d'Aquino family precarious.

Thomas spent his first five years at the family castle under the care of his mother and a nurse. As the youngest son of the family, Thomas was given (*oblatus,* "offered") to the Benedictine abbey of Monte Cassino by his parents at the age of five or six in the firm hope that he would eventually choose the monastic life and become abbot. His earliest training was in the spiritual life, mainly through the Latin psalter, and in the rudiments of reading, writing, and mathematics. The struggle between the pope and the emperor reached a climax in 1239, when Frederick was excommunicated a second time. The imperial troops occupied the abbey, foreigners were expelled, and the young students were sent to one of the Benedictine houses in Naples to attend the imperial university founded in 1224 as a rival to Bologna. At the university, where Thomas remained until 1244, he studied under Master Martin (grammar and logic) and Peter of Ireland (natural philosophy). It was there that he was introduced to Aristotle's philosophy.

By 1243 Thomas was attracted to the Dominicans living nearby at the priory of San Domenico. This order of mendicant friars, founded by Dominic (1170–1221) and confirmed by Pope Honorius III in 1216, was devoted to preaching, study, and the common life. Impressed by their apostolic zeal, poverty, and simplicity and free from obligation, Thomas received the habit in April 1244 at the age of nineteen. Under normal circumstances he would have made his novitiate at San Domenico, but because the friars feared that Thomas's family might intervene forcibly to prevent his entrance to the order, he was sent to Rome. At Rome it was decided that he should go to Paris, and so early in May 1244 he left Rome in the company of John of Wildeshausen, third master of the order, and John's companions, who were traveling to Bologna for the general chapter that met annually at Pentecost.

Learning of her son's entry into a begging order, Teodora, now head of the family, hastened to Naples, then to Rome, only to learn that her son had departed for Bologna. She sent orders to her older son Rinaldo, who was with Frederick's army north of Rome, to intercept Thomas and bring him home by force if necessary. Rinaldo and his escort intercepted the travelers near Acquapendente, north of papal territory, and forced Thomas to return on horseback. Stopping for the night at the family castle of Montesangiovanni in papal territory, the soldiers secured the services of a local prostitute to seduce Thomas, but to no avail. The next day the group rode to Roccasecca, where Thomas was restricted to the castle until Frederick II was excommunicated and deposed by the Council of Lyons on July 17, 1245. By then Teodora and her daughters saw that further attempts to change Thomas's resolve were useless and allowed him to rejoin the friars in Naples, from whence he was sent to Paris.

Arriving at the priory of Saint-Jacques by October 1245, Thomas began his studies at the University of Paris under Albertus Magnus, who was then lecturing on the writings of Dionysius the Areopagite. After three years of study in Paris, Thomas and others accompanied Albertus to Cologne, where a new *studium generale* was to be established, as decreed by the general chapter of Paris in 1248. For the next four years Thomas continued to attend and write down Albert's lectures on Dionysius and his questions on Aristotle's *Ethics.* As Albert's junior bachelor (1250–1252), Thomas lectured cursorily on *Isaiah, Jeremiah,* and *Lamentations.*

The position of the mendicant friars at the University of Paris came under increasingly severe attack from secular masters, particularly William of Saint-Amour. By 1252 the Dominican master general was eager to send promising young men to the university to prepare for inception as master (full professor). Albert convinced the master general to send Thomas, despite his young age, to study for the university chair for non-Parisians. Thomas began his studies under Elias Brunet de Bergerac in the fall of 1252, lecturing on Peter Lombard's *Sentences* for four years. His originality and clarity of thought were conspicuous in his teaching and writing, notably in his commentary on the *Sentences; On Being and Essence*, on the meaning of certain metaphysical terms; and in a short treatise entitled *Principles of Nature.* In the latter work he unequivocally defended (1) a real distinction between essence and existence (*esse*) in all creatures, (2) the pure potentiality of primary matter, (3) absence of matter in spiritual substance (*substantia separata*), (4) participation of all created reality, material and immaterial, in God's being (*esse*), and (5) the Aristotelian dependence of abstracted universals on individually existing material things.

Under tense circumstances in the spring of 1256, Thomas, though underage, was given license to incept by an order of Pope Alexander IV dated March 3. When finally he was allowed to incept, by an order of the pope dated June 17, he and his audience had to be protected by soldiers of Louis IX because the animosity of the town and some students against the mendicants was so great. William of Saint-Amour's antimendicant book *On the Perils of the Last Days*, sent to Rome by the king for examination, was condemned by the pope on October 5, and William was permanently exiled from Paris by the king. Thomas's reply to William's charges (*Contra impugnantes Dei cultum et religionem*), completed in late September or early October, arrived in Rome after the pope had made his decision and, therefore, did not influence the outcome.

Enjoying a respite from the antimendicant polemic, Thomas lectured from 1256 to 1259 on the Bible, held scholastic disputations (*Quaestiones disputatae de veritate*) over three years, preached, and began composing his *Summa contra gentiles* (1259–1264), apparently for Dominican missionaries in Spain and North Africa. This systematic summary in four books is an arsenal of sound and persuasive arguments "against the gentiles," that is, nonbelievers and heretics.

Having served the order's interests in Paris, Thomas returned to Italy where he taught, wrote, and preached from 1259 to 1268. After spending two years in his home priory of Naples, he was assigned to teach at Orvieto (1261–1265), where he lectured to the community on *Job* and was of great service to Pope Urban IV. At the pope's request, he composed the liturgy for the new Feast of Corpus Christi and expressed his views in *Against the Errors of the Greeks* on doctrinal points disputed by Greek and Latin Christians. Having thereby discovered the richness of the Greek patristic tradition, he also began compiling a continuous gloss, or exposition, of the Gospels (*Catena aurea*), made up almost entirely of excerpts from the writings of the Greek and Latin fathers, dedicating the commentary on *Matthew* to Urban IV. In June 1265, the provincial chapter of Anagni assigned Thomas to open a school of theology at Santa Sabina in Rome. Soon realizing that Peter Lombard's *Sentences*, then in common use, was unsatisfactory for young beginners, Thomas projected a three-part survey of Catholic theology (*Summa theologiae*) that would be simpler, more orderly, and more inclusive than other works available. The first part was completed and in circulation by 1268. More subtle questions were disputed in the Roman school in a special series on the power of God (*De potentia*) and on evil (*De malo*). In addition, Thomas lectured on the Bible during this period.

By the end of 1268, Thomas was ordered to return to Paris, as was the Frenchman Peter of Tarentaise (the future Pope Innocent V), to counter a revival of antimendicant sentiment among secular masters. When Thomas and his secretary Reginald of Piperno arrived in Paris early in 1269, Thomas realized that the situation was far more complex and serious than he had assumed. Almost single-handedly he was required to fend off attacks on three fronts: with all mendicants against secular masters opposed to mendicants' being in the university; with a few of his confreres against most of the Dominicans, Franciscans, and secular theologians, opposed to using Aristotle in theology; and with most theologians against young philosophers who tended to promulgate heretical views under the name of Aristotle or his commentator Ibn Rushd (Averroës). Over the next five years Thomas fulfilled his university obligations to lecture on the Bible, to hold disputations, and to preach, while also carrying on a vigorous polemic against the antimendicants, expounding all the major works of Aristotle, writing his *Summa theologiae*, and replying to numerous requests for his opinions.

Revival of the antimendicant controversy under Gérard d'Abbeville and his colleagues at Paris (encouraged by the exiled William) centered largely on the role of evangelical poverty in the spiritual life and on the practice of admitting young boys into their novitiate. Thomas attacked the views of Gérard in his quodlibetal disputations (1269–1271), in two polemical treatises on Christian perfection, and in his *Summa* (2.2.179–189). This phase of the controversy ended with the death of its chief protagonists, William of Saint-Amour on September 13, 1272, and Gérard at Paris that same year on November 8.

On December 10, 1270, thirteen philosophical propositions opposed to the Catholic faith were condemned by Étienne Tempier, bishop of Paris. To prevent such views from developing in the classroom, Thomas undertook a detailed literal commentary on all the main texts of Aristotle then in common use at the University of Paris. It is possible that Thomas began his commentary on *De anima* in Italy, but all the others were written after his return to Paris in 1269, namely, the commentaries on *Physics, On Interpretation, Posterior Analytics, Ethics, Metaphysics, Politics*, and certain others left unfinished at his death. Because all these works of Aristotle were used as textbooks in the arts faculty and had to be taught by the young masters whose best guide to date had been Ibn Rushd, Thomas therefore felt a particular urgency in writing his own commentaries that remained closer to the original sources and within the context of Christian faith. His unfinished expositions of Aristotle's *De caelo, De generatione*, and *Metheora* were among his last writings at Naples.

The extensive second part of the *Summa theologiae* was entirely written at Paris during the intense years 1269 to 1272. This part, later subdivided into two parts, discusses the ultimate goal of human life, namely, eternal life (2.1.1–5) and the means of attaining it, namely, human acts, reason (law), grace, and all the virtues considered in general (2.1) and in particular (2.2) as practiced in various states of life. The third part, begun at Paris, considers the incarnation and life of Christ (3.1–59) and the sacraments, and was left incomplete on the subject of penance when Thomas died.

Shortly after Easter 1272, Thomas left Paris with Friar Reginald for the chapter at Florence, which commissioned him to establish a theological *studium* anywhere he liked in the Roman province. He chose his home priory of Naples, where he subsequently taught, wrote, and preached. After five years of intense activity, however, Thomas had a traumatic experience while celebrating mass in the Chapel of Saint Nicholas on December 6, 1273. Although medieval biographers were uncertain about the nature of this experience, it seems that Thomas suffered a breakdown of some sort. In any case, his productive life had come to an end, and although he did remain physically mobile, he lived as if in a stupor.

Pope Gregory X personally requested that Thomas attend the Second Council of Lyons due to open on May 1, 1274. He also asked him to bring a copy of his treatise *Against the Errors of the Greeks*, composed for Urban IV. Leaving Naples with Reginald and others early in February, Thomas had a serious accident near Maenza in which he hit his head against an overhanging branch and was knocked down. Growing weaker, Thomas asked to stop at the castle of Maenza, home of his niece Francesca, the wife of Annibaldo, count of Ceccano. Lent had already begun on February 14, and Thomas's condition became so serious that he asked to be transported to the nearby Cistercian monastery of Fossanova, where the old abbot Theobald was a member of the Ceccano family. There he received the last rites and died early Wednesday morning March 7, 1274. Thomas's remains stayed at Fossanova until they were transferred by order of Urban V to the Dominican priory in Toulouse on Saturday, January 28, 1369, where they are today. Since the anniversary of Thomas's death always falls in Lent, the Latin church celebrates his feast on January 28.

Thomas had no immediate successors capable of grasping his originality and profundity, although he had many admirers. His labors in Paris were effectively dissipated by the condemnation of 219 various propositions at Paris on March 7, 1277, and of 30 different propositions at Oxford on March 18 that same year. Sixteen propositions of the Paris list reflected the thought of Thomas; three of the Oxford list directly concerned unicity of substantial form in material composites, a pivotal Thomistic thesis. It was not until Thomas's canonization on July 18, 1323, that a new generation of largely self-taught Thomists could begin to teach and develop his teachings freely.

THOUGHT. Thomas Aquinas was first and foremost a theologian whose teachings have been officially endorsed by the Roman Catholic church. Since 1567 Thomas has been considered one of the doctors of the church and has been numbered among the great teachers of antiquity such as Augustine, Jerome, Ambrose, and Gregory I. Moreover, the Latin church has regarded Thomas as the model for all theologians, requiring that his philosophy and his theology be taught in all seminaries and Catholic colleges.

Philosophy. While giving primacy of place and importance to what God has revealed through the Jewish people and through Jesus Christ, Thomas recognized the much larger, though less important, realm of knowledge available to unaided human reason. Unlike many of his contemporaries who merged reason into faith, Thomas emphasized the distinctness and importance of Aristotelian philosophy and the sciences, even for theology. His own strictly philosophical thought is found in his numerous commentaries on Aristotle and in independent treatises. In the manner of his contemporaries in the universities, he adapted his own understanding of Aristotelian ideas, terminology, and methodology to the study of "sacred doctrine," especially in his *Summa theologiae.*

Thomistic "philosophy" is basically Aristotelian, empirical, and realist, or what G. K. Chesterton called "organized common sense." Thomas preferred an order of study that presupposed the liberal arts and mathematics and began with Aristotelian logic, principally *On Interpretation* and the *Posterior Analytics*; moved through natural philosophy, involving all the natural sciences, including psychology; treated moral philosophy, including political science; and concluded with metaphysics, or first philosophy, which today would include epistemology and natural theology.

In logic the Aristotelian categories, syllogisms, and rules of correct reasoning for "demonstration" as distinct from "dialectics" and "sophisms" are considered essential for an accurate understanding of all other disciplines. Of special importance are the meaning of "scientific" knowledge based on "first principles" and the two ways in which both are acquired: experience (*via inventionis*) or education (*via disciplinae*).

In natural philosophy the existence of a physical world and its substantial mutability are taken as self-evident in order to establish the first principles of change: matter (potentiality), form (actuality), and privation (immediate possibility). Natural science is about natural things (not artificial or incidental), things that have within themselves "nature" either as an actual principle (form as a dynamic source of activity) or as a passive principle (matter as receptive of outside forces). The aim of natural science is to understand all natural things through their material, efficient, formal, and final causes. In so doing the naturalist discovers an ultimate, intelligent, efficient, and final cause that is not physical (i.e., not material and not mutable) and is the "first cause" and "agent" of all that is natural. The noblest part of this science is the study of the whole human person composed of matter (body) and form (soul). This study also shows that the human soul has functions, namely, understanding and free choice, that transcend the limitations of animal nature, thereby proving the soul to be immaterial, created, and immortal.

Moral philosophy for Aristotle and Thomas presupposes psychology and deals with human happiness, which is the goal of each person in this life, and the optimum (morally good) means of attaining that goal for the individual, the family, and the body politic. The foundation of both goal and correct means is called the natural law, which is knowable by human reason but open to rejection by the individual. There are four cardinal virtues, or optimum means, for use in every state of life: prudence, justice, fortitude, and temperance. The highest of these is prudence, which binds all virtues together and securely guides humanity to happiness.

Finally metaphysics, or speculative wisdom (natural theology), is about all being-as-such and about the First Cause as the source of all being. For Thomas the most "sublime truth" of this wisdom is the realization that all creatures are composed of a "nature" and a borrowed existence (*esse*), while God's nature alone is "to exist." God is subsistent existence itself (*ipsum esse subsistens*), the Necessary Being that cannot not be. As the highest science, metaphysics has the added task of ordering, defending, and safeguarding all other sciences, speculative and practical. In this role it examines the roots and foundation of all human knowledge (epistemology), natural religion, and public worship.

Theology. Thomistic "theology," which Thomas calls sacred doctrine, is distinct from pure philosophy and depends on the divine gift of faith, which involves the whole realm of revelation, divine law, ecclesial worship, the spiritual life, and human speculation about these. The realm of faith is in the strict sense "*super*-natural" in that its truths, values, and efficacy transcend the realm of "nature." Faith's abilities are freely given by God for human salvation and are beyond the abilities of pure nature (cf. *Rom.* 11:5–6). The content of faith concerns what one must believe (faith) and do (morals) to gain eternal life as revealed by God. The life of faith is a personal sharing by grace of the intimate trinitarian life of God here and hereafter. The efficacy of the life of faith is derived from the passion and death of Jesus Christ, God's only begotten Son. These beliefs and morals are transmitted in history through the Bible and through the living church founded by Christ on Peter and his successors.

Thomas did not divide theology into such modern disciplines as biblical and scholastic, positive and speculative, dogmatic and moral, spiritual and mystical, kerygmatic and academic, and so on. In his day, however, each master in sacred theology lectured on the Bible, presided over scholastic disputations on specific points, and also preached regularly to the university community. Thomas wrote his *Summa theologiae* not as a replacement for the Bible but as an extracurricular aid for beginners who needed an overview of "sacred doctrine." Although the *Summa* is divided into three parts, its conceptual unity is the Dionysian circle of the *exitus* ("going forth") of all things from God and the *reditus* ("return") of all things to God. The First Part considers God and the coming forth of all things from God. The Second and Third parts consider the final goal of human life and the actual return of all things to God. The two parts of the Second Part consider the intrinsic means such as virtues, law, and grace, while the Third Part considers Christ and his sacraments as indispensable extrinsic means to salvation. Without doubt Thomas's most original contribution to theology was the large Second Part, on the virtues and vices, inserted between the original *exitus* and *reditus* found in all contemporary summae of theology. The "Supplement" to the Summa fills out what Thomas left unfinished when he ceased writing on December 6, 1273. It was compiled with scissors and paste by Reginald and other secretaries from Thomas's earlier commentary on Peter Lombard's *Sentences* (4.17–46). Certainly if Thomas had lived to finish the *Summa*, many more developed views would have been written than are now expressed there.

Because theology concerns mysteries revealed by God, it can in no way "prove" or "understand" these or any other mysteries. But it can clarify the terms used, determine what cannot be said, and defend the truth of revealed mysteries against attacks from nonbelievers. Of all the revealed mysteries, Thomas considered two as absolutely basic to the Christian religion: the trinity of persons in one God and the incarnation of the Son of God as true man born of Mary.

For Thomas the supernatural gifts of sanctifying grace and the virtues (faith, hope, love, and the moral virtues) are normally conferred through baptism by water in the name of Jesus or the Trinity of Father, Son, and Holy Spirit. But in an adult the beginnings of this supernatural life are stirred up by God before actual baptism by water. The supernatural life of grace (*gratia*) experienced in this life is, for Thomas, already a foretaste of eternal life (*gloria*) in heaven. The overflow of grace is expressed in good works and in the exercise of all the virtues.

Faith, hope, and love are called "theological" virtues, because they alone have God as their direct object. In the life to come, faith will give way to sight and hope will give way to the possession of God. Love, alone, which Thomas defines as friendship with God, will continue essentially unaltered in heaven in the degree of intensity achieved in this life. This divine friendship, which is none other than the indwelling of the Trinity, is initiated by baptism, nourished by the Eucharist, and increased by prayer and service to one's neighbor. For Thomas, one's place in heaven, or the intensity of beatitude, is determined by the capacity for love developed in this life.

The sources of Thomas's theology are the Vulgate Bible, the life and practice of the church, and the writings of all the available Latin and Greek fathers in Latin translation. The terminology, however, is always traditional, largely philosophical, and often Aristotelian. For this reason it is important to understand such technical terms as matter and form, substance and accidents, essence and existence, nature and operations, and soul and faculties, as well as the four Aristotelian causes, if one is to grasp the meaning of Thomas's exceptionally lucid and simple Latin.

INFLUENCE. Apart from the admiration, love, and respect accorded him by scholars and theologians, Thomas exerted little influence by the time he died in 1274. At Paris his literary and personal efforts could neither stem the tide of heterodoxy among teachers of philosophy nor abate the growing fears of Augustinian theologians against the use of Aristotle or any pagan philosopher in the schools of theology.

From 1278 onward, however, the general chapters of the Dominican order showed an increasing concern that the writings of Thomas be at least respected within the order. By 1309 the chapter required all Dominican lectors to lecture from the works of Thomas, to solve problems according to his doctrine, and to instruct their students in the same. Even before his canonization, Dominicans were obliged to teach according to Thomas's doctrine and the common teaching of the church. In 1279 the Parisian Franciscan William de la Mare compiled a "correctory" (*Correctorium*) of Thomas's writings, indicating therein where Thomas differed from Bonaventure and Augustine. In May 1282 this correctory was made mandatory for all Franciscan teachers, but by 1284 there were five defensive replies by young Dominican teachers, three of whom were Oxonians influenced by the brilliant Thomas Sutton, a self-taught Dominican Thomist. The canonization of Thomas on July 18, 1323, and the lifting in 1325 of the Parisian condemnation insofar as it touched or seemed to touch Thomas removed the foremost barriers to the teaching of his ideas universally. But it was not until the sixteenth century that Thomists began to develop his seminal principles in a notable way. An exception was the French Dominican John Capreolus (1380–1444), "the Prince of Thomists," who in his *Defensiones* on the *Sentences* incisively expounded and defended Thomas's views against Henry of Ghent, Duns Scotus, John of Ripa, William of Ockham, and others.

In the sixteenth century four influential teachers substituted Thomas's *Summa* for the standard Sentences of Peter Lombard: Peter Crokaert in Paris (in 1509); Thomas de Vio Cajetan at Pavia (in 1497), author of an important commentary on the *Summa*, (1507–1522); Konrad Koellin at Heidelberg (1500–1511), author of a commentary on the first two parts of the *Summa* (1512); and Francisco de Vitoria at Salamanca (in 1526) and his many disciples throughout Spain. These Thomists were concerned not so much with defending Thomism as with replying to issues raised by the reformers, resolving new problems of an expanding civilization, and applying Thomas's principles to developments in international law and the treatment of Indians in the New World. By the time of the Council of Trent (1545–1563), most of the outstanding Roman Catholic theologians were Thomists. The influence of Thomas is clear throughout the council's decrees, notably on justification, the sacraments, and the mass. The influential *Roman Catechism*, published by order of Pius V in 1566, was the work of three Dominican Thomists. Pius V declared Thomas a doctor of the church (1567) and ordered that the first *Opera omnia* (the "Piana") be published with the remarkable index (*Tabula aurea*) of Peter of Bergamo at Rome (18 vols., 1570–1571). Since the Piana edition, there have been ten editions of complete works apart from the current critical edition ordered by Pope Leo XIII in 1879 (the "Leonine").

After the Reformation and throughout the scientific and industrial revolutions, there was little interest in Thomistic philosophy or theology outside the decimated Dominican order and scattered groups in Catholic countries. However, a Thomistic revival in Italy and Spain slowly grew and reached its culmination in the encyclical *Aeterni Patris* of Leo XIII (August 4, 1879), urging the study of Thomas's works by all students of theology, and in subsequent legislation by Leo and his successors. This revival focused on Thomistic philosophy as a system capable of countering the effects of positivism, materialism, and secularism on Catholic beliefs and practices. This polemical intention was modified by the attitude of dialogue with the modern world that characterized the approach of the Second Vatican Council (1962–1965). In this spirit Paul VI, in his encyclical on the seventh centenary of Thomas's death (1974), proposed Thomas as a model to theologians, not only with respect to his teachings but with respect to his example of openness to the world and to truth from whatever the source. As a result, there has been increased study and critical reappraisal of Thomas's thought, principles, and methodology. Although Thomism in the restricted sense of a closed system seems no longer tenable, philosophers and theologians of all traditions continue to have recourse to Thomas's thought as a milestone in human thought and to develop his seminal insights in dialogue with modern thought and issues.

SEE ALSO Trent, Council of.

BIBLIOGRAPHY

Works by Thomas Aquinas

Of the ninety or more authentic works of Thomas there have been numerous editions of individual works from 1461 to the present day, over 180 incunabula editions alone. Since the Roman edition of Pius V, *Opera omnia* (1570–1571), there have been more than ten editions or reprints of older standbys, but the only modern critical edition of the *Opera omnia* is the Leonine, 48 vols. to date (Vatican City, 1882–). Both English translations of the *Summa theologiae* (22 vols., London, 1916–1938; bilingual edition, 60 vols., New York, 1964–1976) are far from satisfactory, except for some volumes. Besides the older translation of the *Summa contra gentiles* by the English Dominicans, there is a good edited translation by Anton C. Pegis, *On the Truth of the Catholic Faith*, 4 vols. in 5 (New York, 1955–1957). The most convenient anthologies are *Basic Writings,* 2 vols., edited by Anton C. Pegis (New York, 1945); *Philosophical Texts,* edited and translated by Thomas Gilby (1951; reprint, Durham, N.C., 1982); and *Theological Texts,* edited and translated by Thomas Gilby (1955; reprint, Durham, N.C., 1982). The best single volume sampling of his writings in philosophy with good introductions by Vernon J. Bourke is *The Pocket Aquinas* (New York, 1960).

Works on His Life and Writings

The most complete single volume on Thomas and his writings is my own *Friar Thomas d'Aquino: His Life, Thought, and Works* (1974; reprinted with corrigenda and addenda, Washington, D.C., 1983) with an annotated catalog of authentic writings. Some of the more important biographical documents have been translated and edited by Kenelm Foster in *The Life of Saint Thomas Aquinas* (Baltimore, 1959). All modern studies of the writings must start with the pioneer work of Pierre Mandonnet, *Des écrits authentiques de Saint Thomas d'Aquin* (Fribourg, 1910), Martin Grabmann, *Die Werke,* 3d ed. (Münster, 1949), and some others.

General Works on His Life and Thought

Bourke, Vernon J. *Aquinas' Search for Wisdom.* Milwaukee, 1965. Excellent alternating biographical and doctrinal chapters that should be read carefully to savor the wisdom of Thomas.

Chenu, M.-D. *Toward Understanding Saint Thomas Aquinas.* Chicago, 1964. Indispensable for understanding the medieval context and genre of Thomas's writings.

Chesterton, G. K. *Saint Thomas Aquinas.* London, 1933. A superb appreciation of "the dumb ox" that Gilson and Pegis would have liked to have written, by a natural Thomist.

Copleston, Frederick C. *Aquinas.* Baltimore, 1967. Most appreciated by historians of philosophy.

Gilson, Étienne. *The Christian Philosophy of Saint Thomas Aquinas.* Translated from the fifth edition with a catalog of authentic works by I. T. Eschmann. New York, 1956. Gilson's *chef d'œuvre,* frequently revised over forty years of a distinguished career with all his pet views.

Maritain, Jacques. *Saint Thomas, Angel of the Schools.* London, 1946. Reflections on the life and significance of Thomas by a distinguished modern Thomist.

McInerny, Ralph. *Saint Thomas Aquinas* (1977). Reprint, Notre Dame, 1982. The best short introduction to Thomas and his chief sources: Aristotle, Boethius, and Augustine.

Pegis, Anton C. *Introduction to Saint Thomas Aquinas.* New York, 1948. A handy volume with selections from both *summas* illustrating principal themes of Thomas's thought.

Pieper, Josef. *Guide to Thomas Aquinas.* New York, 1962. A thoughtful invitation to explore the world of Thomas for reflective students.

Sertillanges, A. G. *Saint Thomas Aquinas and His Work* (1933). Reprint, London, 1957. An exciting period piece by a university chaplain in Paris after World War I.

Walz, Angelus M. *Saint Thomas Aquinas: A Biographical Study.* Westminster, Md., 1951. A much-consulted historian's view of Thomas's life and works; see the improved French adaptation by Paul Novarino.

JAMES A. WEISHEIPL (1987)

THOR (ON, Þórr) was presumably the most popular god of the ancient Scandinavian peoples, who conferred upon him such epithets as *ástvinr* ("dear friend") and *fulltrúi* ("trusted friend"). The distribution of his cult is abundantly documented by onomastic evidence; his name is found all over present-day Scandinavia in place-names designating either cult sites or places dedicated to him—woods, fields, hills, brooks, and lakes (de Vries, 1957, pp. 116–120).

Equally abundant are the personal names with *Thor-* as first component. About one-fourth of the immigrants to Iceland had such names, according to the *Landnámabók.* Viking traders and raiders venerated him as their most powerful god and honored him in their new settlements. Local sources report the worship of Þórr by the Norse invaders of Ireland; Þórr's hammer, Mjǫllnir, appeared on the coinage of the Scandinavian rulers of York in the tenth century; there was apparently a temple dedicated to Þórr by Varangian Northmen in Kiev in 1046; the Danes settling in Normandy are said to have invoked "Tur." Even the Lapps, who were strongly influenced by their Germanic neighbors, took Þórr Karl ("old man") into their pantheon as the hammer god Horagalles. Furthermore, artifacts such as Þórr's-hammer amulets bear witness to the strength and survival of his worship even some time after the conversion to Christianity (eleventh century). In this context the Cross of Gosforth in Cumbria, England, is particularly striking, for this essentially Christian symbol bears a graphic representation of one of Þórr's major myths, namely his fishing expedition with the giant Hymir at the rim of the world ocean to catch the cosmic serpent Miðgarðsormr: the scene represents the god "digging his heels so hard into the bottom of the boat" to draw the serpent on board "that both his legs went through it" (Snorri Sturluson, *Gylfaginning* 48).

Adam of Bremen, writing about 1080 and relying on the report of a Christian who had traveled to Sweden, described the temple of Uppsala as having a triad of divine statues: Óðinn, Þórr, and Freyr were worshiped there, but Þórr occupied the central position "because he was the most powerful of them all." This statement, which contradicts Snorri's ranking of Þórr in the second place, after Óðinn, presumably points to the fact that his closeness both to warriors and to peasants gave him more prominence in popular circles than the more "aristocratic" Óðinn. A satirical allusion to the social distribution of the cults of the two gods is recognizable in an exchange between plain, honest Þórr and Óðinn disguised as a ferryman in the Eddic poem *Hárbarzljóð:* "Óðinn gets all the jarls slain by edge of swords, but Þórr gets the breed of thralls." The tradition represented by Adam, however, may also be found in the Old English homily *De falsis diis* (Concerning false gods), commonly ascribed to Ælfric, where Þórr is identified with Jupiter and is "arwurðost ealra ðæra goda" ("the most venerable of all gods"). Several minor sources suggest that Þórr was also able to raise and use winds. For Snorri Sturluson (*Gylfaginning* 21), Þórr s the strongest of the Æsir and the most important among them (after

Óðinn); his domain is Þrúðvangar ("fields of force"), and his home, Bilskirnir (presumably "shining in flashes," a reference to his connection with lightning). He has two goats, Tanngnjóstr ("tooth gnasher") and Tanngrisnir ("grinner"), which pull his chariot; therefore, Þórr is called Ǫkuþórr ("Þórr the charioteer"). He also has three precious objects: his hammer Mjǫllnir, which all giants fear; his "power belt," which doubles his strength; and his iron gauntlets, which he needs to manipulate his hammer. His adventures are so numerous that no one is able to tell them all.

This describes rather well the personality and function of Þórr: he is a characteristic second-function god in the Dumézilian tripartite system, the typical representative of the warrior class, the champion of the gods, the bulwark of the Æsir against the onslaughts of the giants. His whole career illustrates this functional role. Perhaps one of the best examples is the story of his combat with Hrungnir (Snorri Sturluson, *Skáldskaparmál* 3). The sequence of events can be summarized as follows. Having followed Óðinn in a wild gallop into Àsgarðr, the giant Hrungnir is invited by the Æsir to drink with them. His obstreperous behavior soon compels the Æsir to call upon Þórr to put an end to his drunken boasts and threats, but the laws of hospitality prevent the champion of the gods from sealing the giant's fate then and there. As a result, Þórr is challenged to a single combat with Hrungnir at the boundary between the realm of the Æsir and Jǫtunheimr (the land of the giants). To back up Hrungnir in his fight, the giants build the monstrous Mǫkkurkálfi, a huge clay warrior equipped with a mare's heart. Þjálfi, Þórr's astute attendant, persuades Hrungnir that he will be attacked from below, and makes him stand on his shield, exposing him to a fulgurant assault from the sky. Þórr's hammer clashes in midair with the hurled hone of the giant; Mjǫllnir smashes Hrungnir's skull while fragments of whetstone are scattered all around. One lodges in Þórr's head as Hrungnir drops dead over him and has to be removed by Þórr's fantastically strong three-year-old son, Magni. Meanwhile, Mökkurkálfi has ingloriously collapsed under Þjálfi's strokes. A last episode shows how the witch Gróa attempts to remove the piece of Hrungnir's whetstone from Þórr's head but forgets her spells and incantations in the joy of learning that her husband, Aurvandill, has been safely brought home out of the icy North by Þórr.

Snorri's narrative illustrates important features of the ethics and usages of the warrior class: respect for the laws of hospitality (e.g., in spite of Hrungnir's outrageous behavior, Þórr cannot touch him as long as he is a guest in Àsgarðr); taboo on striking down an unarmed adversary (killing him would be an act of cowardice); moral obligation to accept a challenge to a duel; single combat, to be waged in the no-man's-land between two enemy territories. The significance of the dummy (Mǫkkurkálfi) that the giants erect at the location of the duel has been ingeniously explained by Georges Dumézil: Þórr faces and defeats the "stone-hearted" monster, and his "second," Þjálfi, duplicates his exploit by destroying Mǫkkurkálfi. Dumézil sees a warrior initiation pattern in this two-level account, in which Þjálfi reproduces in a realistic terrestrial way the almost cosmic martial exploit of Þórr (Dumézil, 1970, pp 158–159).

His interpretation is supported by a comic episode in *Hrólfs saga kraka* (chapter 23), in which the hero Bǫðvarr Bjarki initiates the coward Hǫttr, making a proper warrior of him. On the eve of the midwinter festival (Yule), King Hrólfr forbids his men to leave his stronghold because an enormous winged troll will appear and kill any champion who challenges him. Bǫðvarr, however, goes out secretly to face the troll, dragging the fearful Hǫttr along. The monster arrives, and while Hǫttr shrinks in the mud in terror, Bǫðvarr dispatches the beast with one thrust of his sword. Picking up Hǫttr, he forces him to drink two gulps of the troll's blood and eat a piece of his heart, after which he engages in a wrestling match with the young man. Hǫttr comes out of this test a truly strong and courageous fighter. They then stand the monster on its feet, as if it were still alive, and return to the king's castle. The following morning, much to the king's surprise, Hǫttr volunteers to go out and "kill" the monster. Ultimately, Hrólfr is not fooled, but he accepts Hǫttr's overnight transformation into a real champion and renames him Hjalti, after the king's sword Gullinhjalti ("golden hilt").

Another well-known adventure of Þórr is narrated in the Eddic *Þrymskviða*. One day Þórr wakes up and realizes to his dismay that Mjǫllnir has been stolen. He dispatches Loki, equipped with Freyja's falcon coat, to Jǫtunheimr to look for it. Loki soon finds out that the giant Þrymr has gotten hold of Þórr's mighty weapon and refuses to return it unless he gets Freyja as a bride in exchange. Freyja does not want to hear anything about marrying the uncouth giant, and the gods assemble in council to look for a solution to Þórr's dilemma. On Heimdallr's advice, they decide that Þórr himself must go to Þrymr, disguised as a bride and escorted by Loki. After their arrival in Þrymr's hall, a lavish meal is served to the travelers from Ásgarðr, but Þórr almost betrays himself by his gluttony. Loki, however, saves the day by stating that "Freyja yearned so much for Jǫtunheimr that she fasted for eight full nights." The situation threatens to deteriorate again when Þrymr attempts to kiss his "bride" and discovers the murderous flames in "her" eyes. Again, Loki finds the proper excuse: "So much did Freyja long to be in Jǫtunheimr that she did not sleep for eight full nights." Then, Þrymr's sister comes to claim her bridal gift, and Þrymr has the hammer Mjǫllnir brought in and placed on his alleged bride's knees, whereupon Þórr grabs his weapon and ruthlessly crushes the skulls of all the giants around him.

No other source duplicates the contents of this remarkable Eddic lay, which achieves its effect with an admirable economy of means and a robust sense of humor, paired with a well-structured scenario and marvelous characterization of the actors in this little drama. Although the poet undoubtedly took his material from older mythological sources, the bal-lad style of the text and the jocular presentation of the argument clearly indicate that the *Þrymskviða* is one of the more recent poems of the Edda. The ludicrous disguise of the champion of the gods is unthinkable in the older tradition, where it would have been completely excluded by the explicit abhorrence of the Æsir for transvestism and other forms of *ergi* ("unmanly behavior"), as illustrated by the *Lokasenna* (23–24), for example.

The text, however, indicates the importance of Þórr's hammer, Mjǫllnir, which is not only associated with the thunderbolt, as its name perhaps indicates (it has been etymologically connected with Russian *molniia* and with Welsh *mellt,* "lightning," but it can also be cognate with Old Norse *mala,* "grind," *mølva,* "crush") and appears to be used to hallow the bride (*Þrymskviða* 30: "brúði at vígja"). This latter function has sometimes been associated with fertility, as the hammer can be considered a phallic symbol, but there is obviously more to the consecration with Þórr's hammer, as the description of Baldr's funeral indicates (Snorri Sturluson, *Gylfaginning* 49): "Þórr vígði bálit með Mjǫllni" ("Þórr hallowed the pyre with Mjǫllnir"). This would be done either to restore the god to life or to protect him from danger on his journey to the world of the dead. Since Baldr does not come back until after Ragnarǫk, the second hypothesis presumably prevails. It is furthermore confirmed by the repeated mention of Þórr as protector of the dead in memorial inscriptions on rune stones, especially in Denmark and southern Sweden, the earliest being found in Rök, East Götland, in the mid-ninth century. Thus, the inscription of Glavendrup (which is found on the Danish island of Fyn and dates to about 900–925) reads: "Þur uiki þas runar" ("May Þórr hallow these runes").

The control of Þórr's hammer over life and death is also illustrated by the following tale about Þórr's goats (*Gylfaginning* 44): One day, while on a journey with Loki, Þórr decided to ask a farmer for hospitality for the night. For the evening meal, Þórr slaughtered his own goats, and after skinning them, cooked them in a cauldron. When the stew was ready, he invited the farmer and his family to share it with him and his travel companion. The next morning, Þórr rose at daybreak and went to the goatskins with the leftover bones. Raising his hammer, Mjǫllnir, he consecrated them, and the goats stood up as if nothing had happened to them. However, one of them was found to be lame in a hind leg. When he noticed it, Þórr realized that a thigh-bone had been split for marrow, and he was angry with the farmer and his household for doing such a stupid thing. The farmer was terrified, and Þórr's angry reproach sounded like a death knell to him. As his frightened family screamed, he begged his dangerous guest for mercy and offered him all he had in compensation. Þórr relented and specified that he would take along the farmer's two children—his son, Þjalfi, and his daughter, Rǫskva—as bond servants.

The association of Þórr with goats is abundantly documented. They pull his chariot; the *Húsdrapá* (st. 3) calls him *hafra njótr* ("user of goats"), and the *Hymiskviða* (st. 31) describes him as *hafra dróttinn* ("lord of goats"). The picture of Þórr riding a vehicle drawn by goats appears repeatedly in the literature (e.g., in *Hauslǫng* 15), and according to a story, perhaps from the late twelfth or early fourteenth century but preserved in *Flateyjarbók* (1387–1390), when king Óláfr Tryggvason entered the pagan temple at Mærin in the Trondheim district, he found a statue of Þórr, adorned with gold and silver, seated on a splendid carriage drawn by finely carved wooden goats (Turville-Petre, 1964, p. 82).

BIBLIOGRAPHY

de Vries, Jan. *Altgermanische Religionsgeschichte,* vol. 2. 2d rev. ed. Berlin, 1957.

de Vries, Jan. *Altnordische Literaturgeschichte,* vol. 2: *Die Literatur von etwa 1150–1300; Die Spätzeit nach 1300.* 2d ed. Berlin, 1967.

Dumézil, Georges. *The Destiny of the Warrior.* Translated by Alf Hiltebeitel. Chicago, 1970.

Lindow, John. "Thor's Duel with Hrungnir." *Alvíssmál* 6 (1996): 3–20.

Lindow, John. "Thor's Visit to Útgarðaloki." *Oral Tradition* 15 (2000): 170–186.

Ljungberg, Helge. *Tor. Undersökningar i indoeuropeisk och nordisk religionshistoria.* vol. 1. Uppsala universitets årsskrift 1947: 9. Uppsala and Leipzig, 1947.

Perkins, Richard. *Thor the Wind-Raiser and the Eyrarland Image.* London, 2001.

Ross, Margaret Clunies. "Þórr's Honour." In *Studien zum Altgermanischen. Festschrift für Heinrich Beck,* edited by Heiko Uecker, pp. 48–76. Berlin and New York, 1994.

Turville-Petre, E. O. G. *Myth and Religion of the North: The Religion of Ancient Scandinavia.* New York, 1964.

EDGAR C. POLOMÉ (1987)
JOSEPH HARRIS (2005)

THOTH was the god of wisdom from Hermopolis in Middle Egypt. According to the Hermopolitan cosmology (which is best known from texts found at other sites), the eight primordial gods representing "hiddenness," "darkness," "formlessness" (?), and the "watery abyss" produced an egg that appeared at Hermopolis when the inundation subsided and from which the creator god appeared and brought everything else into being. When mentioned in the Heliopolitan Pyramid Texts, this creator god was Atum, but in the local Hermopolitan tradition he could have been Thoth.

Thoth was the moon god and as such was the companion of Re, the sun god, but he also had his own following among the stars in the night sky. One mortuary tradition, probably originating at Hermopolis, permitted the dead who knew the correct spells to accompany Thoth in the sky. Thoth was the son of Re, but he also represented the injured eye of the falcon-headed sky god, Horus, whose sound eye was Re. For unknown reasons Thoth is identified with both the ibis and the baboon. He is regularly depicted as a human with the head of an ibis. Baboons often appear in temple reliefs worshiping the sun god, and this association might indicate his subordinate relationship to Re. In the judgment scene of chapter 125 of the *Book of Going Forth by Day*, Thoth as the ibis-headed god presides over and records the weighing of the heart of the deceased owner of the book. A baboon is also represented in this scene seated atop the balance, apparently to ensure its accuracy. Thoth is credited in Egyptian mythology with separating the two contenders, Horus and Seth, as well as with magically restoring Horus's injured eye. He has one of the major supporting roles in much of Egyptian religious literature, and a number of hymns are addressed to him directly, although Re and Osiris are the principal gods discussed and invoked in these texts.

Thoth was renowned for his wisdom and praised as the inventor of writing. The *mdw-ntr* ("god's words," i.e., hieroglyphs) were recognized as perhaps his greatest contribution, and he was frequently shown with brush and papyrus roll in the attitude of the scribes, whose patron he was.

In the eighteenth dynasty several kings took as their throne name *Thothmose* ("Thoth is the one who bore him"). This Thutmosid family included several other members with *ʿiʿḥ* ("moon") in their names, so it is clearly Thoth's position as moon god that is being recalled. Remains of two small temples to Thoth survive in the Theban area, one very late and poorly decorated. Since the eighteenth dynasty was of Theban origin and the son of Amun-Re at Thebes was the moon god, Khonsu, these two moon gods could have been assimilated, but the family could also have chosen the name of the northern god (Thoth) when they moved their residence (capital) to Memphis.

In Egyptian literature there clearly was an ancient tradition concerning the secret knowledge of Thoth. Secret rooms and mysterious books were sought by learned scribes, priests, and princes. This tradition was carried over into some of the Coptic gnostic library tractates, and the question arises whether these were Egyptian or Greek in origin since the Greeks had early identified their god Hermes with Thoth. The origins of the continuing traditions of Hermes Trismegistos and gnosticism can be traced to Egypt, to Thoth, and perhaps even to the Hermopolitan cosmology, but the extent of Egyptian influence on these beliefs remains to be determined.

The great temple of Thoth at Hermopolis has not survived, although its location is known from finds in the area. A large catacomb for the burial of mummified ibises and baboons has been found nearby at the necropolis of Tuna al-Gabal.

See Also Hermes Trismegistos.

Bibliography

Bleeker, C. Jouco. *Hathor and Thoth: Two Key Figures of the Ancient Egyptian Religion.* Leiden, 1973. Issued as a supplement by the periodical *Numen.*

Boylan, Patrick. *Thoth, the Hermes of Egypt.* New York, 1922.

Černý, Jaroslav. "Thoth as Creator of Languages." *Journal of Egyptian Archaeology* 34 (1948): 121–122.

Leonard H. Lesko (1987)

THRACIAN RELIGION.

In ancient Greece the name *Thrakes* referred to most of the inhabitants of the northeastern Balkan Peninsula. Their neighbors to the east were the Scythians; to the west the Pannonians, Dalmatians, and Illyrians; to the north the Balts and the Celts. The name seems to have initially belonged only to the Thracian tribes in close proximity to Greece. Later on, it was extended to related tribes to the north, just as the name *Graeci*, which originally belonged only to a western Greek tribe, was later given by the Romans to all the Hellenes. Nevertheless, the location of the land called Thrake was always restricted to the area south of the Balkan Mountains, principally to the Chalcidice Peninsula.

Thracian Peoples. Nearly two hundred tribes are known under the generic name of Thrakes, of which the most important were the Odrysi, who lived in what is today southeastern Bulgaria; the Dentheleti, north of Macedonia; the Serdi, in Serdica, today the region of Sofia, the capital city of Bulgaria; the Bessi, west of Serdica; the Moesi, between the Balkan Mountains and the river Danube; and the Daco-Getae, who occupied a northern territory approximating modern-day Romania. Other Thracian tribes—the Thyni and Bithyni—settled in Asia Minor. The Phrygians and the Armenians, who originated in the Balkans, were related to them.

History. In the ancient world, the Thracians were, according to Herodotos (fifth century BCE), the most numerous people after the Indians. Thracians are attested in connection with the Trojan War, and they seem to have had a share in the foundation of Troy (in Asia Minor, or modern-day Turkey). Only occasionally did they form larger unions of tribes: the only known confederations are the kingdom of the Odrysi (fifth-fourth centuries BCE), the Geto-Dacian kingdom of Burebista (c. 80–44 BCE), and the Daco-Getic kingdom of Decebalus (87–106 CE). Nonetheless, a certain material and spiritual unity of the Thracians (though not without important inner distinctions) was preserved by several tribes, despite their frequent displacements. Herodotus (*Histories* 5.3) notes that most of the Thracians had kindred customs, with the exception of the Getae, the Trausi, and those living beyond the tribe of the Crestonians.

According to the Greek geographer Strabo (first century BCE), the Getae spoke the same dialect as the other Thracians. Subsequent scholarship has shown, however, that both the culture and the language of the Getae, whom Herodotus calls "the most religious and valiant among the Thracians," were distinct from those of the southern Thracians. Scholars such as Vladimir Georgiev, Ivan Duridanov, and Cicerone

Poghirc have established a clear distinction between two linguistic areas: the Thracian area, in which toponyms ending in *-para*, *-bria*, and *-diza* are dominant, and the Daco-Getic area, in which these endings are replaced by *-dava* and *-sara*. Anthroponyms and phonetic transformation both confirm this distinction. Culturally, the southern Thracians were related to the Iranians, to the Pelasgians, and to some peoples of Asia Minor. They exerted a certain spiritual influence on the Greeks, but they felt, in turn, the decisive impact of Greek civilization. The northern Thracians, the Daco-Getae, were, however, culturally closer to the Illyrians, the Celts, and the Balts. Before the Roman epoch, Greek influence north of the Danube was minimal: in Dacia only thirty Greek inscriptions have been found, representing 1 percent of the more than three thousand Roman inscriptions. In the northern territories the passage from the Hallstatt culture to the La Tène culture was determined by the Celtic invasions during the fourth and third centuries BCE.

Testimonies. The Thracians may be attested in documents written in Linear B, a form of writing used in Mycenaean records dating from the fifteenth to the twelfth century BCE. They are mentioned by Homer and by numerous later Greek and Roman authors. In the fourth century CE, the language of the Thracian tribe of the Bessi was still in use in Christian liturgy. A difficult question is whether any of the Thracian tribes ever used writing. It seems that they did, but only a few records have survived. At least the Geto-Dacians, who formed an impressive theocracy in the first century BCE, seem to have used the Greek and Roman alphabets to transcribe their own language. No document is attested, however, apart from some mysterious inscriptions, each composed of three Greek letters, on stone slabs from the ruins of sanctuaries at Sarmizegetusa Regia (modern-day Gradiştea Muncelului, Romania). In all probability these inscriptions are not marks used by the Greek builders of the sanctuaries but are, instead, numbers related to the complicated astronomical computations of the Dacian priests. Because the slabs were scattered, it has so far been impossible to reconstruct the pattern by which the series of numbers can be read.

The basic sources on Thracian religion are Greek and Roman authors, including Herodotos, Plato, Strabo, the geographer Pomponius Mela, and the Moesian-born Gothic historian Jordanes (sixth century CE). Other sources usually depend on these authors and only occasionally provide important information; a notable exception is the Neoplatonic philosopher Porphyry (third century), who wrote on Zalmoxis. For southern Thrace, Greek votive inscriptions are particularly important; the collection edited by Georgi Mikhailov (1955–1956) contains about 160 names of divinities, together with epithets.

The Thracian regions bordering the Aegean Sea were completely hellenized. The province south of the Balkan Mountains remained under Greek influence even during Roman occupation. The northern regions were decisively influenced by the Romans after being subdued by them: Moesia Superior in 15 CE; Moesia Inferior, along with the Greek Pontic colonies, on the western shore of the Black Sea, in 46 CE; and Dacia in 106 CE. The last speakers of Thracian dialects disappeared from the region south of the Balkan Mountains after the invasion of the Slavs in the sixth century.

Thracian Religion: Some General Features. Religion among the southern Thracians developed along different lines from that of the northern Thracians (the Daco-Getae) owing to what could be called the religious reformation of Zalmoxis in the north. Whether Zalmoxis was a god or a human is an open question, but it can safely be stated that his priests, forming an uninterrupted line of succession that was at times indistinguishable from Daco-Getic kingship, introduced among the northern Thracians religious principles and, later on, scientific speculations that conferred upon their religion a peculiar character. Different sources inform us of the penetration of these ideas among southern Thracians in early times, but Zalmoxis is uncontroversially known as a Gete. It is difficult to speak of a common religious heritage in regard to all Thracian peoples, for different beliefs and customs are attributed to various groups in various sources, but it is easy to recognize in the sources features pertaining to the cult of Zalmoxis. With the exception of Zalmoxis, whose influence extended from the north to the south, all Thracian divinities known in Greece from the fifth century BCE (e.g., Sabazios, Bendis, and Cotys) and the mythic characters to whom the Greeks attributed a Thracian background (e.g., Orpheus and Dionysos) originated among the southern Thracians.

According to Herodotos (5.7) the Thracians worshiped three divinities, corresponding to the Greek Ares, Dionysos, and Artemis, and their kings worshiped a fourth divinity, corresponding to Hermes, to whose posterity they were believed to belong.

As for Ares-Mars, the god of war, Jordanes (*De origine actibusque Getarum* 40–41) confirms his importance among the Getae, in whose land he was supposed to have been born ("apud eos . . . exortum") and to have reigned (cf. Vergil, *Aeneid* 3.35). Prisoners of war were sacrificed to him, and his devotional cults were particularly intense in their affective tones.

Whether Herodotos in his mention of Dionysos was referring to Sabazios is a controversial point, since he could have directly mentioned the name of Sabazios. The same argument applies as well to the goddesses Bendis and Cotys, who are usually identified with Artemis. At the time of Herodotos both of them were known at Athens, and yet the historian did not mention their names in connection with the Thracian Artemis.

Ancient authors attributed to Dionysos himself a Thracian background. In the myth of Dionysos, a Thracian episode, mentioned by Homer (*Iliad* 5.130ff.), is particularly interesting. In numerous variants, it is recounted that the

Thracian king Lykurgos (lit., "wolf's anger") pursues Dionysos, who, in his turn, brings down madness upon the king. The king then either kills himself or is eventually killed by Dionysos. The symbolism of this myth is very complicated. It refers, in all probability, to the cosmic effects of a battle between opposite principles represented by Apollo and Dionysos. As a matter of fact, the wolf is related to Apollo, who is often called Apollo Lukeios, a name referring both to the wolf (Gr., *lukos*) and to light (Gr., *lukē*, "dawn"; Lat., *lux*, "light").

In several variants of the myth, Lykurgos tries to cut down a vine with an ax. Dionysos confuses him so that instead he kills his own son and cuts off one of his own legs. The mythologist Nonnus of Panopolis (fifth century) reports that Lykurgos, an Arab king who pursues Dionysos with an ax in order to kill him, hits one of the Maenads, Ambrosia, who is then changed into a vine. It is difficult to unravel the implications of this myth: while Lykurgos appears to be a vine hater, an enemy of Dionysos, his action may instead simply represent a viticulturist's pruning of his vines. There is nothing typically Thracian in all this, except perhaps the contradictory characterization of Thracians as either vine lovers or vine haters. Strangely enough, the calendar temple in the stronghold at Sarmizegetusa Regia seems to indicate that the Daco-Getic priests under Decebalus were concerned with the vegetative period of the vine, and that this concern was a major element in their culture; yet King Burebista is said to have ordered all vines in his kingdom to be cut down. Is the latter, perhaps, only a wrong assumption on the part of Strabo (*Geography* 7.7–11), who mistakenly expects wine hatred from the spiritualistic, Pythagorean features of Getic religion? This hypothesis deserves further investigation.

As for the Thracian Artemis, both Bendis and Cotys have been identified with this goddess. Bendis appears to be a goddess of marriage, while Cotys, or Kotyto, is an orgiastic Thracian divinity in whose cult men wore women's garments. Her name has been related to the Indo-European **kot-u-* ("avenger"; cf. the Greek *koteo*, "I am angry") and has thus been taken to mean "angry [goddess]" or "[goddess] of fight." Gheorghe Mus,u prefers the etymology "[goddess] energy," from the Indo-European **kued-*, *kuod-* ("stimulate, urge on"). Both Bendis and Cotys were known at Athens from the fifth century BCE onward.

Neither worship of a heavenly god nor the institution of sacred kingship was confined to the northern Thracians. The military historian Polyaenos (second century) reported that the priests of Hera were kings of the tribes of the Kebrenoi and Sykaiboai. One of them, Kosingas, gathered many wooden ladders with the intent, he said, of climbing to heaven in order to indict the Thracians before Hera for their disobedience. Impressed, the Thracians swore to obey his orders.

Two practices that were general among the Thracians rested, in all probability, on religious bases: tattooing and the burial or cremation of living wives together with their dead husbands. Among the Getae, tattooing was probably related to the story of the sufferings once inflicted upon Zalmoxis, and was thus applied to members of certain social categories (e.g., women and slaves) as a sign of suffering. Among the southern Thracians, where only the nobles were tattooed, it must have had another symbolic meaning.

As for the burial or cremation of living widows, archaeological finds confirm the rather puzzling written evidence that the Thracians practiced either one or the other, and sometimes both in the same place. No reasons for this variation are given. Two works based on the findings at several necropolises in Dacia (Protase, 1971; Nicolaescu-Plopsor and Wolski, 1975) have confirmed the concurrent existence of both ritual practices, although cremation prevailed. Wives, sometimes accompanied by their infant children, were sacrificed at the death of their husbands and were buried or cremated in the same tomb. Both Herodotos and Pomponius Mela (*De situ orbis* 2.2.19–20) report that among polygamous Thracians the wives of the deceased vied for the great honor of being killed and buried together with the corpse of their husbands.

Herodotos also reports a three-day exposure of the corpse, followed by animal sacrifices, feasting, mourning, and burial or cremation. To the historian Hellanicus (fifth century BCE) is attributed the information that the animal sacrifices and the banqueting were based on a belief that the deceased would return to the human world to participate in the feast. Pomponius Mela (2.2.18) affirms that some Thracians mourned a child's birth and rejoiced over death. Therefore the feasts following one's death were an expression of collective participation in the happy destiny of the dead. The Getae were not the only Thracians to believe in immortality, but their beliefs, which relate to the cult of Zalmoxis, are better known, for they impressed the Greek authors who came in contact with them after the fifth century BCE.

Strabo (7.3.3) reports that, according to the Stoic Posidonius of Apamea, the Mysians (whom Strabo correctly identifies as the Moesi, i. e., inhabitants of Moesia) practiced vegetarianism, feeding themselves on honey, milk, and cheese. These are called *theosebeis* ("worshipers of the gods") and *kapnobatai* ("walkers on smoke"). Some among the Thracians lived in continence and are recorded as *ktistai* (lit., "founders"). To the latter applies the Homeric epithet *abioi* (lit., "lifeless," i.e., poor), which was attributed to some of the inhabitants of Thrace. The epithet *kapnobatai* may refer to a practice mentioned by Pomponius Mela (2.2.21), according to which some Thracians did not use wine as an intoxicating liquor but instead inhaled smoke from fires upon which had been thrown seeds whose scent provoked exhilaration. The *Lexicon* of Hesychius of Alexandria (fifth or sixth century CE) reports under the word *kanabis* ("hemp") that hemp seeds were burned, and so *Cannabis sativa* may be a plausible identification of the intoxicating plant referred to by Pomponius.

SEE ALSO Geto-Dacian Religion; Zalmoxis.

BIBLIOGRAPHY

The written sources on the religion of the Thracians are contained in *Fontes historiae Dacoromanae,* 2 vols., edited by Virgil C. Popescu et al. (Bucharest, 1964–1970). On Thracian religion in general, Gawrill I. Kazarow's article, "Thrake (Religion)," in *Realencyclopädie der Altertumswissenschaft,* vol. 6 (Stuttgart, 1937), can still be profitably consulted. On Greek votive inscriptions from southern Thrace, Georgi Mikhailov's *Inscriptiones Grecae in Bulgaria repertae,* 4 vols. (Sofia, 1956–1966), is particularly important. On the names of Thracian divinities, see Vladimir Georgiev's "Die thrakischen Götternamen: Ein Beitrag zur Religion der alten Thraker," *Linguistique balkanique* 18 (1975): 5–56. On Thracian funerary practices, see Dumitru Protase's *Riturile funerare la Daci şi Daco-Romani* (Bucharest, 1971), which includes a French summary on pages 183–214, and Dardu Nicolaescu-Plopşor and Wanda Wolski's *Elemente de demografie şi ritual funerar la populaţiile vechi din România* (Bucharest, 1975), which has an English summary on pages 273–292. An extensive bibliography can be found in Mircea Eliade's *Zalmoxis, the Vanishing God: Comparative Studies in the Religions and Folklore of Dacia and Eastern Europe* (Chicago, 1972).

New Sources

Gergova, Diana. "The Find from Rogozen and One Religious Feast in the Thracian Lands. " *Klio* 71 (1989): 36–50.

Gočeva, Zlatozara. "Die Religion der Thraker." *Klio* 68 (1986): 84–91.

Mihailov, Georgi. "Some Problems of Thracian Mythology and Religion." *Journal of Indo-European Studies* 11 (1983): 241–248.

Najderova, Varbinka. "Thracian Paganism and Roman Religions on the Lower Danubian Limes." In *Roman Frontier Studies 1989: Proceedings of the 15th International Congress of Roman Frontier Studies,* ed. by Valerie A. Maxfield and Michael J. Dobson, pp. 291–294. Exeter, U.K., 1991.

IOAN PETRU CULIANU (1987)
CICERONE POGHIRC (1987)
Revised Bibliography

THRACIAN RIDER. The so-called Thracian Rider, a demigod who was the focus of a cult in ancient Thrace, is known principally from sculptures and inscriptions dating from the fourth century BCE to the early fourth century CE. In Greek and Latin inscriptions he is identified simply as "the hero" (*hērōs* or *heros,* usually, but also *hērōn, heron, eron,* etc.). According to Dimiter Detschew (1957, p. 200), the name of the Thracian horseman was probably related to the Thracian term for "hero," **ierus,* or **iarus,* which has Celtic parallels. If so, this linguistic fact reinforces the religious analogies between this Thracian type of divinity and the Greek heroes.

The oldest monuments of the Thracian Rider belong to the fourth century BCE, but his cult was particularly influential in Thrace and in Moesia Inferior (i.e., Lower Moesia, the region of Greco-Roman settlements on the western shore of the Black Sea) during the second and third centuries CE. Roman iconography and inscriptions of that time show that he was identified with Asklepios, Apollo, Dionysos, Silvanus, and other divinities. He bore the epithets *sōtēr* ("savior"), *iatros* ("healer"), and even *megas theos* ("great god"), the last in the city of Odessus (present-day Varna), where he was also known by the Thracian name of Darzalas.

The extant monuments to the Thracian Rider are reliefs and statuettes having either a votive or a funerary character. The horseman is usually represented as riding to the right, toward a tree on which a serpent is coiled. In the inscriptions, Greek and Latin epithets are often added to the generic name of the hero, showing that the cult was adapted to particular heroes, who sometimes were known by Thracian names. The epithets are usually toponyms, names of tribes, or attributes of the horseman.

The names of the worshipers are known from votive inscriptions. It is interesting to note that 61 percent of the worshipers recorded in Moesia Inferior and Dacia (modern Romania and Bessarabia) bore Greek or Greco-Roman names, 34 percent bore Roman names, and only 5 percent bore names of Thracian or Thraco-Roman origin. Accordingly, it can be inferred that the majority of the adepts of the cult in Moesia Inferior were Greek.

Little is known about the cult itself, which was a combination of Greek and Thracian beliefs. At its height it was certainly related to concepts of survival after death and to healing, and it may have involved notions of survival either in the netherworld or in heaven. It was widespread among the population of Thrace and Moesia Inferior, and its devotees included people of various social standings and ethnic backgrounds. So far as we know, the cult never took the form of a mystery religion with secret communities organized in a hierarchy. The cult of the Thracian Rider died away in the first half of the fourth century CE.

SEE ALSO Dacian Riders.

BIBLIOGRAPHY

On the name of the Thracian Rider, see Dimiter Detschew's *Die thrakischen Sprachreste* (Vienna, 1957). For a listing of monuments from southern Thrace, together with an explanation and history of the cult, see Gawrill I. Kazarow's *Die Denkmäler des thrakischen Reitergottes in Bulgarien,* 2 vols. (Budapest, 1938). For a catalog of monuments from Moesia Inferior and Dacia, see Nubar Hampartumian's *Corpus Cultus Equitis Thracii,* vol. 4, *Moesia Inferior (Romanian Section) and Dacia* (Leiden, 1979).

New Sources

Condurachi, Emile. "A propos de la genèse de l'iconographie du cavalier thrace." In *Mythologie gréco-romaine. Mythologies périphériques,* pp. 63–69. Paris, 1981.

Dimitrova, Nora. "Inscriptions and Iconography in the Monuments of the Thracian Rider." *Hesperia* 71 (2002): 209–229.

Gočeva, Zlatozara. "Les traits caractéristiques de l'iconographie du cavalier thrace." In *Iconographie classique et identités régionales,* pp. 237–243. Paris, 1986.

Dimitrova, Nora. "Inscriptions and Iconography in the Monuments of the Thracian Rider." *Hesperia* 71 (2002): 209–229.

Walter, Christopher. "The Thracian Horseman." *Byzantinischen Forschungen* 14 (1989): 657–673.

Hoddinott, Ralf F. "The Thracian Hero at Rogozen." In *Studia Aegaea et Balcanica in Honorem Lodovicae Press*, pp. 157–165. Warsaw, 1992.

IOAN PETRU CULIANU (1987)
CICERONE POGHIRC (1987)
Revised Bibliography

TIAN. A term of basic importance in the worldview and religious life of the Chinese from the remote past to the present, *tian* has two principal senses: as the supreme god of the universe, and as impersonal nature. Often it is not clear in a particular instance which of these meanings is intended, and it may well be that the distinction is vague to the user.

TIAN AS GOD. The root meaning of *tian* is sky or the heavens, the abode of numinous beings. When used without qualifiers the term may denote the supreme deity. The earliest known use of the graph for *tian* occurs in ancient texts of the Zhou period (c. 1111–256 BCE), where it refers to the supreme deity of the Zhou people. In early Zhou times Tian was conceived as the all-powerful, purposeful, apparently anthropomorphic god who sent down blessings or disasters according to whether he was pleased or displeased with human behavior. Politically, Tian was the source of the legitimacy of the king, conferring upon the most righteous man the mandate of Heaven (*tianming*) or withdrawing this mandate from corrupt or unworthy rulers. In this conception of divinity the early Zhou rulers successfully assimilated the supreme god of the preceding Shang dynasty (eighteenth century? to 1111 BCE), called Di, or Shangdi. This assimilation blurred the historical and cultic distinction between the god of the Shang and the god of the Zhou. Subsequently, the terms *haotian* ("heaven of the vast-primal-vital-breath"), or *huangtian* ("august heaven"), and *shangdi* ("supreme ruler") were used interchangeably to denote the greatest power of the universe. As Tian and as Shangdi, this supreme power was conceived of as the creator (*zaowuzhu*). In some texts, including the *Yi jing* (Book of changes), *tian* and *di* (Heaven and Earth) are at least figuratively anthropomorphized as the cosmic father and mother, from whose sexual intercourse all beings are produced.

Worship of Tian, as performed in the elaborate imperial rituals, was forbidden to any but the ruler, as it was the most impressive demonstration of his possession of the mandate of Heaven. But it would hardly have been possible to prevent the people from believing in and expressing their awe of Tian. In the course of time, the notion evolved that the supernatural dimension was an invisible counterpart to the temporal world. Tian was then personified as the emperor of that spirit world who, like the emperor in this world, headed a heavenly bureaucracy of deities. In this role Tian was called Yuhuang Shangdi ("supreme ruler of jadelike augustness"). The common people invoked his aid when in dire trouble, and there were temples in which he was the chief deity. Many homes contained some representation of communication with him, such as an incense brazier. Among the people he was familiarly called Tiangong ("celestial duke") or Laotianye ("old celestial lord").

The omnipresence and concern of Tian with the human world are themes of many proverbs. In some of these, the deity is obviously personified: "Tian's eyes are everywhere, they see all without anyone escaping"; "Man can be fooled, but not Tian"; "Tian punishes the sinner"; "Blessings come from Tian"; "Tian helps those who help themselves"; "Tian knows the good and evil hidden in human hearts." Other sayings, however, are either ambiguous or definitely refer to an impersonal power: "The cyclical revolutions of *tian* cause things to be as they are"; "*Tian* is empty; earth is broad"; "Intelligence is endowed by *tian*"; "There may not be two suns in *tian*"; "It is difficult to go against the Way (*dao*) of *tian*."

The arrival of Buddhism from India and Central Asia at approximately the beginning of the common era introduced new and complicated notions of celestial beings and celestial realms. The Buddhist realms, for example, were divided into the Realm of Desire (*kama-dhatu*), the Realm of Form (*rupadhatu*), and the Realm of Formlessness (*arupyadhatu*). These and other Buddhist realms were called *tian*. In the third and fourth centuries, as Daoism became a cohesive religion, it too developed elaborate notions of supernal realms and called them *tian*. In general, the *tian* of Daoism, variously twenty-eight, thirty-two, or thirty-six in number, were derived from Buddhism, although one novel idea held that counterparts to *tian* existed in the subterranean world. The Daoist *tian* are the abodes of gods and their subordinates, the perfected immortals (*xian*), as well as of the souls of the virtuous dead who will one day attain immortality as perfected beings. The term *tian* also figures in Daoist cosmology, where *xiantian* ("pre-cosmic") and *houtian* ("cosmic," that is, the phenomenal universe) denote stages of evolution that are represented in the performance of liturgical rites.

TIAN AS IMPERSONAL NATURE. The word *tian* often appears in writings of the classical period of philosophy (sixth to third century BCE), where it is used with the connotation "nature." Daoist texts of the period frequently express the idea of *tian* as an impersonal force that produces all natural phenomena. In this usage were blended the ideas of the will of a personal deity and a natural law. Thus, events, in particular, omens, commonly taken to signify the "decree" of *tian*, were here interpreted simply as having occurred spontaneously or of themselves (*tianming ji ziran*). The most forceful assertion of the impersonality of *tian* was made by the Ru (Confucian) scholar Xunzi (fl. c. 298–238 BCE), who denied that *tian* acted in response to human actions or pleas. In his view, *tian* was simply the operation of the physical universe. In another instance of the impersonal use of *tian*, the term refers to something akin to "fate," as in the expression *mingyun de tian* ("Heaven-determined destiny").

As with the anthropomorphic conception of *tian*, the naturalistic interpretation was given its most authoritative expression in the *Yi jing*. There, *tian* is symbolized by the trigram *qian*, and is thus another term for the positive, male, creative principle or force (yang). Its complement is *di*, or earth, symbolized by the trigram *kun*, representing the negative, female, receptive principle or force (yin). The ceaseless, ever-changing interactions and permutations of these complementary principles or forces produce the universe and all beings, and are responsible for their birth, growth, decay, and death.

Although impersonal, the "naturalistic" *tian* has a close functional relationship with man. The classical philosophers see this relationship in a variety of not necessarily reconcilable ways:

- Human life or life span depends upon *tian* (*renzhiming zai tian*).
- Man is a microcosm of the universe, his feet being "square," as earth is, and his head round, as Heaven is.
- Man's nature (*xing*) is conferred at birth by *tian*.
- Man should model himself upon *tian* (*fatian*).
- Since *tian* is impersonal, it is man who acts as the mind (or heart) of *tian*.
- Man and *tian* constantly interact in mutual stimulus and response (a view denied, as we have seen, by Xunzi).
- The function of *tian* is to create, while the function of man is to nurture and bring to perfection those created things.
- *Tian* serves as the moral example for man, who can only attain his complete human development through the discipline of moral steadfastness (*cheng*).

Here again, the concept of *tian* is ambiguous: while moral perfection would seem to be possible only for a person, yet the unfailing regularity, benevolence, and impartiality of *tian* could also be interpreted in moral terms.

In the neo-Confucian movement, which began during the Tang dynasty (618–907) and came to maturity during the Song period (960–1279), philosophers again utilized the term *tian* in various new ways. The neo-Confucian goal may be stated in religious terms as an ultimate self-transformation for the attainment of sainthood or sageliness (*shengren*). Most important was a concept called the *tianli* ("principle of *tian*" or "heavenly principle"), which was interpreted in a number of ways. It stood for the sum of the anciently enunciated virtues of the Confucian tradition; it was a name for the metaphysical substance or embodiment of the *dao* (*xingshang daoti*); it was identified as mind; it was identified as conscience, which produced the innate knowledge of good and evil, right and wrong (*liangxi* or *liangzhi*); it was moral perfection, the very opposite of human desires (*renyu*), a proposition rejected by certain later neo-Confucians; or it designated the totality of all principles, being cosmic Principle. These were some of the concepts the neo-Confucians used in constructing a metaphysics that had been lacking in the ancient Confucian system. They attempted, in this way, to arrive at an understanding of the nature of ultimate reality or the Absolute. In their philosophies, the term *tian* was used for this ultimate reality and also identified with other terms that had the same meaning—*dao*, *li*, *taiji*, and (in Wang Yangming's thought) *xin* ("heart-and-mind"). Although the *tian* of the neo-Confucians was an impersonal metaphysical principle, even in this usage theistic implications were not entirely absent.

SEE ALSO Dao and De; Li; Shangdi; Taiji; Yuhuang.

BIBLIOGRAPHY

There is no monographic treatment of *tian* in English, and the only one in a Western language, Anton Lübke's *Der Himmel der Chinesen* (Leipzig, 1931), is not easily available in many North American libraries. A good overall discussion is found in Alfred Forke's *The World-Conception of the Chinese* (1925; reprint, New York, 1975). On Tian as the god of the Zhou people, see Herrlee G. Creel's "The Origin of the Deity T'ien," in volume 1, appendix C of his *The Origins of Statecraft in China* (Chicago, 1970). On the concept of Tian (i. e., Shangdi) as the supreme deity, see James Legge's *The Notions of the Chinese concerning God and Spirits* (1852; reprint, Taibei, 1971). A suggestive recent interpretation is Ha Tai Kim's "Transcendence Without and Within: The Concept of T'ien in Confucianism," *International Journal for Philosophy of Religion* 3 (Fall 1972): 146–160.

For the role of *tian* in political and social traditions, the definitive treatment is Yang Ch'ing-k'un's *Religion in Chinese Society* (Berkeley, 1961); see the index references s.v. *Heaven*. Proverbs showing generally held notions of *tian* are sampled in Clifford H. Plopper's *Chinese Religion Seen through the Proverb* (1926; reprint, New York, 1969), pp. 23–29, 59–76. Various concepts of *tian* are discussed in H. G. Lamont's "An Early Ninth Century Debate on Heaven," *Asia Major* 18 (1973): 181–208 and 19 (1974): 37–85, although this article is technical and contains considerable extraneous material. An important discussion is found in J. J. M. de Groot's *Les fêtes annuellement célébrées à Émoui (Amoy)*, vol. 1 (1886; reprint, Taibei, 1977), pp. 35–83.

LAURENCE G. THOMPSON (1987)

TIANTAI. The Tiantai tradition of Chinese Māhāyana Buddhism is a lineage centered around the writings of the monk Zhiyi (538–597) and his successors. This tradition is characterized by the emphasis it places on the practice of meditation, its exegetical method, and the centrality it accords the teachings of the *Saddharmapuṇḍarīka Sūtra* (Chin., *Miaofa lianhua jing su*; abbreviated title, *Fahua jing*; the *Lotus Sutra*) and the *Da ban niepan jing* (Skt., *Mahāyāna-parinirvāṇa Sūtra*). The Tiantai tradition forms, together with the Huayan tradition, one of the two major academic and doctrinal systems of Chinese Mahāyāna Buddhism.

ORIGINS. Zhiyi's major meditation text, the *Mohe zhiguan* (The Great Stilling and Insight; T. D. no. 1911), states that the Tiantai lineage began with Huiwen, who transmitted the essence of his enlightenment experience to his disciple Huisi, who in turn instructed Zhiyi. Later Tiantai church history therefore refers to these monks as the first three (Chinese) Tiantai "patriarchs."

Huiwen. Other than the fact that he was active during the Northern Qi period (550–557), little is known of the life of Huiwen. Even late accounts admit that both his place of birth and his dates are unknown. His importance to the tradition derives from his adumbration of certain key concepts that, in the writings of Zhiyi, would become central to Tiantai thought. One source relates that while reading the *Da zhidu lun* (a commentary on the *Prajñāpāramitā Sūtra* in twenty-five thousand slokas that is traditionally attributed to Nāgārjuna) he was struck by a passage that notes, "When one moment of mind obtains all wisdom, the wisdom of the Path, and all species of wisdom, then all of the defilements and their traces are cut off." This concept of "three wisdoms in one mind" (*yxin sanzhi*) became identified in the writings of Zhiyi with his concept of "three insights in one mind" (*yxin sanguan*), a core teaching of the Tiantai system.

This link to the teachings of Nāgārjuna, founder of the Mādhyamika system and perhaps the greatest of all Buddhist thinkers, was later formalized by recognizing him as the tradition's first Indian patriarch and the inspirator of the system as a whole. Such post facto linkage with Indian figures of unquestioned authority was a common means of bestowing legitimacy and prestige upon the Buddhist traditions indigenous to China. Nāgārjuna, in fact, is counted as "first patriarch" of several East Asian Buddhist traditions.

Huisi. The master Huisi was a native of Honan Province; later biographies state that he was born under the Northern Wei on the eleventh day of the eleventh month of 515. At the age of fourteen he entered the monastic life and received full ordination, devoting himself to chanting the text of the *Fahua jing.* At the age of nineteen he had an enlightenment experience while reading the *Miaoshengding jing* (Sutra of Marvelous, Unsurpassed *Samādhi;* otherwise unknown); from this time on he retired to the woods and forests to practice meditation in solitude.

Sometime after this experience Huisi met the master Huiwen and received instruction from him concerning meditation and its concomitant, the experience of enlightenment. Thereafter, he confined his practice to meditation. Tradition alleges that he attained enlightenment only at the point when, dispairing of ever realizing the goal of his practice, Huisi climbed to the top of the monastery wall to throw himself off. The resulting breakthrough he later termed *fahua sanmei,* or "Lotus *samādhi.*"

A recurrent theme in his preaching is summarized in one of his biographies: "The source of enlightenment is not far away, and one's (Buddha) nature, like a sea, is not distant. Only direct your seeking inward upon yourself; do not get enlightenment from another." Huisi died peacefully in 577, at the age of sixty-two.

Some six extant works are attributed to Huisi: the *Dasheng zhiguan famen* (The Mahāyāna Teaching of Stilling and Insight; T. D. no. 1924); the *Zhufa wucheng sanmei famen* (The Teaching of Noncontentious *Samādhi* with Respect to All Phenomena; T. D. no. 1923); the *Sui ciyi sanmei* (The *Samādhi* Attained at Will; *Zokuzōkyō* 2.3); the *Fahua jing anluo xingyi* (The Cultivation of the Anluo Chapter of the Fahua jing; T. D. no. 1926), a work that treats the ethics of a *Lotus* devotee in an era of the decline of the *Dharma,* as outlined in the fourteenth chapter of the Lotus; the *Shou pusa jiehyi* (The Ritual for Receiving the *Bodhisattva* Precepts; *Zokuzōkyō* 2.10); and the *Nanyue sidashi lishi yuanwen* (The Vows of Master Si of Nanyue; T. D. no. 1933). The authenticity of some of these works remains open to scholarly investigation. Attributions, in later catalogs, of some four other inextant works to Huisi may, to judge from the titles of these works, represent a retrospective attempt to ascribe many of the major teachings of Zhiyi to his master's inspiration.

Zhiyi. Zhiyi, the *de-facto* founder of the Tiantai tradition, was born in Jingzhou (present-day Hunan Province) in 538. At the age of seventeen he entered the monastic life under the direction of the master Fazhu of the guoyuan Si in Xiangzhou; after his ordination he began the study of the Vinaya (rules of monastic discipline) with Huikuang, reading at the same time various Mahāyāna texts. Sometime later Zhiyi made a pilgrimage to Mount Taixian, where he went into retreat, reciting the "three Lotus scriptures," the *Fahua jing,* the *Wuliang yi jing,* and the *Puxianguan jing.* He continued his chanting for twenty days, at which time he fully understood the meaning of these texts.

In 560 Zhiyi journeyed to Mount Dasu, where he met Huisi, who was now destined to become his chief instructor. Huisi instructed him in devotions centered around the figure of the *bodhisattva* Samantabhadra (Chin., Puhxian) and in the *Anluo* practices, practices taught in the fourteenth chapter (*Anluoxing pin*) of the *Fahua jing.* Following Zhiyi's enlightenment experience Huisi named him his *Dharma* heir and successor. Thereafter, Zhiyi took up residence in the Waguan Si in Jinling (Nanking), where he was to stay for eight years. During this period he lectured on the *Lotus* and the *Da zhidu lun* and taught a path of gradual meditative cultivation to his disciples. These teachings formed the basis for his *Fajie ziti chumen* (T. D. no. 1925). In 575 he moved to Mount Tiantai, a mountain that was to remain his major headquarters for the rest of his life and from which the tradition derives its name. In 577 Zhiyi and his followers were, by imperial edict, given the tax levies from Shifeng Prefecture (xian), and two clans were indentured to him to provide his community with fuel and water. Sometime in this period Zhiyi lectured on the *Jingming jing* (the *Vimalakīrtinirdeśa*

Sūtra) and the *Jinguangming jing* (a Prajñāpāramitā text); both of these lectures served as the basis for later written works.

In 585 Zhiyi lectured before the last emperor of the Chen dynasty on the *Da zhidu lun.* While in the Chen capital (Jinling) he also lectured on the *Renwang panruo jing* (Sutra of the Benevolent Kings; T. D. no. 246) and admonished the emperor against state intervention in the affairs of the *saṃgha.* In 587 Zhiyi gave a series of lectures on the *Fahua jing* in the Guangze Si; these lectures became the basis for his *Miaofa lianhua jing wenju* (Sentences and Phrases of the *Lotus;* T. D. no. 1718). With the establishment of the Sui dynasty (589–618) and the reunification of China after some three and a half centuries, the area around the two regions of Xiangzhou and Xingzhou was pacified and Zhiyi was able to make a pilgrimage to Mount Lu, a site famous in the history of Pure Land Buddhism. In 591 he administered the *bodhisattva* precepts to the later-to-be second Sui emperor, Prince Guang, in Yangzhou.

In 593 Zhiyi lectured on the *Fahua jing* at the Yuchuan Si, a monastery in Dangyang Prefecture whose construction he had overseen. The transcription of these lectures by Zhiyi's disciple and amanuensis, Guanding, served as the basis of the *Miaofa lianhua jing xuanyi* (The Profound Principles of the *Lotus;* T. D. no. 1716). The following year Zhiyi lectured on the practice of meditation; these lectures, again transcribed by Guanding, formed the basis for the last of his three major works, the *Mohe zhiguan.* In 595, once more at the request of the prince, Zhiyi found himself in the capital, Jinling, where he composed a commentary on the *Vimalakīrti Sūtra* on behalf of his most eminent patron. Soon thereafter, however, inspired by a premonition of impending death, he returned to Tiantai to impart his final teachings to his disciples. These were transcribed under the title *Guanxin lun* (On Visualizing the Mind; T. D. no. 1920). Zhiyi died in the eleventh month of 597.

Although Zhiyi considered himself part of a spiritual lineage that derived ultimately from Nāgārjuna and that had been transmitted through Huiwen and Huisi, the doctrines that have in East Asia been most typically associated with (early) Tiantai are the products of his own skill as a teacher and exegete. His biographies record that Zhiyi was responsible for the construction of some thirty-five monasteries, had fifteen copies of the Tripiṭaka copied and thousands of Buddha images cast, ordained over a thousand monks, some thirty-two of whom became advanced students under his personal guidance, and produced a large number of works on doctrine and meditation. (Forty-six are attributed to him, but a number are clearly later forgeries.)

Also important were the links he established with the Sui ruling house, who saw in Zhiyi's synthesis of diverse strands of the Buddhist tradition a compelling analogue to their own political unification of the empire. Unfortunately, the close relationship enjoyed by Zhiyi with the Sui rulers, and the lavish patronage he and his community received at their hands, were responsible for the school's dramatic loss of prestige in the aftermath of the fall of the Sui in 518. The new dynasty, the Tang, wishing to disassociate itself from Sui policies, naturally eshewed the symbols of religious legitimacy treasured by its predecessor.

DOCTRINE AND PRACTICE. The Tiantai tradition is characterized by the use of an exegetical method developed by Zhiyi and employed by him in his works; all subsequent Tiantai writers employed this same method. Tiantai doctrine is founded upon a particular reading of the *Lotus Sutra,* to which is imported a wide variety of teachings associated with other texts and traditions and an organizational principle whereby the disparate texts and teachings of Mahāyāna Buddhism are seen in the context of an overarjing scheme of revelation and levels of textual interpretation. Although the systematization of this insight into the so-called Five Periods and Eight Teachings doctrine is probably the work of a later hand, the basic inspiration for the system clearly derives from Zhiyi. Three works in particular, all by Zhiyi, are recognized by the tradition as constituting the core and epitome of its teachings.

Miaofa lianhua jing wenzhu. The first of these, the *Miaofa lianhua jing wenzhu* (*Fahua wenzhu,* for short), or *Words and Phrases of the Lotus Sutra,* is based on Zhiyi's lectures at the Guangze Si in 587 on the meaning of key words and phrases in the *Lotus Sutra.* Guanding's compilation and redaction of notes taken at this lecture series were completed in 629.

The *Wenzhu* employs four types of explanation (*sishi*) in commenting on the text:

(1) The explanation according to conditions (*yinyuan shi*), in which the author analyzes the Buddha and his audience and the four "benefits" (*siddhāntas*) produced by this *sūtra* (it leads to joy and happiness, it generates roots of good, it destroys evil, and it enables the devotee to enter into an understanding of the Absolute).

(2) The explanation in which this and all other *sūtras* are analyzed on the basis of the place they occupy in the teachings of the Buddha over his entire lifetime (*yuejiao shi*). The standards for evaluating any teaching are two: whether is it "partial" or "perfect" (i. e., whether it is fully expressive of the insights of the Buddha or only partially so), Hīnayāna or Mahāyāna; and where it is included in the scheme of the Five Periods and the Eight Teachings.

(3) The explanation based on whether the teachings in question constitute the "basic" or "peripheral" message of the *sūtra* (*benji shi*).

(4) The explanation based on the type of meditational practice taught in the *sūtra* (*guanxin shi*).

These four exegetical methods are employed on the *Lotus Sutra* as a whole, and then on each chapter's title and on selected passages from each chapter. The first three explanations are theoretical, the last practical.

Zhiyi divided the contents of the *Lotus Sutra* into three parts, two parts, and a combination of the two. He divided the whole of the scripture into three parts: an introduction (chapter 1), the core teachings (chapter 2 to the first half of chapter 17), and a postscript (the last half of chapter 17 to the end of the work, chapter 28). He also divided the scripture into two parts (based on the *benji shi* method, mentioned above): The first fourteen chapters constitute the fictive or provisional teachings; the second fourteen chapters constitute the basic or absolute level of teaching. Here again, a tripartite analysis is employed against each section. The fictive or provisional teachings are composed of an introduction (chapter 1), a core teaching (chapters 2 to 6), and a postscript (chapters 7 to 14). The basic or absolute teachings are similarly divided into the introduction (the first half of chapter 15), the core teaching (latter half of chapter 15 to the first half of chapter 17), and the postscript (latter half of chapter 17 to the end of the text).

For Zhiyi, the teachings of the first half of the *Lotus* (the first fourteen chapters) center around the promise of salvation for all beings. In this section, the Buddha Śākyamuni reveals that the traditionally articulated soteriological paths (*yānas*)—that of the *śrāvaka*, or "Hīnayāna" devotee, consisting of the teaching and practice of the Four Noble Truths; the pratyekabuddha, or self-enlightened Buddha, epitomized by the teaching of dependent origination (*pratītya-samutpāda*); and the *bodhisattva,* or Mahāyāna practitioner, characterized by the practice of the "perfections" (*pāramitās*)—are only apparently distinct religious paths. In fact, the end of each is nothing less than full and complete Buddhahood; there are not three vehicles to salvation, only one, the *ekabuddhayāna,* or "One Vehicle of the Buddha." This section of the *sūtra* also preaches, according to Zhiyi, that phenomenal existence is identical with the absolute, and that all *dharmas* have real and tangible characteristics.

The second half of the *sūtra* proclaims, however, that Śākyamuni's very appearance in the world is a mere fiction, a device employed, so says Zhiyi, by the one, eternal Buddha to aid in the salvation of all beings. Under this interpretation, the historical Buddha, indeed all Buddhas of the ten directions, are nothing more than emanations of this one Buddha, and their earthly careers—the paradigmatic sequence of birth, renunciation of family life, cultivation of ascetic practices, even the enlightenment and final *nirvāṇa* (*parinirvāṇa*)—mere elements in a great soteriological drama designed to reveal the *Dharma* to sentient beings. For this reason, Zhiyi termed the teachings of the first half of the text provisional; only the latter half constitutes the full revelation of absolute truth.

All subsequent Tiantai writings having the words *wenzhu* in their titles employ the fourfold exegetical method described here.

Miaofa lianhua jing xuanyi. The second of the major works of Zhiyi, the *Miaofa lianhua jing xuanyi,* is primarily an exegesis of the five words in the title of the *sūtra* from five points of view. The exegetical method of this commentary is thus called the "five types of profound principles" (*wuzhong xuanyi*). These five exegetical categories characterize all subsequent Tiantai writings having the term *xuanyi* in their titles and were used to analyze all Buddhist scripture, not merely the *Lotus.* The first explains the name of the *sūtra* (*shiming*); the second is a detailed analysis of its philosophy, a philosophy that may not be necessarily expressed in the text itself (the *bienti* explanation); the third clarifies important points expressed in the body of the text (the *mingzong* explanation); the fourth discusses how the *sūtra* expects persons to act or to think with respect to the teaching presented therein (the *lunyong* explanation); and the fifth evaluates the *sūtra* and ranks it in relationship to the Absolute teachings presented in the Lotus (the *panjiao* explanation). Zhiyi continues with an explanation of the meditational practice taught in the *Lotus,* how the devotee should visualize that the different characteristics of all *dharmas* are all in one's own mind and that this mind actually (not merely potentially) possesses all *dharmas*.

Zhiyi's specific explanation of the meaning of the word *fa* (*dharma*) derives from the explanation that he learned from his master Huisi: The word *fa* includes the aspect of mind, the Buddha, and sentient beings. All these three are at once provisional *and* absolute, a truth that is realized when the devotee sees that he or she and all other sentient beings possess the "ten suchnesses" (*shi rushi*) and the "ten *dharma*dhatus," or realms of rebirth (*shi fajie*). Each realm possesses each of the ten suchnesses for a total of one thousand characteristics, and each one of these one thousand characteristics are empty (*kong*), provisionally existent (*jia*), and both empty and existent at the same time (zhong). This threefold characterization is referred to as the "three wisdoms."

In the last part of the commentary, Zhiyi refutes various theories of early Huayan and Weishi (Yogācāra) masters. He also denies the equality, maintained by many, of the *Lotus Sutra* and the *Huayan jing* and refutes the theories of several early Lotus thinkers.

Mohe zhiguan. The last of the major works of Zhiyi is the *Mohe zhiguan.* Unlike the former two works, which deal primarily with theory and only peripherally with meditation, this work constitutes the core of Tiantai teachings concerning practice. The text of the *Zhiguan* was composed by Zhiyi, but the introduction to the work was written by Guanding. In it, Guanding speaks of the lineage of Tiantai meditational practice and teaching. He speaks of two lineages: The first is taken from the *Fu fazang jing* and posits a line of transmission that begins with the Buddha Śākyamuni and may be traced to the Indian monk Siṃha. This lineage also includes Nāgārjuna. Because it begins with the "golden mouthed" words of the Buddha it is called the "golden mouth lineage." The second lineage is called the "lineage of contemporary masters"; it traces its origin from Nāgārjuna, through Huiwen to Huisi, to Zhiyi.

The Five Periods and the Eight Teachings. One of the most distinctive features of Tiantai thought was its classification of the whole of Śākyamuni's teachings, that is, the whole of Buddhism, into five periods, during which the Buddha is said to have taught different doctrines to different classes of persons. These teachings are further subdivided on the basis of their contents.

The "five periods" (*wushi)* are (1) the Huayan (Skt., Avatamsaka) period, (2) the period of the Ehan, or Agamas, also called the Luyuan (Skt., Mṛgadāva, "Deer Park") period, (3) the Fangdeng (Skt., Vaipulya) period, (4) the Boruo (Skt., Prajñāpāramitā) period; and (5) the Fahua (Skt., Sad*dharma*puṇḍarīka) or *Niepan* (Skt., Nirvāṇa) period. These take their names, as is obvious, from specific scriptures or scriptural collections preached during these eras.

The "eight teachings" (*bajiao*) are two sets of four teachings, so divided on the basis of the method and the type or content of the teaching employed. The first four, the *huayi*, or methods of conversion, are (1) the Sudden Teaching (*dunjiao*), (2) the Gradual Teachings (*jianjiao*), (3) the Secret Teachings (*bimi jiao*), (4) the Indeterminate Teachings (*buding jiao*). The *huafa* teachings, that is, the teachings classified on the basis of their contents, are (1) the Piṭaka Teachings (*zangjiao*), (2) the Common Teachings (*tungjiao*), (3) the Separate Teachings (*biejiao*), and (4) the Perfect Teachings (*yuanjiao*).

When the Buddha Śākyamuni was first enlightened he is reputed to have sat silently for twenty-one days, during which time various emanations from his body are said to have taught several sermons that were later compiled into one work, the *Huayan jing* (*Avataṃsaka Sūtra*). During this twenty-one-day period the Buddha presented the teachings to advanced *bodhisattvas*, the only beings capable of comprehending their lofty contents.

After this twenty-one-day period, the Buddha then spent the next twelve years preaching the Hīnayāna teachings to an audience that was incapable of understanding the "sudden" presentation of the Mahāyāna teachings of the Huayan jing. These Hīnayāna teachings, also called the Āgamas (known in Pali as the Nikāyas), were first preached in the Deer Park (Mṛgadāva) in the town of Sārnāth, a suburb of Banaras, and were intended as an initial step in preparing his listeners for more advanced (i. e., Mahāyāna) teachings. These Hīnayāna discourses were thus deemed expedient (*upāya*) teachings designed to lead the Buddha's hearers eventually to greater understanding of the ultimate or absolute level of the Truth.

Following this, the Buddha then preached for eight years to those followers who had attained the fruit of the Hīnayāna teachings, that is, to *arhats*, in order to bring them to the realization that arhatship does not represent the acme of the religious career. Thus, the Buddha preached a large number of Mahāyāna sermons—represented by such scriptures as the *Weimo jing* (*Vimalakīrtinirdeśa*), the *Shengman jing* (*Śrīmālādevī Sūtra*), the *Jinguang ming jing* (*Suvarṇaprabhāsa Sūtra*)—which were taught, in the words of Zhiyi, "to deprecate the partial and to praise the perfect; to demolish the Hīnayāna, and to praise the Mahāyāna," so that the followers would "be ashamed of the Hīnayāna and long for the Mahāyāna."

Next, the Buddha taught the Prajñāpāramitā (Perfection of Wisdom) teaching of the emptiness of all *dharmas*. This twenty-two year period was followed by the presentation, for the first time since the teachings of the *Huayan jing*, of the absolute truth: For the next eight years the Buddha taught the *Lotus Sutra*. As the Buddha was about to die, his spent his last day and night preaching the *Mahāparinirvāṇa Sūtra*, the *Niepan jing*. In this teaching he emphasized that all beings have the Buddha nature, or the potential to become fully enlightened Buddhas, thus converting those who had remained unswayed by the preaching of the *Lotus Sutra*. In order to remove the delusions of those "of weak capacities among later generations" who would come to have the "false view of extinction and annihilation," he stressed the importance of the Vinaya and its precepts for the moral life, and taught the eternal existence of the Buddha. Because the message and the approximate time period of the preaching of the *Lotus Sutra* and the *Mahāparinirvāṇa Sūtra* were the same, these two scriptures were said to make up a single era.

Zhiyi did not assign any specific number of years to each of these periods; these were first added to this scheme in the early thirteenth century by the scholar-monk Yuansui in his *Sijiaoyi beishi* (*Zokuzōkyō* 2.7.1). This identification with a specific number of years for each period became standard in Tiantai circles, although it was criticized by Zhixu (in his *Jiaoguan kangzong*), the Japanese master Shōshin (in the *Hokkegengi shiki*), and by the seventeenth- and eighteenth-century Japanese masters Fujaku and Hotan.

Of the four methods of conversion, the Sudden Teaching is identified with the Huayan period and the Gradual Teachings with the second, third, and fourth periods. The Secret Teachings are those in which one group of persons is taught the Sudden Teaching and another group is taught a Gradual Teaching, yet neither group realizes that the other has received a different presentation of the teachings. Hence, they are termed "secret [and indeterminate]." But should these two groups realize that each is receiving a different teaching and a different type of spiritual benefit, then the teachings are termed the "[revealed] indeterminate teachings." No specific scriptures are assigned to these last two categories.

The classification of the teachings according to their contents begins with the Piṭaka Teachings, a synonym for the Hīnayāna. In this teaching the Four Noble Truths are taught differently for the *śrāvakas*, *prateyekabuddhas*, and *bodhisattvas*. Then the Four Truths are taught with respect to emptiness and nonarising to these three categories of followers equally. This is termed the Common Teaching. When an unlimited number of Four Truths are taught only to

Mahāyāna *bodhisattvas*, this teaching is coupled with a presentation of the three insights, emptiness (*gu*), provisional existence (*jia*), and the middle, or reconciliation of these two (*zhong*), in a sequential manner. This is the Separate Teaching, as each defilement is cut off separately. When the three insights are taught, cultivated, and realized simultaneously, and when the three defilements are cut off all at once, this is the Perfect Teaching.

The teaching of the Huayan period is the Perfect Teaching, but not exclusively so; it also contains traces of the Separate Teaching. The Deer Park period is devoted exclusively to the Piṭaka Teaching. The third period, the miscellaneous Mahāyāna or Vaipulya period, contains elements of all four teachings, and the fourth period teaches the Perfect Teaching but with strong traces of both the Common and Separate Teachings. In the fifth period, the *Lotus Sutra* is purely the Perfect Teaching, with no admixture of any of the other teachings, whereas the *Mahāparinirvāṇa Sūtra* constitutes a subsidiary teaching, and includes all of the four types of teachings.

Meditation. According to Guanding, Zhiyi's teaching of meditation can be traced to the master Huisi, and comprehends "three types of stilling and insight meditation" (*sanzhong zhiguan*): the gradual attainment of stilling and insight (taught in full in Zhiyi's *Shichan poluomi ziti famen,* T. D. no. 1916), the indeterminate attainment of stilling and insight (represented by his *Liumiao famen,* T. D. no. 1917), and the perfect and sudden attainment of stilling and insight (represented by the *Mohe zhiguan*).

The *Mohe zhiguan* is divided into ten major sections; sections one and seven are further subdivided into important subdivisions. Section one is entitled Dayi, ("great teaching") and is subdivided into (1) generating the *bodhicitta* (in which ten types of good and bad *bodhicitta* are enumerated); (2) cultivating the great practice, in which four types of samādhi are enumerated: the "*samadhi* of perpetual walking," the "*samadhi* of perpetual sitting," the "*samadhi* of half-walking and half-sitting" (which, coupled with the perpetual recitation of the Nembutsu, became important in Japanese Tendai and Pure Land practice), and the "*samadhi* of neither walking nor sitting"; (3) experiencing the great result (i. e., the *saṃbhogakāya*); (4) rending asunder the great snare of doubts, in which the author refutes doubts and objections based on other writings and teachings; and (5) returning to the great source, *nirvāṇa.*

Section two discusses the name (*Stilling and Insight*) of the text. Section three discusses its characteristics; section four states that this practice embraces all *dharmas*; section five discusses whether this practice is partial or perfect; and section six gives some twenty-five external and internal preparations for the practice of meditation. Section seven is entitled "The Real Practice" and is subdivided into ten subdivisions. According to section seven, on the first of the devotee's intensive meditations he or she should meditate on "the three thousand *dharmas* in one instant of mind" (*yinian sanqian*), a practice that has become one of the hallmarks of Tiantai meditation. This teaching states that the devotee's five skandhas presently contain all of the *dharmas* ("the three thousand *dharmas*") of existence. These three thousand are the ten realms of rebirth (hell, *pretas*, animals, *asuras*, humans, *devas*, *śrāvakas*, *pratyekabuddhas*, *bodhisattvas*, and Buddhas) multiplied by the ten "suchnesses," or real, tangible characteristics (nature, external characteristics, body, power, creative ability, causes, conditions, results, recompenses, and the totality of the Absolute), in turn multiplied by the three realms (the realm of sentient beings, their physical lands, and their five *skandhas*).

The remaining portions of section seven elucidate meditational practices designed to remove the influences (*vāsanās*) of one's past *karman.* At this point the *Mohe zhiguan* comes to an abrupt end; that is, it ends at the seventh subdivision of section seven; the remaining sections (eight to ten) are missing, although the names of their titles are known from the introduction to the work: Section eight is concerned with karmic results, section nine with the teachings, and section ten with the general purport. There are two traditional reasons given for this abrupt ending to the text: Either Zhiyi was asked to speak for a certain period of time and his time ran out, or he was beginning to speak of states of attainment that could not be expressed in words. That is to say, if the devotee progressed as far as was already described in the text, the devotee would automatically know the ending of the book.

Introductory manuals. Even though the major writings of the Tiantai tradition are large, voluminous works, early on it became obvious to Zhiyi that his thought would be best presented in shorter epitomes of his teachings. One of the distinctive features of the Tiantai tradition is that it produced a number of one-volume works that present the salient points of Tiantai doctrine in a brief, easy to remember form.

One of the first of these works was Guanding's Tiantai bajiao dayi (The Major Points of the Eight Teachings of the Tiantai; T. D. no. 1930). Another popular one volume introduction to Tiantai thought is the Tiantai sijiaoyi (Kor., *Chŏndee sagyŏngui;* T. D. no. 1931) by the Korean monk Chegwan (Chin., Tiguan). This text is divided into two sections: The first describes the "five periods" (in the teaching career of the Buddha) and the "four teachings" (four types of doctrine preached by Śākyamuni); the second describes the meditational practice of the lineage. With this arrangement the author appears to separate the doctrinal from the practice aspect of the teaching, a point upon which he was criticized by later writers (e.g., Zhihxü).

Another short, one-volume introductory work is the *Jiaoguan kangzong* (T. D. no. 1939) by the Ming dynasty master Zhixu (1599–1655). In this work Zhixu attempts to present the orthodox Tiantai teachings without any admixture of his own interpretations, yet his definition of orthodox Tiantai are the thoughts of the *shanjia* masters of the Song dynasty. This work was written along the lines of Chegwan's *Sagyŏngui,* but whereas Chegwan presents the meditational practices of the various Four Teachings apart from their doctrines, Zhixu stresses the close interrelation between teaching and practice (meditation) in each of the Four Teachings.

Another short introductory work by Zhixu that is still widely read in both China and Japan is the *Fahua lunguan* (A Synopsis of the *Lotus Sutra;* Zokuzōkyō 50). In this work Zhixu adopted Zhiyi's exegetical method and selected passages from Zhiyi's *Fahua xuanyi* and *Fahua wenju* to illustrate the purport of the *sūtra* and its title. He also quotes from these two works to illustrate the teaching of each of the twenty-eight chapters of the *Lotus Sutra.*

Tiantai historiographical works. The Tiantai contribution to Chinese Buddhism is not confined to doctrinal works alone. Two major church histories, the *Fozu tongji* (Comprehensive Record of the Buddha and the Patriarchs; T. D. no. 2035) and the *Shimen chengtong* (*Zokuzokyo* 2.3.5), bear the imprint of Tiantai thought.

The former, composed in 1269 by Zhipan, is a general history of Buddhism in both India and China rendered from the Tiantai point of view. In it are preserved biographies of the Buddha and major patriarchal figures, chronologies of Chinese and Indian church history, histories of rival orders, Tiantai cosmology, accounts of church-state relations, miraculous tales, and the texts of important steles. The work contains much material pertaining to the *shanjiashanwai* debates of the Northern Song period, and is altogether notable for the attention it accords the Pure Land tradition in China, an account of which occupies a full three volumes.

The latter work, the *Shimen chengtong,* is in its present form the work of the Southern Sung master Zongqian, who rewrote the text from an earlier history, the *Zongyuan lu.* It is modeled after secular Chinese historical writings. In its five sections are chronicles of the Buddha and major Indian figures; sectarian lineages; monographs treating such topics as popular customs, social welfare, monastery administration, and so forth; biographies of lesser Tiantai masters; and records of other traditions.

LATER MASTERS. Although Zhiyi represents the lynchpin of Chinese Tiantai, his work was carried on and developed by a succession of later masters whose efforts ensured that Tiantai remained one of the most influential and doctrinally sophisticated traditions of East Asian Buddhism.

Guanding. Zhiyi's successor as abbot and leader of the Tiantai lineage was Guanding (561–632). A native of Zhangan (Zhekyiang Province), Guanding entered the monastic life at the age of six, particularly distinguishing himself in literary studies. He was fully ordained at the age of nineteen. After the death of his ordination master Guanding left the local monastery and went to the Xiuchan Si (later the chief monastery of the Tiantai tradition) on Mount Tiantai, where he met Zhiyi for the first time. It was here that he began his study of the Tiantai meditational practices and doctrinal synthesis established by Zhiyi.

In 583 Guanding accompanied Zhiyi to the Guangze Si in Jinling; here he studied Zhiyi's meditational teachings and was certified as Zhiyi's successor and permanent attendant. In 614 Guanding completed his two-volume commentary on the *Mahāyāna-parinirvāṇa Sūtra,* his *Daniepan jing xuanyi,* and the thirty-three volume comentary on this same scriptures, his *Daniepan jing shu.* With the completion of these works the Tiantai tradition now had complete commentaries on the two most important scriptures in their lineage, the *Lotus Sutra* and the *Mahāyāna-parinirvāṇa Sūtra,* whose doctrines, in the view of Zhiyi and Guanding, make up the "perfect" or "round" teaching (yuanjiao). Guanding's biographer states that, owing to the civil disorder attendent upon the collapse of the Sui, the five years it took him to complete his commentaries were ones of extreme privation.

In his later years Guanding lived in the city of Kuaiji, where he lectured on the *Lotus Sutra.* His biography records that contemporary popular rhyme said that he "surpassed Falang, Huiji, Fayun and Sengyin," the ranking scholar-monks of his day. It was through the efforts of Guanding that the monastery on Mount Tiantai began again to enjoy imperial patronage; Guanding was also responsible for the transcription and propagation of the major and minor works of Zhiyi, thus ensuring their survival for later generations.

In addition to the works mentioned above, Guanding's extant corpus includes the *Guanxin lun shu,* a commentary on Zhiyi's *Guanxin lun;* the *Sui Tiantai Dashi biezhuan,* a one-volume biography of Zhiyi and the primary source for existing knowledge of his life and works; and the *Guoqing bailu.*

Zhanran. Zhanran, counted as the ninth Tiantai patriarch, was born in 711 in Jingxi (present-day Giangsu Province) to a family that had for generations produced Confucian scholars and officials. His biography states that in his youth he excelled in scholarship; at the age of sixteen he developed an interest in Buddhism and began to search out teachers of the faith. His first recorded teacher was Fangyan, who taught him the elements of *zhiguan* meditation. At the age of seventeen he met Xuanlang (later to be counted as the eighth patriarch of the Tiantai tradition), who, it is said, immediately recognized the youth's intelligence and taught him both the doctrines and the meditation techniques of the Tiantai tradition.

For the next twenty years Zhanran, still a layman, devoted himself to the study of Tiantai doctrines, finally becoming ordained in 748. After his ordination, Zhanran journeyed to Kuaiji where he studied the monastic discipline with the Vinaya master Tanyi (Kor., Tamil). Sometime thereafter Zhanran gave a series of lectures on the *Mohe zhiguan* in the Kaiyuan Si in Wujun. Following the death of Xuanlang in 754, Zhanran took upon himself the task of propagating the Tiantai doctrines. This he did by writing commentaries to the three major works of Zhiyi, polemics against the Huayan, Yogācāra, and Chan systems, and short manuals of meditational instruction. His voluminous writings earned him the informal title of *jizhu,* the Master of Commentaries. Zhanran died in 782, and was buried next to the remains of Zhiyi. For his role in propagating Tiantai doctrines at a time of their eclipse Zhanran has been termed "the patriarchal restorer of the Tiantai tradition" (*Tiantai zhongxing zu*). He had some thirty-nine disciples, including Daosui and Xingman, as well as the academician Liang Xiao.

Zhanran's fame rests on his literary works. These include commentaries on Zhiyi's three major works: *Fahua wenju ji* (T. D. no. 1719), *Fahua xuanyi shiqian* (T. D. no. 1717), and the *Zhiguan fuxing zhuanhongjueh* (T. D. no. 1912). In addition to these, Zhanran also reedited the *Niepan shu* and composed three commentaries on the *Weimo jing* (*Vimalakīrtinirdeśa Sūtra*), a selection of significant passages from the *Mohe zhiguan* (his *Zhiguan wenju*), works on Huayan (his *Huayan gumu*), on selected topics in Tiantai doctrine (*Jingang bi lun* and *Shibuer men,* important works in the subsequent Song-dynasty *shanjiashanwai* debates), and a number of introductory manuals of meditation.

Zhili. Zhili, later to be counted as the seventeenth patriarch of the Tiantai tradition, was born in 960 in Siming (Chegiang Province). At the age of six, he lost his mother, and his father sent him to live in a local monastery. It was there, at the age of fourteen, that he received full ordination. At nineteen he began his study of Tiantai doctrine with Yitong (Kor., Ŭitŏng). After Zhili had been with Yitong for one month the master had him lecture on the *Xinjing* (the *Prajñāpāramitāhṛdaya Sūtra*), and after a period of three years Zhili was giving all of his master's lectures. Yitong died in 988; in 991 Zhili took up residence in the Qianfu Si, where he stayed for four years, lecturing on Tiantai doctrines and writings. As his students grew in number the accommodations of the Qianfu Si proved to be too small, so in 995 he moved to the Baoen Yuan; in the following year the abbot of the Baoen Yuan resigned his office and Zhili was able to turn the monastery into a Tiantai teaching center.

Zhili's entire life was devoted to religious instruction. In addition to a voluminous corpus of writings, twenty-three titles by one account, and his lectures on the major Tiantai works and commentaries, he also pursued a rich liturgical and meditative career. He was responsible for the construction of hundreds of monasteries, the mass printing of Tiantai literature, the casting of devotional images, and the inauguration of an "Assembly for the Recitation of the Name of the Buddha and for Giving the Precepts" (*nianfo shijie hui*), convened annually on the fifteenth day of the second month. But Zhili is perhaps best known for his role in the so-called *shanjiashanwai* debates, the seminal Tiantai dispute of the Northern Song period (960–1127).

The *shanjia* ("mountain school," the "orthodox" position) centered around Zhili and his followers; the *shanwai* ("outside the mountain," i. e., non-orthodox) position centered around the monks Qingzhao and Jiyuan. The dispute turned on whether the correct object of meditation should be the "mind as it currently is," defiled and ignorant, or the "true mind," in which case the devotee was to visualize a deity or some other transcendental object in order that the mind might take on the feature of the object of meditation. In the course of the debate the authenticity of various works popularly attributed to Zhiyi and Zhanran was also disputed, so that what came to be at issue was the very question as to which teachings would be recognized as "orthodox" Tiantai doctrine. The debate was joined initially in a series of correspondence between Zhili and his *shanwai* counterparts Wuen, Qingzhao, and Jiyuan. Many of these documents are preserved in Zhili's collected works, the *Siming zunzhe jiaoxing lu* (T. D. no. 1937). In the course of this correspondence Zhili made a case for the everyday mind, replete with defilements as it is, as the proper object of meditation, a point around which a variety of notions concerning the nature of the Absolute also crystallized.

By the time of his death in 1028 Zhili had gathered around him a large number of students, more than thirty of whom were his close disciples. Zhili also personally ordained over seventy monks.

Zhixu. The scholar-monk Zhixu was born in 1599 in the Suzhou district of present-day Giangsu Province. In his youth he was an ardent student of the Confucian classics. Like many of the Confucian scholars of his day, he had an intense dislike for Buddhism and even composed an essay purporting to refute Buddhist doctrine. But at the age of sixteen he chanced to read the *Zizhilu* and the *Zhushuang suibi* of the master Yunqi Zhuhong (1535–1615) and was converted to Buddhism. At nineteen he underwent an enlightenment experience while reading the *Lunyu* (Analects) of Confucius; as his biographer put it, "he was enlightened to the mind (*xinfa*) of Confucius and Yanzi."

In 1638 Zhixu resolved to compose a commentary on the *Fanwan jing* (T. D. no. 1815), the standard Chinese Mahāyāna text treating the precepts. Undecided as to which doctrinal point of view he should adopt in his explanation of the text, he made four tokens in order to practice a rite of divination in front of a Buddha image. On these tokens he wrote "the Huayan tradition," "the Tiantai tradition," "the Weishi tradition," and "my own tradition," respectively, signifying by this last that he would develop his own understanding of the Buddha's teachings. In this rite, the token marked with the Tiantai tradition came to the fore, and from this time onward he composed all of his textual commentaries based on Tiantai principles.

In the summer of 1655 Zhixu fell ill, and on this occasion compiled the *Jingtu shiyao* (Ten Essential Works on the Pure Land), an anthology of ten essays dealing with the Pure Land doctrines. At the end of summer his illness abated and he was then able to complete his *magnum opus,* the forty-four-volume *Yuezang zhijin* and the five-volume *Fahai guanlan.* Later that year his illness returned, whereupon he established a Pure Land religious sodality and composed a set of vows for the group. He also composed some stanzas on seeking rebirth in the Pure Land (the *Qiusheng jingtu jie*). Zhixu died in 1655 at the age of fifty-six; his popular posthumous title was *Lingfeng Yuyi Dashi.* His extant corpus of writings is voluminous: Some forty-six titles appear in various canonical collections and a number of texts still circulate independently. Zhixu's miscellaneous pieces were collected in 1678 by his disciple Chengshi into the ten-volume *Ling feng Yuyi Dashi zonglun.*

Zhixu's corpus includes several works concerned with the *Lengyen jing,* a scripture hitherto not commented upon from the Tiantai standpoint, and works dealing with the precepts, Buddhist logic, different aspects of Buddhist philosophy, many different scriptural commentaries, and interestingly enough, a Buddhist commentary on the Four Books (four Confucian classics) and a ten-volume *Zhouyi chanjie* (a Chan commentary on the *Book of Changes*). Zhixu's largest work is the forty-four-volume *Yuezang zhijin* (Examining the Canon and Determining Its Depth). In this work he comments on every book included in the Buddhist canon, a task he began when he was twenty-nine years old.

Zhixu's text divides the whole of the canon into four parts: Sūtra, Vinaya, Śāstra, and Miscellaneous. The Sūtra section is divided into Mahāyāna Sūtras and Hīnayāna Sūtras, and the Mahāyāna Sūtras are divided on the basis on the Five Periods: Huayan, Vaipulya, Prajñā texts, Lotus-related texts, and Mahāparinirvāṇa texts. The Vaipulya scriptures are divided into Revealed Teachings and Secret Teachings, and the Secret Teachings are further divided into Secret (i. e., Tantric) scriptures and *sādhana* literature.

The Vinaya is here divided into Mahāyāna Vinaya texts and Hīnayāna Vinaya texts. The Sastra section is divided into Mahāyāna Śāstras and Hīnayāna Śāstras. Mahāyāna Śāstras are divided into three: Śāstras that comment on scriptures, sectarian Śāstras, and Śāstras that comment on other Śāstras: this section is also broken down on the basis of those composed in India and those composed in China. The Miscellaneous section is divided into works composed in India and those composed in China, and the section of those works composed in China is divided into fifteen subsections: repentence rituals, Pure Land, Tiantai, Chan, Huayan, Weishi, Tantrism, Vinaya, compilations, biographies, defense of the faith (i. e., polemical writings), glossaries, indices, "prefaces, hymns, poems, and songs," and last, a list of works that *should* be included in the canon. Zhixu comments on a total of 1,773 titles; for each work he gives the name of the translator or author, a summary of its contents, and the names of its chapters. Zhixu's classification of Buddhist scriptures was employed in the printing of the *Dai-Nippon kōtei shukkoku daizōkyō;* the influence of Zhixu's classification can also be found in the internal arrangement of the *Taishō daizōkyō.*

The *Yuezang zhijin* was not published during Zhixu's lifetime. It was first printed by 1669, and was reprinted in 1892 in Nanking. The first full Japanese printing came in 1783, and the work is now included in volume 3 of the *Shōwa hōbō sōmokuroku,* appended to the *Taishō daizōkyō.*

Zhixu also wrote a small work, the *Fahai guanlan* (Drops of Insight into the Sea of Dharma), treating his classification of the canon, which first circulated in a printed edition of 1654. In this work Zhixu divides Buddhist literature into five sections: the Vinaya, texts dealing with "teaching and insight" (Tiantai, Huayan, and Weishi), Chan, the Secret Teachings, and Pure Land works.

SEE ALSO Buddhism, Schools of, articles on Chinese Buddhism and Mahāyāna Philosophical Schools of Buddhism; Buddhist Books and Texts, article on Exegesis and Hermeneutics; Buddhist Meditation; Buddhist Philosophy; Huayan; Nāgārjuna; Nirvāṇa; Tendaishu; Zhiyi.

BIBLIOGRAPHY

Andō Toshio. *Tendai shisōshi.* Kyoto, 1959.

Andō Toshio. *Tendaigaku: Konpon shisō to sono tenkai.* Kyoto, 1968.

Andō Toshio. *Tendaigaku ronshū.* Kyoto, 1975.

Chappell, David, and M. Ichishima. *Tiantai Buddhism: An Outline of the Fourfold Teachings. Honolulu, 1983.*

Fukuda Gyōei. *Tendaigaku gairon.* Tokyo, 1954.

Hazama Jikō. *Tendaishūshi gaisetsu.* Edited by Ōkubo Ryōjun. Tokyo, 1969.

Hibi Senshō. *Tōdai Tendaigaku josetsu.* Tokyo, 1966.

Hibi Senshō. *Tōdai Tendaigaku kenkyū.* Tokyo, 1975.

Hurvitz, Leon N. *Zhiyi (538–597): An Introduction to the Life and Ideas of a Chinese Buddhist Monk.* Brussels, 1962.

Hurvitz, Leon N., trans. *Scripture of the Lotus Blossom of the Fine Dharma.* New York, 1976.

Inaba Enjō. *Tendai shikyōgi shinshaku.* Kyoto, 1925.

Ishizu Teruji. *Tendai jissōron no kenkyū.* Tokyo, 1947.

Magnin, Paul. *La vie et l'œuvre de Huisi: Les origines de la secte bouddhique chinoise du Tiantai.* Paris, 1979.

Sakamoto Yukio. *Hokekyō no shisō to bunka.* Kyoto, 1965.

Sasaki Kentoku. *Tendai kyōgaku.* Kyoto, 1951.

Satō Tetsuei. *Tendai Daishi no kenkyū.* Kyoto, 1961.

Sekiguchi Shindai. *Tendai shoshikan no kenkyū.* Tokyo, 1954.

Shimaji Daitō. *Tendai kyōgakushi.* Tokyo, 1929.

Sun Zhengxin. "Tiantai sixiangdi yuanyuan yu qi texhi." *Xhongguo fojiaoshi lunji* 2 (1956): 687–713.

Weinstein, Stanley. "Imperial Patronage in the Formation of Tang Buddhism." In *Perspectives on the Tang,* edited by Arthur Wright and Denis Twitchett. New Haven, Conn., 1973.

LEO M. PRUDEN (1987)

TIBETAN RELIGIONS

This entry consists of the following articles:

TIBETAN RELIGIONS: AN OVERVIEW

To the Western mind, Tibet has traditionally appeared as a remote yet uniquely fascinating country. Profoundly Buddhist in all aspects of its social, cultural, and religious life, it was, until 1959, dominated by a monastic hierarchy. In the imagination of some, the so-called Land of Snow (as the Tibetans style their country) has also been regarded as the home of mysterious, superhuman beings, *mahatmas*, who, from their secret abodes in the Himalayas, give mystic guidance to the rest of humanity.

As sources become more abundant, a more realistic and complex view of Tibetan history and religion is gaining ground. The following points, which make this clear, should be kept in mind.

First, Buddhism in Tibet is represented by several traditions, monastic "orders," or schools, which have certain basic traits in common but also differ in significant respects. This must be taken into account when reading written sources, since traditional Tibetan historiography (which invariably is religious historiography) tends to reflect the more or less partisan views of the authors.

Second, Buddhism is not the only religion that must be taken into account. Buddhism penetrated into Tibet relatively late—perhaps not before the eighth century CE—and only gradually succeeded in supplanting a well-established indigenous religion that is still only fragmentarily known. Furthermore, from the tenth or eleventh century onward, the various Buddhist orders have existed alongside a religion known as Bon, which, while claiming, certainly not without some justification, continuity with the pre-Buddhist religion, is nevertheless almost indistinguishable from Buddhism in many respects. Bon has retained its own identity to this day. In addition, there remains a vast area of rites and beliefs that are neither specifically Buddhist nor Bon but may be styled "popular religion" or "the religion without a name." There is also a small minority of Tibetan Muslims (who will, however, not be treated in this article).

Third, it should be recognized that *Tibet* is a somewhat ambiguous term. In the present context it can only be used in a meaningful way to refer to an ethnically defined area—including parts of India and Nepal—that shares a common culture and language, common religious traditions, and, to a large extent, a common history. The so-called Tibetan Autonomous Region of China only comprises the western and central parts of Tibet, including the capital, Lhasa. The vast expanses of eastern and northeastern Tibet (Kham and Amdo) have since the 1950s been incorporated into Chinese provinces, but are ethnically and historically entirely Tibetan. Beyond Tibet (thus defined), Tibetan Buddhism is the official religion of Bhutan; until the early years of the twentieth century it reigned supreme in Mongolia; and it is still found among the Buriats, Tuvin, and Kalmuks in Russia. Its spread in the West will be discussed at the end of this article.

The term *Lamaism* is frequently used to refer to Tibetan religion. Tibetans often object to this term, as it could be taken to imply that Buddhism in Tibet is somehow basically different from Buddhism in other parts of Asia. To the extent that the term *Lamaism* points to the important role of the lama (Tib,, *bla ma*), or religious guide and expert in Tibetan religion, it can be said to refer equally to Buddhism and Bon, and thus it retains a certain usefulness. However, as a term intended to describe Tibetan religion as a whole, it remains one-sided and hence misleading.

THE PRE-BUDDHIST RELIGION. When Buddhism was introduced into Tibet in the eighth century, it did not enter a religious vacuum. At present, however, it is not possible to arrive at an adequate understanding of the pre-Buddhist religion because of the incompleteness of the sources.

These sources fall into two categories: ancient and later. Ancient sources are those that predate the collapse of the royal dynasty in the middle of the ninth century. Archaeological sources are practically nonexistent, since only sporadic excavations have been undertaken to date. The royal tombs at 'Phyong rgyas in central Tibet are still prominently visible but were plundered at an early date. The vast majority of the written sources are later than the introduction of Buddhism and thus often show traces of syncretic beliefs. These sources include inscriptions on pillars and bells, manuscripts containing fragments of rituals and myths or of divinatory practices, Buddhist texts that refute the ancient religion, and Chinese chronicles from the Tang dynasty (618-907). The language of these Tibetan texts, however, is archaic and all too often obscure, and the manuscripts themselves are not infrequently in a fragmentary condition.

The later sources date from the twelfth century onward and are found mainly in the historical writings of Buddhism and the Bon religion, which, between them, had by this time been completely successful in an institutional sense at least in replacing the ancient religion. Many indigenous beliefs and practices have persisted until today in the popular, nonmonastic religion, but as they are usually closely intermixed with elements of Buddhism (or, as the case may be, with Bon), it is an exceptionally delicate task to use folk religion as a basis for reconstructing the pre-Buddhist religion.

Thus the picture of pre-Buddhist religion that emerges on the basis of the ancient sources is, unfortunately, fragmentary. Certain rituals, beliefs, and parts of myths may be discerned, but the overall feeling of coherency is lacking, Those elements that are known focus largely on the person of the king. It is safe to assert that the Tibetans, at least from the sixth century onward, if not earlier, had a sacral kingship. The welfare of the country depended on the welfare of the king. Accordingly, rites of divination and sacrifice were performed to protect his life, guarantee his victory in battle, and ensure his supremacy in all things. It is said in the ancient sources that "his helmet is mighty" and his rule "great, firm, supreme," and "eternal." The king "does not change"; he is endowed with "long life."

The king was regarded not only as a vitally important personage but above all as a sacred being. According to a frequently encountered myth, the first king of Tibet descended from heaven ("the sky") and alighted on the summit of a mountain (according to later sources, he made the descent by means of a supernatural rope or ladder). At the foot of the mountain he was received by his subjects. The earliest kings were believed to have ascended bodily to heaven by the same means, thus leaving no corpse behind. Furthermore, the king was assimilated to the sacred mountain itself, just as in later popular religion the distinction between a sacred mountain and the deity residing on it was often blurred.

The myth relates that when the seventh king was killed, funerary rites had to be performed for the first time, In fact, in historical times (i.e., from the sixth century CE onward) huge funerary mounds were erected, assimilated both to the sacred mountains and to the kings, the tombs being given names that consisted of the same elements as those found in the names of the kings themselves. The death of a king was surrounded by elaborate rituals: processions, sacrifices, and the depositing on a lavish scale of all sorts of precious objects in the burial chamber. The officiating priests were known generically as *bon pos*, but apparently there were numerous specialized subgroups. Animals were sacrificed: in particular, sheep, horses, and yaks. The sacrificial sheep seem to have had an important role as guides for the deceased along the difficult road leading to the land of the dead—a land apparently conceived of in terms analogous to that of the living, Servants and officials, perhaps also members of the family, were assigned to the dead king as his "companions"; it is uncertain, however, whether they, too, actually accompanied him to the grave, or, as certain later sources suggest, only lived within the precincts of the tomb for a specified period.

A surviving early text outlines an eschatological cosmology that embodies a cyclical view of time. In a "golden age" plants and animals are transposed from their celestial home to the earth for the benefit of humanity. Virtue and "good religion" reign supreme. However, a demon breaks loose from his subterranean abode and causes a general decline in morals as well as in the physical world. Those who nevertheless follow the path of virtue and honor the gods are led after death to a land of bliss. In the meantime, the world rapidly reaches a point at which everything is destroyed, whereupon a new golden age begins in which the virtuous dead are reborn. Thus the cycle presumably—the text is not explicit—repeats itself.

Little is known of the pantheon of the pre-Buddhist religion. The universe was conceived of as having three levels: the world above (the sky), inhabited by gods (*lha*); the middle world (the earth), the abode of human beings; and the world below (the subterranean world, conceived of as aquatic), inhabited by a class of beings known as *klu* (and later assimilated to the Indian *nāgas*).

According to some sources, the heavenly world above had thirteen levels, inhabited by a hierarchy of male and female deities. Both Chinese sources and epigraphic evidence speak of the sun, the moon, and the stars being invoked as guardians and guarantors of treaties. Sacrifices in the form of various animals were made at the conclusion of the treaty of 822 between China and Tibet. By this time, however, Buddhism had appeared on the scene and the Three Jewels of Buddhism (i.e., Buddha, Dharma, and Sangha) were also invoked. A Buddhist monk with the rank of minister was at the head of the Tibetan delegation.

The subterranean beings, the *klu,* posed a constant danger to humanity, since they were particularly prone to be annoyed by activities that interfered with the surface of the land, such as plowing and digging. The *klu* could cause the eruption of diseases, especially leprosy and dropsy, that could only be cured through rites of atonement and propitiation. However, in determining the details of these rites and in obtaining specific information about the host of demons presumably populating the supernatural world of the ancient Tibetans we are to a large extent reduced to speculation on the basis of later, popular religious practices. Likewise, we meet with the names of various types of deities that are of great importance in later, popular religion: warrior god (*dgra bla*), god of the fireplace (*thab lha*), life god (*srog lha*), god of the land (*yul lha*), and so on.

It is difficult to establish which elements in the pre-Buddhist religion are truly indigenous, The later sources insist that many of the Bon priests came from countries bordering Tibet, in particular, areas to the west. After Buddhism had triumphed, the Tibetans themselves speculated whether the Bonpos were Śaiva adepts from Kashmir. Possible influences emanating from the Iranian world have also been the subject of speculation by Western scholars, so far without conclusive evidence. On the other hand, the importance of the Chinese influence, long ignored, has now been firmly established. The royal tombs have obvious Chinese prototypes, as does the sacredness of the king: he is "god son" (*lha sras*), corresponding to the Chinese emperor, the "Son of Heaven"; he is "sacred and divine" (*'phrul gyi lha*), corresponding to the Chinese *sheng-shen.* This sacredness is manifested in a supernormal intelligence and in the power to act, politically as well as militarily.

It has been suggested that the pre-Buddhist religion was transformed into a coherent political ideology in the seventh century, modeled on the Chinese cult of the emperor. This royal religion was, according to this view, referred to as *gtsug* or *gtsug lag,* a word that was defined as "the law of the gods." However, the later sources, Buddhist and Bonpo, unanimously refer to the ancient religion as Bon, a claim that is supported by recent research. In any case, the cult of the divine kings disappeared together with the organized priesthood.

BUDDHISM. Buddhism was established in Tibet under royal patronage in the eighth century. In the preceding century, Tibet had become a unified state and embarked upon a policy of military conquest resulting in the brief appearance of a powerful Central Asian empire. The introduction of Buddhism was certainly due to the need to provide this empire with a religion that enjoyed high prestige because of its well-established status in the mighty neighboring countries of India and China. The first Buddhist temple was built at Bsam yas (Samyé) in approximately 779; soon afterward the first monks were ordained. From the very start, the Buddhist monks were given economic and social privileges.

When Buddhism was introduced, the Tibetans had a choice as to whether the new religion should be brought from India or China. Modern scholarship has established the important role that China played as a source of Buddhism in the early stages of its history in Tibet. Nevertheless, it was the Indian form of Buddhism that eventually predominated. According to later sources, the Tibetan kings were guided by spiritual considerations and the proponents of Indian Buddhism emerged victorious from a doctrinal debate with Chinese monks representing a form of Chan Buddhism. However, hard political motives were surely equally important: in military and political terms China was Tibet's main rival, and China's influence at the Tibetan court would be unduly increased if it gained control of the powerful Buddhist hierarchy.

In any case, Tibet turned to India for its sacred texts, philosophical ideas, and rituals, in the same way as it had adopted, in the seventh century, an Indian alphabet. Once set on its course, Buddhism rapidly became the dominant religion, suffering only a temporary setback after the collapse of the royal dynasty in 842. In several important respects, Buddhism in Tibet remained faithful to its Indian prototype. It must, of course, be kept in mind that this prototype was, by the seventh and eighth centuries, a form of Mahāyāna Buddhism that was, on the one hand, increasingly dependent on large monastic institutions, and on the other, permeated by Tantric rites and ideas. Both these features—vast monasteries and a pervasive Tantric influence—have remained characteristic of Buddhism in Tibet. Similarly, there has been little development in the realm of philosophical ideas; the Tibetans have, on the whole, been content to play the role of exegetes, commentators, and compilers. However, the political domination that the monasteries gradually obtained was without precedent. A uniquely Tibetan feature of monastic rule was succession by incarnation—the head of an order, or of a monastery, being regarded as the reincarnation (motivated by compassion for all beings) of his predecessor. In other cases, a religious figure might be regarded as the manifestation of a deity (or a particular aspect of a deity). In the person of the fifth Dalai Lama (1617–1682) both ideas were combined. Each Dalai Lama was already regarded as the incarnation of his predecessor; the fifth, who established himself as head of the Tibetan state, also came to be regarded as the emanation or manifestation of the great *bodhisattva* Avalokiteśvara (Tib., Spyanrasgzigs), as have all subsequent Dalai Lamas down to the present, the fourteenth.

The choice of Avalokiteśvara was not made at random. As early as the twelfth or thirteenth century, Avalokiteśvara had come to be regarded in a double respect as the divine protector of Tibet. In the form of an ape he had, in ancient times, assumed the role of progenitor of the Tibetan people in order that the teachings of the Buddha might flourish in Tibet in due course; in the form of the great Tibetan king Srong bstan sgam po, who created the Tibetan empire in the seventh century, Avalokiteśvara had established Buddhism—according to this retrospective view—in the Land of Snow. The Potala Palace in Lhasa, the ancient capital, was built in its present form by the fifth Dalai Lama and made his residence; situated on a hill, it symbolically reestablished the pre-Buddhist connection between the divine king and the sacred mountain.

POPULAR RELIGION. It would be illusory to draw a sharp line of demarcation between popular and monastic religion. Nevertheless, while the study of the Mahāyāna philosophical systems and the performance of elaborate Tantric rites take place within the confines of the monasteries, monks actively participate in a wide range of ritual activities outside the monasteries, and beliefs that do not derive from Buddhism are shared by monks and laypeople alike.

These rites and beliefs may be styled "popular religion," a term that only signifies that it is nonmonastic, traditional, and related to the concerns of laypeople. It does not imply a system representing an alternative to Buddhism (or the Bon religion). For the last thousand years, Buddhist ideas have provided a general cosmological and metaphysical framework for popular religion. In many cases one may also assume that there is continuity with the pre-Buddhist religion, but it is often a delicate task to determine this continuity in precise terms.

Turning, first of all, to elements inspired by Buddhism, the most important—and conspicuous—are undoubtedly the varied and ceaseless efforts to accumulate merit. The law of moral causality (*karman*) easily turns into a sort of balance in which the effect of evil deeds in this life or in former lives may be annulled by multiplying wholesome deeds. While an act of compassion, such as ransoming a sheep destined to be slaughtered, theoretically constitutes the ideal act of virtue, the accumulation of merit generally takes a more mechanical form. Hence the incessant murmuring of sacred formulas (in particular the *mantra* of Avalokiteśvara, "Om mani padme hum"), the spinning of prayer wheels (ranging in size from hand-held wheels to enormous cylinders housed in special buildings), the carving of *mantras* on stones (which may eventually grow into walls several miles in length, so-called *mani*-walls), and the hoisting of banners and strings of flags on which prayers are printed ("prayer flags"). Ritual circumambulation of holy places, objects, and persons is also a distinctly Buddhist, as well as truly popular, practice. Showing generosity toward monks and observing—lightly or scrupulously, as the case may be—the universal precepts of Buddhism (particularly the prohibition against taking the life of any living being, however small) are ethical norms that Tibetans share with all Buddhists.

Pilgrimages constitute an important religious activity: above all to the holy city of Lhasa—sanctified by its ancient temples and (since the seventeenth century) the presence of the Dalai Lama—but also to innumerable monasteries, shrines, and caves in which relics of holy men and women may be seen, honored, and worshiped. Sacred mountains, such as Mount Kailash in western Tibet, attract a stream of pilgrims who circumambulate, perhaps for weeks or months, the holy abode of the chosen deity. The supreme pilgrimage is the long journey to the sacred sites of Buddhism in India and Nepal (Bodh Gayā, Rājagṛha, Lumbinī, Sārnāth); although the flow of pilgrims to India virtually ceased after the thirteenth century, it again became possible in the twentieth century.

Ritual practices, while generally having an overall Buddhist conceptual framework, often contain elements that point back to the pre-Buddhist religion. One such element, frequently met with, is the "ransom" *(glud)* in the form of a small human figurine that is offered as a gesture of propitiation to demons. In the New Year rituals as traditionally practiced in Lhasa, the *glud* was in fact a human scapegoat who was driven out of the city and who, in earlier times, was symbolically killed.

As in other Buddhist countries, regional and local deities have remained objects of worship, generally performed by laypeople. In particular, the deities connected with (or even identified with) sacred mountains, powerful gods of the land (*yul lha*), are worshiped during seasonal festivals with the burning of juniper branches that emit clouds of fragrant smoke; horse races; archery contests; drinking bouts; and songs extolling the might of the deity, the beauty of the land, the fleetness of its horses, and the valor of its heroes. These gods have a martial nature and are accordingly known as enemy gods (*dgra bla*); they are also known as kings (*rgyal po*), Usually they are depicted as mounted warriors, dressed in archaic mail and armor and wearing plumed helmets.

The house ideally reproduces the outside world, and it has its own guardian deities, such as the god of the fireplace (*thab lha*). Care must be taken to avoid polluting the fireplace in any way, as this angers the god. On the flat rooftops are altars dedicated to the "male god" (*pho lha*) and the "female god" (*mo lha*) and a banner representing the enemy god. The "male" and "female" gods are tutelary deities of the household, supervising the activities of its male and female members, respectively. The "enemy god" is —in spite of its name—a deity who protects the entire household or, as a member of the retinue of the local "god of the land," the district. The worship of these gods on the rooftops corresponds to that performed in their honor on mountaintops and in passes: spears and arrows dedicated to them are stacked by the altar and juniper twigs are burned amid fierce cries of victory and good luck.

The person, too, possesses a number of tutelary deities residing in different parts of the body. Every person is also accompanied, from the moment of birth, by a "white" god and a "black" demon whose task it is, after death, to place the white and the black pebbles—representing the good and evil deeds one has done in this life—on the scales of the judge of the dead. The basic opposition between "white" and "black," good and evil, is a fundamental concept in Tibetan popular religion and figures prominently in pre-Buddhist traditions as well. Iranian influences have been suggested, but it seems likely that the Chinese conceptual dichotomy of *yin* and *yang* lies closer at hand.

The ancient cosmological scheme of sky, earth, and underworld remains fundamental in popular religion. In particular, the cult of the *klu*—subterranean or aquatic beings easily irritated by activities such as house building or plowing, which provoke them to afflict people as well as animals with various diseases—remains widespread and provides a direct link to the pre-Buddhist religion.

An important aspect of popular religion (and, indeed, of the pre-Buddhist religion) is the emphasis on knowing the origins not only of the world but of all features of the landscape, as well as of elements of culture and society that are important to man. Tibetans have a vast number of myths centering on this theme of origins; while some of them have a purely narrative function, others serve to legitimate a particular ritual and must be recited in order that the ritual may become effective.

Rites of divination and of healing in which deities "descend" into a male or female medium (*lha pa,* "god-possessed," or *dpa' bo,* "hero") and speak through it are an important part of religious life, and such mediums are frequently consulted. Other, simpler means of divination are also extremely widespread.

A special kind of medium is the *sgrun pa,* the bard who in a state of trance can recite for days on end the exploits of the great hero Gesar. Regarded as an emanation of the *bodhisattva* Avalokiteśvara, Gesar has been approved by the Buddhist hierarchy; but essentially he is a popular, epic hero, a mighty king and warrior. His epic is a storehouse of myths, folklore, and pan-Eurasian narrative motifs, and is widespread outside Tibet in the Hindu Kush and, above all, among the Mongolians. Other visionaries (*'das log*) travel in trance to the Buddhist purgatories, their bodies lying as if dead; on awakening, they give detailed accounts of the punishment awaiting sinners beyond the grave. Still others find hidden "treasures" (*gter ma*) consisting of texts or sacred objects; indeed, this has remained until today an important way of adding to the body of authoritative texts translated from Sanskrit (and, to a lesser extent, from Chinese), for the "treasure-discoverers" (*gter ston*) claim to bring to light texts that have been hidden away (especially by the eighth-century Tantric master Padmasambhava) during times of persecution of Buddhism, to be rediscovered, usually with the assistance of supernatural beings, for the benefit of humanity when the time is ripe. Finally, ecstatics and visionaries point the way to earthly paradises such as the mythical kingdom of Shambhala or to hidden valleys, untouched by man, in the secret recesses of the Himalayas.

Summing up, Tibetan popular religion may perhaps be characterized as an infinitely varied attempt to circumvent, or at least mitigate, the mechanism of the law of moral causality. According to orthodox Buddhist doctrine, this law is inexorable and its justice cannot be avoided; however, since one cannot know what acts one has committed in the past for which one may have to suffer in the future, the intolerable rigor of the law of cause and effect is in practice modified by a religious worldview in which the destiny of the individual also depends on ritual acts and on spiritual beings—benevolent as well as malevolent—who may at least be approached and at best be manipulated.

BON. It has already been noted that a class of ritual experts in the pre-Buddhist religion were known as *bon pos* and that certain early sources indicate that their religion was known as Bon. In any case, the later sources all agree that the pre-Buddhist religion was in fact known as Bon, and these sources tend to describe the struggle between Bon and Buddhism in dramatic terms. This is true not only of the later Buddhist sources but also of texts emanating from a religious tradition, explicitly styling itself Bon, that emerged in the eleventh century, if not before.

While virtually indistinguishable from Buddhism in such aspects as philosophy, monastic life, ritual, and iconographical conventions, this "later" Bon has always insisted that it represents the religion that prevailed in Tibet before the coming of Buddhism. In spite of occasional syncretic efforts on both sides, the Buddhists have tended to regard Bon as heretical, and not infrequently the term *bonpo* has been used in the sense of "heretic," "black magician," and so forth.

Two points about Bon must be made. First, the historical background of the Bon religion that emerged in the eleventh century is far from clear. There is a significant element of continuity with the pre-Buddhist religion, but nothing approaching identity. Second, it is seriously misleading to identify Bon with popular religion in general. On the level of popular religion, followers of Bon and Buddhism alike share the same beliefs and perform, to a very large extent, the same rituals, although details may differ (for example, the Bonpos spin their prayer wheels and perform circumambulations in the opposite direction than the Buddhists do, i.e., counterclockwise; they worship different deities and hence use other *mantras*, and so forth). These correspondences do not represent a case of "perversion," "contradiction," or the like (as has been too hastily suggested), for Bon and Buddhism share the same religious ideals and goals, and they approach them by essentially similar means.

TIBETAN RELIGION TODAY. An overview of Tibetan religion would be incomplete without an attempt to take stock of the situation in the early years of the twenty-first century. The most significant single fact is the downfall of monastic religion. Starting in the 1950s and culminating in the period of the Cultural Revolution in the 1960s and 1970s, the Chinese unleashed a violent antireligious campaign in Tibet that resulted in the total destruction of monastic life. A large number of monks were killed, and the rest were, without exception, defrocked. Most monasteries were razed to the ground, and others were converted into secular buildings such as granaries or army barracks. Vast libraries were destroyed, and ritual objects, Buddha images, and relics were systematically profaned. At the height of the campaign, even the most insignificant expression of religious faith would be severely punished by Chinese soldiers or Red Guards.

The new and more pragmatic policy in China began to take effect in Tibet around 1980. A number of buildings, officially regarded as historical monuments, were carefully restored; a limited number of monks were installed in a number of the largest monasteries: ʿBras-spungs (Drepung) near Lhasa, Bkra shis lhun po (Tashilhunpo) outside Gshis ka rtse (Shigatse), and Bla brang (Labrang) and Sku ʾbum (Kumbum) in eastern Tibet; a few temples were reopened for worship; and hundreds of other monasteries were reconstructed on a voluntary basis by the Tibetans themselves. On the whole, religious activity seems to be tolerated as long as it does not interfere with government policies. Tibet has in fact seen a remarkable resurgence of religious fervor that finds outlet, among other things, in the reconstruction of monasteries and the traditional practices of the popular religion, including extended pilgrimages to sacred mountains and other sites throughout Tibet. Within the limits set by the political and economic conditions imposed on Tibet, it is clear that religious belief and practice remain a fundamental factor in the overall situation in the Land of Snow.

Among the Tibetan refugees in India and Nepal, religious life flourishes, to a large extent along traditional lines. There is a tendency to emphasize monastic life together with those aspects of Buddhism that are common to all Buddhists. In the West, many Tibetan lamas have become highly successful "gurus," and numerous Tibetan Buddhist centers have been established, generally focusing on the teachings of one particular order and emphasizing meditation and ritual rather than conventional, scholastic studies. In exile, the fourteenth Dalai Lama, Bstan ʾdzin rgya mtsho (Tenzin Gyatsho; b. 1935), has become an internationally respected Buddhist figure, a Nobel Peace Prize laureate in 1989 and a guide to the Buddhist way to human happiness and world peace through the development of insight and compassion.

SEE ALSO Avalokiteśvara; Dalai Lama; Gesar; Kingship, article on Kingship in East Asia; Merit, article on Buddhist Concepts; Pilgrimage, article on Tibetan Pilgrimage; Worship and Devotional Life, article on Buddhist Devotional Life in East Asia; Yinyang Wuxing.

BIBLIOGRAPHY

Tibetan religion is a field in which quasi-esoteric literature abounds. However, there are also many works of serious scholarship available to the general reader. The following survey lists titles that are easily available.

General Studies

A classic and still useful introduction to the subject is Charles A. Bell's *The Religion of Tibet* (1931; reprint, Oxford. 1968). More recently, several excellent studies have been published: David L. Snellgrove and Hugh E. Richardson's *A Cultural History of Tibet* (1968; reprint, Boulder, 1980); Rolf A. Stein's *Tibetan Civilization,* translated by J. E. Stapleton Driver (Stanford, Calif., 1972) and republished in a revised French edition as *La civilisation tibétaine* (Paris, 1981); Giuseppe Tucci's *The Religions of Tibet,* translated by Geoffrey Samuel (Berkeley, 1980); Geoffrey Samuel's *Civilized Shamans, Buddhism in Tibetan Societies* (Washington and London, 1993); and Donald S. Lopez Jr. (ed) *Religions of Tibet in Practice* (Princeton, NJ, 1997). A particularly lucid exposition is Anne-Marie Blondeau's "Les religions du Tibet," in *Histoire des religions,* edited by Henri-Charles Puech, vol. 3 (Paris, 1976), pp. 233–329.

Pre-Buddhist Religion

Most studies of the pre-Buddhist religion can be found only in specialized publications. The works of Snellgrove and Richardson, Stein, and Blondeau, however, all contain pertinent discussions based on their own research. A useful study of the early inscriptions is H. E. Richardson's *A Corpus of Early Tibetan Inscriptions* (London, 1985).

Buddhism

Snellgrove and Richardson's work is particularly strong on the formation of the orders and the subsequent political history of the church. Tucci's *The Religions of Tibet* contains a most useful survey of Buddhist doctrine and monastic life. A concise presentation of Tibetan Buddhism is provided in Per Kvaerne's "Tibet: The Rise and Fall of a Monastic Tradition," in *The World of Buddhism: Buddhist Monks and Nuns in Society and Culture,* edited by Heinz Bechert and Richard F. Gombrich (London, 1984), pp. 253–270. For a discussion of ritual and meditation, see Stephan Beyer's *The Cult of Tārā: Magic and Ritual in Tibet* (Berkeley, 1973).

Popular Religion

General surveys of Tibetan popular religion are given by Stein in *Tibetan Civilization* and in Per Kvaerne's "Croyances populaires et folklores au Tibet" in *Mythes et croyances du monde entier,* edited by André Akoun, vol. 4 (Paris, 1985), pp. 157–169, and Satmten G. Karmay, *The Arrow and the Spindle, Studies in History, Myths, Rituals and Beliefs in Tibet* (Kathmandu 1998). A basic reference work is René de Nebesky-Wojkowitz's *Oracles and Demons of Tibet, The Cult and Iconography of the Tibetan Protective Deities* (1956; reprint, Graz, 1975). The reprint edition contains an introduction by Per Kvaerne in which numerous corrections and additions to the earlier edition are provided. A useful supplement to this work is Tadeusz Skorupski's *Tibetan Amulets* (Bangkok, 1983). A major study of ritual texts has been published by Christina Klaus, *Schutz vor den Naturgefahren: Tibetische Ritualtexte aus dem Rin chen gter mdzod ediert, Übersetzt und Kommentiert* (Wiesbaden, 1985). A discussion of Tibetan myths intended for the nonspecialist is provided by Per Kvaerne in a series of articles in *Dictionnaire des mythologies,* edited by Yves Bonnefoy (Paris, 1981), vol. 1, pp. 42–45, 249–252; vol. 2, pp. 194–195, 381–384, 495–497. A survey of the most important pilgrimages is provided in Anne-Marie Blondeau's "Les pèlerinages tibétains," in *Les pèlerinages,* edited by Anne-Marie Esnoul et al. (Paris, 1960), pp. 199–245. A collection of more specialised articles is Alex McKay (ed.) *Pilgrimage in Tibet* (Richmond, Surrey, 1998). The most complete study of Tibetan festivals is Martin Brauen's *Feste in Ladakh* (Graz, 1980).

Among numerous studies published in recent years on the cult of mountains, Toni Huber, *The Cult of Pure Crystal Mountain, Popular Pilgrimage and Visionary Landscape in Southeast Tibet* (New York and Oxford, 1999) is likely to become a standard work.

There is a considerable body of literature on the Gesar epic. The fundamental study is R. A. Stein's *L'épopée et le barde au Tibet* (Paris, 1959). Several translations of the text exist, mainly in the form of summaries. The most easily accessible is probably that of Alexandra David-Neel, *La vie surhumaine de Guésar de Ling* (Paris, 1931), translated with the collaboration of Violet Sydney as *The Superhuman Life of Gesar of Ling* (1933; rev. ed., London, 1959). More scholarly translations are R. A. Stein's *L'épopée tibétaine de Gesar dans la version lamaïque de Ling* (Paris, 1956), and Mireille Helffer's *Les chants dans l'épopée tibétaine de Gesar d'après le livre de la course de cheval* (Geneva, 1977). On visionary journeys to Sambhala and related phenomena, see Edwin Bernbaum's *The Way to Shambhala: A Search for the Mythical Kingdom beyond the Himalayas* (New York, 1980).

Bon

An important translation of a Bon text is David L. Snellgrove's *The Nine Ways of Bon: Excerpts from the gZi-brjid* (1967; reprint, Boulder, 1980). Samten G. Karmay surveys the Bon religion in "A General Introduction to the History and Doctrines of Bon," *Memoirs of the Research Department of the Toyo Bunko,* no. 3 (1975): 171–218. On Bon literature, see Per Kvaerne's "The Canon of the Bonpos," *Indo-Iranian Journal* 16 (1975): 18–56, 96–144. See also the works of Snellgrove and Richardson, Stein, and Blondeau cited above.

Contemporary Religion

Peter H. Lehmann and Jay Ullai's *Tibet: Das stille Drama auf dem Dach der Erde,* edited by Rolf Winter (Hamburg, 1981), and on Bon art and iconography, Per Kvaerne, *The Bon Religion of Tibet, The Icongragphy of a Living Tradition* (London 1995, reprint 2001). The book is remarkable not least for its photographic documentation of the years following the Cultural Revolution. The situation at the end of the twentieth centruy is discussed in Melvyn C. Goldstein and Mathew T. Kapstein (eds.) *Buddhism in Contemprorary Tibet, Religious Revivial and Cultural Identity* (Berkeley, 1998).

PER KVAERNE (1987 AND 2005)

TIBETAN RELIGIONS: HISTORY OF STUDY

Until the 1980s, scholars took a threefold approach to the study of Tibetan religions. First, they used Tibetan materials to supplement Indian and Chinese materials; second, Western scholars were drawn by a fascination with Tibetan Buddhism itself; and third, they studied the numerous Tibetan texts completed since the 1970s by Tibetans who were living either in exile or in Tibet and China. Events and developments of momentous importance for research into the religious life of Tibet occurred during the twentieth century. These events drove some Tibetans into a Western-oriented study of their own religion, brought Western scholars into close contact with learned lamas, and drew scholarly attention to a very early period of Bon and Buddhism in Tibet, while almost simultaneously revealing contemporary practices with a precision and on a scale previously impossible for various political or geographical reasons.

The first event was the discovery in 1905 of Tibetan texts from the eighth to eleventh centuries in a cave along the Silk Road at Dunhuang, China. For the next several years, British, French, Russian, and Japanese scholars were able to study manuscript materials that were much older than those previously known and that were contemporary to the events they described. These materials revolutionized the study of Bon and Buddhism in Tibet, as well as the study of the religious currents flowing through the Tibetan empire from the East and the West. The development of the study of the Dunhuang manuscripts has been of paramount importance in the understanding of Tibetan religions, which for decades had been studied only from a Buddhist perspective, and historically only from a relatively late perspective. Following the studies of Gustave Charles Toussaint and Marcelle Lalou in Paris, one of the most innovative books in this field was *Études Tibétaines dédiées à la mémoire de Marcelle Lalou* (1971), which contained articles by Ariane Macdonald, Rolf A. Stein, and others, and which presented a truly new perspective on the religions of Tibet. The work begun with this volume was later completed by the publication of selections of the Pelliot *Choix de documents tibétains conservés à la bibliothèque nationale* (1978–2001) by Ariane Macdonald, Yoshiro Imaeda, and T. Takeuchi.

The second event was the Chinese invasion of Tibet in the 1950s. Numerous lamas took up residence thereafter in Nepal, northern India, Europe, the United States, and elsewhere. These exiles took some of their vast literature and physical culture with them, and made it accessible to Western scholars. In the late 1980s, Tibetans in China also started to publish a great number of texts through state-owned publishing houses, and later privately. Some of these texts had been previously unknown to many scholars, and they added to the corpus of materials already available.

A third important development occurred in the early 1980s with the relative opening of Tibetan areas, which, along with inexpensive air travel, allowed many researchers to travel and do fieldwork in Tibet. A fourth major development was the advent of the Internet and the digitalization of many Tibetan texts beginning at the end of the twentieth century.

Since the mid-1980s, therefore, there has been no dearth of publications about the religion of Tibet. There has been, however, a shift from a purely philological approach to a more interdisciplinary approach that incorporates history, anthropology, and even art history (numerous exhibitions of Tibetan art have been accompanied by expert catalogues). This shift was certainly the result of scholars being able to travel to Tibet and adjacent areas, and it was also a reflection of the monastic background of some writers. Moreover, the role of women in Tibetan Buddhism, which was all but ignored in earlier writings, became prominent, along with the study of the Bon tradition and Tibetan popular religion, including local cults that are not necessarily Buddhist or have become "buddhicized." These trends in scholarship have profoundly transformed the study of Tibetan religions.

One of the first major contributions to the advancement of the field was the United States Library of Congress project initiated in the 1970s in New Delhi by Gene E. Smith. This program encouraged Tibetans to publish previously unknown texts and disseminate them to academic institutions in the West. Smith added further to the study of the field by establishing the Tibetan Buddhist Resource Center, which promotes research and scholarship in Tibetan Buddhism through digital text and image preservation. Similar projects include the Tsadra Foundation, sponsored by the Trace Foundation, which publishes Tibetan texts and translations. The Trace Foundation has also established the online Latse Contemporary Tibetan Cultural Library, which offers texts and other research materials and sponsors programs for people interested in Tibetan culture. The Tibetan and Himalayan Digital Library, sponsored by the University of Virginia, publishes multilingual and multimedia texts and resources, as well as creative works concerned with the culture and history of Tibet and the Himalayas. Digital versions of the Dunhuang Tibetan documents are available at Old Tibetan Documents Online, a website established by a group of Japanese scholars. Other useful websites include Digital Himalaya, sponsored by Department of Social Anthropology at Cambridge University and the Anthropology Department at Cornell University, and Tibet Visual History Online, sponsored by the Pitt Rivers Museum in Oxford. Such websites are popular with researchers because they include old and previously unavailable footage and photographs, and they constitute a good base for religious studies from an anthropological approach. In 2002, the Tibetology team of the French National Center for Scientific Research inaugurated the first digital academic journal on Tibetan studies: *Revue d'Etudes Tibétaines*. In addition, the major Tibetan religious traditions and lamas have their own websites, where one can find texts, teachings, and photos, as well as polemical writings. In 2003, in Oxford, Tibetologists from all over the world who had gathered for the International Association of Tibetan Studies seminar decided to launch the digital *Journal of the International Association of Tibetan Studies* (JIATS).

The use of the Internet is truly a revolution for a field as previously obscure as the study of Tibetan religions; the Internet allows information to flow even to remote areas of the Tibetan world. The great Western pioneer student of Tibet's religious culture was the Hungarian traveler Alexander Csoma de Körös (c. 1784–1842), some of whose work is still valuable, while that of many of his near-contemporaries is completely outdated. His work parallels that of the founders of Buddhist studies in Europe, who worked from Indian sources. His *Notices on the Life of Shakya, Extracted from the Tibetan Authorities* (1838) is an early work in the field, as is F. Anton von Schiefner's "Eine tibetische Lebensbeschreibung Cakyamuni's, des Begründers des Buddhatums" (*Mémoires de l'academie impériale des sciences de Saint Pétersbourg* 6, 1851).

The best of the early monographs is Emil Schlagintweit's *Buddhism in Tibet, Illustrated by Literary Documents and Objects of Religious Worship* (1863), which deals comprehensively with the Buddhist world in Tibet from its basis in Indian Mahāyāna theory to local customs. Equally rich in data is L. Austine Waddell's *The Buddhism of Tibet, or Lamaism, with its Mystic Cults, Symbolism, and Mythology, and in its Relation to Indian Buddhism* (1895). Giuseppe Tucci's *Die Religionen Tibets* (1970; translated as *Religions of Tibet*, [1980]) is enhanced by Tucci's abundant use of Tibetan sources and his high level of knowledge about the philosophical and historical background of Tibetan religions. One of the most important newer books in the field is *Indo-Tibetan Buddhism: Indian Buddhists and their Tibetan Successors* by David L. Snellgrove (1987). The publication of Gene E. Smith's previously scattered articles and introductions—*Among Tibetan Texts: History and Literature of the Himalayan Plateau* (2001)—has also reinforced the study of Buddhist transmissions in Tibet.

Tibetan scholars have written many works on the introduction and spread of Buddhism in their country and on its origins in India. Studies by European scholars of three such works are particularly important: Schiefner's *Târanâthas Geschichte des Buddhismus in Indien* (1869), a translation of Tāranātha's 1608 *Tibetan-Language History of Buddhism in India*, has sufficient interpretations and explanations by the translator to make it useful for the student of Tibetan Buddhism; and Eugene Obermiller's *History of Buddhism* (1931–1932), a translation of Bu ston's *Chos 'byung*, contains information on Tibet, but Indian subjects predominate. The great achievement in scholarship in this area is George N. Roerich's *The Blue Annals* (1949–1953), a translation of 'Gos Lo tsa ba Gzon nu dpal's *Deb ther snon po*; this classic text describes major developments in Tibet up to the 1470s. Roerich's diligence as a scholar, combined with the various indexes to the text, have made this translation an invaluable reference work.

Another important work is *The Nyingma School of Tibetan Buddhism: Its Fundamentals and History* (1991, 2d ed., 2002), a translation of *Dudjom Rinpoche* by Matthew Kapstein and Gyurme Dorje. Enriched with maps and several indexes, this work is an excellent resource for the history of Buddhism in Tibet, and more particularly for the Rnying ma (Nyingma) school. Austrian, German, and Japanese scholars still lead the field in philological works on the Indian Buddhist texts used by Tibetans, as well as on the Tibetan canons.

A number of works attempting synthetic interpretations of major events or trends in Tibetan religious history appeared in the twentieth century. In particular, Charles Bell's *The Religion of Tibet* (1931) analyzes the history of Buddhism until the early twentieth century, including Tibet's influence on Mongolian Buddhism and the political dimensions of the rule of the Dalai Lamas. In the guise of a description of a series of Tibetan paintings, Tucci's *Tibetan Painted Scrolls* (1949) contains much (well-indexed) material on topics ranging from mythology to iconography that concerns the history of Tibetan religions and sectarian developments.

Eva Dargyay's *The Rise of Esoteric Buddhism in Tibet* (2d ed., 1979) provides data on the Rnying ma pa religious tradition; this work discusses Rnying ma pa's "discovered Treasure" literature and its history. The study of the "discovered" religious writings is now a subfield by itself as a result of access to Tibetan masters and a better knowledge of the transmission lineages. One of the pioneers was Anne-Marie Blondeau, who wrote several articles. Janet Gyatso also published a series of articles on the Treasure movement. Also noteworthy is the *Life and Revelations of Pema Lingpa* (2003) by Sarah Harding and Ganteng Tulku.

The basis of all Buddhist practice is yoga and meditation, and studies of Tibetan versions of such practices with commentaries by learned lamas are appearing in great numbers. Among older established studies that are still frequently consulted, the following are notable either for their lucidity of presentation or their accompanying commentary. Herbert Guenther's translation of Sgam po pa's twelfth-century account of Tibetan religious practice, *The Jewel Ornament of Liberation* (1971), and Guenther's *The Life and Teaching of Nāropa* (1963) on an eleventh-century yogin, are characterized by a sophisticated analysis of the psychology of Buddhist practice. A clear exposition is made by Tenzin Gyatso (Bstan 'dzin rgya mtsho, the fourteenth Dalai Lama) in *The Opening of the Wisdom Eye and the History of the Advancement of Buddhadharma in Tibet* (1966). An analysis of philosophical positions, meditation, and ritual is found in Ferdinand D. Lessing and Alex Wayman's *Mkhas grub rje's Fundamentals of the Buddhist Tantras* (1968), a translation of a fifteenth-century work. Rdzogs chen, a meditative and philosophical teaching common to both the Rnying ma pa and Bon traditions, is explained by Samten Karmay in *The Great Perfection: A Philosophical and Meditative Teaching in Tibetan Buddhism* (1988).

Traditional Buddhist biographies (*rnam thar*) are being used more and more as sources to put meat on the bones of doctrinal studies, but they are also translated into English to cater to an interested audience. Perhaps the best of the earlier efforts is Jacques Bacot's *La vie de Marpa le "traducteur"* (1937). Also worthy of recommendation is Rolf A. Stein's *Vie et chants de 'Brug-pa Kun-legs le yogin* (1972), and of course the different translations of the great saint and poet Mi la ras pa's biography and mystic songs. A more recent study of autobiographical writing in Tibet, especially by visionary yogis, is Janet Gyatso's *Apparitions of the Self: The Secret Autobiographies of a Tibetan Visionary* (1998).

An excellent work intended as a manual for students is *Religions of Tibet in Practice*, edited by Donald Lopez (1997). In addition, *Tibetan Literature: Studies in Genre*, edited by José Cabezón and Roger R. Jackson (1996), covers mainly religious literature.

Westerners who went through Tibetan scholastic education as monks in the 1970s, including Robert Thurman and Jeffrey Hopkins, have published numerous books that provide insight on religious studies in a traditional context. Such works include Georges Dreyfus's *The Sound of Two Hands Clapping: The Education of a Tibetan Buddhist Monk* (2003). Each of these authors holds a chair in religious studies in an American university. Matthieu Ricard, an active monk, contributed to the field with his translation of *The Life of Shabkar: An Autiobiography of a Tibetan Yogin* (1994), as well as his own books and the archiving of the teachings and writings of his lama, Dilgo Khyentse Rinpoche (1910–1991).

In the 1980s, with the importance given to feminist studies in the West, there was a sudden interest in the role that female figures played in Tibetan religions as nuns or partners of lamas, or by themselves. Among the pioneers in translation of women's biographies was Keith Dowman with *Sky Dancer: The Secret Life and Songs of the Lady Yeshe Tsogyel* (1984), and Tsultrim Allione with *Women of Wisdom* (1984). Later, Hanna Havnevik published her dissertation on Tibetan Buddhist nuns, *Karma Lekshe Tsomo, Sisters in Solitude: Two Traditions of Buddhist Monastic Ethics for Women* (1996), and Janice Willis edited *Feminine Ground: Essays on Women and Tibet* (1995). In *Machig Labdrön and the Foundations of Chöd* (1996) Jérôme Edou studied the extraordinary life of this eleventh-century *yoginī*, whose teachings are still practiced today; this work was followed by *The Lives and Liberation of Princess Mandarava*, translated by Lama Chonam and Sangye Khandro (1998)

The Bon religion has been much less studied than Buddhism. Its literature and teachers were not accessible, and some Tibetan Buddhists succeeded in giving early Western visitors a highly inaccurate view of its origins and practices. This trend is now reversed, and by the end of the twentieth century there was great interest in Bon studies, often linked to the Western Tibetan region of Zhang zhung. The field is now flourishing under the impetus of pioneers like Per Kvaerne in Norway and Samten Karmay in France. Bon studies has become linked to the publications program initiated in 2000 by Yasuhiko Nagano at the Ethnological Museum of Osaka; published works include *New Horizons in Bon Studies* (2000), *A Survey of Bonpo Monasteries and Temples in Tibet and the Himalaya* (2003), and *The Call of the Blue Cuckoo: An Anthology of Nine Bonpo Texts on Myths and Rituals* (2002), all edited by Nagano and Karmay. One of the first valuable contributions to the study of Bon mythology and a veritable catalog of the Bon pantheon was A. H. Francke's *gZer mig: A Book of the Tibetan Bonpos*, a translation that was published in five volumes between 1924 and 1949.

Where are the origins of Bon to be sought—beyond Tibet or within? What is its relationship to Buddhism and other religions, in particular to those of Iran? How did Bon evolve? What can be called Bon? These questions are still debated by scholars. Studies on Bon that were particularly valuable include a lengthy essay in Giuseppe Tucci's *Die Religionen Tibets*; Samten Karmay's "A General Introduction to the History and Doctrines of Bon" in *Memoirs of the Research Department of the Toyo Bunko* 33 (1975): 171–218; as well as Karmay's *Treasury of Good Sayings: A Tibetan History of Bon* (1972). An extensive doctrinal text was presented by David L. Snellgrove in *The Nine Ways of Bon: Excerpts from the gZi-brjid* (1967). An important study and the first work on Bon yoga is Per Kvaerne's "Bonpo Studies: The A Khrid System of Meditation," in *Kailash* 1 (1973): 19–50 and 247–332, as well as his important work, *The Bon Religion of Tibet: The Iconography of a Living Tradition* (1995). Dan Martin's *Unearthing Bon Treasures: Life and Contested Legacy of a Tibetan Scripture Revealer* (2001) deals with a Tibetan "text discoverer" and includes a general bibliography of Bon. Martin updated this bibliography in "Bon Bibliography: An Annotated List of Recent Publications," in *Revue d'Etudes Tibétaines* 4 (2003): 61–77, which demonstrates the contemporary strength of Bon studies. Martin joined forces with Per Kvaerne and Yasuhiko Nagano to edit *A Catalogue of the Bon Kanjur* (2003). In addition, Karmay and Nagano edited *A Catalogue of the New Collection of Bonpo Katen Texts* (2001). In France, Jean-Luc Achard is researching the Dzogchen tradition of the Bon and Rnying ma schools. Achard has published several articles in the *Revue d'Etudes Tibétaines,* as well as the book *L'Essence perlée du secret: Recherches philologiques et historiques sur l'origine de la Grande Perfection dans la tradition rNying ma pa* (1999).

The literature and adherents of the normative Buddhism and Bon traditions were the first elements to strike Alexander Csoma de Körös and his successors, and they remain today the center of focus in Tibetology. However, popular religion and its numerous cultic manifestations have increasingly become the topic of studies, especially in Europe since the late 1980s. One such study is Françoise Pommaret's *Les revenants de l'au-delà dans le monde Tibétain: Sources littéraires et traditions vivantes* (1989).

Of course, the interest in Tibet's epic hero, King Gesar, an important figure in popular Tibetan literature and religion, dates back to the eighteenth century when Mongolian-language texts of the epic became known to Western travelers. A comprehensive analysis of the religious and ethnographic data in these materials certainly lies far in the future, but two works may be cited here that analyze different versions of Gesar's life and deeds and thus give an idea of the variety of information available: A. H. Francke's *Der Frühlings- und Wintermythus der Kesarsage: Beiträge zur Kenntnis der vorbuddhistishchen Religion Tibets und Ladakhs* (1902) and Rolf A. Stein's *Recherches sur l'épopée et le barde au Tibet* (1959). The former study shows the influence of the "nature mythology" school of religious studies, while the latter includes sections dealing with Buddhist, Bon, and popular religious influences and motifs. Gesar studies are a subfield in themselves, with Chinese scholars taking a keen interest in the matter.

Among early general studies on popular religion in Tibet, an extensive analysis of the iconography and hierarchical ordering of Tibet's spirits and deities in ritual and literature was René de Nebesky-Wojkowitz's *Oracles and Demons of Tibet* (1956; 2d rev. ed., 1975). Rolf A. Stein's *Tibetan Civilization* (1972) also dwelt on popular religion.

Many anthropologists have studied what is sometimes called shamanist practices in Tibet and the Tibetan areas. Geoffrey Samuel's *Civilized Shamans: Buddhism in Tibetan Societies* (1993) is a challenging and innovative work on the links between Tibetan Buddhism and shamanism. Anthropologists with the opportunity to do fieldwork started studying local deities more or less integrated into Buddhism, as well as different cults and other religious manifestations. These were important in understanding the daily religious life of the people and their relation to their territory. Among different publications, four collections should be noted: *Mandala and Landscape,* edited by A. W. Macdonald (1997); *Reflections of the Mountain: Essays on the History and Social Meaning of the Mountain Cult in Tibet and the Himalayas,* edited by Anne-Marie Blondeau and Ernst Steinkellner (1996); *Tibetan Mountain Deities: Their Cults and Representations,* edited by Blondeau (1998); and *Territory and Identity in Tibet and the Himalayas, Tibetan Studies in Honour of Anne-Marie Blondeau,* edited by Katia Buffetrille and Hildegard Diemberger (2002).

Alex McKay's edition of *Pilgrimage in Tibet* (1998) was another important contribution to the study of religion as practiced by the common people. The history of Tibetan religions must also take into account the numerous publications and translations done in Tibetan Buddhist centers in the West, as well as the biographies of lamas written directly in Western languages. In most cases, such works were not produced as contributions to the field of study, but rather as a means of propagating Buddhist thought. Still, the material they present is often new and interesting for the researcher, while appealing to a wider audience. Two such works that were successful worldwide were *The Words of My Perfect Teacher* by Patrul Rinpoche (1998) and especially *The Tibetan Book of Living and Dying* by Sogyal Rinpoche (2002). Also noteworthy is Philippe Cornu's handy and informative *Dictionnaire encyclopédique du Bouddhisme* (2001).

Religious studies scholars and followers of Tibetan religious traditions have begun engaging in fruitful exchange and interface, although both are often still wary of each other. The academics tend to scorn the disciples' lack of critical approach, and the disciples tend to condescend towards the scholars' lack of "inner understanding" of the religious traditions. A promising development is that Tibetan and Chinese scholars from different research institutes and universities in China have begun to show interest in religious studies, mostly in the Gesar epic and in popular religion. The Tibetan and Chinese scholars concentrate mostly on historical, ethnographic, and sociological subjects. Working as researchers in different academies and institutes, they have good opportunities to publish their studies. They also participate in the seminar of the International Association of Tibetan Studies (IATS), which is held every four years and where they exchange ideas with their Western and Japanese colleagues.

Since the 1980s the amount of written literature and the number of learned informants from all traditions has increased dramatically. Tibetans for the most part feel a great urge to accommodate Western research into their traditions, and many are now working in research institutions in Europe, Japan, and North America. Indeed, Tibetan studies are now awash in resources, and scholars have begun to call into question many of the most important positions that were only recently thought to be firmly established. There is also a new interest in Buddhism as practiced today in Tibet, as evidenced by Melvyn G. Goldstein and Matthew T. Kapstein's *Buddhism in Contemporary Tibet: Religious Revival and Cultural Identity* (1998), which demonstrates that the study of religions of Tibet needs to be envisaged in a cultural and political context.

BIBLIOGRAPHY

An appreciation of the status of modern scholarship can perhaps best be gained by perusing volumes of the Proceedings of the Csoma de Körös Memorial Symposium, as well as the Proceedings of the International Seminar on Tibetan Studies, which are being published regularly. Along with university presses, several private publishing houses, including Wisdom Publications in Boston, Serindia Publications in Chicago, Shambhala Publications in Boston, Snow Lion Publications in Ithaca, N.Y, Padma Publishing in Junction City, California, Prajna Press in Boulder, Colorado, the Tsadra Foundation in New York City, and Dharma Publications in Berkeley, California, as well as the Padma karpo Translation committee in Denmark, are continually releasing books on different aspects of Tibetan Buddhism.

Websites

Digital Himalaya: http://www.digitalhimalaya.com.

Latse Contemporary Tibetan Cultural Library: http://www.latse.org.

Old Tibetan Documents Online: http://www.aa.tufs.ac.jp/~hoshi/OTDO_web/index.html.

Padma karpo translation committee: http://www.tibet.dk/pktc/onlinepubs.htm.

Revue d'Etudes Tibétaines: http://www.digitalhimalaya.com/collections/journals/ret.

Tibet Visual History Online: http://visualtibet.org.

Tibetan and Himalayan Digital Library: http://iris.lib.virginia.edu/tibet.

Tibetan Buddhist Resource Center: http://www.tbrc.org.

Tsadra Foundation: http://www.tsadra.org.

MICHAEL L. WALTER (1987)
FRANÇOISE POMMARET (2005)

TIELE, C. P. (1830–1902), Dutch historian of religions. Cornelis Petrus Tiele studied theology at the University of Amsterdam and was a Remonstrant minister for twenty years (1853–1873). During this time he applied himself to the study of ancient religions and taught himself the Avestan language as well as Akkadian and Egyptian. In 1872 he obtained the Th.D. degree at the University of Leiden; and the following year he became a professor at the Remonstrants' seminary in Leiden, where he taught the history of religions. In 1877, Tiele was appointed to the new chair in history of religions and philosophy of religion at the University of Leiden, in the faculty of theology. He retired in 1900.

Tiele was a pioneer of the "science of religion" and one of the first to offer a historical survey of a number of religions based on the study of source materials. His own research opened up the religions of ancient Iran, Mesopotamia, and Egypt, putting the history of religions on a firm philological-historical basis that was long to be the hallmark of the discipline.

Tiele was much concerned with the broader notion of a "development" of religion, a notion that was natural at a time when evolution and progress were accepted ideas. He saw religion—man's "disposition of the heart toward God"—as a distinct province of life that can be found everywhere, and he was convinced that there is a unity and independence of religious life underlying all its different external forms. The gradual development of the human mind in history implies a parallel development in religion, which is, basically, a progressive expansion of self-consciousness. According to Tiele, the historical changes of the forms of religion show a process of evolution in the course of which the "religious idea" and the religious needs receive an ever fuller and more perfect expression. The historical forms of religion represent different stages of this evolution, in particular from nature religions to ethical religions. The historian of religions has to compare and classify religious phenomena in accordance with the state and direction of their development.

Tiele sharply distinguished all forms of religion from religion itself, and his deeper concern in the study of religion is the question of the real nature and origin of the religion that "reveals" itself in its manifold forms and phenomena. He therefore divides the study of religion into two parts. The first is *morphology*, that is, the inductive study of the phenomena and their changes and transformations as a result of a continuing development. This study requires, among other things, a comparative history of religion.

The second part of the study of religion is *ontology*, the study of the permanent element, beyond and through all changes and passing forms, that is the core and the source of religion. The real nature of religion is under investigation here, and this part of the study demands a deductive reasoning on the basis of what has been reached by means of inductive "empirical" research. The ontological study contains both a phenomenological-analytical part, in which the religious phenomena are studied in each stage of development, and a "psychological-synthetic" part in which the essence and origin of religion are investigated; in fact this stage is philosophical (rather than "psychological") in nature. For Tiele historical, phenomenological, and philosophical questions logically followed from each other. Because Tiele took as his departure the premise that religion fundamentally is a general human phenomenon and that the way in which it has manifested itself as well as the elements of which it is composed are the same always and everywhere, the study of permanently recurring phenomena made sense.

Tiele's history of religions may have been somewhat schematized, but it was dynamic; further, his phenomenology had a dynamic character because of his notion of the development of the human mind. His insistence that religion "manifests" itself in the phenomena, and that this manifestation happens through the activity of the human mind, has an almost modern, phenomenological flavor, like the idea that religions are different expressions of that "religion" that as a tendency slumbers in every person. Religion here is investigated as a human phenomenon, and the unifying factor of all religious phenomena is the human mind.

BIBLIOGRAPHY

For bibliographic data on Tiele's person and work, see my *Classical Approaches to the Study of Religion*, vol. 2, *Bibliography* (The Hague, 1974), pp. 283–286. A noteworthy commemoration by Tiele's colleague P. D. Chantepie de la Saussaye was delivered at the Netherlands Royal Academy of Sciences in 1902 (in Dutch) and republished in the latter's *Portretten en kritieken* (Haarlem, 1909), pp. 82–120.

Three of Tiele's longer works exist in English translation: *Outlines of the History of Religion, to the Spread of Universal Religions*, 7th ed. (London, 1905); *History of the Egyptian Religion*, 2d ed. (London, 1884); and his Gifford Lectures, *Elements of the Science of Religion*, 2 vols. (Edinburgh, 1897–1899).

New Sources

Molendijk, Arie L. "Tiele on Religion." *Numen* 46, no. 3 (1999): 237–268.

Molendijk, Arie L., and Peter Pels, eds. *Religion in the Making: The Emergence of the Sciences of Religion.* Leiden, 1998.

Ryba, Thomas. "Comparative Religion, Taxonomies and 19th-Century Philosophies of Science: Chantepie de la Saussaye and Tiele." *Numen* 48, no. 3 (2001): 309–338.

JACQUES WAARDENBURG (1987)
Revised Bibliography

T'IEN SEE TIAN

T'IEN-T'AI *See* TIANTAI

TIKHON (born Vasilii Ivanovich Belavin; 1865–1925), patriarch of the Russian Orthodox church. Prior to becoming metropolitan of Moscow (1917), Tikhon served as archbishop of Vilna and archbishop of Yaroslavl. Before that he was bishop and archbishop of the Aleutians and North America (1898–1907), laying the foundations of the Orthodox church in America. The Alaskan mission, founded in 1794, was extended and coordinated, so that it was able to grow into an autocephalous church in 1970. Tikhon's plan was to permit the Orthodox of various nations to form a single church, initially dependent on the Russian church, but eventually becoming autocephalous. The goal of a single church in the United States remains to be achieved, its delay being one of the consequences of the Russian Revolution.

Patriarch Tikhon was elected twelve days after the Bolshevik coup by the Great Sobor, or Pomestnyi Sobor (1917–1918), the first assembly of magnitude in the Russian church since the Great Sobor of 1666–1667. His election signaled the successful outcome of a nearly two-hundred-year struggle by the church to emancipate itself from control by the Russian state. Yet, Tikhon and the sobor delegates were aware of the danger in the demise of the provisional government that left the Orthodox church as the only pan-Russian institution to which the masses could turn. The contest that ensued between the church and the Bolsheviks developed into the most extensive persecution experienced by Christians since the days of the Roman emperor Diocletian.

Tikhon's first months as patriarch witnessed the first onslaught of Bolshevik violence when monasteries, cathedrals, and churches were bombarded and desecrated, and priests, bishops, and lay defenders of the church murdered. Tikhon countered through an encyclical urging the Bolsheviks to cease the massacres and telling them that they were doing the work of Satan; he also excommunicated all collaborators in the terror. The encyclical, combined with the reaction to persecution, produced a major groundswell of support for the church. The Bolshevik regime reacted by depriving the church of its legal status, confiscating all its properties and revenues, and launching a holocaust designed to devastate the church and eliminate its legacy in Russian history and culture.

During the persecution the regime pursued two methods of weakening and discrediting the patriarch. First, it supported dissident schismatics who splintered the ecclesiastical administration, and second, it tried to compromise Tikhon with the public in a dispute over the disposition of church values during the famine of 1921–1922. The Living Church, composed of those opposed to restoring traditional canonical authority to the patriarchal office, was created as a result of the schism. Its leaders were allowed to seize the patriarchal palace, the patriarchal administrative offices, and the offices of the metropolitanate of Moscow in May 1922. By this time Tikhon was already under arrest, and leading Moscow clergy had either been tried and condemned to death for inciting the masses "to engage in civil war" or were under indictment for that offense. In the resulting paralysis, the Living Church takeover was accomplished under the guise of providing leadership in unusual circumstances and with the assistance of the secret police. Clergy and bishops who refused to acknowlege the takeover were immediately declared unfrocked by the Living Church administration and arrested, tried, and, in many cases, executed by the secret police.

The takeover coincided with vitriolic attacks upon Tikhon, the hierarchy, and the clergy for refusing to hand over eucharistic vessels for famine relief. Tikhon had already agreed to strip the churches, monasteries, and cathedrals of precious metals and jewels except for the eucharistic vessels. The regime accused the church of hoarding its valuables and launched a massive propaganda attack. Churches were plundered anew, and their defenders arrested and indicted for antistate activities. The Living Church administration went through the motions of deposing Tikhon, and the Soviet government prepared to put him on trial for treason.

A major part of the government's indictment consisted in the accusation that Tikhon was working to overthrow the regime. That accusation was based upon a resolution passed by émigré hierarchs and lay leaders at Karlovci, Yugoslavia, in November 1921, demanding the restoration of the Romanov dynasty. Tikhon had already ordered his faithful and clergy to desist from antistate activities in September 1919 and repudiated the Karlovci statement. He also formally dissolved the émigré church administration in May 1922.

The Soviet regime soon realized that the Living Church did not have the support of the majority of Orthodox believers. Moreover, a general intensification of persecution of the Orthodox church in 1922, during which the popular metropolitan of Petrograd, Benjamin Kazanskii, was tried and executed, produced a deepening of dissatisfaction with Bolshevik rule among the masses. The regime also had put on trial Ioann Cieplak, acting Roman Catholic archbishop in Russia, together with Konstantin Budkiewicz, pastor of the chief Roman Catholic church in Petrograd. The execution of Budkiewicz had raised such an international outcry that the Bolsheviks faltered in their determination to execute the patriarch.

The circumstances led to a compromise. Tikhon wished to meet the Living Church challenge head-on, while the regime was concerned to avoid creating a martyr. Tikhon agreed to issue an encyclical in which he stated his personal loyalty to the Soviet government. He implied that the Living Church, rather than the regime, was the key danger to the Orthodox church. The regime slackened its support for the Living Church and Tikhon was released from prison. However, he was required to live in seclusion in the Donskoi Monastery, where he remained, except for brief hospitalization, until his death on April 7, 1925. While Tikhon contained the damage from the Living Church, he paid the heavy price of being effectively isolated from his shattered flock and of paving the way for further subordination of the Orthodox church to the Soviet regime.

BIBLIOGRAPHY

Cunningham, James W. *Vanquished Hope: The Church in Russia on the Eve of the Revolution.* New York, 1981.

Curtiss, John S. *The Russian Church and the Soviet State, 1917–1950.* Boston, 1953.

Curtiss, John S. *Church and State in Russia: The Last Years of the Empire, 1900–1917.* New York, 1965.

Fletcher, William C. *The Russian Orthodox Church Underground, 1917–1970.* Oxford, 1971.

McCullagh, Francis. *The Bolshevik Persecution of Christianity.* London, 1924.

Nichols, Robert Lewis, and Theofanis Stavrou, eds. *Russian Orthodoxy under the Old Regime.* Minneapolis, 1978.

Pol'skii, Mikhail. *The New Martyrs of Russia.* Montreal, 1972.

Pospielovsky, Dimitry. *The Russian Church under the Soviet Regime, 1917–1982.* 2 vols. Crestwood, N.Y., 1984.

Smolitsch, Igor. *Geschichte der russischen Kirche, 1700–1917.* Leiden, 1964.

Spinka, Matthew. *The Church in Soviet Russia.* Oxford, 1956.

JAMES W. CUNNINGHAM (1987)

TIKHON OF ZADONSK

TIKHON OF ZADONSK (Timofei Savelich Sokolov, or Sokolovskii; 1724–1783), Russian Orthodox bishop and saint. Son of a church reader in the Novgorod province of Russia, the young Sokolov spent his youth in poverty. After graduating from the Novgorod seminary in 1754, he taught Greek and rhetoric until his monastic tonsure and priestly ordination in 1758, when he received the name Tikhon. Having held several academic positions, Tikhon was consecrated suffragan bishop in the Novgorod diocese in 1761 and became bishop of Voronezh in 1763. He retired from episcopal service in 1767 and finally settled in 1769 in the Zadonsk Monastery (hence his popular appellation), where he lived until his death. He was canonized a saint of the Russian Orthodox church on August 13, 1860.

Tikhon surrendered his episcopal ministry for reasons of ill health, probably emotional as well as physical. He was a high-strung person, radically committed to his pastoral work and greatly frustrated in his activities by the ecclesiastical and secular conditions of the imperial Russia of his time. In monastic solitude Tikhon lived a life of continual prayer, reading the Bible (in particular the Gospels, *Psalms,* and Prophets, especially *Isaiah*), as well as the Fathers and saints of the Orthodox church (particularly Chrysostom). He also read Western Christian literature and was particularly interested in the books of the Anglican bishop Joseph Hall and the German Pietist Johannes Arndt, in imitation of whom he wrote his most famous works, *A Spiritual Treasure Collected from the World* and *On True Christianity.* The collected works of Tikhon are in five volumes, including letters, sermons, and instructions of various sorts written mostly for seminarians, pastors, and monastics.

Tikhon regularly attended liturgical church services in the monastery and always participated in the sacraments, but he celebrated in his episcopal rank only at the matins of Christmas and Easter. In his everyday life he practiced great simplicity and poverty. He rarely met with people, particularly those of rank and wealth, and found communication generally very difficult. He did speak with peasants and beggars, however, giving them money, food, and counsel, and he frequently visited prisoners and criminals.

Tikhon was of melancholy spirit until the end of his life, frequently despondent and depressed. He was much given to prayerful lamentation and often wept over the state of the church and the world, particularly within the Russian empire. Even during church services he could be heard weeping and begging God for forgiveness and mercy. His main visual aids to devotion in his monastic cell were not classical Orthodox icons, but Western pictures portraying the passion of Christ in realistic form. Tikhon's life and works had great impact upon subsequent generations in the Russian church, particularly upon intellectuals such as Fedor Dostoevskii, who used Tikhon as a model for figures in his novels, and Bishop Feofan Govorov, known as Feofan the Recluse.

BIBLIOGRAPHY

Numerous editions of Tikhon of Zadonsk's many writings, sermons, and letters were made in nineteenth-century Russia, mostly by the official synodal press in Saint Petersburg. None of Tikhon's major works exists in entirety in any other language but Russian. Extracts of his writings can be found in such works as G. P. Fedotov's *A Treasury of Russian Spirituality* (1950; reprint, Belmont, Mass., 1975). The definitive work on Tikhon in English is Nadejda Gorodetzky's *Saint Tikhon of Zadonsk, Inspirer of Dostoevsky* (1951; reprint, Crestwood, N.Y., 1976). This work contains many long quotations from Tikhon's writings as well as an exhaustive bibliography of writings concerning the man, his life, times, and works.

THOMAS HOPKO (1987)

TIKOPIA RELIGION

TIKOPIA RELIGION. Tikopia is a small island, three miles long and a mile and a half wide. It is part of the political grouping of the Solomon Islands, a thousand-mile chain of islands in the Pacific Ocean. It is also the peak of an old volcano, now largely sunk beneath the sea, and the original vent of the mountain has become a small brackish lake. To the northeast of the island the sacred mountain Reani rises; to the southwest are flat swamplands. The population of around fourteen hundred lives mainly around the western and southern coast of the island. Another six hundred Tikopia have migrated either temporarily or permanently to other parts of the Solomons. Whereas the island is theoretically controlled by the central government of the Solomon Islands, its distance from the seat of government and its general isolation have meant a degree of autonomy in retaining traditional practices and beliefs. The effect of this isolation on its religious practices will be discussed below.

While the majority of islands in the Solomons are peopled by Melanesians, Tikopia is a Polynesian outlier. That is, while it lies outside the true Polynesian triangle in the Pacific Ocean, it shares genetic, linguistic, and cultural traits with Polynesian islands such as Samoa, Tonga, and with the Maori of New Zealand. The major religious beliefs and practices of traditional (i.e., precontact) Polynesia were similar. Traditional Polynesians believed humans had an invisible counterpart or soul that continued its existence after death in an afterworld variously located in the sky or the sea and often composed of a series of heavens. They believed in an analogous life principle in animals and plants. They worshiped gods *(atua)* who had never been human as well as important human ancestors now also regarded as *atua.* Some of these gods could be regarded as departmental deities having responsibility for the sky, the sea, the land, and warfare as well as for elements, like the wind. The *atua* generally were beneficent, but there were also spirit entities that could cause harm.

Traditional Polynesian religion used abstract thought and symbolism. Offerings of food to the gods were made in the belief that the immaterial substance of the food was consumed by the gods but that the actual food could later be eaten by human participants in the rituals. Equally the material symbols of gods and ancestors (statues, significant rocks and trees) were seen as representations or memorials and not actual figurations with specific powers.

Existing knowledge of traditional Polynesian religion is, on the whole, fragmentary and often mediated through the records of missionaries whose duty it was to extirpate these pagan beliefs. Complete conversion of most of Polynesia to Christianity had taken place by the middle of the 1800s. However, Tikopia's isolation and small size made it difficult to find in the early days of Pacific exploration and not worth the effort of exploiting commercially for forced labor or land. This meant that when Raymond Firth carried out his first period of anthropological fieldwork in 1928–1929, the traditional religion was still practiced by three out of the four chiefs and by half the population. Therefore an excellent ethnographic record exists of the traditional ritual cycle, which was referred to as the "Work of the Gods." This summary of traditional Tikopia religious beliefs comes from Firth's extensive writings.

The island is traditionally controlled by four *ariki* (chiefs), heads of patrilineages believed, according to origin myths, to have begun with the birth of four male children to the Atua Fafine (premier female god) and the Atua Lasi (great god). The birth order of the children is reflected in the ranking of the chiefs, and their divine antecedents meant that the chiefs traditionally were regarded as sacred *(tapu).* The body of the chief, and especially his head, is still regarded as *tapu* because of his *mana* or inherent mystical power. In this hierarchically ranked society, *maru* or ritual elders are next below the chiefs. They are men who come from junior chiefly lines. They originally had roles with the *ariki* in the traditional religion, and they still have a political function on the island. Commoners, or *tauarofa,* make up the bulk of the population. Descent is traced patrilineally, and women take no roles in either the politics or the religious practices of the island, although this is changing among those who have left the home island.

TIKOPIA CONCEPTS AND RITUAL. Tikopia religion traditionally rested upon a belief that a set of spiritual beings *(atua)* controlled the fertility of nature and the health and well-being of the people. These *atua* comprised the spirits of dead chiefs and their ritual elders and a number of major gods, most notably the eponymous gods of each clan: the Atua i Kafika, Atua i Tafua, Atua i Taumako, and Atua i Fangarere. The Kafika clan is the senior of the four, and most significant in the Tikopia pantheon was the Atua i Kafika. An elision may have occurred here: the original four brothers were the children of true deities and were themselves deities, but the Atua i Kafika, as he is conceptualized now, was believed to have lived as a mortal man, a chief and a culture hero, responsible for many Tikopian traditional institutions. Killed by an opponent in a struggle for land, he abjured retaliation as he lay dying, and thus morally elevated, he succeeded to the highest position among the gods.

A few female deities were usually highly dangerous to humans: Nau Fiora was preeminent in this group and was believed to have the power to steal the souls of children, thereby killing them. Other female spirits, not deities but also never human, existed in various parts of the island and were sometimes seen benignly leading their spirit children to the sea. However, more dangerous ones existed in the bush and were capable of seducing and killing men. Ideas about gender in the temporal world, where women were conceptualized as powerless but having the potential to be dangerous, were reflected in the spirit world. There were also some other potentially dangerous entities with human origins, such as the spirits of children, either stillborn or miscarried. A child that died before recognizing his or her parents, that is, up to about the age of six weeks after birth, also came into this category, as did occasionally the spirits of young males who had died in accidents. While these spirits could perform mischievous actions by themselves, they were also the ones that often manifested themselves through spirit mediums.

The major gods of the pantheon had several personal names or titles that were held as secret information by the religious leaders, and it was through the ritual invocation of the name that the god could be stimulated to listen to and grant the requests of his worshipers. The deities were on the whole "owned" by different clans and lineages, and although there was some overlap in their attribution, each spirit had a primary social affiliation.

Unlike some of the larger Polynesian groups, the Tikopia had no separate category of priests whose main function was ritual performance. The four chiefs themselves, and their ritual elders, communicated with the gods and ancestor spirits with prayers, invocations, and offerings on behalf of their people. They also performed secular social roles as heads or administrative officers of lineages overseeing clan lands, canoes, and other property. The four *ariki* were the main priests, and each had a primary responsibility for certain crops and elements. The Ariki Kafika had prime responsibility for the success of the yam crop and for the welfare of the island generally. The Ariki Tafua was responsible for the coconut, and he looked out, away from the island, to matters concerning outsiders. The Ariki Taumako was responsible for the taro and for things to do with the sea, while the Ariki Fangarere looked after the breadfruit. This latter chief, for reasons described in the origin story of the birth of the four males, was also connected with disasters like cyclones and drought.

On the whole, commoners were merely supporters in the rituals, providing food and mats and, on some but not all occasions, an audience. However, there were some men (and a few women who had usually passed menopause) who had the potential to go into trance. These mediums were called *vaka atua* (spirit vessels). Their function was more informal and usually involved healing by communicating with some spirit that may have caused sickness. Spirits could also speak through the mediums to express concern at social and interpersonal derelictions. Where the chiefs and ritual elders performed rituals for the larger groups of clan and lineage, the mediums tended to cater to the concerns of families with whom they were connected.

The basic traditional Tikopia religious rite was the presentation of kava to the gods. Kava is the root of *Piper methysticum* that is macerated by pounding or chewing and mixed with water. In modern Tonga, Samoa, and Fiji, kava is prepared and drunk in ceremonies and on social occasions, but traditionally it had a religious function. In Tikopia the kava liquid was hardly drunk at all: it was offered to the gods as a libation poured on to the ground to the accompaniment of prayers for welfare. To perform a kava rite, a chief or elder assumed ritual purity by bathing, and he then donned a special waist cloth and a leaf necklet as a sign of formal religious dedication and set out offerings of bark cloth and food that, with the libations, served as a channel for invoking the spirits. The language used was highly symbolic and honorific; the chief adopted a tone of great humility, pleading poverty and signifying abasement before a god. Using conventional and ritual terms, the chief beseeched the gods to excrete on the earth, the gods' excrement being seen symbolically as all the goods things of the land and the sea.

THE WORK OF THE GODS. A notable feature of Tikopia traditional religion was a collective set of seasonal rites that involved elaborate organization of the community and the assembly of large supplies of food. The title *Work of the Gods* used by the Tikopia to refer to these rituals represented the amount of energy that was required from the people in performing them.

The basic theme of the Work of the Gods was the periodic resacralization of some of the most important elements of Tikopia culture. Under religious auspices, canoes and temples were repaired and rededicated, yams were harvested and replanted, and a red pigment was extracted from turmeric rhizomes and preserved for ritual use. (The turmeric ceremony, *nuanga,* is one of the few elements of traditional ritual to survive the island's conversion to Christianity and will be described below.) Ceremonies were performed for the welfare of the crops and fishing. However, these rituals not only dealt with the technological and economic affairs of the island, they also included a sternly moral public address, under conditions of great sanctity, instructing the people on proper behavior as members of Tikopia society. This included injunctions about birth control, an essential matter on a small island far distant from the next piece of land.

The period ended with ritual dancing in which formal mimetic displays and chanting of archaic songs were succeeded by freer performances by firelight at night in which men and women could indulge in often ribald reference to sexual matters, although still in a highly controlled setting. This aspect of the festival, partly cathartic in nature, was thought to seek the gods' approval of human recreation. Most of the rituals of the Work of the Gods were carried out on *marae,* ceremonial assembly spaces, often outside temples or large meetinghouses.

The Work of the Gods comprised a two-part cycle. It was not strictly calendrical but recognized the two major seasonal alternations: the trade wind period that went from April to October and the monsoon season of sometimes savage cyclones and rain from November to March. The timing of each cycle was based on natural observations, such as the appearance of constellations, especially the Pleiades, the migration of birds, and, for the beginning of the turmeric making, the flowering of the bright red coral tree *(Erithrina sp.).* Each ritual lasted about thirty days and was elaborately organized with much mobilization and exchange of food supplies, drawing the whole community into a vast network of social and economic relationships. Two clear functions of the whole series of religious performances seemed to be to provide occasion for the expression of personal and role status, especially of the chiefs, and to demonstrate communal solidarity.

The Work of the Gods had a special quality of sanctity through traditional authority. No particular myth was told by the Tikopia people to account for the genesis of the ritual cycle. They merely described it as having been instituted by the Atua i Kafika, and the performances of the rituals were regarded as a continuation and replication of the practices the deity had initiated. Therefore every effort was made to see that they were repeated in accurate detail, which required the careful passing on of the rituals from one generation to the next. The cycle began with the burning of a fire stick, and until the ceremony was completed, there was a ban on noise and much secular activity. Each ritual cycle concluded with the lifting of the taboo in a ceremony known as "freeing the land" that was emphasized by deliberate loud noise in contrast to the previous peace. Children ran about shrieking, and men whooped and yelled from the hills as they went about their daily work, making hollow booms by beating the buttresses of giant Tahitian chestnut tree trunks. A detailed description of the rituals is in Firth's *The Work of the Gods in Tikopia* (1940/1967).

CONVERSION TO CHRISTIANITY. Tikopia's relative isolation, as mentioned above, protected the small island from early intrusions by colonizers, traders, and missionaries (who initially contacted the Tikopia in 1858), but the Tikopia themselves discouraged outsiders from settling on their island. This kept missionaries at bay until 1907. Where much of the rest of both Polynesia and Melanesia was missionized by Europeans, Tikopia's first resident missionary was a man from the Banks Islands, a Melanesian. This probably muted to some degree the impact of a new religion. Where the technological superiority (including guns) of Europeans in other parts of the Pacific led to some fairly rapid conversions, in Tikopia the first missionary was not white and not particularly well equipped. The Tikopia gave him a Tikopian name, Pa Pangisi (after Banks), and married him to a Tikopian woman. He spent his whole life with the Tikopia, and his sons underwent the manhood ceremonies of all Tikopia boys.

Pa Pangisi was a missionary for the Melanesian Mission, the Anglican Church in Melanesia. He settled on the leeward side of the island, where one of the four chiefs lived, the Ariki Tafua. This chief converted to Christianity, and a number of commoners belonging to his clan followed him. Pa Pangisi instituted some changes to traditional practices: he discouraged the young men from growing their hair long and joining in the pagan dances. He also insisted on marriage between young people who were in sexual relationships. In this matter, his interpretation, through a Christian lens, of sex outside of marriage failed to take into account the pragmatic Tikopia thinking underlying human relationships. On a small island the necessity to control the population had been recognized in the exhortations of the Work of the Gods. To this end only the eldest son was allowed to marry, "marriage" involving the production of children. Younger sons were allowed to have sexual affairs, but they could not produce offspring, something ensured through abortion or infanticide. Pa Pangisi's insistence on marriage for all sexually active couples led to a population explosion. In about thirty years the population increased 50 percent and led to deaths after a cyclone, when the island's carrying and recuperative capacity was overextended.

The Work of the Gods had also involved the participation of most of the population in the rituals. By 1955 only one of the chiefs, Tafua, had become Christian, but many commoners had converted and were therefore prohibited from joining in the rites of the old beliefs. This meant that the remaining three pagan chiefs did not have sufficient material and human support to carry out the rituals in a manner they thought appropriate. The unity of the people for the good of the land was central to Tikopia belief, and the pagan chiefs, always pragmatists, met and decided that for the good of the land they should convert to Christianity. There are two accounts of the decision to convert.

The first comes from the ethnographic records of Firth and James Spillius, who carried out fieldwork in Tikopia in 1952 and 1953. They recorded that one chief was baptized by Pa Pangisi, who had married into this chief's family, but the other two chiefs insisted that their reception into the Church of Melanesia should be performed by the bishop. A radio message was therefore sent to Honiara asking the bishop to come to Tikopia, and the mission ship, the *Southern Cross,* set out. The two remaining chiefs and nearly all of their clans were thereupon baptized as Anglicans. Only one old woman refused, saying that her husband had died a pagan and she would too. The degree to which there was a deeply felt doctrinal understanding is unknown, although it has been noted that the Ariki Taumako did not intellectually reject his old gods; he just decided not to worship them any longer. Nonetheless the old temples were left to decay, the ritual adzes were destroyed or buried, and new church buildings were constructed in the centers of several villages. The chiefs no longer led the rituals; they were simply members of the congregation. The first priest was the Melanesian Pa Pangisi, but the Tikopia quickly arranged for the education of some of their men as Anglican priests or brothers of the Franciscan order. Priests and catechists in Tikopia have since been largely Tikopian.

The second story of the island's final conversion is consistent with a society taking control of its own history and rewriting it to some degree. This version, recorded in 1980, suggests that, rather than the historical accident of being missionized by Anglicans, a deliberate choice was made. In this version the chiefs looked at all the religions then practiced in the Solomon Islands. They rejected Roman Catholicism on the grounds that the prohibition on priests marrying was an unnatural practice. They rejected Seventh-day Adventism, to which the people of two other Polynesian outliers in the Solomons (Rennell and Bellona) had converted, on the grounds that the dietary restrictions of this religion were unrealistic. The chiefs considered, it was said, that Anglicans were the least trouble and that the island would therefore become Anglican.

With one priest on the island but several churches, the priest moved around the various parishes, named by Anglican tradition after saints. Catechists or senior men of rank could conduct prayer services in the other churches in the priest's absence. The mission ship came once a year for the confirmation of the young, and the priest and other church functionaries were taken off the island once a year for synod.

Various parts of the order of service and some gospels were translated into the Tikopia language, and the communion service was always conducted in the local language. However, accretions that were purely Tikopian crept into the religious practice. Women, allowed no voice in political, economic, or even domestic matters in Tikopia, were not allowed a role in the church, and women's groups like Mothers' Union were actively discouraged. Menstruating women, excluded from traditional rituals and even from dances, were technically prohibited from attending church in that state, something that was seen more as a relief than an exclusion.

The earlier priests were more doctrinally rigid, and ceremonies associated with the Work of the Gods were specifically prohibited. However, by 1980 the turmeric-making ceremony was reinstated. Turmeric is the culinary spice made from the rhizomes of a lilylike plant. The yellow lees from the process are used in food, but the bright orange part of the spice is mixed with coconut oil to make a body and cloth paint. Turmeric was used to mark the body in every life passage ceremony, as well as in the decoration of dancers and their bark-cloth skirts or loincloths. Referred to as "the perfume of the [old] gods," it was traditionally believed to draw the kindly attention of the gods to whatever activity was in progress. During the time it had not been made on the island, turmeric, judged inferior but necessary, was imported from another island. The making of the turmeric in Tikopia involved ritual withdrawal from everyday life and a series of elaborate taboos and restrictions to be followed over the two to three weeks the process took. Once again chiefs or their ritual elders took up their traditional roles in directing the process.

In 1980 the oldest of the four chiefs, the Ariki Taumako, was still alive and was the only one who had taken part in the traditional rituals. His ritual paraphernalia was kept in a small house, which he referred to as a "museum," behind his main dwelling place, and he regularly threw a small offering of food toward the museum. He still remembered and used his invocations to the gods of the sea, who had been the responsibility of his clan when people were to take the interisland ship away from Tikopia. However, he has subsequently died, and two or three generations have passed since the forebears of the present chiefs practiced the old rituals. Their memory exists only in Firth's record.

The interventions by the first missionary in Tikopian birth-control measures resulted in an increase in the population that was unsustainable for the island. From the late 1960s on, people left the island for other parts of the Solomons, forming permanent settlements first in the Russell Islands, later on Makira, and increasingly in the capital of the Solomon Islands, Honiara. There, Tikopia men sometimes married Melanesian women whose exposure to Christianity and practices inclusive of women differed from the Tikopia experience. In the Tikopia village of Nukukaisi on Makira, an in-marrying Melanesian woman became president of the Mothers' Union for the top half of the island. Some Tikopia women (mainly those related to this woman's husband) joined and took responsibility for matters like church linen, something that was not used in Tikopia itself because no money economy existed there. Meanwhile, Tikopia in Honiara have been exposed to a variety of sects, and young men especially have been attracted to religions that provide youth activities such as dances. While Anglicanism remains virtually the only religion on the home island, Tikopia in other parts of the Solomons have begun to espouse other religions, including Jehovah's Witnesses and Mormonism, whereas others have ceased religious observances.

SEE ALSO Atua.

BIBLIOGRAPHY

Firth, Raymond. *We, the Tikopia.* London, 1936.

Firth, Raymond. *The Work of the Gods in Tikopia.* London, 1940; 2d ed. London, 1967.

Firth, Raymond. *The Fate of the Soul: An Interpretation of Some Primitive Concepts.* Cambridge, U.K., 1955.

Firth, Raymond. *History and Traditions of Tikopia.* Memoirs of the Polynesian Society no. 33. Wellington, New Zealand, 1961.

Firth, Raymond. *Tikopia Ritual and Belief.* Boston, 1967.

Firth, Raymond. *Rank and Religion in Tikopia.* Boston, 1970.

Firth, Raymond, and James Spillius. *Study in Ritual Modification: The Work of the Gods in Tikopia in 1929 and 1952.* Royal Anthropological Institute of Great Britain and Ireland Occasional Paper no. 19. London, 1963.

Macdonald, Judith. "The Tikopia and 'What Raymond Said.'" In *Ethnographic Artifacts: Challenges to a Reflexive Anthropology,* edited by Sjoerd R. Jaarsma and Marta A. Rohatynskyj, pp. 107–123. Honolulu, 2000.

RAYMOND FIRTH (1987)
JUDITH MACDONALD (2005)

TILAK, BAL GANGADHAR

TILAK, BAL GANGADHAR (1856–1920), was an Indian political leader. Known by his followers as *Lokamanya,* "revered by the people, " but as the "father of Indian unrest" by the British authorities in India, Tilak had a crucial role in defining Indian nationalism by an appeal to Hindu religious and cultural symbols. He was born on July 23, 1856, in the Ratnagiri district of the Bombay Presidency. His family belonged to the Citpāvan subcaste of Brahmans, members of which had been influential as both religious and secular functionaries under the Marathas, the last indigenous rulers of the region, and Tilak had a proud consciousness of the greatness of Hindu civilization. He began his career in the recently established Fergusson College in Poona, where in 1881 he and his friend G. G. Agarkar established two newspapers: *Kesari,* in Marathi, and *Maratha,* in English. The papers criticized many aspects of British rule and called for a rejuvenation of India's national life.

Tilak's rise to prominence as a nationalist leader must be seen in the context of movements for social and religious reform that had attracted many intellectuals in the Poona region and elsewhere. Many reformers believed, however, in working with the British to bring about gradual political change and in seeking to reform deeply embedded social practices that seemed to have Hindu religious sanction. Tilak did not condone such practices but insisted that freedom from British rule was the first priority, not social or religious reform.

Sometimes Tilak supported, but he also opposed, the Indian National Congress, the organization founded in 1885 that became the chief agent in winning Indian independence. Two characteristics often alienated him from other nationalist leaders: one was his use of Hindu religious symbols as expressions of Indian nationalism, and the other was his acceptance of violence as a legitimate political tool sanctioned by the Hindu tradition.

In two of Tilak's books, *Orion* (1893) and *The Arctic Home of the Vedas* (1903), he argued that the mythic Hindu stories could be interpreted as actual history, thus giving Indians pride in the antiquity of their nationalist narrative. In *Gītā Rahasya* (1915), a commentary on the *Bhagavadgītā*, written while he was imprisoned for sedition, Tilak argued that it was not, as many commentators had interpreted it, a text that encouraged passive devotion to a deity, but, on the contrary, it was a revolutionary call to use violence against oppression. Mahatma Gandhi was later to argue, with Tilak in mind, that the message of the *Bhagavadgītā* was one of nonviolence and love of one's enemies.

Tilak's appeal to the Hindu tradition as a basis for a renewal of Indian greatness and opposition to the British was dramatized in numerous initiatives. One of these was starting festivals to celebrate Śivājī (1621–1680), the great warrior who fought the Mughal emperors, defending Hinduism against the invading Muslims. The implication of the message was not lost on either the Muslim minorities or the British rulers. More directly identified with Hinduism were festivals supported by Tilak in honor of the popular deity Gaṇapati, or Gaṇeśa. These had been in existence as family or local celebrations, but Tilak saw them as a chance for widespread group support for the project for political freedom, for Gaṇapati is the god of new beginnings, a help in overcoming obstacles, and the son of Śiva, the most powerful and potent of the great gods, often pictured as a warrior smiting his enemies. Tilak also joined in the campaign against cow slaughter, arguing that Hindus venerated the cow as a religious symbol. Since Muslims and the British were beef eaters, the campaign had a potent social and political message.

Some of the causes that Tilak supported in the name of Hindu cultural nationalism seemed, not only to the British but also to other Indian intellectuals, reactionary. One was his denunciation of the government when, in 1890, it introduced legislation to raise the permissible age of marriage for girls from ten to twelve. Orthodox Muslim leaders, as well as Hindus, argued that the government was interfering with a practice sanctioned by religion. Then, in 1897, there was an outbreak of bubonic plague in Poona, and the government ordered a house-to-house search under a military officer, W. C. Rand, which Tilak said violated the sanctity of the Hindu home; he also argued that, following the example of Śivājī, violence was justified to protest it. When Rand was assassinated, Tilak was charged with incitement to murder because of his writings, and he was sentenced to eighteen months in prison.

Such activities made Tilak the leading figure in the group within the Indian National Congress that he proudly called the "Extremists," in contrast to the "Moderates," whom he denounced for begging favors from their British overlords when they should be taking by force what was rightfully theirs. He popularized the slogan, "*Swarāj* [self-rule] is my birthright and I will have it." In 1907 he and his group tried to gain control of the annual meeting of the Indian National Congress in Surat, but failed, leading to a split in the organization. In 1908 Tilak was arrested on charges of incitement to violence and sentenced to six years of imprisonment in the unhealthy Andaman Islands, but he survived the ordeal and in 1916 he rejoined the Congress.

At this time, Gandhi arrived on the Indian political scene with a message of nonviolence that rejected Tilak's reading of the *Bhagavadgītā*. Tilak's death in August 1920, just before the Indian National Congress adopted Gandhi's platform of nonviolence, prevented Tilak from questioning the new direction that the nationalist movement was taking. Gandhi's success in subsequent years in persuading Indian nationalists to accept his version of Hinduism as a religion of nonviolence and love overshadowed for many years Tilak's insistence that Hinduism could be the basis for a militant nationalism that would fight to win India's independence. At the beginning of the twenty-first century, however, Tilak's version of militant Hinduism, not Gandhi's pacifism, was dominant in India's political life.

See Also Bhagavadgītā; Brahman; Gandhi, Mohandas; Gaṇeśa; Marathi Religions.

Bibliography

There is no good biography that comprehensively examines Tilak's personal life, political activities, and religious views, and assesses his role in the nationalist narrative. Richard I. Cashman, *The Myth of the Lokamanya: Tilak and Mass Politics in Maharashtra* (Berkeley, 1975), is a scholarly study of aspects of his political activities. Stanley A. Wolpert, *Tilak and Gokhale: Revolution and Reform in the Making of Modern India* (Berkeley, 1962), contrasts his positions with those of his great liberal contemporary and rival, G. K. Gokhale. D. V. Tahmankar, *Lokamanya Tilak: Father of Indian Unrest and Maker of Modern India* (London, 1956), is an authorized biography but gives a fuller picture of Tilak's life and times. G. P. Pradhan, *Lokamanya Tilak* (New Delhi, 1994), is intended to show Tilak as a great patriot and thinker. Examples of Tilak's combination of religious and political thought can be found in B. G. Tilak, *Tilak: His Writings and Speeches*

(Madras, India, 1922). An English translation of his Marathi work is available in *Srimad-Bhagavadgītā-Rahasya*, edited by B. S. Sukthanankar (Poona, India, 1965).

AINSLIE T. EMBREE (2005)

TILĀWAH. Recitation of the sacred words of scripture in Islamic contexts of prayer, liturgy, and public performance is designated by the Arabic terms *tilāwah* and *qirā'ah*. The very name of Muslim scripture, Qur'ān, is a cognate of *qirā'ah* from the finite verb *qara'a*, which means "he read," in the sense of "recited." *Tilāwah* is the more general term for Qur'ān recitation, and its root carries the double sense of "to recite" and "to follow." Thus, the Muslim concept of scripture entails the notion of divine speech meant to be recited, as indeed is the case with several other scriptures, such as the Hindu Vedas and the Jewish Torah. The sacred archetype of Muslim scripture is the Preserved Tablet (*lawḥ maḥfūẓ*, surah 85:22) or Mother of the Book (*umm al-kitāb*, 13:39, 43:4), the heavenly inscription of God's word from which it is believed that scriptures had been sent down to other prophets (e.g., the *torah* to Moses and the gospel to Jesus) and ultimately from which the angel Gabriel recited the Arabic Qur'ān to Muḥammad. This notion of divine speech, preserved and transmitted in heaven and on earth in both written and oral forms, can be traced among Semites to ancient Near Eastern cosmologies. In both its inscribed and its recited Arabic forms, the Qur'ān lies at the heart of Islamic symbolism, ritual, and social experience—indeed, even among many non-Arabic-speaking Muslims.

The tendency of Western scholars to concentrate on problems of textual history and interpretation to the neglect of the contextual modes of oral transmission and performance has resulted in a general failure to appreciate the significance of *tilāwah* in Islamic society. Although the textual form of the Qur'ān is paramount in such areas of classical Muslim scholarship as law (*fiqh*), theology (*kalām*), grammar (*naḥw*), and scriptural commentary (*tafsīr*), it is in its oral form that most Muslims down to the present have learned the Qur'ān.

TILĀWAH AND THE QUESTION OF CANON. In Islam, the problem of establishing an authoritative text was not a question, as it was in Judaism and Christianity, of authorized councils deciding which writings were inspired or otherwise authentic. Materials for the body of scripture (*kitāb*, "book, writing") were from the beginning regarded as simply and exclusively the accurate preservation of Muḥammad's recitation of God's speech, which tradition affirms had circulated orally, and in a less well-assembled form in writing, among contemporaries of the Prophet. Of greater significance was the question of collecting—implying also the arranging—of the Prophet's recitation of *sūrahs* and *āyahs* ("chapters" and "verses"). Tradition assigns the beginning of this task to the Prophet himself and stipulates further that the Qur'anic text was rehearsed in the presence of the angel Gabriel periodically until the revelation ended at the time of Muḥammad's death (632 CE). It is also held that through his secretary, Zayd ibn Thābit (and others), Muḥammad had at least some of the Qur'ān written down during his own lifetime. Various copies (*maṣāḥif*, sg., *maṣḥaf*) of these and the transcription of others were collected by the first two caliphs (Muḥammad's successors as head of the community). Islamic tradition regards the definitive collection ordered by the third caliph 'Uthmān (d. 656), however, as the official copy to which all authoritative copies since that time are traced.

As is often the case when the texts of sacred speech assume written form prior to the development of widespread functional literacy, the *scriptio defectiva* of the earliest transcriptions of the Qur'ān did not present the full and unambiguous script that was later developed for the enunciation, phrasing, and punctuation of each vocable, and it did not provide for other matters of enormous significance for meaning and consistency in oral recitation, such as guidance for phrasing and pauses. *Scriptio plena*, the full and precise system of writing, had neither fully evolved nor was it really necessary in the early stages when the "text" was transmitted primarily in oral form. As a result, slightly different variant readings (recitations) of the written Qur'anic text have existed and been accepted since the formative period of Islam.

Tenth-century Qur'ān scholars, the most famous of whom was Ibn Mujāhid (859–935), analyzed and evaluated the existing variant readings of their day and established the orthodox systems of reciting from the written text attributed to the caliph 'Uthmān (r. 644–656). Tradition accounts for the variations among the reciters, as Ibn Mujāhid's work shows, on the basis of a report (*ḥadīth*) that Muḥammad had been given the Qur'ān to recite according to seven *aḥruf* ("letters"), a term that is sometimes taken to mean the dialects spoken by Arab tribes contemporary with the Prophet. In this view, God revealed the Qur'ān to Muḥammad in the seven dialects of Arabic understood by the various tribes in Arabia, and these phonetic variations account for the different *qirā'āt* of the text of 'Uthmān. The connotation of *aḥruf* as "dialects" is controversial among Islamicists, however. Ibn Mujāhid's work, *Kitāb al-sab'ah* (The Seven Recitations), identified the most renowned orthodox eighth-century reciters of the Qur'ān, and although later authorities boosted to ten and fourteen the number of acceptable recitation systems, Ibn Mujāhid's seven remain the most widely recognized among Muslims today. Disciples of the seven charter reciters promulgated slight variations from their masters; these seven secondary transmitters are known as *rāwīs*, and their traditions of recitation have also survived and found acceptance in the Muslim community.

Thus, for example, in the postscript to the official edition of the Qur'ān printed in Egypt, the editors state that the basic orthography is that of 'Uthmān's copy and that it reflects the phonetic qualities of the oral transmission by the *rāwī* Ḥafṣ (d. 805), whose master was the reciter (*qāri'*, *muqri'*) 'Āṣim (d. 744)—one of Ibn Mujāhid's seven. Many professional reciters know several of the phonetic systems of the classic reciters and their disciples, and they will often repeat a given Qurʾanic phrase in other *qirāʾāt* in order to bring out several possible emphases and meanings allowed by the basic script.

Tilāwah and the Rules of Tajwīd. The significance of acceptable variations in the enunciation of the text is considerable insofar as meaning is established not only by written symbols but also by sounds. Although written texts of the Qurʾān, such as the modern Egyptian edition traced to the *qirāʾah* of ʿĀṣim, are elaborately marked to reflect the phonetic qualities of a given *qirāʾah* and are further coded to guide the reciter in proper phrasing and oral emphasis, the actual art of reciting can be learned properly only from a teacher. This oral, performative, pedagogical context has characterized Qurʾanic studies in Islam since the seventh century. Nonetheless, a considerable literature about the rules that govern recitation has accumulated over the centuries.

Learning to recite the Qurʾān traditionally began in the Qurʾān school (*kuttāb, maktab*), where rote memorization of Qurʾanic passages by children seated around a teacher (*shaykh*) marked the first, and for some the only, stage of formal education. Even with increasing government control of public education in modern times and the changes this has brought about, many contemporary Muslims are attempting to retain some form of the traditional Qurʾān school as an important first stage of Islamic pedagogy. At more advanced levels, students specializing in *tilāwah* learn the rules of *tajwīd*, that is, the rules for rendering correctly the recitation of the Qurʾān (and their application) in more critical learning and performance situations. Again, this is primarily an oral context dominated by a shaykh who has received special training and earned recognition as a reciter. In one of the most popular recitation manuals in use in Cairo today, *tajwīd* is defined as "articulating each letter from its point of articulation, giving it its full value. The intent of *tajwīd* is the reciting of the Qurʾān as God most high sent it down. . . . Knowledge of it is a collective duty, and the practice of it is a duty prescribed for all who wish to recite something from the holy Qurʾān."

Rules for proper recitation are usually printed at the back of the Qurʾān. These include specifications on how to produce the correct phonetic sounds, assimilation of certain juxtaposed phonemes, proper duration of vowel sounds, and sectioning (the rules for pauses and starts in reciting). The first three kinds of rules account for the unique sound of Qurʾanic recitation—a sound that easily distinguishes *tilāwah* from the pronunciation of Arabic for any other purpose. Sectioning allows the reciter to build a cadence or stress a particular phrase through the use of required and optional points of pausing and starting within each verse of the text and through calculated repetition of phrases. The rules of *tajwīd* also cover the proper Arabic formulas used before and after each recitation, such as "I take refuge in God from the evil Satan," followed by the Basmalah, "In the name of God, the merciful, the compassionate." At the completion of each recitation one recites: "The majestic God has spoken truly."

Two general styles of recitation may be distinguished. *Murattal* is the more straightforward type, appropriate for individuals reciting in the context of prayer and private devotions; *mujawwad* refers to the more melodious and ornate styles employed by trained and professional reciters for religious celebrations and public performances. Both *murattal* and *mujawwad* are governed by the rules of *tajwīd*, although *mujawwad* is an art form that takes years to master, and its practitioners receive high recognition in Islamic society.

The term *tilāwah* (which has thus far been used synonymously with *qirāʾah*) has the special connotation, as al-Ghazālī (d. 1111) put it, of being an act of recitation in which the tongue, heart, and mind are equally involved. Thus, *tilāwah* involves three essential ingredients: sound, thought, and emotion. Insofar as the rules of *tajwīd* and the contexts in which they are taught are intended to realize all three factors, Qurʾān recitation cannot be regarded as an empty verbal exercise, a cultural form without content. Muslim literature about *tilāwah* indicates that "the necessary, obligatory recitation is the thoughtful one that engrosses the whole self," or "those who would listen to the Qurʾān with their ears, not attending with their hearts, God faults them for that." The rules of *tajwīd*, then, have to do with sound production in relation to the proper cognitive and emotional responses.

The *tilāwah* literature addresses the rules of *tajwīd* for listening to Qurʾān recitation as well. This dual focus reflects the facts that the Qurʾān is an integral aspect of Muslim piety and worship and that most occasions of Qurʾān recitation entail a speaker/listener social relationship. The reciter's skill and correct frame of mind for his task are to be matched by listeners who likewise are prepared to hear the word of God.

Besides the manuals on *tajwīd*, other sources contributing to the cognitive and intellectual understanding of the Qurʾān include phrase-by-phrase commentaries (*tafsīr*), biographies of the prophet Muḥammad (*sīrāt*), and descriptions of the specific occasions of revelation during Muḥammad's mission *(asbāb al-nuzūl)*. Then too, there are the personal meanings each phrase might symbolize for individual reciters and hearers: when an individual or community feels tempted or threatened by an intrusive outside force or circumstance, for example, a passage about Satan may be recited. In general, the rules of *tajwīd* and Qurʾān recitation are closely connected with these other sources—both literary and social/contextual—of meaning. Any adequate appreciation of the meaning of the Qurʾān would have to involve knowledge of the written text, the commentary literature, the performance of recitation, and the social-ritual contexts—in short, the whole spectrum of Qurʾanic presence in Islamic culture.

The Contexts of Tilāwah. Among the most important settings for Qurʾān recitation are the ritual celebrations appointed by the Muslim calendar. The ninth month, Ramaḍān—the month when Muḥammad's mission was first announced to him with the transmission of the first revelation (surah 96) by the angel Gabriel, and also the month of the obligatory fast—is the occasion for public recitation of one-thirtieth of the text each day in mosques and special gatherings. The written text of the Qurʾān indicates these liturgical divisions with symbols in the margins marking each thirtieth part (*juzʾ*), the halves of each of these, and the quarters of each half. Another set of markings divides the text into seven weekly sections. The apportioning of the text in this fashion is separate from the literary chapter divisions (surahs) and specifically applies to the liturgical and mnemonic functions of reciting.

The actual speed with which a Muslim may choose to recite the entire text (over a month, a week, three days, or even in one night), like the question of which passage to recite on a given occasion, is a matter of personal preference. Various recommendations of the Prophet and his companions on these matters are found in the *ḥadīth* and are quoted in the literature on Qurʾān recitation.

On important calendrical festivals (*ʿuyūd;* sg., *ʿīd),* such as the Prophet's birthday (Mawlid al-Nabī), the Feast of Fast-Breaking (ʿĪd al-Fiṭr, at the end of the month of Ramaḍān), and during the pilgrimage assemblies in Mecca during the twelfth month, Qurʾān recitation also plays an important role. Whereas such public occasions call for the skills of a trained reciter, every Muslim individually recites a portion of the Qurʾān during the five daily prayers. The most frequently recited passage is the brief first surah, the Fātiḥah (Opener).

The Muslim lunar calendar captures in its festivals and holidays the rhythms of sacred history that center around God's revelation to the Prophet and the sacred time of the formation of the Prophet's community (*ummah*) in Mecca and Medina. Another set of social rhythms, the human life cycle, is also celebrated by moments of recitation. The Muslim rites of passage, including birth and naming of the child, circumcision, acquiring the ability to recite the entire Qurʾān from memory, marriage, and death, are normally celebrated among family, friends, and neighbors, and it is common practice to hire a Qurʾān reciter for the edification and enjoyment of those gathered. Numerous political and social occasions also call for a religious blessing attended by Qurʾān recitation. Because Qurʾān recitation in the more ornate *mujawwad* style is also a critical art form, a well-known reciter can attract a large and responsive crowd just to hear him perform his art. Indeed, the ethnomusicological field research of Kristina Nelson has shown that public knowledge and appreciation of different personal styles of *mujawwad* performance are very keen among reciters and their audiences in Egypt today; such intense appreciation of Qurʾān recitation is characteristic of all Muslim societies including regions outside the Arabic-speaking Middle East.

The development of electronic media in the twentieth century has created new contexts for Qurʾān recitation. Tape recordings of the *murattal* and *tajwīd* styles of recitation by famous recent and contemporary reciters are widely available for private and public listening. Cassettes also allow individuals to record their favorite reciter from the radio or at private reciting sessions and to exchange tapes with other connoisseurs. Television stations in Muslim countries typically begin and end each program day with a passage of Qurʾān recitation; as the shaykh recites, the Arabic text rolls down the screen in place of or in addition to the image of the reciter. In some non-Arabic-speaking countries such as Malaysia and Indonesia, a simultaneous translation of the text in the local language may also appear on the screen. Radio, however, is by far the most widely used broadcast medium for Qurʾān recitation today. Most stations broadcast Qurʾān recitation at selected intervals, along with religious poetry, readings of the Prophet's *ḥadīth*, and homiletic materials. Some stations devote programming entirely to Qurʾān recitation and other religious materials, and listeners are able to select times for listening or recording their favorite passages and reciters from broadcast schedules in the print media. Along with reciters famed for their skills and in high demand for public and private recitations in person, those chosen for broadcast performance are carefully screened, and many become well-known personalities in Muslim societies. Given the new media contexts of modern Islam, it is not uncommon, therefore, for someone walking down a street to hear the Qurʾān being recited from several sources at once—from radios and cassette recorders in private homes, small shops, and automobiles, along with those carried by passersby. Throughout the Muslim world students, both male and female, compete in local and national Qurʾān reciting contests, which are decided internationally each year at such renowned centers as al-Azhar University in Cairo.

The contexts of Qurʾān recitation described above have a striking symbolic association with "occasions of revelation" during the sacred time of the Prophet's mission in Mecca and Medina. Recitation then and now belongs to those significant moments in the life of the community that call for enunciation of the divine word. *Tilāwah* is, then, a meaningful speech act governed by rules that situate the speaker and the addressee within the sacred paradigm of God's address to humankind. The recited Qurʾān is, however, no more considered by Muslims to be the actual words of the contemporary reciter than it is attributed to the prophet Muḥammad. The Qurʾān is enthusiastically held to be God's beneficent revelation to the Arabs in the seventh century and, through the Arabs and their language, to the rest of humankind. *Tilāwah* as an Islamic cultural framework embraces not only the sounds but also the cognitive processes of meaning and the emotional responses appropriate to this symbol of divine manifestation. A full appreciation of *tilāwah*, therefore, engages the student of religions with texts, rules, and practices that touch virtually every aspect of Muslim society.

SEE ALSO Dhikr; Qur'ān; Rites of Passage, article on Muslim Rites; Samā'; Tafsīr.

BIBLIOGRAPHY

The standard work on the Qur'ān is by Theodor Nöldeke, Friedrich Schwally, and others, *Geschichte des Qorāns,* 2d rev. ed., 3 vols. (1909-1938; reprint, New York, 1970), of which the third volume by Gotthelf Bergsträsser and Otto Pretzl, *Die Geschichte des Korantexts,* 2d ed. (Leiden, 1938), contains information about Qur'ān recitation. Another standard source of information is Ignácz Goldziher's *Die Richtungen der islamischen Koranauslegung* (1920; reprint, Leiden, 1970), especially pages 1–54. A summary of European scholarship on Qur'ān recitation is presented in Rudi Paret's "Kirā'a," in *The Encyclopaedia of Islam,* new ed. (Leiden, 1960-). Useful information about *tajwīd* may be found in Edward Sell's *The Faith of Islam,* 3d ed. (London, 1907); see appendix A, "'Ilmu't-tajwid."

The most important modern research on Qur'ān recitation has been done by Kristina Nelson; see *The Art of Reciting the Qur'an* (Austin, 1985). Also useful is the *International Congress for the Study of the Qur'an,* series 1, 2d ed., edited by A. H. Johns (Canberra, 1982); see especially Frederick M. Denny's "The *Adab* of Qur'an Recitation: Text and Context," pp. 143–160, and John Bowman's "Holy Scriptures, Lectionaries and Qur'an," pp. 29–37. On Qur'ān recitation in the wider context of Islamic culture, see Frederick M. Denny's "Exegesis and Recitation: Their Development as Classical Forms of Qur'ānic Piety," in *Transitions and Transformations in the History of Religions: Essays in Honor of Joseph M. Kitagawa,* edited by Frank E. Reynolds and Theodore M. Ludwig (Leiden, 1980), pp. 91–123, and my own "Understanding the Qur'an in Text and Context," *History of Religions* 21 (May 1982): 361–384.

Most Muslim works on the Qur'ān are written in Arabic and thus little known in the West except among specialists. An exception is Labib al-Said's *The Recited Koran: A History of the First Recorded Version,* translated and edited by Bernard Weiss, M. A. Rauf, and Morroe Berger (Princeton, 1975).

RICHARD C. MARTIN (1987)

TILLICH, PAUL JOHANNES

TILLICH, PAUL JOHANNES (1886–1965), German-American theologian and philosopher, was born in Starzeddel (now Starosiedle, Poland), in Brandenburg, Germany, on August 20, 1886, the son of a Lutheran pastor. He attended the University of Berlin, from which he received his Ph.D., and the University of Halle, where he received his doctorate in theology. After passing his second theological examination at Halle, he was ordained into the ministry in 1912.

CAREER AND THEORY FORMULATION. During World War I Tillich served as a military chaplain. These years had a profound impact on Tillich's understanding of human reality. The effect of the war's devastation, both physical and spiritual, is reflected in a letter that he wrote in November 1916: "I have become purely an eschatologist [in that] what I, along with others, am experiencing is the actual end of the world of this time." Completing his military service in December 1918, Tillich received his qualification for university teaching (*Habilitation*) at the University of Berlin in 1919. This was also the year in which he published one of his most influential essays, "On the Idea of a Theology of Culture" (*Über die Idee einer Theologie der Kultur*). The essay presented the principles for interpreting culture theologically that Tillich followed throughout his career and that became the basis of a new field of theological study. The guideline that Tillich used for such an interpretation was, in his formulation, that the *Gehalt* (import, or substance) of a cultural work is "grasped in the content (*Inhalt*) by means of the form and given expression." Expressionistic art is an example. In such art, the forms of everyday reality—for example, the human shape or the shapes of everyday objects—are distorted in such a way that this distortion expresses a power, or reality, that manifests itself by the very way in which it breaks through the form and content of the objects. A theology of culture undertakes to interpret the meaning of this "substance" (*Gehalt*), or depth content, which thus breaks through the form into the content. Accordingly, an interpretation of culture always involves a reference to three elements of cultural works: the form, the content (*Inhalt*), and the substance (*Gehalt*).

In the spring of 1929 Tillich accepted a call to teach philosophy and sociology at the Univeristy of Frankfurt. It was there that, in 1933, he published the work that was to cause his emigration to the United States, *Die sozialistische Entscheidung* (*The Socialist Decision*). In content, this was a cautious analysis of socialism and a critique of unrestrained capitalism. It was based upon the idea of *kairos* (right time)—the idea that, even politcally, there are "right" times for accomplishing certain things—and upon an analysis of German democrary as only an abstract, not yet a real, democrary. Tillich drew the conclusion that the time was ripe for a new socialism, specifically, for a religious socialism that could incorporate democracy. National Socialism, however, was not what Tillich envisaged. Hence, the essay also contained a criticism of the totalitarian element in the National Socialist movement, and as a result Tillich became one of the many educated Germans who emigrated under the threat of those years as the movement developed.

Tillich left Germany in October 1933. In February 1934 he began his long teaching career at Union Theological Seminary in New York, remaining there until his retirement in 1955. He then became University Professor at Harvard—a great distinction—and in 1962 he became, with similar distinction, the Nuveen Professor of Theology at the University of Chicago. His last public address, "The Significance of the History of Religions for the Systematic Theologian," delivered at the University of Chicago shortly before his death on October 22, 1965, reflected the direction that his thought had taken toward the questions raised by the encounter of Christianity with other religions. These differed from the questions he had treated in his earlier works because they involved differences in the religious symbols themselves.

Theory of Religion and Symbols. Tillich's major work is the three-volume *Systematic Theology,* in which Tillich undertakes to interpret Christian symbols so as to show how they provide answers to ontological questions. Through the "method of correlation," he shows how the question of the meaning of being (the ontological question) is correlated with the symbol of God as its answer (the theological answer). The symbol *God* is the reality that answers the question of the meaning of being. In the five divisions of *Systematic Theology,* Tillich provides, on the one hand, an analysis of the three basic ways in which the ontological question is asked and, on the other hand, an interpretation of religious symbols in which he shows how the symbols present the reality that answers the question of the meaning of being as such. Simply put, the three basic questions are these: What is the meaning of being itself? What is the meaning of (human) existence? What is the meaning of life? The first question, answered by the symbol *God,* is occasioned by the finitude of human being. The second question, answered by the symbol of Christ, is occasioned by the contradictoriness (estrangement) of the human being—the fact that things are not what they should be and could be. The third question, answered by the symbol of the Spirit, is occasioned by the ambiguity of actual life—the fact that life is a mixture of being and nonbeing, of the good and the bad, of the creative and the destructive. The symbol *God* presents the meaning of the finitude of being; the symbol *Christ* presents the meaning of the contradictoriness of existence; and the symbol *Spirit* presents the meaning of the ambiguity of actual life. The actual human situation is that of life, in which the finitude of being and the contradictoriness of existence as such are always ambiguously mixed. To say that "God," "the Christ," and "the Spirit" are symbols is to say that they actually convey the reality of the answer that they represent. In other words, as a symbol, the word "God" (or the meaning and image borne by that word) actually presents an ultimate meaning in the finitude of being in the world; as a symbol, the word or the image or the history connected with "the Christ" conveys a real power to bear the contradictions and meaninglessness of reality without being overwhelmed by them; and the symbol of "the Spirit" is the actual presence of an unambiguous meaning that can be discerned through the ambiguities of life.

Through this method of correlation, Tillich intended to assign an equal importance to the question of being, which is the main subject matter of philosophy (or ontology), and to God as the symbol in which the meaning of being is present, which is the main subject matter of theology. The correlation between the two is formulated in the statement "God is being-itself." That is to say, what is present in the *symbol* God is also the reality to which the ontological *concept* of being-itself refers.

Besides the method of correlation, Tillich's distinctive contribution to Christian theology lies in three characteristics of his work. The first is his application of the Protestant principle of justification to the realm of theoretical thought. One who doubts the reality of God knows the truth despite that doubt, just as one who sins is justified despite the sin; the reality of God shows itself to the human mind despite the doubt, just as the goodness of God appears in human actions despite their imperfection. The second characteristic of Tillich's theology appears in his theology of culture. This theology of culture is based on the conception that culture itself is capable of expressing, indirectly, the ultimate meaning that is intended by religious faith. Thus, in his analysis of contemporary culture Tillich showed how, as culture, it did express indirectly what religion expresses directly. The third characteristic, which is at the basis of the method of correlation used in *Systematic Theology,* is the idea that philosophy, which asks the question of the meaning of being as such, and religion, which is based upon the reality shown in the symbol of God, cannot be reduced to each other, and they cannot be derived from each other, but they can be "correlated." What human beings seek when they ask the question of the meaning of being can be correlated with what human beings receive through the meaningfulness of religious symbols. Accordingly, Tillich's definition of faith as "ultimate concern"—in the sense of one's being ultimately concerned about that which concerns one unconditionally—implies both the ontological question of the meaning of being and also the symbol *God* as the presence of being-itself, which, as such, is beyond both being and nonbeing.

Tillich's wide influence, especially in the United States, is attributable to the ecumenical character of this theology, to the effectiveness of his teaching, the appeal of his work to professionals as well as to the laity, and, no doubt, to his extraordinary ability to relate theology to the issues of the time.

Bibliography

The most complete biography of Tillich is that of Wilhelm Pauck and Marion Pauck, *Paul Tillich: His Life and Thought,* vol. 1, *Life* (New York, 1976); the projected volume 2 was never published. A highly compact but excellent interpretive study of the unity of his life and thought is the pamphlet by Carl Heinz Ratschow, *Paul Tillich* (Iowa City, 1980). Of several autobiographical sketches, the most helpful one, first published in 1936, was published separately under the title *On the Boundary* (New York, 1966).

Tillich's collected works have been published in German in the *Gesammelte Werke,* 14 vols. (Stuttgart, 1959–1975), and in six supplementary volumes, *Ergänzungsbände* (Stuttgart, 1971–1982). Volume 14 contains an index and bibliography, including a list of unpublished manuscripts in the Tillich Archives at the Harvard Divinity School, Cambridge, Massachusetts, and the Paul-Tillich-Archiv at the University of Marburg, Germany. Among Tillich's major works are *The Socialist Decision* (1933), translated by Frederick Sherman (New York, 1977), *Systematic Theology,* 3 vols. (Chicago, 1951–1963), *What Is Religion?* (New York, 1969), *The Protestant Era* (essays edited by James Luther Adams, Chicago, 1948), *The Courage to Be* (New Haven, Conn., 1952), *Biblical Religion and the Search for Ultimate Reality* (Chicago,

1955), *Theology of Culture* (New York, 1959), *Christianity and the Encounter of the World Religions* (New York, 1963), and *Dynamics of Faith* (New York, 1957), the last of which provides perhaps the best introduction to his thought.

A useful variety of critical and appreciative responses to Tillich's thought is contained in *The Theology of Paul Tillich,* 2d rev. ed., edited by Charles W. Kegley (New York, 1982), with three new essays and a revised bibliography. Responses to his theory of religious symbolism are contained in *Religious Experience and Truth: A Symposium,* edited by Sidney Hook (New York, 1961); included in the volume are two basic essays by Tillich. An excellent brief account of Tillich's religious socialism is John R. Stumme's introduction to the English translation of Tillich's *The Socialist Decision* (New York, 1977). A more recent secondary study is *Mystical Heritage in Tillich's Philosophical Theology,* edited by Gert Hummal and Doris Lax (Münster, 2000).

ROBERT P. SCHARLEMANN (1987 AND 2005)

TIME

SEE CALENDARS; CHRONOLOGY; COSMOGONY; ESCHATOLOGY; ETERNITY; HISTORY; REJUVENATION; SACRED TIME; SYMBOLIC TIME

TIMOTHY AILUROS

TIMOTHY AILUROS (d. 477), known as Timothy II, fifth-century Monophysite theologian who became the first patriarch of the Coptic Church in Alexandria (457–460; 475–477). He was surnamed by his opponents Ailuros ("the cat") because of his small stature and his weasel words and ways. Venerated as a saint by the Coptic Church, Timothy, along with other monophysite patriarchs, was anathematized by the church of Rome under Pope Hormisdas (514–523).

Little is known of Timothy's early life. It is certain that during the Christological controversies of the fifth century he sided with those who rejected the decree of the Council of Chalcedon (451), which defined Christ as "one hypostasis in two natures." The council appointed the orthodox Proterios as patriarch of Alexandria. But the local mob lynched Proterios, and in 457 the Egyptian bishops elected Timothy to succeed him. He served as patriarch for three years, until 460, when he was removed from the patriarchal position and banished. While in exile, Timothy carried on a correspondence against the Chalcedonian decisions and wrote several essays promoting Monophysitism.

Timothy's fate changed again when, upon the death of Emperor Leo I, Basiliskos usurped the throne and turned to the monophysites for support. He reinstated Timothy, who became instrumental in the writing of an encyclical that Basiliskos issued in an attempt to impose Monophysitism as the official Christology of the church. Timothy ruled the church of Alexandria for two more years, until his death in 477. His ecclesiastical policy was characterized both by ambiguity and by fanaticism.

Of Timothy's writings against the Council of Chalcedon three letters have survived in a Syriac translation. A sermon and fragments of his essays have been incorrectly attributed to Timothy III of Alexandria.

BIBLIOGRAPHY

Original writings are available in *Patrologia Graeca,* edited by J.-P. Migne, vol. 86, pt. 1, (Paris, 1860). Useful discussions can be found in Evagrios Scholastikos's Greek-language *Historia ecclesiastica* (2.8–2.11), available as *The Ecclesiastical History of Evagrius,* edited by Joseph Bidez and Léon Parmentier (Amsterdam, 1964), pp. 55–63. See also Konstantinos I. Amantos's *Historia tou Buzantinou kratous,* 2d ed., vol. 1 (Athens, 1953), p. 129.

DEMETRIOS J. CONSTANTELOS (1987)

TINGLEY, KATHERINE

TINGLEY, KATHERINE (1847–1929), was a leader of the Theosophical movement in the United States from 1896 to 1929. She led the organization that established the Point Loma Theosophical Community and was a well-known figure in early-twentieth-century American society.

Tingley was born Catharine Augusta Westcott in Newburyport, Massachusetts, in 1847. According to her own account, she was a dreamy child who enjoyed walking in the woods or along the seashore, engrossed in her imagination. During the Civil War her father equipped and led a company of volunteers to fight for the Union. His unit was transferred to Virginia, and his family followed him. Tingley, as a teenager, witnessed the aftermath of battle, caring for wounded soldiers from both the Union and Confederate armies. Other details of her adolescent and early adult years are sketchy. She married three times, the third time to Philo Tingley. No children resulted from these marriages. By the 1880s she was living in New York City. Like many women from the middle classes of that period, she was interested in various late Victorian, Progressive causes that would improve the quality of life for the urban poor, especially women and children. She was responsible for one or more voluntary establishments that provided food and other relief. Supposedly in the early 1890s, while she was conducting one such operation, she met William Q. Judge (1851–1896), the leader of the Theosophical Society in the United States. Some sources also point to her interest in Spiritualism as a possible context in which she had contact with him.

The Theosophical Society began in 1875 in New York City under the leadership of Helena P. Blavatsky (1831–1891) and Henry Steel Olcott (1832–1907). It attracted urban, middle-class individuals interested in Spiritualism, comparative religions, and the occult. By the time Judge and Tingley met, Theosophical lodges across the United States were growing in size and number. But the most influential leaders of this nationwide movement resided in New York City. They included businessmen, teachers, physicians, and other middle-class, often professionalized, men and women. Judge led many American Theosophical lodges to declare their independence from the worldwide Theosophical Society in 1895. He died the next year. Tingley succeeded him, although the circumstances surrounding her succession remain unclear. Over time, many leaders loyal to Judge shifted their loyalty to her, but not all. Some of the dissenters formed their own Theosophical groups.

Tingley mobilized Theosophists across the United States to work for social reform. Theosophists were responsible for public vegetable gardens, orphanages, halfway houses for prostitutes, job training for the poor, emergency relief, and Theosophical Sunday schools for children, which were originally begun under Judge but expanded under Tingley and called Lotus Circles. The Theosophical response to American soldiers returning from Cuba after the Spanish-American War in 1898 is noteworthy. The United States Army was not prepared to receive the troops who came home weak and ill from tropical diseases. At one such disembarkation point on Long Island, Theosophists led by Tingley staffed a hospital camp where soldiers received food and medical treatment.

In the late 1890s Tingley and the leadership around her took steps toward the establishment of a community of like-minded adults who would provide an education for children based upon Theosophical principles. They selected Point Loma as the location for this community. It was a relatively isolated site a few miles from San Diego, California, with a mild climate and space to expand facilities. American Theosophists led by Tingley believed that they stood on the cusp of a new cycle or age in human history. Ancient souls who had reincarnated countless times in past eons were especially mature and ready to advance spiritually and morally as they appeared in this incarnation as children. This promising cohort required special nurture, and Point Loma was their nursery. Tingley and other adults at Point Loma strictly controlled their children's exposure to the outside world, their diets, their reading material, their physical activities, and their relationships with one another. This system of child-rearing and education was called Raja Yoga, a term that the Theosophists borrowed from Hinduism but invested with their own meaning. In their worldview, Raja Yoga was the holistic education of children in which all of their faculties—spiritual, mental, physical, and emotional—could be cultivated simultaneously. From 1900, when Tingley and others moved to Point Loma, until the community relocated to Covina, California, in 1942, Point Loma Theosophists raised and educated hundreds of children.

Throughout the first three decades of the twentieth century, Tingley made numerous tours of the United States and the world. She set the tone for such travel in 1896 by visiting Theosophical lodges worldwide. Thistour, called the Crusade, was designed to consolidate support for her leadership and establish good working relationships with Theosophists elsewhere. For many years afterward she traveled avidly, publicizing the Point Loma Theosophical Community and advocating a number of social and political causes, especially world peace. During the years immediately preceding World War I she became a noted national and international figure in various peace conferences. Even after the American entry into the war, she continued to advocate peace, and for this reason briefly attracted the attention of the United States government as a possible agent for Germany, although suspicion of Tingley's cooperation with German agents proved unfounded.

Tingley was a high-profile figure, often in the news because of remarks she made at public gatherings or in court cases that included various individuals at Point Loma. Some of these cases dealt with divorces of married couples, some with the settlement of estates left behind by deceased Point Loma residents. In all such instances, Tingley was a witty and feisty participant, yet she maintained a pronounced Victorian respectability consistent with her social class, gender, and generation.

Tingley was praised by Point Loma Theosophists as the rightful successor to Blavatsky and Judge as the leader of world Theosophy, in spite of the opposition to this assertion by other Theosophical organizations. Theosophists claimed that their leaders were granted both paranormal abilities and special authority to teach Theosophical principles by a group of advanced beings called the *masters*, who supervised the great cosmic evolution of souls and worlds. Point Loma Theosophists believed that, as the sanctioned leader, Tingley manifested extraordinary powers of prediction and perception. Her commands were followed without question by those who revered her. She was seen as the mother of the age, as well as the mother of people in this age, especially the suffering and destitute. Maternity defined her particular style of leadership, in contrast to the masculine style of Judge before her, and the more scholarly style of her successor, Gottfried de Purucker (1874–1942). Tingley was a persuasive speaker in an era when public speakers enjoyed widespread popularity and influence in American society. Many of her speeches appeared in the magazines and books printed by Point Loma's press. But within the Point Loma Theosophical tradition, both during and after her lifetime, she was regarded as a great organizer and manager, not a scholar. Her speeches and writings mostly repeated Theosophical ideas already extant, but she articulated them in a way that appealed to late-nineteenth- and early-twentieth-century Americans. She evoked patriotic pride as well as concern for all of humanity; advocated gender distinctions as well as common characteristics of men and women; and argued for children to be both protected and challenged in their nurture. Her genius lay in her ability to tap into American folkways and middle-class discourse about culture, and to intertwine those with Theosophical doctrine.

Tingley was in an automobile accident in Germany in May 1929. As a result of injuries sustained in that accident, she died of illness while convalescing on the island of Visingso, in Sweden, in July 1929. She was eighty-two years of age. Today, the organizational descendant of the Point Loma Theosophical Community is the Theosophical Society, Pasadena, which publishes a bimonthly magazine and Theosophical classics, including the works of Katherine Tingley.

SEE ALSO Blavatsky, H. P.; Judge, William Q; Point Loma Theosophical Community; Theosophical Society.

BIBLIOGRAPHY

Ashcraft, W. Michael. *The Dawn of the New Cycle: Point Loma Theosophists and American Culture.* Knoxville, Tenn., 2002.

Kirkley, Evelyn. "Equality of the Sexes, But. . .: Women in Point Loma Theosophy, 1899–1942." *Nova Religio* 1, no. 2 (1998): 272–288.

Tingley, Katherine. *The Gods Await.* Point Loma, Calif., 1926; rev. ed., Pasadena, Calif., 1992.

Tingley, Katherine. *The Voice of the Soul.* Point Loma, Calif., 1928.

W. MICHAEL ASHCRAFT (2005)

TĪRTHAṂKARAS. According to the Jains, one of the oldest religious communities in India, the *Tīrthaṃkaras* (called *titthagaras* in the Jain canon) are the prophets who periodically teach the world the truth of the imperishable Jain tradition; the term is almost equivalent to *jina* ("victor") or *arhant* ("saint"). The term *tīrtha(ṃ)-kara* refers literally to one who "builds the ford" that leads across the ocean of rebirths and suffering, and thus builds or renews the Jain fourfold community of monks and nuns, laymen and laywomen.

Twenty-four *Tīrthaṃkaras* are said to appear at given periods in selected regions. As they are capable of ultimate spiritual perfection they are thus regarded as having more than a human status. Together with the *cakravartins* (universal sovereigns) and other such heroes, they form the class of the venerated sixty-three personages of the Jain "universal history." They are called *mahāpuruṣas* ("great men") by the Digambaras and *śalākāpuruṣas* ("men with the staff") by the Śvetāmbaras.

MEMBERS OF THE LINEAGE. *Tīrthaṃkaras* are born only in the "middle world" (Madhyadeśa), and there only in the very few *karmabhūmis* (regions where one reaps the fruit of one's actions) of the central continent (Jambūdvīpa): in the southern land of Bhārata (i.e., India), in the northern land of Airāvata, and in half of the central land of Videha. Except in Videha, where conditions differ, they are said to live exclusively during the third and fourth of the six stages of the *avasarpiṇīs* and *utsarpiṇīs*, that is, the descending and ascending halves of the endless temporal cycle, thus at times of mixed happiness and misery.

In Bhārata, the teacher of the present era is Vardhamāna Mahāvīra, the twenty-fourth and last of the series of *Tīrthaṃkaras* in our *avasarpiṇī* half cycle. According to tradition, he was born seventy-five years and eight and one-half months before the end of the fourth period, in which he lived for seventy-two years. Three years after his *nirvāṇa*, allegedly in 523 BCE, the present period began, characterized by misery.

The first *Tīrthaṃkara* was Ṛṣabha, who is said to have been born toward the end of the third period and to have died three and one-half years before its completion. His life span extended over millions of so-called Pūrva years. In the fourth period, after Ṛṣabha and before Mahāvīra, the law was preached by twenty-two *Tīrthaṃkaras*: Ajita, Sambhava, Abhinandana, Sumati, Padmaprabha, Supārśva, Candraprabha, Suvidhi (Puṣpadanta), Śītala, Śreyāṃsa, Vāsupūjya, Vimala, Ananta, Dharma, Śānti, Kunthu, Ara, Malli, Munisuvrata, Nami, (Ariṣṭa)nemi, and Pārśva.

Tradition also gives the lists of their contemporaries in Airāvata, as well as of past and future *Tīrthaṃkaras* of Bhārata. In Videha, the prevailing conditions of happiness mixed with misery are always akin to those of this, the third period in an *avasarpiṇī* half cycle, so that a *Tīrthaṃkara* can be preaching there at any time.

THE CAREER OF A TĪRTHAṂKARA. No soul will become the soul of a *Tīrthaṃkara* unless it has gone through a considerable number of rebirths and has finally practiced exceptional virtues resulting in a special *karman.* The soul is urged by gods to "fall" from its divine mansion and be reborn to practise and propagate the true law. *Tīrthaṃkaras* are usually considered to become incarnate only through male figures; the Śvetāmbaras nevertheless consider the nineteenth, Malli, to be a female, although the Digambaras deny this point.

The career of a *Tīrthaṃkara* conforms to a well-structured pattern, and traditional descriptions of the *Tīrthaṃkaras* provide very few or no distinctive individual characteristics. The biography of a *Tīrthaṃkara* is stereotyped, listing in an almost formulaic sequence the following information: (1) some details of his former existence, (2) the five *kalyāṇas*, or religiously significant moments of his life (i.e., conception, birth, renunciation, attainment of omniscience, *nirvāṇa*), (3) the names of his parents, (4) the number of his followers, (5) the duration of his life, (6) the color of his body (most are golden, but the twentieth and twenty-second are black, the eighth and ninth are white, the sixth and twelfth are red, the twenty-third and another [the nineteenth, according to the Śvetāmbaras, the seventh, according to the Digambaras] are blue-green), (7) his height, (8) his guardian divinities, and (9) the length of time elapsed since his predecessor's *nirvāṇa.* All are born to princely families, and, with two exceptions, are related to the Ikṣvāku dynasty. The conception of a *Tīrthaṃkara* is announced to his mother by a standardized succession of auspicious dreams (fourteen according to the Śvetāmbaras, sixteen according to the Digambaras).

ICONOGRAPHY. Like their biographies, the images of the *Tīrthaṃkaras* are all fundamentally similar. The figures are represented in meditation, either seated cross-legged or standing in a *kāyotsarga* pose (representing a particular type of Jain austerity), with arms stretched slightly apart from the body. Although the canon for the *Tīrthaṃkara* images appears to have been well fixed by the beginning of the common era, there have been some developments through the course of time. After the fifth century, Śvetāmbara icons are characterized by a dhoti (a wrapped garment of draping layers of cloth) and various ornaments; Digambara icons remain naked. Moreover, a series of characteristic marks (*cihnas*) are added to the pedestals in order to distinguish the individual *Tīrthaṃkaras*: Ṛṣabha's symbol is the bull; Nemi's, the conch shell; Pārśva's, the snake; Mahāvīra's, the lion. Representations of Ṛṣabha, Pārśva, and Mahāvīra are particularly numerous; Pārśva is easily recognized by the snake hoods over his head.

The comparative monotony of the *Tīrthaṃkara* images is somewhat striking. These icons, however, are not meant to be picturesque but to suggest omniscient awareness and absolute detachment, serenity.

MYTHIC IMPORTANCE. Despite such uniformity, several *Tīrthaṃkaras* emerge as prominent figures. On the whole, the general trend of the present *avasarpiṇī* implies a notable decline from a golden age and is marked by the considerable shortening of life span, prosperity, and happiness. Thus the legends concerning Ṛṣabha, the "first lord" of this cycle, are of special significance because in them he is shown in a pioneering role.

Ṛṣabha is said to have set the groundwork for civilization: first as a sovereign, when he organized kingdoms and societies, instituted legislation, taught agriculture, fire, cooking, arts and crafts, writing, and arithmetic, and later, when he renounced the world and became the first mendicant, thus shaping the religious life of the present *avasarpiṇī*. These two spheres of influence were further served by two of Ṛṣabha's sons: Bhārata is renowned in Indian tradition as the first *cakravartin* of Bhārata. Bāhubali became a forebearing ascetic and as such has long been revered by the Digambaras, especially in the South, where several impressive monoliths representing this hero were erected. One of the best known is a colossal fifty-seven-foot image towering at the top of one of the hills overlooking Śravaṇa Beḷgoḷa, about one hundred miles northwest of Bangalore.

The twenty-second *Tīrthaṃkara* (Ariṣṭa)nemi, is allegedly related to Kṛṣṇa and the Yādavas. He is extremely popular, especially in Gujarat, where on the sacred Girnar Hills he practiced austerities and eventually understood the ultimate truth, thus achieving enlightenment; after many years he reached final emancipation, *nirvāṇa*, on the same mountain. His revulsion at the sight of the animals awaiting slaughter for his wedding ceremonies as well as his subsequent refusal to marry his betrothed, Rājīmatī, are highly significant and are the subject of many narratives, songs, and paintings that illustrate the greatness of the doctrine of *ahiṃsā*, or noninjury.

Pārśva, the twenty-third *Tīrthaṃkara*, has been regarded by most scholars as possibly being a historical figure. He is said to have lived for a hundred years, some two hundred and fifty years before Mahāvīra, and to have been born in Banaras and ended his life in Bihar on Mount Sameta, which is now also known as Pārasnāth in his honor. He is alleged to have established the "law of four restraints" (*caturyāma-dharma*), which is generally, though not unanimously, considered to be the forerunner of the five "great vows" (*mahāvratas*) followed by Mahāvīra's disciples. Pārśva is associated with serpents and consequently the object of much veneration.

CULTIC LIFE. Immediately after death, the *Tīrthaṃkaras* become *siddhas* ("perfected" souls), and thus became completely inaccessible. But the example they set should be meditated upon, and it is extolled daily when the Jains recite the *Caturviṃśatistava* (Praise of the twenty-four [*Tīrthaṃkaras*]); the images of the *Tīrthaṃkaras* should serve only as meditative supports. Archaeological evidence indicates that this method of worshiping the *Tīrthaṃkaras*, known as *deva-pūjā*, goes back to the first few centuries BCE.

Many lay believers, however, cannot refrain from appealing to superhuman benevolence. They direct their worship and supplications for assistance to the pairs of guardian deities who serve the *Tīrthaṃkaras*. Among the most popular are the snake god Dharaṇendra and his consort Padmāvatī, both of whom flank Pārśva. The Jain teachers, however, have always insisted on the inferior position of these deities and have succeeded in preventing them from usurping the supremacy of the *Tīrthaṃkaras*.

TĪRTHAṂKARAS AND INDIAN RELIGIOUS EXPERIENCE. In Jainism it is clear that the recurrent presence of *Tīrthaṃkaras*, who periodically appear in the human realms in order to preach and show the true law, have a function similar to that of the seven (later twenty-five) Buddhas in Buddhism, and also to that of the Hindu *avatāras* of Viṣṇu. On the other hand, by promoting civilization, the first *Tīrthaṃkara*, Ṛṣabha, recalls the role played by Pṛthu in the epics, by Mahāsammata in Buddhism, and by Prometheus in the Greek and Roman traditions. Thus from many perspectives Jainism offers a coherent system that links the evolutions of time, cosmos, humankind, and the Jain church.

SEE ALSO Ahiṃsā; Cosmology, articles on Hindu Cosmology, Jain Cosmology; Jainism; Mahāvīra.

BIBLIOGRAPHY

The standard books on Jainism provide general information on the *Tīrthaṃkaras*. A comparatively detailed treatment will be found in Helmuth von Glasenapp's *Der Jainusmus: Eine indische Erlösungsreligion* (Berlin, 1925; reprint, Hildesheim, 1964; English translation by S.B. Shrotri: *Jainism. An Indian Religion of Salvation*, Delhi 1998). Padmanabh S. Jaini, *The Jaina Path of Purification.* (Berkeley, Los Angeles London 1979). A substantial although short account is provided by Josef Deleu's "Die Mythologie des Jinismus," in H. W. Haussig's *Wörterbuch der Mythologie* (Stuttgart, 1976), pp. 207–284, esp. pp. 270–273. Various aspects of the *Tīrthaṃkaras*—concept, worship, representation—are considered in several papers of *Approaches to Jaina Studies: Philos-*

ophy, Logic, Ritual and Symbols, edited by N.K. Wagle and Olle Qvarnström (Toronto, 1999).

Sculptures of *Tīrthaṃkaras* are among the most ancient Indian religious images, dating from first to second century CE. Since the eleventh century, illustrated manuscripts (first palm-leaves, later paper manuscripts) represent figures of Jinas and/or depict important moments of their lives. Brightly coloured Jain miniatures (especially in "Western Indian Style"), as well as statues and bas-reliefs are reproduced in Pratapaditya Pal et al., *The Peaceful Liberators: Jain Art from India* (Los Angeles, 1994); Kurt Titze, *Jainism: A Pictorial Guide to the Religion of Non-Violence* (Delhi, 1998); Jan Van Alphen, *Steps to Liberation: 2500 Years of Jain Art and Religion* (Antwerp, 2000). Also see the monograph by José Pereira, *Monolithic Jinas: The Iconography of the Jain Temples of Ellora* (Delhi, 1977).

For the iconography of the *Tīrthaṃkaras*, see Brindavan Chandra Bhattacharya's *The Jaina Iconography*, 2d rev. ed. (Delhi, 1974), and Klaus Bruhn's *The Jina-Images of Deogarh* (Leiden, 1969). The lives of Mahāvīra and the other Jinas are the subject of the *Jiṇacariya*, edited and translated by Hermann Jacobi in *The Kalpasûtra of Bhadrabâhu* (Leipzig, 1879), and of the *Jaina Sûtras*, vol. 1 (London, 1884; reprint, Delhi, 1964). See also *Triṣaṣṭiśalākāpuruṣacaritra*, or *The Lives of the Sixty-three Illustrious Persons by Hemacandra*, 6 vols., translated by Helen M. Johnson (Baroda, 1931–1962). On Ṛṣabha and civilization, see Adelheid Mette's *Indische Kulturstiftungsberichte und ihr Verhältnis zur Zeitaltersage* (Mainz, 1973).

COLETTE CAILLAT (1987 AND 2005)

TITHES. In the ancient Near East lie the origins of a sacral offering or payment of a tenth part of stated goods or property to the deity. Often given to the king or to the royal temple, the "tenth" was usually approximate, not exact. The practice is known from Mesopotamia, Syria-Palestine, Greece, and as far to the west as the Phoenician city of Carthage. Tithing also continued in Christian Europe as a church tithe and as a tax upon Jewish landholdings formerly owned by Christians (or claimed to have been so). Tithes paid in support of parish rectors continued in England into the twentieth century.

Early texts associate the tithe with support of the king and of temples of the royal house (see *Am.* 4:4, 7:1, 7:13; see also Samuel's forecast of actions to be taken by the king, *1 Sm.* 8:15, 8:17). The early biblical references to the tithe in *Genesis* 14:20 and 28:22 are also related to sites where royal shrines were located, such as Jerusalem and Bethel. It is not certain, however, that the tithe originated as a royal levy in support of temples and their personnel.

It is difficult to be sure whether or not the offering of the firstborn of animals and the firstfruits of field and orchard should be treated as a tithe. It seems unlikely, because the two are distinguished in *Numbers* 18 and in *Deuteronomy* 12:17. Moreover, the first fruits of grain and nonanimal products represented only a token amount, which would hardly have corresponded to the tenth or tithe. Firstfruits and tithes are closely related, however, in *Deuteronomy* 26:1–15 and in *Tobit* 1:6–8.

From the time of the monarchy in Israel, and especially from the eighth century forward, the Levites more and more were recognized as the beneficiaries of the tithe. They were not to share in the allotment of land along with the other tribes but were set apart to the service of the Lord (*Nm.* 18, *Dt.* 18:1–8, *Jos.* 21). The Levite cities seem to have been the store cities in which the tithes collected by the Levites were stored (see *Neh.* 10:38), just as the tithes in Mesopotamia were collected by temple personnel and stored in the temples or in their vicinity.

The tithe became the means of livelihood for the Levites during the middle and later periods of the monarchy. Once the city of Jerusalem had been designated by Josiah's reform as the central sanctuary for Israelite worship (622/1 BCE; see *2 Kgs.* 22–23), the need for the tithe to support the Levites at the many local sanctuaries would have disappeared. Accordingly, the law in *Deuteronomy* 14 specifies a quite different character and purpose for the tithe (*Dt.* 14:22–29). The tithe was to be taken to Jerusalem and eaten there before the Lord with rejoicing. It could be converted to money, if need be. And every third year the tithe was to be set aside for meeting the needs of the Levite, the resident alien, the orphan, and the widow. Scholars are divided over the issue of whether or not the text in *Deuteronomy* 14 can be reconciled with those in *Numbers* 18 and *Leviticus* 27.

If the legislation in *Numbers* 18 is later than that in *Deuteronomy* 14, however, the tithe was originally an offering associated with the king and with royal sanctuaries, It was then democratized to become the basis for a celebrative meal before the Lord at the places of worship. After that the priests and Levites claimed the tenth for themselves, with the firstfruits in particular going to the priests and the tithes going to the Levites (*Nm.* 18). Many scholars assign the priestly literary deposit to a period later than that of the Deuteronomic legislation. All acknowledge, however, that the priestly materials contain elements older than *Deuteronomy;* it seems probable that, in this case, the materials found in *Numbers* 18 are the older.

According to *Leviticus* 27:30–33, a distinction is made between those tithes that were redeemable—that is, convertible into silver—and those that were not. Animals were not redeemable, but grain, wine, and oil were. Items that were placed under the ban (Hebrew *cherem*) were never redeemable, and tithed animals, if suitable for offering, also were not redeemable. When a tithe was redeemed, one-fifth of the value was added (*Lv.* 27:31; see also *Lv.* 5:14–16).

With regard to tithes in other parts of the ancient world, Egyptian sources are not informative. There is no indication that the vast temple complexes in ancient Egypt were supported by a tithe. In Greece the situation is different. Numerous references to tithes of the annual harvest and to tithes of spoil taken in battle are known. Delphi, Delos, and Athens are mentioned as recipients of tithe offerings made to the gods. The offering of firstfruits and of tithes seems to have been quite closely associated.

As a part of the Jewish legislation, the tithe becomes fixed and indeed extends beyond the original prescription. The tractates *Terumot* and *Ma'aserot,* along with other talmudic collections, give particulars on postbiblical understandings. The *Book of Tobit* (second century BCE) offers important testimony of the changes in the understanding of the tithe. Tobit reports that when he was a young man, prior to his having been taken captive by the Assyrians and transported to Nineveh, he brought firstfruits, tithes of the produce, and first shearings to Jerusalem. He also gave three tithes: he presented the first tenth to the Levites (as required by *Nm.* 18), offered the second tenth in Jerusalem (as required by *Dt.* 14), and gave the third tenth to the needy (as specified in *Dt.* 14 as well).

In the early church, tithing became a means of securing a livelihood for church leadership, although in the earliest days of the Christian movement tithing seems to have been abandoned entirely in many Christian circles as a practice not in harmony with the Christian divergence from Jewish observances. The tithe remained of great importance for the church as a means of securing a stable institution, providing for ecclesiastical establishments, and offering resources for the care of the poor and the needy. In Judaism the tithe helped the community meet human needs, although complaints were voiced that a "second tithe," amounting to 20 percent (as apparently demanded by the different specifications in *Nm.* 18 and *Dt.* 14), was too heavy a burden on the community. Christian understanding of the tithe has had to combat both an overzealous application of the law of tithing (as some communities have understood it) and the supposition that to provide a tenth of one's goods to the church or to charitable purposes meant that the remainder of one's goods could be used in complete disregard of the claims of Christian stewardship.

SEE ALSO Israelite Law, article on Property Law; Levites.

BIBLIOGRAPHY

Eissfeldt, Otto. *Erstlinge und Zehnte im Alten Testament.* Göttingen, 1916. The classic work, a benchmark in the study of the subject.

Guthrie, Harvey H., Jr. "Tithe." In *Interpreter's Dictionary of the Bible,* vol. 4. New York, 1962; reprint, Nashville, Tenn., 1976.

Levine, Baruch A.. *Leviticus = Vayikra: The Traditional Hebrew Text with the New JPS Translation.* Philadelphia, Pa., New York, Jerusalem, 1988. See especially pp. 199–200.

Levine, Baruch A. *Numbers 1–20: A New Translation with Introduction and Commentary.* Anchor Bible 4A. New York, 1993.

Milgrom, Jacob, *Leviticus 23–27: A New Translation with Introduction and Commentary.* Anchor Bible 3B. New York, 2001. See especially his study of *Leviticus* 27 and the extended comments at the end of the volume.

Tigay, Jeffrey H. *Deuteronomy = Devarim: The Traditional Hebrew Text with the New JPS Translation.* Philadelphia, Pa., New York, Jerusalem, 1996.

Vaux, Roland de. *Les institutions de l'Ancien Testament.* 2 vols. Paris, 1958–1960. Translated by John McHugh as *Ancient Israel: Its Life and Institutions.* 2d ed. New York, 1961; reprint, Grand Rapids, Mich., 1997. See especially pp. 140–141, 380–382, and 403–405.

Vischer, Lukas. "Die Zehntforderung in der Alten Kirche." *Zeitschrift für Kirchengeschichte* 70 (1959): 201–217. Translated by Robert C. Schultz as *Tithing in the Early Church.* Philadelphia, Pa., 1966. Particularly good on the theologians of the early church, but sketchy on the biblical evidence.

Weinfield, Moshe. "Tithe." In *Encyclopaedia Judaica,* vol. 15. Jerusalem, 1971. A thorough and excellent treatment. See also the accompanying article, "Church Tithes," by Bernhard Blumenkranz.

WALTER HARRELSON (1987 AND 2005)

TIV RELIGION. The Tiv, who live in the central Benue valley of Nigeria, have a name for God, Aondo (sky), but are not much interested in him because they say that he is not much interested in them. God, in their view, created the earth and everything within it—including the forces of evil. Then he walked away—the Tiv do not ask where God went.

The Tiv are concerned with health (and with death, the ultimate manifestation of poor health), with fertility of crops, animals, and themselves, and with social harmony. To be healthy, to have plenty, and to live in harmony are natural states. Although the Tiv have some lore about spirits, no spirits manipulate the forces that interfere with these desirable states; Tiv respect their ancestors, but no ancestors manipulate the forces. Rather, the acts and devices of living human beings activate the forces of evil. Tiv ritual is designed to overcome these forces.

The Tiv say that some people grow a substance called *tsav* on their hearts that acts much like a physical organ. *Tsav* is both a sign of and source of special talent or ability, whether musical and artistic, social and political, or the ability to live to old age. One such special talent is to manipulate the forces that repair the society ritually.

Tsav is not present in all people. It becomes enlarged and nefariously powerful in any person who eats human flesh. *Tsav* itself does not tempt its bearers to eat human flesh—but lust for power may. Cannibalism is a metaphor for antisocial misuse of other people, their property, and substance.

The Tiv postulate that some of those with the special talents of *tsav* meet at night as an organization to keep the social and cosmic forces working for the benefit of society as a whole. The *mbatsav* (people with *tsav*) perform rituals to repair the land, but they may, through reckless human emotions such as spite, envy, or fear, use their power (as may any individual with *tsav,* acting alone) for antisocial and deadly purposes that spoil the land. To call the *mbatsav* witches is not accurate, even though they were labeled as such in some of the early literature.

The postulated activities of the *mbatsav,* both for the good of the community and for the evil purposes of some individuals, are associated with certain rituals performed with symbols called *akombo.* This ritual manipulation is called repairing the *akombo.* Those aspects of the natural and social world about which Tiv are most concerned are parceled out among named *akombo,* which exist as amulets, figurines, pots, or plants. Each is associated with a disease (although certain diseases are not associated with *akombo* because the Tiv recognize that some diseases are merely contagious). Each has its own ritual required to activate it or to pacify it. *Akombo,* however, are not personalized and are not spiritualized; they are certainly not gods. They work by forces akin to what Westerners think of as laws of nature.

When Tiv become ill, they assume that an *akombo* is the cause. That means either that some person of ill will who grows *tsav* has ritually manipulated the *akombo* so that it would seize a victim, or else that the victim or one of his or her close kinsmen has performed an act that was precluded by that *akombo* at the time of its creation (usually a commonplace and neutral act, although adultery and battery are prohibited by one or more *akombo*). To determine just which *akombo* is involved, Tiv consult diviners who throw chains of snake bones and pods to determine which *akombo* have been used to cause an illness or create social misfortune.

When the responsible *akombo* is revealed, the Tiv perform rituals to neutralize it. They must also remove the malice that activated it. The latter is achieved by a modest ritual in which every person concerned takes a little water into his or her mouth and spews it out in a spray, signifying that any grudges are no longer effective. Medicines will work only after the ill will is ritually removed and the *akombo* repaired. The ritual for each *akombo* varies, but the climax of all is a prayer that "evil descend and goodness ascend." These rituals are as much group therapy sessions as they are religious acts.

Tiv recognize two major categories of *akombo.* Small *akombo* attack individuals and their farms; their repair demands minor sacrificial animals, usually a chicken. A few small *akombo* require special sacrificial animals such as turtles or valuable ones such as goats or rams. Coins or other forms of wealth can be added to a less valuable sacrificial animal to make it taller and so serve as a more valuable one.

The great *akombo,* on the other hand, attack social groups; they must be repaired either by the elders of the community acting by day, or by a secret group (the same people) acting as the *mbatsav* by night.

At the end of any *akombo* ritual carried out by day, or as the last act of any funeral, the Tiv prepare and break a symbol called *swem.* Made in a potsherd from hearth ashes and symbolic plants, it is held high, then smashed to earth. The ashes, spreading on the breeze, mean that justice spreads through the land and that *swem* will punish evildoers.

Most Tiv claim not to know the details of any *akombo* or its ritual, and all deny knowing that the ritual was carried out at night. But they never postulate that any part of it is a mystery. Somebody knows. Tiv say "God knows" at funerals if they can find no other reason for the death. They mean that they have not yet discovered the human motivation behind the misfortune. But they do not question that the motivation is there and that ultimately it will be detected and either neutralized or punished.

Bibliography

Akiga (Benjamin Akighirga Sai). *Akiga's Story: The Tiv Tribe as Seen by One of Its Members.* 2d ed. Translated and annotated by Rupert East. London, 1965. First edition (1939) contains less material. This work is valuable for Akiga's texts; East's analyses are outdated.

Bohannan, Laura, and Paul Bohannan. *The Tiv of Central Nigeria.* Ethnographic Survey of Africa, Western Africa, part 8. London, 1953. See particularly pages 81–93. This account is brief, and its analysis varies somewhat from the one given in this article, but it is not contradictory.

Bohannan, Paul, and Laura Bohannan. *A Source Notebook on Tiv Religion.* 5 vols. New Haven, Conn., 1969. Field notes for a book that was never written, this work contains a vast amount of ethnographic information but is short on analysis.

Downes, Rupert M. *Tiv Religion.* Ibadan, Nigeria, 1971. Despite its publication date, this study is about Tiv religion as Captain Downes found it in the late 1920s and early 1930s. Downes was a distinguished colonial officer with three months' training in anthropology. His account contains invaluable information, but his analysis is shaky.

New Sources

Ahire, Philip Terdo. *The Tiv in Contemporary Nigeria.* Samaru Zaria, Nigeria, 1993.

Bohannan, Paul. *Justice and Judgment among the Tiv.* Prospect Heights, Ill., 1989.

Burfisher, Mary E. *Sex Roles in the Nigerian Tiv Farm Household.* West Hartford, Conn., 1985.

Jibo, Mvendaga. *Chieftaincy and Politics: The Tor Tiv in the Politics and Administration of Tivland.* New York, 2001.

Makar, Tesemchi. *The History of Political Change among the Tiv in the 19th and 20th Centuries.* Enugu, Nigeria, 1994.

Wegh, Shagbaor F. *Between Continuity and Change: Tiv Concept of Traditional and Modernity.* Lagos, Nigeria, 1998.

Paul Bohannan (1987)
Revised Bibliography

TJURUNGAS. Originally an Aranda word referring to a particular type of secret-sacred object (a stone board bearing engraved designs), the term *tjurunga* has now become generic in anthropological literature and is used to identify a wide variety of Australian Aboriginal religious objects. (The term *tjurunga* also has by now generally replaced the term *churinga* in anthropological writing.) The term covers a wide variety of meanings and can refer not only to the stone and wooden objects to which it was originally restricted but also to bullroarers, ground paintings, ritual poles, headgear, and religious songs (Strehlow, 1947, pp. 84ff.).

Tjurungas and *tjurunga*-type objects are widely distributed throughout central, southern, and western Australia, as well as the Northern Territory. They are usually secret-sacred and may be viewed only by initiated men, although in some cases women too possess religious boards. In all cases, *tjurungas* are closely associated with the mythic and totemic beings of the Dreaming. In the beginning, these beings shaped the physiographic features of the Aboriginal countryside and were, ultimately, responsible for creating human beings, who are regarded as their spiritual descendants. They also established particular Aboriginal social orders and were especially responsible for instituting religious ritual. The Dreaming characters are believed to be as alive today, spiritually, as they were in the past, and their significance continues. It is through the sacred objects that they live on in spiritual form. *Tjurungas* are often considered to represent particular mythic beings, and their engraved designs to represent specific localities and the activities associated with them; some *tjurungas*, however, are undecorated.

Stone *tjurungas* are flat oval platters that vary in size from nine to more than fifty centimeters in length and that, for the most part, are engraved on both sides. Smaller wooden objects are similarly decorated, but they are lenticular in cross section and elongated with rounded ends. Larger boards, between two and three meters in length, are made from tree-trunk sections; they are flat or slightly concave on the incised side and convex on the reverse. Traditionally, the lower incisor of a wallaby's jaw was used to engrave both stone and wooden *tjurungas*, but today steel rasps are used to shape the basic form and chisels to make the design. The act of incising the *tjurunga* is accompanied by songs relevant to the mythological associations of the pattern being made and is itself a ritual act. The knowledge of such songs is held by members of particular local groups, which have the responsibility of maintaining and reproducing the range of emblems and the designs connected with their own territories. Cognate groups collaborate with them in a complex patterning of ritual information between members of a number of similarly constituted social groups.

Tjurungas have a profound religious significance in contemporary desert Aboriginal cultures. Decorated with incised meandering lines, concentric circles, cross-hatching, zigzags, and, more rarely, naturalistic designs of bird and animal footprints and stylized human figures, they represent a compact and conventionalized statement of land occupation, utilization, and ownership, seen in terms of specific areas of land associated with particular mythic beings who in turn have their living representatives today. Beliefs about the origin of *tjurungas* vary according to culture (Davidson, 1953; Strehlow, 1964). Basically, though, it is believed that *tjurungas* were either created by mythic beings or represent tangible aspects of their bodies or something directly associated with them. In virtually all cases a *tjurunga* served as a vehicle in which resided part of a mythic being's spiritual essence. Some stone *tjurungas*, particularly those with well-worn designs or those having none, are regarded as the actual metamorphoses of mythic beings and may be ritually relevant to several sociodialectal groups. Usually, however, a *tjurunga* is personal; it is connected with both men and women and is symbolic of their mythic associations: men look after those belonging to the women of their own local group. As far as men are concerned, *tjurungas* play an important part in conception, initiation, and death.

While the Aranda may manufacture stone *tjurungas*, ensuring that male members of the oncoming generation possess such objects, they basically replicate the older ones according to their particular mythic and topographic type—that is, new *tjurungas* must correspond with those concerning the place of a person's conception and/or local group. In the Western Desert, Aborigines believe that all stone *tjurungas* are of supernatural origin, and these groups manufacture only wooden sacred boards. Small wooden boards or bull-roarers are made and presented to a novice during the final stages of his initiation; they signify his acceptance into the religious life of his people. It is only some years after a man's first initiation that he is introduced to the *tjurungas* of his own group. Later, he may prepare and incise such examples, either alone or in the company of close kin who share the same mythological associations.

The designs that appear on these religious objects are similar to those on spear-throwers, some shields, pearl-shell pendants, and a variety of head ornaments (all of which are used or worn publicly in contrast to the actual ritual objects). Clearly the form of an object and its purpose, rather than the design, indicate whether or not the item is to be regarded as open-sacred or secret-sacred (Berndt, Berndt, and Stanton, 1982, pp. 114–116). The designs depict, through a repetitive but symbolic structure, a particular segment of territory linked to an artist, his mythological connection with it, and some of the physiographic features that characterize this area of land. Moreover, this is usually shown looking from above rather than horizontally from the ground level. This is because mythic beings saw the land in this way. Some Western Desert Aborigines believe that the spirits of men who live a far distance from their own country travel through the sky on their sacred boards during sleep, and they, too, see the country in that way.

The same designs that appear on *tjurungas* are also reproduced in ochers on the bodies of participants in rituals. Depending on the area and the particular ritual being performed, ground structures of furrows and mounds have blood and red ocher superimposed on them and are decorated with feather down: these too represent stylized versions of territories within their mythic context. In such circumstances, *tjurungas* are hung from pole emblems or are worn in the men's headdresses. Since these objects are considered to be ritually and mythologically alive, they signify that the mythic being is actually present in a spiritual form.

The major function of *tjurungas* is to provide a tangible, visible representation of personal and social identity, but it is in fact much more than this. The *tjurunga* affirms and reaffirms a particular group's rights to a specific stretch of country through the land-based associations of mythic personages. These objects are always stored close to the places to which they belong, and such sites fall within different local group territories, the members of which are their custodians. When Aborigines moved away from their own countries as a result of European contact and eventually settled on government and mission stations, they brought some of their sacred objects with them, leaving others behind at their mythic sites. Smaller *tjurungas*, however, are often carried from one place to another when groups gather to hold large rituals that involve both men and women. In the Western Desert, these meetings, in which expressions of hostility are forbidden, are also occasions for settling interpersonal and intragroup disputes and grievances.

Deep reverence and respect are displayed toward all *tjurungas*, whether they are of stone or of wood. For example, fully initiated men may be specially invited to have revealed to them particular boards stored within a repository. This revelation must take place in the presence of a senior man who has the religious right to show them and explain their significance. In such cases, the boards have been prepared by a small group of elders who reanoint them with red ocher mixed with fat: they are treated as if they are living creatures. On approaching the place, the invited men use small branches of leaves to stroke the backs and heads of the sitting elders. This act is said to insulate the power that is believed to be inherent in the *tjurungas* and that can be dangerous to the unprepared. Mythic songs are sung and explained, and the objects are pressed to the bodies of the men who are seeing them for the first time. This action indicates that the men share in their power, which is regarded as eternal and is symbolized by the *tjurunga* objects.

SEE ALSO Dreaming, The.

BIBLIOGRAPHY

Berndt, Ronald M. *Australian Aboriginal Religion.* Leiden, 1974. Provides the first general view of Australian Aboriginal religion. It has iconographical references and is profusely illustrated.

Berndt, Ronald M., and Catherine H. Berndt, with John E. Stanton. *Aboriginal Australian Art: A Visual Perspective.* Sydney, 1982. A comprehensive coverage of traditional and innovative Aboriginal art within its sociocultural context. Illustrated.

Davidson, Daniel S. "The Possible Source and Antiquity of the Slate Churingas of Western Australia." *Proceedings of the American Philosophical Society* 97 (1953): 194–213. Although this article is based on limited materials, it continues to be the only significant study of Western Australian *tjurungas*.

Spencer, Baldwin, and F. J. Gillen. *The Native Tribes of Central Australia.* London, 1899. An early study of central Australian Aboriginal societies. Contains much material from traditions that are no longer extant and is especially rich in descriptions of Aranda ritual.

Strehlow, T. G. H. *Aranda Traditions.* Melbourne, 1947. This provides a discussion of the broad Aranda concept of the term *tjurunga*, with a number of ritual examples.

Strehlow, T. G. H. "The Art of the Circle, Line and Square." In *Australian Aboriginal Art*, edited by Ronald M. Berndt, pp. 44–59. Sydney, 1964. Provides an examination of the iconography of central Australian *tjurungas*, especially those of the Aranda, and also makes comparisons with Western Desert sacred boards.

JOHN E. STANTON (1987)

TLALOC, the pan-Mesoamerican deity of rain and fertility, was named by the Aztec, or Mexica, of Central Mexico. They chose a word derived from the Nahuatl term meaning "he is the embodiment of the earth." Other fertility deities throughout Mesoamerica include Chac among the Maya, Cocijo among the Zapotec, Tzahui among the Mixtec, and Tajin among the Totonac. Many of these deities continue to be worshiped by the contemporary indigenous people of Mesoamerica.

Tlaloc made his first appearance at Teotihuacan between 200 and 700 CE. He is depicted iconographically in murals and temples with round, "goggle" eyes and a fanged mouth. He strongly resembles a jaguar, with predatory features. At Teotihuacan, ideas regarding rain, fertility, wealth, and prestige were combined with human sacrifice and warfare.

More detailed textual information exists regarding Tlaloc during the Mexica period (1325–1521 CE). During the calendar year, which for the Aztec consisted of eighteen twenty-day "months" and five "unlucky days," approximately half of the ceremonies were dedicated to Tlaloc. These ceremonies—such as human sacrifices, fasting, and feasts—focused on topics such as ancestors, food, rain, and fertility. Worship of Tlaloc, therefore, encompassed a wide spectrum of Mesoamerican concerns and articulated more general understandings of the entire cosmology.

Water was an important element in Mesoamerican religions. Its presence in the iconography at ceremonial centers illustrates its material and symbolic importance. The circulation of water through the ceremonial precinct was intimately associated with the deities who were housed in temples there.

According to the Aztec cosmology, all material existence was surrounded by water. In Nahuatl, the language of the

Aztec (still spoken by nearly three million Mexicans), the word for city is *altepetl.* Its literal translation is "water mountain," and it describes the central ceremonial temple that defined the city. Mountains were thought to be containers of water, which made its way from the sea. Tlaloc oversaw the circulation of water through the earth; therefore, human beings propitiated him so that he would release just the right amount of water.

Ritual descriptions emphasized the relationship of the human body and the earth. Both objects were understood to simultaneously be containers of, and surrounded by, liquid. Human flesh was a container for blood, which was understood as a living fluid. During gestation, the human body was surrounded by amniotic fluid. These material aspects of human existence mirrored the Aztec's understanding of their living landscape. Thus, they would perform healing practices, divinatory activity of various sorts, and rituals surrounding childbirth and child-rearing at particular places, where Tlaloc could receive the gifts of human beings.

The material makeup of the human body corresponded with the material makeup of land. Thus Tlaloc, although a rain deity, was also understood to be Tlalteuctli—the "earth lord." His body was likened to that of the crocodile: the ridges of his back were associated with the mountains and ravines, and he was said to float on the primordial saltwater sea. The Tlaloques were "rain dwarfs"; namely, lesser deities associated with various climatological phenomena such as snow, sleet, and lightning.

Tlaloc needed to eat. The ceremonial relationship between human beings and the Tlaloques was primarily based on food exchange. Rain was essential for the development of agriculture in Mesoamerica. In particular, the development of maize cultivation over several thousand years had become the basis for urban culture. Consequently, the Aztec performed ritual strategies for propitiating the rain deities so that they would release adequate amounts of moisture for agricultural bounty. Human beings grew and prospered due to the interaction of earth and water on Tlaloc's body. The Aztec believed that the flesh and blood of human beings, given to Tlaloc through human sacrifice, sustained and regenerated his body. Thus, Tlaloc and the Aztec were in an intimate, reciprocal relationship.

Ceremonial temples, or *altepetl,* were openings to the watery dwelling of the deities.Yet human existence was understood to materially depend on this hidden world of Tlalocan ("the place of Tlaloc"). Ritual activities performed at these places brought human beings into intimate contact with the entire cosmos. Material elements such as earth, water, air, human flesh and blood, trees, and various kinds of animals were understood to be in dynamic interaction with each other.

Since Tlaloc was seen as a living embodiment of the land, whose primary duty was to control the circulation of water both inside and above the earthly plane, the title of "rain deity" is an insufficient description. Attempting to describe the dynamic nature of the ceremonial interactions between the Aztec and Tlaloc as a feeding relationship, one scholar has referred to the mythic world of the Aztec as an "eating landscape."

SEE ALSO Aztec Religion; Cosmology, article on Indigenous North and Mesoamerican Cosmologies; Mesoamerican Religions, article on Formative Cultures.

BIBLIOGRAPHY

Arnold, Philip P. *Eating Landscape: Aztec and European Occupation of Tlalocan.* Niwot, Colo., 1999. Discusses the importance of fertility rites for the Aztec and describes how they meaningfully inhabited their material world.

Broda, Johanna. "Las fiestas Aztecas de los dioses de la luvia: Una reconstruccíon según las fuentes del siglo XVI." *Revista Española de Antropología Americana* 6 (1971): 245–327. Presents a comprehensive outline of rain and fertility gods as described in early colonial sources.

Nicholson, H.B. "Religion in Pre-Hispanic Central Mexico." In *Handbook of Middle American Indians,* vol. 10, *Archaeology of Northern Mesoamerica,* edited by Gordon F. Eckhom and Ignacio Bernal, pp. 395–446. Austin, Tex., 1971. This important article on deities of the Aztec includes a lengthy section on Tlaloc and the Tlaloques.

Sandstrom, Alan R. *Corn Is Our Blood: Culture and Ethnic Identity in a Contemporary Aztec Indian Village.* Norman, Okla., 1991. Sandstrom describes the contemporary understanding of Tlaloc among Nahuatl-speaking people.

PHILIP P. ARNOLD (2005)

TLAXCALAN RELIGION.

What is in the early twenty-first century the Mexican state of Tlaxcala occupies roughly the same territory as the old pre-Hispanic Tlaxcalan confederacy, an alliance of several indigenous principalities independent of the so-called Aztec empire. Its inhabitants were Nahuatl-speaking Indians, and they were the main allies of Hernán Cortés in the Spanish conquest of Mexico from 1519 to 1522. Present-day Tlaxcala is located on the western fringes of the central Mexican highlands. It is the smallest state in the nation, with a population of slightly more than 600,000. Although less than 15 percent of the population still speaks Nahuatl, the ethnic and somatic composition of Tlaxcala is predominantly Indian, and there persists a strong identification with the Indian past.

PRE-HISPANIC BACKGROUND. When the Spaniards arrived in Mexico in 1519 they found a polytheistic religion widespread throughout the area that in the twentieth century came to be known archaeologically and ethnologically as Mesoamerica. Mesoamerica exhibited a rather high degree of cultural uniformity, and in no cultural domain was this more true than in the realm of religion. Thus, Tlaxcalan polytheism was a variant of a pan-Mesoamerican religion, minimally different from, say, Méxica-Aztec, Huastec, Tarascan, Zapotec, or even Maya polytheism.

The main characteristics of Tlaxcalan polytheism were seven:

1. A highly diversified and specialized pantheon, in which hundreds of patron gods and goddesses relating to nearly every human activity, natural phenomenon, or social grouping were arranged in a somewhat hierarchical order
2. A complex and extensive ritual and ceremonial yearly cycle regulated by the calendrical system
3. A sophisticated cosmology and theology centered on the origins and nature of the gods, the creation of humans and the universe, the regulation of humanity's relationship to the gods, the disposition of the dead, and afterlife
4. A religious ideology that emphasized pragmatism in the relationship between humanity and the supernatural at the expense of values and morality, which were almost exclusively an aspect of the social structure in operation
5. An extensive and well-organized priesthood in charge of the administration of religion and several ancillary aspects of the social structure
6. A tremendous emphasis on human sacrifices to the gods and a significant degree of ritual cannibalism
7. A pronounced concern with bloodshed and the dead, and a cult of the dead approaching ancestor worship

Tlaxcalan religion pervaded every significant cultural domain of the confederacy: society, economy, polity, administration, and the military. Indeed, religion was the driving force of Tlaxcalan culture. In many distinct ways, however, Tlaxcalan religion was not that different from Old World polytheistic systems such as those of the Indo-Europeans and the Chinese: the gods were made in the image of humans, and they exhibited the foibles, virtues, and vices of human beings; the gods were hierarchically arranged in an organized pantheon; the social structure of the gods mirrored that of humans, with whom they interacted in a variety of ways; and religion was essentially a pragmatic ritualistic system regulating the relationship between humans and the supernatural.

SYNCRETIC DEVELOPMENT. Tlaxcala was one of the first regions of the continental New World to be subject to systematic efforts to convert its inhabitants. In 1524, the task of indoctrinating the Indian population in the ritual, ceremonial, and theological practices of Roman Catholicism was assigned to the Franciscan friars. For nearly a century the Tlaxcalans were under the religious leadership of the Franciscans. During the second decade of the seventeenth century, the Franciscans were replaced by secular priests and clerics, who continued the catechization of the Indian population. By the end of the seventeenth century, Tlaxcalan Indian Catholicism had essentially crystallized into what it is in the early twenty-first century.

The context of conversion and indoctrination to Catholicism in Tlaxcala can be characterized as "guided syncretism," a policy that the Franciscans consciously followed for two principal reasons: first, to convert the Indians rapidly; and, second, to soften the impact of forced conversion and thus make the new religion more palatable to the masses of the Indian population. This policy of conversion was greatly facilitated by the symbolic, ritual, ceremonial, and formal similarities between the lengthy roster of Catholic saints and the highly diversified Tlaxcalan pantheon. As early as the turn of the seventeenth century, the Tlaxcalan Indians were already practicing a syncretic kind of Catholicism. This was partly the result of the Franciscans' efforts in fostering identifications between the interacting religious traditions, particularly between Tlaxcalan gods and Catholic saints. The same process is evident in the emergence of local (community) religious hierarchies, in which such pre-Hispanic institutions as the priestly houses (*calmecac*) and people's houses (*telpochcalli*) came to interact with such similar Catholic institutions as stewardships (*mayordomías*) and sodalities (*cofradías*). The syncretic process undergone by Tlaxcalan religion from 1524 until approximately the last quarter of the seventeenth century permanently marked Indian Catholicism, and to a lesser extent all rural and urban Catholicism throughout the region.

CONTEMPORARY TLAXCALAN RELIGION. Contemporary Tlaxcalan Catholicism is centered on several institutions: the cult of the saints, the cult of the dead, the *mayordomía* system, the *ayuntamiento religioso* (local religious hierarchy), and the magico-symbolic system. It may be characterized as primarily a type of folk religion; that is, its ritual and ceremonial complex is markedly different from the national Catholic religion of Mexico and is carried on by the *barrios* (quasi-socioreligious units), *hermandades* (brotherhoods), *cofradías,* and other religious institutions of a syncretic nature. The single most important institution in the administration of Tlaxcalan religion is the *república eclesiástica* (ecclesiastic republic), which includes all annually elected officials of the numerous stewardships and the local hierarchy.

One fundamental aspect of Tlaxcalan religion remains unchanged: The present-day folk Catholicism retains the essentially pragmatic and ritualistic character of pre-Hispanic polytheism. The supernatural belief system has one general, predominant aim: to make the individual and the collective world of social existence safe and secure by the proper propitiation of all supernatural forces, regardless of the structural means employed. The relationship between humans and the supernatural, then, is characterized by pragmatic and rather selfish motives for which the individual and the group pay dearly in terms of time and economic and social resources.

Finally, there is a significant magical component to Tlaxcalan religion. It coexists side by side with folk Catholicism and is regulated by the same belief system. Although the practice of magic sometimes merges with folk Catholicism and is part of the syncretic complex, more often it forms a separate system. Witchcraft, sorcery, soul loss, and belief in a series of anthropomorphic or animistic supernaturals constitute the bulk of the magical component. All these practices are of pre-Hispanic origin, but they do contain elements of European and even African witchcraft and sorcery, some of which became syncretized independently of Catholicism.

Bibliography

Pre-Hispanic Polytheism

Carrasco, Pedro. "La sociedad mexicana antes de la Conquista." In *Historia general de México,* vol. 1, edited by Bernardo García Martínez. Mexico City, 1976.

López Austin, Alfredo. *Hombre Dios: Religión y política en el mundo náhuatl.* Mexico City, 1973.

Sahagún, Bernardino de. *Historia general de las cosas de la Nueva España* (compiled 1569–1582; first published 1820). Translated by Arthur J. O. Anderson and Charles E. Dibble as *Florentine Codex: General History of the Things of New Spain,* 13 vols. Santa Fe, N. Mex., 1950–1982.

Syncretic Development

Gibson, Charles. *Tlaxcala in the Sixteenth Century.* New Haven, Conn., 1952.

Nutini, Hugo G., and Betty Bell. *Ritual Kinship,* vol. 1, *The Structure and Historical Development of the Compadrazgo System in Rural Tlaxcala.* Princeton, N. J. 1980.

Contemporary Folk Catholicism

Nutini, Hugo G. *San Bernardino Contla: Marriage and Family Structure in a Tlaxcalan Municipio.* Pittsburgh, 1968.

Nutini, Hugo G. *Ritual Kinship,* vol. 2, *Ideological and Structural Integration of the Compadrazgo System in Rural Tlaxcala.* Princeton, N. J., 1984.

Nutini, Hugo G., and Barry L. Isaac. "Ideology and the Sacro-Symbolic Functions of Compadrazgo in Santa María Belén Azitzimititlán, Tlaxcala, Mexico." *Uomo: Società, tradizione, sviluppo* 1 (1977): 81–120.

Hugo G. Nutini (1987 and 2005)

TOADS See FROGS AND TOADS

TOBACCO.

Now used recreationally throughout the world, tobacco originated in South America as long as eight thousand years ago as a product of two cultivated hybrid species of the genus *Nicotiana, N. rustica* and *N. tabacum.* The genus, which belongs to the nightshade or potato family (Solanaceae), occurs naturally in many parts of the world, including North and South America, Australia, some of the South Pacific Islands, and—with but a single species—Africa. The greatest number is native to North and South America, but even with this relative abundance of nicotine-bearing species, only in one small area of the New World, most likely fertile valleys located between Peru and Ecuador, did early food cultivators discover and make use of the extraordinary effects on mind and body of the powerful alkaloid from which the genus derives its name.

More than likely the early experiments with cross-fertilization that resulted in the two cultivated hybrid species of tobacco, *Nicotiana rustica* and *N. tabacum,* were products of that moment in time when some South American Indians turned from a pure hunting and gathering economy to food cultivation, beginning with the root crop cassava, or manioc. Although all species of the genus contain nicotine, that alkaloid is present in much greater amounts in the two cultigens of ancient lineage, *N. tabacum,* the progenitor of commercial blends, and *N. rustica.* The former is the more variable, with percentages of nicotine content in the leaf ranging from only 0.6 percent to 9.0 percent. In contrast, in a Mexican species of *N. rustica,* the percentage of nicotine was as high as 19 to 20 percent. Although, as Johannes Wilbert notes in his pathbreaking book *Tobacco and Shamanism in South America* (1987), nicotine is distributed throughout the plant, in both species the leaves contain the highest amount, those of *N. rustica* far outstripping the milder species in its capacity to inebriate and addict. Little wonder, then, that the leaves were used either whole or dried and crushed and that *N. rustica* achieved by far the widest distribution as a sacred ecstatic intoxicant among many Native American peoples. Often, especially in South America, it serves as the exclusive vehicle of the shamanic trance, and sometimes it is one of several herbal preparations employed for the altered mental state in which the shaman, it is believed, travels out-of-body to consult with the spirits of the deceased and the gods or to do battle with disease demons and other negative forces on behalf of his or her clients.

Tobacco is sometimes also employed to create an especially receptive state of mind for the application of another psychoactive species with even greater ramifications in the intellectual culture. Thus, to cite just two examples, on their peyote pilgrimages to the north-central Mexican desert, the Huichol Indians of northwestern Mexico, whose most sacred and supernaturally charged plant is peyote, smoke *N. rustica* tobacco wrapped in cornhusks to intensify the effects of the psychoactive cactus. Far to the south, on the north coast of Peru, Mestizo *curanderos* combine tobacco syrup administered through the nostrils with infusions of San Pedro (*Trichocereus pachanoi*), the popular name for a tall, columnar cactus that, like peyote, has mescaline as its primary alkaloid and whose place in Andean shamanism is archaeologically documented as reaching back at least three and half millennia.

It should be emphasized that as many as two hundred major and minor species have been identified in the visionary-therapeutic pharmacopoeias of Native American shamans, the majority in the tropics. Of these, tobacco had the widest distribution even before it became a major item of commerce as a recreational drug in the centuries after Christopher Columbus arrived in the New World. Curiously, despite the rapid pre-Columbian diffusion of tobacco through the Indian Americas, tobacco's cultural role as a visionary intoxicant seems to have stopped at the shores of the Atlantic and the Pacific. Tobacco and the custom of smoking reached West Africa in the 1500s, not long after Columbus's first landfall in the Western Hemisphere, and spread on that continent so quickly that some students of the phenomenon assumed it to be African in origin, reaching the New World with the slave trade, rather than the other way round.

In parts of Africa, notably the Cameroons and Nigeria, tobacco pipes of terra-cotta, metal, and other materials evolved into great sculpture, real masterpieces of portable art and objects of prestige associated with the nobility, great warriors, and priests, with long stems and complex chimneys rivaling in size and volume the monumental pipes of the so-called Mound Builder cultures of prehistoric North America. Both men and women smoked pipes, some with sculptural bowls whose interiors exceed the size of large teacups or coffee cups. Even if the tobacco was of the milder kind, it is hard to believe that the amount of nicotine the smoker absorbed would not have had some effect on consciousness. And yet if African medicine men or shamans used tobacco to contact the spirits, no evidence for it exists. The only possible hint that there was more to African smoking than pleasure or sociability comes from a report by the French anthropologist and Africanist Marcel Griaule (1898–1956). During field research with the Dogon people of Mali, Griaule met an old blind hunter named Ogotemmêli, who was especially knowledgeable in the cosmology and religion of his people. "Having sat down on his threshold," Griaule recounts, "Ogotemmêli scraped in his tobacco pouch and gathered some yellowish dust on the flap. 'Tobacco,' he said, 'clears up the sense of judgment.' And he began to reconstruct the system of the world, for one had to begin with the very beginnings of things" (Griaule, 1970, p. 16).

Tobacco was introduced into Siberia by trade from Russia's possessions in Alaska and the Aleutians—or even earlier; that is, at least by the 1700s. But there are no reliable reports that Siberian shamans adopted it as a ritual intoxicant alongside, or even instead of, the fly agaric mushroom, *Amanita muscaria.* In the Himalayas, on the other hand, Nepalese shamans have added *N. rustica* tobacco to a long list of psychoactive species they classify as "traveling plants" belonging to the god Śiva—"traveling" because they enable the shaman to travel to other worlds. *N. tabacum,* in contrast, is regarded as merely "pleasurable." Both species were introduced in colonial times.

TOBACCO MYTHS. A common theme in the origin mythology of tobacco among Native Americans is that this most widely distributed psychoactive species in the New World was given to the first people by the gods. The gods themselves were believed to require tobacco as their sacred, and even only proper, food. But in making it a gift to humanity they neglected to keep any for their own use—"not even one pipeful," in the words of an elder of the Fox tribe of Wisconsin (Michelson, 1932, p. 127). So they must rely on human beings to give it to them. In exchange, the gods listen to petitions and confer their blessings or, conversely, withhold evil. Reciprocity is thus extended from the social realm to interaction between the spirit world and human beings, whose control over a spirit food fervently desired by the supernaturals gives them some leverage, for the gods are said to be unable to resist it.

The craving for tobacco attributed to the supernaturals can thus also be understood as an extrapolation from human experience, in this case nicotine addiction, especially among tribes whose shamans regularly intoxicated themselves with tobacco. The use of tobacco as smoke, snuff, cuds mixed with lime, or liquid infusions to induce "drunkenness" for the purpose of "communicating with demons" is repeatedly described by sixteenth-century sources from the Caribbean, Mexico, and South America, though in some cases the intoxicating substance was probably not tobacco but another of the many botanical hallucinogens then and now in ritual use.

Wilbert found a particularly complex variety of "tobacco shamanism" among the Venezuelan Warao, whose sacred geography and cosmic architecture are virtually constructed of tobacco smoke and whose shamans smoke themselves into "out-of-body" ecstatic trance states with cane cigarettes three and four feet long. Warao shamans travel to the House of Tobacco Smoke in the eastern part of the universe over a celestial bridge of tobacco smoke conceived of as a channel of energy that guarantees health and abundance on earth as long as the supernaturals continue to be properly fed with tobacco smoke. Wilbert reports that Warao shamans crave tobacco smoke with such "tremendous physiological and psychological urgency" that they are literally sick without it. They believe that the gods likewise await their gift of tobacco with the craving of an addict and will inevitably enter into mutually beneficial relationships with human beings as long as humans provide the gift.

This attribution of addictive craving to the gods probably diffused together with cultivated tobacco itself. The notion dominates tobacco mythology and ritual even among peoples who, like those of the North American Plains and Prairies, customarily reduced the potency of tobacco with such nonpsychoactive plant materials as red willow bark and who, in any event, smoked only small quantities ceremonially in sacred pipes with chimneys of limited interior diameter to please gods and spirits and sanctify the spoken word, never to the point of intoxication.

A significant dichotomy may be noted between the origin mythologies of the cultivated hybrid species *Nicotiana rustica* and the less potent and less widely distributed *N. tabacum,* on the one hand, and the wild species (*N. attenuata, N. bigelovii,* and *N. trigonophylla*) of aboriginal western North America, on the other. While the origin of the Indian species is commonly credited to the divine realm, the latter two species are frequently attributed to the dead, perhaps because, as casuals, these species (like the daturas, which also belong to the Solonaceae) are sometimes seen to grow in disturbed soil (e.g., on graves). In California and the Great Basin they are often highly valued as gifts of the ancestors, but in transitional areas, where both wild and cultivated species are available, the wild varieties are sometimes feared for their association with death.

The oldest evidence thought to point to smoking comes from California, where conical stone pipes dating to circa 4000 BCE have been excavated and where wild tobaccos were widely employed for shamanistic, magico-religious, and medicinal procedures, including the ecstatic trance. The Shoshonean (Uto-Aztecan) Kawaiisu of south-central California used virtually every technique of ingestion reported from South America, including smoking, snuffing, licking, chewing, and swallowing. Likewise, the prophylactic, therapeutic, and metaphysical uses for cultivated species in South America and eastern North America were paralleled by these and other California tribes with the native wild species. The most common method was mixing the pulverized, dried leaves with slaked and powdered lime and either swallowing the mixture dry or liquified or licking and sucking it.

The Kawaiisu participated in the ecstatic-initiatory *toloache (Datura inoxia)* religion common to other California Indians, but tobacco, whose magical potency was given to the first people by the trickster culture hero Coyote, was much more generally employed by them and their neighbors. They used it as a mild-to-potent dream-inducing soporific; as a shamanistic and initiatory intoxicant; or for preventing and curing illness; repelling and killing rattlesnakes; driving away ghosts, monsters, and other threatening supernatural beings; and divining and manipulating the weather.

In North America the widespread function of tobacco to please the spirits is particularly well documented among the Iroquois and Algonquin of the Eastern Woodlands and the Plains and Prairie tribes. Seneca mythology attributes the origin of tobacco (*Nicotiana rustica*) to Awen'hai'i (ancient bodied one), the pregnant daughter of the Great Chief in the Sky, who stripped the heavens of tobacco when she fell onto the newly created earth island through a hole in the sky. This left not only the heavenly powers but the vast company of other spirits that manifest themselves in nature without their most essential divine sustenance. To induce these spirits, which included masters and mistresses of animals and plants as well as the "faces" that appear to hunters in the forest or in dreams and that are represented by the wooden masks of the shamanistic medicine societies of the Iroquois, to act on one's behalf requires the indispensable gift of tobacco.

THERAPEUTIC APPLICATIONS. Though widely employed to trigger the ecstatic visionary trance that is one of the cornerstones of shamanism, tobacco was also deeply embedded in native therapeutics. Almost certainly this was in large part based on observation and experience with the pharmacological effects of nicotine, not only on the human organism but other phenomena in the environment. Answering his own question whether pharmacological science corroborates nicotine therapy and curing practices with tobacco of South American shamans, Wilbert, in a paper published in 1991, lists a whole series of tobacco administrations by shamans that at first sight might be considered "magical" but whose therapeutic efficacy can be pharmacologically demonstrated.

Take, for example, the shaman's breath. Not only in the Americas but wherever shamanism survives, the shaman's breath is considered to have curative, purifying, and strengthening powers. Except in the Arctic, breath is of course invisible, but in the American tropics it is often given form by tobacco smoke. This phenomenon of shamanic practice was noted by the earliest European explorers. Shamans blow both their breath alone and thick clouds of tobacco smoke over their patient and his or her relatives and also fumigate the house. Blowing tobacco smoke is especially valued at the planting season. Before putting their seeds in the ground, farmers ask their shaman to "purify" their seed stock with tobacco smoke to assure a good harvest. Of course, tobacco smoke is sacred and feeds the spirits. But there is more to it than magic or religion: nicotine is a powerful insecticide and vermifuge. German experimenters found that fully 8 percent of the insecticides in tobacco are transferred into tobacco smoke. Seeds fumigated with nicotine against insect pests have in fact been observed to do better than those not so treated.

In treating their patients, shamans not only blow thick clouds of smoke but "capture" the smoke in their cupped hands; direct it into a wound, an aching or extracted tooth, eyes, nose, and mouth; and then massage the affected body parts. In addition curers blow nicotine-laden spittle and soothe aches and pains with tobacco juice. "Looking at these therapeutic practices from the point of view of drug administration," writes Wilbert, one recognizes in them more or less sustained-release mechanisms of application. Tobacco leaves are also used as plasters or compacts. Tobacco therapy thus involves the respiratory, dermal, and even gastrointestinal routes.

In both South America and Mexico, tobacco was also employed in the form of therapeutic enemas. In addition to tobacco, other plants that native peoples invested with sacred power and even divinity were so used. For example, a seventeenth-century Spanish colonial account of therapeutic practices and incantations in a community of speakers of Nahuatl (Aztec) in Guerrero, Mexico, lists therapeutic enemas not only of *piciétl* (tobacco, *Nicotiana rustica*) but of peyote (*Lophophora williamsii*), the little cactus of the north-central Mexican desert whose most important visionary alkaloid is mescaline; an aquatic species of *Datura*; and *ololiuhqui*, the Nahuatl name for the potent seeds of the white-flowering morning glory *Turbina* (form. *Rivea*) *corymbosa*, whose active principles are lysergic acid derivatives related to synthetic LSD.

Native American tobacco lore and therapy thus run counter to modern experience with the effects of tobacco on human health. Of course, Indian tobaccos are truly "organic"—they are cultivated, processed, and ritually employed without chemicals. Shamans often reach great age, including those for whom tobacco is the primary avenue of ecstasy.

Whatever negative effects tobacco intoxication has on the vocal cords, visual acuity, color perception, and so on—and Wilbert lists many of these—have, by way of natural modeling, long since been processed into desirable qualities in the intellectual world of tobacco shamanism. Still, there are no statistics to show whether tobacco shamans fall victim to lung cancer, heart disease, emphysema, or any of the other ills associated in the West with smoking. That Native American peoples are well aware that tobacco can kill is obvious from the many traditions of symbolic death and resurrection through the experience of initiatory intoxication. But there is also the reverse: revitalization, bringing the dead back to life by means of tobacco. This desirable end is dramatically illustrated in the following Seneca myth from upstate New York (Hewitt, 1918):

> In his travels a youth encounters a skeletonized man in a place heaped with the bones of dead people. Skeleton Man tells the youth that the only thing he desires is tobacco, but his pipe and pouch are empty. He sends the youth on a harrowing journey, past or through dangerous obstacles and variations of an ordeal familiar from heroic, funerary, and shamanic mythology—the Symplegades-like "paradoxical passage," that is, clashing rocks, islands, or icebergs that open and close in an instant and through which the hero, the soul, or the shaman must pass. The Seneca youth survives these ordeals and finally reaches a distant place where tobacco is guarded by Seven Sisters and their terrible old mother. Using his *orenda* (spirit power) and trickery, he succeeds in entering the lodge of the female spirits, evading their war clubs and escaping with the magical tobacco. When he returns and fills Skeleton Man's pipe, the bones of the dead people are reclothed with flesh, and the people return to life.

See Also Smoking.

Bibliography

Griaule, Marcel. *Conversions with Ogototemmêli: An Introduction to Dogon Religious Ideas.* London, 1970.

Hewitt, J. N. B., ed. "Seneca Fiction, Legends, and Myths: Part 1." In *Thirty-second Annual Report of the Bureau of American Ethnology,* pp. 37–813. Washington, D.C., 1918. The first volume of a comprehensive collection of Seneca Iroquois oral traditions by a Smithsonian Institution ethnologist and linguist who was a Tuscaloosa, one of the nations of the Iroquois Confederacy.

Meyer, Laure. *Art and Craft in Africa.* Paris, 1995. With numerous photographs in full color, a noted French art historian surveys the high technical and aesthetic qualities of everyday and court arts of one hundred African tribes.

Michelson, Truman. *Notes on the Fox Wapanowiweni.* Smithsonian Institution, Bureau of American Ethnology, Bulletin 105. Washington, D.C., 1932.

Müller-Ebeling, Claudia, Christian Rätsch, and Surenda Bahadur Shahi. *Shamanism and Tantra in the Himalayas.* Rochester, Vt., 2002. With 605 color and black-and-white illustrations, this is a popular but authoritative overview of Nepalese shamans and *tantrikas* and their practices, with special emphasis on psychoactive plants.

Parker, Arthur C. *Seneca Myths and Folk Tales.* Buffalo, N.Y., 1923. An important collection of the oral traditions of his own people, the Iroqouian Seneca of upstate New York, by an ethnologist and New York State archaeologist who served for many years as director of the New York State Museum.

Robicsek, Francis. *The Smoking Gods: Tobacco in Maya Art, History, and* Religion. Norman, Okla., 1978. A richly illustrated study of tobacco and smoking in ancient Maya art, history, and religion.

Ruiz de Alarcón, Hernando. *Treatise on the Heathen Superstitions That Today Live among the Indians of This New Spain, 1629.* Translated and edited by J. Richard Andrews and Ross Hassig. Norman, Okla., 1984.

Wilbert, Johannes. "Tobacco and Shamanistic Ecstasy among the Warao Indians of Venezuela." In *Flesh of the Gods: The Ritual Use of Hallucinogens,* edited by Peter T. Furst, pp. 55–83. New York, 1972. New ed., Prospect Heights, Ill., 1990. A pioneering essay on Warao tobacco shamanism and tobacco cosmology, proposing for the first time that tobacco belongs in the category of the "true" hallucinogens.

Wilbert, Johannes. *Tobacco and Shamanism in South America.* New Haven, Conn., 1987. A pathbreaking study of the ethnology, ethnobotany, and pharmacology of tobacco, the physiological effects of nicotine, and their incorporation in the ideology and practice of shamanism across the South American continent by a UCLA ethnologist whose fieldwork among Indian peoples spans five decades.

Wilbert, Johannes. "Does Pharmacology Corroborate the Nicotine Therapy and Practice of South American Shamanism?" *Journal of Ethnopharmacology* 32 (1991): 179–186. An examination of empirical ethnographic data on indigenous nicotine therapy shows it to compare favorably against experimental clinical studies of nicotine pharmacology and its effects on the human body.

Zigmond, Maurice L. *Kawaiisu Ethnobotany.* Salt Lake City, 1981.

Peter T. Furst (2005)

TOLSTOY, LEO

TOLSTOY, LEO (1828–1910), Russian writer. Leo Nikolaevich Tolstoy was born on his family's estate of Yasnaia Poliana (Bright Meadow), in Tula Province. His parents, both from the high aristocracy, died in his early boyhood. Tolstoy was a melancholy child, self-centered but filled with the desire to be a better person.

He entered the University of Kazan in 1844, planning to become a diplomat, but left the university in 1847 without taking a degree. That same year, he inherited Yasnaia Poliana and went there to live. In 1849 he opened a school for the village children and was one of its teachers. At this time, as later, he was strongly under the influence of Rousseau.

Tolstoy volunteered in 1851 for army service in the Caucasus, and he subsequently took part in the Crimean War (1854–1856) in the Danube region and at Sevastopol. He left the army in 1856 and returned to Yasnaia Poliana.

By the following year he had published a semi-autobiographical trilogy on his childhood and youth and a group of short stories on the war in the Caucasus and at Sevastopol. These works soon brought him fame.

Tolstoy made the first of two trips to western Europe in 1857 and was repelled by the absence of spiritual values and the materialism he found there. In Paris he witnessed a public execution and from it concluded that all governments were immoral. During his second trip abroad in 1860 his favorite brother, Nikolai, who had tuberculosis, died in Tolstoy's arms. The next year Tolstoy returned to Russia and resumed teaching at the Yasnaia Poliana school.

In 1862 Tolstoy married Sof'ia Andreevna Bers, eighteen years old. They had thirteen children, of whom five died. The first decade of his marriage was the happiest time of his life. During this period he wrote *War and Peace* (1863–1869).

Tolstoy's concern with moral development and religion was evident from his childhood. At the age of nineteen he wrote out rules of behavior for himself that were close to the precepts of his later Christianity. In 1855 he wanted to found a new religion, free of dogma and mysticism. Happiness would be achieved not in heaven but on earth, by following the voice of one's conscience. His letters from the 1850s on, and his literary works from *Childhood* (1852) to *Anna Karenina* (1873–1877), reflect the development of his ideas.

Beginning in the early 1870s, Tolstoy engaged in a moral and religious quest that was to continue until the end of his life. He had begun reading Schopenhauer in 1867 and was influenced by Schopenhauer's negative view of life. In the fall of 1869, while on a trip to buy land, he stopped at the provincial town of Arzamas, staying overnight at an inn. There, in the middle of the night, he had a terrifying vision of death. From this time on, Tolstoy was obsessed with thoughts of his own death—although earlier works, like *Three Deaths* (1859), were witness that the problem of death had been on his mind for years. It was this obsession that led to his search for a viable religious faith, one that would make life worth living and would reconcile him to the bitter fact that he too must die.

Tolstoy's spiritual crisis began during the writing of *Anna Karenina* and lasted until 1879. It is mirrored in the seekings of Levin, the novel's hero, and is akin to the spiritual quest that had occupied Pierre Bezukhov, the hero of *War and Peace.* But whereas *War and Peace* had ended in optimism, in *Anna Karenina* a dark force seems to take over. Levin cannot accept a materialist explanation for his life. That would be "the mockery of Satan," the power that remains in the universe if there is no God. This power is Schopenhauer's blind force of will, the same force that destroys Anna. Levin thinks that suicide is the only possible escape from his situation.

In *A Confession,* which he wrote from 1879 to 1882, Tolstoy described his own crisis. Reason and the sciences gave him no answer to his questions, which marriage and family life had stifled only temporarily. He read extensively, but the thinkers he studied—Socrates, Solomon, Buddha, Schopenhauer—all concluded that life was an evil and that the greatest good was to free oneself of one's existence. Tolstoy then turned to the peasants. He saw that their simple faith in God gave their life meaning. They did not fear death, which they regarded as the natural outcome of life. Tolstoy concluded that the answer was simply to believe, without reasoning. Belief in God and in the possibility of moral perfection made life meaningful. The peasants' faith, however, was bound up with Orthodox ritual and dogma, which Tolstoy could not accept. He ended *A Confession* promising to study the scriptures and the church's doctrines in order to separate the truth in them from falsehood.

Tolstoy taught himself Greek and Hebrew in order to read the biblical texts in the original. In his *Translation and Harmony of the Four Gospels* (1880–1881) he rearranged the Gospels, rewriting or eliminating material he thought incomprehensible or untrue. Miracles, including the resurrection, were discarded. Tolstoy's version presented the tenets of Christianity as he saw them. He said that this book was the most important thing he had written. The other promised work, *A Criticism of Dogmatic Theology* (also 1880–1881), was an attack on the Orthodox church. In it, Tolstoy examined the church's doctrines and said they were distortions of the true teachings of Christ, who had wanted only love, humility, and forgiveness.

His next book, *What I Believe* (1882–1884), was a summing-up of Tolstoy's creed. He listed in it five commandments of Christ: (1) do not be angry; (2) do not lust; (3) do not swear oaths; (4) do not resist evil with force; (5) love all persons without distinction. Observance of these rules would transform life on earth by putting an end to courts of law, governments, and wars between nations. Tolstoy's other religious and moralistic works, such as *On Life* (1887) and *The Kingdom of God Is within You* (1892–1893), contained essentially the same ideas as the earlier ones. All of these books, including *A Confession,* were banned by the censor, but they circulated in underground editions or were published abroad and smuggled into Russia.

Tolstoy's new religion was essentially a system of personal ethics, the same rules he had been trying to live by since boyhood. The church, he said, had obscured true Christianity with ritual, miracles, and symbols. It tried to keep from people the true Christ, a man and not a divine being, who wanted to unite men in peace and make them happy. Tolstoy's Christianity was based primarily on the sermon on the mount, and especially on Christ's principle of turning the other cheek (*Mt.* 5:38–42). God had placed the light of conscience within each person. By heeding their inner voice, people would act with simple truthfulness and love and would achieve happiness. The only way to combat evil was by a constant effort at self-perfection, not by opposing the evil of others with force. If each person does good whenever possible, evil will die of itself. Nonresistance to evil became Tolstoy's main tenet.

But Tolstoy's Christianity did not bring him peace and did not end his search, any more than Levin's quest in *Anna Karenina* had ended with his conversion. Never believing in personal immortality, Tolstoy was not able to accept death's physical finality and the thought of his own physical annihilation. He returned again and again to the theme of death, which continued to haunt him. Efforts to include death in his vision of harmony on earth by viewing it as a peaceful merging with nature warred with flashes of nihilism. Only in his last years did he make his peace with death.

After his conversion Tolstoy condemned his own pre-1878 fiction, saying that it contained morally bad feelings. He resumed writing literary works in the mid-1880s, but they had changed. He now used a bare, plain style that would be accessible to every reader. Tolstoy wrote two kinds of works, both fundamentally tracts: short stories for peasants and children that presented his views on love and nonviolence, and longer stories for the educated reader, such as *The Death of Ivan Il'ich* (1886), *Kreutzer Sonata* (1889), *The Devil* (1889), and *Father Sergii* (1890–1891). He still had all his literary force, but the joy in life that had animated his earlier fiction was gone; the longer stories are dominated by gloomy, strong passions. Most of them express a hatred of the flesh, the source of life and of death.

Tolstoy's last work to be published in his lifetime was *Resurrection* (1899). It depicts the moral regeneration of Nekhliudov, a nobleman whose early debauchery had ruined the life of a young servant girl. In prison, Nekhliudov observes a religious service during which the priest, after giving communion, "took the cup back with him behind the partition and drank all the remaining blood and finished all the remaining pieces of God's flesh." Because of the heretical passages in *Resurrection* and his attacks on the church and state, the Holy Synod excommunicated Tolstoy in 1901. On the day the decree was announced, a cheering crowd of supporters gathered around his house.

By the 1880s Tolstoy had numerous disciples in Russia and abroad, many of them misfits or half-mad. One of his followers, Vladimir Chertkov, gained increasing influence over him. Tolstoy's disciples regarded him as a living saint, and Yasnaia Poliana became a goal of pilgrimages. Groups of Tolstoyans formed who tried to live by his ideas. All these groups eventually fell apart. (Many of the early *kibbutsim* in Palestine, however, were inspired by the ideology of a Russian-Jewish Tolstoyan, Aharon David Gordon.) Tolstoy continued to write in the final years of his life, expressing his views on most of the social, religious, and political issues of the day. He corresponded with Mohandas K. Gandhi, and Gandhi's doctrine of *satyagraha* was an adaptation of Tolstoy's nonresistance to evil.

Tolstoy's relations with his wife had deteriorated as he became more and more preoccupied with religion. Friction between her and Chertkov made Tolstoy's life at home unbearable and led to his flight from Yasnaia Poliana in late October of 1910. He had long wanted to live quietly in solitude. On the train journey he fell ill and was taken to the stationmaster's house at Astapovo, where he died on November 7.

While Tolstoy's religious writings are peripheral to his literary achievements, his art is unimaginable without the moral and religious vision that informs it. Perhaps he cheated death better than he knew; as artist and seeker he has continued, generation after generation, to attract passionate adherents, and Yasnaia Poliana remains a focus of pilgrimages from all over the world.

In one of his Sevastopol stories, Tolstoy had written: "The hero of my narrative, whom I have tried to render in all its beauty and who was, is, and always will be beautiful, is truth." Tolstoy's brother Nikolai had said that in a certain spot at Yasnaia Poliana there was a green stick on which was written a secret that would destroy evil in men and make them happy. As a boy, Tolstoy searched in the bushes at Yasnaia Poliana for this stick. Much later, he wrote: "I believe that this truth exists, and that it will be disclosed to men and will give them what it promises." According to his wish, Tolstoy was buried at the place where he thought the green stick was hidden.

Bibliography

Aldanov, Mark. *Zagadka Tolstogo* (1923). Reprint, Providence, R.I., 1969.

Christian, R. F. *Tolstoi: A Critical Introduction.* London, 1969.

Eikhenbaum, Boris. *Lev Tolstoi.* 2 vols. Leningrad, 1928.

Maude, Aylmer. *The Life of Tolstoi.* 2 vols. London, 1929–1930.

Noyes, George Rapall. *Tolstoi* (1918). Reprint, New York, 1968.

Rolland, Romain. *Vie de Tolstoï.* Paris, 1928.

Tolstoy, Alexandra. *Tolstoi: A Life of My Father.* New York, 1953.

Weisbein, Nicolas. *L'évolution religieuse de Tolstoï.* Paris, 1960.

Sylvia Juran (1987)

TOLTEC RELIGION.

In pre-Columbian central Mexico, *Tolteca* literally meant "people living at a place named Tollan [i.e., among the rushes]." However, even then the name had no single application, and it has none today. Because there was more than one place called Tollan, the word *Toltec* refers not to a single culture or religion, but rather to at least five specific groups of people, all belonging to Postclassic Mesoamerica: (1) the inhabitants of what is now the archaeological site of Tula de Allende near Mexico City, (2) the inhabitants or, more precisely, the elite, called Toltec-Maya, of Chichén Itzá, Yucatán, (3) the inhabitants of Tollan as it is described in central Mexican historical documents of the sixteenth century, (4) militant leading groups in other parts of Mesoamerica claiming descent from a place called Tollan, (5) members of various, often quite different, ethnic groups, all bearing the typological name Tolteca, that migrated to central Mexico. In addition, the term *Toltec* was generally applied to any person who exhibited extraordinary skills, arts, or wisdom.

The present article discusses, in turn, each of these five groups, which overlap only to a certain degree. The familiar hybrid picture of "Toltec," resulting from an unsophisticated merging commonly found in overall descriptions, can no longer be supported. Presumably there never existed either a single, homogeneous Toltec culture or, consequently, a single Toltec religion. But many traits are certainly common to various of the above-mentioned "Toltecs," including religious traits. In this article, common features will be stressed, but the reader should be aware that they are not necessarily all elements of one coherent whole.

Toltecs of Tula. The rather extensive archaeological site of Tula de Allende in the modern Mexican state of Hidalgo, 75 kilometers north-northwest of Mexico City, has been excavated professionally since 1940. Its main ceremonial center, Tula Grande, flourished from about 950 to 1200 CE (dates established by ceramic crossties but only very few radiocarbon readings). In its final shape, Tula Grande consisted of some ten hectares of magnificently arranged buildings, surrounded by ten to twelve square kilometers of living quarters. So far, Tula-Toltec religion can be reconstructed only from the archaeological remains of the main ceremonial center. In contrast to buildings of the earlier metropolitan civilization of the region, Teotihuacan, Tula-Toltec religious buildings were designed for the full participation of large groups of people, who gathered in pillared halls, or colonnades, along one side of the huge central square. Different types of benches along the walls of the colonnades suggest that they were intended for groups of people of varying rank, although all participants probably belonged to the social elite. Numerous bas-reliefs show them dressed as warriors and aligned in rows, emphasizing their function in the cult as a homogeneous group: no single person is highlighted.

Archaeological vestiges indicate that the ceremonies of the Tula-Toltecs focused on the strange effigies known as chacmools. These are approximately lifesize sculptures of a reclining male figure dressed in some of the paraphernalia of a warrior, but clearly no warrior himself. He holds an object, perhaps a receptacle, over his belly and glares with sharply turned face at approaching worshipers. Despite recent attempts to interpret the chacmools as the stones on which human sacrifice was made, their specific function is as yet unknown. The practice of human sacrifice, however, was not uncommon among the Tula-Toltecs. The practice seems to be addressed metaphorically in endlessly repeated sculptural reliefs depicting eagles devouring human hearts. There are also frequent allusions in the reliefs to death in the form of skulls and bones.

More difficult to establish from archaeological data is the deity to whom the devotion of the presumed caste of warriors was directed. Most probably it was that highly complex being that in Tula is metaphorically depicted by a combination of reptilian, avian, and human elements: the face of a man with circular, spectacle-like eyes is shown looking out of or emerging from open reptilian jaws. The figure, depicted *en face*, is surrounded by feathers and supports itself on legs with birdlike claws. Despite clear analogies, this hybrid being is not the famous feathered serpent, which in Tula architecture is represented only as a subordinate element.

Another quite different aspect of Tula-Toltec religious activities centered on a ritual ball game, which is generally believed to have been important as a symbolic reenactment of cosmic movement. In Tula Grande at least three giant ball courts existed, but there is no basis for any extensive interpretation.

Toltec-Maya. Similar to Tula-Toltec culture in its essential expression, Toltec-Maya also seems to have been restricted to a single, extremely important place: Chichén Itzá in north-central Yucatán. The great resemblances between Chichén Itzá and Tula, 850 kilometers away, as the crow flies, are a commonplace in Mesoamerican archaeology, although the site of origin of these particular traits has not been definitively established. Chichén Itzá was always an important center of late Classic Puuc Maya, which toward its final period (c. 900 CE) exhibited an increased extra-Mayan influence. Subsequent development, to be found only at Chichén Itzá, shows a merging of traditional and newly introduced elements, the latter having been found so far only in Tula. The center of the Toltec-Maya city covers some thirty hectares, the general outline very much resembling that of Tula: large courts, colonnades, and ball courts. The more abundant and detailed iconography and a historical tradition, albeit a faint one, give the picture a little more color: the dominant social stratum, that of the warriors, is principally the same as in Tula, but a wider variety of grades is displayed.

The central deity of Toltec-Maya culture at Chichén Itzá is depicted, as in Tula, as the man-reptile-bird combination. The image is omnipresent, but there are practically no variations to provide deeper insight, although sometimes artists misinterpreted the stereotyped picture and made it look like a heavily adorned warrior with his pectoral and feathered headdress. The theme itself is an old Maya one: a man's head emerging from a snake's mouth. It is already known in Classic Maya representations and is frequent in the Puuc-style ruins, where the feathered rattlesnake is also common. Colonial sources call this mythological animal *k'uk'ulkan* ("quetzal-feathered serpent") and mention a famous leader of Chichén Itzá who bore this name and who is said to have "returned" to central Mexico. A person intimately associated with this feathered serpent serves as the focus of a story with a mythical flavor, the wording of which is unknown but which is depicted with considerable detail in various Chichén Itzá temples. The sculptural narration makes clear that this feathered serpent was the center of devotion for the Toltec-Maya elite.

There is evidence, however, that the feathered serpent did not occupy the paramount place in the Toltec-Maya pantheon. Not infrequently, what seems to be a supreme deity is depicted seated on a low throne-bench in the shape of a jaguar before a giant sun disk designed in the manner of central Mexico. This theme demonstrates the preoccupation of Toltec-Maya religion with the sun, which is presumably also the main concern of the ritual ball game. Based on central Mexican analogies, long rows of reliefs of strangely reclined warriors have been interpreted in relation to the sun cult: the sun that passed beneath the earth during the night had to be revived every morning through rituals executed by the warriors.

To the water deities was directed a special cult peculiar to Chichén Itzá: on certain occasions, human beings were thrown into the sacred cenote (natural well) and drowned to appease the rain gods or to act as intermediaries between them and men. The continuing belief in the old Maya water god Chac is clearly visible in the large masks with elongated noses that adorn the corners and facades of most temples, sometimes together with the bird-snake-man motif.

A great variety of human sacrifice was practiced among the Toltec-Maya, in contrast to earlier Maya times. The sheer quantity of victims, whose skulls were displayed on special racks, is impressive. Striking, too, is the constant presence of the death symbol on buildings, as well as on warriors' clothing. The act of human sacrifice is frequently depicted, not only in the metaphorical form of wild beasts (symbolizing warriors) feeding on human hearts but also in naturalistic representations found on the interior walls of temples and along the field of the ball court. In the latter, the decapitation of the leader of the losing team is depicted. The rubber ball of the game in this scene is a symbol of glorious death, and snakes emerging from the victim's neck symbolize precious blood.

These are examples of the abundant metaphorical motifs, also seen in the chacmools and the images of feathered serpents, whose interpretation is fraught with difficulties. Chichén Itzá clearly presents a syncretic religion in which the veneration of old Maya water gods mingles with foreign solar-astral ideas. Everything points to the martial rituals as being associated with the elite warrior group, or "Toltecs," whereas the cult of the water deities is likely to have been connected with the commoners, the Maya farmers.

TOLTECS OF TOLLAN XICOCOTITLAN. Although identified by Jiménez Moreno with Tula de Allende, the famous Tollan Xicocotitlan referred to in colonial sources is not this town alone. As epithet or name, the word *Tollan* has been used to designate other famous cities, and the description of this Tollan corresponds—if to any place on earth at all—more to Classic Teotihuacan than to Tula de Allende. As described in the written sources, Tollan Xicocotitlan was a sort of paradise. Thanks to their prudence, the inhabitants of Tollan possessed everything they needed in abundance, including maize and cotton, precious stones, and gold.

They worshiped only one god, whom they called Quetzalcoatl ("quetzal-feathered serpent"), a name also given to the highest priest of the deity. This god did not require any sumptuous service and reportedly abhorred human sacrifice (although scholars believe that these accounts were designed to please the Spanish missionaries and divert from historical truth). People were admonished to offer their god only serpents, flowers, and butterflies. They considered their incomparable wisdom, science, skill, and arts as emanating from their god and strictly obeyed the orders given by Quetzalcoatl and voiced by his priest. The god, resembling a monster, lay like a fallen rock, as one source says, in his temple on the top of a tall pyramid. He had a long beard. He—or perhaps his priest—repeatedly made autosacrifice by bleeding himself with sharp thorns, thus becoming a prototype for all later priests in central Mexico.

This account, given to the sixteenth-century Spanish missionary and historian Bernardino de Sahagún by educated Indians, is incompatible in its details not only with the ecological situation of Tula but also with a warrior-dominated society like that of archaeological Tula. It seems to correspond to earlier times, when the idea of a divine feathered serpent was developed or introduced in Teotihuacan iconography and later refined and elaborated in places like Xochicalco and Cacaxtla. On the other hand, Sahagún and other sources tell the story of a famous ruler of Tollan Xicocotitlan, who, confusingly enough, bore the title of Quetzalcoatl in addition to his personal name Topiltzin ("our beloved prince") and the name of the date of his birth, Ce Acatl. Details of his origin, genealogy, and life are contradictory. He may have belonged to the Nonoalca, the culturally (and perhaps politically) dominant group of multiethnic Tollan Xicocotitlan. Scholars assume that the Nonoalca migrated from the southern Veracruz region, where they had been in contact with a more sophisticated civilization, which would explain their opinion of themselves and of Quetzalcoatl as the incarnation of cultural superiority.

One of the more important virtues of the people of Tollan Xicocotitlan was their forthrightness. According to Sahagún, they spoke thus: "It is so, it is true, yes, no." But the very personification of their integrity— Topiltzin himself, the Quetzalcoatl—was attacked by three demons, two of them bearing the names of later, Aztec deities (Huitzilopochtli and Titlacahuan, that is, Tezcatlipoca), although they do not seem to have been identical with them. One should refrain from interpreting this incident as the mythic rendering of an antagonistic struggle between divine principles or between two religious factions practicing and opposing human sacrifice. Topiltzin was eventually overthrown, and consequently one disaster after the other befell his city. Finally he had to gather his followers and leave the place. It is generally accepted that part of the story reflects internal dissent in Xicocotitlan between Nonoalca and Tolteca-Chichimeca, another constituent ethnic group.

From here on, history once more becomes legend. On his flight, Topiltzin Quetzalcoatl worked miracles in many places. Eventually, on reaching the Veracruz coast, he either burned himself and became the morning star, or, according to other versions, he walked or sailed on a raft, miraculously made by intertwining serpents, to the mythical land Tlapallan, where he may have died. After his departure from Xicocotitlan, Topiltzin was replaced by a more secular ruler, Huemac, perhaps Topiltzin's kinsman, who himself was also persecuted by the demons and who finally fled to a cave where he killed himself or disappeared—the sources are hopelessly contradictory on this point. Huemac, too, assumed divinity, as lord of the underworld.

Conquerors of "Toltec" Affiliation. In various parts of Mesoamerica during early Postclassic times a local population had to submit to small groups of militant immigrants. These usurpers, who showed positive "Toltec" traits, established themselves as ruling elites. In the case of the Quiché and Cakchiquel Maya in highland Guatemala, the respective elites claimed descent from a mythical place of origin called Tulán, far to the north, and ethnic affiliation with those they called the Yaqui (Nahuatl-speaking Mexicans). After their initial migration the Quiché settled for a long time near the Laguna de Términos on the Gulf of Mexico and later continued their migration into the Guatemalan highlands. They carried with them a "sacred bundle"—in Mesoamerica generally considered the very essence of their god and the sacrosanct symbol of ethnic identity—which they were given by Nacxitl at Tulán. Nacxitl or Acxitl is one of the names of Quetzalcoatl, according to central Mexican sources.

Quiché tradition of the sixteenth century, amply preserved in their "sacred book," the *Popol Vuh*, relates that at Tulán their four ethnic subdivisions had each been given tribal deities: Tohil, Avilix, Hacavitz, and Nicacatah. The most powerful, Tohil, who was identified by the *Popol Vuh* with Quetzalcoatl, was the possessor of fire; he offered this cultural achievement to other starving tribes at the price of using them as victims for human sacrifice, hitherto unknown at Tulán. The other tribes thus came under Quiché dominance, which they unsuccessfully tried to shake off.

The creation myth recorded at length in the *Popol Vuh* is generally considered an adaptation of central Mexican (Toltec) prototypes: here, the creation of the world in various stages of completion is referred to as the work of Tepeu and Cucumatz (Gucumatz). The name *Tepeu* recalls the ruler of Tollan, named Totepeuh (*to* is a Nahuatl possessive prefix), sometimes referred to as the father of Topiltzin or Huemac; the name *Cucumatz* is a literal translation of *Quetzalcoatl* into Quiché. The account of the *Popol Vuh* also gives deep insight into the wide corpus of legends of the Quiché that do not seem to be of Toltec origin.

TOLTECA CHICHIMECA. As a rule, central Mexican ethnic groups have ample traditions regarding their migration to their present homes. Most of these refer to a place of origin at Chicomoztoc (Seven Caves), and they count Tollan among their stopping places during their long migration. This holds true for the inhabitants of Cholula (Chollollan) in the Puebla valley. They report in the monumental *Historia Tolteca-Chichimeca* that their forefathers, bearing the characteristic name Tolteca-Chichimeca, had to leave the decaying Tollan. Before starting off, their messenger-priest asked the god of Chollollan, then already a famous place of pilgrimage, for permission to settle in his city, which was granted. The god is referred to in the Nahuatl text as Quetzalcoatl Nacxitl Tepeuhqui and is addressed as Tloque' Nahuaque' (Lord of Proximity and Vicinity), the omnipresent deity. The allusion of the source to Quetzalcoatl as already present in Chollollan seems to indicate that well before the fall of Tollan the god's cult had begun to spread, certainly fostered by "Toltec" groups, into wider parts of central Mexico.

CONCLUSION. Only a few characteristic elements common to various facets of "Toltec" religion can be singled out so far: a supreme deity, Quetzalcoatl, who gave his name to priests and rulers; a cult dominated by eagles and jaguars (i.e., the warriors); a ritual ball game as reenactment of cosmic processes; and the importance of human sacrifice. These traits, whose roots go back far into Classic times, survived, sometimes altered or obscured, into late Postclassic times. For example, Quetzalcoatl ceded his rank to the Aztec Tezcatlipoca, the former being reduced to a mere wind god while the latter assumed titles peculiar to the "Toltec" Quetzalcoatl. Thus many religious descriptions in the colonial sources contain "Toltec" nuclei, although they are often barely recognizable.

SEE ALSO Quetzalcoatl.

BIBLIOGRAPHY

No special treatment of Toltec religion in any form has yet been published. The most comprehensive study of the Toltecs, written from an ethnohistoric point of view but making full use of available archaeological data, is Nigel Davies's *The Toltecs* (Norman, Okla., 1977). The subsequent period and developments are covered in detail by the same author in *The Toltec Heritage* (Norman, Okla., 1980), an expanded version of his *Los Mexicas, primeros pasos hacia el imperio* (Mexico City, 1973). There is no published synthesis yet of archaeological work at Tula de Allende, but Jorge R. Acosta's "Los Toltecs," in *Los señoríos y estados militaristas* (Mexico City, 1976), can be profitably consulted. The Toltec-Maya period of Chichén Itzá is summarized, although not very satisfactorily, in Román Piña Chan's *Chichén Itzá, la ciudad de los brujos del agua* (Mexico City, 1980).

The Quiché text of the *Popol Vuh* has been translated many times. *Popol Vuh: The Sacred Book of the Ancient Quiché Maya*, translated by Delia Goetz and Sylvanus G. Morley from the Spanish edition of Adrián Recinos (Norman, Okla., 1950), was the standard English version until it was superseded by the more scholarly work of Munro S. Edmonson in *The Book of Counsel: The Popol Vuh of the Quiché Maya* (New Orleans, 1971). A recommendable interpretation of this highly important text is, however, still lacking.

New Sources

Brumfel, Elizabeth M. "Huitzilopochtli's Conquest: Aztec Ideology in the Archeological Record." *Cambridge Archaeological Journal* 8 (1998): 3–14.

Davies, Nigel. *Aztec Empire: The Toltec Resurgence.* Norman, Okla., 1987.

Graulich, Michel. *Myths of Ancient Mexico.* Translated by Bernard R. Ortiz and Thelma Ortiz de Montellano. Norman, Okla., 1997.

Hers, Marie-Areti. *Toltecas in tierras chichimecas.* Mexico City, 1989.

Rolingson, Martha Ann. *Toltec Mounds and Plum Bayou Culture: Mound D Excavations.* Fayettville, Ark., 1998.

Rolingson, Martha Ann, ed. *Emerging Patterns of Plum Bayou Culture: Preliminary Investigations of Toltec Mounds Research Project.* Fayettville, Ark., 1982.

Sánchez, Victor. *Toltecs of the New Millennium.* Translated by Robert Nelson. Santa Fe, N.M., 1996.

HANNS J. PREM (1987)
Revised Bibliography

TOMBS. In many European languages, to speak of "the tomb" is synecdochically to speak of death. In other places this is not true, since mortuary rites do not involve anything resembling a tomb. Moreover, where they exist, there are a wide variety of structures that may be described as tombs.

TOMBLESS DEATH RITUALS. There are ethnographic instances where corpses are simply abandoned. When a death occurs in the camps of some of the hunting and gathering peoples of the Kalahari Desert, there is an outpouring of grief, but nevertheless the band rapidly decamps leaving the corpse just as it lay at the moment of dying. There is a ritual response in that the site is avoided for years afterwards, but it is about as minimal a response as can be imagined. Corpses abandoned in this way are generally disposed of by carrion creatures, most commonly hyenas. Across much of Africa, hyenas are the subject of black humor, since they are always ready to devour the injured or dig up shallow graves.

The same theme of disposal as carrion is found in the Tibetan practice of "sky burial," in which corpses are ritually butchered by a caste of death specialists, and fed to vultures. What this expresses in the starkest possible terms is the Buddhist contempt for the body, whose transience stands in contrast to the eternal verities of the spiritual world. The Jain "towers of the dead" use vultures in the same way, but the doctrinal emphasis is on avoiding pollution of the earth.

If these cases seem obscure, consider the ancient Hindu tradition of cremation, still followed by millions of people in Northern India. The purpose is to allow the corporeal elements to return to their origins—vision to the sun, feeling to the air, and so on. Consequently, rather than retaining the ashes, they are cast into rivers so that they can be dispersed. The most auspicious river of all is the Ganges, and the temples and burning *ghats* of Benares are a major focus of Hindu ritual.

IMPERIAL MORTUARY COMPLEXES. At the opposite end of the spectrum, there are examples of royal tombs constructed on such a vast scale that they constitute some of the most spectacular finds of archaeology. When Chinese archaeologists began in the 1970s to probe the mound associated with the Qin Emperor Shi Huangdi, the first to unify the Chinese into one state, they discovered a series of vaults containing an estimated seven thousand life-size terra-cotta statues comprising an entire army of infantry, cavalry, crossbowmen, and charioteers. The figures are extremely lifelike, each face different and thought to have been modeled from life. They comprise a stunning artistic and technical triumph, but it is not clear what ideology lay behind the complex, especially as it was not imitated by subsequent emperors. At first sight it seems to reflect the megalomania of an emperor who evidently thought that he could ride into the afterlife at the head of his army, but there were also sociological effects that may or may not have been part of the emperor's intentions. The organizational challenge of such a project was appropriate to a new state in the process of establishing its infrastructure, especially as it must have trained thousands of artisans in pottery techniques for which China has ever since been famous. Moreover, it augmented a national cult focused on the emperor.

Much the same argument could be made about the massive pyramids of Giza in Egypt. Although the pyramids were all built within a century near the beginning of the pharaonic state, they can also be placed within the context of a religion that developed over several millennia. The most famous archaeological discovery of the 1920s was the tomb of a relatively unimportant pharaoh of the eighteenth dynasty obscure enough to have avoided the attention of grave robbers in antiquity. By comparison with the temple complexes of other pharaohs, Tutankhamen's tomb was modest. Nevertheless, it contained a fabulous storehouse of treasures, including enough furniture to equip a small palace. As is demonstrated by the tombs in the Valley of the Nobles at Luxor, such grandeur was not restricted to pharaohs.

GRAVE GOODS. The Qin emperor's soldiers and Tutankhamen's furniture are examples, if remarkable ones, of the practice commonly found all over the world of entombing useful or valuable objects with a corpse. It is often argued that such grave goods are among the earliest prehistoric evidence of ritual activity, and that they demonstrate belief in an afterlife. This does not, in fact, follow. Other motives are possible, such as the desire to prevent the further use of objects sentimentally associated with the deceased. Even so, grave goods often do imply an equipping of the dead. For instance, in parts of Borneo there is an elaborated theory of the journey of the dead to the afterlife by canoe. Consequently, paddles and sun hats are often hung from the sides of mausoleums. These grave goods are of little intrinsic value, and in a similar fashion even humble graves are often found to contain pottery or tools.

Archaeologists are also familiar with finding valuables in gravesites. Often these are goods originating from far away, and so give evidence of ancient trade. Examples are the shell disks and embossed copper sheets found in mounds throughout central North America, and the gold and precious stones found across much of the Middle East. It is a safe assumption that such valuables were not taken out of circulation lightly, but it is often unclear exactly what the goal was. There may have been an element of sacrifice, especially where animals or even humans were immolated at the graveside. In accordance with that conception, in many places grave goods must be broken before they can be transmitted to the other world.

Hierarchy and Tomb Elaboration. Diversity in grave goods from tombs of the same period is often taken by archaeologists as evidence of differences in the social status of the living, and hence a measure of social hierarchy. There are, as usual, exceptions that undermine the validity of the inference. For instance, the funerals of the kings of Bali, an island in Indonesia, were theatrical displays of pomp and hierarchy, yet the king's ashes ended up strewn on the sea according to the Hindu origins of the ancient empire of Majapahit. Noble Balinese families that had lost a member in the previous few years took the opportunity to participate in the grand cremation rites, so that the only graves that remained were those of commoners. Again, the kings of the Shilluk of southern Sudan had no tombs because it was intolerable that the king should die. Since the king's vitality was associated with that of the whole nation, signs of frailty meant that he had to be suffocated by his own wives, or so it was said. However the king died, his body was simply left where it lay, and the door of the hut walled up with bricks. Until the new king was installed, the spirit of the nation passed into an effigy kept for the purpose. Consequently, mortuary structures provide no evidence of the existence of the state. As a further example, Saudi kings are buried in plain graves facing Mecca as a gesture of humility before Allāh.

Nevertheless, it remains true that the tombs most characteristic of a place or an epoch are often those of the elite, especially where there is intense status competition. In Iron Age northern Europe, warrior kings tried to establish their lineages by building impressive tumuli containing stone-lined vaults and passageways. The size of the artificial hill was physical proof of a king's ability to muster numerous followers. A striking variant was the ship burials that have proved such a treasure trove for archaeologists and were particularly appropriate to images of death as a voyage. Ship symbolism is in fact widely found in connection with tombs, and particularly with coffins that resemble dugout canoes.

Primary and Secondary Storage. Tumuli or burial mounds often became ritual centers, incorporating subsequent interments. This was especially true when they were associated with secondary treatment of the dead. This involves the temporary storage of a corpse while the flesh decays from the bones, with final entombment of the bones at a later date.

The technique was employed in ancient times across the Mississippi region. At Cahokia in present-day Illinois, there are over a hundred flat-topped earth mounds, the largest of which is one hundred feet high. The mounds show traces of wooden buildings on top, which probably included charnel houses where corpses were left to rot until the remains were ready for burial in the mound. There are also graves containing whole skeletons, the remains of burials of particularly prestigious people. Bundles of bones were also brought from elsewhere, to produce a complex pattern of interment in one mound. The Cahokia site supported a dense population, but dispersed populations in less fertile regions of the Appalachian Mountains also built mounds, which grew over many generations by accretion of new bones and earth. Exposure platforms were widely used across North America, the corpse dressed and equipped suitably for the gender and role of the deceased.

Secondary treatment is by no means restricted to the Americas. It is found in parts of Southeast Asia and in New Guinea, where corpses are laid out on platforms or set behind domestic fireplaces to dry out. In rural Greece the burial of corpses is only temporary. After some years, the grave is dug up and the bones stored in a communal ossuary. The same process in monastic communities in southern Europe produced crypts lined with anonymous skulls and femurs neatly arranged in patterns—a dramatic expression of death as the great leveler. In other cases in Europe, the removal of bones from communal graveyards to make room for others is the fate of paupers buried at public expense.

Burials, Tombstones, Vaults, and Mausoleums. Simple earth burial is often associated with those on the lower rungs of a social hierarchy. It may be argued that this is a matter of practical expedience, the most rapid way to dispose of corpses before putrescence sets in. The carnage of a battle or a lethal epidemic makes mass graves necessary. At Cahokia, however, immediate burial was a privilege of a small elite, whereas paupers in southern Europe were lucky to rest undisturbed in their graves. In the Christian tradition, earth burial is the norm for rich and poor, in accordance with the doctrine of the resurrection of the body. Moreover, missionaries have exported Christian practices to the indigenous populations of Africa, the Americas, and Asia. The spread of Islam has had the same effect, so that burial is now more universal than it was in previous centuries.

Accordingly, tombstones provide the most familiar of death monuments. They are found in many varieties, from stones or plain slabs covering a grave to elaborate sculptures. The commonest are headstones inscribed with brief accounts of the deceased, but changing fashions have sometimes produced much more elaborate and imposing structures. In parts of the Islamic world, grave markers are nothing more than short wooden posts, carved in abstract or floral designs, but elsewhere the same process of elaboration has occurred as in Christian cemeteries.

Such changes of fashion date back to classical antiquity. Until sometime in the first century, Romans of any respectability were cremated, and their ashes stored in barrel-vaulted brick and masonry chambers, with niches in the walls to contain urns. Such was the expense of building them that subscribers joined funeral cooperatives called *collegia.* Meanwhile, the poor and slaves were disposed of casually in pits, initially on the Esquilline Hill. Beginning in the first century, Romans began to copy Greek fashions of inhumation, which had long been the practice throughout the eastern Mediterranean. The motivation appears to have been display, since Greek funerary monuments had developed from amphorae over graves to structures elaborately decorated with an eclectic iconography, including sphinxes and winged lions. Roman versions can still be seen along the Via Appia, some originally displaying bas-relief portraits of the occupants. Also to be seen in Rome are the catacombs of the early Christian era, which represent a continuation of the Middle Eastern practice of burial in caves or rock-cut tombs.

Underground vaults are another common development from simple earth burial, and not only in the Mediterranean. In much of sub-Saharan Africa, graves are roofed with logs before being covered over.

A stone vault built above ground is usually described as a mausoleum, after the massive tomb of King Mausolus in Asia Minor. In central Borneo, ironwood mausoleums were constructed on top of large pilings. Sometimes thirty feet or more high and delicately carved in swirling designs, they are the premier artistic achievements of the region. They may contain coffins, large jars used for corpses, or smaller ones for bones collected after secondary treatment, with sometimes a dozen or more sets of remains in one aerial chamber. Adjacent to them are simple earth burials.

Location of Tombs and Location of the Dead. There are striking differences from culture to culture in where tombs are located in relation to the community. In New Britain, corpses were buried directly under the floor of the house, with the explicit aim of keeping the dead with their kinsmen. Pressure from missionaries and colonial authorities forced an end to the practice, but the dead are still buried as close to their houses as possible. In parts of eastern Indonesia, corpses were buried under the dance ground in the middle of the village. Moreover, kin and neighbors were required to sit by uncomplaining during a long wake because bodily corruption was seen as a positive process that allowed the deceased to return to mother earth. At the same time the dead were associated with ancestral villages in the mountains, so that they had a complex multiple presence for the living.

In Borneo, the elaborate mausoleums described above were sited across the river from communal longhouses, so that flowing water formed a barrier between the living and the dead. The mausoleums were described as houses of the dead; they were raised on pilings like the longhouse, and no one entered this village of the dead without very good reasons for fear that the inhabitants would see the intrusion as the arrival of a new member. This perception was contradicted, however, by long sacred chants at the funeral that took the deceased on a riverine journey to the land of the dead. Consequently, the dead were seen as simultaneously both near and far, and that mystery contributed much to the power and drama of indigenous ritual. The entire community of ancestors was invited to funerals by other chants, but great care was taken to disentangle them from the living after the deceased was delivered to them.

Archaeological data from China show evidence of burials beneath the house, but in recent centuries the living have been careful not to live near graveyards for fear of unquiet ghosts. However, in many Chinese communities, both in China and abroad, ancestors figure prominently in the rituals of extended kin groups, and they are represented by tablets in special ancestor temples. Moreover, the location of the tombs is thought to have a major influence, and the ancient techniques of feng shui, or "wind and water," are designed to site deceased family members so that they deflect evil and funnel blessings towards the living.

Reliquaries, Stupas, and Cenotaphs. A special case of the ambiguous presence of the dead is provided by holy relics. In medieval Europe there was a brisk trade in body parts supposedly belonging to saints, and they were handled lovingly and stored in valuable reliquaries. Yet the virtue of the relics is, to say the least, doctrinally obscure. The saints are presumably in heaven, and there is no reason why their blessing should somehow inhere in their blood or bones. The paradox is sharper in Buddhism, but from its beginnings relics of the Buddha have been enshrined in large stupas that became centers of pilgrimage. Officially, relics, like statues, have no power other than to provide a focus of individual meditation, yet they have become national symbols. When the Portuguese conquered Sri Lanka they seized the relic housed in the Temple of the Tooth in Kandy, ground it into powder and threw it in the sea. But faith is not so easily destroyed. Within a short time the relic was miraculously rediscovered by a fisherman in his net and restored to its rightful place. Even when there are no remains in a tomb, it may become a national symbol, as with the Cenotaph in London, which honors the dead of both world wars.

Changing Styles of Tombs in England and the United States. Since the eighth century, graveyards in England were located within settlements next to the parish church. Consequently, villagers attending services were reminded of their forebears, now resting under the protection of the church. The elaboration of grave markers also served to remind them of the local social order. Throughout the Middle Ages, senior clerics tried to prohibit burials inside the church, which were seen as desecrating. One thirteenth-century prelate grumbled that such was the clutter of memorials that the graveyard appeared to have moved inside the church. It was difficult, however, to refuse landowners who patronized churches so that they could be buried there. Life-sized effigies were not unusual atop grand family tombs.

The urbanization accompanying the industrial revolution changed this pattern. City churches could no longer provide space, and graveyards had to be moved to the outskirts of cities, where they were often overtaken by further expansion. Consequently, graveyards became an issue of urban planning, although authorities were slow to respond. In the Victorian era, this changed under the influence of a new sentimentalization of death and the afterlife. Graveyards became "cemeteries," a term derived from the Greek *koimeterion* (a sleeping place), which were filled with fanciful architecture imitating Roman and Egyptian motifs.

A similar development occurred in the United States. In New England the Puritan tradition meant that graveyards were treated as mere necessities, and all affectation in burials was frowned on. Further south, things were not much different, and visitors to the colonies remarked on the chaotic state of graveyards in New York and Philadelphia. In the nineteenth century the rural cemetery movement set out to change this start of affairs. Their best-known achievement is Mount Auburn cemetery outside Boston, which is beautifully landscaped with tombs discretely set into hillocks. A Swedish visitor remarked, "A glance at this cemetery almost excites a wish to die." A parallel innovation was the embalming of corpses, which originated during the Civil War so that distant families could take their sons home for burial. By the mid-twentieth century the entombing of embalmed corpses had become standard among Americans, whether newly immigrant or long established. Cemeteries were made efficient by insetting tombstones flat on the ground to allow regular mowing, but underneath these neat lawns lay massive concrete vaults and luxuriously furnished steel coffins. Cremation came into vogue at the end of the twentieth century, but an archaeologist of the future would certainly conclude that American notions of death paralleled those of the ancient Egyptians.

SEE ALSO Caves; Death; Funeral Rites; Pyramids, overview article; Towers.

BIBLIOGRAPHY

Cotterell, Arthur. *The First Emperor of China: The Greatest Archeological Find of Our Time.* New York, 1981.

Metcalf, Peter, and Richard Huntington. *Celebrations of Death: The Anthropology of Mortuary Ritual.* 2d ed. Cambridge, U.K., 1991.

Morley, John. *Death, Heaven, and the Victorians.* Pittsburgh, 1971.

Morris, Ian. *Death Ritual and Social Structure in Classical Antiquity.* Cambridge, U.K., 1992.

Stannard, David, ed. *Death in America.* Philadelphia, 1974.

PETER METCALF (2005)

TOMOL.

The indigenous people of the central California coast now collectively known as the Chumash are known in ethnographic circles for their unique use of the plank canoe, or *tomol,* a vessel that was not only instrumental in the Chumash exploitation of their marine resources, but served to solidify the complex regional trade system whose influence was felt far beyond the Chumash interaction sphere. However, for some contemporary Chumash, this important item of material culture reaches beyond its practical value and into the realm of prime symbol, tapping into the essence of Chumash culture and religious orientation and encompassing a nexus of meaning surrounding issues of dependence upon nature, belief in the reciprocity of social life, and the world view of the people.

THE CHUMASH. In classical times, the Chumash were never a discreet linguistic or cultural entity. They lived in a geographic area along the California coast from roughly Topanga Canyon in the south to Estero Bay in the north, extending east to the western edge of the San Joaquin Valley, and in the northern Channel Islands. The people who have come to be known as the Chumash inhabited numerous relatively autonomous villages, each with its own internal political structure, the largest of which acted as capital cities for smaller village collectives. These individual city-states supported several dialects of the Hokan linguistic family, first identified by anthropologist Alfred Kroeber in 1925 and named, for the most part, for the missions in the areas encompassed by the dialects, namely the Ventureño, Barbareño, Ineseño, Purisimeño, Obispeño, and the additional Emigdiano, Cuyama, and Island dialects. While these dialects have been identified as branches of the Hokan linguistic family tree, they in fact operated much like distinct languages. This, in turn, has given rise to the notion that the various regional entities actually operated as distinct tribes in their own right, but with the necessary economic and sociopolitical system that would unite a region into a relatively cohesive network.

The regional federations consisted of smaller villages, which varied in population from sixty to over a thousand people, each presided over by a chief, or *wot.* The smaller villages owed their allegiance to a major chief for the region who resided in a capital village, enabling him to control the production and redistribution of the goods within his villages, thereby strengthening the federation's position among the other regions. Perhaps the key feature of this complex of inter-regional trade is the presence of specialized craft guilds, or brotherhoods, both within the villages and extending into a regional alliance of like craft specialists. These guilds were fraternal in nature, with the knowledge needed to produce the various products of these guilds passed on to subsequent generations via familial ties.

These specializations standardized the production of a number of important elements of Chumash material life, including baskets, obsidian projectile points, plant fiber cordage, shell bead money, and especially the plank canoe known as the *tomol.* In fact, the most powerful of these guilds was the brotherhood of the *tomol,* with its members in possession of high social status, important links to the religious leadership (*'antap*), and unprecedented access to the political leadership, as well. The *tomol,* with its powerful brotherhood, was the glue that held the entire system together. In order to fully understand the importance of the *tomol* and the brotherhood in classical times, it is necessary to analyze the region's economy prior to the Spanish arrival.

TRADE AND TRAVEL. As the Chumash interaction sphere exists within a coastal zone and encompasses some eight to ten thousand years (since, roughly, the recession of the last coastal ice- age permafrost), it should not be construed as a stable environment. Changes in rainfall patterns and sea surface temperatures and their resulting impacts on terrestrial and ocean resources prompted the Chumash to rely upon a complex trade system in order to mitigate against shortfalls. As Daniel Larson and his colleagues state in "Missionization Among the Coastal Chumash of Central California":

> As Chumash population levels increased there was a greater dependence on exchange of food from one settlement to the next. This reciprocity allowed groups to meet their provisioning needs when there were shortfalls within a village's cachment. As populations continued to grow, subsistence strategies expanded and intensified, settlements became increasingly interdependent, and mutual trade became critical to subsistence success. Tied to the mutual trading relationship was a hierarchical political system involving chiefs who acted as brokers in the exchange relationships. They were also responsible for the scheduling of feasts, ceremonies, and celebrations, which were essential to intervillage social interaction and conflict resolution. (p. 264)

The *tomol* was the tool par excellence for the maintenance of this system of trade, enabling the reciprocal exchange of goods and ideas and galvanizing the network of interdependence that contemporary Chumash see as fundamental to their ethical system. Owing to its role as facilitator for the trade system, the *tomol* represents an investment of time, ingenuity, and resource management techniques. In addition to requiring an estimated 180 to 540 person-days of labor to complete, not to mention great amounts of skill in order to produce a sea-worthy vessel, the raw materials for the *tomol* represent sometimes years of careful management before they ever make it to the production level.

The key ingredients of the canoe are, of course, wood, with redwood driftwood (washed down from the northern California coast) being the most prized; natural fiber cordage for lashing the planks together as well as for tether and anchor lines; a mixture of asphaltum (naturally occurring petroleum deposits and pine pitch) for caulking and sealing; and the assorted tools (adzes, drills, etc.) for the manufacturing process. These raw materials are employed as a result of preproduction processes such as gathering (or purchasing via the aforementioned trade system), preparation (curing and planking the wood), knowledge of availability (in the case of asphaltum deposits); and ongoing resource management.

This last point is especially true with regard to stands of red milkweed (*Asclepias fascicularis*) and/or dogbane (*Apocynum canabis*) for the approximately one mile of cordage needed for the finished *tomol*. In this last case, contemporary Chumash assert that the availability of large amounts of this important resource depended upon management. Chumash ethnobotanist Julie Cordero states that the plant simply will not occur in useable stands if merely left to its own growth patterns. Clearly, the *tomol* required a vast amount of personnel and resource management before the manufacturing even began.

PADDLING AS PRACTICE. This system does not stop at the production level. Crew responsibilities and the environmental knowledge required for safe travel are also important. It is this last point that provides the clearest metaphorical connection between the contemporary *tomol* crew and their classic predecessors. The rowing of a relatively small vessel in the hazardous Santa Barbara Channel requires great skill and teamwork for safety and efficiency. Individual paddlers must be physically capable, mentally adroit, and socially connected to the other paddlers for the safe and successful operation of the *tomol*.

The nature of the vessel is such that individual balance while compensating for the movement of the other paddlers and synchronous strokes of the paddles are key for the smooth movement of the canoe. For this to occur, it is optimal that the crew be experienced with the other members so they will be aware of their style and physical types and their various strengths and weaknesses, and for the formation of personal bonds of trust, as the process, even in the contemporary context, is not without some measure of risk. It is precisely this relationship-building, among both paddlers and non-paddling support and building crews, that gives the Chumash involved in paddling the *tomol* the tangible elements for understanding the underlying ethos viewed as uniquely Chumash.

In the process of learning the behaviors and skills required for the rowing of the *tomol,* the contemporary Chumash have also begun to fashion a rhetorical system within which the *tomol* protocol, as well as the actual requirements for paddling, are transmitted to others. This oratory ranges from practical concerns regarding canoe operation to ontological statements of emotive quality that are seen as pertinent to living a proper life. Maintenance of the tomol is liked to maintenance of interpersonal relationships. Paddling together is connected to bonds of trust, interdependence, and ancestral honor. Suffice it to say that, in the reprise of canoe culture for the Chumash, the *tomol* provides both an exemplar of the entire ethos seen as essentially Chumash, as well as an opportunity to express through practice what it is that comprises the particular Chumash ethic.

The *tomol,* for the Chumash who are involved in the revival of their maritime culture, provides a key symbol of an ancient ethos that navigated its way through some ten thousand years of history, through many transformations in climate, and continues to provide a vessel with which they can carry their children into a future that regards their past as continually present.

SEE ALSO North American Indians, article on Indians of California and the Intermountain Region.

BIBLIOGRAPHY

Arnold, Jeanne. "Complex Hunter-Gatherer-Fishers of Prehistoric California: Chiefs, Specialists, and Maritime Adaptations of the Channel Islands" *American Antiquity* 57, no. 1 (1992): 60–84.

Blackburn, Thomas. *December's Child: A Book of Chumash Oral Narratives.* Berkeley, Calif., 1975.

Bourdieu, Pierre. *The Logic of Practice.* Stanford, Calif., 1980.

Johnson, John R. "Chumash Social Organization: An Ethnohistoric Perspective." Ph.D. diss., University of California, Santa Barbara, 1988.

Larson, Daniel O., John R. Johnson, and Joel C. Michaelsen. "Missionization Among the Coastal Chumash of Central California: A Study of Risk Minimization Strategies." *American Anthropologist* 96, no. 2 (1994): 263–299.

Ortner, Sherry B. "On Key Symbols." In *Reader in Comparative Religion,* edited by William A. Lessa and Evon Z. Vogt. New York, 1973.

Swidler, Ann. "Culture in Action: Symbols and Strategies." *American Sociological Review* 5 (1986): 273–286.

DENNIS F. KELLEY (2005)

TÖNNIES, FERDINAND (1855–1936), German sociologist. Tönnies provided elaborate definitions of branches of sociology long before it was recognized as an academic discipline.

Ferdinand Julius Tönnies's academic preparation for his work as sociologist was uncommonly broad. In 1877 he received his doctorate in classical philology. Beginning his teaching career at the University of Kiel in 1881, he successively taught philosophy, economics, statistics, and sociology, and meanwhile published many articles on public policies. From 1909 to 1933 he was president of the German Sociological Society (founded by him along with Georg Simmel, Werner Sombart, and Max Weber). Having been publicly opposed to rising National Socialism and anti-Semitism, he was later illegally discharged from this post by the Hitler regime.

In 1887 he published his most famous book, a typological study, *Gemeinschaft und Gesellschaft* (translated as *Community and Society,* 1957). Outside Germany the reputation of this work overshadowed his other important writings such as those on Thomas Hobbes, on Karl Marx, on custom and morals, and on public opinion. Employing his dichotomous ideal types, *Gemeinschaft* ("community") and *Gesellschaft* ("society"), he attempted to define fundamentally different kinds of human relationships in their dimensions and structures. He took into account biological and psychological as well as institutional perspectives, and he expounded the typology with impressive erudition and poetic imagination. He leaned heavily on English literature from Hobbes to Herbert Spencer and Henry Maine. He compared his typology to Maine's distinction between status and contract.

For Tönnies, all social groupings are willed creations manifesting different kinds of human will. He saw these differentiations in terms of another dichotomy. On the one hand is a common "natural will" consisting of life forces associated with instincts, emotions, and habits, forming personal bonds and obligations that engender an unconscious sense of organic unity and solidarity of persons and groups. On the other hand is a deliberate, consciously purposeful "rational will" manifest in the impersonal pursuit of individual and group interests. In the rational will is a combination of motifs issuing from romanticism and rationalism. These differentiations become evident also in religion. (In his later period he envisaged the possibility of a nondogmatic universal religion to unite humankind.)

The "natural will" of community is integrative; the "rational will" of society is pluralistic and segmental, reaching its peak in capitalism. Both kinds of will are always present in some form or degree, but Tönnies favored a community-oriented socialism.

Some critics have seen these typological dichotomies an inimical to strictly empirical studies. Typology, they say, should not replace historiography, though the latter requires the former. Tönnies was aware of the danger of oversimplification and reduction in one's view of social reality. This becomes readily evident in his sharp critique of statisticians.

In his early essay on Spinoza, "Studie zur Entwicklungsgeschichte des Spinozas" in *Vierteljahrsschrift für wissenschaftliche Philosophie* (1883), Tönnies spoke of the emphasis on will as revealing a philosophy (stimulated by Arthur Schopenhauer) that he called "voluntarism," which entails the recognition of the primacy of will over intellect, and which is applicable to psychology, epistemology, and metaphysics. His old friend Friedrich Paulsen in his *Einleitung in die Philosophie* (1892) spelled out the conception of voluntarism in psychological terms. Paul Tillich in *Socialist Decision* (1933) adapted Tönnies's concepts of community and society. William James was so enthusiastic about Paulsen's book that he provided a lengthy introduction for the English edition, and one can see voluntaristic elements in James's concept of the "will to believe."

BIBLIOGRAPHY

Cahnman, Werner J., ed. *Ferdinand Tönnies: A New Evaluation; Essays and Documents.* Leiden, 1973.

Wirth, Louis. "The Sociology of Ferdinand Tönnies." *American Journal of Sociology* 32 (1926): 412–422.

New Sources

Bickel, Cornelius. *Ferdinand Tönnies: Soziologie als skeptische Aufklärung zwischen Historismus und Rationalismus.* Opladen, Germany, 1991.

JAMES LUTHER ADAMS (1987)
Revised Bibliography

TORAH. It is no exaggeration to claim that the term *torah* is the quintessential symbol in Judaism. The present essay approaches this symbol from a variety of linguistic, historical, and phenomenological points of view. The discussion is divided into nine basic parts. The first of these offers basic etymological orientation to the semantic range of the term *torah* in classical Hebrew usage. Parts two to four address the problem of the nature and origins of the diverse sorts of writings that have come to be called *torah* in Judiasm. With the literary survey of *torah* complete, we then move to a survey of the ideological perspectives that Jews in various times and places have used to explain the meaning and the authority of *torah.* Part eight traces the profound role that the value of Torah study has played in the history of Judaism. The final part addresses the ritual functions of the book of the Torah as physical object.

ETYMOLOGY AND BASIC MEANINGS. The Hebrew noun *torah* is formed from the linguistic stem *y-r-h.* This stem has a complex semantic history, bearing at least three distinct senses: "to throw or shoot," "to water," and "to proclaim or instruct." Some nineteenth-century scholars held that the stem has a primary setting in the context of divination practices, as in the casting of lots (e.g., *Jos.* 18:6). Indeed in Akkadian a closely related stem underlies the noun, *tertu,* which refers to an oracular directive or instruction. Nevertheless, in contemporary times, there has been no firm consensus about the linguistic history of the term *torah* prior to its characteristic usages in the Hebrew Bible and associated ancient Hebrew literature. In these sources, *torah* bears the primary sense of "teaching" or "instruction." Depending upon the context, *torah* can refer to the orally imparted wisdom of parents (*Prv.* 1:8, 4:2) as well as to the teachings of formal instructors, including sages (*Prv.* 13:14), priests (*Dn.* 17:11), or prophets (*Dn.* 1:5). Very commonly it refers to messages delivered by the God of Israel to prophetic spokespersons, usually in the form of auditory disclosures of the divine voice (*Is.* 30:9). Especially in the biblical book of *Deuteronomy,* and at key junctures in the historical accounts of the books of Joshua through 2 Kings (e.g., *Jos.* 8:31, 2 *Kgs.* 14:6, 23:25), "the book of the Torah of Moses" (*sefer torat mosheh*) refers to a written collection of hortatory teachings and legal instructions. Equivalent terms, apparently referring to a complete document, are "the book of the Torah of YHWH" (*sefer torat yhwh;* e.g., *Neh.* 9:3) and "the book of the Torah of God" (*sefer torat ʾelohim;* e.g., *Jos.* 24:26). According to *Deuteronomy,* these teachings were copied by Moses in response to the divine command and deposited for posterity in the ark that housed the stone covenantal tablets received on Sinai/Horeb (*Dn.* 31:24-26). The author of the biblical book of *Nehemiah,* writing sometime between the fifth and the fourth centuries BCE, assumed that the scroll read by the priestly scribe, Ezra, in the covenant-renewal ceremony described in *Nehemiah* 8:1 and following, was a copy of this very same book of the Torah. It is represented as the written testimony of a covenantal relationship between the Israelite nation and the God of Israel, who redeemed it from slavery in the time of Moses and promises to restore Israel's fortunes in the future in return for full loyalty to the norms contained within the Torah (*Neh.* 9:6-10:31).

THE LITERARY FORMAT OF THE CANONICAL TORAH. In the authoritative version known for well over 2000 years, the Torah refers collectively to the first five books in the canon of the Hebrew Bible. Ancient Jewish translations of the Hebrew Bible into Greek (i.e., the *Septuagint,* c. 250 BCE and later), which form the textual basis of the Christian Old Testament, refer to these five books collectively as the Pentateuch ("the Five Books"). Greek-speaking Jews commonly referred to this collection by the term *ho nomos* ("the Law"; e.g., 2 *Mc.* 15:9, *Rom.* 7:1). Through the mediation of Christianity, deeply influenced by the usages of Greek-speaking Jews, it has become common in Western culture to conceive of the Torah as a law code and of *torah* as "law." More properly, the Torah founded in the Hebrew Bible is an extended narrative that contains law codes. In traditional Jewish usage, the general noun torah—without the definite article—refers broadly to any authoritative religious teaching—legal, ethical, or theological.

Neither ancient Hebrew copies of the Torah nor modern scrolls used in Jewish worship identify either the Torah as a whole or its separate books by name. In traditional Jewish usage the title of each book is drawn from Hebrew words that appear in their first sentences: *Bereshit* ("In the beginning"), *Shemot* ("Names"), *Vayiqrʾa* ("And he called"), *Bamidbar* ("In the wilderness"), and *Devarim* ("Words"). In Christian usage, the titles are drawn from Latin renderings of the Septuagint's Greek titles that allude broadly to the theme of each work. These are the origins of the terms routinely used in Christian communities. English translations of the Old Testament, for example, list the titles of the Pentateuchal books as *Genesis* (Gr. *Genesis*); *Exodus* (Gr. *Exodos*); *Leviticus* (Gr. *Leuitikon*); *Numbers* (Gr. *Arithmoi);* and *Deuteronomy* (Gr. *Deuteronomion*).

Modern readers of the Torah in Hebrew will find it in two forms: as a printed book in the larger collection of a printed Hebrew Bible or as a handwritten scroll used in synagogue rituals which call for reading from the Torah in public. Scholars, perhaps, will have consulted medieval handwritten copies of the Torah that take the form of codices—separate leaves of parchment or other writing material bound together into a book. The format of the scroll is the most ancient and is found in the earliest surviving fragmentary copies of parts of the Torah that have been found among the Dead Sea Scrolls. These fragments, over eighty in number, offer evidence of the state of the text as early as the mid-second century BCE. They also show that the books of the Torah, like other writings presently included in the canon of the Hebrew Bible, circulated in a variety of versions, many of which differ from that found in the official scriptural canon. It is not clear how early the five books comprising the Torah were routinely copied together on one scroll. Nevertheless, Jewish and early Christian literary sources from the beginning of the Common Era assume that all five books formed a single literary entity.

The Contents of the Canonical Torah. The canonical version of the Torah is a complex narrative work of extremely sophisticated composition. No simple outline of the plot of the Torah can do justice to its complexity. Major and minor themes and subplots are skillfully woven throughout the five books so that passages in one book are alluded to or even quoted in others (e.g., *Ex.* 16:2-3 and *Nm.* 11:4-6). The thematic unity of the Torah, then, fully justifies the rabbinic view that the books must be copied on a single scroll (B.T., *Git.* 60a). The following summary suggests the overall coherence of the Torah's narrative across the five books in which the story is told.

The Torah's master theme organizes diverse stories and collections of laws into a theologically coherent statement as well as a compelling historical narrative. The Torah is a history of the expressions of divine love for Israel and of Israel's inability to accept and respond to that love. The theme is given a universal significance in the first eleven chapters of *Genesis,* a complete literary unit that forms a prologue describing the origins of the world in God's creative speech (*Gn.* 1:1-2:4) and the early history of humanity. These chapters describe various forms of human rebellion from the time of the primordial man and woman, Adam and Eve (*Gn.* 2:4-3:24) and continuing through their descendants: Cain's murder of his brother, Abel (*Gn.* 4:1-16); the violence of Noah's generation that led to the destruction of nearly all life (*Gn.* 6-9); and the insolence of the generation that sought to invade the heavens by building a tower in Babel (*Gn.* 11:1-10).

This history of human rebellion foreshadows the Torah's depiction of God's relationship with the family of Abraham and his descendants through his son, Isaac, and grandson, Jacob. *Genesis* chapters 12 to 36 describe various covenantal promises sealed between God and these Patriarchs (*Gn.* 12:1-4, 15:1-21, 17:1-14, 22:15-19, 26:23-25, 28:10-15). Essential to these is the promise of the Land of Canaan as the eventual dwelling place of the Israelite people. Thematically, this Land recalls the original Garden in which Adam and Eve lived and from which they were expelled due to their rebellion. It is to be the place in which God and his human partners dwell together in harmony. But as the Torah's narrative unfolds, it becomes clear that Israel is no less susceptible than the original humans to the urge to defy God. Each patriarch lives in the Land for a time, and each is tested with various hardships that require him to leave the Land. Ultimately, through a combination of famine and certain intrigues involving a plot by Jacob's eleven sons against their brother Joseph, all of Jacob's descendants migrate to Egypt (*Gn.* 37-50), abandoning entirely the Land promised to them through their ancestor, Abraham.

The book of *Exodus* opens (chapter 1) with a description of the enslavement of Jacob's descendants to the Egyptian Pharaoh. The focus of chapters 2 to 4 is the figure of Moses, a son of Hebrew slaves, spared from death and raised in the royal household, who discovers his true identity and is called upon by God to lead Israel out of slavery into a formal covenant of servitude to God himself. Chapters 5 to 15 trace the negotiations of Moses and his brother, Aaron, with Pharaoh for the release of Israel from slavery. They also describe Israel's liberation through the visitation of plagues against Egypt, culminating in the death of firstborn sons. Moses brings the freed slaves to a wilderness mountain chosen by God—Sinai—and there concludes a covenant-making ceremony that includes the revelation to Moses and Israel of the legal terms of covenantal service to God (chapters 19-24). At this point Israel is in full possession of the covenant revelation and anticipates rapid entry in the Land of Canaan, where its terms are to be fulfilled.

With a few crucial narrative interruptions, the details of these covenantal laws extend from chapter 25 of *Exodus,* through the entire book of *Leviticus,* and into the first ten chapters of *Numbers.* The first narrative interruption in this extensive collection of laws is of great importance to the Torah's overall theme of human rebellion against divine love. *Exodus* chapter 32 describes how Israel, just having seen the saving power of God in his punishment of Egypt, initially rebels against the terms of its covenant at Sinai. The very first divine statement of the covenantal terms was the commandment to avoid worship of any image as a divinity and to devote cultic service exclusively to the God who redeemed Israel from Egyptian servitude (*Ex.* 20:1-4). Nevertheless, when Moses is delayed on Sinai in discourse with God, Israel coerces Aaron to supply a cultic icon in the form of a golden calf to serve as a focus of religious devotion. Although Israel atones for this violation, and God's anger is appeased, a pattern of disloyalty familiar from the first chapters of Genesis has been reestablished.

The book of *Numbers,* from chapter 11, resumes the theme of Israel's inability to be loyal to the terms of the divine covenant. It repeatedly offers stories that illustrate Israel's lack of trust in God's power. The most important illustration comes in chapters 13 and 14. Two years after the liberation from slavery, Moses has lead Israel to the border of the Land promised to Abraham. In response to God's word, he sends spies into the Land to help prepare the invasion. But the spies are intimidated by the might of the Canaanite nations living there and convince Israel not to invade. The divine response to this lack of trust is to force Moses to lead Israel on a wilderness journey lasting thirty-eight years, during which the entire generation of adults that refused to enter the Land dies off. Only thereafter is Israel brought again to the Moabite territory adjacent to the Land, with a new generation prepared to take the Land and divide it among the tribal descendants of Jacob's sons (chapters 35-36).

The book of *Deuteronomy* opens with Moses delivering an extended speech to Israel, assembled on the banks of the Jordan River. Moses recounts the history of God's redemptive acts and Israel's ungrateful or rebellious responses, repeating and elaborating on stories told in Exodus and Numbers. He reviews the covenantal laws delivered on Sinai and elaborates in many cases upon their performance. He repeatedly underscores the fact that Israel's covenant with God entails both a blessing and a curse (e.g., *Dt.* 11:26-30, 28:1-68). If Israel obeys the covenantal laws in the Land it will prosper there; but disobedience will be punished by war and exile from the Land. Finally Moses writes down all God has told him in a document called the Book of the Torah of Moses. Deuteronomy closes with final words of dire prediction as well as hopeful blessings placed in Moses' mouth (chapters 32-33). At the end, in chapter 34, Moses dies and passes on the leadership of the people to his disciple Joshua. With this the Torah concludes, its readers fully aware of the eventual fulfillment of Moses' most dire predictions.

The Formation of the Canonical Torah. The canonical Torah described above contains many instances of Moses writing down utterances delivered by God. Readers both ancient and modern have wondered about the relation of the Torah-text found in the Hebrew Bible to the various documents that Moses is asserted to have written at divine dictation. Indeed, it is not unusual to read in the Torah that Moses wrote down "*this* Torah" or "*these* words" in response to a divine utterance. But careful readers also note that the antecedent of such expressions can be interpreted plausibly as the immediately preceding divine utterances—or perhaps the book of *Deuteronomy* itself—rather than a series of five books beginning with the creation of the world and ending with the death of Moses. Nevertheless, virtually all Jewish writings known to have been composed during the later Second Temple period (c. 400 BCE-70 CE) assume that the Torah which Moses received and copied is identical to the five books found in Torah scrolls. But in some writings, such as the preamble to the noncanonical book of *Jubilees* (c. 160 BCE), it is also assumed that the received Torah is incomplete; Moses received other revelations on Sinai as well and wrote them down. These, too, should share the authority of the Torah of Moses. The early rabbinic sages, in traditions formulated from the second through the fourth centuries CE, also believed in the Mosaic origin of the canonical text. But noticing a host of chronological discrepancies and other textual problems, they debated the possibilities that the original revelations were received and transcribed by Moses in an order that is no longer preserved in the canonical version (*Mekh.Yish.*, to *Ex.* 15:9). Others suggested that the last verses of *Deuteronomy* describing the death of Moses were written by his disciple, Joshua (B.T., *Bava Bat.* 14b-15a).

The issue of the Mosaic authorship of the canonical text of the Torah has been a particular focus of modern literary-historical scholarship since at least the seventeenth century. The fundamental assumption of modern scholarship is that the Torah, like all texts, is an essentially human product composed by authors immersed in specific historical situations. Proper interpretation of the Torah, then, involves critical study of the text, reading it for literary, stylistic, and linguistic clues to the historical setting in which it was composed. This assumption has freed historians from traditional Jewish and Christian claims about the Torah's Mosaic origins, and inspired them to propose a host of theories about the historical setting of the Torah's composition and the persons or groups responsible for its creation. Since the middle of the nineteenth century, the most influential historical reconstructions of the composition of the Torah have been associated with the Documentary Hypothesis proposed, most notably by the German scholar Julius Wellhausen (1844-1918) and refined by generations of later scholars.

As its name indicates, the Documentary Hypothesis holds that the canonical Torah is a composite literary creation composed, in part, of written documents that are more ancient than the final five-volume narrative into which they have been incorporated. These documents may have originated in oral narrative or legal traditions, but for the most part circulated in ancient Israelite priestly and scribal circles as written sources. Most versions of the hypothesis identify four specific sources, each with its own geographical and chronological point of origin, and each representing a distinct point of view regarding theology, politics, and, most importantly, the early history of Israel as a covenant people. The canonical Torah was created by editors who selected and combined elements from each of these sources in light of their own views about the history of Israel's covenant relationship to its God.

Most versions of the Documentary Hypothesis identify the four documentary sources as follows. The oldest source, often regarded as originating by the ninth century BCE, is a collection of stories reflecting many of the historical interests of the canonical Torah: stories about early humanity, the Israelite patriarchs, and the events surrounding the liberation from Egypt. It is characterized by a preference for the proper name, *YHWH*, in reference to the God of Israel. It also has a particular interest in events located in the southern part of the Land of Israel. It is called the *J-source*, an indication of its Judean origins and its preference for the divine name (spelled *jhwh* in German). Scholars usually identify its creators as a school of scribes associated with the Davidic dynasty in Jerusalem.

The second major documentary source is identified as the *E-source*. This reflects its tendency to prefer the divine title *ʾelohim* ("God") in reference to the God of Israel, and a greater degree of interest in depicting the Patriarchs as founders of worship sites in the northern part of the Land of Israel, also known as Ephraim. Most scholars regard E as a fragmentary source used to supplement and comment on basic elements of the J-source. Presumably it was composed in the northern part of the Land of Israel prior to the destruction of the Northern Israelite Kingdom by the Assyrians in 722 BCE. When Ephraimite refugees migrated south to the Davidic Kingdom they brought their traditions with them. Over time they were incorporated into the J-source traditions to produce a richer and more complex narrative. Some scholars designate this blended document as JE.

The *Priestly* or *P-source* stems, as its name indicates, from priestly writers associated with the Temple in Jerusalem. Like J and E, P contains narratives that comment on primeval human history, the Patriarchal era, and experience of liberation. But its distinctive contribution is enormous and includes detailed collections of legal codes focusing largely, but hardly exclusively, on cultic rules of sacrifice, matters of cultic purity, sexual and dietary behavior, and other matters concerned with the separation of the Israelite community from various sources of ritual contamination. These are richly represented in Leviticus and Numbers in particular. The P-source was at first thought by scholars to be relatively recent, even postexilic in composition. Most opinion holds that it is probably pre-exhilic in origin, although it may incorporate certain revisions and additions stemming from postexilic priestly editors.

The final source of the Torah, according to the Documentary Hypothesis, survives in the Torah largely intact as the book of Deuteronomy. It is called D. Most regard it as having been composed by 621 BCE in order to justify, in terms of Mosaic authority, King Josiah's program for a reform of Israelite cultic practices. Its continual preoccupation is that Israel's tenure on the Land is dependent upon total opposition to idolatry in all its forms and the destruction of non-Israelite shrines throughout the Land. In its present form, Deuteronomy is the introduction to a larger historical work, called by scholars the Deuteronomic History, extending from the scriptural books of Joshua through 2 Kings. Deutronomy closes with Moses' prediction of Israel's failure to heed the covenant, and the Deuteronomic History concludes with a description of the destruction of Jerusalem and the deportation of its royal house and priests. Accordingly, most scholars argue that D and the history attached to it are preexilic works completed in the wake of Jerusalem's destruction and the onset of the period of exile.

There remains in the twenty-first century no universal consensus about precisely how to divide the canonical Torah into the constituent four source documents. Debates continue as well regarding the dating and identity of the authors—whether individuals or "schools"—that stand behind the sources. Most contemporary scholars accept the view that the final work of editing the various sources into their present form must have been done sometime between the destruction of Jerusalem in 587 BCE and the career of the priest, Ezra (c. 450-398 BCE), depicted in the books of Ezra and Nehemiah as imposing the laws of the Torah of Moses upon the Judean community.

Also in contemporary times, the Documentary Hypothesis has been subject to some heated criticism by historians who regard as implausible the hypothesis's principle scenario: that the Torah was created by an editorial team that took apart and recombined elements of earlier written sources. Many contemporary students of oral tradition in ancient scribal cultures, like those of ancient Israel and early Judaism, acknowledge that written sources may lie behind both narrative and legal parts of the Torah. But they have also observed that the so-called "scissors and paste" method of composition proposed by the Documentary Hypothesis has no parallel in other ancient literary traditions. These depend heavily upon orally transmitted material, much of which undergoes transformation due to numerous public performances. This neglect of the oral-traditional dimension of the Torah, when combined with the failure of documentary critics to reach total consensus on the range of each documentary source, has drawn charges that the method of documentary analysis is too subjective to provide a definitive historical account of the composition of the Torah. Nevertheless, at the beginning of the twenty-first century no other theory of the Torah's origins and composition has won a consensus among contemporary academic historians of ancient Israel's literature.

TORAH AS REVELATION. As much as the term Torah is etymologically linked to the idea of teaching, it is in all forms of Judaism linked rhetorically to the idea of revelation, i.e., teaching that stems from a transmundane source. Like the other monotheistic religions originating in the Middle East (i.e., Christianity and Islam), Judaism is grounded in claims to possess revealed texts or doctrines. Since at least the early Second Temple period, the text of the Torah of Moses has served as the paradigmatic revelation. Specifically, the document inscribed on the scroll of the Torah stems from a disclosure of God's love and will to Moses. But this is not to say that Judaism in all times and places has had a single conception of revelation or of how the Torah found in the canon of Scripture and in other more recent writings is related to the actual words disclosed to Moses.

The writings of Palestinian Jewish scribes from the Second Temple period, whose pens produced dozens of books represented as revelations disclosed to ancient prophets and sages from Abraham to Ezra, commonly accepted a stenographic model of revelation derived from the depictions of Moses found throughout the Torah itself (e.g., 4 *Ezr.* 14:37-48). Just as ancient authors commonly dictated their books to scribal copyists, so God dictated his teachings to his prophetic scribe, Moses. Some Second Temple scribal circles, however, asserted that Moses had written down more of the divine revelation than was contained in the scroll anchoring the growing collection of scriptural literature. Both the book of *Jubilees*, many copies of which were found among the Dead Sea Scrolls, and the singular *Temple Scroll*, represent themselves as records of revelation to Moses. Presumably, the authors or groups promoting these works as revelation affirmed that they, no less than the canonical Torah, constituted authoritative, divinely authorized teaching.

Despite the popularity of the stenographic model of revelation in Palestinian scribal circles, there is at least one Jewish source from the late Second Temple period that suggests a rather different view. In the opinion of Philo (15 BCE–45 CE), a philosophically trained Jew who thrived in the Greco-Roman culture of Alexandria, Egypt, Moses was more than the copyist of the Torah. Rather, in Philo's view, Moses was the author of the Torah (e.g., *On the Sacrifices of Abel and Cain,* 12, 94). He wrote his book in a state of philosophical closeness to God that constituted prophetic illumination. In Philo's view, Moses' narratives and laws are the external form that concealed the deeper philosophical truths taught long after Moses' death by Socrates and Plato. Only by application of allegorical methods of interpretation, Philo held, could the philosophical content of the Torah be recovered. This content, only alluded to allegorically in the concrete text of the Torah's stories and laws, constituted for Philo the true revelation to Moses. The revelation of the Torah was the perception of philosophical truth disclosed to the human mind in a state of prophetic ecstasy (e.g., *On the Sacrifices of Abel and Cain,* 78).

Medieval Jewish thinkers, entirely independently of Philo, would revive the idea of the Torah as an allegory whose truths had to be decoded through appropriate interpretive systems. But they would do so in a way deeply influenced by Rabbinic Judaism, the form of Judaism that grew to dominate Mediterranean and Middle Eastern Jews from the second century CE until the rise of Islam in the seventh century. In its classical form, as found in the later Talmudic literature of Late Antiquity, the rabbinic theory of revelation is grounded in three basic conceptions.

The first is that "Torah is from Heaven" (M. *San.* 10:1)—that is, the God of Israel is the exclusive source of the Torah. In holding this view, the rabbinic sages shared the views of generations of Palestinian Jewish scribes before them, who regarded Moses as a kind of stenographer taking dictation from the God of Israel. The sages also accepted another element of Second Temple Jewish thought, the idea that certain writings produced after the time of Moses were disclosed to religious teachers—prophets in the line of Mosaic authority but subordinate to him in status—whose writings were the result of inspiration by the "holy spirit" (*ruah haqodesh*: e.g., B.T., *Meg.* 7a). Rabbinic discussion of the extent of the canon of the Hebrew Bible revolved in part around the criterion of inspiration (T. *Yad.* 2:14). Thus the relatively recent book of Daniel, composed around 167 BCE, is included within the rabbinic scriptural canon on the basis of its attribution to an ancient seer from the Exilic period. But an older work, a collection of wise sayings from the pen of the Temple Scribe Yeshua ben Sirach (included in Christian collections of the Apocrypha as the *Wisdom of ben Sira,* c. 180 BCE), was not included in the rabbinic canon, despite its popularity among rabbinic sages as a source of wisdom.

The third key element in the rabbinic conception of revelation is that the Sinaitic revelation to Moses included two intertwined but discrete bodies of teaching. One of these, the actual scroll of the Torah of Moses (and by extension, later books included in the rabbinic scriptural canon), was called the written Torah (e.g., *Tanh.-Bub.*, to Ex. 19:1). But in addition, God had disclosed an unwritten body of knowledge which alone could unlock the secrets of the written Torah. This unwritten revelation is called the oral Torah (e.g., *Avot Nat.,* A:15). Other Jewish groups of the Second Temple period had asserted the existence of books of revelations that were not contained in the Torah of Moses. But the rabbinic claim is unique in insisting that this revelation was not found in books, but only available as oral tradition learned at the feet of rabbinic sages themselves. Indeed, in rabbinic terminology, the "study of Torah" (*talmud torah*) refers specifically to the study of the written and oral Torah, for Torah had become the comprehensive term denoting the entirety of teachings recognized by rabbinic tradition as authoritative. By early medieval times, rabbinic scribes and teachers had come to preserve oral Torah in discrete written compilations, most importantly, the Mishnah and its Talmudic commentaries. These were routinely memorized by rabbinic disciples, whose discussions and inquiries into the texts of oral Torah continued the oral tradition despite the use of writing in its preservation.

Torah as Law and Ontological Principle. The term *torah,* in addition to its specific sense of "teaching" and the more comprehensive suggestion of "revealed teaching," has also served to convey the concept of "legal rule." This meaning is already well attested in the Hebrew Bible (e.g., *Nm.* 19:14). It is confirmed as well in the penchant of Greek-speaking Jews and early Christians to refer to their collection of scriptures as "the Law" (*ho nomos*; *Matt.* 5:17). Within classical rabbinic Judaism, the written Torah served as a fundamental source of civil and ritual law. Rabbinic sages, functioning as jurisprudents, interpreted and applied the law within the traditional framework of the oral Torah.

A homiletic passage of the Babylonian Talmud (B.T.) (*Mak.* 24a) asserts that God had revealed in the written Torah no less than 613 specific commandments (*mitsvot;* sing. *mitsvah*). The Talmud nowhere lists these commandments, a task that would be taken up by many medieval legal codifiers. Nevertheless, the conceptual tools and interpretive principles for identifying these commandments and applying them in practical affairs were transmitted in the oral Torah tradition (e.g., the *Bar. Yish.*). These yielded the authoritative procedures (*halakhot;* sing. *halakhah*) for embodying the commandments in the covenant life of Israel. In practice, the legal force of a commandment in the written Torah was delimited exclusively by the meaning ascribed to it in the halakhic tradition of the oral Torah, regardless of what the semantic meaning of the commandment might suggest. Thus, to take a famous example, the written Torah's commandment to take "an eye for an eye" in the case of damages caused by negligence (*Ex.* 21:23) is defined halakhically to mean that the responsible party must compensate the victim financially for his or her loss (e.g., *Mek. Yish.* to *Ex.* 21:23).

The most decisive development in rabbinic conceptions of Torah as a legal system was the emergence of various attempts to systematically organize the vast legal discussions of the Talmudic literature into manageable codes that could serve the needs of rabbinic courts and educated laity. First in the Islamic world, and then in Latin Christendom, rabbinic scholars produced a series of influential halakhic collections. These experimented with a variety of organizational formats. The *She'iltot* of Rabbi Aha (c. 750), for example, organized halakhic norms in tandem with the rabbinically prescribed Torah readings for the Sabbath which served as their sources. Others, such as the halakhic digest of Rabbi Isaac Al-Fasi (1013-1103), followed the traditional sequence of Talmudic tractates, extracting essential halakhic conclusions from the give-and-take of the debates within which the Talmud had preserved them. The most innovative and encyclopedic attempt at codification was the *Mishneh Torah,* composed by Moses ben Maimon ("Maimonides," 1135-1204). He organized all of rabbinic halakhah within the framework of fourteen major topical headings, each of which included several subheadings, all arranged in scrupulous logical sequence. Subsequent codes, such as Rabbi Jacob ben Asher's *'Arb'a Turim* (fourteenth century) and Rabbi Joseph Caro's *Shulhan 'Arukh* (sixteenth century) revised Maimonides's comprehensive organizational categories. They also narrowed Maimonides's scope, focusing only upon halakhic norms that governed the daily life of individuals and the community as a corporate entity. Thus, vast halakhic topics that depended upon the existence of the Jerusalem Temple were excluded, despite their extensive treatment by Maimonides. The primary categories developed in the *'Arb'a Turim* have become conventional in later rabbinic halakhic thinking until contemporary times. They are *'Orakh Hayyim* (laws governing the liturgical cycle of the day, week, and year); *Yoreh De'ah* (ritual laws, such as the dietary restrictions, that signify the holiness of the Jewish community); *Hoshen Mishpat* (the topics of civil and criminal law); and *'Even Ha'ezer* (*halakhot* governing the contraction, duration, and dissolution of marriage).

In addition to this halakhic-jurisprudential development of the meaning of Torah as "law," classical rabbinic tradition also suggested that Torah constituted a kind of law of being, "a precious instrument through which the world was created" (M. *Avot* 3:14). The thought was driven home vividly in midrashic settings, in which the Torah was likened to an architect's blueprint that proved indispensable to the builder of a palace *(Ber. Rab.* 1:1) or claimed to have existed for 947 generations prior to the creation of the world (B.T., *Zev.* 116a). Such suggestions that the Torah in some sense preceded the creation of the world entailed, of course, a radical disassociation of Torah, conceived as a principle of being, from the specific writings found in books. Torah, in the context of such discussions, now denoted an ontological principle that transcended the existence of the historical Torah of Moses, even as the latter pointed toward and symbolized that ontological reality.

The jurisprudential and ontological developments of the idea of Torah among the sages of Late Antiquity provided the foundations upon which medieval rabbinic intellectuals, responding to larger movements in Islamic and Christian thought and piety, created fresh formulations of these themes. Many of these formulations were inspired by polemical interactions. The pioneering figure in the Jewish philosophical tradition, Rabbi Sa'adia ben Joseph (882-942) produced his masterpiece, *The Book of Opinions and Beliefs,* in part as an effort to demonstrate to rationalist critics the rationality of the Torah as a legal system stemming from God and disclosed in its complete and final form to Israel's prophets. Deeply influenced by the rationalist Islamic school known as the Mut'azilite Kalam, Sa'adia hoped to use the Kalam's own rigorous methodology to demonstrate the intellectual sufficiency of Torah as a comprehensive source of divine knowledge. Building upon traditional Talmudic distinctions between pragmatic rules (*mishpatim*) and inscrutable divine decrees (*huqqim*), Sa'adia argued that both were absolutely essential in the context of the Torah as revelation. Laws self-evidently necessary for social order, such as the prohibition against murder (*Ex.* 20:13), were entirely susceptible to rational explanation. Apparently absurd requirements, such as the injunction against certain types of foods (e.g. *Lv.* 11:1ff.), on the other hand, required revelationbecause unaided reason would never discover them as the will of God. In this sense, the rational laws of the Torah are a crucial part of revelation because they inspire confidence in the inscrutable divine will that commands as well the nonrational prohibitions and injunctions of the Torah (*Book of Beliefs and Opinions,* III.3–5).

Reflection on the rationality of the Torah as a source of law, a characteristic leitmotif of the Jewish philosophical tradition since the time of Sa'adia, reached its high point in the work of Maimonides. An Aristotelian critic of the Kalam, Maimonides argued for the complete rational intelligibility of all of the laws of the Torah. He did so both by philosophical argument and jurisprudential demonstration. Maimonides' great codification of the *halakhah,* discussed above, demonstrated the rational integrity and complete harmony of the entire body of written and oral Torah. By contrast, Maimonides' principal philosophical work, the *Guide of the Perplexed,* offered a powerful defense of the rationality of the Torah as a guide to the perfection of human beings as creatures of God. He rejected earlier distinctions, such as those of Sa'adia, between rational and nonrational commandments, arguing instead for the conceptual cogency of the entire system of revealed law as developed in the oral Torah. Acknowledging that the rationality of some commandments was more immediately clear than others, he insisted that the Torah's law remains the most complete and incomparable disclosure of the divine will in human language (*Guide of the Perplexed* III:26-28).

When thinking about the ontological dimension of the Torah, thinkers such as Sa'adia and Maimonides hesitated to subscribe to the idea of the Torah as a pre-existent ontological principle that pervaded creation. In their view, to speak of the Torah pre-existing the world was tantamount to questioning the fundamental belief that God created the world from nothing. Torah could reflect, as law, the mind and will of God, but it could not be conceived as something co-eternal with God. This type of ontological thinking about Torah, in fact, became characteristic of the qabbalistic tradition, a distinctly antiphilosophical movement of Spanish and southern French pietists that began to take shape in the eleventh through thirteenth centuries.

Qabbalists such as Rabbi Todros Abulafia (1220-1298, writing in *ʾOtsar Hakavod*, to *Shab.* 28b), tended to reject as hubris the Maimonidean idea that the human mind could justify divine commandments through the exercise of reason. All of the 613 commandments—the reasonable as well the absurd—were profound mysteries fulfilling some hidden purpose in the economy of creation. In qabbalistic thought, which reprised certain neo-Platonic themes that had originally inspired Jewish philosophers as well, thinking about the Torah as law and ontological principle was, in fact, elegantly combined. The pioneering Talmudist, biblical interpreter, and qabbalist Rabbi Moses ben Nahman ("Nahmanides," 1194-1270), asserted in the introduction to his commentary on the Torah that the Torah is nothing less than the being of God in linguistic form, a series of divine names. Reflecting such conceptions, writers such as Azriel of Gerona (early thirteenth century) conceived the 613 commandments of the halakhic tradition metaphorically as the "limbs" of God, each limb corresponding to an appropriate human limb for which that commandment was destined (*Per. Ag.*, 37). On this view, the "reason" for the commandments had nothing to do with rational justification of the divine will. Rather, a Jew's performance of commandments according to their halakhic prescriptions effected a communication of being between God and his creatures (e.g., *Zoh.* II: 165b). The *Zohar*, a canonical expression of thirteenth-century Qabbalah, expressed this principle as a kind of axiom: "Three dimensions of being are bound up with each other—the Blessed Holy One, Torah, and Israel" (*Zoh.* III:73a). That is to say, Torah is at one and the same time a system of law and the root of all existence. By enacting the law, Israel unifies the limbs of God into their ideal configuration, thus bringing blessing to the world (*Zoh.* II:85b).

The qabbalistic unification of Torah as law with Torah as a principle of being proved immensely influential. The Jewish philosophical tradition, which had never engaged more than a relatively small minority of Jews, would essentially die out by the sixteenth century. But from the thirteenth century onward, qabbalistic ideas transmitted in the *Zohar* and by its exegetical interpreters came to dominate much of the rabbinic intellectual leadership. Indeed, one of the last great Jewish philosophers, Hasdai Crescas (1340-1410), was himself deeply sympathetic to the Qabbalah's insistence that the Torah could not be comprehended by human rationality. Qabbalistic perspectives on Torah are also represented in the writings of later intellectual leaders, such as Rabbi Isaac Abarbanel (1437-1508), Rabbi Moses Alshekh (c. 1590), Rabbi Haim Vital (1542-1620), the Maharal of Prague (Rabbi Judah Loewe ben Betsalel: 1525-1609) and the Vilna Gaon (Rabbi Elijah ben Solomon: 1720-1797). The writings of Rabbi Haim Vital and the Maharal were particularly influential in the development of Eastern European Hasidism, a revivalist movement founded in the eighteenth century. The idea of Torah as an ontological principle of being is richly represented in the early Hasidic writings of such influential masters as Rabbi Shneʾur Zalman of Liady (1745-1813), author of *Tanya*, and Rabbi Menahem Nahum of Chernobyl (1730-1797), the author of *Meʾor ʿEnayim*.

Torah as a Record of Jewish Moral and Historical Experience. In the contemporary world it is still possible to find communities of Jews remaining ideologically committed to stenographic conceptions of the revelation of the Torah. For the most part, such Jews structure their behavior exclusively in light of the oral Torah's halakhic tradition as defined in the *Shulhan ʿArukh*, and regard the Torah as a creative principle at the heart of reality. But they consider themselves—and are so considered by most other Jews—as ultra-orthodox rejectionists, opposed to all influences of Western civilization upon Judaism. Accordingly, their intellectual impact upon the thought of Jews more accepting of modern civilization has tended to be minimal. Of far greater influence in most forms of contemporary Jewish thinking about the Torah are intellectual traditions that emerged in the context of modern European Protestant religious thought and went on to shape much of the intellectual style of modernity. These include in particular an ethical universalism associated with the philosopher Immanuel Kant (1724-1804), a romantic focus on personal religious experience stemming from the work of the theologian Friedrich Schleiermacher (1768-1834), and an idealist search for the patterns of historical development that achieved influential formulation in the philosophy of G. W. F. Hegel (1770-1831).

These traditions stand behind three fundamental shifts in Jewish thinking about the Torah in the past two centuries. The first, inspired by Kant, is the shift from conceiving Torah as a legal instrument requiring absolute obedience to conceiving it as a source of eternal moral values and ethical norms. Thinkers following in this tradition include, among others, Moritz Lazarus (1824-1903), Hermann Cohen (1842-1918), and Leo Baeck (1873-1956), all of whom found the essence of Judaism to be in the Torah as the first historical expression of ethical monotheism. The Torah remains essential, in this view, as an ongoing inspiration to moral seriousness and universal ethical concern on the part of the Jewish people. The ritual and civil laws of the Torah are no longer literally binding upon Jews, although the ethical values informing them abide.

The second shift, inspired by Schleiermacher, moves the traditional notion of revelation in the direction of personal subjectivity, transforming the giving of the Torah from an historical event to a moral and psychological experience. For much of modern Jewish religious thought, the Torah is conceived as a written record of the profound personal religious experiences enjoyed by Israel's prophets and still retrievable for the modern reader through the proper interpretation of the text. A brilliant and influential exponent of this view was Abraham Geiger (1810-1874), the founder of Reform Judaism. In the middle of the twentieth century, the existentially oriented philosophical and hermeneutical writings of Martin Buber (1878-1965) brought this theme to the attention of a wide audience. Buber focused upon revelation as the matrix of an I-Thou relationship with God as the Eternal Thou. He was famous for insisting that the laws of the Torah could only constitute revelation if they were subjectively experienced as commandments by the individual.

Finally, the third shift involves a revision of the relationship of the Torah to historical and cultural processes. Classically, the Torah is transhuman and originates with God. For most modern Jewish thinkers, the Torah—both as a collection of texts and as a system of values—is a tradition that developed in accord with historical processes and under a variety of cultural influences. This shift can ultimately be traced back to the influence of Hegel's notion of history as the temporal unfolding of an eternal Absolute Spirit that would eventually come, through the dialectical patterns intrinsic to the logic of its own being, to a complete self-consciousness of itself. This conception was first applied to the history of Judaism by Nahman Krochmal (1785-1840). He viewed the Torah in dialectical terms as both the product of historical Jewish experience and the eternal, ideal structure of that experience. The influential writings of the twentieth-century philosopher Franz Rosenzweig (1886-1929) take issue with much of Hegelian idealism, but remain deeply committed to the concept of the eternality of the Torah as a unique structure of Jewish being and consciousness. Rosenzweig's interchange of letters with Buber over the nature of the Torah's commandments as revelation remains a crucial signpost in the history of modern Jewish thinking about the Torah.

Throughout the twentieth century, modern Jewish religious thought in the United States, Europe, and the State of Israel has elaborated upon the Torah as a source of Jewish ethics, a record of Jewish religious insight, and a product of Jewish historical and cultural experience. For the most part, this conversation has proceeded without the contribution of those Jews, mostly of Eastern European and Middle Eastern origin, who for a variety of reasons have rejected modern culture in principle. A singular exception is Rabbi Joseph B. Soloveitchik (1903-1992), descendant of a prestigious family of Lithuanian Talmudists, and the principal mid-twentieth-century exponent of modern Orthodox Judaism. Fully conversant with the Kantian, Scheiermachian, and Hegelian foundations of modern theology, Soloveitchik devoted himself to constructing a workable theory of the continued authority of the halakhic tradition of written and oral Torah over Jewish life. For Soloveitchik, the halakhic tradition embodies an historically given and existentially grounded mode of human consciousness. Intellectual mastery and scrupulous observance of Torah—paradigmatically, the tradition of received halakhic norms—enables Jews to transform their broken human existence in accordance with the ideal construct of human personhood imagined for all humanity at the time of creation.

At the beginning of the twentieth-first century, Torah continues to occupy a central place in Jewish religious discourse. All of the traditional themes of modern Jewish conceptions of the Torah—the ethical, the personalist, and the historicist—have their exponents and these conceptions continue to be refined in both popular and academic writings. A potentially significant development in more recent decades is the emergence of an explicitly "postmodernist" style of Jewish thought inspired by developments in European philosophy and literary studies associated with a movement known as "Deconstruction." Emanuel Levinas (1905-1995), the French author of both philosophical works and Talmudic commentaries, has been influential in this trend, particularly among American thinkers. The principle tendency of Jewish postmodernism is to expose the ideological underpinnings of the primary pillars of modern thought in general—its claim to ethical ultimacy and historically comprehensive vision. By depriving modern thought of its absolute authority over values and visions of the past, Jewish postmodernists have begun to experiment with new ways of engaging the texts of Torah—broadly conceived now as the entire sum of texts that disclose dimensions of Jewish existence. It remains to be seen how these new ways of reading will influence Jewish conceptions of Torah in coming decades.

TORAH STUDY AS A FORM OF JUDAIC PIETY. A famous rabbinic text included in the rabbinic ritual for daily morning blessings concludes its list of praiseworthy acts with the phrase "and the study of Torah overrides all of them" (*talmud torah keneged kulam*: P.T., *Pe'ah* 1:1). This phrase summarizes the centrality of Torah study in rabbinic Judaism. To a certain degree the study of the Torah of Moses is given a high evaluation in a variety of Second Temple-period Jewish settings (cf. *Ps.* 119, Preface to the *Wisdom of ben Sira*, and *Rule of the Community*, QS 6:6-8). But in rabbinic Judaism, which coalesced over a century after the destruction of the Jerusalem Temple in 70 CE, Torah study came to occupy a new role. It was conceived as a form of piety which, on a par with formal public worship, substituted for the vanished sacrificial service performed in ancient times by the Jerusalem priesthood (B.T., *Meg.* 16b). Both activities were regarded by sages as world-sustaining acts which, like sacrifice itself, drew divine energy into the world and ensured its being (e.g., M. *Avot* 1:2). Indeed, it is not uncommon for rabbinic sages to suggest that Torah study may be even more important than prayer and performance of other commandments as a form of sacrificial worship (e.g., B.T., *Qid.* 40b). Like public prayer, however, *talmud torah* was conceived by rabbinic sages as a paradigmatically male form of divine service (B.T., *Qid.* 29a). Accordingly, for most of the history of rabbinic Judaism, Torah study has been primarily a male activity, deemed crucial in the shaping of masculine Jewish identity.

The character of Torah study in classical rabbinic times can be inferred from careful study of the surviving rabbinic literature. It is clear, first of all, from the remarkable facility of midrashic literature in finding the most obscure biblical texts to make an exegetical point, that many rabbinic sages had full recall of virtually the entire canon of the written Torah. Indeed, a common form of Palestinian rabbinic entertainment included competitions in stringing the most impressive list of biblical verses under specific themes (P.T., *Hag.* 2:2). The disciples of sages were also expected to master the emerging tradition of oral Torah. Whereas written versions of such crucial texts as the Mishnah may have circulated as early as the third century, the preferred way to study oral Torah was by hearing the text recited by a teacher or an official text-memorizer (B.T., *Git.* 60b). Disciples would rehearse their oral texts prior to examination by a master, often using distinctive tunes (T. *Oh.*16:8) or other mnemonic techniques (B.T., *Hor.*12a) as an aid to memorization. The master would then review not only the orallymemorized text (B.T., *ʿEruv.* 54b), but engage the student in extemporaneous analysis of the text in comparison with other texts on connected themes (B.T., *Bava Qam.* 117a).

The rabbinic disciple-communities of late antiquity were rather small circles associated with individual sages. Torah study in this setting was, therefore, part of an evolving relationship between teacher and student. In medieval times the expansion of the rabbinic community and the consequent production of written compendia of the Talmudic tradition engendered important changes in the character of Torah study. Large institutionalized schools of rabbinic education (*yeshivot*; sing. *yeshivah)* were created and the study of a fixed text, often encountered primarily in written form, began to replace the process of oral memorization. By the tenth century, written commentaries by especially influential masters (e.g., Rabbi Hananʾel ben Hushiʾel of Kairouan, Rashi of Troyes) began to circulate in manuscript copies as part of the Torahcurriculum and came as well to be regarded as part of the oral Torah.

The emergence of print technology in the late fifteenth century was embraced by rabbinic authorities as providential, for it enabled the wide dissemination of both the written and the oral Torah in uniform formats that transcended local textual differences and scribal practices. The expansion of profound Talmudic scholarship in sixteenth- through seventeenth-century Eastern Europe was in part enabled by the production of printed copies of rabbinic literature for use in the great *yeshivot.* Thanks to printers, the prodigious memories encouraged by Talmudic learning were aided by the production of text editions in which identical, clearly printed words could be found on the exact same page of hundreds of copies of a given rabbinic work throughout the Jewish world. Whereas this premium on memorization led at times to a rather arid academicism, various educational reforms renewed rigorous conceptual analysis of Talmudic discourse under various pedagogical theories until well into the nineteenth century.

The premium on memorized mastery of the written text and its commentaries, in conjunction with distinct methodological approaches derived from nineteenth- and twentieth-century innovators, continues to be the distinguishing trait of *yeshivah*-grounded Torah study in contemporary Orthodox and Hasidic centers of Torah study throughout the world. Curricula vary depending upon the specific ideological commitments of distinct communities. For example classical Hasidic sources are not commonly taught in *yeshivot* founded by anti-Hasidic authorities. Nevertheless, the core of contemporary Torah study remains the Babylonian Talmud and the commentaries printed on its margins and in the appendices to each printed volume. Closely associated with study of the Talmud is careful analysis of the traditional medieval codes, particularly those of Maimonides, Rabbi Jacob ben Asher, and Rabbi Joseph Caro, with their panoply of associated commentaries and supercommentaries. A recent innovation in many contemporary *yeshivot* is the inclusion within the curriculum of explicitly theological studies (*hashqafah*). Examples might include the more philosophical passages of Maimonides's *Mishneh Torah,* works of classical Qabbalah, or works of ethical self-scrutiny stemming from the nineteenth-century Musar movement founded by Rabbi Israel Salanter (1786-1866).

Among contemporary Jews, the primacy of Torah study as a Judaic religious value is felt even beyond the circles of traditional *yeshivot.* The explosion of electronic media and an ongoing industry in the translation of classical Judaica into a variety of languages has enabled the creation of novel settings for popular as well as advanced Torah study. Similarly, the revolutionary achievements of feminism in Western culture have affected most Jewish communities. Since the latter half of the twentieth century, Torah study was made widely available to women in the more liberal religious denominations. Most recently, certain Orthodox communities in both the United States and the State of Israel have experimented with opening advanced Torah study to women.

Contemporary Jewish communities of any size will have multiple outlets for the study of Jewish history and tradition at diverse levels in synagogues or community centers. Many of these, based upon Western educational models, take the form of classes for children and adults on various themes and include the study of the written and oral Torah in the original languages and in accessible translations. Whereas such contexts do not yet provide the comprehensive technical mastery and ideological *élan* of Orthodox *yeshivot,* they testify to the continued significance of Torah study as a form of Jewish identification.

TORAH SCROLL AS AN OBJECT OF RITUAL DEVOTION. The Torah in Judaism is more than a subject of study. The scroll of the Torah, read aloud in the synagogue liturgies of the Sabbath, holy days, and at other prescribed occasions, is Judaism's most important ritual object. It is invested with a numinous quality—*qedushah* ("holiness")—which, like other ritual objects described in the anthropological studies of tribal cultures around the world, is conceived both as a source of charisma and as something deeply vulnerable to violation. The *qedushah* invested in the scroll must therefore be protected. This protection is afforded by ritual activities that surround all aspects of its handling.

The ritualization of the scroll begins even prior to its first use in public synagogue worship. Complex halakhic requirements surround every stage of its creation. These govern the preparation of the hides and inks used by the scribe, the shapes of the letters used in writing, the spellings of the words in the text, and the paragraphing of textual units. The scribe, who must copy the text letter-by-letter from another suitable scroll, will have rinsed his hands prior to setting to work to ensure the requisite degree of bodily purity. Women whose menstrual cycles render them ritually unclean for certain periods of each month may not serve as scribes for this reason.

Once it is ready for use, a Torah scroll must still be protected from defilement through contact with sources of impurity, including the hands of synagogue worshipers. The means of protecting the scroll also serve a second function of drawing attention to and beautifying it. It is wrapped in a finely made, embroidered sheath or case. Often it will be adorned as well with finely wrought silver crowns and breastplates. Thus protected from random touching, the scroll is stored in a specially designed, ornate cabinet at the very front of the synagogue. This cabinet is normally called the *ʾaron haqodesh* ("the holy ark") and recalls the box in which Moses placed the stone tablets that represented the covenant between Israel and God.

The formal liturgy of reading the Torah in public is also deeply enmeshed in ritual performances. These call to mind the charismatic *qedushah* of the scroll and, at the same time, assimilate the empirical, existing scroll in the synagogue to the Torah of Moses revealed on Sinai and stored in the original holy ark. When, at the appropriate liturgical moment, the ark is opened, the entire congregation must rise to attention, as if royalty had entered the room. At this point the worshippers recite in unison a verse from the Torah: "And when the Ark began to move, Moses said: 'Arise, O Lord, and scatter your enemies, and may those who hate you flee from before you'" (*Nm.* 10:35). The scroll is then borne around the synagogue in a solemn procession accompanied by the singing of texts from the book of Psalms. During this procession, worshippers engage in formal acts of adoration—particularly, touching the sheath with a prayer shawl or prayer book, and kissing the place on the shawl or book that touched the Torah. At the end of the procession, the scroll is brought to a reading table, usually in the front of the congregation or in its very midst. It is carefully removed from its sheath and placed on the table, covered by a protecting cloth.

The actual reading of the Torah, commencing at this point, is equally surrounded by ritual performances. Depending upon the occasion, anywhere from three to seven congregants will be honored with an "ascent" (*ʿaliyah*) to the Torah. The term *ascent* intentionally recalls Moses' ascent to Sinai. During these ascents a preselected passage will be read aloud, normally by a professional reader. Each person who ascends to the Torah recites, before and after the reading, a benediction of thanks to God for the privilege of having received the Torah. During the reading, the reader keeps track of the text with a silver or wood pointer (*yad),* so as to avoid touching the scroll. At the conclusion of the final ascent, the Torah, now unfurled to expose a minimum of three columns of its text, is raised high in the hands of a designated congregant. At this the congregation points to the scroll and intones the following formula from the Torah itself (*Dn.* 4:44): "This is the Torah which Moses placed before the children of Israel at God's command, by Moses' hand." The scroll is then rolled, returned to its sheath, and carried in a second adorational procession back to its storage place in the ark.

Like all sacred objects, Torah scrolls can become defiled and disqualified for liturgical use (*pasul).* For example, constant use over the years may cause ink to chip from the scroll, rendering a word illegible. This is sufficient to prevent the scroll from being read until the ink is restored by a duly qualified scribe. Tears in the parchment and other minor repairs may also be made to restore the scroll to service. But if a scroll suffers massive irreparable damage—as in a fire or other disaster—the scroll is retired from use. In some communities, a defiled scroll is afforded the honor due to a human corpse and buried. In others it is stored in a special storage area (*Genizah*) with other damaged books that contain the divine name and, therefore, cannot be intentionally destroyed.

Bibliography

Amir, Yehoshua. "Authority and Interpretation of Scripture in the Writings of Philo." In *Mikra: Text, Translation, Reading and Interpretation of the Hebrew Bible in Ancient Judaism and Early Christianity,* edited by Martin Jan Mulder, pp. 421–454. Philadelphia, 1988.

Campbell, Antony F., and Mark A. O'Brien, eds. *Sources of the Pentateuch: Texts, Introductions, Annotations.* Minneapolis, 1993.

Goodblatt, David. *Rabbinic Instruction in Sasanian Babylonia.* Leiden, Netherlands, 1975.

Heller, Marvin J. *Printing the Talmud: A History of the Earliest Printed Editions of the Talmud.* Brooklyn, 1992.

Jaffee, Martin S. *Torah in the Mouth: Writing and Oral Tradition in Palestinian Judaism, c. 200 BCE–400 CE.* New York, 2001.

Kanarfogel, Ephraim. *Jewish Education and Society in the High Middle Ages.* Detroit, 1991.

Kellner, Menachem. *Dogma in Medieval Jewish Thought: From Maimonides to Abravanel.* Oxford, 1986.

Leiman, Sid Z. *The Canonization of Hebrew Scripture: The Talmudic and Midrashic Evidence.* Hamden, Conn., 1976.

Matt, Daniel. "The Mystic and the Mizwot." In *Jewish Spirituality From the Bible Through the Middle Ages,* edited by Arthur Green, pp. 367–404. New York, 1986.

Morgan, Michael L. *Dilemmas in Modern Jewish Thought: The Dialectics of Revelation and History.* Bloomington, Ind., 1992.

Najman, Hindy. *Seconding Sinai: The Development of Mosaic Discourse in Second Temple Judaism.* Leiden, 2003.

Neusner, Jacob. *Torah: From Scroll to Symbol in Formative Judaism.* Philadelphia, 1985.

Niditch, Susan. *Oral World and Written Word: Ancient Israelite Literature.* Louisville, Ky., 1996.

Posner, Raphael, and Israel Ta-Shema, eds. *The Hebrew Book: An Historical Survey.* Jerusalem, 1975.

Ray, Eric. *Sofer: The Story of a Torah Scroll.* New York, 1998.

Scholem, Gershom. "The Meaning of the Torah in Jewish Mysticism." In *On the Kabbalah and its Symbolism,* by Gershom Scholem, translated by Ralph Mannheim, pp. 32–86. New York, 1969.

Urbach, Ephraim E. *The Halakhah: Its Sources and Development.* Translated by Ralph Posner. Masada, Israel, 1986.

Whybray, R. N. *The Making of the Pentateuch: A Methodological Study.* Sheffield, U.K., 1987.

MARTIN S. JAFFEE (2005)

TORAH SHEBEʾAL PEH SEE ORAL TORAH

TORAJA RELIGION.

TORAJA RELIGION. The Sa'dan Toraja, a people numbering about 325,000, live in Tana Toraja, the mountainous northern part of the southwest peninsula of the Indonesian island of Sulawesi (formerly Celebes). The name *Sa'dan* is derived from the Sa'dan River, the main stream in the region. *Toraja* is a contraction of *To-ri-aja* ("men of the mountains"), a name given the people by their Bugis neighbors. Following local customs, we refer to these people as Toraja.

The region of approximately 3,180 square kilometers, originally heavily forested, has been changed by cultivation. The few remaining forests cover slopes unsuitable for cultivation. The principal means of subsistence is agriculture. Rice, cassava, and maize are the staples; coffee and cloves are the principal cash crops. Animal husbandry is practiced on a large scale, but only the breeding of pigs is of economic importance. The buffalo, a status symbol, is rarely used for work in the fields. The animal has primarily a ritual function, for the superior type of death feast demands the sacrifice of about a hundred buffalo.

Social change began with the introduction of coffee growing and the coffee trade in the last quarter of the previous century. The subduing of the Toraja country by the Dutch (1906), the period of the Japanese occupation (1942–1945), and the independence of Indonesia (1945) accelerated this process. Tourism, a recent development, has brought further change. The school system introduced by the Dutch government and missionaries opened a new world for a people who had known only an oral tradition. Tana Toraja became the missionary field of the Reformed Alliance of the Dutch Reformed Church and half of the population has been converted to Christianity.

THE "BELIEF OF THE OLD." The autochthonous religion of the Toraja is called Aluk To Dolo (*to dolo* literally means "people bygone"), that is, "belief of the old," or "rituals of the ancestors." In this religion, ancestor cult, myth, and ritual are intertwined. During the celebration of major rituals, the *to minaa,* a priest well versed in tribal lore and history, recites the lengthy litany of the tribe's origins. He tells of how the cosmos and the gods came into being, how man, his food plants, and animals had originated in heaven and were brought down when the first nobleman descended to earth, landing on a mountain. The *to manurun,* that is, the person of status who descended from heaven, brought with him the entire social order and a complete heavenly household, including a house, slaves, animals, and plants. With the *to manurun* also came priests: the *to minaa,* the *to burake* (the highest rank of religious functionary), the rice priest, and the medicine man. The death priest, however, is not mentioned. The descent of a nobleman was believed to have occurred several times in Toraja history. With regional variations these main themes are found throughout Tana Toraja.

THE TRIPARTITE COSMIC WORLD. In the Toraja view, the cosmos is divided into three parts: the upper world, the world of mankind (earth), and the underworld. In the beginning, however, heaven and earth were one expanse of darkness, united in marriage. With their separation came light. Several gods sprang from this mythical marriage. Puang Matua ("the old lord") is the principal god and the deity of heaven. Pong Banggai di Rante ("the master of the plains") is the god of the earth. Gaun ti Kembong ("the swollen cloud"') resides between heaven and earth. Indo' Belo Tumbang ("the lady who dances beautifully") is the goddess of the medicine that cures the sick in the Maro ritual. Pong Tulak Padang is the Toraja Atlas; he carries the earth, not on his shoulders but in the palms of his hands. Together with Puang Matua in the upper world he keeps earth, the world of mankind, in equilibrium, separating night from day. His bad-tempered spouse, Indo' Ongon-ongon, however, upsets the equilibrium by causing earthquakes when she is in a bad mood. She is much feared, as is Pong Lalondong ("the lord who is a cock"). Puya ("the land of souls") lies in the southwest under the earth's surface. The underworld and upper world have other deities, and there are also *deata* (deities, ghosts) residing on earth and in rivers, canals, wells, trees, and stones. Eels are revered as fertility symbols.

THE BIPARTITE DIVISION OF THE RITUALS. By observing the rules of deities and ancestors, man observes his part in maintaining the equilibrium between the upper worlds and the underworlds. He does so by means of rites and rituals. Rituals are divided into two spheres, one of the east, the Rising Sun or Smoke Ascending (Rambu Tuka), and the other of the west, the Setting Sun or Smoke Descending (Rambu Solo'). The north is associated with the east, the south with the west. Rituals of the Rising Sun are those celebrating joy and life. This category includes birth, marriage, rice ceremonies, and feasts for the well-being of the family, the house, and the community. Ceremonies for healing the sick are also rituals of the Rising Sun; yet to the extent that sickness poses a danger to the community the rituals of healing share some traits with those of the Setting Sun. The Setting Sun ritual is associated with darkness, night, and, of course, with death. With the exception of the healing rituals, the ritual spheres of east and west are kept quite distinct from one another.

The most important ritual of the eastern sphere is the Bua' feast, a ceremony for a whole territory, the Bua' community. During this feast the *burake*—in some districts a priestess, in others a priest who is considered a hermaphrodite—implores the gods of heaven to bestow their benevolence on the community. Another feast of importance is the Merok, held for the welfare of a large family. At the center of the Merok is the *tongkonan*, the dwelling founded by the family's first ancestor. The most important of these houses are the ones considered to have been founded by a *to manurun*. These major rituals of the east have their ritual counterparts in high-ranking death feasts. Ritualizing the dead is a major focus of Toraja culture. A ranking order in funerals exists that corresponds to the status of the deceased. Toraja society is a stratified one, with much emphasis laid on the display of wealth. By the efforts and the devotion of the family, and through the expenditure lavished on buffalo, entertainment, and care of the death priest, the deceased of rank will reach Puya. After being judged by Pong Lalondong he climbs a mountain and reaches heaven. There he will occupy a place among the deified ancestors, who form a constellation that guards mankind and the rice. Thus the spheres of death and life, notwithstanding an apparent opposition, meet each other.

SEE ALSO Southeast Asian Religions, article on Insular Cultures.

BIBLIOGRAPHY

Bigalke, Terance Williams. *A Social History of Tana Toraja, 1875–1965.* Ann Arbor, 1981.

Jannel, Claude, and Frédéric Lontcho. *Laissez venir ceux qui pleurent: Fête pour un mort Toradja (Indonésie).* Place and date of publication not given. Includes translations of Toraja poems by Jeannine Koubi.

Koubi, Jeannine. *Rambu Solo', la fumée descend.* Paris, 1982.

Lanting, H. Th. "Nota van den Controleur van Makale/ Rantepao." In *Memorie van Overgave,* Archives of the Netherlands Ministry of Home Affairs. The Hague, 1926.

Nobele, E. A. J. "Memorie van Overgave betreffende de Onderafdeeling Makale." *Tijdschrift/Bataviaasch Genootschap van Kunsten en Wetenschappen* 60 (1926): 1–144.

Nooy-Palm, Hetty. *The Sa'dan-Toraja: A Study of Their Social Life and Religion.* 2 vols. The Hague, 1986.

Veen, Hendrik van der. *Tae' (Zuid-Toradjasch) Nederlandsch Woordenboek.* The Hague, 1940.

Volkman, Toby, "The Riches of the Undertaker." *Indonesia* 28 (1979): 1–16.

New Sources

Chambert-Loir, H., A. Reid, and Australian National University. *The Potent Dead: Ancestors, Saints and Heroes in Contemporary Indonesia.* Honolulu, 2002.

Klass, M., and M. K. Weisgrau. *Across the Boundaries of Belief: Contemporary Issues in the Anthropology of Religion.* Boulder, Colo., 1999.

Kobong, T. *Evangelium und Tongkonan: Eine Untersuchung über die Begegnung zwischen christlicher Botschaft und der Kultur der Toraja.* Hamburg, 1989.

Kotilainen, E. M. *When the Bones are Left: A Study of the Material Culture of Central Sulawesi.* Helsinki, 1992.

Yampolsky, P., and Masyarakat Seni Pertunjukan Indonesia. *Sulawesi Festivals, Funeral and Work.* Washington, D.C., 1999.

HETTY NOOY-PALM (1987)
Revised Bibliography

TORQUEMADA, TOMÁS DE (1420–1498),

Spanish inquisitor. Tomás de Torquemada, nephew of Juan de Torquemada (1388–1468), the celebrated Dominican theologian, canonist, and cardinal, was born at Valladolid and as a youth entered the Order of Preachers. For twenty-two years he was prior of the Dominican convent of Santa Cruz at Segovia. In 1474 he was appointed confessor to Queen Isabella I of Castile, and later he performed the same service, nominally at least, for King Ferdinand V of Aragon.

By a brief of February 11, 1482, Pope Sixtus IV named Torquemada, along with ten other Dominicans, to replace former officers of the Spanish Inquisition who had been charged with corrupt practices. On August 2, 1483, Torquemada was appointed grand inquisitor for the kingdoms of Castile and León; a few months later his authority was extended to Catalonia, Aragon, Valencia, and Majorca. He forthwith established tribunals at Seville, Cordova, Jaén, and Villarreal (later transferred to Toledo). Between 1484 and 1498 he set down the basic procedure of the Inquisition in a series of *instrucciónes*—fifty-four articles in all—that guided the activities of succeeding grand inquisitors. These were published in 1576.

Torquemada, though himself descended from Jewish forebears, was particularly harsh in carrying out the mandate of the Inquisition against crypto-Jews (Marranos), Jews who continued to practice Judaism in secret after their forced conversion to Christianity. In 1492 he supported, and perhaps promoted, the expulsion of the Jews from the newly united Spain. Complaints about his severity moved Pope Alexander VI in 1494 to add four colleagues to his judicial bench, but as early as the next year they were accused of financial misconduct, and there was no discernible change in the Inquisition's practices after Torquemada's retirement or even after his death.

Torquemada became, and has remained, the personification of religious intolerance at its worst. It is believed that as many as two thousand people were burned to death under his regime, and many thousands of others suffered imprisonment, confiscation of their property, and various other forms of harassment and indignity. Papal efforts to moderate the inquisitorial zeal in Spain were usually ineffectual, because the Spanish Inquisition, as Torquemada fashioned it, was an instrument to secure the racial and religious uniformity that was a primary concern of the Catholic kings and of Spanish policy for a long time afterward.

BIBLIOGRAPHY

Two classic works include treatments, hostile, of Torquemada: Henry C. Lea's *A History of the Inquisition in Spain*, 4 vols. (1907; reprint, New York, 1966), and Juan Antonio Llorente's *Discurso sobre el orden de procesar en los tribunales de Inquisición* (Paris, 1817); an English translation and abridgment of Llorente's work (London, 1823) has been many times reprinted. A good brief study is A. S. Turberville's *The Spanish Inquisition* (1932; reprint, London, 1949), and a popular account of a special subject is Thomas Hope's *Torquemada, Scourge of the Jews* (London, 1939).

MARVIN R. O'CONNELL (1987)

TORTOISES SEE TURTLES AND TORTOISES

TOSAFOT [FIRST EDITION].

Tosafot is the Hebrew word that designates the glosses printed alongside the commentary of Rashi (Rabbi Shelomoh ben Yitsḥaq, eleventh-century French sage and commentator) in most editions of the Babylonian Talmud. Yet these *tosafot* are only a fraction of those composed by the French and German scholars (tosafists) of the twelfth and thirteenth centuries. The descendants of Rashi and his students edited his commentaries and added glosses to them. Even after these additions became much more extensive than the original commentaries, they continued to be called *tosafot* (additions). The *tosafot* emerged from disputations in the Talmudic academies that were recorded by teachers or by students under their direction. Students traveled from place to place recording the novel interpretations of their rabbis, and an academy of study acquired a good name based on the collections of *tosafot* available there.

EMERGENCE OF THE *TOSAFOT*. The beginnings of this new literary form are discernible already in the commentaries of Rashi's son-in-law Yehudah ben Natan, and even more so in the commentaries of his other son-in-law, Me'ir ben Shemu'el, and those of the latter's son, Rashbam (Rabbi Shemu'el ben Me'ir), who wrote addenda to Rashi's commentaries on the Talmud. The new style can be seen also in the works of Riva' (Rabbi Yitsḥaq ben Asher), who was Rashi's student in Troyes, France, and who later settled in Speyer, in southwestern Germany. While Rashi's commentaries generally explain each *sugyah* (Talmudic discussion of a specific subject) where it occurs (i.e., on the same page), in the works of these others the dialectical and polemic tendency and the trend to comparison predominate.

In the establishment and perfection of the distinctive style of the *tosafot* a decisive influence was exercised by Rashi's grandson, Ya'aqov ben Me'ir, known as Rabbenu ("our teacher") Tam (after *Genesis* 25:27). With his immense breadth of knowledge and his sharp and penetrating mind, Tam influenced the scholars of his generation. The students who came to learn with him in his academy in Ramerupt adopted his method of study. His students were subsequently active in all regions of France, in England, in the communities on the Rhine, and in southern Germany, Bohemia, Carinthia, and Hungary, and in Kiev. Many others who never studied under him personally accepted his authority as binding and were influenced by his method.

Rabbenu Tam's successor was his nephew, generally known by the acronym Riy (Rabbi Yitsḥaq [ben Shemu'el]). Students flocked to Riy's academy in Dampierre from every country in Europe that was inhabited by Jews, including Spain. Moses Nahmanides, known as Ramban (Rabbi Mosheh ben Naḥman), the thirteenth-century rabbi and commentator from Barcelona, described the influence of Rashi and his successors thus: "The French sages . . . they are our teachers, they the instructors; they reveal to us everything that is hidden" (*Dina' de-garmi*, intro.). The academy of Riy could be considered the forge of the *tosafot*. His work and that of his disciples established the method for writing *tosafot:* verification of the text of the Talmud and clarification and analysis of each *sugyah* through comparison of parallel passages in the Babylonian Talmud with the rest of the halakhic and aggadic sources, thus uncovering and resolving contradictions and fixing methodological principles. Few of Riy's *tosafot* have reached us in their original formulations, but they were included in the collections compiled by his students—his son Elḥanan, Rash (Rabbi Shimshon [ben Avraham]) of Sens and his brother Yitsḥaq, Yehudah ben Yitsḥaq of Paris (also known as Rabbi Yehudah Sir Leon), Eli'ezer ben Shemu'el of Verona, Barukh ben Yitsḥaq of Worms, and others. Riy's teachings were recorded in their works and, through them, in the *tosafot* of later generations.

TYPES OF *TOSAFOT*. The greatest of the teachers edited collections of their *tosafot*, but their disciples did not consider these closed collections. On the one hand, they abridged long *tosafot*, while on the other, they added to the collections more recent *novellae*. As a result, the students appended glosses in the margins of the *tosafot*, which copyists subsequently introduced into the body of the text.

The disciples of Riy did not simply record his teachings. Moreover, they did not all study with him at the same time, and later students often added to the *tosafot* of their predecessors the new explanations that grew out of their discussions and decisions of their master, which were rendered to them orally or in writing. Even within the works of given individuals we can sometimes discern development. The *tosafot* of Rash of Sens to tractate *Ketubbot* (modern edition, Jerusalem, 1973) were compiled, it would seem, when he was still young. In them the teachings of his teacher Riy are exceptionally predominant, and one can still sense in his style the give and take of the discussion in the academy. In contrast, the second edition of his *tosafot* to tractate *ʿAvodah Zarah* (modern edition, New York, 1969) exhibit little of the style of disputation characteristic of most *tosafot;* they are instead rather similar to the style of the Rash in his Mishnah commentaries.

Authority in the academies of the tosafists was not institutionalized; there was no well-defined hierarchy within them. Whoever could demonstrate exceptional capabilities and great erudition gained authority, but this authority was constantly subject to the challenges and criticism of younger scholars and students.

With the passage of time, different styles of *tosafot* developed. Some scholars were content to record their critical notes on famous *tosafot,* such as those of Rash of Sens. This is what Elʿazar of Worms (the author of *Sefer ha-roqeaḥ*) and Berakhiyah of Nicole (modern-day Lincoln, England) did. In contrast, after the burning of the Talmud in Paris in 1244, there is a clearly discernible tendency, especially in the academy at Évreux, to compose *tosafot shiṭah*—a presentation of the Talmudic *sugyah* together with various explanations of it and the discussions of tosafists. One such *shiṭah* from Évreux on tractate *Nazir* was published from a manuscript in New York in 1974.

Toward the end of the thirteenth century, in the wake of the emigration of many of the sages of northern France and the increasing persecutions in Germany, original creativity among the scholars became rarer, while the collection of existing *tosafot* became more widespread. The great compilers, whose works spanned the entire Talmud, were Perets of Corbeil, Eliʿezer of Touques, and Asher ben Yeḥiʾel. The *tosafot* of Perets of Corbeil were extant in Italy until the time of the printing of the Talmud, and they also reached Spain. Eliʿezer of Touques abridged and edited the *tosafot* compiled by Rash of Sens, added to them from other collections, and appended his own *novellae* in the margins. His *tosafot* quickly spread through France and Germany.

When Asher ben Yeḥiʾel, known as Rabbenu Asher (also as Roʾsh), left Germany, he brought with him to Spain collections of *tosafot* from the collections of Riy and Rash of Sens and copied them almost unchanged, occasionally adding an explanation of his teacher, Meʾir ben Barukh, known as Maharam of Rothenburg. Rabbenu Asher prepared this work in order to present the community of scholars in Spain with an important collection of the teachings of the outstanding scholars of France. His son Yaʿaqov (that is, Yaʿaqov ben Asher), author of the halakhic codex *Arbaʿah Ṭurim,* wrote to a German scholar who was preparing to come to Spain: "Bring whatever books you have, whether commentaries of Rashi, or *gemaraʾ*, or other works, but you needn't bring the *tosafot,* for they only learn the *shiṭah* of my father and teacher, may the memory of the righteous be a blessing." These *tosafot* did not spread beyond Spain, though, and they were subsequently dispersed abroad (especially to Italy and the Ottoman Empire) with the exiles from Spain. While the scholars of Germany and Poland remained unaware of their existence, for us these *tosafot* are an important source for reconstructing the original formulation of the *tosafot* of Riy and his disciples.

The aforementioned compilations sealed a period of nearly two hundred years of creativity. The earlier *tosafot* were superseded by the later collections, but many of the former were preserved by individuals, some of whom copied from them into their own compilations and collections. This phenomenon can be observed in various collections: the catalogs of decisions and *responsa,* like *Or Zaruʿa,* compiled by Yitsḥaq ben Mosheh of Vienna, and the *Mordekhai* of Mordekhai ben Hillel; in the *Haggahot Maymuniyyot* and the *Teshuvot Maymuniyyot* of the school of Maharam; the collections of exegesis of the Pentateuch (such as *Daʿat zeqenim, Hadar zeqenim, Moshav zeqenim,* and *Minḥat Yehudah*); and in manuscripts. All of these works help us to identify the editors of extant collections of *tosafot* and the authors of anonymous interpretations recorded in them.

PRINTING OF THE *TOSAFOT.* The spread of the *tosafot* encouraged printers of the Talmud to print these commentaries alongside the commentary of Rashi, which were already being printed alongside the Talmudic text. Yehoshuʿa Shelomoh first printed the *tosafot* to tractate *Berakhot* in Soncino, Italy, in 1484. By 1519 his nephew Gershom Soncino had printed twenty-three tractates with *tosafot.* The Bomberg Press in Venice (1520–1523) generally copied the *tosafot* from the Soncino edition, but they corrected them from manuscripts. After that time, the *tosafot* were printed in every edition of the Talmud, except in some early Eastern editions, until the *gemaraʾ*, the commentary of Rashi, and *tosafot* came to be studied as a single unit, referred to as GePeT (from *gemaraʾ*, *perush Rashi,* and *tosafot*).

EDITING OF THE *TOSAFOT.* Examination of the *tosafot* printed in standard editions of the Talmud in relation to other collections that have been printed or preserved in manuscript and in comparison with other sources demonstrates that the standard *tosafot* originated in various academies and at different times. A summary of the conclusions that can be drawn about the origins of the *tosafot* of the various tractates can be found in table 1.

THE METHOD OF INTERPRETATION IN THE *TOSAFOT.* Despite the diversity and the convoluted process of development of all the various collections, the *tosafot* nevertheless share a common method of explication, for they all are characteristically dialectical and critical. These methodological foundations, as drawn by Rabbenu Tam and Riy, remained fixed, with variation only in the quality of their employment. On the one hand, the tosafists themselves adopted the style of discussion of the amoraim and developed special techniques by which to express it; on the other hand, they traced and criticized the way in which the amoraim used this style.

Origins of the Tosafot

B. T. Tractate	Origins Of Tosafot
Berakhot	A reworking of the *tosafot* of Yehudah ben Yitshaq of Paris, including material added by his students, edited by a German scholar who studied in the academy at Évreux.
Shabbat	Edited by Eli`ezer of Touques. The editing of the final section (from page 122b) was never completed.
`Eruvin	Compiled by Shimshon ben Avraham of Sens (Rash), edited by students of Yitshaq ben Avraham (known as Ritsba').
Pesahim	Edited by Eli`ezer of Touques. The first nine chapters are based on the *tosafot* of Shimshon ben Avraham of Sens while chapter 10 is based on the *tosafot* of Yehi'el of Paris.
Yoma'	Edited by Me'ir ben Barukh of Rothenburg.
Sukkah	Compiled by Shimshon ben Avraham of Sens.
Beitsah	Edited by a disciple of Perets of Corbeil.
Ro'sh ha-Shanah	Compiled by Shimshon ben Avraham of Sens.
Ta`anit	Late *tosafot,* apparently from the fourteenth century.
Megillah	Edited by Yehudah ben Yitshaq of Paris.
Mo`ed Qatan	Edited by Shemu'el ben Elhanan, grandson of Yitshaq ben Shemu'el.
Hagigah	Edited by Mosheh of Évreux, based on the *tosafot* of Elhanan and Yehudah ben Yitshaq of Paris.
Yevamot	Edited by Eli`ezer of Touques based upon the *tosafot* compiled by Shimshon ben Avraham of Sens up to chapter 12; from there, based primarily on the *tosafot* of Yehudah ben Yitshaq of Paris.
Ketubbot	Edited by Eli`ezer of Touques but without a final editing; apparently a first edition.
Nedarim	Edited by a student of Perets of Corbeil, based on the *tosafot* of Évreux.
Nazir	Edited by a student of Perets of Corbeil based upon the *shitah* of Yitshaq of Évreux.
Sotah	German *tosafot,* edited by a disciple of Yehudah and Me'ir, the sons of Qalonimos.
Gittin	Edited by Eli`ezer of Touques.
Qiddushin	*Tosafot* from Évreux, from the end of the thirteenth century.
Bava' Qamma'	Edited by Eli`ezer of Touques based upon the *tosafot* of Yehudah ben Yitshaq of Paris.
Bava' Metsi`a'	Edited by Eli`ezer of Touques, based on the *tosafot* of Elhanan, Shimshon ben Avraham of Sens, and German students of the disciples of Yitshaq ben Shemu'el.
Bava' Batra'	Until page 144a, edited by Eli`ezer of Touques based on the *tosafot* of Shimshon ben Avraham of Sens, Mosheh of Évreux, and Yitshaq ben Mordekhai (known by the acronym Rivam), who worked under the supervision of Ya`aqov ben Me'ir; after page 144a, the primary source was the *tosafot* of a disciple of Yitshaq ben Shemu'el.
Sanhedrin	*Tosafot* from the school of Perets of Corbeil, based on the *tosafot* compiled by Shimshon ben Avraham.
Makkot	Edited during the lifetime of Perets of Corbeil.
Shavu`ot	Edited by Eli`ezer of Touques, after the *tosafot* of Elhanan of Sens.
`Avodah Zarah	Edited by a disciple of Perets of Corbeil, who copied unchanged the tosafot of Shemu'el of Falaise, who had drawn from the *tosafot* of Yehudah ben Yitshaq of Paris, whose explanations were in accordance with the *tosafot* of Elhanan, son of Yitshaq ben Shemu'el. The *tosafot* of Elhanan, composed around 1182, were in fact used as a major source for all the aforementioned *tosafot* on *`Avodah Zarah.*
Horayot	German *tosafot,* based primarily on the explanations of Simhah of Speyer.
Zevahim	Compiled and edited by Barukh ben Yitshaq of Worms.
Menahot	Compiled by Shimshon ben Avraham of Sens.
Hullin	Edited by Eli`ezer of Touques, based on the *tosafot* compiled by Shimshon ben Avraham of Sens and the *tosafot* of Yehudah ben Yitshaq of Paris.
Bekhorot	Compiled by Shimshon ben Avraham of Sens.
`Arakhin	*Tosafot* from Évreux, edited by a disciple of Shemu'el of Évreux's son.
Temurah	*Tosafot* from Évreux, the handiwork of a different editor.
Keritot	Edited by a disciple of Yitshaq ben Shemu'el.
Me`ilah	Edited by a disciple of Perets of Corbeil during the life of his master.
Qinnim	German *tosafot,* used as sources for the *tosafot* of Yitshaq ben Asher and Ya`aqov ben Yitshaq ben Eli`ezer ha-Levi (known as Ya`avets).
Niddah	Edited by Eli`ezer of Touques, based on the *tosafot* of Shimshon ben Avraham of Sens and other disciples of Yitshaq ben Shemu'el.

TABLE 1.

Every single line of the Talmud was analyzed acutely and tested, sometimes by uncovering contradictions between it and other statements in the sources, and sometimes by drawing from it the most extreme inferences and conclusions possible. Precisely because they perceived the Talmud to be the eternal source of halakhic decision, the tosafists considered it incumbent upon them to compare, to question, and to solve contradictions between the cases in the contradictory sources by formulating "distinctions" (*ḥilluqim*). In this manner they hoped to advance the determination of the *halakhah* by supplementing what was already explicit in the Talmud.

The efforts of the tosafists were directed toward the verification of the accurate text of the Talmud. Rabbenu Tam condemned those who emended texts in order to remove difficulties and problems, and he and his disciples developed a whole methodology for textual criticism. The principles and explanations they elaborated to explain the development of defective texts anticipated modern philology.

In their work supplementing the commentary of Rashi and expanding its bounds, the tosafists had at their disposal a number of additional sources, such as the commentaries of Ḥanan'el ben Ḥushi'el and the Talmudic dictionary, *Sefer ha-ʿarukh*, of Natan ben Yeḥi'el, an eleventh-century rabbi. They relied primarily on their broad knowledge of the classical sources, however, including not only the Babylonian Talmud but also the Tosefta, the halakhic and aggadic *midrashim*, and the Palestinian Talmud (Jerusalem Talmud). While using these works the tosafists also contributed toward the establishment of their correct versions and toward a better understanding of their contents. Nevertheless, the tosafists' main aim remained the clarification of every *sugyah* of the Babylonian Talmud from all possible angles, including the testing of the logical arguments, distinctions, and classifications that they posited and the marshaling of support for their conclusions. All this activity was directed toward the attempt to see every subject and problem in its widest context. Every dictum of the *tosafot* demonstrates the extent to which the tosafists had assimilated the way of learning embodied in the Babylonian Talmud; they studied until they were willing and able to comment on what is the "way of the *sugyah*" and what is the "method of the Talmud." Taken together, the principles governing their study constitute a complete methodology. Their formulations describe the use of the "rules for expounding scripture"; the relationship between the Talmud and *baraitot* (teachings of the tannaim that were not included in the Mishnah); the proper identification of tannaim and amoraim; the proper definition of the terms of the *sugyah*; the order of the Mishnah; and the editing of the Talmud. In this aspect of their endeavor, also, several of the tosafists' conclusions anticipated modern research.

The Method of *Tosafot* in Deciding *Halakhah*. The tosafists did not ignore the normative aim of the Talmudic discussions. Although their comments generally do not explicitly contain halakhic summaries or decisions, the clarification of the various strains of Talmudic thought nevertheless essentially contributed to the formation of the *halakhah*. This fact justifies the work of the author of *Pisqei tosafot* (The decisions of *tosafot*)—whether he was Rabbenu Asher or his son Yaʿaqov—who abstracted the halakhic decision from each dictum of *tosafot*. Indeed, the later rabbinic authorities (decisors) learned much practical *halakhah* from the *tosafot*.

While the tosafists used the books and *responsa* of the geonim and the halakhic codices of the decisors, such as Rif (Rabbi Yitsḥaq Alfasi), the Talmud remained for them the primary source, and they evaluated the decisions of the geonim and the decisors in its light. Rabbenu Asher explained: "Who is as great in our estimation as Rashi, may the memory of the righteous be a blessing, who enlightened the entire Diaspora with his commentary? Nevertheless his descendants Rabbenu Tam and Riy, may their memories be a blessing, disagreed with him in many instances and refuted his positions, for the Torah is known as 'the *torah* of truth,' so we do not allow flattery of anyone" (commentary to *San.* 4.6). Likewise he wrote elsewhere, "[We do not flatter the geonim] for respecting any subject not explicitly dealt with in the Talmud which Rav Ashi and Ravina' edited, anyone can rise and build up [arguments], even if he opposes the conclusions of the geonim" (*Responsa* 54.10).

The tosafists' method of study provided them with powerful tools to harmonize, circumvent, and redefine, but nevertheless their contemporary reality, with all its conflicting claims and conditions, sometimes asserted itself as a challenge to their methods. The tosafists had to take account of "everyday occurrences" and justify "generally accepted custom." Thus, just as they found means to abrogate laws and customs well supported in the sources, they likewise managed to include within the system of *halakhah* late developments that were without a basis in the sources. To a certain extent, the willingness to venture bold new explanations was a function of the differing personalities of the tosafists, who differed from one another in their personal inclinations and in their spiritual characteristics. However, they were united in their intention to continue the formulation and further the organic development of the Talmudic project as a way of life.

The Tosafists and the Glossarists. Several scholars have noted the similarity between the method of the Scholastics and that of the tosafists. Some of these scholars speak in terms of influence, but the spiritual meeting ground between Christians and Jews took place in biblical exegesis; there is no hint of direct contact in the fields of law and *halakhah*. The *tosafot* were not known to the glossarists, nor were the tosafists familiar with the works of the Roman and canonical legal scholars. Nevertheless, comparison of the *tosafot* and the glosses shows similarities both in the way they came into being and in details of terminology and presentation. Both presume that contradictions in the sources could and must be resolved, whether by distinguishing the cases from one another or by clarifying differences in the time, place, and social position of the various personalities. The way in which the *tosafot* spread and the way in which they were studied also parallel the success of the activities of the glossarists of both Roman and canon law. Despite the differences between the political and social contexts of the Jewish and Christian communities, which lived in a constant, unequal struggle with one another, their assumptions and aspirations were similar. Both communities acknowledged the authority of the Bible and considered themselves commanded to draw from it instruction for their day-to-day existence. Thus both communities greatly esteemed the intellectual ability, sharpwittedness, and breadth of knowledge that made it possible to solve contradictions and deal with social change in the context of the tradition.

THE INFLUENCE OF THE *TOSAFOT*. *Tosafot* came to occupy a central role in the system of study and education of the Jews. It is true that Yehudah Löw ben Betsal'el (known as Maharal of Prague) bitterly decried the teaching of *tosafot* to children, but only few paid any attention to his objections, and until the modern period the traditional schoolbook remained *gemara'*, the commentary of Rashi, and *tosafot.* In the more advanced stages of education the *tosafot* were learned not only in relationship to the Talmud but also as independent sources whose own internal contradictions required resolution. In the fourteenth and fifteenth centuries, the circles of Yisra'el Isserlein, Ya'aqov Molin, Yosef Qolon, and Yitsḥaq Stein in Germany devoted much energy to deriving positions implied by *tosafot.* The *tosafot* stood in the center of the course of study of the Polish and the Turkish scholars. In Vlorë, Albania, scholars of the sixteenth century debated about the *tosafot,* which they called "the short profundities of Touques." In the contract of Italian rabbis, the rabbi "accept[ed] upon himself the obligation to come to the synagogue and teach the *tosafot* for an hour or more before the afternoon prayer."

Suspicion of casuistry and excessive exhibition of sharpwittedness were concerns already of the first tosafists. Rabbenu Tam, who understood the power and possibilities of casuistry as few others did, decried "casuists" who find "bundles and bundles" of answers to every question. In similar fashion, Mosheh al-Ashqar (1462–1542) declared himself against "those who scrutinize the words of the *tosafot* and say senseless things about the redundancies in their language" (*Responsa* 29–30). The influence of the methodology of *tosafot* far exceeded the tendency toward dialectics that arose in their study. This influence is clear in the works of the decisors, in the responsa, and in the works of *novellae* of interpreters trying to get at the simple sense of the text, as well as in various aspects of modern Talmudic research.

BIBLIOGRAPHY

Research on the *tosafot* first concentrated on biography and bibliography. Leopold Zunz edited a list of tosafists and sages mentioned in *tosafot* that appears in his book *Zur Geschichte und Literatur* (Berlin, 1845), in which he refers to the manuscript of the important book by Heimann J. Michael, *Or ha-ḥayyim* (Frankfurt, 1891). Isaac H. Weiss discussed the activities of the tosafists in *Dor dor ve-dorshav,* vol. 4 (Vienna, 1887); he also wrote a monograph on Rabbenu Tam that appeared in *Beit Talmud,* 3 (1883). Heinrich Gross gathered important information about the French tosafists in his book *Gallia Judaica* (Amsterdam, 1897). Abraham Epstein's criticism of the book, printed in the *Monatsschrift für Geschichte und Wissenschaft des Judenthums* (MGWJ) 41 (1897): 464–480, is especially valuable. A similar work, dealing with the German sages, is *Germania Judaica,* published in two parts, edited by Marcus Brann et al. (Frankfurt, 1917–1934). Victor Aptowitzer devotes a long chapter to this subject in his *Mavo' le-sefer ha-Ra'vyah* (Jerusalem, 1938). The principles of the Talmud described in *tosafot* were collected by P. Buchholtz in his article "Die Tossafisten als Methodologen," *MGWJ* 38 (1894): 342–359. On the methodology of the tosafists, see Chaim Tchernowitz's article "Lederekh ha-limmud shel ba'alei ha-tosafot," in *Festschrift Adolf Schwarz,* edited by Samuel Krauss (Berlin, 1917). Following publication of my book *Ba'alei ha-tosafot* (Jerusalem, 1956), there ensued intensive activity in the publishing of *tosafot*; most of the newly published works were from manuscripts that had never been printed, but new editions of *tosafot* that had previously been published in corrupt editions also appeared. There have also been a number of studies of the historical and social reality discernible through the compilations of the tosafists, as well as works on their ideas and influence. A summary is given in Salo W. Baron's *A Social and Religious History of the Jews,* vol. 9, 2d ed., rev. & enl. (New York, 1965). A full bibliography can be found in the expanded and corrected fourth edition of my book mentioned above (Jerusalem, 1980).

E. E. URBACH (1987)
Translated from Hebrew by Akiva Garber

TOSAFOT [FURTHER CONSIDERATIONS].

Research conducted during the early twenty-first century focuses on identifying and evaluating more precisely the distinctions between northern French and German Tosafists, integrating newly discovered collections of *Tosafot* texts and bringing to the fore Tosafists whose writings and contributions have not been fully assessed, reconsidering the extent of Christian intellectual influences on Tosafist methods, and examining the non-Talmudic disciplines with which the Tosafists were significantly engaged.

DIFFERENCES BETWEEN FRANCE AND GERMANY. *Tosafot* texts produced in northern France failed to cite leading German scholars who were active circa 1200 (with barely an exception), including those who authored prominent books such as Judah b. Qalonymus of Spires (d. 1199; *Sefer Yihusei Tanna'im va-Amora'im*), Eliezer b. Joel ha-Levi (1160 to 1165–c. 1235; *Sefer Rabiah*), Barukh of Mainz (1150–1221; the no longer extant *Sefer ha-Hokhmah*), Eleazar of Worms (1176–1238; *Sefer Roqeah*), and Simhah of Speyer (c. 1230; the partially extant *Seder Olam*). At the same time, these German works cite few northern French Tosafists after Rabbenu Tam (c. 1100–1171) and his immediate students. Between the years 1170 and 1220 students from Germany did not study with northern French Tosafists (as they did before and after this period) and vice versa. During this period German Tosafists are known as leading judges and judicial figures. In this context they produced extensive works that dealt primarily with monetary law. Two examples (that are no longer extant) are Ephraim of Regensburg's (d. c. 1175) *Arba'ah Rashim* and Barukh of Mainz's *Sefer ha-Hokhmah.*

On the other hand, the Tosafists of northern France, who undoubtedly participated as judges in cases of monetary law and in the preparation and adjudication of bills of divorce, are rarely identified as such. They are known as *rashei yeshivah* (heads of academies), whose power and reputation derived mainly from their ability to put forward overarching interpretations and novellae (*hiddushim*), rather than from any role that they played as communal judges. The period of disengagement between the northern French and German centers ends only in the days of R. Isaac ben Moses (1180–1250; *Or Zarua'*) and his student, R. Meir of Rothenburg (1220–1293), who spent a significant amount of time studying in northern France. The mid-thirteenth-century Tosafist study hall at Evreux, France, that appears to represent an amalgam between the Talmudic methodology of the Tosafists of northern France and the educational critique and ethical imperatives of the German pietists, should also be noted in this regard.

The *Tosafot* that were produced in these different centers throughout the twelfth and thirteenth centuries employed somewhat different methodologies as well. German *Tosafot* (and *halakhic* writings) take into account a wider selection of Talmudic and rabbinic literature (e.g., *midreshei halakhah va-'aggadah*) than did their counterparts in northern France. Northern French *Tosafot* most often focused on penetrating analyses of relevant texts within the Babylonian Talmud in particular (seeing themselves as a continuation of the methodology of the Amoraim), while German dialectic is milder. In the end, however, the northern French *Tosafot* form dominated. The three leading *Tosafot* collections from the late thirteenth century, *Tosafot Tukh* (Turcheim, Germany), *Tosafot ha-Rosh*, and *Tosafot Rabbenu Perez*, were essentially collections of earlier northern French material (even as all the editors had German roots).

During the twelfth century northern French Tosafists produced *Tosafot* comments almost exclusively, while German Tosafists produced a wider spectrum of *halakhic* works and self-standing texts that contained Talmudic commentary as well. The production of *halakhic* works in northern France at the turn of the twelfth century and into the thirteenth (such as Barukh b. Isaac's [d. 1211] *Sefer ha-Terumah* and Moses of Coucy's [c. 1240] *Sefer Mizvot Gadol*) may reflect the influence of the German pietists with regard to the primacy of practical *halakhah* as well as the notion that a period of great literary creativity is most often followed by one of collection and assessment. The thirteenth century also saw the collection and compilation of earlier *Tosafot* texts, with R. Isaac (Ri) of Dampierre's (d.c. 1200) student Samson of Sens (1150–1230) as one of the first and most prominent examples. Manuscript discoveries in the last decade show, however, that unlike other students of Ri who presented *Tosafot* interpretations that their students then copied and edited, Samson composed his own *Tosafot* interpretations and intended them as an organized work that could be cross-referenced from one tractate to another. Another leading student of Ri, Judah Sirleon (d. 1224), is the first to cite Maimonides, Moses (Mosheh ben Maimon, 1135/8–1204) in his *Tosafot.* Judah's successor, R. Yehi'el of Paris (d.c. 1265), also produced material in the style of *Tosafot*, although his teachings are cited most often in the form of *halakhic* and ritual decisions (*pesaqim*).

Northern French Tosafists generally did not preserve their *responsa* or *pesaqim*, while their German counterparts did. German Tosafists consulted and communicated much more frequently with each other and collected and preserved more faithfully the writings of their Tosafist predecessors from both northern France and Germany. German *Tosafot* were produced by Moses Taku (c. 1230), Simhah of Speyer, Judah b. Qalonymus of Speyers, and Eleazar of Worms, as well as Meir of Rothenburg. Tosafists in Germany, perhaps under the influence of the German pietists, also tended to produce more commentaries than their French counterparts to those tractates that were taught or studied less frequently, such as those included in *Seder Qodashim.*

Although it has been assumed that the genre of *Tosafot* originated in northern France during the mid-twelfth century, the earliest such activity is actually to be found in the work of the German scholar R. Isaac b. Asher (Riga) of Spires (d.c. 1130), who flourished a full generation earlier that Rashi's (R. Solomon b. Isaac, 1040-1100) grandsons, Rabbenu Tam and Rashbam (1085–1174). There is, however, an important stylistic or methodological distinction between them. While Riba functioned more like a judge, who tried to decide between the various possible positions by pushing aside or ferreting out as much material as possible that was not centrally relevant, the early Tosafists in northern France sought to bring together similar *sugyot* to encourage comparisons (as a lawyer might typically do).

It was, however, in northern France that the classical form of *Tosafot* proliferated. Ri, who was Rashi's great-grandson, transformed the Tosafist method from a tool of the elite that was to be used only by the greatest of scholars (such as Rabbenu Tam and his closest students), to the predominant method of learning in study halls throughout northern France. From the days of Ri a series of northern French Tosafists expressed the notion that authoritative Torah study and Talmudic readings and rulings are not solely the property or province of the teacher but belong equally to his students as well who, on the basis of their analysis of underlying Talmudic and rabbinic texts, may "outsmart" or emend the conclusions of the teachers.

All these newly highlighted distinctions between Germany and northern France can account for a number of systemic differences in *halakhic* rulings and outlook between the two regions. At the same time, their commonly held customs, basic methodologies, and interpretational values often led to an unwavering consensus, whether in specific practices and matters of belief, or in the need to formulate valid *halakhic* justifications for economic and other societal practices that appeared prima facie to contradict Talmudic law. To be sure, the issue of intentionality in developing these justifications has been the subject of renewed, vigorous discussion in recent years, just as it was when Urbach's *Ba'alei ha-Tosafot* first appeared.

Urbach essentially reverses his original position on possible Christian influences on Tosafist dialectic, whether by canon lawyers and masters of theology or by Christian scholars of Roman law, in the revised edition of his work. Then, after adducing additional parallels in method and terminology, Urbach concludes that it is difficult to argue for more than zeitgeist. Disparate geographic centers and differences in textual valence were at the core of the critiques of Urbach's original view. More recent research suggests that the argument for influence should not be abandoned. New paradigms, such as the jurists at Pavia, have been suggested. In addition the presence of nascent dialectic at the *yeshivah* in Worms already in the last quarter of the eleventh century (not to mention the presence of critical dialectic within the Talmud itself) lessened the role that external influence would have to play. Influences transmitted by passing personal contacts and conversations rather than through literary sources must also be considered.

Although Urbach notes at various points in his work that certain Tosafists produced writings that were not related to *Tosafot* texts or *halakhic* treatises, the impression fostered by his presentation is that Tosafists were involved only marginally in these other disciplines. So-called Tosafist Torah commentaries (*perushei Ba'alei ha-Tosafot 'al ha-Torah*) are mentioned by Urbach mostly because they also contained parallel or reworked *Tosafot* texts to the Talmud. At the end of his long and nuanced discussion of the *Tosafot* corpus of Ri, Urbach writes that Ri and his son, R. Elhanan (d. 1184), "tried their hand" at the composition of liturgical poems (*piyyutim*), referring the reader to the listings of Leopold Zunz (1794–1886) for details. Urbach refers only in passing to Abraham b. Azri'el of Bohemia (c. 1230), a student of Eleazar of Worms better known for his large and important treatise of *piyyut* commentary *'Arugat ha-Bosem* (which Urbach edited as well) than as a Talmudist. This further supports the perception that Tosafists did Talmud and legal studies, while other disciplines were handled by specialists, a change from the situation in Ashkenaz before the First Crusade when leading scholars typically embraced several different disciplines.

Current research is beginning to question this supposition. Although the impact of twelfth-century legalism caused some Tosafists (and leading ones at that) to focus exclusively on Talmudic and *halakhic* texts and studies, manuscript evidence and a concomitant reevaluation of published texts suggest that others displayed interest in virtually the same variety of disciplines as did their Ashkenazic predecessors from the pre-Crusade period. The more than two hundred manuscript collections of *perushei Ba'alei ha-Tosafot 'al ha-Torah* have barely been analyzed by modern scholarship. Many of them do contain a large amount of Talmudic and *halakhic* material. But at the same time, some display a much greater interest in forms of simple or literal biblical interpretation (*peshat*) than has been imagined.

To be sure, there is greater interest in the *peshat* approach favored by the Tosafist and biblical commentator Yosef b. Isaac Bekhor Shor of Orleans (d.c. 1200) than in the more radical *peshat* of the earlier northern French Tosafist and biblical scholar Rashbam. Also, the Tosafist biblical collections or compilations of the mid- and late thirteenth century often blend (and perhaps blur) *peshat* interpretations with unrestrained midrashic- or *gematria*-based comments. Nonetheless, it is possible to identify a group of Tosafists writing in the late twelfth and early thirteenth centuries that cultivated *peshat* interpretations on their own terms, while also serving as a kind of super-commentary to Rashi. In this role they were interested in verifying not only the Talmudic and midrashic underpinnings of Rashi's Torah commentary, but also his approach to *peshat* and his consistency as a *peshat* exegete. Among these figures are Jacob of Orleans (d. 1189), Isaiah di Trani the Elder (d. c. 1240), and Moses of Coucy. Interestingly, they are joined by R. Yehudah he-Hasid (d. 1217) in a number of the exoteric biblical comments that have been attributed to him. At the same time, Tosafist figures such as Rashbam's brother, Rabbenu Tam, and Ri Samson and R. Samson of Sens (d. 1204) play almost no role in these endeavors.

A similar reevaluation has also been undertaken with regard to the writing of liturgical poetry. Some scholars suggest that no *piyyut* was composed by northern French Tosafists after Rabbenu Tam. Although German Tosafists and rabbinic scholars such as Ephraim of Regensburg, Menahem of Worms (d. 1204), Barukh of Mainz, and Meir of Rothenburg out-produced northern French Tosafists by far in this realm in terms of quantity, a number of northern French Tosafists including Elhanan the son of Ri, Yosef Bekhor Shor (of Orleans), Tuvyah of Vienne (d.c. 1260), and Isaac of Chinon (c. 1250) produced particular genres or patterns of *piyyutim*, suggesting that their involvement was intentional and focused. In any case the German Tosafists just noted appear to have received Spanish material in this discipline (as was the case with respect to biblical interpretation in the preceding discussion). As will be seen shortly, a number of German Tosafists who composed *piyyutim* were also involved with mystical teachings. Lesser-known Tosafist figures such as Avigdor Katz of Vienna and Samuel b. Abraham of Boppard (d.c. 1250) also composed *piyyutim*.

Strong ascetic tendencies and related interest in mysticism and magic were demonstrated in both Germany and northern France during the twelfth and thirteenth centuries, once again, primarily on the basis of texts and fragments still in manuscript. For these disciplines, the direction of influence extends from Ashkenaz to Provence and Spain (as was the case for Talmudic studies). Tosafists display awareness of and interest in ancient Jewish mystical texts, including *Sefer Yezirah* and especially *Hekhalot* literature. They wished to understand the secrets of the Divine Names, the use of Divine Names for magical purposes, and the mystical functioning of the heavenly realm. Although Rashbam and Rabbenu Tam in northern France and R. Eliezer b. Nathan (Raban) of Mainz (c. 1090–1170; who were aware of some of these teachings as well) tried to play them down, they were embraced by leading Tosafists (including Ri) in the second half of the twelfth century and became even more prominent through the thirteenth century, culminating in the figure of Maharam of Rothenburg). The influence of the German pietists in cultivating these disciplines also appears to have been significant, although French figures such as Ezra the (*ha-Navi*) of Moncontour (d.c. 1200 and other students of Ri suggest that there was an independent core of influence as well that perhaps extended back to Elijah of Paris (d.c. 1130) in the early twelfth century.

All of this has implications for the way(s) that anthropomorphism was approached and understood in medieval Ashkenaz, which in turn impacts on the realities behind the Maimonidean controversy. In any event, rabbinic culture in medieval Ashkenaz during the Tosafist period was clearly broader and more variegated than has been thought, although Talmudic interpretation and *halakhic* writings remained the Tosafists' most important areas of endeavor and achievement.

See Also Ashkenazic Hasidism; Halakhah, article on History of Halakhah; Judaism, article on Judaism in Northern and Eastern Europe to 1500; Rabbinate, article on The Rabbinate in Pre-Modern Judaism.

Bibliography

Emanuel, Simcha. "The Lost Halakhic Books of the Tosafists" (in Hebrew). Ph.D. dissertation, Hebrew University of Jerusalem, 1993.

Emanuel, Simcha. "Biographical Data on R. Barukh b. Isaac" (in Hebrew). *Tarbiz* 69 (2000): 423–440.

Emanuel, Simcha. "Rabbi Barukh of Mainz: Portrait of a Scholar as Reflected in the Fragments of His Writings" (in Hebrew). *Issues in Talmudic Research.* Conference commemorating the fifth anniversary of the passing of Ephraim E. Urbach, Jerusalem, 2001.

Kanarfogel, Ephraim. *Jewish Education and Society in the High Middle Ages.* Detroit, Mich., 1992.

Kanarfogel, Ephraim. *Peering through the Lattices: Mystical, Magical, and Pietistic Dimensions in the Tosafist Period.* Detroit, Mich., 2000.

Kanarfogel, Ephraim. "Religious Leadership during the Tosafist Period." In *Jewish Religious Leadership: Image and Reality*, edited by Jack Wertheimer, pp. 265–305. New York, 2004.

Reiner, Rami. "Rabbenu Tam's Northern French Teachers and German Students" (in Hebrew). Master's thesis, Hebrew University of Jerusalem, 1997.

Shoshana, Abraham, ed. *Tosafot Yeshanim ʿal Massekhet Yevamot* (in Hebrew). Jerusalem, 1994.

Sussmann, Yaacov. "The Scholarly Oeuvre of Professor Ephraim Urbach" (in Hebrew). In *Ephraim Elimelech Urbach: A Bio-Bibliography*, edited by David Assaf, pp. 7–62. Jerusalem, 1993.

Ta-Shma, Israel. *Ritual, Custom, and Reality in Franco-Germany, 1000–1350* (in Hebrew). Jerusalem, 2000a.

Ta-Shma, Israel. *Talmudic Commentary in Europe and North Africa* (in Hebrew). Jerusalem, 2000b.

Ta-Shma, Israel. *Collected Studies: Rabbinic Literature in the Middle Ages* (in Hebrew). Vol. 1, *Ashkenaz.* Jerusalem, 2004.

Ephraim Kanarfogel (2005)

TOSEFTA See MISHNAH AND TOSEFTA

TOTEMISM is the systematic symbolization of social entities (individuals, social units) through concrete phenomenal images, often natural species, and the development of these symbols into relationships of identity, power, and common origin. The term *totem* derives from *dotem*, a term used by the Ojibwa, an Algonquin people of North America, to denote clan membership. As a concept, totemism has been treated in two distinct senses, or phases, of anthropological theory. In the first, or evolutionary sense, it was postulated as an institution of primitive thought, a necessary stage of religious conceptualization that all peoples must pass through in the course of cultural evolution. This notion was developed by such theorists as James G. Frazer and Émile Durkheim, and it was the subject of a definitive critique by Alexander A. Goldenweiser. The second, more modern sense of the term might be called its "systematic" sense, one that allows for a wide range of variance in culture-specific schemes of symbolization and classification and that approaches the significance of totemism through its relationship to these schemes. This modern sense informs the viewpoint of Claude Lévi-Strauss's critique *Totemism* (1963) and forms the basis for his subsequent idea of a "science of the concrete" (*The Savage Mind*, 1966).

The first sense of totemism tends to exaggerate its unitary aspects and make of it something of a universal primitive institution; the second tends to dissolve it into general issues of denomination and symbolism and to underplay the distinctiveness of the term and the usages to which it refers.

Instances of the naming of clans for natural species among North American peoples were known long before the practice came to be called totemism. By the time the origin, significance, and definition of totemism became a major topic of controversy among theorists of tribal religion, the area of ethnographic exemplification had shifted from the Americas to central Australia. This shift was in part a consequence of the splendid ethnography of Baldwin Spencer and Francis James Gillen, but it also coincided with the widespread adoption of the evolutionist notion of the "psychic unity of mankind." According to this idea, human culture was essentially unitary and universal, having arisen everywhere through the same stages, so that if we could identify a people who were "frozen" into an earlier stage, we would observe modes of thought and action that were directly ancestral to our own. Australia, a continent populated originally by hunting and gathering peoples alone, seemed to furnish examples of the most primitive stages available.

Together with the concept of taboo, and perhaps also that of *mana*, totemism became, for the later cultural evolutionists, the emblem (or perhaps the "totem") of primitive thought or religion—its hallmark, and therefore also the key to its suspected irrationality. The origin and significance of totemism became the subject of widespread theoretical speculation during the first two decades of the twentieth century. Much of the early theorization developed along the lines of E. B. Tylor's conception of the evolution of the soul (for example, totemic species as representations or repositories of the soul), or as literalizations of names (as in Herbert Spencer's hypothesis that totems arose from an aberration in nicknaming).

The controversy over totemism reached its peak after the publication of Frazer's *Totemism and Exogamy* (1910). In that work, Frazer distinguished totemism, as implying a relationship of equality or kinship with the totem, from religion, as a relationship with higher powers. He emphasized the solidarity function of totemism, which knits people into social groups, as a contribution to the "cause of civilization." Frazer's speculation concerning the origin of totemism, however, came more and more to reflect the particulars of his Australian exemplars. From an initial theory identifying the totem as a repository for a soul entrusted to it for safekeeping, Frazer turned to an explanation based on the Intichiuma rites of central desert Aborigines, in which each subgroup is responsible for the ritual replenishment of some (economically significant) natural species. The idea of the economic basis of totemism was later revived, in simplified form, by Bronislaw Malinowski. Finally, Frazer developed the "conception theory" of totemism, on the model of the Aranda people of central Australia, according to which a personal totem is identified for a child by its mother on the basis of experiences or encounters at the moment she becomes aware that she is pregnant. A creature or feature of the land thus "signified" becomes the child's totem.

In 1910, Goldenweiser, who had studied under Boas, published "Totemism: An Analytical Study," an essay that became the definitive critique of "evolutionary" totemism. Goldenweiser called into question the unitary nature of the phenomenon, pointing out that there was no necessary connection between the existence of clans, the use of totemic designations for them, and the ideology of a relationship between human beings and totemic beings. Each of these phenomena, he argued, could in many cases be shown to exist independently of the others, so that totemism appeared less an institution or religion than an adventitious combination of simpler and more widespread usages.

Despite the acuity and ultimate persuasiveness of Goldenweiser's arguments, the more creative "evolutionary" theories appeared in the years after the publication of his critique. Like Frazer's theory, Durkheim's conception of totemism is exemplified primarily through Australian ethnography. Durkheim viewed totemism as dominated by what he called a quasi-divine principle (Durkheim, 1915, p. 235), one that turned out to be none other than the representation of the social group or clan itself, presented to the collective imagination in the symbolic form of the creature that serves as the totem. Totemism, then, was a special case of the argument of *Elementary Forms of the Religious Life*, a work stating that religion is the form in which society takes account of (reveres, worships, fears) its own collective force.

Sigmund Freud included the concept of totemism, as an exemplar (like the notion of taboo) of contemporary ideas of primitive thought, in his psychodynamic reassessment of cultural and religious forms. Freud's *Totem and Taboo* (1918) projected human culture as the creative result of a primal oedipal guilt. The totem was selected and revered as a substitute for the murdered father, and totemic exogamy functioned as an expiatory resignation on the part of the sons of claims to the women freed by the murder of the father.

In the last major theoretical treatment of "evolutionary" totemism, Arnold van Gennep argued, against Goldenweiser, that its status as a particular combination of three elements did not disqualify totemism's integrity as a phenomenon. Yet Gennep rejected the views of Durkheim and other social determinists to the effect that totemic categorization was based on social interests. Anticipating Lévi-Strauss, who based his later views on this position (Lévi-Strauss, 1966, p. 162), Gennep saw totemism as a special case of the more general cultural phenomenon of classification, although he did not pursue the implications of this position to the degree that Lévi-Strauss did.

Claude Lévi-Strauss's modern critique effectively concludes the attack on evolutionary totemism begun by Goldenweiser, although it aims at the term *totemism* itself. In *Totemism* (1963), Lévi-Strauss critically reviews the history of the subject and reaches the conclusion that totemism is the illusory construct of an earlier period in anthropological theory. Reviewing the more recent ethnographic findings of writers like Meyer Fortes and Raymond Firth, he arrives at the proposition that it is the differences alone, among a series of totemic creatures, that serve to distinguish the corresponding human social units. He disavows, in other words, any sort of analogic relationship (of substance, origin, identity, or interest) between a totem and its human counterpart, and he thus reduces totemism to a special case of denomination or designation. This leaves unexplained (or reduces to mere detail) perhaps the bulk of the ethnographic material to totemism, concerned as it is with special ties and relationships between totem and human unit. In order to deal with this question, Lévi-Strauss developed, in *The Savage Mind* (1966), his notion of the "science of the concrete," in which totemic "classifications" are but a special instance of a more widespread tradition of qualitative logic. Thus Lévi-Strauss is able to substitute the systematic tendencies of an abstract classifying schema for the specific relations between a totem and its social counterpart.

What is the place of totemism in the life of an ongoing community? Consider the Walbiri, an Aboriginal people of the central Australian desert. Walbiri men are divided into about forty lines of paternal descent, each associated with a totemic lodge devoted to the lore and ritual communication with an ancestral Dreaming totem (kangaroo, wallaby, rain, etc.). When they enact the Dreaming rituals, the men are believed to enter the "noumenal" phase of existence (Meggitt, 1972, p. 72) and to merge with the totemic ancestors themselves. Here the analogies between human beings and totemic creatures are sacramentally transformed into identities, made ritually into real relationships of mutual origin and creation, so that men of the different lodges actually belong to different totemic species. When the ritual is concluded, however, they return to everyday "phenomenal" existence and reassume their human character, so that the totemic designations revert to mere names, linked to respective moieties, linked subsections, and other constituents of the complex Walbiri social structure.

Thus the "noumenal phase" of Walbiri life, the ritual state, is constituted by the analogies drawn between human beings and their totems, whereas in the "phenomenal phase" these analogies collapse into arbitrary labels. Only in the latter phase does Lévi-Strauss's proposition about the "differences alone" being the basis for coding human groups apply, for, as human beings, the members of these subsections and moieties can marry one another's sisters and daughters, something that different species cannot do. Within the same culture, in other words, totemic distinctions can serve either as "labels," to code the differences or distinctions among human groups, or, by expanding into metaphoric analogues, accomplish the religious differentiation of men into different "species."

The totemic symbolization of social units is, in many cultures, integrated into a larger or more comprehensive categorial or cosmological scheme, so that the totemic creatures themselves may be organized into broader categories. Among the Ojibwa of North America, totems are grouped according to habitat (earth, air, or water). Aboriginal Australia is distinctive in carrying this tendency to the extreme of "totem affiliation," in which all the phenomena of experience, including colors, human implements, traits, weather conditions, as well as plants and animals, are assigned and grouped as totems (Brandenstein, 1982, p. 87). These universalized systems, in turn, are generally organized in terms of an overarching duality of principles. Brandenstein identifies three of these—quick/slow, warm/cold, and round/flat (large/small)—as generating, in their various permutations and combinations, the totemic-classificatory systems of aboriginal Australia (ibid., pp. 148–149). A similarly comprehensive system is found among the Zuni of the American Southwest, for whom totemic clans are grouped in respective association with seven directional orientations (the four directions, plus zenith, nadir, and center), which are also linked to corresponding colors, social functions, and, in some cases, seasons.

At the other extreme is individuating, or particularizing totemism, for the individual is also a social unit. Among the Sauk and Osage of North America, traits, qualities, or attributes of a clan totem will be assigned to clan members, as personal names, so that members of the Black Bear clan will be known for its tracks, its eyes, the female of the species, and so on (Lévi-Strauss, 1966, p. 173). Among the Kujamaat Diola of Senegal, on the other hand, individuals are totemized secretly through relationships with personalized animal doubles, which are produced by defecation from their own bodies, and which live in the bush near their dwellings (Sapir, 1977). Among the Usen Barok of New Ireland, individual names are taken from plant or animal manifestations of the essentially formless *masalai*, or tutelary clan spirit. Wherever personal names are conceived of as a relation between the bearer of the name and some phenomenal entity, we can consider naming itself to be a form of individual totemism.

Totemic individuation of this sort, in which the character of the name itself bears a specific relational significance, occurs frequently in the naming of modern sports teams, and in formal or informal national symbols, such as the eagle or the bear. Totemism has been proposed as the antecedent of the syncretistic religion of ancient Egypt, with possible indirect connections to the Greco-Roman pantheon. Predynastic Egypt was subdivided into a large number of local territorial units called nomes, each identified through the worship of a particular theriomorphic deity. As the unification of Egypt involved the political joining of these nomes, so the evolution of Egyptian religion led to the combining of the totemic creatures into compound deities such as Amun-Re ("ram-sun"), or Re-Harakhte ("sun-hawk"). There are possible archaic connections of these theriomorphic deities, with Homeric Greek divinities: for example, the cow Hathor with the "ox-eyed Hera." Alternatively, of course, these divinities may have acquired such characterizations as the heritage of an indigenous totemism.

Totemism may not be the key to "primitive thought" that Frazer, Durkheim, and Freud imagined it to be, but the use of concrete phenomenal images as a means of differentiation is not easily explained away as merely another mode of designation, or naming. Wherever social units of any kind—individuals, groups, clans, families, corporations, sports teams, or military units—are arrayed on an equal footing and in "symmetrical" opposition to one another, the possibility arises of transforming a mere quantitative diversity into qualitative meaning through the use of concrete imagery. Diversity is then not merely encoded but instead enters the dimension of meaning, of identity as a concrete, positive quality.

Whenever we speak of a sports team as the Braves, Indians, Cubs, or Vikings, or speak of the Roman, American, German, or Polish eagle, or consider Raven, Eagle, and Killer Whale clans, we make the differences among the respective units something more than differences, and we give each unit a center and a significance of its own. Whenever this occurs, the possibility arises of developing this significance, to a greater or lesser degree, into a profound relationship of rapport, communion, power, or mythic origin. Viewed in this light, the "totems" of a social entity become markers and carriers of its identity and meaning; to harm or consume the totem may well, under certain cultural circumstances, become a powerful metaphor for the denial of qualitative meaning. When theorists of totemism sought to explain the phenomenon solely in terms of the food quest, marriage restrictions, coding, or classification, they subverted the force of cultural meaning to considerations that would find an easier credibility in a materialistically and pragmatically oriented society, "consuming," as it were, meaning through its markers and carriers.

The ostensibly "primitive" character of totemism is an illusion, based on a tendency of literate traditions to overvalue abstraction and to reduce the rich and varied spectrum of meaning to the barest requirements of information coding. In fact abstract reference and concrete image are inextricably interrelated; they imply each other, and neither can exist without the other. Certainly, peoples whose social organizations lack hierarchy and organic diversity (e.g., social class or the division of labor) tend to develop and dramatize a qualitative differentiation through the imagery of natural species, whereas those whose social units show an organic diversity need not resort to a symbolic differentiation. The choice, however, is not a matter of primitiveness or sophistication but rather of the complementarity between social form and one of two equally sophisticated, and mutually interdependent, symbolic alternatives.

See Also Anthropology, Ethnology, and Religion; Australian Indigenous Religions, overview article; Warlpiri Religion.

Bibliography

Brandenstein, C.-G. von. *Names and Substance of the Australian Subsection System.* Chicago, 1982. A comprehensive, comparative analysis of totemic categories in relation to Australian social organizaiton.

Durkheim, Émile. *The Elementary Forms of the Religious Life* (1915). Reprint, New York, 1965. The classic work on the social origin and conception of religion; totemism plays a prominent part in the argument.

Frazer, James G. *Totemism and Exogamy.* 4 vols. London, 1910. The work that established totemism as a central issue in the era of historical anthropology. Well written, but an exercise in a dated style of anthropological speculation.

Freud, Sigmund. *Totem and Taboo.* New York, 1918. The heuristic psychoanalytic "origin myth" of society, its neuroses and taboos; theoretical speculation on totemism at the apex of its popularity outside of anthropological circles.

Goldenweiser, Alexander A. "Totemism: An Analytical Study." *Journal of American Folk-Lore* 23 (1910): 179–293. The classic critique on the "evolutionary" concept of totemism, valid even in relation to works published years afterward.

Lévi-Strauss, Claude. *Le totémisme aujourd'hui.* Paris, 1962. Translated into English by Rodney Needham as *Totemism* (Boston, 1963). The modern critique of totemism, written from a symbolic point of view; a classic of the structuralist approach.

Lévi-Strauss, Claude. *The Savage Mind.* London, 1966. A development of the idea of totemism as denomination into the notion of a "science of the concrete."

Meggitt, M. J. "Understanding Australian Aboriginal Society: Kinship Systems of Cultural Categories." In *Kinship Studies in the Morgan Centennial Year,* edited by Priscilla Reining, pp. 64–87. Washington, D.C., 1972. An account by a noted ethnographer of the complexities of Australian Aboriginal social conceptualization.

Sapir, J. David. "Fecal Animals: An Example of Complementary Totemism." *Man,* n.s. 12 (April 1977): 1–21. A contemporary study of a highly unusual form of individual totemism and its philosophical implications.

New Sources

Adler, Alfred, Bernard Juillerat, and Marie Mauzé. *Totémismes.* Ivry, France, 1998.

Morphy, Howard. "Myth, Totemism and the Creation of Clans." *Oceania* 60, no. 4 (1990): 55–64.

Ratha, S. N. "Rethinking Totemism: Man-nature Relationship in Maintaining the Ecological Balance." *Man in India* 70, no. 3 (1990): 245–252.

Schwartz, Theodore. "Culture Totemism: Ethnic Identity, Primitive and Modern." In *Ethnic Identity: Creation, Conflict, and Accommodation.* Walnut Creek, Calif., 1995.

Shapiro, Warren. "Claude Lévi-Strauss meets Alexander Goldenweiser: Boasian Anthropology and the Study of Totemism." *American Anthropologist* 93, no. 3 (1991): 599–610.

Silverman, Eric Kline. "Gender of the Cosmos: Totemism, Society and Embodiment in the Sepik River." *Oceania* 67, no. 1 (1996): 30–49.

Roy Wagner (1987)
Revised Bibliography

TOTONAC RELIGION. In the city of Zempoala (Cempoallan), situated in what is today the state of Veracruz, Mexico, the Totonac people were the first to receive Europeans to the great land mass of continental America. The year was 1519 and the Spanish conquest of Mexico had begun. At that time the Totonac occupied a strip of land flanked by the Atlantic Ocean and the Sierra Madre Oriental, between the Cazones River in the north and La Antigua River near the present port of Veracruz. Two important Totonac ceremonial centers existed in this territory. The first, El Tajín, was located in the north and had ceased to function before the arrival of the Spanish. The second, Zempoala, is reputed to have been populous when the Spanish arrived; soon after, it witnessed the collapse of its idols and their replacement with the Christian cross.

Well before the Conquest, the Totonac people had extended even farther south, to the margins of the Papaloapan River. The Nahuatl-speaking Aztec had, however, reduced the extent of the Totonac's southern territories, and at the time of the Spanish arrival Zempoala, the Totonac capital, was paying tribute to its Aztec rulers. By this time Nahuatl was the lingua franca in the region, and thus the Spanish priests used Nahuatl terms to describe Totonac religion, a practice still common among scholars today.

At present some one hundred thousand Totonac-speaking people survive in the northern part of their original territory between the states of Puebla and Veracruz. Linguistically, the Totonac are related to the Zoqueano- and Mayan-speaking peoples. However, there is no evidence connecting the religion and culture of the Totonac to those of the Maya and the Zoqueano. Our understanding of the Totonac religion is based upon archaeological evidence primarily from Zempoala, El Tajín, and Puebla, and upon analysis of early descriptions provided by Fray Bartolomé de Las Casas and Fray Andrés de Olmos.

EVIDENCE FROM ZEMPOALA. According to Las Casas, who relied on information supplied by a young page of Cortés, daily homage was paid in Zempoala to the Sun (Chichiní in Totonac), who was the creator of all other gods. Early in the morning seven priests would attend the temple. One of the priests would gaze skyward, paying reverence to the Sun before bathing the Sun's image, as well as the images of other gods, in incense. On ceremonial occasions nobles and officials would go to the temple to worship. According to Las Casas, every Saturday everyone was obliged to gather in the atrium of the temple to pray. Scholars now believe that this took place every fifth day. There, the nobles and principal dignitaries mutilated themselves before their gods by passing numerous straws through incisions made in various parts of their bodies. Las Casas mentions in particular tongues, thighs, and ears. The act of bleeding was a mechanism of purification.

At the winter solstice an important festival was celebrated during which eighteen people, men and women, were sacrificed. Eighteen is also the number of *veintenas* (Span., "set of twenty," i.e., "months" composed of twenty days each) into which the Mesoamerican year was divided. The human sacrifice took place at midnight; the hearts of the victims were ground into the mouths of the principal idols. Blood was the food of the Sun. The persons sacrificed were messengers sent to plead with the Sun to send his son to liberate the Totonac from the practices imposed on them by the Aztec. (Fine illustrations of human sacrifice are to be found in the reliefs at El Tajín.) Similar practices were followed at Zempoala for at least two other important festivals. The flesh of the victims was eaten by dignitaries and a few other influential people. Besides this elitist communion, there existed a practice popular among men who were more than twenty-six years of age: every six months they consumed a paste prepared from the blood of infants' hearts, seeds from plants grown in the temples, and a milky latex from the *Castilla elastica* tree. This sacrament was called *yoliaimtlaqualoz*, a Nahuatl word meaning "food for the soul."

Another regular custom was a confession of sins, called *maiolcuita* in Nahuatl. A person would retire to some isolated spot and confess his wrongdoings aloud. According to Las Casas, penitents would often wring their hands and cry out in anguish with such conviction that it was, in his words, a custom "well worth consideration."

The Totonac had a goddess, the consort of the sun god, whose temple was high in the sierra. She received sacrifices of decapitated animals and birds as well as offerings of herbs and flowers. Her name was Tonacayohua, which means "preserver of the flesh" in Nahuatl. In contrast to many other Mesoamerican cultures, the Totonac did not believe the Sun's consort to be the Moon, since Totonac tradition considered both the Sun and the Moon to be male deities. The Totonac's hope, reported by Las Casas, that the sun god would intercede by sending his son to liberate them from servitude to the Aztec's gods, who required human sacrifice, may well have been a Christian interpretation of Totonac belief. Similarly, although the Sun, the Moon, and the planet Venus together figure prominently in the paintings in the temple of Las Caritas in Zempoala, it is improbable that the Totonac viewed these three celestial deities as forming a unified Trinity.

In the same city a temple was dedicated to Xolotl, the twin brother of Quetzalcoatl. These brothers were personifications of the different manifestations of the planet Venus as Morning Star and Evening Star.

To the south of Zempoala, large sculptures were erected of women who had died during their first childbirth. Such women were venerated, their deaths being seen as equivalent to the deaths of soldiers killed while taking prisoners (new servants for the Sun). Called *cihuateteo* (Nah., "deified women") by the Aztec, they were responsible for transporting the Sun on his course across the sky. Statuettes from the same area provide evidence that human beings were flayed in homage to a god similar to the Aztec deity Xipe Totec; the sacrifice was made to ensure a bountiful harvest.

EVIDENCE FROM EL TAJÍN AND PUEBLA. The relief sculptures among the archaeological remains of El Tajín reveal the existence of another god, Huracán (whence the English word *hurricane*). While in Zempoala Huracán is represented as a *chacmool*, a reclining anthropomorphic figure, in El Tajín he is represented as a one-legged deity whom I consider analogous to Tezcatlipoca. From the Sierra Madre near El Tajín, Olmos reported the existence of (and denounced) a god called Chicueyozumatli ("8 Monkey"), to whom homage was paid at a time near that of the Christian festival of Easter. Like Huracán, Chicueyozumatli is analogous to Tezcatlipoca. Huracán was also equivalent to the god Tajín himself; this storm god survives today among the Totonac, who give him various names, including Trueno Viejo (Span., "old thunder"), Aktsini', and Nanahuatzin.

It was also from the Sierra Madre that the Spanish first reported a festival, called Calcusot by the Totonac, which was held in November for the remembrance of the dead. This festival was widespread among the indigenous peoples of Mexico and survives today in a modified form celebrated on All Souls' Day.

Religious beliefs bore upon sexual practices. Totonac priests were required to maintain celibacy. The high priest and the secondary priest were responsible for the circumcisions of month-old boys, and they also broke the hymens of infant girls. Priests would recommend that mothers repeat the latter operation once their daughters had reached the age of six. Through Olmos we also know that those seeking good health for some relative would refrain from sexual contact for eighty days before making their petition. The general regard for abstinence is demonstrated in a popular tale in which an old man arrives too late for a competition as a result of his libertine ways. The winner of the competition is transformed into the Sun; the old man is transformed into the Moon.

Several popular tales today constitute the remnants of the Totonac religion. In the area of Zempoala the Totonac language is no longer spoken, but in the area of El Tajín (present-day Papantla de Olarte) it still survives. Here the Totonac religious tales have become syncretized with Roman Catholic beliefs. One example is that the Sun and Jesus Christ are often considered to be the same. Another example is that Saint John and the god Tajín (or Trueno Viejo) are also identified as the same. The spread of Catholic (and, more recently, Protestant) religion continues to break down the original Totonac religion.

See Also Tezcatlipoca.

Bibliography

Las Casas, Bartolomé de. *Apologética historia de las Indias.* Madrid, 1909.

Olmos, Andrés de. "Proceso seguido por Fray Andrés de Olmos en contra del cacique de Matlatlán." *Archivo general de la nación* (Mexico City) 3 (1912): 205–215.

Torquemada, Juan de. *Monarquía indiana.* 3d ed. Mexico City, 1975.

Williams-García, Roberto. "Trueno Viejo = Huracán = Chac Mool." *Tlatoani* (Mexico City) 8–9 (1954): 77.

Williams-García, Roberto. "Una visión del mundo totonaquense." In *Actes du Quarante-deuxième Congrès international de americanistes*, vol. 9–B, pp. 121–128. Paris, 1979.

New Sources

Cuentos totonacos: antología (Totonac tales: anthology). Mexico City, 2000.

Culturas prehispánicas del Golfo (Pre-hispanic cultures in the gulf). Veracruz, Mexico, 1999.

Espejo, Alberto, Moraima Marín, and Rosalía Hernández. *Cuentos y leyendas de la region de Naolinco* (Tales and legends of the Naolinco region). Veracruz, Mexico, 1996.

Garma Navarro, Carlos. *Protestantismo en una comunidad totonaca de Puebla, México* (Protestantism and a Totonac community in Puebla, Mexico). Mexico City, 1987.

Ortiz Espejel, Benjamín. *Cultura asediada: espacio e historia en el trópico veracurano, el caso del Totonacapan* (Besieged culture: space and history in the Veracruz tropics, the case of the Totonac). Mexico City, 1995.

Roberto Williams-Garcia (1987)
Translated from Spanish by Robert Allkin
Revised Bibliography

TOUCHING.

In religious usage touching often implies more than simple physical contact with the hands or other parts of the body. One may confer a touch to heal or assert power, to convey or obtain grace, or to consecrate or constrain a person or object.

Healing Touch. A classic instance of touching is recorded in the first three Gospels. They relate that a woman who had had an issue of blood for twelve years came behind Jesus in a crowd and touched the fringe of his garment. According to Luke, Jesus asked, "Who touched me?" and added, "I perceive that power has gone out from me" (*Lk.* 8:45–46). When the woman saw that she was hidden despite the pressing crowd, she fell down before Jesus and declared that she had been immediately healed. As a charismatic healer, Jesus laid his hands upon sick folk, touched lepers, and put his fingers into the ears of a deaf mute and touched his tongue; he also put his spittle on the eyes of a blind man and twice laid hands on his eyes to effect a cure (*Mk.* 8:22–26).

In the Hebrew scriptures, the prophet Elisha is said to have laid himself upon the corpse of a child and to have put his mouth on the child's mouth, his eyes on his eyes, and his hands on his hands. The child's flesh became warm, and the prophet got up and then again stretched himself upon the body. Then the child sneezed seven times and opened his eyes (*2 Kgs.* 4:34–35). The prophet Isaiah, after having had a vision of God "high and lifted up," confessed his own sinfulness, whereupon a seraph flew to him with a live coal from the heavenly altar and touched his mouth with it to purge his iniquity (*Is.* 6:1–7).

Not only the touch of a sacred person but the touch of anything connected with him could exercise healing power. The New Testament reports that the shadow of Peter was sought by the sick, who were brought into the street to be cured as he passed by (*Acts* 5:15). And miracles were wrought not only by the hands of Paul but by the clothes that were taken from his body and given to the sick, whereupon diseases and possession by evil spirits went out of them (*Acts* 19:12).

The disciples of Jesus healed the sick by anointing them with oil (*Mk.* 6:13), and the elders of the church were instructed to pray for the sick and anoint them with oil in the name of the Lord (*Jas.* 5:14–15). From this developed what came to be called the unction of the sick, in some Eastern and Western churches, and extreme unction (a sacrament) in the Roman Catholic church. To the accompaniment of prayer, anointing oil is administered to the eyes, ears, nose, lips, hands, and feet of the sick person "for the health of body and soul." This rite is to be distinguished from the viaticum ("provision for a journey") of Holy Communion, which is administered to those near death.

Although Islam affirms that Muḥammad was a man and that the one miracle he wrought was the Qurʾān, devotees have credited the Prophet with a healing touch. Al-Bakhārī recorded that when one of Muḥammad's companions broke his leg, the Prophet passed his hands over the limb, whereupon it seemed as if nothing had ever been wrong with it. A woman brought him her son who was possessed, and Muḥammad stroked the boy's breast and prayed until the lad vomited and was healed. The Prophet even had power over nature: a palm tree that was one of the pillars of his mosque is said to have shouted out until it almost split, whereupon the Prophet embraced it until it calmed down and was quiet again.

In ancient and preliterate societies, power is attributed to the touch of healers, priests, and shamans. Doctors of the Ndembu of Zambia, for example, encircle a patient's hut and bring medicines of roots and leaves. The patient's chest and shoulders are washed, and then the doctor catches him by the little finger and directs him to a fire to warm himself. Still holding the patient's little finger, the doctor gives him a rattle, and after a while the patient begins to tremble and dance. A helper puts his hands on the patient's shoulders while the doctor places a medicine basket on the patient's head; after further dancing, the patient is led backward into his own hut to rest and recover.

The practice of touching an animal in order to transfer evil to it is illustrated in the Bible. The priest Aaron was instructed to take two goats into the wilderness, one to be sacrificed as a sin offering and the other to be given as a scapegoat to ʿAzaʾzel, a desert demon. The priest placed his hands on the head of the second goat, confessing over it the sins of the people, and sent it off to wander in the wilderness (*Lv.* 16:7–10, 21). In West Africa, a mother of twins who had died took a goat by the horns and placed her forehead three times against it in order to transfer her evil to it. Then the animal was sent away to wander outside the village.

In Asia and North America, both medicine men and shamans alike have performed functions of healing by touching. Although the shaman may utilize the curative properties of plants and animals or may massage patients, many illnesses are regarded as spiritual, that is, caused by injury to the soul. Thus the shaman's method is meant to restore the soul, and this he accomplishes by ascending to the heavens or descending to the underworld in a trance. If he perceives the disease to have been caused by a foreign body, visible or invisible, he may extract it by sucking the part of the body that he saw while in a trance, sucking the skin either directly or through a bone or wooden tube. The shaman then dances and afterward may paint magical designs on the patient's body or instruct the patient's family on how this is to be done.

In Japan, Nakayama Miki (1778–1884), founder of the Tenrikyō religion, sought to heal sick people by giving them food or one of her belongings. As the numbers of her followers increased, she prepared amulets to give them. Relatives of the sick consulted her and brought with them some of the afflicted one's clothes. She took them in her hands and breathed on them, and it was said that recovery followed at once. Miki also distributed to her disciples pieces of paper on which she had breathed, and when the demand on her became too great she granted this power of breath to her chosen disciples.

TOUCHES OF POWER OR REVERENCE. According to the *Laws of Manu,* a Hindu high-caste student must clasp the feet of his teacher both at the beginning and at the end of each lesson in the Vedas, crossing his hands so that he touches the left foot with his left hand and the right foot with his right hand. Similarly, he should touch the feet of his teacher's wife and the wife of his teacher's brother, if she is of the same caste (*Manu* 2.72, 132, 217).

Down to modern times, the physical presence of a teacher or guru has been treasured above books or learning, since true knowledge, power, and even divinity come through him. Sometimes the guru sits before his disciple in silence, and the latter squats with eyes closed. The guru may eventually touch the disciple's forehead or gaze into his eyes, and thus power is felt to pass from one to the other.

In daily religious practice, a devout Hindu asks pardon from the earth for touching it with his feet as he rises from bed. When he is ready for worship, he invokes his god by *nyāsa,* "placing" or "fixing" the presence of the divinity in his body by holding the right hand successively in front of the mouth, eyes, ears, nostrils, top of the head, forearms, navel, and back. The touching is accompanied by recitation of a mantra, a scriptural text, and prayers that the gods who protect different parts of the body may each take up his special place. *Nyāsa* is also performed on images to install the gods within them. With bunches of sacred grass, the breast of the image is touched to install Brahma, the hand is touched to install Indra, the feet for Viṣṇu, and other parts for the appropriate gods.

In Sri Lanka, Buddhists perform comparable rites. In the presence of a superior, one joins the hands in reverence, bows or kneels, and even touches the ground with the forehead or touches the feet of the person saluted. Similar reverence is accorded images of the Buddha and other holy figures. The "eye festival," which is held on completion of an image of the Buddha, is an elaborate ritual performed to ensure that the gaze of the image does not fall directly on the craftsman who paints in the eyes. He looks into a mirror to see the eyes as he paints them, thus avoiding the dangerous gaze; afterward he is led blindfolded from the room, and the covering is removed only when his eyes will fall on something harmless, such as water.

In Buddhist myth and imagery occurs the symbolic gesture (*mudrā*) of the Buddha "touching the ground" (Bhūmiśparsa Mudrā). There are several versions of this event. In one version, the Buddha at the point of attaining perfection was warned that he would be attacked by demons. So he pointed to the ground with his finger and called on the gods of the earth to rise up and kill the demons. In another version, the demon king Māra claimed the Buddha's throne and summoned his troops as witnesses. The Buddha then touched the earth as his witness, and it proclaimed his right to the throne. Yet other accounts call this symbolic gesture the *mudrā* of the defeat of Māra, or touching the earth to oblige its gods to swear eternal fealty. Touching the ground has the meaning of repressing evil and also of calling the earth to witness. The five fingers of the left hand hold the Buddha's robe at the level of the breast, and with the right hand five fingers touch or press the earth. In Buddhist imagery, this gesture is a distinctive sign of the historical Buddha, Śākyamuni, whereas other gestures in images and pictures are common to several Buddhas.

An Islamic tradition, from al-Bukhārī, says that once, when there was only a little food, Muḥammad blessed it until there was enough for a great multitude. This is similar to the gospel accounts of Jesus praying, blessing, and breaking five loaves of bread for five thousand people. Another Islamic narrative says that once, when the followers of Muḥammad were thirsty, he put his hand into a bucket and water gushed out from between his fingers like a spring. One follower said that the Prophet came to him in a dream and kissed his cheek, so that when he awoke the house was full of scent.

In Christianity, laying on of hands is said to communicate power. The Gospels record that parents brought children to Jesus in order that he might touch them. He brushed aside the protective barrier formed by the disciples and, taking the children in his arms, "he blessed them, laying his hands upon them" (*Mk.* 10:16). The Gospels record that the first Christian apostles chose deacons to help in secondary duties, laid hands on them, and prayed, whereupon the deacons became filled with power. Peter and John laid their hands on converts so that they would receive the Holy Spirit (*Acts* 6:6). The magician Simon tried to buy this power so that the Spirit might also descend on those on whom he laid his hands (*Acts* 8:18–19). Paul and Barnabas had hands laid on them for success in a special mission, but a warning to Timothy to "lay hands suddenly on no man" shows that care was needed in such dedication.

Commission to service by laying on hands, especially in the ordained ministry of the church, has continued through the ages. It is practiced by nonepiscopal and free churches as well as by those that claim an unbroken apostolic and episcopal succession transmitted through this sacred touch. In the Church of England, the ordination of priests by the episcopal touch gives power as well as office, as reflected in these words from the traditional *Book of Common Prayer:* "Receive the Holy Ghost for the office and work of a priest in the Church of God, now committed unto thee by the imposition of our hands." In the consecration of a bishop, other bishops lay hands on his head and exhort him to "stir up the grace of God which is given thee by this imposition of our hands." At the investiture of a high-caste Hindu, the candidate passes from low or neutral status to that of a "twice-born." The central rite is the Upanayana, the "donning of the sacred thread," nowadays confined usually to boys, although in former times girls also were invested with this symbol of rebirth. While the preceptor recites appropriate texts, the candidate, facing the sun, slips the cotton threads over his head and across his breast. The teacher puts his right hand on the right side of the boy, alternately touching the candidate's shoulder and his own breast while exhorting obedience and unity of mind. The teacher then takes the boy's right hand into his own and asks him his "old name"; he then gives him a "new name" (which is uttered only at this ceremony). When the candidate is finally considered ceremonially pure, he performs *nyāsa,* touching his own head, eyes, nostrils, hands, arms, limbs, and other parts of his body to purify them all. The third finger of the right hand is considered the most auspicious, and, with it, the newly "twice-born" man touches some of the ashes of the sacred fire that is burning nearby and puts them on his forehead, throat, and right shoulder and over his heart. Then he is blessed and bows to his teacher and all his elders.

Not only prophets and healers but secular rulers have been credited with a potent touch, thereby expressing the divinity that "doth hedge a king." European kings touched their subjects who suffered from scrofula, also called "the king's evil," a swelling of the glands that supposedly was cured by the royal touch. French kings had done this since ancient times, and the custom was introduced to England in the eleventh century by the saintly Edward the Confessor. In the late fifteenth century, Henry VII, perhaps to encourage support for his claim to the throne, instituted a ceremony for touching persons suffering from scrofula and presented the afflicted with gold coins; in the seventeenth century, Charles I distributed silver pieces for the sufferers to touch. From then until 1719, the Anglican *Book of Common Prayer* contained an office called At the Healing, in which the monarch laid hands on the assembled infirm persons and put gold or silver about their necks while a chaplain recited the following prayer: "God give a blessing to this work, and grant that these sick persons on whom the king lays his hands may recover." The practice of royal touching to gain popular support reached its peak in England under Charles II, who reigned from 1660 to 1685. Charles touched nearly one hundred thousand people. According to Thomas Macaulay, "in 1684, the throng was such that six or seven of the sick were trampled to death." A short time later, William III called the practice "a silly superstition," though his wife and coregent, Mary II, continued it. Queen Anne, who reigned from 1702 to 1714, was the last British monarch to practice royal touching. James Boswell recorded in his biography of Samuel Johnson that the infant Johnson had been taken to be touched by Queen Anne because he had a disfigured face, "his mother yielding to the superstitious notion, which, it is wonderful to think prevailed so long in this country, as to the virtue of the regal touch." Queen Anne's touch, however, had no effect on the young Johnson, and Boswell teased him that "his mother had not carried him far enough, she should have taken him to Rome." A practice comparable to the royal healing touch is the washing of feet performed on Maundy Thursday by notable people in imitation of Christ's washing his disciples' feet. The practice took its name from the Latin *mandatum,* the translation of the "new commandment" that is given in *John* 13:34. Popes, bishops, and kings practiced the ablution; the pope would wash the feet of his cardinals or, in modern times, the feet of selected poor men. In England, kings did such washing until the reign of James II in the late seventeenth century. Specially minted "Maundy money" is still distributed by the monarch to certain old people during a religious ceremony that takes place at a different cathedral in England each year on Maundy Thursday, the Thursday before Easter.

Power in the royal touch, look, or presence is attested in many places. In the *Laws of Manu* the presence of the king, like the sun, is said to burn eyes and hearts, and nobody on earth can even gaze on him; even an infant king is a deity in human form. The monarch's responsibilities are great, and he must conquer his own senses if he is to require obedience from others. The king rules by the rod but must do no bodily injury unjustly. If he fights his foes in battle, he must not strike with poisonous weapons or smite one who surrenders. His highest duty is to protect his subjects and gratify with a kindly reception all who come to see him.

West African kings often wore beaded veils over their faces, a practice that seems to be very ancient, from the evidence of bronze masks with holes for veils. To look directly at a king's face or to receive his unveiled gaze were considered equally dangerous. For the monarch to point at or touch a commoner might be seen as either a mark of favor or of danger.

In China, the physical obligations of a king were detailed by the Confucian scholar Tung Chung-shu, who stated that the monarch must personally grasp a plow handle and plow a furrow, pluck mulberries and feed silkworms, and break new ground to increase the supply of grain. As the representative of Heaven, the king formally touched the plow or sickle to initiate the harvest. In Japan, to this day the emperor cuts the first rice of the harvest. Photographs in public newspapers show him dressed in shirt, suspenders, and trousers, harvesting rice. The rice he has cut is sent to the central Shinto shrines at Ise.

KISSING AND HANDSHAKING. Kissing is a form of close touching, a sign of reverence as well as of greeting or affection. It is performed on human beings and objects alike. The Bible's report that the prophet Elijah was assured that there were in Israel seven thousand people who had not kissed the god Baal indicates that the Canaanite and Phoenician custom of kissing the images of their gods was being practiced by the Israelites. The prophet Hosea also spoke despairingly of the Israelites kissing silver idols of calves. The Greeks and Romans also kissed images of their gods, and early Christians were persecuted for refusing to make such homage.

The ancient Hebrews kissed the floor of the Temple. Jews still kiss the scroll of the Torah when they are about to read it, and they kiss any holy book if it has been accidentally dropped. When the Torah scrolls are taken around the synagogue in procession, worshipers touch them and then place their hands on their own breasts. When a Jew puts on a prayer shawl, he kisses it, and upon entering or leaving a room, Jews may kiss or touch a *mezuzah,* the miniature container holding several verses of scripture that is affixed to a doorpost. At the Western Wall in Jerusalem, worshipers handle and kiss pieces of paper on which they write prayers and that they then put into cracks in the wall.

In the celebration of the Mass, Roman Catholic priests kiss the altar and the corporal cloth on which the sacred elements are laid. A priest also kisses the cross on a stole before he puts it on. In both Eastern and Western churches, ritual kissing is also performed with relics and with books of the gospel, crosses, candles, palm branches, vestments, and utensils of the liturgy. In British courts, oaths are sworn by taking the Bible or another holy book in ungloved hands; formerly the book was kissed.

Images and icons are popular objects of the kiss. In Saint Peter's Church in Rome, the toe of a statue of the apostle has been partly worn away by the kisses of devotees. In Ireland, the kissing of the Blarney Stone is a modern tourist attraction that may look back to prehistoric times. Part of the ritual of the Islamic pilgrimage to Mecca is kissing the Black Stone, which is set in the wall of the Kaʿbah. Because the crowds are vast, some pilgrims use long sticks to touch the stone, or from a distance they simulate a gesture of touching and afterward pass their hands over their faces while praising God and his prophet. In the opposite corner of the Kaʿbah is another stone, which it was the Prophet's custom to touch. When the crowd prevents a pilgrim from touching it, he says a prayer for blessing and forgiveness. Followers of the late shah of Iran may still be observed kissing his portrait, and the same gesture of reverence is offered to pictures of his rival, the Ayatollah Khomeini.

The Second Psalm (2:11) exhorts Israelite worshipers to "kiss [the Lord's] feet," no doubt an act of homage. This carried over to the kissing of kings' and popes' feet. In India, to kiss the feet or take the dust of the feet upon one's own head is a sign of submission and reverence. A farewell kiss to the dead is an old practice, one that was sometimes forbidden. It is still practiced in an attenuated form by touching the coffin.

In the Islamic world, kissing the shoulder, the foot, or, especially, the hand of a holy man is believed to communicate spiritual benefit. The water in which saints have washed their hands confers grace, and schoolboys may drink the water they have used to wash the board on which they write passages from the Qurʾān, in order that they may learn the text more easily. The saliva of a holy man is said to have medicinal value, and schoolboys are thought to learn their lessons better when their teachers spit into their mouths.

The kiss of peace became a distinctive Christian ritual: both Paul and Peter exhorted their readers to "salute one another with a holy kiss," but by the time of Tertullian, in the second century, it was ruled that men should kiss only men and women should kiss only women, to prevent suggestions of scandal. The kiss had a sacramental value. It was an outward sign of spiritual union or blessing: bishops were given a kiss at their consecration and kings at their coronation. The practice of the kiss of peace has been revived in modern times, either by shaking hands and uttering a phrase of peace or, for the less reserved, by giving a holy kiss.

The shaking of hands may also transfer grace or mark privilege. In Morocco, when equals meet they may join hands in salutation, and then each person will kiss his own hand. Among the West African Ashanti, during intervals of dancing, priests walk around the circle of spectators, and each places his right hand between the extended palms of the person saluted. The right hand is usually considered the proper or fortunate one, and the Ashanti may refuse to take a gift or even the payment of a debt from the left hand of the giver. In Latin, the word for left is *sinister,* and the Greeks euphemistically called the left the "well-named" side in order to avert bad luck. Shaking with the left hand, or with a finger bent back, is practiced by special societies and copied by Freemasons and Boy Scouts.

TOUCHING PROHIBITED. On the negative side, the prohibition against touching may be as important as the act itself. Usually it serves to save a person from contamination. When Moses brought the Israelites to Mount Sinai, he alone went up into the presence of God. Although the people were sanctified by ritual washing, they were exhorted not to touch the mountain or its border, for "whosoever touches the mount shall surely be put to death" (*Ex.* 19:12). The elaborate regulations described in *Leviticus* include many prohibitions against touching objects and people that were deemed sacred or dangerous. Touching any unclean thing would bring guilt and pollution and would require purgation by the presentation of a sin offering and an atonement effected by a priest. Touching a dead body was considered particularly dangerous, and there are repeated warnings against such action. The power of blood was always perilous, and touching a menstruating woman or anything she sat on required washing and the presentation of a sin offering. Because blood was considered the life or soul, prohibitions against its consumption were imposed on Jews, and this rule was extended to Muslims as well.

The Bible also strictly forbade touching to harm, or even to suggest disrespect for, a sacred object or person. When Uzzah put out his hand to steady the Ark, "God smote him" (*2 Sm.* 6:7). The Bible records God's command, "touch not mine anointed, and do my prophets no harm," a sentiment echoed in the vicar of Bray's damnation of those who "touch the Lord's anointed"—a reference to the execution of Charles I. An example of reverential and perhaps numinous prohibition against touching is found in the words of the risen Christ to Mary: "Touch me not" (*Jn.* 20:17). There are many other examples of religious figures who kept themselves from being touched. When Nakayama Miki felt herself to be filled with divinity and chosen for a special mission, she separated herself from the common people. She ordered that a separate fire and separate vessels be used to cook her food, and she wore only red robes to show that she was not an ordinary person. This emphasized the numinous value of the amulets that she gave to her faithful, since she claimed to be the mediatrix between God and men, saying, "I must be set aside and live in a special and separate room."

SEE ALSO Blood; Kashrut; Power; Scapegoat; Tenrikyō.

BIBLIOGRAPHY

Among the countless books on Christian teaching and life that may be consulted on themes related to touching, special reference may be made to *A New Dictionary of Christian Theology,* edited by Alan Richardson and John Bowden (London, 1983), and to the oft-reprinted *Oxford Dictionary of the Christian Church,* edited by F. L. Cross (Oxford, 1957). See also *Touching* by Ashley Montagu (New York, 1971). Islamic rituals of pilgrimage and prayers are described by Ahmad Kamal in *The Sacred Journey* (New York, 1961). Victor Turner describes "religious processes" among the Ndembu of Zambia in *The Drums of Affliction* (Oxford, 1968), and Henry van Straelen's *The Religion of Divine Wisdom* (Tokyo, 1954) gives an account of the history and rituals of Tenrikyō. *The Rites of the Twice-Born* (1920; reprint, New Delhi, 1971) by Margaret S. Stevenson is probably still the most detailed and readable account of Indian high-caste life and practices. *Mudra* (New York, 1960) by E. Dale Saunders is an illustrated study of symbolic gestures in Buddhist sculpture. A valuable study of the rites and symbols associated with kissing is *The Kiss Sacred and Profane: An Interpretive History of Kiss Symbolism and Related Religio-Erotic Themes* (Berkeley, Calif., 1969) by Nicholas J. Perella. Shamanic activities in a variety of cultures are described at length by Mircea Eliade in *Shamanism,* rev. & enl. ed. (New York, 1964), and perhaps the most exhaustive account of particular Islamic customs is to be found in Edward Westermarck's *Ritual and Belief in Morocco,* 2 vols. (1926; reprint, New Hyde Park, N.Y., 1968).

GEOFFREY PARRINDER (1987)

TOURISM AND RELIGION. Tourism and its associated practices interact with religious life and the institutions of religion in virtually every corner of the world. From Amish communities of rural Pennsylvania to the snowy summits of Mount Fuji in Japan, from the mysterious ruins of Machu Picchu in the Peruvian Andes to the monumental pyramids of Giza in Egypt, from Chartres in France to the Western Wall in Jerusalem, millions of tourists seek out places of religion every year. The relationship between religion and tourism, however, amounts to far more than places of religion that host tourist visitors. In fact, there are at least three broad approaches to understanding this relationship: spatial, historical, and cultural. Each of these illuminates different implications for religious life when tourists enter a sacred precinct.

SPATIAL RELATIONS BETWEEN RELIGION AND TOURISM. Tourists and religious adherents often occupy the same spaces; consequently, they both play a role in attributing meanings to these spaces and in sustaining the sacred character of sites that host both casual and deeply committed visitors. In fact, the religious meanings that make a place sacred also make the site a meaningful destination for tourists. At the same time, however, tourists and religious practitioners usually have very different attachments to and understandings of these sacred spaces.

Spaces become sacred according to the historical, social, and cultural contexts of particular religious traditions. The holy nature of Mecca, for instance, cannot be understood apart from the historical and sociocultural contexts of Islam. Indeed, the close identification between Islam and its most sacred city make them nearly indistinguishable. Likewise, the shrine at Tepeyac, which houses the sacred image of the Virgin of Guadalupe in Mexico City, gains its auspicious powers from the miraculous appearance of the Virgin there; these powers, however, also derive from the historical circumstances of colonial relations between European Christians and Native American converts, as well as from the racial, ethnic, gender, and socioeconomic dynamics of subsequent generations of Catholic worshippers at the site. Both of these cases demonstrate how places are made holy according to particular religious traditions and the spatial practices that sustain their sacred character.

Tourists, on the other hand, arrive with a different set of spatial practices embedded in their own peculiar historical, social, and cultural contexts. Unlike religious practices related to particular sacred spaces, however, the spatial practices of tourists rely on modern conventions of travel and aesthetics practiced in the context of global capitalism. Hence, they make these spaces into touristic places that remain distinct from the sacred places of religious people. At Tepeyac, for instance, the sacredness sustained in veneration of the Virgin of Guadalupe appears to a touristic sensibility in terms of aesthetics, history, and the exotic otherness of unfamiliar cultic behaviors. Thus, the space of Tepeyac becomes simultaneously a place of religious practice and a place of touristic indulgence.

Places of both religion and tourism range from the predominantly religious to the predominantly touristic. As an example of the former, the prohibition of non-Muslims in Mecca keeps Islam's most holy city free from purely touristic travelers, although the touristic imagination of non-Muslims makes it a desirable, if improbable, destination. In contrast, Uluru in Australia, the world's largest monolith, retains its mythic significance as a sacred site for Aboriginal people, but it is best known for the striking beauty of its ethereal hues. A half million annual visitors make the journey deep into the Australian interior to view the giant outcropping set in the stark outback landscape.

Between the extremes of predominantly religious and predominantly touristic lies a great variety of religious places that host significant numbers of tourist visitors. These places range from the ancient to the contemporary, from auspicious features of the natural landscape to glass and steel architectural structures, from remote spots far from human habitation to the centers of the world's most densely populated urban areas. In addition, tourists seek out religious events that include regularly performed rituals, special dedicatory events, festivals, and carnivals. There seems no end to the types and locales of religious sites and celebrations that appeal to the curiosities of touristic travelers.

Among the most auspicious of places that tourists seek out are natural features regarded as sacred by one or more religious traditions. Mount Fuji, for example, looms above the Japanese landscape as a sacred monument in both the Shintō and Buddhist traditions; at the same time, the mountain serves as one of Japan's most recognizable icons for tourists. Caves, on the other hand, tend to appeal to visitors more for their ancient artwork associated with prehistoric religions rather than for their inherent sacredness. At places like Lascaux in France and the Altamira caves of northern Spain, visitors can tour exact replicas of the caverns complete with detailed copies of their ancient paintings, even though entrance into the caves themselves is restricted at both sites.

Tourists also visit the architectural ruins of places where ancient peoples practiced their religions. Among the most famous of these sites are the remains of structures built by the Egyptian, Greek, Roman, and other civilizations of the ancient Mediterranean world. Similarly in Indonesia, travelers can visit the restored Buddhist temple of Borobudur. Prehistoric sites in the Americas include the monumental pyramids and other sacred structures of Teotihuacan in central Mexico, and the Inca ceremonial center of Machu Picchu in Peru remains a favorite stop for tourists.

Places where contemporary people continue to practice their religion also capture the attention of tourists. Tourists can view the Dome of the Rock, one of the holiest sites for Muslims in the ancient city of Al-Quds (Jerusalem). Also in Jerusalem, an ancient ruin that remains an active place of religious practice for Jews is the Western Wall of the Temple Mount, popularly known as the Wailing Wall. In Rome, holy places of Christianity abound; among the most popular are St. Peter's Basilica and other sites of the Vatican. In Japan, the Ise temple complex, the most sacred site of the Shintō religion, is a favorite destination for tourists.

Tourists often take more interest in witnessing religions in practice than in merely viewing the places of religion. A visit to a church, temple, mosque, or shrine becomes more meaningful and fulfilling if a ritual or some other event happens to be occurring at the time of the visit. Special celebrations and religious festivals generate even more enthusiasm among visitors. Widely known festivals such as Carnival in Rio de Janeiro in Brazil or Mardi Gras in New Orleans in the United States attract huge crowds every year. But smaller, lesser-known celebrations often have greater appeal for travelers. Visitors in China intent on experiencing authentic Chinese culture may have more interest in a local village's Lantern Festival than in a large celebration that is widely promoted in tourist literature.

There is no end to the places and events of religion that tourists visit each year, and an attempt to list all the possible religious attractions for travelers would prove futile. Indeed, outsiders visit religious sites and witness religious activities virtually everywhere. Many of these visitors do not regard themselves as religious practitioners or pilgrims; they come as tourists, modern consumers of religious culture. Certainly, a good number find themselves actively participating in religious practices at the places they visit, but at the same time they rarely falter in pursuit of their touristic objective to have authentic, aesthetically pleasing experiences.

Historical Relations between Religion and Tourism. It is tempting to suggest that tourism has its roots in religious pilgrimage. In fact, as categories of practice and experience, pilgrimage and tourism are easily confused. In contemporary settings, pilgrims often engage in touristic activities; like tourists, they take photographs of the places they visit, they purchase souvenirs and gifts, and they avail themselves of the same transportation and lodging accommodations that tourists use. At the same time, tourists who visit religious sites, including pilgrimage destinations, sometimes find themselves participating in religious practices, and many so-called tourists are overtaken by feelings that can be described as religious at sites regarded as sacred. Thus, it is easy to confuse the experience of the tourist with that of the pilgrim.

Yet despite the difficulty of distinguishing between them, the practice of tourism has origins largely independent of the traditions of religious pilgrimage. By 1780, when the term *tourist* first appeared in the English language, conventions of recreational and educational travel in the Western world already had established themselves with more than two centuries of development. In fact, the history of touristic practices follows on the same historical forces that challenged the traditional authority of Christianity and consequently led to the demise of pilgrimage in much of northern Europe. These include the rise of humanism beginning in Renaissance Italy and spreading northward; the Protestant reformations of the sixteenth century that shook the foundations of traditional church authority in Christian Europe; and the Enlightenments of the seventeenth and eighteenth centuries, which introduced new models of political authority and modern forms of subjectivity. Along with their profound impact on European societies in general, these movements also changed the expectations and requirements for an educated citizenry. Sara Warneke (1995, p. 30) notes that, instead of a pure scholasticism pursued in earlier times, the Renaissance education sought to prepare students for a life of service to their community, their prince, and their state; this often included stays in foreign states to learn firsthand the culture and politics of other societies. By the second half of the sixteenth century, significant numbers of travelers were leaving their homelands in hopes of gaining the educational benefits of a continental journey.

Following the Thirty Years' War of the seventeenth century, travelers settled into a conventional pattern of educational travel that would be the basis for what became known in the eighteenth century as the Grand Tour. Not unlike their counterparts in the sixteenth and seventeenth centuries, participants in the Grand Tour sought education and refinement. But tourism changed over the course of the eighteenth century. Early in the century a classical view of the Grand Tour dominated, most typically involving young men traveling with an entourage of servants and tutors to selected European destinations, most often Paris and Italy, to finish their education and practice the refinements of cultivated society. But in the second half of the century, as Jeremy Black (1992, p. 300) points out, the classical model became less typical as more people traveled for enjoyment and amusement. Black goes on to note that although many aristocratic families continued to send their sons abroad for education and social finishing, the emphasis on education declined as tourism joined in the growing European fascination with leisure activities (p. 303).

By the time of Napoleon's defeat at Waterloo in 1815, travel practices in Europe were undergoing significant changes that precluded a return to the heyday of the Grand Tour. Steamships and railroad service allowed for more convenient, more enjoyable, and less time-consuming tours of the Continent. And although tourist travel throughout most of the nineteenth century remained primarily a privilege of wealthy classes, the growth of railroad transportation made travel available to at least a few members of the middle classes. In the twentieth century, however, mass production of automobiles, along with a trend toward shorter workweeks, allowed greater numbers from all but the lowest socioeconomic classes to indulge in regular, if infrequent, tourist travels. Air travel has extended the range of the twenty-first-century tourist to every continent on earth, and space travel has even taken tourists even beyond the earth's atmosphere.

From the very beginning of tourism's history, tourists have held a fascination with religion. Early travelers of the European Renaissance regularly visited churches, cathedrals, shrines, and other religious sites in their studies of the art, architecture, culture, and history of the nations they visited. On occasion, Renaissance travelers also condemned the practices of the religious people they encountered at such places. In fact, the humanist Desiderius Erasmus (1466?–1536) signaled a pivotal moment between Christian pilgrimage and the beginnings of religious tourism with his colloquy "A Pilgrimage for Religion's Sake," which first appeared in 1526, with an anonymous English translation appearing a decade later as "The Pilgrimage of Pure Devotion." Erasmus traveled as a secular visitor to various pilgrimage sites where he had little patience for traditional religious practices; indeed, his observations and subsequent criticisms of pilgrims reflected the groundswell of intellectual, political, and religious reforms sweeping Europe at the time.

The tension between practices of the earliest tourists and those of their pilgrim counterparts, as exemplified in Erasmus's essay, has continued into the twenty-first century. In fact, pilgrimage sites remain favorite tourist destinations even today. Nonreligious visitors frequent such popular Christian pilgrimage destinations as Lourdes in France, Santiago de Campostela in Spain, and the Basilica of the Virgin of Guadalupe in Mexico. In the Hindu tradition, Benares, India, serves as a favorite destination of tourists, and Buddhist stupas throughout Asia attract both religious and nonreligious travelers. In these auspicious religious places, pilgrims become tourists even as tourists fancy themselves as pilgrims. A cultural understanding of tourism, however, reveals that the appeal of religion as a desirable attraction for tourist visitors extends beyond the confusion between tourist and pilgrim. In fact, tourism as a modern cultural practice transforms religious places, rituals, artifacts, and people into objects for touristic consumption.

Cultural Relations between Religion and Tourism. Tourism amounts to a set of cultural practices aimed most often at aesthetically pleasing experiences of unfamiliar places and peoples. Tourists encounter cultural otherness by leaving their familiar surroundings, but touristic practices tend to domesticate unfamiliar places and novel experiences by making them into objects of consumption. In this regard, tourism exemplifies modernity; in particular, its conventions, habits, and discursive concerns rely on and respond to the forces of modern capitalism, especially in its emphasis on consumption, its tendency toward globalization, and its aesthetic proclivities. Put simply, tourists are practitioners of modernity. Moreover, tourism has become pervasive in modern life. Not only do modern people travel far more than ever before, but as some commentators insist, they are tourists most of the time, even in their own homes and communities. Indeed, touristic practices pervade the modern way of life.

On the other hand, tourists rank among the most maligned of modern subjects. In fact, derogating tourists is a part of being a tourist; Jonathan Culler (1981, p. 130) notes the somewhat ironic fact that tourists gain esteem by denying their status as a tourist; indeed, there is always someone else less adept in the arts of modern travel whom one can disparage as "tourist," elevating oneself as something better than a tourist. Consequently, maligning others conceals one's own touristic inclinations and practices, even as it makes one a better tourist.

Being a better tourist, then, involves having only a discreet engagement with touristic practices. At the most fundamental level, these practices rely on the technologies, networks, and discourses that constitute modern travel practices in general. Travel practices can be defined as any practice, discourse, or circumstance that either necessitates translocal movements or that generates a desire for travel and encourages people to travel; besides tourism, these practices also encompass migration, business and trade, military deployments, research excursions, family visitations, and many other forms of and motives for travel. The practices themselves involve various modes of transportation, most commonly airlines, trains, buses, and automobiles. They also include communication networks that facilitate travel, especially telecommunications and the Internet, but also television and radio broadcast media, newspapers and magazines, and other forms of mass communication. Other aspects of the modern practice of travel include banking networks that allow convenient and trustworthy currency exchange; accommodations for lodging and food services; and any other services or products that meet the needs and desires of modern travelers.

Besides modern infrastructures and services that make global travel possible, convenient, and comfortable, touristic practices participate in modern discourses that make travel desirable. Foremost among these is a discourse on experience. In fact, as a discursive category, experience serves tourism as an epistemological mode of knowing the world in a modern way. This includes equating authenticity with truth and interpreting experiences as meaningful by aestheticizing landscapes, cultures, events, cities, villages, and even entire societies. In fact, touristic discourse attributes aesthetic qualities to anything and everything that travelers might encounter. Indeed, tourists everywhere seek out and expect the most authentic and aesthetically pleasing experiences possible.

The emphasis on experience in touristic discourse aligns tourism with religion in the modern world. Robert Sharf (1998, p. 95) points out that theologians and scholars of religion invoke the category of experience in dealing with two peculiarly modern challenges to traditional religious authority: empiricism and cultural pluralism. Indeed, the claim of authentic religious experience forestalls critiques of religious authority on strictly objective, empirical grounds. At the same time, cross-cultural similarities of religious experiences lend a universal authority to the category of religion beyond the limited claims of particular religious traditions. In a similar fashion, touristic experiences, at once both authentic and aesthetic, confer validity, authority, and meaningfulness on the modern traveler.

As a modern practice, however, tourism submits these experiences to a thoroughgoing process of commodification. Every sight, sound, and taste; every locale and event; indeed every experience available to modern travelers becomes subject to a system of exchange that commodifies them in aesthetic terms for touristic consumption. Tourists are hyperconsumers of aestheticized culture, including religion. In fact, religious people themselves oftentimes adopt touristic practices to commodify their religion for touristic consumption. They do this not only for financial gain, but also to proselytize, and in many cases religious groups capitalize on touristic attention simply to present themselves and their religion publicly in the best possible light. For example, the Church of Jesus Christ of Latter-day Saints takes advantage of touristic interest at Temple Square in Salt Lake City to tell the Mormon story in heroic terms and to draw visitors into the church's missionary process. On the other hand, numerous churches in Europe pay for their upkeep and improvements by charging admission to visitors and by operating retail shops where tourists can purchase souvenirs and religious paraphernalia.

This process of commodification highlights the implications of the encounter between religion and tourism. Nearly all religious people in the world today must contend with the challenges that modernity presents to long-standing traditions, and tourists bring those challenges into the sacred spaces of the world's religions. By involving themselves in the touristic discourse on experience, both authentic and aesthetically pleasing, religious people conform to conventional assumptions about the role of religion in the modern world even as they assert the validity and power of their religious traditions and values in modern terms. At the same time, tourists experience religious life according to their own assumptions, expectations, and desires. Consequently, most tourists rarely appreciate the uniqueness and complexity of the religious practices and traditions they observe in their touristic travels. On the other hand, viewing tourism from the perspective of its spatial dimensions, understanding its historical origins, and regarding it as a cultural phenomenon of the modern world obviates a simple dichotomy between religion and tourism. Differentiating religious people and tourists in strictly oppositional terms becomes more difficult when considering the many dimensions of their relationship. Indeed, tourism and religion are not mutually exclusive, and in fact they often reside together in individuals who remain at once both tourists and religious adherents.

BIBLIOGRAPHY

Adler, Judith. "Origins of Sightseeing." In *Travel Culture: Essays on What Makes Us Go*, edited by Carol Traynor Williams, pp. 3–23. Westport, Conn., 1998. Adler discusses the historical shift in tourism in the modern Western world from an emphasis on texts to a focus on images and visuality.

Black, Jeremy. *The British Abroad: The Grand Tour in the Eighteenth Century.* New York, 1992. This is one of the most thorough historical studies of the European Grand Tour.

Bremer, Thomas S. *Blessed with Tourists: The Borderlands of Religion and Tourism in San Antonio*, Chapel Hill, N.C., 2004. This case study explores religion and tourism in San Antonio, Texas.

Brockman, Norbert C. *Encyclopedia of Sacred Places.* Santa Barbara, Calif., 1997. A compendium of places throughout the world regarded as sacred, all of which host tourist visitors.

Clifford, James. *Routes: Travel and Translation in the Late Twentieth Century.* Cambridge, Mass., 1997. An anthropologist's analysis of travel as a vehicle for modern understandings of culture.

Crick, Malcolm. "Representations of International Tourism in the Social Sciences: Sun, Sex, Sights, Savings, and Servility." *Annual Review of Anthropology* 18 (1989): 307–344. An examination of how social-scientific studies tend to represent international tourism.

Culler, Jonathan. "Semiotics of Tourism." *American Journal of Semiotics* 1, nos. 1–2 (1981): 127–140. This essay regards tourists as semioticians and offers a semiotic analysis of authenticity in touristic discourse.

Eco, Umberto. *Travels in Hyper Reality: Essays.* Translated by William Weaver. San Diego, Calif., 1986. Particularly in the title essay of this collection, Eco examines tourism from a semiotic perspective with attention to questions of authenticity and what he calls "the absolute fake."

Franklin, Adrian, and Mike Crang. "The Trouble with Tourism and Travel Theory?" *Tourist Studies* 1, no.1 (2001): 5–22. A brief overview of tourism as a subject of academic study; attempts to theorize about touristic phenomena.

Hibbert, Christopher. *The Grand Tour.* London, 1987. A historical study of the European Grand Tour.

Judd, Dennis R., and Susan S. Fainstein, eds. *The Tourist City.* New Haven, Conn., 1999. A collection of essays on urban tourism that draws attention to the ways that the tourist industry defines, organizes, and commodifies touristic experiences.

Kirshenblatt-Gimblett, Barbara. *Destination Culture: Tourism, Museums, and Heritage.* Berkeley, Calif., 1998. A cultural study of heritage tourism. Especially useful is the essay "Exhibiting Jews," which discusses representations of Jews and Judaism at world's fairs.

MacCannell, Dean. *The Tourist: A New Theory of the Leisure Class.* 3d ed. Berkeley, Calif., 1999. This is a classic sociological study of tourists and tourism from a structuralist perspective.

Sears, John F. *Sacred Places: American Tourist Attractions in the Nineteenth Century.* New York, 1989. A historical study of the emergence of American tourist destinations in the nineteenth century; Sears demonstrates the connection between tourism and American identity.

Sharf, Robert H. "Experience." In *Critical Terms for Religious Studies*, edited by Mark C. Taylor, pp. 94–116. Chicago, 1998. Sharf discusses the category of "experience" as it relates to religious practices and the academic study of religion.

Smith, Valene L., ed. *Hosts and Guests: The Anthropology of Tourism.* 2d ed. Philadelphia, 1989. A collection of anthropological essays on tourists and the people who inhabit tourist destinations.

Stowe, William W. *Going Abroad: European Travel in Nineteenth-Century American Culture.* Princeton, N.J., 1994. A historical and literary analysis of nineteenth-century American tourists in Europe and how their travels and travel writing contributed to personal and collective identities.

Urry, John. *The Tourist Gaze: Leisure and Travel in Contemporary Societies.* Newbury Park, Calif., 1990. A sociological study of tourism that applies a Foucauldian understanding of "gaze" to the social, historical, economic, and cultural implications of touristic practices.

Warneke, Sara. *Images of the Educational Traveller in Early Modern England.* New York, 1995. This book examines early modern English travels to the European continent for educational purposes; the conventions of educational travel served as a historical precedent for later practices of tourism.

THOMAS S. BREMER (2005)

TOWERS. Strictly speaking, a *tower* is any architectural structure that is high in proportion to its lateral dimensions. Broadening that definition, tower here will be understood to be any architectural structure whose religious meaning is related to its lofty vertical dimension. This entry will refer to this quality as vertical aspiration, which, while inexact, at least sets towers apart from merely massive structures. Towers have no single explanation but betray a variety of meanings that show clearly the ingenious fertility of the religious imagination and offer a challenge to the interpreter, especially in cases where there is a paucity of written sources. Their meanings are not fixed but can change over time.

The Egyptian pyramid, one of the earliest examples of tower building, is essentially a funerary monument used to inter and glorify deceased pharaohs, yet the pyramid is not simply a gigantic tombstone. Because of the divinization of the ruler, it is also a structure that houses a sacred presence. The obelisk, originally a monument to the sun god Re, later became a popular architectural feature in Europe and North America. The ziggurat of ancient Mesopotamia was a multistoried structure surmounted by a temple, where gods were worshipped, annual rites were performed, and the authority of the ruler was confirmed; it was a place of communication between upper and lower worlds.

The Zarathushtrian *dokhma*, often translated as "tower of silence," has an entirely different meaning. These towers are twenty- to thirty-foot cylindrical funerary structures that continue to be used in the twenty-first century by the small Parsi population of South Asia and Iran (e.g., Mumbai, ancient Yazd). Because earth, fire, and water are sacred and because the more common means of disposing of the dead (burial, cremation, interment) would pollute these elements, bodies of the deceased are placed over grates at the summit of the tower, through which body fluids and rain can pass until the vultures and sun leave nothing but bones. The towers therefore prevent pollution of the sacred elements, thus protecting the living and also becoming passageways for the dead from this life to eternity.

STUPA AND PAGODA. The basic form of the Buddhist stupa was a hemispherical earthbound dome built to house the sacred relics of the Buddha or his disciples and to be the focus of ritual circumambulation or meditation by devotees. The group at Sāñcī in central India remains the best surviving example of this genre. Although stupas were not conceptually towers in their original form, reliefs on Indian Buddhist buildings already depict the stupa in the second to third centuries CE with a vertical character. Early stupas in Nepal, such as that of Carumati, show a towerlike elongation of the *harmikā* (the finial above the dome of the stupa). Generally the vertical elongation took place as the stupa form crossed central Asia, and by the time it entered China in the later Han dynasty (25–220 CE) it had become a true tower.

The Chinese Buddhist pagoda represents a culmination of this development, becoming a multistoried building that ascended at times to dizzying heights, as does the Fogong monastery pagoda at Yingxian, built in 1056. At 550 feet it is still the tallest wooden structure in the world. Since earlier Chinese architecture was horizontal in character, with rare examples of multistory buildings, the pagoda suggests an aspiration for transcendence not found previously. Yet in its original meaning the lofty pagoda signifies the same as its architectural opposite, the earthbound stupa. It is a structure built to house and honor the relics of the Buddha. At the same time it acquired a wealth of new meanings over a long history in China and elsewhere in East Asia. Built to house the living presence of deity in the form of the Buddha's remains, it was at first the principal worship space in early Chinese Buddhist architecture. The Yongning Temple at Loyang, built in 516 CE, for example, had the pagoda sited at the center of the temple complex. Later the pagoda shared its centrality on the main axis of a monastic or temple compound with the Great Buddha hall just behind it. As time passed the Buddha hall became the main place of worship, and the pagoda declined in importance and came to be situated outside and behind the monastic or temple complex. Ritual circumambulation of the stupa was replaced by circumambulation of the Buddha image.

The pagoda acquired other meanings, becoming an imposing sign of Buddhist presence in China, a demonstration of the merit of the emperors and wealthy patrons who were able to fund such a project, a "guiding tower" to lead pilgrims toward their destination, and a funerary structure built to house the ashes of cremated monks. Finally, the pagoda was fully "domesticated" as a familiar element in the Chinese landscape, a site for popular rituals and a protective element in the complex system of fengshui (geomancy) that sought to balance *qi* (vital energy) that flowed in patterns across the surface of the earth. Yet older meanings were rarely lost. At the pagoda of the Temple of the Buddha's Tooth outside Beijing, post-Communist crowds still come as pilgrims, kowtowing as they ascend the steps to revere the sacred relic and worship the Buddha.

ŚIKHARA. By the fifth century CE the Indian Śilpa Sāstra texts had formally designated the tower or *śikhara* as the most prominent architectural statement for the Hindu temple (i.e., *vimāna,* that which is "well measured") and the crowning achievement for the idea of *pratibimba* (the creation of divine regions). The *śikhara* served at least three functions: as denoting generally sacred space, as a sacred mountain that denotes the dwelling place of the deity, and as a vehicle that carries the deity into the presence of the people and the people into the presence of the deity. The Śilpa Sāstra texts also suggest that those who build temples will not only be prosperous and have peaceful reigns but will have sons to succeed them and care for the funerary rites. Thus the reigning dynasties had great incentives to build these towering temples to the gods.

The Hindu temple as a whole became the architectural form of the *vāstupuruṣa maṇḍala,* the locus where the divine being (*puruṣa*) dwells. It is almost always built on an east-west axis, with the entrance from the east and the tower above the western end. Underneath the tower is the inner sanctum, the *garbagṛha,* the dwelling place of the deity. Along the roof of the *vimāna* from entrance to *śikhara* are gradually ascending towers that imitate the sacred Himalayas, the ultimate dwelling place of the gods and goddesses on earth. Surmounting the *śikhara* on all temples is a *kalaśa,* or water pot, signifying the eternal bathing (*abhiseka*) of the tower by the holy waters of the Ganges River. In the northern- or *nāgara*-style the temple tower is convex, with an *āmalaka* or fruit of the Indian gooseberry (*Emlica officinalis*) immediately below the *kalaśa.* The southern- or Dravida-style tower is concave and has a small stupa (*stūpīka*) below the *kalaśa* symbolizing the cosmic dome over the dwelling of the deity.

Most temples were constructed as places where *brahman* priests could perform *pūja,* ritual worship on behalf of the king and his realm, reminding the people of the king's power and divine right to rule. Temples thus became centers of political, social, and cultural as well as religious activities. As the towers became higher in both North and South India, this sense of dominance was enhanced. The architectural climax of this movement is evident in the Bṛhadeśvara temple of the early eleventh century CE Cōḻa king, Rājarāja, of Thanjavur in South India. Towering 210 feet above the base of the temple, the *śikhara* is as high as the technology of the period would allow, and it remains the tallest temple tower in all of India. The eighty-ton *stūpīka* that crowns the *śikhara* is the largest single stone employed by Indian architecture on any temple tower.

Following the Cōḻa period the temple tower that marked the holy of holies began to lose its vertical dominance in the south, whereas the *goparam,* or gateway to the temple precincts, achieved ascendancy. By the sixteenth and seventeenth centuries, at the temple cities of Śrīraṅgam and Madurai, the gateways reached as much as fourteen stories into the sky and could be seen for miles around as one approached the city. Here both resident and visitor entered the sacred precincts and were at the same time reminded of the king's power to protect his people. As many of the *śikharas* had done in earlier times, these towers assumed a didactic function, visualizing in hundreds of sculpted images various mythic narratives of the lives of the gods for the mostly nonliterate population.

The Indian temple *śikhara* as mountain–sacred city exhibits its most extravagant forms and highest ornamentation in the Hindu temple complexes of the Khmers of Cambodia (e.g., Angkor Wat) and the Buddhist temple tower complex at Borobudur in Java. The latter combines the stupa idea with Hindu *śikhara* towers in imitation of the holy mountain range of the Himalayas with Mount Meru as the center peak. At Borobudur pilgrims are guided through a ritual of ascension from the lower and outer precincts until they reach the central stupa representing Mount Meru, the culmination of their journey.

CHRISTIAN CHURCHES. The architecture of the Christian churches provides the principal example of towers in Europe, and their development is a revealing history in stone. In the earliest pre-architectural stage, the *ecclesia* was simply the gathering of believers in crypts or private homes. In the post-Constantinian period Christians adopted the Roman basilica, a secular and civic building, as a place for worship. Two developments followed, both containing the seeds for the vertical development that occurred in the following centuries. The central domed structure of Byzantine classical style that developed from the circular plan of the martyrium and baptistery gained height and size, resulting in an interior space that was homologized to the universe of time and space. Standing firmly on the earth in the present, the worshiper could look upward at the dome of the church as a symbol of the heaven to come. The iconography of Christ, the Virgin, and saints, often portrayed against a background of gold mosaic, enhanced this impression. The Romanesque church of western Europe, a development of the basilica form into a cruciform plan, showed the first high vaulting and spires, then developed into the Gothic style, the epitome of vertical aspiration. Without drawing out the distinctions between spire, steeple, belfry, and bell tower, it is clear that from the twelfth century on architects strove for luminosity, lightness, and majestic height in their cathedrals.

The French Gothic cathedrals of Chartres, Reims, and Amiens seem to push the vertical aspiration to its material and architectural limit. Whether as the domed eastern style or the lofty vaulted western style, the change in meaning is clear. From a gathering of people in an ordinary secular structure, believers took their place in an increasingly hierarchically demarcated church building: the bishop's throne, the apse for the clergy, the communion railing separating lay from religious. Jesus became a lordly king; Mary, his mother, became a grand queen of both worlds. The upper stories of the towering churches carried worshipers in spirit to this higher realm. At the same time these "towers" marked the earthly splendor of the dwelling place of the divine presence and the place where God was most fittingly worshiped.

The churches acquired a host of other meanings. Not only did they house divinity, they were images of divinity as the body of Christ crucified. Many, such as Westminster Abbey in London, served funerary purposes as crypts for the royalty, nobility, and high clergy, whose funds had built, supported, and maintained the churches. They were the sites of colorful pageantry and elaborate ritual, where the secular and sacred often mixed indistinguishably. They housed the relics of the saints; hermits attached themselves to certain churches like barnacles to anchors; and pilgrims flocked to them seeking miracles, sometimes creating new meanings and discomfiting ecclesiastical authorities. These churches also became symbols of civic pride, with cities vying with other cities to have the largest, highest, or most costly cathedral. All of these factors, together with many others, must be considered if one wishes to interpret the meaning of Christian churches.

Minar. In Islam the *minar* towers over the landscape as a reminder of the obligation of Muslims to pray five times a day in conformity with the second pillar (prayer) of the religion. Traditionally the muezzin or prayer caller would climb the *minar* at the prescribed times, projecting his voice over village or city to remind Muslims of their duty to pray. *Minars* also mark off a significant ritual space for worshipers, as *minars* are most often positioned at the four corners of the mosque where Muslims come to pray, at least once a week on Fridays, and where they may gather periodically for other important social occasions.

Minars normally stand as slender towers (thus the French *minarette*) rising above the domed mosques, though in parts of Asia the *minars* took on enormous proportions, as, for example, at the Emin mosque in Turpan in China, where the tower, like a huge inverted ice cream cone, dwarfs its companion mosque. At least once in Islamic history the *minar* symbolism was changed into a blatant expression of political and military power. Q'tub-ud-din, the twelfth-century central Asiatic conqueror of India, built the original Q'tub *minar* some 238 feet high as a symbol of his victory over North India. It remains the tallest *minar* in the Islamic world.

Mesoamerican Structures. Though tall, narrow structures are rare in pre-Columbian Mesoamerica (the multistoried palace at Palenque is the outstanding exception), the abundant pyramidal temples of that region are suitably construed as towers. Often inaccurately contrasted with the Egyptian pyramids as architecture for the living instead of for the dead, the comparison is not exact, for many of the Mesoamerican structures, such as the Temple of Inscriptions at Palenque, had burial chambers within them. Imitating mountains and generally conforming to the Eliadean paradigm of the *axis mundi,* they were considered to mark the center of the earth, the site of creation, and could be described as places where the three worlds were connected. The pyramids were often linked with nearby cenotes (sacred wells), their contrasting meanings of upper- and underworld mutually reinforcing one another.

The Temple of the Sun at Teotihuacán was considered a mountain where celestial gods, terrestrial deities of fertility and plenty, and underworld beings met. The temple, and the entire city around it, was oriented to the place where the setting sun on the summer solstice touched the horizon. The great pyramid of Cholula was built over a spring (underworld), and its iconography, including the feathered serpent motif, indicate that it was a place of communication between the lower and upper worlds, the worlds of humans and the gods. The Castillo pyramid at Chichén Itzá, with its famous descending serpent, is the best-known expression of this motif and a veritable compendium of cosmic, astral, and calendrical correlations; at the same site the Caracol, a circular pillbox rather than pyramidal configuration, provides a similarly prominent variation on the tower theme. Tenochtitlán of the Aztecs had its Templo Major, the twin pyramid sites for worship of the god of war, Huitzilopochtli, and the god of rain, Tlaloc, referring to mountains in the mythic history of the Aztecs. The pyramids of Mayan Tikal in the Peten area are the most vertical in feeling, with sharply inclined steps leading to a temple platform. The temple in turn was surmounted by a *cresteria* (comb) rising high above the back wall of the temple, adding to the impression of height. The priests would have performed rites of worship with the people watching from far below.

The Mesoamerican pyramids show cosmic orientation and astronomical and calendrical correlations and are generally built in layered levels, manifesting a stratification expressive of the hierarchical societies that produced them. Besides being sites to worship the gods, the pyramids offered a ritual stage to carry out rites of warfare and human sacrifice and to dramatize the coronations that established sovereignty and claimed divine authority and purified and renewed the community. As with church architecture, their forms are quite similar from place to place, while their meaning has changed from one historical period and culture (e.g., Toltec, Maya, Aztec) to another.

Modern Towers. The U.S. Capitol and the Washington Monument obelisk in Washington, D.C., stand as symbols of American civic religion. The Capitol was planned as the center of the city, and it manifests the same spatial metaphors as the Byzantine church, with its dome showing the first president in the heavenly realms and a crypt below the rotunda floor originally intended for his burial. The Washington Monument's towering height, together with its mysterious and nontextual character, has captured the central place in the popular American imagination. It stands in the middle of the city's ritual core, with the Capitol, the White House, and the Lincoln and Jefferson Memorials cardinally placed on its four sides.

Perhaps it is the skyscraper, more than any other building, that symbolizes the city since the nineteenth century. And while lacking sacrality, skyscrapers are not without symbolic power. When the Twin Towers of the World Trade Center in New York were destroyed on September 11, 2001, the terrorists were attacking a symbol of U.S. financial dominance. But subsequent events have cast a religious aura over the site, making it into a place of martyrdom and heroic self-sacrifice, a shrine to the mythical best qualities in the American spirit. Public and private rituals, the placing of flowers, a lone flag flying over the debris, notes, names, and other signs of grief all transformed the site almost immediately into a shrine. Though some events were orchestrated public expressions of grief, most of the actions enacted there were spontaneous. The changed significance of the site is a clear example of the mutability of meaning noted in towers everywhere. No architectural meaning is final. A purely secular building may become a sacred one, and the rituals that have and will be performed at the site will influence the reception of whatever structure succeeds the former monument to financial power.

SEE ALSO Architecture; Axis Mundi; Basilica, Cathedral, and Church; Mountains; Pyramids, overview article; Sacred Space; Stupa Worship; Temple; Tombs.

BIBLIOGRAPHY

Bloom, Jonathan. *Minaret: Symbol of Islam.* Oxford, U.K., 1989.

Carrasco, Davíd, Lindsay Jones, and Scott Sessions, eds. *Mesoamerica's Classic Heritage: From Teotihuacan to the Aztecs.* Boulder, Colo., 2000.

Eliade, Mircea. *Images and Symbols: Studies in Religious Symbolism.* Translated by Philip Mairet. New York, 1961.

Gendrop, Paul, and Doris Heyden. *Pre-Columbian Architecture of Mesoamerica.* Translated by Judith Stanton. New York, 1974.

Giedion, Sigfried. *The Eternal Present: A Contribution on Constancy and Change,* vol. 2: *The Beginnings of Architecture.* Washington, D.C., 1964.

Harle, J. C. *The Art and Architecture of the Indian Subcontinent.* 2d ed. New Haven, Conn., 1994.

Kramrisch, Stella. *The Hindu Temple.* Calcutta, 1946.

Prache, Anne. *Cathedrals of Europe.* Ithaca, N.Y., 2000.

Rowland, Benjamin. *The Art and Architecture of India: Buddhist, Hindu, Jain.* 3d rev. ed. Baltimore, Md., 1967.

Wu, Nelson I. *Chinese and Indian Architecture: The City of Man, the Mountain of God, and the Realm of the Immortals.* New York, 1963.

Xinian Fu, Daiheng Guo, Xujie Liu, Guxi Pan, Yun Qiao, and Dazhang Sun. *Chinese Architecture.* Edited by Nancy S. Steinhardt. New Haven, Conn., 2002.

JEFFREY F. MEYER (2005)
J. DANIEL WHITE (2005)

TRADITION. The word *tradition* comes from the Latin noun *traditio* (handing over), which derives from the verb *tradere* (hand over, deliver). *Traditio* corresponds closely to the Greek *paradosis,* which also comes from a verb *(paradidomi)* meaning "hand over." *Traditio* and *paradosis* can be used literally or figuratively, in the latter case often to mean "teaching" or "instruction." *Traditio* and *paradosis* were commonly used in this sense by Latin and Greek Christian theologians to denote the body of teachings preserved and handed down by the church as "the Catholic faith." In the modern study of religion, however, a broader and more differentiated concept of tradition must be employed.

THE CONCEPT OF TRADITION. Culture depends on teaching and learning, and teaching and learning presuppose a tradition. The concept of tradition thus applies to all fields of culture, including science, arts and letters, education, law, politics, and religion.

A belief or practice in any field of culture may be said to be a tradition to the extent that it is received from the hands, lips, or the example of others rather than being discovered or invented; that it is received on the assumption that the authors and transmitters are reliable and therefore the tradition valid; and that it is received with the express command and conscious intention of further transmission without substantial change. Hence, as a source of knowledge, tradition is to be distinguished from rumor and fashion. Rumor and fashion, although received from others, are not necessarily assumed to be reliable or to merit transmission without alteration; on the contrary, they invite speculation and elaboration. Tradition, purporting to embody a fixed truth from an authoritative source, demands faithfulness and obedience.

Established traditions command respect because of their relative antiquity and the presumed trustworthiness of their authors and transmitters. Sacred traditions provide a link between the origin and destiny of things. The ancient Greek poet and prophet Hesiod in his *Theogony* says that the Muses, the daughters of Zeus, "inspired me with a divine voice to tell of the things that are to come and the things that were before" (ll. 31–32). Similarly, the sacred traditions of all religions offer access to beginnings and insight into endings that personal experience and unaided reason cannot supply.

Sacred traditions sometimes tell of a golden age in the past. They preserve glimmers of the glorious age and establish beliefs, practices, and institutions to help people cope with the "iron age" of the present. At other times, traditions anticipate the attainment of a glorious future age, which they portray in prophecies. And sacred traditions often address past and future together. In all three cases, a view of time as something that can be recapitulated, or at least held in synoptic vision long enough to lend perspective on the present, underlies the concept of sacred tradition. The work of seizing time through myth or prophecy explains the critical importance of memory in religious traditions. Memory defies time and change. "Remember!" is the first commandment of tradition.

The second commandment is "Trust!" which in practice means "Obey!" Obedience to authorities who are deemed trustworthy is indispensable to the working of tradition because tradition is by definition something received from others. Within the community of tradition, obedience is validated by the benefits a person derives, or expects to derive, from following the tradition. From the outside, however, and especially from a modern critical perspective, the obedience tradition requires (and inspires) may appear to be confining, even oppressive. The discussion of tradition in the modern study of religion has been much affected by this clash of perspectives.

The concept of tradition in religion may be applied to the means by which norms of belief and practice are handed down (e.g., bards, books, chains of teachers, institutions) or to the norms themselves. This article is concerned with the norms, whereas the word *transmission* refers to the means by which traditional norms are handed down. The distinction between tradition and transmission is not absolute, however. Religions typically resist it, especially if it is used to justify attempts to abstract the supposed essence of a religion from its historic vehicles and forms of expression. Because tradition is by definition an indirect source of knowledge, the forms in which traditional knowledge is transmitted cannot be cast away without risking loss of content, because the content is not accessible or verifiable from contemporary sources. To the extent that it is immediately accessible, it ceases to be traditional in the strict sense of the word.

A sense of tradition as normative is a basic element in all religious systems, whether or not formal concepts of tradition exist. When formal concepts appear, they may be broad or specialized, depending on their function in the system and the degree of differentiation among the sources of religious belief and practice. Often the sense of tradition as normative is expressed by a broad collective reference to authoritative teachers or compendia: "the fathers," "the elders," "the sages," "the poets." An evolution from broad to specialized concepts can sometimes be discerned. In early Catholic Christianity, for example, the concept of tradition embraced all the formal sources of belief and practice handed down by the church, including the Holy Scriptures. Only much later, and only in the Western as distinct from the Eastern church, did "tradition" come to signify the extrabiblical (ecclesiastical) sources in particular, at which point the "problem" of scripture and tradition could arise. In Sunnī Islam, by contrast, the formal concept of tradition, the *sunnah* (custom, example) of the Prophet, became more specialized as a result of the formation of a closed collection of traditions—the six books of *ḥadīths*, or stories of the Prophet, compiled in the third and fourth centuries AH (ninth and tenth centuries CE) and eventually accepted as authoritative throughout Sunnī Islam.

Even more specialized cases are presented by two words meaning "tradition" in Judaism, *Masora* and *Qabbalah,* which come from verbs meaning "hand down" and "receive," respectively. The verbs are used at the beginning of the early rabbinic *Ethics of the Fathers* (*Avot* 1.1) with reference to the handing down of the Torah from God to Moses, Moses to Joshua, Joshua to the elders, and so on. However, the nouns Masora and Qabbalah eventually came to be used not for tradition in the comprehensive sense but for specialized traditions: Masora for the exegetical traditions governing the transmission of the Hebrew text of the Holy Scriptures (hence "Masoretic text" for the canonical version of the Hebrew Bible), Qabbalah for the mystical and esoteric traditions of Judaism. The function of specialized concepts is to sharpen the definition of tradition in selected areas, not to diminish the scope of tradition as a comprehensive norm. In religions with highly specialized concepts of tradition, much that is traditional falls outside the formal concepts without being any less traditional for that reason.

In addition to occurring in the practice of religion, the concept of tradition appears also in the modern study of religion, where it is used descriptively rather than normatively and often rather loosely. Sometimes the word is little more than a synonym for the name of a religion, as when "Islamic tradition" simply denotes "Islam." This way of speaking may be questioned to the extent that it singles out traditionality as the most basic characteristic of a religion.

More problematic in relation to normative concepts of tradition is the pluralism reflected in some uses of the descriptive concept, as when "Chinese tradition" is applied collectively to the several religious systems of China or "Christian tradition" is used to group together conflicting normative versions of Christianity (Orthodox, Catholic, Lutheran, and so on). In some cases the modern descriptive concept of tradition fosters research into what might be called "deep tradition"—cultural patterns and values so basic to a civilization that they are not formally stated in the classical tradition and may not even be clearly recognized by the bearers of the tradition. The concern of some modern scholars of India with the problem of defining the "Indianness" of India—the deposit of culture underlying the many different normative traditions of India—is a case in point. In this case the notion of "Indian tradition" hypothesizes a unity that remains to be found and described. Such unities are difficult to define and are rejected by many scholars as mystifications meriting no more credence than "the Russian soul," "the Oriental mind," or other cultural stereotypes. Nevertheless, the presentiment of continuity in the world's great civilizations is powerful enough to motivate continuing research on "deep tradition."

TYPES OF TRADITIONS. Traditions may be verbal or nonverbal. Nonverbal traditions include traditional artifacts (e.g., icons, monuments, symbolic objects), sites, designs, gestures, postures, customs, and institutions. Nonverbal traditions cannot exist in isolation from verbal traditions, for the latter are needed to interpret them. However, nonverbal traditions possess a measure of autonomy in relation to verbal traditions because verbal interpretations can never completely penetrate the "thickness" of traditional objects or, in the case of religious objects, their presumed sacrality. Far from being dependent on specific verbal interpretations, nonverbal traditions typically host multiple or successive interpretations without losing their identity or traditional status. The persistence of nonverbal traditions in relative autonomy over against the interpretations attached to them is a good example of traditionality: the ascription of value to something by virtue of the fact that it has been handed down from early times on good authority.

Oral and written tradition. Verbal traditions may be oral or written. Although the distinction pertains first of all to the means of transmission rather than to tradition, the substance of traditions is affected by the differences between oral and written transmission.

First, the forms of expression used in traditions are dictated in part by the means available. Some forms, such as hymns, proverbs, riddles, and folk tales, are essentially oral. They may be written down, but writing does not open the way to a fuller realization of the form. Other forms, such as chronicles, law codes, and commentaries, depend on writing or are fully realized only in writing. Some of the most important forms of expression used in traditions, such as mythology and epic poetry, may reach a high level of development in either mode.

Second, oral tradition is a much older phenomenon than written tradition and precedes it in the formative period of traditions, even after the invention of writing. This fact suggests that written traditions themselves are shaped in part by oral traditions. In many literate religious traditions, for example, scriptural and pedagogical titles recall and even purport to re-create an oral system of communication. Thus, *Qur'ān* means "recitation." The title of the first book of rabbinic law, *Mishnah,* comes from a verb meaning "repeat" and refers to pedagogy based on oral recitation. *Upaniṣad,* a name for books of philosophical and esoteric teaching in Vedic tradition, comes from Sanskrit words meaning "sit down before [a teacher]." An accomplished monk in early Buddhism was called a *bahusuta,* "one who has heard much." The Greek word *euangelion,* "gospel" or "good news," means news in the literal sense of something proclaimed aloud in the hearing of the general public.

Third, oral tradition exists mainly in performance, while written tradition exists also in objective form apart from its applications. The relative independence of written texts stimulates the development of intellectuality and greatly increases the possibilities of dissemination in a fixed form. At the same time, writing involves significant dangers for a tradition. When a tradition is put into writing, its inconsistencies become more evident. It may not be an exaggeration to say that the quickened intellectuality that accompanies written traditions arises first of all from the need to address the inconsistencies that the writing down of a tradition exposes. Also, the independence of written texts opens the way to the use of traditional materials in ways not intended by traditional authorities, ways that are remote from the "living word" actualized in pedagogy and cult. To be sure, a written tradition is not further removed from the living word than an oral tradition insofar as the latter is understood as a tradition in the strict sense. Tradition, oral or written, is the word handed down by others—the vehicle of the living word but not the living word itself. Nevertheless, the organic connection of oral tradition with performance guarantees the close proximity of tradition to the living word, whereas in the case of written tradition the connection is not as direct and greater pains must be taken to regulate the use of traditions.

Many moral and religious teachers have felt anxiety about writing. In the *Phaedrus,* for example, Plato has Socrates tell a story about a wise Egyptian king who, in reply to the god who offered the Egyptians the gift of writing as "a drug to produce memory and wisdom," observed that the invention was more likely to produce just the opposite, because those who came to depend on it would tend to seek wisdom in an external source rather than having to look within their own souls, and so they would "seem wise without being wise" (*Phaedrus* 274c–275).

Fourth, oral and written traditions coexist and influence each other even after many authoritative sources of tradition have been committed to writing. Oral tradition is not a stage that is outgrown with the arrival of written tradition. Even after it has been replaced by writing as the chief means of transmission, oral tradition continues to thrive in the form of customs, folklore, popular preaching, storytelling, esoteric speculation, practical applications of religion to everyday life, and other manifestations of traditional mentality. The text of the *Book of Exodus* was well established by ʿAqivaʾ ben Yosef's day, but that did not prevent the rabbi and his colleagues from arguing about the number and size of the frogs sent against Egypt in the famous plague (B.T., *San.* 67b). People love to talk, and talk preserves and extends itself by means of oral tradition. Sometimes oral tradition even generates new bodies of written tradition, as in the case of the oral Torah canonized in the rabbinic law codes, the Mishnah and the Talmud.

The importance of oral tradition in the history of traditions has been widely recognized in the modern study of religion. In particular, the concept of oral tradition has been used by scholars seeking to reconstruct the origins and early history of religious traditions. Unfortunately, the methodological problems of applying the concept of oral tradition are severe. Except for the data supplied by modern anthropologists and ethnographers from direct observation, the evidence for oral tradition must be extracted from written sources. Scholarly opinion thus divides along a spectrum running from skepticism about the possibility of ever isolating the original oral layer of a written tradition to more confident approaches based on literary and rhetorical analysis and the selective application of archaeological evidence.

Scripture and tradition. Many classical religious systems make a formal distinction between scripture and tradition. *Scripture* refers to divinely revealed texts; *tradition* refers to revelation mediated by human teachers. The distinction tends to be clear enough in practice. Thus Catholic Christians have no trouble distinguishing between the New Testament writings and the creeds and canons of the church councils; Muslims do not confuse the *sunnah* of the Prophet with the Qurʾān delivered by him. Yet the distinction between scripture and tradition is a difficult one to make in theory. It does not turn on the difference between divine revelation and human teaching, for in most religions authoritative tradition is reverenced almost as much as scripture as a conduit of revelation. Furthermore, the theoretical priority of scripture over tradition rarely translates into a higher degree of binding force in practice.

To some extent the distinction between scripture and tradition reflects the history of canonization in a religion. When a canon of scripture is definitively closed, authoritative teaching accruing thereafter is "tradition." Even so, the relationship must not be construed as a mere serial progression, least of all as a purely exegetical relationship, as if tradition were in essence commentary on a body of scripture that antedates it. Traditions often manifest a significant degree of independence from scripture for a variety of reasons: their origin in a time prior to the canonization of scripture, the diversity of sources embodied in tradition as opposed to the more restricted sources constituting a written canon, and the reference of tradition to basic religious functions not adequately treated by scripture, such as liturgy or law.

Beyond providing a source of religious authority in addition to scripture, tradition plays an indispensable role in the appropriation of scriptural sources. Scripture cannot be used if it cannot be interpreted, and every use (liturgical, legal, theological) implies an interpretation. Interpretation, however, requires a framework and accepted rules of discourse that scripture by itself cannot supply. They are supplied by tradition. Thus there arises a practical dependence of scripture on tradition. Dependence need not imply diminished regard for the authority of scripture. While the critical historian might view a hermeneutical tradition as a device for overcoming the piecemeal character or obscurity of scripture, the pious mind will regard it as the only conceivable means by which to gain access to the vast and awe-inspiring contents of divine revelation—the means established by divine authority as opposed to human ingenuity. In the eyes of piety there is no contradiction between an appreciation of the grandeur and sufficiency of scripture and a recognition of the crucial role of interpretation. The aim of interpretation is not to threaten but to preserve and protect scriptural revelation: "Tradition [Masora] is a fence to the Torah" (*Avot* 3.14).

Nevertheless, conflicts between scripture and tradition are bound to arise because of differences in provenance, time of origin, and ideological tendency. In every religion with a body of scripture, there will be traditions lacking scriptural warrant or even contradicting the plain sense of scripture, and there will be beliefs and practices mandated by scripture with no living function in the tradition. While exegetical ingenuity can go a long way toward resolving these conflicts, the problem of scripture and tradition cannot be settled by exegesis alone. From the outset, a conciliatory assumption of harmony between scripture and tradition must be made to support the work of exegesis and interpretation; otherwise the situation of the interpreter would be impossible, for scripture and tradition always diverge enough to make reconciliation impossible without the antecedent assumption of an ultimate harmony. This assumption is itself a *traditum,* a thing handed down and explicitly confessed by religious traditions with respect to their scriptures. The determination to affirm the harmony of scripture and tradition suggests that scripture has a significance that goes beyond its substantive contents, namely as an object of traditional loyalty, a badge of affiliation, and a symbol of continuity.

The role of the Vedic scriptures in Hinduism affords a good example. The Vedas were for a long time not scripture in the strict sense of the word because they were transmitted orally, but they played a quasi-scriptural role long before being committed to writing. In scriptural form they enjoy theoretical priority over the books of tradition (*smṛti*; literally, "remembered") that were produced later. A wide gulf separates the religion of the Vedas from that of later Hindu tradition. The Vedas present a religion of animal sacrifice and of meat-eating, intoxicant-drinking priests; a worldview that knows nothing of the cycle of rebirth (*saṃsāra*) and little of the theory of action (*karman*); a cult without temple worship; and a pantheon in which many of the most popular gods and heroes of later Hinduism play little or no role. Nevertheless the books of *smṛti* consistently avow loyalty to the Vedas, and conciliatory explanations of departures from Vedic ways are offered. As Louis Renou put it, "The Veda is precisely the sign, perhaps the only one, of Indian orthodoxy" (Renou, 1960, vol. 6, pp. 2–3). In the religious history of India a crucial line of division separates the continuators of Vedic tradition from groups, such as the Jains and Buddhists, who broke with the tradition in principle. Among the continuators a community of tradition existed, despite many differences of doctrine and practice. Between the continuators and the others there was not a community of tradition, despite many historical and cultural affinities.

Tradition and Religious Originators. For a number of reasons the consciousness of standing in a sacred tradition is a typical feature of the outlook of originating figures in the history of religion. First, bearers of a new prophecy, revised values, or new loyalties must address their audience in terms the latter understands. The terms have to be drawn from a shared tradition. A classic example is in the *Book of Exodus* in the connection the prophet Moses proclaims between the God Yahveh, whose name he is commanded to reveal to the Israelite slaves, and "the God of your fathers, the God of Abraham, the God of Isaac, and the God of Jacob," that is to say the God or gods of ancient tradition (*Ex.* 3:13–15; cf. *Ex.* 6:2–3).

Second, religious originators must be able to reflect upon their own experiences. Affording a means of achieving distance from the immediate present, tradition provides a framework for interrogation, interlocution, interpretation, and evaluation, without which reflection would be impossible. For example, early in his prophetic ministry Muḥammad experienced visions that he later came to regard as encounters with the archangel Gabriel, the figure thereafter identified by Muslims as the agent of Qurʾanic revelation. Scholars have pointed out, however, that the only reference to Gabriel as a revealer in the Qurʾān occurs in a late *Medinan sūrah* (2:97–98) and that the descriptions of visions in earlier *sūrahs* (53:1–18, 81:15–25) are vague about the identity of the being Muḥammad encountered. In other words, it appears that an angelological tradition, not invented by Muḥammad but accepted by him at some point, served the Prophet (and later Islam) as a way of understanding his early experiences.

Third, the consciousness of standing in a sacred tradition supports religious originators who break with the sacred traditions of their contemporaries and coreligionists. The originator's sense of tradition makes the break bearable and keeps it from being episodic or nihilistic. So, for example, the Apostle Paul, preaching a break with the Jewish law on the basis of faith in the gospel of Jesus Christ, was greatly aided by his conviction that he represented a tradition of faith authenticated by the law itself in its testimonies concerning Abraham (*Rom.* 3–4; *Gal.* 3–4).

The complexity of the relationship of religious originators to tradition can be seen in Jesus' confrontation with Jewish tradition as presented in the Synoptic Gospels. That presentation has decisively shaped the way the problem of tradition and innovation has been understood in the history of Christianity and even in modern scholarship. The German sociologist Max Weber (1864–1920), in his famous discussion of charismatic leadership, was thinking of the rhetorical dichotomies of Jesus when he wrote, "From a substantive point of view, every charismatic authority would have to subscribe to the proposition, 'It is written . . . but I say unto you,'" and when he wrote, "Hence, in a revolutionary and sovereign manner, charismatic domination transforms all values and breaks all traditional and rational norms: 'It has been written . . . but *I* say unto you'" (Weber, 1978, vol. 1, p. 243, vol. 2, p. 1115; cf. *Mt.* 5:21—48). Actually, in *Matthew,* Jesus does not say "It is written" but "You have heard that it was said to the men of old," but he then proceeds to quote from the Torah. Thus the confrontation is indeed between a written law and a living master. Jesus is also shown in the Synoptic Gospels to be sovereign over the sacred oral tradition claimed by the Pharisees, as when he reproached them saying, "You leave the commandment of God, and hold fast the tradition of men" (*Mk.* 7:8; cf. *Mt.* 15:1–9).

Nevertheless, Jesus' relation to Jewish tradition is misconstrued if one assumes that at bottom it was dichotomous. Throughout the Gospels, including the passages cited above, there is much evidence of continuity: "Think not that I have come to abolish the law and the prophets; I have come not to abolish them but to fulfill them" (*Mt.* 5:17). The theme of continuity has often been muted by the anti-Judaic tendencies of much historical Christianity, including nineteenth- and twentieth-century liberal theology, which made a sharp distinction between the "legalistic" religion of the Jews and the "spiritual" religion of Jesus. Weber's discussion of charisma also tends to emphasize the break with tradition in the work of Jesus, as well as that of other prophets, military heroes, and messianic figures. Weber's emphasis is justifiable given his aims, namely the clarification of pure ("ideal") types. Abstractly considered, a charismatic leader always stands against tradition. He or she offers his or her followers something new and lays claim to a highly personal kind of authority, whereas "authority will be called traditional if legitimacy is claimed for it and believed in by virtue of the sanctity of age-old rules and powers" (Weber, 1978, vol. 1, p. 226). In historical reality, however, charismatic leaders always possess notions of tradition that play a crucial role in their own thinking and in their relationships with followers and with the general public. Thus Jesus, in the ostensibly anti-Mosaic teachings of *Matthew* 5 (e.g., vv. 21–22: "You have heard that it was said to the men of old, 'You shall not kill; and whoever kills shall be liable to judgment.' But I say to you that every one who is angry with his brother shall be liable to judgment") was probably not trying to invalidate the law of Moses but simply demanding behavior radically consistent with it. Jesus also frequently cited traditional authorities in his confrontation with the Pharisees, as when he cited the Prophet Isaiah to support his condemnation of "your tradition" (hand washing before meals) in *Mark* 7:6–7 (cf. *Mt.* 15:7–9; *Is.* 29:13). Here the condemnation of a certain understanding of tradition is itself supported by an appeal to tradition, as Jesus draws an analogy between his conflict with the Pharisees and the conflicts of the prophets of Israel with the religious establishment of an earlier day. Even conflicts with tradition are molded by tradition.

Charismatic prophets who attack the sacred traditions of their contemporaries are not the only type of originators in the history of religion. Sociable teachers of virtue who accept the commonly received forms of tradition but reinterpret their contents are also important. Originators of this type often make a conscious effort to deny the novelty of their message. Confucius is a good example. A powerful originator who reoriented Chinese tradition, Confucius achieved a remarkable humanization of the substance of Chinese religion in his doctrine of "humanity" (*jen*). Yet he vigorously denied that there was anything new in his work. "I transmit but do not innovate; I am truthful in what I say and devoted to antiquity" (*Analects* 7.1, Lau translation). Confucius's words and deeds were designed to authenticate this claim. He was scrupulous in his observance of the established rites, devoted himself to traditional poetry and music, took the worthies of antiquity as his models, and showed reverence for the spirit world and for heaven.

The approach of Socrates to tradition, at least in Plato's quasi-canonical version, runs parallel to that of Confucius in an important way, though with an equally important difference. The difference lies in the method—dialectic—which allows for the critical interrogation of received tradition in a spirit quite foreign to Confucius's approach. The parallel lies in Socrates' insistence that he had neither new truths to teach people nor access to a special or secret source of truth, but simply wanted to clarify the traditional values—justice, goodness, piety—that most people accept on faith but cannot define or defend when challenged to do so. Thus throughout Plato's portrait of Socrates there is a tension between the critique and the affirmation of Greek tradition. Socrates is depicted as a man who respects and participates in the common forms of tradition even as he demolishes the arguments of pretentious and incompetent apologists, such as Euthyphro, Ion, and Agathon. The *Republic*, for example, although it contains the sharpest attack on Greek tradition in Plato's dialogues, namely the critique of Homer and Hesiod for "badly portraying the nature of gods and heroes" (*Republic* 377e), opens with Socrates telling how he went down to Piraeus to pray to a goddess during a religious festival and ends with him recounting a myth of gods and heroes (the myth of Er).

THE FORMATION OF TRADITIONS. A general theory of the formation of religious traditions has eluded scholars of religion despite the large body of specialized scholarship on the formative periods of many world religions. The difficulty is related to the conflict between the modern critical view of tradition as a historical product and the religious concept of tradition as a body of inviolate sacred canons transcending time and change. The application of historical and philological analysis to sacred traditions never fails to demonstrate their dependence on historical determinants. Yet the critical analysis of sacred traditions, if carried to the point of radical relativism, fails to account for the most distinctive fact of all: the continuity of certain sacred traditions with the capacity, however limited, to preserve themselves in a world of time and change.

The dynamics of traditionalism and relativism are further complicated by the instability of critical-historical theory itself. The annals of the modern study of religion abound with examples of theories that at one time commanded a substantial scholarly consensus but subsequently collapsed, not because they were opposed by religious traditionalists but because they were rejected by a new generation of critical scholars. For several decades of the twentieth century, for example, students in the reputable Protestant theological schools of Europe and North America were taught to view the Pentateuch through the lens of the "tradition history" school of Albrecht Alt, Gerhard von Rad, and Martin Noth. These scholars regarded the Pentateuch as the product of the expansion of smaller yet well-defined units of traditional material dating in some cases from as far back as the Middle Bronze Age (2100–1600 BCE). Toward the end of the twentieth century this theory gave way to a view of the Pentateuch as a much later body of material reflecting the party struggles of the waning years of the Israelite monarchy (seventh–sixth centuries BCE) and owing relatively little to canonical forms handed down from earlier periods. The revisionist view itself is susceptible to revision, of course, not least because it tends to evade rather than settle the issue of tradition. While emphasizing the decisive role of political and religious elites in the fashioning of the Pentateuch, the revisionists concede that the elites did not create their material from nothing but worked with an antecedent "body of lore (myths, legends, laws, etc.)," "a basic core of stories, traditions, and so on," or a "body of diverse traditional material" (Van Seters, 1998, pp. 8–9, 14). If so, then an account of the history of these traditions is demanded. The category of tradition, marginalized by criticism of "tradition history," enters the picture again.

Political determinism, namely the view that traditions are formed by elites as a means of legitimating power and privilege, has been a powerful factor in modern theoretical reflection on the formation of religious traditions. Attention focused originally on clerical elites who, as Enlightenment rationalists supposed, invented the apparatus of religious tradition to exploit the ignorant masses. Beginning with the French Revolution the role of secular political elites also came under scrutiny, as critics of "ideology" exposed the cozy relations between church, throne, and aristocracy. As monarchical and aristocratic power declined in the nineteenth century, ideological criticism was directed against the new power elite, namely the middle class. The feminist criticism of tradition took shape in the same historical context. A related form of political determinism reverses the terms, suggesting that certain traditions were formed by oppressed groups as a way of contesting established power structures, whether through a revolutionary assault or through some sort of exodus from them. Such a view has been particularly influential in the interpretation of the Hebrew Bible, in presentations of the ethics and "politics" of Jesus in the New Testament, and in liberation theology.

Delineating the connections between traditions and power elites has proved complicated enough to prevent the emergence of a generally accepted analysis. That power elites manipulate traditions and play a role in maintaining them has been clearly established by three centuries of critical analysis. What is not so clear is the extent to which traditions are the invention of power elites. The difficulty lies in the concept of legitimation. The legitimation, via tradition, of arrangements favorable to a power elite works only as long as the tradition is actually perceived as escapsulating a truth that transcends the elite. If the target audience—including the power elite itself—loses faith in the objective or unconstructed truth of a tradition, the latter quickly becomes useless for political as well as all other purposes. Legitimation thus proves to be an ambiguous concept: it combines political and transpolitical elements without clarifying the relationship between them.

The persistence of the tao-tʿai pattern (the animal mask or dragon figure) in traditional Chinese ritual and art can serve as an example of the dilemma faced by the interpreter of any enduring tradition. Widely disseminated by the Shang rulers of China in the second millennium BCE, especially as a motif on the bronze ritual vessels of the period, the tao-tʿai and related patterns have been called "signs or emblems of Shang authority" (Hsu and Linduff, 1988, p. 19). Yet the origins of the pattern are almost certainly to be looked for in a shamanistic spirituality that long predated the Shang. Moreover, when the Chou dynasty overthrew the Shang in the late twelfth century BCE, the new rulers perpetuated the classical pattern, thereby showing that they and their audience regarded it not as a Shang emblem but as a tradition of general validity, a channel of truth. Even if one can show that the meaning of the tao-tʿai changed significantly in the course of its long history, the persistence of the ancient template as a form for the discovery of new meaning is itself a highly significant fact about Chinese religion and thought, an example of a certain kind of traditionality.

An important contribution to study of the formation of traditions has been made by Eric Hobsbawm, Terence Ranger, and others who have investigated "the invention of tradition" in modern times. Careful to distinguish their subject from tradition in a more comprehensive sense, these critics focus on the conscious production of new rituals in response to the social, political, and ecological upheavals created by modern capitalism. Invented traditions are designed to establish or symbolize social cohesion in an environment where traditional communal bonds have been disrupted or revolutionized. Typically modern communities, such as new nation-states, awakened ethnicities, labor unions, voluntary organizations, environmentalist groups, gender-based associations, and others, invent traditions as a way of justifying their novelty. Often this takes the form of embracing "traditions" that appear to be old but are in fact quite new. The Romantic movement, with its interest in premodern folk culture, was an important source of ideas for inventors of traditions. Archaeology and anthropology also contributed by stimulating interest in prehistoric civilization.

Efforts to promote the cult of goddesses (or the Goddess) in Europe and North America are a good example of the invention of tradition. The critical framework of modern goddess religiosity is provided by the feminist critique of patriarchalism and the environmentalist critique of capitalism and modern technology. The positive religious content is drawn from the work of archaeologists, such as Marija Gimbutas, who seek to reconstruct the goddess-centered spirituality of a putatively pre-patriarchal period of European civilization. The limitations of the enterprise derive from the difficulty of determining the actual significance of goddess motifs in their original context, given the absence of written sources.

In addition to political theories, linguistically based theories of the formation of tradition have been influential in the modern study of religion. Here traditionality is seen not just as the product of social and political interests but as something inherent in the very structure of human understanding. This view of tradition is connected with the linguistic turn in the human sciences in the twentieth century. Many twentieth-century thinkers lost confidence in Enlightenment rationalism with its search for an unmediated starting point of knowledge and focused instead on the medium in which human beings actually think and communicate. The concreteness of language seemed to provide a surer foundation for a theory of human understanding than metaphysical notions, such as self, substance, or God. In Anglo-American thought the linguistic turn generated analytic philosophy; in continental European thought it produced philosophical hermeneutics and postmodernism. The contribution of analytic philosophers to the theory of tradition has been modest. Continental philosophers on the other hand, especially Martin Heidegger, Hans-Georg Gadamer, Paul Ricoeur, and Jacques Derrida, have had an enormous impact. By rejecting "pure" experience and insisting on the radically historical, interested, necessarily biased character of all human expression, these thinkers stimulated a new respect for tradition to the extent that tradition manifests the predicament of human understanding generally. If all human expression (ideas, values, symbols, and so on) is, in effect, a commentary on its own temporal situation (including the other human expressions found in its situation), then one may say that all human expression functions in and as a tradition of some kind.

Ironically, reverence for tradition played little part in the rise of philosophical hermeneutics and postmodernism. Heidegger viewed his philosophical project as a revolutionary break with the entire tradition of Western philosophy and theology since Plato, a view not unconnected with the European fascist project of leaping beyond modernity into a radically new historical epoch. The "post" in *postmodernism* encodes the same idea of an irrevocable break with the Western tradition. However, by rejecting the Enlightenment project of modernity, philosophical hermeneutics and postmodernism stimulated a fresh look at the premodern value systems the Enlightenment rejected, including historic religious traditions. Heidegger's more moderate heirs in the following generation, especially Gadamer and Ricoeur, have played a particularly prominent role in recasting the discussion of tradition.

IDEALIZATION AND CANONIZATION. All religious traditions construct pictures of their own formative periods. The pictures are built up over time by the retrospective projection of religious ideals onto the history of the tradition. Such pictures must not be accepted as literal descriptions of the formation of a tradition. Their function is to stress the unity and continuity of tradition, whereas the critical history of any tradition in the formative period never fails to reveal breaks, conflicts, and a diversity of views and practices.

An example of an idealized picture of the formative period of a tradition is the picture of the early Christian church in the *Acts of the Apostles*, a New Testament work composed in the last third of the first century. The picture of the church in *Acts* was shaped in part by the proto-Catholic ideal of a single apostolic church, and it contributed to the spread of this ideal in the following decades. *Acts* depicts a worldwide church directed from Jerusalem by twelve apostles governing alongside elders who are not identified as apostles, such as Jesus' brother James. Much attention is devoted to the missionary work of Paul, who is not identified as an apostle except in *Acts* 14. Stress is placed on Paul's cooperation with the Jerusalem church and on the harmony of his views with those of Peter, the only apostle to receive a substantial amount of attention in *Acts*. Matters that would tend to qualify the general impression of a unified church leadership, such as the nature of the relationship between the twelve apostles, Paul, and James, are not clarified. The picture in *Acts* is at variance with the evidence preserved in Paul's letters. Paul does not hesitate to call himself an apostle, does not deal with a group of twelve apostles in Jerusalem, records a sharp conflict with Peter (*Gal.* 2:11–14), and in general gives the impression of a more independent relationship to the Jerusalem Church than the one ascribed to him by *Acts*.

The idealization of tradition by later canonizers stands in tension not only with protean historical experience but with living traditions originating prior to the canonization of the tradition. No religious tradition springs onto the scene already possessing the canonical structures that will hold it together in the long run. Nevertheless, nascent tradition must be defined and held together in some way in the circles where it is received. In these circles the legacy of charismatic leaders who can claim a direct link to the originating source of sacred tradition plays an important role, as do beliefs and practices validated by custom and oral tradition. Local centers of living tradition developing independently and without much central coordination are the original hearths of tradition. Examples are the regional schools of law in early Islam (e.g., Medinese, Iraqi, Syrian), the metropolitan churches in early Christianity (e.g., Antioch, Alexandria, Rome), and the various monastic disciplines elaborated by the Buddha's successors around a common core but admitting significant differences of practice and eventually belief. The fixing of canons in a tradition necessarily breeds conflict with the original local centers of living tradition. Conflict would be inevitable even if the work of later canonizers were free of ideological or regional bias, which is rarely the case. The function of canonization is to generalize and standardize, that of living tradition to affirm and develop inherited beliefs and practices.

Yet it must not be thought that canonization represents nothing but the regimentation of tradition by a central authority. Canonization is a process that presupposes a significant measure of consensus among the centers of living tradition to begin with. Without it the canonization of a tradition could not be successful but would result in division. An example of division is the split in the order of monks at the second Buddhist council, said to have been held at Vaisali about a century after the Buddha's death. Catholic Christianity and Sunnī Islam, on the other hand, are examples of extremely successful efforts of broad-based canonization, accomplished in each case during the first three to four centuries of the religion's existence. The consolidation of broad segments of Judaism in late antiquity on the basis of the Talmud is another example of canonization carried out in a religious environment that modern scholarship has shown to be far more diverse than formerly supposed.

If canons are by definition clear, communicable, and relatively easy to identify once the process of canonization has been completed, the consensus presupposed by canonization is more difficult to locate and define. The concept of consensus is further complicated by the fact that some religious traditions possess their own particular concepts of consensus, such as the concept of the consensus (*ijmāʿ*) of the law schools in early Islam. While concepts of consensus in religious systems function primarily as ideals, the ideals usually preserve evidence of the fact that the formation of the tradition was not the work of a single religious center dictating canons to the periphery but resulted from the simultaneous emergence of distinct living traditions whose informal agreement on fundamentals was the sine qua non of the formal consolidation of tradition at a later time.

A good example of these dynamics is seen in the evolution of the *sunnah*, or tradition, in early Islam. In the third and fourth centuries AH (ninth and tenth centuries CE) the *sunnah* of the Prophet received its classic form in the six canonical books of *ḥadīths*, or stories of the Prophet, eventually accepted by Sunnī Muslims. How these books were produced is not a mystery. They were the leading works to emerge from decades of travel, research, and discussion by learned seekers of *ḥadīths* who undertook to discriminate between sound and spurious reports and whose methodology—the testing of the chain of transmission *(isnād)* of each report—was rigorous, even though modern critical historians would question some of the criteria applied. However, to suppose that one has explained the formation of the *sunnah* upon rendering an account of the work of the seekers of *ḥadīths* is to fail to address more basic and difficult questions:

what was the connection between the *ḥadīth* material on which the seekers worked and the living traditions of Islam before their time, and what factors of consensus operating in earlier times paved the way for their work?

Much modern Western scholarship on *ḥadīth* and the closely related subject of early Islamic law stresses the breaks between the work of the canonizers and earlier Islam. It is pointed out that the transmission of *ḥadīths* with a certifying *isnād* was a late phenomenon and that there is reason to doubt that *ḥadīths* were formally transmitted at all in the first century of Islam. It is sometimes questioned whether the Prophet left any *sunnahs*, or traditions, apart from the Qurʾān. Above all it is pointed out that the schools of law, whose roots went back to early times, looked upon the later *ḥadīth* movement as a disruptive force that threatened their own understanding of the *sunnah* as the tradition of the law schools (rather than of the Prophet himself) and undermined the ideal of consensus.

Some modern scholars, however, notably Fazlur Rahman in *Islam* (1979), have pointed out the ultimate irrationality of a critical historiography that bars the assumption of continuity in early Islam, since the consolidation of the *sunnah* and the integration of the traditional law schools into Sunnī tradition cannot be imagined without assuming significant elements of continuity and consensus at work from early times. Thus Rahman holds that, from the beginning, *sunnah* could not have meant the *sunnah* of the law schools alone but must have focused on the Prophet, at least in intention, even if "it was not so much like a path as like a riverbed which continuously assimilates new elements." Accordingly, transmission of the *sunnah* would have taken the form of a "'silent'or 'living' tradition" rather than a formal discipline (Rahman, 1979, pp. 54–55). The later *ḥadīth* movement formalized and, so to speak, professionalized the *sunnah.* But the movement was successful, in Rahman's opinion, because the concept of "the *sunnah* of the Prophet" had always been the implied ideal of Muslim practice, and also because a fixed corpus of *ḥadīths* provided a more solid basis on which to build a pan-traditional ("Sunnī") consensus than did the ideal of the consensus of the law schools.

Beyond their role in the formative period of traditions, groups oriented toward a traditional consensus often play a significant role in the regulation or reformation of traditions. Brahman castes in many parts of Hindu India may be cited as an example of tradition-minded regulators. An important group of brahmans even goes by the name of Smārtas (from *smṛti,* "tradition"), or "traditionists."

For an example of tradition-minded reformers, one may point to the Pharisees in Judaism in late antiquity. Scholarly debate continues over how best to classify the Pharisees as a religious group and how to define their role in the reorganization of Judaism culminating in the canonization of the Mishnah and Talmud. In the twentieth century, George Foot Moore, Louis Finkelstein, and other scholars propounded a view of the Pharisees as representatives of a "normative Judaism" that served as the foundation for later rabbinic tradition. Subsequent scholarship has richly documented the religious diversity of Judaism in late antiquity, the influence of Hellenistic culture on the Pharisees themselves, and the role of parties other than the Pharisees in the making of rabbinic Judaism. The result has been to give rise to a revisionist view of the Pharisees almost diametrically opposed to the earlier one. Far from being seen as the bearers of "normative Judaism," the Pharisees are presented as simply one sect among many in the religiously complicated world of Judaism around the beginning of the Common Era. That the name *Pharisee* may have originally meant "sectarian" lends support to this view.

Yet the revisionist view has its problems. The conceptual problem is how to distinguish between sectarians and traditionists. If all religious activists in a given setting are "sectarians," then none of them are. To put it another way, the term *sect* in the history of religion has meaning only in contrast to *church* or similar terms denoting broad-based traditional structures emphasizing consensus and continuity. To be sure, the distinction between sectarians and traditionists is a relative one, but without it one cannot speak about some basic differences between religious groups. For example, the difference between the Pharisees on the one hand and the early Christians and the community at Qumran (where the Dead Sea Scrolls were discovered) on the other was a difference of kind, not just degree. The latter two were sects: small bands of devotees living apart from the ordinary world in a closely knit commune (Qumran) or preaching a radical new prophecy with its own novel cult (Christians). Moreover, Christians and Qumranians lived in the expectation of an approaching cosmic cataclysm that would put an end to the historic Judaism of their day. Long before the destruction of the Second Temple in 70 CE, these groups had broken with Jerusalem and the Temple by reinterpreting Jewish tradition in terms of their own sources of illumination. The Pharisees too were innovators, but they had a completely different orientation to tradition. What set the Pharisees apart from Christians and Qumranians was the assumption of continuity with the historic institutions of Judaism, including the Temple, and the stress on realizing the goals of piety in the everyday world, without new prophecies and without a new cult.

THE MULTIFORMITY OF CLASSICAL TRADITIONS. Classical traditions are multiform. Multiformity results from the adaptation of traditions to the variegated quality of human experience, including religious experience. Nestor, the voice of tradition in the Homeric poems, describes the problem exactly: "The gods do not give people all things at the same time" (*Iliad* 4.320). Talents, tastes, values, social and political roles, age, gender, and station in life vary among individuals and groups. Tradition is called upon to unite what experience divides, so that the old can communicate with the young, the intellectual with the illiterate, the urbanite with the rustic, the priest with the flock, the prince with the pauper. Unity is sought not through regimentation but through the multiform elaboration of tradition. Multiformity in turn makes it possible for tradition to play a number of mediating roles in a civilization: to apply religious values flexibly, to mediate conflicts between different sets of values, to host creative interaction between different theoretical viewpoints, and so on. The multiformity of classical traditions stops short of radical pluralism, however. In the end, every tradition recognizes a hierarchy of values.

Several kinds of multiformity can be seen in the history of classical traditions. One kind results from the sociocultural differentiation of a tradition. Using terms that subsequently found wide application in the study of religion, the anthropologist Robert Redfield, in his *Peasant Society and Culture* (1956), called the two basic forms of tradition resulting from this type of differentiation "the great tradition" and "the little tradition." The great tradition is literate, reflective, cultivated by specialists working in cities, schools, temples, monasteries, and the like. The little tradition is typically illiterate, customary, embodied in the common beliefs and practices of the mass of ordinary folk. Scholars and cultivated practitioners of religion have always recognized that classical and popular religion diverge, yet this recognition seldom led to advances in understanding because of the tendency to regard popular religion as a "lower" form of expression. The contribution of modern anthropological studies of religion has been to show, first, that popular religion is just as much a tradition as classical religion, a tradition that can achieve high levels of organization, complexity, and "rural cosmopolitanism"; and second, that the interaction between great and little forms of tradition is a dynamic one in which the little tradition not only receives from the great but also contributes to it. Great and little traditions are, as Redfield put it, "two currents of thought and action, distinguishable, yet ever flowing into and out of each other" (Redfield, 1956, p. 72). Redfield's distinction has been criticized by other anthropologists for oversimplifying "great" and "little" traditions and for underestimating the degree to which ordinary believers are conversant with their great tradition via nonliterary means, such as icons, oral tradition, preaching, rituals, and authority structures (Tambiah, 1970, pp. 3–4, 367–377). But these criticisms do not so much refute the distinction as suggest a more nuanced version of it. Almost no responsible scholar of religion wishes to return to the privileging of text-based religiosity and the neglect of demotic factors.

A second kind of multiformity in classical traditions develops from the recognition of the multiplicity of paths to religious fulfillment. Classical Hinduism, for example, distinguishes at least three valid paths to the goal of liberation (*mokṣa*): the path of knowledge (*jñāna mārga*), the path of devotion to a personal God (*bhaktimārga*), and the path of ritual and dutiful action in the world (*karma-mārga*). It is fairly clear that the paths originated at different times and in different circles and that they evolved in relative independence of each other. Furthermore there has never been a consensus in Hinduism about the relative merits of the paths. Monist philosophers unanimously proclaim the superiority of the path of knowledge, and their control of much of the higher philosophical literature of Hinduism has led some observers to assume that this appraisal is shared by most Hindus. Yet in the fervor of communion with God, the devotionalist does not doubt the superiority of the devotional path, nor in all probability has the majority of Indians doubted the practical superiority of dutiful action in the world. Thus the idea that the three paths are expressions of a common aspiration cannot be explained as the natural outcome of the paths themselves but must be seen as a *traditum* in its own right—a tradition of handing down distinct paths in association with each other on the assumption of their mutual coherence. The assumption is an act of faith, since a systematic doctrine reconciling the different paths has never been accepted by all Hindus.

The Hebrew Scriptures constitute another *traditum* embodying a multiplicity of ways to religious insight. In Judaism and Christianity this multiplicity, while recognized, has not been emphasized in ways that would threaten strict monotheism or ecclesiastical unity. Nevertheless, the religious multiformity of the Bible has always been exploited by Jewish and Christian traditionists. Certainly the Bible would be a far less usable book if it admitted only the normative religion of priests and legists, only the charismatic religion of the prophets, only the Logos of the wise men, or only the devotionalism of the psalmist or if it lacked the rage of Job, the skepticism of *Ecclesiastes*, the eroticism of the *Song of Songs*. Nothing is more characteristic of the Hebrew Scriptures as a *traditum* than the transmission of many ways of theological insight together in a single canon of law, prophets, and writings. Historically, the various forms of religion represented in the Bible originated in relative independence from each other and were cultivated selectively by different groups. One must not project back into the ancient period a general fraternization of priests, legists, prophets, wise men, cult singers, and skeptics united in the praise of the Lord of Israel. Their solidarity in witness to and celebration of the One—the "Bible" as distinguished from its component parts—was the contribution of tradition.

Other kinds of multiformity result from the adaptation of a tradition to stages of life and degrees of religious virtuosity. An example is the classical Hindu doctrine of the four *āśramas*, or stages of life (celibate student, householder, forest hermit, wandering ascetic). In the classical doctrine the four *āśramas* are seen as successive stages through which a pious male of the twice-born castes will pass in the course of his life. It appears, however, that the distinction between the *āśramas* antedates the notion that they represent "stages" in a coherent succession. In any case only a minority of Hindu householders have ever passed beyond the second stage, and many hermits and ascetics in the history of Indian religion were never householders. The doctrine of the *āśramas* appears to be an attempt on the level of ideals to reconcile the world-affirming, dutiful religion of the Indian family system with the renunciationist religiosity of ascetic and mystical virtuosos. The contribution of tradition is the assumption that the four *āśramas* are coherently related to each other, and that respect and communication are therefore possible among their representatives. The reach of Hindu tradition is thereby significantly expanded.

A special adaptation of tradition to stages of life is represented by forms of religion connected with dying and the treatment of the dead. In all societies these matters are regulated chiefly by tradition, because neither reason nor experience can offer much guidance. By establishing a role in death, a tradition secures a place for itself in life, because people's lives will be affected by the way they expect to die. In Japan, for example, Buddhism has traditionally been the religion of funerals, and only at the grave does it come close to being the universal religion of the Japanese people. Still its special authority over death is one of the ways Buddhism gains visibility and prestige in Japanese tradition as a whole.

In some religions the distinction between the religion of virtuosos and that of ordinary people is built into the fundamental structure of the tradition. Buddhism is a case in point. In its first century Buddhism was a religion of monks that, although moderate in comparison with other asceticisms in its day, proposed a way of life incompatible with life as a householder in the everyday world. Yet Buddhism managed to establish itself as the dominant religious tradition in several Asian societies. It achieved its hegemony not by abandoning monasticism but by developing a mode of lay religious participation distinct from the monastic one yet in harmony with it: laypeople are invited to earn "merit" by providing food, clothing, dwellings, and other services for monks. The rewards of this exchange for the laity are ritual protection against the chaotic forces of the universe, enhanced moral clarity in this life, and a better birth in the next life. This "domestication" of Buddhism, as Todd T. Lewis has called it, had a profound effect not only on Buddhist societies but on Buddhist monasticism itself (Lewis, 2000, pp. 3–4). While the Western scholarly stereotype of the Buddhist monk as a detached seeker of transcendental enlightenment (*nirvāṇa*) can certainly be documented, the large majority of Buddhist monks seem to have been more concerned with such sociable pursuits as collecting and disseminating parables, conducting rituals, and preaching for the edification of the community as a whole. Indeed it is hard to imagine how Buddhism could have been such a successful religion if most of its monks had followed the more detached way. The dialectic of multiformity and community occurs in one form or another in every religious tradition.

MYSTICISM, ESOTERICISM, AND TRADITION. Mysticism and esotericism are forms of religious expression that present special problems for classical traditions. *Mysticism* is the cultivation of closeness to or union with the divine or ultimate. It may or may not involve special doctrines; it always involves special techniques. *Esotericism* is the study and application of "secret" teachings of a speculative (e.g., theosophical, cosmological, eschatological) or practical (e.g., magical, occult) sort. Mysticism and esotericism need not overlap, although they often do. The genius of classical religious traditions is nowhere better seen than in their capacity to host mysticism and esotericism, if not always as honored traditions within the tradition at least as a traditionally tolerated religious "night life."

Experience is the goal of mysticism regardless of the means employed, which range from strict asceticism through sociable middle ways to antinomian abandon. In essence, mysticism is not a matter of tradition, since experience cannot be received from or handed on to others. Mysticism is a matter of insight or perception, not texts, doctrines, or rules. However, because mysticism is interesting to most religious communities, and because human beings need to communicate about the things that interest them, mysticism typically generates formal mystical traditions, which may grow to an imposing size and complexity even against the wishes of a saintly originator. Formal mystical traditions are canons applied specifically to adepts or aspirants, such as myths of foundation, sacred histories, chains of authoritative transmitters, initiatory rites, techniques of devotion and ecstasy, sayings, texts, and rules regulating physical functions. As a general rule, once a mystical tradition is formed, little vagueness or laxity in its application is tolerated even though the goal of mysticism remains personal experience. In fact the canons of mystical traditions tend to be even more rigorously defined and enforced than those of mainstream traditions. This is partly because of the elite character of mystical traditions—rules can be more strictly enforced when applied to a few; partly because of the central role of the spiritual master in many mystical traditions, a role commanding a high degree of obedience from aspirants and apprentices; and also perhaps because of the need to guard against the explosive forces of unstructured mysticism. In madness and in method the traditional mystic is not unlike a classical Ṣūfī poet: God-intoxicated yet still mindful of the meters.

Whereas the interaction between mysticism and host traditions is extremely complex, the history of religion supports the generalization that the two need each other. Mysticism needs a host tradition as a source of vocabulary and symbols. Even though the meaning of these may be revised by the mystics who use them, without them the mystics would not be understood by anyone. In addition, the reserve shown to mystics by the authorities of a host tradition, beyond safeguarding the interests of the latter, is generally healthy for mystics because it challenges them to clarify their goals and refine their methods. As a rule the nemesis of mysticism is not too much structure but too little.

Mysticism can renew tradition. Cadmus and Tiresias, personages representing the Greek political and religious establishment in Euripides' play *The Bacchae*, gave good advice to every established tradition when they counseled the young ruler of Thebes, Pentheus, to admit the revels of the god Dionysos into the city, maintaining that incorporation of the cult would fortify tradition and enhance the prestige of the ruling house. If Pentheus disregarded his elders' advice with disastrous consequences to himself and his city, established traditions in the history of religion have usually heeded it. Traditions may also strengthen their links with popular culture by patronizing mystics. In spite of the elitism involved in a formal mystical discipline, many mystics have been rather sociable individuals, and they have almost always found favor with the popular strata. Among other things, this has made mystics and ascetics effective agents of mission in religious traditions with missionary ambitions.

Conflicts between mystics and host traditions are common and may be severe. In the sixth century certain Palestinian monks, seekers of union with Christ through mental prayer, claimed that they would achieve "equality with Christ" in the restoration of all things at the end of time, for which reason they were called Isochrists or "Equal-to-Christers." They were expelled from their monastery, and the doctrines supporting their position were condemned by the Council of Constantinople (553 CE). The great Muslim mystic al-Ḥallāj was executed in Baghdad in 922 CE for claiming "I am the Truth" (i.e., God). In both cases, however, the conflict was precipitated more by the doctrinal implications of verbalized claims than by the practices or experiences that prompted the claims. The suppression of the Isochrists did not stop the spread of the mysticism of mental prayer in Eastern Orthodox monasteries; it simply showed that certain claims could not be expressed in public and probably should not be entertained in private, even if inspired by mystical experiences. Similarly many a Ṣūfī after al-Ḥallāj has doubtless thought "I am the Truth" but has not said it or has said it in figurative language, with an appropriate gloss, or in the secrecy of the heart.

As a general rule, mystics and traditionists tend to recognize their mutual interest in avoiding direct conflict, or at least in finding ways to routinize it. Moreover, the way is always open for creative individuals to experiment with means of uniting mysticism and tradition. Individuals who succeed in this enjoy great popularity in their tradition. One may point to al-Ghazālī, who achieved fame in eleventh-century Islam as a doctor of law and a Ṣūfī adept; to Gregory Palamas, the fourteenth-century bishop of Thessalonica, who employed the refined intellectual traditions of Greek Orthodox theology to defend the radical experientialism of rustic monks; and to the Indian philosopher Rāmānuja (eleventh to twelfth century), who, using the texts and methods of Vedānta, attempted to reconcile monism with the experientially based claims of devotionalists in a "qualified nondualism." In most cases the theoretical differences between mysticism and the doctrines of its host tradition are great enough to put an absolute synthesis beyond reach. But tradition does not require synthesis; mediation is enough.

Esotericism is concerned with teachings rather than experience, although mystical and esoteric currents mingle in the history of religion. The basis of esotericism in religion is the claim to possess secret or otherwise special traditions from an authoritative source—traditions that support speculation, occult practices including magic, or both. The possession of secret traditions may provide the basis for independence from other religious groups or for the existence of an elite group within a larger host tradition. Among the reasons given to justify secrecy are that most people are too simple or too perverse to understand true teachings or that the withholding of secrets is part of a providential plan to be revealed in the future. Also at work is the natural desire to avoid enraging the guardians of normative tradition by undercutting their authority in public. The threat of conflicts is real because esotericists always claim access to authoritative sources beyond those of normative tradition. So, for example, certain masters of Jewish Qabbalah claimed access through secret tradition to a primordial revelation from Adam or to texts composed by biblical patriarchs and other ancient worthies. Such claims compromised the singularity of the Torah received from Moses, and therefore also the authority of the Orthodox rabbis. Similarly, the teaching authority of Catholic Christian bishops was threatened by the belief of Gnostics that the inner meaning of the gospel was handed down by the apostles to an elite of spiritual and intellectual Christians, not to the church as a whole.

Like mystics, esotericists generally steer away from direct conflicts with traditional authorities and aim instead at accommodation. Rarely a religion in its own right, esotericism needs an exoteric tradition in order to define itself. The common tradition is enriched by the multiformity. One of the most important contributions of modern research on Qabbalah, for example, has been to show that many forms of esotericism were deeply embedded in the soil of Palestinian Judaism from early times and developed within the framework of the Talmudic tradition. This is not to deny that influences from other religions and from popular culture helped shape Qabbalah. But influences have consequences in the history of religion because they resonate with the needs and themes of established traditions. Esotericists, for the most part, are less interested in reshaping traditional piety than in heightening its intensity by focusing on specific values and goals within it. The "paradoxical emphasis on the congruence of intuition and tradition" that Gershom Scholem observed in Qabbalah is typical of the approach of most esotericists to their host traditions (Scholem, 1978, p. 3).

TRADITION AND CHANGE. Religious traditions are not hostile to change, provided the new can be integrated with the old through reform or renewal. Integration is difficult to accomplish in practice, and religious traditions rarely make the effort except when compelled to do so by a crisis of some sort. In critical situations, however, when the outward authority or inner coherence of tradition is at stake, religious traditions can demonstrate a vitality that contrasts sharply with their apparent inertia at other times. There is no paradox here. One of the primary functions of religious traditions is to provide direction in times of change. A sense of tradition, allowing for the old to be appreciated as ever new and the new to be received as clarifying or fulfilling the old, serves to check the chaotic potential of change. Of course, traditions may be overwhelmed by a crisis of catastrophic proportions, such as the European conquest of the Americas. Even in these cases, however, features of the displaced tradition often survive under the auspices of the successor tradition, usually on the popular level in the form of an ongoing little tradition.

While religious traditions are not necessarily opposed to reform or renewal, revolutionary change is a different matter. By definition, a tradition is opposed to changes that abrogate the link with the past preserved in its fundamental *tradita.* The completely new is intolerable in a traditional religion. Even prophetic religions promising new and wondrous things typically do so in a way that reflects the mind of tradition. Prophets depend on traditions of expectation—that is, patterned ways of seeking and announcing the new—and they use traditional paradigms to make sense of new developments. The Prophet Isaiah heralded the fall of Babylon and the liberation of the Judean exiles in his day as "new things . . . created now, not long ago" (*Is.* 48:6–7). But the rhetoric of novelty did not keep him from understanding the liberation as a new Exodus and the liberator as the same Lord who stood for Israel in ancient times.

Before modern times, the greatest challenges to religious traditions came not from antireligious or nonreligious value systems but from rival religious traditions. The coexistence of different religious traditions in the same societies for long periods of time was also a source of change. While the interaction of religious traditions before modern times has not yet been studied in great detail, there is plenty of evidence to suggest that the boundaries between traditions were much more permeable than either the guardians of tradition or their modern detractors suppose. Wilfred Cantwell Smith went so far as to propose a "history of religion in the singular" based on the countless ideas, stories, practices and accoutrements that have found their way into many different religious traditions (Smith, 1981, p. 3). Smith's paradigm is the legend of the Christian saint Josaphat (or Joasaph), the young Asian prince who abandoned his opulent, cocoon-like circumstances to seek salvation as a monk. The legend is the story of Siddhārtha Gautama, the Buddha, and it entered the repertoire of medieval Christianity from the East through an Islamic intermediary. By such a route did the Buddha become a Christian saint.

There is general agreement that the pace of religious change has quickened in recent centuries as a result of the economic, social, political, and intellectual changes summed up in the term *modernization.* The problem of tradition and modernity concerns the fate of traditional value systems, including religious traditions, in a world shaped by modern science and market capitalism and the ideologies and technologies resulting from them, such as liberalism, nationalism, socialism, and biological and social engineering. Despite numerous studies of the problem of modernization in particular societies, however, there is little consensus among scholars about the lasting effects of modernity on religious traditions.

When the problem began to be studied by social scientists in the nineteenth century, progressivist ideologies, liberal or socialist, shaped the discussion. Most critics assumed that tradition was fated to give way to modernity, either at a stroke or through gradual evolution. This view received a great deal of support from the spectacle of antitraditional, Marxist revolutions coming to power in Russia and China in the twentieth century. In the late twentieth century and the early twenty-first century, however, with the worldwide collapse of Communism and the decline of secularist regimes in the Islamic world and elsewhere, more attention has been given to the persistence of religious traditions. Evidence has also been adduced to show that in many societies modernization actually reinforces and even reinvigorates certain aspects of tradition, as, for example, when modern technologies of communication make it possible for religious groups to promote their messages with unprecedented militancy (e.g., Protestant Christian and Islamic fundamentalism), or when economic and political revolutions result in power and prominence for groups whose outlook remains deeply traditional (e.g., Hindu nationalism). In many places modernizing ideologies actually appear to require an alliance with tradition, including religious tradition, in order to promote their goals. The central role of nationalism in the contemporary world is a good example of this type of linkage. Nationalism owes its dynamism to the fact that whereas it promotes essentially secular values, it also serves to reaffirm traditional solidarities.

Postmodernism has attempted a resolution of the problem of tradition and modernity by declaring modernity, as such, to be over. Modernity in this context means the Enlightenment project of reforming the world on the basis of science, natural law (human rights), and a common human rationality. Postmodernism rejects this universalism in principle on the grounds of the endless plurality of human cultures and the unfinalizability of discourse. Although postmodernism was invented by radically secularized philosophical elites, its critique of Enlightenment liberalism has been embraced by some apologists for religious tradition according to the principle "my enemy's enemy is my friend." Yet the use of postmodernism to defend religious tradition is problematic. The world-historical religious traditions are universalist in principle, and it is hard to see in the final analysis how a case for them can be based on radical relativism. Postmodernists respond to this criticism by asserting that supposedly universalist or "great" traditions are in fact a vast congeries of essentially local and constantly changing beliefs and practices. There is truth in this assertion, but also a problem. Classifications such as "Christian," "Muslim," "Buddhist," and the like appear to count for something in the traditions that claim these names. Religious communities seem to aspire to identification with a great tradition, no matter how embedded they are in their local context. To be sure, there are several great traditions, not just one. But this multiplicity can be interpreted in a number of ways, including some that cohere with the universalism of the traditions themselves.

The postmodernist assertion that modernity is over can also be questioned. The claim seems to ignore the large body of evidence summed up in the term *globalization*. Globalization, as Peter Berger has observed, is "a continuation, albeit in an intensified and accelerated form, of the perduring challenge of modernization" (Berger and Huntington, 2002, p. 16). The forces of globalization—science, market capitalism, individualism—are expanding, not contracting in the world, and religious traditions everywhere are struggling to come to terms with them. The religious fundamentalisms that are often cited as evidence of the collapse of modernity are in fact just one of a number of responses to modernity, their stridency and extremism marking them as untraditional phenomena. While globalization occurs in diverse forms, there are enough similarities among its forms to suggest that it is indeed a global process. In short, whereas postmodernist critics have significantly refined the discussion of modernity by discrediting simplistic theories, the case is by no means closed.

For the time being the best approach is probably to recognize that the problem of tradition and modernity is part of the religious situation of contemporary civilization and not likely to be resolved, or even greatly altered, in the near future. The naive progressivism of the early theorists of modernization has been abandoned by most scholars, but the general problem stands. Given globalizing trends, the continuators of tradition may be expected to go on experiencing threats to their identities, including some that arise from within their own traditions as modernizing tendencies insinuate themselves even there. Yet the work of the globalizers is also full of tensions, and these are likely to intensify as idealistic enthusiasm for modern visions gives way to the difficulty of putting these visions into practice. Globalizers risk losing the way to the future for lack of a connection with the past. A steady orientation in any field of endeavor seems to require traditions: traditions inherited from premodern times, new traditions of modernity's own making, or new cultural syntheses combining elements of both.

SEE ALSO Canon; Folk Religion; Ḥadīth; Memorization; Oral Tradition; Popular Religion; Reform; Revival and Renewal; Scripture; Sunnah.

BIBLIOGRAPHY

Edward Shils's *Tradition* (Chicago, 1981) is an excellent introduction to the concept of tradition, although the book does not contain a specialized discussion of tradition in religion. Josef Pieper's *Überlieferung: Begriff und Anspruch* (Munich, 1970) is a good introduction to religious and theological dimensions of the concept. The lectures by Jaroslav Pelikan, *The Vindication of Tradition* (New Haven, Conn., 1984), offer a lively if brief defense of the centrality of tradition in religion and culture. The broad influence of Robert Redfield's concept of tradition makes his *Peasant Society and Culture: An Anthropological Approach to Civilization* (Chicago, 1956) required reading, especially chap. 3, "The Social Organization of Tradition." The most influential sociological discussion of tradition is Max Weber's in *Economy and Society: An Outline of Interpretive Sociology*, 2 vols., edited by Guenther Roth and Claus Wittich (Berkeley, Calif., and London, 1978). The seminal essay by T. S. Eliot, "Tradition and the Individual Talent," in *The Sacred Wood: Essays on Poetry and Criticism* (London, 1920), pp. 47–59, reprinted in *Selected Essays*, 3d ed. (New York, 1950), pp. 13–22, is also essential reading.

For the contribution of philosophical hermeneutics to the discussion of tradition, one should consult the two masters of the discipline, Hans-Georg Gadamer, *Truth and Method*, translated by Joel Weinsheimer and Donald G. Marshall, 2d rev. ed. (New York, 1989); and Paul Ricoeur, *Hermeneutics and the Human Sciences: Essays on Language, Action, and Interpretation*, edited and translated by John B. Thompson (Cambridge, U.K., and New York, 1981). For an overview see Jean Grondin, *Introduction to Philosophical Hermeneutics*, translated by Joel Weinsheimer (New Haven, Conn., and London, 1994).

On oral tradition one may begin with Jan Vansina's *Oral Tradition: A Study in Historical Methodology* (Chicago, 1965), a rigorous discussion of the value of oral tradition as a historical source; and Walter J. Ong, *Orality and Literacy: The Technologizing of the Word* (London and New York, 2002). The fundamental work on oral poetic tradition is Albert Bates Lord's *The Singer of Tales* (Cambridge, Mass., 1960). For a more recent treatment see Ruth Finnegan, *Oral Poetry: Its Nature, Significance, and Social Context* (Bloomington, Ind., 1992). On oral tradition in the Hebrew Bible see Eduard Nielsen's *Oral Tradition: A Modern Problem in Old Testament Introduction*, with a foreword by Harold H. Rowley (Chicago, 1954); and Susan Niditch, *Oral World and Written Word: Ancient Israelite Literature* (Louisville, Ky., 1996).

A large literature exists on the concept and practice of tradition in particular religions. The best of these works shed light not only on the traditions under investigation but on traditionality in general. On goddesses in prehistoric Europe see Marija Gimbutas, *The Civilization of the Goddess*, edited by Joan Marler (San Francisco, 1991). Douglas A. Knight, ed., *Tradition and Theology in the Old Testament* (Philadelphia, 1977), is a good collection of essays on tradition in the Hebrew Bible. James A. Sanders's *Torah and Canon* (Philadelphia, 1972) is a suggestive discussion of tradition and canonicity. See also John Van Seters, "The Pentateuch," in *The Hebrew Bible Today: An Introduction to Critical Issues*, edited by Steven L. McKenzie and M. Patrick Graham (Louisville, Ky., 1998), pp. 3–49. For contrasting approaches to tradition in rabbinic Judaism see Jacob Weingreen, *From Bible to Mishna: The Continuity of Tradition* (New York, 1976); and Jacob Neusner, *Early Rabbinic Judaism: Historical Studies in Religion, Literature, and Art* (Leiden, Netherlands, 1975), especially chap. 1, "The Meaning of Oral Torah, with Special Reference to Kelim and Ohalot." On tradition in mystical Judaism see Gershom Scholem, *Kabbalah* (New York, 1974).

On tradition in the history of Christianity one cannot do better than to consult Jaroslav Pelikan, *The Christian Tradition: A History of the Development of Doctrine,* 4 vols. (Chicago, 1971–1989). Yves M.-J. Congar, *Tradition and Traditions: An Historical and a Theological Essay* (New York, 1967), is a another masterful treatment by one of the intellectual leaders of the Second Vatican Council. One should also consult the classic that inspired both Pelikan and Congar, John Henry Newman's *An Essay on the Development of Christian Doctrine* (New York, 1845). For Orthodox Christian approaches see John Meyendorff, *Living Tradition: Orthodox Witness in the Contemporary World* (Crestwood, N.Y., 1978); Constantine Scouteris, "Paradosis: The Orthodox Understanding of Tradition," *Sobornost* 4, no. 1 (1982): 30–37; and Michael Plekon, ed., *Tradition Alive: On the Church and the Christian Life in Our Time: Readings from the Eastern Church* (Lanham, Md., 2003). See also the critical assessment by Paul Valliere, *Modern Russian Theology: Bukharev, Soloviev, Bulgakov: Orthodox Theology in a New Key* (Edinburgh, U.K., and Grand Rapids, Mich., 2000), chap. 15, "Conclusion: The Limits of Tradition."

A probing discussion of tradition in Islam is in Fazlur Rahman's *Islam,* 2d ed. (Chicago, 1979), chaps. 3, "Origins and Development of the Tradition," and 4, "The Structure of the Law." Rahman's critique of the analysis of Islamic tradition by Western scholars illuminates the problem of continuity in religion in general. Similarly Robert Lingat's study of tradition (*smṛti*) in Hinduism, *The Classical Law of India,* translated with additions by J. Duncan M. Derrett (Berkeley, Calif., 1973), provides insights into the workings of any system of norms based on tradition. See also Louis Renou, *Études védiques et pāṇinéennes,* vol. 6 (Paris, 1960).

On tradition in early Chinese civilization, see K. C. Chang, *Art, Myth, and Ritual: The Path to Political Authority in Ancient China* (Cambridge, U.K., and London, 1983); Cho-Yun Hsu and Katheryn M. Linduff, *Western Chou Civilization* (New Haven, Conn., and London, 1988); and Aihe Wang, *Cosmology and Political Culture in Early China* (Cambridge, U.K., 2000). The complex interaction between religious tradition and social systems in Buddhism is explored by S. J. Tambiah, *Buddhism and the Spirit Cults in North-East Thailand* (Cambridge, U.K., 1970); Melford E. Spiro, *Buddhism and Society: A Great Tradition and Its Burmese Vicissitudes,* 2d ed. (Berkeley, Calif., 1982); and Todd T. Lewis, *Popular Buddhist Texts from Nepal: Narratives and Rituals of Newar Buddhism* (Albany, N.Y., 2000).

On tradition and change in modern times, see Robert N. Bellah, "Epilogue: Religion and Progress in Modern Asia," in *Religion and Progress in Modern Asia,* edited by Robert N. Bellah (New York, 1965), pp. 168—229; and Eric J. Hobsbawn and Terence Ranger, eds., *The Invention of Tradition* (Cambridge, U.K., 1983). Lloyd I. Rudolph and Susanne Hoeber Rudolph, *The Modernity of Tradition: Political Development in India* (Chicago, 1967), is a classic study of the role of tradition in modern politics. Milton Singer, *When a Great Tradition Modernizes: An Anthropological Approach to Indian Civilization,* with a foreword by M. N. Srinivas (New York, 1972), is another fine work on tradition and modernity in South Asia. The tenacious reader will be rewarded by working through Joseph Richmond Levenson's *Confucian China and Its Modern Fate: A Trilogy,* 3 vols. (Berkeley, Calif., 1958–1968). Donald H. Shively, ed., *Tradition and Modernization in Japanese Culture* (Princeton, N.J., 1971), is a good collection of essays on tradition and change in early modern Japan. Paul Heelas, ed., with the assistance of David Martin and Paul Morris, *Religion, Modernity, and Postmodernity* (Oxford, U.K., and Malden, Mass., 1998), provides a sampling of postmodernist perspectives on issues of tradition and modernity.

From the growing literature on the cultural and religious impact of globalization, see Arjun Appadurai, ed., *Globalization* (Durham, N.C., and London, 2001); Peter L. Berger and Samuel P. Huntington, eds., *Many Globalizations: Cultural Diversity in the Contemporary World* (Oxford, U.K., 2002); and Mark Juergensmeyer, ed., *Global Religions: An Introduction* (New York, 2003), which includes a helpful bibliography. In the same connection, William Ernest Hocking's suggestive typology of the interaction between religious traditions in *Living Religions and a World Faith* (New York, 1940) is receiving fresh attention, as is Wilfred Cantwell Smith's *Towards a World Theology: Faith and the Comparative History of Religion* (Philadelphia, 1981).

PAUL VALLIERE (1987 AND 2005)

TRANSCENDENCE AND IMMANENCE. According to *Webster's New International Dictionary of the English Language,* second edition, unabridged, to transcend is to "ascend beyond, excel." The term is used of the "relation of God to the universe of physical things and finite spirits, as being . . . in essential nature, prior to it, exalted above it, and having real being apart from it." *Immanence,* defined as "presence in the world . . . in pantheism is thought of as uniform, God . . . equally present in the personal and the impersonal, in the evil and the good. According to theism, immanence occurs in various degrees, more in the personal than the impersonal, in the good than in the evil."

It is clear that *transcendence* is a value term expressing the unique excellence of God, because of which worship—utmost devotion or love—is the appropriate attitude toward the being so described. It is less obvious that *immanence* is a value term, but *ubiquity,* "being everywhere," comes closer to expressing a unique property. If God is everywhere in the world and also in some sense beyond the world, then God certainly surpasses all ordinary objects of respect or love.

"Prior to the universe" seems to suggest a time when God was alone, with no cosmos of creatures to relate to—first a creator not actually creating, then one creating. But it also might mean that there was a different universe before our own. Origen thought God had created an infinity of universes in succession and never lacked relation to some actual creatures. We see a partial return to that position in Alfred North Whitehead's hypothesis of "cosmic epochs," each with its own natural laws. Whitehead held that having a universe, some universe or other, is, in principle, inherent in God's nature and not subject to divine choice. What may be subject to such choice are the particular laws that will govern a cosmic epoch about to arise. God's "real being apart from the universe" means, in such a view, a vantage apart from our current universe, not apart from all universes. Not every theologian agrees with those who think to compliment God by affirming divine freedom to have simply no creatures. The objection to this once-popular view is that since any creatures are better than none (that being as such is primarily good and only secondarily bad is a classical doctrine), God would be making the worst possible choice by not creating at all. Freedom to do this seems nonsensical when affirmed of God.

In what sense is God *in* the universe? The suggestion in *Webster's*, attributed to "idealists," is that the divine presence is "like that of a conscious self in the world of that self." Or, attributed to "realists," it is like "that of a self in its organism and its behavior." The latter suggestion makes Plato a realist, for it was he who in the West first thought of God as the World Soul, whose body is the entire cosmos of nondivine things and persons. This proposal (in the *Timaeus*) was, however, seldom followed until recent times, and was rejected by Whitehead. In this I take Whitehead to have been mistaken. The relation of mind to body in human (and other) animals is the relation of mind to physical reality, to "matter," that we most directly and surely know. If our thoughts do not influence our behavior, then we know nothing of any influence of mind or spirit on the physical world. David Hume pointed this out in his *Dialogues concerning Natural Religion* through the character Cleanthes.

REALISTIC IDEALISM. The idealist view referred to above is less obviously intelligible. Does our mere contemplation of the world make us immanent in that world? When we remember past experiences, does that put our present consciousness back into those experiences? If I think of someone in Hong Kong, does that put me in Hong Kong? The form of idealism referred to by *Webster's* definition is no longer widely held. It is the data of an awareness that are in the awareness, not vice versa. If this realistic principle—accepted by the theistic metaphysicians Charles S. Peirce and Whitehead, who in some respects are properly called idealists—is sound, then it is the creatures' awareness of God, not God's awareness of them, that constitutes the divine presence in the universe. And if God is universally present, then the creatures universally are, however inadequately, aware of God, who is the universal object as well as the universal subject. This implies, as Peirce and Whitehead held, as did Henri Bergson and some other recent theists, that every creature has some form of awareness, even if it be nothing more than some mode of feeling. For those of this persuasion, dualism and materialism are both inconsistent with a well-thought-out theism.

Unfortunately, the term *idealism* is still often applied to the now antiquated doctrine presupposed by the editors of *Webster's*. Few changes of opinion are more definite or important than the shift, in this century, in the way the relations of mind or experience to its data are conceived. Indeed, the alternative to idealism is no longer realism but the choice between dualism and materialism. A "realistic idealism" makes perfectly good sense. And Plato was both realist and idealist, except insofar as, like all ancient Greeks, he was unable to escape dualism and materialism entirely. No one in the West knew how to conceive mind, or awareness, as a universal property of creatures until Leibniz, the true founder of realistic idealism, made his distinction between dynamic singulars and aggregates or groups of singulars. (The singulars he called monads, but this term tends to connote some further doctrines peculiar to Leibniz that are no longer accepted, even by those strongly influenced by Leibniz, so far as the problem of mind and matter is concerned.) In Asia, where Leibniz has not as yet had much influence, there seems to be no comparably well-articulated doctrine of realistic idealism that can be called theistic.

The distinction between dynamic singulars—all of which are sentient—and their groups or aggregates depends, for Leibniz, on the primitive form of the atomic theory then entertained by physicists and also upon the discovery by Leeuwenhoek of the realm of microscopic animals. With a stroke of genius, Leibniz generalized this and held that larger animals consist of smaller animals (in a generalized sense), thus anticipating the cell theory established much later. Leibniz may well have realized the philosophical meaning of Leeuwenhoek's discoveries better than some philosophers do now. He made a realistic idealism at last possible and thereby freed theism from one of its greatest difficulties, enabling it to give a positive explanation of the divine ubiquity.

GOD'S DUALLY TRANSCENDENT LOVE. Whitehead's theory of prehension (or "feeling of feeling"), applied to God and all creatures, makes God the universally prehending and universally prehended subject, feeling all and felt by all. Hence God is in all and all is in God. Since creaturely prehensions are those of subjects in principle inferior to God, they feel God inadequately, whereas God, in principle superior to all, feels the creatures and their mostly unintellectual feelings with ideal adequacy. Although each creature contains God and God contains each creature, the divine containing is unqualified, but the creaturely containing is more or less drastically qualified. Thus, for theism, God is present "in various degrees" in the parts of the universe, but the creatures are wholly present to God. As Berdiaev urges, the most pertinent question is not "Is God in the world?" but rather "Is the world in God?" The Pauline saying, that in God "we live and move and have our being," can be taken literally without necessarily implying pantheism.

To say that God feels the feelings of all creatures is to contradict the doctrine of classical theism that God is impassible, wholly unaffected by others. Anselm said that God was not compassionate, although the effects of the divine being were *as if* God were compassionate. What this amounts to, for some of us, is that the New Testament saying "God is love" is untrue, yet the effects of God's nature upon us are what they would be if God loved us. We here confront a deep divergence between that theism pervasive in Scholasticism (with Bonaventure producing the most thoroughgoing attempt to interpret divine love), and found also in medieval Islamic and Jewish writings, and the theism that I call neoclassical, which has been set forth by some recent philosophers and theologians (e.g., Nikolai Berdiaev, Alfred North Whitehead, Rudolf Otto, Otto Pfleiderer, John Oman, Alfred Ernest Garvie, and Edgar S. Brightman). Whitehead's assertion that "to attribute mere happiness to God is a profanation" hints at this rejection of Anselm's doctrine, and his further statement that "God is the fellow sufferer who understands" makes the contrast quite clear. Berdiaev is no less plain on this point.

The denial that love, however generalized, can characterize deity is implied by Plato, who, in his *Symposium*, interprets love as the longing for absolute beauty and hence a confession of imperfection. The nearest Plato comes to attributing love to God is to say that there is no envy in the divine nature, and hence God is willing to have creatures sharing existence with him. Plato does definitely attribute to God knowledge of the creatures, whereas Aristotle denies this. All his deity thinks is the generic nature of thinking itself, totally free from the contingency and particularity that go with individuals in the world.

In India, the Advaita Vedāntins, often regarded as the orthodox Hindus, thought of the highest and only genuine reality as beyond anything that could be called love. The latter is a social relation, presupposing a plurality of subjects in space and time, whereas *brahman* is without temporal or spatial plurality. In India, however, there are also various proponents of pluralism. Ramanuja and Madhva are the most obvious examples, but there are others whose views show striking analogies to the Western "process" view, the greatest single representative of which is Whitehead. To appreciate adequately the strength of the worldwide effort to find something greater and better, or more real, than love at its best, we need to relate the issue to the problem of anthropomorphism. We human animals are social, and it has with some justice been said that an absolutely nonsocial animal does not exist. God, however, is in principle superior to any animal. God is uniquely excellent, without possible rival or equal.

The Christian doctrine of the Trinity is an attempt to have it both ways. In some sense, the Son and Holy Spirit are equal to God the Father; in some sense God is supreme. The three divine persons could love each other, even were there no creatures. This doctrine is too paradoxical to be defended apart from revelation. Apart from some such doctrine, either God does not love anyone or the being in principle superior to all conceivable others loves these lesser beings. Even with the trinitarian doctrine, the question remains relevant: must not God, conceived by analogy to what we know of ordinary beings (and how else can we conceive anything?), cherish the creatures? If we can sympathize with children and other kinds of animals, must God view them and us with mere indifference? If so, was not Aristotle right in saying that God does not know particular, contingent individuals because they are "not worth knowing"?

EXTREMIST AND MIDDLE-GROUND STRATEGIES. History shows two ways of approaching philosophical disagreement. One way, in practice taken by some of the wisest philosophers, is to suspect extreme views and look for a "middle way" between opposite extremes. Some of the ancient Buddhists did this explicitly. With regard to transcendence and immanence, one extreme is gross anthropomorphism, taking God to be, as Matthew Arnold put it, "a magnified, nonnatural man." The opposite extreme is to say, as Karl Barth once did (he later partly rescinded the statement), that God is "wholly other" than ourselves. The middle way is to look for a difference in principle between God and all else and yet also, consistent with this, a resemblance in principle between God and all other beings. Many philosophers and theologians have more or less consciously proceeded in this fashion, and two of these, Plato and Whitehead, have been especially successful (at least according to some scholars strongly influenced by Whitehead). However, conditions in the ancient world were unfavorable to this side of Plato; and for many centuries a quite different way was taken in the West (beginning with Aristotle and the theologian Philo Judaeus).

In India, also, it was not a middle way that was the mainstream of thought. Instead, an extremist strategy was followed, though with some inconsistency. It was taken for granted that truth is an extreme with error its opposite. The maxim, without ever being so stated, perhaps, was "Let us find the view that is most hopelessly wrong and affirm the opposite." That the God of all the worlds is like a localized and mortal animal, dependent for its very existence on an environment, is clearly wrong, the absurd error of anthropomorphism. So, let us deny of God, or the supreme reality, all traits that animals and still lesser beings have in common, and, by achieving the opposite of anthropomorphism in characterizing God, we will come as close to the truth as is in our power. All animals and lesser beings are finite, changeable, subject to influence by others, complex, and have feelings as well as thoughts (if they have the latter). Let us say, therefore, that God is infinite, unchangeable in every way, wholly impassible, immune to influence by others, wholly simple, incapable of feeling, but with purely intellectual knowledge (whatever that may be). It was David Hume who first indicated the possible fallacy in all this. What is to guarantee that, when we have denied all that constitutes reality as we experience it, anything is left to distinguish God from mere nonentity? The famous negative way, the *via negativa*, must, after all, be supplemented by something positive, or we may end up worshiping a mere nothing or a mere verbal formula.

As a matter of fact, the premise of the negative way—its characterization of beings in the world—is seriously inaccurate. What is common to ordinary individuals is only inadequately or ambiguously described as finite, changeable, subject to influence by others, and complex. Furthermore, the distinction between awareness as feeling and awareness as pure thought or knowledge is problematic. What thought or knowledge would be without feeling is not something that our experience makes transparently obvious. Finally, we animals are not simply finite; each of us is a mere *fragment* of the finite. The entire cosmos may be spatially finite; and even a beginningless past would be in a sense finite compared to the infinity of all that is conceivable. It is very well arguable that no knowledge of finite things could, without contradiction, be considered absolutely infinite. Hence an all-knowing God must be in some sense or respect finite.

Similarly, knowledge of the contingent must be contingent. What we are and what God cannot be is fragmentary. The divine finitude must encompass at least the world's finitude and also its infinity in whatever sense the world is infinite. Yes, we are affected by others, but it is just as true that we affect others. We are cause and effect; the question is, does it even make sense to view God as the cause of all and the effect of nothing? As Aristotle said, knowledge of contingent things is conditioned by the reality of the things known. The all-knowing cannot be simply and in every sense uncaused, unconditioned.

The alternative to the negative way is the doctrine of dual transcendence, according to which God in principle excels over others both in the sense that the divine nature is uniquely absolute and infinite and in the sense that it is uniquely relative and finite. If we could not be absolute (independent) or infinite in the divine sense, neither could we be relative or finite in the divine sense. Nor need it be contradictory to attribute both of these contrasting properties to God. Contradiction occurs only if a subject is said to have a property and a contrary property in the same respect; otherwise contradiction does not obtain. And if it be said that since God is simple, God cannot contain a duality, the reply is ready: the divine simplicity is itself only one side of the duality of transcendence. In Whitehead's view, God's "primordial nature" is simple (I would say even simpler than Whitehead makes it) but God's "consequent nature" is the most complex reality there is. The complex can include the simple.

It was said above that "changeable" is an inadequate or ambiguous characterization of things other than God. There are changes for the better, for the worse, and neutral changes. Animals are open to good changes—growth, enrichment of experience—but also to bad ones—decay, impoverishment. To demand that God be, in every respect, immutable is to imply that there is no form of the capacity to change without which a being would be defective, or even a mere abstraction, not a concrete, actual being. The divine excellence requires immunity to negative change, to loss or degeneration; but does it require an incapacity for any and every kind of good change, every kind of increase in value? Plato (not the scriptures) proposed the argument "God must be perfect, hence any change would have to be either for the worse or without value, meaningless." This argument presupposes for its force that we have a positive idea of a maximum of value such that no additional value would be possible. Plato's phrase for such an unincreasable, unsurpassable value was "absolute beauty." What this is neither Plato nor anyone else has told us. An analysis of aesthetic principles strongly suggests that given any conceivable beauty there could be a greater beauty. If this be so, Plato's argument proves nothing.

Another ambiguity or problematic concept in the negative way was the idea that dependence was necessarily a defect distinguishing ordinary things from God. This excludes knowledge from God, if indeed Aristotle, or anyone else, can tell us what "to know" means. In addition there are two kinds of dependence, only one of which is obviously a weakness, this being dependence for very existence and essential properties. Denying this radical dependence of God for very existence leaves quite open the possibility of a dependence for qualities not necessary to the divine existence. If there is any genuine freedom in the creatures, they will do things they might not have done. God will know what they have done, but (as the Socinians saw long ago) this knowledge cannot be essential to God's very existence. Rather, had a creature done something other than what it did, God would have had correspondingly different knowledge other than the knowledge he does have. If the word *knowledge* is given an honest meaning, one can consistently assert the compatibility of creaturely freedom with divine knowledge only if one admits divine knowledge without which God could and would—had the world been otherwise—have existed as God, incapable of error and ignorance. Total independence of others entails not knowing these others. Plato did not know us and was independent of us; we know Plato and *therefore* are not wholly independent of Plato.

Step by step, the reasoning of simple or nondual transcendence has been examined by this and other writers. It seems lacking in cogency. To understand the steady loss of support by philosophers (beginning with Hume and Kant) for classical theism (which denies dual transcendence), this lack of cogency is important. Belief in the divine uniqueness can survive the admission that it is not change but certain kinds of change, not dependence but certain kinds of dependence, that are excluded by the divine excellence. That the issue is worldwide and intercultural is remarkably well illustrated by the following coincidences.

In a year—I think the very month or week—in which I was thinking and writing about how God in some senses is changing, yet also in other senses unchanging, a man from India delivered a sermon in the chapel of the University of Chicago, with which I was connected for twenty-seven years. He was Radhakamal Mukerji, a leading sociologist of India, but also a writer on mysticism. He said in his sermon that God is unchanging in "ethical" goodness but increases in "aesthetic" value, which I took to mean in the richness or beauty of the divine experience of the world as new creatures come into being. This distinction between ethical value as capable of an absolute maximum and aesthetic value as an open infinity with no upper maximum was exactly the conclusion I had come to before hearing or knowing Mukerji. Also before this, I had had a somewhat similar intercultural experience, which was confirmed again long after Mukerji's visit. It involved two monks of the modern Bengali sect of Hinduism whose views harmonized with the idea of a deity both unchanging and yet in some respects changing. One of these monks, Ma-kanam Brata Brahmachari, who did his doctoral dissertation under me, quoted a representative of his sect who wrote of God: "Lo, the cup is eternally full, yet it grows without ceasing." When this man began talking to me about "love" as a theological term I asked him what he meant by the word. "I mean," he said, "the consciousness of consciousness, the thinking of thinking, the . . . of. . . ." I am not sure, but he may have said, "the feeling of feeling." If he did, the analogy with Whitehead was close. In his dissertation he writes: "God is more than the absolute." Of course, for a mere negative like *nonrelative* by itself constitutes no sufficient account of any actuality. Plato is not relative to us, but that is Plato's total ignorance of us; we constitute nothing of Plato's being, whereas, by his knowledge of and hence relativity to them, Parmenides and many others whom he did know contributed much to his wonderfully comprehensive awareness.

The Reality of Divine Love. Finally, I want to focus on the proposition "God is love." Mortimer Adler has recently explained why, although he is convinced that an intelligent divine being exists as creator of all, he does not think it can be demonstrated that this being is benevolent or loving. One may, however, question the distinction drawn here between divine intelligence and divine love. If God is to know us, God must know our feelings. How can feelings be known except by feelings? Can mere intellect (whatever that is—perhaps a computer) know feelings while having none of its own? And if God has feelings, what kind of feelings? Envy, malice, conceit, hatred, inferiority complexes? What have these to do with all-encompassing intelligence? For me, this is a wholly absurd combination of ideas. By embracing in knowledge all the qualities of reality, God possesses all that anyone possesses by way of value, so what could envy mean? Hatred would be baseless, since by willing the suffering of creatures God would be willing divine sharing in these sufferings. Whitehead's wonderfully simple formula of "feeling of feeling" as a basic element in knowledge excludes any ground for Adler's dilemma. To know others without intuiting their feelings is scarcely knowledge at all, and such an ability would hardly seem likely as an essential quality of an indestructible cosmic subject upon which all others radically depend. Simple atheism would be more reasonable than affirming such a God, so far as I can see. To give intelligence cosmic and everlasting scope, but to deny such scope to love, seems a discordant mixture of notions. Or is Advaita Vedānta and the doctrine of *māyā* the alternative to love? We think we exist as individuals, but really only *brahman* exists, spaceless and timeless. We are appearances of *brahman*, although *brahman* is unaware of us. Or does *brahman* constitute us by dreaming us? I have a different theory of dreams, and so had Bergson. Perhaps we can leave the doctrine of *māyā* to the Indians, who are by no means in agreement on the subject.

It is fair to add that there is no agreement in the West on the reality of divine love. Can a fragment of reality comprehend the encompassing? I feel entirely confident that if love cannot encompass all, including creaturely hatred as a degenerate case of love (the total lack of which is mere indifference), then nothing positively conceivable by such as we are can do so either.

If no form of theism escapes difficulties, puzzles it cannot solve, questions to which it finds no convincing answer, this is perhaps to be expected. A god easily understood is not God but a fetish, an idol. Dual transcendence removes some of the traditional paradoxes, especially if we include a clear doctrine of freedom as well as of more or less humble forms of sentience and feeling for all dynamic singulars in nature. Peirce had already done this before Whitehead took creativity as the ultimate category, applicable in the uniquely, divinely excellent form to God and in humbler forms to all creatures. But still there are puzzles. Change in God seems to imply, and Berdiaev hints at this, a divine kind of time. But how to relate this timelike aspect of God to worldly time is a problem that overwhelms me with a sense of incompetence. Physicists have their own difficulties with time, and without a mathematical competence beyond that of most of us one can scarcely begin to understand these difficulties, let alone overcome them.

By attributing freedom as well as minimal sentience to even the least single creatures (particles, atoms), the classical atheistic argument from evil loses its cogency. The details of nature are decided not by God but by the creatures concerned, by atoms, molecules, bacteria, single-celled animals, and many-celled animals, including human beings. And if it be said that God, in deciding to have free creatures instead of unfree creatures, is indirectly responsible for evil, the reply is that for the new type of idealism "unfree creature" is an ill-formed formula. As God is supreme freedom, ordinary singular beings are instances of less than supreme freedom, not of total lack of freedom. To be is to create, to decide what is otherwise undecided. Decision making, freedom, cannot be monopolized. Supreme freedom would have nothing to do were there not also less exalted forms of freedom. Genuine power is not power over the powerless. No single agent ever decides exactly what happens. The new physics (and even classical physics as interpreted by Clerk Maxwell, Reichenbach, Peirce, Whitehead, Sudarshan, and others) seems to harmonize better with this doctrine than did classical physics as it was usually interpreted by philosophers.

The present climate of opinion suggests the need for reconsidering many an old controversy and for questioning not only certain assumptions of classical theologians but also some of those of classical atheists or agnostics, including Hume, Kant, Marx, Comte, Russell, and Nietzsche. Not all contemporary forms of theism can be refuted by antiquated forms of skeptical argument.

Religion is a two-story affair, to adapt a phrase from James Feibleman. It is in part an empirical and historical matter, concerned with contingent fact about human nature and traditions. The idea of God, however, is nonempirical and metaphysical. Dealing as they do with what is eternal and necessary, including the eternal and necessary aspects of God, metaphysical statements are true if they make coherent sense and false otherwise. To admit that one has no idea of the answers is to imply that one has no idea of the question; for they are either self-answering or else confused. It is humanly difficult to admit this confusion. If one could clearly see that and how one is confused, would one still be confused? I feel confident there will be other writers in this collective enterprise whose confusions will contrast with mine. And there is something to be said for making one's partialities explicit.

See Also Anthropomorphism; Attributes of God; Pantheism and Panentheism; Sky; Supreme Beings; Theism.

Bibliography

My article "Pantheism and Panentheism" in this encyclopedia deals with closely related topics; its bibliography is relevant here. My *Omnipotence and Other Theological Mistakes* (Albany, N.Y., 1984) is a somewhat popular, nontechnical presentation of my own version of the idea of God as supreme love exalted above ordinary love by dual transcendence. My article "Transcendence" appears in *An Encyclopedia of Religion*, edited by Vergilius Ferm (New York, 1945), pp. 791–792; see also in the same work my articles "Hume, David," "Omnipotence," "Omnipresence," and "Perfect, Perfection," as well as Herman Hausheer's "Fechner, Gustav Theodor."

For a distinguished Jewish theologian's idea of God, see John C. Merkle's *The Genesis of Faith: The Depth Theology of Abraham Joshua Heschel* (New York, 1985); see also Heschel's *God in Search of Man: A Philosophy of Judaism* (New York, 1955). Heschel's view is remarkably close to the neoclassical view, although both doctrines were worked out independently. Edgar S. Brightman's *The Problem of God* (Nashville, 1930) is an approximation to the dual transcendence view; see also Brightman's *A Philosophy of Religion* (1940; Westport, Conn., 1969), especially chapters 7, 10, and 11, for a fine historical sketch of the idea that God must have finite as well as infinite aspects. Brightman's conceptualization is in line with the trend to turn away from the extremist strategy that prevailed from Aristotle to early modern times toward a middle-ground strategy, in which God is neither exclusively infinite nor exclusively finite but is, in suitable divine ways, both.

New Sources

Faulconer, James E., ed. *Transcendence in Philosophy and Religion.* Bloomington, 2003.

Hyland, Drew A. *Finitude and Transcendence in Platonic Dialogue.* Albany, 1995.

Polakola, Jolana. *Searching for the Divine in Contemporary Philosophy: Tensions between the Immanent and the Transcendent.* Translated by Jan Veleska. Lewiston, N.Y., 1999.

Roy, Louis. *Transcendent Experiences: Phenomenology and Critique.* Toronto, 2001.

Seligman, Adam B. *Modernity's Wager; Authority, and Transcendence.* Princeton, N.J., 2000.

Stone, Jerome Arthur. *The Minimalist Vision of Transcendence: A Naturalist Philosophy of Relgion.* Albany, N.Y., 1992.

Charles Hartshorne (1987)
Revised Bibliography